August 21–24, 2011
San Diego, California, USA

Association for
Computing Machinery

Advancing Computing as a Science & Profession

KDD'11

Proceedings of the 17th ACM SIGKDD Conference on

Knowledge Discovery and Data Mining

Sponsored by:

ACM SIGKDD and ACM SIGMOD

Association for
Computing Machinery

Advancing Computing as a Science & Profession

The Association for Computing Machinery
2 Penn Plaza, Suite 701
New York, New York 10121-0701

ISBN: 978-1-4503-0934-9 (Digital)

ISBN: 978-1-4503-1256-1 (Print)

Additional copies may be ordered prepaid from:

ACM Order Department
PO Box 30777
New York, NY 10087-0777, USA

Phone: 1-800-342-6626 (USA and Canada)
+1-212-626-0500 (Global)
Fax: +1-212-944-1318
E-mail: acmhelp@acm.org
Hours of Operation: 8:30 am – 4:30 pm ET

Printed in the USA

General Chair's Welcome Message

It is my great honor and pleasure to welcome you to ACM SIGKDD's *17th Annual Conference on Knowledge Discovery and Data Mining, KDD2011,* being held in San Diego, California, from August 21 through August 24, 2011. This year's KDD Conference continues its tradition of being the premier forum for the sharing of leading edge research results and industrial experiences of KDD theory, technology, and applications, among it's multi-disciplinary participants from academia, government, and industry. The KDD2011 organization committee has worked hard to help organize this year's conference, and to ensure that it maintains its pre-eminent position as the top worldwide conference for dissemination of cutting edge technical progress of this community.

The science and business of extracting actionable insights from data has never been more important. We are experiencing an explosion of data, and the consequent interest in analyzing this information in a timely and rigorous fashion. Data and content volumes are expected to grow exponentially in the next decade. Much of the new growth is expected to dominantly come from unstructured content; documents, images, audio and video. These trends are setting up the stage for a fascinating set of new research challenges, and simultaneously driving the need for accelerated deployment of our research advances, ranging from algorithmic advances in core modeling and learning techniques, to scalable methods for parallel and distributed mining of massive scale data, to new paradigms for consumption and delivery of the analytic insights. It is my hope that attendees at this conference will be able to sense and appreciate the impressive progress our community is making in addressing these challenges.

We have made a few changes this year to the traditional KDD conference format, to address the growing interest in this technology. The conference will begin as always with workshops and tutorials on Sunday, and then we have a full 3-day program for the main body of the conference. The extended 3-day main program has allowed us to include additional keynote plenary talks and make space for some exciting new content. We are launching a new track this year, called the Industry Practice Expo. The aim of the IPE track is to bring in eminent practitioners of KDD from industry to share with the participants their in depth experiences on what it means to successfully deploy working instances of high impacting KDD solutions.

You will get to read more details of the technical program in the forewords from our Program Chairs. Industry/Government Application Chairs, and Industry Practice Expo Chairs. I would like to truly thank and appreciate all the hard work put in by the entire organization committee of the conference. In addition, no conference can be run on its own today without the generous support from our industry and government sponsors. I wish to thank them all. Special thanks to ACM and SIGKDD for providing solid support in all matters, organizational and financial. Finally, thanks to all of you, conference attendees and participants, for your continued endorsement of this important venue. Enjoy the conference!

Chid Apte
KDD2011 General Chair
IBM Research, Yorktown Heights, NY, USA

ACM SIGKDD 2011 Program Chairs' Welcome

The KDD conference has come a long way from its origins as an IJCAI workshop in Detroit in 1989, evolving into a full-fledged research conference in 1995, with continued growth since – were it publicly traded it would have been an excellent investment over the years. This year we received a record 714 submissions to the research program, from which 126 papers were accepted, 56 as talks and 70 as posters, for an aggregate acceptance rate of 17.6% (quite similar to recent years). As a comparative example, twelve years ago in 1999, when this conference was also held in San Diego, there were 280 papers submitted to the research program and 52 were accepted as talks or posters.

The success and growth of the KDD conference over the past two decades has paralleled the broader emergence of machine learning and data mining as major areas of research in academia and industry. Among the academic conferences, the KDD conference has typically more of an emphasis on applications when compared to sibling conferences such as NIPS and ICML. Yet it is important to keep in mind that the successes of data mining and machine learning depend not only on successful applications. It is the *synergy* of research and application that drives our field forward - one without the other will wither. This synergy is also what makes our field vibrant and fun – who among us knew while listening to lectures on linear algebra or probability in high-school or college that we would later apply these ideas to discover information from data as diverse as Web pages, medical images, movie ratings, and climate records.

The breadth of topics covered in this year's research program is correspondingly diverse, including social networks, privacy, text mining, predictive modeling, time-series forecasting, spatial data analysis, and more. We are very fortunate to have 4 world-class keynote speakers this year, providing expert overviews of the latest advances in optimization, Web mining, causality, and bioinformatics. If you have not heard these speakers before you have a treat in store – and if you have heard them speak before, then you already know not to miss any of these 4 talks. The panel discussion on Wednesday afternoon on data mining prize competitions is also well worth your attention – participants include several of the world's leading authorities on this topic.

The process of whittling down the initial 714 submissions to the final set of 126 accepted papers required the coordination and time of a large number of willing volunteers. The program committee (PC) consisted of over 350 reviewers (PC members) and 37 senior PC members. In the first phase each submitted paper was automatically assigned to 3 reviewers (after a bidding process) and to a single senior PC member. Once the reviews from each of the 3 reviewers were completed, the senior PC members had the option of initiating a discussion for any of their papers, e.g., if there was significant divergence in scores among reviewers, or if a paper was on the borderline of being accepted. Following the discussion phase, the senior PC members provided a recommendation score for each paper in terms of its suitability for acceptance, and (optionally) a short meta-review. In the final phase, we (the program chairs) analyzed all of this information, starting with the obvious accept and reject decisions, and then gradually focusing in more detail on the papers near the borderline, seeking additional reviews and input from the PC and senior PC members where appropriate. It is quite likely that in hindsight some worthy papers may have been rejected as part of this process – these errors are an unfortunate reality of modern computer science conferences, and hard to avoid when a very large number of decisions have to be made over a short time span based on a subjective reviewing process.

We made a number of changes to the reviewing and decision process this year compared to recent years. For example, we jettisoned the author-response phase – there are certainly some merits to be gained by allowing such a phase, but we felt that the aggregate time and effort spent by authors and reviewers in total often outweighs the specific gains obtained for a relatively small number of individual papers. We also added a conditional accept phase – of the 126 accepted papers, 43 had been identified by 2 or more the reviewers as needing significant improvement in writing (typos, grammar, etc). These papers were duly revised and resubmitted by the authors (in some cases with multiple iterations) until we felt that they were ready for publication in the proceedings. Our decision to include this extra round of revision came from our observation that the quality of writing has deteriorated in recent years at computer science conferences - it is increasingly common to encounter poorly written papers in published proceedings. This reflects poorly on our field and motivated our desire to try to improve the writing quality this year. Our attempts are likely to have been only partly successful, but we nonetheless encourage chairs and authors for future conferences to continue to raise the bar for writing quality.

We conclude with some well-deserved words of thanks to the large supporting cast. We are extremely grateful to the PC members and senior PC members for volunteering their time to help in the reviewing process. Diligent peer review is an essential cornerstone for research progress – we thank you all for the many detailed and conscientious reviews that were generated. Last year's program chairs, Andrew Tomkins and Qiang Yang, were generous in providing us with advice and expertise based on lessons learned in 2010. Professor Jie Tang and his colleagues at Tsinghua volunteered their time and effort to provide valuable rankings of papers for reviewers during the bidding process. We would also like to convey our sincere thanks to the staff who run the Microsoft CMT system – they were more than willing to answer questions and help us at all times during the submission, reviewing, and decision process. And finally we would like to thank all of our colleagues on the KDD 2011 organization committee who were a pleasure to work with and without whom we would not have a conference.

Let the 17th ACM SIGKDD conference begin – we hope you enjoy it!

Joydeep Ghosh and Padhraic Smyth
ACM SIGKDD 2011 Program Chairs

Foreword to the Industrial/Government Track

The 2011 Industrial/Government track continued the revitalization that began in 2010 by clearly focusing on three areas of applied KDD work that are the sources of value to industrial and government organizations: (1) deployed applications, (2) knowledge discoveries, and (3) emerging applications. These areas build on the results of KDD research by applying the results of such research to enable the construction of novel and useful applications, the discovery of novel, interesting and useful knowledge, and the extension and application of research results to specific real world problems of interest. Papers were solicited and reviewed in these three areas:

- Deployed KDD systems that are providing real value to industry, government, or other organizations or professions. These deployed systems could support ongoing knowledge discovery or could be applications that employ discovered knowledge, or some combination of the two.

- Discoveries of knowledge with demonstrable value to industry, government, or other users (e.g., scientific or medical professions). This knowledge must be "externally validated" as interesting and useful; it can not simply be a model that has better performance on some traditional KDD metric such as accuracy or area under the curve.

- Emerging applications and technology that provide insight relevant to the above value propositions. These emerging applications must have clear user interest and support to distinguish them from KDD research papers, or they must provide insight into issues and factors that affect the successful use of KDD technology and methods. Papers that describe infrastructure that enables the large-scale deployment of KDD techniques also are in this area.

Industry/Government track papers not only document and recognize significant accomplishments in these three areas, but also provide feedback to KDD researchers about needs, constraints, and applicability of KDD algorithms, methods and techniques in the real world. Our emphasis was on papers that advance the understanding of practical, applied, or pragmatic issues related to the use of KDD technologies in industry and government settings and highlight new research challenges arising from attempts to create such real KDD applications. We encouraged potential authors to address these issues and challenges in the Call for Papers and the accompanying Author Instructions (see http://www.kdd.org/kdd2011/author_instructions_industry.shtml)

Our review process began with a validation by the reviewers that the authors correctly classified their paper's area – to ensure that the paper was reviewed according to the applicable criteria for that area – and a check that all required elements for that area were addressed in the paper. These required elements were:

- Deployed KDD case studies describe deployed projects with measurable benefits that include KDD technology. These papers must clearly describe the industry or government problem that is solved, the overall architecture of the deployed system, the data sources used, the reasons for the choices of particular KDD technologies, how KDD technologies solved the problem, the particular KDD process embodied by the deployed application, the use and payoff of the application, the costs to develop the application, the maintenance plan, and the number and types of users.

- Papers that describe discoveries of knowledge must clearly state what data sources and background knowledge were used, what data mining algorithms were tried, what overall KDD process was used, what the new discovered knowledge is, how the new knowledge was validated, and what the value to the industry or government is of such newly discovered knowledge. Note that this category is intended for significant discoveries of domain knowledge that were enabled by KDD technologies and processes, and not for reporting of KDD research results.

- Emerging application and technology papers discuss prototype applications, tools for focused domains or tasks, useful techniques or methods, useful system architectures, scalability enablers, tool evaluations, or integration of KDD with other technologies. Such papers must clearly explain the requirements arising from the particular industry or government setting for which the application is being developed and from the particular databases on which the application is based. These papers must also identify how the emerging solution is using KDD technologies to address these requirements, the deployment plan, and the evaluation methodology and metrics for the emerging application. Pragmatic issues and considerations include important practical and research considerations, approaches, and architectures that enable successful applications. This category may include comparative evaluations of different KDD technologies for particular application problems. Preferences will be given to papers whose insights may generalize to other domains or problems. Product advertisements will not be accepted.

Specific review criteria included:

- Value/Payoff: What are the measurable benefits of the deployed application, the value of the newly discovered knowledge, or the generalizable insights from the emerging application?
- Cost: What is the cost/effort of the reported project? (To develop and maintain the application or to discover the new knowledge)
- External Significance: Is there clear evidence that the application problem being addressed and the KDD solution matters to an identified external set of users?
- External Validity: Is the knowledge discovered/used by the application externally validated? (This can be demonstrated by its use by a business, government, or profession; by publication in a peer-reviewed domain journal, or other means)
- Does the paper thoroughly describe the data sources and background knowledge used?
- Does the paper thoroughly describe the selection, use, appropriateness and effectiveness of the KDD technologies and/or data mining algorithms?
- Does the paper describe the KDD process enabled by the application or used to discover knowledge?
- Novelty/Originality: Does the work apply KDD technology to a new problem? Does it develop or apply a new type of KDD technology to an existing problem? Does it apply KDD technology to achieve a better result than with previous technology?

- Technical soundness: Does the paper show an accurate understanding of KDD research and technology? Does it identify relevant past work? Does it appropriately match techniques to problem characteristics?
- Evaluation: Is the reported work carefully evaluated? Is it statistically sound? Are the results compared to appropriate baselines? To other approaches and solutions? To previously reported work? Are its claims supported?
- Deployment/Use: Is there clear evidence that the application is deployed or on a path to deployment, or that the discovered knowledge will be used?
- Clarity: Is the paper written clearly? Is it organized logically? Are there sufficient figures and tables to illustrate its main points? Is it accessible to readers without specialized domain knowledge? Is it accessible to readers from different technical specialties and application domains?
- Does the paper contain insights or results that will generalize or apply to other domains or is it specialized to a particular domain?
- Will the paper be accessible to non-specialists in the particular domain?

Overall, we reviewed 73 papers and accepted 26, of which 9 describe deployed applications, 3 knowledge discoveries, and 14 emerging applications. The application areas cover a broad range, including finance, security, internet, text mining, science, retail, medical, and social, showing the many different fields to which KDD is being applied and adding value.

We hope you find these papers interesting and look forward to continued improvements in the use of KDD techniques to provide real value to industry and government.

Ted Senator and Michael Zeller
Industrial/ Government Track Program Chairs

Foreword to the KDD 2011 Industry Practice Expo

It is our distinct honor to welcome you to the inaugural Industry Practice Expo track at the KDD conference. The Industry Practice Expo features invited talks from leading experts who have developed and deployed successful, large-scale data mining applications and systems in their respective fields. We trust that this opportunity for the KDD community to hear directly from the experts will start a new era of cross-fertilization of ideas in knowledge discovery and data mining from various disciplines.

The field of Knowledge Discovery and Data Mining has matured tremendously over the past 15 years. This advancement in the field is duly reflected in the KDD conference publications describing the leading edge research and industry/government applications. At the planning meeting for KDD 2011, Usama Fayyad, the SIGKDD chairman, proposed starting a new track that would complement the already well-established Research and Industry/Government tracks at the KDD conference and showcase the successes and best-practices of applications and systems of knowledge discovery and data mining in various industries. While the Research and Industry/Government tracks would continue their excellent work featuring the latest advances in the field via peer-reviewed publications, the Industry Practice Expo track would feature invited talks from leading experts who would otherwise not publish in the KDD Research or Industry/Government tracks either because of time-constraints or because they are from industries where their work is publicized in forums other than the KDD conference. Armed with this mandate we started on an almost year long journey to conceive, implement, and present to you the inaugural KDD Industry Practice Expo.

We have kept our ambitions very high right from the beginning and have aspired to bring together a group of leading-experts to deliver a series of technical talks focusing on innovative and leading-edge, large-scale applications and systems of data mining in areas such as finance, health-care, bio-informatics, public policy, infrastructure (transportation, utilities, etc.), telecommunications, social media, and computational advertising. We wanted to select the talks that will inspire and motivate fellow members of our KDD community by spreading awareness of various seminal, innovative, and proven applications of knowledge discovery and data mining, sharing key insights and best-practices, and introducing new problems, challenges, and methodologies. We have been immensely fortunate to have the opportunity of working with an advisory committee for the Industry Practice Expo. The committee comprises of individuals who are luminaries in their own right and have generously devoted their time and energies in guiding us through the process. We are extremely grateful for their advice, constant support and encouragement.

We have selected a great panel of speakers who represent a broad cross-section of KDD applications and systems across multiple industries. In putting together this Industry Practice Expo track we have taken the time and effort to get to know each potential speaker well, carefully reviewed their work to better understand their contributions and ensure that the material they present would be interesting and valuable to the KDD audience. We would like to thank all of our speakers for their time and patience as we went through the vetting process and for graciously accepting our invitation to present their work at the KDD conference.

We warmly welcome you to the inaugural KDD Industry Practice Expo and hope that you will enjoy it and find it useful in your professional endeavors. Your suggestions and comments are very welcome.

Best regards,

Rajesh Parekh and Ying Li
Industry Practice Expo Track co-chairs

Table of Contents

Session A1: Matrix Factorization

Session A1: Graph Analysis

Session A2: Web User Modeling

Session A2: User Modeling

Session A2: Online Data and Streams

Session A4: Emerging 2

Session A4: Emerging 3

Session B1: Text Mining 1

Session B1: Text Mining 2

Session B1: Privacy

Session B2: Social Networks

Session B2: Theory

Session B2: Frequent Sets

Session C1: Text Mining

Session C1: Unsupervised Learning

Session C1: Graph Mining

Session C2: Scalability

Session C2: Predictive Modeling

Demonstration Track

Industrial Practice Expo Track

Poster Session

ACM SIGKDD 2011 Conference Organization

General Chair:	*Chid Apte (IBM Research)*
Program Co-Chairs:	*Joydeep Ghosh (UT Austin)* *Padhraic Smyth (UC Irvine)*
Industry/Government Track Co-Chairs:	*Ted Senator (SAIC)* *Michael Zeller (Zementis)*
Industry Practice Expo Co-Chairs:	*Ying Li (Microsoft)* *Rajesh Parekh (Groupon)*
Sponsorship Chair:	*Balaji Krishnapuram (Siemens)*
Student Awards Chair:	*Jimeng Sun (IBM Research)*
SIGKDD Chair:	*Usama Fayyad (ChoozOn Corporation)*
Tutorials Chair:	*Deepak Agarwal (Yahoo!)*
Workshops Co-Chairs:	*Ian Davidson (UC Davis)* *Jennifer Dy (Northeastern)*
Posters Chair:	*Sofus A. Macskassy (Fetch Technologies)*
Publicity Co-Chairs:	*Rayid Ghani (Accenture)* *Yan Liu (USC)*
Publications Co-Chairs:	*Jie Tang (Tsinghua University)* *Alexandru Niculescu-Mizil (NEC Laboratories America)*
Web Co-Chairs:	*Melissa Carroll (IBM Research)* *David Eis (Princeton University)*
Exhibits and Demos Co-Chairs:	*Natasha Balac (UC San Diego)* *Hui Xiong (Rutgers)*
Local Arrangements Chair:	*Nancy Davis (ION)*
Registrations Chair:	*Claudia Perlich (Media6Degrees)*
Treasurer:	*Vikas Sindhwani (IBM Research)*
KDD Cup Co-Chairs:	*Gideon Dror (Yahoo!)* *Yehuda Koren (Yahoo!)* *Markus Weimer (Yahoo!)*
KDD Awards Chair:	*Osmar Zaiane (Alberta)*
KDD Research Paper Awards Chairs:	*Andrew Tomkins (Google)* *Rich Caruana (Microsoft)*

KDD'11 Research Track Program Committees

Senior Program Committee:

Niall Adams (Imperial College)
Charu Aggarwal (IBM)
Arindam Banerjee (University of Minnesota)
Rich Caruana (Microsoft)
Corinna Cortes (Google)
Gautum Das (University of Texas, Arlington)
Charles Elkan (University of California, San Diego)
Johannes Gehrke (Cornell University)
Aristides Gionis (Yahoo! Barcelona)
Dimtrios Gunopulos (University of Athens)
Jiawei Han (UIUC)
George Karypis (University of Minnesota)
Yehuda Koren (Yahoo! Research)
Jure Leskovec (Stanford University)
David Madigan (Columbia University)
Chris Meek (Microsoft Research)
Katarina Morik (University of Dortmund)
Zoran Obradovic (Temple University)
Srini Parthasarathy (The Ohio State University)
Jian Pei (Simon Fraser University)
Raghu Ramakrishnan (Yahoo! Research)
Matt Richardson (Microsoft)
Saharon Rosset (Tel Aviv University)
Sunita Sarawagi (IIT, Bombay)
Arno Siebes (Utrecht University)
Alex Smola (Yahoo! and ANU)
Ramakrishnan Srikant (Google)
Evimaria Terzi (Boston University)
Andrew Tomkins (Google)
Alex Tuzhilin (New York University)
Wei Wang (University of North Carolina, Chapel Hill)
Stefan Wrobel (Fraunhofer IAIS & University of Bonn)
Eric Xing (Carnegie Mellon University)
Qiang Yang (Hong Kong UST)
Philip Yu (University of Illinois, Chicago)
Mohammed Zaki (RPI)
Zhi-Hua Zhou (Nanjing University)

Program Committee:

Naoki Abe (IBM T.J. Watson Research Center)
James Abello (DIMACS/Rutgers University)
Sreangsu Acharyya (University of Texas, Austin)
Ryan Adams (University of Toronto)
Foto Afrati (National Technical University of Athens)
Eugene Agichtein (Emory University)
Mohammad Al Hasan (IUPUI)
Aijun An (York University)
Aris Anagnostopoulos (Sapienza University of Rome)
Christoforos Anagnostopoulos (University of Cambridge)
Annalisa Appice (University Aldo Moro of Bari)
Arthur Asuncion (Uviversity of California, Irvine)
Sitaram Asur (Hewlett Packard Labs)
Vassilis Athitsos (University of Texas, Arlington)
Amir Atiya (Cairo University)
Lars Backstrom (Cornell University)
Tony Bagnall (University of East Anglia)
James Bailey (University of Melbourne)
Tim Bailey (University of Queensland)
Sugato Basu (Google Research)
Stephen Bay (Deloitte Consulting)
Roberto Bayardo (Google)
Paul Bennett (Microsoft Research)
Bettina Berendt (University of Leuven)
Tanya Berger-Wolf (University of Illinois at Chicago)
Pavel Berkhin (Microsoft)
Michele Berlingerio (KDD Lab, ISTI-CNR, Pisa)
Michael Berthold (University of Konstanz)
Chiru Bhattacharya (IISc)
Mikhail Bilenko (Microsoft Research)
Mustafa Bilgic (Illinois Institute of Technology)
Marina Blanton (University of Notre Dame)
Francesco Bonchi (Yahoo! Research)
Edwin Bonilla (CSIRO)
Karsten Borgwardt (Max Planck Insitute)
Henrik Bostrom (Stockholm University)
Ulf Brefeld (Yahoo! Barcelona)
Gavin Brown (University of Manchester)
Wray Buntine (NICTA)
Deng Cai (Zhejiang University)
Rui Cai (Microsoft Research, Beijing)
Toon Calders (Technische Universiteit Eindhoven)
Carlos Castillo (Yahoo!)
Deepayan Chakrabarti (Yahoo! Research)
Ed Chang (Google)
Jonathan Chang (Facebook)

Joerg Sander (University of Alberta)
Purnamrita Sarkar (University of California, Berkeley)
Shin'ichi Satoh (National Institute of Informatics)
D. Sculley (Google)
Thomas Seidl (RWTH Aachen University)
Dennis Shasha (NYew York University)
Shashi Shekhar (University of Minnesota)
Dou Shen (Buzzlabs)
Luo Si (Purdue University)
Kevin Small (Tufts University)
Mauro Sozio (Max Planck, Saarbrucken)
Myra Spiliopoulou (Otto-von-Guericke-Universityersitaet Magdeburg)
Suvrit Sra (Max Planck Institute)
Rohini Srihari (University at Buffalo, State University of New York)
Harald Steck (Bell-Labs, Alcatel-Lucent)
Michael Steinbach (University of Minnesota)
David Stern (Microsoft Research Cambridge)
L. Venkata Subramaniam (IBM Research - India)
Masashi Sugiyama (Tokyo Institute of Technology)
Jimeng Sun ((IBM T.J. Watson Research Center)
Neel Sundaresan (eBay Research Labs)
Einoshin Suzuki (Kyushi University)
Pang-Ning Tan (Michigan State University)
Jie Tang (Tsinghua University)
Dacheng Tao (University of Technology, Sydney)
Yufei Tao (Chinese University of Hong Kong)
Dimitris Tasoulis (Winton Capital)
Shirish Tatikonda (IBM Almaden Research Center)
Bo Thiesson (Microsoft Research)
HangHang Tong (IBM T.J. Watson Research Center)
Volker Tresp (Siemens)
Panayiotis Tsaparas (Microsoft Research)
Grigorios Tsoumakas (Aristotle University of Thessaloniki)
Allan Tucker (Brunel University)
Michael Turmon (JPL)
Duygu Ucar (Stanford University)
Naonori Ueda (NTT Communication Science Labs)
Antti Ukkonen (Yahoo!)
Lyle Ungar (University of Pennsylvania)
Jaideep Vaidya (Rutgers University.)
Laurens van der Maarten (University of California, San Diego and TU, Delft)
Michalis Vazirgiannis (Athens University of Economics & Business)
Jean-Philippe Vert (Mines Paris Tech and Curie Institute)
Vassilios Verykios (University. of Thessaly)
Vishy Vishwanathan (Purdue University)
Michalis Vlachos (IBM Research)
Chris Volinsky (AT&T Labs - Research)
Jilles Vreeken (University of Antwerp, Belgium)
Slobodan Vucetic (Temple University)
Haixun Wang (Microsoft Asia)
Xuanhui Wang (Yahoo! Labs)
Charles Ward (Stony Brook University)
Markus Weimer (Yahoo! Research)
Gary Weiss (Fordham University)
Sholom Weiss (IBM Research)
Ran Wolff (University of Haifa)
Raymond Chi-Wing Wong (Hong Kong University of Science and Technology)
Weng-Keen Wong (Oregon State University)
Xindong Wu (University of Vermont)
Yanghua Xiao (Fudan University)
Hui Xiong (Rutgers University)
Guirong Xue (Shanghai Jiaotong University)
Kenji Yamanishi (University of Tokyo)
Jun Yan (Microsoft Research Asia)
Xifeng Yan (University of California, Santa Barbara)
Jieping Ye (Arizona State University)
Dit-Yan Yeung (Hong Kong University of Science and Technology)
Xiaoxin Yin (Microsoft Research)
Jeffrey Xu Yu (Chinese University of Hong Kong)
Lei Yu (Binghamton University)
Shipeng Yu (Siemens Medical Solutions)
Yisong Yue (Carnegie Mellon University)
Bianca Zadrozny (IBM Research Brazil)
Carlo Zaniolo (University of California, Los Angeles
Demetris Zeinalipour (University of Cyprus)
Filip Zelezny (Czech Technical University)
Hongyuan Zha (Georgia Tech)
Aidong Zhang (University at Buffalo)
Kun Zhang (Max Planck Institute)
Min-Ling Zhang (Southeast University)
Nan Zhang (George Wash. U)
Zhongfei (Mark) Zhang (SUNY Binghamton)
Jun Zhu (Carnegie Mellon University)
Xingquan Zhu (University of Technology, Sydney)
Arthur Zimek (LMU Munich)

KDD'11 Industry/Government Program Committee

John Akred (Accenture)
Richardo Baeza-Yates (Yahoo! Research)
Michael Berthold (KNIME)
Kanishka Bhaduri (NASA)
Eric Bloedorn (MITRE - USA)
Rainer Burkhardt (JgenCy)
Deng Cai (Zhejiang University)
Katrina Carter-Journet (NASA)
Hong Cheng (The Chinese University of Hong Kong)
David Duling (SAS)
Marty Ellingsworth (ISO Innovative Analytics)
Nancy Grady (Science Applications International Corporation)
Shawndra Hill (Wharton School of Business)
Steven Hillion (Greenplum/EMC)
Derek Hao Hu (Hong Kong UST)
Jianying Hu (IBM T.J. Watson Research Center)
Sergei Israilev (Jabiru Ventures)
Ron Karidi (Microsoft (Israel Innovation Labs)
Mei Kobayashi (IBM Research Lab, Tokyo)
Christoph Lingenfelder (IBM)
Nathan Nan Liu (Hong Kong UST)
David Lo (Singapore Management University)
Jack Lucas (US Government)
Jamie MacLennan (Predixion Software)
Gideon Mann (Google)
Dawn Martin (NASA)
Gabor Melli (Simon Fraser University)
Theodore Omtzigt (Stillwater Supercomputing)
Sinno JIalin Pan (HKUST)
Wei Peng (Xerox)
Ralf Rantzau (Truviso)
Karl Rexer (Rexer Analytics)
Neal Rothleder (MITRE)
Ramendra Sahoo (Citi)
Ashok Savasere (SAS)
Dawit Seid (SAS)
Nitin Sharma (Groupon)
Ali Shaykhian (NASA)
Dou Shen (BuzzLabs)
Jiaqiang Shen (Pearson Education)
Jian-Tao Sun (Microsoft Research)
AC Surendran (Microsoft)
Arun Swami (Google)
Wayne Thompson (SAS)
Hanghang Tong (Carnegie Mellon University)
Ramasamy Uthurusamy (GM)
Peter Van der Putten (Pegasystems & Leiden University)
Ranga Vatsavai (Oak Ridge National Labs)
Andrew Veal (Government Communications HQ, UK)
Dave Vennergrund (Delta Solutions)
Stefan Weber (Siemens AG)

ACM SIGKDD 2011 Industry Practice Expo Advisory Committee & Additional Reviewers

ACM SIGKDD KDD 2011 Sponsors & Supporters

Sponsors:

KDD.org

ACM SIGMOD

Supporters

Microsoft Research

SDSIC Software is Everywhere

Google

media6degrees

IBM

eBay Research Labs

SAIC

Yahoo! Labs

25th Anniversary Machine Learning

Morgan & Claypool Publishers

Arnetminer

Salford Systems

CRC Press Taylor & Francis Group

Cambridge University Press

Opera Solutions

StatConsulting

odysci

KNIME

NSF

Keynote Talk

Convex Optimization: From Embedded Real-Time To Large-Scale Distributed

Stephen Boyd
Electrical Engineering Department
Stanford University
Stanford, CA 94305, USA
boyd@stanford.edu

Abstract

Convex optimization has emerged as useful tool for applications that include data analysis and model fitting, resource allocation, engineering design, network design and optimization, finance, and control and signal processing. After an overview, the talk will focus on two extremes: real-time embedded convex optimization, and distributed convex optimization. Code generation can be used to generate extremely efficient and reliable solvers for small problems, that can execute in milliseconds or microseconds, and are ideal for embedding in real-time systems. At the other extreme, we describe methods for large-scale distributed optimization, which coordinate many solvers to solve enormous problems.

Categories and Subject Descriptors: G.1.6 [Numerical Analysis]: Optimization
General Terms: Theory

Bio

Stephen P. Boyd is the Samsung Professor of Engineering, and Professor of Electrical Engineering in the Information Systems Laboratory at Stanford University. He also has a courtesy appointment in the Department of Management Science and Engineering, and is member of the Institute for Computational and Mathematical Engineering. His current research focus is on convex optimization applications in control, signal processing, and circuit design.

Professor Boyd received an AB degree in Mathematics, summa cum laude, from Harvard University in 1980, and a PhD in EECS from U. C. Berkeley in 1985. He holds an honorary doctorate from Royal Institute of Technology (KTH), Stockholm. In 1985 he joined the faculty of Stanford's Electrical Engineering Department.

He is the author of many papers and three books: Linear Controller Design: Limits of Performance (with Craig Barratt, 1991), Linear Matrix Inequalities in System and Control Theory (with L. El Ghaoui, E. Feron, and V. Balakrishnan, 1994), and Convex Optimization (with Lieven Vandenberghe, 2004). His group has produced several open source tools, including CVX (with Michael Grant), a widely used parser-solver for convex optimization.

KDD'11, August 21–24, 2011, San Diego, California, USA.
ACM 978-1-4503-0813-7/11/08.

Keynote Talk

Internet Scale Data Analysis

Peter Norvig
Google
1600 Amphitheatre Parkway
Mountain View, CA 94043, USA
peter@norvig.com

Abstract

This talk covers techniques for analyzing data sets with up to trillions of examples with billions of features, using thousands of computers. To operate at this scale requires an understanding of an increasing complex hardware hierarchy (e.g. cache, memory, SSD, another machine in the rack, disk, a machine in another data center, ...); a model for recovering from inevitable hardware and software failures; a machine learning model that allows for efficient computation over large, continuously updated data sets; and a way to visualize and share the results.

Categories and Subject Descriptors: H.2.8 [Database Management]: Database Applications - *Data Mining*
General Terms: Algorithms

Bio

Peter Norvig is a Fellow of the American Association for Artificial Intelligence and the Association for Computing Machinery. At Google Inc he was Director of Search Quality, responsible for the core web search algorithms from 2002-2005, and has been Director of Research from 2005 on.

Previously he was the head of the Computational Sciences Division at NASA Ames Research Center, making him NASA's senior computer scientist. He received the NASA Exceptional Achievement Award in 2001. He has served as an assistant professor at the University of Southern California and a research faculty member at the University of California at Berkeley Computer Science Department, from which he received a Ph.D. in 1986 and the distinguished alumni award in 2006. He has over fifty publications in Computer Science, concentrating on Artificial Intelligence, Natural Language Processing and Software Engineering, including the books Artificial Intelligence: A Modern Approach (the leading textbook in the field), Paradigms of AI Programming: Case Studies in Common Lisp, Verbmobil: A Translation System for Face-to-Face Dialog, and Intelligent Help Systems for UNIX. He is also the author of the Gettysburg Powerpoint Presentation and the world's longest palindromic sentence.

KDD'11, August 21–24, 2011, San Diego, California, USA.
ACM 978-1-4503-0813-7/11/08.

Keynote Talk
Cancer Genomics

David Haussler
Center for Biomolecular Science and Engineering
University of California Santa Cruz
Santa Cruz, CA 95064, USA
haussler@soe.ucsc.edu

Abstract

Throughout life, the cells in every individual accumulate many changes in the DNA inherited from his or her parents. Certain combinations of changes lead to cancer. During the last decade, the cost of DNA sequencing has been dropping by a factor of 10 every two years, making it now possible to read most of the three billion base genome from a patient's cancer tumor, and to try to determine all of the thousands of DNA changes in it. Under the auspices of NCI's Cancer Genome Atlas Project, 10,000 tumors will be sequenced in this manner in the next two years. Soon cancer genome sequencing will be a widespread clinical practice, and millions of tumors will be sequenced. A massive computational problem looms in interpreting these data.

First, because we can only read short pieces of DNA, we have the enormous problem of assembling a coherent and reliable representation of the tumor genome from massive amounts of incomplete and error-prone evidence. This is the first challenge. Second, every human genome is unique from birth, and every tumor a unique variant. There is no single route to cancer. We must learn to read the varied signatures of cancer within the tumor genome and associate these with optimal treatments. Already there are hundreds of molecularly targeted treatments for cancer available, each known to be more or less effective depending on specific genetic variants. However, targeting a single gene with one treatment rarely works. The second challenge is to tackle the combinatorics of personalized, targeted, combination therapy in cancer.

Categories and Subject Descriptors: J.3 [Life and Medical Sciences]: Biology and Genetics
General Terms: Algorithms, Human Factors, Theory

Bio

David Haussler's research lies at the interface of mathematics, computer science, and molecular biology. He develops new statistical and algorithmic methods to explore the molecular function and evolution of the human genome, integrating cross-species comparative and high-throughput genomics data to study gene structure, function, and regulation. He is credited with pioneering the use of Hidden Markov Models (HMMs), Stochastic Context-Free Grammars, and discriminative kernel method for analyzing DNA, RNA, and protein sequences. He was the first to apply the latter methods to the genome-wide search for gene expression biomarkers in cancer, now a major effort of his laboratory.

As a collaborator on the international Human Genome Project, his team posted the first publicly available computational assembly of the human genome sequence on the internet on July 7, 2000. Following this his team developed the UCSC Genome Browser, a web-based tool that is used extensively in biomedical research and serves as the platform for several large-scale genomics projects, including NHGRI's ENCODE project to use omics methods to explore the function of every base in the human genome (for which UCSC serves as the Data Coordination Center), NIH's Mammalian Gene Collection, NHGRI's 1000 genomes project to

KDD'11, August 21–24, 2011, San Diego, California, USA.
ACM 978-1-4503-0813-7/11/08.

explore human genetic variation, and NCI's Cancer Genome Atlas project to explore the genomic changes in cancer.

His group's informatics work on cancer genomics provides a complete analysis pipeline from raw DNA reads through the detection and interpretation of mutations and altered gene expression in tumor samples. His group collaborates with researchers at medical centers nationally, including members of the Stand Up To Cancer "Dream Teams" and the Cancer Genome Atlas, to discover molecular causes of cancer and pioneer a new personalized, genomics-based approach to cancer treatment.

He co-founded the Genome 10K Project to assemble a genomic zoo - a collection of DNA sequences representing the genomes of 10,000 vertebrate species - to capture genetic diversity as a resource for the life sciences and for worldwide conservation efforts.

Haussler received his Ph.D. in computer science from the University of Colorado at Boulder. He is a member of the National Academy of Sciences and the American Academy of Arts and Sciences and a fellow of AAAS and AAAI. He has won a number of awards, including the 2009 ASHG Curt Stern Award in Human Genetics, the 2008 Senior Scientist Accomplishment Award from the International Society for Computational Biology, the 2006 Dickson Prize for Science from Carnegie Mellon University, and the 2003 ACM/AAAI Allen Newell Award in Artificial Intelligence.

Investigator, Howard Hughes Medical Institute Distinguished Professor, Biomolecular Engineering, University of California, Santa Cruz Scientific Co-Director, California Institute for Quantitative Biosciences (QB3) Director, Center for Biomolecular Science & Engineering.

Keynote Talk
The Mathematics of Causal Inference

Judea Pearl
Computer Science Department
University of California Los Angeles
Los Angeles, CA 90024, USA
judea@cs.ucla.edu

Abstract

I will review concepts, principles, and mathematical tools that were found useful in applications involving causal and counterfactual relationships. This semantical framework, enriched with a few ideas from logic and graph theory, gives rise to a complete, coherent, and friendly calculus of causation that unifies the graphical and counterfactual approaches to causation and resolves many long-standing problems in several of the sciences. These include questions of causal effect estimation, policy analysis, and the integration of data from diverse studies. Of special interest to KDD researchers would be the following topics:

1. The Mediation Formula, and what it tells us about direct and indirect effects.
2. What mathematics can tell us about "external validity" or "generalizing from experiments"
3. What can graph theory tell us about recovering from sample-selection bias.

Categories and Subject Descriptors: G.m [Mathematics of Computing]: Miscellaneous
General Terms: Theory

Bio

Judea Pearl is a professor of computer science and statistics at the University of California, Los Angeles. He is a graduate of the Technion, Israel, and has joined the faculty of UCLA in 1970, where he currently directs the Cognitive Systems Laboratory and conducts research in artificial intelligence, causal inference and philosophy of science. He has authored three books: Heuristics (1984), Probabilistic Reasoning (1988), and Causality (2000;2009). A member of the National Academy of Engineering, and a Founding Fellow the American Association for Artificial Intelligence (AAAI), Judea Pearl is the recipient of the 2008 Benjamin Franklin Medal for Computer and Cognitive Science and this year's David Rumelhart Prize from the Cognitive Science Society.

KDD'11, August 21–24, 2011, San Diego, California, USA.
ACM 978-1-4503-0813-7/11/08.

CHIRP: A New Classifier Based on Composite Hypercubes on Iterated Random Projections *

Leland Wilkinson†
Department of Computer Science
University of Illinois at Chicago
leland.wilkinson@systat.com

Anushka Anand
Department of Computer Science
University of Illinois at Chicago
aanand2@lac.uic.edu

Dang Nhon Tuan
Department of Computer Science
University of Illinois at Chicago
tdang@cs.uic.edu

ABSTRACT

We introduce a classifier based on the L^∞ norm. This classifier, called CHIRP, is an iterative sequence of three stages (projecting, binning, and covering) that are designed to deal with the curse of dimensionality, computational complexity, and nonlinear separability. CHIRP is not a hybrid or modification of existing classifiers; it employs a new covering algorithm. The accuracy of CHIRP on widely-used benchmark datasets exceeds the accuracy of competitors. Its computational complexity is sub-linear in number of instances and number of variables and subquadratic in number of classes.

Categories and Subject Descriptors

H.2.8 [**Database Applications**]: Data mining

Keywords

Supervised Classification, Random Projections

1. INTRODUCTION

Supervised classifiers face some serious obstacles. First, there is the *curse of dimensionality*: nearest neighbors in high-dimensional spaces diverge exponentially with dimension. A second problem is *computational complexity*: polynomial-time algorithms are infeasible in high-dimensional spaces. A third problem is *separability*: for some point sets in a vector space (e.g., a 2D disk surrounded by a ring) there exists no homeomorphism that will allow separation of regions using hyperplanes in the codomain.

There have been numerous approaches to overcoming these problems, such as hybrid classifiers [15, 39] or reduction of dimensionality through principal components, k-means clustering [13], or random projections [42].

*Supported by NSF/DHS grant DMS-FODAVA-0808860.

†Systat Software Inc. and Department of Computer Science, University of Illinois at Chicago

KDD'11, August 21–24, 2011, San Diego, California, USA.

Our algorithm is an integrated solution that addresses all of these problems. CHIRP is a classifier that was designed to address the curse of dimensionality and exponential complexity by using projection, binning, and covering in a sequential framework. For class-labeled points in high-dimensional space, CHIRP employs computationally-efficient methods to construct 2D projections and sets of rectangular regions on those projections that contain points from only one class. CHIRP organizes these sets of projections and regions into a decision list for scoring new data points.

CHIRP is a nonparametric, ensemble classifier that does not need to be customized for each data set, making it ideal for handling diverse data sets without prior knowledge of their structure. Its average prediction accuracy over a wide range of data sets exceeds that of competitive classifiers, especially ones that have sensitive parameters like kernel types, bandwidths, pruning criteria, etc.

CHIRP is based on a visual analytics framework [6] using what we call Composite Hypercube Description Regions (CHDRs) that can be used to define local and large-scale structures.

1.1 Composite Hypercube Description Regions (CHDRs)

While the union of open spherical balls is used to define a basis for the L^2 Euclidean metric topology, we can alternatively use balls based on other L^p metrics. For CHIRP, we employ the L^∞ or *sup* metric:

$$||x||_\infty = sup(|x_1|, |x_2|, \dots |x_n|)$$

when we search for neighbors. In this search, we are looking for all neighbors of a point at the center of a hypercube of fixed size in a vector space. Because we are concerned with finite-dimensional vector spaces in practice, we will use $max()$ instead of $sup()$ from now on.

Definition 1. A *hypercube description region* (HDR) is the set of points less than a fixed distance from a single point (called the *center*) using the L^∞ norm. A weighted hypercube description region is an HDR that uses the positively weighted L^∞ norm:

$$||x||_\infty = max(w_1|x_1|, w_2|x_2|, \dots w_n|x_n|).$$

We will assume the term HDR refers to this more general case. Our use of weights implies that different points in a high-dimensional space can have different weights defining their hypercubes.

Definition 2. A *composite hypercube description region* (CHDR) is the set of points inside the union of zero or more hypercube description regions.

The CHDR is the structure we use to define a region containing points belonging to a single class or to no class. CHDRs are defined for any number of dimensions in a finite-dimensional vector space. For scalability, we have limited them to two dimensions. The VisClassifier[6] algorithm assembled a set of 2D projections and used CHDRs to capture human visual interactions in order to classify a high-dimensional dataset. Following those promising results, we have subsequently removed humans from the loop and we grow CHDRs using an iterated covering algorithm. Figure 1 shows an example of a CHDR covering a 2D projection of the Orange10 dataset used in our tests later in this article. The CHDR represented by the blue region of the figure is a composition of rectangles extending out to the edges of the frame.

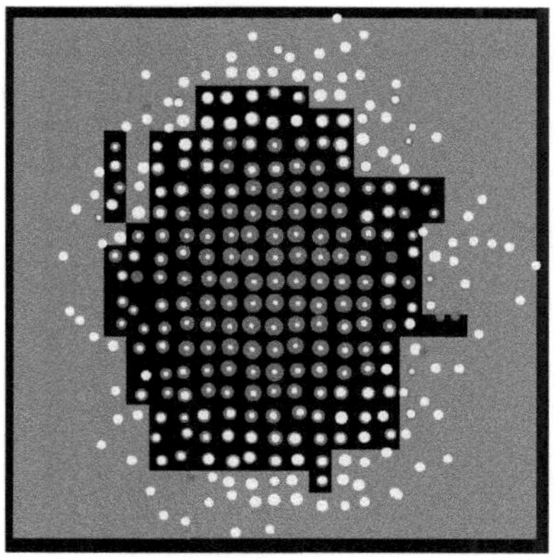

Figure 1: A CHDR covering class instances at the periphery of a projected random spherical distribution. Data are the Orange10 dataset from [19]. The data have been binned into a 24×24 grid with the size of each dot proportional to the count of instances in each bin. Yellow is used to represent the currently selected class; gray represents all other classes. All-yellow dots represent bins containing only current class instances. All-gray dots represent bins containing only other-class instances. Gray dots with yellow centers and yellow dots with gray centers represent mixed-class bins. The CHDR (a union of rectangles) is colored blue; it covers bins such that the odds of covering current class instances vs. all other instances are maximized.

1.2 CHIRP Constructs a List of CHDRs

Each CHDR constructed by CHIRP is based on a different random 2D projection. The algorithm is a one-against-all classifier [12]. For each class C_k in a training set, we (a) compute a 2D projection, (b) bin the projected data values in a 2D rectangular segmentation, and (c) cover bins containing mostly instances of C_k with a CHDR. We iterate over classes until we are unable to find bins pure enough to classify remaining instances in the training set.

The result of this process is a list of CHDRs that can be used to score new data points. A point is assigned to the first CHDR in the list that contains it. If no CHDR contains the point, it is assigned to the closest CHDR in the list using smallest point-to-rectangle L^∞ distance.

CHIRP is an ensemble classifier. We run it m times and score a testing instance based on simple-majority, equally-weighted vote. In this paper, we use $m = 7$. Increasing m improves accuracy (with diminishing gains), but at the expense of time.

Although CHIRP employs some well-known ideas, the combination of them described in this paper results in a classifier that is novel and coherent. We will first discuss related work, then present the algorithm, and finally present performance comparisons between CHIRP and competitors. We will argue, in conclusion, that the success of CHIRP is due to the statistical properties of its components and the way they are combined.

2. RELATED WORK

Perhaps the most widespread use of rectangular description regions is in recursive partitioning trees [10, 30]. These methods partition a space into nested rectangular regions that are relatively homogeneous over the values of a predicted variable. Our approach differs from these models, however, because it is not restricted to a partitioning. Our description regions need not be disjoint or exhaustive.

Several teams have developed projection-pursuit classifiers [25, 14, 21]. These efforts exploit the flexibility of affine projections but have failed to ameliorate the computational complexity of projection pursuit.

Researchers have used hyperboxes for classification through neural networks [34], mixed integer programming [41], set covering [28], and decision lists [35, 4]. These approaches can be slow to converge on larger datasets. Most importantly, the hyperbox researchers restrict their method to 2D axis-parallel (pairs of features) projections, so their utility is limited.

Finally, various researchers have used compositions of rectangles (unions and products) to characterize the results of unsupervised classification [5, 3, 11, 16, 17, 29]. The primary focus of these researchers has been to develop rapid scoring methods that can be implemented inside a database through the use of rectangles. We will discuss some of this work in more detail as we describe the CHIRP algorithm in the next sections.

3. CHIRP TRAINING

The CHIRP training algorithm consists of three stages – *projecting*, *binning*, and *covering*. We will describe these stages in detail in this section. First, however, we will summarize preliminary data processing steps similar to those employed in other classifiers.

3.1 Preliminary Processing (Transforming and Normalizing)

We begin by reading n rows and p columns of a training dataset X. We code numerical values as double precision numbers and string values as integers. We assume numerical values are derived from *continuous variables* and string values from *categorical variables*, although numerals can be treated as strings if so designated. We use the terms *feature* and *variable* interchangeably to mean a mapping of a set of objects to a set of values.

We next transform extremely skewed variables. We compute standardized skewness and kurtosis on each raw variable and sort the standardized values. We then sequentially test each element in these lists by adjusting the 99th percent critical value drawn from the standard normal distribution in order to control the false discovery rate [8]. If a standardized skewness or kurtosis value exceeds this adjusted critical value, we apply our transformation.

Our transformation is a folded square root:

$$t(x) = sgn(x)sqrt(abs(x))$$

This flexible transformation accommodates instances such as non-negative, positively-skewed data based on log-normal, Poisson, gamma, or exponential processes (counts, incomes, etc.), as well as long-tailed data from double-exponential, Cauchy, and similar distributions.

Our goal in transforming is to improve our chances of discovering class separation in relatively dense regions. This is especially important because we will use binning (a form of segmentation) to compress our data. Without transformation, highly-skewed densities might concentrate in only one or two bins. The logic behind this is similar to the rationale for using linearizing transformations in support vector machines.

After transforming, we normalize the data by rescaling each variable (feature) to the unit interval. The next three subsections describe the three stages that comprise the core of the CHIRP algorithm. We iterate these three stages cyclically over classes until we are unable to classify remaining training data. Each iteration is a one-against-all classification step involving the current class vs. other classes.

3.2 Projecting

We will be binning 2D projections of variables in the hope of locating dense and well-separated class distributions. To do this, we generate a candidate list of 1D projections, pick the best of these based on a separation measure for the current class, and pair the best to make a set of 2D projections.

Before projecting, however, we need to scale categorical variables in order to project them into the same subspace with continuous variables. To scale categorical variables, we use a strategy derived from the latent class model [24]. For a given categorical variable, we count the unclassified instances of the current class in each category. We divide this count by the total count of unclassified instances in each category. Finally, we replace integer category values with the corresponding proportions based on these two counts.

Next, we generate a set of 1D projections using three-valued vectors with elements

$$u_j \in \{-1, 0, 1\}, j = 1, \ldots, p.$$

Of the p projection weights, r are zero and the remainder are split evenly between -1 and 1.

Choosing r depends on p. When p is small ($p \leq 50$), we apply random projections with zero and nonzero weights. Otherwise, we apply random projections after constraining $p - 50$ weights to be zero. Our choice of 50 is guided by results in [20] and [27].

3.2.1 *Small* p.

If p is small, we choose $r = p/4$, $r = p/2$, or $r = 3p/4$. We decide among the three alternatives by generating three random projections (using these r values) and choosing the one with the largest value of a separation statistic S. For a projection, our separation statistic is the distance of the current-class projected mean $\bar{x}_c$ from the closest other-class projected mean $\bar{x}_k$:

$$S = \min_{k \neq c}(d_{\bar{x}_c, \bar{x}_k})$$

3.2.2 *Large* p.

If p is large, we set $p - 50$ weights to zero before doing our random projections on the remaining features the same way we do for small p. In this case, we need to determine which features are constrained to have zero weights. To decide, we compute the class-separation statistic S on each variable. We sort all features on this statistic and we constrain the $p - 50$ features with the smallest class-separation statistics to have zero weights. This process is a form of feature selection, but unlike other applications that use feature selection to pre-process large datasets, we employ it *inside* our iterations. Different features are likely to be selected on different iterations because class means change as points are removed from the training set.

Unit-weighting our projections is a form of regularization [19, 38]. Regularized estimators increase bias in order to reduce prediction error. We discuss this aspect further in the Appendix.

3.3 Binning

The next step in the process is to pair our best 1D projections and bin currently unclassified instances into a bin matrix for each pair. We base the number of bins for each 2D projection on a formula in [37]. Given n instances, we compute the marginal number of bins b using

$$b = 2\ log_2(n)$$

This formula produces a few more bins than optimal statistical estimates for binning normal and mildly skewed distributions [32, 44]. Traditional methods assume a homogeneous distribution, however, which is clearly not the case in classification.

Next, we rank our $b \times b$ 2D bin matrices on a purity measure. For a given target class C_k, our purity measure is

$$P_k = \sum_{i=1}^{b}\sum_{j=1}^{b} n_{i,j} I_{i,j}(C_k)$$

where

$$I_{i,j}(C_k) = \begin{cases} 1 & n_{i,j} = n_{i,j,k} \\ 0 & otherwise \end{cases}$$

In other words, we sum the counts across all bins whose total counts of points falling in them ($n_{i,j}$) are due only to class C_k counts ($n_{i,j,k}$). We want our purity measure to count only pure bins, because our fitting method will be especially greedy. The more pure bins we can eliminate early in the process, the better chance we have of seeing well-separated other classes later.

To recapitulate our current status: we have generated a small number of 1D random projections sorted on our separation measure S and we have paired them to make a set of 2D projections. We then have chosen the best of these 2D projections based on our bin purity measure P. We are now working with the upper tail of the extreme-value distribution of binned, unit-weighted random projections ordered on a bin purity measure. We now will cover these binned

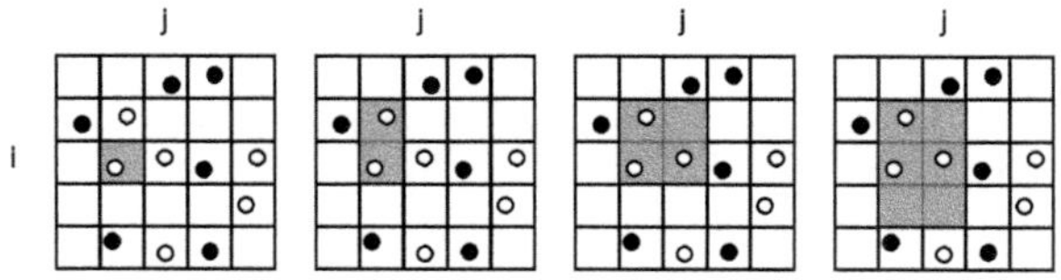

Figure 2: Growing a Hypercube Description Region (HDR) on a binned 2D projection. Each point is located at the centroid of the instances in each cell. Hollow symbols represent bins containing only instances of the current class. Solid symbols represent bins containing at least one instance of another class.

projections with rectangles and pick the cover that most improves our training-set classification.

3.4 Covering

The last stage in each iteration involves covering pure bins in order to define a classification region for a given class C_k. Our cover is a CHDR, which is a list of HDRs. Each CHDR is uniquely associated with a class label.

3.4.1 Growing a CHDR

We grow a CHDR on a given 2D bin matrix with a recursive algorithm. Figure 2 shows how this process works. For a given pure bin element $b_{i,j}$, we grow an HDR covering the bin and its pure neighbors by expanding upward ($b_{.,j+1}$), rightward ($b_{i+1,.}$), downward ($b_{.,j-1}$), and leftward ($b_{i-1,.}$) in a spiral path. In other words, we sequentially expand each side of the current rectangle by one bin-row or bin-column whose length is equal to the length of that side. We cease expanding in any of the four directions when the odds ratio of current-class vs. other-class instances inside the covering rectangle begins to decrease. This strategy tends to result in squarish rectangles that cover pure or empty bins, similar to an approach in [3].

We grow an HDR for each of the bins in the 2D bin matrix. For each HDR we record the number of instances of the current class that we have covered. We pick the HDR that results in the largest current-class count. Finally, if the current-class count in the HDR exceeds 10, we add the HDR to the current CHDR list for that 2D projection. This 10 is not a magic number. It is based on a rule-of-thumb for a slippage test [40].

Once we compute an HDR, we mark bins that it covers. Then we iterate this procedure over the 2D bin matrix starting with uncovered bins until we can find no HDRs that meet Tukey's criterion. The resulting set of HDRs is a CHDR for a 2D bin matrix.

3.5 Iterating

We iterate through classes in cyclical order. For each iteration, we pick a new target class and repeat our three stages (*projecting, binning, covering*). This means recalculating all the statistics within these stages. Fortunately, these are one-pass calculations, so the iterations are fairly rapid. We terminate iterations when no CHDR can be constructed according to our rules.

4. CHIRP SCORING

To score a new instance, we transform and rescale a new point. Then we pass through the list of CHDRs. For each CHDR, we project the point using the stored projections from the training data. Then we pass through the list of rectangles for that CHDR. The first rectangle to enclose our projected testing point determines the classification.

If no enclosing rectangle is encountered by the end of the list, we assign the point to the nearest rectangle in the CHDR list. This computation involves finding the shortest L^∞ distance between a point and a rectangle. Because the perimeter of a CHDR is a zero level set for a naive density estimator based on the union of rectangular polygons [33], this point-to-rectangle distance is asymptotically a nearest-neighbor statistic.

This scoring algorithm is based on a decision list [31]. Unlike trees, decision lists do not require traversal of the entire depth in order to score new instances (unless, of course, a cover is not encountered).

5. PERFORMANCE

In this section we will discuss two different aspects of CHIRP performance: accuracy and efficiency. We conducted an experiment to evaluate CHIRP against a comprehensive set of competitive classifiers. We first summarize the experimental design and then present results for accuracy and efficiency.

5.1 Datasets

We tested CHIRP and other classifiers on 20 datasets from the UCI Machine Learning Repository [7], [19], and other sources. Table 1 summarizes prominent aspects of these datasets.

5.2 Challenges

There are three reasonable questions for proponents of particular classifiers who conduct evaluation experiments: 1) Have they "cherry-picked" their datasets to make their classifiers look effective? 2) Have they included a sufficient number of datasets to provide reasonable statistical power for their conclusions? and 3) Have they tested their classifiers against a sufficient number of competitors to insure their claims are generalizable?

In response to the first question, we selected these particular datasets for their structural variety; each represents a different challenge for classifiers. We tried not to bias the results by picking two or more datasets with a similar structure. These datasets include examples of missing values (Horse), mixed categorical and continuous variables (Adult), mixed binary variables (Cover), small n (number of instances), large n, small p (number of variables), large p, ($n \ll p$) (Cancer), small g (number of groups), large g, relatively small training set (Poker, Segment) and disparate within-and-between-groups data densities (discrete, continuous, mixed, convex, non-convex (Orange10). Almost all the test datasets are real, and each has been widely tested on numerous classifiers.

In response to the second question, we included 20 datasets. This number enabled relatively narrow confidence intervals on our error results. The median width of our confidence intervals for standardized errors was .6. We should mention, in addition, that the distributions of the standardized errors within classifiers are relatively symmetrical, so our use of the t-distribution to construct confidence intervals is justified..

In response to the third question, we added CHIRP to

Table 1: Characteristics of Datasets

	Training	Testing	Attributes	Groups	Categorical Vars	Continuous Vars
Abalone	2,088	2,089	8	3	No	Yes
Adult	32,561	16,281	14	2	Yes	Yes
Cancer	144	54	16,063	14	No	Yes
Cover	11,340	569,672	54	7	Yes	Yes
Credit	345	345	14	2	No	Yes
Horse	300	68	22	2	Yes	Yes
Madelon	2,000	600	500	2	No	Yes
Optdigits	3,823	1,797	64	10	Yes	Yes
Orange10	5,000	50,000	10	2	No	Yes
Page Blocks	4,000	1,473	10	5	No	No
Pendigits	7,494	3,498	16	10	No	Yes
Poker	25,010	1,000,000	10	10	No	Yes
Satellite	4,435	2,000	36	6	No	Yes
Segment	210	2,100	19	7	No	Yes
Shuttle	43,500	14,500	9	7	No	Yes
Spect	80	187	22	2	Yes	No
Swiss Roll	1,000	1,000	3	2	No	Yes
Vehicle	679	167	18	4	No	Yes
Vowel	528	462	10	11	No	Yes
Waveform	300	500	21	3	No	Yes

the Weka data mining workbench [45]. Then we tested every classifier in Weka Version 3.6.1, omitting classifiers that could not deal with all 20 datasets (because they were specialized or were not scalable to the larger datasets). This left a total of 50 classifiers. We included hybrid and meta classifiers as well, even though these are not direct competitors because they do not rest on a single geometric model. Tests were run on a 2.5 GHz Intel Core 2 Duo Macintosh Powerbook with Macintosh OS X Version 10.5.7 and Java Version 1.5.0 running in a 2GB partition. The full experiment took almost three weeks of continuous CPU time. To the best of our knowledge, this is one of the most comprehensive experimental evaluations of classifiers since the Statlog Project [23, 36, 1]. We also examined published error rates for non-Weka classifiers on these datasets and found almost all of them to lie in the range of our findings (except for specialized classifiers such as [26], which can perform extraordinarily well on specific types of datasets).

5.3 Accuracy

We computed a variance components analysis on the error rates for every classifier across datasets. Dataset and Classifier were treated as random factors. The effects of both factors were highly significant ($p < .001$). Consequently, we standardized the error statistics within dataset for our final analysis.

Figure 3 summarizes the error performance for all classifiers. (Tables of these data are available on the senior author's website.) CHIRP has the lowest standardized error of all classifiers and a relatively small variance. CHIRP is not only extraordinarily accurate but also unusually consistent across a wide range of data scenarios.

Figure 4 shows the performance of all the classifiers on these datasets. CHIRP is highlighted in red. No other family of classifiers (SVMs, Trees, ...) had the lowest or near-lowest error on as many datasets as did CHIRP.

5.4 Efficiency

CHIRP makes one pass through n rows of the training data to compute data limits and basic statistics. For each of the g classes, it makes an additional pass through the data to construct 25 2D bin matrices. CHIRP sorts this bin-matrix list and picks the top 5 candidate 2D bin matrices. It iterates through this process t times, adding a CHDR to the decision list at each step. Thus, we should expect

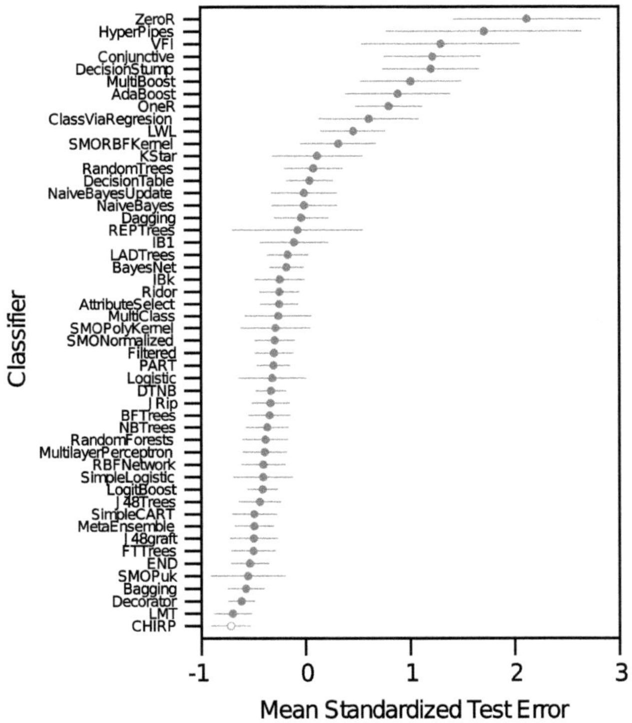

Figure 3: Average standardized error rates and associated 95% confidence intervals for CHIRP and Weka Version 3.6.1 classifiers. Default parameter values were used for all classifiers.

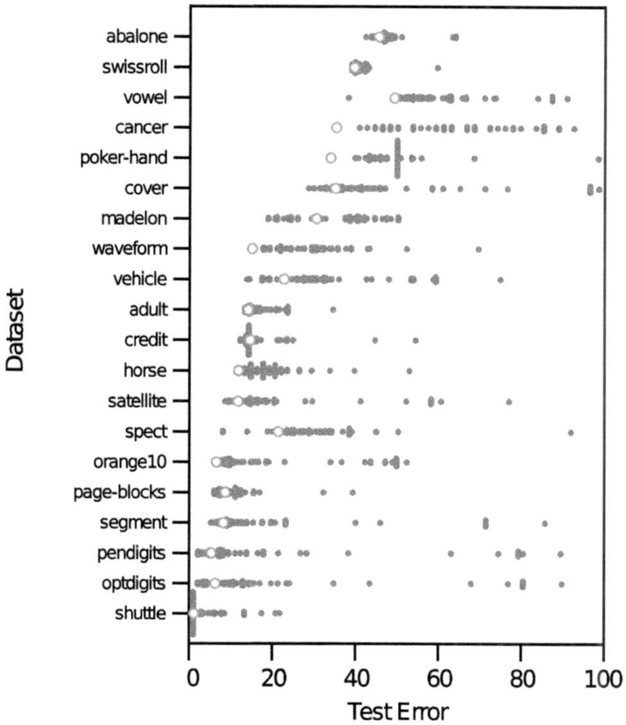

Figure 4: Errors for CHIRP (in red) and the other classifiers (in blue) on 20 test datasets.

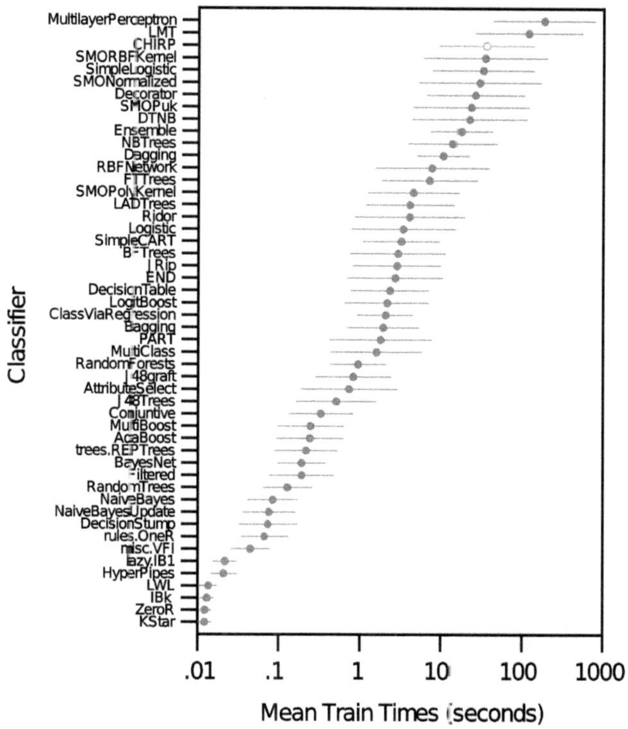

Figure 5: Mean training times and associated 95% confidence intervals for CHIRP and Weka Version 3.6.1 classifiers.

CHIRP to be $O(npgt)$ in time. To test this expectation, we did a simulation.

We generated Gaussians for $n = \{500, 5000, 50000\}$ and $p = \{20, 40, 60, 80, 100\}$, and $g = \{2, 4, 6, 8, 10\}$. In each of the 75 datasets, the first g Gaussians had unit variance with centroids located at the corners of a $(g-1)$-simplex with edges of length 7. Values for the remaining $p - g$ variates were $N(\mathbf{0}, \mathbf{I})$. We ran CHIRP once on each dataset.

The times are fit well ($R = .962$, with well-behaved residuals) with the simple linearized model:

$$E[\log(t)] = -10.34 + 0.94\log(n) + 1.66\log(g) + 0.68\log(p)$$

Our empirical results indicate that CHIRP is sublinear in n and p and subquadratic in g.

Figure 5 shows the training times for CHIRP and the other classifiers. Not surprisingly, some of the worst performing classifiers in Figure 3 are the fastest to train. The converse is not always true, however. The Multilayer Perceptron classifier was the least efficient to train, yet its performance was in the middle of the pack. CHIRP's closest rival in performance, Logistic Model Trees, was significantly slower in training.

CHIRP is slower to train than many of the other classifiers in part because it is an ensemble classifier. In a parallel computing environment, each thread would run concurrently, so this would not be an issue. The longest training time (rules-DTNB on Madelon) was 38 hours. The longest training time for CHIRP was 2.6 hours on Poker Hand. The longest time for an SVM was 15 hours (SMOPuk on Adult).

Figure 6 shows the testing times per instance for CHIRP and the other classifiers. In contrast to its training performance, CHIRP falls in the fastest group of classifiers, with performance that is not significantly worse than decision trees (although its standard error is larger). Interestingly, the support vector machines are generally the slowest in testing; the SVM with the lowest overall error (SMOPuk) is among the slowest performers in a testing environment.

Again, scoring could be speeded up for CHIRP by parallelizing the voting. The longest scoring time for an instance was 4 minutes (lazyKStar on Satellite). The longest scoring time for CHIRP was 2 seconds (on Satellite). The longest scoring time for an SVM was 22 seconds (SMOPuk on Satellite). These longer times are problematic, because scoring times of more than a few seconds would be impractical for online applications. By contrast, CHIRP is a good candidate for online classification in a time-critical environment.

6. DISCUSSION

Our experiment provides clear evidence that CHIRP outperforms competitive classifiers across a wide range of datasets. We intend to pursue the question of why this is true in further research, although we designed each stage using well-established findings from the statistical and machine-learning literature. What is unique about CHIRP is how these components are assembled. We need to investigate theoretically how these components interact. We also need to investigate whether extending projections to 3D can improve performance without sacrificing scalability.

We do have several preliminary answers to the question of why CHIRP works so well, however. First, CHIRP handles nonconvex, discrete and disjoint densities by covering instead of partitioning. We suspect (but have not yet proven) that covering requires fewer rectangles than partitioning in

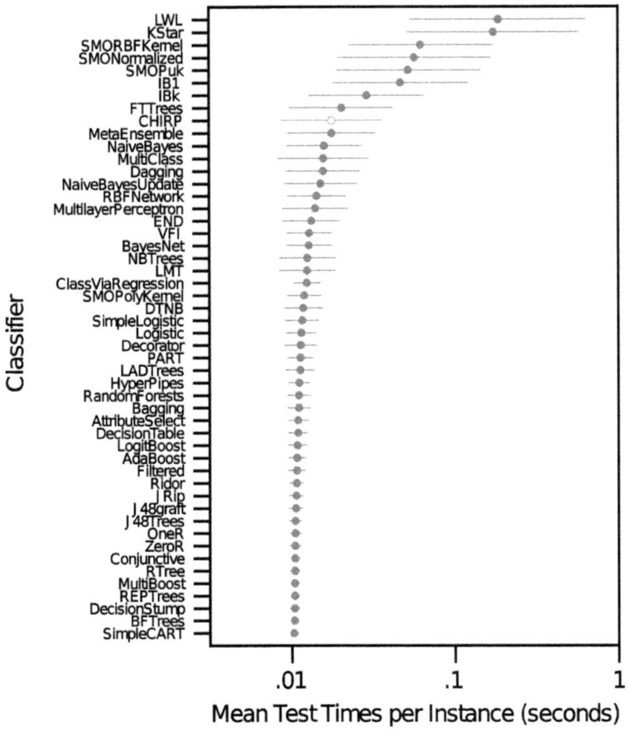

Figure 6: Mean testing times per instance and associated 95% confidence intervals for CHIRP and Weka Version 3.6.1 classifiers.

the case of certain topologies (such as the Orange10 or Waveform datasets). Second, its categorical scaling algorithm allows us to combine discrete and continuous densities to search for homogeneous joint regions. Third, CHIRP is an ensemble classifier. Its use of random projections naturally lends itself to a voting architecture. Fourth, CHIRP uses affine instead of axis-parallel projections; other set-covering classifiers do not employ this technique. Fifth, its two fitness measures used for ranking projections (the class separation measure S and the bin purity measure P) target different aspects of densities. The S measure values projections with large margins; the P measure values projections with compact subsets. "Good" projections missed by one are likely to be found by the other. Finally, CHIRP embeds its projections and covers *inside* its iterations; we have, for the first time, used projections and covers recursively. This architecture contributes to the ability of CHIRP to peel away sets of exterior points that obscure other sets in the core of a density. This peeling is adaptive; CHIRP responds to the topology of the conditional density as it shrinks in size and changes shape on each iteration.

CHIRP can have difficulty with certain higher-dimensional densities as its covers are confined to 2D projections. Its ability to peel off subsections of higher-dimensional densities mitigates against this weakness, but there are some configurations it cannot exploit. Like all classifiers, CHIRP cannot outperform everyone on every dataset. Our future direction is to leverage the 2D aspect that motivated this approach to develop a new visualization to explore the "interesting" separating projections used by the classifier. With the strength and flexibility of CHIRP experimentally shown here, we can now use its framework to get a visual understanding of the class-separating relationships in the data and the inner workings of the classifier.

7. CONCLUSION

CHIRP is a relatively efficient classifier with average accuracy superior to other classifiers commonly associated with good performance on benchmark datasets. Its virtues are:

- Categorical variables expend only one degree-of-freedom. We scale categorical variables on each iteration, so there is no dummy-coding to inflate dimensionality.
- The performance is linear in complexity on n or p. It is subquadratic on g (the number of classes), but solution times are practical for up to a hundred classes.
- CHIRP does not depend on sensitive adjustable parameters (convergence criteria, kernel types, bandwidths, pruning schedules, etc.). We tested this assertion by assessing its performance over a wide range of parameter settings. Most importantly, none of the potentially settable CHIRP parameters was adjusted to optimize performance on a specific dataset in our training or testing.
- CHIRP had the lowest average standardized testing error rate and achieved the lowest error rate on more datasets than did any other classifier. Clearly, these datasets were not selected to favor CHIRP; we included well-known datasets designed to present classifiers with the broadest variety of challenges.
- CHIRP is readily parallelizable at the random projection stage and/or voting stage.
- CHIRP is tiny. Its JAR file is under 50K in size. The algorithm iterates over three simple steps.
- CHIRP is a novel algorithm; it is not a hybrid classifier. This fact would tend to support the idea that CHIRP can contribute relatively independent classification information to the results of other classifiers.

Given these distinctive features and its fundamental differences from other classifiers, CHIRP is uniquely suited for applications where there is limited *a priori* knowledge of the structure of the dataset.

8. REFERENCES

[1] M. R. Abdullah, K.-A. Toh, and D. Srinivasan. A framework for empirical classifiers comparison. In *Industrial Electronics and Applications*. IEEE, 2006.

[2] D. Achlioptas. Database-friendly random projections. In *PODS '01: Proceedings of the twentieth ACM SIGMOD-SIGACT-SIGART symposium on Principles of database systems*, pages 274–281, New York, 2001. ACM.

[3] R. Agrawal, J. Gehrke, D. Gunopulos, and P. Raghavan. Automatic subspace clustering of high dimensional data for data mining applications. In *Proceedings of the 1998 ACM SIGMOD*, pages 94–105, 1998.

[4] J. Aguilar, J. Riquelme, and M. Toro. Decision queue classifier for supervised learning using rotated hyperboxes. In *Proceedings of the 6th Ibero-American Conference on AI: Progress in Artificial Intelligence*, volume 4045 of *Lecture Notes in Computer Science*, pages 326–336. Springer, 1998.

[5] B. Alpern and L. Carter. The hyperbox. In *Proceedings of the IEEE Information Visualization 1991*, pages 133–134, 1991.

[6] A. Anand, L. Wilkinson, and D. N. Tuan. An L-infinity norm visual classifier. In *ICDM*, pages 687–692, 2009.

[7] A. Asuncion and D. Newman. UCI machine learning repository. `http://www.ics.uci.edu/~mlearn/MLRepository.html`, 2007.

[8] Y. Benjamini and Y. Hochberg. Controlling the false discovery rate: A practical and powerful approach to multiple testing. *Journal of the Royal Statistical Society, Series* B, 57:289–300, 1995.

[9] P. Bickel and E. Levina. Some theory for Fisher's linear discriminant function, 'naive Bayes', and some alternatives when there are many more variables than observations. *Bernoulli*, 10:989–1010, 2004.

[10] L. Breiman, J. Friedman, R. Olshen, and C. Stone. *Classification and Regression Trees.* Wadsworth, Belmont, CA, 1984.

[11] S. Bu, L. V. S. Lakshmanan, and R. T. Ng. MDL summarization with holes. In *VLDB '05: Proceedings of the 31st international conference on Very large data bases*, pages 433–444. VLDB Endowment, 2005.

[12] T. G. Dietterich and G. Bakiri. Solving multiclass learning problems via error-correcting output codes. *Journal of AI Research*, 2:263–286, 1995.

[13] C. Ding and X. He. K-means clustering via principal component analysis. In *ICML '04*, page 29, New York, NY, USA, 2004. ACM.

[14] T. E. Flick, L. K. Jones, R. G. Priest, and C. Herman. Pattern classification using projection pursuit. *Pattern Recognition*, 23:1367–1376, 1990.

[15] Y. Freund and R. E. Schapire. A decision-theoretic generalization of on-line learning and an application to boosting. In *EuroCOLT '95*, pages 23–37, London, UK, 1995. Springer-Verlag.

[16] B. Gao. *Hyper-rectangle-based discriminative data generalization and applications in data.* PhD thesis, Simon Fraser University, 2002.

[17] B. J. Gao and M. Ester. Turning clusters into patterns: Rectangle-based discriminative data description. In *ICDM '06: Proceedings of the Sixth International Conference on Data Mining*, pages 200–211, Washington, DC, USA, 2006. IEEE Computer Society.

[18] Y. Guo, T. Hastie, and R. Tibshirani. Regularized discriminant analysis and its application in microarrays. *Biostatistics*, 1:1–18, 2005.

[19] T. Hastie, R. Tibshirani, and J. H. Friedman. *The Elements of Statistical Learning: Data Mining, Inference, and Prediction.* Springer, New York, 2001.

[20] C. Hegde and R. Baraniuk. Random projections for manifold learning. In *NIPS 2007: Proceedings of the 2007 conference on Advances in neural information processing systems*, Cambridge, MA, USA, 2007. MIT Press.

[21] L. O. Jimenez and D. A. Landgrebe. Projection pursuit for high dimensional feature reduction: paralleland sequential approaches. In *Geoscience and Remote Sensing Symposium, 1995. IGARSS '95*, volume 1, pages 148–150, 1995.

[22] W. B. Johnson and J. Lindenstrauss. Lipschitz mapping into Hilbert space. *Contemporary Mathematics*, 26:189–206, 1984.

[23] R. King, C. Feng, and A. Sutherland. Statlog: comparison of classification algorithms on large real-world problems. *Applied Artificial Intelligence*, 9, 1995.

[24] P. F. Lazarsfeld and N. Henry. *Latent Structure Analysis.* Houghton Mifflin, Boston, 1968.

[25] E.-K. Lee, D. Cook, S. Klinke, and T. Lumley. Projection pursuit for exploratory supervised classification. *Journal of Computational and Graphical Statistics*, 14:831–846, 2005.

[26] P. Li. Robust LogitBoost and Adaptive Base Class (ABC) LogitBoost. In *UAI 2010 Proceedings.* IEEE, 2010.

[27] P. Li, T. J. Hastie, and K. W. Church. Very sparse random projections. In *KDD '06: Proceedings of the 12th ACM SIGKDD International Conference on Knowledge Discovery and Data Mining*, pages 287–296, New York, NY, USA, 2006. ACM.

[28] M. Marchand and J. Shawe-Taylor. The set covering machine. *Journal of Machine Learning Research*, 3:723–746, 2002.

[29] K. Q. Pu and A. O. Mendelzon. Concise descriptions of subsets of structured sets. *ACM Transactions on Database Systems*, 30(1):211–248, 2005.

[30] J. R. Quinlan. *C4.5: Programs for Machine Learning (Morgan Kaufmann Series in Machine Learning).* Morgan Kaufmann, 1993.

[31] R. L. Rivest. Learning decision lists. *Machine Learning*, 2:229–246, 1987.

[32] D. W. Scott. On optimal and data-based histograms. *Biometrika*, 66:605–610, 1979.

[33] B. Silverman. *Density Estimation for Statistics and Data Analysis.* Chapman & Hall, New York, 1986.

[34] P. K. Simpson. Fuzzy min-max neural network, i: Classification. *IEEE Transactions on Neural Networks*, 3:776–786, 1992.

[35] M. Sokolova, N. Japkowicz, M. Marchand, and J. Shawe-taylor. The decision list machine. In *Advances in Neural Information Processing Systems 15*, pages 921–928. MIT Press, 2003.

[36] A. Statnikov, C. F. Aliferis, I. Tsamardinos, D. Hardin, and S. Levy. A comprehensive evaluation of multicategory classification methods for microarray gene expression cancer diagnosis. *Bioinformatics*, 21(5):631–643, 2005.

[37] H. A. Sturges. The choice of a class interval. *Journal of the American Statistical Association* 21:65–66, 1926.

[38] R. Tibshirani. Regression shrinkage and selection via the lasso. *Journal of the Royal Statistical Society, Series* B, 58:267–288, 1995.

[39] R. Tibshirani and T. Hastie. Margin trees for high-dimensional classification. *Journal of Machine Learning Research*, 8:637–652, 2007.

[40] J. Tukey. A quick, compact, two-sample test to Duckworth's specifications. *Technometrics*, pages 31–48, 1959.

[41] F. Üney and M. Türkay. A mixed-integer programming approach to multi-class data classification problem. *European Journal of Operational Research*, 173:910–920, 2006.

[42] S. S. Vempala. *The Random Projection Method.* American Mathematical Society, Providence, RI, USA, 2004.

[43] H. Wainer. Estimating coefficients in linear models: It don't make no nevermind. *Psychological Bulletin*, 83(2):213–217, 1976.

[44] M. P. Wand. Data-based choice of histogram bin width. *The American Statistician*, 51(1):59–64, 1997.

[45] I. H. Witten, E. Frank, L. Trigg, M. Hall, G. Holmes, and S. J. Cunningham. Weka: Practical machine learning tools and techniques with Java implementations. In *Proceedings of the ICONIP/ANZIIS/ANNES'99 Workshop on Emerging Knowledge Engineering and Connectionist-Based Information Systems*, pages 192–196, 1999.

APPENDIX

Suppose there are two normal populations with respective $p \times 1$ mean vectors $\boldsymbol{\mu_1}$ and $\boldsymbol{\mu_2}$ and common $p \times p$ covariance matrix $\boldsymbol{\Sigma}$. Without loss of generality, we will assume that $\boldsymbol{\mu_1} = -\boldsymbol{\mu_2}$. The two-group Linear Discriminant Analysis (LDA) classification algorithm assigns a new point $\mathbf{x}$ to the group with the smaller Mahalanobis distance

$$(\mathbf{x} - \boldsymbol{\mu}_i)^T \boldsymbol{\Sigma}^{-1} (\mathbf{x} - \boldsymbol{\mu}_i), i = 1, \dots, 2$$

Equivalently, if the Fisher linear discriminant function

$$\delta_F(\mathbf{x}) = \boldsymbol{\Sigma}^{-1} (\boldsymbol{\mu_1} - \boldsymbol{\mu_2})^T \mathbf{x}$$

is negative, we assign $\mathbf{x}$ to the first group, otherwise to the second.

Because we do not usually know $\boldsymbol{\mu_1}$ or $\boldsymbol{\mu_2}$ or $\boldsymbol{\Sigma}$, we customarily estimate them via maximum likelihood on n observations of sample data and employ the discriminant function

$$d_F(\mathbf{x}) = \widehat{\boldsymbol{\Sigma}}^{-1} (\hat{\boldsymbol{\mu}}_1 - \hat{\boldsymbol{\mu}}_2)^T \mathbf{x}$$

for our classification rule.

When $p > n$, the maximum likelihood estimate of $\boldsymbol{\Sigma}$ cannot be computed because the conventional matrix estimator is singular. Classical remedies for computing the linear discriminant function in these cases include using a Moore-Penrose inverse or selecting a subset of the p variables (features) to get our estimate.

Alternatively, we can assume $\boldsymbol{\Sigma} = \sigma^2 \mathbf{I}$. In this case, the estimated discriminant function passes through $\hat{\boldsymbol{\mu}}_1$ and $\hat{\boldsymbol{\mu}}_2$ and the decision rule based on the linear discriminant function is equivalent to a Naive Bayes rule. Bickel and Levina [9] prove that the Naive Bayes classification rule substantially outperforms the Fisher linear discriminant rule under broad conditions when the number of variables grows faster than the number of observations. This gives us some confidence that we do not substantially increase prediction error by ignoring covariance structure when searching for maximum separation of means in higher-dimensional spaces.

Suppose we now replace the discriminant function coefficients with unit weights

$$d_U(\mathbf{x}) = \mathbf{u}^T \mathbf{x},$$

where $u_i \in \{-1, 0, 1\}$. Suppose also that we choose unit weights that produce the greatest spread between sample means on the $d_U(\mathbf{x})$ discriminant function. The number of possible weights we must consider before making this choice is $\frac{1}{2}(3^p - 1)$. (The $\frac{1}{2}$ is due to the symmetry of $d_U(\mathbf{x})$ around zero).

The following lemma gives us the upper bound of the angle between the optimal unit-weight vector $d_U(\mathbf{x})$ and the Fisher discriminant vector $d_F(\mathbf{x})$.

LEMMA 1. *Let U be the set of all non-null $p \times 1$ vectors $\mathbf{u}$, where $u_i \in \{-1, 0, 1\}$. Let $\mathbf{x}$ be a $p \times 1$ vector in $\boldsymbol{R}^p$. Let $\mathbf{u_x}$ be the element of U that is closest in angle to $\mathbf{x}$. Then for any $\mathbf{x}$, the maximum possible angle between $\mathbf{u_x}$ and $\mathbf{x}$ is*

$$\theta_{max} = \arccos\left(1 / \sqrt{p^2 - 2\sum_{m=1}^{p} \sqrt{m}\sqrt{m-1}}\right)$$

For $p = 50$, for example, using $d_U(\mathbf{x})$ instead of $d_F(\mathbf{x})$ will shrink the values of $\hat{\boldsymbol{\mu}}_1$ and $\hat{\boldsymbol{\mu}}_2$ projected on $d_F(\mathbf{x})$ toward zero by a factor of approximately .3. The gains from this type of shrinkage are discussed in [43, 19, 38, 18] and elsewhere. It belongs to a class of regularization methods that, relative to maximum likelihood estimators like $d_F(\mathbf{x})$, are more resistant to outliers and have lower prediction error in new samples.

In practice, we cannot expect to find the projection $d_U(\mathbf{x})$ with the greatest separation of means because it is impractical to search over $\frac{1}{2}(3^p - 1)$ weight vectors for large p. We can get close, however, by taking advantage of the Johnson-Lindenstrauss Theorem [22]. This theorem states that if a metric on X results from an embedding of X into a Euclidean space, then X can be embedded in R^k with distortion less than $1 + \epsilon$, where $k = O(\epsilon^2 log|X|)$. Remarkably, this embedding is achieved by projecting onto a random k-dimensional subspace. Because our discriminant rule depends on a similarity transformation of Euclidean distances, we can logarithmically reduce the complexity of the problem through random projections.

Johnson-Lindenstrauss was originally proven for Gaussian weights, but Achlioptas [2] showed that unit-weighted projections do not jeopardize accuracy in approximating distances. Furthermore, Hastie et al. [27] showed that unit random weights for most purposes can be made very sparse with the following probabilities:

$$u_j = \begin{cases} 1 & \text{with probability} \quad \frac{1}{2\sqrt{p}} \\ 0 & \text{with probability} \quad 1 - \frac{1}{\sqrt{p}} \\ -1 & \text{with probability} \quad \frac{1}{2\sqrt{p}} \end{cases}$$

In sum, we get lower prediction-error, robustness, scalability, and better approximation to the maximum-separation vector by using random unit weights in CHIRP. Furthermore, by constructing 2D projections from these random 1D projections and using (possibly) non-convex set covers on them, we substantially outperform LDA and other classifiers when the normality assumption is not plausible.

Supervised Learning for Provenance-Similarity of Binaries

Sagar Chaki, Cory Cohen, and Arie Gurfinkel
Carnegie Mellon Software Engineering Institute
4500 Fifth Avenue, Pittsburgh, PA, USA
{chaki,cfc,arie}@sei.cmu.edu

ABSTRACT

Understanding, measuring, and leveraging the similarity of binaries (executable code) is a foundational challenge in software engineering. We present a notion of similarity based on provenance – two binaries are similar if they are compiled from the same (or very similar) source code with the same (or similar) compilers. Empirical evidence suggests that provenance-similarity accounts for a significant portion of variation in existing binaries, particularly in malware. We propose and evaluate the applicability of classification to detect provenance-similarity. We evaluate a variety of classifiers, and different types of attributes and similarity labeling schemes, on two benchmarks derived from open-source software and malware respectively. We present encouraging results indicating that classification is a viable approach for automated provenance-similarity detection, and as an aid for malware analysts in particular.

Categories and Subject Descriptors

D.2.7 [**Software Engineering**]: Distribution, Maintenance, and Enhancement—*Restructuring, reverse engineering, and reengineering*

General Terms

Algorithms, Measurement, Security

Keywords

Binary Similarity, Classification, Software Provenance

1. INTRODUCTION

Binary similarity is an important area of software engineering research. Techniques for checking binary similarity find applications in areas ranging from code clone detection [18] and software birthmarking [7], to malware analysis [20] and software virology [12]. Several notions of similarity have been proposed and studied in the literature. Our focus is the similarity, which we call *provenance-similarity*, that arises from the fact that many binaries are the result of compiling "similar" source code with "similar" compilers. The term provenance indicates that the similarity originates not only from the source of the binaries, but also from the (compilation) process by which they were derived.

The major application area for provenance-similarity is malware analysis and virology. Empirical evidence [20] suggests that the vast majority of existing malware belong to a relatively small number of "families" of related instances. For example, a 2006 Microsoft report [3] states that *over 97,000* malware variants were detected in the first six months of 2006. At the same time, according to Symantec [19] and Microsoft [3], the typical number of malware families encountered in any six month period is a *few hundred*. In fact, the Microsoft report (see Figure 1 of [20]) further indicates that the 7 and 25 most common families account for over 50% and 75%, respectively, of detected malware instances.

There are several reasons to believe that many malware families consist of provenance-similar instances. Similarity in source code stems from two factors. First, malware authors reuse old programs – it is very unlikely that the 1,131,335 (presumed) malicious executables with unique MD5 checksums collected by CERT in the final quarter of 2010 were all written from scratch in 92 days. Second, many malware families – such as Aliser [1] – generate new instances by changing a data element (e.g., an encryption key, etc.), but not other parts of the source code. In addition, similarity in generative compilers arises because a small number of related compilers are used to produce the vast majority of malware. For example, we scanned a collection of malware available within CMU CERT and found that of all the malware whose generative compilers are known with reasonable certainty, about 60% were compiled with Microsoft Visual C++, about 25% with Delphi, and most of the rest with Microsoft Visual Basic. Such limited variability in compiler and source code suggests that provenance-similarity is a pervasive feature in malware.

Current approaches to checking provenance-similarity of binaries are largely manual (e.g., forensic analysis done by a malware analyst). While good tools are available for binary disassembly and visualization (e.g., IDAPro [14]), most of the technical analysis is still manual, and, therefore, non-scalable. Automated analysis tools, when available, are either not robust (i.e., they have high false positive and false negative rates) or inefficient. Therefore, developing an automated, robust, and efficient approach for checking provenance-similarity is an important and open problem. Addressing this problem is the subject of our paper.

We begin with a definition of provenance-similarity.

KDD'11, August 21–24, 2011, San Diego, California, USA.

Provenance-similarity between two binaries implies similarity in not only the source code from which they were derived, but also in the compilers used to generate them. We define two binaries B_1 and B_2 to be *provenance-similar* if: (i) B_1 and B_2 have been compiled from the same (or very similar) source code; and (ii) B_1 and B_2 have been generated by closely related compilers (or the same compilers with different compilation flags).

Note that our definition excludes the situations where the source code of B_1 and B_2 are very different, such as when B_1 is derived from B_2 via a major patch, or when B_1 and B_2 are radically different implementations of the same functionality, e.g., merge-sort and bubble-sort. We also exclude cases where the compilers involved are very different (e.g., Visual C++ versus GCC). These problems are beyond the scope of this paper.

To understand the challenges in detecting provenance-similarity, consider Microsoft Visual C++. As a security feature to guard against buffer-overflow attacks, the compiler is able to generate extra code that checks for stack integrity at runtime, and aborts if an integrity violation is detected. However, the exact code generated depends on the compiler context, which includes factors such as the compilation flags used (e.g., `/GS` to enable the security feature), the version of the compiler, calling conventions, etc. Consider two binaries, B_1 and B_2, generated from the same source code by Microsoft Visual C++ under different contexts, and therefore containing different code for runtime buffer-overflow checks. A typical problem is to detect the provenance-similarity of B_1 and B_2 in a robust and efficient manner.

Developing a Robust and Efficient Provenance-Similarity Checker. In the general context of binary similarity, the following two main approaches have been proposed:

(a) *Syntactic* approaches compare signatures [8] or feature vectors [18, 21] extracted from the syntactic binary structure. They resemble techniques used by anti-virus tools, and thus are efficient. However, they are not robust, and are foiled by even minor syntactic differences in binaries.

(b) *Semantic* approaches compute and compare "mathematical" descriptions of the semantic meaning of binaries [11, 15]. They are precise, but require considerable manual interaction, and computationally expensive technology for symbolic and mathematical reasoning (e.g., term-rewriting, symbolic simulation, and theorem proving), and thus have limited practicability and scalability.

In this paper, we investigate the use of classification to develop a robust and efficient binary similarity checker (BSC) for provenance-similarity. Classification is particularly suitable for problems where: (i) closed form solutions are hard to develop, and (ii) a solver can be "learned" using a training set composed of positive and negative samples. Both conditions apply to provenance-similarity.

Provenance-Similarity as a Classification Problem. At a high-level, a BSC is a "black box" that accepts a pair of binaries B_1 and B_2 as input, and outputs "yes" if B_1 and B_2 are similar, and "no" otherwise. This is clearly a *binary classification* problem. However, to be effective, a classification-based BSC must be trained properly and use the right classification technology. Moreover, proper training requires good features that are efficiently computable from binaries. We address these challenges, and make the following specific contributions.

Features. First, we develop a suite of "semantic" and "syntactic" attributes (a.k.a. features) (cf. Sec. 4). Semantic features capture the effect of a binary's execution on specific components of the hardware state, viz., registers and memory locations. Syntactic features represent groups of instruction opcodes occurring contiguously in the binary. They are derived from n-grams and n-perms [20]. Second, we extend these features two pairs of binaries to capture the *difference* between two binaries, and not a single binary in isolation.

Benchmark. While malware is a major target domain for provenance-similarity, it is extremely challenging to develop good sample (i.e., training and testing) sets from malware due to the lack of information on source code and generative compilers. Our second contribution is a benchmark (cf. Sec. 5) for provenance-similarity using a benchmark derived from 14 commonly downloaded SourceForge projects, containing more than 21 million LOC.

Empirical Evaluation. Finally, we do a systematic evaluation of classification for provenance-similarity over both open-source and malware benchmarks. Our main results are: (i) we compare a suite of classifiers implemented in WEKA [22] on the open-source benchmark, and find RandomForest [4] to be the most effective; (ii) for the malware benchmark, we develop a suite of labeling schemes that do not require source-level information; we show very good classification using these labels and RandomForest; we argue that this implies applicability of classification for provenance-similarity in domains, such as malware, without reliable source-level information; (iii) we compare semantic and syntactic attributes, and show that 1-grams are almost as effective as semantic features, while being much less expensive to compute. Our experiments and results are presented in Sec. 6.

Function Similarity. We focus on similarity between binary "functions" instead of complete binaries. Intuitively, a function is a binary fragment that results from the compilation of a procedure or method at the source code level. We choose functions because: (i) they are the smallest externally identifiable units of behavior generated by compilers; (ii) similarity at the function level is desirable for further analysis; indeed, malware of similar provenance, will rarely be identical everywhere, but instead share important functions; thus, malware analysts look for common functions to judge if two binaries are related; also, information about function similarity are useful for clustering and as building blocks for measuring similarity at the binary level; and (iii) we were able to use extensive function-based malware datasets from CERT for our experimentation.

The rest of this paper is structured as follows. In Sec. 2, we survey related work. Sec. 3, we formalize our notion of functions. In Sec. 4, we present our semantic and syntactic features, and the procedures for extracting them from function descriptions. In Sec. 5, we present a benchmark derived from open-source software, and our methodology for deriving testing and training sets from the benchmark. In Sec. 6, we present our experiments and results. In Sec. 7, we conclude.

2. RELATED WORK

A number of different approaches have been proposed for binary similarity. For example, several researchers have used feature vector comparison to detect code clones [18], and to protect against malware [21]. Gao et al. [11] use a control-flow based analysis that combines graph isomorphism, symbolic simulation, and theorem proving to detect semantic differences in binaries. Apel et al. [2] propose metrics for measuring similarity of malware. Dullien et al. [9] and Flake [10] investigate approaches to compare binaries at the level of graphs derived from their syntax. None of these approaches use supervised learning. Also, they require ultimately the selection of a threshold to decide similarity. In contrast, we use supervised learning to automatically compute a threshold that is appropriate for the target binaries.

Rosenblum et al. [17] propose the use of machine learning to extract *compiler provenance* from binaries. The goal of compiler provenance is to correctly identify the compiler that was used to generate a target binary. Rosenblum et al. use a specific type of machine learning technology, called the linear chain conditional random field. They also rely on syntactic features, known as idiom-features. The research presented in this paper is different in terms of both the problem – we consider provenance similarity between two binaries – and the solution – we explore a wide variety of classification techniques, and semantic features, to discover the most effective solution.

Hu et al. [13] present an approach to index malware based on the syntactic call-graph structure of programs. Our approach is complementary since it focuses on features extracted from semantic behavior of functions. Ye et al. [23] use clustering to categorize malware. In contrast, we focus on using classification.

Cohen et al. [8] explore the use of cryptographic hashes to study program similarity. A possible basis for semantic function signatures are "mathematical functions" extracted [15] from binaries to describe their behavior. In contrast to these signature-based approaches, our approach is based on supervised learning.

A number of researchers have developed techniques, such as alias analysis [5] and interface identification [6], for binaries. These techniques are crucial for identifying functions and their boundaries, a problem that is orthogonal to our goal of developing effective techniques for binary similarity.

3. FUNCTIONS

In this section, we present the notion of functions we use for this research. We write $Dom(X)$ to denote the domain of a mapping X. We write $X \hookrightarrow Y$ to denote a (possibly partial) mapping from X to Y with a finite domain. Intuitively, a function is a partial mapping from addresses to instructions, together with a starting address. We assume a totally ordered set $Addr$ of addresses, viz. the set of 32-bit unsigned integers, and a set $Inst$ of instructions, each comprising of an opcode, and one or more operands.

DEFINITION 1. *A function is a pair* $(Body, Start)$ *where: (i) the partial mapping* $Body : Addr \hookrightarrow Inst$ *is its body, and (ii)* $Start \in Dom(Body)$ *is its starting address.*

In general, a function body is non-contiguous, and comprises of a set of instruction blocks that are dispersed throughout the binary. This is true of code generated by state-of-the-art compilers and obfuscators which relocate and reorganize code fragments in non-trivial ways. In practice, however, many functions are *contiguous*, i.e., their bodies consist of a single sequence of instructions spanning a contiguous range of addresses. For such functions, we now present a more concrete definition.

Address a	Instruction $i = Body(a)$	$\epsilon(i)$	$\pi(i)$
100026E3	push dword [ebp+0x8]	FF7508	FF7508
100026E6	lea eax,[ebp-0x208]	8D85F8FDFFFF	8D85F8FDFFFF
100026EC	push eax	50	50
100026ED	lea eax,[ebp-0x308]	8D85F8FCFFFF	8D85F8FCFFFF
100026F3	push dword 0x10006470	6870640010	6800000000
100026F8	push eax	50	50
100026F9	call [0x1000509c]	FF159C500010	FF1500000000
100026FF	add esp,0x10	83C410	83C410
10002702	mov esi,0x100078d2	BED2780010	BE00000000
10002707	push esi	56	56
10002708	call [0x10005064]	FF1564500010	FF1500000000
1000270E	mov edi,[0x1000501c]	8B3D1C500010	8B3D00000000
10002714	test eax,eax	85C0	85C0
10002716	jz 0xa	7408	7408

Figure 1: A basic block of an example function, with ϵ and π mapping.

Representing Contiguous Functions as Byte-Sequences. Let Str be the set of finite-length byte sequences (or strings), and $\bullet$ be concatenation. Let $\epsilon : Inst \mapsto Str$ and $\pi : Inst \mapsto Str$ be mappings such that: **(INJ)** ϵ is injective, and **(PIC)** $\pi(i_1) = \pi(i_2)$ iff i_1 and i_2 differ only in their address operands. Intuitively, $\epsilon(i)$ and $\pi(i)$ are the exact and position-independent representations of i, respectively. For a contiguous function $f = (Start, Body)$, let $A = \langle a_1, \dots, a_n \rangle$ be the sequence of addresses obtained by sorting $Dom(Body)$ in increasing order, and $I = \langle i_1, \dots, i_n \rangle$ be the sequence of instructions such that: $\forall 1 \leq k \leq n \cdot i_k = Body(a_k)$. Then, the *exact*, $f.EB$, and *position-independent*, $f.PB$, representations of f are:

$$f.EB = \epsilon(i_1) \bullet \cdots \bullet \epsilon(i_n) \qquad f.PB = \pi(i_1) \bullet \cdots \bullet \pi(i_n) .$$

EXAMPLE 1. *Figure 1 shows a basic block of a function* f *with starting address* 100025E2, $Body$, ϵ *and* π. *Note that while the function starts at* 100025E2, *the basic block displayed in the figure starts at* 100026E3. *There are additional addresses in the function both before and after the displayed basic block. The mapping* $\epsilon(i)$ *follows the Intel IA-32 instruction definitions, and, thus, satisfies* **(INJ)**. *The mapping* $\pi(i)$ *is obtained by replacing the bytes in* $\epsilon(i)$ *which represent address operands with zeros, and, thus, satisfies* **(PIC)**. *For instructions* i *at addresses* 100026F3, 100026F9, 10002702, 10002708, *and* 1000270E, $\epsilon(i) \neq \pi(i)$ *because the operand bytes corresponding to an address have been replaced with zeros in* $\pi(i)$. *Instructions at addresses* 100026F9, 10002708, *and* 1000270E *have operands which are easily identified as memory dereferences by the type of the operand, while the operands for the instructions at addresses at* 100026F3 *and* 10002702, *can only be identified as addresses by the observation that the values of these operands fall inside the defined range of addresses for the program. This heuristic approach is occasionally flawed (e.g., in invalid truncated programs), but we don't believe this detail is relevant to our results. For all remaining instructions,* $\epsilon(i) = \pi(i)$ *since* i *does not have any address operands. Finally,* $f.EB$ *and* $f.PB$ *are, respectively, the concatenation of the elements of the third and fourth columns.*

Our approach assumes a reliable way to extract functions from executables. Identifying function boundaries in binaries is a complex and open problem. This is especially true for obfuscated (i.e., packed and/or encrypted) malware. These issues are beyond the scope of this paper.

4. ATTRIBUTES

Recall that our BSC classifies function pairs into two groups – similar (the "yes" group), and dissimilar (the "no" group). We now present our approach to extract attribute vectors from a function pair (f_1, f_2). Since we are interested in the degree of similarity between f_1 and f_2, each attribute captures the difference between f_1 and f_2 along some dimension. More specifically, the attribute vector is constructed as follows:

1. We apply a function-level attribute extraction scheme $\mathcal{A}$ to extract two attribute vectors: $\vec{v_1} = \mathcal{A}(f_1)$ and $\vec{v_2} = \mathcal{A}(f_2)$. We assume that all attributes extracted by $\mathcal{A}$ are numeric.

2. We construct the attribute vector for (f_1, f_2), denoted by $\mathcal{A}^{\Delta}(f_1, f_2)$, by taking the pointwise difference of $\vec{v_1}$ and $\vec{v_2}$. That is:

$$\forall 1 \leq i \leq |\vec{v_1}| \cdot \mathcal{A}^{\Delta}(f_1, f_2)[i] = \vec{v_1}[i] - \vec{v_2}[i], .$$

   Note that $\mathcal{A}^{\Delta}$ is asymmetric, i.e., in general, $\mathcal{A}^{\Delta}(f_1, f_2) \neq \mathcal{A}^{\Delta}(f_2, f_1)$. It is possible to make $\mathcal{A}^{\Delta}$ symmetric by ordering each function pair such that $f_1.EB < f_2.EB$.

We now present two function-level attribute extraction schemes, which we use for our experiments:

1. A *semantic* approach based on the effect of executing the function on a hardware state.

2. A *syntactic* approach based on n-grams and n-perms [21] – this approach represents existing work on attribute vector extraction from binaries, and serves as a point of comparison. In Sec. 6, we show empirically that classification with semantic attributes outperforms classification with syntactic attributes.

4.1 Semantic Attributes

The semantic attribute vector of a function f, denoted by $SemAtt(f)$, is a vector of values of semantic attributes. $SemAtt(f)$ represents the effect of executing f on a state of the hardware. Moreover, semantic attributes are defined so that if $SemAtt(f_1)$ and $SemAtt(f_2)$ are similar, then the executions of f_1 and f_2 have similar effects. We assume that every function f has a control flow graph $f.CFG$, and that each execution of f follows a specific path in $f.CFG$. The process of extracting a semantic attribute vector from a path in $f.CFG$ involves simulation, sign abstraction, and counting abstraction. We now present this process in detail.

4.1.1 Extracting Attribute Vectors from Paths

Let $\mathsf{SymConst} = \{v_0, v_1, \dots\}$ be a denumerable set of symbolic constants. Let $\pm$ denote the set of signs $\{+, -\}$ and $\mathbb{N} = \{1, 2, \dots\}$ be the set of numerals representing natural numbers. Symbolic expressions, denoted by SymExp, are linear combinations of symbolic constants (with unit or zero coefficient) and integers. Formally, their syntax has the following BNF form:

$$\mathsf{SymExp} := \pm\mathsf{SymConst} \mid \pm\mathbb{N} \mid \pm\mathsf{SymConst} \pm \mathbb{N}$$

Symbolic State. Let $\mathsf{Reg} = \{r_0, r_1, \dots\}$ be a denumerable set of virtual registers, and $\mathsf{Mem} = \{m_0, m_1, \dots\}$ be a denumerable set of memory locations. A symbolic state is a pair (R, M) where: (i) $R : \mathsf{Reg} \hookrightarrow \mathsf{SymExp}$ maps registers to the symbolic values of their contents; and (ii) $M : \mathsf{Mem} \hookrightarrow \mathsf{SymExp} \times \mathsf{SymExp}$ maps memory locations to the symbolic values of their addresses and contents.

Sign Abstraction. The sign abstraction of a symbolic expression e, denoted by $\mathsf{Sign}(e)$, is an element of Σ, where $\Sigma = (\pm \cup \{0\}) \times (\pm \cup \{0\}) \setminus \{(0,0)\}$. Intuitively, $\mathsf{Sign}(e)$ is obtained by removing all symbolic constants and numerals from e, and replacing any missing component with 0. Formally, it is defined as follows:

$$\mathsf{Sign}(q\ v) = (q, 0) \quad \mathsf{Sign}(q\ n) = (0, q) \quad \mathsf{Sign}(q\ v\ q'\ n) = (q, q')$$

where $q, q' \in \pm$, $v \in \mathsf{SymConst}$, and $n \in \mathbb{N}$. Note that $\{(0,0)\}$ is not a valid sign abstraction, and $|\Sigma| = 8$. Sign abstraction extends to pairs of symbolic expressions in the natural manner: $\mathsf{Sign}(x, y) = (\mathsf{Sign}(x), \mathsf{Sign}(y))$.

Sign-Abstract State. Applying sign abstraction to a symbolic state $s = (R, M)$ results in the sign-abstract state $\mathsf{Sign}(s)$. Formally, $\mathsf{Sign}(s)$, is a pair of functions $(R^{\#}, M^{\#})$ such that for $f = R, M$, the following holds:

$$Dom(f) = Dom(f^{\#}) \bigwedge \forall x \in Dom(f) \cdot f^{\#}(x) = \mathsf{Sign}(f(x))$$

Counting Abstraction. Let $f : X \hookrightarrow \Sigma$ be any mapping. The counting abstraction of f, denoted by $\mathsf{Count}(f)$ is the vector of numbers defined as follows. First we order the elements of $\pm \cup \{0\}$ strictly as: $- < 0 < +$. This induces the following strict ordering on Σ:

$$(x, y) < (x', y') \iff (x' < x') \vee (x = x' \wedge y < y')$$

Let $\vec{\Sigma}$ be the vector of elements of Σ induced by the above strict ordering on Σ. Thus, $\vec{\Sigma}[1] = (-,-)$ and $\vec{\Sigma}[8] = (+,+)$. Then, $\mathsf{Count}(f)$ is the vector such that:

$$\mathsf{Count}(f)[i] = |\{x \in X \mid f(x) = \vec{\Sigma}[i]\}|$$

In other words, the i-th element of $\mathsf{Count}(f)$ is the number of elements of $Dom(f)$ that are mapped by f to the i-th element of $\vec{\Sigma}$. Note that $\mathsf{Count}(f)$ always has 8 elements.

For any pair $x = (x_1, x_2)$, let us write $\mathsf{Fst}(x)$ and $\mathsf{Snd}(x)$ to mean x_1 and x_2 respectively. Let $f : X \mapsto \Sigma \times \Sigma$ be any mapping. Then the two functions $\mathsf{Fst}(f), \mathsf{Snd}(f)$ are defined as follows:

$$\forall x \in X \cdot \mathsf{Fst}(f)(x) = \mathsf{Fst}(f(x)) \wedge \mathsf{Snd}(f)(x) = \mathsf{Snd}(f(x))$$

We write $\vec{x} \bullet \vec{y}$ to denote the concatenation of vectors $\vec{x}$ and $\vec{y}$. The counting abstraction of a sign abstract state $s^{\#} = (R^{\#}, M^{\#})$, denoted by $\mathsf{Count}(s^{\#})$, is the vector of numbers defined as follows:

$$\mathsf{Count}(s^{\#}) = \mathsf{Count}(R^{\#}) \bullet \mathsf{Count}(\mathsf{Fst}(M^{\#})) \bullet \mathsf{Count}(\mathsf{Snd}(M^{\#}))$$

In other words, we apply counting abstraction to the registers, memory addresses, and memory data, and concatenate the resulting vectors. Note that $\mathsf{Count}(f^{\#})$ always has 24 elements. Intuitively, each index of $\mathsf{Count}(f^{\#})$ corresponds to a different a semantic attribute.

Post-Condition. A path p in $f.CFG$ is a sequence of assembly instructions. The post-condition of p, denoted by $\mathsf{Post}(p)$, is a symbolic state representing the hardware configuration after the execution of p. The exact value of $\mathsf{Post}(p)$ depends on the semantics of the instructions in p. In our experiments, we rely on the ROSE [16] infrastructure to compute $\mathsf{Post}(p)$.

EXAMPLE 2. *Consider the path p with three instructions* `inc ax`, `inc ax`, *and* `mov [bx] ax`. *Thus, p increments register* `ax` *twice, and then copies the contents of* `ax` *into the memory location whose addresses is stored in* `bx`. *Then,* $\mathsf{Post}(p) = (R, M)$ *where:*

$$R(r_0) = +v_0 + 2 \qquad R(r_1) = +v_1$$
$$M(m_0) = (+v_1, +v_0 + 2)$$

Note that r_0 *and* r_1 *represent registers* `ax` *and* `bx`, *respectively. Also,* v_0 *and* v_1 *are the initial values of* `ax` *and* `bx`, *respectively. Finally,* m_0 *is the memory location whose address is stored in* `bx`. *Also,* $\mathsf{Sign}(\mathsf{Post}(p)) = (R^\#, M^\#)$ *where:*

$$R^\#(r_0) = (+,+) \qquad R^\#(r_1) = (+,0)$$
$$M^\#(m_0) = ((+,0),(+,+))$$

Recall that $\vec{\Sigma}[7] = (+,0)$ *and* $\vec{\Sigma}[8] = (+,+)$. *Therefore,* $\mathsf{Count}(\mathsf{Sign}(\mathsf{Post}(p))) = \vec{x} \bullet \vec{y} \bullet \vec{z}$, *where:*

$$\vec{x}[7] = \vec{x}[8] = \vec{y}[7] = \vec{z}[8] = 1\ ,$$

and all other elements of $\vec{x}$, $\vec{y}$, *and* $\vec{z}$ *are zero.*

Extracting Attribute Vectors from Paths. The semantic attribute vector of a path p, denoted by $SemAtt(p)$, is defined as follows:

$$SemAtt(p) = \mathsf{Count}(\mathsf{Sign}(\mathsf{Post}(p)))$$

4.1.2 Extracting Attribute Vectors from Functions

Let f be a function represented by the byte sequence $f.EB$. The attribute vector $SemAtt(f)$ is constructed from $f.EB$ as follows:

1. $f.EB$ is parsed and the control flow graph $f.CFG$ is constructed. In our implementation, we use the ROSE [16] infrastructure to perform this step.
2. In general, $f.CFG$ has cycles, and therefore infinitely many paths. We use a bounded-depth-first-search traversal to extract $\#p$ paths of depth at most $\#d$ from $f.CFG$. The search is randomized, i.e., successors for traversal are picked randomly. For our experiments, we use $\#p = 50$ and $\#d = 50$. Note that since the number of possible paths is exponential in $\#d$, we limit $\#p$ as well. Let P be the set of paths extracted.
3. From each $p \in P$, we construct $SemAtt(p)$ as defined in the previous section. Note, $|SemAtt(p)| = 24$.
4. Let $\uplus$ be the element-wise addition of two vectors, i.e.,
   $$\forall i \cdot (\vec{x} \uplus \vec{y})[i] = \vec{x}[i] + \vec{y}[i]$$
   Then, we compute $SemAtt(f)$ as follows:
   $$SemAtt(f) = \biguplus_{p \in P} SemAtt(p)$$

Increasing $\#p$ or $\#d$ also increases the time to extract semantic attributes. Empirically, we found $\#p = 50$ and $\#d = 50$ to be a good tradeoff. For example, to extract semantic attributes from a random sample of 541 functions in our benchmark using $\#p = 50$ and $\#d = 50$, the time required is 95 mins. When $\#d$ is increased to 100, the time is 165 mins, a 74% jump. However, the number of attributes for which values differ between the two cases is only about 1.2% of the total number of attributes.

EXAMPLE 3. *Let* f *be a function such that* $f.CFG$ *has two paths* p_1 *and* p_2. *Let* p_1 *be the same as* p *from Example 2. Therefore,* $SemAtt(p_1) = \mathsf{Count}(\mathsf{Sign}(\mathsf{Post}(p_1))) = \vec{x} \bullet \vec{y} \bullet \vec{z}$, *where:*

$$\vec{x}[7] = \vec{x}[8] = \vec{y}[7] = \vec{z}[8] = 1\ ,$$

and all other elements of $\vec{x}$, $\vec{y}$, *and* $\vec{z}$ *are zero.*

Let p_2 *have 4 instructions* `mov [ax] bx`, `dec ax`, `mov bx 10`, `mov [ax] bx`. *Then,* $\mathsf{Post}(p_2) = (R, M)$ *where:*

$$R(r_0) = +v_0 - 1 \qquad R(r_1) = +10$$
$$M(m_0) = (+v_0, +v_1) \qquad M(m_1) = (+v_0 - 1, +10)$$

Note that r_0 *and* r_1 *represent registers* `ax` *and* `bx`, *respectively. Also,* v_0 *and* v_1 *are the initial values of* `ax` *and* `bx`, *respectively. The addresses of memory locations* m_0 *and* m_1 *are stored in* `ax` *initially and finally, respectively. Also,* $\mathsf{Sign}(\mathsf{Post}(p_2)) = (R^\#, M^\#)$ *where:*

$$R^\#(r_0) = (+,-) \qquad R^\#(r_1) = (0,+)$$
$$M^\#(m_0) = ((+,0),(+,0)) \qquad M^\#(m_1) = ((+,-),(0,+))$$

Recall that $\vec{\Sigma}[5] = (0,+)$ *and* $\vec{\Sigma}[6] = (+,-)$. *Therefore,* $SemAtt(p_2) = \mathsf{Count}(\mathsf{Sign}(\mathsf{Post}(p_2))) = \vec{x} \bullet \vec{y} \bullet \vec{z}$, *where:*

$$\vec{x}[5] = \vec{x}[6] = \vec{y}[6] = \vec{y}[7] = \vec{z}[5] = \vec{z}[7] = 1\ ,$$

and all other elements of $\vec{x}$, $\vec{y}$, *and* $\vec{z}$ *are zero. Finally,* $SemAtt(f) = SemAtt(p_1) \uplus SemAtt(p_2) = \vec{x} \bullet \vec{y} \bullet \vec{z}$, *where:*

$$\vec{x}[5] = \vec{x}[6] = \vec{x}[7] = \vec{x}[8] = 1 \qquad \vec{y}[6] = 1$$
$$\vec{z}[5] = \vec{z}[7] = \vec{z}[8] = 1 \qquad \vec{y}[7] = 2$$

and all other elements of $\vec{x}$, $\vec{y}$, *and* $\vec{z}$ *are zero.*

Implementation Details. For our empirical evaluation, we generalize semantic attributes as follows. First, we split registers into three sub-categories: general-purpose, segment, and flag – based on their use by the compiler. We apply sign and counting abstractions separately to each category. Since now there are 3 types of registers in addition to memory addresses and data, $|SemAtt(p)| = |\Sigma \times (3+2) = 40$ for any path p. Second, we consider three ways of combining the elements of $SemAtt(p)$ to obtain an element of $SemAtt(f)$ – sum (as described above), minimum, and maximum. We also consider splitting up a path at call-sites, and replacing a counting abstraction with a 0-1 abstraction (i.e., replacing all counts greater than 0 with 1). In all, we have 36 possible combinations, leading to $40 \times 36 = 1440$ attributes.

4.2 Syntactic Attributes

We present two flavors of syntactic attributes, based on n-grams and n-perms [20], respectively. Let Mnem be the sequence of x86 instruction mnemonics, and Mnem^n be the set of sequences of n elements drawn from Mnem. Let $\vec{\mathsf{Mnem}}^n$ be the vector of elements of Mnem^n ordered lexicographically. For any positive value of n, the n-gram vector of f, denoted by $NGram_n(f)$, is computed as follows:

1. Parse $f.EB$ to construct of sequence of assembly instructions $I = \langle i_1, \ldots, i_k \rangle$. Extract the mnemonic from each instruction to obtain a sequence of mnemonics $M = \langle m_1, \ldots, m_k \rangle$. In our implementation, this step is performed using ROSE.

2. Then, $NGram_n(f)$ is the vector of $|\vec{\mathsf{Mnem}}^n|$ numbers, such that for any $1 \leq i \leq |\vec{\mathsf{Mnem}}^n|$, $NGram_n(f)[i]$ equals the number of times $\vec{\mathsf{Mnem}}^n[i]$ occurs as a subsequence of M.

EXAMPLE 4. *Let* $\mathsf{Mnem} = \{\mathtt{inc}, \mathtt{dec}, \mathtt{mov}\}$. *Then,* $\vec{\mathsf{Mnem}}^2 = \{\mathtt{inc}\cdot\mathtt{inc}, \dots, \mathtt{mov}\cdot\mathtt{mov}\}$. *Let f be a function such that $f.EB$ leads to the following sequence of mnemonics:* $M = \langle \mathtt{mov}, \mathtt{inc}, \mathtt{inc}, \mathtt{mov}, \mathtt{dec}, \mathtt{mov} \rangle$. *For any* $x \in \vec{\mathsf{Mnem}}^2$, *let us write $NGram_2(f)[x]$ to mean $NGram_2(f)[i]$ such that* $\vec{\mathsf{Mnem}}^2[i] = x$. *Then,*

$$NGram_2(f)[\mathtt{mov}\cdot\mathtt{inc}] = NGram_2(f)[\mathtt{inc}\cdot\mathtt{inc}] = 1$$
$$NGram_2(f)[\mathtt{inc}\cdot\mathtt{mov}] = NGram_2(f)[\mathtt{mov}\cdot\mathtt{dec}] = 1$$
$$NGram_2(f)[\mathtt{dec}\cdot\mathtt{mov}] = 1$$

and all other elements of $NGram_2(f)$ are 0.

For any positive value n, the n-perm vector of f is denoted by $NPerm_n(f)$. n-perm vectors are similar to n-gram vectors, except that ordering is ignored.

EXAMPLE 5. *For the* Mnem *and f in Example 4, we have,*

$$NPerm_2(f)[\mathtt{inc}\cdot\mathtt{mov}] = NPerm_2(f)[\mathtt{dec}\cdot\mathtt{mov}] = 2$$
$$NPerm_2(f)[\mathtt{inc}\cdot\mathtt{inc}] = 1$$

and all other elements of $NPerm_2(f)$ are 0.

Detailed evaluation of our attributes is presented in Sec. 6.2.

5. TRAINING AND TESTING SETS

Since our training and testing sets are constructed using the same procedure, we refer to them simply as sample sets. A (N^+, N^-)-sample set – consisting of N^+ "yes" samples and N^- "no" samples – is constructed as follows:

1. First, we construct a benchmark $\mathcal{B}$ comprising of sets of provenance-similar functions.
2. Next, using $\mathcal{B}$, we create N^+ and N^- random samples belonging to "yes" and "no" classes respectively. The final result is the union of all the samples obtained.

We now describe these two steps in more detail.

5.1 Benchmark Construction

Our benchmark $\mathcal{B}$ consists of a set of clusters, where each cluster is a set of provenance-similar and contiguous functions. $\mathcal{B}$ was constructed as follows:

1. We manually selected a set of 14 open-source software packages (containing collectively over 21 million LOC) available at SourceForge (`http://www.sf.net`) that are among the most downloaded, written in C/C++, and executable on Windows. Each software yielded a set of clusters by the following steps.
2. The software was compiled with Microsoft Visual Studio 2003 .NET, 2005, and 2008 on Windows XP SP3.
3. The binaries were processed with IDAPro 5.6 [14] together with custom Python extensions to extract a set of functions. We write $f.Name$ to mean the compiler-generated name of a function f. We use this name to relate functions across the different compilers, as described in the next step.

Table 1: Benchmark summary: KLoC = Kilo Lines of Code; BSz = size of binaries in MB; #Cl = no. of equivalence classes; Avg, StD, Med = mean, standard deviation and median of equivalence class sizes.

Software	KLoC	BSz	#Cl	Avg	StD	Med
`7zip`	153	2.4	2992	4.4	9.4	3
`cppunit`	36	26.4	616	15.2	128.4	3
`flac`	78	5.1	269	4.4	8.4	3
`net-snmp`	395	5.9	1507	4.6	62.4	3
`notecase`	48	0.8	228	4.7	7.8	3
`NppExec`	35	3.8	888	4.1	6.6	3
`ogl`	285	3.0	1205	2.6	17.7	2
`poco`	268	4.8	3745	5.1	61.5	3
`speed`	154	0.3	376	2.9	3.9	3
`tcl`	251	8.9	872	2.9	1.0	3
`tightvnc`	138	3.7	1455	5.4	48.9	3
`tinyxml`	7	1.4	639	4.2	18.9	3
`ultravnc`	183	6.0	1414	7.4	33.9	2
`wincvs`	154	27.3	1646	9.8	63.8	3

4. Recall that $f.PB$ is the position-independent byte-representation of a function f. The functions were clustered into equivalence classes induced by the reflexive-transitive closure of the following relation $\mathcal{R}$:

$$f_1 \mathcal{R} f_2 \iff f_1.Name = f_2.Name \vee f_1.PB = f_2.PB$$

Thus, we assume that if $f_1 \mathcal{R} f_2$, then f_1 and f_2 are provenance-similar. Alternatively, we assume that two provenance-dissimilar functions have different names *and* position-independent byte representations.

5. An equivalence class c was discarded if it satisfied the following condition:

$$|c| = 1 \bigvee \mathrm{Max}_{f \in c}|f.EB| < 50$$

This eliminates equivalence classes that are: (i) singleton – since, as we see later, singletons are not useful in generating "yes" samples; and (ii) have no functions with bodies larger than 50 bytes – since we believe that classification is not applicable to detect similarity between very small functions. The cutoff of 50 was chosen empirically.

6. Each remaining equivalence class yields a cluster.

Table 1 summarizes our benchmark $\mathcal{B}$. A median of (mostly) 3 indicates that the most common case is, as expected, one function for each of the 3 compilers. The number of equivalence classes, averages and standard deviations vary widely, indicating that we have a good mix of clusters in terms of their sizes.

5.2 Sample Set Construction

We now present our approach to construct a (N^+, N^-)-sample set from $\mathcal{B}$. When constructing (either "yes" or "no") samples, we ignore function pairs (f_1, f_2) such that $f_1.PB = f_2.PB$[1], since, by assumption, such function pairs

[1]Without this restriction, the overall trend in our results is similar, but with even higher F-measures.

are already provenance-similar, and hence need not be classified. In the following, Ψ is a scheme to extract feature vectors from function pairs, as described in Sec. 4.

First, to construct a "yes" sample, we use procedure **PickYes**, consisting of the following steps: (i) Randomly pick a cluster $c \in \mathcal{B}$. Recall that c contains at least two functions. (ii) Randomly pick two distinct functions $f_1, f_2 \in c$ s.t. $f_1.PB \neq f_2.PB$. (iii) Output $\Psi(f_1, f_2)$ labeled with "yes". Next, to construct a "no" sample, we use procedure **PickNo**, consisting of the following steps: (i) Randomly pick two distinct clusters $c_1, c_2 \in \mathcal{B}$. (ii) Randomly pick two functions $f_1 \in c_1$ and $f_2 \in c_2$. (iii) Output $\Psi(f_1, f_2)$ labeled with "no". Finally, to construct the desired (N^+, N^-)-sample set, we repeat **PickYes** N^+ times, **PickNo** N^- times, and collect together the resulting samples.

The benchmark $\mathcal{B}$ consists of over six million functions, divided into 17,852 clusters. Therefore, we have over 36×10^{12} possible samples available for training and testing. In our experiments, we use sample sets consisting of an equal proportion of "yes" and "no" samples. Thus, we say "(n_1, n_2)-classification" to mean a classification with a $(\frac{n_1}{2}, \frac{n_1}{2})$-training set, and a $(\frac{n_2}{2}, \frac{n_2}{2})$-testing set.

Since our testing and training sets are randomly created, we repeat our experiments several times, and use the averages of the measurements for our conclusions. Specifically, for any metric M, we say "M of $(n_1 \diamond k_1, n_2 \diamond k_2)$-classification" to mean the average of the values of M for $k_1 \times k_2$ classifications, done by: (i) selecting k_1 random training sets of size n_1, and for each training set, (ii) learning a classifier and testing it with k_2 random testing sets of size n_2. We use three main metrics for our evaluation – the F-measure, training time, and testing time.

6. EXPERIMENTAL RESULTS

We performed three types of experiments: learner selection, feature selection, and to judge the applicability of our approach to detect similarity in malware. All experiments were performed on a quad-core 2.8 GHz machine. Each session (training or testing) was run with a time limit of 1800s and a memory limit of 700MB. Our benchmark and tools are available at `http://www.contrib.andrew.cmu.edu/user/schaki/binsim`.

6.1 Learner Selection

These experiments were done with the semantic attributes – i.e., with $\Psi = SemAtt^{\Delta}$ – on our open-source benchmark $\mathcal{B}$. We first evaluated 24 classifiers implemented in the WEKA [22] tool (version 3.6.2). For each classifier, we used the default WEKA configuration, and measured F for a $(10000 \diamond 5, 20000 \diamond 5)$-classification. We observed a clear separation between the classifiers: seven are effective – having F-measures ≥ 0.875; the rest are ineffective – having F-measures around ≈ 0.5 (like random guessing). The results for the 7 effective schemes, in order of decreasing F-measure, are summarized in Table 2.

Comparing Effective Schemes. Next, we compared the performance of the 7 effective schemes. The IBk and J48graft schemes are eliminated immediately. They have worse performance – lower F-measure, and higher training and testing times – compared to RandomForest. We evaluated each of the remaining 5 schemes using a series of $(N \diamond 5, 2N \diamond 5)$-classifications, where the value of N was varied from 10000 to 30000 in increments of 2000. The results

Table 2: Comparison of various classifiers on a $(10000 \diamond 5, 20000 \diamond 5)$-classification. F-measure = avg/stdev; Train = training time (avg/stdev in secs); Test = testing time (avg/stdev in secs).

Classifier	F-measure	*Train*	*Test*
RandomForest	0.928/0.002	19.41/0.23	4.56/0.075
J48graft	0.909/0.002	97.96/6.28	6.52/0.301
J48	0.900/0.003	93.74/4.95	3.34/0.056
Ridor	0.895/0.005	266.7/27.1	2.79/0.045
REPTree	0.887/0.003	22.15/0.64	3.08/0.044
RandomTree	0.876/0.003	5.72/0.13	3.89/0.123
IBk	0.861/0.003	164.6/2.97	459.0/26.6

are summarized in Figure 2. All classifiers show increasing F-measures with increasing N. However, RandomForest is the clear winner. All classifiers also require more testing and training time with increasing N. In particular, Ridor's training is most expensive, and it times out for training sets of size 24,000 and up. Overall, we conclude that RandomForest is the most effective classifier.

RandomForest. Next, we evaluated RandomForest by varying its three parameters – **(P1)** number of trees, **(P2)** number of attributes, and **(P3)** tree depth.

First, we performed $(N \diamond 5, 2N \diamond 5)$-classifications with increasing **P1**, and with N ranging from 5 to 150. Figure 3-(top) summarizes the F-measures we observed. The F-measure improves rapidly with increasing **P1** up to $N = 20$, then improves very slowly till $N = 40$. For $N > 40$, the improvement tapers off, and is difficult to ascertain.

Next, we performed $(N \diamond 5, 2N \diamond 5)$-classifications with increasing **P2**, and with different N. Figure 3-(bottom) summarizes the F-measures we observed. As expected, the F-measure improves with increasing **P2**, but the gains taper off after about 12.

Finally, we performed $(N \diamond 5, 2N \diamond 5)$-classifications with increasing **P3** – starting at 0 (which indicates unlimited depth), and moving up to 80 in increments of 10 – and with different N. We saw that **P3** ≥ 20 is required for an F-measure within 0.1 of the F-measure with unlimited **P3**. However, at **P3** $= 20$, the training and testing times are similar to those with unlimited **P3**. Therefore, unlimited **P3** is the optimal choice.

In all cases, training and testing times increase monotonically with the values of **P1**, **P2**, **P3**, and N.

6.2 Feature Selection

Next, we compared $SemAtt^{\Delta}$, $NGram_n{}^{\Delta}$ and $NPerm_n{}^{\Delta}$ for $n = \{1, 2\}$ using our open-source benchmark $\mathcal{B}$. We evaluated their performances using a series of $(N \diamond 5, 2N \diamond 5)$-classifications, where the value of N was varied from 10000 to 30000 in increments of 2000. Table 3 shows our results. We see that $NGram_1{}^{\Delta} (= NPerm_1{}^{\Delta})$ is superior to $SemAtt^{\Delta}$ in terms of training and testing times, and almost as good in terms of F-measure. Feature extraction with $NGram_1{}^{\Delta}$ is also less expensive than $SemAtt^{\Delta}$ (e.g., about one day vs. a week for our open-source benchmark). A combination of $SemAtt^{\Delta}$ and $NGram_1{}^{\Delta}$ improves negligibly over $SemAtt^{\Delta}$ alone.

As expected, classification with $NGram_2{}^{\Delta}$ and $NPerm_2{}^{\Delta}$ is slower than with $NGram_1{}^{\Delta}$ due to a greater number of attributes. However, surprisingly, it is

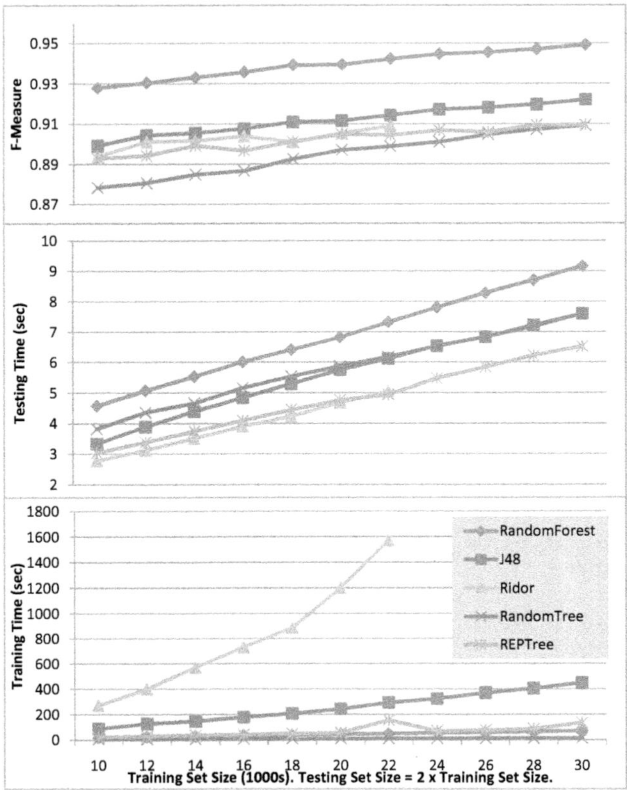

Figure 2: Comparison of effective classifiers; legend at the bottom applies to all charts.

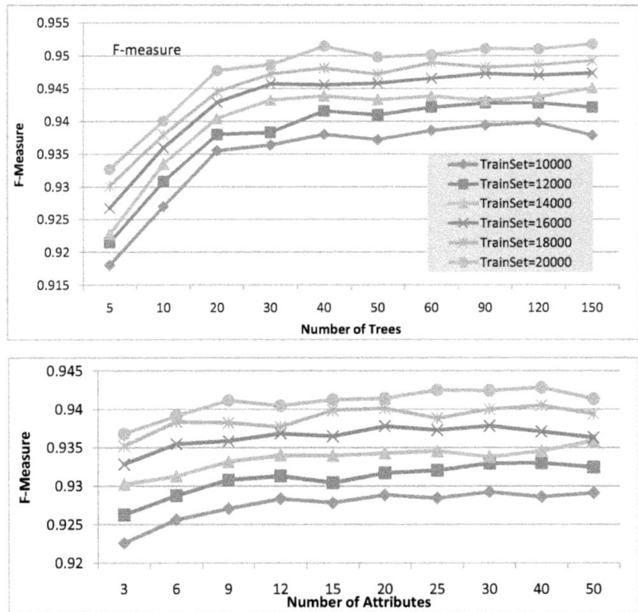

Figure 3: Performance of RandomForest with different tree numbers (top) and attribute numbers (bottom); legend at the top applies to both charts.

Table 4: Malware families in our benchmark; #Ehashes and #Phashes = no. of unique exact and position-independent function byte representations.

Name	#Files	#Funcs	#Ehashes	#Phashes
F1	9	6631	1889	487
F2	265	80831	15512	1766
F3	308	9360	2363	1070
F4	7	2410	1053	704
F5	10	1090	112	112
F6	38	5159	3053	346
F7	22	10887	4384	1790
F8	27	10815	431	395
F9	18	1259	1055	581
F10	9	792	180	62
F11	24	49318	19241	1251
F12	6	2400	416	102

also worse in terms of F-measure. This indicates that counts of pairs of adjacent instruction mnemonics characterize a function less well than the counts of single mnemonics. We believe that one reason for this is instruction reordering due to compiler optimizations and changes in source code, the two sources of provenance similarity. The same set of instructions, upon reordering, will lead to different $NGram_2{}^{\Delta}$ and $NPerm_2{}^{\Delta}$, but the same $NGram_1{}^{\Delta}$. Overall, we believe $NGram_1{}^{\Delta}$ is the best choice if time is limited, and $SemAtt^{\Delta}$ is best otherwise.

Recall that $\mathcal{A}^{\Delta}$ computes the element-wise difference of function-level attribute vectors. We also evaluated $\mathcal{A}^{\Delta}$ against another approach – denoted by $\mathcal{A}^{\bullet}$ – that simply concatenates the two function-level vectors. Specifically,

$$\mathcal{A}^{\bullet}(f_1, f_2) = \mathcal{A}(f_1) \bullet \mathcal{A}(f_2) \qquad [\bullet \text{ denotes concatenation}]$$

Note that $\mathcal{A}^{\bullet}(f_1, f_2)$ has more attributes than $\mathcal{A}^{\Delta}(f_1, f_2)$, and captures information about the difference between f_1 and f_2 less directly. Empirically, we found $SemAtt^{\Delta}$ to be superior to $SemAtt^{\bullet}$, as shown in Table 3.

6.3 Applicability to Malware

To judge the applicability of classification to detect similarity in malware, we experimented with a benchmark $\mathcal{M}$ derived from 12 malware families from the CERT database. To ensure that we only consider true families, we picked a dozen candidates from cases on which a suite of anti-virus tools all agree in their family identification. The details of the families are presented in Table 4.

The main problem with malware is designing a good labeling function for training provenance-similarity. Since source-level information is rarely available, it is difficult to automatically decide if two functions are similar (or not) with high confidence. While the labeling problem for malware is beyond the scope of our paper, as a starting point, we experimented with a labeling function – denoted L^{PIC} – based on position-independent (PIC) byte representations. Specifically, L^{PIC} labels an attribute vector derived from a function pair (f_1, f_2) "yes" iff f_1 and f_2 have the same PIC byte representation. We don't claim that L^{PIC} is the best possible labeling function for malware similarity. However, we believe that it is a good approximation to the extent that if classification with L^{PIC} is not accurate, it will likely be inaccurate with a better labeling function as well.

We created sample sets using our benchmark $\mathcal{M}$ and L^{PIC}, and performed a series of $(N\diamond5, 2N\diamond5)$-classifications, where the value of N was varied from 10000 to 30000 in increments of 2000. We repeated our experiments with

Table 3: Comparison of $SemAtt^{\triangle}$, ${NGram_n}^{\triangle}$, and $SemAtt^{\bullet}$; $SA+NG_1 = SemAtt+NGram_1$; N = size of training set; Tr = Avg. training time (s); Te = Avg. testing time (s).

N	$SemAtt^{\triangle}$			${NGram_1}^{\triangle}$			$(SA+NG_1)^{\triangle}$			${NGram_2}^{\triangle}$			${NPerm_2}^{\triangle}$			$SemAtt^{\bullet}$		
	F	Tr	Te	F	Tr	Te	F	Tr	Te	F	Tr	Te	F	Tr	Te	F	Tr	Te
10K	0.929	19	4.6	0.919	17	3.3	0.930	22	4.8	0.884	90.9	5.5	0.880	83	5.1	0.905	39	9.1
12K	0.930	25	5.1	0.924	22	3.5	0.933	29	5.3	0.890	118	6.1	0.889	98	5.6	0.909	52	10.5
14K	0.933	28	5.5	0.928	25	3.8	0.935	33	5.8	0.894	145	6.8	0.894	120	6.2	0.914	58	11.9
16K	0.936	34	6.0	0.931	28	4.1	0.939	40	6.3	0.900	155	7.2	0.899	125	6.7	0.918	70	13.2
18K	0.939	40	6.4	0.935	33	4.4	0.943	46	6.8	0.904	185	7.8	0.904	158	7.2	0.922	82	14.6
20K	0.939	45	6.8	0.937	37	4.6	0.944	56	7.3	0.908	211	8.4	0.907	171	7.8	0.926	94	16.0
22K	0.942	50	7.3	0.938	40	4.8	0.947	60	7.8	0.913	233	9.4	0.912	190	8.3	0.926	99	17.5
24K	0.945	55	7.8	0.942	46	5.0	0.947	67	8.3	0.915	261	9.8	0.914	224	9.2	0.928	112	18.7
26K	0.946	60	8.3	0.944	49	5.2	0.949	73	8.8	0.918	292	10.0	0.918	236	9.4	0.932	125	20.0
28K	0.947	63	8.7	0.945	51	5.4	0.950	84	9.4	0.922	310	10.6	0.920	257	9.6	0.935	138	21.6
30K	0.949	73	9.2	0.948	58	5.7	0.952	89	9.8	0.924	362	11.3	0.924	285	10.1	0.936	146	23.0

$SemAtt^{\triangle}$ and ${NGram_1}^{\triangle}$. In all cases, we got a high F-measure (0.998), indicating that classification is a promising approach for provenance-similarity in malware.

7. CONCLUSION

In this paper, we explore the use of classification to detect provenance-similarity of binaries. Specifically, we use classification to predict if a pair of functions is "similar" or "dissimilar". Our classification uses features that capture the difference between the target function pair. We evaluate our approach on a benchmark derived from open-source software, with encouraging results. Preliminary experiments also indicate that classification is a promising approach to detect malware similarity. A major challenge with malware is the difficulty of obtaining sufficiently many samples with reliable similarity labeling. We believe that semi-supervised learning is a promising avenue in addressing this issue.

8. REFERENCES

[1] Aliser worm. `http://www.sophos.com/security/analyses/viruses-and-spyware/w32aliserdam.html`.

[2] M. Apel, C. Bockermann, and M. Meier. Measuring similarity of malware behavior. In *Proc. of LCN*, 2009.

[3] M. Braverman, J. Williams, and Z. Mador. Microsoft security intelligence report: January–June 2006, 2006. `http://microsoft.com/downloads/details.aspx?FamilyId=1C443104-5B3F-4C3A-868E-36A553FE2A02`.

[4] L. Breiman. Random Forests. *Machine Learning*, 45(1):5–32, 2001.

[5] D. Brumley and J. Newsome. Alias analysis for assembly. Technical report CMU-CS-06-180[R], Carnegie Mellon University, Pittsburgh, 2006.

[6] J. Caballero, N. M. Johnson, S. McCamant, and D. Song. Binary code extraction and interface identification for security applications. Technical report UCB/EECS-2009-133, University of California, Berkeley, Berkeley, CA, October 2009.

[7] S. Choi, H. Park, H. il Lim, and T. Han. A Static Birthmark of Binary Executables Based on API Call Structure. In *Proc. of ASIAN*, 2007.

[8] C. Cohen and J. Havrilla. Function Hashing for Malicious Code Analysis, 2009. `www.cert.org/research/2009research-report.pdf`.

[9] T. Dullien and R. Rolles. Graph-based comparison of Executable Objects. In *Proc. of SSTIC*, 2005.

[10] H. Flake. Structural Comparison of Executable Objects. In *Proc. of DMIVA*, 2004.

[11] D. Gao, M. K. Reiter, and D. X. Song. BinHunt: Automatically Finding Semantic Differences in Binary Programs. In *Proc. of ICICS*, 2008.

[12] M. Hayes, A. Walenstein, and A. Lakhotia. Evaluation of malware phylogeny modelling systems using automated variant generation. *Journal in Computer Virology (JCV)*, 5(4):335–343, November 2009.

[13] X. Hu, T. Chiueh, and K. G. Shin. Large-scale malware indexing using function-call graphs. In *Proc. of CCS*, 2009.

[14] IDA Pro. `http://www.hex-rays.com/idapro`.

[15] R. Linger, S. Prowell, and K. Sayre. Computing the behavior of malicious code with function extraction technology. In *Proc. of CSIIRW*, 2009.

[16] ROSE. `http://rosecompiler.org`.

[17] N. E. Rosenblum, B. P. Miller, and X. Zhu. Extracting compiler provenance from program binaries. In *Proc. of PASTE*, 2010.

[18] A. Sæbjørnsen, J. Willcock, T. Panas, D. J. Quinlan, and Z. Su. Detecting code clones in binary executables. In *Proc. of ISSTA*, 2009.

[19] Symantec. Symantec internet security threat report: Trends for January 06–June 06, 2006. `http://www.symantec.com/enterprise/threatreport/index.jsp`.

[20] A. Walenstein and A. Lakhotia. The Software Similarity Problem in Malware Analysis. In *Duplication, Redundancy, and Similarity in Software*, volume 06301 of *Dagstuhl Seminar Proceedings*, 2007.

[21] A. Walenstein, M. Venable, M. Hayes, C. Thompson, and A. Lakhotia. Exploiting Similarity Between Variants to Defeat Malware: "Vilo" Method for Comparing and Searching Binary Programs. In *Proc. of BLACKHAT DC*, 2007.

[22] WEKA website. `http://www.cs.waikato.ac.nz/ml/weka`.

[23] Y. Ye, T. Li, Y. Chen, and Q. Jiang. Automatic malware categorization using cluster ensemble. In *Proc. of KDD*, 2010.

Trading Representability for Scalability: Adaptive Multi-Hyperplane Machine for Nonlinear Classification

Zhuang Wang
Knowledge and Decision Systems
Siemens Corporate Research
Princeton, NJ, USA
zhuang.wang@siemens.com

Nemanja Djuric
Department of Computer and Information Sciences
Temple University
Philadelphia, PA, USA
nemanja.djuric@temple.edu

Koby Crammer
Department of Electrical Engineering
The Technion
Haifa, Israel
koby@ee.technion.ac.il

Slobodan Vucetic
Department of Computer and Information Sciences
Temple University
Philadelphia, PA, USA
vucetic@temple.edu

ABSTRACT

Support Vector Machines (SVMs) are among the most popular and successful classification algorithms. Kernel SVMs often reach state-of-the-art accuracies, but suffer from the curse of kernelization due to linear model growth with data size on noisy data. Linear SVMs have the ability to efficiently learn from truly large data, but they are applicable to a limited number of domains due to low representational power. To fill the representability and scalability gap between linear and nonlinear SVMs, we propose the Adaptive Multi-hyperplane Machine (AMM) algorithm that accomplishes fast training and prediction and has capability to solve nonlinear classification problems. AMM model consists of a set of hyperplanes (weights), each assigned to one of the multiple classes, and predicts based on the associated class of the weight that provides the largest prediction. The number of weights is automatically determined through an iterative algorithm based on the stochastic gradient descent algorithm which is guaranteed to converge to a local optimum. Since the generalization bound decreases with the number of weights, a weight pruning mechanism is proposed and analyzed. The experiments on several large data sets show that AMM is nearly as fast during training and prediction as the state-of-the-art linear SVM solver and that it can be orders of magnitude faster than kernel SVM. In accuracy, AMM is somewhere between linear and kernel SVMs. For example, on an OCR task with 8 million highly dimensional training examples, AMM trained in 300 seconds on a single-core processor had 0.54% error rate, which was significantly lower than 2.03% error rate of a linear SVM trained in the same time and comparable to 0.43% error rate of a kernel SVM trained in 2 days on 512 processors. The results indicate that AMM could be an attractive option when solving large-scale classification problems. The software is available at `www.dabi.temple.edu/~vucetic/AMM.html`.

KDD'11, August 21–24, 2011, San Diego, California, USA.

Categories and Subject Descriptors

I.5.2 [**Pattern Recognition**]: Design Methodology—*Classifier design and evaluation*

General Terms

Algorithms, Performance, Experimentation

Keywords

Large-scale learning, Nonlinear classification, Stochastic gradient descent, Support vector machines

1. INTRODUCTION

In the environment where new large-scale problems are emerging in various disciplines and pervasive computing applications are becoming more common, there is an urgent need for machine learning algorithms that can achieve high accuracy in computationally efficient way. Support Vector Machines (SVMs) [7] provide a powerful paradigm for solving complex classification problems. However, this ability comes at the price of significant computational costs. There has been active research over the last decade to improve efficiency of SVM training [23, 27, 3, 22, 6, 10, 16, 18, 9, 2, 28, 21, 25, 5, 19, 26, 24] and today's state-of-the-art solvers are able to tackle data sets having hundreds of thousands or even millions of highly dimensional examples. Despite the recent advances, there is a fundamental limitation of SVMs with nonlinear kernels that prevents applying them on truly large data sets or data streams. This is a well documented and understood property that on the noisy or highly nonlinear data sets, the size of SVM model, measured in the number of support vectors, grows linearly with number of training examples [20]. This limitation could explain the recent increased interest in linear SVMs whose model size remains fixed regardless of the data size. However, this comes at a price of significantly reduced representational power of linear SVMs.

As a result, there is a large scalability and representability gap between linear and kernel SVMs. On the kernel SVM side, recent empirical results show that training on data with millions of examples can take days even when using parallel processing techniques and result in a classifier consisting of hundreds of thousands of support vectors. On the linear SVM side, training on such large data takes only seconds on a regular PC and results in a single weight vector as the final classifier. The scalability and short prediction time of linear SVMs make them popular in applications such as text categorization, where examples are sufficiently high dimensional to make the classification problem nearly linearly separable. However, in many other applications, high representational power of kernel SVMs makes them significantly more accurate than linear SVMs. Filling the representability and scalability gap between linear and nonlinear classification is the challenge we intend to address in this paper.

We propose the Adaptive Multi-hyperplane Machine (AMM), a fast learning algorithm applicable to large-scale nonlinear classification problems, which provides a computationally efficient alternative to kernel SVMs. The AMM model consists of a set of weights, each assigned to one of the classes, and it predicts based on the class of weight that provides the largest prediction. The idea of using multiple weights for classification can be traced back to the multi-class SVM [8], which assigns a single weight to each class and predicts the class whose weight gives the largest prediction. By defining the cost function as the regularized margin-based training error, the resulting learning problem becomes convex and can be solved by standard tools of convex optimization. An extension of this idea that allows multiple weights per class has been originally proposed in [1]. Since each weight defines a hyperplane, we refer to this approach as the Multi-hyperplane Machine (MM). There are two important properties of the MM approach. The first is that the resulting optimization problem is nonconvex, such that only convergence to a local optimum can be guaranteed. The second is that it has higher representational power than the single-hyperplane approach. It has been demonstrated experimentally that the benefits of increased representational power outweigh problems with nonconvexity and that MM could accurately solve nonlinear classification problems.

There are two issues that prevent use of MM on large-scale classification problems. The first is that it uses a Sequential Minimal Optimization (SMO) [14] based training algorithm, which is a batch solver that is not suitable for large-scale data. Another is that it requires a user to pre-specify the number of weights per class. Since the optimal number of weights depends on a particular classification problem, this creates a need to select this hyperparameter using an expensive cross-validation procedure. The proposed Adaptive MM approach addresses both of these issues, which makes it practically applicable to very large-scale nonlinear classification problems, as will be illustrated in the experiments.

AMM achieves its computational efficiency through the Stochastic Gradient Descent (SGD), a popular optimization technique that has recently attracted much interest as an alternative to the traditional batch-mode convex optimization for training of SVMs on large-scale data (e.g. [18]). SGD works by sampling labeled examples one at a time and updating the model through (sub-)gradient descent over the instantaneous objective function. Its sequential access to data makes it very suitable for large-scale or online learning. We will show analytically that our implementation of SGD allows AMM to converge to a local optimum, a property shared by the MM.

Table 1: Summary of notation

$\mathbf{x}$	Instance
y	Label
t, n	Indexes for $\mathbf{x}$
$\mathbf{W}$	Weight matrix
$\mathbf{w}_{i,j}$	j-th weight vector of i-th class (column vector)
i, j, k, z	Indexes for $\mathbf{w}$
$A^{(t)}$	A at the t-th iteration
$P(\mathbf{W})$	Objective function parameterized by $\mathbf{W}$
$P(\mathbf{W}\|\mathbf{z})$	Function of $\mathbf{W}$ given the fixed $\mathbf{z}$
$P^{(t)}(\mathbf{W})$	Instantaneous version of $P(\mathbf{W})$ upon $(\mathbf{x}_t, y_t)$
$\mathbf{W}^*$	The optimal solution of min$P(\mathbf{W}\|\mathbf{z})$

AMM addresses the problem of selection of number of weights by an adaptive procedure that allows SGD algorithm to automatically select an appropriate number of weights. Specifically, the SGD algorithm starts with a single zero weight assigned to each class and adds new weights as necessary. On simple problems such as linear or near-linear classification, the number of weights remains low, while it can become relatively high on more complex problems. Since the generalization error of AMM grows with the number of weights, as shown by an extension of the generalization theorem from [1], AMM also contains a pruning mechanism that removes small weights, such that it provably results in only a minor degradation in optimization accuracy. In addition to improving generalization error, pruning is also useful because it reduces the cost of training and prediction.

With efficient training and prediction, comparable to linear SVM, and the ability to solve nonlinear classification problems, similar to kernel SVM, AMM fills the scalability and representability gap between linear and nonlinear classification. As such, AMM can be an appealing option when solving large-scale nonlinear classification problems.

2. PRELIMINARIES

In this paper we focus on multi-class problems. To facilitate reading, the main notation used in the paper is summarized in Table 1. Let us assume we are given a set of training examples $S = \{(\mathbf{x}_n, y_n), n = 1, ..., N\}$, where instance $\mathbf{x}_n \in \mathbb{R}^D$ is a D-dimensional feature vector and $y_n \in \mathcal{Y} = \{1, ..., M\}$ is the multi-class label. The goal is to learn a function $f : \mathbb{R}^D \rightarrow \mathcal{Y}$ that accurately predicts the label of new instances. Next, we will give an overview of multi-class SVMs proposed in [8] and their extension, the Multi-hyperplane Machine (MM) proposed in [1]. This overview will provide the necessary background needed for description of the proposed AMM algorithm, given in Section 3.

2.1 Multi-Class SVM

In multi-class SVM [8], the model $f(\mathbf{x})$ is of the form

$$f(\mathbf{x}) = \text{argmax}_{i \in \mathcal{Y}} g(i, \mathbf{x}), \quad (1)$$

where

$$g(i, \mathbf{x}) = \mathbf{w}_i^T \mathbf{x} \quad (2)$$

is parameterized by the weight vector $\mathbf{w}_i \in \mathbb{R}^D$ of the i-th class. Thus, the predicted label of $\mathbf{x}$ is the class of the weight vector that achieves the maximum value $g(i, \mathbf{x})$. By concatenating all the class-specific weight vectors, we can construct

$$\mathbf{W} = [\mathbf{w}_1 \ \mathbf{w}_2 \ ... \ \mathbf{w}_M]$$

as the $D \times M$ weight matrix representing $f(\mathbf{x})$. Under this setup, the multi-class SVM problem was defined in [8] as

$$\min_{\mathbf{W}} P(\mathbf{W}) \equiv \frac{\lambda}{2}||\mathbf{W}||^2 + \frac{1}{N}\sum\nolimits_{n=1}^{N} l(\mathbf{W}; (\mathbf{x}_n, y_n)), \quad (3)$$

where $\lambda > 0$ is a regularization parameter that trades off the model complexity defined as the Frobenius norm on $\mathbf{W}$,

$$||\mathbf{W}||^2 = \sum\nolimits_{i \in \mathcal{Y}} ||\mathbf{w}_i||^2,$$

and the margin-based training loss

$$l(\mathbf{W}; (\mathbf{x}_n, y_n)) = \max\left(0, 1 + \max_{i \in \mathcal{Y} \setminus y_n} g(i, \mathbf{x}_n) - g(y_n, \mathbf{x}_n)\right). \quad (4)$$

It can be seen from (4) that the training loss is zero if the prediction from the correct class is larger by at least one than the maximal prediction from the incorrect classes; otherwise, linear penalty is charged.

2.2 Multi-Hyperplane Machine

In order to increase the expressiveness of the classifier, Aiolli and Sperduti [1] extended the multi-class SVM by allowing multiple weights per class. Let us denote $\mathbf{w}_{i,j}$ as the j-th weight of the i-th class and let us assume that the i-th class has a total of b_i weights. By redefining $g(i, \mathbf{x})$ from (2) as

$$g(i, \mathbf{x}) = \max_j \mathbf{w}_{i,j}^T \mathbf{x}, \quad (5)$$

the classifier $f(\mathbf{x})$ from (1) returns the associated class of the weight with the maximal prediction. With this modification to multi-class SVM, the training loss (4) equals zero if the maximal prediction from the weights of the correct class is by at least one larger than any prediction from weights of the incorrect classes.

We can now concatenate all weights and define

$$\mathbf{W} = \left[\ \mathbf{w}_{1,1} ... \mathbf{w}_{1,b_1} \ | \ \mathbf{w}_{2,1} ... \mathbf{w}_{2,b_2} \ | \ ... \ | \ \mathbf{w}_{M,1} ... \mathbf{w}_{M,b_M} \ \right] \quad (6)$$

where $b_1, ..., b_M$ are the numbers of weights assigned to each of the classes and each block in (6) is a set of class-specific weights. Given this setup, $\mathbf{W}$ is learned by solving the optimization problem (3) where $g(i, \mathbf{x})$ is defined as in (5) and the model complexity is calculated as the Frobenius norm on $\mathbf{W}$ from (6). We call this algorithm the Multi-hyperplane Machine (MM).[1]

We should note that although the MM algorithm allows using different number of weights (i.e. b_i) for different classes, due to practical difficulties in determining these numbers, in [1] all classes are assigned the same number of weights b. This can be suboptimal since, depending on their distribution, different classes might require different numbers of weights.

[1]In [1] this algorithm was called the Multi-Prototype SVM.

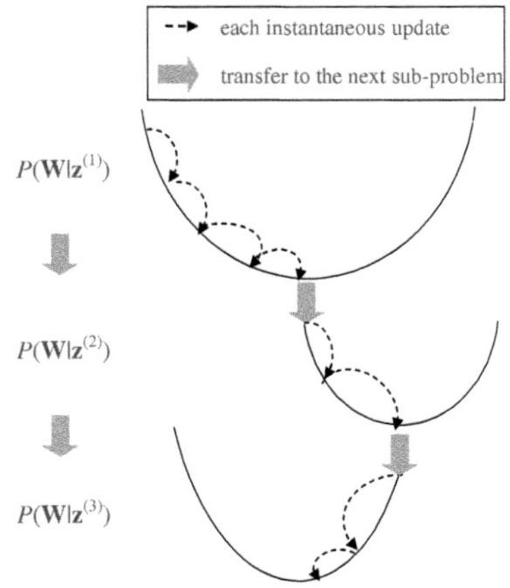

Figure 1: Convergence of MM training

2.3 MM Training

Let us consider finding the optimal MM weight matrix (6) by minimizing (3). As explained in [1], the cost function $P(\mathbf{W})$ is nonconvex and finding the global optimum cannot be guaranteed. To find a local optimum, an iterative procedure was proposed that solves a series of convex upper bounds of $P(\mathbf{W})$. The convex-approximated problem is defined as

$$\min_{\mathbf{W}} P(\mathbf{W}|\mathbf{z}) \equiv \frac{\lambda}{2}||\mathbf{W}||^2 + \frac{1}{N}\sum\nolimits_{n=1}^{N} l_{cvx}(\mathbf{W}; (\mathbf{x}_n, y_n); z_n), \quad (7)$$

where the non-convex loss function l in (3) is replaced by its convex upper bound

$$\begin{aligned} &l_{cvx}(\mathbf{W}; (\mathbf{x}_n, y_n); z_n) \\ &= \max\left(0, 1 + \max_{i \in \mathcal{Y} \setminus y_n} g(i, \mathbf{x}_n) - \mathbf{w}_{y_n, z_n}^T \mathbf{x}_n\right) \end{aligned}, \quad (8)$$

that replaces the concave term $-g(y_n, \mathbf{x}_n)$ in (4) with the convex term $-\mathbf{w}_{y_n, z_n}^T \mathbf{x}_n$. Element z_n of vector $\mathbf{z} = [z_1 ... z_N]$ determines which weight from the correct class of n-th example is used to calculate (8). Values $\mathbf{z}$ are fixed during optimization of (7).

The resulting MM algorithm can be described in the following way. At step $r = 1$, initialize $\mathbf{z}^{(1)}$, typically by random weight assignment. Then, solve the convex optimization problem (7) to find model weights as

$$\mathbf{W}^* = \arg\min_{\mathbf{W}} P(\mathbf{W}|\mathbf{z}^{(r)}).$$

Then, at step $(r+1)$, recalculate assignments $\mathbf{z}$ such that the objective function is minimized,

$$\mathbf{z}^{(r+1)} = \arg\min_{\mathbf{z}} P(\mathbf{W}^*|\mathbf{z}). \quad (9)$$

This can be achieved by calculating $z_n^{(r+1)}$ as

$$z_n^{(r+1)} = \arg\max_k (\mathbf{w}_{y_n,k}^*)^T \mathbf{x}_n, \quad (10)$$

which is the correct class weight that gives the highest prediction on n-th example. The procedure of optimizing $\mathbf{W}$ and reassigning $\mathbf{z}$ is then repeated until convergence to a local optimum. The convergence is guaranteed because each step of the algorithm leads to a decrease of the objective function $P(\mathbf{W}|\mathbf{z})$. Convergence of MM is illustrated in Figure 1, where it can be seen that

$$\min_{\mathbf{W}} P(\mathbf{W}|\mathbf{z}^{(r)}) \geq \min_{\mathbf{W}} P(\mathbf{W}|\mathbf{z}^{(r+1)}).$$

3. ADAPTIVE MULTI-HYPERPLANE MACHINE (AMM)

In this section we describe the AMM algorithm. We start by describing AMM training using Stochastic Gradient Descent (SGD). Then, we explain that SGD allows us to easily address the problem of selecting the number of class-specific weights. After pointing out that the generalization error increases with the number of weights, we propose a pruning strategy that allows reducing the generalization error while having a provably small negative impact on the optimization. Finally, we propose a simplified version of AMM that is suitable for online learning.

3.1 Solving the Sub-Problem (7)

We propose an SGD algorithm to solve the convex optimization problem (7). The SGD is initialized with the zero weight matrix $\mathbf{W}^{(1)} = \mathbf{0}$ and it reads examples one by one and modifies the weight matrix accordingly. Let us for now assume that there are b_i weights for each class. Upon receiving example $(\mathbf{x}_t, y_t) \in S$ at t-th round, $\mathbf{W}^{(t)}$ is updated using the sub-gradient of the instantaneous objective on t-th example defined as

$$P^{(t)}(\mathbf{W}|\mathbf{z}) \equiv \frac{\lambda}{2}||\mathbf{W}||^2 + l_{cvx}(\mathbf{W}; (\mathbf{x}_t, y_t); z_t).$$

As seen, the instantaneous objective differs from (7) in that it only calculates the convex loss on t-th example. The model weights are updated in the negative direction of the sub-gradient as

$$\mathbf{W}^{(t+1)} = \mathbf{W}^{(t)} - \eta^{(t)}\nabla^{(t)}, \tag{11}$$

where $\eta^{(t)} = 1/(\lambda t)$ is the learning rate and the sub-gradient matrix $\nabla^{(t)}$ is defined as

$$\nabla^{(t)} = \left[\begin{array}{c|c|c|c} \nabla^{(t)}_{1,1} \ldots \nabla^{(t)}_{1,b_1} & \nabla^{(t)}_{2,1} \ldots \nabla^{(t)}_{2,b_2} & \ldots & \nabla^{(t)}_{M,1} \ldots \nabla^{(t)}_{M,b_M} \end{array}\right] \tag{12}$$

where $\nabla^{(t)}_{i,j} = \nabla_{\mathbf{w}^{(t)}_{i,j}} P^{(t)}(\mathbf{W}^{(t)}|\mathbf{z})$ is a column vector. If convex loss $l_{cvx}(\mathbf{W}; (\mathbf{x}_t, y_t); \mathbf{z}_t)$ equals zero, then $\nabla^{(t)}_{i,j} = \lambda \mathbf{w}^{(t)}_{i,j}$; otherwise,

$$\nabla^{(t)}_{i,j} = \begin{cases} \lambda \mathbf{w}^{(t)}_{i,j} + \mathbf{x}_t, & \text{if } i = i_t,\ j = j_t \\ \lambda \mathbf{w}^{(t)}_{i,j} - \mathbf{x}_t, & \text{if } i = y_t,\ j = z_t \\ \lambda \mathbf{w}^{(t)}_{i,j}, & \text{otherwise,} \end{cases} \tag{13}$$

where

$$i_t = \arg\max_{k \in \mathcal{Y} \backslash y_t} g(k, \mathbf{x}) \quad \text{and} \quad j_t = \arg\max_{k} (\mathbf{w}^{(t)}_{i_t,k})^T \mathbf{x}_t.$$

The update rule (11) can be summarized as follows. At every round, all model weights are reduced towards zero. In addition, if the convex loss on the t-th example is positive, then the class weight from the true class indexed by z_t, $\mathbf{w}^{(t)}_{y_t,z_t}$, is moved towards $\mathbf{x}_t$, while the class weight with the maximum prediction from the remaining classes $\mathbf{w}^{(t)}_{i_t,j_t}$ is moved away from $\mathbf{x}_t$. The SGD updates are summarized in Algorithm 1 (Steps 4-7).

Algorithm 1 Training Algorithm for AMM

Input: Training set S, the regularization parameter λ
Output: $\mathbf{W}^{(t)}$
Initialize: $\mathbf{W}^{(1)} = \mathbf{0}$, $t = 1, r = 1$;

1: initialize $\mathbf{z}^{(1)}$; /* *Build 1-st sub-problem* $P(\mathbf{W}|\mathbf{z}^{(1)})$ */
2: **repeat**
3: /* *Solve each sub-problem* $P(\mathbf{W}|\mathbf{z}^{(r)})$*: lines* $4 \sim 7$*/
4: **repeat**
5: $(\mathbf{x}_t, y_t) \leftarrow t$-th example from S;
6: compute $\mathbf{W}^{(++t)}$ using (11);
7: **until** (enough epochs)
8: compute $\mathbf{z}^{(++r)}$ using (9); /* *Reassign* $\mathbf{z}$ */
9: **until** $(\mathbf{z}^{(r+1)} == \mathbf{z}^{(r)}$ or enough epochs)

The convergence to the global optimum of the convex subproblem (7) by SGD can be shown by the following theorem. Without the loss of generality, let us assume $||\mathbf{x}|| \leq 1$.

THEOREM 1. *Run the SGD update rule (11) to solve the optimization problem (7). Let* $\mathbf{W}^*$ *be the optimal solution of (7). Then we have*

$$\frac{1}{T}\sum_{t=1}^{T} P^{(t)}(\mathbf{W}^{(t)}|\mathbf{z}) - \frac{1}{T}\sum_{t=1}^{T} P^{(t)}(\mathbf{W}^*|\mathbf{z}) \leq \frac{8(\ln(T)+1)}{\lambda T}.$$

The proof of Theorem 1 is in the Appendix. The theorem tells that when T is large the averaged instantaneous loss of the algorithm converges towards that of the optimal solution. The following corollary can be obtained by following the proof of Theorems 2 and 3 from [18].

COROLLARY 1. *Assume that the conditions stated in Theorem 1 hold and for all* t $(\boldsymbol{x}_t, y_t)$ *is i.i.d. sampled from* S. *Let* $\delta \in (0, 1)$. *Then, with probability of at least* $1 - \delta$, *we have*

$$P(\mathbf{W}^{(T)}|\mathbf{z}) \leq P(\mathbf{W}^*|\mathbf{z}) + \frac{8(\ln(T)+1)}{\delta \lambda T}.$$

The corollary tells that when T is large the weight matrix $\mathbf{W}^{(t)}$ converges to the optimal solution in the limit and that the convergence rate is inversely proportional to the confidence parameter δ.

3.2 Number of Weights

As mentioned in Section 2.2, a drawback of MM is the need to pre-specify the number of model weights. In our AMM algorithm that uses SGD, we address this issue by simply setting the number of weights per class to infinity. Let us discuss the consequences of this idea.

First, we should observe that SGD initializes all model weights to zero. At t-th round, zero weight $\mathbf{w}_{i,j}$ becomes non-zero only if the convex loss $l_{cvx}(\mathbf{W}; (\mathbf{x}_t, y_t); z_t)$ is positive and either (i) $i = i_t$ and $j = j_t$ (the largest prediction from nonzero weights of incorrect classes is less than zero) or (ii) $i = y_t$ and $j = z_t$ (the assigned weight from true class is zero). Therefore, at most two zero weights can become nonzero at each round. In practice, as the AMM classifier improves during training, it will become less likely that any zero weight satisfies either condition (i) or (ii). On more complex and noisy data sets, we can expect to have more nonzero weights than on the simpler classification problems.

Second, let us discuss the implementation issue of storing an infinite number of model weights. We address it by storing all nonzero weights and a single reserved zero weight per class. Any time a zero weight becomes nonzero, we create a space for the newly created nonzero weight. In this way, a compact storage is achieved that is equivalent to storing an infinite number of weights.

3.3 Generalization Error

We now discuss the generalization error of the learned AMM model. Let us denote by b_i the number of AMM weights for i-th class, which is the sum of all its nonzero weights plus one for the reserved zero weight. In [1], the authors derived a generalization error of MM model under the assumption that training data can be separated by the model. Their proof follows the framework of Decision Directed Acyclic Graph (DDAG) [15] and the techniques used in [8]. The proof was based on the assumption that each class has equal number of weights. Here, we provide an extension of the proof in case when the number of weights per class varies.

By considering the classification process of AMM model as a DDAG with $\frac{1}{2}\sum_{i=1}^{M} b_i \sum_{j\neq i}^{M} b_j$ nodes, and following the proof of Lemma 3 in [1], we can obtain a margin-based bound. By upper bounding the margin-relevant terms by the norm of model weights, we have the following error bound.

THEOREM 2. *Suppose we are able to correctly classify an i.i.d sampled training set S using the AMM model*

$$\mathbf{W} = [\mathbf{w}_{1,1} \ldots \mathbf{w}_{1,b_1} \mathbf{w}_{2,1} \ldots \mathbf{w}_{2,b_2} \ldots \mathbf{w}_{M,1} \ldots \mathbf{w}_{M,b_M}],$$

then we can upper bound the generalization error with probability greater than $1-\delta$ *as*

$$\frac{130}{N}\left(||\mathbf{W}||^2 B \log(4eN)\log(4N) + \log(\frac{2(2N)^K}{\delta})\right),$$

where $B = \sum_{i=1}^{M} b_i + 1 + b_{\max}^2 - b_{\max} - b_{\min}$, $K = \frac{1}{2}\sum_{i=1}^{M} b_i \sum_{j\neq i}^{M} b_j$, $b_{\min} = \min_{i=1,\ldots,M}\{b_i\}$ *and* $b_{\max} = \max_{i=1,\ldots,M}\{b_i\}$.

Theorem 2 shows that the generalization error is proportional to $||\mathbf{W}||^2 B$ and that it can be reduced either by reducing the model weight norm or the number of weights. This clearly suggests that AMM should attempt to use as few nonzero weights as possible. This conclusion is a motivation for weight pruning strategy proposed next.

3.4 Weight Pruning

Every round of SGD training results in shrinking AMM model weights towards zero. As a result, the class weights that are rarely updated can become very small and start resembling zero weights. Such weights are typically generated during initial stages of training when AMM model is less accurate or during model updates caused by noisy examples. Since, by Theorem 2, nonzero weights negatively impact the generalization error, and since replacing small weights with zero weights is not likely to significantly influence AMM accuracy, we propose a pruning step that occasionally removes weights with sufficiently small norms. In addition to reducing the generalization error, weight removal is beneficial from computational viewpoint because it can speed-up both training and prediction and reduce model size.

The pruning step can be formulated as

$$\mathbf{W}^{(t+1)} \leftarrow \mathbf{W}^{(t+1)} - \Delta\mathbf{W}^{(t)}, \tag{14}$$

where $\Delta\mathbf{W}^{(t)}$ is a sparse matrix of the same size as $\mathbf{W}^{(t+1)}$ whose nonzero columns correspond to removed weights. For example, if $\mathbf{w}_{i,j}^{(t)}$ is removed, $\Delta\mathbf{w}_{i,j}^{(t)} = \mathbf{w}_{i,j}^{(t)}$, and all other columns of $\Delta\mathbf{W}^{(t)}$ are zero. In AMM, pruning is performed periodically after every k rounds and only on the weights that are below a threshold. The following theorem analyzes the impact of pruning on the convergence of SGD.

THEOREM 3. *Consider the SGD update rule (11). Let* $\mathbf{W}^*$ *be the optimal solution of the problem (7). Define a pruning constant* $c \geq 0$ *and execute the pruning step (14) after each* k *iterations with* $\Delta\mathbf{W}^{(t)} \leq c/((t-1)\lambda)$. *Then we have*

$$\frac{1}{T}\sum_{t=1}^{T} P^{(t)}(\mathbf{W}^{(t)}|\mathbf{z}) - \frac{1}{T}\sum_{t=1}^{T} P^{(t)}(\mathbf{W}^*|\mathbf{z}) \leq \frac{(8+c)(\ln(T)+1)}{\lambda T} + \frac{2(4+c)c}{k\lambda}.$$

The proof is in the Appendix. Theorem 3 quantifies the upper bound on the difference between the averaged instantaneous loss of the AMM with pruning and the optimal solution. It can be seen that the gap is proportional to the pruning threshold c and inversely proportional to the pruning interval k. When $c = 0$, Theorem 3 is equivalent to Theorem 1. Large c and small k correspond to a more aggressive pruning that enforces a simpler classifier but with a wider gap with the optimal solution; while small c and large k shrink the gap but lead to larger AMM model. Next, we state the following important property of pruning.

PROPOSITION 1. *Let us consider the case where pruning (14) is executed after each* k *iterations with threshold* c. *Let us consider a weight which is being updated at least* c *times through the first two cases in (13) during the previous* k *iterations. It can be shown that such weight will not be pruned.*

We omit the proof due to lack of space. The Proposition 1 provides a very useful interpretation of the effect of the pruning threshold c in Theorem 3. To be consistent with Theorem 3, pruning in AMM is implemented as follows: every k rounds, AMM weights are pruned starting from the one with the smallest norm, and continued as long as the cumulative Frobenius norm of the pruned weights is below threshold $c/((t-1)\lambda)$.

3.5 Online AMM

AMM described in Algorithm 1 is suitable for offline application where the whole data set is residing on a computer and multiple passes through the data are allowed. This is due to the procedure that iteratively solves an approximate convex problem (7) and recalculates assignments $\mathbf{z}$ on the whole data set. Here, we propose a modification of AMM that allows its use in an online setting, where the data set is observed sequentially in a single pass. Online AMM calculates assignment of the incoming t-th example as

$$z_t = \arg\max_k((\mathbf{w}_{y_t,k}^{(t)})^T \mathbf{x}_t)$$

and updates $\mathbf{W}^{(t)}$ to $\mathbf{W}^{(t+1)}$ using SGD (11) with this assignment. The resulting online training procedure is summarized in Algorithm 2.

Algorithm 2 Online Algorithm

Input: Training set S, the regularization parameter λ
Output: $\mathbf{W}^{(t)}$
Initialize: $\mathbf{W}^{(1)} = \mathbf{0}$, $t = 1$

```
repeat
    (x_t, y_t) ← t-th example from S;
    calculate z_t by (10);
    update W^(++t) by (11);
until (data set exhausted)
```

The main difference between the offline (Algorthm 1) and online (Algorithm 2) versions of AMM is that the online version does not wait for convergence of (7) but changes the assignment $\mathbf{z}$ after every update of SGD. As a result, instead of having to periodically calculate assignment $\mathbf{z}$ on the whole data set, it only has to be done on the single incoming example. This allows a single-pass AMM training, and it also leads to savings in computational speed and memory. The price to be paid is that convergence of online AMM to a local optimum cannot be guaranteed, because the online AMM greedily minimizes the non-convex instantaneous objective (3). As will be seen from the experimental results, the online AMM behavior is very similar to the offline AMM. Coupled with computational efficiency, ease of implementation, and applicability for stream learning, this makes online AMM a highly attractive learning algorithm.

3.6 Implementation Details

A naïve implementation of the update rule (11) would require $\mathcal{O}(D)$time for weight shrinking $(1 - \eta^{(t)}\lambda)\mathbf{w}_{i,j}^{(t)}$ and $\mathcal{O}(D)$ time to perform weight update. This computational burden is unnecessary when instances are highly dimensional and sparse (e.g. in text/image data). To circumvent this problem we apply an approach used to speed-up linear SVM training [18] that represents $\mathbf{w}_{i,j}$ as $\mathbf{w}_{i,j} = s_{i,j}\mathbf{v}_{i,j}$, where $s_{i,j}$ is a scalar and $\mathbf{v}_{i,j} \in \mathbb{R}^D$. In this case, the update rule can be decomposed into $s_{i,j}^{(t)} \leftarrow (1 - \eta^{(t)}\lambda)s_{i,j}^{(t)}$ and $\mathbf{v}_{i,j}^{(t)} \leftarrow \mathbf{v}_{i,j}^{(t)} \pm \eta^{(t)}/s_{i,j}^{(t)}\mathbf{x}_t$ in time only proportional to the number of non-zero features in $\mathbf{x}_t$.

4. EXPERIMENTS

In this section, we evaluate the proposed batch and online AMM algorithms and compare them with the large-scale Kernel and Linear SVM algorithms on several large real-life data sets. The competing algorithms are listed as follows:

- **LibSVM**[4] A popular SMO-based SVM solver which is scalable to hundreds of thousands examples.
- **LaSVM**[3] A large-scale online SVM algorithm that accesses one example at a time.
- **P-packSVM**[28] An SVM solver that parallelizes the SGD style training on multiple processors.
- **Pegasos**[18] The state-of-the-art Linear SVM solver which is based on SGD.
- **Poly 2 SVM by Liblinear**[5] A fast solver for Polynomial degree 2 kernel SVM. The algorithm explicitly expresses the feature space as a set of attributes and then trains Liblinear on the transformed data. However, it is only scalable to very sparse or low dimensional data.

A summary of datasets[2] is shown in Table 2.

For Algorithm 1, instead of a random assignment, we initialized $\mathbf{z}^{(1)}$ by a single scan of data using Online AMM, which sequentially sets each element of $\mathbf{z}^{(1)}$ as in (10). Our preliminary results showed it worked better than the simple random initialization approach. We used the epoch-based stopping criteria[3] for SGD for each sub-problem. Since all studied data sets were large we used only 1 epoch before reassigning the weights. We stopped training after 5 passes through the data. We ran online AMM using a single pass of the data. In addition, we also explored performance of online AMM when 5 passes through data. This allowed us to compare online and batch AMM. The pruning step with $k = 10,000$ and $c = 10$ was used with Algorithms 1 & 2 in all the experiments.

The training error and training time of LibSVM, LaSVM, P-packSVM and Poly 2 SVM were taken from recently published results in [5, 12, 28]. For Pegasos and the proposed batch and online AMM algorithms, we selected the regularization parameter λ through cross-validation. The considered range was $\lambda = 10^{-2}, ..., 10^{-7}$. We repeated all the experiments five times, each with randomly shuffled training data. Mean and standard deviation of each set of experiments are reported. All the training examples were normalized such that all attributes were within range $[-1, +1]$. Both batch and online AMM algorithms were implemented in C++. Unless otherwise stated, all the experiments were run using a 3.0GHz Intel Xeon processor with 16G memory on Linux.

The generalization error and the training time of all the algorithms on large datasets are summarized in Table 3. Due to the large computational costs of Kernel SVM training on the largest datasets from our collection, no previous results are reported (to the best of our knowledge), so we use NA to mark these cases in the table. The original MM algorithm [1] is also not scalable to any of the studied large datasets, so it is not included in the comparison.

Batch vs. Online First, let us compare two versions of AMM. We can see that batch AMM achieved lower generalization error than its online sibling at the expense of significantly longer training time that occasionally was more than one order of magnitude longer. The difference in accuracy depends on the difficulty of the datasets. Considering that online AMM used only a single pass of the data, its slightly degraded generalization error is understandable.

AMM vs. Linear SVM Comparing the generalization error of AMM with Linear SVM, we can see that both AMM algorithms significantly outperformed Linear SVM on 5 out of 7 datasets. Considering training time, online AMM had comparable training time to Linear SVM and batch AMM was somewhat slower. Considering prediction time, Table 4 lists the number of weights in the AMM classifiers that dictate prediction time and memory needed to store the

[2] url dataset [13] is available at `http://www.sysnet.ucsd.edu/projects/url/`; all the others are available at `http://www.csie.ntu.edu.tw/~cjlin/libsvmtools/datasets/`

[3] As suggested in [2]. [18] uses a predefined threshold on the objective value as the stopping criteria. However, this threshold can vary from case to case.

Table 2: **Summary of large datasets**

Datasets	#train	#test	#dim	#class	non-zero %	file size	domain
a9a	32,561	16,281	123	2	11.3%	2M	social survey
ijcnn	49,990	91,701	22	2	66.7%	7.5M	time series
webspam	280,000	70,000	254	2	41.9%	327M	web text
rcv1_bin	677,399	20,242	47,236	2	0.2%	35M	news text
url	1,976,130	420,000	3,231,961	2	0.004%	1.7G	Internet data
mnist8m_bin	8,000,000	10,000	784	2	19.3%	18G	OCR images
mnist8m_mc	8,000,000	10,000	784	10	19.3%	18G	OCR images

Table 3: Error rate and training time comparison with large-scale algorithms (RBF SVM is solved by LibSVM unless specified otherwise. Poly2 and LibSVM results are from [5]).

Datasets	Error rate (%)					Training time (seconds)[1]				
	AMM *batch*	AMM *online*	Linear (Pegasos)	Poly2 SVM	RBF SVM	AMM *batch*	AMM *online*	Linear (Pegasos)	Poly2 SVM	RBF SVM
a9a	15.03±0.11	16.44±0.23	15.04±0.07	14.94	14.97	2	0.2	1	2	99
ijcnn	2.40±0.11	3.02±0.14	7.76±0.19	2.16	1.31	2	0.1	1	11	27
webspam	4.50±0.24	6.14±1.08	7.28±0.09	1.56	0.80	80	4	12	3,228	15,571
mnist_bin	0.53±0.05	0.54±0.03	2.03±0.04	NA	0.43[2]	3084	300	277	NA	2 days[2]
mnist_mc	3.20±0.16	3.36±0.20	8.41±0.11	NA	0.67[3]	13864	1200	1180	NA	8 days[3]
rcv1_bin	2.20±0.01	2.21±0.02	2.29±0.01	NA	NA	1100	80	25	NA	NA
url	1.34±0.21	2.87±1.49	1.50±0.39	NA	NA	400	24	100	NA	NA

[1] excludes data loading time.
[2] achieved by parallel training P-packSVMs on 512 processors; results from [28].
[3] achieved by LaSVM; results from [12].

classification model. These numbers divided by the number of classes directly reflect the increased prediction time of AMM as compared to Linear SVM. We can see that AMM classifiers are around one order of magnitude slower than Linear SVM, which has $\mathcal{O}(MD)$ prediction time. This is very impressive result considering that AMM achieves significantly lower error rate than Linear SVM. This indicates that AMM is superior to linear SVM because it provides a better tradeoff between accuracy and speed in all but the most resource-constrained applications.

AMM vs. Kernel SVM Comparison against Poly2 SVM on three relatively small datasets (a9a, ijcnn, webspam) shows that AMM had similar error rates as Poly2 SVM, while achieving several orders of magnitude faster training. Also, the $\mathcal{O}(MD)$ prediction time of AMM is much more favorable than the $\mathcal{O}(MD^2)$ prediction time of Poly2 SVM. By comparing AMM with RBF SVM on 5 low-dimensional datasets (where RBF SVM's results were reported in the previous literature), we can see that AMM has somewhat lower $(0.1\%-2.9\%)$ but still comparable error rate. Particularly, on the two largest datasets (mnist8m_bin and mnnist8m_mul), the error rate achieved by AMM after running on a single processor for a couple of hours is very competitive to P-packSVM's classifier trained in 2 days on 512 processors and LaSVM's classifier trained in 8 days on a single processor. These results show that the AMM algorithms are appealing alternative to kernel SVMs when learning from very large data.

Train Online AMM in Batch Mode Table 3 lists Online AMM results when it was run with a single pass through the data. We also performed experiments when it was allowed to make multiple passes through the data. The detailed results on the two largest datasets for the multi-pass Onine AMM are shown in Figure 2. The top left and bottom left panels in Figure 2 show the evolution of the error rate and the total training time as a function of the number of epochs (one epoch denotes a full pass through the data). We can see that the error rate rapidly decreases during the first epoch and that it continues to improve slightly after the first epoch. The training time increases linearly, as expected. The results suggests that, if the training time is not of major concern and if data could be stored in memory, multiple accesses to the training data should be recommended. The top right and bottom right panels of Figure 2 show the number of AMM weights as training progresses. In addition to the current number of weights, the panels also show the total number of weights created and pruned at any stage of training process. It can be seen that the pruning has the desired effect of controlling the total number of model weights without negatively influencing the error rate.

5. CONCLUSIONS

Recent advances in large-scale learning resulted in many successful algorithms for linear classification. However, creating sufficiently efficient kernel SVM is still an open problem that prevents its application on the largest data sets. This study aimed at filling the scalability and representability gap between linear and kernel SVMs. We presented two multi-hyperplane algorithms for multi-class classification that have several favorable features: fast training and prediction, simple implementation, ability to represent nonlinear concepts, and theoretical justification of their proper-

Table 4: The number of weights in the classifiers

Datasets	a9a	ijcnn	webspam	mnist8m_bin	mnist8m_mc	rcv1	url
batch AMM	11±1	11±1	13±2	20±1	65±2	22±2	4±0
online AMM	16±2	15±1	10±1	13±1	61±3	44±5	5±1

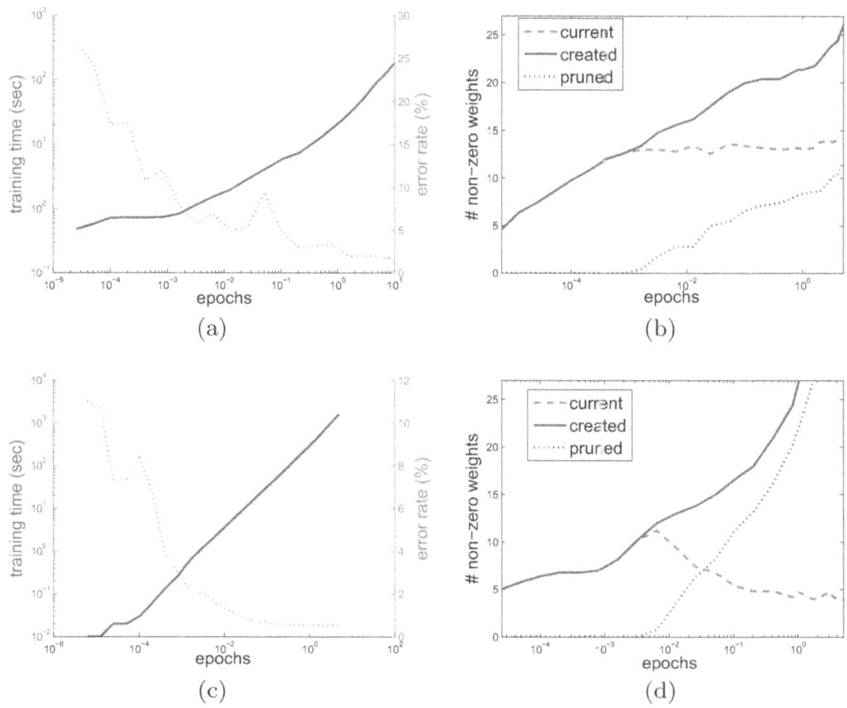

Figure 2: Detailed results on url data (upper two panels) and mnist8m_bin data (lower two panels)

ties. Experimental comparison with the state-of-the-art linear and kernel SVMs on large data sets showed that AMM classifiers provide an interesting tradeoff between these two major classes of algorithms. In addition to being an attractive option when solving large-scale classification problems, AMM could also be useful as a data exploration tool. When faced with a new large-scale classification problem, AMM could be trained together with linear SVM and if its error rate is significantly lower, it could indicate that the problem is nonlinear and that more computationally costly but more powerful classification algorithms should be considered.

6. ACKNOWLEDGMENTS

Authors thank Yu Liang (Temple Univ.) for implementing the first version of the algorithms and Kai Zhang (Siemens Corporate Research) for proofreading the manuscript. N. Djuric and S. Vucetic were supported by the U.S. National Science Foundation Grant IIS-0546155. K. Crammer is a Horev Fellow, supported by the Taub Foundations.

7. REFERENCES

[1] F. Aiolli and A. Sperduti. Multi-class classification with multi-prototype support vector machines. *Journal of Machine Learning Research*, 2005.

[2] A. Bordes, L. Bottou, and P. Gallinari. Sgd-qn: careful quasi-newton stochastic gradient descent. *Journal of Machine Learning Research*, 2009.

[3] A. Bordes, S. Ertekin, J. Weston, and L. Bottou. Fast kernel classifiers for online and active learning. *Journal of Machine Learning Research*, 2005.

[4] C.-C. Chang and C.-J. Lin. Libsvm: a library for support vector machines, http://www.csie.ntu.edu.tw/ cjlin/libsvm. 2001.

[5] Y.-W. Chang, K.-W. C. C.-J. Hsie and, M. Ringgaard, and C.-J. Lin. Training and testing low-degree polynomial data mappings via linear svm. *Journal of Machine Learning Research*, 2010.

[6] R. Collobert, F. Sinz, J. Weston, and L. Bottou. Trading convexity for scalability. In *International Conference on Machine Learning*, 2006.

[7] Cortes and Vapnik. Support-vector networks. *Machine Learning*, 1995.

[8] K. Crammer and Y. Singer. On the algorithmic implementation of multiclass kernel-based vector machines. *Journal of Machine Learning Research*, 2001.

[9] C.-J. Hsieh, K.-W. Chang, C.-J. Lin, S. S. Keerthi, and S. Sundararajan. A dual coordinate descent method for large-scale linear svm. In *International Conference on Machine Learning*, 2008.

[10] T. Joachims. Training linear svms in linear time. In

ACM SIGKDD Conference on Knowledge Discovery and Data Mining, 2006.

[11] J. Kivinen, A. J. Smola, and R. C. Williamson. Online learning with kernels. *IEEE Transactions on Signal Processing*, 2002.

[12] G. Loosli, S. Canu, and L. Bottou. Training invariant support vector machines using selective sampling. *Large Scale Kernel Machines, Cam-bridge, MA, MIT Press*, 2007.

[13] J. Ma, L. K. Saul, S. Savage, and G. M. Voelker. Identifying suspicious urls: An application of large-scale online learning. In *International Conference on Machine Learning*, 2009.

[14] J. Platt. Fast training of support vector machines using sequential minimal optimization. *Advances in kernel methods - support vector learning, MIT Press*, 1998.

[15] J. Platt, N. Cristianini, and J. S. Taylor. Large margin dags for multiclass classification. In *Advance in Nueral Information Processing Systems*, 2000.

[16] A. Rahimi and B. Recht. Random features for large-scale kernel machines. In *Advance in Nueral Information Processing Systems*, 2007.

[17] S. Shalev-Shwartz and Y. Singer. Logarithmic regret algorithms for strongly convex repeated games (technical report). The Hebrew University, 2007.

[18] S. Shalev-Shwartz, Y. Singer, and N. Srebro. Pegasos: primal estimated sub-gradient solver for svm. In *International Conference on Machine Learning*, 2007.

[19] S. Sonnenburg and V. Franc. Coffin : a computational framework for linear svms. In *International Conference on Machine Learning*, 2010.

[20] I. Steinwart. Sparseness of support vector machines. *Journal of Machine Learning Research*, 2003.

[21] C. Teo, S. V. N. Vishwanathan, A. J. Smola, and Q. V. Le. Bundle methods for regularized risk minimization. *Journal of Machine Learning Research*, 2010.

[22] I. W. Tsang, J. T. Kwok, and P.-M. Cheung. Core vector machines: fast svm training on very large data sets. *Journal of Machine Learning Research*, 2005.

[23] S. V. N. Vishwanathan, A. J. Smola, and M. N.Murty. Simplesvm. In *International Conference on Machine Learning*, 2003.

[24] Z. Wang, K. Crammer, and S.Vucetic. Multi-class pegasos on a budget. In *International Conference on Machine Learning*, 2010.

[25] Z. Wang and S.Vucetic. Online training on a budget of support vector machines using twin prototypes. *Statisitcal Analysis and Data Mining Journal*, 2010.

[26] H.-F. Yu, C.-J. Hsieh, K.-W. Chang, and C.-J. Lin. Large linear classification when data cannot fit in memory. In *ACM SIGKDD Conference on Knowledge Discovery and Data Mining*, 2010.

[27] T. Zhang. Solving large scale linear prediction problems using stochastic gradient descent. In *International Conference on Machine Learning*, 2004.

[28] Z. A. Zhu, W. Chen, G. Wang, C. Zhu, and Z. Chen. P-packsvm: parallel primal gradient descent kernel svm. In *IEEE International Conference on Data Mining*, 2009.

APPENDIX

Unified Proof of Theorems 1 & 3: First, we rewrite the update rule of SGD with the optional pruning step as $\mathbf{W}^{(t+1)} \leftarrow \mathbf{W}^{(t)} - \eta^{(t)}\partial^{(t)}$, where $\partial^{(t)} = \nabla^{(t)} + E^{(t)}$ and $E^{(t)} = \mathbf{0}$ if no pruning is used. The relative progress towards the optimal solution $\mathbf{W}^*$ at t-th round $D^{(t)}$ can be lower bounded as

$$\begin{aligned} &D^{(t)} = ||\mathbf{W}^{(t)} - \mathbf{W}^*||^2 - ||\mathbf{W}^{(t)} - \eta^{(t)}\nabla^{(t)} - \eta^{(t)}E^{(t)} - \mathbf{W}^*||^2 \\ &= -(\eta^{(t)})^2||\partial^{(t)}||^2 + 2\eta^{(t)}(E^{(t)})^T(\mathbf{W}^{(t)} - \mathbf{W}^*) \\ &+2\eta^{(t)}(\nabla^{(t)})^T(\mathbf{W}^{(t)} - \mathbf{W}^*) \\ &\geq_1 -(\eta^{(t)})^2G^2 - 2\eta^{(t)}||E^{(t)}||\tfrac{4+c}{\lambda} \\ &+2\eta^{(t)}\left(P^{(t)}(\mathbf{W}^{(t)}) - P^{(t)}(\mathbf{W}^*) + \tfrac{\lambda}{2}||\mathbf{W}^{(t)} - \mathbf{W}^*||^2\right). \end{aligned} \tag{15}$$

In $\geq_1$, we assume there is a constant $G \geq 0$ such that $||\partial^{(t)}|| \leq G$ and we will quantify G later on. For the second term, we first bound $\mathbf{W}^{(t)}$ as

$$\begin{aligned} &||\mathbf{W}^{(t)}|| \leq ||(1 - \eta^{(t-1)}\lambda)\mathbf{W}^{(t-1)}|| + 2\eta^{(t-1)} + ||\Delta\mathbf{W}^{(t-1)}|| \\ &\leq \tfrac{t-2}{t-1}||\mathbf{W}^{(t-1)}|| + \tfrac{2}{(t-1)\lambda} + \tfrac{c}{(t-1)\lambda} \\ &\leq \tfrac{1}{t-1}||\mathbf{W}^{(0)}|| + \tfrac{2(t-1)}{(t-1)\lambda} + \tfrac{(t-1)c}{(t-1)\lambda} = \tfrac{2+c}{\lambda}, \end{aligned}$$

and then use triangle inequality to bound $||\mathbf{W}^{(t)} - \mathbf{W}^*|| \leq (2+c)/\lambda + 2/\lambda$ by using the fact $||\mathbf{W}^*|| \leq 2/\lambda$ according to the result in [11]. Then, we bound the third term using function $P^{(t)}(\mathbf{W}^{(t)})$'s λ-strong convexity [17].

Dividing both sides of inequality (15) by $2\eta^{(t)}$ and rearranging, we obtain

$$\begin{aligned} &P^{(t)}(\mathbf{W}^{(t)}) - P^{(t)}(\mathbf{W}^*) \leq \tfrac{D^{(t)}}{2\eta^{(t)}} - \tfrac{\lambda}{2}||\mathbf{W}^{(t)} - \mathbf{W}^*||^2 \\ &+\tfrac{\eta^{(t)}G^2}{2} + \tfrac{(4+c)||E^{(t)}||}{\lambda}. \end{aligned} \tag{16}$$

Summing over all t, we get

$$\begin{aligned} &\sum_{t=1}^{T} P^{(t)}(\mathbf{W}^{(t)}) - \sum_{t=1}^{T} P^{(t)}(\mathbf{W}^*) \leq \sum_{t=1}^{T} \tfrac{D^{(t)}}{2\eta^{(t)}} \\ &- \sum_{t=1}^{T} \tfrac{\lambda}{2}||\mathbf{W}^{(t)} - \mathbf{W}^*||^2 + \tfrac{G^2}{2}\sum_{t=1}^{T}\eta^{(t)} + \tfrac{(4+c)}{\lambda}\sum_{t=1}^{T}||E^{(t)}||. \end{aligned}$$

We bound the first and second terms in inequality (16) as

$$\begin{aligned} &\tfrac{1}{2}\sum_{t=1}^{N}\left(\tfrac{D^{(t)}}{\eta^{(t)}} - \lambda||\mathbf{W}^{(t)} - \mathbf{W}^*||^2\right) = \tfrac{1}{2}\Big((\tfrac{1}{\eta^{(1)}} - \lambda)||\mathbf{W}^{(1)} \\ &-\mathbf{W}^*||^2 + \sum_{t=2}^{N}\left(\tfrac{1}{\eta^{(t)}} - \tfrac{1}{\eta^{(t-1)}} - \lambda\right)||\mathbf{W}^{(t)} - \mathbf{W}^*||^2 \\ &-\tfrac{1}{\eta^{(N)}}||\mathbf{W}^{(T+1)} - \mathbf{W}^*||^2\Big) \\ &=_1 -\tfrac{1}{2\eta^{(N)}}||\mathbf{W}^{(T+1)} - \mathbf{W}^*||^2 \leq 0. \end{aligned} \tag{17}$$

In $=_1$, the first and second terms vanish after plugging $\eta_t \equiv 1/(\lambda t)$. Next, we bound the third term in inequality (16) according to the divergence rate of harmonic series,

$$\frac{G^2}{2}\sum_{t=1}^{T}\eta^{(t)} = \frac{G^2}{2\lambda}\sum_{t=1}^{T}\frac{1}{t} \leq \frac{G^2}{2\lambda}(\ln(T) + 1). \tag{18}$$

Then, we quantify G as

$$||\partial^{(t)}|| \leq ||\nabla^{(t)}|| + ||E^{(t)}|| \leq (\lambda||\mathbf{W}^{(t)}|| + 2) + 2 + c \leq 6 + c \equiv G.$$

If no pruning is used, $||E^{(t)}|| = 0$. For the iterations when the pruning is executed, we bound $||E^{(t)}||$ as $||E^{(t)}|| \leq 2c$ using the bound on $\Delta\mathbf{W}^{(t)}$. Combining inequality (17) with (18) and dividing two sides of inequality by T, we get the stated bounds as in Theorems 1 and 3.

An Improved GLMNET for L1-regularized Logistic Regression

Guo-Xun Yuan
Dept. of Computer Science
National Taiwan University
Taipei 106, Taiwan
r96042@csie.ntu.edu.tw

Chia-Hua Ho
Dept. of Computer Science
National Taiwan University
Taipei 106, Taiwan
b95082@csie.ntu.edu.tw

Chih-Jen Lin
Dept. of Computer Science
National Taiwan University
Taipei 106, Taiwan
cjlin@csie.ntu.edu.tw

ABSTRACT

GLMNET proposed by Friedman et al. [1] is an algorithm for generalized linear models with elastic net. It has been widely applied to solve L1-regularized logistic regression. However, recent experiments indicated that the existing GLMNET implementation may not be stable for large-scale problems. In this paper, we propose an improved GLMNET to address some theoretical and implementation issues. In particular, as a Newton-type method, GLMNET achieves fast local convergence, but may fail to quickly obtain a useful solution. By a careful design to adjust the effort for each iteration, our method is efficient regardless of loosely or strictly solving the optimization problem. Experiments demonstrate that the improved GLMNET is more efficient than a state-of-the-art coordinate descent method.

Categories and Subject Descriptors

I.5.2 [**Pattern Recognition**]: Design Methodology—*Classifier design and evaluation*

General Terms

Algorithms, Performance, Experimentation

1. INTRODUCTION

Logistic regression is a popular classification method in machine learning. Recently, L1-regularized logistic regression is widely used because it can generate a sparse model. Given a set of instance-label pairs $(\boldsymbol{x}_i, y_i)$, $i = 1, \ldots, l$, $\boldsymbol{x}_i \in \mathbf{R}^n$, $y_i \in \{-1, +1\}$, L1-regularized logistic regression solves the following unconstrained optimization problem:

$$\min_{\boldsymbol{w}} \quad f(\boldsymbol{w}) \equiv \|\boldsymbol{w}\|_1 + C\sum_{i=1}^{l} \log(1 + e^{-y_i \boldsymbol{w}^T \boldsymbol{x}_i}), \tag{1}$$

where $\|\cdot\|_1$ denotes the 1-norm. The regularization term $\|\boldsymbol{w}\|_1$ is used to avoid overfitting the training data, while the other term is the sum of training losses. The user-defined parameter $C > 0$ is used to balance the regularization and loss terms. Different from the 2-norm regularization, the 1-norm regularization gives a sparse solution of (1).

A difficulty for solving (1) is that $\|\boldsymbol{w}\|_1$ is not differentiable. Many optimization approaches have been proposed; for example, [2, 3, 4, 5, 6]. Recently, Yuan et al. [7] made a comprehensive comparison among state-of-the-art algorithms and software for L1-regularized logistic regression and SVM. They conclude that coordinate descent (CD) methods perform better than others for large sparse data (e.g., document data). In particular, CD methods can quickly obtain a useful solution.

In [7], the method GLMNET by Friedman et al. [1] is included for comparison and the performance is reasonably well. GLMNET is a Newton-type approach by iteratively minimizing the second-order approximation. The result in [7] indicates that GLMNET has fast local convergence, but may spend too much time in early iterations. Thus, different from CD methods, GLMNET could not quickly obtain a useful model. Further, in [7], the existing GLMNET implementation failed to solve two large problems.

In this paper, we propose an improved GLMNET called newGLMNET. Our contributions are as follows. First, we modify GLMNET to be under a general framework in [8] for establishing the theoretical convergence. Second, we address some implementation concerns in GLMNET. In particular, by a careful design to adjust the effort for each iteration, our method is efficient for both loosely and strictly solving the optimization problem. Third, we show that the CD method recommended by [7] may be inefficient for dense data (i.e., each instance contains many non-zero feature values). The reason is that compared to newGLMNET and GLMNET, in a similar number of operations, CD methods need much more exponential/logarithmic operations.

We define notation and discuss some basic properties of (1). The logistic loss is twice differentiable, so most existing approaches use the gradient and the Hessian of the second term in (1): By defining

$$L(\boldsymbol{w}) \equiv C\sum_{i=1}^{l} \log(1 + e^{-y_i \boldsymbol{w}^T \boldsymbol{x}_i}),$$

the gradient and Hessian of $L(\boldsymbol{w})$ are respectively

$$\begin{aligned} \nabla L(\boldsymbol{w}) &= C\sum_{i=1}^{l} (\tau(y_i \boldsymbol{w}^T \boldsymbol{x}_i) - 1) y_i \boldsymbol{x}_i \quad \text{and} \\ \nabla^2 L(\boldsymbol{w}) &= C X^T D X, \end{aligned} \tag{2}$$

where $\tau(s)$ is the derivative of the logistic loss $\log(1 + e^s)$:

$$\tau(s) = \frac{1}{1 + e^{-s}},$$

KDD'11, August 21–24, 2011, San Diego, California, USA.

$D \in \mathbf{R}^{l\times l}$ is a diagonal matrix with

$$D_{ii} = \tau(y_i \boldsymbol{w}^T \boldsymbol{x}_i)\left(1 - \tau(y_i \boldsymbol{w}^T \boldsymbol{x}_i)\right),$$

and

$$X \equiv \begin{bmatrix} \boldsymbol{x}_1^T \\ \vdots \\ \boldsymbol{x}_l^T \end{bmatrix} \in \mathbf{R}^{l\times n}.$$

From standard convex analysis, $\boldsymbol{w}^*$ is optimal for problem (1) if and only if $\boldsymbol{w}^*$ satisfies the optimality conditions.

$$\begin{cases} \nabla_j L(\boldsymbol{w}^*) + 1 = 0 & \text{if } w_j^* > 0, \\ \nabla_j L(\boldsymbol{w}^*) - 1 = 0 & \text{if } w_j^* < 0, \\ -1 \leq \nabla_j L(\boldsymbol{w}^*) \leq 1 & \text{if } w_j^* = 0. \end{cases} \tag{3}$$

Equivalently, $\boldsymbol{w}^*$ is optimal if and only if the minimum-norm sub-gradient at $\boldsymbol{w}^*$ is zero.

$$\nabla^S f(\boldsymbol{w}^*) = \mathbf{0}, \tag{4}$$

where

$$\nabla_j^S f(\boldsymbol{w}) \equiv \begin{cases} \nabla_j L(\boldsymbol{w}) + 1 & \text{if } w_j > 0, \\ \nabla_j L(\boldsymbol{w}) - 1 & \text{if } w_j < 0, \\ \text{sgn}(\nabla_j L(\boldsymbol{w})) \max(|\nabla_j L(\boldsymbol{w})| - 1, 0) & \text{if } w_j = 0. \end{cases}$$

This paper is organized as follows. Section 2 discusses a framework of decomposition methods by [8]. The CD method recommended by [7] and GLMNET by [1] can be considered as examples of this framework. We also point out some theoretical and implementation issues of GLMNET. In Section 3, we propose an improved GLMNET called newGLMNET. Experiments in Section 4 shows the superiority of newGLMNET. Section 5 concludes this work.

2. DECOMPOSITION METHODS

Decomposition methods are a commonly-used optimization approach by iteratively solving smaller sub-problems. At each iteration of a decomposition method, a set J of working variables is chosen and the following sub-problem is solved:

$$\min_{\boldsymbol{d}} \quad f(\boldsymbol{w} + \boldsymbol{d}) - f(\boldsymbol{w}) \quad \text{subject to} \quad d_j = 0 \quad \forall j \notin J, \tag{5}$$

where

$$f(\boldsymbol{w} + \boldsymbol{d}) - f(\boldsymbol{w}) = L(\boldsymbol{w} + \boldsymbol{d}) - L(\boldsymbol{w}) + \|\boldsymbol{w} + \boldsymbol{d}\|_1 - \|\boldsymbol{w}\|_1.$$

Only variables in J are updated at each iteration. If $\boldsymbol{d}$ is an optimal solution of (5), then $\boldsymbol{w}$ is updated by

$$w_j \leftarrow w_j + d_j, \forall j \in J.$$

There are two key issues of a decomposition method: one is the selection of the working set J; the other is how to solve the sub-problem (5). Practically, because the smaller sub-problem (5) may be still hard, most existing decomposition methods only approximately solve (5).

Tseng and Yun [8] study a general decomposition method CGD (Coordinate Gradient Descent) for L1-regularized problems. They assume that at each iteration, a second-order approximation to $L(\boldsymbol{w} + \boldsymbol{d}) - L(\boldsymbol{w})$ is used. Specifically, given a symmetric positive-definite matrix $H^k \in \mathbf{R}^{n\times n}$ approximating the Hessian matrix $\nabla^2 L(\boldsymbol{w}^k)$ and a working set $J^k \subseteq \mathcal{N} = \{1, \ldots, n\}$ at the kth iteration, CGD solves the following quadratic sub-problem:

$$\min_{\boldsymbol{d}} \quad q_k(\boldsymbol{d}) \equiv \nabla L(\boldsymbol{w}^k)^T \boldsymbol{d} + \frac{1}{2}\boldsymbol{d}^T H^k \boldsymbol{d} + \|\boldsymbol{w}^k + \boldsymbol{d}\|_1 - \|\boldsymbol{w}^k\|_1$$
$$\text{subject to} \quad d_j = 0 \quad \forall j \notin J^k, \tag{6}$$

where $\boldsymbol{w}^k$ is the current iterate.

Many methods are available to select the working set J. A common rule is to choose working variables in a cyclic manner. That is, elements of the sequence $\{\{1\}, \{2\}, \ldots, \{n\}\}$ repeatedly take turns to serve as the working set J. The cyclic rule for choosing working variables is often called the Gauss-Seidel rule. Besides, because the gradient reveals the closeness to an optimal solution, some methods, called Gauss-Southwell rules, select J based on the gradient information. The concept is extended in [8] by checking the relationship between $\boldsymbol{d}(J)$ and $\boldsymbol{d}(\mathcal{N})$, which are optimal solutions of (6) using J and $\mathcal{N}$ as working sets, respectively. For example, one rule selects J satisfying

$$\|\boldsymbol{d}(J)\|_\infty \geq v\|\boldsymbol{d}(\mathcal{N})\|_\infty, \tag{7}$$

where $v \in (0, 1)$.[1]

To ensure the convergence, [8] conducts line search after obtaining an optimal solution $\boldsymbol{d}$ of (6). A step size $\lambda \in \{\beta^i \mid i = 0, 1, \ldots\}$ is found such that $\lambda\boldsymbol{d}$ satisfies the following sufficient decrease condition:

$$\begin{aligned} &f(\boldsymbol{w}^k + \lambda\boldsymbol{d}) - f(\boldsymbol{w}^k) \\ \leq &\sigma\lambda\left(\nabla L(\boldsymbol{w}^k)^T \boldsymbol{d} + \gamma\boldsymbol{d}^T H^k \boldsymbol{d} + \|\boldsymbol{w}^k + \boldsymbol{d}\|_1 - \|\boldsymbol{w}^k\|_1\right), \end{aligned} \tag{8}$$

where $0 < \beta < 1$, $0 < \sigma < 1$, and $0 \leq \gamma < 1$. The overall procedure is in Algorithm 1. Under some assumptions, [9] proved the asymptotic convergence and the local linear convergence of Algorithm 1.

Algorithm 1 A decomposition framework by [8] for L1-regularized logistic regression

1. Given $\boldsymbol{w}^1$. Choose a strategy for selecting working sets. Given $0 < \beta, \sigma < 1$ and $0 \leq \gamma < 1$.
2. For $k = 1, 2, 3, \ldots$
   - Choose an H^k and a working set J^k.
   - Get $\boldsymbol{d}^k$ by solving the sub-problem (6).
   - Compute $\lambda = \max\{1, \beta, \beta^2, \ldots\}$ such that $\lambda\boldsymbol{d}^k$ satisfies (8).
   - $\boldsymbol{w}^{k+1} = \boldsymbol{w}^k + \lambda\boldsymbol{d}^k$.

In the rest of this section, we discuss two examples of Algorithm 1. One is a CD method recommended by [7] and the other is GLMNET [1]. The latter is what we would like to improve upon in this paper, while the former is used for comparison.

2.1 Size of Working Set is One: Cyclic Coordinate Descent Method

This method cyclically selects a singleton working set $J = \{j\}$, where $j = 1, \ldots, n$. We describe the specific version in [7]. The sub-problem (6) has only one variable:

$$\min_z \quad q_k(z\boldsymbol{e}_j), \tag{9}$$

[1]We explain why (7) indirectly uses gradient information. If the 1-norm term is not considered and H^k is diagonal, then $\boldsymbol{d}(\mathcal{N})$ is a "scaled" gradient with $d_j(\mathcal{N}) = -\nabla_j L(\boldsymbol{w}^k)/H_{jj}^k$. Thus, (7) selects indices with larger scaled gradient values.

where $e_j = [\underbrace{0, \ldots, 0}_{j-1}, 1, 0, \ldots, 0]^T$ is an indicator vector and

$$q_k(ze_j) = \nabla_j L(w^k)z + \frac{1}{2}H_{jj}^k z^2 + |w_j^k + z| - |w_j^k|. \quad (10)$$

Because of only one variable in (9), [7] considers the exact Hessian matrix to have $H_{jj}^k = \nabla_{jj}^2 L(w^k)$. It is well known that (9) has a simple closed-form solution

$$d = \begin{cases} -\frac{\nabla_j L(w^k)+1}{H_{jj}^k} & \text{if } \nabla_j L(w^k) + 1 \le H_{jj}^k w_j^k, \\ -\frac{\nabla_j L(w^k)-1}{H_{jj}^k} & \text{if } \nabla_j L(w^k) - 1 \ge H_{jj}^k w_j^k, \\ -w_j^k & \text{otherwise.} \end{cases} \quad (11)$$

Because (11) gives a Newton direction, [7] refers to this setting as CDN (CD method using one-dimensional Newton directions). By setting $\gamma = 0$, the sufficient decrease condition (8) in the line search procedure is reduced to

$$f(w^k + \lambda de_j) - f(w^k) \le \sigma\lambda \left(\nabla_j L(w^k)d + |w_j^k + d| - |w_j^k|\right). \quad (12)$$

Because CDN is a special case of Algorithm 1, any limit point of the sequence $\{w^1, w^2, \ldots\}$ is an optimum of (1).

We discuss the computational complexity of CDN. While solving (9) by (11) takes a constant number of operations, calculating $\nabla_j L(w^k)$ and $\nabla_{jj}^2 L(w^k)$ for constructing the sub-problem (9) is expensive. From (2),we need $O(nl)$ operations for obtaining $w^T x_i, \forall i$. A common trick to make CD methods viable for classification problems is to store and maintain $w^T x_i, \forall i$. [7] stores $e^{w^T x_i}$ instead and updates the values by

$$e^{w^T x_i} \leftarrow e^{w^T x_i} \cdot e^{\bar{\lambda} d x_{ij}}, \forall i, \quad (13)$$

where $\bar{\lambda}$ is the step size decided by the line search procedure and d is the optimal solution of (9). If $e^{w^T x_i}, \forall i$ are available, the evaluation of $\nabla_j L(w^k)$ and $\nabla_{jj}^2 L(w^k)$ in (10), and $f(w^k + \lambda de_j)$ in (12) takes $O(l)$ operations. Therefore, the complexity of one cycle of n CD steps is:

$$n \times (1+ \text{ \# steps of line search}) \times O(l). \quad (14)$$

We call the n CD steps to update $w_1, \ldots, w_n$ as a cycle, which will be frequently used in our subsequent analysis and experiments.

We discuss two implementation techniques in [7]. A conventional CD method sequentially minimizes $q_k(ze_j)$ in the order of $\{1, \ldots, n\}$. Many past works have indicated that solving n sub-problems in a random order leads to faster convergence. Thus, [7] uses a randomly permuted sequence $\pi(1), \ldots, \pi(n)$ as the order of solving n sub-problems.

The second technique is shrinking. Because problem (1) has a sparse solution, [7] heuristically removes some zero elements during the optimization procedure. They use the following property to conjecture zero elements in an optimal solution: From (3), if w^* is optimal for (1), then

$$-1 < \nabla_j L(w^*) < 1 \quad \text{implies} \quad w_j^* = 0. \quad (15)$$

Assume the previous CD cycle contains iterates $w^{k-|\bar{J}|+1}, \ldots, w^k$, where elements in $\bar{J} = \{\bar{j}_1, \ldots, \bar{j}_{|\bar{J}|}\}$ were updated. That is, $\bar{J}$ corresponds to variables remained in the beginning of the current cycle. Then, at the current cycle, sequentially an element $j \in \bar{J}$ is checked and removed if

$$w_j^{k+t-1} = 0 \quad \text{and} \quad -1 + \frac{M}{l} < \nabla_j L(w^{k+t-1}) < 1 - \frac{M}{l}, \quad (16)$$

where t is the iteration index for the current cycle and

$$M \equiv \max\left(\left|\nabla_{\bar{j}_1}^S f(w^{k-|\bar{J}|})\right|, \ldots, \left|\nabla_{\bar{j}_{|\bar{J}|}}^S f(w^{k-1})\right|\right). \quad (17)$$

If (16) does not hold, then a CD iteration is conducted to update w_j. After all elements in $\bar{J}$ have been processed, a smaller subset J is obtained and passed to the next cycle. Note that in (16), we have $t = 1, \ldots, |J|$ instead of $1, \ldots, |\bar{J}|$ because some elements in $\bar{J}$ may have been removed.

Because (15) holds only for an optimal solution, in (16), through the value M, we use a slightly smaller interval than $(-1, 1)$. Note that M uses the minimum-norm sub-gradient to measure the maximum violation of the optimality condition in the previous CD cycle, so the size of interval is self-adjusted. The calculation of M is in a sequential manner because, for updating w_j, we only calculate $\nabla_j L(w)$ and can easily obtain $\nabla_j^S f(w)$. We never need the whole vector $\nabla L(w)$.

2.2 Size of Working Set is Full

An extreme setting of Tseng and Yun's framework [8] is to update all variables at every iteration. That is, we consider a working set $J = \mathcal{N} = \{1, \ldots, n\}$. Because (7) holds if $J = \mathcal{N}$, this selection is a special Gauss-Southwell rule. The method GLMNET by Friedman et al. [1] can be considered as an example. GLMNET supports different choices of H^k, but here we discuss the setting of using $H^k = \nabla^2 L(w^k)$. Then, (6) becomes the second-order approximation of (5) and a Newton direction is obtained.

For the sake of computational efficiency, GLMNET does not conduct line search after solving (6). Therefore, seriously speaking it is not an example of Algorithm 1. Also, the convergence is in question. In Section 3, we will add line search back and conduct proper changes to ensure the convergence. Further, we experimentally show in Section 4 that these changes do not cause any inefficiency.

Many optimization methods can be applied to solve the sub-problem (6). Friedman et al. [1] consider a cyclic coordinate descent method, so the procedure for solving sub-problem (6) is almost the same as CDN in Section 2.1. Indeed, it is simpler because (6) is a quadratic problem. Sequentially, d's values are updated by minimizing the following one-variable function:

$$\begin{aligned} & q_k(d + ze_j) - q_k(d) \quad (18) \\ = & |w_j^k + d_j + z| - |w_j^k + d_j| + \nabla_j \bar{q}_k(d)z + \frac{1}{2}\nabla_{jj}^2 \bar{q}_k(d)z^2, \end{aligned}$$

where

$$\bar{q}_k(d) \equiv \nabla L(w^k)^T d + \frac{1}{2} d^T H^k d$$

represents the smooth terms of $q_k(d)$ and plays a similar role to $L(w)$ for (1). We have

$$\nabla_j \bar{q}_k(d) = \nabla_j L(w^k) + (\nabla^2 L(w^k)d)_j, \nabla_{jj}^2 \bar{q}_k(d) = \nabla_{jj}^2 L(w^k). \quad (19)$$

Since (18) is in the same form as (10), it can be easily solved by (11). Regarding the line search required in Algorithm 1, because (18) is exactly solved, the sufficient decrease condition (8) holds with $\lambda = 1$ and $\gamma = 1/2$.[2] Thus, line search is not needed.

Because an iterative procedure (CD method) is used to solve the sub-problem (6), GLMNET contains two levels of iterations. An "outer iteration" corresponds to the process from $\boldsymbol{w}^k$ to $\boldsymbol{w}^{k+1}$, while the "inner" level consists of CD iterations for solving (6). For an algorithm involving two levels of iterations, the stopping condition of the inner iterations must be carefully designed. A strict inner stopping condition may cause the algorithm to take a prohibitive amount of time at the first outer iteration. Alternatively, a loose inner condition leads to an inaccurate solution of (6) and possibly lengthy outer iterations. GLMNET terminates the CD procedure by checking if $\boldsymbol{d}$ is still significantly changed. That is, in a cycle of n CD steps to update $d_1, \ldots, d_n$, the corresponding changes $z_1, \ldots, z_n$ satisfy

$$\max_j (\nabla^2_{jj} L(\boldsymbol{w}^k) \cdot z_j^2) \leq \epsilon_{\text{in}}, \tag{20}$$

where ϵ_{in} is the inner stopping tolerance. For the outer stopping condition, similarly, GLMNET checks if $\boldsymbol{w}$ is still significantly changed. Let $\boldsymbol{w}^{k+1} = \boldsymbol{w}^k + \boldsymbol{d}^k$. GLMNET stops if the following condition holds:

$$\max_j (\nabla^2_{jj} L(\boldsymbol{w}^{k+1}) \cdot (d_j^k)^2) \leq \epsilon_{\text{out}}, \tag{21}$$

where ϵ_{out} is the outer stopping tolerance. GLMNET uses the same value for inner and outer tolerances; i.e., $\epsilon_{\text{in}} = \epsilon_{\text{out}}$. We will propose better settings in Section 3 and show experiments in Section 4.

We discuss the computational complexity of GLMNET. At each CD step, most operations are spent on calculating $\nabla_j \bar{q}_k(\boldsymbol{d})$ and $\nabla^2_{jj} \bar{q}_k(\boldsymbol{d})$ in (19). Note that $\nabla^2_{jj} \bar{q}_k(\boldsymbol{d}) = \nabla^2_{jj} L(\boldsymbol{w}^k), \forall j$ can be pre-calculated before the CD procedure. For $\nabla_j \bar{q}_k(\boldsymbol{d})$, from (2),

$$(\nabla^2 L(\boldsymbol{w}^k)\boldsymbol{d})_j = C \sum_{t=1}^{n} \sum_{i=1}^{l} X^T_{ji} D_{ii} X_{it} d_t = C \sum_{i=1}^{l} X^T_{ji} D_{ii} (X\boldsymbol{d})_i.$$

Thus, if $X\boldsymbol{d}$ (i.e., $\boldsymbol{x}_i^T \boldsymbol{d}, \forall i$) is maintained and updated by

$$(Xd)_i \leftarrow (Xd)_i + X_{ij} z, \ \forall i,$$

then calculating $\nabla_j \bar{q}_k(\boldsymbol{d})$ costs $O(l)$ operations.[3] Therefore, the CD method for (6) requires

$$O(nl) \text{ operations for one cycle of } n \text{ CD steps.} \tag{22}$$

GLMNET applies a shrinking technique to obtain a smaller sub-problem (6). That is, some $\boldsymbol{w}$'s elements are conjectured to be already optimal, so the working set J becomes only a subset of $\mathcal{N}$. At the kth iteration, GLMNET conducts the following loop to sequentially solve some smaller sub-problems.

While (`TRUE`)

- Conduct one cycle of n CD steps. Let J include those d_j's which still need to be changed.
- If (20) holds, then `break`.
- Use CD to solve a sub-problem with the working set J until (20) holds.

[2]Now $q_k(\boldsymbol{d})$ is minimized, so in (8) $f(\cdot)$ is replaced by $q_k(\cdot)$ and $L(\cdot)$ is replaced by $\bar{q}_k(\cdot)$.

[3]This is like how $e^{\boldsymbol{w}^T \boldsymbol{x}_i}, \forall i$ are handled in Section 2.1.

The working set J chosen in the above procedure excludes the following elements satisfying the optimality conditions of $\min_z q_k(\boldsymbol{d} - z\boldsymbol{e}_j) - q_k(\boldsymbol{d})$:

$$\nabla_j \bar{q}_k(\boldsymbol{d}) + 1 = 0 \quad \text{if } w_j^k + d_j > 0, \tag{23}$$

$$\nabla_j \bar{q}_k(\boldsymbol{d}) - 1 = 0 \quad \text{if } w_j^k + d_j < 0, \tag{24}$$

$$-1 \leq \nabla_j \bar{q}_k(\boldsymbol{d}) \leq 1 \quad \text{if } w_j^k + d_j = 0. \tag{25}$$

This shrinking method differs from (16) of CDN in several aspects. First, (16) shrinks only zero elements. Second, while (25) is similar to (16), CDN uses an interval slightly smaller than $(-1, 1)$. Thus, (23)–(25) are more aggressive in removing variables. In Section 3.5, we will propose a setting similar to (16) for GLMNET.

3. AN IMPROVED GLMNET: NEWGLMNET

As discussed in Section 2.2, GLMNET lacks theoretical convergence properties. In this section, we propose an improved GLMNET to have the asymptotic convergence. Moreover, we carefully address some implementation concerns. We refer to the improved algorithm as newGLMNET.

3.1 Positive Definite H^k

The convergence proof in [8] requires that H^k in (6) is positive definite. However, from (2), $H^k = \nabla^2 L(\boldsymbol{w}^k)$ in GLMNET is only positive semi-definite. For example, if X has dependent columns, then $\nabla^2 L(\boldsymbol{w}^k)$ is not positive definite. To make GLMNET a case in the framework [8], we slightly enlarge the diagonal elements of $\nabla^2 L(\boldsymbol{w}^k)$:

$$H^k \equiv \nabla^2 L(\boldsymbol{w}^k) + \nu \mathcal{I}, \tag{26}$$

where $\nu > 0$ is a small positive value and $\mathcal{I} \in \mathbf{R}^{n \times n}$ is an identity matrix.

3.2 Line Search and Asymptotic Convergence

For computational efficiency, GLMNET omits the line search procedure after obtaining the Newton direction. Thus, the function value may not be decreasing. To use the convergence result in [8], we include the line search procedure. Experiments in Section 4 show that in almost all cases, $\lambda = 1$ satisfies the sufficient decrease condition (8). Thus, the line search procedure does not introduce extra cost. We prove that all conditions needed in [8] are satisfied, so any limit point of $\{\boldsymbol{w}^k\}$ generated by newGLMNET is an optimal solution of (1). The proof is omitted due to space limit.

3.3 CD Method for Solving Sub-problem (6)

As shown in Section 2.2, the CD method for the quadratic problem (6) is simpler than CDN for (1) because each one-variable function can be exactly minimized and line search is not needed. Thus, following an analysis similar to that in Section 3.2, any limit point of the CD procedure is an optimum of (6).

The similarity to CDN implies that two implementation tricks discussed in Section 2.1 can be applied. We discuss the shrinking implementation in detail in Section 3.5.

3.4 An Adaptive Inner Stopping Condition

We mentioned in Section 2.2 that the inner tolerance must be carefully decided. For example, under GLMNET's current setting of $\epsilon_{\text{in}} = \epsilon_{\text{out}}$, if users specify a small ϵ_{out}, a huge amount of time is needed for the first outer iteration.

For newGLMNET, we propose an adaptive inner stopping condition. The design principle is that in the early stage, newGLMNET should behave like CDN to quickly obtain a reasonable model, while in the final stage, newGLMNET should achieve fast local convergence by using Newton-like directions. In a cycle of updating $\boldsymbol{d}$'s n variables, we assume that $\boldsymbol{d}^1, \ldots, \boldsymbol{d}^n$ are sequentially generated and from $\boldsymbol{d}^j$ to $\boldsymbol{d}^{j+1}$, the jth element is changed. Then, we propose the following inner stopping condition by checking the minimum-norm sub-gradient:

$$\sum_{j=1}^{n} |\nabla_j^S q_k(\boldsymbol{d}^j)| \leq \epsilon_{\text{in}}. \tag{27}$$

Note that we do not need to calculate the whole $\nabla^S q_k(\boldsymbol{d}^j)$. Instead, $\nabla_j^S q_k(\boldsymbol{d}^j)$ is easily available via $\nabla_j \bar{q}_k(\boldsymbol{d}^j)$ in (19).

If at one outer iteration, the condition (27) holds after only one cycle of n CD steps, then we reduce ϵ_{in} by

$$\epsilon_{\text{in}} \leftarrow \epsilon_{\text{in}}/4. \tag{28}$$

That is, the program automatically adjusts ϵ_{in} if it finds that too few CD steps are conducted for minimizing $q_k(\boldsymbol{d})$. Therefore, we can choose a large ϵ_{in} in the beginning.

We use an outer stopping condition similar to (27):

$$\sum_{j=1}^{n} |\nabla_j^S f(\boldsymbol{w}^k)| \leq \epsilon_{\text{out}}. \tag{29}$$

3.5 A Two-level Shrinking Scheme

Sections 2.1 and 2.2 have discussed shrinking schemes for CDN and GLMNET, respectively. Following the nature of newGLMNET, we propose a two-level shrinking scheme: the outer level removes some $\boldsymbol{w}$'s elements so that a smaller sub-problem (6) is solved; the inner level is applied to remove elements in $\boldsymbol{d}$ so that (6) becomes an even smaller problem.

In the beginning of each outer iteration, we remove w_j if

$$w_j^k = 0 \quad \text{and} \quad -1 + \frac{M^{\text{out}}}{l} < \nabla_j L(\boldsymbol{w}^k) < 1 - \frac{M^{\text{out}}}{l},$$

where

$$M^{\text{out}} \equiv \max\left(\left|\nabla_1^S f(\boldsymbol{w}^{k-1})\right|, \ldots, \left|\nabla_n^S f(\boldsymbol{w}^{k-1})\right|\right).$$

This setting is different from (23)–(25) in several aspects. First, because we must calculate $\nabla_j L(\boldsymbol{w}^k)$ in the beginning of the kth iteration, we do not need a special cycle of n CD steps in GLMNET. Note that $\nabla^S f(\boldsymbol{w}^k)$ can be easily obtained via $\nabla L(\boldsymbol{w}^k)$ and used for obtaining M^{out} of the next iteration.[4] Second, like (17), M^{out} is used to adjust the shrinking scheme from a conservative setting in the beginning to an aggressive setting in the end.

As indicated in Section 2.2, the CD procedure in each GLMNET's outer iteration for solving (6) is very similar to CDN for (1). Thus, we can apply CDN's shrinking scheme to the inner loop of newGLMNET. Assume the previous cycle of CD steps contains points $\boldsymbol{d}^{r-|\bar{J}|+1}, \ldots, \boldsymbol{d}^r$, where elements in the set $\bar{J} = \{\bar{j}_1, \ldots, \bar{j}_{|\bar{J}|}\}$ were updated. That is, $\bar{J}$ corresponds to variables remained in the beginning of the current cycle. Then, at the current cycle, sequentially an element $j \in \bar{J}$ is checked and removed if

$$w_j^k + d_j^{r+t-1} = 0 \quad \text{and} \quad -1 + \frac{M^{\text{in}}}{l} < \nabla_j \bar{q}_k(\boldsymbol{d}^{r+t-1}) < 1 - \frac{M^{\text{in}}}{l}, \tag{30}$$

[4]If $k = 1$, $\nabla^S f(\boldsymbol{w}^{k-1})$ is not available. We set $M^{\text{out}} = \infty$, so no variables are shrunk at the first outer iteration.

Algorithm 2 newGLMNET with two-level shrinking

1. Given $\boldsymbol{w}^1$, ϵ_{in}, and ϵ_{out}. Choose a small positive number ν. Choose $\beta \in (0,1)$, $\gamma \in [0,1)$, and $\sigma \in (0,1)$.
2. Let $M^{\text{out}} \leftarrow \infty$.
3. For $k = 1, 2, 3, \ldots$ (outer iteration)
   - Let $J \leftarrow \{1, \ldots, n\}$, $M \leftarrow 0$, and $\bar{M} \leftarrow 0$.
   - For $j = 1, \ldots, n$
     - Calculate H_{jj}^k, $\nabla_j L(\boldsymbol{w}^k)$ and $\nabla_j^S f(\boldsymbol{w}^k)$.
     - If $w_j^k = 0$ (outer-level shrinking)
       * If $|\nabla_j L(\boldsymbol{w}^k)| < 1 - M^{\text{out}}/l$
         $J \leftarrow J \backslash \{j\}$.
     - $M \leftarrow \max(M, |\nabla_j^S f(\boldsymbol{w}^k)|)$.
     - $\bar{M} \leftarrow \bar{M} + |\nabla_j^S f(\boldsymbol{w}^k)|$.
   - If $\bar{M} \leq \epsilon_{\text{out}}$
     `return` $\boldsymbol{w}^k$.
   - Let $M^{\text{out}} \leftarrow M$ and $M^{\text{in}} \leftarrow \infty$.
   - Let $T \leftarrow J$ and $\boldsymbol{d} \leftarrow \boldsymbol{0}$.
   - For $p = 1, 2, 3, \ldots, 1000$ (inner iteration)
     - Let $m \leftarrow 0$ and $\bar{m} \leftarrow 0$.
     - For $j \in T$
       * Let $\nabla_{jj}^2 \bar{q}_k(\boldsymbol{d}) = H_{jj}^k$. Calculate $\nabla_j \bar{q}_k(\boldsymbol{d})$ and $\nabla_j^S q_k(\boldsymbol{d})$.
       * If $w_j^k + d_j = 0$ (inner-level shrinking)
         · If $|\nabla_j \bar{q}(\boldsymbol{d})| < 1 - M^{\text{in}}/l$
           $T \leftarrow T \backslash \{j\}$.
       * Else
         · $m \leftarrow \max(m, |\nabla_j^S q(\boldsymbol{d})|)$.
         · $\bar{m} \leftarrow \bar{m} + |\nabla_j^S q(\boldsymbol{d})|$.
         · $d_j \leftarrow d_j + \arg\min_z q(\boldsymbol{d} + z\boldsymbol{e}_j) - q(\boldsymbol{d})$.
     - If $\bar{m} \leq \epsilon_{\text{in}}$
       * If $T = J$ (inner stopping)
         `break`.
       * Else (active set reactivation)
         $T \leftarrow J$ and $M^{\text{in}} \leftarrow \infty$.
     - Else
       $M^{\text{in}} \leftarrow m$.
   - If $p = 1$, then $\epsilon_{\text{in}} \leftarrow \epsilon_{\text{in}}/4$.
   - Compute $\lambda = \max\{1, \beta, \beta^2, \ldots\}$ such that $\lambda \boldsymbol{d}$ satisfies (8). $\boldsymbol{w}^{k+1} = \boldsymbol{w}^k + \lambda \boldsymbol{d}$.

where t is the iteration index for the current cycle and

$$M^{\text{in}} \equiv \max\left(\left|\nabla_{\bar{j}_1}^S q_k(\boldsymbol{d}^{r-|\bar{J}|})\right|, \ldots, \left|\nabla_{\bar{j}_{|\bar{J}|}}^S q_k(\boldsymbol{d}^{r-1})\right|\right).$$

If (30) does not hold, element j remains.[5] Then, a regular CD iteration is conducted by solving (18) to obtain $\bar{z}$ and generating $\boldsymbol{d}^{r+t} = \boldsymbol{d}^{r+t-1} + \bar{z}\boldsymbol{e}_j$. After the whole set $\bar{J}$ has been processed, a smaller subset J is obtained and we move to the next cycle.[6] The overall procedure of newGLMNET with two-level shrinking is shown in Algorithm 2.

3.6 Analysis on the Number of Exponential and Logarithmic Operations

Algorithms for logistic regression involve exponential and logarithmic operations, each of which is much more expensive than one multiplication/division. It is important to

[5]Note that in (30), $t = 1, \ldots, |J|$ instead of $1, \ldots, |\bar{J}|$; see the explanation in Section 2.1.
[6]Similar to the way to initialize M^{out}, for the first CD cycle, we set $M^{\text{in}} = \infty$.

Table 1: Number of exp/log operations in a cycle of n coordinate descent steps.

One cycle of n CD steps	CDN	newGLMNET
Total # of operations (dense data)	$O(nl)$	$O(nl)$
# exp/log (dense data)	$O(nl)$	$\leq O(l)$
Total # of operations (sparse data)	$O(\text{nnz})$	$O(\text{nnz})$
# of exp/log (sparse data)	$O(\text{nnz})$	$\leq O(l)$

check how many exp/log operations are required in an algorithm because a high proportion of exp/log operations may substantially influence the performance. We analyze both CDN and newGLMNET by checking each cycle of n CD steps. We make an assumption that the number of line search steps in CDN is small (e.g., one or two). Table 1 shows the number of total operations and the number of exp/log operations. From (14) and (22), CDN and newGLMNET both require $O(nl)$ total operations in a cycle. However, their numbers of exp/log operations are very different. In CDN, because $e^{\boldsymbol{w}^T\boldsymbol{x}_i}\ \forall i$ must be updated in (13), $O(l)$ exp operations are needed at each CD iteration. In line search, calculating $f(\boldsymbol{w}^k + \lambda \boldsymbol{d}\boldsymbol{e}_j)$ in (12) takes $O(l)$ log operations. Thus, $O(nl)$ exp/log operations are needed in one cycle. In contrast, because $q_k(\boldsymbol{d})$ in (6) has no exp/log terms, the CD procedure in newGLMNET does not require any exp/log operations. To construct (6) in the beginning of each outer iteration, from (2), $O(l)$ exp operations are required. Because several cycles are used to solve (6), we can say that each cycle shares no more than $O(l)$ exp operations.

Therefore, CDN's $O(nl)$ exp/log operations are much more than newGLMNET's $O(l)$. The difference becomes smaller for sparse data because CDN's $O(nl)$ is replaced by $O(\text{nnz})$, where nnz is the total number of non-zero elements in X (i.e., training data). From this analysis, we expect that CDN suffers from many slow exp/log operations if data are dense and n is not small. This result will be clearly observed in Section 4. A related discussion on exp/log operations for L2-regularized problems is in [10].

Besides, newGLMNET is also superior to CDN in terms of the cost of line search. More analysis appears in the long version of the paper [11, Section 4].

4. EXPERIMENTS

In this section, we investigate the performance of CDN, GLMNET, and newGLMNET. All these methods can be easily extended to solve logistic regression with a bias term b:

$$\min_{\boldsymbol{w},b} \quad \|\boldsymbol{w}\|_1 + C\sum\nolimits_{i=1}^{l} \log(1+e^{-y_i(\boldsymbol{w}^T\boldsymbol{x}_i+b)}). \qquad (31)$$

Because the GLMNET implementation solves (31) instead of (1), in our comparison, (31) is used. We do not consider other methods because in [7], CDN is shown to be the best for sparse data.

4.1 Data Sets and Experimental Settings

We use eight data sets in our experiments. Five of them (news20, rcv1, yahoo-japan, yahoo-korea, and webspam) are document data sets. The other three data sets come from different learning problems: gisette is a handwriting digit recognition problem from NIPS 2003 feature selection challenge; epsilon is an artificial data set for Pascal large scale learning challenge in 2008; KDD2010-b includes student performance prediction data for a tutoring system and is used for the data mining competition KDD Cup 2010. All document data sets are instance-wisely normalized, so the length of each instance is one. For non-document data, gisette is feature-wisely scaled to the $[-1, 1]$ interval, and epsilon is feature-wisely scaled to $N(1, 0)$ and then instance-wisely normalized. KDD2010-b is preprocessed in [12].

We prepare training and testing sets for each problem. For gisette and KDD2010-b, we use their original training and test sets. For others, we randomly split data to one fifth for testing and the remaining for training.

We choose the parameter C in (31) by five-fold cross validation on the training set. All methods then solve (31) with the best C to obtain the model for prediction. Table 2 shows the statistics and the best C of all data sets. We can clearly see that two data sets (epsilon and gisette) are very dense, while others are sparse.

Next, we describe software information and parameter settings in our experiments.

- CDN: this coordinate descent method is described in Section 2.1. In the line search procedure, we use $\sigma = 0.01$ and $\beta = 0.5$. The C/C++ implementation is included in LIBLINEAR (version 1.7), which is available at `http://www.csie.ntu.edu.tw/~cjlin/liblinear/oldfiles/`; see the implementation document [13] for more details.
- newGLMNET: an improved GLMNET is described in Section 3. For the positive definiteness of H^k, we set $\nu = 10^{-12}$ in (26). To check the sufficient decrease condition (8), we use $\beta = 0.5$, $\gamma = 0$, and $\sigma = 0.01$. We choose the initial $\epsilon_{\text{in}} = \|\nabla^S f(\boldsymbol{w}^1)\|_1$. The C/C++ implementation is included in LIBLINEAR (version 1.8).
- GLMNET: this method is described in Section 2.2. GLMNET is implemented in Fortran with an R interface. The source code (version 1.5.3) is available at `http://cran.r-project.org/web/packages/glmnet/`. GLMNET uses the regularization parameter $\lambda = 1/(Cl)$ instead of C. We ensure that the equivalent settings have been made in our experiments.

GLMNET offers an option to find a solution path $\{\boldsymbol{w}^{C_1}, \ldots, \boldsymbol{w}^{C_*}\}$ of an increasing parameter sequence $\{C_1, \ldots, C_*\}$. It applies a warm start technique so that the optimal solution of the previous C_{i-1} is used as the initial point for the current C_i. The number of outer iterations should be small because of a more accurate initial point. GLMNET authors suggest that finding a solution path may be faster than solving a single optimization problem under a fixed C. [1, Section 2.5]. We refer to this approach as GLMNETpath and include it for comparison. By their default setting, we consider a parameter sequence of length 100 starting from the smallest C_1 such that $\boldsymbol{w}^{C_1} = \boldsymbol{0}$. Given our desired parameter C_*, a geometric sequence is generated by a fixed ratio between successive C values..

We set the initial $\boldsymbol{w}^1 = \boldsymbol{0}$ for all methods. All experiments are conducted on a 64-bit machine with Intel Xeon 2.0GHz CPU (E5504), 128KB L1 cache, 1GB L2 cache, and 32GB main memory. We use GNU C/C++/Fortran compilers (version 4.4.1) and the optimization flag is properly set.

4.2 Running Time Comparison

We begin with checking the change of function values along the running time. We show in Figure 1 pairs of (time, function value) by gradually reducing the stopping toler-

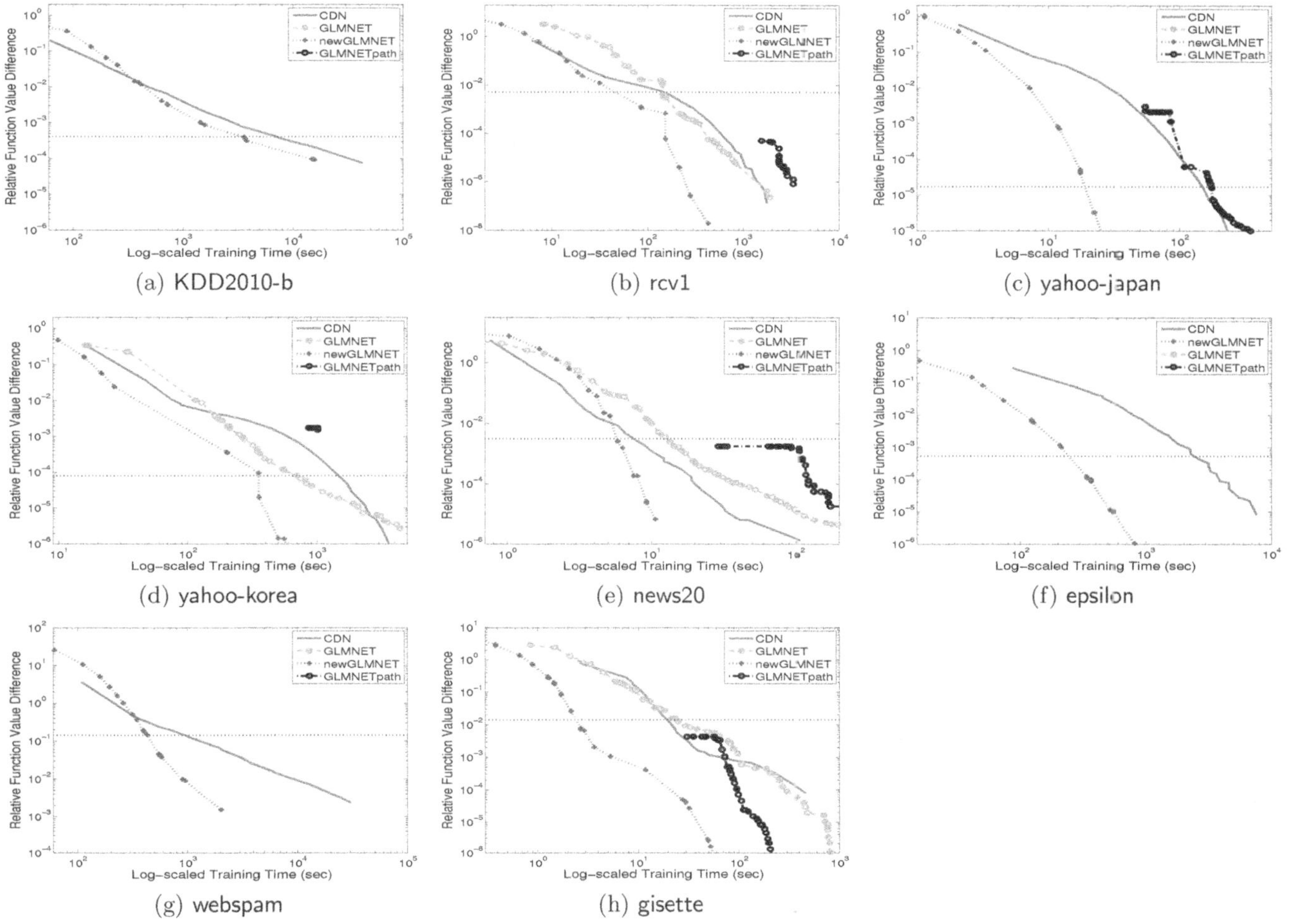

Figure 1: Relative difference to the optimal function value versus training time. Both x-axis and y-axis are log-scaled. GLMNET and GLMNETpath failed to generate some results because of either memory problems or lengthy running time.

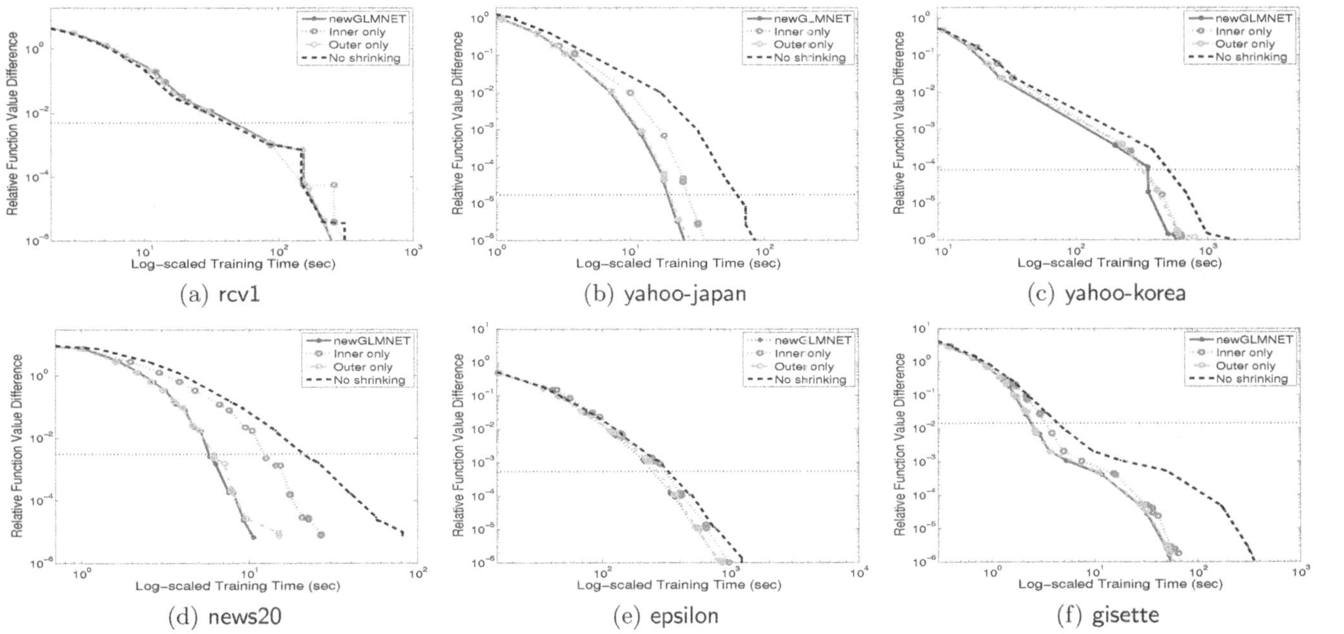

Figure 2: Effect of two-level shrinking. "Inner only" ("Outer only") indicates that only inner-level (outer-level) shrinking is conducted.

Table 2: Data statistics and the best parameter C. Data sets are sorted by the number of nonzero elements per instance in the training data. We conduct five-fold cross validation on the training set to select C in $\{2^k \mid k = -4, -3, \ldots, 6\}$. All data sets except yahoo-japan and yahoo-korea are available at `http://www.csie.ntu.edu.tw/~cjlin/libsvmtools/datasets/`.

Data set	#data train	#data test	#features	#nonzeros in training	#nonzeros per instance	C
KDD2010-b	19,264,097	748,401	29,890,095	566,345,888	29	0.5
rcv1	541,920	135,479	47,236	39,625,144	73	4
yahoo-japan	140,963	35,240	832,026	18,738,315	133	4
yahoo-korea	368,444	92,110	3,052,939	125,190,807	340	4
news20	15,997	3,999	1,355,191	7,281,110	455	64
epsilon	400,000	100,000	2,000	800,000,000	2,000	0.5
webspam	280,000	70,000	16,609,143	1,043,724,776	3,727	64
gisette	6,000	1,000	5,000	29,729,997	4,955	0.25

ance.[7] The x-axis is the log-scaled training time and the y-axis is the relative difference to the optimal function value:

$$\frac{f(\boldsymbol{w}) - f^*}{f^*},$$

where $\boldsymbol{w}$ is the solution under the specified tolerance and f^* is the optimal function value. Because f^* is not available, we obtain an approximation by running newGLMNET with a small stopping tolerance

$$\epsilon_{\text{out}} = \epsilon \cdot \min(\#\text{pos}, \#\text{neg})/l \cdot \|\nabla^S f(\boldsymbol{w}^1)\|_1, \tag{32}$$

where $\epsilon = 10^{-8}$, and #pos and #neg indicate the numbers of positive and negative labels in the training set, respectively. The horizontal dotted line in Figure 1 indicates the relative function difference by running CDN using LIBLINEAR's default stopping tolerance with $\epsilon = 0.01$ in (32). The point where a method's curve passes this horizontal line roughly indicates the time needed to obtain an accurate enough solution.

From Figure 1, if the optimization problem is loosely solved using a large ϵ_{out}, CDN is faster than newGLMNET and GLMNET. This result is reasonable because CDN uses a greedy setting to sequentially update variables. In contract, in each outer iteration, newGLMNET uses only a fixed H^k. If using a smaller ϵ_{out}, newGLMNET surpasses CDN and achieves fast local convergence. For dense data (epsilon and gisette), newGLMNET is always better than CDN. Take epsilon as an example. In Figure 1(f), to reach the horizontal line, newGLMNET is ten times faster than CDN. This huge difference is expected following the analysis on the number of exp/log operations in Section 3.6.

From results above the horizontal lines in Figure 1, we see that newGLMNET is faster than GLMNET in the early stage. Recall that GLMNET sets $\epsilon_{\text{in}} = \epsilon_{\text{out}}$, while newGLMNET uses an adaptive setting to adjust ϵ_{in}. Because a large ϵ_{in} is considered in the beginning, newGLMNET can compete with CDN in the early stage by loosely solving (6). We use an example to further illustrate the importance to properly choose ϵ_{in}. By running GLMNET with the default $\epsilon_{\text{out}} = 10^{-4}$ on news20 and rcv1, the training time is 20.10 and 758.82 seconds, respectively. The first outer iteration already takes 6.99 seconds on news20 and 296.87 on rcv1. A quick fix is to enlarge the initial ϵ_{in}, but the local convergence in the later stage may be slow. A better inner stopping condition should be adaptive like ours so that the sub-problem (6) can be solved properly at each outer iteration.

[7]For GLMNET and newGLMNET, the tolerance means the outer tolerance ϵ_{out} in (21). For GLMNETpath, under any given ϵ_{out}, a sequence of problems (1) is solved.

In Figure 1, GLMNET and GLMNETpath failed to generate some results because of either memory problems or lengthy running time. This indicates that a careful implementation is very important for large-scale problems. We also observe that GLMNETpath is not faster than GLMNET. Another drawback of GLMNETpath is that it is hard to quickly obtain an approximate solution. That is, regardless of ϵ_{out} specified, a sequence of problems (1) still needs to be solved.

We have checked the relationship between the testing accuracy and the training time. The comparison result, not presented due to space limit, is similar to that in Figure 1.

Recall we added a line search procedure in newGLMNET. We find that the sufficient decrease condition (8) holds for $\lambda = 1$ in all cases. In contrast, CDN spends considerable time on line search.

In summary, because of the proposed adaptive inner stopping condition, newGLMNET takes both advantages of fast approximation in the early stage like CDN and of fast local convergence in the final stage like GLMNET.

4.3 Effect of Exp/log Operations

In Table 2, we sort data sets according to nnz/l, which is the average number of non-zero values per instance. The purpose is to see the effect of exp/log operations, where CDN needs $O(\text{nnz})$ and GLMNET needs $O(l)$ operations per cycle of n CD steps, respectively. Clearly, for the two dense data (epsilon and gisette), newGLMNET is much faster. Because many other issues affect the running time, we focus on the first CD cycle and present running time in Table 3. Clearly, for dense data, CDN's exp/log operations are much more expensive than other operations, so the total time is longer than that of newGLMNET. This result indicates that CDN is not competitive for data with a large nnz/l.

4.4 Effect of Shrinking

We compare newGLMNET implementations with/without shrinking in Figure 2, which shows that shrinking significantly improves the running time. The outer-level shrinking is particularly useful. Interestingly, from [7, Figure 9] and Figure 2, shrinking is more effective for newGLMNET than CDN.

5. DISCUSSIONS AND CONCLUSIONS

In newGLMNET, a CD method is applied to solve the sub-problem (6). Using the property that CD involves simple

Table 3: Timing analysis of the first cycle of n CD steps. Time is in seconds. (*: dense data)

Data set	CDN		newGLMNET	
	exp/log	Total	exp/log	Total
KDD2010-b	21.72 (30.7%)	70.80	3.88 (6.9%)	56.50
rcv1	4.61 (73.8%)	6.25	0.12 (5.3%)	2.20
yahoo-japan	1.47 (70.9%)	2.08	0.03 (4.2%)	0.71
yahoo-korea	10.65 (66.3%)	16.06	0.08 (1.2%)	6.66
news20	0.21 (27.3%)	0.76	0.003 (0.5%)	0.60
epsilon*	64.98 (73.0%)	89.07	0.09 (0.8%)	11.15
webspam	72.89 (66.6%)	109.39	0.06 (0.1%)	41.10
gisette*	1.66 (66.8%)	2.49	0.002 (0.6%)	0.27

and cheap updates, we carefully adjust the stopping condition for sub-problems. Then, newGLMNET is competitive with a CD method like CDN in the early stage, but becomes a Newton method in the end. This design is similar to "truncated Newton" methods in optimization. While CD seems to be a good choice for solving the sub-problem, whether there are better alternatives is an interesting future issue.

In this work, we not only improve GLMNET's theoretical properties, but also successfully address many implementation issues. The proposed newGLMNET is more stable and efficient for large-scale L1-regularized logistic regression. The implementation is included in LIBLINEAR (version 1.8).

6. ACKNOWLEDGMENTS

The authors thank anonymous reviewers for helpful comments. This work was supported in part by the National Science Council of Taiwan via the grant 98-2221-E-002-136-MY3.

7. REFERENCES

[1] J. Friedman, T. Hastie, and R. Tibshirani, "Regularization paths for generalized linear models via coordinate descent," *Journal of Statistical Software*, vol. 33, no. 1, pp. 1–22, 2010.

[2] A. Genkin, D. D. Lewis, and D. Madigan, "Large-scale Bayesian logistic regression for text categorization," *Technometrics*, vol. 49, no. 3, pp. 291–304, 2007.

[3] K. Koh, S.-J. Kim, and S. Boyd, "An interior-point method for large-scale l1-regularized logistic regression," *Journal of Machine Learning Research*, vol. 8, pp. 1519–1555, 2007.

[4] G. Andrew and J. Gao, "Scalable training of L1-regularized log-linear models," in *Proceedings of the Twenty Fourth International Conference on Machine Learning (ICML)*, 2007.

[5] J. Liu, J. Chen, and J. Ye, "Large-scale sparse logistic regression," in *Proceedings of The 15th ACM SIGKDD International Conference on Knowledge Discovery and Data Mining*, pp. 547–556, 2009.

[6] M. Schmidt, G. Fung, and R. Rosales, "Fast optimization methods for l1 regularization: A comparative study and two new approaches," in *Proceedings of European Conference on Machine Learning*, pp. 286–297, 2007.

[7] G.-X. Yuan, K.-W. Chang, C.-J. Hsieh, and C.-J. Lin, "A comparison of optimization methods and software for large-scale l1-regularized linear classification," *Journal of Machine Learning Research*, vol. 11, pp. 3183–3234, 2010.

[8] P. Tseng and S. Yun, "A coordinate gradient descent method for nonsmooth separable minimization," *Mathematical Programming*, vol. 117, pp. 387–423, 2009.

[9] S. Yun and K.-C. Toh, "A coordinate gradient descent method for l1-regularized convex minimization," *Computational Optimizations and Applications*, vol. 48, no. 2, pp. 273–307, 2011.

[10] K.-W. Chang, C.-J. Hsieh, and C.-J. Lin, "Coordinate descent method for large-scale L2-loss linear SVM," *Journal of Machine Learning Research*, vol. 9, pp. 1369–1398, 2008.

[11] G.-X. Yuan, C.-H. Ho, and C.-J. Lin, "An improved GLMNET for l1-regularized logistic regression and support vector machines," tech. rep., National Taiwan University, 2011.

[12] H.-F. Yu, H.-Y. Lo, H.-P. Hsieh, J.-K. Lou, T. G. McKenzie, J.-W. Chou, P.-H. Chung, C.-H. Ho, C.-F. Chang, Y.-H. Wei, J.-Y. Weng, E.-S. Yan, C.-W. Chang, T.-T. Kuo, Y.-C. Lo, P. T. Chang, C. Po, C.-Y. Wang, Y.-H. Huang, C.-W. Hung, Y.-X. Ruan, Y.-S. Lin, S.-D. Lin, H.-T. Lin, and C.-J. Lin, "Feature engineering and classifier ensemble for KDD cup 2010," in *JMLR Workshop and Conference Proceedings*, 2011. To appear.

[13] R.-E. Fan, K.-W. Chang, C.-J. Hsieh, X.-R. Wang, and C.-J. Lin, "LIBLINEAR: A library for large linear classification," *Journal of Machine Learning Research*, vol. 9, pp. 1871–1874, 2008.

Integrating Low-Rank and Group-Sparse Structures for Robust Multi-Task Learning

Jianhui Chen, Jiayu Zhou, Jieping Ye
Computer Science and Engineering, Center for Evolutionary Medicine and Informatics, The Biodesign Institute, Arizona State University, Tempe, AZ 85287
{Jianhui.Chen, Jiayu.Zhou, Jieping.Ye}@asu.edu

ABSTRACT

Multi-task learning (MTL) aims at improving the generalization performance by utilizing the intrinsic relationships among multiple related tasks. A key assumption in most MTL algorithms is that all tasks are related, which, however, may not be the case in many real-world applications. In this paper, we propose a robust multi-task learning (RMTL) algorithm which learns multiple tasks simultaneously as well as identifies the irrelevant (outlier) tasks. Specifically, the proposed RMTL algorithm captures the task relationships using a low-rank structure, and simultaneously identifies the outlier tasks using a group-sparse structure. The proposed RMTL algorithm is formulated as a non-smooth convex (unconstrained) optimization problem. We propose to adopt the accelerated proximal method (APM) for solving such an optimization problem. The key component in APM is the computation of the proximal operator, which can be shown to admit an analytic solution. We also theoretically analyze the effectiveness of the RMTL algorithm. In particular, we derive a key property of the optimal solution to RMTL; moreover, based on this key property, we establish a theoretical bound for characterizing the learning performance of RMTL. Our experimental results on benchmark data sets demonstrate the effectiveness and efficiency of the proposed algorithm.

Categories and Subject Descriptors

H.2.8 [**Database Management**]: Database Applications - Data Mining

General Terms

Algorithms

Keywords

Multi-task learning, robust, low-rank patterns, group-sparsity

1. INTRODUCTION

Multi-task learning (MTL) aims at improving generalization performance by utilizing the intrinsic relationships among multiple tasks. One key assumption in most of the existing MTL algorithms is that all tasks are correlated via a certain structure, which, for example, includes hidden units in neural networks [7], a common prior in a hierarchical Bayesian model [3, 29, 35, 37], parameters in Gaussian process covariance [17], kernels and regularizations [10], and common feature representation [1, 9, 2, 27, 16, 34]. Under such an assumption, the knowledge learned from one task is transferable to the other tasks and learning multiple tasks simultaneously generally leads to improved performance.

In many real-world applications involving multiple tasks, it is usually the case that a group of tasks are related while some other tasks are irrelevant to such a group. Simply pooling all tasks together and learning them simultaneously under a presumed structure may degrade the overall learning performance. It is thus desirable to identify irrelevant (outlier) tasks in the development of the multi-task learning algorithms. Learning multiple tasks under this setting is usually referred to as robust multi-task learning [36].

Recently robust multi-task learning has received increasing attention in the areas of data mining and machine learning. In [30, 33, 13], the task clustering (TC) approach is proposed for discovering the common structures in multiple learning tasks. The main idea behind the TC algorithms is to cluster similar tasks into different groups and constrain the tasks from the same group to share the same model representation or parameters. In [36, 38], multivariate student t-processes and their generalization are proposed for distinguishing good tasks from noisy or outlier tasks. The t-processes-based MTL algorithms model the relationship of multiple tasks using a task covariance matrix and they are robust by nature as t-process is implicitly an infinite Gaussian mixture. In [26, 14], the block-sparse structures ($\ell_{1,\infty}$-norm or $\ell_{2,1}$-nrom) are employed to extract essential features shared across the tasks and hence improve the robustness of the learning algorithms.

In this paper, we propose a robust multi-task learning (RMTL) algorithm which learns multiple tasks simultaneously as well as identifies the irrelevant (outlier) tasks. Specifically, our proposed RMTL algorithm captures the relationship of multiple related tasks using a low-rank structure and meanwhile identifies the outlier tasks using a group-sparse structure. The proposed RMTL algorithm is formulated as a non-smooth convex (unconstrained) optimization problem in which the least squares loss is regularized by a nonnegative linear combination of the trace norm and the $\ell_{1,2}$-norm. The optimization problems involving the trace norm and the $\ell_{1,2}$-norm can be routinely reformulated as semi-definite programs or second-order cone programs, both of which, however, are not scalable to large-scale data. We propose to adopt the accelerated proximal method (APM) for solving the proposed RMTL formulation efficiently. One key component in applying APM for solving RMTL is the computation of the associated proximal op-

KDD'11, August 21–24, 2011, San Diego, California, USA.

erator, which is a non-smooth optimization problem involving two optimization variables. The associated proximal operator can be shown to admit an analytic solution. We also conduct theoretical analysis on the performance bound of the composite regularization in RMTL. We first present key properties of the optimal solution to RMTL (Lemma 4.3). We then present an assumption associated with the prescribed training samples and the geometric structures of the matrices of interest; based on this assumption, we derive a performance bound for the combined regularization for multi-task regression (Theorem 4.1). We conduct simulations on benchmark data sets to demonstrate the effectiveness and efficiency of the proposed algorithm.

Notation Denote $\mathbb{N}_m = \{1, \cdots, m\}$. For any $A = [a_1, \cdots, a_m] \in \mathbb{R}^{d \times m}$, let $a_i \in \mathbb{R}^d$ be the i-th column of A; denote by $\|a_i\|_2$ the ℓ_2-norm of a_i; let $\|A\|_{\infty,2} = \|a_j\|_2$, where $j = \arg\max_i \|a_i\|_2$; let $\|A\|_{1,2} = \sum_{i=1}^m \|a_i\|_2$; let $\{\sigma_i(A)\}_{i=1}^r$ be the set of non-zero singular values in non-increasing order, where $r = \text{rank}(A)$; denote by $\|A\|_2 = \sigma_1(A)$ and by $\|A\|_* = \sum_{i=1}^r \sigma_i(A)$ the operator norm and the trace norm of A, respectively.

2. ROBUST MTL FRAMEWORK

Assume that we are given m (regression) learning tasks. Each task is associated with a set of training data

$$\{(x_1^i, y_1^i), \cdots, (x_{n_i}^i, y_{n_i}^i)\} \subset \mathbb{R}^d \times \mathbb{R}, \; i \in \mathbb{N}_m, \tag{1}$$

and a linear predictive function f_i as

$$f_i(x_j^i) = w_i^T x_j^i \approx y_j^i, \; x_j^i \in \mathbb{R}^d, \; y_j^i \in \mathbb{R}, \tag{2}$$

where i and j index the task and the training sample respectively, w_i is the weight vector, n_i and d denote the training sample size and the feature dimensionality respectively.

We consider the multi-task learning setting where multiple tasks are divided into two groups, i.e., the related tasks group and the irrelevant (outlier) tasks group. We consider a composite structure which couples the related tasks using a low-rank structure and identifies the outlier tasks using a group-sparse structure. Denote the transformation matrix of the m tasks by $W = [w_1, \cdots, w_m] \in \mathbb{R}^{d \times m}$. Specifically, W is given by the direct summation of a low-rank matrix $L = [l_1, \cdots, l_m] \in \mathbb{R}^{d \times m}$ (of a smaller set of basis factors), and a group-sparse (column-sparse) matrix $S = [s_1, \cdots, s_m] \in \mathbb{R}^{d \times m}$ (of zero-vectors in the columns). The weight vector of the i-th task can be expressed as

$$w_i = l_i + s_i, \; l_i \in \mathbb{R}^d, \; s_i \in \mathbb{R}^d, \; i \in \mathbb{N}_m, \tag{3}$$

where l_i and s_i are from the aforementioned low-rank structure and the group-sparse structure, respectively.

We propose a robust multi-task learning formulation (RMTL) to learn multiple tasks simultaneously as well as identify the irrelevant outlier tasks. Mathematically, RMTL is formulated as

$$\min_{L,S} \; \mathcal{L}\left((l_i + s_i)^T x_j^i, y_j^i\right) + \alpha\|L\|_* + \beta\|S\|_{1,2}, \tag{4}$$

where the trace norm regularization term encourages the desirable low-rank structure in the matrix L (for coupling the related tasks), and the $\ell_{1,2}$-norm regularization term induces the desirable group-sparse structure in the matrix S (for identifying the outlier tasks), α and β are non-negative trade-off parameters, and $\mathcal{L}(\cdot, \cdot)$ represents the commonly used least squares loss function. Note that the empirical evaluation of the (averaged) least square loss of the m tasks over the prescribed training data can be expressed as

$$\mathcal{L}\left((l_i + s_i)^T x_j^i, y_j^i\right) = \sum_{i=1}^m \sum_{j=1}^{n_i} \frac{1}{mn_i}\left((l_i + s_i)^T x_j^i - y_j^i\right)^2. \tag{5}$$

Our motivation behind the proposed RMTL formulation in Eq. (4) is as follows: if the i-th task is from the related tasks group, s_i is expected to be a zero-vector and hence w_i obeys the specified low-rank structure constraint; on the other hand, if the i-th task is from the outlier tasks group, s_i is expected to be non-zero and w_i is equal to a direct sum of l_i and the non-zero s_i.

The RMTL formulation in Eq. (4) is an unconstrained convex optimization problem with a non-smooth objective function. Such a problem is difficult to solve directly due to the non-smoothness in the trace norm and the $\ell_{1,2}$-norm regularization terms.

The proposed RMTL formulation in Eq. (4) subsumes several representative algorithms as special cases. As $\beta \to +\infty$, RMTL is degenerated into

$$\min_{L} \; \sum_{i=1}^m \sum_{j=1}^{n_i} \frac{1}{mn_i}\left(l_i^T x_j^i - y_j^i\right)^2 + \alpha\|L\|_*. \tag{6}$$

The formulation in Eq. (6) is essentially the least squares regression with trace norm regularization, in which multiple learning tasks are coupled via a low-rank structure. On the other hand, as $\alpha \to \infty$, RMTL is degenerated into

$$\min_{S} \; \sum_{i=1}^m \sum_{j=1}^{n_i} \frac{1}{mn_i}\left(s_i^T x_j^i - y_j^i\right)^2 + \beta\,|S\|_{1,2}. \tag{7}$$

The formulation in Eq. (7) is essentially a variant of the ridge regression with the smooth term $\sum_{i=1}^m \|s_i\|^2$ replaced by the non-smooth term $\sum_{i=1}^m \|s_i\|$. In such a formulation, the multiple tasks are decoupled and each task can be learned (optimized) via

$$\min_{s_i} \; \frac{1}{mn_i} \sum_{j=1}^{n_i} \left(s_i^T x_j^i - y_j^i\right)^2 + \beta\|s_i\|_2.$$

Note that similar low-rank and group-sparse structures are studied from a different perspective in [32, 12], which focus on decomposing a given data matrix into a unique sum of a low-rank structure and a column-sparse structure and providing a theoretical guarantee for existence and uniqueness of the decomposition.

3. ACCELERATED PROXIMAL METHOD

In this section, we consider to solve the RMTL formulation in Eq. (4) using the accelerated proximal method (APM) [4, 24, 25]. APM has attracted extensive attentions in the machine learning and data mining communities [20, 19, 15, 8, 18, 21] due to its optimal convergence rate among all first-order techniques and its ability of dealing with large-scale non-smooth optimization problems. Note that in this paper, we focus on discussing the key ingredient of APM, i.e. the proximal operator and its efficient computation; the detailed description of APM can be found in [4, 24, 25].

3.1 Proximal Operator

For the optimization problem in Eq. (4), we symbolically denote its variables by

$$Z = \begin{bmatrix} L \\ S \end{bmatrix}, \; L \in \mathbb{R}^{d \times m}, \; S \in \mathbb{R}^{d \times m},$$

and denote the smooth and non-smooth components of its objective function respectively by

$$f(Z) = \mathcal{L}\left((l_i + s_i)^T x_j^i, y_j^i\right), \quad g(Z) = \alpha\|L\|_* + \beta\|S\|_{1,2}. \tag{8}$$

To solve Eq. (4), APM maintains two sequences of variables: a feasible solution sequence $\{Z_k\}$ and a searching point sequence $\{\widehat{Z}_k\}$. The general scheme of APM can be described as below: at the k-th iteration of APM, the solution point Z_{k+1} can be computed via

$$Z_{k+1} = \arg\min_{Z} \frac{\gamma_k}{2} \left\| Z - \left(\widehat{Z}_k - \frac{1}{\gamma_k} \nabla f(\widehat{Z}_k) \right) \right\|_F^2 + g(Z), \quad (9)$$

where $\widehat{Z}_k$ denotes a searching point constructed from a linear combination of Z_k and Z_{k-1} from previous iterations, and $\nabla f(\widehat{Z}_k)$ denotes the derivative of the smooth component $f(\cdot)$ in Eq. (8) at $\widehat{Z}_k$, γ_k specifies the step size which can be appropriately determined by iteratively increasing its value until the inequality

$$f(Z_{k+1}) \leq f(\widehat{Z}_k) + \langle \nabla f(\widehat{Z}_k), Z_{k+1} - \widehat{Z}_k \rangle + \frac{\gamma_k}{2} \|Z_{k+1} - \widehat{Z}_k\|_F^2, \quad (10)$$

is satisfied. The procedure in Eq. (9) is commonly referred to as the proximal operator [23]. The efficient computation of the proximal operator is critical for the practical convergence of APM, as it is involved in each iteration of the APM algorithm.

3.2 Proximal Operator Computation

For the optimization problem in Eq. (4), its proximal operator can be expressed as an optimization problem of the general form

$$\min_{L_z, S_z} \quad \|L_z - L_{\hat{z}}\|_F^2 + \|S_z - S_{\hat{z}}\|_F^2 + \hat{\alpha}\|L_z\|_* + \hat{\beta}\|S_z\|_{1,2}, \quad (11)$$

where $\hat{\alpha} = \frac{2\alpha}{\gamma_k}$ and $\hat{\beta} = \frac{2\beta}{\gamma_k}$. It can be easily verified that the optimization of L_z and S_z in Eq. (11) are decoupled. Moreover, the optimal solution to Eq. (11) admits an analytic form as presented below.

Computation of L_z The optimal L_z to Eq. (11) can be obtained by solving the following optimization problem:

$$\min_{L_z} \quad \|L_z - L_{\hat{z}}\|_F^2 + \hat{\alpha}\|L_z\|_*. \quad (12)$$

The computation procedure above is equal to the matrix shrinkage operator discussed in [6, 11]. In essence it applies soft-thresholding to the non-zero singular values [28] of $L_{\hat{z}}$ as summarized in the following theorem.

THEOREM 3.1. *Given an arbitrary $L_{\hat{z}}$ in Eq. (12), let $rank(L_{\hat{z}}) = r$ and denote the singular value decomposition (SVD) of $L_{\hat{z}}$ in the reduced form as*

$$L_{\hat{z}} = U_{\hat{z}} \Sigma_{\hat{z}} V_{\hat{z}}^T, \quad \Sigma_{\hat{z}} = diag\left(\{\sigma_i\}_{i=1}^r\right)$$

where, $U_{\hat{z}} \in \mathbb{R}^{d \times r}$ and $V_{\hat{z}} \in \mathbb{R}^{m \times r}$ consist of orthonormal columns, $\Sigma_{\hat{z}} \in \mathbb{R}^{r \times r}$ is diagonal, and $\{\sigma_i\}_{i=1}^r$ represent the non-zero singular values. Then the optimal L_z^* to Eq. (12) is given by

$$L_z^* = U_{\hat{z}}\, diag\left(\left\{ \sigma_i - \frac{1}{2}\hat{\alpha} \right\}_+ \right) V_{\hat{z}}^T,$$

where $\{e\}_+ = \max(e, 0)$.

The dominating cost in solving Eq. (12) lies in the compact SVD operation on the matrix $L_{\hat{z}} \in \mathbb{R}^{d \times m}$ ($m \ll d$ in general MTL settings).

Computation of S_z The optimal S_z to Eq. (11) can be obtained by solving the following optimization problem:

$$\min_{S_z} \quad \|S_z - S_{\hat{z}}\|_F^2 + \hat{\beta}\|S_z\|_{1,2}. \quad (13)$$

It can be easily verified that in Eq. (13) the column vectors of S_z can be optimized separately. Specifically, each vector of the optimal S_z to Eq. (13) can be obtained via solving a subproblem in the form

$$\min_{s} \quad \|s - \hat{s}\|_2^2 + \hat{\beta}\|s\|_2. \quad (14)$$

It can be verified that the optimization problem above admits an analytic solution [19] as summarized in the following lemma.

LEMMA 3.1. *Let s^* be the optimal solution to the optimization problem in Eq. (14). Then s^* is given by*

$$s^* = \begin{cases} \hat{s}\left(1 - \frac{\hat{\beta}}{2\|\hat{s}\|_2}\right) & \|\hat{s}\|_2 > \frac{\hat{\beta}}{2} \\ 0 & 0 \leq \|\hat{s}\|_2 \leq \frac{\hat{\beta}}{2} \end{cases}.$$

The computation cost of solving Eq. (13) is relatively small compared to the cost of solving Eq. (12).

4. THEORETICAL ANALYSIS

In this section, we derive a performance bound for the proposed RMTL formulation in Eq. (4). This performance bound can be used to theoretically evaluate how well the integration of the low-rank structure and the group-sparse structure can estimate the multiple tasks (the ground truth of the linear predictive functions). Note that in the following analysis, for simplicity we assume that the training sample sizes for all tasks are the same; the derivation below can be easily extended to the setting where the training sample size for each task is different.

Assume that the linear predictive function associated with the i-th task satisfies

$$y_j^i = f_i(x_j^i) + \delta_{ij} = w_i^T x_j^i + \delta_{ij}, \; i \in \mathbb{N}_m, \; j \in \mathbb{N}_n, \quad (15)$$

where $\{(x_j^i, y_j^i)\}$ are the training data pairs of the i-th task, and $\delta_{ij} \sim \mathcal{N}(0, \sigma_\delta^2)$ is a stochastic noise variable. For the i-th task, denote its training data matrix X_i and its label vector y_i respectively by

$$X_i = [x_1^i, \cdots, x_n^i] \in \mathbb{R}^{d \times n}, y_i = [y_1^i, \cdots, y_n^i]^T \in \mathbb{R}^n, i \in \mathbb{N}_m. \quad (16)$$

Denote the empirical evaluation of the i-th task f_i over the training data $\{x_j^i\}$ and the associated noise vector δ_i respectively by

$$\hat{f}_i = [f_i(x_1^i), \cdots, f_i(x_n^i)]^T \in \mathbb{R}^n, \; \delta_i = [\delta_{i1}, \cdots, \delta_{in}]^T \in \mathbb{R}^n. \quad (17)$$

It follows that Eq. (15) can be expressed in a compact form as

$$y_i = \hat{f}_i + \delta_i, \; i \in \mathbb{N}_m. \quad (18)$$

Moreover, the optimization problem in Eq. (4) can be rewritten as

$$(\widehat{L}_z, \widehat{S}_z) = \arg\min_{L,S} \frac{1}{mn} \sum_{i=1}^{m} \|X_i^T(l_i + s_i) - y_i\|_2^2 + \alpha\|L\|_* + \beta\|S\|_{1,2}, \quad (19)$$

where $\widehat{L}_z = [\hat{l}_1, \cdots, \hat{l}_m]$ and $\widehat{S}_z = [\hat{s}_1, \cdots, \hat{s}_m]$ are the optimal solution pair obtained via solving Eq. (19).

4.1 Basic Properties of the Optimal Solution

We present some basic properties of the optimal solution pair defined in Eq. (19); these properties are important building blocks for our following theoretical analysis. We first define two operators, namely $\mathcal{Q}$ and its complement $\mathcal{Q}_\perp$, on an arbitrary matrix pair (of the same size), based on Lemma 3.4 in [28].

LEMMA 4.1. *Given any L and $\widehat{L}$ of the same size $d \times m$, let rank$(L) = r \leq \min(d, m)$ and denote the SVD of L as*

$$L = U \begin{bmatrix} \Sigma & \mathbf{0} \\ \mathbf{0} & \mathbf{0} \end{bmatrix} V^T,$$

where $U \in \mathbb{R}^{d\times d}$ and $V \in \mathbb{R}^{m\times m}$ are orthogonal, and $\Sigma \in \mathbb{R}^{r\times r}$ is diagonal consisting of the non-zero singular values on its main diagonal. Let

$$U^T(\widehat{L} - L)V = \begin{bmatrix} M_{11} & M_{12} \\ M_{21} & M_{22} \end{bmatrix},$$

where $M_{11} \in \mathbb{R}^{r\times r}$, $M_{12} \in \mathbb{R}^{r\times(m-r)}$, $M_{21} \in \mathbb{R}^{(d-r)\times r}$, and $M_{22} \in \mathbb{R}^{(d-r)\times(m-r)}$. Define $\mathcal{Q}$ and $\mathcal{Q}_\perp$ on $\widehat{L} - L$ as

$$\mathcal{Q}(\widehat{L}-L) = U \begin{bmatrix} M_{11} & M_{12} \\ M_{21} & \mathbf{0} \end{bmatrix} V^T, \mathcal{Q}_\perp(\widehat{L}-L) = U \begin{bmatrix} \mathbf{0} & \mathbf{0} \\ \mathbf{0} & M_{22} \end{bmatrix} V^T.$$

Then rank$(\mathcal{Q}(\widehat{L}-L)) \leq 2r$, $L\mathcal{Q}_\perp^T(\widehat{L}-L) = L^T\mathcal{Q}_\perp(\widehat{L}-L) = 0$.

The results in Lemma 4.1 imply a condition under which the trace norm on a matrix pair is additive. From Lemma 4.1 we can verify

$$\|L + \mathcal{Q}_\perp(\widehat{L} - L)\|_* = \|L\|_* + \|\mathcal{Q}_\perp(\widehat{L} - L)\|_*, \qquad (20)$$

for arbitrary L and $\widehat{L}$ of the same size. As a direct consequence of Lemma 4.1, we derive a bound on the trace norm of the matrices of interest as summarized below (the detailed proof is provided in the Appendix).

COROLLARY 4.1. *For an arbitrary matrix pair $\widehat{L}$ and L, the following inequality holds*

$$\|\widehat{L} - L\|_* + \|L\|_* - \|\widehat{L}\|_* \leq 2\|\mathcal{Q}(\widehat{L} - L)\|_*.$$

Analogous to the bound on the trace norm derived in Corollary 4.1, we derive a bound on the $\ell_{1,2}$-norm of the matrices of interest. Denote by $\mathcal{C}(S)$ the set of indices corresponding to the non-zero columns of the matrix S as

$$\mathcal{C}(S) = \{i : s_i \neq 0,\ i \in \mathbb{N}_m\}, \qquad (21)$$

and by $\mathcal{C}_\perp(S)$ the associated complement (the set of indices corresponding to the zero columns). Denote by $\widehat{S}_{\mathcal{C}(S)}$ the matrix of the same columns as $\widehat{S}$ on the index set $\mathcal{C}(S)$ and of zero columns on the index set $\mathcal{C}_\perp(S)$, i.e., $\widehat{S}_{\mathcal{C}(S)} = [\tilde{s}_1, \cdots, \tilde{s}_m]$, where $\tilde{s}_i = \hat{s}_i$ if $i \in \mathcal{C}(S)$ and $\tilde{s}_i = \mathbf{0}$ if $i \in \mathcal{C}_\perp(S)$. The bound on the $\ell_{1,2}$-norm is summarized below (the detailed proof is provided in the Appendix).

LEMMA 4.2. *Given a matrix pair S and $\widehat{S}$ of the same size, the following inequality holds*

$$\|\widehat{S} - S\|_{1,2} + \|S\|_{1,2} - \|\widehat{S}\|_{1,2} \leq 2\|(\widehat{S} - S)_{\mathcal{C}(S)}\|_{1,2}. \qquad (22)$$

We now present some important properties of the optimal solution in Eq. (19) as summarized in the following lemma.

LEMMA 4.3. *Consider the optimization problem in Eq. (19) for $m \geq 2$ and $n, d \geq 1$. Let X_i and y_i be defined in Eq. (16), and f_i and δ_i be defined in Eq. (17). Assume that all diagonal elements of the matrix $X_iX_i^T$ are equal to 1 (features are normalized). Take the regularization parameters α and β as*

$$\frac{\alpha}{\sqrt{m}}, \beta \geq \lambda,\ \lambda = \frac{2\sigma_\delta}{nm}\sqrt{d+t}, \qquad (23)$$

where $t > 0$ is a universal constant. Then with probability of at least $1 - m\exp\left(-\frac{1}{2}\left(t - d\log\left(1+\frac{t}{d}\right)\right)\right)$, for a global minimizer $\widehat{L}_z, \widehat{S}_z$ in Eq. (19) and any $L, S \in \mathbb{R}^{d\times m}$, we have

$$\frac{1}{nm}\sum_{i=1}^m \|X_i^T(\hat{l}_i + \hat{s}_i) - f_i\|_2^2 \leq \frac{1}{nm}\sum_{i=1}^m \|X_i^T(l_i + s_i) - f_i\|_2^2 + \alpha\|\mathcal{Q}(\widehat{L}_z - L)\| + \beta\|(\widehat{S}_z - S)_{\mathcal{C}(S)}\|_{1,2}, \qquad (24)$$

where $\hat{l}_i$ and $\hat{s}_i$ (l_i and s_i) are the i-th columns of $\widehat{L}_z$ and $\widehat{S}_z$ (L and S), respectively.

PROOF. From the definition of $(\widehat{L}_z, \widehat{S}_z)$ in Eq. (19), we have

$$\frac{1}{nm}\sum_{i=1}^m \|X_i^T(\hat{l}_i + \hat{s}_i) - y_i\|_2^2 \leq \frac{1}{nm}\sum_{i=1}^m \|X_i^T(l_i + s_i) - y_i\|_2^2$$
$$\alpha\|L\|_* + \beta\|S\|_{1,2} - \alpha\|\widehat{L}_z\|_* - \beta\|\widehat{S}_z\|_{1,2}.$$

By substituting Eq. (18) into the inequality above and rearranging all terms, we have

$$\frac{1}{nm}\sum_{i=1}^m \|X_i^T(\hat{l}_i + \hat{s}_i) - f_i\|_2^2 \leq \frac{1}{nm}\sum_{i=1}^m \|X_i^T(l_i + s_i) - f_i\|_2^2 + \alpha(\|L\|_* - \|\widehat{L}_z\|_*) + \beta(\|S\|_{1,2} - \|\widehat{S}_z\|_{1,2}) + \frac{2}{nm}\sum_{i=1}^m \langle \hat{l}_i - l_i, X_i\delta_i\rangle + \frac{2}{nm}\sum_{i=1}^m \langle \hat{s}_i - s_i, X_i\delta_i\rangle. \qquad (25)$$

Next we compute upper bounds for the terms $\frac{2}{nm}\sum_{i=1}^m\langle \hat{l}_i - l_i, X_i\delta_i\rangle$ and $\frac{2}{nm}\sum_{i=1}^m\langle \hat{s}_i - s_i, X_i\delta_i\rangle$ in Eq. (25), respectively. Define a set of random events $\{\mathcal{A}_i\}$ as

$$\mathcal{A}_i = \left\{\frac{2}{nm}\|X_i\delta_i\|_2 \leq \lambda\right\},\ \forall i \in \mathbb{N}_m.$$

For each $\mathcal{A}_i$, define a set of random variables $\{v_{ij}\}$ as

$$v_{ij} = \frac{1}{\sigma_\delta}\sum_{k=1}^n x_{jk}^i\delta_{ik},\ j \in \mathbb{N}_d,$$

where x_{jk}^i denotes the (j,k)-th entry of the data matrix X_i. Since all diagonal elements of the matrix $X_iX_i^T$ are equal to 1, it can be shown that $\{v_{i1}, v_{i2}, \cdots, v_{id}\}$ are i.i.d. Gaussian variables obeying $\mathcal{N}(0,1)$ (Lemma 1 in the Appendix). We can also verify that $\sum_{j=1}^d v_{ij}^2$ is a chi-squared random variable with d degrees of freedom. Moreover taking λ as in Eq. (23), we have

$$\Pr\left(\frac{2}{nm}\|X_i\delta_i\|_2 > \lambda\right) = \Pr\left(\sum_{j=1}^d\left(\sum_{k=1}^n x_{jk}^i\delta_{ik}\right)^2 \geq \frac{\lambda^2n^2m^2}{4}\right)$$
$$= \Pr\left(\sum_{j=1}^d v_{ij}^2 \geq d + t\right) \leq \exp\left(-\frac{1}{2}\mu_d^2(t)\right),$$

where $\mu_d(t) = \sqrt{t - d\log\left(1+\frac{t}{d}\right)}$ $(t > 0)$, and the last inequality above follows from a concentration inequality (Lemma 2 in the Appendix). Let $\mathcal{A} = \bigcap_{i=1}^m \mathcal{A}_i$. Denote by $\mathcal{A}_i^c$ the complement of each event $\mathcal{A}_i$. It follows that

$$\Pr(\mathcal{A}) \geq 1 - \Pr\left(\bigcup_{i=1}^m \mathcal{A}_i^c\right) \geq 1 - m\exp\left(-\frac{1}{2}\mu_d^2(t)\right).$$

Under the event $\mathcal{A}$, we derive a bound on the term $\frac{2}{nm}\sum_{i=1}^{m}\langle \hat{l}_i - l_i, X_i\delta_i\rangle$ as

$$\frac{2}{nm}\sum_{i=1}^{m}\langle \hat{l}_i - l_i, X_i\delta_i\rangle \leq \frac{2}{nm}\sum_{i=1}^{m}\|\hat{l}_i - l_i\|_2\|X_i\delta_i\|_2$$

$$\leq \lambda\sum_{i=1}^{m}\|\hat{l}_i - l_i\|_2 \leq \alpha\|\widehat{L}_z - L\|_*, \quad (26)$$

where the first inequality above follows from Cauchy-Schwarz inequality and the second inequality follows from

$$\sum_{i=1}^{m}\|\hat{l}_i - l_i\|_2 \leq \sqrt{m\sum_{i=1}^{m}\|\hat{l}_i - l_i\|_2^2} = \sqrt{m}\|\widehat{L}_z - L\|_F \leq \sqrt{m}\|\widehat{L}_z - L\|_*.$$

Similarly under $\mathcal{A}$, we also derive a bound on the term $\frac{2}{nm}\sum_{i=1}^{m}\langle \hat{s}_i - s_i, X_i f_i\rangle$ as

$$\frac{2}{nm}\sum_{i=1}^{m}\langle \hat{s}_i - s_i, X_i\delta_i\rangle \leq \frac{2}{nm}\sum_{i=1}^{m}\|\hat{s}_i - s_i\|_2\|X_i\delta_i\|_2 \leq \beta\|\widehat{S}_z - S\|_{1,2}. \quad (27)$$

Moreover we bound the right side of Eq.(25) using the results from Eqs. (26) and (27). It follows that

$$\frac{1}{nm}\sum_{i=1}^{m}\|X_i^T(\hat{l}_i+\hat{s}_i)-\hat{f}_i\|_2^2 \leq \frac{1}{nm}\sum_{i=1}^{m}\|X_i^T(l_i+s_i)-\hat{f}_i\|_2^2 +$$
$$\alpha(\|\widehat{L}_z-L\|_*+\|L\|_*-\|\widehat{L}_z\|_*)+\beta(\|\widehat{S}_z-S\|_{1,2}+\|S\|_{1,2}-\|\widehat{S}_z\|_{1,2}).$$

Finally by applying Corollary 4.1 and Lemma 4.2 together with the inequality above, we complete the proof. □

4.2 Performance Bound

We present a performance bound of the proposed RMTL formulation in Eq. (19). This bound measures how well the multi-task learning scheme (via the integration of the low-rank structure and the $\ell_{1,2}$-norm structure) can estimate the linear predictive functions in Eq. (15).

We begin with some notations. Let $X \in \mathbb{R}^{md\times mn}$ be a block-diagonal matrix with its i-th block formed by the matrix $X_i \in \mathbb{R}^{d\times n}$ ($i \in \mathbb{N}_m$). Define a diagonalization operator $\mathcal{D}$ on an arbitrary $\Omega = [\omega_1, \omega_2, \cdots, \omega_m] \in \mathbb{R}^{d\times m}$: $\mathcal{D}(\Omega) \in \mathbb{R}^{md\times m}$ is a block diagonal matrix with its i-th block formed by the column vector $\omega_i \in \mathbb{R}^d$. Let $\mathcal{F} = [\hat{f}_1, \cdots, \hat{f}_m]$, where $\hat{f}_i$ is defined in Eq. (17). Therefore we can rewrite Eq. (24) in a compact form as

$$\frac{1}{T}\|X^T\mathcal{D}(\widehat{L}_z+\widehat{S}_z)-\mathcal{D}(\mathcal{F})\|_F^2 \leq \frac{1}{T}\|X^T\mathcal{D}(L+S)-\mathcal{D}(\mathcal{F})\|_F^2$$
$$+\alpha\|\mathcal{Q}(\widehat{L}_z - L)\|_* + \beta\|(\widehat{S}_z - S)_{\mathcal{C}(S)}\|_{1,2}, \quad (28)$$

where $T = nm$. We next introduce our assumption over a restricted set. The assumption is associated with training data X and the geometric structure of the matrices of interest.

ASSUMPTION 4.1. *For a matrix pair Γ_L and Γ_S of size d by m, let $s \leq \min(d, m)$ and $q \leq m$. We assume that there exist constants $\kappa_1(s)$ and $\kappa_2(q)$ such that*

$$\kappa_1(s) \triangleq \min_{\Gamma_L,\Gamma_S\in\mathcal{R}(s,q)} \frac{\|X\mathcal{D}(\Gamma_L+\Gamma_S)\|_F}{\sqrt{T}\|\mathcal{Q}(\Gamma_L)\|_*} > 0, \quad (29)$$

$$\kappa_2(q) \triangleq \min_{\Gamma_L,\Gamma_S\in\mathcal{R}(s,q)} \frac{\|X\mathcal{D}(\Gamma_L+\Gamma_S)\|_F}{\sqrt{T}\|(\Gamma_S)_{\mathcal{C}(S)}\|_{1,2}} > 0, \quad (30)$$

where the restricted set $\mathcal{R}(s,q)$ is defined as

$$\mathcal{R}(s,q) = \Big\{\Gamma_L, \Gamma_S \in \mathbb{R}^{d\times m} \,|\, \Gamma_L \neq 0, \Gamma_S \neq 0,$$
$$\textit{rank}(\mathcal{Q}(\Gamma_L)) \leq s, \ |\mathcal{C}(\Gamma_S)| \leq q\Big\},$$

and $\mathcal{C}(\cdot)$ is defined in Eq. (21), and $|\widehat{C}|$ denotes the number of elements in the set $\widehat{C}$.

The assumption in Eqs. (29) and (30) can be implied by several sufficient conditions as in [5]. Due to the space constraint, the details are omitted. Note that similar assumptions are used in [22] for deriving a certain performance bound for a different multi-task learning formulation.

We present the performance bound of the RMTL formulation in the following theorem.

THEOREM 4.1. *Consider the optimization problem in Eq. (19) for $m \geq 2$ and $n, d \geq 1$. Take the regularization parameters α and β as in Eq. (23). Then with probability of at least $1 - m\exp\left(-\frac{1}{2}\left(t - d\log\left(1+\frac{t}{d}\right)\right)\right)$, for a global minimizer $\widehat{L}_z, \widehat{S}_z$ in Eq. (19), we have*

$$\frac{1}{T}\|X\mathcal{D}(\widehat{L}_z+\widehat{S}_z)-\mathcal{D}(\mathcal{F})\|_F^2 \leq (1+\epsilon)\inf_{L,S}\frac{1}{T}\|X\mathcal{D}(L+S)-\mathcal{D}(\mathcal{F})\|_F^2$$
$$+\mathcal{E}(\epsilon)\left(\frac{\alpha^2}{\kappa_1^2(2r)} + \frac{\beta^2}{\kappa_2^2(c)}\right), \quad (31)$$

where inf *is taken over all $L, S \in \mathbb{R}^{d\times m}$ with rank$(L) \leq r$ and $|\mathcal{C}(S)| \leq c$, and $\mathcal{E}(\epsilon) > 0$ is a constant depending only on ϵ.*

PROOF. Denote $\Gamma_L = \widehat{L}_z - L$ and $\Gamma_S = \widehat{S}_z - S$. It follows from Eq. (28) that

$$\frac{1}{T}\|X^T\mathcal{D}(\widehat{L}_z+\widehat{S}_z)-\mathcal{D}(\mathcal{F})\|_F^2 \leq \frac{1}{T}\|X^T\mathcal{D}(L+S)-\mathcal{D}(\mathcal{F})\|_F^2$$
$$+\alpha\|\mathcal{Q}(\Gamma_L)\|_* + \beta\|(\Gamma_S)_{\mathcal{C}(S)}\|_{1,2}. \quad (32)$$

Given $\mathcal{Q}(\Gamma_L) \leq 2r$ (from Lemma 4.1) and $|\mathcal{C}(S)| \leq c$, we derive upper bounds on $\alpha\|\mathcal{Q}(\Gamma_L)\|_*$ and $\beta\|(\Gamma_S)_{\mathcal{C}(S)})\|_{1,2}$ over the restrict set $\mathcal{R}(2r, c)$ based on Assumptions 4.1, respectively. It follows from Eq. (29) in Assumption 4.1 that

$$2\alpha\|\mathcal{Q}(\Gamma_L)\|_* \leq \frac{2\alpha}{\kappa_1(2r)\sqrt{T}}\|X\mathcal{D}(\Gamma_L+\Gamma_S)\|_F \leq \frac{2\alpha}{\kappa_1(2r)\sqrt{T}}$$
$$\left(\|X\mathcal{D}(\widehat{L}_z+\widehat{S}_z)-\mathcal{D}(\mathcal{F})\|_F + \|X\mathcal{D}(L+S)-\mathcal{D}(\mathcal{F})\|_F\right) \leq$$
$$\frac{\alpha^2\tau}{\kappa_1^2(2r)} + \frac{1}{\tau T}\|X\mathcal{D}(\widehat{L}_z+\widehat{S}_z)-\mathcal{D}(\mathcal{F})\|_F^2 + \frac{\alpha^2\tau}{\kappa_1^2(2r)} +$$
$$\frac{1}{\tau T}\|X\mathcal{D}(L+S)-\mathcal{D}(\mathcal{F})\|_F^2, \quad (33)$$

where the last inequality above follows from $2ab \leq a^2\tau + b^2\frac{1}{\tau}$ for $\tau > 0$. Similarly, we have

$$2\beta\|(\Gamma_S)_{\mathcal{C}(S)}\|_{1,2} \leq \frac{\beta^2\tau}{\kappa_2^2(c)} + \frac{1}{\tau T}\|X\mathcal{D}(\widehat{L}_z+\widehat{S}_z)-\mathcal{D}(\mathcal{F})\|_F^2 +$$
$$\frac{\beta^2\tau}{\kappa_2^2(c)} + \frac{1}{\tau T}\|X\mathcal{D}(L+S)-\mathcal{D}(\mathcal{F})\|_F^2. \quad (34)$$

Substituting Eqs. (33) and (34) into Eq. (32) and setting $\tau = 2+\frac{4}{\epsilon}$, we obtain

$$\frac{1}{T}\|X\mathcal{D}(\widehat{L}_z + \widehat{S}_z) - \mathcal{D}(\mathcal{F})\|_F^2$$
$$\leq \frac{\tau+2}{\tau-2}\|X\mathcal{D}(L+S) - \mathcal{D}(\mathcal{F})\|_F^2 + \frac{2\tau^2}{\tau-2}\left(\frac{\alpha^2}{\kappa_1^2(2r)} + \frac{\beta^2}{\kappa_2^2(c)}\right)$$
$$= (1+\epsilon)\|X\mathcal{D}(L+S) - \mathcal{D}(\mathcal{F})\|_F^2 + \mathcal{E}(\epsilon)\left(\frac{\alpha^2}{\kappa_1^2(2r)} + \frac{\beta^2}{\kappa_2^2(c)}\right),$$

where $\mathcal{E}(\epsilon) = \epsilon(\frac{1}{2} + \frac{1}{\epsilon})^2$. This completes the proof. □

The performance bound described in Eq. (31) can be refined by choosing specific values for the regularization parameters α and β: it can be verified that the component $\frac{\alpha^2}{\kappa_1^2(2r)} + \frac{\beta^2}{\kappa_2^2(c)}$ is minimized if α and β are chosen to be proportional to $\kappa_1^2(2r)$ and $\kappa_2^2(c)$, respectively.

5. EXPERIMENTS

In this section, we evaluate the proposed RMTL formulation in Eq. (4) in comparison with other representative algorithms for multi-task learning; we also conduct numerical studies on the APM algorithm in comparison with the commonly used proximal method (PM) [25, 24] for solving RMTL. All algorithms are implemented in Matlab. Note that for numerical accuracy consideration, we solve the RMLT formulation with its objective function multiplied by nm, where m and n correspond to the task number and the sum of the sample sizes for all tasks, respectively.

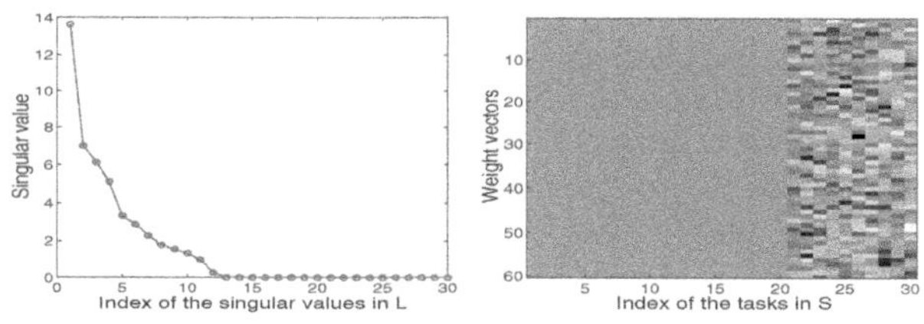

Figure 1: Demonstration of the extracted low-rank and group structures: the left plot shows the singular values of the low-rank component L (the last 18 singular values are zero); the right plot demonstrates the structure of the group-sparse component S (the first 20 columns are zero-vectors). In the right plot the grey area corresponds to the pixels of zero-value.

5.1 Demonstration of Extracted Structures

We apply the RMTL algorithm on a synthetic data set and then demonstrate the extracted low-rank and group-sparse structures. The synthetic data is constructed as follows: set the task number $m = 30$, the size of the training samples for each task $n_i = 50$, and the feature dimensionality of the training samples $d = 60$; generate the entries of the training data $X_i \in \mathbb{R}^{d\times n_i}$ (for the i-th task) randomly from the distribution $\mathcal{N}(0, 25)$; generate the entries in the low-rank component L (of size $d \times m$) randomly from $\mathcal{N}(0, 16)$ and then set its smallest 20 singular values at 0; generate the entries in the group-sparse component S (of size $d \times m$) randomly from $\mathcal{N}(0, 20)$ and then set its first 20 columns as zero-vectors; construct the response (target) vector of each task as $y_i = X_i^T(L+S) + \delta_i \in \mathbb{R}^{n_i}$ ($i \in \mathbb{N}_m$), where each entry in the vector δ_i is randomly generated from $\mathcal{N}(0, 1)$. Under this experimental setting, we construct 20 related tasks as well as 10 outlier tasks, where each task is associated with 50 training samples of feature dimensionality 60.

In Figure 1, we present the low-rank component L and the group-sparse component S obtained by solving RMTL with $\alpha = 50$ and $\beta = 10$. From the left plot of Figure 1, we can observe that the matrix L (of size 60×50) has 12 non-zero singular values; this result is consistent with our problem setting of using a low-rank structure to capture the tasks relationship. From the right plot of Figure 1, we can observe that the first 20 columns (corresponding to the related tasks) in S are zero vectors, while the last 10 columns (corresponding to the outlier tasks) are non-zero vectors. The results in Figure 1 empirically demonstrate the effectiveness of RMTL.

5.2 Performance Evaluation of RMTL

We evaluate the RMTL algorithm on multi-task regression problems in comparison with other representative algorithms including ridge regression (Ridge), least squares with ℓ_1-norm regularization (Lasso), least squares with trace norm regularization (TraceNorm), least squares with low-rank and sparse structures regularization (Sparse-LowRank) [8], and convex multi-task feature learning (CMTL) [2]. The normalized mean squared error (nMSE) and the averaged mean squared error (aMSE) are employed as the regression performance measures as used in previous studies [2, 38]. Note that nMSE is defined as the mean squared error (MSE) divided by the variance of the target vector; aMSE is defined as MSE divided by the squared norm of the target vector. We adopt APM to solve RMTL and terminate APM when the relative change of the objective values in two successive iterations is smaller than 10^{-5}. We use the School data[1] and the SARCOS data[2] for the experiments.

The School data consists of the exam scores of 15362 students from 139 secondary schools; each student is described by 27 attributes such as gender and ethnic group. The exam score prediction of the students can be cast into a multi-task regression (learning) problem: we are given 139 tasks (schools), where each task has a different number of samples (students) and each sample has 27 features (attributes). We randomly select 10%, 20%, and 30% of the samples (from each task) to form the training set and use the rest of the samples as the test set. The experimental results averaged over 15 random repetitions are presented in Table 1. From the presented results, we have the following observations: (1) RMTL outperforms all other competing algorithms in terms of nMSE and aMSE; (2) the multi-task learning algorithms (TraceNorm, Sparse-LowRank, CMTL, and RMTL) outperform the single-task learning algorithms (Ridge and Lasso) in terms of both nMSE and aMSE; (3) the performance of CMTL is similar to that of TraceNorm; this result may be due to the use of similar penalty terms in CMTL and TraceNorm.

The SARCOS data is collected for an inverse dynamics prediction problem for a seven degrees-of-freedom anthropomorphic robot arm. This data consists of 48933 observations corresponding to 7 joint torques; each of the observations is described by 21 features including 7 joint positions, 7 joint velocities, and 7 joint accelerations. Our goal is to construct mappings from each observation to 7 joint torques. We randomly select 50, 100, 150 observations to form 3 training sets and accordingly randomly select 5000 observations to form 3 test sets. The experimental results averaged over 15 random repetitions are presented in Table 2. From the experimental results, we have the following observations: (1) RMTL performs better than or compares competitively to all other competing algorithms in terms of both nMSE and aMSE; (2) the multi-task learning algorithms (TraceNorm, Sparse-LowRank, CMTL,

[1] http://www.cs.ucl.ac.uk/staff/A.Argyriou/code/
[2] http://www.gaussianprocess.org/gpml/data/

Table 1: Performance comparison of the six competing algorithms in terms of the normalized MSE (nMSE) and the averaged MSE (aMSE) with standard deviation using the School data. All parameters of the six methods are determined via cross-validation and the reported regression performance is averaged over 15 random repetitions. Note that a smaller value of nMSE and aMSE represents better regression performance.

Measure	training ratio	Ridge	Lasso	TraceNorm	Sparse-LowRank	CMTL	Robust MTL
nMSE	10%	1.0398 ± 0.0038	1.0261 ± 0.0132	0.9359 ± 0.0370	0.9175 ± 0.0261	0.9413 ± 0.0021	$\mathbf{0.9130 \pm 0.0039}$
	20%	0.8773 ± 0.0043	0.8754 ± 0.0194	0.8211 ± 0.0032	0.8126 ± 0.0132	0.8327 ± 0.0039	$\mathbf{0.8055 \pm 0.0103}$
	30%	0.8171 ± 0.0090	0.8144 ± 0.0091	0.7870 ± 0.0012	0.7657 ± 0.0091	0.7922 ± 0.0052	$\mathbf{0.7600 \pm 0.0032}$
aMSE	10%	0.2713 ± 0.0023	0.2682 ± 0.0036	0.2504 ± 0.0102	0.2419 ± 0.0081	0.2552 ± 0.0032	$\mathbf{0.2330 \pm 0.0018}$
	20%	0.2303 ± 0.0003	0.2289 ± 0.0051	0.2156 ± 0.0015	0.2114 ± 0.0041	0.2131 ± 0.0071	$\mathbf{0.2018 \pm 0.0025}$
	30%	0.2165 ± 0.0021	0.2137 ± 0.0012	0.2089 ± 0.0012	0.2011 ± 0.0022	0.1922 ± 0.0102	$\mathbf{0.1822 \pm 0.0014}$

Table 2: Performance comparison of the six competing algorithms in terms of nMSE and aMSE with standard deviation using the SARCOS data.The experimental setting is similar to the one described in Table 1.

Measure	training size	Ridge	Lasso	TraceNorm	Sparse-LowRank	CMTL	Robust MTL
nMSE	50	0.2454 ± 0.0260	0.2337 ± 0.0180	0.2257 ± 0.0065	0.2127 ± 0.0033	0.2192 ± 0.0016	$\mathbf{0.2123 \pm 0.0038}$
	100	0.1821 ± 0.0142	0.1616 ± 0.0027	0.1531 ± 0.0017	0.1495 ± 0.0023	0.1568 ± 0.0037	$\mathbf{0.1456 \pm 0.0138}$
	150	0.1501 ± 0.0054	0.1469 ± 0.0028	0.1318 ± 0.0053	$\mathbf{0.1236 \pm 0.0004}$	0.1301 ± 0.0034	0.1245 ± 0.0015
aMSE	50	0.1330 ± 0.0143	0.1228 ± 0.0083	0.1122 ± 0.0064	0.1073 ± 0.0026	0.1156 ± 0.0011	$\mathbf{0.0982 \pm 0.0026}$
	100	0.1053 ± 0.0096	0.0907 ± 0.0023	0.0805 ± 0.0026	0.0793 ± 0.0047	0.0852 ± 0.0013	$\mathbf{0.0737 \pm 0.0083}$
	150	0.0846 ± 0.0045	0.0822 ± 0.0014	0.0772 ± 0.0023	$\mathbf{0.0661 \pm 0.0062}$	0.0755 ± 0.0025	0.0674 ± 0.0014

and RMTL) outperform the single-task learning algorithms (Ridge and Lasso) in terms of both nMSE and aMSE. We also observe that Sparse-LowRank has a similar performance to RMTL. In Sparse-LowRank, incoherent low-rank and (ℓ_1-norm based) sparse structures [8] are used to capture the task relatedness as well as identify discriminative features for each task. These results imply that allowing each task to independently select discriminative features may improve the robustness of the algorithm.

5.3 Sensitivity Studies on RMTL

We conduct a sensitivity study on the proposed RMTL formulation. In particular, we study how the regularization parameters and the training sample size affect the regression performance of RMTL in terms of nMSE and aMSE, respectively.

Effect of the Regularization Parameters For this experiment, we randomly select 10% of the School data as the training set and use the rest of the data as the test set. By fixing $\beta = 100$ as well as varying the value of α in α-value set, i.e., $[50 : 50 : 500]$, we study how the parameter α affects the regression performance of RMTL. Similarly, by fixing $\alpha = 150$ as well as varying the value of β in β-value set of $[20 : 5 : 115]$, we study how the parameter β affects the regression performance of RMTL. In Figure 2, we present the regression performance (averaged over 15 random repetitions) of RMTL in terms of nMSE (1st and 3rd plots) and aMSE (2nd and 4th plots) for each pair of (α, β). From Figure 2, we can observe that both nMSE and aMSE change with different settings of (α, β); we can also observe that the best performance of RMTL for a fixed α (or a fixed β) is obtained by setting β in the middle of β-value set (or setting the value of α in the middle of α-value set).

Effect of the Training Ratio For this experiment, we randomly select $\{10\%, 20\%, \cdots, 80\%\}$ of the School data as the training set and use the rest of the data as the test set. We study how the the training sample size (in terms of the training ratio) affects the regression performance of RMTL. Note that the regularization parameters α and β are determined via double cross-validation. The experimental results are presented in Figure 3. We can observe that by increasing the training ratio, both the nMSE and aMSE decrease; this result is consist with our expectation that more training data will lead to more accurate predictive model and hence better generalization performance.

5.4 Numerical Studies on APM

We conduct numerical studies on APM in comparison with PM for solving RMTL in terms of the computation time (in seconds) and the iteration number. We randomly select 10% of the School data for the following experiments. The experimental setting is described as follows: we stop PM when the change of the objective value in two successive iterations is smaller than 10^{-i} and record the attained objective value; such a value is then used as the stopping criterion in APM, that is, we stop APM when the attained objective value in APM is equal to or smaller than the one previously obtained from PM; we vary the stopping criterion of PM in the set $\{10^{-i}\}_{i=1}^{6}$ and record the required computation time and iteration number for both PM and APM. From the experimental results presented in Figure 4, we have the following observations: (1) APM requires less computation time and iteration number than PM for attaining the same objective value; (2) both APM and PM require more computation time and a larger iteration number if the stopping criterion is set as a smaller value (higher accuracy).

6. CONCLUSION

In this paper, we propose a robust multi-task learning (RMTL) algorithm which learns multiple tasks simultaneously as well as identifies the outlier tasks. The proposed RMTL algorithm captures the task relationships using a low-rank structure, and simultaneously identifies the outlier tasks using a group-sparse structure. RMTL is formulated as a non-smooth convex (unconstrained) optimization problem in which the least square loss is regularized by a combination of the trace norm regularization and the $\ell_{1,2}$-norm regularization. We propose to adopt the accelerated proximal method (APM) for solving this optimization problem and develop efficient algorithms for computing the associated proximal operator. We also conduct a theoretical analysis on the proposed RMTL formulation. In particular, we derive a key property of the optimal solution to RMTL; based on the key property, we establish

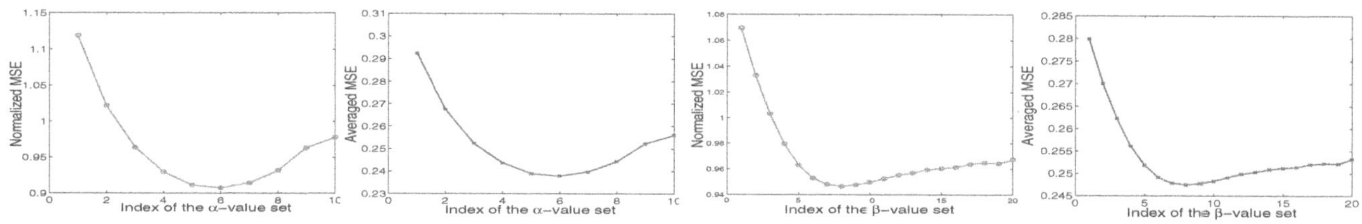

Figure 2: Sensitivity study on RMTL: study the effect of the parameters α and β in terms of nMSE (1st and 3rd plots) and aMSE (2nd and 4th plots), respectively. For the first two plots, we set $\beta = 100$ and vary α in the α-value set $[50 : 50 : 500]$; for the last two plots, we set $\beta = 150$ and vary β in the β-value set $[20 : 5 : 115]$.

a theoretical performance bound to characterize the learning performance of RMTL. Our experimental results on benchmark data sets demonstrate the effectiveness and efficiency of the proposed algorithms. In the future, we plan to apply the proposed RMTL to other real world applications such as Alzheimer's disease study and *Drosophila* gene expression images analysis.

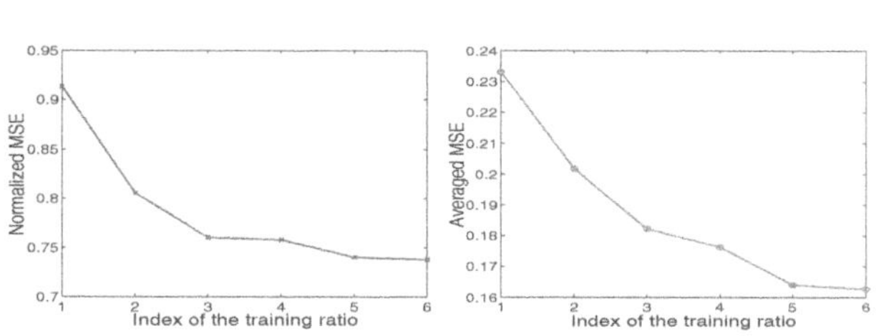

Figure 3: Sensitivity study on RMTL: study the effect of the training ratio in terms of nMSE (left plot) and aMSE (right plot), respectively. The regularization parameters are determined via double cross-validation. The i-th coordinate on the x-axis corresponds to the training ratio $i \times 10\%$.

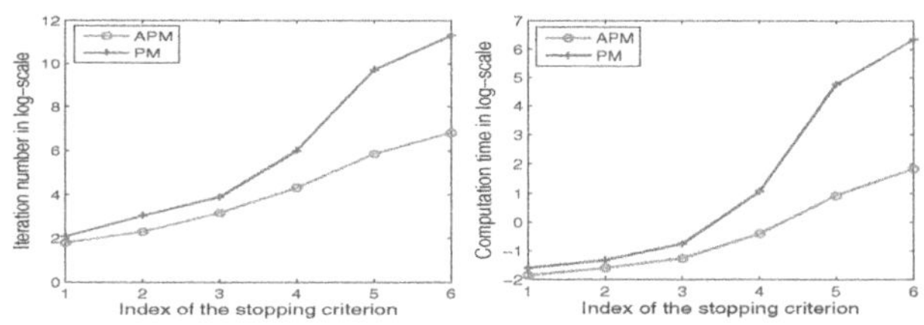

Figure 4: Computation cost comparison of APM and PM in terms of the iteration number (left plot) and the computation time in seconds (right plot) for solving RMTL. The i-th coordinate on the x-axis corresponds to the stopping criterion 10^{-i}.

Acknowledgment

This research is sponsored in part by NSF IIS-0953662 and NSF CCF-1025177.

APPENDIX

Proof of Corollary 4.1

PROOF. From Lemma 4.1, we have

$$\widehat{L} - L = \mathcal{Q}(\widehat{L} - L) + \mathcal{Q}_\perp(\widehat{L} - L)$$

for any matrix pair L and $\widehat{L}$. It follows that

$$\begin{aligned} \|\widehat{L}\|_* &= \|L + \mathcal{Q}(\widehat{L} - L) + \mathcal{Q}_\perp(\widehat{L} - L)\|_* \\ &\geq \|L + \mathcal{Q}_\perp(\widehat{L} - L)\|_* - \|\mathcal{Q}(\widehat{L} - L)\|_* \\ &= \|L\|_* + \|\mathcal{Q}_\perp(\widehat{L} - L)\|_* - \|\mathcal{Q}(\widehat{L} - L)\|_*, \end{aligned}$$

where the inequality above follows from the triangle inequality and the last equality above follows from Eq. (20). Moreover,

$$\begin{aligned} &\|\widehat{L} - L\|_* + \|L\|_* - \|\widehat{L}\|_* \\ \leq\, &\|\widehat{L} - L\|_* + \|L\|_* - \left(\|L\|_* + \|\mathcal{Q}_\perp(\widehat{L} - L)\|_* - \|\mathcal{Q}(\widehat{L} - L)\|_*\right) \\ \leq\, &2\|\mathcal{Q}(\widehat{L} - L)\|_*. \end{aligned}$$

We complete the proof of this corollary. □

Proof of Lemma 4.2

PROOF. From the definition of $\mathcal{C}(S)$ in Eq. (21), we have

$$S_{\mathcal{C}_\perp(S)} = \mathbf{0}, \quad \|(\widehat{S} - S)_{\mathcal{C}_\perp(S)}\|_{1,2} = \|\widehat{S}_{\mathcal{C}_\perp(S)}\|_{1,2}.$$

It follows that

$$\begin{aligned} &\|(\widehat{S} - S)_{\mathcal{C}_\perp(S)}\|_{1,2} + \|S\|_{1,2} - \|\widehat{S}\|_{1,2} \\ =\, &\|\widehat{S}_{\mathcal{C}_\perp(S)}\|_{1,2} + \|S\|_{1,2} - \|\widehat{S}\|_{1,2} \\ =\, &\|S_{\mathcal{C}(S)}\|_{1,2} - \|\widehat{S}_{\mathcal{C}(S)}\|_{1,2} \\ \leq\, &\|(S - \widehat{S})_{\mathcal{C}(S)}\|_{1,2} = \|(\widehat{S} - S)_{\mathcal{C}(S)}\|_{1,2}. \end{aligned}$$

By substituting the equation above into the left side of Eq. (22), we complete the proof of this lemma. □

LEMMA 1. *Let $\delta_1, \delta_2, \cdots, \delta_n$ be a random sample of size n from the Gaussian distribution $\mathcal{N}(0, \sigma)$. Let $x_1, x_2, \cdots, x_n$ satisfy $x_1^2 + x_2^2 + \cdots + x_n^2 = 1$. Denote a random variable v as*

$$v = \frac{1}{\sigma}\sum_{i=1}^{n} x_i \delta_i.$$

Then v obeys the Gaussian distribution $\mathcal{N}(0, 1)$.

PROOF. Since $\{\delta_i\}$ are mutually independent, the mean of the random variable v can be computed as

$$\mathbb{E}(v) = \mathbb{E}\left(\frac{1}{\sigma}\sum_{i=1}^{n} x_i \delta_i\right) = \frac{1}{\sigma}\sum_{i=1}^{n} x_i \mathbb{E}(\delta_i) = 0.$$

Similarly, the variance of v can be computed

$$\mathbb{E}(v - \mathbb{E}(v))^2 = \mathbb{E}\left(\frac{1}{\sigma^2}\sum_{i=1}^{n} x_i^2 \delta_i^2\right) = \frac{1}{\sigma^2}\sum_{i=1}^{n} x_i^2 \mathbb{E}(\delta_i^2) = 1,$$

where the first equality follows from $\mathbb{E}(\delta_i \delta_j) = 0 \ (i \neq j)$. Using the fact that the sum of Gaussian random variables is Gaussian distributed, we complete the proof of this lemma. □

LEMMA 2. *Let $\mathcal{X}_p^2$ be a chi-squared random variable with p degrees of freedom. Then*

$$\Pr\left(\mathcal{X}_p^2 \geq p + \pi\right) \leq \exp\left(-\frac{1}{2}\left(\pi - p\log\left(1+\frac{\pi}{p}\right)\right)\right), \pi > 0.$$

PROOF. From Theorem 4.1 in [31], we approximate the chi-square distribution using a normal distribution as

$$\Pr\left(\mathcal{X}_p^2 \geq q\right) \leq \Pr\left(\mathcal{N}_{0,1} \geq z_p(q)\right), \ q > p,$$

where $\mathcal{N}_{0,1} \sim \mathcal{N}(0,1)$ and $z_p(q) = \sqrt{q - p - p\log\left(\frac{q}{p}\right)}$. It is known that for $x \sim \mathcal{N}(0,1)$, the inequality $\Pr(x \geq t) \leq \exp(-\frac{t^2}{2})$ holds. Therefore we have

$$\Pr\left(\mathcal{X}_p^2 \geq q\right) \leq \exp\left(-\frac{1}{2}z_p^2(q)\right).$$

By substituting $q = p + \pi \ (\pi > 0)$ into the inequality above, we complete the proof of this lemma. □

A. REFERENCES

[1] R. K. Ando and T. Zhang. A framework for learning predictive structures from multiple tasks and unlabeled data. *Journal of Machine Learning Research*, 6:1817–1853, 2005.

[2] A. Argyriou, T. Evgeniou, and M. Pontil. Convex multi-task feature learning. *Machine Learning*, 73(3):243–272, 2008.

[3] B. Bakker and T. Heskes. Task clustering and gating for bayesian multitask learning. *Journal of Machine Learning Research*, 4:83–99, 2003.

[4] A. Beck and M. Teboulle. A fast iterative shrinkage-thresholding algorithm for linear inverse problems. *SIAM Journal of Imaging Science*, 2:183–202, 2009.

[5] P. J. Bickel, Y. Ritov, and A. B. Tsybakov. Simultaneous analysis of lasso and dantzig selector. *Annals of Statistics*, 37:1705–1732, 2009.

[6] J.-F. Cai, E. J. Candes, and Z. Shen. A singular value thresholding algorithm for matrix completion. *SIAM Journal on Optimization*, 20(4):1956–1982, 2010.

[7] R. Caruana. Multitask learning. *Machine Learning*, 28(1):41–75, 1997.

[8] J. Chen, J. Liu, and J. Ye. Learning incoherent sparse and low-rank patterns from multiple tasks. In *KDD*, 2010.

[9] J. Chen, L. Tang, J. Liu, and J. Ye. A convex formulation for learning shared structures from multiple tasks. In *ICML*, 2009.

[10] T. Evgeniou, C. A. Micchelli, and M. Pontil. Learning multiple tasks with kernel methods. *Journal of Machine Learning Research*, 6:615–637, 2005.

[11] D. Goldfarb and S. Ma. Convergence of fixed point continuation algorithms for matrix rank minimization. *Submitted to Foundations of Computational Mathematics.*

[12] D. Hsu, S. Kakade, and T. Zhang. Robust matrix decomposition with outliers. arXiv:1011.1518, 2010.

[13] L. Jacob, F. Bach, and J.-P. Vert. Clustered multi-task learning: A convex formulation. In *NIPS*, 2008.

[14] A. Jalali, P. Ravikumar, S. Sanghavi, and C. Ruan. A dirty model for multi-task learning. In *NIPS*, 2010.

[15] S. Ji and J. Ye. An accelerated gradient method for trace norm minimization. In *ICML*, pages 457–464, 2009.

[16] S. Kim and E. P. Xing. Tree-guided group lasso for multi-task regression with structured sparsity. In *ICML*, 2010.

[17] N. D. Lawrence and J. C. Platt. Learning to learn with the informative vector machine. In *ICML*, 2004.

[18] J. Liu, J. Chen, and J. Ye. Large-scale sparse logistic regression. In *KDD*, 2009.

[19] J. Liu, S. Ji, and J. Ye. Multi-task feature learning via efficient l2,1-norm minimization. In *UAI*, pages 339–348, 2009.

[20] J. Liu, S. Ji, and J. Ye. *SLEP: Sparse Learning with Efficient Projections.* Arizona State University, 2009.

[21] J. Liu, L. Yuan, and J. Ye. An efficient algorithm for a class of fused lasso problems. In *KDD*, 2010.

[22] K. Lounici, M. Pontil, A. B. Tsybakov, and S. van de Geer. Taking advantage of sparsity in multi-task learning. In *COLT*, 2008.

[23] J.-J. Moreau. Proximité et dualité dans un espace hilbertien. *Bull. Soc. Math. France*, 93:273–299, 1965.

[24] A. Nemirovski. *Efficient Methods in Convex Programming.* Lecture Notes, 1995.

[25] Y. Nesterov. *Introductory Lectures on Convex Programming.* Lecture Notes, 1998.

[26] F. Nie, H. Huang, X. Cai, and C. Ding. Efficient and robust feature selection via joint l21-norms minimization. In *NIPS*, 2010.

[27] G. Obozinski, B. Taskar, and M. I. Jordan. Multi-task feature selection. In *Technical report, Dept. of Statistics, UC Berkeley*, 2006.

[28] B. Recht, M. Fazel, and P. A. Parrilo. Guaranteed minimum rank solutions to linear matrix equations via nuclear norm minimization. *SIAM Review*, (3):471–501, 2010.

[29] A. Schwaighofer, V. Tresp, and K. Yu. Learning gaussian process kernels via hierarchical bayes. In *NIPS*, 2004.

[30] S. Thrun and J. O'Sullivan. Discovering structure in multiple learning tasks: The TC algorithm. In *ICML*, 1996.

[31] D. L. Wallace. Bounds on normal approximations to student's and the chi-square distributions. *Annals of Mathematical Statistics*, 30(4):1121–1130, 1959.

[32] H. Xu, C. Caramanis, and S. Sanghavi. Robust pca via outlier pursuit. In *NIPS*, 2010.

[33] Y. Xue, X. Liao, L. Carin, and B. Krishnapuram. Multi-task learning for classification with dirichlet process priors. *Journal of Machine Learning Research*, 8:35–63, 2007.

[34] X. Yang, S. Kim, and E. P. Xing. Heterogeneous multitask learning with joint sparsity constraints. In *NIPS*, 2009.

[35] K. Yu, V. Tresp, and A. Schwaighofer. Learning gaussian processes from multiple tasks. In *ICML*, 2005.

[36] S. Yu, V. Tresp, and K. Yu. Robust multi-task learning with *t*-processes. In *ICML*, 2007.

[37] J. Zhang, Z. Ghahramani, and Y. Yang. Learning multiple related tasks using latent independent component analysis. In *NIPS*, 2005.

[38] Y. Zhang and D.-Y. Yeung. Multi-task learning using generalized t process. In *AISTATS*, 2010.

Model Order Selection for Boolean Matrix Factorization

Pauli Miettinen
Max Planck Institute for Informatics
Saarbrücken, Germany
pmiettin@mpi-inf.mpg.de

Jilles Vreeken
Dept. of Mathematics and Computer Science
Universiteit Antwerpen, Belgium
jilles.vreeken@ua.ac.be

ABSTRACT

Matrix factorizations—where a given data matrix is approximated by a product of two or more factor matrices—are powerful data mining tools. Among other tasks, matrix factorizations are often used to separate global structure from noise. This, however, requires solving the 'model order selection problem' of determining where fine-grained structure stops, and noise starts, i.e., what is the proper size of the factor matrices.

Boolean matrix factorization (BMF)—where data, factors, and matrix product are Boolean—has received increased attention from the data mining community in recent years. The technique has desirable properties, such as high interpretability and natural sparsity. But so far no method for selecting the correct model order for BMF has been available. In this paper we propose to use the Minimum Description Length (MDL) principle for this task. Besides solving the problem, this well-founded approach has numerous benefits, e.g., it is automatic, does not require a likelihood function, is fast, and, as experiments show, is highly accurate.

We formulate the description length function for BMF in general—making it applicable for any BMF algorithm. We extend an existing algorithm for BMF to use MDL to identify the best Boolean matrix factorization, analyze the complexity of the problem, and perform an extensive experimental evaluation to study its behavior.

Categories and Subject Descriptors

H.2.8 [**Database management**]: Database applications–*Data mining*

General Terms

Theory, Algorithms, Experimentation

1. INTRODUCTION

A typical task in data mining is to find observations and variables that behave similarly. Consider, for instance, the standard example of supermarket basket data. We are given transactions over items, and we want to find groups of transactions and groups of items such that we can (approximately) represent our data in terms of these groups, instead of the original transactions. Such representation is called a low-dimensional representation of the data, and is usually obtained using some form of matrix factorization.

In matrix factorizations the input data (represented as a matrix) is decomposed into two (or more) factor matrices. Usually the aim is to have low-dimensional factor matrices whose product approximates the original matrix well. By imposing different constraints, one obtains different factorizations. Perhaps the two best-known factorizations are Singular Value Decomposition (SVD), closely related to Principal Component Analysis (PCA), and Non-negative Matrix Factorization (NMF). SVD and PCA restrict the factor matrices to be orthogonal, while NMF requires the data and the factor matrices to be non-negative.

When the input data is Boolean, (that is, contains only 0s and 1s, as is typical with supermarket basket data), one can apply Boolean Matrix Factorization (BMF). Similarly to NMF, it restricts the factor matrices for added interpretability and sparsity. In BMF, the factor matrices are required to be Boolean, i.e., contain only 0s and 1s. Also the matrix product is changed, from normal to Boolean. As a consequence, it is possible that BMF obtains smaller reconstruction error than SVD for the same decomposition size—something that NMF, by definition, cannot do [20]. Furthermore, it can be shown that for sparse Boolean matrices, there is always a sparse exact factorization [21].

But no matter what factorization method one applies, one always has to solve the model order selection problem: what is the correct number of latent dimensions? In some situations the answer is obvious, for example, if a user wants to have a three-dimensional representation of the data (say, for visualization). But when the user wants a good description of the structure in the data, selecting the number of latent dimensions comes down to the question: what is structure and what is noise.

Whereas various methods have been proposed to answer this question for non-Boolean matrix factorization, varying from statistical methods based on likelihood scores (such as the Bayesian Information Criterion, BIC) to subjective analysis of error (so-called elbow methods), there is no known applicable method for selecting the model order for BMF (other than visual analysis of errors).

In this paper, we study the model order selection problem in the framework of BMF. To that end, we merge two orthogonal lines of research, namely those of Boolean matrix factorizations and Minimum Description Length (MDL) principle. We formulate description length functions that can be used for model order selection with any BMF algorithm. We then extend an existing algorithm for BMF to use MDL in an effective way, and via extensive experimental evaluation we show that using our description length formulation, the algorithm is able to identify the correct number of latent dimensions in synthetic and real-world BMF tasks.

2. RELATED WORK

Matrix factorization methods such as Singular Value Decomposition (SVD) [13] or Non-negative Matrix Factorization (NMF) [29] are ubiquitous in data mining and machine learning. Two of the most popular uses for matrix factorizations are separating structure and noise, and learning missing values of matrices.

Boolean matrix factorizations have been studied extensively in combinatorics (see, e.g., [25] and references therein). The use of Boolean factorizations in data mining was proposed in [22], and they are related to many other data mining methods (see below for some related work and [20] for more). Outside data mining, Boolean factorizations have found application in, e.g., finding roles for access control [33, 36].

The Asso algorithm to solve BMF was proposed by Miettinen et al. [22]. Later, Lu et al. [19] proposed a heuristic based on a mixed-integer-programming formulation. Independently, Belohlavek and Vychodil [1] gave an algorithm for computing the Boolean rank of a matrix based on solving the Set Cover problem. At worst case this algorithm can take exponential time and does not guarantee any non-trivial approximation factor, but recently it was shown that with certain sparsity constraints, the algorithm runs in polynomial time and provides a logarithmic approximation guarantee [21].

Matrix factorizations have a long history in various fields of science. SVD and its close relative PCA have been of particular importance. Hence, it is no surprise that many methods for model order selection for these two decompositions have been proposed. One of the earliest suggestions was the Guttman–Kaiser criterion, dating back to the Fifties (see [41]). In that criterion, one selects those principal vectors that have corresponding principal value greater than 1. It is perhaps not surprising that this simple criterion has shown to perform poorly [41]. Another often-used method is Cattell's scree test [2], where one selects the point where the ratio between two consecutive singular values (in descending order) is high. Usually, this is done by visual analysis, but automated methods have also been proposed (e.g., [42]).

Since these two classical methods, researchers have proposed many alternative methods. For example, in a probabilistic framework one can use Bayesian model selection (e.g. [23, 32]). For BMF, however, it would be very hard, if not impossible, to construct a good likelihood function. Yet another approach is to use cross validation. While this is perhaps mostly used when learning missing values of the matrix, it can also applied to the noise removal. Assumption is that when the model order is too high, the factors start to specialize to noise, and hence, the cross-validation error increases. Normally, hold-out set would contain either rows or columns, but not both. Recently, Owen and Perry [28] proposed a method to leave out a sub-matrix. The method is based on the assumption that the remaining matrix has the same rank as the original matrix, as this is needed to fit the factors to the test data.

The concept of intrinsic dimension of the data is related to the model order. While often the intrinsic dimension refers to the number of variables needed to explain the data completely (e.g., the rank of a matrix), also noise-invariant approaches have been studied [30]. Tatti et al. [34] defined intrinsic dimensionality to Boolean data based on fractal dimensions.

As discussed by Faloutsos and Megalooikonomou [8], the Minimum Description Length principle [14] is a powerful, well-founded, and natural approach to data mining, as it allows us to clearly identify the most succinct and least redundant model for a dataset. As such, MDL has been successfully employed for a wide range of data mining tasks, including, for example, discretization [9], imputation [37], and clustering [4, 16].

Basically, a Boolean matrix factorization gives us a group of patterns (the left-hand matrix $\mathbf{B}$) and their occurrences (the right-hand matrix $\mathbf{C}$). As such, BMF essentially describes the data with a *set of patterns*. Therefore, pattern set mining techniques are related.

KRIMP [38] pioneered the use of MDL for identifying good pattern sets, and selects that group of frequent itemsets that describes the data best. LESS [15] and PACK [35] follow a similar approach, but respectively describe data using low-entropy sets and decision trees. A major difference between these methods and BMF is that rows are only covered using subsets of that row, and approximate matches are not allowed. Further, KRIMP and LESS do not allow overlap between patterns covering the same row. All three typically return many more, and much more specific, patterns than BMF.

Summarization, proposed by Chandola et al. [3], is a compression-based approach that identifies a group of itemsets such that each transaction is summarized by one itemset with as little loss of information as possible. Wang and Parthasararthy [40] find summary sets, i.e., sets of itemsets such that each transaction is (partially) covered by the largest itemset that is frequent. In BMF, however, we do not require every row to be modeled by at least one factor.

More closely related to BMF is Tiling [12], which essentially employs the well known greedy set-cover algorithm to iteratively cover the data with that itemset that covers the most uncovered 1s in the data. Kontonasios and De Bie [17] iteratively discover the most interesting 'noisy tile', where they define interestingness through a local MDL score. Unlike our situation, it does not return a model for the data, but rather orders a given collection of itemsets.

3. NOTATION

Before we introduce the theory behind our approach, we introduce the notation we will use throughout the paper.

Throughout this paper, we identify the datasets with Boolean matrices. Matrices are denoted by upper-case bold letters ($\mathbf{A}$). Vectors are lower-case bold letters ($\mathbf{a}$). If $\mathbf{A}$ is an n-by-m Boolean matrix, $|\mathbf{A}|$ denotes the number of 1s in it, i.e., $|\mathbf{A}| = \sum_{i,j} a_{ij}$. We extend the same notation to Boolean vectors. The scalar product of two vectors $\mathbf{x}$ and $\mathbf{y}$ is denoted as $\langle \mathbf{x}, \mathbf{y} \rangle$.

Let $\mathbf{X}$ be n-by-k and $\mathbf{Y}$ be k-by-m Boolean matrices (i.e., $\mathbf{X}$ and $\mathbf{Y}$ take values from $\{0, 1\}$). Their *Boolean matrix product*, $\mathbf{X} \circ \mathbf{Y}$, is the Boolean matrix $\mathbf{Z}$ with $z_{ij} = \bigvee_{l=1}^{k} x_{il} y_{lj}$.

If $\mathbf{X}$ and $\mathbf{Y}$ are two n-by-m Boolean matrices, we have the following element-wise matrix operations. The *Boolean sum* $\mathbf{X} \vee \mathbf{Y}$ is the normal matrix sum with addition defined as $1 + 1 = 1$. The *Boolean subtraction* $\mathbf{X} \ominus \mathbf{Y}$ is the normal element-wise subtraction with $0 - 1 = 0$. Notice that this does not define an inverse of Boolean sum, as $1 + 1 - 1 = 0$. The *Boolean element-wise product* $\mathbf{X} \wedge \mathbf{Y}$ is defined as normal element-wise matrix product. The *exclusive or* $\mathbf{X} \oplus \mathbf{Y}$ is the normal matrix sum with addition defined as $1 + 1 = 0$ (i.e., addition is done over the field $\mathbb{Z}_2$).

The *Boolean rank* of an n-by-m Boolean matrix $\mathbf{A}$, $\text{rank}_B(\mathbf{A})$, is the least integer k such that there exists an n-by-k Boolean matrix $\mathbf{B}$ and a k-by-m Boolean matrix $\mathbf{C}$ for which $\mathbf{A} = \mathbf{B} \circ \mathbf{C}$.

Matrices $\mathbf{B}$ and $\mathbf{C}$ are *factor matrices* of $\mathbf{A}$, and the pair $(\mathbf{B}, \mathbf{C})$ is the (approximate) *Boolean factorization* of $\mathbf{A}$. Lastly, all logarithms are of base 2, and we employ the usual convention that $0 \log 0 = 0$.

4. BOOLEAN MATRIX FACTORIZATION

In this section we introduce Boolean matrix factorization (BMF) and give a short description of Asso, one of the existing algorithms for Boolean matrix factorization.

4.1 BMF, a brief primer

In Boolean matrix factorization, the goal is to (approximately) represent a Boolean matrix as the Boolean product of two Boolean matrices. The crux is the Boolean product: as the product is not over a field, but over a semiring $(0, 1, \vee, \wedge)$, Boolean matrix factorizations have some unique properties. For example, the Boolean rank of a matrix $\mathbf{A}$ can be only a logarithm of the normal matrix rank of $\mathbf{A}$ [25]. As a consequence, Boolean factorizations can yield smaller reconstruction error than factorizations of same size done under the normal arithmetic. Unfortunately, unlike normal rank, computing the Boolean rank is NP-hard [27], and even approximation is hard [22] (although recent work shows that logarithmic approximations can be obtained by assuming sparsity [21]).

But even assuming we could compute the Boolean rank efficiently, this is rarely what we actually want. Similarly to normal rank, one would assume that most of the real-world data matrices have full or almost full Boolean rank, due to noise; instead, we often want to have a low-rank approximation of a matrix. Such approximation is usually interpreted to contain the latent structure of the data, while the error it causes is regarded as the noise. When the target rank is given, we have the Boolean matrix factorization problem:

PROBLEM 1 (BMF). *Given n-by-m Boolean matrix $\mathbf{A}$ and integer k, find n-by-k Boolean matrix $\mathbf{B}$ and k-by-m Boolean matrix $\mathbf{C}$ such that $\mathbf{B}$ and $\mathbf{C}$ minimize*

$$|\mathbf{A} \oplus (\mathbf{B} \circ \mathbf{C})| \,. \tag{1}$$

Unsurprisingly, also this optimization problem is NP-hard, and has strong inapproximability results in terms of multiplicative and additive errors (see [20]). But there is also another, more fundamental problem: the formulation of the BMF problem requires us to have *a priori* knowledge on k, the Boolean rank of the decomposition. With the structure/noise interpretation above, this means that we have to have *a priori* knowledge of the dimensionality of the latent structure—something we most likely do not have.

This problem is, by no means, unique to BMF. Indeed, the same issue underlies any matrix factorization method. And also in clustering, for example, we have to deal with the same problem, known as the model order selection problem. The main contribution of this paper is to provide a method to (approximately) solve the model order selection problem in the BMF framework.

4.2 The Asso Algorithm

Knowing the latent dimensionality of the data is usually not enough—we also want to know the latent factors, i.e., we want to solve the BMF problem. As the problem is NP-hard, even to approximate well, we will solve it using a heuristic approach. We have opted to use an existing algorithm for BMF, called Asso [22]. We chose to use Asso as previous studies have shown it performs reasonably well [21, 22, 33], and because the algorithm is hierarchical, i.e., the rank-$(k-1)$ decomposition gives the first $k-1$ columns of $\mathbf{B}$ (and first $k-1$ rows of $\mathbf{C}$) of rank-k decomposition. The latter property is particularly useful when doing the model order selection, as we will see later. We emphasize, though, that the proposed model order selection method is not bound to any specific algorithm for BMF.

For the sake of completeness, we provide a quick explanation of how Asso works. For more detailed explanation, see [20, 22]. The name of Asso stems from it using pairwise association accuracies to generate so-called candidate columns. More precisely, Asso generates an n-by-n matrix $\mathbf{X} = (x_{ij})$ with $x_{ij} = \langle \mathbf{a}_i, \mathbf{a}_j \rangle \,/\, \langle \mathbf{a}_j, \mathbf{a}_j \rangle$ where $\mathbf{a}_i$ is the jth row of $\mathbf{A}$. That is, x_{ij} is the association accuracy for rule $\mathbf{a}_j \Rightarrow \mathbf{a}_i$.

The columns of $\mathbf{B}$ are selected from the columns of $\mathbf{X}$, after the latter have been rounded to Boolean columns. The threshold t for the rounding is a user-specified parameter. The selection of columns of $\mathbf{B}$ happens in a greedy fashion: each not-used column of rounded $\mathbf{X}$ is tried, and the selected column is the one that maximizes the gain, defined being the number of newly-covered 1s of $\mathbf{A}$ minus the number of newly-covered 0s of $\mathbf{A}$. Element a_{ij} is newly-covered if $(\mathbf{B} \circ \mathbf{C})_{ij} = 0$ before adding the new column to $\mathbf{B}$. The row of $\mathbf{C}$ corresponding to the column of $\mathbf{B}$ is build using the same technique: if the gain of using the new column of $\mathbf{B}$ to cover a column of $\mathbf{A}$ is positive, then the corresponding element of the new row of $\mathbf{C}$ is set to 1; otherwise it is 0.

As Asso never tracks back its decisions, it clearly has the desired hierarchical property. But Asso also requires the user to set an extra parameter: the rounding threshold t. Selecting this parameter can be daunting, as it is hard to anticipate the difference it makes to the factorization. To solve this problem, we will use our model order selection mechanism to slightly larger question of *model selection* and in addition to selecting the best k, we also select the best t.

5. MDL FOR BMF

In this section we give our approach for selecting model orders for BMF by the Minimum Description Length principle.

5.1 MDL, a brief primer

The MDL (Minimum Description Length) [14, 31] principle, like its close cousin MML (Minimum Message Length) [39], is a practical version of Kolmogorov complexity [18]. All three embrace the slogan *Induction by Compression*. For MDL, this principle can be roughly described as follows.

Given a set of models[1] $\mathcal{H}$, the best model $H \in \mathcal{H}$ is the one that minimizes

$$L(H) + L(D \mid H)$$

in which $L(H)$ is the length, in bits, of the description of H, and $L(D \mid H)$ is the length, in bits, of the description of the data when encoded with H.

This is called two-part MDL, or *crude* MDL. As opposed to *refined* MDL, where model and data are encoded together [14]. We use two-part MDL because we are specifically interested in the compressor: the factorization that yields the best compression. Further, although refined MDL has stronger theoretical foundations, it cannot be computed except for some special cases. Note that MDL requires the compression to be *lossless* in order to allow for fair comparison between different $H \in \mathcal{H}$.

To use MDL, we have to define what our models $\mathcal{H}$ are, how a $H \in \mathcal{H}$ describes a database, and how all of this is encoded in bits. Note, however, that with MDL we are only interested in the length of the description, and not in the encoded data itself. That is, we are only concerned with the length of the used codes, and do not have to materialize the codes themselves.

5.2 Encoding BMF

We now proceed to define how we can use MDL to identify the best Boolean factorization $(\mathbf{B}, \mathbf{C})$ for a given dataset $\mathbf{A}$.

Recall that an essential requirement of MDL is that the encoding is lossless. That is, whether or not a factorization $(\mathbf{B}, \mathbf{C}) \in \mathcal{H}$ for $\mathbf{A}$ is exact, we need to be able to reconstruct $\mathbf{A}$ without loss. We do this by explicitly encoding the difference, or error, between the original data $\mathbf{A}$ and its approximation as given by the Boolean product of its factor matrices $\mathbf{B}$ and $\mathbf{C}$, i.e., $\mathbf{B} \circ \mathbf{C}$. That is, we

[1] MDL-theorists talk about *hypothesis* in this context, hence the $\mathcal{H}$.

define error matrix $\mathbf{E}$ for $\mathbf{A}$, $\mathbf{B}$, and $\mathbf{C}$, to be the unique Boolean matrix of dimensions n-by-m such that

$$\mathbf{E} = \mathbf{A} \oplus (\mathbf{B} \circ \mathbf{C})\,. \tag{2}$$

Vice versa, when we are given matrices $\mathbf{B}$, $\mathbf{C}$, and $\mathbf{E}$ we can reconstruct $\mathbf{A}$ without loss. Then, the total compressed size $L(\mathbf{A}, H)$, in bits, for a Boolean dataset $\mathbf{A}$ and a Boolean matrix factorization $H = (\mathbf{B}, \mathbf{C})$, with $H \in \mathcal{H}$, is defined as

$$L(\mathbf{A}, H) = L(H) + L(\mathbf{E})\,, \tag{3}$$

where $\mathbf{E}$ follows from $\mathbf{A}$ and H, using Eq. 2. Following the MDL principle, the best factorization for $\mathbf{A}$ is found by minimizing Eq. 3. As we will discuss later, this is not as simple as it sounds. But let us first discuss how we encode H and $\mathbf{E}$, or most importantly, how many bits this requires.

We start by defining how to compute the number of bits required for a factorization $H = (\mathbf{B}, \mathbf{C})$, of dimensions n-by-k and k-by-m, for $\mathbf{B}$ and $\mathbf{C}$ respectively, as

$$L(H) = L(n) + L(m) + L(k) + L(\mathbf{B}) + L(\mathbf{C})\,. \tag{4}$$

That is, we encode the dimensions n, m, k, and then the content of the two factor matrices. By explicitly encoding the dimensions of the matrices, we can subsequently encode matrices $\mathbf{B}$ and $\mathbf{C}$ using an optimal prefix code [5]. To encode m and k, we use the Elias-Delta code, which is a Universal code for integers [5]. A Universal code is a code that can be decoded unambiguously without requiring the decoder to have any background information, but for which the expected length of the code words are within a constant factor of the true optimal code [14]. Elias-Delta coding requires

$$L(x) = \log(x) + \log\log(x) \tag{5}$$

bits to encode an integer x. Note that, as desired, $L(n) + L(m)$ is constant between any $(\mathbf{B}, \mathbf{C}) \in \mathcal{H}$ with $\mathbf{B} \circ \mathbf{C}$ of dimensions n-by-m. (Which is the case when we regard Boolean matrix factorizations of an n-by-m matrix $\mathbf{A}$.)

As we want the selection for the best factorization to depend strictly on the structure of the factorization and the error it introduces —and do not want to introduce any bias to small k by the encoding of the value of k—we do not encode k using the ED code (Eq. 5). Instead, we use a fixed number of bits, i.e., block-encoding, which gives us

$$L(k) = \log(\min(m, n))\,. \tag{6}$$

This gives us a number of bits in which we can encode values for k up to the minimum of m and n. Note that larger values do not make sense in BMF, as for $k = \min(m, n)$ there already is a trivial factorization $(\mathbf{B}, \mathbf{C})$ of $\mathbf{A}$ with $\mathbf{B} = \mathbf{A}$ and $\mathbf{C}$ the identity-matrix, or vice-versa.

With the dimensions encoded, we continue by encoding the factor matrices $\mathbf{B}$ and $\mathbf{C}$. To not introduce bias between different factors, these are encoded per factor. That is, we encode $\mathbf{B}$ per row and $\mathbf{C}$ per column. For transmitting the Boolean values of each factor we use an optimal prefix code, for which Shannon entropy, $-\log P(x)$, gives us the optimal code lengths. In order to use this optimal code, we need to first encode the probability $p_1^{\mathbf{b}_i} = P(1 \mid \mathbf{b}_i) = |\mathbf{b}_i|/n$ of encountering 1 in column i of $\mathbf{B}$. As the maximum number of 1s in a column of $\mathbf{B}$ is n, we need k times $\log(n)$ bits to encode these probabilities. This gives us, for $\mathbf{B}$ of n-by-k,

$$L(\mathbf{B}) = k\log(n) + \sum_{i=1}^{k} \left(|\mathbf{b}_i| l_1^{\mathbf{b}_i} + (n - |\mathbf{b}_i|) l_0^{\mathbf{b}_i}\right) \tag{7}$$

in which $k\log(n)$ is the number of bits to transmit the number of 1s in each column vector $\mathbf{b}_i$, and

$$l_1^{\mathbf{b}_i} = -\log(\frac{|\mathbf{b}_i|}{n}) \quad \text{and} \quad l_0^{\mathbf{b}_i} = -\log(\frac{n - |\mathbf{b}_i|}{n})$$

are the optimal prefix code lengths for 1 and 0, respectively, for vector $\mathbf{b}_i$ corresponding to the ith column of $\mathbf{B}$.

Analogously, we encode $\mathbf{C}$, of k-by-m, per row and have

$$L(\mathbf{C}) = k\log(m) + \sum_{j=1}^{k} \left(|\mathbf{c}_j| l_1^{\mathbf{c}_j} + (m - |\mathbf{c}_j|) l_0^{\mathbf{c}_j}\right) \tag{8}$$

with

$$l_1^{\mathbf{c}_j} = -\log(\frac{|\mathbf{c}_j|}{m}) \quad \text{and} \quad l_0^{\mathbf{c}_j} = -\log(\frac{m - |\mathbf{c}_j|}{m})$$

where $\mathbf{c}_j$ corresponds the jth row of $\mathbf{C}$.

With the above definitions we now have all elements to calculate $L(H)$. By H, the receiver knows $\mathbf{B}$ and $\mathbf{C}$, and only needs $\mathbf{E}$ to be able to lossless reconstruct $\mathbf{A}$. We will now discuss four increasingly involved alternatives for encoding $\mathbf{E}$; we will explore their quality experimentally in Section 6.

5.2.1 Encoding E: Naïve Factors

As we are scoring Boolean matrix factorizations, it would be natural to also encode the entries of $\mathbf{E}$ as a factorization, e.g., such that $\mathbf{E} = \mathbf{F} \circ \mathbf{G}$. Of course, we have to keep in mind that $\mathbf{B}$ and $\mathbf{C}$ encode the structure in $\mathbf{A}$, whereas $\mathbf{E}$ encodes the noise, and noise by definition is unstructured. Hence, we have to encode each 1 in $\mathbf{E}$ in a separate factor, i.e., separate columns/rows in $\mathbf{F}$ and $\mathbf{G}$. The amount of bits this requires is given by

$$\begin{aligned} L_f(\mathbf{E}) = \log mn + |\mathbf{E}| \Big(&- (n-1)\log\left(\frac{n-1}{n}\right) - \log\left(\frac{1}{n}\right) \\ &- (m-1)\log\left(\frac{m-1}{m}\right) - \log\left(\frac{1}{m}\right)\Big) \end{aligned} \tag{9}$$

in which we essentially use the same encoding for the factors as in Eq. 7 and 8 (but with the extra knowledge that every row/column in the factor matrices contains only one 1). We refer to this encoding as the Naïve Factor encoding for $\mathbf{E}$.

Quick analysis of this encoding tells us it is monotonically increasing for larger error, which is good, but also that we are spending too many bits, as we essentially encode full rows and columns, whereas we only want to transmit the locations of the 1s in $\mathbf{E}$.

5.2.2 Encoding E: Naïve Indices

This observation suggests that we should simply transmit the coordinates of the 1s in $\mathbf{E}$. Clearly, this takes $\log m + \log n$ bits per entry. Then,

$$L_i(\mathbf{E}) = |\mathbf{E}|\,(\log m + \log n)\,, \tag{10}$$

gives us the total cost for transmitting $\mathbf{E}$. We refer to this encoding as Naïve Indices.

It saves us bits compared to Naïve Factors, albeit a marginal amount, and hence by MDL it is a better encoding. Further, it is monotonically increasing with the amount of 1s in $\mathbf{E}$.

5.2.3 Encoding E: Naïve Exclusive-Or

Although perhaps counter-intuitive, typically we can encode $\mathbf{E}$ more succinctly if we transmit the whole matrix instead of just the 1s. That is, we can save bits by transmitting, in a fixed order, and using an optimal prefix code, not only the 1s but also the 0s.

We do this by first transmitting the number of 1s in $\mathbf{E}$, i.e., $|\mathbf{E}|$, in $\log mn$ bits, which allows the receiver to calculate the probability $p_1^{\mathbf{E}} = \frac{|\mathbf{E}|}{mn}$, and hence, the optimal prefix codes for 1 and 0. Then, using these codes, and in a fixed order, we transmit the value of every cell of $\mathbf{E}$. The total number of bits required by this approach, which we refer to as Naïve XOR, is given by

$$L_n(\mathbf{E}) = \log mn + |\mathbf{E}|\, l_1 + (mn - |\mathbf{E}|)l_0 \;, \qquad (11)$$

where the lengths of the codes for 1 and 0 respectively are

$$l_1 = -\log p_1^{\mathbf{E}} \quad \text{and} \quad l_0 = -\log(1 - p_1^{\mathbf{E}}) \;.$$

By this approach, we consider every cell in $\mathbf{E}$ independently, yet, importantly, with regard to $p_1^{\mathbf{E}}$. This means that L_n is not strictly monotonic with regard to the number of 1s in $\mathbf{E}$, as once $p_1^{\mathbf{E}} > (1 - p_0^{\mathbf{E}})$, adding 1s to $\mathbf{E}$ decreases its cost. In practice, however, this is not a problem, as it only occurs if $\mathbf{A}$ is both extremely large and extremely dense, yet contains so little structure that encoding it in factors costs more bits than one gains. Besides a pathological case, this situation could be avoided by spending 1 extra bit to indicate whether we are encoding $\mathbf{E}$ or its Boolean inverse—a cost that is dwarfed by the total number of bits to describe $\mathbf{E}$.

5.2.4 *Encoding* $\mathbf{E}$*: Typed Exclusive-Or*

Our last refinement is to differentiate between noise in the part of $\mathbf{E}$ that falls within the modeled part of $\mathbf{A}$, i.e., the 1s we have modeled but do not occur in $\mathbf{A}$, $\mathbf{E}^- = \mathbf{E} \wedge (\mathbf{B} \circ \mathbf{C})$, and those 1s that are part of $\mathbf{A}$ but not included in the model, i.e., $\mathbf{E}^+ = \mathbf{E} \ominus (\mathbf{B} \circ \mathbf{C})$. Trivially, this gives us $\mathbf{E} = \mathbf{E}^+ \vee \mathbf{E}^-$. We refer to this approach as Typed XOR.

We encode each of these two parts analogously to Naïve XOR, but can transmit the number of 1s in the additive and subtractive parts in respectively $\log(mn - |\mathbf{B} \circ \mathbf{C}|)$ and $\log|\mathbf{B} \circ \mathbf{C}|$ bits. We define the probability of a 1 in $\mathbf{E}^+$ as $p_1^+ = |\mathbf{E}^+| \,/ (mn - |\mathbf{B} \circ \mathbf{C}|)$, and similarly for $\mathbf{E}^-$, $p_1^- = |\mathbf{E}^-| \,/\, |\mathbf{B} \circ \mathbf{C}|$. When we combine this, we can calculate the number of bits required to encode $\mathbf{E}$ by the Typed XOR encoding as

$$L_x(\mathbf{E}) = L(\mathbf{E}^+) + L(\mathbf{E}^-) \qquad (12)$$

where

$$L(\mathbf{E}^+) = \log(mn - |\mathbf{B} \circ \mathbf{C}|) + |\mathbf{E}^+|\, l_1^+ + (mn - |\mathbf{B} \circ \mathbf{C}| - |\mathbf{E}^+|) l_0^+$$

and

$$L(\mathbf{E}^-) = \log(|\mathbf{B} \circ \mathbf{C}|) + |\mathbf{E}^-|\, l_1^- + (|\mathbf{B} \circ \mathbf{C}| - |\mathbf{E}^-|) l_0^-$$

respectively give the number of bits to encode the additive and subtractive parts of $\mathbf{E}$. We calculate l_1^+, l_0^+, l_1^-, l_1^- analogous to how we calculate l for Naïve XOR.

Like Naïve XOR, in general this encoding is monotonically increasing for larger error $|\mathbf{E}|$. However, it is more efficient than its naïve cousin when the noise is not uniformly distributed over the modeled and not modeled parts of $\mathbf{A}$. That is, when the probability of a 1 being part of a true pattern being recorded as a 0 is not equal to the probability of a true 0 being recorded as a 1. Clearly, in many situations this may be the case.

By making a choice for one of the four encoding strategies of $\mathbf{E}$, we can now calculate the total compressed size $L(\mathbf{A}, H)$ for a dataset $\mathbf{A}$ and its factorization. As out of the four strategies, Typed XOR compresses $\mathbf{E}$ most efficiently given the available information, we expect it to be the best choice for identifying the correct model order. In Section 6 we will empirically evaluate performance, but first we discuss the complexity of finding the factorization that minimizes $L(\mathbf{A}, H)$.

5.3 Computational Complexity

Finding the minimum description length Boolean matrix factorization is a computationally hard task. To start with, the shortest encoding corresponds to the Kolmogorov complexity, which is non-computable. But even when we try to minimize some given encoding, like one of the above, the problem does not necessarily become easy. In particular, we cannot have a polynomial-time algorithm that minimizes the description length in *any* given encoding.

PROPOSITION 1. *Unless* P = NP, *there exists no polynomial-time algorithm that, given an encoding length function* L *and an* n*-by-*m *Boolean matrix* $\mathbf{A}$, *finds Boolean matrices* $\mathbf{B}$ *and* $\mathbf{C}$ *such that* $L(\mathbf{A}, (\mathbf{B}, \mathbf{C}))$ *is minimized.*

PROOF. Consider function $L(\mathbf{A}, H) = L(H) + L(\mathbf{E})$ that has $L(H) < L(\mathbf{E})$ for any $\mathbf{E}$ with $|\mathbf{E}| > 0$. Furthermore, let $L(H)$ be such that if $\mathbf{B}$ is n-by-k and $\mathbf{B}'$ is n-by-k' with $k < k'$, then $L(\mathbf{B}) < L(\mathbf{B}')$ (and same for $\mathbf{C}$). (Such encoding could, for example, encode every value of $\mathbf{B}$ and $\mathbf{C}$ with one bit, and then send more than $2nm$ bits for each 1 in $\mathbf{E}$.) Then clearly, if $\mathbf{B}$ and $\mathbf{C}$ are such that $\mathbf{A} = \mathbf{B} \circ \mathbf{C}$ and they are as small as possible, they also minimize $L(\mathbf{A}, H)$. But if such $\mathbf{B}$ is n-by-k, then we know that $\mathrm{rank}_B(\mathbf{A}) = k$. As finding the Boolean rank of $\mathbf{A}$ is NP-complete problem, if a polynomial-time algorithm can minimize L, it must be that P = NP. □

The encoding used in the above proof is, of course, something we would not use in practice. Also, Proposition 1 does not say that *all* encoding lengths would be hard to minimize (indeed, it is not very hard to come up with an encoding that is trivial to minimize). What Proposition 1 does say, however, is that if we can minimize some encoding length in polynomial time, that must be because of some specific properties of the encoding (or because P = NP).

With MDL in general, and our encodings specifically, we have the problem that the total encoded size is not monotonic with regard to addition and removal of factors—or, moving of 1s from $\mathbf{E}$ into the factors. Adding a factor always costs bits, but depending on how many 1s it replaces, and how much error it introduces, it may or not lead to a decrease of the total encoded size. Another problem with the more efficient XOR encodings is that introducing error at one iteration influences the cost of introducing error later on: a locally optimal decision may turn out to be quite bad. Moreover, there is no usable structure that we can exploit for a direct search for the MDL-optimal BMF.

Intuitively, however, it would make a good heuristic to iteratively minimize the MDL cost by finding the factor that will save us most bits. This means that we are essentially trying to move as many 1s possible from $\mathbf{E}$ into a new factors in $\mathbf{B}$ and $\mathbf{C}$, while keeping the complexity of those factors in mind. (In fact, the MDL optimal factorization can be the same as the zero-error factorization, the latter known to be NP-hard to compute in general.) Basically, this strategy means minimizing the error, while favoring factors with short description lengths. If we drop the latter, non-monotonic requirement, our strategy is to minimize error, which is the same strategy Asso follows to solve BMF heuristically, and is one reason why we choose to employ Asso here.

5.4 Merging MDL and Asso

The most straightforward way to decide the model order, given an encoding method, is to compute the BMF for each value of k, and to report the k at which $L(\mathbf{A}, H)$ was found to be minimal. This naïve strategy, however, may be very slow in practice, as, if we do not set a maximum k ourselves, we would have to re-start $\min(n, m)$ times—with n and m in the order of thousands, this would mean a significant computational task. But here the hierarchical nature of Asso comes to help: instead of having to re-start every time, we can start by computing the first factor, compute its description length, add the second factor, compute the new encoded length, and so on. To compute $L(\mathbf{A}, H)$, we can use the fact that at any point we know the cost of encoding the previous $k-1$ factors, and thus only have to compute the cost for the new factor. Further, as Asso calculates per step how much it reduces the error, we can use this information when encoding the error matrix.

As we minimize the error, we cannot guarantee that the description length is a convex function with respect to k. Nevertheless, if we assume the cost to be approximately convex we can implement an early-stopping criterion: stop the algorithm if compression has not improved during the last c steps.

The benefits of using Asso with MDL are not restricted to only selecting the model order. Recall that Asso requires a user-provided parameter t to generate the candidate factors. Selecting the value for this parameter can be a daunting task. Here MDL also helps: by computing the decompositions for different values of t, we can select the pair (k, t) that minimizes the total description length. Hence, we can use MDL not only for BMF model order selection in general, but also for BMF model selection.

6. EXPERIMENTS

In this section we experimentally evaluate how well our description length functions identify the correct model orders. While we naturally also investigate the factors discovered at these orders, note that this is not specifically the topic of this paper; rather, our main concern is the model order selection.

We implemented the scoring models and the Asso algorithm in Matlab/C, and provide the source code for research purposes together with the generator for the synthetic data.[2]

6.1 The Other Option: Cross Validation

We selected 10-fold cross-validation (CV) as our benchmark method. As we are not trying to predict missing values, hold-out data are columns of the original data. While CV is an appealing and simple approach, it has one major drawback in the context of BMF: generalizing the column factors to the hold-out data is NP-hard. Namely, finding the best possible way to express the given column with the factors is called Basis Usage Problem, and is known to be NP-hard even to approximate better than with superpolylogarithmic factor [20]. To solve this problem, we used the same greedy process used by Asso (see Section 4.2). The overall error for each k and t was averaged over the folds, and the parameters that gave the least average error were selected.

Notice that we cannot use Owen and Perry's bi-cross-validation approach [28], as their method to generalize the learned factors to test data does not apply to BMF.

6.2 Synthetic Data

We start our experimental analysis in a controlled environment by using synthetic data. For these experiments, we generate n-by-m matrices, in which we plant k random itemsets, of random cardinality, and random frequency. We also add noise to the matrix by flipping values from 0 to 1, and vice-versa, with respective probabilities of n^+ and n^-.

[2]http://www.mpi-inf.mpg.de/~pmiettin/src/mdl4bmf.zip

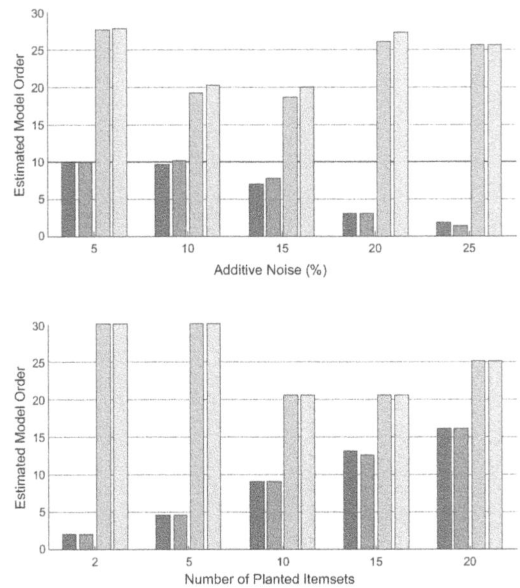

Figure 1: Model order estimates for varying amounts of additive noise (top, true $k = 10$) and varying true model order (bottom). The bars represent the estimates of, from left to right, Typed XOR, Naïve XOR, Naïve Indices, and Naïve Factor. All values averaged over 5 datasets.

First, we investigate sensitivity to noise. To this end, for n^+ from 5% to 25% in steps of 5%, we generate 5 matrices of 8000-by-100 planting 10 random itemsets, each of random cardinality between 4 and 6, and random frequency between 10% and 40%. We fix n^- to 5%. Note that at the highest noise levels, more than twice as many 1s are due to noise than to structure. For each of these datasets, we run Asso for k from 1 to 30, and t from 0.1 to 0.9 in increments of 0.025. For each of the $30 \times 32 = 960$ factorizations this gives us per dataset, we calculate $L(\mathbf{A}, H)$ for each encoding, and per encoding we record the values for k associated with the minimal encountered description length. For the same datasets, we also estimate k by running Asso with 10-fold cross-validation.

In this experiment, as well as in all other experiments, cross-validation always always estimates k to full-rank. Hence, we draw the conclusion that CV does not give good estimates in combination with Asso, and is not a good choice for solving the BMF model order selection problem, and do not further report on it (but see Section 7 for discussion why CV fails).

In the top graph of Figure 1 we plot the average k per encoding strategy for each level of noise. We see that Naïve Factor and Naïve Indices perform equal, and over-estimate k strongly. Naïve XOR and Typed XOR do provide very good estimates: exact at 5% and 10%, still very good at 15%, and underestimate when the large majority of the 1s in the data are due to noise at 20% and 25%.

While under-estimation is clearly preferred to over-estimation—we do not want to model noise—yet it does raise the question whether the effect is due to the scoring function or the search strategy; by iteratively minimizing error, Asso may simply not consider any H of correct k that remotely resemble the true model, and hence, making it impossible to detect the correct model order.

To see what is the case, we manually compare the encoded sizes of the true model to that of the best model found by Asso. The results are clear: for low noise, Asso finds models that compress as well as the true model, sometimes even better, e.g., by not to modeling damaged parts of a structure. Unsurprisingly, the discovered itemsets match the underlying model very well.

For high noise levels, on the other hand, we see that Asso returns models that compress worse, typically requiring 10% more bits. The discovered itemsets, however, do consist of combinations of the true itemsets; specifically, those with relatively large overlap in items and rows. So, while the true itemsets are in fact detected, by the iterative minimization of error, Asso does not report them separately. Hence, it is clear that the scoring function performs very well; even for the highest levels of noise, the true model compresses much better, and hence, if it (or any model remotely resembling it) would be considered, the model order would be identified correctly.

Next, we experiment for varying model orders. We again generate matrices of 8000-by-100, and plant random itemsets of cardinality between 2 and 10 and frequencies between 10% and 40%, fixing n^+ to 10%, and n^- to 5%. We experiment with datasets in which we plant 2, 5, 10, 15, and 20 itemsets. The bottom graph of Figure 1 shows the averaged results for each of these datasets. We see again that the Factor and Indices encodings overestimate, and may dismiss these as good encodings for the model order selection problem. The much more efficient XOR encodings, on the other hand, do consistently give very good estimates. Only for 20 planted itemsets we see a slight under-estimation, of which inspection shows is again due to overlap (due to chance, and the small number of columns, i.e., 100) between itemsets, which makes Asso's greedy strategy group some of these together. (Also, for $k = 10$, we note that Naïve Indices is either correct *or* strongly overestimates.)

These two experiments show that Naïve XOR and Typed XOR provide highly accurate BMF model order estimates, even for large amounts of noise and densely populated matrices. Further experiments show these encodings also identify k accurately for datasets of varying density, numbers of columns, and data rows. As over all experiments, Typed XOR gives the best results, we will use this encoding for the remainder of this section.

6.3 Real Data

Now that we know that the model order is accurately identified for synthetic data, we proceed to real data. We first consider 7 datasets, most of which are publicly available. The 859-by-3933 *Abstracts* dataset represents the words for all abstracts of the accepted papers at the ICDM conference up to 2007, where the words have been stemmed and stop words removed [17]. The 6980-by-19 *DBLP* dataset contains records of in which of the 19 conferences the 6980 authors had published. The dataset is collected from the DBLP database[3] and it is pre-processed as in [20]. *Dialect* is a 1334-by-506 presence data of dialectical linguistic properties in 506 Finnish municipalities [7]. The *DNA Amplification* data, of 4590-by-392, contains information on DNA copy number amplifications. Such copies activate oncogenes and are hallmarks of nearly all advanced tumors [26]. Amplified genes represent attractive targets for therapy, diagnostics and prognostics. This dataset exhibits a banded structure [11]. The *Mammals* presence data[4] consists of presence records of 124 European mammals within 2183 geographical areas of 50 × 50 kilometers [24]. *Newsgroups* is a subset of the *20Newsgroups* dataset,[5] containing, for 400 posts from 4 newsgroups[6], the usage of 800 words. Finally, the 501-by-139 *Paleo* dataset consists of fossil records per location.[7]

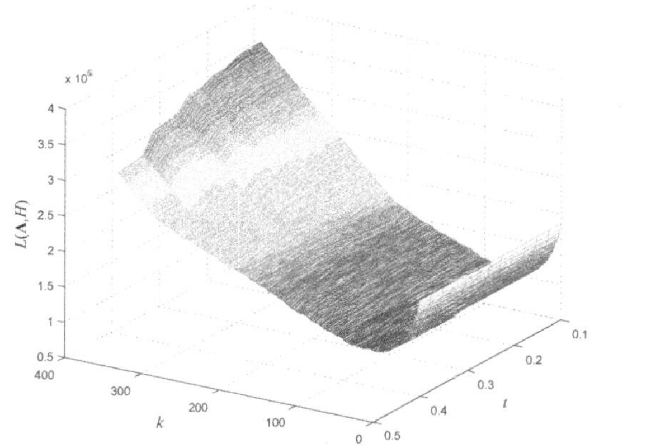

Figure 2: A 3D plot of the number of bits (y-axis), for varying values of k (x-axis) and t (z-axis) for the *DNA* dataset. Minimal description length attained at $k = 57$ and $t = 0.325$.

Before we discuss the identified model orders, we look at the sensitivity to Asso's parameter t. In Figure 2, we plot a typical example of the space of total encoded lengths, $L(\mathbf{A}, H)$. For the *DNA* data, we show all $L(\mathbf{A}, H)$ for every considered k and t. The figure shows the landscape to be a valley, with extreme high values for overly complex and overly simplistic models, and the model order is to be found in the distinct minimum around $k = 57$; which is the value for k at which $L(\mathbf{A}, H)$ for Asso is minimized. Further, the plot tells us that t does not (strongly) influence the detected model order k. Over all considered datasets the landscape is of similar shape, with the exception of the highly noisy synthetic data. Hence, in practice, we can do with a coarse sweep over t.

In Figure 3 we show, for each of the datasets, the total encoded size per k, fixing t to the value at which the minimum description length was found. The identified model orders (i.e., values for k at which the minimum was reached) are given in each figure. As the plots show, our description length function is close-to-convex for Asso's greedy heuristic search. This means that the early-stop criterion c can validly be employed. It also suggests that binary search might be a valid search strategy for non-hierarchical algorithms.

As mentioned above, the purpose of these experiments is to assess the quality of our model-order selection approach, not that of BMF or Asso per se. Nevertheless, we have to analyze whether the selected model orders make sense, and can best do this by investigating the factors Asso discovers at the identified model orders.

For the *DBLP* dataset, our method proposes $k = 4$. This yields four disjoint sets of conferences as row factors: (1) SIGMOD, VLDB, ICDE, (2) SODA, FOCS, STOC, (3) KDD, PKDD, ICDM, and (4) ICML, ECML. These four factors clearly correspond to four different field of computer science, namely (1) databases, (2) theoretical computer science, (3) data mining, and (4) machine learning. The suggested number of factors for *Newsgroups*, 17, might seem high given that the data is about four newsgroups. But it would be overly simplistic to assume that each newsgroup could be represented with just one (or even two) topic. Instead, there are some general topics (i.e., factors containing words appearing across the data, such as 'question'), and three to four subtopics per newsgroup. The estimate for *DNA*,

[3] `http://www.informatik.uni-trier.de/~ley/db/`

[4] Available for research purposes from the Societas Europaea Mammalogica at `http://www.european-mammals.org`

[5] `http://people.csail.mit.edu/jrennie/20Newsgroups/`

[6] The authors are grateful to Ata Kabán for pre-processing the data; the pre-processing in explained in [20]

[7] NOW public release 030717, available from `http://www.helsinki.fi/science/now/` [10].

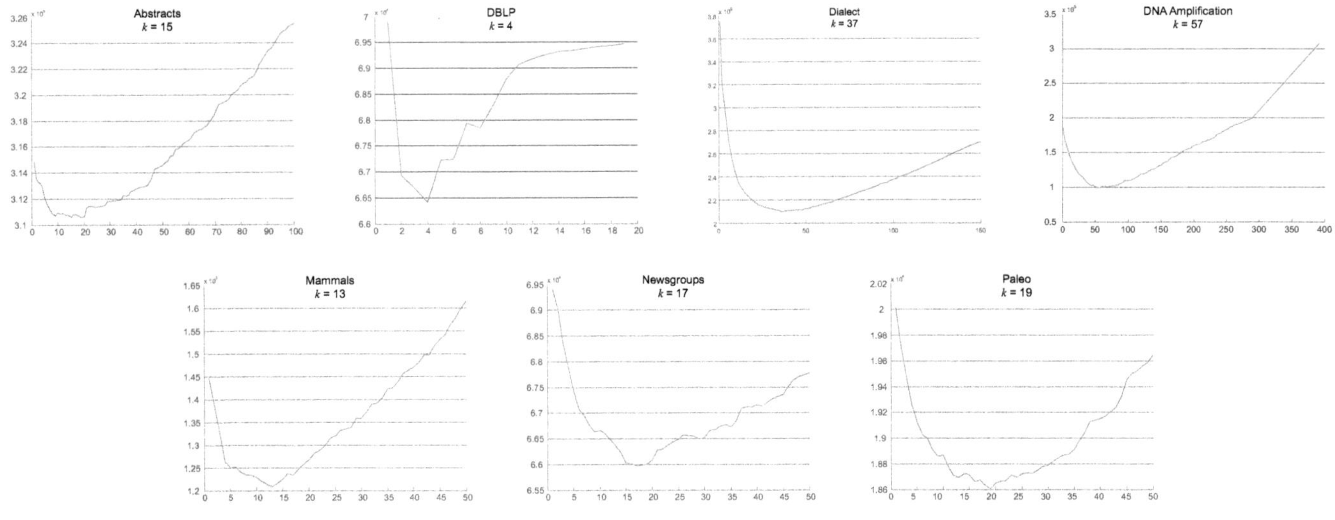

Figure 3: MDL score per k for, from left to right: (top row) *Abstracts*, *DBLP*, *Dialect*, *DNA*, (bottom row) *Mammals*, *Newsgroups*, and *Paleo*. Value for t fixed per dataset to value at which the minimal description length is found over all t and k.

$k = 57$, returns factors that model the known chromosomal regions (or, bands [11]) of interest very well [26], only missing some of the smallest itemsets. What comes to *Paleo* ($k = 19$), Tatti et al. [34] computed its normalized correlation dimension to be 15. While this normalized correlation dimension has no direct connection to BMF, we consider it interesting that these two methods designed for Boolean data give rather similar results. Even more so, as Tatti et al. [34] report that explaining 90% of the variance with PCA requires 79 factors.

We also checked the error curves for these data sets. In most of the cases, error decreases smoothly as k increases, and hence we cannot find any 'elbow' that would suggest the model order.

We also experimented with *NSFAbstracts* dataset. The data[8] contains 4894 terms used in 12 841 project abstracts. The preprocessing is explained in [20]. The resulting data is extremely sparse (0.9%).The model selection procedure resulted to $t = 0.8$ and $k = 1848$. Here, k is of course too large for humans to interpret the factors. Yet, it seems that the data indeed requires quite large k, as the model cost decreases steeply when k is increased. Furthermore, using PCA, 1848 factors explain only about 69% of the variance, and in order to explain at least 90% of the variance, PCA needs to have 3399 factors. While these numbers are not directly comparable, they do indicate that the data has very complex structure (e.g., very little overlap between the rows). This can, at least partly, explain also the need for high k with BMF.

7. DISCUSSION

The experiments show our approach to solve the BMF model order selection problem by MDL works very well. By the MDL principle, and hence by employing the most efficient encoding for the error matrix, Typed XOR, we find highly accurate estimates.

We also applied cross-validation. While intuitively appealing, it failed to produce any reasonable results. Why was that? There are (at least) two possible reasons. First, generalizing the learned factors to new columns is a hard problem, as we already mentioned. But it might be that cross-validation fails even if we could generalize in an optimal way. The problem is that when we generalize to new columns (or rows), we do not have to use all factors. The consequence is most obvious in hierarchical decompositions, such as those returned by Asso: adding a new factor reduces the error on training data, but it will never increase the error on test data (if it would, we would not use it to explain the test data). This is not special to Boolean factorizations, as similar behavior has been reported with PCA [6].

Of our error matrix encoding strategies, the inefficient Naïve Factor and Naïve Indices do not work well in practice—except when noise is low and a model closely resembling the true model is offered. Naïve XOR and Typed XOR, on the other hand, consistently provide highly accurate model order estimates. Neither overestimate model complexity, and naturally provide underestimation in high-noise situations; highly desirable properties for model (order) selection. As it is the most efficient encoding, our overall recommendation is to use Typed XOR to encode $\mathbf{E}$.

Experiments on real data show that meaningful factors are discovered at the selected model orders, as well as that the score is near-convex. This means that, even for the heuristic BMF algorithm we employed in our experiments, we can confidently employ a greedy early-stopping criterion.

We did not investigate data-to-model codes in this paper. Such codes are very efficient, and hence we expect these to work badly with Naïve Factors and Naïve Indices, while not providing significant benefits compared to the current encoding when used with Typed XOR. Space constraints, however, prevent us from exploring these hypotheses here.

Finally, we note that our encoding length functions are easily adaptable for different variations of BMF, such as Boolean column subset-selection [20] and dominated BMF [21].

8. CONCLUSION

We proposed a general solution to the model order selection problem for Boolean matrix factorization. By the Minimum Description Length principle, we formulate the number of bits required to lossless encode the model and the error it introduces, and report the order of the model for which this sum is minimized. We empirically evaluated its performance in combination with the Asso BMF algorithm. The experiments show that the correct model orders are reliably selected for varying amounts of noise and model orders, and

[8] `http://kdd.ics.uci.edu/databases/nsfabs/nsfawards.html`

moreover, that the models at which the MDL score is minimized consist of meaningful factors.

Future work includes the development of good heuristics that optimize the MDL score directly, instead of the error, when finding Boolean matrix factorizations of a given rank, as well as further analysis of the complexity of problem.

Acknowledgements

Jilles Vreeken is supported by a Post-Doctoral Fellowship of the Research Foundation – Flanders (FWO).

9. REFERENCES

[1] R. Belohlavek and V. Vychodil. Discovery of optimal factors in binary data via a novel method of matrix decomposition. *J. Comp. Sys. Sci.*, 76(1):3–20, 2010.

[2] R. Cattell. The scree test for the number of factors. *Multivar. Behav. Res.*, 1:245–276, 1966.

[3] V. Chandola and V. Kumar. Summarization – compressing data into an informative representation. *Knowl. Inf. Syst.*, 12(3):355–378, 2007.

[4] R. Cilibrasi and P. Vitanyi. Clustering by compression. *IEEE Trans. Inform. Theory*, 51(4):1523–1545, 2005.

[5] T. Cover and J. Thomas. *Elements of Information Theory, 2nd ed.* John Wiley and Sons, 2006.

[6] C. T. dos S. Dias and W. J. Krzanowski. Model selection and cross validation in additive main effect and multiplicative interaction models. *Crop Sci.*, 43:865–873, 2003.

[7] S. M. Embleton and E. S. Wheeler. Finnish dialect atlas for quantitative studies. *J. Quant. Ling.*, 4(1–3):99–102, 1997.

[8] C. Faloutsos and V. Megalooikonomou. On data mining, compression and Kolmogorov complexity. *Data Min. Knowl. Disc.*, 15:3–20, 2007.

[9] U. Fayyad and K. Irani. Multi-interval discretization of continuous-valued attributes for classification learning. In *Proc. UAI'93*, pages 1022–1027, 1993.

[10] M. Fortelius et al. Neogene of the old world database of fossil mammals (NOW), 2003. http://www.helsinki.fi/science/now/.

[11] G. C. Garriga, E. Junttila, and H. Mannila. Banded structure in binary matrices. In *Proc. KDD'08*, pages 292–300, 2008.

[12] F. Geerts, B. Goethals, and T. Mielikäinen. Tiling databases. In *Proc. DS'04*, pages 278–289, 2004.

[13] G. H. Golub and C. F. Van Loan. *Matrix Computations*. JHU Press, 1996.

[14] P. D. Grünwald. *The Minimum Description Length Principle*. MIT Press, 2007.

[15] H. Heikinheimo, J. Vreeken, A. Siebes, and H. Mannila. Low-entropy set selection. In *Proc. SDM'09*, 2009.

[16] E. Keogh, S. Lonardi, and C. A. Ratanamahatana. Towards parameter-free data mining. In *Proc. KDD'04*, pages 206–215, 2004.

[17] K.-N. Kontonasios and T. De Bie. An information-theoretic approach to finding noisy tiles in binary databases. In *Proc. SDM'10*, 2010.

[18] M. Li and P. Vitányi. *An Introduction to Kolmogorov Complexity and its Applications*. Springer-Verlag, 1993.

[19] H. Lu, J. Vaidya, and V. Atluri. Optimal Boolean matrix decomposition: Application to role engineering. In *Proc. ICDE'08*, pages 297–306, 2008.

[20] P. Miettinen. *Matrix Decomposition Methods for Data Mining: Computational Complexity and Algorithms*. PhD thesis, University of Helsinki, 2009.

[21] P. Miettinen. Sparse Boolean matrix factorizations. In *Proc. ICDM'10*, pages 935–940, 2010.

[22] P. Miettinen, T. Mielikäinen, A. Gionis, G. Das, and H. Mannila. The discrete basis problem. *IEEE Trans. Knowl. Data Eng.*, 20(10):1348–1362, 2008.

[23] T. P. Minka. Automatic choice of dimensionality for PCA. In *Proc. NIPS'00*, pages 598–604, 2001.

[24] A. J. Mitchell-Jones, G. Amori, W. Bogdanowicz, B. Krystufek, P. J. H. Reijnders, F. Spitzenberger, M. Stubbe, J. B. M. Thissen, V. Vohralik, and J. Zima. *The Atlas of European Mammals*. Academic Press, 1999.

[25] S. D. Monson, N. J. Pullman, and R. Rees. A survey of clique and biclique coverings and factorizations of $(0, 1)$-matrices. *Bulletin of the ICA*, 14:17–86, 1995.

[26] S. Myllykangas, J. Himberg, T. Böhling, B. Nagy, J. Hollmén, and S. Knuutila. DNA copy number amplification profiling of human neoplasms. *Oncogene*, 25(55), 2006.

[27] D. S. Nau, G. Markowsky, M. A. Woodbury, and D. B. Amos. A mathematical analysis of human leukocyte antigen serology. *Math. Biosci.*, 40:243–270, 1978.

[28] A. B. Owen and P. O. Perry. Bi-cross-validation of the SVD and the nonnegative matrix factorization. *Ann. Appl. Stat.*, 3(2):564–594, Jun 2009.

[29] P. Paatero and U. Tapper. Positive matrix factorization: A non-negative factor model with optimal utilization of error estimates of data values. *Environmetrics*, 5:111–126, 1994.

[30] V. Pestov. An axiomatic approach to intrinsic dimension of a dataset. *Neural Networks*, 21(2-3):204–213, 2008.

[31] J. Rissanen. Modeling by shortest data description. *Automatica*, 14(1):465–471, 1978.

[32] M. Schmidt, O. Winther, and L. Hansen. Bayesian non-negative matrix factorization. In *Proc. ICA'09*, volume 5411 of *LNCS*, pages 540–547, 2009.

[33] A. Streich, M. Frank, D. Basin, and J. Buhmann. Multi-assignment clustering for Boolean data. In *Proc. ICML'09*, pages 969–976, 2009.

[34] N. Tatti, T. Mielikainen, A. Gionis, and H. Mannila. What is the dimension of your binary data? In *Proc. ICDM'06*, pages 603–612, 2006.

[35] N. Tatti and J. Vreeken. Finding good itemsets by packing data. In *Proc. ICDM'08*, pages 588–597, 2008.

[36] J. Vaidya, V. Atluri, and Q. Guo. The role mining problem: Finding a minimal descriptive set of roles. In *Proc. SACMAT*, pages 175–184, 2007.

[37] J. Vreeken and A. Siebes. Filling in the blanks – KRIMP minimisation for missing data. In *Proc. ICDM'08*, pages 1067–1072, 2008.

[38] J. Vreeken, M. van Leeuwen, and A. Siebes. Krimp: Mining itemsets that compress. *Data Min. Knowl. Discov.*, 19(2):176–193, 2010. 10.1007/s10618-010-0202-x.

[39] C. Wallace. *Statistical and inductive inference by minimum message length*. Springer-Verlag, 2005.

[40] J. Wang and G. Karypis. On efficiently summarizing categorical databases. *Knowl. Inf. Syst.*, 9(1):19–37, 2006.

[41] K. Yeomans and P. Golder. The Guttman–Kaiser criterion as a predictor of the number of common factors. *The Statistician*, 31(3):221–229, 1982.

[42] M. Zhu and A. Ghodsi. Automatic dimensionality selection from the scree plot via the use of profile likelihood. *Comp. Stat. & Data Anal.*, 51(2):918–930, 2006.

Rank Aggregation via Nuclear Norm Minimization

David F. Gleich*
Sandia National Laboratories†
Livermore, CA
dfgleic@sandia.gov

Lek-Heng Lim‡
University of Chicago
Chicago, IL
lekheng@uchicago.edu

ABSTRACT

The process of rank aggregation is intimately intertwined with the structure of skew-symmetric matrices. We apply recent advances in the theory and algorithms of matrix completion to skew-symmetric matrices. This combination of ideas produces a new method for ranking a set of items. The essence of our idea is that a rank aggregation describes a partially filled skew-symmetric matrix. We extend an algorithm for matrix completion to handle skew-symmetric data and use that to extract ranks for each item. Our algorithm applies to both pairwise comparison and rating data. Because it is based on matrix completion, it is robust to both noise and incomplete data. We show a formal recovery result for the noiseless case and present a detailed study of the algorithm on synthetic data and Netflix ratings.

Categories and Subject Descriptors

H.3.5 [**Information Storage and Retrieval**]: On-line information Services—*Web-based services*; G.1.3 [**Numerical analysis**]: Numerical Linear Algebra—*Singular value decomposition*

General Terms

Algorithms

Keywords

nuclear norm, skew symmetric, rank aggregation

1. INTRODUCTION

One of the classic data mining problems is to identify the important items in a data set; see Tan and Jin [2004] for an interesting example of how these might be used. For this task, we are concerned with rank aggregation. Given a series of votes on a set of items by a group of voters, rank aggregation is the process of permuting the set of items so that the first element is the best choice in the set, the second element is the next best choice, and so on. In fact, rank aggregation is an old problem and has a history stretching back centuries [Condorcet, 1785]; one famous result is that any rank aggregation requires some degree of compromise [Arrow, 1950]. Our point in this introduction is not to detail a history of all the possible methods of rank aggregation, but to give some perspective on our approach to the problem.

Direct approaches involve finding a permutation explicitly – for example, computing the Kemeny optimal ranking [Kemeny, 1959] or the minimum feedback arc set problem. These problems are NP-hard [Dwork et al., 2001, Ailon et al., 2005, Alon, 2006]. An alternate approach is to assign a score to each item, and then compute a permutation based on ordering these items by their score, e.g. Saaty [1987]. In this manuscript, we focus on the second approach. A key advantage of the computations we propose is that they are *convex* problems and efficiently solvable.

While the problem of rank aggregation is old, modern applications – such as those found in web-applications like Netflix and Amazon – pose new challenges. First, the data collected are usually cardinal measurements on the quality of each item, such as 1–5 stars, received from voters. Second, the voters are neither experts in the rating domain nor experts at producing useful ratings. These properties manifest themselves in a few ways, including skewed and indiscriminate voting behaviors [Ho and Quinn, 2008]. We focus on using aggregate pairwise data about items to develop a score for each item that predicts the pairwise data itself. This approach eliminates some of the issues with directly utilizing voters ratings, and we argue this point more precisely in Section 2.

To explain our method, consider a set of n items, labeled from 1 to n. Suppose that each of these items has an unknown intrinsic quality $s_i : 1 \leq i \leq n$, where $s_i > s_j$ implies that item i is better than item j. While the s_i's are unknown, suppose we are given a matrix $\boldsymbol{Y}$ where $Y_{ij} = s_i - s_j$. By finding a rank-2 factorization of $\boldsymbol{Y}$ (there is no rank-1 skew-symmetric factorization), for example

$$\boldsymbol{Y} = \mathbf{s}\mathbf{e}^T - \mathbf{e}\mathbf{s}^T, \tag{1}$$

we can extract unknown scores. The matrix $\boldsymbol{Y}$ is skew-symmetric and describes any score-based global pairwise ranking. (There are other possible rank-2 factorizations

*Supported by the Natural Sciences and Engineering Research Council of Canada and the Dept. of Energy's John von Neumann fellowship.

†Sandia National Laboratories is a multi-program laboratory managed and operated by Sandia Corporation, a wholly owned subsidiary of Lockheed Martin Corporation, for the U.S. Department of Energy's National Nuclear Security Administration under contract DE-AC04-94AL85000.

‡Supported by NSF CAREER Award DMS 1057064

Table 1: Notation for the paper.

Sym.	Interpretation
$\mathcal{A}(\cdot)$	a linear map from a matrix to a vector
$\mathbf{e}$	a vector of all ones
$\mathbf{e}_i$	a vector with 1 in the ith entry, 0 elsewhere
$\lVert\cdot\rVert_*$	the nuclear norm
$\boldsymbol{R}$	a rating matrix (voters-by-items)
$\boldsymbol{Y}$	a fitted or model pairwise comparison matrix
$\hat{\boldsymbol{Y}}$	a measured pairwise comparison matrix
Ω	an index set for the known entries of a matrix

of a skew-symmetric matrix, a point we return to later in Section 3.1.)

Thus, given a measured $\hat{\boldsymbol{Y}}$, the goal is to find a minimum rank approximation of $\hat{\boldsymbol{Y}}$ that models the elements, and ideally one that is rank-2. Phrased in this way, it is a natural candidate for recent developments in the theory of matrix completion [Candès and Tao, 2010, Recht et al., 2010]. In the matrix completion problem, certain elements of the matrix are presumed to be known. The goal is to produce a low-rank matrix that respects these elements – or at least minimizes the deviation from the known elements. One catch, however, is that we require matrix completion over skew-symmetric matrices for pairwise ranking matrices. Thus, we must solve the matrix completion problem inside a structured class of matrices. This task is a novel contribution of our work. Recently, Gross [2010] also developed a technique for matrix completion with Hermitian matrices.

With a "completed" matrix $\boldsymbol{Y}$, the norm of the residual $\|\hat{\boldsymbol{Y}} - \boldsymbol{Y}\|$ gives us a certificate for the validity of our fit – an additional piece of information available in this model.

To continue, we briefly summarize our main contributions and our notational conventions.

Our contributions.

- We propose a new method for computing a rank aggregation based on matrix completion, which is tolerant to noise and incomplete data.
- We solve a structured matrix-completion problem over the space of skew-symmetric matrices.
- We prove a recovery theorem detailing when our approach will work.
- We perform a detailed evaluation of our approach with synthetic data and an anecdotal study with Netflix ratings.

Notation.

We try to follow standard notation conventions. Matrices are bold, upright roman letters, vectors are bold, lowercase roman letters, and scalars are unbolded roman or Greek letters. The vector $\mathbf{e}$ consists of all ones, and the vector $\mathbf{e}_i$ has a 1 in the ith position and 0's elsewhere. Linear maps on matrices are written as script letters. An index set Ω is a group of index pairs. Each $\omega \in \Omega$ is a pair (r, s) and we assume that the ω's are numbered arbitrarily, i.e. $\Omega = \{\omega_1, \ldots, \omega_k\}$. Please refer to Table 1 for reference.

Before proceeding further, let us outline the rest of the paper. First, Section 2 describes a few methods to take voter-item ratings and produce an aggregate pairwise comparison matrix. Additionally, we argue why pairwise aggregation is a superior technique when the goal is to produce an ordered list of the alternatives. Next, in Section 3 we describe formulations of the noisy matrix completion problem using the nuclear norm. In our setting, the LASSO formulation is the best choice, and we use it throughout the remainder. We briefly describe algorithms for matrix completion and focus on the SVP algorithm [Jain et al., 2010] in Section 3.1. We then show that the SVP algorithm preserves skew-symmetric structure. This process involves studying the singular value decomposition of skew-symmetric matrices. Thus, by the end of the section, we've shown how to formulate and solve for a scoring vector based on the nuclear norm. The following sections describe alternative approaches and show our recovery results. At the end, we show our experimental results. In summary, our overall methodology is

$$\begin{gathered}\text{Ratings } (= \boldsymbol{R}) \\ \Downarrow (\S 2) \\ \text{Pairwise comparisons } (= \boldsymbol{Y}) \\ \Downarrow (\S 3) \\ \text{Ranking scores } (= \mathbf{s}) \\ \Downarrow \text{(sorting)} \\ \text{Rank aggregations.}\end{gathered}$$

An example of our rank aggregations is given in Table 2. We comment further on these in Section 6.3.

Finally, we provide our computational and experimental codes so that others may reproduce our results: `https://dgleich.com/projects/skew-nuclear`

2. PAIRWISE AGGREGATION METHODS

To begin, we describe methods to aggregate the votes of many voters, given by the matrix $\boldsymbol{R}$, into a measured pairwise comparison matrix $\hat{\boldsymbol{Y}}$. These methods have been well-studied in statistics [David, 1988]. In the next section, we show how to extract a score for each item from the matrix $\hat{\boldsymbol{Y}}$.

Let $\boldsymbol{R}$ be a voter-by-item matrix. This matrix has m rows corresponding to each of the m voters and n columns corresponding to the n items of the dataset. In all of the applications we explore, the matrix $\boldsymbol{R}$ is highly incomplete. That is, only a few items are rated by each voter. Usually all the items have a few votes, but there is no consistency in the number of ratings per item.

Instead of using $\boldsymbol{R}$ directly, we compute a pairwise aggregation. Pairwise comparisons have a lengthy history, dating back to the first half of the previous century [Kendall and Smith, 1940]. They also have many nice properties. First, Miller [1956] observes that most people can evaluate only 5 to 9 alternatives at a time. This fact may relate to the common choice of a 5-star rating (e.g. the ones used by Amazon, eBay, Netflix, YouTube). Thus, comparing pairs of movies is easier than ranking a set of 20 movies. Furthermore, only pairwise comparisons are possible in certain settings such as tennis tournaments. Pairwise comparison methods are thus natural for analyzing ranking data. Second, pairwise comparisons are a relative measure and help reduce bias from the rating scale. For these reasons, pairwise comparison methods have been popular in psychology, statistics, and social choice theory [David, 1988, Arrow, 1950]. Such methods have also been adopted by the learning to rank community; see the contents of Li et al. [2008]. A final advantage of pairwise methods is

Table 2: The top 15 movies from Netflix generated by our ranking method (middle and right). The left list is the ranking using the mean rating of each movie and is emblematic of the problems global ranking methods face when infrequently compared items rocket to the top. We prefer the middle and right lists. See Section 6 and Figure 4 for information about the conditions and additional discussion. LOTR III appears twice because of the two DVDs editions, theatrical and extended.

Mean	Log-odds (all)	Arithmetic Mean (30)
LOTR III: Return ...	LOTR III: Return ...	LOTR III: Return ...
LOTR I: The Fellowship ...	LOTR I: The Fellowship ...	LOTR I: The Fellowship ...
LOTR II: The Two ...	LOTR II: The Two ...	LOTR II: The Two ...
Lost: Season 1	Star Wars V: Empire ...	Lost: S1
Battlestar Galactica: S1	Raiders of the Lost Ark	Star Wars V: Empire ...
Fullmetal Alchemist	Star Wars IV: A New Hope	Battlestar Galactica: S1
Trailer Park Boys: S4	Shawshank Redemption	Star Wars IV: A New Hope
Trailer Park Boys: S3	Star Wars VI: Return ...	LOTR III: Return ...
Tenchi Muyo! ...	LOTR III: Return ...	Raiders of the Lost Ark
Shawshank Redemption	The Godfather	The Godfather
Veronica Mars: S1	Toy Story	Shawshank Redemption
Ghost in the Shell: S2	Lost: S1	Star Wars VI: Return ...
Arrested Development: S2	Schindler's List	Gladiator
Simpsons: S6	Finding Nemo	Simpsons: S5
Inu-Yasha	CSI: S4	Schindler's List

that they are much more complete than the ratings matrix. For Netflix, $\boldsymbol{R}$ is 99% incomplete, whereas $\boldsymbol{Y}$ is only 0.22% incomplete and most entries are supported by *many* comparisons. See Figure 1 for information about the number of pairwise comparisons in Netflix and MovieLens.

More critically, an incomplete array of user-by-product ratings is a strange matrix – not every 2-dimensional array of numbers is best viewed as a matrix – and using the rank of this matrix (or its convex relaxation) as a key feature in the modeling needs to be done with care. Consider, if instead of rating values 1 to 5, 0 to 4 are used to represent the exact same information, the rank of this new rating matrix will change. Furthermore, whether we use a rating scale where 1 is the best rating and 5 is worst, or one where 5 is the best and 1 is the worst, a low-rank model would give the exact same fit with the same input values, even though the connotations of the numbers is reversed.

On the other hand, the pairwise ranking matrix that we construct below is invariant under monotone transformation of the rating values and depends only on the degree of relative preference of one alternative over another. It circumvents the previously mentioned pitfalls and is a more principled way to employ a rank/nuclear norm model.

We now describe five techniques to build an aggregate pairwise matrix $\hat{\boldsymbol{Y}}$ from the rating matrix $\boldsymbol{R}$. Let α denote the index of a voter, and i and j the indices of two items. The entries of $\boldsymbol{R}$ are $R_{\alpha i}$. To each voter, we associate a pairwise comparison matrix $\hat{\boldsymbol{Y}}^{\alpha}$. The aggregation is usually computed by something like a mean over $\hat{\boldsymbol{Y}}^{\alpha}$.

1. **Arithmetic mean of score differences** The score difference is $Y_{ij}^{\alpha} = R_{\alpha j} - R_{\alpha i}$. The arithmetic mean of all voters who have rated both i and j is
$$\hat{Y}_{ij} = \frac{\sum_{\alpha}(R_{\alpha i} - R_{\alpha j})}{\#\{\alpha \mid R_{\alpha i}, R_{\alpha j} \text{ exist}\}}.$$
These comparisons are translation invariant.
2. **Geometric mean of score ratios** Assuming $\boldsymbol{R} > 0$, the score ratio refers to $Y_{ij}^{\alpha} = R_{\alpha j}/R_{\alpha i}$. The (log) geometric mean over all voters who have rated both i and j is
$$\hat{Y}_{ij} = \frac{\sum_{\alpha}(\log R_{\alpha i} - \log R_{\alpha j})}{\#\{\alpha \mid R_{\alpha i}, R_{\alpha j} \text{ exist}\}}.$$
These are scale invariant.
3. **Binary comparison** Here $Y_{ij}^{\alpha} = \operatorname{sign}(R_{\alpha j} - R_{\alpha i})$. Its average is the probability difference that the alternative j is preferred to i than vice versa
$$\hat{Y}_{ij} = \Pr\{\alpha \mid R_{\alpha i} > R_{\alpha k}\} - \Pr\{\alpha \mid R_{\alpha i} < R_{\alpha j}\}.$$
These are invariant to a monotone transformation.
4. **Strict binary comparison** This method is almost the same as the last method, except that we eliminate cases where users rated movies equally. That is,
$$\hat{Y}_{ij}^{\alpha} = \begin{cases} 1 & R_{\alpha i} > R_{\alpha j} \\ - & R_{\alpha i} = R_{\alpha j} \\ -1 & R_{\alpha i} < R_{\alpha j}. \end{cases}$$
Again, the average Y_{ij} has a similar interpretation to binary comparison, but only among people who expressed a strict preference for one item over the other. Equal ratings are ignored.
5. **Logarithmic odds ratio** This idea translates binary comparison to a logarithmic scale:
$$\hat{Y}_{ij} = \log \frac{\Pr\{\alpha \mid R_{\alpha i} \geq R_{\alpha j}\}}{\Pr\{\alpha \mid R_{\alpha i} \leq R_{\alpha j}\}}.$$

3. RANK AGGREGATION WITH THE NUCLEAR NORM

Thus far, we have seen how to compute an aggregate pairwise matrix $\hat{\boldsymbol{Y}}$ from ratings data. While $\hat{\boldsymbol{Y}}$ has fewer missing entries than $\boldsymbol{R}$ – roughly 1-80% missing instead of almost 99% missing – it is still not nearly complete. In this section, we discuss how to use the theory of matrix completion to estimate the scoring vector underlying the comparison matrix $\hat{\boldsymbol{Y}}$. These same techniques apply even when $\hat{\boldsymbol{Y}}$ is

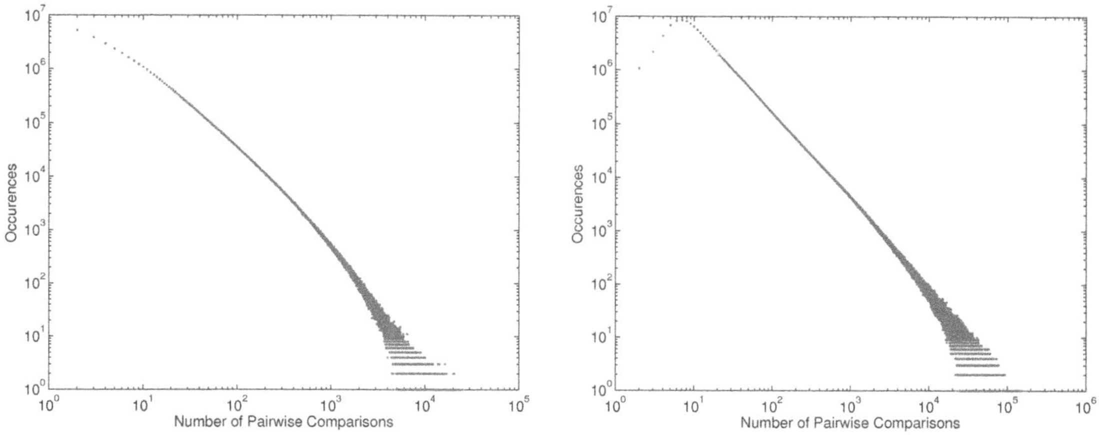

(a) MovieLens - 85.49% of total pairwise comparisons

(b) Netflix - 99.77% of total pairwise comparisons

Figure 1: A histogram of the number of pairwise comparisons between movies in MovieLens (left) and Netflix (right). The number of pairwise comparisons is the number of users with ratings on both movies. These histograms show that most items have more than a small number of comparisons between them. For example, 18.5% and 34.67% of all possible pairwise entries have more than 30 comparisons between them. Largely speaking, this figure justifies dropping infrequent ratings from the comparison. This step allows us to take advantage of the ability of the matrix-completion methods to deal with incomplete data.

not computed from ratings and is measured through direct pairwise comparisons.

Let us now state the matrix completion problem formally [Candès and Recht, 2009, Recht et al., 2010]. Given a matrix $\boldsymbol{A}$ where only a subset of the entries are known, the goal is to find the lowest rank matrix $\boldsymbol{X}$ that agrees with $\boldsymbol{A}$ in all the non-zeros. Let Ω be the index set corresponding to the known entries of $\boldsymbol{A}$. Now define $\mathcal{A}(\boldsymbol{X})$ as a linear map corresponding to the elements of Ω, i.e. $\mathcal{A}(\boldsymbol{X})$ is a vector where the ith element is defined to be

$$[\mathcal{A}(\boldsymbol{X})]_i = X_{\omega_i}, \tag{2}$$

and where we interpret X_{ω_i} as the entry of the matrix $\boldsymbol{X}$ for the index pair $(r, s) = \omega_i$. Finally, let $\mathbf{b} = \mathcal{A}(\boldsymbol{Y})$ be the values of the specified entries of the matrix $\boldsymbol{Y}$. This idea of matrix completion corresponds with the solution of

$$\begin{array}{ll} \text{minimize} & \text{rank}(\boldsymbol{X}) \\ \text{subject to} & \mathcal{A}(\boldsymbol{X}) = \mathbf{b}. \end{array} \tag{3}$$

Unfortunately, like the direct methods at permutation minimization, this approach is NP-hard [Vandenberghe and Boyd, 1996].

To make the problem tractable, an increasingly well-known technique is to replace the rank function with the nuclear norm [Fazel, 2002]. For a matrix $\boldsymbol{A}$, the nuclear norm is defined

$$\|\boldsymbol{A}\|_* = \sum_{i=1}^{\text{rank}(\boldsymbol{A})} \sigma_i(\boldsymbol{A}) \tag{4}$$

where $\sigma_i(\boldsymbol{A})$ is the ith singular value of $\boldsymbol{A}$. The nuclear norm has a few other names: the Ky-Fan n-norm, the Schatten 1-norm, and the trace norm (when applied to symmetric matrices), but we will just use the term nuclear norm here. It is a convex underestimator of the rank function on the unit spectral-norm ball $\{\boldsymbol{A} : \sigma_{\max}(\boldsymbol{A}) \leq 1\}$, i.e. $\|\boldsymbol{A}\|_* \leq \text{rank}(\boldsymbol{A})\sigma_{\max}(\boldsymbol{A})$ and is the largest convex function with this property. Because the nuclear norm is convex,

$$\begin{array}{ll} \text{minimize} & \|\boldsymbol{X}\|_* \\ \text{subject to} & \mathcal{A}(\boldsymbol{X}) = \mathbf{b} \end{array} \tag{5}$$

is a convex relaxation of (3) analogous to how the 1-norm is a convex relaxation of the 0-norm.

In (5) we have $\mathcal{A}(\boldsymbol{X}) = \mathbf{b}$, which is called a noiseless completion problem. Noisy completion problems only require $\mathcal{A}(\boldsymbol{X}) \approx \mathbf{b}$. We present four possibilities inspired by similar approaches in compressed sensing. For the compressed sensing problem with noise:

$$\text{minimize } \|\mathbf{x}\|_1 \quad \text{subject to } \boldsymbol{A}\mathbf{x} \approx \mathbf{b}$$

there are four well known formulations: LASSO [Tibshirani, 1996], QP [Chen et al., 1998], DS [Candès and Tao, 2007] and BPDN [Fuchs, 2004]. For the noisy matrix completion problem, the same variations apply, but with the nuclear norm taking the place of the 1-norm:

LASSO

$$\begin{array}{ll} \text{minimize} & \|\mathcal{A}(\boldsymbol{X}) - \mathbf{b}\|_2 \\ \text{subject to} & \|\boldsymbol{X}\|_* \leq \tau \end{array}$$

DS

$$\begin{array}{ll} \text{minimize} & \|\boldsymbol{X}\|_* \\ \text{subject to} & \sigma_{\max}(\mathcal{A}^*(\mathcal{A}(\boldsymbol{X}) - \mathbf{b})) \leq \mu \end{array}$$

QP Mazumder et al. [2009]

$$\text{minimize} \quad \|\mathcal{A}(\boldsymbol{X}) - \mathbf{b}\|_2^2 + \lambda \|\boldsymbol{X}\|_*$$

BPDN Mazumder et al. [2009]

$$\begin{array}{ll} \text{minimize} & \|\boldsymbol{X}\|_* \\ \text{subject to} & \|\mathcal{A}(\boldsymbol{X}) - \mathbf{b}\|_2 \leq \sigma \end{array}$$

Returning to rank-aggregation, recall the perfect case for the matrix $\boldsymbol{Y}$: there is an unknown quality s_i associated with each item i and $\boldsymbol{Y} = \mathbf{s}\mathbf{e}^T - \mathbf{e}\mathbf{s}^T$. We now assume that the pairwise comparison matrix computed in the previous section approximates the true $\boldsymbol{Y}$. Given such a $\hat{\boldsymbol{Y}}$, our goal is to complete it with a rank-2 matrix. Thus, our objective:

$$\begin{array}{ll} \text{minimize} & \|\mathcal{A}(\boldsymbol{X}) - \mathbf{b}\|_2 \\ \text{subject to} & \|\boldsymbol{X}\|_* \leq 2 \quad \text{and} \quad \boldsymbol{X} = -\boldsymbol{X}^T \end{array} \tag{6}$$

where $\mathcal{A}(\cdot)$ corresponds to the filled entries of $\hat{\boldsymbol{Y}}$. We adopt the LASSO formulation because we want $\text{rank}(\boldsymbol{X}) = 2$, and $\|\boldsymbol{X}\|_*$ underestimates rank as previously mentioned. This problem only differs from the standard matrix completion problem in one regard: the skew-symmetric constraint. With a careful choice of solver, this additional constraint comes "for-free" (with a few technical caveats). It should also be possible to use the skew-Lanczos process to exploit the skew-symmetry in the SVD computation. The problem remains convex because these new equality constraints are linear.

3.1 Algorithms

Algorithms for matrix completion seem to sprout like wild-flowers in spring: Lee and Bresler [2009], Cai et al. [2008], Toh and Yun [2009], Dai and Milenkovic [2009], Keshavan and Oh [2009], Mazumder et al. [2009], Jain et al. [2010]. Each algorithm fills a slightly different niche, or improves a performance measure compared to its predecessors.

We first explored crafting our own solver by adapting projection and thresholding ideas used in these algorithms to the skew-symmetrically constrained variant. However, we realized that many algorithms do not require any modification to solve the problem with the skew-symmetric constraint. This result follows from properties of skew-symmetric matrices we show below.

Thus, we use the SVP algorithm by Jain et al. [2010]. For the matrix completion problem, they found their implementation outperformed many competitors. It is scalable and handles a LASSO-like objective for a fixed rank approximation. For completeness, we restate the SVP procedure in Algorithm 1.

Algorithm 1 Singular Value Projection [Jain et al., 2010]: Solve a matrix completion problem. We use the notation $\Omega(\boldsymbol{X})$ to denote output of $\mathcal{A}(\boldsymbol{X})$ when $\mathcal{A}(\cdot)$ is an index set.

INPUT index set Ω, target values $\mathbf{b}$, target rank k, maximum rank k, step length η, tolerance ε
1: Initialize $\boldsymbol{X}^{(0)} = 0$, $t = 0$
2: REPEAT
3: Set $\boldsymbol{U}^{(t)}\boldsymbol{\Sigma}^{(t)}\boldsymbol{V}^{(t)T}$ to be the rank-k SVD of a matrix with non-zeros Ω and values $\Omega(\boldsymbol{X}^{(t)}) - \eta(\Omega(\boldsymbol{X}^{(t)}) - \mathbf{b})$
4: $\boldsymbol{X}^{(t+1)} \leftarrow \boldsymbol{U}^{(t)}\boldsymbol{\Sigma}^{(t)}\boldsymbol{V}^{(t)T}$
5: $t \leftarrow t + 1$
6: UNTIL $\|\Omega(\boldsymbol{X}^{(k)}) - \mathbf{b}\|_2 > \varepsilon$

If the constraint $\mathcal{A}(\boldsymbol{X}) = \mathbf{b}$ comes from a skew-symmetric matrix, then this algorithm produces a skew-symmetric matrix as well. Showing this involves a few properties of skew-symmetric matrices and two lemmas.

We begin by stating a few well-known properties of skew-symmetric matrices. Let $\boldsymbol{A} = -\boldsymbol{A}^T$ be skew-symmetric. Then all the eigenvalues of $\boldsymbol{A}$ are pure-imaginary and come in complex-conjugate pairs. Thus, a skew-symmetric matrix must always have even rank. Let $\boldsymbol{B}$ be a square real-valued matrix, then the closest skew-symmetric matrix to $\boldsymbol{B}$ (in any norm) is $\boldsymbol{A} = (\boldsymbol{B} - \boldsymbol{B}^T)/2$. These results have elementary proofs. We continue by characterizing the singular value decomposition of a skew-symmetric matrix.

LEMMA 1. *Let $\boldsymbol{A} = -\boldsymbol{A}^T$ be an $n \times n$ skew-symmetric matrix with eigenvalues $i\lambda_1, -i\lambda_1, i\lambda_2, -i\lambda_2, \ldots, i\lambda_j, -i\lambda_j$, where $\lambda_i > 0$ and $j = \lfloor n/2 \rfloor$. Then the SVD of $\boldsymbol{A}$ is given by*

$$\boldsymbol{A} = \boldsymbol{U} \begin{bmatrix} \lambda_1 & & & & & & \\ & \lambda_1 & & & & & \\ & & \lambda_2 & & & & \\ & & & \lambda_2 & & & \\ & & & & \ddots & & \\ & & & & & \lambda_j & \\ & & & & & & \lambda_j \end{bmatrix} \boldsymbol{V}^T \tag{7}$$

for $\boldsymbol{U}$ and $\boldsymbol{V}$ given in the proof.

PROOF. Using the Murnaghan-Wintner form of a real matrix [Murnaghan and Wintner, 1931], we can write

$$\boldsymbol{A} = \boldsymbol{X}\boldsymbol{T}\boldsymbol{X}^T$$

for a *real-valued* orthogonal matrix $\boldsymbol{X}$ and *real-valued* block-upper-triangular matrix $\boldsymbol{T}$, with 2-by-2 blocks along the diagonal. Due to this form, $\boldsymbol{T}$ must also be skew-symmetric. Thus, it is a block-diagonal matrix that we can permute to the form:

$$\boldsymbol{T} = \begin{bmatrix} 0 & \lambda_1 & & & \\ -\lambda_1 & 0 & & & \\ & & 0 & \lambda_2 & \\ & & -\lambda_2 & 0 & \\ & & & & \ddots \end{bmatrix}.$$

Note that the SVD of the matrix

$$\begin{bmatrix} 0 & \lambda_1 \\ -\lambda_1 & 0 \end{bmatrix} = \begin{bmatrix} 0 & 1 \\ 1 & 0 \end{bmatrix} \begin{bmatrix} \lambda_1 & 0 \\ 0 & \lambda_1 \end{bmatrix} \begin{bmatrix} -1 & 0 \\ 0 & 1 \end{bmatrix}.$$

We can use this expression to complete the theorem:

$$\boldsymbol{A} = \underbrace{\boldsymbol{X} \begin{bmatrix} 0 & 1 & & & \\ 1 & 0 & & & \\ & & 0 & 1 & \\ & & 1 & 0 & \\ & & & & \ddots \end{bmatrix}}_{=\boldsymbol{U}} \begin{bmatrix} \lambda_1 & & & & \\ & \lambda_1 & & & \\ & & \lambda_2 & & \\ & & & \lambda_2 & \\ & & & & \ddots \end{bmatrix} \underbrace{\begin{bmatrix} -1 & 0 & & & \\ 0 & 1 & & & \\ & & -1 & 0 & \\ & & 0 & 1 & \\ & & & & \ddots \end{bmatrix} \boldsymbol{X}^T}_{=\boldsymbol{V}^T}.$$

Both the matrices $\boldsymbol{U}$ and $\boldsymbol{V}$ are real and orthogonal. Thus, this form yields the SVD of $\boldsymbol{A}$. □

We now use this lemma to show that – under fairly general conditions – the best rank-k approximation to a skew-symmetric matrix is also skew-symmetric.

LEMMA 2. *Let $\boldsymbol{A}$ be an n-by-n skew-symmetric matrix, and let $k = 2j$ be even. Let $\lambda_1 \geq \lambda_2 \geq \ldots \geq \lambda_j > \lambda_{j+1}$ be the magnitude of the singular value pairs. (Recall that the previous lemma showed that the singular values come in pairs.) Then the best rank-k approximation of $\boldsymbol{A}$ in an orthogonally invariant norm is also skew-symmetric.*

PROOF. This lemma follows fairly directly from Lemma 1. Recall that the best rank-k approximation of $\boldsymbol{A}$ in an orthogonally invariant norm is given by the k largest singular values and vectors. By assumption of the theorem, there is a gap in the spectrum between the kth and k+1-st singular value. Thus, taking the SVD form from Lemma 1 and truncating to the k largest singular values produces a skew-symmetric matrix. □

Finally, we can use this second result to show that the SVP algorithm for the LASSO problem preserves skew-symmetry in all the iterates $\boldsymbol{X}^{(k)}$.

Algorithm 2 Nuclear Norm Rank Aggregation. The SVP subroutine is given by Algorithm 1.

INPUT ranking matrix $\boldsymbol{R}$, minimum comparisons c

1: Compute $\boldsymbol{Y}$ from $\boldsymbol{R}$ by a procedure in Section 2.
2: Discard entries in $\boldsymbol{Y}$ with fewer than c comparisons
3: Let Ω be the index set for all retained entries in $\boldsymbol{Y}$ and $\mathbf{b}$ be the values for these entries
4: $\boldsymbol{U}, \boldsymbol{S}, \boldsymbol{V}$ = SVP(index set Ω, values $\mathbf{b}$, rank 2)
5: Compute $\mathbf{s} = (1/n)\boldsymbol{U}\boldsymbol{S}\boldsymbol{V}^T\mathbf{e}$

THEOREM 3. *Given a set of skew-symmetric constraints* $\mathcal{A}(\cdot) = \mathbf{b}$, *the solution of the* LASSO *problem from the* SVP *solver is a skew-symmetric matrix* $\boldsymbol{X}$ *if the target rank is even and the dominant singular values stay separated as in the previous lemma.*

PROOF. In this proof, we revert to the notation $\mathcal{A}(\boldsymbol{X})$ and use $\mathcal{A}^*(\mathbf{z})$ to denote the matrix with non-zeros in Ω and values from $\mathbf{z}$. We proceed by induction on the iterates generated by the SVP algorithm. Clearly $\boldsymbol{X}^{(0)}$ is skew-symmetric. In step 3, we compute the SVD of a skew-symmetric matrix: $\mathcal{A}^*(\mathcal{A}(\boldsymbol{X}^{(k)}) - \mathbf{b})$. The result, which is the next iterate, is skew-symmetric based on the previous lemma and conditions of this theorem. □

The SVP solver thus solves (6) for a fixed rank problem. A final step is to extract the scoring vector $\mathbf{s}$ from a rank-2 singular value decomposition. If we had the exact matrix $\boldsymbol{Y}$, then $(1/n)\boldsymbol{Y}\mathbf{e} = \mathbf{s} - (\mathbf{s}^T\mathbf{e})/n\mathbf{e}$, which yields the score vector centered around 0. The outcome that a rank-2 $\boldsymbol{U}\boldsymbol{\Sigma}\boldsymbol{V}^T$ from SVP is not of the form $\mathbf{s}\mathbf{e}^T - \mathbf{e}\mathbf{s}^T$ is quite possible because there are many rank-2 skew-symmetric matrices that do not have $\mathbf{e}$ as a factor. If we had a full-but-inconsistent pairwise comparison matrix $\boldsymbol{Y}$, then using a Borda count $\mathbf{s} = (1/n)\boldsymbol{Y}\mathbf{e}$ provides *the best least-squares approximation* to $\mathbf{s}$ [Jiang et al., 2010]. Formally, $(1/n)\boldsymbol{Y}\mathbf{e} = \operatorname{argmin}_{\mathbf{s}} \|\boldsymbol{Y}^T - (\mathbf{s}\mathbf{e}^T - \mathbf{e}\mathbf{s}^T)\|$. This discussion justifies using the scoring vector $\mathbf{s} = (1/n)\boldsymbol{U}\boldsymbol{\Sigma}\boldsymbol{V}^T\mathbf{e}$ derived from this completed matrix.

Our complete ranking procedure is given by Algorithm 2.

4. OTHER APPROACHES

Now, we briefly compare our approach with other techniques to compute ranking vectors from pairwise comparison data. An obvious approach is to find the least-squares solution $\min_{\mathbf{s}} \sum_{(i,j)\in\Omega}(Y_{i,j} - (s_i - s_j))^2$. This is a linear least squares method, and is exactly what Massey [1997] proposed for ranking sports teams. The related Colley method introduces a bit of regularization into the least-squares problem [Colley, 2002]. By way of comparison, the matrix completion approach has the same ideal objective, however, we compute solutions using a two-stage process: first complete the matrix, and then extract scores.

A related methodology with skew-symmetric matrices underlies recent developments in the application of Hodge theory to rank aggregation [Jiang et al., 2010]. By analogy with the Hodge decomposition of a vector space, they propose a decomposition of pairwise rankings into *consistent*, *globally inconsistent*, and *locally inconsistent* pieces. Our approach differs because our algorithm applies without restriction on the comparisons. Freeman [1997] also uses an SVD of a skew-symmetric matrix to discover a hierarchical structure in a social network.

We know of two algorithms to directly estimate the item value from ratings [de Kerchov and van Dooren, 2007, Ho and Quinn, 2008]. Both of these methods include a technique to model voter behavior. They find that skewed behaviors and inconsistencies in the ratings require these adjustments. In contrast, we eliminate these problems by using the pairwise comparison matrix. Approaches using a matrix or tensor factorization of the rating matrix directly often have to determine a rank empirically [Rendle et al., 2009].

The problem with the mean rating from Netflix in Table 2 is often corrected by requiring a minimum number of rating on an item. For example, IMDB builds its top-250 movie list based on a Bayesian estimate of the mean with at least 3000 ratings (`imdb.com/chart/top`). Choosing this parameter is problematic as it directly excludes items. In contrast, choosing the minimum number of comparisons to support an entry in $\boldsymbol{Y}$ may be easier to justify.

5. RECOVERABILITY

A hallmark of the recent developments on matrix completion is the existence of theoretical *recoverability* guarantees (see Candès and Recht [2009], for example). These guarantees give conditions under which the solution to the optimization problems posed in Section 3 *is or is nearby* the low-rank matrix from whence the samples originated. In this section, we apply a recent theoretical insight into matrix completion based on operator bases to our problem of recovering a scoring vector from a skew-symmetric matrix [Gross, 2010]. We only treat the noiseless problem to present a simplified analysis. Also, the notation in this section differs slightly from the rest of the manuscript, in order to match the statements in Gross [2010] better. In particular, Ω is not necessarily the index set, $\imath$ represents $\sqrt{-1}$, and most of the results are for the complex field.

The goal is this section is to apply Theorem 3 from Gross [2010] to skew-symmetric matrices arising from score difference vectors. We restate that theorem for reference.

THEOREM 4 (THEOREM 3, GROSS [2010]). *Let* $\boldsymbol{A}$ *be a rank-r Hermitian matrix with coherence* ν *with respect to an operator basis* $\{\boldsymbol{W}_i\}_{i=1}^{n^2}$. *Let* $\Omega \subset [1, n^2]$ *be a random set of size* $|\Omega| > O(nr\nu(1+\beta)(\log n)^2)$. *Then the solution of*

$$\begin{array}{ll} \text{minimize} & \|\boldsymbol{X}\|_* \\ \text{subject to} & \operatorname{trace}(\boldsymbol{X}^*\boldsymbol{W}_i) = \operatorname{trace}(\boldsymbol{A}^*\boldsymbol{W}_i) \quad i \in \Omega \end{array}$$

is unique and is equal to $\boldsymbol{A}$ *with probability at least* $1 - n^{-3}$.

The definition of coherence follows shortly. On the surface, this theorem is useless for our application. The matrix we wish to complete is not Hermitian, it's skew-symmetric. However, given a real-valued skew-symmetric matrix $\boldsymbol{Y}$, the matrix $\imath\boldsymbol{Y}$ is Hermitian; and hence, we will work to apply this theorem to this particular Hermitian matrix.

The following theorem gives us a condition for recovering the score vector using matrix completion. As stated, this theorem is not particularly useful because $\mathbf{s}$ may be recovered from noiseless measurements by exploiting the special structure of the rank-2 matrix $\boldsymbol{Y}$. For example, if we know $Y_{i,j} = s_i - s_j$ then given s_i we can find s_j. This argument may be repeated with an arbitrary starting point as long as the known index set corresponds to a connected set over the indices. Instead we view the following theorem as providing intuition for the noisy problem.

Consider the operator basis for Hermitian matrices:

$$\mathcal{H} = \mathcal{S} \cup \mathcal{K} \cup \mathcal{D} \text{ where}$$
$$\mathcal{S} = \{1/\sqrt{2}(\mathbf{e}_i\mathbf{e}_j^T + \mathbf{e}_j\mathbf{e}_i^T) : 1 \le i < j \le n\};$$
$$\mathcal{K} = \{\imath/\sqrt{2}(\mathbf{e}_i\mathbf{e}_j^T - \mathbf{e}_j\mathbf{e}_i^T) : 1 \le i < j \le n\};$$
$$\mathcal{D} = \{\mathbf{e}_i\mathbf{e}_i^T : 1 \le i \le n\}.$$

THEOREM 5. *Let* $\mathbf{s}$ *be centered, i.e.,* $\mathbf{s}^T\mathbf{e} = 0$. *Let* $\boldsymbol{Y} = \mathbf{s}\mathbf{e}^T - \mathbf{e}\mathbf{s}^T$ *where* $\theta = \max_i s_i^2/(\mathbf{s}^T\mathbf{s})$ *and* $\rho = ((\max_i s_i) - (\min_i s_i))/\|\mathbf{s}\|$. *Also, let* $\Omega \subset \mathcal{H}$ *be a random set of elements with size* $|\Omega| \ge O(2n\nu(1+\beta)(\log n)^2)$ *where* $\nu = \max((n\theta + 1)/4, n\rho^2)$. *Then the solution of*

$$\begin{array}{ll} \text{minimize} & \|\boldsymbol{X}\|_* \\ \text{subject to} & \operatorname{trace}(\boldsymbol{X}^*\boldsymbol{W}_i) = \operatorname{trace}((\imath\boldsymbol{Y})^*\boldsymbol{W}_i), \quad \boldsymbol{W}_i \in \Omega \end{array}$$

is equal to $\imath\boldsymbol{Y}$ *with probability at least* $1 - n^{-\beta}$.

The proof of this theorem follows directly by Theorem 4 if $\imath\boldsymbol{Y}$ has coherence ν with respect to the basis $\mathcal{H}$. We now show this result.

DEFINITION 6 (COHERENCE, GROSS [2010]). *Let* $\boldsymbol{A}$ *be* $n \times n$, *rank-r, and Hermitian. Let* $\boldsymbol{U}\boldsymbol{U}^*$ *be an orthogonal projector onto* range$(\boldsymbol{A})$. *Then* $\boldsymbol{A}$ *has coherence* ν *with respect to an operator basis* $\{\boldsymbol{W}_i\}_{i=1}^{n^2}$ *if both*

$$\max_i \operatorname{trace}(\boldsymbol{W}_i\boldsymbol{U}\boldsymbol{U}^*\boldsymbol{W}_i) \le 2\nu r/n, \text{ and}$$
$$\max_i \operatorname{trace}(\operatorname{sign}(\boldsymbol{A})\boldsymbol{W}_i)^2 \le \nu r/n^2.$$

For $\boldsymbol{A} = \imath\boldsymbol{Y}$ with $\mathbf{s}^T\mathbf{e} = 0$:

$$\boldsymbol{U}\boldsymbol{U}^* = \frac{\mathbf{s}\mathbf{s}^T}{\mathbf{s}^T\mathbf{s}} - \frac{1}{n}\mathbf{e}\mathbf{e}^T \text{ and } \operatorname{sign}(\boldsymbol{A}) = \frac{1}{\|\mathbf{s}\|\sqrt{n}}\boldsymbol{A}.$$

Let $\boldsymbol{S}_p \in \mathcal{S}$, $\boldsymbol{K}_p \in \mathcal{K}$, and $\boldsymbol{D}_p \in \mathcal{D}$. Note that because sign$(\boldsymbol{A})$ is Hermitian with no real-valued entries, both quantities trace$(\operatorname{sign}(\boldsymbol{A})\boldsymbol{D}_i)^2$ and trace$(\operatorname{sign}(\boldsymbol{A})\boldsymbol{S}_i)^2$ are 0. Also, because $\boldsymbol{U}\boldsymbol{U}^*$ is symmetric, trace$(\boldsymbol{K}_i\boldsymbol{U}\boldsymbol{U}^*\boldsymbol{K}_p) = 0$. The remaining basis elements satisfy:

$$\operatorname{trace}(\boldsymbol{S}_p\boldsymbol{U}\boldsymbol{U}^*\boldsymbol{S}_p) = \frac{1}{n} + \frac{s_i^2 + s_j^2}{2\mathbf{s}^T\mathbf{s}} \le (1/n) + \theta$$
$$\operatorname{trace}(\boldsymbol{D}_p\boldsymbol{U}\boldsymbol{U}^*\boldsymbol{D}_p) = \frac{1}{n} + \frac{s_i^2}{\mathbf{s}^T\mathbf{s}} \le (1/n) + \theta$$
$$\operatorname{trace}(\operatorname{sign}(\boldsymbol{A})\boldsymbol{K}_p)^2 = \frac{2(s_i - s_j)^2}{n\mathbf{s}^T\mathbf{s}} \le (2/n)\rho^2.$$

Thus, $\boldsymbol{A}$ has coherence ν with ν from Theorem 5 and with respect to $\mathcal{H}$. And we have our recovery result. Although, this theorem provides little practical benefit unless both θ and ρ are $O(1/n)$, which occurs when $\mathbf{s}$ is nearly uniform.

6. RESULTS

We implemented and tested this procedure in two synthetic scenarios, along with Netflix, movielens, and Jester joke-set ratings data. In the interest of space, we only present a subset of these results for Netflix.

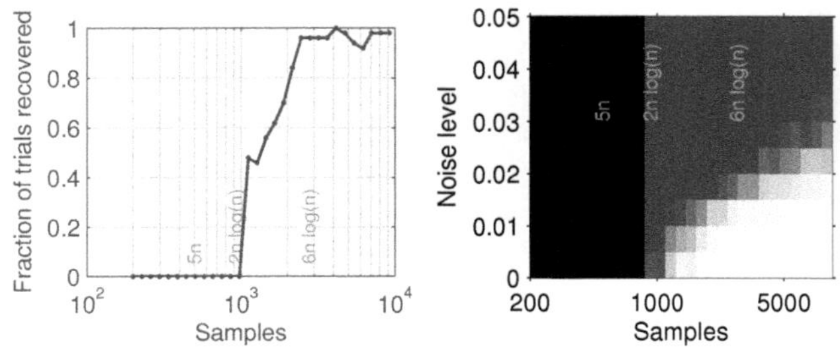

Figure 2: An experimental study of the recoverability of a ranking vector. These show that we need about 6n log n entries of Y to get good recovery in both the noiseless (left) and noisy (right) case. See §6.1 for more information.

6.1 Recovery

The first experiment is an empirical study of the recoverability of the score vector in the noiseless and noisy case. In the noiseless case, Figure 2 (left), we generate a score vector with uniformly distributed random scores between 0 and 1. These are used to construct a pairwise comparison matrix $\boldsymbol{Y} = \mathbf{s}\mathbf{e}^T - \mathbf{e}\mathbf{s}^T$. We then sample elements of this matrix uniformly at random and compute the difference between the true score vector $\mathbf{s}$ and the output of steps 4 and 5 of Algorithm 2. If the relative 2-norm difference between these vectors is less than 10^{-3}, we declare the trial recovered. For $n = 100$, the figure shows that, once the number of samples is about $6n \log n$, the correct $\mathbf{s}$ is recovered in nearly all the 50 trials.

Next, for the noisy case, we generate a uniformly spaced score vector between 0 and 1. Then $\boldsymbol{Y} = \mathbf{s}\mathbf{e}^T - \mathbf{e}\mathbf{s}^T + \varepsilon\boldsymbol{E}$, where $\boldsymbol{E}$ is a matrix of random normals. Again, we sample elements of this matrix randomly, and declare a trial successful if the *order* of the recovered score vector is identical to the true order. In Figure 2 (right), we indicate the fractional of successful trials as a gray value between black (all failure) and white (all successful). Again, the algorithm is successful for a moderate noise level, i.e., the value of ε, when the number of samples is larger than $6n \log n$.

6.2 Synthetic

Inspired by Ho and Quinn [2008], we investigate recovering item scores in an item-response scenario. Let a_i be the center of user i's rating scale, and b_i be the rating sensitivity of user i. Let t_i be the intrinsic score of item j. Then we generate ratings from users on items as:

$$R_{i,j} = L[a_i + b_i t_j + E_{i,j}]$$

where $L[\alpha]$ is the discrete levels function:

$$L[\alpha] = \max(\min(\operatorname{round}(\alpha), 5), 1)$$

and $E_{i,j}$ is a noise parameter. In our experiment, we draw $a_i \sim N(3,1)$, $b_i \sim N(0.5, 0.5)$, $t_i \sim N(0.1, 1)$, and $E_{i,j} \sim \varepsilon N(0,1)$. Here, $N(\mu, \sigma)$ is a standard normal, and ε is a noise parameter. As input to our algorithm, we sample ratings uniformly at random by specifying a desired number of average ratings per user. We then look at the Kendall τ correlation coefficient between the true scores t_i and the output of our algorithm using the arithmetic mean pairwise aggregation. A τ value of 1 indicates a perfect ordering correlation between the two sets of scores.

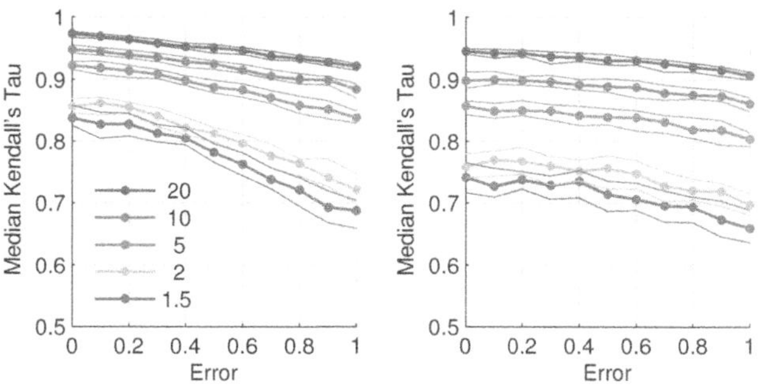

Figure 3: The performance of our algorithm (left) and the mean rating (right) to recovery the ordering given by item scores in an item-response theory model with 100 items and 1000 users. The various thick lines correspond to average number of ratings each user performed (see the in place legend). See §6.2 for more information

Figure 3 shows the results for 1000 users and 100 items with 1.1, 1.5, 2, 5, and 10 ratings per user on average. We also vary the parameter ε between 0 and 1. Each thick line with markers plots the median value of τ in 50 trials. The thin adjacency lines show the 25th and 75th percentiles of the 50 trials. At all error levels, our algorithm outperforms the mean rating. Also, when there are few ratings per-user and moderate noise, our approach is considerably more correlated with the true score. This evidence supports the anecdotal results from Netflix in Table 2.

6.3 Netflix

See Table 2 for the top movies produced by our technique in a few circumstances using all users. The arithmetic mean results in that table use only elements of $\boldsymbol{Y}$ with at least 30 pairwise comparisons (it is a `am all 30` model in the code below). And see Figure 4 for an analysis of the residuals generated by the fit for different constructions of the matrix $\hat{\boldsymbol{Y}}$. Each residual evaluation of Netflix is described by a code. For example, `sb all 0` is a strict-binary pairwise matrix $\hat{\boldsymbol{Y}}$ from all Netflix users and $c = 0$ in Algorithm 2 (i.e. accept all pairwise comparisons). Alternatively, `am 6 30` denotes an arithmetic-mean pairwise matrix $\hat{\boldsymbol{Y}}$ from Netflix users with at least 6 ratings, where each entry in $\hat{\boldsymbol{Y}}$ had 30 users supporting it. The other abbreviations are `gm`: geometric mean; `bc`: binary comparison; and `lo`: log-odds ratio.

These residuals show that we get better rating fits by only using frequently compared movies, but that there are only minor changes in the fits when excluding users that rate few movies. The difference between the score-based residuals $\|\Omega(\mathbf{s}\mathbf{e}^T - \mathbf{e}\mathbf{s}^T) - \mathbf{b}\|$ (red points) and the SVP residuals $\|\Omega(\boldsymbol{U}\boldsymbol{S}\boldsymbol{V}^T) - \mathbf{b}\|$ (blue points) show that excluding comparisons leads to "overfitting" in the SVP residual. This suggests that increasing the parameter c should be done with care and good checks on the residual norms.

To check that a rank-2 approximation is reasonable, we increased the target rank in the SVP solver to 4 to investigate. For the arithmetic mean (6,30) model, the relative residual at rank-2 is 0.2838 and at rank-4 is 0.2514. Meanwhile, the nuclear norm increases from around 14000 to around 17000. These results show that the change in the fit is minimal and our rank-2 approximation and its scores should represent a reasonable ranking.

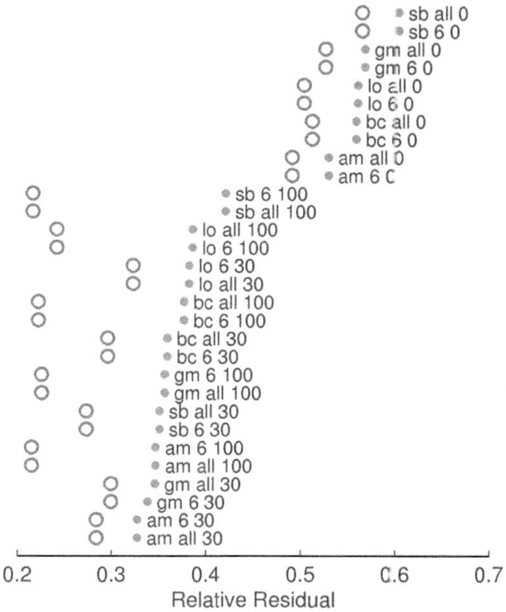

Figure 4: The labels on each residual show how we generated the pairwise scores and truncated the Netflix data. Red points are the residuals from the scores, and blue points are the final residuals from the SVP algorithm. Please see the discussion in §6.3.

7. CONCLUSION

Existing principled techniques such as computing a Kemeny optimal ranking or finding a minimize feedback arc set are NP-hard. These approaches are inappropriate in large scale rank aggregation settings. Our proposal is (i) measure pairwise scores $\hat{\boldsymbol{Y}}$ and (ii) solve a matrix completion problem to determine the quality of items. This idea is both principled and functional with significant missing data. The results of our rank aggregation on the Netflix problem (Table 2) reveal popular and high quality movies. These are interesting results and could easily have a home on a "best movies in Netflix" web page. Such a page exists, but is regarded as having strange results. Computing a rank aggregation with this technique is not NP-hard. It only requires solving a convex optimization problem with a unique global minima. Although we did not record computation times, the most time consuming piece of work is computing the pairwise comparison matrix $\boldsymbol{Y}$. In a practical setting, this could easily be done with a MapReduce computation.

To compute these solutions, we adapted the SVP solver for matrix completion [Jain et al., 2010]. This process involved (i) studying the singular value decomposition of a skew-symmetric matrix (Lemmas 1 and 2) and (ii) showing that the SVP solver preserves a skew-symmetric approximation through its computation (Theorem 3). Because the SVP solver computes with an explicitly chosen rank, these techniques work well for large scale rank aggregation problems.

We believe the combination of pairwise aggregation and matrix completion is a fruitful direction for future research. We plan to explore optimizing the SVP algorithm to exploit the skew-symmetric constraint, extending our recovery result to the noisy case, and investigating additional data.

Acknowledgements. The authors would like to thank Amy Langville, Carl Meyer, and Yuan Yao for helpful discussions.

References

N. Ailon, M. Charikar, and A. Newman. Aggregating inconsistent information: ranking and clustering. In *STOC '05*, pages 684–693, 2005. doi: 10.1145/1060590.1060692.

N. Alon. Ranking tournaments. *SIAM J. Discret. Math.*, 20 (1):137–142, 2006. doi: 10.1137/050623905.

K. J. Arrow. A difficulty in the concept of social welfare. *J. Polit. Econ.*, 58(4):328–346, 1950. http://jstor.org/stable/1828886.

J.-F. Cai, E. J. Candès, and Z. Shen. A singular value thresholding algorithm for matrix completion. *arXiv*, math.OC:0810.3286v1, 2008. http://arxiv.org/abs/0810.3286.

E. Candès and T. Tao. The Dantzig selector: Statistical estimation when p is much larger than n. *Ann. Stat.*, 35(6): 2313–2351, 2007. doi: 10.1214/009053606000001523.

E. J. Candès and B. Recht. Exact matrix completion via convex optimization. *Found. Comput. Math.*, 9(6):717–772, 2009. doi: 10.1007/s10208-009-9045-5.

E. J. Candès and T. Tao. The power of convex relaxation: Near-optimal matrix completion. *IEEE Trans. Inform. Theory*, 56(5):2053–2080, 2010. doi: 10.1109/TIT.2010.2044061.

S. S. Chen, D. L. Donoho, and M. A. Saunders. Atomic decomposition by basis pursuit. *SIAM J. Sci. Comp.*, 20(1): 33–61, 1998. doi: 10.1137/S1064827596304010.

W. N. Colley. Colley's bias free college football ranking method: The Colley matrix explained. Technical report, Princeton University, 2002.

J.-A.-N. d. C. Condorcet. *Essai sur l'application de l'analyse à la probabilité des décisions...* de L'imprimerie Royale, Paris, 1785. http://gallica2.bnf.fr/ark:/12148/bpt6k417181.

W. Dai and O. Milenkovic. Set: an algorithm for consistent matrix completion. *arXiv*, 2009. http://arxiv.org/abs/0909.2705.

H. A. David. *The method of paired comparisons.* Number 41 in Griffin's Statistical Monographs and Courses. Charles Griffin, 1988. ISBN 0195206169.

C. de Kerchov and P. van Dooren. Iterative filtering for a dynamical reputation system. *arXiv*, cs.IR:0711.3964, 2007. http://arXiv.org/abs/0711.3964.

C. Dwork, R. Kumar, M. Naor, and D. Sivakumar. Rank aggregation methods for the web. In *WWW '01*, pages 613–622, New York, NY, USA, 2001. ACM. ISBN 1-58113-348-0. doi: 10.1145/371920.372165.

M. Fazel. *Matrix rank minimization with applications.* PhD thesis, Stanford University, 2002. http://faculty.washington.edu/mfazel/thesis-final.pdf.

L. C. Freeman. Uncovering organizational hierarchies. *Computational and Mathematical Organization Theory*, 3 (1):5–18, 1997. doi: 10.1023/A:1009690520577.

J.-J. Fuchs. Recovery of exact sparse representations in the presence of noise. In *ICASSP '04*, volume 2, pages ii–533–6 vol.2, 2004. doi: 10.1109/ICASSP.2004.1326312.

D. Gross. Recovering low-rank matrices from few coefficients in any basis. *arXiv*, cs.NA:0910.1879v5, 2010. http://arxiv.org/abs/0910.1879.

D. E. Ho and K. M. Quinn. Improving the presentation and interpretation of online ratings data with model-based figures. *Amer. Statist.*, 62(4):279–288, 2008. doi: 10.1198/000313008X366145.

P. Jain, R. Meka, and I. Dhillon. Guaranteed rank minimization via singular value projection. In *NIPS 23*, pages 937–945, 2010. http://books.nips.cc/papers/files/nips23/NIPS2010_0682.pdf.

X. Jiang, L.-H. Lim, Y. Yao, and Y. Ye. Statistical ranking and combinatorial hodge theory. *Mathematical Programming*, 127(1):1–42, 2010. doi: 10.1007/s10107-010-0419-x.

J. G. Kemeny. Mathematics without numbers. *Daedalus*, 88 (4):577–591, 1959. http://jstor.org/stable/20026529.

M. G. Kendall and B. B. Smith. On the method of paired comparison. *Biometrika*, 31(3-4):324–345, 1940. doi: 10.1093/biomet/31.3-4.324.

R. H. Keshavan and S. Oh. A gradient descent algorithm on the grassman manifold for matrix completion. *arXiv*, 2009. http://arxiv.org/abs/0910.5260.

K. Lee and Y. Bresler. Admira: Atomic decomposition for minimum rank approximation. *arXiv*, 2009. http://arxiv.org/abs/0905.0044.

H. Li, T.-Y. Liu, and C. Zhai, editors. *SIGIR '08 Workshop: Learning to Rank for Information Retrieval.* 2008. http://research.microsoft.com/en-us/um/beijing/events/lr4ir-2008/PROCEEDINGS-LR4IR%202008.PDF.

K. Massey. Statistical models applied to the rating of sports teams. Master's thesis, Bluefield College, 1997.

R. Mazumder, T. Hastie, and R. Tibshirani. Regularization methods for learning incomplete matrices. *arXiv*, 2009. http://arxiv.org/abs/0906.2034v1.

G. A. Miller. The magical number seven, plus or minus two: Some limits on our capacity for processing information. *Psychol. Rev.*, 101(2):343–352, 1956. doi: 10.1037/h0043158.

F. D. Murnaghan and A. Wintner. A canonical form for real matrices under orthogonal transformations. *PNAS*, 17 (7):417–420, 1931. http://www.pnas.org/content/17/7/417.full.pdf+html.

B. Recht, M. Fazel, and P. A. Parrilo. Guaranteed minimum-rank solutions of linear matrix equations via nuclear norm minimization. *SIAM Review*, 52(3):471–501, 2010. doi: 10.1137/070697835.

S. Rendle, L. Balby Marinho, A. Nanopoulos, and L. Schmidt-Thieme. Learning optimal ranking with tensor factorization for tag recommendation. In *KDD '09*, pages 727–736. ACM, 2009. doi: 10.1145/1557019.1557100.

T. L. Saaty. Rank according to Perron: A new insight. *Math. Mag*, 60(4):211–213, 1987. http://jstor.org/stable/2689340.

P.-N. Tan and R. Jin. Ordering patterns by combining opinions from multiple sources. In *KDD '04*, pages 695–700. ACM, 2004. doi: 10.1145/1014052.1014142.

R. Tibshirani. Regression shrinkage and selection via the lasso. *J. R. Stat. Soc. Ser. B Stat. Methodol.*, 58(1):267–288, 1996. http://www.jstor.org/stable/2346178.

K.-C. Toh and S. Yun. An accelerated proximal gradient algorithm for nuclear norm regularized linear least squares problems. *Opt. Online*, 2009. http://www.optimization-online.org/DB_FILE/2009/03/2268.pdf.

L. Vandenberghe and S. Boyd. Semidefinite programming. *SIAM Rev.*, 38(1):49–95, 1996. doi: 10.1137/1038003.

Large-Scale Matrix Factorization with Distributed Stochastic Gradient Descent

Rainer Gemulla[1] Peter J. Haas[2] Erik Nijkamp[2] Yannis Sismanis[2]

[1]Max-Planck-Institut für Informatik
Saarbrücken, Germany
rgemulla@mpi-inf.mpg.de

[2]IBM Almaden Research Center
San Jose, CA, USA
{phaas, enijkam, syannis}@us.ibm.com

ABSTRACT

We provide a novel algorithm to approximately factor large matrices with millions of rows, millions of columns, and billions of nonzero elements. Our approach rests on stochastic gradient descent (SGD), an iterative stochastic optimization algorithm. We first develop a novel "stratified" SGD variant (SSGD) that applies to general loss-minimization problems in which the loss function can be expressed as a weighted sum of "stratum losses." We establish sufficient conditions for convergence of SSGD using results from stochastic approximation theory and regenerative process theory. We then specialize SSGD to obtain a new matrix-factorization algorithm, called DSGD, that can be fully distributed and run on web-scale datasets using, e.g., MapReduce. DSGD can handle a wide variety of matrix factorizations. We describe the practical techniques used to optimize performance in our DSGD implementation. Experiments suggest that DSGD converges significantly faster and has better scalability properties than alternative algorithms.

Categories and Subject Descriptors

G.4 [**Mathematics of Computing**]: Mathematical Software—*Parallel and vector implementations*

General Terms

Algorithms, Experimentation, Performance

Keywords

distributed matrix factorization, stochastic gradient descent, MapReduce, recommendation system

1. INTRODUCTION

As Web 2.0 and enterprise-cloud applications proliferate, data mining algorithms need to be (re)designed to handle web-scale datasets. For this reason, low-rank matrix factorization has received much attention in recent years, since it is fundamental to a variety of mining tasks that are increasingly being applied to massive datasets [8, 12, 13, 15, 16]. Specifically, low-rank matrix factorizations are effective tools for analyzing "dyadic data" in order to discover and quantify the interactions between two given entities. Successful applications include topic detection and keyword search (where the corresponding entities are documents and terms), news personalization (users and stories), and recommendation systems (users and items). In large applications (see Sec. 2), these problems can involve matrices with millions of rows (e.g., distinct customers), millions of columns (e.g., distinct items), and billions of entries (e.g., transactions between customers and items). At such massive scales, distributed algorithms for matrix factorization are essential to achieving reasonable performance [8, 9, 16, 20]. In this paper, we provide a novel, effective distributed factorization algorithm based on stochastic gradient descent.

In practice, exact factorization is generally neither possible nor desired, so virtually all "matrix factorization" algorithms actually produce low-rank approximations, attempting to minimize a "loss function" that measures the discrepancy between the original input matrix and product of the factors returned by the algorithm; we use the term "matrix factorization" throughout to refer to such an approximation.

With the recent advent of programmer-friendly parallel processing frameworks such as MapReduce, web-scale matrix factorizations have become practicable and are of increasing interest to web companies, as well as other companies and enterprises that deal with massive data. To facilitate distributed processing, prior approaches would pick an embarrassingly parallel matrix factorization algorithm and implement it on a MapReduce cluster; the choice of algorithm was driven by the ease with which it could be distributed. In this paper, we take a different approach and start with an algorithm that is known to have good performance in non-parallel environments. Specifically, we start with stochastic gradient descent (SGD), an iterative optimization algorithm that has been shown, in a sequential setting, to be very effective for matrix factorization [13]. Although the generic SGD algorithm (Sec. 3) is not embarrassingly parallel and hence cannot directly scale to very large data, we can exploit the special structure of the factorization problem to obtain a version of SGD that is fully distributed and scales to extremely large matrices.

The key idea is to first develop (Sec. 4) a "stratified" variant of SGD, called SSGD, that is applicable to general loss-minimization problems in which the loss function $L(\theta)$ can be expressed as a weighted sum of "stratum losses," so that $L(\theta) = w_1 L_1(\theta) + \cdots + w_q L_q(\theta)$. At each iteration, the algorithm takes a downhill step with respect to one of the stratum losses L_s, i.e., approximately in the direction of the negative gradient $-L'_s(\theta)$. Although each such direction is "wrong" with respect to minimization of the overall loss L, we prove that, under appropriate regularity conditions, SSGD

KDD'11, August 21–24, 2011, San Diego, California, USA.

will converge to a good solution for L if the sequence of strata is chosen carefully. Our proof rests on stochastic approximation theory and regenerative process theory.

We then specialize SSGD to obtain a novel distributed matrix-factorization algorithm, called DSGD (Sec. 5). Specifically, we express the input matrix as a union of (possibly overlapping) pieces, called "strata." For each stratum, the stratum loss is defined as the loss computed over only the data points in the stratum (and appropriately scaled). The strata are carefully chosen so that each stratum has "d-monomial" structure, which allows SGD to be run on the stratum in a distributed manner. The DSGD algorithm repeatedly selects a stratum according to the general SSGD procedure and processes the stratum in a distributed fashion. Importantly, both matrix and factors are fully distributed, so that DSGD has low memory requirements and scales to matrices with millions of rows, millions of columns, and billions of nonzero elements. When DSGD is implemented in MapReduce (Sec. 6) and compared to state-of-the-art distributed algorithms for matrix factorization, our experiments (Sec. 7) suggest that DSGD converges significantly faster, and has better scalability.

Unlike many prior algorithms, DSGD is a generic algorithm in that it can be used for a variety of different loss functions. In this paper, we focus primarily on the class of factorizations that minimize a "nonzero loss." This class of loss functions is important for applications in which a zero represents missing data and hence should be ignored when computing loss. A typical motivation for factorization in this setting is to estimate the missing values, e.g., the rating that a customer would likely give to a previously unseen movie. See [10] for a treatment of other loss functions.

2. EXAMPLE AND PRIOR WORK

To gain understanding about applications of matrix factorizations, consider the "Netflix problem" [3] of recommending movies to customers. Netflix is a company that offers tens of thousands of movies for rental. The company has more than 15M customers, each of whom can provide feedback about their personal taste by rating movies with 1 to 5 stars. The feedback can be represented in a feedback matrix such as

$$\begin{array}{c} \\ \textit{Alice} \\ \textit{Bob} \\ \textit{Charlie} \end{array} \begin{array}{c} \begin{array}{ccc} \textit{Avatar} & \textit{The Matrix} & \textit{Up} \end{array} \\ \begin{pmatrix} ? & 4 & 2 \\ 3 & 2 & ? \\ 5 & ? & 3 \end{pmatrix} \end{array}.$$

Each entry may contain additional data, e.g., the date of rating or other forms of feedback such as click history. The goal of the factorization is to predict missing entries (denoted by "?"); entries with a high predicted rating are then recommended to users for viewing. This matrix-factorization approach to recommender systems has been successfully applied in practice; see [13] for an excellent discussion of the underlying intuition.

The traditional matrix factorization problem can be stated as follows. Given an $m \times n$ matrix $\boldsymbol{V}$ and a rank r, find an $m \times r$ matrix $\boldsymbol{W}$ and an $r \times n$ matrix $\boldsymbol{H}$ such that $\boldsymbol{V} = \boldsymbol{W}\boldsymbol{H}$. As discussed previously, our actual goal is to obtain a low-rank approximation $\boldsymbol{V} \approx \boldsymbol{W}\boldsymbol{H}$, where the quality of the approximation is described by an application-dependent loss function L. We seek to find

$$\underset{\boldsymbol{W},\boldsymbol{H}}{\operatorname{argmin}}\, L(\boldsymbol{V}, \boldsymbol{W}, \boldsymbol{H}),$$

i.e., the choice of $\boldsymbol{W}$ and $\boldsymbol{H}$ that give rise to the smallest loss. For example, assuming that missing ratings are coded with the value 0, loss functions for recommender systems are often based on the *nonzero squared loss* $L_{\text{NZSL}} = \sum_{i,j:\boldsymbol{V}_{ij} \neq 0} (\boldsymbol{V}_{ij} - [\boldsymbol{W}\boldsymbol{H}]_{ij})^2$ and usually incorporate regularization terms, user and movie biases, time drifts, and implicit feedback.

In the following, we restrict attention to loss functions that, like L_{NZSL}, can be decomposed into a sum of *local losses* over (a subset of) the entries in $\boldsymbol{V}_{ij}$. I.e., we require that the loss can be written as

$$L = \sum_{(i,j) \in Z} l(\boldsymbol{V}_{ij}, \boldsymbol{W}_{i*}, \boldsymbol{H}_{*j}) \qquad (1)$$

for some *training set* $Z \subseteq \{1, 2, \ldots, m\} \times \{1, 2, \ldots, n\}$ and *local loss function* l, where $\boldsymbol{A}_{i*}$ and $\boldsymbol{A}_{*j}$ denote row i and column j of matrix $\boldsymbol{A}$, respectively. Many loss functions used in practice—such as squared loss, generalized Kullback-Leibler divergence (GKL), and L_p regularization—can be decomposed in such a manner [19]. Note that a given loss function L can potentially be decomposed in multiple ways. In this paper, we focus primarily on the class of *nonzero decompositions*, in which $Z = \{(i,j) : \boldsymbol{V}_{ij} \neq 0\}$. As mentioned above, such decompositions naturally arise when zeros represent missing data. Our algorithms can handle other decompositions as well; see [10].

To compute $\boldsymbol{W}$ and $\boldsymbol{H}$ on MapReduce, all known algorithms start with some initial factors $\boldsymbol{W}_0$ and $\boldsymbol{H}_0$ and iteratively improve them. The $m \times n$ input matrix $\boldsymbol{V}$ is partitioned into $d_1 \times d_2$ blocks, which are distributed in the MapReduce cluster. Both row and column factors are blocked conformingly:

$$\begin{array}{c} \\ \boldsymbol{W}^1 \\ \boldsymbol{W}^2 \\ \vdots \\ \boldsymbol{W}^{d_1} \end{array} \begin{array}{c} \begin{array}{cccc} \boldsymbol{H}^1 & \boldsymbol{H}^2 & \cdots & \boldsymbol{H}^{d_2} \end{array} \\ \begin{pmatrix} \boldsymbol{V}^{11} & \boldsymbol{V}^{12} & \cdots & \boldsymbol{V}^{1d_2} \\ \boldsymbol{V}^{21} & \boldsymbol{V}^{22} & \cdots & \boldsymbol{V}^{2d_2} \\ \vdots & \vdots & \ddots & \vdots \\ \boldsymbol{V}^{d_1 1} & \boldsymbol{V}^{d_1 2} & \cdots & \boldsymbol{V}^{d_1 d_2} \end{pmatrix} \end{array},$$

where we use superscripts to refer to individual blocks. The algorithms are designed such that each block $\boldsymbol{V}^{ij}$ can be processed independently in the map phase, taking only the corresponding blocks of factors $\boldsymbol{W}^i$ and $\boldsymbol{H}^j$ as input. Some algorithms directly update the factors in the map phase (then either $d_1 = m$ or $d_2 = n$ to avoid overlap), whereas others aggregate the factor updates in a reduce phase.

Existing algorithms can be classified as *specialized algorithms*, which are designed for a particular loss, and *generic algorithms*, which work for a wide variety of loss functions. Specialized algorithms currently exist for only a small class of loss functions. For GKL loss, Das et al. [8] provide an EM-based algorithm, and Liu et al. [16] provide a multiplicative-update method. In [16], the latter MULT approach is also applied to squared loss and to nonnegative matrix factorization with an "exponential" loss function. Each of these algorithms in essence takes an embarrassingly parallel matrix factorization algorithm developed previously and directly distributes it across the MapReduce cluster. Zhou et al. [20] show how to distribute the well-known alternating least squares (ALS) algorithm to handle factorization problems with a nonzero squared loss function and an optional weighted L_2 regularization term. Their approach requires a double-partitioning of $\boldsymbol{V}$: once by row and once by column. Moreover, ALS requires that each of the factor matrices $\boldsymbol{W}$ and $\boldsymbol{H}$ can (alternately) fit in main memory. See [10] for details on the foregoing algorithms.

Generic algorithms are able to handle all differentiable loss functions that decompose into summation form. A simple approach is distributed gradient descent (DGD) [9, 11, 17], which distributes gradient computation across a compute cluster, and then performs centralized parameter updates using, for example, quasi-Newton methods such as L-BFGS-B [6]. Partitioned SGD approaches make use of a similar idea: SGD is run independently and in parallel on partitions of the dataset, and parameters are averaged after each pass over the data (PSGD [11, 18]) or once at the end (ISGD [17, 18, 21]). These approaches have not been applied to matrix factorization before. Similarly to L-BFGS-B, they exhibit slow convergence in practice (see Sec. 7) and need to store the full factor matrices in memory. This latter limitation can be a serious drawback: for large factorization problems, it is crucial that both matrix and factors be distributed. Our present work on DSGD is a first step towards such a *fully distributed* generic algorithm with good convergence properties.

3. STOCHASTIC GRADIENT DESCENT

In this section, we discuss how to factorize a given matrix via standard SGD. We also establish basic properties of this stochastic procedure.

3.1 Preliminaries

The goal of SGD is to find the value $\theta^* \in \Re^k$ ($k \geq 1$) that minimizes a given loss $L(\theta)$. The algorithm makes use of noisy observations $\hat{L}'(\theta)$ of $L'(\theta)$, the function's gradient with respect to θ. Starting with some initial value θ_0, SGD refines the parameter value by iterating the stochastic difference equation

$$\theta_{n+1} = \theta_n - \epsilon_n \hat{L}'(\theta_n), \tag{2}$$

where n denotes the step number and $\{\epsilon_n\}$ is a sequence of decreasing step sizes. Since $-L'(\theta_n)$ is the direction of steepest descent, (2) constitutes a noisy version of gradient descent.

Stochastic approximation theory can be used to show that, under certain regularity conditions [14], the noise in the gradient estimates "averages out" and SGD converges to the set of stationary points satisfying $L'(\theta) = 0$. Of course, these stationary points can be minima, maxima, or saddle points. One may argue that convergence to a maximum or saddle point is unlikely because the noise in the gradient estimates reduces the likelihood of getting stuck at such a point. Thus $\{\theta_n\}$ typically converges to a (local) minimum of L. A variety of methods can be used to increase the likelihood of finding a global minimum, e.g., running SGD multiple times, starting from a variety of initial solutions.

In practice, one often makes use of an additional projection Π_H that keeps the iterate in a given constraint set H. For example, there is considerable interest in nonnegative matrix factorizations [15], which corresponds to setting $H = \{\,\theta : \theta \geq 0\,\}$. The projected algorithm takes the form

$$\theta_{n+1} = \Pi_H\big[\theta_n - \epsilon_n \hat{L}'(\theta_n)\big]. \tag{3}$$

In addition to the set of stationary points, the projected process may converge to the set of "chain recurrent" points [14], which are influenced by the boundary of the constraint set H.

3.2 SGD for Matrix Factorization

To apply SGD to matrix factorization, we set $\theta = (\boldsymbol{W}, \boldsymbol{H})$ and decompose the loss L as in (1) for an appropriate training set Z and local loss function l. Denote by $L_z(\theta) = L_{ij}(\theta) = l(\boldsymbol{V}_{ij}, \boldsymbol{W}_{i*}, \boldsymbol{H}_{*j})$ the local loss at position $z = (i,j)$. Then $L'(\theta) = \sum_z L'_z(\theta)$ by the sum rule for differentiation. DGD methods (see Sec. 2) exploit the summation form of $L'(\theta)$ at each iteration by computing the local gradients $L'_z(\theta)$ in parallel and summing them. In contrast to this exact computation of the overall gradient, SGD obtains noisy gradient estimates by scaling up *just one* of the local gradients, i.e., $\hat{L}'(\theta) = NL'_z(\theta)$, where $N = |Z|$ and the training point z is chosen randomly from the training set. Algorithm 1 uses SGD to perform matrix factorization.

Algorithm 1 SGD for Matrix Factorization

Require: A training set Z, initial values $\boldsymbol{W}_0$ and $\boldsymbol{H}_0$
  while not converged **do** /* *step* */
    Select a training point $(i,j) \in Z$ uniformly at random.
    $\boldsymbol{W}'_{i*} \leftarrow \boldsymbol{W}_{i*} - \epsilon_n N \frac{\partial}{\partial \boldsymbol{W}_{i*}} l(\boldsymbol{V}_{ij}, \boldsymbol{W}_{i*}, \boldsymbol{H}_{*j})$
    $\boldsymbol{H}_{*j} \leftarrow \boldsymbol{H}_{*j} - \epsilon_n N \frac{\partial}{\partial \boldsymbol{H}_{*j}} l(\boldsymbol{V}_{ij}, \boldsymbol{W}_{i*}, \boldsymbol{H}_{*j})$
    $\boldsymbol{W}_{i*} \leftarrow \boldsymbol{W}'_{i*}$
  end while

Note that, after selecting a random training point $(i,j) \in Z$, we need to update only $\boldsymbol{W}_{i*}$ and $\boldsymbol{H}_{*j}$, and do not need to update factors of the form $\boldsymbol{W}_{i'*}$ for $i' \neq i$ or $\boldsymbol{H}_{*j'}$ for $j' \neq j$. This computational savings follows from our representation of the global loss as a sum of local losses. Specifically, we have used the fact that

$$\frac{\partial}{\partial \boldsymbol{W}_{i'k}} L_{ij}(\boldsymbol{W}, \boldsymbol{H}) = \begin{cases} 0 & \text{if } i \neq i' \\ \frac{\partial}{\partial \boldsymbol{W}_{ik}} l(\boldsymbol{V}_{ij}, \boldsymbol{W}_{i*}, \boldsymbol{H}_{*j}) & \text{otherwise} \end{cases} \tag{4}$$

and

$$\frac{\partial}{\partial \boldsymbol{H}_{kj'}} L_{ij}(\boldsymbol{W}, \boldsymbol{H}) = \begin{cases} 0 & \text{if } j \neq j' \\ \frac{\partial}{\partial \boldsymbol{H}_{kj}} l(\boldsymbol{V}_{ij}, \boldsymbol{W}_{i*}, \boldsymbol{H}_{*j}) & \text{otherwise} \end{cases} \tag{5}$$

for $1 \leq k \leq r$. SGD is sometimes referred to as *online learning* or *sequential gradient descent* [4]. Batched versions, in which multiple local losses are averaged, are also feasible but often have inferior performance in practice.

One might wonder why replacing exact gradients (GD) by noisy estimates (SGD) can be beneficial. The main reason is that exact gradient computation is costly, whereas noisy estimates are quick and easy to obtain. In a given amount of time, we can perform many quick-and-dirty SGD updates instead of a few, carefully planned GD steps. The noisy process also helps in escaping local minima (especially those with a small basin of attraction and more so in the beginning, when the step sizes are large). Moreover, SGD is able to exploit repetition within the data. Parameter updates based on data from a certain row or column will also decrease the loss in similar rows and columns. Thus the more similarity there is, the better SGD performs. Ultimately, the hope is that the increased number of steps leads to faster convergence. This behavior can be proven for some problems [5], and it has been observed in the case of large-scale matrix factorization [13].

4. STRATIFIED SGD

In this section we develop a general stratified stochastic gradient descent (SSGD) algorithm, and give sufficient conditions for convergence. In Sec. 5 we specialize SSGD to obtain an efficient distributed algorithm (DSGD) for matrix factorization.

4.1 The SSGD Algorithm

In SSGD, the loss function $L(\theta)$ is decomposed into a weighted sum of q (> 1) "local" loss functions:

$$L(\theta) = w_1 L_1(\theta) + w_2 L_2(\theta) + \ldots + w_q L_q(\theta), \tag{6}$$

where we assume without loss of generality that $0 < w_s \leq 1$ and $\sum w_s = 1$. We refer to index s as a *stratum*, L_s as the *stratum loss* for stratum s, and w_s as the *weight* of stratum s. In practice, a stratum often corresponds to a part or partition of some underlying dataset. In this case, one can think of L_s as the loss incurred on the respective partition; the overall loss is obtained by summing up the per-partition losses. In general, however, the decomposition of L can be arbitrary; there may or may not be an underlying data partitioning. Also note that there is some freedom in the choice of the w_s; they may be altered to arbitrary values (subject to the constraints above) by appropriately rescaling the stratum loss functions. This freedom gives room for optimization.

SSGD runs standard stochastic gradient descent on a single stratum at a time, but switches strata in a way that guarantees correctness. The algorithm can be described as follows. Suppose that there is a (potentially random) *stratum sequence* $\{\gamma_n\}$, where each γ_n takes values in $\{1,\ldots,q\}$ and determines the stratum to use in the nth iteration. Using a noisy observation $\hat{L}'_{\gamma_n}$ of the gradient L'_{γ_n}, we obtain the update rule $\theta_{n+1} = \Pi_H\big[\theta_n - \epsilon_n \hat{L}'_{\gamma_n}(\theta_n)\big]$. The sequence $\{\gamma_n\}$ has to be chosen carefully to establish convergence to the stationary (or chain-recurrent) points of L. Indeed, because each step of the algorithm proceeds approximately in the "wrong" direction, i.e., $-L'_{\gamma_n}(\theta_n)$ rather than $-L'(\theta_n)$, it is not obvious that the algorithm will converge at all. We show in Sec. 4.2 and 4.3, however, that SSGD will indeed converge under appropriate regularity conditions provided that, in essence, the "time" spent on each stratum is proportional to its weight.

4.2 Convergence of SSGD

Appropriate sufficient conditions for the convergence of SSGD can be obtained from general results on stochastic approximation in Kushner and Yin [14, Sec. 5.6]. We distinguish step-size conditions, loss conditions, stratification conditions, and stratum-sequence conditions. Step-size conditions involve the sequence $\{\epsilon_n\}$: It has to approach 0 at the "right speed" in that $\epsilon_n \to 0$, $\sum_{i=1}^n \epsilon_i \to \infty$, and $\sum_{i=0}^n \epsilon_i^2 < \infty$ as $n \to \infty$. I.e., ϵ_n approaches 0 slowly enough so that the algorithm does not get stuck far away from the optimum, but fast enough to ensure convergence. The simplest valid choice is $\epsilon_n = 1/n$. A sufficient set of loss conditions is that the constraint set H in which L is defined is a hyperrectangle and that L is bounded and twice continuously differentiable on H.[1] Regarding stratification, we require that the estimates $\hat{L}'_s(\theta)$ of the gradient $L'_s(\theta)$ of stratum s are unbiased, have bounded second moment for $\theta \in H$, and do not depend on the past. See [10] for a more precise statement of these conditions, which are satisfied in most matrix factorization problems. Finally, we give a sufficient condition on the stratum sequence.

CONDITION 1. *The step sizes satisfy* $(\epsilon_n - \epsilon_{n+1})/\epsilon_n = O(\epsilon_n)$ *and the* γ_n *are chosen such that the directions "average out correctly" in the sense that, for any* $\theta \in H$,

$$\lim_{n\to\infty} \epsilon_n \sum_{i=0}^{n-1} [L'_{\gamma_i}(\theta) - L'(\theta)] = 0$$

almost surely.

For example, if ϵ_n were equal to $1/n$, then the n-th term would represent the empirical average deviation from the true gradient over the first n steps.

If all conditions hold, then the sequence $\{\theta_n\}$ converges almost surely to the set of limit points of the "projected ODE"

$$\dot{\theta} = -L'(\theta) + z$$

in H, taken over all initial conditions. Here, z is the minimum force to keep the solution in H [14, Sec. 4.3]. As shown in [14], the limit points consist of the set of stationary points of L in H ($z = 0$), as well as a set of chain-recurrent points on the boundary of H ($z \neq 0$). In our setting, the limit point to which SSGD converges is typically a good local minimum of the loss function (Sec. 7), and the crux of showing that SSGD converges is showing that Condition 1 holds. We address this issue next.

4.3 Conditions for Stratum Selection

The following result gives sufficient conditions on $L(\theta)$, the step sizes $\{\epsilon_n\}$, and the stratum sequence $\{\gamma_n\}$ such that Condition 1 holds. Our key assumption is that the sequence $\{\gamma_n\}$ is *regenerative* [2, Ch. VI], in that there exists an increasing sequence of almost-surely finite random indices $0 = \beta(0) < \beta(1) < \beta(2) < \cdots$ that serves to decompose $\{\gamma_n\}$ into consecutive, independent and identically distributed (i.i.d.) cycles $\{C_k\}$,[2] with $C_k = \{\gamma_{\beta(k-1)}, \gamma_{\beta(k-1)+1}, \ldots, \gamma_{\beta(k)-1}\}$ for $k \geq 1$. I.e., at each $\beta(i)$, the stratum is selected according to a probability distribution that is independent of past selections, and the future sequence of selections after step $\beta(i)$ looks probabilistically identical to the sequence of selections after step $\beta(0)$. The length τ_k of the kth cycle is given by $\tau_k = \beta(k) - \beta(k-1)$. Letting $I_{\gamma_n = s}$ be the indicator variable for the event that stratum s is chosen in the nth step, set $X_k(s) = \sum_{n=\beta(k-1)}^{\beta(k)-1} (I_{\gamma_n = s} - w_s)$ for $1 \leq s \leq q$. It follows from the regenerative property that the pairs $\{(X_k(s), \tau_k)\}$ are i.i.d. for each s. The following theorem asserts that, under regularity conditions, we may pick any regenerative sequence γ_n such that $\mathrm{E}[X_1(s)] = 0$ for all strata.

THEOREM 1. *Suppose that* $L(\theta)$ *is differentiable on* H *and* $\sup_{\theta\in H} |L'_s(\theta)| < \infty$ *for* $1 \leq s \leq q$ *and* $\theta \in H$. *Also suppose that* $\epsilon_n = O(n^{-\alpha})$ *for some* $\alpha \in (0.5, 1]$ *and that* $(\epsilon_n - \epsilon_{n+1})/\epsilon_n = O(\epsilon_n)$. *Finally, suppose that* $\{\gamma_n\}$ *is regenerative with* $\mathrm{E}[\tau_1^{1/\alpha}] < \infty$ *and* $\mathrm{E}[X_1(s)] = 0$ *for* $1 \leq s \leq q$. *Then Condition 1 holds.*

The condition $\mathrm{E}[X_1(s)] = 0$ essentially requires that, for each stratum s, the expected fraction of visits to s in a cycle equals w_s. By the strong law of large numbers for regenerative processes [2, Sec. VI.3], this condition—in the presence of the finite-moment condition on τ_1—is equivalent to requiring that the long-term fraction of visits to s equals w_s. The finite-moment condition is typically satisfied whenever the number of successive steps taken within a stratum is bounded with probability 1.

PROOF. Fix $\theta \in H$ and observe that

$$\epsilon_n \sum_{i=0}^{n-1} (L'_{\gamma_i}(\theta) - L'(\theta)) = \epsilon_n \sum_{i=0}^{n-1} \sum_{s=1}^{q} (L'_s(\theta) I_{\gamma_i = s} - L'_s(\theta) w_s)$$
$$= \sum_{s=1}^{q} L'_s(\theta) \epsilon_n \sum_{i=0}^{n-1} (I_{\gamma_i = s} - w_s).$$

Since $|L'_s(\theta)| < \infty$ for each s, it suffices to show that $n^{-\alpha} \sum_{i=0}^{n-1} (I_{\gamma_i = s} - w_s) \xrightarrow{\text{a.s.}} 0$ for $1 \leq s \leq q$. To this end, fix s and denote by $c(n)$ the (random) number of complete cycles up to step n. We have $\sum_{i=0}^{n} (I_{\gamma_i = s} - w_s) = \sum_{k=1}^{c(n)} X_k(s) + R_{1,n}$, where $R_{1,n} = \sum_{i=\beta(c(n))}^{n} (I_{\gamma_i = s} - w_s)$. I.e., the sum can be broken up into sums over complete cycles plus a remainder term corresponding to a sum over a partially completed cycle. Similar calculations let us write $n = \sum_{k=1}^{c(n)} \tau_k + R_{2,n}$, where $R_{2,n} = n - \beta(c(n)) + 1$.

[1]Points at which the loss is non-differentiable may arise in matrix factorization, e.g., when l_1-regularization is used. SSGD can handle with this phenomenon using "subgradients" [14, Sec. 5.6].

[2]The cycles need not directly correspond to strata. Indeed, we make use of strategies in which a cycle comprises multiple strata.

Thus

$$\frac{\sum_{i=0}^{n}(I_{\gamma_i=s}-w_s)}{n^\alpha}=\frac{\sum_{k=1}^{c(n)}X_k(s)+R_{1,n}}{\left(\sum_{k=1}^{c(n)}\tau_k+R_{2,n}\right)^\alpha}$$
$$=\frac{\sum_{k=1}^{c(n)}X_k(s)}{c(n)^\alpha}\left(\frac{\sum_{k=1}^{c(n)}\tau_k}{c(n)}+\frac{R_{2,n}}{c(n)}\right)^{-\alpha}$$
$$+\frac{R_{1,n}/c(n)^\alpha}{\left(\sum_{k=1}^{c(n)}\tau_k/c(n)+R_{2,n}/c(n)\right)^\alpha}. \tag{7}$$

By assumption, the random variables $\{X_k(s)\}$ are i.i.d. with common mean 0. Moreover, $|X_k(s)| \le (1+w_s)\tau_k$, which implies that $\mathrm{E}\,[\,|X_1(s)|^{1/\alpha}\,] \le (1+w_s)^{1/\alpha}\,\mathrm{E}\,[\,\tau_1^{1/\alpha}\,] < \infty$. It then follows from the Marcinkiewicz-Zygmund strong law of large numbers [7, Th. 5.2.2] that $n^{-\alpha}\sum_{k=1}^{n}X_k(s) \xrightarrow{\text{a.s.}} 0$. Because each regeneration point, and hence each cycle length, is assumed to be almost surely finite, it follows that $c(n) \xrightarrow{\text{a.s.}} \infty$, so that $\sum_{k=1}^{c(n)}X_k(s)/c(n)^\alpha \xrightarrow{\text{a.s.}} 0$ as $n \to \infty$. Similarly, an application of the ordinary strong law of large numbers shows that $\sum_{k=1}^{c(n)}\tau_k/c(n) \xrightarrow{\text{a.s.}} \mathrm{E}\,[\,\tau_1\,] > 0$. Next, note that $|R_{1,n}| \le (1+w_s)\tau_{c(n)+1}$, so that $R_{1,n}/c(n)^\alpha \xrightarrow{\text{a.s.}} 0$ provided that $\tau_k/k^\alpha \xrightarrow{\text{a.s.}} 0$. This latter limit result follows from a Borel-Cantelli argument; see [10] for details. A similar argument shows that $R_{2,n}/c(n) \xrightarrow{\text{a.s.}} 0$, and the desired result follows after letting $n \to \infty$ in the rightmost expression in (7). □

The conditions on $\{\epsilon_n\}$ in Theorem 1 are often satisfied in practice, e.g., when $\epsilon_n = 1/n$ or when $\epsilon_n = 1/\lceil n/k \rceil$ for some $k > 1$ with $\lceil x \rceil$ denoting the smallest integer greater than or equal to x (so that the step size remains constant for some fixed number of steps, as in Algorithm 2 below). Similarly, a wide variety of strata-selection schemes satisfy the conditions of Theorem 1. Examples include (1) running precisely cw_s steps on stratum s in every "chunk" of c steps, and (2) repeatedly picking a stratum according to some fixed distribution $\{\,p_s > 0\,\}$ and running cw_s/p_s steps on the selected stratum s. Certain schemes in which the number of steps per stratum is random are also covered by Theorem 1; see [10]. In Sec. 6, we discuss variants on these schemes that are particularly suitable for practical implementation in the context of DSGD.

5. THE DSGD ALGORITHM

Classic, sequential SGD as in Sec. 3 cannot be used directly for rank-r factorization of web-scale matrices. We can, however, exploit the structure of the matrix factorization problem to derive a scalable distributed SGD algorithm. The idea is to specialize the SSGD algorithm, choosing the strata such that SGD can be run on each stratum in a distributed manner. We first discuss the "interchangeability" structure that we will exploit for distributed processing within a stratum.

5.1 Interchangeability

In general, distributing SGD is hard because the individual steps depend on each other: from (3), we see that θ_n has to be known before θ_{n+1} can be computed. However, in the case of matrix factorization, the SGD process has some structure that we can exploit. We focus throughout on loss-minimization problems of the form $\text{minimize}_{\theta\in H}\, L(\theta)$ where the loss function L has *summation form*: $L(\theta) = \sum_{z\in Z} L_z(\theta)$.

DEFINITION 1. *Two training points* $z_1, z_2 \in Z$ *are* interchangeable *with respect to a loss function* L *having summation form if for all* $\theta \in H$*, and* $\epsilon > 0$,

$$L'_{z_1}(\theta) = L'_{z_1}(\theta - \epsilon L'_{z_2}(\theta))$$
$$\textit{and} \quad L'_{z_2}(\theta) = L'_{z_2}(\theta - \epsilon L'_{z_1}(\theta)). \tag{8}$$

Two disjoint sets of training points $Z_1, Z_2 \subset Z$ *are interchangeable with respect to* L *if* z_1 *and* z_2 *are interchangeable for every* $z_1 \in Z_1$ *and* $z_2 \in Z_2$.

As described in Sec. 5.2 below, we can swap the order of consecutive SGD steps that involve interchangeable training points without affecting the final outcome.

Now we return to the setting of matrix factorization, where the loss function has the form $L(\boldsymbol{W},\boldsymbol{H}) = \sum_{(i,j)\in Z} L_{ij}(\boldsymbol{W},\boldsymbol{H})$ with $L_{ij}(\boldsymbol{W},\boldsymbol{H}) = l(\boldsymbol{V}_{ij},\boldsymbol{W}_{i*},\boldsymbol{H}_{*j})$. The following theorem gives a simple criterion for interchangeability, and follows directly from (4) and (5); see [10] for more details.

THEOREM 2. *Two training points* $z_1 = (i_1, j_1) \in Z$ *and* $z_2 = (i_2, j_2) \in Z$ *are interchangeable with respect to any loss function* L *having summation form if they share neither row nor column, i.e.,* $i_1 \ne i_2$ *and* $j_1 \ne j_2$.

It follows that if two blocks of $\boldsymbol{V}$ share neither rows or columns, then the sets of training points contained in these blocks are interchangeable.

5.2 A Simple Case

We introduce the DSGD algorithm by considering a simple case that essentially corresponds to running DSGD using a single "d-monomial" stratum (see Sec. 5.3). The goal is to highlight the technique by which DSGD runs the SGD algorithm in a distributed manner within a stratum. For a given training set Z, denote by $\boldsymbol{Z}$ the corresponding *training matrix*, which is obtained by zeroing out the elements in $\boldsymbol{V}$ that are not in Z; these elements usually represent missing data or held-out data for validation. In our simple scenario, Z corresponds to our single stratum of interest, and the corresponding training matrix $\boldsymbol{Z}$ is block-diagonal:

$$\begin{array}{c} \\ \boldsymbol{W}^1 \\ \boldsymbol{W}^2 \\ \vdots \\ \boldsymbol{W}^d \end{array}
\begin{array}{c} \begin{array}{cccc} \boldsymbol{H}^1 & \boldsymbol{H}^2 & \cdots & \boldsymbol{H}^d \end{array} \\
\begin{pmatrix} \boldsymbol{Z}^1 & 0 & \cdots & 0 \\ 0 & \boldsymbol{Z}^2 & \cdots & \vdots \\ \vdots & \vdots & \ddots & 0 \\ 0 & \cdots & 0 & \boldsymbol{Z}^d \end{pmatrix} \end{array}, \tag{9}$$

where $\boldsymbol{W}$ and $\boldsymbol{H}$ are blocked conformingly. Denote by Z^b the set of training points in block $\boldsymbol{Z}^b$. We exploit the key property that, by Th. 2, sets Z^i and Z^j are interchangeable for $i \ne j$. For some $T \in [1,\infty)$, suppose that we run T steps of SGD on $\boldsymbol{Z}$, starting from some initial point $\theta_0 = (\boldsymbol{W}_0, \boldsymbol{H}_0)$ and using a fixed step size ϵ. We can describe an instance of the SGD process by a *training sequence* $\omega = (z_0, z_1, \ldots, z_{T-1})$ of T training points. Define $\theta_0(\omega) = \theta_0$ and $\theta_{n+1}(\omega) = \theta_n(\omega) + \epsilon Y_n(\omega)$, where the update term $Y_n(\omega) = -NL'_{\omega_n}(\theta_n(\omega))$ is the scaled negative gradient estimate as in standard SGD. We can write

$$\theta_T(\omega) = \theta_0 + \epsilon\sum_{n=0}^{T-1} Y_n(\omega). \tag{10}$$

To see how to exploit the interchangeability structure, consider the subsequence $\sigma_b(\omega) = \omega \cap Z^b$ of training points from block $\boldsymbol{Z}^b$; the subsequence has length $T_b(\omega) = |\sigma_b(\omega)|$. The following theorem asserts that we can run SGD on each block independently, and then sum up the results.

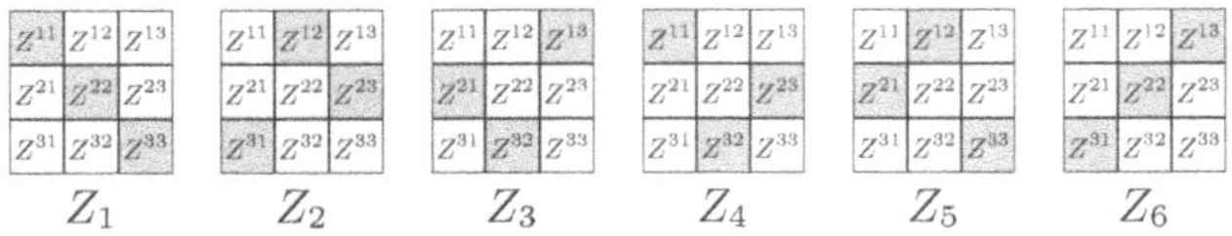

Figure 1: Strata for a 3×3 blocking of training matrix $\boldsymbol{Z}$

THEOREM 3. *Using the definitions above,*

$$\theta_T(\omega) = \theta_0 + \epsilon \sum_{b=1}^{d} \sum_{k=0}^{T_b(\omega)-1} Y_k(\sigma_b(\omega)). \tag{11}$$

See [10] for a complete proof. The idea is to repeatedly invoke Th. 2 and Def. 1 to show that, if the mth training point in the combined sequence corresponds to the kth training point from block $\boldsymbol{Z}^b$, then the update terms coincide: $Y_m(\omega) = Y_k(\sigma_b(\omega))$. Applying this result to all of the blocks establishes a one-to-one correspondence between the update terms in (10) and in (11).

We now describe how to exploit Theorem 3 for distributed processing on MapReduce. We block $\boldsymbol{W}$ and $\boldsymbol{H}$ conformingly to $\boldsymbol{Z}$—as in (9)—and divide processing into d independent map tasks $\Gamma_1, \ldots, \Gamma_d$ as follows. Task Γ_b is responsible for subsequence $\sigma_b(\omega)$: It takes $\boldsymbol{Z}^b$, $\boldsymbol{W}^b$, and $\boldsymbol{H}^b$ as input, performs the block-local updates $\sigma_b(\omega)$, and outputs updated[3] factor matrices $\boldsymbol{W}^b_{\text{new}}$ and $\boldsymbol{H}^b_{\text{new}}$. By Theorem 3, we have $\boldsymbol{W}' = (\boldsymbol{W}^1_{\text{new}} \cdots \boldsymbol{W}^d_{\text{new}})^{\mathrm{T}}$ and $\boldsymbol{H}' = (\boldsymbol{H}^1_{\text{new}} \cdots \boldsymbol{H}^d_{\text{new}})$, where $\boldsymbol{W}'$ and $\boldsymbol{H}'$ are the matrices that one would obtain by running sequential SGD on ω. Since each task accesses different parts of both training data and factor matrices, the data can be distributed across multiple nodes and the tasks can run simultaneously.

In the foregoing development, we used the fact that $\boldsymbol{Z}$ is block-diagonal only to establish interchangeability between blocks. This means that Theorem 3 and the resulting distributed SGD scheme also applies when the matrix is not block-diagonal, but can be divided into a set of interchangeable submatrices in some other way. We now exploit this fact to obtain the overall DSGD algorithm.

5.3 The General Case

We now present the complete DSGD matrix-factorization algorithm. The key idea is to stratify the training set Z into a set $S = \{ Z_1, \ldots, Z_q \}$ of q strata so that each individual stratum $Z_s \subseteq Z$ can be processed in a distributed fashion. We do this by ensuring that each stratum is "d-monomial" as defined below. The d-monomial property generalizes the block-diagonal structure of the example in Sec. 5.2, while still permitting the techniques of that section to be applied. The strata must *cover* the training set in that $\bigcup_{s=1}^{q} Z_s = Z$, but overlapping strata are allowed. The parallelism parameter d is chosen to be greater than or equal to the number of available processing tasks.

DEFINITION 2. *A stratum Z_s is d-*monomial *if it can be partitioned into d nonempty subsets $Z_s^1, Z_s^2, \ldots, Z_s^d$ such that $i \neq i'$ and $j \neq j'$ whenever $(i,j) \in Z_s^{b_1}$ and $(i',j') \in Z_s^{b_2}$ with $b_1 \neq b_2$. A training matrix $\boldsymbol{Z}_s$ is d-*monomial *if it is constructed from a d-monomial stratum Z_s.*

There are many ways to stratify the training set according to Def. 2. In our current work, we perform *data-independent blocking*; more advanced strategies may improve the speed of convergence further. We first randomly permute the rows and columns of $\boldsymbol{Z}$, and then create $d \times d$ blocks of size $(m/d) \times (n/d)$ each; the factor matrices $\boldsymbol{W}$ and $\boldsymbol{H}$ are blocked conformingly. This procedure ensures that the expected number of training points in each of the blocks is the same, namely, N/d^2. Then, for a permutation $j_1, j_2, \ldots, j_d$ of $1, 2, \ldots, d$, we can define a stratum as $Z_s = Z^{1j_1} \cup Z^{2j_2} \cup \cdots \cup Z^{dj_d}$, where the *substratum* Z^{ij} denotes the set of training points that fall within block $\boldsymbol{Z}^{ij}$. Thus a stratum corresponds to a set of blocks; Fig. 1 shows the set of possible strata when $d = 3$. In general, the set S of possible strata contains $d!$ elements, one for each possible permutation of $1, 2, \ldots, d$. Note that different strata may overlap when $d > 2$. Also note that there is no need to materialize these strata: They are constructed on-the-fly by processing only the respective blocks of $\boldsymbol{Z}$.

Given a set of strata and associated weights $\{w_s\}$, we decompose the loss into a weighted sum of per-stratum losses as in (6): $L(\boldsymbol{W}, \boldsymbol{H}) = \sum_{s=1}^{q} w_s L_s(\boldsymbol{W}, \boldsymbol{H})$. (As in Sec. 3.2, we suppress the fixed matrix $\boldsymbol{V}$ in our notation for loss functions.) We use per-stratum losses of form

$$L_s(\boldsymbol{W}, \boldsymbol{H}) = c_s \sum_{(i,j) \in Z_s} L_{ij}(\boldsymbol{W}, \boldsymbol{H}), \tag{12}$$

where c_s is a stratum-specific constant; see the discussion below. When running SGD on a stratum, we use the gradient estimate

$$\hat{L}'_s(\boldsymbol{W}, \boldsymbol{H}) = N_s c_s L'_{ij}(\boldsymbol{W}, \boldsymbol{H}) \tag{13}$$

of $L'_s(\boldsymbol{W}, \boldsymbol{H})$ in each step, i.e., we scale up the local loss of an individual training point by the size $N_s = |Z_s|$ of the stratum. For example, from the $d!$ strata described previously, we can select d disjoint strata $Z_1, Z_2, \ldots, Z_d$ such that they cover Z; e.g., strata Z_1, Z_2, and Z_3 in Fig. 1. Then any given loss function L of the form (1) can be represented as a weighted sum over these strata by choosing w_s and c_s subject to $w_s c_s = 1$. Recall that w_s can be interpreted as the "time" spent on each stratum in the long run. A natural choice is to set $w_s = N_s/N$, i.e., proportional to the stratum size. This particular choice leads to $c_s = N/N_s$ and we obtain the standard SGD gradient estimator $\hat{L}'_s(\boldsymbol{W}, \boldsymbol{H}) = N L'_{ij}(\boldsymbol{W}, \boldsymbol{H})$. As another example, we can represent L as a weighted sum in terms of all $d!$ strata; in light of the fact that each substratum Z^{ij} lies in exactly $(d-1)!$ of these strata, we choose $w_s = N_s/\big((d-1)!N\big)$ and use the value of $c_s = N/N_s$ as before.

The individual steps in DSGD are grouped into *subepochs*, each of which amounts to processing one of the strata. In more detail, DSGD makes use of a sequence $\{(\xi_k, T_k)\}$, where ξ_k denotes the *stratum selector* used in the kth subepoch, and T_k the number of steps to run on the selected stratum. Note that this sequence of pairs uniquely determines an SSGD stratum sequence as in Sec. 4.1: $\gamma_1 = \cdots = \gamma_{T_1} = \xi_1$, $\gamma_{T_1+1} = \cdots = \gamma_{T_1+T_2} = \xi_2$, and so forth. The $\{(\xi_k, T_k)\}$ sequence is chosen such that the underlying SSGD algorithm, and hence the DSGD factorization algorithm, is guaranteed to converge; see Sec. 4.3. Once a stratum ξ_k has been selected, we perform T_k SGD steps on Z_{ξ_k}; this is done in a parallel and distributed way using the technique of Sec. 5.2. DSGD is shown as Algorithm 2, where we define an *epoch* as a sequence of d subepochs. As will become evident in Sec. 6 below, an epoch roughly corresponds to processing the entire training set once.

When executing DSGD on d nodes in a shared-nothing environment such as MapReduce, we only distribute the input matrix once. Then the only data that are transmitted between nodes during subsequent processing are (small) blocks of factor matrices. In our implementation, node i stores blocks $\boldsymbol{W}^i, \boldsymbol{Z}^{i1}, \boldsymbol{Z}^{i2}, \ldots, \boldsymbol{Z}^{id}$ for $1 \leq i \leq d$; thus only matrices $\boldsymbol{H}^1, \boldsymbol{H}^2, \ldots, \boldsymbol{H}^d$ need be transmitted. (If the $\boldsymbol{W}^i$ matrices are smaller, then we transmit these instead.)

[3] Since training data is sparse, a block $\boldsymbol{Z}^b$ may contain no training points; in this case we cannot execute SGD on the block, so the corresponding factors simply remain at their initial values.

Algorithm 2 DSGD for Matrix Factorization

Require: $\boldsymbol{Z}, \boldsymbol{W}_0, \boldsymbol{H}_0$, cluster size d
  $\boldsymbol{W} \leftarrow \boldsymbol{W}_0$ and $\boldsymbol{H} \leftarrow \boldsymbol{H}_0$
  Block $\boldsymbol{Z}$ / $\boldsymbol{W}$ / $\boldsymbol{H}$ into $d \times d$ / $d \times 1$ / $1 \times d$ blocks
  while not converged **do** /* *epoch* */
    Pick step size ϵ
    for $s = 1, \ldots, d$ **do** /* *subepoch* */
      Pick d blocks $\{\boldsymbol{Z}^{1j_1}, \ldots, \boldsymbol{Z}^{dj_d}\}$ to form a stratum
      for $b = 1, \ldots, d$ **do** /* *in parallel* */
        Run SGD on the training points in $\boldsymbol{Z}^{bj_b}$ (step size $= \epsilon$)
      end for
    end for
  end while

Since, by construction, parallel processing within the kth selected stratum leads to the same update terms as for the corresponding sequential SGD algorithm on Z_{ξ_k}, we have established the connection between DSGD and SSGD. Thus the convergence of DSGD is implied by the convergence of the underlying SSGD algorithm.

6. DSGD IMPLEMENTATION

In this section, we discuss practical methods for choosing the training sequence for the parallel SGD step, selecting strata, and picking the step size ϵ. As above, a "subepoch" corresponds to processing a stratum and an "epoch"—roughly equivalent to a complete pass through the training data—corresponds to processing a sequence of d strata.

Training sequence. When processing a subepoch (i.e., a stratum), we do not generate a global training sequence and then distribute it among blocks. Instead, each task generates a *local* training sequence directly for its corresponding block. This reduces communication cost and avoids the bottleneck of centralized computation. Practical experience suggests that good results are achieved when (1) the local training sequence covers a large part of the local block, and (2) the training sequence is randomized. To process a block $\boldsymbol{Z}^{ij}$, we randomly select training points from $\boldsymbol{Z}^{ij}$ such that each point is selected precisely once. This approach ensures that many different training points are selected while at the same time maximizing randomness; see [10] for further discussion. Note that Theorem 1 implicitly assumes sampling with replacement, but can be extended to cover the foregoing strategy as well. (In brief, redefine a stratum to consist of a single training point and redefine the stratum weights w_s accordingly.)

Update terms. When processing a training point (i, j) during an SGD step on stratum s, we use the gradient estimate $\hat{L}'_s(\theta) = NL'_{ij}(\theta)$ as in standard SGD; thus $c_s = N/N_s$ in (13). For (i, j) picked uniformly and at random from Z_s, the estimate is unbiased for the gradient of the stratum loss $L_s(\theta)$ given in (12).

Stratum selection. Recall that the stratum sequence (ξ_k, T_k) determines which stratum is chosen in each subepoch and how many steps are run on the stratum. We choose training sequences such that $T_k = N_{\xi_k} = |Z_{\xi_k}|$; i.e., we make use of all the training points in each selected stratum. Moreover, we pick a sequence of d strata to visit during an epoch such that the strata jointly cover the entire training set; the sequence is picked uniformly and at random from all such sequences of d strata. This strategy is analogous to that for intra-block training-point selection. Taking the scaling constant c_s in (12) as N/N_s, it can be seen that this strategy is covered by Theorem 1, where each epoch corresponds to a regenerative cycle. We argue informally as follows. Recall that if Theorem 1 is to apply, then w_s must correspond to the long-term fraction of steps run on stratum Z_s. This means that all but d of the weights are zero, and the remaining weights satisfy $w_s = N_s/N$. The question is then whether this choice of w_s leads to a legitimate representation of L as in (6). One can show that $\{w_s\}$ satisfies (6) for all $\boldsymbol{Z}$ and L of form (1) if and only if $\sum_{s:Z_s \supseteq Z^{ij}} w_s c_s = 1$ for each substratum Z^{ij}. This equality holds for the above choices of w_s and c_s.

Step sizes. The stochastic approximation literature often works with step size sequences roughly of form $\epsilon_n = 1/n^\alpha$ with $\alpha \in (0.5, 1]$; Theorem 1 guarantees asymptotic convergence for such choices. To achieve faster convergence over the finite number of steps that are actually executed, we use an adaptive method for choosing the step size sequence. We exploit the fact that—in contrast to SGD in general—we can determine the current loss after every epoch, and thus can check whether the loss has decreased or increased from the previous epoch. We then employ a heuristic called *bold driver*, which is often used for gradient descent. Starting from an initial step size ϵ_0, we (1) increase the step size by a small percentage (say, 5%) whenever the loss decreases over an epoch, and (2) drastically decrease the step size (say, by 50%) if the loss increases. Within each epoch, the step size remains fixed. Given a reasonable choice of ϵ_0, the bold driver method worked extremely well in our experiments. To pick ϵ_0, we leverage the fact that many compute nodes are available, replicating a small sample of $\boldsymbol{Z}$ (say, 0.1%) to each node and trying different step sizes in parallel. Specifically, we try step sizes $1, 1/2, 1/4, \ldots, 1/2^{d-1}$; the step size that gives the best result is selected as ϵ_0. As long as the loss decreases, we repeat a variation of this process after every epoch, trying step sizes within a factor of $[1/2, 2]$ of the current step size. Eventually, the step size will become too large and the loss will increase. Intuitively, this happens when the iterate has moved closer to the global solution than to the local solution. At this point, we switch to the bold-driver method for the rest of the process.

7. EXPERIMENTS

We compared various factorization algorithms with respect to convergence, runtime efficiency, and scalability. Overall, the convergence speed and result quality of DSGD was on par or better than alternative methods, even when these methods are specialized to the loss function. Due to space limitations we report on only a few representative experiments; see [10] for detailed results.

7.1 Setup

We implemented DSGD on top of MapReduce, along with the best-of-breed PSGD, DGD, and ALS methods; see Sec. 2. The DGD algorithm uses the L-BFGS quasi-Newton method as in [9]. DSGD, PSGD, and L-BFGS are generic methods that work with a wide variety of loss functions, whereas ALS is restricted to quadratic loss. We used two different implementations and compute clusters: one for in-memory experiments and one for large scaling experiments on very large datasets using Hadoop.

The in-memory implementation is based on R and C, and uses R's `snowfall` package to implement MapReduce. It targets datasets that are small enough to fit in aggregate memory, i.e., with up to a few billion nonzero entries. We block and distribute the input matrix across the cluster before running each experiment (as described at the end of Sec. 5.3). The factor matrices are communicated via a centralized file system. The R cluster consists of 8 nodes, each running two Intel Xeon E5530 processors with 4 cores at 2.4GHz each. Every node has 48GB of memory.

The second implementation is based on Hadoop [1], an open-source MapReduce implementation. The Hadoop cluster is equipped with 40 nodes, each with two Intel Xeon E5440 processors and 4

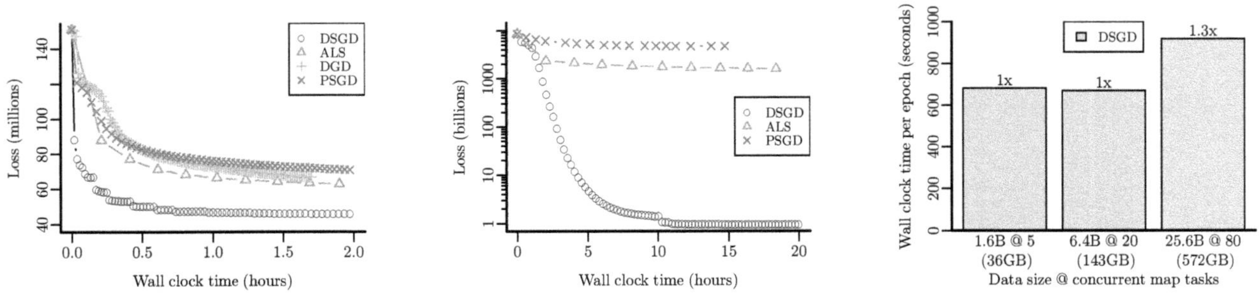

(a) Netflix data (NZSL, R cluster @ 64) (b) Synth. data (L2, $\lambda = 0.1$, R cluster @ 64) (c) Scalability (Hadoop cluster)

Figure 2: Experimental results

cores at 2.8GHz and 32GB of memory. We employ a couple of Hadoop-specific optimizations; see [10].

For our experiments with PSGD and DSGD, we used adaptive step-size computation based on a sample of roughly 1M data points, eventually switching to the bold driver. The time for step-size selection is included in all performance plots.

We used the Netflix competition dataset [3] for our experiments on real data. This dataset contains a small subset of movie ratings given by Netflix users, specifically, 100M anonymized, time-stamped ratings from roughly 480k customers on roughly 18k movies. For larger-scale performance experiments, we used a much larger synthetic dataset with 10M rows, 1M columns, and 1B nonzero entries. We first generated matrices $\boldsymbol{W}^*$ and $\boldsymbol{H}^*$ by repeatedly sampling values from the $N(0, 10)$ distribution. We then sampled 1B entries from the product $\boldsymbol{W}^*\boldsymbol{H}^*$ and added $N(0, 1)$ noise to each sample, ensuring that there existed a reasonable low-rank factorization. We always centered the input matrix around its mean. The starting points $\boldsymbol{W}_0$ and $\boldsymbol{H}_0$ were chosen by sampling entries uniformly and at random from $[-0.5, 0.5]$; we used the same starting point for each algorithm to ensure fair comparison. Finally, for our scalability experiments, we used the Netflix competition dataset and scaled up the data in a way that keeps the sparsity of the matrix constant. Specifically, at each successive scale-up step, we duplicated the number of customers and movies while quadrupling the number of ratings (nonzero entries). We repeat this procedure to obtain matrices between 36GB and 572GB in size. Unless stated otherwise, we use rank $r = 50$.

We focus here on two common loss functions: plain nonzero squared loss $L_{\text{NZSL}} = \sum_{(i,j)\in Z}(\boldsymbol{V}_{ij} - [\boldsymbol{W}\boldsymbol{H}]_{ij})^2$ and nonzero squared loss with L2 regularization $L_{\text{L2}} = L_{\text{NZSL}} + \lambda(\|\boldsymbol{W}\|_{\text{F}}^2 + \|\boldsymbol{H}\|_{\text{F}}^2)$. For our experiment on synthetic data and L_{L2}, we use a "principled" value of $\lambda = 0.1$; this choice of λ is "natural" in that the resulting minimum-loss factors correspond to the "maximum a posteriori" Bayesian estimator of $\boldsymbol{W}$ and $\boldsymbol{H}$ under the Gaussian-based procedure used to generate the synthetic data. Results for other loss functions (including GKL loss) are given in [10].

All of our reported experiments focus on *training* loss, i.e., the loss over the training data, since our emphasis is on how to compute a high quality factorization of a given input matrix as efficiently as possible. The *test* loss, i.e., how well the resulting factorized matrix predicts user ratings of unseen movies, is an orthogonal issue that depends upon, e.g., the choice of loss function and regularization term. In this regard, we re-emphasize that the DSGD algorithm can handle a wide variety of loss functions and regularization schemes. (In fact, we found experimentally that the loss performance of DSGD relative to other factorization algorithms looked similar for test loss and training loss.)

7.2 Relative Performance

We evaluated the relative performance of the matrix factorization algorithms. For various loss functions and datasets, we ran 100 epochs—i.e, scans of the data matrix—with each algorithm and measured the elapsed wall-clock time, as well as the value of the training loss after every epoch. We used 64-way distributed processing on 8 nodes (with 8 concurrent map tasks per node).

Representative results are given in Figs. 2a and 2b. In all our experiments, DSGD converges about as fast as—and, in most cases, faster than–alternative methods. After DSGD, the fastest-converging algorithms are ALS, then DGD, then PSGD. Note that each algorithm has a different cost per epoch: DSGD ran 43 epochs, ALS ran 10 epochs, DGD ran 61 epochs, and PSGD ran 30 epochs in the first hour of the Netflix experiment. These differences in runtime are explained by different computational costs (highest for ALS, which has to solve $m + n$ least-squares problems per epoch) and synchronization costs (highest for PSGD, which has to average all parameters in each epoch). We omit results for DGD in Fig. 2b because its centralized parameter-update step ran out of memory.

Besides the rate of convergence, the ultimate training-loss value achieved is also of interest. DGD will converge to a good local minimum, similarly to DSGD, but the convergence is slow; e.g., in Fig. 2a, DGD was still a long way from convergence after several hours. With respect to PSGD, we note that the matrix-factorization problem is "non-identifiable" in that the loss function has many global minima that correspond to widely different values of $(\boldsymbol{W}, \boldsymbol{H})$. Averages of good partition-local factors as computed by PSGD do not correspond to good global factors, which explains why the algorithm converged to suboptimal solutions in the experiments. Finally, ALS, which is a specialized method, is outperformed by DSGD in the experiments shown here, but came close in performance to DSGD in some of our other experiments [10]. Unlike the other algorithms, we are unaware of any theoretical guarantees of convergence for ALS when it is applied to nonconvex optimization problems such as matrix factorization. This lack of theoretical support is perhaps related to ALS's erratic behavior. In summary, the overall performance of DSGD was consistently more stable than that of the other two algorithms, and the speed of convergence was comparable or faster.

We also assessed the impact of communication overheads on DSGD by comparing its performance with standard, sequential SGD. Note that we could not perform such a comparison on massive data, because SGD simply does not scale to very large datasets, e.g., our 572GB synthetic dataset. Indeed, even if SGD were run without any data shuffling, so that data could be read sequentially, merely reading the data once from disk would take hours. We therefore compared SGD to 64-way DSGD on the smaller Netflix dataset.

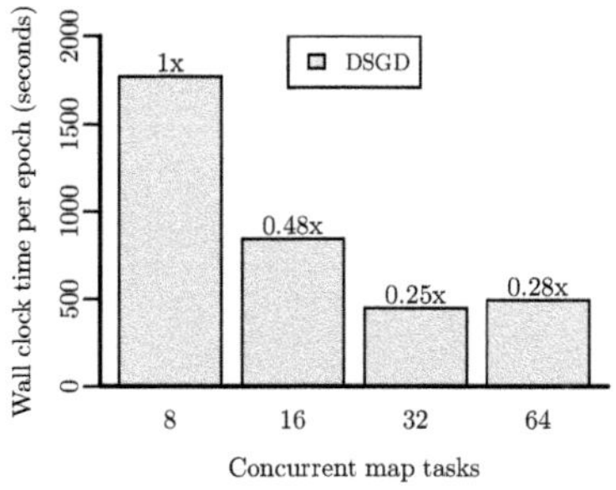

Figure 3: Speed-up experiment (Hadoop cluster, 143GB data)

Here, SGD required slightly fewer epochs than DSGD to converge. This discrepancy is a consequence of different randomizations of the training sequence: SGD shuffles the entire dataset, whereas DSGD shuffles only strata and blocks. The situation was reversed with respect to wall-clock time, and DSGD converged slightly faster than SGD. Most of DSGD's processing time was spent on communication of intermediate results over the (slow) centralized file system. Recent distributed processing platforms have the potential to reduce this latency and improve performance for moderately-sized data; we are currently experimenting with such platforms.

7.3 Scalability of DSGD

We next studied the scalability of DSGD in our Hadoop environment, which allowed us to process much larger matrices than on the in-memory R cluster. In general, we found that DSGD has good scalability properties on Hadoop, provided that the amount of data processed per map task does not become so small that system overheads start to dominate.

Figure 2c shows the wall-clock time per DSGD epoch for different dataset sizes (measured in number of nonzero entries of V) and appropriately scaled numbers of concurrent map tasks (after @-sign). The processing time initially remains constant as the dataset size and number of concurrent tasks are each scaled up by a factor of 4. As we scale to very large datasets (572GB) on large clusters (80 parallel tasks), the overall runtime increases by a modest 30%. This latter overhead can potentially be ameliorated by improving Hadoop's scheduling mechanism, which was a major bottleneck.

A similar observation is made in Figure 3, where we depict the speedup performance when the number of ratings (nonzero entries) is fixed at 6.4B (143GB) and the number of concurrent map tasks is repeatedly doubled. DSGD initially achieves roughly linear speed-up up to 32 concurrent tasks. After this point, speed-up performance starts to degrade. The reason for this behavior is that, when the number of map tasks becomes large, the amount of data processed per task becomes small—e.g., 64-way DSGD uses 64^2 blocks so that the amount of data per block is only $\approx$ 35MB. The actual time to execute DSGD on the data is swamped by Hadoop overheads, especially the time required to spawn tasks.

8. CONCLUSION

We have developed a stratified version of the classic SGD algorithm and then refined this SSGD algorithm to obtain DSGD, a distributed matrix-factorization algorithm that can efficiently handle web-scale matrices. Experiments indicate its superior performance. In future work, we plan to investigate alternative loss functions, such as GKL, as well as alternative regularizations. We also plan to investigate both alternative stratification schemes and emerging distributed-processing platforms. We will also extend our techniques to other applications, such as computing Kohonen maps.

9. REFERENCES

[1] Apache Hadoop. `https://hadoop.apache.org`.

[2] S. Asmussen. *Applied Probability and Queues*. Springer, 2nd edition, 2003.

[3] J. Bennett and S. Lanning. The Netflix prize. In *KDD Cup and Workshop*, 2007.

[4] C. M. Bishop. *Pattern Recognition and Machine Learning*. Information Science and Statistics. Springer, 2007.

[5] L. Bottou and O. Bousquet. The tradeoffs of large scale learning. In *NIPS*, volume 20, pages 161–168. 2008.

[6] R. H. Byrd, P. Lu, J. Nocedal, and C. Zhu. A limited memory algorithm for bound constrained optimization. *SIAM J. Sci. Comput.*, 16(5):1190–1208, 1995.

[7] Y. S. Chow and H. Teicher. *Probability Theory: Independence, Interchangeability, Martingales*. Springer, 2nd edition, 1988.

[8] A. S. Das, M. Datar, A. Garg, and S. Rajaram. Google news personalization: scalable online collaborative filtering. In *WWW*, pages 271–280, 2007.

[9] S. Das, Y. Sismanis, K. S. Beyer, R. Gemulla, P. J. Haas, and J. McPherson. Ricardo: Integrating R and Hadoop. In *SIGMOD*, pages 987–998, 2010.

[10] R. Gemulla, P. J. Haas, E. Nijkamp, and Y. Sismanis. Large-scale matrix factorization with distributed stochastic gradient descent. Technical Report RJ10481, IBM Almaden Research Center, San Jose, CA, 2011. Available at www.almaden.ibm.com/cs/people/peterh/dsgdTechRep.pdf.

[11] K. B. Hall, S. Gilpin, and G. Mann. MapReduce/Bigtable for distributed optimization. In *NIPS LCCC Workshop*, 2010.

[12] T. Hofmann. Probabilistic latent semantic indexing. In *SIGIR*, pages 50–57, 1999.

[13] Y. Koren, R. Bell, and C. Volinsky. Matrix factorization techniques for recommender systems. *IEEE Computer*, 42(8):30–37, 2009.

[14] H. J. Kushner and G. Yin. *Stochastic Approximation and Recursive Algorithms and Applications*. Springer, 2nd edition, 2003.

[15] D. D. Lee and H. S. Seung. Learning the parts of objects by non-negative matrix factorization. *Nature*, 401(6755):788–791, 1999.

[16] C. Liu, H.-c. Yang, J. Fan, L.-W. He, and Y.-M. Wang. Distributed nonnegative matrix factorization for web-scale dyadic data analysis on mapreduce. In *WWW*, pages 681–690, 2010.

[17] G. Mann, R. McDonald, M. Mohri, N. Silberman, and D. Walker. Efficient large-scale distributed training of conditional maximum entropy models. In *NIPC*, pages 1231–1239. 2009.

[18] R. McDonald, K. Hall, and G. Mann. Distributed training strategies for the structured perceptron. In *HLT*, pages 456–464, 2010.

[19] A. P. Singh and G. J. Gordon. A unified view of matrix factorization models. In *ECML PKDD*, pages 358–373, 2008.

[20] Y. Zhou, D. Wilkinson, R. Schreiber, and R. Pan. Large-scale parallel collaborative filtering for the Netflix Prize. In *AAIM*, pages 337–348, 2008.

[21] M. A. Zinkevich, M. Weimer, A. J. Smola, and L. Li. Parallelized stochastic gradient descent. In *NIPS*, pages 2595–2603, 2010.

Diversity in Ranking via Resistive Graph Centers

Avinava Dubey
IBM Research India
avinava.dubey@gmail.com

Soumen Chakrabarti
IIT Bombay
soumen@cse.iitb.ac.in

Chiranjib Bhattacharyya
IISc Bangalore
chiru@csa.iisc.ernet.in

ABSTRACT

Users can rarely reveal their information need in full detail to a search engine within 1–2 words, so search engines need to "hedge their bets" and present diverse results within the precious 10 response slots. Diversity in ranking is of much recent interest. Most existing solutions estimate the marginal utility of an item given a set of items already in the response, and then use variants of greedy set cover. Others design graphs with the items as nodes and choose diverse items based on visit rates (PageRank). Here we introduce a radically new and natural formulation of diversity as finding centers in resistive graphs. Unlike in PageRank, we do not specify the edge resistances (equivalently, conductances) and ask for node visit rates. Instead, we look for a sparse set of center nodes so that the effective conductance from the center to the rest of the graph has maximum entropy. We give a cogent semantic justification for turning PageRankthus on its head. In marked deviation from prior work, our edge resistances are learnt from training data. Inference and learning are NP-hard, but we give practical solutions. In extensive experiments with subtopic retrieval, social network search, and document summarization, our approach convincingly surpasses recently-published diversity algorithms like subtopic cover, max-marginal relevance (MMR), GRASSHOPPER, DIVRANK, and SVMDIV.

Categories and Subject Descriptors

H.3 [**Information storage and retrieval**]: Information Search and Retrieval

General Terms

Algorithms, Performance

Keywords

graph, conductance, diversity, ranking

1. INTRODUCTION

Learning to rank is an active area of machine learning and data mining research [18]. Queries are short (1–2 words) and are often an incomplete excerpt of the user's information need. For example, many person names are ambiguous. User attention drops off steeply with rank, and they rarely look beyond the first 10 or 20 hits.

Together, these two phenomena make *diversity* a critical requirement. The goal of the search engine is to "hedge its bets" and present a variety of response items within scarce screen real estate (10–20 top-ranking positions), so as to minimize the (expected) number of users who abandon the search without satisfying their information need.

Depending on the application, diversity of response items may be interpreted in different ways. For person name queries on the Web, search engines usually return home pages of different people sharing the name. For queries related to broad topics, diversity may mean adequate coverage of subtopics. For commerce search over laptops or cameras, users may expect a faceted or tabular view of models and attributes. In extractive document summarization, a minimal amount of non-repetitive text must be extracted from given documents. Here the items are typically sentences.

1.1 Prior art

The diversity motive clearly requires a global item selection strategy, because the desirability of including an item in a query response obviously depends on other items, even if its intrinsic relevance does not. This central observation has led to two major approaches to diversity.

In the *cover* approach, the marginal worth of including an item in the response is evaluated as some function of the information it contains that is not elsewhere in the response. Subtopic coverage [29], max-marginal relevance (MMR) [4] and submodular coverage [17, 16] are examples of this paradigm where the marginal utility is designed by hand. SVMDIV [28] and INDSTRSVM [15] learn the marginal utility of subtopic coverage of documents from training data.

In the *Markov walk* approach, a graph is designed with nodes representing items. Weighted edges represent some form of similarity between items that is designed by hand, using domain knowledge. The resulting graph is often called a *resistive* graph, with edges having resistance (equivalently, *conductance* representing transition probabilities). Random walk processes are defined on the graph. Nodes are included in the response based on visit rates [19] or expected numbers of visits before absorption [32].

A recent, third approach to diversity uses proprietary click-through data [2] from search engines, sometimes in online settings [23]. The basic idea is that if clusters of users click to different pages after querying a person name, we know that future responses to the query should be diversified. For this approach to succeed, enough users should see diverse URLs to click in the first place, which means that "cold-start diversity" remains an important problem.

Here we focus on the first two approaches, and describe the most closely related work in more detail in Section 2.

1.2 Our contributions

Our work began by recognizing some limitations in the cover and Markov walk paradigms above.

- In the cover approach, at test time, how one item covers (thus rendering redundant) another item is not directly visible. Therefore, one cannot create features for the units of coverage, even if these are known during training (as in subtopic queries).
- The Markov walk approach can potentially get around

- this problem by directly comparing items without reference to the units of coverage. However, existing work hardwires edge weights rather than learn them.
- Markov walks express *associativity* [1]: a node i with large score linking to node j pulls up the score of j. However, diversity demands *dissociative* decisions: if i and j are both relevant and very similar, we should pick only one of them.

The last-mentioned disconnect between the semantics of diversity and the Markov walk approach has led to somewhat contrived fixes that we will discuss in Section 2.

Our main contribution is GCD (graph center diversity), a new framework for diversity. Roughly speaking, GCD finds a sparse teleport [12] for an associative Markov walk to have a high-entropy stationary distribution. It is semantically well-motivated and more effective in practice than existing algorithms. GCD is novel in several key ways:

- In standard Markov walks [12, 26], walk parameters, including the teleport vector, are inputs and node scores are the output. In contrast, in our new framework, the *teleport is the output*. We know of no other attempts to use Markov walks in this fashion. This critical role reversal allows us to reuse associative graphs for diversity, while avoiding their conceptual limitation.
- In Markov walk approaches, walk parameters are hand-designed and hardwired. In contrast, we learn the walk parameters from an expressive parameter space, using training data.
- Our framework incorporates attention decrease with rank ("presentation bias") in a natural way.

Somewhat unsurprisingly, inference in GCD is NP-hard. However, simple and practical heuristics work well. The framework is presented in Section 3. Inference is discussed in Section 4. Training the parameters is discussed in Section 5. The training problem has some resemblance to structured learning [27], but with additional complications. GCD has some similarity with maximizing diffusion of influence in networks [13] but the latter involves dynamic models. GCD is reminiscent of centerpiece subgraphs [25]. Their goal is not diversity, but salient hub nodes connecting a *small* set of query nodes, and walk parameters are not learnt.

In Section 6 we report on experiments with the TREC subtopic task, queries on the IMDB graph of movies, actors, and countries, and the DUC document summarization task. All data sets are public and have been used to evaluate recent algorithms. We show that the elegance of GCD is corroborated by substantially better diversity as evaluated by the end applications.

2. RELATED WORK

2.1 Marginal relevance

Carbonell *et al.* [4] were among the earliest to note the potential conflict between relevance and diversity and offer a trade-off. Given query q and a set of documents S already reported, maximum marginal relevance (MMR) proposes greedily choosing document $\arg\max_{d \notin S} \lambda \operatorname{sim}_1(d,q) - (1-\lambda)\max_{d' \in S} \operatorname{sim}_2(d,d')$ as the next document, for suitably designed similarity functions $\operatorname{sim}_1, \operatorname{sim}_2$ and tuned parameter λ. Zhang *et al.* [31], Chen *et al.* [5] and Guo *et al.* [11] offer probabilistic and/or mixture model formulations addressing the same basic issue.

2.2 Subtopic coverage

Zhai *et al.* [29] proposed subtopic coverage as a diversification objective and demonstrated effective algorithms on the TREC interactive track. In the learning-to-rank literature, Yue and Joachims [28] proposed a structured learning framework SVMDIV for diverse topic coverage, by using features that capture word coverage signals as surrogates of topic coverage. INDSTRSVM [15] propose additional constraints to encourage diversity and balance appropriate for the specific application of summarization. SVMDIV and INDSTRSVM stand out as among very few diversity approaches that learn from a powerful hypothesis space.

2.3 Submodular subset selection

An approach related to MMR [17, 16] represents items as nodes V in a graph, edges with weights w_{ij} representing similarity, and seeks a subset $S \subset V$ to maximize $\sum_{i \in S, j \in V \setminus S} w_{ij}$ (or a similar function) while minimizing the redundancy or self-similarity $\sum_{i,j \in S, i \neq j} w_{ij}$. I.e., they maximize the first term minus λ times the second, as in MMR. Such objectives are *submodular*, affording approximation guarantees from simple greedy algorithms. Despite using a graph representation, this approach has no connection with associative Markov walks. Enhanced with item sizes c_i and a budget constraint $\sum_{i \in S} c_i \leq B$, submodular subset selection has been shown to be particularly suited for document summarization. Similar subset selection has been used to summarize blogs [8]. That paper requires a fixed and known notion of how each blog posting covers subtopics, which precludes its application in our settings. It also proposes an online algorithm to learn preference weights of individual users on the fixed subtopics, but this has no connection with our learning algorithm.

2.4 Random walk variations

Closest to our proposal here are the following papers, each of which represents the documents to be (re)ranked as nodes in a graph with edges representing similarity.

Zhang *et al.* [30] design an "affinity graph" between items (documents) to be ranked. Suppose $C(j|i)$ is the probability of transition from item i to j. $C(j|i)$ is large if most words in i are also in j, reducing the novelty of i. They first compute PageRank on the affinity graph. The initial scores of items are set to their PageRanks. Then, in a loop, they remove the document j with the largest score $s(j)$, and reduce the score of linked documents i by $s(j)\,C(j|i)$. Although it uses a PageRank computation, this approach is very similar in spirit to marginal relevance.

Zhu *et al.*'s GRASSHOPPER algorithm [32] also sets up a random walk with transition probabilities related to similarity between items. They find the top-ranking item using conventional personalized PageRank [12], but then make the corresponding node a *sink*, i.e., having no outbound transition edges. The resulting graph no longer has a meaningful stationary distribution (the PageRank of the sink state will be 1), so they compute the expected number of visits to each node before the random walk is absorbed into the sink node. The node with most visits is the second-ranked node. Then they make the second node a sink as well and continue the process. This is the graph analog to the $k = 1$ case of Chen and Karger [5, Section 7.1].

The latest example of this style of formulation is DIVRANK [19], which proposes a random walk with *time-variant* transition probabilities $C_T(j|i)$ at time T:

$$C_T(j|i) = (1-\lambda)r(j) + \lambda \frac{C_0(j|i)N_T(j)}{\sum_k C_0(k|i)N_T(k)}$$

where $N_T(j)$ is the (random) number of times node j has been visited up to time T and r is a multinomial teleport distribution. This translates into

$$p_{T+1}(j) = (1-\lambda)r(j) + \lambda \sum_i \frac{C_0(j|i)N_T(j)}{\sum_k C_0(k|i)N_T(k)} p_T(i)$$

Unfortunately $N_T(i)$ must be approximated with point estimates to keep the computation practical. Mei *et al.* argue that the above implements a "rich gets richer" effect as in preferential attachment [3]: through random choice and/or asymmetry in the graph neighborhood, one node will emerge the "winner" in each tightly connected subgraph. This strategy achieves the same end as Zhang *et al.*'s [30] discounting of information richness through the affinity graph.

Other uses of such random walks exist [6], but walk parameters are again hardwired, and the results are used to define similarity between items which is then used in the formulation.

Despite differences in specifics, much is in common across the above techniques [30, 32, 19]. In all cases a graph is defined with edges representing similarity, and a random walk is formulated with parameters that are predefined and hardwired. We argue that diversity has no semantic foundation in visit rates of random surfers and rich-gets-richer phenomena. *Diversity is not the outcome of a social process.* Diversity is a *desirable property of a ranking* that we should seek when query intent is uncertain.

2.5 Associative vs. dissociative graph models

If nodes (documents) are labeled relevant or irrelevant, all graphs defined above would have *associative edge potentials* in graphical model terminology [14], i.e., neighboring nodes will tend to have the same label. This is just a restatement of the cluster hypothesis in IR, and has been used for collective (associative) ranking using the undirected graph Laplacian [21]. Let a_{ij} be the similarity between items i, j, $b(i)$ a non-collective score wrt the query, and $f(i)$ the final score we seek. Laplacian techniques seek to minimize $\sum_{i,j} a_{ij}\big(f(i) - f(j)\big)^2 + \diamondsuit \sum_i \big(f(i) - b(i)\big)^2$, i.e., we want scores $f(i)$ to be "smooth" across edges while not differing much from the local scores $b(i)$. PageRank corresponds to a directed version of the Laplacian [1], but the edges continue to be associative.

In contrast, diversity calls for *dissociative* edge potentials. Let the node labels now be "report" vs. "do not report". Relevance is now a *node potential* [14] rather than a node label: in the absence of edges, relevant nodes should be reported and vice versa. But if an edge (i, j) represents a strong similarity and i, j are both relevant, then the diversity principle dictates that the labels across the edge be *different* rather than the same. It is therefore unsurprising that the above attempts to use an associative network in an essentially dissociative labeling task result in an uneasy fit.

While dissociative graphical models are a more natural expression of the diversity objective, they are computationally intractable [14]. In contrast, PageRank and Laplacian smoothing can be implemented efficiently via power iterations and quadratic optimization, respectively.

This raises the central question addressed in this paper: Can we retain the simplicity and efficiency of associative Markov walks while making dissociative ranking decisions?

3. DIVERSITY AS TELEPORT SEARCH

In this section we introduce the GCD diversity framework. First we list the notation and facts about PageRank used hereafter. In what follows, i, j represent nodes (interchangeably, items to be ranked) in a graph. Let the number of nodes in the graph be N.

- $C(j|i)$ is the probability of walking from node i to j. We will also write it as a matrix element $C(j,i)$ (note the transposition).
- $\alpha \in (0,1)$ is the probability of walking, and $1-\alpha$ is the probability of teleporting, at any step.
- When a teleport happens, the destination is node i with probability $r(i)$; r is a multinomial teleport distribution.
- The resulting PageRank vector is called $p(\alpha, C, r)$ and satisfies the recurrence $p(\alpha, C, r) = \alpha C p(\alpha, C, r) + (1-\alpha)r$, which solves to $p(\alpha, C, r) = (1-\alpha)(\mathbb{I} - \alpha C)^{-1} r$, where $\mathbb{I}$ is the identity matrix.

We will denote $(1-\alpha)(\mathbb{I} - \alpha C)^{-1}$ as the the $N \times N$ matrix M.

3.1 From random surfer to teleported searcher

In standard (personalized) PageRank, α, C, r are fixed, and the search engine uses $p(\alpha, C, r)$ as an estimate of the prestige of pages. I.e., the actions of the random surfer determine the score and rank assigned by the search engine.

However, by now, the surfer's predominant access path into the Web is initiated by a search. Search engine rankings form a narrow peephole (typically $K = 10$ links at a time) through which users explore the Web. (Search engines greatly influence visit and link rates of Web pages. Increased visibility via high PageRank can lead to more visits and links, which can set up a feedback [9] and delay or prevent prominence of newcomer pages.)

3.1.1 Reversing the role of teleport r

In successfully using an associative graph model for dissociative ranking, our key insight is to regard teleport as the *output* of the search engine as against an *input* to its ranking processes. Suppose we regard the $K = 10$ links returned by the search engine in response to a query as defining a teleport vector. The user then uses these response links to teleport to some of these pages. From there the user can locate other similar pages using a variety of devices:

- Following explicit hyperlinks
- Acquiring vocabulary by reading documents and composing further queries
- Consulting topic directories and hubs to locate related pages

Thus, the search engine's initial response sets off a diffusion process through which the user experiences a subset of the corpus.

3.1.2 Omniscient view of relevance, b

The search engine, meanwhile, has analyzed tens of billions of pages and has an "omniscient" view of the relevance of a document to the user's query. Fixing the query, the omniscient relevance score of document i is denoted $b(i)$. In a typical linear scoring framework, this is just $x_{qi}^\top w$, where w is a scoring model vector and x_{qi} is a vector space representation of document i for query q.

In vector space cosine scoring, $x_{qi}^\top w$ is already scaled to lie between 0 and 1, with a score of 0 representing complete irrelevance. (If this does not hold for the raw scores, a variety of transformations, such as the logit function, can be used.) We rescale document scores so that the scores of all documents add up to 1, thereby making b a multinomial distribution. To summarize:

> The goal of the search engine is to choose teleport r so as to make the "teleported searcher" visit node i with probability close to $b(i)$.

3.2 Teleport profile: Modeling rank bias

To start with, we can assume that the user samples each of the K links provided by the search engine uniformly at random. Under this assumption the teleport vector r induced by the search engine output will have exactly K nonzero elements, each equal to $1/K$.

It is now established [10, 22] that user attention to ranked responses is heavily skewed toward top ranks. Accordingly, we can use a *decaying profile* for teleport r. We insist that the K nonzero values be $a_1, \ldots, a_K$ summing to 1, with $a_1 \geq \cdots \geq a_K$. Here are some profiles we evaluated.

Uniform: This is the simplest option, $a_k = 1/K$.

Exponential: $a_k \propto 2^{-k}$, motivated by clickthrough rates [10].

Reciprocal: $a_k \propto 1/k$, motivated by mean average precision and mean reciprocal rank [18].

Logarithmic: $a_k \propto 1/\log k$, motivated by the NDCG ranking accuracy measure [18].

In all cases, the K nonzero *values* in teleport r are predetermined; the search engine must find K nodes and order them from $1, \ldots, K$ so that the design of r can be completed.

As a single profile policy across all queries and data sets, the logarithmic profile worked consistently better than other profiles in our experiments. However, it is conceivable that different kinds of queries (e.g., navigational vs. informational) may benefit from different profiles. This is an interesting direction for future work.

3.3 Exploiting linearity and PPVs

As we have seen, given teleport r, conductance matrix C, and walk probability α, the PageRank vector $p = (1-\alpha)(\mathbb{I} - \alpha C)^{-1} r = Mr$, say. This means that p is a linear function of r. If we denote this functional dependency as p_r, we have $p_{cr} = cp_r$ for $c \in \mathbb{R}$, and $p_{r_1+r_2} = p_{r_1} + p_{r_2}$.

A special class of teleport vectors, called *impulse teleports*, reset to one node with probability 1. The impulse teleport to node i is written δ_i, where $\delta_i(i) = 1$ and $\delta_i(j) = 0$ for all $j \neq i$. The PageRank for δ_i, called the *personalized PageRank vector* for node i and denoted PPV_i, is simply $p(\delta_i)$.

Suppose we precompute PPV_i for all nodes i. PPV_i is the ith column of M, written M^i. Then, given an arbitrary teleport vector r, we can express $p_r = \sum_j M^j r(j)$, using the linearity property.

3.3.1 The divergence objective

The problem thus reduces to the following: Given multinomial probability vectors M^i, $i = 1, \ldots, N$ and scalars $a_1, \ldots, a_K$ adding up to 1, find indices $i_1, \ldots, i_K$ such that

$$\textstyle\sum_{k=1}^{K} a_k M^{i_k} \approx b, \tag{1}$$

where b is the omniscient relevance. In place of "$\approx$" above, in an implementation, we would seek to

$$\min_{i_1,\ldots,i_K} \left\| b - \textstyle\sum_{k=1}^{K} a_k M^{i_k} \right\| \tag{2}$$

where for $\|\cdots\|$ we can use L_1, L_2, KL, or some other suitable notion of divergence.

3.3.2 The entropy objective

An important special case is when all $b(i)$ are equal. E.g., for each query in the well-known subtopic search data set (Section 6.1), a set of (only) relevant documents is provided. In the GCD framework, it is reasonable to want the teleported searcher to visit all these relevant documents at the same rate. A similar situation holds in the IMDB data set (Section 6.2) where the goal is to rank actors by prestige while maintaining diversity (uniform distribution) over countries. If b is uniform and KL divergence is used, (2) turns into maximizing the entropy of $\sum_{k=1}^{K} a_k M^{i_k}$.

Additional notation. Let the D dimensional probability simplex be denoted by $\mathcal{S}_D = \{p | \sum_{d=1}^{D} p_d = 1, p_d \geq 0\}$. Let the entropy $H(p) = -\sum_{d=1}^{D} p_d \log p_d$ where $p \in \mathcal{S}_D$. D can be any positive integer. The Kullback-Leibler divergence is defined as $\text{KL}(p, p') = \sum_{d=1}^{D} p_d \log \frac{p_d}{p'_d}$ for $p, p' \in \mathcal{S}_D$.

4. INFERENCE

There are now two questions remaining.

Inference. If α, C, b are fixed, how should the search engine design a sparse ($K = 10$ non-zeros, say) teleport $r \in \mathcal{S}_N$ such that the teleported searcher visits items at rates prescribed by b? This section focuses on this question. I.e., the output of inference is an optimal r^*, expressed as the choices of $\{i_k\}$ in (2).

Training. Suppose we are given an inference algorithm together with training data, i.e., graph instances with r^* specified. The goal of training or learning is to fit C on each graph such that the output of the inference algorithm is (close to) r^*, or at least, the inference algorithm outputs some $\tilde{r}$ achieving an objective close to that obtained with r^*. Our goal is to avoid hardwired notions of similarity between items as in much of the related work. Section 5 studies this problem.

4.1 Hardness

Proposition 1. *Even with uniform profile a, maximizing the entropy of $\sum_{k=1}^{K} a_k M^{i_k}$ is NP-hard.*

Proof. Given an exact-cover-by-3-sets (X3C [20]) instance with a universe $[T] = \{1, \ldots, T\}$ of elements (3 divides T exactly) and sets indexed $n \in [N]$, the decision version of X3C asks if there exist $K = T/3$ sets whose union is $[T]$, and each element is covered exactly once. We prepare our matrix M which will be of size $T \times N$. Each column corresponds to a set; rows corresponding to elements in the set are set to $1/3$, rest 0s. Suppose an X3C exists. This can be used to produce an r with fill $T/3$, each element being $3/T$, such that Mr is a column vector of T elements, each equal to $1/T$. The entropy is $\log T$. Suppose an X3C does not exist. Then any choice of K columns of M will leave at least one element uncovered. The form of the objective is $-\sum_i (1/T) \log p_i$, where at most $T-1$ p_i values can be positive. So the best bet is to make them all $1/(T-1)$, for an entropy of $\frac{T-1}{T} \log(T-1)$ which is strictly less than $\log T$. □

Proposition 2. *With uniform profile a and using L_2 divergence, solving (2) for arbitrary b is NP-hard.*

Proof. This follows from the hardness of finding sparse solutions to linear least-square problems [20]. □

4.2 Heuristics

Given the hardness results, it is reasonable to try a greedy search. We collect K columns from the N columns of PPV matrix M from the input set successively, in each step choosing that vector which minimizes the divergence or maximizes the entropy. The procedure is shown in Figure 1.

input: PPV matrix M; $a_1 \geq \cdots \geq a_K > 0$; reference b
output: sequence S of K columns chosen from M
initialize $S = \varnothing$
for $k = 1, 2, \ldots, K$ **do**
  for each $i \in [1, N] \setminus S$ **do**
    tentatively include column i in S
    compute $\psi = \frac{\sum_{s=1}^{|S|} a_s M^s}{\sum_{s=1}^{|S|} a_s}$
    record $\|\psi - b\|$
  choose best column and commit inclusion in S

Figure 1: Greedy teleport selection.

One way to estimate the gap between the greedy solution and the optimal is to bound the optimal using a relaxed integer program. Let $z_{ki} \in \{0, 1\}$ be decision variables indicating if the ith item (column) is placed at rank k, where $i = 1, \ldots, N$ and $k = 1, \ldots, K$. The basic constraints on z_{ki} are

$$\forall k: \quad \textstyle\sum_i z_{ki} = 1 \qquad (3)$$

(exactly one item in each rank, assuming $n \geq k$), and

$$\forall i: \quad \textstyle\sum_k z_{ki} \leq 1 \qquad (4)$$

(each item goes to at most one rank among $1, \ldots, K$). Once z_{ki} are relaxed to $[0, 1]$, the generic divergence or entropy objectives lead to a convex optimization that can be efficiently executed.

5. LEARNING GRAPH CONDUCTANCE

In this section we discuss the design of our edge weights, and how these are learnt from data. Some salient properties of our approach are summarized below.

- Unlike prior work, we do not work with a single graph. We overlay *one graph per feature* to define edge conductance.
- The per-feature graphs are combined through a learning process.

Wherever associative graph models have been used to enhance diversity, edge conductance $C(j|i)$ have been hardwired and fixed by design. A common design has been to make $C(j|i)$ directly related to $\text{sim}(i, j)$. If $\text{sim}(i, j) \in \mathbb{R}_+$, as is the case in TFIDF cosine or Jaccard similarity,

$$C(j, i) = \frac{\text{sim}(i, j)}{\sum_{j'} \text{sim}(i, j')}. \qquad (5)$$

has been frequently used. There is only one kind of edge conductance.

5.1 Edge features

Given nodes i and j, there may be multiple notions of symmetric similarity or asymmetric coverage between them. Each such notion is said to be a *feature*, indexed by $f \in [1, F]$. We will end this subsection with examples of features that we use. For each feature f, we get a conductance matrix C_f.

Now there are (at least) two ways to combine information from the per-feature conductance matrices into a single one. The first way is to use a convex combination on C_f, i.e., let $C = \sum_f \lambda_f C_f$, where $\lambda_f \geq 0$ and $\sum_f \lambda_f = 1$, i.e., $\lambda \in \mathcal{S}_F$. The resulting matrix C is also stochastic, so now we can use $M = (1 - \alpha)(\mathbb{I} - \alpha C)^{-1}$ as usual. This creates a mixture of Markov walks and then finds the corresponding PPV matrix M, which sounds more natural. However, observe that the parameters to be learnt, λ, get involved in M as a matrix inverse, which makes the optimization over λ extremely complicated. Guided by preliminary experiments, we pursue an alternate parametrization:

$$M_f = (1 - \alpha)(\mathbb{I} - \alpha C_f)^{-1}, \quad M(\lambda) = \sum_f \lambda_f M_f. \qquad (6)$$

This parametrization simplifies the training procedure and is the focus of the study in the enusing paragraphs.

5.1.1 Conventional symmetric similarity features

Most Markov walk based diversity algorithms [32, 19] start with a symmetric edge weight based on some measure of similarity between the edge endpoints i, j. Specifically, they use cosine similarity between documents or sentences in some vector space. Other variations like (weighted) Jaccard may also be used. The raw edge weight is divided by the total outbound edge weight from a node to get outgoing transition probabilities, as shown in (5).

5.1.2 Asymmetric coverage features (MinSim)

Consider subtopic retrieval and a document i that is a concatenation of documents j_1 and j_2. Then i is a good center, and, to bring this out, i should have high probability transitions to j_1, j_2. The converse need not, and perhaps should not hold.

This intuition (also see [30]) led us to the "MinSim" feature. Fix a word, and suppose it occurs n_i, n_j times in document i, j where there is a directed edge (i, j). Then we say that the word contributes $\min\{1, n_i/n_j\}$ to the edge (i, j). I.e., if i contains the word as many times as j, i completely covers j as far as this word is concerned. (For $n_j = 0$ MinSim is defined to be 0.)

We can now aggregate signals from different words in various ways. We did this by taking a simple average or a weighted averages of the MinSim scores, the weights being inverse document frequency (IDF) [24].

5.1.3 Projecting out query information

The items we are (re)ranking for diversity are all assumed to be fairly relevant to the query. In case of subtopic retrieval, we expect that all documents in the relevant set contains some or most of the query words. One may argue that, in computing edge features, we should ignore query words. This is easy because we allow any number of potentially redundant edge features. I.e., we can compute edge features including or excluding query words, and retain both sets of features.

5.1.4 Encoding other application signals

Earlier work on extractive document summarization [32, 19] have observed and exploited that good summary sentences tend to come disproportionately from early parts of documents. They biased their teleport r by choosing $r(k) \propto k^{-0.25}$ where k is the rank of the sentence in a document (0.25 was found by hand-tuning). In our case, we can simply devise an additional edge feature and corresponding conductance matrix (details in Section 6.3).

5.2 Learning feature weights

During training, each instance consists of a graph skeleton, together with M_f for each feature f. For the subtopic retrieval task, an instance corresponds to a query. For the summarization task, an instance is one or more related documents that need to be summarized together. For each instance, we are also given one or more optimal, sparse teleport vectors r^*. The job of the learner is to fit a suitable λ to combine the M_fs. As a simple baseline we will start with all λ_f equal, and compare it with more elaborate algorithms.

The input data to the learner is $\{(q, M_{q,f}, r_q^*)\}$ where q is a query or task unit, M_{qf} the PPV matrix for query q and feature f, and r_q^* is/are one (or more near-) perfect teleports. For the qth query $M_q(\lambda) = \sum_f \lambda_f M_{qf}$ is a matrix and r_q^* be a given vector vector such that

$p_f^q = M_{qf} r_q$ and $p_f^{q*} = M_{qf} r_q^*$, where $p_f^q, p_f^{q*} \in \mathcal{S}_N$.

q is omitted when fixed or clear from context. We want to select λ so that, for each query, the entropy corresponding to r^* to exceed the entropy of any other (non-optimal) teleport r. I.e., we want $H(M_q r_q^*) \geq H(M_q r)$.

5.2.1 *Entropy maximization (MaxEnt) heuristic*

Ensuring $H(Mr^*) \geq H(Mr)$ is nontrivial. As an early heuristic, we could just try to maximize the lhs. Consider the quantity

$$H(Mr^*) = H\left(\textstyle\sum_f \lambda_f M_f r^*\right) = H\left(\textstyle\sum_f \lambda_f p_f^*\right),$$

say, where p_f^* are *known* multinomial vectors. Because H is concave, this is a benign optimization, and can be efficiently solved. We call this the MaxEnt trainer.

5.2.2 *Exponentiated gradient (EG) approach*

We are also given an inference procedure which, given a query and the weights λ (6), outputs $\hat{r}_q$, a good if not ideal teleport. Unfortunately, the inference problem is NP hard, and can only be solved approximately. At this point it is unclear how to choose a λ to help the inference algorithm return a *good* r, given a new test query. In this section we propose a loss function and an associated subgradient based online procedure for learning λ.

5.2.2.1 *Loss function.*

In Section 4 we discussed a greedy inference algorithm which computes r with large $H(M_q(\lambda)r)$. However, the ground truth r^* may not equal r as obtained from the inference procedure.

If the inference algorithm for a fixed λ gives us r_q such that $H(M(\lambda)r_q) \geq H(M(\lambda)r_q^*)$, then clearly we need to try to improve λ. This immediately motivates a loss

$$\sum_q \Delta(r_q, r_q^*;\ \lambda) = \sum_q [H(M(\lambda)r_q) - H(M(\lambda)r_q^*)]_+ \quad (7)$$

where $[c]_+ = \max\{0, c\}$. This loss is minimum if $H(M(\lambda)r_q) \leq H(M(\lambda)r_q^*)$ for all q. The problem of minimizing this loss as a function of λ is not easy as the loss is non-convex. In the sequel we derive a convex upper bound and derive a *prox* function based algorithm [7] for solving the problem in an online setup.

5.2.2.2 *Optimizing the loss.*

Let us rewrite the argument in the *max* function as a *difference* of two convex functions, specifically note that $\Delta(r_q, r_q^*;\ \lambda) = \max\{0, -G_q(\lambda) + G_q^*(\lambda)\}$ where $G_q(\lambda) = -H(Mr_q)$ and $G_q^*(\lambda) = -H(Mr_q^*)$. Because H is concave, G is convex in λ. Let $p(\lambda) = \sum_f \lambda_f p_f^q$ and $p^*(\lambda) = \sum_f \lambda_f p_f^{q*}$. We approximate G by its global under-estimator:

$$G_q(\lambda) \geq \hat{G}_q(\lambda) = -H\left(\sum_{i=1}^{d} \lambda_i^0 p_i^t\right) + u(\lambda^0)^\top(\lambda - \lambda^0),$$

where $u_j(\lambda) = \sum_j (1+\log p_j(\lambda)) p_{ij}^t$. This motivates a convex loss function which upperbounds Δ. Specifically,

$$\Delta(r_q, r_q^*, \lambda) \leq l_q(\lambda) \left(= \max\left(0, G_q^*(\lambda) - \hat{G}_q(\lambda)\right)\right).$$

One can minimize l_q as a function of λ. Though the problem is convex, one cannot invoke gradient based procedure for this purpose as l_q is not differentiable We exploit the fact that l_q is sub-differentiable and propose a subgradient based algorithm suited for the online setting. We use the subgradient

$$g_q(\lambda) = \begin{cases} 0, & \hat{G}_q(\lambda) \geq G_q^*(\lambda) \\ \nabla_\lambda G_q^*(\lambda) - u(\lambda^0), & \text{otherwise.} \end{cases}$$

Here $g_q(\lambda)_i = \sum_{j=1}^n (1 + \log p_j^*(\lambda)) p_{ij}^{q*}$. This immediately implies that

$$l_q(\lambda) - l_q(\lambda') \leq (\lambda - \lambda')^\top g_q(\lambda) \quad (8)$$

Consider the online setup where queries are processed one after another. Let there exist

$$\lambda^* = \arg\min_{\lambda \in \mathcal{S}_F} L_T(\lambda) \left(= \frac{1}{T}\sum_{q=1}^{T} l_q(\lambda)\right).$$

We define the *regret* R as $R(\lambda_1, \ldots, \lambda_T) = L(\lambda_1, \ldots, \lambda_T) - L_T(\lambda^*)$ where $L(\lambda_1, \ldots, \lambda_T) = \frac{1}{T}\sum_{q=1}^T l_q(\lambda_q)$.

Proposition 3. *Let there exist m such that*

$$m \geq \|g_q(\lambda)\|_\infty \quad \forall \lambda \in \mathcal{S}_F \quad (9)$$

Then the iteration

$$\lambda_{t+1} = \arg\min_{\lambda \in \mathcal{S}_d} \mathrm{KL}(\lambda, \lambda_t) + \eta(\lambda - \lambda_t)^\top \nabla_{\lambda_t} l_t(\lambda_t) \quad (10)$$

ensures that $R(\lambda_1, \ldots, \lambda_T) \leq 2m\sqrt{\frac{\log F}{T}}$ *provided* $\eta = \sqrt{\frac{\log F}{m^2 T}}$.

Proof. The proof follows Duchi *et al.* [7]. As a consequence of (8), it is immediate to see that

$$R = \frac{1}{T}\sum_{t=1}^{T}(l_t(\lambda_t) - l_t(\lambda^*)) \leq \frac{1}{T}\sum_{t=1}^{T}(\lambda_t - \lambda^*)^\top g_t(\lambda). \quad (11)$$

The goal would then be to upperbound the rhs. To this end see that the iteration (10) leads to updates of the form $\lambda_{(q+1)i} = \frac{\lambda_{qi}}{Z}\exp(-\eta g_q(\lambda)_i)$ where Z is chosen so that lhs sums to 1 over i. For such a choice of λ_{t+1} one can prove

$$\mathrm{KL}(\lambda^*, \lambda_t) - \mathrm{KL}(\lambda^*, \lambda_{t+1}) \geq \eta(\lambda_t - \lambda^*)^\top g_t - \eta^2 m^2 \quad (12)$$

See that the LHS simplifies to

$$= -\log\left(\sum_k \lambda_{tk}\exp\left(-\eta\left(\nabla l_t(\lambda_t)\right)_k\right)\right) - \eta\lambda^{*\top}\nabla l_t(\lambda_t).$$

Exploiting $e^x \leq 1 + x + x^2$ for $|x| \leq 1$, and assuming that $\eta|g_{qi}| \leq 1$,

$$\log\left[\sum_k \lambda_{qk}\exp(-\eta g_{qk})\right] \leq \log\left[1 - \eta\lambda^\top g_q + \eta^2\sum_{i=1}^n \lambda_{qi} g_{qi}^2\right]$$

$$\leq \log(1 - \eta\lambda^\top g_t + m^2\eta^2) \leq -\eta\lambda^\top g_t + \eta^2 m^2.$$

The last two inequalities follow because log is monotonically increasing and is upperbounded by the identity function which proves the claim.

Using (12) and summing over all t we get

$$\sum_{t=1}^{T}(\lambda_t - \lambda^*)^\top g_t \leq \tfrac{1}{\eta}\left(\mathrm{KL}(\lambda^*, \lambda_1) - \mathrm{KL}(\lambda^*, \lambda_{t+1})\right) + \eta m^2.$$

Dropping the second term in RHS we obtain the inequality

$$\sum_{t=1}^{T}(\lambda_t - \lambda^*)^\top g_t \leq \frac{1}{\eta}\mathrm{KL}(\lambda^*, \lambda_1) + \eta T m^2$$

Taking $\lambda_1 = \vec{1}/F$, where $\vec{1}$ is a vector of all 1s, yields $\mathrm{KL}(\lambda, \lambda_1) \leq \log F$. Finally the bound is proved by noting that the minimum of $\frac{a}{\eta} + b\eta$ is obtained at $\eta = \sqrt{\frac{a}{b}}$ and the optimum value is $2\sqrt{ab}$. □

The learning algorithm tries to minimize $\Delta(r_q, r_q^*; \lambda)$ by minimizing a convex upper-bound in an online setup. The minimization is not easy as it yields a non-differentiable objective but the problem is finessed by a *prox* function approach [7].

6. EXPERIMENTS

We compared GCD with most of the recent coverage/novelty [4, 29, 28] and Markov walk [32, 19] based diversity algorithms. We explored three application areas with public data sets, reported in separate subsections next.

6.1 Diverse subtopic retrieval

In the TREC 6–8 interactive tracks, each query is associated with a set of subtopics and a set of relevant documents, and each document is marked with the set of subtopics for which it is relevant. This data set has been used earlier by Zhai *et al.* [29] and Yue *et al.* [28]. The subtopics and their coverage is used to compute diversity-cognizant recall and precision scores for retrieval algorithms, but the algorithms are not supposed to know subtopic coverage information.

We used the following edge features:

- Average MinSim coverage of one document by another, weighted by word IDF in the corpus of relevant documents for each query.
- Symmetric cosine and Jaccard similarity between documents.

Each query is associated with only relevant (to at least one subtopic) documents. Thus, as in Yue *et al.* [28], the relevance issue is thereby fixed for all algorithms, and only their effect on diversity is studied. We used a uniform b. For training, r^* was obtained using greedy set cover given the subtopic/s covered by each relevant document.

For evaluation, we used standard S-recall and S-precision originally proposed by Zhai *et al.* [29] for such data. Let $\mathrm{SubTopics}(d)$ be the subtopics for which document d is relevant, and let a query have τ subtopics. The S-recall at rank K is $\frac{1}{\tau}\left|\bigcup_{k=1}^{K} \mathrm{SubTopics}(d_k)\right|$. Let $\mathrm{MinRank}(\pi, r)$ be the smallest rank at which S-recall of r is achieved by a ranking π. Then S-precision at recall r is $\frac{\mathrm{MinRank}(\pi^*, r)}{\mathrm{MinRank}(\pi, r)} \in [0, 1]$, where π^* is the optimal order. Let $\mathrm{SubTopicsUpto}(k) = \bigcup_{\kappa=1}^{k} \mathrm{SubTopics}(d_\kappa)$ and $\mathrm{NewTopics}(d_k) = \mathrm{SubTopics}(d_k) \setminus \mathrm{SubTopicsUpto}(k-1)$. Then the S-MAP (mean average precision) at rank K is defined as $\sum_{k=1}^{K} \frac{\mathrm{NewTopics}(d_k)}{\tau\, k}$, a direct analog of standard MAP.

6.1.1 Accuracy of diversification

As a summary view, Figure 2 shows S-precision vs. S-recall for most of the recent algorithms. GCD stands out as dominating other algorithms over almost all recall levels. DivRank is excellent at small recall, and, given its simplicity, MMR is surprisingly good at larger recall.

Figure 3 shows subtopic-aware MAP (mean average precision) or S-MAP against rank of responses. Our GCD approach is clearly superior at all ranks. SVMdiv and DivRank are the runners-up.

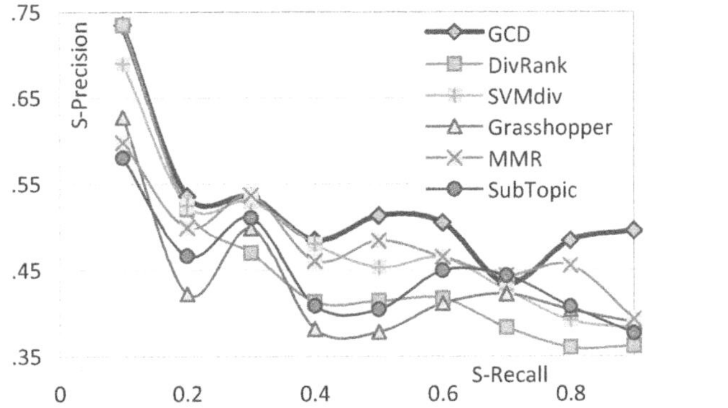

Figure 2: S-precision vs. S-recall, subtopic retrieval.

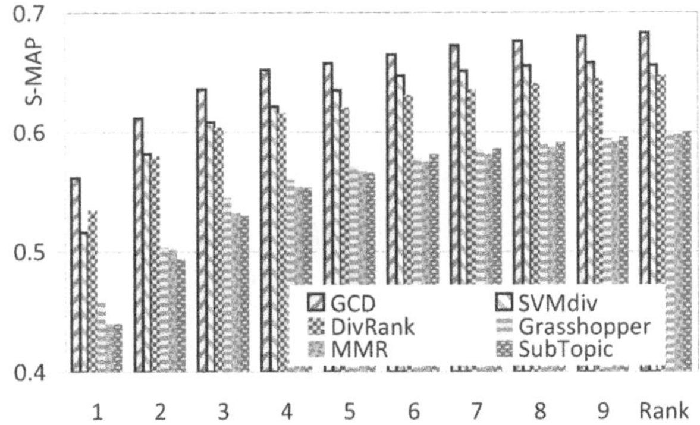

Figure 3: Subtopic-aware MAP (S-MAP).

6.1.2 Inference quality

Greedy search (Section 4.2) was used throughout. We did spot-checks on 17 queries, comparing relaxed integer program (Section 4.2) entropy (upper bound) with greedy entropy; average upper bound ÷ greedy was **1.0089**; it was less than 1.008 for 16 queries.

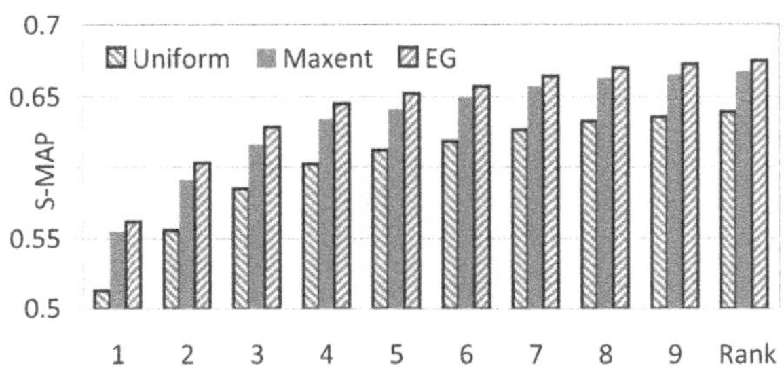

Figure 4: Effect of training λ.

6.1.3 Effect of training

In Figure 4 we show test S-MAP at ranks 1–10 after various forms of training λ. The baseline is no training, with all λ_f equal, i.e., giving equal importance to all M_f matrices. The second set of bars correspond to the MaxEnt trainer described in Section 5.2.1. The final set of bars corresponds to the exponentiated gradient (EG) trainer described in Section 5.2.2. MaxEnt training shows a substantial benefit beyond using a uniform λ, and EG training further improves on that. The typical training time per instance of GCD is less than 10 seconds, while for SVMdiv it is over 3 hours.

6.1.4 Ablation study

In GCD we changed both the edge representation and the algorithm. Compared to DivRank and Grasshopper,

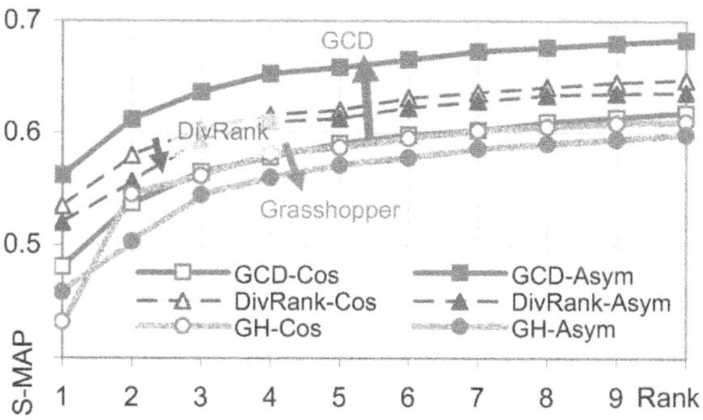

Figure 5: Ablation study.

how much of the accuracy gains shown by GCD are because of a different graph, and how much of it is because of a different, trainable algorithm? Figure 5 shows that moving from symmetric cosine to asymmetric MinSim greatly helps GCD, while it hurts DivRank and Grasshopper. In fact, GCD with cosine is worse than DivRank. This highlights the unified nature of our formulation.

6.2 Ranking in social networks

Grasshopper [32] introduced a diversity task quite distinct from subtopic retrieval and document summarization. It involves the IMDB database, represented as a graph with actors as nodes. Associated with each actor is a set of movies where s/he worked. Edges between actors nodes can be designed in various ways, depending on symmetric overlap (cosine, Jaccard) or asymmetric coverage (MinSim) in terms of movies associated with the endpoint nodes. Unseen by the algorithms, each actor is also associated with a country. The data involves 3452 actors, 1027 movies, and 47 countries.

Each algorithm has to rank the actors by some notion of network prestige. Since high-prestige actors work in many movies, we expect that, as we collect more actors down the ranked list, we will rapidly increase the number of associated movies. If the ranking of actors is also diverse, we would expect to collect countries rapidly as well.

Figure 6 shows the number of distinct countries and movies associated with a prefix of top-ranked actors from the lists returns by various algorithms, where parameters were chosen to maximize the performance of each algorithm. DivRank works well, but the diversity of GCD dominates others wrt both movies and countries.

6.3 Document summarization

Earlier diversity algorithms [32, 19] were evaluated on sentence-level document summarization. The goal is to return a set of sentences that have low redundancy among themselves, and "covers" well the rest of the sentences in the document/s being summarized. Representing sentences as nodes and symmetric similarity or asymmetric coverage as edges between sentence pairs makes it natural to apply Grasshopper, DivRank and GCD.

Prior work recognized that earlier sentences in documents are more likely to be included in good summaries, and encoded this in their teleport vectors. In GCD, since the teleport is our *output*, we need a different device. Within a document, sentence number i links to all sentences numbered $j > i$, and the last sentence loops back to the first one. This corresponds to the realistic reader/surfer model of reading a document starting at a given sentence, getting

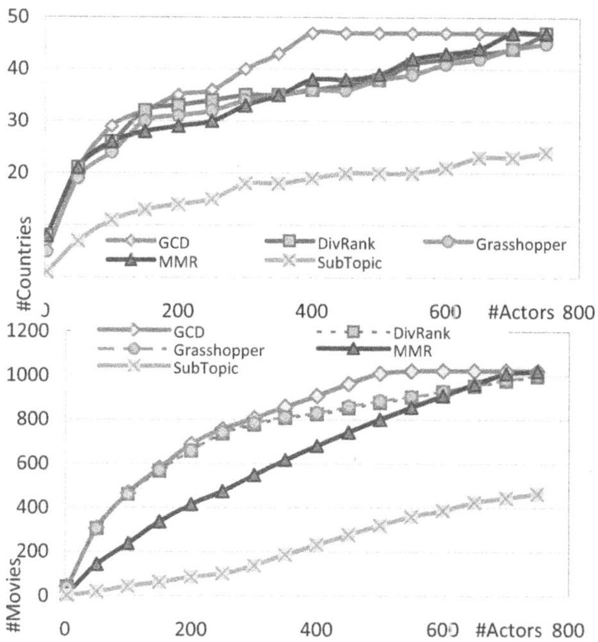

Figure 6: Simultaneous diverse country and movie coverage as a function of number of top actors.

bored with some probability at each subsequent sentence and teleporting away.

The DUC 2004 data set includes human-written, *non-extractive* summaries with associated ROUGE-1 scores [32]. We exhaustively searched the documents for sets of sentences that have ROUGE-1 scores close to the human summaries, and use these sets to define r^* for training. We used the 50 labeled instances as defined by Task-2 of DUC 2004, randomly split into 30 training and 20 test instances.

Algorithm	Train	Test
MMR [4]	.324	.32
SubTopic [29]	.32	.323
Grasshopper [32]	.341	.33
DivRank [19]	.353	.345
GCD	.365	**.369**
Submodular [16]	.389	**.373**
Optimal	.421	.407

Figure 7: Document summarization accuracy.

Figure 7 shows ROUGE-1 scores for different algorithms. GCD fares better than MMR, SubTopic, Grasshopper and DivRank. Submodular beats GCD by only **0.004** in test data. Here, GCD did not use information about sentence length and summary budget (in words or bytes), whereas Submodular did. Leveling the playing field and comparing them again is left for future work.

6.4 Typical training and inference time

Recent work on diversity focuses more on formulation and quality than speed. In particular, evaluating M_f through matrix inversion can be expensive. On the TREC subtopic data set, SVMDiv takes over three hours to train. As a ballpark estimate, for executing the average query, SVMDiv takes 1s, GCD and Zhai *et al.*'s subtopic algorithms take 2s each, Grasshopper takes 4s, and DivRank takes 3s. For IMDB, query times compare as Zhai < GCD < DivRank ≪ Grasshopper. Thus, although none of these algorithms are well suited for large-scale real-time deployment, GCD is quite competitive wrt prior art.

7. CONCLUSION

The starting point of our work was to recognize that diversity algorithms [32, 19] modeled around PageRank had no plausible generative or phenomenological explanation. Meanwhile, SVMDiv [28] can be trained to recognize topic coverage, and NetRank [1] can train graph conductances. The key difference between NetRank and this work is that here we are after *dissociative* selection, which is achieved by the graph center search. In this process, we gave an alternative, sound theoretical foundation of diversity around associative graph models. Giving inference guarantees and extending to clickthrough data are natural directions of future work.

Acknowledgment. Thanks to Andrew Goldberg and Qiaozhu Mei for help with data sets and Yisong Yue for help with SVMDiv. Thanks to the reviewers for helping us improve the presentation.

8. REFERENCES

[1] A. Agarwal and S. Chakrabarti. Learning random walks to rank nodes in graphs. In *ICML*, 2007.

[2] R. Agrawal, S. Gollapudi, A. Halverson, and S. Ieong. Diversifying search results. In *WSDM Conference*, pages 5–14, 2009.

[3] A.-L. Barabási and R. Albert. Emergence of scaling in random networks. *Science*, 286:509–512, 1999.

[4] J. Carbonell and J. Goldstein. The use of MMR, diversity-based reranking for reordering documents and producing summaries. In *SIGIR Conference*, pages 335–336, 1998.

[5] H. Chen and D. Karger. Less is more: probabilistic models for retrieving fewer relevant documents. In *SIGIR Conference*, pages 429–436, 2006.

[6] A. Das Sarma, S. Gollapudi, and S. Ieong. Bypass rates: reducing query abandonment using negative inferences. In *SIGKDD Conference*, pages 177–185, 2008.

[7] J. Duchi, S. Shalev-Shwartz, Y. Singer, and A. Tewari. Composite objective mirror descent. In *COLT*, pages 14–26, 2010.

[8] K. El-Arini, G. Veda, D. Shahaf, and C. Guestrin. Turning down the noise in the blogosphere. In *SIGKDD Conference*, pages 289–298. ACM, 2009.

[9] A. Frieze, J. Vera, and S. Chakrabarti. The influence of search engines on preferential attachment. *Internet Mathematics*, 3(3):361–381, 2006–2007.

[10] L. A. Granka, T. Joachims, and G. Gay. Eye-tracking analysis of user behavior in www search. In *SIGIR Conference*, pages 478–479, 2004.

[11] S. Guo and S. Sanner. Probabilistic latent maximal marginal relevance. In *SIGIR Conference*, pages 833–834, 2010. Poster.

[12] G. Jeh and J. Widom. Scaling personalized web search. In *WWW Conference*, pages 271–279, 2003.

[13] D. Kempe, J. M. Kleinberg, and É. Tardos. Influential nodes in a diffusion model for social networks. In *ICALP*, pages 1127–1138, 2005.

[14] D. Koller and N. Friedman. *Probabilistic Graphical Models: Principles and Techniques.* MIT Press, 2009.

[15] L. Li, K. Zhou, G.-R. Xue, H. Zha, and Y. Yu. Enhancing diversity, coverage and balance for summarization through structure learning. In *WWW Conference*, pages 71–80, Apr. 2009.

[16] H. Lin and J. Bilmes. Multi-document summarization via budgeted maximization of submodular functions. In *HLT Conference*, pages 912–920, Stroudsburg, PA, USA, 2010. Association for Computational Linguistics.

[17] H. Lin, J. Bilmes, and S. Xie. Graph-based submodular selection for extractive summarization. In *Automatic Speech Recognition and Understanding Workshop*, 2009.

[18] T.-Y. Liu. Learning to rank for information retrieval. Tutorial at SIGIR, 2008.

[19] Q. Mei, J. Guo, and D. Radev. DivRank: the interplay of prestige and diversity in information networks. In *SIGKDD Conference*, pages 1009–1018, 2010.

[20] B. K. Natarajan. Sparse approximate solutions to linear systems. *SIAM Journal on Computing*, 24(2):227–234, apr 1995.

[21] T. Qin, T.-Y. Liu, X.-D. Zhang, D.-S. Wang, W.-Y. Xiong, and H. Li. Learning to rank relational objects and its application to Web search. In *WWW Conference*, pages 407–416, 2008.

[22] F. Radlinski and T. Joachims. Active exploration for learning rankings from clickthrough data. In *SIGKDD Conference*, pages 570–579, 2007.

[23] F. Radlinski, R. Kleinberg, and T. Joachims. Learning diverse rankings with multi-armed bandits. In *ICML*, pages 784–791, 2008.

[24] G. Salton and M. J. McGill. *Introduction to Modern Information Retrieval.* McGraw-Hill, 1983.

[25] H. Tong and C. Faloutsos. Center-piece subgraphs: Problem definition and fast solutions. In *SIGKDD Conference*, 2006.

[26] H. Tong, C. Faloutsos, and J.-Y. Pan. Fast random walk with restart and its applications. In *ICDM*, 2006.

[27] I. Tsochantaridis, T. Joachims, T. Hofmann, and Y. Altun. Large margin methods for structured and interdependent output variables. *JMLR*, 6(Sep):1453–1484, 2005.

[28] Y. Yue and T. Joachims. Predicting diverse subsets using structural SVMs. In *ICML*, pages 271–278, 2008.

[29] C. X. Zhai, W. W. Cohen, and J. Lafferty. Beyond independent relevance: methods and evaluation metrics for subtopic retrieval. In *SIGIR Conference*, pages 10–17, 2003.

[30] B. Zhang, H. Li, Y. Liu, L. Ji, W. Xi, W. Fan, Z. Chen, and W.-Y. Ma. Improving web search results using affinity graph. In *SIGIR Conference*, SIGIR '05, pages 504–511, New York, NY, USA, 2005. ACM.

[31] Y. Zhang, J. Callan, and T. Minka. Novelty and redundancy detection in adaptive filtering. In *SIGIR Conference*, pages 81–88, 2002.

[32] X. Zhu, A. B. Goldberg, J. Van, and G. D. Andrzejewski. Improving diversity in ranking using absorbing random walks. In *HLT-NAACL*, pages 97–104, 2007.

Collective Graph Identification

Galileo Mark Namata
Dept. of Computer Science
University of Maryland
College Park, MD 20742, USA
namatag@cs.umd.edu

Stanley Kok
Dept. of Computer Science
University of Maryland
College Park, MD 20742, USA
skok@cs.umd.edu

Lise Getoor
Dept. of Computer Science
University of Maryland
College Park, MD 20742, USA
getoor@cs.umd.edu

ABSTRACT

Data describing networks (communication networks, transaction networks, disease transmission networks, collaboration networks, etc.) is becoming increasingly ubiquitous. While this observational data is useful, it often only hints at the actual underlying social or technological structures which give rise to the interactions. For example, an email communication network provides useful insight but is not the same as the "real" social network among individuals. In this paper, we introduce the problem of *graph identification*, i.e., the discovery of the true graph structure underlying an observed network. We cast the problem as a probabilistic inference task, in which we must infer the nodes, edges, and node labels of a hidden graph, based on evidence provided by the observed network. This in turn corresponds to the problems of performing *entity resolution*, *link prediction*, and *node labeling* to infer the hidden graph. While each of these problems have been studied separately, they have never been considered together as a coherent task. We present a simple yet novel approach to address all three problems simultaneously. Our approach, called C^3, consists of Coupled Collective Classifiers that are iteratively applied to propagate information among solutions to the problems. We empirically demonstrate that C^3 is superior, in terms of both predictive accuracy and runtime, to state-of-the-art probabilistic approaches on three real-world problems.

Categories and Subject Descriptors

H.2.8 [**Database Management**]: Database Applications—*Data Mining*

General Terms

Algorithm, Design, Experimentation, Performance

Keywords

entity resolution, link prediction, collective classification, semi-supervised learning

1. INTRODUCTION

In recent years, there has been a surge of interest in network analysis applied to diverse domains including social networks, technological networks, biological networks and more. In part, this interest is driven by the burgeoning growth in the amount of digital information describing network data that is available including e-mail, citation collections, epidemiological data, and social media. Such data contain a wealth of information (e.g., key individuals, communities, and contagion trends) that, when uncovered, can help to create better predictive models and help elucidate general laws governing network evolution. However, the available network data is typically noisy, observational, and, while it provides useful signal for uncovering the underlying sociological or technological network, it is not the *same* thing.

We define the process of discovering the hidden structure which gives rise to observational network data as the problem of *graph identification*. Figure 1 illustrates an example of inferring a social network (Figure 1(b)) from an email communication network (Figure 1(a)). We refer to the observational network data as the *input graph*, and the hidden network of interest as the *output graph*. Graph identification uncovers the hidden network by simultaneously solving three problems:

Entity resolution: merging nodes in the input that refer to the same entity, e.g., "Do `Neil Smith` and `N. Smith` refer to the same person?".

Link prediction: inferring the links between nodes in the output graph, often based on links in the input graph, e.g., "Does an employer-employee relationship exist between Anne and Robert?".

Node labeling: determining the label of nodes in the output graph, e.g., "Is Neil a CEO, manager or assistant?".

In addition to constructing the hidden output graph, graph identification involves constructing the mapping from nodes in the input graph to nodes in the output graph (Figure 1(c)).

Each task informs the others, and by solving them simultaneously, we allow information to propagate among them to obtain better solutions. For example, in a bibliographic domain, predicting whether one paper cites another (link prediction) allows us to determine whether two papers cite common papers. Co-citation helps us to decide whether they have the same topic (node labeling), which in turn aids in ascertaining whether they are the same paper (entity resolution). This last information in turn helps to determine the citation links from the two papers to other papers, closing the information propagation loop. While previous work [19,

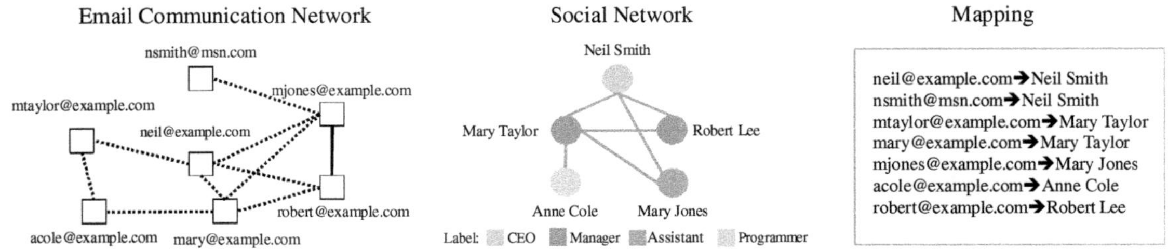

(a) (b) (c)

Figure 1: Input and output of graph identification. (a) Input graph representing a communication network where the nodes are email addresses and the edges are email communications. (b) Output graph representing the social network identified by graph identification. The nodes correspond to people and the edges to employee-manager relationships. The people are also labeled with their roles. (c) Mapping from input to output nodes.

13, 29, 3, 28, 2, 25] has addressed each of these tasks separately, to our knowledge, we are the first to efficiently address them simultaneously.

To address the problem of graph identification, we present the C^3 (Coupled Collective Classifiers) algorithm. C^3 defines a probabilistic model to capture the dependencies within each task as well as the relational interactions among all three. While it is conceptually possible for standard probabilistic inference algorithms to jointly solve all three tasks within the framework of our model, in practice they are too computationally expensive for large real-world datasets. C^3 uses an iterative procedure that simultaneously solves all three tasks. It begins by using a local classifier based solely on observed information in the input graph to solve each task independently. Then it iteratively propagates these solutions among the three tasks by means of relational features that capture the interactions within and among the tasks. Empirically, we observed that by propagating information, C^3 improved predictive accuracy by as much as 48%. To further tailor C^3 as a practical approach, we designed it to address the real-world scenario where it is costly to obtain fully labeled network data. C^3 adopts a *semi-supervised* learning algorithm that can exploit training data with only a small fraction of labeled examples.

The remainder of the paper is organized as follows. We begin with a background review in Section 2. Then we describe C^3 in detail (Section 3) and report our experiments (Section 4). Next we discuss related work (Section 5). Finally, we conclude with future work (Section 6).

2. BACKGROUND

Throughout the paper, we use an uppercase letter to represent a random variable (e.g., Y) and a lowercase letter (e.g., y) to represent its value. Bold letters represent a vector or set (e.g., $\mathbf{Y}$) and their values (e.g., $\mathbf{y}$).

A *Markov random field* (also known as *Markov network*) encodes a joint distribution over a set of random variables $\mathbf{Y}$. Let $\mathcal{C}$ denote a set of subsets (or cliques) of the random variables, and let $\mathbf{Y}_c$ denote the random variables in a subset c. For each $c \in \mathcal{C}$, we have an associated *potential* $\phi_c(\mathbf{Y}_c)$, which is a non-negative function defined over the joint domain of $\mathbf{Y}_c$. The Markov random field defines the following distribution:

$$P(\mathbf{y}) = \frac{1}{Z} \prod_{c \in \mathcal{C}} \phi_c(\mathbf{y}_c) \tag{1}$$

where $Z = \sum_{\mathbf{y}'} \prod_{c\in\mathcal{C}} \phi_c(\mathbf{y}'_c)$ is a normalization constant. The potential functions are often represented more compactly as a log-linear combination over a set of features: $\phi_c(\mathbf{y}_c) = \exp\left(\sum_i w_i f_i(\mathbf{y}_c)\right) = \exp\left(\mathbf{w}_c \cdot \mathbf{f}_c(\mathbf{y}_c)\right)$. In this case, Equation 1 can be equivalently expressed as

$$P(\mathbf{y}) = \frac{1}{Z} \exp\left(\sum_{c\in\mathcal{C}} \mathbf{w}_c \cdot \mathbf{f}_c(\mathbf{y}_c)\right). \tag{2}$$

In many applications, we are interested in conditional distributions where a subset of the variables $\mathbf{X}$ are provided as *evidence*, and we predict a set of *target* variables $\mathbf{Y}$. A *conditional Markov network* defines the distribution $P(\mathbf{y} \mid \mathbf{x}) = \frac{1}{Z(\mathbf{x})} \prod_{c\in\mathcal{C}} \phi_c(\mathbf{x}_c, \mathbf{y}_c)$, where the partition function $Z(\mathbf{x})$ now depends on $\mathbf{x}$: $Z(\mathbf{x}) = \sum_{\mathbf{y}'} \prod_{c\in\mathcal{C}} \phi_c(\mathbf{x}_c, \mathbf{y}'_c)$. Note that evaluating the above equation requires that we compute $Z(\mathbf{x})$, which in turn, requires that we sum over all possible assignments to $\mathbf{y}'$. Since this is exponential in $|\mathbf{Y}|$, computing $Z(\mathbf{x})$ and hence the equation are generally intractable.

A common approximation is the pseudolikelihood [1]:

$$\begin{aligned} P^*(\mathbf{y} \mid \mathbf{x}) &= \prod_i P(y_i|\mathbf{y}_{-i}, \mathbf{x}) \\ &= \prod_i \frac{\exp\left(\sum_{c\in\mathcal{C}:y_i\in\mathbf{y}_c} \mathbf{w}_c \cdot \mathbf{f}_c(\mathbf{x}_c, \mathbf{y}_c)\right)}{Z(\mathbf{y}_c \setminus y_i, \mathbf{x})} \end{aligned} \tag{3}$$

where $\mathbf{y}_{-i} = y_1, \ldots, y_{i-1}, y_{i+1}, \ldots, y_m$ and $Z(\mathbf{y}_c \setminus y_i, \mathbf{x}) = \sum_{y_i} \exp\left(\sum_{c\in\mathcal{C}:y_i\in\mathbf{y}_c} \mathbf{w}_c \cdot \mathbf{f}_c(\mathbf{x}_c, \mathbf{y}_c)\right)$. Note that we only sum over the possible values of y_i. Hence evaluating the normalization constants of all terms only requires time that is linear in $|\mathbf{Y}|$.

3. COUPLED COLLECTIVE CLASSIFIERS

C^3 takes a graph $(\mathbf{V}, \mathbf{E})$ as input where $\mathbf{V}$ and $\mathbf{E}$ are respectively a set of vertices and directed edges[1]. Each vertex

[1] C^3 extends straightforwardly to graphs with more than one

$v \in \mathbf{V}$ represents a reference to an entity, and each edge $(v_i, v_j) \in \mathbf{E}$ represents an interaction between references v_i and v_j. Each node v_i in the input graph has associated attributes A_i. For example, if a node represents a reference to a paper, the attributes may describe the words which appear in the paper. Edges (v_i, v_j) may also have associated attributes, denoted A_{ij}. An example of an edge attribute is the number of emails sent on a communication link from person v_i to v_j. We use $\mathbf{A} = \{A_i\} \cup \{A_{ij}\}$ where $i, j = 1, \ldots, |\mathbf{V}|$ to denote the attributes of all input nodes and edges.

C^3 jointly performs the three tasks of entity resolution, link prediction and node labeling. For entity **R**esolution, we define binary random variables $\mathbf{R} = \{R_{ij}\}$ where $i, j = 1, \ldots, |\mathbf{V}|$ and R_{ij} is an indicator variable denoting whether references V_i and V_j are co-referent. For **L**ink prediction, we define binary random variables $\mathbf{L} = \{L_{ij}\}$ where $i, j = 1, \ldots, |\mathbf{V}|$ and L_{ij} is an indicator variable denoting whether there is a link, or edge, from V_i to V_j, in the output graph[2]. For **N**ode labeling, we define random variables for each node representing its label $\mathbf{N} = \{N_i\}_{i=1}^{|\mathbf{V}|}$ and $N_i \in \{1, 2, \ldots, k\}$ where k is the number of possible label values.

We partition each set of variables into a set representing variables that are *observed* (i.e., evidence), and a set representing variables that are *predicted* (i.e., are target variables). We denote observed variables as $\mathbf{R}_o$, $\mathbf{L}_o$, and $\mathbf{N}_o$, and target variables as $\mathbf{R}_p$, $\mathbf{L}_p$, $\mathbf{N}_p$, where $\mathbf{R} = \mathbf{R}_o \cup \mathbf{R}_p$, $\mathbf{L} = \mathbf{L}_o \cup \mathbf{L}_p$ and $\mathbf{N} = \mathbf{N}_o \cup \mathbf{N}_p$. In addition, attributes $\mathbf{A}$ and edges $\mathbf{E}$ in the input graph are also assumed to be observed. Thus $\mathbf{R}_o$, $\mathbf{L}_o$, $\mathbf{N}_o$, $\mathbf{A}$ and $\mathbf{E}$ constitute evidence, i.e., $\mathbf{X} = \mathbf{R}_o \cup \mathbf{L}_o \cup \mathbf{N}_o \cup \mathbf{A} \cup \mathbf{E}$. The target variables $\mathbf{Y}$ are made up of the predicted variables, i.e., $\mathbf{Y} = \mathbf{R}_p \cup \mathbf{L}_p \cup \mathbf{N}_p$.

Given the above definitions and using Equation 3, we can represent the joint probability over the target variables $\mathbf{R}_p, \mathbf{L}_p, \mathbf{N}_p$ given evidence $\mathbf{X}$ as follows:

$$P^* (\mathbf{r}_p, \mathbf{l}_p, \mathbf{n}_p \mid \mathbf{x}) = \left(\prod_{r_p \in \mathbf{r}_p} P(r_p | \mathbf{y} \backslash r_p, \mathbf{x})\right)\left(\prod_{l_p \in \mathbf{l}_p} P(l_p | \mathbf{y} \backslash l_p, \mathbf{x})\right)\left(\prod_{n_p \in \mathbf{n}_p} P(n_p | \mathbf{y} \backslash n_p, \mathbf{x})\right). \tag{4}$$

3.1 Features

C^3 makes use of two kinds of features: *local* and *relational*. Local features capture the dependencies between a single predicted variable and evidence. For example, in a bibliographic domain, a local feature $f(N_i, A_i)$ represents how the topic N_i of a paper i depends on its content words A_i. Relational features capture the interaction between multiple predicted variables. We further differentiate between two kinds of relational features: *intra-relational* and *inter-relational*. Intra-relational features help in propagating information among variables of one task, whereas inter-relational features aid in disseminating information among variables of different tasks. For example, for node labeling the intra-relational feature $f(N_i, \{N_{ij}\}_{\forall j:(v_i,v_j) \in \mathbf{E}})$ represents the condition that the label of node N_i depends on the predicted label of its *observed* neighbors along edges $\mathbf{E}$ in the input graph, and the inter-relational feature $f(N_i, \{N_{ij}\}_{\forall j:L_{ij}=1})$ represents the condition that the label of node N_i depends on the predicted label of its *inferred* neighbors along edges L in the output graph. Similarly, for entity resolution, we may have an intra-relational feature $f(R_{ij}, \{R_{ik}, R_{jk}\}_{\forall k:R_{ik}=R_{jk}=1})$ representing the condition that nodes i and j are likely to be co-referent if they have a common neighbor k that they are predicted to be co-referent with. And we may have an inter-relational feature $f(R_{ij}, N_i, N_j)$ expressing the condition that nodes i and j are likely to be co-referent if their inferred node labels N_i and N_j are the same.

kind of edge and hypergraphs. We focus on the case of a single edge type for simplicity of presentation.

[2]In practice, we do not instantiate all the $|\mathbf{V}|^2$ variables in $\mathbf{R}$ and $\mathbf{L}$. Section 4 describes how we use filtering techniques to only create variables for pairs that have some possibility of being co-referent/linked.

Note that a wide gamut of dependencies can be cast in terms of C^3's features. This is essential for graph identification because it allows us to exploit the diverse set of dependencies which have been proposed for each of the underlying tasks. Previous work in entity resolution, for example, has proposed using a variety of attribute similarity measures between potentially co-referent pairs of nodes [6]. Similarity measures have also been proposed to quantify the set similarity of "neighborhoods" of pairs of nodes [2]. Common definitions of a node's neighborhood include adjacent nodes, all nodes within a given shortest path distance, and all nodes which have an adjacent node in common (e.g., all papers which cite some common subset of papers). All of these definitions can be captured in our framework.

Work in link prediction also makes use of features based on attribute and neighborhood similarity. These features capture the assumption that many networks are homophilic, i.e., similar nodes are likely to share a link. Link prediction features also tend to rely on topology-based characteristics which capture the structural similarity (e.g., degree) or proximity (e.g., existence of paths) between two potentially adjacent nodes [13]. In multi-relational networks, link prediction may rely on features based on the attributes of links between the same pair of nodes (e.g., attributes of a communication edge between people imply something about their social relationship). For node labeling, features traditionally include the observed attributes of the given node, as well as observed and predicted values of nodes in its neighborhood. Table 1 contains more examples of local and relational features, and shows the diversity of features that we used in our experimental evaluation.

We use $\mathcal{F}$ to denote the set of features used by C^3, and $\mathbf{y}_f$ to denote the random variables used in the definition of features $f \in \mathcal{F}$. Then, from Equation 3 and Equation 4, we can represent the joint probability over the target variables $\mathbf{R}_p, \mathbf{L}_p, \mathbf{N}_p$ as follows:

$$P^* (\mathbf{r}_p, \mathbf{l}_p, \mathbf{n}_p \mid \mathbf{x}) = \prod_{y \in \mathbf{r}_p \cup \mathbf{l}_p \cup \mathbf{n}_p} \frac{\exp\left(\sum_{f \in \mathcal{F}: y \in \mathbf{y}_f} w_f \cdot f(\mathbf{x}_f, \mathbf{y}_f)\right)}{Z(\mathbf{y}_f \backslash y, \mathbf{x})}. \tag{5}$$

3.2 Weight Learning

Observe that Equation 4 decomposes into three terms, one for each of the $\mathbf{R}_p$, $\mathbf{L}_p$ and $\mathbf{N}_p$ target variables. A feature that is defined over more than one type of variable appears in more than one of the terms with the same weight (e.g., $f(\mathbf{R}_p, \mathbf{L}_p, \mathbf{x})$ appears in both $\prod_{r_p \in \mathbf{r}_p} P(r_p | \mathbf{y} \backslash r_p, \mathbf{x})$ and $\prod_{l_p \in \mathbf{l}_p} P(l_p | \mathbf{y} \backslash l_p, \mathbf{x})$). We simplify the equation further by assuming that the appearances of such a feature in a term

Table 1: Features used for entity resolution (ER), link prediction (LP), and node labeling (NL) for CORA, CITESEER, and ENRON. The evidence and inferred variables used in each features are in italics. We define two nodes V_i and V_j as *transitively co-referent* if there exists a co-reference path along *observed* and *predicted co-reference* edges between V_i and V_j.

Task	Type	Feature Description
		CORA/CITESEER Citation Network
ER	Local	· Jaccard similarity of *observed words* over nodes
		· Jaccard similarity of the set of nodes adjacent via *observed edges*
	Intra-Rel.	· Jaccard similarity of the set of nodes adjacent via *observed edges* to *observed* and *predicted transitively co-referent nodes*
		· Indicator for whether or not there is a co-reference path along *observed* and *predicted co-reference* edges between nodes
	Inter-Rel.	· Jaccard similarity of the set of nodes adjacent via *observed* and *predicted citation edges*
		· Jaccard similarity of the set of nodes adjacent via *observed* and *predicted citation edges* to *observed* and *predicted transitively co-referent nodes*
		· For each possible label value pair, an indicator variable for the *observed* or *predicted labels* of the nodes
LP	Local	· Jaccard similarity of *observed words* over nodes
		· Indicator variable of matches of *observed words* at both nodes
	Intra-Rel.	· Indicator variable for the existence of nodes adjacent to both nodes via *observed edges*
		· Indicator variable for the existence of nodes adjacent to both nodes via *observed* and *predicted citation edges*
	Inter-Rel.	· For each possible label value pair, an indicator variable for the *observed* or *predicted labels* of the nodes
		· Transitive existence of edge due to *observed* and *predicted citation edges* in *observed* and *predicted transitively co-referent nodes*
NL	Local	· *Observed words* of node
	Intra-Rel.	· For each possible label value, the % of nodes adjacent via *observed edges* with this *observed* and *predicted label*
	Inter-Rel.	· For each possible label value, the % of nodes adjacent via *observed* and *predicted citation edges* with this *observed* and *predicted label*
		· For each possible label value, the % of nodes which are *observed* and *predicted transitively co-referent* with this *observed* and *predicted label*
		ENRON Email Communication and Social Network
ER	Local	· String similarity of *observed email addresses*
		· Percent similarity of *observed word usage*
	Intra-Rel.	· Indicator for whether or not there is a co-reference path along *observed* and *predicted co-reference* edges between nodes
		· Jaccard similarity of the nodes adjacent via *observed communication edges*
		· Jaccard similarity of the nodes adjacent to *observed* and *predicted transitively co-referent nodes* via *observed communication* edges
	Inter-Rel.	· For each possible label value pair, an indicator variable for the *observed* or *predicted labels* of the nodes
		· Jaccard similarity of the nodes adjacent to *observed* and *predicted transitively co-referent nodes* via *observed* and *predicted managerial edges*
LP	Local	· Indicator variable of *observed words* in shared communications
		· Number of *observed communications* sent or received
	Intra-Rel.	· Indicator variable of *observed* and *predicted managerial edges* between nodes adjacent via *observed incoming and/or outgoing communication edges*
	Inter-Rel.	· For each possible label value pair, an indicator variable for the *observed* or *predicted labels* of the nodes
		· Transitive existence of edge due to *observed* and *predicted managerial edges* in *observed* and *predicted transitively co-referent nodes*
NL	Local	· *Observed words* in communications
		· Number of *observed communications* sent and/or received
	Intra-Rel.	· For each label, the % of nodes adjacent via *observed incoming and/or outgoing communication edges* with this *observed* and *predicted label*
		· For each label, the % of *observed communications* with nodes adjacent via *observed incoming and/or outgoing communication edges* with this *observed* and *predicted label*
	Inter-Rel.	· For each label, the % of nodes adjacent via *observed* and *predicted managerial edges* with this *observed* and *predicted label*
		· For each label, the % of *observed* and *predicted transitively co-referent nodes* with this *observed* and *predicted label*

are distinct from those in another term, thus allowing the weights of the feature to be different. This simplifies the weight learning algorithm by allowing it to find the optimal weights for each term separately.

In C^3, we are interested in inferring the most likely assignment of the variables (also known as the *maximum a posteriori* state). Hence, for each term $\prod_{v \in \mathbf{v}} P(v|\mathbf{y} \setminus v, \mathbf{x})$ ($\mathbf{v} \in \{\mathbf{r}_p, \mathbf{l}_p, \mathbf{n}_p\}$), we want to find feature weights that maximize the ratio $\frac{P(v|\mathbf{y}\setminus v,\mathbf{x})}{P(v'|\mathbf{y}\setminus v',\mathbf{x})}$ between the conditional probability of each correct assignment v and every incorrect assignment v'. Taking logs of the ratio, we see that we are equivalently maximizing the *margins* $\sum_{f\in\mathcal{F}:v\in\mathbf{y}_f} w_f \cdot (f(\mathbf{x}_f,\mathbf{y}_f\setminus v,v) - f(\mathbf{x}_f,\mathbf{y}_f\setminus v,v'))$ for each $v\in\mathbf{v}$ and $v'\neq v$, i.e.,

$$\begin{aligned}&\text{maximize } \gamma \ \text{ s.t. } \textstyle\sum_{f\in\mathcal{F}} w_f^2 \leq 1 \text{ and}\\ &\forall v\in\mathbf{v},\ \forall v'\neq v\ \ \Delta f_{(\mathbf{x}_f,\mathbf{y}_f)}(v,v')\geq\gamma\end{aligned}$$

where $\Delta f_{(\mathbf{x}_f,\mathbf{y}_f)}(v,v') = \sum_{f\in\mathcal{F}:v\in\mathbf{y}_f} w_f \cdot (f(\mathbf{x}_f,\mathbf{y}_f\setminus v,v) - f(\mathbf{x}_f,\mathbf{y}_f\setminus v,v'))$.

Applying a standard transformation to eliminate γ and introducing slack variables ξ_v to allow some constraints to be violated to accommodate non-linearly-separable data, we get:

$$\begin{aligned}&\text{minimize } \tfrac{1}{2}\textstyle\sum_{f\in\mathcal{F}} w_f^2 \ + \ K\sum_{v\in\mathbf{v}}\xi_v \ \text{ s.t.}\\ &\forall v\in\mathbf{v},\ \forall v'\neq v\ \ \Delta f_{(\mathbf{x}_f,\mathbf{y}_f)}(v,v')\geq 1-\xi_v\end{aligned}$$

where K is a constant. The above is precisely the optimization that a multi-class support vector machine (SVM) [7] performs[3]. Hence we train three SVMs, one for each of the $\mathbf{R}_p$, $\mathbf{L}_p$, and $\mathbf{N}_p$ variables.

Thus far, we have assumed that training data is fully observed, i.e., we know the ground truth values of all **R**, **L**, and **N** variables. For large real-world networks, this is an impractical assumption because the ground truth values are seldom readily available and it is too costly to manually label them. Hence, we focus on the more realistic scenario of *semi-supervised* learning where only a small portion of the variables are observed.

One difficulty with partially observed data is that we cannot compute the values of relational features containing unlabeled variables. We solve this problem by first using the observed variables to train a new set of SVMs containing only local features, one SVM for each of the $\mathbf{R}_p$, $\mathbf{L}_p$, and $\mathbf{N}_p$ variables. Next these are used to infer the values of the target variables (recall that their values are not observed). With these inferred values, we can evaluate the relational features involving predicted variables, and hence learn feature weights that optimize the margins for the originally observed variables. Algorithm 1 contains the pseudocode for C^3's weight learning.

Even though we have derived the SVM optimization for C^3, we would like to emphasize that C^3 can easily be used with other classifiers (logistic regression, naive Bayes, etc.).

3.3 Inference

Algorithm 2 gives the pseudocode for C^3's inference procedure. Given a set of target variables $\mathbf{Y} = (\mathbf{R}_p, \mathbf{L}_p, \mathbf{N}_p)$ and evidence $\mathbf{x}$, we begin by using a local SVM (i.e., one containing only local features) learned by Algorithm 1 to infer the values of each of the $\mathbf{R}_p, \mathbf{L}_p$, and $\mathbf{N}_p$ variables. At this point, the variable assignments are based solely on the evidence $\mathbf{x}$. The algorithm then proceeds to capture the dependencies between the variables. It iteratively evaluates the relational features using the variable values inferred in the previous iteration, and then infers new variable values for the current iteration. The algorithm terminates when the variable values converge or when a user-specified maximum number of iterations is reached.

Given an assignment of values to the predicted variables, we can construct an output graph. We create an entity node in the output graph for each collection of co-referent references. We also create edges between the entities based on whether the majority of their corresponding variables **L**, defined over their references, indicate that the entities are linked. Finally, we can assign the label to an entity based on the values in **N** corresponding to its references. It is possible that assignments to these variables are inconsistent (i.e., N_i may not equal N_j even though references i and j are predicted co-referent). In these cases, we can define a procedure to resolve the inconsistencies prior to generating the output graph (e.g., enforce transitivity over co-referent pairs, add edges between entities whose references have an edge, and taking the mode label over the labels of its references). For the evaluation in this paper, we evaluate only over the predicted variables **Y**; because we do not have appropriate ground truth to test against, we do not perform this additional set of steps.

[3]We use a multi-class SVM rather than a binary-class one because the node-labeling variables **N** can be assigned to one of more than two possible values.

Algorithm 1 C^3 Semi-supervised Weight Learning

input: $\mathbf{f}^{local}$, a set of local features
$\mathbf{f}^{relational}$, a set of relational features
$\mathbf{y}^{observed}$, values of observed variables
$\mathbf{Y}^{predicted}$, predicted variables
$\mathbf{x}$, evidence variables
output: $\mathbf{w}$, weights of $\mathbf{f}^{local}\cup\mathbf{f}^{relational}$
$\mathbf{w}^{local}$, weights of $\mathbf{f}^{local}$
calls: $LearnWeights(\mathbf{f},\mathbf{y},\mathbf{x},C)$, which returns weights of features $\mathbf{f}$ given observed variables $\mathbf{y}$, evidence $\mathbf{x}$ and classifier C
$InferValue(Y,\mathbf{f},\mathbf{w},\mathbf{x},C)$, which returns the MAP value of variable Y given features $\mathbf{f}$, their weights $\mathbf{w}$, evidence $\mathbf{x}$ and classifier C

```
w^local ← LearnWeights(f^local, y^observed, x, SVM)
for each Y ∈ Y^predicted
    y^predicted ← InferValue(Y, f^local, w^local, x, SVM)
f ← f^local ∪ f^relational
w ← LearnWeights(f, y^observed, x ∪ y^predicted, SVM)
return (w, w^local)
```

Algorithm 2 C^3 Inference

input: $\mathbf{Y}$, target variables
$\mathbf{x}$, evidence
$\mathbf{f}$, a set of local and relational features
$\mathbf{w}$, weights of features in $\mathbf{f}$
$\mathbf{f}^{local}$, a set of local features
$\mathbf{w}^{local}$, weights of features in $\mathbf{f}^{local}$
$maxIter$, maximum number of iterations
output: $\mathbf{y}$, values of target variables
calls: $InferValue(Y,\mathbf{f},\mathbf{w},\mathbf{x},C)$, which returns the MAP value of variable Y given features , their weights $\mathbf{w}$, evidence $\mathbf{x}$, and classifier C

```
i ← 0
for each Y ∈ Y
    y^i ← InferValue(Y, f^local, w^local, x, SVM)
repeat
    i ← i + 1
    for each Y ∈ Y
        y^i ← InferValue(Y, f, w, x ∪ {y^(i-1) \ y^(i-1)}, SVM)
until i = maxIter or y values converge
return y^i
```

4. EXPERIMENTAL EVALUATION

We evaluate our approach using two types of networks: citations networks and email communication networks.[4]

Citation Networks We evaluate on two datasets, CORA and CITESEER [25]. In a citation network, nodes represent papers and directed edges represent citations. The CORA network contains 2708 nodes with 5428 edges. The CITESEER network contains 3312 nodes with 4732 edges. The nodes of both networks also contain, after pruning, 500 binary attributes representing the presence of a word in a paper, as well as a label indicating the topic of a paper (7 possible labels in CORA and 6 in CITESEER). Because noisy versions of these networks are not readily available[5], we create noisy versions of these graphs (i.e., input graphs) which attempt to mimic the types of noise likely encountered during the extraction of a network from multiple sources.

We create an input network by first adding a "reference" paper for a paper entity each time that paper is cited. For each reference, we copy the words from the corresponding entity, but introduce noise, with probability η_{attr}, by replacing the observed word with a randomly chosen word that did not occur in that paper. Next, for the citation links between the entity papers, we create a citation edge between each each reference, and introduce noise by replacing a percentage of the edges, η_{edge}, chosen randomly, with random edges between previously unconnected input nodes. These edges simulate the edges that may be encountered in a noisy extraction process. In our experiments, we used settings of η_{attr} and η_{edge} at 0.2, 0.3, and 0.4 (denoted Low, Medium, and High Noise, respectively).

For entity resolution and link prediction, because the inferences are made over pairs of nodes, there are important scalability issues. If done naively, both entity resolution and link prediction require $O(|V|^2)$ predictions. Clearly this will be intractable for all but the smallest of graphs. In both tasks, a filtering step is often applied to limit the potential pairs that are considered [17, 29]. This is crucial for making the algorithm scalable, and has been shown to improve the accuracy of the predictions. The filtering step is referred to as *blocking* [8] or *canopies* [17]. Any method that can quickly identify the potential pairs while minimizing the false negatives can be used. In our setting, the blocking criterion for entity resolution filters potential pairs as nodes which have at least two nodes, adjacent via edges in the input graph, in common. For link prediction, the blocking criterion filters potential pairs as nodes which have an extracted edge between them. Note that while this substantially reduces the number of potential pairs, in our experiments there remain up to 120,000 pairs for entity resolution and 34,000 pairs for link prediction.

Email Communication Network The second type of network we evaluate over is a corporate communication and social network, based on the ENRON dataset [10]. The input graph is an email communication network where the nodes correspond to email addresses, directed edges represent emails sent from one email address to another, and edge attributes indicate the words used and the number of communications between those email addresses. The output graph is a social network where the nodes represent people, edges indicate a managerial relationships, and the node labels indicate people's titles. We also have annotations on which email addresses belong to the same person. The full network consists of 211 email address nodes with 2837 directed communication edges corresponding to 146 individuals with 5 job title labels and 139 managerial relationships among them. Candidate pairs for entity resolution are limited to pairs of email addresses which are at most a distance three away in the communication network. Similarly, candidate managerial relationships are limited to pairs of nodes which share a communication edge.

The evaluation for these networks is semi-supervised; we train on the observed part of the network and predict the remaining parts of the network. We varied the percentage of missing annotations over the reference labels for node labeling and the potential pairs for entity resolution and link prediction, evaluating at 25%, 50%, and 75% for CORA and CITESEER and 20%, 30%, and 40% for the much smaller ENRON network (denoted Low, Medium, and High, respectively). We construct five random samples for each setting (and each noise level for CORA and CITESEER) using stratified snowball sampling.

4.1 Evaluation

We evaluated C^3 on the three networks using the features defined in Table 1. We used the LibSVM [4] implementation and set $maxIter = 10$ in Algorithm 2. We evaluated entity resolution, link prediction, and node labeling performance using the average F1 performance over the predictions for the target variables $\mathbf{Y}$, defined in Section 3. We also examined the average training, testing, and overall runtime for each of the approaches by defining variants of C^3 which use different subsets of full set of features. In the first variant, LOCAL, we use only features based on the observed attributes of the nodes (i.e., words, email address string). This is equivalent to commonly used approaches for entity resolution, link prediction, and node labeling which make predictions independently and base predictions on only observed attributes [4, 6]. The second variant, INTRA, performs C^3 using only the relational features which capture the intra-dependencies of the predictions (dependencies on predictions of the same type). This variant allows us to study the relative impact of capturing the collective propagation among target variables of the same type. The INTRA variant is also representative of approaches which perform collective entity resolution, collective link prediction, and collective node labeling as separate, unrelated tasks [19, 28, 2].

We also compare against two popular approaches to performing inference involving multiple tasks: PIPELINE and Markov Logic Networks (MLN) [22]. The PIPELINE approach performs tasks one at a time and in a fixed order. At each stage of the PIPELINE, we perform collective inference for a particular task only, using a similar learning and inference procedure to C^3 for comparability, but with the intra-relational features for that task and the inter-relational features from tasks which occurred earlier. Consequently, while the intra-dependencies are captured at each stage, the flow of information in PIPELINE does not allow earlier stages to use the predictions of later stages. This baseline is sen-

[4]Additional information about the datasets, features, and settings used for these experiments are available from http://www.cs.umd.edu/projects/linqs/c3.

[5]We note that while there are annotations for entity resolution (e.g., [2, 27]), link prediction (e.g., [13]), and node labeling (e.g., [25]) available, we are unable to use them directly since they are over different subsets of the network.

sitive to ordering so we consider all possible orderings (six in total for the three tasks in graph identification). Due to space, we only present the performance of the best possible ordering (denoted PIPELINE*). The other approach we compare to, MLN, is a state-of-the-art joint inference model proposed by Richardson and Domingos [22]. For this comparison, we use an open source implementation of MLN called Alchemy[11].[6] Because dependencies in MLN are represented using first order logic, we define first order logic formulae to mimic features defined in Table 1. We explored various data representations and parameters for Alchemy, including the option to perform MAP or marginal inference, and present the results for the best performing combination in terms of both runtime and performance.

4.2 Results

We present the overall F1 performance (representing the average over the entity resolution, link prediction, and node labeling F1 performances) over the multiple levels of noise and annotation in Table 2. The best performance for each set is indicated in bold. We also perform statistical significance tests, using a paired-t test with significance > 95%, over the F1 values for all pairs of approaches. The results are summarized in Table 3. The table indicates the number of times one approach, shown in each row, significantly outperforms another approach, shown in the columns. In Table 4, we list the average training, testing, and overall runtimes for a representative subset of the CORA experiments. These experiments were run on a single server with dual Intel Xeon 2.66Ghz processors and 48GB of memory. All implementations are in Java except for Alchemy which is in C++.

Comparing the performances of all the approaches, we see that C^3 is overall the best performing. C^3 is the best performing in all but one of the columns and in that single instance, the difference is not statistically significant. Looking at Table 3, we see that C^3 significantly outperforms all the other approaches in most cases while there are no instances where C^3 does significantly worse than any other algorithm. Next, looking at the approaches which exploit varying subsets of the dependencies within and among the different tasks, we see that LOCAL has the worst performance, followed by INTRA, and PIPELINE*. The trend in performance is directly correlated with the amount of intra- and inter-dependencies used by each approach; the more intra- and inter-dependencies are exploited, the better the overall performance. In addition, while increasing the number of dependencies used in the models increases runtime, we see that the difference in runtime is minimal compared to the performance improvement.

Relating the performance of the INTRA and LOCAL approaches, we see that making use of the intra-dependencies can, by itself, significantly improve performance. This is consistent with previous work which looked at these tasks in isolation and shows the importance of exploiting these types of dependencies. Similarly, comparing the relative performance of the INTRA to the PIPELINE* and C^3 approaches, we find that further making use of the inter-dependence yields a comparable, if not larger, improvement in performance with little impact on overall runtime. While using the inter-dependencies in these tasks has not been widely studied, the results show the importance of these types of dependencies. Relative to the PIPELINE* approach, we found the best performing PIPELINE* to be a competitive baseline in both performance and runtime. We note, however, that there is a significant variance in the performance of PIPELINE* based on the ordering of the tasks. Successful application of the PIPELINE* requires the non-trivial task of identifying which ordering is optimal which we accomplish by evaluating all possible orderings (generally requiring six times more runtime than C^3). Our C^3 approach, on the other hand, requires no ordering yet still significantly outperforms even the best performing PIPELINE* in all but three, statistically insignificant, cases.

Comparing the performance of the two joint models, we find that C^3 significantly outperforms MLN performance while being an order of magnitude faster. We found that despite multiple attempts to optimize the MLN, the performance of MLN in our experiments remained relatively poor. One possibility for this is that there is insufficient training data for the MLN weight learning given the number of dependencies and features involved. We may also need to look at extensions of the basic MLN model [30, 9]. Understanding the causes of the poor MLN performance and addressing those issues is part of our future work. Our experience with MLN, however, highlights the challenge in efficiently and successfully modeling all the dependencies to jointly infer the tasks involved in graph identification, and the advantages of using a simpler approach based on collections of coupled classifiers.

[6]We had to modify Alchemy to improve its efficiency when grounding its large underlying Markov network.

5. RELATED WORK

Graph identification is related to domain-specific problems such as information extraction in natural language processing [24], network mapping in computer networks [26], and biological network inference in bioinformatics [16]. While graph identification may provide a unifying paradigm for these problems and others, there are some important differences as well. Information extraction traditionally infers structured output from unstructured text (e.g., newspaper articles, emails), while graph identification is specifically focused on inferring structured data (i.e., the output graph) from other structured data (i.e., the input graph, perhaps produced from a noisy information extraction process). Network mapping and biological network inference are also related to graph identification, but they are mainly concerned with inferring only network topology.

There is significant prior work exploring the components of graph identification individually; representatives include work on collective classification (which we refer to as *node labeling*) [15, 18, 25], link prediction [13, 29, 5], and entity resolution [28, 2, 31]. More recently, there is work that looks at various ways these tasks are inter-dependent and can be modeled jointly [29, 23, 32, 21]. To our knowledge, however, previous work has not formulated the complex structured prediction problem as interacting components in order to collectively infer a graph.

Our iterative approach is similar in spirit to the iterative classification algorithm (ICA) presented by Neville and Jensen [19] and the link-based classification work by Lu and Getoor [14]. It is also related to work on relational dependency networks (RDN) [20] and stacked inference [12], which also use local conditional classifiers. In a RDN, a joint probability distribution is estimated using a variant of Gibbs sampling over the predicted local conditional distributions.

Table 2: Overall F1 performance (representing the average over the entity resolution, link prediction, and node labeling F1 performance) on the different models. Bold indicates the highest value in a given column. C^3 is the best performing in all but one statistically insignificant case.

		CITESEER			CORA			ENRON
% Unknown		Low Noise	Medium Noise	High Noise	Low Noise	Medium Noise	High Noise	
Low	MLN	0.512	0.449	0.382	0.435	0.367	0.329	0.098
	LOCAL	0.648	0.526	0.409	0.682	0.557	0.390	0.352
	INTRA	0.678	0.574	0.468	0.747	0.631	0.507	0.426
	PIPELINE*	0.705	0.612	0.505	0.779	0.676	0.565	0.451
	C^3	**0.713**	**0.621**	**0.519**	**0.790**	**0.688**	**0.577**	**0.465**
Medium	MLN	0.373	0.399	0.385	0.352	0.373	0.310	0.089
	LOCAL	0.698	0.592	0.482	0.735	0.626	0.466	0.379
	INTRA	0.736	0.642	0.545	0.801	0.703	0.581	0.420
	PIPELINE*	0.756	0.672	0.579	0.830	0.745	0.641	0.440
	C^3	**0.763**	**0.679**	**0.588**	**0.837**	**0.753**	**0.649**	**0.457**
High	MLN	0.202	0.177	0.168	0.180	0.182	0.177	0.077
	LOCAL	0.713	0.619	0.507	0.744	0.648	0.502	0.388
	INTRA	0.748	0.668	0.568	0.805	0.716	0.592	0.441
	PIPELINE*	0.764	0.692	0.599	0.829	0.756	0.653	**0.458**
	C^3	**0.768**	**0.695**	**0.602**	**0.836**	**0.761**	**0.656**	0.455

Table 3: Each row indicates the number of times the approach, in each row, significantly outperforms the average overall performance of the approaches in each column, over all three levels of noise and three levels of sampling (a maximum of 9 pairwise comparisons for CORA and CITESEER and a maximum of 3 for ENRON).

	CITESEER					CORA					ENRON				
	MLN	LOCAL	INTRA	PIPELINE*	C^3	MLN	LOCAL	INTRA	PIPELINE*	C^3	MLN	LOCAL	INTRA	PIPELINE*	C^3
MLN	-	0	0	0	0	-	0	0	0	0	-	0	0	0	0
LOCAL	9	-	0	0	0	9	-	0	0	0	3	-	0	0	0
INTRA	9	9	-	0	0	9	9	-	0	0	3	2	-	0	0
PIPELINE*	9	9	9	-	0	9	9	9	-	0	3	3	0	-	0
C^3	9	9	9	8	-	9	9	9	9	-	3	3	2	2	-

Table 4: Average training, testing, and overall runtimes (in minutes) for each model over a subset of the experiments on CORA. PIPELINE* does not include the runtime of other orderings that are needed to identify the optimal one.

	Train Time	Test Time	Overall Time
MLN	535.0	45.3	580.3
LOCAL	3.6	0.3	3.9
INTRA	11.3	10.9	22.2
PIPELINE*	12.6	12.7	25.3
C^3	14.5	13.3	27.9

In stacked inference, classifiers retrained at every iteration are "stacked" such that the output of one classifier is used to augment the feature space and serves as input to another. We explored both approaches and found that in the semi-supervised setting described here they did not perform as well as C^3. Also, previous work in these methods have mainly looked only at the problem of node labeling, using simple aggregations for relational features. C^3 is a generalization of these approaches which use coupled classifiers to perform multiple tasks simultaneously, as well as using a richer set of relational features including aggregate, set similarity, and path-based features.

6. CONCLUSION

Graph identification is an important emerging problem. As more observational data describing networks becomes available, the need to properly map from the observational data to the "true" underlying social, technical or biologic network of scientific interest grows in importance. Correctly identifying these networks from noisy data before they are further analyzed is of huge importance. Not only do the inferred networks prevent us from drawing erroneous conclusions, they expedite our analysis as they are often orders of magnitude smaller than the observed ones. The problem is extremely challenging, in terms of propagating information correctly, training the models appropriately, and evaluating the results. In this work, we have formulated this problem as a probabilistic inference problem, and shown how to combine the results of entity resolution, link prediction, and node labeling in a coherent manner. We developed C^3 which can capture the intra- and inter-relational dependencies and showed that it can achieve significant performance gains over existing approaches. There is much room for further exploration; for example applying graph identification to evolving networks, studying convergence and complexity properties, exploring the use of other algorithms and models for graph identification, and applying the algorithm to other types of network data. In this paper, we have shown that a simple and intuitive coupled collective classification approach can be effective in this complex, highly inter-dependent, prediction problem.

7. ACKNOWLEDGMENTS

This work was supported by NSF Grant # IIS-0746930 and AFRL contract # FA8750-10-C-0191.

8. REFERENCES

[1] J. Besag. Statistical analysis of non-lattice data. *The Statistician*, 24:179–195, 1975.

[2] I. Bhattacharya and L. Getoor. Collective entity resolution in relational data. *ACM Transactions on Knowledge Discovery from Data*, 1:1–36, 2007.

[3] V. R. Carvalho and W. W. Cohen. On the collective classification of email "speech acts". In *Proceedings of the ACM SIGIR Conference on Research and Development in Information Retrieval*, 2005.

[4] C.-C. Chang and C.-J. Lin. *LIBSVM: a library for support vector machines*, 2001. Software available at `http://www.csie.ntu.edu.tw/~cjlin/libsvm`.

[5] A. Clauset, C. Moore, and M. E. J. Newman. Hierarchical structure and the prediction of missing links in networks. *Nature*, 453:98, 2008.

[6] W. W. Cohen, P. Ravikumar, and S. E. Fienberg. A comparison of string distance metrics for name-matching tasks. In *Proceedings of the IJCAI Workshop on Information Integration*, 2003.

[7] K. Crammer, Y. Singer, N. Cristianini, J. Shawe-taylor, and B. Williamson. On the algorithmic implementation of multiclass kernel-based vector machines. *Journal of Machine Learning Research*, 2:2001, 2001.

[8] I. P. Fellegi and A. B. Sunter. A theory for record linkage. *Journal of the American Statistical Association*, 64(328):1183–1210, 1969.

[9] T. Huynh and R. Mooney. Max-margin weight learning for markov logic networks. In W. Buntine, M. Grobelnik, D. Mladenic, and J. Shawe-Taylor, editors, *Machine Learning and Knowledge Discovery in Databases*, volume 5781 of *Lecture Notes in Computer Science*, pages 564–579. Springer Berlin / Heidelberg, 2009.

[10] B. Klimt and Y. Yang. Introducing the enron corpus. In *Conference on Email and Anti-Spam*, 2004.

[11] S. Kok, M. Sumner, M. Richardson, P. Singla, H. Poon, and P. Domingos. The alchemy system for statistical relational ai. Technical report, Department of Computer Science and Engineering, University of Washington, Seattle, WA, 2006.

[12] Z. Kou and W. Cohen. Stacked graphical models for efficient inference in markov random fields. In *Proceedings of the SIAM International Conference on Data Mining*, 2007.

[13] D. Liben-Nowell and J. Kleinberg. The link prediction problem for social networks. In *Proceedings of the ACM Conference on Information and Knowledge Management*, 2003.

[14] Q. Lu and L. Getoor. Link-based classification using labeled and unlabeled data. In *Proceedings of the ICML Workshop on the Continuum from Labeled to Unlabeled Data in Machine Learning and Data Mining*, 2003.

[15] S. A. Macskassy and F. Provost. Classification in networked data: A toolkit and a univariate case study. *Journal of Machine Learning Research*, 8:935–983, 2007.

[16] S. Martin, D. Roe, and J.-L. Faulon. Predicting protein-protein interactions using signature products. *Bioinformatics*, 21:218–226, 2005.

[17] A. McCallum, K. Nigam, and L. Ungar. Efficient clustering of high-dimensional data sets with application to reference matching. In *Proceedings of the ACM SIGKDD International Conference On Knowledge Discovery And Data Mining*, 2000.

[18] L. McDowell, K. M. Gupta, and D. W. Aha. Cautious inference in collective classification. In *Proceedings of the AAAI Conference on Artificial Intelligence*, 2007.

[19] J. Neville and D. Jensen. Iterative classification in relational data. In *Proceedings of the AAAI Workshop on Learning Statistical Models from Relational Data*, 2000.

[20] J. Neville and D. Jensen. Relational dependency networks. *Journal of Machine Learning Research*, 8:653–692, 2007.

[21] H. Poon and P. Domingos. Joint unsupervised coreference resolution with markov logic. In *Proceedings of the Conference on Empirical Methods in Natural Language Processing*, 2008.

[22] M. Richardson and P. Domingos. Markov logic networks. *Machine Learning*, 62:107–136, 2006.

[23] D. Roth and W. Yih. A linear programming formulation for global inference in natural language tasks. In *Proceedings of the Conference on Computational Natural Language*, 2004.

[24] S. Sarawagi. Information extraction. *Foundations and Trends in Databases*, 1(3):261–377, 2008.

[25] P. Sen, G. M. Namata, M. Bilgic, L. Getoor, B. Gallagher, and T. Eliassi-Rad. Collective classification in network data. *AI Magazine*, 29(3):93–106, 2008.

[26] R. Sherwood, A. Bender, and N. Spring. Discarte: a disjunctive internet cartographer. *SIGCOMM Computer Communication Review*, 38(4):303–314, 2008.

[27] P. Singla and P. Domingos. Multi-relational record linkage. In *Proceedings of the ACM SIGKDD International Conference On Knowledge Discovery And Data Mining*, 2004.

[28] P. Singla and P. Domingos. Entity resolution with markov logic. *IEEE International Conference on Data Mining*, 21:572–582, 2006.

[29] B. Taskar, M.-F. Wong, P. Abbeel, and D. Koller. Link prediction in relational data. In *Proceedings of the Conference on Neural Information Processing Systems*, 2003.

[30] J. Wang and P. Domingos. Hybrid markov logic networks. In *Proceedings of the AAAI Conference on Artificial Intelligence*, pages 1106–1111, 2008.

[31] M. Wick, A. Culotta, K. Rohanimanesh, and A. McCallum. An entity-based model for coreference resolution. In *Proceedings of the SIAM International Conference on Data Mining*, 2009.

[32] M. L. Wick, K. Rohanimanesh, K. Schultz, and A. McCallum. A unified approach for schema matching, coreference and canonicalization. In *Proceedings of the ACM SIGKDD International Conference On Knowledge Discovery And Data Mining*, 2008.

Semi-Supervised Ranking on Very Large Graphs with Rich Metadata

Bin Gao
Microsoft Research Asia
No. 5, Danling Street
Beijing, 100080, P. R. China
bingao@microsoft.com

Tie-Yan Liu
Microsoft Research Asia
No. 5, Danling Street
Beijing, 100080, P. R. China
tyliu@microsoft.com

Wei Wei*
School of Computer Science and Technology
Huazhong University of Science and Technology
Wuhan, 430074, P. R. China
weiwei8329@gmail.com

Taifeng Wang
Microsoft Research Asia
No. 5, Danling Street
Beijing, 100080, P. R. China
taifengw@microsoft.com

Hang Li
Microsoft Research Asia
No. 5, Danling Street
Beijing, 100080, P. R. China
hangli@microsoft.com

ABSTRACT

Graph ranking plays an important role in many applications, such as page ranking on web graphs and entity ranking on social networks. In applications, besides graph structure, rich information on nodes and edges and explicit or implicit human supervision are often available. In contrast, conventional algorithms (e.g., PageRank and HITS) compute ranking scores by only resorting to graph structure information. A natural question arises here, that is, how to *effectively and efficiently* leverage all the information to more accurately calculate graph ranking scores than the conventional algorithms, assuming that the graph is also very large. Previous work only partially tackled the problem, and the proposed solutions are also not satisfying. This paper addresses the problem and proposes a general framework as well as an efficient algorithm for graph ranking. Specifically, we define a semi-supervised learning framework for ranking of nodes on a very large graph and derive within our proposed framework an efficient algorithm called Semi-Supervised PageRank. In the algorithm, the objective function is defined based upon a Markov random walk on the graph. The transition probability and the reset probability of the Markov model are defined as parametric models based on features on nodes and edges. By minimizing the objective function, subject to a number of constraints derived from supervision information, we simultaneously learn the optimal parameters of the model and the optimal ranking scores of the nodes. Finally, we show that it is possible to make the algorithm efficient to handle a billion-node graph by taking advantage of the sparsity of the graph and implement it in the MapReduce logic. Experiments on real data from a commercial search engine show that the proposed algorithm can outperform previous algorithms on several tasks.

*This work was performed when the third author was an intern at Microsoft Research Asia.

KDD'11, August 21–24, 2011, San Diego, California, USA.

Categories and Subject Descriptors

H.3.3 [**Information Storage and Retrieval**]: Information Search and Retrieval; H.5.4 [**Information Interface and Presentation**]: Hypertext/Hypermedia.

General Terms

Algorithm, Experimentation, Theory

Keywords

Page importance, PageRank, MapReduce.

1. INTRODUCTION

Graph ranking is one of the key technologies in applications like web search and social computing. Traditionally, PageRank [7, 17] and HITS [15] algorithms and their variants [13, 16, 19] are exploited in the task, most of which only make use of the link structure information. That is why these algorithms are also known as link structure analysis. Nowadays, extremely large graphs with billions or even trillions of nodes have been created, and a large amount of information has also been accumulated around the graphs. The information is also varied, and includes user behavior data and rich metadata associated with the graphs. For example, in web search, data on users' browsing history of web pages has been collected which can be viewed as humans' supervision on page importance ranking (intuitively, the more visits a page has the more important it is). In addition, web pages contain URLs, contents, anchor texts, tags assigned by users, etc., which can also be useful signals for determining the quality, richness, and freshness of web pages and thus for performing page importance ranking. Similarly, information on edges is helpful as well, such as the type of the hyperlinks and the number of transitions on the hyperlinks.

Thus, graph ranking faces a significant challenge: that is, how to effectively leverage all the useful information to perform better graph ranking and to do it efficiently in order to handle billion-node or trillion-node graphs.

Previous work only partially addressed the challenge. Several approaches have been proposed to incorporate supervision information into the learning process to guide graph ranking [2, 3, 4, 9, 10, 18, 22, 23]. However, these algorithms still have the following issues. (i) Only the graph structure is considered in the algorithms, and some of the useful information on the graph is ignored. (ii) Most algorithms require computations which are expensive in terms of both time and space (nearly $O(n^3)$, where n is the number of nodes), and the algorithms become intractable when the scale of the problem is large.

In this paper, we propose a semi-supervised learning framework for graph ranking to tackle the challenge. In the framework, a graph is no longer considered a simple collection of nodes and edges. Instead, we assign each node and each edge a feature vector, representing meta information about the node and the edge. The ranking model ranks the nodes according to the meta information contained in the graph representation as well as the information from human supervision. Ranking of nodes and learning of model parameters are conducted at the same time and in a theoretically sound way, by minimizing a graph-based objective function with regard to parameterized models of the meta information, subject to constraints from the supervision information.

In addition, we propose an efficient algorithm called *Semi-Supervised PageRank* (SSP), within the framework. Specifically, we (i) define the graph-based objective function using a Markov random walk (similarly as in PageRank); (ii) define the transition probability of the Markov process using a parametric model containing features on edges, and define the reset probability using a parametric model containing features on nodes; (iii) define the constraints as pairwise preferences from supervision information; and (iv) obtain the optimal parameters and optimal ranking result simultaneously by minimizing the graph-based objective function subject to the constraints. Furthermore, by leveraging the fact that graphs are usually sparse, we implement the optimization process in nearly linear complexity with regard to the number of edges. We also show how to parallelize the algorithm using the MapReduce logic [12].

We have conducted experiments on different ranking tasks and with different graph data sets (up to billions of nodes) to test the performance of the proposed algorithm. The experimental results show that our proposed SSP algorithm can outperform existing algorithms on anti-spam and relevance ranking in search. Furthermore, the proposed algorithm can handle billion-scale graphs while most other algorithms cannot. These results demonstrate the advantages of the proposed algorithm.

To sum up, the contributions of the paper are as below. (i) We have proposed a novel learning problem, i.e., ranking on a very large graph with rich metadata, and developed a general framework to address the problem. (ii) We have developed the SSP algorithm, which has very good ranking performance and can scale up to rank billions of nodes. (iii) We have performed an empirical study on state of the art page ranking algorithms using billion-scale web graphs, which is, as far as we know, the largest-scale experiment reported in the literature.

The rest of the paper is organized as follows. The proposed semi-supervised learning framework is presented in Section 2. The SSP algorithm is introduced in Section 3. The related work is discussed in Section 4. In Section 5, we show that several related algorithms actually correspond to special cases of the proposed framework. Experimental results are reported in Section 6. Conclusions and future work are given in the last section.

2. SEMI-SUPERVISED LEARNING FRAMEWORK FOR GRAPH RANKING

In this section, we define a general framework for semi-supervised graph ranking, which enables us to develop powerful graph ranking algorithms.

We first propose a new representation of a graph. Traditionally, a graph is defined as a tuple $\mathcal{G}'(V, E, W)$, where V is a node set, E is an edge set, and W is a weight matrix on the edges in E. In this definition, only the skeleton of the graph can be described, and rich information about the nodes and edges cannot be expressed. To tackle the problem, we propose defining a graph using the following new representation, $\mathcal{G}(V, E, X, Y)$. That is, a graph still contains a node set V with n nodes and an edge set E with m edges. In addition, we also have a set of edge features $X = \{x_{ij}\}$ and node features $Y = \{y_i\}$, which can encode information in the graph. More specifically, for each edge from node i to node j, there is an l-dimensional feature vector $x_{ij} = (x_{ij1}, x_{ij2}, \cdots, x_{ijl})^T$; and for each node i, there is an h-dimensional feature vector $y_i = (y_{i1}, y_{i2}, \cdots, y_{ih})^T$. Usually, l and h are small numbers as compared to the scale of the graph.

The edge weight in traditional graph representation can be regarded as an edge feature. In addition, one can have many other edge features. For example, in web search, the intra-site or inter-site property of an edge (hyperlink) can be a valuable edge feature. Similarly, one can have many node features. Again in web search, the quality, content, and freshness of a node (web page) can be useful node features.

To sum up, in the framework, a graph consists of graph structure V and E, edge features X, and node features Y. The graph structure defines the global relationship among nodes, edge features represent the local relationships between any two nodes, and node features describe the properties of individual nodes. They are all useful information for graph ranking.

Next, we define the semi-supervised graph ranking framework as follows,

$$\min_{\omega \geq 0, \phi \geq 0, \pi \geq 0} R(\pi; f(\omega, X), g(\phi, Y)) \quad s.t.\ S(\pi; B, \mu) \geq 0. \tag{1}$$

Here, we represent the ranking scores of nodes in graph $\mathcal{G}(V, E, X, Y)$ as an n-dimensional vector π. Furthermore, we introduce parameter vectors ω and ϕ for the node and edge features, and the corresponding functions $f(\omega, X)$ and $g(\phi, Y)$. The constraints on ω, ϕ, and π are $\omega \geq 0$, $\phi \geq 0$, and $\pi \geq 0$. Note that here by using "≥ 0", we mean that all the elements in the vector are non-negative and at least one element is positive. We will explain these components in the following subsections.

2.1 Objective Function

The objective function in the newly-defined framework takes the following form:

$$R(\pi; f(\omega, X), g(\phi, Y)).$$

This objective function can be understood as a graph-based smoothing function for ranking scores π. It ensures that the ranking scores π are consistent with the information contained in the graph in an *unsupervised* learning process. For example, we can use the Markov random walk model to build the smoothing function. The transition probability of the Markov process is defined with $f(\omega, X)$, the parametric model based on edge features, and the reset probability is defined with $g(\phi, Y)$, the parametric model based on node features. Then the smoothing function requires that the ranking scores should be as close to the stationary distribution of the *parametric* Markov process as possible. More details about this example will be introduced in Section 3.

2.2 Constraints

The constraints in the framework take the following form:

$$S(\pi; B, \mu) \geq 0,$$

where matrix B encodes supervision information, and μ denotes weights on samples of supervision information.

The constraints require that the ranking scores π should be consistent with supervision information as much as possible. Learning with regard to the constraints is performed in a *supervised* manner. In contrast, learning with regard to the objective function is performed in an *unsupervised* manner. We therefore call (1) a *semi-supervised* framework for graph ranking.

Matrix B can represent different types of supervision information, such as binary labels, pairwise preferences, partial order, and even total order. For example, pairwise preferences can be labeled by human annotators or mined from users' implicit feedback. In this case, B is a r-by-n matrix with 1, -1, and 0 as elements, where r is the number of preference pairs. Each row of B represents a pairwise preference $u \succ v$, meaning that node u is preferred to node v. The corresponding row of B has 1 in u's column, -1 in v's column, and zeros in the other columns. Accordingly, the constraints can be specified as below, where e is an r-dimensional vector with all its elements equal to 1.

$$S(\pi; B, \mu) = -\mu^T(e - B\pi) \geq 0. \quad (2)$$

For binary labels (e.g., in web search, spam pages and junk pages may correspond to label zero while good pages correspond to label one), partial order, or total order, it is not difficult to convert them to a number of pairwise preference relations and then use constraints similar to (2).

2.3 Equivalent Optimization Problem

For ease of computation, we convert the constraints into a loss function and add it into the objective function (1), obtaining the following equivalent optimization problem.

$$\min_{\omega \geq 0, \phi \geq 0, \pi \geq 0} \alpha R(\pi; f(\omega, X), g(\phi, Y)) - (1-\alpha) S(\pi; B, \mu), \quad (3)$$

where $0 \leq \alpha \leq 1$. By solving Problem (1) or (3), we can obtain the optimal ranking scores π^* as well as the optimal parameters ω^* and ϕ^*.

3. SEMI-SUPERVISED PAGERANK

In this section, we propose an efficient algorithm named *Semi-Supervised PageRank* (SSP) under the general framework. This algorithm demonstrates, as a showcase, that we can successfully address the challenge to graph ranking presented in Section 1.

3.1 Objective Function and Constraints

In SSP, we define the objective function using the same principle as in PageRank. Specifically, one step of the Markov random walk in PageRank can be written as below,

$$\tilde{\pi} = dP_0^T \pi + (1-d) r_0, \quad (4)$$

where P_0 is the transition matrix, r_0 is the reset probability, and d is the damping factor. We introduce parameters to both the transition matrix and the damping factor, and define the loss of $\|\tilde{\pi} - \pi\|^2$ as the objective function,

$$R(\pi; f(\omega, X), g(\phi, Y)) = \|df(\omega, X)\pi + (1-d)g(\phi, Y) - \pi\|^2. \quad (5)$$

Here $f(\omega, X)$ plays the same role as P_0^T does in the original PageRank algorithm (4). For ease of understanding, we rewrite it as $P^T(\omega, X)$ (or sometimes $P^T(\omega)$ or P^T for compact reading) to show that it is a parametric transition probability matrix. Each element $p_{ij}(\omega)$ in $P(\omega)$ represents the transition probability from node i to node j, which is determined by the model of edge features with parameter ω. For example, we can use linear combination, i.e.,

$$p_{ij}(\omega) = \begin{cases} \frac{\sum_k \omega_k x_{ijk}}{\sum_j \sum_k \omega_k x_{ijk}}, & \text{if there is an edge from } i \text{ to } j, \\ 0, & \text{otherwise.} \end{cases} \quad (6)$$

That is, only the transition probability for an existing edge in the graph is non-zero[1], and the value is determined by the edge features. We will only change the weight of an existing edge including assigning zero weight, but will not add new edges to the graph. This can keep the graph sparse.

Here $g(\phi, Y)$ plays the same role as r_0 in the original PageRank algorithm (4). We also rewrite it as $r(\phi, Y)$ (or sometimes $r(\phi)$ or r for compact reading) to show that it is a parametric reset probability vector. Each element $r_i(\phi)$ in $r(\phi)$ represents the reset probability of node i, which is determined by the model of node features with parameter ϕ. For example, we can once again use linear combination, i.e.,

$$r_i(\phi) = \phi^T y_i. \quad (7)$$

Suppose the constraints are based on pairwise preferences.[2] We then obtain the following optimization problem.

$$\min_{\omega \geq 0, \phi \geq 0, \pi \geq 0} \{\alpha \|dP^T(\omega)\pi + (1-d)r(\phi) - \pi\|^2 + (1-\alpha)\mu^T(e - B\pi)\}. \quad (8)$$

One may think about whether it is possible to move the constraints $\omega \geq 0$, $\phi \geq 0$, and $\pi \geq 0$ into the objective function and formalize the problem as non-constrained optimization. It is not an appropriate formulation, however. This is because the features and ranking scores must be non-negative in the current problem and the three constraints

[1] To avoid rank sink, if a node has no outlink edges, we will assume it links to all nodes.

[2] As mentioned before, all kinds of supervision information can be converted to pairwise preferences.

must be strictly satisfied. The non-negative conditions will not be guaranteed when included in the objective function. In fact, in our formulation we need to conduct boundary detection for ω, ϕ, π in each iteration to ensure that they are non-negative. By solving this problem[3], we can obtain the optimal ω^*, ϕ^*, and π^*, and use them to rank the nodes in the graph. In the next sub-sections, we will show how to efficiently solve this optimization problem.

3.2 Solving the Optimization Problem

For ease of explanation, we use $G(\omega, \phi, \pi)$ to denote the objective function in (8),

$$G(\omega,\phi,\pi) = \alpha\|dP^T(\omega)\pi + (1-d)r(\phi) - \pi\|^2 + (1-\alpha)\mu^T(e - B\pi). \quad (9)$$

We use the gradient descent method to minimize $G(\omega, \phi, \pi)$. The partial derivatives of $G(\omega, \phi, \pi)$ with respect to ω, ϕ, and π can be calculated as below,

$$\frac{\partial G}{\partial \omega} = 2\alpha d[P^T\pi \otimes \pi - \pi \otimes \pi + (1-d)r \otimes \pi]^T \frac{\partial vec(P)}{\partial \omega^T}, \quad (10)$$

$$\frac{\partial G}{\partial \phi} = 2\alpha(1-d)[(1-d)r + dP^T\pi - \pi]\frac{\partial r}{\partial \phi}, \quad (11)$$

$$\frac{\partial G}{\partial \pi} = 2\alpha[(dPP^T - dP - dP^T + I)\pi - (1-d)(I-dP)r] - (1-\alpha)B^T\mu. \quad (12)$$

Operator $\otimes$ represents the Kronecker product, and operator $vec(\cdot)$ denotes the expansion of a matrix to a long vector by its columns. For the last fractions in (10) and (11), we have,

$$\frac{\partial vec(P)}{\partial \omega^T} = \begin{pmatrix} \frac{\partial p_{11}}{\partial \omega_1} & \cdots & \frac{\partial p_{11}}{\partial \omega_l} \\ \vdots & \ddots & \vdots \\ \frac{\partial p_{n1}}{\partial \omega_1} & \cdots & \frac{\partial p_{n1}}{\partial \omega_l} \\ \vdots & \ddots & \vdots \\ \frac{\partial p_{1n}}{\partial \omega_1} & \cdots & \frac{\partial p_{1n}}{\partial \omega_l} \\ \vdots & \ddots & \vdots \\ \frac{\partial p_{nn}}{\partial \omega_1} & \cdots & \frac{\partial p_{nn}}{\partial \omega_l} \end{pmatrix} \text{ and } \frac{\partial r}{\partial \phi} = \begin{pmatrix} \frac{\partial r}{\partial \phi_1} \\ \vdots \\ \frac{\partial r}{\partial \phi_i} \\ \vdots \\ \frac{\partial r}{\partial \phi_h} \end{pmatrix} \quad (13)$$

If $p_{ij}(\omega)$ is a linear function of the edge features, its partial derivatives with respect to ω_k will be,

$$\frac{\partial p_{ij}}{\partial \omega_k} = \frac{x_{ijk}\sum_j\sum_k \omega_k x_{ijk} - (\sum_k \omega_k x_{ijk})(\sum_j x_{ijk})}{(\sum_j\sum_k \omega_k x_{ijk})^2}. \quad (14)$$

With the above derivatives, we can iteratively update ω, ϕ, and π by means of gradient descent. The corresponding algorithm is given in Figure 1, where ρ is the learning rate and ϵ controls the stopping condition. Note that the problem does not have a unique minimum. We may compute the original PageRank for the graph and use it as the initial value of π.

[3]Note that we do not add $\sum_i \pi_i = 1$ as a constraint to the optimization problem. In our mind, though this constraint looks necessary if π is supposed to be a probability distribution in PageRank, it is not so necessary if we use it for ranking, where the absolute value of π_i is not very important as long as the relative order is preserved.

Input: X, Y, B, μ, l, h, n, ρ, ϵ, α.
Output: Node ranking score π^*

Algorithm:

1. Set $s = 0$, initialize $\pi_i^{(0)}$ $(i = 1, \cdots, n)$, $\omega_k^{(0)}$ $(k = 1, \cdots, l)$, and $\phi_t^{(0)}$ $(t = 1, \cdots, h)$.
2. Calculate $P^{(s)} = P(\omega^{(s)})$, $r^{(s)} = r(\phi^{(s)})$, and $G^{(s)} = G(\omega^{(s)}, \phi^{(s)}, \pi^{(s)})$.
3. Update $\pi_i^{(s+1)} = \pi_i^{(s)} + \rho\frac{\partial G^{(s)}}{\partial \pi_i^{(s)}}$, $\omega_k^{(s+1)} = \omega_k^{(s)} + \rho\frac{\partial G^{(s)}}{\partial \omega_k^{(s)}}$, and $\phi_t^{(s+1)} = \phi_t^{(s)} + \rho\frac{\partial G^{(s)}}{\partial \phi_t^{(s)}}$.
4. Force $\pi_i^{(s+1)}$, $\omega_k^{(s+1)}$, $\phi_t^{(s+1)}$ to 0, if they are negative.
5. Normalize $\pi_i^{(s+1)} \leftarrow \frac{\pi_i^{(s+1)}}{\sum_{j=1}^n \pi_j^{(s+1)}}$, $\omega_k^{(s+1)} \leftarrow \frac{\omega_k^{(s+1)}}{\sum_{j=1}^l \omega_j^{(s+1)}}$, and $\phi_t^{(s+1)} \leftarrow \frac{\phi_t^{(s+1)}}{\sum_{j=1}^h \phi_j^{(s+1)}}$.
6. Calculate $G^{(s+1)} = G(\omega^{(s+1)}, \phi^{(s+1)}, \pi^{(s+1)})$, if $G^{(s)} - G^{(s+1)} < \epsilon$, stop and output $\pi^* = \pi^{(s+1)}$; else $s = s + 1$, jump to step 2.

Figure 1: The Learning Process of the SSP Algorithm.

3.3 Efficient Implementation

Next, we efficiently implement the algorithm, by using the common fact that graphs in practice tend to be sparse.

By defining $\pi' = P^T\pi$ and $\pi'' = \pi' - \pi$, and conducting some simple mathematical transformations, we can reduce the partial derivative on π to,

$$\frac{\partial G}{\partial \pi} = 2\alpha[d(P\pi'' - \pi'') + (1-d)(\pi - r + dPr)] - (1-\alpha)B^T\mu. \quad (15)$$

In order to compute (15), only three steps of matrix-vector multiplications are needed: $P^T\pi$, $P\pi''$, and Pr. Similarly, the computations in (10) and (11) can also be simplified with the help of π' and π'', i.e.,

$$\frac{\partial G}{\partial \omega} = 2\alpha d\{[\pi'' + (1-d)r] \otimes \pi\}^T \frac{\partial vec(P)}{\partial \omega^T}. \quad (16)$$

$$\frac{\partial G}{\partial \phi} = 2\alpha(1-d)[(1-d)r + d\pi' - \pi]\frac{\partial r}{\partial \phi}. \quad (17)$$

Since the graph is sparse, in (16), we only need to compute the non-zero blocks in the Kronecker product and the left partial derivative vector in (13). Suppose there are m edges in the graph, then the cost is proportional to m. In general, the computational complexity of the proposed Semi-Supervised PageRank algorithm is only of order $O(ml + n)$.

Moreover, we can parallelize the algorithm using MapReduce. MapReduce [12] is a programming model for parallelizing large-scale computations on a distributed computer cluster. It reformulates the logic of a computation task to a series of Map and Reduce operations. The map operation takes a <key, value> pair, and emits one or more intermediate <key, value> pairs. Then all values with the same intermediate key are grouped together into a <key, valuelist> pair, where valuelist contains all values associated with the same key. The reduce operation reads a <key, valuelist> pair and emits one or more new <key, value> pairs.

There are mainly two kinds of large-scale computation prototypes in SSP, i.e., matrix-vector multiplication and Kronecker product of vectors on a sparse graph. These proto-

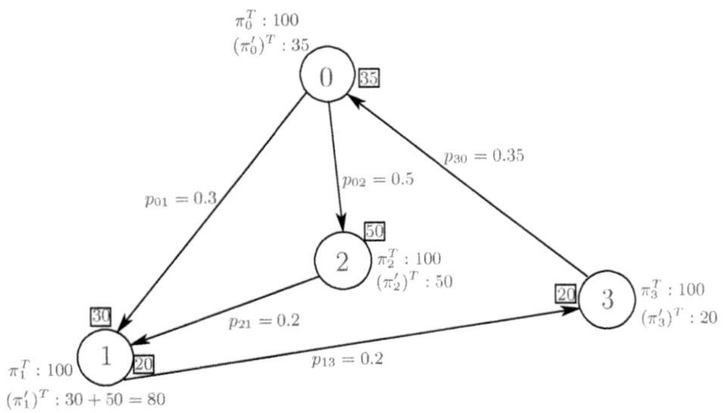

Figure 2: Matrix P is built from the graph, in which element p_{ij} is defined as the normalized edge weight from node i to node j. The product $\pi^T P$ can be interpreted as the data propagation process on the graph. $\pi^T \Rightarrow (\pi')^T$.

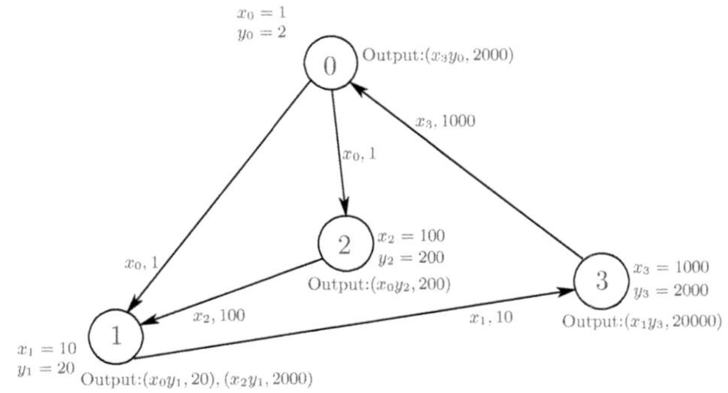

Figure 3: Kronecker product of two vectors is trying to compute $x_i y_j$ under the constraint of graph structure. We can propagate x_i along graph edges, so as to filter necessary x_i to multiply y_j. The process can be implemented by two MapReduce processes.

types can be written in the below MapReduce logic, in which we denote O_i as the outlink node set of node i, and I_i as the inlink node set of node i.

3.3.1 Matrix-Vector Multiplication

We take $\pi' = P^T \pi$ as example. It can be equally written as $(\pi')^T = \pi^T P$. The computation can be performed using a graph based propagation process. That is, we first take π^T as a meta data of node i, and then pass π^T from node i to each of its connected node j by multiplying p_{ij}. By aggregating all the incoming values on each node j, we can get the new $(\pi')^T$. The process can be implemented as below (refer to Figure 2).

Map: Take graph record $< i, \{j, p_{ij}\}, j \in O_i >$ and $< i, \pi_i >$ as input. Map input on j, such that tuples with the same j are shuffled to the same machine in the form of $< j, \{\pi_i p_{ij}\}, \forall j \in O_i >$.

Reduce: Take $< j, \{\pi_i p_{ij}\}, \forall i \in I_j >$ and emit $< j, \pi'_j >$, where $\pi'_j = \sum_{\forall i \in I_j} \pi_i p_{ij}$.

3.3.2 Kronecker Product of Vectors on a Sparse Graph

Suppose x and y are both n-dimensional vectors, we want to compute the Kronecker product $z = x \otimes y$ (z is an n^2-dimensional vector) of them on a sparse graph, i.e., we need to compute $x_i y_j$ only if there is an edge from page i to page j in the graph. We do not want to look up the sparse graph to determine whether we need to compute $x_i y_j$. The solution is to take x_i, y_i as the meta data of node i in the graph, and pass x_i from node i to its connected nodes. After that, we can aggregate the incoming x_i to node j. By multiplying y_j with all x_i received on node j, we can get all necessary $x_i y_j$. The operations can be implemented as below (refer to Figure 3).

Map-I: Take graph record $< i, \{j, p_{ij}\}, j \in O_i >$ and $< i, x_i >$ as input. Map input on j, such that tuples with the same j are shuffled to the same machine in the form of $< j, (i, x_i) >$.

Reduce-I: Take $< j, (i, x_i), \forall i \in I_j >$, and emit $< j, \{(i, x_i), i \in I_j\} >$.

Map-II: Map $< j, \{(i, x_i), i \in I_j\} >$ and $< j, y_j >$ on j, such that tuples with the same j are shuffled to the same machine in the form of $< j, \{y_j, (i, x_i), i \in I_j\} >$.

Reduce-II: Take $< j, \{y_j, (i, x_i), i \in I_j\} >$, and emit $< i, j, x_i y_j >$.

Besides this, there are some other operations in the SSP algorithm that can also be written in the MapReduce logic, including vector normalization, vector addition (and subtraction), and the gradient updating rules. As the implementations are trivial, we will not give unnecessary details.

3.4 Advantages

As has been seen so far, the SSP algorithm has the following advantages. (i) It can naturally leverage all the information useful for graph ranking, including meta information on graphs and supervision information from humans. (ii) It has a nearly linear time complexity with respect to the number of edges, and thus can scale up to very large graphs. (iii) It employs a parametric model, which has a generalization ability. In fact, with our algorithm, the ranking model can be learned from one graph (or one part of a graph) and applied to the other graphs (or the other parts of a graph).

4. RELATED WORK

In the framework we defined in Section 2, graph structure, edge features, and node features are all considered. If only a part of them are used, we obtain several variants of the objective function. Most recent work on graph ranking can be understood as optimizing such special cases, as shown below.[4] It is obvious that these special cases are not as powerful as the general case using the Type (a) objective function in Table 1.

(i) LiftHITS [10] corresponds to optimizing the Type (d) objective function defined based upon the HITS algorithm, subject to constraints of binary labels derived from user feedback. It cannot leverage information carried by node and edge features, neither can it expand to very-large-scale graphs. When 'lifting' the authority of one node, many corresponding sparse rows in the link matrix will become dense. The problem will become more severe when 'lifting' the authority of multiple nodes. As a result, the computation of the eigenvectors of the link matrix will be prohibitively expensive.

(ii) Adaptive PageRank [22] alters the PageRank scores of nodes according to feedback from humans, using an optimization technique. It corresponds to optimizing the Type (d) objective function subject to constraints of the pairwise

[4]We present the detailed derivations in Section 5.

Table 1: Different forms of the objective function.

TYPE	EDGE	NODE	FORM	EXAMPLE METHODS
(a)	$\surd$	$\surd$	$R(\pi; f(\omega, X), g(\phi, Y))$	Semi-Supervised PageRank
(b)	$\surd$		$R(\pi; f(\omega, X))$	
(c)		$\surd$	$R(\pi; g(\phi, Y))$	
(d)			$R(\pi)$	LiftHITS, Adaptive PageRank, NetRank, Laplacian Rank

preferences. It does not use the edge features, and it has high time complexity. This is because it requires computing the inverse of the link matrix during its optimization process. The authors have proposed grouping nodes into clusters, to reduce the complexity. However, to make effective use of human supervision, the number of clusters cannot be too small and thus the issue has not been fundamentally solved.

(iii) NetRank [9, 3] learns the parameters of the Markov random walk on the graph according to supervision information. It corresponds to optimizing the Type (d) objective function subject to the constraints of the pairwise preferences. The method does not leverage the node and edge features; and it is also inefficient, because it needs to compute successive matrix multiplications multiple times at each step of the optimization process.

(iv) Laplacian Rank [24, 4, 18, 23] formulates the supervised graph ranking problem as that of minimizing a combination of an empirical loss and a graph Laplacian based regularization term. It corresponds to optimizing the Type (d) objective function subject to the constraints of the pairwise preferences. In addition to not being able to use the node and edge features, it cannot scale up due to the necessity of computing the pseudo-inverse of the Laplacian matrix in the optimization process.

To sum up, these previous methods cannot make effective use of information on the nodes and edges, and/or cannot scale up to very large graphs.

In addition, there are some other works on classification or link prediction on graphs with metadata. SPA [11] is a graph node classifier based on kernel smoothing trained by semi-supervised learning. It leverages the information from both the labeled nodes and the relationship between labeled and unlabeled nodes. WITCH [1] is a spam page classifier based on graph regularization. It exploits both the graph structure and the web page content to learn a linear classifier using an SVM-like objective function. Supervised Random Walks [5] combines the network structure with node and edge attributes, and uses the attributes to supervise a random walk on the graph in link prediction. All these works are not for graph ranking, and thus it is not appropriate to make a comparison of them with the current work.

5. DISCUSSION

We show that several previous graph ranking algorithms actually correspond to special cases of the proposed framework in (1) or another form (3).

5.1 LiftHITS

Suppose a link matrix M specifies the connectivity between nodes, i.e., $M_{ij} \neq 0$ if there is a link from node i to node j; $M_{ij} = 0$, otherwise. Then the authority scores π can be iteratively computed by $\pi' = M^T M\pi$ in HITS. If we let $S(\pi; B, \mu) = B(\pi' - \pi)$, and use a Type (d) objective function $R(\pi) = \|\pi' - M^T M\pi\|$, then Problem (1) will become

$$\begin{array}{ll} \min_{\pi \geq 0} & \|\pi' - M^T M\pi\| \\ s.t. & B(\pi' - \pi) \geq 0, \end{array} \tag{18}$$

where matrix B specifies the nodes that should be 'lifted" in the next iteration.

The above formulation is equivalent to the LiftHITS method proposed in [10]. In other words, LiftHITS is a special case of the general framework, in which the Type (d) objective function and the constraints of binary labels are used.

5.2 Adaptive PageRank

If we let $S(\pi; B, \mu) = B\pi - \xi$, where $\xi > 0$ is a slack vector, and adopt a Type (d) objective function $R(\pi) \equiv R(\pi(\eta)) = \|\pi(\eta) - \bar{\pi}\|$, where π and $\bar{\pi}$ are computed from the graph structure, then Problem (1) will become

$$\begin{array}{ll} \min_{\pi \geq 0} & \|\pi(\eta) - \bar{\pi}\| \\ s.t. & B\pi \geq \xi,\ \xi \geq 0 \\ & \bar{\pi} = (1-d)(I - dP)^{-1}e \\ & \pi(\eta) = (1-d)(I - dP)^{-1}\eta \\ & \eta \geq 0. \end{array} \tag{19}$$

where P is the transition matrix derived from the graph, d is the damping factor in PageRank, and η is a n-dimensional parameter vector for the nodes in the graph.

The above formulation exactly corresponds to the Adaptive PageRank method proposed in [22]. In other words, Adaptive PageRank is a special case of the general framework, in which the Type (d) objective function and the constraints of the pairwise preferences are used.

5.3 NetRank

Suppose the transition matrix is parameterized by different types of edges, i.e., edge (i, j) belongs to type $t(i, j)$. If type t has an associated weight $w(t)$, the weight of edge (i, j) will be $w(t(i, j))$. Thus one possible formulation of the parametric transition matrix can be written by

$$P_{ij}(t) = \frac{w(t(i,j))}{\sum_j w(t(i,j))}. \tag{20}$$

If we set $\alpha = 0$ and let $S(\pi; B, \mu) = -e^T(e - B\pi)$, Problem (3) will become as follows,

$$\begin{array}{ll} \min_{\pi \geq 0} & \sum_{i \prec j} (1 + \pi_i - \pi_j) \\ s.t. & \pi = (P^T(t))^H \pi^{(0)}. \end{array} \tag{21}$$

where $\pi^{(0)}$ is a vector whose elements all equal $\frac{1}{n}$, and H is the iteration number of matrix multiplication.

The above problem corresponds to one formulation of the NetRank method [9]. In other words, NetRank is a special case of the general framework, in which the Type (*d*) objective function and the constraints of the pairwise preferences are used.

5.4 Laplacian Rank

If we define the Type (*d*) objective function using the Laplacian of the graph, i.e., $R(\pi) = \pi^T L \pi$, where

$$L = I - \frac{\Pi^{1/2} P \Pi^{-1/2} + \Pi^{-1/2} P^T \Pi^{1/2}}{2} \quad (22)$$

is the Laplacian for the directed graph, and Π is a diagonal matrix with $\Pi_{ii} = \bar{\pi}_i$ ($\bar{\pi}$ has the same definition as in Section 5.2), use the pairwise preferences as the constraints, and set $\alpha = \frac{1}{2}$, Problem (3) will become,

$$\begin{array}{ll} \min_{\pi \geq 0} & \frac{1}{2}\pi^T L \pi + \frac{1}{2}\sum_{(i,j)} \mu_{ij}\xi_{ij} \\ s.t. & \pi_i - \pi_j \geq 1 - \xi_{ij}, \xi_{ij} \geq 0. \end{array} \quad (23)$$

This is exactly the Laplacian Rank method discussed in [24, 4, 18, 23].[5] In this regard, we say Laplacian Rank is a special case of the general framework, in which the Type (*d*) objective function and the constraints of the pairwise preferences are used.

6. EXPERIMENTAL RESULTS

In the experiments, we use page importance ranking on web graphs to evaluate the performance of our proposed SSP algorithm.

Two web graphs of different scales are used. The pages on both graphs belong to the ".uk" domain.

- The first graph, denoted as G_1, is the website graph from the Web Spam Challenge [8, 25], which contains 114,529 nodes and 1,836,441 edges. Some websites in the dataset G_1 are labeled as "spam" or "non-spam", and the labeled data is partitioned into a training set (with 222 spam sites and 3,776 non-spam sites) and a test set (with 122 spam sites and 1,933 non-spam sites).
- The second graph, denoted as G_2, is from a commercial web search engine, which contains about 1.4 billion pages and 15.6 billion edges. Together with the graph, a dataset of queries and their associated web pages are also provided. The dataset is partitioned into a training set (with millions of queries collected from the query log in October 2009) and a test set (with about 2000 queries sampled from the query log in November 2009). In the training set, the click-through count of each page is given as the implicit judgment on its relevance to the query. In the test set, each document is manually labeled as "relevant" or "irrelevant."

For each edge in the graphs, we extract ten features, including (1) the type of the edge (i.e., intra-site or inter-site), (2) the inlink number of the source node of the edge, (3) the outlink number of the source node of the edge, (4) the inlink number of the destination node of the edge, (5) the outlink number of the destination node of the edge, (6) the URL depth of the source node of the edge, (7) the URL depth of the destination node of the edge, (8) the URL length of the source node of the edge, (9) the URL length of the destination node of the edge, and (10) the weight (link number) of the edge. For each node, we extract five features, including (1) the inlink number of the node, (2) the outlink number of the node, (3) the number of two-step neighbors, (4) the URL depth of the node, and (5) the URL length of the node.

[5]The work in [18] used an alternate form of Laplacian Rank in label propagation for classification, and used an alternate form of PageRank in graph ranking.

Table 2: Number of spam websites over buckets.

No.	# of Websites	PageRank	AP	SSP
1	150	2	0	0
2	537	2	0	0
3	1257	1	1	0
4	2660	2	8	2
5	4788	4	7	8
6	8344	12	7	9
7	13708	7	16	12
8	20846	13	33	27
9	29008	19	25	42
10	33231	60	25	22

The parameters for our algorithm are set empirically as follows: (i) μ is set to a vector whose elements are all equal to 1; (ii) ρ is set to 0.1; (iii) ϵ is set to 10^{-12}; (iv) α is set to 0.5. In our experiments, the SSP algorithm converges within 30 iterations.

We run the experiments on a cluster of 40 Rackable C2004 servers each with a quad-core CPU and 8 gigabytes memory. We test two baseline algorithms in addition to our algorithm: PageRank and Adaptive PageRank (AP for short). We are not able to test LiftHITS, NetRank, and Laplacian Rank in our computer cluster, because these algorithms are computationally very demanding. Even in a more powerful computing environment, these algorithms could hardly handle a dataset like G_1 or G_2. In the experiments, the damping factors for SSP, PageRank, and AP are all heuristically set to 0.85. For AP, we conduct clustering on the nodes, with each cluster containing about 10,000 nodes, following the proposal in [22]. Even with clustering, AP can only run on G_1. Therefore we only report the result of AP on G_1. Note that we do not consider the efficient implementations of personalized PageRank [14] such as those in [21] as baselines. The reason is that such personalized PageRank methods largely depend on the preference assumption, like the topic bias in topic-sensitive PageRank[13], which does not hold in the general setting of SSP.

6.1 Anti-Spam

We use the spam labels in the training set of G_1 as supervision information to train different page importance ranking methods, and evaluate the ranking results on the test set to see whether the methods are good at anti-spam.

In order to train SSP and AP, we create pairwise preferences from the spam labels (i.e., non-spam websites are preferred to spam websites). We evaluate the ranking performance using spam bucket distribution. Specifically, given an algorithm, we sort all the websites in G_1 in the descending order of their ranking scores given by the algorithm. Then we put these sorted websites into 10 buckets.[6] The numbers of the labeled spam websites in the test set over the buckets

[6]The buckets are partitioned based on the scores given by the algorithm. That is, the sum of the scores in each bucket is 10% of the total score.

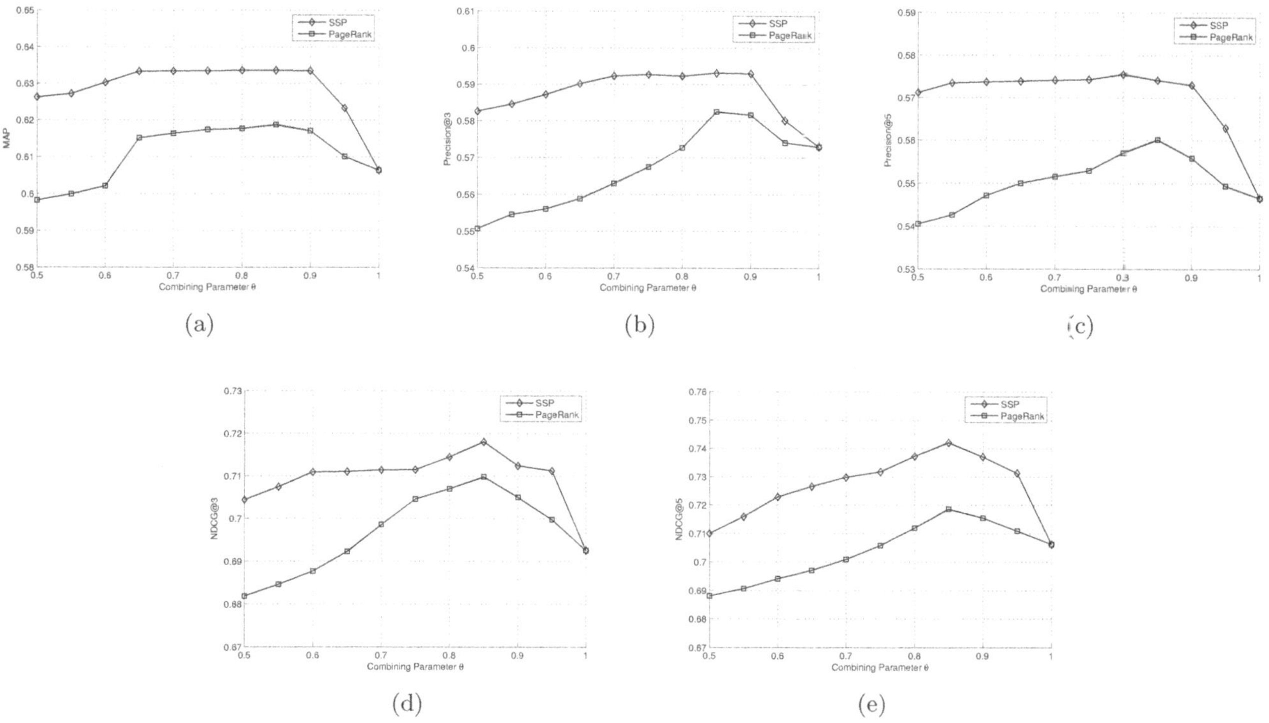

Figure 4: (a) Search performance in terms of MAP. (b) Search performance in terms of Precision@3. (c) Search performance in terms of Precision@5. (d) Search performance in terms of NDCG@3. (e) Search performance in terms of NDCG@5.

for different algorithms are listed in Table 2. Considering that the goal of spammers is to promote the ranking positions of their websites, a ranking algorithm with good anti-spam ability should remove as many spam sites from the top buckets as possible. For the websites in the bottom buckets, as their page importance scores are very low, whether they are spam or not does not make much difference.

From the table, we have the following observations: (i) AP performs better than PageRank, for AP can take advantage of supervision information while PageRank is an unsupervised algorithm. (ii) SSP outperforms AP, for SSP can leverage more information than AP. Specifically, SSP integrates graph structure, edge features, node features, and supervision information into the ranking mechanism, while AP does not consider using edge features and node features. Therefore, SSP can successfully remove more spam websites from the top buckets, compared to the two baselines.

6.2 Relevance Ranking

In web search, the retrieved pages for a given query are often ranked according to two factors: content relevance and page importance. Without loss of generality, we use a linear combination of these two factors to produce the final ranking result,

$$\theta Score_{relevance} + (1-\theta) Score_{importance}, \qquad (24)$$

where $0 \leq \theta \leq 1$ is the combining parameter. In our experiments, we use BM25 [20] to generate the relevance score, and the importance score is calculated by different algorithms under investigation. The corresponding relevance ranking performances are evaluated in terms of MAP [6], Precision@k [6], and NDCG@k [6] on the test set.

As mentioned above, since G_2 is extremely large, only PageRank and SSP can run on the data. For SSP, we construct pairwise preferences from the click-through counts. That is, if the number of clicks of a page for all the queries in the training data is larger than that of the other page, we will create a pairwise constraint on the two pages. PageRank does not use any training data since it is an unsupervised algorithm. After a ranking model is trained by an algorithm, we compute the importance scores of all the pages in G_2 using the ranking model. We then combine the importance score and relevance score to rank the pages in the test set.

MAP of the ranking results are shown in Figure 4 (a). Precision @3, 5 of the ranking results are shown in Figure 4 (b) and (c). NDCG@3, 5 of the ranking results are shown in Figure 4 (d) and (e). From the figures, we can see that SSP consistently outperforms PageRank, with all θ values, and in terms of all evaluation measures. The explanation for the better performance of SSP is as follows. By leveraging more helpful information (e.g., node and edge features, supervision information), SSP can achieve better performance than PageRank in page importance ranking.

To summarize the experimental results, SSP outperforms the baseline algorithms on several tasks and in several evaluation measures, and can handle billion-scale graphs very well.

7. CONCLUSIONS AND FUTURE WORK

In this paper, we have defined a semi-supervised learning framework for graph ranking on a very-large-scale graph, and developed an efficient algorithm named Semi-Supervised PageRank (SSP) within the framework. The new algorithm can make effective use of supervision information, leverage rich information on the graph, and scale up to very-large-scale problems. Our experimental results have shown that the proposed algorithm can outperform baseline algorithms on graph ranking.

For future work, we plan to investigate the following issues. (i) We will try advanced optimization techniques like conjugate gradient method to minimize the objective function in Semi-Supervised PageRank, instead of using the simple gradient descent method. (ii) We plan to try other forms of objective functions, so as to extend the idea of SSP to other algorithms such as Semi-Supervised HITS. (iii) We will consider improving SSP using both labeled and unlabeled data as in conventional semi-supervised learning. Currently, the preference matrix B only contains known preference pairs; we may extent B to cover all pairs (both known pairs and unknown pairs) and also predict the relationship of the unknown pairs in the learning process. (iv) We will conduct more comprehensive studies to investigate the sensitivity of the parameters in the model.

8. REFERENCES

[1] J. Abernethy, O. Chapelle, and C. Castillo. Web spam identification through content and hyperlinks. In the proceedings of AIRWeb'08, 2008.

[2] A. Agarwal and S. Chakrabarti. Learning random walks to rank nodes in graphs. In the proceedings of the 24th International Conference on Machine Learning (*ICML*), pages 9-16, 2007.

[3] A. Agarwal, S. Chakrabarti, and S. Aggarwal. Learning to rank networked entites. In the proceedings of the 12th ACM SIGKDD International Conference on Knowledge Discovery and Data Mining, pages 14-23, 2006.

[4] S. Agarwal. Ranking on graph data. In the proceedings of the 23th International Conference on Machine Learning (*ICML*), pages 25-32, 2006.

[5] L. Backstrom and J. Leskovec. Supervised Random Walks: Predicting and Recommending Links in Social Networks. In the proceedings of the 4th ACM International Conference on Web Search and Data Mining (*WSDM*), pages 635-644, 2011.

[6] R. Baeza-Yates and B. Ribeiro-Neto. *Modern Information Retrieval.* Addison Wesley, ISBN-13: 978-0201398298, May 1999.

[7] S. Brin and L. Page. The anatomy of a large-scale hypertextual Web search engine. In *Computer Networks and ISDN Systems*, volume 30, issue 1-7, pages 107-117, 1998.

[8] C. Castillo, D. Donato, L. Becchetti, P. Boldi, S. Leonardi, M. Santini, and S. Vigna. A reference collection for web spam. In *SIGIR Forum*, volumn 40, issue 2, pages 11-24, 2006.

[9] S. Chakrabarti and A. Agarwal. Learning parameters in entity relationship graphs from ranking preferences. In the proceedings of the 10th European Conference on Principles and Practice of Knowledge Discovery in Databases (*PKDD*), volume 4213, pages 91-102, 2006.

[10] H. Chang, D. Cohn, and A. K. McCallum. Learning to create customized authority lists. In the proceedings of the 17th International Conference on Machine Learning (*ICML*), pages 127-134, 2000.

[11] M. Culp and G. Michailidis. Graph-based semisupervised learning. IEEE Transactions on Pattern Analysis and Machine Intelligence, VOL. 30, No. 1, pages 174-179, 2008.

[12] J. Dean and S. Ghemawat. MapReduce: Simplified Data Processing on Large Clusters. In the proceedings of the 6th Symposium on Operating System Design and Implementation (*OSDI*), 2004.

[13] T. H. Haveliwala. Topic-sensitive PageRank. In the proceedings of the 11th International World Wide Web Conference (*WWW*), 2002.

[14] T. Haveliwala, S. D. Kamvar, and G. Jeh. An Analytical Comparison of Approaches to Personalizing PageRank. Stanford University, Preprint, 2003.

[15] J. M. Kleinberg. Authoritative sources in a hyperlinked environment. In the proceedings of the 9th Annual ACM-SIAM Symposium on Discrete Algorithms (*SODA*), pages 668-677, 1998.

[16] T. Kolda and B. Bader. The TOPHITS Model for Higher-Order Web Link Analysis. In the proceedings of the 4th Workshop on Link Analysis, Counterterrorism and Security, in conjunction with the 6th SIAM International Conference on Data Mining (*SDM*), 2006.

[17] L. Page, S. Brin, R. Motwani, and T. Winograd. The PageRank citation ranking: bringing order to the web. Technical report, Stanford Digital Library Technologies Project, 1998.

[18] D. Rao, and D. Yarowsky. Ranking and semi-supervised classification on large scale graphs using map-reduce. In the proceedings of the 4th International Joint Conference on Natural Language Processing of the Asian Federation of Natural Language Processing (*ACL-IJCNLP*), 2009.

[19] M. Richardson and P. Domingos. The intelligent surfer: probabilistic combination of link and content information in PageRank. In the proceedings of the 16th Annual Conference on Neural Information Processing Systems (*NIPS*), 2002.

[20] S. E. Robertson. Overview of okapi projects. *Journal of Documentatioin*, volumn 53, issue 1, pages 3-7, 1997.

[21] T. Sarlos, A. A. Benczur, K. Csalogany, D. Fogaras, and B. Racz. To randomize or not to randomize: space optimal summaries for hyperlink analysis. In the proceedings of the 15th International World Wide Web Conference (*WWW*), pages 297-306, 2006.

[22] A. C. Tsoi, G. Morini, F. Scarselli, M. Hagenbuchner, and M. Maggini. Adaptive ranking of Web pages. In the proceedings of the 12th International World Wide Web Conference (*WWW*), pages 356-365, 2003.

[23] M. Xie, J. Liu, N. Zheng, D. Li, Y. Huang, and Y. Wang. Semi-supervised graph-ranking for text retrieval. In the proceedings of the 4th Asia Infomation Retrieval Symposium (*AIRS*), pages 256-263, 2008.

[24] D. Zhou, J. Huang, and B. Scholkopf. Learning from labeled and unlabeled data on a directed graph. In the proceedings of the 22th International Conference on Machine Learning (*ICML*), pages 1041-1048, 2005.

[25] http://www.yr-bcn.es/webspam/datasets/uk2007/

Benefits of Bias: Towards Better Characterization of Network Sampling

Arun S. Maiya
Dept. of Computer Science
University of Illinois at Chicago
arun@maiya.net

Tanya Y. Berger-Wolf
Dept. of Computer Science
University of Illinois at Chicago
tanyabw@cs.uic.edu

ABSTRACT

From social networks to P2P systems, network sampling arises in many settings. We present a detailed study on the nature of biases in network sampling strategies to shed light on how best to sample from networks. We investigate connections between specific biases and various measures of structural representativeness. We show that certain biases are, in fact, beneficial for many applications, as they "push" the sampling process towards inclusion of desired properties. Finally, we describe how these sampling biases can be exploited in several, real-world applications including disease outbreak detection and market research.

Categories and Subject Descriptors

H.2.8 [**Database Management**]: Database Applications—*Data Mining*

General Terms

Algorithms; Experimentation, Measurement

Keywords

sampling, bias, social network analysis, complex networks, graph mining, link mining, online sampling, crawling

1. INTRODUCTION AND MOTIVATION

We present a detailed study on the nature of biases in network sampling strategies to shed light on how best to sample from networks. A *network* is a system of interconnected entities typically represented mathematically as a graph: a set of vertices and a set of edges among the vertices. Networks are ubiquitous and arise across numerous and diverse domains. For instance, many Web-based social media, such as online social networks, produce large amounts of data on interactions and associations among individuals. Mobile phones and location-aware devices produce copious amounts of data on both communication patterns and physical proximity between people. In the domain of biology also, from neurons to proteins to food webs, there is now access to large networks of associations among various entities and a need to analyze and understand these data.

With advances in technology, pervasive use of the Internet, and the proliferation of mobile phones and location-aware devices, networks under study today are not only substantially larger than those in the past, but sometimes exist in a decentralized form (e.g. the network of blogs or the Web itself). For many networks, their global structure is not fully visible to the public and can only be accessed through "crawls" (e.g. online social networks). These factors can make it prohibitive to analyze or even access these networks in their entirety. How, then, should one proceed in analyzing and mining these network data? One approach to addressing these issues is *sampling*: inference using small subsets of nodes and links from a network.

From epidemiological applications [13] to Web crawling [7] and P2P search [47], network sampling arises across many different settings. In the present work, we focus on a particular line of investigation that is concerned with constructing samples that match critical structural properties of the original network. Such samples have numerous applications in data mining and information retrieval. In [29], for example, structurally-representative samples were shown to be effective in inferring network protocol performance in the larger network and significantly improving the efficiency of protocol simulations. In Section 7, we discuss several additional applications. Although there have been a number of recent strides in work on network sampling (e.g. [3,25,29,34]), there is still very much that requires better and deeper understanding. Towards this end, we conduct a detailed study on *network sampling biases*. There has been a recent spate of work focusing on *problems* that arise from network sampling biases including how and why biases should be avoided [1,15,20,30,46,47]. Our work differs from much of this existing literature in that, for the first time in a comprehensive manner, we examine network sampling bias as an *asset to be exploited*. We argue that biases of certain sampling strategies can be advantageous if they "push" the sampling process towards inclusion of specific properties of interest. Our main aim in the present work is to identify and understand the connections between specific sampling biases and specific definitions of structural representativeness, so that these biases can be leveraged in practical applications.

Summary of Findings. We conduct a detailed investigation of network sampling biases. We find that bias towards high *expansion* (a concept from expander graphs) offers several unique advantages over other biases such as those to-

KDD'11, August 21–24, 2011, San Diego, California, USA.

ward high degree nodes. We show both empirically and analytically that such an expansion bias "pushes" the sampling process towards new, undiscovered clusters and the discovery of wider portions of the network. In other analyses, we show that a simple sampling process that selects nodes with many connections from those already sampled is often a reasonably good approximation to directly sampling high degree nodes and locates well-connected (i.e. high degree) nodes significantly faster than most other methods. We also find that the breadth-first search, a widely-used sampling and search strategy, is surprisingly among the most dismal performers in terms of both discovering the network and accumulating critical, well-connected nodes. Finally, we describe ways in which some of our findings can be exploited in several important applications including disease outbreak detection and market research. A number of these aforementioned findings are surprising in that they are in stark contrast to conventional wisdom followed in much of the existing literature (e.g. [2,13,30,41,42]).

2. RELATED WORK

Not surprisingly, network sampling arises across many diverse areas. Here, we briefly describe some of these different lines of research.

Network Sampling in Classical Statistics. The concept of sampling networks first arose to address scenarios where one needed to study hidden or difficult-to-access populations (e.g. illegal drug users, prostitutes). For recent surveys, one might refer to [19,28]. The work in this area focuses almost exclusively on acquiring unbiased estimates related to variables of interest attached to each network node. The present work, however, focuses on inferring properties related to the *network itself* (many of which are not amenable to being fully captured by simple attribute frequencies). Our work, then, is much more closely related to *representative subgraph sampling*.

Representative Subgraph Sampling. In recent years, a number of works have focused on *representative subgraph sampling*: constructing samples in such a way that they are condensed representations of the original network (e.g. [3,25,29,32,34]). Much of this work focuses on how best to produce a "universal" sample representative of *all* structural properties in the original network. By contrast, we subscribe to the view that no single sampling strategy may be appropriate for all applications. Thus, our aim, then, is to better understand the *biases* in specific sampling strategies to shed light on how best to leverage them in practical applications.

Unbiased Sampling. There has been a relatively recent spate of work (e.g. [20,22,47]) that focuses on constructing uniform random samples in scenarios where nodes cannot be easily drawn randomly (e.g. settings such as the Web where nodes can only be accessed through crawls). These strategies, often based on modified random walks, have been shown to be effective for various frequency estimation problems (e.g. inferring the proportion of pages of a certain language in a Web graph [22]). However, as mentioned above, the present work focuses on using samples to infer structural (and functional) properties of the *network itself*. In this regard, we found these unbiased methods to be less effective during preliminary testing. Thus, we do not consider them and instead focus our attention on other more appropriate sampling strategies (such as those mentioned in *representative subgraph sampling*).

Studies on Sampling Bias. Several studies have investigated *biases* that arise from various sampling strategies (e.g. [1,15,30,31,46]). For instance, [46] showed that, under the simple sampling strategy of picking nodes at random from a scale-free network (i.e. a network whose degree distribution follows the power law), the resultant subgraph sample will *not* be scale-free. The authors of [1,31] showed the converse is true under traceroute sampling. Virtually all existing results on network sampling bias focus on its negative aspects. By contrast, we focus on the *advantages* of certain biases and ways in which they can be exploited in network analysis.

Property Testing. Work on sampling exists in the fields of combinatorics and graph theory and is centered on the notion of *property testing* in graphs [38]. Properties such as those typically studied in graph theory, however, may be less useful for the analysis of *real-world* networks (e.g. the exact meaning of, say, k-colorability [38] within the context of a social network is unclear). Nevertheless, theoretical work on property testing in graphs is excellently surveyed in [38].

Other Areas. Decentralized search (e.g. searching unstructured P2P networks) and Web crawling can both be framed as network sampling problems, as both involve making decisions from subsets of nodes and links from a larger network. Indeed, network sampling itself can be viewed as a problem of information retrieval, as the aim is to seek out a subset of nodes that either individually or collectively match some criteria of interest. Several of the sampling strategies we study in the present work, in fact, are graph search algorithms (e.g. breadth-first search). Thus, a number of our findings discussed later have implications for these research areas (e.g. see [39]). For reviews on decentralized search both in the contexts of complex networks and P2P systems, one may refer to [27] and [49], respectively. For examples of connections between Web crawling and network sampling, see [7,9,42].

3. PRELIMINARIES

3.1 Notations and Definitions

We now briefly describe some notations and definitions used throughout this paper.

Definition 1. $G = (V, E)$ is a *network* or *graph* where V is set of vertices (or nodes) and $E \subseteq V \times V$ is a set of edges (or links among the nodes).

Definition 2. A *sample* S is a subset of vertices, $S \subset V$.

Definition 3. $N(S)$ is the *neighborhood* of S if $N(S) = \{w \in V - S : \exists v \in S \; s.t. \; (v, w) \in E\}$.

Definition 4. G_S is the *induced subgraph* of G based on the sample S if $G_S = (S, E_S)$ where the vertex set is $S \subset V$ and the edge set is $E_S = (S \times S) \cap E$. The induced subgraph of a sample may also be referred to as a *subgraph sample*.

3.2 Datasets

We study sampling biases in a total of twelve different networks: a power grid (PowerGrid [50]), a Wikipedia voting network (WikiVote [33]), a PGP trust network (PGP [6]), a citation network (HEPTh [33]), an email network (Enron [33]), two co-authorship networks (CondMat [33] and

AstroPh [33]), two P2P file-sharing networks (Gnutella04 [33] and Gnutella31 [33]), two online social networks (Epinions [33] and Slashdot [33]), and a product co-purchasing network (Amazon [33]). These datasets were chosen to represent a rich set of diverse networks from different domains. This diversity allows a more comprehensive study of network sampling and thorough assessment of the performance of various sampling strategies in the face of varying network topologies. Table 1 shows characteristics of each dataset. All networks are treated as undirected and unweighted.

Network	N	D	PL	CC	AD
PowerGrid	4941	0.0005	19	0.11	2.7
WikiVote	7066	0.004	3.3	0.21	28.5
PGP	10,680	0.0004	7.5	0.44	4.6
Gnutella04	10,876	0.0006	4.6	0.01	7.4
AstroPh	17,903	0.0012	4.2	0.67	22.0
CondMat	21,363	0.0004	5.4	0.70	8.5
HEPTh	27,400	0.0009	4.3	0.34	25.7
Enron	33,696	0.0003	4.0	0.71	10.7
Gnutella31	62,561	0.00008	5.9	0.01	4.7
Epinions	75,877	0.0001	4.3	0.26	10.7
Slashdot	82,168	0.0001	4.1	0.10	12.2
Amazon	262,111	0.00003	8.8	0.43	6.9

Table 1: Network Properties. **Key:** *N= # of nodes, D= density, PL = characteristic path length, CC = local clustering coefficient, AD = average degree.*

4. NETWORK SAMPLING

In the present work, we focus on a particular class of sampling strategies, which we refer to as *link-trace sampling*. In *link-trace sampling*, the next node selected for inclusion into the sample is always chosen from among the set of nodes directly connected to those already sampled. In this way, sampling proceeds by tracing or following links in the network. This concept can be defined formally.

Definition 5. Given an integer k and an initial node (or seed) $v \in V$ to which S is initialized (i.e. $S = \{v\}$), a *link-trace sampling* algorithm, $\mathcal{A}$, is a process by which nodes are iteratively selected from among the current neighborhood $N(S)$ and added to S until $|S| = k$.

Link-trace sampling may also be referred to as *crawling* (since links are "crawled" to access nodes) or viewed as *online* sampling (since the network G reveals itself iteratively during the course of the sampling process). The key advantage of sampling through link-tracing, then, is that complete access to the network in its entirety is *not* required. This is beneficial for scenarios where the network is either large (e.g. an online social network), decentralized (e.g. an unstructured P2P network), or both (e.g. the Web).

As an aside, notice from Definition 5 that we have implicitly assumed that the neighbors of a given node can be obtained by visiting that node during the sampling process (i.e. $N(S)$ is known). This, of course, accurately characterizes most real scenarios. For instance, neighbors of a Web page can be gleaned from the hyperlinks on a visited page and neighbors of an individual in an online social network can be acquired by viewing (or "scraping") the friends list.

Having provided a general definition of *link-trace sampling*, we must now address *which* nodes in $N(S)$ should be preferentially selected at each iteration of the sampling process. This choice will obviously directly affect the properties of the sample being constructed. We study seven different approaches - all of which are quite simple yet, at the same time, ill-understood in the context of real-world complex networks.

Breadth-First Search (BFS). Starting with a single seed node, the BFS explores the neighbors of visited nodes. At each iteration, it traverses an unvisited neighbor of the *earliest* visited node [14]. In both [30] and [42], it was empirically shown that BFS is biased towards high-degree and high-PageRank nodes. BFS is used prevalently to crawl and collect networks (e.g. [41]).

Depth-First Search (DFS). DFS is similar to BFS, except that, at each iteration, it visits an unvisited neighbor of the most *recently* visited node [14].

Random Walk (RW). A random walk simply selects the next hop uniformly at random from among the neighbors of the current node [37].

Forest Fire Sampling (FFS). FFS, proposed in [34], is essentially a probabilistic version of BFS. At each iteration of a BFS-like process, a neighbor v is only explored according to some "burning" probability p. At $p = 1$, FFS is identical to BFS. We use $p = 0.7$, as recommended in [34].

Degree Sampling (DS). The DS strategy involves greedily selecting the node $v \in N(S)$ with the highest degree (i.e. number of neighbors). A variation of DS was analytically and empirically studied as a P2P search algorithm in [2]. Notice that, in order to select the node $v \in N(S)$ with the highest degree, the process must know $|N(\{v\})|$ for each $v \in N(S)$. That is, knowledge of $N(N(S))$ is required at each iteration. As noted in [2], this requirement is acceptable for some domains such as P2P networks and certain social networks. The DS method is also feasible in scenarios where 1) one is interested in efficiently "downsampling" a network to a connected subgraph, 2) a crawl is repeated and history of the last crawl is available, or 3) the proportion of the network accessed to construct a sample is less important.

SEC (Sample Edge Count). Given the currently constructed sample S, how can we select a node $v \in N(S)$ with the highest degree *without* having knowledge of $N(N(S))$? The SEC strategy tracks the links from the currently constructed sample S to each node $v \in N(S)$ and selects the node v with the most links from S. In other words, we use the degree of v in the induced subgraph of $S \cup \{v\}$ as an approximation of the degree of v in the original network G. Similar approaches have been employed as part of Web crawling strategies with some success (e.g. [9]).

XS (Expansion Sampling). The XS strategy is based on the concept of expansion from work on expander graphs and seeks to greedily construct the sample with the maximal expansion: $\text{argmax}_{S:\,|S|=k} \frac{|N(S)|}{|S|}$, where k is the desired sample size [23, 40]. At each iteration, the next node v selected for inclusion in the sample is chosen based on the expression:

$$\underset{v \in N(S)}{\text{argmax}} \, |N(\{v\}) - (N(S) \cup S)|.$$

Like the DS strategy, this approach utilizes knowledge of $N(N(S))$. In Sections 5.3 and 6.2, we will investigate in detail the effect of this expansion bias on various properties of constructed samples.

5. EVALUATING REPRESENTATIVENESS

What makes one sampling strategy "better" than another? In computer science, "better" is typically taken to be structural *representativeness* (e.g. see [25, 29, 35]). That is, samples are considered better if they are more representative of structural properties in the original network. There are, of course, numerous structural properties from which to choose, and, as correctly observed by Ahmed et al. [4], it is not always clear which should be chosen. Rather than choosing arbitrary structural properties as measures of representativeness, we select specific measures of representativeness that we view as being potentially useful for real applications. We divide these measures (described below) into three categories: Degree, Clustering, and Reach. For each sampling strategy, we generate 100 samples using randomly selected seeds, compute our measures of representativeness on each sample, and plot the average value as sample size grows. (Standard deviations of computed measures are discussed in Section 5.4. Applications for these measures of representativeness are discussed later in Section 7.) Due to space limitations and the large number of networks evaluated, for each evaluation measure, we only show results for two datasets that are illustrative of general trends observed in all datasets. However, full results are available as supplementary material.[1]

5.1 Degree

The degrees (numbers of neighbors) of nodes in a network is a fundamental and well-studied property. In fact, other graph-theoretic properties such as the average path length between nodes can, in some cases, be viewed as byproducts of degree (e.g. short paths arising from a small number of highly-connected hubs that act as conduits [5]). We study two different aspects of degree (with an eye towards real-world applications, discussed in Section 7).

5.1.1 Measures

Degree Distribution Similarity (DistSim)**.** We take the degree sequence of the sample and compare it to that of the original network using the two-sample Kolmogorov-Smirnov (K-S) D-statistic [34], a distance measure. Our objective here is to measure the agreement between the two degree distributions in terms of both shape and location. Specifically, the D-statistic is defined as $D = \max_x\{|F(x) - F_S(x)|\}$, where x is the range of node degrees, and F and F_S are the cumulative degree distributions for G and G_S, respectively [34]. We compute the distribution similarity by subtracting the K-S distance from one.

Hub Inclusion (Hubs)**.** In several applications, one cares less about matching the *overall* degree distribution and more about accumulating the highest degree nodes into the sample quickly (e.g. immunization strategies [13]). For these scenarios, sampling is used as a tool for information retrieval. Here, we evaluate the extent to which sampling strategies accumulate hubs (i.e. high degree nodes) quickly into the sample. As sample size grows, we track the proportion of the top K nodes accumulated by the sample. For our tests, we use $K = 100$.

5.1.2 Results

Figure 1 shows the *degree distribution similarity* (DistSim) and *hub inclusion* (Hubs) for the Slashdot and Enron datasets. Note that the SEC and DS strategies, both of which are biased to high degree nodes, perform best on *hub inclusion* (as expected), but are the *worst* performers on the DistSim measure (which is also a direct result of this bias). (The XS strategy exhibits a similar trend but to a slightly lesser extent.) On the other hand, strategies such as BFS, FFS, and RW tend to perform better on DistSim, but worse on Hubs. For instance, the DS and SEC strategies locate the majority of the top 100 hubs with sample sizes less than 1% in some cases. BFS and FFS require sample sizes of over 10% (and the performance differential is larger when locating hubs ranked higher than 100). More importantly, no strategy performs best on *both* measures. This, then, suggests a tension between goals: constructing small samples of the most well-connected nodes is in conflict with producing small samples exhibiting representative degree distributions. More generally, when selecting sample elements, choices resulting in gains for one area can result in losses for another. Thus, these choices must be made in light of how samples will be used - a subject we discuss in greater depth in Section 7. We conclude this section by briefly noting that the trend observed for SEC seems to be somewhat dependent upon the quality and number of hubs actually present in a network (relative to the size of the network, of course). That is, SEC matches DS more closely as degree distributions exhibit longer and denser tails (as shown in Figure 2). We will revisit this in Section 6.3. (Other strategies are sometimes affected similarly, but the trend is much less consistent.) In general, we find SEC best matches DS performance on many of the social networks (as opposed to technological networks such as the PowerGrid with few "good" hubs, lower average degree, and longer path lengths). However, further investigation is required to draw firm conclusions on this last point.

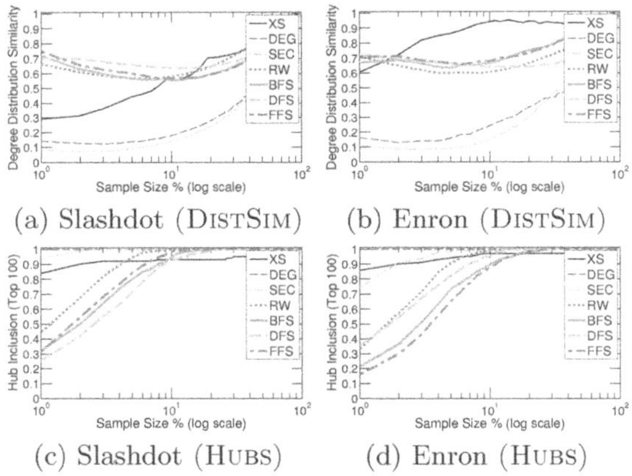

(a) Slashdot (DistSim) (b) Enron (DistSim)

(c) Slashdot (Hubs) (d) Enron (Hubs)

Figure 1: Evaluating (DistSim) and (Hubs). Results for remaining networks are similar.

5.2 Clustering

Many real-world networks, such as social networks, exhibit a much higher level clustering than what one would expect at random [50]. Thus, clustering has been another graph property of interest for some time. Here, we are interested in evaluating the extent to which samples exhibit the level of clustering present in the original network. We employ two notions of clustering, which we now describe.

5.2.1 Measures

Local Clustering Coefficient (CCloc)**.** The local clustering coefficient [43] of a node captures the extent to which

[1]Supplementary material for this paper is available at:
`http://arun.maiya.net/papers/supp-netbias.pdf`

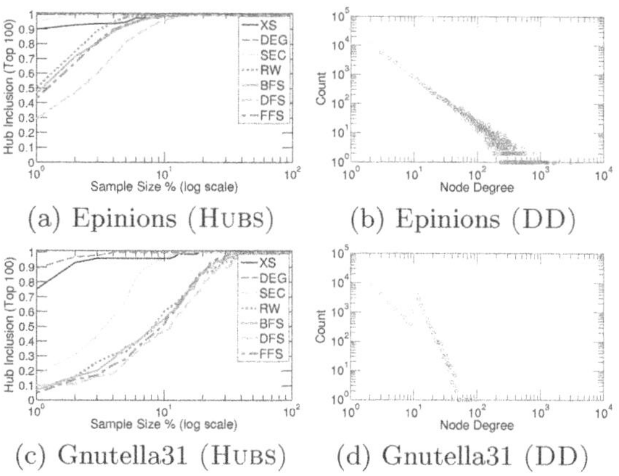

(a) Epinions (HUBS) (b) Epinions (DD)

(c) Gnutella31 (HUBS) (d) Gnutella31 (DD)

Figure 2: Performance of SEC on HUBS (shown in green on left) is observed to be dependent on the tail of the degree distributions (DD). SEC matches DS more closely when more and better quality hubs are present. For HUBS, SEC generally performs best on the social networks evaluated.

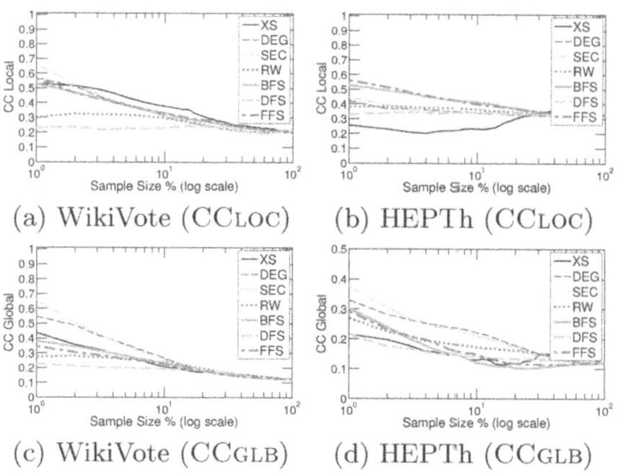

(a) WikiVote (CCLOC) (b) HEPTh (CCLOC)

(c) WikiVote (CCGLB) (d) HEPTh (CCGLB)

Figure 3: Evaluating CCGLB and CCLOC.

the node's neighbors are also neighbors of each other. Formally, the local clustering coefficient of a node is defined as $C_L(v) = \frac{2\ell}{d_v(d_v-1)}$ where d_v is the degree of node v and ℓ is the number of links among the neighbors of v. The average local clustering coefficient for a network is simply $\frac{\sum_{v \in V} C_L(v)}{|V|}$.

Global Clustering Coefficient (CCGLB). The global clustering coefficient [43] is a function of the number of triangles in a network. It is measured as the number of closed triplets divided by the number of connected triples of nodes.

5.2.2 *Results*

Results for clustering measures are less consistent than for other measures. Overall, DFS and RW strategies appear to fare relatively better than others. We do observe that, for many strategies and networks, estimates of clustering are initially higher-than-actual and then gradually decline (see Figure 3). This agrees with intuition. Nodes in clusters should intuitively have more paths leading to them and will, thus, be encountered earlier in a sampling process (as opposed to nodes not embedded in clusters and located in the periphery of a network). This, then, should be taken into consideration in applications where accurately matching clustering levels is important.

5.3 Network Reach

We propose a new measure of representativeness called *network reach*. As a newer measure, *network reach* has obviously received considerably less attention than Degree and Clustering within the existing literature, but it is, nevertheless, a vital measure for a number of important applications (as we will see in Section 7). *Network reach* captures the extent to which a sample *covers* a network. Intuitively, for a sample to be truly representative of a large network, it should consist of nodes from diverse portions of the network, as opposed to being relegated to a small "corner" of the graph. This concept will be made more concrete by discussing in detail the two measures of *network reach* we employ: *community reach* and the *discovery quotient*.

5.3.1 *Measures*

Community Reach (CNM and RAK). Many real-world networks exhibit what is known as *community structure*. A *community* can be loosely defined as a set of nodes more densely connected among themselves than to other nodes in the network. Although there are many ways to represent community structure depending on various factors such as whether or not overlapping is allowed, in this work, we represent community structure as a *partition*: a collection of disjoint subsets whose union is the vertex set V [18]. Under this representation, each subset in the partition represents a community. The task of a community detection algorithm is to identify a partition such that vertices within the same subset in the partition are more densely connected to each other than to vertices in other subsets [18]. For the criterion of *community reach*, a sample is more representative of the network if it consists of nodes from more of the communities in the network. We measure *community reach* by taking the number of communities represented in the sample and dividing by the total number of communities present in the original network. Since a community is essentially a cluster of nodes, one might wonder why we have included *community reach* as a measure of *network reach*, rather than as a measure of *clustering*. The reason is that we are slightly less interested in the structural details of communities detected here. Rather, our aim is to assess how "spread out" a sample is across the network. Since community detection is somewhat of an inexact science (e.g. see [21]), we measure *community reach* with respect to two separate algorithms. We employ both the method proposed by Clauset et al. in [12] (denoted as CNM) and the approach proposed by Raghavan et al. in [45] (denoted as RAK). Essentially, for our purposes, we are defining communities simply as the output of a community detection algorithm.

Discovery Quotient (DQ). An alternative view of *network reach* is to measure the proportion of the network that is *discovered* by a sampling strategy. The number of nodes discovered by a strategy is defined as $|S \cup N(S)|$. The *discovery quotient* is this value normalized by the total number of nodes in a network: $\frac{|S \cup N(S)|}{|V|}$. Intuitively, we are defining the *reach* of a sample here by measuring the extent to which it is one hop away from the rest of the network. As we will discuss in Section 7, samples with high *discovery quotients* have several important applications. Note that a simple greedy algorithm for coverage problems such as this has a well-known sharp approximation bound of $1 - 1/e$ [16,39]. However, link-trace sampling is restricted to selecting subsequent sample elements from the current neighborhood $N(S)$ at each iteration, which results in a much smaller search space. Thus, this approximation guarantee can be shown not to hold within the context of link-trace sampling.

5.3.2 Results

As shown in Figure 4, the XS strategy displays the overwhelmingly best performance on all three measures of *network reach*. We highlight several observations here. First, the extent to which the XS strategy outperforms all others on the RAK and CNM measures is quite striking. We posit that the expansion bias of the XS strategy "pushes" the sampling process towards the inclusion of new communities not already seen (see also [40]). In Section 6.2, we will analytically examine this connection between expansion bias and *community reach*. On the other hand, the SEC method appears to be among the least effective in reaching different communities or clusters. We attribute this to the fact that SEC preferentially selects nodes with many connections to nodes already sampled. Such nodes are likely to be members of clusters already represented in the sample. Second, on the DQ measure, it is surprising that the DS strategy, which explicitly selects high degree nodes, often fails to even come close to the XS strategy. We partly attribute this to an overlap in the neighborhoods of well-connected nodes. By explicitly selecting nodes that contribute to *expansion*, the XS strategy is able to discover a much larger proportion of the network in the same number of steps - in some cases, by actively sampling comparatively *lower* degree nodes. Finally, it is also surprising that the BFS strategy, widely used to crawl and explore online social networks (e.g [41]) and other graphs (e.g. [42]), performs quite dismally on all three measures. In short, we find that nodes contributing most to the expansion of the sample are unique in that they provide specific and significant advantages over and above those provided by nodes that are simply well-connected and those accumulated through standard BFS-based crawls. These and previously mentioned results are in contrast to the conventional wisdom followed in much of the existing literature (e.g. [2,13,30,41,42]).

5.4 A Note on Seed Sensitivity

As described, link-trace sampling methods are initiated from randomly selected seeds. This begs the question: How sensitive are these results to the seed supplied to a strategy? Figure 5 shows the standard deviation of each sampling strategy for both *hub inclusion* and *network reach* as sample size grows. We generally find that methods with the most explicit biases (XS, SEC, DS) tend to exhibit the least seed sensitivity and variability, while the remaining methods (BFS, DFS, FFS, RW) exhibit the most. This trend is exhibited across all measures and all datasets.

6. ANALYZING SAMPLING BIASES

Let us briefly summarize two main observations from Section 5. We saw that the XS strategy dramatically outperformed all others in accumulating nodes from many different communities. We also saw that the SEC strategy was often a reasonably good approximation to directly sampling high degree nodes and locates the set of most well-connected nodes significantly faster than most other methods. Here, we turn our attention to analytically examining these observed connections. We begin by briefly summarizing some existing analytical results.

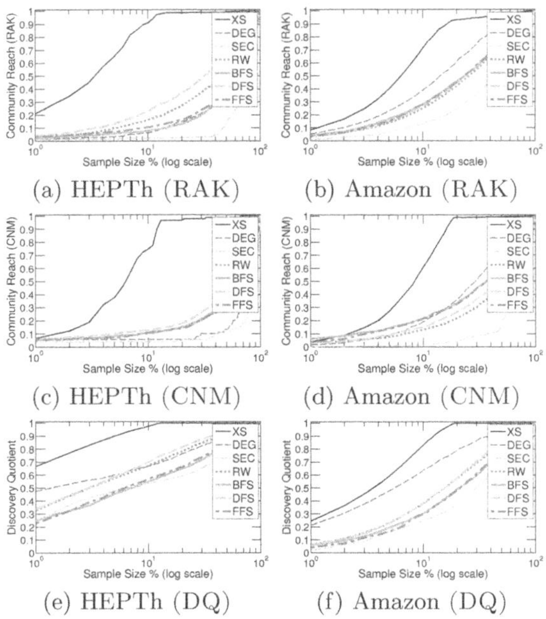

(a) HEPTh (RAK) (b) Amazon (RAK)
(c) HEPTh (CNM) (d) Amazon (CNM)
(e) HEPTh (DQ) (f) Amazon (DQ)

Figure 4: Evaluating *network reach*. Results for remaining networks are similar with XS exhibiting superior performance on all three criteria.

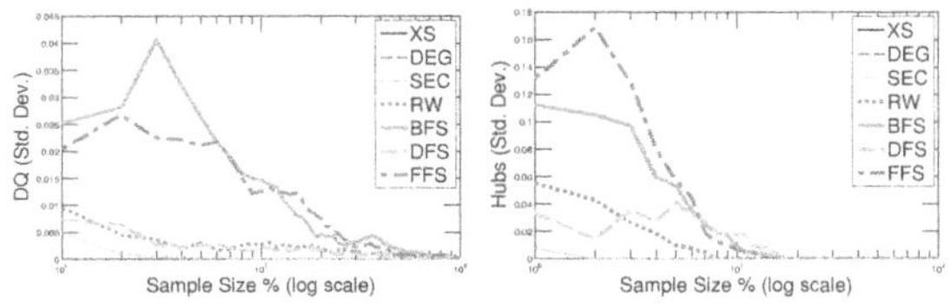

(a) Epinions (DQ) (b) Epinions (HUBS)

Figure 5: Standard deviation for DQ and HUBS on Epinions network. Results are similar for remaining networks.

6.1 Existing Analytical Results

Random Walks (RW). There is a fairly large body of research on random walks and Markov chains (see [37] for an excellent survey). A well-known analytical result states that the probability (or *stationary* probability) of residing at any node v during a random walk on a connected, undirected graph converges with time to $\frac{d_v}{2 \cdot |E|}$, where d_v is the degree of node v [37]. In fact, the *hitting time* of a random walk (i.e. the expected number of steps required to reach a node beginning from any node) has been analytically shown to be directly related to this stationary probability [24]. Random walks, then, are naturally biased towards high degree (and high PageRank) nodes, which provides some theoretical explanation as to why RW performs slightly better than other strategies (e.g. BFS) on measures such as *hub inclusion*. However, as shown in Figure 1, it is nowhere near the best performers. Thus, these analytical results appear only to hold in the limit and fail to predict actual sampling performance.

Degree Sampling (DS). In studying the problem of searching peer-to-peer networks, Adamic et al. [2] proposed and analyzed a greedy search strategy very similar to the DS sampling method. This strategy, which we refer to as a degree-based walk, was analytically shown to quickly find the highest-degree nodes and quickly cover large portions of scale-free networks. Thus, these results provide a theoretical explanation for performance of the DS strategy on measures such as *hub inclusion* and the *discovery quotient*.

Other Results. As mentioned in Section 2, to the best of our knowledge, much of the other analytical results on sampling bias focus on *negative* results [1,15,30,31,46]. Thus, these works, although intriguing, may not provide much help in the way of explaining *positive* results shown in Section 5.

We now analyze two methods for which there are little or no existing analytical results: XS and SEC.

6.2 Analyzing XS Bias

A widely used measure for the "goodness" or the strength of a community in graph clustering and community detection is *conductance* [26], which is a function of the fraction of total edges emanating from a sample (lower values mean stronger communities):

$$\varphi(S) = \frac{\sum_{i\in S, j\in \overline{S}} a_{ij}}{\min(a(S), a(\overline{S}))}$$

where a_{ij} are entries of the adjacency matrix representing the graph and $a(S) = \sum_{i\in S}\sum_{j\in V} a_{ij}$, which is the total number of edges incident to the node set S.

It can be shown that, provided the conductance of communities is sufficiently low, sample expansion is directly affected by community structure. Consider a simple random graph model with vertex set V and a community structure represented by partition $C = \{C_1, \ldots, C_{|C|}\}$ where $C_1 \cup \ldots \cup C_{|C|} = V$. Let e_{in} and e_{out} be the number of each node's edges pointing within and outside the node's community, respectively. These edges are connected uniformly at random to nodes either within or outside a node's community, similar to a configuration model (e.g., [11]). Note that both e_{in} and e_{out} are related directly to conductance. When conductance is lower, e_{out} is smaller[2] as compared to e_{in}. The following theorem expresses the link between expansion and *community reach* in terms of these inward and outward edges.

THEOREM 1. *Let S be the current sample, v be a new node to be added to S, and n be the size of v's community. If $e_{out} < \frac{|V|(e_{in})^2}{n(|V|+e_{in}|S|)}$, then the expected expansion of $S\cup\{v\}$ is higher when v is in a new community than when v is in a current community.*

PROOF. Let X_{new} be the expected value for $|N(\{v\}) - N(S) \cup S|$ when v is in a new community and let X_{curr} be the expected value when not. We compute an upper bound on X_{curr} and a lower bound on X_{new}.

[2]Suppose conductance of a vertex set Y is $\varphi(Y)$, the total number of edges incident to Y is e, and e_{in} and e_{out} are random variables denoting the inward and outward edges, respectively, of each node (as opposed to constant values). Then, $\mathbb{E}(e_{out}) = \frac{e\varphi(Y)}{|Y|}$ and $\mathbb{E}(e_{in}) = \frac{2e(1-\varphi(Y))}{|Y|}$. If $\varphi(Y) < \frac{2}{3}$, then $\mathbb{E}(e_{out}) < \mathbb{E}(e_{in})$. (In this example, the expectations are over nodes in Y only.)

Deriving X_{curr}: Assume v is affiliated with a current community already represented by at least one node in S. Since we are computing an upper bound on X_{curr}, we assume there is exactly one node from S within v's community, as this is the minimum for v's community to be a *current* community. By the linearity of expectations, the upper bound on X_{curr} is $e_{out} + \frac{(n-e_{in})e_{in}}{n}$, where the term $\frac{(n-e_{in})e_{in}}{n}$ is the expected number of nodes in v's community that are both linked to v *and* in the set $V - (N(S) \cup S)$.

Deriving X_{new}: Assume v belongs to a new community not already represented in S. (By definition, no nodes in S will be in v's community.) Applying the linearity of expectations once again, the lower bound on X_{new} is $e_{in} - e_{out}|S|\frac{e_{in}}{|V|}$, where the term $e_{out}|S|\frac{e_{in}}{|V|}$ is the expected number of nodes in v's community that are both linked to v *and* already in $N(S)$.

Solving for e_{out}, if $e_{out} < \frac{|V|(e_{in})^2}{n(|V|+e_{in}|S|)}$, then $X_{new} > X_{curr}$. □

Theorem 1 shows analytically the link between expansion and community structure - a connection that, until now, has only been empirically demonstrated [40]. Thus, a theoretical basis for performance of the XS strategy on *community reach* is revealed.

6.3 Analyzing SEC Bias

Recall that the SEC method uses the degree of a node v in the induced subgraph $G_{S\cup\{v\}}$ as an estimation for the degree of v in G. In Section 5, we saw that this choice performs quite well in practice. Here, we provide theoretical justification for the SEC heuristic. Consider a random network G with some arbitrary expected degree sequence (e.g. a power law random graph under the so-called $G(\mathbf{w})$ model [11]) and a sample $S \subset V$. Let $d(\cdot,\cdot)$ be a function that returns the expected degree of a given node in a given random network (see [11] for more information on *expected* degree sequences). Then, it is fairly straightforward to show the following holds.

PROPOSITION 1. *For any two nodes $v, w \in N(S)$, if $d(v,G) \geq d(w,G)$, then $d(v, G_{S\cup\{v\}}) \geq d(w, G_{S\cup\{w\}})$.*

PROOF. The probability of an edge between any two nodes i and j in G is $\frac{d(i,G)\cdot d(j,G)}{\Delta}$ where $\Delta = \sum_{m\in V} d(m,G)$. Let $\delta = d(v, G_{S\cup\{v\}}) - d(w, G_{S\cup\{w\}})$. Then,

$$\delta = \sum_{x\in S} \frac{d(x,G)\cdot d(v,G)}{\Delta} - \sum_{x\in S} \frac{d(x,G)\cdot d(w,G)}{\Delta} \quad (1)$$

$$= (d(v,G) - d(w,G)) \sum_{x\in S} \frac{d(x,G)}{\Delta} \quad (2)$$

Since $\delta \geq 0$ only when $d(v,G) \geq d(w,G)$, the proposition holds. □

Combining Proposition 1 with analytical results from [2] (described in Section 6.1) provides a theoretical basis for observed performance of the SEC strategy on measures such as *hub inclusion*. Finally, recall from Section 5.1.2 that the extent to which SEC matched the performance of DS on HUBS seemed to partly depend on the tail of degree distributions. Proposition 1 also yields insights into this phenomenon. Longer and denser tails allow for more "slack" when deviating from these expectations of random variables (as in real-world link patterns that are not purely random).

7. APPLICATIONS FOR OUR FINDINGS

We now briefly describe ways in which some of our findings may be exploited in important, real-world applications. Although numerous potential applications exist, we focus here on three areas: 1) Outbreak Detection 2) Landmarks and Graph Exploration 3) Marketing.

7.1 Practical Outbreak Detection

What is the most effective and efficient way to predict and prevent a disease outbreak in a social network? In a recent paper, Christakis and Fowler studied outbreak detection of the H1N1 flu among college students at Harvard University [10]. Previous research has shown that well-connected (i.e. high degree) people in a network catch infectious diseases earlier than those with fewer connections [13, 17, 51]. Thus, *monitoring* these individuals allows forecasting the progression of the disease (a boon to public health officials) and *immunizing* these well-connected individuals (when immunization is possible) can prevent or slow further spread. Unfortunately, identifying well-connected individuals in a population is non-trivial, as access to their friendships and connections is typically not fully available. And, collecting this information is time-consuming, prohibitively expensive, and often impossible for large networks. Matters are made worse when realizing that most existing network-based techniques for immunization selection and outbreak detection assume full knowledge of the global network structure (e.g. [36, 48]). This, then, presents a prime opportunity to exploit the power of *sampling*.

To identify well-connected students and predict the outbreak, Christakis and Fowler [10] employed a sampling technique called *acquaintance sampling* (ACQ) based on the so-called friendship paradox [10, 13, 51]. The idea is that random neighbors of randomly selected nodes in a network will tend to be highly-connected [13, 17, 51]. Christakis and Fowler [10], therefore, sampled random friends of randomly selected students with the objective of constructing a sample of highly-connected individuals. Based on our aforementioned results, we ask: Can we do better than this ACQ strategy? In previous sections, we showed empirically and analytically that the SEC method performs exceedingly well in accumulating hubs. (It also happens to require less information than DS and XS, the other top performers.) Figure 6 shows the sample size required to locate the top-ranked well-connected individuals for both SEC and ACQ. The performance differential is quite remarkable, with the SEC method faring overwhelmingly better in quickly zeroing in on the set of most well-connected nodes. Aside from its superior performance, SEC has one additional advantage over the ACQ method employed by Christakis and Fowler. The ACQ method assumes that nodes in V can be selected uniformly at random. It is, in fact, dependent on this [13]. (ACQ, then, is *not* a link-trace sampling method.) By contrast, SEC, as a pure link-trace sampling strategy, has no such requirement and, thus, can be applied in realistic scenarios for which ACQ is unworkable.

7.2 Marketing

Recall from Section 5.3 that a community in a network is a cluster of nodes more densely connected among themselves than to others. Identifying communities is important, as they often correspond to real social groups, functional groups, or similarity (both demographic and not) [18]. The ability to easily construct a sample consisting of members from diverse groups has several important applications in marketing. Marketing surveys often seek to construct stratified samples that collectively represent the diversity of the population [28]. If the attributes of nodes are not known in advance, this can be challenging. The XS strategy, which exhibited the best *community reach*, can potentially be very useful here. Moreover, it has the added power of being able to locate members from diverse groups with absolutely no *a priori* knowledge of demographics attributes, social variables, or the overall community structure present in the network. There is also recent evidence to suggest that being able to construct a sample from many different communities can be an asset in effective word-of-mouth marketing [8]. This, then, represents yet another potential marketing application for the XS strategy.

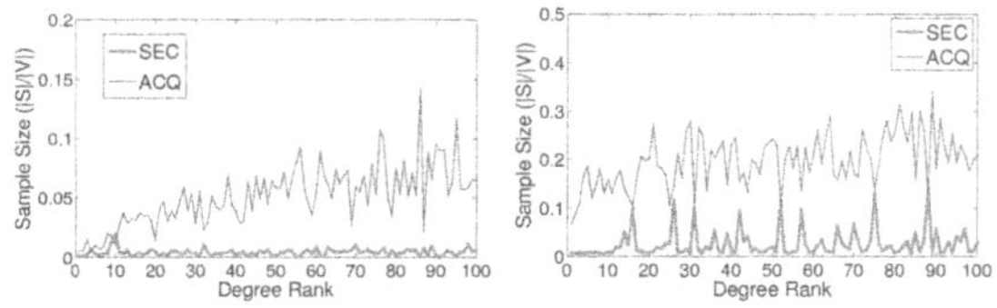

(a) Slashdot (b) CondMat

Figure 6: Comparison of SEC and ACQ on quickly locating well-connected individuals (lower is better). SEC far surpasses ACQ. Results are similar for every network.

7.3 Landmarks and Graph Exploration

Landmark-based methods represent a general class of algorithms to compute distance-based metrics in large networks quickly [44]. The basic idea is to select a small sample of nodes (i.e. the landmarks), compute offline the distances from these landmarks to every other node in the network, and use these pre-computed distances at runtime to approximate distances between pairs of nodes. As noted in [44], for this approach to be effective, landmarks should be selected so that they *cover* significant portions of the network. Based on our findings for *network reach* in Section 5.3, the XS strategy overwhelmingly yields the best *discovery quotient* and covers the network significantly better than any other strategy. Thus, it represents a promising landmark selection strategy. Our results for the *discovery quotient* and other measures of *network reach* also yield important insights into how graphs should best be explored, crawled, and searched. As shown in Figure 4, the most prevalently used method for exploring networks, BFS, ranks low on measures of *network reach*. This suggests that the BFS and its pervasive use in social network data acquisition and exploration (e.g. see [41]) should possibly be examined more closely.

8. CONCLUSION

We have conducted a detailed study on sampling biases in real-world networks. In our investigation, we found the BFS, a widely-used method for sampling and crawling networks, to be among the worst performers in both discovering the network and accumulating critical, well-connected hubs. We also found that sampling biases towards high expansion tend to accumulate nodes that are uniquely different from those that are simply well-connected or traversed during a BFS-based strategy. These high-expansion nodes tend to be in newer and different portions of the network not already encountered by the sampling process. We further demonstrated that sampling nodes with many connections from those already sampled is a reasonably good approximation to sampling high degree nodes. Finally, we demonstrated several ways in which these findings can be exploited in real-world application such as disease outbreak detection and marketing. For future work, we intend to investigate ways in which the top-performing sampling strategies can be enhanced for even wider applicability. One such direction is to investigate the effects of alternating or combining different biases into a single sampling strategy.

9. REFERENCES

[1] D. Achlioptas, A. Clauset, D. Kempe, and C. Moore. On the bias of traceroute sampling: or, power-law degree distributions in regular graphs. In *STOC '05*.

[2] L. A. Adamic, R. M. Lukose, A. R. Puniyani, and B. A. Huberman. Search in power-law networks. *Physical Review E*, 64(4):046135+, Sept. 2001.

[3] N. K. Ahmed, F. Berchmans, J. Neville, and R. Kompella. Time-based sampling of social network activity graphs. In *MLG '10*.

[4] N. K. Ahmed, J. Neville, and R. Kompella. Reconsidering the Foundations of Network Sampling. In *WIN '10*.

[5] A.-L. Barabasi and R. Albert. Emergence of Scaling in Random Networks. *Science*, 286(5439):509–512, Oct. 1999.

[6] M. Boguñá, R. P. Satorras, A. D. Guilera, and A. Arenas. Models of social networks based on social distance attachment. *Physical Review E*, 70(5):056122+, Nov. 2004.

[7] P. Boldi, M. Santini, and S. Vigna. Do Your Worst to Make the Best: Paradoxical Effects in PageRank Incremental Computations. In *WAW '04*.

[8] T. Cao, X. Wu, S. Wang, and X. Hu. OASNET: an optimal allocation approach to influence maximization in modular social networks. In *SAC '10*.

[9] J. Cho, H. G. Molina, and L. Page. Efficient crawling through URL ordering. *Computer Networks and ISDN Systems*, 30(1–7):161–172, 1998.

[10] N. A. Christakis and J. H. Fowler. Social Network Sensors for Early Detection of Contagious Outbreaks. *PLoS ONE*, 5(9):e12948+, Sept. 2010.

[11] F. Chung and L. Lu. Connected Components in Random Graphs with Given Expected Degree Sequences. *Annals of Combinatorics*, 6(2):125–145, Nov. 2002.

[12] A. Clauset, M. E. J. Newman, and C. Moore. Finding community structure in very large networks. *Physical Review E*, 70(6):066111+, Dec. 2004.

[13] R. Cohen, S. Havlin, and D. ben Avraham. Efficient Immunization Strategies for Computer Networks and Populations. *arXiv:cond-mat/0207387v3*, Dec. 2003.

[14] T. H. Cormen, C. E. Leiserson, R. L. Rivest, and C. Stein. *Introduction to Algorithms*. McGraw-Hill Science / Engineering / Math, 2nd edition, Dec. 2003.

[15] E. Costenbader. The stability of centrality measures when networks are sampled. *Social Networks*, 25(4):283–307, Oct. 2003.

[16] U. Feige. A threshold of ln n for approximating set cover. *J. ACM*, 45(4):634–652, July 1998.

[17] S. L. Feld. Why Your Friends Have More Friends Than You Do. *The Am. J. of Sociology*, 96(6):1464–1477, 1991.

[18] S. Fortunato. Community detection in graphs. *arXiv:0906.0612v2 [physics.soc-ph]*, Jan. 2010.

[19] O. Frank. *Models and Methods in Social Network Analysis (Structural Analysis in the Social Sciences)*, chapter 3. Cambridge University Press, Feb. 2005.

[20] M. Gjoka, M. Kurant, C. T. Butts, and A. Markopoulou. A Walk in Facebook: Uniform Sampling of Users in Online Social Networks. *arXiv e-print (arXiv:0906.0060v3)*, Feb. 2011.

[21] B. H. Good, Y.-A. de Montjoye, and A. Clauset. Performance of modularity maximization in practical contexts. *Physical Review E*, 81(4):046106+, Apr. 2010.

[22] M. R. Henzinger, A. Heydon, M. Mitzenmacher, and M. Najork. On near-uniform URL sampling. In *WWW '00*.

[23] S. Hoory, N. Linial, and A. Wigderson. Expander Graphs and Their Applications. *Bull. Amer. Math. Soc*, 43, 2006.

[24] J. Hopcroft and D. Sheldon. Manipulation-resistant reputations using hitting time. In *WAW'07*.

[25] C. Hubler, H.-P. Kriegel, K. Borgwardt, and Z. Ghahramani. Metropolis Algorithms for Representative Subgraph Sampling. In *ICDM '08*.

[26] R. Kannan, S. Vempala, and A. Vetta. On clusterings: Good, bad and spectral. *J. ACM*, 51(3):497–515, May 2004.

[27] J. Kleinberg. Complex Networks and Decentralized Search Algorithms. In *International Congress of Mathematicians (ICM)*, 2006.

[28] E. D. Kolaczyk. *Statistical Analysis of Network Data*, chapter 5. Springer, 2009.

[29] V. Krishnamurthy, M. Faloutsos, M. Chrobak, J. Cui, L. Lao, and A. Percus. Sampling large Internet topologies for simulation purposes. *Computer Networks*, 51(15):4284–4302, Oct. 2007.

[30] M. Kurant, A. Markopoulou, and P. Thiran. On the bias of BFS. *Arxiv e-print (arXiv:1004.1729v1)*, Apr. 2010.

[31] A. Lakhina, J. W. Byers, M. Crovella, and P. Xie. Sampling Biases in IP Topology Measurements. In *INFOCOM '03*.

[32] S. H. Lee, P. J. Kim, and H. Jeong. Statistical properties of sampled networks. *Physical Review E*, 73(1):016102+, Jan. 2006.

[33] J. Leskovec. Stanford Large Network Dataset Collection. http://snap.stanford.edu/data/.

[34] J. Leskovec and C. Faloutsos. Sampling from large graphs. In *KDD '06*.

[35] J. Leskovec, J. Kleinberg, and C. Faloutsos. Graphs over Time: Densification Laws, Shrinking Diameters and Possible Explanations. In *KDD '05*.

[36] J. Leskovec, A. Krause, C. Guestrin, C. Faloutsos, J. VanBriesen, and N. Glance. Cost-effective outbreak detection in networks. In *KDD '07*.

[37] L. Lovasz. Random Walks on Graphs: A Survey. *Combinatorics: Paul Erdos is 80*, II, 1994.

[38] L. Lovasz. Very large graphs. *arXiv:0902.0132v1 [math.CO]*, Feb. 2009.

[39] A. S. Maiya and T. Y. Berger Wolf. Expansion and search in networks. In *CIKM '10*.

[40] A. S. Maiya and T. Y. Berger-Wolf. Sampling Community Structure. In *WWW '10*.

[41] A. Mislove, M. Marcon, K. P. Gummadi, P. Druschel, and B. Bhattacharjee. Measurement and analysis of online social networks. In *IMC '07*.

[42] M. Najork. Breadth-first search crawling yields high-quality pages. In *WWW '01*.

[43] M. E. J. Newman. The structure and function of complex networks. *SIAM Review*, 45:167–256, Mar. 2003.

[44] M. Potamias, F. Bonchi, C. Castillo, and A. Gionis. Fast shortest path distance estimation in large networks. In *CIKM '09*.

[45] U. N. Raghavan, R. Albert, and S. Kumara. Near linear time algorithm to detect community structures in large-scale networks. *Physical Review E*, 76(3):036106+, Sept. 2007.

[46] M. P. H. Stumpf, C. Wiuf, and R. M. May. Subnets of scale-free networks are not scale-free: Sampling properties of networks. *PNAS*, 102(12):4221–4224, Mar. 2005.

[47] D. Stutzbach, R. Rejaie, N. Duffield, S. Sen, and W. Willinger. On unbiased sampling for unstructured peer-to-peer networks. *IEEE/ACM Trans. Netw.*, 17(2):377–390, 2009.

[48] H. Tong, B. A. Prakash, C. Tsourakakis, T. E. Rad, C. Faloutsos, and D. H. Chau. On the Vulnerability of Large Graphs. In *ICDM '10*.

[49] D. Tsoumakos and N. Roussopoulos. Analysis and comparison of P2P search methods. In *InfoScale '06*.

[50] D. J. Watts and S. H. Strogatz. Collective dynamics of 'small-world' networks. *Nature*, 393(6684):440–442, June 1998.

[51] E. W. Zuckerman and J. T. Jost. What Makes You Think You're so Popular? Self-Evaluation Maintenance and the Subjective Side of the "Friendship Paradox". *Social Psychology Quarterly*, 64(3), 2001.

Scalable Distributed Inference of Dynamic User Interests for Behavioral Targeting

Amr Ahmed, Yucheng Low
School of Computer Science, CMU
Carnegie Mellon University
Pittsburgh, PA 15213, USA
{amahmed,ylow}@cs.cmu.edu

Mohamed Aly, Vanja Josifovski,
Alexander J. Smola
Yahoo! Research, Santa Clara, CA 95051, USA
{aly, vanjaj, smola}@yahoo-inc.com

ABSTRACT

Historical user activity is key for building user profiles to predict the user behavior and affinities in many web applications such as targeting of online advertising, content personalization and social recommendations. User profiles are temporal, and changes in a user's activity patterns are particularly useful for improved prediction and recommendation. For instance, an increased interest in car-related web pages may well suggest that the user might be shopping for a new vehicle.In this paper we present a comprehensive statistical framework for user profiling based on topic models which is able to capture such effects in a fully *unsupervised* fashion. Our method models topical interests of a user dynamically where both the user association with the topics and the topics themselves are allowed to vary over time, thus ensuring that the profiles remain current.

We describe a streaming, distributed inference algorithm which is able to handle tens of millions of users. Our results show that our model contributes towards improved behavioral targeting of display advertising relative to baseline models that do not incorporate topical and/or temporal dependencies. As a side-effect our model yields human-understandable results which can be used in an intuitive fashion by advertisers.

Categories and Subject Descriptors

I.2.6 [**ARTIFICIAL INTELLIGENCE**]: Learning; G.3 [**PROBABILITY AND STATISTICS**]:

General Terms

Algorithms, Experimentation

Keywords

Computational Advertising, Distributed Inference, Large-scale, Online Inference, User Modeling

1. INTRODUCTION

Computational advertising, content targeting, personalized recommendation, and web search, all benefit from a detailed knowledge of the interests of the user in order to personalize the results and improve relevance. For this purpose, user activity is tracked by publishers and third parties through browser cookies that uniquely identify the user visits to web sites. A variety of different actions are associated with each user as web page visits, search queries, etc. They are distilled into a compact description of the *user profile.*

In this paper we focus on generation of compact and effective user profiles from the history of user actions. One of the key challenges in this task is that the user history is a mixture of user interests over a period of time. In order to reason about the user, the personalization layer needs to be able to separate between the distinct interests to avoid degrading the user experience.

The framework presented in this paper is based on topic models. It is able to capture the *user interests* in an *unsupervised* fashion. We demonstrate the effectiveness of this framework for the *audience selection* task in display advertising. Audience selection is one of the core activities in display advertising where the goal is to select a good target for a particular campaign.

There are several challenges with topical analysis of the user action streams. First, for a production strength system, the analysis has to scale to hundreds of millions of users with tens, if not hundreds of actions daily. Most of the topical analysis models are computationally expensive and cannot perform at this scale. The second issue is that of time dependence: Users' interests change over time and it is this change that proves to be commercially very valuable since it may indicate purchase intents. For example, if a user suddenly increases the number of queries for the Caribian and cruises, this may indicate interest in a cruise vacation. The appearance of this new topic of interest in the user's stream of actions can be predictive of his interest. Furthermore, there are external effects that may govern user behavior. For instance, an underwater oil spill does not convert users into deep sea exploration aficionados yet it affects search behavior and thus needs to be filtered out.

Finally, generating good features that *describe* user behavior does not necessarily translate into good features that are *predictive* of commercially relevant decisions. In other words, we ultimately want to obtain discriminatively useful features. Hence we would like to obtain a user profiling algorithm which has at least *the potential* of being adapted to the profiling task at hand.

We propose a coherent approach using Bayesian statistics to achieve all those goals and we show that it excels at

KDD'11, August 21–24, 2011, San Diego, California, USA.

the task of predicting user responses for display advertising targeting. In summary our contributions are as follows:

- We develop a Bayesian approach for online modeling of user interests.
- Our model incrementally adapts both the user-topic associations and the topic composition based on the stream of user actions.
- We show how topic models can be used for improved targeting for display advertising, an application requiring analysis of *tens of millions* of users in real time.

2. FRAMEWORK AND BACKGROUND

We begin by spelling out the intuition behind our model in qualitative terms and describe the concepts behind the statistical model capable of addressing core profile generation issues, which we will address below and in Section 3:

- unsupervised topic acquisition
- dynamic topic descriptions
- dynamic user topical description
- filtering-out of global events

When categorizing user behavior it is tempting to group users into categories. That is, one might aim to group users together based on their (similar) behavior. While this has been used successfully in the analysis of user data [1] it tends to be rather limited when it comes to large numbers of users and large amounts of behavioral data: With millions of users it makes sense to use more than 1000 clusters in order to describe the user behavior. However, an inflation of clusters decreases the interpretability of the clusters considerably. Secondly, we would like to exploit sharing of statistical strength between clusters, e.g. if a number of clusters contain users interested in Latin music one would like to transfer modeling knowledge between them.

This can be addressed by topic models such as Latent Dirichlet Allocation (LDA) [6]. There objects (users) are characterized by a mixture of topics (interests). It is intuitively clear that such a topical mixture may carry considerably more information. For instance, even if we are allowed to choose only two out of 1000 topics we can already model 500,000 possible combinations. In other words, we can model the same variety of observations in a considerably more compressed fashion than what would be needed if we wanted to describe things in terms of clusters. The other key advantage of such models is that they are fully *unsupervised*. That is, they require *no* editorial data. Instead, they build the entire model by attempting to describe the data available. A key benefit in this setting is that it allows us to cover the entire range of interests rather than only those that an editor might be aware of. As a result this method is not language and culture specific. In the following we will be using the words topic and interest interchangeably.

Our strategy is thus to describe users as a mixture of topics and to assume that each of their actions is motivated by choosing a topic of interest first and subsequently a word to describe that action from the catalog of words consistent with that particular interest. For the purpose of this paper the **user actions** are either to issue a query or view an object (page, search result, or a video). We represent each user as a *bag of words* extracted from those actions and we use the term *user action* to denote generating a **word** from this bag. For instance, when issuing a query, each word in

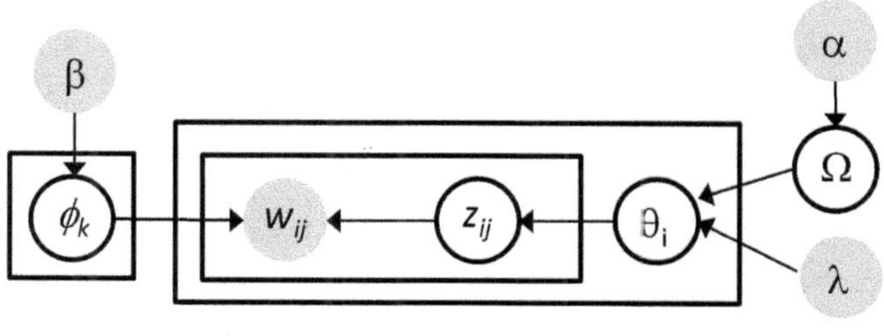

Figure 1: Latent Dirichlet Allocation.

the query is an action. Similarly, when viewing a video, each tag of the video represents an action, and when viewing a page, each word in the title of the page is an action.

In the following subsections we first review Latent Dirichlet Allocation (LDA) and then give an equivalent Polya-Urn scheme representation which will serve as the basis for the time-varying model described later in the paper.

2.1 Latent Dirichlet Allocation

LDA was introduced by [6] for the purpose of document modeling. The associated graphical model is given in Figure 1. In it, the variables w_{ij} correspond to the j-th action of user i that we observe. All remaining variables are considered latent, i.e. they are unobserved.
The associated graphical model of LDA assumes a static setting in which the order of the actions of each user w_{ij} is irrelevant. θ_i represents user i's specific distribution over topics (interests), and ϕ_k represents the topic distribution over words. Typically one chooses for $p(\theta_i|\lambda\Omega)$ and for $p(\phi_k|\beta)$ Dirichlet distributions, hence the name Dirichlet Allocation. The full generative process is specified as follow:

1. Draw once $\Omega|\alpha \sim \mathrm{Dir}(\alpha/K)$.
2. Draw each topic $\phi_k|\beta \sim \mathrm{Dir}(\beta)$.
3. For each user i:
   (a) Draw topic proportions $\theta_i|\lambda, \Omega \sim \mathrm{Dir}(\lambda\Omega)$.
   (b) For each word
      (a) Draw a topic $z_{ij}|\theta_d \sim \mathrm{Mult}(\theta_i)$.
      (b) Draw a word $w_{ij}|z_{ij}, \phi \sim \mathrm{Multi}(\phi_{z_{ij}})$.

K denotes the number of topics. The above generative process factors out the global distribution over topics into two parts: Ω and λ. Ω is a normalized vector, i.e., a probability distribution and represents the prior distribution over topics (interests) across users, and is sampled from a symmetric Dirichlet prior parametrized by α/K. λ on the other hand, is a scalar, and controls how each user's distribution over interests might vary from the prior distribution. This factored representation is critical for the rest of this paper.

2.2 A Polya-Urn Representation of LDA

In order to make explicit how the above LDA generative process captures local and global users' interests, we present an equivalent representation obtained by integrating out the global topic distribution Ω and the user-specific topic distribution θ. Let us assume that user i has generated $j-1$ actions and considering generating action j. Among those $j-1$ actions, let n_{ik} represent the number of actions expressing interest k. To generate action j the user might choose to either repeat an old interest with probability proportional to n_{ik} (and increment n_{ik}) or to consider a totally new interest with probability proportional to λ. In the former case, the user action is controlled by the user's mindset, and in the latter case the new interest is decided by considering the global frequency of interests across all users. We let m_k represent the global frequency by which interest k is expressed across users. Thus, user i can select to express interest k with probability proportional to $m_k + \alpha/K$ and increment m_k as well as n_{ik}. This allows the model to capture the fact that not every action expressed by the user represents a genuine user's interest. For example, a user might search for articles about the oil spill just because of the large buzz created about this incident. In summary we have

$$P(z_{ij} = k | w_{ij} = w, \text{rest}) \\ \propto \left(n_{ik} + \lambda \frac{m_k + \frac{\alpha}{K}}{\sum_{k'} m_{k'} + \alpha} \right) P(w_{ij}|\phi_k) \quad (1)$$

In the literature, this model is known as the hierarchical Polya-Urn model [5] in which previously expressed interests have a *reinforcing* effect of being re-expressed either at the user-level or across users. Moreover, this model is also equivalent to a *fixed-dimensional* version of the hierarchical Dirichlet process (HDP) [25]. In Figure 2 we graphically show this representation. The static model is equivalent to a single vertical slice (with no prior over m nor n). This figure makes explicit that every visit to the global process by user i creates a new table which is denoted by a big circle. Thus m_k represents the total number of tables associated with topic k across all users. Note that in the standard HDP metaphor, to generate an action j, one first selects a table proportional to its popularity (or a new table with probability $\propto \lambda$), and then generates the action from the topic associated with the selected table. The process described above is strictly equivalent since the probability of choosing topic k under this standard HDP metaphor is thus equal to the number of words assigned to all tables serving topic k (which we denoted by n_{ik}). In Section 3, we will describe the time-varying version of this process.

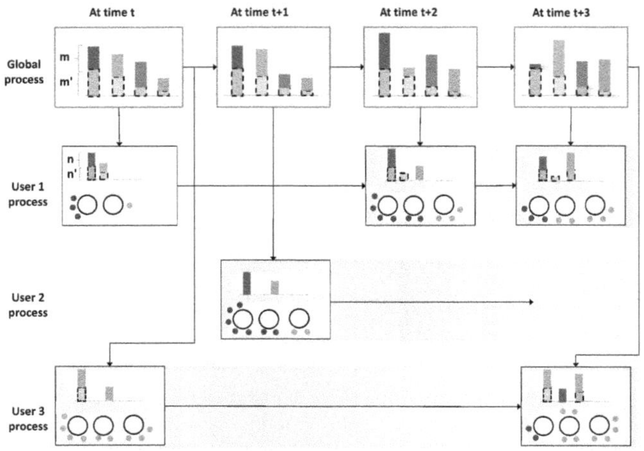

Figure 2: A time-varying hierarchical Polya-urn representation of the TVUM process (can also be regarded as a fixed-dimensional,fully-evolving recurrent Chinese restaurant franchise process [3]). Here (unlink in [3]) all levels are evolving. The top level represents the global process that captures the global topic trends. Each row gives the process for a given user. Each bar represents a topic's popularity (either global popularity m, or user-specific popularity n). The dotted (bottom) part of each bar represents the prior ($\tilde{m}$ for global topic prior, and $\tilde{n}$ for user-specific topic prior). To avoid clutter, we only show first-order dependencies, however, the global process evolves according to an exponential kernel and the user-specific processes evolve according to a multi-scale kernel as shown in Figure 3. Note here also that user interactions are sparse and users need not appear at all days nor enter in the system in the same day. Finally, small circles in user processes represent words according to topics.

3. TIME-VARYING USER MODEL

We now introduce our model — the Time-Varying User Model (TVUM). In Section 2.1, we assumed that user actions are fully exchangeable, and that user's interests are fixed over time. It is reasonable though to assume that a user's interests are not fixed over time, instead, we may assume that the proportions change and that new interests may arise. For instance, after the birth of a baby users will naturally be interested in parenting issues and their preferences in automobiles may change. Furthermore, specific projects, such as planning a holiday, purchasing a car, obtaining a mortgage, etc. will lead to a marked change in user activity. In the classical document context of LDA this is the equivalent of allowing the topics contained in a document to drift slowly as the document progresses. In the context of users this means that we assume that the daily user interest distribution is allowed to drift slowly over time.

We divide user actions into epochs based on the time stamp of the action. The epoch length depends on the nature of the application and can range from a few minutes to a full day. Figure 2 depicts the generative process of TVUM. User actions inside each epoch are modeled using an epoch-specific, fixed-dimensional hierarchical Polya-Urn model as described in Section 2.2. As time goes by, three aspects of the static model change: the global distribution over interests, the user-specific distribution over interests and the topic distribution over words ϕ. We address each of which in the following subsections and then summarize the full process in Section 3.4.

3.1 Dynamic Global Interests

The global trend of interests change over time. For example, the release of the iPhone 4 results in an increase in the global interest of the 'mobile gadgets' topic (intent) for a few days or weeks to follow. To capture that, we use a similar idea to that introduced in [3] and stipulate that the popularity of an interest k at time t depends both on the topic usages at time t, m_k^t, and on its historic usages at previous epochs, where the contribution of the previous epochs is summarized as $\tilde{m}_k^t$. We use exponential decay with kernel parameter κ defined as follows:

$$\tilde{m}_k^t = \sum_{h=1}^{t-1} \exp^{\frac{h-t}{\kappa}} m_k^h. \quad (2)$$

3.2 Dynamic User's Interests

Now we turn to model the dynamics in the user-specific interests. The topic trends of a given user n_{ik} is now made dependent on time via n_{ik}^t. This is after all, the very variable that we wish to estimate. We could use the same exponential decay idea that we used in modeling the change in the global trends of interests, however, the change in the user's interests over time is rather more complicated. Consider the set of actions observed from user i up to time $t-1$ as depicted in Figure 3. For simplicity, assume that all of these actions are words from queries. Each day, we observe a set

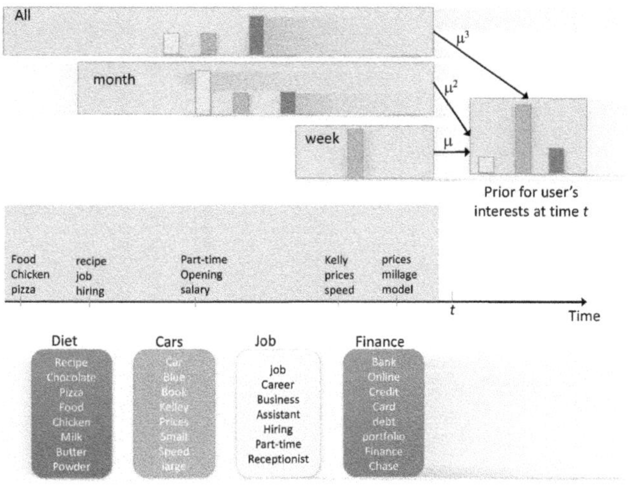

Figure 3: An illustration describing how TVUM captures users' long and short-term interests.

of queries issued by the user. In the figure we also list a set of 4 interests (topics). For each topic, we give the top words in its distribution as recorded in ϕ. What could be the expected interests of the user at time t? To answer this question, we observe that we can factor out the interests of the user into short-term interests and long-term (or persistent) interests. For example, this user has a long-term interest in Diet (Food) related materials. From the user history we can also discern two transient short-term interests localized on time: one over finding a job and the other over buying a car. To discover the long-term interests of the user, we could count the frequency of expressing interest k across the whole user history. This gives the long-term interests of the user. As depicted in Figure 3, this shows that the user has a long-term interest over Diet. Similarly we could compute the same quantity for the recent week and month to get the short-term interests of the user. As shown in Figure 3, it is clear that in the recent month, the user was mainly looking for a job and then started to look for a car in the recent week. Thus to get the *expected* user-specific's popularity over interests $\tilde{\mathbf{n}}_i^t$ for user i at time t, we combine these three levels of abstractions using a weighted sum

$$\tilde{n}_{ik}^t = \mu_{\text{week}}\, \tilde{n}_{ik}^{t,\text{week}} + \mu_{\text{month}}\, \tilde{n}_{ik}^{t,\text{month}} + \mu_{\text{all}}\, \tilde{n}_{ik}^{t,\text{all}}. \quad (3)$$

Here $\tilde{n}_{ik}^t$ is our estimate for user i's interest over topic k at time t, and $\tilde{n}_{ik}^{t,\text{week}} = \sum_{h=t}^{t-7} n_{ik}^h$, n_{ik}^h is the frequency of expressing interest k by user i at time h, and $\tilde{n}^{t,\text{week}}$ is just the sum of these frequencies over the past week. The other two quantities $\tilde{n}^{t,\text{all}}$ and $\tilde{n}^{t,\text{month}}$ are defined accordingly over their respective time ranges. The set of weights μ gives the contribution of every abstraction to the final estimate. In Figure 3, we show the final estimate at time t and it shows that we expect that the user will continue to look for cars, might still look for 'diet' related content, or with some probability considers a new job. There are a few observations here. First, if we had used an exponential decay as we employed for modeling the global trends, the model would have forgotten quickly about the user's long-term interest in 'diet'. This happens because the user history is sparse and the time between the user's activities might range from days to weeks. However, for modeling the change in the global trends of topics, it is enough to consider the preceding days to get a good estimate about the future: if an interest starts to fade, it is likely that it will die soon unless the data at future days tells us something else. The second observation is that $\tilde{\mathbf{n}}_i^t$ is not enough to capture what the user will look for at time t, as the user might still consider a new interest. For example, the user might develop an interest in obtaining a loan to finance his new car purchase. To model this effect, we combine the aforementioned prior with the global distribution over interests, as we will detail in Section 3.4, to generate the user actions at time t.

Finally, it is hard to fit or tune three different weights as in (3), thus we use $\mu_{\text{week}} = \mu, \mu_{\text{month}} = \mu^2$ and $\mu_{\text{all}} = \mu^3$, where $\mu \in [0, 1]$. For values of μ close to 0, more weight is given to the short-term interests and for values of μ close to 1 a uniform weight is given to all levels which implies more weight given to the long-term interests as they are aggregates over a longer time period. μ could be either optimized per user or set to a default value for all users.

3.3 Dynamic Topics

The final ingredient in our model is rendering the topics themselves dynamic. Indeed as we observe more user interactions, we expect the topic distribution over words to change in response to world events like the release of a new car. This feature is related to earlier work in dynamic topic models [7, 3] which uses non-conjugate logistic normal priors (which are challenging during inference) and [16] which uses multi-scale priors similar to Figure 3. Our approach here resembles [16] but with a simpler form for the prior. We achieve this dynamic effect by making the topic distribution over words ϕ_k time dependent, i.e. we have ϕ_k^t which now depends on the smoothing prior $\tilde{\beta}_k^t$ in addition to the static prior β. The component $\tilde{\beta}_{kw}^t$ of $\tilde{\beta}_k^t$ depends on a decayed version of the frequencies of observing word w from topic k at times $1 : t-1$. This is similar to the way we modeled the dynamics of the global distribution over interests, and we use an exponential decay kernel parametrized by κ_0:

$$\tilde{\beta}_{kw}^t = \sum_{h=1}^{t-1} \exp^{\frac{h-t}{\kappa_0}} n_{kw}^h, \quad (4)$$

Here n_{kw}^h is the frequency of observing word w from topic k at day h. Finally, we have $\phi_k^t \sim \text{Dir}\left(\tilde{\beta}_k^t + \beta\right)$

Note that the decision to *add* β to the above prior enforces that the components of the prior corresponding to new words (i.e. words that have $\tilde{\beta}_{kw}^t = 0$) is nonzero and as such new words can appear as time goes by.

3.4 Model Summary

We now put all the pieces together and give the full generative process of TVUM. Consider generating action j for user i at time t. User i can choose an interest k with probability proportional to $n_{ik}^t + \tilde{n}_{ik}^t$ and then increments n_{ik}^t. Alternatively, the user can choose a new interest with probability proportional to λ. To select this new interest, he considers the global trend of interests across users: he select interest k with probability proportional to $m_k^t + \tilde{m}_k^t + \alpha/K$ and increment m_k^t as well as n_{ik}^t. Finally the user generates the word w_{ij}^t from topic k's distribution at time t, ϕ_k^t. Putting everything together, we have

$$P(z_{i_j}^t = k | w_{ij}^t = w, \text{rest})$$
$$\propto \left(n_{ik}^t + \tilde{n}_{ik}^t + \lambda \frac{m_k^t + \tilde{m}_k^t + \frac{\alpha}{K}}{\sum_{k'} m_{k'}^t + \tilde{m}_{k'}^t + \alpha} \right) P(w_{ij}^t | \phi_k^t) \quad (5)$$

In fact, taking the limit of this model as $K \to \infty$ we get the recurrent Chinese restaurant franchise process as in [3] albeit with all levels being evolved and with different level-specific time-kernels. In [3] only the top level evolves since a given document does not persist across time epochs. Moreover, our fixed-dimensional approximation is more amenable for distributed inference and is still not highly affected by the number of topics as we will demonstrate in the experiments.

3.5 Inference

The problem of inferring interests for millions of users over several months is formidable and it considerably exceeds the scale of published work on scalable topic models including [23]. As a result exact inference, even by sampling, is computationally infeasible: for instance, in a collapsed sampler along the lines of [13, 26] the temporal interdependence of topic assignments would require inordinate amounts of computation even when resampling single topic assignments for user actions: it affects all actions within a range of one month if we use a correspondingly long dependence model to describe the topic and interest evolution.

A possible solution is to use Sequential Monte Carlo (SMC) methods such as those proposed by [9] for online inference of topic models. The problem is that due to the long-range dependence the particles in the SMC estimator quickly become too heavy, so we need to rebalance and resample fairly frequently. This problem is exacerbated by the sheer amount of data — we need to distribute the inference algorithm over several computers. This means that whenever we resample particles we need to transfer and update the state of many computers. Such an approach very quickly becomes infeasible and we need to resort to further approximations.

We make the design choice of essentially following an inference procedure. That is, we only perform forward inference through the set of dependent variables for each time step and we attempt to infer $\mathbf{z}^t$ only given estimates and observations for $t' \leq t$. This allows us to obtain improving results as time progresses, alas at the expense of rather suboptimal estimates at the beginning of the inference chain.

A second reason to use forward sampling is practicality: data keeps on arriving at the estimator and we obviously would like to update the user profiles as we go along. This is only feasible if we need not revisit old data constantly while new data keeps on arriving. Our setting allows effectively for an online sampling procedure where we track the current interest distribution and the nature of interests relative to incoming data. Thus to summarize, our inference procedure incrementally runs a *fast* batch MCMC over the data at epoch t given the state of the sampler at earlier epochs.

Sampling Details

Our sampler resembles the collapsed, direct-assignment sampler with augmented representation as described in [25]. We collapse the topic multinomials (ϕ^t) and compute the posterior over $\mathbf{z}^t$ given assignments to hidden variables at previous epochs. As noted in (5), sampling z would couple topic indicators across all users via $\mathbf{m^t}$: recall from Figure 2 that m_k^t is the number of tables across all users serving topic k. This fact is undesirable especially when users are distributed across machines. To remedy this, we augment the representation by instantiating and sampling the global topic distribution at time time, i.e. Ω^t. Thus the sampler alternate between sampling $\mathbf{z}^t, \mathbf{m^t}$, and Ω_t. It should be noted that

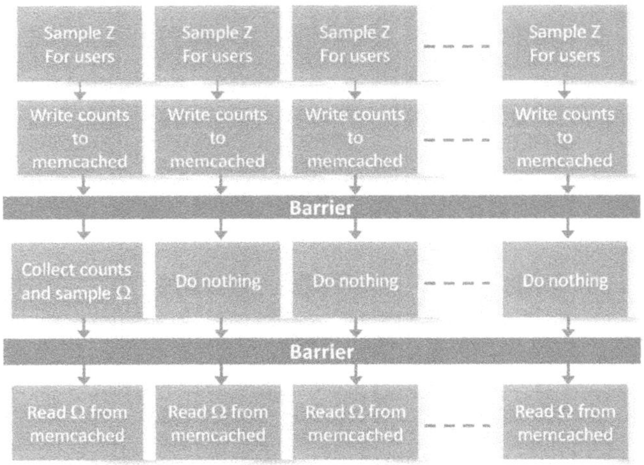

Figure 4: Synchronization during a sampling cycle.

collapsing ϕ^t also introduces coupling across users, however we deal with that using the architecture of [23].

Sampling z_{ij}^t: The conditional probability for z_{ij}^t has the same structure as in LDA albeit with the previously defined compound prior. We have,

$$P(z_{ij}^t = k | w_{ij}^t = w, \Omega^t, \tilde{\mathbf{n}}_i^t)$$
$$\propto \left(n_{ik}^{t,-j} + \tilde{n}_{ik}^t + \Lambda\Omega^t\right) \frac{n_{kw}^{t,-j} + \tilde{\beta}_{kw}^t + \beta}{\sum_l n_{kl}^{t,-j} + \tilde{\beta}_{kl}^t + \beta} \tag{6}$$

where n_{kw}^t is the number of times a word w was sampled form topic k (this is known as the topic-word matrix). Λ denotes the influence of the common activity distribution. The superscript $-j$ means excluding the contribution of word j. The structure of (6) allows us to utilize the efficient sparse sampler described in [26] which in fact was another reason to our choice of using the augmented representation, i.e. for instantiating Ω^t.

Sampling m_k^t: Since our sampler does not explicitly maintain the word-table assignments, we need to sample $m_k^t = \sum_i m_{ik}^t$. Where m_{ik}^t is the number of tables in user i's process serving topic k. This last quantity m_{ik}^t follows what is called the Antoniak distribution [25]. A sample from this distribution can be obtained as follows. First, set $m_{ik}^t = 0$, then for $j = 1 \cdots n_{ik}^t$, flip a coin with bias $\frac{\lambda\Omega_k^t}{j-1+\lambda\Omega_k^t}$, and increment m_{ik}^t if the coin turns head. The final value of m_{ik}^t is a sample from the Antoniak distribution. Recall that n_{ik}^t is the number of words expressing interest k from user i at time t.

Sampling Ω^t: By examining the structure of (1) and (5) and the equivalence between the construction in Section 2.2 and LDA, it is straightforward to see that

$$P(\Omega^t | \mathbf{m}^t, \tilde{\mathbf{m}}^t) \sim \text{Dir}(\tilde{\mathbf{m}}^t + \mathbf{m}^t + \alpha/K).$$

This constitutes a **single** Gibbs cycle. For each time epoch (day) we iterate this cycle **100 times** over all active users in that day. 100 iterations were enough due to 1) the small size of user observations at each day, and 2) the informative prior from earlier days.

Systems Aspects

To be able to apply the model to tens of millions of users, we use a distributed implementation following the architecture in [23]. The state of the sampler comprises the topic-word

set	days	users	vocabulary	campaigns	size
1	56	13.34M	100K	241	242GB
2	44	33.5M	100K	216	435GB

Table 1: Basic statistics of the data used.

counts matrix, and the user-topic counts matrix. The former is shared across users and is maintained in a distributed hash table using `memcached` [23]. The later is user-specific an can be maintained locally in each client. We distribute the users at time t across N clients. Each client executes a foreground thread to implement (6) and a background thread that synchronizes its local copy of the topic-word counts matrix with the global copy in memcached. As shown in Figure 4, after this step, Ω^t and m_k^t should be sampled. However, sampling Ω^t requires a *reduction* step across clients to collect and sum m_{ik}^t. First, each client writes to memcached its contribution for m_k^t (which is the sum of the values of m_{ik}^t for users i assigned to this client), then the clients reach a *barrier* where they wait for each other to proceed to the next stage of the cycle. We implemented a sense-reversing barrier algorithm which arranges the nodes in a tree and thus has a latency that scales logarithmically with N [21]. After this barrier, all counts are in memcached and as such one client sums these counts to obtain $\mathbf{m}^t$, uses it to sample Ω^t, and finally writes the sampled value of Ω^t back to the memcached. All other clients wait for this event (signaled via a barrier), and then read the new value of Ω^t and this finalizes a single cycle.

4. EXPERIMENTS

- We show that the discovered user interests are effective when used as features for behavioral targeting. This holds both in the sense of generating *interpretable* features and in the sense of generating *predictive* models.
- Secondly we demonstrate the scalability of our inference algorithm across both the number of machines and number of users. In particular we demonstrate that our algorithm is capable of processing tens of millions of users. This is over 10 times larger than the datasets analyzed by [23] who only discuss LDA.
- Third, we show that our model and inference algorithm are robust to a wide range of parameter settings. Hence it applies to a wide range of problems without the need to excessively hand-tune its parameters.

4.1 Datasets and Tasks

We used two datasets each of which spans approximately two months. The exact dates of each dataset are hidden for privacy reasons. In each case we collected a set of adcampaigns and sampled a set of users who were shown ads in this campaign during the covered time period. For each user, we represented the users' interaction history as a sequence of tokens. More precisely, the user *is represented* at day t as *a bag of words* comprising the queries they issued at this day and the textual *content* of the pages they view on this day. This constitutes the input to all the models discussed in the following subsections. Thus all datasets are Yahoo! privacy policy compliant, since we don't retain the precise page the user viewed on Yahoo! Sports (for instance) but rather retain only the description of the page at a higher level in terms of words extracted from the content.

For evaluation purposes, we also collect the user's response to individual ads: the ads they converted on (positive response); and the ads they ignored either by not clicking or

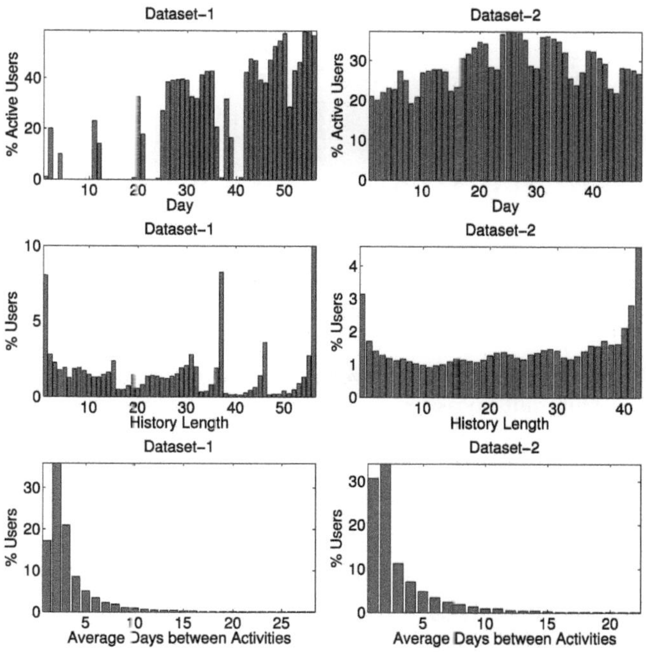

Figure 5: Characteristics of the data sets.

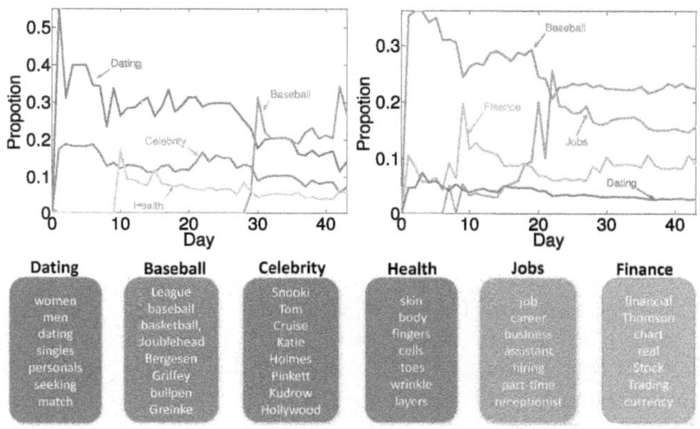

Figure 6: Dynamic interests of two users.

not converting post-click (negative response). We used the users' responses to ads in the last week of the dataset as a test set and the remaining responses as a training set. The characteristics of each dataset are shown in Figure 5 and Table 1. As evident from Figure 5, the first dataset is sparser than the second which presents a challenge for any model.

Our task is to build a model based on users' history that can predict whether or not a user will convert given an ad. We break this problem in two parts. First, we translate the user's history into a feature-vector profile using the TVUM and other baselines. Second, the profiles are used to build an SVM model that is evaluated over the test set using the area under the ROC curve as a metric.

4.2 Interpretability

Figure 6 qualitatively illustrates our model. For each user we plot the interest distribution over 6 salient topics. For each topic we print the top words as recorded in ϕ. The top part of the figure shows the dynamic interest of two users (User A — left; User B — right) as a function of time. Our model discovers that A has a *long-term* interest in dating, health, and celebrity albeit to a varying degree.

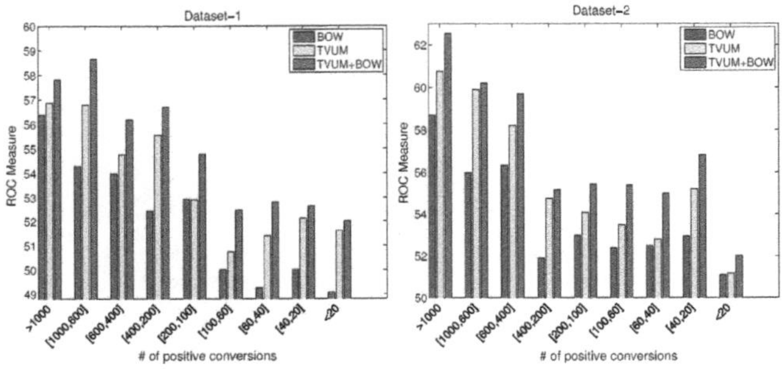

Figure 7: Performance vs. number of conversions.

In the last 10 days, A developed a *short-term* interest in baseball, quite possibly due to the global rise in interest in baseball (within our dataset). On the other hand B has a *long-term* interest in sports and finance; B was interested in dating in the first week, and was mainly looking for jobs in the last month. These discovered time-varying features for each user are useful for timely targeting of users with products. The following experiments buttress this intuition.

4.3 Performance

To show that the proposed **TVUM** is effective for extracting user interest we compare it to two baselines: a bag of words model **(BOW)** which does *not* incorporate any topical or temporal dependencies, and a **static LDA** model which incorporates topical information but *no* time dependence. The bag of words (BOW) model just outputs the concatenation of the user history up until time t as its representation of the user's interest at time t. This is in fact a very strong baseline. One advantage of the TVUM is that it is capable of processing user data in an online fashion, that is, we may estimate the user interest distribution one day at a time, sweeping through the dataset.

The training data for the SVM consists of the user's distribution over intent at time t (or a bag of words alternatively) and the user's response to the ad. For the TVUM, we used the following default parameters:[1] we set the number of topics $K = 200, \beta = 0.01, \mu = e^{-1} \approx .6, \kappa = \kappa_0 = \lambda = 1$.

In Figure 7, we show a comparison between this BOW baseline and the TVUM as a function of the number of positive conversions in each campaign. In this figure, we also show a third model that combines the BOW features with the TVUM features. As evident, our model improves over the baseline in both datasets across all the campaigns. We observe that, in general, the number of positive examples in ad campaigns is scarce. Therefore, models that feature a compact representation of the user's history overall perform better and can leverage the BOW features to further improve its performance. We can also notice from this figure that the gain over the BOW baseline is larger in campaigns with medium to small number of conversions. We also experimented with a variation of the BOW baseline featuring **BOW+time decay**. In this variation of BOW, we use an *exponential decay* of the form $a^{t'-t}$ over the *word counts* in the BOW baseline such that distant history will be given less weight at time t, however, the best result in this case was obtained when $a = 1$ (i.e. ignoring time), thus our model was able to leverage temporal information in a better way.

[1]It is possible to learn μ for users with long history (greater than two weeks). The likelihood of μ is Drichlet-multinomial compound and μ can be learnt using gradient descent. We leave this as a future work.

Table 2: Average ROC measure (TVUM: time-varying user model, BOW: bag of words baseline).

	BOW	TVUM	TVUM+BOW	LDA+BOW
dataset 1	54.40	55.78	**56.94**	55.80
dataset 2	57.03	58.70	**60.38**	58.54

Table 3: Time (in minutes) per a Gibbs iteration

topics		50	100	200
dataset 1	50 machines	0.7	0.9	1.2
dataset 2	100 machines	0.9	1.1	1.5

Table 4: Effect of # topics on predictive accuracy.

	topics	TVUM	TVUM + BOW
dataset 1	50	55.32	56.01
	100	55.5	56.56
	200	**55.8**	**56.94**
dataset 2	50	59.10	60.40
	100	**59.14**	**60.60**
	200	58.7	60.38

Table 5: The effect of the topic-decay parameter on the performance of TVUM+BOW.

Decay(κ_0)		none	1	2	3
dataset 1	200 topics	56.2	**56.94**	56.51	56.51
dataset 2	100 topics	**60.68**	60.60	60.40	60.40

To summarize the performance of each model over all campaigns, we give in Table 2 a weighted average of the ROC measure across campaigns, where the weight of each campaign is proportional to the number of positive examples in the campaign.

Finally, Table 2 also shows a comparison with a static LDA model+BOW features. Due to the large scale of this dataset, we can not apply batch LDA directly over it. Instead, we sampled 2M users from the training set and built a static LDA model over them. Then, we used variational inference to infer our estimate of the user's interest at time t, where t can be in the training or test set. Note here that LDA does not have the notion of a user in the model in a sense that when predicting the user's history at time t_1 and later at t_2, the user history up until time t_1 and time t_2 are presented as separate documents to the model. As evident from Table 2, our model beats static LDA on both datasets due to its ability to model time, and to maintain a coherent representation of the user as a time-evolving entity (note that in this application of predicting conversion, an increase of 1-2 points of the ROC measure is considered significant)

4.4 Speed and Efficiency

One key advantage of our model is its ability to process data in an online and distributed fashion. This allows us to process data at a scale quite unlike any system that we are aware of. Rather than processing a small number of millions of documents (i.e. users) [27, 28] while requiring a large cluster of computers, and rather than being able to process tens of millions of documents without time dependence [23], we are able to process tens to hundreds of millions of users in a dynamic fashion at a speed of **two hours per day** of data being processed. This is quite a significant improvement and makes topic models suitable for Yahoo's user base.

Table 3 provides the time for a single Gibbs-sampling iteration for different number of topics and using different number of machines. Since dataset 2 is almost double the size of dataset 1 in terms of the number of users, we doubled the number of machines when processing dataset 2. As shown in this table, the time per iteration is almost the same across the two datasets. The slight increase in time for dataset 2 arises because of the cost of synchronization and inter-client communications which was kept low thanks to the logarithmic complexity of the tree-based barrier algorithm.

4.5 Sensitivity Analysis

We evaluate the results' sensitivity to the model's parameters. Bayesian models depend on the specification of the parameters which encode our prior belief. However, no matter what prior is used, as long as the prior does not exclude the correct answer, the model can reach the true conclusion as the size of the dataset increases (which is true in our application). We first study the effect of the number of topics and then the effect of the decay parameter κ_0 for the topic distribution over words. The effect of κ was negligible.

Number of Topics: We varied the number of topics in the range 50, 100, 200. Results are presented in Table 4. From these tables, we first observe that the effect on the final performance is not quite large in both datasets. This is largely due to the fact that our inference algorithm optimizes over the topic's global distribution Ω which allows it to adapt the *effective* number of topics for each dataset [29]. For dataset 1, the performance increases as we add more topics. This is due to the sparsity and inhomogeneity of this dataset. Thus, the arrival of new users at each day requires more topics to model their intents properly. Whereas dataset 2 was more homogeneous, and as such, 100 topics were enough. We recommend setting the number of topics in the low hundreds for behavioral targeting applications.

Topic-Distribution Decay: Decaying the topic's word distribution has two important roles. First, it allows the model to recover from a poor initial estimate, and second, it enables the model to capture drifts in the topic's focus. As shown in Table 5 this feature helps in the first dataset due to the initial poor estimate of the topics in the first few days because of the low number of available users. However for the second homogeneous dataset, the performance *slightly* increases if we turn this feature off. We recommend setting κ_0 to a value between 1 and 3. It is possible to learn this parameter, however, this requires the storage of all the past topic distributions over time which is prohibitive in terms of storage requirements. In our implementation, because of the form of the decay function, we only need to discount the topic-word counts at the end of each day and use this as the initial estimate for the following day.

5. RELATED WORK

The emergence of the web has allowed for collection and processing of user data magnitudes larger than previously possible. This has resulted in a spike of interest in user data analysis and profile generation as reported in [10, 12, 17, 19]. Profile generation has been reported for a few different applications. In [24] the authors describe profiles for search personalization. Here, the authors build profiles based on the query stream of the user and users similar to it. The authors also report an alternative that is based on the relevance feedback approaches in information retrieval over the documents that the user have perceived as relevant. Both techniques are orthogonal to the work presented in this paper and could be used to produce a potentially richer set of of features that will serve as an input to the topical analysis.

User profile generation is also studied in other online settings and also for content recommendation (e.g., [14, 18, 20]). Most of these focus on detecting the user's short term vs long term interest and using these in the proposed application. In our case, we blend the short term and long term interests into a single profile. A survey of user profile generation can be found in [12].

In the area of audience selection, Provost et al. [22] have recently shown that user profiles can be built based on co-visitation patterns of social network pages. These profiles are used to predict the performance of brand display advertisements over 15 campaigns. In [10] the authors discuss prediction of clicks and impressions of events (queries, page views) within a set of predefined categories. Supervised linear poisson regression is used to model these counts based on a labeled set of user-class pairs of data instances.

While there are many profile generating algorithms satisfying a partial set of requirements outlined in this paper we are unaware of methods covering the entire range of the desiderata. In the topical analysis area, there are many predictive algorithms which try modeling the observed data via static generative model. The examples include singular value decomposition of the (user, action) matrix thus yielding a technique also known as Latent Semantic Indexing [11] or more advanced techniques such as Probabilistic Latent Semantic Indexing [15] or Latent Dirichlet Allocation [6]. However, while reducing the dimensionality of the space (the number for unique features), LSI and PLSI yield a dense vectorial representation. All of these approaches are static in terms of the user and to be able to apply new data we need to recompute the topical model from scratch. Finally, several models exist in the literature that could accommodate the evolution of topic global trends, topic distribution over words [7, 16] and the number of topics [3]. However, we are not aware of *any* attempts to model the intra-document drift of topics which corresponds to a user in our application – which is the *main contribution* of this paper.

6. CONCLUSION

In this paper, we addressed the problem of user profile generation for behavioral targeting. We presented a time-varying hierarchical user model that captures both the user's long term and short term interests. While models of this nature were not known to scale for web-scale applications, we showed a streaming distributed inference algorithm that both scales to tens of millions of users and adapts the inferred user's interest as it gets to know more about the user. Our learnt user representation was experimentally proven to be effective in computational advertising.

There are several directions for future research. First, we focused in this paper on the dynamic aspect of user profiles, and integrated all available user actions into a single vocabulary. While this approach seems promising, it would be beneficial to model each facet of the user action independently perhaps using a different language model for each facet. It is also possible to build a supervised model as in [8] that uses the users' responses to historical ads in inferring the user's interests.

7. REFERENCES

[1] D. Agarwal and S. Merugu. Predictive discrete latent factor models for large scale dyadic data. *KDD*, 2007.

[2] A. Ahmed and E. P. Xing. Dynamic non-parametric mixture models and the recurrent chinese restaurant process In *SDM*, pages 219–230. SIAM, 2008.

[3] A. Ahmed and E. P. Xing. Timeline: A dynamic hierarchical dirichlet process model for recovering birth / death and evolution of topics in text stream. In *UAI*, 2010.

[4] A. Asuncion, P. Smyth, and M. Welling. Asynchronous distributed learning of topic models. In *NIPS*, pages 81–88. MIT Press, 2008.

[5] D. Blackwell and J. MacQueen. Ferguson distributions via polya urn schemes. *The Annals of Statistics*, 1973.

[6] D. Blei, A. Ng, and M. Jordan. Latent Dirichlet allocation. *JMLR*, 3:993–1022, 2003.

[7] D. M. Blei and J. D. Lafferty. Dynamic topic models. In *ICML*, volume 148, pages 113–120. ACM, 2006.

[8] D. M. Blei and J. D. McAuliffe. Supervised topic models. In *NIPS*. MIT Press, 2007.

[9] K. R. Canini, L. Shi, and T. L. Griffiths. Online inference of topics with latent dirichlet allocation. In *AISTATS*, 2009.

[10] Y. Chen, D. Pavlov, and J. F. Canny. Large-scale behavioral targeting. In *KDD*, pages 209–218, 2009.

[11] S. Deerwester, S. T. Dumais, G. W. Furnas, T. K. Landauer, and R. Harshman. Indexing by latent semantic analysis. *Am. Soc. for Information Science*, 41, 1990.

[12] S. Gauch, M. Speretta, A. Chandramouli, and A. Micarelli. User profiles for personalized information access. In *LNCS 4321*, Springer, 2007.

[13] T.L. Griffiths and M. Steyvers. Finding scientific topics. *PNAS*, 101:5228–5235, 2004.

[14] A. Hassan, R. Jones, and K. L. Klinkner. Beyond DCG: User behavior as a predictor of a successful search. In *WSDM 2010*, pages 221–230, 2010.

[15] T. Hofmann. Unsupervised learning by probabilistic latent semantic analysis. *Machine Learning*, 2001.

[16] T. Iwata, T. Yamada, Y. Sakurai, and N. Ueda. Online multiscale dynamic topic models. In *KDD*, 2010.

[17] H. R. Kim and P. K. Chan. Learning implicit user interest hierarchy for context in personalization. In *IUI*, 2003.

[18] R. Kumar and A. Tomkins. A characterization of online search behavior. In *WWW*, 561–570, 2010.

[19] L. Li, Z. Yang, B. Wang, and M. Kitsuregawa. Dynamic adaptation strategies for long-term and short-term user profile to personalize search. In *ADWM*, 2007.

[20] L. Li, W. Chu, J. Langford, and R. Schapire. A contextual bandit approach to personalized news article recommendation. In *WWW*, 661–670, 2010.

[21] J. Mellor-Crummey and M. L. Scott. Algorithms for scalable synchronization on shared-memory multiprocessors. *ACM TOCS*, 9(1):21–65, February 1991.

[22] F. J. Provost, B. Dalessandro, R. Hook, X. Zhang, and A. Murray. Audience selection for on-line brand advertising: privacy-friendly social network targeting. In *KDD*, pages 707–716, 2009.

[23] A.J. Smola and S. Narayanamurthy. An architecture for parallel topic models. In *VLDB*, 2010.

[24] K. Sugiyama, K. Hatano, and M. Yoshikawa. Adaptive web search based on user profile constructed without any effort from users. In *WWW*, pages 675–684, 2004.

[25] Y. Teh, M. Jordan, M. Beal, and D. Blei. Hierarchical dirichlet processes. *JASA*, 2006.

[26] L. Yao, D. Mimno, and A. McCallum. Efficient methods for topic model inference on streaming document collections. In *KDD'09*, 2009.

[27] Y. Wang, H. Bai, M. Stanton, W. Chen, and E. Chang. PLDA: Parallel latent dirichlet allocation for large-scale applications. In *Proc. of 5th International Conference on Algorithmic Aspects in Information and Management*, 2009.

[28] D. Newman, A. Asuncion, P. Smyth and M. Welling. Distributed Algorithms for Topic Models. In *Journal of Machine Learning Research*, 2009.

[29] H. Wallach, D. Mimno and A. McCallum. Rethinking LDA: Why Priors Matter. In *Advances in Neural Information Processing Systems 22*, 2009.

Multiple Domain User Personalization

Yucheng Low
Carnegie Mellon University
Pittsburgh, PA 15213, USA
ylow@cs.cmu.edu

Deepak Agarwal
Yahoo! Research
Santa Clara, CA 95051, USA
dagarwal@yahoo-inc.com

Alexander J. Smola
Yahoo! Research
Santa Clara, CA 95051, USA
alex@smola.org

ABSTRACT

Content personalization is a key tool in creating attractive websites. Synergies can be obtained by integrating personalization between *several* Internet properties. In this paper we propose a hierarchical Bayesian model to address these issues. Our model allows the integration of multiple properties without changing the overall structure, which makes it easily extensible across large Internet portals. It relies at its lowest level on Latent Dirichlet Allocation, while making use of latent side features for cross-property integration. We demonstrate the efficiency of our approach by analyzing data from several properties of a major Internet portal.

Categories and Subject Descriptors

I.2.6 [**Computing Methodologies**]: ARTIFICIAL INTELLIGENCE—*Learning*; G.3 [**Mathematics of Computing**]: PROBABILITY AND STATISTICS

General Terms

Algorithms, Experimentation

Keywords

Latent Dirichlet Allocation, User Profiling, Domain Integration, Parallel Statistical Inference

1. INTRODUCTION

The rapid growth of the World Wide Web results in a tremendous amount of information available to people. To prevent information overload, many collaborative filtering and recommendation systems [1, 19, 8, 3, 2] have been developed to filter the information stream and display only information the user may be interested in. Such methods have been successfully deployed in various settings ranging from movies (Netflix) to music (iTunes, last.fm) and books (Amazon).

A problem with existing recommendation systems is that they generally require some amount of user interaction to be recorded before personalization is possible.[1] For instance, a movie recommendation system will need a user to provide preference information for some movies, before it is possible to provide personalized recommendation of other movies; likewise, a news portal will require a number of page views before an interest profile of the user can be constructed. In the meantime, the user will experience poor recommendation results. This is known as the **cold-start** problem. Many methods have been developed to tackle this problem typically by making use of additional information about the user (such as age, gender and occupation) [2]. A variation of the cold-start problem is where new items are added to the system (say for instance, a new movie). In this case either prior information about the item is available, or feature based approaches can also be used [13, 17].

In this paper, we propose a solution to the cold-start problem by combining user information across multiple domains(properties). We construct a hierarchical Bayesian model which integrates recommendation systems over multiple different domains (such as the frontpage of an Internet portal and its news site) and makes use of the user's interactions in one set of domain to immediately provide a personalized experience in other domains the user may have never interacted with. Note that the domains may operate over different "vocabularies". For instance, this model could be used to infer that a person interested in sports news (at a news webpage) is also interested in buying sports apparel (at a store) even if no metadata matching is provided for the store items. Our contributions include:

- A novel graphical model formulation of the user personalization problem which is easily *extensible* and allows integration over an unlimited number of domains.
- A scalable distributed inference procedure which allows the model to scale to millions of users.
- Demonstrating excellent predictive performance on a large real-world dataset.

Outline: We begin with a detailed description of the estimation and the model associated with it in Sections 2 and 3. This is followed in Section 4 by details on how to implement the sampler efficiently. Experimental results are reported in Section 5 and we conclude with a discussion and an outlook towards more advanced user modeling techniques.

KDD'11, August 21–24, 2011, San Diego, California, USA.

[1]User could be either a browser cookie or registered Yahoo! id. No personally identifiable user information was available in the data analyzed.

2. MODEL

2.1 Data Integration

Data integration between different sites is a key problem and challenge for large Internet portals. For instance, for a content provider such as Yahoo, Google or Microsoft, serving specialized content sites such as search, news, advertising, a portal, instant messaging, photos, video, cars, dating, etc. it is highly desirable to be able to leverage information from one site on the other. Some of the benefits from such an approach are:

- We can use information gained about a user on one site to provide personalized content right from the beginning on a second site, too. This addresses issues with the cold-start problem.
- We can use such information for improving the overall recommendation accuracy even for users which visit several sites frequently.
- Cross property information helps with abuse detection.
- Personalization can be used for recommending other properties.

Naively we could simply attempt to address the problem by having one joint set of user specific features that are shared by all properties and which are modified based on the user behavior. However, this approach is problematic for a number of reasons:

1. Users may exhibit different site-specific behavior which may only partially relate to the big picture about them. For instance, a user may well fancy himself as an expert in medieval numismatics on an answering site, yet at the same time he may exhibit some more mainstream preferences on the other sites. This means that we need to *allow* for the possibility of rather diverse and incoherent behavior between sites, and thus additional site-specific personalization, in our model.
2. It must be easy to add sites to the profiling system without the need to re-engineer the model of the already integrated sites. This is a practical imperative since in reality Internet properties are launched, bought or sold and our model must accommodate these requirements efficiently.
3. The framework needs to allow for different levels of sophistication in the model across different sites. That is, while some properties might only be willing to use a simple demographic targeting approach, others may be open to using an advanced Bayesian approach such as Latent Dirichlet Allocation [4].

In this paper we propose a flexible model that addresses all of these concerns in a principled fashion, namely by means of directed graphical models [14]. Its main structure is given in the diagram of Figure 1.

There are two basic use cases for such a model. In the first use case, each domain already has an existing personalization system. This model could then be used to provide for each user an "initialization prior" allowing personalization on the first visit to a new domain. In the second use case, the existing personalization system can be directly integrated into the hierarchical model, allowing personalization in different domains to be inferred jointly, potentially improving performance. The second use case is of course preferred.

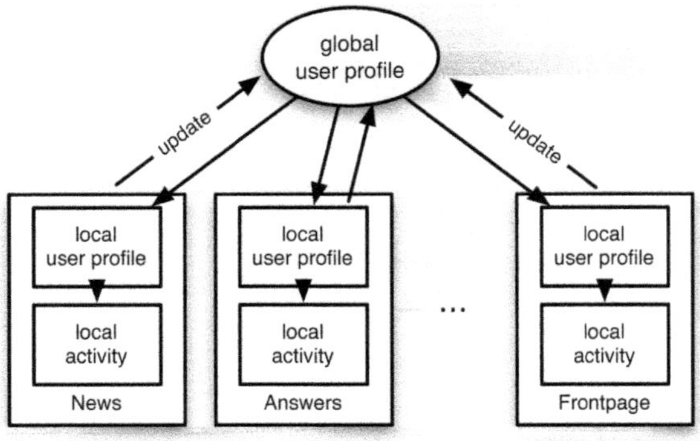

Figure 1: The high level structure of the proposed hierarchical statistical model. All properties share (and update) a joint profile vector. In addition to that, each property may keep a local model of the user's behavior in order to adapt to the possibly idiosyncratic activities of a user on a given site.

2.2 Formal Definition

In the following we denote by U the set of users in the system and let $|U|$ be the number of users. Furthermore let D be the set of personalization domains, such as News, Answers, Frontpage or Movies. Each user $u \in U$ interacts with one or more domains $d \in D$ producing a sparse list of tokens $W_{du} \subseteq \mathcal{W}_d$. Note that the space $\mathcal{W}_d$ can be different from domain to domain. For instance, in the News domain, this could be the text of the documents viewed, while in the Movies domain, this could be the list of movies rated. Additionally, let D_u denote the set of domains the user interacted with. Note that the number of domains a user interacts with is variable. So is the number of interactions per site.

The task is to predict each user's preferences in all domains. We would like to estimate the user's future behavior in domains the user has visited; while simultaneously predicting the user's preferences in domains the user have never visited. The latter is clearly the more difficult task. Such a situation may occur when say a dedicated News-reader first accesses the Movie rental site. We would like to provide **both** personalized news recommendations as well as predict the movies the user may be interested in; even if the user has never rented any movies before. Here we will focus on the cold-start problem while noting that the multiple-site personalization problem is contained in it. Formally, for each user $u \in U$, predict W_{du} where $d \notin D_u$.

As measures for the accuracy of the estimator we use a) the increase in log-likelihood by combining several domains, i.e. the increase in statistical prediction accuracy by combining several domains; b) the increase in the cosine similarity score when using several domains for improved personalization. Before we discuss the design of the graphical model associated with Figure 1 let us evaluate some alternatives.

2.3 Alternatives

Joint parameter vector:

Inferring two or more domains jointly is difficult due to the different domain spaces $\mathcal{W}_d$. The simplistic solution of combining all the domains by letting the domain be $\bigcup_{d \in D} \mathcal{W}_d$ is undesirable as it restricts the model excessively. Such a model will not deal well with often rather different amounts of data per domain.

For instance, if we naively combine Movie and News by using article headlines for the News domain, and movie titles for the Movies domain, the model would infer that a person interested in Sports news, must also be interested in Sports movies, and a person interested in Political news must also be interested political documentaries. The model will have difficulties modeling users who are interested in Political news and Action movies since it ignores the fact that users may exhibit different personalities on different domains.
Secondly, if we combine search queries and page views we might end up with several orders of magnitude more tokens in the case of page views. Simply combining both datasets would give queries only a minuscule weight and consequently underestimate their importance as relevant user features.

Joint action space: Another possibility is to combine the domains in a way such that tokens from one domain do not interfere with tokens from the other domain. For instance, this could be done in the Movie and News example by append the numeral "1" to every word in the movie title, and appending the numeral "2" to every word in the news title. Forcing the "dictionary" of both domains to be different, but inferring a joint model naively will resolve the case described in the previous paragraph, but still will not lead to a desirable solution. There are several issues.

- The "model complexity" of the domains could be very different. For instance, the number of tokens in the News domain could be significantly greater than the number of tokens in the Movie domain. Inferring them jointly will cause the latent factors will be largely dominated by the News. Moreover, the problem of recommending movies might be considerably harder than that of recommending news, requiring a richer latent representation.
- The modeling complexity could grow rapidly with the number of domains. For instance, we could observe that the News domain alone could be modeled with 10 latent factors, while the Movie domain could be modeled with 5 latent factors. However, when inferred jointly, the number of latent factors required could be much larger than $10+5 = 15$ since there could be one group of users who are interested in Political news and Action movies, as well as another group of users who are interested in Political news and Horror movies. These would have to be modeled as different latent factors, resulting in potentially a multiplicative increase in the number of factors necessary to build an accurate model. This model therefore does not provide the scalability necessary to extend to a large number of domains.

Independent Parameter Vector: This model trivially solves both problems mentioned above, simply by modeling each domain on its own. However, such an approach entire defeats the purpose of integration. In the following we propose a modification of this model to allow for cross-domain personalization.

2.4 Hierarchical Latent Model

Our model resolves these problems by adding an additional layer of latent parameters. We begin by assuming that each user has a hidden **latent feature vector** x_u which completely describes the user's *global* preferences and interests. Each domain also has a hidden **latent domain matrix** λ_d. Furthermore we assume that for each property d the user u also exhibits local traits, say θ_{du}. We assume that the local traits θ_{du} characterize the actions W_{du} that we observe. This yields the following generative model:

1. For all properties d do
   (a) Sample trait vector λ_d
2. For all users u do
   (a) Sample user trait x_u
   (b) For all properties d do
      i. Sample $\theta_{du}|x_u, \lambda_d$
      ii. Sample user actions $W_{du}|\theta_{du}$

In other words, the joint distribution is given by

$$p(\lambda, x, \theta, W) = \prod_d p(\lambda_d) \prod_u p(x_u) \prod_{d,u} p(\theta_{du}|x_u, \lambda_d) p(W_{du}|\theta_{du})$$

This has the advantage that we can express the distribution of the global user vector in terms of its local parameter estimates only. Moreover, the distribution factorizes, that is we have

$$p(x_u|\text{rest}) \propto p(x_u) \prod_d p(\theta_{du}|x_u, \lambda_d). \quad (1)$$

3. STATISTICAL FORMULATION

To make further progress we need to specify the distributions involved in $p(\lambda, x, \theta, W)$. Specifically we use Latent Dirichlet Allocation [4] (LDA) to describe $p(W_{du}|\theta_{du})$ and we subsequently employ a latent variant of "upstream conditioning" [11] to couple properties into a joint graphical model. We first begin with an explanation of plain LDA.

3.1 Latent Dirichlet Allocation

One model for estimating user behavior is to assume that users have a number of interests and that their actions are given by a combination of said interests. For instance, if we had a model describing which websites are visited by users interested in politics and which websites are visited by users interested in automobiles then we could easily infer the activity pattern of a user interested in both topics, simply by mixing the topical interest patterns of both.

Such a model is considerably more flexible than, say, an attempt to cluster users: in the latter case we would need to generate clusters for each and every *combination* of interests. Even worse, interests can be expressed to various degrees, so a simple model clustering users as being interested in cars may not be sensitive enough to infer whether users are die-hard car fanatics or whether they just exhibit a fleeting interest in automobiles.

LDA addresses this issue as follows: each user is endowed with a topic mixture θ_u that is drawn from some Dirichlet distribution $\text{Dir}(\alpha)$. Subsequently, for each user action, we draw a topic z_{ui} from the user-specific topic distribution θ_u and finally, we draw an action w_{ui} from the action distribution associated with topic z_{ui}. The action distributions φ_k themselves are drawn from a Dirichlet distribution. The parameters α and β are priors that adjust how nonuniform

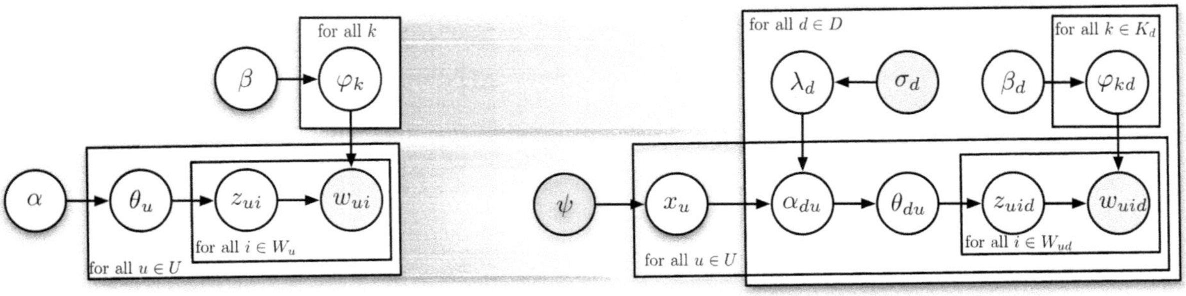

Figure 2: Left: Latent Dirichlet Allocation. This model covers the behavior of users u, as expressed in the actions w_{ui} on a single property. Right: Hierarchical Model with LDA applied to all properties. Each property has a characterization vector λ_d and each user is endowed with a global personalization vector x_u. σ_d and ψ are priors for these personalization terms.

the topic distributions and the word distributions are. We obtain [4]

$$p(w, z, \theta, \varphi|\alpha, \beta) \tag{2}$$
$$= \prod_k p(\varphi_k|\beta) \prod_u p(\theta_u|\alpha) \prod_{i \in W_u} p(z_{ui}|\theta_u) p(w_{ui}|z_{ui}, \varphi)$$

Large scale inference for (2) presents a significant challenge and there are only few published results on how to apply LDA to millions of instances (i.e. users). We use the approach of [18] for distributed collapsed inference and build on this framework. Before going into details regarding large scale estimation let us extend (2) in the spirit of Figure 1.

3.2 Upstream Coupling

The key to combining different properties is to make the prior α depend on both the property and the global features of the user. That is, instead of fixing α we assume that $\alpha_{du}|x_u, \lambda_d$ where x_u is the global user feature and λ_d is the site specific trait.

More specifically, to interact with a domain, a nonnegative[2] **user-domain feature vector** α_{du} is produced by computing the logistic transfer function $\text{lgt}(\lambda_d x_u)$ where

$$\text{lgt}(y) = \log\left[1 + e^y\right]. \tag{3}$$

In other words, α_{du} is computed by multiplying the user's **latent feature vector** with the domain's **latent domain matrix** and passed through a non-linear transform to enforce positivity. Note that the choice of lgt is somewhat arbitrary as there are many ways to project from $(-\infty, \infty)$ to $[0, \infty)$. In [11] this is done by exponentiation. However, we found exponentiation to be difficult to work with as its steep gradients cause numeric instabilities in inference. Hence we chose lgt for its simplicity. If sparsity in α is desirable, other possibilities such as Huber or L1 loss can be considered.

The **user-domain feature vector** is a description of how the user may interact with a given domain and can be interpreted freely by the domain specific model. As already outlined above we use LDA [4] as the domain specific model. However, note that the design of the model (Figure 1) does not require this assumption. As further elaborated in Sec. 7, many alternate generative procedures could be used. In particular, the model permits different procedures to be used for different domains, allowing the model to take advantage of domain-specific properties.

Essentially, the user's **latent feature vector** can be interpreted as a "super-topic" in the same spirit as [12]. Each column in the **latent domain matrix** can then be interpreted as the distribution of topics inside the super-topic. Multiplying these two latent parameters together will therefore produce a distribution over topics within the domain, which can then be used as a prior (α_{du}) for the actual topic distribution of the user's interaction within the domain.

Note that this model allows us to have different degrees of complexity in different domains: while the dimensionality of the global latent space is fixed via $x_u \in \mathbb{R}^k$, we may have different numbers of topics on different properties via $\lambda_d x_u$, simply by choosing different dimensions for different λ_d. This makes sense from a modeling perspective — some properties may only see small amounts of a user's activity (e.g. it is unlikely that on a cars site we may care much about the interest of a user in medieval numismatics). In summary the generative process is as follows:

1. For all properties d do
   (a) Generate **latent domain matrix** $\lambda_d \sim \mathcal{N}(0, \sigma_d)$
2. For all users u do
   (a) Generate **latent feature vector** $x_u \sim \mathcal{N}(0, \psi)$
   (b) For all visited properties $d \in D_u$ do
      i. Let **user-domain feature vector** be
      $$\alpha_{du} = \text{lgt}(\lambda_d x_u)$$
      ii. Draw user-domain topic distribution
      $$\theta_{du} \sim \mathcal{D}(\alpha_{du})$$
      iii. for each observed token $i \in W_{du}$
         A. Draw topic $z_{dui} \sim \mathcal{MN}(\theta_{du})$
         B. Draw word $w \sim \mathcal{MN}(\phi_{z_{dui}})$

The graphical model is in Fig. 2. We observe that if all user and domain latent parameters are known, i.e. if λ and x are observed, each domain essentially reduces to an instance of LDA. This therefore provides a relatively straightforward inference scheme.

3.3 Inference

We make the observation that once all λ and x are fixed, the model is essentially equivalent to having $|D|$ independent LDA models, where users are documents, and where

[2]Non-negativity of the coefficients α is needed to encode a valid Dirichlet prior on the topic distribution.

the topic prior is different for each document. We can therefore perform collapsed sampling in a similar manner as in [7] by integrating out θ and φ, and sampling z. In addition we sample x using Langevin diffusion. The λ parameter is optimized using L-BFGS [9]. We describe (the rather technical) details below. They are not essential to understanding the experiments but they matter for the purpose of reproducibility of the results. After integrating over θ, the complete likelihood $P(z, \lambda, x)$ of the model is given by

$$\prod_{d,u:d\in D_u} \frac{\Gamma(\sum_{t_d} \operatorname{lgt}(x_u^T \lambda_{d,t_d}))}{\Gamma(\sum_{t_d} \operatorname{lgt}(x_u^T \lambda_{d,t_d}) + n_{du})} \prod_{t_d} \frac{\Gamma(\operatorname{lgt}(x_u^T \lambda_{d,t_d}) + n_{t|du})}{\Gamma(\operatorname{lgt}(x_u^T \lambda_{d,t_d}))} \tag{4}$$

$$\prod_{d,t_d,k} \frac{1}{2\pi\sigma_k^2} \operatorname{lgt}\left(\frac{-\lambda_{d,t_d,k}^2}{2\sigma_k^2}\right) \prod_{u,k} \frac{1}{2\pi\psi_k^2} \operatorname{lgt}\left(-\frac{x_{u,k}^2}{2\psi_k^2}\right)$$

Note that this is very similar to [11, Eq. (1)], but with user-properties instead of documents, and different choices for λ and x. Let $\operatorname{dlgt}(y) := \partial_y \operatorname{lgt}(y)$ be the derivative of the logistic transfer function. In this case the derivative of the log likelihood with respect to $\lambda_{p,t_p,k}$, i.e. $\partial_{\lambda_{p,t_p,k}} \log P(z, \lambda, x)$ is given by

$$-\frac{\lambda_{d,t_d,k}}{\sigma_k^2} + \sum_{u:d\in D_u} x_{u,k} \operatorname{dlgt}\left(x_u^T \lambda_{d,t_d}\right) \times \tag{5}$$

$$\left[\Psi\left(\sum_{t_d} \operatorname{dlgt}\left(x_u^T \lambda_{d,t_d}\right)\right) - \Psi\left(\sum_{t_d} \operatorname{dlgt}\left(x_u^T \lambda_{d,t_d}\right) + n_{du}\right)\right.$$
$$\left. + \Psi\left(\operatorname{dlgt}\left(x_u^T \lambda_{d,t_d}\right) + n_{t|du}\right) - \Psi\left(\operatorname{dlgt}\left(x_u^T \lambda_{d,t_d}\right)\right)\right]$$

We use this equation to optimize λ using L-BFGS. The derivative $\partial_{x_{u,k}} \log P(z, \lambda, x)$ with respect to $x_{u,k}$ is similar:

$$-\frac{x_{u,k}}{\psi_k^2} + \sum_{u:d\in D_u} \sum_{t_d} \lambda_{p,t_d,k} \operatorname{dlgt}\left(x_u^T \lambda_{p,t_d}\right) \times \tag{6}$$

$$\left[\Psi\left(\sum_{t_d} \operatorname{dlgt}\left(x_u^T \lambda_{p,t_d}\right)\right) - \Psi\left(\sum_{t_d} \operatorname{dlgt}\left(x_u^T \lambda_{d,t_d}\right) + n_{du}\right)\right.$$
$$\left. + \Psi\left(\operatorname{dlgt}\left(x_u^T \lambda_{d,t_d}\right) + n_{t|du}\right) - \Psi\left(\operatorname{dlgt}\left(x_u^T \lambda_{d,t_d}\right)\right)\right]$$

This equation allows us to sample each $x_{u,k}$ using a Langevin Diffusion sampler.

3.4 Langevin Sampler

The Langevin Diffusion sampler [15] is essentially a Metropolis-Hastings sampler with a Gaussian proposal shifted in the direction of the gradient: Where the current value of $x_{u,k}$ is $x_{u,k}^t$ (sample value at time t), we propose the new value:

$$y_{u,k} = x_{u,k}^t + \frac{\sigma^2}{2} \frac{\partial \log P(z, \lambda, x)}{\partial x_{u,k}}\bigg|_{x_{u,k}^t} + N(0, \sigma^2)$$

Where the notation $\frac{\partial \log P(z,\lambda,x)}{\partial x_{u,k}}|_{x_{u,k}^t}$ means to take the partial derivative of $\log P(z, \lambda, x)$ against the variable $x_{u,k}$ (Eq. (6)) and evaluate it at the value $x_{u,k}^t$.

We then compute the acceptance ratio:

$$r = \frac{\exp\left\{-\left\|x^t{}_{u,k} - y_{u,k} - \frac{\sigma^2}{2}\frac{\partial \log P(z,\lambda,x)}{\partial x_{u,k}}|_{y_{u,k}}\right\|^2 \Big/ 2\sigma^2\right\}}{\exp\left\{-\left\|y_{u,k} - x_{u,k}^t - \frac{\sigma^2}{2}\frac{\partial \log P(z,\lambda,x)}{\partial x_{u,k}}\Big|_{x_{u,k}^t}\right\|^2 \Big/ 2\sigma^2\right\}}$$

Then update $x_{u,k}^t$ to the proposed value $y_{u,k}$ with probability $\min(r, 1)$:

$$x_{u,k}^{t+1} = \begin{cases} y_{u,k} & \text{with probability } \min(r,1) \\ x_{u,k}^t & \text{with probability } 1\text{-}\min(r,1) \end{cases}$$

4. IMPLEMENTATION

To run experiments on large datasets, it is necessary to make use of large scale distributed processing. We therefore implemented the model by extending the distributed LDA implementation from [18]. The extension is relatively straightforward due to the similarities to regular LDA. The main contributions we made to the implementation is a distributed L-BFGS solver, as well as a novel way to initialize the distributed sampler which accelerates convergence significantly.

An overview of our approach is provided in Algorithm 1. Firstly, the set of users are equally partitioned among the P machines in the cluster. Each machine then initializes each user with a random **latent feature vector**, and uses the Distributed Initialization procedure described in Sec. 4.2 to provide the initial topic assignments to each observed token, producing local word-topic counts. A set of `Memcached` servers[3] are used to synchronize the local word-topic counts with the global word-topic counts. See [18] for details on the communication between nodes. The **latent domain matrix** is initialized by having one machine generate the random matrix, writing it into `Memcached`, and all remaining machines reading from it.

The sampler then proceeds as described in [18], with the exception that the user's latent feature vector must be sampled, and the latent domain matrices are optimized periodically (every 15 iterations in the pseudo-code in Alg. 1).

4.1 Distributed L-BFGS solver

The latent domain matrices are optimized using a distributed L-BFGS solver. We first observe that the gradient of the log-likelihood of the model with respect to the domain matrices λ can be written as a sum over all the users in the dataset. This naturally means that the gradient can be computed in a fully distributed fashion, collected and summed on one machine, which then performs the actual L-BFGS update. This procedure is however further complicated by the Armijo line-search stage of the L-BFGS solver, which requires the log-likelihood and and the gradient to be recomputed repeatedly for different values of λ. This requires a close level of coordination among all the machines which is not immediately provided by the `memcached` framework.[4]

[3]`Memcached` is a fast distributed (key, value) storage system

[4]One might suspect that the entire algorithm could be efficiently implemented in Hadoop MapReduce. However, convergence of the sampling algorithm is severely hampered if all inter-process communication is deferred to the Reduce phase. Moreover, the barriers between iterations can lead to considerable performance penalties. For a detailed discussion see [18].

Algorithm 1 Sampling executed on each machine.

```
for Each user u in this machine's partition do
  Initialize u's latent feature vector
  for Each domain d ∈ D_u the user interacted with do
    for Each observed token w ∈ W_du do
      Sample w's topic using the procedure in Sec. 4.2
    end for
  end for
end for
if I am Machine 0 then
  Initialize latent domain matrices
  Store latent domain matrices into Memcached
else
  Initialize latent domain matrices from Memcached
end if
for i = 1 to #sampling iterations do
  if i mod 15 = 0 then
    \\ Optimize every 15 iterations
    Optimize latent domain matrices using
          distributed L-BFGS
  end if
  for Each user u in this machine's partition do
    Sample u's latent feature vector using
          Langevin Diffusion
    Sample the topic in each observed token in u
  end for
end for
```

Algorithm 2 Pseudo-code of Distributed L-BFGS Solver

```
Compute the local gradient g Using Eq. (5)
Compute the local log likelihood l Using Eq. (4)
Perform distributed sum over g and l
if I am machine 1 then
  Compute L-BFGS step Δ using g and l
  Update λ
  broadcast λ
else
  receive broadcast λ
end if
\\ Armijo Line search
while True do
  Compute the local gradient g' Using Eq. (5)
  Compute the local log likelihood l' Using Eq. (4)
  Perform distributed sum over g' and l'
  if I am machine 1 then
    Test Armijo and Wolfe conditions using g' and l'
    if Armijo conditions satisfied then
      return
    else
      Decrease step-size and update λ
      broadcast λ
    end if
  else
    Wait for Machine 1
  end if
end while
```

To implement this algorithm, we must first re-implement three standard distributed programming primitives within the memcached environment. The three primitives are the **barrier**, **sum** and **broadcast**.

The **barrier** is a function which provides "sequentialization" of execution across a distributed program. When a process call the **barrier** function, the process will stop execution and pause. The **barrier** function only returns when all machines in the distributed system enter the **barrier**. A common use-case for the **barrier** is to "wait" for all processors to complete a particular task, before going on to the next task. We implement a version of the sense-reversing barrier algorithm described in [10].

The distributed **sum** function (or more generally also known as **reduce** or **fold**) simply collects and aggregates a value posted by each machine. Each machine p calls the **sum** function with a particular value v_p. The function then returns with the sum of all the values $(v_1+v_2+\cdots+v_{P-1}+v_P)$. We implement this operation by having each machine write its value v_p to a `memcached`. A **barrier** is then called to guarantee that all machines have completed the write. Machine 1 then reads all the values from `memcached`, sums them and writes back to `memcached`. Another **barrier** is used here to ensure that the write is completed. Then all machines reads the resultant value from from `memcached`.

The **broadcast** operation allows one machine to send a value to all the other machines in the network. This operation is similar to the **sum** operation. Combining these operations, we can write the distributed L-BFGS solver in pseudo-code in Alg. 2.

4.2 Distributed Initialization

The standard way to initialize an LDA sampler is to sample the topic of each new word from a uniform distribution. However, this results in slow convergence. A more effective way of initializing the sampler is to perform online sampling [5]. That is, the topic of each new word is sampled by conditioning on all the words seen so far. This procedure is easy when performed on a single machine, but is extremely complex to implement in a distributed setting as the global topic counts will need to be synchronized very frequently.

A plausible alternative is to have each machine perform the online sampling process independently using only the local topic counts. This however, produces poor initializations as each machine could assign very different topics to the same word resulting in a uniform topic distribution when the topic counts are aggregated across all the machines.

Instead, we propose a simple solution: We perform online sampling independently on each machine as described above. However, when we sample a topic for a new word w, instead of using a random number generator, we use $hash\,(w + \#\text{occurrences of w seen so far})$.

This procedure is equivalent to constructing a different pseudo-random generator for each unique word, and that this generator is seeded identically across all the machines. This algorithm does not correspond to a true online-LDA initialization, but it simply "correlates" the random number generator across all machines, encouraging similar topic distributions for each word. An advantage of this procedure is that it does not require any communication between the machines, allowing for a simple implementation.

5. TWO DOMAIN EXPERIMENTS

We tested the model on a large real world dataset comprising a random subsample of 5.6 million users who interacted with Yahoo! News and Yahoo! Frontpage for a week. We record "click-through" information for each user. That is to say, when the user clicks on a Frontpage link, we record the words in the link. Likewise, when the user clicks on a News article, we record the words in the article.

The goal is to predict how a new user might interact with Frontpage, given the user's past interactions with News (and vice versa). The problem is made particularly difficult since only 1% of all the users in our dataset interacted with both Yahoo! News and Yahoo! Frontpage.

To perform holdout testing, we selected 20% of the users who interacted with both domains and hide the user's interaction with one of the properties when training the model. The model can then be used to predict the user's interaction with the hidden property. Where α_{du} is the user-domain feature vector, we note that the predicted word distribution $P(w_{du}|\alpha)$ is simply proportional[5] to $\varphi \times \alpha_{du}$. We evaluate accuracy using the cosine similarity score between the predicted word distribution $P(w_{du}|\alpha)$ and the true observed word distribution w_{du}.

$$\frac{\langle w_{du}, \varphi \times \alpha_{du} \rangle}{|w_{du}| \times |\varphi \times \alpha_{du}|}$$

We tested against a simple baseline, which is the mean-prediction formed by averaging the word distribution across all the user-interactions within the domain. This intuitively represents the "average" user. We do not test against nearest-neighbor methods as they require large amounts of computation to evaluate each new user and do not scale well to large dataset sizes. We also do not consider the method of combining all the domains into a single LDA model (joint parameter vector and joint action space in Sec. 2.3) to be viable models due to the significant difference in the domain types for the three-domain experiment of Section 6.

Using 100 topics to model FrontPage and 400 topics to model News, we plot in Fig. 3(a) the model log-likelihood $P(w, z)$ across sampling iterations. We compare the likelihood curves obtained when varying the dimensionality of the latent feature vector. As expected, running independent LDA on both domains (equivalent to using a 0 length latent feature vector) produces the lowest log-likelihood. Increasing the dimensionality of the latent feature vector from 0 to 25 allows the model to fit the data better, resulting in a higher log-likelihood. Further increasing to 50 increase log-likelihood slightly, though we observe diminishing returns.

Next in Fig. 3(b) we plot the % improvement in hold-out accuracy over baseline prediction. We observe significant gains in holdout accuracy for both Front Page and News. Increased model complexity (by increasing the number of latent features) appears to overfit slightly, resulting in decreased hold out accuracy.

Fig. 3(b) also suggests that it is easier to predict FrontPage preferences from News preferences than vice versa. This is expected since the size of News vocabulary is about 4 times larger than the size of the FrontPage vocabulary. Each interaction with a News article also produces significantly more tokens. Moreover, the range of stories on the FrontPage is considerably more constrained than the set of news events. Hence there is less information to be gained from knowing which FrontPage story a given user viewed.

Next, since $\lambda_{\text{news}} x_i$ is the topic "preference" for user i in the News domain, and $\lambda_{\text{fp}} x_i$ is the topic "preference" for

[5]This simple identity holds for Dirichlet priors in the absence of any additional data since it forms a conjugate prior to the multinomial mixture.

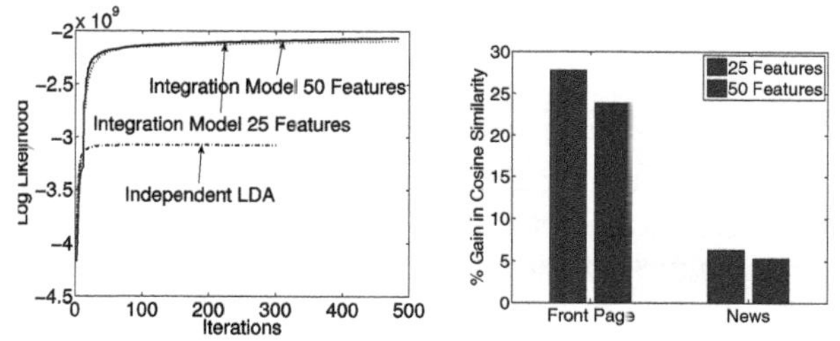

(a) Two Prop Log Likelihood (b) Two Prop Holdout

Figure 3: (a) Two Property FrontPage + News model log- likelihood over iterations using 100 topics for FrontPage and 400 topics for News. Each curve corresponds to using a user latent feature vector of different lengths. The "Independent LDA" is the log-likelihood of running LDA independently on both domains and is equivalent to using a latent feature vector of length 0. As expected, increased dimensionality of the latent feature vector results in increased log-likelihood. (b) Two Property FrontPage + News Hold out accuracy improvement over baseline for different number of latent features.

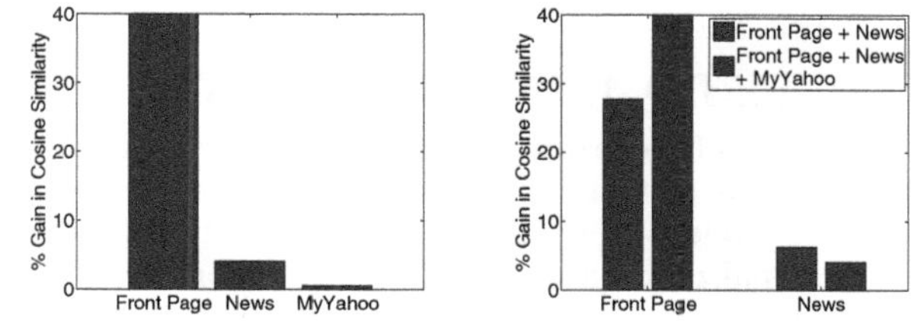

(a) Three Prop. Holdout (b) 2 vs 3 Prop Holdout

Figure 4: (a) Three Property FrontPage + News + myYahoo Holdout Accuracy. (b) Comparing Frontpage and News holdout accuracy for the two domain model and the three domain model

user i in the Frontpage, we can use $\sum_x (\lambda_{\text{news}} x)(\lambda_{\text{fp}} x)^T$ to estimate the correlation between the topics across News and Frontpage. Using this, we can infer that for a person who is interested in a particular topic on Frontpage, what other topics might he be interested in when he visits News.

A minor problem with this procedure is that it can be hard to factor out strong "background preferences". That is, a Frontpage topic which **everyone** is interested in, might appear to be strongly correlated with almost all other News topics. However, we still obtain interpretable results.

In Table 1, we demonstrate this for two random selected topics in Frontpage, and their top correlated topic in News. For instance, the first row suggests that people interested in reading about science articles on Frontpage might also be interested in reading about Avatar (a science fiction movie) on the News website. And people interested in the Oscars might also be interested in reality TV shows.

In Table 2, we demonstrate the reverse. For two randomly selected topics in News, what are their top correlated topics in Frontpage. The first row suggests that people interested in technology, might also be interested in college graduate earnings. In the second row, we encounter the strong "background preference" problem as stated earlier. Here we try to infer the Frontpage preferences of a user who is interested reading about the healthcare debate on News. If we look at the top correlated topic, we might infer that the user is

FrontPage	News
bacteria, fight, super, struggling, developed, doctors, resistant, lethal, virtually, drugs, antibiotic, competitors, chad	film, movie, movies, films, director, story, avatar, james, time, hollywood, big, make, hes
sandra, oscar, oscars, red, carpet, bullock, golden, gown, bullocks, nominee, bestactress, sparkles, stunning	vienna, bachelor, jake, pavelka, giraldi, finale, show, stars, dancing, love, season, time, abc

Table 1: Given a particular frontpage topic (left column), the top correlated news topic (right column). The first row suggests that people interested in science might also be interested in Avatar (a science fiction movie).

News	Frontpage
iphone, apple, app, apps, ipod, google, store, apples, android, mac, mobile, touch, ipad	college, year, earn, years, 000, bestpaid, average, 129, colleges, graduates, ten, alums, schools
health, care, bill, obama, president, rep, house, republican, senate, news, sen, democrats, fox	drafts, player, nfl, scouts, team, riskiest, peril, bryant, dez, pick, talented, nba, james home, bank, facing, ceo, gomez, eviction, rosalina, bought, cleaning, foreclosed, client, janitor, offices captured, inside, mountain, terrorist, observers, impresses, alqaidas, complexity, base, features, hideout, size, special

Table 2: Given a news topic (left column), the top correlated frontpage topic (right column). For the second row, the top three topics are provided.

interested in reading about sports. However, including the second and third most correlated topics, we see that the user might also be interested in banking and terrorism articles.

6. THREE DOMAIN EXPERIMENT

We next extend the model further by including a third domain: MyYahoo; demonstrating the scalability and extensibility of the model. To our knowledge this is first attempt at user personalization across three different domains.

For the myYahoo domain, we only record the **id's** of the articles the user clicked on. This makes the problem significantly harder as the article id's have no semantic significance. We selected 5.6 million users from the same date range as the previous experiment. 5.5% of the users interact with two or more domains. We selected 10% of the users who interacted with two or more domains for holdout testing.

We trained the model on the dataset, using 50 latent features and plot the % improvement in holdout accuracy over baseline prediction in Fig. 4(a). We demonstrated improvement for both Frontpage and News, as well as an insignificant improvement in MyYahoo. This is to be expected due to the lack of semantic information in the MyYahoo domain and due to the comparatively small number of applications provided on MyYahoo.

Next, in Fig. 4(b), we compare the holdout accuracy for FrontPage and News between the 3-domain model and the 2-domain model. Each model was tested with 25, 50 and 75 latent features and the best setting for each model was used. The 2-domain model required only 25 latent features and increasing the feature count further results in overfitting, while the 3-domain model continues to improve in performance up to 50 latent features. We observe that even with the limitations of the MyYahoo data, including the third domain still improves holdout performance significantly on Frontpage prediction (while incurring a small drop for News).

7. EXTENSIONS

The model is designed to be a highly **generic** model for user personalization, supporting a variety of extensions.

Firstly, the design of the model does not require all the user features x to be latent. Instead, we may combine our model with the upstream conditioning of [11] which immediately allows us to add observed variables. For instance, one could use geographical location (via the IP address or via HTML5) as a fully observed user feature. Alternatively, the model also permits the use of features which are not observed for all users (such as gender). The latter case is particularly interesting as the model would then try to infer the feature value for the remaining users. For instance, the model would try to infer the gender of user if the user's gender is not observed.

Next, the model does not require the use of LDA within a domain. The inference process is highly modular with regards to each domain, and permits any domain model to be used as long as a log-likelihood derivative with respect to x can be computed.

- This could permit the model to provide cross-domain personalization into unusual domains such as personalized spam filtering.
- We could use a Gaussian latent matrix factorization model [16], replacing the discrete set of topics by a continuous (low dimensional) factorization.
- We could employ a factorization akin to the Indian Buffet Process [6] which uses a binary latent variable representation instead of a finite (sparse) set of topics.

Also, since the model places no restriction on the number of domains it can personalize over, the model could, with little effort, be used as a back-end to connect other generative user-personalization schemes.

8. CONCLUSION

In this work, we designed a new model for providing user personalization across two or more domains and demonstrated its efficacy on a large real-world dataset comprising of data from Yahoo News, Yahoo FrontPage and MyYahoo, obtaining significant gains in prediction accuracy. The model we developed is **highly extensible** and observed user features such as geographical location and gender can be integrated. Furthermore, the model treats each domain in a **modular** fashion, allowing other generative user personalization schemes to be connected easily. Finally, we provide a scalable inference procedure with a novel initialization scheme, allowing the model to scale to millions of users.

9. REFERENCES

[1] J. Abernethy, F. Bach, T. Evgeniou, and J.-P. Vert. A new approach to collaborative filtering: Operator estimation with spectral regularization. *Journal of Machine Learning Research*, 10:803–826, March 2009.

[2] D. Agarwal and B.-C. Chen. Regression-based latent factor models. In J.F. Elder, F. Fogelman-Soulié, P.A. Flach, and M.J. Zaki, editors, *Proceedings of the 15th ACM SIGKDD International Conference on Knowledge Discovery and Data Mining*, pages 19–28. ACM, 2009.

[3] J. Basilico and T. Hofmann. Unifying collaborative and content-based filtering. In *Proc. Intl. Conf. Machine Learning*, pages 65–72, New York, NY, 2004. ACM Press.

[4] D. Blei, A. Ng, and M. Jordan. Latent Dirichlet allocation. *Journal of Machine Learning Research*, 3:993–1022, January 2003.

[5] K. R. Canini, L. Shi, and T. L. Griffiths. Online inference of topics with latent dirichlet allocation. In *Proceedings of the Twelfth International Conference on Artificial Intelligence and Statistics (AISTATS)*, 2009.

[6] T. Griffiths and Z. Ghahramani. Infinite latent feature models and the indian buffet process. In *NIPS*, 2005.

[7] T.L. Griffiths and M. Steyvers. Finding scientific topics. *Proceedings of the National Academy of Sciences*, 101:5228–5235, 2004.

[8] Y. Koren, R.M. Bell, and C. Volinsky. Matrix factorization techniques for recommender systems. *IEEE Computer*, 42(8):30–37, 2009.

[9] Dong C. Liu and Jorge Nocedal. On the limited memory BFGS method for large scale optimization. *Mathematical Programming*, 45(3):503–528, 1989.

[10] John M. Mellor-Crummey and Michael L. Scott. Algorithms for scalable synchronization on shared-memory multiprocessors. *ACM Transactions on Computer Systems*, 9(1):21–65, February 1991.

[11] D. M. Mimno and A. McCallum. Topic models conditioned on arbitrary features with dirichlet-multinomial regression. In D. A. McAllester and P. Myllymäki, editors, *UAI, Proceedings of the 24th Conference in Uncertainty in Artificial Intelligence*, pages 411–418. AUAI Press, 2008.

[12] D.M. Mimno, W. Li, and A. McCallum. Mixtures of hierarchical topics with pachinko allocation. In Z. Ghahramani, editor, *International Conference on Machine Learning*, volume 227, pages 633–640. ACM, 2007.

[13] Seung-Taek Park, David Pennock, Omid Madani, Nathan Good, and Dennis DeCoste. Naïve filterbots for robust cold-start recommendations. In Tina Eliassi-Rad, Lyle H. Ungar, Mark Craven, and Dimitrios Gunopulos, editors, *KDD*, pages 699–705. ACM, 2006.

[14] J. Pearl. *Causality: Models, Reasoning and Inference*. Cambridge University Press, 2001.

[15] C. Robert and G. Casella. *Monte Carlo Statistical Methods*. Springer, second edition, 2004.

[16] R. Salakhutdinov and A. Mnih. Bayesian probabilistic matrix factorization using markov chain monte carlo. In W.W. Cohen, A. McCallum, and S.T. Roweis, editors, *Machine Learning, Proceedings of the Twenty-Fifth International Conference (ICML 2008), Helsinki*, volume 307, pages 880–887. ACM, 2008.

[17] Andrew I. Schein, Alexandrin Popescul, Lyle H. Ungar, and David M. Pennock. Methods and metrics for cold-start recommendations. In Micheline Beaulieu, Ricardo Baeza-Yates, Sung Hyon Myaeng, and Kalervo Järvelin, editors, *Proceedings of the 25th annual international ACM SIGIR Conference on Research and Development in Information Retrieval*, pages 253–260, New York, August 11–15 2002. ACM Press.

[18] A.J. Smola and S. Narayanamurthy. An architecture for parallel topic models. In *Very Large Databases (VLDB)*, 2010.

[19] M. Weimer, A. Karatzoglou, Q. Le, and A. Smola. Cofi rank - maximum margin matrix factorization for collaborative ranking. In J.C. Platt, D. Koller, Y. Singer, and S. Roweis, editors, *Advances in Neural Information Processing Systems 20*. MIT Press, Cambridge, MA, 2008.

Click Shaping to Optimize Multiple Objectives

Deepak Agarwal, Bee-Chung Chen, Pradheep Elango, Xuanhui Wang
Yahoo! Labs
Sunnyvale, CA
{dagarwal,beechun,elango,xhwang}@yahoo-inc.com

ABSTRACT

Recommending interesting content to engage users is important for web portals (e.g. AOL, MSN, Yahoo!, and many others). Existing approaches typically recommend articles to optimize for a single objective, i.e., number of clicks. However a click is only the starting point of a user's journey and subsequent downstream utilities such as time-spent and revenue are important. In this paper, we call the problem of recommending links to jointly optimize for clicks and post-click downstream utilities *click shaping*. We propose a multi-objective programming approach in which multiple objectives are modeled in a constrained optimization framework. Such a formulation can naturally incorporate various application-driven requirements. We study several variants that model different requirements as constraints and discuss some of the subtleties involved. We conduct our experiments on a large dataset from a real system by using a newly proposed unbiased evaluation methodology [17]. Through extensive experiments we quantify the tradeoff between different objectives under various constraints. Our experimental results show interesting characteristics of different formulations and our findings may provide valuable guidance to the design of recommendation engines for web portals.

Categories and Subject Descriptors

H.3.5 [**Information Storage and Retrieval**]: Online Information Services

General Terms

Algorithms, Design

Keywords

Multi-objective, click shaping, constrained optimization

1. INTRODUCTION

Searching and browsing are two dominant ways to access information on the Web. While searching to obtain specific content of interest is ubiquitous, a significant amount of time is also spent on browsing the web for content items that are trendy, interesting and eclectic. Examples include visits to a sports site like ESPN to find the latest game updates, browsing the Yahoo! Front Page to read interesting articles, and so on. Hence, it is important to recommend interesting content items that delight and engage users.

Online digital content is easy to create and access. This provides a rich inventory of widely varying quality on the Web, and underscores the need to develop algorithmic methods that can prune low quality content in order to surface the engaging ones. However, such an approach depends on the metrics that we are interested in optimizing for. Prior work typically approach this problem by considering a single metric – the click through rate (CTR) on the recommended content (e.g., [3, 8] and references therein). While CTR is a reasonable proxy for content popularity and simple to measure, such an approach ignores nuances that are involved in measuring other metrics that are often of interest to website owners. For instance, time-spent on the content page is an important engagement metric reported by comScore[1], it is known to be indicative of users' satisfaction in other scenarios such as search [18, 6]. Furthermore, website owners may also consider non-engagement metrics like advertising revenue on the content page. Often, these metrics are in conflict and optimizing for one may deteriorate some others. For example, increasing CTR at the expense of total time-spent is perhaps detrimental and indicative of inferior user experience. Thus, recommending items to obtain an appropriate tradeoff among several metrics is an important research problem.

Consider the Today Module on Yahoo! Front Page in Figure 1 as a concrete example. Articles are selected from a live content pool for display on the four module positions. Of the four positions, the F1 position has the maximum exposure. An article in the content pool links to a page on some other Yahoo! property like News, Finance, and Sports. Thus Yahoo! Front Page is like a distribution channel that routes users to various other Yahoo! pages. Hence a click on the Today Module is associated with downstream metrics like time-spent and revenue that accrues post-click. Although optimizing total clicks on Today Module can boost overall *supply* to different Yahoo! pages, in the presence of significant inter-property variance in downstream metrics, optimizing for clicks alone may lead to an undesirable supply distribution. For instance, maximizing for total clicks may divert more user visits to a low revenue entertainment site at the expense of a higher revenue finance site. It is perhaps desirable to change the content serving scheme to obtain a larger fraction of clicks on finance articles without losing too many clicks overall. This is an example of optimizing for multiple objectives when recommending articles (items) to users. Intuitively when we optimize for different objectives, the clicks on the Today Module that generate visits to different Yahoo! properties

[1] http://www.comscore.com/

KDD'11, August 21–24, 2011, San Diego, California, USA.

Figure 1: Today Module on Yahoo! Front Page

are *shaped* by the recommendation system. Hence we refer to this problem of recommending items to users to jointly optimize for clicks and post-click downstream utilities *click shaping*.

In this paper we propose a multi-objective programming (MOP) approach [20] for click shaping. The goal of such click shaping in our application scenarios is to obtain significant improvements in some downstream metrics (e.g., revenue or time-spent) by forgoing a small fraction of total click volume that is obtained through the status quo scheme that maximizes for CTR alone. We formulate the problem in a constrained optimization framework. Such a formulation can naturally incorporate various application-driven business requirements. A range of solutions that compute the amount of click loss incurred to barter a certain improvement in downstream metrics is given by the multi-objective programming approach. The solution embraced by the website owner depends on the application scenario and business strategy. We believe that quantifying such tradeoffs among multiple competing objectives provide non-trivial insights to the design of recommendation engines and can help with better decision-making. Specifically we make the following contributions in this paper:

- We propose *click shaping*, a novel twist to content recommendation that incorporates both click-throughs and other downstream metrics in a multi-objective programming (MOP) framework. In particular, we formulate MOPs of different flavors that tradeoff total clicks with downstream engagement metrics like time-spent. We show that for recommending content on large web portal pages that distribute traffic to several downstream pages, click shaping provides opportunities to effectively tradeoff multiple downstream metrics.

- We introduce variants that ensure "fairness" when routing visits to different properties (domains). Our fairness objective ensures that the gains in engagement are shared in a fair way among different domains. Such constraints are important in a portal setting where the downstream properties are heterogeneous. Furthermore, our fairness objective also helps in normalizing for scale effects whereby engagement metrics may have sharp differences in scale across different properties. Imposing such constraints presents additional computational challenges. We show several of our constrained MOPs can be efficiently solved through convex optimization techniques [21].

- Through replay experiments [17] on logs obtained via a randomized serving scheme on the Today Module, we provide unbiased performance comparison for different MOPs. Our data analysis is conducted with two metrics – clicks and time-spent. Solutions obtained for MOPs under different constraints provide interesting insights. We show that significant gains in downstream engagement is possible by losing small fraction of clicks. We also show the behavior of click shaping in the presence of fairness objective. We provide interesting insights obtained through extensive data analysis.

2. PROBLEM SETUP

For the sake of concreteness, we define our problem in the setting of the Today Module on Yahoo! Front Page in Figure 1. Our methodology can be easily applied to other multi-objective recommendation settings. Today Module provides users with interesting, timely, and informative articles every day. At each time point, there is a candidate pool of live articles created through editorial oversight, the pool is frequently refreshed to keep up with timely and trendy articles. For every visit to the Yahoo! Front Page, articles selected from the live content pool are recommended on the Today Module with the goal of optimizing some objective(s).

Notations: Formally, at each epoch t, the set of live articles is denoted by $\mathcal{A}_t = (A_1, \cdots, A_{n_t})$. Each article $j \in \mathcal{A}_t$ belongs to one of K different Yahoo! properties (e.g., News, Finance, Sports, etc). Supply to a given Yahoo! property is significantly influenced by the links clicked in the Today Module and provides a good setup for our study. Let $\mathcal{P} = \{P_1, ..., P_K\}$ denote the set of properties and $j \in P_k$ means the landing page of article j belongs to property P_k. Users are assumed to be clustered into m segments: $\mathcal{S} = \{S_1, \cdots, S_m\}$, this is an important assumption for methods discussed in this paper. We discuss various user segmentation schemes in Section 5. Let p_{ijt} denote the probability (CTR) that a user in segment i would click article j when it is displayed in epoch t, and let d_{ijt} denote the time that the user would spend on the landing property of article j if she clicks the article. Other downstream utilities (single or multiple) can be easily incorporated in our framework, we focus only on time-spent in this paper for the sake of illustration. Note that if the goal is to optimize for a single objective (maximize clicks or time-spent, but not both), the optimal solution is to recommend the article with the highest p_{ijt} (or $p_{ijt} \cdot d_{ijt}$) to users in segment i.

Explore/exploit: Content optimization is an explore/exploit problem. To optimize for any metric, we need to estimate the performance of each candidate article in terms of that metric. Without displaying an article to any user, it is difficult to know the performance of that article. Models may be built to predict article performance based on article features; however they may be worse than a simple method that directly computes the metric from online data (e.g., computing click-through rate using the clicks and views of the article) [3]. The explore/exploit problem for a single objective is well studied (e.g., [3]). Developing explore/exploit methods for multiple objectives that ensure certain notion of optimality is non-trivial. In this paper we assume some explore/exploit scheme is running in the system. In particular, we use a simple scheme — ϵ-greedy, which has been empirically shown to achieve good performance [24]. This scheme works as follows: We serve a small fraction of randomly selected user visits with articles selected uniformly at random from the current content pool in order to collect data for every article (explore population). For the remaining visits, we serve the article with the highest estimated CTR if the goal is to maximize clicks (exploit population). With multiple objectives, the serving scheme for the exploit population is different from that of displaying the highest CTR article as we shall see later in this paper.

Serving scheme: Given multiple objectives and constraints, our goal is to construct a serving scheme that can be used to serve articles to users in the exploit population. For each epoch t, a serving scheme uses information obtained before the epoch to decide an allocation plan $\mathbf{x}_t = \{x_{ijt} : i \in \mathcal{S}, j \in \mathcal{A}_t\}$, where x_{ijt} is the fraction of visits in user segment i to be served with article j in epoch t. Obviously the fractions are non-negative and lie on the article simplex for each user segment, i.e., $x_{ijt} \geq 0$ and $\sum_j x_{ijt} = 1$. Given $\mathbf{x}_t$, an incoming user in epoch t is assigned to the appropriate user segment and an article is served through a multinomial draw from the article simplex of the segment. Different optimization methods generate different allocation plans according to different criteria. For example, the click maximization method would set x_{ij^*t} to 1 if j^* has the highest estimated CTR among all the articles and 0 for the remaining articles. Soft clustering of users also works with our formulation and in this case the allocation vector of a user is a weighted sum of cluster-specific allocation vectors. User clusters can also change over time, for ease of exposition we assume they are fixed.

Offline evaluation: The best way to evaluate a content optimization method is to run controlled live experiments on small fractions of randomly selected user visits on the Yahoo! Front Page. However, such a method is expensive and not feasible in practice for a battery of schemes that one may want to test. Hence, we take recourse to an offline evaluation methodology that works on logged data collected retrospectively [17, 14]. This offline evaluation method can give us *unbiased* and *replicable* comparison. We provide a brief description of the scheme below.

The logged data must be collected from a serving scheme that selects each article from the pool with some *known, non-zero* probability. In our case, we collect view and click events from an experiment where articles are displayed uniformly at random to a small randomly selected user population. We shall refer to this as the *random bucket*. The selection probability of each article is $1/n_t$ at epoch t; this avoids the need to estimate selection probabilities from a non-randomized scheme and also ensures each article is shown a large number of times.

Each view event in our logged data consists of the user segment ID and article ID displayed at F1. For each click event, in addition to user segment ID and article ID, we also record the time-spent (or any other downstream metric of interest) on the landing property. All the events are ordered temporally. The replay evaluation works as follows. It goes through each epoch sequentially. At epoch t, we perform the following steps:

1. Compute the expected CTR and time-spent for each (user segment i, article j) pair. The estimates are computed using all data before epoch t.

2. Compute the allocation plan $\mathbf{x}_t$ for the multiple objective optimization (MOP) under consideration.

3. For each event in t, if the user segment = i, we draw an article j^* from the current pool according to probability x_{ijt}. If the article served in the logged data matches j^*, we record this matched event; otherwise we ignore it.

At the end of this process, we compute CTR and time-spent metrics based on the recorded events and it can be shown these estimates are unbiased [17, 14]. Note that all the matched events for a serving scheme give us a sample of user activities for that scheme. Different serving schemes have different sets of matched events. However, because each article in the random bucket has an equal probability to be displayed to users, the number of matched view events for any serving scheme is expected to be the same. A better serving scheme to optimize CTR can match more click events. We can thus compute the overall CTR and time-spent from these matched events and use these metrics to compare different serving schemes. As emphasized before, under mild assumptions such an evaluation provides an unbiased estimate of performance with small variance when we use large amounts of data.

3. OBJECTIVE DEFINITIONS

In this section we introduce various objectives to be optimized in our multi-objective programming (MOPs). We only consider content serving on a single position (the F1 position on Today Module); optimizing for multiple positions is more involved and part of future work.

We consider two different objectives – (a) total clicks and (b) total time-spent on landing properties. These objectives are standard engagement metrics and commonly reported by companies like comScore; they play a crucial role in forming advertiser perception and measuring website performance. Also from a user satisfaction perspective, it is important to encourage downstream engagement with content in addition to clicks. For instance, the presentation of a link (captions, images, etc) may sometimes boost click-rates without generating high engagement; our MOP approach helps avoid such artifacts by simultaneously optimizing for both downstream engagement and CTR. We work with the two metrics mentioned above to illustrate the main ideas on a real world application.

Let N_t denote the total number of visits during epoch t. Also let $\boldsymbol{\pi}_t = (\pi_{1t}, \cdots, \pi_{mt})$ denote the fraction of visits in different user segments. Obviously, $\sum_{i \in \mathcal{S}} \pi_{it} = 1$ and $N_t \pi_{it}$ is the total number of visits to segment i. In a MOP, $\boldsymbol{\pi}_t$ can be estimated easily based on user visits in past epochs. We now describe the objectives below. Since we solve MOP separately for each epoch, we drop suffix t from the notations. For example, $\mathbf{x} = \{x_{ij}\}$ is the allocation plan for the current epoch.

- **Total clicks**: Note that $N\pi_i x_{ij}$ denotes the number of displays of article j in segment i; thus the total number of clicks in the epoch is

$$\mathit{TotalClicks}(\mathbf{x}) = N \sum_{i \in \mathcal{S}} \sum_{j \in \mathcal{A}} \pi_i x_{ij} p_{ij} \tag{1}$$

- **Total time-spent**: Recall that d_{ij} is the mean of the time-spent by a user in segment i on the landing property of article j after a click; hence the total time-spent is

$$\mathit{TotalTime}(\mathbf{x}) = N \sum_{i \in \mathcal{S}} \sum_{j \in \mathcal{A}} \pi_i x_{ij} p_{ij} d_{ij} \tag{2}$$

Before defining our MOPs, we first consider the **click optimization scheme** with the serving algorithm that solely maximizes total clicks (overall CTR); this algorithm serves as the baseline that our MOPs will be compared to. Let $\{z_{ij}\}$ denote a serving scheme that maximizes only for CTR. Then,

$$z_{ij} = \begin{cases} 1 & \text{when } j = \arg\max_J p_{iJ} \\ 0 & \text{otherwise} \end{cases} \tag{3}$$

We use *TotalClicks** and *TotalTime** to denote the value of objectives for the click maximization scheme; they are constants in our MOPs.

4. OPTIMIZATION MODELS

In this section we discuss different ways of formulating multi-objective optimization problems. In general multi-objective problems can be solved by a number of multi-criteria programming techniques [20]. These include solving a single objective that is a weighted average of multiple objectives or using goal programming where the objectives are optimized sequentially with constraint(s) that previous objectives retain a certain fraction of their optimal value [12].

4.1 Scalarization

Assume *TotalClicks* and *Downstream* are the two objectives of interest where *Downstream* can be *TotalTime* or other downstream metrics of interest. To construct the allocation plan, we find the $\mathbf{x}$ that maximizes

$$\lambda \cdot \mathit{TotalClicks}(\mathbf{x}) + (1-\lambda) \cdot \mathit{Downstream}(\mathbf{x}),$$

where $\lambda \in [0,1]$ represents the tradeoff between total clicks and downstream engagement; with a smaller λ we lose more clicks and obtain better downstream engagement. It is easy to see that the solution is given by

$$x_{ij} = \begin{cases} 1, & \text{if } j = \arg\max_J \lambda \cdot p_{iJ} + (1-\lambda) \cdot p_{iJ} d_{iJ} \\ 0, & \text{otherwise} \end{cases} \quad (4)$$

The tradeoff between objectives for a constant λ may vary significantly across epochs. In fact in some epochs the loss in clicks could be significant, this maybe a problem in some application scenario. However, the ability to lose a significant number of clicks in some epochs to obtain substantial gains in engagement may lead to better results over a long time horizon. We shall refer to this scheme as a scalarized multi-objective program, or **s-MOP**. Such an approach is attractive when the website owner is interested in a weighted combination of multiple objectives and it does not hurt if any one of them deteriorates significantly. Since the objectives are both linear, one drawback of this approach is the inability to explore all possible points on the Pareto optimal curve ([21] Chapter 7), it may miss out some interesting solutions. Another drawback of this method is that it is not easy to introduce application-driven business constraints.

4.2 Constrained Optimization

We now describe the constrained optimization approach to our multi-objective problem. This is important when website owners are interested in optimizing for multiple objectives but under certain constraints. This is the case in our problem. For instance, too much variation in click loss changes the downstream supply and could have an adverse impact on advertising. It is also not desirable to get overall lifts in downstream metrics by significantly changing the supply to different properties from the status quo. Hence, constrained optimization provides a reasonable approach in our application scenario.

4.2.1 g-MOP: Global Constrained Optimization

We begin with the simplest version of MOP that involves constrained optimization of objectives at the global level. We will call them global multi-objective programs or **g-MOP**s since they involve objectives that are "global". For our two-objective problem, we obtain the design variable $\mathbf{x}$ as the solution to the following optimization problem. We note that $\{x_{ij}\}$s are always non-negative and on the simplex for each i; thus, we do not mention it explicitly in describing our MOPs.

$$\begin{aligned} &\text{maximize } \mathit{Downstream}(\mathbf{x}) \\ &\quad \text{s.t. } \mathit{TotalClicks}(\mathbf{x}) \geq \alpha \cdot \mathit{TotalClicks}^* \end{aligned} \quad (5)$$

where $\alpha \in [0,1]$, and *Downstream* in this paper is *TotalTime*. Here we want to obtain maximum improvement in downstream engagement ensuring the percentage loss in total click volume in no more than $(1-\alpha)$. Since maximizing total clicks is the normative serving scheme in general, it is reasonable for website owners to control this loss. We also note that solutions to g-MOPs will show lower variation in number of clicks lost per epoch relative to s-MOP described earlier. In fact, one can interpret the constraint imposed per epoch in g-MOP as inducing a different tradeoff parameter λ_t in s-MOP for epoch t. Hence constrained g-MOPs can find solutions on the Pareto curve that are missed by s-MOP. With *Downstream* $=$ *TotalTime* in Equation 5, it is easy to see that the optimal $\mathbf{x}$ to this problem can be obtained by a standard linear program solver.

4.2.2 ℓ-MOP: Localized Constrained Optimization

As mentioned before, the g-MOP formulation is reasonable when landing pages in different properties are homogeneous. This is hardly true in practice; the layout of the landing page on a property may have a significant influence on the distribution of d_{ij}s. For instance, suppose we have two pages — an entertainment page with several video links and a finance stock ticker page. The distribution of time-spent for the video page is stochastically larger than the finance page. Maximizing downstream engagement may simply take away clicks from finance and route it to video page. In fact the situation may get worse — we take away highly engaged users on finance and route them to video where they engage less than a typical video page user. To avoid such effects, we solve g-MOPs under additional constraints. We refer to these as **ℓ-MOPs** and not surprisingly, the ℓ-MOPs come in various flavors depending on the objective being maximized and the constraints being imposed. We motivate the constraints that define the ℓ-MOPs below.

Let us assume the articles have been grouped based on landing page characteristics. We use the property grouping $\{P_1, \cdots, P_K\}$ described earlier to illustrate in this paper; some other grouping may be important in other applications. Our first formulation to address the inter-property heterogeneity maximizes the minimum value of total engagement across properties subject to constraint on click loss. By maximizing the minimum, we ensure "fairness" since all properties receive the benefit of losing clicks on the portal page. Before defining our constrained optimization problems, we introduce some new notations.

Let $\mathit{Obj}(P, \mathbf{x})$ denote the value of the objective restricted to property P, and let $\mathit{Obj}^*(P)$ denote the objective value on property P under the click maximization scheme where *Obj* can be *TotalClicks*, *TotalTime*, or some other objective of interest. To normalize engagement metrics across properties and create a single "currency", we measure engagement improvement for a property P_k by the ratio $\frac{\mathit{Obj}(P_k,\mathbf{x})}{\mathit{Obj}^*(P_k)}$ We are now ready to mathematically state our ℓ-MOP to ensure "fairness".

MaxMin ℓ-MOP:

$$\begin{aligned} &\text{maximize}_{\mathbf{x}} \min_k \{\frac{\mathit{Downstream}(P_k, \mathbf{x})}{\mathit{Downstream}^*(P_k)}\} \\ &\quad \text{s.t. } \mathit{TotalClicks}(\mathbf{x}) \geq \alpha \cdot \mathit{TotalClicks}^* \end{aligned} \quad (6)$$

When *Downstream* $=$ *TotalTime*, the objective function is concave and hence can be solved by convex programming techniques. However it is not differentiable, so it is difficult to solve it directly. We use a standard trick in convex programming that transforms the problem to the epigraph form [21]. The epigraph for this program is given by

$$\begin{aligned} &\text{maximize } \beta \\ &\text{s.t. } \frac{\mathit{Downstream}(P_k, \mathbf{x})}{\mathit{Downstream}^*(P_k)} \geq \beta, k = 1, ..., K \\ &\quad \mathit{TotalClicks}(\mathbf{x}) \geq \alpha \cdot \mathit{TotalClicks}^* \end{aligned}$$

It is easy to see that the above is a linear program.

Relaxed ℓ-MOP: Although the MaxMin formulation encourages the benefits of click loss to be shared among properties, the socialistic nature may impose constraints that are too strict. In fact, it may not be possible to get significant gains in downstream engagement under such strict constraints in some applications. Furthermore, portal owners may not care to improve engagement metrics of some properties; only a handful may be more important than others. They may be satisfied with increasing total engagement by ensuring engagement of important properties does not deteriorate compared to the status quo. We can encourage such behavior by introducing property level constraints but still maximizing aggregate engagement. The number of properties subject to such constraints can also vary. Formally our optimization problem is described below.

$$\begin{aligned} \text{maximize}_{\mathbf{x}}\ & \textit{Downstream}_1(\mathbf{x}) \\ \text{s.t. } & \textit{Downstream}_2(P_k, \mathbf{x}) \geq \textit{Downstream}_2^*(P_k), k \in \mathcal{I} \\ & \textit{TotalClicks}(\mathbf{x}) \geq \alpha \cdot \textit{TotalClicks}^* \end{aligned} \tag{7}$$

where *Downstream*$_1$ and *Downstream*$_2$ can be the same or different (in this paper they are both *TotalTime*), and $\mathcal{I}$ is the set of properties that are constrained. When this set is empty we fall back to g-MOP and when it includes all properties, we have tight constraints but these are still more relaxed than MaxMin ℓ-MOP. Instead of constraining the properties to improve, we can also relax and provide a lower bound to the maximum possible deterioration (it is easy to incorporate such constraints). The solution techniques for this class of problem again depends on the combination of downstream engagement objective *Downstream*$_1$ and downstream engagement constraint *Downstream*$_2$. For total time-spent constraints, all variants of constrained ℓ-MOPs can be solved using linear programming!

5. STATISTICAL MODELS

In previous sections, we assume that π_{it}, p_{ijt} and d_{ijt} are given. In our application, we solve MOPs by "plugging-in" the expected values estimated from a statistical model. Note that our formulation requires clustering the users into segments, hence we focus on segmented CTR (and time-spent) model in this paper. Since our optimization problem involves constraining click-loss, we create user segments that are most predictive for estimating click-rates and use these to estimate time-spent. Gains are significant if there is wide variation in average time-spent across articles for a given user segment.

5.1 User Segmentation

Each user is characterized by a feature vector consisting of demographics (age and gender) and affinity to different behavioral categories (such as sports, finance or entertainment) based on cookie activities throughout the Yahoo! network. In this paper, we illustrate with user segments constructed using a few strategies. We consider three segmentation schemes:

- Age-gender: segments are obtained based on user age and gender.
- Attribute-based: unsupervised k-means clustering on the attribute vectors based on age, gender and behavioral affinities.
- Activity-based: unsupervised k-means that cluster users based on their estimated click activities on different articles.

For age-gender segmentation, we discretize age into 10 groups and have 3 gender groups (male, female, and unknown), and thus we have 30 segments. Obtaining clusters using attribute-based k-means is straightforward. For the activity-based k-means, we collected large amounts of historic click data. A simple approach is to construct a vector for each user based on the articles the user clicked. However, this does not work so well since the distribution of user visits is heavy tailed - a small number of users have many clicks and a large fraction of users have few clicks. This imbalance makes it difficult to construct user profiles directly from clicks. We build a separate logistic regression model for each article based on user attributes and use the *predicted* CTR values on each article to compose the activity vectors. Specifically, let $\mathbf{a}_u$ denotes attribute vector for user u, then the click probability on article j for user u is $\theta_{uj} = \frac{1}{1+\exp(-\mathbf{a}_u \cdot \eta_j)}$, where η_j for article j is estimated through a logistic regression for article j based on all the users who clicked (positive examples) or viewed j without clicks (negative examples). This gives us an activity-based profile for user u based on θ_{uj} for a set of articles in the historic data. We then cluster the users into segments by applying k-means on these profiles. A similar approach was used in [7] with article categories instead of articles which implicitly assumed a constant affinity for a given user for all articles in a given category. We found wide variations in user affinities for articles within a category, hence the profiles used in this paper are at the article level.

For online serving, each user will be classified to a user segments based on their corresponding article profile vectors. We note that creating such a profile for historic articles that are no longer in the pool is not a problem for us since we can always predict θ_{uj} for any user on any article j (old or new). For all k-means based clustering, a centroid is kept for each cluster and a user is assigned to the nearest one. In this paper, we use the cosine similarity and the k-means algorithm proposed in [10, 9]

5.2 Estimation of π_{it}, p_{ijt} and d_{ijt}

Given user segments, both user population π_{it} and time-spent d_{ijt} are estimated based on moving average over historical data. For example, given all the epochs before t, we collect all click events for article j from user segment i. Each click event has a time-spent value and d_{ijt} is estimated as the average time-spent over all the clicks.

For CTR estimation, recall that p_{ijt} denotes the CTR of user segment i on article j at epoch t. In [2], we showed that the Gamma-Poisson model performs well for estimating CTR on such segmented models. Let n_{ijt} denote the number of times we show article j to user segment i at time t. Let c_{ijt} denote the number of clicks that resulted from these n_{ijt} page views. For simplicity, assume CTR does not change much over time in a user segment; thus we drop index t in p_{ijt} (for the extension that captures temporal dynamics, see [2]). The Gamma-Poisson model assumes

$$\begin{aligned} c_{ijt} &\sim \text{Poisson}(p_{ij}\, n_{ijt}) \\ p_{ij} &\sim \text{Gamma}(\text{mean}{=}\mu_i, \text{size}{=}\gamma_i), \end{aligned}$$

where μ_i is the CTR of user segment i on a random article according to our prior belief, and γ_i is the equivalent sample size of the prior belief (intuitively, this prior belief represents information equivalent to γ_i page views and $\gamma_i\mu_i$ clicks). Effectively, the Gamma-Poisson model is a "smoothed" counting model which estimates p_{ijt} as

$$\hat{p}_{ijt} = \left(\gamma_i\mu_i + \sum_{\tau<t} c_{ij\tau}\right) / \left(\gamma_i + \sum_{\tau<t} n_{ij\tau}\right).$$

If we have little data the estimate will be close to the prior μ_i; with more data the estimate will be close to maximum likelihood.

6. EXPERIMENTS

In this section we report experimental results on Yahoo! Front Page Today Module data.

Data: Our data set is derived from Yahoo! web server logs which record the view and click information of users who interact with the Today Module on the Yahoo! Front Page. We collected such click and view data from a random bucket (defined in Section 2) of the Today Module during August 2010. Around 2 million view events were collected on average on a daily basis. To compute downstream time-spent, we also collected post-click information on all the pages that a user visited within Yahoo! after clicking on a Today Module article.[2] We use the first $1/3$ of the data to learn the user segmentation. The remaining $2/3$ of the data is used to compare different algorithms based the replay methodology described in Section 2 that provides unbiased estimates.

Metrics: We define the time-spent d_{ij} of a user in segment i after clicking article $j \in P_k$ as the length (in second) of the *session* of the user's events that starts from the click and ends at the last page view inside property P_k, before the user either leaves the property or has no activity for more than 30 minutes. For confidentiality reasons, we cannot reveal the total number of clicks or total time-spent. Thus, we only report the relative CTR and relative time-spent as defined below. After running a replay experiment using serving scheme A, we compute the average number of clicks per view p_{A} (i.e., CTR) and the average time-spent per view q_{A}. Fixing one baseline algorithm B, we report the performance of algorithm A by two ratios: CTR ratio $\rho_{\text{CTR}} = \frac{p_{\mathsf{A}}}{p_{\mathsf{B}}}$ and TS ratio $\rho_{\text{TS}} = \frac{q_{\mathsf{A}}}{q_{\mathsf{B}}}$.

6.1 Results on Segmentation

Comparison of segmentation methods: In this set of experiments, we report the performance of different algorithms in terms of CTR and TS ratios by using the click optimization model with age-gender segmentation as the baseline algorithm B. We first compare different segmentation methods using both the s-MOP and g-MOP algorithms in Figure 2. In this figure, the α (click-constraint parameter) values used are $\{1, 0.99, 0.97, 0.95, 0.93, 0.9, 0.85, 0.8, 0\}$ for g-MOP and we vary λ (tradeoff in scalarization approach) from 1 to 0 with decrements of 0.1. Each specific parameter value gives us a pair of CTR ratio and TS ratio. The tradeoff curves are thus obtained by varying these two parameters respectively for s-MOP and g-MOP. We have 30 segments in age-gender model. For all k-means-based clusters (feature and activity based), we also set the number of clusters m to 30. Each method is represented by a curve; the higher and more to the right the curve is, the better the performance. From this figure we make the following observations:

(1) The activity-based segmentation significantly outperforms the other two methods, while the age-gender segmentation is slightly better than the attribute-based k-means method which clusters users based only on their features. This shows that a carefully designed user segmentation is crucial component of our method. Our activity-based method can segment users much better because it uses click information (one of our objective) to construct clusters. On the contrary, the attribute-based method that uses only user profile features is less effective. The age-gender model though simple, still achieves better results than attribute-based k-means method.

[2]By users we mean an anonymized browser-cookie. There is no personally identifiable information in the data used in our experiments.

Method	CTR ratio		TS ratio	
	mean	stdev	mean	stdev
s-MOP (λ=0.60)	0.9580	0.0316	1.0850	0.0480
g-MOP (α=0.97)	0.9604	0.0242	1.0830	0.0376

Table 1: Temporal variance of s-MOP and g-MOP.

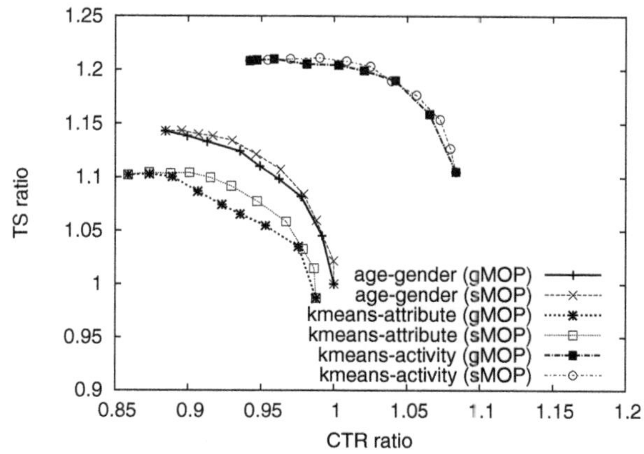

Figure 2: Comparison of user segmentation methods.

(2) The bottom right end point of each curve corresponds to $\alpha = 1$ or $\lambda = 1$, i.e., the performance of the click optimization model. As we decrease the α values, we move up and to the left; the CTR ratio becomes smaller but the TS ratio becomes larger. For example, for the activity-based segmentation, comparing $\alpha = 1$ and $\alpha = 0.97$, we increase the TS ratio from 1.10 to 1.20 (8.1% lift) and decrease the CTR ratio from 1.08 to 1.04 (3.8% drop). This means both s-MOP and g-MOP effectively tradeoff clicks for time-spent. For all the 3 curves, we observe similar trends and the curves become flat towards the end as expected.

(3) We observe that s-MOP achieves better tradeoff than g-MOP, especially with a less effective user segmentation. As described earlier, the α constraint imposed per epoch in g-MOP can be interpreted as introducing a different tradeoff parameter λ_t in s-MOP for each epoch t. The parameter α uniformly bounds the CTR loss for the worst case over all the epochs while λ bounds the CTR loss on average. Thus, given the same CTR loss, we anticipate that the temporal variance in CTR loss and TS gain will be large. To verify this, for each epoch, we compute the CTR ratio of s-MOP and g-MOP: $\frac{p_{\lambda=0.6}}{p_{\lambda=1}}$, $\frac{p_{\alpha=0.97}}{p_{\alpha=1}}$ and their TS ratios $\frac{q_{\lambda=0.6}}{q_{\lambda=1}}$, $\frac{q_{\alpha=0.97}}{q_{\alpha=1}}$ based on the activity-based segmentation. We compute the mean and standard deviation of these four sets of values over all epochs and summarize them in Table 1. From the table, we clearly observe that the variances of both CTR ratio and TS ratio in s-MOP are significantly larger than g-MOP. In some epochs, s-MOP loses more clicks to obtain better gains in time-spent, g-MOP on the other hand is more stable in its tradeoff behavior over epochs. This shows the desirable properties of constrained optimization, if significant deviation from the status quo CTR is not desirable during most time periods, one should take recourse to constrained optimization.

Number of clusters: We study the impact of varying the number of clusters m in the activity-based segmentation scheme on the tradeoffs between clicks and time-spent. In Figure 3, we plot tradeoff curves for different values of m using g-MOP. As evident, choosing number of clusters has a significant impact on performance. If m is small, the clusters might get coarse and lead to biased CTR and time-spent estimates for items within clusters. Increasing the

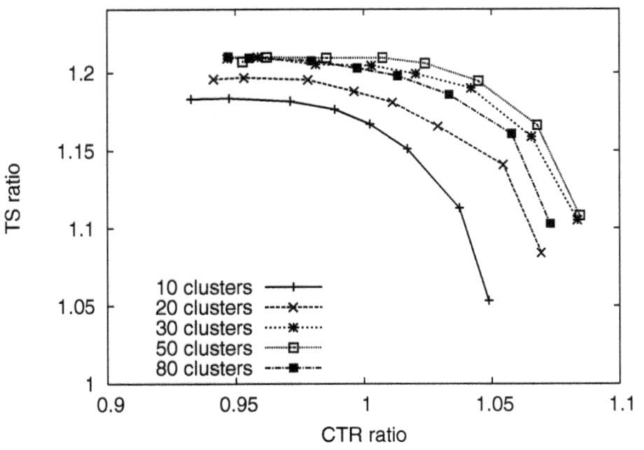

Figure 3: The impact of the number of user segments using activity-based k-means.

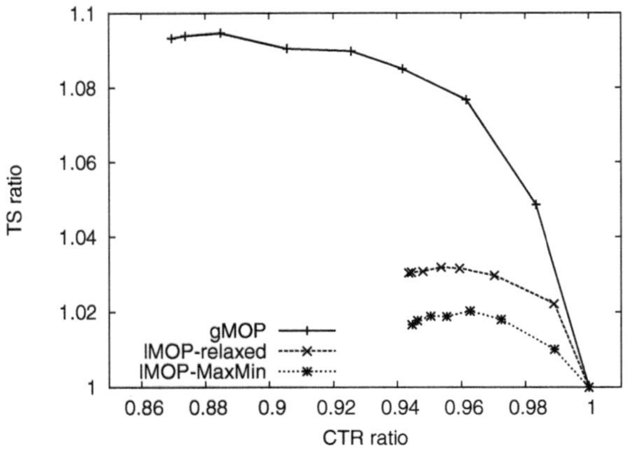

Figure 4: Comparison of different constrained optimization formulation.

number of clusters leads to high variance and deteriorates performance. As can be seen from Figure 3, in our experiments, the optimal m is between 30 and 50.

6.2 Results on Different Formulations

In this section, we compare three different formulations: g-MOP, ℓ-MOP-relaxed, and ℓ-MOP-MaxMin. For segmentation, we report results only from activity-based k-means with $m = 30$ in the following experiments. The CTR ratio and TS ratio are computed using the click optimization model with the activity-based segmentation as the baseline B.

Tradeoff comparison: We first compare the tradeoff curves of the three formulations in Figure 4. In this figure, we can see that g-MOP improves time-spent significantly with a small loss in CTR. However, when we impose the per-property constraints in ℓ-MOP-relaxed, the time-spent gains become much smaller. ℓ-MOP-MaxMin has the least time-spent gain among the 3 formulations. For example, when we set $\alpha = 0.97$, the TS ratio of these 3 methods are 1.08, 1.03 and 1.02. This is because after imposing per-property constraints, we have less freedom to move clicks from one property to another even when there is a property that has higher average time-spent. The ℓ-MOP-MaxMin model is more constrained since it aims to improve every property simultaneously.

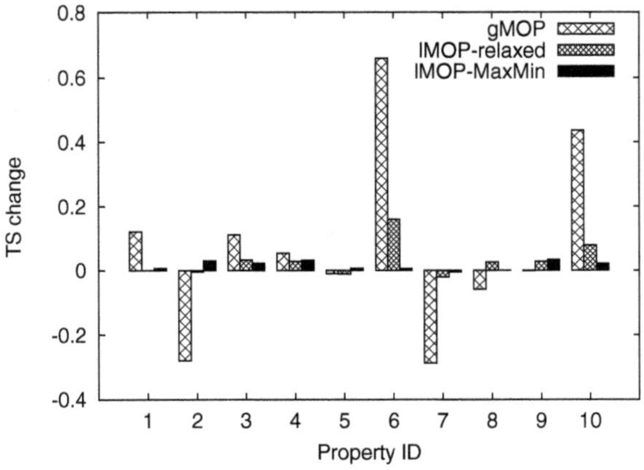

Figure 5: Time-spent difference before and after click shaping given the same amount of CTR loss.

	g-MOP	ℓ-MOP-relaxed	ℓ-MOP-MaxMin
click	0.2750	0.0637	0.0361
time-spent	0.2764	0.0504	0.0134

Table 2: Comparison of the standard deviation over the most popular 10 properties.

Both ℓ-MOP-relaxed and ℓ-MOP-MaxMin impose property-level constraints. We show the impact of these constraints in Table 2. We select the top 10 popular properties, and for each of these properties we compute per-property total click and time-spent relative difference between $\alpha = 0.97$ and $\alpha = 1$ for all the 3 formulations using $\frac{t_{\alpha=0.97} - t_{\alpha=1}}{t_{\alpha=1}}$. We then compute the standard deviations for each formulation across all 10 properties. From this table, we can see that the variance for g-MOP is much higher than ℓ-MOP-relaxed and ℓ-MOP-MaxMin. To further illustrate the variance, we plot the relative difference of time-spent for the 10 properties in Figure 5. From this figure, we can see that the difference across properties for g-MOP vary quite a bit. For example, for a given amount of click loss, some properties can gain more than 60% in time-spent whereas some properties lose around 30% in time spent. On the other hand, ℓ-MOP-relaxed and ℓ-MOP-MaxMin have relatively low variation across properties; no property loses total time-spent significantly. This underlines the effectiveness of including per-property level constraints in our MOPs. The figure also illustrates the fairness of ℓ-MOP-MaxMin - all properties experience similar time-spent gains.

Fewer property constraints: We showed two extreme cases where we either do not have any per-property constraints or we apply the constraints on all properties. In reality, some constraints are more important for certain business purpose. We show the results of selectively applying the constraints on a subset of properties. In Figure 6 and Table 3, we show the results of ℓ-MOP-relaxed with constraints applied to the top 3, 5, 7 properties that have the largest number of views in our data set. Clearly when we reduce the number of constraints, we can achieve much better gains in time-spent with the same loss in clicks. On the other hand as shown in Table 3, the variance in time-spent gain across top 10 properties becomes larger when we enforce fewer constraints.

Example: To understand how clicks are shaped, we compare the time-spent distribution based on ℓ-MOP-relaxed in Figure 7 before and after click shaping on two properties. We discretize the

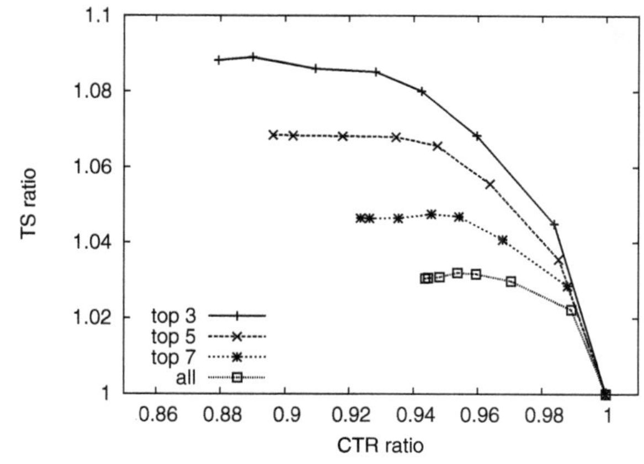

Figure 6: Impact of number of constraints on ℓ-MOP-relaxed.

	Top 3	Top 5	Top 7	All
click	0.2372	0.1792	0.1501	0.0637
time-spent	0.2424	0.1818	0.1506	0.0504

Table 3: Comparison of the standard deviation over properties for ℓ-MOP-relaxed with different number of per-property constraints.

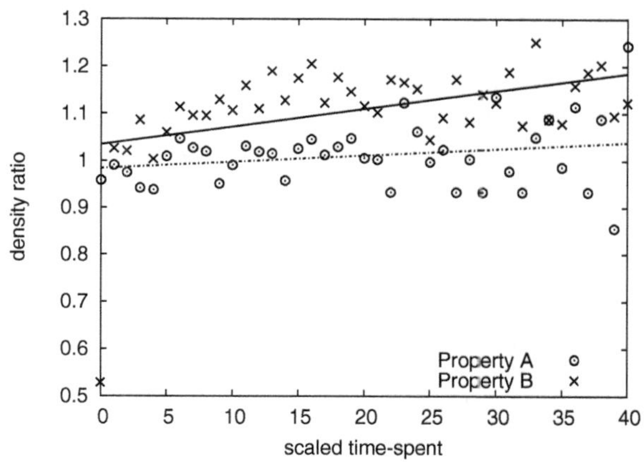

Figure 7: Time-spent distribution ratio between click shaping and status quo.

time-spent values into multiple bins and compute the percentage of clicks that fall into each bin. Let $P_{\alpha=1}(b)$ and $P_{\alpha=0.97}(b)$ be proportional to the number of clicks in bin b before ($\alpha = 1$) and after ($\alpha = 0.97$) click shaping, we plot the ratio $\frac{P_{\alpha=0.97}(b)}{P_{\alpha=1}(b)}$ against the time-spent bins in Figure 7. We also fit a regression line to each property. It can be seen that both lines have positive slope (0.004 for Property B and 0.002 for Property A) and this shows the percentage ratio increases with increase in time-spent. This means that after click shaping, we reduce the number of clicks that result in lower time-spent but increase the number of clicks with more time-spent for each property. This is expected behavior from our formulation and more desirable because more engaged articles (measured by time-spent) are recommended by our algorithms. The fact that this behavior is empirically supported in real world application provides a good validation of our theoretical formulation.

7. RELATED WORK

It is commonplace to measure user interaction with websites through multiple metrics such as number of page views, number of unique user visits, and total time-spent. Such metrics are routinely reported by companies like comScore and have profound impact on advertiser perception. Most of the previous methods on Web content optimization (e.g., [3, 8, 2, 1, 16]) focus on a single metric: number of clicks. The problem is often formulated as a multi-armed bandit problem [5, 15, 4]. However, to the best of our knowledge, no prior work has attempted to provide methods that simultaneously optimize a combination of various engagement metrics.

Some instances of tradeoffs among multiple objectives are discussed in online advertising. For instance, auctions in sponsored search incorporate both revenue (bid) and ad quality (measured through CTR) in ranking ads [19]. The multi-objective programming pursued in this area is simple – rank ads by product of bid and CTR. In fact, this rule is a special case of s-MOP with $\lambda = 0$ in our formulation. Recent works on display advertising also consider multi-objective programming to simultaneously optimize for revenue of remnant inventory and overall ad quality delivered to advertisers participating in the guaranteed display ads marketplace [11]. Another work that is somewhat related incorporates both CTR and ad quality in ranking ads for sponsored search [22]. The authors define a new measure called *bounce rate* to capture ad quality by inferring abandonment rate on ad landing pages. However, the study is more focused on ways to predict bounce rates and multi-objective optimization is not the main focus. Other papers such as [13] considered constraints such as limited supply of the items in a collaborative filtering setting and [23] studied several objectives in learning to rank. Both of these are in a static setting and thus the whole problem setup is different from our online recommendation.

We note that there is a rich and mature literature on multi-objective programming [20]. We are not contributing new techniques to this body of work. Instead, we have shown the utility of such approaches in simultaneously optimizing for several engagement metrics when recommending content on large Web portals in an online manner.

8. CONCLUSIONS AND FUTURE WORK

In this paper we proposed click shaping, an effective way to recommend content on large portal pages to optimize simultaneously for multiple engagement metrics. We formulated our problem in a constrained optimization framework which can naturally incorporate application-driven business requirement. In particular, we introduced a novel fairness objectives that aims to distribute gains in engagement in a fair way among heterogeneous domains and showed how this can be modeled in our framework. Through extensive data analysis on logged events, we provided unbiased estimates of performance for various flavors of our MOP under different constraints. Our data analysis reveals interesting characteristics of different formulations with tradeoffs among multiple metrics. We provide intuitive explanations of how clicks get shaped that in turn provides valuable guidance to the design of online recommendation engines.

Large variations in downstream engagement metrics provide more opportunities for lucrative tradeoffs; we are currently exploring methods to create fine grained user segments directly to maximize multiple objectives. Our MOP shows that imposing per epoch constraints is stringent when the goal is to obtain good performance over a larger time window. How to formulate solutions that ensure such long-term constraints but provide a per-epoch plan is a challenging problem.

9. REFERENCES

[1] D. Agarwal, B.-C. Chen, and P. Elango. Explore/exploit schemes for web content optimization. In *Proceedings of the Ninth International Conference on Data Mining*, 2009.

[2] D. Agarwal, B.-C. Chen, and P. Elango. Spatio-temporal models for estimating click-through rate. In *WWW*, pages 21–30, 2009.

[3] D. Agarwal, B.-C. Chen, P. Elango, and et al. Online models for content optimization. In *NIPS*, 2008.

[4] P. Auer, N. Cesa-Bianchi, and P. Fischer. Finite-time analysis of the multiarmed bandit problem. *Machine Learning*, 47(2–3):235–256, 2002.

[5] D. A. Berry and B. Fristedt. *Bandit Problems: Sequential Allocation of Experiments*. Monographs on Statistics and Applied Probability. Chapman and Hall, 1985.

[6] G. Buscher, L. van Elst, and A. Dengel. Segment-level display time as implicit feedback: a comparison to eye tracking. In *Proceedings of the 32nd international ACM SIGIR conference on Research and development in information retrieval*, pages 67–74, 2009.

[7] W. Chu, S.-T. Park, T. Beaupre, N. Motgi, A. Phadke, S. Chakraborty, and J. Zachariah. A case study of behavior-driven conjoint analysis on yahoo!: front page today module. In *KDD*, pages 1097–1104, 2009.

[8] A. Das, M. Datar, A. Garg, and S. Rajaram. Google news personalization: scalable online collaborative filtering. In *Proceedings of the 16th international conference on World Wide Web*, pages 271–280. ACM, 2007.

[9] I. S. Dhillon, J. Fan, and Y. Guan. Efficient clustering of very large document collections. In V. K. R. Grossman, C. Kamath and R. Namburu, editors, *Data Mining for Scientific and Engineering Applications*. Kluwer Academic Publishers, 2001. Invited book chapter.

[10] I. S. Dhillon and D. S. Modha. Concept decompositions for large sparse text data using clustering. *Machine Learning*, 42(1):143–175, Jan 2001.

[11] E.Vee, S.Vassilvitski, and J.Shanmugasundaran. Optimal online assignment with forecasts. In *EC*, 2010.

[12] J. P. Ignizio. *Goal programming and extensions*. Lexington Books, 1976.

[13] T. Jambor and J. Wang. Optimizing multiple objectives in collaborative filtering. In *Proceedings of the fourth ACM conference on Recommender systems*, pages 55–62, 2010.

[14] J. Langford, A. Strehl, and J. Wortman. Exploration scavenging. In *ICML*, pages 528–535, 2008.

[15] J. Langford and T. Zhang. The epoch-greedy algorithm for contextual multi-armed bandits. In *Advances in Neural Information Processing Systems 20*, 2008.

[16] L. Li, W. Chu, J. Langford, and R. E. Schapire. A contextual-bandit approach to personalized news article recommendation. In *Proceedings of the Nineteenth International Conference on World Wide Web*, 2010.

[17] L. Li, W. Chu, J. Langford, and X. Wang. Unbiased offline evaluation of contextual-bandit-based news article recommendation algorithms. In *WSDM*, 2011.

[18] C. Liu, R. W. White, and S. T. Dumais. Understanding web browsing behaviors through weibull analysis of dwell time. In *SIGIR*, pages 379–386, 2010.

[19] R.Fain and J.Pederson. Sponsored search: A brief history. *Bulletin of American Society of Information and Technology*, 32:12–13, 2006.

[20] R.Steuer. *Multi-criteria optimization: theory, computation, and application*. Wiley, 1986.

[21] S.Boyd and L.Vandenberghe. *Convex Optimization*. Cambridge University Press, 2004.

[22] D. Sculley, R. G. Malkin, S. Basu, and R. J. Bayardo. Predicting bounce rates in sponsored search advertisements. In *KDD*, pages 1325–1334, 2009.

[23] K. M. Svore, M. N. Volkovs, and C. J. C. Burges. Learning to rank with multiple objective functions. In *WWW*, 2011.

[24] J. Vermorel and M. Mohri. Multi-armed bandit algorithms and empirical evaluation. In *In European Conference on Machine Learning*, pages 437–448. Springer, 2005.

Response Prediction Using Collaborative Filtering with Hierarchies and Side-information

Aditya Krishna Menon*
University of California, San Diego
La Jolla, CA, USA
akmenon@ucsd.edu

Krishna-Prasad Chitrapura
Yahoo! Labs
Bengaluru, Karnataka, India
pkrishna@yahoo-inc.com

Sachin Garg
Yahoo! Labs
Bengaluru, Karnataka, India
gsachin@yahoo-inc.com

Deepak Agarwal
Yahoo! Research
Santa Clara, CA, USA
dagarwal@yahoo-inc.com

Nagaraj Kota
Yahoo! Labs
Bengaluru, Karnataka, India
nagarajk@yahoo-inc.com

ABSTRACT

In online advertising, response prediction is the problem of estimating the probability that an advertisement is clicked when displayed on a content publisher's webpage. In this paper, we show how response prediction can be viewed as a problem of *matrix completion*, and propose to solve it using matrix factorization techniques from *collaborative filtering* (CF). We point out the two crucial differences between standard CF problems and response prediction, namely the requirement of predicting probabilities rather than scores, and the issue of confidence in matrix entries. We address these issues using a matrix factorization analogue of logistic regression, and by applying a principled confidence-weighting scheme to its objective. We show how this factorization can be seamlessly combined with explicit features or *side-information* for pages and ads, which let us combine the benefits of both approaches. Finally, we combat the extreme sparsity of response prediction data by incorporating *hierarchical information* about the pages and ads into our factorization model. Experiments on three very large real-world datasets show that our model outperforms current state-of-the-art methods for response prediction.

Categories and Subject Descriptors

H.3.5 [**Information Storage and Retrieval**]: Online Information Services

General Terms

Algorithms, Design, Experimentation

Keywords

Response prediction, collaborative filtering, hierarchies

*Work done while first author was interning at Yahoo! Bangalore.

KDD'11, August 21–24, 2011, San Diego, California, USA.

1. THE RESPONSE PREDICTION PROBLEM

Online advertising involves the interaction between two entities: *publishers* (e.g. AOL, Yahoo), who own and manage webpages, and *advertisers* (e.g. Pepsi, Nike), who have products that they wish to market to users of the publishers' webpages via ads. A fundamental monetary paradigm in this form of advertising is *pay-per-click*. Here, each advertiser places a bid for their ad to be placed on a publisher's webpage, and pays the bid amount to the publisher only if the ad was selected to be displayed (referred to as a *view*) and subsequently clicked by a user. Amongst many competing ads, the publisher chooses to display the ad with the highest *expected revenue*, which is the ad's bid amount multiplied by the probability that it is clicked. This probability is known as the clickthrough rate (CTR) of an ad, and its reliable estimation is crucial for a publisher to maximize revenue. The task of estimating this probability is known as *response prediction*, or *CTR estimation*.

Response prediction is a challenging problem for at least two reasons. First, the majority of ads have limited or no past history on a particular publisher page. This *sparsity* obviously hinders simple CTR estimation, and necessitates a principled way to exploit correlations in the data. Second, as most ads are clicked very infrequently, we have to predict the probability of a *rare event*, which is very challenging. In both situations, it is beneficial to exploit known *hierarchical information* about pages and ads. This refers to a pre-defined hierarchy for both entities, where for example, the set of all ads is partitioned according to the campaigns they belong to, the campaigns are in turn divided according to the advertisers running the campaigns and so on. (See Figure 1 for an example.) These hierarchies encode correlations between the CTRs – for example, two ads shown as part of the same campaign will have similar CTRs – and so are very useful in deriving reliable probability estimates when historical data is limited.

Existing methods for response prediction are based either on training standard classifiers on explicit features for pages and ads, or on statistical smoothening over baseline estimates. In this paper, we propose a novel approach to the problem based on *collaborative filtering* (CF). This is a technique used in recommender systems, where the input is a matrix of user-by-item preference scores, where most entries are missing. Each non-missing entry is a numeric score telling us how much a user likes an item. The desired output is a set of predicted scores for the missing entries, so that we can recommend for each user some new items that she might like. We show the natural connection between this problem and response prediction, where we think of pages as users, ads as items, and the entries of the matrix as the historical CTRs for (page, ad) pairs, while pointing out two differences between the problems: (i) response prediction requires the predicted CTRs to be meaningful probabilities, and (ii) our goal in response prediction is to not only fill-in the missing CTRs in this matrix, but also *smoothen* the CTRs for which there is limited historical data. This requires respecting the *confidence* in the matrix entries. Further, from a modelling perspective, the aforementioned problem of data sparsity in response prediction necessitates a careful mechanism for exploiting all available information. To address these differences, we begin by showing how a *matrix factorization* model can meet the basic requirements for response prediction, using simple extensions that have been studied in the CF literature. This extended factorization model is capable of incorporating explicit page and ad features, known in the CF literature as *side-information*. We give a simple iterative scheme by which the side-information can be used to refine our model's performance. We then show how the factorization model can be made to exploit *hierarchical information* about pages and ads. This novel extension allows the model to mitigate the challenge of data sparsity, and constitutes the main contribution of the paper. Our resulting model may be optimized using stochastic gradient descent, allowing it to scale to datasets with several billion matrix entries. Experiments on three real-world datasets show that our model improves on the performance of state-of-the-art response prediction models, and demonstrates the model's scalability.

2. BACKGROUND AND RELATED WORK

There are three main relevant areas of research for this paper: response prediction, hierarchical constraints and collaborative filtering. Before proceeding, we fix the notation used in this paper.

2.1 Notation and terminology

Given a matrix $X \in \mathbb{R}^{m \times n}$, we denote the (i, j)th entry of the matrix by X_{ij} and the jth column of the matrix by X_j. We call each pair (i, j) a *dyad*. We denote the Frobenius norm of a matrix by $||X||_F := \sqrt{\sum_i ||X_i||_2^2}$. If X has entries that are unobserved or missing, we denote these by "?". We let $\mathcal{O} = \{(i, j) : X_{ij} \neq \text{"?"}\}$ be the set of observed entries for the matrix X.

Response prediction. We are interested in predicting probabilities given the interaction between (web)pages $\mathcal{P} = \{1, \ldots, m\}$ and ads $\mathcal{A} = \{1, \ldots, n\}$, where each entity is represented by a unique identifier. Given a page i and an ad j, we would like to predict $P_{ij} = \Pr[\text{Click}|i, j]$. The available historical data consists of matrices $C, V \in \mathbb{Z}^{m \times n}$, representing the number of *clicks* and *views* respectively that have been observed for particular (page, ad) pairs. Specifically, V_{ij} tells us how many times ad j was shown on publisher's ith page, and C_{ij} says how many times it was clicked once shown. By definition, we must have $C_{ij} \leq V_{ij}$.

Hierarchies. We use $\mathcal{H}^X$ to denote a *hierarchy* over objects in the set X. A hierarchy is a directed graph $(\mathcal{V}, \mathcal{E})$ with a *level* based structure: there is an injective function $\ell^X : \mathcal{V} \to \{1, \ldots, D^X\}$, where D^X is the *depth* of the hierarchy, such that a node $u \in \mathcal{V}$ can only have edges to nodes $v \in \mathcal{V}$ with $\ell^X(v) = \ell^X(u) + 1$. Further, every node in levels $\{1, \ldots, D^X - 1\}$ has at least one outgoing edge. The leaf nodes in level D^X correspond to the elements of X. Finally, we constrain that there is only one node $v \in \mathcal{V}$ with $\ell^X(v) = 1$, which we call the *root node*. Figure 1 represents an example of such a hierarchy over ads, where $D^X = 4$. We let $|\mathcal{H}^X| = |\mathcal{V}|$ denote the number of nodes in the hierarchy $\mathcal{H}^X$.

We refer to the set of parents for a node u by $\text{Par}(u)$. A hierarchy is a *tree* if and only if every non-root node has exactly one parent. Any two nodes u, u' with a common parent are called *siblings*. We refer to the set of paths from the root node to a node u by $\text{Path}(u)$.

2.2 Response prediction

The introduction described the basic monetary paradigm in computational advertising, where an advertiser pays a publisher for every user click. Response prediction was cast as the problem of estimating the fundamental quantity of interest in this setting, which is the probability of an ad being clicked. Recently, new response types have been adopted by advertisers, where the payout happens not when a user clicks on an ad, but only when she performs an action (called a *conversion*) after the ad is displayed. The action could be buying a product, filling out a form, *et cetera*. Accurate estimation of the probability for all response types is crucial to select the ad with highest expected revenue. "Response prediction" is therefore a blanket term that includes prediction for all three types of user response. However, the specific type of conversion does not change the modelling problem, and so for the rest of the paper, we will assume we are dealing with click events for simplicity.

With this is mind, consider the problem of predicting $P_{ij} = \Pr[\text{Click}|\text{View}; i, j]$. Given historical data, arguably the simplest solution is the maximum likelihood estimate (MLE), P^{MLE}:

$$P_{ij}^{\text{MLE}} := \begin{cases} \frac{C_{ij}}{V_{ij}} & \text{if } V_{ij} \neq 0 \\ ? & \text{else.} \end{cases} \quad (1)$$

The "?" denotes that the MLE is undefined when $V_{ij} = 0$, since we have no historical data for the particular (page, ad) pair. Thus, the MLE is unusable if $V_{ij} = 0$. Similarly, if $V_{ij} \neq 0$ but is small, then the MLE is very noisy: for example, if an ad has been shown 5 times on a page and received 0 clicks, a CTR estimate of 0 is intuitively too extreme. As these two cases are the majority in practice, we need a different estimate $\hat{P}$ that *smoothens* the MLE to make it more reliable. There are three properties any estimator $\hat{P}$ should satisfy: (i) it should provide estimates when $V_{ij} = 0$, (ii) it should provide smoothened estimates when $V_{ij} \neq 0$ but is small, and (iii) it should output meaningful probabilities in $[0, 1]$. Note however that the MLE is *consistent*, meaning that as $V_{ij} \to \infty$, $P_{ij}^{\text{MLE}} \to P_{ij}$. This implies that any estimator $\hat{P}_{ij}$ should ideally *converge to the MLE when V_{ij} is sufficiently large*.

Existing learning methods for response prediction can be categorized as feature-based or MLE-based. Feature-based methods build prediction models based on explicit features of an ad and a page, also known as *side-information*. These could include the textual content of an ad, its placement on the webpage, *et cetera*. Many existing feature based methods build prediction models using the logistic regression family [17, 8]. MLE-based methods smoothen the raw MLE via statistical models of clicks and views, with a popular choice being the Gamma-Poisson model [5, 2].

2.3 Hierarchical constraints

Pages and ads can often be organized into pre-defined hierarchies. For example, the set of all ads can be categorized according to the advertiser who made the ad. Each advertiser in turn typically instruments a series of campaigns in which to display the ads, each with differing markets and goals. This means that there is a tree-like structure to the ads: Root → Advertiser → Campaign → Advertisement. See Figure 1 for a simple example of an ad hierarchy. Notice that hierarchies are not necessarily trees, since an ad may be shown as part of multiple campaigns, for example.

Hierarchical structure encodes useful prior knowledge about CTRs. For example, the CTRs of all ads from the same campaign tend to correlated with one another. So, if a particular (page, ad) pair has

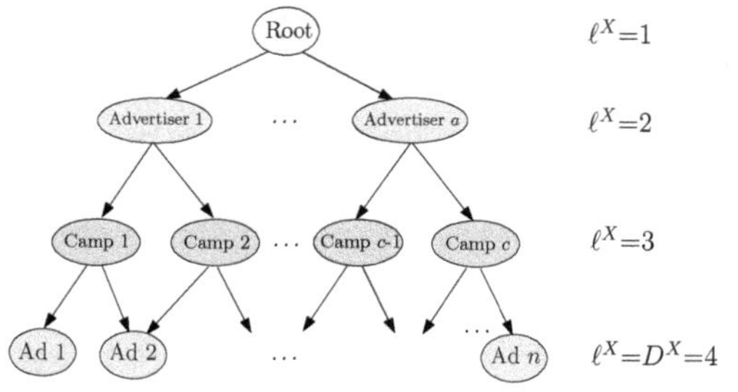

Figure 1: Hierarchical structure for advertisers.

only a few views, but the siblings of the ad have many views, then the reliability of its estimate can be increased by "borrowing" from the siblings' probability estimates in some principled manner. Hierarchical information has been successfully used in previous work on response prediction. [3] enforces relationships between estimates for (page, ad) pairs using a Markov model based on the hierarchy. The state-of-the-art LMMH model in [2] stores a separate weight ϕ_{ij} for each pair of nodes (i, j) in the page and ad hierarchies, and the click probability is modelled as a product of weights for all pairs of nodes on the respective hierarchy paths for i and j. The key idea here is *fallback*: if a (page, ad) pair (i, j) has an insufficient number of views, then the model sets ϕ_{ij} to 1, causing a fall back onto the probability estimates of parent nodes.

2.4 Collaborative filtering

Given a database of users and their preferences for various items, recommender systems aim to suggest to users new items that they will probably like, but have not already consumed. A canonical example is movie recommendation, a problem popularized by the Netflix challenge [1]. Collaborative filtering is a very successful approach to this problem, which makes recommendations based solely on the preference database: the fundamental intuition is that "similar" users will have "similar" preference, where "similar" refers to a latent notion that is *learned* by the model.

Formally, our input is an incomplete matrix $X \in \mathbb{R}^{m \times n}$ of user-item preferences, where most X_{ij} entries are missing. Our goal is to fill in these missing entries with predicted scores. The state of the art in collaborative filtering is *matrix factorization*: X is modelled as $X \approx \alpha^T \beta$, where $\alpha \in \mathbb{R}^{k \times m}$ and $\beta \in \mathbb{R}^{k \times n}$ and k is the number of *latent features* [12]. Conceptually, each α_i represents a feature vector for users, and each β_j a feature vector for items. The simplest factorization model is to solve the optimization [19]

$$\min_{\alpha,\beta} \frac{1}{|\mathcal{O}|} \sum_{(i,j)\in\mathcal{O}} (X_{ij} - \alpha_i^T \beta_j)^2 + \Omega(\alpha,\beta) \qquad (2)$$

where $\Omega(\alpha,\beta) = \frac{\lambda_\alpha}{2}||\alpha||_F^2 + \frac{\lambda_\beta}{2}||\beta||_F^2$. The first term makes the model parameters predictive of the observed entries. The second term is a *regularizer* that prevents overfitting on the observed entries. Penalizing the α and β weights by their ℓ_2 norm is equivalent to imposing a Gaussian prior on them [9, p. 64].

2.5 Our contributions

There are two main contributions to this paper. First, we present a novel approach to response prediction based on matrix factorization techniques from collaborative filtering. This model uses both latent features as well as side-information in the form of page and ad features. Ours is not a mere black-box application of collaborative filtering, however: as we will discuss subsequently, matrix factorization models such as Equation 2 are inadequate for response prediction, and require fundamental modifications. We additionally propose an iterative procedure to leverage the complementary nature of latent and explicit features. To our knowledge, the only prior work on using collaborative filtering for response prediction is [6], but it uses mixture-model approaches that have been superseded by matrix factorization. While [6] concludes that these mixture-models do not deal with the rare event problem in response prediction data, our model demonstrates state-of-the-art performance.

Second, we provide a principled way to incorporate hierarchies into matrix factorization methods for collaborative filtering. The modelling details here are very different from how hierarchies are used in existing response prediction models, since our approach is based on a different foundation. There has been work on exploiting hierarchical information in the CF literature, but only using neighbourhood models [22, 23], and so the modelling details are again completely different. Note also that such approaches are not applicable to response prediction for the same reasons that apply to standard factorization methods, which we discuss in Section 3.

3. RESPONSE PREDICTION VIA MATRIX FACTORIZATION

We now discuss how response prediction can be solved using ideas from collaborative filtering (CF). We start by addressing why a black-box application of CF techniques is insufficient.

3.1 Differences between CF and response prediction

Recall that the goal in response prediction is to construct an estimator $\hat{P}$ of the CTR that satisfies the three requirements outlined in Section 2.2. If we treat the matrix P^{MLE} as our input, then requirement (i) asks us to fill in the missing entries of this matrix. We observe an immediate connection between this task and CF: if we treat pages as users, ads as items, and the entries of P_{ij}^{MLE} as being an "affinity" score of the (page, ad) pair (i, j), then we are trying to predict the affinity for (page, ad) pairs for which there is no historical data. Applying CF to solve this problem is based on the intuition that "similar" ads will demonstrate "similar" CTRs on a given page, where "similar" is some notion that is *learned* by a mathematical model.

With this connection in place, it might appear that response prediction can be solved by just feeding P^{MLE} as the input to a collaborative filtering model, such as matrix factorization. However, a standard matrix factorization $P^{\text{MLE}} \approx \alpha^T \beta$ as in Equation 2 does *not* meet requirements (ii) and (iii): it does not output valid probabilities in $[0, 1]$, and it completely ignores the issue of confidence for entries with a few views. This necessitates fundamental changes to the factorization framework, which we detail below.

3.2 Confidence-weighted factorization

We can think of the problem of estimating $\Pr[\text{Click}|\text{View}; i, j]$ as an analogue of the binary classification problem of estimating $\Pr[y = 1|x]$. If we consider a click to be a "positive" event, and a non-click a "negative" event, we can think of the dyad (i, j) as comprising C_{ij} *duplicated* positive labels, and $V_{ij} - C_{ij}$ duplicated negative labels. Therefore, we have constructed a two dimensional table, where each cell consists of several binary labels. [13] constructs a similar table, but unlike our setting uses it in conjunction with explicit features for pages and ads.

There are now two problems to solve: we need to compute the probability of each individual label in the table being positive or negative, and we need to deal with the fact that there are multiple such labels per cell. For the first problem, suppose for the moment that each cell (i,j) has a single binary label X_{ij}. We now assume that for a fixed set of page latent vectors α, the probability of a positive label arising for ad j may be modelled via logistic regression with a weight vector β_j, giving us $P^{\text{MF}}_{ij} = \sigma(\alpha_i^T \beta_j)$. This is clearly symmetric to assuming that for a fixed set of ad vectors β, the probability of a positive label for a page i has the given form. If we now optimize over α,β jointly, we get the modified factorization model

$$\min_{\alpha,\beta} \frac{1}{|\mathcal{O}|} \sum_{(i,j)\in\mathcal{O}} \big(-X_{ij} \log P^{\text{MF}}_{ij}(\alpha,\beta) - (1_{ij} - X_{ij}) \log(1 - P^{\text{MF}}_{ij}(\alpha,\beta))\big) + \Omega(\alpha,\beta), \quad (3)$$

where $\Omega(\alpha,\beta) = \frac{\lambda_\alpha}{2}||\alpha||_F^2 + \frac{\lambda_\beta}{2}||\beta||_F^2$ as in Equation 2. The above objective can be thought of as replacing the square-loss in Equation 2 with the more appropriate logistic loss for binary data. Models of this type have been recently studied in the collaborative filtering literature, such as in the RLFM model [4], which optimizes parameters in a Bayesian manner. In statistics, similar models have been considered in the context of modelling edges in graphs [10]. SGD optimization of the above has been proposed in the LFL model [15], of which the above is a special case for binary inputs, and the FIP model [21]. Finally, [18] proposed a similar model for collaborative filtering, where P^{MF}_{ij} was further scaled to constrain predictions to lie in a finite interval.

In the above, each α_i represents a latent feature vector for pages, and each β_j a latent vector for ads. This assumes a *low rank* structure to P, which induces correlations between the matrix entries. This sharing of parameters allows us to smoothen probability estimates: even if a particular (page, ad) pair (i,j) has a few views, we can still reliably estimate $\hat{P}_{ij}$ by estimating α_i from all other ads shown on the page, and β_j from all other pages the ad is shown on.

The remaining problem is how to deal with the multiple entries in each cell of the table. Noting the connection of the above model to logistic regression, the duplicated labels in the table are analogous to having the same example x appear several times in a supervised learning task, each time with a different labels. Logistic regression can easily be performed on such a dataset, and it is straightforward to check that the number of duplicated labels merely appear as weights in the likelihood term. The same holds in our problem, and so we get the objective

$$F(\alpha,\beta;C,V) = \frac{1}{|\mathcal{O}|} \sum_{(i,j)\in\mathcal{O}} \big(-C_{ij} \log P^{\text{MF}}_{ij} - (V_{ij} - C_{ij}) \log(1 - P^{\text{MF}}_{ij})\big) + \Omega(\alpha,\beta). \quad (4)$$

where P^{MF} is understood to be a function of α,β . This objective clearly takes into account confidence in the entries: if a dyad has small V_{ij}, then very little weight is placed on the likelihood term that measures its probability of click. The form of the objective is somewhat similar to that of [11], which targets CF datasets where there are no negative ratings. However, that paper uses a factorization of the form $X \approx \alpha^T\beta$, which as mentioned earlier does not output valid probabilities. Further, our objective is motivated by a principled construction of a table of positive and negative labels from the C, V matrices.

The objective in Equation 4 is differentiable, and may be optimized using stochastic gradient descent (SGD). This allows us to scale to very large datasets. The variations to the basic objective that we describe in subsequent sections will not affect differentiability, and so they will all be amenable to SGD training. As with the standard objective in Equation 2, the objective in Equation 4 is non-convex and thus SGD optimization only finds a local minima. Empirically, this local minima is found to have good predictive performance on test data.

3.3 Is factorization better than other methods?

Our confidence-weighted factorization overcomes the limitations of MLE. First, it can make predictions for (page, ad) pairs with no historical views. Second, even when there are historical views, it returns a *smoothened* estimate that is learned from multiple (page, ad) pairs, which has lesser variance than the raw MLE value. One caveat is that our method is *not* guaranteed to converge to the MLE as $V_{ij} \to \infty$, simply because the true probability P_{ij} may not be expressible as $\sigma(\alpha_i^T\beta_j)$. However, since we noted that our optimization can be thought of as using the logistic loss, which is a *proper loss* function [7], we can expect our estimates to be meaningful approximations of P_{ij}. In Section 6 we will demonstrate that empirically, given a large enough number of latent features k, our model converges to the MLE solution when V_{ij} is large.

Recall from Section 2.2 that existing methods for response prediction are based on either explicit features or MLE smoothing. We will see what potential advantages the other methods have over the factorization, and use these to guide extensions to our model. Looking at the feature-based methods, the obvious difference to our basic factorization model is that we learn *latent* features from the historical data, and use these to make predictions. In standard collaborative filtering problems, latent features are typically much more expressive than explicit features, because they can capture subtle correlations in the data [16]. However, the features used in response prediction – for example, the spatial placement of the ad on a webpage, the time it was displayed, *et cetera* – are known to be highly influential to CTR by themselves, and so a similar conclusion cannot obviously be made here. Instead, the approaches should be seen as *orthogonal* solutions that should be combined.

Compared to simple statistical models for smoothening the MLE, one advantage of the factorization approach is that we can learn a rich latent structure by choosing a sufficiently large number of latent features k. However, the state-of-the-art LMMH technique [2] warrants a closer study. LMMH is based on two ingredients. First, the results of a baseline model only using features (such as logistic regression) are used to compute an expected number of clicks $\hat{C}_{ij}$ for each dyad. Next, one fits a log-linear model on the clicks C and *expected* clicks $\hat{C}$ under some statistical assumptions about the data. This log-linear model is fitted by exploiting *hierarchical* information for the pages and ads. This information is treated separately from the other features (such as placement of an ad) because of its special structure: specifically, as we noted in Section 2.3, the hierarchy for an ad directly encodes information about correlations amongst CTRs. The reason is that this is a high-dimensional categorical variable, whose outcomes appear amongst multiple cells in the data matrix. The use of hierarchies helps LMMH handle the extreme sparsity problem quite effectively.

With this understanding, we now study two important extensions to the factorization model in turn: how to incorporate side-information, and how to incorporate hierarchies. The resulting model will be shown to have superior performance to both LMMH and the feature-based methods. Table 1 provides a summary of the components of our final model.

4. INCORPORATING SIDE-INFORMATION

As discussed earlier, pages and ads possess explicit features other than just their unique identifiers, such as the content of the ad, its placement on the page, *et cetera*. In collaborative filtering, such features are known as *side-information*. Side-information is primarily useful for making predictions in *cold-start* settings, where

Method	Section	Key idea
Confidence-weighted factorization	Section 3.2	$P_{ij}^{\text{MF}} \approx \sigma(\alpha_i^T \beta_j)$ with confidence determined by C_{ij}, V_{ij}
Fusion with side-information	Section 4.1	$P_{ij}^{\text{SI}} \approx \sigma(\alpha_i^T \beta_j + w^T x_{ij})$ for side-information given in x_{ij}
Iterative refinement	Section 4.2	$P_{ij}^{\text{MLE}} \rightarrow P_{ij}^{\text{SI}}$ and confidence weighted factorization repeated
Hierarchy regularization	Section 5.1	$\alpha_i \sim \mathcal{N}(\alpha_{\text{Par}(i)}, \lambda_\alpha^{-1} I), \beta_j \sim \mathcal{N}(\beta_{\text{Par}(j)}, \lambda_\beta^{-1} I)$
Agglomerate fitting	Section 5.2	$\alpha_i \sim \mathcal{N}(\alpha_{\text{Par}(i)}, \lambda_\alpha^{-1} I), \beta_j \sim \mathcal{N}(\beta_{\text{Par}(j)}, \lambda_\beta^{-1} I)$; $C, V \rightarrow C^{\text{Agg}}, V^{\text{Agg}}$
Residual fitting	Section 5.3	$\alpha_i \rightarrow \sum_{u \in \text{Path}(i)} \alpha_u, \beta_j \rightarrow \sum_{v \in \text{Path}(j)} \beta_u$
Hybrid hierarchical model	Section 5.4	Hierarchy regularization + Agglomerate fitting + Residual fitting

Table 1: Summary of the various components of the model used in this paper.

we have a dyad involving an object that was unobserved during training; for example, we may have an ad that has never been displayed before. In response prediction, the explicit features are strongly predictive of the CTR, as demonstrated by the fact that methods based just on explicit features were until recently the state-of-the-art [17]. It is thus prudent to incorporate this information into the factorization model for improved accuracy.

4.1 A joint factorization and feature model

Several ways of combining latent and explicit features have been studied in the collaborative filtering literature. We will use a simple scheme employed by the LFL [15] and FIP models [21], where we have a linear combination of the latent features and explicit features:

$$P_{ij}^{\text{MF}} = \sigma(\alpha_i^T \beta_j + w^T x_{ij}),$$

where x_{ij} consists of the explicit features for the dyad (i, j). It is clear that our predictions will now be influenced by the side-information, with w measuring the relative importance of the explicit features over the latent features. One now optimizes for the latent vectors α, β as well as the weights w. Training the augmented model can be done in an alternating fashion as suggested in [15]. We describe a simplified version of this process: first, note that the model may be rewritten as

$$P_{ij}^{\text{MF}} = \sigma(\left[1; w\right]^T \left[\alpha_i^T \beta_j; x_{ij}\right]), \tag{5}$$

This can be seen as a logistic regression model where the matrix factorization estimates $\alpha_i^T \beta_j$ are treated as additional *input features* that are augmented with x_{ij}. This suggests a simple learning strategy: first, we train the standard factorization model, yielding estimates P^{MF}. This step is equivalent to assuming that $w \equiv 0$. Now we fix $\alpha_i^T \beta_j$, and just optimize over w. This can be done by feeding the features $x'_{ij} = \left[\alpha_i^T \beta_j; x_{ij}\right]$ into a standard logistic regression model. The resulting solution, P^{SI}, predicts the click probability using both latent structure as well as side-information, thus enjoying the benefits of both approaches.

4.2 An iterative refinement procedure

Given the above model, a simple iterative procedure can be applied to further improve performance. Let us rewrite the confidence weighted factorization model of Equation 4 as

$$\min_{\alpha, \beta} \frac{1}{|\mathcal{O}|} \sum_{(i,j) \in \mathcal{O}} -V_{ij} \left(P_{ij}^{\text{MLE}} \log P_{ij}^{\text{MF}} - \right.$$
$$\left.(1 - P_{ij}^{\text{MLE}}) \log(1 - P_{ij}^{\text{MF}})\right) + \Omega(\alpha, \beta). \tag{6}$$

Earlier, we motivated the above as a sensible way to incorporate confidence into the factorization model. However, the model is limited by the historical data: recall that if a cell has a small to medium number of views, then P_{ij}^{MLE} will be noisy. This means that our confidence weighting is *itself* noisy. Ideally, we would like to weight each entry by the true probability P_{ij}, which is the optimal measure of confidence to guide our factorization model. But of course, if we knew this quantity, our learning would be complete. Yet this motivates the following EM-style procedure: we take the predictions from our above model, P_{ij}^{SI}, and use these in place of P_{ij}^{MLE} in the above equation. We now *re-learn* our confidence-weighted factorization model using these new confidences. The idea is that since P_{ij}^{SI} is a more reliable estimate of the true probability that P_{ij}^{MLE}, the factorization model is encouraged to focus its modelling efforts on the "right" dyads. We can now iterate by feeding the results of the newly learned factorization into a logistic regression model, and use the resulting estimates $\hat{P}_{ij}^{SI}$ as a fresh set of confidence weights. This process may be repeated till convergence. This scheme exploits the complementary properties of the two models so that by improving the outputs of one model, we can feed in more reliable inputs to the other.

We note a similarity to the previously discussed approach followed in LMMH, with two subtle but important differences: (i) LMMH uses a feature-based model to generate the initial refinement of the data, based on which further smoothing is applied. By contrast, we apply the *factorization* as the first step to refine the data, and feed this into the feature-based model; and (ii) We iterate the process till convergence. Distinction (ii) can naturally be expected to improve performance, a fact we verify empirically. We argue that distinction (i) is important, because our factorization approach yields much more reliable estimates than a feature-based method if we have even a small amount of historical data, as observed in [16]. The smoothing applied in the first phase fundamentally affects the overall performance, because only if the results of the first model are sufficiently rich does the second stage phase gain a significant advantage over modelling the training data as-is. Put another way, LMMH is made to solve the difficult problem of fitting the residual of an only moderately reliable feature-based model. By contrast, in our case the second phase involves a much simpler task, since most of the structure is already captured by the factorization. These intuitions will be empirically corroborated in Section 6.

5. INCORPORATING HIERARCHIES

Recall that the other ingredient behind the success of existing response prediction methods is the use of hierarchical information to overcome the extreme data sparsity. We now look how this can be incorporated into our factorization model. There are three basic ideas: (i) *hierarchical regularization*, where we keep a latent vector for each node in the page and ad hierarchies, and enforce priors based on this to induce correlations; (ii) *agglomerate fitting*, where we refine (i) by constructing more informative priors based on agglomerating subtrees in the hierarchy; and (iii) *residual fitting*, where we use fit the residual of the basic factorization using appropriate latent vectors in the hierarchy. Each of the methods modifies different parts of the objective function in Equation 4 (as noted earlier, without altering differentiability). The methods can in fact be used in *conjunction* with each other, and thus represent different facets of a larger approach to incorporating hierarchies. We will return to this matter after first discussing the methods in detail.

5.1 Hierarchical regularization

Our first idea is to let every node in the hierarchy possess its *own* latent vector, and use this to construct priors that constrain the latent vectors. For simplicity, we will use the notation α_i to denote the appropriate vector associated with the node i, and similarly for β_j: in Figure 2, $\beta_1, \ldots, \beta_n$ represent the latent vectors for ads as before, while $\beta_{n+1}, \ldots, \beta_{n+c}$ represent the latent vectors for the campaigns, and so on. When we refer to the matrix α, it is now in $\mathbb{R}^{|\mathcal{H}^P| \times k}$, and similarly for β.

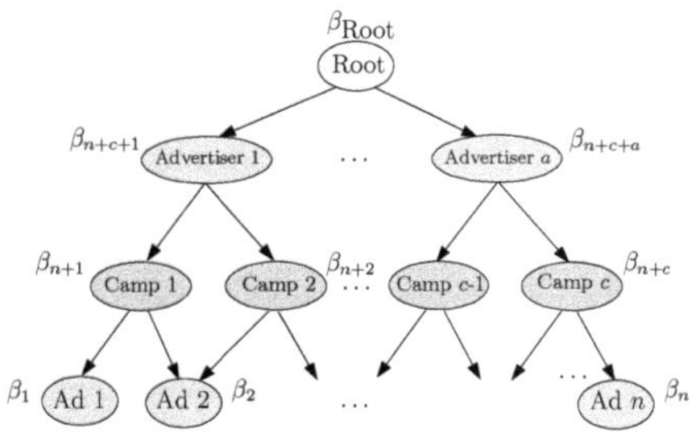

Figure 2: Each node in the hierarchy has a latent vector.

Recall that the standard ℓ_2 regularizer on α,β corresponds to placing a zero-mean Gaussian prior on them, i.e. $\alpha_i \sim \mathcal{N}(0, \lambda_\alpha^{-1} I)$. With the above setup, we impose *hierarchical priors* on the latent vectors, such that each latent vector has a prior so that it behaves like its parent in expectation:

$$\alpha_{\text{Root}} \sim \mathcal{N}(0, \lambda_{\text{Root}}^{-1} I), \forall i \in \mathcal{H}^P - \{\text{Root}\} \alpha_i \sim \mathcal{N}(\alpha_{\text{Par}(i)}, \lambda_\alpha^{-1} I) \tag{7}$$

To find the joint prior over α, note that given its parent, a node is conditionally independent of all higher level nodes. Thus, we replace the standard regularizer in Equation 4 by

$$\Omega(\alpha,\beta) = \frac{\lambda_\alpha}{2} \sum_{i \in \mathcal{H}^P} ||\alpha_i - \alpha_{\text{Par}(i)}||_2^2 + \frac{\lambda_\beta}{2} \sum_{j \in \mathcal{H}^A} ||\beta_j - \beta_{\text{Par}(j)}||_2^2 + \frac{\lambda_R}{2}(||\alpha_{\text{Root}}||_2^2 + ||\beta_{\text{Root}}||_2^2). \tag{8}$$

The regularizer helps in estimating vectors when there are few corresponding views. Suppose there are two siblings u, v with a common parent, and that node u has only a few views while node v has many views. For v, the dominating term in the objective will be the loss function, so its parameters will be optimized to be predictive for the CTR. For u, the regularizer will dominate and push its latent vector to be similar to the parent node. In turn, the parent is encouraged to be close to its children, and so u, v are indirectly encouraged to be similar to each other. This means that u will "borrow strength" from v.

The above easily handles hierarchies that are not trees: instead of the prior mean being a parent node's latent vector, we can use the *average* of all parents' vectors. This approach has a total of $(|\mathcal{H}^P| + |\mathcal{H}^A|)k$ parameters. In practice, hierarchies are often bottom-heavy, so that $|\mathcal{H}^X| = O(|X|)$. Thus we learn roughly the same number of parameters as in the standard setting. Of course, the constant in the $O(\cdot)$ makes a difference in two ways: it adds the risk of overfitting, and it potentially increases the number of local optima. We will empirically verify that neither of these risks are seriously manifested in practice.

5.2 Agglomerate fitting

In the previous section, the latent vectors for non-leaf nodes only appear in the regularizer, and hence are only indirectly affected by the click and view data. Intuitively, by making them directly depend on the data, they will serve as more informative priors for the leaf nodes. To do this, we use the hierarchy to *agglomerate* the click/view data across many pages and ads, and try to predict this data using the appropriate latent vectors. For example, for a (page, campaign) pair (i, c), we agglomerate the clicks/views for all children of c when shown on page i. We model the resulting data using the vectors α_i and β_c. This will learn a sensible prior for the children's latent vectors.

Formally, we construct the Cartesian product of the hierarchies, $G := \mathcal{H}^P \times \mathcal{H}^A$. Any $(u, v) \in G$ is a tuple of nodes from the page and ad hierarchies, and we associate with it the aggregated clicks of all its children:

$$C^{\text{Agg}}(u, v) = \sum_{(u',v'):(u,v) \in \text{Par}((u',v'))} C^{\text{Agg}}(u', v').$$

The base case is when both u and v are leaf nodes in the respective hierarchies, so that $C^{\text{Agg}}(u, v)$ is the standard click value C_{ij}. We repeat the same process for the views. We now have click and view matrices $C^{\text{Agg}}, V^{\text{Agg}} \in \mathbb{R}^{|\mathcal{H}^P| \times |\mathcal{H}^A|}$. We optimize the objective of Equation 4 using $F(\alpha,\beta; C^{\text{Agg}}, V^{\text{Agg}})$ along with the regularizer Ω of Equation 8. Therefore, every latent vector appears in both the objective and the regularizer. Figure 3 illustrates how we can think of the new matrices as being augmentations of the original C, V.

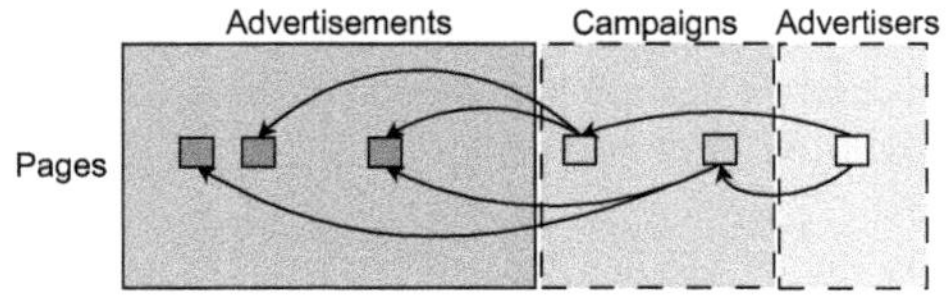

Figure 3: Illustration of the agglomeration process. Arrows denote that the clicks/views are added up.

There is a subtle problem with implementing agglomerative fitting as-is: the clicks and views of individual (page, ad) pairs will be "drowned out" by the ones corresponding to parent nodes, and our predictions will no longer be fine-grained for each individual pair. Concretely, consider some page i, an ad j, and the ad's campaign c. Then, the number of clicks/views for the (page, campaign) pair (i, c) will be greater than the clicks/views for the (page, ad) pair (i, j), by construction of the agglomerated click and view matrices. Since the model of Equation 4 is confidence weighted by the number of views, we will essentially ignore the contributions of the (page, ad) pairs. One fix to this problem is to train our model in stages. Letting α^{Par} and β^{Par} denote the latent vectors for non-leaf nodes, we perform the following steps:

1. Learn α,β with $\alpha^{\text{Par}}, \beta^{\text{Par}}$ fixed. This is the standard factorization model of Equation 4.
2. Learn $\alpha^{\text{Par}}, \beta^{\text{Par}}$ with α,β fixed. This asks the parent nodes to be predictive for the agglomerated data, but *using* the already learnt vectors for pages and ads e.g. when we predict for a (page, campaign) pair.

3. Relearn α,β with α^{Par}, β^{Par} fixed. This asks us to respect the hierarchical prior when reconstructing the data matrix. Since the parent nodes are not optimized at this stage, we do not overfit on the agglomerated entries. We can use the result of step (1) as initialization here.

One can think of this process as using hierarchies to give a principled way of finding good local optima for α,β .

5.3 Residual fitting

The previous extensions all enforce similarity among parameters based on the hierarchy, but finally use the prediction $\sigma(\alpha_i^T \beta_j)$. A sensible idea is to modify this prediction itself based on the hierarchy. Specifically, for the pair (i, j), we use the prediction $\sigma(\tilde{\alpha}_i^T \tilde{\beta}_j)$, where $\tilde{\alpha}$, $\tilde{\beta}$ modify the original vectors α,β based on the hierarchy. A simple choice is the additive model

$$\tilde{\alpha}_{ik} = \alpha_{ik} + \sum_{u \in \text{Path}(i)-\{i\}} \alpha_{uk}$$

and similarly for $\tilde{\beta}$. Here, the fine-grained latent features for each page are modelled as corrections over coarser latent features of parent nodes, which may be thought of as *bias* terms. This technique easily generalizes to non-tree hierarchies if we use the average latent vector of all parent nodes on a *per-level* basis.

5.4 Putting it all together: a hybrid method

We can easily combine the ideas of the previous sections to create the following hybrid approach: (i) our prediction for dyad (i, j) involves all latent vectors along the respective paths in the hierarchy, (ii) we impose hierarchical priors on the latent vectors, and (iii) we force the latent vectors for parent nodes to be predictive for agglomerated data. We later demonstrate that empirically, this hybrid performs significantly better than any of its individual components. We also note that the hybrid can be easily augmented with additional side-information using the framework detailed in Section 4.

5.5 Handling cold-start pages and ads

We quickly comment on how the hierarchical extensions let us estimate the latent vectors for a cold-start page or ad. As a simple example, suppose there are several pages that share a common parent node. Suppose one of them, page i, has no past history. Then, if we use hierarchical regularization, α_i will only appear in the regularization term Ω in Equation 8. Thus, it optimized by setting it equal to $\alpha_{\text{Par}(i)}$. If this parent node is estimated via agglomerative fitting, it will be a good representative of the common structure between the siblings of i. Therefore, we will be able to make reasonable predictions for page i on test data. This argument holds equally for entities that are "almost cold-start" i.e. which have extremely limited past history. Having inferred the latent vectors in this manner, we can now employ the framework of Section 4.

6. EXPERIMENTS

Our experiments address several questions: (i) how well does the basic confidence-weighted factorization model perform compared to existing response prediction methods?, (ii) do the hierarchical extensions improve performance?, and (iii) does exploiting latent features and side-information offer noticeable performance gains? To answer these questions, we conducted experiments on three very large real-world datasets, which shows our model is highly scalable and that it outperforms current state-of-the-art methods. MATLAB code for our methods is available online at [14].

6.1 Datasets used

Our datasets were collected from Yahoo! traffic streams. (Unfortunately, we cannot release our datasets due to their proprietary nature.) To mirror the real-world prediction problem, the train-test splits in all our datasets is done in a temporal manner, so that the events in the training set occur before those in the test set. All splits were conducted 20 times to ensure the significance of our results. Since the datasets are proprietary, we cannot report the corresponding number of pages and ads, clicks and views, nor the number of days used to construct the train-test split. Instead, we just report the number of nonzero records (≥ 1 view) in the train and test sets.

We used the same three datasets as [2]. These datasets each involve the interaction between ads and pages, and differ in the nature of the interaction. The first data set, **Click**, records the event of an ad being clicked when shown on a page. Both pages and ads have a two level hierarchy in this dataset. The second dataset, **PVC**, measures how many users performed a pre-determined action after *viewing* an ad. Finally, the post-click conversion dataset (**PCC**) measures how many users performed a pre-determined action after *clicking* an ad. Both **PVC** and **PCC** have four level ad hierarchies, and the same two level page hierarchy as with **Click**. Of the three datasets, **PVC** is the sparsest, since post-view conversions are generally difficult to measure. There are $\sim$(90B, 3B) (train, test) records for **Click**, $\sim$(7B, 250M) for **PVC**, and $\sim$(500M, 20M) for **PCC**. The three datasets also include *interaction features* for the user involved in each interaction (e.g. the age and gender of the user that clicks on an ad, how recently the ad was shown to the user, *et cetera*).

6.2 Methods used

We implemented the confidence-weighted factorization of Section 3 (denoted "CWFact" in our figures), two of our hierarchical extensions (denoted "Agglomerative", and "Residual"), and the hybrid hierarchical method of Section 5.4 (denoted "Hybrid"). (The hierarchical regularization method in Section 5.1 by itself showed similar performance to CWFact, as is essentially subsumed by Agglomerative.) The basic versions of these methods did not include explicit features, and are purely based on matrix factorization. We additionally ran the CWFact and Hybrid methods with side-information using the joint model of Section 4, and denote these methods by "CWFact+LogReg" and "Hybrid+LogReg". Finally, the method "Hybrid+LogReg++" used the iterative scheme detailed in Section 4.2, where we iteratively use the model's predicted number of clicks as input to a residual model. We ran this model till convergence.

We trained all models using stochastic gradient descent (SGD), and used the MapReduce code from the Apache Mahout project (`http://mahout.apache.org/`) to scale to the challenging sizes of the datasets. We parallelized the optimization by fixing the page latent features α_i and then optimizing for the advertisement latent features β_j using SGD. This optimization of each individual β_j can be done in parallel. Once the estimates of the β_j's converged, we fixed their values and optimized the α_i's in parallel; this alternating scheme was repeated until convergence. For the hierarchical regularization scheme, we optimized the parameters level-by-level based on the hierarchy. Thus, for the initial optimization of advertisement features β_j, the campaign features were fixed and regularization was done towards these fixed latent features. Once optimization of the advertisements concluded, the campaign features were optimized with regularization towards fixed advertiser features, and so on.

Regarding parameter selection, we picked the strengths of regularization λ_α, λ_β by cross-validation. Due to space limitations, we cannot show results for a range of latent feature dimensions, k, and instead just show results for $k = 100$. Qualitatively, we found that the gains of our model were modest with a much smaller value of $k = 10$, indicating that it is important to choose a sufficiently large number of latent features to capture the structure in the data.

We compare to three state-of-the-art methods, discussed earlier in Section 2.2. The first is the model of [2], denoted "LMMH". The second and third are variants of a logistic regression model that uses explicit features for pages and ads, similar to [17]. Prior to LMMH, these models were the state-of-the-art for response prediction [17]. We fed these logistic methods input features derived from the page and ad hierarchies. For example, each ad has its corresponding advertiser ID as a categorical feature. The first variant of logistic regression, "LogReg", just used all the raw features as input. The second variant, "LogRegHash", also uses *cross-features* of pages and ads. To mitigate the dramatic increases in the number of features, following [2], we applied the hashing trick of [20] to compress the features into a smaller number of bins.

6.3 Evaluating performance

We use the standard performance metric of Bernoulli log-likelihood, which measures how well the predicted CTRs match the CTR on the test set. For a test set $\mathcal{T}$ of (page, ad) pairs with clicks and views $C^{\mathcal{T}}, V^{\mathcal{T}}$, given the model's predictions $\hat{P}_{ij}$, the log-likelihood is:

$$\mathcal{L} = - \sum_{(i,j) \in \mathcal{T}} \log \hat{P}_{ij}^{C_{ij}^{\mathcal{T}}} (1 - \hat{P}_{ij})^{(V_{ij}^{\mathcal{T}} - C_{ij}^{\mathcal{T}})}.$$

Again, for confidentiality reasons we cannot report raw log-likelihood numbers for any method. Hence, on all datasets we report the % lift in likelihood over the appropriate baselines.

6.4 Results on large-scale datasets

Our results are summarized in Figure 4. We see that for all datasets, the Hybrid+LogReg++ model gives the best log-likelihood lift, in particular outperforming LMMH in terms of average lift, and with a consistently lower standard deviation. The multiple iterations used in Hybrid+LogReg++ are seen to have a useful boost over Hybrid+LogReg, which by itself outperforms LMMH on all but PCC, where LMMH performs marginally better. This shows that the combination of factorization, hierarchies and side-information gives state-of-the-art performance. Note also that the good performance of Hybrid+LogReg shows that it is not just the multiple iterations that give us the advantage over LMMH. A closer study reveals the value of each of these components in our final model. The importance of using hierarchies is demonstrated by the surprisingly poor performance of the basic CWFact model, which is outperformed by even the simple LogReg models. However, these feature-based models are in turn significantly outperformed by the Hybrid method that adds hierarchies to the factorization. Note also that the Hybrid method always manages to significantly improve over the individual Agglomerative and Residual sub-models. Yet, we conclude that it imperative to have a model that *combines* latent features and side-information, because the Hybrid method by itself is merely competitive with LMMH; it is only when we add side-information to the factorization that we start to see improvements.

For our models that used both latent features and side-information, we found that the LogReg component invariably put relatively little weight on the standard features, meaning that the factorization "feature" was considered most important. This is expected, since the factorization model by itself is strongly predictive of the CTR. To further analyze the interplay between the factorization and side-information, Figures 5a and 5b gives log-log plots of the ratio of predictions of the Hybrid+LogReg++ model and the LogReg model to the test set CTR, ordered by increasing number of views on the training set. The flat line in black is the optimal solution where the model prediction matches the test set CTR, and both are displayed on the same y-range for ease of comparison. (Recall that we are unable to report exact view numbers for our datasets. Hence, in both plots, we removed identifying information about the number of views on the x-axis.) There are two striking characteristics in the plots: first, the Hybrid+LogReg++ model has significantly less variance than LogReg, which shows that its factorization component helps the LogReg component by capturing most of the structure in the data through latent features. Second, the Hybrid+LogReg++ model converges much quicker to the true CTR than LogReg model in terms of number of views. This shows that our model can successfully smoothen at a much greater degree of sparsity in the training data, corresponding to dyads with a few number of views. As we noted earlier, similar behaviour has been observed for standard collaborative filtering data [16].

Finally, to see how the performance of Hybrid+LogReg++ varies across each iteration, Figure 5c shows the lifts on the **Click** dataset after each iteration. An iteration here refers to a single application of both the Hybrid and LogReg models, using the results of the previous iteration as input. The results are encouraging: we almost always improve the log-likelihood as we run the model for more iterations. (We observed similar results on the other datasets.) This shows that with minimal added cost, the simple iterative scheme of Section 4 offers further gains for our framework.

7. CONCLUSION AND FUTURE WORK

This paper showed how we can improve on the state-of-the-art in response prediction using a novel approach based on collaborative filtering. Our model is based on a matrix factorization that learns latent structure from the data, and additionally exploits side-information in the form of page and ad features. We proposed an iterative procedure to further exploit the complementary nature of latent and explicit features. Finally, we showed how to incorporate hierarchical information for pages and ads into our model. Experimental results on Yahoo! traffic data show that our method outperforms existing response prediction approaches, and that it can handle high amounts of sparsity in the training data.

There are several avenues for future work. First, the matrix factorization model proposed here uses MAP estimates of the weight vectors. A Bayesian approach involving marginalization of these parameters would be useful, though it poses challenges due to the interdependencies between parameters. Second, it is important to address other real-world complexities that arise in response prediction, such as the fact that ad behaviour is time-varying.

8. REFERENCES

[1] Netflix prize. http://www.netflixprize.com/.

[2] D. Agarwal, R. Agrawal, R. Khanna, and N. Kota. Estimating rates of rare events with multiple hierarchies through scalable log-linear models. In *KDD '10*, pages 213–222, New York, NY, USA, 2010. ACM.

[3] D. Agarwal, A. Z. Broder, D. Chakrabarti, D. Diklic, V. Josifovski, and M. Sayyadian. Estimating rates of rare events at multiple resolutions. In *KDD '07*, pages 16–25, New York, NY, USA, 2007. ACM.

[4] D. Agarwal and B.-C. Chen. Regression-based latent factor models. In *KDD '09*, pages 19–28, New York, NY, USA, 2009. ACM.

[5] D. Agarwal, B.-C. Chen, and P. Elango. Spatio-temporal

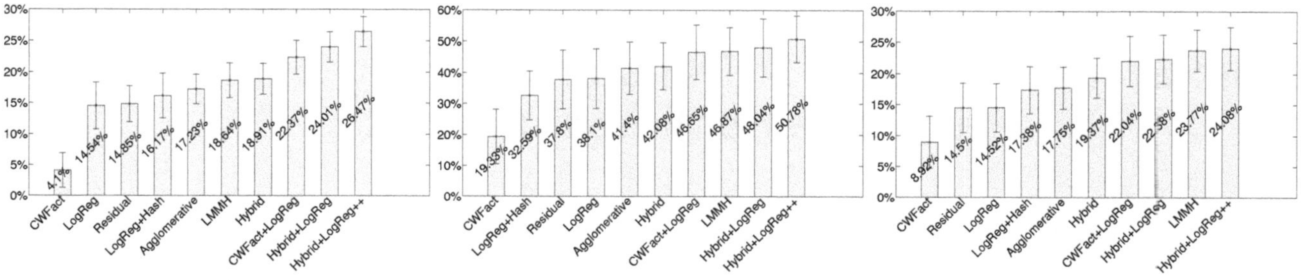

(a) Click. (b) PVC. (c) PCC.

Figure 4: Log-likelihood lifts on large-scale datasets.

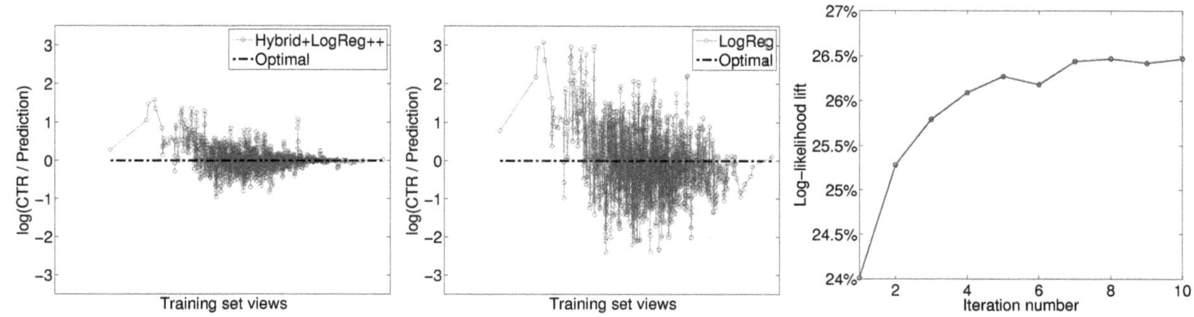

(a) Hybrid+LogReg++ versus test CTR. (b) LogReg versus test CTR. (c) Per-iteration lift.

Figure 5: Analysis of factorization model's performance on Click. See text regarding the missing axes in (a) and (b).

models for estimating click-through rate. In *WWW '09*, pages 21–30, New York, NY, USA, 2009. ACM.

[6] S. Banerjee and K. Ramanathan. Collaborative filtering on skewed datasets. In *WWW '08*, pages 1135–1136, New York, NY, USA, 2008. ACM.

[7] A. Buja, W. Stuetzle, and Y. Shen. Loss functions for binary class probability estimation: Structure and applications. Unpublished manuscript, 2005.

[8] T. Graepel, J. Q. Candela, T. Borchert, and R. Herbrich. Web-scale Bayesian click-through rate prediction for sponsored search advertising in Microsoft's Bing search engine. In *ICML '10*, pages 13–20, 2010.

[9] T. Hastie, R. Tibshirani, and J. Friedman. *The Elements of Statistical Learning*. Springer Series in Statistics. Springer New York Inc., New York, NY, USA, 2001.

[10] P. D. Hoff. Bilinear mixed-effects models for dyadic data. *Journal of the American Statistical Association*, 100:286–295, March 2005.

[11] Y. Hu, Y. Koren, and C. Volinsky. Collaborative filtering for implicit feedback datasets. In *ICDM '08*, pages 263–272, Washington, DC, USA, 2008. IEEE Computer Society.

[12] Y. Koren, R. M. Bell, and C. Volinsky. Matrix factorization techniques for recommender systems. *IEEE Computer*, 42(8):30–37, 2009.

[13] Y. Lifshits and D. Nowotka. Estimation of the click volume by large scale regression analysis. In *CSR*, pages 216–226, 2007.

[14] A. K. Menon. Code for experiments. `http://cseweb.ucsd.edu/~akmenon/code`.

[15] A. K. Menon and C. Elkan. A log-linear model with latent features for dyadic prediction. In *ICDM*, 2010.

[16] I. Pilászy and D. Tikk. Recommending new movies: even a few ratings are more valuable than metadata. In *RecSys '09*, pages 93–100, New York, NY, USA, 2009. ACM.

[17] M. Richardson, E. Dominowska, and R. Ragno. Predicting clicks: estimating the click-through rate for new ads. In *WWW 07*, pages 521–530, New York, NY, USA, 2007. ACM.

[18] R. Salakhutdinov and A. Mnih. Probabilistic matrix factorization. In *NIPS*, 2007.

[19] G. Takács, I. Pilászy, B. Németh, and D. Tikk. Scalable Collaborative Filtering Approaches for Large Recommender Systems. *Journal of Machine Learning Research*, 10:623–656, 2009.

[20] K. Weinberger, A. Dasgupta, J. Langford, A. Smola, and J. Attenberg. Feature hashing for large scale multitask learning. In *ICML '09*, pages 1113–1120, 2009.

[21] S. Yang, B. Long, A. Smola, N. Sadagopan, Z. Zheng, and H. Zha. Like like alike – joint friendship and interest propagation in social networks. In *WWW*, 2011.

[22] C.-N. Ziegler, G. Lausen, and J. A. Konstan. On exploiting classification taxonomies in recommender systems. *AI Communications*, 21(2-3):97–125, 2008.

[23] C.-N. Ziegler, G. Lausen, and S.-T. Lars. Taxonomy-driven computation of product recommendations. In *Proceedings of the thirteenth ACM international conference on Information and knowledge management*, CIKM '04, pages 406–415, New York, NY, USA, 2004. ACM.

From Bias to Opinion: A Transfer-Learning Approach to Real-Time Sentiment Analysis

Pedro H. Calais Guerra, Adriano Veloso, Wagner Meira Jr., Virgílio Almeida
Universidade Federal de Minas Gerais, Brazil
{pcalais,adrianov,meira,virgilio}@dcc.ufmg.br

ABSTRACT

Real-time interaction, which enables live discussions, has become a key feature of most Web applications. In such an environment, the ability to automatically analyze user opinions and sentiments as discussions develop is a powerful resource known as *real time sentiment analysis*. However, this task comes with several challenges, including the need to deal with highly dynamic textual content that is characterized by changes in vocabulary and its subjective meaning and the lack of labeled data needed to support supervised classifiers. In this paper, we propose a transfer learning strategy to perform real time sentiment analysis. We identify a task – *opinion holder bias prediction* – which is strongly related to the sentiment analysis task; however, in constrast to sentiment analysis, it builds accurate models since the underlying relational data follows a stationary distribution.

Instead of learning textual models to predict content polarity (i.e., the traditional sentiment analysis approach), we first measure the bias of social media users toward a topic, by solving a relational learning task over a network of users connected by endorsements (e.g., retweets in Twitter). We then analyze sentiments by *transferring* user biases to textual features. This approach works because while new terms may arise and old terms may change their meaning, user bias tends to be more consistent over time as a basic property of human behavior. Thus, we adopted user bias as the basis for building accurate classification models. We applied our model to posts collected from Twitter on two topics: the 2010 Brazilian Presidential Elections and the 2010 season of Brazilian Soccer League. Our results show that knowing the bias of only 10% of users generates an F1 accuracy level ranging from 80% to 90% in predicting user sentiment in tweets.

Categories and Subject Descriptors

H.2.8 [**Database Management**]: Database Applications—*Data Mining*

General Terms

Algorithms, Experimentation

Keywords

Social Media, Relational Learning, Sentiment Analysis, Opinion Mining, Transfer Learning

1. INTRODUCTION

The rise of text-based social media channels has fueled data miners with torrents of opinion-based data on the most diverse topics and entities. Blogs, microblogs and online social networks are constantly flooded with opinions about a multitude of topics such as politics, sports and other "buzz" topics that pop up daily on news media. The ability to automatically distinguish positive and negative content in streams of opinion-based data enables the creation of valuable real-time applications that monitor public opinion and summarize the aggregated sentiment of online society [13].

In this work, we argue that current state-of-the-art sentiment analysis strategies are not effective for mining opinions in this new, challenging environment. Traditionally, sentiment analysis (also known as *opinion mining*) algorithms have been designed for static and well-controlled scenarios that target analysis of reviews of products and services [26, 28]. In those scenarios, pre-defined lists of positive and negative words (i.e., lexicons) and traditional supervised machine learning techniques have been quite successful [28]. However, the real-time sentiment classification of opinion-based content on general topics discussed in social media, on a real time basis, is particularly challenging for two reasons:

1. **Data dynamicity:** Topics such as sports competitions and electoral disputes exhibit an inherent dynamic nature, caused by the *sub-events* that take place during the monitoring of the major event. Further, real time sentiment analysis needs to deal with textual data that exhibits significant *concept drift* and a *non-stationary* distribution, which both changes the characteristics of the sentiment analysis task and degrades prediction quality over time. For example, at least 50 different high-volume discussion threads arose during the US 2008 Elections [17], moreover, they could not be predicted in advance, such as the "lipstick on a pig" discussion, that resulted on the largest number of posts. Another example occurred during the 2010 Brazilian Presidential Elections when a scandal involving a close assistant of one of the candidates was unveiled in the middle of the electoral process, unleashing a large volume of unpredicted negative comments.

2. **Lack of labeled data:** Traditional machine learning strategies for sentiment analysis require training samples in order to build text-based models. However, the high volume and sparsity of sentiment stream data may render vast amounts of labeled examples unfeasible, thus compromising the potential of typical supervised learning strategies.

In this work we propose a novel strategy to address these challenges. Our strategy is based on the premises that opinion holders tend to express their opinions *multiple times*, and they are usually *consistent* in doing so. In other words, positive and negative opinions are not randomly expressed by people. For instance, someone who supports a candidate in an election will tend to post positive comments about him and negative comments about his/her adversaries on a regular basis. Technically, we say that opinion holders exhibit a varying degree of *bias*. Social theories argue that bias is an inherent feature of human behavior, which is characterized by a lack of appropriate balance, neutrality and critical doubt in argumentation [29]; one of the most clear manifestations of bias is when someone supports one side too strongly or too often [15].

In the context of social media, we develop a strategy for real-time sentiment analysis based on the *opinion holder bias prediction*, which has two main assumptions. First, users express their opinions through *endorsements*, that is, interactions among users in which one user implicitly agrees with another. We emphasize that endorsements are transactional, and such structured data is easier to deal with than textual data, enabling a more effective learning process. Second, as mentioned above, for the majority of users, bias is a *consistent, robust* characteristic of their behavior. While text content may be influenced by external factors, such as new terms that enter a topic discussion, user biases are less prone to external perturbations, unless users actually change their opinion, which is usually a relatively long process.

It is interesting to note that because opinions on a topic are not independent from the opinion holders who write them, determining user biases also addresses another objective of our study, which is to develop a *transfer learning framework* [25] strategy to analyze sentiment in social media content. Starting with the original target task $\mathcal{T}_t$ (i.e., *real time sentiment analysis*), which lacks labeled data and faces concept drift, we define *opinion holder bias prediction* as a source task $\mathcal{T}_s$ and then map solutions from $\mathcal{T}_s$ to $\mathcal{T}_t$. It is rather intuitive that user biases may significantly improve the task of mining user opinions, but so far no sentiment analysis models have been based on that information. In addition to proposing this model, we address two key related questions: (i) How can the sociological definition of bias be implemented into a social media platform by only considering social interactions among users? (ii) How can bias information be converted into information on the sentiment that is associated with the generated content?

In summary, the main contributions of our work are as follows:

- We identify the user bias mining problem as a suitable *source task* $\mathcal{T}_s$ that is suitable for a transfer-learning strategy for real time sentiment analysis of social media content; the task focuses on the robustness and consistency of user opinions about a given topic.
- We propose and evaluate a solution to the user bias mining problem in social media in terms of a relational learning problem. Our solution exploits *endorsements* among users.
- We propose a simple unsupervised knowledge transfer approach to analyze sentiment in social media discussions based on the propagation of user bias quantifications to textual features, enabling text classifiers to use timely information on the sentiment associated with new terms arising in discussions and thus dealing with the lack of labeled training data and the non-stationary data distribution of textual content to some extent.
- We evaluate our approach using two datasets collected from Twitter [16], which is a microblogging service that disseminates user opinions and comments in real time. We analyzed two major events in Brazil: the 2010 Brazilian Presidential Elections and the 2010 season of the Brazilian National Soccer League. Our results show that knowing the bias of 10% of users is sufficient to reach an F1 accuracy level ranging from from 80% to 90% in predicting user sentiment in tweets.

2. RELATED WORK

In this section, we review some previous work on sentiment analysis and opinion holder bias prediction.

Sentiment Analysis. Sentiment analysis and opinion mining research have focused on static and well-controlled scenarios, mainly extracting opinions from product and service reviews. Two broad categories of opinion analysis strategies can be identified in the literature: lexicon-based and classification-based [11] strategies. Lexicon-based approaches use lists of words containing positive and negative terms to compute the overall polarity of the document by counting the occurrence of those terms [28]. A clear disadvantage of this strategy is that lexicons are domain-dependent and the effort needed to generate lists of words may be high.

Sentiment analysis has also been addressed as a traditional supervised learning task, with relative success. Different text classification algorithms have been applied to learn from word co-occurences and linguistic features to determine the sentiment contained in documents [14, 28]. Moreover, it has been used conjunction with pre-defined lexicons to assess sentiment in political and movie review blogs [22].

More recently, the increasing availability of opinion-based data in real time has motivated some studies that have analyzed sentiments in streaming data, specially over Twitter. Some approaches are as simple as the manual classification of tweets and lexicons of positive and negative words to monitor the debate performance of candidates in the 2008 US Elections [6] [24]. While lexicons may provide sentiment analysis on an aggregated level, their coverage in terms of content is usually low because in complex contexts such as elections and sports, content is often ironic, contains subtle comments and refers to specific terms that only make sense at a specific time; it often lacks expressions of clear polarity such as "I love it" or "I hate it".

Standard classification techniques have also been tested on Twitter [2], as have stream classification techniques such as the Multinomial Naive Bayes and the Stochastic Gradient Descent [3]. The major drawback of these approaches is that they require labeled data, which are very costly to obtain on a regular basis in a volume large enough to properly address concept drift. Further, active and semi-supervised strategies aim at reducing labeling and training efforts [5], but they still require training data to be sampled from a stationary distribution. In addition to that, in microblogs such as Twitter, the small document lengths restrict the possibility of using co-occurrence among terms and other standard text mining techniques to assign classes from an initial set of labeled documents.

Bias. Bias has been extensively studied by sociologists as a characteristic of people or entities that exhibit one or more of the following characteristics [29]: (i) a lack of proper balance and neutrality in argumentation, (ii) a lack of proper critical doubt, (iii) a particular position of the arguer regarding a subject, and (iv) a personal interest from the arguer in the outcome of the argument or discussion. We can find bias in almost any scenario where opinions are expressed, and one of the most common types of bias is political or ideological bias [15], In news media, selection bias guides decisions regarding of events are covered, while description bias is related to the veracity of the media coverage [7]. Given the subjective nature of bias, one key question here involves measuring bias. One strategy to measure media bias is to count the number of times a particular media outlet cites various sources, and compare this to the citation rates of those sources by congressmen; this approach, for instance, unveiled a strong liberal bias in the US news media [23]. In social media, bias has mainly been studied with respect to blogs. Some studies categorize political blogs according to their political bias and analyze the communication patterns and network structure that different political views induce [1]. Bias in political blogs has also been used to predict the bias of political articles in the online news media [10], by counting the number of liberal and conservative blogs that cite each article. These studies focus on the study of bias on the domain of blogs and on two main groups of blogs (liberal and conservative). In this paper, we extend these studies by analyzing bias on a microblog platform and considering an additional domain (i.e., sports).

Our Work. This paper lies between the two fields described above. We propose a *transfer learning* approach for real time sentiment analysis that connects both the abovementioned tasks. Transfer learning is applicable when a task is hard to solve (e.g., due to lack of labeled data or when the data becomes quickly outdated), but the task may benefit from knowledge obtained from similar tasks or domains [18, 25]. Experiments and techniques that apply transfer learning to sentiment analysis are relatively new; some recent works developed *domain adaptation* techniques, which comprise a special case of transfer learning when labeled data is available for one domain but absent in the target domain. This technique has been applied to transfer knowledge acquired from the analysis of opinions about a certain class of products (e.g., movie reviews) to classify documents about other products (e.g., books) [4, 18].

Transfer learning is an appealing strategy to provide real time sentiment analysis, because the availability of labeled data is even more limited than in classical scenarios such as product review. Moreover, text-based models can become quickly outdated because of the dynamic nature of online discussions. Furthermore, a similar domain with labeled data is not easy to find, as any comparable domain would present the same drawbacks. We then present a novel transfer learning approach for real time sentiment analysis: instead of learning text-based models to predict document polarity, we solve a different (but related) problem (i.e., social media user bias prediction) and then *transfer* the knowledge acquired to sentiment analysis algorithms. In contrast to recent domain adaptation efforts, in which the source task still involves dealing with textual data, the source task is chosen to provide consistent, robust patterns of user behavior in order to support the target task.

3. QUANTIFYING USER BIAS IN SOCIAL MEDIA

In this section we describe how we use social media endorsements to quantify user bias towards a topic. We start by discussing which types of information may indicate endorsement, and then we present our model of user bias prediction, we include an the opinion agreement graph and discuss how it can be used to quantify user bias.

3.1 User Endorsements in Social Media

As mentioned above, user endorsements express a user's support of a specific opinion which coincides with that user's bias. One piece of basic information that is frequently exploited as evidence of potential agreement between social network users is the social relationship that connects them. However, these relationships may not represent endorsements *per se*, because bias is topic-dependent, and two persons who are connected through a relationship may agree regarding a certain topic but disagree with respect to another topic. Even within a specific topic, social ties are not definitive evidence of agreement between users; in the 2010 Brazilian Presidential Elections, for example, about half of the users who followed one of the top two candidates in Twitter also followed the other. While this may indicate neutrality in some cases, we believe that a significant fraction of such users where actually following his or her preferred candidate and monitoring the other.

As compared to social ties, *social interactions* (such as the exchange of messages between users) have been shown to be stronger indicators of link strength among users [30]. Furthermore, interactions are usually associated with *content*; thus, they may be categorized into specific topics, unlike social ties.

Most social media platforms support *endorsement interactions*, through which a user explicitly agrees with other user with respect to certain content. In Twitter, *retweets* are endorsements in which a user propagates a message posted by another user to their list followers, while in Facebook users may explicitly support a content (and, indirectly, the user who generated it) by clicking on the "Like" button. Endorsements may be represented as a directed graph, where an edge (u,v) represents that user u has endorsed user v. Figure 1 shows an example of an endorsement graph. Nodes A and B are highlighted; their significance will be clarified later in this section.

3.2 Modeling User Bias Prediction

Our proposal to model user bias is based on the premise that similar users share a similar bias. Thus, before we analyze sentiments, we first determine the most similar users based on individual endorsements.

We model the user bias prediction problem as a *relational learning problem* [12]. More specifically, we treat it as a *within-network classification problem*, where the goal is to classify the nodes of a partially labeled network [21]. Assuming that there are K possible sides that a user may support regarding a given topic (e.g., candidates, parties or football clubs), we represent each user u as a *bias vector* $\vec{B_u} = [B_{u1}, ..., B_{uK}]$, where each B_{ui} quantifies the bias of user u towards side i. We expect that neutral users are equally distant (or close) to all sides, while biased users should be closer to one side (or a selection of sides) than others.

Formally, given K sides, a set of users U, a set of relationships E, and a set $A \subset U$, which contains users with known bias, we define the problem of predicting user bias as the estimation of $B_{ui}, \forall u \in U, 1 \leq i \leq K$.

Most methods proposed so far for addressing this problem infer the missing information in aggregate based on the hypothesis that linked or nearby nodes are likely to have the same labels [20]. However, a major challenge in our scenario is to determine the training set A, not only because bias quantifications are usually not available as ground truth, but also because quantifying bias is a subjective assessment for humans. More specifically, judging whether social media users are "too biased" towards one side of the discussion or "just a bit biased" is simply not feasible. That is, manually assigning a bias measure for a significant set of users is costly and not practical.

3.3 The Opinion Agreement Graph

We address the challenge of determining user bias by introducing a new graph, which we call the Opinion Agreement Graph (OAG), where neighbors (i.e., users that are close in the graph) tend to be similar. The rationale behind OAG is that the weight of an edge between two users should quantify both the intensity of their endorsement relative toward a given set of users, and the intensity of the endorsement of a given set of users toward them. We call those measures active and passive similarity, respectively, and they are calculated using frequent pattern mining techniques [27], as follows. The active similarity comes from a "database" $\mathcal{D}_\alpha$ of "transactions" where each transaction contains the users who endorsed a given user. For each pair of users (u, v) we define its active similarity $\alpha(u, v)$ as the *lift* of pair (u, v) in $\mathcal{D}_\alpha$. Lift is a standard metric of interest in association rule mining that captures how surprising a relationship among two items is, by comparing the frequency of their co-occurrence to the *expected* frequency of their co-occurrence, assuming that they are independent from one another [27]. Notice that the use of lift is compatible with the sociological definition of bias, which indicates biased behavior when someone supports one side or someone too strongly or too often [15].

The passive similarity ($\rho(u, v)$) of each pair of users (u, v) is calculated in the same way; the only difference is that $\mathcal{D}_\rho$, which is the passive database, contains the users endorsed by a given user in each transaction. Passive similarity is important for measuring bias using data beyond's user direct endorsements the direct control of the user: even if he/she does not endorse any content/user, we can assess his/her bias using the bias of users who endorse him/her. This is particularly useful to quantify the bias of news media profiles, which usually never endorse any content but must be evaluated based on how they are interpreted by the other users.

We then define the *Opinion Agreement Graph* $G(V, E)$ which contains pair-wise similarity information, where V is the set of vertices so that each vertex is associated with a user (item) from $\mathcal{D}_\alpha \cup \mathcal{D}_\rho$, and E is the set of weighted edges that represent relationships between pairs of users, with weight $E_{u,v}$ = mean($\alpha(u, v) + \rho(u, v)$).

In Figure 2, we show the resulting OAG calculated from endorsements (u, v) from Figure 1. Solid lines connect users that share an active bias similarity, and dashed lines represent passive biases.

Note that the semantics of an edge in the OAG is richer than a directed edge in the original endorsement graph: instead of simply showing that a given user endorsed another user, an edge in the OAG captures the strength of the similarity relationship of two users based on the set of users *as a whole.*

It is interesting to note that the different criteria used to define edges generate a graph topology that makes explicit relationships that were hidden in the original endorsement graph. Node 6, which is apparently a sink in Figure 1, now emerges as an important bridge between nodes A and B. Nodes 1, 2, 3 and 4, which share only one edge in the endorsement graph (i.e., an endorsement of user 2 by user 1), now form a dense sub-graph because they commonly endorse nodes 5 and A. The OAG also connects nodes that are not mutually reachable in the endorsement graph, such as pairs (5,6), (8,10), and (6,11). Node 7, however, does not appear in OAG, because it does not have common neighbors in terms of either incoming or outgoing edges.

Attractors. There usually are a few users that are clearly biased toward one or more sides of a discussion, based on prior knowledge. For example, in a political discussion, the official profiles of candidates and parties are expected to only express opinions that are favorable to their side. We label users whose bias is clearly identifiable as representative of a particular side in a discussion as *attractors*. In Figures 1 and 2, nodes A and B are assumed to be attractors. We associate each side i of a topic discussion with a set of attractors $A_i = [A_{i1}, \dots, A_{ij}]$, which are the nodes associated with the users chosen to represent that side.

Attractors serve as reliable sources of bias knowledge, and they allow us to determine the bias of other users. The bias of each node is its *proximity* from attractors that represent that side to all users

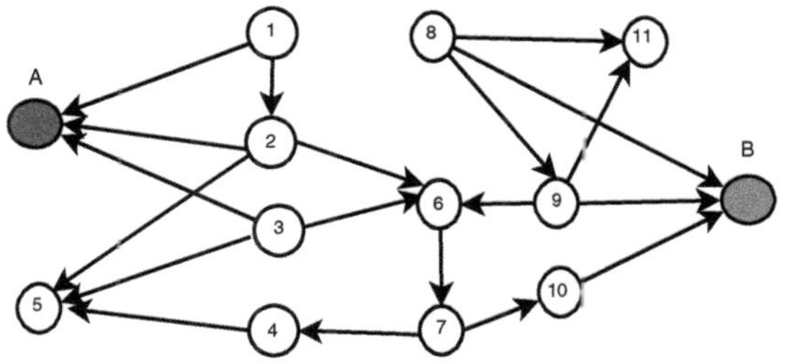

Figure 1: An hypothetical endorsement graph.

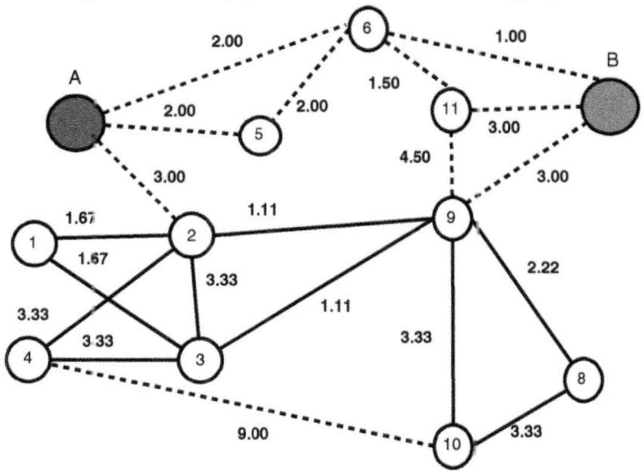

Figure 2: An OAG for endorsements from Figure 1, which connects users who endorse and are endorsed by common sets of users, respectively represented by solid and dashed lines. Edge weights are calculated based on the lift of the relationship between u and v. For example, nodes 9 and 11 are endorsed by the same users at a rate 4.5 times higher than expected. In constrast to the endorsement graph, edges in AOG are undirected and capture the global opinion of the whole network on the proximity of the users they connect.

in U. There are several strategies to determine this proximity; we used random walk to measure of proximity among nodes, due to its capacity to capture the multi-faceted relationship between nodes in a graph [8]. Formally,

$$B_{ui} = RandomWalk(G, A_i, u) \tag{1}$$

Our approach is in accordance with recent studies that demonstrate that using few seeds can be an effective strategy for propagating labels in graphs [9, 19]. Our scenario is particularly suitable for such a strategy because of the high consistency of the relationships we create, which indicate that the connected pair of users commonly endorse and/or are commonly endorsed by a *group* of users, in constrast to the original endorsement graph, in which any user endorsing another user creates a path in the graph. Furthermore, the edges in OAG are undirected, what turns the analysis of connectivity among users simpler and more effective.

Neutral user normalization. In a traditional within-network learning setting, a node linked to a large number of neighbors from class C_1 and a small number of neighbors from class C_2 will mostly likely be assigned to class C_1, which will be acceptable for most applications. In our scenario, however, we must consider that different sides of a discussion may have different strength levels in a social media platform, and thus they may differentially affect user bias values. In other words, it is not reasonable to directly compare proximities calculated from different starting distributions; the network, as a whole, may be more inclined to a subset of sides. To address this problem, we define the *neutral user* $\vec{N}$ as a user who endorses all other users, and has been endorsed by all other users. The bias vector $\vec{N}$ captures the global tendency of the network and is used to adjust all biases by a component-wise division:

$$\vec{B_u} = \frac{\vec{B_u}}{\vec{N}} \quad (2)$$

In the OAG shown in Figure 2, let A and B be attractors that represent two sides of a discussion, e.g., two candidate profiles. To predict the bias of users 1 to 11 regarding those two sides, we compute the random walk proximity of A and B towards each of those users. The resulting bias vector of each user is plotted in Figure 3. Note that nodes 9 and 11 are closer to B, while node 2 has a clear preference for attractor A. In particular, the direction of the bias vector indicates the bias of the user with respect to each attractor, whereas its magnitude captures the intensity of user activity. Thus, we have different patterns of neutrality: users who strongly support two or more sides, and users who strongly advocate against all sides.

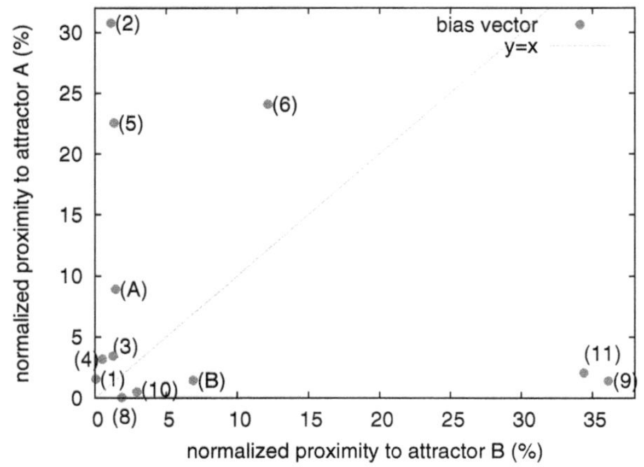

Figure 3: Bias vectors calculated as random walks from attractors.

4. CASE STUDY: POLITICAL AND SPORTS DISCUSSIONS IN TWITTER

We use the strategy introduced in Section 3 to quantify user bias in online discussions about two major events that took place in Brazil in 2010: the Presidential Elections and the Brazilian First Division Soccer League season. Both events were heavily debated on *Twitter*, which is a popular microblogging system that allow users to exchange short messages that are instantly made available to the set of users who follow the message's originator [16]. It is worth noticing that our proposal assumes that there is some polarity in the discussions as a basis for determining user bias, and these two scenarios are clearly polarized, discussed below.

The Brazilian presidential election campaign was held from June to October 2010, and two candidates led the polls since July 2010: Dilma Rousseff and Jose Serra. Rousseff and Serra each had more than 500,000 followers on Twitter, and both tried to use the system as one of the main means of communication with their voters. After the election came to a second round, Dilma Rousseff won the runoff with 56% of the vote.

In Table 1, we show a general overview of the two datasets considered in this work. The data collection of each dataset was performed using the Twitter API[1]; data was collected by focusing on the entities involved in each topic. In the `Elections-BR` dataset, the entities were the names of the two candidates starting in July 2010 and leading up to the 2010 Brazilian Presidential Elections (i.e., Dilma Rousseff and Jose Serra). To build the `Soccer` dataset, we considered the 12 most popular Brazilian soccer teams, which played on the Brazilian 2010 First Division Soccer League. In both domains, we can observe that a significant fraction of users endorsed tweets of others, using the retweet mechanism that propagates a tweet from one user to all of another user's followers.

[1] available at http://apiwiki.twitter.com/

Table 2 shows some statistics from the Opinion Agreement Graph for both datasets. The graphs considered only users who were involved in at least five endorsements. Note that a fraction of edges are a combination of active and passive similarities.

	Elections-BR	**Soccer**
number of nodes (users)	34,678	172,398
number of active bias edges	460,808	4,426,235
number of passive bias edges	607,331	886,895
number of active+passive bias edges	143,052	146,935
average degree	21.41	35.72
average edge weight	161.27	306.33

Table 2: Opinion Agreement Graph Statistics.

In their respective domains, the official profiles of candidates and soccer clubs are natural attractors. After computing the vector of proximities relative to these attractors and plotting the results in Figures 4 and 5, the high degree of polarization in the discussions on both topics becomes clear. Regarding the Brazilian Elections (Figure 4), at least 76% of users have a clear inclination towards one of the candidates. In the case of Twitter users who comment about soccer, the vast majority of users have a clear inclination towards one specific team (Figure 5).

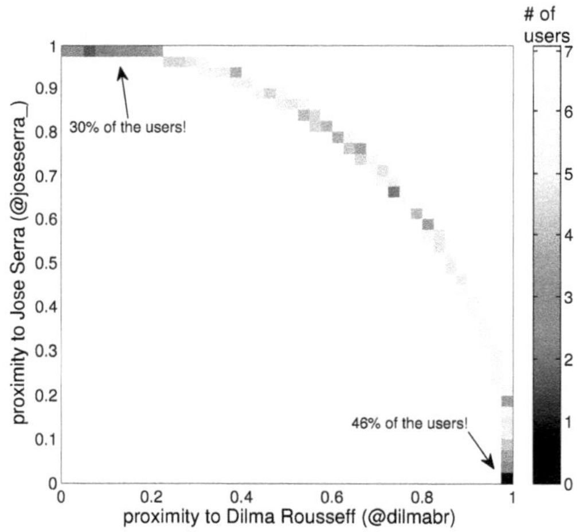

Figure 4: Bias vectors for the 2010 Brazilian Presidential Elections discussions. At least 76% of users are much closer to one side than the other, indicating a clear political bias.

Bias consistency. We empirically evaluate the robustness and consistency of our bias quantification of user tendencies. The intuition is that, given that users exhibit consistently a biased behavior, we should infer similar bias of a user based on two different samples of his/her endorsements.

We divided the set of endorsements into two sets; the first set comprised all of the endorsements observed during the first half of the data collection period, and the second set comprised the other

	Elections-BR	Soccer
period	2009-12-18 to 2010-10-03	2010-05-08 to 2010-09-07
entities	2 candidates	12 football clubs
number of tweets	7,707,192	8,828,520
number of retweets	2,511,779 (32.6% of tweets)	1,866,593 (21.1% of tweets)
number of users	1,022,396	1,633,537
number of users retwitting posts	489,214 (47.8% of users)	584,685 (35.7% of users)
number of retweeted users	179,441 (17.5% of users)	337,352 (20.6% of users)
avg. number of unique users retweeted by each user	16.41	5.54
avg. number of unique users that have retweeted each user	6.24	3.43

Table 1: General Overview of the Datasets.

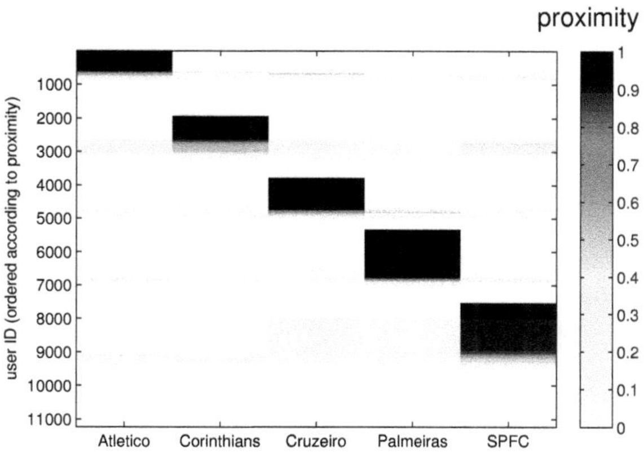

Figure 5: Bias vectors of users towards soccer teams. Supporters of Brazilian teams Atletico, Corinthians, Cruzeiro, Palmeiras and SPFC are identified. Users close to all teams are likely to be commentators or neutral media vehicles.

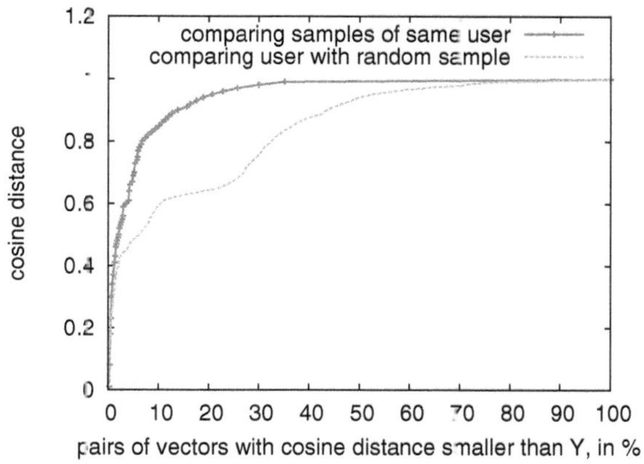

Figure 6: Small changes in user bias vectors calculated from different samples indicate robustness of user bias patterns in the ELECTIONS-BR dataset.

half. We then calculated the bias vector for all users in each set. We computed two bias measures for the second set. One considers the original pairs (u, v) of endorsements, and the other considers randomized endorsements. We then compute the cosine distance between each pair of vectors associated with each user from both sets, for users who were involved in endorsements in both sets. In Figure 6, we plot the cumulative distribution of the cosine distance for the two scenarios (that is, the original and randomized sets). Due to space constraints, we only show our analysis for the political discussion, but results were similar for the sports discussions.

Note that for more than 90% of users, vectors calculated from the two samples presented a high cosine similarity, greater than 0.80. However, when we compare bias vectors generated from the first set to the randomized samples from the second set, they are no longer similar. This means that, for the majority of users, the direction of their bias vectors does not change significantly across time but rather reflects the robustness and consistency of user behavior. Thus, it is not crucial to update the Opinion Agreement Graph and bias quantifications as new endorsements are observed, and as such, this task may simply be done at regular intervals. In addition, if the bias of a small sample of users is known, sentiment analysis based on that information is already possible, as we will show in the next section.

5. EXPLOITING USER BIAS FOR REAL-TIME SENTIMENT ANALYSIS

In this section we introduce our transfer-learning strategy for analyzing sentiments. The input is a constant flow of triplets in the form of $< author, d, e >$, where *author* is the opinion holder who wrote message d, which mentions an entity e. The goal is to predict the *polarity* $p = \{+, -\}$ of message d toward e. As discussed, there are several challenges in performing such a task and the dominant approach relies on extracting textual patterns from messages and exploiting these patterns to predict polarity.

User bias, in contrast, provides information that is more robust to these challenges, as it is more consistent than typical textual information (recall Figure 6 from Section 4). Thus, we propose an alternate approach that is based on transfer learning [25]. More specifically, we first solve a *source task* (denoted as τ_s), which involves estimating the bias of some users. This bias information is then *transferred* to the *target task* (denoted as τ_t), which is to predict the polarity of messages referencing entity e.

Propagating bias across terms. We transfer information from task τ_s to task τ_t by assuming that term t will be *positive* toward entity e if it is adopted more frequently by users biased toward entity e than by users of different sides in tweets that mention e. Similarly, t will be *negative* to entity e if it is adopted by a large number of users who oppose that entity, in contrast with the number of supporters of e. Neutral content is expected to be endorsed by both sides. To validate this intuition, in Figure 7 we plot the bias vector associated with users that referred to three different web pages in their tweets: a YouTube video with positive comments about Jose Serra (Figure 7a), an official video from Dilma Rousseff's campaign (Figure 7b), and a general news article about the 2010 Presidential Elections (Figure 7c).

In order to transform user bias into term bias, we take into account the bias vector associated with each user that used term t. A

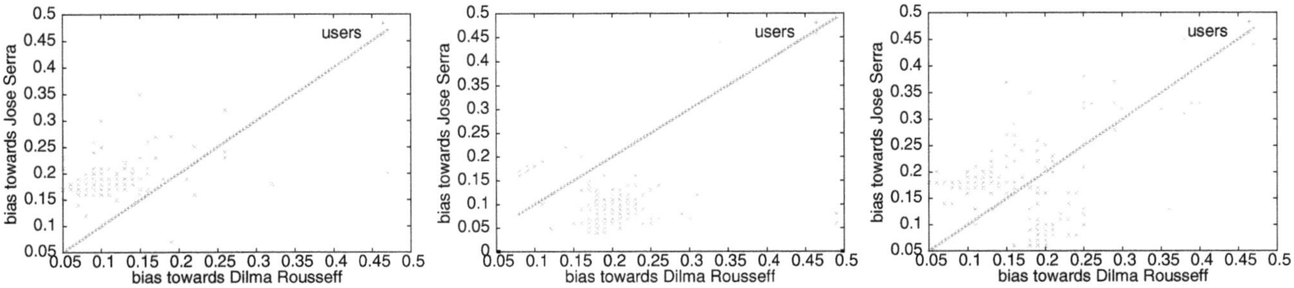

(a) positive term for Jose Serra (b) positive term for Dilma Rousseff (c) neutral term

Figure 7: User bias vectors for three different contents, which show that user bias is a good predictor of term polarity.

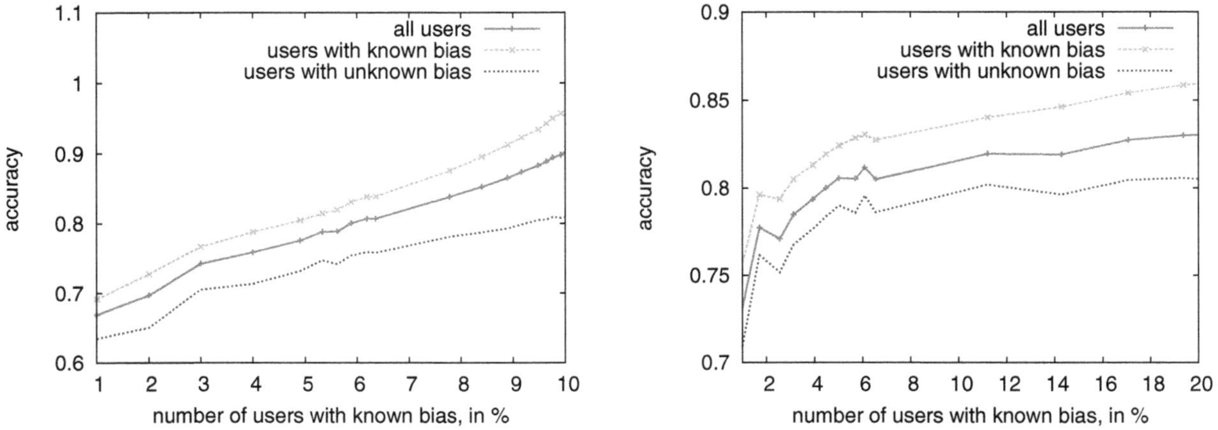

Figure 8: F1-accuracy level for different ratios of users with known bias. Left - ELECTIONS-BR dataset. Right - SOCCER dataset. As the ratio of users of known bias increases, the F1-measure increases, even for tweets posted by users with unknown bias.

possible unsupervised approach is to compute the sum vector of all users present in the Opinion Agreement Graph that refer to entity e by adopting term t:

$$\vec{B}_{t,e} = \sum_{u \in V} \vec{B}_u \qquad (3)$$

Note that this computation *propagates* user bias information to all messages that contain at least one term adopted by a user with known bias, thereby revealing the judgement of the content produced by users with unknown bias. This is important because it is expected that information on user bias will be available for only a portion of users, since many users are never involved in endorsement interactions, as shown in Table 1.

Dealing with concept drift. When a term is adopted for the first time, it will have the same bias as the corresponding user who adopted it. As new messages pass through the stream, $\vec{B}_{t,e}$ is updated incrementally. As such, users collectively judge new terms, referring to them (or not) in their messages. To predict the polarity of a message d, we first convert the bias vector of each term present in a message into *polarity probabilities*. Given the bias vector $\vec{B}_{t,e}$, and that $\vec{B}_{t,e,e}$ represents the strength of component e in $\vec{B}_{t,e}$, we calculate the probability that term t refers positively to entity e according to Equation 4.

$$\hat{p}(polarity = +|t,e) = \frac{B_{t,e,e}}{||\vec{B}_t||} \qquad (4)$$

Note that we compare the strength of bias to e in $\vec{B}_{t,e}$ with the magnitude of the bias vector. Specifically, $\hat{p}(polarity = -|t,e)$ may be calculated as 1 - $\hat{p}(polarity = +|t)$. To predict message polarity, we may adopt various strategies to combine those probabilities. Limited to 140 characters, Twitter messages are short, thus, we exploit a simple strategy for predicting message polarity, which is to consider the term of highest polarity in each tweet: $polarity = argmax(\hat{p}(polarity = x|t))$.

In Figure 8, we analyze the performance of our transfer learning approach as the fraction of users whose known bias varies. We report performance numbers using the $F1$ measure. To generate ground truth with respect to messages, we combined manual labeling with automatic labeling for messages containing tags that clearly indicated a preference for a specific entity. To make our evaluations fair, we removed all tags used to generate our labels from message content. We can see that the F1-measure increases as the proportion of users with known bias increases, up to a point at which F1 stabilizes. When the bias of 15% of users commenting on politics is known, the F1-measure equals 85%, while in the corresponding case for soccer, F1 is 90%. Note that the F1-measure for posts from users with unknown bias also increases as we transfer bias from a greater number of users, what further demonstrates the applicability of our user–term bias transfer approach.

Comparison with SVM. We now compare the F1-measure provided by our bias-based sentiment analysis model against the same metric provided by a typical SVM classifier. We chose SVM because it has already been successfully applied to various sentiment

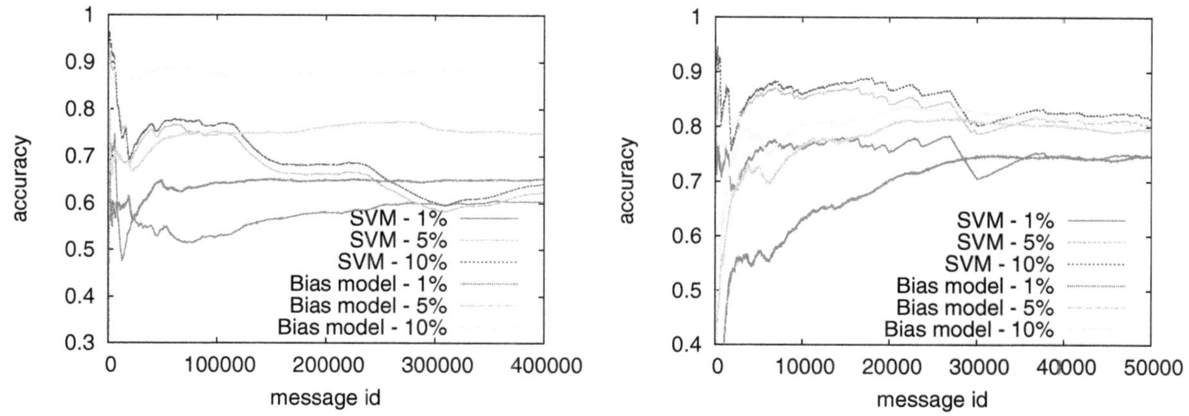

Figure 9: Bias-based model versus SVM classifier. Left - `ELECTIONS-BR` dataset. Right - `SOCCER` dataset.

analysis application scenarios, including the analysis of tweets [2, 28]. In order to execute this experimental comparison, we split each dataset into two partitions. The first partition is used for training, and it is comprised of the first 10% of tweets from each dataset. The second partition is used to validate each approach. Our comparison involves the execution of different training configurations. More specifically, each execution uses 10%, 50% or 100% of the training partition. For SVM, the training partition was used to train textual-based models, while for our bias-based model, we only considered endorsements in order to compute the OAG and generate bias assessments for users. When we compared the results on a chronologically ordered set of labeled tweets (i.e., the test partition), as shown in Figure 9, some important observations arise. We can note that the SVM F1-measure decreases across time for both datasets, which is evidence of changes in the textual feature distribution. In constrast, the bias-based sentiment classifier is able to mantain a stable F1-measure, as it incrementally incorporates bias information on new terms by propagating user bias. Indeed, the bias model performs better than SVM for the `ELECTIONS-BR` dataset, and it exhibits a similar F1-measure for the `SOCCER` dataset, even though is does not require labeled textual data, as in SVM.

Sentiment during a soccer match game. In order to demonstrate the capability of our sentiment analysis approach in analyzing the reactions of microblog users during live events, we have chosen to follow the buzz generated on Twitter during one of the most exciting matches of the Brazilian 2010 Soccer Season, which pitted team "Cruzeiro" against "Atletico Mineiro", two fierce rivals. Atletico won by 4-3, scoring three goals in the first half. In Figure 10, we plot positive and negative comments for each team during the game. Positive and negative comments were shown along the Y-axis. We have highlighted the timing of the goals with numbers (in black for Atletico Mineiro and in white for Cruzeiro). Note that positive comments tend to coincide with the timing of the goals, and are targeted at the team who scored. At 36', Cruzeiro conceded a third goal, and at that point, we detected a burst of negative comments about the team. Note that due to Atletico Mineiro's good game, almost no negative comments toward the team were observed during entire game. After the game finished, a spike of positive comments about Atletico was detected, at 95'.

6. CONCLUSIONS AND OUTLOOK

Real time sentiment analysis is a difficult task; labeled data is usually not available to support supervised classifiers, and debate about monitored topics may turn into unpredictable discussions.

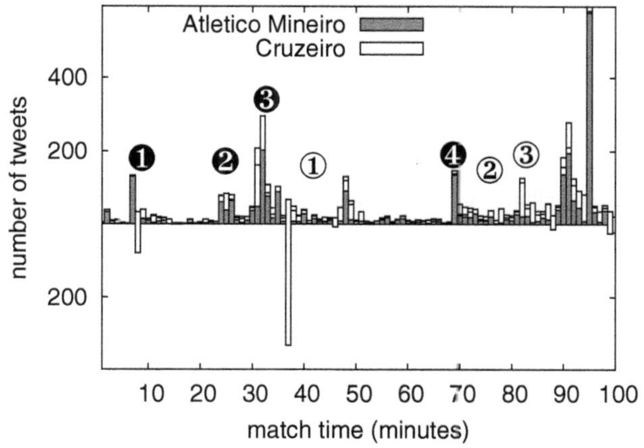

Figure 10: Stacked histogram showing sentiment variation during the Brazilian National Soccer League game Atletico Mineiro 4 – 3 Cruzeiro. Comment peaks coincide with goals.

Our contribution to the field of sentiment analysis addresses those challenges by proposing a novel transfer learning approach to topic-based real time sentiment analysis. We identify a suitable source task (that is, *opinion holder bias prediction*), which is motivated by sociological theories that argue that humans tend to have consistently biased opinions. We model this problem as a relational learning task by leveraging the network structure induced by the mutual endorsements among social media users. We then devise a simple and effective knowledge transfer strategy that propagates user bias to terms associated with user content. Then, term biases are combined to compute the overall content polarity.

Our work has demonstrated that the consistency in human bias enables robust, real time sentiment analysis without labeled text data, on topics in which polarization among user opinions occurs (such as politics and sports). By knowing the bias of only 10% of users who commented about those topics in Twitter, we were able to correctly classify the polarity of 80% to 90% of the tweets.

Our next step is to incorporate bias information into state-of-the art sentiment analysis algorithms. Furthermore, we want to evaluate the applicability of our strategy to contexts with lower degrees of polarization, such as sentiment analysis of product review data, and we hope to derive theoretical guarantees regarding performance based on the degree of polarization among opinion holders.

Acknowledgments

This work was partially supported by CNPq, CAPES, FAPEMIG, FINEP, InWeb and by UOL (`www.uol.com.br`) through its Research Scholarship Program, Proc. Number 20110215235100.

7. REFERENCES

[1] L. A. Adamic and N. Glance. The political blogosphere and the 2004 U.S. election: divided they blog. In *LinkKDD '05: Proceedings of the 3rd international workshop on Link discovery*, pages 36–43, New York, NY, USA, 2005. ACM.

[2] A. Bermingham and A. F. Smeaton. Classifying sentiment in microblogs: is brevity an advantage? In *Proceedings of the 19th ACM international conference on Information and knowledge management*, CIKM '10, pages 1833–1836, New York, NY, USA, 2010. ACM.

[3] A. Bermingham and A. F. Smeaton. Crowdsourced real-world sensing: sentiment analysis and the real-time web. In *AICS 2010 - Sentiment Analysis Workshop at Artificial Intelligence and Cognitive Science*, 2010.

[4] J. Blitzer, M. Dredze, and F. Pereira. Biographies, bollywood, boom-boxes and blenders: Domain adaptation for sentiment classification. In *Proceedings of the 45th Annual Meeting of the Association of Computational Linguistics*, Prague, Czech Republic, 2007. Assoc. for Computational Linguistics.

[5] O. Chapelle, B. Schölkopf, and A. Zien. Semi-supervised learning. MIT Press, 2006.

[6] N. A. Diakopoulos and D. A. Shamma. Characterizing debate performance via aggregated twitter sentiment. In *Proceedings of the 28th international conference on Human factors in computing systems*, CHI '10, pages 1195–1198, New York, NY, USA, 2010. ACM.

[7] J. Earl, A. Martin, J. D. McCarthy, and S. A. Soule. The use of newspaper data in the study of collective action. volume 30, pages 65–80. Annual Review of Sociology, 2004.

[8] F. Fouss, A. Pirotte, J.-M. Renders, and M. Saerens. Random-walk computation of similarities between nodes of a graph with application to collaborative recommendation. *IEEE Trans. on Knowl. and Data Eng.*, 19:355–369, 2007.

[9] B. Gallagher, H. Tong, T. Eliassi-Rad, and C. Faloutsos. Using ghost edges for classification in sparsely labeled networks. In *Proceeding of the 14th ACM SIGKDD international conference on Knowledge discovery and data mining*, KDD '08, New York, NY, USA, 2008. ACM.

[10] M. Gamon, S. Basu, D. Belenko, D. Fisher, M. Hurst, and A. C. König. Blews: Using blogs to provide context for news articles. In *In Proceedings of the 2nd International AAAI Conference on Weblogs and Social Media (ICWSM)*, 2008.

[11] S. Gerani, M. J. Carman, and F. Crestani. Proximity-based opinion retrieval. In *Proceeding of the 33rd international ACM SIGIR conference on Research and development in information retrieval*, SIGIR'10, pages 403–410, New York, NY, USA, 2010. ACM.

[12] L. Getoor and B. Taskar. *Introduction to Statistical Relational Learning (Adaptive Computation and Machine Learning)*. The MIT Press, 2007.

[13] B. J. Jansen, M. Zhang, K. Sobel, and A. Chowdury. Twitter power: Tweets as electronic word of mouth. *J. Am. Soc. Inf. Sci. Technol.*, 60:2169–2188, November 2009.

[14] W. Jin, H. H. Ho, and R. K. Srihari. Opinionminer: a novel machine learning system for web opinion mining and extraction. In *Proceedings of the 15th ACM SIGKDD international conference on Knowledge discovery and data mining*, KDD '09, New York, NY, USA, 2009. ACM.

[15] M. Kienpointner and W. Kindt. On the problem of bias in political argumentation : an investigation into discussions about political asylum in Germany and Austria. *Journal of Pragmatics*, 5(27):555–585, 1997.

[16] H. Kwak, C. Lee, H. Park, and S. Moon. What is twitter, a social network or a news media? In *WWW '10: Proceedings of the 19th international conference on World wide web*, pages 591–600, New York, NY, USA, 2010. ACM.

[17] J. Leskovec, L. Backstrom, and J. Kleinberg. Meme-tracking and the dynamics of the news cycle. In *Proceedings of the 15th ACM SIGKDD international conference on Knowledge discovery and data mining*, KDD '09, pages 497–506, New York, NY, USA, 2009. ACM.

[18] T. Li, V. Sindhwani, C. H. Q. Ding, and Y. Z. 0005. Bridging domains with words: Opinion analysis with matrix tri-factorizations. In *SDM*, pages 293–302, 2010.

[19] F. Lin and W. W. Cohen. Semi-supervised classification of network data using very few labels. In *ASONAM*, pages 192–199, 2010.

[20] S. A. Macskassy and F. Provost. A simple relational classifier. In *Proceedings of the Second Workshop on Multi-Relational Data Mining (MRDM-2003) at KDD-2003*, pages 64–76, 2003.

[21] S. A. Macskassy and F. Provost. Classification in networked data: A toolkit and a univariate case study. *J. Mach. Learn. Res.*, 8:935–983, December 2007.

[22] P. Melville, W. Gryc, and R. D. Lawrence. Sentiment analysis of blogs by combining lexical knowledge with text classification. In *Proceedings of the 15th ACM SIGKDD international conference on Knowledge discovery and data mining*, KDD '09, New York, NY, USA, 2009. ACM.

[23] J. Milyo and T. Groseclose. A measure of media bias. Working Papers 0501, Department of Economics, University of Missouri, Jan. 2005.

[24] B. O'Connor, R. Balasubramanyan, B. Routledge, and N. Smith. From tweets to polls: Linking text sentiment to public opinion time series. In *Proceedings of the Int'l AAAI Conference on Weblogs and Social Media*, 2010.

[25] S. J. Pan and Q. Yang. A survey on transfer learning. *IEEE Transactions on Knowledge and Data Engineering*, 22:1345–1359, 2010.

[26] B. Pang and L. Lee. Opinion mining and sentiment analysis. *Foundations and Trends in Information Retrieval*, 2(1-2):1–135, 2008.

[27] P. Tan, Steinbach, M., and V. Kumar. *Introduction to Data Mining, (First Edition)*. Addison-Wesley Longman Publishing Co., 2005.

[28] P. D. Turney. Thumbs up or thumbs down? semantic orientation applied to unsupervised classification of reviews. In *Proceedings of the 40th Annual Meeting on Assoc. for Computational Linguistics*, ACL '02, Morristown, NJ, USA, 2002. Assoc. for Computational Linguistics.

[29] D. Walton. Bias, critical doubt, and fallacies. Number 28, pages 1–22. Argumentation and Advocacy, 1991.

[30] R. Xiang, J. Neville, and M. Rogati. Modeling relationship strength in online social networks. In *Proceedings of the 19th international conference on World Wide Web*, WWW '10, pages 981–990, New York, NY, USA, 2010. ACM.

User Reputation in a Comment Rating Environment

Bee-Chung Chen, Jian Guo*, Belle Tseng and Jie Yang
Yahoo! Labs, Santa Clara, CA
*Harvard University
{beechun,belle,jielabs}@yahoo-inc.com, *jguo@hsph.harvard.edu

ABSTRACT

Reputable users are valuable assets of a web site. We focus on user reputation in a comment rating environment, where users make comments about content items and rate the comments of one another. Intuitively, a reputable user posts high quality comments and is highly rated by the user community. To our surprise, we find that the quality of a comment judged editorially is almost uncorrelated with the ratings that it receives, but can be predicted using standard text features, achieving accuracy as high as the agreement between two editors! However, extracting a pure reputation signal from ratings is difficult because of data sparseness and several confounding factors in users' voting behavior. To address these issues, we propose a novel bias-smoothed tensor model and empirically show that our model significantly outperforms a number of alternatives based on Yahoo! News, Yahoo! Buzz and Epinions datasets.

Categories and Subject Descriptors

H.3.4 [**Systems and Software**]: User profiles and alert services; G.3 [**Mathematics of Computing**]: Probability and Statistics

General Terms

Algorithms, Experimentation, Human Factors, Measurement

1. INTRODUCTION

The success of social media applications, such as news groups, blogs, online forums, question-answering systems, and social news services, depends highly on the quality and attractiveness of the contributions from regular users. Usually, good contributions are produced by a relatively small set of "reputable" users and consumed by a large user population. Intuitively, one can use a reputation score to quantify how good a user is at producing good contributions. At a high level, we distinguish between two types of reputation scores in a web system, *external scores* and *internal scores*. External (or public) reputation scores are user facing, and usually used to incentivize users for desired behavior; e.g., Yahoo! Answers displays the points that a user earned to recognize those who provided good answers. The key problem is how to design a good reward and incentive mechanism. This is an important problem, but this paper is devoted to another equally important problem, namely estimating internal reputation scores from data. Internal reputation scores are not revealed to users, but used to support internal applications. They are useful for at least the following use cases: (1) *Ranking and recommendation:* Content items (i.e., user contributions) can be ranked or recommended based on the author's reputation. Users can also be recommended to follow their content based on their reputation scores. These scores can also be used in any ranking algorithms as features. (2) *Content enrichment:* Media portals can use the contribution from reputable users to enrich existing content pages. For example, a news site can add related tweets from reputable users to a news article page. (3) *Crowdsourcing:* To reduce costs, it may be desirable for media portals to give some regular users privilege to curate (add value to) their content pages and moderate (manage) user contributions and the contributors. Reputable users are good candidates for such tasks. (4) *Abuse detection:* Reputable users are not likely to abuse the system. Reputation scores can be important features to improve abuse detectors. Also, reputable users may help report spam for removal.

Although we are interested in user reputation in any UGC (user-generated content) systems and the methods developed in this paper may also be applied to them, we ground our study in a particular kind of UGC environment, namely the comment rating environment where users make comments about content items and rate (e.g., thumb up or down) the comments of one another. The reasons are two-fold: (1) Focusing on a specific environment allows us to better understand the notion of reputation since discussion of reputation is usually not meaningful without a specific purpose and context [10, 42]. (2) Almost all UGC systems have an environment to allow users to express their opinions through comments. Thus, the scope of this study is not limited to the specific comment rating environment that we investigate — the results are useful for almost all UGC systems.

To determine the reputation score of a user, we identify two important and quite distinct dimensions:

- *Quality* of the comments that the user makes, which is defined by a set of guidelines that incorporate relevance, usefulness, abusiveness, writing quality, etc., and can be judged by human editors.

KDD'11, August 21–24, 2011, San Diego, California, USA.

- *Support* that the user receives from the user community, which is estimated from the rating data.

Originally, we focused on comment quality and would like to identify users who make high quality comments by appropriately aggregating the ratings that they receive. However, to our surprise, we find that the quality of a comment and the ratings on the comment are almost uncorrelated. Also to our surprise, we find that standard features extracted from comment text can be used to predict quality-based reputation scores with accuracy as high as the agreement between two trained editors (with rank correlation around 0.4 in terms of Kendall's tau). This result suggests that, even for trained editors, it is not easy to have high agreement to what means by high quality, and a few standard text features are sufficient to capture what they agree to. Therefore, we turn our focus to understanding what user ratings stand for. Further investigation reveals that users usually give high ratings to the opinions or viewpoints that they support irrespective of the quality; e.g., supporters of President Obama almost always give pro-Obama comments high ratings. Thus, the level of support that a user receives from the user community is an important notion of user reputation in the comment rating environment, almost orthogonal to quality.

However, it is challenging to quantify the level of support that a user receives based on biased rating data. If we were able to require all users to rate all comments, the average rating that a user receives (i.e., the average rating on all of his/her comments from all users) would be the level of support that he/she receives from the user community. We call this the unobserved *true support score* of a user. However, each user j usually only receives ratings from a small and biased subset of users. For example, the subset of users may happen to include only users who share the same opinion as user j. One of our main technical contributions is to address how to approximate the true support score using sparse and biased rating data.

Any reputation system is subject to gaming and attack. A rigorous solution to this issue is future work.

Contributions and Outline: Specifically, we make the following contributions:

- *Difference between comment quality and ratings:* In Section 2, we define comment quality and show the surprising lack of correlation between quality and ratings based on more than ten thousand editorially labeled comments on Yahoo! News and Yahoo! Buzz. To our knowledge, this lack of correlation has not been reported before. In Section 3, we also show that standard machine-learning models with standard text features can achieve high accuracy for predicting quality-based user reputation, whereas rating-based methods (including PageRank on the rating graph) fail miserably.
- *Average rating over the entire user community as a support-based reputation score:* In Section 4, we define support-based user reputation and propose a simple method to approximate the true support score based on a rating prediction model built on rating data. To our knowledge, this approach to defining user reputation has not been studied before. Since users interact with one another in multiple contexts (e.g., politics vs. entertainment), we further break down support scores by contexts.
- *Bias-smoothed tensor model:* In Section 5, we develop a novel latent factor model for multi-context rating prediction. This model is based on a rating-generation assumption especially suited for estimating user reputation in a comment rating environment. Interesting, the true support score corresponds to the author-reputation factor in the model, which represents reputation after removing a number of confounding factors. In Section 6, we show strong empirical performance of the proposed model.

We conclude and discuss related work in Section 7.

2. EDITORIAL AND RATING DATA

Users who make high quality comments are valuable. It is sometimes believed that, by appropriately aggregating the ratings, we can find those users. In this section, we define the quality-based reputation score, and show that user ratings are almost uncorrelated with comment quality.

Data: We collected comment rating data from Yahoo! Buzz (Y!Buzz) and Yahoo! News (Y!News) during a 3-month period. Users on these sites can post comments on articles and rate the comments of one another by thumb-up votes (positive ratings) and thumb-down votes (negative ratings). We say that user i gives user j a rating if i gives a rating to j's comment. The Y!Buzz dataset includes 1.8M comments authored by 217K users and 11M ratings given by 184K users. The Y!News dataset includes 9M comments authored by 1.6M users and 67M ratings given by 1.5M users.

2.1 Defining Quality Scores

We define the quality score of a comment based on a set of editorial guidelines, and the quality score of a user is obtained by averaging the quality scores of his/her comments. Specifically, we asked Yahoo! editors (who are hired and trained to label web pages for different tasks) to label each comment using the following five labels:

- *Excellent:* Expert opinion, superb quality, thoughtful, voice of reasoning, very useful.
- *Good:* Somewhat useful/thoughtful, informative, interesting, good quality.
- *Fair:* No meaningful/valuable point, but not harmful.
- *Bad:* Irrelevant to the context (article and other comments), bad writing.
- *Abuse:* In violation of terms of service, e.g., spam, harassment, adult content.

A set of example comments for each of the five labels is also given to the editors to help distinguish different labels. We then assign numerical scores to these labels: Excellent=2, Good=1, Fair=0, Bad=−1, and Abuse=−2. We tried other ways of mapping levels to numerical scores and did not observe any significant difference in any of our results. The quality-based reputation score of a user is the average score of the comments posted by the user. The average is, in fact, computed base on 10 labeled comments per user. In total, we collected 13,700 editorial labels on comments in Yahoo! Buzz and 3,000 on comments in Yahoo! News.

2.2 Difference between Quality and Ratings

At first glance, one might think user ratings should have some correlation with quality scores. However, we find that these two do not correlate well. To understand the correlation, we randomly select 707 Yahoo! Buzz users who re-

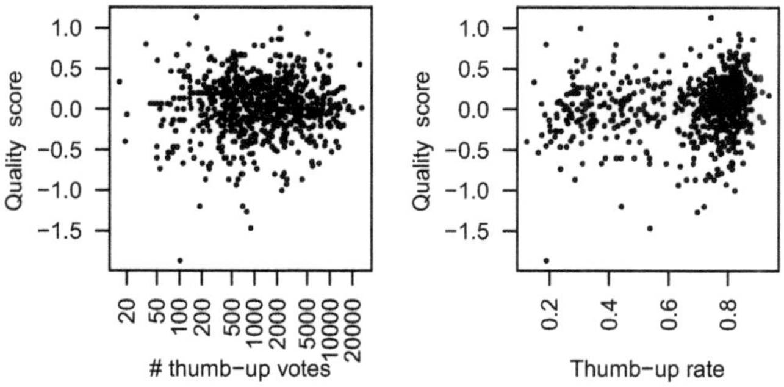

Figure 1: Editorial score vs. rating-based score

ceived at least 100 ratings. Note that on Yahoo! Buzz, users rate comments by thumb-up (positive rating) or thumb-down (negative rating) votes. For each of these user, we obtain his/her quality score and two versions of simple rating-based scores: *#thumb-up votes* of a user is the number of thumb-up votes that the user receives, and the *thumb-up rate* is the user's #thumb-up votes divided by the total number of votes that he/she receives. We also tried different kinds of denominators for thumb-up rate, e.g., number of comments he/she posts, number of unique user rated his/her comments, etc, and observe no significant difference. Figure 1 shows the scatter plots that compare the quality scores to these two rating-based scores. Each point represents one user. If quality scores correlate well with rating-based scores, we should see points along the diagonal line. However, the points in the two plots are almost random, showing lack of correlation between the quality and rating-based scores. The same behavior is observed in Yahoo! News. In Section 3, we will show that more complicated ways of using user ratings to predict quality scores (including a PageRank-style method) also fail to be useful. After inspecting the comments of those users, we find that:

- Editors rate a comment based on the guidelines.
- Users vote for whatever they support. For example, a low quality comment that supports President Obama may draw many thumb-up votes from his supporters. Likewise, a high quality comment that supports President Obama may draw many thumb-down votes from people who are against him.

The above two criteria are very different.

3. PREDICTING QUALITY SCORES

We now apply machine-learning methods to predict quality scores and show that standard text features can capture comment quality to the level of the agreement between two different editors who independently judge those comments.

Features: We extract the following sets of features from a comment: (1) *Length:* Numbers of total words, unique words and characters in a comment. (2) *Lexical diversity:* Number of unique words divided by number of words. (3) *Textual similarity:* Similarity between the comment and the article that the comment is about. We include cosine similarity and jaccard similarity. (4) *Bad words:* We collected hundreds of words considered bad in comments and count the number of bad words in the comment. (5) *Spellcheck:* Percentage of words in the comment that are not in a standard English dictionary. (6) *Readability:* Three readability scores [28, 11, 16]. (7) *Capital words:* Percentage of capital words, percentage of capital characters. (8) *Rating:* Numbers of thumb-up and thumb-down votes, thumb-up rate.

Table 1: Accuracy of Quality Score Prediction

Model	Rank correlation			
	Yahoo! Buzz		Yahoo! News	
	use vote	no vote	use vote	no vote
Random Forest	0.4164	0.4049	0.4601	0.4684
GBRank	0.4054	0.4016	0.4554	0.4515
Linear model	0.3926	0.3901	0.4706	0.4619
Two editors	0.4157		0.4280	
PageRank	0.0576		-0.0368	

Models: We build and compare a number of machine-learning models: Random forest [8], GBRank [44] and linear regression model. Each model takes the features of a comment as the input and predict the editorial score of that comment. The predicted reputation score of a user is the average of the predicted scores of his/her comments.

PageRank: As PageRank-style methods are frequently used to identify authority or reputation, we include an edge-weighted version of PageRank in our comparison. Rating data can be represented as a graph. We draw an edge from user i to user j if i gives a rating to the comment of j. Let n_{ij}^{+} and n_{ij}^{-} denote the number of positive ratings (thumb-up) and the number of negative ratings (thumb-down) that i gives j. We try several different ways of defining edge weights w_{ij}. The first is an unweighted version; i.e., $w_{ij} = 1$ if $n_{ij}^{+} > 0$; otherwise, $w_{ij} = 0$. Then, we consider $w_{ij}(b_0, b_1, b_2) = \lfloor b_0 + b_1 n_{ji}^{+} - b_2 n_{ji}^{-} \rfloor$; with different settings of b_0, b_1, b_2, we can obtain different weighting schemes. We tune b_0, b_1, b_2 and the damping factor settings heavily and only report the result of the best setting. This heavy tuning may lead to overfitting. However, what we will see is that even overfitted PageRank cannot predict quality scores.

Evaluation: To evaluate the accuracy of a model, we first rank the users by their predicted quality scores and then determine how well it correlates with the ranking produced by the editor-labeled ground-truth quality scores. A rank correlation metric (Kendall's tau) is used to measure the accuracy. If the two ranked lists are the same, the rank correlation is 1. If the model just randomly predicts scores, we get 0. We show the 5-fold cross validation results in Table 1. To understand the importance of ratings in a model, we compare a version of the model that uses rating features (the "use vote" column) to a version that does not (the "no vote" column). To understand how good a rank correlation value (e.g., 0.41) is, we asked two editors to label the same set of comments independently and compute two quality scores for each user in the selected set. The rank correlation between two editors is shown in Table 1. As can be seen, the performance of the models are as good as the agreement between two editors. In the Yahoo! News case, surprisingly our models produce better rank correlations than the agreement between two editors. This is unexpected, but possible because our models are trained and tested based on quality scores given by a single editor per comment (though different comments may be judged by different editors), but the two editors make independent judgment without looking at the labels generated by each other.

Discussion: We first note that PageRank fails miserably even after heavy tuning. Next, by comparing the "use vote" column with the "no vote" column, we find that rating-based features almost add no value to quality prediction models. Finally, we note that the rank correlation 0.41~0.42 between two editors is not very high. We did refine the guidelines after each round of judgment by going through some examples; however, no significant improvement is observed. Table 1 suggests that our text features almost completely capture what different editors think in common in terms of comment quality.

4. SUPPORT-BASED REPUTATION

As discussed in Section 2.2, users' ratings show their support for different opinions or viewpoints, instead of comment quality. Thus, the level of support that a user receives from the user community is an important notion of reputation in a comment rating environment. Because users interact with one another in multiple contexts (e.g., topics or content categories), it is useful to quantify support level on a per-context basis. In this section, we define support-based reputation scores or simply called *support scores*.

Contexts: A user has different levels of expertise and different degrees of interest in different areas, thus receiving different levels of support. A single score for each user is usually insufficient. For example, a user who receives a high level of support in the context of politics may not receive any support in the context of entertainment. Thus, it is usually desirable to break comments down by *contexts*, which may be topics, categories, etc., and estimate a support score for each user in each context. Now, the question is what should be the contexts in which we estimate support scores. In this paper, we define the set of contexts to be the set of the topic categories that Yahoo! Buzz and Yahoo! News use to classify news articles. Specifically, the context of a comment is the category of the news article that the comment is about, and the context of a rating is the context of the rated comment. Example categories include Business, Entertainment, Health, Lifestyle, Politics, Technology, Sports, etc. These categories are also what the users use to find content items on the sites, and thus, are reasonable choices to define support scores on. If the categories are not available, one can apply topic discovery techniques (e.g., Latent Dirichlet Allocation [5]) to assign topics to comments.

Notation: The rating data consists of a set of observed ratings. We say that user i gives user j a rating (or user i rates user j) if i gives a rating to a comment authored by user j. We call i the rater and j the author. Let y_{ijk} denote the rating that user i gives user j in context k, and $\mathcal{U}$ denote the set of all users in the comment rating environment.

True support score: We define the *true support score* s_{jk} of user j in context k as the average rating that user j would receive in context k from all users, i.e., $s_{jk} = \sum_{i \in \mathcal{U}} y_{ijk}/|\mathcal{U}|$, where $|\mathcal{U}|$ denote the size of set $\mathcal{U}$. For example, consider a binary rating environment (e.g., thumb-up vs. thumb-down). The true support score of user j is proportional[1] to the total number of users who would rate user j positively if we were able to require all users to rate user j. It is a very natural and ideal definition of support. It is also interesting to note that true support scores are not sensitive to gaming and attacks since it involves a summation over the entire user base (as long as attackers do not control a large fraction of users). However, these scores are not computable from rating data because each user j usually only receives ratings from a small subset of users.

[1] The denominator of a true support score is a constant.

Challenges: It is challenging to estimate the true support scores. One simple approach would be to compute the support score of user j in context k as the average rating over the small subset of users who have rated user j in context k. The major issues with this approach are:

- *Data sparseness:* Because the subset is small, this average is usually unreliable.
- *Biased sample:* Even if the user subset is large enough to compute a reliable average number, it may not be a representative sample of the entire user base. For example, this subset of users may happen to include only users who like one another (e.g., friends), or users who share the same viewpoint as user j in the context.

Prediction-based support score: One conceptually simple approach to approximate the true support score is to use a rating-prediction model — whenever we see an unobserved (voter i, author j, context k) triple, we use the predicted rating $\hat{y}_{ijk}$, which is output from the model. The accuracy of these predicted support scores are directly linked to the accuracy of the rating-prediction model used; the better the model, the better the scores. However, averaging over all users can still be quite computationally intensive; nevertheless, one may simply use a large enough random sample to compute the average. In the next section, we propose a novel rating-prediction model that is accurate and does not require this averaging process to obtain support scores.

5. BIAS-SMOOTHED TENSOR MODEL

In this section, we introduce a novel latent factor model for rating prediction, which is useful for extracting context-specific reputation scores from rating data. This model is motivated by the observation that users' ratings are usually generated according to several factors:

- *Author reputation:* The comments made by reputable users tend to receive high ratings.
- *Rater bias:* Some users rate more positively than others.
- *Agreement in opinions:* Some users vote positively (or negatively) on a comment because they agree (or disagree) with the opinion in the comment, even when the comment has no useful information (e.g., "Obama is great").

To extract pure reputation scores (author reputation) from rating data, it is important to remove the effect of confounding factors (rater bias and agreement in opinions). For example, a positive vote from a user who always rates user j positively should carry little weight when computing user j's reputation score. Interestingly, as we will see later, the author reputation factor with the effect of confounding factors removed corresponds to the true support score.

5.1 Model

Notation: In addition to ratings, we may also have features for users. Since we always use i to denote a rater and j to denote an author, we abuse the notation a bit by using $\boldsymbol{x}_{ik}$ to denote user i's feature vector when he/she acts as a rater in context k and $\boldsymbol{x}_{jk}$ to denote user j's feature vector when he/she acts as an author in context k.

Model specification: We assume that each rating y_{ijk} is generated according to (1) the rater bias α_{ik} of user i in context k, (2) the author reputation factor β_{jk} of user j in context k and (3) the similarity between the opinions of the two users in context k, which is modeled as a tensor product $\langle \boldsymbol{v}_i, \boldsymbol{v}_j, \boldsymbol{w}_k \rangle = \sum_\ell v_{i\ell} v_{j\ell} w_{j\ell}$ of the opinion factor vectors $\boldsymbol{v}_i$, $\boldsymbol{v}_j$ of the two users and a context-specific weight vector $\boldsymbol{w}_k$. We use $\dim(v)$ to denote the number of dimensions of the opinion factor vector of a user. Mathematically, we assume:

$$y_{ijk} \sim N(\mu_{ijk},\ \sigma_y^2) \text{ or Bernoulli}(1/(1+\exp\{-\mu_{ijk}\}))$$
$$\mu_{ijk} = \alpha_{ik} + \beta_{jk} + \langle \boldsymbol{v}_i, \boldsymbol{v}_j, \boldsymbol{w}_k \rangle$$

For numeric ratings, we use the Gaussian distribution denoted by N(mean,var); for binary ratings, we use the Bernoulli distribution and the standard logistic transformation. We then specify the prior distributions of the factors:

$$\alpha_{ik} \sim N(\boldsymbol{g}_k' \boldsymbol{x}_{ik} + q_k \alpha_i,\ \sigma_{\alpha,k}^2), \qquad \alpha_i \sim N(0,1) \qquad (1)$$
$$\beta_{jk} \sim N(\boldsymbol{d}_k' \boldsymbol{x}_{jk} + r_k \beta_j,\ \sigma_{\beta,k}^2), \qquad \beta_j \sim N(0,1) \qquad (2)$$
$$\boldsymbol{v}_i \sim N(\boldsymbol{0},\ \sigma_v^2 I), \qquad \boldsymbol{w}_k \sim N(\boldsymbol{0}, I) \qquad (3)$$

These priors describe the generation process of the factors. We first generate a global rater-bias factor α_i for user i from the standard Gaussian. Then, the expected value of the context-specific factor $E[\alpha_{ik}]$ for context k is determined by a linear function $\boldsymbol{g}_k' \boldsymbol{x}_{ik} + q_k \alpha_i$ of the global factor α_i and features $\boldsymbol{x}_{ik}$, where $\boldsymbol{g}_k$ and q_k are the context-specific regression weights. The actual context-specific factor α_{ik} is then generated by adding a Gaussian random effect to $E[\alpha_{ik}]$ to allow deviation from the linear function. β_{jk} is generated in a similar way, where β_j is the global author-reputation factor for user j, and $\boldsymbol{d}_k$ and r_k are the regression weights for context k. For the opinion-related factors $\boldsymbol{v}_i$ and $\boldsymbol{w}_k$, we just put a Gaussian zero-mean prior, assuming no opinion preference a priori. We call this model the *bias-smoothed tensor model,* because the per-user context-specific "bias" terms in the model (i.e., α_{ik} and β_{jk}) are "smoothed" based on the global factors (i.e., α_i and β_j). We note that this model can be thought of as a significant extension to [18] by adding regression-based hierarchical priors to the per-user bias terms.

To summarize, given a rating dataset $\boldsymbol{y} = \{y_{ijk}\}$, we will learn the factors $\boldsymbol{\eta} = \{\alpha_{ik}, \beta_{jk}, \alpha_i, \beta_j, \boldsymbol{v}_i, \boldsymbol{w}_k\}$ and prior parameters (regression weights and variances) $\boldsymbol{\Theta} = \{\boldsymbol{g}_k, \boldsymbol{d}_k, q_k, r_k, \sigma_y^2, \sigma_{\alpha,k}^2, \sigma_{\beta,k}^2, \sigma_{v,k}^2\}$ from the data. Note that it is appropriate to set the prior variances of α_i, β_j and $\boldsymbol{w}_k$ to 1, because q_k, r_k and $\boldsymbol{v}_i$ are learned from data; if we scale up the variance of α_i, q_k will automatically be scaled down, since they are not separable in $q_k \alpha_i$.

Special case: Smoothed reputation-only model: To better understand the above model, it is instructive to study a simplified special case. Let us keep only the author-reputation factors and set others to zero (thus called reputation-only model); i.e.,

$$\mu_{ijk} = \beta_{jk}, \quad \beta_{jk} \sim N(\boldsymbol{d}_k' \boldsymbol{x}_{jk} + r_k \beta_j,\ \sigma_{\beta,k}^2), \quad \beta_j \sim N(0,1)$$

This model handles the data sparseness issue, but does not address the sample bias issue (discussed in Section 4). To understand how it handles data sparseness, we note that if we have a lot of rating data for user j in context k, the author-reputation factor β_{jk} would mostly depend on the observed data. However, if the data is sparse, β_{jk} would be influenced by the rating data of user j in other contexts and the user features $\boldsymbol{x}_{jk}$. In fact, β_{jk} would be "shrunk" toward $\boldsymbol{d}_k' \boldsymbol{x}_{jk} + r_k \beta_j$. The second term $r_k \beta_j$ combines information from other contexts; β_j is intuitively a weighted average over β_{jk} and the weight of context k depends on $\sigma_{\beta,k}^2$, which is learned from data. The first term $\boldsymbol{d}_k' \boldsymbol{x}_{jk}$ is the prediction based on features $\boldsymbol{x}_{jk}$ and the weight vector $\boldsymbol{d}_k$ is learned from data; when the features are predictive, the number of ratings required to achieve good accuracy would be small. Intuitively, the potentially unstable β_{jk} is "smoothed" based on a regression on β_j and $\boldsymbol{x}_{jk}$. The full model also enjoys this nice property.

Opinion factors: To understand why $\langle \boldsymbol{v}_i, \boldsymbol{v}_j, \boldsymbol{w}_k \rangle$ represents agreement between opinions, consider another simplified special case where $\dim(v) = 1$ and $\boldsymbol{w}_k = 1$. Intuitively, positive v_i means a positive opinion on an issue; negative v_i means a negative opinion on the issue; and the absolute value of v_i represents the strength of the opinion. If v_i and v_j are both positive or both negative, $\langle \boldsymbol{v}_i, \boldsymbol{v}_j, \boldsymbol{w}_k \rangle = v_i' v_j$ is high (at least a positive number); otherwise, it is low (a negative number). The prior $v_i \sim N(0, \sigma_v^2 I)$ will "shrink" v_i toward zero, meaning if we do not have much data for a user, we do not associate him/her with a strong opinion. The extension from $\dim(v) = 1$ to n allows the model to capture opinions on multiple latent issues. Ideally, each context should have a different set of issues. This would lead to a high dimensionality problem; e.g., if we have m contexts and n issues per context, then $\dim(v) = mn$. The extension from fixing $\boldsymbol{w}_k = 1$ to learning $\boldsymbol{w}_k$ from data allows us to reduce the dimensionality by assuming that the agreement between two users in context k is determined by applying a context-specific weight vector $\boldsymbol{w}_k$ to the global latent opinion profiles $\boldsymbol{v}_i$, $\boldsymbol{v}_j$ of the two users.

5.2 Predicted Support Scores

Let $\hat{y}_{ijk}$ be the predicted rating that user i would give user j in context k, $\bar{\alpha}_k = \sum_i \alpha_{ik}/|\mathcal{U}|$ and $\bar{\boldsymbol{v}} = \sum_i \boldsymbol{v}_i/|\mathcal{U}|$. For simplicity, we first consider the Gaussian model. The predicted support score for user j in context k is

$$\hat{s}_{jk} = \sum_{i \in \mathcal{U}} \hat{y}_{ijk}/|\mathcal{U}| = \beta_{jk} + \bar{\alpha}_k + \langle \bar{\boldsymbol{v}}, \boldsymbol{v}_j, \boldsymbol{w}_k \rangle$$

Efficient computation: Notice that $\bar{\alpha}_k$ and $\bar{\boldsymbol{v}}$ are sufficient statistics for computing $\hat{s}_{jk}$. We only need to compute $\bar{\alpha}_k$ and $\bar{\boldsymbol{v}}$ once; after that, the computation of $\hat{s}_{jk}$ does not involve any averaging.

Removing global opinion bias: Sometimes it is useful to force $\bar{\boldsymbol{v}} = 0$, meaning that we believe, after averaging over all users, there is no global opinion bias. After training, this can be done by defining the following factors: $\boldsymbol{v}_i^{\text{new}} = \boldsymbol{v}_i - \bar{\boldsymbol{v}}$, $\alpha_{ik}^{\text{new}} = \alpha_{ik} + \langle \boldsymbol{v}_i^{\text{new}}, \bar{\boldsymbol{v}}, \boldsymbol{w}_k \rangle$ and $\beta_{jk}^{\text{new}} = \beta_{jk} + \langle \boldsymbol{v}_j^{\text{new}}, \bar{\boldsymbol{v}}, \boldsymbol{w}_k \rangle$. It can be shown that

$$\mu_{ijk} = \alpha_{ik}^{\text{new}} + \beta_{jk}^{\text{new}} + \langle \boldsymbol{v}_i^{\text{new}}, \boldsymbol{v}_j^{\text{new}}, \boldsymbol{w}_k \rangle + c_k,$$

where c_k is a constant, and $\bar{\boldsymbol{v}}^{\text{new}} = 0$.

Confounding factor removal: Consider the case where $\bar{\boldsymbol{v}} = 0$ or $\bar{\boldsymbol{v}}^{\text{new}} = 0$. We ignore the superscript for succinctness. Then, $\hat{s}_{jk} = \beta_{jk} + \bar{\alpha}_k$. Since $\bar{\alpha}_k$ is a constant, the predicted support score is basically the author-reputation factor β_{jk}.

Logistic model: For the logistic model, the correspondence is not that direct. However, since reputation scores are used to rank users, the absolute values of the scores are not important. Thus, we may redefine the support score s_{jk} to be the average log-odds (instead of probability or predicted rating) that other users would rate user j positively in context k. Then, the above discussion applies.

5.3 Fitting Procedure

We use the Monte Carlo EM algorithm [6] to fit the model. The EM algorithm iterates between an E-step and an M-step until convergence. Let $\hat{\mathbf{\Theta}}^{(t)}$ denote the current estimated value of the set of prior parameters $\mathbf{\Theta}$ (defined in Section 5.1) at the beginning of the tth iteration.

- **E-step:** We take expectation of the complete data log likelihood with respect to the posterior of latent factors $\boldsymbol{\eta}$ conditional on the observed data $\boldsymbol{y}$ and the current estimate of $\mathbf{\Theta}$; i.e., compute
$$f_t(\mathbf{\Theta}) = E_{\boldsymbol{\eta}\sim\Pr(\boldsymbol{\eta}\,|\,\boldsymbol{y},\hat{\mathbf{\Theta}}^{(t)})}[\log\Pr(\boldsymbol{y},\boldsymbol{\eta}\,|\,\mathbf{\Theta})]$$
as a function of $\mathbf{\Theta}$, where the expectation is taken over the posterior distribution of $(\boldsymbol{\eta}\,|\,\boldsymbol{y},\hat{\mathbf{\Theta}}^{(t)})$, which is not in closed-form, thus, approximated by Monte Carlo mean.
- **M-step:** We maximize the expected complete data log likelihood from the E-step to obtain updated values of $\mathbf{\Theta}$; i.e., find $\hat{\mathbf{\Theta}}^{(t+1)} = \arg\max_{\mathbf{\Theta}} f_t(\mathbf{\Theta})$.

Note that the actual computation in the E-step is to generate sufficient statistics for computing $\arg\max_{\mathbf{\Theta}} f_t(\mathbf{\Theta})$, so that we do not need to scan the raw data every time when we need to evaluate $f_t(\mathbf{\Theta})$. At the end, we obtain a maximum likelihood estimate of $\mathbf{\Theta}$, i.e.,

$$\arg\max_{\mathbf{\Theta}}\Pr(\boldsymbol{y}\,|\,\mathbf{\Theta}) = \arg\max_{\mathbf{\Theta}}\int\Pr(\boldsymbol{y},\boldsymbol{\eta}\,|\,\mathbf{\Theta})\,d\boldsymbol{\eta},$$

modulo local maximums and Monte Carlo errors. We then can use the estimated $\hat{\mathbf{\Theta}}$ to obtain the posterior distribution of the factors $(\boldsymbol{\eta}\,|\,\boldsymbol{y},\hat{\mathbf{\Theta}})$. For simplicity, we only describe the algorithm to fit the Gaussian model. The logistic model for binary response is fitted using variational approximation [22]. For convenience, we provide the formulas of $\log\Pr(\boldsymbol{y},\boldsymbol{\eta}\,|\,\mathbf{\Theta})$ and $E_{\boldsymbol{\eta}}[\log\Pr(\boldsymbol{y},\boldsymbol{\eta}\,|\,\mathbf{\Theta})]$ in the appendix.

5.4 E-Step

We use a Gibbs sampler to draw L samples of the factors and compute the Monte Carlo mean.

Draw α_i and α_{ik}: Now, consider that all the other factors are given. Let $o_{ijk} = y_{ijk} - \beta_{jk} - \langle\boldsymbol{v}_i,\boldsymbol{v}_j,\boldsymbol{w}_k\rangle - \boldsymbol{g}_k'\boldsymbol{x}_{ik}$ and $\alpha_{ik}^* = \alpha_{ik} - \boldsymbol{g}_k'\boldsymbol{x}_{ik}$. Then, we have

$$o_{ijk}\sim N(\alpha_{ik}^*,\,\sigma_y^2),\ \alpha_{ik}^*\sim N(q_k\alpha_i,\,\sigma_{\alpha,k}^2),\ \alpha_i\sim N(0,1)$$

Let $\mathcal{J}_{ik}$ denote the set of authors that user i has rated in context k. Let $\boldsymbol{o}_{ik} = \{o_{ijk}\}_{\forall j\in\mathcal{J}_{ik}}$. Since all the distributions are normal, the distribution of $(\alpha_i|\boldsymbol{o}_{ik})$ is also normal, and can be obtained by $\int p(\alpha_i,\alpha_{ik}^*\,|\,\boldsymbol{o}_{ik})\,d\alpha_{ik}^*$. Let $\rho_{ik} = (1+|\mathcal{J}_{ik}|\,\sigma_{\alpha,k}^2/\sigma_y^2)^{-1}$. We have

$$E[\alpha_i\,|\,\boldsymbol{o}_{ik}] = Var[\alpha_i\,|\,\boldsymbol{o}_{ik}]\left(\rho_{ik}\,q_k\sum\nolimits_{j\in\mathcal{J}_{ik}}\tfrac{o_{ijk}}{\sigma_y^2}\right)$$
$$Var[\alpha_i\,|\,\boldsymbol{o}_{ik}] = \left(1+\tfrac{q_k^2}{\sigma_{\alpha,k}^2}(1-\rho_{ik})\right)^{-1}$$

Then, letting $\boldsymbol{o}_i = \{\boldsymbol{o}_{ik}\}_{\forall k}$, we obtain the distribution of $(\alpha_i\,|\,\boldsymbol{o}_i)$, which is normal with

$$E[\alpha_i\,|\,\boldsymbol{o}_i] = Var[\alpha_i\,|\,\boldsymbol{o}_i]\left(\sum\nolimits_k\tfrac{E[\alpha_i\,|\,\boldsymbol{o}_{ik}]}{Var[\alpha_i\,|\,\boldsymbol{o}_{ik}]}\right)$$
$$Var[\alpha_i\,|\,\boldsymbol{o}_i] = \left(1+\sum\nolimits_k\left(\tfrac{1}{Var[\alpha_i\,|\,\boldsymbol{o}_{ik}]}-1\right)\right)^{-1}$$

Now, we draw α_i from this distribution. Then, for each k, we draw α_{ik} from the distribution of $(\alpha_{ik}\,|\,\alpha_i,\boldsymbol{o}_i)$, which is normal with

$$E[\alpha_{ik}\,|\,\alpha_i,\boldsymbol{o}_i] = V_{ik}^{(\alpha)}\left(\tfrac{q_k\,\alpha_i}{\sigma_{\alpha,k}^2}+\sum\nolimits_{j\in\mathcal{J}_{ik}}\tfrac{o_{ijk}}{\sigma_y^2}\right)+\boldsymbol{g}_k'\boldsymbol{x}_{ik}$$
$$Var[\alpha_{ik}\,|\,\alpha_i,\boldsymbol{o}_i] = V_{ik}^{(\alpha)} = \left(\tfrac{1}{\sigma_{\alpha,k}^2}+\tfrac{1}{\sigma_y^2}|\mathcal{J}_{ik}|\right)^{-1}$$

Draw β_j and β_{jk}: This is similar to the previous case.

Draw $\boldsymbol{v}_i$: For each user i, draw $\boldsymbol{v}_i$ from $(\boldsymbol{v}_i\,|\,\text{Rest})$, which is normal, for all i. Note that "Rest" here denote all the other factors. Let $\mathcal{I}_{ik}$ denote the set of users that user i receives ratings from. Let $o_{ijk} = y_{ijk} - \alpha_{ik} - \beta_{jk}$ and $\boldsymbol{v}_{jk} = \boldsymbol{v}_j\circ\boldsymbol{w}_k$, meaning element-wise product.

$$E[\boldsymbol{v}_i\,|\,\text{Rest}] = V_i^{(v)}\left(\sum\nolimits_{j\in\mathcal{J}_{ik}}\tfrac{o_{ijk}\boldsymbol{v}_{jk}}{\sigma_y^2}+\sum\nolimits_{j\in\mathcal{I}_{ik}}\tfrac{o_{jik}\boldsymbol{v}_{jk}}{\sigma_y^2}\right)$$
$$Var[\boldsymbol{v}_i\,|\,\text{Rest}] = V_i^{(v)} = \left(\tfrac{I}{\sigma_v^2}+\sum\nolimits_{j\in(\mathcal{J}_{ik}\cup\mathcal{I}_{ik})}\tfrac{\boldsymbol{v}_{jk}\boldsymbol{v}_{jk}'}{\sigma_y^2}\right)^{-1}$$

Draw $\boldsymbol{w}_k$: For each context k, draw $\boldsymbol{w}_k$ from $(\boldsymbol{w}_k\,|\,\text{Rest})$, which is normal, for all k. Let $\mathcal{U}_k = \{(i,j) : \text{user } i \text{ gives user } j \text{ a rating in context } k\}$ and $o_{ijk} = y_{ijk} - \alpha_{ik} - \beta_{jk}$.

$$E[\boldsymbol{w}_k\,|\,\text{Rest}] = V_k^{(w)}\left(\sum\nolimits_{(i,j)\in\mathcal{U}_k}\tfrac{o_{ijk}(\boldsymbol{v}_{ik}\circ\boldsymbol{v}_{jk})}{\sigma_y^2}\right)$$
$$Var[\boldsymbol{w}_k\,|\,\text{Rest}] = V_k^{(w)} = \left(I+\sum\nolimits_{(i,j)\in\mathcal{U}_k}\tfrac{(\boldsymbol{v}_{ik}\circ\boldsymbol{v}_{jk})(\boldsymbol{v}_{ik}\circ\boldsymbol{v}_{jk})'}{\sigma_y^2}\right)^{-1}$$

5.5 M-Step

We use the following notations: $\hat{a}$ and $\hat{V}[a]$ to denote the posterior mean and variance of factor a, and $\hat{V}[a,b]$ to denote the covariance between factor a and b, which are computed as the sample mean, variance, covariance based on the Monte Carlo samples obtained in the E-step.

Estimating $(\boldsymbol{g}_k, q_k, \sigma_{\alpha,k}^2)$: Let $\boldsymbol{\theta}_k = (q_k,\boldsymbol{g}_k)$, $\boldsymbol{z}_{ik} = (\hat{\alpha}_i,\boldsymbol{x}_{ik})$, $\Delta_i = \text{diag}(\hat{V}[\alpha_i],\mathbf{0})$ and $\boldsymbol{c}_{ik} = (\hat{V}[\alpha_{ik},\alpha_i],\mathbf{0})$. We want to find $\boldsymbol{\theta}_k$ and $\sigma_{\alpha,k}$ that minimize

$$\tfrac{1}{\sigma_{\alpha,k}^2}\sum\nolimits_i\left((\hat{\alpha}_{ik}-\boldsymbol{\theta}_k'\boldsymbol{z}_{ik})^2+\boldsymbol{\theta}_k'\Delta_i\boldsymbol{\theta}_k-2\boldsymbol{\theta}_k'\boldsymbol{c}_{ik}+\hat{V}[\alpha_{ik}]\right)$$
$$+\ N_k\,\log\sigma_{\alpha,k}^2,$$

where N_k is the number of raters in context k. By setting the derivative to zero, we obtain

$$\hat{\boldsymbol{\theta}}_k = \left(\sum\nolimits_i(\Delta_i+\boldsymbol{z}_{ik}\boldsymbol{z}_{ik}')\right)^{-1}\left(\sum\nolimits_i(\boldsymbol{z}_{ik}\hat{\alpha}_{ik}+\boldsymbol{c}_{ik})\right)$$
$$\hat{\sigma}_{\alpha,k}^2 = \left((\hat{\alpha}_{ik}-\hat{\boldsymbol{\theta}}_k'\boldsymbol{z}_{ik})^2+\hat{\boldsymbol{\theta}}_k'\Delta_i\hat{\boldsymbol{\theta}}_k-2\hat{\boldsymbol{\theta}}_k'\boldsymbol{c}_{ik}+\hat{V}[\alpha_{ik}]\right)\,/\,N_k$$

Estimating $(\boldsymbol{d}_k, r_k, \sigma_{\beta,k}^2)$: Similar to the previous case.

Estimating σ_v^2 and σ_y^2: Let R and N denote the total numbers of ratings and users. We obtain $\hat{\sigma}_v^2 = (\sum_i\text{trace}(\hat{V}[\boldsymbol{v}_i])+\hat{\boldsymbol{v}}_i'\hat{\boldsymbol{v}}_i)/(N\dim(v))$ and $\sigma_y^2 = ((y_{ijk}-\hat{\mu}_{ijk})^2+\hat{V}[\mu_{ijk}])/R$.

6. EXPERIMENTAL RESULTS

We show strong empirical performance of our model in this section. One novel aspect of our model is the use of a regression-based hierarchical prior (Equation 1 and 2) to link to the global factor. We first evaluate this component by considering a special case, the smoothed reputation-only model. Next, we show that the full bias-smoothed tensor model outperforms a number of competitive models. Finally, we show that, by removing bias, we see a higher correlation between the predicted support scores and the quality scores.

6.1 Smoothed Reputation-Only Model

We use the Y!Buzz and Y!News datasets described in Section 2 to evaluate this model. The ratings in these two datasets are thumb-up and thumb-down votes. Thus, we would like to see whether the regression-based hierarchical prior can help improve thumb-up rate prediction in the presence of data sparseness. Each dataset has 10 contexts, which are the content categories. Note that for users who receive many votes, their *observed thumb-up rates*, defined as number of thumb-up / total vote, would be very close to their true thumb-up rates. Thus, we select (user, category) pairs that receive at least 50 votes, for users who have data in at least 4 categories, and treat the observed thumb-up rates for such pairs as the ground truth. We only evaluate our model based on these ground-truth pairs.

We use 5-fold cross validation to compare the following methods: (1) *Constant:* The constant model predicts every (user, category) pairs to have the same value, which is the average thumb-up rate in the test set. (2) *Per-user average:* This model computes the average thumb-up rate for each user (ignoring contexts) based on the training data, and then predict the user's thumb-up rates in unobserved contexts as this user-specific average rate. (3) *Hierarchical-only:* This is the smoothed reputation-only model without the regression part; i.e., $\beta_{jk} \sim N(\beta_j,\ \sigma^2_{\beta,k})$. (4) *Regression & hierarchical:* This is the smoothed reputation-only model; i.e., $\beta_{jk} \sim N(\boldsymbol{d}'_k \boldsymbol{x}_{jk} + r_k \beta_j,\ \sigma^2_{\beta,k})$. We measure the model accuracy using the root mean squared error (RMSE) between the predicted thumb-up rate and the observed thumb-up rate. The result is in the following table.

	RMSE	
Method	Buzz	News
Regression & hierarchical	0.1049	0.1488
Hierarchical-only	0.1142	0.1504
Per-user average	0.1222	0.1537
Constant	0.1901	0.1789

We note that the order of the four methods according to their accuracies are the same in all five folds — the difference is significant. On the Yahoo! Buzz data, Regression & hierarchical reduces the error by 45% from Constant, 14% from Per-user average and 8% from Hierarchical-only. On the Yahoo! News data, the error reduction is smaller. This is probably due to the fact that our current News categories are automatically extracted from article URLs (not editorially labeled) and thus noisier than Buzz categories (which are editorially labeled). Thus, the data does not provide precise context information for the model to take advantage.

6.2 Rating Prediction

Since the bias-smoothed tensor model is a rating-prediction model, we compare its performance to other rating prediction models. Our goal is not to show that our model beats the best of all rating prediction methods, but to demonstrate that, by incorporating the rating behavior on comments, we can achieve better performance than general-purpose state-of-the-art methods. After all, any rating prediction model can be used to predict support scores. In addition to Y!News and Y!Buzz datasets, we also use the Epinions dataset [32]; although it is not a comment rating dataset, it is publicly available and can be used to compare different rating prediction methods. Since reputable users should have certain level of activity, we only select users who authored at least 30 comments to be included in the Y!News and Y!Buzz experiments. For the Epinions experiment, we only select authors who posted at least 10 reviews and received at least 100 ratings; we also create binary ratings by setting rating values ≥ 5 to 1 and otherwise 0. We use the 10 content categories as the contexts for Y!News and Y!Buzz, and the top 10 verticals as the contexts for Epinions.

We compare the following four methods: (1) *BST*: the proposed bias-smoothed tensor model. (2) *BSM*: a simplified version of BST, called bias-smoothed matrix factorization. Instead of tensor factorization, we do matrix factorization; i.e., $\mu_{ijk} = \alpha_{ik} + \beta_{jk} + \boldsymbol{v}'_i \boldsymbol{v}_j$. (3) *GMF*: the global matrix factorization model, which does not use the context information; i.e., $\mu_{ijk} = \alpha_i + \beta_j + \boldsymbol{v}'_i \boldsymbol{u}_j$. We also tried using $\boldsymbol{v}'_i \boldsymbol{v}_j$ instead of $\boldsymbol{v}'_i \boldsymbol{u}_j$ and observed no significant difference. (4) *SMF*: the separate matrix factorization model, where we perform independent matrix factorization for each context; i.e., $\mu_{ijk} = \alpha_{ik} + \beta_{jk} + \boldsymbol{v}'_{ik} \boldsymbol{u}_{jk}$ without hierarchical prior on α_{ik} and β_{jk}. Again, we also tried using $\boldsymbol{v}'_{ik} \boldsymbol{v}_{jk}$ instead of $\boldsymbol{v}'_{ik} \boldsymbol{u}_{jk}$ and observed no significant difference. Let Model.n (e.g., BST.5) denote a model with dim(v)=n (i.e., n opinion factors per user). We only report the best dim(v) for each method found in tuning. The mixed-membership stochastic blockmodel (MMSB) [3] is also tried on the rating graph (if user i rates user j positively (or negatively), we create a positive (or negative) edge from i to j). We slightly modified MMSB to take negative edges (instead of assuming no edge means negative). However, we observe that MMSB has much worse accuracy than the above factorization methods. To make the plots cleaner, we do not plot its performance.

Since the ratings are binary, we measure the performance of different methods by AUC (area under ROC curve) [7]; higher AUC means better accuracy. To understand how different methods handle data sparseness, when we compute the test-set AUC numbers, we only consider (author, context) pairs, each of which receives $\leq N$ ratings in the training set. We then vary N from 0 to 10, so that the performance of a method is represented by a curve. These AUC curves are shown in Figure 2 for the three datasets. As can be seen, BST has the best performance across the three datasets. On the Epinions dataset, BST and BSF are indistinguishable, suggesting that the interaction behavior between users is similar across all contexts. By comparing BST to SMF and GMF, we see a big gain by using regression-based hierarchical priors.

6.3 Support vs. Quality

Although we saw lack of correlation between ratings and quality, here we show that, by removing bias, we can increase the correlation. The rank correlation between the predicted support scores and editor-labeled quality scores are shown in the following table.

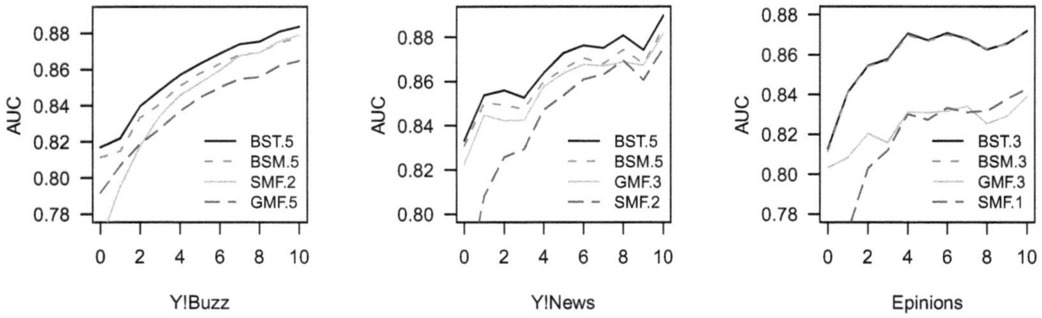

Figure 2: AUC of different rating prediction methods as a function of different data-sparseness levels

Model	Buzz	News
No opinion factor (dim(v)=0)	0.0817	0.0900
Use opinion factor (dim(v)=1)	0.1264	0.1328

As can be seen, having the opinion factors in the model (that removes the effect of opinion bias) significantly improves the rank correlation. Interestingly, different numbers of option factors do not make a difference. Comparing to Table 1, we see that our predicted support scores (based purely on ratings without using any editorial data) have much better performance than PageRank, but much worse than models trained using editorial labels. This worse performance is again due to the inherent difference between quality and support as discussed in Section 2.2.

7. CONCLUSION AND RELATED WORK

We study the problem of how to estimate user reputation in a comment rating environment and provide three novel contributions: (1) We find surprising lack of correlation between comment quality and user ratings, which has not been reported before. (2) We provide a new approach to estimating support-based reputation scores. (3) We propose a novel latent factor model that captures the generation behavior of comment ratings. In the following, we discuss prior work related to these contributions.

Quality vs. Ratings: Text quality is a heavily studied problem [40]. The most related studies are those on quality of UGC items, e.g., blogs [17], reviews [29, 12, 30], answers [2] and others [20]. On the rating behavior side, votes on reviews and answers are a popular topic [9, 29, 2]. Specifically, an exploratory analysis of votes on reviews is reported in [9]. Liu et al. [29] found three biases of user votes in reviews and developed a classifier based on text features. However, they did not try to model these biases or confounding factors as we do. Lu et al. [30] proposed an ℓ_2-regularization model to improve review quality prediction by incorporating user profiles and social networks, and Hsu et al. [20] proposed an SVM-based supervised ranking algorithm to rank comment qualities. Talwar et al. [39] found that a user's rating partly reflects the difference between true quality and prior expectation of quality in a hotel review dataset. Agichtein et al. [2] found that ratings are useful for predicting answer quality, unlike what we found in comments. To our knowledge, the sharp difference between quality and ratings in a comment rating environment has not been studied before.

Definition of reputation: External (user facing) reputation scores are used to incentivize users for desired behavior. A few examples are [35, 37]. These scores are usually count-based and have to be simple so that users can easily understand them. However, our focus is on internal scores. In this area, many graph-based approaches have been proposed based on PageRank [19, 23], trust/distrust propagation [15, 45], mutual reinforcement propagation between user reputation scores and content quality [4, 33] and frequent patterns [14]. In addition, Agarwal et al. [1] also proposed a graph-based algorithm to identify influential bloggers. Zhang et al. [43] conducted an extensive study comparing different scoring-based and graph-based reputation estimation methods using a Java online forum. While most existing graph-based approaches ignore the presence of confounding factors, Shin et al. [38] proposed a propagation algorithm trying to separate user sociability from reputation. Statistical models are also used to identify reputable users. For example, Maeno [31] developed a model for covert node discovery in social networks and applied it to identifying suspicious logs. Kuter [27] proposed a trust inference algorithm that uses a probabilistic sampling technique to estimate the confidence in the trust information from some designated sources. See Jøsang et al. [24] and Farmer et al. [10] for surveys of reputation methods. Different from the above work, we define a conceptually simple, but *unobserved* support score and address the challenges of computing the score using statistical models.

Latent factor models: We reduce the problem of estimating support scores to a rating prediction problem and develop a novel latent factor model. Although any rating prediction model can be used, we have shown strong performance of ours. Our model is a significant extension to [18] by adding regression-based hierarchical priors to the per-user bias terms. Rating prediction is a hot problem in recommender systems. Factorization methods [36, 25] are very competitive methods if not the best. Our goal is not to show that our model beats the best of rating prediction methods, but to demonstrate that, by incorporating the rating behavior in comments, we can achieve better performance than general-purpose state-of-the-art methods.

Other related work: We note that the problem of finding reliable users in crowdsourcing is an interesting line of research [21, 34, 41]. Exploratory analysis of comment rating environments includes [26, 13].

8. REFERENCES

[1] N. Agarwal, H. Liu, L. Tang, and P. S. Yu. Identifying the influential bloggers in a community. In *WSDM*, 2008.

[2] E. Agichtein, C. Castillo, D. Donato, A. Gionis, and G. Mishne. Finding high-quality content in social media. *Proceedings of the international conference on Web search and web data mining - WSDM '08*, 2008.

[3] E. M. Airoldi, D. M. Blei, S. E. Fienberg, and E. P. Xing. Mixed membership stochastic blockmodels. *JMLR*, 2008.

[4] J. Bian, Y. Liu, D. Zhou, E. Agichtein, and H. Zha. Learning to recognize reliable users and content in social media with coupled mutual reinforcement. In *WWW*, 2009.

[5] D. M. Blei, A. Y. Ng, and M. I. Jordan. Latent dirichlet allocation. *JMLR*, 3, 2003.

[6] J. Booth and J. Hobert. Maximizing generalized linear mixed model likelihoods with an automated monte carlo EM algorithm. *J.R.Statist. Soc. B*, 1999.

[7] A. P. Bradley. The use of the area under the roc curve in the evaluation of machine learning algorithms. *Pattern Recognition*, 1997.

[8] L. Breiman. Random forests. *Machine learning*, 2001.

[9] C. Danescu-niculescu mizil, J. Kleinberg, and L. Lee. How Opinions are Received by Online Communities : A Case Study on Amazon.com Helpfulness Votes. *WWW*, 2009.

[10] R. Farmer and B. Glass. *Building Web Reputation Systems.* Yahoo Press, 2010.

[11] R. Flesch. A new readability yardstick. *Journal of Applied Psychology*, 1948.

[12] A. Ghose and P. G. Ipeirotis. Estimating the Helpfulness and Economic Impact of Product Reviews : Mining Text and Reviewer Characteristics. *TKDE*, 2009.

[13] V. Gómez, A. Kaltenbrunner, and V. López. Statistical analysis of the social network and discussion threads in slashdot. In *WWW*, 2008.

[14] A. Goyal, F. Bonchi, and L. V. Lakshmanan. Discovering leaders from community actions. In *CIKM*, 2008.

[15] R. Guha, R. Kumar, P. Raghavan, and A. Tomkins. Propagation of trust and distrust. In *WWW*, 2004.

[16] R. Gunning. *The Technique of Clear Writing.* 1952.

[17] R. Hellmann, J. Griesbaum, and T. Mandl. Quality in blogs: How to find the best user generated content. In *Business Information Systems.* 2010.

[18] P. D. Hoff. Bilinear mixed-effects models for dyadic data. *J. of the Amer. Stat. Ass.*, 2005.

[19] L. Hong and Z. Yang. Incorporating participant reputation in community-driven question answering systems. In *Symposium on Social Intelligence and Networking*, 2009.

[20] C.-F. Hsu, E. Khabiri, and J. Caverlee. Ranking comments on the social web. In *International Conference on Computational Science and Engineering*, 2009.

[21] P. G. Ipeirotis, F. Provost, and J. Wang. Quality Management on Amazon Mechanical Turk. *KDD The Human Computation Workshop*, 2010.

[22] T. S. Jaakkola and M. I. Jordan. Bayesian parameter estimation via variational methods. *Statistics and Computing*, 2000.

[23] Jianshu Weng, et al. Twitterrank: finding topic-sensitive influential twitterers. In *WSDM*, 2010.

[24] A. Jøsang, R. Ismail, and C. Boyd. A survey of trust and reputation systems for online service provision. *Decision Support Systems*, 2007.

[25] Y. Koren. Collaborative filtering with temporal dynamics. *Commun. ACM*, 2010.

[26] J. Kunegis, A. Lommatzsch, and C. Bauckhage. The slashdot zoo: Mining a social network with negative edges. In *WWW*, 2009.

[27] U. Kuter. Sunny: A new algorithm for trust inference in social networks using probabilistic confidence models. In *AAAI*, 2007.

[28] G. H. M. C. Laughlin. SMOG Grading ŮŰ a New Readability Formula. *Journal Of Reading*, 1969.

[29] J. Liu, et al. Low-Quality Product Review Detection in Opinion Summarization. *EMNLP-CoNLL*, 2007.

[30] Y. Lu and P. Tsaparas, et al. Exploiting social context for review quality prediction. In *WWW*, 2010.

[31] Y. Maeno. Node discovery in a networked organization. In *Intl Conf on Sys., Man and Cyber.*, 2009.

[32] P. Massa and P. Avesani. Trust metrics in recommender systems. In *Computing with Social Trust*, 2009.

[33] M. G. Noll, et al. Telling experts from spammers: Expertise ranking in folksonomies. In *SIGIR*, 2009.

[34] V. C. Raykar, et al. Learning From crowds. *JMLR*, 2010.

[35] P. Resnick and Z. Richard. *Trust Among Strangers in Internet Transactions: Empirical Analysis of eBay's Reputation System.* Elsevier Science, 2002.

[36] R. Salakhutdinov and A. Mnih. Probabilistic matrix factorization. In *NIPS*, 2008.

[37] J. Schneider, et al. Disseminating trust information in wearable communities. In *HUC*, 2000.

[38] H. Shin, et al. Separating the reputation and the sociability of online community users. In *SAC*, 2010.

[39] A. Talwar, R. Jurca, and B. Faltings. Understanding user behavior in online feedback reporting. In *EC*, 2007.

[40] S. Valenti, F. Neri, and A. Cucchiarelli. An Overview of Current Research on Automated Essay Grading. *Journal of Information Technology Education*, 2003.

[41] P. Welinder, S. Branson, S. Belongie, and P. Perona. The Multidimensional Wisdom of Crowds. *NIPS*, 2010.

[42] P. Windley, K. Tew, and D. Daley. A framework for building reputation systems. In *WWW*, 2007.

[43] J. Zhang, et al. Expertise networks in online communities: structure and algorithms. In *WWW*, 2007.

[44] Z. Zheng, H. Zha, K. Chen, and G. Sun. A regression framework for learning ranking functions using relative relevance judgments. In *SIGIR*, 2007.

[45] C.-N. Ziegler and G. Lausen. Propagation models for trust and distrust in social networks. *Info. Sys. Frontiers*, 2005.

Appendix: Let R = #observed rating, N_k = #raters and M_k = #authors in context k. The complete data log likelihood of bias-smoothed tensor model is:

$$
\begin{aligned}
&2 \log \Pr(\mathbf{y}, \boldsymbol{\eta} \mid \boldsymbol{\Theta}) = \text{ some constant} \\
&- R \log \sigma_y^2 - \sum_{ijk} (y_{ijk} - \alpha_{ik} - \beta_{jk} - \langle \boldsymbol{v}_i, \boldsymbol{v}_j, \boldsymbol{w}_k \rangle)^2 / \sigma_y^2 \\
&- \sum_k N_k \log \sigma_{\alpha,k}^2 - \sum_k \sum_i (\alpha_{ik} - \boldsymbol{g}_k' \boldsymbol{x}_{ik} - q_k \alpha_i)^2 / \sigma_{\alpha,k}^2 \\
&- \sum_k M_k \log \sigma_{\beta,k}^2 - \sum_k \sum_j (\beta_{jk} - \boldsymbol{d}_k' \boldsymbol{x}_{jk} - r_k \beta_j)^2 / \sigma_{\beta,k}^2 \\
&- \sum_i \left(\dim(v) \log \sigma_v^2 + \|\boldsymbol{v}_i\|^2 / \sigma_v^2 \right) - \sum_i \alpha_i^2 - \sum_j \beta_j^2 - \sum_k \|\boldsymbol{w}_k\|^2
\end{aligned}
$$

Use the notation defined in Section 5.5. The expected log likelihood (over $\boldsymbol{\eta}$) is

$$
\begin{aligned}
&2\, E_{\boldsymbol{\eta}}[\log \Pr(\mathbf{y}, \boldsymbol{\eta} \mid \boldsymbol{\Theta})] = \text{ some constant} \\
&- R \log \sigma_y^2 - \sum_{ijk} \left((y_{ijk} - \hat{\mu}_{ijk})^2 + \hat{V}[\mu_{ijk}] \right) / \sigma_y^2 \\
&- \sum_k N_k \log \sigma_{\alpha,k}^2 - \sum_k M_k \log \sigma_{\beta,k}^2 \\
&- \sum_k \sum_i \frac{(\hat{\alpha}_{ik} - g_k' x_{ik} - q_k \hat{\alpha}_i)^2 + \hat{V}[\alpha_{ik}] - 2 q_k \hat{V}[\alpha_{ik}, \alpha_i] + q_k^2 \hat{V}[\alpha_i]}{\sigma_{\alpha,k}^2} \\
&- \sum_k \sum_j \frac{(\hat{\beta}_{jk} - d_k' x_{jk} - r_k \hat{\beta}_j)^2 + \hat{V}[\beta_{jk}] - 2 r_k \hat{V}[\beta_{jk}, \beta_j] + r_k^2 \hat{V}[\beta_j]}{\sigma_{\beta,k}^2} \\
&- \sum_i \left(\dim(v) \log \sigma_v^2 + \left(\hat{\boldsymbol{v}}_i' \hat{\boldsymbol{v}}_i + \mathrm{trace}(\hat{V}[\boldsymbol{v}_i]) \right) / \sigma_v^2 \right)
\end{aligned}
$$

Selecting a Comprehensive Set of Reviews

Panayiotis Tsaparas
Search Labs
Microsoft Research
panats@microsoft.com

Alexandros Ntoulas*
Zynga
San Francisco, CA
antoulas@zynga.com

Evimaria Terzi†
Boston University
evimaria@cs.bu.edu

ABSTRACT

Online user reviews play a central role in the decision-making process of users for a variety of tasks, ranging from entertainment and shopping to medical services. As user-generated reviews proliferate, it becomes critical to have a mechanism for helping the users (information consumers) deal with the information overload, and presenting them with a small comprehensive set of reviews that satisfies their information need. This is particularly important for mobile phone users, who need to make decisions quickly, and have a device with limited screen real-estate for displaying the reviews. Previous approaches have addressed the problem by ranking reviews according to their (estimated) helpfulness. However, such approaches do not account for the fact that the top few high-quality reviews may be highly redundant, repeating the same information, or presenting the same positive (or negative) perspective. In this work, we focus on the problem of selecting a *comprehensive* set of few high-quality reviews that cover many different aspects of the reviewed item. We formulate the problem as a maximum coverage problem, and we present a generic formalism that can model the different variants of review-set selection. We describe algorithms for the different variants we consider, and, whenever possible, we provide approximation guarantees with respect to the optimal solution. We also perform an experimental evaluation on real data in order to understand the value of coverage for users.

Categories and Subject Descriptors

H.3.3 [**Information Search and Retrieval**]: [Selection Process]; H.2.8 [**Database Management**]: Database applications—*Data Mining*

General Terms

Algorithms, Experimentation, Theory

Keywords

Review Selection, Set Cover, Greedy Algorithms

*Work done while the author was at Microsoft Research.
†Work done while visiting Search Labs.

1. INTRODUCTION

Online user reviews are an invaluable resource for making informed decisions for a variety of tasks such as purchasing products, booking flights and hotels, selecting restaurants, or picking movies to watch. Sites like `Yelp.com` and `Epinions.com` have created a viable business as review portals, while part of the popularity and success of `Amazon.com` and `TripAdvisor.com` is attributed to their extensive user reviews. The benefit of user reviews is that they are voluminous and comprehensive: multiple people, with different needs, different viewpoints, and different experiences review the same item, composing collectively a picture that is rich in detail and diverse in perspective.

At the same time, this information abundance can be overwhelming to the users. In `Amazon.com`, for popular products such as digital cameras, there are typically several hundreds of reviews, many of which are fraudulent, uninformative, or repetitive. Typical online users do not have the patience to go through all of them to sort out the ones with useful information content. To address this problem, most online portals allow the users to rate reviews according to their helpfulness, and there has been substantial amount of research in automatically estimating the quality of a review [19, 29, 9, 10, 32, 17, 15, 20].

Such approaches produce a score for each review, or an ordered list of reviews. However, they do not account for the redundancy in the content of the reviews, or the fact that some important aspects of the reviewed item may not be covered at all by the top results. For example, all top reviews may be highly informative about the long-range zoom of a new camera, but mention nothing about how easy it is to use, or to carry. Similarly, for a restaurant, the most helpful reviews may be detailed about the quality of the food, but mention nothing about the ambiance of the place, or how kid-friendly it is.

Furthermore, an ordered list of reviews does not necessarily represent all different viewpoints (e.g., positive vs. negative) of the item reviewed. There is experimental evidence [9] that users tend to consider helpful (and vote them as such) the reviews that agree with the average item rating. As a result the top reviews are more likely to represent a single viewpoint. Users usually need to explicitly filter on the review rating in order to get a diverse set of opinions.

Therefore, ordering reviews according to their user-defined, or algorithmically-estimated quality does not guarantee that there is a small set of reviews that covers the different aspects of an item with diverse viewpoints. The need for such compact and comprehensive information becomes critical in the case of mobile phone users. In mobile phones, screen real-estate and time resources are even more sparse, and users need helpful information to make quick decisions as they do not have the luxury to carefully go through multiple reviews. Instead, they want to quickly browse through a few reviews and get a well rounded view of how good a product is, whether they are likely to enjoy a film, or whether the restaurant that is two blocks away has good vegetarian dishes. Therefore, the few reviews that they will read should have high information content and cover the aspects of an item with diverse opinions.

In this paper we consider the *review set selection* problem where given a set of reviews for a specific item, we want to select a comprehensive subset of small size. The notion of comprehensiveness is defined with respect to the attributes of the product and the viewpoints of the reviews. Given a review of a specific item, we assume that we have the following information: (a) the attributes of the item that are discussed in the review; (b) the quality of the review; (c) the viewpoint of the review (e.g., positive or negative). The selected subset should cover as many attributes of the item as possible, while containing reviews of high quality, which offer different viewpoints for the attributes of the product. We formalize this intuition as a *maximum coverage* problem, and we show how we can extend existing algorithms for maximizing coverage to address our requirements.

In this paper we make the following contributions:

- We formulate the review set selection problem as a coverage problem and we define a generic formalism that can be used to model the different variations of our problem. The GROUP-COVERAGE problems we define in Section 2 are novel, and have not been previously studied.
- We provide a theoretical analysis of the coverage problems we consider, and describe efficient algorithms for review selection. Whenever possible, we provide approximation guarantees for the proposed algorithms.
- We perform an experimental analysis of the algorithms on real data, and we study the value of coverage to users by conducting a user study on Amazon Mechanical Turk.

The rest of the paper is structured as follows. In Section 2, we define the coverage formalism, and model our selection problem. In Section 3, we provide a theoretical analysis of the different coverage variants we consider; we give algorithms for each one of these variants in Section 4. In Section 5, we present the experimental analysis. In Section 6, we present the related work, and we conclude in Section 7 with a discussion about possible extensions of our framework.

2. COVERAGE PROBLEM FORMULATION

We now show how to formulate the review set selection problem as a maximum coverage problem and we define different variants of the problem that we will consider. Consider a given item x, e.g., a product, that has a set of attributes $\mathcal{A} = \{a_1, a_2, ..., a_m\}$. Let $\mathcal{R} = \{r_1, ..., r_n\}$ be a set of reviews for item x. We assume that each review r is associated with a subset $\mathcal{A}_r \subseteq \mathcal{A}$ of attributes of x: these are the attributes that are discussed in review r for item x. We also say that review r *covers* attribute a if $a \in \mathcal{A}_r$. We use $\mathcal{R}_a$ to denote the set of reviews in $\mathcal{R}$ that cover attribute a.

Now, let $\mathcal{S} \subseteq \mathcal{R}$ denote a subset of reviews. We assume a *coverage scoring function* $f(\mathcal{S}, a)$ that assigns a score to attribute a given the subset $\mathcal{S}$. Intuitively, the scoring function measures the the benefit we obtain from covering attribute a with set $\mathcal{S}$. Let $\mathcal{A}_\mathcal{S}$ denote the union of attributes covered by the reviews in set $\mathcal{S}$, $\mathcal{A}_\mathcal{S} = \cup_{r \in \mathcal{S}} \mathcal{A}_r$. We define the function f such that $f(\mathcal{S}, a) = 0$ for all attributes $a \notin \mathcal{A}_\mathcal{S}$. Therefore, in order to define f, given a set $\mathcal{S}$, we only need to specify the value $f(\mathcal{S}, a)$ for the attributes $a \in \mathcal{A}_\mathcal{S}$.

We now define the following generic *coverage* problem, parametrized by the coverage scoring function f.

PROBLEM 1 (COVERAGE(f)). *Given a set of attributes $\mathcal{A}$ and a set of reviews $\mathcal{R}$ for an item x, an integer budget value k, and a coverage scoring function f, find a subset of reviews $\mathcal{S} \subseteq \mathcal{R}$ of size $|\mathcal{S}| = k$ that maximizes*

$$F(\mathcal{S}) = \sum_{a \in \mathcal{A}} f(\mathcal{S}, a)$$

We will refer to function $F(\mathcal{S})$ as the *cumulative coverage scoring function*, and it is defined with respect to the coverage scoring function f.

This broad definition allows us to define different coverage problems by varying the coverage scoring function f. In the simplest case, the scoring function f assigns the same score to all attributes covered by the set $\mathcal{S}$. We use f_u to denote this scoring function and we have that $f_u(\mathcal{S}, a) = 1$ for all $a \in \mathcal{A}_\mathcal{S}$. We use F_u to denote the corresponding cumulative scoring function, and we denote the COVERAGE(f_u) problem as UNIT-COVERAGE. The UNIT-COVERAGE problem asks for a set of k reviews that cover as many attributes as possible; it is also known in the literature as the MAX-COVERAGE problem [12].

Assume now that we are given a quality function $q : \mathcal{R} \rightarrow [0, 1]$ that maps a review r to a real number $q(r)$ that measures the *quality*, or *helpfulness*, of the review. This value may be present in our data (for example, via users voting for the quality of different reviews), or it may be inferred algorithmically. Given the quality values, we would like our selected subset to contain reviews that have high quality, while at the same time cover as many different attributes of a product as possible. The coverage scoring function should then give higher score to a pair $(\mathcal{S}, a)$ if the attribute a is covered by a review of high quality. Let $\mathcal{S}_a$ denote the set of reviews in $\mathcal{S}$ that cover a, that is, $\mathcal{S}_a = \mathcal{S} \cap \mathcal{R}_a$ Given the quality function q, we define the coverage scoring function f_q, as follows:

$$f_q(\mathcal{S}, a) = \max_{r \in \mathcal{S}_a} q(r)$$

That is, the coverage score of attribute a is the highest review quality among the reviews that cover a. Note that the scoring function f_u (and the COVERAGE(f_u) problem) is a special case of the f_q (and COVERAGE(f_q)) when $q(r) = 1$ for all reviews. Similar to before, we use F_q to denote the cumulative scoring function with respect to f_q. We refer to the COVERAGE(f_q) problem as the QUALITY-COVERAGE problem.

Assume now that we can partition the reviews into g groups, $\mathcal{R} = \{\mathcal{R}^1, ..., \mathcal{R}^g\}$. In our work, we assume that each group $\mathcal{R}^i$ contains reviews of the same viewpoint. When $g = 2$ we have a positive and a negative viewpoint, while for $g > 2$ we have a finer granularity of viewpoints. Given this partition, we now require the selected subset to represent all different groups.

For a subset $\mathcal{S}$ of reviews, let $\mathcal{S}^i = \mathcal{S} \cap \mathcal{R}^i$ denote the set of reviews in $\mathcal{S}$ that belong to group $\mathcal{R}^i$. Let f denote a *base* scoring function that is applied to each group (e.g., this can be either f_u, or f_q). We define the group coverage scoring function as follows:

$$f_g(\mathcal{S}, a) = \min_{i=1...g} f(\mathcal{S}^i, a) \quad (1)$$

By using the min operator in the definition of the f_g function in Equation 1, we guarantee that the score of an attribute that is not covered by all groups is zero. Therefore, in order to obtain benefit for a given attribute we need the attribute to be covered by all different groups. Again, we use F_g to denote the cumulative coverage scoring function, and we will refer to the COVERAGE(f_g) problem as the GROUP-COVERAGE problem. To the best of our knowledge this is the first time that the GROUP-COVERAGE problem is defined. Maximum coverage with groups has been considered in [7] but in this case they require that only one review can be selected from each group.

We will define the group coverage function f_g using f_u or f_q as the base scoring functions. When necessary to discriminate between the two, we will use f_{gu} to denote the group coverage function defined with respect to f_u, and f_{gq} to denote the group coverage function defined with respect to f_q. We use F_{gu} and F_{gq} to denote the corresponding cumulative functions, and GROUP-UNIT-COVERAGE and GROUP-QUALITY-COVERAGE to denote the corresponding problems.

The COVERAGE(f_g) problem requires that the selected subset $\mathcal{S}$ covers each attribute a from all possible viewpoints. We can relax this requirement, by replacing the min operator in the f_g function, by a sum operator. We thus have the following scoring function:

$$f_s(\mathcal{S}, a) = \sum_i f_q(\mathcal{S}^i, a) \tag{2}$$

We use F_s to denote the corresponding cumulative scoring function, and we refer to the COVERAGE(f_s) as the SOFT-COVERAGE problem. Similar to before, we define scoring (cumulative) functions f_{su} (F_{su}) and f_{sq} (F_{sq}) depending on the choice of the basis function. We will refer to the corresponding problems as SOFT-UNIT-COVERAGE and SOFT-QUALITY-COVERAGE.

3. ANALYSIS OF COVERAGE

We will now analyze the complexity of the different variants of the COVERAGE problem.

For the simple unit coverage scoring function f_u, the UNIT-COVERAGE problem corresponds to the MAX-COVERAGE problem. In the MAX-COVERAGE problem, given a universe of elements $\mathcal{A} = \{a_1, ..., a_m\}$, and a collection of sets $\mathcal{R} = \{r_1, ..., r_n\}$, and an integer budget value k, we are looking for a set $\mathcal{S} \subseteq \mathcal{R}$ of size k, such that the set of elements in $\mathcal{A}$ that are covered by the sets in $\mathcal{S}$ is maximized. This is identical to the definition of the COVERAGE(f_u) problem where the elements are attributes, and the sets are reviews. The MAX-COVERAGE problem is known to be NP-hard [12]. Since functions f_q, f_g and f_s contain f_u as a special case, it follows that the QUALITY-COVERAGE, GROUP-COVERAGE and SOFT-COVERAGE problems are also NP-hard.

Since getting an optimal solution is hard, we turn to approximation algorithms. If OPT(X) is the benefit of the optimal solution for a maximization problem on an input instance X, and ALG(X) is the benefit of algorithm ALG on instance X, we say that ALG is an α-approximation algorithm, if $\frac{\text{OPT}(X)}{\text{ALG}(X)} \geq \alpha$ for all possible input instances X.

The MAX-COVERAGE (UNIT-COVERAGE) problem is known to have a simple $(1 - 1/e)$-approximation algorithm [12]. The algorithm proceeds in k iterations, where in each iteration a new review is added to the result set. The algorithm chooses the next review to be added in a greedy fashion each time selecting the review that covers most of the attributes that have not already been covered. The proof for the approximation factor relies on the fact that the cumulative scoring function F_u that we want to maximize is *monotone* and *submodular*. Let $2^{\mathcal{R}}$ denote the powerset of the set $\mathcal{R}$. The function $F : 2^{\mathcal{R}} \rightarrow \Re$ is monotone if for every $\mathcal{S}, \mathcal{T} \in 2^{\mathcal{R}}$, such that $\mathcal{S} \subseteq \mathcal{T}$, $F(\mathcal{S}) \leq F(\mathcal{T})$. The function F is submodular, if it has the *diminishing returns* property: for every $\mathcal{S}, \mathcal{T} \in 2^{\mathcal{R}}$, such that $\mathcal{S} \subseteq \mathcal{T}$, and every $r \in \mathcal{R}$,

$$F(\mathcal{S} \cup \{r\}) - F(\mathcal{S}) \geq F(\mathcal{T} \cup \{r\}) - F(\mathcal{T})$$

That is, the *incremental gain* of adding an element to a set decreases as the size of the set increases. When looking for a subset of reviews of size k that maximizes a submodular function F, the greedy algorithm that each time adds the review r that maximizes the incremental gain to the existing set is $(1 - 1/e)$-approximate.

It is very easy to show that all cumulative functions are monotone. The function F_u is known to be submodular. We can prove the following lemma for function F_q.

LEMMA 1. *The function* $F_q(\mathcal{S}) = \sum_{a \in \mathcal{A}_\mathcal{S}} f_q(\mathcal{S}, a)$ *is submodular.*

We omit the proof due to space constraints. The submodularity of F_q is also discussed in [4]. The submodularity of F_s follows directly from that of F_q. The review sets $\mathcal{R}^i$ for the different groups are disjoint. Therefore, the gain in F_s of adding review $r \in \mathcal{R}^i$ to a multi-group set of reviews $\mathcal{S}$ is the same as the gain in F_q of adding review r to the set $\mathcal{S}^i$. Since we know that F_q is submodular it follows that F_s is also submodular.

We can prove that the F_g function is *not* submodular.

LEMMA 2. *The function* $F_g(\mathcal{S})$ *is not submodular.*

PROOF. We consider the case where the f_g function is defined with respect to f_u, and we assume that there are just two groups $\{\mathcal{R}^1, \mathcal{R}^2\}$. For a given set of reviews $\mathcal{S}$, we use $\mathcal{A}_\mathcal{S}$ to denote the set of attributes that are covered by at least one review in $\mathcal{S}$, that is, $f_u(\mathcal{S}, a) = 1$. Let $C_\mathcal{S} \subseteq \mathcal{A}_\mathcal{S}$ denote the set of attributes in $\mathcal{A}_\mathcal{S}$ for which $f_g(\mathcal{S}, a) = 1$, that is, they are are covered by a review from both groups, and let $U_\mathcal{S} \subseteq \mathcal{A}_\mathcal{S}$ denote the set of attributes in $\mathcal{A}_\mathcal{S}$ for which $f_g(\mathcal{S}, a) = 0$, that is they are covered by reviews of only one of the two groups. We say that the attributes in $C_\mathcal{S}$ are *fully* covered, while the attributes in $U_\mathcal{S}$ are *partially* covered. Without loss of generality, we assume that all attributes in $U_\mathcal{S}$ are covered (only) by reviews in group $\mathcal{R}^1$.

Consider now another set of reviews $\mathcal{T} \supseteq \mathcal{S}$, such that $C_\mathcal{T} = C_\mathcal{S}$, and $U_\mathcal{T} \supset U_\mathcal{S}$, and assume that the attributes in $U_\mathcal{T} \setminus U_\mathcal{S}$ are covered (only) by reviews in group $\mathcal{R}^1$ Let $r \in \mathcal{R}^2$ be a review from group 2, such that $\mathcal{A}_r = U_\mathcal{T}$. We have $F_g(\mathcal{S} \cup \{r\}) - F_g(\mathcal{S}) = |U_\mathcal{S}|$. On the other hand, $F_g(\mathcal{T} \cup \{r\}) - F_g(\mathcal{T}) = |U_\mathcal{T}| > |U_\mathcal{T}|$. It follows that $F_g(\mathcal{S})$ is not submodular. □

In fact, we can show that the GROUP-COVERAGE problem contains as a special case the DENSEST k-SUBGRAPH (DKS) problem for bipartite graphs. In the DKS problem, given a bipartite graph G we want to find a set of k vertices, such that the number of edges in the induced subgraph is maximized. The approximation-ratio of the DKS is unresolved. It is known that there is no Polynomial-Time Approximation Scheme (PTAS), and the best known approximation algorithm has approximation ratio $O(n^{1/4})$ [3]. It is not known if there is a $O(n^\epsilon)$ approximation algorithm for $\epsilon \geq 0$. A constant factor approximation for the COVERAGE(f_g) would imply a constant factor approximation for DKS.

To reduce GROUP-COVERAGE to the DKS problem, we consider again the case of two groups ($g = 2$), where all reviews have uniform quality. We create a bipartite graph $G = (V_1, V_2, E)$, where the left side V_1 contains one node for each review $r \in \mathcal{R}^1$ in group 1, while V_2 contains one node for each review $r \in \mathcal{R}^2$ in group 2. We create an edge (r_1, r_2), if reviews r_1 and r_2 share a covered attribute, that is $\mathcal{A}_{r_1} \cap \mathcal{A}_{r_2} \neq \emptyset$. The edge $e = (r_1, r_2)$ is associated with the edge attribute-set $\mathcal{A}_e = \mathcal{A}_{r_1} \cap \mathcal{A}_{r_2}$. Then, the GROUP-COVERAGE becomes the problem of finding k vertices in G, such that the cardinality of the union of the edge attribute-sets in the induced subgraph is maximized. In the special case where each edge is associated with exactly one attribute, and all edge attribute-sets are disjoint, this is exactly the DKS problem on a bipartite graph.

4. ALGORITHMS FOR COVERAGE

We now present our algorithms for the different variants of the COVERAGE problem. For the coverage scoring functions f_u, f_q, and f_s, since the resulting cumulative functions F_u, F_q, and F_s are submodular, we use a greedy algorithm that is easy to implement, and it is theoretically proven to produce a solution that is a constant-factor approximation of the optimal.

Let $\Delta_{\mathcal{S}}(r) = F(\mathcal{S} \cup \{r\}) - F(\mathcal{S})$ denote the incremental gain in the cumulative score function F when adding review r to the set $\mathcal{S}$. The algorithm proceeds in k iterations, incrementally building the review set, by adding one review at the time. Let $\mathcal{S}_i$ denote the set of reviews constructed in iteration i, where $\mathcal{S}_0 = \emptyset$. At iteration i, given the set of reviews $\mathcal{S}_{i-1}$, we compute for each review $r \in \mathcal{R} \setminus \mathcal{S}_{i-1}$ the incremental gain $\Delta_{\mathcal{S}_{i-1}}(r)$ and we select the one with the maximum value to generate $\mathcal{S}_i$. The outline of the greedy algorithm is shown in Algorithm 1 and it is parametrized by the scoring function f (and the corresponding cumulative function F).

Algorithm 1 The GREEDY algorithm

Input: Set of reviews $\mathcal{R} = \{r_1, ..., r_n\}$; Set of attributes $\mathcal{A} = \{a_1, ..., a_m\}$; Integer budget value k; Scoring function f.
Output: A set of reviews $\mathcal{S} \subseteq \mathcal{R}$ of size k.

$\mathcal{S}_0 = \emptyset$
for all $i = 1, ..., k$ **do**
  for all $r \in \mathcal{R} \setminus \mathcal{S}_{i-1}$ **do**
    Compute $\Delta_{\mathcal{S}_{i-1}}(r)$
  end for
  $r_i = \arg\max_{r \in \mathcal{R} \setminus \mathcal{S}_{i-1}} \Delta_{\mathcal{S}_{i-1}}(r)$
  $\mathcal{S}_i = \mathcal{S}_{i-1} \cup \{r_i\}$
end for
return $\mathcal{S}_k$

Applying the GREEDY algorithm to the GROUP-COVERAGE problem is not straightforward. Due to the requirement that each attribute should be covered by at least g reviews (one from each group), adding a single review r to a review set $\mathcal{S}$ incurs no benefit, unless there are already $g-1$ reviews in $\mathcal{S}$ from all other groups that cover the same attribute(s) as r. For an attribute a, we have that $f_g(\mathcal{S}, a) > 0$ if and only if the set $\mathcal{S}$ contains a *tuple* $t = (r^1, ..., r^g)$ of g reviews, such that review r^i belongs to group $\mathcal{R}^i$, and all reviews in t cover attribute a. In this case, we say that the tuple t *fully* covers attribute a. For the attributes in $\mathcal{A}_t$ that are not fully covered, we say that they are *partially* covered by tuple t.

We propose a greedy algorithm for the GROUP-COVERAGE problem that selects tuples of reviews instead of individual reviews, thus guaranteeing that at each step it incurs non-zero gain, if this is possible. Let $\mathcal{T} = \mathcal{R}^1 \times \cdots \times \mathcal{R}^g$ denote the set of all possible tuples. Given a set of reviews $\mathcal{S}$, and a tuple $t \in \mathcal{T}$, let $\Delta_{\mathcal{S}}(t)$ denote the incremental gain of adding the reviews in tuple t to the set $\mathcal{S}$. Also let $C_{\mathcal{S}}(t) = |t \setminus \mathcal{S}|$ denote the number of reviews contained in t that are not in $\mathcal{S}$; $C_{\mathcal{S}}(t)$ captures the *cost* of adding tuple t to the set $\mathcal{S}$. The tuples with cost within the remaining review budget are *candidate* tuples. The algorithm proceeds greedily, at each step adding to the output review set $\mathcal{S}$ the candidate tuple t that maximizes the gain-to-cost ratio $\Delta_{\mathcal{S}}(t)/C_{\mathcal{S}}(t)$. We also experimented with maximizing just the gain $\Delta_{\mathcal{S}}(t)$ of the newly introduced tuple, but this algorithm performed worse experimentally, so we omit any further discussion.

When adding a tuple in our set, we obtain an immediate gain, but we also create a potential for future gains, by introducing attributes that are only partially covered. We take into account the potential of a tuple in order to break ties between tuples with equal gain. For example, if we have a two tuples t_1, t_2 which both have the same gain-to-cost ratio, but the set of attributes partially covered by reviews in t_1 is larger than that of t_2, then we should prefer t_1 over t_2 since we expect future additions to give higher gains at a lower cost.

Formally, for a tuple t, let U_t denote the set of attributes that are partially covered by tuple t. We define the *potential* of t with respect to $\mathcal{S}$ as $P_{\mathcal{S}}(t) = |U_t \setminus \mathcal{A}_{\mathcal{S}}|$, that is, the number of attributes partially covered by t that are not already partially or fully covered by $\mathcal{S}$. We use the potential to break the ties between tuples with the same gain-to-cost ratio. We observed experimentally that this modification can improve the performance of the algorithm significantly.

Algorithm 2 outlines the new greedy algorithm. In line 8 of the algorithm we find the *set* of tuples that have the maximum gain-to-cost ratio, and then in line 9, we select the one with the maximum potential. If there are still ties, we break them by selecting a tuple arbitrarily.

Algorithm 2 The t-GREEDY algorithm.

Input: Set of reviews $\mathcal{R} = \{r_1, ..., r_n\}$ and groups $\{\mathcal{R}^1, ..., \mathcal{R}^g\}$; Set of attributes $\mathcal{A} = \{a_1, ..., a_m\}$; Integer budget value k; Scoring function f_g
Output: A set of reviews $\mathcal{S} \subseteq \mathcal{R}$ of size k.

1: Compute $\mathcal{T} = \mathcal{R}^1 \times \cdots \times \mathcal{R}^g$
2: $\mathcal{S} = \emptyset$
3: **while** $|\mathcal{S}| < k$ **do**
4:   $b = k - |\mathcal{S}|$
5:   **for all** $t \in \mathcal{T}$ **do**
6:     Compute $\Delta_{\mathcal{S}}(t)$, $C_{\mathcal{S}}(t)$, $P_{\mathcal{S}}(t)$
7:   **end for**
8:   $T = \arg\max_{t: C_{\mathcal{S}}(t) \leq b} \Delta_{\mathcal{S}}(t)/C_{\mathcal{S}}(t)$
9:   $t = \arg\max_{t \in T} P_{\mathcal{S}}(t)$
10:   $\mathcal{S} = \mathcal{S} \cup t$
11: **end while**
12: return $\mathcal{S}$

5. EXPERIMENTAL ANALYSIS

In this section we perform an experimental analysis of our algorithms. The goals of the analysis are two-fold: to quantitatively compare the different algorithms over different measures, and understand when each algorithm performs better; to qualitatively compare the algorithms by performing a user study.

5.1 Datasets

For our analysis we use real data which are publicly available from the Bing shopping portal. The Bing shopping portal aggregates reviews from multiple sites such as Amazon and CNET. We consider a collection of 4,362 products, over three categories: Digital Cameras, Cell Phones, and MP3 Players. This amounts to 129,783 reviews in total.

For each review, we have the content of the review, the rating of the review for the product, and the *helpfulness* votes for the review, from the users in the site. A helpfulness vote can be either positive or negative. We use the fraction of positive votes over the total number of votes as a measure of the *quality* of the review. We intentionally choose to make the quality of a review to be algorithm-independent, so as to understand the effect of our selection algorithms without having to account for the effects of quality estimation. In a real application scenario, where not all reviews have sufficient number of helpfulness votes (or any at all), some algorithm for estimating the quality of the review [19, 29, 9, 10, 32, 17, 15, 20] can be utilized to obtain a quality value.

From the collection of products and reviews, we prune away products that have less than 20 reviews so as to make the selection process meaningful. We also prune reviews with less than 10 votes in total, since for these reviews we consider that we do not have sufficient evidence to determine the quality of the review.

For the attribute extraction we use the attributes extracted from the Bing search engine for the "Product Scorecard". There are 96 total possible attributes for category Digital Cameras, 84 attributes for category Cell Phones, and 68 attributes for category MP3 Players. The attributes include a broad range of characteristics of the products such as "ease of use", "battery life", "sound quality", "image quality", "screen" and more. To avoid spurious attribute references, we consider that a review covers an attribute if it is mentioned at least twice in the review, and we only keep attributes that are covered by at least two reviews of the product. On average each review covers 4 attributes, and there are 20.7 distinct attributes per product. We note that our selection algorithms are independent of the attribute extraction algorithm. Any off-the-shelf (such as [13, 14, 6]), or custom-built attribute extraction algorithm can be used.

We use the product ratings to define groups of reviews. We consider the case where we have two groups: positive reviews, and negative reviews. Ratings take discrete values between 1 and 5. Following the convention in the Amazon.com site, we consider a review to be positive if the rating is 4 or 5, and negative if it is 3 or less. To avoid the effect of outliers, we create a group only if it contains at least three reviews. Otherwise we assume a single group.

5.2 Algorithms

We consider six different algorithms one for each variation of the COVERAGE problem. The algorithms are all greedy, as described in Section 4. More specifically we have the following algorithms.

GREEDY-U, GREEDY-Q, GREEDY-SU, GREEDY-SQ: The greedy Algorithm 1 that optimizes the F_u, F_q, F_{su} and F_{sq} cumulative score functions respectively.

GREEDY-GU, GREEDY-GQ: The greedy Algorithm 2 that optimizes the F_{gu} and F_{gq} cumulative score functions respectively.

In addition to the greedy algorithms we also compare against the following baselines.

TOPQLTY: Sort the reviews according the their quality and select the top-k reviews. To aid the TOPQLTY algorithm in the comparisons with the greedy algorithms with respect to coverage, we break ties in quality using the number of attributes covered by the reviews.

TOPLEN: Sort the reviews according to length, and select the top-k reviews. This is meant to serve as a natural basic baseline. Longer reviews are also expected to be of higher quality and cover more attributes.

RANDOM: The RANDOM algorithm selects randomly k reviews. This is meant to serve as a sanity check in order to calibrate the results of the other algorithms. We perform 1000 runs for the RANDOM algorithm, and take the average performance of the algorithm.

For all the runs we set the value of k to be 5. We consider this to be a reasonable number of reviews that can give a thorough picture of a product. Furthermore, in the mobile applications we envision, where the screen and time resources are limited, we do not expect the user to be able to read more than five reviews.

5.3 Quantitative Evaluation

The goal of this section is to study how our algorithms perform with respect to coverage metrics, and compare them against the baseline algorithms, and each other. As coverage metrics, we consider all the different coverage scoring functions that we defined. For the following, we use UCOV to denote the *unit coverage* value of the F_u function; QCOV to denote the *quality coverage* value of the F_q function; GUCOV to denote the *group coverage* value of the F_{gu} function; GQCOV to denote the *group quality coverage* value of the F_{gq} function; SUCOV to denote the *soft coverage* value of the F_{su} function; and SQCOV to denote the *soft quality coverage* value of the F_{sq} function. For a given set we also compute the *average review quality* QLTY of the set. Note that for each metric there is a corresponding greedy algorithm that aims at maximizing this metric. We call this the *target* metric of the greedy algorithm.

In order to be able to aggregate or compare values across different products, we normalize the coverage values by the maximum possible coverage value that can be obtained if we include in our set *all* of the reviews (i.e., set $k = n$). For the QLTY metric the maximum is achieved by the TOPQLTY algorithm. Table 1 shows the average normalized measures for all algorithms, and the standard deviation. For the RANDOM algorithm, we compute for each product the average over the 1000 random samples, and then we compute the average of the averages, and the standard deviation over the averages.

The following high-level observations emerge from the analysis of Table 1. First, all algorithms perform on average better than the random baseline (with the exception of TOPQLTY on GUCOV), although there are cases where the values are within the standard deviation interval.

Second, each greedy algorithm achieves the best value on the target metric (the value in bold), although for some metrics (e.g., UCOV) there are other algorithms that are close. This indicates that the greedy heuristics, although not optimal, do a good job at optimizing the function at hand.

Third, the normalized coverage values are high. The greedy algorithms achieve at least 83% of the maximum possible for their target metric, and as high as 98% for the GREEDY-U on the unit coverage metric. This indicates that our premise that there is a small subset of reviews that covers the attributes of a product and the different viewpoints of the reviews is valid in practice, and thus it makes sense to look for such a set.

We investigate further the results in Table 1, and we perform some statistical tests to better quantify the difference between the different algorithms. For each algorithm, each metric, and each product we compute the *empirical p-value* of the output value against the RANDOM algorithm. Let COV_{ALG} denote the value of algorithm ALG for the coverage metric COV. Let COV_i denote the value of the i-th random trial of the RANDOM algorithm. We define the empirical p-value of the COV_{ALG} measurement as

$$p(\text{COV}_{\text{ALG}}) = \frac{1}{N_S} \sum_{i=1}^{N_S} \mathbb{I}(\text{COV}_i \geq \text{COV}_{\text{ALG}})$$

where N_S is the number of RANDOM samples ($N_S = 1000$) in our experiments, and $\mathbb{I}$ is an indicator function that is 1 if the predicate is true and zero otherwise. The p-value is the fraction of random trials for which the RANDOM algorithm achieves a value on COV greater or equal than COV_{ALG}. We consider the value COV_{ALG} to be statistically significant if the p-value is less than 0.05, meaning that we can reject the *null hypothesis* that the value was generated by a random process with confidence greater than 95%.

	UCOV	QCOV	GUCOV	GQCOV	SUCOV	SQCOV	QLTY
GREEDY-U	**0.98** (0.04)	0.90 (0.09)	0.27 (0.24)	0.26 (0.24)	0.73 (0.11)	0.70 (0.12)	0.83 (0.11)
GREEDY-Q	0.97 (0.05)	**0.96** (0.06)	0.21 (0.26)	0.21 (0.27)	0.70 (0.12)	0.73 (0.12)	0.92 (0.07)
GREEDY-GU	0.72 (0.27)	0.66 (0.26)	**0.84** (0.14)	0.77 (0.17)	0.62 (0.15)	0.55 (0.16)	0.80 (0.12)
GREEDY-GQ	0.71 (0.27)	0.70 (0.28)	0.82 (0.15)	**0.83** (0.15)	0.61 (0.15)	0.58 (0.16)	0.86 (0.11)
GREEDY-SU	0.95 (0.07)	0.87 (0.11)	0.77 (0.17)	0.70 (0.18)	**0.86** (0.10)	0.79 (0.13)	0.80 (0.11)
GREEDY-SQ	0.95 (0.07)	0.93 (0.08)	0.71 (0.20)	0.72 (0.19)	0.84 (0.10)	**0.84** (0.11)	0.89 (0.08)
TOPQLTY	0.74 (0.19)	0.77 (0.17)	0.14 (0.23)	0.15 (0.25)	0.52 (0.18)	0.58 (0.18)	**1.00** (0.00)
TOPLEN	0.88 (0.11)	0.84 (0.13)	0.31 (0.30)	0.31 (0.30)	0.68 (0.14)	0.68 (0.15)	0.85 (0.11)
RANDOM	0.61 (0.11)	0.54 (0.12)	0.16 (0.08)	0.14 (0.07)	0.43 (0.11)	0.40 (0.11)	0.77 (0.08)

Table 1: Mean and standard deviation of the performance measures for the different algorithms

We compute the p-values for all algorithms, all metrics, and all products. Then, for each algorithm and each metric, we compute the fraction of products for which we have a p-value greater than 0.05. This is the fraction of products for which there is a probability at least 5% that a random selection of k reviews can produce a metric value greater or equal to that of the algorithm. We call this the *null-hypothesis fraction* (or simply the fraction).

Table 2 shows the null-hypothesis fraction for all algorithm and metric pairs. We observe that all algorithms achieve fraction zero, or close to zero, for their target metric. Therefore, the performance of the algorithms cannot be viewed as a random artifact. The few products for which we have high p-value for the GREEDY-U and GREEDY-Q algorithms correspond to cases where the number of attributes to be covered is small, and they can be covered with one or two reviews.

We observe higher fraction values for the other algorithm-metric combinations. High null-hypothesis fraction values correspond also to low normalized coverage metric values in Table 1. These are the metrics for which the algorithm performs worse. We have the highest fraction (worst performance) values for the greedy coverage algorithms GREEDY-U and GREEDY-Q when evaluated against the group coverage metrics GUCOV and GQCOV, and the group coverage algorithms GREEDY-GU and GREEDY-GQ when evaluated against the UCOV and QCOV metrics. In these cases, we have high p-values for more than 50% of the products, and for as many as 83.6% of the products for the case of the GREEDY-Q algorithm against the GUCOV metric. This is expected since the target metric of the algorithm, and the evaluation metric are qualitatively very different, and optimizing one does not offer any guarantees for the other. On the other hand, for metrics that are related, such as UCOV and QCOV the corresponding greedy algorithm performs well on both metrics. The soft coverage metrics (and the corresponding algorithms) sit somewhere in between these two extremes and as a result we obtain relatively good performance for these metrics for all greedy algorithms, while the corresponding greedy algorithms perform relatively well on all metrics.

To better understand the relationship between the different algorithms and metrics we perform pairwise comparisons between the different algorithms. What we want to understand is whether some of the algorithms we consider are redundant and their results could be obtained by some of the other variations. For example for the UCOV metric, the performance of the GREEDY-Q is very similar to that of the GREEDY-U; is it the case that we can obtain similar coverage with the GREEDY-Q algorithm?

To measure the similarity between the different algorithms we compute the average pairwise intersection of the output reviews. The results are shown in Table 3. The resulting matrix is asymmetric since there are cases that one algorithm may output less than k results. Entry $(\text{ALG}_i, \text{ALG}_j)$ contains the average (over products) fraction of reviews in the returned results of algorithm ALG_i that appear in the results of algorithm ALG_j. The table indicates high overlap between pairs of algorithms that have similar underlying intuition such as the different quality versions of the greedy heuristics, or the soft and non-soft counterparts. The intersection can be as high as 81%. However, this similarity is not statistically significant. For a coverage metric COV, and the corresponding greedy algorithm ALG that optimizes this metric, let $\overrightarrow{\text{COV}_{\text{ALG}}}$ denote the vector of COV values of algorithm over all products. We performed a paired t-test between $\overrightarrow{\text{COV}_{\text{ALG}}}$ and $\overrightarrow{\text{COV}_{\text{ALG}'}}$ for every other algorithm ALG' to determine if the vectors come from a distribution with the same mean. The significance tests indicate that this is not the case with confidence 95%. Therefore, the similarity between the algorithms is not statistically significant.

Finally, it is interesting to understand the relationship between coverage and quality. From the TOPQLTY row of Tables 1 and 2 we see that high quality does not guarantee high coverage. The TOPQLTY algorithm achieves very low coverage values (and high null-hypothesis fraction values) for all metrics. For the GUCOV metric, the performance of TOPQLTY is actually worse than that of RANDOM. Surprisingly the TOPLEN algorithm performs better than TOPQLTY with respect to all coverage metrics. One possible explanation is that longer reviews are more likely to cover more attributes. On the flip side, the greedy coverage algorithms have high null-hypothesis fraction (low performance) values for the QLTY metric. The algorithms that perform best are GREEDY-Q, GREEDY-SQ and GREEDY-GQ that take quality into account in their optimization criterion. Out of these GREEDY-GQ performs the worst, probably due to the hard constraint it imposes on covering every attribute from both groups.

The disconnect between quality and coverage implies that in our set selection we need to balance between these two competing metrics. In the following section we study how the preferences of the users align between these two metrics.

5.4 Qualitative Analysis

In the previous section we investigated how the algorithms perform under different coverage measures, and how they compare to each other. We will now perform a user study to understand how useful the selected sets are to actual users. Our goal is to determine whether the set of reviews produced by a given algorithm for a given product would enable the users to make an informed buy/not-buy decision on the product.

To this end, we ran an experiment with a set of workers from Amazon's Mechanical Turk. For our task we selected a set of 25 products from our dataset for which we can create a positive and negative group. This was necessary in order to have a fair com-

	UCov	QCov	GUCov	GQCov	SUCov	SQCov	Qlty
Greedy-U	**0.98%**	3.43%	74.59%	70.49%	7.38%	9.02%	88.24%
Greedy-Q	6.37%	**0.49%**	83.61%	77.87%	23.77%	11.48%	40.20%
Greedy-GU	57.35%	56.86%	**0.00%**	0.82%	51.64%	61.48%	91.67%
Greedy-GQ	61.27%	54.90%	0.00%	**0.00%**	54.10%	50.82%	60.78%
Greedy-SU	13.24%	17.16%	1.64%	3.28%	**0.00%**	2.46%	89.71%
Greedy-SQ	17.65%	3.43%	14.75%	9.84%	0.82%	**0.00%**	53.43%
TopQlty	83.33%	51.96%	90.16%	86.89%	80.33%	59.02%	**1.47%**
TopLen	48.53%	34.80%	68.85%	61.48%	42.62%	35.25%	67.65%

Table 2: Null hypothesis fraction for the different algorithms and different performance measures

	Greedy-U	Greedy-Q	Greedy-GU	Greedy-GQ	Greedy-SU	Greedy-SQ	TopQlty	TopLen
Greedy-U	100%	67.78 %	65.29 %	54.13 %	82.99 %	66.04 %	31.20 %	50.90 %
Greedy-Q	57.48 %	100%	44.90 %	64.04 %	53.28 %	80.96 %	51.22 %	49.21 %
Greedy-GU	61.58 %	50.29 %	100%	76.67 %	80.92 %	66.95 %	28.01 %	46.31 %
Greedy-GQ	44.18 %	63.12 %	69.97 %	100%	62.29 %	81.09 %	37.39 %	46.22 %
Greedy-SU	75.77 %	57.18 %	79.00 %	66.95 %	100%	73.18 %	28.18 %	48.24 %
Greedy-SQ	53.66 %	78.38 %	58.86 %	79.41 %	66.94 %	100%	43.94 %	49.78 %
TopQlty	23.82 %	47.16 %	23.53 %	35.10 %	24.51 %	42.25 %	100%	34.61 %
TopLen	39.80 %	46.08 %	39.41 %	44.31 %	42.25 %	48.63 %	34.61 %	100%

Table 3: Average result intersection between different algorithms

parison among all the algorithms. We created a HIT (Human Intelligence Task) for every algorithm and product combination. In each HIT we present the worker with the name of the product, a link to a web page describing the product, and the review set output by the algorithm. For each review we display the text of the review and the rating of the product. We then asked the workers to evaluate the set of reviews produced by each of the algorithms in terms of how informed they felt in making a buy/not-buy decision after reading the set of reviews. More specifically the users were asked to select one of the options of "perfectly informed", "well informed", "somewhat informed" or "not informed at all". We assigned each one of these options a score from 0 ("not informed at all") up to 3 ("perfectly informed") and we requested 18 workers for each algorithm-product combination. For each algorithm, the review set consists of 5 reviews for each product ($k = 5$). To eliminate spam and minimize noise, out of these 18 workers we kept the 5 which spent the most time during their task (and thus we were relatively certain that they had done a thorough job in reading the reviews).

The first column of Table 4 shows the average user satisfaction score for each algorithm, computed over all workers and over all products. The higher the score (with a maximum of 3.00) the more informed the users felt after reading the reviews. Our first observation is that the performance of all algorithms is comparable. Surprisingly, the TopQlty does not perform as well as one would expect. In our experiment, selecting the top-5 reviews with the highest quality does not produce informative reviews. This could possibly be attributed to a perceived redundancy in the results of the TopQlty algorithm. The algorithm that performs best is the TopLen algorithm, indicating a user preference towards more lengthy reviews. With the exception of the Greedy-GU and Greedy-GQ algorithms, our greedy heuristics perform well; they outperform the TopQlty algorithm, and achieve performance close to that of the TopLen. This result indicates that coverage is important to the users, and it should be accounted for when selecting a small set of reviews to present. The "soft" versions of the algorithms perform slightly better (although the difference is rather small) indicating that representing different viewpoints in the results is a desirable property. The Greedy-GU and Greedy-GQ algorithms performed the worst among our greedy algorithms. This is mostly due to the hard requirement of covering attributes from both viewpoints, which results in a more restrictive selection. As a result these algorithms perform worse compared to their "soft" counterparts, i.e., Greedy-SU and Greedy-SQ respectively.

To further study the tradeoff between coverage and quality we also performed an additional Mechanical Turk experiment, where we asked the users to compare our greedy algorithms against the TopQlty algorithm. In the task we showed the users two sets of reviews, and asked them to select the one that they felt gave them more information about the product. We assigned the task to 18 workers, out of which we selected again the 5 best as before, and we measured the average difference of workers that prefer the greedy algorithm over the TopQlty algorithm minus those that prefer TopQlty over the greedy. The results we obtain are shown in the second column of Table 4, and are consistent with the average user satisfaction. The greedy algorithms are preferred over TopQlty and TopLen wins the comparisons with the highest margin. In this experiment, the value of introducing the review quality in the greedy optimization stands out more clearly. These experiment confirm our finding that coverage and viewpoint diversity are important to the users, together with review quality.

6. RELATED WORK

The set selection problem we consider in this paper is closely related to the quality estimation, and ranking of reviews. Ranking can be viewed as another way to obtain a small set of reviews by selecting the top-k best reviews and we compare our algorithms against a ranking approach. There has been substantial amount of research in this area [19, 29, 9, 10, 32, 17, 15, 20]. In all of these works, the output is a score for each review, or an ordering of the reviews. Our work is different in that we are trying to select a *set* of reviews that collectively perform well, rather than score each individual review.

	User Satisfaction	Average Difference over TOPQLTY
GREEDY-U	2.10	1.02
GREEDY-Q	2.10	1.74
GREEDY-GU	1.98	0.20
GREEDY-GQ	1.94	0.46
GREEDY-SU	2.13	0.78
GREEDY-SQ	2.11	1.44
TOPLEN	2.26	2.84
TOPQLTY	1.98	0.00

Table 4: Average results in our user study.

There is also substantial amount of work on opinion summarization [14, 13, 31, 22, 21, 23]. The overall goal is to extract aspects (or features) of an product, and a short piece of text that summarizes the opinions on the different aspects. This is different from our approach where we want to find a subset of reviews that best captures the different aspects of a product. Our work is to a large extent complimentary to this work.

The most related work to ours is a recent work by Lappas and Gunopoulos [16] where they consider the problem of finding a small set of reviews that cover *all* product attributes, while preserving the distribution of positive and negative reviews. This is similar to our problem definition, However, our formulation is different from that in [16], since we look for a set of fixed size, and our goal is to cover attributes from both the positive and negative viewpoint, rather than preserve the viewpoint distribution. This difference leads to a different optimization problem, and as a result, to different algorithmic challenges.

Our problem is also related to *query result diversification* where the goal is to produce a ranking of the query results that cover as many *query intents* as possible. There is substantial amount of work in this area [1, 8, 11, 30, 2, 25, 28, 26, 27]. In this case, the goal is to return search results that are as orthogonal as possible and still relevant to the input query. This goal is usually formulated as an optimization problem that tries to maximize two competing measures: relevance and diversity. In our setting maximizing diversity is not an end in itself; we are content with non-orthogonal reviews as long as they collectively have high coverage of attributes. In the case of the GROUP-COVERAGE problem, we want reviews from different viewpoints to work together to cover the attributes of the item, which is substantially different from the traditional diversification setting.

At a high level the problem we consider is similar to work on *document summarization via sentence extraction* where the goal is to pick a set of sentences that summarize a given document. Despite this high-level similarity, there are fundamental differences in the problem definition. Traditional document summarization (e.g., MMR [5] and Mead [24]) focus on designing scoring functions for candidate sentences: every sentence is scored independently of other sentences and the output contains a collection of highly scored sentences. These scoring functions do not take into account the interaction between sentences. In our case, we select sets of reviews rather than scoring each review separately.

The combinatorial version of the document-summarization problem has been only considered lately by Liu et al. [18]. In this case, the goal is to pick a set of sentences that collectively cover as many document topics and, at the same time have the minimum possible topical overlap. This formulation is different from the one we consider here: we do want high-coverage reviews, but we do not want them to be necessarily orthogonal to each other, and we also want to represent all possible viewpoints. As a result, the objective function and the corresponding optimization problem we consider are different from the one considered by Liu et al. [18]. Overall, although some special cases of the COVERAGE problem have been considered in the past for review-corpora management, our work is the first to provide and analyze the formalism in its full generality, including the GROUP-COVERAGE problem.

7. DISCUSSION AND CONCLUSIONS

In this paper we studied the problem of selecting a small subset of reviews from a large collection of reviews for a product, such that we cover the different attributes of the product with high quality content that represents different viewpoints. We provide a generic framework for formulating coverage problems that capture these requirements. We proposed algorithms for these problems, and studied their theoretical properties. We performed experiments, and showed that our algorithms achieve performance that is statistically significant. Our user study indicates that attribute coverage and viewpoint diversity are properties that appeal to users.

There are several interesting extensions of our work, and connections with different domains. First, in this paper we work with product reviews, but our generic framework can be applied to other domains as well. One such domain is news and updates. In this setting, we have a collection of articles about a specific event, or storyline. Each article covers specific aspects of the event, has some quality, and a specific viewpoint (e.g., conservative vs. progressive). We want to select a small subset of articles of high quality, that cover as many aspects of the event as possible and present all different viewpoints. This problem can be naturally modeled using the coverage formalism we introduced in this paper. This formulation can also be applied to the case that instead of articles we have tweets, or facebook updates about a specific event, person, or URL.

Another interesting extension of our work is the case where the attributes of the product that we want to cover are not statically predefined, but rather defined dynamically by the user. In this case, we are looking for the smallest set of reviews that covers all the specified attributes. We can easily modify our framework to handle this case, and the same greedy algorithms are still applicable to the minimization problem. For some of these algorithm we can again obtain approximation guarantees. Note that the user-defined attributes could be in the form of queries, rather than be selected from a fixed pool of attributes. It is not clear what results should be returned by a search engine when handling a *collection* of queries, rather than a single query. Our work provides a possible approach for addressing this question.

Finally, our formulation allows for additional complexity that we did not explore in this paper due to size limitations. First, it is easy to incorporate the importance of attributes in our optimization criteria, if such information is available. Second, in our formulation we assumed that each review belongs to a specific group, for example positive or negative. It is though possible that the same review covers some attributes positively, and some attributes negatively. Our framework can be easily extended to handle this case, and our greedy group algorithms naturally generalize to this case.

Acknowledgements

We would like to thank Kunal Talwar for helpful discussions on the complexity of GROUP-COVERAGE. We would also like to thank Pei Yue, Raghuram Rajagopal, Rama Shenai, and Stuart Marshal with their help in getting the review data.

8. REFERENCES

[1] R. Agrawal, S. Gollapudi, A. Halverson, and S. Ieong. Diversifying search results. In *WSDM*, pages 5–14, 2009.

[2] Y. Azar, I. Gamzu, and X. Yin. Multiple intents re-ranking. In *Proceedings of the 41st annual ACM symposium on Theory of computing*, STOC '09, 2009.

[3] A. Bhaskara, M. Charikar, E. Chlamtac, U. Feige, and A. Vijayaraghavan. Detecting high log-densities: an $(^{1/4})$ approximation for densest -subgraph. In *STOC*, pages 201–210, 2010.

[4] G. Calinescu, C. Chekuri, M. Pál, and J. Vondrák. Maximizing a submodular set function subject to a matroid constraint (extended abstract). In *IPCO*, pages 182–196, 2007.

[5] J. G. Carbonell and J. Goldstein. The use of MMR, diversity-based reranking for reordering documents and producing summaries. In *SIGIR*, pages 335–336, 1998.

[6] G. Carenini, R. T. Ng, and E. Zwart. Extracting knowledge from evaluative text. In *Proceedings of the 3rd international conference on Knowledge capture*, K-CAP '05, pages 11–18, New York, NY, USA, 2005. ACM.

[7] C. Chekuri and A. Kumar. Maximum coverage problem with group budget constraints and applications. In *APPROX-RANDOM*, pages 72–83, 2004.

[8] H. Chen and D. R. Karger. Less is more: probabilistic models for retrieving fewer relevant documents. In *SIGIR*, pages 429–436, 2006.

[9] C. Danescu-Niculescu-Mizil, G. Kossinets, J. Kleinberg, and L. Lee. How opinions are received by online communities: a case study on amazon.com helpfulness votes. In *WWW '09*, pages 141–150, New York, NY, USA, 2009. ACM.

[10] A. Ghose and P. G. Ipeirotis. Designing novel review ranking systems: predicting the usefulness and impact of reviews. In *ICEC '07*, pages 303–310, New York, NY, USA, 2007. ACM.

[11] S. Gollapudi and A. Sharma. An axiomatic approach for result diversification. In *WWW*, pages 381–390, 2009.

[12] D. Hochbaum, editor. *Approximation algorithms for NP-hard problems.* PWS Publishing Company, 1997.

[13] M. Hu and B. Liu. Mining and summarizing customer reviews. In *KDD*, pages 168–177, 2004.

[14] M. Hu and B. Liu. Mining opinion features in customer reviews. In *AAAI*, pages 755–760, 2004.

[15] S.-M. Kim, P. Pantel, T. Chklovski, and M. Pennacchiotti. Automatically assessing review helpfulness. In *EMNLP*, pages 423–430, Sydney, Australia, July 2006.

[16] T. Lappas and D. Gunopulos. Efficient confident search in large review corpora. In *ECML/PKDD (2)*, pages 195–210, 2010.

[17] J. Liu, Y. Cao, C.-Y. Lin, Y. Huang, and M. Zhou. Low-quality product review detection in opinion summarization. In *EMNLP-CoNLL*, pages 334–342, 2007. Poster paper.

[18] K. Liu, E. Terzi, and T. Grandison. Highlighting diverse concepts in documents. In *SDM*, pages 545–556, 2009.

[19] Y. Liu, X. Huang, A. An, and X. Yu. Modeling and predicting the helpfulness of online reviews. In *ICDM*, pages 443–452, 2008.

[20] Y. Lu, P. Tsaparas, A. Ntoulas, and L. Polanyi. Exploiting social context for review quality prediction. In *WWW*, 2010.

[21] Y. Lu and C. Zhai. Opinion integration through semi-supervised topic modeling. In *WWW*, pages 121–130, 2008.

[22] Y. Lu, C. Zhai, and N. Sundaresan. Rated aspect summarization of short comments. In *WWW*, pages 131–140, 2009.

[23] A.-M. Popescu, B. Nguyen, and O. Etzioni. Opine: Extracting product features and opinions from reviews. In *HLT/EMNLP*, 2005.

[24] D. Radev, T. Allison, S. Blair-Goldensohn, J. Blitzer, A. Çelebi, S. Dimitrov, E. Drabek, A. Hakim, W. Lam, D. Liu, J. Otterbacher, H. Qi, H. Saggion, S. Teufel, M. Topper, A. Winkel, and Z. Zhang. MEAD - a platform for multidocument multilingual text summarization. In *LREC 2004*, Lisbon, Portugal, May 2004.

[25] F. Radlinski, P. N. Bennett, B. Carterette, and T. Joachims. Redundancy, diversity and interdependent document relevance. *SIGIR Forum*, 43(2):46–52, 2009.

[26] F. Radlinski, R. Kleinberg, and T. Joachims. Learning diverse rankings with multi-armed bandits. In *ICML*, pages 784–791, 2008.

[27] D. Rafiei, K. Bharat, and A. Shukla. Diversifying web search results. In *WWW*, 2010.

[28] A. Slivkins, F. Radlinski, and S. Gollapudi. Learning optimally diverse rankings over large document collections. In *ICML*, 2010.

[29] O. Tsur and A. Rappoport. Revrank: a fully unsupervised algorithm for selecting the most helpful book reviews. In *ICWSM*, 2009.

[30] E. Vee, U. Srivastava, J. Shanmugasundaram, P. Bhat, and S. Amer-Yahia. Efficient computation of diverse query results. In *ICDE*, pages 228–236, 2008.

[31] H. Wang, Y. Lu, and C. Zhai. Latent aspect rating analysis on review text data: a rating regression approach. In *KDD*, pages 783–792, 2010.

[32] Z. Zhang and B. Varadarajan. Utility scoring of product reviews. In *CIKM '06*, pages 51–57, New York, NY, USA, 2006. ACM.

Enabling Fast Prediction for Ensemble Models on Data Streams

Peng Zhang[†,⋆], Jun Li[†], Peng Wang[†], Byron J. Gao[‡], Xingquan Zhu[§], Li Guo[†,⋆]

[†] Institute of Computing Technology, Chinese Academy of Sciences, Beijing, 100190, China
[⋆] National Engineering Laboratory for Information Content Security, Beijing, China
[‡] Department of Computer Science, Texas State University - San Marcos, TX 78666-4616, USA
[§] QCIS, Faculty of Eng. & IT, University of Technology, Sydney, NSW 2007, Australia
{zhangpeng, lijun, wpeng, guoli}@ict.ac.cn, bgao@txstate.edu, xqzhu@it.uts.edu.au

ABSTRACT

Ensemble learning has become a common tool for data stream classification, being able to handle large volumes of stream data and concept drifting. Previous studies focus on building accurate prediction models from stream data. However, a linear scan of a large number of base classifiers in the ensemble during prediction incurs significant costs in response time, preventing ensemble learning from being practical for many real world time-critical data stream applications, such as Web traffic stream monitoring, spam detection, and intrusion detection. In these applications, data streams usually arrive at a speed of GB/second, and it is necessary to classify each stream record in a timely manner. To address this problem, we propose a novel *Ensemble-tree* (E-tree for short) indexing structure to organize all base classifiers in an ensemble for fast prediction. On one hand, E-trees treat ensembles as spatial databases and employ an *R-tree* like height-balanced structure to reduce the expected prediction time from linear to sub-linear complexity. On the other hand, E-trees can automatically update themselves by continuously integrating new classifiers and discarding outdated ones, well adapting to new trends and patterns underneath data streams. Experiments on both synthetic and real-world data streams demonstrate the performance of our approach.

Categories and Subject Descriptors

H.2.8 [**Database Management**]: Database Applications—*Data Mining*

General Terms

Algorithm, Performance

Keywords

Stream data mining, stream classification, ensemble learning, spatial indexing, concept drifting

1. INTRODUCTION

Data stream classification represents one of the most important tasks in stream data mining [1]. Compared to traditional classification, data stream classification faces two additional challenges: large/increasing data volumes and drifting/evolving concepts [27, 32]. To address these challenges, many ensemble-based models have been proposed recently, including weighted classifier ensembles [14, 26, 31, 16, 35], incremental classifier ensembles [4], classifier and cluster ensembles [33], to name a few. While these models vary from one to another, they share the same fundamental idea: *using divide-and-conquer techniques to handle large volumes of stream data with concept drifting*. Specifically, these ensemble models partition continuous stream data into small data chunks, build one or multiple light-weight base classifier(s) from each chunk, and combine all base classifiers in different ways for prediction. Such an ensemble learning design enjoys a number of advantages such as scaling well, adapting quickly to new concepts, low variance errors, and ease of parallelization. As a result, it has become one of the most popular techniques in data stream classification.

Existing works on ensemble learning in data streams mainly focus on building accurate ensemble models. Prediction efficiency has not been concerned mainly because (1) Prediction typically takes linear time, which is sufficient for undemanding applications. (2) Existing works only consider combining a small number of base classifiers, *e.g.*, no more than 30 [14, 32, 33, 35, 35]. However, there are increasingly more real world applications where stream data arrive intensively in large volumes. In addition, the hidden patterns underneath data streams may change continuously, which requires a large number of base classifiers to capture various patterns and form a quality ensemble. Such applications call for fast sub-linear prediction solutions.

Motivating example. In online Web page stream monitoring, ensemble learning can be used to identify malicious pages from normal pages, both arriving continuously, in real time. We implemented a detection system on a Linux machine with 3GHz cpu and 2GB memory. Each day, a batch of base classifiers are trained using decision trees (C4.5 algorithm [22, 30]) with all base classifiers combined to classify pages in the next day. In our experiments, in total 120 days of stream data [19] were used.

The curve in Fig. 1 summarizes our experimental results, showing the typical linear relationship between prediction time and ensemble size. For example, an ensemble with 50 members takes 0.083 second to classify a page. Suppose that the Web page stream flows 10,000 pages per second, which is common for backbone networks. Then, monitoring all stream records requires a sophisticated parallel computing architecture having 830 processors!

To achieve sub-linear prediction, a practical approach is to explore shared patterns among all base classifiers. Without loss of

KDD'11, August 21–24, 2011, San Diego, California, USA.

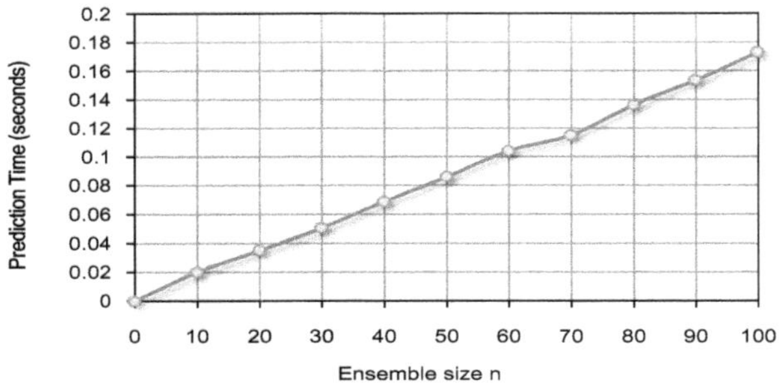

Figure 1: Prediction time vs. ensemble size

generality, suppose that the base classifiers are built using decision trees. Then, each base classifier is comprised of a batch of *decision rules*. Each decision rule covers a rectangular area in the decision space, and can be considered as a *spatial object* in the decision space. This way, each base classifier is converted to a batch of spatial objects, and an ensemble model is converted to a *spatial database* as shown in Fig. 2. By doing so, the problem can be reduced to exploring shared patterns among all the spatial objects (base classifiers) in the spatial database (ensemble model).

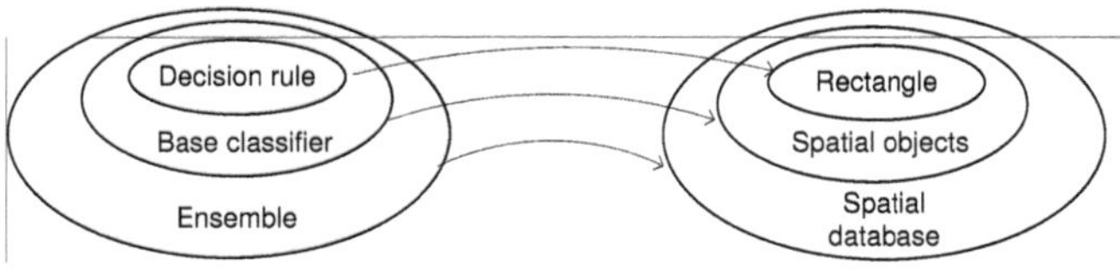

Figure 2: Mapping an ensemble model to a spatial database.

Spatial databases have been extensively studied in the past several decades. Many spatial indexing structures exist that utilize shared patterns among spatial data to reduce query and update costs [11]. Examples include *R-tree* [12], *R*-tree* [25], *R+-tree* [23], *M-tree* [6], to name a few [24]. Generally speaking, these methods can be used to index ensemble models. However, compared to traditional spatial databases, indexing ensemble models has its unique characteristics that pose non-trivial technical challenges:

- **Complex indexing objects.** Existing spatial indexing methods are designed for *conventional spatial data* such as image, map, and multimedia data. The indexing objects for ensemble models are *decision rules* with much richer information, including class labels, class probability distribution, and weights of classifiers.
- **Different objectives.** Conventional spatial indexing aims at fast retrieval and updating of spatial data. Ensemble model indexing aims at fast prediction of incoming stream records.
- **Changing data distributions.** Due to concept drifting, hidden patterns underneath stream data change continuously. Thus a decision region in ensemble models may be associated with different class labels.

In light of these challenges, in this paper we propose a novel *Ensemble-tree* (E-tree for short) structure that organizes base classifiers in a height-balanced tree structure to achieve logarithmic time complexity for prediction. Technically, an E-tree has three key operations: (1) Search: traverse the E-tree to classify an incoming stream record x; (2) Insertion: Integrate new classifier member into the E-tree; (3) Deletion: Remove the outdated classifier from the E-tree. As a result, E-tree approach not only guarantees a logarithmic time complexity for prediction, but also able to adapt to new trends and patterns in stream data.

The rest of the paper is structured as follows. Section 2 introduces the ensemble indexing problem. Section 3 describes the main structure and key operations of E-trees. Section 4 studies the theoretical aspects of E-trees. Section 5 reports experiments. Section 6 surveys the related work. We conclude the paper in Section 7.

Table 1: The five base classifiers in Example 1.

ID	Decision Rules
C_1	if $(r_1 \le 1.5) \wedge (r_2 \le 1.5)$ then abnormal; otherwise normal
C_2	if $(0.5 \le r_1 \le 2) \wedge (0.5 \le r_2 \le 2)$ then abnormal; otherwise normal
C_3	if $(1 \le r_1 \le 2.5) \wedge (1 \le r_2 \le 2.5)$ then abnormal; otherwise normal
C_4	if $(2.5 \le r_1 \le 4) \wedge (2.5 \le r_2 \le 4)$ then abnormal; otherwise normal
C_5	if $(3.5 \le r_1 \le 5) \wedge (3.5 \le r_2 \le 5)$ then abnormal; otherwise normal

2. PROBLEM DESCRIPTION

Formally, consider a two-class data stream S consisting of an infinite number of records $\{(x_i, y_i)\}$, where $x_i \in \mathbb{R}^d$ is a d-dimensional attribute vector, and $y_i \in \{normal, abnormal\}$ is the class label, which is invisible unless the sample is properly labeled. Suppose that we have built n base classifiers $C_1, C_2, \cdots, C_n$ from historical stream data using a decision tree algorithm (such as C4.5). All the n base classifies are combined together as an ensemble classifier E. Each base classifier C_i $(1 \le i \le n)$ is comprised of l decision rules R_{ij} $(1 \le j \le l)$ represented by conjunction literals (*i.e.*, rules are expressed as "*if...then...*"). Then, there are $N = n \times l$ decision rules in the ensemble E. The **aim** of this paper is to generate accurate prediction for an incoming stream record x, using the ensemble model E, with sub-linear time complexity $O(log(N))$.

In order to achieve this goal, we first convert each base classifier C_i $(1 \le i \le n)$ into a batch of spatial objects o_{i_j} $(1 \le j \le l)$. This way, the ensemble model E is converted to a spatial database A_E containing all spatial objects o_{i_j} $(1 \le i \le n, 1 \le j \le l)$. As a result, the original problem is reduced to *classifying each incoming stream record x by searching over the spatial database* A_E.

In the following we use Example 1 to illustrate the mapping from the ensemble model E to the spatial database A_E. This example will be used throughout the paper.

Example 1. Consider a Web monitoring stream S having two classes (normal and abnormal). Suppose that each stream record has two attributes r_1, r_2, where $r_i \in [0, 5]$, and the most recent five base classifiers $C_1, C_2, \cdots, C_5$ built along the stream are incorporated in the ensemble model E, with decision rules for the base classifiers listed in Table 1. For simplicity, each classifier contains one literal clause (in an if-then expression) corresponding to the target abnormal class. The goal is to classify each incoming record x using the ensemble E.

Now we demonstrate the conversion of the ensemble model E to a spatial database A_E. As shown in Fig. 3, the whole decision space is a two-dimensional rectangle $A = (0, 0, 5, 5)$. For each base classifier, a small gray rectangle is used to represent its decision rule for the target abnormal class. Besides, due to concept drifting, the gray rectangles associated with the five classifiers drift from the bottom left corner to the upper right corner in the decision space A. By doing so, the ensemble model can be represented by a batch of spatial objects (*i.e.*, the gray rectangles) generated from all base classifiers. These spatial objects constitute the spatial database A_E. Given a small circle $x = (4, 4)$ as an incoming record, we want to classify x as accurate and as fast as possible by searching over A_E.

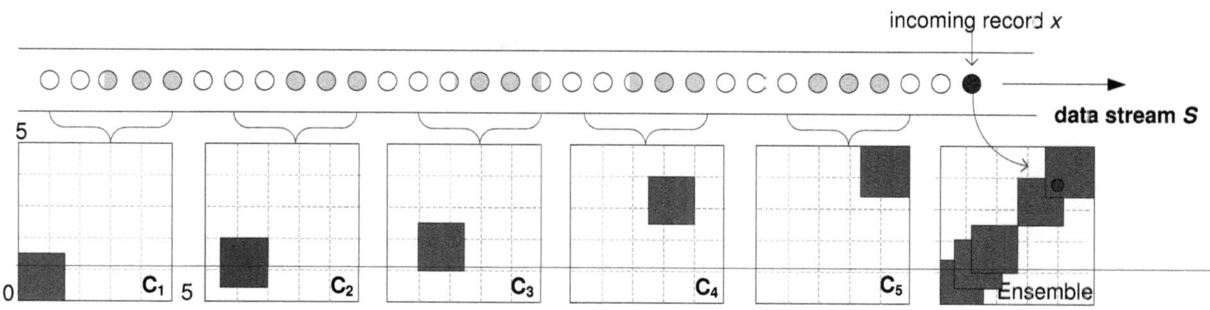

Figure 3: Mapping ensemble E in Example 1 to spatial database A_E.

3. THE E-TREE INDEXING STRUCTURE

In this section, we introduce the E-tree data structure and the three key operations, *Search*, *Insertion*, and *Deletion* for maintaining E-trees.

3.1 The basic structure of E-trees

An E-tree, as shown in Fig. 4, is a height-balanced tree mainly consisting of two components: (1) an *R-tree* like structure T on the right-hand side storing all decision rules of the ensemble, and (2) a *table structure* on the left-hand side storing all the classifier-level information of the ensemble, such as IDs and weights of the classifiers. The two structures are connected together by linking each classifier in the table to its corresponding decision rules in the tree.

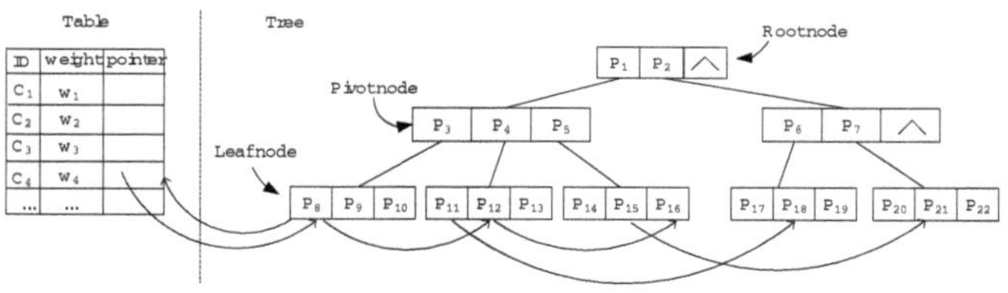

Figure 4: An illustration of E-tree (some links are omitted).

The tree structure consists of two different types of nodes: leaf nodes and pivot nodes. Similar to R-trees, each leaf node contains a batch of decision rules that are located in a heavily overlapping area in the decision space. Each decision rule can be represented as a special type of spatial object of the following form

$$(I, classifier\_id, sibling), \qquad (1)$$

where I denotes a rectangle bounding the decision rule, $classifier\_id$ denotes the classifier generating the decision rule, and $sibling$ denotes the memory address of the next decision rule generated by the same classifier. Generally, a decision rule covers a closed space $I = (I_0, I_1, \cdots, I_d)$ with each I_i representing a closed bounded interval along dimension i. On the other hand, a pivot node in the tree structure contains entries in the form of

$$(I, child\_pointer), \qquad (2)$$

where I is the smallest rectangle covering all the decision rules in its child nodes, and *child_pointer* references its child node. Every non-root node contains between m and M entries. The root node has at least two entries unless it is a leaf.

The table structure contains information about all base classifiers in an ensemble model with each entry denoted as follows:

$$(classifier\_id, weight, pointer), \qquad (3)$$

where the first item represents the classifier ID in the ensemble, the second item represents the classifier's weight, and the last item denotes the memory address of its first component decision rule in the tree structure.

While R-trees index conventional spatial objects such as image, map, and multimedia data, E-trees index a new type of spatial data, decision rules, with the following constrains:

- All decision rules make built in a continuous attribute space. In case that a discrete attribute is observed, we can convert it to a continuous attribute by severely penalizing its difference. For example, if a binary attribute r_3 $(True, False)$ appears in Example 1, and the decision rule in C_1 is "*if* $(r_1 \leq 1.5) \wedge (r_2 \leq 1.5) \wedge (r_3 = True)$ *then abnormal; otherwise normal*", the decision rule in C_2 is "*if* $(0.5 \leq r_1 \leq 2) \wedge (0.5 \leq r_2 \leq 2) \wedge (r_3 = False)$ *then abnormal; otherwise normal*", then the first decision rule on abnormal class will be $(0, 0, 0, 1.5, 1.5, 0)$, while the second one will be $(0.5, 0.5, 1, 2, 2, 1)$. However, any change of r_3 will be heavily penalized by assigning a much heavier weight.

- Each decision rule covers a closed space. In case a decision rule covers only a partially-closed space, a lower or upper bound of the decision space will be added to make it closed. For example, in Example 1, decision rule R_{11} from classifier C_1 is a half-closed rule $(r_1 \leq 1.5) \wedge (r_2 \leq 1.5)$, then the lower bound $r_1 = 0, r_2 = 0$ will be added to make it a closed space $(0 \leq r_1 \leq 1.5) \wedge (0 \leq r_2 \leq 1.5)$. Moreover, if a decision rule covers only k $(k < d)$ dimensions, it will be expanded over the remaining $(d - k)$ dimensions. For example, for a decision rule defined in partially closed space as follows:

  $\mathcal{R} = (0 \leq r_1 \leq 1.5)$

  We will expand $\mathcal{R}$ to a closed space as

  $\mathcal{R}' = (0 \leq r_1 \leq 1.5) \wedge (0 \leq r_2 \leq 5)$.

- All decision rules are "hard" decisions. For example, a Web page has 100% chance of being malicious or not. Therefore, there are no explicit items in Eqs.(1) and (2) to define the posterior class distributions.

- We only consider binary classification. Moreover, we only index decision rules from one class (the minor class containing fewer decision rules). For multi-class classification, an intuitive method is to combine multiple E-trees together by using a one-against-one or one-against-all strategy.

Example 2. Fig. 5 shows the E-tree structure for the ensemble model used in Example 1. For simplicity, some links from leaf nodes to the table structure are omitted.

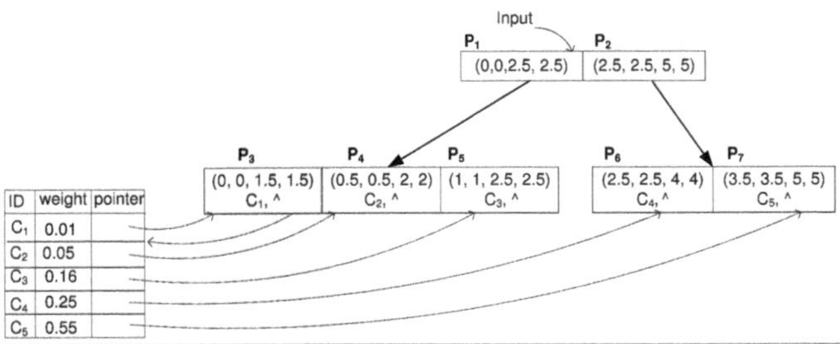

Figure 5: E-tree for the ensemble model in Example 1.

3.2 Search operation

Each time a new record x arrives, a search operation is invoked to predict a class label for x. The algorithm first traverses the E-tree and finds decision rules in the leaf node(s) covering record x. Then it calculates the class label for x by combining decisions from all the retrieved decision rules using Eq. (4),

$$y_x = sgn(\Sigma_{i=1}^{u} w_i P(C_{index}|x),\ \gamma), \tag{4}$$

where y_x denotes the class label of x, u is the total number of retrieved decision rules covering x, $sgn(a, \gamma)$ is a threshold function that decides x's class label by comparing a and γ, and C_{index} is the indexing class in the tree. Recall that only the minor class with fewer decision rules is indexed in E-trees. For instance, in Example 1, C_{index} represents the abnormal class. $P(C_{index}|x)$ is a "hard" posterior probability of either 0 or 1.

Algorithm 1 lists detailed procedures of the search operation. The algorithm performs a depth-first search over the tree. To derive a class label for x, it first traverses along the branches whose rectangles cover x, and then calculates the class label for x using Eq. (4). In the following, we use Example 3 derived from Example 1 to explain the search process.

Example 3. Suppose $x = (4, 4)$ is an incoming record as shown in Example 1, and the parameter γ in Eq. (4) is 0.5. The search algorithm first compares x with entries P_1 and P_2 in the root node, and then descends along entry P_2 that covers x. After that, it finds that both entries (P_6 and P_7) in P_2's child cover x. Next, it obtains the weights for entries P_6 and P_7 in the table structure through their *classifier_id* entries. Based on these results, the probability of x belonging to the abnormal class can be calculated as follow:

$$w_4 P(abnormal|x) + w_5 P(abnormal|x) = 0.75 > 0.5.$$

Therefore, x is predicted as abnormal. In this example, at worst four comparisons will be used (P_1, P_2, P_6, and P_7). Compared to a linear scan that needs five comparisons, E-tree achieves a 20% improvement.

3.3 Insertion operation

Insertions are used to integrate new base classifiers into the ensemble model, so that the ensemble model can adapt to new trends and patterns in data streams. Algorithm 2 lists detailed procedures of the insertion operation. When a new classifier C arrives, a new entry associated with C is added into the table structure. Meanwhile, its decision rules R are inserted into the tree structure one by one, and linked together by their pointer entries.

Inserting R into the tree structure is similar to the insertion operation in R-trees. First, a *searchLeaf(R, T)* function is used to find a leaf node to insert each decision rule R. This function searches from the root node, and traverses the branches covering R. Once a leaf node (e.g., P_L) is found, the algorithm will investigate whether node P_L has spare room for inserting R. If it contains less than

Algorithm 1: Search

```
Input : E-tree T, stream record x, parameter γ
Output: x's class label y_x
Initialize(stack) ;   // initialize a stack for search
U ← ∅ ;               // U records all rules covering x
P ← T.tree.root ;     // get the root of the tree
foreach entry R ∈ T do
    push(stack, R) ;
while stack ≠ ∅ do
    e ← pop(stack) ;
    if e is an entry of a leaf then
        U ← U ∪ e ;
    else
        P ← e.child ;
        foreach entry e ∈ P do
            if x ∈ e then
                push (stack, e) ;
foreach entry e ∈ U do
    find its weights in the table structure ;
y_x ← Call Eq. (4) to calculate x's class label ;
Output y_x ;
```

M entries, then R will be successfully inserted, and a function *updateParentNode(P_L)* will be invoked to revise the corresponding entry in the parent node to cover the minimum bounding rectangle of the new node. On the other hand, if node P_L is full, a *splitNode(P_L)* function will be invoked to split the current leaf node.

The most critical step in the insertion operation is node splitting. Similar to R-trees, by principle *the total area of the two covering rectangles after a split should be minimized.* Compared to existing methods, node splitting in E-trees faces a new challenge which is that a decision rule may contain discrete attributes that can not be changed during area enlargement. To solve this problem, a much heavier weight is assigned to each discrete attribute during node splitting to avoid enlargement or shrinkage. Formally, when a new entry R is added into node P incurring a split, the following objective function should be optimized,

$$< P_L, P_R >= argmin_{<X,Y>|X,Y \in R \cup P}\ (X.I + Y.I,) \tag{5}$$

where X and Y are variables, and P_L and P_R are the new nodes containing R and all entries in P. Obviously, solving Eq. (5) requires investigation of all possible groupings of all nodes in $R \cup P$, and thus is an NP-hard problem. In other words, when M is large, Eq. (5) is very hard to solve. Then, a greedy heuristic would first randomly select two entries in $R \cup P$ that has the largest distance, and then cluster all the remaining $m - 1$ entries in $R \cup P$ into the given two classes.

In the following we use Example 4 to explain the insertion and node splitting of the five classifiers in Example 1. This process is also illustrated in Fig. 6. Due to the page limit, we omit the table structure in the E-tree.

Example 4. We insert the five classifier in Example 1 one by one. Suppose parameters $M = 3$ and $m = \lfloor \frac{M}{2} \rfloor = 1$. The first three classifiers can be inserted by simply adding them to the root node. Upon inserting C_4, the number of entries in the root node is four, which exceeds M. Thus, the greedy splitting algorithm with initial points $(0, 0, 1, 1)$ and $(2.5, 2.5, 4, 4)$ will be invoked to partition the root node into two leaf nodes. Besides, a new root node with two entries is generated to index the two leaf nodes. In the end, C_5 is

Algorithm 2: Insertion

Input : E-tree T, classifier C, parameters m, M
Output: Updated E-tree T'

$P \leftarrow T.tree.root$; `// get the root of the tree`
foreach *decision rule* $R \in C$ **do**
  $L \leftarrow searchLeaf(R, P)$; `// leaf node L contains R`
  if $L.size < m$ **then**
    $L \leftarrow L \cup R$;
    $T' \leftarrow updateParentNode(L)$;
  else
    $< P_L, P_R > \leftarrow splitNode(L, R)$;
    $T' \leftarrow adjustTree(T, P_L, P_R)$;
Insert C into the table structure ;
Output T' ;

inserted into the right leaf node directly as the node size is smaller than M.

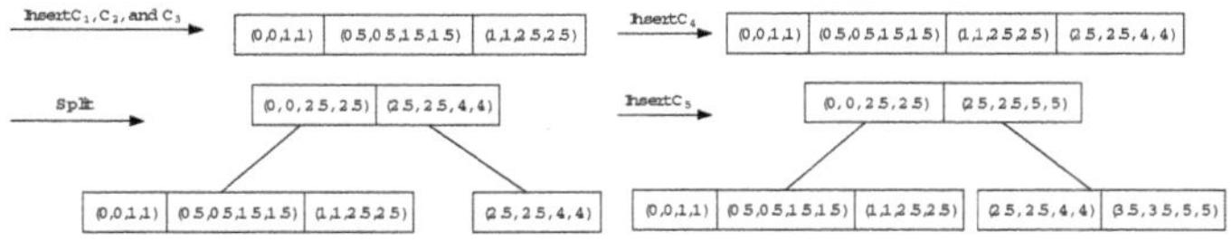

Figure 6: Inserting the five classifiers in Example 1 to E-tree.

3.4 Deletion operation

The deletion operation discards outdated classifiers when the E-tree reaches its capacity. For example, if the largest classifier size is set to four in Example 1, C_1 will be discarded from the E-tree when C_5 arrives.

Possibly two different deletion methods can be adopted. The first one resembles deletions in B-trees. It merges the under-full nodes to one of the siblings resulting in the least area increase. The second one resembles deletions in R-trees and performs *delete-then-insert*. It first deletes the under-full node, then inserts the remaining entries into the tree using the insertion operation.

The second method is advantageous in that: (1) It is easy to implement. (2) Re-insertion will incrementally refine the spatial structure of the tree. In addition, it has been shown [12] that the B-tree method may cause excessive node splits. Therefore, we use the second method for our deletion operation. Specifically, if a classifier C needs to be deleted from the E-tree, we first find its classifier ID in the table structure using function *searchClassifier(C, A)*, and then delete its component decision rules by traversing the pointer entries. After each deletion, if a leaf node has less than m entries, the node will be deleted and re-inserted into the E-tree. The update will propagate to the upper level unless the $[m, M]$ condition is met. Algorithm 3 gives the details of the deletion operation.

3.5 Ensemble learning with E-trees

Fig. 7 shows the architecture of ensemble learning with E-trees on data streams. The training module maintains an E-tree that is constantly updated by calling the *insertion* and *deletion* operations. The prediction module contains a synchronized copy of the E-tree to make online predictions by calling the *search* operation.

For each incoming stream record, on one hand, the prediction module will call the search operation to predict its class label. On the other hand, the record will be stored in a buffer of the training module, where it will be labeled by experts (either human experts

Algorithm 3: Deletion

Input : E-tree T, classifier C, parameters m, M
Output: Updated E-tree T'

$P \leftarrow T.tree.root$; `// get the root of the tree`
$A \leftarrow T.table.ref$; `// get the reference in the table`
$R \leftarrow searchClassifier(C, A)$; `// get C from table A`
$P \leftarrow R.pointer$;
while $P \neq \emptyset$ **do**
  $L \leftarrow P.node()$; `// leaf node L contains rule P`
  $q \leftarrow P.sibling$;
  $L' \leftarrow deleteEntry(L, P)$;
  if $L'.size < m$ **then**
    $T' \leftarrow deleteNode(T, L')$; `// recursive deletion`
    foreach *entry* $e \in L'$ **do**
      $T' \leftarrow insertRule(e, T)$;
  $P \leftarrow q$;
Output T' ;

or intelligent labeling machines). Note that the labeling process is time-consuming, and only a small portion of incoming records can be labeled. In order to provide uniform labeling, a practical approach is to set a sampling frequency parameter that matches the labeling speed. Once the buffer gets full, all the labeled records will be used to build a new classifier, which is inserted into the E-tree by calling the insertion operation. In case the E-tree is full, an outdated classifier will be deleted by calling the deletion operation. The updated E-tree will be synchronized to the E-tree copy in the prediction module.

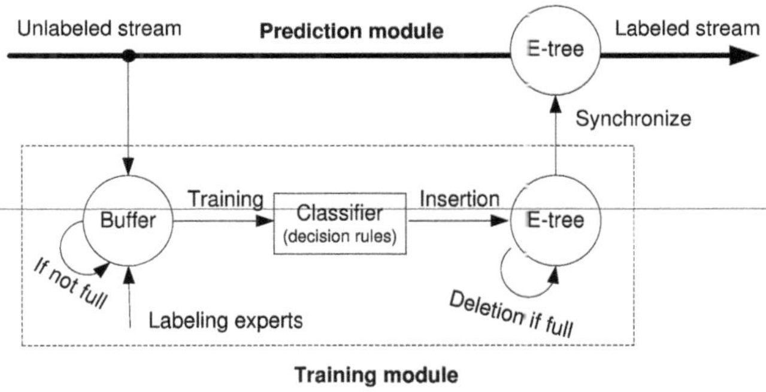

Figure 7: Architecture of Ensemble Learning with E-trees.

4. THEORETICAL ANALYSIS OF E-TREES

In this section, we provide theoretical study on the properties and performance of E-trees. In classifying a stream record x using an E-tree, the ideal scenario is that all target decision rules covering x are located in one single leaf node. This way, the search algorithm only needs to traverse one path down the tree to make the final prediction for x. On the other hand, in the worst scenario, if the target decision rules span all the leaf nodes, the search algorithm has to traverse all possible pathes in order to classify x. In light of this observation, the key to analyzing E-tree's performance is to estimate the probability that x's target decision rules are located in one single leaf node.

Assume decision rules are mutually independent (dependency between rules will only improve E-tree's performance as will be discussed shortly), the probability that two rules are located in the same leaf node is proportional to the overlapping region between two hyper-rectangles representing the two rules. Thus, the problem becomes that given a set of decision rules, how to estimate the size of their overlapping region?

To answer this question, consider two decision rules R_a and R_b in the $d-$ dimensional space $S = S_1 \times S_2 \times \cdots \times S_d$, where $S_i \in [0, s_i]$, $1 \leq i \leq d$. Since not all rules cover all the d-dimensions, rules R_a and R_b may overlap on some dimensions. Without loss of generality, assume rule R_a is defined on r_a dimensions $S_1 \times S_2 \times \cdots \times S_{r_a}$, with the ith $(1 \leq i \leq r_a)$ dimension S_i spanning in a_i region (out of the whole domain $[0, s_i]$), and rule R_b is defined on r_b dimensions $S_{1'} \times S_{2'} \times \cdots \times S_{r_b}$, with the jth $(1 \leq j \leq r_b)$ dimension S_j spanning in b_j region. Due to the temporal correlations of data streams, it is often the case that R_a and R_b overlap on r $(r < r_a, r < r_b)$ dimensions. Then, we have Theorem 1 as follows:

THEOREM 1. *Given two decision rules R_a and R_b, the probability that they are located in the same leaf node $\mathcal{P}$ is*

$$\mathcal{P} \propto \prod_{i=1}^{r} \frac{a_i \cdot b_i}{s_i \cdot s_i} \prod_{j=r+1}^{r_a} \frac{a_j}{s_j} \prod_{k=r+1}^{r_b} \frac{b_k}{s_k}. \tag{6}$$

PROOF. Obviously, for each of the first r common dimensions, S_i, the common region between the two rules on this dimension is the overlapping region between a_i and b_i, which is equivalent to the expectation of observing a joint event a_i and b_i, as $E(a_i \wedge b_i)$. Because observing a_i out of the whole domain $[0, s_i]$ is a_i/s_i, and R_a and R_b are assumed to be independently generated, we have

$$E(a_i \wedge b_i) = E(a_i) \cdot E(b_i) = \frac{a_i \cdot b_i}{s_i \cdot s_i}. \tag{7}$$

For any of the remaining $r_a - r$ dimensions for rule R_a (*i.e.*, the jth, $r \leq j \leq r_a$ dimension), it spans in a region a_j. For rule R_b, it spans over the whole s_j region (Recall in Section 3.1, a disclosed decision rule will be spanned over the whole undefined attribute space). As a result, the common region between the two rules in s_j is given as

$$E(a_j) = \frac{a_j}{s_j}. \tag{8}$$

Similarly, for decision rule R_b, the shared interval on the $k^{th}, 1 \leq k \leq r_b$ dimension is b_k/s_k. Because dimensions and rules are assumed to be independent, the total overlapping area can be calculated by multiplying all the above three terms, as defined in Theorem 1. □

Assume that an incoming record has t target decision rules that are mutually independent, the probability that all these rules being located in the same leaf node is proportional to

$$\mathcal{P}' = (\prod_{i=1}^{r} \frac{a_i \cdot b_i}{s_i \cdot s_i} \prod_{j=r+1}^{r_a} \frac{a_j}{s_j} \prod_{k=r+1}^{r_b} \frac{b_k}{s_k})^{t-1}. \tag{9}$$

5. EXPERIMENTS

In this section, we present extensive experiments on both synthetic and real-world data streams to validate the performance of E-trees with respect to prediction time, memory usage, and prediction accuracy. All experiments were conducted on a Linux machine with 3GHz CPU and 2GB memory. The E-tree source code can be downloaded from *http://streammining.org*.

Benchmark data streams. Three real-world streams and one synthetic steam from the UCI repository were used [2]. Table 2 lists the real streams after using the F-Score feature selection [5]. All

Table 2: Real-world data streams

Name	Instances	Attributes (Feature selection)	Areas
intrusion detection	4000000	11	Security
spam detection	460001	15	Security
malicious url detection	488420	14	Security

of them are binary classification problems. Due to the page limit, please refer to [2] for detailed descriptions. The synthetic stream is similar to Example 1. It was generated as follows. First, we randomly generated a collection of stream data $\{\cdots, (x_i, y_i), \cdots\}$, where $x_i \in \mathbb{R}^d$ is a d-dimensional vector with the j^{th}element $x_{ij} \in [0, 1]$, and $y_i \in \{normal, abnormal\}$ is the class label. Thus the decision space is a d-dimensional hyper-cube. The class of each stream record was defined by the rule that if $a \leq x_i \leq b$, where $a \in [0, 1]^d, b \in [0, 1]^d, a_i < b_i$ for each $i \in [1, d]$, then "abnormal"; otherwise, "normal". That is to say, we defined a small sub-cube in the decision space as the abnormal class. To simulate concept drifting, after generating a data chunk of D records, we randomly selected its $j^{th}, (1 \leq j \leq d)$ dimension a_j, b_j to change to $a_j + u\alpha, b_j + u\alpha$, where $u = \{-1, 1\}$ controls the direction of the change and $u = -1$ with 50% probability. If the upper or lower bound of the decision space is reached, u will change it value. For simplicity, we initially set $\alpha = 0.1$ and $b - a = 0.5$.

Benchmark methods. We implemented four benchmark methods for comparison purposes. (1) Global E-tree (**GE-tree**). In this method, there is no upper bound on the number of base classifiers in an ensemble. For each new base classifier, GE-tree simply integrates it into the ensemble and deletions are never invoked. (2) Local E-tree (**LE-tree**). Different from GE-tree, LE-tree sets an upper bound on the ensemble size. Once the upper bound is reached, the oldest classifier will be removed from the ensemble Obviously, E-trees are in the LE-tree category. (3) Global Ensemble (**G-Ensemble**). In this method, a traditional linear scan is used during prediction. Classifiers will be added into the ensemble model continuously without deletions. (4) Local Ensemble (**L-Ensemble**). Similar to LE-tree, an upper bound on the ensemble size is set. In all the four methods, C4.5 was used to generate decision rules from data streams. All the decision rules are "hard" decisions.

Measures. Three measures were used. (1) Time cost. By using a height-balanced tree to index all classifiers in the ensemble, E-trees are expected to achieve a much lower computational cost than typical ensemble models. (2) Memory cost. E-trees are expected to consume a larger yet affordable memory space. (3) Accuracy. E-trees are expected to achieve the same prediction accuracy as original ensemble models.

Experimental results. We compared the four methods under different parameter settings on number of classifiers n, parameter M, and the target indexing class. By default the chunk size was set to 10000, parameter γ was set to 0.5, the ensemble size was set to 30 for the local methods and 100 for the global methods. Besides, all base classifiers were weighted by an averaging weighting scheme.

Parameter M. This parameter controls the node size and is the most important one for E-trees. If a node contains more than M entries, node splitting will be invoked. Ideally, M should be set such that splits do not happen when the entries in a node heavily overlap each other. Fig. 8 shows E-tree's performance with respect to different M values on both synthetic and real-world data streams. From the results we have the following observations. When M increases at the very early stage (e.g., from 10 to 30), both the prediction time and memory cost decrease significantly. After that, the

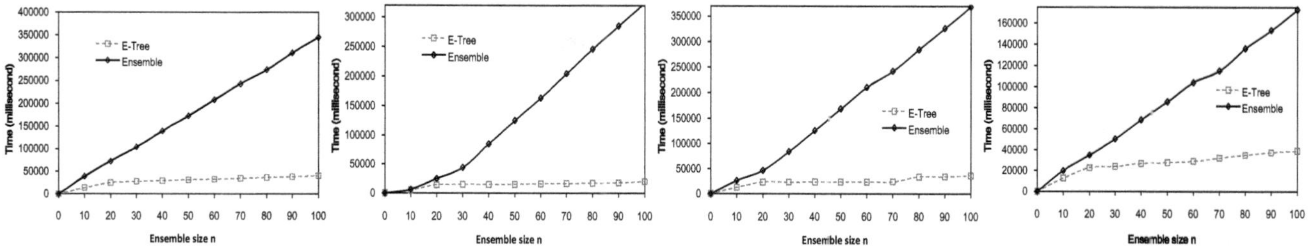

(a) Syn-10 (b) Intrusion detection (c) Spam detection (d) Malicious URL detection

Figure 9: E-trees vs. original ensemble models with respect to prediction time. We can observe that E-trees significantly reduced the prediction time.

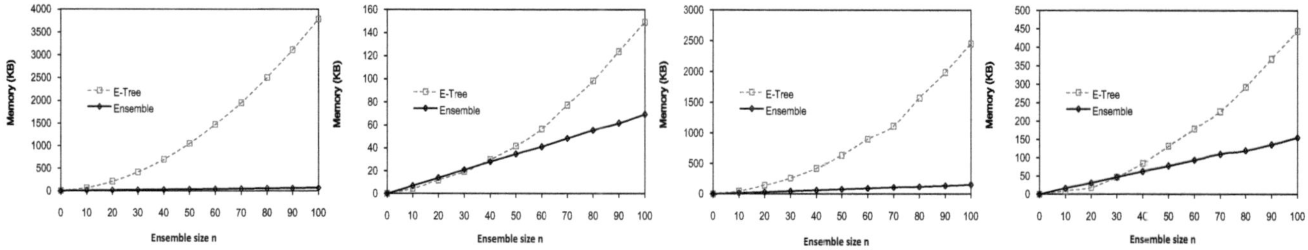

(a) Syn-10 (b) Intrusion detection (c) Spam detection (d) Malicious URL detection

Figure 10: E-trees vs. original ensemble models with respect to memory consumption. We can observe that E-trees consume larger yet affordable memory space.

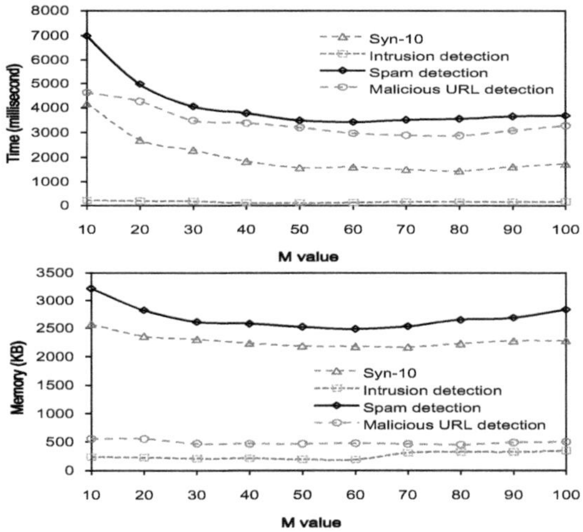

Figure 8: Comparisons with respect to different M values.

benefit becomes marginal and then turns negative with increasing M. For example, in the spam data set, when M increases from 10 to 40, the prediction time drops sharply from 6990ms to 3780ms, meanwhile the memory cost also drops quickly from 3218KB to 2520KB. On the other hand, when M increases from 60 to 100, both the prediction and memory costs increase.

To see why, increasing M at an early stage reduces the numbers of pivot nodes and leaf nodes. As a result, entries that overlap heavily can be stored in the same node, leading to reduced search and storage costs. However, when M continues to increase, entries that slightly overlap with each other will be mistakenly stored in the same node, leading to extra comparisons on each node and increased search time. Therefore, a satisfactory M value should

Table 3: Indexing different classes

Data stream	Class	Rules	LE-tree Time (ms)	LE-tree Mem. (KB)	GE-tree Time (ms)	GE-tree Mem. (KB)
Syn-10	Abnormal	**1234**	**1659**	**70.25**	**4712**	**3082**
	Normal	2238	3149	81.69	5921	4085
Intrusion detection	Abnormal	2308	1250	20.8	4850	340.50
	Normal	**20**	**62**	**1.50**	**169**	**114.90**
Spam detection	Spam	1172	4362	46.38	6532	3458
	Non-spam	**1089**	**3484**	**46.29**	**5933**	**2547.07**
Malicious URL detection	Malicious	**168**	**1099**	**35.04**	**1206**	**147.26**
	Benign	177	2815	37.52	3166	149.48

neither be too large nor too small. In the following experiments M was set to 30.

Ensemble size n. To evaluate how E-trees improve on predicting efficiency, we compared the LE-tree and GE-tree methods by varying ensemble size n. From the results in Fig. 9 and Fig. 10, we can come to two important conclusions: (1) E-trees can significantly reduce the prediction cost. For example, in the malicious URL detection data stream, when n = 100, E-tree took 39166ms to classify a record, about four times faster than the original ensemble model, which took 172937ms. (2) As far as the memory cost is considered, E-trees consumes larger yet affordable memory space comparing to the original ensemble models.

Target indexing class. As discussed in Section 3.1, for a binary classification problem, E-trees only index decision rules from the target class. Which class should be selected as the target class? To answer this question, we conducted a series of experiments presented in Table 3. From the results we can observe that, indexing the minor class will enhance E-tree's performance. For example, in the intrusion detection data stream, there are 20 decision rules for "normal" and 2308 for "abnormal". It is obvious that indexing "normal" will significantly reduce the prediction time. Thus, for

Table 4: Comparisons among benchmark methods

Data stream	LE-tree			L-Ensemble			GE-tree			G-Ensemble		
	Time (ms)	Memory (KB)	Error (%)	Time (ms)	Memory (KB)	Error (%)	Time (ms)	Memory (KB)	Error (%)	Time (ms)	Memory (KB)	Error (%)
Syn-5	**1712**	12.29	4.37	32360	**1.67**	4.37	3001	2320.97	4.01	345140	121.42	4.01
Syn-10	**1659**	70.25	7.05	37125	**1.63**	7.05	4712	3082	6.41	345140	690.42	6.41
Intrusion	**62**	1.50	1.03	337	**0.93**	1.03	169	114.90	0.96	444.50	107.76	0.96
Spam	**3484**	46.29	8.28	47406	**3.15**	8.28	5933	2547.07	9.18	368969	155.17	9.18
URL	**1099**	35.04	5.64	35890	**0.93**	5.64	1206	147.26	5.64	136891	78.27	5.64
Adult	**6523**	80.80	19.66	20361	**6.37**	19.66	7452	2135.06	19.59	449078	800.14	19.59
Magic	**3145**	40.45	7.18	36250	**3.07**	7.18	7263	1378.14	4.74	336880	401.40	4.74
Winered	**3657**	46.50	22.32	31250	**3.57**	22.32	11220	632.56	23.38	305950	463.10	23.38
Winewhite	**3031**	118.50	23.43	38120	**2.95**	23.43	8849	5825.37	23.43	350640	1070.60	23.43
Census	**782**	261.70	5.77	133600	**0.76**	5.77	1153	9375	5.73	1234840	2518.80	5.73

binary classification the minor class should be chosen as the target class.

Comparisons among benchmark methods. We compared the four benchmark methods on 10 data sets as shown in Table 4. From the results, we can observe that: (1) LE-tree performs better than GE-tree with respect to both prediction time and memory cost. For example, in the Syn-10 data stream, LE-tree is nearly three times faster than GE-tree, meanwhile takes less memory space. (2) LE-tree performs better than L-Ensemble with respect to prediction time. Besides, LE-tree achieves the same prediction accuracy with L-Ensemble. For example, in the URL data stream, LE-tree only takes 3% prediction time of L-Ensemble, but achieves the same prediction error rate 5.60%. On the other hand, although LE-tree consumes more memory than L-Ensemble, it is still an efficient method, continuously deleting outdated classifiers to release memory space. This guarantees that LE-tree will not be too large to be stored in main memory. (3) LE-tree performs better than G-Ensemble with respect to prediction time and memory cost. It is obvious that E-tree, which indexes the most recent classifiers, will perform better than G-Ensemble, which linearly scans all historical classifiers during prediction.

6. RELATED WORK

Stream classification. Existing data stream classification models can be categorized into two groups: online / incremental models [8, 7] and ensemble learning [14, 26, 31, 16, 10, 36, 33, 4]. The former aims to build a single sophisticated model that can be continuously updated. Examples include the Very Fast Decision Tree (VFDT) model and the incremental SVM model. Ensemble learning employs a divide-and-conquer strategy. It first splits continuous data streams into small data chunks, and then builds light-weight base classifiers for these chunks. Ensemble models scale well to large volumes of stream data, adapt quickly to new concepts, achieve a lower variance error, and are easy to be parallelized [4]. Due to these advantages, ensemble learning has become a common tool for data stream classification.

Stream indexing. A stream classification model can be considered as a special query model that queries for class labels of incoming stream records. However, it differs from traditional query models, such as *aggregate query* [3] that aims to obtain statistical results from data streams, and *boolean expression query* [28, 20] where queries appear as DNF or CNF expressions [28]. Classification queries involve more complex *if-then* rules that may contain both continuous and discrete attributes. They also have to face decision conflicts due to concept drifting. These differences lead to different indexing techniques. Other stream indexing methods exist that index multimedia data [17] or micro-clusters [21] on data streams. However, none of them considers the problem of indexing classifiers for anytime data stream classification.

Spatial indexing. The E-tree originates from the R-tree. The R-tree has been extensively studied in the past several decades, and many variants have been proposed to enhance its performance, such as the R^**-tree* [25], R^+*-tree* [23], *Hilbert R-tree* [15], and *SS-tree* [29]. The techniques in these works can be employed to enhance E-tree's performance.

Ensemble pruning. For the purpose of reducing computational and memory costs, ensemble pruning [34, 18] searches for a good subset of all ensemble members that performs as well as the original ensemble. A basic assumption in ensemble pruning is that all the base models in the ensemble share a unique global probability distribution. Thus, some base models can be discarded from the ensemble to reduce prediction costs. However, in dynamic data streams, concepts change continuously, and it is very difficult to predict which base model(s) can be discarded from the ensemble.

7. CONCLUSIONS

Ensemble learning has become a common tool for data stream classification. However, existing ensemble models perform a linear scan of all base classifiers during prediction, which is increasingly inadequate for many real world applications that involve large volumes of data steams with concept drifting and require timely responses. To address this problem, we proposed a novel E-tree indexing structure to organize the base classifiers, achieving $O(log(N))$ time prediction for incoming stream records. Comprehensive experiments on both synthetic and real-world data streams demonstrated the performance of E-trees for stream classification.

In this study, base classifiers are trained using decision trees and decision rules can be represented as spatial objects in the decision space. In case that base classifiers are trained using other non-axis-parallel classification models such as support vector machines, k nearest neighbors or neural networks, rule extraction can be applied to extract if-then rules from such black-box models [9, 13]. Then, these models can also be converted to spatial objects and indexed using E-trees.

The main contributions of this study are twofold: (1) We are the first to formulate and address the prediction efficiency problem for ensemble models on data streams, which is a legitimate research problem well motivated by increasing real-world applications. (2) Our solution converts ensemble models into spatial databases and applies spatial indexing techniques to achieve sub-linear prediction. This novel technique can be extended to other data stream classification models besides ensemble learning, or general classification models that require timely prediction.

8. ACKNOWLEDGMENTS

This research was partially supported by the National Science Foundation of China (NSFC) under Grant No.61003167, Basic Research Program of China (973 Program) under Grant No.2007CB311100, the Texas Norman Hackerman Advanced Research Program under Grant No.003656-0035-2009, and Australian Research Council (ARC) Future Fellowship under Grant No.FT100100971.

9. REFERENCES

[1] C. Aggarwal. *Data Streams: Models and Algorithms*. Springer, 2006.

[2] A. Asuncion and D. Newman. *UCI Machine Learning Repository*. Irvine, CA, 2007.

[3] S. Babu and J. Widom. Streamon: An adaptive engine for stream query processing. In *Proc. of SIGMOD 2004*.

[4] A. Bifet, G. Holmes, B. Pfahringer, R. Kirkby, and R. Gavalda. New ensemble methods for evolving data streams. In *Proc. of KDD 2009*.

[5] C.-C. Chang and C.-J. Lin. *LIBSVM: a library for support vector machines, Software available at: http://www.csie.ntu.edu.tw/ cjlin/libsvm*, 2001.

[6] P. Ciaccia, M. Patella, and P. Zezula. M-tree: An efficient access method for similarity search in metric spaces. In *Proc. of VLDB 1997*.

[7] C. Domeniconi and D. Gunopulos. Incremental support vector machine construction. In *Proc. of ICDM 2001*.

[8] P. Domingos and G. Hulten. Mining high-speed data streams. In *Proc. of KDD 2000*.

[9] G. Fung, S. Sandilya, and R. Rao. Rule extraction from linear support vector machines. In *Proc. of KDD 2005*.

[10] J. Gao, W. Fan, and J. Han. On appropriate assumptions to mine data streams: analysis and practice. In *Proc. of ICDM 2007*.

[11] R. Guting. An introduction to spatial database systems. *VLDB Journal*, 3(4), 1994.

[12] A. Guttman. R-trees: A dynamic index structure for spatial searching. In *Proc. of SIGMOD 1984*.

[13] B. Huysmans and J. Vanthienen. Using rule extraction to improve the comprehensibility of predictive models. *Technical report, FETEW Research Report KBI-0612, K.U.Leuven*, 2006.

[14] H.Wang, W. Fan, P. Yu, and J. Han. Mining concept-drifting data streams using ensemble classifiers. In *Proc. of KDD 2003*.

[15] I. Kamel and C. Faloutsos. Hilbert r-tree: An improved r-tree using fractals. In *Proc. of VLDB 1994*, pages 500–509.

[16] J. Kolter and M. Maloof. Using additive expert ensembles to cope with concept drift. In *Proc. of ICML 2005*.

[17] Z. Liu, S. Parthasarathy, A. Ranganathan, and H. Yang. Near-optimal algorithms for shared filter evaluation in data stream systems. In *Proc. of SIGMOD 2008*, pages 133–145.

[18] Z. Lu, X. Wu, X. Zhu, and J. Bongard. Ensemble pruning via individual contribution ordering. In *Proc. of KDD 2010*, pages 871–880.

[19] J. Ma, L Saul, S. Savage, and G. Voelker. Identifying suspicious urls: An application of large-scale online learning In *Proc. of ICML 2009*.

[20] A. Machanavajjhala, E. Vee, M. Garofalakis, and J. Shanmugasundaram. Scalable ranked publish/subscribe. In *Proc. of VLDB 2008*.

[21] C. B. Philipp Kranen, Ira Assent and T. Seidl. The clustree: indexing micro-clusters for anytime stream mining. *Knowledge and Information Systems*, 2010.

[22] J. Quinlan. *C4.5: Programs for Machine Learning*. Morgan Kaufmann Publishers, 1993.

[23] T. Sellis, C. N. Roussopoulos, and Faloutsos. The r^+-tree: A dynamic index for multi-dimensional objects. In *Proc. of VLDB 1997*.

[24] T. Sellis, N. Roussopoulos, and C. Faloutsos. Multi-dimensional access methods: Trees have grown everywhere. In *Proc. of VLDB 1997*.

[25] T. Sellis, N. Roussopoulos, and C. Faloutsos. The r^*-tree: An efficient and robust access method for points and rectangles. In *Proc. of SIGMOD 1990*.

[26] W. N. Street and Y. Kim. A streaming ensemble algorithm (sea) for large-scale classification. In *Proc. of KDD 2001*.

[27] A. Tsymbal. The problem of concept drift: definitions and related work. *Available online: http://scss.tcd.ie/publications/tech-reports/reports.04/TCD-CS-2004-15.pdf*.

[28] S. Whang and H. Molina. Indexing boolean expressions. In *Proc. of VLDB 2009*.

[29] D. White and R. Jain. Similarity indexing with the ss-tree. In *Proc. of IEEE ICDE 1996*.

[30] P. Winston. Available online: www2.cs.uregina.ca/ dbd/cs831/notes/ml/dtrees/c4.5/tutorial.html. 1992.

[31] P. Zhang, X.Zhu, Y. Shi, L.Guo, and X. Wu. Robust ensemble learning for mining noisy data streams. *Decision Support Systems*, 50(2):469–479, 2011.

[32] P. Zhang, X. Zhu, and Y. Shi. Categorizing and mining concept drifting data streams. In *Proc. of KDD 2008*.

[33] P. Zhang, X. Zhu, J. Tan, and L. Guo. Classifier and cluster ensembles for mining concept drifting data streams. In *Proc. of IEEE ICDM 2010*.

[34] Y. Zhang, S. Burer, and W. Street. Ensemble pruning via semi-definite programming. *Journal of Machine Learning Research*, 7(2006):1315–1338, 2006.

[35] X. Zhu, P. Zhang, X. Lin, and Y. Shi. Active learning from stream data using optimal weight classifier ensemble. *IEEE Transactions on System, Man, Cybernetics, Part B*, 40(4):1–15, 2010.

[36] X. Zhu, P. Zhang, X. Wu, D. He, C. Zhang, and Y. Shi. Cleansing noisy data streams. In *Proc. of ICDM 2008*, pages 1139 - 1144.

Online Active Inference and Learning

Josh Attenberg
Polytechnic Institute of NYU
Brooklyn, NY
josh@cis.poly.edu

Foster Provost
NYU Stern School of Business
New York, NY
fprovost@stern.nyu.edu

ABSTRACT

We present a generalized framework for *active inference*, the selective acquisition of labels for cases at prediction time in lieu of using the estimated labels of a predictive model. We develop techniques within this framework for classifying in an online setting, for example, for classifying the stream of web pages where online advertisements are being served. Stream applications present novel complications because (i) at the time of label acquisition, we don't know the set of instances that we will eventually see, (ii) instances repeat based on some unknown (and possibly skewed) distribution. We combine ideas from decision theory, cost-sensitive learning, and online density estimation. We also introduce a method for on-line estimation of the utility distribution, which allows us to manage the budget over the stream. The resulting model tells which instances to label so that by the end of each budget period, the budget is best spent (in expectation). The main results show that: (1) our proposed approach to active inference on streams can indeed reduce error costs substantially over alternative approaches, (2) more sophisticated online estimations achieve larger reductions in error. We next discuss simultaneously conducting active inference and active *learning*. We show that our expected-utility active inference strategy also selects good examples for learning. We close by pointing out that our utility-distribution estimation strategy can also be applied to convert pool-based active learning techniques into budget-sensitive online active learning techniques.

Categories and Subject Descriptors: H.2.8 [**Database Management**]: Database Applications—data mining; I.2.6 [**Artificial Intelligence**]: Learning—induction; I.5.1 [**Pattern Recognition**]: Models—statistics

General Terms: Algorithms, Design, Human Factors

Keywords: active inference, machine learning, active learning, on-line advertising, micro-outsourcing

The authors thank AdSafe Media for data and support. Foster Provost thanks NEC for a Faculty Fellowship.

KDD'11, August 21–24, 2011, San Diego, California, USA.

1. INTRODUCTION

When making decisions under uncertainty with data-driven models, we often have the option of directing (costly) human resources to help improve the process, for example by hand-labeling carefully selected data instances. Active learning methods try to select the instances to label that will best improve the modeling for a given cost. In this paper we study a complementary problem. *Active inference* involves carefully selecting instances to label at the time of use of a predictive model ("prediction time" or "inference time").

In many applications it is desirable to incur some cost to improve decision making by bypassing the model's decisions in favor of a human's. This choice may be a result of the model's uncertainty about a particular case, or alternatively, because assigning a label to a certain case will impart some improvement on other decisions. As a first contribution of this paper, we present a general framework for such *active inference.* This framework has prior approaches for inference-time label acquisition as special cases. The main generalizations of prior settings are threefold: (i) instances can be drawn with replacement from some distribution;[1] (ii) there may be a limited budget for labeling,[2] and (iii) the set of instances that will eventually be seen may not be known when a particular labeling decision needs to be made.

As our main application we will consider learning and inference on data streams, a problem setting which can exhibit all three of these characteristics. As a motivating example consider the problem of building classifiers for "safe" online advertising: helping advertisers to control the content adjacent to their advertisements. Certain categories of objectionable content such as hate speech and pornography are at odds with the carefully crafted images associated with most brands. Given a stream of impression opportunities, a safe advertising system is tasked with classifying each page as acceptable or objectionable, with the goal of preventing ads from occurring on objectionable pages. Figure 1 presents a typical distribution over web page occurrences in a production safe advertising system. In such a highly skewed setting, a few pages appear extremely frequently in the impression stream. However, most pages occur very infrequently. Given the extreme sensitivity to objectionable content, as well as to large numbers of falsely blocked good web pages, it is clear that not all pages should warrant equal effort—some pages may be sufficiently sensitive or frequent to have their own

[1]In practice, this distribution may be far from uniform.
[2]The budget constrains the number of examples that may be labeled.

hard-set ground-truth labels (within some labeling budget). However, at any point in time the set of pages to-be-seen is unknown, a scenario that is especially likely upon the introduction of a new impression stream to the advertising system. Note that these properties are not exclusive to the safe advertising problem: similar difficulties may be faced by classification problems in web search, spam detection, online ad targeting, error detection in complex systems, and others, where instances for prediction appear in streams with repetition.

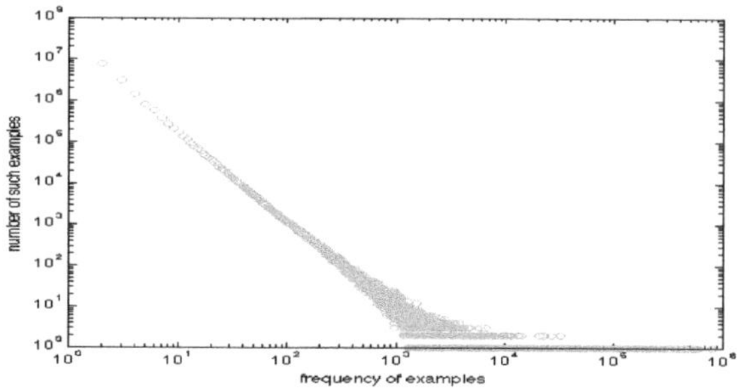

Figure 1: A histogram of impression frequencies of web pages sampled from a single day's ad traffic. Such skewed distributions on page views are typical in online advertising.

Ideally, one would like to apply the limited labeling budget to the most "useful" examples appearing in a stream. However, this task is complicated by the necessity of performing various estimates, and combining these into a higher-level estimation. The estimates include the expected per-example benefit from acquiring a ground truth label and using this label as a substitute for the model's predictions, and the expected number of times the example will appear in the future. More subtly, on top of this we also have to estimate the distribution of *utilities* that we will see, so we can plan how to spend the budget. The resulting model tells which instances to label so that by the end of the budget period, the budget has been best spend (in expectation).

We present a solution to this active inference problem using a framework for online utility-distribution estimation ("UDE") and test this method on eight different classification problems from a real streaming classification application. The main results show that: (1) active inference on streams can indeed reduce error cost substantially over not doing the online estimation, and (2) more sophisticated online estimation provides more reduction in error.

To close the paper we discuss relationships with active learning: What if you need to learn the model at the same time you are doing the active inference? In our original workshop position paper on active inference [1], we conjectured that a technique like the one we present and analyze below (which we had not yet designed completely or implemented) not only would be an effective active inference strategy, but also would be a potentially effective online active *learning* strategy for the online setting, and therefore that it should provide a strong baseline against which more sophisticated AI+AL strategies can be compared. We now provide initial supporting evidence.

As a final, suggestive, contribution we also discuss how the overall online utility estimation framework provides a new way to look at *online* active learning: it can be used to take any active learner that selects examples based on scoring each example in a pool (as most active learners do), and convert it to an online or stream-based active learner.

2. ACTIVE INFERENCE

Similar to work on active learning, this paper assumes that at a cost we can acquire accurate label information on selected cases. The difference is that here we acquire labels at prediction time, enabling the acquisition of "ground truth" labels as a supplement or substitute to the predictions of error-prone statistical models. The objective of this "active inference" is to reduce the total cost incurred by the predictive system. This section provides a framework for active inference for classification tasks. This framework generalizes prior work on prediction time label acquisition, including active inference for collective classification and techniques for classification with a reject option. Later, we develop techniques within this framework for performing online active inference (from streams) as another special case with its own unique characteristics and complications.

At first it might seem that prediction-time acquisition of training labels would not make sense: if labels are available for the instances being processed, then why perform potentially error-prone statistical inference in the first place? While "ground truth" labels are likely to be preferable to statistical prediction, we cannot ignore the cost/benefit context. Acquisition of ground truth labels may be more costly than simply making a model-based prediction, and there may be a limited budget for labeling.

The classification task can be formalized as: given a set of n discrete classes, $c^j \in \mathcal{C}, j = 1 \dots n$, instances, x_i, are drawn from some distribution, each with an associated class label $y_i = c \in \mathcal{C}$, drawn according to some $p(y = c|x)$. A classifier estimates this hidden class value, y_i, ideally in a way that minimizes some cost function, $\text{cost}(c^k|c^j)$—the penalty for predicting $y_i = c^k$ when in fact the true label is c^j [14]. Consider a model capable of predicting the posterior probability distribution over $\mathcal{C}$ conditioned on a given x_i, $\hat{p}(y_i = c|x_i) = f(x_i)$.[3] Based on this estimated posterior distribution, one can choose a particular classification $\hat{y}_i$ which will minimize an *expected* misclassification cost (or *loss*):

$$L(x_i, \hat{y}_i) = \sum_{c' \in \mathcal{C}} \hat{p}(y_i = c'|x_i)\text{cost}(\hat{y}_i|c')$$

More generally, an instance x_i may be presented repeatedly. Let $\phi(x_i)$ denote the number of times a given example x_i appears during a particular period of prediction time, the embodiment a sequence of draws *with replacement* from some distribution $p(x_i)$.[4] For a set of instances $\mathbb{T}$ that would be encountered by a classifier during this time period, the

[3]For instance in the case of our motivating example, given a web page, estimate the probability that page is objectionable.

[4]For this paper we will simplify and consider x_i to be a unique case that repeats verbatim in the stream, such as a particular web page, a particular query string in web search classification, a particular spam email, etc. This is different, for example, from two distinct web pages i and j that have the same feature representation. On one hand, this unique-case condition can be enforced trivially whenever an identifier or key exists (or can be generated) for the instance, such as the web page's URL or the hash value of the text of an email, which can be included in x_i. On the other

expected misclassification cost is:

$$\mathcal{L}_{\mathbb{T}} = \sum_{x_i \in \mathbb{T}} \phi(x_i) \min_c \sum_j \hat{p}(c^j|x_i)\text{cost}(c|c^j) \quad (1)$$

Note that for the pool-based setting typical in the literature (e.g., in most cross-validation experiments) $\phi(x_i) = 1$ for all x_i and can thus be ignored.[5]

Given a budget B for acquiring instance labels during a given time period, a predefined cost function, $\text{cost}(c^k|c^j)$ and a given cost structure, $q(x)$, revealing the expense of acquiring the label for each instance at prediction time, the objective of a general active inference strategy is to select a set of examples for which to acquire labels, $\mathcal{A}$, such that the expected *total* classification cost is minimized, adhering to the budget constraints:

$$\mathcal{A} = \arg\min_{\mathcal{A}' \subset \mathbb{T}} \mathcal{L}_{\mathbb{T} \setminus \mathcal{A}'} + \sum_{x_i \in \mathcal{A}'} q(x_i) \quad (2)$$
$$\text{s.t. } B \geq \sum_{x_i \in \mathcal{A}'} q(x_i)$$

The idea that we may defer the prediction task for certain cases to a human expert has been studied extensively as "classification with a reject option." This setting tends to focus on the balance between the expected misclassification cost, $L(x_i, \hat{y}_i)$, and the cost associated with "rejecting" the inferred classification, $q(x_i)$.

In the simplest case, imagine an unlimited budget for label acquisition, where no repetition occurs, and the labels of all examples are independent. Further assume symmetric error costs; w.l.o.g., $\text{cost}(c^k|c^j) = 1$ when $c^k \neq c^j$, with a cost of 0 otherwise. In this case, it is straightforward to show [10, 9] that the optimal "reject" policy, the set $\mathcal{A}$ offering a minimum reject rate for a given expected error probability (or, equivalently, minimizing the expected error probability for a given reject rate), is given by:

$$\mathcal{A} = \left\{ x_i \| \min_c \hat{p}(y_i = c|x_i) > q(x_i) \right\} \quad (3)$$

As would be expected, very large query costs tend to obviate the usefulness of the reject option; indeed the reject option would never be exercised when $q(x_i) > \frac{1}{2}$. (It it optimal to always query the oracle when $q(x_i) = 0$.) Of course the uniform misclassification costs assumed above are seldom realistic. Extending the reject rule of Chow to the case of asymmetric misclassification costs, Herbei and Wegkamp [20] show that the optimal $\mathcal{A}$ is given by:

$$\mathcal{A} = \left\{ x_i \| \min_{\hat{y}} L(x_i, \hat{y}_i) > q(x_i) \right\} \quad (4)$$

To our knowledge, classification with a reject option has not been extended to the stream setting. Observing examples sequentially presents several challenges to an active inference strategy. Instances may repeat, thereby multiplying otherwise small individual expected losses into significant cumulative penalties. Perhaps more difficult, the set of possible examples is unknown, and the distribution from which instances are drawn must also be estimated. Furthermore, a finite budget must be managed over time; it is suboptimal simply to use the thresholds described above, because the budget may be exhausted early, on low-margin cases. The development we present below might be seen as an on-line, stream-based, budget-sensitive version of the reject option. However, the repeating of examples might stretch the "reject" idea: rather than rejecting cases that (we believe) will show up in the future, we *invest in them.*

The active inference framework presented in Equation 2 also is a generalization of a framework presented previously [6] in the context of *collective* active inference [22, 6, 7, 8]. When examples are interrelated (e.g., in a network), collective inference may take advantage of relational autocorrelation in the labels to improve predictive performance beyond that achieved by treating the instances as i.i.d.[6] Since with collective inference, inferred labels affect each other, errors in inference can propagate. Thus, if one has a budget for human labeling at inference time, it may be spent on carefully selecting the examples to label such that the collective generalization performance is maximally improved [22].

In the active inference model we have presented so far (more will come), the generalization over the model of [6] is the addition of $\phi(x)$. In many applications we repeatedly make decisions about some instances; whether or not we take $\phi(x)$ into account can substantially change the cases we would want to label, when the distribution is not uniform. We are not extending the prior active inference methods in this paper; the on-line, stream setting that we introduce next requires a different set of techniques from the collective, network setting. A very interesting line of future work would be to find solutions for the combined setting. For example, the web pages that arrive in a stream are indeed interlinked in a network that exhibits relational autocorrelation in the class variable (objectionable pages are more likely to be linked to other objectionable pages, cf., [12]).

3. ACTIVE INFERENCE ON DATA STREAMS

A main contribution of this paper is the extension of active inference to the data stream setting. Here, active inference has a unique set of challenges that are beyond the capabilities of current methods. The primary differentiating factor of online active inference is that examples are typically drawn *with replacement* from some (unknown) process, $p(x)$.

In practical applications like web classification, $p(x)$ often exhibits a highly skewed, power-law-like distribution (cf., Figure 1). Due to this instance repetition, misclassification costs multiply; particular examples with a small individual expected loss may becoming quite costly over time. In the pool-based setting typically discussed in the machine learning literature, $\phi(x)$ would be known and fixed. In such cases, the strategy presented in Equation 2 may be applied directly.

However, the primary use case we are concerned with in this paper is when $p(x)$ is unknown—such as in the context of classifying a stream—requiring estimating it from

hand, this simplification presents limitations. For example, we may want to consider a webpage to be the same webpage even if there are minor modifications to the text that cause the feature vector to change slightly. Similarly, in other applications, there may be an entity that repeats, but with different feature vectors (e.g., different transactions from an entity that is either fraudulent or not), and we want to make decisions at the entity level, not the transaction level [15]. We leave the generalization of the setting to future work.

[5]Or, given the unusual case of a multiset, a pool of examples that exhibits repetition, $\phi(x)$ can be computed exactly by simply counting occurrences in the data.

[6]This networked inference setting is related to work on selecting a subset of sensors to activate in a sensor network [17].

the data and continually updating it during the inference process to ensure/maintain accuracy. We describe how we will do this in Section 3.2, leaving a thorough evaluation of online density estimation and its interplay with active inference for future work.

It is important to note that the notion of "density" presented by having to estimate $p(x)$ is different from the notion of "density" employed in "density-senstive" active learning (e.g., [26, 21]). In the former case (this paper), $p(x_i)$ represents the probability of "drawing" x_i from the data-generating process (d.g.p.). In the active learning work, the "density" corresponds to the likelihood of drawing from the d.g.p. *other* examples similar to x_i, so that choosing x_i for learning will be worthwhile. We are not aware of active learning work that explicitly considers $p(x)$. In turn, in this paper we do not consider how the more general geometry of the problem space might be taken into account for active inference. It is an open question as to what problem characteristics would induce the rate of incidence of examples (e.g., in a stream), $p(x)$, to be correlated to the similarity between the examples themselves.

A second complication of the stream setting is that the (reduction in) cost associated with a particular x_i must be extrapolated into the future, and appropriately discounted. A third, related complication is that we will need a framework relating the budget to the stream (and to the discounting). Do we have a fixed budget for the future (foreseeable or not)? Do we have a budget-per-unit time? This of course will be application dependent. For the development of the rest of the paper, we deal with these two related complications by assuming that we are given a budget for a given time period (or a budget-per-unit-time), and that we can ignore discounting: either because we really are most concerned with this immediate time period (a "square-wave" discount function), or because the discounting affects $p(x)$ uniformly, so weighting by $p(x)$ implicitly deals with the discounting. In our experience, having a budget for a particular time period is a typical application setting. For example, a business may budget so many dollars per month for human labeling of web pages. Next month there will be a new (possibly different) budget. We assume for the rest of this development that we know enough about the rate of seeing examples over the budget period that we can directly translate $\hat{p}(x_i)$ to $\hat{\phi}(x_i)$, the estimated frequency of seeing example x_i over the budget period.

A fourth and more insidious complication is that in the stream setting we do not actually know $\mathbb{T}$, the set of x_i's that we will see over a particular time period, nor even the total set of (realisable) x_i's that we might actually see. If x_i is a web page described by a bag-of-terms representation (for example), we certainly don't expect to see every possible x_i. Thus it is awkward, and may be ineffective, to treat $\mathcal{A}$ simply as a set of examples (as we could in the pool setting discussed briefly above). We would like to take the more general notion of $\mathcal{A}$ being a decision strategy that will incorporate $\hat{\phi}(x_i)$ and $\hat{p}(y_i = c|x_i)$ to produce a decision whenever an x_i presents itself: should we spend some of our budget to acquire its label? We now discuss this in greater depth.

3.1 Utility Distribution Estimation

Given the cost structure presented above, the estimated expected benefit of acquiring y_i for instance x_i is

$$\hat{\mathcal{U}}(x_i) = \hat{\phi}(x_i)L(x_i, \hat{y}_i) - q(x_i) \quad (5)$$

As with online estimation of $\hat{p}(x)$, we can add another layer of estimation, and treat $\hat{\mathcal{U}}(x_i)$ as a random variable upon which we can induce a density estimate. Let $\hat{\psi}(\hat{\mathcal{U}})$ be our estimated probability (density) function over the different possible expected utilities for the various x_i drawn in accordance with $p(x)$.

Now we can formulate a proposed general active inference acquisition strategy: label all x_i for which $\hat{\mathcal{U}}(x_i) \geq \tau$, that is, label all instances with a sufficiently high estimated utility. This threshold should be set in such a way as to exhaust the budget per epoch, in expectation:

$$\tau = \arg\max_{\tau'} \int_{\tau'}^{\infty} \hat{\psi}(\hat{\mathcal{U}})d\hat{\mathcal{U}} \quad (6)$$

constrained such that $\int_x p_1(x)\mathbb{I}_{\tau'}(x)q(x) \leq B$. Here $p_1(x)$ is the probability of seeing the argument at least once. If we expect N observations during the the budget period, we could estimate $p_1(x) = 1 - (1 - p(x))^N$, making the simplifying assumption that each subsequent draw is conditionally independent from other observations in the stream, given $p(x)$. Here $\mathbb{I}_{\tau'}(x)$ is 1 whenever $\hat{\mathcal{U}} \geq \tau'$, and 0 otherwise. Although Equation 6 could be simplified to choosing the minimum τ after each observation, leaving the rest implicit, the presented form illustrates the notion of a distribution of utilities of observed examples, from which we would like to choose the upper tail. We call such a utility-thresholding strategy *online utility-distribution estimation.* We will call this active inference strategy based upon online utility-distribution estimation *Active Inference with Utility Distribution Estimation*, or simply AI-UDE.

3.2 Online Density Estimation

Returning briefly to the problem of estimating $\hat{p}(x)$ on the fly, let us note that while appropriately choosing an estimatation model for $\hat{p}(x)$ is certainly critical to the performance of an active inference strategy, in this paper we leave a thorough evaluation of online density estimators and their associated influence on active inference for future work. Instead, we present two techniques as a baseline. Hopefully it will be clear that improved density estimation will only make the active inference techniques better. The two techniques considered in this paper are:

Dirichlet Multinomial (DMN) The simplest density estimation technique for this problem is a maximum likelihood estimation for the multinomial distribution over the instances. As this will over-estimate the probability on those cases that we observed more frequently just by chance, we instead use the posterior of a Dirichlet-multinomial distribution with a uniform prior. Specifically, we use the typical "add-α" smoothing: $p_\alpha(x_i) = \frac{f_{x_i}+\alpha}{\sum_j f_{x_j}+N\alpha}$, where N is the number of examples seen. For all experiments in this paper, we set $\alpha = 1$.

Good-Turing (SGT) The main drawback of methods like DMN is that they assume to know $\mathbb{T}$ at any point in time. As described above, we don't know what instances we will see, nor the total space of realisable instances. Especially with long-tail distributions, these instances could make up a substantial portion of the probability mass. Multinomial methods will thus overestimate the actual $p(x_i)$ and $\phi(x_i)$ for the already seen x_i's.

Good-Turing methods [18] explicitly account for the unobserved probability mass when estimating the probability/frequency for each example observed at least once. Specifically, $\hat{\phi}(x_i) = (f_{x_i}+1)\frac{E(n_{f_{x_i}+1})}{E(n_{f_{x_i}})}$, where n_{f_x} represents the number of examples observed f_x times; the height of the corresponding bin in a histogram. Good-Turing techniques are a family of smoothing estimators for computing estimating the quantity $E(n_{C(\cdot)})$.

Here we follow the Simple Good Turing (SGT) method [11] where to estimate $E(n_{C(\cdot)})$ an interpolation is performed on the empirical histogram, fitting a least-squares regression on the log-log scale. For a complete explanation, see [16].

4. EXPERIMENTAL SETUP

To demonstrate the effectiveness of active inference we compared methods on real-world stream data from the domain of safe online advertising. These data sets consist of placement opportunities (web pages) for ads observed in a stream. For experimentation, the pages were labeled along four distinct "safety" categories: adult content, hate speech, inappropriate alcohol content, and content related to illegal drugs. Each category poses a distinct learning and inference challenge, all with differing levels of skew with base rates ranging from $10,000:1$ to $1,000,000:1$ in the data stream.

Taking the cross product of four classification tasks with two data streams, we consider eight distinct brand safety sub-problems. The use case considered thus far involves the application of an existing (pre-trained) predictive model to the problem of example selection for inference. To facilitate this in an experimental setting, each category utilized a model trained using a separate, held-out, labeled data set, ensuring consistency across all active inference methods considered. In each case, all methods are given a burn-in period of $200,000$ unlabeled observations, allowing the density estimators to get some rough idea of the nature of the distribution under consideration.[7] After this burn-in, the density estimators continue to "learn," incorporating each new observation into a refined estimator for $\hat{\phi}(x)$.[8] Note that the burn-in period of $200,000$ is somewhat arbitrary: a larger or smaller burn-in does not alter the qualitative conclusions presented herein. However, the rates of divergence for the techniques compared varies. A cost ratio of $10,000:1$ is used, capturing the very severe consequences of having advertisements appear adjacent to inappropriate content. The data were drawn from two distinct time periods:

September 2010. A stream of $77,932,679$ ad impressions were taken from ad traffic on a single day in September, 2010, out of which $448,282$ distinct web pages were sampled (uniformly at random). All impressions from this sample set of web pages are considered.

January 2011. A stream of $189,096,009$ ad impressions were taken from a single day in January 2011. From this stream, $466,858$ unique web pages were sampled and the occurrences of these pages in the impression stream were recorded.

Budget-sensitive stream-based experiments require a setting more complex than traditional cross-validation experiments. Preliminary experiments suggest that the qualitative results are not sensitive to the particular choices made, but we have not yet conducted a large-scale sensitivity analysis. The budget is allocated in epochs of $25,000$ observations; each active inference technique is given a budget for selecting twenty-five examples for labeling per epoch. We assume the query cost $q(x_i)$ to be constant and small enough that the budget can be exhausted for all techniques (to avoid that additional complexity). For each technique, if an instance is encountered subsequently in the stream, it is classified directly using the already-purchased ground-truth label.[9] For examples without ground-truth labels, the model's predicted class distribution is used via the cost-sensitive calculation described in Section 2. In all strategies, if for any reason (e.g., poor utility-distribution estimation) the budget is not expended during a particular epoch, it is added to the budget of the next epoch. This is done to eliminate any disadvantage a particular strategy may have due to unused budget, isolating the quality of the selections themselves in the evaluation. However, all optimizations are performed on a per-epoch basis—effectively ignoring the impact of such remainders when performing selections.

Class probability estimation is performed with logistic regression trained using stochastic gradient descent and feature hashing [28]. These choices were based on efficiency during training and induction, critical given the massive numbers of experimental runs performed in this work, and the ability to naturally learn sequentially, a property which we will leverage in Section 6. Smaller-scale experiments indicate that the main findings are independent of the type of model induction technique used (indeed the chosen learning technique is quite competitive). Note, given appropriately selected training data, predictive models seem to perform well on this paper's classification tasks; e.g., for adult content AUC is around 0.97 (and it can be much higher with significantly larger training sets). The devil's detail is that the tremendous class skew still can leave precision wanting.

We compare the following active inference strategies.

Random. Randomly select k examples for labeling during each epoch. If the number of observations to be seen in each budget epoch can be approximated in advance, this strategy simply selects k instances uniformly.

First. Select the first not-yet-labeled examples encountered during each epoch until the budget is depleted. Under certain distributions, First may be a very strong competitor: it maximizes the opportunity for each acquired label to be utilized for direct inference. In addition, the examples appearing first may be those examples with the greatest frequency (or not, depending on the skew of the distribution $p(x)$).

Active Inference with Utility Distribution Estimation (AI-UDE). Here we use the full expected utility-distribution estimation based on our proposed framework: $\mathcal{U}(x_i) = \phi(x_i)L(x_i,\hat{y}_i) - q(x_i)$, including cost-sensitive expected utility, online density estimation, and the online utility-distribution estimation proposed in Equations 2 and 6. Unless noted otherwise, for all AI techniques density estimation is performed using DMN with $\alpha = 1$; we return to SGT later.

AI-Frequency (AI-Freq). Here we turn off the loss por-

[7]In this case, a long tailed distribution such as the one presented in Figure 1.

[8]Rather than storing the examples themselves, unique identifiers (in the case of the ad safety problem, a URL) are used to maintain frequency information. The same identifiers are used to look up stored labels from the active inference process, giving the proposed process a small memory footprint.

[9]Additionally, these labels could optionally be used to supplement the training data available to the model, potentially reducing the future error rate. We explore this scenario in Section 6.

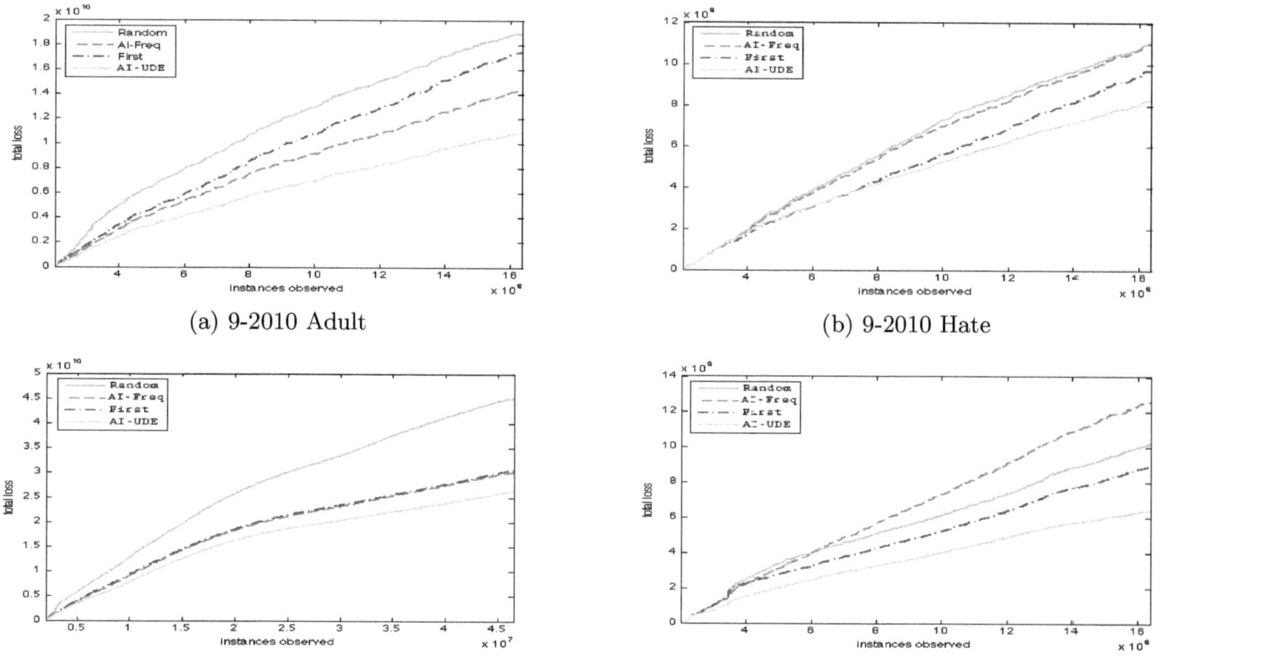

(a) 9-2010 Adult (b) 9-2010 Hate

(c) 1-2011 Adult (d) 9-2010 Alcohol

Figure 2: Active inference comparison on four datasets, representing the qualitative behavior on all the stream datasets.

tion of the UDE calculation, setting $\mathcal{U}(x_i) = \phi(x_i)$. While labeling the most frequent examples is simple in a pool-based multiset, such selection is non-trivial in the stream setting. For example, even if I get enough data to estimate $\phi(x_i)$ well for a particular x_i, how do I know whether this is going to be one of the *most frequent* x's? Fortunately, our online utility-distribution estimation framework given by Equation 6 solves this problem as well.

AI-Loss Only (AI-Loss). Here the frequency $\phi(x)$ is ignored for the purpose of utility-distribution estimation, using only $\mathcal{U}(x_i) = L(x_i, \hat{y}_i) - q(x_i)$. This represents the extension of prior strategies that do not use frequency estimation, one of the main novel contributions of the AI-UDE approach. This can be considered an application of cost-sensitive classification with a reject option to the setting where the example space is only partially observed, utilizing the online UDE framework of Equation 6.

5. RESULTS

Figure 2 presents experimental results on four domains; these represent the qualitative behavior over all eight. With few exceptions (e.g., Figure 2(c)), the active inference strategies utilizing online utility-distribution estimation outperform those that do not. This suggests that there is benefit to estimating the distribution on the utility space for budgetary planning.

The full-blown utility-distribution estimation strategy (AI-UDE) dominates in all eight cases, offering the most promising results among all the strategies. In some cases AI-UDE yields a reduction in misclassification cost of 20% to 30% in comparison to the next-best strategy. Thus even the suboptimal (and likely inaccurate) online density estimators are sufficient to provide useful selections for these problems.

Considering only $\phi(x)$ in utility estimates (AI-Freq) still provides very promising loss results. Even without the rest of the expected utility calculation, being able to estimate $\phi(x)$ online—and importantly reason about its overall distribution online (Equation 6)—can provide for a competitive active inference strategy. This seems to be due to the long-tailed distributions, where some instances are much more frequent than others, and on these even very small errors multiply quickly. However, AI-Freq is not as consistent as AI-UDE; sometimes selection based solely on the frequency and frequency-distribution estimations is less effective than competing strategies. This may be due to high skew observed in the conditional distribution $p(y|x)$ in addition to that observed in $p(x)$. Such a skew may result in AI-Freq selecting only negative examples ($c = 0$), the likely "default" classification, which would therefore result in labeling many examples the model would already classify correctly.

We left the results from AI-Loss out of the figures. This strategy, meant to represent an online extension of prior methods for prediction-time label acquisition, was not competitive with the other selection heuristics considered and severely reduced the interpretability of the graphs. The poor performance seems to be due to the strictly loss-based approach having a tendency to choose outliers, singletons in terms of $\phi(x)$. (These often seem to be the cases for which the model is most uncertain, and therefore for which the frequency-ignorant expected utility of labeling them is highest.) In the stream, labeling singleton instances offers minimal reduction in misclassification cost. This suggests caution should be taken in direct applications of reject inference to data streams with repeated instances.

To provide some sensitivity analysis, we varied the budget and misclassification cost in a narrower experimental setting. Specifically, we selected a subset of 35,000 pages extracted from the real stream, with an 80 to 1 class skew for adult content. Over ten folds of cross-validation, a power law distribution ($\alpha = 2$) was induced on the testing portion of each fold in order to simulate the actual skewed $p(x)$. Then for the experiments that follow we assume that $\phi(x)$ is estimated perfectly. Thus we can focus on how much value the frequency and the loss components add, without being

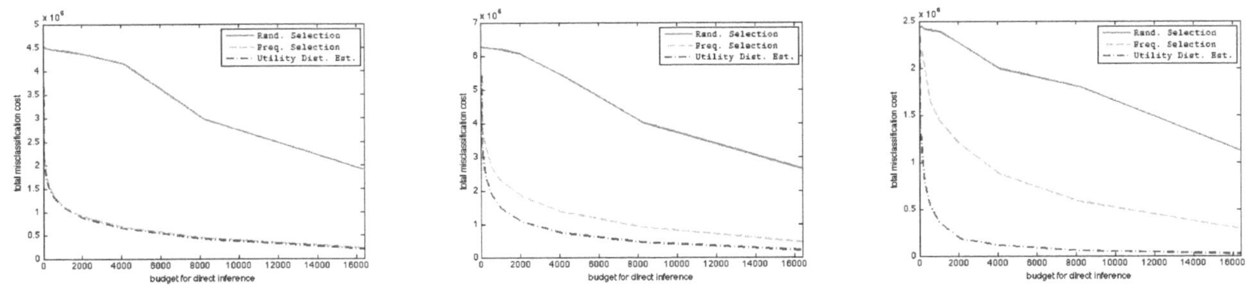

(a) 10 to 1 (b) 100 to 1 (c) 1,000 to 1

Figure 3: Total incurred costs for different instance selection strategies for different given budgets, B

confounded by errors in the online density estimation (more on that later).[10] Here we assume that the per-query labeling cost $q(x_i) = 1$ for all x_i.

Figure 3 compares the total loss of Random, AI-Freq, and AI-UDE while varying the total available budget (along the horizontal axes) and varying the false-positive error cost (across the three panes) from 10 to 100 to 1,000 times the false-negative error cost.

From these experiments we see two things. First, no matter what the budget, active inference provides a substantial reduction in total loss. Second, given this power-law distribution, it is only for the larger cost ratios that the utility component adds value; for the 10 : 1 cost ratio AI-Freq and AI-UDE are essentially equivalent. It should be clear that this is just a demonstration: for a uniform distribution, the utility component obviously would dominate for any non-trivial cost ratio (assuming the probability estimation is good enough). On the power-law distribution, when the costs are high enough, both components make substantial contributions, and the full-blown AI-UDE gives a much larger loss reduction than AI-Freq.

6. ACTIVE INFERENCE AND LEARNING

What we have presented so far is only half the story. While many stream-based active inference settings may begin with a satisfactory model in order to perform statistical predictions,[11] in other applications we need to learn the model simultaneously with making predictions. In addition, as long as we are acquiring labels, we may want to improve the model. Countless prior papers on active learning (AL) have demonstrated the benefit of carefully choosing instances to label for training. In some applications there may be separate budgets for active inference and for labeling for training. However, even then the active inference selections will produce more potential training data. Therefore, we should consider how to allocate a single budget so as to get the best overall performance, taking into account both (active) inference and (active) learning. A full development being well beyond the scope of this paper, we present some interesting insights into the interplay of these two label demands, and demonstrate the striking generality of the online utility-distribution estimation strategy presented in Equation 6.

Similar to our setting, online active learning is concerned with selecting instances for labeling from a stream, where the current model is applied to the subsequent stream. Helmbold and Panizza [19] first looked at the tradeoffs between the cost of errors and the costs of labels in online active learning. Subsequently there have been several proposed techniques for "label efficient" techniques including b-sampling [5], and a logistic confidence model [24]. Online active learning research does not address the use of labels for direct inference, nor is repetition in the instance stream accounted for explicitly.[12] There also has been much work in "pool-based" active learning [25]. Many (not all) AL techniques formulate a usefulness score for instances, and then select or sample instances based on this score. The most commonly used family of AL techniques measures usefulness in terms of model uncertainty, with the score ranging from the similarity of the estimated probabilities of the two most likely classes, to the entropy or variance of an ensemble of constituent models, to the distance from a separating hyperplane. Roughly: get more labels on instances near the decision boundary. (Note the similarity to reject inference described above.)

Initially it appears that for our setting only online active learning approaches are appropriate, because the pool-based approaches presume that you score all the examples in the pool first in order to select among them. However, the utility term, $\mathcal{U}(x)$ from Equation 6 could instead denote any AL usefulness score! Then the online utility-distribution estimation procedure we introduced and applied for active inference above will instead estimate the distribution of active learning usefulness scores across the stream. Thus, it can be used to apply arbitrary score-based active learning techniques to the online/stream setting.

In fact, consider AI-UDE presented above. The full-blown AI-UDE can be thought of as generalized uncertainty sampling (cf. [23]) for streams with different error costs, repetition, unknown $p(x)$, and the need for budget management.

Proposition: *The active inference strategy of selecting the instance x_i with largest $\hat{\psi}(x_i)$ selects the same instance as uncertainty sampling under conditions of uniform (estimated) instance frequency, uniform query cost, and uniform error cost.*

Proof: The proof proceeds simply by unwinding the derivation above in Section 2 (See [1] for details). □

The generalization to different error costs generalizes uncertainty sampling in the same way reject inference was generalized (see Section 2). The other generalizations make intuitive sense in our setting as well: prefer to spend the labeling budget on instances, ceteris paribus, if they would be more costly to get wrong, if labeling them is particularly

[10]Note that by assuming we know $\phi(x)$ we've factored out the key components of the stream; this now is pool-based active inference where there may be replication in the pool.

[11]For instance, in safe advertising an objectionability model may already exist when encountering new advertising partner, with a very different impression stream.

[12]This only scratches the surface of online active learning. For example, recently, Beygelzimer et al. [4] made a significant theoretical and empirical advance in importance-weighted active learning.

cheap, and/or if they are particularly likely to "reappear." To our knowledge no prior work has weighted uncertainty sampling by $p(x)$ or, equivalently, $\phi(x)$ (cf., the discussion above on density-sensitive AL).

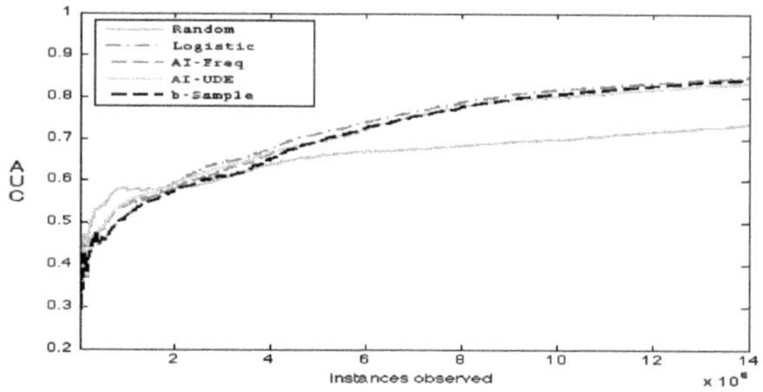

(a) AUC of Training Only

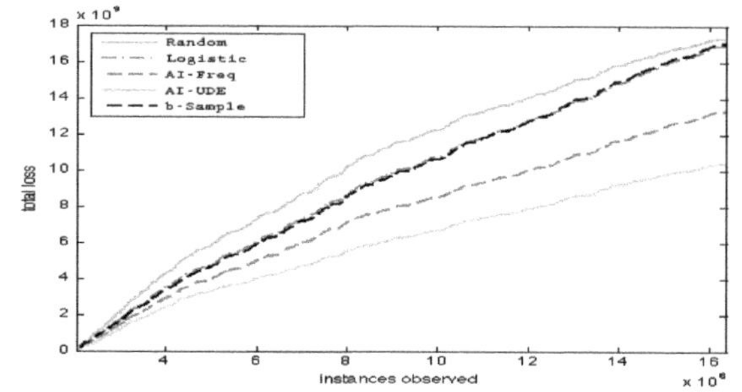

(b) Loss Experienced by Learning and Induction

Figure 4: A comparison of active learning strategies with our proposed active inference strategies

Figure 4(a) compares the ROC area (AUC) of *learning* with the online AI strategy AI-UDE and the online AL strategies b-sampling and logistic sampling (discussed above). This experiment is performed on the Sept. 2010 adult classification data set. As before using 200,000 unlabeled examples to burn-in a DMN density estimator, a completely untrained model is deployed and trained only on those instances selected via each acquisition strategy.[13] In line with our conjecture, the AI-UDE strategy indeed chooses examples that accelerate learning over random selection, as one would expect with an effective active learning technique. Surprisingly, the dedicated online active learning techniques provide only marginal additional improvement (at best). This provides suggestive evidence in support of our conjecture that AI-UDE is a solid candidate for active *learning* in stream settings.

Finally, let's put everything together. If AI-UDE did so well for active learning, perhaps the online AL strategies will do very well for active inference. Figure 4(b) presents the same label acquisition strategies applied to the same problem—starting as in the AUC results with the untrained model. However, now we see the effect on *total misclassification loss* if each strategy is used for AI and AL (otherwise, the same setup as the main results presented earlier). Unlike with the AUC results, here the AI and AL strategies do not perform comparably. For simultaneous AI+AL, AI-UDE dominates. This is clearly due to the focus on active inference, since we saw that the underlying models are comparable (at least in terms of AUC). These results are suggestive that active inference techniques like AI-UDE should be considered more broadly for reducing overall loss in stream applications needing online active learning.

7. CONCLUSIONS & LIMITATIONS

This paper addresses the problem of prediction-time label acquisition, presenting a framework that generalizes both classification with a reject option and existing work in active inference. Within this framework, we presented the problem of online active inference, a real problem faced in applications such as our running example of web-page classification for safe advertising. The results on stream data from several safe-advertising problems demonstrates that online active inference has the potential to reduce the cost of inference substantially under skewed error costs and example frequency distributions. A key to success is the online estimation of two different quantities: (i) the frequency distribution and (ii) the distribution of utilities that will be encountered.

The expected-loss-minimizing active inference strategy we introduced turns out to be a generalization of traditional uncertainty sampling, as discussed in Section 6, and is quite effective when one also must (actively) *learn* the predictive model simultaneously with using it for inference. Furthermore, our framework for online estimation of the utility distribution provides the tooling to extend many batch-mode active learning strategies into the online setting.

While this work presents several advances in the development of prediction-time label acquisition techniques, there are a number of limitations that provide a fallow field for future research. Based on what we have seen so far, the largest potential for improvement in the active inference results may be from improved online density estimation. We used DMN extensively in the experimental portion of this work due to its speed of estimation for the very large-scale runs conducted for the main results. However, smaller-scale experiments show SGT yielding superior density estimation at the cost of speed. We see this in Figure 5, which shows Random, AI-UDE with DMN, AI-UDE with SGT, and AI-UDE with perfect ("oracle") estimation of $\phi(x)$. The current density estimation seems to get about half the total possible improvement in performance, and we see that SGT improves over DMN, but not substantially. Further improvements may be realized via techniques more sophisticated than SGT, or possibly by conditional density estimation (i.e., taking x into account). Note that the oracle estimation case probably is an unachievable "floor" on performance, since we have to observe the stream of data to do the online estimation.

Relatedly, there is an exploration/exploitation tradeoff in utility-distribution estimation. Because we are estimating $p(x_i)$ on the fly, it may be the case that for a particular x_i we first use the model to classify it for a while, and then eventually acquire its label. When are we certain enough to label, rather than wait "one more" time? The current models make this decision implicitly as they learn $p(x)$, but

[13]The overall performance figures are fairly low for this application—the best methods achieving an AUC of approximately 0.8 after an accumulation of 14,000 labeled examples from over 14 million observations. This domain, with such extreme class skew, needs much larger training sets or special example selection regimes to get the best possible accuracies; typical active learning strategies have trouble finding positive examples [3, 2].

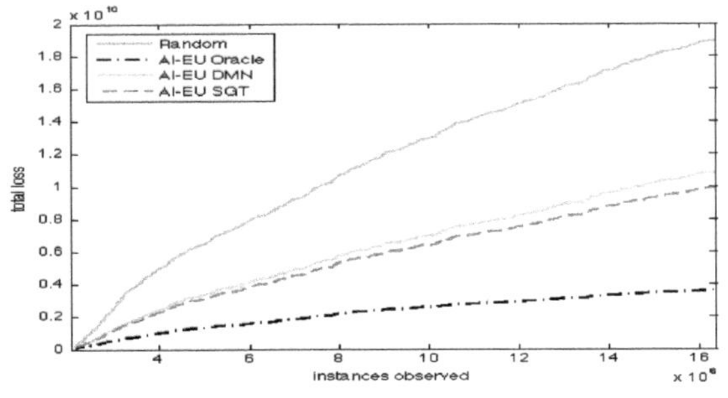

Figure 5: Comparing the AI-UDE strategy with different density estimation techniques, including perfect estimation

perhaps the decision could be improved with a confidence-interval strategy like that of [13]. More generally, the budget needs to be managed over the stream, trading off several competing desires. Labeling pages early both maximizes the value of those particular labels and maximizes the value to model induction. Labeling later allows better estimation of $p(x)$, and therefore may increase the value of the active inference.

Relatedly, this work assumes labels are made available instantly upon request. Incorporating a delay between requests and data acquisition is an important direction for future work, and a matter of practical importance. For example, it may be that waiting t time units only ends up shifting the curve up, because t is short enough that the expected additional loss will essentially be constant. Furthermore, this is just one possible budget framework.

We assume that $p(x)$ is static. Many realistic settings have a dynamic $p(x)$: new instances appear not only because they simply are rare, but because they actually are new. The dynamics of this change can be abrupt, with instances rising rapidly in popularity: e.g., new popular web pages or new popular search terms (e.g., "Egypt riots").

We have made the usual assumption that labeling is error-free. However, in reality for the applications we are considering the labeling will be done by error-prone humans, for example via a micro-outsourcing system, and the active inference procedure should take that into account. For example repeated labeling [27] becomes a strategy that must be considered. This adds wonderful complexity to active inference. There no longer is a clear switch from model-based inference to human-based inference. Now we need to consider the fusion of different evidence, acquired at different costs, at different times. The model's estimation could be seen as just another labeling source; for certain examples it may even be more accurate than an average human labeler.

Despite these limitations, we hope that the techniques and results presented in this paper have made significant progress toward the development of systems that manage labeling budgets as well as possible in real-world, stream-based, online prediction systems.

8. REFERENCES

[1] J. Attenberg and F. Provost. Active inference and learning for classifying streams. In *BL-ICML '10: Workshop on Budgeted Learning*, 2010.

[2] J. Attenberg and F. Provost. Inactive Learning? Difficulties Employing Active Learning in Practice. *SIGKDD Explorations*, 12(2):36–41, 2010.

[3] J. Attenberg and F. Provost. Why label when you can search? Strategies for applying human resources to build classification models under extreme class imbalance. In *KDD*, 2010.

[4] A. Beygelzimer, S. Dasgupta, and J. Langford. Importance weighted active learning. In *Proc of the 26th Intl Conf on Machine Learning*, ICML '09, 2009.

[5] N. C. Bianchi, C. Gentile, and L. Zaniboni. Worst-case analysis of selective sampling for linear classification. In *J. Mach. Learn. Res.*, volume 7, pages 1205–1230, 2006.

[6] M. Bilgic and L. Getoor. Effective label acquisition for collective classification. In *Proceeding of the 14th ACM SIGKDD international conference on Knowledge discovery and data mining*, KDD '08, pages 43–51. ACM, 2008.

[7] M. Bilgic and L. Getoor. Reflect and correct: A misclassification prediction approach to active inference. *ACM Trans. Knowl. Discov. Data*, 3, December 2009.

[8] M. Bilgic and L. Getoor. Active Inference for Collective Classification. In *AAAI*, 2010.

[9] C. Chow. On optimum recognition error and reject tradeoff. *IEEE Transactions on Information Theory*, 16(1):41–46, January 1970.

[10] C. K. Chow. An Optimum Character Recognition System Using Decision Functions. *IEEE Transactions on Electronic Computers*, (4):247–254, December 1957.

[11] K. Church and W. Gale. A comparison of the enhanced Good-Turing and deleted estimation methods for estimating probabilities of English bigrams. *Computer Speech & Language*, 5(1):19–54, January 1991.

[12] B. D. Davison. Topical locality in the web. In *Proceedings of the 23rd annual international ACM SIGIR conference on Research and development in information retrieval*, SIGIR '00, pages 272–279, New York, NY, USA, 2000. ACM.

[13] P. Donmez, J. G. Carbonell, and J. Schneider. Efficiently learning the accuracy of labeling sources for selective sampling. In *Proceedings of the 15th ACM SIGKDD international conference on Knowledge discovery and data mining*, KDD '09, pages 259–268, New York, NY, USA, 2009. ACM.

[14] C. Elkan. The Foundations of Cost-Sensitive Learning. In *IJCAI*, pages 973–978, 2001.

[15] T. Fawcett and F. Provost. Activity monitoring: Noticing interesting changes in behavior. In *In Proceedings of the Fifth ACM SIGKDD International Conference on Knowledge Discovery and Data Mining*, pages 53–62, 1999.

[16] W. A. Gale. Good-Turing smoothing without tears. *Journal of Quantitative Linguistics*, 2, 1995.

[17] D. Golovin, M. Faulkner, and A. Krause. Online distributed sensor selection. In *Information Processing in Sensor Networks*, pages 220–231, 2010.

[18] I. J. Good and G. H. Toulmin. The number of new species, and the increase in population coverage, when a sample is increased. *Biometrika*, 43(1-2):45–63, June 1956.

[19] D. Helmbold and S. Panizza. Some label efficient learning results. In *COLT '97: Proceedings of the tenth annual conference on Computational learning theory*. ACM, 1997.

[20] R. Herbei and M. H. Wegkamp. Classification with reject option. *Can J Statistics*, 34(4):709–721, 2006.

[21] H. T. Nguyen and A. Smeulders. Active learning using pre-clustering. In *ICML*, 2004.

[22] M. J. Rattigan, M. Maier, and D. Jensen. Exploiting Network Structure for Active Inference in Collective Classification. Technical Report 07-22, University of Massachusetts Amherst, 2007.

[23] M. Saar-Tsechansky and F. Provost. Decision-Centric active learning of Binary-Outcome models. *INFORMATION SYSTEMS RESEARCH*, 18(1):4–22, Mar. 2007.

[24] D. Sculley. Online active learning methods for fast label-efficient spam filtering. In *Fourth Conf. on Email and AntiSpam*, 2007.

[25] B. Settles. Active learning literature survey. Computer Sciences Technical Report 1648, University of Wisconsin–Madison, 2009.

[26] B. Settles and M. Craven. An analysis of active learning strategies for sequence labeling tasks. In *Proceedings of the Conference on Empirical Methods in Natural Language Processing*, EMNLP '08, pages 1070–1079, Stroudsburg, PA, USA, 2008. Association for Computational Linguistics.

[27] V. S. Sheng, F. Provost, and P. G. Ipeirotis. Get another label? improving data quality and data mining using multiple, noisy labelers. In *KDD '08*, 2008.

[28] K. Weinberger, A. Dasgupta, J. Attenberg, J. Langford, and A. Smola. Feature hashing for large scale multitask learning. In *ICML '09*, 2009.

Unbiased Online Active Learning in Data Streams

Wei Chu[*]
Microsoft
Redmond, WA, USA
chu.wei@microsoft.com

Martin Zinkevich
Yahoo! Labs
Sunnyvale, CA, USA
maz@yahoo-inc.com

Lihong Li
Yahoo! Labs
Sunnyvale, CA, USA
lihong@yahoo-inc.com

Achint Thomas
Yahoo! Labs
Sunnyvale, CA, USA
aothomas@yahoo-inc.com

Belle Tseng
Yahoo! Labs
Sunnyvale, CA, USA
belle@yahoo-inc.com

ABSTRACT

Unlabeled samples can be intelligently selected for labeling to minimize classification error. In many real-world applications, a large number of unlabeled samples arrive in a streaming manner, making it impossible to maintain all the data in a candidate pool. In this work, we focus on binary classification problems and study selective labeling in data streams where a decision is required on each sample sequentially. We consider the unbiasedness property in the sampling process, and design optimal instrumental distributions to minimize the variance in the stochastic process. Meanwhile, Bayesian linear classifiers with weighted maximum likelihood are optimized online to estimate parameters. In empirical evaluation, we collect a data stream of user-generated comments on a commercial news portal in 30 consecutive days, and carry out offline evaluation to compare various sampling strategies, including unbiased active learning, biased variants, and random sampling. Experimental results verify the usefulness of online active learning, especially in the non-stationary situation with concept drift.

Categories and Subject Descriptors

G.3 [**Probabilities and Statistics**]: Probabilistic Algorithms (including Monte Carlo); I.5.2 [**Pattern Recognition**]: Design Methodology—*Classifier design and evaluation*

General Terms

Algorithms, Experimentation, Performance

[*]The work was done when WC was with Yahoo! Labs.

KDD'11, August 21–24, 2011, San Diego, California, USA.

Keywords

Active Learning, Adaptive Importance Sampling, Unbiasedness, Bayesian Online Learning, Data Streaming

1. INTRODUCTION

Active learning holds the promise of reducing the amount of labeled data in supervised learning required to reach a certain level of performance such as classification accuracy. Many of the successful applications are for the pool-based scenario [20], where a *static* collection of unlabeled data are given, from which a subset are chosen for labeling. In other situations where unlabeled examples arrive sequentially, *stream-based* active learning [5, 7] is more appropriate. Since the size of the data stream is often large (and even unbounded) in real-world applications, it is impractical to store all unlabeled data and then run active learning. Rather, an online algorithm has to decide, for the current unlabeled datum, whether to query its label or not. It is typically not allowed to query labels for data *in the past.*

Generally, the subset of data chosen for labeling are *biased* in the sense that they do *not* faithfully represent the original distribution of data. Therefore, optimizing a classifier based on this biased labeled set is problematic, especially in problems where the positive and negative classes are not separable. In the literature, importance sampling (IS) has been applied to reweight labeled data to remove the bias (e.g., [2, 4]). As with most importance-sampling-based methods, controlling variance is crucial for producing reliable classifiers in active learning.

As a motivating application, consider the detection of abusive user-generated content (UGC) on the Web. Common forms of UGC abuse include *commercial spam*, *offensive language*, *adult content*, etc. UGC abuse detection is challenging for many reasons. First, at Yahoo!, UGC is extremely diverse and Yahoo! receives millions of items a day, rendering it impractical for human arbitrators to examine every posted item. Because abusers can probe the detection system to determine what items are posted, they can easily bypass static, hand-coded detection rules. Machine-learned, automated detection is thus necessary. Second, similar to email spam detection, patterns of abuse evolve over time in a possibly adversarial manner. Therefore, the traditional train-once-and-deploy mode almost surely fails, as is confirmed by our analysis in Section 6. A natural solution to tackle these challenges is to periodically retrain an abuse classifier by including new, publicly visible UGC as training data, whose labels are provided by paid human editors. Active learning can be used to reduce the editor's labeling efforts as new unlabeled data arrive.

This work has two contributions: we apply an online active learning paradigm [2] in a domain which is not IID, and develop a new algorithm using the importance weighting principle. This is the first paper that applies online active learning to a truly dynamic problem. Whereas [2] used a sequence of data drawn uniformly at random from the MNIST data set, we try to discriminate between commercial spam and good comments in user-generated content. We begin by establishing that the dataset has concept drift. Then, we show how online active learning is affected by this drift by comparing its performance on the data in its original order versus running the algorithm on a shuffled variant of the data. What this paper shows is that online active learning is more powerful in real dynamic problems than in environments where data arrives IID. This analysis is done using the probit model [3] to classify examples. We come up with an online update variant based on [15] that can handle weighted examples through an approximation technique. We also study a time-decay variant of the probit model.

2. PROBLEM SETTINGS

Let us denote by $\mathcal{X}$ the feature space and by $\mathcal{Y}$ the label space of input samples. An unknown distribution over $\mathcal{X}\times\mathcal{Y}$ is denoted by $p(\mathbf{x}, y)$, where $\mathbf{x}$ denotes a column vector of features and $y \in \{+1, -1\}$ in binary classification problems. Let $p(y|\mathbf{x};\theta)$ be a predictive model parameterized by θ.

To optimize θ, we need a criterion to evaluate the goodness of a value of θ. Usually, the criterion is defined as

$$R(\theta) = \int\int G(\mathbf{x}, y; \theta) p(\mathbf{x}, y) dy d\mathbf{x}$$

where $G(\mathbf{x}, y; \theta)$ is a measurement function over samples. For instance, in the empirical risk minimization (ERM) framework, $G(\mathbf{x}, y; \theta)$ is usually a loss function, and the integral above is approximated by an empirical risk

$$\hat{R}_n = \frac{1}{n}\sum_{i=1}^{n} G(\mathbf{x}_i, y_i; \theta), \qquad (1)$$

using n samples drawn i.i.d. from $p(\mathbf{x}, y)$.

In the setting of online active learning (a.k.a. selective labeling and selective sampling), we observe unlabeled samples $\mathbf{x}$ from $p(\cdot)$ sequentially, whereas an agent reveals y upon our request on $\mathbf{x}$. We deliberately select a subset of unlabeled samples for labeling, thus the resulting set of labeled samples might be distributed differently from $p(\mathbf{x})$.

When the labeled samples are drawn from an instrumental distribution $q(\mathbf{x}, y)$, according to the importance sampling principle, the empirical risk can be evaluated with reweighted labeled samples as follows,

$$\hat{R}_{n,q} = \frac{1}{\sum_{i=1}^{n} \frac{p(\mathbf{x}_i, y_i)}{q(\mathbf{x}_i, y_i)}} \sum_{i=1}^{n} \frac{p(\mathbf{x}_i, y_i)}{q(\mathbf{x}_i, y_i)} G(\mathbf{x}_i, y_i; \theta). \qquad (2)$$

Since the instrumental distribution $q(\mathbf{x}, y)$ can be factorized by $p(y|\mathbf{x})q(\mathbf{x})$ in this case, the objective is then simplified to

$$\hat{R}_{n,q} = \frac{1}{\mathcal{B}}\sum_{i=1}^{n} \beta_i G(\mathbf{x}_i, y_i; \theta), \qquad (3)$$

where $\beta_i = \frac{p(\mathbf{x}_i)}{q(\mathbf{x}_i)}$ and $\mathcal{B} = \sum_{i=1}^{n} \beta_i$. Note that $\beta_i \propto \frac{1}{q(\mathbf{x}_i)}$ if $\mathbf{x}_i$ is i.i.d. from $p(\mathbf{x})$.

2.1 Sampling Distribution

There is a strong connection between online active learning and adaptive importance sampling (AIS) [17]. A popular approach in AIS finds an optimal q to minimize risk variance: $q^* = \arg\min_q E_{\mathbf{x}\sim q}\left[\left(\hat{R}_{n,q} - E_{\mathbf{x}\sim q}\left[\hat{R}_{n,q}\right]\right)^2\right]$, where the samples are drawn from $q(\mathbf{x})$. The following propositions ensure the soundness of (3).

PROPOSITION 1. *(Unbiasedness) If* $\beta_i = \frac{p(\mathbf{x}_i)}{q(\mathbf{x}_i)}$, *then we have:*
(1) $E_{\mathbf{x}\sim q}[\beta_i] = 1$;
(2) $E_{\mathbf{x}\sim q}[\mathcal{B}] = n$;
and
(3) $E_{\mathbf{x}\sim q}[\beta_i G(\mathbf{x}_i, y_i; \theta)] = R(\theta)$.

PROPOSITION 2. *(Asymptotic Variance) For* $\hat{R}_{n,q}$ *in (3), we have* $\sqrt{n}\left(\hat{R}_{n,q} - R(\theta)\right) \to N(0, \sigma_q^2)$
where $\sigma_q^2 = \int \left(\frac{p(\mathbf{x})}{q(\mathbf{x})}\right)^2 (G(\mathbf{x}, y; \theta) - R(\theta))^2 q(\mathbf{x}) d\mathbf{x}$.

In brief, Proposition 1 is a direct consequence of the definition of β_i. Proposition 2 follows from known results for the "Delta method" [17, 19, 22]. AIS minimizes the variance estimate σ_q^2 above using $q^*(\mathbf{x}) \propto p(\mathbf{x})|G(\mathbf{x}, y; \theta) - R(\theta)|$. However, we do not know y in online active learning when making label request decisions. $G(\mathbf{x}, y; \theta)$ could be estimated by expected estimate, i.e., $\hat{G}(\mathbf{x}; \theta) = \sum_{y'} p(y'|\mathbf{x}; \theta) G(\mathbf{x}, y'; \theta)$. $R(\theta)$ could also be estimated by the current $\hat{R}_{n,q}$. In practice, if the expected risk is close to 0, we may simply choose $q^*(\mathbf{x}) \propto p(\mathbf{x})|\hat{G}(\mathbf{x}; \theta)|$ with the estimate above.

As a special case, the measurement function $G(\mathbf{x}, y; \theta)$ in (1) can be chosen as $-\log p(y|\mathbf{x}; \theta)$, and the risk minimizer is equivalent to the Maximum Likelihood estimate. For the importance-weighted version (3), the minimizer is then equivalent to the Maximum Weighted Likelihood estimate.

3. ONLINE BAYESIAN PROBIT

In the ERM framework, stochastic gradient descent [24] is commonly applied to updating the model parameters θ. Given a weighted labeled sample $(\mathbf{x}_i, y_i, \beta_i)$ at time t, the update rule is $\theta_{t+1} = \theta_t + \eta\beta_i \frac{\partial G(\mathbf{x}_i, y_i; \theta)}{\partial \theta}$, where θ_t and θ_{t+1} denote the current and new parameters, respectively, and η the step size. Note that the selection probability β_i becomes a scaling factor of the step size. It is nontrivial to identify an appropriate step size and iteration number in stochastic gradient descent. Sometimes all labeled samples need be stored for periodic batch learning.

In this work, we resort to online Bayesian learning to maintain the posterior distribution of the weight vector in linear classifiers. For simplicity, we focus on linear models for problems involving binary classification. Denote by $\mathbf{w}$ the weight vector of the linear model at time t, and the function value is given by $\mathbf{x}^\top\mathbf{w}$. The distribution of $\mathbf{w}$ is modeled as a multi-variate Gaussian distribution with mean μ_t and covariance Σ_t:

$$p(\mathbf{w}_t) = N(\mathbf{w}; \mu_t, \Sigma_t). \qquad (4)$$

Often, $\mu_0 = \mathbf{0}$ and $\Sigma_0 = \mathbf{I}$ are used for initialization. Suppose a labeled sample $(\mathbf{x}_i, y_i)$ is available for training at time t. The likelihood function is the *probit* function defined as:

$$\mathcal{P}(y_i|\mathbf{x}_i, \mathbf{w}) = \Phi(y_i \mathbf{x}_i^\top \mathbf{w}), \tag{5}$$

where $\Phi(z) = \int_{-\infty}^{z} N(v; 0, 1)\, dv$ is the cumulative distribution function of the standard Gaussian distribution. By Bayes' theorem, the posterior distribution of $\mathbf{w}$ is proportional to the product of the likelihood in (5) and the prior distribution in (4):

$$p(\mathbf{w}|\mathbf{x}_i, y_i) \propto \mathcal{P}(y_i|\mathbf{x}_i, \mathbf{w}) N(\mathbf{w}; \mu_t, \Sigma_t). \tag{6}$$

Unfortunately, the posterior is non-Gaussian. In practice, the first two moments of $\mathbf{w}$ are often used to construct a Gaussian approximation. Here, our approximation is based on a variational approach known as Adaptive Density Filter (ADF) [12, 15]. Given a posterior distribution p, ADF finds a Gaussian approximation that matches the first two moments of p. Specifically, let $N(\mathbf{w}; \mu_{t+1}, \Sigma_{t+1})$ be the target Gaussian, whose parameters $\{\mu_{t+1}, \Sigma_{t+1}\}$ are chosen to minimize the Kullback-Leibler divergence:

$$\min \mathbf{KL}\left(\Phi(y_i \mathbf{x}_i^\top \mathbf{w}) N(\mathbf{w}; \mu_t, \Sigma_t) \| N(\mathbf{w}; \mu_{t+1}, \Sigma_{t+1})\right).$$

This optimization problem can be solved analytically by moment matching up to the second order, yielding:

$$\mu_{t+1} = \mu_t + \alpha\,(\Sigma_t \mathbf{x}_i) \tag{7}$$

$$\Sigma_{t+1} = \Sigma_t - \delta\,(\Sigma_t \mathbf{x}_i)(\Sigma_t \mathbf{x}_i)^\top \tag{8}$$

where

$$\alpha = \frac{y_i}{\sqrt{\mathbf{x}_i^\top \Sigma_t \mathbf{x}_i + 1}} \frac{N(z)}{\Phi(z)}$$

$$\delta = \frac{1}{\sqrt{\mathbf{x}_i^\top \Sigma_t \mathbf{x}_i + 1}} \frac{N(z)}{\Phi(z)} \left(\frac{N(z)}{\Phi(z)} + z\right)$$

with $z = \frac{y_i \mathbf{x}_i^\top \mu_t}{\sqrt{\mathbf{x}_i^\top \Sigma_t \mathbf{x}_i + 1}}$. If the dimension of $\mathbf{x}_i$ is high, the covariance matrix Σ_t can be restricted to be *diagonal*. This restriction corresponds to the idea of mean-field approximation; see [9] for a successful application of this method in a search engine setting. Then, the parameter update above takes $\mathcal{O}(d)$ time on average, where d is the average number of non-zero features. Hereafter, we focus on diagonal covariance matrices only.

In online active learning, unlabeled samples come in sequentially. For an unlabeled sample, we may use the current classifier's predictive distribution on the label to decide whether to request its label. Given parameters $\theta = \{\mu_t, \Sigma_t\}$ of the classifier at time t, the predictive distribution for sample $\mathbf{x}$ is given by: $\mathcal{P}(y|\mathbf{x}; \theta) = \int \Phi(y\mathbf{x}^\top \mathbf{w}) N(\mathbf{w}; \mu_t, \Sigma_t)\, d\mathbf{w}$, where $\Phi(y\mathbf{x}^\top \mathbf{w})$ is the probit likelihood and $N(\mathbf{w}; \mu_t, \Sigma_t)$ is the approximate posterior distribution of $\mathbf{w}$ at time t. The integral can be exactly computed by

$$\mathcal{P}(y = +1|\mathbf{x}; \theta) = \Phi\left(\frac{\mathbf{x}^\top \mu_t}{\sqrt{\mathbf{x}^\top \Sigma_t \mathbf{x} + 1}}\right). \tag{9}$$

In the ERM framework, class label prediction is based on function value only (e.g., $\mathbf{x}^\top \mathbf{w}$ or $\Phi(\mathbf{x}^\top \mathbf{w})$). To visualize the conceptual difference between the predictive probability in (9) and the function-value-only prediction, we present a synthetic case in two-dimensional feature space in Figure 1.

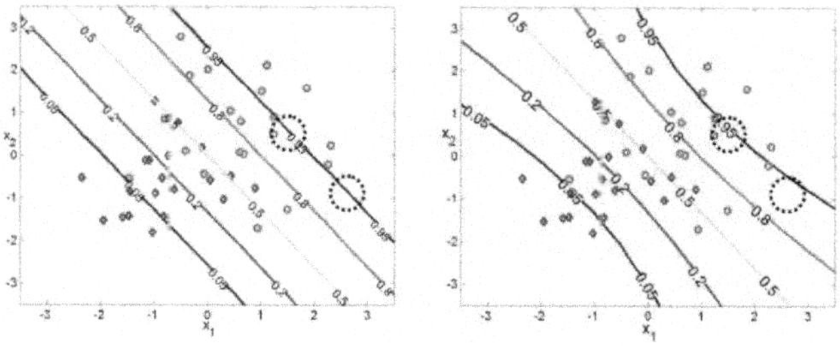

Figure 1: An illustration on predictive probabilities (right) in contrast with function values (left).

The red circles and blue diamonds represent the labeled samples of two classes used for training. In the right graph, the contour curves are indexed with predictive probabilities of the class of red circles. In the left graph, the contour curves are indexed with confidence level of belonging to the class of red circles based on function values only. The two dotted circles in black indicate two regions of interest where unlabeled samples come from. One region is about the center of red circles with predictive probability 0.95, and another region is a bit far away from training samples. In function-value-only prediction, the latter region is also predicted with probability 0.95 because of the hyper-plane determined by $\mathbf{w}$, whereas the predictive probability in (9) lowers the confidence on the latter region. The advantage comes from the quadratic term $\mathbf{x}^\top \Sigma_t \mathbf{x}$ in the denominator, which tends to be large on regions far from training samples. In some high-dimensional feature spaces, the difference on predictive uncertainty could be more significant. Even when the covariance matrix Σ_t is constrained to be diagonal, different attributes could have different uncertainties.

To summarize, three critical advantages are identified for online Bayesian learning:

- The step size per example can be computed analytically using ADF, without the need for a line search or learning rate tuning;
- Consistency in predictive class probabilities, which can be utilized by Bayesian decision theory to find optimal cutoffs for various utility functions;
- Model uncertainty is explicitly considered, which makes active learning more sensible on novel samples, especially in high-dimensional spaces.

3.1 Weighted Likelihood

Online active learning induces a stochastic process that selects unlabeled samples with certain probability for labeling. The selected samples come from an instrumental distribution $q(\cdot)$ rather than $p(\cdot)$, the distribution of interest. We use the weighted likelihood bootstrap sampling procedure [16] to select the samples to be sent for labeling. Suppose we obtain a labeled sample $(\mathbf{x}_i, y_i, \beta_i)$ through online active learning, where β_i denotes the sampling probability of $\mathbf{x}_i$. The weighted likelihood function is then defined by

$$\mathcal{P}(y_i|\mathbf{x}_i, \mathbf{w}, \beta_i) = \mathcal{P}^{\beta_i}(y_i|\mathbf{x}_i, \mathbf{w}) \tag{10}$$

where $\beta_i = \frac{1}{q(\mathbf{x}_i)}$ is the importance weight. Asymptotic properties of maximum weighted likelihood estimators have been studied [22]. In this section, we give approximate update rules coupled with weighted likelihood to update the model in an online fashion. The variational approximation as in (7) and (8) finds an optimal Gaussian approximation. Now we attempt to find a Gaussian approximation, parameterized by $\check{\mu}_{t+1}$ and $\check{\Sigma}_{t+1}$, which is adjusted to the weighted likelihood as in (10). Based on the approximation $N(\mathbf{w}; \mu_{t+1}, \Sigma_{t+1})$ and the weight β_i in weighted likelihood [9], we have

$$\check{\Sigma}_{t+1}^{-1} - \Sigma_t^{-1} = \beta_i(\Sigma_{t+1}^{-1} - \Sigma_t^{-1})$$

$$\check{\Sigma}_{t+1}^{-1}\check{\mu}_{t+1} - \Sigma_t^{-1}\mu_t = \beta_i(\Sigma_{t+1}^{-1}\mu_{t+1} - \Sigma_t^{-1}\mu_t)$$

Reorganizing terms, we reach the following update rules:

$$\check{\Sigma}_{t+1} = \Sigma_{t+1}(\beta_i\Sigma_t + (1-\beta_i)\Sigma_{t+1})^{-1}\Sigma_t \quad (11)$$

$$\check{\mu}_{t+1} = \check{\Sigma}_{t+1}(\beta_i\Sigma_{t+1}^{-1}\mu_{t+1} + (1-\beta_i)\Sigma_t^{-1}\mu_t) \quad (12)$$

These rules are in the same spirit of the scaling effect on step size in stochastic gradient descent in the ERM framework.

3.2 Dynamics

So far the model assumes a stationary data distribution $p(\mathbf{x}, y)$ and then the variance on weights would converge towards zero as labeled samples increase. Gradually, the model would stop learning. We are handling time series patterns in data streams, so that the model we have investigated should be capable of adapting to changes in *non-stationary* situations. If we can access all historical labeled samples, we can introduce a decay factor to decrease the influence on the posterior from outdated samples. This decay can be achieved by down-weighting the likelihood of such out-of-date samples. However, in online active learning, we cannot store all training samples for revisiting their weighted likelihood. Fortunately we can introduce a memory loss factor on the current model, the prior distribution of $\mathbf{w}$ at time t. Then the joint likelihood becomes

$$\mathcal{P}^{\beta_i}(y_i|\mathbf{x}_i, \mathbf{w})N^{\gamma}(\mathbf{w}; \mu_t, \Sigma_t)$$

where γ is the loss factor and $0 \ll \gamma \leq 1$. Dynamics corrections can be derived analogously as in (11) and (12) by replacing the 1's by γ.

3.3 Sampling Distribution

According to Proposition 2, the instrumental distribution $q(\cdot)$ should be proportional to the entropy estimate. Since the current model may deviate from the truth, we introduce a tolerance parameter ϵ to reflect misclassification rate, where $0 \leq \epsilon \ll 1$, so that the predictive probability becomes

$$\check{p}(y|\mathbf{x}; \theta) = \epsilon + (1 - 2\epsilon)p(y|\mathbf{x}; \theta),$$

where the predictive probability $p(y|\mathbf{x}; \theta)$ is defined as in (9). The instrumental distribution we applied in this work is defined as follows:

$$q(\mathbf{x}) = \sum_y -\check{p}(y|\mathbf{x}; \theta)\log_2(\check{p}(y|\mathbf{x}; \theta)). \quad (13)$$

The right panel of Figure 2 plots example curves of the labeling probability again the function value $\mathbf{x}^\top\mathbf{w}$ for a fixed $\epsilon = 0.1$ and different values of $\sigma^2 = \mathbf{x}^\top\Sigma\mathbf{x}$. The left panel plots the labeling probability given by [4], which is based on function values only: $q(\mathbf{x}) \propto \frac{b}{b+|\mathbf{x}^\top\mathbf{w}|}$. Both instrumental distributions in Figure 2 are conceptually similar while the key difference lies in our method's capability of modifying labeling probability based on prediction uncertainty.

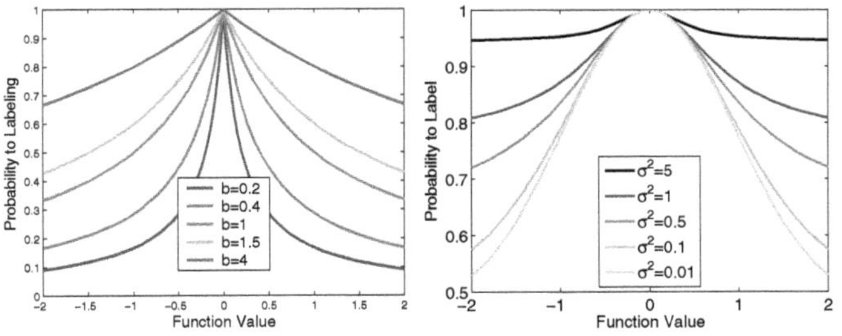

Figure 2: Label selection probabilities based on function value (left) and entropy (right).

Algorithm 1 Online Active Learning with Bayesian Probit

Input: data stream $\{\mathbf{x}_1, \mathbf{x}_2, \ldots\}$, classifier $\theta = \{\mu, \Sigma\}$
$t \leftarrow 0$, $\mu \leftarrow \mathbf{0}$, $\Sigma \leftarrow \mathbf{I}$
repeat
  $t \leftarrow t + 1$, $H_t \leftarrow p(+1|\mathbf{x}_t; \theta)$,
  sample $\tau \sim \mathcal{U}_{(0,1)}$
  if $\tau < q(\mathbf{x}_t)$ **then**
    acquire label y_t
    update model $\{\mu, \Sigma\}$ by $(\mathbf{x}_t, y_t, \beta_t)$
  end if
until the end of data stream
Output: $\{\mu, \Sigma\}$ and predictive probabilities $\{H_1, H_2, \ldots\}$

Algorithm 1 summarizes our algorithm for online active learning based on the techniques discussed in this section.

4. DISCUSSION

When we make IID assumptions on non-IID data, there can be undesirable consequences. In this section, we discuss two simple examples of what can go wrong. In particular, we ask:

1. Is there an example of a problem where shuffling the data would not improve performance, but training only on early data would?
2. Is there an example of a problem where shuffling the data would improve performance?

The first example is straightforward. To connect it to the spam problem, we call it the novel spam attack problem.

EXAMPLE 1. ***The Novel Spam Attack Problem:*** *Over N days, there are N distinct messages in the dataset: no distinct message shares any features with another distinct message. The first distinct message occurs on the first day k times, the second distinct message occurs on the second day k times, etc. The label of each distinct message is random.*

Note that once a message has been seen and labeled, it will never be misclassified again. Thus, an algorithm that memorizes examples will make $N/2$ mistakes. If the data is shuffled, this will not improve the result, because there is no way to generalize between distinct messages. On the other hand, an algorithm that trains only on the first day will get the first day right, but will at best in expectation make $(N-1)k/2$ mistakes on the rest of the data.

A second example shows where shuffling does have an impact. It focuses on a known spammer approach, where they create e-mails that would be misclassified by the current classifier, but keep the problem separable. It is related to a classic problem in online learning, that the VC dimension can be low while the mistake bounds are infinite. Consider learning a threshold on the $[0, 1]$ interval.

EXAMPLE 2. ***Spammer Splitting the Difference:*** *Define* $\mathcal{X} = [0, 1]$*. Let a be the highest value of a negative example seen so far (or 0 if no negative example has seen so far), and b the lowest value of a positive example seen so far (or 1 if no positive example has been seen so far). The next instance is* $\frac{a+b}{2}$*, and the probability that it is positive is* $\frac{1}{2}$*.*

This is an example when, given the examples in order, there is almost nothing to be done. Even though all positive examples have higher values than the negative ones, the positive examples monotonically decrease in the instance space, and the negative examples monotonically increase. But when the examples are shuffled, it becomes much easier, for this monotonicity can be leveraged. If, when you see an example x, you have seen another example x' with a positive label where $x > x'$, then x is positive. Similarly, if you have seen another example x'' with a positive label where $x < x''$, then x is negative. Define p to be the number of positive examples, and $\{x_1 \dots x_p\}$ to be the positive examples in order of arrival. So, if we consider shuffling the positive indices, we only get a positive examples wrong if it is the highest number seen so far. From folklore, if you shuffle the numbers from 1 to p, the number of times you see a number higher than any you have seen so far is $\Theta(\log p)$ times. Thus, if there are m examples, then one will make $\Theta(m)$ mistakes if the data is unshuffled, but if the data is shuffled, then one will make $\Theta(\log m)$ mistakes.

Thus, the ability for spammers to push closer and closer to the boundary over time can be incredibly powerful. However, note that if shuffling improves performance directly, this implies a connection between spam attacks. If spam attacks were completely novel, then shuffling would not improve performance.

5. RELATED WORK

Given unlabeled examples, two types of active learning scenarios exist [20]. In the *pool-based* scenario (e.g., [13]), a *static* set of unlabeled examples are given, from which a subset is chosen for labeling. The setting considered in the present paper falls into the other scenario known as *stream-based* [5, 7], in which the learner has to decide, for each example in the data stream, whether to query a label (and then updates the classifier if a label is obtained). For applications like UGC abuse detection where examples arrive sequentially, the stream-based model is more natural.

Many heuristics exist for scoring the *informativeness* of unlabeled examples in active learning, including those based on uncertainty sampling [13], the principle of maximal disagreement [8, 21], model variance minimization [6, 23], and version/model space pruning [1, 5, 14], etc. Most relevant to this work is probably the heuristic based on estimated error reduction [10, 18], where an unlabeled example is scored based on the estimated reduction in the classification error if that example is labeled and included in the training set. However, most of these selection criteria are deterministic. Hence, the labeled training data can represent a distribution that is very different from the original data distribution, which introduces bias in the learning process. In contrast, our active learning scheme is probabilistic, so that importance weighting is easily incorporated to remove bias in the labeled data. This property is crucial as it ensures that the learned classifier is optimized against the right distribution.

The idea of using importance weighting for de-biasing has been used in prior work. [4] combines probabilistic selective sampling in Perceptron-like algorithms. However, these algorithms do not explicitly control variance, so the mistake bounds become larger as variance increases. The IWAL algorithm [2], on the other hand, guarantees bounded variance by a careful specification of the labeling probabilities, but calculating the probabilities is expensive except for special cases. Our algorithm takes a further step and directly relates the labeling probabilities to the variance of the risk of the final classifier, and the probabilities are easier to compute.

Regarding metrics in online learning, it is worth noting that [11] has shown that the AUC measure has a fundamental limitation since it implicitly uses different misclassification cost distributions for different classifiers. To overcome the incoherence in terms of misclassification costs, a valid alternative to the AUC was proposed.

6. EXPERIMENTAL RESULTS

This section reports experimental results on commercial spam moderation in UGC to verify the usefulness of the proposed algorithm for online active learning. We implemented online probit regression model with diagonal covariance matrix as in [9] as the classifier. For comparison purposes, three unbiased active learning strategies were implemented to couple with the Bayesian classifier:

- Entropy-based criteria: The sampling probability is a function of entropy estimate as in (13), see the right graph in Figure 2;
- Function-value-based criteria: The sampling probability is defined as $\frac{b}{b+|\mathbf{x}^\top \mathbf{w}|}$ proposed by [4], see the left graph in Figure 2;
- Random: As a baseline approach, a fraction of samples are selected randomly to labeling.

We have also implemented their corresponding biased variants, i.e. selected samples are equally weighted rather than $\frac{1}{q(\mathbf{x})}$, to show the advantages of ensuring unbiasedness.

6.1 Settings

We give a brief introduction to data collection, and then highlight temporal concept drift in the data stream.

6.1.1 UGC Spam Detection

On a commercial news portal, users are allowed to post comments to discuss news articles. Around the end of 2010, we selected a subset of UGC to human editors for commercial spam detection. The data collection lasted 30 days. The selection rule was kept unchanged in the 30 days. Human editors manually examined the comment content and gave a label such as clean, commercial spam or other types of abuse. Based on the editorial labels, we collected clean UGC and commercial spam UGC into our data set. Our goal here is to build an online classifier to distinguish commercial spam from clean UGC. The UGC samples are indexed by submission timestamp as in time series. We extracted features from UGC text content only, including text analysis results, named entities and TFIDF. There are about 0.26 million UGC samples and 0.27 million features in the data set. The feature vector of a UGC sample is usually sparse, containing about 90 non-zero elements on average. The daily commercial spam rate is about 1% ~ 5%. It should be noted that the spam rate in our data set does not represent the real-world spam rate in the commercial news portal at all, though daily spam patterns have been well preserved in the sample selection procedure.

6.1.2 Evaluation Methodology

The samples from the first day were used to train a binary classifier as an initial model, and the samples from the remaining days were used for evaluation. The UGC data set contains evaluation data from 29 days. The samples in the remaining days were sorted by the time that the comment was posted. The online Bayesian classifiers in all candidate models were initialized by the first-day model in the same way. The simulation was then carried out as follows: (a) The classifier takes the next sample in the data stream and makes a prediction on its label, named as a one-step-ahead prediction; (b) the active learning algorithm decided whether to acquire the editorial label or not; (c) if label acquisition was requested, the editorial label was revealed without any delay and a model update was executed by the online classifier using the labeled sample as in Section 3.1; (d) steps (a), (b) and (c) were repeated until the end of the data stream.

To evaluate generalization performance, we took the results of one-step-ahead predictions in the simulation, i.e. the output H in Algorithm 1, and computed the following metrics:

- Negative logarithm of predictive probability (NLP) is defined as $\frac{1}{N}\sum_{i=1}^{N} -\log p(y_i|\mathbf{x}_i)$ where $p(y_i|\mathbf{x}_i)$ is the predictive probability given by the classifier as in (9). NLP is 0 for a perfect classifier;
- Area under ROC (AUC) is a popular performance metric to measure the quality of predictive ordering on classification datasets. In our experiments, predictive ordering was determined by sorting the predictive probabilities $p(y_i = +1|\mathbf{x}_i)$ in descending order. AUC is 1 for perfect ordering and 0.5 for random guessing;
- Weighted loss (WL) is defined as $c_n * FN + c_p * FP$ where c_n and c_p are pre-fixed cost scalar, FN is the number of false negative predictions, and FP is the number of false positive predictions. Based on Bayesian decision theory, the optimal threshold is $c_p/(c_p + c_n)$ rather than 0.5 in the cost-sensitive setting, i.e. the classifier yields positive label if $p(y_i = +1|\mathbf{x}_i) \geq c_p/(c_p + c_n)$, otherwise negative label.[1] In the following case study, we set $c_n = 9$ and $c_p = 1$. This tradeoff makes sense in user generated data, because if a comment is blocked, then a real person becomes immediately aware that his or her comment was blocked and can try again, and if spam gets through, then many readers are inconvenienced.

To veil business-sensitive information, we only report *relative gains* over the baseline performance of the first-day initial model. For NLP and WL, the relative gain is defined as 1-Score/Baseline, while for AUC it is Score/Baseline-1. In all cases, a larger metric implies better performance.

[1] We assume our classifier's predictive probability is correct. The loss to give away positive label (but the true label is negative) is $c_p(1 - p(y_i = +1|\mathbf{x}_i))$, whereas the loss of negative label is $c_n p(y_i = +1|\mathbf{x}_i)$. The losses incurred by the two opposite actions are balanced only when $p(y_i = +1|\mathbf{x}_i) = c_p/(c_p + c_n)$.

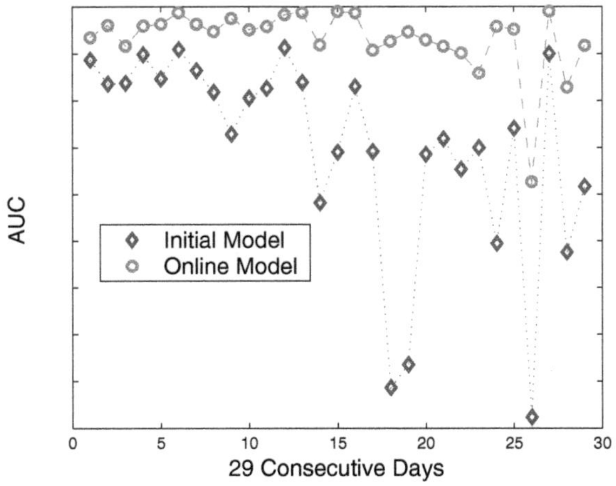

Figure 3: Initial vs. Online model on daily AUC.

γ	AUC	NLP	WL
1.0	0.04161	0.5373	0.7116
0.99999	0.04217	0.5451	0.7135
0.99995	0.04312	0.5676	0.7428
0.9999	0.04388	0.5750	0.7468
0.9995	0.03832	0.4426	0.5871
0.999	0.03065	0.2857	0.3816

Table 1: Online learning performance with decay.

6.1.3 Pattern Change

To illustrate the existence of concept drift or pattern change in our data set, we compared the initial model against an online classifier on the evaluation data. The initial model was built using the first day's data and was kept unchanged in the test. The online classifier was updated as in Algorithm 1 but without selective labeling in the simulation, i.e., every label is revealed in time. We present the comparisons in Figure 3 as empirical evidence. We observed that the initial model suffers by performance degradation especially after 10 days indicating a change in the data. The online classifier is capable of learning pattern changes in a timely manner to handle the changing data over time. The existence of concept drifting in the data stream is further verified in Section 6.3.

6.1.4 Memory Decay Factor

We also compared online classifiers with different decay factors on the UGC evaluation data. The decay factor was varied from 1.0 to 0.999. In Table 1, we report three performance metrics for four online classifiers. Note that in this study, selective labeling was not involved. We revealed sample labels to the classifier for online model update after every one-step-ahead prediction. We observed that the online classifier with a decay factor of 0.99999 or 0.9999 yields better performance than the online classifier without memory decay. The best performance is achieved with decay factor

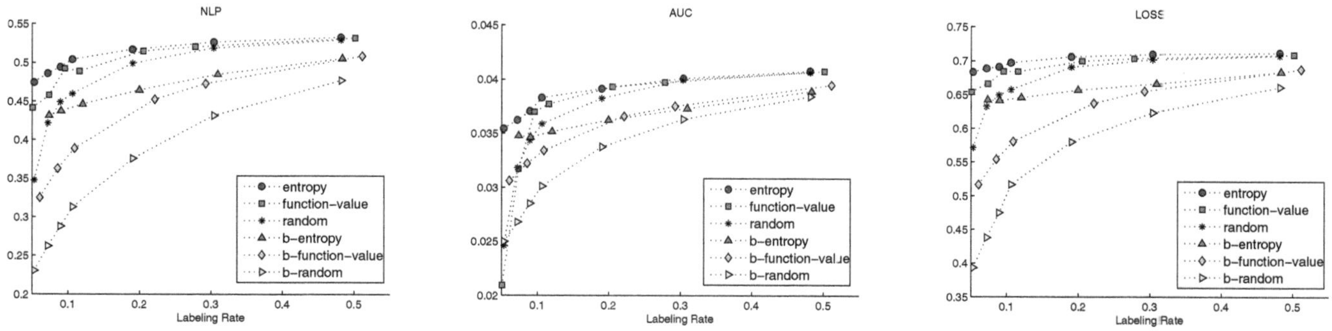

Figure 4: Generalization performance at different labeling rates.

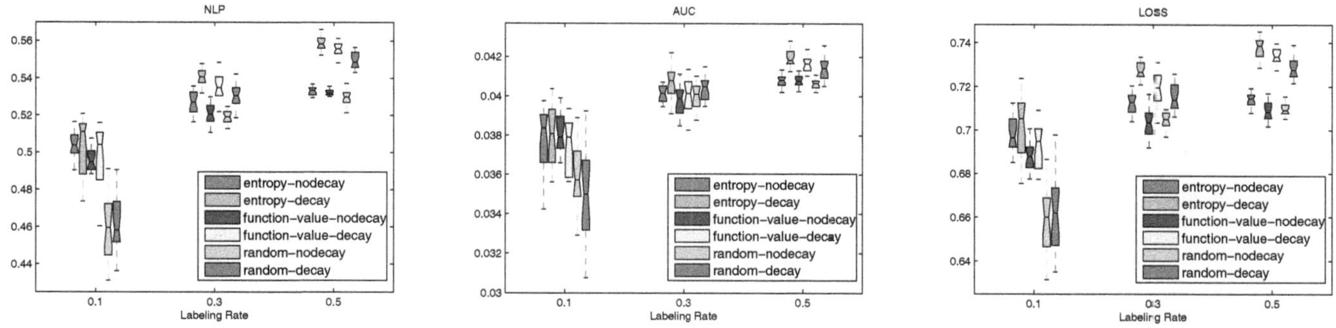

Figure 5: Generalization performance with and without the decay factor. For each different labeling rate in each plot, the three labeling strategies from left to right are entropy-based, function-value-based, and random; the results with and without decaying for each strategy are listed side-by-side. The box has lines at the lower quartile, median, and upper quartile values.

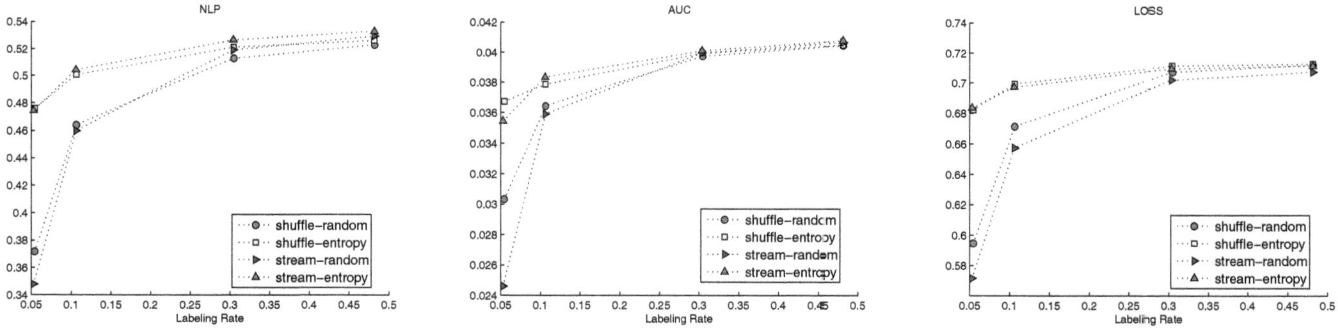

Figure 6: Generalization performance on shuffled data vs. on data stream, at different labeling rates.

0.9999. When the factor goes down to 0.9995, the performance becomes worse than that without memory decay. We also observed that the three metrics, NLP, AUC and WL, are consistently correlated. The benefits we observed from the decay factor also support the conjecture that there are temporal changes of the spam pattern or input distribution in the one-month UGC data stream.

6.2 Online Active Learning

We tested six candidate models of the online probit classifier. These six models were realized by combining three active learning strategies (entropy-based criteria, the function-value-based criteria, and random selection), with two bias types (unbiased and biased). The six candidate models were initialized by the same first-day model. The labeling rate in entropy-based algorithms is controlled by the tolerance parameter ϵ. We varied ϵ from 0.1 to 0.0025, and the resulting label rate decreased from 50% to 5%. The labeling rate in function-value-based algorithms is controlled by the parameter b. We varied b from 4 to 0.2 and the resulting label rate decreased from 50% to 5% as well. We explicitly specified selection rates in the random models at the rates realized by the entropy models. We report our results averaged over 20 trials on the evaluation data.

Figure 4 presents the results (for various metrics) of each model *without decay* on the evaluation data. Each graph presents generalization results of the six models at different labeling rates ranging from 5% to 50%, averaged over 20 trials.

Figure 5 presents the results (for various metrics) for the unbiased models with decay factor 0.9999 on the evaluation data stream. Each boxplot present generalization results of the six models at three labeling rates, 10%, 30% and 50%, averaged over 20 trials.

The three biased models yield inferior performance, compared to their unbiased counterparts. In general the unbiased models converge faster to the optimal than the biased models. In Figure 4, the optimal performance is bounded by the online learning result without decay factor $\gamma = 1$ given in Table 1. The gap between the biased and unbiased random model emphasizes the well-known fact that the learning rate is critical in online sequential learning. Around a labeling rate of 0.7, the biased entropy model can catch up with the unbiased random model. Within the three biased models, we found that the function-value and entropy models are consistently better than the random model at all labeling rates. When the labeling rate is below 20%, the entropy model performs significantly better than the function-value model. Within the three unbiased models, we found that the function-value and entropy models are consistently better than the random model. When the labeling rate is above 20%, although the function-value and entropy models are usually better than the random model, the difference is insignificant. The entropy model performs significantly better than the function-value model when the labeling rate is below 10%, as shown in Figure 5. In Figure 5, we observed that the active learning algorithms with memory decay are capable of achieving superior performance on the three metrics, especially when the labeling rate is greater than 30%. The boxplot graphs in Figure 5 also visualize performance results of the three unbiased active learning models for the 20 trials. When the labeling rate is 10%, the entropy-based model without decay is significantly better than the function-value-based model on both NLP and LOSS metrics.

6.3 Shuffled Data

In the last set of experiments, we compared active learning results on shuffled data with those on the data stream in its original order. We randomly shuffled the evaluation data to generate a new data stream, and then report the performance of the entropy model and the random model on the shuffled data. Both models are run without decay for the purpose of comparison. We present the generalization performance averaged over 20 trials, at different labeling rates ranging from 5% to 50%. The performances of the random model on the two data sets reveal the intrinsic difficulty of the two learning tasks. Since the random model consistently yields better metrics on the shuffled data when the labeling rate is below 30%, we believe that classification on the original data stream is more difficult than on the shuffled data. The underlying reason might be due to something similar to Example 2, but it is hard to know for sure. The learning tasks become even harder as the label rate decreases. On the two tasks, the entropy-based active learning approach performs consistently better than the random model. We also observed that the entropy model yields comparable results on both cases. If we look at the 0-1 loss, while the shuffled problem seems to be significantly harder given a random sampling of data, it seems that the active learning algorithm does equally well on both problems. This demonstrates that the lift obtainable in the original online problem is higher than that obtained in the shuffled problem. Thus, in this dynamic environment, active learning provides more benefits than in the stationary analogue of the problem.

7. CONCLUSIONS

In this work, we studied online active learning in dynamic problems with potentially adversarial concept drifts. It is shown, using real UGC data from a news portal at Yahoo!, that active learning is powerful for reducing labeling efforts in dynamic problems. Furthermore, motivated by practical challenges in spam detection from user generated content, we proposed and tested an online Bayesian algorithm that can handle sample weighing and forgetting, both of which are required by online active learning. Empirical results show the effectiveness of the algorithm.

The promising results in the paper raise a few important questions. First, it is interesting to analyze regret or mistake bounds for online active learning algorithms, similar to those developed for stationary problems (e.g., [4]), when there is concept drift. Obviously, little can be hoped for if arbitrary concept drifts are allowed, so reasonable assumptions are necessary. Second, we haven't studied how to adapt the value of γ in online model updates, which is an important question in practice. Third, pool-based and stream-based scenarios represent two extremes of practical situations. In reality, it is often possible, and even advantageous, to keep a small amount of unlabeled data as to-be-labeled candidates for the data stream case, so that the algorithm can revisit not-so-old examples to decide whether or not their labels are required. It is not straightforward to ensure unbiasedness in such hybrid architectures.

For future work, it is interesting to carry out controlled experiments on simulated datasets in which the concept drift process is predefined, to verify that online active learning is more powerful in dynamic environments. It is also worth comparing our approach to stochastic gradient decent. Finally, the labeling rate in online active learning is indirectly controlled through tolerance parameters in a highly nonlinear fashion, which may lead to prohibitive workload for labeling occasionally. The impact of realistic constraints in label acquisition needs to be investigated as well.

8. ACKNOWLEDGEMENTS

We appreciate the support from Pramod Khincha's engineer team in data collection.

9. REFERENCES

[1] M.-F. Balcan, A. Beygelzimer, and J. Langford. Agnostic active learning. In *Proceedings of the*

Twenty-Third International Conference on Machine Learning (ICML-06), pages 65–72, 2006.

[2] A. Beygelzimer, S. Dasgupta, and J. Langford. Importance weighted active learning. In *Proceedings of the Twenty-Sixth International Conference on Machine Learning (ICML-09)*, pages 49–56, 2009.

[3] C. I. Bliss. The calculation of the dosage-mortality curve. *Annals of Applied Biology*, 22:134–167, 1935.

[4] N. Cesa-Bianchi, C. Gentile, and L. Zaniboni. Worst-case analysis of selective sampling for linear classification. *Journal of Machine Learning Research*, 7:1205–1230, 2006.

[5] D. A. Cohn, L. Atlas, and R. Ladner. Improving generalization with active learning. *Machine Learning*, 15(2):201–221, 1994.

[6] D. A. Cohn, Z. Ghahramani, and M. I. Jordan. Active learning with statistical models. *Journal of Artificial Intelligence Research*, 4:129–145, 1996.

[7] I. Dagan and S. P. Engelson. Committee-based sampling for training probabilistic classifiers. In *Proceedings of the Twelfth International Conference on Machine Learning (ICML-95)*, pages 150–157, 1995.

[8] Y. Freund, H. S. Seung, E. Shamir, and N. Tishby. Selective sampling using the query by committee algorithm. *Machine Learning*, 28(2–3):133–168, 1997.

[9] T. Graepel, J. Q. Candela, T. Borchert, and R. Herbrich. Web-scale Bayesian click-through rate prediction for sponsored search advertising in Microsoft's Bing search engine. In *Proceedings of the Twenty-Seventh International Conference on Machine Learning (ICML-10)*, pages 13–20, 2010.

[10] Y. Guo and R. Greiner. Optimistic active-learning using mutual information. In *Proceedings of the Twentieth International Joint Conference on Artificial Intelligence (IJCAI-07)*, pages 823–829, 2007.

[11] D. J. Hand. Measuring classifier performance: a coherent alternative to the area under the roc curve. *Machine Learning*, 77:103–123, 2009.

[12] N. D. Lawrence, M. Seeger, and R. Herbrich. Fast sparse Gaussian process methods: The informative vector machine. In S. Becker, S. Thrun, and K. Obermayer, editors, *Advances in Neural Information Processing Systems 15*, pages 609–616, 2002.

[13] D. D. Lewis and W. A. Gale. A sequential algorithm for training text classifiers. In *Proceedings of the Seventeenth Annual International ACM-SIGIR Conference on Research and Development in Information Retrieval (SIGIR-94)*, pages 3–12, 1994.

[14] D. J. C MacKay. Information-based objective functions for active data selection. *Neural Computation*, 4(4):590–604, 1992.

[15] T. P. Minka. *A family of algorithms for approximate Bayesian inference*. Ph.D. thesis, Massachusetts Institute of Technology, January 2001.

[16] M. A. Newton and A. E. Raftery. Approximate Bayesian inference by the weighted likelihood bootstrap. Technical Report No. 199, Department of Statistics, University of Washington, March 1991.

[17] M.-S. Oh and J. O. Berger. Adaptive importance sampling in Monte Carlo integration. *Journal of Statistical Computation and Simulation*, 41:143–168, 1992.

[18] N. Roy and A. McCallum. Toward optimal active learning through sampling estimation of error reduction. In *Proceedings of the Eighteenth International Conference on Machine Learning (ICML-01)*, pages 441–448, 2001.

[19] C. Sawade, N. Landwehr, S. Bickel, and T. Scheffer. Active risk estimation. In *Proceedings of the Twenty-Seventh International Conference on Machine Learning (ICML-10)*, pages 951–958, 2010.

[20] B. Settles. Active learning literature survey. Technical Report 1648, Department of Computer Sciences, University of Wisconsin-Madison, January 2009.

[21] H. S. Seung, M. Opper, and N. Tishby. Query by committee. In *Proceedings of the Fifth Annual Conference on Computational Learning Theory (COLT-92)*, pages 287–294, 1992.

[22] X. Wang, C. van Eeden, and J. V. Zidek. Asymptotic properties of maximum weighted likelihood estimators. *Journal of Statistical Planning and Inference*, pages 37–54, 2004.

[23] T. Zhang and F. J. Oles. A probability analysis on the value of unlabeled data for classification problems. In *Proceedings of Seventeenth International Conference on Machine Learning (ICML-00)*, pages 1191–1198, 2000.

[24] M. Zinkevich. Online convex programming and generalized infinitesimal gradient ascent. In *Proceedings of the Twentieth International Conference on Machine Learning (ICML-03)*, pages 928–936, 2003.

Learning to Trade Off Between Exploration and Exploitation in Multiclass Bandit Prediction

Hamed Valizadegan
Department of Computer Science
University of Pittsburgh
Pittsburgh, USA
hamed@cs.pitt.edu

Rong Jin
Department of Computer Science and Engineering
Michigan State University
East Lansing, PA, USA
rongjin@cs.msu.edu

Shijun Wang
Radiology and Imaging Sciences
National Institute of Health
USA
wangshi@cc.nih.gov

ABSTRACT

We study multi-class bandit prediction, an online learning problem where the learner only receives a partial feedback in each trial indicating whether the predicted class label is correct. The exploration vs. exploitation tradeoff strategy is a well-known technique for online learning with incomplete feedback (i.e., bandit setup). Banditron [8], a multiclass online learning algorithm for bandit setting, maximizes the run-time gain by balancing between exploration and exploitation with a fixed tradeoff parameter. The performance of Banditron can be quite sensitive to the choice of the tradeoff parameter and therefore effective algorithms to automatically tune this parameter is desirable. In this paper, we propose three learning strategies to automatically adjust the tradeoff parameter for Banditron. Our extensive empirical study with multiple real-world data sets verifies the efficacy of the proposed approach in learning the exploration vs. exploitation tradeoff parameter.

Categories and Subject Descriptors

I.2 [**Artificial Intelligence**]: Learning

General Terms

Theory, Algorithms

Keywords

Online Learning, Bandit Feedback, Multi-class Classification, Exploration vs. Exploitation

1. INTRODUCTION

The exploitation vs. exploration tradeoff strategy has been widely used to develop online learning techniques when the feedback provided to the learner is bandit, i.e. the learner only receives the cost of its action but not the cost of other possible actions. Exploration refers to taking an action that is not recommended by the current model (classifier). It allows the learner to explore the environment (opponent), receive the feedback for different actions, and consequentially gain new knowledge from the environment. Exploitation refers to taking the best action according to the current statistical model in order to maximize the gain. These two objectives are complementary, but opposite: exploration leads to the maximization of the gain in the long run at the risk of losing short term reward, while exploitation maximizes the short term gain at the price of losing the gain over the long run. A careful tradeoff between these two objectives is important to the success of any online learner utilizing the combined strategy [17].

The exploitation vs. exploration tradeoff strategy was originally designed for the multi-armed bandit problem [15] where a slot machine has multiple arms and the player needs to choose the arm with minimum cost (or maximum gain). In each trial, after choosing one arm, the learner receives the cost (award) for the selected arm, but does not know the cost (or award) of the other arms. Under this bandit setting, the learner is required to find the best (possibly mixed) arm in a repeated game. The learner can also be equipped with side information in order to identify the best arm more efficiently. Recently, this technique has been successfully applied to online multi-class classification with partial feedback. Unlike the typical setup of online learning where the learner receives the correct class assignment for an input pattern after making prediction, in online multi-class leaning with partial feedback, the learner only receives an incomplete feedback that indicates if the predicted class is correct. This problem is also referred to as Multiclass Bandit Prediction [8] and has found applications in several domains, including online advertisement and recommender systems [12].

Banditron [8], an algorithm that was recently developed for multi-class bandit prediction, utilizes the exploration vs. exploitation tradeoff technique to handle the challenge of the partial feedback for online multi-class learning. This tradeoff is explicitly captured by a single parameter $\gamma \in (0, 0.5)$ in Banditron: with probability $1-\gamma$, the learner will predict the most likely class label based on the current classification model (exploitation), and with probability γ, the learner will randomly choose one of the remaining class labels for prediction (exploration). Figure 1 shows the performance of Banditron for three different data sets by varying the value of γ. It is clear that the performance of Banditron strongly depends on the value of γ and it is therefore important to develop strategies to automatically tune this parameter. In-

KDD'11, August 21–24, 2011, San Diego, California, USA.

tuitively, at the beginning of the learning stage, due to the fact that the classification model is trained by a small number of examples, we would expect it to perform poorly. As a result, it may be more desirable to have more exploration and consequentially set γ to a large value. As the learning procedure proceeds, after the classification model is updated with sufficiently large number of examples, we expect it to make accurate prediction. As a result, it is desirable to decrease the value of γ and consequentially reduce the amount of exploration with increasing number of training examples. Theoretically, as suggested by [8][1], the choice of $\gamma = \rho(\frac{DK}{t})^{1/3}$ minimizes the mistake bound given (i) the complexity measure D of optimal W in the Frobenius norm of W, (ii) the number of classes K and (iii) the noise level ρ[2]. One major problem with this choice of γ is that it does not depend on the performance of the online classifier, as we would expect a small amount of exploration (i.e., small γ) is needed when the online learner makes accurate prediction. This is because the optimal γ is obtained by minimizing the upper bound for the number of mistakes. Since most mistake bounds are concerned with the asymptotical behavior of an online learning algorithm, it tends to be very loose. As a consequence, the resulting γ is only optimal in the asymptotical sense, not necessarily for finite horizons. To further support our argument, in Figure 1, we also include the error rates of online multi-class bandit prediction using $\gamma = \rho(\frac{DK}{t})^{1/3}$ highlighted by horizonal lines. Here, we set $D = 2|W_p|_F^2$ and $\rho = \ell(W_P)/T$ where W_p is the classifier learned by the Perceptron[3]. It is clear that the error rates of using this γ are far from the true optimals.

This paper is organized as follows. Section 2 reviews the related work to this study. After a short description of Banditron algorithm in Section 3, we propose three different methods to automatically learn the tradeoff parameter γ in Sections 3.2, 3.3, and 3.4. Section 4 shows the efficacy of the proposed approaches through an extensive experimental study. Section 5 concludes this work with future directions.

2. RELATED WORK

Online multi-class learning in bandit setting has been recently received increasing interests [9, 8, 11, 2]. It is closely related to the multi-armed bandit problem [14, 1, 6], where the exploitation vs. exploration tradeoff is used [19, 5, 13]. The multi-armed bandit cannot be applied directly to online multi-class bandit prediction because they do not exploit any side information, such as the feature vector of training examples. Langford et al. extended the multi-armed bandit setting to the case where side information is used to make a better prediction [9]. They refer to the new setting as "contextual bandit problem" and introduced the epoch-greedy algorithm and derived its regret bound. Kakade et al. introduced an efficient algorithm for multiclass bandit prediction that is efficient and guarantees certain regret bound [8], which utilizes the exploitation vs. exploration technique. Wang et al. developed a general potential based framework from which Banditron is a special case [18]. The major problem with Banditron is that its performance could be sensitive to the parameter that trades off between exploration and exploitation, as shown in Fig 1. To the best of our knowledge, this is the first study that aims to learn the tradeoff parameter for multi-class bandit problem.

[1]Corollary 3 in [8].

[2]In [8], it is assumed that there exists a $\rho \in (0,1)$ such that $\sum_{i=1}^T \ell_t(W) \leq \rho T$, where $\ell_t(W)$ is a convex loss function.

[3]Assuming that we already know the classifier learned by Perceptron

3. OPTIMIZING THE TRADEOFF BETWEEN EXPLORATION AND EXPLOITATION

3.1 Preliminaries

Algorithm 1 shows Banditron [8]. At round t, Banditron receives sample $\mathbf{x}_t$ and predicts a class label $\widetilde{y}_t$ for $\mathbf{x}_t$. It then receives an incomplete (bandit) feedback $[y_t = \widetilde{y}_t]$, where $[y_t = \widetilde{y}_t]$ is an indicator function that outputs 1 if $y_t = \widetilde{y}_t$ and zero otherwise, and updates its classification model accordingly.

Banditron can be considered as the multi-class perceptron [16] adapted for the bandit setting using the exploitation vs. exploration tradeoff strategy. Similar to the Perceptron algorithm, it computes label $\widehat{y}_t$ after receiving an example x_t using a linear model W. However, due to the bandit feedback, extra (randomization) steps are performed to predict $\widetilde{y}_t$ based on the exploitation vs. exploration tradeoff strategy (Steps 7-8): with probability $1-\gamma_t$ it predicts class label $\widehat{y}_t$ and with probability γ_t it chooses one random class label for prediction. After receiving the partial feedback $[y_t \neq \widetilde{y}_t]$, the algorithm computes the update matrix $x_t\delta_t$ which, on average, is equivalent to the update matrix used in Perceptron for the full feedback setting. We denote by M the number of mistakes made by algorithm for all the trials, i.e. $M = \sum_{t=1}^T [\widetilde{y}_t \neq y_t]$.

In our study, we assume a linear model for each class, denoted by $W = (\mathbf{w}_1, \ldots, \mathbf{w}_K) \in \mathbb{R}^{d\times K}$, although the extension to nonlinear classifiers using kernel trick is straightforward. We denote by $W_1, \ldots, W_T$ the sequence of linear classifiers generated by an online learning algorithm over the trials. Our analysis is based on bounding the number of mistakes made by the online learning algorithm when compared to U, an arbitrary linear classifier. Since the proposed framework is a stochastic algorithm, we will focus on the expectation of the mistake bound. We denote by $\ell_t(W)$ the multi-class hinge loss of classifier W on the training example $(\mathbf{x}_t, y_t)$, defined as

$$\ell_t(W) = \ell\left(\max_{k\neq y} \mathbf{w}_k^\top \mathbf{x}_t - \mathbf{w}_{y_t}^\top \mathbf{x}_t\right)$$

where $\ell(z) = \max(0, z+1)$. Theorem 1 gives the mistake bound of the Banditron algorithm that is slightly different from the original work. It provides the foundation for deriving the strategies to learn the tradeoff parameter γ.

THEOREM 1. *Let K be the number of classes. After running over a sequence of examples $\mathbf{x}_1, \ldots, \mathbf{x}_T$, with $\|\mathbf{x}_t\|_2 \leq 1$ for all t, the expected number of mistakes made by Banditron, denoted by $\mathrm{E}[M]$, is bounded as follows*

$$\begin{aligned}\mathrm{E}[M] &\leq |U|_F^2 + \sum_{t=1}^T \ell_t(U) + \mathrm{E}\left[\sum_{t=1}^T \gamma_t\right] \\ &+ \mathrm{E}\left\{\sum_{t=1}^T \gamma_t[\widehat{y}_t = y_t] + \sum_{t=1}^T \frac{K}{\gamma_t}[\widehat{y}_t \neq y_t]\right\} \quad (1)\end{aligned}$$

where U is any arbitrary weight matrix (classifier) and $\{\gamma_t\}_{t=1}^T$ are sampling probabilities of trials.

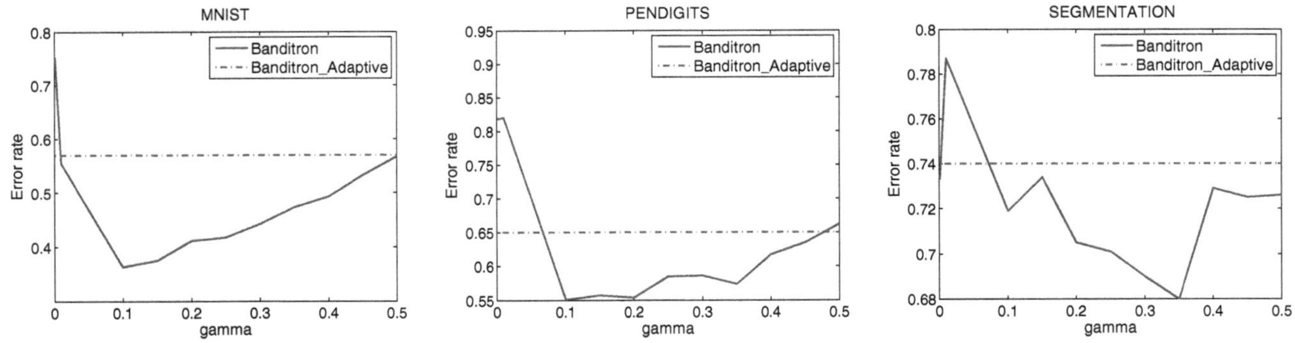

Figure 1: The error rates of Banditron with different choice of γ for three different data sets

---

Algorithm 1 The Banditron Algorithm

Set $W^0 = \mathbf{0}$
for $t = 1, \ldots, T$ **do**
  Receive $\mathbf{x}_t \in \mathbb{R}^d$
  Compute $\widehat{y}_t = \arg\max_{1 \leq k \leq K} \mathbf{x}_t^\top \mathbf{w}_k^{t-1}$
  Choose sampling probability γ_t
  Set $p_k = (1-\gamma_t)[k = \widehat{y}_t] + \gamma_t/K, k = 1, \ldots, K$
  Sample $\widetilde{y}_t$ by distribution $\mathbf{p} = (p_1, \ldots, p_K)$.
  Predict $\widetilde{y}_t$ and receive feedback $[y_t = \widetilde{y}_t]$
  Compute $\delta_t = \mathbf{1}_{\widehat{y}_t} - \mathbf{1}_{\widetilde{y}_t}\frac{[y_t=\widetilde{y}_t]}{p_{\widetilde{y}_t}}$ where $\mathbf{1}_k$ stands for the vector with all its elements being zero except its kth element is 1.
  Compute $W^t = W^{t-1} - \mathbf{x}_t \delta_t^\top$
end for

PROOF. Following the gradient descent framework for online learning [3], we have the following bound when $\widehat{y}$ is used as the predictor:

$$
\begin{aligned}
& \sum_{t=1}^T [\widehat{y}_t \neq y] \left(\ell_t(W_{t-1}) - \ell_t(U)\right) \\
\leq \; & \sum_{t=1}^T [\widehat{y}_t \neq y] \langle U - W_{t-1}, \nabla \ell_t(W) \rangle \\
= \; & \sum_{t=1}^T \langle U - W_{t-1}, \mathrm{E}_t[W_t - W_{t-1}] \rangle \\
= \; & \frac{1}{2} \sum_{t=1}^T \mathrm{E}\Big[|U - W_{t-1}|_F^2 - |U - W_t|_F^2 + |W_t - W_{t-1}|_F^2 \Big] \\
= \; & \frac{1}{2}|U - W_0|_F^2 + \mathrm{E}\left[\frac{1}{2} \sum_{t=1}^T |W_{t-1} - W_t|_F^2 \right] \\
\leq \; & \frac{1}{2}|U|_F^2 + \frac{1}{2} \sum_{t=1}^T \mathrm{E}\left[|\delta_t|_F^2 \right] \\
\leq \; & \frac{1}{2}|U|_F^2 + \mathrm{E}\left\{ \sum_{t=1}^T \gamma_t [\widehat{y}_t = y_t] + \sum_{t=1}^T \frac{K}{\gamma_t} [\widehat{y}_t \neq y_t] \right\}
\end{aligned}
$$

In the above, the first inequality follows directly the convexity of the loss function, the first equality follows the relationship $\mathrm{E}_t[\mathbf{x}_t \delta_t^\top] = \nabla \ell_t(W)$ [18], the second inequality follows $|\mathbf{x}_t|_2 \leq 1$, and the last inequality follows Lemma 5 of [8].

We complete the proof by using the following relationships

$$
\sum_{t=1}^T \mathrm{E}[\widehat{y}_t \neq y_t] \leq \sum_{t=1}^T [\widehat{y}_t \neq y_t] \ell_t(W)
$$

$$
\mathrm{E}[M] \leq \sum_{t=1}^T \mathrm{E}[\widehat{y}_t \neq y_t] + \sum_{t=1}^T \gamma_t
$$

□

Remark I:.

By scaling U and $\ell(z)$ as follows

$$
U \to \eta U, \; \ell(z) \to \ell_\eta(z) = \max(0, \eta + z)
$$

we generalize Theorem 1 as

$$
\begin{aligned}
\mathrm{E}[M] \leq & \sum_{t=1}^T t\ell_t(U) + \mathrm{E}\left[\sum_{t=1}^T \gamma_t \right] \\
& + \frac{\eta}{2}|U|_F^2 + \frac{1}{\eta}\mathrm{E}\left\{ \sum_{t=1}^T \gamma_t [\widehat{y}_t = y_t] + \sum_{t=1}^T \frac{K}{\gamma_t} [\widehat{y}_t \neq y_t] \right\}
\end{aligned}
$$

By minimizing over scaling factor η, we have

$$
\begin{aligned}
\mathrm{E}[M] \leq & \sum_{t=1}^T \ell_t(U) + \mathrm{E}\left[\sum_{t=1}^T \gamma_t \right] \\
+ & \; |U|_F \sqrt{2\mathrm{E}\left\{ \sum_{t=1}^T \gamma_t [\widehat{y}_t = y_t] + \sum_{t=1}^T \frac{K}{\gamma_t} [\widehat{y}_t \neq y_t] \right\}} \quad (2)
\end{aligned}
$$

which the same inequality used by [8] to obtain the mistake bound.

Given the bound provided in Theorem 1, the optimal set of sampling probabilities $\{\gamma_t\}_{t=1}^T$ will be obtained by minimizing the mistake bound stated in Theorem 1, i.e.

$$
\mathcal{L} = \sum_{t=1}^T \frac{K}{\gamma_t} [\widehat{y}_t \neq y_t] + \sum_{t=1}^T \gamma_t (1 + [\widehat{y}_t = y_t])
$$

However $[\widehat{y}_t \neq y_t]$ and $[\widehat{y}_t = y_t]$ are not provided explicitly in the partial feedback, making it impossible to obtain γ_t by directly minimizing the upper bound. Note that in the previous studies, this difficulty is resolved by bound $[\widehat{y}_t = y_t] \leq 1$, leading to the choice of γ_t independent from the prediction performance of the online classifier. To address the difficulty, we approximate $[\widehat{y}_t \neq y_t]$ and $[\widehat{y}_t = y_t]$ by two biased estimators μ_t and τ_t, respectively:

- Approximate $[\widehat{y}_t = y_t]$ by $\mu_t = 2[\widehat{y}_t = \widetilde{y}_t][\widetilde{y}_t = y_t]$. This is because

$$\begin{aligned} [\widehat{y}_t = y_t] &= \mathrm{E}_t\left[\frac{[\widehat{y}_t = \widetilde{y}_t][\widetilde{y}_t = y_t]}{p_{\widetilde{y}_t}}\right] \\ &\le \mathrm{E}_t\left[\frac{[\widehat{y}_t = \widetilde{y}_t][\widetilde{y}_t = y_t]}{1-\gamma_t}\right] \\ &\le \mathrm{E}_t\left[\mu_t\right] \end{aligned}$$

Note that in the last step, we use the fact $\gamma_t \le 1/2$.

- Approximate $[\widehat{y}_t \neq y_t]$ by $\tau_t = 1 - [\widehat{y}_t = \widetilde{y}_t][\widetilde{y}_t = y_t]$

$$\begin{aligned} [\widehat{y}_t \neq y_t] &= 1 - [\widehat{y}_t = y_t] \\ &\le 1 - \mathrm{E}_t\left[[\widehat{y}_t = \widetilde{y}_t][\widetilde{y}_t = y_t]\right] \\ &= \mathrm{E}_t[\tau_t] \end{aligned} \quad (3)$$

Using μ_t and τ_t allows us to compute the two quantities without have to know $[\widehat{y}_t = y_t]$ or $[\widehat{y}_t \neq y_t]$. However, it is infeasible to use μ_t and τ_t for approximation because both of them require knowing y_t. We address this difficulty by approximating μ_t and τ_t with the average of μ and τ over all the trials up to the time t, i.e., replacing μ_t and τ_t with $\sum_{i=1}^{t-1}\mu_i/(t-1)$ and $\sum_{i=1}^{t-1}\tau_i/(t-1)$, respectively. Combining with the trivial bounds that $[\widehat{y}_t = y_t] \le 1$ and $[\widehat{y}_t \neq y_t] \le 1$, in the following subsections, we consider three strategies for approximating $[\widehat{y}_t = y_t]$ and $[\widehat{y}_t \neq y_t]$

- $[\widehat{y}_t \neq y_t] \le \tau_t$ and $[\widehat{y}_t = y_t] \le \mu_t$
- $[\widehat{y}_t \neq y_t] \le 1$ and $[\widehat{y}_t = y_t] \le \mu_t$
- $[\widehat{y}_t = y_t] \le 1$ and $[\widehat{y}_t \neq y_t] \le \tau_t$

In order to generate a general family of functions for γ_t, we introduce the concept of *good support function*, which is the key gradient for defining the tradeoff parameter.

DEFINITION 2. *A function $\omega(z)$ defined in the domain of $z \ge 0$ is called a* **good support function** *if it satisfies the following conditions: (a) $\omega(z)$ is concave for $z \ge 0$ and $\omega(0) \ge 0$, (b) $\omega(z)$ is monotonically increasing, i.e., $\omega'(z) > 0$, for $z \ge 0$, (c) $\omega(z)$ is Lipschitz continuous with Lipschitz constant L, i.e., $\omega'(z) \le L$, for $z \ge 0$, and (d) there exists a constant $\rho \ge 1$ such that for any $t \ge 0$ and $z \ge 0$, we have $\omega'(z) \le \rho^t \omega'(z+t)$.*

The discussion below allows us to connect the definition of good support function to the desired properties of γ_t.

- Given Property (a), it is easy to conclude that $\omega'(z)$ is a non-decreasing function of z, $\omega'(z+t) \le \omega'(z)$ or $\frac{1}{\omega'(z)} \le \frac{1}{\omega'(z+t)}$ for $t \ge 0$. This non-increasing property of $\omega'(z)$ also allows us to define non-increasing γ_t that is bounded between 0 and $1/2$.

- Property (b) allows us to have $\omega(z) \le \omega(z+t)$ or $\frac{1}{\omega(z+t)} \le \frac{1}{\omega(z)}$ for $t \ge 0$, another important quantity for deriving the mistake bound.

- Property (c) and (d) allow us to upper-bound $\omega'(z)$ by a constant L and by $\omega'(z+t)$ for $t \ge 0$.

The following proposition gives examples of good support function.

PROPOSITION 1. *(1) $\omega(z) = (a+z)^\lambda$, with $\lambda \in (0,1]$ and $a > 0$, is a good support function, with Lipschitz constant $L = \lambda a^{\lambda-1}$, and $\rho = e^{(1-\lambda)/a}$, and (2) $\omega(z) = \ln(a+z)$ with $a > 0$ is a good support function, with $L = 1/a$, and $\rho = e^{1/a}$.*

PROOF. We only show the result for $\omega(z) = (a+z)^\lambda$. A similar derivation can be applied to $\omega(z) = \ln(a+z)$. For Lipschitz continuous constant L, we have

$$L = \max_{z\ge 0} \frac{\lambda}{(a+z)^{1-\lambda}} = \lambda a^{\lambda-1}$$

For ρ, we have

$$\frac{(a+z+t)^{1-\lambda}}{(a+z)^{1-\lambda}} \le (1+t/a)^{1-\lambda} \le e^{t(1-\lambda)/a}$$

leading to $\rho = e^{(1-\lambda)/a}$. □

3.2 Finding Optimal γ using μ_t and τ_t

Using $[\widehat{y}_t = y_t] \le \mu_t$ and $[\widehat{y}_t \neq y_t] \le \tau_t$, we approximate $\mathcal{L}$ by

$$\widehat{\mathcal{L}} = \sum_{t=1}^T \frac{K}{\gamma_t}\tau_t + \sum_{t=1}^T \gamma_t(\mu+1).$$

To bound $\widehat{\mathcal{L}}$, we introduce two good support functions $\omega_1(z)$ and $\omega_2(z)$, with $\omega_1'(z) \ge \omega_2'(z)$ for any $z \ge 0$, and define γ_t as follows

$$\gamma_t = \frac{\omega_2'\left(\sum_{i=1}^{t-1} 1+\mu_i\right)}{2\omega_1'\left(\sum_{i=1}^{t-1}\tau_i\right)} \quad (4)$$

We have $\gamma_t \le 1/2$ for any t because

$$\gamma_t \le \frac{\omega_1'\left(\sum_{i=1}^{t-1} 1+\mu_i\right)}{2\omega_1'\left(\sum_{i=1}^{t-1}\tau_i\right)} \le \frac{\omega_1'\left(\sum_{i=1}^{t-1}\tau_i\right)}{2\omega_1'\left(\sum_{i=1}^{t-1}\tau_i\right)} = \frac{1}{2}$$

The first inequality follows $\omega_1'(z) \ge \omega_2'(z)$, and the last step follows the property $\tau_i \le 1$ and the fact that $\omega_1'(z)$ is non-increasing in z. In addition, since $\omega_1'(z)$ and $\omega_2'(z)$ are non-increasing functions of z, γ_t is decreasing in μ_t and increasing in τ_t, implying that the algorithm gives a large amount of exploration when the classifier makes a number of mistakes, and a small amount of exploration when the classifier encounters only a few prediction errors. The following proposition shows key properties for γ_t in Equation 4.

PROPOSITION 2. *Given γ_t defined in (4), we have the following inequalities:*

$$\begin{aligned} \sum_{t=1}^T \gamma_t &\le \frac{\rho_2\omega_2(T)}{2\omega_1'\left(\sum_{t=1}^T \tau_t\right)} \\ \sum_{t=1}^T \gamma_t\mu_t &\le \frac{\rho_2^2\omega_2\left(\sum_{t=1}^T \mu_t\right)}{2\omega_1'\left(\sum_{t=1}^T \tau_t\right)} \\ \sum_{t=1}^T \frac{K}{\gamma_t}\mu_t &\le \frac{2K\rho_1\omega_1\left(\sum_{t=1}^T \tau_t\right)}{\omega_2'\left(\sum_{t=1}^T 1+\mu_t\right)} \end{aligned}$$

where ρ_1 and ρ_2 are the constants defined respectively for the good support functions ω_1 and ω_2.

PROOF. Define $A_t = \sum_{i=1}^t \tau_i$. We have

$$\begin{aligned}\sum_{t=1}^T \frac{K}{\gamma_t}\tau_t &= \sum_{t=1}^T \frac{2K\omega_1'(A_{t-1})\tau_t}{\omega_2'\left(\sum_{i=1}^{t-1} 1+\mu_i\right)} \\ &= \sum_{t=1}^T \frac{2K\omega_1'(A_{t-1})(A_t - A_{t-1})}{\omega_2'\left(\sum_{i=1}^{t-1} 1+\mu_i\right)} \\ &\leq \frac{2K\sum_{t=1}^T \omega_1'(A_{t-1})(A_t - A_{t-1})}{\omega_2'\left(\sum_{i=1}^{T} 1+\mu_i\right)}\end{aligned}$$

where the inequality follows that ω_2' is a non-increasing function. Since

$$\begin{aligned}\sum_{t=1}^T \omega_1'(A_{t-1})(A_t - A_{t-1}) &\leq \rho_1 \sum_{t=1}^T \omega_1'(A_t)(A_t - A_{t-1}) \\ &\leq \rho_1 \sum_{t=1}^T \omega_1(A_t) - \omega_1(A_{t-1}) \\ &\leq \rho_1 \omega_1(A_T),\end{aligned}$$

we have the first inequality. In the above, the first step follows the definition of good support functions (i.e. $\omega_1'(A_{t-1}) \leq \rho_1\omega_1'(A_t)$), the second step is due to the concavity of ω_1 and the last step is due to $\omega_1(0) \geq 0$. Combining the above results produces the first inequality in the proposition. Similar to the first inequality, for the second inequality, we define $B_t = \sum_{i=1}^t \mu_i$ and have

$$\begin{aligned}\sum_{t=1}^T \gamma_t\mu_t &= \sum_{t=1}^T \frac{\omega_2'(B_{t-1}+t-1)}{2\omega_1'(A_{t-1})}\mu_t \\ &\leq \frac{\sum_{t=1}^T \omega_2'(B_{t-1})(B_t - B_{t-1})}{2\omega_1'(A_T)} \\ &\leq \frac{\sum_{t=1}^T \rho_2^2\omega_2'(B_t)(B_t - B_{t-1})}{2\omega_1'(A_T)} \\ &\leq \frac{\rho_2^2\omega_2(B_T)}{2\omega_1'(A_T)}\end{aligned}$$

The second equality follows $\omega_2'(B_{t-1}) \leq \rho_2^{\mu_t}\omega_2'(B_t)$ and $\mu_t \leq 2$. The same analysis is applied to show the last inequality. □

THEOREM 3. *Let $\omega_1(z)$ and $\omega_2(z)$ be two good support functions with $\omega_1'(z) \geq \omega_2'(z)$ for any $z \geq 0$. By running Algorithm 1 with γ_t set as in Eq. (4), we have the following bound for the expected number of misclassified examples:*

$$\begin{aligned}\mathrm{E}[M] &\leq \sum_{t=1}^T \ell_t(U) + \frac{\rho_2\omega_2(T)}{2\omega_1'(T)} \\ &+ |U|_F\left(\sqrt{\frac{2\rho_1 K\omega_1(3T)}{\omega_2'(3T)}} + \rho_2\sqrt{\frac{\omega_2(2T)}{2\omega_1'(2T)}}\right)\end{aligned}$$

where ρ_1 and ρ_2 are the constants of two good support functions.

PROOF. The proof is straightforward by using the result in Remark I, Proposition 2, inequality $\sqrt{a+b} \leq \sqrt{a}+\sqrt{b}$, and the properties of good support functions. □

COROLLARY 4. *Suppose γ_t is in Eq. (4) with $\omega_1(z) = (1+z)^{\lambda_1}$ and $\omega_2(z) = (1+z)^{\lambda_2}$, where $\lambda_1, \lambda_2 \in (0,1]$ and $\lambda_1 = \lambda_2 + 1/3$. By running Algorithm 1, we have the following bound for the expected number of misclassified examples:*

$$\begin{aligned}\mathrm{E}[M] &\leq \sum_{t=1}^T \ell_t(U) + \frac{\rho_2}{\lambda_2+\frac{1}{3}}(1+T)^{\frac{2}{3}} \\ &+|U|_F\left(\sqrt{\frac{\rho_2 e^{\frac{1}{3}}K}{\lambda_2}}(1+3T)^{\frac{2}{3}} + \frac{\rho_2}{\sqrt{\lambda_2+\frac{1}{3}}}(1+2T)^{\frac{1}{3}}\right)\end{aligned}$$

where $\rho_2 = e^{1-\lambda_2}$. This bound is of $O(T^{2/3})$ and similar to the bound of the original Banditron.

Remark II:.
Although the mistake bounds given in Theorem 3 and Corollary 4 are not better than the result derived in the previous study, we emphasize that the analysis of mistake bound is often loose because its focus is to obtain the asymptotical behavior of the learner. The key advantage of the tradeoff parameter γ_t defined in Eq. 4 is its capability of adapting to the classification performance (i.e., μ_t and τ_t) of the learner, making it intuitively more attractive.

3.3 Finding Optimal γ using μ_t

Using $[\widehat{y}_t \neq y_t] \leq 1$ and $[\widehat{y}_t = y_t] \leq \mu_t$, we upper bound $\mathcal{L}$ by

$$\widehat{\mathcal{L}} = \sum_{t=1}^T \frac{K}{\gamma_t} + \sum_{t=1}^T \gamma_t(1+\mu_t)$$

Given a good support function $\omega(z)$, we define γ_t as

$$\gamma_t = \frac{1}{2L}\omega'\left(\sum_{i=1}^{t-1} 1+\mu_i\right) \tag{5}$$

It is straightforward to see $\gamma_t \in [0, 1/2]$. Since $\omega(z)$ is a concave function, $\omega'(z)$ is a non-increasing function of z, leading to a decreasing value for γ_t as more and more training examples have been classified correctly. The following proposition shows key properties for γ_t in (5).

PROPOSITION 3. *Given γ_t defined in (5), we have the following inequalities:*

$$\begin{aligned}\sum_{t=1}^T \gamma_t\mu_t &\leq \frac{\rho^2}{2L}\omega\left(\sum_{t=1}^T \mu_t\right) \\ \sum_{t=1}^T \gamma_t &\leq \frac{\rho}{2L}\omega(T) \\ \sum_{t=1}^T \frac{K}{\gamma_t} &\leq \frac{2KLT}{\omega'\left(\sum_{t=1}^T 1+\mu_t\right)}\end{aligned}$$

The proof is almost identical to that for Proposition 2.

THEOREM 5. *Let $\omega(z)$ be a good support function. By running Algorithm 1 with γ_t set as in Eq. (5), we have the following bound for the expected number of mistakes made by the algorithm:*

$$\mathrm{E}[M] \leq \sum_{t=1}^T + \frac{\rho\omega(T)}{2L} + |U|_F\left(\rho\sqrt{\frac{\omega(2T)}{2L}} + \sqrt{\frac{2KLT}{\omega'(3T)}}\right)$$

The following corollary directly follows from Proposition 1 and Theorem 5.

COROLLARY 6. *By running Algorithm 1 with γ_t as in Eq. (5) and $\omega(z) = (1+z)^\lambda$, where $\lambda \in (0, 1]$, we have the following bound for the expected number of classification mistakes:*

$$\begin{aligned} \mathrm{E}[M] \quad &\leq \quad \sum_{t=1}^{T} \ell_t(U) + \frac{e^{1-\lambda}}{2\lambda}(1+T)^\lambda \\ &+ \quad |U|_F \left(\frac{e^{1-\lambda}}{\sqrt{2\lambda}}(1+2T)^{\frac{\lambda}{2}} + \sqrt{2K}(1+T)^{\frac{1-\lambda}{2}} T^{\frac{1}{2}} \right) \end{aligned}$$

When $\lambda = 2/3$, we have $\mathrm{E}[M] = O(T^{2/3})$ which is the same convergence rate as Banditron.

3.4 Finding Optimal γ using τ_t

Similar to the approach presented in the previous sections, we set γ_t as

$$\gamma_t = \frac{\omega_2'(t)}{2\omega_1'\left(\sum_{i=1}^{t-1} \tau_i\right)} \quad (6)$$

where $\omega_1(z)$ and $\omega_2(z)$ are two good support functions and $\omega_1'(z) \geq \omega_2'(z)$. It is easy to verify that $\gamma_t \in (0, 1/2]$ due to the properties of a good support function. The proposition below allows us to bound $\sum_{t=1}^{T} \gamma_t$ and $\sum_{t=1}^{T} K/\gamma_t$.

PROPOSITION 4. *Given the construction of γ_t in (6), we have the following inequalities:*

$$\begin{aligned} \sum_{t=1}^{T} \frac{K}{\gamma_t}\tau_t \quad &\leq \quad 2K\rho \frac{\omega_1\left(\sum_{t=1}^{T} \tau_t\right)}{\omega_2'(T)} \\ \sum_{t=1}^{T} \gamma_t \quad &\leq \quad \frac{\omega_2(T)}{2\omega_1'\left(\sum_{t=1}^{T} \tau_t\right)} \end{aligned}$$

PROOF. Similar to Proposition 2 and 3. □

THEOREM 7. *Let $\omega_1(z)$ and $\omega_2(z)$ be two good support functions. By running Algorithm 1 with γ_t set as in Eq. (6), we have the following bound for the number of misclassified examples $M = \sum_{t=1}^{T} [\widehat{y}_t \neq y_t]$:*

$$\begin{aligned} \mathrm{E}[M] \quad &\leq \quad \sum_{t=1}^{T} \ell_t(U) + \frac{\omega_2(T)}{2\omega_1'\left(\sum_{t=1}^{T} \tau_t\right)} \\ &+ \quad |U|_F \left(\sqrt{\frac{\omega_2(T)}{2\omega_1'(T)}} + \sqrt{2K\rho_1 \frac{\omega_1(T)}{\omega_2'(T)}} \right) \end{aligned}$$

PROOF. The proof directly follows Theorem 1 and Proposition 4. □

The following corollary directly follows from the result of Proposition 1 and Theorem 7.

COROLLARY 8. *By running Algorithm 1 with γ_t in Eq. (6) and $\omega_1 = (1+z)^{\lambda_1}$ and $\omega_2 = (1+z)^{\lambda_2}$ with $\lambda_1, \lambda_2 \in (0, 1]$, we have the following bound for the expected number of misclassified examples*

$$\begin{aligned} \mathrm{E}[M] \leq &\sum_{t=1}^{T} \ell_t(U) + \frac{1}{2\lambda_1}(1+T)^{\lambda_2+1-\lambda_1} \\ &+|U|_F \left(\sqrt{\frac{1}{2\lambda_1}}(1+T)^{\frac{\lambda_2+1-\lambda_1}{2}} + \sqrt{\frac{2ke^{1-\lambda_1}}{\lambda_2}}(1+T)^{\frac{\lambda_1+1-\lambda_2}{2}} \right) \end{aligned}$$

with $\lambda_1 = \lambda_2 + \frac{1}{3}$ we have $E[M] = O(T^{2/3})$ which is of the same rate as Banditron.

4. EXPERIMENTS

In this section, we conduct experiments on several real-word data sets to validate the proposed strategies for balancing the tradeoff between exploration and exploitation.

4.1 Data Set

Several real-world data sets from UCI data repository [7] and LIBSVM web page [4] are used in our study as described in the following. Notice that for some of these data sets, there were two separate sets, one for training and one for testing. We only used the training set in our experiments.

- **RCV1**. RCV1 consists of 15,564 of training documents for text categorization. Each document is a news report from Reuters [10], represented by a vector of 47,236 dimension, and belongs to one of the 53 classes.
- **MNIST**. MNIST contains grey scale images of size 28×28 for hand written digits. It contains 60000 training samples, each represented by 780 features.
- **Protein**. Protein has 17766 samples, represented by 357 features and three classes.
- **Letter**. Letter contains 15000 instances of 26 characters, represented by 16 features.
- **optdigits**. This is a normalized bitmaps of handwritten digits from 30 people that contains 3823 instances, each represented by 8 × 8 features.
- **pendigits**. This is another digits collection containing 7495 samples, each with 16 features.
- **Nursery**. Originally developed to rank applications for nursery school, it has 12960 records, each represented by 8 features belonging to one of 4 classes (we removed one class that only had two samples).
- **Isolet**. Isolet contains 7797 spoken alphabet with 617 attributes and 26 classes.
- **Abalone**. Developed to predict the age of abalone from physical measurement, it contains 4177 records, each represented by 8 features and one of the 29 classes.
- **Car**. This data set contains 1728 samples, each represented by 6 features and one of the four classes.
- **Waveform**. Waveform data set contains 5000 samples of three classes, each represented by 21 features.
- **RedWineQuality**. This data set contains 1599 red wine records, each represented by 11 features and one of the 6 classes.
- **RedWineQuality**. WhiteWineQuality contains 4898 white wine records, each represented by 11 features and one of the 7 classes.
- **Segmentation**. The image Segmentation data set contains 2310 samples. Each sample is represented by 19 features and belongs to one of the 7 classes.

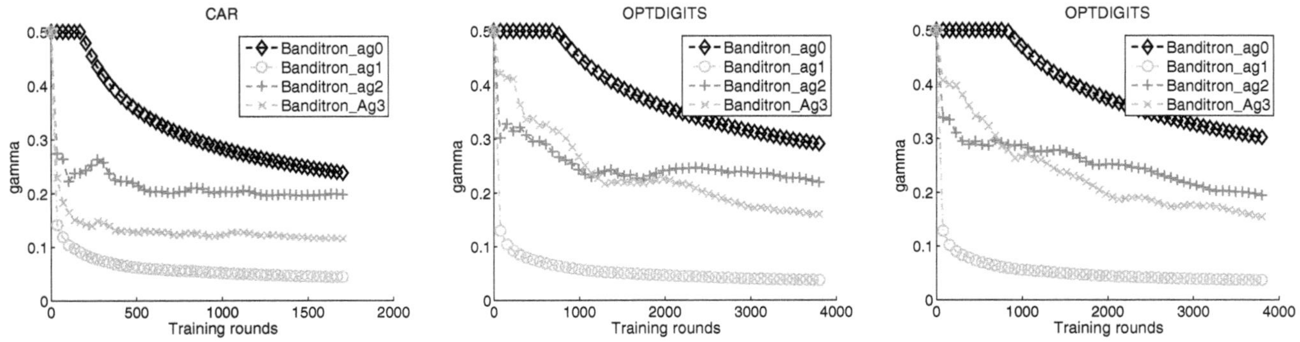

Figure 2: Behavior of γ in different methods for data sets, Car and Optdigits. There are two figures for Optdigits to stress that the proposed methods adapt γ based on the sequence of the samples over trials.

4.2 Experimental Settings

We refer to the algorithms developed in Sections 3.2, 3.3, and 3.4 as **Banditron_ag3**, **Banditron_ag1** and **Banditron_ag2**. To evaluate the classification performance of the three proposed learning strategies for exploitation vs. exploration tradeoff parameter γ, we compare them with three different version of Banditron, namely, **Banditron_Worst**, **Banditron_Best**, and **Banditron_ag0**. **Banditron_Worst** and **Banditron_Best** are Banditron algorithm when γ is set to the worst and best value for a given data. The worst and best γ are found from the predefined set $S = \{0.001, 0.01, 0.1, 0.15, 0.2, 0.25, 0.3, 0.35, 0.4, 0.45, 0.5\}$. **Banditron_ag0** is the Banditron with the adaptive $\gamma_t = \min(0.5, \rho(\frac{DK}{t})^{1/3})$ as suggested in [8] for the general agnostic case. We used $D = 2|W_p|_F^2$ and $\rho = \ell(W_P)/T$ where W_p is the classifier learned by the Perceptron [4]. We repeat each experiment 50 times by generating random sequences of instances and report the average accumulate error rates, which are computed as the ratio of the number of misclassified samples to the number of samples received so far. For all three proposed methods in all the experiments, we use similar good support functions $\omega(z) = \omega_1(z) = \omega_2(z) = (1+z)^\lambda$ with $\lambda = 0.1$ for a fair comparison. Also notice that the result is stable for most of these data sets with different values of λ.

4.3 Experimental results

To study the behavior of different learning algorithms over trials, we show the average error rates of all the methods over the entire online process in Figure 3. First notice that there is big gap between Banditron_worst and Banditron_Best in all data sets that emphasizes that the Banditron algorithm can perform very poorly if γ is not set appropriately.

We observe that overall the proposed algorithms exhibit similar or better learning rates as the Banditron algorithm with the optimal γ. In particular, banditron_ag2 and banditron_ag3 yields the best performance among the algorithms in comparison. In most of the data sets, banditron_ag2 and banditron_ag3 perform significantly better than banditron_ag0 which suggests that $\gamma_t = \min(0.5, \rho(\frac{DK}{t})^{1/3})$ is not a good adaptive choice (even with the assumption that Perceptron setting for variables D and ρ is known). As a few examples, notice that the final error rate of banditron_ag0 is 56% versus 37% error rate of banditron_ag2, banditron_ag3 and banditron_best for MNIST data set. For Optdigits data set, the final error rate of banditron_ag2 and banditron_ag3 is 56% which is significantly low compared to 59% error rate of banditron_best and banditron_ag0. The latter example also suggests that our adaptive strategy is better than the Banditron with a single best γ.

Although better than banditron_worst, the performance of banditron_ag1 is not comparable to that of the other methods for most of the cases. This can be explained by the inherited difference between banditron_ag1 and the other two proposed approaches. Unlike banditron_ag2 and banditron_ag3 where two good support functions are introduced to determine γ_t, the γ_t defined in banditron_ag1 is determined by a single good support function. As a result, we have a better control of the value for γ over time in banditron_ag2 and banditron_ag3 by a trade-off between two functions: one which is the decreasing function of time and the other which is the increasing function of the number of misclassified examples.

Figure 2 shows how γ changes during the learning process for different algorithms for two data sets, car and optdigits. We also plot two different runs of optdigits to see how the proposed methods is sensitive to the order of presented samples. Notice that unlike banditron_ag0 that constantly decreases the value of γ, the proposed methods are more adaptive. More particularly, banditron_ag2 and banditron_ag3 update γ based on the performance of Banditron over trials, and if needed, they increase the value of γ. Moreover, the proposed methods are sensitive to the sequence of the samples, and chooses the best updating rule based on how samples presented over trials and how much the learning process in Banditron succeeded so far.

5. CONCLUSION

In this work, we study the problem of optimizing the exploration-exploitation tradeoff in the context of multi-class bandit prediction. We proposed three different strategies to automatically tune the tradeoff parameter used by the Banditron algorithm. We showed through extensive experimental study that the proposed approaches are effective in adjusting the exploration-exploitation tradeoff. In particular, we found that **banditron_ag2** and **banditron_ag3** achieve similar or better performance compared to Banditron with the best value for γ. In the future, we plan to exploit other approaches for balancing the exploration-exploitation tradeoff other than the ϵ-greedy strategy applied in Banditron.

[4]We also tried $\gamma_t = 0.5t^{-1/3}$. The proposed approach consistently produces better result than $\gamma_t = 0.5t^{-1/3}$ as well.

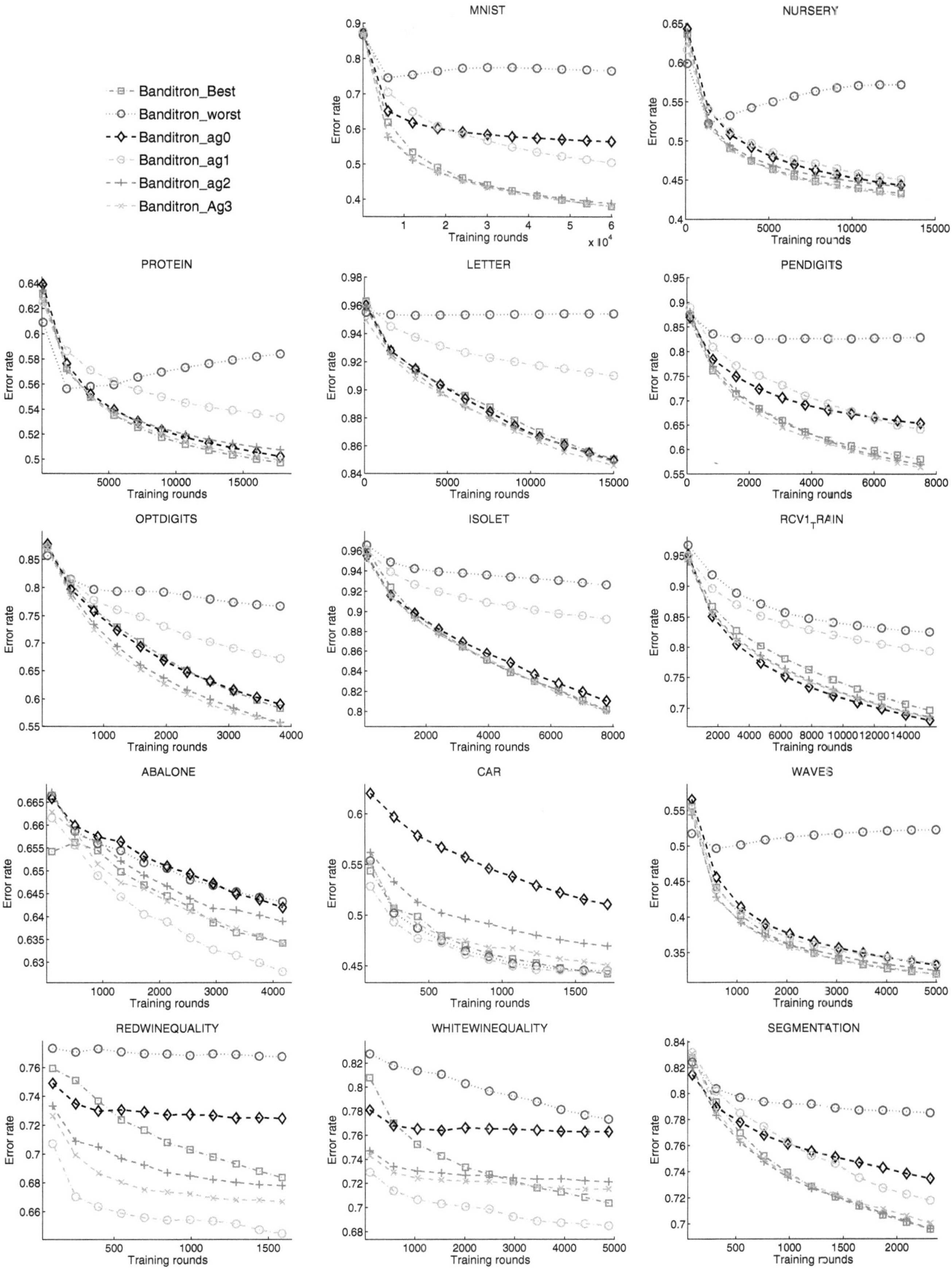

Figure 3: The error rates of different methods over trials. Each point on a curve is the average results of 50 randomly generated sequences of data.

6. ACKNOWLEDGEMENT

This work is supported in part by National Science Foundation (IIS-0643494), and the Office of Navy Research (N00014-09-1-0663).

7. REFERENCES

[1] Peter Auer, Nicolò Cesa-Bianchi, and Paul Fischer. Finite-time analysis of the multiarmed bandit problem. *Machine Learning*, 47(2-3):235–256, 2002.

[2] Alina Beygelzimer, John Langford, Lihong Li, Lev Reyzin, and Robert E. Schapire. An optimal high probability algorithm for the contextual bandit problem. *Computational Research Repository*, abs/1002.4058, 2010.

[3] N. Cesa-Bianchi and G. Lugosi. *Prediction, learning, and games.* Cambridge Univ Pr, 2006.

[4] Chih-Chung Chang and Chih-Jen Lin. Libsvm : a library for support vector machines, 2001.

[5] Eyal Even-Dar, Shie Mannor, and Yishay Mansour. PAC bounds for multi-armed bandit and markov decision processes. In *COLT '02: Proceedings of the 15th Annual Conference on Computational Learning Theory*, pages 255–270, 2002.

[6] Eyal Even-Dar, Shie Mannor, and Yishay Mansour. Action elimination and stopping conditions for the multi-armed bandit and reinforcement learning problems. *Journal of Machine Learning Research*, 7:1079–1105, 2006.

[7] A. Frank and A. Asuncion. UCI machine learning repository, 2010.

[8] Sham M. Kakade, Shai Shalev-Shwartz, and Ambuj Tewari. Efficient bandit algorithms for online multiclass prediction. In *ICML 2008: Proceedings of the 25th international conference on Machine learning*, pages 440–447, 2008.

[9] John Langford and Zhang Tong. The epoch-greedy algorithm for contextual multi-armed bandits. In *NIPS 2007: Proceeding of the 20th Annual Conference on Neural Information Processing System*, 2007.

[10] D. D. Lewis, Y. Yang, T. Rose, and F. Li. Rcv1: A new benchmark collection for text categorization research. *Journal of Machine Learning Research*, 5:361–397, 2004.

[11] Lihong Li, Wei Chu, John Langford, and Robert E. Schapire. A contextual-bandit approach to personalized news article recommendation. In *WWW '10: Proceedings of the 19th international conference on World wide web*, pages 661–670, New York, NY, USA, 2010. ACM.

[12] Wei Li, Xuerui Wang, Ruofei Zhang, Ying Cui, Jianchang Mao, and Rong Jin. Exploitation and exploration in a performance based contextual advertising system. In *KDD 2010: Knoledge Discovery and Data Mining*, pages 27–36, 2010.

[13] Shie Mannor and John N. Tsitsiklis. The sample complexity of exploration in the multi-armed bandit problem. *Journal of Machine Learning Research*, 5:623–648, 2004.

[14] Herbert Robbins. some aspects of the sequential design of experiments. *Bulletin of the American Mathematical Society*, 58:527–535, 1952.

[15] Herbert Robins. Some aspects of the sequential design of experiments. *Bull. Amer. Math. Soc.*, 58(5):527–535, 2010.

[16] F. Rosenblatt. The perceptron: a probabilistic model for information storage and organization in the brain. *Psychological review*, 65:386–408, 1958.

[17] Joannès Vermorel and Mehryar Mohri. Multi-armed bandit algorithms and empirical evaluation. In *In European Conference on Machine Learning*, pages 437–448. Springer, 2005.

[18] Shijun Wang, Rong Jin, and Hamed Valizadegan. A potential-based framework for online multi-class learning with partial feedback. In *ISTATS 2010: Artificial Intelligence and Statistics*, 2010.

[19] C. Watkins. *Learning from delayed Rewards.* PhD thesis, Cambridge, 1989.

Linear Scale Semantic Mining Algorithms in Microsoft SQL Server's Semantic Platform

Kunal Mukerjee
Microsoft
Redmond, WA, USA
+1-425-703-6009
kunalm@microsoft.com

Todd Porter
Microsoft
Redmond, WA, USA
+1-425-703-5337
tporter@microsoft.com

Sorin Gherman
Microsoft
Redmond, WA, USA
+1-425-538-4725
soring@microsoft.com

ABSTRACT

This paper describes three linear scale, incremental, and fully automatic semantic mining algorithms that are at the foundation of the new Semantic Platform being released in the next version of SQL Server. The target workload is large (10 – 100 million) Enterprise document corpuses. At these scales, anything short of linear scale and incremental is costly to deploy. These three algorithms give rise to three weighted physical indexes: Tag Index (top keywords in each document); Document Similarity Index (top closely related documents given any document); and Semantic Phrase Similarity Index (top semantically related phrases, given any phrase), which are then query-able through the SQL interface. The need for specifically creating these three indexes was motivated by observing typical stages of document research, and gap analysis, given current tools and technology at the Enterprise. We describe the mining algorithms and architecture, and also outline some compelling user experiences that are enabled by the indexes.

Categories and Subject Descriptors

H.2.8 [**Database Management**]: Database Applications – *data mining, statistical databases.*

General Terms: Algorithms.

Keywords

Semantic Platform, semantic mining, linear scale, incremental, keyword extraction, document similarity

1. INTRODUCTION

Managing unstructured and structured data in separate systems leads to many problems, such as consistency control, synchronizing backups, and supporting multiple systems. Increasingly, this pain drives users to move unstructured data into relational databases. Such unstructured data includes files (e.g., office documents, PDFs), large text fragments (e.g., emails, wiki pages, forum comments), etc.

KDD'11, August 21–24, 2011, San Diego, California, USA.

As users store more documents in databases, it is critical that databases help manage them. Doing so effectively requires more than storing and retrieving bits; it requires providing access to the information in documents. To illustrate, suppose a consumer products company keeps corporate documents in a database. These documents describe which employees work on which products, how products are related, how they compare to the competition, etc. However, if the database treats these documents merely as opaque bits, users cannot query this information. To address this, we introduce the Semantic Platform for SQL Server, which mines and then exposes structured concepts within unstructured data to database queries, by building three physical indexes: 1) Tag Index (TI), which can return the top keywords, given a document; 2) Document Similarity Index (DSI), which can return the most closely related documents, given any document; and 3) Semantic Phrase Similarity Index (SPSI), which returns the top semantically related phrases, given any phrase.

The view from one level up is that in SQL Server, we are building a tightly streamlined and integrated Document Understanding Platform, comprising Integrated Full Text Search (IFTS) and Semantic Platform for documents, under a unified functional surface of SQL language extensions. We avoid creating an entirely separate syntax for Semantic Platform, by merely extending the IFTS syntax that is already familiar to many customers. The processing flow and algorithms are highly optimized so that documents are crawled, parsed and mined in a unified, 1-pass algorithm. The algorithm is incremental, and efficiently updates the index as the corpus evolves over time (increments may be triggered both manually and automatically). The Full-Text Index (FTI) is one output, in order to satisfy the needs of document search. Simultaneously, document level semantics are mined into the three new indexes: TI, DSI and SPSI, without needing to re-crawl and re-parse the original documents.

Additionally, the user does not have to go through any special configuration steps in order to tell the system about their data, e.g. set up special classifiers, etc. Everything involved in mining these indexes, figuring out what are the semantic concepts contained in the document corpus, how they cluster, etc., is fully automatic and inherent to the system. This means that we have created a very low barrier to entry for users of the document understanding system.

We conducted experiments to verify two main properties: linear scalability and quality. Results show that building the FTI, TI, and DSI is linear and highly scalable. Also, experimental results show that both TI and DSI produce very competitive precision numbers when compared to other methods.

The rest of the paper is organized as follows: The rest of Section 1 describes related products and algorithms, and then describes how we used customer and scenario focused design to help guide our design. In Section 2, we describe the overall architecture and components. Experimental results are described in detail in Section 3. We describe some potential applications in Section 4. We conclude with future work in Section 5.

1.1 Related Products and Algorithms

Starting in February 1990, the NSF has been publishing a set of goals for database research and commercialization every 5 years. The NSF prospectus [12] clearly identifies the need to cover IR over unstructured and semi-structured data and document processing, as a large emerging need for future database product lines. Fifteen years later we have Full-Text Search trending towards mainstream in multiple database product lines including Microsoft SQL Server; Oracle acquiring OpenText in 2008, etc.

We are currently at the cusp of widespread adoption of document IR in the database, as predicted by leading NSF researchers. In the Enterprise space, Oracle, PostgreSQL, Microsoft and others are competing in order to become entrenched players in the space of Document Understanding. Oracle's Open Text [10] has created integration with Share Point and Microsoft Duet (Office + SAP). Oracle Open Text offers a broad based document strategy, providing good support for web docs, via their Red Dot component, and over semi-structured data, by way of LiveLink. Semi-structured search is also supported with LiveLink ECM [10]. Microsoft's primary products in the space of document understanding include SharePoint and FAST, and also in-database IFTS, which has been offered for a few releases now.

At the algorithmic level, two semantic mining classics are Latent Semantic Indexing (LSI) [5] and Latent Dirichlet Allocation (LDA) [2]. These have been extensively used and built upon, in both Enterprise and Web based search. There are a number of approaches for extracting relevant keywords from a document, e.g. [3].

The main advantages of our semantic mining algorithms over the existing algorithms are that our algorithms scale linearly with the size of data, as we show in the results section, and they are incremental. All of these are essential ingredients for mining large (e.g. 10 to 100 million) Enterprise document corpuses and keeping the indexes "fresh" as the corpus evolves over time.

In [4] the authors propose a language-independent means of gauging topical similarity in unrestricted text, using character level n-grams and a simple vector-space technique to infer categorization and similarity. By contrast, we bootstrap our system with fairly large and complete statistical language models (LM), and work with ngrams over LM words that are output by the word breakers in our system [6], to cheaply inject high level structural and contextual constraints into our feature space very early on (almost at the outset). This saves compute time for our system.

In a related work also based on character level n-grams [3], the authors are motivated to construct a highlight/abstract extraction system that does not rely on any language-specific resources such as stemmers and stop lists, whereas the scenario is exactly opposite for IFTS and Semantic Platform in SQL Server, where the language is explicitly identified, and space constraints are not as tight. So we do employ stop lists, stemmers and sophisticated LMs as relatively cheap components from our perspective, to reduce CPU load, which aligns better with the more imperative aspects of our typical customer workload.

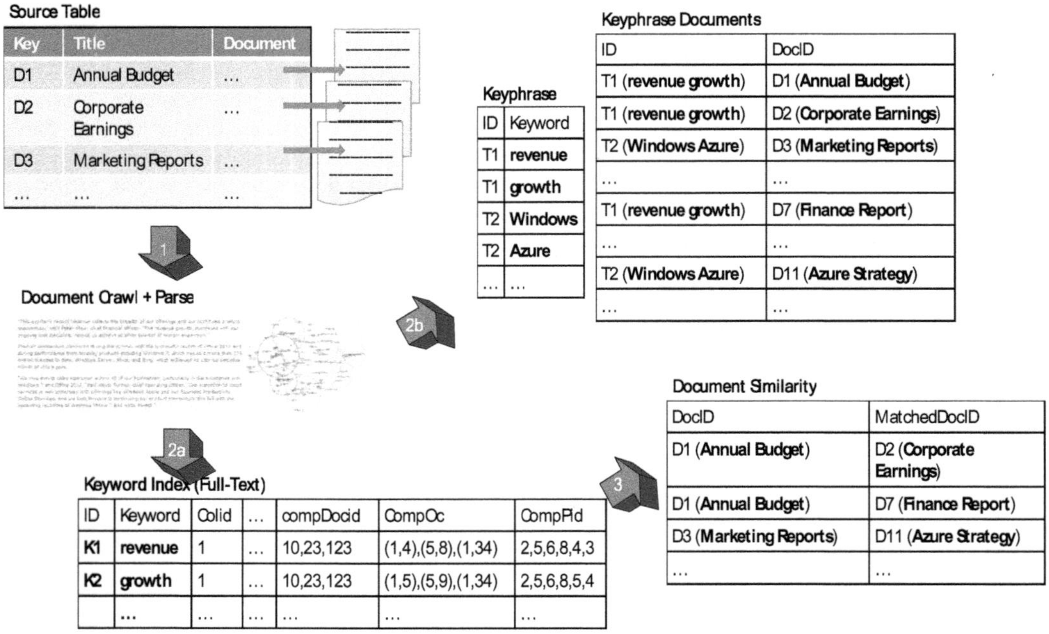

Figure 1. System design directly mirrors typical customer activities in researching large document corpuses: 1) FT1 enables full text search, returning references to the most relevant documents; 2) The next step is to query top documents for most relevant keywords and phrases – this is facilitated by T1; 3) The subset of interesting documents is used to query all related documents, using the DSI; and 4) Search terms are refined by way of SPSI (not shown here) – this takes us back to step 1.

In [7] the authors do inject language specific resources; they go one step further and use a knowledge model based on training a space of concepts on Wikipedia. Their Explicit Semantic Analysis (ESA) system reports good correlation with subjective evaluation, and also has the advantage of working over a vector space that makes intuitive sense compared to the above character-based vector space methods. However, at the Enterprise (the primary domain for SQL Server), a lot of the information tends to be very domain-specific, technical, and full of jargon and acronyms. For this reason we construct a system that does use a vector space of language ngrams, but stops short of constructing a vector space over a generic knowledge model, because we have found that these tend to be too generic. An adaptive knowledge model is more interesting for our purpose, however there are several engineering as well as Test challenges to this, given that database users tend to value determinism and reproducibility very highly.

For document similarity, our approach is close to the classic vector space model [11]. We use cosine-similarity over the documents represented in the vector space of weighted keywords, and use LM entropy to boost semantic salience to correlate well with subjective evaluation.

Our approach to phrase similarity is close to [8]. Whereas their objective is to ultimately use the phrase graph to infer document similarity, ours is to infer a semantic thesaurus that incorporates transitive relationships between phrases. We also focus on scalability aspects and linear approximation whilst generating a transitively closed phrase graph, because linear scale is pretty much a hard pre-requisite for SQL Server's customer base.

Most important from our perspective is the fact that our mining algorithms are tightly integrated as a cohesive system such that the documents are parsed or incrementally scanned in a single pass, and all the data flows linearly through the entire system to create the three new indexes, plus the already existing FTI. Additionally, the one pre-existing and three new indexes are created and maintained to directly support four very fundamental customer needs and interactions, which are described next. This makes the end-to-end system highly optimized, and ensures that all functionality and end outputs are directly motivated by customer requirements.

1.2 Customer and Scenario Focused Design

Customer focus groups reveal that the following is a common work flow of events and actions when perusing and researching a document corpus, as depicted in Figure 1: 1) First, the user, by now very accustomed to using search engines, starts by searching the corpus for an idea, a word or a phrase; 2) Next, when the search returns a number of "hits" comprising Enterprise documents, the user needs to quickly skim the top results for their content without reading the entire document – this is an important differentiator for the Enterprise user as opposed to the user of web search, because Enterprise documents may be hundreds of pages long, whereas web pages are short enough to be scanned rapidly; 3) When a small number of candidate documents have been identified, the user wishes to round off their search by querying for all documents that are related to those exemplars – without this the research would not be complete; and 4) Finally, the user may wish to re-submit a search by refining the search terms, typically by seeking out *semantically related* words or phrases. For instance, "Google" may translate into {search engine, relevance} by way of ordinary thesaurus lookup; however, a semantically related term for "Google", when mined over a corpus of Microsoft documents, might result in "competition".

With the results of step 4, the user returns once more to step 1, and the process refines and repeats until the research is completed. The fundamentals of system design of Semantic Platform follow almost directly from the above work flow. Internally, we provide four physical indexes to support the above queries. 1) FTI, already available in past releases of SQL Server, enables searching of words and phrases; 2) TI summarizes each document into its top phrases; 3) DSI finds the top related documents to a given document; and 4) SPSI provides semantically related phrases to a given phrase.

The family of mining algorithms that processes a large enterprise document corpus linearly and incrementally to produce the above four indexes, constitutes a significant advance in the state of art, because they may be applied to unify the search and semantic inference processing suites of a significantly large number of Enterprise products. With modifications to handle spam and account for web-specific relevance characteristics such as hyperlink count (page rank), they may become interesting for search engines. Our algorithms can provide substantial savings of capital expenditure as well as reduce document crawl- to-index availability, i.e. end-to-end throughput and latency of these products may be improved.

In this paper, we present the Semantic Platform being released in the next version of SQL Server – and encourage people to try it out. This paper specifically describes the underlying mining algorithms of Semantic Platform, and provides a brief outline of the SQL extensions and new user experiences that are easy to build by querying these indexes.

2. SEMANTIC MINING ALGORITHMS AND ARCHITECTURE

In this section, we first show the system level block diagram, which shows how all the algorithmic pieces of IFTS and Semantic Platform fit, and how data flows through the tightly combined IFTS and Semantic Platform system end-to-end. Next, we will provide details on the three new Semantic mining algorithms.

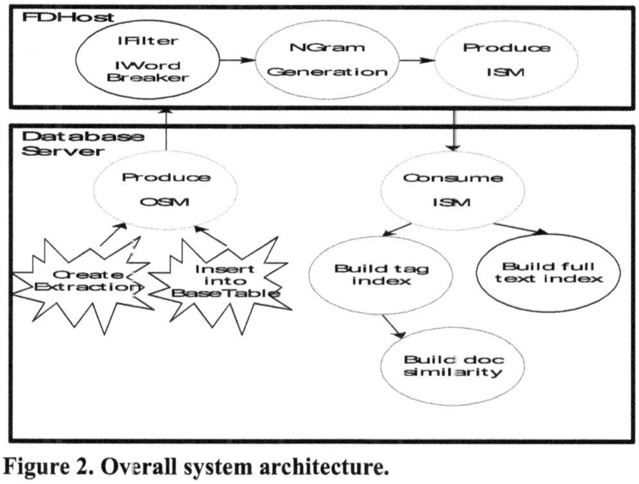

Figure 2. Overall system architecture.

2.1 Top Level System Diagram

Figure 2 shows how all the pieces fit at the system level. We start with a table in SQL database, where one column contains references (e.g. URIs) to actual documents. If the source of the data resides in a relational database, the primary key in the relational table or view goes in the main document index key field. Once the extraction process is created and launched by the user, the documents are crawled and parsed in a separate process called FDHost, which runs as a service, hosting third party DLLs such as IFilters and word breakers, which crack open the document formats, e.g. *.doc, *.pdf, and extract words and word sequences (ngrams). Shared memory is used for inter-process communications between the database server processes. Once the ngrams have been received back in the database server process, the TI and FTI are built and/or incremented concurrently. After the TI has been built, it is in turn used as the source to construct the DSI. After DSI is built or incremented, the whole process is complete.

Due to the close integration of the Semantic mining platform with the pre-existing Full Text Search pipeline, the cost/effort to develop and maintain this architecture is moderate. We took 8 months with a team of 6 Developers, 5 Testers and 1 Program Manager to productize the system from start to finish.

2.2 Mining the Semantic Phrase Similarity Index (Graph)

N.B: *This index is not being shipped in the next version of SQL Server, but in a subsequent release to be determined by Microsoft.*

In this section we first describe the top level objectives of the information we are trying to mine, to clarify for the reader, fundamental differences with related approaches like [8]. Whereas the end objective in [8] is to infer document similarity, our objective is to infer a phrase similarity graph that is approximately closed under transitive closure, and has near-linear time computational requirement.

2.2.1 Top Level Objective: Semantic Thesaurus

The overall objective of mining the semantic SPSI is to derive a semantic thesaurus which embodies the inferred semantic space over phrases used at the Enterprise.

For example, given a Microsoft corpus of documents, I would like "Google" to translate into things like "search engine", "ad revenue", etc., that I would normally get from a Thesaurus lookup, but additionally, also get "competition". In case the corpus is mainly discussing the competition between these companies, I want "competition" to be heavily weighted. I also wish to discover so-called latent relationships [5] between words and phrases, such that if A → B with a high weight and B → C with a high weight, then I wish to infer the A → C relationship. Most importantly, I wish to construct the mining algorithm to scale linearly, be incremental, and possible to integrate tightly into the overall FTI and Semantic Platform architecture outlined in Section 2.1.

The SPSI algorithm consists of eight stages, numbered S1 – S8 in

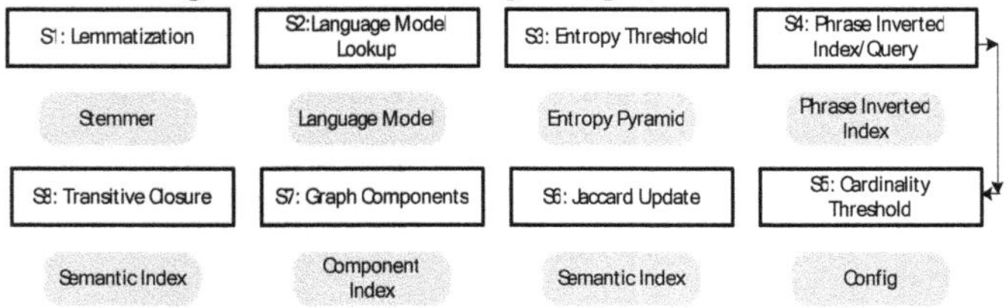

Figure 3. SPSI mining algorithm: Stages S1-S8 and data structures that go with them.

Figure 3. Corresponding to each stage is a data structure abstraction, as shown in the figure.

To facilitate understanding this algorithm, we will re-use a worked example from [15]. Consider that the document corpus we are working with contains the following three documents, with ids: D_1, D_2 and D_3.

D_1: "Cat ate cheese"

D_2: "Mouse ate cheese too"

D_3: "Cat ate mouse too"

In S1, which does tokenization and lemmatization into base forms, we transform the corpus thus:

D_1: "cat **eat** cheese"

D_2: "mouse **eat** cheese too"

D_3: "cat **eat** mouse too"

In S2 we simply substitute LM ids for each word (or ngram), so that the rest of the algorithm works with integers. This makes the processing more efficient than working with strings. However, for ease of explanation, we will revert back to using strings for the remainder of this worked example.

D_1: 2022, 788, 4077

D_2: 16788, 788, 4077, 345

D_3: 2022, 788, 16788, 345

In S3, where we use an LM to filter out the low entropy words in the language, we end up with the following:

D_1: "cat ~~**eat**~~ cheese"

D_2: "mouse ~~**eat**~~ cheese ~~**too**~~"

D_3: "cat ~~**eat**~~ mouse ~~**too**~~"

We preprocess the text using LMs to derive entropy sliced pyramids (ESP). The top levels of these pyramids contain the most salient semantic entities. Lower levels of the ESP contain progressively more terms, and the lowest level contains everything and can be used for full text search. ESP essentially gives us a multi-resolution decomposition of the data, and imposes the priority/scale constraints that the top levels of the pyramid contain both the most semantically valuable as well as least quantity of data, which means we can "skim off the top" and compute only the most salient information, entities and

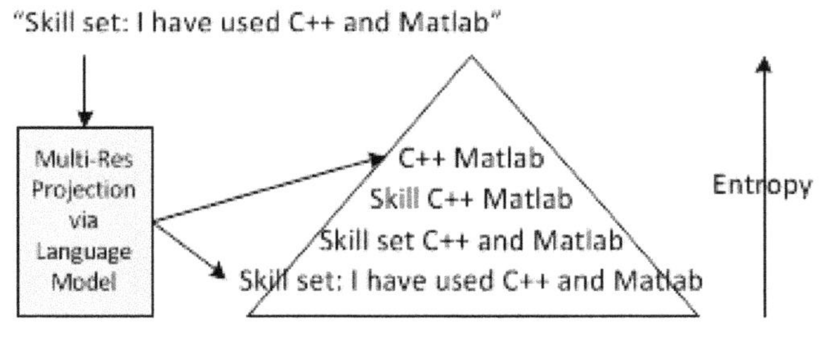

Figure 4. Entropy sliced pyramid structure. Each level contains all terms at or above the entropy threshold for that level. We may decide to truncate the pyramid at some level if we only need it for semantic indexing, otherwise we go all the way to the bottom for full text indexing.

relationships faster than the rest. This mechanism enables us to deal very effectively with information at scale. Figure 4 shows an example of using an ESP on the incoming text (presumably from a resume): "Skill set: I have used C++ and MATLAB".

In S4, we create the inverted ngram index, as shown below:

"cat": {D_1, D_3}

"cheese": {D_1, D_2}

"mouse": {D_2, D_3}

"cat cheese": {D_1}

"mouse cheese": {D_2}

"cat mouse": {D_3}

Here it's worth mentioning that we only used 1, 2, and 3-grams.

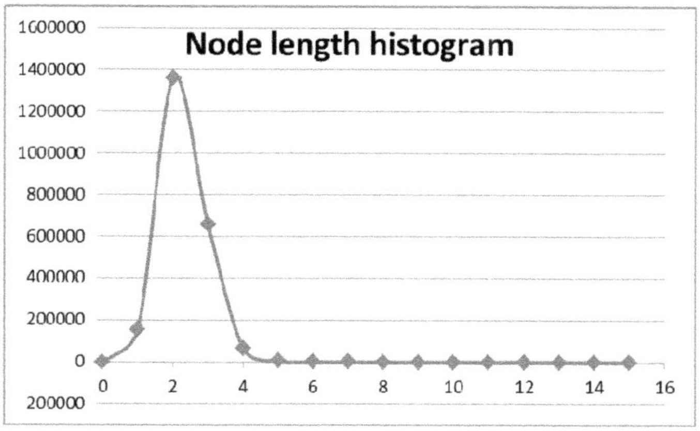

Figure 5. Ngram node length histogram mined from a 3000 doc corpus

There is a big space/disk cost to using high order ngrams, and we repeatedly found evidence of diminishing returns for ngrams longer than 3 in a number of large (Enterprise) corpuses. This is shown in Figure 5.

In S5 we filter out sets with cardinality less than some threshold. For example, in our running example, we may filter out the sets: "cat cheese", "mouse cheese" and "cat mouse" because they are all singletons. Sometimes singleton sets are indicative of noise, and they are rarely useful in linking semantically similar content.

In S6, we create weighted adjacency lists, using the Jaccard metric: $J(D_1,D_2)=\frac{|D_1\bigcap D_2|}{|D_1\bigcup D_2|}$. This provides a notion of semantic nearness between any two ngrams, as the count of documents they are both present, over those where at least one is present. In our running example, the pairwise Jaccard metric applied to the surviving ngrams produces the following output, which is an Adjacency Matrix:

cat: {(cheese, 0.33), (mouse, 0.33), (cat cheese, 0.5), (cat mouse, 0.5)}

cheese: {(cat, 0.33), (mouse, 0.33), (cat cheese, 0.5), (mouse cheese, 0.5)}

mouse: {(cat, 0.33), (cheese, 0.33), (mouse cheese, 0.5), (cat mouse, 0.5)}

cat cheese: {(cat, 0.5), (cheese, 0.5)}

mouse cheese: {(cheese, 0.5), (mouse, 0.5)}

cat mouse: {(cat, 0.5), {mouse, 0.5)}

For S6, we compute the Jaccard graph that relates all pairs of ngram nodes incrementally, with each incoming document, as described below.

Induction Hypothesis: Graph is Jaccard complete (i.e. all pairs have distance given by the Jaccard metric) after we have seen the $(i-1)^{th}$ document.

Induction Step: We only partially update the graph to change numerators and denominators of only the "active ngrams" – these are the ngrams that occur in the ith document. After the update step the graph is once more Jaccard complete.

In the following we outline the steps of the fast Jaccard update algorithm on receiving the ith document.

1. Represent the incoming document as a set of ngrams: Doc(i) = {ng_{j1}, ng_{j2}, …, ng_{jn}};
2. Mark previously unseen and previously seen ngrams, creating the set partitions: $Doc(i) = Seen(i)\bigcup Unseen(i)$;
3. Insert the unseen set into the Adjacency Matrix, the unseen rows become: Doc(i), all numerators and denominators = 1;
4. For each ngram in the Seen set, append the Unseen set, and initialize all numerator = denominator = 1;
5. For each ngram in Seen set, update the old row with denominator++; and if the old word is in Doc(i) then numerator++.

Step S7 is actually an optimization/pre-processing step to speed up S8, and so we first describe S8, which is the transitive closure over the graph obtained from S6.

At the output of S6, we have a pairwise connected weighted graph represented by the adjacency matrix. From this it is possible to compute connected components and semantic clusters and neighborhoods. Indeed, that is what we do in S7. However, in order to capture the latent semantic relationships, it is necessary to consider transitive relationships between ngram nodes. If we fail to do that, the semantic inference available from the entire process tends to be locked into "vocabulary silos".

We compute the transitive closure over this graph using the classic Floyd-Warshall algorithm, by defining the relaxation step to be the maximum over edge weight between vertices *i*, *j*, and intermediate vertex *k*: *e(i, k) x e(k, j)*. This exposes the latent semantic relationships, and gives us functional equivalence with LSI. The end result is an entity relatedness graph with edge weights representing relationship strengths between any pair of vertices. Note that our edge weights are symmetrical, and so we only need to deal with the upper triangular half of the adjacency matrix, discounting diagonal entries (each node is trivially related to itself).

Theorem: Given a Graph *G*, defining the relaxation step on an edge connecting vertices V_i and V_j as: $e(i, j) = \text{Max}\{e(i, j), e(i, k) \times e(k, j)\}$ where the base edge weights represent Jaccard similarity, is necessary and sufficient to induce transitive closure over *G*, exposing latent semantic relationships.

Proof: If Jaccard similarity is considered as an approximation of probability that nodes V_i and V_j are related, and if the relationship between any two (non-identical) pairs of vertices (e.g. $\{V_i, V_j\}$ and $\{V_i, V_k\}$) is independent, then their joint probability is the result of multiplying independent probabilities. But this is the same as multiplying edge weights stemming from Jaccard similarity.

To complete the running example, here are the outputs of the Transitive Closure step. Latent relationships that emerge after transitive closure are highlighted.

cat: {(cheese, 0.33), (mouse, 0.33), (cat cheese, 0.5), (cat mouse, 0.5), **(mouse cheese, 0.165)**}

cheese: {(cat, 0.33), (mouse, 0.33), (cat cheese, 0.5), (mouse cheese, 0.5), **(cat mouse, 0.165)**}

mouse: {(cat, 0.33), (cheese, 0.33), (mouse cheese, 0.5), (cat mouse, 0.5), **(cat cheese, 0.165)**}

cat cheese: {(cat, 0.5), (cheese, 0.5), **(mouse, 0.165), (mouse cheese, 0.25), (cat mouse, 0.25)**}

mouse cheese: {(cheese, 0.5), (mouse, 0.5), **(cat, 0.165), (cat cheese, 0.25), (cat mouse, 0.25)**}

cat mouse: {(cat, 0.5), {mouse, 0.5), **(cheese, 0.165), (cat cheese, 0.25), (mouse cheese, 0.25)**}

2.2.2 *Transitive Closure Optimizations (S7)*

Transitive Closure on a graph is an expensive $O(N^3)$ operation. We outline a series of optimizations that reduce the end-to-end complexity.

First, we *enforce sparseness* on the graph from S6 by clamping weights, e(i,j), that are less than a *sparseness threshold*, T, to zero: *If (e(i, j) < T e(i, j)) = 0, then e(i,j) = 0.*

We next run connected components algorithm on the sparse graph. Connected components is O(N). Once the M components are identified, the transitive closure on the entire graph reduces to running transitive closure on the M components. Thus, we transform the overall complexity from $O(N^3)$ to $O(\sum_{i=0}^{M} n_i^3)$.

A spin-off data structure of connected components is the *Component Index*, which is actually a hierarchy of embedded sub-components, corresponding to different values of sparseness threshold. This enables us to work with components and clusters later on.

We now state without formal proof, a conjecture based on substantive empirical evidence, that actually results in completely eliminating the expensive transitive closure operation for large corpuses. ***Either transitive closure is necessary and the document set is small, in which case it is cheap to compute; or transitive closure is asymptotically unnecessary*** (and can therefore be entirely eliminated), beyond filling in the pair-wise Jaccard similarities, when the document set is large.

Intuitive Explanation: Consider documents relating Obama and the US presidency. These are likely to be many. Consider documents relating Obama and basketball. These are likely to be few. In a small collection there may not be any single document commenting on relationships between the office of the President of USA and basketball. However, if a sufficiently large document set is constructed, then there is a high chance that some document does talk about how presidents relate to the game of basketball.

This intuitively explains why the net contribution of transitive closure, or latent relationships, in general, may be expected to diminish as we approach very large document sets.

Experimental Evidence: We now present the experimental evidence (Figure 6) which shows that the contribution of the weight deltas due to the transitive closure step seems to follow roughly an exponential decay curve as the corpus size increases. We have found that this generalizes over a variety of different Enterprise (e.g. SharePoint design document repository) and academic corpuses (e.g. New England Journal of Medicine).

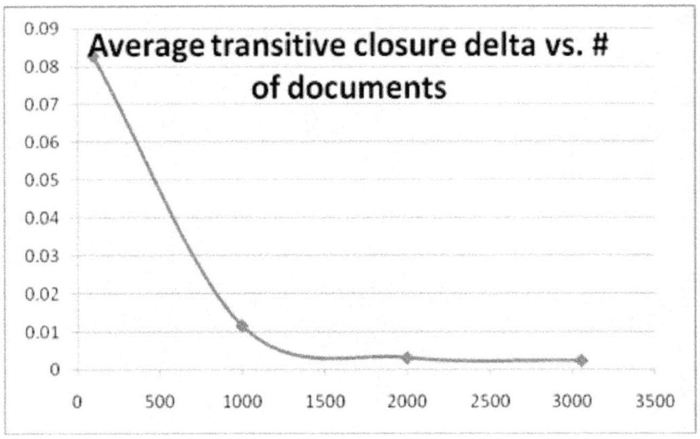

Figure 6. Contribution of Transitive Closure diminishes for large document corpuses.

2.3 Mining the Tag Index

The primary objective of mining the tag index (TI) is the need to summarize long enterprise documents (sometimes 200 – 500 pages long) into their top few key words and phrases. This is very important in order to support the search experience, because the user might otherwise find search results, which are links to long documents, very time consuming to go through. Good tag indexing therefore directly results in productivity gains for the user of an enterprise search based system such as IFTS.

The TI mining algorithm is based on a LM and weight and threshold functions. TI is the output of the algorithm: given a document id, the TI returns a list of its top N key phrases, each with a weight signifying relative importance in the document.

The data flowing into the TI mining algorithm is shown in the system block diagram above (Figure 2). The TI mining algorithm is kept simple for scalability purposes, and is based on cross-entropy: we compare the word distributions from the LM (which contains expected distributions) to the word distribution from the current document. We score the ngrams based on how much more frequently they appear in a document, compared to their expected frequency as computed based on LM. This can be viewed as an approximation to Term Frequency Inverse Document Frequency (TFIDF) weighting, but we are replacing the inverse document frequency portion with the LM frequency. This enables our algorithm to be corpus independent, which is essential for Enterprise document corpuses that are getting new documents daily – we do not want to re-compute the TI every time this occurs. Also, our algorithm is not machine learning based, so there is no training phase, it can be used without the need of a good corpus representative sample data set for initial training.

A caveat is that for short documents the word distributions are not very reliable. Therefore, we take into account document length as well. For all ngrams in any document that are considered as a possible tag, the algorithm requires: 1) Ngram frequency in the document; and 2) Ngram frequency in the language. This is either directly available in the LM, or is inferred from the LM, by treating words as i.i.d and adding their log probabilities.

The pseudo-code for extracting keywords is provided below.

```
ExtractTopNKeyPhrases(doc)
{
  languageModel <- SelectLanguageModel(doc)
  candidates <- Empty topN priority queue
  for each ((ngram, locations) in doc) do
    score = CrossEntropy(
```

```
            doc.GetSize(),
            locations.Length,
                // ngram frequency in doc
            languageModel.Frequency(ngram)
          );
      Candidates.Add(ngram, score);
  end for
  return topN candidates by descending score
}

ComputeCrossEntropy(docSize, docFrequency,
                        LMFrequency)
= (docFrequency/docSize) x (BASE^Log10(LMFrequency))
```

2.4 Mining the Document Similarity Index

The DSI mining algorithm works with a populated and stable TI as its input/data source. The end output of the algorithm is an index which can be queried by any given document id, and returns the top N other documents which share common highly ranked key phrases with the given document, with connection weights for each related document.

We only consider up to top K′ candidate documents that we consider for similarities (to avoid the $O(N^2)$ CPU issue), and only top K (where $K \leq K'$) of those similarities will be stored. This allows us to avoid the $O(N^2)$ space issue. This greedy heuristic can be summarized as: given the target doc T, we have the list of keywords in descending order by their relative weight within T given by the TI; we start exploring the keywords list top-down and we find the documents where these keywords are also highly weighted; we stop when we have found K′ such documents, or we finished exploring the keywords list for doc T; those K′ documents are our candidates.

Given two documents, doc_1 and doc_2, the TI gives us the list of tags and corresponding weights for each:

Doc_1: {(tag_{11}, $weight_{11}$), (tag_{12}, $weight_{12}$),..., (tag_{1k}, $weight_{1k}$)}

Doc_2: {(tag_{21}, $weight_{21}$), (tag_{22}, $weight_{22}$),..., (tag_{2k}, $weight_{2k}$)}

We use cosine-similarity to compute the similarity between two documents, as shown below:

$$CosineSimilarity(doc_1, doc_2) = DotProduct(doc_1, doc_2) / (Norm(doc_1) * Norm(doc_2))$$

where:

$$DotProduct(doc_1, doc_2) = \Sigma\{Weight(tag, doc_1) * Weight(tag, doc_2)\}$$

for each tag that is common to doc_1 and doc_2, and

$$Norm(doc_i) = \sqrt{\sum Weight(tag, doc_i)^2}$$ for each tag in doc_i.

The pseudo-code for the DSI mining algorithm is provided below.

```
ExtractTopKDocumentSimilarities(TagIndex TI)
{
  for each (unprocessed docId) do
    // Step 1: Find top K' candidates
    topK'Candidates=SelectSimCandidates(TI,
                                    docId);
    // Step 2: Find similarities,
    //         relative to candidates
    resultsHeap <- EmptyHeap(size=K);
    for each (candidateId in topK') do
      similarity=CosineSimilarity(T, docId,
                                candidateId);
      resultsHeap.Add(candidateId,
                          similarity);
    end for
    // Step 3: Select top K results
    for each (candidateId,similarity) in
                                resultsHeap do
      DSI.WriteRow(docId,candidateId,
                                similarity);
    end for
  end for
}
```

The details of the `SelectSimCandidates` function are provided in pseudo-code.

```
SelectSimCandidates(TI, docId)
{
  resultSet = Empty(Map<int, double>);
  for each (tag, weight1) in TI(docId) do
    for each ((candidateId, weight) in
        (select topK' docs from TI[tag]) do
      if (candidateId ∉ resultSet)
        resultSet.Add(candidateId, 0.0);
      end if
      resultSet[candidateId]+=weight1*weight2;
    end for
  end for
  return top K items in resultSet;
}
```

3. EXPERIMENTAL RESULTS

Traditional accuracy metrics for full text search and web search are Precision and Recall [1]. Whereas the precision of semantic search is good, the recall is expected to be somewhat poor in comparison to full text search products, because we follow transitive links to other documents.

For our tagging experiment, we used the social tagging dataset culled from Delicious that was used in [9]. There are two versions of the TI algorithm that we tested - the normal algorithm and a filtered version (Filtered TI). The filtered version takes the keywords produced by the TI and then filters out keywords that do not appear in the document a minimum number of times normalized by the document length. We compare our results to corpus dependent machine learning methods: KEA [14], Linear Support Vector Machine (SVM) and Ranking Support Vector Machine (Ranking SVM) [9]. For details on parameter settings, test/training splits, etc., please see [9]. We also compare our results to the standard Term Frequency (TF) and TFIDF methods. Table 1 shows our results based on the Precision at 5 (P @ 5) and Precision at 10 (P @ 10) metrics.

The results are quite promising. Without filtering, TI produces results that are approximate to TFIDF, but in a corpus independent way. Once we filter TI, we achieve results that surpass TF and TFIDF and, in fact, are closing in on KEA. The advantage is that our method scales linearly. One interesting result is that TF performed better than TFIDF, which could be due to the small corpus size (600). Overall, the results show that TI provides a solid foundation upon which DSI can be built.

Table 1. Precision results for our algorithm (TI and Filtered TI) compared to others

	P @ 5	P @ 10
TI	**0.289**	**0.221**
TFIDF	0.295	0.23
TF	0.34	0.267
Filtered TI	**0.38**	**0.27**
KEA	0.437	0.31
SVM	0.469	0.323
Ranking SVM	0.495	0.349

For document similarity precision performance, we constructed a corpus of 2500 documents scraped from Wikipedia. The corpus consisted of 25 topics, each with 100 documents each. Sample topics include "american actors", "american singers", and "national football league players". Note, some of the documents belonged in two categories, such as an actor that was also a singer. This negatively affects precision results for all methods including DSI. To test the precision, we took a single document from each of the topics and used it as the query document, and then we obtained the top 10 most similar documents. Then precision numbers at 1, 3, 5, and 10 were calculated. We compared our results to the traditional Cosine similarity measure (CosSim) based on TFIDF [1].

The results in Table 2 show that DSI provides a similar precision level to CosSim, but does so in linear time instead of in $O(N^2)$ time, and is completely corpus independent, unlike CosSim. This is a big win for customers whose workloads are in the millions of documents, anything other than linear will simply not be feasible at such scale.

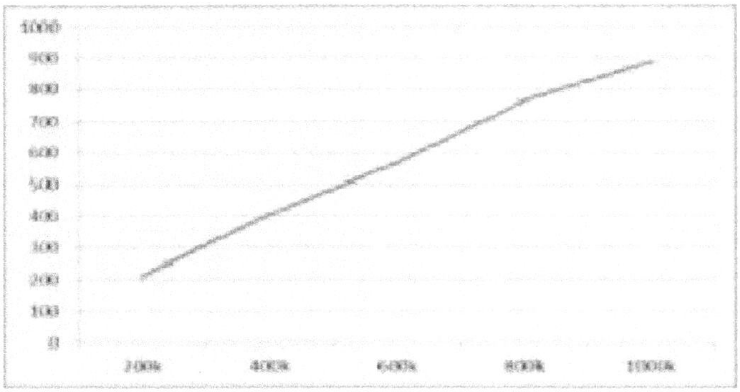

Figure 7. Total execution time in seconds versus total number of documents.

Table 2. Precision results for DSI and CosSim

	P @ 1	P @ 3	P @ 5	P @ 10
DSI	0.8	0.8	0.79	0.78
CosSim	0.8	0.82	0.83	0.82

Figure 7 shows how FTI, TI and DSI mining stack up in terms of end-to-end execution time (i.e. sum total of computing all three indexes) on a real customer workload sampled at 200k document increments, with an average sample size of 40KB per document in plain text format. The test machine had 32GB of RAM and a DOP of 32. The results clearly show linear scaling. Pre-release bits of this product were released to a restricted set of users, and have been well received, with one Microsoft internal and one external customer showing intent to adopt.

4. APPLICATIONS

Based on mining the SPSI (Section 2.1), we propose to enable a set of concept-centric information navigation experiences (Figure 8). This enables the user to browse a document collection by following links through concepts, rather than through document names or a sequence of search queries – especially useful in large document collections where individual documents are large, e.g. at the Enterprise. In Figure 9, we show how the semantic graph may be used to enhance the Windows Explorer user experience.

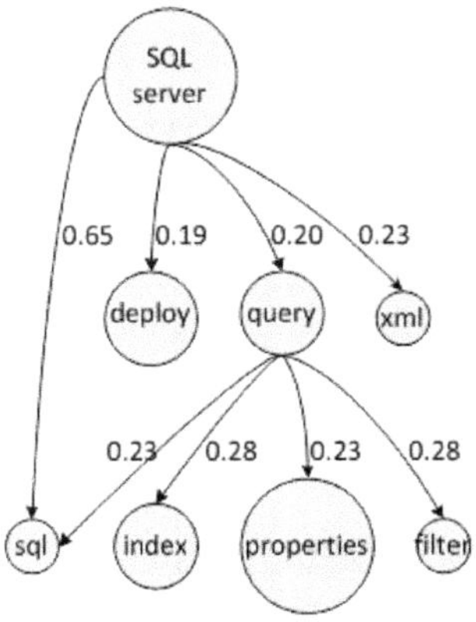

Figure 8. Exploring a concept graph

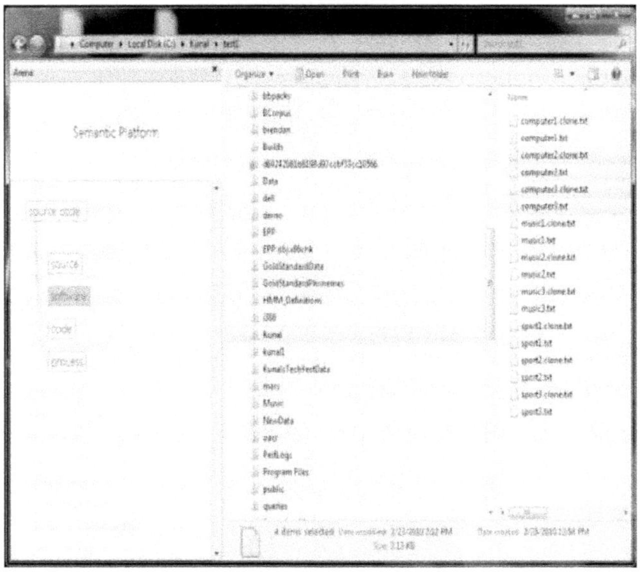

Figure 9. Exploring mined concepts in a file system. When a concept is browsed on the left, the corresponding files are highlighted on the right.

5. CONCLUSIONS

We have described the semantic mining algorithms that lie at the core of Semantic Platform, which is being released in the next version of SQL Server, and shown that they scale linearly with large document corpuses. The combination of the four indexes facilitates the process and work flow of browsing, searching and researching information at the Enterprise, where documents can be large compared to web pages. It also enables new and intuitive user experiences along the lines of browsing concepts that are contained in documents instead of the documents themselves, e.g. using filenames.

Future work includes keyword precision improvements for the TI by utilizing additional corpus independent features such as first occurrence and phrase distribution [9]. Additionally, for the DSI, exploring different candidate document selection strategies and document similarity functions being researched; these could yield gains in performance and precision. We also plan to expose more tuning knobs to better control the degree of completeness of DSI results. Adaptive language modeling is yet another promising future direction when mining Enterprise document corpuses.

6. REFERENCES

[1] Baeza-Yates, R., and Ribeiro-Neto, B., Modern Information Retrieval, Addison-Wesley, 1999.

[2] Blei, D. M., Ng, A. Y., and Jordan, M., Latent Dirichlet allocation, Journal of Machine Learning Research No. 3, pp. 993 – 1022.

[3] Cohen, J. D., Highlights: Language- and domain independent automatic indexing terms for abstracting, Journal of the American Society of Information Science, Volume 46, Issue 3, pp. 162-174, April 1995.

[4] Damashek, M., Gauging similarity with N-grams: Language-independent categorization of text, Science 267, Feb. 1995.

[5] Deerwester, S., et al., Improving Information Retrieval with Latent Semantic Indexing, Proceedings of the 51st Annual Meeting of the American Society for Information Science 25, 1988, pp. 36–40.

[6] Full Text Search Overview (http://msdn.microsoft.com/en-us/library/ms142571.aspx).

[7] Gabrilovich, E., Markovitch, S., Computing semantic relatedness using Wikipedia-based explicit semantic analysis, in Proceedings of the 20th International Joint Conference on Artificial Intelligence, 2007.

[8] Hammouda, K., M., Kamel, M., S., Document Similarity using a Phrase Indexing Graph Model, Journal of Knowledge and Information Systems, Vol. 6, Issue 6, November 2004.

[9] Jiang, X., Hu, Y., Li, H., A Ranking Approach to Keyphrase Extraction, Microsoft Research Technical Report, 2009.

[10] McNabb, K., Moore, C., and Levitt, D., Open Text Leads ECM Suite Pure Plays, The Forrester Wave Vendor Summary, Q4 2007.

[11] Salton, G., Wong, A., Yang, C. S., "A Vector Space Model for Automatic Indexing", Communications of the ACM, vol. 18, nr. 11, pages 613-620, 1975.

[12] Silberschatz, A., Stonebraker, M., and Ullman, J., Database Research: Achievements and Opportunities into the 21st Century. Technical Report, Stanford, 1996.

[13] Tan, P-N , Steinbach, M., and Kumar, V., Introduction to Data Mining, 2005.

[14] Witten, I.H., Paynter, G. W., Frank, E., Gutwin, C., and Nevill-Manning. C., G., KEA: Practical automatic keyphrase extraction, Proc. DL '99, pp. 254-256.

[15] Zamir, O., and Etzioni, O., Web Document Clustering: A Feasibility Demonstration, in Proc. ACM SIGIR'98, 1998.

Combining File Content and File Relations for Cloud Based Malware Detection

Yanfang Ye
Comodo Security Solutions
Beijing, 100082, P.R.China
yanfang@comodo.com

Tao Li
School of Computer Science
Florida International University
Miami, FL, 33199, USA
taoli@cs.fiu.edu

Shenghuo Zhu
NEC Laboratories America
Cupertino, CA, 95129, USA
zsh@sv.nec-labs.com

Weiwei Zhuang
Xiamen University
Xiamen, 361005, P.R.China
zhuangweiwei@gmail.com

Egemen Tas, Umesh Gupta
Comodo Security Solutions
New Jersey, NJ, 07310, USA
{egemen,umesh}@comodo.com

Melih Abdulhayoglu
Comodo Security Solutions
New Jersey, NJ, 07310, USA
melih@comodo.com

ABSTRACT

Due to their damages to Internet security, malware (such as virus, worms, trojans, spyware, backdoors, and rootkits) detection has caught the attention not only of anti-malware industry but also of researchers for decades. Resting on the analysis of file contents extracted from the file samples, like Application Programming Interface (API) calls, instruction sequences, and binary strings, data mining methods such as Naive Bayes and Support Vector Machines have been used for malware detection. However, besides file contents, relations among file samples, such as a "Downloader" is always associated with many Trojans, can provide invaluable information about the properties of file samples. In this paper, we study how file relations can be used to improve malware detection results and develop a file verdict system (named "Valkyrie") building on a semi-parametric classifier model to combine file content and file relations together for malware detection. To the best of our knowledge, this is the first work of using both file content and file relations for malware detection. A comprehensive experimental study on a large collection of PE files obtained from the clients of anti-malware products of Comodo Security Solutions Incorporation is performed to compare various malware detection approaches. Promising experimental results demonstrate that the accuracy and efficiency of our Valkyrie system outperform other popular anti-malware software tools such as Kaspersky AntiVirus and McAfee VirusScan, as well as other alternative data mining based detection systems. Our system has already been incorporated into the scanning tool of Comodo's Anti-Malware software.

Categories and Subject Descriptors

I.2.6 [**Artificial Intelligence**]: Learning; D.4.6 [**Operating System**]: Security and Protection - Invasive software

KDD'11, August 21–24, 2011, San Diego, California, USA.

General Terms

Algorithms, Experimentation, Security

Keywords

cloud based malware detection, file content, file relation, semi-parametric model for learning from graph

1. INTRODUCTION

1.1 Cloud Based Malware Detection

Malware is software designed to infiltrate or damage a computer system without the owner's informed consent (e.g., virus, worms, trojans, spyware, backdoors, and rootkits) [23]. Numerous attacks made by the malware pose a major security threat to Internet users [8]. Hence, malware detection is one of the internet security topics that are of great interest [4, 25, 13, 15, 19, 20, 27, 24]. Currently, the most significant line of defense against malware is anti-malware software products, such as Kaspersky, MacAfee and Comodo's Anti-Malware software. Typically, these widely used malware detection software tools use the signature-based method to recognize threats. Signature is a short string of bytes, which is unique for each known malware so that its future examples can be correctly classified with a small error rate.

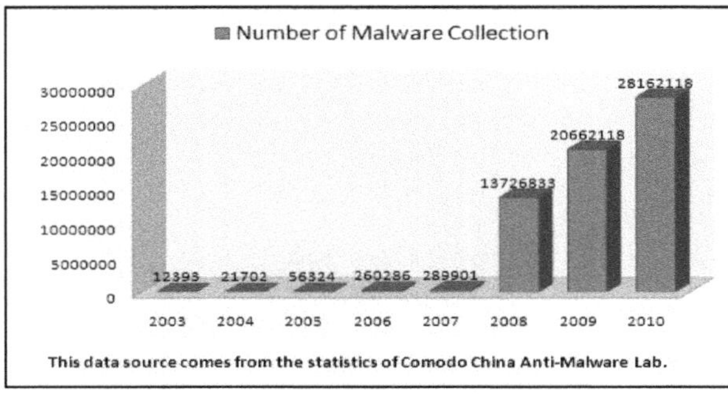

Figure 1: The Increment of Malware Samples (Data source: Comodo China Anti-Malware Lab).

However, driven by the economic benefits, malware writers quickly invent counter-measures against proposed malware analysis tech-

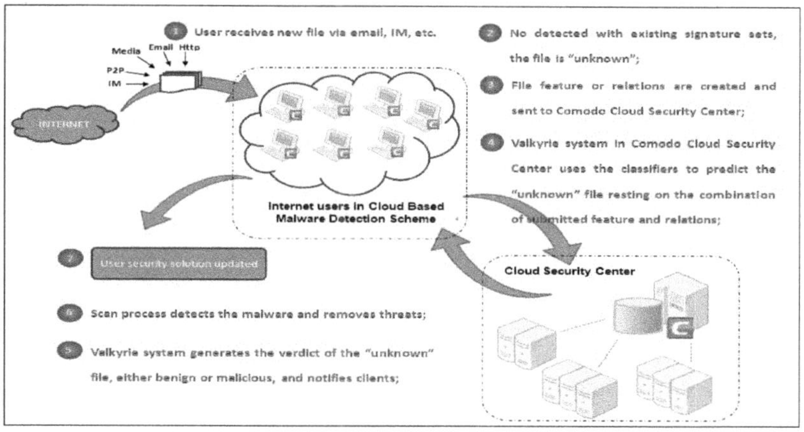

Figure 2: The Workflow of Comodo Cloud Based Malware Detection Scheme.

niques, chief among them being automated obfuscation [20]. Because of automated obfuscation, today's malware samples are created at a rate of thousands per day. Figure 1 shows the increasing trend of malware samples in P.R.China from Year 2003 to Year 2010 (this data is provided by Comodo China Anti-Malware Lab). It can be observed that the number of malware samples has increased sharply since 2008. In fact the number of malware samples in 2008 alone is much larger than the total sum of previous five years.

Nowdays malware samples increasingly employ techniques such as polymorphism [2], metamorphism [1], packing, instruction virtualization, and emulation to bypass signatures and defeat attempts to analyze their inner mechanisms [20]. In order to remain effective, many Anti-Malware venders have turned their classic signature-based method to ***cloud*** (server) based detection. The work flow of the cloud based detection method adopted by Comodo Security Solutions Incorporation is shown in Figure 2.

The work flow of this cloud based malware detection scheme can be described as follows:

1. On the client side, users may receive new files from emails, media or IM(Instant Message) tools when they are using the Internet.

2. Anti-malware products will first use the signature set on the clients for scanning. If these new files are not detected by existing signatures, then they will be marked as "unknown".

3. In order to detect malware from the unknown file collection, file features (like file content as well as the file relations) are extracted and sent to Comodo Cloud Security Center.

4. Based on these collected features, the classifier(s) on the cloud server will predict and generate the verdicts for the unknown file samples, either benign or malicious.

5. Then the cloud server will send the verdict results to the clients and notify the clients immediately.

6. According to the response from the cloud server, the scanning process can detect new malware samples and remove the threats.

7. Due to the fast response from the cloud server, the client users can have most up-to-date security solutions.

To sum-up, using the cloud-based architecture, malware detection is now conducted in a client-server manner: authenticating valid software programs from a whitelist and blocking invalid software programs from a blacklist using the signature-based method at the client (user) side, and predicting any unknown software (i.e., the gray list) at the cloud (server) side and quickly generating the verdict results to the clients within seconds. The gray list, containing unknown software programs which could be either benign or malicious, was usually authenticated or rejected manually by malware analysts before. With the development of the malware writing techniques, the number of file samples in the gray list that need to be analyzed by malware analysts on a daily basis is constantly increasing. For example, the gray list collected by the Anti-Malware Lab of Comodo Security Solutions Incorporation usually contains about 500,000 file samples per day. Therefore, there is an urgent need for anti-malware industry to develop intelligent methods for efficient and effective malware detection at the cloud (server) side.

Recently, many research efforts have been conducted on developing intelligent malware detection systems [4, 25, 13, 15, 19, 20, 27, 24]. In these systems, the detection process is generally divided into two steps: *feature extraction* and *classification*. In the first step, various features such as Application Programming Interface (API) calls [27] and program strings [13, 19, 18] are extracted to capture the characteristics of the file samples. In the second step, intelligent classification techniques such as decision trees [17], Naive Bayes, and associative classifiers [24, 13, 19, 27] are used to automatically classify the file samples into different classes based on computational analysis of the feature representations. These intelligent malware detection systems are varied in their use of feature representations and classification methods. For example, IMDS [27] performs association classification on Windows API calls extracted from executable files, while Naive Bayes methods on the extracted strings and byte sequences are applied in [19].

These intelligent techniques have isolated successes in classifying particular sets of malware samples, but they have limitations that leave a large room for improvement. In particular, none of these techniques have taken the relationships among file samples into consideration for malware detection. Simply treating file programs as independent samples allows many off-the-shelf classification tools to be directly adapted for malware classification. However, the relationships among file samples may imply the interdependence among them and thus the usual ***i.i.d*** (independent and identical distributed) assumption may not hold for malware samples. As a result, ignoring the relations among file samples is a significant limitation of current malware classification methods.

1.2 Relations Among File Samples

For malware detection, the relations among file samples provide invaluable information about their properties. Here we use some examples for illustration. Based on the collected file lists from clients, we construct a co-occurrence graph to describe the relations among file samples. Generally, two files are related if they are shared by many clients (or equivalently, file lists). As shown in Figure 3, we can observe that the file "yy(1).exe" is associated with many trojans which are marked as purple color. Actually, this "yy(1).exe" file is a kind of Trojan-Downloader malware. Trojan-Downloader refers to any malicious software that downloads and installs multiple unwanted applications of adware and malware from remote servers. Malware samples of this type are spread from malicious websites or by emails as attachments or links, and are installed secretly without the user's consent. Therefore, from the relations shown in Figure 3, we can infer that if an ***unknown*** file always co-occurs with many kinds of trojans in users' computers, then most likely, it is a malicious Trojan-Downloader file.

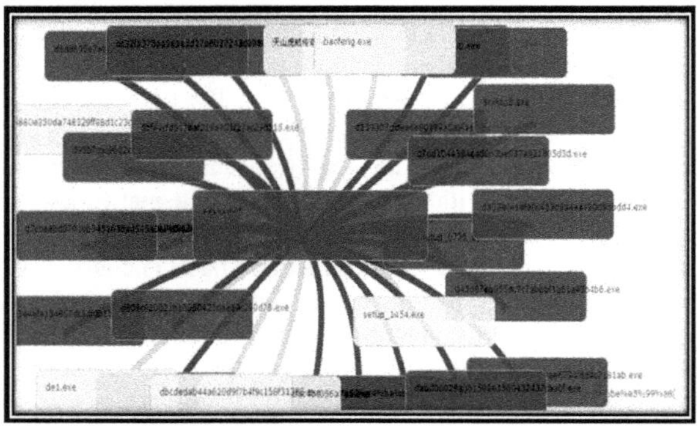

Figure 3: File Relations Between a Trojan-Downloader and its Related Trojans.

Another example showing the relations among benign files is illustrated in Figure 4. From Figure 4, we can observe that an unknown file "everest.exe" can be possibly recognized as benign since it is always associated with known benign files marked in green color. Actually, this "everest.exe" is a benign system diagnostic application which always co-occurs with its related Dynamic Link Library files, such as, "everest_start.dll", "everest_mondiag.dll", "everest_rcs.dll" and so on.

Sometime it is not easy to determine whether a file is malicious or not solely based on file content information itself. According to the experience and knowledge of our anti-malware experts, file relations among samples can be a novel and practical feature representation for malware detection. Some malware samples may have stronger connections with benign files than malicious ones. In such cases, those file samples might be infected files. Actually, these unexpected relations can be filtered and removed, because the infected samples can be detected independently using the infected file detector which is developed by our anti-malware experts.

1.3 Combining File Content and File Relation

To improve the performance of file sample classification for malware detection, in this paper, we utilize both file content and file relation information. However, relation information and file content have different properties. Relation information provides a graph structure in the data and induces pairwise similarity between objects while the file content provides inherent characteristic information about the file samples. Although both the relation information and file content can be used independently to classify file samples, classification algorithms that make use of them simultaneously should be able to achieve a better performance.

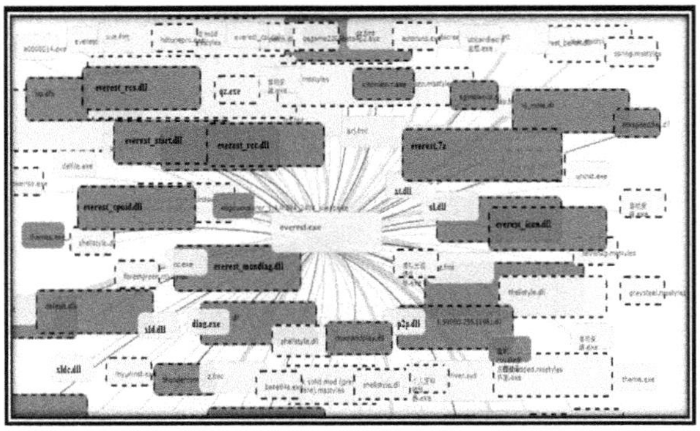

Figure 4: File Relations Between a Benign Application and its Related Dynamic Link Library files.

The problem of combining content information and relation information (i.e., link information) have been widely studied for web document categorization in data mining and information retrieval community [26, 9]. The approaches for combining content and link information generally fall into two categories: (1) feature integration which treats the relation information as additional features and enlarges the feature representation [3, 11, 16]; and (2) Kernel Integration which integrates the data at the similarity computation or the Kernel level [10, 14]. However, both types of approaches have limitations: feature integration may degrade the quality of information as file relations and file content typically have different properties, while kernel integration fails to explore the correlation and the inherent consistency between the content information and the relation information [31].

1.4 Contributions of Our Paper

In this paper, we propose a semi-parametric classification model for combining file content and file relations. The semi-parametric model consists of two components: a parametric component reflecting file content information and a non-parametric component reflecting file relation information. The model seamlessly integrates these two components and formulates the classification problem using the graph regularization framework. Our model can be viewed as an extension of recently developed joint-embedding approaches which aims to seek a common low-dimensional embedding via joint factorization of both the content and relation information [31, 5, 30]. However, different from the joint-embedding approaches, our model does not explicitly infer the embedding and is directly optimized for classification. We develop a file verdict system (named "Valkyrie") using the proposed model to integrate file content and file relations for malware detection. To the best of our knowledge, this is the first work of using both file content and file relations for malware detection. In short, our developed Valkyrie system has the following major traits:

- *Novel Usage of File Relation:* Different from previous studies for malware detection, we not only make use of file content, but also use the file relations for malware detection.
- *A Principled Model for Combining File Content and File Relations:* We propose a semi-parametric classification model

to seamlessly combine file content and file relation, and formulate the classification problem using the graph regularization framework.

- *A Practical Developed System for Real Industry Application:* Based on 37,930 clients, we obtain 30,950 malware samples, 225,830 benign files and 434,870 unknown files from Comodo Cloud Security Center. We build a practical system for malware detection and provide a comprehensive experimental study.

All these traits make our Valkyrie system a practical solution for automatic malware detection. The case studies on large and real daily malware collection from Comodo Cloud Security Center demonstrate the effectiveness and efficiency of our Valkyrie system. As a result, our Valkyrie system has already been incorporated into the scanning tool of Comodo's Anti-Malware software.

1.5 Organization of The Paper

The rest of this paper is organized as follows. Section 2 presents the overview of our Valkyrie system. Section 3 describes the feature extraction and representation; Section 4 introduces the proposed semi-parametric model combining file content and file relations together for malware detection; In Section 5, using the daily data collection obtained from Comodo Cloud Security Center, we systematically evaluate the effectiveness and efficiency of our Valkyrie system in comparison with other proposed classification methods, as well as some of the popular Anti-Malware software such as Kaspersky and NOD32. Section 6 presents the details of system development and operation. Section 7 discusses the related work. Finally, Section 8 concludes the paper.

2. SYSTEM ARCHITECTURE

Figure 5 shows the system architecture of our Valkyrie system. We briefly describe each component below.

- **Training:**

  1. **User File List and File Sample Collector:** It collects the file lists from the clients which contain the potential relations between file samples, together with the file samples.
  2. **File Content Feature Exactor:** Besides its high extraction efficiency compared with dynamic feature representation methods, Application Programming Interfaced (API) calls can well reflect the behaviors of program code pieces. Therefore, our developed file content feature extractor extracts the API calls from the collected malicious and benign Windows Portable Executable (PE) files. (See Section 3.1 for details.)
  3. **File Relation Feature Exactor:** Based on the collected file lists from clients, a co-occurrence graph is constructed to describe the file relations. Note that many unexpected relations (like relations between infected samples and benign files) are removed using infected file detectors. (See Section 3.2 for details.)
  4. **Semi-Parametric Model Based Classifier:** Our proposed semi-parametric model integrates file content and relation information and formulates the classification problem using the graph regularization framework. (See Section 4 for details.)

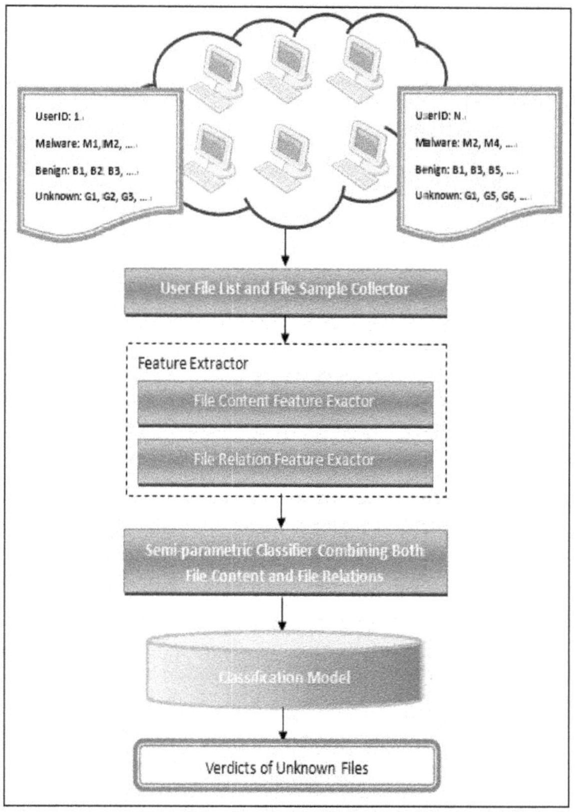

Figure 5: The System Architecture of Valkyrie.

- **Prediction:** On the clients, our Comodo Anti-Malware software products authenticate valid software from a whitelist and block invalid software from a blacklist using the signature-based method. The gray list, containing unknown software programs which could be either normal or malicious, is then fed into our Valkyrie system. After file content and file relation feature extractions, the semi-parametric model is applied to the gray list for prediction.

3. FEATURE EXTRACTION

Our Valkyrie system is performed directly on Windows Portable Executable (PE) codes. PE is designed as a common file format for all flavor of Windows operating system, and PE malware are in the majority of the malware rising in recent years [27]. In this section, we will introduce both file content and file relation feature extraction methods we adopted.

3.1 File Content

We extract the Application Programming Interface (API) calls from the Import Tables [27] of collected malicious and benign PE files, convert them to a group of 32-bit global IDs (for example, the API "MAPI32.MAPIReadMail" in encoded as 0X00000F12) as the content features, and stores these features in the signature database. A sample file content signature database is shown in Figure 6, in which there are 6 fields: record ID, PE file name, file type ("-1" represents benign file while "1" is for malicious file), called APIs name, called API ID, the total number of called API functions.

3.2 File Relations

Based on the collected file lists from clients, we construct a

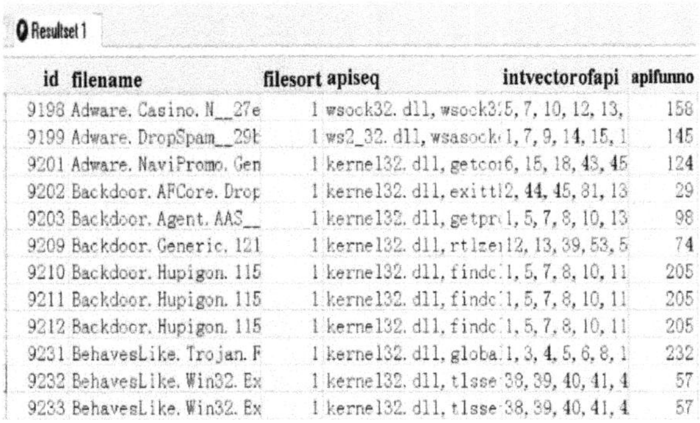

Resultset 1

id	filename	filesort	apiseq	intvectorofapi	apifunno
9198	Adware. Casino. N__27e	1	wsock32. dll, wsock3	5, 7, 10, 12, 13,	158
9199	Adware. DropSpam__29t	1	ws2_32. dll, wsasock	1, 7, 9, 14, 15, 1	145
9201	Adware. NaviPromo. Gen	1	kernel32. dll, getco	6, 15, 18, 43, 45	124
9202	Backdoor. AFCore. Drop	1	kernel32. dll, exitt	2, 44, 45, 81, 13	29
9203	Backdoor. Agent. AAS__	1	kernel32. dll, getpr	1, 5, 7, 8, 10, 13	98
9209	Backdoor. Generic. 121	1	kernel32. dll, rtlze	12, 13, 39, 53, 5	74
9210	Backdoor. Hupigon. 115	1	kernel32. dll, findc	1, 5, 7, 8, 10, 11	205
9211	Backdoor. Hupigon. 115	1	kernel32. dll, findc	1, 5, 7, 8, 10, 11	205
9212	Backdoor. Hupigon. 115	1	kernel32. dll, findc	1, 5, 7, 8, 10, 11	205
9231	BehavesLike. Trojan. F	1	kernel32. dll, globa	1, 3, 4, 5, 6, 8, 1	232
9232	BehavesLike. Win32. Ex	1	kernel32. dll, tlsse	38, 39, 40, 41, 4	57
9233	BehavesLike. Win32. Ex	1	kernel32. dll, tlsse	38, 39, 40, 41, 4	57

Figure 6: Sample File Content Features in the Signature Database.

co-occurrence graph to describe the relations among file samples. Generally, two files are related if they are shared by many clients (or equivalently, file lists). Note that many unexpected relations (like relations between infected samples and benign files) are first removed using infected file detectors.

The co-occurrence graph is defined as $G =< V, E >$ where V is the set of file samples. Given two file samples v_i and v_j, let S_i be the set of file lists containing v_i and S_j be the set of file lists containing v_j. Then the similarity between v_i and v_j is computed as

$$sim(v_i, v_j) = \frac{|S_i \cap S_j|}{|S_i \cup S_j|}, \tag{1}$$

where $|S|$ denotes the size of a set S. If the similarity between a pair of file samples is greater than 0, then there is an edge between them and E is the set of edges between vertices.

An example graph is shown in Figure 7 illustrating the real relations between some file samples, where the size of each edge indicates its weight.

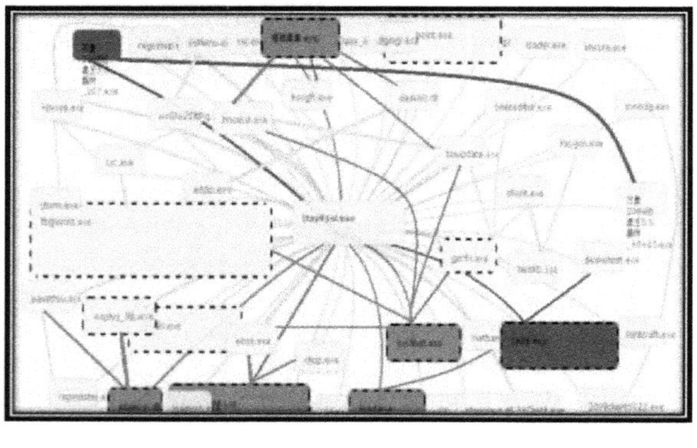

Figure 7: An example graph of real relations between some file samples (purple color-malware samples, green color-benign files, transparent color-unknown files).

4. A SEMI-PARAMETRIC MODEL FOR COMBINING FILE CONTENT AND FILE RELATIONS

In this section, we propose a semi-parametric model to combine file content and file relations for classification using the graph regularization framework. The semi-parametric model consists of two components: a parametric component reflecting file content information and a non-parametric component reflecting file relation information.

Let $\mathbf{f}$ be a vector, each of whose elements is the label (i.e., malicious or benign) of a file example to be predicted. The vector $\mathbf{f}$ can be generated from two parts, parametric and non-parametric ones. The parametric component follows a linear model, $\mathbf{X}^\top\mathbf{w}$, where each column of matrix $\mathbf{X}$ is the content feature vector of a file example, and $\mathbf{w}$ is the coefficients. The non-parametric part is just a vector of $\mathbf{h}$, each element of which corresponds to a value of a file example. Combining two parts, we have $\mathbf{f} = \mathbf{X}^\top\mathbf{w} + \mathbf{h}$.

Now considering the labeling information vector $\mathbf{y}$. Let $y_i = 1$ if the i-th file sample is malicious, $y_i = -1$ if the i-th file sample is benign, $y_i = 0$ if the i-th file sample is unlabeled. We can use hinge loss for labeled file samples as in Support Vector Machine, or use L_2 loss for labeled data as in Least Square problems. For simplicity, we follow [29] to use L_2 loss on all data points, i.e. $\|\mathbf{y}-\mathbf{f}\|^2$. We also consider the global consistency on the co-occurrence graph [29], $\mathbf{f}^\top\mathbf{L}\mathbf{f}$, where the symmetric matrix $\mathbf{L}$ is the normalized Laplacian of the graph. Thus the total loss is

$$\frac{1}{2}\|\mathbf{y} - \mathbf{f}\|^2 + \frac{\alpha}{2}\mathbf{f}^\top\mathbf{L}\mathbf{f}, \tag{2}$$

where α is the weight for combining two parts of information, adding $\frac{1}{2}$ is just for convenience.

To limit the model complexity, we add the regularization terms for $\mathbf{w}$ and $\mathbf{h}$, which are

$$\frac{1}{2\beta}\mathbf{w}^\top\mathbf{w} + \frac{1}{2\gamma}\mathbf{h}^\top\mathbf{h}, \tag{3}$$

where β and γ are the regularization parameters.

Putting Eq. (2) and Eq. (3) together, we have optimization problem:

$$\min_{\mathbf{f},\mathbf{w},\mathbf{h}} \ \frac{1}{2}\|\mathbf{y} - \mathbf{f}\|^2 + \frac{\alpha}{2}\mathbf{f}^\top\mathbf{L}\mathbf{f} + \frac{1}{2\beta}\mathbf{w}^\top\mathbf{w} + \frac{1}{2\gamma}\mathbf{h}^\top\mathbf{h} \tag{4}$$

subject to $\mathbf{f} = \mathbf{X}^\top\mathbf{w} + \mathbf{h}$.

To solve Eq. (4), we introduce Lagrange multiplier $\boldsymbol{\xi}$.

$$\begin{aligned}\mathcal{L}(\mathbf{f}, \mathbf{w}, \mathbf{h}; \boldsymbol{\xi}) &= \frac{1}{2}\|\mathbf{y} - \mathbf{f}\|^2 + \frac{\alpha}{2}\mathbf{f}^\top\mathbf{L}\mathbf{f} + \frac{1}{2\beta}\mathbf{w}^\top\mathbf{w} \\ &\quad + \frac{1}{2\gamma}\mathbf{h}^\top\mathbf{h} + \boldsymbol{\xi}^\top(\mathbf{f} - \mathbf{X}^\top\mathbf{w} - \mathbf{h}).\end{aligned}$$

As $\frac{\partial\mathcal{L}}{\partial\mathbf{w}} = 0$, $\frac{\partial\mathcal{L}}{\partial\mathbf{h}} = 0$, $\frac{\partial\mathcal{L}}{\partial\boldsymbol{\xi}} = 0$, and $\frac{\partial\mathcal{L}}{\partial\mathbf{f}} = 0$, we have

$$\mathbf{w} = \beta\mathbf{X}\boldsymbol{\xi} \tag{5}$$

$$\mathbf{h} = \gamma\boldsymbol{\xi} \tag{6}$$

$$\mathbf{f} = \mathbf{X}^\top\mathbf{w} + \mathbf{h} \tag{7}$$

$$\mathbf{y} = \mathbf{f} + \alpha\mathbf{L}\mathbf{f} + \boldsymbol{\xi} \tag{8}$$

Plugging Eqs. (5,6) into Eq. (7), we have

$$\mathbf{f} = (\beta\mathbf{X}^\top\mathbf{X} + \gamma\mathbf{I})\boldsymbol{\xi},$$

or

$$\boldsymbol{\xi} = (\beta\mathbf{X}^\top\mathbf{X} + \gamma\mathbf{I})^{-1}\mathbf{f}.$$

Plugging it into Eq. (8), we have

$$\mathbf{f} = \left[\mathbf{I} + \alpha\mathbf{L} + (\beta\mathbf{X}^\top\mathbf{X} + \gamma\mathbf{I})^{-1}\right]^{-1}\mathbf{y}. \tag{9}$$

This model is an extension of [29] by consider the parametric part. Note that if there are no content features, then $f = h$ and this model reduces to traditional semi-supervised learning. Different from [31] and [30], this model does not infer the embedding.

Computation Issues: We need to solve

$$\left[\mathbf{I} + \alpha\mathbf{L} + (\beta\mathbf{X}^\top\mathbf{X} + \gamma\mathbf{I})^{-1}\right]\mathbf{f} = \mathbf{y} \quad (10)$$

Let the size of $\mathbf{X}$ be $p \times n$, where p is the number of feature and n is the number of instances, the average nonzeros element of $\mathbf{L}$ be κ. As long as $p \ll n$, we can follow the Woodbury identity, and Eq. (10) becomes

$$\left[(1+\gamma^{-1})\mathbf{I} + \alpha\mathbf{L} - \gamma^{-1}\mathbf{X}(\gamma\beta^{-1}\mathbf{I} + \mathbf{X}\mathbf{X}^\top)^{-1}\mathbf{X}^\top\right]\mathbf{f} = \mathbf{y} \quad (11)$$

To solve Eq. (11), we can use conjugate gradient descent method. Computing $\mathbf{X}\mathbf{X}^\top$ is $O(np^2)$, the inverse of $(\gamma\beta^{-1}\mathbf{I} + \mathbf{X}\mathbf{X}^\top)$ is $O(p^3)$, and we precompute $(\gamma\beta^{-1}\mathbf{I}+\mathbf{X}\mathbf{X}^\top)^{-1}\mathbf{X}^\top$ with $O(np^2 + p^3)$. In each iteration of conjugate gradient descent, we compute $\left[(1+\gamma^{-1})\mathbf{I} + \alpha\mathbf{L} - \gamma^{-1}\mathbf{X}(\gamma\beta^{-1}\mathbf{I} + \mathbf{X}\mathbf{X}^\top)^{-1}\mathbf{X}^\top\right]\mathbf{v}$ for some $\mathbf{v}$. The computation of each iteration is $O(n(p+\kappa))$. The convergence rate depends on the condition number of the LHS matrix of Eq. (11).

5. EXPERIMENTAL RESULTS AND ANALYSIS

In this section, we conduct three sets of experimental studies using our data collection obtained from Comodo Cloud Security Center to fully evaluate the performance of our developed Valkyrie system: (1) In the first set of experiments, we evaluate the effectiveness of file content based classifier and file relation based classifier for malware detection; (2) In the second part of experiments, we evaluate our proposed semi-parametric model based classifier by comparing it with alternative methods for combining file content and file relations. (3) In the last set of experiments, we compare our Valkyrie system with some of the popular anti-malware software products such as Kaspersky Anti-Virus, MaAfee VirusScan, Bitdefender.

5.1 Experimental Setup

We measure the malware detection performance of different classifiers using the following evaluation measures:

- **True Positive (TP)**: the number of samples correctly classified as malicious files.
- **True Negative (TN)**: the number of samples correctly classified as benign files.
- **False Positive (FP)**: the number of samples mistakenly classified as malicious files.
- **False Negtive (FN)**: the number of samples mistakenly classified as benign files.
- **Accuracy (ACY)**: $\frac{TP+TN}{TP+TN+FP+FN}$
- **Recall (RC)**: $\frac{TP+TN+FP+FN}{TheNumberOfTotalFileCollection}$.

The dataset we obtained from Comodo Cloud Security Center includes 37,930 user file lists that describe file relations between 30,950 malware samples, 225,830 benign files and 434,870 unknown files (analyzed by the anti-malware experts of Comodo Security Lab, 39,138 of them are malware, while 395,732 of them are benign files). We also have the file relation information for all the file samples. Using the feature extraction methods described in Section 3, based on this data collection, 1) resting on the API calls extracted from the known file samples, we obtain 210,850 training file content vectors (since part of the file samples' Import Table are invalid, 23,610 malicious files can be effectively extracted their API calls, while 187,240 benign samples are successfully extracted) with 86,757 dimensions; 2) from the collected user file lists, after excluding the unexpected relations (like relations between infected samples and benign files), we construct a graph including 248,986 vertices (29,006 represent malicious files, while 219,980 represent benign samples) with 356,134 edges.

All the experimental studies are conducted under the environment of Windows 7 operating system plus Intel(R) Core(TM) i3 CPU and 4 GB of RAM.

5.2 Comparisons of File Content and File Relation Based Classifiers

In this set of experiments, we evaluate the effectiveness of malware detection results based on different feature representations: file content and file relations. The large collection of file sample data along with the high dimensionality and sparseness requires the classification methods for malware detection to be scalable and robust. With the advantage of handling large feature space without overfitting, Support Vector Machine (SVM) has shown state-of-art results in classification problems [22, 12, 28]. Therefore, in this section, we use SVM [7] as the base classifier. For file content based classification, SVM is applied on the features of API calls. For file relation based classification, we treat file relations as the features for each file sample, i.e., the i-th feature is the similarities with the i-th file sample. Linear SVM [7] is used in both cases and the regularization parameter of SVM is selected using cross-validation.

From Table 1 and Figure 8, we observe that the accuracy of file relation based classifier is similar to file content based classifier, while the recall of the file relation based classifier greatly outperforms the file content based classifier for unknown file verdicts.

Training	TP	FP	TN	FN	ACY	RC
F_Content	23,585	32	187,208	25	0.9997	0.8211
F_Relation	27,018	880	219,100	1,988	0.9885	0.9696
Testing	TP	FP	TN	FN	ACY	RC
F_Content	23,358	2,230	236,196	6,423	0.9677	0.6168
F_Relation	25,969	6,880	312,100	9,988	0.9525	0.8162

Table 1: Comparisons of File Content and File Relation Based Classifiers. Remark: "F_Content"-File Content based Classifier, "F_Relation"-File Relation based Classifier.

5.3 Comparisons of Different Classifiers Combining File Content and File Relation

In this section, we compare our semi-parametric model with the following methods of combining file relations and file content information: (1) SVM on feature integration: We combine the content features and the relation features and then apply SVM on the enlarged feature space. We use different weights for these two sets of features and the weights are selected using cross-validation. (2) SVM on kernel integration: We average the linear kernel on the content and the relation similarity (note that the co-occurrence graph can be viewed as a kernel) and apply SVM on the composite kernel. (3) joint-factorization: We use the supervised joint matrix factorization on both the content and relation information and then perform SVM on the resulting low dimensional embedding. For

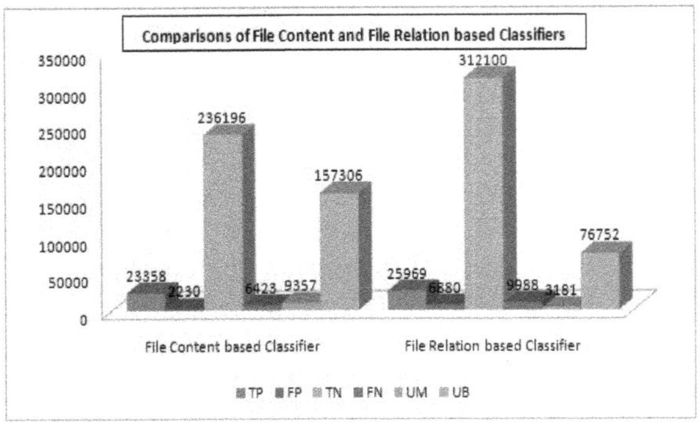

Figure 8: Comparisons of File Content and File Relation Based Classifiers. Remark: "UM"-the number of malware from unknown file collection still unrecognized by classifier, "UB"–the number of benign files from unknown file collection still unrecognized by classifier.

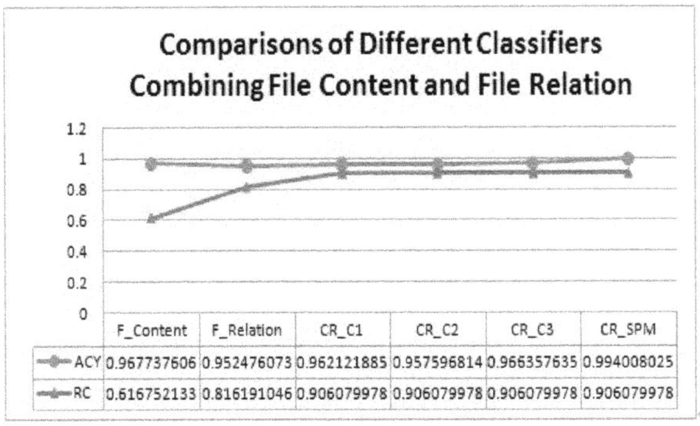

Figure 9: Comparisons of Different Classifiers Combining File Content and File Relation. Remark: "F_Content"-File Content based Classifier, "F_Relation"-File Relation based Classifier, "CR_C1"-SVM on Feature Integration, "CR_C2"-SVM on Kernel Integration, "CR_C3"-Joint-factorization Classifier, "CR_SPM"-our proposed Semi-Parametric Model.

more details on this method, please refer to [31]. For our semi-parametric model, the parameters α, β, and γ are all set to 0.1.

The results as shown in Table 2 and Figure 9 demonstrate that: (1) Combining file relation with file content can improve the classification effectiveness for malware detection; (2) Combining file relation with file content, our proposed semi-parametric model based classifier outperforms other alternative methods.

Testing	TP	FP	TN	FN	ACY	RC
F_Content	23,358	2,230	236,196	6,423	0.9677	0.6168
F_Relation	25,969	6,880	312,100	9,988	0.9525	0.8162
CR_C1	29,002	7,454	350,100	7,471	0.9621	0.9061
CR_C2	28,123	8,358	349,196	8,350	0.9576	0.9061
CR_C3	30,789	7,572	349,982	5,486	0.9664	0.9061
CR_SPM	34,675	563	356,991	1,798	0.9940	0.9061

Table 2: Comparisons of Different Classifiers Combining File Content and File Relation. Remark: "F_Content"-File Content based Classifier, "F_Relation"-File Relation based Classifier, "CR_C1"-SVM on Feature Integration, "CR_C2"-SVM on Kernel Integration, "CR_C3"-Joint-factorization Classifier, "CR_SPM"-our proposed Semi-Parametric Model.

AV.	TP	FP	TN	FN	ACY	RC
Kasp	27,954	711	0	0	0.9752	0.0659
Nod32	26,589	923	0	0	0.9665	0.0633
Mcafee	23,951	1,011	0	0	0.9595	0.0574
BD	28,763	780	0	0	0.9736	0.0679
Avira	29,009	1,887	0	0	0.9389	0.0710
Valkyrie	34,675	563	356,991	1,798	0.9940	0.9061

Table 3: The malware detection results of different AV software products on the collection with 434,870 unknown files.

5.4 Comparisons with Different AV Venders

In this section, we apply Valkyrie system in real applications to evaluate its malware detection effectiveness and efficiency on the daily data collection described in Section 5.1.

5.4.1 Comparisons of Detection Effectiveness between Different AV Venders

Based on 434,870 unknown files (analyzed by the anti-malware experts of Comodo Security Lab, 39,138 of them are malware, while 395,732 of them are benign files), we first compare the malware detection effectiveness of Valkyrie system with some of the popular AV products, like Kaspersky(Kasp), NOD32, Mcafee, Bitdefender(BD) and Avira. For comparison purpose, we use all of the Anti-Virus scanners' latest versions of the base of signature on the same day(Feb 14th, 2011). Table 3 and Figure 10 show that the malware detection effectiveness of our Valkyrie outperforms other popular AV products based on our huge data collection.

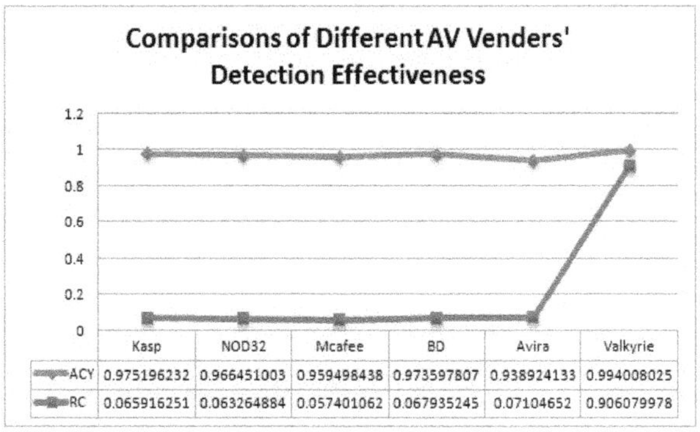

Figure 10: The comparisons of malware detection results of different AV software products on the collection with 434,870 unknown files.

5.4.2 *Comparisons of Detection Efficiency between Different AV Venders*

In this set of experiments, we compare the detection efficiency of our developed Valkyrie system with different AV scanners. The results in Figure 11 illustrate that our Valkyrie system achieves much higher efficiency than other popular scanners when being executed in the same environment, due to its high efficient feature extraction ways and novel detection scheme.

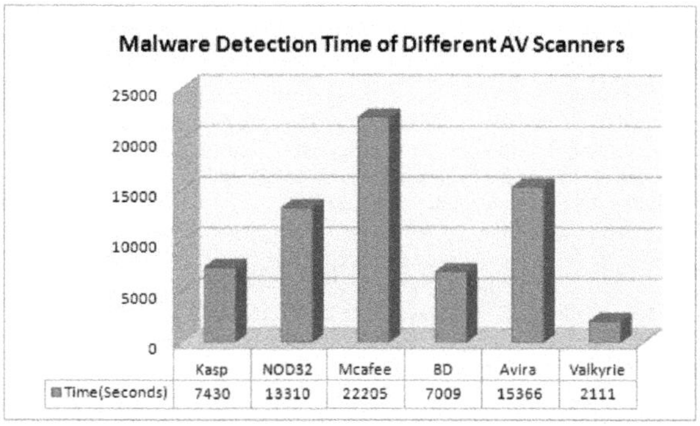

Figure 11: The comparisons of malware detection efficiency of different AV software on 434,870 file collection.

All of these traits make it possible for real anti-malware industry application. The Valkyrie system has been incorporated into the Comodo Anti-Malware products.

6. SYSTEM DEVELOPMENT AND OPERATION

Till now, by adopting our proposed classification method, the system has been extended to combine file relations and various kinds of file content representations, such as, program strings, instructions, functions extracted from export table and so on. We now totally have 15 classifiers combining file relations and 15 different file content representations. Figure 12 shows the real file verdict service (http://valkyrie.comodo.com) for pubic which integrates our developed Valkyrie system. For the development of the Valkyrie system, Comodo has spent over $550K, $150K of which is on the hardware equipment. The system monitors 15 classifiers that verify functionality and availability and is managed in a revision control system. Over 40 anti-malware analysts at Comodo Cloud Security Center are utilizing the system on the daily basis. In practice, a human analyst has to spend at least 8 hours to manually analyze 100 file samples for malware detection. Using the Valkyrie system, the analysis of about 500,000 file samples (including feature extraction and prediction) can be performed within 8 hours using 5 servers. The high efficiency of our Valkyrie system can greatly save human labors and reduce the staff cost. This would benefit over 8 million Internet users of Comodo's client anti-malware products.

7. RELATED WORK

7.1 Malware Detection

With the development of malware industry and the sharp increase of the number of malware samples, most of the Anti-Malware Venders have switched from signature-based detection methods to the cloud based scheme. In the cloud based malware detection scheme, anti-Malware Venders authenticate valid software programs from a whitelist and block invalid software programs from a blacklist using signature-based method on the clients, collect and predict a large number of unknown software programs (i.e., the gray list) on the cloud (server), and quickly generate the verdict results and send to the clients within seconds. As the number of file samples in the gray list increasing rapidly with the development of the malware writing techniques, there is an urgent need for anti-malware industry to apply intelligent techniques on the cloud side for automatic malware detection. Using these intelligent techniques, the detection process is generally divided into two steps: *content feature extraction* and *classification*. The detection performance is critically dependent on the set of extracted features and the classifier [18].

Figure 12: File Verdict Service for Pubic Integrated Valkyrie System.

Content Feature Extraction: For content feature extraction, there are mainly two types of methods [23]: static and dynamic feature extraction. Compared with dynamic feature extraction methods, static feature extraction methods are easier and less expensive [27]. In addition, according the statistics from Comodo Cloud Security Center, over 80% of the collected file samples in our work can be represented by static features, while just about 40% of the file samples can run dynamically. Therefore, we use static feature extraction in our work. There are many different kinds of static features [8], such as Application Programming Interface (API) calls, binary string, and file instructions, each has its own advantages and disadvantages. In our work, we extract Application Programming Interface (API) calls from the collected malicious and benign PE files since they can well reflect the behavior of program code pieces.

Classification: For classification, over the last couple of years, many data mining and machine learning approaches have been adopted for malware detection [21, 4, 25, 13, 15, 19, 20, 27, 24]. Neural Networks as well as immune system are used by IBM for computer virus recognition [21]. Naive Bayes method, Support Vector Machine(SVM), decision tree and associative classification methods are applied to detect new malicious executables in previous studies [13, 19, 24, 27].

However, all of these methods are applied on the file content features. Sometimes, according to file content itself, it is not easy to determine whether a file is malicious or not solely based on the file content. Recently, a malware detection system based on large-scale graph inference using file relationships is developed in [6]. To improve the detection performance, in our work, we use both the file content and file relation information for classification.

7.2 Combining Content Information and Link Information

The problem of combining content information and relation information (i.e., link information) have been widely studied for web document categorization in data mining and information retrieval community [26]. Early approaches for combining content information and link information fall into two general categories: (1) feature integration [3, 11, 16]: this approach enlarges the feature representation to incorporate all data and produce a unified feature space. In particular, the relation information is viewed as additional features/attributes. However, since file relations and file content have different properties, direct feature integration may degrades the quality of information. (2) Kernel Integration [10, 14]: The data is kept in their original form and they are integrated at the similarity computation or the Kernel level. In other words, relation similarity and content similarity are combined directly. One drawback of the kernel integration is that it does not fully explore the correlation and the inherent consistency between the content information and the relation information. Recently Joint-Embedding approaches are proposed to address the limitations of the above two types of approaches [31, 5, 30]. These Joint-Embedding approaches first seek a common low-dimensional embedding via joint factorization of both the content and relation information and then perform classification in the transformed space. In our work, we propose a semi-parametric classification model for combining file content and file relations. Our model can be regarded as an extension of Joint-Embedding approaches. However, different from the joint-embedding approaches, our model does not explicitly infer the embedding and is directly optimized for classification.

8. CONCLUSION

In this paper, we study how file relations can be used to improve malware detection results for a large collection of file samples and develop a file verdict system (named "Valkyrie") based on a semi-parametric classification model to combine file content and file relations together for malware detection. To the best of our knowledge, this is the first work of using both file content and file relations for malware detection. Empirical studies on large and real daily data sets collected by Comodo Cloud Security Center illustrate that our Valkyrie system outperforms other malware classification methods as well as some of the popular AV products. The system has been incorporated into the Comodo's Anti-Malware products.

Acknowledgement

The work of T. Li is partially supported by the US National Science Foundation under grants IIS-0546280 and DMS-0915110.

9. REFERENCES

[1] P. Beaucamps and E. Filiol. Metamorphism, formal grammars and undecidable code mutation. In *Journal in Computer Science, 2 (1)*, pages 70–75, 2007.

[2] P. Beaucamps and E. Filiol. On the possibility of practically obfuscating programs towards aunified perspective of code protection. In *Journal in Computer Virology, 3 (1)*, 2007.

[3] S. Chakrabarti, B. Dom, and P. Indyk. Enhanced hypertext categorization using hyperlinks. *SIGMOD Rec.*, 27:307–318, June 1998.

[4] M. Christodorescu, S. Jha, and C.Kruegel. Mining specifications of malicious behavior. In *Proceedings of ESEC/FSE'07*, pages 5–14, 2007.

[5] D. Cohn and T. Hofmann. The missing link - a probabilistic model of document content and hypertext connectivity. In *Advances in Neural Information Processing Systems 13*, 2001.

[6] D. Chau, C. Nachenberg, J. Willhelm, A. Wright and C. Faloutsos. Polonium: Tera-scale graph mining and inference for malware detection. In *Proccedings of SIAM International Conference on Data Mining (SDM) 2011*, 2011.

[7] R. Fan, K. Chang, C. Hsieh, X. Wang, and C. Lin. Liblinear: A library for large linear classification. *J. Mach. Learning Res.*, 9:1775–1778, 2008.

[8] E. Filiol. Computer viruses: from theory to applications. In *Springer, Heihelberg*, 2005.

[9] M. Fisher and R. Everson. When are links useful? experiments in text classification. In *ECIR*, 2003.

[10] T. Joachims, N. Cristianini, and J. Shawe-Taylor. Composite kernels for hypertext categorisation. In *ICML*, 2001.

[11] P. Kolari, T. Finin, and A. Joshi. Svms for the blogosphere: Blog identification and splog detection. In *AAAI Spring Symposium on Computational Approaches to Analysing Weblogs*, 2006.

[12] A. Kolcz, X Sun, and J Kalita. Efficient handling of high-dimensional feature spaces by randomized classifier ensembles. In *SIGKDD*, 2002.

[13] J. Kolter and M. Maloof. Learning to detect malicious executables in the wild. In *SIGKDD*, 2004.

[14] A. Maguitman, F. Menczer, H. Roinestad, and A. Vespignani. Algorithmic detection of semantic similarity. In *WWW*, 2005.

[15] M. Bailey, J. Oberheide, J. Andersen, Z. M.Mao, F. ahanian, and J. Nazario. Automated classification and analysis of internet malware. *RAID 2007, LNCS*, 4637:178–197, 2007.

[16] H. Oh, S. Myaeng, and M. Lee. A practical hypertext catergorization method using links and incrementally available class information. In *SIGIR*, 2000.

[17] J.R. Quinlan. C4.5. programs for machine learning. In *San Mateo, CA: Morgan Kaufmann*, 1993.

[18] D. K. S. Reddy and A. K. Pujari. N-gram analysis for computer virus detection. *J Comput Virol*, pages 231–239, 2006.

[19] M. Schultz, E. Eskin, and E. Zadok. Data mining methods for detection of new malicious executables. In *Proccedings of 2001 IEEE Symposium on Security and Privacy*, pages 38–49, 2001.

[20] A. Sung, J. Xu, P. Chavez, and S. Mukkamala. Static analyzer of vicious executables (save). In *Proceedings of the 20th Annual Computer Security Applications Conference*, 2004.

[21] G.J. Tesauro, J.O. Kephart, and G.B. Sorkin. Neural network for computer virus recognition. In *IEEE Expert, 11:5-6)*, 1996.

[22] I.W. Tsang, J.T. Kwok, and P.M. Cheung. Core vector machines: Fast svm training on very large data sets. *J. Mach. Learn. Res.*, 6:363–392, 2005.

[23] U. Bayer, A. Moser, C. Kruegel, and E. Kirda. Dynamic analysis of malicious code. *J Comput Virol*, 2:67–77, May 2006.

[24] J. Wang, P. Deng, Y. Fan, L. Jaw, and Y. Liu. Virus detection using data mining techniques. In *Proccedings of ICDM'03)*, 2003.

[25] X. Jiang and X. Zhu. vEye: behavioral footprinting for self-propagating worm detection and profiling. *Knowledge and Information System*, 18(2):231–262, 2009.

[26] Y. Yang, Seán Slattery, and R. Ghani. A study of approaches to hypertext categorization. *J. Intell. Inf. Syst.*, 18:219–241, March 2002.

[27] Y. Ye, D. Wang, T. Li, and D. Ye. IMDS: Intelligent malware detection system. In *SIGKDD*, 2007.

[28] H. Yu, J. Yang, and J. Han. Classifying large data sets using svms with hierarchical clusters. In *SIGKDD*, 2003.

[29] D. Zhou, O. Bousquet, T. N. Lal, J. Weston, and B. Scholkopf. Learning with local and global consistency. In *Advances in Neural Information Processing Systems 16*, 2004.

[30] D. Zhou, S. Zhu, K. Yu, X. Song, B. L. Tseng, H. Zha, and C. Lee Giles. Learning multiple graphs for document recommendations. In *WWW*, 2008.

[31] S. Zhu, K. Yu, Y. Chi, and Y. Gong. Combining content and link for classification using matrix factorization. In *SIGIR*, 2007.

High-Precision Phrase-Based Document Classification on a Modern Scale

Ron Bekkerman
LinkedIn Corporation, USA
rbekkerman@linkedin.com

Matan Gavish
Stanford University, USA
gavish@stanford.edu

ABSTRACT

We present a document classification system that employs lazy learning from labeled phrases, and argue that the system can be highly effective whenever the following property holds: most of information on document labels is captured in phrases. We call this property *near sufficiency*. Our research contribution is twofold: (a) we quantify the near sufficiency property using the Information Bottleneck principle and show that it is easy to check on a given dataset; (b) we reveal that in all practical cases—from small-scale to very large-scale—manual labeling of phrases is feasible: the natural language constrains the number of common phrases composed of a vocabulary to grow *linearly* with the size of the vocabulary. Both these contributions provide firm foundation to applicability of the phrase-based classification (PBC) framework to a variety of large-scale tasks. We deployed the PBC system on the task of *job title classification*, as a part of LinkedIn's data standardization effort. The system significantly outperforms its predecessor both in terms of precision and coverage. It is currently being used in LinkedIn's ad targeting product, and more applications are being developed. We argue that PBC excels in high explainability of the classification results, as well as in low development and low maintenance costs. We benchmark PBC against existing high-precision document classification algorithms and conclude that it is most useful in *multilabel* classification.

Categories and Subject Descriptors

H.3.5 [**Information Storage and Retrieval**]: Online Information Services—*Web-based services*

General Terms

Standardization

Keywords

Multilabel text classification, high-precision classification, large-scale classification

KDD'11, August 21–24, 2011, San Diego, California, USA.

1. INTRODUCTION

Automatic classification of text documents plays a preeminent role in numerous industrial and academic data mining applications. Text classification has been explored for two decades at least [7], and machine learning techniques have proved successful for a variety of text classification scenarios [10, 14]. There are four possible text classification setups:

• ***Eager learning* from labeled documents**—the most common setup, in which a generic machine learning classifier is trained on a set of labeled documents.

• ***Lazy learning* [1] from labeled documents**—a case-based classifier (e.g. k-nearest neighbors) is build based on labeled documents. This setup is fairly rare in the text domain as it is highly inefficient in many practical cases.

• **Eager learning from labeled features**—usually coupled with learning from labeled documents (see, e.g. [6]).

• **Lazy learning from labeled features**—an ensemble of decision-stump-like classifiers is constructed, each of which is triggered if a document contains a certain feature, such as a word or a phrase (i.e. an *n*gram of words). This setup is in the focus of our paper—we term it *Phrase-Based Classification (PBC)*. Variations of PBC have been studied for years in Information Retrieval (see, e.g. [8]). PBC is very natural for *multilabel* text classification (when each document may belong to a number of classes), as a number of decision stumps may be triggered for a document. Another advantage of PBC is in *explainability* of classification results, which is an important feature of commercial text classification systems: the fact that a document d is categorized into a class c can be easily explained by the fact that d contains a phrase t that was manually categorized into c.

Obviously, PBC is not the ultimate solution for every text classification task. In this paper, we characterize the class of tasks in which PBC is set for success. We introduce the property of *near-sufficiency*: the information about a document's class label is mostly concentrated in a few *n*grams (usually noun phrases) occurring in the document. Intuitively, the near-sufficiency property holds if the categorized documents are short (such as news headlines, helpdesk requests, Twitter tweets, Quora questions, LinkedIn user profile summaries, etc)—just because short documents have little content beyond a few phrases. Still, longer texts can hold this property as well.[1] In Section 2 we formalize this property in terms of the Information Bottleneck principle [12].

[1]A (rather extreme) example would be to categorize pieces of code according to the programming language this code was written in. Regardless of the code's length, just a few keywords may be enough to reveal the class label accurately.

Despite that text classification in general, and PBC in particular, have been around for a while, the field has lately enjoyed a fresh breeze of change, caused by two factors:

- **A quantum leap in the data scale.** The social media boom brings huge amounts of textual content on the daily basis. Blogs, reviews, news feeds, and status updates (such as tweets) are often publicly available and ready for mining. Analyzing hundreds of millions or even billions text items is the modern reality. However, their vast majority is unlabeled and thus intensive manual labeling is often necessary.
- **Availability of cheap editorial resources (Crowdsourcing).** Companies such as Amazon (mturk.com), Samasource, CrowdFlower, and others provide means for quickly labeling large-scale data. Crowdsourcing can also be used for evaluating classification results. The cost of labeling a data instance can be as low as a fraction of a cent. Apparently though, the quality of crowdsourcing results is in many cases quite low. Some workers are underqualified, some simply cannot stay in focus for long, and therefore their output is often noisy and inconsistent. This causes some frustration among researchers who apply crowdsourcing to text classification (see, e.g. [13]). Nevertheless, manual labeling of hundreds of thousands data instances (which was impractical just a few year ago) is now perfectly practical.

We introduce Phrase-Based Multilabel Classification as a process consisting of the following steps: (a) given a dataset D and a set of classes C, construct a *Controlled Vocabulary* V of words relevant for categorizing D into C; (b) from the dataset D, extract a set T of frequently used phrases that are composed out of words from V; (c) categorize phrases T into C via crowdsourcing; (d) map each document d onto a subset of phrases from T and assign d into a subset of classes based on classification of the phrases. In Section 4 we describe the phrase-based classification in greater details.

Crowdsourcing classification of phrases has two important advantages. First, humans are very good at categorizing short pieces of text. If properly trained, human annotators can perform the task accurately and fairly quickly—mostly based on their common knowledge. In contrast, to create a common knowledge base in an automatic classification system is notoriously difficult (see, e.g. [9]). Second, humans are much better than machines at multilabel classification. Questions such as *"How many classes does a data instance belong to?"* or *"Should this data instance be assigned to any class?"* are usually easy for a human annotator.

We see three potential drawbacks of crowdsourcing classification of phrases. First, crowdsourcing classification would never be consistent—we apply quite a heavy-lift consistency check on the crowdsourcing results (see Section 4). Second, human annotators cannot cope with too many classes.[2] Third, the number of phrases to be labeled might be overwhelmingly large and infeasible for human annotation, even in a crowdsourcing setup.

In Section 3, we reveal that crowdsourcing classification of phrases is actually feasible in all practical situations: the natural language imposes a (very restrictive) upper bound on the effective number of phrases which can possibly be composed out of a controlled vocabulary. Based on a language model estimated over a huge text collection, we discover that the effective number of phrases grows linearly—rather than exponentially—in the vocabulary size. To the best of our knowledge, this is an observation that has not been made before. It allows extremely high-precision classification of multimillion document collections that obey the near-sufficiency property.

We implemented phrase-based classification at LinkedIn on the task of *Job Title Classification*. The task is to categorize job titles of LinkedIn users into a couple of dozen classes according to a job function performed by those titles' holders. In Section 5, we describe the developed system—it dramatically increased precision and coverage of the previous version of job title classification. Our offline evaluation shows that we achieve about 95% classification precision. In Section 6, we compare our phrase-based classification with Support Vector Machine (SVM) classification [4], and show that our method significantly outperforms four SVM versions on the multilabel job title classification task.

Our system has been successfully deployed in LinkedIn's ad targeting product.[3] Increasing the coverage resulted in increasing the user profile inventory available for targeting, which had a direct revenue impact.

Our contributions can be summarized as follows. First, we formalize the near-sufficiency property of the data that guarantees high-precision phrase-based classification (PBC). Second, we show that PBC will always be feasible, and not shy of dealing with multimillion and potentially billion data instance collections. Last, we present a working use case of phrase-based classification on LinkedIn data, and provide insights on building a successful PBC system.

2. PHRASE-BASED CLASSIFICATION

2.1 Problem Setup

The problem of multilabel text classification is defined as follows. Each document from an unlabeled corpus D is to be categorized into one or more classes from a class set C. More formally, a rule $L : D \to 2^C$ is to be learned from training data. Also available is a labeled test set $D_{test} = \{(d_i, C_i^*)\}$, where $|D_{test}| \ll |D|$ and each $C_i^* \subset C$ is a set of d_i's ground truth classes. Performance of the classification rule L is evaluated on the test set by comparing each $L(d_i)$ with C_i^*.

In classic text categorization, the rule L is learned given a training set D_{train} of documents and their labels. However, the categorization framework does not restrict the training set to contain only documents. This paper deals with *phrase-based classification (PBC)*—a text classification framework in which the training data consists of labeled *phrases*, or *n*grams, extracted from the (unlabeled) documents.[4]

2.2 The Property of Near Sufficiency

It is sometimes possible to identify a collection of words (which we term *Controlled Vocabulary, V*), such that the collection of *n*grams composed from V is a feature set that contains enough information about the document labels to allow high-precision classification using these features alone. In this section, we formalize and quantify this property.

Let T denote the set of all *n*grams ($n = 1, 2, \ldots$) from a controlled vocabulary V that are commonly used in a document collection D. In large-scale corpora, $|T| \ll |D|$ for any reasonable choice of V, that is, the size of the phrase feature

[2]However, if the classification is done for a user-facing product, too many classes are not necessary because the end users will not be able to cope with them either.

[3]`http://www.linkedin.com/advertising`

[4]We will be using terms *phrase* and *ngram* interchangeably.

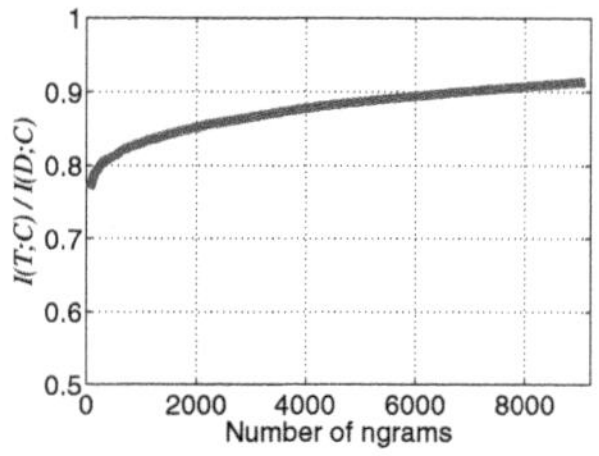

Figure 1: $I(T;C)$ as a percentage of $I(D;C)$ in the LinkedIn test data (see Section 5) plotted over the number of $n$grams in T. The $n$grams are sorted in the descending order of their frequency.

set is significantly smaller than the number of documents. In Section 3, we show that $|T|$ is always small enough to be feasible for manual classification.

In order to measure the extend to which a given collection of phrases T is *sufficient* for classification (i.e. the extend to which we can replace any document by a set of extracted phrases without significantly increasing misclassification rate), we appeal to the Information Bottleneck principle [12]. See [11] for a recent survey of this approach. Information Bottleneck considers an input variable X and an output variable Y. (In our case, the document variable is input and the class variable is output). The value of Y is to be estimated given an observation X. In order to compress the variable X to a simpler variable, or a variable with fewer levels, a variable T is sought (in our case, the *phrase* variable) which achieves an optimal tradeoff between sufficiency for Y (attributed by a high value of the *mutual information* $I(T;Y)$) and simplicity of representation (attributed by a low value of $I(X;T)$). The Data-Processing Inequality [5] states that $I(X;Y) \geq I(T;Y)$ so that the compressed variable T cannot hold more information on Y than the original variable X. As shown in [11], whenever the $I(X;Y) = I(T;Y)$ equality holds, T is a *sufficient statistic* for Y. In other words, all the information for estimating Y is in the reduced variable T.[5] However, we do not expect the equality to hold in many practical cases.

Definition 1. *Let D with $L : D \rightarrow 2^C$ be a labeled document corpus, and V a controlled vocabulary. We say that the phrases T constructed from V are* ϵ-nearly-sufficient *for L, if $I(T;C) \geq (1-\epsilon)I(D;C)$ for some $\epsilon > 0$.*

To measure *near-sufficiency* of a candidate phrase collection T, we need to define a joint probability distribution based on the labeled corpus $D_{test} = (D, C)$ and the control vocabulary V. Put the uniform distribution on D. Let $\mathbf{DC}$ be the document-class matrix where $\mathbf{DC}_{i,j} = 1$ if document d_i belongs to class c_j and 0 otherwise. Let $\widetilde{\mathbf{DC}}$ be the row-normalized version of $\mathbf{DC}$. We think about $\widetilde{\mathbf{DC}}$ as an empirical conditional distribution of labels given document. Now let $\mathbf{DT}$ be the document-phrase matrix with $|T|$ columns and let $\widetilde{\mathbf{DT}}$ be its row-normalized version. Consider the joint distribution $p(D, C, T)$. It is easy to check that the marginal joint distribution $p(D, C)$ documents-classes is given by $\widetilde{\mathbf{DC}}/|D|$ and that the marginal joint distribution $p(T, C)$ of phrases-classes is given by $\widetilde{\mathbf{DT}}^\top \widetilde{\mathbf{DC}}/|D|$. This allows us to compute the mutual information $I(D;C)$ between the "original" documents variable and the class variable, and the mutual information $I(T;C)$ between the "compressed" variable (i.e phrases) and the class variable. The closer $I(T;C)$ is to $I(D,C)$, the more sufficient T is for classification, prompting the use of our phrase-based classification method. Note that this criterion is easy to check in practice.

The test set of the LinkedIn data (see Section 5) holds the near-sufficiency property, in the sense that $\frac{I(T;C)}{I(D;C)} > 0.9$ for a labeled data set of size 19000, controlled vocabulary of size 1485, and the set of phrases of size 9111 (see Figure 1). It is important to note that in the LinkedIn dataset, using the controlled vocabulary itself (i.e. unigrams) is not enough for a successful classification. Indeed, $\frac{I(V;C)}{I(D;C)} = 0.53$, which suggests that most of the information is concentrated in phrases T rather than in single words V. This implies that we cannot avoid the tedious process of labeling phrases, where unfortunately $|T| \gg |V|$. Luckily, labeling phrases is feasible, which we prove in Section 3 below.

3. FEASIBILITY OF PHRASE LABELING

Since our classification framework is heavily dependent on the manual process, we need to make sure that the process will be manageable in a generic case: the number of $n$grams to annotate will not exceed human capabilities. We are only interested in annotating those $n$grams that are *frequent enough* in the language—otherwise we will lose generality of our framework.[6] Despite that the combinatorial number of all possible $n$grams made of words from a vocabulary V is growing exponentially with n (the length of $n$gram), it is quite obvious that the language will not allow most of them to be frequently used. Let us show that the number of *frequent enough* $n$grams is reasonably small in all practical settings. First, let us explain what we mean by "frequent enough" $n$grams.

Definition 2. *We define the* frequency *of a set X to be the frequency of its least frequent item: $F(X) = \min_{x \in X} F(x)$.*

We say that a set T consists of frequent enough $n$grams if $F(T) \geq F(V)$, i.e. the set of $n$grams is as frequent as the vocabulary out of which those $n$grams were composed. Here we solely aim at conditioning the frequency of T on the frequency of the controlled vocabulary. We might have imposed a different condition, e.g. $F(T) \geq \frac{F(V)}{\alpha}$ where $\alpha > 1$. This would lead to similar results but make our reasoning more complicated after introducing an extra parameter α.

To show that the set T of frequent enough $n$grams is feasibly small, we make use of the Web 1T dataset.[7] The Web 1T data was released by Google in 2006. It consists of frequency counts of unigrams, bigrams, trigrams, fourgrams, and fivegrams, calculated over a dataset of *one trillion* tokens. The

[5] In fact, in the unilabel classification scenario, Shamir et al. [11] prove that the misclassification rate of the maximum conditional likelihood rule using the reduced variable T instead of the full variable D decreases *exponentially* with the number of labeled points—with $I(T;Y)$ in the exponent.

[6] Obviously, we can artificially limit the number of $n$grams to be labeled. For example, we can take a list of only ten thousand most frequent $n$grams. This will hurt the coverage though, as many documents would not be mapped onto any $n$gram from the list.

[7] `http://www.ldc.upenn.edu/Catalog/CatalogEntry.jsp?catalogId=LDC2006T13`

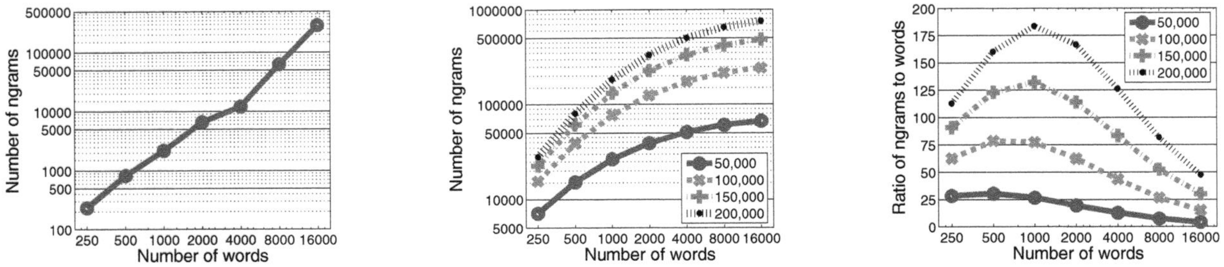

Figure 2: (left) $|T^*|$ as a function of $|V^*|$; (mid) $|T^{**}|$ as a function of $|V^{**}|$; (right) $\frac{|T^{**}|}{|V^{**}|}$ as a function of $|V^{**}|$.

data is large enough to be a good model of a natural language.[8] The unigram portion of the Web 1T data consists of about 7.3M words (we lowercased letters and ignored punctuation), with their frequency counts in a range from about $2 \cdot 10^{10}$ down to $2 \cdot 10^2$. Needless to say, most of these words are not in our lexicons. In fact, only the upper 50K or so contain words that are in our everyday use.

We preprocessed the data by first omitting *n*grams that appeared less than 1000 times in the Web 1T data, removing stopwords and alphabetically sorting words in each *n*gram (which leads to ignoring the words' order). For example, given a fivegram *"of words from the dictionary"*, we removed stopwords *of*, *from*, and *the*—and then alphabetically sorted the remaining words into a bigram *"dictionary words"*. We ended up with about 2.5M (distinct) unigrams, 13M bigrams, 10M trigrams, 4M fourgrams, and 1.4M fivegrams.

To establish the upper bound on the number of frequent enough *n*grams, we first ask the question what would be a vocabulary of size k out of which the *maximal* number of *n*grams can be composed. Obviously, this is an NP-hard problem, as we would need to construct $\binom{N_1}{k}$ vocabularies, where N_1 is the number of unigrams in our data. We apply a greedy approximation. Let $T = U(V)$ be the set of *n*grams composed out of a vocabulary V, where U is an *n*gram construction function, provided to us by the natural language. Let $V = U^{-1}(T)$ be the vocabulary out of which the set of *n*grams T is composed. First, we take a set T^* of all the most frequent *n*grams in the Web 1T data, such that $|V^*| = |U^{-1}(T)| = k$, i.e. the underlying vocabulary V^* is of size k. Second, we take a set $\widehat{T}^* = U(V^*)$ of all *n*grams composed of V^*, which is as frequent as V^* itself, i.e. $F(\widehat{T}^*) \geq F(V^*)$. This way, we assure that $T^* \subseteq \widehat{T}^*$. The fact that *n*gram frequencies follow a power law—and that $\widehat{T}^*$ contains *all* the most frequent *n*grams—guarantees high quality of our approximation.

In Figure 2 (left), we plot $|\widehat{T}^*|$ as a function of $|V^*|$. As we can see on the plot, $|\widehat{T}^*| = |V^*|^\beta$, where the exponent β is very small: $1 \leq \beta < 1.3$. This leads us to the conclusion that the language will only allow a reasonably small number of frequent enough *n*grams, to be composed out of vocabularies of reasonably small sizes.

The procedure for creating a vocabulary V^* described above is artificial, and quite unrealistic in practice. While this does not matter for establishing the upper bound, we can tighten it if we apply a more natural scenario. We start with an observation that controlled vocabularies are usually built of words that come from the same topic (or a few topics). We simulate the creation of a topic-oriented controlled vocabulary V^{**} in the following process: we first sample a word w_1 from a multinomial distribution defined over the set V_m of m most frequent words in the Web 1T data. The word w_1 plays the role of a seed for the topic of V^{**}. Then we add a second word $w_2 \in V_m$ that is most co-occurring with w_1, and we add a third word $w_3 \in V_m$ that is most co-occurring with $\{w_1, w_2\}$, and so on until we populate our vocabulary V^{**} with k most co-occurring words.[9] We then build the *n*grams $T^{**} = U(V^{**})$, such that $F(T^{**}) \geq F(V_m)$—the *n*grams are as frequent as the space of words from which V^{**} was built (note that $F(V_m) \leq F(V^{**})$). To overcome the non-determinism of seeding the topic, we repeat the process 10 times and report on the mean and standard error.[10]

We probe various sizes k of the controlled vocabulary, from 250 to 16,000 words. This spans over arguably the entire spectrum of possibilities, as a set of 250 words appears to be too small for a high-quality controlled vocabulary, while a set of 16,000 is larger than the entire lexicon of an average language speaker. We also probe different values of m—the number of most frequent words from which V^{**} is built. We tried four values of m: 50K, 100K, 150K, and 200K. We argue that the utility of using $m >$ 200K is very low, as words in the tail of that list are completely obscure, and therefore useless from the generalization point of view.

Our results are shown in Figure 2 (middle): we plot $|T^{**}|$ over $|V^{**}|$ and see that it looks curvy on the log-log scale, which may imply that the number of *n*grams is no longer super-linear in the number of underlying words. To verify this claim, we expose an additional view of the same data: we plot $\gamma = \frac{|T^{**}|}{|V^{**}|}$ over $k = |V^{**}|$, and show that $\gamma < 200$ for all realistic values of k and m, which leads to the following formal result:

COROLLARY 3. *The natural language imposes a linear dependency between the number of words in a controlled vocabulary V and the number of frequent enough ngrams composed out of words from V.*

We observe an interesting saturation effect on the right plot: for large vocabularies ($k > 1000$), the γ ratio decreases. We can explain this as follows: high-frequency words are well represented in vocabularies of any size. Low-frequency

[8]In our future work, we plan to utilize the newly released Books *n*gram dataset `http://ngrams.googlelabs.com`.

[9]The fact that the words in V^{**} highly co-occur with each other assures that V^{**} is built around a particular topic—which is more realistic than in our previous setup. The fact that the words co-occur *as much as possible* allows us to establish the *upper bound* on the number of *n*grams composed out of V^{**}.

[10]The standard error is too small to be visible on our plots.

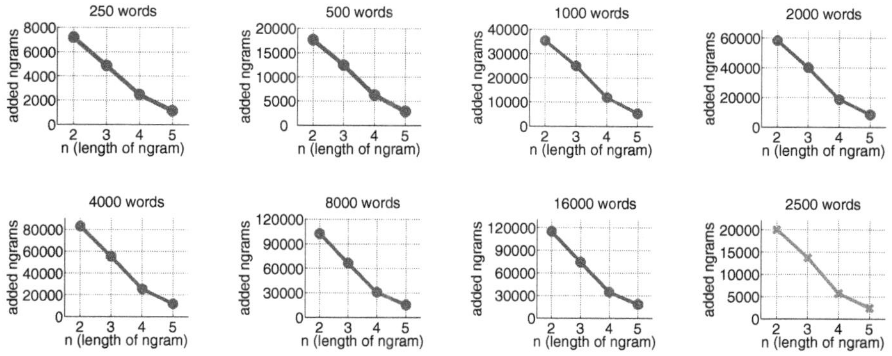

Figure 3: Additions to the set of $n$grams T, as obtained from portions of the Web 1T data, sorted from bigrams to fivegrams. The last plot is for the real-world controlled vocabulary.

words, however, are mostly represented in large vocabularies. Ngrams that contain lower-frequency words are even less frequent—they fall below our threshold, which leads to fewer $n$grams in T^{**} per word in V^{**}.

One could argue that since the Web 1T data does not contain frequencies of high-order $n$grams (above fivegrams), then the data is not complete and no conclusion can be made on the overall number of frequent enough $n$grams composed out of words in V. While the data is not complete indeed, we are confident that it contains enough information to let us reason about the total size of T. Figure 3 justifies our claim. The figure shows the number of $n$grams added after every processing step: first, after scanning Web 1T bigrams, then after scanning trigrams, then fourgrams and fivegrams. As we see from the plots, the number of $n$grams to be added goes down dramatically as the $n$grams' order goes up. It can be easily explained by the fact that the probability of an $n$gram to be frequent enough decreases exponentially with the $n$gram's length. As the number of added $n$grams is already small at the fivegram landmark, we do not anticipate a significant addition to the total size of T that would come from higher-order $n$grams.

The first seven of the eight plots in Figure 3 show the $n$gram addition data over the same values of k as in Figure 2. The last, eighth plot shows an example of a real-world V of size 2500—the one described in Section 5—with the frequency constraint $F(U(V)) \geq F(V)$. While the curve behaves very similarly to the previous seven curves, the overall number of $n$grams is about 3–4 times lower, as compared to the artificial setups with $k = 2000$ and $k = 4000$. This implies that our upper bound is actually not very tight.

4. ARCHITECTURE OF PHRASE-BASED CLASSIFICATION SYSTEM

In this section we propose a system for phrase-based classification, which achieves very high precision (see Section 5) and outperforms popular classification methods (Section 6). The system is composed of two modules: offline and online. The offline module aims at constructing and labeling phrases which are then used in the online module for categorizing documents. Clearly, the online module is optimized for throughput such that most of the heavy data processing is done in the offline module.

4.1 Offline Process of Phrase Classification

The schematic view of the phrase classification module is shown in Figure 4. Let us walk over the module's components one-by-one.

Agree upon the Taxonomy of Classes C. Each classification system that is built in response to a particular business need in a commercial organization starts with defining the taxonomy of classes. Any text corpus can be categorized into a variety of class taxonomies, however not all of them fit well the data at hand. If our data consists of, say, people's job titles, but our classes are models of Japanese cars, then we will fail to meet the system's coverage requirement. A good taxonomy is constructed in a negotiation between business and technology groups within the organization. Note that the success of this step as well as most of the next steps could not be achieved without the involvement of a *Content Manager*—a domain expert who is in charge of keeping the data organized and presented in the best possible way.

The next step in the process is to **Create a Controlled Vocabulary** V of words that are supposed to characterize classes in the taxonomy. Controlled vocabularies are routinely used in computational linguistics to investigate particular language patterns, as well as in library science to organize and index knowledge. In our case, the creation of a controlled vocabulary is a semi-manual feature selection process where, at first, words in the dataset are sorted in the descending order of their frequency, and then the content manager scans through the sorted list and uses his/her domain expertise to decide whether a word can be included or not. Tools can be built to improve productivity of this work, given a particular task at hand.

Once we agreed on the content of the controlled vocabulary, the next step is to **Build Phrases** T. We are only interested in $n$grams of words from V that frequently reappear in the data (rare phrases are useless from the generalization point of view). We ignore the order of words in phrases, so that, for example, *text classification* and *classification (of) text* will be considered the same phrase.[11] In Section 3, we proved that the language will not let the set T be too large for manual labeling. The process of building the set T can be fully automatic: (a) extract all phrase candidates from the data D; (b) sort them by frequency; (c) cut off the least frequent ones. We have to take care of the following issues:

- **Filter out compound phrases.** We can use NLP

[11]One may argue that in some cases the order of words is actually crucial, e.g. *Paris Hilton* and *Hilton, Paris* are not the same. However, those cases are rare from the statistical point of view, and therefore for all practical purposes words' ordering can be ignored in text classification (see, e.g. [2]).

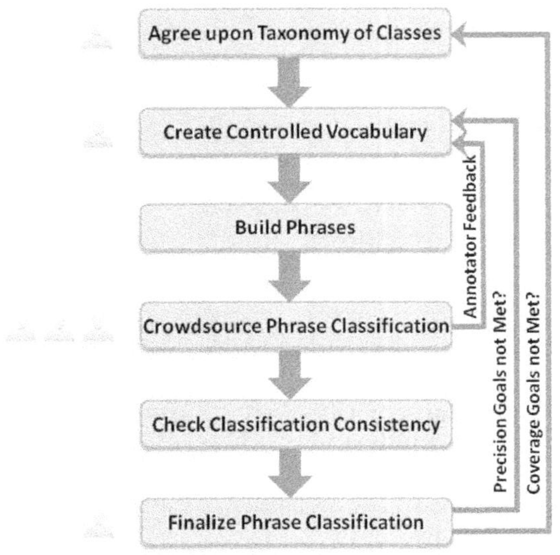

Figure 4: Phrase Classification. A single human icon means involvement of the content manager; multiple human icons mean crowdsourcing.

techniques (such as *shallow parsing*), to identify phrases that are frequent enough, but are clearly composed of two (or more) stand-alone phrases. For example, a phrase *"Machine Learning or Information Retrieval"* can be frequent enough, but keeping *machine learning* and *information retrieval* in one phrase might distract our annotators, who may make an arbitrary decision whether the phrase belong to one class, two classes, or none.

• **Filter out too specific phrases.** Some phrases, such as, e.g. *"Content-Based Collaborative Filtering"*, can be frequent enough in the data but too specific for an annotator to understand their meaning. It makes more sense to remove such phrases given that a more general phrase (i.e. *collaborative filtering*, in this example) is in T.

• **Filter out near duplicate phrases.** Some phrases, such as *"Recommendation System"* and *"Recommender System"*, are practically identical—not only in their form but also in their meaning. We may use *Levenshtein distance* to identify those pairs and then reason whether one of them can be mapped on the other. Some help from the content manager may be needed with this task.

Now, when we have a feasible number of phrases, we can **Crowdsource Phrase Classification**. Crowdsourcing sounds simple but it is actually not. A straightforward approach would be to submit the task to a crowdsourcing tool, asking the workers to assign each phrase[12] into zero, one, or more classes from the predefined set C. If priced properly, the task will be done quickly but chances are strong that the results will be unsatisfactory (in some cases, practically random). The voting mechanism (i.e. let a number of workers annotate each phrase and then take the majority vote) does not seem to help much as the mode sometimes emerges from a seemingly uniform distribution. The mechanism of *qualification tests* (which a worker needs to pass in order to take the task) is helpful though. The best results are achieved when (a) trust is established between the requester and every worker; and (b) every worker is well educated about the task to be performed.

As a byproduct of the classification process, workers can detect nonsensical phrases, as well as undesired words in the controlled vocabulary. Their feedback can be plugged back into the system and necessary changes can be made.

Even when the workers are well trained for the task, the results are likely to have two issues: *systematic errors* and *consistency errors*. A systematic error occurs when the majority of workers make the same incorrect decision. Systematic errors are hard to discover and fix. One way to reduce the systematic error rate is to choose workers of different backgrounds and geographic locations, and use the voting mechanism. Fortunately, systematic errors are not very common.

Consistency errors are more common, but also easier to tackle. A consistency error occurs when one choice is made for an item, and a different choice for a similar item. Consistency errors occur even when the voting mechanism is used. When the consensus of voters is weak, it is often enough for a single worker to make an inconsistent choice, in order to introduce a consistency error. To dramatically reduce the consistency error rate, it is desirable for each worker to perform the *entire* task. This increases the systematic error rate, but—again—those are quite rare. Even when each worker performs the entire task, consistency errors are common, primarily because people do not remember all the choices they have made. Another approach to reduce the consistency error rate is to present the workers with sets of similar items. Even then, the results are rather inconsistent.

This observation leads us to the next step in the pipeline: **Check Classification Consistency**. We represent each phrase t as a feature vector over the aggregated Bag-Of-Words of all documents mapped onto t. This representation is supposed to be dense enough for machine learning to be applied. If it is still too sparse, we can make use of additional data, such as, e.g., documents hyperlinked from our dataset D (e.g. shared links in tweets, etc).

Once represented as a feature vector, each phrase passes a consistency check, which utilizes a simple k-nearest neighbors (kNN) model: each phrase t_i is assigned to a class c_i^{knn} based on the class majority vote of its neighbors in the vector space. Whenever $c_i^{knn} \in C_i$, where C_i is a set of classes obtained for t_i via the manual classification, we consider the classification to be consistent. A more interesting case is when $c_i^{knn} \notin C_i$. Crowdsourcing the task of deciding between c_i^{knn} and C_i is unlikely to produce good results, as people are bad at choosing between two legitimate options.[13]

We use an SVM model as the judge. We train it on the consistently categorized phrases and apply it to the unresolved cases. Since SVM model is fundamentally different from the kNN model (one is eager learning, another is lazy learning), we believe that the two models are unlikely to produce a systematic error. If the SVM judgement c_i^{svm} falls within $\{c_i^{knn}\} \cup C_i$, we go with the SVM result. If not, we declare the case too difficult and leave t_i uncategorized.

By this, we approach the last step of the pipeline: **Finalize Phrase Classification**. Even after such an elaborated error detection process, some problems may remain in the phrase classification results. It turns out however that spot-checking the existing classification results is a much easier

[12]Despite that we do not preserve words' ordering in the phrases, we need to present them to annotators in the form that is most commonly used in our data.

[13]We created a test of 20 such cases and asked over 200 workers to take it—none of them passed a 75% accuracy barrier.

task for a human than coming up with the original classification. The content manager can do a good job of fixing last issues by simply scanning through the created phrase classification. Of course, not all the issues can be detected this way. However, this process can go on long after the classification system is deployed. Given that the phrase classification task is by no means large-scale, it has the potential of eventually converging to the 100% precision.

4.2 Online Process of Document Classification

The online part of the PBC system is to map each document to a subset of phrases from T, and then the document classes are obtained by a simple look-up of classes of the corresponding phrases. Since the set of phrases T was created out of most common phrases in the data D, many documents from D will be mapped onto at least one phrase. The mapping process is fully automatic, and fairly similar to the process of creating T. For each document d_i, we (a) extract controlled vocabulary words $V_i = V \cap d_i$; (b) given V_i, construct all possible phrases $T_i \subset T$; and (c) filter some irrelevant phrases if any. The latter step would also incorporate some shallow NLP, for example, if the document is *"Text Analytics and Image Classification"*, then we must not map it onto the phrase *text classification*. Note that before we start the mapping process, we need to perform some preprocessing, such as taking care of word misspellings and abbreviations—to be mapped onto their full, correct form.

Another important aspect of the document-to-phrases mapping is that we would prefer mapping documents onto the most specific phrases available (filtering in the offline process prevents us from getting too specific). For example, if a document is mapped onto three phrases: *text*, *classification*, and *text classification*, then we would choose the more specific phrase (*text classification*) and filter out the others. This is done because the more specific the phrase is, the more precise decision the annotator can make.

5. JOB TITLE CLASSIFICATION SYSTEM

Our use case for testing the proposed PBC methodology is classification of LinkedIn users' job titles. On their professional profiles, LinkedIn users are free to specify their job titles in any form they wish. For example, we found almost 40,000 different ways in which users specified a title *"Software Engineer"*.[14] Table 1 shows a few very common cases.

A showcase task we describe here is to categorize the job titles into a few dozens of classes according to job functions. Examples of the classes can be *Engineering, Marketing, Sales, Support, Healthcare, Legal, Education*, etc. For the offline module (phrase classification), we used a dataset of about 100M job titles. Obviously, many of the titles repeat in the data, especially those generic titles such as *"Manager"*, *"Director"* etc. After we lowercased all titles and identified duplicates, we created a dataset of unique titles which turned out to be about 5 times smaller than our original dataset. Let us first discuss the offline part of our PBC implementation:

- **Agree upon Taxonomy of Classes.** The set of classes was provided by the business owner which we accepted.
- **Create Controlled Vocabulary.** There are three most important types of words in job titles: (a) job names, such as *engineer*, *president*, *comedian* etc; (b) seniority words, e.g. *senior*, *junior*, *principal*; and (c) function words, such as *sales*, *research*, *financial* etc. Seniority words are the smallest bucket; function words are the largest bucket. Altogether, our controlled vocabulary consists of about 2500 words. Also, we created a translation look-up table, where abbreviations, common misspellings, and foreign language words were translated into the controlled vocabulary words.

Note that classification of foreign titles is quite straightforward because our domain is very narrow: simple word-by-word translation usually creates a meaningful English phrase that annotators can successfully categorize. Two corner cases that we needed to take care of are translation of one word into multiple words (typical in German), and translation of multiple words into one word (typical in French).

- **Build Phrases.** Titles got cleaned by filtering out words that did not belong to our controlled vocabulary, and applying translations. Following our recipe in Section 4, we split compound titles (such as *"Owner/Operator"*), got rid of too specific titles, and deduplicated the resulting list. We then selected a few dozens of thousands most common cleaned titles to be our set of phrases (we called them *standardized titles*). Examples of standardized titles are *software engineer*, *senior software engineer*, *software developer*, *java programmer* etc. We verified that the list of standardized titles was comprehensive enough to cover the spectrum from very common to relatively rare titles. Practically every non-compound title that consisted of the controlled vocabulary words and appeared in our dataset more than a couple hundred times was added to the standardized title list.
- **Crowdsource Phrase Classification.** Classification of the standardized titles was the pivotal step in the project. It was critical for us to perform the job with the highest possible precision, so we decided not to outsource it. Instead, we chose the annotators to be LinkedIn employees. To reduce a possible systematic error, we needed to hire annotators of diversified backgrounds. Together with that, we had to minimize the effort of educating and training our annotators, so we organized them in groups. We created two groups of annotators in two separate geographic regions, and asked each annotator to label the entire set of standardized titles. After the task was completed, we applied the voting mechanism and found that about 15% of the standardized titles could not gain the majority vote (i.e. no class was chosen for those titles by the majority of annotators). We then performed two rounds of disambiguation and finally came to a consensus classification of every standardized title in the list.
- **Check Classification Consistency.** As described in Section 4, we applied the kNN model and found out that about 25% of the standardized title classifications were not consistent with the kNN model results. We then applied the SVM model as a judge and resolved most of the inconsistency cases. We left uncategorized the cases when SVM produced a result that differed from both the kNN result and the original manual classification result.
- **Finalize Phrase Classification.** It turned out that the process of finalizing the standardized title classification was very important for the success of the project. Spot-checking revealed a number of systematic errors and consistency errors. After the classification got finalized, the new challenge was to evaluate the standardized title classification results. We could not use our annotators for evaluating their own work. Therefore, we hired a different group of annota-

[14]We did not include various subgroups of software engineers, nor software developers / programmers, in this count.

software engineer	trainee software engineer	software enginer	software engineer / consultant
software engg	software engineer trainee	software engineer (contractor)	software engineer co-op
sw engineer	sw eng	software engineer (intern)	software enggineer
software eng	software engeneer	software engineer	ingénieur logiciel
s/w engineer	consultant software engineer	software engineer/consultant	s/w engr
software engineer intern	software engr	sw engg	soft engineer
software engineer ii	software engineer i	intern software engineer	soft eng
software enginner	ingeniero de software	software engineeer	software engineer/architect
s/w engg	software engineer iv	soft engg	software engineer/project manager
software engineer iii	software engineer consultant	software engineer (consultant)	sw engr
software engineering	software engineer (contract)	software engineer in test	software engineer/developer
sofware engineer	s/w eng	software engineer 2	engenheiro de software

Table 1: A small sample of common ways to specify a job title "Software Engineer" on LinkedIn user profiles.

tors, who evaluated 25% of standardized title classifications and estimated the classification precision at 98%.

The online process of mapping original titles onto the standardized titles is fairly simple. For each original title, we first applied word translations and filtered out words that did not belong to our controlled vocabulary. Out of the remaining words, we composed all possible standardized titles from our list. We then applied three NLP heuristics to get rid of problematic mappings. For example, we avoided mapping a compound title *"Senior Engineer / Project Manager"* onto a standardized title *senior project manager*. We also removed generic mappings if more specific ones were available. For example, if a title was mapped onto both *senior software engineer* and *software engineer*, we removed the latter. The resulting mapping achieved more than 95% coverage on our dataset of about 100M titles.

A challenging task was to evaluate the precision of the mapping. We used one of the commercial crowdsourcing providers for this task. The provider evaluated a large set of mappings, where the evaluation set of original titles was sampled from the original title distribution (such that more common titles had a higher probability to get selected). Given the high level of duplications in our data, the evaluation set covered about 40% of all titles in our dataset. The evaluation estimated the mapping precision at 97%.

Given the precision of standardized title classification (98%), the lower bound on precision of the overall (original job title) classification process is 97%*98% = 95%. It is a lower bound because an original title can be incorrectly mapped onto a standardized title that happens to belong to the same class as the original title. We succeeded in achieving our precision goals. However, we could not meet our coverage goals which stood at 90%, because for many standardized titles (usually generic ones, such as *"Manager"*) there was no appropriate class in C. Obviously, coverage does not only depend on the system but also on the data and the taxonomy of classes, which makes the coverage goals rather vulnerable. Our system's coverage currently stands at 80%. Higher coverage can be achieved either by introducing new data classes, or by mapping the input data to more specific phrases—those that *can* be categorized.

6. COMPARISON WITH SVM

A legitimate question is how well would the traditional text classification tools cope with the problem of job title classification. As we now have an order of a hundred million job titles categorized with 95% precision, we can use any portion of this data to train a classifier and compare its results with those we obtained with PBC.

We use the SVM classifier for this comparison. Note that SVM is not a strawman—it is one of the best classification models available, particularly well suited for text (see, e.g. [14]). We followed [3] to set up a multilabel SVM framework. We used SVMlight[15] with parameters $c = 0.1$ and $j = 2$ which were chosen based on our prior knowledge.

We train an SVM on a portion of the job title data, then test it on the *entire* data and compare the classes assigned by the SVM with the classes assigned by PBC. If the SVM is within the 90 percentile from PBC, we can say that the document-based classification results are comparable with the phrase-based classification results. However, if the SVM results are farther from those of PBC, we can claim that the SVM does a poor job (given that PBC is 95% accurate).

We propose two quality measures of the classification results: a tolerant and an aggressive:

- **Partial Match.** For each data instance d_i, we choose a *single* class c_i^{svm} that has the maximal confidence score among those obtained by one-against-all binary classifiers. Note that the maximal score can actually be negative. Then we consider d_i to be successfully categorized if $c_i^{svm} \in C_i$ (i.e. if c_i^{svm} is among classes assigned by PBC). In this setup, we apply $k+1$ binary classifiers, where the extra classifier is for "No Class"—we compose an artificial class of instances that PBC did not assign to any class.
- **Full Match.** For each data instance d_i, we build a set C_i^{svm} of classes that have positive confidence scores. We then consider d_i to be successfully categorized if $C_i^{svm} = C_i$ (i.e. SVM classes and PBC classes are identical). In this setup, we do not need an extra class for "No Class".

We used the standard Precision, Recall, and F1 measures in both setups, as obtained on the entire data D, besides instances that were not covered by PBC. Note that this way the SVM is evaluated on both the training and testing data simultaneously—and it is a rare case when this is *not* a problem: since we start from scratch (no labeled data is initially provided), it does not matter which instances are categorized manually and which automatically, as soon as the results can be fairly compared. And we achieve fair comparison by training the SVM on the *same number* of instances as were manually labeled in the PBC process.

We tested four options for applying SVMs: (a) train on the set of standardized titles T, and test on D while taking into account only features from T, that is, only our controlled vocabulary V; (b) the same, but apply the word translation lookup table, for mapping some extra features of data D onto V; (c) train on the most common titles in D; (d) train on titles sampled from the title distribution over

[15]http://svmlight.joachims.org/

Setup	Multiclass SVM trained on:	Partial Match			Full Match		
		Precision	Recall	F-measure	Precision	Recall	F-measure
(a)	*standardized titles*	91.2%	83.6%	87.2%	80.9%	65.5%	72.4%
(b)	*standardized titles with word translations*	94.0%	92.1%	93.0%	82.4%	73.6%	77.8%
(c)	*most frequent titles*	95.4%	88.2%	91.7%	83.0%	73.4%	77.9%
(d)	*randomly chosen titles*	95.1%	88.0%	91.4%	80.7%	73.7%	77.1%

Table 2: SVM results on the job title classification task. SVM results are good on single-class classification (partial match columns), but are poor on multilabel classification (full match columns).

D. The reason for choosing those options was that, in traditional text classification, option (d) would be the default one, option (c) could be plausible, but options (a) and (b) would not be available. Our goal is to see whether the domain knowledge provided in V and the translation table can improve the SVM classification results.

Our findings are summarized in Table 2. The *Partial Match* results are very good, which proves again that the SVM classifier is strong. The *Full Match* results are much poorer. They suggest that SVMs are not able to identify all the classes an instance can belong to, while phrase-based classification copes with this problem very gracefully. Among the four training options, option (a) turned to be the worst one, which can be easily explained by the fact that T (without word translations) had the minimal number of features among the four setups. However, whenever word translations got added (option (b)), this setup became the leader, which suggests that the domain knowledge is helpful for SVM classification. Options (c) and (d) performed remarkably similarly, which was rather predictable, given that sampling from the title distribution (option (d)) would heavily prefer most common titles (option (c)).

7. DISCUSSION

In this paper, we show that phrase-based classification (PBC) can achieve extremely high precision (95%) with reasonable coverage (80%, improvable) on a large-scale text collection of over 100M instances. We characterize the class of data on which PBC can be successful (the data that satisfies the near-sufficiency property), and prove that PBC will be feasible on data of virtually any size, once crowdsourcing is used—the natural language prevents the annotation task from being overwhelmingly large. The development cost of our deployed PBC system is low (2 person years plus annotation expenses), and so is the maintenance cost (which boils down to periodically updating the controlled dictionary as well as the pool of categorized phrases).[16] Overall, we proposed a classification framework that can be directly applied to other tasks, with success guaranteed.

We believe that the main advantage of the deployed system is in the right use of human labor: domain expertise of the content manager combined with common knowledge of the crowd is leveraged in intuitive, single-action tasks such as "choose a word", "categorize a phrase", and "check a phrase/category pair".

We note that crowdsourcing is not a panacea, and is actually a much more complex task than it would have expected. Without a consistency check, the crowdsourcing classification results would be rather poor. Consider our job title classification use case, for which we hired two groups of annotators. Since we now have all final results, we can see how well each group did as compared to the final results. It turns out that one group achieved 73.2% F-measure in the *Full Match* setup (see Section 6), while the other group achieved 76.7% F-measure. Together they achieved 79.3% F-measure. This implies that the two-step consistency check contributed over 20% to the F-measure, bringing success to the entire framework.

[16] Within half a year of no maintenance, the coverage of our job title classification system decreased only by 0.3%, which assures its sustainability.

8. REFERENCES

[1] D. Aha, editor. *Lazy learning.* Kluwer Academic Publishers, 1997.

[2] R. Bekkerman and J. Allan. Using bigrams in text categorization. Technical Report IR-408, CIIR, UMass Amherst, 2004.

[3] R. Bekkerman, R. El-Yaniv, N. Tishby, and Y. Winter. Distributional word clusters vs. words for text categorization. *JMLR*, 3:1183–1208, 2003.

[4] B. Boser, I. Guyon, and V. Vapnik. A training algorithm for optimal margin classifiers. In *Proceedings of COLT*, pages 144–152, 1992.

[5] T. M. Cover and J. Thomas. *Elements of Information Theory.* Wiley, 1991.

[6] G. Druck, G. Mann, and A. McCallum. Learning from labeled features using generalized expectation criteria. In *Proceedings of SIGIR*, 2008.

[7] D. D. Lewis. An evaluation of phrasal and clustered representations on a text categorization task. In *Proceedings of SIGIR*, pages 37–50, 1992.

[8] E. Riloff and W. Lehnert. Information extraction as a basis for high-precision text classification. *ACM Transactions on Information Systems*, 12, 1994.

[9] M. Sahami and T. Heilman. A web-based kernel function for measuring the similarity of short text snippets. In *Proceedings of WWW*, 2006.

[10] F. Sebastiani. Machine learning in automated text categorization. *ACM Computing Surveys*, 34, 2002.

[11] O. Shamir, S. Sabato, and N. Tishby. Learning and generalization with the information bottleneck. *Theoretical Computer Science*, 411:2696–2711, 2010.

[12] N. Tishby, F. Pereira, and W. Bialek. The information bottleneck method. In *Proceedings of the 37-th Annual Allerton Conference*, pages 368–377. 1999.

[13] P. Wais, S. Lingamneni, D. Cook, J. Fennell, B. Goldenberg, D. Lubarov, and D. Martin. Towards building a high-quality workforce with mechanical turk. In *Proceedings of Workshop on Computational Social Science and the Wisdom of Crowds*, 2010.

[14] T. Zhang and F. Oles. Text categorization based on regularized linear classification methods. *Information Retrieval*, 4(1):5–31, 2001.

Activity Analysis Based on Low Sample Rate Smart Meters

Feng Chen[1] Jing Dai[2] Bingsheng Wang[3] Sambit Sahu[4] Milind Naphade[5] Chang-Tien Lu[6]

[1, 3, 6] Computer Science Department, Virginia Tech
7054 Haycock Road
Falls Church, VA
{[1]chenf, [3]claren89, [6]ctlu} @vt.edu

[2, 4, 5] Watson Research Center, IBM
19 Skyline Drive
Hawthorne, NY
{[2]jddai, [4]sambits, [5]naphade} @us.ibm.com

ABSTRACT

Activity analysis disaggregates utility consumption from smart meters into specific usage that associates with human activities. It can not only help residents better manage their consumption for sustainable lifestyle, but also allow utility managers to devise conservation programs. Existing research efforts on disaggregating consumption focus on analyzing consumption features with high sample rates (mainly between 1 Hz ~ 1MHz). However, many smart meter deployments support sample rates at most 1/900 Hz, which challenges activity analysis with occurrences of parallel activities, difficulty of aligning events, and lack of consumption features. We propose a novel statistical framework for disaggregation on coarse granular smart meter readings by modeling fixture characteristics, household behavior, and activity correlations. This framework has been implemented into two approaches for different application scenarios, and has been deployed to serve over 300 pilot households in Dubuque, IA. Interesting activity-level consumption patterns have been identified, and the evaluation on both real and synthetic datasets has shown high accuracy on discovering washer and shower.

Categories and Subject Descriptors

H.2.8 [Database Management]: Database Applications

General Terms

Algorithms, Design, Experimentation, Performance

Keywords

Smart Meter, Low Sample Rate, Disaggregation, Classification, Hidden Markov Model, Gaussian Mixture Model.

1. INTRODUCTION

Sustainability and design of sustainable technologies have become urgent and important priority for cities given the unprecedented level of resource demand - water, energy, transit, healthcare, public safety - to every imaginable service that makes a city attractive and desirable. At the same time, digital reification of cyber-physical world has been possible with widespread penetration of sensing and monitoring technologies. These two important catalysts have fuelled significant interest and cross organizational collaboration among researchers, industries, urban planners, and government. A lot of technology and research has recently focused on leveraging information from such digital reification of cyber-physical world to help manage various services more efficiently. Our paper takes a step in that direction - examines the feasibility and provides innovative approaches towards influencing people's consumption behavior. More precisely, we provide activity analysis based on smart water meter readings.

Given the real world constraints, we research the feasibility of activity analysis to identify activities from smart utility meter readings. Our study is based on the hypothesis that consumption activities disaggregated from meter readings will empower residents with appropriate insights to influence and shape their behavior. This has been rightly validated through a city-wide survey [1] followed by four-month-long experimentation with a real city [2]. In addition, from disaggregated consumption, utility managers can design and assess conservation programs, and prioritize energy-saving potential retrofits.

Research on disaggregating electricity or water load has been conducted on smart meter readings with fine granularity (mainly between 1 Hz ~ 1MHz). Existing approaches identify appliances/ fixtures based on analyzing steady state or transient state change in real-time consumption. However, they are not suitable for many existing smart meter infrastructure.

Real-world deployments of smart meters are designed for utility billing and some basic analysis requirement, but many of them are not suitable for consumption disaggregation. Smart meters transmit consumption readings using wireless protocols, which consume battery and have dependency on physical environments. Although the meters can sample at a rate even higher than 1MHz, many of existing deployments have chosen to accumulate to 15 min or even longer intervals to ensure reliable data transmission. However, physical environment may still affect the data transmission. This scenario brings the following challenges to consumption disaggregation: 1) Parallel usage activities, e.g., a toilet flush and shower in the same 15 minute interval. 2) Difficulty of aligning usage events temporally, e.g., a shower may appear in one or two intervals. 3) Lack of features, i.e., only aggregated consumption and start time of each interval can be used to identify usage activity. An example of such water meter data and expected disaggregated activities is illustrated in Figure 1.

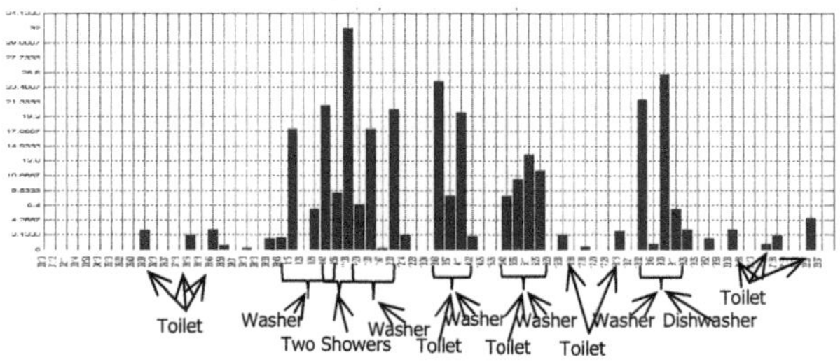

Figure 1. An Example of Data and Disaggregated Activities.

To handle these challenges, we have designed a novel statistical framework for activity analysis on coarse granular smart water meter readings, and deployed it as a component in Smarter Water Service for Dubuque, IA. In this framework, fixture characteristics, household behavior, and activity correlations are utilized to disaggregate consumption. To implement this framework, we propose two approaches to identify activities. The first approach applies hidden Markov model to capture the relationship among consumption events and hidden activities. The second approach utilizes classification techniques to learn from labeled activities, and a Gaussian mixture model is used for disaggregation. The proposed approaches have been validated using both real-world water consumption and synthetic datasets. The experiments have demonstrated the capability of the proposed disaggregation framework, illustrated the appropriate sample rate for disaggregation in various applications, and revealed interesting usage insights from 300+ pilot households. In summary, the major contributions of this work include:

- Providing activity-level consumption insights to residents and the city management team to support decision making.
- Designing a general disaggregation framework with two implementations for different scenarios.
- Exploring appropriate smart meter sample rate to enable consumption disaggregation.
- Revealing interesting consumption patterns from the disaggregation results.

This paper is organized as follows: Section 2 illustrates the application deployment for the proposed approach, and introduces the related challenges. A novel general statistical framework for disaggregation is proposed in Section 3. The detailed implementations for water consumption disaggregation are described in Section 4. Section 5 evaluates the performance of the proposed approaches under different scenarios with real-world and synthetic datasets and demonstrates some interesting findings from the pilot households. The related work is reviewed in Section 6. Finally, Section 7 concludes our work with future directions.

2. BACKGROUND & PROBLEM

2.1 Application Deployment

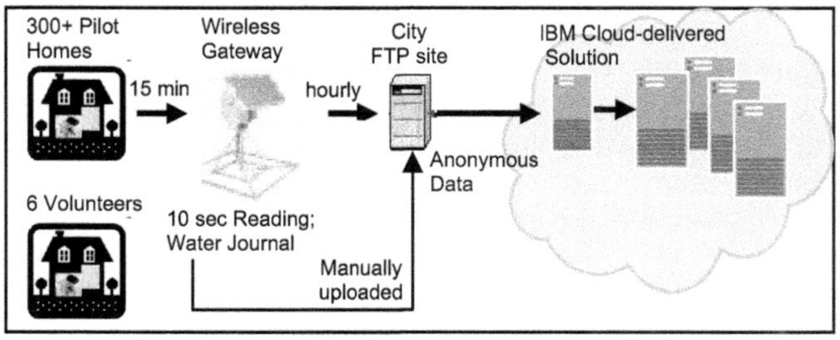

Figure 2. Data Acquisition.

The activity analysis is an important function provided in Smarter Water Service based on smart water meters. The deployed environment of our smart water meter infrastructure is shown in Figure 2. Since August 2010, over 300 pilot households have volunteered to install Neptune R900 smart water meters [3] with UFR (Unmeasured Flow Reducer), which transmit a new aggregated reading roughly every 15 minutes through 900MHz wireless connection. Each aggregated reading is broadcasted repeatedly within the entire interval to ensure the success of transmission. Wireless gateways have been deployed in the city to collect these readings, attach timestamps, and send to a data center through 3G network every hour. In addition, 6 volunteer households had applied data logger which records water consumption every 10 seconds, and had done water usage activity journaling accordingly for a week. All the meter readings have been anonymized and sent to IBM Computing Cloud for analytics.

The software architecture of the deployment is visualized in Figure 4. The smart meter data are first cleaned and transformed by InfoSphere Information Server®(IIS), and then stored in a Smart Meter Database managed by DB2®. On top of this database, Cognos® is utilized to provide OLAP functions such as consumption metric and pattern monitoring; a java-based module is developed to perform advanced analytics functions such as disaggregation and prediction. IBM WebSphere Application Server®(WAS) hosts the service layer to allow users interact with the services. In addition, a community engagement component plays the role of motivating residents through competition and collaboration via multiple media channels. The whole system, as a $850K deployment engagement with Dubuque, IA, has been deployed on IBM Smarter Cities Sustainable Model Cloud, and provides services to residents (300+ pilot households) and the city management team (about 10 government employees)[2].

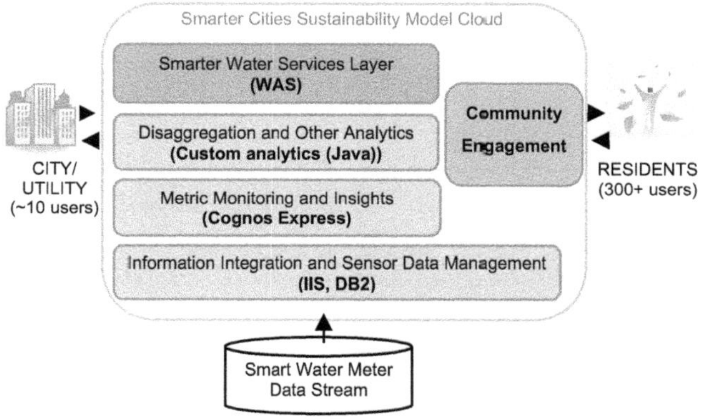

Figure 4. Smarter Water Service Architecture.

The main objective of this Smarter Water Service is to provide affective services that can help the volunteers modify their behavior to be more sustainable, in other words, let the residents know what they need to know to change their behavior. To achieve that goal, one important process is to reveal disaggregated water consumption, so that the users can know where in their houses they could conserve water, and sustainable operations or investment can be suggested. As a component of Smarter Water Service, activity analysis shared the computing resources with the other custom analytics. It works as a backend service that outputs activity-level consumption distribution reports every month from 15-minute aggregated consumption. This component will continuously provide consumption insights as part of the Smarter Water Service, and will be updated by enhancing learning ability and expanded to the expected 4000 households with hourly readings by 2013.

A preliminary summary has shown 6.6% normalized accumulative consumption reduction in 8 weeks after the Smarter Water Service was published in September 2010. In addition, a survey conducted in December 2010 showed that since September,

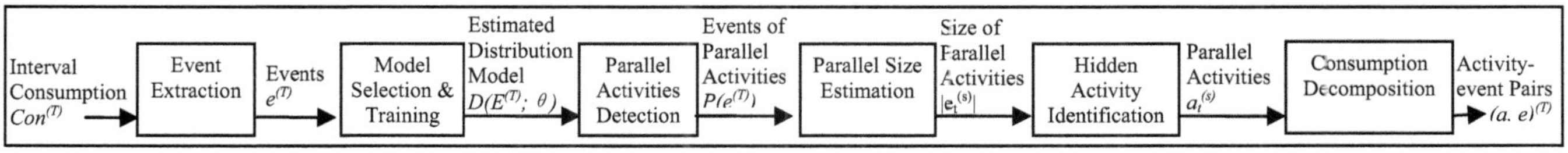

Figure 3. Disaggregation Framework.

out of 64 respondents, 15 households had fixed leaks, 13 respondents had shortened their showers, and 14 purchases on water-efficient toilet/appliances had been made.

2.2 Problem & Definitions

The problem of disaggregation from coarse granular smart water meter readings can be informally described as follows:

Problem: *Given a sequence of aggregated interval water consumption* $\boldsymbol{Con}^{(T)} = (Con_1, ..., Con_T)$, *where* Con_i *refers to the aggregated water consumption at the i-th time interval, the proposed solution should return a set of activities* $((A_1, E_1), ..., (A_k, E_k))$ *that are most likely to cause the aggregated consumption* $\boldsymbol{Con}^{(T)}$, *where* A_i *refers to an activity state (e.g., washer, shower, or toilet uses), and* E_i *refers to an observation (event) of water consumption for this activity state and is represented by a vector of event features, including total water consumption and start/end time intervals.*

The related terms and their definitions are summarized in Table 1, and will be used in the rest of the paper. We use capital letters to denote random variables and small letters to denote observations.

Table 1. Terms & Definitions.

Term	Symbol	Definition
Consumption	Con	Amount of water used in terms of gallons.
Interval	Int	The time period between 2 consecutive meter readings.
Activity	A	Integer value that represents one of the following: sink, toilet, shower, and washer.
Event	E	A vector of features to represent an event. The event features include total consumption, start/end time, etc.
Event sequence	$(E_1, ..., E_T)$	A sequence of events occurs in a time window (e.g., 24 hours), where T is the number of events.
Parallel activities	$(A_{t1}, ..., A_{ts})$	s activities occur together in event E_t
Events of parallel activities	$P(E^{(T)})$	A set of events in $(E_1, ..., E_T)$ generated by parallel activities.
Parallel sub-events	$(E_{t1}, ..., E_{ts})$	A set of parallel sub-events whose aggregation generates the event E_t. Each sub-event E_{ti} is generated by a single activity A_{ti}.

2.3 Research Challenges

General challenges for usage disaggregation from single main meter include the following: 1) Appliances/fixtures with similar consumption patterns, e.g., certain sink usage and a toilet flush; 2) Appliances/fixtures with multiple settings, e.g., normal, dedicated, and permanent of a washer; 3) Load variation, e.g., low, medium, and full load of a washer, or length of showers; 4) Multiple cycles, e.g., washer and dishwasher; 5) Lack of real-world ground truth, i.e., hard to collect sufficient labeled data from consumers. Disaggregation with the above challenges can be treated as a real-world classification problem.

In addition, the specific application scenario introduced in the previous section brings more challenges because of the coarse granularity and unstable reading intervals caused by unreliable communication. These limitations cause: 1) Parallel usage activities, e.g., two toilet flushes and a shower in the same 15 minute interval. 2) Difficulty of aligning usage events temporally, e.g., a shower may appear in one or two intervals. 3) Lack of features, i.e., only aggregated consumption and start time of each interval can be used to identify usage activity. These specific challenges make the task of water usage disaggregation more than a classification problem and difficult to solve.

The existing disaggregation approaches focus on analyzing steady state or transient state changes. They cannot handle the specific challenges in this scenario, because no steady state or transient state can be detected with such a low sample rate.

2.4 Observations

Due to the challenges discussed, the aggregated consumption of each interval alone surely cannot provide confident disaggregation results. We need to investigate the available ground truth on what other factors may help improve the disaggregation accuracy. After a study over the activity journaling from the volunteers, we have found three useful characteristics of water usage activities: fixture-dependant, household-dependant, and time-dependant.

2.4.1 *Fixture-dependant Pattern*

Each fixture category has its own usage pattern in term of consumption and duration that can be used to distinguish it from the others. Specifically, the amount of water consumed in a toilet flush usually fell in several small ranges between 1.5 ~ 5 gallons, and was consistent for a specific toilet. A load of washer generally lasted between 30~60 minutes, and consisted of multiple cycles with similar water usage. Showers had consistent flow rate most of the time, and lasted from 5 minutes to 15 minutes in most cases. Sink usage was usually short in time and low in consumption. These patterns can help briefly categorize the usage events. For example, any interval with flow rate lower than 0.1 gallons per 15 minutes can be filtered out as sink usage. However, using a fixture specification library is not enough to identify parallel activities, or to deliver customized models for each household.

2.4.2 *Household-dependant Pattern*

Activity patterns heavily depend on the fixture models and occupants of a specific household. For example, households with kids generally spent more time on shower every day; households with open leaks showed continuous usage for a long time; some households have 3 toilets and each has a different specification. Therefore, each household needs to be modeled separately to ensure accurate disaggregation. These models can be learned from historical consumption records and household profiles if available.

2.4.3 *Time-dependant Pattern*

According to human behavior, some activities may happen frequently during a specific time period, which can be used to distinguish ambitious water usage. One interesting example of such pattern is shower. Most of the labeled showers happened either close to the first event of usage in the morning or close to the first event after work. Although toilet flush occurred almost any time in a day, it was less frequent in working hours and midnight than the rest of a day. Not only time of day, but also day of week has been found drawing impacts on activity patterns. An example could be washer usage which happened mostly during weekends in some households. In addition, some activities are found temporally associated. For instance, a toilet flush in many cases was followed by a short sink usage for hand washing. According to the time-dependant activity patterns, timestamps of usage events should be able to improve disaggregation results significantly.

3. A NEW STATISTICAL DISAGGREGATION FRAMEWORK

Coarse granular smart meter readings cause a large portion of parallel activities, and disaggregation of parallel activities has become a critical and important challenge. This section introduces a new General Disaggregation Framework (GDF) to address the disaggregation problem. As illustrated in Figure 3, the GDF framework applies six phases to disaggregate water consumption. The work flow is described as follows:

Phase 1 Event extraction: Given a sequence of aggregated interval consumption $\boldsymbol{Con}^{(T)} = (Con_1, ..., Con_T)$, the intervals with continuous consumption are grouped to generate events where each represents one activity or parallel activities. The output of this phase is an event observation sequence of a given time window: $\boldsymbol{e}^{(T)} = (e_1, e_2, \dots, e_T)$. Hence, $\boldsymbol{e}^{(T)}$ is regarded as one observation of the event random variables $\boldsymbol{E}^{(T)} = (E_1, E_2, \dots, E_T)$. Each event E_i may be generated by a hidden activity (A_i) or several parallel hidden activities $(A_{i1}, \dots, A_{is})$.

Phase 2 Model selection and training: Select an appropriate stochastic model $\boldsymbol{D}(\boldsymbol{E}^{(T)}; \boldsymbol{\theta})$, such as *HMM* or *GMM*, and estimate parameters $\widehat{\boldsymbol{\theta}}$ based on historical labeled or unlabeled observations.

Phase 3 Parallel activity detection: Given the estimated stochastic model $\boldsymbol{D}(\boldsymbol{E}^{(T)}; \widehat{\boldsymbol{\theta}})$, the events with parallel activities $\boldsymbol{P}(\boldsymbol{e}^{(T)})$ can be identified from anomalous events $\boldsymbol{O}(\boldsymbol{e}^{(T)})$. Anomalous events can be obtained using leave-one-out test, i.e., $\boldsymbol{O}(\boldsymbol{e}^{(T)}) = \{e_t \mid e_t \in \boldsymbol{R}(\boldsymbol{E}^{(-t)} = \boldsymbol{e}^{(-t)}, \alpha)\}$, where $\boldsymbol{E}^{(-t)} = (E_1, \dots, E_{t-1}, E_{t+1}, \dots, E_T)$, $\boldsymbol{e}^{(-t)} = (e_1, \dots, e_{t-1}, e_{t+1}, \dots, e_T)$. $\boldsymbol{R}(\cdot)$ refers to the outlying region of normal event E_t that is defined based on the conditional distribution of $[E_t \mid \boldsymbol{E}^{(-t)} = \boldsymbol{e}^{(-t)}]$ and a confidence level α (e.g., 0.99). The calculation of outlying regions based on *HMM* and *GMM* models will be discussed in Section 4. This phase assumes all anomalous events are generated due to parallel activities. An anomalous event may also be generated by true abnormal activities such as a shower lasting more than an hour. However, it is difficult to differentiate these only based on coarse granular meter readings. Hence, we only consider parallel activities.

Phase 4 Parallel size estimation: For each anomalous event observation $e_t \in O(\boldsymbol{e}^{(T)})$, the number of parallel activities that generate e_t can be estimated by

$$s = \min\{s \mid e_t \in \boldsymbol{R}_{Agg}^{-}(\boldsymbol{E}^{(-t)} = \boldsymbol{e}^{(-t)}, Agg(E_{t1}, \dots, E_{ts}), \alpha)\} \quad (1)$$

where $\{E_{t1}, \dots, E_{ts}\}$ refers to the parallel activities (random variables) whose aggregation generates the event e_t, $Agg\ (\cdot)$ refers to the vector of aggregated features, and $\boldsymbol{R}_{Agg}^{-}(\cdot)$ refers to the normal region of the aggregated features $Agg(E_{t1}, \dots, E_{ts})$. $Agg(E_{t1}, \dots, E_{ts})$ returns aggregated features, such as the total water consumption, the earliest start time, and the latest end time of the sub-events $\{E_{t1}, \dots, E_{ts}\}$. The reason of selecting the minimal s is that heavy consumption (a washer load) can always be decomposed into a large number of small activities (e.g., toilet flushes), which is not reasonable.

Phase 5 Hidden activity identification: For each abnormal event $E_t \in O(E^T)$, given s, the estimated size of parallel activities, this phase estimates the disaggregated activities $\{a_{t1}, \dots, a_{ts}\}$:

$$(a_{t1}, \dots, a_{ts}) = \arg\max_{(a_{t1}, \dots, a_{ts}) \in \{1, \dots, m\}^s} \Pr(A_{t1} = a_{t1}, \dots, A_{ts} = a_{ts} \mid \boldsymbol{E}^{(-t)} = \boldsymbol{e}^{(-t)}, \text{Agg}(E_{t1}, \dots, E_{ts}) = e_t), \quad (2)$$

where m is the total number of activity types (e.g., shower, washer).

Phase 6 Consumption decomposition: Given the hidden parallel activities $\{a_{t1}, \dots, a_{ts}\}$ estimated in Phase 5, the related water consumption of these hidden activities can be estimated as:

$$\begin{aligned}(Con(e_{t1}), \dots, Con(e_{ts})) \quad (3)\\ = \arg\max_{Con(e_{t1}), \dots, Con(e_{ts})} L(Con(E_{t1}) = Con(e_{t1}), \dots, Con(E_{ts})\\ = Con(e_{ts}) \mid \boldsymbol{E}^{(-t)} = \boldsymbol{e}^{(-t)}, A_{t1} = a_{t1}, \dots, A_{tm}\\ = a_{ts}, Agg(E_{t1}, \dots, E_{ts}) = e_t),\end{aligned}$$

where L is the likelihood function, and $Con(e_{ti})$ is the consumption feature of the sub-event observation e_{ti}, i $= 1, \dots, s$.

To evaluate the correctness of *GDF*, we have the theorem as:

Theorem: *Given a sequence of aggregated consumption intervals* $\boldsymbol{Con}^{(T)} = (Con_1, \dots, Con_T)$, *GDF is able to identify true hidden activities* $((A_1, E_1), \dots, (A_k, E_k))$ *of* $\boldsymbol{Con}^{(T)}$, *if the following assumptions are satisfied: a) In Phase 1, The events can be correctly identified and the features extracted are sufficient; b) The distribution* $\boldsymbol{D}(\boldsymbol{E}^{(T)}; \boldsymbol{\theta})$ *is correctly selected and estimated; c) All anomalous events are due to parallel activities; d) The minimal s selected in Phase 4 is correct.*

Proof Sketchy: The four conditions stated above assure that the built statistical model by *GDF* is consistent with the true distribution of hidden activities of $\boldsymbol{Con}^{(T)}$. It follows that the activities identified by *GDF* are most probable results and should be consistent with true hidden activities.

4. DISAGGREGATION APPROACHES

This section presents two approaches based on *GDF* to handle different disaggregation scenarios. When there is no sufficient training data available, which is true in many real-world scenarios, we propose an approach to learn hidden relationship among consumption events and activities without user input based on hidden Markov model (*HMM*). When labeled activities are available for training, we design the second approach to construct statistical models using classification techniques and disaggregate parallel activities using Gaussian mixture model (*GMM*).

4.1 HMM-based Approach

This section presents an implementation of *GDF* based on *HMM*. It is trained based on unlabeled data and performs disaggregation without user input. For the purpose of simplicity, each event E_i is represented by a single feature, the total water consumption. Other features, such as start/end time intervals, and duration can be included to this approach in a straightforward manner.

4.1.1 Event Extraction (GDF Phase 1)

The key challenge of event extraction is the segmentation process. Without labeled historical data, it is necessary to define a set of heuristic rules to generate meaningful events based on domain knowledge. The basic criterion is to keep adjacent interval consumption in a single event if they possibly relate to one activity or parallel activities. This is to avoid the situation where one activity is divided to two separate events, which is not recoverable in our approach. If two nonparallel activities are mistakenly grouped to one event, they can still be identified in the consequent disaggregation process.

Similar to the idea of hierarchical clustering, a bottom-up based segmentation algorithm is proposed as follows:

Step 1: Preprocessing. Remove leaking effects, and filter out all zero-consumption intervals.

Step 2: Initialization. Regard each left interval as one event. Then we have the sequence of initial events $(e_1, \dots, e_k)$, where k is the number of nonzero consumption intervals.

Step 3: Merging heavy events. Define a water consumption threshold ϑ (e.g., 5.5 gallons for 15-minute-size intervals). For each continuous event pair (e_i, e_{i+1}), if $Con(e_i) > \vartheta$ and $Con(e_i) > \vartheta$, merge e_i and e_{i+1}. Repeat until no such pair exists.

Step 4: Merging light events. For each event e_i with $Con(e_i) > \vartheta$, if $0 < Con(e_{i-1})$, then merge e_i and e_{i-1}. Similarly, if $0 < Con(e_{i+1})$, then merge e_i and e_{i+1}. If there is an event e_i with $0 < Con(e_i)$, and both $Con(e_{i-1})$ and $Con(e_{i+1})$ greater than ϑ, then e_i is merged to the segment with the smallest consumption.

Step 5: Merging peak events. Merge two peak events $(Con(e_i), Con(e_j))$ if $dist(e_i, e_j) \leq \tau$, where $dist(e_i, e_j) = t_{start}(e_j) - t_{end}(e_i)$, and $t_{start}(\cdot)$ and $t_{end}(\cdot)$ refer to the start and end time of an event respectively. We define an event as a peak if its total water consumption is greater than a threshold γ (e.g., 20 gallons). This step is specifically designed for fixtures like washers, which consists of multiple peaks with more than 15 minutes empty cycle (no water consumption) between peaks.

4.1.2 HMM Parameter Estimation (GDF Phase 2)

A hidden Markov model is usually trained based on EM algorithm, which can only guarantee local optimum. Given a large number of parameters to be estimated in a HMM model, including the number of hidden states, the initial probabilities, the emission distribution of each state, and the transition matrix, it is critical to find appropriate initial settings for these parameters. By empirical evaluation, we decided a mixture model of three Gaussians for sink events, and Gaussian models for other activity events. This section presents a heuristic based approach to seek initial settings for each household based on generic domain knowledge:

Step 1: Toilet identification. Hierarchical clustering is applied on events to identify toilet clusters. By domain knowledge, toilet clusters could be identified by requiring the cluster size to be greater than 3 times the total number of days in the training data, and the consumption standard deviation smaller than 0.5 gallons.

Step 2: Sink identification. Sink events can be identified as the events with consumption lower than $(\mu_i - 2 * \sigma_i)$, where μ_i and σ_i are the mean and standard deviation of the toilet cluster with the smallest mean consumption in all toilet clusters.

Step 3: Frequent pattern identification. After removing sink events and toilet clusters, hierarchical clustering is applied on the remaining events to identify other qualified clusters. In order to control the HMM complexity, we only keep the 12 clusters with the smallest standard deviation.

Step 4: Cluster labeling. This step gives labels to the qualified clusters based on predefined rules such as a shower usage should be within 5~25 gallons. If some clusters are still not labeled, we label these clusters as "others", which may relate to some unknown activity state or frequent combination of parallel activities.

Step 5: Anomaly removal. The anomalous events are identified based on a Gaussian mixture distribution estimated from qualified clusters. These outliers will impact the training of HMM, therefore they are removed from training data.

Step 6: Probability estimation. Regarding each qualified cluster as a hidden state, we can get the number of hidden states, the mean and standard deviation of each hidden state. The transition matrix and initial probabilities can be estimated based on labeled events.

4.1.3 Disaggregation and Labeling (GDF Phase 3-6)

First, several notations are defined as follows. The set of activity states is $\{1, \ldots, m\}$, D is an m by m transition matrix, π is the initial probability of the m states, $p_i(e_t) = Pr(E_t = e_t \mid A_t = i)$, and $u_i(t) = Pr(A_t = i)$. For the purpose of simplicity, we assume that each event E_t conditioned on activity state A_t follows a Gaussian distribution $[E_t|A_t = i] \sim \mathcal{N}(\mu_i, \sigma_i^2)$. Note that the following derivations can also be straightforwardly extended to Gaussian mixture distributions.

Let $P(e) = \begin{bmatrix} p_1(e) & 0 & 0 \\ 0 & \ldots & 0 \\ 0 & 0 & p_s(e) \end{bmatrix} \in \mathbb{R}^{s \times s}, \alpha_t = \Pr(e_1, \ldots, e_t, A_t) \in \mathbb{R}^s,$
$\alpha_t(a_t) = \alpha_t = \Pr(e_1, \ldots, e_t, A_t = a_t) \in \mathbb{R}, \beta_t = \Pr(e_{t+1}, \ldots, e_T|A_t) \in \mathbb{R}^s,$
$\beta_t(a_t) = \Pr(e_{t+1}, \ldots, e_T|A_t = a_t) \in \mathbb{R}$, and $B_t = DP(e_t)$.

The *HMM* implementations of *GDF* Phase 3 to 6 are as follows:

GDF Phase 3: Parallel activity detection

The probability density function

$$P\left(E_t = e \mid E^{(-t)} = e^{(-t)}\right) = \frac{\alpha_{t-1}^T DP(e)\beta_t}{\alpha_{t-1}^T D\beta_t} = \sum_i w_i(t)p_i(e),$$

where $w_i(t) = \frac{d_i(t)}{\sum_{j=1}^m d_j(t)}, d_i(t) = [\alpha_{t-1}^T D]_i [\beta_t]_i$. It indicates that $\left[E_t = e \mid E^{(t)} = e^{(-t)}\right]$ follows a *GMM*:

$$\left[E_t = e \mid E^{(-t)} = e^{(-t)}\right] \sim \sum_i w_i(t)\mathcal{N}(x|\mu_i, \sigma_i^2)$$

The outlying region of the *GMM* model can be calculated as

$$\boldsymbol{R}(\boldsymbol{e}^{(-t)}, \alpha) = \left\{e \,\middle|\, |e - \mu_{k^*}| > \sigma_{k^*}\Phi^{-1}\left(\frac{1-\alpha}{2}\right)\right\},$$

where k^* is the Gaussian component closest to e, and $\Phi(\cdot)$ is the cumulative density function (CDF) of a standard Gaussian distribution. Here, we assume that the statistics of outlying events are dominated by the component closest to the observation. This outlying region estimation has been justified in [4] using extreme value statistics.

GDF Phase 4: Parallel size estimation

The probability density function

$$P\left(E_{t1} = e_{t1}, \ldots, E_{ts} = e_{ts} \mid \boldsymbol{e}^{(-t)}\right) = \frac{\alpha_{t-1}^T \prod_{i=1}^s \{DP(e_{ti})\}\beta_t}{\alpha_{t-1}^T D^s \beta_t}$$
$$= \sum_{(l_1, \ldots, l_s) \in \{1, \ldots, m\}^s} w_{l_1, \ldots, l_s} P_{l_1}(e_{t1}) \cdots P_{l_m}(e_{ts}),$$

where $w_{l_1, \ldots, l_m}$ is the weight that can be calculated based on the form $\{\alpha_{t-1}^T \cdot \prod_{i=1}^s \{DP(e_{ti})\} \cdot \beta_t\} / \alpha_{t-1}^T D^s \beta_t$.

It implies that

$$\left[E_{t1}, \ldots, E_{ts} \mid \boldsymbol{E}^{(-t)} = \boldsymbol{e}^{(-t)}\right] \sim$$
$$\sum_{(l_1, \ldots, l_s) \in \{1, \ldots, m\}^s} w_{l_1, \ldots, l_s} \mathcal{N}\left(\left[\mu_{l_1}, \ldots, \mu_{l_s}\right]^T, \mathrm{diag}(\sigma_{l_1}^2, \ldots, \sigma_{l_s}^2)\right)$$

By linear transformation, we have that

$$\left[E_{t1} + \cdots + E_{ts} \mid \boldsymbol{E}^{(-t)} = \boldsymbol{e}^{(-t)}\right] \sim$$
$$\sum_{(l_1, \ldots, l_s) \in \{1, \ldots, m\}^s} w_{l_1, \ldots, l_s} \mathcal{N}\left(\sum_{k=1}^s \mu_{l_i}, \sum_{k=1}^s \sigma_{l_i}^2\right).$$

Note that here $Agg(E_{t1}, \ldots, E_{tm}) = E_{t1} + \cdots + E_{ts}$. Since $\left[Agg(E_{t1}, \ldots, E_{tm}) \mid \boldsymbol{E}^{(-t)} = \boldsymbol{e}^{(-t)}\right]$ follows a Gaussian mixture distribution, the normal region $\boldsymbol{R}_{Agg}^-(\cdot)$ can be estimated similarly as in the above *GDF* Phase 3.

GDF Phase 5: Hidden activity identification

The probability density function

$$\Pr\left(A_{t1} = a_{t1}, \ldots, A_{ts} = a_{ts} \mid \boldsymbol{E}^{(-t)} = \boldsymbol{e}^{(-t)}, E_{t1} + \cdots + E_{ts} = e_t\right) =$$
$$\frac{\alpha_{t1}(a_{t1}) \prod_{i=1}^{s-1} \Pr(a_{t(i+1)}|a_{ti}) \Pr(\sum_k E_{tk} = e_t|a_{t1}, \ldots, a_{ts}) \beta_{ts}(a_{ts})}{L_T},$$

where L_T is the likelihood of the whole sequence and can be neglected when solving the problem (2). Note that the random variables $E_{t1}, \ldots, E_{ts}$ are independent to each other given their hidden activity states $A_{t1}, \ldots, A_{ts}$. The probability density function $\Pr(\sum_k E_{tk} = e_t|a_{t1}, \ldots, a_{ts})$ can be calculated by simple linear transformation of independent Gaussian random variables.

GDF Phase 6: Consumption decomposition

Given the hidden activity states $\{a_{t1}, \ldots, a_{ts}\}$, we have that

$$[E_{t1}, \ldots, E_{ts} \mid a_{t1}, \ldots, a_{ts}] \sim \mathcal{N}(\boldsymbol{\mu}, \boldsymbol{\Sigma}),$$

where $\boldsymbol{\mu} = \left[\mu_{a_{t1}}, \ldots, \mu_{a_{ts}}\right]^T, \boldsymbol{\Sigma} = \mathrm{diag}(\sigma_{a_{t1}}^2, \ldots, \sigma_{a_{ts}}^2)$. The optimal solution of the problem (3) can be obtained as [5]

$$[e_{t1}, \ldots, e_{ts}]^T = \boldsymbol{\mu} - \boldsymbol{\Sigma}^{-1}\mathbf{1}^T(\mathbf{1}^T\boldsymbol{\Sigma}\mathbf{1})^{-1}(\mathbf{1}^T\boldsymbol{\mu} - e_t).$$

4.2 Classification-GMM-based Approach

Different from the *HMM*-based approach, this section presents a mixed model approach to the disaggregation problem that requires labeled data for training. It first applies a classification model (e.g., support vector machine, neural network, and *k*-nearest neighbor classifier) to classify each event as a single activity, or a known frequent combination of parallel activities, or an unknown infrequent combination of parallel activities. For the events classified to the last category (unknown infrequent combinations), it applies an implementation of the *GDF* framework based on *GMM* to disaggregate parallel activities.

Assume that we are given a sequence of aggregated interval consumption $\boldsymbol{Con}^{(T_1)} = (Con_1^*, \ldots, Con_{T_1}^*)$ and the related hidden activities $((a_1^*, e_1^*), \ldots, (a_k^*, e_k^*))$ as the labeled training data. The objective is to build a model on $\boldsymbol{Con}^{(T_1)}$ that can identify unknown hidden activities $((a_1, e_1), \ldots, (a_k, e_k))$ of a new aggregated intervals consumption sequence $\boldsymbol{Con}^{(T)} = (Con_1, \ldots, Con_T)$.

4.2.1 Event Extraction (GDF Phase 1)

This phase first applies the same procedure as in Section 3.2.1 to identify a sequence of events. Here each e_i has six features, which include the start time, duration, total consumption, minimal interval consumption, maximal interval consumption, and number of peaks.

4.2.2 Classification (GDF Phase 2)

The event extraction phase returns an event sequence $(e_1, \ldots, e_k)$, where each e_i is represented by a vector of six features ($e_i \in \mathbb{R}^6$). Note that all the features are mapped to real type values, in order to apply classification models such as SVM and neural network.

Here, we neglect the dependencies between events and treat $(e_1, \ldots, e_k)$ as a set of independent training instances: $\{e_1, \ldots, e_k\}$. Based on the labels $(a_1^*, e_1^*), \ldots, (a_k^*, e_k^*)$, it is able to identify hidden activities of each event e_i. To decide class labels, not only single activities (e.g., toilet, shower, and washer) are treated as distinct classes, but also frequent combinations of parallel activities are regarded as distinct classes. The current setting is that frequent parallel activities should occur at least once per week.

4.2.3 GMM-based Disaggregation (GDF Phase 3-6)

After the classification process, each event has been labeled as a single activity, or known/unknown combination of parallel activities. For parallel activities, a *GMM*-based implementation of the *GDF* framework is proposed to disaggregate parallel activities. The basic procedures are as follows:

Based on the labels of training events $\{e_1, \ldots, e_k\}$, it is able to collect training instances for each activity state, such as toilet, shower, and washer. For simplicity, in this disaggregation step, we only consider a single feature (the total water consumption), for each event e_i. Each single-activity related event (E_t) can modeled by a Gaussian mixture distribution as $E_t \sim \sum_{i=1}^{m} \pi_i \mathcal{N}(\mu_i, \sigma_i^2)$, where π_i is the prior probability of the activity state i, and $\mathcal{N}(\mu_i, \sigma_i^2)$ is the event distribution of activity i.

Given an event e_t that is classified as parallel activities, the objective is to identify the most probable hidden activities $((a_{t1}, e_{t1}), \ldots, (a_{ts}, e_{ts}))$ with $Agg(e_{t1}, \ldots, e_{ts}) = e_t$. Here the aggregation function Agg is the summation function $\sum(\cdot)$. The *GDF* disaggregation framework can be employed here, which can be regarded a simplified case of HMM based approach. Readers are referred to [15] for detailed specifications.

5. EVALUATION & FINDINGS

The framework has been implemented using JDK 1.5 and deployed in the Custom Analytics Layer of the Smarter Water Service (Figure 4). Pie charts of activity consumption distribution are generated to illustrate how each fixture has been used on monthly basis. From the Smarter Water Service layer interface, the residents can browse their own consumption distribution; meanwhile, the government agency and utility manager can explore how water has been consumed by each activity at regional level.

Both HMM-based and GMM-based approaches have been implemented and evaluated. Specifically, for the GMM-based approach, we have assessed three classification methods, k-Nearest Neighbor classification (kNN-GMM), Artificial Neural Network (ANN-GMM), and Support Vector Machine (SVM-GMM) accordingly. Given the available labeled activities, the evaluation focused on identifying toilet flushes, showers, and washer loads.

To evaluate the effectiveness of consumption disaggregation on identifying these activities, we adopted three metrics, *precision*, *recall*, and *F-measure*. The major reason of using these metrics is that the disaggregation evaluation is similar to an information retrieval process, where subsets of intervals represent certain true activities and the testing results are also subsets of intervals labeled as activities. The metrics need to capture not only how many labels are matched, but also how many true activities are missed and how many false labels are placed. These metrics are defined as follows: *Precision* refers to the portion of matched activities within the corresponding disaggregation results; *Recall* refers to the portion of matched activities within the corresponding true activities; *F-measure* is the harmonic mean of precision and recall.

To evaluate the proposed disaggregation solution, we have applied both HMM-based and GMM-based approaches on the consumption of 6 volunteer households, as well as 50 simulation datasets that were generated based on their labeled consumption. In addition, we varied the sample rate in these datasets to investigate its impact on disaggregation results. The correlation between sample rate and effectiveness can provide guidance to future planning and deployment of human activity analysis applications.

Due to the lack of labeled activities from most of the pilot households, we only applied the HMM-based model to analyze activities of the 300+ pilot households. Some interesting patterns discovered can illustrate common human behavior characteristics.

5.1 Datasets

A real-world dataset was collected from 6 volunteer households. It consists of 1/10 Hz water reading and the corresponding usage journaling records for 7 days. The usage journaling was input manually by these volunteers, so it always has approximated timestamps and missing activities, which introduce inaccuracy which needs to be handled carefully. Note that these households came from various demographic categories and showed significantly different consumption patterns. A summary of labeled activities from one volunteer is listed in Table 2 as an example.

Table 2. Water Journaling of One Household.

Fixture	Occurrences	Total Amount	Percentage
Shower 1	5	71	7%
Shower 2	5	57	6%
Washer	9	366	38%
Toilet 1	43	217	24%
Toilet 2	33	68	7%
Others (sink & unlabeled)	N/A	186	19%

50 simulation datasets were generated by simulating occurrences and corresponding consumption of activities according to their distributions in the labeled dataset from the 6 volunteer households. Firstly, from the labeled activities, the number of instances of each activity in a week was estimated using Poisson distribution. Each instance was randomly assigned to a day and time according to the distributions of labeled activities in day-of-week and time-of-day domains. These distributions were captured by activity occurrence histograms generated from labeled activities and smoothed by kernel density. Once date and start time of an instance was determined, its consumption and duration was randomly picked from a dictionary of the corresponding labeled activities. Finally, consumption noise of each day was randomly picked from 42 (6

households * 7 days) samples, of which each contains unlabeled consumption (<2 gallons) of a whole day. In this way, simulated consumption data for 6 months were generated in each dataset.

A live dataset was constructed from the 15-min consumption of all the pilot households since August 2010. This dataset has inconsistent reading intervals all the time, missing readings due to communication failure, and even water leaks that can impair the disaggregation results.

5.2 Parameter Settings & Baseline Methods

For HMM-based approach, the major settings are as follows: 1) in GDF Phase 1 (event extraction) Step 3 (merging heavy events), the threshold ϑ was set to 5.5 gallons; 2) in GDF Phase 1 (event extraction) Step 5 (merging peak events), the thresholds τ and γ were set to 15 minutes and 20 gallons, respectively; 3) in GDF Phase 2 (HMM parameter estimation) Step 4 (cluster labeling), the clusters with mean consumption between 1.2 gallon and 6 and frequency greater than two times per day were labeled as toilets; the clusters with mean consumption between 8 and 30 were labeled as showers; the clusters with mean consumptions between 30 and 55 gallons were labeled as washers; the clusters with frequency smaller than 1 times per day were disregarded; and the left clusters were labeled as "others"; 4) the number of states in *HMM* was decided automatically (See GDF Phase 2 step 3). Note that all the preceding parameters were decided based on domain experiences.

For kNN-GMM-based approach, the event extraction phase was the same as that in HMM-based approach. Note that the same event extraction process was also used in all other compared approaches. The kNN classifier used in the experiments was provided by MATLAB-2008a Bioinformatics Toolbox. One major parameter is the number of nearest neighbors used in the classification. We applied 10-folder cross validation to select the best k from the candidate values from 5 to 15.

For ANN-GMM-based approach, the neural network classifier was provided by MATLAB 2008a Neural Network Toolbox. We used one-per-class cording for multiclass classification. In one-per-class coding, each output neuron is designated the task of identifying a given class. The output code for that should be 1 at this neuron and 0 for others. We used Levenberg-Marquardt backpropagation, which is the default training algorithm in MATLAB. 10-folder cross validation was used to select the best parameter "the number of hidden layers" in the range from 2 layers to 8 layers. Other parameters were the default settings. Note that, another popular training algorithm is "Gradient descent back propagation" with two major parameters "learning rate" and "the number of hidden layers". We have also tried this training algorithm in experiments. But results indicate that the Levenberg-Marquardt backpropagation method is more accurate and efficient. For SVM-GMM-based approach, the SVM classifier was provided by LIBSVM [6]. We used the popular radial basis function as the kernel function. There are two parameters including cost (c) and gamma (g). These two parameters were tuned by 10-folder cross validations, and the best parameters was selected from different combinations of the cost parameter (c) range: $log_2(c) = 1{:}0.25{:}5$, and the gamma parameter (g) range: $log_2(g) = -7{:}0.25{:}-1$. We used the "one-against-one" method for multiclass classification.

Two baseline approaches, named random-pick and knapsack based, were applied to evaluate the effectiveness of the above four proposed methods. The random-pick method is described as follows: First, conduct the same event extraction as in HMM-based method; second, the events with consumption smaller than 2 gallons are labeled as sink uses; third, the left events are randomly labeled to toilet, shower, and washer uses.

The knapsack based method is described as follows: First, conduct the same event extraction as in HMM-based method; second, knapsack each segment to the best combination of the following activities: "Toilet-old (1.6 gallons)", "Toilet-new (4 gallons)", "Shower-Low-flow (15 gallons)", "Shower-Standard (30 gallons)", "Laundry (50 gallons)", and "Sink (<=1.6)".

5.3 Effectiveness Comparison

To demonstrate the effectiveness of proposed approaches, we used the labeled activities from water journaling and the simulation datasets as ground truth, and compared the proposed approaches. The comparison was conducted among 4 versions of disaggregation approaches, HMM, kNN-GMM, ANN-GMM, and SVM-GMM; and the two baseline solutions, random pick and knapsack. Cross validation was applied to find the best parameters for the corresponding classification methods.

As shown in Table 3, all the proposed approaches achieved about 95% precision on shower identification, while the recall was relatively low (77~81%). It was because the deviation of shower consumption is very high in real life. In many cases, consumption of a shower may be similar to that of two toilet flushes, or a front-load washer. Therefore, some true showers could not be correctly identified. But once an activity is labeled as a shower, it's very likely to be true. Although these four methods performed similarly on labeling showers, SVM-GMM achieved the highest scores.

Table 3. Precision, Recall, and F-measure on Simulation Data.

Precision, Recall, F-measure	**Toilet** Mean (Standard Deviation)	**Shower** Mean (Standard Deviation)	**Washer** Mean (Standard Deviation)
HMM	0.7704 (0.08), 0. 6651 (0.04), 0.7110 (0.04)	0.9471 (0.04), 0.7883 (0.04), 0.8594 (0.03)	0.7839 (0.06), 0.9610 (0.04), 0.8620 (0.04)
kNN-GMM	0.7291 (0.07), 0.8552 (0.03), **0.7850 (0.04)**	0.9552 (0.02), 0.7723 (0.05), 0.8530 (0.03)	0.8536 (0.06), 0.8937 (0.09), 0.8702 (0.06)
ANN-GMM	0.5982 (0.05), 0.8709 (0.03), 0.7075 (0.04)	0.9584 (0.03), 0.7670 (0.06), 0.8505 (0.04)	0.8554 (0.08), 0.8994 (0.12), 0.8710 (0.09)
SVM-GMM	0.4669 (0.07), 0.8873 (0.02), 0.6086 (0.06)	0.9622 (0.02), 0.8057 (0.05), **0.8761 (0.03)**	0.8613 (0.06), 0.9329 (0.06), **0.8940 (0.04)**
Random Pick	0.1022 (0.03), 0.0531 (0.01) 0.0699 (0.02)	0.1514 (0.03), 0.1608 (0.04) 0.1560 (0.03))	0.0737 (0.02), 0.3237 (0.10) 0.1201 (0.07)
Knapsack	0.0655 (0.01), 0.1534 (0.02) 0.0918 (0.02)	0.4570 (0.05), 0.3294 (0.05), 0.3828 (0,05)	0.8619 (0.16), 0.3516 (0.13) 0.4995 (0.19)

Different to shower, washer loads were disaggregated with very high recall (89~96%), and relatively low precision (78~86%). Generally, cloth washer is the heaviest and meanwhile the least frequent activity on water consumption in a household. Based on the specifications and settings of a washer, its water consumption is usually consistent. That's the reason why almost all of the washer instances can be learned and identified. On the other hand, a washer usage usually crosses multiple intervals. This usage pattern may be similar to certain combinations of other consumption. Therefore, some other consumption was classified as washer by the disaggregation approaches. In overall, SVM-GMM achieved the best overall performance, and HMM got the highest recall.

Detecting toilet flushes is the most difficult task comparing to shower and washer. Because toilet usage typically happens very frequently and costs a small amount of water, it is hard to be distinguished from sink usage in 15-minute interval, or be identified when combined with heavy activities such as a shower or a washer load. All the four approaches had F-measure between 61% and 78%. HMM was the only approach with precision higher than recall. KNN-GMM performed the best in terms of F-measure.

Due to the small number of training data (<= 4 days per house), GMM-based approaches failed to disaggregate consumption on the volunteer households. As shown in Table 4, HMM perfectly identified the washer usage, and disaggregated showers with high scores. The F-measure for toilet disaggregation with HMM only achieved 55%, although still much better than the baselines.

Table 4. Precision, Recall, and F-measure on Volunteers.

Precision, Recall, F-measure	Toilet Mean (Standard Deviation)	Shower Mean (Standard Deviation)	Washer Mean (Standard Deviation)
HMM	0.516 (0.27), 0.597 (0.17) **0.5536 (0.22)**	0.831(0.138), 0.818 (0.144), **0.8244 (0.14)**	1 (0), 1 (0) **1 (0)**
Random Pick	0.20 (0.18), 0.19 (0.08) 0.1949 (0.13)	0.08 (0.09), 0.19 (0.16) 0.1126 (0.17)	0.07 (0.09), 0.29 (0.34) 0.1128 (0.27)
Knapsack	0.20 (0.10), 0.904 (0.01) 0.3275 (0.05)	0.52 (0.34), 0.47 (0.16) 0.4937 (0.25)	0.44 (0.52), 0.23 (0.27) 0.3021 (0.39)

5.4 Impact of Sample Rate

Choosing an appropriate sample rate for smart meter deployment is a very important decision that may affect hardware and maintenance cost. This set of experiments can provide practical suggestions from the requirement of activity analysis. Reading intervals of the simulation datasets were varied from 15 min to 3 hours in this set of experiments to evaluate its impact on the accuracy of disaggregation results. Both HMM and GMM methods were evaluated in this set of experiments. SVM-GMM was selected to represent GMM, because it had shown practically good accuracy and efficiency in previous experiments. As suggested in Figure 5, both 15 and 30 min intervals provide acceptable results. 1 hour interval supports fair disaggregation of washer and shower, but cannot identify more than half of toilet flushes.

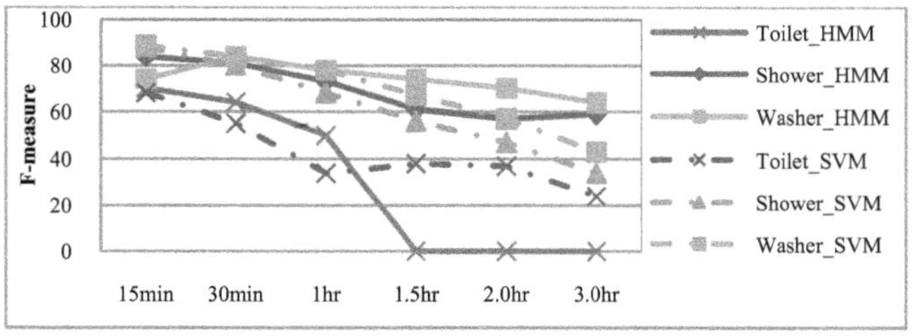

Figure 5. Impact of Interval Length.

5.5 Disaggregation for Pilot Households

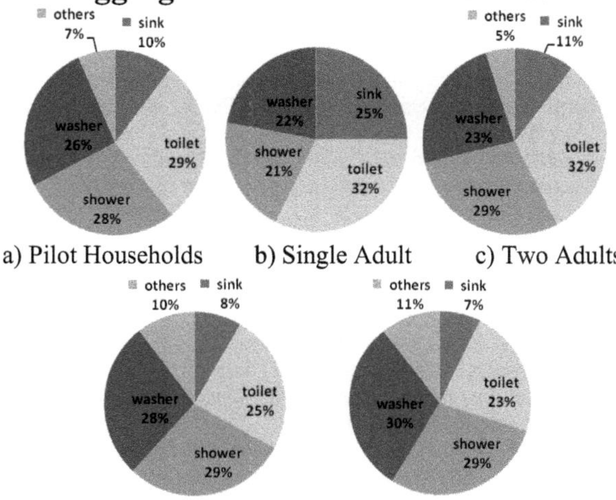

a) Pilot Households b) Single Adult c) Two Adults

d) Households with Kids e) Households with Toddlers

Figure 6. Distribution vs. Demographic Info.

The proposed HMM-based approach has been applied on 300+ pilot households with 15 minute meter readings. Hidden Markov models were constructed for each household, and water consumption since August 2010 was disaggregated into activities to provide insights to residents and the city management team. Some interesting usage patterns discovered from the disaggregation results are illustrated in the following paragraphs.

By combining with demographic survey results, we first summarize the consumption distribution of different types of households in pie charts as shown in Figure 6. Each pie chart shows the portion of water each activity used by a given group of households. The consumption that cannot be disaggregated is included in category 'others'. The consumption distribution of all the pilot households is illustrated in Figure 6 a), where toilet and shower used about 30% each, and washer used about 25%. Households with single occupant (Figure 6 b)) showed different usage pattern, where shower only consumed 21% of the overall usage and washer reduced to 22%. Figure 6 c) shows the pie chart for households with two adults only. Compared to the single adult households, households of two adults consumed significantly higher in shower. On the other hands, kids in general caused more washer usage. As shown in Figure 6 d) and e), households with kids brought washer usage to 28%, and more specifically, households with toddlers had increased washer usage further to 30%. By comparison, a resident can easily figure out on which activity his or her household needs more efforts to conserve water.

Temporal patterns of washer and shower usage have been identified from the disaggregation results. As shown in Figure 7, the pilot households preferred to use washer in weekends, and each weekday there was about 0.9 load per household in average. Not only the number of loads, but also the size of each load increased in weekends. Figure 7 b) illustrates that each load on Saturday used 9% more water than a load on Tuesday or Wednesday. This is reasonable because usually heavy laundry is saved to weekends.

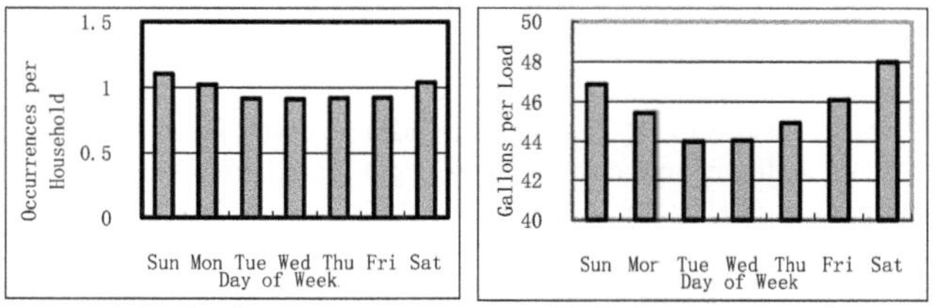

a) Daily Occurrences b) Gallons per Load

Figure 7. Washer Usage vs. Day of Week.

Similar to washer, as can be seen in Figure 8 a), more showers happened during the days in weekends. However, interestingly, an average shower on Sunday used the least water in a week, which was 10% less than one on Saturday. Furthermore, a shower on Friday consumed the highest amount of water in a week. It seemed that people wanted to relax and enjoyed longer showers on Friday, while the stress from work arrived early on Sunday.

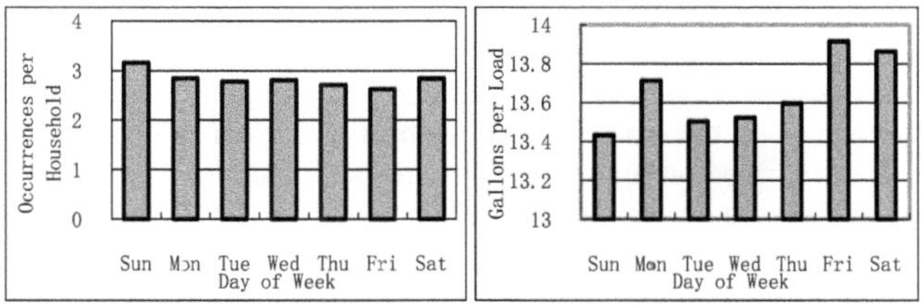

a) Daily Occurrences b) Gallons per Load

Figure 8. Shower vs. Day of Week.

Figure 9 demonstrates the time of day distributions of shower and washer across the pilot households. As expected, the peaks of showers happened during 8~9 am and 6~7 pm in a day, which are before and after work. Washer usage showed a similar distribution in b), although the pm peak was not significant. That consistency could be explained as that many washer loads occurred right after a shower to handle the changed clothes.

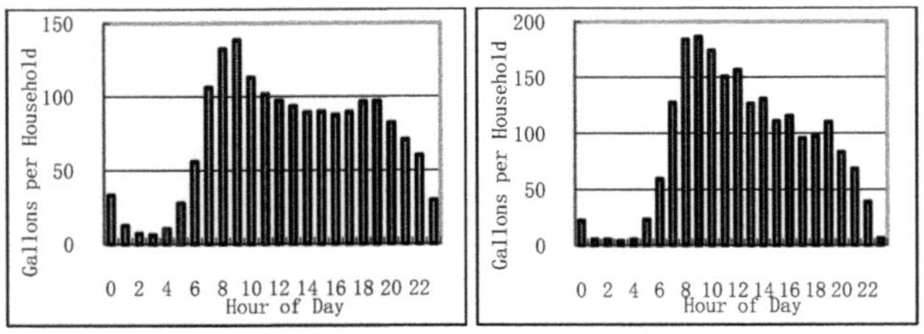

a) Shower b) Washer Usage

Figure 9. Shower/Washer vs. Time of Day.

6. RELATED WORK

Non-intrusive load monitoring has been proposed based on analyzing steady state change and transient state change. So far most of the research effort has been focused on electricity load disaggregation with high sample rate [7-13]. A power meter with high sample rate (>= 1Hz) can identify most of the state changes of multiple metrics (e.g., power, reactive power, voltage, and harmonics) caused by individual appliances in a real-world home. Based on state change of current and voltage, a non-intrusive load monitoring approach [7] was proposed to determine power consumption of individual appliances. An electrical noise sensor has been used to disaggregate consumption by running SVM on transient noise of turning on and off appliances [8]. By measuring voltage of each outlet in a house, one approach [12] applied kNN and SVM to classify appliances. This approach collected peak, average, and RMS of voltage of a single target with 4kHz sample rate, and achieved best results using an NN classifier. An NN-based disaggregation approach has been proposed to identify appliances with 90% accuracy using only the main power meter [9, 13]. The features it used consist of power, reactive power, voltage RMS, and harmonics for state transition. RECAP has recently been proposed using artificial neural network (ANN) to disaggregate electricity usage [11]. Features including power factor, peak and RMS of voltage and current were aggregated every minute and analyzed in a 3-layer ANN. To extract better features, Matrix Pencil [10] has been proposed to model each signal as complex plan, and use residues and poles as features for disaggregation. Improved disaggregation results have been demonstrated.

Compared with electricity disaggregation, residential water disaggregation has attracted much less research effort. To the best of our knowledge, there has not been any design that can disaggregate water consumption either using a single water meter or from a sample rate lower than 500Hz. Microphone-based sensors were applied on major water pipes (cold inlet, hot inlet, and sewing) to recognize usage activities [14]. Combining the timestamps that these microphones detect noise, the authors identified most of the water usages. However, this approach has difficulties to disaggregate concurrent activities and cannot determine water volume. Integration of a water meter and a network of accelerometers [15] has been proposed to estimate the flow rates based on pipe vibration. This approach has been applied in laboratory environments to disaggregate water usage. To avoid accessing water pipes, an approach using pressure sensor on main source [16] was proposed to identify fixtures. This approach applies hierarchical classifiers to first detect valve open and close events, and then label fixtures. Due to the 1 kHz sample rate, it can clearly capture *on* and *off* signals of fixtures from water pressure.

7. CONCLUSION

This paper describes a design and deployment of activity disaggregation using low sample rate smart water meters in Dubuque, IA. In the proposed general disaggregation framework, fixture characteristics, household behavior, and activity correlations are modeled to disaggregate water consumption. Implementations based on Hidden Markov Model and Gaussian Mixture Model have been developed accordingly to provide insights for helping residents improve their behavior and supporting utility manager's decision making. Evaluation on both real and simulation datasets have demonstrated the effectiveness of the disaggregation approaches, and revealed some interesting patterns from pilot households. Future efforts may include providing user annotation interface to support learning from feedback; and expanding the disaggregation service to electricity smart meters.

8. ACKNOWLEDGEMENTS

The authors would like to gratefully acknowledge the collaboration from the Information Services Department of City of Dubuque on smart meter data transmission; and the support from Dubuque 2.0, an NGO, for engaging the volunteer households.

9. REFERENCES

[1] Dubuque2.0, "Inspiring Sustainability," 2010.

[2] T. Woody, "Smart Water Meters Catch On in Iowa," in *The New York Times* New York City, 2010.

[3] NeptuneTechnologyGroup, "R900 RF Wall or Pit MIU Product Sheet," 2009.

[4] S. J. Roberts, "Novelty Detection using Extreme Value Statistics," *IEE-VISP,* vol. 146, pp. 124-129, Jun. 1999.

[5] H. Rue, "Fast Sampling of Gaussian Markov Random Fields," *JRSS: Series B,* vol. 63, pp. 325-338, 2001.

[6] C. C. Chang and C. J. Lin, "LIBSVM: a library for support vector machines," 2001.

[7] G. W. Hart, "Nonintrusive Appliance Load Monitoring," *Proceedings of the IEEE,* vol. 80, pp. 1870 - 1891, Dec. 1992.

[8] S. N. Patel, T. Robertson, J. A. Kientz, M. S. Reynolds, and G. D. Abowd, "At the Flick of a Switch: Detecting and Classifying Unique Electrical Events on the Residential Power Line," in *ACM-ICUC*, Innsbruck, Austria, 2007, pp. 271-288.

[9] M. Berges, E. Goldman, H. S. Matthews, and L. Soibelman, "Learning Systems for Electric Consumption of Buildings," in *ASCE International Workshop on Computing in Civil Engineering*, Austin, TX, 2009, pp. 1-10.

[10] H. Najmeddine, K. E. K. Drissi, C. Pasquier, C. Faure, K. Kerroum, T. Jouannet, M. Michou, and A. Diop, "Smart metering by using "Matrix Pencil"," in *IEEE EEEIC*, Prague, Czech Republic, 2010, pp. 238-241.

[11] A. G. Ruzzelli, C. Nicolas, A. Schoofs, and G. M. P. O'Hare, "Real-Time Recognition and Profiling of Appliances through a Single Electricity Sensor," in *IEEE SECON*, Boston, MA, 2010, pp. 1-9.

[12] T. Saitoh, T. Osaki, R. Konishi, and K. Sugahara, "Current Sensor Based Home Appliance and State of Appliance Recognition," *SICE JCMSI,* vol. 3, pp. 86-93, Mar. 2010.

[13] M. Berges, E. Goldman, H. S. Matthews, and L. Soibelman, "Enhancing Electricity Audits in Residential Buildings with Nonintrusive Load Monitoring," *Journal of Industrial Ecology,* vol. 14, pp. 844-858, Oct. 2010.

[14] J. Fogarty, C. Au, and S. E. Hudson, "Sensing from the Basement: A Feasibility Study of Unobtrusive and Low-Cost Home Activity Recognition," in *ACM UIST*, Montreux, Switzerland, 2006, pp. 91-100.

[15] Y. Kim, T. Schmid, Z. M. Charbiwala, J. Friedman, and M. B. Srivastava, "NAWMS: Nonintrusive Autonomous Water Monitoring System," in *ACM SenSys*, Raleigh, NC, 2008, pp. 309-322.

[16] J. Froehlich, E. Larson, T. Campbell, C. Haggerty, J. Fogarty, and S. N. Patel, "HydroSense: Infrastructure-Mediated Single-Point Sensing of Whole-Home Water Activity," in *ACM ICUC*, Orlando, FL, 2009, pp. 235-244.

Estimating the Number of Users behind IP Addresses for Combating Abusive Traffic

Ahmed Metwally and Matt Paduano
Google Inc
1600 Amphitheatre Pkwy, Mountain View, CA 94043 USA
{metwally, mattp}@google.com

ABSTRACT

This paper addresses estimating the number of the users of a specific application behind IP addresses (IPs). This problem is central to combating abusive traffic, such as DDoS attacks, ad click fraud and email spam. We share our experience building a general framework at Google for estimating the number of users behind IPs, called hereinafter the sizes of the IPs. The primary goal of this framework is combating abusive traffic without violating the user privacy. The estimation techniques produce statistically sound estimates of sizes relying solely on passively mining aggregated application log data, without probing machines or deploying active content like Java applets. This paper also explores using the estimated sizes to detect and filter abusive traffic. The proposed framework was used to build and deploy an ad click fraud filter at Google. The first 50M clicks tagged by the filter had a significant recall of all tagged clicks, and their false positive rate was below 1.4%. For the sake of comparison, we simulated a naïve IP-based filter that does not consider the sizes of the IPs. To reach a comparable recall, the naïve filter's false positive rate was 37% due to aggressive tagging.

Categories and Subject Descriptors

H.2.8 [**Database Management**]: Database applications—*Data mining*; C.2.0 [**Computer Communication Networks**]: General—*security and protection*

General Terms

Algorithms, Experimentation, Measurement, Security

Keywords

IP Size Estimation, Abusive Traffic Filtering, Advertisement Click Fraud, Real Data Experiments

1. INTRODUCTION

Simple conventional mechanisms for abuse detection that rely on source IPs set a limit, i.e., filtering threshold, on the IP activity within a time period. Once the limit is reached by an IP, either the IP traffic gets filtered for the rest of that time period, or the IP gets blacklisted for several consecutive periods. These techniques typically set the same threshold for all IPs. Setting an aggressive threshold yields a high false positive rate since some IPs have numerous users behind them and are hence expected to send relatively large traffic volumes. Setting a conservative threshold yields a high false negative rate, since the threshold becomes ineffective for distributed attacks where IPs send relatively little traffic. This work tailors the thresholds to the sizes of the IPs. It proposes a new framework for timely estimation of the number of users behind IPs with high enough accuracy to reduce false positives and with high enough coverage in the IP space to reduce false negatives.

We define the sizes of the IPs based on two dimensions: application and time. Each application has a specific size associated with each IP depending on the number of human users using this application. For Google, the query size of an IP is the number of human users querying the search engine, which may differ from the number of users clicking ads or the number of users sending emails to the Google email service. Thus, sizes should be estimated using the log files of the application whose activity is subject to estimation.

The other dimension for defining the sizes is time. The number of human users behind an IP changes over time, like when the IP observes a flash crowd, i.e., an unexpected surge in usage, or gets reassigned to households and/or companies. The size estimates should be issued frequently enough to cope with the frequent size changes. This calls for a short estimation time period. Conversely, the estimation period should be long enough to yield enough IP coverage, as well as enough traffic per IP to produce statistically sound sizes.

Estimation Challenges and Methodology

While estimating the sizes of individual IPs has ramifications on the security field, the primary concern is violating the user privacy. To preserve the user privacy, the proposed techniques estimate sizes of IPs using the application-level log files. First, the application users are assumed to be only temporarily identified, e.g., with cookie IDs in the case of HTTP-based log files. Thus, no Personally Identifiable Information, such as the name or the email address, is revealed. Second, no individual machines are tracked. Third, the framework uses application log data aggregated at the IP-level. Over 30% of dynamic IPs are reassigned every one to three days [19], and thus an IP is considered a temporary identification of a user. In addition, the majority of the

KDD'11, August 21–24, 2011, San Diego, California, USA.

users share IPs. This is illustrated by Fig. 1 that shows the distribution of 10M random IPs (from Google ad click log files) shared by 26.9M total estimated ad users.

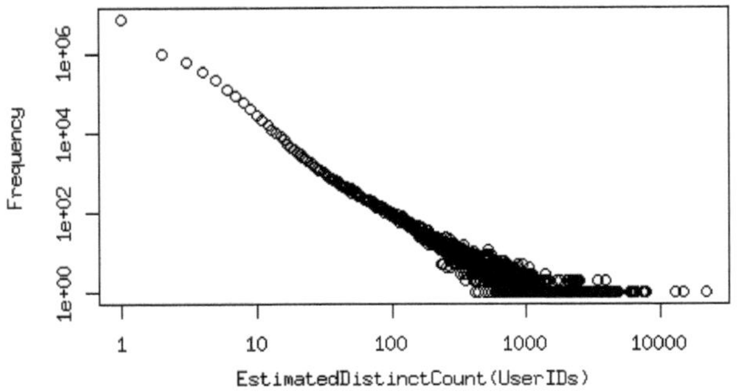

Figure 1: The estimated sizes of 10M random IPs.

Estimating sizes from the log files is not straightforward. Naïve counting of distinct user identifications, e.g., cookie IDs or "user agents" (UAs), per IP fails to accurately estimate sizes. Corporate NAT devices usually have the same UA on all hosts. Similarly, an Internet cafe host is used by several users sharing the same user ID. Meanwhile, small IPs can masquerade as large IPs by clearing or farming cookies, and overwriting UAs in HTTP requests. Therefore, estimating sizes by distinct counting of cookies and UAs may result in over-estimation or under-estimation. Filtering traffic based on these inaccurate sizes yields high false negatives and high false positives, respectively.

Instead, this paper proposes using the log files to build statistical models that are later used for estimating sizes. However, this approach poses some challenges.

1. The log files do not contain only legitimate traffic. The existence of abusive traffic entries in these files degrades the quality of the models and the estimated sizes. To avoid such quality degradation, the models should be built only from the traffic of the trusted users[1]. This introduces a sampling bias in the traffic used to build the models. To mitigate this bias later in the estimation phase, only the trusted traffic of each IP[2] during a period, p, is used to estimate its size for p (§ 2.).
2. The sizes of the IPs change due to legitimate reasons, such as reassignments, flash crowds and business-week cycles. For an estimation period, p, the log files cannot be finalized before the end of p. They are then analyzed to produce estimates after each IP has already made its activities during p. Hence, estimated sizes are always lagging behind real-time sizes. Meanwhile, real-time abuse detection needs the estimates when p begins. This lag reduces the filtering accuracy when an IP legitimately changes size (§ 4).

[1]Trusted users, identified by cookie IDs for example, are typically those whose activity was rarely tagged as abusive by any existing filter. If this is the only deployed filter, trusted users can be alternatively defined as those with some signature of good traffic, where the definition of good traffic is application-dependent. For combating ad click fraud, trusted cookies can be defined as those with a relatively high conversion rate, where conversions are rare but trusted post-click activities, like purchases from the advertisers.

[2]Traffic entries tagged by filters are logged in abusive log files. Both trusted and untrusted traffic entries exist in the log files. Only untrusted entries exist in the abusive log files.

Given the above challenges, our contributions can be better laid down into the following three efforts:

1. building statistical models for size estimation in an autonomous, passive and privacy-preserving way from aggregated log files (§ 3),
2. devising a distributed efficient algorithm that examines previous size estimates, and produces a predicted size for each possible IP for a period p before p begins to mitigate the deleterious effects of lag (§ 4), and
3. setting traffic filtering thresholds based on the sizes without any manual intervention (§ 5).

The cycle and the interdependencies between these three processes is summarized in § 2.

2. THE SIZE ESTIMATION CYCLE

The cycle of size estimation and filtering is laid out in this section. The basic cycle consists of four processes that communicate via log files and size lookup tables. For period p, the inputs and outputs of the real-time traffic event logging, estimation, predictions, and real-time abuse detection processes are formalized in relations 1, 2, 3, and 4, respectively.

$$\textit{traffic}_p \xrightarrow{\textit{RT-Log(p)}} \textit{log-files}_p \quad (1)$$

$$\textit{log-files}_p \ltimes_{entry} \textit{abusive-log-files}_p \xrightarrow{\textit{Est(p)}} \textit{estimates-table}_p \quad (2)$$

$$\forall_{i=p-w-1}^{p-2} \textit{estimates-table}_i \xrightarrow{\textit{Prd(p)}} \textit{predictions-table}_p \quad (3)$$

$$\textit{traffic}_p \ltimes_{IP} \textit{predictions-table}_p \xrightarrow{\textit{RT-Abuse-Dtct(p)}} \textit{abusive-log-files}_p \quad (4)$$

Real-time logging, denoted *RT-Log(p)* in rel. 1, finalizes the traffic $\textit{log-files}_p$ as $p+1$ starts. Next, the $\textit{log-files}_p$ are consumed, among other input, by the estimation process, *Est(p)*, to produce the $\textit{estimates-table}_p$ mapping IPs that issued traffic during p to their estimated sizes (rel. 2). Next, the algorithm for predicting sizes, *Prd(p + 2)*, consumes the *estimates-tables* from a sliding window of length w periods[3], $p-w+1$ through p, to produce the $\textit{predictions-table}_{p+2}$. We assume that before the beginning of $p+2$, this prediction process, *Prd(p+2)*, completes and produces the $\textit{predictions-table}_{p+2}$, mapping IPs to their predicted sizes of period $p+2$.

The *estimates-tables* that contributed to $\textit{predictions-table}_p$ are shown in rel. 3. The $\textit{predictions-table}_p$ is used by the real-time abuse detection process, denoted *RT-Abuse-Dtct(p)* in rel. 4, to produce the $\textit{abusive-log-files}_p$ for p. The $\textit{abusive-log-files}_p$ contain the IDs of the traffic entries in $\textit{log-files}_p$ identified as abusive. The $\textit{abusive-log-files}_p$ are joined with the $\textit{log-files}_p$ by *Est(p)* to disregard the abusive traffic entries, and produce estimates based solely on legitimate traffic (rel. 2). While this joining makes estimation exclusively based on non-abusive traffic, care should be taken to avoid over-filtering of legitimate traffic.

This over-filtering caveat is best clarified by an example. Let IP 10.1.1.1 be stable at an estimated size of 1 for the periods $p-w$ through $p-1$, and then suddenly observes a flash

[3]The length, w, of the estimates window should be long enough to span cycles in the activities of the IPs such that *Prd(.)* considers legitimate cyclic size changes. Conversely, w should not be excessively large not to include very old sizes unrepresentative of future sizes. In our system, the estimates window was set to span several weekly cycles.

crowd during period p. *Prd(p+1)*, which runs during period p, is agnostic to this flash crowd and predicts a size of 1 for period $p+1$. Hence, *RT-Abuse-Dtct(p+1)* filters the majority of the traffic from 10.1.1.1. When the *log-files*$_{p+1}$ and the *abusive-log-files*$_{p+1}$ are joined, most of the traffic from this IP is not considered for estimation, and *Est(p + 1)* underestimates its size. Since the *estimates-table*$_{p+1}$ are fed back into *Prd(p+3)*, 10.1.1.1 continues to have a small predicted size, and to be overfiltered in $p+3$. To mitigate over-filtering caused by this hysteresis loop, only the egregiously abusive traffic is disregarded for the purpose of estimation[4].

The estimation and prediction phases have been assumed so far to run together in less than $l = |p|$, the period length. This introduced a *lookahead delay* of $2l$. That is, the output of *RT-Log(p)* is not used by *RT-Abuse-Dtct(.)* before $p+2$. The longer the *lookahead delay*, the higher the chance of filtering based on inaccurate sizes. Enhancements to the basic cycle to reduce the *lookahead delay* are discussed in Appendix A. We next discuss the *Est(.)*, *Prd(.)* and *RT-Abuse-Dtct(.)* phases in § 3, § 4 and § 5, respectively.

3. ESTIMATION DETAILS

In the sequel, a user is defined as an entity that generates average activity of a trusted human for a specific application over a particular time period of length l. It is assumed that cookie IDs in the log files temporarily identify trusted users. Models of the average activity built from cookie IDs are influenced by the noise of users sharing or frequently clearing cookies. The log entries of one cookie ID may show the activity of one or more users, or part of the activity of one user. Thus, these cookie IDs do not perfectly represent real users. This phenomenon is a part of the trusted user activity, and is hard to separate from the log files.

Moreover, there is natural variance in the users' activity that can result in size estimation errors. However, this risk is lower for large IPs, where the absolute estimation errors are operationally more significant. The estimation error decreases as the IP traffic increases, as verified in § 3.4.

Next, two main classes for building models are presented: the rate estimators (§ 3.1) and the features diversity estimators (§ 3.2). Combining estimates is described in § 3.3.

3.1 The Rate Estimators Class

This class of estimators relies on the activity rate of an IP to estimate the number of users behind it. For any activity, if the trusted-user activity rate is verified to follow a Poisson distribution, then from the properties of the distribution, the size of an IP can be estimated based on its activity rate.

For a Poisson distribution with rate λ, the probability of having k log entries from a single user within one period is given by $f(k, \lambda l) = \frac{(\lambda l)^k e^{-\lambda l}}{k!}$. The sum of Poisson random variables with parameters $\lambda_1, \ldots, \lambda_M$ is a Poisson random variable with $\lambda = \sum_{i=1}^{M} \lambda_i$. For the estimated activity, the average trusted-user rate, λ_m, can be used to estimate the sizes of IPs. An IP with M users is expected to have a rate of $M \times \lambda_m$. More formally stated, the Maximum Likelihood Estimator (MLE) of the number of users behind an IP is $\frac{\lambda_{IP}}{\lambda_m}$, where λ_{IP} is the rate of activity of the IP.

To estimate the average unknown trusted-user rate of activity, the straightforward way is to calculate the MLE of λ_m, the average number of activity entries per trusted cookie per time period. A more practical method that is less susceptible to outliers is to construct the distribution of rates, and use its median or mode as λ_m. An empirical c-confidence interval on estimated size is given by $[\frac{\lambda_{IP}}{\lambda_{hi}}, \frac{\lambda_{IP}}{\lambda_{lo}}]$, where c is the fraction of the trusted users' rates between λ_{lo} and λ_{hi}.

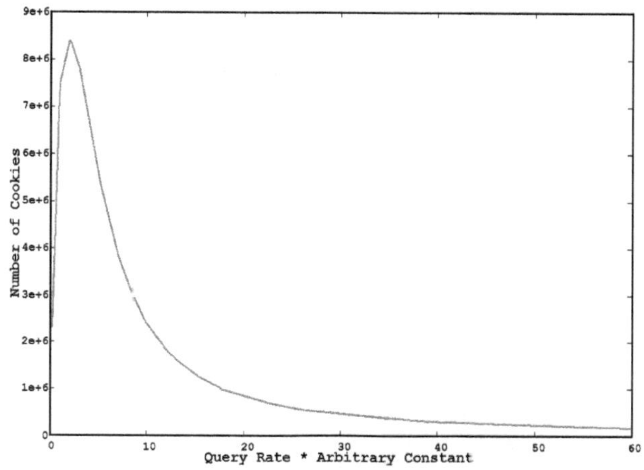

Figure 2: The query rate distribution PDF.

Taking the number of users who query Google as an example, Fig. 2 shows the query rate distribution of $\approx$ 100M highly trusted cookies[5]. A median of 7, and an interquartile interval $[\lambda_{0.25}, \lambda_{0.75}]$ of $[3, 24]$ can be used for estimation.

3.2 The Features Diversity Estimators Class

This class of estimators builds a regression model of the numbers of trusted cookies behind IPs, i.e., the baseline of *measured sizes*, as related to the *explanatory diversity* of their traffic feature(s). For example, after a linear model is built of how the *measured sizes* of IPs relates to their distinct queries, the same model can then be used to estimate the query size of any IP from its number of distinct queries.

The *explanatory diversity* of feature(s) can be quantified in several ways. One simple way is counting its distinct values in the IP traffic. More sophisticated ways include calculating the perplexity and the compressibility of the sequence of the feature in the IP traffic. A feature, X (e.g., the query) in the traffic of an IP typically assumes several values, $x_1, x_2, \ldots$ (all the possible query phrases). The perplexity of a feature is calculated as $Perp(X, b) = b^{H_b(p)}$, where b is some base and $H_b(p) = \sum_x p(x) \log_b(\frac{1}{p(x)})$ is the entropy of the distribution of feature X in the IP traffic[6].

A training sample of $\approx$ 10M IPs, was collected to build a linear regression model of the number of users as related

[4]We have defined egregious traffic as the traffic that was filtered by another filter already deployed at Google. However, as a guideline if this is the only deployed filter, egregious traffic can be defined as the traffic filtered using a threshold h times higher than the normal threshold for the size of the source IP, where $h > 1$. Selecting h involves a trade-off. As h increases, filtering abusive traffic is reduced, which could later contribute to overestimating sizes of abusive IPs. Building attacks slowly over time exploits this vulnerability. As h decreases, the filter becomes less vulnerable, but produces more false positives since the estimation cycle becomes less responsive to unforeseen legitimate changes in sizes.

[5]Due to the sensitive nature of the exact distribution, the rate is scaled by an arbitrary constant.

[6]Perplexity was verified on several datasets to exhibit linear relationship with the numbers of trusted cookie IDs behind IPs (*measured sizes*). Entropy does not exhibit this quality.

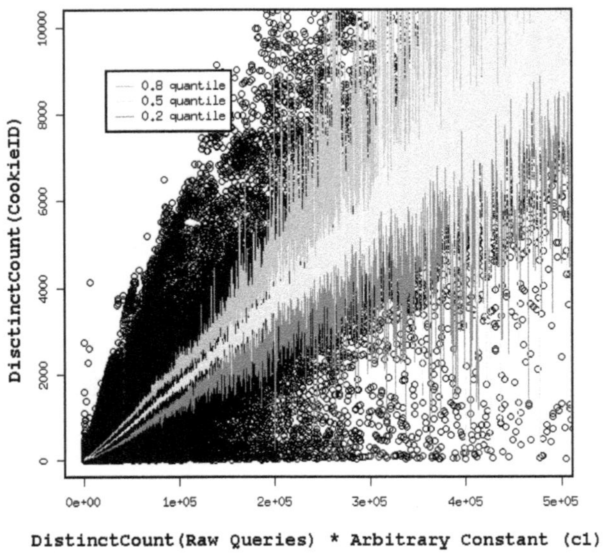

(a) The distinct count of queries scattered with user count.

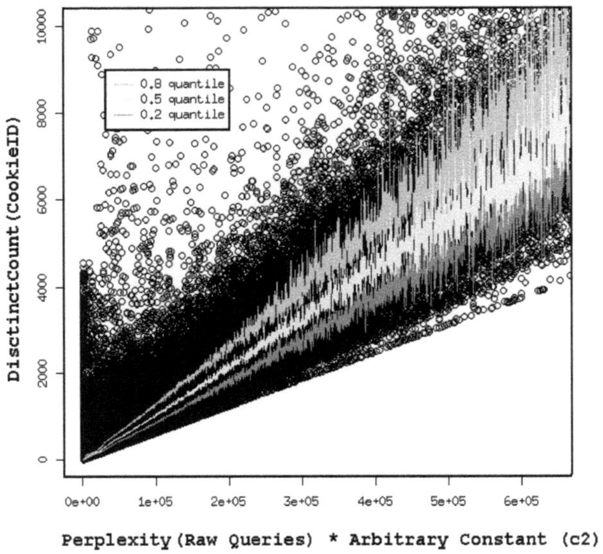

(b) The perplexity of queries scattered with user count.

Figure 3: The scatter plots of query diversity and the number of users.

to the query diversity quantified using distinct counting and perplexity. The data used to build the regression model for query sizes is plotted in Fig. 3. In Fig. 3, each circle represents one, or multiple overlapping sampled IP(s). Each circle shows the distinct number of trusted cookies querying Google, and the distinct count (Fig. 3(a)) and perplexity (Fig. 3(b)) of the queries issued by these trusted cookies[7].

Because models are built from log files aggregated at the level of IPs, and the overwhelming majority of IPs have very few trusted cookies behind them, sampling noise can cause issues. If a random training sample is selected, the few IPs with large *measured sizes*, i.e, the IPs with numerous trusted cookies, can be easily missed out. To avoid under-representing IPs with large *measured sizes*, stratified sampling is used [16]. IPs are bucketed into disjoint classes by their *measured sizes*. The number of samples from each class should represent this class in the global sample by the same proportion of that class in the global IPs population.

From Figures 3(a) and 3(b), some observations can be made about the stratified sample of IPs. First, the relationship between the *measured sizes*, i.e, the number of trusted cookies, and query diversity shows high heteroscedasticity. That is, the variance of the *measured sizes* increases with the distinct count (Fig. 3(a)) and perplexity (Fig. 3(b)) of queries. To build the model, instead of ordinary least squares linear regression, quantile regression [8] is used[8], since it is less susceptible to outliers.

The second observation is the data density decreases almost exponentially as the *explanatory diversity* increases. Using quantile regression to build the regression model on all the data yields models whose accuracy highly favors the dense areas of the low values of the *explanatory diversity*, and demonstrates low accuracy bias towards IPs with large *measured size*, where the accuracy is more critical. To build an estimation model that does not strongly favor dense regions, the high disparity in the data density should be normalized by giving all values of the *explanatory diversity* roughly the same weight. For a quantile, q, let the *q-quantile-curve* be the set of the q-quantile points of the *measured sizes* across all values of the *explanatory diversity* on the x-axis. Let the slopes of the lines that best fit the *q_{lo}-quantile-curve*, *0.5-quantile-curve* and *q_{hi}-quantile-curve* be $\theta_{q_{lo}}$, $\theta_{0.5}$ and $\theta_{q_{hi}}$, respectively, and $q_{hi} - q_{lo} = c$. Then, the estimated size of an IP whose *explanatory diversity* value is ρ_{IP} is $\rho_{IP} * \theta_{0.5}$; the size of the IP is in the range $[\rho_{IP} * \theta_{q_{lo}}, \rho_{IP} * \theta_{q_{hi}}]$ with confidence c.

For example, in Fig. 3, the *quantile-curves* of 0.2, 0.5 and 0.8, are plotted. Each point on the *0.5-quantile-curve* in Fig. 3(a) constitutes the median of the *measured sizes* on the y-axis for its corresponding value of distinct query count on the x-axis. The number of unique queries from an IP scaled by $\theta_{0.5}$ is its estimated query size.

3.3 Combining Estimates

For each IP, individual estimates are calculated based on its traffic rate and diversity, as discussed in § 3.1 and § 3.2. Even more, these two classes of estimators produce multiple individual estimates if the application has multiple "sub-activities". Taking the Google social network service as an example, a user can do several sub-activities like updating status, or sharing links. Each one of these sub-activities can be used for size estimation based on its rate and diversity.

When building the estimation models, the individual estimates are linear-regressed against the baseline of *measured sizes* to calculate the *combining weights* that are later used to calculate the *overall estimated sizes* when doing estimation. The *overall estimated sizes* are expected to have higher confidence and less error variance than any individual size estimate; and should serve as a general purpose size for the application whose activity is subject to estimation.

[7]Due to the sensitive nature of the exact distribution, the x-axes of Fig. 3 are scaled, and the perplexity is calculated with two bases, $b1 \neq b2$, as $Perp(X, b_1, b_2) = b_1^{H_{b_2}(p)}$.

[8]A q-quantile regression applied to a dataset fits a hyperplane that lies under roughly q of the points.

Preliminary filtering can be carried out at this stage. Since each IP typically has multiple individual estimates, high variance in these estimates is a strong signal for focusing on a specific activity, which is usually abusive. For instance, IPs that have noticeably high rates of issuing friend requests, and uncommonly low rates of status updates could be suspicious. IPs with high variance in their individual estimates are ignored when building the estimation models and have their traffic tagged as abusive during the filtering phase. The simplest method for setting a threshold on the variance is to measure the variances of all the IPs, calculate the standard deviation of the variances, and set the threshold at 2 or 3 times the standard deviation. More robust methods for setting this threshold are currently under investigation.

3.4 Gauging Estimation Accuracy

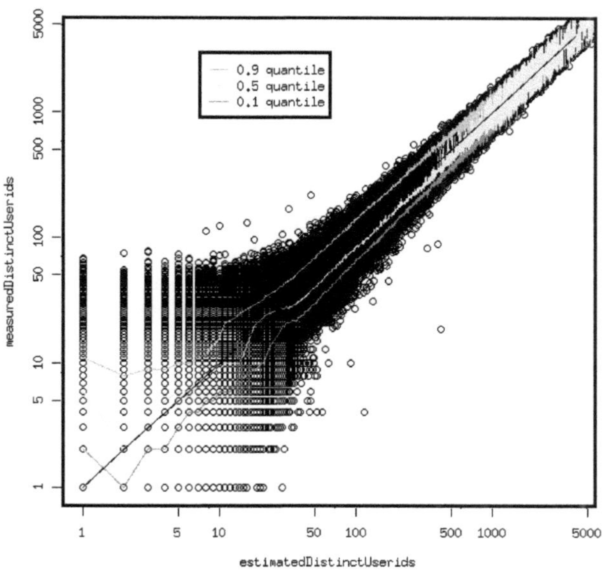

Figure 4: The estimated vs. measured query sizes.

Assessing the accuracy of the estimation process is done by using the estimation models on a testing set that is different from the training set. Only the traffic from the trusted cookies are used to produce the *overall estimated sizes* of the IPs in the testing set. These estimates are compared against the baseline *measured sizes*, the number of trusted cookies behind these IPs. For the purpose of modeling and gauging accuracy, only the traffic from the trusted cookies are used to produce the size estimates, and traffic from the non-trusted cookies is ignored. However, in reality, all the traffic is used to estimate the total number of users, and not only the trusted cookies users.

The sizes and the 0.1, 0.5 and 0.9 *quantile-curves* are plotted in Fig. 4 with logarithmic axes, where each circle represents one, or multiple overlapping IP(s). The line passing though the point $(1, 1)$ with slope 1 (drawn in black) represents perfect estimation. The median *quantile-curve* is almost overlapping with perfect estimation for estimates above 1, and 80% of the estimates are close to perfect estimation.

While from a statistical perspective it is undesirable to have estimation accuracy biases, it was purposeful for larger IPs, where the relative estimation errors are operationally more significant, to be more accurate. To achieve that, the sampling of the training IPs was stratified, and quantile regression on the *quantile-curves* was used to fit the models.

4. PREDICTION DETAILS

As discussed in § 2, the *estimates-tables* produced by the *Est(.)* phase over a window of size w are input to the *Prd(.)* phase. To reduce the *lookahead delay*, the prediction algorithm was developed with high focus on efficiency.

4.1 The Size Prediction Alternative Approaches

Predicting the size of every possible IP based on its previous size estimates is a gigantic web-scale time series analysis problem.

Typically, a time series prediction is carried out by doing a weighted average of the previous w values, where the weights are usually calculated offline using regression analysis. This is effective with time series with high autocorrelation where the current state is a function of previous states and white noise. This is customarily combined with smoothing, such as moving averages, to reduce noise, yielding the commonly known autoregressive moving average (ARMA) models [7].

Other alternatives for predicting sizes include nonparametric regression, like Spline curves [6]. The accuracy of these techniques depends largely on the number of iterations used to fit some model. This computational cost is still acceptable if the modeling is done offline.

There are several challenges with applying conventional time series procedures for predicting sizes of IPs. First, the time series of sizes are non-stationary. The time series of each IP does not follow the same distribution over time due to, among other factors, the reassignments of over 30% of the dynamic IPs every one to three days [19]. Such abrupt and unforeseen changes to sizes cause lack of stationarity, which limits the application of some techniques, like ARMA.

The second and bigger challenge is the estimates of each IP form a time series that should be analyzed to produce a prediction for this IP. Given the high heterogeneity in the behavior of IPs according to numerous factors including their assignments, time-zones and sizes, building a one-size-fits-all predictive model based on a sample of IPs becomes impracticable. Therefore, a specialized and efficient prediction algorithm is sought. While the time series literature does not strictly apply to this problem, the *PredictSizes* algorithm, described in § 4.4, employs some concepts from seasonal autoregressive integrated moving average (ARIMA) models.

At a high level, for each IP, *PredictSizes* predicts its size in isolation based on its latest w size estimates. For each IP, the *PredictSizes* algorithm performs three main functions. First, it analyzes the periodicity of the size estimates, since it has been consistently observed that the activity of IPs is periodic (§ 4.2). Second, for each periodicity, *PredictSizes* analyzes a sliding window of estimates and seeks their representative stable size by doing iterative variance reduction until the estimates lie within an acceptable confidence interval (§ 4.3). Third, it combines the estimates of all periodicities.

4.2 Considering Multiple Size Periodicities

Considering the periodicity of IP activity is imperative. Periodicities of the sizes of the IPs were discovered by selecting a sample of IPs, and applying Discrete Fourier Transform to each. The terms with the highest coefficients are the periodicities used by the *PredictSizes* algorithm [3]. For the vast majority of IPs, most of their sizes were noticed to have diurnal and weekly periodicities. These periodicities were especially clear for the IPs of school districts and large institutes, as informed by the Whois databases [18].

PredictSizes fetches the estimates of several periodicities, e.g., diurnal and weekly, for each IP to produce its prediction. For n periodicities, $s_1 < s_2 < \cdots < s_n$, *PredictSizes* considers the most recent w_i estimates s_i periods apart, for $1 \leq i \leq n$. For example, to estimate the sizes of IPs in six hours with all the sliding windows having length 10, $s_1 = 1$, $s_2 = 4$ and $s_3 = 28$, *PredictSizes* is considering the last 10 six-hour contiguous estimates, as well as the same-slot estimates of the last ten days and the last ten weeks.

4.3 Iterative Variance Reduction

PredictSizes deals with the sizes time series of each periodicity of each IP in isolation. It then combines the predictions from all the periodicities of an IP as discussed in § 4.4.

For time series predictions, it is typical to do simple trend analysis using simple linear regression with time as the explanatory dimension to show consistent increase or decrease over time (allowing for some white noise) [7]. The trend is then used for extrapolation. However, based on analysis of numerous IPs, time series of size periodicities almost never show strong trends within the window of estimates used for predictions. Moreover, using trend analysis hurts IPs that have drastic size change, since false trends result in erroneous predictions. Hence, *PredictSizes* assumes a stable value for each periodicity time series. The stable value, the representative statistic on the time series, is calculated using the *StableSize* function and is produced as the prediction.

For simplicity, the *StableSize* algorithm deals with each periodicity time series as a set. For each time series, *StableSize* does iterative variance reduction by removing outlier estimates that contribute the most to the variance until the ratio of the width of the confidence interval to the mean falls below a specific bound. The truncated mean of the remaining sizes is declared the stable size of this time series.

At each iteration, *StableSize* calculates the standard deviation, mean and the width of the c-confidence interval on the mean of the time series. The element that contributes the most to the variance is the farthest from the mean. This element can be identified in constant time by checking which of the maximum and the minimum elements are farther from the set mean and deleting it in each iteration. Each time an extreme element is deleted, the new mean and variance are incrementally accurately updated in constant time [17]. The most costly process is then identifying the extreme elements, which can be done efficiently using a minmax heap.

The algorithm fails if the time series exhibits little stability, due to abrupt size changes or due to the weakness of this periodicity compared to others. It bails out once the fraction of the discarded elements exceeds some threshold.

4.4 The PredictSizes Algorithm

Since *PredictSizes* deals with each periodicity of each IP separately, it can be massively parallelized using the Mapreduce framework [14], as the size estimates are stored in files sharded by the period IDs and IPs. The algorithm combines all the stable sizes of all the periodicities using a *Combiner* function that also does sanity checks on the predicted sizes.

The main factor that influences the choice of the *Combiner* is the loss function of the predictions, which is application-dependent. In its simplest form, a *Combiner* can be a simple statistic, such as the mean, truncated mean, median, max or min. For instance, when sizes are used for service optimization, the mean statistic minimizes the expected loss under the mean squared error loss function. Another alternative for *Combiner* functions is using a weighted average of the stable sizes, where the weights are inversely proportional to the fraction of size outliers (extreme estimates) discarded by the *StableSize* function for each periodicity. More involved analysis entails doing a regression of the size estimates of a particular period (as the expected *predicted size*) as related to the stable sizes from individual periodicities (as *explanatory sizes(s)*). However, such a regression-based *Combiner* can be easily influenced by the heterogeneity of IPs discussed in § 4.1, such as time-zones.

The *Combiner* algorithm ensures that the predicted size agrees with the stable sizes of all the periodicities. A simple solution was implemented that does two sanity checks. First, it checks that the predicted size is within some factor of the stable size for each periodicity. Second, it checks that the predicted size is within a specific quantile range of all the stable sizes. If the predicted size does not conform to the *Combiner* sanity check, the IP is deemed unstable, and no predicted size is produced for it. In our experiments, these simple sanity checks proved to be very effective in detecting abrupt legitimate size changes early on, and hence reducing the false positives caused by over-filtering legitimate traffic.

4.5 Evaluating Predictions

To evaluate the proposed predictions algorithm, an experiment was run on three months worth of query data log files. Two metrics were measured. The first metric is, for every period p, the agreement of the predicted sizes of the IPs with their estimated sizes during p (§ 4.5.1). The second metric is the *coverage*, the ratio of IPs in the traffic in period p that had predictions (§ 4.5.2).

4.5.1 Prediction Accuracy

To assess the prediction accuracy, a random sample of 10M IPs was collected. The relative ratio, *predicted size / estimated size*, is shown in Fig. 5, where each circle represents one, or multiple overlapping IP(s).

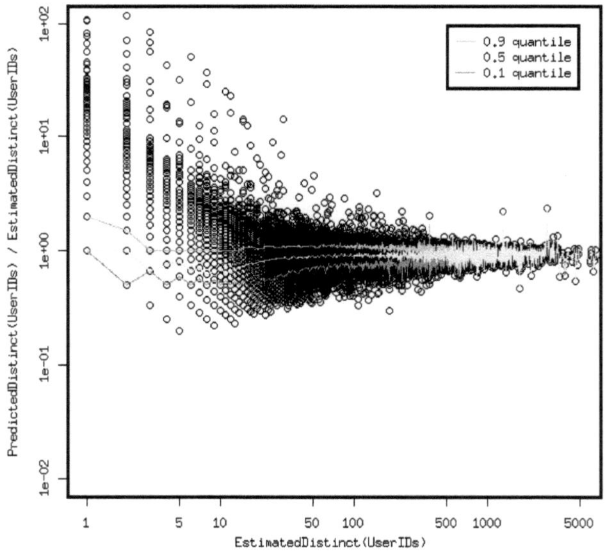

Figure 5: The relative ratio in predicting query sizes by the estimated sizes.

98% of the absolute errors are between −4 and 2, and 54% of the predictions are exact. The mean absolute error

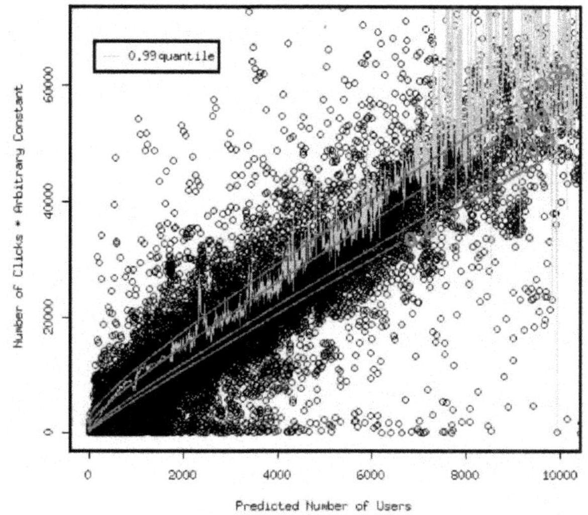

Figure 6: The CDF of a given number of clicks from a given number of users in red lines. The empirical CDF of a given number of clicks from a given estimated number of users in blue.

is −0.149. All the quantiles with a step of 0.001 were calculated. The topmost four 0.001 quantiles are 5282, 5, 4 and 3, and the bottommost quantiles are −6870, −12, −8, −7. Based on Whois databases, the IPs that caused the largest absolute errors belonged to large commercial ISPs with several netblocks and diverse customer bases. These IPs probably changed sizes due to reassignment.

From Fig. 5, among all the predicted sizes, 98% were within a factor of 2 of the estimated size. The topmost four 0.001 quantiles of the relative ratios were 5283, 4, 4 and 3, and the bottommost quantiles were 0.2, 0.4, 0.4 and 0.44.

Since the largest relative ratio was as high as 5283, it was concerning that reassignments of IPs and flash crowds can result in predicted sizes that are significantly smaller than the estimated sizes. The *IP-period* instances[9] showing this behavior in these three months were counted. No IP showed this behavior for more than 2 periods, owing to the 2 period *lookahead delay* discussed in the framework cycle (§ 2) and the *Combiner* algorithm sanity checks (§ 4.4). Only 33 *IP-period* instances, , composed of 21 IP's, had a relative ratio greater than 500. Some IP's spanned 2 periods. Only ≈ 4700 *IP-period* instances from only ≈ 3000 IPs had a relative ratio greater than 100. These anomalies are very insignificant compared to the number of IPs observed over three months.

The relative ratio is broken down by the estimated sizes in Fig. 5. The comparisons of measured vs estimated sizes are quantitatively similar to the comparisons of estimated vs predicted sizes. The line that passes through the y-axis point 1 with slope 0 represents perfect predictions. Clearly, the median *quantile-curve* is almost overlapping with the perfect predictions line for medium and large values of estimated sizes. In addition, 80% of the predictions lie in the vicinity of perfect predictions. Most importantly, the accuracy of the predictions increases as the estimated size increases, where the accuracy is more operationally desired.

4.5.2 Predictions Coverage

For predictions to be effective, they should have high *coverage*, i.e., a high ratio of the IPs in the traffic have predictions. There are several factors that contribute to the predictions coverage, such as the stability of the estimated sizes of the IPs, the diversity of the IPs that visit the application provider, the length of the estimation period and the length of the sliding windows of estimates used for prediction.

The coverage of the three-month experiments dropped below 95% on two days, and never dropped below 93%. The coverage of the click sizes was also examined. The click-coverage averaged around 65%, and never dropped below 61%. Since the number of queries is at least one order of magnitude more than the clicks, the query traffic is expected to come from more IPs, which better cover the IP space than the click traffic. Hence, the probability any IP generates traffic on two distinct *IP-period* is higher for queries than clicks, which explains the higher query-coverage.

5. THRESHOLD-BASED FILTERING

Thanks to the high accuracy and coverage of the estimation and prediction phases discussed in § 3 and § 4, respectively, a threshold-based traffic filter, *RT-Abuse-Dtct(.)*, was built based on the predicted sizes of the IPs. The ad click filter built at Google caps the number of clicks per IP at a specific threshold and filters any extra clicks.

5.1 Selecting the Filtering Threshold

The distribution of the number of trusted users (cookies) who generate N traffic log entries per period is reused when setting the filtering thresholds. Normalizing this distribution yields the PDF of the number of entries from the average trusted user. This PDF is convolved with itself M times to get the distribution of the number of entries from M users[10]. This distribution is then numerically integrated to produce a CDF of the number of entires from M users.

For the application of ad click filtering, the number of trusted users who click N times per period is used. The shape of this distribution is extremely similar to the corresponding query distribution in Fig. 2. The CDF contour lines for the 0.8, 0.9, 0.99 and 0.999 quantiles were calculated and are plotted in Fig. 6 in red for $1 \leq M \leq 10K$. The *q-quantile-curve* at size M indicates the number of clicks M trusted users should not exceed with probability q. For instance, from Fig. 6, 99% of the IPs with an estimated size of 2000 should generate clicks less than ≈ 1480[11]. Using a *q-quantile-curve* as the threshold, only $1 - q$ of IPs with any given size have their clicks filtered. Therefore, q can be set based on how aggressive the filter is designed to be.

To check the combined accuracy of the estimation and prediction phases, the numbers of clicks from IPs with predicted sizes were analyzed. A sample of 1M IPs were selected at random, and their numbers of clicks are plotted in Fig. 6 with the 0.99-*quantile-curve* plotted in blue. Comparing the red and blue curves in Fig. 6 shows the theoretical and the empirical calculations of the 0.99-*quantile-curve* agree. This proves the accuracy of the proposed framework and the threshold selection mechanism.

Notice that while models exclusively built from the traffic of trusted users may be biased, reusing the distribution of the activity of the trusted users to select the filtering

[9] An *IP-period* instance is the size of one IP in one period.

[10] This convolution is done by performing Fast Fourier Transform (FFT) on the single-user distribution, raising the result to the Mth power, and taking the inverse FFT.

[11] The number of clicks is scaled by an arbitrary constant.

threshold mitigates such bias. Practically, both modeling and traffic filtering are done in the domain of trusted users.

5.2 Filter Evaluation

A sensitivity analysis on the parameter q was carried out. The value of q was varied and the filtered traffic as well as the false positives were measured. For the purpose of this paper, the false positives are calculated as the ratio of conversion rate from the tagged clicks to the conversion rate from all the ad traffic[12]. A conversion is a trusted post-click activity, like a purchase from the advertisers. While conversions are useful for evaluating filters, they are less useful for directly detecting fraud in real time, since they are scarce and delayed events.

When q was set to 0.999, the filtering rate was significantly higher than $1 - q$. Most of the filtered traffic entries were false positives. As q approached 0.99, the filtering rate was slightly higher than $1 - q$, with a low ratio of false positives. While the absolute number of false positives did not decrease as q decreased, the ratio of the false positives to the filtered traffic dropped drastically. As q approached 0.95, both the absolute number of false positives and their ratio to the filtered traffic increased quickly due to aggressive filtering. Hence, the threshold quantile was set at 0.99.

The discovered false positives were consistently due to unforeseen reassignments of IPs and flash crowds. For instance, the top 10 IPs causing false positives had predicted sizes significantly smaller than their estimated sizes. These false positives were reduced significantly by detecting abrupt legitimate size changes early on using the prediction sanity checks discussed in § 4.4.

The overlap between proposed filters and existing filters is a useful metric customarily measured at Google. Multiple filtering layers provide defense in depth against abuse. Among the first 50M clicks tagged by the filter, 99.55% of them overlapped with other filters. While the marginal gain of this filter is small, the filter is highly valuable as a very accurate safety net and as a verifier of other filters.

The false negatives, the clicks tagged only by other filters, decreased monotonically with q. Most of the false negatives occurred due to two reasons: botnet attacks with few clicks per IP, and attacks from IPs with no predicted sizes. To address the first reason, we are currently generalizing this filter to multi-dimensions. We are investigating thresholds on the number of clicks per IP across some dimension(s), such as the query term. This allows for setting tighter thresholds at a finer granularity. For the second reason of false negatives, we analyzed the coverage of the predicted click sizes. While the coverage of the predicted click sizes was around 65%, the number of clicks whose IPs had predicted sizes was roughly 78% due to the non-uniform distribution of the number of clicks from different IPs. To increase the recall of the filter, we are currently evaluating using a default high threshold for IPs with no predicted sizes.

The filter was deployed on all the ad traffic at Google, and had a significant recall of all the clicks tagged by all the filters. Analyzing and monitoring the filtered traffic of the deployed filters is customary at Google to retune the thresholds based on the natural changes in global traffic patterns. Among these 50M clicks, the rate of false positives was $\approx$ 1.4%, which surpasses many other deployed filters.

[12]A significant ratio of advertisers share conversion information with Google.

For the sake of comparison, we simulated a naïve filter that does not consider the sizes of the IPs. It tags clicks from IPs based on a fixed threshold. It was difficult to force the naïve filter to have exactly the same recall of the developed filter. However, to achieve comparable recall, the threshold of the naïve filter had to be set for aggressive tagging, which yielded a false positive rate of 37%.

6. RELATED WORK

To the best of our knowledge, this is the first work that mines Internet traffic to estimate sizes of IPs. This work complements the prior work on the dynamics of IPs and classifying them [2, 4, 5, 9]. Only some of the recent work on combating abusive traffic based on the source IPs [1, 10, 11, 13, 15, 19, 20] have considered the nature of IPs, e.g., the rate of reassignment, but not the sizes of IPs.

The work that is most related to estimating sizes of IPs deals with counting the hosts behind NAT devices [2, 4, 9, 12]. Bellovin presented a technique for counting the hosts behind a NAT using the `IPid` field in [2]. The technique relies on the host operating system sequentially incrementing the `IPid` field for each successive packet. Hence, the number of unique `IPid` streams from a specific IP can be used as an estimate of the number of hosts. This technique is limited by the resolution of the `IPid` field. Even more, the `IPid` field is not incremented sequentially in modern operating systems. Furthermore, in the measurements reported in [4], less than 5% of the sampled NATs sent multiple `IPid` streams.

The focus of [4] was identifying middle-boxes and classifying them as NAT devices and Proxies by learning the internal IPs of the hosts using active web content. However, this technique underestimates the sizes by the ratio of users not collaborating with the research effort. It also fails if a NAT box has a hierarchy of NAT devices behind it, where collisions, and hence under-estimation can happen.

In [9], Kohno *et al.* investigated using clock skews for identifying hosts behind NAT devices, where the clock skew is the ratio of the actual clock frequency to the nominal one. Typically, the clock skew of a host is stable within 1-2 $\mu s/s$. Given that the difference between the clock skews of different hosts goes up to 50 $\mu s/s$, hosts can be fingerprinted by their clock skews. The number of hosts behind a NAT device can then be passively estimated by counting distinct fingerprints from this NAT device. However, the accuracy of this technique is highly limited by the collisions between clock skew identities. For instance, [12] could only extract 4-6 bits of host identification using clock skews.

This work is different in scope, goal and methodology from these in [2, 4, 9]. The proposed techniques are not restricted to NAT devices to achieve high IP coverage. The proposed framework neither probes machines for pseudo-identification, nor does it deploy active content, which can be intrusive, and is hence worrisome for some users. The goal of this work is filtering abusive traffic according to the source IPs, while preserving the user privacy.

7. CONCLUSION

This paper is an example of how to mine traffic at an aggregate level in order to balance combating abusive traffic and preserving user privacy. It shares our experience:

1. building statistical models for estimating the number of application users behind IPs,

2. devising a sizes prediction algorithm, and
3. setting traffic thresholds based on the predicted sizes.

The framework has been deployed on Google live traffic for combating click fraud. While sharing this new framework could be inspiring, details of the signals and parameters used were concealed to preserve their effectiveness.

The proposed framework is general, and can be applied to a wide spectrum of applications to estimate a population of users who are not permanently identified. The framework only assumes the existence of a body of trusted users, whose activities are used to build models for size estimation. These models are known only to the application/service providers. When applied for abuse detection, the framework leverages such knowledge to give an advantage to the providers over the attackers in the arms race. The traffic filtering is also general, since most of the filtering is threshold-based, and is hence agnostic to the traffic nature.

Our future work focuses on applying the framework to more types of abuse, such as excessive service sign-ups, which have less traffic and lower coverage in the IP space. One approach being explored is using IP classification techniques [5, 19, 20] to improve the filtering coverage in the lack of high IP space coverage in the traffic. In addition, we are currently exploring other more sophisticated abuse detection and combating approaches that compare how the distribution of sizes of IPs per entity, e.g., the query term, to the aggregate background distribution of sizes of IPs.

Acknowledgment

We thank Adel El-Atawy, Adrian Isles, Amgad Zeitoun, Algis Rudys, Christos Faloutsos, John Hawkins, Kourosh Gharachorloo, Michael McNally, Mohamed Elfeky and the rest of the ad traffic quality team for the useful discussions and help with the deployment.

8. REFERENCES

[1] D. Anderson, C. Fleizach, S. Savage, and G. Voelker. Spamscatter: Characterizing Internet Scam Hosting Infrastructure. In *Proceedings of the 16th USENIX Security Symposium*, pages 135–148, 2007.

[2] S. Bellovin. A Technique for Counting NATted hosts. In *Proceedings of the 2nd ACM SIGCOMM IMW Workshop on Internet measurment*, pages 267–272, 2002.

[3] P. Bloomfield. *Fourier Analysis of Time Series: An Introduction.* Wiley-IEEE, 2004.

[4] M. Casado and M. Freedman. Peering Through the Shroud: The Effect of Edge Opacity on IP-Based Client Identification. In *Proceedings of the 4th ACM/USENIX NSDI Symposium on Networked Systems Design and Implementation*, pages 173–186, 2007.

[5] M. Freedman, M. Vutukuru, N. Feamster, and H. Balakrishnan. Geographic Locality of IP Prefixes. In *Proceedings of the 5th ACM SIGCOMM IMC Conference on Internet Measurement*, pages 13–13, 2005.

[6] J. Friedman. Multivariate Adaptive Regression Splines. *Annals of Statistics*, 19(1), 1991.

[7] J. Hamilton. *Time series analysis.* Princeton University Press, illustrated edition, 1994.

[8] R. Koenker and K. Hallock. Quantile Regression. *Journal of Economic Perspectives*, 15(4):143–156, 2001.

[9] T. Kohno, A. Broido, and K. Claffy. Remote Physical Device Fingerprinting. In *Proceedings of the 26th IEEE S&P Symposium on Security and Privacy*, pages 211–225, 2005. An extended version appeared in the IEEE Transactions on Dependable and Secure Computing, 2(2):93–108, 2005.

[10] A. Metwally, D. Agrawal, and A. El Abbadi. DETECTIVES: DETEcting Coalition hiT Inflation attacks in adVertising nEtworks Streams. In *Proceedings of the 16th WWW International World Wide Web Conference*, pages 241–250, 2007.

[11] A. Metwally, F. Emekçi, D. Agrawal, and A. El Abbadi. SLEUTH: Single-pubLisher attack dEtection Using correlaTion Hunting. *Proceedings of the VLDB Endowment*, 1(2):1217–1228, 2008.

[12] S. Murdoch. Hot or Not: Revealing Hidden Services by their Clock Skew. In *Proceedings of the 13th ACM CCS conference on Computer and Communications Security*, pages 27–36, 2006.

[13] T. Peng, C. Leckie, and K. Ramamohanarao. Proactively Detecting Distributed Denial of Service Attacks Using Source IP Address Monitoring. In *Proceedings of the 3rd International IFIP-TC6 Networking Conference*, pages 771–782, 2004.

[14] R. Pike, S. Dorward, R. Griesemer, and S. Quinlan. Interpreting the Data: Parallel Analysis with Sawzall. *Scientific Programming*, 13(4):277–298, 2005.

[15] A. Ramachandran, N. Feamster, and S. Vempala. Filtering Spam with Behavioral Blacklisting. In *Proceedings of the 14th ACM CCS Conference on Computer and Communications Security*, pages 342–351, 2007.

[16] G. Snedecor and W. Cochran. *Statistical Methods.* Wiley, John & Sons, Incorporated, eighth edition, 1991.

[17] D. West. Updating Mean and Variance Estimates: An Improved Method. *Communications of the ACM*, 22(9):532–535, 1979.

[18] Whois.net. Domain Research Tool. http://www.whois.net.

[19] Y. Xie, F. Yu, K. Achan, E. Gillum, M. Goldszmidt, and T. Wobber. How Dynamic are IP Addresses? In *Proceedings of the 22nd ACM SIGCOMM Conference on Applications, Technologies, Architectures, and Protocols for Computer Communications*, pages 301–312, 2007.

[20] L. Zhuang, J. Dunagan, D. Simon, H. Wang, and J. Tygar. Characterizing Botnets from Email Spam Records. In *Proceedings of the 1st Usenix LEET Workshop on Large-Scale Exploits and Emergent Threats*, pages 1–9, 2008.

APPENDIX

A. CYCLE ENHANCEMENTS

Some enhancements are applicable to the basic cycle in § 2 to reduce the *lookahead delay* introduced by the estimation phase. First, we introduce $Est_d(p)$ that divides the periods into d sub-periods, $p_1, \ldots, p_d$ of length $\frac{l}{d}$. Hence, preliminary processing can be done once a sub-period ends, and the intermediary results from all the d sub-periods can be combined together into $estimates\text{-}table_p$. The lower bound on the *lookahead delay* is hence reduced from $l\left(1 + \left\lceil \frac{|Est(.)|+|Prd(.)|}{l} \right\rceil\right)$ to $l + (l/d)\left\lceil \frac{|Est_d(.)|+|Prd(.)|}{(l/d)} \right\rceil$[13].

The estimation period can also be defined as a sliding window over sub-periods. Hence, $d-1$ sub-periods would be shared by any two consecutive periods. This amortizes the preliminary processing on several cycles. As d increases, $Est_d(.)$ is expected to run in less time than $Est(.)$ as long as the benefits of producing preliminary results and amortizing their processing outweigh the cost of combining them.

The main advantage of the sliding window model is producing estimates roughly d times more frequently than the basic cycle. Let $PrelimEst_d(.)$ be the preliminary processing of any sub-period, and $Comb_d(.)$ be the combining of d the sub-periods results, then the sliding window model reduces the *lookahead delay* to $(l/d)\left(1 + \left\lceil \frac{|PrelimEst_d(.)|+|Comb_d(.)|+|Prd(.)|}{(l/d)} \right\rceil\right)$. Therefore, for low traffic-volume applications, l can be increased proportionally to produce sound estimates from more traffic. Experimentation is needed to set the value of l and d based on the IPs' coverage in the traffic, and the processing power available.

[13] Each process run time is assumed consistent over time.

Data-driven Multi-touch Attribution Models

Xuhui Shao*
Turn, Inc.
835 Main St.
Redwood City, CA 94063
xuhui.shao@turn.com

Lexin Li†
Department of Statistics
North Carolina State University
Raleigh, NC 27695
li@stat.ncsu.edu

ABSTRACT

In digital advertising, attribution is the problem of assigning credit to one or more advertisements for driving the user to the desirable actions such as making a purchase. Rather than giving all the credit to the last ad a user sees, multi-touch attribution allows more than one ads to get the credit based on their corresponding contributions. Multi-touch attribution is one of the most important problems in digital advertising, especially when multiple media channels, such as search, display, social, mobile and video are involved. Due to the lack of statistical framework and a viable modeling approach, true data-driven methodology does not exist today in the industry. While predictive modeling has been thoroughly researched in recent years in the digital advertising domain, the attribution problem focuses more on accurate and stable interpretation of the influence of each user interaction to the final user decision rather than just user classification. Traditional classification models fail to achieve those goals.

In this paper, we first propose a bivariate metric, one measures the variability of the estimate, and the other measures the accuracy of classifying the positive and negative users. We then develop a bagged logistic regression model, which we show achieves a comparable classification accuracy as a usual logistic regression, but a much more stable estimate of individual advertising channel contributions. We also propose an intuitive and simple probabilistic model to directly quantify the attribution of different advertising channels. We then apply both the bagged logistic model and the probabilistic model to a real-world data set from a multi-channel advertising campaign for a well-known consumer software and services brand. The two models produce consistent general conclusions and thus offer useful cross-validation. The results of our attribution models also shed several important insights that have been validated by the advertising team.

We have implemented the probabilistic model in the production advertising platform of the first author's company, and plan to implement the bagged logistic regression in the next product release. We believe availability of such data-driven multi-touch attribution metric and models is a breakthrough in the digital advertising industry.

*Xuhui Shao is Chief Technology Officer, Turn, Inc.

†Lexin Li is the corresponding author and Associate Professor, Department of Statistics, North Carolina State University.

KDD'11, August 21–24, 2011, San Diego, California, USA.

Categories and Subject Descriptors

I.6.5 [**Computing Methodologies**]: Simulation and Modeling, Model Development

General Terms

Algorithms, Performance, Theory

Keywords

Digital Advertising, Multi-touch Attribution Model, Bagged Logistic Regression

1. INTRODUCTION

Digital advertising started 16 years ago as a new media where traditional print ads can appear [1]. When internet continues to grow with an exploding rate, advertising industry embraced digital advertising and has made it a $40 Billion a year mega industry in US alone. Digital advertising's appeal is not only in its ability to precisely target different groups of consumers with customized ad messages and ad placements, but probably more importantly in its ability to track responses and performances almost instantaneously.

Advertising campaigns are often launched across multiple channels. Traditional advertising channels include outdoor billboard, TV, radio, newspapers and magazines, and direct mailing. Digital advertising channels include search, online display, social, video, mobile and email. In this article, we focus on the digital advertising channels. Typically multiple advertising channels have delivered advertisement impressions to a user. When the user then makes a purchase decision or signs up to a service being advertised, the advertiser wants to determine which ads have contributed to the user's decision. This step is critical in completing the feedback loop so that one can analyze, report and optimize an advertising campaign. This problem of interpreting the influence of advertisements to the user's decision process is called the attribution problem.

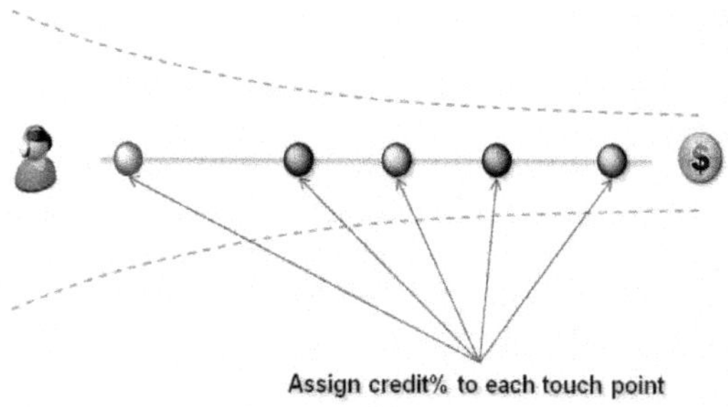

Figure 1: An illustration of multi-touch attribution problem.

The goal of attribute modeling is to pin-point the credit assignment of each positive user to one or more advertising touch point, which is illustrated in Figure 1. The resulting user-level assignment can be aggregated along different dimensions including media channel to derive overall insights. Attribution modeling is not to be confused with marketing mix modeling (MMM), which is limited to the temporal analysis of marketing channels and can not perform any inference at the user level or any dimensions other than marketing channel.

To determine which media channel or which ad is to be credited, initially a simple rule was developed and quickly adopted by the online advertising industry: The last ad the user clicked on before he made the purchase or sign up decision, or say, conversion, gets 100% of the credit. This "last-click win" model was extended to include "last-view win" if none of the ads was clicked within a reasonable time window before user conversion. We call both these two models "last-touch attribution" (LTA), where "touch" or touch point is defined to be any ad impression, click or advertising related interaction the user has experienced from the advertiser. The last-touch attribution model is simple. However, it completely ignores the influences of all ad impressions except the last one. It is a highly flawed model as pointed out by [2].

Alternatively, the concept of multi-touch attribution (MTA) model has been recently proposed, where more than one touch point can each have a fraction of the credit based on the true influence each touch point has on the outcome, i.e., user's conversion decision. Atlas institute, a division of Microsoft Advertising first proposed the notion of MTA [2]. However, in that paper and other related research from Microsoft Atlas, there is no proposal for how to assign the percentage of credit statistically based on the campaign data.

Clearsaleing is a consulting company specialized in attribution analysis, whose attribution model assigns equal fraction of credits to the first and the last touch point, and collectively all the touch points in between [3]. While a data-driven custom model is described as available upon request, the methodology of the custom model is not publicized.

Another company, C3 Metric, also offers a rule-based MTA model [4]. But like [3], their model assigns credit to certain touch points simply based on the temporal order of touch points and with fixed percentages. In our opinion, because user's decision process is largely dependent on the advertiser, the product offer, and how advertising messages and creative design are structured, a desirable attribution model should be campaign-specific and be driven by a solid statistical analysis of user response data.

In addition to the lack of a true data-driven MTA model, a good metric to evaluate different MTA models is not available either. Intuitively, a good MTA model should have a high degree of accuracy in correctly classifying a user as positive (with a conversion action) or negative (without a conversion action). Equally or more important in digital advertising is that, a good MTA model should provide a stable estimation of individual variable's (for example, media channel) contribution. Unlike predictive models, the stability of the estimation is especially important here because attribution model determines the performance metric for the ad campaign. Every advertising company and every advertising tactic ultimately are judged by the performance metric set forth in the attribution model. Having stable and reproducible result is by definition what a performance metric needs to be. Ideally the attribution model should be easy to interpret as the results of attribution analysis are often used to derive insights to the ad campaign and its optimization strategy.

Although in recent years predictive modeling has been thoroughly researched in the digital advertising domain, for example in [5] and [6], the focus has been on the classification accuracy. The resulting models, many generated from a black-box type predictive approach, are very hard to interpret. Furthermore, little attention has been paid to the stability issue of the variable contribution estimate. There is also the problem of variable correlation when one tries to interpret the model coefficients directly, which was discussed in section 4.4.2 of [7].

In this paper, we first propose a new bivariate metric. One component of this metric measures the variability of the estimate, and the other measures the accuracy of classifying the positive and negative users. We then develop a bagged logistic regression model, which we show achieves a comparable classification accuracy as a usual logistic regression, but a much more stable estimate of individual variable contributions. We also propose a simple and intuitive probabilistic model to compute the attribution of different variables based on a combination of first and second order conditional probabilities. We evaluate both models using the proposed bivariate metric, and find the two generate consistent results. We then analyze a large advertising campaign data set, which has 72.5 million anonymized users with over 2 billion ad impressions coming from search, display, social, email and video channels over a four-week period. As for implementation, the probabilistic model has been deployed in the production advertising system of the first author's company. The bagged logistic regression model is currently being developed for future product release in the production system.

The rest of the paper is organized as follows. We present the bivariate metric in Section 2, and the two data-driven multi-touch attribution models in Section 3. We evaluate the empirical performance the proposed models in Section 4. We conclude the paper with a discussion.

2. A BIVARIATE METRIC

It is always of interest to identify if a user is to make a

purchase or sign up for a service based on his exposure to various advertisement channels. This is a typical classification problem, where the outcome is binary, with positive meaning a user is to make a purchase action and negative meaning otherwise, and the covariates are the number of touch points of different channels. Towards that end, we employ the usual misclassification error rate as part of an evaluation metric for an MTA model.

On the other hand, human behavior is complex and the user data are highly correlated. As a consequence, a simple MTA model, e.g., a usual logistic regression, could have highly variable estimate which would make the model difficult to interpret. In addition, the high collinearity in attributes also causes strong variables to suppress weaker, correlated variables as described in Section 4.4.2 of [7]. Therefore we aim to capture the variability of an MTA model in our model evaluation metric. Towards that goal, we employ the notion of standard deviation and also take advantage of the fact that the advertising campaign data almost always have a large number of users.

More specifically, we first obtain a random subset of samples of both positive and negative users as a training data set, then another random subset as a testing data set. To avoid having too few positive users in the samples, we fix the ratio of positive versus negative users. In our numerical analysis, we have experimented this ratio with 1 : 1 and 1 : 4 and the two yield very similar results. For brevity we only report the results based on 1 : 4 ratio below. We then fit an MTA model to the training data. We record the contribution of each advertisement channel, i.e., the coefficient estimate, from the fitted MTA model. We also evaluate the fitted model on the independent testing data and record the misclassification error rate.

We then repeat the above process multiple times in order to compute the standard deviation of individual coefficient estimates across multiple repetitions. We report the average of all standard deviations across different channels as the variability measure (V-metric), and the average of misclassification error rates across data repetitions as the accuracy measure (A-metric). We evaluate an MTA model based upon the bivariate metric of both the variability and the accuracy (the V-A-metric). A small A-metric indicates that the model under investigation has a high accuracy of predicting the active or inactive user, while a small V-metric indicates that the model has a stable estimate. Ideally a good MTA model should have both metrics small.

3. MULTI-TOUCH ATTRIBUTION MODELS

3.1 A Bagged Logistic Regression

There have been intensive research on classification modeling in the literature. Some well known examples include support vector machines [8], neural networks [10], and other unique methods designed for online advertising in [6] and [9]. See [7], [10] and [11] for a good review. Most of those methods generate a complex model, some of which are of a black-box type. The resulting classification boundary is rather flexible, so it can achieve a competent classification accuracy. However, in attribution modeling, it is more of a concern to obtain a model that is stable and relatively easy to interpret, so that advertisers can develop a clear strategy to optimize their resource allocations and optimization among multiple advertising channels.

The bagging approach as a meta learning method was first proposed in [12]. One of the most popular bagged approaches is random forest [13] where decision tree models are stacked to increase performance and robustness. Bagged logistic regression is not of much interest in terms of predictive modeling, since it is more productive to combine nonlinear models in order to increase the prediction accuracy. It has been shown to be outperformed by the tree-based method [14]. On the other hand, the bagging approach possesses the ability to isolate variable collinearity, as discussed in Section 15.4.1 of [7].

In our context of attribution modeling, we combine the commonly used logistic regression, which is simple and easy to interpret, and the bagging idea, which is to help reduce the estimation variability due to the highly correlated covariates. This results in the bagged logistic regression, which retains the ease of interpretation of a simple logistic model, whereas achieving a stable and reproducible estimation result. More specifically, the bagged logistic regression is fitted using the following steps.

Step 1. For a given data set, sample a proportion p_s of all the sample observations and a proportion p_c of all the covariates. Fit a logistic regression model on the sampled covariates and the sampled data. Record the estimated coefficients.

Step 2. Repeat Step 1 for M iterations, and the final coefficient estimate for each covariate is taken as the average of estimated coefficients in M iterations.

The sample proportion p_s, the covariate proportion p_c, and the number of iterations M are the parameters of the bagged logistic regression. We will examine their choices in detail in Section 4. Our observations are that, for a range of values of p_s and p_c that are not close to either 0 or 1, the bagged logistic regression yield similar results. Besides, the results are not overly sensitive to the choice of M. When evaluating the model using the proposed V-A-metric, we find that, the bagged logistic regression achieves a very similar misclassification rate (A-metric) but enjoys a much smaller variability (V-metric) compared to a usual logistic regression, which is desirable for attribution modeling.

3.2 A Simple Probabilistic Model

In addition to the bagged logistic regression model, we also develop a probabilistic model based on a combination of first and second-order conditional probabilities. This new model is even simpler than a logistic model. Such a model simplicity translates into both low estimation variability and ease of interpretation, meanwhile it trades off accuracy. As such, compared to the bagged logistic model, we expect the new model would achieve a smaller V-metric but a larger A-metric. Our numerical analysis confirms this expectation.

The probabilistic model is generated using the following steps:

Step 1. For a given data set, compute the empirical probability of the main factors,

$$P(y|x_i) = \frac{N_{positive}(x_i)}{N_{positive}(x_i) + N_{negative}(x_i)} \tag{1}$$

and the pair-wise conditional probabilities

$$P(y|x_i, x_j) = \frac{N_{positive}(x_i, x_j)}{N_{positive}(x_i, x_j) + N_{negative}(x_i, x_j)}, \quad (2)$$

for $i \neq j$. Here y is a binary outcome variable denoting a conversion event (purchase or sign-up), and $x_i, i = 1, \ldots, p$, denote p different advertising channels. $N_{positive}(x_i)$ and $N_{positive}(x_i)$ denote the number of positive or negative users exposed to channel i, respectively, and $N_{positive}(x_i, x_j)$ and $N_{negative}(x_i, x_j)$ denote the number of positive or negative users exposed to both channels i and j.

Step 2. The contribution of channel i is then computed at each positive user level as:

$$\begin{aligned} C(x_i) &= p(y|x_i) + \frac{1}{2N_{j\neq i}} \sum_{j\neq i} \Big\{ p(y|x_i, x_j) \\ &\quad - p(y|x_i) - p(y|x_j) \Big\}, \end{aligned} \quad (3)$$

where $N_{j\neq i}$ denotes the total number of j's not equal to i. In this case it equals to N-1, or the total number of channels minus one (the channel i itself) for a particular user.

The model is essentially a second-order probability estimation. Due to the similarly designed advertising messages and user's exposure to multiple media channels, there are a fair amount of overlapping between the influences of different touch points. Therefore it is critically important to include the second-order interaction terms in the probability model. Theoretically we can go to the third-order, fourth-order interactions or higher. However, the number of observations with the same third-order interaction drops significantly for even a data set as large as the one analyzed in Section 4. Therefore, it is of little practical use to attempt to estimate the empirical probability with the third or higher order. Furthermore, we make an important assumption in the probability model in that the net effect of the second-order interaction goes evenly to each of the two factors involved. Based on the Occam's Razor principle, we feel this is the minimal assumption we need to make without any data evidence to suggest otherwise. Focusing on the first and second-order terms also helps to reduce any assumption to a minimum – for example, trying to split the effect in the third-order interactions can be more hazardous than in the second-order interactions.

In Section 4, we will employ both the bagged logistic regression model and the probabilistic model to analyze the same advertising campaign data set for overall attribution results across all main media channels. Our results show that, while there are small differences, the general conclusion is consistent between the two models.

The reason that we consider more than one model is the following. Digital advertising relies on a fair amount of subjectivity. Having two different modeling approaches give advertiser the flexibility to choose. The bagged logistic regression model is more accurate and more flexible with a larger number of covariates. It is slightly more difficult to interpret. On the other hand, the probabilistic model is less accurate but much more intuitive to interpret. In addition, the result from both models can cross-validate the general conclusion reached in the overall advertising campaign analysis.

4. NUMERICAL ANALYSIS

4.1 Data Background

In this section, we analyze a large advertising campaign data set using both proposed methods. This is a 2010 advertising campaign of a consumer software and services company. The campaign ran over a four week period. The size of the data set is over 300GB compressed. We sampled one-third, i.e., 72.5 million anonymous users. In total these 72.5 million users received over 2 billion ad impressions coming from search, display, social, email and video channels over a four-week period. Because search advertising is priced as pay-per-click model, only search clicks are reported for each user. Furthermore, more than a dozen advertising networks or equivalent media buying channels are involved in delivering identically designed advertisements. In our study, there are 39 channels in total. It is an unresolved but critically important problem for the advertiser to determine the true effectiveness of each media buying channels. This attribution analysis is not only important for ranking the effectiveness of the channels, but also in deriving insights so that different optimization tactic can be deployed under different circumstances. We apply the bagged logistic regression model and the simple probabilistic model to analyze this data.

4.2 Bagged Logistic Regression Analysis

In this section we examine the empirical performance of the bagged logistic regression model, and compare with the usual logistic regression using the V-A-metric. In addition, we also examine the choice of the tuning parameters in the bagged logistic regression. The simulation setup is based upon the following scheme.

Step 1. Randomly sample a subset of N users as the training data. We choose $N = 50,000$, and the ratio between the active and inactive users is $1:4$. (The results for the ratio of $1:1$ are very similar, so are omitted for brevity.) This leads to 10,000 randomly selected active users and 40,000 inactive users.

Step 2. Randomly sample another independent subset of N users as the testing data.

Step 3. Fit the bagged logistic regression to the training data, with the pre-specified sample proportion p_s and the covariate proportion p_c, and obtain the coefficient estimate.

Step 4. Fit the usual logistic regression to the training data, and obtain the coefficient estimate.

Step 5. Evaluate the misclassification error rate of both regression models on the testing data.

Step 6. Repeat Steps 1 to 5 for $S = 100$ times. Compute the V-A-metric for both regression models. Because each sampling is random, all data have chance of being selected as training or testing data.

We set the sample proportion as $p_s = 0.25, 0.5$ and 0.75, and the covariate proportion as $p_c = 0.25, 0.5$ and 0.75, respectively. Table 1 reports the results. It is seen from the table that, when p_s and p_c are both close to zero, the bagged

Table 1: **Comparison of the bagged logistic regression (BLR) and the usual logistic regression (LR) in terms of the V-A-metric.**

			p_c					
			0.25		0.50		0.75	
			V-metric	A-metric	V-metric	A-metric	V-metric	A-metric
p_s	0.25	LR	2.053	0.091	1.934	0.091	2.006	0.091
		BLR	0.257	0.142	0.688	0.093	0.824	0.091
	0.50	LR	1.913	0.091	2.115	0.091	1.972	0.091
		BLR	0.284	0.147	0.672	0.093	1.039	0.091
	0.75	LR	1.868	0.091	2.053	0.091	1.968	0.091
		BLR	0.327	0.147	0.743	0.093	1.294	0.091

logistic model achieves a substantially smaller V-metric but also a worse A-metric compared to the usual logistic model. When p_s and p_c take some value in the middle range of zero and one, e.g., when $p_s = 0.5$ and $p_c = 0.5$, we clearly see that the bagged model achieves a variability measure that is much smaller than the variability of the usual logistic model, whereas the accuracy measure of the two models become almost identical. As p_s and p_c increase closer to one, the bagged model exhibits a A-metric that is essentially identical to that of the usual logistic model, but with a lower V-metric. As such we recommend to choose p_s and p_c to take values around 0.5 if both the variability and the accuracy are of the concern. For the number of iterations M, we have experimented with a number of values and observe the same qualitative patterns. For brevity, we only report in Table 1 the results based on $M = 1000$ iterations. We also note that the V-metric for the usual logistic regression varies a little although it does not depend on the varying parameters p_s and p_c. This is due to the random sampling variation, which to some extent reflects how variable the usual logistic model can be for the advertising data — even a random subset of samples would cause visible estimation variation.

4.3 Probabilistic Model Analysis

We next apply the simple probabilistic model to the same data set, and we evaluate the model with the V-A-metric. The resulting V-metric is 0.026, whereas the A-metric is 0.115. Comparing with the results in Table 1, we see that the probabilistic model achieves a very low variability due to its deterministic logic and simple model structure. On the other hand, its misclassification rate is higher than the bagged logistic model, which again is intuitively attributable to the low model complexity. These observations reflect the well known bias-variance tradeoff. Although more complicated models, e.g., a higher order probabilistic model, could improve estimation accuracy, it would also induce higher variation. Besides, higher order models are often computationally infeasible for ad data of such a scale.

We also compare the bagged logistic regression model and the simple probabilistic model in terms of MTA user-level assignment. For the bagged logistic model, we take the linear term $\hat{\beta}' x_i$ as the contribution of the channel i, where $\hat{\beta}$ denotes the coefficient estimate based on the bagged model. For the simple probabilistic model, we use equation (3) to compute user-level assignment for each channel. We resample the data $S = 100$ times, and show the box plot for the two models in Figure 2. First, we observe that the two models yield very similar patterns, suggesting a good agreement of the two models. Second, the bagged logistic regression model exhibits a relatively low variability across data re-sampling, whereas the simple probabilistic model shows a even smaller variability due to its model simplicity.

We also comment that, for ease of comparison, we choose the simplest feature construction scheme for all the models, i.e., we only encode the presence of each channel as a binary variable. The actual model can take on more complex features such as the creative design, web-site category, time of advertisement, frequency of the user's exposure to the same ad, among others. While the scaling constants are different, both proposed models have a computation complexity of $O(p^2 N)$, where p is the number of dimensions and N is the data sample size. These additional variables have been implemented in the production environment of the first author's company with the help of a cluster of multi-core Linux servers. The general conclusion reached in this paper extends well to those more complex models.

4.4 Interpretation of the Results

We presented the user-level attribution analysis to the advertising team. Some interesting observations were made when comparing the MTA model with advertiser's existing LTA model. The comparison is show in Table 2 for a subset of channels that are of particular interests to the advertising team. As seen from the table, for search click, email click, retail email click and social click, MTA and LTA get very similar numbers. Essentially these types of user initiated responses are both: highly correlated to the final purchase decision; and temporally occurring very close to the purchase decision.

On the other hand, the effectiveness of display ad networks are widely different. Overall, display ads (or banner ads) are undervalued by the LTA model since these ad impressions are usually further away in time from the purchase action than, say, search click. In addition, some ad networks (for example, Network G) are doing much better and some (for example, Network A) are doing much worse. This may be attributed to a trick some ad networks play in gaming the LTA model. It is called "cookie bombing" where large amount of low-cost almost invisible ads are shown to large amount of users. While these impressions do not have much real influence on user's decision, they appear quite often as the last ad impression user "sees" and therefore gets the credit from LTA model.

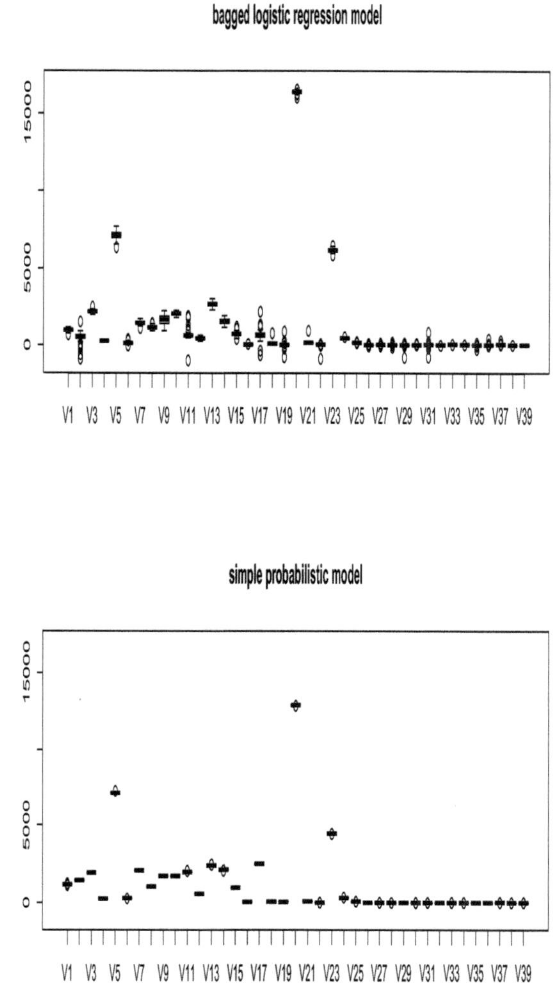

Figure 2: MTA user-level assignment for the bagged logistic regression model and the simple probabilistic model.

Our models provided some important insights that helped the advertiser to gauge the true effectiveness of each media channel and root out those gaming tactics. By this change alone, it is estimated that the advertiser can improve the overall campaign performance by as much as 30%.

5. DISCUSSION

In this article we proposed two statistical multi-touch attribution models. We also proposed a bivariate metric that can be used to evaluate and select a data-driven MTA model. We consider the main body of this work falls under descriptive or interpretive modeling, a field that has been largely ignored in comparison to predictive modeling. For digital advertising, having the right attribution model is critically important as it drives performance metric, advertising insights and optimization strategy. We believe our work makes some useful and unique contribution in this field.

Current state-of-the-art attribution models are represented by [2], [3] and [4]. Comparing to our proposed models, none of the existing publicized models are statistically derived from the advertising data in question. To apply those models, one needs to either rely on some universal rule that would result in identical assignment regardless of advertisers or user context ([3] and [4]), or one needs to come up with some subjective assignment rule oneself based on human intuition. By contrast, our methods are data-driven and are based upon the most relevant advertising data, and as such are believed to be more accurate and objective.

The probabilistic model is currently deployed in the production environment of the first author's company. It is the industry's first data-driven multi-touch attribution model commercially available to the best of our knowledge. Because of this, at the time of this writing, a number of top-5 media holding companies and several Fortune 100 advertisers have signed up to test this MTA model. We are also planning to develop and deploy the bagged logistic regression model as a follow-up version so that advertisers can choose either model to focus more on accuracy or more on interpretation.

While we believe both methods are statistically sound, to make MTA models useful for digital advertising requires additional heuristics in the following areas:

1. Select the right dimensions to model on. Introducing unnecessary dimensions would introduce noise and make results difficult to interpret.

2. Control the dimensionality and cardinality. Higher dimensionality and cardinality would either significantly increase the amount of data needed for statistical significance or drown out the important conclusions.

Table 2: The MTA user-level attribution analysis.

Channel	MTA Total	LTA Total	Difference
Search Click	17,494	17,017	97%
Email Click	6,938	7,340	106%
Display Network A	5,567	8,148	146%
Display Network G	2,037	470	23%
Display Network B	1,818	1,272	70%
Display Trading Desk	1,565	1,367	87%
Display Network C	1,494	1,373	92%
Display Network D	1,491	1,233	83%
Email View	1,420	458	32%
Display Network E	1,187	1,138	96%
Brand Campaign	907	1,581	174%
Social	768	1,123	146%
Display Network H	746	284	38%
Display Network F	673	787	117%
Display Network I	489	136	28%
Retail Email Click	483	491	102%
Display Network J	222	92	41%
Retail Email	168	110	66%
Social Click	133	153	115%
Video	58	31	54%

3. Carefully encode variables so that domain knowledge could help choose a compact yet effective model.

There are a number of avenues for future research. First, bagging process is a wrapper method that can be applied to many types of learning machines. For example Random Forrest [13] is a very popular bagged decision tree model. We choose logistic regression for the ease of implementation and the simple interpretation of the coefficients. One area of the future development is to extend this MTA framework to other learning machines so that we can choose a more powerful learning method while still be able to easily derive the user-level attribution assignment. Another area of development is in formalizing the heuristics needed for building specific types of MTA models that can address typical digital advertising questions such as budget allocation, cross-channel optimization, and message sequencing. The third area is in incorporating the MTA model into predictive advertising models. Attribution model defines the success metric of each advertising campaign. Because of the dominance of the LTA model, many predictive models used today are influenced by it. New predictive models are needed when advertisers start to adopt the new attribution model.

6. REFERENCES

[1] D'Angelo, F. Happy Birthday, Digital Advertising! 2009. `http://adage.com/digitalnext/post?article_id=139964`

[2] Chandler-Pepelnjak, J. Atlas Institute, Microsoft Advertising. Measuring ROI Beyond the Last AD. `http://www.atlassolutions.com/uploadedFiles/Atlas/Atlas_Institute/Published_Content/dmi-MeasuringROIBeyondLastAd.pdf`.

[3] Clearsaleing Inc. Clearsaleing Attribution Model. `http://www.clearsaleing.com/product/accurate-attribution-management/`

[4] C3 Metric, Inc. What is C3 Metric. `http://c3metrics.com/executive-summary/`

[5] Provost, F., Dalessandro, B., Hook, R., Zhang, X., and Murray, A. Audience Selection for On-line Brand Advertising: Privacy-friendly Social Network Targeting. In *Proceedings of the Fifteenth ACM SIGKDD International Conference on Knowledge Discovery and Data Mining*, 2009.

[6] Li, W., Wang, X., Zhang, R., Cui, Y., Mao, J., and Jin, R. Exploitation and Exploration in a Performance Based Contextual Advertising System. In *Proceedings of the Fifteenth ACM SIGKDD International Conference on Knowledge Discovery and Data Mining*, 2010.

[7] Hastie, T., Tibshirani, R., and Friedman, J. *The Elements of Statistical Learning: Data Mining, Inference and Prediction*, 2nd Edition, Springer, New York, 2009.

[8] Cortes, C., and Vapnik, V. Support-Vector Networks. *Machine Learning*, 20, 273-297, 1995.

[9] Jin, X., Li, Y., Mah, T., and Tong, J. Sensitive Webpage Classification for Content Advertising. In *Proceedings of the 1st international workshop on Data mining and audience intelligence for advertising*, 2007.

[10] Bishop, C.M. *Neural Networks for Pattern Recognition*, Oxford University Press, 1996.

[11] Bishop, C.M. *Pattern Recognition and Machine Learning*, Springer, 2007.

[12] Breiman, L. Bagging Predictors. *Machine Learning*, 24, 123-140, 1996.

[13] Breiman, L. Random Forests. *Machine Learning*, 45, 5-32, 2001.

[14] Perlich, Cl, Provost, F., and Simonoff, J.S. Tree Induction vs. Logistic Regression: A Learning-Curve Analysis. *Journal of Machine Learning Research*, 4, 211-255, 2003.

Bid Landscape Forecasting in Online Ad Exchange Marketplace

Ying Cui, Ruofei Zhang, Wei Li, Jianchang Mao
Yahoo! Labs
4401 Great America Parkway
Santa Clara, CA, 95054
{ycui,rzhang,lwei,jmao}@yahoo-inc.com

ABSTRACT

Display advertising has been a significant source of revenue for publishers and ad networks in online advertising ecosystem. One important business model in online display advertising is Ad Exchange marketplace, also called non-guaranteed delivery (NGD), in which advertisers buy targeted page views and audiences on a spot market through real-time auction. In this paper, we describe a bid landscape forecasting system in NGD marketplace for any advertiser campaign specified by a variety of targeting attributes. In the system, the impressions that satisfy the campaign targeting attributes are partitioned into multiple mutually exclusive samples. Each sample is one unique combination of quantified attribute values. We develop a divide-and-conquer approach that breaks down the campaign-level forecasting problem. First, utilizing a novel star-tree data structure, we forecast the bid for each sample using non-linear regression by gradient boosting decision trees. Then we employ a mixture-of-log-normal model to generate campaign-level bid distribution based on the sample-level forecasted distributions. The experiment results of a system developed with our approach show that it can accurately forecast the bid distributions for various campaigns running on the world's largest NGD advertising exchange system, outperforming two baseline methods in term of forecasting errors.

Categories and Subject Descriptors

H.2.8 [**Database Management**]: Database Applications - data mining; H.3.5 [**Information Storage and Retrieval**]: On-line Information Services

General Terms

Algorithms, Experiments, Measurement, Performance

Keywords

Online display advertising, Ad Exchange marketplace, bid landscape forecasting

1. INTRODUCTION

Online advertising has become a major industry. In 2009, despite the total advertising expenditures in U.S. declined 12.3% due to economic recession, online display advertising geared up 7.3% [10]. Such a tremendous growth is logically due to the need of online advertisers for both brand awareness and direct responses. Most publishers sell their premium ad inventories to the highest-paying advertisers through their direct sales channel on a guaranteed basis, called guaranteed delivery (GD). By this way, inventories must be delivered systematically to achieve the desired impression goals committed by the publisher's direct sales force. On the other hand, publishers usually sell their remaining ad space on a non-guaranteed basis through their direct sales channel, as well through their indirect sales channel, typically through an online auction mechanism. This market place is called non-guaranteed delivery (NGD). It takes the advantage of ad networks and ad exchanges that provide a bidding platform for buyers to bid for ad impressions.

NGD is a dynamic system which relies heavily on the bidding price. On a specific publisher, the number of available impressions is relatively stable, that is, the overall user visits during a certain period will not change much. Thus, the actual impression delivered for an ad campaign mostly depends on its winning rate, which is decided by the bidding pricing and the demand landscape in the marketplace. The role of bid landscape forecasting in NGD is to predict the bid price distribution that a given ad campaign would fetch on the display advertising exchange marketplace. It's much needed to provide a bid landscape (distribution) forecasting on how many impressions an advertiser can win if bidding at a certain bid amount. This functionality is very useful for advertisers to obtain budget guidance as well as for the publishers to allocate NGD traffic and set price for their inventories [13].

The major difficulties of NGD bid landscape forecasting lie in forecasting for new or changed ad campaigns, and forecasting the winning rate on an unseen bid value. Another difficulty lies in the variety of ad campaign targeting attributes. For every campaign, there is a targeting profile describing all its targeting attributes. Advertisers can change or add new targeting attributes at any time to the profile. For example, an advertiser's targeting may include users in certain geographic locations regardless of age, while excludes some publishers; or the advertiser can target at users who are interested in movie at a specified time, and change to target at users interested in sports later. In addition, different combinations of targeting attribute values have different supply/demand and thus different competitiveness in the NGD marketplace, which leads to different bid landscapes. Figure 1 shows a bid landscape example of two consecutive months from one sample campaign in a real display ad network, represented by cumulative density function (CDF). The CDF value at a certain bid amount indicates how much traffic the advertiser can win if bidding at this price. As clearly shown in the figure, the shapes of the two curves differ distinctly, and the CDF value of month 1 changed almost at all bid price in month 2. The changes in the distribution are mostly caused by the changes of targeting attributes. Therefore, direct prediction of each campaign which contains targeting to many different attributes is not effective, we need a more general way to estimate the winning bid distribution at finer granularity based on the campaign/advertiser's specific targeting attributes.

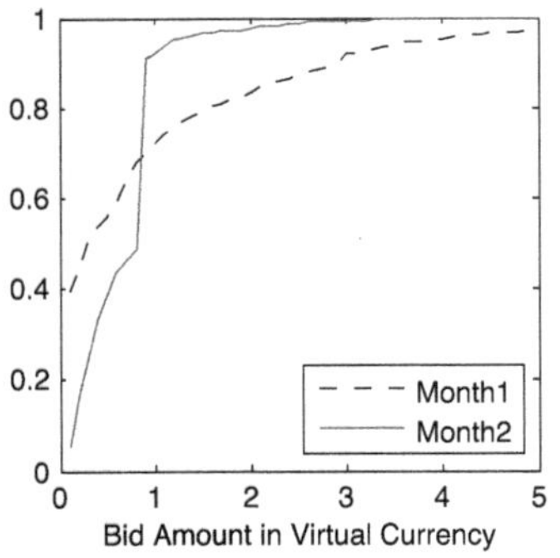

Figure 1: Actual cumulative histograms for two consecutive months of a sample campaign

In this paper, we develop a bid landscape forecasting system for NGD ad exchange marketplace to provide bidding guidance for both publishers and advertisers. Instead of direct prediction of each campaign, we break down the problem to perform forecasting on each combination of targeting attribute values, namely a sample, to meet the variety of advertisers' targeting requirements. In the targeting profile of each campaign, every targeting attribute can have multiple values. We define a sample as a unique combination of targeting attribute values. For example, for a campaign with following target profile: target to publisher P1 and P2, male users in age (18-23) or (30-35). We have several samples to represent it. S1: publisher=P1, gender=male, age in (18-23); S2: publisher=P2, gender=male, age in (18-23). S3: publisher=P1, gender=male, age in (30-35); and S4: publisher=P2, gender=male, age in (30-35). We produce the estimated bid for each sample, using non-linear regression with gradient boosting decision tree (GBDT) [7]. Because history information is very important in sample-level bid forecasting, a novel star-tree data structure is introduced to store it. A template matching method is designed to deal with the low coverage in exact match for history search. It also has the advantage of smoothing the low confidence history measures caused by data sparseness. Then we propose a mixture-of-log-normal model to generate campaign-level bid landscape forecasting based on the sample-level estimated statistics. The experiment results show that our system can accurately forecast the bid distribution for targeting profiles with various targeting attributes running on the world's largest NGD advertising exchange system.

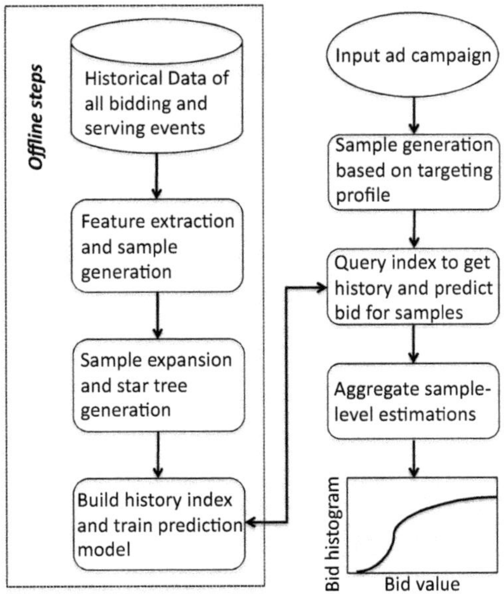

Figure 2: NGD bid landscape forecasting system

The rest of the paper is organized as follows. In the next section, we give an overview of the proposed bid landscape forecasting system architecture. The details of the developed approach is presented in Section 3. In Section 4, we discuss the evaluation results of our system running on a real world display ad exchange. The related works is summarized in Section 5. Finally, we conclude the paper with future work in Section 6.

2. OVERVIEW OF THE NGD BID LANDSCAPE FORECASTING SYSTEM

Given an advertiser campaign, directly tracking the historical bid histogram to perform forecasting is not applicable because if the advertisers' targeting profiles have changed or are going to change, the winning bid value in the marketplace could change accordingly. Therefore, we develop a three-step divide-and-conquer approach for our NGD bid landscape forecasting system. First, each campaign is decomposed into samples based on their targeting, then we perform forecasting on the finer sample-level granularity. In the end, the sample-level estimations are aggregated using model fitting to predict the bid landscape at campaign level. The whole procedure is summarized in Figure 2.

The entire NGD bid landscape forecasting system can be roughly divided into two parts, offline process and online serving. In the offline process, we perform data preprocessing, feature extraction, history index building and prediction model training. In a typical NGD display advertising system, every bidding and serving event, including the ad opportunity, winner of this auction and the user viewed this ad impression is logged. Every ad opportunity is described by its attributes, including url, publisher, ad position; and user demographic, geo location information; while the winner information includes winning bid value, actual payout etc. Typically, there are a myriad of targeting attributes. Most of them are complex boolean targeting logic rules to match the ad inventory advertisers want to target. Thus, feature selection is a crucial factor in the system. There

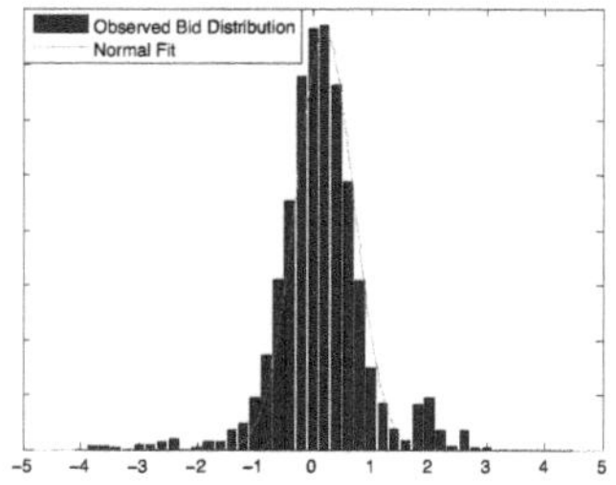

Figure 3: The log of winning bid prices of a sample on the NGD marketplace as fitted with normal distribution

are several possible ways to evaluate features, such as decision tree based method [2] or feature weighting by relevance [8]. In this work, we select a subset of features by the Fast-Correlation Based Filtering (FCBF) method proposed in [14] because of its efficiency in dealing with large amount of features. FCBF is a deterministic algorithm to eliminate attributes that are either uncorrelated with the target value, or redundant when considered along with other attributes that have higher correlation with the target value. It enables us to cut down the feature search time considerably, since we are able to search a limited subset of the space while having reasonably high confidence that a representative sample of the entire space are covered. It computes the correlation between features and target values in terms of symmetric uncertainty (SU), defined as:

$$SU(X,Y) = 2\frac{IG(X|Y)}{H(X)+H(Y)}, \quad (1)$$

where IG is the information gain, and H is the entropy. $IG(X|Y)$ measure the additional information of X provided by Y, and $IG(X|Y) = IG(Y|X)$. SU is a normalized measure of IG compensating for IG's bias on feature cardinality. After selecting a subset of the features, we aggregate the historical data according to them for sample generation and star tree expansion, which will be described in detail in the next section. The history index is built for all paths in the star tree. With the data stored in the star tree, we train and validate our prediction model.

In an online serving session, when an advertiser call comes, samples are generated according to the targeting logics described in its targeting profile. Then we query the history index to get history bid information for every sample. The history features together with the samples' targeting attribute values are fed to the prediction model. The estimated parameters of bid distribution for each sample is then obtained. Finally, the sample-level estimations are aggregated to get the bid distribution for the campaign of the ad call.

3. NGD BID LANDSCAPE FORECASTING

In the NGD marketplace, the bid values of most samples exhibit heavy-tailed distributions. While the vast majority of prices are low, there are significant numbers of opportunities that fetch higher bids. After taking the log of the bid values, the distribution can be reasonably approximated by a normal distribution. See Figure 3 for an example. Based on this assumption, the problem of estimating sample-level bid distribution is reduced to estimating the bid mean and standard deviation (std) of log-normal distribution. In this section, we concentrate on star tree expansion with runtime lookup via templates, sample-level bid mean and std prediction, and aggregation of sample-level estimation to get bid distribution for every ad campaign.

3.1 Online Bid History Lookup

Two important features we use to forecast bid mean and std for a sample are its historical bid mean and std. Therefore we need to build a history lookup table for every possible combination of targeting attribute values. This task can be achieved in two steps. In the first step, we introduce a bid star tree to expand our observed samples to cover as much targeting space as possible. In the second step, we retrieve the bid history for testing samples by searching in the tree with the help of templates. In this section, we will explain the bid star tree expansion and how to select templates for runtime lookup.

3.1.1 Bid Star Tree Expansion

Bid history lookup table can be organized into a tree structure, where each level corresponds to one targeting attribute and each path represents a sample. An example tree is shown on the left side of Figure 4. There are three targeting attributes $TA1$, $TA2$ and $TA3$ so each path has a length of three. $TA1$ can have two values: a_1 and a_2; $TA2$ can have one: b_1; and $TA3$ can have two: c_1 and c_2. We observe three unique samples in history: $a_1b_1c_1$, $a_1b_1c_2$ and $a_2b_1c_1$. The three leaf nodes at the bottom store the corresponding bid mean and std values. Note that when a sample has no impression observed (e.g. $a_2b_1c_2$), it is not included in the tree. The bid history lookup table is generated by populating observed impressions into the tree structure.

This simple structure works well for samples with sufficient histories but has several limitations. First of all, if a testing sample is never observed before, we are unable to find its history in the tree. In addition, there are a large number of rare samples whose bid are too sparse to be reliable. Therefore we need to introduce a smoothing mechanism to deal with unseen or rare samples. Another scenario that the simple lookup tree cannot handle is when a testing sample consists of a special "targeting all" value for one or more attributes. This value means that the advertiser does not care about a particular attribute and any value for that attribute is considered as a match.

In order to solve these problems, we introduce a "star" value for each targeting attribute. This value is used to represent "targeting all" for that attribute as well as those with few or no histories. For each internal node in the lookup tree, we add one star node as its child. If the star node is not at the bottom level, we also add additional nodes as its children as if it were a normal node. An example is shown on the right side of Figure 4. New edges are added in bold lines. Now one impression can match multiple paths in the tree. For example, an impression with values $a_1b_1c_1$ matches paths $***$, $**c_1$, $*b_1*$, $*b_1c_1$, a_1**, a_1*c_1, a_1b_1* and $a_1b_1c_1$. This impression will be considered in the bid mean and std calculation of all those paths. The star nodes play an important role in smoothing. For example, if we want to look up the history for $a_2b_1c_2$ in the tree shown in Figure 4, we cannot find an exact match because this sample is new. But we may choose a similar path a_2b_1* or $*b_1c_2$ for approximation. In addition, we can remove the paths with very few impressions because their bid history is

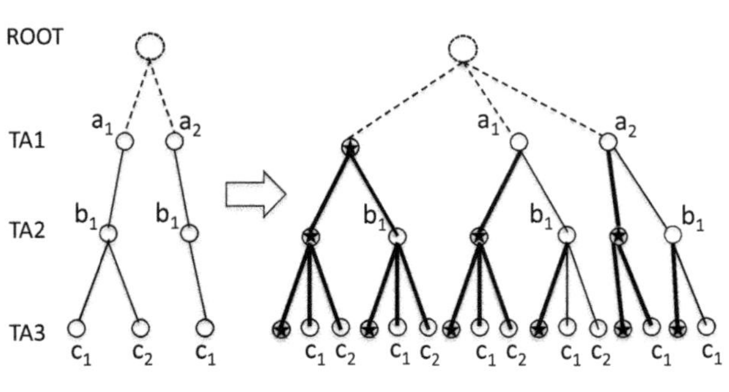

Figure 4: Bid star tree expansion. Left: original bid tree build by raw events. Right: bid star tree by star value expansion

too sparse, and rely on similar star paths for more reliably bid estimation. By doing so, we also reduce the storage space significantly. Another advantage of the star tree is to support the "targeting all" values easily. When a testing sample consists of such a value, we just need to replace it with a star and look up the tree like regular samples.

3.1.2 History Lookup via Templates

While the star tree provides smoothed estimation for bid history and supports the "targeting all" value, it also introduces a new challenge, i.e., how to find the most similar path to a testing sample. In the ideal case, the testing sample can find a path exactly match itself. If an exact matched path does not exist, we still want to find a path which shares the largest number of most important targeting attribute values. Templates are introduced for the purpose of finding the most similar path in the star tree, when there is no exact match. There are two matching types for each targeting attribute: one is exact match, denoted as "v" match; the other is star match since star value means "targeting all" and is considered a match for any value, denoted as "*" match. A template is defined as a combination of matching types for each targeting attribute. D targeting attributes lead to D-dimensional templates. For one example, we have a template $T_k = [T_{k1}T_{k2}\dots T_{kd}\dots T_{kD}]$ where $T_{kd} \in \{*, v\}$ and a sample s_i. When we apply T_k to mask s_i, denoted as "$s_i' = s_i \oplus T_k$". If $T_{kd} = v$, the dth original targeting attribute value of s_i (s_{id}) remain unchanged; while $T_{kd} = *$, s_{id} is changed to star in the output s_i'. If s_i' exists in the tree, we get a matching path for s_i. For the star tree shown in Figure 4, if $s_i = a_2b_1c_2$ and $T_k = [vv*]$, $s_i' = a_2b_1*$ is a matching path for s_i. We define the similarity score between s_i and s_i' as $simScore(s_i, s_i') = \sum_{d=1}^{D} \lambda_d \delta(s_{id}, s_{id}')$, where λ_d is the feature importance of the dth targeting attribute (TA_d). $\delta(s_{id}, s_{id}')$ equals 1 if $s_{id} = s_{id}'$ for TA_d and 0 otherwise. The similarity score is calculated as the overall weight of retained attributes. To measure the feature importance λ_d, we use SU defined in Eq.(1) because it is non-negative and normalized to the range [0,1], i.e., $\lambda_d = SU(TA_d, bid)$. Accordingly, we can assign a quality score to any template T_k as $qualityScore(T_k) = \sum_{d=1}^{D} \lambda_d \delta(T_{kd}, v)$. Because if T_k has "v" at the dth dimension, i.e. $T_{kd} = v$, its masked output is guaranteed to equal to the original sample for the dth targeting attribute value. It is also clear that the all "v" template keeps all the original targeting attribute values and thus has the highest quality. Therefore, high quality templates assure high similarity between their masked outputs and the original sample.

Algorithm 1 Training algorithm for template selection

1. Function templateSelection(trainingSamples s_i, imp_i,
   featureWeight λ, numberTemplate K)
2. qualityScore=(0)
3. **for each** possible template T_k, $k \in \{1, 2, \dots, 2^D\}$
4. $qualityScore(T_k) = \sum_{d=1}^{D} \lambda_d \delta(T_{kd}, v)$
5. sort $\{T_k\}$ by qualityScore in decreasing order $\rightarrow \{T_{sorted}\}$
6. coverageScore=(0);
7. **for each** $s_i, i \in \{1, 2, \dots, N\}$
8. $T_{tmp} = T_1$ in $\{T_{sorted}\}$
9. **while** ($s_i \oplus T_{tmp}$ not exist)
10. $T_{tmp} \leftarrow$ next T_k in $\{T_{sorted}\}$
11. $coverageScore(T_{tmp}) = coverageScore(T_{tmp}) + imp_i$
12. sort $\{T_k\}$ by coverageScore
    $\{T_{selected}\} \leftarrow$ top K templates
13. **if** (all-star template $\notin \{T_{selected}\}$)
    replace the last in $\{T_{selected}\}$ with all-star template
14. **return** $\{T_{selected}\}$

Finding the most similar path via template is by no means an easy task because runtime history lookup is subject to the curse of dimensionality even with tens of dimensions. For example, for a star tree with 20 targeting attributes, there will be 2^{20} possible templates. In the worst case, we may need to scan the outputs from all the templates for a match, and end up with stars for all dimensions. This is not practical in a real system. It is desirable to find a small set of templates, which can limit the search space as well as retain the similarity between samples and their matching paths in the tree as high as possible. We develop an algorithm to solve this problem, as shown in Algorithm 1.

The input of this algorithm consists of a set of D-dimensional training samples $\{s_1, s_2, \dots, s_N\}$, the aggregated numbers of impressions for each sample $\{imp_1, imp_2, \dots, imp_N\}$, feature importance values of the D targeting attributes $\lambda = (\lambda_1, \dots, \lambda_D)$ and the number of templates we want to select K. Note that the samples used here are held-out data that are not used in building the star tree. More specifically, we use samples from time period t_1 to build the star tree and samples from time period t_2 to select templates. The aggregated impressions imp_i are also calculated from t_2 events.

The criteria for template set selection are high quality and high coverage. As shown by lines 2-4 in Algorithm 1, we first compute the quality score for every possible template. Then the templates are sorted by quality score in decreasing order. For each sample s_i, we sequentially mask it with templates from the sorted list. If the output path $s_i \oplus T$ exists in the star tree, we stop and update the coverage score for template T. The detailed calculation is shown in lines 6-11. Finally, the templates are sorted by coverage score and the top K templates are selected. If there is a tie, the template with a higher quality score is chosen. All-star template is a special template because any sample is guaranteed to have at least one matching path in the star tree (all-star path) by masking to it. Then if it is not in the selected template set, we add it in to replace the last one.

We perform the template selection training offline. Although it seems time consuming in searching the outputs of sample s masked by all templates, most of the time, it will stop at the first several templates. And in our system, the search in Algorithm 1 line 9-10 is not performed template by template; instead, we query the star tree with the outputs from tens of templates in parallel. Also because the selected template set changes very slow from time to time, we only need to train it once for several months. For online history lookup, we mask an incoming sample with all the templates selected, typically around 30, and send all the outputs in parallel to query the history star tree. From all the existing paths, we choose the one whose template has the highest quality score. The bid history stored in its leaf node will then be retrieved.

3.2 Bid Forecasting using Gradient Boosting Decision Trees

In our experiments it shows that although historical features are very important, other user features and publisher features also have strong impact on the bid values. To exploit those features effectively we use regression method for bid mean and std forecasting. In the regression formalization, those ad opportunity features also act as a smoothing factor for samples with sparse history. Gradient boosting decision trees (GBDT) [4, 5, 7] model is used for the regression because it is especially effective for prediction based on a large number of potentially interacting categorical and continuous variables. This is particularly desirable as almost all of our targeting attributes are categorical. It can be shown that GBDT, a weighted additive expansion of weak trees, can produce an excellent fit of the predicted values to the observed values, even if the specific nature of the relationships between the predictor variables and the dependent variable of interest is very complex (nonlinear in nature).

From the statistics point of view, regression problem can be formulated as follows: given a set of training samples $\{(\mathbf{x}_i, y_i)\}_{i=1}^{N}$ with $\mathbf{x}_i \in \mathcal{X}$ and $y_i \in \mathcal{Y}$, the goal is to find a function $F^*(\mathbf{x})$ that maps $\mathcal{X}$ to $\mathcal{Y}$, such that the expected value of some specified loss function ℓ over the joint distribution of all $(y, \mathbf{x})$-values is minimized

$$F^*(\mathbf{x}) = \arg\min_{F(\mathbf{x})} E_{y,\mathbf{x}}\{\ell(y, F(\mathbf{x}))\}.$$

GBDT generates a prediction model in the form of an ensemble of a sequence of simple decision trees as base learner, where each successive tree is learned for prediction residuals of the preceding trees. We use least square gradient boosting tree, which performs least-squares residual fitting, with a square-error loss function. Assume that the scaling parameter is incorporated in the base learner $h(\mathbf{x}; \mathbf{a})$, with F_0 be the sample average, the splitting variables $\mathbf{a}$ and $F(\mathbf{x})$ are updated at each step m:

$$F_0(\mathbf{x}) = \frac{1}{N}\sum_{i=1}^{N} y_i$$

$$\mathbf{a_m} = \arg\min_{\mathbf{a}} \sum_{i=1}^{N} [y_i - F_{m-1}(\mathbf{x}_i) - h(\mathbf{x}_i; \mathbf{a})]^2 \tag{2}$$

$$F_m(\mathbf{x}) = F_{m-1}(\mathbf{x}) + h(\mathbf{x}; \mathbf{a_m}).$$

There are many advantages of using the least-square boosting tree for our prediction problem. For example, no normalization is needed when using different types of features. The tradeoff between runtime efficiency and accuracy can be easily achieved by truncating the number of trees used in the model. Feature importance is also a byproduct of the boosted trees model because it performs greedy feature search when selecting splitting features. The boosting tree prediction also has good scalability, it can be easily extended if we add new features as regressors. In our experiments, we also demonstrate the effectiveness of using the powerful tool - GBDT for sample-level prediction in Section 4.2.1.

Algorithm 2 Pseudocode for online bid landscape forecasting

Function getBidHistogram(campaign CP, templates $\{T_k\}_{k=1}^{K}$, history bid star tree, GBDT model)
  matching samples $\{s_1, s_2, \ldots, s_N\} \leftarrow$ CP's targeting profile

  for each $s_i \in \{s_1, s_2, \ldots, s_N\}$
    $\{s_i^{(1)}, s_i^{(2)}, \ldots, s_i^{(K)}\} = s_i \oplus$ all T $\in \{T_k\}_{k=1}^{K}$
    query history tree for all $s_i^{(k)}$ in parallel
    $s_i' \leftarrow$ exist$(s_i^{(k)})$ with max quality score,
      get historical bid mean $\tilde{E}(s_i')$ and std $\tilde{std}(s_i')$
    $(\hat{E}[s_i], \hat{std}[s_i]) \leftarrow GBDT(s_{i1}, \ldots, s_{iD}, \tilde{E}(s_i'), \tilde{std}(s_i'))$
    $(\hat{\mu_i}, \hat{\sigma_i}^2) \leftarrow (\hat{E}[s_i], \hat{std}[s_i])$ by Equation 4

  histogram(CP) $\leftarrow$ mixture of $s_i \sim Log - \mathcal{N}(\hat{\mu_i}, \hat{\sigma_i}^2)$
  return histogram(CP)

3.3 Aggregation of Sample-level Estimation

From the observation that the sample winning bid values are log normal distributed, the campaign level bid distribution is modeled by a mixture of log normals, with each component be a log-normal distribution of sample-level estimated bid mean and std. To formalize, the probability of the data given a finite mixture model (FMM) [9] is $P(X|\Theta) = \sum_{j=1}^{C} \pi_j P(X|\theta_j)$, where π_j is the prior probability (or mixture proportion) of each component and θ_j is the model parameter, C is the total number of mixture components. In our model, the bid distribution of each sample s is a mixture component, $x = bid(s) \sim Log - \mathcal{N}(\mu, \sigma^2)$,

$$f_s(x; \mu, \sigma) = \frac{1}{x\sigma\sqrt{2\pi}} e^{\frac{-(lnx-\mu)^2}{2\sigma^2}}, x > 0;$$

the probability density function of campaign level bid price X can be represented by:

$$f(X|x; \theta_1, \theta_2, \ldots, \theta_C; \pi_1, \pi_2, \ldots, \pi_C) = \sum_{j=1}^{C} \pi_j \frac{1}{x\sigma_j\sqrt{2\pi}} e^{\frac{-(lnx-\mu_j)^2}{2\sigma_j^2}}, \tag{3}$$

where $0 < \pi_j < 1$, and $\sum_{j=1}^{C} \pi_j = 1$.

We take the weighted sum of the probability density function of sample-level bid to estimate the campaign-level bid distribution. The sample level bid distribution is represented by its mean $E[s]$ and std $std[s]$ in the original linear space, we can simply get the parameters μ and σ of log normal distribution via:

$$\mu = ln(E[s]) - \frac{1}{2} ln(1 + \frac{std[s]^2}{E[s]^2})$$

$$\sigma^2 = ln(1 + \frac{std[s]^2}{E[s]^2}) \tag{4}$$

The weights of each mixture component π_j are assigned based on different metrics for each sample, such as the number of expected available impressions. Alternatively, π_j can also be learned to maximize log-likelihood [3]. Our experiment shows that the finite mixture model we proposed is particularly well-suited to the representation of the campaign-level bid distribution.

Our divide-and-conquer approach for campaign level bid landscape forecasting is summarized in Algorithm 2. Note that in the online process, the for-loop in lines 3-8, estimation of each sample bid mean $\hat{E}(s_i)$ and std $\hat{std}(s_i)$ is conducted in parallel on a distributed computing infrastructure. This makes the whole procedure very fast so that the estimated bid histogram can be returned in real time.

4. EXPERIMENTS

In this section, we discuss the experiments we conducted to validate our approach. We apply our method to an industry leading NGD exchange system and conduct extensive evaluation with real online event log data and advertising campaigns.

4.1 Data Set

We collect the actual bid events from three consecutive time periods, t_1, t_2 and t_3, sampled from the world's largest NGD exchange system, RightMedia Exchange. In our experiment, each time period t contains 30 days. We forecast the bid distribution in a certain time period based on the data from the previous time period. To be specific, we train a prediction model using t_1 and t_2 data, and testing the model on the forecasting of t_3 bid distribution.

In the daily NGD bid event log, we recorded the information of every auction on both publisher side and user side. Users are anonymized to hide personal identifiable information. We also record the most important bid related attributes, such as winning bid value, pricing type, advertiser payout. From these bid events, we performed feature selection as explained in Section 2, and selected 15 targeting attributes in our experiments, including user age, gender, geo location, segments, ad position, ad size, publisher page categories and others. Based on these targeting attributes, we aggregated the bid events in t_1 and t_2 respectively into raw samples without "*", and record the bid mean and std of each sample. Then we expand two bid star trees for t_1 and t_2 based on their raw samples as described in Section 3.1.1. For each time period t, there are 15 billion impressions and we aggregated them to about 5M number of unique raw samples, each is a combination of the 15 targeting attribute values. After star tree expansion, we have approximately 120M number of distinct leaf nodes/samples in each tree. Post pruning is performed with an impression threshold of 200 in order to remove the rare samples for the uncertainty of their bid mean and std. Finally, 30M leaf nodes are left in each tree.

For the sample-level forecasting, we trained GBDT regression models using samples in t_2 bid star tree. 10-fold cross validation is conducted to avoid over-fitting. According to the method described in Algorithm 1, we selected 30 templates with samples in t_1 and t_2 periods as training samples. Our testing data are composed of 1800 campaigns randomly sampled from t_3 period. We expanded these campaigns into samples, searched their bid history in t_2 star tree, and fed them to the trained GBDT model to get the sample-level estimated bid mean and std. Finally, these estimations were combined to generate campaign-level bid distribution. We compared our forecasted bid landscape of t_3 to the empirical bid histogram of the same period for evaluation.

Table 1: Sample level error for bid mean

Bid Range	Samp (%)	avg $\|err_i\|$	90%I (err_i)	avg $\|rerr_i\|$ %	90%I $rerr_i(\%)$
$[0-0.1)$	4.45	0.02	[-0.04 0.04]	34.18	[-61.99 70.06]
$[0.1-0.2)$	3.61	0.04	[-0.10 0.06]	29.46	[-65.17 43.00]
$[0.2-0.3)$	3.46	0.07	[-0.17 0.09]	29.29	[-66.21 35.63]
$[0.3-0.4)$	3.59	0.10	[-0.22 0.11]	27.06	[-62.41 31.30]
$[0.4-0.5)$	4.54	0.11	[-0.26 0.14]	25.35	[-58.64 30.39]
$[0.5-0.6)$	4.23	0.14	[-0.33 0.17]	25.79	[-59.72 30.77]
$[0.6-0.8)$	6.20	0.19	[-0.43 0.19]	27.26	[-62.01 26.72]
$[0.8-1.0)$	5.83	0.24	[-0.55 0.30]	26.72	[-61.26 33.32]
$[1.0-1.5)$	13.35	0.31	[-0.71 0.44]	24.85	[-57.28 35.25]
$[1.5-2.0)$	12.04	0.38	[-0.89 0.56]	21.76	[-50.99 32.08]
$[2.0-3.0)$	23.80	0.43	[-1.02 0.55]	17.32	[-41.44 22.68]
$[3.0-5.0)$	14.29	0.59	[-1.37 0.31]	16.19	[-36.86 8.19]
$[5.0-\infty)$	0.63	1.99	[-3.25 -0.73]	34.60	[-47.47 -21.73]

Table 2: Sample level error for bid std

Bid Range	Samp (%)	avg $\|err_i\|$	90%I (err_i)	avg $\|rerr_i\|$ %	90%I $rerr_i(\%)$
$[0-0.1)$	4.45	0.05	[-0.15 0.09]	40.12	[-85.55 64.10]
$[0.1-0.2)$	3.61	0.10	[-0.26 0.12]	31.74	[-71.23 35.29]
$[0.2-0.3)$	3.46	0.12	[-0.31 0.16]	30.08	[-68.12 34.04]
$[0.3-0.4)$	3.59	0.14	[-0.35 0.21]	29.40	[-65.99 40.51]
$[0.4-0.5)$	4.54	0.15	[-0.37 0.25]	27.24	[-61.00 42.50]
$[0.5-0.6)$	4.23	0.18	[-0.43 0.27]	26.42	[-59.99 39.88]
$[0.6-0.8)$	6.20	0.22	[-0.53 0.30]	25.29	[-58.77 34.74]
$[0.8-1.0)$	5.83	0.24	[-0.58 0.32]	23.42	[-55.27 32.25]
$[1.0-1.5)$	13.35	0.26	[-0.65 0.33]	21.39	[-51.16 27.63]
$[1.5-2.0)$	12.04	0.28	[-0.70 0.34]	18.82	[-45.35 23.74]
$[2.0-3.0)$	23.80	0.26	[-0.65 0.37]	15.74	[-38.12 24.39]
$[3.0-5.0)$	14.29	0.24	[-0.61 0.45]	13.64	[-31.90 26.46]
$[5.0-\infty)$	0.63	0.50	[-0.97 1.19]	23.33	[-37.47 54.98]

4.2 Results and Discussions

In this section, to demonstrate the effectiveness of our approach, we present the detailed results of our experiments. Because the NGD bid landscape forecasting system requires accurate prediction of bid distribution for each campaign, we also conduct comparisons of our divide-and-conquer approach to two baseline approaches on campaign-level bid histogram estimation. Note that all bid values used in the experiments are in virtual currency, due to the sensitive nature of the revenue related bid information. The numbers shown are the actual bid amount in US dollar multiplied by a scaling factor.

4.2.1 Sample-level Forecasting Error

First, we study the sample-level forecasting error of our system. Two GBDT models are trained for bid mean and bid std separately. There are 30 million of unique sample in our testing data (period t_3), including those star nodes. We randomly sampled 10% of them and compute the estimation error $err_i = \hat{y}_i - y_i$ and relative error $rerr_i = (\hat{y}_i - y_i)/y_i$, where $\hat{y}_i$ is our estimation and y_i is the actual value. We present the average absolute value of these two error metrics with their 90% confidence interval. The 90% interval is a range that 90% of the testing samples have their error in that range. The numerical results are shown in table 1 for bid mean estimation, and table 2 for bid std estimation with respect to each bid range shown in the first column. The bid range is obtained according to the actual bid mean. The second column shows the percentage of samples falls in each bid range. From the tables we can see that there are fewer samples with smaller bid values and more samples with high bid values. This tells us that samples are more diversi-

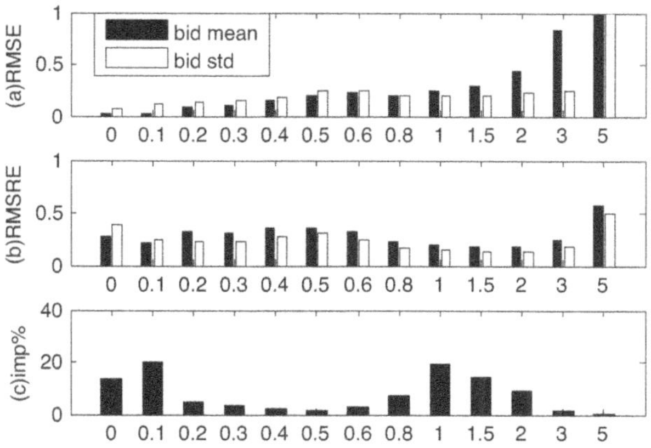

Figure 5: Impression-weighted sample level estimation error for mean and std. The x-axis: bins by actual bid value; the y-axis: (a).RMSE (b).RMSRE and (c).impression percentage for each bin.

fied with high bid values, because the advertisers' targeting include some specific attribute values which are expensive. For example, they may target at users who are interested in diamonds or automobiles. When bid value is less than 1, the number of samples are rather flat because the advertisers' targeting basically are those common attributes. We also found that the relative error becomes smaller as the bid value increases for both bid mean and std, and the confidence interval becomes tight. When the actual bid value is small, even a little bit over-estimate will result in high relative error. Despite very few outliers with bid greater than 5, our forecasting tends to be more acurate when the actual bid value is high.

Because our bid landscape is built on each impression level, we are also interested in the impression weighted errors. In our GBDT training, samples are not equally weighted. From our past experience, popular targeting attributes in the previous month has high possibility to remain popular in the following month. Therefore, we use history impressions as sample weights because we want to have smaller errors for samples with high-volume traffic. To measure sample-level forecasting error, we use impression-weighted root-mean-sqaured error (RMSE) and impression-weighted root-mean-squared relative error (RMSRE), defined as:

$$RMSE = \sqrt{\sum_{i=1}^{N} I_i(\hat{y_i} - y_i)^2 / \sum_{i=1}^{N} I_i}$$

$$RMSRE = \sqrt{\sum_{i=1}^{N} I_i(\frac{\hat{y_i} - y_i}{y_i})^2 / \sum_{i=1}^{N} I_i} \quad (5)$$

where $\hat{y_i}$ is the estimation and y_i is the actual value, N is the total number of samples and I_i is number of impressions of the ith sample. Within each bid range, we aggregate the impression weighted square-error into a single measure to further show the overall predictive power of our system.

The statistics of impression-weighted errors are presented in Figure 5, with black bars for bid mean and white bars for bid std. We use the same bid bin as above. For example, bin 0 contains samples with actual bid mean in [0 - 0.1). Subfigure(a) shows the RMSE at each bin. Basically, the RMSE of bid mean increases with bid value. Although the RMSE of bid mean jumps when the true bid value is greater than 2, the RMSRE remains small, as shown in Subfigure(b). Subfigure (b) shows the RMSRE of predicted bid mean and std. Subfigure(c) describes the traffic distribution in terms of impression percentage in each bin. Most of the traffic has the true bid value within 0 to 0.2 or 0.8 to 2. This gives us a clue of our advertiser behavior. They can be classified into two groups, one just targets at the general categories which is relatively cheap, with a goal of receiving large number of impressions; while the other targets at some specific segments with high value, very likely to be defined by the advertiser itself, and is willing to pay more. This is also shown by that although both groups share about 35% of the total impressions, the latter has unique samples over 10 times the former as shown in Tables 1 and 2. We use impression I_i in t_2 period as data wights to train our GBDT model, and subfigures(b)-(c) demonstrate that in prediction of t_3, samples with high impressions have smaller errors in $RMSRE$. Bid range [0.1 0.2) and [0.8 2] have 70% traffic, and the RMSRE is less than 20%. While the errors seem to be high for bid values in [3 5) and [5 ∞], the impressions are only 1.43% and 0.02% of the total traffic respectively.

We also conduct a comparison between GBDT prediction and direct forecast using history bid average for each sample. The latter has about 15% and 25% higher overall impression weighted RMSE and RMSRE respectively. This is because those samples without an exact match in the history bid star tree will pick the bid average from a star node, and the bid values, although smoothed, may be different from the actual bid values. Besides historical features, other features, such as publishers, ad position and user segments are also very important features. The accuracy of simply using the historical sample bid mean and std, to predict new combination of target attributes/samples, is inferior to that of our regression model based approach.

4.2.2 Campaign-level Forecasting Error

After obtaining the sample-level estimated bid mean and std, we use the mixture-of-log-normal model described in Section 3.3 for campaign-level bid landscape forecasting. We also present two baseline methods for comparison as follows to benchmark our system forecasting accuracy:

Baseline method 1: This method directly uses the empirical bid distribution of $t2$ period as the estimated bid distribution of $t3$ period. It actually copies the recent historical bid distribution if available. Note that baseline 1 has no generalization ability to predict a new campaign without history. We compare the proposed method to this baseline method in order to show that the "divide step", which breaks each campaign's targeting profile into samples, is quite necessary and powerful.

Baseline method 2: Because direct estimation of the bid value for each impression is not realistic, we performed sample-level bid estimation as described in Section 4.2.1. Utilizing the estimated average bid of each sample, we perform a rough counting to get the distribution for each line. Without any assumption of the sample-level bid distribution, we treat each impression belonging to a certain sample to have the same bid amount as the average bid of this sample. We count the number of impressions at each bid amount and generate the final distribution. By the comparison of

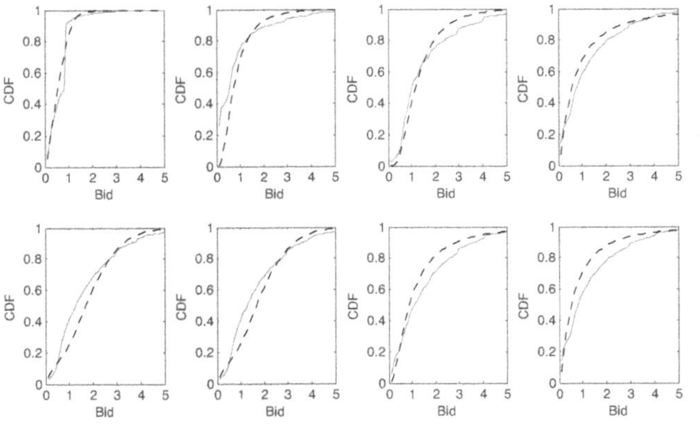

Figure 6: The estimated cumulative density function vs. the actual cumulative density function. Solid line: actual bid CDF; dotted line: estimated CDF.

our method to this baseline method, we demonstrate the superiority of the proposed mixture model of log-normals.

For the 1800 campaigns we sampled from t_3 data, we study the actual histogram of bid versus our estimated distribution. These campaigns cover about 2/3 of the leaf nodes stored in the bid star tree. Since the estimated distribution is used to calculate the winning rate, which is more interesting to the advertisers and publishers, we use cumulative density function (CDF) to represent the histogram.

The bid distributions of eight randomly selected campaigns are shown in figure 6. As expected, our estimated CDF curve is smoother because it is obtained from a close form distribution of mixtures. For the actual bid CDF, we used 50 bins from 0 to 5, with each bin a 0.1 increase, and counted the actual percentage of the traffic falling in each bin. We can see that our approach can generate the CDF close to the actual CDF. The 4 subfigures shown in the top row of figure 6 demonstrate that we can accurately predict the bid landscape, while the subfigures at the bottom row show higher errors. Our predictions tend to under-estimate the winning rate when the bid value is low, and over-estimate the winning rate when the bid value is high as shown in curves at the bottom. But clearly, the estimated distributions share roughly the same shape as the actual curves, and follow the actual bid in a decent range. The actual histogram shown in the top left-most in Figure 6 is for the same campaign shown in Figure 1. By our method, we are able to forecast its bid distribution very well.

The overall errors distribution of the 1800 campaigns are shown in Figures 7. We compute the average of error err_i and relative error $rerr_i$ in each bid bin. Similar to sample-level forecasting accuracy evaluation, we also provide their 90% confidence interval to show the low variance of our system. The average error distributions are shown on the left and relative error distribution are shown on the right. The two subfigures on the top are the results generated by our proposed divide-and-conquer (DC) method; the middle subfigures are from baseline method 1; the two subfigures at the bottom are obtained from baseline method 2. For our DC method, the major error lies in the bins with small bid value. When the bid value increases, the error bound becomes tighter. When the bid is greater than 0.4, the interval becomes quite small. For baseline method 1, only 1309 (72.72%) testing campaigns find their history in $t2$ period, and our testing error is calculated on these campaigns.

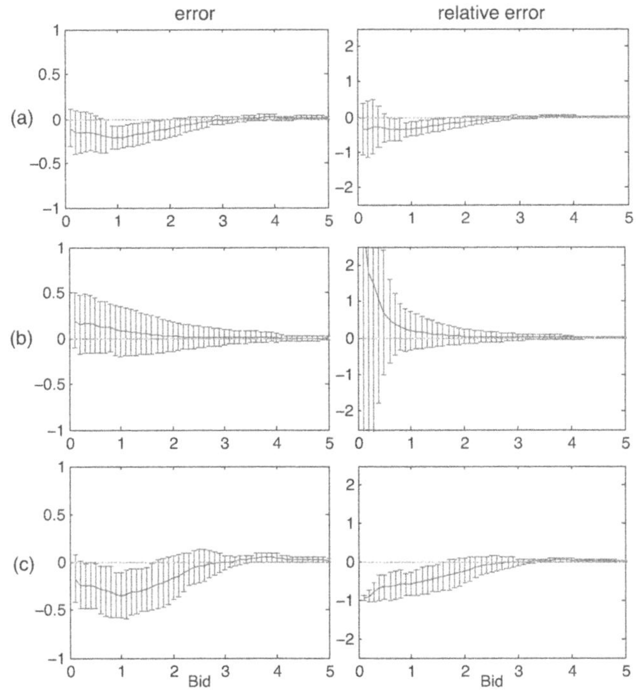

Figure 7: The error and relative error distribution for testing campaigns in each bin. (a). our proposed DC method; (b). baseline method 1; (c). baseline method 2. Left: error distribution; Right: relative error distribution for testing campaigns.

Moreover, among these campaigns with $t2$ appearance, only 815 (62.26%) campaigns remain their targeting profile unchanged. The new coming campaigns and changed campaigns make very high prediction errors. The error value is higher and the error bound is much wider. Baseline method 2 uses rough counting of the impressions with sample-level estimated bid. With sample-level estimation, the error is much smaller compared to baseline method 1. However, the results show serious under-estimation when the bid amount is small. The error bound is also considerably wider than that of our DC method. Beside smaller average error and relative error, the tighter error bounds in subfigure (a), show that the estimated cumulative histogram created by our DC method are more trustable.

We compute the RMSE and RMSRE for each campaign using Eq. (5), with y_i be the CDF value at bid bin i. The average RMSE and RMSRE with their std over all lines are summarized in Table 3. For the 1800 testing campaigns, the RMSRE of our method is only 34.5% of baseline method 1 and 61.5% of baseline method 2; and std is only 5.24% of baseline method 1 and 61.6% of baseline method 2. We also conduct chi-sqaure goodness of fit test at the 0.05 significance level to check if the observed actual bids fit the mixture model we proposed. 1630/1800 campaigns pass the test, counting for 90.56%. This again demonstrates the effectiveness and robustness of our forecasting system.

5. RELATED WORK

Until recently, there has not been much attention paid to the forecasting system in display advertising. The focus has

Table 3: Campaign-level average and std of RMSE and RMSRE for testing campaigns

Method	avg (RMSE)	std (RMSE)	avg (RMSRE)	std (RMSRE)
DC method	0.1204	0.0379	23.51%	4.53%
baseline 1	0.1695	0.0688	67.88%	86.47%
baseline 2	0.1974	0.0498	38.21%	7.36%

largely been on forecasting in search related online advertising, such as prediction of click-through-rate or impressions in sponsored search and content match [11, 1, 12]. Due to the very different objectives and mechanisms of search related advertising and display advertising, these techniques can not be applied directly. More closely related, in display advertising, some ad networks provide certain forecasting functionalities for guaranteed delivery (GD). Because in GD most campaigns are from large advertisers with relatively stable targeting attribute values and their ads are mostly shown on large publishers, time series models are typically applied to predict impressions. Unfortunately, those systems are proprietary thus no public evaluations are reported in the literature. Moreover, the method proposed in [6] estimates the distribution of highest bid for bidding agent of GD to meet the advertiser goal; and the system developed in [13] involves forecasting of available impressions to optimize inventory allocation between GD and NGD advertising campaigns. To the best of our knowledge, we have found no prior work on a complete bid landscape forecasting system for NGD. The advantage of our method is that it allows greater flexibility for advertisers in the design and implementation of their display advertising campaigns. Our system provides a powerful tool in prediction of the bid distribution with the advertisers' varying targeting and bid amount in the NGD marketplace, which is quite dynamic in nature.

6. CONCLUSION AND FUTURE WORK

The goal of NGD bid landscape forecasting is to forecast the bid distribution for any advertising campaign in NGD exchange system. In this paper, we propose a general divide-and-conquer approach to solve this problem in real time. An input campaign is decomposed to samples according to the attribute values in its targeting profile. Using sample history stored in a novel bid star tree, we forecast the sample-level distribution by a non-linear regression model. Finally, sample-level estimates are aggregated using a mixture-of-log-normal model to generate bid distribution estimation for the ad campaign. The proposed approach offers both scalability and generality.

We evaluate our NGD bid landscape forecasting system experimentally using real data and campaigns collected from the world's largest NGD exchange system. The results demonstrate that the forecasting system we developed can predict the bid distribution effectively. Comparisons with two baseline methods show the superiority of our system in the measure of both forecasting accuracy and robustness. In future work, we will extend the system to long-term forecasting by designing time series method to model long term trend and seasonality patterns in bid evolution. Another future work is to develop campaign recommendation algorithms on top of bid landscape forecasting. By suggesting targeting attributes to advertisers, they could optimize their campaigns on the NGD marketplace to reach their ROI goals and other objectives more effectively.

7. REFERENCES

[1] D. Agarwal, A. Z. Broder, D. Chakrabarti, D. Diklic, V. Josifovski, and M. Sayyadian. Estimating rates of rare events at multiple resolutions. In *KDD '07: Proceedings of the 13th ACM SIGKDD international conference on Knowledge discovery and data mining*, pages 16–25, New York, NY, USA, 2007. ACM.

[2] C. Cardie. Using decision trees to improve case-based learning. In *In Proceedings of the Tenth International Conference on Machine Learning*, pages 25–32. Morgan Kaufmann, 1993.

[3] A. P. Dempster, N. Laird, and D. B. Rubin. Maximum likelihood from incomplete data via the em algorithm. *Journal of the Royal Statistical Society. Series B (Methodological)*, 39:1–38, 1977.

[4] J. H. Friedman. Stochastic gradient boosting. *Computational Statistics and Data Analysis*, 38:367–378, 1999.

[5] J. H. Friedman. Greedy function approximation: A gradient boosting machine. *Annals of Statistics*, 29:1189–1232, 2000.

[6] A. Ghosh, B. I. Rubinstein, S. Vassilvitskii, and M. Zinkevich. Adaptive bidding for display advertising. In *WWW '09: Proceedings of the 18th international conference on World wide web*, pages 251–260, New York, NY, USA, 2009. ACM.

[7] T. Hastie, R. Tibshirani, and J. H. Friedman. Chapter 10. boosting and additive trees. In *The elements of statistical learning: data mining, inference, and prediction*, pages 337–384. New York: Springer, 2009.

[8] K. Kira and L. A. Rendell. A practical approach to feature selection. In *ML '92: Proceedings of the Ninth International Workshop on Machine Learning*, pages 249–256, San Francisco, CA, USA, 1992. Morgan Kaufmann Publishers Inc.

[9] G. J. McLachlan and D. Peel. *Finite Mixture Models*. New York: Wiley, 2000.

[10] K. Media. U.S. Advertising Expenditures Declined 12.3 Percent in 2009, 2009. http://www.businesswire.com/news/home/20100317005458/en/Kantar-Media-Reports-U.S.-Advertising-Expenditures-Declined.

[11] M. Richardson, E. Dominowska, and R. Ragno. Predicting clicks: estimating the click-through rate for new ads. In *WWW '07: Proceedings of the 16th international conference on World Wide Web*, pages 521–530, New York, NY, USA, 2007. ACM.

[12] X. Wang, A. Broder, M. Fontoura, and V. Josifovski. A search-based method for forecasting ad impression in contextual advertising. In *WWW '09: Proceedings of the 18th international conference on World wide web*, pages 491–500, New York, NY, USA, 2009. ACM.

[13] J. Yang, E. Vee, S. Vassilvitskii, J. Tomlin, J. Shanmugasundaram, T. Anastasakos, and O. Kennedy. Inventory allocation for online graphical display advertising. Technical Report YL-2010-004, Yahoo! Labs., aug 2010.

[14] L. Yu and H. Liu. Feature selection for high-dimensional data: A fast correlation-based filter solution. In *Proceedings of the Twentieth International Conference on Machine Learning (ICML-2003)*, pages 856–863, 2003.

Detecting Adversarial Advertisements in the Wild

D. Sculley
Google, Inc.
dsculley@google.com

Matthew Eric Otey
Google, Inc.
otey@google.com

Michael Pohl
Google, Inc.
mpohl@google.com

Bridget Spitznagel
Google, Inc.
drsprite@google.com

John Hainsworth
Google, Inc.
hainsworth@google.com

Yunkai Zhou
Google, Inc.
yunkaiz@google.com

ABSTRACT

In a large online advertising system, adversaries may attempt to profit from the creation of low quality or harmful advertisements. In this paper, we present a large scale data mining effort that detects and blocks such adversarial advertisements for the benefit and safety of our users. Because both false positives and false negatives have high cost, our deployed system uses a tiered strategy combining automated and semi-automated methods to ensure reliable classification. We also employ strategies to address the challenges of learning from highly skewed data at scale, allocating the effort of human experts, leveraging domain expert knowledge, and independently assessing the effectiveness of our system.

Categories and Subject Descriptors

I.5.4 [**Computing Methodologies**]: Pattern Recognition—*Applications*

General Terms

Experimentation

Keywords

online advertisement, data mining, adversarial learning

1. INTRODUCTION

The multi-billion dollar online advertising industry continues to grow [15]. This growth is fueled by users who find that online advertisements yield high quality, trustworthy content, as provided by millions of good-faith advertisers. However, in this favorable landscape a small number of *adversarial advertisers* may seek to profit by attempting to promote low quality or untrustworthy content via online advertising systems. Our goal is to detect and block these motivated adversaries, protecting users and ensuring that online advertisement remains a trustworthy source of commercial information.

KDD'11, August 21–24, 2011, San Diego, California, USA.

The problem of detecting adversarial advertisements is complicated by scale. With millions of advertisers and billions of advertiser landing pages,[1] automated detection methods are clearly needed. However, unlike many data-mining tasks in which the cost of false positives (FP's) and false negatives (FN's) may be traded off, in this setting both false positives and false negatives carry extremely high misclassification cost. Thus, both FP and FN rates must be driven toward zero, even for difficult edge cases.

The need for extreme reliability at scale necessitates the use of both automated and semi-automated methods in a tiered system. Automated detection methods, based on high-precision, large-scale machine learning methods, are able to handle the bulk of the detection work. High-recall models are then used in semi-automated fashion to guide the effort of expert humans who can resolve hard edge cases. Together, these approaches form the basis of a system that quickly and reliably identifies adversarial advertisements and blocks them from serving.

1.1 Challenges

This paper presents the full anatomy of the multi-tiered data mining system currently deployed at Google for detecting and blocking adversarial advertisements, and is intended to serve as a detailed case study. This study is structured around the following key challenges:

- **High cost of both FP's and FN's.** In our setting, both FP's and FN's have high cost; we cannot trade off one against the other. Using a combination of automated and semi-automated effort helps drive both FP and FN rates towards zero.

- **Minority-class and multi-class issues.** The vast majority of ads are from good-faith advertisers; thus detecting adversarial advertisements presents a difficult class imbalance issue [6]. This challenge is compounded by the presence of many different classes of adversarial advertisements, described in Section 2.

- **Training many models at scale.** At a high level, our system may be viewed as an ensemble composed of many large-scale component models. Each of these models must be frequently trained, evaluated, calibrated, and monitored; an efficient paradigm for this effort is presented in Section 3.

[1]The *ad landing page* is the web page to which a user is directed after clickling on an ad.

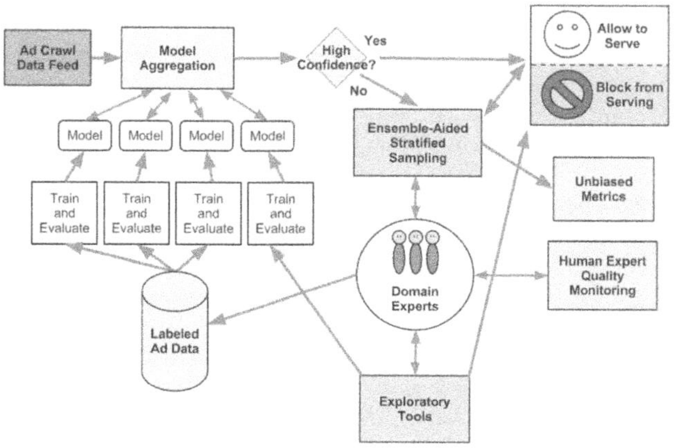

Figure 1: System-Level Architecture. Our system relies both on automated detection using large-scale learning and semi-automated detection in which learned models direct the effort of human experts.

- **Capturing expert knowledge.** To cope with constantly evolving adversarial tactics, our system needs to be able to capture and leverage expert knowledge quickly and efficiently. Using experts to label examples is one such method. Section 5 details additional approaches including the use of active learning, providing exploratory tools to experts, and enabling experts to develop rule-based models for fast response.

- **Allocating expert effort for multiple concurrent goals.** Expert effort is required not only for handling edge-cases, but also for providing training data and unbiased evaluation metrics. Section 4 presents an ensemble-aided stratified sampling approach to achieve these multiple goals simultaneously.

- **Independent evaluation.** Because we rely on human experts for ground truth, regular independent evaluations are critical to ensure that our ground truth understanding is accurate and comprehensive (see Section 6).

1.2 System Architecture

A high-level overview of our system architecture is given in Figure 1. The main source of data for our system is provided by a feed of advertisement data, including a crawl of the ad landing pages themselves. Because the crawl is responsible for fetching the contents of billions of ad landing pages and is a massive system in its own right, a detailed description of the crawl system is outside the scope of this work.

Each ad is evaluated by a large number of deployed models. The decisions from the models are aggregated; if there is a high-confidence decision of `block` or `allow`, this decision is put into serving. If the automated models are unable to provide a high-confidence decision, the ad may be shown to human experts as part of our ensemble-aided stratified sampling process (see Section 4). Human experts may also develop models using automated assistance, or use exploratory tools to find adversarial cases and add this data to our system. Because ad content may change dynamically over time, we record a snapshot of all features for an ad at the moment it is labeled by a human so that our repository of labeled data is contextually accurate.

2. BACKGROUND: ADVERSARIAL ADVERTISEMENTS

To our knowledge, adversarial advertisements have not yet been widely studied in the literature (see Section 7). In this section, we clarify the problem area by describing some representative categories of adversarial advertisements that we have encountered in practice. Note that this section is a partial listing intended to guide the reader's intuition for this paper; official policies are available online via the Google AdWords Help Center [13].

- **Counterfeit goods.** Some adversaries attempt to sell counterfeit or otherwise fraudulent goods while representing the goods as authentic.

- **Misleading or inaccurate claims.** This class of adversarial advertisements attempt to make claims that are unrealistic or scientifically impossible, such as a weight-loss plan promising extreme weight loss without exercise or dieting.

- **User safety issues.** Some adversaries attempt to profit by causing the user some form of harm, such as with false financial or medical claims.

- **Phishing.** Adversaries may attempt to obtain sensitive personal information by disguising their site to look like another site.

- **Arbitrage.** Advertisements whose sole or primary purpose is to direct the user to additional advertisements add little or no value to the user experience, in contrast to ads that provide useful content.

- **Unclear or deceptive billing.** Advertisements that list inaccurate or deceptive pricing, or which obscure the pricing or billing method, can constitute adversarial attempts to profit from false pretenses.

- **Malware.** Some adversaries attempt to direct users to landing pages where they might unwittingly download malware, badware, or other malicious software.

3. LEARNING METHODS

We now turn to the details of our learning-based approaches to detecting adversarial advertisements, starting with an examination of the features available for learning. We then describe the approaches we use to cope with the particular form of hierarchical multi-class classification required in this setting, including methods for dealing with highly skewed class imbalance. We present a simple MapReduce framework for training such models at scale, and conclude this section with an examination of practical considerations that must be addressed in a live production setting.

3.1 Features

Feature engineering is a key component of effective data mining; the following is a listing of the features extracted from advertisements during training and classification.

- **Natural language features** are extracted from the text of advertisement keywords, creatives, and landing pages. These include term-level features, and semantically related terms and topic-level features using methods similar to [9] and [3].

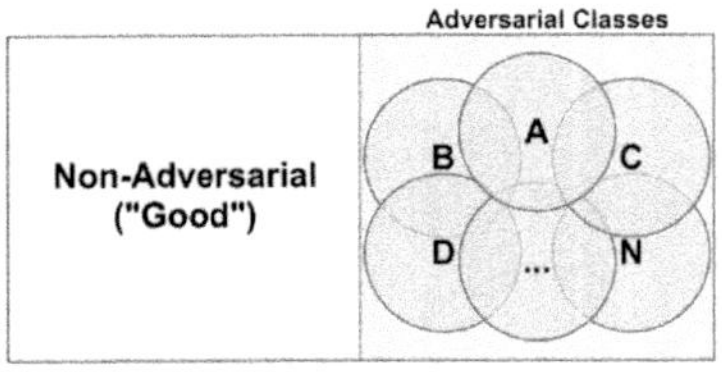

Figure 2: Class Structure. There is a clear distinction between `adversarial` and `non-adversarial`, but members of the `adversarial` classes overlap in places.

- **String-based features** are intended to avoid the possibility that adversaries may exploit alternate spellings or typographical manipulation to avoid detection. We incorporate features that allow inexact string matching, similar in spirit to [30].
- **Structural features** are extracted from the structural layout of the landing page.
- **Page-type features** are given by sub-classifiers that determine the general landing page type, such as a blog posting or a list of shopping results.
- **Crawl-based features** are extracted from the results of the http fetch of the landing page.
- **Link-based features** are based on links and redirects from the landing page.
- **Non-textual content-based features** yield information about the image, video, or other multimedia content on the page.
- **Advertiser account-level features** provide various information that may help identify suspicious or gaming behavior from adversaries.
- **Policy-specific features** include a variety of proprietary hand-crafted features that help to identify violations in particular policy areas.

3.2 Multi-Class and Minority-Class Issues

As described in Section 2, this problem area is inherently multi-class. For policy reasons, it is important to determine the exact category or categories for a given example, rather than a binary `adversarial` or `non-adversarial` classification. This problem is made more challenging by the fact that the vast majority of ads are `non-adversarial`, making each adversarial category an extreme minority class.

Our automated classification methods include a variety of inherently multi-class classifiers, including nearest neighbor approaches, naive-bayes variants, and semi-supervised graph-based algorithms. Because these methods are well known [2], we will not describe them further here.

Interestingly, the most effective methods we have found are based on sets of binary-class linear classifiers deployed as per-class classifiers, including linear support vector machines (SVM's) [16, 28], linear rank-based SVM's [17, 26], and linear models in cascades [33]. These methods will be the focus of this section.

3.2.1 One-vs-Good Multi-Class Classification

Typical strategies for performing k-class multi-class classification with binary classifiers include the *one-vs-all* method of training k individual models to distinguish each class from all other classes, and the *one-vs-one* method of training $\binom{k}{2}$ models to distinguish each class from each other class [14].

The class labels in our setting have a special structure. There is a single large class of `non-adversarial` (or "good") ads, and then a large number of possibly overlapping `adversarial` classes (see Figure 2). This setting naturally suggests a multi-class decomposition that we call *one-vs-good*, in which for each of $k-1$ adversarial classes, a model is trained to distinguish that class from members of the `non-adversarial` class only. This allows overlapping classes to be detected by examining the output of all models. In situations where several classes overlap significantly, we found it useful to train additional models to distinguish all members of the high-overlap set from the `non-adversarial` class.

3.2.2 Learning-to-Rank Methods for Classification

Linear SVM's have been found to be highly effective at high dimensional classification tasks similar to those encountered here, such as text classification [17]. Linear SVM's are trained by solving the following optimization problem:

$$\min_{\mathbf{w}} \frac{\lambda}{2}||\mathbf{w}||^2 + L(\mathbf{w}, D)$$

Here, $\mathbf{w} \in \mathbb{R}^d$ is a d-dimensional linear weight vector and λ is a regularization parameter controlling model complexity. $L(\mathbf{w}, D)$ is the total hinge-loss of $\mathbf{w}$ over the labeled training data $D = ((\mathbf{x}_1, y_1), \ldots, (\mathbf{x}_m, y_m))$ given by $\sum_{i=1}^{m} \max(0, 1 - y_i\langle \mathbf{w}, \mathbf{x}_i\rangle)$. Each labeled example contains a feature vector $\mathbf{x} \in \mathbb{R}^d$, and a class label $y \in \{-1, +1\}$. Linear SVM's may be trained efficiently using stochastic gradient descent variants such as the Pegasos SVM algorithm [28].

However, in cases of extreme class imbalance, linear SVM's have been found to give less than ideal results [21]. One approach is to set per-class weights on the loss function to emphasize the importance of the minority class [21], but we have found (in accordance with prior work [18, 26]) that using a pairwise objective function both improves results and eliminates the need to tune special per-class weights.

In the binary-class case, we refer to this pairwise method as the ROC Area SVM, or ROC-SVM. An ROC-SVM is trained by solving the following optimization problem:

$$\min_{\mathbf{w}} \frac{\lambda}{2}||\mathbf{w}||^2 + L(\mathbf{w}, P)$$

Here, P is the set of all *candidate pairs* in the original data set D. A candidate pair contains one $\mathbf{x}_p$ member of the positive class and one $\mathbf{x}_n$ member of the negative class, and is used to construct a labeled pairwise example $((\mathbf{x}_p - \mathbf{x}_n), +1)$. The ROC-SVM may be trained efficiently (despite the quadratic number of candidate pairs) using stochastic gradient descent and an indexed sampling scheme; see [26].[2]

Results. Using ROC-SVM instead of a standard Pegasos SVM improves recall by as much as 15% at our high-precision threshold for automated blocking of adversarial advertisements.

[2]Open source code for (single-machine) ROC-SVM using SGD is freely available `http://code.google.com/p/sofia-ml`.

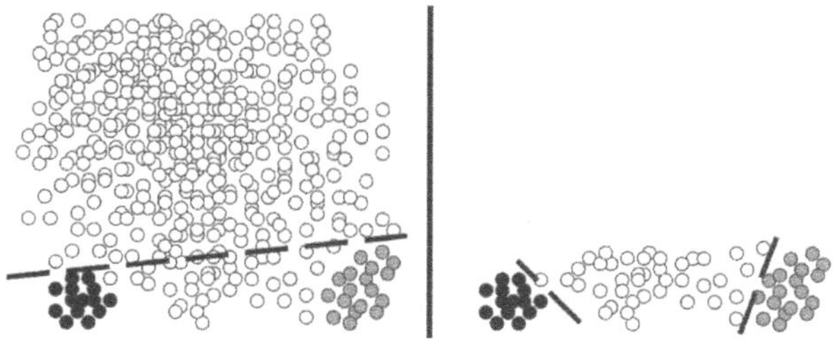

Figure 3: Visualizing Cascades. The vast majority of easy, good ads are filtered out by a high-recall coarse model (left). Finely-grained models then detect specific adversarial classes (right).

3.2.3 *Cascade Models*

The single model ROC-SVM approach works well for a number of adversarial classes, but other classes are more difficult to classify at the high-precision levels needed for automated blocking. For these cases, we use a more sophisticated methodology based on cascades.

The basic cascade framework uses a series of models, each of which rejects a portion of the data space, as illustrated in Figure 3. This approach has been particularly successful in the field of computer vision for tasks such as face recognition [33] and email spam filtering [37]. In theory, there is no limit to the number of stages that may be applied (and boosting approaches may result in dozens of stages). In practice, tuning a large number of cascade stages requires significant manual effort, creating a heavy maintenance burden.

After experimenting with a range of multi-stage configurations, we found a simple strategy that achieves good results with minimal system complexity. We use a single coarse model, common to all of our cascade models, trained to distinguish `adversarial` from `non-adversarial` with high recall. We then train a set of more finely-grained models to detect each of these more difficult classes with high precision, using the one-vs-good framework (see Figure 4).

Cascade models are particularly susceptible to problems of over-fitting. We have found tightly regularizing the coarse-level model to be effective. (Another approach uses cross-validation on the training data [37], but it is then non-trivial to combine the models in stages in a principled way.) The coarse model is tightly L1-regularized (see Section 3.3.2), inducing sparsity that keeps the memory footprint of this coarse model relatively small; this is an important consideration when dealing with billions of features. The sub-models are each trained on data sets that are much reduced in size due to the coarse-level filtering, reducing their size significantly as well.

Results. Representative results for three difficult per-class cascade models are given in Figure 5. (Note that the precision and recall values given in these graphs have been linearly transformed to obscure sensitive data; the relative performance trends remain unchanged.) In general, the cascade models give excellent improvement in recall at high precision levels (the upper-left corner of each graph), in comparison with a single ROC-SVM model for the same class problem. Note that in cases where the precision/recall curves cross (at lower precision levels, used for prioritizing human expert effort) we can always use the better of the two models in the different regions.

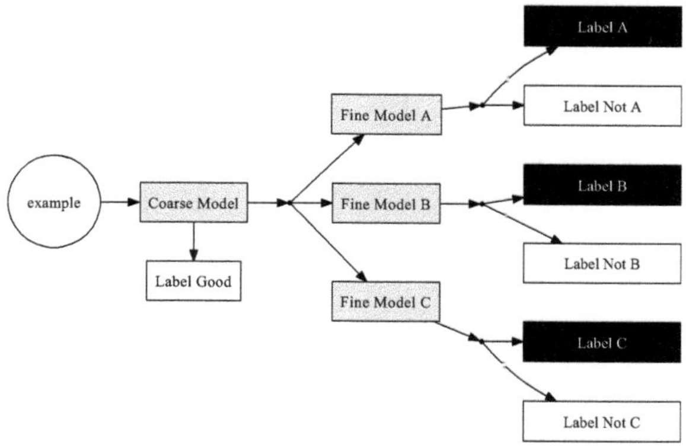

Figure 4: Multi-Class Cascade Framework. The coarse model filters out examples that are clearly `non-adversarial`. The remainder are passed to a set per-class models for fine-grained classification.

3.3 Large-Scale Training

By some standards, the data sets used to train our models may be seen as large (measured in terabytes); we need an efficient methodology for frequent training of dozens or hundreds of models. By enforcing sparsity during training, we ensure that the resulting models fit in memory on a single machine. This allows us to deploy an efficient stochastic gradient descent (SGD) training paradigm in a MapReduce[3] setting for fast model training.

3.3.1 *MapReduce SGD*

Solving optimization problems such as those presented in Section 3.2.2 may be done efficiently using SGD, which quickly converges to approximate solutions that are highly satisfactory from a machine learning perspective [4, 28]. SGD is an iterative solver, sequentially examining data points one at a time in a random order. The basic SGD training paradigm for linear SVM [38] is given in Algorithm 1.

Algorithm 1 Training Linear SVM using SGD.

1: $\mathbf{w}_0 \leftarrow 0$
2: **for** $i = 1$ to t **do**
3: $(\mathbf{x}, y) \leftarrow \text{RandomExample}(D)$
4: $\eta \leftarrow \text{GetLearningRate}(t)$
5: **if** $y\langle \mathbf{w}_{i-1}, \mathbf{x}\rangle < 1.0$ **then**
6: $\delta \leftarrow 1$
7: **else**
8: $\delta \leftarrow 0$
9: **end if**
10: $\mathbf{w}_i \leftarrow (1 - \eta\lambda)\mathbf{w}_{i-1} + \delta\eta y \mathbf{x}$
11: **end for**
12: **return** $\mathbf{w}_t$

In general, each iteration is fast to compute when $\mathbf{x}$ is sparse, and can be completed in $O(s)$ time where s is the number of non-zero elements in $\mathbf{x}$. The Pegasos SVM variant includes a step that projects $\mathbf{w}$ into an L2-ball of fixed radius after step 10; this may be done in O(1) time with appropriate data structures [28]. The number of iterations t may be large, but is provably independent of the number of training examples, making the SGD framework ideal for

[3]MapReduce is a paradigm for "embarrassingly parallel" tasks, widely used in cluster-based computing [8].

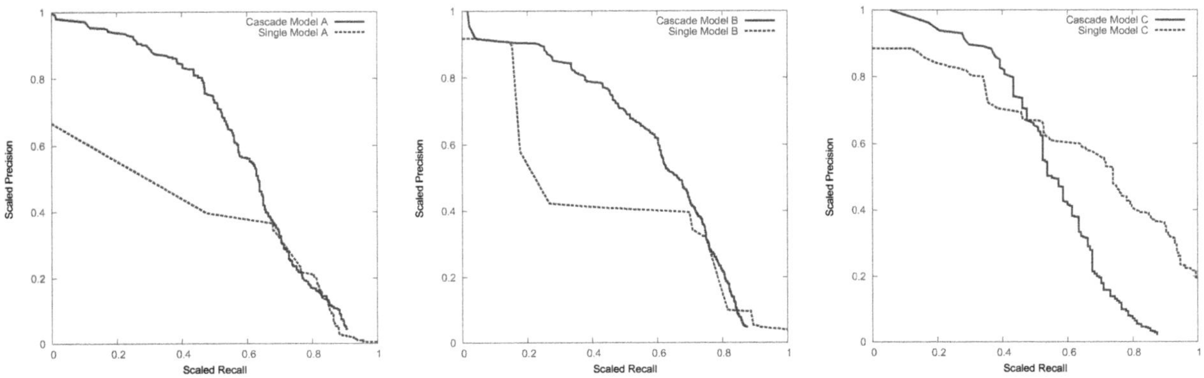

Figure 5: Cascade Models vs. Single Models. Values from three representative adversarial category identification tasks show that using cascade methodology significantly improves recall at low false positive rates. (Note that precision and recall values have been linearly transformed to protect sensitive data.)

large-scale learning [28, 4]. For example, only a few CPU seconds are required for training on data sets that are considered large in the academic literature, such as RCV1 [21]. But because SGD is a sequential online methodology, it is non-trivial to parallelize SGD training across multiple machines. Approaches that have been analyzed include message passing approaches [23], lazy distributed updates [39], training on multiple independent samples of the data [40], and performing multiple chained MapReduce steps [35]. However, these methods all add significant complexity to a relatively simple learning algorithm, and in some cases adversely impact model quality or give only limited incremental benefit as more machines are added.

Interestingly, we have observed that the main cost of SGD training is actually *reading and parsing data from disk*; this can be orders of magnitude more expensive than the actual training. Langford *et al.* have found it effective to reduce this cost by using a specialized data format, which significantly reduces disk-read times [19]. This observation allows us to parallelize our training effort with a simpler approach than those described above. As shown in Figure 6 our approach is summarized as follows:

- **Do expensive work in parallel.** The expensive work of parsing, filtering, labeling, transforming, and encoding data can all be done independently in parallel. We use hundreds of machines in the Map phase. The output of the Map phase is labeled training data that is efficiently compressed.

- **Do cheap work sequentially.** Because our models are small enough to fit in memory, a single Reduce machine can perform the SGD training quickly once the data has been properly prepared and formatted. This eliminates the need for expensive message passing or synchronization.

This framework allows us to train models within minutes on large data sets, and is used for both ROC-SVM training and for training our cascade models. A similar framework is used for evaluating models on holdout test data.

3.3.2 Controlling Model Size

The learned models must be small enough to fit in memory on a single machine; we use two strategies for keeping model size suitably restricted.

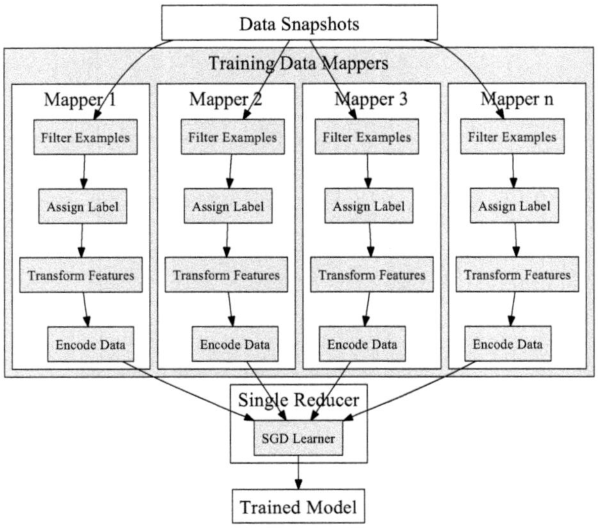

Figure 6: SGD learning via MapReduce. Preprocessing is parallelized; training is sequential.

The first of these is to use a feature-hashing approach similar in spirit to that of [36]. If we think of $\mathbf{w} \in \mathbb{R}^d$ as a set of key-value pairs where many values are exactly 0, then it is efficient to store the non-zero values in a hash map. Hashing the keys ensures that the model size will not grow beyond a certain bound. We have found that ignoring collisions does not degrade model performance, in line with results from [36] and keeps model size manageable.

The second strategy is to encourage sparsity in the learned model, so that many weight values are indeed exactly 0. We follow a projected-gradient methodology similar to that of [10], projecting $\mathbf{w}$ to an L1-ball of a specified radius after updates. This is done every k steps, after step 10 in Algorithm 1. The exact L1-projection of [10] was somewhat slow, so we use a simpler and faster approximate projection given in Algorithm 2. The method of Duchi *et al.* uses an approach similar to randomized median finding to find the exact value of τ that is used to project a given vector $\mathbf{w}$ onto an L1-ball of radius at most λ. We make do with using a value of τ that is guaranteed to cause the $||\mathbf{w}||_1$ to converge to radius at most λ after repeated calls. In practice, we find this work well, is fast to compute, and is easier to tune than the truncated gradient approach of [20].

Algorithm 2 Approximate projection to L1-ball of radius at most λ. Repeated calls to this projection will converge to radius λ.

$c \leftarrow \max(\lambda - ||\mathbf{w}||_1, 0)$
$d \leftarrow ||\mathbf{w}||_0$
$\tau \leftarrow \frac{c}{d}$
for each non-zero element i of $\mathbf{w}$ **do**
  $s \leftarrow sign(\mathbf{w}_i)$
  $\mathbf{w}_i \leftarrow s * \max(|\mathbf{w}_i - \tau|, 0)$
end for

3.4 Model Management

It is worth briefly looking at some of the engineering issues involved in maintaining a large-scale data mining system with many component models. Our management strategies include performing automated model calibration, establishing effective automated monitoring of live models, and bundling useful information into models.

3.4.1 Calibration

As models are re-trained over time, the semantic meaning of their output scores may drift or vary, resulting in constant adjustment of decision thresholds. To avoid the need for manual threshold adjustment, we automatically calibrate each model so that its final output is an actual probability estimate rather than an arbitrary score.

Recall that each linear model $\mathbf{w}$ scores a given example $\mathbf{x}$ using a scoring function $f(\mathbf{x}) = \langle \mathbf{w}, \mathbf{x} \rangle$. We learn a calibration function $c(\cdot)$ using holdout validation data to ensure that $c(f(\mathbf{x})) = Pr[y_{\mathbf{x}} = 1]$. This ensures that scores from different model versions may be interpreted along the same natural scale.

3.4.2 Monitoring

In a live production setting, it is critical to monitor the quality and output of models. Our first level of monitoring involves a set of precision/recall tests that each model must pass, based on holdout test data, whenever the model is re-trained. If the model fails these tests, the new version is not pushed to production. Second, we monitor the input features, to make sure that in aggregate the distribution of values is relatively stable. We need to be alerted if our input features or signals were to vary significantly, as this would cause changed behavior from our models. Third, we monitor model output scores to detect drift in distribution of values. A sudden drift would be a warning of a change somewhere in our system. We also monitor the actual decision rates in addition to the score distributions, to ensure we are aware of any sudden changes there. Finally, we monitor the overall system quality, based on data from our ensemble-aided stratified sampling pipeline, as described in Section 4.

3.4.3 Bundling Model Data

It is clear that a model needs to know how to classify examples. But what else should a model know how to do? Over time, we have found that it is useful to bundle a surprisingly large amount of information together into a model object. In particular, a model should know how to do the following:

- **Filter** out examples that should be ignored, for example if they are in the wrong language.
- **Transform** features as needed, including scaling, discretizing, etc.
- **Label** training data as a positive or a negative, and distinguish test data from training data.
- **Report** the parameters that were used to train it, so that the model may be re-trained if needed.
- **Score** an example using a feature vector $\mathbf{w}$.
- **Calibrate** its output scores onto a consistent scale.

Together, these requirements define a somewhat broader view of a "model" than is generally considered in academic literature, which often only discuss the weight vector $\mathbf{w}$. We have found bundling this data together reduces system complexity and eases the burden of managing and maintaining a large number of models in production.

4. ENSEMBLE-AIDED STRATIFIED SAMPLING

Acquiring hand-labeled data represents a significant cost, requiring expert judgement to navigate intricate policies and to recognize a wide variety of clever adversarial attacks. Our pilot experiments testing low-cost, crowd-sourced rater pools showed that crowd-sourcing was not a viable option to achieve labels of the needed quality for production use. Thus, we rely on more expensive, specially trained expert raters. It is therefore critical that we make the most efficient use of this limited resource.

In this section, we detail an ensemble-aided approach to stratified sampling that helps allocate rater effort efficiently to achieve multiple distinct goals.

4.1 Multiple Needs for Hand-Labeled Data

In machine learning literature, it is common to focus on gathering hand-labeled data only for the purpose of model training. But in our real-world setting, there are actually several important and distinct areas in our system that require hand-labeled data from expert raters. These are:

- **Catching hard adversaries.** Human judgement is needed to provide a final verdict on cases which are too difficult for automated methods to classify with high precision.
- **Improving learned models.** Hand-labeled data is needed to train models, and to keep the models current as adversarial methods change over time. Examples which are most beneficial for improved models (such as may be selected by various active learning strategies [32]) may be different from hard adversaries, above.
- **Detecting new trends.** It is helpful to prioritize the review of new ads, so that new trends from adversaries are quickly detected both by our automated systems and by our human domain experts.
- **Maximizing impact.** Because expert human-rater capacity is expensive and limited, it is desirable to maximize the impact by focusing on advertisements that have high impression counts.

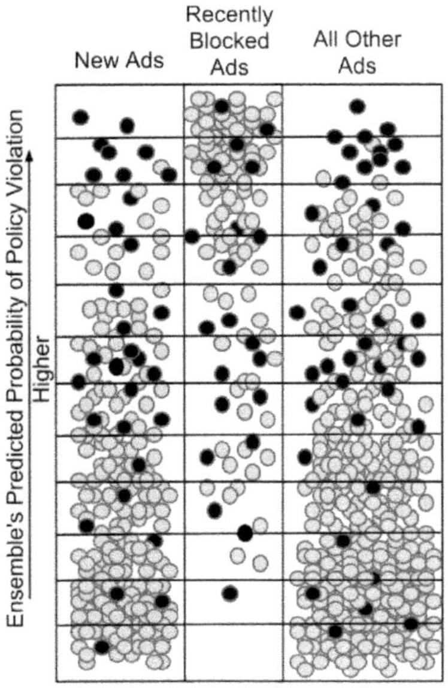

Figure 7: Ensemble-Aided Stratified Sampling. Ads in a given language are binned based on probability estimates from an ensemble. Grey and black circles represent un-sampled and sampled ads, respectively.

- **Providing unbiased metrics.** Hand rated data should be able to provide unbiased estimates for model-level and system-level precision and recall. The naive approach to gathering unbiased evaluation data would be to hand rate a uniform sample of ads. However, this would waste effort because the vast majority of ads are not adversarial. Sampling ads to achieve the other goals above results in biased evaluation data; by constructing the sample in a careful manner we can later remove the sample bias when computing metrics.

Not surprisingly, these different goals are largely disjoint, making it non-trivial to determine which ads should be selected for human rating.

4.2 Ensemble-Aided Stratification

We considered various forms of model-aided sampling [25], using learned models to induce a sampling bias towards more useful ads for human rating. We first tried to define an aggregate "utility" score based on these different factors, but it was unclear how to combine (or in some cases even how to measure) these different quantities. We also considered framing this problem in a bandit setting; however, McMahan and Streeter show that the use of bandit algorithms is problematic for selecting data for model-training due to the non-stationarity of the underlying models [24].

Our approach is to stratify the data across several different dimensions, as shown in Figure 7. First, ads in each language are considered separately. Within a given language, ads are divided into three categories, `new ads` that are less than t hours old, `recently blocked ads` that have been caught and turned off within the last t hours, and `all other ads` that have been actively served over the last t hours.

To aggregate the scores from the many different models in production, we train an ensemble model [2] for the given language, using the output scores of each of the m models as features for the ensemble. We use a binary-class (`adversarial` vs. `non-adversarial`) linear ROC-Area SVM to train

Algorithm 3 Priority Sampling Ads from a Bin. We use the following priority-sampling algorithm from [11] to select ads from a given bin for near-optimally low variance.

```
for each advertisement i with impressions w_i do
    pick p_i uniformly at random from (0, 1]
    let priority q_i = w_i / p_i
end for
sort all ads by their priority q
let τ equal the (k + 1)-th highest priority
for each of the k highest priority ads do
    let effective weight w'_i = max(w_i, τ)
end for
exclude all other ads from the sample for this bin
```

the ensemble, and calibrate its output scores as described in Section 3.4.1. The score from the ensemble-model is used to divide the ads in each category into uniformly spaced score-bins containing different numbers of ads.

This coarse binning allows us to explicitly decide how many ads to select from each bin in order to balance the differing goals listed in Section 4.1. Selecting sites from mid-probability bins is akin to uncertainty sampling [32], and provides benefit for model training. Selecting ads from higher probability bins in the `new ads` or `all other ads` categories gives priority to catching adversaries that have not yet been detected automatically. Selecting some ads from every bin ensures coverage of the entire data space.

4.3 Priority Sampling from Bins

Assuming we have decided to select k ads from a given bin, how should we choose which k to pick from that bin? Ideally, we would like a low-variance estimate of the impression-weighted total of each class of adversarial advertisement from the given bin; however, impression counts vary dramatically across ads, following a heavy-tail distribution.

In this heavy-tail setting, using uniform sampling to select ads within a bin is a poor strategy, resulting in high variance estimates [11]. Using an intuitive sampling proportional to impression-count strategy is better, but far from optimal [11]. Instead, we use the Priority Sampling strategy of Duffield *et al.* which has been proven to yield near-optimally low variance estimates for arbitrary subset sums [11]. This strategy is reviewed in Algorithm 3.

The variance from an estimate based on k samples selected with this strategy is provably at least as low as the variance of $k+1$ samples selected with the (computationally infeasible) optimal strategy [31]. It also has the attractive quality of tending to prioritize very-high impression ads for review to maximize impact of human effort while maintaining good coverage of the long tail.

Results. Using our ensemble-aided stratified sampling approach instead of the naive approach of separate samplings increased the effective impact of our human experts by 50%, and reduced the latency required to compute unbiased metrics by an order of magnitude with no added cost.

5. LEVERAGING EXPERT KNOWLEDGE

We have found it critical to leverage the knowledge of human experts to help detect evolving adversarial advertisements. Here, data mining methods provide automated guidance, ensuring the most effective use of human effort.

5.1 Active Learning

Experts periodically detect new categories of bad ads, or particular emerging trends, for which it is useful to develop a new model. Lacking initial training data, we have found that margin-based uncertainty sampling (akin to the `simple` strategy of Tong and Koller [32]) has been an effective methodology for rapid development of new models, often requiring only a few dozen hand-labeled examples.

5.2 Exploring for Adversaries

Attenberg *et al.* recently reported that in cases of extreme class imbalance, traditional active learning strategies may fail from difficulty in locating any members of the proposed positive class. They suggested using information retrieval systems in such cases, allowing expert users to search for positive examples guided by their intuition.

Independently, we have also found that providing a search-based interface for expert users provides valuable automated assistance for finding new examples of adversarial advertisements. Because this search-based tool is used by experts, it has been practical to augment standard keyword-based search with a variety of feature-based filters (using many of the features listed in Section 3.1). This allows experts to make guided searches in real time, based on their intuition and a large store of informative data.

5.3 Rule-Based Models

Coming from a machine-learning background, it has surprised us that our experts have proven capable of developing hand-crafted, rule-based models with extremely high precision. Enabling such models to be served in production provides a rapid response mechanism to new adversarial attacks, and gives an effective means of injecting expert knowledge directly into our system.

Because such models do not adapt over time, we have developed automated monitoring of the effectiveness of each rule-based model; models that cease to be effective are removed. Although rule-based models only account for less than 4% of the overall system impact, they provide an important capability to respond to new classes of adversarial attacks within minutes of discovery.

6. INDEPENDENT EVALUATION

Finally, we examine the data challenge of evaluating the human components of our system.

6.1 Monitoring Human Rater Quality

Because human ratings are used as our ground truth, it is critical to measure how reliable these ratings are. To establish this, we regularly evaluate the precision and recall of our base-level raters, using higher-level experts to re-rate a sample of ratings from each lower-level rater. We also regularly double-check these results using an independent set of higher-level experts. This allows us both to assess the performance of the base-level raters and to measure our confidence in those assessments.

6.2 Monitoring User Experience

The different levels of human experts described above are all paid and carefully vetted experts, and as such may have a viewpoint that does not always align with the perception of common users. To ensure that we get an accurate reading of real user perception, we additionally perform regular large-scale evaluations using an approach similar to crowdsourcing [29]. These evaluations are used to calibrate our understanding of real user perception and ensure that our system continues to protect the interests of actual users. The aggregate results from these independent evaluations have consistently shown strong agreement with our human expert opinion.

7. RELATED WORK

To our knowledge, the general problem of detecting adversarial advertisements has not previously been studied. In the most closely related work, Attenberg *et al.* detected *unsafe* advertisements, such as those containing adult content or hate speech, and used a search-based methodology over active-learning for model training [1]. We consider a broader range of adversarial advertisements, including many that are often difficult for non-experts to distinguish from good-faith advertisements without aid.

The field of email spam filtering has a large body of literature on the use of data mining for blocking adversarial messages (see [12] for an informative survey). The problem of adversarial advertisement detection differs in several ways, including the multi-class nature of the problem, the minority class difficulties, the presence of dynamically changing content, and the need for trained expert human raters.

Dalvi *et al.* attempt to learn classifiers in adversarial situations by modeling the adversaries [7], but accurately modeling motivated adversaries is problematic in real-world settings. Lowd and Meek point out that in a publicly-facing system, adversaries may attempt to reverse-engineer the model via membership queries [22]. Our inclusion of semi-automated methods involving human effort helps to minimize the effectiveness of such strategies.

Crowd-sourcing efforts like reCAPTCHA [34] attempt to use the effort of anonymous users to block abuse on the web. This approach is difficult in the case of advertisements because it would be problematic to keep motivated adversaries from poisoning the signal. Sculley *et al.* explored the use of aggregate user-based signals such as *bounce-rate* for determining user satisfaction [27], but this approach is unsuitable for making per-advertisement decisions with high precision due to signal noise. Various approaches such as that of Chakrabarti *et al.* have used click-feedback to determine ad *relevance* [5], but for adversarial advertisements relevance is a secondary factor compared to user safety.

8. REFERENCES

[1] J. Attenberg and F. J. Provost. Why label when you can search?: alternatives to active learning for applying human resources to build classification models under extreme class imbalance. In *KDD*, 2010.

[2] C. M. Bishop. *Pattern Recognition and Machine Learning*. Springer-Verlag New York, Inc., 2006.

[3] D. M. Blei, A. Ng, and M. Jordan. Latent dirichlet allocation. *JMLR*, 3, 2003.

[4] L. Bottou and O. Bousquet. The tradeoffs of large scale learning. In *Advances in Neural Information Processing Systems 20*. 2008.

[5] D. Chakrabarti, D. Agarwal, and V. Josifovski. Contextual advertising by combining relevance with click feedback. In *WWW '08: Proceeding of the 17th international conference on World Wide Web*, 2008.

[6] N. V. Chawla, N. Japkowicz, and A. Kotcz. Editorial: special issue on learning from imbalanced data sets. *SIGKDD Explor. Newsl.*, 6, June 2004.

[7] N. Dalvi, P. Domingos, Mausam, S. Sanghai, and D. Verma. Adversarial classification. In *Proceedings of the tenth ACM SIGKDD international conference on Knowledge discovery and data mining*, KDD '04, 2004.

[8] J. Dean and S. Ghemawat. Mapreduce: simplified data processing on large clusters. *Commun. ACM*, 51, January 2008.

[9] S. Deerwester, S. Dumais, T. Landuaer, G. Furnas, and R. Harshman. Indexing by latent semantic analysis. *Journal of the American Society of Information Science*, 1990.

[10] J. Duchi, S. Shalev-Shwartz, Y. Singer, and T. Chandra. Efficient projections onto the l1-ball for learning in high dimensions. In *ICML '08: Proceedings of the 25th international conference on Mach ine learning*, 2008.

[11] N. Duffield, C. Lund, and M. Thorup. Priority sampling for estimation of arbitrary subset sums. *J. ACM*, 54, December 2007.

[12] J. Goodman, G. V. Cormack, and D. Heckerman. Spam and the ongoing battle for the inbox. *Commun. ACM*, 50(2), 2007.

[13] Landing page and site policies. Google AdWords Help Center, 2011. `http://goo.gl/XcbPO`.

[14] C.-W. Hsu and C.-J. Lin. A comparison of methods for multiclass support vector machines. *Neural Networks, IEEE Transactions on*, 13(2), Mar. 2002.

[15] IAB internet advertising revenue report, 2010. `http://www.iab.net/media/file/IAB_report_1H_2010_Final.pdf`.

[16] T. Joachims. Making large-scale support vector machine learning practical. 1999.

[17] T. Joachims. Optimizing search engines using clickthrough data. In *KDD '02: Proceedings of the eighth ACM SIGKDD international conference on Knowledge discovery and data mining*, 2002.

[18] T. Joachims. A support vector method for multivariate performance measures. In *ICML '05: Proceedings of the 22nd international conference on Machine learning*, 2005.

[19] J. Langford. Vowpal wabbit. Open source release, 2007. `http://hunch.net/~vw/`.

[20] J. Langford, L. Li, and T. Zhang. Sparse online learning via truncated gradient. *J. Mach. Learn. Res.*, 10, 2009.

[21] D. D. Lewis, Y. Yang, T. G. Rose, and F. Li. RCV1: A new benchmark collection for text categorization research. *J. Mach. Learn. Res.*, 5, 2004.

[22] D. Lowd and C. Meek. Adversarial learning. In *Proceedings of the eleventh ACM SIGKDD international conference on Knowledge discovery in data mining*, KDD '05, 2005.

[23] G. Mann, R. McDonald, M. Mohri, N. Silberman, and D. Walker. Efficient large-scale distributed training of conditional maximum entropy models. In *Advances in Neural Information Processing Systems 22*. 2009.

[24] H. B. McMahan and M. Streeter. Tighter bounds for multi-armed bandits with expert advice. In *COLT '09: 22nd Annual Conference on Learning Theory*, 2009.

[25] C.-E. Särndal, B. Swensson, and J. Wretman. *Model Assisted Survey Sampling*. Springer, 2003.

[26] D. Sculley. Large scale learning to rank. In *NIPS 2009 Workshop on Advances in Ranking*, 2009.

[27] D. Sculley, R. G. Malkin, S. Basu, and R. J. Bayardo. Predicting bounce rates in sponsored search advertisements. In *KDD '09: Proceedings of the 15th ACM SIGKDD international conference on Knowledge discovery and data mining*, 2009.

[28] S. Shalev-Shwartz, Y. Singer, and N. Srebro. Pegasos: Primal estimated sub-gradient solver for SVM. In *ICML '07: Proceedings of the 24th international conference on Machine learning*, 2007.

[29] R. Snow, B. O'Connor, D. Jurafsky, and A. Y. Ng. Cheap and fast—but is it good?: evaluating non-expert annotations for natural language tasks. In *Proceedings of the Conference on Empirical Methods in Natural Language Processing*, EMNLP '08, 2008.

[30] S. Sonnenburg, G. Rätsch, and B. Schölkopf. Large scale genomic sequence svm classifiers. In *ICML '05: Proceedings of the 22nd international conference on Machine learning*, 2005.

[31] M. Szegedy. The DLT priority sampling is essentially optimal. In *Proceedings of the thirty-eighth annual ACM symposium on Theory of computing*, STOC '06, 2006.

[32] S. Tong and D. Koller. Support vector machine active learning with applications to text classification. *J. Mach. Learn. Res.*, 2, March 2002.

[33] P. Viola and M. Jones. Rapid object detection using a boosted cascade of simple features. *CVPR: IEEE Computer Society Conference on Computer Vision and Pattern Recognition*, 1:511, 2001.

[34] L. von Ahn, B. Maurer, C. McMillen, D. Abraham, and M. Blum. reCAPTCHA: Human-based character recognition via web security measure. September 2008.

[35] M. Weimer, S. Rao, and M. Zinkevich. A convenient framework for efficient parallel multipass algorithms. In *NIPS 2010 Workshop on Learning on Cores, Clusters and Clouds*, 2010.

[36] K. Weinberger, A. Dasgupta, J. Langford, A. Smola, and J. Attenberg. Feature hashing for large scale multitask learning. In *Proceedings of the 26th Annual International Conference on Machine Learning*, ICML '09, 2009.

[37] W. Yih, J. Goodman, and G. Hulten. Learning at low false positive rates. In *Proceedings of the Third Conference on Email and Anti-Spam (CEAS)*, 2006.

[38] T. Zhang. Solving large scale linear prediction problems using stochastic gradient descent algorithms. In *ICML '04: Proceedings of the twenty-first international conference on Machine learning*, 2004.

[39] M. Zinkevich, A. Smola, and J. Langford. Slow learners are fast. In *Advances in Neural Information Processing Systems 22*. 2009.

[40] M. Zinkevich, M. Weimer, A. Smola, and L. Li. Parallelized stochastic gradient descent. In *Advances in Neural Information Processing Systems 23*. 2010.

Applying Data Mining Techniques to Address Disaster Information Management Challenges on Mobile Devices

Li Zheng, Chao Shen, Liang Tang, Tao Li, Steve Luis, Shu-Ching Chen
School of Computing and Information Sciences, Florida International University
11200 S.W. 8th Street, Miami, Florida, 33199, U.S.A.
{lzhen001, cshen001, ltang002, taoli, luiss, chens}@cs.fiu.edu

ABSTRACT

The improvement of Crisis Management and Disaster Recovery techniques are national priorities in the wake of man-made and nature inflicted calamities of the last decade. Our prior work has demonstrated that the efficiency of sharing and managing information plays an important role in business recovery efforts after disaster event. With the proliferation of smart phones and wireless tablets, professionals who have an operational responsibility in disaster situations are relying on such devices to maintain communication. Further, with the rise of social media, technology savvy consumers are also using these devices extensively for situational updates. In this paper, we address several critical tasks which can facilitate information sharing and collaboration between both private and public sector participants for major disaster recovery planning and management. We design and implement an **All-Hazard Disaster Situation Browser (ADSB)** system that runs on Apple's mobile operating system (iOS) and iPhone and iPad mobile devices. Our proposed techniques create a collaborative solution on a mobile platform using advanced data mining and information retrieval techniques for disaster preparedness and recovery that helps impacted communities better understand the current disaster situation and how the community is recovering. Specifically, hierarchical summarization techniques are used to generate brief reviews from a large collection of reports at different granularities; probabilistic models are proposed to dynamically generate query forms based on user's feedback; and recommendation techniques are adapted to help users identify potential contacts for report sharing and community organization. Furthermore, the developed techniques are designed to be all-hazard capable so that they can be used in earthquake, terrorism, or other unanticipated disaster situations.

Categories and Subject Descriptors

H.2.8 [**Database Applications**]: Data mining; H.3.3 [**Information Search and Retrieval**]: Clustering; H.3.5 [**Online Information Services**]: Web-based services; H.4 [**Information Systems Applications**]: Miscellaneous.

General Terms

Algorithms, Design, Management.

Keywords

Data Mining, Disaster Information Management, Hierarchical Summarization, Dynamic Query Form, User Recommendation

1. INTRODUCTION

Business closures caused by disasters can cause millions of dollars in lost productivity and revenue. A study in Contingency Planning and Management shows that 40% of companies that were shut down by a disaster for three days failed within 36 months. Thin margins and lack of a well-designed and regularly tested disaster plan make companies, particularly small businesses, especially vulnerable [1]. We believe that the solution to better disaster planning and recovery is one where the public and private sectors work together to apply world class computing tools to deliver the right information to the right people at the right time facilitating the work of those feverishly restoring a community's sense of normalcy.

Over the last four years, our disaster management team at Florida International University has cooperated closely with experts and participants from South Florida Emergency Management and industry partnership, such as Wal-Mart, Office Depot, Wachovia, T-Mobile, Ryder Systems and IBM among others. The collaboration provides us with the opportunity to gain the insight of the way South Florida public and private sector entities manage and exchange information in a disaster situation. We have designed and implemented a web-based prototype of a Business Continuity Information Network (BCIN) system (www.bizrecovery.org) utilizing the data processing power of advanced information technologies for disaster planning and recovery under hurricane scenarios. It can largely help people discover, collect, organize, search and disseminate real-time disaster information [5,6].

1.1 Assimilating Information Exchange Needs in Major Disasters

Our study of the hurricane disaster information management domain has revealed two interesting yet crucial information management issues that present similar challenges in other disaster management domains.

The first issue is that reconstructing or creating information flow becomes intractable in domains where the stability of information networks is fragile and can change frequently. On the other hand, important information networks often carry and store critical information between parties, which dominates the flow of resources and information exchanges. The consequence is that the ability and the efficiency of communication degrade once critical networks are disrupted under disaster impact and people may not have alternative path to pursue so that they can consume information or restore their connections. For instance, once power is disabled and uninterruptable power supplies are drained after hurricane, computing and networking equipment will fail unless preventative measures are taken. However, maintaining a fuel-consuming generator is not always available in advance or after such events.

Another issue we observe is the human need to consume a large volume of disaster situational information. Reading and assimilating situational information is very time consuming and has a high probability of exposure to redundant information. For instance, it is very common for multiple information channels to publish the same situational information in a repetitive fashion.

Therefore, to quickly re-assemble or create information flow for multi-party coordination activities during disaster situations, technologies that are able to extract information of recent updates, deliver information without conflicts or irrelevance and represent information of preference are needed.

Based on our long-standing collaboration with Miami-Dade County Emergency Management and private sector business continuity planners, we understand that professionals from both sides have those needs not only under hurricane scenarios but also under many other major disaster situations. To summarize, in disaster situations, the information delivery should be able to support users' complex information needs and approximately tailored to the situation and the tasks. As a result, the information should be synthesized from heterogeneous sources, be tailored to specific contexts or tasks at hand, and be summarized for effective delivery, and be immediately useful for making decision.

1.2 Motivation for Developing on a Mobile Platform

In January 2009, a few months after Hurricane Ike (the third most costly hurricane in US history [2]) impacted the city of Houston, TX, our team was invited by FEMA to attend a meeting of public and private sector stakeholders. At that meeting, we asked emergency managers and business continuity professionals about the role technology played in the recovery process of the city. Most attendees agreed that mobile phones where being used extensively for voice, SMS and data based services despite the spotty coverage by various cellular carriers. At the National Hurricane Conference that same year, technical staff of the American Red Cross conveyed their use of mobile phones in the wake of mid-west river floods. The Red Cross shipped cell phones to affected areas so that staff had communication capabilities to address logistical needs. Despite the flooding impact, cellular carriers were capable of providing adequate cellular service. In both cases we heard similar reasons for using mobile phones:

1. **The devices are portable** (pocket sized) and do not have to be hand carried like a laptop which is considered a burden in the field.
2. **The devices can operate without electrical power for long periods of time** making it easier to operate in areas with limited access to power.
3. **The devices can be used for different modalities of communication.** For example, an SMS message can be sent to someone who has actionable information that is needed urgently to solicit an immediate response versus an email that can be replied at the convenience of the receiver.
4. **Native mobile apps make it easy to enter information** from the phone instead of having to use phone's web browser to access a website.

Recent consumer trends suggest that mobile phones are being used extensively for situational updates to social networking services like Facebook, Twitter, and many other photo sharing, blogging, location aware services [22]. From the information services perspective, acquiring data from a mobile phone can be more media rich since the phone has image, video and sound recording capabilities. Data acquired from the mobile phone is typically transmitted with geo-location data that makes it easy to organize data spatially.

In summary, professionals who have an operational responsibility in disaster situations are relying on mobile phones to maintain communications, update status and share situational information. Consumers, too, are finding mobile devices convenient for sharing information about themselves and what is going on in their lives. By using a mobile platform we can build native applications which utilize onboard sensors, rich media, and simplified user interface to engage users in a way they feel most comfortable to share such information in a disaster situation.

In this paper, built on our previous work, we design and implement an **All-Hazard Disaster Situation Browser (ADSB)** system running on mobile platforms which uses advanced data mining and information retrieval techniques to address the important information management needs in major disaster situations.

1.3 Research Challenges and Proposed Solutions

During prototyping ADSB to integrate those critical features into the mobile platform, we have identified the following three key tasks to fully utilize the advantages and overcome the limitations of major mobile devices.

1. Design and develop effective and interactive information summarization methods to help users understand large collection of reports. It is typically difficult for readers to extract useful information from a large quantity of documents. Multi-document summarization provides users with a tool to effectively extract important and related ideas of current situations. However, previous text summarization techniques gave users a set of sentences based on user query. The summarization is fixed once the query is determined. Note that mobile devices are generally with a small display and limited input capabilities. An interactive summarization interface is needed to help users navigate collected information at different granularities, and locate their target information more efficiently.

2. Design and develop intelligent information delivery techniques to help users quickly identify the information they need. The data is collected through many different channels and belongs to different categories. During disaster preparation and recovery, users do not have the time and patience to go through the system to find the information they want. Structured information can be of important value to help people make decisions by providing them with actionable and concrete information representation and exploration. However, navigating the large result set on the mobile device is particularly inefficient. An interactive tabular interface can largely help users filter useful information by adapting changing query conditions and user feedbacks.

3. Design and develop dynamic community generation techniques for reports recommendation and user group organization. In information sharing tasks, identifying a group of recipients to which a certain type of information is conveyed to can highly improve the efficiency of communication and gain valuable feedback. But on mobile device, managing the groups of friends within the limited display often makes user miss highly related friends. User recommendation techniques can offer a user such convenience by automatically and interactively generating potential recipients for different pieces of information. In addition, user recommendation techniques can help users effectively and dynamically organize user groups according to various information sharing tasks.

In general, to accomplish these three goals, ADSB utilizes the latest advances in database, data mining, and information extraction technologies, to create a user friendly, information-rich service on mobile platform in disaster management and recovery domain. It also acts as an infusive channel for better sharing, integration, extraction, and processing of business continuity information.

In particular, to address task 1, we apply hierarchical summarization to automatically extract the status information from a large document set and also provide a hierarchical view to help users browse information at different granularities. To address task 2, we create a user interface called the Dynamic Query Form to improve information exploration quality. It captures users' interests by interactively allowing them to refine and update their queries. To address task 3, we use transactional recommendation history combined with textual content to explore the implicit relationship among users.

ADSB is essentially a collaborative platform for preparedness and recovery that helps disaster impacted communities to better understand what the current disaster situation is and how the community is recovering. This achievement is paramount, as we have seen, in the aftermath of disasters like Hurricanes Katrina and Andrew, communities disintegrating because faith in the process of recovery is lost. The analytical power of our solutions is designed to be all hazards capable so that they can be used in earthquake, terrorism, or other unanticipated disaster events.

The rest of the paper is organized as follows. Section 2 presents the overview of ADSB system; Section 3 describes the hierarchical summarization module in detail. Affinity Propagation is used to build the hierarchical summaries; Section 4 discusses the dynamic query form module. We propose probabilistic models to dynamically generate query forms based on user's feedback; Section 5 describes the user recommendation module. The algorithm for ranking users' interaction preference is implemented by considering the transaction information and the textual content; Section 6 describes the system evaluation and data crawling strategies; Finally, Section 7 concludes the system development and operation.

2. ADSB OVERVIEW

ADSB is a collaborative solution on mobile platform designed for information sharing, integration, extraction, and processing. It can help the user efficiently identify, organize, and deliver important information. In ADSB, registered users can submit reports by typing plain texts as well as attach resources of other formats such as PDF and Doc. The system users can also tag those reports to manage their interested information or post comments to interact with other users. ADSB provides hierarchical summaries generated from user specified keywords to briefly capture important information. Also, a set of suggested query forms helps the users efficiently refine the query results. At last, users can also organize their important friends into groups according to different information management tasks. Figure 1 illustrates the system architecture. **A video demonstration accompanying the paper is available at http://users.cis.fiu.edu/~taoli/ADSB-Demo/demo.htm. Details of system functionalities can be obtained from the video.**

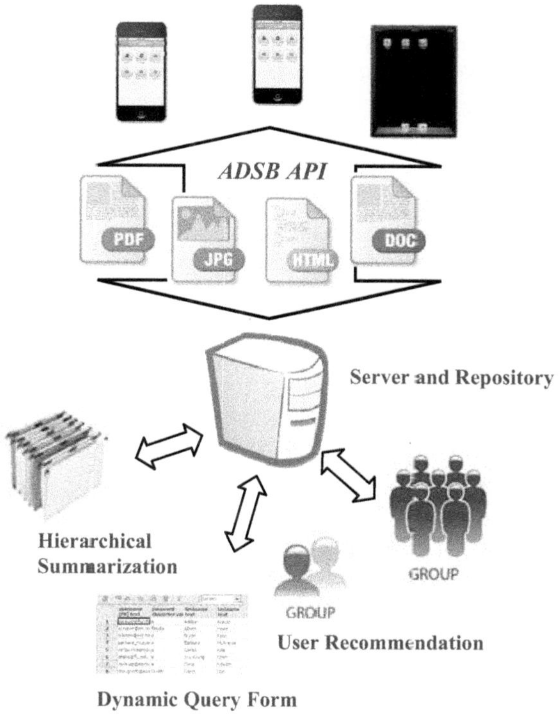

Figure 1. ADSB System Architecture

2.1 ADSB System Components

Based on the experience of developing our prototype we have designed series of components necessary for practical information exploration and exchange:

Report List: A personalized list of reports, which are related to the users interests and current most important news posted onto the system. A user can sort through the reports either in chronological order or by personalized recommendation settings.

Report Detail: It is a comprehensive view where all information related to each individual report will be displayed. It is designed to support various formats of text sources such as PDF, HTML, plain text and others. Users can also retrieve related images, post new comments and add tags. The report sharing interface dynamically generates a user list based on the specific report content to share an interesting report with others.

Advanced Search: Users can obtain summarized information by submitting keywords in the advanced search interface. Each query (consists of one or more keywords) will return a summarization (several sentences). Each sentence corresponds to a certain aspect, which allows users to further drill-down or scroll-up operation along hierarchical summaries.

Dynamic Query Form: It is implemented in the way to satisfy those dynamic and heterogeneous query desires by covering attribute sets and annotation attributes associated with different reports. The user can refine query conditions and select related query results to generate more concrete and related query forms.

Community Management: Community is defined as a set of users that have a specific relationship between each other. Also, it is an important channel to obtain related information and monitor how the situation evolves with respect to an event. An interactive approach is implemented to improve experiences in which a user can freely group contacts from a recommended contact list rather than being forced to navigate the user list repeatedly.

We illustrate those important components in Figure 2.

2.2 ADSB Architecture

2.2.1 ADSB API

ADSB adopts the open source REST (REpresentational State Transfer) framework named Restlet which is a lightweight, comprehensive and fully Java implemented web architecture model designed for both server and client Web applications[3,4].

The implementation of the ADSB API is entirely HTTP-based and follows CRUD (Create, Read, Update and Delete) rules by specifying a corresponding HTTP response code. As a Restful resource, ADSB API supports both XML and JSON formats. Due to the simplicity and flexibility of Restlet framework, ADSB API allows us to:

- Conveniently interact with multiple information domains.
- Quickly create components and functions based on information management processes.
- Improve end-user programmability and configurability.
- Can be easily released to third party clients to embed our data service into different application.

2.2.2 ADSB's Major Modules

The above-mentioned system information processing and representation functionalities are integrated with the following three critical modules: Hierarchical Summarization, Dynamic Query Form and User Recommendation.

Hierarchical Summarization: ADSB system provides users with reports summaries which are generated from multiple reports. The Affinity propagation method is applied on the sentence similarity graph to build hierarchical summaries in an agglomerative way. The exemplar generated by affinity propagation for each sub-cluster can be used as a summary of that cluster. Details of summarization approaches are discussed in Section 3.

Dynamic Query Form: After obtaining document graph and attribute graph which represent relationships among document set and attribute set respectively, we iteratively calculate similarities between documents and attributes separately by running the random walk model. The suggested query condition can be generated based on each given document and previously selected attributes. Details are discussed in Section 4.

User Recommendation: ADSB provides an interface for users to share a single report with other people. Such sharing transactions are good indications of users' preferences and can help us identify meaningful users groups. We utilize the transactional hyper-graph and the textual content to generate the suggested user list by ranking the interaction preference of each user based on the given report and the selected user seeds. The details will be described in Section 5.

These modules are tightly integrated to provide a cohesive set of services and constitute a holistic effort on developing a data-driven solution for disaster management and recovery.

Figure 2. ADSB Screen Shots of Important Components

* iPhone implementation has the same style with iPad but without rich visual abilities, such as the split view.

3. HIERARCHICAL SUMMARIZATION

ADSB allows users to search reports by keywords or query forms like traditional information systems. To give a brief view of the latest information that the user is interested in, we develop the hierarchical multi-document summarization method to generate the hierarchical summaries of reports. In our summarization, we use the Affinity Propagation (AP) [17] clustering method to build a hierarchical structure for sentences of related reports.

3.1 Affinity Propagation

The input of the Affinity Propagation algorithm is the sentence similarity graph defined as $G<V, E>$: V is the set of vertices with each vertex, called data point, representing a sentence. E is the set of edges. Let $s(i,k)$ be the similarity between two distinct points i and k, indicating how well that the data point k is suitable to be the exemplar of point i. Specially, $s(i,i)$ is the preference of a sentence i to be chosen as the exemplar. In the algorithm, there are two kinds of messages passing between data points: the responsibility and the availability.

The responsibility $r(i,k)$ is computed as follows,

$$r(i,k) \leftarrow s(i,k) - \max_{\{k' \neq k\}}\{a(i,k') + s(i,k')\}.$$

The responsibility $r(i,k)$ is passing from i to candidate exemplar k. It reflects the accumulated evidence for how well point k suits to be the exemplar for point i against other candidate exemplars.

The availability $a(i,k)$, is computed as follows,

$$a(i,k) \leftarrow min\{0, r(k,k) + \sum_{i' \in V, i' \notin \{i,k\}} \max\{0, r(i',k)\}.$$

The availability $a(i,k)$ is passing from the candidate exemplar k to point i, reflecting the accumulated evidence for how appropriate it would be for point i to choose point k as its exemplar, considering the support from other points which share point k as exemplar. Whereas the responsibility updating lets all candidate exemplars compete for the ownership of a data point, the availability updating gathers evidence from data points to measure the goodness of each candidate exemplar.

The self-availability $a(k,k)$ is updated as follows:

$$a(k,k) \leftarrow \sum_{i' \in V, i' \neq k} \max\{0, r(i',k)\}.$$

This message reflects accumulated evidence of point k being an exemplar based on the positive responsibilities sent to candidate exemplar k from other points.

All availabilities are initialized to zero: $a(i,k) = 0$. After the updating converges, availabilities and responsibilities are combined to identify exemplars. For point i, its corresponding exemplar is obtained by maximizing the following expression:

$$k^* = \arg\max_k \{a(i,k) + r(i,k)\}.$$

We choose AP for the following reasons:

- AP can find clusters with much lower error than other clustering methods, such as the k-means method.
- AP performs efficiently on sparse similarity graph, which is the case of document space. The running time for iterations is linear to the number of edges in the graph.
- AP takes a real number as input, called preference for each data point. The preference quantifies the likelihood of it being chosen as exemplar. Thus the prior and heuristic knowledge can be used to associate different sentence with different preference.
- AP identifies exemplars for each cluster or group which can be naturally used as the summary sentence for the cluster.

3.2 Hierarchical Summarization on Affinity Propagation

For the sentences in related reports, $\{s_1, s_2, \cdots, s_n\}$, we want to build a hierarchical clustering structure, exemplars of clusters are used as the summary. In an agglomerative way, starting from all the sentences, then the exemplars, we recursively apply affinity propagation until the number of exemplars is small enough. To conduct the affinity propagation algorithm, we specify the preference for each sentence and similarity between sentences as the input of the algorithm.

3.2.1 Sentence Preference

We define the preference of a sentence i to be chosen as an exemplar using the following scores.

Language Model score L: For sentence i, L_i is calculated as the logarithmic probability of sentence i using unigram model training on the reports $\{s_1, s_2, \cdots, s_n\}$. Generally, a short sentence which has more frequent words in the reports would have a higher score.

LexPageRank score P: LexPageRank proposed by [18] calculates the Page Rank score for sentences on the sentence similarity matrix. The score measures the prestige in sentence networks assuming that the sentences that are similar to many of the other sentences in a cluster are more prestigious to the topic. Since the original LexPageRank can be interpreted as the probability in random walk theory, we use the logarithmic version to make it in a same scale with the Language Model score.

Freshness score F: In our application, users are generally more interested in latest information, we calculate the freshness score of sentence i as

$$F_i = -e^{a_i},$$

where a_i is the *age* in term of number of days the document contains the sentence i.

Finally, the preference of s_i is the sum of the three feature scores with a scaling parameter:

$$s(i,i) = L_i + D_i + F_i.$$

3.2.2 Sentence Similarity

Sentence similarity $s(i,j)$ indicates how well the data point with index j is suited to be the exemplar for data point i. In our case, it means how likely sentence i can be summarized by sentence j. If sentence i and sentence j have non-stop word overlaps, we calculate $s(i,j)$ by the log-likelihood of sentence i given that its exemplar is sentence j.

$$s(i,j) = log\, P(i|j).$$

To calculate the conditional probability, a unigram language model is trained on sentence j by using the Dirichlet smoothing. Then the probability of sentence i is calculated by using the language model.

4. DYNAMIC QUERY FORM

In ADSB, each report is associated with a set of attributes, such as the report location, date, or annotations added by the creator. Such structural information allows users to execute relational queries on reports. For example, we want to find those reports which are about hurricanes from year 1990 to 2010 and hurricane centers' latitudes are above 30 degrees latitude. Hence, our ADSB system applies query forms for users to satisfy the relational queries.

Traditional query forms are statically embedded in the system by developers or database administrators. Those static query forms are used for the static database schema. However, in ADSB, different reports have different sets of attributes. For example, the hurricane report and earthquake report own two very distinct sets of attributes. Furthermore, the associated values of annotation attributes that are created by the user at runtime may not be consistent. Therefore, it is impossible to design a static and fixed query form to cover all those attributes. In ADSB, we implement dynamic query form to satisfy those dynamic and heterogeneous query desires.

Previous research on database query forms focuses on how to automatically generate the query form from the data distribution or query history [12,13,14,15]. However, different users can have different query desires. How to capture the current user's interests and construct appropriate query forms is the key challenge for query form generation which has not been solved yet.

4.1 Problem Formulation

Query forms are designed to return the user's desired results. The metric of the goodness of a query form is based on two traditional measures for evaluating the quality of the query results. One is *precision*, which is the fraction of results returned by the query form desired by the user. The other is *recall*, which is the fraction of desired results contained in the results.

Let $F = (\mathbf{A}_F, \sigma_F)$ be a query form with a set of query conditions σ_F and a set of displaying attributes $\mathbf{A}_F$. Let D be the set of all reports in the database. $|D|$ is the number of reports. $P_u(.)$ is the distribution function of user interests. $P_u(d)$ is the user interest for a report d, and $P_u(\mathbf{A}_F)$ is the user interest for an attribute subset $\mathbf{A}_F$. $P(\sigma_F|d)$ is the probability of query condition σ_F being satisfied by d, i.e., $P(\sigma_F|d) = 1$ if d is returned by F and $P(\sigma_F|d) = 0$ otherwise. Then, given a query form $F = (\mathbf{A}_F, \sigma_F)$, the *expected precision*, *expected recall* and *expected fscore* of F are defined as follows:

$$Precision_E(F) = \frac{\sum_{d\in D} P_u(d)P_u(A_F)P(\sigma_F|d)}{\sum_{d\in D} P(\sigma_F|d)},$$

$$Recall_E(F) = \frac{\sum_{d\in D} P_u(d)P_u(A_F)P(\sigma_F|d)}{\sum_{d\in D} P_u(d)\, P_u(A)},$$

$$FScore_E(F) = \frac{(1+\beta^2)\cdot Precision_E(F)\cdot Recall_E(F)}{\beta^2\cdot Precision_E(F)\cdot Recall_E(F)},$$

where $A_F \subseteq A$, $\sigma_F \in \sigma$, β is a parameter defined by the user and β is usually set to 2.

$FScore_E(.)$ is the metric in ADSB system to evaluate the overall goodness of a query form. The problem of our dynamic query form is how to construct a query form $\hat{F}$ that maximizes the goodness metric $FScore_E(.)$, i.e.,

$$\hat{F} = \underset{F}{\operatorname{argmax}}\, FScore(F).$$

4.2 Method Description

It is impractical to construct an optimal query form $\hat{F}$ at the very beginning, since we do not know which reports and attributes are desired by the user. In other words, estimating $P_u(d)$ and $P_u(\mathbf{A}_F)$ is difficult.

ADSB system provides an iterative way for the user to interactively enrich the query form. Figure 3 shows the work-flow of our dynamic query form system. At each iteration, ADSB computes a ranked list of query form components for users, and then lets users make the choice for their query form. Those query form components are ranked by the metric $FScore_E(F)$.

There are two types of query form components: attribute display and query condition.

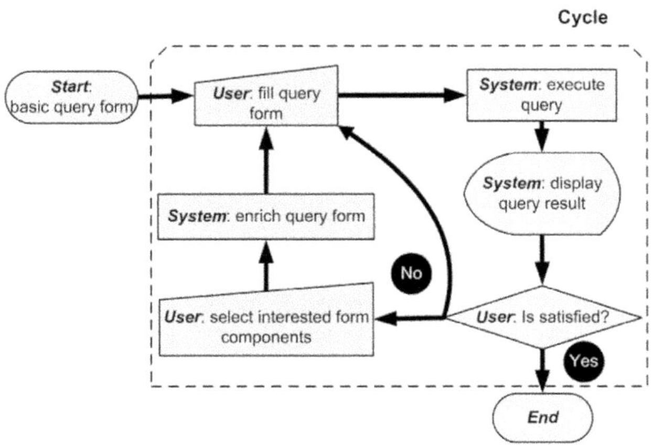

Figure 3. Flowchart of Dynamic Query Form

Assume the current query form is F_i in the flowchart, and the next query form is F_{i+1}. In order to compute $FScore_E(F_{i+1})$, we have to estimate $P_u(d)$, $P_u(\mathbf{A}_{F+1})$ and $P(\sigma_{F+1}|d)$. The estimation is based on user behaviors when interacting with the ADSB system. Let D_{uf} be the set of reports viewed by the users. We assume those reports are interesting to the current user, then

$$P_u(d) = \sum_{d'\in D_{u,f}} P_u(d|d')P_u(d').$$

We use the random walk model to compute the relevance score between reports as the value of $P_u(d|d')$ [16]. Figure 4 shows an example of the *report graph*, where d_i is report i, w_{ij} is the weight of report i and report j, i,j=1,2,.... w_{ij} is computed by how many attributes and values are commonly shared by the two reports.

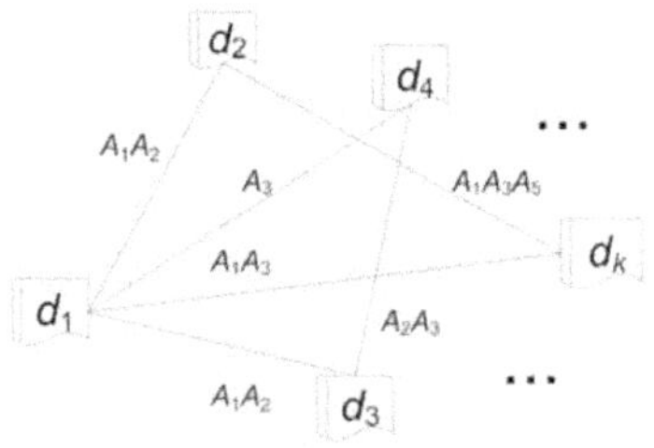

Figure 4. Report Graph

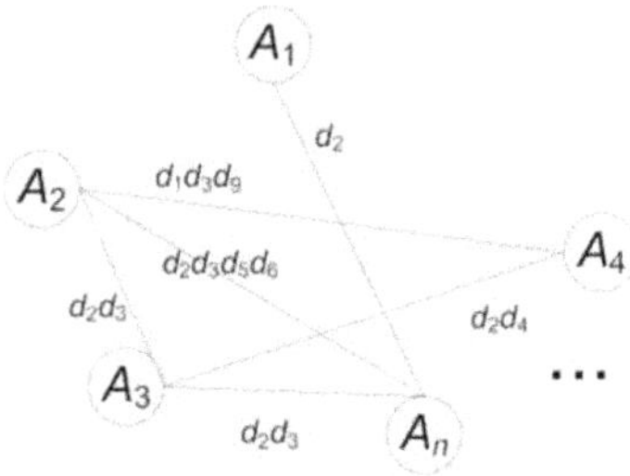

Figure 5. Attribute Graph

Suppose A is displaying an attribute we suggest for query form F_{i+1}. So $\boldsymbol{A}_{f_{i+1}} = A \cup \boldsymbol{A}_{F_i}$, where $A \in \boldsymbol{A}$, $A \notin \boldsymbol{A}_{F_i}$. $\boldsymbol{A}_{F_i}$ can be obtained in the current query form F_i.

$$P_u(\boldsymbol{A}_{F_{i+1}}) = P_u(A|\boldsymbol{A}_{F_i})\, P_u(\boldsymbol{A}_{F_i}).$$

We also estimate $P_u(A|\boldsymbol{A}_{F_i})$ by using random walk model on the *attribute graph* as shown in Figure 5. The nodes of the attribute graph are report attributes, and the edges are common reports. So the weight of the edge *ij* is computed by how many reports both own the two attributes *i* and *j*.

Suppose *s* is a query condition we suggest for query form F_{i+1}. So $\sigma_{F_{i+1}} = s \wedge \sigma_{F_i}$, where *s* is a single query condition for attribute A_s, $A_s \in \mathbf{A}$. σ_{F_i} can be obtained in the current query form F_i. For each report $d \in D$, $P(\sigma_{F_{i+1}}|d) = P(s|d)\,P(\sigma_{F_i}|d)$. It is very time-consuming to find the best *s* by brute-force search on all $P(s|d)$. So we pre-compute the $P(s|d)$ and store it in the database.

5. USER RECOMMENDATION

ADSB's user recommendation component provides an interface for the user to explore other users' recommendations or share reports with other people. It is also a tool to help the user quickly identify sets of users with shared interests. It is designed by considering each individual's transactional sharing history, textual content of each transaction and timeliness of interaction to provide each user with a personalized information sharing experience.

Related work during past years has been applied to email communication networks analysis to find important persons, identifying frequent communication pattern and detecting communities based on transactional user relationships [7,8,9, 10,11]. Those techniques can prevent a user from forgetting to add important recipients, avoid costly misunderstandings, and communication delays. Carvalho et al. [10] introduced several supervised learning models to predict the score of each user associated with a given email content. By aggregating TF-IDF vector of each email that a user was related to (by To, CC or BCC), it can predict the score of a new email to such user. However, it was not aware of the different importance of emails for senders and recipients. Horn et al. [11] explicitly associated higher weights to senders, and also consider user-interaction graph as a directed hyper-graph. It focused on the time and frequency of interactions but ignored the content information involved in each email, which could be an important indication of potential related users.

In ADSB, there are three practical considerations motivating the user recommendation: 1. To share information to the right/related people, users need an intelligent tool to help them auto-generate a recipient list which covers active users who could be highly interested in specific information; 2. Identifying meaningful groups of users is tough work, so users prefer efficient ways to organize contacts instead of navigating the contact list repeatedly; 3. It could be more effective and straightforward for one user to access information that others think it is important to him rather than finding it by himself.

So, ADSB system addresses the above-mentioned issues by considering both user interactions and textual information. In practice, we provide dynamic user suggestion for news recommendation and community recommendation interface to help our system users organize their critical partnerships.

5.1 Transactional Interactions

In ADSB, an interaction or transaction is defined as the process of a user sharing a report with one or more other users. So, the reports sharing transaction database can be treated as a hyper-graph with each node representing a registered user and a set of edges created at the same time from one node to a set of nodes representing an occurred transaction. There are three important factors associated with each edge:

Time: The time that the transaction happened. It indicates the importance of recency. In general, the more recently a transaction happens, the more important the report is to those users involved.

Direction: The relation of an interaction. An edge pointed from node A to node B indicating that A shares some information with a set of users including B. The direction indicates that the shared information is more important to the sender than to receivers.

Textual Content: Each transaction is associated with some certain textual content, so the content of an edge means that someone thinks such content is important or related to some group of users.

In practice, a personalized user recommendation requires the algorithm to identify potential users who have frequent and active interactions with the sender and are also interested in some certain topics. In completion of two recommendation tasks, we extend both [10] and [11] by taking the direction, timeliness and textual content of the interaction into consideration to generate 1) a suggested user list for specific report and 2) a suggested user list for specified seeds (users).

5.1.1 User Groups

There could be multiple transactions associated with a specified user and each transaction involves a group of users, as shown in Figure 6.

Even though transactions may include the same sender and receivers, they are treated as unique in the transactional hyper graph since they are associated with unique timestamps. Despite the textual content of each transaction, the contribution of each group made to current user seeds can be easily evaluated by Interaction Rank proposed in [11].

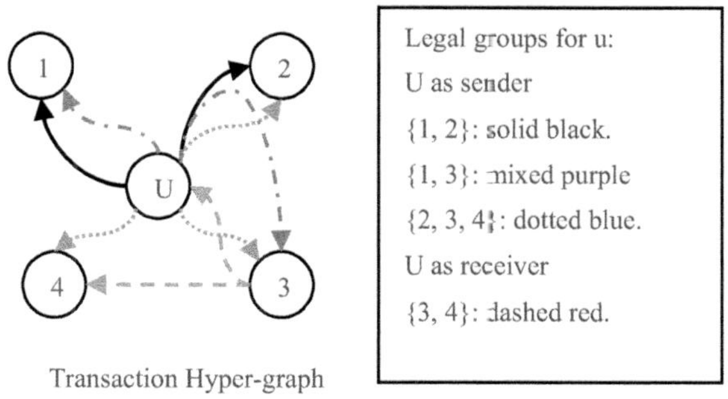

Figure 6. Transactional User Groups

5.1.2 User Profile

To build the user profile, we consider textual content in all transactions related to the user. Carvalho [10] introduced a centroid vector-based representation which aggregates all related documents to build a user profile. In our method, we consider transaction directions and assign document sending weight $\mathcal{W}_s$ or receiving weight $\mathcal{W}_r$ respectively. We use term frequency-inverse document frequency (TF-IDF) transformation to represent textual content as a vector. So the user profile can be represented as:

$$profile(u) = \mathcal{W}_s \cdot \sum_{d \in S(u)} tfidf(d) + \mathcal{W}_r \cdot \sum_{d \in R(u)} tfidf(d),$$

where $tfidf(d)$ is defined as

$$tfidf(d)_i = TFIDF(d)_i^{\ t},$$

$t = \frac{time(now)-time(n)}{\lambda}$ indicates a over-time exponential decay of each document's contribution. $S(u)$, $R(u)$ are sets of documents which sent and received by u respectively. So, for a report d, user u 's preference to this report can be simply generated by computing the cosine similarity between the users profile and the TF-IDF vector of d as:

$$preference(u,d) = cos\left(profile(u), ts_{tfidf}(d)\right).$$

Practically, user profile is stored separately and will not be updated in each calculation. Typically, it will be updated when there is new event announced or regularly every few days.

5.1.3 Algorithm

We extended the friend-finding algorithm proposed in [11] to generate a list of user recommendations by aggregating the groups' contribution to a user and considering the relevance between users and reports. Algorithm is described in Figure 7. Score of each user in the list represents the interaction preference with respect to the given user and report.

```
Input:  u, the user; d, the report, and S, the seeds
Output:  R, recommended user list
1. G ← GetTransactionalGroups(u)
2. R ← ∅
3. for each group g ∈ G
4.     for each user c ∈ g, c ∉ S
5.       if c ∉ R
6.             R [c] ← 0
7.       R [c] ← R [c] + GroupScore(c, S, g, d)
     or  [c] ← R [c] + CommunityScore(c, S, g)
```

Figure 7. Suggesting User Routine

5.2 Group Contribution

From the algorithm described in Table 5.1, the interaction preference of a user is the aggregated value of the contribution that each transaction made to the user. There are two types of contribution measurements with respect to different tasks. We use group score and community score to represent contributions for report sharing and community user recommendation respectively.

5.2.1 Group Score

The group contribution $\mathcal{GC}$ described below represents the contribution that a user group contributes on the user. There are two situations considered, 1) In order to suggest users related to a document, we consider the preference (similarity) between the document and a user; 2) In order to help user form a meaningful group, we consider the similarity between users. We defined $\mathcal{GC}$ as an aggregated score of users' preferences to a specific document considering the direction and timeliness of each interaction.

For the first situation, we use similarities between each user in a group with report d:

$$\mathcal{GC}(d,g) = w_s \cdot \sum_{i \in O(u,g)} s(i,d)^t + w_r \cdot \sum_{i \in I(u,g)} s(i,d)^t,$$

where $s(i,d) = \sum_{u \in i} preference(u,d)$.

For the second situation, we simply modified the $\mathcal{GC}(d,g)$ as $\mathcal{GC}(c,g)$ and $s(i,d)$ as

$$s(i,c) = \sum_{u \in i} cos\big(profile(u), profile(c)\big),$$

to calculate similarity without document information.

In both situations, $O(u,g)$ and $I(u,g)$ are sets of sending and receiving interactions/transactions which user u was involved.

5.2.2 Recommend Users with Report

Recommending a report to group of users involves historic recommendation transactions and the report's textual content. The score that a transaction contributes to a user is the aggregation of preferences of a group of users to the given report:

$$\boldsymbol{GroupScore}\,(c,\mathcal{S},g,d) = \begin{cases} \mathcal{GC}(d,g), \text{if } \mathcal{S} \cap g \neq \emptyset; \\ 0, \quad otherwise. \end{cases}$$

5.2.3 Recommend Users for Communities

Recommending users to form communities involves historic transactions without textual information. The score that a transaction contributes to a user is the aggregation of similarities between the user and users in the group:

$$\boldsymbol{CommunityScore}\,(c,\mathcal{S},g) = \begin{cases} \mathcal{GC}(c,g), \text{if } \mathcal{S} \cap g \neq \emptyset; \\ 0, \quad otherwise. \end{cases}$$

By specifying a couple of users as seeds, our recommendation components can dynamically generate more users related to the given textual content and list of users with high concurrence.

6. DATA COLLECTION AND EVALUATION

The data sources used in our project can be broadly divided into two categories based on the temporal characteristics: static data sources and dynamic data sources. Static data sources include historical data from Miami-Dade Office of Emergency Management (EOC). Dynamic data sources include (a) situation reports from Miami-Dade EOC and participating companies illustrating the current status of threat, ongoing operations and goals/objectives for preparation and recovery efforts; (b) open/closure status about roadways/highways/bridges and other infrastructure such as Fuel, Power, Transportation, Emergency Services (Fire Stations, Police Stations etc.), Schools and Hospitals; (c) Reports crawled from FEMA [20] web site about twenty major disasters happened since year 2000; and (d) tweets posted in August 2010 by using Twitter API [19] from dozens of active accounts.

Evaluation is conducted on two levels: algorithm evaluation and system evaluation.

To evaluate the algorithms used in our system we use standard performance metrics used in the research literature and carefully compare our algorithms with existing work when applicable.

Our system evaluation process consists of presenting the system to our community of emergency managers, business continuity professionals and other stakeholders for feedback and performing community exercises. The community exercises involve a real time simulation of a disaster event and are integrated into an existing exercise that the community conducts for readiness each year. This evaluation exposes information at different time intervals and asks the community to resolve different scenarios by using the tool developed. The evaluation conducted takes on the form of a "table-top" exercise in which information injects provide details about the current disaster situation and specify potential goals and course of action. In return, the participant uses the system to gather information to best assess the situation and provide details about the actions they will take. We gather information from the user about what information they found to derive their conclusions or lack thereof. This information allows us to better understand how those techniques overall improve the information effectiveness.

Feedbacks from our users are overwhelming positive and suggest that our system can be used not only to share the valuable actionable information but to pursue more complex tasks like business planning and decision making. There are also many collaborative missions that can be undertaken on our system which allows public and private sector entities to leverage their local capacity to serve the recovery of the community. Our initial work has been recognized by FEMA (Federal Emergency Management Agency) Private Sector Office as a model in assistance of Public-Private Partnerships [21].

7. SYSTEM OPERATION AND CONCLUSION

FIU has spent over $600K in the development of the application and has received over $400K in sponsored research or industry donation. The system is utilized by over 100 companies in local communities and County emergency agencies in the south Florida area, which facilitates the collaboration on their mutual interest of disaster preparedness, response and recovery and benefits. The system is monitored 24/7 via scripts that verify application, database, web server, and hardware availability. The system is managed in a revision control system and is running through a test suite that validates key functionality such as report submission, keyword searching, and dynamic queries.

The potential impact of this research on the economy is enormous. A study by the Insurance Information Institute (III) shows that significant economic impacts can result from even minor events; an event that forced the permanent closure of just 1% of businesses in Broward, Miami-Dade, and Monroe Counties (the South Florida tri-county area) would result in 13,500 lost jobs, over $1.8 billion in lost sales, and over $414 million in lost payroll for the first year. Our analysis shows that, if our system helps 5% of the companies in the South Florida area to speed up their hurricane recovery by 1 week, it will prevent more than $200 million dollars of non-property economic losses that would result from that week's closure [6].

8. ACKNOWLEDGMENTS

This work is supported by NSF grant HRD-0833093 and DHS grant 2009-ST-062-000016. We thank Jesse Domack, Mark Oleson and Jason Allen for their work in the system development and testing.

9. REFERENCES

[1] The Conference Board. Preparing for the worst: A guide to business continuity planning for mid-markets. Executive Action Series, February 2006.

[2] R. Berg. Hurricane Ike Tropical Cyclone Report. NHC. Retrieved 2009-09-12.

[3] Wikipedia. http://en.wikipedia.org/wiki/Restlet

[4] R.T. Fielding, (2000), Architectural Styles and the Design of Network-based Software Architectures, Doctoral dissertation, University of California, Irvine.

[5] V. Hristidis, S. Chen, T. Li, S. Luis, and Y. Deng. Survey of data management and analysis in disaster situations. The Journal of Systems and Software, 83:1701–1714, 2010.

[6] L. Zheng, C. Shen, L. Tang, T. Li, S. Luis, S. Chen, and V. Hristidis. Using data mining techniques to address critical information exchange needs in disaster affected public-private networks, KDD '10, pages 125–134, 2010.

[7] M.D. Choudhury , W. A. Mason , Jake M. Hofman , Duncan J. Watts, Inferring relevant social networks from interpersonal communication, Proceedings of the 19th international conference on World wide web, April 26-30, 2010.

[8] I. Kahanda and J. Neville. Using transactional information to predict link strength in online social networks. In Proceedings of the Third International Conference on Weblogs and Social Media (ICWSM), June 2009.

[9] S. Yoo , Y. Yang , F. Lin , I. Moon, Mining social networks for personalized email prioritization, Proceedings of the 15th ACM SIGKDD international conference on Knowledge discovery and data mining, June 28-July 01, 2009, Paris, France.

[10] V. R. Carvalho , W.W. Cohen, Ranking users for intelligent message addressing, Proceedings of the IR research, 30th European conference on Advances in information retrieval, March 30-April 03, 2008, Glasgow, UK.

[11] I. Horn, A. Leichtberg, N. Leiser, Y. Matias, and R. Merom. Suggesting friends using the implicit social graph. In Proceedings of KDD-2010, pages 233–242.

[12] M. Jayapandian and H.V. Jagadish. Automated creation of a forms-based database query interface. In Proceedings of VLDB 2008, pages 695-709.

[13] M. Jayapandian and H.V. Jagadish. Expressive query specification through form customization. In Proceedings of EDBT 2008, pages 416-427.

[14] M. Jayapandian and H.V. Jagadish. Automating the design and construction of query forms. IEEE TKDE 21(10): 1389-1402, 2009.

[15] P.P. Talukdar, M. Jacob, M.S. Mehmood, K. Crammer, Z. G. Ives, F. Pereira, and S. Guha. Learning to create data-integrating queries. In Proceedings of VLDB 2008, pages 785-796.

[16] H. Tong, C. Faloutsos, and J. Pan. Fast random walk with restart and its application. In Proceedings of ICDM 2006, pages 613-622.

[17] B.J. Frey and D. Dueck, Clustering by passing messages between data points. Science. 2007

[18] G. Erkan and D.R. Radev, Lexpagerank: Prestige in multi-document text summarization. In Proceedings of EMNLP, 2004.

[19] Twitter API, http://apiwiki.twitter.com.

[20] FEMA, http://www.fema.gov.

[21] FEMA Public Private Partnership Models. http://www.fema.gov/privatesector/ppp_models.shtm. under Miami-Dade County.

[22] comScore Press Events. http://www.comscore.com/Press_Events/Press_Releases/2010/3/Facebook_and_Twitter_Access_via_Mobile_Browser_Grows_by_Triple-Digits. March 3, 2010.

Enhancing Investment Decisions in P2P Lending: An Investor Composition Perspective

Chunyu Luo[1,2], Hui Xiong[2], Wenjun Zhou[3], Yanhong Guo[1], Guishi Deng[1]

[1]Faculty of Management and Economics, Dalian University of Technology, China
E-mail: luochy@gmail.com, guoyh@dlut.edu.cn, denggs@dlut.edu.cn

[2]Management Science and Information Systems Department, Rutgers University, USA
E-mail: hxiong@rutgers.edu

[3]Department of Statistics, Operations and Management Science, University of Tennessee, USA
E-mail: wzhou7@gmail.com

ABSTRACT

P2P lending, as a novel economic lending model, has imposed new challenges about how to make effective investment decisions. Indeed, a key challenge along this line is how to align the right information with the right people. For a long time, people have made tremendous efforts in establishing credit records for the borrowers. However, information from investors is still under-explored for improving investment decisions in P2P lending. To that end, we propose a data driven investment decision-making framework, which exploits the investor composition of each investment for enhancing decisions making in P2P lending. Specifically, we first build investor profiles based on quantitative analysis of past performances, risk preferences, and investment experiences of investors. Then, based on investor profiles, we develop an investor composition analysis model, which can be used to select valuable investments and improve the investment decisions. To validate the proposed model, we perform extensive experiments on the real-world data from the world's largest P2P lending marketplace. Experimental results reveal that investor composition can help us evaluate the profit potential of an investment and the decision model based on investor composition can help investors make better investment decisions.

Categories and Subject Descriptors

H.2.8 [**Database Management**]: Database Applications—*Data Mining*

General Terms

Algorithms, Design, Experimentation

Keywords

P2P Lending, Investor Profile, Investor Composition

1. INTRODUCTION

P2P lending, or online social lending, allows individuals to directly lend to and borrow from each other on an Internet-based platform, without the participation of traditional financial intermediaries. In this marketplace, borrowers submit applications for loans, called lists, and then lenders bid on them. If the total dollar amount requested by a list is fulfilled within a limited time period, the list will become a loan. Typically, a lender would like to spread his money across many different loans to help reduce risk, and a loan is usually funded by many lenders. In recent years, advances in P2P lending markets have enabled new research opportunities with the availability of massive amounts of P2P transaction data. For instance, Prosper.com [1], the world's largest P2P lending marketplace with more than one million members and over 2.1 billion in funded loans, has provided the investors with large amounts of transaction data for investment analysis.

As an emerging market for investment, P2P lending has imposed new challenges in decisions making. While tremendous efforts have been made to establish credit records for borrowers, the information from investors remains under-explored for improving investment decisions in P2P lending. Indeed, in the field of behavioral finance [29, 2], it has been found that investors make different investment decisions due to differences in knowledge structures, information sources, cognitive development, and behavioral preferences. For many-to-many investment relationships, such as stock market and P2P lending market, different investors can have different investment preferences and different investees (i.e. stocks, P2P loans, etc.) could be funded by different types of investors. In other words, the investor composition of an investee–the group of investors who invest on this investee–can exhibit certain characteristics, some of which can be quantified by various statistics. Therefore, it is promising to exploit investor composition for improving investment decisions in P2P lending.

As a matter of fact, composition analysis, or structure analysis, has been an important and commonly used method in finance and economics. For example, the portfolio composition [23] evaluates a portfolio of assets, each having different risks and returns, to reduce risk for a give level of return. Similarly, the capital structure [24] has been considered as an important indicator of a firm's financial position. In addition, the board composition [19] has been considered as one of the important factors on a firm's overall performance. However, since P2P lending is an emerging investment field, the research methods and types of data being collected are still under development. As a result, the problem of how to exploit investor composition for enhancing investment decisions is still under-explored.

The P2P lending marketplace can be modeled as a bipartite graph with investors and loans on either side. This graph represents many-to-many investment relationships between investors and loans. Therefore, each loan may be funded by multiple lenders, and each lender invests on many different loans. In this paper, we exploit such relationships for analyzing investor composition, based on which we build a data-driven investment decision-making framework for enhancing investment decisions in P2P lending.

Furthermore, we perform the quantitative analysis of the past performances, risk preferences, and investment experiences of investors and build investor profiles including various segments of investors with different characteristics. Then, based on investor profiles, we develop an investor composition analysis model which can be used to estimate the profit potential of each investment. Finally, we demonstrate the effectiveness of the proposed investment composition analysis through extensive experiments on a real-world P2P lending dataset. Experiment results reveal that the investor composition can effectively indicate investment values, and the investor composition model can improve the profit potential of investment in P2P lending.

Overview. The rest of this paper is organized as follows. An overview of related work is provided in Section 2. We define the bipartite investment network and analyze investor profiles in Section 3. Section 4 provides an investor composition analysis model to quantitatively analyze investor composition. In Section 5, an investor composition driven investment decisions model is proposed. Section 6 presents experiments with real-world data for validating the effectiveness of the proposed investment decision model. Finally, we conclude the work in Section 7.

2. RELATED WORK

P2P lending, as a novel economic lending model, has been studied extensively in the literature in recent years. For instance, Hulme and Wright [15] provided an in-depth treatment of the social lending subject from multiple perspectives. Freedman and Jin [10] have investigated whether social networks solve the information asymmetry problem in peer-to-peer lending. They found that the estimated return of group loans is lower than those of non-group loans due to lender's learning and the elimination of group leader rewards. Wang et al. [33] provided an overview of the concept of people-to-people lending, a relatively new e-commerce phenomenon that has the potential to radically change the structure of the loan segment of the financial industry. Lauri and Jeffrey [25] developed a borrower decision aid system, which helps the borrowers quantify their strategic options, such as starting interest rate, and the amount of loan to request. The role of financial intermediaries on the P2P online market was analyzed by Berger and Gleisner [3], which demonstrates that the recommendation of a borrower significantly enhances credit conditions, and the intermediary's bid on a credit listing has a crucial impact on the resulting interest rate. Benjamin and Robert [6] build a theoretical framework for the evaluation and design of community reputation systems. Katherine and Sergio [17] examined the behavior of lenders and find that, while there exists high variance in risk-taking between individuals, many transactions represent sub-optimal decisions on the part of lenders. Garman et al. [12] made the case that lenders' search for listings to bid on is an integral part of the lenders' behavior. Ryan et al. [28] analyzed the correlation between variables and regression models using real-world data.

Traditional loan evaluation techniques also relate to P2P lending when we study from the investor's perspective. One goal of these techniques is to distinguish good loan applications from bad applications. These techniques can be roughly categorized into five groups: statistical models, operational research methods, artificial intelligence techniques, hybrid approaches, and ensemble models [8]. For instance, statistical models include logistic regression [35, 32], linear discriminate analysis [26], k-nearest neighbor (KNN) [5], classification tree [9], Markov chain [11] and survival analysis [31]. Operations research methods include linear programming [22] and quadratic programming [4]. Artificial intelligence techniques include neural networks [16], Support Vector Machines (SVMs), Genetic algorithms [7] and genetic programming [14]. Hybrid approaches include fuzzy systems and neural networks [21], fuzzy systems and support vector machines [34] and neural networks and multivariate adaptive regression spines [18]. For ensemble models, the neural network ensemble is a typical example [36].

As a novel financial model that involves diverse elements, P2P lending renders lots of research opportunities and challenges that are currently under-explored. Specially, we view P2P lending as a many-to-many investment network, and study investment decisions from the investor's point of view. In this paper, we exploit investor composition as an investment decisions aid in P2P lending.

3. INVESTOR PROFILES

In this section, we define the bipartite investment network and analyze investor profiles.

3.1 Investment Network

Many modern investment relations can be modeled as many-to-many relation. For example, in the stock market, most investors hold many different stocks and each stock is owned by many investors. In P2P lending, investors diversify their investment by allocating money on many different loans, and a loan can gain investments from many different investors. In this section, we use a bipartite network to describe the many-to-many investment relationship between investors and investees.

Bipartite network is widely used to model the relationship among two types of entities [13, 30, 20]. In P2P lending, we consider the following two different types of entities. **investors** are the people who provide capital to selective loans, also known as "lenders". **Investees** are the loans that need to be financed. In P2P lending, a borrower may submit multiple loan requests. Instead of considering borrowers for credit risk analysis, we consider each individual loan as a separate Investee, since each loan has a different set of investors available for composition analysis.

In the following, we describe the construction of the bipartite investment network with basic notations. Suppose there are m investors $U = \{u_1, u_2, u_3, ..., u_m\}$ and n investees $V = \{v_1, v_2, v_3, ..., v_n\}$. We can build a bipartite investment network $G = \{U, V, E\}$, where U and V are vertices on the two sides, and $E = \{e_{11}, e_{12}, ..., e_{ij}, ..., e_{mn}\}$ are the edges connecting them. Each edge, e_{ij}, represents the amount investor u_i has lent to investee v_j. Specially, $e_{ij} = 0$ if investor u_i has never lent to investee v_j.

We define investors' investment weight w_{ij} as the ratio of u_i's investment on v_j to the total amount of u_i's all investments in the investment network $G = \{U, V, E\}$, as written in Equation (1):

$$w_{ij} = \frac{e_{ij}}{\sum_{j=1}^{n} e_{ij}} \tag{1}$$

Similarly, we also define investees' investment weight λ_{ij} as the ratio of u_i's investment in v_j to the total amount which v_j' gain from all investors in the investment network $G = \{U, V, E\}$, as written in Equation (2):

$$\lambda_{ij} = \frac{e_{ij}}{\sum_{i=1}^{m} e_{ij}} \tag{2}$$

An illustration of such bipartite graph and investment weights is shown in Figure 1 below.

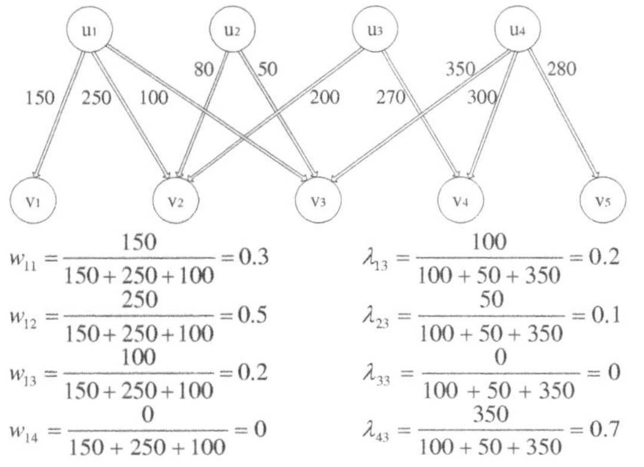

Figure 1: An Example Bipartite Investment Network.

In P2P lending, based on investor's investment data and investee's performance data, we can construct a whole bipartite investment network that provides the basis to quantitatively analyze investor profile and investor composition.

3.2 Investor Profile Analysis

In order to analyze investor composition, we should first understand the investors' behavior. In this section, we study how to quantitatively analyze investors' past performance, risk preference, and investment experience in order to build investor profiles.

Based on past investment behavior of an investor, it is possible to build a profile to represent his/her proficiency in making successful investments. We consider an investor's profile from three aspects: past performance, risk preference, and investment experience. In this section, we describe the computation formulas for synthesizing each of the three aspects into a numerical measure.

An investor in the P2P lending marketplace typically has multiple investments, each of which may have a different rate of return. Let R_j represent the rate of return of loan v_j. Since loans can be paid back in full, or default with partial or no payment, the rate of return R_j can be negative. The past investment performance $\bar{R}_i$ of investor u_i is measured by a weighted average of investment returns, as written in Equation (3):

$$\bar{R}_i = \sum_{j=1}^{n} w_{ij} R_j \tag{3}$$

where $w_{ij} = \frac{e_{ij}}{\sum_{j=1}^{n} e_{ij}}$ is the ratio of u_i's investment on v_j to the total amount of u_i's all investments in the investment network $G = \{U, V, E\}$.

Standard deviation is often used to quantify risk [23]. For each investor u_i, we define investment risk preferences, P_i, as the standard deviation of investment rates of returns, as written in Equation (4):

$$P_i = \sqrt{\sum_{j=1}^{n} w_{ij} \left(R_j - \bar{R}_i\right)^2} \tag{4}$$

It is reasonable to believe that the more past investments, the more experience an investor has acquired in the P2P lending marketplace. For each investor u_i, we define his/her investment experience as the number of previous investments. In P2P lending, given an investment network, the degree of a node u_i, denoted as E_i, is the number of edges that have one end attached to the node. We can compute investment experience E_i using Equation (5):

$$E_i = \# \{e_{ij} | \forall e_{ij} \neq 0\} \tag{5}$$

where # represents the cardinality of a set.

3.3 An Example of the Investor Profile

An example that computes an investor profile is shown in Figure 2. In this figure, investor u_1 has invested \$500 in total on three loans v_1, v_2 and v_3. The invested amounts are \$150 for v_1, \$250 for v_2 and \$100 for v_3, respectively. So the corresponding investment weights are $w_{11} = \$150/\$500 = 0.3$, $w_{12} = \$250/\$500 = 0.5$ and $w_{13} = \$100/\$500 = 0.2$. Suppose the loans' rates of return are $R_1 = 0.1$, $R_2 = 0.2$ and $R_3 = -0.4$, respectively, we can calculate the past investment performance as $\bar{R}_1 = 0.05$. Similarly, we can find risk preference $P_1 = 0.23$ and experience $E_1 = 3$.

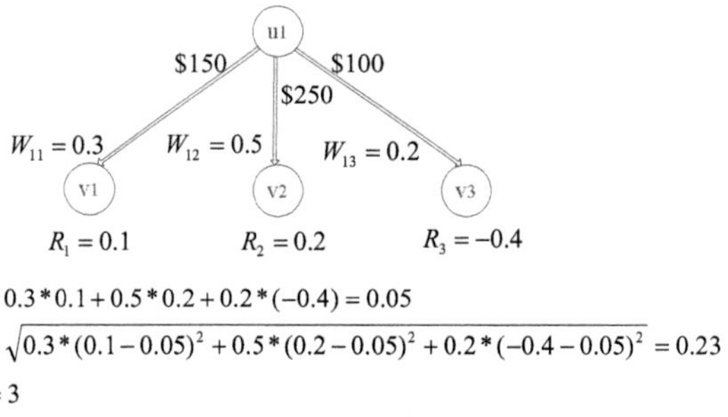

Figure 2: An Example of the Investor Profile.

In summary, in this section, we have used the bipartite investment network to describe the many-to-many investment relationship, and quantitatively analyze past investment performance, risk preference and investment experience. Analysis of investor profile provides the basis on which we can analyze investor composition.

4. INVESTOR COMPOSITION

In a many-to-many investment relationship, the investor composition of an investee, a group of investors who invest on this investee, may exhibits certain characteristics, some of which can be quantified by statistics. In this section, we study the quantitative evaluation of investees by their composition of investors.

As the typical scenario in a bipartite network, an investor can invest across many different investees, and an investee can be funded by a number of different investors. The group of investors who invested on the same investee is called the *investor composition* of the investee. For investee v_j, its investor composition C_j can be written as:

$$C_j = \{u_i | \forall e_{ij} \neq 0\} \tag{6}$$

An example of the investor composition is shown in Figure 3, where there are four investor composition C_1, C_2, C_3 and C_4 corresponding to four different investees v_1, v_2, v_3 and v_4. It is obvious that each investor composition contains a different combination of investors, who may have different past investment history.

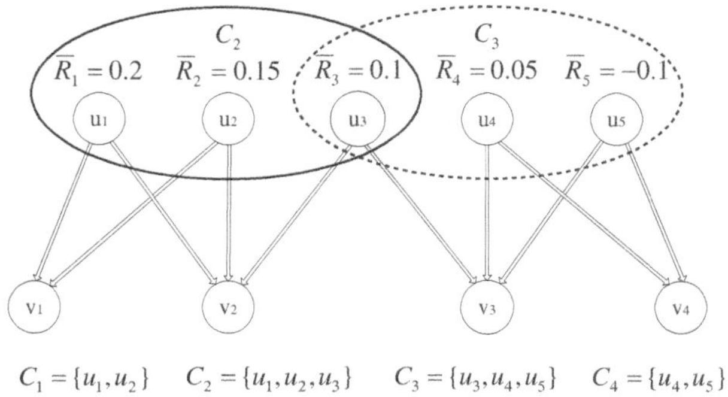

Figure 3: An Example of the Investor Composition.

In following subsections, we study how to quantitatively analyze the investor composition for a investee, which can be applied for investment decisions in P2P lending.

4.1 Investor Composition Analysis

Since each investor has several aspects in their profiles, we consider these aspects accordingly when evaluating the investor composition of an investee. Also, we propose a combined measure for easier comparison across all investees.

4.1.1 Composition of Investor Performances

For each investee v_j, we define composition of investor performance CR_j as the average past investment performance of investors who invest on this investee v_j, weighted by the amount invested, as shown in Equation (7). We have

$$CR_j = \sum_{i=1}^{m} \lambda_{ij} \bar{R}_i \tag{7}$$

where $\lambda_{ij} = \frac{e_{ij}}{\sum_{i=1}^{m} e_{ij}}$ is the ratio of u_i's investment in v_j to the total amount which v_j' gain from all investors in the investment network $G = \{U, V, E\}$. $\bar{R}_i$ is the past investment performance of investor u_i.

Composition of investor performance CR_j is the average past investment performance of investors who invest to investee v_j. An investee that gains investment from good investors who have good past investment performance is a more worthwhile to invest, because we believe a good investor will make more correct investment decisions.

4.1.2 Composition of Investor Risk Preferences

Viewing each investee as a portfolio of investors, we can evaluate the risk of an investee based on risk preferences of individual investors [23, 27]. For each investee v_j, we define composition of investor risk preferences CP_j as the standard deviation of all investors' risk preferences P_i who invest on this investee v_j. For each investee v_j, we can compute composition of risk preferences CP_j using Equation (8) below:

$$CP_j = \sqrt{\sum_{i=1}^{m} (\lambda_{ij}^2 P_i^2 + 2 \sum_{k=1}^{m-i} (J_{ik} \lambda_{ik} \lambda_{i,i+k} P_i P_{i+k}))} \tag{8}$$

where J_{ik} is the correlation between investor u_i and u_k.

We estimate J_{ik} according to similarity in past investments. For any two investors, the more proportion of investment on the same investee, the higher investment similarity they have. For example, in P2P lending, if two investors have invested on exactly the same set of loans, the correlation between them is 1; if they have never invested on any loan in common, their correlation is 0. Here, we compute J_{ik} using Jaccard coefficient between investors u_i and u_k:

$$J_{ik} = \frac{D_{ik}}{D_i + D_k - D_{ik}} \tag{9}$$

where D_i is the total number of past investments by investor u_i, D_k is the total number of past investments by investor u_k, D_{ik} is the number of past investments that investors u_i and u_k have in common (i.e. on the same investee).

4.1.3 Investor Composition Score

We consider investor composition score as a comprehensive measure of return per unit of risk in an investment [29]. For each investee v_j, we define score of investor composition CS_j as the ratio of composition of investor performance CR_j to composition of investor risk preferences CP_j:

$$CS_j = \frac{CR_j}{CP_j} \tag{10}$$

where CR_j is given in (7) and CP_j is given in (8).

Score of investor composition CS_j is a synthetic index that takes into account both the investor performance CR_j and risk preferences CP_j. In P2P lending, a loan having a composition of high investor performance does not necessarily mean that it is a valuable loan, since higher risk might be involved. Only loans with high CR_j and low CP_j are of best investment value.

4.2 An Example of Investor Composition

An example of investor composition analysis is shown in Figure 4, where we specifically analyze the investor composition of investees v_2 and v_3. By calculating CR_2 and CR_3, we can see that CR_2 is much higher than CR_3. It means that the average past investment performance of v_2's investors is better than those of v_3's. If we were to decide whether to invest in v_2 or v_3 by following the investment decisions made by other investors, we would trust those having consistently better performance in the past. So in this case, it is reasonable to believe that v_2 promises more returns than v_3 according to investors' "voting." Also, we notice that the comprehensive risk of v_2, CP_2, is lower than that of v_3. With higher return and lower risk, investee v_2 has a higher investor composition score CS_2, which indicates that v_2 is more worthwhile to invest on.

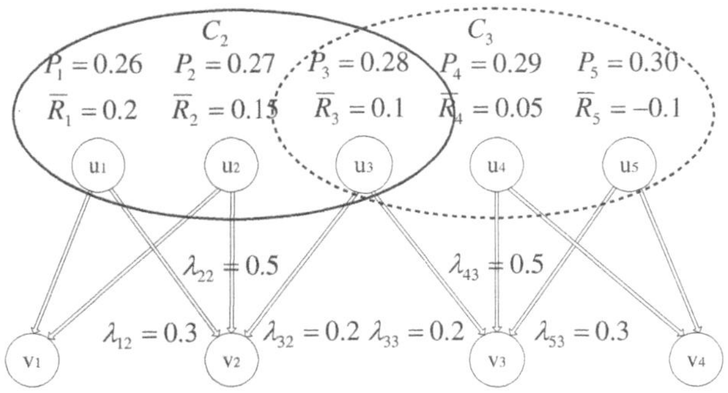

$$CR_2 = 0.3*0.2+0.5*0.15+0.2*0.1 = 0.155$$
$$CR_3 = 0.2*0.1+0.5*0.05+0.3*(-0.1) = 0.015$$
$$CP_2 = 0.165 \qquad CP_3 = 0.179$$
$$CS_2 = 0.939 \qquad CS_3 = 0.084$$

Figure 4: An Illustration of Investor Composition Analysis.

5. INVESTMENT DECISIONS MODEL

The goal of investment decisions is to find the best subset of investees. In this section, we describe how to apply investor composition analysis for investment decisions.

5.1 Model Description

In P2P lending market, investors face many loans which can be chosen at the same time. A common task for the investors would be to find out the list of investment candidates. In our proposed model, the investors find candidates through investor composition analysis of the loans.

Figure 5 describes the computation and decisions process. The whole process can be divided into three phases. In the first phase, the goal is to build investor profiles. In this phase, past investment performance, risk preference and investment experience of investors are calculated to form the profiles of the investors. The second phase is investor composition analysis. Each investee will receive a score by investor composition. Finally, the last phase is to aid the investment decisions by identifying top investees as the candidate set.

There are two input datasets in the model. *DataSetH* is the past investment transactions that include all investors' past investment behaviors, which is used for building investor profile. *DataSetN* is the current investment status that contains information of all loans waiting to be funded. The investment decisions model will find out the investment candidates based on investment composition analysis.

In the process of building investor profiles, based on past investment data, $BuildNet(DataSetH)$ builds a past investment network to gain the rate of return of loan R_j, investors' investment weight w_{ij}, investors' investment times D_i and same investment times between investors D_{ik}. Then for each investor, we calculate the past investment performance $\bar{R}_i$, the investment risk preferences P_i and the investment experience E_i using Equations in section 6.2. Deposit the Jaccard correlation coefficient J_{ij} will be used in process of investor composition analysis, we have to calculate J_{ij} based on investors' past investment data using Equation (9).

In the process of investor composition analysis, based on current investment data, $BuildNet(DataSetN, \alpha, \beta)$ is used to construct the current investment network and gain inestees' investment weight λ_{ij}. *DataSetN* is current investment data and parameters α, β are used to filter investors

Input: DataSetH: past investment datasets
DataSetN: current investment datasets
α: minimum number of previous investments
β: the ratio of investee fulfillment
γ: the first γ percent to be the investment candidate set I
Output:
I: the investment candidate set

1. **Initializations**
2. **Build Investor Profile**
   (1) $(R_j, w_{ij}, D_i, D_{ik})$ = BuildNet(DataSetH)
   (2) **For** i from 1 to m
   (3) **Begin**
   (4) $\bar{R}_i = \sum_{j=1}^{n} w_{ij} R_j$
   (5) $P_i = \sqrt{\sum_{j=1}^{n} w_{ij} (R_j - \bar{R}_i)^2}$
   (6) $E_i = D_i \quad J_{ij} = \frac{D_{ik}}{D_i + D_k - D_{ik}}$
   (7) **End for**
3. **Investors Composition Analysis**
   (1) λ_{ij} = BuildNet(DataSetN, α, β)
   (2) **For** j from 1 to n
   (3) **Begin**
   (4) $CR_j = \sum_{i=1}^{m} \lambda_{ij} \bar{R}_i$
   (5) $CP_j = \sqrt[2]{\sum_{i=1}^{m} \left(\lambda_{ij}{}^2 P_i{}^2 + 2 \sum_{k=1}^{m-i} (J_{ik} \lambda_{ik} \lambda_{i,i+k} P_i P_{i+k})\right)}$
   (6) $CS_j = \frac{CR_j}{CP_j}$
   (7) **End for**
4. **Gain Investment Candidate Set**
   (1) Vr = Ranking(V, CS_j)
   (2) I = Subset(Vr, γ)
5. **Output I**

Figure 5: Investment Decisions Model.

and loans. The parameter α is used to filter investors by keeping those with more investments than α. Accordingly the parameter β is used to filter loans with more fulfillment rate than β and less than 1. Furthermore, for each investor, we calculate composition of investor performance CR_j, composition of investor performance CR_j and score of investor composition CS_j using Equations in section 4.1.

In the process of investment decisions, we rank all loans according to score of investor composition CS_j from the highest to the lowest, then choose the top γ proportion of investees as the candidate set.

5.2 Description of Parameters

Parameter α is the minimum requirement on the investor's experience, or more specially, the number of investments in historical data. This is reasonable since the more investments in the past, the better we can estimate and predict future investment returns, due to reduced variability given more observations.

The parameter β represents the ratio of acquired amount of the investee to the total amount requested. To make use of the investor composition driven investment decisions model, one constraint has to be that the investee's requested amount has already been partially financed. In other words, there are investors who have already invested some money on the investee, but not all the requested amount has been fulfilled. Obviously, we have $0 \leq \beta \leq 1$. The larger β, the more trustable the expert preference will be, yet the smaller investment opportunity will remain.

The parameter γ is the size of proportion of candidate set to all investees. In the process of prediction, investment decisions model uses certain proportion of the most preferred investees to be the candidate set. The choice of γ could be specified by the users according to size and variability of their investments.

The choices of parameters β and γ are usually determined by the users according to their investment needs and experiences. In the following, we discuss the adaptive choice of α based on the statistical foundations.

We formulate the choice of the minimum requirement on the investor's experience as a sample size problem. As we know, for random variable X, in order to estimate the mean μ, using the sample mean $\bar{x}$ from n random samples from a distribution with variance σ^2, by central limit theorem, the confidence interval for given confidence level would be $(\bar{x} - B, \bar{x} + B)$, where $B = u_\alpha \frac{\sigma}{\sqrt{n}}$. Typically $u_\alpha = 1.96$ with confidence level 0.95. Suppose that the success or failure of an investment (i.e. the loan being paid or default) by an investor follows a Bernoulli distribution with success probability p, we observe his investments for n times. We can compute the confidence interval with $B = u_\alpha \sqrt{p(1-p)/n}$.

Furthermore, we define the investment reliability of investor as:

$$R = 1 - \frac{B}{p} = 1 - u_\alpha \sqrt{\frac{1-p}{p*n}}. \qquad (11)$$

The relationship between the minimum number of investments α and the investor reliability R can be illustrated in Figure 6. It can be seen that the larger α, the smaller proportion of investors will be selected. In that situation, since the minimum investment experience standards are higher, fewer investors will be selected, resulting in a smaller set of higher quality investors with respect to reliability. Thus we say that the choice of parameter α has to consider a tradeoff between investors' reliability and the number of investors to be selected when constructing the current investment network. Such considerations provide basic guidelines when building a investment decisions model in practice.

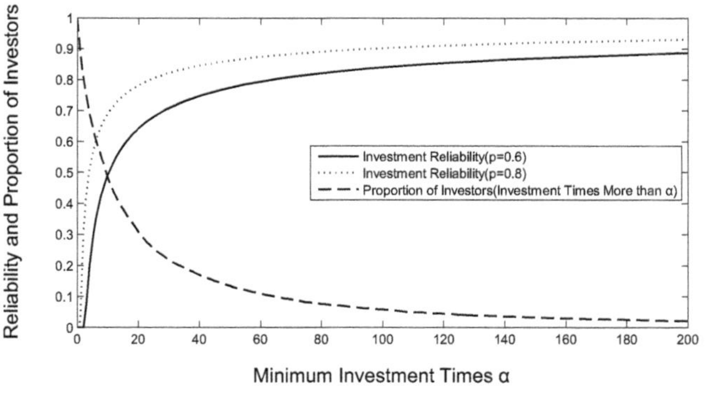

Figure 6: Investor Experience and Reliability.

6. EXPERIMENTAL RESULTS

In this section, we validate our model by showing empirical results on real-world P2P lending datasets. In the following, we will describe the data, show the distributions of the statistics, analyze the effectiveness of using investor composition as an indicator, and compare the performance of our model against baselines. We find that investor composition can effectively indicate investment value and in turn, help investors make better decisions.

6.1 Experiment Data

The experiments are based on the public dataset from Prosper.com[1], which includes six relational data tables. The `Members` and `Groups` data tables contain users' basic registration information and member groups. The `Credit Profile` table contains borrowers' personal credit information. The `Listings` table contains information about loans request. The `Loans` and `Bids` tables are the most important for modeling, and are described in more detail below.

Loans The loans table contains all information about loans, such as loan amount, interest rate and payment status (i.e. paid, late, or default). This table is the most important to evaluate the performance of a loan.

Bids The bids table contains the time and amount of each investment by investors on each loan. We can learn each investor' number of investments and amount invested on each loan. We can also know whether each loan has been fulfilled. This information is the basis to build a whole investment network.

In order to verify the effectiveness of our model, we only use investments whose payment information is available. In this dataset, there are 7968 loans in *DataSetH* for building investor profiles, and 4781 loans in *DataSetN* for computing investor composition.

6.2 Empirical Statistics

It is well known in behavior finance that investors will make different investment decisions because of differences in knowledge structures, information sources, cognitive development, and behavioral preferences. Therefore, we first show that different investors have different profiles in P2P lending.

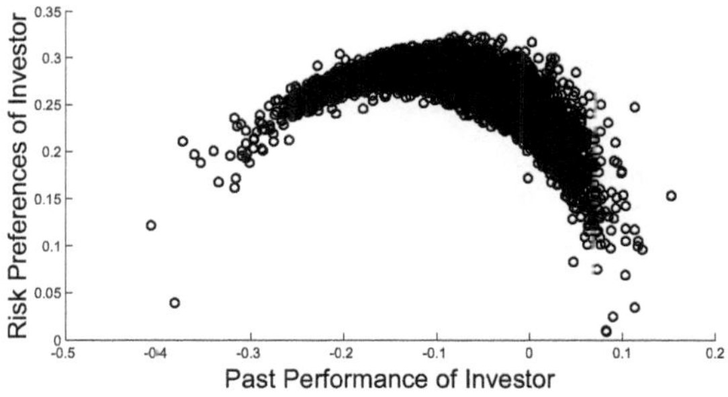

Figure 7: Scatter Plot of Investor Profiles.

Different aspects of investor profiles, i.e. past performance, risk preference and investment experience, are shown in Figure 8. Using the techniques mentioned in Section 3, we can show the distribution of these quantitative measures. It is not surprising to find that investment experience has a skewed distribution, where there are fewer investors having a large number of past investments. In order to show stable statistics on each investor's past performance and risk,

[1]http://www.prosper.com/tools/DataExport.aspx

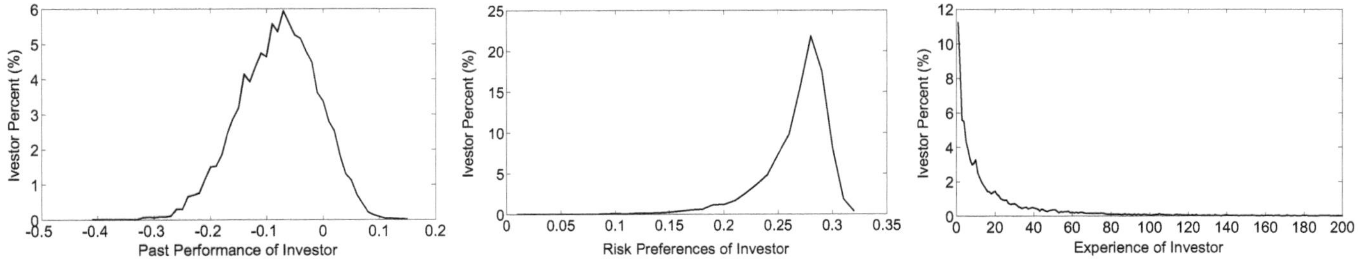

(a) Past Performance (Experience> 20) (b) Risk Preferences (Experience> 20) (c) Experience

Figure 8: Distribution of Investor Profiles.

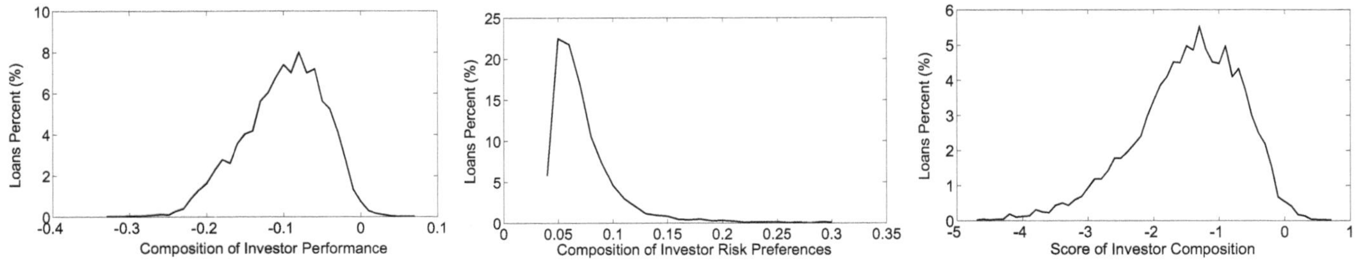

(a) Composition of Performance (b) Composition of Risk (c) Composition Score

Figure 9: Distributions of Investor Composition of Loans.

we show these statistics only for investors having at least 20 past investments. Figure 7 shows the scatter plot of investor's performance versus risk. The data points seem to lie on a curved shape, and we can tell that the best performing investors have lower risk than many others.

Furthermore, since each loan can be funded by different investors, we expect investor composition of different loans to have different statistical characteristics, as shown in Figure 9. It is interesting to see that the composition risk of a loan (Figure 9(b)) is generally lower than the risk of an individual investor (Figure 8(b)). This reflects the idea of reducing risk by diversification.

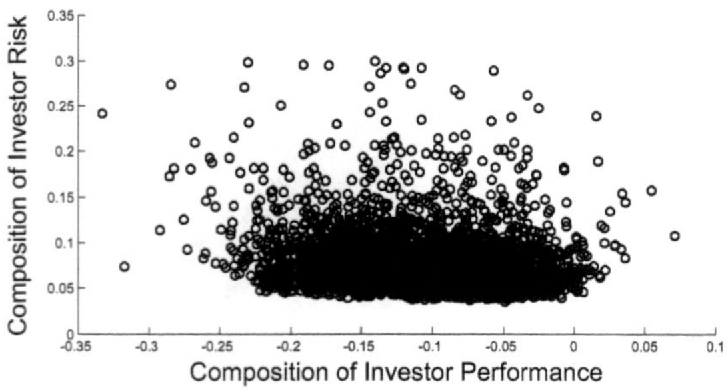

Figure 10: Scatter Plot of Composition Scores.

Similar to investor's risk and return, we show a scatter plot of each loan's risk versus return in Figure 10. In the figure, we can see that most of the loans' risk levels are minimized at a given performance level, and there are much fewer loans with higher risk.

6.3 Investor Composition as An Indicator

In this subsection, we show that the score of investor composition, as studied in Section 4.1, can indicate the performance of loans in P2P lending.

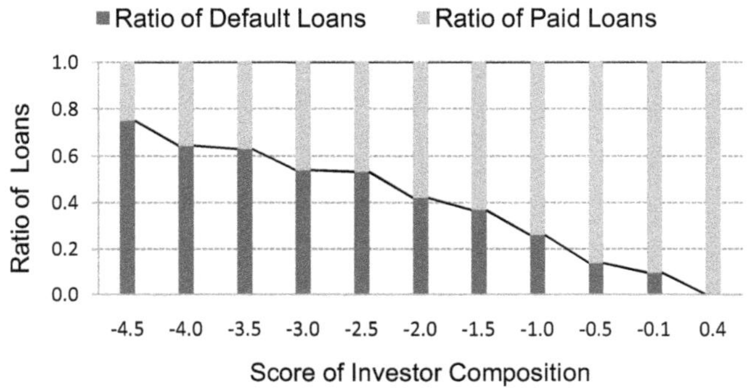

Figure 11: The Default Rate by Investor Composition Scores.

We first group loans based on their score of investor composition, and compare the default rate of loans within each group (Figure 11). We can tell a consistent decreasing trend in the proportion of loans that are default, when the investor composition score increases. This shows intuitively that a higher investor composition score might indicate a lower probability that the loan will become default.

On the other hand, we divide loans into two groups: the paid group and the default group, and then compare the distribution of investor composition scores, as shown in Figure 12 and Table 1. The box-plot shows that the investor composition scores of paid loans is overall higher than those of default loans. As shown in Table 1, the p-value is below 0.001, indicating that the difference is significant.

6.4 Decisions Model by Investor Composition

In Section 5, we proposed an investment decisions model based on investor composition analysis to help investors make better investment decisions. In this subsection, we find em-

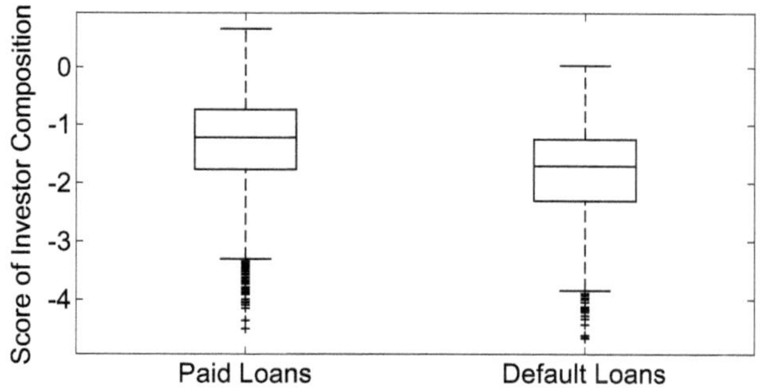

Figure 12: Distributions of Investor Composition Scores by Loans Status.

Table 1: Significance Test between Groups

Group	Mean	Std. Dev.	t-statistic	p-Value
Paid	−0.871	0.5027	24.95	< 0.001
Default	−1.248	0.5097		

pirical evidence to show the effectiveness of our model and the influence of different parameters.

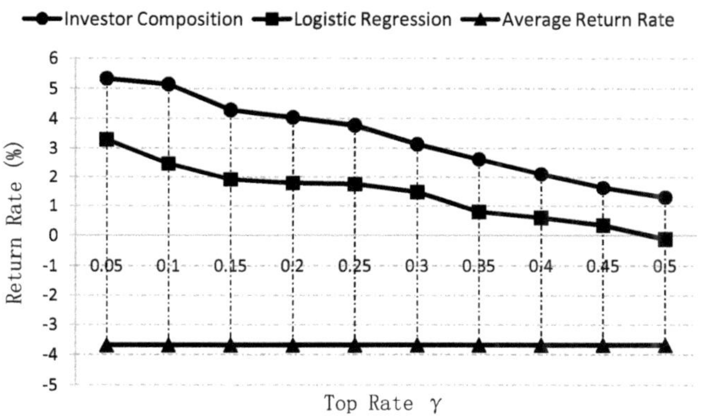

Figure 13: A Comparison of Rate of Return.

In P2P lending, our investment decisions model identifies a ranking of loans, from best loans to worst ones, according to the scores of investor composition. Investors can then choose the top ones as the candidate set. In Figure 13, we compare the rate of return by our model against two baselines. One baseline is the average rate of return by investing on all loans. We can see that without selectively picking good quality loans from the whole pool of all loans, we expect to have a negative rate of return. On the other hand, we compare with candidate selection by logistic regression model, which is the most commonly used on personal loans risk analysis [8, 32]. Based on default probability computed by logistic regression and interest rate, loans are ranked by decreasing expected rate of return. We find that with different values of γ, where γ is the percentage of top loans to invest on, the candidates chosen by our model have consistently higher rate of return than logistic regression.

We compare the performance of our model with different values of the parameter α, which is the minimum investor experience. Experiment results in Figure 14 show the performance of model with $\alpha = 20$ or $\alpha = 30$ is better than one with $\alpha = 0$ or $\alpha = 90$. As discussed in Section 5.2, the choice of parameter α is a tradeoff between investors' reliability and the number of investors who will be chosen to construct current investment network.

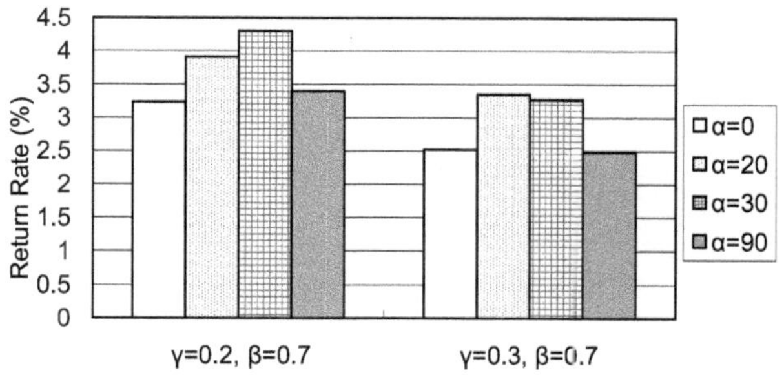

Figure 14: Return Rates with Different α.

Furthermore, we compare the performance of model with different values of the parameter β, as shown in Figure 15. For a loan, the parameter β represents the ratio of acquired amount to the total amount requested. It is make sense that for larger β, our model prefers a larger number of investors when analyzing investor composition, which results in better performance on the rate of return.

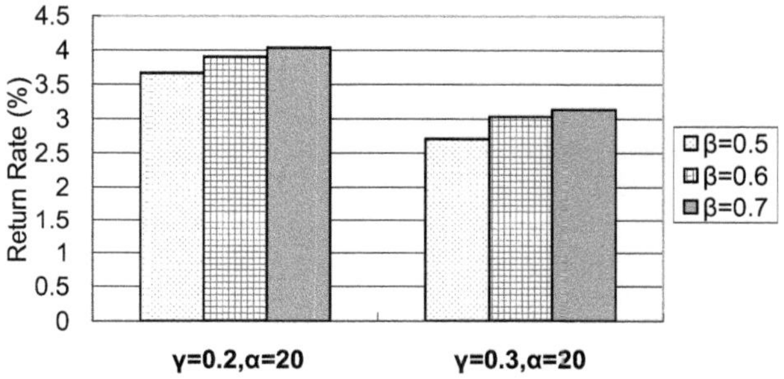

Figure 15: Return Rates with Different β.

Overall, as shown in the experiments with different parameters, our model gains consistently higher rate of return than the average rate of return in the market.

7. CONCLUSION

In this paper, we designed a data driven investment decision-making framework, which exploits the investor composition of each investment for enhancing decisions making in P2P lending. Specifically, we first built investor profiles based on quantitative analysis of past performances, risk preferences, investment experiences and reliability of investors. Then, based on investor profiles, we developed an investor composition analysis model, which can be used to select valuable investments and improve the investment decisions. Experimental results on real-world P2P lending data revealed that the investor composition model could effectively indicate the investment value and this investor composition model can significantly improve the investment performances.

8. ACKNOWLEDGMENTS

This work was supported in part by Natural Science Foundation of China (No. 70972059, 70890080, 70890083), National Science Foundation (No. CCF-1018151) and Fund of Ministry of Education of China (No. 10YJC630065).

9. REFERENCES

[1] Prosper Marketplace. *http://www.prosper.com*, 2006.

[2] N. Barberis and R. Thaler. A survey of behavioral finance. *Handbook of the Economics of Finance*, 1:1053–1128, 2003.

[3] S. Berger and F. Gleisner. Emergence of financial intermediaries in electronic markets: The case of online p2p lending. *Business Research*, 2(1):39–65, 2009.

[4] V. Bugera, H. Konno, and S. Uryasev. Credit cards scoring with quadratic utility functions. *Journal of Multi-Criteria Decision Analysis*, 11(4-5):197–211, 2002.

[5] S. Chatterjee and S. Barcun. A nonparametric approach to credit screening. *Journal of the American statistical Association*, 65(329):150–154, 1970.

[6] B. Collier and R. Hampshire. Sending mixed signals: multilevel reputation effects in peer-to-peer lending markets. In *Proceedings of the 2010 ACM conference on Computer supported cooperative work*, pages 197–206. ACM, 2010.

[7] V. DESAI, D. Conway, J. CROOK, and G. OVERSTREET. Credit-scoring models in the credit-union environment using neural networks and genetic algorithms. *IMA Journal of Management Mathematics*, 8(4):323, 1997.

[8] G. Dong, K. Lai, and J. Yen. Credit scorecard based on logistic regression with random coefficients. *Procedia Computer Science*, 1(1):2457–2462, 2010.

[9] D. Feldman and S. Gross. Mortgage default: classification trees analysis. *The Journal of Real Estate Finance and Economics*, 30(4):369–396, 2005.

[10] S. Freedman and G. Jin. Do social networks solve information problems for peer-to-peer lending? evidence from prosper.com. *Working Papers*, 2008.

[11] H. Frydman, J. Kallberg, and D. Kao. Testing the adequacy of Markov chain and mover-stayer models as representations of credit behavior. *Operations Research*, 33(6):1203–1214, 1985.

[12] S. Garman, R. Hampshire, and R. Krishnan. A Search Theoretic Model of Person-to-Person Lending. 2008.

[13] P. Holme, F. Liljeros, C. Edling, and B. Kim. Network bipartivity. *Physical Review E*, 68(5):56107, 2003.

[14] J. Huang, G. Tzeng, and C. Ong. Two-stage genetic programming (2SGP) for the credit scoring model. *Applied Mathematics and Computation*, 174(2):1039–1053, 2006.

[15] M. Hulme and C. Wright. Internet based social lending: Past, present and future. *Social Futures Observatory*, pages 1–115, 2006.

[16] H. Jensen et al. Using neural networks for credit scoring. *Managerial Finance*, 18(6):15–26, 1993.

[17] K. Krumme and S. Herrero-Lopez. Do Lenders Make Optimal Decisions in a Peer-to-Peer Network? In *Proceedings of the IEEE/WIC/ACM Int'l Joint Conf. on Web Intelligence and Intelligent Agent Technology*, pages 124–127. IEEE Computer Society, 2009.

[18] T. Lee, I. Chen, et al. A two-stage hybrid credit scoring model using artificial neural networks and multivariate adaptive regression splines. *Expert Systems with Applications*, 28(4):743–752, 2005.

[19] J. Linck, J. Netter, and T. Yang. The determinants of board structure. *Journal of Financial Economics*, 87(2):308–328, 2008.

[20] Y. Liu, L. Xiao, and L. Ni. Building a scalable bipartite P2P overlay network. *IEEE Transactions on Parallel and distributed systems*, pages 1296–1306, 2007.

[21] R. Malhotra and D. Malhotra. Differentiating between good credits and bad credits using neuro-fuzzy systems. *European Journal of Operational Research*, 136(1):190–211, 2002.

[22] O. Mangasarian. Linear and nonlinear separation of patterns by linear programming. *Operations Research*, 13(3):444–452, 1965.

[23] H. Markowitz and H. Markowitz. *Portfolio selection: Efficient diversification of investments*. Wiley, 1991.

[24] F. Modigliani and M. Miller. The cost of capital, corporation finance and the theory of investment. *The American Economic Review*, 48(3):261–297, 1958.

[25] L. Puro, J. Teich, H. Wallenius, and J. Wallenius. Borrower Decision Aid for people-to-people lending. *Decision Support Systems*, 49(1):52–60, 2010.

[26] E. Rosenberg and A. Gleit. Quantitative methods in credit management: a survey. *Operations research*, 42(4):589–613, 1994.

[27] M. Rubinstein. Markowitz's" portfolio selection": A fifty-year retrospective. *The Journal of finance*, 57(3):1041–1045, 2002.

[28] J. Ryan, K. Reuk, and C. Wang. To Fund Or Not To Fund: Determinants Of Loan Fundability in the Prosper. com Marketplace. *WP, The Standord Graduate School of Business*, 2007.

[29] R. Shiller. From efficient markets theory to behavioral finance. *The Journal of Economic Perspectives*, 17(1):83–104, 2003.

[30] W. Souma, Y. Fujiwara, and H. Aoyama. Complex networks and economics. *Physica A: Statistical Mechanics and its Applications*, 324(1-2):396–401, 2003.

[31] M. Stepanova and L. Thomas. Survival analysis methods for personal loan data. *Operations Research*, 50(2):277–289, 2002.

[32] L. Thomas. *Consumer credit models: pricing, profit and portfolios*. Oxford University Press, USA, 2009.

[33] H. Wang, M. Greiner, and J. Aronson. People-to-People Lending: The Emerging E-Commerce Transformation of a Financial Market. *Value Creation in E-Business Management*, pages 182–195, 2009.

[34] Y. Wang, S. Wang, and K. Lai. A new fuzzy support vector machine to evaluate credit risk. *Fuzzy Systems, IEEE Transactions on*, 13(6):820–831, 2005.

[35] J. Wiginton. A note on the comparison of logit and discriminant models of consumer credit behavior. *Journal of Financial and Quantitative Analysis*, 15(03):757–770, 1980.

[36] L. Yu, S. Wang, K. Lai, and L. Zhou. *Bio-Inspired Credit Risk Analysis: Computational Intelligence with Support Vector Machines*. Springer Verlag, 2008.

From Market Baskets to Mole Rats: Using Data Mining Techniques to Analyze RFID Data Describing Mole Rat Behavior

Dan P. McCloskey[1,2], Michael E. Kress[3,7], Susan P. Imberman[4,7], Igor Kushnir[5], Susan Briffa-Mirabella[2,6]
1. Dept. Psychology 2. CSI/IBR Center for Developmental Neuroscience, 3. Vice President of Technology Systems, 4. Dept. Computer Science 5. Masters Program in Neuroscience, 6. Program in Neuroscience, Department of Biology, The Graduate Center at CUNY 7. Doctoral Program Computer Science the Graduate Center at CUNY
College of Staten Island, 2800 Victory Blvd, Staten Island, NY 10314
Correspondence to: susan.imberman@csi.cuny.edu

ABSTRACT
The use of new technologies, such as RFID sensors, provides scientists with novel ways of doing experimental research. As scientists become more technologically savvy and use these techniques, the traditional approaches to data analysis fail given the huge amounts of data produced by these methods. In this paper we describe an experiment in which colonies of naked mole rats were tagged with RFID transponders. RFID sensors were strategically placed in the mole rat caging system. The goal of this experiment was to document and analyze the interactions between animals. The huge amount of data produced by the sensors was not analyzable using the traditional methods employed by behavioral neuroscience researchers. Computational methods used by data miners, such as cluster analysis, association rule mining, and graphical models, were able to scale to the data and produce knowledge and insight that was previously unknown. This paper describes in detail the experimental setup and the computational methods used.

Categories and Subject Descriptors
J. Computer Applications J.4 SOCIAL AND BEHAVIORAL SCIENCES *Psychology*

H. Information Systems H.2 DATABASE MANAGEMENT H.2.8 Database applications Data Mining

General Terms
Algorithms, Measurement, Experimentation,

Keywords
cluster analysis, association rule mining, maximal frequent itemsets, visualization, RFID

1. INTRODUCTION
The study of animal behavior can take place in a variety of settings. Animals can be observed in their natural environment (Field Studies) and data collected can be as low-tech as birdwatchers recording data from banded birds who land in their back yard, or as high tech as real-time GPS tracking of individual animals as they migrate thousands of miles. In the laboratory setting, the study of animal behavior has been considerably low tech.

Most laboratory measurements of animal behavior involve animals (typically rats or mice) that are placed in a maze environment while an experimenter quantifies behavioral events (e.g. maze choices) either directly, or through video recording. This approach has been questioned for its external validity, as brain and behavior have been shown to be quite sensitive to environment and experience. Therefore, removing animals from their home environment may cause inaccurate measurement of behavior (See [27] for discussion).

An alternative approach to removing animals from their housing environments and measuring behavior in a novel and artificial setting, is to capture behavior in the housing environment. This approach has the advantage of limiting animal stress and behavioral response to the artificiality of the testing experience. It also allows for the analysis of behavior across multiple time scales (seconds to weeks). Recent developments in automated video-oriented animal behavior analysis have allowed for the advanced detection of abnormalities in transgenic mouse models [14]. However these behavior detection systems have the limitation that animals are housed individually, which can be stressful for most rodents [26].

An area of growing interest in behavioral neuroscience is the study of social behaviors, with respect to how the brain is modified in various conditions such as autism [10]. While social approach behavior (investigating a caged unfamiliar animal) can be automated in an artificial maze environment [11], no studies to date have attempted to measure social behavior over long periods of time in the animal's own housing environment. Studying animals in this way may be important if the processes that drive social behavior in a novel location with an unfamiliar animal, differ from those that drive social behavior in a familiar setting with familiar animals. Traditionally, behavioral scientists use automated video systems, but these systems are incapable of distinguishing multiple laboratory animals, particularly over long periods of time in a complex housing environment.

Our research in this area therefore required a system that was able to deliver a snapshot of the location of multiple animals in a complex housing environment. While this system should be useful for the study of both rats and mice, we wanted to develop a system that could also measure activity in a specific laboratory animal, the naked mole rat. Naked mole rats (NMR) are highly social rodents with colonies that can grow to 75 in a single housing environment. We were interested in knowing the locations of each animal, with a sub second time resolution, over a period of days.

Our solution to this problem was to quantify social behavior using the premise that animals that spend more time in the presence of other animals are more social than animals that spend more time alone. To quantify these behaviors, an RFID (radio frequency identification) system, consisting of transponders and readers, was used. RFID provides automatic identification of physical objects using radio waves. Because each RFID transponder has a unique ID, an unlimited number of animals could be tracked within the same housing environment. Our initial question was, "Which mole rats socially interacted with each other?" To answer this, we developed a system based on the methods reported by Kritzler and colleagues to track mouse behavior [17,18,19]. The underlying premise was that mole rats tagged with transponders that socialized with each other, would be located in the proximity of the same reader. The major problem encountered was that the data generated by this system was too massive to be analyzed using the traditional methods by behavioral scientists.

The organization of this paper outlines our approach as follows: Section 2 outlines the experimental design and the software used for data capture. Section 3 details the data mining algorithms used for data analysis and the results. Section 4 discuses our conclusions and we summarize in section 5.

2. EXPERIMENTAL DESIGN

2.1 Animal Model

The naked mole rat (*Heterocephalus Glaber*) is one of 18 species of African mole-rats, which belong to the hystricognath suborder of rodents. Of all African mole-rats, the naked mole rats inhabit some of the harshest environmental habitats in the arid regions of central and eastern Ethiopia, central Somalia, and Kenya. Naked mole-rats are highly successful in the wild, and are in no danger of extinction at this time. They have adapted by evolving skills to work together, including skills for social tolerance and cooperation in large groups. They have the largest colony size of any social vertebrate, which averages about 75 animals in the wild, and the largest litter size of any mammal [4,25]. The colony is maintained through a cooperative breeding system, with fewer than 5% of the animals achieving reproductive status in their lifetime. These animals are one of only two mammalian species (both African mole rats) with a eusocial reproductive hierarchy similar to that of bees, termites, or ants. The non-breeding animals cooperate in caring for young (retrieval, licking, grooming, and provision of food), and protecting and maintaining the colony [20]. Cooperative behaviors and social activity among subordinate animals allows for the study of social behaviors that do not appear to be confounded by mating behavior or the goal of procreation, and permits shared housing of dozens of animals in the same environment. Naked mole rats are exclusively subterranean and maintain an extensive burrow system, with 3-4 km of tunnels, used to identify tuber food sources. The animals also maintain communal nest and toilet chambers that are areas of high social interaction. Figure 1 shows an example of two naked mole rats in their laboratory housing environment.

While previous studies have examined interactions of pairs of animals temporarily removed from their housing environment [9], or activity patterns of animals living in isolation [23], the present study was designed to measure activity and social behavior in the intact, unperturbed colony. Therefore, the results from these analyses would provide the first evidence of group behavior dynamics of a naked mole rat colony. It was hypothesized that within each colony of naked mole rats, there would be measurable differences in the level of social behavior.

2.2 RFID Tracking in home environment

Each naked mole rat in the animal laboratory was implanted subcutaneously with a Trovan Unique radio frequency identification transponder (transponder size 11.5 x 2.2mm; MicrochipID Lake Zurich, IL) in March 2010. The transponders are passive and therefore do not require batteries, and should not need to be replaced during the lifespan of the animal (over 28 years in captivity, the longest living rodent on Earth; [5]). In each colony, animals are housed in 3 standard mouse tub cages connected by over 7 meters of clear polycarbonate tubing (50.8 mm inner diameter) with stationary circular RFID antennae (100 mm inner diameter) placed around the tubing at multiple locations, and connected to a backend computer (See Figure 2).

The dataset used for the current analyses were collected from 3 separate colonies of naked mole rats (n = 16, 22, and 38 animals respectively). Colonies were physically separated from each other, so the analyses should show no interaction between animals of different colonies, thus validating the experimental model and the analytical techniques.

The RFID tracking system consists of a tag, a reader, and a backend computer (See Figure 3). Below is a list of each component along with a description of that component.

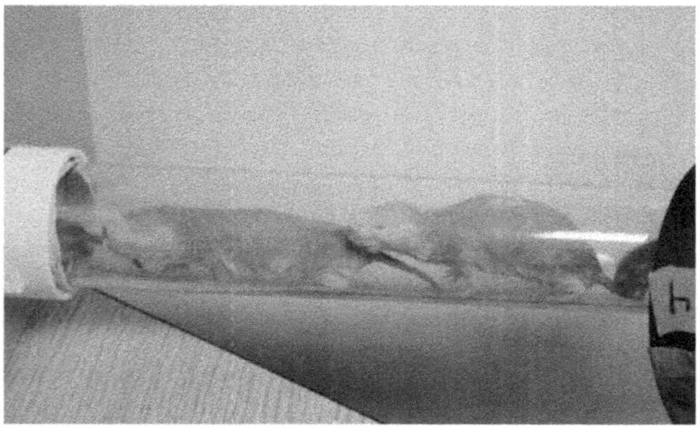

Figure 1: Image of 2 adult naked mole rats from the Degas colony traveling into the nest chamber after passing through antenna number 4. The animal to the rear is the queen of the colony, the only reproductively active female.

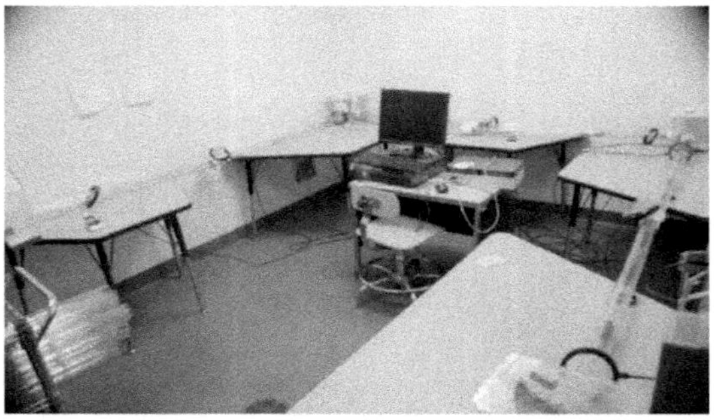

Figure 2: Arrangement of Degas colony semi-natural environment with chambers (toilet chamber on bottom right) connecting tunnels, antennae, and the backend computer for compiling data.

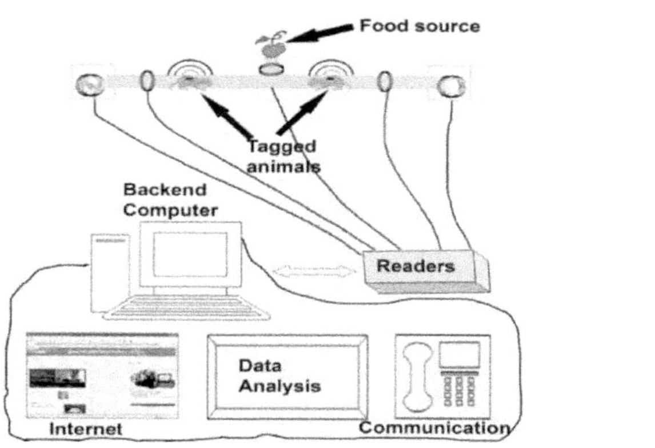

Figure 3: Schematic of how RFID is used to track movement of individual animals in the colony.

• Tag (transponder): stores identifying data of a physical object, to which it is attached (animals).

• Reader: placed at multiple places within the housing system gets data from tag and communicates with backend computer.

• Backend computer system consisting of RFID middleware, applications, hosts databases: processes information from the reader, and connects to the enterprise network, and to the Internet

The backend computer, which was connected to a series of Trovan LID 650 readers (MicrochipID, Lake Zurich, IL), updated a text file each time an animal passed through one of the 10 antennae. The event in the text file included the animal ID (unique 10 digit alphanumeric code), time of entry, and reader number (1-10). Text files containing 24 hours of data entries were parsed using Matlab, by location (antenna) and a state matrix identifying the last known location for each animal was processed for each event.

3. DATA METHODOLOGY AND RESULTS

As mentioned above, the goal of the current study was to measure animal social behavior. Traditional approaches for this type of measurement involve recording the amount of time a test animal spends in the area of a maze where another animal resides during a 15 minute test period [11]. With a total number of dyads in a group equal to N(N-1)/2, traditional social approach behavior nalysis for a colony of 33 animals would require 7,920 minutes of behavioral observation.

The alternative approach is to monitor the amount of time animals spend in each possible dyad at specific locations in the housing environment. However, this process would require mining or summarizing very large datasets. We present here several successful methods in data mining and summary data analysis.

3.1 Cluster Analysis

Hierarchical and K-means clustering techniques were implemented with the goals of organizing or partitioning the data, respectively, such that animals that spend time in the same location are homogenous and animals with different location preferences are well-separated. Clusters were determined using iterative functions in Matlab based on the state matrix dataset. Figure 4 shows a histogram organized by the results of a K-means cluster analysis, with the bars representing the normalized frequency of "visits" (y axis) by each animal (1-76, x axis) to each reader location (1-10, z axis).

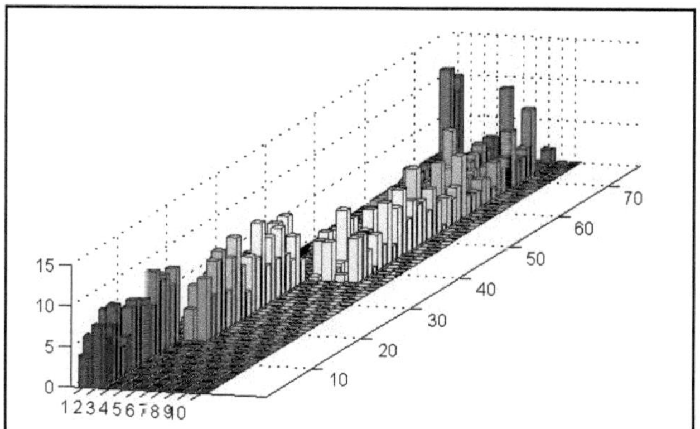

Figure 4: Location frequency-duration histogram computed in Matlab for each of 76 animals in three colonies (X axis) tracked at 10 different locations (Z axis) over a 24 hour period (114,000 RFID events). The Y axis is a normalized duration period. Animals are clustered using a k- means cluster (k=3). The results show some variability in place preferences for animals within a colony. Bar colors are used to distinguish individual animals.

This type of analysis is beneficial as it utilizes the entire dataset, including every movement of each animal during the 24-hour recording period. It also is a useful tool to identify animals with similar "place preferences", demonstrated here by the separation of the three colonies into different clusters. However, although two animals may have the same place preference, these clustering techniques will not indicate whether two animals were in the same place at that same time. Therefore, while we found clustering useful for identifying common and unusual patterns of behavior, we were limited in the conclusions we could draw regarding social behavior.

3.2 Adjacency Matrix Sampling

The second approach was to generate a consensus structure of the network organization using multiple adjacency matrices. Adjacency matrices are n x n matrices constructed such that for time *T*, if animals *i* and *j* are indicated at the same reader location then the *ij*th cell is equal to 1 and if animal *k* is in a different location then both the *ik*th and *jk*th cells are equal to 0. The adjacency matrix is undirected and symmetrical such that for adjacency matrix *A*: $A_{ij} = A_{ji}$.

Adjacency matrices can be easily graphed using statistical (R) or graphical (Gephi) software, where the vertices (nodes) are represented by polygons, and the edges are represented by lines connecting a node. This type of graphical representation of social relationship, often referred to as a sociogram, is common in the field of social network analysis [9,25]. Thus, in the example above, the sociogram would show nodes representing animals *i,j* and *k*, with lines connecting nodes *i* and *j*, but with node *k* not connected to either *i* or *j*.

Clearly, choosing a single time-point may not be a good measure of social behavior, as animals *i* and *j* may be merely passing each other at the same location at time *T*, and not interacting at all. Therefore, a more reliable indicator of social behavior would require multiple time points sampled during the 24 hour period. To this end, we created adjacency matrices at 100 random time points during the 24 hour data acquisition period, and created a consensus matrix using the centralgraph routine in the sna package in R [7]. This function calculates the mean dichotomized adjacency matrix of the 100 sample matrices.

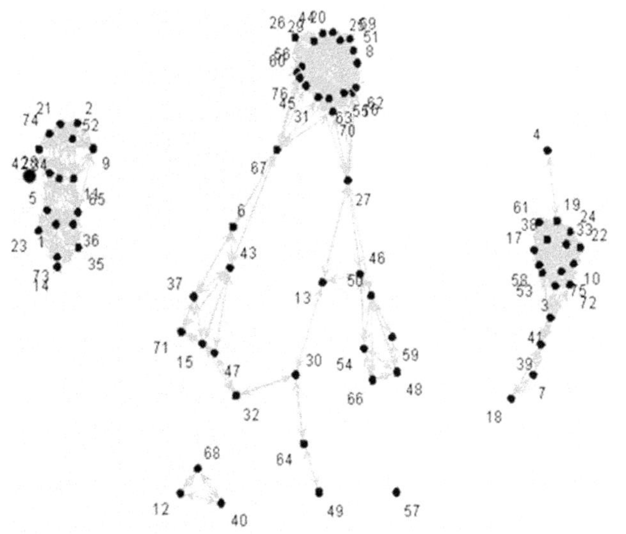

Figure 5: Sociogram computed in R using the centralgraph function representing the average interactions from 100 randomly sampled adjacency matrices from the data used in Figure 4.

Figure 5 shows a sociogram of the centralgraph using the same data used to create the histogram in Figure 4. Once again, separate colonies can be easily identified using this analysis. This form of analysis is powerful in that it also allows for secondary measures of the strength of each dyad (indicated by edge weight) and each animal's involvement in the network, for example, the degree of centrality (number of edges to other nodes) or eigenvector centrality (number of edges to other node weighted by edge weight). These measures have been summarized elsewhere [8,12,25].

One difficulty in this type of analysis, however, is deciding what the appropriate sample size is to represent the population of social interactions. Here, we used 100 random sampled time points over a 24-hour period, but without any scientific basis for the number of samples or length of the recording period. To avoid this problem, a scalable data mining procedure, which is not prone to sampling bias, may be advantageous.

3.3 Association Rule Mining

Association rule mining has been used in market basket analysis for finding groups of items that are purchased together. Each store transaction corresponds to groups of items in a customer's market basket. This results in sets of items that are frequently purchased together, along with rules to the effect that, "customers that buy cereal are likely to buy milk". These rules hold with minimum statistical significance and confidence. Our goal for this study was to find mole rats that group together, given readings captured from a reader. There seemed a natural mapping from the traditional association rule market basket problem to the groupings defined by the readings from the RFID system. One can think of the readers as corresponding to the cash register scanner in a store, the groups of mole rats captured at each reader corresponding to a market basket transaction, and the results yielding frequent groups of mole rats that socialize together, along with rules to the effect of, "when animals 5 and 6 are together we are likely to see animal 8 as well".

More formally, given a set $I = \{ i_1, i_2, i_3, \ldots i_n \}$ of items, a transaction is a subset X of I. A Subset of the items in a transaction is also a subset of I and is called an itemset. A

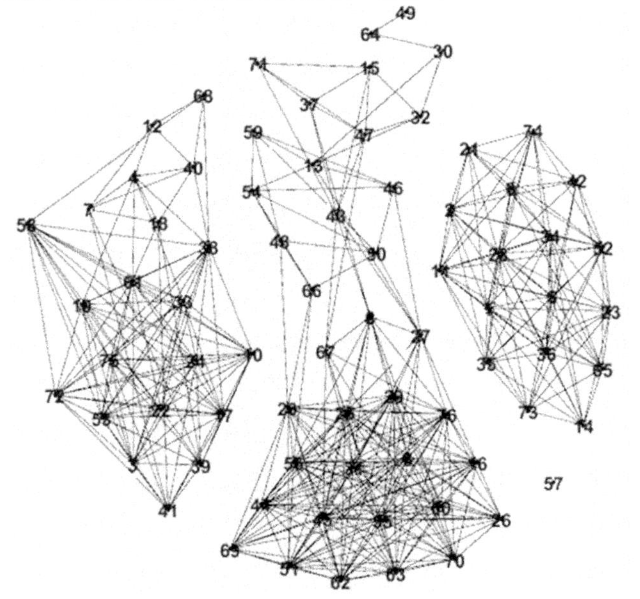

Figure 6: Gephi file sociogram based on maximal frequent itemsets from the same datafile shown in Figure 5. Notice that the three colonies are once again separated, and that the colony identity of some animals in Figure 5 has been resolved.

frequent itemset is a subset of I that satisfies some minimum percentage of transactions. This value is known as the support of the itemset. Support is an indication of the itemset's statistical significance. Let X and Y be subsets of I such that $X \cap Y = \phi$. An association rule is a probabilistic implication $X \Rightarrow Y$. Given an association rule $X \Rightarrow Y$ as defined above, the support of the rule is the support of the itemset defined by $X \cup Y$. The confidence of a rule is the number of transactions that satisfy the itemset defined by $X \cup Y$ divided by the number of transactions that satisfy X. A rule that has support above a user defined minimum called *minsup* and confidence above s user defined minimum called *minconf* is an interesting association rule [1,2,3].

Recently there has been a focus on mining sets of itemsets that are representative of the set of frequent itemsets. Mining frequent itemsets can become cost prohibitive in dense datasets with long patterns of 20 items or more. For these types of datasets research has focused on mining closed frequent itemsets [21,22,24] and maximal itemsets [6,13]. Given a frequent itemset X, X is a closed frequent itemset if there exists no $Y \supset X$ such that the support of Y equals the support of X. A frequent set X is a maximal frequent itemset if for all supersets Y of set X, set Y is infrequent. [13] The frequent itemsets are a superset of the closed frequent itemsets, which in turn are a superset of the maximal frequent itemsets.

Since we were looking to find sets of animals that socialize, it made sense to look at the maximal frequent itemsets rather than the rules these itemsets defined. For instance, rat5 $\Rightarrow$ rat24 has no different confidence measure than rat24 $\Rightarrow$ rat5 since both rat24, and rat5 would trigger the same reader at the same time if they collocated. We chose to find the maximal frequent itemsets since these coded for a less redundant set of items. [28]

With direction from the domain expert, we found all maximal itemsets with a minimum support of 40%, the interpretation being, find all groups of mice that socialize at least 40% of the time. For the dataset containing 76 mole rats, 369 maximal itemsets were found. Klemettinen et. al.[16] describe a method of visualizing association rules using a graphical representation. Attributes are represented by nodes, and the directed arcs between these represent the rules. Building on this, we represented the maximal itemsets generated for the naked mole rat domain by an undirected graph. Given that each animal is represented by a node, the itemsets code for undirected edges between animals within the same itemset. Itemsets can be graphically connected to each other via common items. For example, given maximal itemset {6, 25, 29} and maximal itemset {6, 31} we can see that animal 6 associates with animals 25, 29, and 31. Figure 6 shows the undirected graph found from the maximal frequent itemsets. Note that the results are generally similar to those in Figure 5, but that association rule mining resolves some issues, such as the colony identity of animals 12, 40, and 68. Animal 57 lived in the same colony as animals 7, 18, 4 (etc) but the co-localization of this animal with colony mates was too infrequent to create an edge in either the adjaceny matrix or association rule mining analyses.

4. CONCLUSIONS

The measurement of the social behavior of laboratory animals has become more in demand in recent years as investigators seek to understand the neural mechanisms of autism and schizophrenia [10]. Traditional methods used to study social behavior lack external validity as the testing environment is artificial and may be confounded by the stress of encounters with unfamiliar animals. These methods are also time consuming and not well-suited for the study of large groups of animals.

The current study used multiple complementary approaches to measure the social organization of large groups of RFID tracked laboratory animals in the home environment. This approach is advantageous, as it improves external validity, and can accommodate large groups. However, the very large datasets created by RFID tracking pose new problems for researchers in the field of behavioral neuroscience.

Multiple solutions were attempted to solve the problem of drawing task-relevant conclusions from these large data sets. First, hierarchical and K-series mean clustering techniques were used to demonstrate groups of animals with similar location preferences. While this approach is useful to demonstrate patterns of behavior, it is not conclusive whether animals shared the same space at the same time.

Our next approach was to create a central graph based on multiple (>100) animal-location adjacency matrices created from random time points throughout the day. This technique is useful for identifying which animals share the same space, and is amenable to social network graphing and analysis (i.e. degree of centrality), but is problematic in that large preliminary datasets must be analyzed before assessing how much sampling is enough to accurately depict the true social relationships.

Our final approach, the association rule mining approach, is advantageous because it uses the whole dataset and thus avoids the issues of sampling bias or inadequacy. As shown here, the output of this analysis is also amenable to graphing in social network analysis programs and analysis of social network statistics.

Together, these results show, for the first time that despite having nearly identical genetic backgrounds, siblings in a naked mole rat colony show measureable differences in the level of social behavior. This validates the use of this technology as a new approach to measuring social behavior in the laboratory animal.

5. SUMMARY

Jim Gray of Microsoft Research defined *eScience* as the intersection between IT and scientists. He goes on to define a fourth paradigm of scientific inquiry as being "data intensive science". The work proposed in this paper is a prime example of the kinds of results one can obtain when pairing scientists with computer scientists.

This work provides a template for using automated data collection tools to measure social behavior in large groups. The experiments demonstrated here were "proof-of-concept" in nature to confirm that animals housed in physically separated environments would appear as separate social networks in our analyses, but they also yielded information about the differing levels of social behavior within each colony.

For future work, we are recording single colonies with higher spatial resolution (~25 cm inter-reader distances) and have achieved even greater understanding of the role of individual animals in the larger social network. These methods are also being applied to a more traditional laboratory animal species, the Long Evans rat, with similar success.

Because of the temporal nature of the data, we will investigate the application of additional data mining techniques such as sequential temporal data analysis, and social network analysis to this experimental dataset. These analytical methods allow us to answer questions such as, "How long are animal groups associating with each other?, Do social groups congregate only in one area or do they socialize in other maze areas as well?, and Which animal is initiating a social interaction?" The technology and analytical tools provides a breadth of possibilities in this area, opening up the investigation of behaviors that were too difficult to be previously analyzed.

These analyses yielded informative results because they allowed for the measurement of multiple animals simultaneously. To our knowledge, this social network approach has not been used previously to identify group behavior dynamics in laboratory animals. Based on this combination of methods, we intend to compare brain features of more social and less social animals from the same colony, with a long-term goal to understand neural correlates of social behavior deficits.

6. ACKNOWLEDGMENTS

This research was supported, in part, under National Science Foundation Grants CNS-0958379 and CNS-0855217, PSC-CUNY grant 62323-00-40, the Dormitory Authority of the State of New York, and the City University of New York High Performance Computing Center. We thank Dr. Bruce Goldman for generous donation of the naked mole rat colonies and Dr. Xiowen Zhang for advice on designing the RFID tracking system

7. REFERENCES

[1] Agrawal, R., Imielinski, T., and Swami, A. 1993. Mining association rules between sets of items in large databases. *In Proc. ACM SIGMOD* (pp. 207-216).

[2] Agrawal, R., and Srikant, R. 1994. Fast Algorithms for Mining Association Rules. *IBM Res. Rep.* RJ9839. IBM Almaden.

[3] Agrawal, R., Mannila, H., Srikant, R., Toivonen, H. and Verkamo, A. I. 1996. Fast Discovery Of Association Rules. In U. Fayyad, G. Piatetsky-Shapiro, P. Smyth, & R. Uthurusamy

(Eds.), *Advances in Knowledge Discovery and Data Mining* (pp. s 307-328). AAAI/MIT Press.

[4] Brett, R. A. 1991. The population structure of naked mole-rat colonies. In P. W. Sherman, J. U. M. Jarvis & R. D. Alexander (Eds.), *The Biology of the Naked Mole Rat* (pp. 97- 136) Princeton, NJ: Princeton University Press.

[5] Buffenstein, R. 2008. Negligible senescence in the longest living rodent, the naked mole-rat: Insights from a successfully aging species. *Journal of Comparative Physiology.B, Biochemical, Systemic, and Environmental Physiology,* 178(4), 439-445.

[6] Burdick, D. , Calimlim, M. , Flannick, J. , Gehrke, J. , and Yiu., T. 2005. MAFIA: A Maximal Frequent Itemset Algorithm, *IEEE Transactions on Knowledge and Data Engineering,* 17(11), p.1490-1504. [doi>10.1109/TKDE.2005.183]

[7] Butts, C.T., 2000 The sna package for the R statistical computing system. *Software Library*, Pittsburgh, PA.

[8] Butts, C.T., 2008. Social network analysis: A methodological introduction. *Asian Journal of Social Psycholog.* 11, 13-41.

[9] Clarke, F.M., and Faulkes, C.G., 1999. Kin discrimination and female mate choice in the naked mole-rat Heterocephalus glaber. *Proceedings of the Royal Society of London B*; 266 (1432), 1995-2002.

[10] Crawley, J.N., 2000. What's wrong with my mouse?, Wiley–Liss, New York.

[11] Crawley, J. 2007. Mouse behavioral assays relevant to the symptoms of autism. *Brain Pathology*;17:448–459.

[12] Freeman, L.C., 1979. Centrality in social networks: Conceptual clarification. *Social Networks* 1(3), 223-258.

[13] Gouda, K., and Zaki,, M.J. 2001. Efficiently mining maximal frequent itemsets. *ICDM, First IEEE International Conference on Data Mining* (p. 163).

[14] Goulding,E.H., Schenk, A.K,. Juneja, P., MacKay, A.W., Wade, J.M., and Tecott, L.H. 2008. A robust automated system elucidates mouse home cage behavioral structure. *Proceedings of the National Academy of Sciences of the United States of America* 105: 20575–20582.

[15] Hey, T., Tansley, S., Tolle, K. eds 2009. The Fourth Paradigm: Data-Intensive Scientific Discovery ,Microsoft Research.

[16] Klemettinen, M. Mannila, H., Ronkainen, P., Toivonen, H., and A. Verkamo, I., 1994. Finding interesting rules from large sets of discovered association rules. In Proceedings of the third international conference on Information and knowledge management (CIKM '94), Nabil R. Adam, Bharat K. Bhargava, and Yelena Yesha (Eds.). ACM, New York, NY, USA, 401-407.

[17] Kritzler, M., Lewejohann, L., and Krüger, A. 2007. Analysing movement and behavioural patterns of laboratory mice in a semi natural environment based on data collected via RFID-technology. *Proceedings of the Workshop on Behaviour Monitoring and Interpretation*: 17-28

[18] Kritzler, M., Jabs, S., Kegel, P., and Krüger, A. 2008. Indoor tracking of laboratory mice via an RFID-tracking framework. In *Proceedings of the first ACM international workshop on Mobile entity localization and tracking in GPS-less environments (MELT '08). ACM, New York, NY, USA,*

[19] Lewejohann, L., Hoppmann, A.M., Kegel, P., Kritzler, M., Kruger, A., and Sachser, N. 2009. Behavioral phenotyping of a murine model of alzheimer's disease in a seminaturalistic environment using RFID tracking. *Behavioral Research Methods* 41:850-856.

[20] O'Riain, M.J., Jarvis, J.U., Alexander, R., Buffenstein, R., and Peters, C. 2000. Morphological castes in a vertebrate. *Proceedings of the National Academy of Sciences of the United States of America*, 97(24), 13194-13197

[21] Pasquier, N., Bastide, Y., Taouil, R., & Lakhal, L. 1999. Discovering Frequent Closed Itemsets for Association Rules. In *Proceedings of the 7th international Conference on Database theory*. In C. Beeri & P. Buneman (Eds.), (LNCS 1540, pp. 398-416).

[22] Pei, J., Han, J., & Mao, R. 2000. CLOSET, An efficient algorithm for mining frequent closed itemsets. In *Proc. 2000 ACM SIGMOD Int.Workshop Data Mining and Knowledge Discovery (DMKD00)* (pp. 11-20).

[23] Riccio, A.P., and Goldman, B.D. 2000. Circadian rhythms of body temperature and metabolic rate in naked mole-rats. *Physiology and Behavior*; 71 (1-2), 15-22.

[24] Wang, J. , Han, J., and Pei, J.. 2003. CLOSET+: searching for the best strategies for mining frequent closed itemsets. In *Proceedings of the ninth ACM SIGKDD international conference on Knowledge discovery and data mining* (KDD '03). ACM, New York, NY, USA, 236-245

[25] Wasserman, S., and Faust, K. 1994. *Social network analysis: Methods and applications*. Cambridge; New York: Cambridge University Press.

[26] Weiss, I.C. Pryce, C.R., Jongen-Relo, A.L., Nanz-Bahr, N.I., and Feldon, J. 2004. Effect of social isolation on stress-related behavioural and neuroendocrine state in the rat, *Behavioral Brain Research,* 152 279–295.

[27] Würbel, H. 2002. Behavioral phenotyping enhanced - beyond (environmental) standardization. Genes, Brain and Behavior 2002; 1: 3-8

[28] Zaki, M. J. 2000. Generating non-redundant association rules. In *Proceedings of the Sixth ACM SIGKDD international Conference on Knowledge Discovery and Data Mining* (Boston, Massachusetts, United States, August 20-23, 2000).

A Pattern Discovery Approach to Retail Fraud Detection

Prasad Gabbur, Sharath Pankanti, Quanfu Fan, and Hoang Trinh
Exploratory Computer Vision Group, IBM Research
19 Skyline Drive, Hawthorne, NY 10532
pgabbur@email.arizona.edu, {sharat, qfan, trinhh}@us.ibm.com

ABSTRACT

A major source of revenue shrink in retail stores is the intentional or unintentional failure of proper checking out of items by the cashier. More recently, a few automated surveillance systems have been developed to monitor cashier lanes and detect non-compliant activities such as fake item checkouts or scans done with the intention of deriving monetary benefit. These systems use data from surveillance video cameras and transaction logs (TLog) recorded at the Point-of-Sale (POS). In this paper, we present a pattern discovery based approach to detect fraudulent events at the POS. Our approach is based on mining time-ordered text streams, representing retail transactions, formed from a combination of visually detected checkout related activities called *primitives* and barcodes from TLog data. Patterns representing single item checkouts, i.e. anchored around a single barcode, are discovered from these text streams using an efficient pattern discovery technique called *Teiresias*. The discovered patterns are used to build models for true and fake item scans by retaining or discarding the anchoring barcodes in those patterns respectively. A pattern matching and classification scheme is designed to robustly detect non-compliant cashier activities in the presence of noise in either the TLog or the video data. Different weighting schemes for quantifying the relative importance of the discovered patterns are explored: *Frequency*, *Support Vector Machine (SVM)* and *Frequency+SVM*. Using a large scale dataset recorded from retail stores, our approach discovers semantically meaningful cashier scan patterns. Our experiments also suggest that different weighting schemes result in varied false and true positive performances on the task of fake scan detection.

Categories and Subject Descriptors: I.5.4 [Pattern Recognition]: Applications—*computer vision, text processing*

General Terms: Security

Keywords: Retail, Security, Sweethearting, Pattern discovery, Teiresias

KDD'11 August 21–24, 2011, San Diego, California, USA.

1. INTRODUCTION

A major source of revenue shrink in retail stores is the intentional or unintentional failure of proper checking out of items by the cashier. It is estimated to cause billions of dollars in revenue losses each year [8]. In the case of an intentional failure, it is referred to as *sweethearting* between a cashier and a customer as both intend to derive monetary benefit from it. More recently a few automated surveillance systems have been developed to monitor cashier lanes and detect non-compliant activities. These systems use data from surveillance video cameras and transaction logs (TLog) recorded at the Point-of-Sale (POS). Video-based [8, 1, 2] systems visually monitor the activities of a cashier around the Point-of-Sale to detect item checkouts and verify them using TLog data. Being able to detect as many non-compliant events as possible while keeping the number of false alarms low is key to the successful deployment of these systems. It is a challenging problem to optimize the two conflicting objectives due to variations and noise within the input data streams.

Instead of using the two streams (video and TLog) of data separately, we posit that much can be learned about the nature of an item scan performed by a cashier by combining them into a single stream. This is because most item checkouts are normal (no fraud) and a barcode is registered in the TLog. By analyzing visual information around the registered barcode events, it is possible to model variations in the cashier's activities for checking out an item. This is helpful in detecting non-compliant cashier activities more robustly in the presence of noise in either the TLog or the video data.

Video-based systems usually make use of complex analytics to detect and monitor cashier activities [7]. Many of these approaches make adhoc assumptions such as only a constrained set of activities being performed by a cashier during retail transactions. Real-world data presents a number of challenges to such approaches due to those assumptions being violated very often. Computer vision systems are based on extracting visual features from input video streams. Recently, there has been some work in transforming videos into a sequence of discrete features [11] and applying text-based data mining algorithms on the resulting streams. This has opened up new possibilities for looking at video data in a different light in order to infer useful knowledge. Text-based algorithms are simpler and faster than many sophisticated video analysis techniques. But their potential in addressing some of the vision challenges have not been explored. In this work, we propose a text-based approach to analyzing

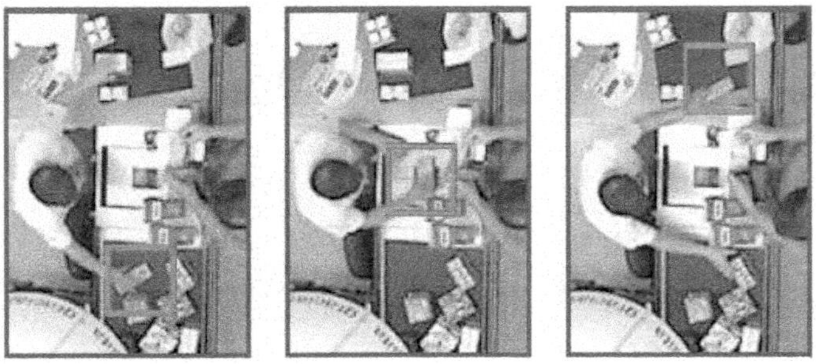

1: A typical checkout involves the pickup (P), scan (S) and drop (D) of the item of interest. Each such action is detected as a *primitive* by a motion-based primitive detector (See Section 3.1).

videos represented as time-ordered discrete features called *primitives* in the context of a retail surveillance application.

A retail transaction involves the checkout of a set of items the customer intends to buy. Ideally, each checkout event can be thought of as comprising three sub-events or primitives: Pickup (P), Scan (S), and Drop (D) in that temporal order, as illustrated in Fig. 1. A visual compliance approach [7] is designed to detect these sub-events in a video and group them into PSD triplets corresponding to visual scans of items. A visual scan with an associated barcode confirms a valid checkout, otherwise it is a potential candidate for a fraud or operational error. We refer to a valid checkout as a *true* or *visual scan* and a fraud or operational error as a *fake scan*.

Usually the output of the primitive and event detection modules is not a single PSD triplet for every checkout. Some of the sub-events may be repeated more than once or may not even be detected due to various reasons. One common situation arises when a cashier has difficulty scanning the item in a single attempt and ends up doing multiple scans resulting in repeated S primitives for a single item. Therefore the primitive sequence output by the detection system is usually noisy with repetitions and/or no occurrences of one or more of the P, S and D primitives. This poses difficulties to any approach looking for the presence of a PSD triplet corresponding to an item checkout. A more robust method accounting for missing and repeated primitives is needed.

In what follows, a paradigm for visual compliance based on pattern discovery and matching is proposed. A brief description of the proposed approach is given in Section 2. The details of the various steps involved including pattern discovery and matching, primitive classification and true/fake scan detection are given in Sections 3 and 4. Section 5 describes a few weighting schemes to quantify the relative importance of the discovered patterns for classification. Experimental details and results are given in Section 6 followed by a brief discussion of the results in Section 7 and conclusions in Section 8.

2. OUR APPROACH

Various patterns of item checkouts are discovered using an efficient pattern discovery algorithm called *Teiresias* [12]. The input to the pattern discovery algorithm are text strings formed from temporally ordering the output of the primitive detectors and the TLog data. By treating the barcode as another primitive, the alphabet set from which the text strings are formed has a cardinality of four: $\{P, S, D, B\}$. The output of the pattern discovery algorithm is a set of patterns within the input strings that are repeated at least a minimum number of times across those strings. Only those patterns that have a single barcode B primitive within them and with particular configurations of the other three primitives around it are selected and the others are discarded. Practically most item checkouts in retail transactions are genuine and fake checkouts are very rare. With this assumption, the selected patterns are representative of single item checkouts and model the variations in the process of checking out an item represented as a combination of discrete primitives. Conceptually, a fake scan or a fraudulent item checkout is similar in essence to a genuine checkout except that a barcode is not registered in the TLog. So a model representing fake scans is derived from the model for true scans by discarding the barcode primitives from the pattern set. For the sake of convenience, we term the models corresponding to true and fake scans as *positive* and *negative* models respectively.

The positive and negative models are used to detect the presence of any fake scans within a new transaction with the help of a pattern matching and classification scheme. Each primitive within the transaction stream is assigned a vote by each of the patterns in the positive and negative groups when they match a certain neighborhood of that primitive. Following a Bayesian approach, these votes are transformed into posterior likelihoods of the primitive being a part of a true or a fake scan. A classification based on maximum posterior likelihood (above a certain minimum confidence level) is done to assign the primitive to the most likely class. Finally a grouping of the classified primitives based on their class labels and temporal adjacency leads to a segmentation of the transaction stream into true and fake scans.

3. CHECKOUT PATTERN DISCOVERY

More details of the primitive detection and pattern discovery steps are given in the following subsections.

3.1 Primitive Detection

To detect primitives: Pickup (P), Scan (S), and Drop (D) from the retail video stream, we implement an efficient vision technique proposed in [14]. The approach is based on the observation that each primitive P, S, D follows a specific motion pattern - each primitive is an in/out process in which the cashier's hand enters and exits a region of interest (ROI). To detect hand motion, a hand color model is first adaptively learned by continuously collecting hand pixel examples. Based on this model, each pixel in the motion map computed by frame differencing is classified as hand pixel or not, to form a hand motion map for each video frame. This map explicitly captures the hand motion robustly in the presence of motion noise from belt movement, background changes, and customer interactions. A hierarchical finite state machine (FSM) is then applied to deterministically check whether or not the hand motion follows the predefined in/out pattern corresponding to each primitive. After the primitives P, S, D are detected, these are combined with the barcode primitives (B) from the TLog data to form a temporally ordered text string of $\{P, S, D, B\}$, which is used as input string to the pattern discovery algorithm.

3.2 TEIRESIAS

Teiresias [12] is a widely used algorithm for discovering repeated patterns across finite alphabet streams. It was originally developed for discovering rigid patterns in biological sequences, eg., motifs in amino acid sequences. However, it has been applied to problems in other domains such as spam filtering [13] and intrusion detection [18] in UNIX processes. Teiresias discovers all unique $< L, W >$ *maximal* patterns having a certain minimum support K within a given set of alphabetic sequences. A $< L, W >$ pattern is defined to be one in which every sub-pattern of length W or more has at most $(W - L)$ wildcard characters, the others are alphabets. The term *maximal* implies that the discovered patterns cannot be made more specific without reducing their support sets within the input streams. The computational complexity of the algorithm is seen to scale quasi-linearly with the size of the output patterns, hence making it a very efficient pattern discovery tool.

3.3 Patterns in retail transactions

The Teiresias pattern discovery algorithm is used to discover patterns that are representative of genuine item scans within retail transactions. In our system, a transaction is a stream of P, S, D and B primitives, where the ordering is determined by their occurrence in time. Since a typical item checkout involves picking, scanning and then dropping it, some representative patterns that correspond to this process would be $PSBD$, $PBSD$ or $PSDB$, allowing for time delays in primitive detection or barcode registration. In reality, there are a number of other patterns that are possible due to noisy primitive streams rendered by the primitive detector and TLog data. Some typical examples include:

1. Multiple scan: An item is scanned more than once before a successful barcode registration. Representative patterns in this case might be $PSDSBD$, $PSDSDSBD$, and many more.

2. Late barcode: A successful scan but a delay in the arrival of barcode might result in patterns such as $PSDB$, $PSDPSB$, etc. Such patterns might also result from items which have to be manually registered at the POS without scanning. Examples include organic produce such as vegetables and fruits.

3. Parallel scan: Following a successful scan, an item is dropped after the next item in the pickup queue is picked up. This can be represented using $PSPBD$, $PSBPD$ and so on.

Variations in the patterns representing item scans are captured by mining primitive streams, resulting from transactions, for patterns that repeat across transactions. Most of the item checkouts in transactions are true scans with a barcode being registered for each scan. Therefore patterns that are repeated across transactions and have a single barcode (B) primitive within them can be thought of as corresponding to true scans. We seek such patterns by first discovering unique maximal $< L, W >$ patterns with support at least K from a set of transactions, employing the Teiresias algorithm. This process is repeated for a few different $L = W$ values to capture representative patterns of different lengths, i.e., with different levels of noise embedded in them. Setting $L = W$ ensures that the resulting patterns do not have any wildcard characters so that exact pattern matching can be done using those patterns. For the experiments in this work, the $L = W$ values range from 3 to 10. We choose a conservative value for K (2) so that even patterns that are repeated only once are captured. From the resulting set, only those patterns that match the regular expression $P[PSD] * B[PSD] * D$ are retained. These are all the single barcode (B) patterns that start with a pickup (P) and end in a drop (D) primitive with any possible number and arrangement of P, S and D primitives between them.

Some of the patterns discovered by Teiresias are representative of different possible ways an item checkout occurs at the POS. Table 1 lists the first eight patterns based on their repeatability across transactions used for pattern discovery along with the number of transactions in which they occur. Upon visual inspection of the corresponding videos, the patterns $PBSD$ and $PSBD$ represent idealized item checkouts involving one each of the P, S, D and B primitives in them. $PDBSD$, $PBSPD$, and $PDBSPD$ are representative of overlaps between checkouts of two successive items. $PDBSD$ indicates that the drop of the previous item occurs in parallel or after the pickup of the next item, whose barcode is included in the pattern. Similarly, $PBSPD$ represents picking up the next item while or before dropping off the current item, whose barcode forms a part of the pattern. These are instances of parallel scanning. Parallel scanning of the current item with both the previous and the next one results in the pattern $PDBSPD$, with the B primitive corresponding to the current item. The other patterns in the table result from a missing S primitive in one or more of the cases described above. Similarly, we found that multiple scanning was represented by the patterns: $PDSDSBD$ and $PDSDBSD$, although they did not occur in as many transactions (19 and 53 respectively) as the patterns above.

3.4 Reducing pattern redundancy

The output of the Teiresias algorithm is a set of unique maximal patterns for a particular setting of the $< L, W >$ parameter values. We capture various levels of noise in the representation of a true scan by discovering patterns with different settings for $L = W$. This leads to some redundancy in the discovered pattern set in that a few patterns are repeatedly discovered for two different settings of $L = W$ and there are overlaps between some patterns. One example of an overlapping pair of patterns is PSB and SBD, which form sub-patterns of the canonical true scan pattern $PSBD$. This might be the result of slightly different support sets for the two patterns caused by a missing P or a D primitive in one of the scans within the input transactions. Repetitions are easily taken care of by retaining only the unique patterns. One possible way to account for overlaps is to find all pairs of patterns with overlaps among them and stitch them together into longer and longer patterns in an iterative process. But this has a high likelihood of reducing the support set of the resulting longer patterns relative to the component patterns if the component patterns did not come from a single parent pattern. This is not desirable because each of the overlapping patterns may uniquely represent a true scan with some missing primitives.

In order to address redundancy due to overlapping patterns, we do a pattern-transaction co-occurrence analysis, which is similar to Latent Semantic Analysis [6] used in the area of information retrieval. A pattern-transaction co-occurrence matrix C is constructed, where each row in the matrix corresponds to a unique discovered pattern and each column to an input transaction used for pattern discovery. The $(i, j)$the entry of the matrix is a count of the number of times pattern i appears in the jth transaction. Usually C is a sparse matrix with a few positive entries scattered among zeros. Each row of this sparse matrix can be thought of as a representation of the corresponding pattern in a space of dimensionality equal to the number of transactions used for pattern discovery. In general, these dimensions are not uncorrelated. So a measure of similarity among patterns such as the correlation coefficient cannot be reliably computed in this space. Singular Value Decomposition is performed on the co-occurrence matrix C resulting in the following factorization of C

$$C = U\Sigma V^T \tag{1}$$

where U and V are orthogonal matrices of size $m * m$ and $n * n$, assuming C is of size $m * n$, i.e., there are a total of m patterns discovered from a set of n transactions. Σ is a rectangular matrix with only non-zero elements along its diagonal, which correspond to singular values. The columns of U and V are the eigenvectors of CC^T and C^TC respectively. Choosing only the first k largest singular values and the corresponding eigenvectors leads to the best rank k approximation of C in the least squares sense. Further, each row of matrix U is a representation of the corresponding pattern (in C) in an orthogonalized space.

Since the number of transactions n is usually much smaller than the number of patterns m, there are only n non-zero singular values in the SVD of C. Therefore only the first n columns of U comprise a full representation of the patterns in an orthogonal space while allowing a complete reconstruction of C. Correlation coefficient computed in this space is a more reliable measure of similarity between patterns based on their co-occurrence within the transactions. We use this measure for clustering patterns together that have a high correlation among them. A greedy agglomerative clustering scheme is adopted, where the patterns are first ordered in the decreasing order of their total number of occurrences. Then all the patterns that have a high correlation (> 0.5) with the most repeated pattern are put into one cluster. This is repeated with the next available most repeated pattern and so on until all patterns are exhausted. Each cluster is then represented by the most occurring pattern among its members. Only the cluster representatives are used for pattern matching.

4. PATTERN MATCHING AND CLASSIFICATION

The patterns derived from the above procedure define a model for true scans, which we refer to as the *positive* model for the sake of convenience. It can be hypothesized that fake scans are similar to true scans but without the registration of a barcode. With this assumption, a corresponding *negative* model is constructed for fake scans by eliminating the B primitive from the true scan patterns. Two tables are built, one corresponding to true scans (positive) and the other corresponding to fake scans (negative). The two tables contain the same set of patterns except for the barcode primitive being deleted from each pattern in the negative set. Given a primitive stream from a new transaction, each primitive in the stream is assigned a true or fake scan label based on a pattern matching and classification procedure using the two pattern sets. Each pattern in the positive set contributes a positive vote to every primitive of any corresponding substring it matches within the transaction stream. Similarly negative votes are accumulated for each primitive based on how many patterns in the negative set exactly match a substring containing the primitive. These votes are used for classifying the primitives as described below.

4.1 Classif cation

Each primitive p in the input transaction stream is assigned a true (T) or a fake (F) scan label depending on the number of votes it has accumulated for the two categories. In order to do this classification, a Bayesian framework is adopted. Let S_T and S_F denote the sets of all true and fake scan patterns respectively. Then the likelihood of the primitive p being a part of a true scan can be written as

$$P(T|p) \propto P(T, p) \tag{2}$$

Similarly, the likelihood of p belonging to a fake scan is given by

$$P(F|p) \propto P(F, p) \tag{3}$$

We define the joint likelihoods $P(T, p)$ and $P(F, p)$ to be the probabilities of the *context* of p belonging to the set S_T and S_F respectively.

$$P(T, p) \equiv P(p - context \in S_T) \tag{4}$$

$$P(F, p) \equiv P(p - context \in S_F) \tag{5}$$

where $p - context$ is used to denote the context or neighborhood of p. Each of the above likelihoods are proportional to the number of patterns in S_T and S_F respectively that match a sub-string containing p. If we denote the positive and negative votes accumulated by p with $Votes_T(p)$ and $Votes_F(p)$ respectively, then

$$P(p - context \in S_T) \propto Votes_T(p) \tag{6}$$

$$P(p - context \in S_F) \propto Votes_F(p) \tag{7}$$

Appropriate normalization of the cumulative votes of the primitive p for the two categories yields the posterior probabilities $P(T|p)$ and $P(F|p)$. The primitive is assigned to the class with the maximum posterior likelihood given it is above a certain threshold value.

4.2 True and fake scan detection

Classification of a transaction's primitive stream results in a class label (T or F) for those primitives whose posterior likelihoods for the respective class are above the chosen threshold. Other primitives remain unclassified. This usually results in continuous stretches of T's and F's with unclassified primitives in between them. One continuous stretch of T or F labels need not necessarily correspond to a single true or fake scan respectively. A segmentation like procedure groups subsets of adjacent primitives that are assigned T labels into true scans. This is achieved by choosing a B primitive within each such subset as the anchor for the corresponding true scan. Other primitives such as P, S and D that form a part of the true scan are searched for locally, i.e., the nearest ones to the anchoring B primitive within a small window. The size of the window is limited to the set of non-B primitives around the anchor, which have been classified as belonging to the class T. Only one P, S and D primitive is assigned to a true scan.

Among the available P's and S's within a window, preference is given to the ones that occur closest to B but earlier in the stream. On the other hand, a D that is closest to B but occurs later in the stream is preferably assigned to the true scan. In the absence of a P, S or D primitive within the neighborhood window of an anchoring B, a new such primitive is created and assigned to the true scan. Similar grouping is performed to detect fake scans using S primitives labeled as belonging to class F as anchors and searching for the nearest P and D primitives. In order to keep the number of false positives manageable, we assume that at least one each of P, S and D primitives should be present to provide enough evidence for a fake scan and that two successive fake scans be at least 3 seconds apart.

5. WEIGHTING VOTES

Within a transaction stream, a primitive is assigned a vote by each of the patterns matching a sub-string containing the primitive. A voting scheme where each pattern contributes the same vote to the matching primitives might not be optimal. Our goal is to be able to reliably distinguish true scans from fake scans based on the discovered patterns. Not all the patterns contain the same amount of information to distinguish between the two classes. There may still be some redundancies left among patterns filtered out by co-occurrence analysis. Therefore it is not guaranteed that each pattern contributes independent information relative to others in the set. Further some of the patterns may even be noisy, eg., resulting from missing or multiple primitive detections for single pickup, scan or drop events during transactions. A weighting scheme where patterns that carry independent information and are the most important for classification are weighted more relative to others is desirable. We experiment with two weighting schemes that assign different relative votes to the patterns.

5.1 Frequency weights

This is a simple weighting scheme where each pattern is assigned a weight inversely proportional to the number of times it occurs across all the transactions used for pattern discovery. This is mostly an empirical weighting scheme driven by experimentation. We tried different heuristic schemes that were based on the frequency of patterns and the size of their clusters in the co-occurrence analysis (Section 3.4). Among them, this simple weighting scheme led to the best results in terms of the number of falsely detected fake scans relative to the total number of detected true scans.

A possible reason might be that smaller patterns tend to occur more frequently than longer ones among our discovered patterns. Using a uniform voting scheme, the smaller patterns have a higher influence in the classification decision of a majority of primitives because smaller patterns match more sub-strings than longer ones. Further each pattern in the negative (F) class is one primitive shorter than its counterpart in the positive class. All these factors contribute to an increased number of short noisy primitive segments that are assigned to the negative (F) class. With the inverse frequency based voting scheme, longer (less frequent) patterns influence the classification decision of many primitives leading to longer, less noisy segments of continuous T or F labels. However, this scheme causes many genuine fake scans to be missed, based on our experiments (See Section 6). In order to circumvent this problem, we designed a weighting scheme where the weights were derived from a classifier trained to distinguish true from fake scans using ground truth data.

5.2 Support Vector Machine (SVM) weights

Support Vector Machine (SVM) [15, 3] is used in a variety of classification problems because of a number of its favorable properties including superior generalization ability. A two-class SVM estimates a hyperplane separating the training points in a feature space such that the margin between the hyperplane and the two classes is maximized. Assuming a linear kernel SVM, the weights are indicative of how useful the corresponding features are for the purpose of classification. This has been used for feature selection [5, 9]. We exploit this property of SVMs to learn the relative importance of the discovered patterns for classifying a primitive into true or fake scan based on the matches to its context. In order to achieve this, we sample a set of training points belonging to true and fake scan classes and map them onto a feature space with dimensionality equal to the number of patterns. The training points are a set of primitive strings centered around the B primitive for a true scan and the S primitive for a fake scan.

The B primitive locations of true scans are randomly sampled from the set of transaction streams used for training leaving out those transactions which have a fake scan in them. Note that we hand labeled the locations of the fake scans in our transaction streams by a visual inspection of the corresponding videos. There are a total of 13 fake scans in our data consisting of 1660 transactions. The number of randomly sampled true scan points from training data is in the order of a few hundreds. There is a large imbalance in the number of training points for the two classes. Training on such data leads to a SVM that is biased towards the class with the larger size [10]. A number of approaches have been proposed for SVM training in the presence of a large imbalance in data for the two classes. These methods either undersample the majority class [17], oversample the minority class [4] or adjust the SVM margin to reduce the bias towards majority class [16, 10].

Our use of SVM is to learn a weight for each of the feature dimensions, corresponding to a pattern, that quantifies the importance of that pattern for classification. It is desirable to have a non-negative weight for each pattern so that they can be easily interpreted. In order to avoid the data imbalance effects and to ensure positive weights, we learn a zero-bias SVM with a particular mapping of the true and fake scans into a feature space. The mapping is such that the true scan points always lie in the positive hyper-quadrant and the fake scan points in the negative hyper-quadrant. A hyper-quadrant refers to the extension of a quadrant in a 2D space to a higher dimensional space. So the positive hyper-quadrant is the set of all points with only positive coordinates and similarly for the negative hyper-quadrant. The sampled true scan points are matched with the set of patterns in the positive set to obtain a feature vector for each of these points. Only the dimensions corresponding to the patterns with exact matches are set to suitable non-zero positive values and the others are zero. Similarly the feature vectors for fake scan points are obtained by pattern matching with the negative set of patterns. However the values for the dimensions with exact matches are set to suitable negative values in this case. Fig. 2 illustrates the mapping and

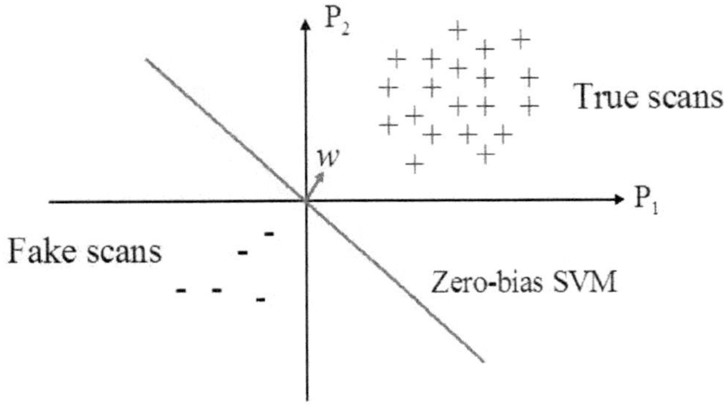

2: A zero-bias SVM for classifying true scan points from fake scans. The mapping of points is such that true scan samples always lie in the positive quadrant and the fake scan samples in the negative quadrant. There are very few fake scan samples relative to the number of true scan samples. The SVM weights are all positive and quantify the relative importance of the feature dimensions (P_1 and P_2) for classification.

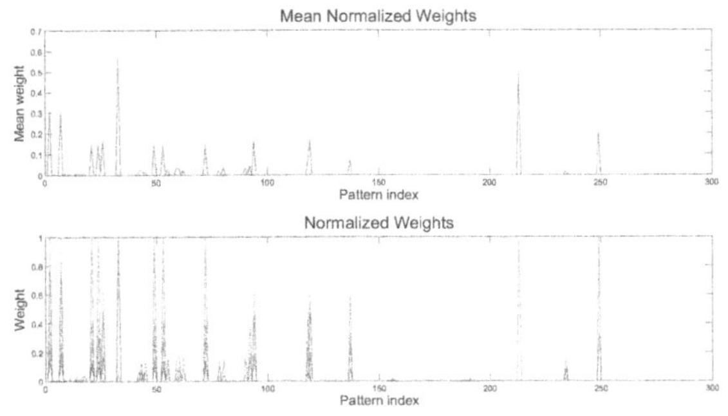

3: (Below) SVM weights after normalization (maximum value 1) for each random split of the available data. The learned weights for the different splits are superimposed. (Above) Averaged weights across all the random splits. The weights imply relative importance of patterns for the task of classification. Clearly, some patterns are more important than others.

the SVM geometry in a 2D space corresponding to patterns P_1 and P_2.

The available data within a training set (3 lanes) (See Section 6) is split into two equal parts randomly (approx. 250 true scans and 2-3 fake scans) with one half used for SVM training and the other half held out for testing the learned classifier. SVMs are trained with 100 different such random splits and the weights are averaged to obtain the final weights. Considering one training division of all the data, Fig. 3 shows the normalized weights after SVM training using each of the 100 random splits of the data and also the averaged weights across those splits.

The mapping into the feature space can be done in many different ways. Our experiments favored an asymmetric mapping scheme between the true and fake scan training points. In this scheme, the positive value assigned to a match between a true scan and a pattern is proportional to the frequency of the pattern. On the other hand the same negative value is assigned to all the fake scan point and pattern matches regardless of the pattern. Such a mapping causes true scan points that match to only a few of the patterns occurring less frequently to be moved more towards the origin in the feature space relative to others. Since the SVM hyperplane passes through the origin it seems that points matching to less frequent patterns are most likely to be the support vectors, which influence the final weights. This has a tendency to favor lesser number of false positives in our experiments. Table 1 shows the SVM weights obtained by averaging the learned normalized mean SVM weights across all the divisions of the data from 6 lanes into 3 training and 3 held-out lanes (See Section 6.1). Interestingly, the two idealized checkout patterns ($PBSD$ and $PSBD$) have the most significant average SVM weights among the above, implying their usefulness for classification.

5.3 Combining frequency and SVM weights

The SVM-based weights emphasize those patterns that are useful for distinguishing true and fake scan points within the training data. Interestingly, these weights also lead to an increased number of genuine fake scan detections (true positives) within the held-out data relative to using the frequency weights (Section 6). However the false positive performance of the classifier using SVM weights is worse compared to that using the frequency weights. This suggests an interesting possibility of combining the two weights such that the combined weights help achieve a better false positive performance relative to the SVM weights and better true positive performance relative to the frequency weights. The combined weights are obtained by summing the SVM and frequency weights, thereby reinforcing only those frequently occurring short patterns that are useful for classification. For convenience, these weights are referred to as *(Frequency+SVM)* weights.

6. EXPERIMENTS

6.1 Data

Video data recorded from 6 lanes of a retail store during one business day (approx. 16 hrs) of transactions was used for all the experiments reported in this work. During this period, 18 different cashiers checked out a total of about 32,969 registered items within 1660 transactions. The video data was transformed into discretized and time ordered primitives and merged with the barcode events from the TLog data. Primitive streams corresponding to transactions on 3 of the lanes were chosen for discovering patterns as described in Section 3.3. The same set of patterns were used for all the experiments reported here. The entire data was divided into two parts (3 lanes each). These two sets are referred to as *training* and *held-out* lanes respectively. All such divisions ($\binom{6}{3} = 20$) were considered and the results were averaged across the divisions. Note that the frequency weights remain the same for all the data divisions resulting in the same true and fake scan detections unlike the other two weighting schemes. Only the held-out statistics change across those divisions. Similarly for the unweighted Teiresias and all patterns (Section 6.2). The data from all the lanes was manually evaluated by six human subjects for the presence of sweethearting activities or operational errors leading to the failure of barcode registration for the corresponding items. A total of 13 such events were found.

Pattern	#Repeats across transactions	Average SVM weight
PBD	1584	0.005
$PBSD$	1302	0.593
$PDBD$	782	0.009
$PBPD$	774	0.010
$PBSPD$	734	0.127
$PDBSD$	629	0.127
$PSBD$	590	0.597
$PDBSPD$	585	0.014

1: The first eight most repeated patterns across all transactions used for pattern discovery by Teiresias. Each of those pattern's number of repeats (transactions in which they occur) and the learned average SVM weight are reported in the second and third columns respectively. $PBSD$ and $PSBD$ represent idealized item checkouts and also have the most significant average SVM weights. Other patterns represent parallel scans between successive items and scans with a missing S primitive. See text for more details.

6.2 All patterns

Our model for true scans is a set of discovered primitive patterns with different combinations of P, S and D primitives anchored around a single B primitive. The discovered set of patterns capture possible variations of the P, S and D primitives within a true scan based on a finite amount of training data. It is a natural question to ask whether the discovered set of patterns capture all such possible variations. In order to address this we designed an experiment considering all possible combinations of the P, S and D primitives around a single B primitive to model a true scan. The number of such patterns is finite since we consider patterns within a certain range of lengths (m to n) and is given by

$$\#Patterns = \sum_{i=m}^{n} i(3)^{i-1} \tag{8}$$

Considering patterns with lengths in the range 3 to 10 (see Section 3.3) results in a total of 280476 patterns. This is a large number relative to the set of 270 patterns discovered by Teiresias followed by reduction with co-occurrence analysis. Therefore a *brute force* approach considering all possible patterns is computationally expensive. However it helps quantify how much of the variation in true scans is not captured by the patterns discovered from training data.

6.3 Performance measures

We evaluate the true and fake scan detection performances using various patterns and weighting schemes on held out data using two measures: true positive recall rate and false positive detection rate. True positive recall rate for a set of lanes is defined as the total number of detected genuine fake scans relative to the total number of them found by human evaluators. The false positive rate across a set of lanes is defined as the total number of detected fake scans as a fraction of the total number of detected true scans on those lanes. The modified definitions above allow us to see the differences between different methods given the rarity of genuine fake scans in the data and the variations in the number of true scan detections across methods.

6.4 Results

As described in Section 4.1, each primitive in a transaction stream is assigned a true or fake scan label based on whether its maximum posterior likelihood for the corresponding class exceeds a certain threshold. We vary this threshold value from 0.5 to 0.9 in steps of 0.1 and plot the true and fake scan detection performances. The number of detected true (or visual) and fake scans for data from the held out lanes of one particular division of all the data is plotted in Fig. 4. In addition to the above, the detection of genuine fake scans is an important measure of performance. Fig. 5a shows the average true positive recall rate for the held out lanes across all the 20 divisions of the entire data along with the standard errors. The average false positive rates and their standard errors for the held out lanes across all the training/held-out divisions is plotted in Fig 5b.

7. DISCUSSION

Based on the plot of Fig. 4a, we see that the true (or visual) scan detection using Teiresias patterns is quite stable across the entire range of classifier thresholds. This implies that the posterior probabilities resulting from the pattern matching are high for the true class primitives regardless of the weighting scheme used. Using all patterns leads to increased uncertainty in assigning a primitive to either of the two classes as is evident from the drastic reduction in the number of both true and fake scan detections with increasing classifier threshold. This suggests that using more patterns to model cashier checkout activities is not always beneficial with the proposed pattern matching and classification scheme but learning from data is helpful.

From Fig. 4b, the false positive detection rate decreases with increasing classifier threshold in the case of unweighted Teiresias patterns and all patterns but remains relatively constant using any of the weighting schemes. This suggests that using weighted votes, the confidence in classifying a primitive into the fake scan class is usually higher as implied by the posterior likelihoods. Among all the weighting schemes, SVM weights lead to an increased false positive rate (7.5% to 8.8%) for all classifier threshold values. The other two weighting schemes have a false positive rate within about 4.0% to 6.3%. The range is much larger, between 3.3% to 10 1% for the unweighted Teiresias and all patterns. A similar analysis of the results (Table 2) from a state-of-the-art video-based surveillance system [7, 8] on the same dataset resulted in an average false positive rate of 4.4% with a standard error of 0.12%. Note that similar to our case of frequency weighted votes, there is no true notion of held out data in this case as the detections remain the same for all the divisions.

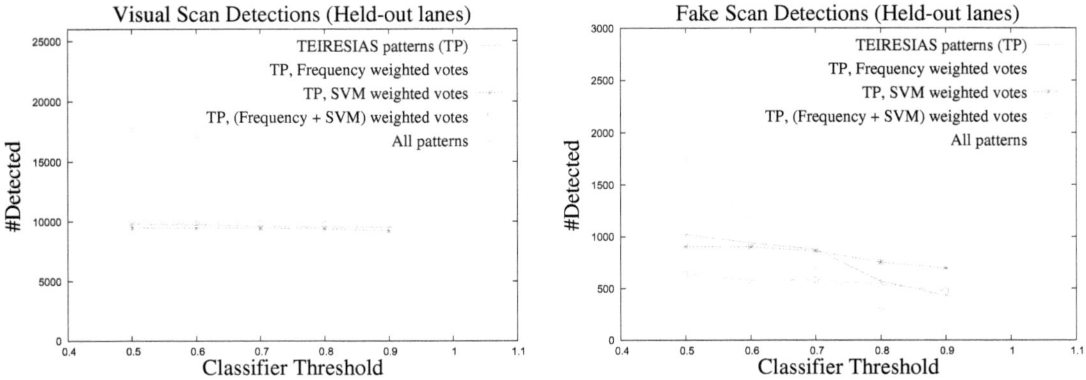

(a) True (Visual) Scan Detections (b) Fake Scan Detections

4: True (visual) and fake scan detection performances on transactions of the held-out lanes of one particular division of the entire data into training/held-out sets. The total #detections are plotted separately for the true (left) and fake(right) scans as a function of the classification threshold. The various curves are for results using the Teiresias patterns without any weighting or the same patterns using different weighting schemes (See Section 5). A curve for the brute force method of considering all possible patterns is also plotted (See Section 6.2). The total number of successfully registered items is 18,357.

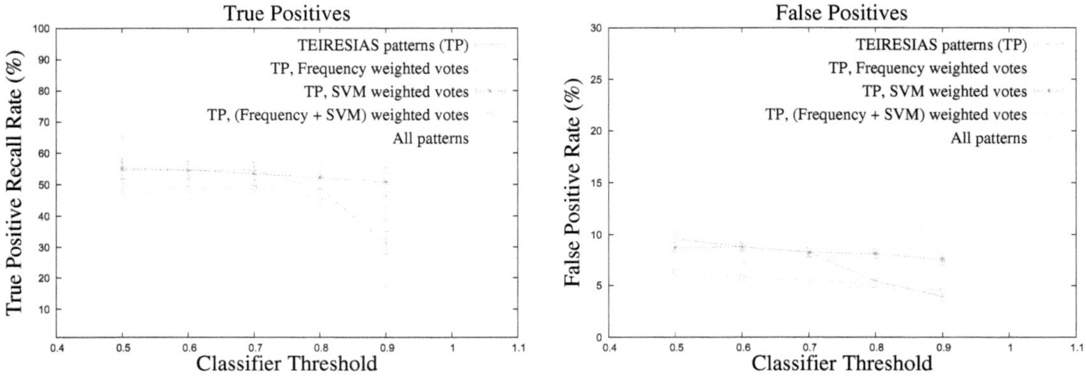

(a) True Positive Recall Rate (b) False Positive Rate

5: Average true positive recall rate (left) as a function of classifier threshold for the various methods (weighted, unweighted Teiresias patterns and all patterns). True positive rate is defined to be the fraction of all the human annotated fake scans detected by the particular method. The curves show the averaged rates across all the held-out sets of the 20 divisions of the entire data into training and held-out sets. Similarly, the average false positive rate (right) across the held-out lanes for the different pattern sets and weighting schemes is plotted. False positive rate is the number of detected false positives as a fraction of the total number of detected true scans. The vertical bars in the above plots are the standard errors of the corresponding means.

Lane	1	2	3	4	5	6
#Visual scans	2497	2186	4463	3195	3533	4244
#Fake scans (FS)	67	176	209	145	114	165
#True positives	1	1	1	1	2	2
#Ground truth FS	3	2	1	1	4	2

2: Detection statistics of the video-based system across the 6 lanes. The number of manually detected or ground truth fake scans (FS) for each lane are also shown in the bottom row.

From the plot of Fig. 5a, we observe that the SVM weighting scheme helps achieve the best true positive detection performance across the entire range of classifier thresholds (50.8% to 55.2%). Using unweighted Teiresias patterns results in a similar performance (54.5%) but only for lower values of the classifier threshold. On the other hand, the frequency weighting scheme results in a relatively smaller average true positive recall rate (38.1% to 47.1%). Combining the two weighting schemes in an additive fashion results in an average true positive recall rate ranging between 38.3% to 49.4%. The corresponding statistic for the video-based surveillance system is 63.6% with a standard error of 3.01%. We would like to point out that the video-based system uses the time duration of primitives in more ways than is being made use of in our approach.

8. CONCLUSIONS

In this paper we address the problem of detecting fake item checkouts by cashiers in retail stores. A new detection framework is proposed by merging data from video and TLog streams recorded at the POS. Using an efficient pattern discovery technique called Teiresias, we learn variable patterns of cashier checkout activity and use them to build simple complementary models for true and fake item checkouts. These models are employed in a pattern matching and classification scheme to detect fake scans robustly in the presence of noise in either video or TLog data. We experiment with a few different weighted voting schemes for the discovered patterns and compare the true and false positive detection performances. Our results suggest that a pattern frequency based weighting scheme leads to reduced false positive rates while a SVM weighting scheme results in higher true positive detection rates. A hybrid scheme combining the two weights in an additive manner helps achieve a trade-off between the two.

We compared the performance of our system with a state-of-the-art video surveillance system and obtained similar performances in terms of false positive detections. This is achieved without making use of the time information of the primitives in any systematic way as is already being done by the video-based system. This is perhaps also the reason for a slightly inferior true positive detection rate in our case relative to theirs. Our future work will include utilizing this information in various stages of our algorithm. We also intend to deploy the proposed system in a few retail stores for checkout lane monitoring.

9. ACKNOWLEDGMENTS

We would like to thank Sachiko Miyazawa, Jiyan Pan and Juan Moreno for their efforts in annotating the video data.

10. REFERENCES

[1] http://www.stoplift.com.

[2] http://www.agilenceinc.com.

[3] C. M. Bishop. *Pattern Recognition and Machine Learning*. Springer, 2006.

[4] N. Chawla, K. Bowyer, L. Hall, and W. Kegelmeyer. Smote: Synthetic minority over-sampling technique. *Journal of Artificial Intelligence Research*, 16:321–357, 2002.

[5] Y. L. Cun, J. S. Denker, and S. A. Solla. Optimal brain damage. In *Advances in Neural Information Processing Systems 2*, pages 598–605, San Francisco, CA, USA, 1990. Morgan Kaufmann Publishers Inc.

[6] S. Deerwester, S. T. Dumais, G. W. Furnas, T. K. Landauer, and R. Harshman. Indexing by latent semantic analysis. *Journal of the American Society for Information Science*, 41:391–407, 1990.

[7] Q. Fan, R. Bobbitt, Y. Zhai, A. Yanagawa, S. Pankanti, and A. Hampapur. Recognition of repetitive sequential human activity. *Computer Vision and Pattern Recognition, IEEE Computer Society Conference on*, 0:943–950, 2009.

[8] Q. Fan, A. Yanagawa, R. Bobbitt, Y. Zhai, R. Kjeldsen, S. Pankanti, and A. Hampapur. Detecting sweethearting in retail surveillance videos. In *Proceedings of the 2009 IEEE International Conference on Acoustics, Speech and Signal Processing*, ICASSP '09, pages 1449–1452. IEEE Computer Society, 2009.

[9] I. Guyon, J. Weston, S. Barnhill, and V. Vapnik. Gene selection for cancer classification using support vector machines. *Machine Learning*, 46(1-3):389–422, 2002.

[10] T. Imam, K. Ting, and J. Kamruzzaman. z-svm: An svm for improved classification of imbalanced data. *AI 2006: Advances in Artificial Intelligence*, 4304:264–273, 2006.

[11] J. R. Kender, M. L. Hill, A. P. Natsev, J. R. Smith, and L. Xie. Video genetics: a case study from youtube. In *Proceedings of the International Conference on Multimedia*, MM '10, pages 1253–1258, New York, NY, USA, 2010. ACM.

[12] I. Rigoutsos and A. Floratos. Combinatorial pattern discovery in biological sequences: The TEIRESIAS algorithm [published erratum appears in Bioinformatics 1998;14(2):229]. *Bioinformatics*, 14(1):55–67, February 1998.

[13] I. Rigoutsos and T. Huynh. Chung-kwei: a pattern-discovery-based system for the automatic identification of unsolicited e-mail messages (spam). In *First Conference on Email and Anti-Spam*, 2004.

[14] H. Trinh, Q. Fan, S. Pankanti, P. Gabbur, J. Pan, and S. Miyazawa. Detecting human activities in retail surveillance using hierarchical finite state machine. In *ICASSP*, 2011.

[15] V. Vapnik. *Statistical Learning Theory*. Wiley Interscience, 1998.

[16] K. Veropoulos, C. Campbell, and N. Cristianini. Controlling the sensitivity of support vector machines. In *Proceedings of the International Joint Conference on AI*, pages 55–60, 1999.

[17] F. Vilarino, P. Spyridonos, P. Radeva, and J. Vitria. Experiments with svm and stratified sampling with an imbalanced problem: Detection of intestinal contractions. *Lecture Notes in Computer Science*, 3687:783–791, 2005.

[18] A. Wespi, M. Dacier, and H. Debar. Intrusion detection using variable-length audit trail patterns. In *In Proceedings of the 2000 Recent Advances in Intrusion Detection*, pages 110–129. Springer-Verlag, 2000.

Driving with Knowledge from the Physical World

Jing Yuan[1,2], Yu Zheng[2], Xing Xie[2], Guangzhong Sun[1]

[1]School of Computer Science and Technology, University of Science and Technology of China

[2]Microsoft Research Asia, Building 2, No. 5 Danling Street, Haidian District, Beijing, P.R. China 100090

yuanjing@mail.ustc.edu.cn, {yuzheng, xingx}@microsoft.com, gzsun@ustc.edu.cn

ABSTRACT

This paper presents a Cloud-based system computing *customized* and *practically* fast driving routes for an end user using (historical and real-time) traffic conditions and driver behavior. In this system, GPS-equipped taxicabs are employed as mobile sensors constantly probing the traffic rhythm of a city and taxi drivers' intelligence in choosing driving directions in the physical world. Meanwhile, a Cloud aggregates and mines the information from these taxis and other sources from the Internet, like Web maps and weather forecast. The Cloud builds a model incorporating day of the week, time of day, weather conditions, and individual driving strategies (both of the taxi drivers and of the end user for whom the route is being computed). Using this model, our system predicts the traffic conditions of a future time (when the computed route is actually driven) and performs a self-adaptive driving direction service for a particular user. This service gradually learns a user's driving behavior from the user's GPS logs and customizes the fastest route for the user with the help of the Cloud. We evaluate our service using a real-world dataset generated by over 33,000 taxis over a period of 3 months in Beijing. As a result, our service accurately estimates the travel time of a route for a user; hence finding the fastest route customized for the user.

Categories and Subject Descriptors

H.2.8 [**Database Management**]: Database Applications - *data mining, Spatial databases and GIS*;

General Terms

Algorithms, Experimentation

Keywords

Driving directions, trajectory, traffic prediction, cyber-physical.

1. INTRODUCTION

Finding fast driving routes saves both the time of a driver and energy consumption (as traffic congestion wastes a lot of gas). Meanwhile, people are more likely to choose public transportation if they can know in advance that the practically quickest driving route to a destination is still slower than the public transportation. Therefore, this service is important for both end users and governments aiming to ease traffic and protect environment. Google and Bing Maps have provided the service of finding the fastest driving path in terms of the speed constraints of a road segment. However, the practical travel time of a driving route is usually different from the result calculated based solely on speed constraints. Although real-time traffic conditions are posted on some road segments, this is meant as basic information and is not incorporated into driving direction services. It is frustrating to traverse a road segment which was fast when being checked on a map while becomes very crowded when being actually driven.

Essentially, the time that a driver traverses a route depends on three aspects: 1) The physical feature of a route, such as distance, the number of traffic lights and direction turns; 2) The time-dependent traffic flow on the route; 3) A user's drive behavior. Given the same route, cautious drivers will likely drive slower than those driving aggressively. Also, users' drive behaviors vary in their progressing driving skills and experiences. E.g., traveling on an unfamiliar route, a user has to pay attention to the road signs, hence drive relatively slowly. Thus, a good routing service should consider these three aspects (routes, traffic and drivers), which are far beyond the scope of the shortest path computing.

Usually, big cities have a large number of taxicabs traversing in urban areas. To enable efficient taxi dispatch and monitoring, taxis are usually equipped with a GPS sensor, which enables them to report on their location to a server at regular intervals, e.g., 2~3 minutes. That is, a lot of GPS-equipped taxis already exist in major world cities, generating a huge volume of GPS trajectories every day [12][13][26]. Intuitively, taxi drivers are experienced in finding the quickest driving routes based on their knowledge. When selecting a route, they usually consider multiple factors including distance, traffic flows and signals, etc. Consequently, these taxi trajectories already have the knowledge of experienced drivers, physical routes and traffic conditions.

In this paper, we propose a cloud-based cyber-physical system for computing practically fast routes for a particular user, using a large number of GPS-equipped taxis and the user's GPS-enabled phone. First, GPS-equipped taxis are used as *mobile* sensors probing the traffic rhythm of a city in the *physical* world. Second, a *Cloud* in the *cyber* world is built to aggregate and mine the information from these taxis as well as other sources from the Internet like weather forecast. The mined knowledge includes the intelligence of taxi drivers in choosing driving directions and traffic patterns on road surfaces. Third, the knowledge in the *Cloud* is used in turn to serve Internet users and ordinary drivers in the *physical* world. Fourth, a *mobile* client, typically running in a user's GPS-phone, accepts a user's query, communicates with the *Cloud*, and presents the result to the user. The mobile client gradually learns a user's driving behavior from the user's driving routes and supports the *Cloud* to customize the fastest route for the user. The contribution of our work lies in three aspects:

- Using the intelligence of taxi drivers and traffic patterns mined from a large number of taxi trajectories, we propose a routing service which self-adapts to a particular user's driving behavior and customizes the fastest path for the user.
- We infer the future traffic conditions on a road using an *m*th-order Markov model considering both the historical traffic patterns and present traffic flow mined from taxi trajectories. Then, the predicted future traffic condition is integrated into the proposed routing service. We evaluated

KDD'11, August 21–24, 2011, San Diego, California, USA.

the prediction model with Beijing taxi data as well as Singapore traffic data, and found a better performance over some well-known methods using historical patterns or real-time traffic alone like T-Drive [26] and ARIMA [10]. Using a high dimensional embedding approach, we can conduct this model online.

- We built our system with a real dataset generated by 33,000 taxis in a period of 3 months, and evaluated the system with extensive experiments in both effectiveness and efficiency.

The remainder of this paper is organized as follows. Section 2 gives an overview of our system. Section 3 presents our driving direction service. Section 4 details the processes of traffic condition prediction. Section 5 reports on major experimental results followed by some discussions. Finally, we summarize the related work in Section 6 and draw conclusions in Section 7.

2. PRELIMINARY

In this section, we define some terms used in this paper and give an overview of our work.

Definition 1 (*Taxi Trajectory*): A taxi trajectory Tr is a sequence of GPS points pertaining to one trip. Each point p consists of a longitude, latitude and a timestamp $p.t$. That is, $Tr: p_1 \rightarrow p_2 \rightarrow \cdots \rightarrow p_n$, where $0 < p_{i+1}.t - p_i.t < \Delta T$ $(1 \leq i < n)$. ΔT defines the maximum sampling interval between two consecutive points.

Definition 2. (*Road Segment*): A road segment r is a directed (one-way or bidirectional) edge that is associated with a direction symbol ($r.dir$), two terminal points ($r.s$, $r.e$), and a list of intermediate points describing the segment using a polyline. If $r.dir$ =one-way, r can only be traveled from $r.s$ to $r.e$, otherwise, people can start from both terminal points, i.e., $r.s \rightarrow r.e$ or $r.e \rightarrow r.s$. Each road segment has a length $r.length$ and a speed constraint $r.speed$, which is the maximum speed allowed on this road segment.

Definition 3. (*Route*): A Route R is a set of consecutive road segments, $R: r_1 \rightarrow r_2 \rightarrow \cdots \rightarrow r_n$, where $r_k.end = r_{k+1}.start$, $1 \leq k < n$. The start point and end point of a route can be represented as $R.s = r_1.s$ and $R.e = r_1.e$.

Figure 1 shows the framework of our system which consists of two parts: knowledge discovery and service providing.

Knowledge discovery: This part is comprised of two steps, offline mining and online inference. 1) In the first step, we mine the accumulated historical data, including taxis trajectories and weather condition records, and build four landmark graphs respectively corresponding to different weather conditions (normal and severe weather) and day types (weekday and weekend). This mining step runs offline and not very often, e.g., every month. Here, a landmark is defined as a road segment that has been frequently traversed by taxis, and an edge connecting two landmarks represents the frequent transition of taxis between the two landmarks. Each edge in these landmark graphs is associated with a distribution of travel time learned from the taxi trajectories. Such landmark graphs can well model taxi drivers' intelligence in finding driving directions and traffic patterns on road surfaces. 2) In the online inference step, we calculate the real-time traffic on landmark edges according to the recently received taxi trajectories, and infer future traffic conditions in terms of the real-time traffic and the corresponding landmark graph. This process is conducted every 10-20 minutes.

Service providing: As shown in the left part of Figure 1, this process is comprised of five steps. 1) A user submits a query, consisting of a start point q_s, a destination q_d, a departure time t and a custom factor $\boldsymbol{\alpha}$, from a GPS-enabled mobile phone. Here, t can be a future time and $\boldsymbol{\alpha}$ is a vector, which represents how fast the user typically drives on different landmark edges. $\boldsymbol{\alpha}$ is set by a default value at the very beginning and is gradually updated in later services. 2) Using our time-dependent routing algorithm, the *Cloud* computes the fastest driving route for the user according to the received query. This routing algorithm uses the traffic condition at the time when the road was actually driven. This future condition is constantly computed in the online inference. 3) The *Cloud* sends the computed driving route along with the distributions of travel times on each landmark edge contained in the driving route to the user's mobile phone. 4) The GPS-phone records a GPS trajectory when the user really traverses the route. 5) The user's phone computes a new $\boldsymbol{\alpha}$ based on the recorded trajectory and the travel time distributions sent from the *Cloud*.

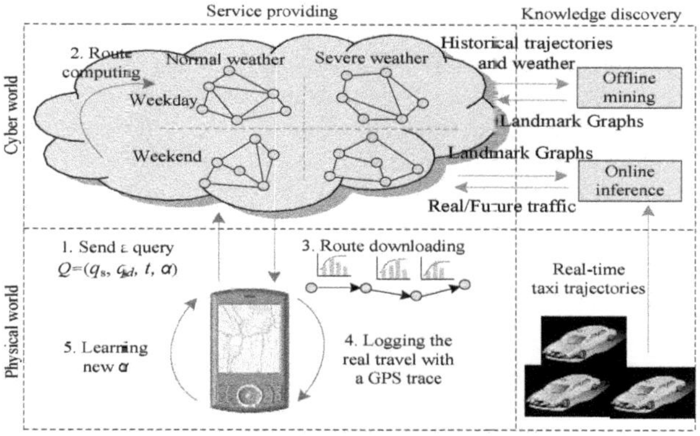

Figure 1: The framework our system

3. KNOWLEDGE DISCOVERY

3.1 Offline Mining

3.1.1 Modeling Taxi Trajectories

In practice, to save energy and communication loads, taxis usually report on their locations in a very low frequency, like 2-5 minutes per point. This increases the uncertainty of the routes traversed by a taxi [20][27]. Also, we cannot guarantee that there are sufficient taxis traversing on each road segment anytime even if we have a large number of taxis. That is, we cannot directly estimate the speed pattern of each road segment based on taxi trajectories.

In our method, we first partition the GPS log of a taxi into some taxi trajectories representing individual trips according to the taximeter's transaction records. Then, we employ our IVMM algorithm [27], which has a better performance than existing map-matching algorithms when dealing with the low-sampling-rate trajectories, to project a GPS point onto a road segment where the point was recorded. As a result, each taxi trajectory is converted to a sequence of road segments.

Based on the preprocessed taxi trajectories, we detect the top-*k* frequently traversed road segments, which are termed as *landmarks*. First, the sparseness and low-sampling-rate of the taxi trajectories do not support us to directly calculate the travel time for each road segment while we can estimate the traveling time between two landmarks (which have been frequently traversed by taxis). Second, the notion of landmarks follows the natural thinking pattern of people. For instance, the typical pattern that people introduce a route to a driver is like this "*take I-405 South at NE 4th Street, then change to I-90 at exit 11, and finally exit at Qwest Field*". Instead of giving turn-by-turn directions, people prefer to use a sequence of landmarks (like *NE 4th Street*) that highlight key directions to the destination.

After detecting the landmarks, we define the transition between two landmarks as below:

Definition 4. (*Transition*): Given a trajectory archive, a time threshold t_{max}, two landmarks u, v, arriving time t_a, leaving time t_l, we say $s = (u, v; t_a, t_l)$ is a transition if the following conditions are satisfied:

(I) There exists a trajectory $Tr: p_1 \rightarrow p_2 \rightarrow \cdots \rightarrow p_n$, after map matching, Tr is mapped to a road segment sequence $(r_1, r_2, \ldots, r_n)$. $\exists i, j,\ 1 \leq i < j \leq n$ s. t. $u = r_i;\ v = r_j$.

(II) $r_{i+1}, \ldots, r_{j-1}$ are not landmarks.

(III) $t_a = p_i.t;\ t_l = p_j.t$ and the *travel time* of this transition $t_l - t_a \leq t_{max}$.

Let S_{uv} be the set of the transitions connecting (u, v). If $S_{uv} \neq \emptyset$, we say $e = (u, v; \mathcal{T}_{uv})$ is a candidate edge, where

$$\mathcal{T}_{uv} = \{(t_a, t_l) |\ (u, v;\ t_a, t_l) \in S_{uv}\}$$

records all the historical arriving and leaving times. The frequency of e is the average number of transitions recorded per day, denoted as $e.freq$. Given a minimum frequency threshold δ, e is a landmark edge if $e.freq \geq \delta$. If no ambiguity arises, we denote the landmark edge by e_{uv}. Later, we connect all the landmark edges and construct a *landmark graph* defined as follows:

Definition 5. (*Landmark Graph*): A landmark graph $G_l = (V_l, E_l)$ is a directed graph that consists of a set of landmarks V_l (conditioned by k) and a set of landmark edges E_l conditioned by δ and t_{max}.

We observe (from the taxi trajectories) that different weekdays (e.g., Tuesday and Wednesday) almost share similar traffic patterns while the weekdays and weekends have different traffic patterns. We also find that the traffic pattern varies in weather conditions. Therefore, we respectively build different landmark graphs for weekday and weekend, and for normal and severe weather conditions, like storm, heavy rain, and snow. In total, 2×2 = 4 landmark graphs are built. The weather condition records are crawled from a weather forecast website.

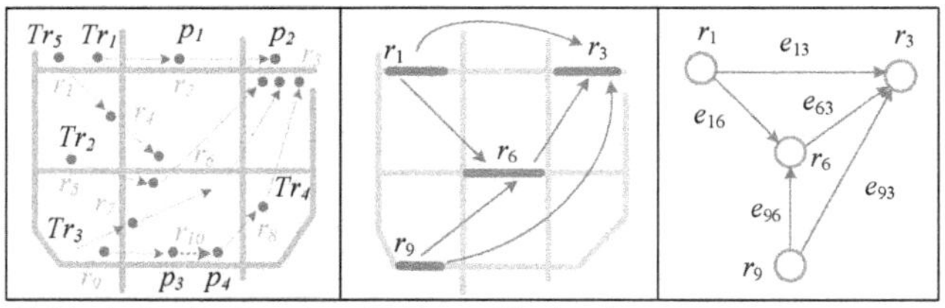

A) Matched taxi trajectories B) Detected landmarks C) A landmark Graph

Figure 2. An example of building landmark graph

Figure 2 illustrates an example of building a landmark graph. If we set k = 4, the top-4 road segments (r_1, r_3, r_6, r_9) with more projections are detected as landmarks. Note that the consecutive points (like p_3 and p_4) from a single trajectory (Tr_4) can only be counted once for a road segment (r_{10}). This aims to handle the situation that a taxi was stuck in a traffic jam or waiting at a traffic light where multiple points may be recorded on the same road segment (though being traversed once). As shown in Figure 2 (C), after the landmark detection, we convert each taxi trajectory from a sequence of road segments to a landmark sequence, and then connect two landmarks with an landmark edge if the transitions between these two landmarks conform to Definition 5 (supposing δ =1 in this example). We propose the landmark graph to model 1) the intelligence of the experienced drivers and 2) traffic flow patterns on road surfaces during a period of historical time.

3.1.2 Mining Taxi Drivers' Knowledge

Given the transition set S_{uv} of a landmark edge e_{uv}, we aim to estimate the time-dependent travel time of e_{uv}. Figure 3 A) plots all the travel times of the transitions pertaining to a real landmark edge (on weekdays over 3 months). Clearly, the travel times gather around some values (like a set of clusters) rather than a typical Gaussian distribution. This may be induced by 1) the different number of traffic lights encountered by different drivers, 2) the different routes chosen by different drivers traveling the landmark edge, and 3) drivers' personal behavior, skills and preferences. Therefore, different from existing methods [14][22] regarding the travel time of an edge as a single-valued function based on time of day, we regard a landmark edge's travel time as a set of distributions corresponding to different time slots.

Intrinsically, different roads have different time-variant traffic patterns. That is, we cannot use a predefined time partition for all the landmark edges. Here, we employ our VE-Clustering algorithm proposed in [26] to automatically learn a proper time partition for each landmark edge based on the information entropy of the data (travel times) associated with a landmark edge. This approach consists of two phases: V-Clustering and E-Clustering. The first phase clusters the travel times pertaining to a landmark edge into several categories based on the variance of the travel times. The second phase utilizes the information gain to automatically learn a proper time partition such that in each time slot the distribution of travel time is relatively stable. As a result, the travel times of each landmark edge haven been divided into some portions (pertaining to different time slots), which are ready for distribution computing.

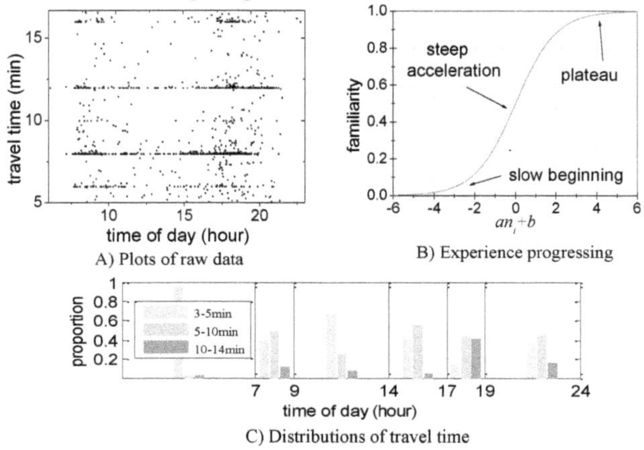

Figure 3. Learning travel time distributions from raw data

Differentiate taxi drivers' experiences: Intuitively, different taxi drivers have different knowledge in different regions of a city (especially a big city). Drivers are more likely to find out smart driving routes in a region they are very familiar with. Meanwhile, this familiarity and experience will change over the times that a driver has traveled in the region. So, when calculating the distribution of the travel times, we differentiate taxi drivers' experience based on the times they have traversed the edge.

Suppose a landmark edge e_{uv} was traversed by N different taxi drivers. Accordingly, the transition set S_{uv} can be categorized into N sample spaces. After VE-Clustering, the time of day is partitioned into several time slots. Let $\mathcal{D}_i$ be the travel time distribution (of a time slot) computed only based on the sample from a taxi driver i, denoted as

$$\mathcal{D}_i = \begin{pmatrix} 1 & 2 & \ldots & k \\ p_1^i & p_2^i & \ldots & p_k^i \end{pmatrix} \quad (1)$$

where (1, 2, … , k) stand for k different travel time clusters of this landmark edge and p_k^i represents the proportion of cluster k in taxi driver i's sample space. The progress of a driver's familiarity with a landmark edge is modeled using a Sigmoid learning curve [16] (as shown in Figure 3 B), defined as:

$$f(n_i) = \frac{1}{1+e^{-(an_i+b)}}; \tag{2}$$

where $f(n_i)$ is the familiarity, a, b are the coefficients, and n_i is the times that the driver i has traversed the landmark edge. $an_i + b$ is the linear transformation which maps n_i from [*min*, *max*] to [-6, 6], where *min* and *max* respectively represent the minimum and maximum number of transitions (generated by all the drivers) on this landmark edge. Then distribution of this time slot, denoted by $\mathcal{D}$, is computed by the weighted average:

$$\mathcal{D} = \begin{pmatrix} 1 & 2 & \dots & k \\ \sum w_i p_1^i & \sum w_i p_2^i & \dots & \sum w_i p_k^i \end{pmatrix}, \tag{3}$$

Where w_i is a normalized familiarity of the driver i, calculated as

$$w_i = \frac{f(n_i)}{\sum_{i=1}^{N} f(n_i)}. \tag{4}$$

Using this method, we obtain the travel time distribution of each time slot for each landmark edge. For example, as shown in Figure 3 C), in the time slot 9-14, over 60 percent of drivers traverse the landmark edge in 3-5 minutes (the green bar), while about 30 percent of drivers need 5-10 minutes (the yellow bar) and the rest of them even spends 10-14 minutes (the red bar).

3.2 Online Inference

In this section, we infer the traffic condition at a future time (*F*) in terms of the landmark graphs built from historical data (*H*) and real-time traffic flow calculated based on recently received taxi trajectories (*R*). In short, $H + R \rightarrow F$. In our method, we model this problem as an mth-order Markov chain, and implement the model on-the-fly using a high-dimensional embedding approach.

Table 1 Notations

τ	Traffic updating frequency	φ	Delay (future) time
x_t	A traffic condition at time t	Ω	The collection of x_t
$\mathbf{X}$	Traffic condition space	$\mathbf{S}$	A finite state space
$\mathbf{F}(x)$	A discretization function $\mathbf{F}: \mathbf{X} \rightarrow \mathbf{S}$	Y_i	A random variable in $\mathbf{S}$ space.
y_i	Realization of Y_i, y_i=$\mathbf{F}(x_{t_i}) \in \mathbf{S}$.	m	Order of a Markov chain
$\mathbf{P}^{(h)}$	h-step-ahead transition matrix of the mth-order Markov chain in $\mathbf{S}$ space		
$\mathbb{P}^{(h)}$	h-step-ahead transition matrix of the first-order Markov chain in $\mathbf{S}^m$ space		
$P_{a \rightarrow b}^{(h)}$	h-step-ahead transition probability of a Markov chain from state a to state b.		

3.2.1 *Modeling Traffic Condition*

We track the traffic condition $x_{t_1}, x_{t_2}, \dots, x_{t_n}$ at each time stamp t_i, as shown in Figure 4. Here, x can be the average velocity that vehicles can traverse on a road segment, or the average travel time of a landmark edge. This time series of real-time traffic can be calculated based on the recently received taxi trajectories and/or road sensors, using some approaches. One method is calculating the average speed or travel time of the samples on a road.

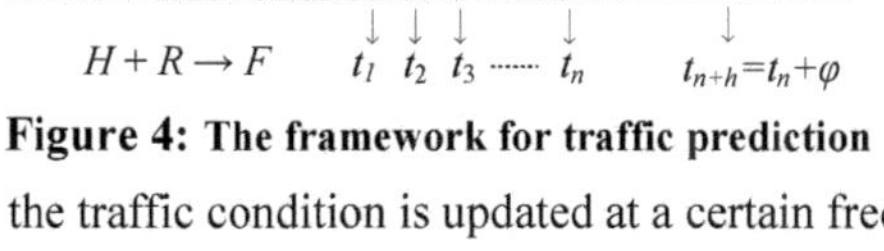

Figure 4: The framework for traffic prediction

Typically, the traffic condition is updated at a certain frequency τ,

$$\tau = t_{j+1} - t_j \qquad j = 1,2,\dots,n-1. \tag{5}$$

Given the accumulated historical traffic conditions $\mathbf{\Omega}$, we aim to predict the traffic condition at a future time $t_n + \varphi$, where

$$\varphi = h\tau, \qquad h=1, 2, \dots \tag{6}$$

In practice, the *delay* φ is configured by user-sending queries, whereas τ is often determined by a traffic monitoring system.

Since the traffic condition is usually presented to end users using discrete states, we map the continuous x_t value into a finite state space $\mathbf{S}$ by a *discretization function* $\mathbf{F}: \mathbf{X} \rightarrow \mathbf{S}$. For example, after the VE-Clustering algorithm, the travel times of transitions pertaining to a landmark edge are discretized into a cluster set, which can be regarded as the state space. After the discretization, $x_{t_1}, x_{t_2}, \dots, x_{t_n}$ is converted into a state sequence, which can be considered as the realization of a stochastic process $\{Y_i | Y_i \in \mathbf{S}\}_{i=1}^{n}$, where each Y_i is a random variable. Intuitively, the traffic condition at t_i usually depends on the time a short period before t_i, e.g., 1-2 hours, i.e., the past m states. Hence, we model this stochastic process as an mth-order Markov chain [24], stated as:

$$P(Y_n = y_n | Y_1 = y_1, Y_2 = y_2, \dots, Y_{n-1} = y_{n-1})$$
$$= P(Y_n = y_n | Y_{n-m} = y_{n-m}, \dots, Y_{n-1} = y_{n-1}) \tag{7}$$

$\forall y_i \in \mathbf{S}$, $i = 1,2,\dots,n$. Thus, for simplicity, we define our problem as: Predict the distribution of Y_{m+h} given the realization of $\{Y_i\}_{i=1}^{m}$, i.e., compute the h-step-ahead transition probability

$$P(Y_{m+h} = y_{m+h} | Y_1 = y_1, Y_2 = y_2, \dots, Y_m = y_m), \tag{8}$$

3.2.2 *High Dimensional Embedding*

Our solution is comprised of the following four steps:

***Step* 1**: Compute 1-step-ahead transition matrix of the mth-order Markov chain in $\mathbf{S}$ space using the Bayesian probability model.

We denote the h-step-ahead transition probability

$$P(Y_{m+h} = y'_m | Y_1 = y_1, Y_2 = y_2, \dots, Y_m = y_m),$$

by notation $P_{y_1, y_2, \dots, y_m \rightarrow y'_m}^{(h)}$. Then the h-step-ahead transition matrix of the mth-order Markov chain is denoted by

$$\mathbf{P}^{(h)} = \{P_{y_1, y_2, \dots, y_m \rightarrow y'_m}^{(h)}\}_{|\mathbf{S}|^m \times |\mathbf{S}|} \tag{9}$$

For $h = 1$, we can compute the 1-step-ahead transition matrix $\mathbf{P} = \mathbf{P}^{(1)}$ based on the Bayesian probability theory. That is,

$$P_{y_1, y_2, \dots, y_m \rightarrow y'_n}^{(1)} = \frac{P(Y_1 = y_1, Y_2 = y_2, \dots, Y_m = y_m | Y_{m+1} = y'_m) P(Y_{m+1} = y'_m)}{\sum_{j \in \mathbf{S}} P(Y_{m+1} = j)\, P(Y_1 = y_1, Y_2 = y_2, \dots, Y_m = y_m | Y_{m+1} = j)}$$
$$= \frac{|\{x_{t_i} \in \Omega | F(x_{t_i}) = y_1, \dots, F(x_{t_{i+m}}) = y'_m\}|}{|\{x_{t_i} \in \Omega | F(x_{t_i}) = y_1, \dots, F(x_{t_{i+m-1}}) = y_m\}|}. \tag{10}$$

The numerator and denominator of Equation 10 are calculated based on the statistics in the historical data when implementing.

***Example* 1**. Figure 5 shows an exemplary 1-step-ahead transition matrix $\mathbf{P} = \mathbf{P}^{(1)}$, where $m = 2$ and the state space is S={1, 2} (1 could be the normal traffic and 2 could indicate a traffic jam). For instance, the element (at row 11 and column 2) $P_{11 \rightarrow 2}$= 0.205 is the transition probability from $\{Y_1 = 1; Y_2 = 1\}$ to $Y_3 = 2$. The value of $P_{11 \rightarrow 2}$ is calculated according to Equation 10.

$$\begin{array}{c} \\ 11 \\ 12 \\ 21 \\ 22 \end{array} \begin{array}{c} \begin{array}{cc} 1 & 2 \end{array} \\ \begin{pmatrix} 0.795 & 0.205 \\ 0.957 & 0.043 \\ 0.523 & 0.477 \\ 0.880 & 0.120 \end{pmatrix} \end{array}$$

Figure 5: $\mathbf{P} = \mathbf{P}^{(1)}$

$$\begin{array}{c} \\ 11 \\ 12 \\ 21 \\ 22 \end{array} \begin{array}{c} \begin{array}{cccc} 11 & 12 & 21 & 22 \end{array} \\ \begin{pmatrix} 0.795 & 0.205 & 0 & 0 \\ 0 & 0 & 0.957 & 0.043 \\ 0.523 & 0.477 & 0 & 0 \\ 0 & 0 & 0.880 & 0.120 \end{pmatrix} \end{array}$$

Figure 6: $\mathbb{P} = \mathbb{P}^{(1)}$

***Step* 2**: Embed the mth-order Markov chain into an $\mathbf{S}^m$ space by binding the consecutive m variables from $\{Y_i\}_{i=1}^{n}$ into a vector.

Basically, when h >1, we can still use Equation 10 to compute the h-step-ahead transition matrix. However, this process is very time consuming as we need to scan the whole sample space $\mathbf{\Omega}$ many times for different h. Instead, we compute the h-step-ahead probability by mapping the mth-order Markov chain $\{Y_j\}$ from a space **S** into an m dimensional space $\mathbf{S}^m$ according to Lemma 1, as illustrated in Figure 7.

LEMMA 1. *Let* $\vec{Y}_j = \{Y_j, Y_{j+1}, \dots, Y_{j+m-1}\}$ *be a random vector of dimension* m*, where* $\{Y_j\}_{j=0}^{\infty}$ *is a* mth-*order Markov chain in the space* **S***, then* $\{\vec{Y}_j\}_{j=1}^{\infty}$ *is a* 1st-*order Markov chain in the space* $\mathbf{S}^m$.

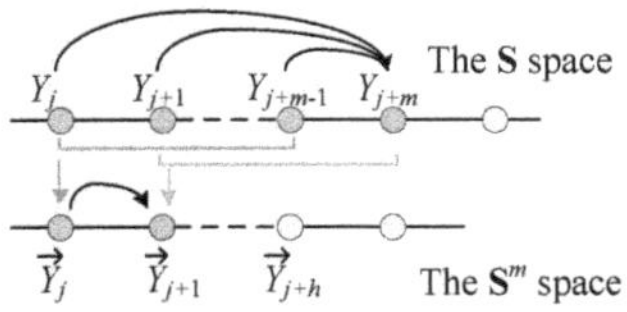

Figure 7: Mapping an *m*th-order Markov chain from S to $\mathbf{S}^m$ spaces

***Step* 3**: Compute the h-step-ahead transition matrix $\mathbb{P}^{(h)}$ of the converted Markov chain in the $\mathbf{S}^m$ space.

According to Lemma 1, $\{\vec{Y}_j\}_{j=1}^{\infty}$ is a 1st-order Markov chain in the $\mathbf{S}^m$ space. We denote the h-step-ahead transition matrix in $\mathbf{S}^m$ by:

$$\mathbb{P}^{(h)} = \{P^{(h)}_{y_1,y_2,\dots,y_m \to y'_1,y'_2,\dots y'_m}\}_{|\mathbf{S}|^m \times |\mathbf{S}|^m} \quad (11)$$

for $\forall y_j, y_j' \in \mathbf{S}$, j=1, 2,..., m.

Let $\mathbb{P} = \mathbb{P}^{(1)} = \{P^{(1)}_{y_1,y_2,\dots,y_m \to y'_1,y'_2,\dots y'_m}\}_{|\mathbf{S}|^m \times |\mathbf{S}|^m}$ be the 1-step-ahead transition matrix of $\vec{Y}_j$ in the embedded space $\mathbf{S}^m$, i.e.,

$$P^{(1)}_{y_1,y_2,\dots,y_m \to y'_1,y'_2,\dots y'_m} = P(\vec{Y}_{j+1} = \{y'_1, y'_2, \dots y'_m\} | \vec{Y}_j = \{y_1, y_2, \dots, y_m\})$$

$$= \begin{cases} P_{y_1,y_2,\dots,y_m \to y'_m} & \text{if } \{y_2, y_3, \dots, y_m\} = \{y'_1, y'_2, \dots y'_{m-1}\} \\ 0 & \text{else} \end{cases} \quad (12)$$

where $P_{y_1,y_2,\dots,y_m \to y'_m}$ is the element on row $y_1, y_2, \dots, y_m$ and column y'_m of the transition matrix **P**.

According to the the Chapman-Kolmogorov equation [15], the h-step-ahead transition matrix for $\vec{Y}_j$ is $\mathbb{P}$ multiplied by itself h times, i.e., $\mathbb{P}^{(h)} = \mathbb{P}^h$. So, $P^{(h)}_{y_1,y_2,\dots,y_m \to y'_1,y'_2,\dots y'_m}$ is an element of $\mathbb{P}^h$ at the row $y_1, y_2, \dots, y_m$ and column $y'_1, y'_2, \dots y'_m$.
Note that this property does not hold for the original mth-order Markov chain. That's the reason why we embed the mth-order Markov chain into the $\mathbf{S}^m$ space.

***Example* 2**. Figure 6 presents the 1-step-ahead transition matrix $\mathbb{P}$, which is constructed by applying Equation (12) to the matrix **P** shown in Figure 5. For example,

$$P_{11\to12} = P(\vec{Y}_{j+1} = \{1,2\} | \vec{Y}_j = \{1,1\})$$
$$= P(Y_{j+1} = 1, Y_{j+2} = 2 | Y_j = 1, Y_{j+1} = 1) = P_{11\to2} = 0.205. \text{ Yet,}$$

$$P_{11\to21} = P(\vec{Y}_{j+1} = \{2,1\} | \vec{Y}_j = \{1,1\})$$
$$= P(Y_{j+1} = 2, Y_{j+2} = 1 | Y_j = 1, Y_{j+1} = 1) = 0,$$

Since Y_{j+1} =2 and $Y_{j+1} = 1$ never appear in the historical data $\mathbf{\Omega}$.

***Step* 4**: Compute the h-step-ahead transition matrix $\mathrm{P}^{(h)}$ in **S** space based on the $\mathbb{P}^{(h)}$.

Given $\mathbb{P}$ and $\mathbb{P}^{(h)}$, the h-step-ahead transition matrix of $\{Y_j\}$ in the **S** space can be computed directly as follows.

***Example* 3**. Figure 8 presents the matrix $\mathbb{P}^{(5)}$=$\mathbb{P}^5$, i.e., $\mathbb{P}$ to the power of 5, which is the 5-step-ahead transition matrix of $\{\vec{Y}_j\}$ in the $\mathbf{S}^2$ space (m=2). In the original **S** space, note

$$P^{(5)}_{11\to1} = P^{(5)}_{11\to11} + P^{(5)}_{11\to21} = 0.566 + 0.203 = 0.769,$$

Where $P^{(5)}_{11\to11}$ and $P^{(5)}_{11\to21}$ are obtained from $\mathbb{P}^5$. In this way, we compute other elements in $\mathbf{P}^{(5)}$, shown in Figure 9.

Formally, we have

	11	12	21	22
11	0.566	0.221	0.203	0.010
12	0.517	0.179	0.290	0.014
21	0.565	0.247	0.179	0.009
22	0.520	0.188	0.279	0.013

Figure 8: $\mathbb{P}^{(5)} = \mathbb{P}^5$

	1	2
11	0.769	0.231
12	0.807	0.193
21	0.744	0.256
22	0.799	0.201

Figure 9: $\mathbf{P}^{(5)}$

$$P^{(h)}_{y_1,y_2,\dots,y_m \to y'_m} = \begin{cases} \sum_{y'_{m-h+1},\dots,y'_{m-1}} P^{(h)}_{y_1\dots y_m \to y_{h+1},\dots,y_m,y'_{m-h-1},\dots,y'_{m-1},y'_m} & \text{if } h < m \\ \sum_{y'_1,\dots,y'_{m-1}} P^{(h)}_{y_1\dots y_m \to y'_1,\dots,y'_{m-1},y'_m} & \text{if } h \geq m \end{cases} \quad (13)$$

In this way, we only need to pre-compute the 1-step-ahead transition matrix $\mathbf{P}^{(1)}$ of $\{Y_j\}$ in **S** space while $\mathbb{P}^{(h)}$ and $\mathbf{P}^{(h)}$ can be calculated online (h >1), which is more efficient than using a Bayesian probability model like Equation 10. The time cost for computing the matrix $\mathbf{P}^{(h)}$ is $O(h \cdot |\mathbf{S}|^{\varepsilon m})$, where ε < 2.376 [4]. In the implementation, since both m and $|\mathbf{S}|$ (number of states) are small (e.g., $m \leq 3$; $|\mathbf{S}| \leq 5$), the online computation is affordable. To further improve the efficiency, we can compute $\mathbf{P}^{(h)}$ with some small h=2, 3 in advance.

As a result, we obtain the future traffic condition (a distribution of states) φ ahead of the present time. The value (a representative travel time) of a state can be calculated in terms of the mean of the samples pertaining to the state. Though in our system this condition is represented as a distribution of travel times associated with a landmark edge at time $t + \varphi$, the method can be generally applied to other datasets and traffic prediction problems.

4. SERVICE PROVIDING

This section details the service providing process, which consists of 5 steps, as shown in the left part of Figure 1:

1) *Query Sending*. A user sends a query $(q_s, q_d, t_d, \boldsymbol{\alpha})$ to the Cloud. Specifically, $\boldsymbol{\alpha} = (\alpha_1, \alpha_2, \dots, \alpha_k)$, $\forall \alpha_i \in \boldsymbol{\alpha}$, $0 < \alpha_i \leq 1$ (typically stored in a mobile phone) is a custom factor indicating how fast a user usually drives on the ith landmark edge, and k denotes the number of landmark edges. The larger the value α_i has, the faster the user drives on the ith edge. Initially, each α_i can be set as a default value, and be gradually adapted to the user's driving habits in terms of the user's driving paths collected later.

2) *Route Computing*. In this step, the Cloud first chooses a proper landmark graph according to the day type and weather of the departure time t_d . Then, a two-stage routing algorithm is performed to find out a time-dependent fastest route. In the first stage, we search the landmark graph (see Figure 2 C for an instance) for a rough route represented by a sequence of landmarks, using a time-dependent routing algorithm, like [5]. For example, Figure 10 A) depicts the travel time distribution of a landmark edge i in a given time slot, where (c_1~c_5) denotes 5 categories of travel times. Then, we convert this distribution into a cumulative frequency distribution function and fit it with a continuous cumulative frequency curve [3] depicted in Figure 10 B). Given a user's custom factor α_i= 0.7 of this landmark edge, we can particularly determine the travel time of the user on this landmark edge and in this time slot. Note that the traffic conditions (travel time distributions) on a landmark edge at a future time are computed using the method proposed in Section 3.2. For instance, we can respectively pre-calculate the travel time distribution of a landmark edge at the time that is 15, 30, 45, and 60 minutes later then the present time. Then, in the routing algorithm, we can choose the distribution of the time slots according to the time that the user will arrive at the landmark edge.

In the second stage, we perform a detailed routing that finds the fastest path (based on speed constraints) connecting consecutive landmarks in the rough route generated in the first stage. This two-stage routing algorithm is even more efficient than existing methods. First, the rough routing on a landmark graph is very fast as a landmark graph is only a subset of the original road network. Second, the search space of the detailed routing becomes smaller than before as the distance between two landmarks is shorter than that between the original start and end points.

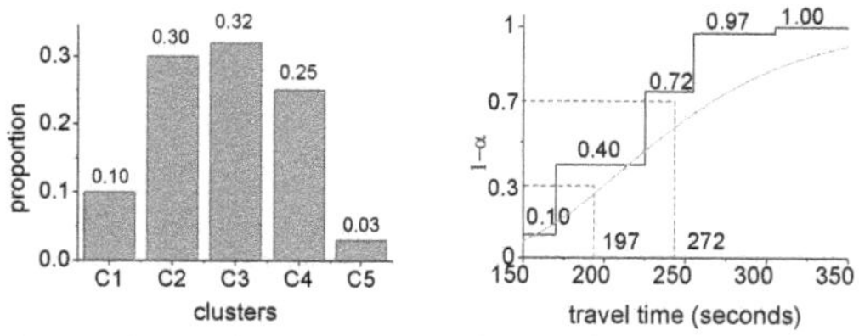

A) Travel time distribution B) Cumulative frequency distribution

Figure 10: Travel time w.r.t. custom factor

3) ***Route Downloading*** **and 4)** ***Path Logging***. The Cloud sends the computed driving routes along with the travel time distributions of the landmark edges contained in the driving route to the phone. Later, the mobile phone logs the user's driving path with a GPS trajectory, which will be used to recalculate the user's custom factor $\boldsymbol{\alpha}$. The more a driver uses this system, the deeper this system understands the driver; hence, a better driving direction service can be provided.

5) ***Adapting custom factor***. For simplicity, we choose one $\alpha_i \in \boldsymbol{\alpha}$ to demonstrate the updating process. Initially, we assign α_i a default value, e.g., 1.0. Let $\alpha_i^{(M)}$ be the α_i the client sent to the cloud at the M-th query, and $CDF_i(t)$ be the cumulative distribution function (refer to Figure 10B for an example) of the ith landmark edge. After traveling, we calculate the real travel time of the landmark edges $T_i^{(M)}$ by the recorded GPS traces. Then the mobile client computes the new custom factor by:

$$\widetilde{\alpha}_i^{(M)} = CDF_i\left(T_i^{(M)}\right) \tag{14}$$

To obtain a stable value for α_i, we need to study the most recent n driving routes of a user instead of a single trip. Meanwhile, the most recent driving paths should be more valuable in calculating α_i than those distant past. Therefore, we compute the new α_i by using a weighted moving average(WMA) shown as below

$$\alpha_i^{(M+1)} = \frac{\sum_{j=1}^{n} j\widetilde{\alpha}_i^{(M-n+i)}}{\sum_{j=1}^{n} j} = \frac{2}{n(n+1)}\sum_{j=1}^{n} j\widetilde{\alpha}_i^{(M-n+j)} \tag{15}$$

where n is the window size of the moving average.

In the next query, the $\alpha_i^{(M+1)}$ will be sent to the Cloud. Note that both path recording and $\boldsymbol{\alpha}$ learning are performed in a user's mobile phone. Therefore, the user's privacy is preserved.

5. Evaluation

Considering that the travel time of a driving route depends on route, traffic and driver, we evaluated the following two aspects in the experiments. 1) Does our method precisely predict the future traffic conditions? 2) Does our method learn a user's diver behavior accurately and estimate the travel time of a route for the user precisely? If the answers are yes, our service is valuable.

5.1 Datasets

Taxi Trajectories: We build our system using GPS trajectories generated by 33,000 taxis over a period of 3 months. The total distance of the dataset is over 400 million kilometers and the total number of GPS point reaches 790 million. The average sampling interval of the dataset is 3.1 minutes and the average (Euclidian) distance between two consecutive points is about 600 meters.

Road Network: The adaptive routing is based on the road network of Beijing which has 106,579 road nodes and 141,380 segments.

Singapore traffic data: This dataset includes the updates (in a frequency of every 26 minutes on average) of traffic conditions on 50 road segments in Singapore from Nov. 1- Dec. 13 (43 days).

5.2 Evaluation on Traffic Prediction

Framework: 1) Prediction on a landmark edge: We use the taxi trajectories of the first two months as a training set (for offline mining) and choose 12 days, consisting of 6 workdays and 6 weekends, from the trajectories of the third month as a test set. 6 out of the 12 days had normal weather conditions, and the remainder had severe weather conditions. We use the expectation of the travel times as a predictor calculated based on the inferred distribution. The ground truth of a given landmark edge is computed in terms of the average travel time of the transitions (from the test dataset) pertaining to the landmark edge in the time slot to be inferred. 1,000 landmark edges with over 10 transitions are chosen for the evaluation. 2) Prediction on a road segment: We also test the performance of our method predicting traffic on road segments, using the Singapore traffic data.

Baselines: We compare our $H + R$ approach with two baseline methods: 1) H method (T-Drive [26]). This method selects the travel time distribution from the historical traffic patterns according the time slot to be inferred, and then transfer the distribution into a travel time expectation. 2) R method (ARIMA [10], whose order is determined using AIC criterion). This is a well-known baseline method predicting the traffic conditions on a landmark edge (or a road segment) in terms of the samples (e.g., taxi trajectories) received a certain time (e. g, 1 or 2 hours) earlier than the time to be inferred.

Measurements: To quantify the accuracy of the traffic inference, we use the *root mean square error* (RMSE) defined as:

$$\text{RMSE} = \sqrt{\frac{1}{M}\sum_i (x_i - \hat{x}_i)^2} \tag{16}$$

where x_i is the real travel time, $\hat{x}_i$ is the predicted travel time and M is the number of predictions. Using this measurement, we study the performance of our approach changing over φ. If not specified, the default m is 2, i.e., second-order Markov Model.

Figure 11 a) shows the overall RMSE (the lower, the better) with φ =90min, τ=15min, between 2pm-7pm on weekdays. Clearly, $H + R$ outperforms both the H and R methods, especially in the rush hours (6pm-7pm), in which the traffic patterns (likely affected by multiple factors) change significantly and in complex ways; hence becomes difficult to predict for the baseline methods. Generally speaking, our method models a set of historical traffic patterns (for a landmark edge) conditioned by the recent traffic flows, $P(H|R)$. Therefore, our method chooses different H patterns to predict future traffic in terms of the R. However, the stand alone H method only has one pattern corresponding to a given time slot.

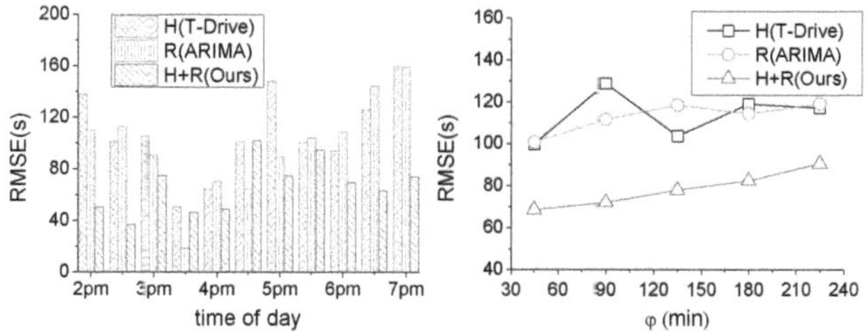

a) w.r.t. time of day($\boldsymbol{\varphi}$=90min) b) w.r.t. $\boldsymbol{\varphi}$ ($\boldsymbol{\tau}$ =30min)

Figure 11: RMSE of different methods

Figure 11 b) plots the RMSE changing over φ with τ=30 minutes. As the delay φ increases, the performance of these approaches decreases while our approach has smaller RMSE (about a 30-second gap) than the competing methods. In short, given the same prediction error, our method is more capable of predicting traffic conditions at a farther time than *H* and *R* methods.

Figure 12 a) visualizes the distribution of residual error of the three methods, where $H + R$ has a clear advantage over *H* and *R*. Figure 13 investigates the performance varying in the order m, of our Markov model. Obviously, the 2nd-order model outperforms the 1st-order model because the traffic condition of a future time t depends on not only the state right before t but also a sequence of traffic states in the near past of t. However, the larger m we select, more data and heavier computation are needed. In practice, it is not necessary to choose a very large m given that the traffic condition does not rely on the distant past.

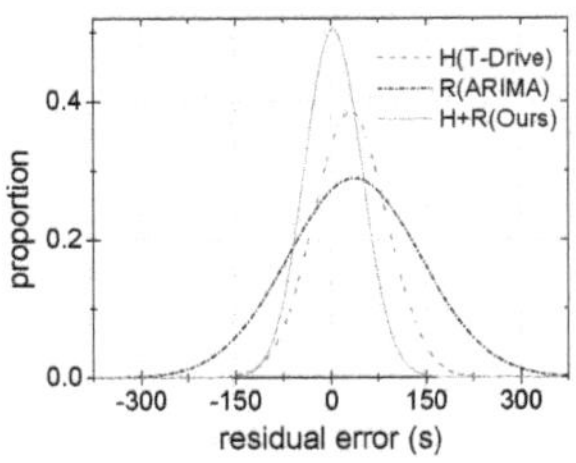

Figure 12: Distribution of residual error

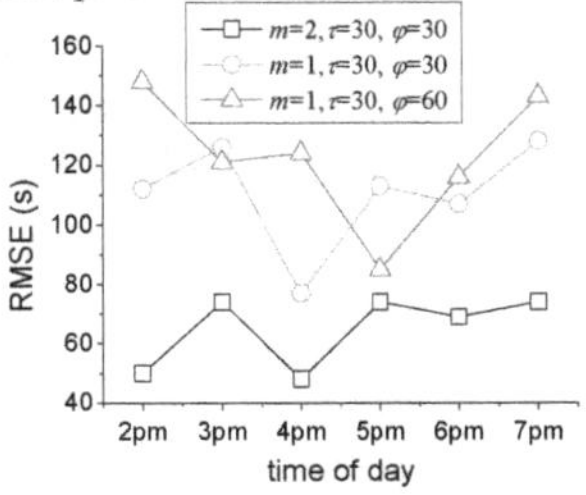

Figure 13. RMSE vs φ

Table 2 shows the RMSE of our method (with or without considering the weather) in predicting the future traffic conditions, using the time slot 6pm-7pm of the test days having a severe weather condition. Clearly, weather information brings significant benefit to our model. Given limited space we do not present more.

Table 2: RMSE considering weather information

φ (min)	with weather (s)	without weather (s)
30	**90.6**	106.6
60	**98.6**	107.1
90	**97.7**	140.4

Figure 14 shows the overall precision of the predictions on road segments using the Singapore traffic data. Here, the traveling speed of a road is discretized into four classes representing different volumes of traffic flows according to a pre-defined schema, e.g., green denotes >40km/h and yellow represents 20-40km/h. Though both ours and the *H* method outperform the *R* method, our approach did not show clear advantages over the *H* method according to the aggregated results (over 50 segments). But, our method does have a significantly better performance than the two baselines when predicting the traffic conditions on some road segments. So, we further explore these road segments, aiming to reveal the features (of roads) supporting our method.

Methods	Precision (over φ)	
	90min	120min
H(T-Drive)	0.686	0.689
R(ARIMA)	0.643	0.651
Ours	**0.683**	**0.688**

Figure 14: Overall precision of predictions on road segments

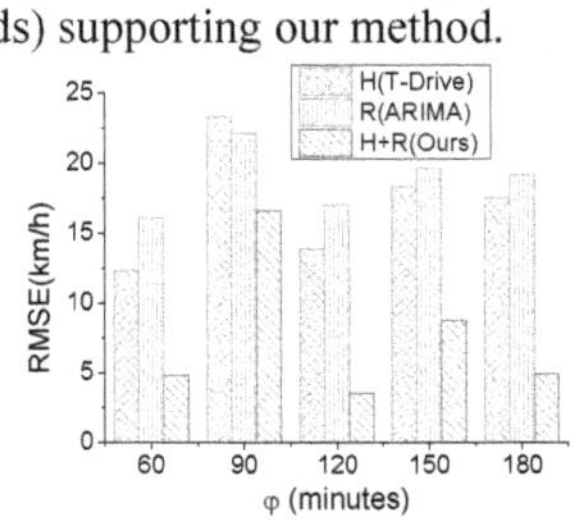

Figure 15: RMSE of the road

The Shrewsbury road, which is one of the good road segments (for ours), has a relatively complex linking structure in the road network, denoted as a blue segment in Figure 16 A). There are five kinds of directions and throughput that can happen at one of its terminal points (refer to the white arrows illustrated in Figure 16 B). Hence, the traffic pattern on this road becomes more complex and difficult to model. This claim is further justified by the traffic conditions plotted in Figure 16 C) where the travel speed is chaotic and disorderly over time of day. Neither *H* nor *R* can handle such a situation very well, and thus drops behind ours, as shown in Figure 15.

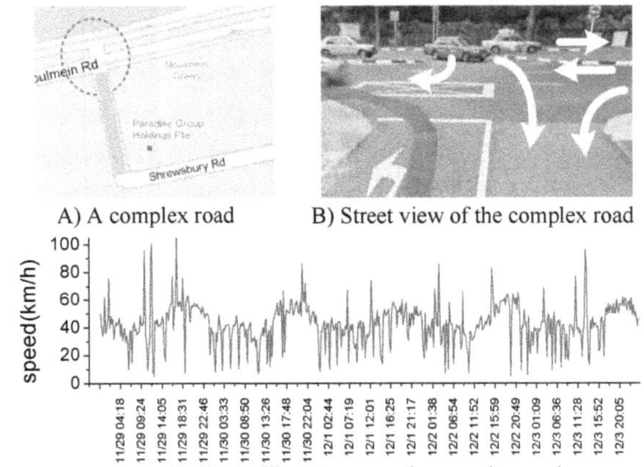

A) A complex road B) Street view of the complex road

C) The traffic patterns on the complex road

Figure 16: Traffic pattern study on Shrewsbury road

W.r.t. the road segments where our method is no better than the baselines, we found they have simple connecting structures in the road network. As demonstrated in Figure 17, Pan Island Expy is a straight road segment with only one link (to other road segments) at its terminal points (refer to Figure 17 A)). Thus, the traffic pattern on this road becomes similarly periodical and easy to predict (see Figure 17 B)) for the baselines. However, insufficient data (only 43 days) affects the precision of our model in inferring multiple $P(H|R)$.

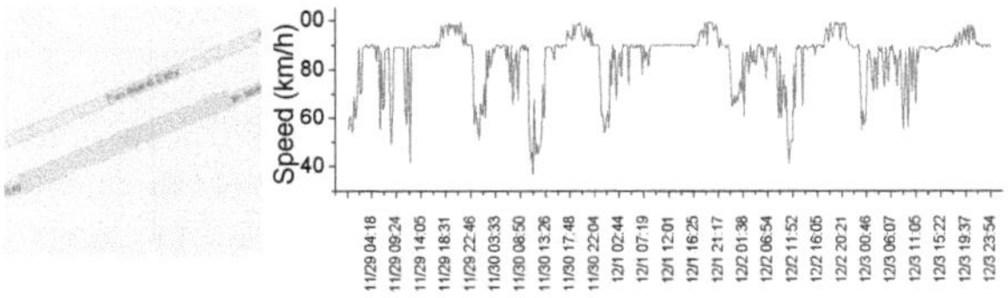

A) A simple road B) The traffic patterns on the simple road

Figure 17: Traffic pattern study on Pan Island Expy road

As shown in Table 3, we further studied the average number of links connecting to a terminal point (node) in both the Beijing landmark graph and Singapore roads. Since a landmark (in Beijing data) usually has more links than a road segment (from Singapore), our method has a better overall performance on the Beijing dataset. Meanwhile, our method is more capable of predicting road segments with relatively more links to others. Given sufficient data, our method will show a higher performance.

Table 3: Average number of links at a terminal point

Datasets	On all segments	On good segments
Beijing landmark	3.1	8.7
Singapore	1.9	2.5

5.3 Evaluation on Routing

It is very difficult to *directly* evaluate whether a customized route (provided by our system) for a real user is the actually fastest one due to the following two reasons. First, a user can only drive on one route at a given time. You would never know if other routes are better (for the user) than the driven one. Requesting a different user to travel another route simultaneously would bring unexpected factors (caused by their different drive behaviors and knowledge) to the evaluation. Second, it is not reasonable to request a single user to drive two different routes separately since the user can learn from their past driving experiences. So, the route driven later will benefit from the first test.

To address the above challenges, instead of directly finding the fastest driving route for a particular user, we first record the routes the user has driven with GPS logs and then estimate the travel time of these routes based on our method and baselines respectively, using the GPS logs as ground truths. More specifically, by mapping a route R to a landmark graph, we convert R into a sequence of landmark edges: $e_1, e_1, \ldots, e_n$. Then, we measure the accuracy of the estimation using the absolute percentage error (APE), defined as Equation (17).

$$\text{APE} = \frac{\sum_i^n |t(e_i) - \hat{t}(e_i)|}{\sum_i^n t(e_i)} \quad (17)$$

where $t(e_i)$ and $\hat{t}(e_i)$ are the real and predicted travel times of e_i.

Here, we use two users' 1-year GPS logs (released in GeoLife dataset [28][29]) to determine the ground truth of the exact road segments a driver traversed and corresponding travel times. As proved in [26], T-Drive outperforms major routing services, such as speed-constraint-based and real-time-traffic-based methods, we only compare our approach with T-Drive here. Initially, we set α=1.0 on all the landmark edges for our method.

Figure 18 illustrates the self-adaptive process for learning user A's custom factor $\boldsymbol{\alpha}$ on two different routes. First, the estimated travel time of our method gradually becomes accurate (measured by APE) and converges as the user A traverses these two routes more, showing advantage beyond that using a fixed $\boldsymbol{\alpha}$. For instance, when the user A traversed Route1 over 20 times, the APE of our method decreases to 0.15 while that of a fixed α = 1.0 is still 0.3. Choosing a small α = 0.3, T-Drive has a relatively minor APE in the first several days, however, it drops behind our method after user A has traveled the route several times. This is because a user's driving behavior changes over the times she has traveled a route. Second, the user A has different drive behaviors on these two routes. For example, our method can reach an APE of 0.15 after the user A traversed Route2 10 times while Route1 needs to be traversed 20 times before APE approaches 0.15.

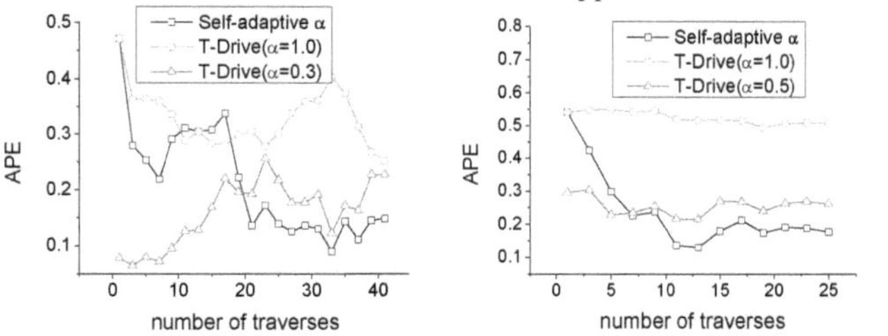

(a) Route1 (b) Route2

Figure 18: Self-learning user A's custom factor

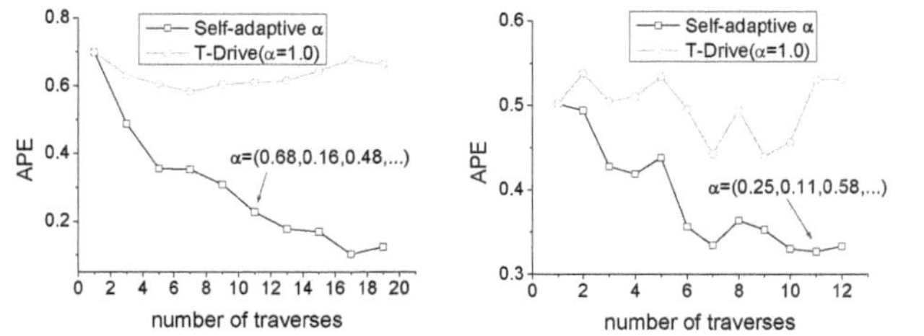

(a) User A (b) User B

Figure 19: Learning different two users' factors on the same route

Figure 19 plots the self-tuning processes of two users traversing the same route, demonstrating the fact that different users have different custom factors tuned in different ways. For instance, we see the clear difference between these two users' $\boldsymbol{\alpha}$ after they traversed the route 11 times. Note that $\boldsymbol{\alpha}$ is a vector rather than a single value and a route could include several landmark edges. According to these results, we should neither use the same custom factor for different users nor set a consistent factor for a particular user on different routes. Additionally, the custom factor of a user is dynamic and changes over the user's driving experiences and skills on a road. So, our self-adaptive routing out-performs T-Drive which is better than other major services.

Efficiency: Besides being effective, our system is also efficient due to the following reasons. First, a landmark graph is only a subset of the original road network (8% in node size, 16% in edge size). So, the rough routing on the landmark graph is very fast. Also, a rough route indicating the key directions reduces the search area on a road network and enables parallel computing when performing the detailed routing [26]. Second, the high dimensional embedding approach speeds up the traffic prediction tremendously, as depicted in Figure 20. After calculating the 1-step transition matrix which has the same computation with the statistic-based approach, our method computes the h-step ($h \geq 2$) very efficiently. The time cost shown in Figure 21 is an average time on calculating six transitions, h =1-6. Third, we only include the items (about 0.1% of $|\boldsymbol{\alpha}|$ according to a study) with significant changes, sending a query to the *Cloud*. To reveal the performance of our method (regardless of system design), we test our system on a single server with 2.67GHz CPU and 16GB RAM (using a single thread without optimization) in the *Cloud*, as shown in Figure 21. The mobile client is running on a Windows smartphone with 1GHz CPU and GPRS connection. Roughly, we can answer 1,000 queries per second using 30 (24-core) servers in a Cloud.

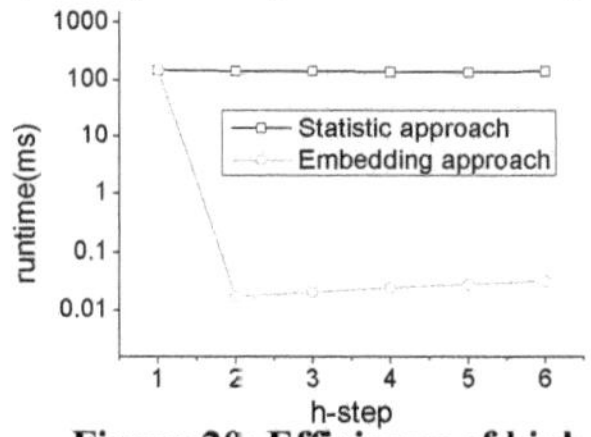

Figure 20: Efficiency of high dimensional embedding

Mobile	T	Cloud	T
Query send	144 ms	Predict traffic	25 ms
Results down	287 ms	Route compute	326 ms
Learning new $\boldsymbol{\alpha}$	20 us	Build landmark	6h

Figure 21: Time cost study on operations of our system

6. RELATED WORK

6.1 Traffic Estimation

There are a few projects [1][2][9][11][12][25] aiming to learn historical traffic patterns, estimate real-time traffic flows and forecast future traffic conditions on some road segments in terms of floating car data [23], such as GPS trajectories as well as Wi-Fi and GSM signals. However, these methods are road-segment-level inferences, which predict the traffic conditions on individual road segments with enough samples. Although our prediction model can also be used on a road segment, our work differs from the above methods in the following aspects. First, by using the landmark graphs, our work well models the city-wide traffic conditions from low sampling-rate trajectories (e.g., 3-5minutes per sample), and enables a real routing service. Second, the routing service considers the driver behavior both of an end user (for whom the route is being computed) and taxi drivers. Third, according to the experimental results our prediction model outperforms competing methods, such as ARIMA [10].

6.2 Smart Routing

To optimize taxi drivers' income, literatures [7][19] has proposed route recommendation services for a taxi driver by analyzing fleet trajectories. Here, they focus on taxi drivers' pick-up behavior in creating higher profit (e.g., how to easily find passengers). So, a normal end user cannot benefit from the recommended routes. Meanwhile, the traffic conditions are not involved in their systems.

Papers like [17][18][21] present work that aims to provide personalized routes according to a user's driving preferences in choosing a road, using user-computer interaction or implicit modeling. The recommended routes from these works are not optimized by travel time. Different from these works, the route we recommend to a driver is the practically fastest one customized for a particular driver, considering both traffic conditions of a future time (when the computed route will be actually traversed) and the behavior of the driver. Other factors, like day of the week, and weather conditions, are also considered in our routing model.

Existing work [6][8][26] also aims to use user-generated GPS trajectories to improve routing services. The work presented in this paper significantly differs from those examples, especially our previous publication T-Drive [26] in the following five aspects. 1) T-Drive does not consider the drive behavior of end users for whom a route is computed. Also, a user's mobile phone does not provide any knowledge of the user. But, our method self-learns different users' drive behaviors (varying in different roads and the times they traversed a road) according to the recent GPS logs, automatically and gradually, in their own mobile phones. The interaction between *mobile* and *Cloud* enables us to find the *practically* fastest driving route *customized* for a user. 2) T-Drive only employs the historical traffic patterns in the routing process. However, we infer the traffic conditions at a future time (when a road is actually driven) based on the historical patterns and real-time traffic flow. The future traffic conditions are involved in the routing. 3) We incorporate other resources from the Web, like weather condition records, into the routing model. 4) We differentiate different taxi drivers' knowledge in different regions. This helps us better model the traffic patterns and taxi drivers' knowledge in choosing a route. 5) Given the above differences, we estimate the travel time of a route more precisely than T-Drive according to the extensive evaluations; our method hence can find better driving routes for a particular user.

7. CONCLUSION

This paper describes a system for computing shortest-time driving routes using traffic information and driver behavior. Specifically, the system mines historical traffic patterns (from GPS trajectories generated by taxicabs) and incorporates recent real-time traffic information (from the same fleet or road sensors) to predict future traffic conditions at the time when the computed route is actually driven. The system incorporates day of the week, time of day, weather conditions, and individual driving strategies (both of the fleet drivers and of the end user for whom the route is being computed). We build our system with a real-world dataset generated by over 33,000 taxis in Beijing, and evaluate our services with extensive experiments and in-the-field studies. The prediction model is also tested using a Singapore traffic dataset. The results show that: 1) our prediction method considering both historical patterns and real-time traffic, $H + R$, outperforms the approaches separately using H and R in predicting the future traffic conditions, especially, in handling road segments with relatively more links (to other segments). The proposed high dimensional embedding method speeds up the 2nd-order Markov model and enables the online traffic prediction. 2) Our system accurately estimates the travel time of a driving route for a particular user by self-tuning the custom factors (on different roads) for the user in terms of the user's historical GPS logs. So, we can find *practically* fast routes *customized* for a particular user.

In the future, we plan to learn a user's driver behavior in a mobile phone, with a more efficient, accurate and advanced method.

8. REFERENCE

[1] Bejan, A., I., Gibbens, R., J., Evans D., Beresford, A., R., Bacon, J., Friday A. Statistical Modelling and Analysis of Sparse Bus Probe Data in Urban Areas, In Proc. ITS, 2010.

[2] Castro-Neto, M., Jeong, Y. S., Jeong, M., K., Han, L., D. Online-SVR for short-term traffic prediction under typical and atypical traffic conditions. Expert systems with applications. 36, 2009

[3] Chhikara, R., S., inverse L. F. L. The inverse Gaussian distribution: theory, methodology, and applications, 1989.

[4] Coppersmith, D., Winograd S. Matrix multiplication via arithmetic progressions. Journal of symbolic computation; 1990:251--280.

[5] Ding, B., Yu, J. X., Qin, L. Finding time-dependent shortest paths over large graphs. In Proc. EDBT; 2008:205-216.

[6] Fawcett, J. and P. Robinson, Adaptive Routing for Road Traffic. IEEE Computer Graphics and Applications, 2000. 20(3): p. 46-53.

[7] Ge, Y., Xiong, H., Tuzhilin, A., Xiao, K., Gruteser M., Pazzani M. J. An Energy-Efficient Mobile Recommender System. In Proc. KDD 2010.

[8] Gonzalez H., Han J., Li X., Myslinska M., Sondag J. P. Adaptive fastest path computation on a road network: A traffic mining approach. In Proc. VLDB, 2007.

[9] Guehnemann A., Schaefer R. P., Thiessenhusen K. U., Wagner P. Monitoring traffic and emissions by floating car data. Institute of transport studies Australia, 2004.

[10] Hamilton J. Time series analysis: Princeton University Press, 1994.

[11] Herrera, J. C., Work, D. Ban, X., Herring, R. Jacobson, Q. and Bayen, A. Evaluation of traffic data obtained via GPS-enabled mobile phones: the *Mobile Century* field experiment. *Transportation Research C*, 18, pp. 568–583, 2010.

[12] Herring R., Hofleitner A., Abbeel P., Bayen A. Estimating arterial traffic conditions using sparse probe data. In Proc. ITS, 2010.

[13] Hunter T., Herring R., Abbeel P., Bayen A. Path and travel time inference from GPS probe vehicle data. In Proc. Neural Information Processing Systems foundation (NIPS), 2009.

[14] Kanoulas E., Du Y., Xia T., D. Z. Finding fastest paths on a road network with speed patterns. In Proc. ICDE, 2006.

[15] Karlin S., Taylor H. M. A first course in stochastic processes, 1975.

[16] Leibowitz, N., Baum, B., Enden, G., Karniel, A. The exponential learning equation as a function of successful trials results in sigmoid performance, Journal of Mathematical Psychology, 54(3):338-340, 2010.

[17] Letchner J., Krumm J., and Horvitz E., Trip Router with Individualized Preferences (TRIP): Incorporating Personalization into Route Planning, In Proc. IAAI, 2006.

[18] Liu B. Route Finding by using knowledge about the road network. IEEE Trans. on systems, man and cybernetics. 27 (4), 1997.

[19] Liu, L., Andris, C., Biderman, A., Ratti, C. Uncovering cabdrivers' behavior patterns from their digital traces. Computers, Environment and Urban Systems, 2010.

[20] Lou, Y., Zhang, C., Zheng, Y., Xie, X., Huang, Y. Map-matching for low-sampling-rate GPS trajectories. In Proc. ACM SIGSPATIAL GIS, 2009.

[21] McGinty, L. and Smyth, B. Turas: A Personalized Route Planning System. In Proc. Sixth Pacific Rim International Conference on AI, PRICAI, 2000.

[22] Orda, A., Rom R. Shortest-path and minimum-delay algorithms in networks with time-dependent edge-length. JACM; 1990:625.

[23] Pfoser D. Floating Car Data. Encyclopedia of GIS 2008

[24] Raftery A. E. A model for high-order Markov chains. Journal of the Royal Statistical Society. Series B (Methodological); 1985:528--39.

[25] Thiagarajan A., et al. VTrack: accurate, energy-aware road traffic delay estimation using mobile phones. In Proc. of the 7th ACM Conference on Embedded Networked Sensor Systems, 2009.

[26] Yuan J., Zheng Y., Zhang C. Y., Xie W., Xie, X., Sun, G., Huang, Y. T-Drive: Driving Directions Based on Taxi Trajectories. In Proc. ACM SIGSPATIAL GIS, 2010.

[27] Yuan J., Zheng Y., Zhang C. Y., Xie X. An Interactive-Voting based Map Matching Algorithm. In Proc. MDM, 2010.

[28] Zheng, Y., Chen, Y., Xie, X., Ma, W., Y. GeoLife2.0: A Location-Based Social Networking Service. In Proc. MDM 2009.

[29] Zheng, Y., Xie, X., Ma, W., Y. GeoLife: A Collaborative Social Network-ing Service among user, location and trajectory. IEEE Data Engineering Bulletin, 2010. 33(2), 2010, pp. 32-40

Interactive Learning for Efficiently Detecting Errors in Insurance Claims

Rayid Ghani
Accenture Technology Labs
Chicago, IL, USA
rayid.ghani@gmail.com

Mohit Kumar
Accenture Technology Labs
Chicago, IL, USA
mohit.x.kumar@accenture.com

ABSTRACT

Many practical data mining systems such as those for fraud detection and surveillance deal with building classifiers that are not autonomous but part of a larger interactive system with an expert in the loop. The goal of these systems is not just to maximize the performance of the classifier but to make the experts more efficient at performing their task, thus maximizing the overall Return on Investment of the system. This paper describes an interactive system for detecting payment errors in insurance claims with claim auditors in the loop. We describe an interactive claims prioritization component that uses an online cost-sensitive learning approach (more-like-this) to make the system efficient. Our interactive prioritization component is built on top of a batch classifier that has been trained to detect payment errors in health insurance claims and optimizes the interaction between the classifier and the domain experts who are consuming the results of this system. The goal is to make these auditors more efficient and effective as well as improving the classification performance of the system. The result is both a reduction in time it takes for the auditors to review and label claims as well as improving the precision of the system in finding payment errors. We show results obtained from applying this system at two major US health insurance companies indicating significant reduction in claim audit costs and potential savings of \$20-\$26 million/year making the insurance providers more efficient and lowering their operating costs. Our system reduces the money being wasted by providers and insurers dealing with incorrectly processed claims and makes the healthcare system more efficient.

Categories and Subject Descriptors

H.2.8 [**Database Management**]: Database Applications—*Data Mining*; H.4.2 [**Information Systems Applications**]: Types Of Systems—*Decision Support*

General Terms

Algorithms, Measurement, Performance

Keywords

Interactive machine learning, Health insurance claims, cost sensitive learning, budgeted learning, error detection, quality control

1. INTRODUCTION

Many deployed data mining systems such as those for fraud detection and surveillance deal with building classifiers (or predictors) that are not deployed in isolation but are part of a larger interactive system with an expert in the loop. Typically, once the models are trained, these systems score a large amount of new data and present the experts with a ranked list of cases to review and verify. These experts are often expensive, and have limited time and attention. Fraud Detection, Intrusion Detection, Medical Diagnosis, Information Filtering, and Video Surveillance are some examples where these systems are currently being used to aid experts in finding cases of interest to them. All of these applications involve a limited number of labeled examples with a high cost of labeling, and a large number (millions) of unlabeled examples, with majority of them being negative (skewed class distribution). These kinds of applications have attracted a lot of research attention from the data mining community but typical data mining research in these application areas has focused on making the classifiers more accurate when in fact, the business goal of these systems is not just to maximize the performance of the classifier but to make the experts more efficient at performing their task.

This paper deals with the problem of predicting (and reducing) payment errors when processing health insurance claims. The goal is to minimize errors by predicting which claims are likely to have errors, and presenting the highly scored ones to human auditors so that they can be corrected before finalization and payment.

Reducing payment errors in health insurance claims has a direct impact on making healthcare more affordable for consumers. Health insurance costs across the world have increased alarmingly in recent years which is forcing insurance companies to reduce their administrative costs and decrease insurance premiums. The typical process for insured healthcare in the US is that a patient goes to a service provider (medical facility) for the necessary care and the provider files a claim with the patient's health insurance company for the services provided. The insurance company then pays the service provider based on multiple complex factors including eligibility of the patient at time of service, coverage of the procedures in the benefits, contract status with the provider etc. Payment errors made by insurance companies while processing claims often result in re-processing of the claim. This extra administrative work to re-process claims is known as *rework* and accounts for a significant portion of the administrative costs of health insurance providers. These errors also have a direct monetary impact in terms of the insurance company paying more or less than what it should have. [1] estimates from a large insurance plan covering 6 million members had $400 million in identified overpayments. In our discussions with major insurance companies, we have found that these errors can result in loss of revenue of up to $1 billion each year. In addition to the direct monetary impact, there is also an indirect monetary impact since employees need to be hired to *rework* the claim and answer phone calls regarding them. According to estimates by an Accenture study, 33% of the administrative workforce is directly or indirectly related to rework processing. These statistics make the problem of rework prevention extremely important and valuable to the healthcare industry and motivated the work described in this paper.

In an earlier paper [5], we described our *batch* system for predicting errors in insurance claims. When we deployed the batch system described in [5] and tested it with auditors from a large US health insurer, we got encouraging classification results but also noticed several problems that affected the efficiency of the auditors (and hence the overall system) when interacting with our rework prediction system.

Issue 1: Context Switching Costs: The auditors were provided with the ranked list of claims that were scored highly by the trained classifier. They started from the top of that list and worked their way down. One problem they experienced was high switching costs when moving from claim to claim. This switching cost arose from the fact that the auditors spent considerable time (up to 20 minutes) reviewing a claim to figure out whether it was an error or a correctly processed claim. Once they had investigated that claim, they were given the next claim (from the ranked list) that was often completely different (both in terms of the *reason* for flagging and in terms of the procedures or diagnosis) from the previous one. At a later stage, they would be given a claim that was lower down in the ranked list but was scored highly by the classifier for *similar* reasons as an earlier claim. Unfortunately, by that time, they have already gone through enough different claims that they need to redo the investigation and the time it takes them to label it is the same as the earlier ones.

Issue 2: Intuitive Explanations of model predictions for each claim: The interface we designed for the auditors highlighted data fields in the claim form that had high scores using the hyperplane that was learned by our classifier (SVM). Even though the weights learned by the SVM result in a classifier that provides high classification accuracy, they were not necessarily intuitive (and accurate) as an explanation for the auditors.

Both of these issues stemmed from the fact that our system was designed to optimize the classification performance of the system, and not necessarily to optimize the return on investment of the overall system which includes the auditors in the loop. We were using classification accuracy (in the top n% scored claims) to measure the overall performance of the system instead of the business metric of interest which should have been related to the cost savings due to the more efficient use of the auditors. This led us to the real metric that needed to be maximized in our system (and many other similar data mining systems) - that is the number of incorrectly paid claims (both in terms of volume and dollar spend) prevented per dollar of audit spend (the ROI). In fact, it is certainly possible to have a system with lower overall classification accuracy but higher ROI. One way of achieving that is to decrease the time it would take to audit a claim. This could be done by generating intuitive explanations that make it faster (hence cheaper) to audit claims, or by ordering the scored claims so the next claim audited is not necessarily the next most likely erroneous claim but one that is similar to the previous one (possibly with a lower score) and faster to audit. Both of these approaches would result in more claims audited in a given amount of time which could result in a higher overall ROI for the system.

Taking these issues into account, we focused on building an interactive claims prioritization component that makes our batch system more efficient using an online cost-sensitive learning approach (more-like-this). Our interactive prioritization component is built on top of a batch classifier that has been trained to detect payment errors in health insurance claims and optimizes the interaction between the classifier and the auditors who are consuming the results of this system. The goal is to make these auditors more efficient and effective as well as improving the observed classification performance of the system. The result is both a reduction in time it takes for the auditors to review and label claims as well as improving the precision of the system in finding payment errors.

We show results obtained from applying this system at two major US health insurance companies indicating significant reduction in claim audit costs and multi-million dollar savings making the insurance providers more efficient and lowering their operating costs. The Rework Prevention Tool that is the basis of our work in this paper is part of Accenture's Claims Administration Offering which is currently deployed at many of the larger health insurance companies in the US. The results so far show potential savings of over $20-$26 million each year for a typical insurer. This reduces the money being wasted by providers and insurers dealing with incorrectly processed claims and makes the healthcare system more efficient. Although our work is specific to insurance claims, our interactive prioritization component is designed to be generic enough to take as input the results of any batch classifier and re-prioritize the results in order to optimize the interaction between the classifier and the domain experts, thus resulting in a higher ROI.

2. RELATED WORK

There are some vendors such as Enkata that provide tools to analyze past claims in order to discover root causes for claims rework but these tools do not predict future rework using data mining techniques and help prevent errors automatically. Typically, these tools help with understanding the factors correlated with historical rework and require managers to fix the back-end system.

In general, claims processing is not an area where data mining techniques have been widely used. A lot of the work in claims has focused on fraud detection which is a related but different area. [4] mentioned a system for detecting health-care provider fraud in electronically submitted claims developed at Travelers Insurance. Health claim fraud is very different from Rework identification because the characteristics of fraudulent claims and Rework claims are different. Often, there is not much labeled data available for fraud and the magnitude of fraud is also typically smaller. Similarly, related work in the area of credit card fraud [3] is also different from Rework identification as the data characteristics and expectations are different. There has been some work in the area of claim overpayment identification [1] which is a subproblem of Rework identification as Rework constitutes both overpayment and underpayment of claims. Also the approach taken in the system is dependent on client-specific 'edits' or rule-based scenarios by training the models for each scenario. This makes the approach less generalizable as it requires the designing of these client scenarios or rules.

Tools that are available for predicting errors in claims and more generally for interactive data mining tasks (such as fraud detection, intrusion detection, surveillance, medical diagnosis) focus on maximizing the classification performance instead of maximizing the ROI of the overall system (that includes domain experts in the loop).

The research community has focused on some aspects of tasks which have experts in the loop. There has been research work in the areas of active learning and cost-sensitive active learning [17], [8], [12] where the aim is to minimize the overall cost of training an accurate model, recognizing that the annotation costs are not constant across instances, and can vary considerably. A related area is active feature acquisition where the goal is to select the most informative features to obtain during training [14]. Budgeted learning [6], [10] where the goal is to learn the most accurate 'active classifier' based on a fixed learning budget for acquiring training data which is also related to the idea of Exploitation/Exploration from Reinforcement Learning. [16] provides an excellent survey of the latest advancements in the field of Active learning. None of the research work we are aware of has focused on the task we are tackling, that is taking the results of a batch classifier and of post-processing classification results to optimize the efficiency of domain experts in reviewing these results.

3. BACKGROUND

We give a brief overview of our batch system here and more details can be found in [5]. We formulate the problem of rework prediction as an interactive classification problem and produce a ranked list of claims that need to be manually reviewed. Figure 1 gives a generalized view of the claims processing pipeline. Claims are created by service providers and submitted to the insurance company. They go through automatic validation checks and then the appropriate pricing is applied to the claims using benefit rules and contracts. This takes place automatically in some cases and in other cases, manual intervention is required. Once the pricing is applied, claims get finalized and payment is sent to the service provider. The system we describe in this paper is the module placed after the pricing is applied to detect potential issues with the claim before it is finalized so it can be corrected before payment is sent.

3.1 System Overview

We worked with domain experts to come up with requirements that would make a rework prediction solution practical and useful for insurance companies. Our system consists of the following components: Data Collection, Feature Construction, Model Learning and Selection, Item Scoring, Explanation Generation, User Feedback, and User Interface. We only give a brief description of our baseline system here since details are given in [5]. We obtain data from health insurance companies along with the labels: **rework** or **correct**. The claims assigned the label *rework* are those that were manually examined in the past and contained errors. Those assigned the label *correct* are ones that were manually examined in the past and found to be correct. Once the data is collected and labeled, feature construction is the next step that takes place. There are four classes of information in each claim: Member information, Provider information, Claim Header, and Claim Line Details. Our features are extracted from these classes of information. Overall, we end up with approximately 15,000 categorical and numerical features to build our models.

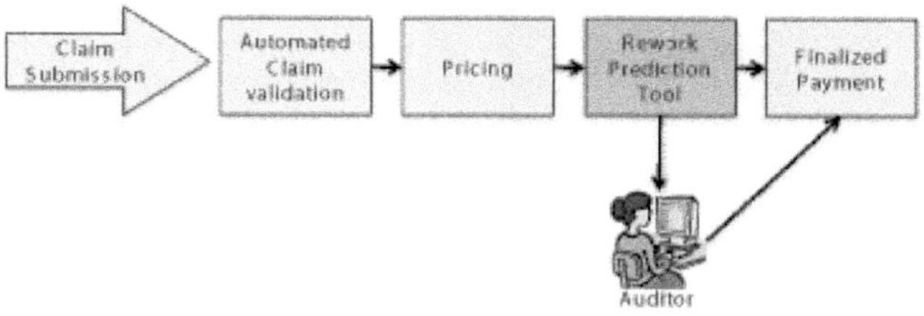

Figure 1: Claim Processing Pipeline

We chose SVMs as the main learning algorithms after experimenting with other classifiers such as decision trees and logistic regression. We also experimented with different versions of SVMs including SVMperf [9], Pegasos, LibSVM [2], and Sofia [15]. Since we have more than 238,000 features after creating binary features from the categorical data, we experimented with frequency-based feature selection techniques which made our system more efficient both in terms of execution time and storage requirements.

Accurately identifying rework and presenting it to auditors is one aspect of our system. Another equally important aspect is to give the auditors the ability to quickly determine if the claim being presented to them is rework or not. Currently, auditors in most companies are given a claim without any hints about why a claim could be rework. In our experiences working with auditors at several companies, a full audit of a claim without any hints as to why a claim is being flagged as rework could take up to an hour. We want to *explain* the predictions of the classifier to the auditor to reduce the time it takes them to determine the label of the claim. In our case, we use the feature weights learned by the SVM to generate the explanations. [13] have also used a similar approach to perform feature selection by retaining features with high weights.

We also get feedback from auditors to improve future predictions. We obtain claim level feedback (labels of examples) as well as feature-level feedback using the user interface we have developed. We worked with teams of auditors to design an interface that was similar to what auditors typically use (a claim form) when auditing the claim but enhanced it with some new features. Figure 2 shows a screenshot of the user interface for the auditors. This interface provides the auditors with a list of claims in their work queue with a rework likelihood score assigned to each claim that is generated by the classifier. In addition, we use the influence

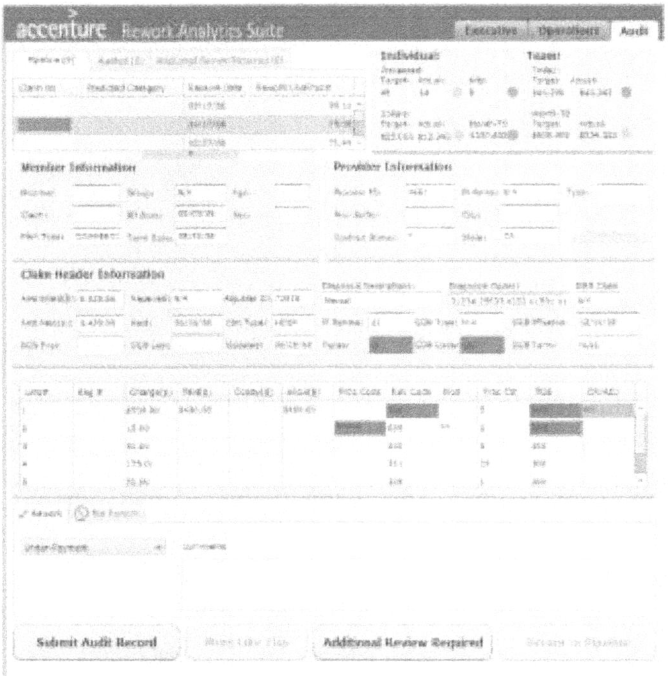

Figure 2: User Interface with the Auditor view (sensitive PHI fields are blanked out).

scores described earlier to highlight the data fields. The intensity of the highlight color is proportional to the influence score assigned by the classifier. This feature has been designed to focus the attention of the auditor to the influential data fields and help them audit the claim faster. We also allow the auditors to click on any field to *unhighlight* it (if it's highlighted) or to highlight it and give us feedback that field is influential (or not).

4. ONLINE COST-SENSITIVE LEARNING

When we did a pilot deployment of the system described in the previous section at a large US health insurance company, we got encouraging results but also noticed several problems that affected the efficiency of the auditors when interacting with our rework prediction system.

Context Switching Costs: We used the confidence of the SVM classifier to rank new claims. The auditors were then provided with the ranked list of claims and started from the top of that list and worked their way down auditing the claims. One problem they experienced was high switching costs when moving from example to example. This switching cost arose from the fact that the auditors spent considerable time (up to 20 minutes) reviewing a claim to figure out whether it was a positive or a negative example. Once they had investigated (and labeled) that claim, they were given the next claim (from the ranked list using the SVM confidence scores) that was often completely different (in terms of the *reason* for flagging) from the previous one. At a later stage, they would be given a claim that was lower down in the ranked list but was scored highly by the classifier for *similar* reasons as an earlier claim. Unfortunately, by that time, they have already gone through enough different claims that they need to redo the investigation and the time it takes them to label it is the same as the earlier ones. We hypothesize that if we can group similar claims together, it would reduce the *context switching* and help make the reviewing times shorter.

Low Precision when reviewing Top 2% scored claims: Based on the class distribution, claim volumes, auditor workload, and audit times, we determined that it's optimal to manually review top 2% of the claims that are scored by our classifier, making precision at 2% the metric we optimize[1]. The scores assigned by the SVM to the top few percent of the claims are fairly similar which results in poor ranking at the top of this list. Also, based on the feedback we got from the auditors, we found that as they went down the list reviewing the claims, they encountered several series of consecutive claims that were all negative examples (and often for similar reasons). We hypothesize that this was because the ranking was purely based on SVM scores and did not have any notion of diversity. Again, grouping similar claims together could help group a lot of these negative examples together and improve the performance of the human auditors.

Intuitive Explanations: The interface we designed for the auditors highlight data fields in the claim form that had high scores using the hyperplane that was learned by the SVM. Even though the weights learned by the SVM result in a classifier that provides high classification accuracy, they were not necessarily intuitive as an explanation for the auditors.

Batch Retraining/Learning: Because we are dealing with a system that is interactive with costly human auditors in the loop, we do not have the time to retrain the system (in real-time) after each claim is reviewed by the auditors. The long wait time that is required for retraining makes the process too expensive since the auditors have to be idle during that time. This situation forces us to deal with the tradeoff between potentially better results (by retraining after every new label) and maximizing the use of the auditor time (by retraining after a certain number of new labels have been acquired).

4.1 Interactive Claims Prioritization using Online Cost-Sensitive Learning

The four issues described above caused us to think about approaches that could take the results of the classifier and process them in order to improve the overall ROI of the system. That formed the basis of our Claims Prioritization strategy that uses online cost-sensitive learning in order to maximize the efficiency of the auditors while helping them achieve their goal of finding errors in insurance claims. The efficiency of the auditors is not just a function of the accuracy of the system but also the time it takes them to review a claim. Reducing the time it takes to review an example (claim) is an understudied area which is not often discussed in KDD research literature and is important when dealing with interactive business applications where the experts are expensive and have limited time. We describe our online cost-sensitive learning framework that focuses on reducing the overall time experts spend on labeling (verifying or correcting) examples provided to them by a classifier. We deal with the scenario where a batch classifier has been trained to predict errors in claims and focus on optimizing the interaction between the classifier and the auditors who are

[1]More details on that are in [5]

consuming the results of this predictor. The goal is to make these auditors more efficient and effective in performing their task as well as eventually improving the system over time.

4.1.1 More-Like-This Strategy

Our *More-Like-This* (MLT) strategy (Algorithm 1) is motivated by the context switching costs, low precision, and explanation issues described above. The goal of this strategy is to group the scored claims into clusters that contain claims that have been scored highly for *similar* underlying reasons. This allows us to provide the auditors with a cluster of claims that are both highly likely to be *rework* (errors) and can also be audited very quickly with small incremental audit costs. The cost gets reduced because once the auditors have invested the effort in reviewing the first couple of claims in a cluster, the rest of the claims will have similar labels due to similar reasons. At the same time, this technique also allows us to ignore a large number of claims that are similar to each other and are in fact correct claims (negative examples) but have been incorrectly ranked highly by the classifier. This is done by our online strategy where we rank the clusters using a variety of metrics (described later) and give the auditors a few claims from a cluster. If the claims are verified by the auditors as being errors, we continue giving them claims from that cluster. Otherwise, we move on the next cluster thus avoiding a large number of highly scored claims that were in fact negative. This strategy also implicitly provides the auditors with an *explanation* for the classification by providing them with other claims that are similar to what they have just labeled. MLT works as a post-processing step on new (unlabeled) claims that have already been scored by the trained classifier.

Algorithm 1: Online More-Like-This Algorithm

Require: a labeled set of claims L and an unlabeled set U

1. Train classifier C on L
2. Label U using classifier C
3. Select the top m% scored unlabeled claims U_T (we use m=10 in our case)
4. Cluster the examples $U_T \bigcup L$ into k clusters
5. Rank the k clusters using a cluster-based ranking function (described in the next section)
6. For each cluster in the ranked cluster list
   (a) Rank the claims within the cluster based on their informativeness of the quality of the cluster
   (b) For each claim in the ranked list within the cluster
      i. Query human auditor for the label of the claim
      ii. Move to the next cluster if the evaluation metric (we use precision in our experiments) calculated over claims labeled so far in the cluster falls below threshold P

The intuition behind our MLT approach is to use a supervised classifier like SVM to initially provide a rough partitioning of the scored examples and then use a clustering algorithm to do more finer-grained partitions. The function of clustering is to take the examples that are scored highly by the classifier and group similar ones together, hopefully creating clusters that correspond to claims that have similar underlying *reasons* for being errors. Our two-step approach of post-ranking (or classification) clustering is also potentially useful in cases where there are different underlying subgroups (or reasons) in the positive class that may be disjoint which could create issues for a binary classifier (unless multiclass labels are available).

In Step 3, we use m=10% for our experiments which selects the top 10% of the claims. Setting m=100% would be equivalent to clustering all the examples without taking into account the classifier scores. Intuitively, we would choose m based on the class priors and the budget available for reviewing the claims.

In Step 4, we vary k (number of clusters) from 200 to 2800 and settle for $|U|/100$. The higher the number of clusters, the more coherent/similar each group will be which can decrease the audit time and provide better explanations but increases the number of clusters to examine. Another tradeoff is that the larger the number of clusters the test examples may be split in different clusters thus not resulting in reduction of context-switch cost. We use Cluto[11] to perform the clustering.

In Step 5, we experiment with a variety of metrics to rank the clusters described in the next section. These ranking metrics are a function of the number of positive examples (from L in the cluster), the mean score assigned by the classifier to the unlabeled examples U in this cluster, the ratio of the positive to negative labeled examples (from L), the inter-cluster similarity score of the cluster, and the intra-cluster similarity of the cluster.

To rank the claims for review within a cluster (in Step 6a), we use the score assigned by the classifier as the metric in our experiments. This is just one example of a metric that can be used. Other metrics we plan to experiment with include distance from the centroid of the cluster (to select prototypical examples from a cluster first), and sample selection metrics from active learning literature (based on uncertainty sampling for example). In Step 6b(ii), we use precision as the metric and set the threshold to 30%. This is chosen empirically based on the baseline precision scores and the class distribution.

4.1.2 Pool-based Active Learning

The *More-Like-This* (MLT) strategy is designed to reduce the time it takes to review (or label) a claim and also to provide the auditors with immediate rewards. We also use active learning strategies to improve the future performance of the system. We use the standard pool-based active learning setting and use different sample selection strategies such as density-based and uncertainty sampling. This approach is potentially not immediately rewarding to the human auditors and focuses on future improvement of the classifier.

For density-based sampling, we calculate cosine similarity between each pair of claims and use the average similarity of each claim to all the other claims as a measure of density. For uncertainty sampling, we use the absolute value of the SVM score (distance from the SVM margin) as a measure of uncertainty.

4.1.3 Hybrid Active Learning with More-Like-This

The two strategies mentioned above have potentially competing goals. More-Like-This is designed to be of immediate benefit to the auditors by giving them claims that are highly scored and quick to audit, thus increasing their short-term

ROI. The Active Learning strategies are designed to maximize future improvement of the system and not necessarily providing claims to the auditors (in the short-term) that would be errors. In fact, the uncertainly sampling strategy is designed to present claims to the auditor for which the classifier is least confident about with the promise of improvement in the future. The tradeoff between the two previous strategies motivates a strategy that combines the benefits of both of them. We propose three different approaches to implement this hybrid strategy.

MLT-then-Active: This strategy performs MLT clustering as described in Section 4.1.1 but then uses active learning (with different sample selection metrics) to select examples to provide to the user for review and labeling.

Hybrid Sample Scoring: Hybrid Sample Scoring strategy assigns a score to every unlabeled example based on both strategies. Each example gets a score using active learning (which indicates it's utility in improving future classifier performance) as well as with the More-Like-This strategy (which indicates it's immediate utility). We can then use a weighted combination of these scores to create a final ranking.

Online Hybrid Learning: This hybrid strategy treats the two strategies independently and alternates among them based on the recent past, availability of expert resources, and business needs.

We have discussed these strategies with domain experts in claims processing and have found them to be quite receptive to the last strategy as a tradeoff. In the results with the pilot deployments presented in this paper, we don't use any hybrid strategies but we believe that these can be highly effective and are currently running experiments to evaluate their suitability in practical situations.

5. EXPERIMENTAL RESULTS

5.1 Data and Experimental Setup

We present results from two pilots with major US health insurance companies that were conducted using the system described in this paper during the past year. From the first company, we started with approximately 25 million claims spanning 2 years. Of these 25 million claims, 379,000 had been manually labeled through various audit processes. In this labeled data set, around 65% claims were Rework (errors) and the rest were Correct. It is important to remember that this distribution does not hold in the operational world since the labeled data has a skewed class distribution. For the second company, we got approximately 40 million claims spanning 12 months. Of these 40 million claims, 150000 had been manually audited and found to be either Rework or not. In this set, around 80% claims were Rework and the rest Correct. Since SVMs are not able to handle categorical data we create binary features from the categorical features resulting in around 238,500 and 215,000 features respectively for the two cases.

We ran two pilots with large US health insurance companies to evaluate the prioritization component described in this paper. The pilots involved a team of auditors from the insurance companies where we gave the auditors a set of claims to audit based on system's recommendations and the different strategies described in the previous section. In this paper, we will not describe the entire pilot but just a part of the larger evaluation that motivated and verified the More-Like-This strategy. We give detailed results with a second set of offline experiments that were designed to analyze our strategies in more detail.

5.2 Live System Deployment

We compared the improvement due to the interactive prioritization strategies described in this papers in our pilots. For the first pilot, the baseline system precision was 29% where the auditors audited 200 claims and found 58 claims to be Rework. With More-Like-This strategy, we obtained a hit rate of 55% where the auditors audited 307 claims and found 169 claims to be Rework. Thus we got a 90% improvement over the baseline system. The average audit time per claim was reduced from 3 min 55 sec for the baseline system to 2 min 52 sec for More-Like-This strategy (27% relative reduction in time). The reduction in time for auditing as well as the improvement in precision is statistically significant with $p << 0.001$ for Student's T-Test. We also ran further experiments over a period of 3 weeks with two auditors to validate some of our results.

For the second pilot, we obtained a baseline system precision of 19% where the auditors audited 221 claims and found 42 to be Rework. With More-Like-This strategy, we achieved a hit rate of 51% where 1119 claims were audited and 573 were found to be Rework. This represents a 170% relative improvement over the baseline strategy. The average time to audit was reduced from 5 min 47 sec for the baseline system to 3 min 43 sec for More-Like-This strategy (36% relative reduction in time). As observed for the first pilot, the reduction in time for auditing as well as improvement in precision is statistically significant with $p << 0.001$ for Student's T-Test.

The business benefit of these results are described in more detail in section 6 and show potential savings on 20–26 million/year for a typical US health insurance provider.

5.3 Offline experiments

Due to the high cost and limited availability of the auditors, we limited the live audits using only the strategies that we thought would work the best. To conduct further in-depth analysis of different strategies described in this paper, we ran a large number of offline experiments. These experiments were performed 5-fold cross-validation on a claims data from last 5 months with 70,179 claims having 52% positive claims.[2]. Since the distribution of the positive class is skewed in historical data we create the test cases in each fold with 5% positive examples as follows. We select all the negative examples belonging to the fold and then exclusively sample from the remaining examples so that the test data has 5% positive examples. We keep creating test cases until we exhaust all the positive examples in the fold. Thus each test fold has same negative examples but unique positive examples. In our case, we got 4 folds with 20 test cases and 1 fold with 19 test cases with the desirable 5% positive class ratio.

[2]Since we wanted to run multiple detailed experiments, we had to select a smaller dataset for practical runtime considerations

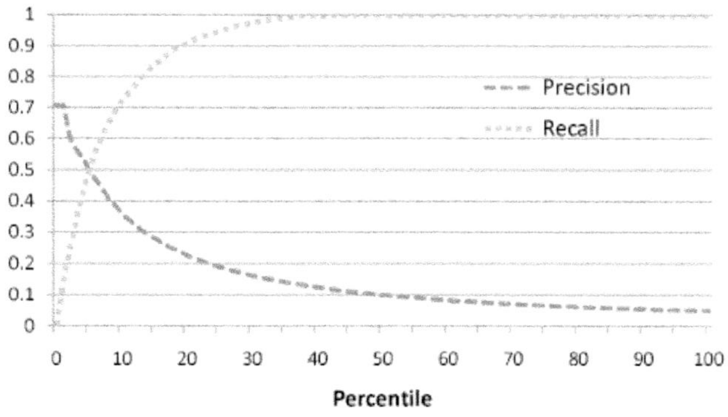

Figure 3: Precision Recall averaged over five folds with approx 20 test sets in each fold

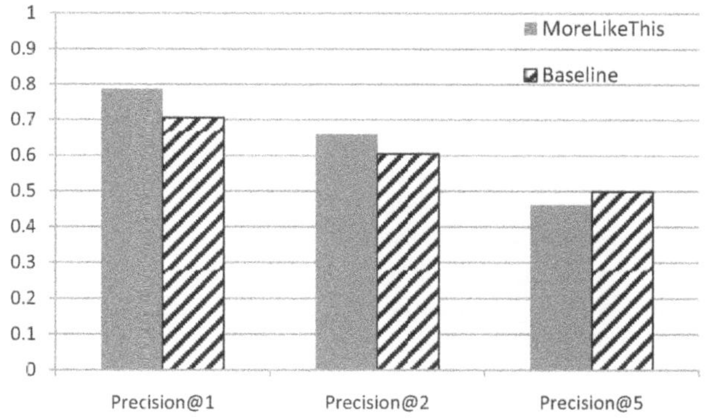

Figure 4: Performance comparison of More-Like-This strategy with Baseline strategy for different metrics

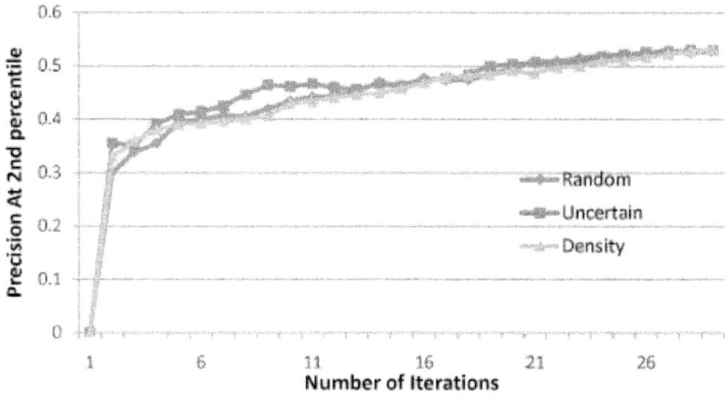

Figure 5: Performance curve for different active learning strategies

5.3.1 Metrics

The audit capacity for typical insurance companies is approximately 2% of the total daily volume of the claims, which means that given their current audit resources they can only review up to 2% of the incoming claims every day. Standard metrics such as accuracy, precision, or recall are useful in comparing different models and approaches, but not enough to minimize the number of claim errors, which is the eventual metric. Based on the audit capacity and discussions with domain experts, we decided that we need a metric that evaluates performance for the top 2-5% scored claims to maximize benefits in real scenarios. Hence, we use Precision (or hit rate) at 2nd Percentile as our metric. This is similar to the evaluation metric, Precision at top 10 documents, popularly used in the Information Retrieval community. In our experimental framework, we do have the flexibility to modify the metric easily and do model selection based on different metrics. In the results reported below, we show precision recall graphs where appropriate, as well as our precision at top 2% metric when comparing different models.

5.3.2 Is our system accurate?

We ran five fold validation experiments where each fold has approx 20 test sets with 5% Rework ratio to show the effectiveness of our baseline system. Figure 3 shows the Precision-Recall graph for this experiment averaged over five folds with approx 20 test sets each. The average precision at 2nd percentile is 60.5%. Compared to the 2-5% hit rate that the insurance companies get in their auditing practice currently, this is a significant boost in performance.

5.3.3 How well does More-Like-This work?

We use the More-Like-This strategy on top of the baseline system. We experimented with varying the number of clusters (k ranging from 200 to 2800), the clustering algorithms (Repeated Bisections, Repeated Bisections with global optimization and direct k-way clustering), and different cluster ranking metrics as described in Section 4.1.1. We used CLUTO [11] for the clustering.

The best performance was achieved with a cluster size of 500 with repeated bisection clustering algorithm. The ranking criterion for the clusters was ratio of training Rework to Correct claims in a cluster followed by mean prediction score for test claims. Figure 4 shows the performance improvement over the baseline system. We obtain 9% relative improvement for Precision at 2nd percentile, which is the metric that we want to optimize. The improvement is statistically significant with $p << 0.001$ for paired, two-tailed Student's T-test.

5.3.4 How well do typical Active sample selection strategies work?

We experimented with the typical pool-based Active sample selection strategies (uncertainty and density based sampling) along with the baseline random sampling in a batch learning setting. The results are shown in Figure 5. We notice that the performance is quite similar for the different strategies. This result is not too surprising as has previously pointed out by [7] that standard strategies applied myopically in batch learning setting are often worse than random querying.

6. BUSINESS BENEFITS

The work presented in this paper is targeted to increase the overall ROI of the system which we earlier defined as number of incorrectly processed claims identified per dollar of audit cost. The real business metrics behind the system are more complex and we give more details in this section.

Every claim that gets processed and paid incorrectly results in extra costs for the insurance company in various ways. If a claim is underpaid (provider is paid less than the correct amount), the service provider files a dispute with the insurance company. The dispute gets reviewed by the insurance company, and if it is indeed an error, the insurance company sends the additional payment with an interest penalty amount. While the claim is in this dispute review process, the patient and the provider continue calling the customer service center for the insurance company asking for status, resulting in call center costs. According to estimates by an Accenture study, 33% of the administrative workforce is directly or indirectly related to rework processing. Typical costs for insurance companies for these functions because of underpayments are:

- Dispute reviews/audits and adjustments: $10 million/year
- Provider Service Calls: $40 million/year
- Patient Service Calls: $50 million/year
- Interest Payments to Providers: $5 million/year

If a claim is overpaid (provider is paid more than the correct amount), in some cases the provider returns the excess money. In many cases, the insurance company ends up losing the money because they do not have a mechanism of identifying these overpayments. In cases where they do identify them, they have to go through a recovery process which results in additional costs. [1] estimates from a large insurance plan covering 6 million members had $400 million in identified overpayments making it a major source of waste in the US healthcare system.

6.1 Business Value of the Interactive Prioritization Strategy

Based on the costs we described above, we determine the business value of the prioritization strategy presented in this paper on top of the batch system. In our two pilots, the prioritization strategy resulted in 25-40% reduction in audit time per claim while at the same time increasing the relative hit rate by 90-170% (from 29% to 55% for company 1 and from 19% to 51% for company 2). Given that a typical insurance company spends $10 million/year in audits, 25-40% reduction in audit time results in $2.5-4 million/year in savings. Also, the industry estimates that 10% claims end up being paid incorrectly (which we call rework rate). Based on the rework rate of 10% and the absolute increase in hit rate results in 26-32% of additional incorrect claims being caught before being paid reducing the service calls and interest payments by $27-$33 million/year. This total of **$30-$37 million/year** in savings does not even include the medical cost savings that insurance companies will receive because they won't lose money in overpayments. That number is typically hard to quantify since the total is unknown but is known to be a large amount (in the 100s of millions). It's also important to note that these savings are estimates per year for each insurance company. Accenture is currently in discussions with most of the major health insurance companies in the US about this system that we have been developing thus increasing the overall impact on reduction of waste in the US healthcare system. The goal is to reduce the waste in the healthcare system by making claims processing more accurate and reducing the money being wasted by providers and insurers dealing with incorrectly processed claims.

7. CONCLUSIONS

This paper describes an interactive system for detecting payment errors in insurance claims with claim auditors in the loop reviewing the highly scored claims. Our main contribution is an interactive claims prioritization component that makes the system efficient using an online cost-sensitive learning approach (more-like-this). Our interactive prioritization component is built on top of a batch classifier that has been trained to detect payment errors in health insurance claims and optimizes the interaction between the classifier and the domain experts who are consuming the results of this system. The goal is to make these auditors more efficient and effective as well as improving the performance of the system over time. The result is both a reduction in time it takes for the auditors to review and label claims as well as improving the system in finding payment errors. We show results obtained from applying this system at several major US health insurance companies show significant reduction in claim audit costs and $20-$26 million each year (for typical US health insurance providers) making the insurance providers more efficient and lowering their operating costs. This reduces the money being wasted by providers and insurers dealing with incorrectly processed claims and makes the healthcare system more efficient.

In addition to the impact on the healthcare industry, we believe that this also highlights interesting research directions for the KDD community by focusing on reducing the time it takes to label an example, especially when combined with traditional active learning strategies. This setting occurs in many practical deployments of data mining systems. Although our work is specific to insurance claims, our interactive prioritization component is designed to be generic enough to take as input the results of any batch classifier and re-prioritize the results in order to optimize the interaction between the classifier and the domain experts, thus resulting in a higher ROI for many interactive data mining systems such as those for fraud detection, surveillance, intrusion detection among others.

8. REFERENCES

[1] A. Anand and D. Khots. A data mining framework for identifying claim overpayments for the health insurance industry. In *Proceedings of INFORMS Workshop on Data Mining and Health Informatics*, 2008.

[2] C. C. Chang and C. J. Lin. *LIBSVM: a library for support vector machines*, 2001. Software available at `http://www.csie.ntu.edu.tw/~cjlin/libsvm`.

[3] C. Curry, R. L. Grossman, D. Locke, S. Vejcik, and J. Bugajski. Detecting changes in large data sets of payment card data: a case study. In *Proceedings of KDD*, 2007.

[4] U. M. Fayyad, G. Piatetsky-Shapiro, P. Smyth, and R. Uthurusamy, editors. *Advances in knowledge discovery and data mining*. AAAI, 1996.

[5] R. Ghani, M. Kumar, and Z.-S. Mei. Data mining to predict and prevent errors in health insurance claims processing. In *Proceedings of KDD*, 2010.

[6] S. Guha and K. Munagala. Approximation algorithms for budgeted learning problems. In *Proceedings of ACM symposium on Theory of computing (STOC)*, 2007.

[7] Y. Guo and D. Schuurmans. Discriminative batch mode active learning. In *Proceedings of NIPS*, 2008.

[8] R. Haertel, K. Seppi, E. Ringger, and J. Carroll. Return on investment for active learning. In *Proceedings of the NIPS Workshop on Cost-Sensitive Learning*, 2008.

[9] T. Joachims. Training linear svms in linear time. In *Proceedings of KDD*, 2006.

[10] A. Kapoor and R. Greiner. Learning and classifying under hard budgets. In *Proceedings of ECML*, 2005.

[11] G. Karypis. Cluto - a clustering toolkit. Computer sciences technical report, University of Minnesota, 2002.

[12] D. D. Margineantu. Active cost-sensitive learning. In *Proceedings of International Joint Conference on Artificial Intelligence*, 2005.

[13] D. Mladenic and J. Brank. Feature selection using linear classifier weights: interaction with classification models. In *Proceedings of SIGIR*, 2004.

[14] M. Saar-Tsechansky, P. Melville, and F. Provost. Active feature-value acquisition. In *Management Science*, 2009.

[15] D. Sculley. Combined regression and ranking. In *Proceedings of KDD*, 2010.

[16] B. Settles. Active learning literature survey. Computer Sciences Technical Report 1648, University of Wisconsin–Madison, 2009.

[17] B. Settles, M. Craven, and L. Friedland. Active learning with real annotation costs. In *Proceedings of the NIPS Workshop on Cost-Sensitive Learning*, 2008.

NIMBLE: A Toolkit for the Implementation of Parallel Data Mining and Machine Learning Algorithms on MapReduce

Amol Ghoting, Prabhanjan Kambadur, Edwin Pednault, and Ramakrishnan Kannan
IBM Thomas J. Watson Research Center, Yorktown Heights, NY
{aghoting, pkambadu, pednault, ramkrish}@us.ibm.com

ABSTRACT

In the last decade, advances in data collection and storage technologies have led to an increased interest in designing and implementing large-scale parallel algorithms for machine learning and data mining (ML-DM). Existing programming paradigms for expressing large-scale parallelism such as MapReduce (MR) and the Message Passing Interface (MPI) have been the *de facto* choices for implementing these ML-DM algorithms. The MR programming paradigm has been of particular interest as it gracefully handles large datasets and has built-in resilience against failures. However, the existing parallel programming paradigms are too low-level and ill-suited for implementing ML-DM algorithms. To address this deficiency, we present NIMBLE, a portable infrastructure that has been specifically designed to enable the rapid implementation of parallel ML-DM algorithms. The infrastructure allows one to compose parallel ML-DM algorithms using reusable (serial and parallel) building blocks that can be efficiently executed using MR and other parallel programming models; it currently runs on top of Hadoop, which is an open-source MR implementation. We show how NIMBLE can be used to realize scalable implementations of ML-DM algorithms and present a performance evaluation.

Categories and Subject Descriptors

D.2.2 [**Design Tools and Techniques**]: Software libraries

General Terms

Design, Performance, Algorithms

Keywords

Data mining, Machine learning, MapReduce, Tasks

1. INTRODUCTION

In the last decade, advances in data collection and storage technologies have allowed organizations to accumulate vast amounts of data. Organizations, ranging from small Internet companies to large businesses, are collecting terabytes of data on a daily basis with the intent of understanding and improving their business processes. Hence, there is a growing need to run machine learning and data mining (ML-DM) algorithms on very large datasets. To complicate matters, recent trends in hardware have brought new challenges to the programming community; multi-core and many-core systems have become ubiquitous and advances in single-threaded processor performance have reached a standstill. Increasing dataset sizes and the shift towards parallel scaling in hardware have necessitated that ML-DM algorithms be parallelized in the immediate future.

While the need for parallelization in ML-DM is evident, few solutions to satisfy this need exist today. For more than two decades, parallel database products such as those offered by IBM, Oracle, Teradata, and Netezza have provided a partial means to realize a parallel implementation of ML-DM algorithms. However, it is difficult to restructure parallel ML-DM algorithms to suit the declarative SQL-based programming interface exposed by these database products. Furthermore, large-scale installations of these products are extremely expensive and are not an affordable option in most cases. Consequently, the past few years have seen researchers moving to parallelization of ML-DM based on imperative specification that use open-source products. One approach has been to use low-level abstractions for parallelization such as those provided by Pthreads [10], OpenMP [9], TBB[5], and PFunc [19] for shared-memory systems, and MPI [8] for distributed-memory systems. As these programming abstractions originated in the high performance computing community, they are expressive and powerful, but are arcane; hence, they make implementation cumbersome.

In recent years, an increasing number of programmers have migrated to the MapReduce (MR) programming model. The MR programming model was designed to simplify the processing of large files on a parallel system through user-defined Map and Reduce primitives. A MR job consists of two phases — a Map phase and a Reduce phase. During the Map phase, the user-defined Map primitive transforms the input data into $(key, value)$ pairs in parallel. These pairs are stored and then sorted by the system so as to accumulate all $values$ for each key. During the Reduce phase, the user-defined Reduce primitive is invoked on each unique key with a list of all the $values$ for that key; usually, this phase is used to perform aggregations. Finally, the results are output in the form of $(key, value)$ pairs. Each key can be processed in parallel during the Reduce phase. Hadoop [1], an open-source implementation of the MR programming model, has emerged as a vastly popular platform for parallelization in industry and academia. A user can perform parallel computations by submitting one or more MR jobs to Hadoop. One of the key advantages of Hadoop is that it is capable of running on large commodity clusters and recovering from both data as well as compute node failures. Companies like Facebook, Yahoo!, Amazon, Baidu, AOL, and IBM use Hadoop on a daily basis. Furthermore, many data management platforms such as HBase [2], Hive [3], PIG [22], and JAQL [6] build off it as well. Hence, we conjecture that Hadoop will be a stable, growing, and well-maintained platform.

While the above mentioned programming models are very popular in their particular domains, we believe that they have a set of limitations that make them ill-suited to the implementation of parallel ML-DM algorithms. To get a better grasp of these limitations, we first characterize the requirements of the ML-DM community when it comes to implementing their parallel algorithms.

Parallelization with limited effort: Efficient parallelization of an existing sequential implementation of an algorithm is a non-trivial process as factors such as communication, data management, and scheduling have to be carefully considered[1]. Parallelization using existing frameworks such as PThreads [10], OpenMP [9], TBB [5], and PFunc [19] for shared-memory systems, and MPI [8] for distributed-memory systems is time-consuming and requires in-depth knowledge of parallel programming. Most of these frameworks have been designed for "optimal parallelization"; that is, they allow the user to control data placement, scheduling, and communication so as to realize the best possible parallel implementation. However, the requirements of ML-DM researchers and developers are different — they need a means to both implement and evaluate their algorithms in a limited amount of time and they do not necessarily want to spend time concentrating on an "optimal parallelization". Therefore, ML-DM researchers and developers have shied away from implementing parallel versions of their algorithms. Ideally, parallel implementation should require little additional work relative to the sequential implementation; this requires that the parallelization interface should support programming patterns that are typically used during sequential implementation. For example, serial implementations of decision tree induction typically follow a divide-and-conquer approach and operate by first finding the best splitting criterion for a dataset, then partitioning the dataset on this criterion, and finally recursively processing these partitions until the recursion terminates. In this case, to make things simple and natural for the implementer, the parallelization framework should support recursive programming patterns.

Support for rapid prototyping: The knowledge discovery process is iterative in nature — researchers and users often need to evaluate a variety of algorithms before picking the most effective algorithm for a given task. Typically, algorithms tend to have several common components; thus, the parallelization framework should allow the programmer to reuse as much of their existing code as possible to facilitate rapid prototyping. For example, consider the implementation of a parallel ensemble method such as bagging [12] that uses the above mentioned decision tree induction algorithm for its base classifier. Bagging generates several random samples of the training data and builds a different classifier using each of these random samples to create an ensemble of classifiers. It then takes the majority class label from the labels predicted by each individual classifier on the test data to produce the final prediction. Ideally, one should be able to compose a parallel bagging predictor using a parallel random sampler and a pluggable parallel classifier.

Domain-specific parallelization: Most of the parallelization platforms that we have mentioned in this Section are generic; that is, they can efficiently parallelize applications from a wide variety of application domains. However, their genericity comes at a high price — these parallelization frameworks require that the parallelization be expressed at a very low-level. As the implementers of ML-DM algorithms often do not have expertise in low-level parallel programming, it is essential that the parallelization framework employed to parallelize ML-DM algorithms be domain-specific. Furthermore, given the varying nature of ML-DM workloads, the framework should support efficient parallelization of both compute and I/O-intensive workloads.

We believe that no existing parallelization infrastructure, including MR, is capable of addressing all these requirements. As is, MR programming is very low level and the implementation process continues to be time consuming. Its one-input, two stage data flow is extremely rigid and does not directly match with the nature of ML-DM computations. Its deficiencies are as follows:

- Users need to write custom code to manage larger computations that require multiple MR jobs (e.g., iterative and recursive computations). Also, they are responsible for managing data across jobs and scheduling these jobs.
- When multiple computations can be performed inside a single MR job, users are responsible for co-scheduling and pipelining these computations inside a single job.

These factors lead to code that is difficult to maintain and reuse. Furthermore, the burden of optimizing these executions falls in the hands of the implementer. Ideally, the parallel programming tools should be palatable to the ML-DM community and the optimization strategies should be aligned with the nature of parallel ML-DM algorithms.

To address these challenges, we present an infrastructure named NIMBLE whose programming abstractions have been designed with the intention of parallelizing ML-DM computations. These programming abstractions allow users to specify data parallel, iterative, task parallel, and even pipelined computations. Furthermore, NIMBLE provides built-in support to process data stored in a variety of formats; it also allows facile implementation of custom data formats. The abstraction and optimization strategies have been designed hand-in-hand to deliver high performance on MR based runtimes — the infrastructure however is portable and can support other runtimes (e.g., MPI, X10). NIMBLE is fully implemented and is being used by programmers at IBM Corporation and will be available for public consumption in the immediate future.

The rest of this paper is organized as follows. Details of the NIMBLE interface are presented in section 2. The runtime and the execution engine are presented in section 3. Sample implementations and their performance evaluations are presented in section 4. Related work is presented in section 5 and conclusions in section 6

2. SOFTWARE ARCHITECTURE

The primary goal of NIMBLE is to enable rapid development of parallel ML-DM algorithms that run portably on distributed- and shared-memory machines. To realize this goal, every design decision in NIMBLE is geared towards both productivity and portability; e.g., NIMBLE is implemented in JAVA, a high productivity language. In this section, we describe the design of NIMBLE in detail.

Software architecture overview: NIMBLE is organized into three distinct layers (Figure 1): (1) The *User API layer*, which provides the programming interface to the users. It primarily consists of abstract classes that allow users to represent *tasks* and directed acyclic graphs (DAGs) of tasks to express dependencies between tasks. A task can take one or more datasets as input, may process the input in parallel, and produce one or more datasets as output. Additionally, NIMBLE's API also provides means to allow users to spawn other tasks/DAGs from inside other tasks and wait on their completion.

[1]There are a small class of embarrassingly parallel algorithms, which can be parallelized without much effort.

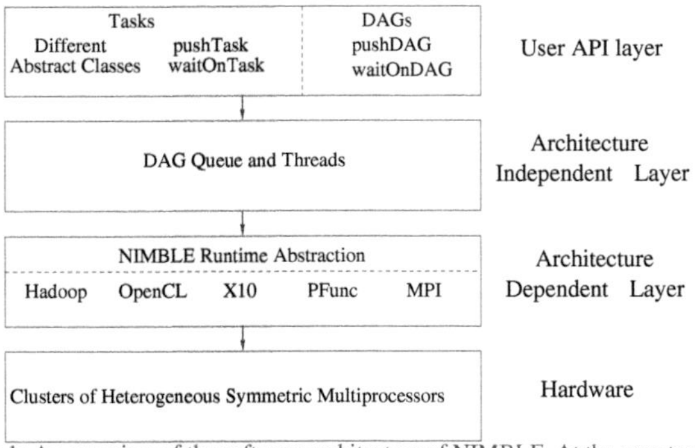

Figure 1: An overview of the software architecture of NIMBLE. At the very top is the user-level API, followed by the architecture independent DAG control layer. The last layer is the architecture dependent layer that allows portable execution of NIMBLE programs.

(2) The *Architecture independent layer*, which acts as the middleware between the user specified tasks/DAGs, and the underlying architecture dependent layer. The primary structures in this layer are a DAG queue along with worker threads that process this queue to ensure progress. This layer is primarily responsible for the smart scheduling of tasks and DAGs, and delivering the completion notifications of these tasks and DAGs to the users. (3) The *Architecture dependent layer*, which consists of harnesses that allow NIMBLE to run portably on various runtimes. Currently, NIMBLE only supports execution on the Hadoop platform.

Software view of hardware: NIMBLE presents a master/slave perspective of the hardware to the user-level tasks (Figure 2). In this model, the main thread of execution begins on the master node. When a task is spawned, depending on its requirements, it is either directly executed on the master node or the task and its data are split into smaller chunks and each chunk is executed on a different slave node (i.e., a different virtual address space). This allows NIMBLE to use a single physical machine as both the master and slave nodes.

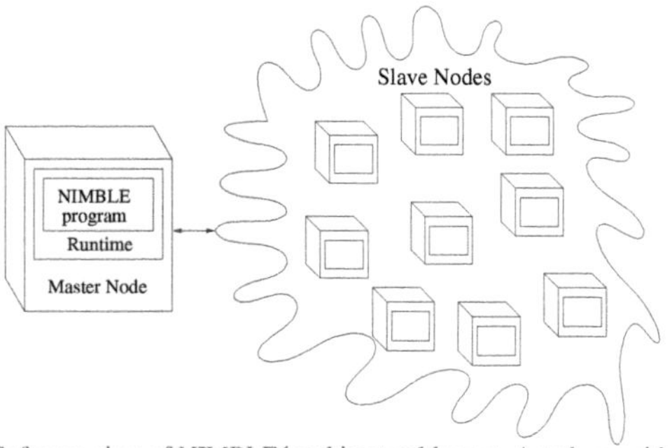

Figure 2: Software view of NIMBLEś architectural layout. A task can either execute on the master node, or be split and executed among slave nodes. Split tasks do not share any state as they execute in disjoint virtual address spaces.

User API layer: The primary mechanism for users to express an algorithm is by implementing one or more tasks. A task represents an independent, reusable piece of computation. In programming terms, a task is a JAVA class that is a subclass of one of the abstract task classes provided by NIMBLE. Several abstract task types are provided; each of which represents a different control/-data flow (Figure 3); also each abstract class has some properties that dictate its co-scheduling eligibility. NIMBLEś tasking model is designed to let users write simple, reusable components that can be composed together to implement a wide variety of algorithms at a high-level of abstraction; thus NIMBLE effectively decouples the functionality provided by the task from its execution.

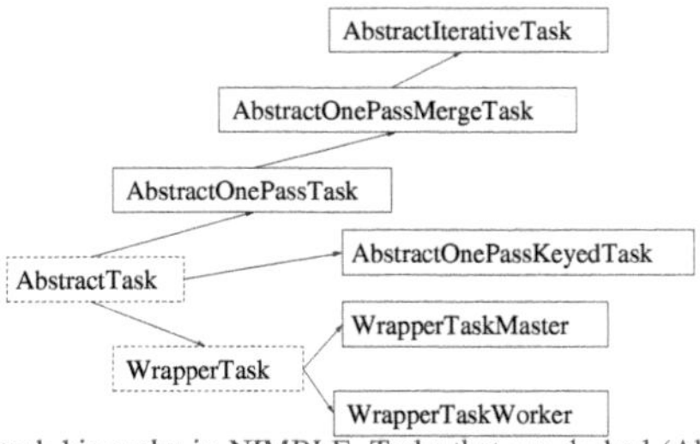

Figure 3: The task hierarchy in NIMBLE. Tasks that are dashed (AbstractTask and WrapperTask) are not directly extensible. The rest of the tasks can be extended by the users to create their own custom tasks.

All NIMBLE tasks derive from AbstractTask; however, this class is not directly extensible by the users. In NIMBLE tasks can be divided into one of two kinds: *Data tasks* that have at least one input dataset and can generate one or more output datasets, and *Non-Data tasks* that represent pure computations and have neither input nor output datasets.

AbstractOnePassTask, AbstractOnePassMergeTask, AbstractOnePassKeyedTask, and AbstractIterativeTask are all examples of data tasks. Specifically, they can access their input datasets in parallel and write to one or more output datasets in parallel. There are two types of datasets, *regular datasets* and *keyed datasets*. Regular datasets consist of one or more records that are independent, and hence, can be processed one record at a time. Keyed datasets will be described shortly. All the data tasks have initializeTask () and finalizeTask () methods. The initializeTask () method is called at the beginning of a task's execution and is executed only once on the master node before commencing with the data parallel execution on the slave nodes. Similarly, the finalizeTask () method is invoked only once on the master node after a task has completed processing all its input data. We now describe the individual data tasks in more detail.

```
Input: t: task
Output: taskSet: A set of tasks
dataPartition = partition(getInputDatasets(t));
taskSet = ∅;
/* Create as many tasks as data partitions */ ;
foreach partition ∈ dataPartition do
    t' = makeReplica(t);
    setInputData(t', partition);
    taskSet = taskSet ⋃ t';
/* Process each partition */ ;
foreach task ∈ taskSet do
    foreach dataset ∈ getInputDatasets(task) do
        foreach record ∈ getRecords(dataset) do
            t.processRecord(dataset, record);
return taskSet;
```

Algorithm 1: executeTask

AbstractOnePassTask is the simplest of the data tasks (see Algorithm 2) and it requires users to implement a processRecord() method. Once the initializeTask () method is invoked on the master node, conceptually, the data is broken into a number of partitions. We make a copy of the task for each of these partitions, and then process each partition with its associated copy of the task. The partition is processed by feeding the task one record at a time using the processRecord() method (see Algorithm 1). The task also has the ability to write to one or more output datasets inside the processRecord() method. Once all the partitions are processed, we invoke the finalizeTask () method on the original task. While this programming abstraction does not make parallelism explicit, it emulates a doAcross() loop over the entire data, where each partition is processed in parallel. An example of an operation that maps well to AbstractOnePassTask is matrix scaling, which can be carried out independently on each element.

```
Input: t: task
t.initializeTask();
executeTask(t);
t.finalizeTask();
```

Algorithm 2: executeOnePassTask

AbstractOnePassMergeTask extends AbstractOnePassTask with an additional mergeTasks() method (see Algorithm 4); this method can be used to merge/aggregate the state of all the tasks that processed independent partitions of data during processRecord(). The mergeTasks() method is akin to a *reduction* operation, hence can be invoked on two or more instances of a task in parallel; it is an ideal candidate when partial results computed during processRecord() need to be accumulated. For example, consider computing the mean of all the elements of a sparse matrix, which would involve accumulating both the number of non-zeros and the sum of all values in each partition during processRecord(). The mergeTasks() method can then be used to merge all the partial results and produce the final result.

```
Input: taskSet: A set of tasks
Output: t: A merged task
t = pop(taskSet);
foreach t' ∈ taskSet do
    t.mergeTasks(t');
return t;
```

Algorithm 3: mergeTasks

```
Input: t: task
t.initializeTask();
taskSet = executeTask(t);
t = mergeTasks(taskSet);
t.finalizeTask();
```

Algorithm 4: executeOnePassMergeTask

AbstractIterativeTask extends AbstractOnePassMergeTask by adding iterative control flow using beginIteration () and endIteration () methods (see Algorithm 5). Iterations continue till the beginIteration () method returns false. The endIteration () method is invoked at the end of every iteration to perform computations to setup the following iterations. AbstractIterativeTask task should be used for the specification of iterative, data parallel computations. Consider the implementation of k-Means clustering in NIMBLE — beginIteration () returns true till convergence is reached. processRecord() is used to assign data points to one of k centers and maintain sufficient statistics, mergeTasks() is used to accumulate sufficient statistics across partitions, and endIteration () is used to compute the new k centers (see Section on k-Means clustering).

```
Input: t: task
t.initializeTask();
while t.beginIteration() do
    taskSet = executeTask(t);
    t = mergeTasks(taskSet);
    t.endIteration();
t.finalizeTask();
```

Algorithm 5: executeIterativeTask

AbstractOnePassKeyedTask is used to process keyed datasets, where each record is associated with a key. AbstractOnePassKeyedTasks require that their input records be sorted on each key across all their input datasets. The task is then provided with all records across all datasets that match a certain key through the reduceRecord() method. When all the records with the same key have been reduced, NIMBLE invokes finishProcessingForCurrentKey() to help which allows key-wide reduction. This task should be used for the specification of data parallel computations where aligned access to one more inputs is needed. For example, consider the addition of two matrices — we need to ensure that we add elements with the same row and column indices; this requires a sort operation.

Non-data tasks derive from WrapperTask. As these are designed to represent computations without data access, depending on where the task is to be executed, one can either use WrapperTaskMaster tasks (for execution on the master node) or WrapperTaskWorker tasks (for execution on a slave node). The WrapperTaskMaster can be used to implement work flows consisting of other serial and parallel tasks. The WrapperTaskWorker can be used to embed existing binaries that can be executed on the slaves node. It allows one to leverage task parallelism using existing binaries.

```
Input: t: task
t.initializeTask();
keyedDatasets = getInputDatasets(t);
/* Sort all datasets on key */;
sortedKeyedDatasets = sortOnKey(keyedDatasets) ;
foreach key ∈ sortedKeyedDatasets do
    foreach dataset ∈ getInputDatasets(t) do
        foreach record ∈ getRecords(key, dataset) do
            t.reduceRecord(key,dataset,record);
        t.finishProcessingForCurrentKey();
t.finalizeTask();
```

Algorithm 6: executeOnePassKeyedTask

Task Spawning: In NIMBLE, tasks can spawn and wait on completion of their spawned tasks. The outputs of any completed task can be piped in as input to the spawned task as well. As has been noted, a task represents data parallel computations; with the ability for tasks to spawn other tasks, NIMBLE also supports task parallelism. In fact, NIMBLEś API elegantly supports algorithms that require both task and data parallelism concurrently. An example where task spawning is beneficial is the implementation of divide-and-conquer algorithms, such as decision tree induction algorithms. Task spawning also facilitates the writing of reusable parallel codes – each task should be used to represent an independent piece of computation and tasks can spawn other tasks akin to function calls in programming languages to realize reusable parallel codes.

DAGs of tasks: NIMBLE supports the chaining of tasks to create task DAGs and ensures their efficient execution; this is an important feature of NIMBLE that promotes modular design of reusable tasks without sacrificing performance. Unlike task spawning, where the dependency between tasks is available only when a task is executed, by task chaining, the dependencies between tasks are made explicit *a priori*. The benefit of making these dependencies available early is that NIMBLEś runtime system can co-schedule many of these chained tasks inside a single MR job, thereby minimizing the number of I/O scans and the overheads of starting MR jobs. An example where specifying DAGs of tasks is beneficial is the implementation of matrix computations, which are common when implementing ML-DM algorithms.

One issue that arises when dealing with DAGs of tasks is that of data alignment. As a rule, an AbstractOnePassKeyedTask requires its input to be sorted on its input datasets' keys. However, once inputs have been sorted, a parent task of type AbstractOnePassKeyedTask does not need to have its output re-sorted before feeding its output to its children provided that it has not altered the alignment of the keys. Thus, each edge in a DAG has a property that specifies whether the input to a task needs to be sorted or can be used as is. The benefit of this property is that it allows one to co-schedule AbstractOnePassKeyedTasks in a situation where one provides the input to the other without having to sort on the keys.

In summary, the NIMBLEś API layer exposes an abstraction that allows programmers to express different forms of parallelism without requiring explicit data management, communication, or scheduling. This allows users to write near serial code, while reaping the benefits of parallel execution. Furthermore, NIMBLE encourages composition of complex algorithms using smaller parallel building blocks. Algorithms that have been written against this API are then presented to the lower layers that orchestrate execution on Hadoop while managing control and data.

Datasets: An important aspect of using NIMBLE involves moving data in and out of tasks. In NIMBLE, all data are treated as a stream of records (essentially black boxes); the only requirement being that records must be convertible to and from strings (TextRecords) or bytes (BinaryRecords). To facilitate users, NIMBLE provides several adaptors that allow data stored in many popular formats to be used without any modifications. For example, NIMBLE has built-in support for LibSVM [13] and several other sparse matrix formats such as (i, j, v), and compressed sparse row/column (CSR/CSC) formats. Furthermore, it is trivial to write adaptors that allow use of data stored in any format (text or binary) with NIMBLE.

3. RUNTIME

One of the primary goals of NIMBLE is to enable the user's algorithms to run on a wide-variety of parallel platforms in a performance-portable fashion. In order to realize this goal, NIMBLEś runtime is split into two parts; the architecture independent layer, and the architecture dependent layer. Figure 1 depicts the high-level structure of the runtime composition of NIMBLE; the user's applications always interact with the architecture independent layer, ensuring complete portability. In this section, we briefly describe the architecture independent layer. In addition, we also describe the Hadoop architecture dependent layer, which allows NIMBLE applications to run on the Hadoop MR framework.

Architecture independent layer: This light-weight layer sits between the user programs and runtime platforms such as Hadoop, MPI, and X10. It consists of a DAG queue and a thread pool; threads wait for users to push DAGs or individual tasks into the DAG queue. As there is a single DAG queue that services all the threads in the thread pool, the architecture independent layer of NIMBLE can be thought of as a *work-sharing* environment. Once a thread pulls a DAG from the DAG queue, it executes it to completion using the pre-specified architecture dependent layer. [2] Algorithm 7 shows the naive version of the loop run by each architecture independent thread. Briefly, each thread gets a runtime (e.g., the Hadoop architecture dependent layer) and the DAG queue as input; then, it continually removes DAGs from this queue and executes them. DAGs are executed by repeatedly extracting the maximal sub DAG that can be executed by the given runtime as one job and executing it (see Section on Co-scheduling of tasks).

The Hadoop architecture dependent layer: The primary goal of this layer is to provide the services needed by the architecture independent layer; i.e., allowing smooth execution of NIMBLE programs on the underlying framework. To enable running NIMBLE applications for a specific runtime, we need to implement an interface for that runtime, which can take NIMBLE DAG specifications and execute these DAGs as efficiently as possible. We selected Hadoop as the target runtime for our first architecture dependent

[2] Individual tasks are internally wrapped around in a DAG for uniformity.

```
Input: Q: queue of DAGs, R: Architecture-specific runtime
while not shutdown() do
    repeat
        d = getNextDAG(Q);
    until not d = NULL ;
    while executionIncomplete(d) do
        s = getExecutableSubDAG(R, d);
        s = executeDAG(R, s);
        reintegrateDAG(d, s);
```

Algorithm 7: runArchitectureIndependentThread

layer because of its inherent support for handling large datasets, which are an important consideration for data mining and machine learning algorithms. Briefly, each architecture dependent layer has to expose the following functionality: (1) co-scheduling individual tasks found in the DAG using one or more jobs, (2) executing the job, which includes piping intermediate outputs between tasks, and (3) returning the executed DAG (with changed internal state) back to the architecture independent layer.

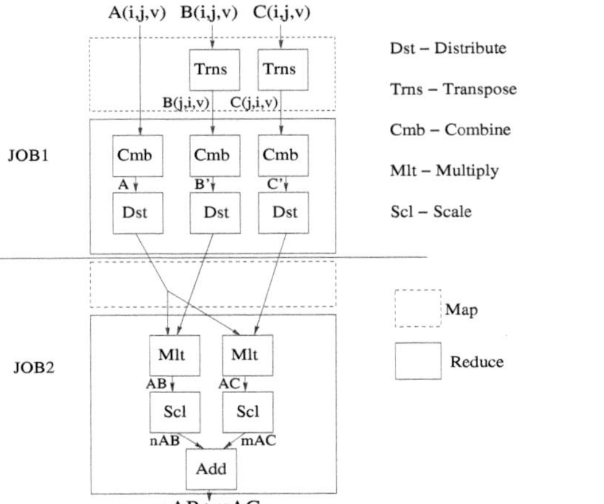

Figure 4: Co-scheduling for a naive implementation of the matrix equation $n \times A \times B + m \times A \times C$ such that the entire operation is completed in two MR jobs.

Co-scheduling of tasks: An important advantage of NIMBLE is its ability to design an entire application as a series of encapsulated, reusable tasks. However, executing each individual task as a separate "job" can result in excessive startup costs and lost opportunities for data reuse between tasks. To alleviate such performance bottlenecks, NIMBLE allows users to spawn and execute entire DAG computations instead of just individual tasks. Apart from being an elegant and powerful programming abstraction, the ability to spawn and execute DAG computations also allows NIMBLE to co-schedule appropriate tasks within a DAG in a single MR operation, thereby overcoming the high overhead involved in executing Hadoop jobs. However, there is not a one to one correlation between the user-level DAGs and those that can be executed by Hadoop in one MR job. In this section, we describe the algorithms used to select the maximal sub-DAG from the user-level DAG that can be executed as one MR job.

Consider the execution of the computation $X = (n \times A \times B + m \times A \times C)$, where A, B, and C are sparse square matrices represented in the (i, j, v) format, and n and m are scalars. One way to compute this equation using MR is to first convert the matrices from their (i, j, v) representation into individual compressed sparse rows (CSR); of course, matrices B and C, are first transposed into (j, i, v) before converting them into their CSR format. Once this step is complete, we have A, B^T, and C^T represented as CSR vectors; now, the given equation can be computed quite easily. The DAG of the tasks that are involved in computing X is shown in

```
Input: DAG D
Output: List of executable tasks.
execTaskSet = ∅;
repeat
    noNewAdditions = true;
    foreach task t ∈ unchosenTaskList(D) do
        removeDependencies(t, executableTaskSet);
        if noUnsatisfiedDependency(t) then
            execTaskSet = execTaskSet ⋃ t;
            if instanceOf(OnePassKeyedTask,t) or
            (instanceOf(OnePassTask,t) and lastParentPhase(t) ==
            reduce) then
                setExecutionPhase(t, reduce);
            else
                setExecutionPhase(t, map);
            markTaskAsChosen(t);
            noNewAdditions = false;
until noNewAdditions ;
return execTaskSet;
```

Algorithm 8: getExecutableSubDAG

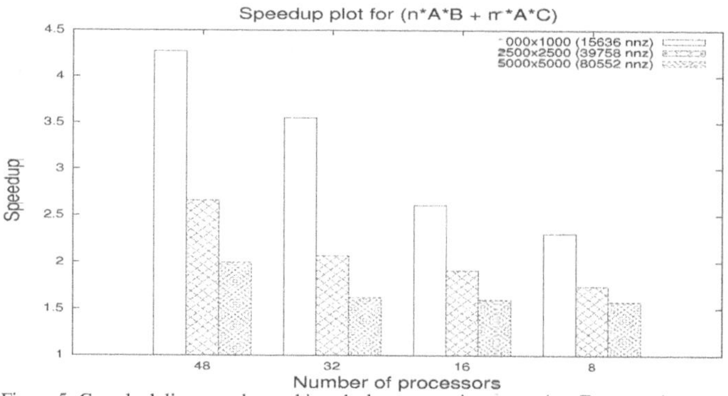

Figure 5: Co-scheduling speedups achieved when computing $(n \times A \times B + n \times A \times C)$, where A, B, and C are sparse matrices. Matrix multiplication was carried out (naively) using the inner-product formulation. Number of non-zeros in each matrix are given in brackets. The experiments were run on IBM's Nadal cluster (see Section 4).

Figure 4. The matrix transpose is calculated by using two separate task types; the Transpose task is of type AbstractOnePassTask; it takes (i, j, v) entries as input and generates (j, i, v) entries that are keyed on j, the original column numbers. The Combine task is of type AbstractOnePassKeyedTask that takes these (j, i, v) matrix elements and recombines them to form CSR column-vectors. The next task is to distribute the matrices A, B^T, and C^T so that $A \times B$ and $A \times C$ can be computed using inner products. This is done using the Distribute task of type AbstractOnePassTask which takes in a row-vector and generates an output dataset, which is keyed based on the row-number. In addition, the Distribute task also replicates the right hand side (matrices B^T and C^T) so that each row in B^T and C^T (i.e., each column of B and C) is sent to each row of A. The next tasks are self-explanatory; the two Multiply tasks of type AbstractOnePassKeyedTask compute $A \times B$ and $A \times C$ one row at a time respectively. Similarly, the two Scale tasks of type AbstractOnePassTask compute $n \times A \times B$ and $m \times A \times C$ respectively, and finally the Add task of type AbstractOnePassKeyedTask adds the two results from the Scale tasks together to compute X.

If each task in the above DAG were executed as an individual MR job, it would take 13 MR jobs to compute X; since many elements are needlessly read from and written to the disk multiple times, a large overhead is incurred. For example, A is common in computing $A \times B$ and $A \times C$; the result of these computations can be directly streamed to be scaled and added up resulting in computation of X without ever having to write intermediate results to disk. This intuitive execution is precisely what NIMBLE achieves, thereby computing X in just two MR jobs (see Figure 4). This has two benefits: (a) we only pay Hadoop's overhead cost once and (b) we directly pipe data from one task to another *in memory* as long as both tasks are executing in the same phase (i.e., Map or Reduce).

Algorithms 8 and 9 elaborate on the exact procedure used to pick the maximal sub-DAG in a DAG that can be executed in one MR job. From the time a DAG is spawned for execution until it has completed its execution, NIMBLE's runtime engine repeatedly queries getExecutableSubDAG() to get the maximal executable sub-DAG of the spawned DAG. When invoked, getExecutableSubDAG() returns a list of tasks that can be run in the Map phase and a list of tasks that can be run in the Reduce phase of the MR job. This is achieved by first adding all those tasks in the DAG that have no dependencies (as checked by noUnsatisfiedDependency()) to the appropriate list (all but tasks of type AbstractOnePassKeyedTask are marked as Map phase tasks). Once these initial tasks are added to the Map and the Reduce task lists, we iterate over the remaining tasks until a fixed point is reached (i.e., no new tasks are added). Additional tasks are added by judiciously removing dependencies that are satisfied by the execution of the tasks that are already in the Map and the Reduce task lists. This procedure is shown in removeDependencies() and the logic is as follows. If a child task t_c depends on the completion of a parent task t_p, then we mark such an edge as satisfied *iff* t_c can be executed after t_p in the same MR job. As can be seen in Algorithm 9, marking an edge (t_p, t_c) as satisfied depends on the *type* of both t_p and t_c. When t_p is a AbstractIterativeTask, we cannot mark any of its outgoing edges as satisfied because the termination criteria is determined only at runtime. When t_p is a AbstractOnePassTask, all its outgoing edges can be marked as satisfied because t_p can be completely executed in the Map or Reduce phase. When t_p is a AbstractOnePassMergeTask, an edge to t_c, which is a AbstractOnePassKeyedTask, can be marked as satisfied because t_p's execution can be completed during the Reduce phase, and t_c can be completely executed after t_p in completed in the same Reduce phase. Finally, when both t_p and t_c are AbstractOnePassKeyedTasks, an edge from t_p to t_c can be marked as satisfied *iff* t_p's output is aligned with t_c's input — in other words, if the output of t_p does not have to be sorted again. Once the maximal sub-DAG is found, the tasks in this sub-DAG are executed in topological order. Note that tasks of type WrapperTask do not appear in Algorithms 8 and 9 because they have no input or output. Hence, they are perceived as singleton nodes in the DAG.

Figure 5 presents the speedups achieved by co-scheduling tasks when executing the task DAG shown in Figure 4. By co-scheduling tasks, we consistently get speedups across all matrix sizes. For smaller matrices, the speedups are significant as most of the execution time can be attributed to the I/O overhead involved in MR. As the number of computations required increase, the speedups are lower as the execution time is dominated by the $O(n^3)$ operations required for matrix multiplication. The importance of co-scheduling tasks is more pronounced when the executions are I/O bound — which is true for a large class of ML-DM algorithms.

Executing a DAG: After selecting the maximally executable sub-DAG, the Hadoop architecture dependent layer first determines all the inputs that are needed for the current sub-DAG to execute, and creates output file paths for all the leaf tasks' outputs. Once this is done, the job is submitted to Hadoop with our custom Map and Reduce classes; these classes know how to read the $(key, value)$ pairs that are inputs to both the Map and the Reduce phases, interpret these pairs as records and marshal them to the tasks that need these inputs. Since we execute more than one task in both the Map and the Reduce phases, the NIMBLE Hadoop layer also redirects the intermediate output from the non-leaf tasks to other tasks.

```
Input: t_c: task, T: set of tasks
foreach task t_p ∈ T do
    if isParent(t_p,t) and not instanceOf(IterativeTask,t) then
        if instanceOf(OnePassMergeTask, t_p) then
            if instanceOf(OnePassKeyedTask,t_c) or
            (instanceOf(OnePassTask,t_c) and not
            instanceOf(OnePassMergeTask, t_c)) then
                markEdgeAsSatisfied(t_p,t_c);
        else
            if instanceOf(OnePassTask,t_p) then
                if getExecutionPhase(t_p) == reduce then
                    if (instanceOf(OnePassKeyedTask, t_c) and
                    alignedWithParents(t_c)) or
                    instanceOf(OnePassTask, t_c) then
                        markEdgeAsSatisfied(t_p,t_c);
                else
                    markEdgeAsSatisfied(t_p,t_c);
            else
                if instanceOf(OnePassKeyedTask,t_p) then
                    if instanceOf(OnePassKeyedTask,t_c) &&
                    alignedWithParents(t_c) then
                        markEdgeAsSatisfied(t_p,t_c);
                    else
                        if (instanceOf(OnePassTask,t_c) and not
                        instanceOf(OnePassMergeTask, t_c)) then
                            markEdgeAsSatisfied(t_p,t_c);
```

Algorithm 9: removeDependencies

Returning the executed task: In NIMBLE users express computation as tasks, which are JAVA objects. As these tasks are executed in Hadoop by replicating the objects, the state in each of these tasks may need to be merged and returned to the users. This is done in the following manner. At the end of the Map phase, the tasks that were used in that Mapper are emitted as values with a special set of keys ($taskKeys$). These are directed to a set of reducers who proceed to merge these tasks together and write the serialized, partially merged tasks to the file system. These partially merged tasks are then recreated in memory on the master node by de-serializing the tasks and merging them to finally create a single task that is returned to the user.

4. ALGORITHMS AND EVALUATIONS

To demonstrate the expressiveness of NIMBLE, we detail the implementation of two popular data mining algorithms — k-Means Clustering and Pattern Growth-based Frequent Itemset Mining. We also evaluate the performance of these algorithms together with three other data mining algorithms – k-Nearest Neighbors, Random Decision Trees, and RBRP-based Outlier Detection (implementation details omitted due to space constraints) – to illustrate gains in productivity and performance. Experiments were performed on IBM's Nadal cluster, which has 48 processors distributed across 12 nodes with 4 GB of RAM per processor. All the nodes were running RHEL 5 (kernel 2.6.18-164.el5) with IBM Java v1.6.0 and Hadoop 0.20.2.

k-Means Clustering: Given a dataset D consisting of n data points, each with d dimensions, the data clustering problem is to partition this dataset into k subsets such that each subset behaves "well" under some measure. The popular k-Means clustering algorithm can be briefly described as follows. First, it begins with k random centers, $C^0 = \{C_1^0, \cdots, C_k^0\}$. Next, for each of the n data points, it finds its closest center in C^0 and maintains the sum of all points and number of points that were assigned to each center. The data points are partitioned into k subsets based on their closest centers. The center of mass for each of these k subsets is used to find the new set of k centers, $C^1 = \{C_1^1, \cdots, C_k^1\}$. This process continues iteratively until we encounter an iteration i such that the centers C^i and $C^{(i+1)}$ are identical.

It is well known that data parallelization is a means of parallelizing k-Means clustering. A parallel implementation of k-Means clustering in NIMBLE is provided in Figure 6. k-Means clustering is implemented using just one class that extends AbstractIterativeTask. The initializeTask () method is used to initialize the centers randomly. The beginIteration () method returns true provided the process has not converged. The processRecord() method is responsible for assigning each data point to its closest center and maintaining sufficient statistics that will be used to determine the new centers. The mergeTasks() method sums up the sufficient statistics. The endIteration () method computes new centers based on the accumulated sufficient statistics and also checks for convergence. The finalizeTask () method is used to output centers after convergence. Looking at this example, it is evident that NIMBLE provides a natural and near-serial way of implementing algorithms. The only additional method needed for parallelization is the mergeTasks() method that is straightforward to implement in this case. Data management, communication, and control are absent. The implementation is far more succinct relative to the corresponding MR implementation that would span several classes and require explicit data management (to provide input and read output of a MR job) and job submission for each iteration of k-Means clustering.

```
class kMeansTask extends AbstractIterativeTask {
  float [][] kCenters = new float [k][dimensions];
  float [][] newkCenters = new float [k][dimensions];
  int [] kPoints = new int [k];
  float [][] kSumPoints = new float [k][dimensions];
  boolean converged = false;
  public void initializeTask() {initializeCenters(kCenters);}
  public boolean beginIteration() {return converged;}
  public void processRecord(BasicRecordI record) {
    final int closestCenter = findClosestCenter(kCenters,record);
    ++(kPoints[closestCenter]);
    for (int i = 0; i < record.getNumFields(); i++) kSumPoints[closestCenter][i] += record[i];
  }
  public void mergeTasks(AbstractBasicTask mergeTask) {
    for (int i = 0; i < kCenters.length; i++) {
      for (int j = 0; j < kCenters[i].length; j++)
        kSumPoints[i][j] += ((KMeansTask)mergeTask).kSumPoints[i][j];
      kPoints[i] += ((KMeansTask)mergeTask).kPoints[i];
    }
  }
  public void endIteration() {
    for (int i = 0; i < newkCenters.length; i++)
      for (int j = 0; j < newkCenters[i].length; j++)
        newkCenters[i][j] = kSumPoints[i][j] / kPoints[i];
    converged = (difference(newkCenters, kCenters) < THRESHOLD) ? true: false;
    kCenters = newkCenters;
  }
  public void finalizeTask() { outputCenters(kCenters); }
}
```

Figure 6: k-Means Clustering using NIMBLE

Frequent Pattern Mining: Frequent pattern mining, also known as frequent itemset mining (FIMI), plays an important role in a range of data mining tasks. The frequent pattern mining problem was formulated by Agrawal *et al.* [11] for association rule mining. Briefly, the problem description is as follows: Let $I = \{i_1, i_2, \cdots, i_n\}$ be a set of n items, and let $D = \{T_1, T_2, \cdots, T_m\}$ be a set of m transactions, where each transaction T_i is a subset of I. An itemset $i \subseteq I$ of size k is known as a k-itemset. The *support* of i is $\sum_{j=1}^{m}(1 : i \subseteq T_j)$, or informally speaking, the number of transactions in D that have i as a subset. The frequent pattern mining problem is to find all $i \in D$ that have *support* greater than a minimum support value.

Our parallel FIMI implementation in NIMBLE uses a pattern growth approach that is similar to the one proposed by Li *et al.* [21] and is provided in Figure 7. The approach extends all the given prefixes in the input dataset by 1 and prunes away infrequent extensions. It then groups these extended prefixes and builds a projected dataset for each group. Finally, it recursively invokes the same task on these projected datasets until no more extensions are possible. The recursive implementation of FIMI in NIMBLE needs a single class called fimiTask that extends AbstractIterativeTask. The task performs two iterations. In the first iteration, the processRecord() method maintains counts for items as extensions of all itemsets in prefixes. Then the mergeTasks() method is used to aggregate counts across tasks. Finally, the endIteration() method is used to prune infrequent extensions, group frequent extensions into itemsetGroups, and allocate datasets for each group in itemsetGroups. In the second iteration, the processRecord() method projects the input dataset for each group in itemsetGroups. Finally, the endIteration() method *spawns* a child task for each group in itemsetGroups, provided it can be extended.

Looking at this example, as was the case with k-Means, the implementation is natural, succinct, and near-serial – the only additional method needed for parallelization is the mergeTasks() method that is straightforward to implement in this case. Furthermore, support for recursion does indeed simplify implementation.

```
class fimiTask extends AbstractIterativeTask {
  int iteration = 0;
  HashMap<Vector<Long>,HashMap<Long,Long>> itemCounts=
        new HashMap<Vector<Long>,HashMap<Long,Long>>();
  Vector<Vector<Vector<Long>>> itemsetGroups=new Vector<Vector<Vector<Long>>>();
  //Projected datasets for an itemset group
  HashMap<Integer,OutputDataset> itemsetProjectedDatasets =
        new HashMap<Long, OutputDataset>();
  Vector<Vector<Long>> prefixes;
  public boolean beginIteration() {return (iteration == 0 || iteration == 1) ? true: false;}
  public void processRecord(BasicRecordI record) {
    if(iteration == 0) countItems(record,itemCounts);
    else if(iteration == 1) {
      for (int i=0; i < itemsetGroups.size(); i++)
        project(itemsetGroups.get(i),record,itemsetProjectedDatasets.get(i));
    }
  }
  public void mergeTasks(AbstractBasicTask mergeTask) {
    if(iteration == 0) mergeItemCounts(itemCounts, ((fimiTask)mergeTask).itemCounts);
  }
  public void endIteration() {
    if(iteration == 0){
      pruneInfrequentItems(itemCounts);
      groupItems(itemsetGroups, itemCounts);
      for (int i= 0; i<itemsetGroups.size();i++){
        SparseDataset od = new SparseDataset();
        itemsetProjectedDatasets.put(i,od);
      }
    } else if (iteration == 1) {
      for (int i= 0; i<itemsetGroups.size();i++){
        fimiTask childTask = new fimiTask();
        childTask.prefixes = new Vector <Vector<Long>>();
        childTask.prefixes.addAll(itemsetGroups.get(i));
        childTask.addInputDataset(itemsetProjectedDataset.get(i));
        if (childTask.prefixes.size > 0 && itemsetProjectedDataset.get(i).hasRecords())
          this.getTaskQueue().pushTask(childTask);
      }
    }
    ++iteration;
  }
```

Figure 7: Frequent Pattern Mining using NIMBLE

***k*-Nearest Neighbors:** Given a dataset, the k-Nearest Neighbors (k-NN) algorithm finds the k nearest neighbors for each point in the dataset Nearest neighbors can be computed using any distance metric; for our implementation we used euclidean distances. k-NN is often used in machine learning as a simple classification mechanism where each unlabeled item is labeled based on a majority vote of the labels of its nearest neighbors. The process of calculating k-NN for each data point consists of computing the distance from that point to every other point and maintaining a $MaxHeap$ that keeps track of only the k nearest neighbors of the point. The procedure followed to compute k-NN is an iterative one and is implemented as an AbstractIterativeTask. During each iteration, we perform distance computations to find the k nearest neighbors for a subset of the data points by streaming through and measuring distances against all other data points. This process continues iteratively until we have determined the k nearest neighbors of all input points.

Random Decision Trees: We implemented a classifier based on Random Decision Trees [15] in NIMBLE. The algorithm constructs multiple decision trees randomly. When constructing each tree, the algorithm picks a feature randomly when expanding a node without any purity check (such as information gain). When picking a categorical feature, it ensures that the feature-value combination has not been chosen previously on the path from that node to the root node. Continuous features on the other hand can always be chosen and are set with a random threshold. We stop expanding a node when the number of instances that reach that node are below a threshold. The approach is implemented using an AbstractIterativeTask – each task builds one random decision tree. The task initializes a subset of the nodes of the tree randomly based on the range of values of the features and then gathers the number of instances in the training set that reach each node in the tree. Nodes that are not reached by a sufficient number of instances are pruned away. Nodes that can be further expanded are grown with a new random subtree and this process continues iteratively until the process terminates.

Outlier Detection: We implemented the RBRP algorithm [16] for distance-based outlier detection in NIMBLE. The algorithm operates in two phases. The first phase partitions the dataset into bins such that points that are closer to each other are more likely to be assigned to the same bin. Every point is assigned to exactly one bin and each bin must be less than a certain size. The second phase finds outliers in each bin separately and then merges these outliers into a global set of outliers. Both these phases have been parallelized using an AbstractIterativeTask.

Performance Evaluation: The results of our performance evaluation for all five algorithms are provided in Figure 8. The speedup numbers are relative to the execution time measured when using 8 processors. Thus, the maximum possible speedup when using 48 processors is 6. k-Means clustering was evaluated using large synthetic datasets – 10D-100M implies a 10 dimensional dataset with 100 million points. FIMI was evaluated using a large synthetic dataset (T10I4D100M) with 100 million transactions and a large real dataset (Webdocs) with 1.7 million transactions. k-NN was evaluated using the MNIST [20] datasets that have dimensionality 784 and the number points were varied from 20K to 60K. Random decision trees and RBRP were evaluated using large synthetic datasets – the naming convention for their datasets is same as that used for the k-Means datasets. It is easy to see that the NIMBLE implementations are indeed efficient and speedup improves with increasing dataset size and dimensionality.

5. RELATED WORK

Although there has been extensive research into *ad-hoc* parallelization of ML-DM algorithms for over two decades, we focus our attention on efforts that have looked at building a generic framework for parallelizing ML-DM algorithms. Jin and Agrawal

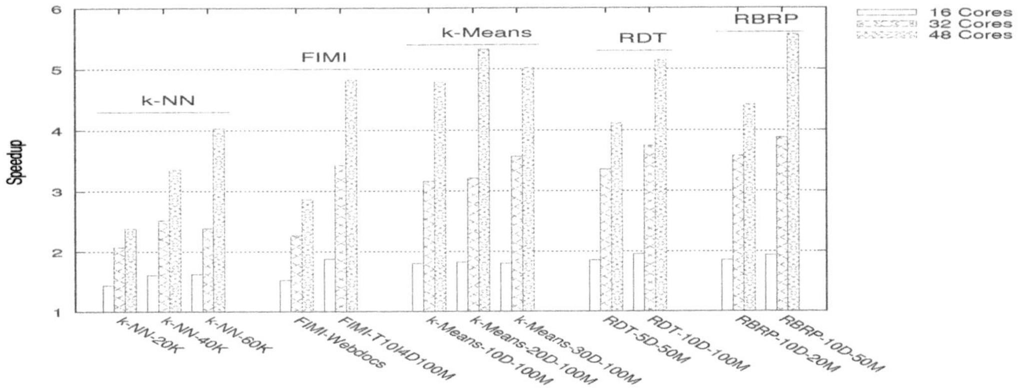

Figure 8: Speedup for algorithms implemented in NIMBLE. Speedup is relative to execution time on 8-cores.

[18] first studied the problem of building a common framework for implementing parallel data mining algorithms. They showed that these algorithms share a common structure that is amenable to MR-type parallelization. Based on this structure, the authors presented an interface for data parallelization of these algorithms that requires one to make simple modifications to sequential code to realize a parallelization. However, in addition to data parallelism, NIMBLE provides task parallelism, task DAGs, and efficient execution of these DAGs, which results in greater I/O efficiency. IBM's Parallel Machine Learning Toolbox (PML) [4] incorporates an infrastructure for implementing and running ML-DM algorithms on large parallel systems by leveraging aggregate memory for data storage and fast collective communication to perform reductions. However, unlike NIMBLE, PML does not support task parallelism.

Recently, the MR abstraction has been used to implement parallel machine learning algorithms. Chu *et al.* [14] have used MR to express a class of machine learning algorithms that fit the Statistical-Query model. In another study, Panda *et al.* presented a framework for the implementation of decision tree ensembles [23] on top of MR. We have already discussed the deficiencies of using MR for implementing parallel ML-DM algorithms.

Implementations such as Dryad [17] and Dryad-LINQ [24] support DAG-based abstractions for implementing ML-DM algorithms. While the DAG-based abstraction permits rich computational dependencies, it does not naturally express iterative, data parallel, task parallel, and dynamic data driven algorithms that are prevalent in ML-DM. Furthermore, Dryad's DAG abstraction is far too low level and we can in fact use it as an alternative runtime to Hadoop in NIMBLE. Apache's Mahout project [7] is closely related to NIMBLE in that it provides a library of machine learning implementations; however, it does not provide an infrastructure for the specification of parallel ML-DM algorithms.

6. CONCLUSION

In this paper, we presented NIMBLE, a novel, domain-specific parallelization framework that allows rapid development of parallel ML-DM algorithms. In particular, NIMBLE has been designed to scale to large datasets and processor counts as its runtime targets (e.g., Hadoop) are themselves scalable. NIMBLE cleanly separates process choreography and control from actual analytics. This allows algorithm designers to focus more on algorithmic issues and worry less about parallelization issues. Furthermore, we have designed a DAG execution engine that optimizes execution of DAGs of tasks by packing as many tasks as possible into one runtime job. Results on several algorithms demonstrate both the efficiency and the ease of use of NIMBLE.

7. REFERENCES

[1] Hadoop. `http://hadoop.apache.org`.

[2] HBase. `http://hadoop.apache.org/hbase`.

[3] Hive. `http://hadoop.apache.org/hive`.

[4] IBM Parallel Machine Learning Toolbox. `http://www.alphaworks.ibm.com/tech/pml`.

[5] Intel Threading Building Blocks. `http://www.threadingbuildingblocks.org`.

[6] JAQL. `http://www.jaql.org`.

[7] Mahout. `http://lucene.apache.org/mahout/`.

[8] MPI. `http://www.mpi-forum.org`.

[9] OpenMP. `http://www.openmp.org`.

[10] PThreads. `https://computing.llnl.gov/tutorials/pthreads`.

[11] R. Agrawal et al. Mining association rules between sets of items in large databases. *ACM SIGMOD*, 22(2), 1993.

[12] L. Breiman. Bagging predictors. *Machine Learning*, 24(2), 1996.

[13] C.-C. Chang and C.-J. Lin. *LIBSVM: a library for support vector machines*, 2001.

[14] C. Chu et al. Map-reduce for machine learning on multicore. In *NIPS*, 2007.

[15] W. Fan et al. A general framework for accurate and fast regression by data summarization in random decision trees. In *ACM SIGKDD*, 2006.

[16] A. Ghoting et al. Fast mining of distance-based outliers in high-dimensional datasets. *DMKD*, 16(3), 2008.

[17] M. Isard et al. Dryad: distributed data-parallel programs from sequential building blocks. In *SIGOPS Operating System Review*, 2007.

[18] R. Jin and G. Agrawal. Shared Memory Parallelization of Data Mining Algorithms: Techniques, Programming Interface, and Performance. In *SDM*, 2002.

[19] P. Kambadur et al. PFunc: Modern Task Parallelism For Modern High Performance Computing. In *SC*, 2009.

[20] Y. LeCun et al. Gradient-based learning applied to document recognition. In *Intelligent Signal Processing*, 2001.

[21] H. Li et al. Pfp: parallel fp-growth for query recommendation. In *ACM RecSys*, 2008.

[22] C. Olston et al. Pig latin: a not-so-foreign language for data processing. In *ACM SIGMOD*, 2008.

[23] B. Panda et al. PLANET: massively parallel learning of tree ensembles with MapReduce. *Proceedings of the VLDB Endowment*, 2(2), 2009.

[24] Y. Yu et al. DryadLINQ: A System for General-Purpose Distributed Data-Parallel Computing Using a High-Level Language. In *OSDI*, 2008.

Classification of Proxy Labeled Examples for Marketing Segment Generation

Dean Cerrato
Akamai Technologies
8 Cambridge Center
Cambridge, MA 02142
617-444-3000
dcerrato@akamai.com

Rosie Jones
Akamai Technologies
8 Cambridge Center
Cambridge, MA 02142
617-444-3000
rejones@akamai.com

Avinash Gupta
Akamai Technologies
8 Cambridge Center
Cambridge, MA 02142
617-444-3000
avgupta@akamai.com

ABSTRACT

Marketers often rely on a set of *descriptive segments*, or qualitative subsets of the population, to specify the audiences of targeted advertising campaigns. For example, the descriptive segment "Empty Nesters" might describe a desirable target audience for extended vacation package offers.

While some segments may be easily described and generated using demographic data as ground truth, others such as "Soccer Moms" or "Urban Hipsters" reflect a combination of demographic and behavioral attributes. Ideally, these attributes would be available as the basis for ground truth labeling of a classifier training set or even direct member selection from the population. Unfortunately, ground truth attributes are often scarce or unavailable, in which case a proxy labeling scheme is needed.

We devise a method for labeling a population according to criteria based on a postulated set of shopping behaviors specific to a descriptive segment. We then perform supervised binary classification on this labeled dataset in order to discover additional identifying patterns of behavior typical of labeled positives in the population. Finally, the resulting classifier is used to perform selection from the population into the segment, extending reach to cookies who may not have exhibited the postulated behaviors but likely belong in the segment.

We validate our approach by comparing a descriptive segment trained on ground truth to one trained on behavioral attributes only. We show that our behavior-based approach produces classifiers having performance comparable to that of a classifier trained on the ground truth data.

Categories and Subject Descriptors

I.5.2 [**Pattern Recognition**]: Design Methodology – *Classifier design and evaluation.*

General Terms

Algorithms, Experimentation.

Keywords

Marketing segments, classification, computational advertising, rules, RIPPER.

1. INTRODUCTION

We describe our efforts to design a supervised classification algorithm that determines membership for a group of descriptive marketing segments in the absence of ground truth demographic data.

1.1 Motivation

Descriptive marketing segments are a familiar way to specify targeted audiences for on-line advertising campaigns; for example, a purveyor of fast food might find it desirable to display coupon ads to young people of a certain age who attend college, i.e., members of the College Students descriptive segment.

Ideally, comprehensive demographic data would be available from which to deduce segment membership for members of the population, but often this is not the case. In fact, some descriptive segments have a significant subjective component (e.g., Trend-setters) that cannot be inferred directly from hard quantitative data.

In the absence of ground truth, it becomes necessary to define a proxy definition for segment membership derived from available data, which in an on-line context is presumed to be related to web surfing behavior. Once such a definition is created, it can be used to proxy label the population.

A naïve proxy labeling scheme would be to restrict segment membership to visitors to certain websites or pages; indeed, this is often the approach taken by marketing operations.

Our work refines and extends this approach, recasting it as a supervised classification problem that yields a variety of solutions having a range of performance characteristics relating to descriptive segment population size and targeting precision.

1.2 Business Context

The Advertising Decision Systems (ADS) group at Akamai maintains a confidential cooperative network of advertising partners for whom we track visitor traffic and target on-line advertisements. In particular, our Descriptive Segments product offering enables partners to target ads to specific types of on-line shopper [2].

Users are identified using anonymous web browser cookies. For the purpose of identifying descriptive segment members, we have access to web shopping data collected at both the website and department levels. For the purpose of this study, we also use a set of limited demographic data. Each user is represented by an anonymous identifier, and no attempt is made to connect any identifier with a real-world person. Browsing history for each cookie comprised a set of every distinct department-level web location they had visited, from our confidential cooperative network of shopping sites. All data was collected in accordance with Akamai's privacy policy [4] and the privacy policies of the sites visited by the cookies.

Marketing intuition affords us a starting point in identifying websites and departments that are relevant to the various descriptive segments, particularly the murkier ones.

A significant hard constraint on our solution arises from the targeting system: segment membership is bestowed via disjunctive normal form (DNF) rulesets, in terms of antecedents of the form "this cookie visited Site A" or "this cookie visited Department B" or their negations.

Other, softer constraints on the ruleset solutions are: the number of rules per ruleset should not be too large; and as few as possible rules should fire for any given cookie (this would adversely affect the ability of operations to optimize the system on-the-fly).

Finally, the ability to "tune" the *reach* (number of segment members) and targeting precision of the rulesets is highly desirable.

1.3 Related Work

Market segmentation refers to the differentiation of sub-types of customers who would prefer different kinds of products. Most applications of machine learning to market segmentation have focused on predicting purchase behavior. In our work, we are using as our target psycho-demographic descriptions of target audiences. Thus in most cases we do not have labeled instances.

Machine learning has been successfully applied to learning customer segmentation when the target is to identify responders. One piece of previous work focused on using SVMs to learn user preferences in the taste of beef [7] – here a kernel-based similarity function based on clustering finds groups of users with similar tastes. Other work has combined machine learning and expert opinions to perform market segmentation of performing arts audiences [1]. Florez-Lopez et al [8] showed that decision trees out-performed statistical approaches on their task of predicting caravan insurance purchasers. This approach [10] of automatically finding users with similar behavior is referred to in marketing as "look-alike" modeling. Büchner and Mulvenna [5] combine marketing domain expertise with on-line data sources to discover user patterns. In [11], Perlich and Huange analyze relational database structure to discover relationships relevant in CRM contexts.

1.4 Roadmap

Consistent with the requirements for papers submitted under the Industry Track: Emerging area, our work represents the development of a KDD-based prototype solution designed to address a specific industry problem subject to a special set of constraints arising from data availability and legacy system limitations.

This Section has introduced the problem in the particular context of our business operations and constraints. Section 2 presents a more thorough explication of the KDD-based binary classification approach using proxy labeled examples. In Section 3, we define our modeling and evaluation methodologies. In Section 4, we display some resulting rulesets and present performance metrics, which are discussed in Section 5. Sections 6 and 7 offer thoughts for future work and a recap of our conclusions.

2. SOLUTION APPROACH

The primary challenge is to define a subjective yet reasonable proxy labeling scheme to identify positive examples for segment membership. From there, the supervised classification problem may be solved and the solutions evaluated.

2.1 Proxy Labeling Scheme

At the heart of our definition of segment membership is the *indicator set*, or the set of websites (*indicator sites*) and departments (*indicator departments*) deemed relevant to the descriptive segment. For example, a Luxury segment member might be relatively likely to visit a *haute couture* website or the fine jewelry page of a department store website. The indicator set should span the shopping domain of the typical segment member.

Candidates for inclusion in the indicator set are initially drawn from marketing intuition but may extend to sites and departments found during, say, searches for relevant substrings in site and department titles.

Cookies with a history of activity in the indicator set are candidates for segment membership. A minimum *threshold* is defined that can be set in order to vary the strictness of the labeling criteria, i.e., cookies who have visited at least *threshold* distinct indicator sites (including parent sites of indicator departments) receive a positive label. In general, one would expect that higher thresholds result in a smaller but more precise set of positive labels.

The indicator set criterion can be supplemented by demographic criteria if such data are available. For example, an augmented labeling scheme might select as positives those cookies who meet the indicator set criteria *and* fall within a certain desired demographic.

2.2 Ruleset Generation

A supervised binary classification algorithm is needed to create a rule-based model as described. Initially, we considered an association rule approach for itemset discovery and subsequent mapping to descriptive segments; in fact, the Apriori algorithm [2] was run on some preliminary trial data, but found to be inappropriate to the problem, since a) we're defining the segments up front and wish to model them explicitly, and b) Apriori seeks to discover all itemsets satisfying a set of minimum coverage and accuracy requirements, which turns out to be rather memory intensive past a certain modest data set size (~10,000 examples).

The definitive algorithm for this task is the RIPPER algorithm [6]. RIPPER is a supervised binary classification algorithm that generates DNF rulesets. During training, RIPPER iteratively grows and prunes a set of rules in order to maximize coverage of the minority class on a *grow* fold of the training data while minimizing classification error on a *prune* fold; an optimization phase then replaces and revises underperforming rules. RIPPER has been shown to be robust and fairly efficient. Our work utilizes JRip, the Weka [9] implementation of RIPPER.

2.3 Performance Metrics

In addition to good prediction performance on the test dataset, the rulesets generated should satisfy a set of business requirements.

2.3.1 Prediction Performance

The typical metrics derived from the confusion matrix serve as our benchmarks. We mainly consider true-positive-rate (TPR) and false-positive-rate (FPR) on the test data:

$$TPR = \frac{\text{\# positives selected (true positives)}}{\text{\# positives}}$$

$$FPR = \frac{\text{\# negatives selected (false positives)}}{\text{\# negatives}}$$

TPR should significantly exceed FPR, an indication of preferential selection of actual positive examples over negatives:

$$require\ TPR >> FPR$$

An (FPR, TPR) duple maps to a point on an ROC curve. Thus, when TPR >> FPR, the model identifies positives better than random selection. (If we were able to vary the strictness of selection by a ruleset, we could sweep out an entire ROC curve; unfortunately for rulesets, selection is boolean and this is not the case.)

Over the population as a whole, the marketing department will find targeting precision and reach to be of most interest, where

$$precision = \frac{\#\,true\ positives}{\#\,selected}$$

serves as the "accuracy" measurement, and reach is simply the number of cookies selected for membership in the descriptive segment.

We find it helpful to compute the *normalized* precision, or *gain*, relative to the baseline precision of the random selection method, which simply equals the frequency of the positive class in the population, or *response rate*:

$$gain = \frac{precision}{response\ rate}$$

2.3.2 *Precision vs. Reach Trade-off*

Depending on the descriptive advertising campaign, the focus might be on precise targeting or extensive reach or some of both. In general, the two are mutually exclusive: to increase reach, you must select less suitable cookies, which decreases precision.

Therefore, it is important to provide a way to tune the precision/reach trade-off. Unfortunately, rulesets perform a binary selection; thus, there is no segment membership score that can be thresholded to vary the selection. This is addressed by generating multiple rulesets with varying precision and reach statistics; it is then up to the marketing department which ruleset they shall use.

2.3.3 *Rule Overlap*

Because of legacy constraints on the way descriptive segments are operationalized, it is important that the number of rules that fire for a typical cookie not exceed one or two (preferably one); multiple rules firing means multiple campaign treatments for that cookie. By matching one cookie with multiple rules, there can be unintended negative consequences; e.g., the daily limit on ad impressions for that cookie may be exceeded, causing them to saturate on ad creative and thus become unresponsive; and decreased reach as ad impressions intended for distinct viewers are exhausted on repeat impressions to the same people.

We have no direct control over rule overlap, although RIPPER rulesets generally begin with large-coverage rules followed by additional, smaller-coverage rules that fill in the gaps. Therefore, we check overlap of all rulesets to verify that this requirement is satisfied.

2.3.4 *Intuitive Appeal*

Just as the indicator set is based on subjective descriptive criteria, so must every ruleset pass intuitive muster by discovering behaviors typical of the (intended) members of that segment, and hopefully avoiding any that are contraindicated.

3. METHODOLOGY

3.1 Data Sources

A data set of 20 million browser cookies and their browsing history was drawn randomly from the (much larger) overall population. The bulk of the modeling effort focused on this data.

In addition, an independent, anonymous subset of roughly 280,000 cookies and their browsing history was associated with a small set of demographic features (procured from an external source and joined to our data via an automated cookie-matching process). Separate modeling runs involving demographically-enhanced positive definitions were thus possible.

Browsing history was redacted for all sites and departments opting to exclude their data from analysis.

3.2 Definition of Positives

Five descriptive segments of interest were modeled, each of a different type: Brides-To-Be, Moms-With-Kids, Luxury, Trend-setters, and College Students.

3.2.1 *Indicator Set Selection*

For each descriptive segment, an indicator set was selected based initially on marketing expertise and then extended and filtered based on various methods.

For each of the marketing indicator sites, cosine similarity was computed for every other site in the network (based on co-occurrence of visitors), with the most similar sites also considered for indicator set membership based on visitor volume and relevance to the descriptive segment.

Sets of terms related to the descriptive segment concept were enumerated (e.g., "kids", "wedding", "diamond") and used to perform substring matching on the names of sites and departments; matching sites and departments were added to the indicator set depending on visitor volume.

Finally, sites and departments whose data was excluded from analysis were removed from the indicator sets.

3.2.2 *Threshold Variation*

Positives were defined for various threshold values, creating a range of strictness criteria for labeling. Threshold values typically ran from 1 through 3 or 4 depending on the descriptive segment.

3.2.3 *Enhancement Using Demographic Data*

Demographic age range data was used to enhance the positive definition for the College Students descriptive segment. An additional criterion – Age between 18 and 24 – was added to the indicator site criterion. The smaller demographic dataset was thus labeled for generation of College Students rulesets.

A purely demographic Moms-With-Kids positive definition was constructed from Age, Gender, and Child-In-Household features. This labeling was applied to the demographic dataset for generation of Moms-With-Kids rulesets. Positives met the criteria of Age between 20 and 49 + Gender = Female + Child-In-Household = True; negatives were those for whom feature values were available but who failed one or more criteria; the remaining cookies were ignored for training purposes.

3.3 Modeling Procedure

3.3.1 *Down-Sampling*

After proxy labeling the datasets, the data was down-sampled in order to reduce total dataset size and to bring the number of negatives closer to the number of positives.

It was observed that large variations in down-sampling ratios (neg:pos) can affect ruleset size, as larger ratios afford more opportunity to prune rules, resulting in smaller, more precise rulesets.

Higher down-sampling ratios were generally allowed for higher (i.e., stricter) thresholds where the number of positives was generally low, thus magnifying the precision of the resulting rulesets.

For lower thresholds, the down-sampling ratio was automatically lowered by the algorithm in order to control the total dataset size and to increase reach.

In all cases, the number of positives was forced to be less than the number of negatives, so that the positive class remained the minority class for purposes of modeling with RIPPER. Thus, the down-sampling ratio never fell below 1.0.

3.3.2 Feature Set Preparation

The feature set consisted of ~20,000 sites and departments possibly having been visited, with the exception of those that were opted-out of analytics use.

Site and department features (and their children) appearing in the indicator set were stricken from the feature set.

Finally, the feature set was reduced to the top 1000 features ranking highest in terms of InfoGain score. (This was performed by Weka.)

3.3.3 RIPPER Modeling in Weka

The down-sampled dataset was passed to Weka for JRip ruleset generation. All parameters were left at their default values, except for "Tweights" (the minimum allowed coverage for a rule) which was varied automatically by the outer modeling loop until a ruleset having between 7-10 rules was found.

Weka applied a stratified 2/1 train/test split to the data and returned train and test performance statistics.

3.3.4 Generation of Multiple Rulesets

Multiple rulesets were generated for the current descriptive segment with the goal of providing a range of precision and reach options. An outer loop varied the pre-specified thresholds, whereas down-sampling ratios were varied automatically (as described previously). In a few trials, the pre-defined indicator sets were iteratively augmented with newly "discovered" sites/departments from the latest ruleset to generate the next ruleset, stopping when gain fell too low or reach stopped increasing sufficiently.

Added to each ruleset was a "Rule 0", equivalent to a positive definition based on the ruleset's indicator set with a threshold of 1. This is a necessary addition prior to production, since the rulesets as generated will never have perfect recall, yet we do not want to exclude any labeled positives from the descriptive segment.

3.4 Performance Measurement

TPR >> FPR was checked for the Weka test split of every ruleset to ensure good discrimination between positives and negatives.

The rulesets were "sniff tested" for intuitive appeal by looking for newly discovered behaviors typical of the descriptive segment and verifying that no suspicious rules had been created. Rulesets were also verified to be between 7-10 rules.

The rulesets were applied to the entire 20 million-cookie datasets; TPR and FPR were confirmed to be approximately equal to those for the Weka test split. Performance statistics were extrapolated upwards to the entire large population, and gain and reach computed for each ruleset. The set of rulesets was confirmed to provide a range of precision/reach trade-off options.

Rule overlap was computed for each ruleset, confirming that the large majority of cookies fired only one or two rules per ruleset.

4. RESULTS

4.1 Proxy Labeling Using Demographic Data

4.1.1 Pure Demographic Ground Truth

The Moms-With-Kids indicator set-based rulesets were compared with that segment's demographic-based ruleset, which can be viewed as a best-case ruleset having been trained on approximate ground truth data.

In terms of TPR and FPR on the demographic ground truth data, performance was only slightly worse than best-case for the lower-precision rulesets, i.e., those generated from threshold values of 1 and 2 (Table 1):

Table 1. Comparison of Low-precision vs. Best-Case

Ruleset	TPR	FPR
thresh = 1	47.20%	38.93%
thresh = 2	43.53%	35.60%
best-case	44.45%	30.21%

Specifically, the threshold (1,2) indicator set-based rulesets had comparable TPR but somewhat elevated FPR, suggesting that, at least for this segment, the indicator set was a reasonable proxy for ground truth as long as it was not too strictly applied.

For the threshold (3,4) rulesets, both TPR and FPR fell significantly, revealing that it was unrealistic to expect those segment members to have visited that many distinct indicator sites (Table 2):

Table 2. Comparison of High-precision vs. Best-Case

Ruleset	TPR	FPR
thresh = 4	3.34%	1.73%
thresh = 3	7.71%	5.56%
best-case	44.45%	30.21%

When applied to the indicator set-based data, the demographic ruleset showed significantly higher reach than the indicator set-based rulesets (Table 3):

Table 3. Comparison of Low-precision vs. Best-Case. Reach is normalized.

Ruleset	Reach
thresh = 2	1.00
thresh = 1	2.04
best-case	4.28

This supports the suspicion that reach may be fundamentally limited by indicator set visitor volume, whereas ground truth labeling does not suffer from this effect.

4.1.2 Demographically Enhanced Proxy Labeling

The addition of the demographic age range criterion to the College Students indicator set-based labeling scheme appears to have shifted the precision vs. reach trade-off towards higher precision (Table 4):

Table 4. Adding Age Criterion Effect on Precision/Reach. Reach is normalized.

	no Age-range	w/Age-range
Reach	1.46	1.00
Precision	48.4%	54.2%
Gain	15.8	17.6

This should be expected, since the additional demographic criterion makes for a stricter positive definition.

4.1.3 True Positive Rate vs. False Positive Rate

For all descriptive segments, we observed that TPR >> FPR for the Weka test splits for all proxy labeled rulesets, indicating a high degree of discrimination between positive and negative examples. For the Brides-To-Be segment (Table 5):

Table 5. TPR >> FPR on Weka Test Split

	TPR (Weka)	FPR (Weka)
Ruleset 1	50.30%	0.30%
Ruleset 2	57.60%	0.80%
Ruleset 3	52.30%	2.40%
Ruleset 4	72.30%	7.70%

This pattern persisted when the rulesets were applied to the full non-down-sampled set of 20 million examples (Table 6):

Table 6. TPR >> FPR on Population

	TPR (population)	FPR (population)
Ruleset 1	46.45%	0.15%
Ruleset 2	53.69%	0.32%
Ruleset 3	44.56%	0.79%
Ruleset 4	59.93%	2.63%

However, the difference in TPR and FPR was much less pronounced whenever the Moms-With-Kids ground truth-labeling was used either as the training data for the ruleset (Table 7) or as the test data for any of the rulesets (cf. Tables 1 and 2).

Table 7. Ground Truth Ruleset Applied to Indicator Set Test Data

Test Data	TPR	FPR
threshold = 4	61.27%	10.26%
threshold = 3	58.91%	10.25%
threshold = 2	52.03%	10.21%
threshold = 1	22.07%	10.07%

It would appear that the ground truth-agnostic case (where a ruleset trained on proxy labeled positives is evaluated on proxy labeled test data) is an easier problem than either a) selecting proxy labeled positives using a ruleset trained on ground truth, or b) selecting ground truth positives using either type of ruleset.

4.1.4 Precision vs. Reach

For each descriptive segment, it was possible to generate multiple rulesets exhibiting a range of precision and reach when applied to the entire population. As expected, high precision was associated with low reach and vice versa. For the Brides-To-Be segment, for example, precision and reach were varied by using different combinations of threshold and down-sampling ratio (Table 8):

Table 8. Precision vs. Reach in Brides-To-Be Rulesets

Brides-To-Be	Ruleset 1	Ruleset 2	Ruleset 3	Ruleset 4
Threshold	3	3	2	2
Down-Ratio	50	20	5	2
Reach Ratio	1.0	2.1	5.1	17.3
Precision	7.89%	4.60%	2.41%	0.99%
Gain	180.2	104.9	54.9	22.6

Reach is defined as the number of users matching the segment with a given ruleset. We use the first ruleset as the baseline, and give reach relative to it.

The higher threshold (3) results in higher precision and reduced reach. For a given threshold, the higher down-sampling ratio makes more negatives available to be used in pruning and therefore increases precision and reduces reach also. (Precision is computed for the dataset where threshold = 2 and down-sampling ratio = 2.)

For Luxury, precision and reach tend to behave similarly as threshold and down-sampling ratio are varied; for some reason, however, threshold = 4 actually becomes *less* precise (Table 9):

Table 9. Precision vs. Reach in Luxury Rulesets

Luxury	Ruleset 1	Ruleset 2	Ruleset 3	Ruleset 4
Threshold	4	3	2	1
Down-Ratio	50	50	8.5	1
Reach	1.0	0.69	4.6	21.0
Precision	43.29%	51.27%	23.33%	8.34%
Gain	23.3	27.5	12.5	4.5

Regardless of segment, reach becomes difficult to increase beyond a certain point where threshold = 1, down-ratio is small, and the indicator set is using all available relevant sites and departments.

4.1.5 Rule Overlap

For all rulesets, multiple rules tend not to fire for the vast majority of cookies. A typical distribution of #rules-fired for a ruleset shows that ~80% of cookies fire only a single rule (Figure 1):

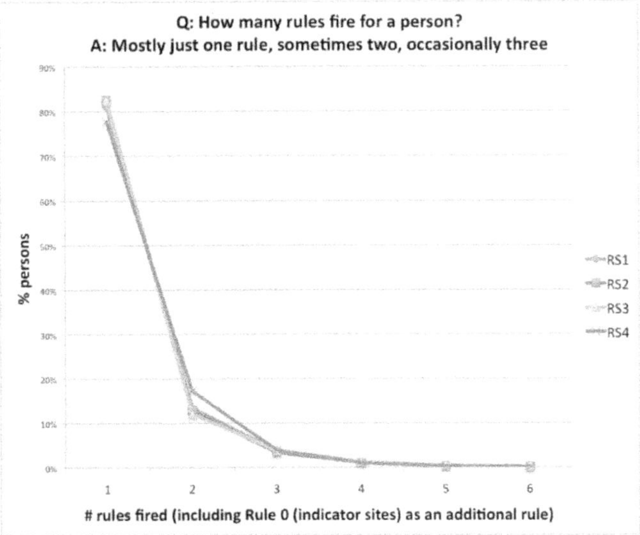

Figure 1. Rule overlap is minimal

4.1.6 Intuitive Ruleset Appeal

The degree to which the rulesets made intuitive sense varied across descriptive segments.

For the Brides-To-Be and Moms-With-Kids segments, at least some of the rules could be interpreted as behaviors expected from members of the descriptive segment. In particular, their more precise rulesets found relevant sites and departments that weren't included in the indicator set, or combinations of sites and departments that characterized a relevant behavior. This was less true for the lower precision rulesets, as more of the rules "cast a wide net" by selecting from sites that weren't strongly relevant to the segment, but weren't irrelevant either.

The most precise ruleset for Brides-To-Be appears to describe shopping for invitations, floral arrangements, and wedding favors; there's even a rule for bride who is adding housewares to her registry (Table 10).

Table 10. Ruleset for Brides-To-Be (Rule 0 = indicator set)

Rule	Antecedents
0	Crafts-Hobbies-1, Speciality-and-Gifts-8, Seasonal-1
1	Personalized-Gift-Site-1 ∧ Housewares-1
2	Housewares-1 ∧ Digital-Printing-4:10 Great Product Offers
3	Housewares-1:Tabletop ∧ ¬Housewares-1:Gift Registry
4	Personalized-Gift-Site-1:Home page
5	Digital-Printing-3 ∧ Housewares-1
6	Flowers-Gifts-1 ∧ Digital-Printing-4
7	Department-Store-1:Classic Collections ∧ Housewares-1:Furniture
8	Housewares-1: Search ∧ Housewares-1: Gift Registry ∧ Housewares-1: Home page
9	Digital-Printing-4: Any page ∧ Digital-Printing-3: Home page

This indicator set for Brides-To-Be contains three very strongly wedding-oriented sites; this situation is somewhat ideal.

The indicator set for the Moms-With-Kids descriptive segment is likewise composed of relevant kid-oriented sites. In this case, we had more sites to select into the indicator set. The resulting ruleset discovers some kid-related departments, and contains rules for moms who are shopping for personalized items that aren't business cards, and moms who are shopping for health and wellness items (Table 11).

Table 11. Moms-With-Kids Ruleset (Rule 0 = indicator set)

Rule	Antecedents
0	Toys-1, Digital-Printing-2, Kids-Clothing-1, Toys-2, Toys-3, Kids-Gear-1, Furniture-1, Kids-Gear-2, Speciality-and-Gifts-1, Kids-Clothing-2
1	Housewares-1: Home Page
2	Clothing-1 ∧ Shoes-1: Home Page
3	Clothing-2: Home page
4	Clothing-1: Girls
5	Housewares-1 ∧ Digital-Printing-4
6	Clothing-3: Kids
7	Clothing-1: Boys
8	Shoes-1: Home page ∧ Department-Store-1
9	Personalized-Gift-Site-2 ∧ Digital-Printing-4 ∧ ¬Digital-Printing-4:Business Cards
10	Health-and-Wellness-1 ∧ ¬Health-and-Wellness-2: Home page

Keep in mind that the indicator set elements are excluded from the feature set, so ruleset generation is restricted to building rules from a less richly relevant set of features.

For the ground truth-labeled Moms-With-Kids examples, all sites and segments are included in the feature set. Two of the indicator sites are discovered when training with demographic data and a common clothing brand (Table 12), but overall many of the rules differ.

This suggests that ground truth demographic data for Moms-with-Kids leads to different shopping behavior than our Platonic Concept of a Mom-with-Kid, who shops for children's clothing and toys. Both had similar precision, when evaluated on the demographic data, but focus on different parts of the space. It calls into question whether we should be marketing to the true demographic or the population whose shopping patterns we wish to target.

Note rules 12 and 13 in the demographic based ruleset for Moms-With-Kids in Table 11. Negations are included for Home Improvement and Electronics, perhaps ruling out Dads or Handy-Moms. On the other hand, the indicator site method does not exclude these patterns – shopping for children's items is sufficient.

The concept behind the Luxury descriptive segment is somewhat diffuse; consequently, applying the indicator set method to this segment was more problematic, as "luxurious" behavior can take many different forms.

Table 12. Moms-With-Kids Ruleset (Ground Truth)

Rule	Antecedents
1	Clothing-2
2	Telecom-1
3	Kids-Clothing-1
4	Clothing-4
5	Clothing-5
6	Shoes-2
7	Fast-Food-1
8	Automotive-1 ∧ ¬Home-Improvement-1 ∧ ¬Specialty-and-Gifts-2
9	Clothing-6 ∧ ¬Specialty-and-Gifts-2
10	Clothing-14 ∧ ¬Specialty-and-Gifts-2
11	Toys-3 ∧ ¬Specialty-and-Gifts-2
12	Toys-1 ∧ ¬Electronics-1 ∧ ¬Specialty-and-Gifts-2 ∧ ¬Home-Improvement-1
13	Department-Store-3 ∧ ¬Home-Improvement-1 ∧ ¬Electronics-2 ∧ ¬Clothing-1 ∧ ¬Specialty-and-Gifts-2

The highest-precision ruleset for Luxury discovers a few departments that are vaguely indicative of extravagance or expensiveness (Table 13); perhaps the nicest surprise is the exclusion of shoppers at Clothing-6:Apartment (a youthful budget-oriented site) from Rule 5. However, the ruleset as a whole isn't as convincing as those for Brides-To-Be or Moms-With-Kids (Table 4).

Table 13. Luxury Ruleset (Rule 0 = indicator set)

Rule	Antecedents
0	Cosmetics-1, Speciality-and-Gifts-4, Shoes-5, Speciality-and-Gifts-5, Speciality-and-Gfts-6, Clothing-9, Speciality-and-Gifts-7, Clothing-10, Clothing-11, Clothing-12, Department-Store-2
1	Department-Store-1:Sales & Values
2	Housewares-1:Check out
3	Department-Store-1: Jewelry
4	Clothing-6 ∧ Shoes-4
5	Clothing-6 ∧ Department-Store-1 ∧ ¬Clothing-6:Apartment
6	Clothing-7 ∧ Shoes-3
7	Clothing-13 ∧ Housewares-1
8	Department-Store-1 ∧ Clothing-7
9	Clothing-8
10	Housewares-2:Gifts

The College Students segment and the Trend-setters segment yield similarly vague but not entirely off-the-mark rulesets.

5. DISCUSSION

5.1 Successes

5.1.1 Performance Metrics

Given our method for generating proxy labels for the training and test data, the remainder of the model building process has been fairly successful in terms of the prediction performance of the rulesets that were generated. All rulesets rated well in terms of TPR >> FPR and small ruleset overlap. We generated rulesets of the desired size and provided multiple rulesets per descriptive segment so that a choice of precision vs. reach was available.

5.1.2 Validation on "Ground Truth"

We were able to validate that, for the Moms-With-Kids segment, some of the rulesets created using the indicator set positive criteria performed almost as well on approximate ground truth labeled data as did the "best-case" ruleset that was trained on the same type of data.

5.2 Shortcomings

5.2.1 Upper Limit on Reach

Maximum reach for each ruleset was gotten by reducing the threshold and down-sampling ratio to their most lenient values. Beyond that, this method only allows reach to be increased by either making the rulesets larger (i.e., increasing the maximum allowed number of rules) or by increasing the size of the indicator set (to create more positives).

Increasing the maximum ruleset size was not an option; however, some attempts were made to increase indicator set size both manually and automatically (by adding discovered sites and departments in rulesets to the indicator set), but the affects on reach were small.

It may be that, if indeed there are more ground truth positives in the population than we are finding, our method is fundamentally limited by the numbers of visitors to the relevant websites. This would be especially true for descriptive segments that are less behaviorally oriented towards on-line shopping, or at least to the categories of e-commerce sites appearing in our network.

5.2.2 Believability of Rulesets

Despite the good predictive performance of the rulesets on the labeled data, the bottom line of this exercise is whether or not the rulesets are selecting ground truth positives. The scenario as postulated precludes ever knowing for sure, at least until the rulesets are operationalized and other streams of performance data are created. In the absence of any approximate ground truth to help validate future rulesets, a subjective assessment of the rulesets themselves will hold much weight.

As we have seen, some descriptive segments received unsuprising rulesets and some did not. It must be reiterated that a surprising ruleset does not necessarily indicate an invalid one – Luxury shoppers may indeed pay frequent visits to the somewhat more down-market Shoes-4 and Shoes-3; but this subjective assessment may in fact determine whether a ruleset is accepted by marketing for production. In the end, we must *believe* in our solution.

6. FUTURE WORK

The several challenges encountered during this exercise may be remedied somewhat by some different approaches to the problem.

6.1 Alternative Labeling Schemes

The way in which indicator sets were created and used to label examples could be improved.

6.1.1 Categorized Indicator Sets

Indicator sets would be chosen as before but categorized; thresholding would be employed across the categories to require that shopping behavior span a number of categories.

6.1.2 Weighting of Examples

In addition to assigning a binary class to each example, a weight could also be assigned based on the degree to which the example satisfies the selection criteria. For example, the number of indicator sites a cookie has visited could serve as the weight.

The RIPPER algorithm in Weka allows training with weighted examples; rule coverage is computed as the sum of the weights of the examples that fire the rule. Consequently, examples that were more confidently labeled as positives and negatives would drive ruleset creation.

6.2 Extending the Set of Positives

Increasing reach will probably involve increasing the number of positive examples in the data.

6.2.1 Iterative Labeling by Ruleset Positives

Using the current indicator set approach for initial labeling, generate a ruleset. Next, redefine the set of labeled positives in the data as the union of the existing positives and the ruleset positives. Generate another ruleset and repeat. Stop when reach is sufficiently high or precision falls too low. Start with a bootstrap indicator set that is conservative and precise.

7. CONCLUSIONS

We have shown that shopping data is a reasonable proxy for demographic and behavioral data for the task of identifying customer segments for marketing. For computational efficiency, RIPPER is a more appropriate tool than Apriori, when our task is to learn DNF rules for a pre-defined target. We also find that when evaluated against ground truth demographic data, our rules trained on positives labeled with shopping data have similar true and false positive rates. We may learn an interesting lesson when we look at the details of rules learned, and contrast rules learned from demographic training data with rules trained on shopping positives: the demographic data may indeed focus a little too precisely on the technical definition of segment membership, while shopping data allows us to find others with similar shopping behavior, even if their demographics step outside stereotypes.

8. ACKNOWLEDGMENTS

Thanks to Brian Mancuso for help with data processing. Thanks also go out to our friends on the sales and marketing side: Avi Spivack, Amy Deneson, and Kym Insana. Special thanks to Danner Stodolsky for brainstorming and feedback.

9. REFERENCES

[1] Maria M. Abad-Grau, Maria Tajtakova, Daniel Arias-Aranda. 2009. Machine Learning Methods for the Market Segmentation of the Performing Arts Audiences. *International Journal of Business Environment, Volume 2, Number 3 / 2009.* 356-375.

[2] ADS Descriptive Segments. Akamai Technologies, Advertising Decision Systems. http://www.akamai.com/html/solutions/ads_descriptive_segments.html

[3] Rakesh Agrawal, Ramakrishnan Srikant. 1994. Fast Algorithms for Mining Association Rules in Large Databases. *Proceedings of the 20th International Conference on Very Large Databases.* 487-499.

[4] Akamai Technologies Privacy Policy. http://www.akamai.com/html/policies/index.html

[5] A. G. Büchner, M. D. Mulvenna. 1998. Discovering Internet Marketing Intelligence Through Online Analytical Web Usage Mining. *ACM SIGMOD Record (special issue on electronic commerce), ISSN 0163-5808, 27(4).* 54-61.

[6] William W. Cohen. 1995. Fast Effective Rule Induction. *International Conference on Machine Learning, 1995.* 115-123.

[7] Jorge Díez, Juan José Del Coz, Carlos Sañudo, Pere Albertí, Antonio Bahamonde. 2005. A Kernel Based Method for Discovering Market Segments in Beef Meat. *Proceedings of the 16th European Conference on Machine Learning – 9th European Conference on Principles and Practice of Knowledge Discovery in Databases, ECML/PKDD 2005.* 462-469.

[8] Raquel Florez-Lopez, Juan Manuel Ramon-Jeronimo. 2009. Marketing Segmentation Through Machine Learning Models: An Approach Based on Customer Relationship Management and Customer Profitability Accounting. *Social Science Computer Review (2009), Volume 27, Issue 1.* 96-117.

[9] Mark Hall, Eibe Frank, Geoffrey Holmes, Bernhard Pfahringer, Peter Reutemann, Ian H. Witten. 2009. The WEKA Data Mining Software: An Update. *SIGKDD Explorations, Volume 11, Issue 1.*

[10] D. Iacobucci, P. Arabie, A. Bodapati. 2000. Recommendation Agents on the Internet. *Journal of Interactive Marketing, 14(3), Summer.* 2-11.

[11] Perlich, C., and Z. Huang. Relational Learning for Customer Relationship Management. *International Workshop on Customer Relationship Management: Data Mining Meets Marketing.* NYU 2005

Ameliorating Buyer's Remorse

Rakesh Agrawal
Search Labs
Microsoft Research
rakesha@microsoft.com

Samuel Ieong
Search Labs
Microsoft Research
saieong@microsoft.com

Raja Velu*
School of Management
Syracuse University
rpvelu@syr.edu

ABSTRACT

Keeping in pace with the increasing importance of commerce conducted over the Web, several e-commerce websites now provide admirable facilities for helping consumers decide *what* product to buy and *where* to buy it. However, since the prices of durable and high-tech products generally fall over time, a buyer of such products is often faced with a dilemma: Should she buy the product now or wait for cheaper prices?

We present the design and implementation of Prodcast, an experimental system whose goal is to help consumers decide *when* to buy a product. The system makes use of forecasts of future prices based on price histories of the products, incorporating features such as sales volume, seasonality, and competition in making its recommendation. We describe techniques that are well-suited for this task and present a comprehensive evaluation of their relative merits using retail sales data for electronic products. Our back-testing of the system indicates that the system is capable of helping consumers time their purchase, resulting in significant savings to them.

Categories and Subject Descriptors

H.2.8 [**Database Management**]: Database Applications—*Data Mining*; J.4 [**Social and Behavioral Sciences**]: Economics

General Terms

Experimentation, Algorithms, Economics

Keywords

Forecasting, Recommendation, Prodcast

---

*Work done while author was visiting Search Labs.

KDD'11, August 21–24, 2011, San Diego, California, USA.

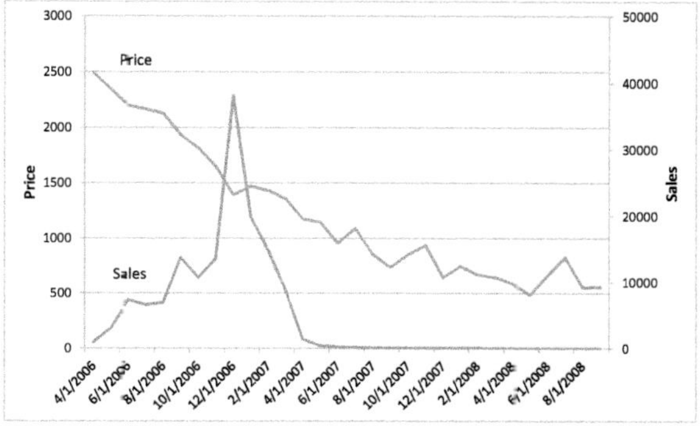

(a) Price & sales history of Samsung LCD TV LN4051D

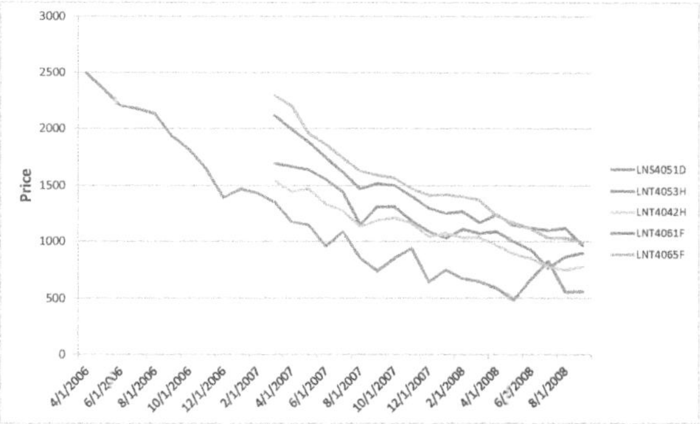

(b) Prices of comparable Samsung LCD TVs

Figure 1: Price and sales data of Samsung LCD TVs (Source: NPD)

1. INTRODUCTION

The prices of durable and high-tech products generally fall over time as firms continually introduce products that have enhanced features [13, 17]. As an illustration of how product prices evolve, let us consider the category of LCD TVs, and focus on the TVs made by Samsung between 2006 and 2008. Figure 1(a) shows the price and sales of a particular model, LNS4051D (40 inch Widescreen LCD HDTV). This product first appeared in the market in April 2006. Its sales first increased, peaking in December 2006, and then decreased rapidly until Spring when new models were introduced. Meanwhile, its price declined steadily. The price histories of five comparable models of TVs made by Samsung are shown in Figure 1(b). They also demonstrate similar declining trend.

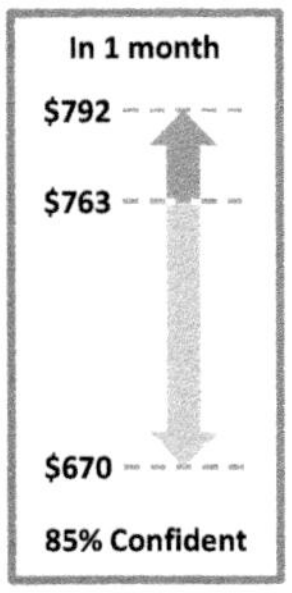

Figure 2: Presenting forecasts to Consumers

Buyers of durable products often suffer from a sense of regret after having made a purchase. While the origin of this remorse can be traced to various factors [5], buyers often agonize whether they could have bought the product for a cheaper price just by waiting for some time. The low-price guarantees advertised by merchants are of little avail because of the loop holes and the hassle costs associated with enforcing the compliance [9].

We present a system that we call Prodcast, which has been designed to ameliorate buyer's remorse by providing expected price movement information to a consumer interested in buying a particular product. The system forecasts future prices based on price history of the product, incorporating factors such as sales volume, seasonality, and competitive products. This information is encapsulated and presented to the user in the form of a widget as illustrated in Figure 2.

This schematic allows a consumer to learn not only about the direction of future price change, but also distributional aspects of the change. These are important information especially in the context of consumer durables, as prices generally exhibit a downward trend, and the key to making good timing decisions is in knowing the magnitude and likelihood of the change. In this specific example, the current price of the product is at $763. In one month's time, the system is 85% certain that prices will be between $670 and $792, with the likelihood of a price drop outweighing potential price increase by about 3-to-1.

We describe techniques that are well-suited for this application domain and present a comprehensive evaluation of their relative merits using retail sales data for electronic products. Our back-testing of the system indicates that the system is capable of helping consumers time their purchase, resulting in significant savings to them.

The rest of the paper is organized as follows. We begin with a discussion of related work in Section 2. In Section 3, we give an overview of the architecture of Prodcast, and discuss how the system is evaluated. Focusing on the question of how best to forecast future product prices, we describe a number of methods that we considered in our evaluation in Section 4. We present a large-scale experiment using real-life data to compare the performances of these methods in Section 5. We conclude with the main insights gained from the experiments in Section 6.

2. RELATED WORK

The inspiration for Prodcast came from the the pioneering work of Etzioni *et al.* for making wait or buy recommendation for airline tickets [8]. The authors develop models to forecast airfare and make recommendations once the consumer reveals the travel date and the points of origin and destination. Price data for particular flights was gathered from the web, and features such as number of hours until departure and the current prices are extracted from the raw data. Various data mining algorithms including Rule Learning, Q-Learning and time series methods are applied to mine the data. The quality of the predictive models is evaluated by quantifying the savings that each model would generate. While all the methods resulted in net savings, a model that combines the forecasts made by the various methods produced maximum savings.

There is a crucial difference in the nature of durable products and airline tickets that makes the two problems very different. In the case of a durable product, a user derives utility from owning and using the product over time, hence if a user defers the purchase, she suffers a *loss of use* while waiting. This cost must be factored into the decision. In contrast, a user derives utility from using an airline ticket for travel. There is no loss in utility if a user obtains the ticket now or later, provided that the ticket is obtained prior to the date of travel. Hence, the problem of deciding when to buy a ticket depends only on whether prices are likely to increase or decrease, whereas the problem of deciding when to buy a durable good depends also on the speed and the magnitude of the changes, as trade-offs between potential price drops and loss of use are made.

Few websites tackle the problem of helping consumers with deciding when to purchase consumer durables. The site Nextag provides just a price history and the current prices with various vendors. A recent site, Gazaro, provides price history for consumer durables and advocates when a product is ready to be purchased. Based on description from its website, its methodology considers factors such as competition, volatility, and price trends from both online and brick and mortar retailers. The problem it addresses is closer in spirit to ours. However, there is no published paper on the techniques or the quality of the recommendations.

There has been a number of studies in the marketing literature on how product prices evolve over time. These studies typically examine the question from the viewpoints of the manufacturers. Prices are believed to evolve in a way related to the lifecycle of a product. The theory of experience curves states that the unit cost of production declines over time as a manufacturer gains experience in the production of a product, and the relationship is non-linear. This model has been successfully applied to model electronic goods prices in [6]. However, the analysis was at a category level and do not directly apply to our setting as our focus is on price evolution at a product level. There has also been work that combines experience curves with demand models [7]. For a review of pricing research in marketing, see [14, 15].

In summary, existing work in marketing research provides evidence that product prices do not behave like random walks, but rather follow definite patterns that depend on the product lifecycles. We believe that by considering prices, sales, and competition, we should be able to produce good price forecasts that can help consumers make more informed decisions on when to buy a product.

There is a large body of related work in statistics on forecasting methods. The classical approach is based on time-series analysis [2]. More recently, Hyndman *et al.* have achieved much success on data sets from forecasting com-

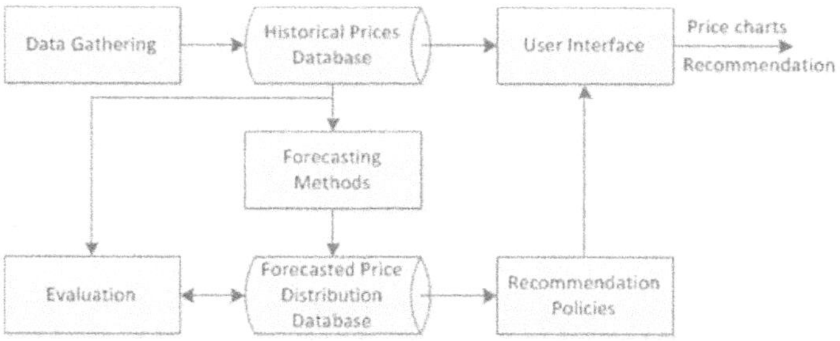

Figure 3: Overview of the Prodcast system

petitions (known as the M-competitions [11]) based on a smoothing-based approach [10]. We compare a number of methods that utilize these approaches in this paper, investigate to what extents product prices can be predicted, and find out what additional information can help with the prediction.

3. SYSTEM DESIGN

We provide an overview of the Prodcast system in Figure 3. The system consists of five major components:

Data Gathering. The data gathering component is responsible for collecting product prices and other information that can help with predicting price changes such as sales volume data. Our present implementation is based on data feeds, and performs basic outlier detection to identify potential data entry errors. An alternative implementation could obtain price data by scraping e-commerce retailer websites. The resulting data are stored in a historical prices database.

Forecasting Methods. The forecasting component is responsible for making forecasts of future prices based on the data gathered about the products. The methods take as input price histories and other information such as sales volume, and produces a distribution over future prices. The results are stored in a forecasted price distribution database, both for evaluation and as an input to the recommendation policies. We focus on this component in this paper, describe a number of methods for this problem and conduct a systematic evaluation of these methods over a real-life data set.

Recommendation Policies. The recommendation component is responsible for making buy-or-wait recommendations to the users based on the forecasted price distribution and user preference parameters. This is a component separate from the forecasting component, as given the same forecasts, the recommendation may be different depending on the user preferences.

User Interface. The user interface component is responsible for providing users with price-related information of the product. In response to a query for a product, the component renders a price chart depicting the price history of the product, and also produces a graphical display of the forecast prices as illustrated in Figure 2. For user interested in receiving a customized recommendation for when to buy the product, the interface further elicits certain preference parameters and provides those as input to the recommendation policies, which can then act as a service that alerts the user when to buy the product.

Evaluation. The evaluation component is responsible for running periodic evaluation of the forecasting methods, and keeping track of their historical performances. It makes use of the archive data, splits them into training and test sets, and measures the performance of the system. It helps to select the best method for predicting prices for each product.

3.1 Problem Description

Consider a consumer who has selected a particular durable product to buy, and is deciding whether to purchase the product now or at a future time period. The consumer is described by two parameters: a value θ that measures her utility for the product, and a value λ that captures her *loss of use* of the product while she waits. If she purchases the product now, she gains a utility of θ; if she purchases in the future time period, she gains a utility of $(\theta - \lambda)$. The loss of use parameter captures the important characteristic of durable products that they provide value to the consumers over their lifetime. Its introduction presents a trade-off between buying now and waiting that was not captured by past work in the domain of airfare and tickets.

Let the current price of the product be p. If we know the price of the product in the future time period, say p', the problem would be simple. We can simply compare between the net utility of buying the product now, $(\theta - p)$, and that of buying in the future, $(\theta - \lambda - p')$, and choose accordingly based on which value is higher. The problem is that we do not know the future price. The role of the forecasting methods is to make use of historical data to make forecasts of the future price.

Let the historical prices of the product be $\mathbf{p}$, and other relevant historical data, such as sales and competition, be $\mathbf{S}$. We define the recommendation problem as follows.

Definition 1 (Buy-or-wait Recommendation Problem)**.** Given consumer parameters θ and λ, the current price of the product p, and historical data $\mathbf{p}$ and $\mathbf{S}$, recommend to the consumer whether she should buy the product now or wait to buy it in the future period.

Given historical prices $\mathbf{p}$ and historical data $\mathbf{S}$, suppose the forecasting method produces a forecasted distribution of the future prices D. A natural recommendation policy is to take as input consumer parameters θ and λ, the current price p and the forecasted distribution D and recommends the consumer to buy if

$$\theta - p \geq \theta - \lambda - \mathbb{E}_{p' \sim D}[p'] \ ,$$

where $\mathbb{E}_{p' \sim D}$ denotes the expectation of p' drawn according to distribution D. This policy tacitly assumes that the consumer is *risk-neutral*, and attempts to maximize the expected utility of the consumer based on the forecasts.

In general, a recommendation policy may take into account additional information such as the risk attitude of the consumers. It may require as input not only the mean forecast of the future price, but also possibly its entire distribution. Thus, we impose a requirement on the forecasting methods to generate distribution of forecasts as their output. Fortunately, as we will see in Section 4.1, there exists a general approach to generate forecast distributions from mean forecasts.

To determine the performance of the recommendation system, we measure the utility consumers have if they follow the recommendations made. Suppose we are given a set of n problem instances, where the i-th instance is given by $(\theta^i, \lambda^i, p^i, \mathbf{p}^i, \mathbf{S}^i)$ and p'^i which denotes the realized price in the future time period. Denote the recommendation of the system for the i-th instance by rec^i. The performance of the system is defined as

$$\sum_{i=1}^{n} \begin{cases} (\theta^i - p^i) & \text{if rec}^i \text{ is buy now} \\ (\theta^i - \lambda^i - p'^i) & \text{if rec}^i \text{ is wait} \end{cases} . \quad (1)$$

4. FORECASTING METHODS

We now describe a number of forecasting methods that we explore in this study. We first describe the notations for this section and a general technique to produce distribution of forecasts from methods that only produce mean forecasts. We then describe a number of methods that only use past prices for predicting future prices. We next look into how additional signals, such as seasonality, sales, and competition, can be incorporated into the forecasts. Finally, we describe methods that aggregate forecasts.

4.1 Preliminaries

Recall that the input to the forecasting methods are price histories $\mathbf{h}$ and additional historical data $\mathbf{S}$. For concreteness, we denote the length of the history by s. Hence, $\mathbf{h} = (p_1, p_2, \ldots, p_s)$ and $\mathbf{S} = (S_1, S_2, \ldots, S_s)$. Thus, the price p_s constitutes the current price according to our problem formulation in Section 3.1, and the objective of the methods is to come up with a distribution of prices for time $(s+1)$.

In the proceeding, some methods may use only a subset of the history. Let the history up to time t, $t \le s$, be denoted $\mathbf{h}_t$ and $\mathbf{S}_t$. For clarity, we denote the overall history analogously by $\mathbf{h}_s$ and $\mathbf{S}_s$.

Under the framework presented in Section 3.1, forecasting methods are required to output a *distribution* of future prices. We now describe a simple and parsimonious approach to convert methods that only produce mean forecasts to ones that produce distribution of forecasts. We apply this approach to all the methods described in this section.

Given price history $\mathbf{h}_s$ and meta-data $\mathbf{S}_s$, let the mean forecast according to method A of the price at time $s+1$ be denoted $\mu_1^A(\mathbf{h}_s, \mathbf{S}_s)$. The historical *in-sample sum of squared errors*, SE_1^A, is defined as

$$SE_1^A(\mathbf{h}_s, \mathbf{S}_s) = \frac{1}{s} \sum_{t=1}^{s} \left(\mu_1^A(\mathbf{h}_{t-1}, \mathbf{S}_{t-1}) - p_t \right)^2 .$$

The distribution at time $s+1$ is then given by a Gaussian distribution with mean $\mu_1^A(\mathbf{h}_s, \mathbf{S}_s)$ and variance $SE_1^A(\mathbf{h}_s, \mathbf{S}_s)$. This distribution is consistent with the interpretation that method A maximizes the likelihood of the observed data under normally distributed errors.

4.2 Methods that Only Use Prices

We consider two main classes of methods. One class include heuristic methods that are based on smoothing the data. Another class include autoregressive models that are based on time series analysis. They have been used extensively in forecasting [2, 10]. We review these methods in this subsection for completeness.

4.2.1 Smoothing Methods

We consider three smoothing methods in this study. All three methods depend on certain parameters that control the amount of smoothing. We learn these parameters by maximizing likelihood of observing the historical prices.

Moving Average (MA). Given a window size parameter w, for history $\mathbf{h}_s$, the mean forecast of the price at time $s+1$ equals

$$\mu_1^{MA}(\mathbf{h}_s) = \begin{cases} (1/w) \sum_{i=0}^{w-1} p_{s-i} & \text{if } s > w \\ \text{undefined} & \text{otherwise} \end{cases} .$$

The window size parameter controls how much smoothing is done. A larger window size increases the amount of smoothing performed on the history.

Exponential Smoothing (Exp). Given a decay parameter α ($0 < \alpha < 1$) and a seed value $\hat{p}$, for history $\mathbf{h}_s$, the mean forecast of the price at time $s+1$ is defined as an exponentially weighted sum of past prices, i.e.,

$$\begin{aligned} \mu_1^{Exp}(\mathbf{h}_s) &= \alpha p_s + (1-\alpha)\mu_1^{Exp}(\mathbf{h}_{s-1}) \\ &= \alpha \sum_{i=1}^{s} (1-\alpha)^{s-i} p_i + (1-\alpha)^s \hat{p} \end{aligned}$$

and for $s = 0$, $\mu_1^{Exp}(\mathbf{h}_s) = \hat{p}$. The decay parameter controls how much the method weighs recent data compared to past data. Smaller values of α increases the weight placed on historical prices.

Holt's Method (Holts). The Holt's method is a generalization of exponential smoothing. Given a level decay parameter α, a growth decay parameter β, and seed values of level and growth, $\hat{\ell}$ and $\hat{b}$, the mean forecast of the price at time $s+1$ is defined by the set of update equations, i.e.,

$$\mu_1^{Holts}(\mathbf{h}_s) = \ell_s + b_s$$

where for $s \ge 1$,

$$\begin{aligned} \ell_s &= \alpha p_s + (1-\alpha)\mu_1^{Holts}(\mathbf{h}_{s-1}) \\ b_s &= \beta(p_s - \ell_{s-1}) + (1-\beta) b_{s-1} \end{aligned}$$

and for $s = 0$, $\mu_1^{Holts}(\mathbf{h}_s) = \hat{\ell}$ and $b_s = \hat{b}$. Note that when β and b_1 are set to 0, the method is the same as exponential smoothing.

4.2.2 Autoregressive (AR) Models

Autoregressive models are a family of models that predict future values as linear combinations of past values. The model is specified by the number of past terms the future values depend on (known as its *order*). An autoregressive model of order k, AR(k), is described by the equation

$$p_t = \sum_{i=1}^{k} \beta_i p_{t-i} + \epsilon_t \quad (2)$$

where ϵ_t are normally distributed errors. The parameters β are estimated by linear regression. Under our framework, for history $\mathbf{h}_s$, $\mu_1^{AR(k)}(\mathbf{h}_s) = p_{s+1} = \sum_{i=1}^{k} \beta_i p_{s-i+1}$.

For product prices, one may want to model price changes rather than price levels. This can be achieved by taking the differences between successive values in the series, i.e.,

$$\Delta_t = p_t - p_{t-1} .$$

The differences Δ_t is then modeled by an autoregressive model. We denote an autoregressive model of order k over the differences by AR-Diff(k).

The order of the model and whether to difference the series is often selected heuristically. In our experiments, we try a number of models to find what works best for our problem.

One advantage of AR models is its extensibility. One can easily incorporate additional signals by adding the signals to the relationship in Equation (2). Such extensions are considered later in this section.

4.3 Modeling Seasonality

Seasonality refers to *cyclical* variations in the sequence of data being modeled. For example, consumer spending often exhibits seasonality (higher in November and December due to holiday shopping).

Classical methods for estimating seasonality require at least two full cycles of data [10]. They do not readily apply to our problem. This is because the length of a cycle for our problem is 12 months, whereas the length of the lifecycle of a typical electronic product is between 18 and 30 months, as estimated using the data set described further in Section 5. Thus, these methods could at best help with forecasts for the last few months of a product about to be discontinued, and are not sufficiently applicable to our problem.

We propose to model seasonality by grouping together products that are similar to the one in question. This allows us to learn seasonality at an aggregate level and apply it to the individual products. Let P denote a set of products and L denote the number of time units per cycle (e.g., 12 months or 52 weeks per year). First, we compute the relative change in prices for each product i in P, $d_t^i = (p_t^i / p_{t-1}^i) - 1$. Next, we compute the average change per period, $\bar{d}_t$, by averaging over the individual changes d_t^i. We then compute the average change in each time unit within a cycle, i.e., for $j < L$,

$$\text{season}_j = \text{Average}\Big(\{\bar{d}_t \mid t \bmod L = j\}\Big) .$$

Finally, we compute a *seasonal effect* by subtracting the average overall change from s_j, i.e.,

$$\text{season}_j^* = \text{season}_j - \frac{1}{L}\sum_{i=0}^{L-1} \text{season}_j$$

To make use of seasonal effects in forecast, for each product, we first *detrend* the product prices by computing

$$p_t^* = p_t / (1 + \text{season}_{f(t)}^*)$$

where $f(t)$ selects the corresponding season for time t. This has the effect of accounting for the price changes that can be explained by seasonal fluctuations. Forecasting is then performed over the new time series $\mathbf{p}^*$. To recover the actual value, the mean forecast for time s is multiplied by the seasonal effect $(1 + \text{season}_{f(s)}^*)$.

This procedure leaves open the question of how to select a similar set of products. We explore this question experimentally in Section 5.

4.4 Incorporating Sales Volume

Based on past studies in marketing research, sales volume is an important factor in determining product prices [6]. We propose two approaches to incorporating sales volume in making the forecasts.

In one approach, we add sales volume data to Equation (2) as part of a regression model. In our study, we add the sales volume data from a number of past periods corresponding to the order of the AR model.

In another approach, we use sales volume data to help determine the "stage" of the lifecycle of a product, and learn a separate AR model for each stage. We use autoregressive trees (AR Trees), proposed in [12], for this purpose. Intuitively, the AR tree approach combines decision trees with AR model. Like a decision tree, each of the internal nodes of the tree splits the data based on some criteria, in this case by sales volume. At the leaf node, an autoregressive model is learned for the data that are classified to the node.

4.5 Incorporating Competition

Competition among products exists in many forms, such as through price or feature differentiation. In this study, we focus on price competition. Given a set of competing products P to the product in question, we propose three approaches to capture the competition. These approaches are based on creating correlated time series that are added to an autoregressive model as additional regression variable(s). They differ in how these time series are generated.

Top k competitors. Create a set of k time series to be added to the AR model by selecting k products from P that minimizes the in-sample sum of squared errors for the product in question. We consider the top 1 competitor in the experiments.

Average competition. Create a single time series by taking the average price over all products in P. The motivation behind this approach is to capture the overall competition from the market.

Principal Component Analysis (PCA). Create a set of k time series by selecting the first k eigenvectors that correspond to the principal component analysis of the prices of all products in P. Formally, form a matrix M where each column corresponds to the prices of a product in P, and each row corresponds to the prices for a given time index. Perform an eigen decomposition of matrix M (i.e., run PCA). This can be interpreted as identifying the variables that best explains the variation in the data [1]. By adding the eigenvectors as regressors, the approach attempts to incorporate signals that help to explain price changes. To make this approach comparable to the other two in experiments, we add only the principal eigenvector so that each method adds only one additional time series in its regression.

4.6 Aggregating Forecasts

A number of studies in statistics and machine learning has found that aggregating forecasts can often lead to better performances than individual forecasts [3, 4, 16]. We consider three approaches to aggregation in this study, all of which has been successfully used in the literature.

Average. Take the simple average of the forecasts to produce the mean of the forecast. This approach tends to be robust to outliers that may skew the distribution.

Regression. Use past data to learn a linear combination of the forecasts that minimizes empirical error. This approach adapts to the data and can serve as means to selecting the best method.

Inverse Variance. Take a weighted average of the forecasts inversely proportional to the variance (and hence, sample error) of the forecasts. This places less weights on forecasts that have high sample errors historically.

5. EXPERIMENTS

To find out what forecasting methods work best for predicting product prices, and how to incorporate additional sources of signals such as seasonality, sales volume, and competition, we conduct a large-scale empirical study in the electronic goods domain. We start out with using only price data for forecasting, then tested different ways to incorporate each source of signals, and finally consider ways to aggregate the forecasts.

5.1 Data

We obtained monthly price and sales volume data for four categories of electronic products—Televisions, Digital cameras, Camcorders, and Printers—between January 2005 and September 2008. The data is obtained from NPD, a commercial data provider, and is based on sales registered in about ten major retail chains across the US. Prices are computed as the volume-weighted average prices of the products at the checkout registers of these stores.

The evaluation period is from June 2008 to September 2008. Products for which the month-to-month change in prices is greater than 4 times (i.e., more than 300% increase or 75% decrease) are filtered out, as we believe these are due to data entry errors. After this preprocessing step, there are about 1,200 products in the data set. Over the evaluation period, the value of products sold per month was worth about 380 million dollars. The weighted average month-to-month decrease in product prices is about 3.5%, with a standard error of about 5%. Most of the time series are short, with between 18 and 30 data points. These are considered challenging problems in time series analysis due to data sparsity.

5.2 Methodology

We evaluate the methods by measuring the performance of the system as given by Equation (1) in Section 3.1. For each product in the dataset, we generate four problem instances corresponding to each of the four months between June 2008 and September 2008. The consumer parameters for each problem instance are chosen as follows. The value of the product θ is chosen to be 5% higher than the current price when a consumer first gets interested in buying the product. The loss of use λ is expressed as a fraction of the value θ. This fraction, which we call *loss of use ratio*, is chosen to be between 2.5% and 4.5%. These values are consistent with past studies on consumer discount rates for electronic goods, which can be interpreted as proxies for the loss of use [18].

To normalize the results, we report the performance relative to the maximum possible utility that a consumer can obtain with perfect foresight. This maximum is unachievable in practice due to the stochastic nature of price changes. Nonetheless, it helps us gauge how close we are to the best possible result. For the chosen consumer parameters, a 1% difference in relative performance corresponds to about 1.1 million dollars in utility for the data under consideration. A 70% relative performance corresponds to about 77 million dollars in utility.

5.3 Results

5.3.1 Methods that Only Use Prices

We first consider forecasting methods that only use past prices in making a forecast. These include the three smoothing methods presented in Section 4.2.1, with parameters selected by maximizing likelihood (MA-MLE, Exp-MLE, Holts-MLE), and three autoregressive models with different orders

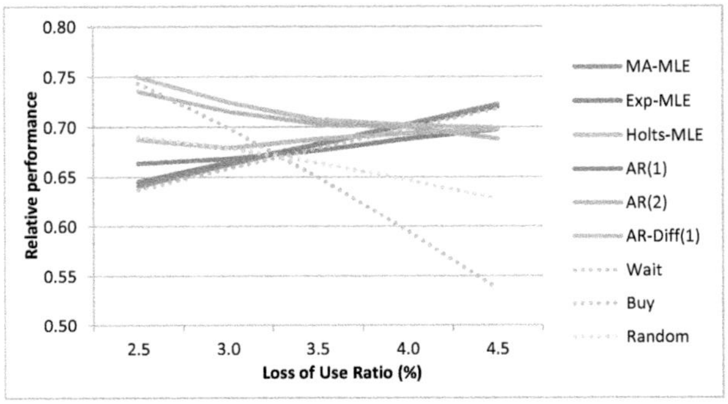

Figure 4: Relative performances of forecasting methods that use only prices, compared to baselines.

and differencing (AR(1), AR(2), AR-Diff(1)). For comparison, we also report the performance obtained when a consumer always buys the product right away (Buy), always waits to buy the product (Wait), and randomly choose between buying now or waiting (Random). The results are presented in Figure 4. The key observations are:

- The best performing methods are Holt's methods and AR(2). They outperform all three baselines by an average of 5% over the entire range, and with the exception at the extremes when wait is better at a discount rate of 2.5% and buy is better at a discount rate of 4.5%, they are better than all three baselines. Both methods share a similar characteristic in that they consider how prices have *changed* in the past period. This turns out to be important for our application.
- The performances of MA-MLE and Exp-MLE closely mirror that of the buy baseline in the entire range. This is because the forecasts made by both methods are close to the price in the preceding time period, corresponding to a small window parameter w and a large decay parameter α respectively. As a result, the recommendation using either forecast is to buy, except for the rare cases where the methods have identified a definite trend.
- AR(2) outperforms both AR(1) and AR-Diff(1). This is likely because AR(2) uses more data than the other two models, and hence produces more accurate forecasts. However, increasing the orders further to incorporate yet more data could lead to overfitting. Indeed, we observe worse performances for AR models of higher order (not shown in figure to avoid clutter).

5.3.2 Modeling Seasonality

In Section 4, we proposed an approach to model seasonality that depends on how products are grouped together to estimate seasonal trends. We consider two groupings in this section. In one, we group all electronic products together to learn a global seasonal trend. In another, we group together products by their category to learn category-specific seasonal trends. The seasonal effects we learn under these groupings are shown in Figure 5.

We observe that category-specific trends exhibit higher variability compared to the global trend. For all trends, the seasonal effects fluctuate within a fairly small band (between -1.5% and +1.5%) between January and October. There is a

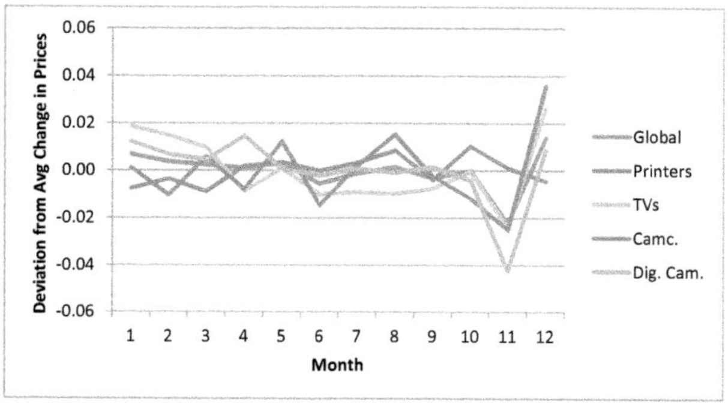

Figure 5: Global and category-specific seasonalities of product prices.

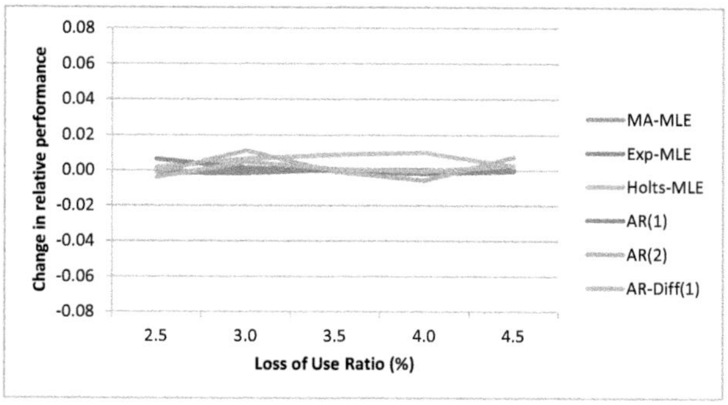

Figure 6: *Change* in relative performance after correcting for a global seasonal trend. Results for that of category-specific seasonal trends are similar.

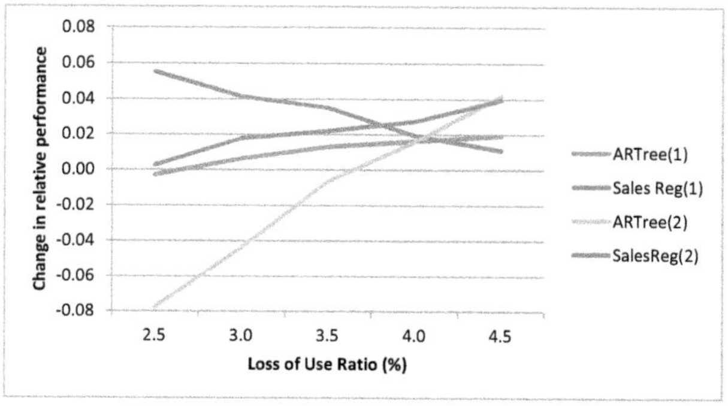

Figure 7: *Change* in relative performance when sales are incorporated in AR models.

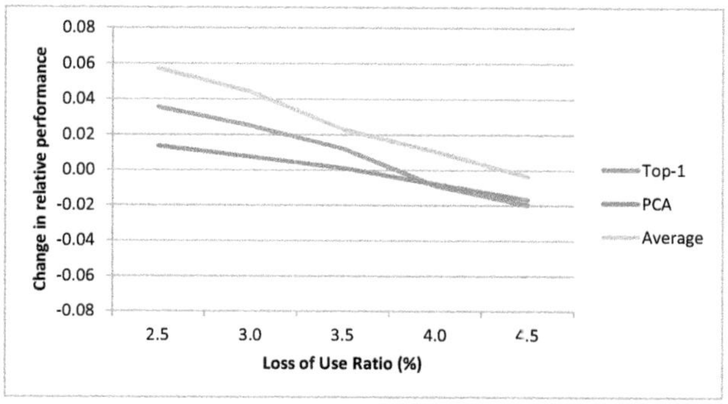

Figure 8: *Change* in relative performance when competition is incorporated.

large seasonal effect that leads to larger-than-expected price drops in November, follow by smaller-than-expected drops in December. The trends do depend on the category. Printers, for example, exhibit a relatively stable trend throughout.

Next, we incorporate these trends to our forecasting methods. The changes in relative performances after incorporating a global seasonal trend are shown in Figures 6. The results using category-specific trends are similar and omitted for brevity.

We observe that the relative performances for all of the methods remain almost the same after incorporating the seasonal trends. It is not surprising because from June to September, the months over which performance is evaluated, we observe relatively little seasonal effects in Figure 5. We expect a larger gain in performance for November and December. As there are only three full years of data, we were unable to verify the hypothesis due to data sparsity.

5.3.3 Incorporating Sales Volume

In Section 4, we presented two approaches that use sales volume data to help predict future prices. Both methods extend the AR models but differ in how sales data is used. Under the AR Tree approach, sales data is used to segment the AR model into piece-wise linear region. Under the regression approach, sales data are treated as independent variables in a regression against future prices. We present the results of extending the AR(1) and the AR(2) models under both approaches in Figure 7.

We observe that with the exception of extending the AR(2) model using AR Tree, incorporating sales lead to higher relative performances, in some cases fairly significant improvements. For both models, the AR Tree approach lags behind the regression approach. To understand how the two approaches differ, we compare the recommendations according to the AR models and their extensions. We find that the regression approach disagrees on about 20% of the products. It finds better recommendations in about 75% of the time, explaining its success. On the other hand, the AR tree approach disagrees on about 40% of the products. It finds better recommendations in only about half the time. Hence, the improvement in relative performances is less, and in some cases the relative performance is actually worse.

5.3.4 Incorporating Competition

We presented three different methods to incorporate competition in Section 4. In this experiment, we treat all products within a given category as competition, as we lack detailed product specification to perform more refined groupings of products. The results of extending the AR(1) model are presented in Figure 8.

We observe that taking the average prices of all products within a category gives the largest gain in relative performances among all three methods of incorporating competition. There is a general downward trend for all three methods as discount rates increase. Examining the recommendation in more detail, it appears that including competition often leads to lower price forecast, and hence an increased likelihood to recommend wait to the consumer. This leads to worse relative performances as discount rate increases since waiting is likely to earn less utility at higher discount rates.

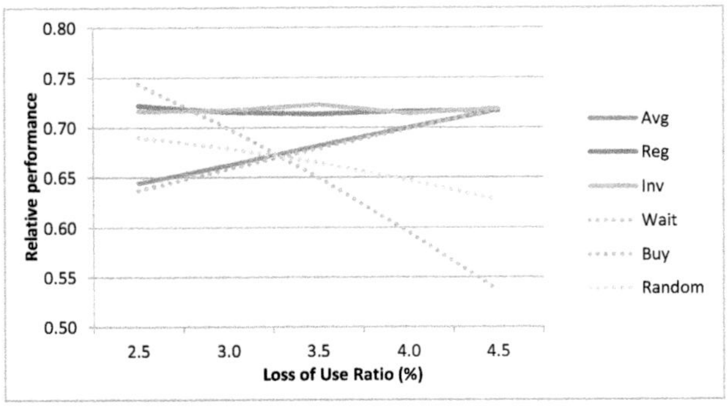

Figure 9: Relative performances of aggregating forecasts from four constituent methods (Holts-MLE, SalesReg(2), MA-MLE, AR-Diff(1)).

5.3.5 *Aggregating Forecasts*

We now consider whether aggregating forecasts can improve performances. We select a number of forecasting methods to aggregate based on their performance and how much they differ from one another. Adding more varied forecast may help to complement the shortcomings of one another. Based on the experiments, we selected Holt's methods and sales incorporated through regression (SalesReg(2)) as these are the two best individual methods. From the first set of experiments, we found that both MA-MLE and AR-Diff(1) perform reasonably well, and exhibit qualitatively different behavior as their performances improve as discount rate increases. The results based on the three aggregation methods of averaging (Avg), regression (Reg), and inverse variance (Inv) are presented in Figure 9.

We observe that aggregating forecasts by regression and inverse variance both outperform aggregating forecasts by averaging. The performances of the former two are comparable to the best individual method in the group (SalesReg(2)), but deliver more consistent performances over the entire range of discount rates and outperform all three baselines in almost all cases. We conclude from this experiment that aggregating forecasts is a robust approach to ensuring good performances.

5.3.6 *Sensitivity to Value Parameter*

For the above experiments, the value of the product θ has been chosen to be 5% higher than the current price when a consumer first gets interested in buying the product. Varying this parameter does not change the relative ordering among the forecasting methods, but it has an effect on the total expected utility the system generates for its users and the relative performances. When θ is 4% higher than the current price, the relative performance of the best method becomes 68%; when θ is 6% higher, the relative performance becomes 76%. This trend is because as θ gets smaller, there is an increased likelihood that a wait recommendation may lead to negative utility. This can be avoided with perfect foresight, hence the relative performance of all methods, including the best one, decreases. Nonetheless, the gap between the best method and the baselines remain consistent at about 5% of relative performance.

6. CONCLUDING REMARKS

We presented Prodcast, an experimental system that is designed to ameliorate buyer's remorse by providing recommendations to consumers on when to buy a durable product. It complements the facilities provided by existing e-commerce websites that help consumers decide what product to buy and where to buy it. We gave an overview of the system architecture, and described a framework for evaluating the system based on the expected utility it generates for the users. Focusing on the question of what forecasting methods work well for this application domain, we systematically compared a large number of forecasting methods based on smoothing and time series analysis. We analyzed additional signals such as seasonality, sales volume, and competition to see to what extent they can help to predict product prices. We also investigated various methods for combining forecasts. Our best method achieves a relative performance of about 72% compared to the optimal decision with perfect foresight. It outperforms the best baseline by about 5% in our dataset. This confirms that the proposed system can generate significant utilities to users shopping for durable products.

We have gained a number of insights from our experimental study using real-life data. First, we found that forecasting methods that use both the change in prices and the past price level, such as Holt's methods and AR(2) models, do well in this domain. Due to data sparsity, methods that use more past data than these methods end up doing worse as a result of overfitting. Second, the relatively short time series present a challenge to traditional approaches to modeling seasonality. By aggregating across multiple products, we discover a trend that is born out by experience, i.e., prices tend to drop more than expected in November. These seasonal effects may help to improve forecasts for the holiday seasons. Third, both sales volume and competition are sources of signals that can be leveraged to improve performance. However, the degree of improvements depends on how these signals are used. Based on our experiment, sales are best incorporated through regression, and competition through averaging. Finally, while we do not see gains in performances by aggregating forecasts compared to the best forecasting method, aggregating forecasts can smooth out the performances across different discount rates, and alleviate the need to explicitly select a specific method.

Some interesting directions for future work are as follows. In this paper, we have considered the problem of recommending whether to buy now or in the next time period. Depending on the length of a time period, we may want to consider the more general problem of buying now or some time in the future several periods from now. This requires extending the forecasting techniques studied to produce multi-period forecasts.

In our experiments, we have relied on data obtained from a commercial vendor. To obtain more timely data, one may want to crawl the data from online retailers. This introduces challenges on how to ensure the quality of the data, and how to aggregate the data, which are at the levels of individual offers, to reflect the prices of the underlying products.

7. REFERENCES

[1] C. M. Bishop. *Pattern Recognition and Machine Learning*. Springer, 2006.

[2] G. Box, G. M. Jenkins, and G. Reinsel. *Time Series Analysis: Forecasting and Control*. Prentice Hall, 3rd edition, 1994.

[3] R. T. Clemen. Combining forecasts: A review and annotated bibliography. *Int. J. Forecasting*, 5:559–583, 1989.

[4] R. T. Clemen, A. H. Murphy, and R. L. Winkler. Screening probability forecasts: Contrasts between choosing and combining. *Int. J. Forecasting*, 11:133–146, 1995.

[5] W. H. Cummings and M. Venkatesan. Cognitive dissonance and consumer behavior: A review of the evidence. In M. J. Schlinger, editor, *Advances in Consumer Research Volume 2*, pages 21–32. Association for Conusmer Research, 1975.

[6] R. N. Dino. Forecasting the price evolution of new electronic products. *J. Forecasting*, 4:39–60, 1985.

[7] R. J. Dolan and A. P. Jeuland. Experience curves and dnamic demand models: Implications for optimal pricing strategies. *J. Marketing*, 45:52–62, 1981.

[8] O. Etzioni, R. Tuchinda, C. A. Knoblock, and A. Yates. To buy or not to buy: mining airfare data to minimize ticket purchase price. In *Proceedings of KDD*, pages 119–128, 2003.

[9] M. Hviid and G. Shaffer. Hassle costs: The achilles heel of price-matching guarantees. *J. Economics & Management Strategy*, 8(4), 1999.

[10] R. J. Hyndman, A. B. Koehler, J. K. Ord, and R. D. Snyder. *Forecasting with Exponential Smoothing*. Springer, 2008.

[11] S. Makridakis and M. Hibon. The M3-competition: results, conclusions and implications. *Int. J. Forecasting*, 16(4):451–476, 2000.

[12] C. Meek, D. M. Chickering, and D. Heckerman. Autoregressive tree models for time-series analysis. In *Proceedings of SIAM Int. Conf. on Data Mining*, 2002.

[13] H. Nair. Intertemporal price discrimination with forward-looking consumers: Application to the US market for console video-games. *Quant. Market. and Econ.*, 5:239–292, 2007.

[14] S. S. Oren. Comments on "pricing research in marketing: The state of the art". *J. Business*, 57:61–64, 1984.

[15] V. R. Rao. Pricing research in marketing: The state of the art. *J. Business*, 57:39–60, 1984.

[16] R. E. Schapire. A brief introduction to boosting. In *Proceedings of IJCAI*, 1999.

[17] I. Song and P. K. Chintagunta. A micromodel of new product adoption with heterogenous and forward-looking consumers: Application to the digital camera category. *Quant. Market. and Econ.*, 1:371–407, 2003.

[18] R. S. Winer. Discounting and its impact on durables buying decision. *Marketing Letters*, 8:109–118, 1997.

Experiences with Mining Temporal Event Sequences from Electronic Medical Records: Initial Successes and Some Challenges

Debprakash Patnaik[1]
patnaik@vt.edu

Patrick Butler[1]
pabutler@vt.edu

Naren Ramakrishnan[1]
naren@cs.vt.edu

Laxmi Parida[2]
parida@us.ibm.com

Benjamin J. Keller[3]
bkeller@emich.edu

David A. Hanauer, MD[4]
hanauer@umich.edu

[1]Department of Computer Science and Discovery Analytics Center, Virginia Tech, VA 24061
[2]IBM T.J. Watson Research Center, Yorktown Heights, NY 10598
[3]Department of Computer Science, Eastern Michigan University, Ypsilanti, MI 48197
[4]Department of Pediatrics and Communicable Diseases, University of Michigan, Ann Arbor, MI 48109

ABSTRACT

The standardization and wider use of electronic medical records (EMR) creates opportunities for better understanding patterns of illness and care within and across medical systems. Our interest is in the temporal history of event codes embedded in patients' records, specifically investigating frequently occurring sequences of event codes across patients. In studying data from more than 1.6 million patient histories at the University of Michigan Health system we quickly realized that frequent sequences, while providing one level of data reduction, still constitute a serious analytical challenge as many involve alternate serializations of the same sets of codes. To further analyze these sequences, we designed an approach where a partial order is mined from frequent sequences of codes. We demonstrate an EMR mining system called EMRView that enables exploration of the precedence relationships to quickly identify and visualize partial order information encoded in key classes of patients. We demonstrate some important nuggets learned through our approach and also outline key challenges for future research based on our experiences.

Categories and Subject Descriptors

J.3 [**Computer Applications**]: Life and Medical sciences—*Medical information systems*; H.2.8 [**Information Systems**]: Database Management—*Data mining*

General Terms

Algorithms, Design, Management

Keywords

Medical informatics, Temporal data mining, Partial orders.

1. INTRODUCTION

The increased use of electronic medical records (EMRs) to capture standardized patient information creates an opportunity to better understand both patterns of illness among similar patients, as well as patterns of care within and across medical systems. While the first allows us to identify "fingerprints" of clinical symptoms that may help us capture the progression toward catastrophic clinical transitions, the second can help us understand how diagnoses and procedures are applied within and across different clinical settings.

Two primary categories of information embedded in an EMR are referred to as ICD and CPT codes. ICD 9 (International Classification of Diseases and Related Health Problems, v9) is a popular classification system used in health care which is also heavily used for a wide variety of research activities [7]. This system is primarily intended to code signs, symptoms, injuries, diseases, and conditions. CPT (Current Procedural Terminology) refers to a similar categorization of medical procedures performed on a patient. CPT codes are 5 digit numeric codes, which are published by the American Medical Association. The purpose of this coding system is to provide uniform language that accurately describes medical, surgical, and diagnostic services (including radiology, anesthesiology, and evaluation/management services of physicians, hospitals, and other health care providers). There are about 20,000 distinct ICD 9 codes and about 10,000 CPT codes in use today. Thus an electronic medical record consists, in its most basic sense, of an interleaved sequence of diagnostic (ICD) and procedure (PCT) codes assigned to the patient every time he/she received care along with other associated test reports and doctor's notes.

An EMR is intrinsically temporal in nature yet research on temporal data mining in medical records is scarce. This work seeks to fill this void. Our goal is to extract clinically relevant *sequences* of event codes embedded in the patient histories of more than 1.6 million subjects of the University of Michigan's health system. A straightforward implementation of sequential mining approaches [20] does help provide one level of data reduction, but the resulting sequences are still too many for human consumption because they are permutations or nearly permutations of each other representing different serializations of the same sets of codes. For instance, it is more likely to see a diagnosis of cardiac ischemia before an aortic coronary bypass, but there are patients for which these occur in the opposite order. It is also not satisfactory to simply lump together codes on the evidence of multiple permutations, because not all sequences are equally likely. We therefore present an approach to derive a partial order from frequent sequences of codes, along with a tool called EMRView that supports exploration of these orders based on a physician's selections of supporting sequences.

2. INITIAL EXPLORATION

After obtaining approval from the Institutional Review Board at the University of Michigan Medical School, we organized a dataset of information about 1.6 million patients in the health system. The actual medical records contained about 100 million time stamped ICD 9 and CPT 4 codes and also other categories of data such as doctor's notes, test results, prescriptions and x-ray images. There are two main concerns in using these other categories of data. The first is to ensure the privacy of the patients concerned. With freeform text this is a very hard problem to address. The second concern pertains to transcribing the handwritten notes into electronic form before they can be analyzed. Hence we began our initial focus on the encoded procedure and diagnostic codes.

First, we replaced patient medical record numbers with artificial research identifiers not tied to the medical record. Time intervals were then used to replace specific dates (thus, resetting the start of a patient's record to time zero). See Table 1 for an example. These codes represented over 10 years of clinical encounters in our electronic medical record system. Data was securely transferred to Virginia Tech for analysis. Specific details of the data are shown in Table 2. The range of the number of entries/codes per patient varies from 1 to 10K, i.e., there were many patients with few isolated visits and also patients who have received their entire lifetime of care from the particular healthcare provider. These and other power law behaviors are shown in Fig. 1. Some patient records extend over 20 years! In terms of the diagnostic and procedure codes, there are over 40 million and 38 million entries respectively of each type of code in the data.

After a preliminary analysis, we decided to focus exclusively on the diagnostic (ICD) codes. The reason for this decision is that most of the procedure codes (CPT) appear to have been initiated in response to a diagnosis and hence actually served as proxy for conditions. This aided in simplifying the search for patterns downstream although we run the risk of missing infrequent classes of relationships (e.g., the administration of a procedure causing a complication down the road).

Let us denote the medical record of the ith patient as an ordered sequence of diagnostic codes:

$$S_i = \langle (E_1, t_1), \ldots, (E_j, t_j), \ldots, (E_{|S_i|}, t_{|S_i|}) \rangle$$

where E_j is the jth diagnostic code and t_j is the associated time stamp. An entire EMR database consisting of several patient records is denoted by $\mathcal{D} = \{S_1, \ldots, S_{|\mathcal{D}|}\}$.

One interesting characteristic of the data was observed when we plotted the distribution of time differences between consecutive diagnostic codes across all records (see Fig. 2). Note the different modes at multiples of 7 days, an artifact of how followup visits to the health care provider are typically scheduled.

Table 1: Example EMR.

Patient ID	Code	Type	Desc.	Timestamp (in days)
149970	99243	CPT	Office consultation	0
149970	145.9	ICD	Malignant neoplasm of mouth, unspecified.	0
149970	88321	CPT	Microslide consultation.	1
149970	792.9	ICD	Other nonspecific abnormal findings in body substances.	1

Table 2: Characteristics of the EMR database.

Property	Value
Number of patients	1,620,681
Number of diagnostic (ICD) codes	41,186,511
Number of procedure (CPT) codes	38,942,605
Max. number of codes in a record	10,430
Min. number of codes in a record	1
Max. span of a record in days	8202 days≈ 22.5 years
Min. span of a record in days	1

Finally, just as stopword elimination is employed in information retrieval, we conducted 'stopcode elimination' to remove diagnostic codes that are too frequently used. Specifically, codes that surfaced in more than 0.49% of patient records were eliminated (the most frequent code surfaced in 9% of patients).

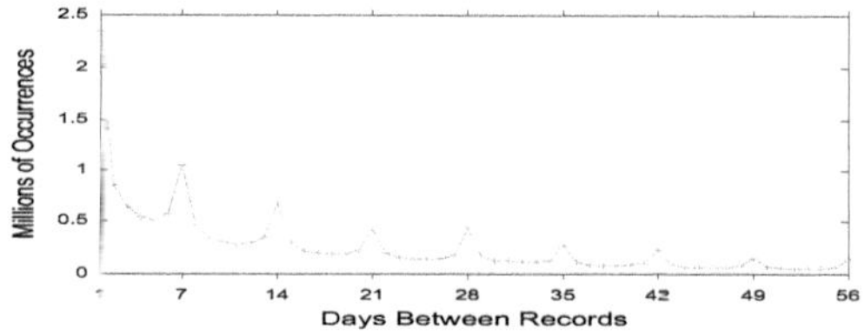

Figure 2: Distribution of interarrival times

3. METHOD OVERVIEW

Figure 3 provides an overview of our proposed methodology for unearthing partial orders from EMR data. There are three broad stages: i) mining parallel episodes, ii) tracking serial extensions, and iii) learning partial orders.

Mining parallel episodes: Parallel episodes are very similar to itemsets but take temporal information into account in the form of expiry constraints. We present a counting algorithm in Section 4.1 that discovers parallel episodes which are frequent above a given threshold. It is well known that patterns with support higher than a threshold may not always be interesting because certain high frequency items can randomly co-occur. Hence, we apply the maximum entropy principle[13] to predict the support of an episode and examine the actual support to impart a score of significance. This score is used to order episodes and is carried out offline.

Tracking serial extensions: After mining a set of frequent parallel episodes, we find order information embedded in these frequently co-occurring sets of diagnostic codes. The intuition behind searching for order is to unearth potential evidence (or lack thereof) for sequentiality in the data. For a n sized frequent parallel episode, there could potentially be $n!$ permutations exhibited in the data.

Learning partial orders: The set of all serial extensions determined in the previous step is compacted into a partial

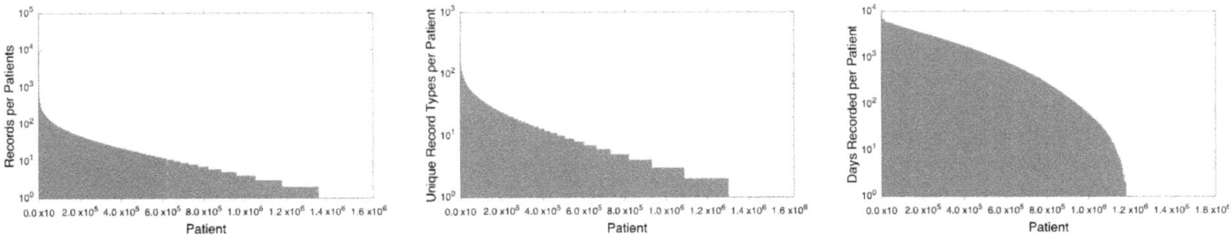

(a) No. of ICD codes per record (b) No. of distinct ICD codes per record (c) Span of record in days

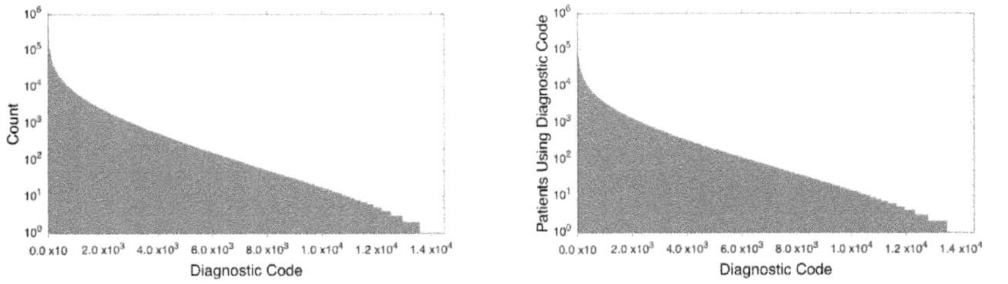

(d) No. of occurrences of an ICD code (e) No. of patients assigned an ICD code

Figure 1: Plots of various distributions seen in the real EMR data.

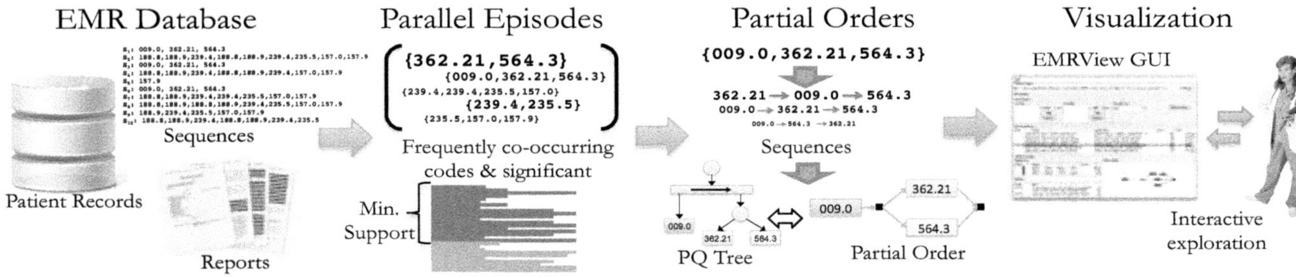

Figure 3: Overview of the proposed EMR analysis methodology.

order using a special PQ tree algorithm. PQ trees[3] enable an expressive class of partial orders to be learnt and the user has the flexibility to interactively aid the search for partial orders by selecting the set of extensions to be modeled. This part of the procedure is thus interactive so that the medical professional can iteratively generalize and specialize partial orders in order to arrive at an understanding of the underlying orders.

4. FREQUENT EPISODE MINING

In this section we briefly review the frequent episode mining framework and related terminology.

DEFINITION 4.1 (GENERAL EPISODE). *An episode α is defined as a tuple $\{V_\alpha, \leq_\alpha\}$, where $V_\alpha \subseteq \mathcal{A}$, $\mathcal{A}$ is the set all symbols (i.e. diagnostic codes). The relation $\leq_\alpha$ defines an ordering of the codes in V_α. A general episode is a partial order over V_α.*

For example, consider an episode α given by $V_\alpha = \{A, B, C\}$ with $A \leq_\alpha B$ and $A \leq_\alpha C$. This defines an episode where A must occur before B and C but (B, C) can occur in any order and can be denoted as $A \rightarrow (BC)$.

DEFINITION 4.2 (SERIAL EPISODE). *A serial episode is an ordered sequence of symbols/codes. It represents a total order where for any pair $a_i, a_j \in V_\alpha$ and $a_i \neq a_j$, either $(a_i \leq_\alpha a_j)$ or $(a_j \leq_\alpha a_i)$ holds.*

An example of a serial episode is $A \rightarrow B \rightarrow C$ where the relation $\leq_\alpha$ is such that $A \leq_\alpha B$, $A \leq_\alpha C$ and $B \leq_\alpha C$.

DEFINITION 4.3 (PARALLEL EPISODE). *A parallel episode is an unordered set of symbols/codes i.e. $\leq_v = \phi$.*

A sequence S supports an episode α, if $V_\alpha \subseteq \{A_i : A_i \in S\}$ and for no pair A_j preceding A_i in S, $A_i \leq_\alpha A_j$ holds. In other words, the order of the symbols in S does not violate the precedence order encoded by $\leq_\alpha$. The support of α is the fraction of sequences in D that support it. In addition, an expiry constraint T_X can be specified for episodes which requires that the symbols in S that constitute an occurrence of the episode occur no further than T_X time units apart from each other.

EXAMPLE 4.4. *Consider an EMR dataset of 4 sequences (Fig. 4). The highlighted codes constitute occurrences of the parallel episode (ABC) (in S_1,S_2,S_3 and S_4), serial episode $A \rightarrow B \rightarrow C$ (in S_2 and S_3), and the partial order $A \rightarrow (BC)$. Later we shall use this example to illustrate our method.*

4.1 Parallel Episodes with Expiry

Frequent episode mining follows the Apriori-style itemset mining algorithm: the set of n-size frequent episodes are used to generate the $(n+1)$-size candidate episodes. The counting algorithm then determines the support of each candidate episode over the database of ordered sequences D.

S_1: W, U, C, I, B, C, K, A, Y, E, K, J, H, A
S_2: K, J, A, D, K, E, W, K, B, C, R, H
S_3: Q, T, B, J, A, C, O, J, B, A, C, K, F, N, F
S_4: L, M, A, N, C, V, J, H, B, I, U, W, G, B, G, G

Figure 4: Database of four sequences S_1, S_2, S_3 and S_4. The time-stamps are not shown. Note that *support*$(ABC) = 4/4$, *support*$(A \to B \to C) = 2/4$ **and** *support*$(A \to (BC) = 3/4$.

Typically, frequent episode mining is carried out over one long sequence of time-stamped events. In a database of ordered sequences, episodes essentially reduce to sequential patterns [1] so that support is defined as the fraction of sequences that have the pattern as a subsequence. Our expiry constraint gives us an additional handle to control the explosion in candidates besides the support threshold.

Algorithm 1 Count parallel episodes of size-k.

Input: Set of candidate k size parallel episodes C, Sequence database D, Expiry time constraint T_X, Min support θ.
Output: Set of frequent parallel of episodes with counts.
$\mathcal{A}$ = Set of all codes in episodes in C
Initialize $waits[A] = \phi, \forall A \in \mathcal{A}$
for all $\alpha \in C$ **do**
  Set $count[\alpha] = 0$
  Set $wait\_count[\alpha, A] = 1$ and $T[\alpha, A] = \phi, \quad \forall A \in \alpha$
  Add α to $waits[A]$
for all $S \in D$ **do**
  for all $(E, t) \in S$ **do**
    for all $\alpha \in waits[E]$ **do**
      Update $wait\_count[\alpha, E] = 0$ and $T[\alpha, E] = t$
      for all $A \in \alpha$ **do**
        if $(t - T[\alpha, A] > T_X)$ **or** $sid(A)! = S.id$ **then**
          $wait\_count[\alpha, E] = 1$
      if $(\sum_{A \in \alpha} wait\_count[\alpha, A]) = 0$ **then**
        $count[\alpha] = count[\alpha] + 1$
        Reset $wait\_count(\alpha, A) = 1, \forall A \in \alpha, \forall \alpha \in C$
return $\{\alpha, count(\alpha) : count(\alpha) \geq \theta|D|\}$

Algorithm 1 sketches the counting algorithm for parallel episodes with expiry time constraint. The algorithm makes one pass of the database to determine the support of all episodes in the set of candidates. It uses a hash-map data structure to efficiently reference episodes that need to be updated for each code seen in a sequence. The data structure $wait\_count[.]$ tracks the codes that are remaining to complete an occurrence and $T[.]$ stores the latest time stamp of each code. Note that tracking the latest time-stamp ensures that the span of the resulting occurrence is minimum. Hence we correctly track all episode occurrences that satisfy the expiry constraint.

4.2 Significance of parallel episodes

We utilize the maximum entropy formulation introduced in [30] to assess significance of our episodes. Consider an n-size parallel episode $\alpha = \{E_1, \ldots, E_n\}$, where E_i's are the diagnostic codes. Let Ω be the sample space of all n-size binary vectors and has a distribution $p : \Omega \to [0, 1]$. In the context of the database D, $p(\omega)$ gives the fraction of the sequences which support the binary vector ω where each 0/1 represents the presence or absence of the corresponding code E_i in a sequence. We compute the empirical distribution q_α over ω using the support of α and those of its sub-episodes. Example 4.5 illustrates the use of inclusion-exclusion principle to obtain q_α.

Example 4.5 (Empirical distribution). *Consider a 3-size parallel episode ABC. If ABC is frequent, all the sub-episode supports are known. Table 3 illustrates the computation of the empirical distribution q_{ABC} using the inclusion-exclusion principle over support (σ) of subepisodes.*

Table 3: Computing the empirical distribution q_α

A B C	Distribution q_{ABC}
0 0 0	$\sigma(\phi) - \sigma(A) - \sigma(B) + \sigma(AB) - \sigma(C) + \sigma(AC) + \sigma(BC) - \sigma(ABC)$
0 0 1	$\sigma(C) - \sigma(AC) - \sigma(BC) + \sigma(ABC)$
0 1 0	$\sigma(B) - \sigma(AB) - \sigma(BC) + \sigma(ABC)$
0 1 1	$\sigma(BC) - \sigma(ABC)$
1 0 0	$\sigma(A) - \sigma(AB) - \sigma(AC) + \sigma(ABC)$
1 0 1	$\sigma(AC) - \sigma(ABC)$
1 1 0	$\sigma(AB) - \sigma(ABC)$
1 1 1	$\sigma(ABC)$

We estimate the distribution p for α using only the support of its sub-episodes. This is done by estimating the maximum entropy distribution p_α^{ME} (defined in Eq 1) that represents a log-linear model.

$$p_\alpha^{ME}(\omega) = \frac{1}{Z_\alpha} \exp\left(\sum \lambda_i f_i(\omega)\right) \quad (1)$$

Here each factor $f_i(w)$ is an indicator function:

$$f_i(w) = I(\omega \text{ covers } i^{th} \text{ subepisode of } \alpha)$$

We learn the maximum entropy model under the constraint that the expectations $\mathbb{E}\langle f_i \rangle = \langle$support of ith proper subepisode of $\alpha\rangle$. We use the KL-divergence measure between the empirical distribution and the maximum entropy distribution estimated using only subepisodes to score the significance of α (Eq 2).

$$score(\alpha) = \sum_\omega q_\alpha(\omega) \log \frac{q_\alpha(\omega)}{p_\alpha^{ME}(\omega)} \quad (2)$$

A higher score implies that the support of the episode is more surprising given the subepisodes. This significance score is used to rank the discovered patterns.

4.3 Tracking sequential extensions

After mining the lattice of frequent parallel episodes, we make another pass through the data to record the number of times different linear (serial) extensions of each frequent parallel episode occur in the data. This is illustrated below for the sequences in Example 4.4.

Example 4.6 (Sequential Extensions). *Consider the parallel episode (ABC). There are $3! = 6$ possible permutations or serial extensions of this episode. Now consider the sequences shown in Example 4.4, where only 3 of the 6 permutations of (ABC) are seen in the data. The supports of these sequences is noted below.*

$A \to B \to C : 2/4; \quad A \to C \to B : 1/4; \quad B \to C \to A : 1/4$

5. LEARNING PARTIAL ORDERS

At this stage, we have mined sets of frequent episodes that are permutations of each other, e.g. $A \to B \to C$, $A \to C \to B$ and $B \to C \to A$. Since the parallel episode (ABC) and each of these serial episodes is known to be frequent in the data, we aim to find a partial order that describes these sequences (and as few other sequences as possible). A trivial solution is the already obtained null partial order: (ABC) which, besides covering the above three extensions, also covers $B \rightarrow A \rightarrow C$, $C \rightarrow A \rightarrow B$, and $C \rightarrow B \rightarrow A$. A better solution is the partial order $(A(BC))$ which describes only one other sequence in addition to above: $C \rightarrow B \rightarrow A$.

Mining partial orders is a difficult problem in general because the space of partial orders grows very quickly with alphabet size. As a result, researchers have proposed focusing on special cases of partial orders (e.g., series-parallel) to make the problem tractable [21]. Here, we present a PQ tree approach[16] for finding a recursive partial order over the set of frequent serial episodes over the same set of symbols.

In the context of sequential data, a sequence S is *compatible* with a partial order α, if for no pair a_2 preceding a_1 in S, $a_1 \leq_\alpha a_2$ holds in α. In other words, the order of the elements in S does not violate the precedence order encoded by $\leq_\alpha$. A compatible S is also called an *extension* of $\leq_\alpha$. Sequence S is called a complete extension of $\leq_\alpha$ when S contains all the elements of V_α. In the episodes framework, only a complete extension is considered to support the episodes α. We shall define S' as the subsequence of S that is still a complete extension of α but contains only the elements of V_α. Subsequently, we shall refer to S' as the serial extension of α in the sequence S and denote it as $S' \in \alpha$.

A partial order can be represented by a directed graph where each edge (a_1, a_2) represents the relation $a_1 \leq_\alpha a_2$. Since the relation $\leq_\alpha$ is antisymmetric, it is easy to see that this graph is acyclic (i.e., a DAG). Further, the transitive reduction G'_α of the graph G_α also encodes the partial order α such that when $a_1 \leq_\alpha a_2$, there is a directed path from a_1 to a_2 in G'_α.

5.1 Maximal partial order problem

It is easy to see that S is a serial extension of the parallel episode α where $\leq_\alpha = \phi$ for any sequence S on the alphabet V_α. Also if $S \in \alpha(V_\alpha, \leq_\alpha)$, then $S \in \beta(V_\alpha, \leq_\beta)$ where $(\leq_\beta \subset \leq_\alpha)$. Thus it is natural to talk about a *maximal* partial order. We identify the following problem:

PROBLEM 1. *Given a set $\mathcal{S}$ of sequences S_i, $1 \leq i \leq m$, each of length n defined over the same alphabet, find a maximal partial order α such that all $S_i \in \alpha$ and this does not hold for any partial order β with $V_\alpha = V_\beta$ and $(\leq_\beta \supset \leq_\alpha)$.*

Here maximality implies that: given a pair (a_i, a_j), if a_i precedes d_j in *all* the given m sequences then $(a_i \leq_\alpha a_j)$ must hold. A straightforward approach to solving the problem is to collect all pairs (a_1, a_2) such that a_1 precedes a_2 in *all* sequences $s_i \in \mathcal{S}$ and then construct a (transitive reduction) DAG from these pairs.

5.2 Excess in partial orders

Consider $s_1 = \langle a\,b\,c\,d \rangle$ and $s_2 = \langle d\,c\,b\,a \rangle$. Notice that no pair of characters preserve the order in s_1 and s_2, hence the only partial order that s_1 and s_2 do not violate is shown in Figure 5(a). However, any permutation of the characters $\{a, b, c, d\}$ also does not violate this partial order.

Let $A(\alpha)$ be the set of all complete extensions $s \in \alpha$. Thus it is clear that the partial order captures some but not all the subtle ordering information in the data and the maximal partial order α of $\mathcal{S}$ is such that $A(\alpha) \supseteq \mathcal{S}$. The gap, $A(\alpha) \setminus \mathcal{S}$ is termed *excess*. One way to handle excess in partial order is allowing for multiple partial orders, say α_1

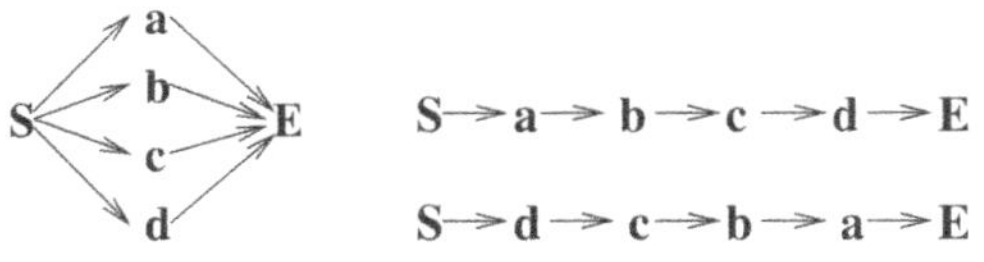

(a) α_0 (b) α_1 and α_2

Figure 5: (a) One partial order, α_0 and (b) two partial orders, α_1, α_2 representing $s_1 = \langle a\,b\,c\,d \rangle$ and $s_2 = \langle d\,c\,b\,a \rangle$.

and α_2 in Figure 5(b). Clearly, given S, there has to be a balance between the number of partial orders and the excess in the single maximal partial order α_0.

It is easy to see that given n distinct sequences, n partial orders (chains or total orders) give zero excess. Obviously this is not an acceptable solution, and a trade off between excess and the number of multiple partial orders needs to be made. However getting an algorithmic handle on this combinatorial problem, using excess, is non trivial. Other researchers have assumed further restrictions, e.g., Mannila and Meek [21] restrict their partial orders to have an MSVP (minimal vertex series-parallel) DAG. Their aim is to count the size of of $A(\alpha)$ (number of complete extensions of α) since they are looking for a probabilistic model of an underlying generator.

5.3 Handling excess with PQ structures

We illustrate this approach starting with an example.

EXAMPLE 5.1. *Let $\mathcal{S} = \{\langle abcdegf \rangle, \langle bacedfg \rangle, \langle acbdefg \rangle, \langle edgfabc \rangle, \langle degfbac \rangle\}$. It is easy to see that the maximal partial order is α_0 shown in Figure 6. In α_1, the alphabet is augmented with $\{\mathbf{S}_1, \mathbf{E}_1, \mathbf{S}_2, \mathbf{E}_2, \mathbf{S}_3, \mathbf{E}_3\}$ to obtain a tighter description of $\mathcal{S}$.*

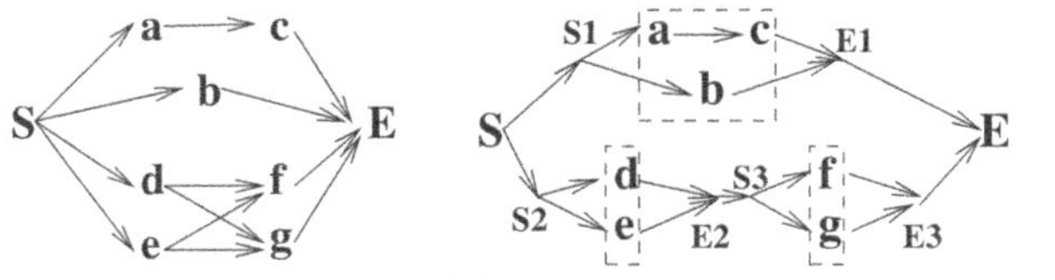

(a) Partial order, α_0 (b) Augmented partial order, α_1

Figure 6: α_1 is a specialization of α_0: If $S \in \alpha_1$, then $S \in \alpha_0$, but not *vice-versa*. If $S = \langle abdefcg \rangle$, then $S \in \alpha_0$ but $S \notin \alpha_1$.

Here the solution to handling excess is to augment the alphabet V_α with $\mathcal{O}(|V_\alpha|)$ characters in the maximal partial order DAG, G_α. Let this new set be V'_α. All complete extension S' are now on $(V_\alpha \cup V'_\alpha)$ and can be easily converted to S on V_α by simply removing all the symbols $\mathbf{S}_k, \mathbf{E}_k \in V'_\alpha$.

The boxed elements in Figure 6 are clusters of symbols that *always* appear together, i.e., are uninterrupted in $\mathcal{S}$. Our scheme exploits this property to reduce excess. We use the systematic representation of these recursive clusters in reducing excess in partial orders. The recursive (order) notation of clusters is naturally encoded by a data structure called the PQ tree [3]. The equivalence of this order notation to a PQ structure, denoted by T_c, along with efficient algorithms is discussed in [16].

A PQ tree is a rooted tree whose internal nodes are of two types: P and Q. The children of a P node occur in no particular order while those of a Q node must appear either

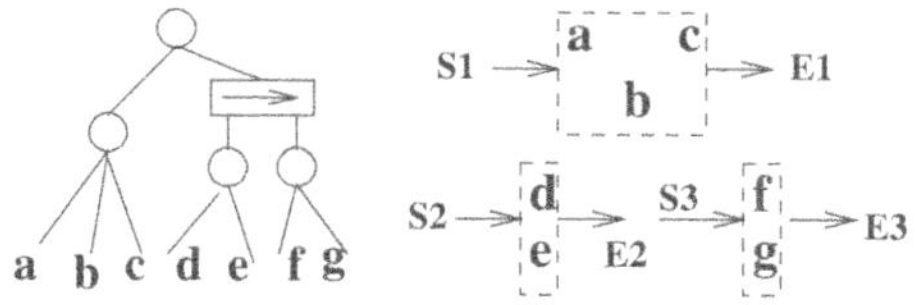

(a) (b)

Figure 7: (a) The minimal consensus oriented PQ structure for the data in Example 5.1. (b) The P nodes as placed in parallel and the Q nodes are placed serially.

in a strict left to right or right to left order. We designate a P node by a circle and a Q node by a rectangle. The leaves of T_c are labeled bijectively by the elements of $\mathcal{S}$. The *frontier* of T_c, denoted by $Fr(T_c)$, is the permutation of the elements of $\mathcal{S}$ obtained by reading the labels of the leaves from left to right. Two PQ trees T_c and $T_{c'}$ are equivalent, denoted $T_c \equiv T_{c'}$, if one can be obtained from the other by applying a sequence of the following transformation rules: (1) Arbitrarily permute the children of a P node, and (2) Reverse the children of a Q node. $\mathcal{C}(T_c)$ is defined as follows: $\mathcal{C}(T_c) = \{Fr(T_{c'}) | T_{c'} \equiv T_c\}$. An *oriented PQ tree* is a tree where all the Q nodes are oriented similarly (in our case left-to-right).

Given $\mathcal{S}$, the *minimal consensus PQ Tree* is a structure that captures all the common clusters that appear in each $s \in \mathcal{S}$. A linear time algorithm, $\mathcal{O}(|\mathcal{S}|\,|V_\alpha|)$, to compute this tree is discussed in [16]. We make a simple modification (not discussed here) in the algorithm to give oriented PQ (oPQ) trees where each Q node follows the strict left-to-right order. The number of augmented alphabet pairs $\mathbf{S}_k, \mathbf{E}_k$, in the augmented DAG correspond to the number of internal nodes in a PQ tree.

Algorithm 2 PQ Tree construction

Input: A set of sequences $\mathcal{S}$ each consisting of all symbols in V.
Output: A minimal consensus PQ Tree T_c for $\mathcal{S}$.

```
Compute common intervals in sequences S = C_Π using algorithm in [10].
Initialize T_c = {Universal tree}
for all c ∈ C_Π do
    T_c = REDUCE(T_c, c){See reference [3]}
return T_c
```

To summarize, given $\mathcal{S}$, our scheme works as follows: (1) We first construct the minimal consensus oriented PQ tree T_c of $\mathcal{S}$ using Algorithm 2. (2) For each internal P node we construct an instance of Problem 1 and construct the maximal partial order. (3) Using the PQ structure of step (1) we combine all the maximal partial order DAGs of (step 2), with augmented characters $\mathbf{S}_k, \mathbf{E}_k$ for each to obtain the augmented maximal partial order.

Figure 7 shows the steps on the data of Example 5.1. (a) shows the minimal consensus oriented PQ tree for the input data. Then the P nodes are arranged in parallel and the Q nodes are arranged serially as shown in (b). For each cluster, the partial order problem is solved and the resulting DAG is shown in Figure 6(b).

6. EMRVIEW

In this section we describe the features of the EMRView graphical user interface (GUI) software that serves as a partial order exploration tool. The parallel episode mining algorithm runs offline to generate a set of frequent parallel episodes for a user-defined support threshold. The parallel episodes are ordered in decreasing order of the significance score discussed earlier. This allows the user to focus his attention on the most surprising patterns in the data first. The offline mining algorithm also determines the support of the sub-sequences in the EMR sequences that constitute the occurrences of the given parallel episode. We learn a partial order over a subset of these sequences chosen so as to account for a sufficient fraction of the support of the parallel episode. This partial order brings out the ordering information embedded in the EMR data and is displayed via its Hasse diagram.

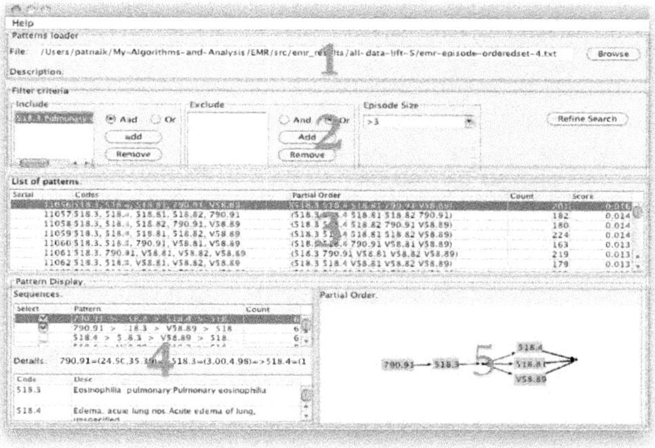

Figure 8: EMRView tool showing different panels of the interface.

Pattern loader (Panel 1): The offline result of parallel episode mining together with counts of the sequences constituting the occurrences of each parallel episode is loaded into the visualization tool. The tool also allows reading data in compressed/zip format.

Filtering results (Panel 2): For the parameters noted in the result section, the number of frequent parallel episodes is over 10,000. Looking through each of the parallel episodes and its supporting subsequences can be a daunting task. The EMRView tool allows the user to filter the list of episodes based on multiple criteria. The user can specify a set of diagnostic codes that must be present in the reported episodes with the option for enforcing all or any of the codes. Similarly the user can specify a set of diagnostic codes that must not be present. Further the user can specify the size of episodes that must be displayed.

A specially designed search dialog is presented to the user to select diagnostic codes. This dialog allows the user to search for the codes by entering either text describing the diagnostic code or the code if available. One could also pick codes by browsing through the hierarchy of the ICD codes. Figure 9 shows the search dialog illustrating the different options available for finding and adding diagnostic codes.

Result display (Panel 3): The filtered parallel episodes are displayed here. The first column gives an identifier for the row. The second column shows the list of

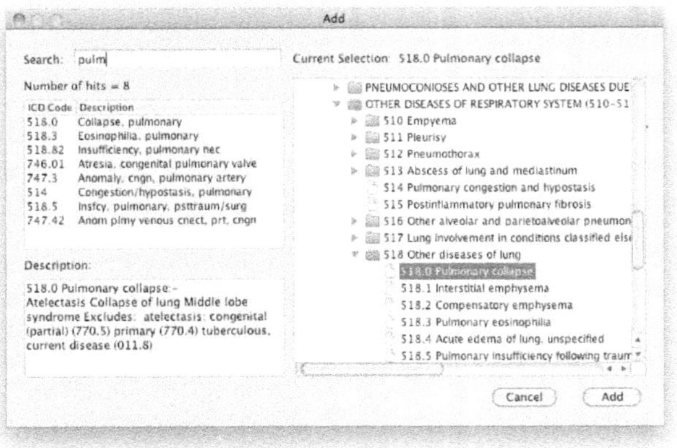

Figure 9: EMRView diagnostic code lookup interface.

codes in the parallel episode. Since there is no order imposed on the codes, we sort them in alphabetical order. The third column displays a partial order learnt from the set of sequences which together account for 75% of the support of the parallel episode. The same set of sequences are shown selected by default in Panel 4. Note that these sequences are ordered in descending order of support. The forth and fifth columns present the support (or count) and significance scores respectively. The rows are presorted in decreasing order of the significance score.

Pattern display (Panel 4): This panel lists the sequences (more appropriately subsequence of the EMR sequences) that constitute the occurrences of the parallel episode. This panel is populated when the user selects a parallel episode in Panel 3. The sequences are listed in decreasing order of support. By default, sequences are selected until the sum of their support values exceeds a threshold of 75% of the total support of the parallel episode. The rationale is that these are likely the most important orders encountered in the data for the parallel episode under consideration. The partial order learnt from the selected sequences is displayed in the adjacent panel. In addition the user can select/deselect sequences. The partial order is updated online to reflect the selection. This puts the user in control of selecting sequences he deems useful and the algorithm summarizes them into a compatible partial order.

7. RESULTS AND CLINICAL RELEVANCE

For the current study we chose to discover temporal patterns that occurred within a consecutive 200 day (6.5 month) period at support level $\geq 10^{-4}$. We did not identify any truly novel patterns but were able to discover many that reflect the capabilities of our algorithm and the power of our partial order discovery methodology.

Figure 10 shows the progression from a general diagnosis of hip pain to a subsequent diagnosis of osteoarthritis and a femur fracture, ultimately requiring a hip replacement. The code 719.68 is rather nonspecific but is typical of diagnosis codes used for routine care, especially when uncertainty exists in the final diagnosis.

Another set of patterns related to sinusitis are shown in Figures 11(a) and 11(b). In both of these sequential patterns, an initial diagnosis (deviated septum or nasal polyps) leads to various chronic sinusitis diagnoses. The sequence in Figure 11(a) occurred 102 times among the patient population, whereas the two sequences shown in Figure 11(b) occurred collectively 27 times. Similar sequences could also be found in the dataset with varying frequencies.

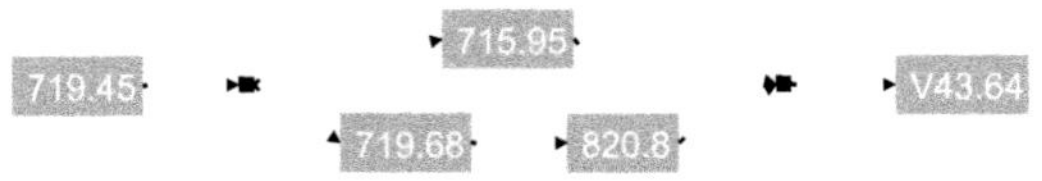

Figure 10: A five-sequence pattern demonstrating an initial diagnosis of pelvic pain (719.45) followed by the variable sequence of (a) a poorly defined joint symptom (719.68); (b) a femoral neck fracture (820.8); and (c) pelvic osteoarthritis (715.95), with a final common pathway converging on a hip joint replacement (V43.64).

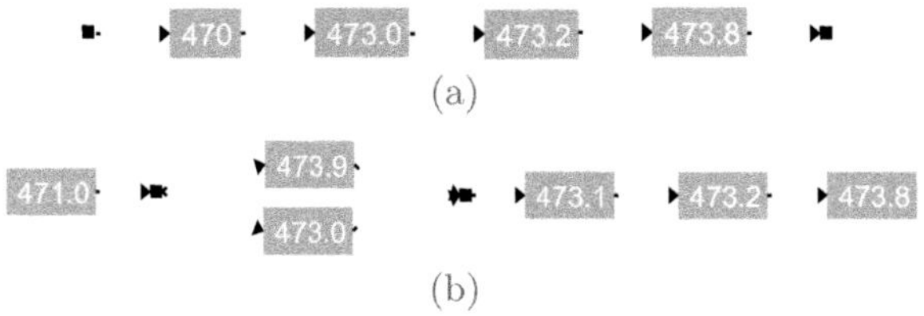

Figure 11: Sequences showing events leading to a sinusitis diagnosis. In (a) a deviated septum (470) leads to maxillary sinusitis (473.0), followed by ethmoidal sinusitis (473.2), and then a non-specific sinusitis diagnosis (473.8). In (b) nasal polyps (471.0) leads to maxillary sinusitis (473.0) or a non-specific sinusitis (473.9), followed by frontal sinusitis (473.1), then ethmoidal sinusitis (473.2) and finally another non-specific sinusitis (473.8).

Some sequences converged on a diagnosis or event, whereas others diverged. This can be seen in Figures 12(a) and 12(b). Figure 12(a) shows events related to arm fractures at a school playground (representing 84 distinct patients), whereas Figure 12(b) shows events related to an initial pylenonephritis (kidney infection) event with subsequent diagnoses of calculi (stones) in the kidneys and urinary tracts. In this context, a convergence means requiring a particular diagnosis before continuing to make other diagnoses.

The clinical relevance of the above patterns is quite immediate. For instance, the presence of osteoarthritis is a recommended, although controversial, indication for performing a hip joint replacement after the occurrence of a femoral neck fracture[9, 28, 18]. It is possible to imagine that someday clinicians may wish to interrogate their local data with EMRView to determine local patterns of care in order to answer questions such as "At our institution, what is our routine process of care for patients with a finding of osteoarthritis who subsequently develop a femoral neck fracture?" A key component in such a query would be to include the temporal concept of "subsequently" so that the timing of the fracture in relation to the other relevant diagnoses can be taken into account.

The observations regarding sinusitis are also interesting, and support the use of EMRView for hypothesis generation.

(a) (b)

Figure 12: Sequences that converge onto a common event or diverge from a common event. The elements stacked vertically were found to occur interchangeably in the patterns found, suggesting that the specific ordering does not matter. In (a) A fall from playground equipment (E884.0) was associated in time with a lower humerus fracture(812.40) as well as a supracondylar humerus fracture (812.41), but all ended up with a follow-up exam for the healed fracture (V67.4). The diagram in (b) shows an initial pylenonephritis event (590.00) occurring, followed by the diagnoses of kidney calculus (e.g., stone) (592.0), ureter calculus (592.1), and non-specific urinary calculus (592.9).

It is well known that maxillary sinus is the most common site for such an infection to occur, followed by the ethmoid sinus (87% vs. 65%, respectively) [14], but it is worthwhile to note that in our observations, for the sequences that contained the codes for both maxillary (473.0) and ethmoidal sinusitis (473.2) the maxillary preceded the ethmoidal in the vast majority of cases. It may be that a severe maxillary sinusitis can often lead to an ethmoid infection with the reverse sequence being less common, or it may simply be that maxillary sinusitis is easier to diagnose and only later is an ethmoid sinusitis diagnosed in the same patient. It is also noteworthy that this temporal pattern occurred when the initial diagnoses was a deviated septum as well as with nasal polyps. It is unclear why this temporal pattern emerged. At least one source has reported that about 75% of all polyps are located in the ethmoid sinuses [19], which raises the question why the sinusitis was still primarily occurring in the maxillary sinuses first.

Among the other events we reported, the relationship between arm/humerus fractures and falls from school playground equipment is well documented in the literature [17, 11]. Nevertheless, monitoring how such patterns over time change at a specific medical center might allow for the detection of playgrounds that are especially dangerous, or perhaps the success of safety programs implemented to prevent such accidents. The relationship between pyelonephritis (kidney infections) and urinary system calculi also has important implications. As outlined in a recent report, using ultrasound to discover the calculi may be a useful tool when such infections are diagnosed since calculi may be a complicating factor in the management of the infections [4].

8. RELATED WORK

Many studies have explored temporal patterns in clinical data: some have focused on extracting temporal patterns from natural language descriptions in clinical documents [27, 8] whereas others have used coded administrative data, similar to the data we used [6, 2]. Reis et al. [26] used Bayesian models to predict future risks of abuse based on past episodes. They theorized that such a system could provide an early warning for clinicians to identify patients at high risk for future abuse episodes. Others have used temporal data mining to explore patterns related to specific diseases such as diabetes [5] or specific time frames such as adverse events following immunizations in a large cohort of nearly a million children in Denmark [29].

Plaisant and colleagues [25] built into the Microsoft Amalga software a user interface to help visualize patient specific temporal patterns. This did not involve data mining and the interface itself was significantly different from EMRView. More closely related, however, was the methodology and interface built by Moskovitch and Shahar [23] to identify and visualize temporal patterns in clinical data which was applied to a dataset of about 2000 patients with diabetes. More broadly, several published papers discuss the challenges faced in analyzing EMR data starting from data integration aspects [15] to privacy issues [22]. Interest in the KDD community has blossomed recently, e.g., in [31], a multi label classifier is proposed that learns inter-code relationships from clinical free text. In another study it has been shown that using the entropy of ICD9 codes it is possible to categorize diseases as chronic or acute [24]. Our work is novel in the application to a large scale database of EMRs to mine frequent and significant episodes, in the new partial order discovery algorithm, and in the development of EMRView based on user needs.

9. DISCUSSION

Our exercise in using temporal data mining to identify clinically relevant patterns in medical record data did demonstrate the feasibility of the approach. We were able to find hundreds of patterns using real world data that had been collected as a part of routine care. The clinical relevance of the patterns helps to confirm the validity of our mining algorithms.

Our current analysis brings about many future challenges for temporal mining in EMRs. For instance, thus far we have limited the time frame for analysis to 200 days. While this has the advantage, at least theoretically, of yielding greater clinical relevance between events that are temporally correlated, the disadvantage is the danger of missing correlated events that are far apart. Asbestos exposure and subsequent development of lung diseases is one such example [12]. Automatically identifying intervals for analysis is one area of research.

A second major issue with our analysis is that it is easier to obtain the data then it is to explore or assign meaning to the results. There is nothing intrinsic in the data itself to inform if a temporal sequence is novel, important, or even clinically valid. From our initial analysis the results do seem to be valid, but there is no existing database of clinical medicine with which to computationally compare our findings. The more frequently occurring patterns are probably a reflection of an event occurring more frequently among our population. But it may very well be that the less frequently occurring events are the ones that are not well described in the literature and may represent novel discoveries. Finding a scalable approach to explore this space is still an open question.

Last, while we did have nearly 100 million events with which to detect patterns, these codes still represent only a tiny fraction of the clinical parameters that are relevant to each patient. Many clinical details were not present in the dataset that might have a significant impact on the interpretation of the results. It will be important to develop methods to incorporate these additional data into the data mining algorithms to extract more meaningful results in the future.

Acknowledgements

This work is supported in part by the Institute for Critical Technology and Applied Science, Virginia Tech and by US NSF grant CCF-0937133.

Availability of source code

The software is available at http://nostoc.cs.vt.edu/emr-view.

10. REFERENCES

[1] R. Agrawal and R. Srikant. Mining sequential patterns. In *11th ICDE*, pages 3—14, Taipei, Taiwan, 1995.

[2] R. Bellazzi et al. Methods and tools for mining multivariate temporal data in clinical and biomedical applications. In *Conf Proc IEEE Eng Med Biol Soc.*, pages 5629–32, 2009.

[3] K. Booth and G. Lueker. Testing for the Consecutive Ones Property, Interval Graphs, and Graph Planarity using PQ-tree Algorithms. *JCSS*, 13(3):335–379, 1976.

[4] K. C. Chen, S. W. Hung, V. K. Seow, C. F. Chong, T. L. Wang, Y. C. Li, and H. Chang. The role of emergency ultrasound for evaluating acute pyelonephritis in the ed. *Am J Emerg Med*, Apr 2010.

[5] S. Concaro et al. Temporal data mining for the assessment of the costs related to diabetes mellitus pharmacological treatment. In *AMIA Annu Symp Proc.*, pages 119–123, 2009.

[6] S. Concaro et al. Mining health care administrative data with temporal association rules on hybrid events. *Methods Inf Med*, 50(2), Dec 2010.

[7] C. De Coster et al. Identifying priorities in methodological research using ICD-9-CM and ICD-10 administrative data: report from an international consortium. *BMC Health Serv Res.*, 6:77, Jun 2006.

[8] J. Denny et al. Extracting timing and status descriptors for colonoscopy testing from electronic medical records. *J Am Med Inform Assoc.*, 17(4):383–8, Jul-Aug 2010.

[9] W. L. Healy and R. Iorio. Total hip arthroplasty: optimal treatment for displaced femoral neck fractures in elderly patients. *Clin Orthop Relat Res*, (429):43–48, Dec 2004.

[10] S. Heber and J. Stoye. Finding all common intervals of k permutations. In *Proc. of the 12th CPM'01*, pages 207–218, London, UK, UK, 2001. Springer-Verlag.

[11] A. W. Howard, C. Macarthur, L. Rothman, A. Willan, and A. K. Macpherson. School playground surfacing and arm fractures in children: a cluster randomized trial comparing sand to wood chip surfaces. *PLoS Med*, 6(12), Dec 2009.

[12] E. Jamrozik, N. de Klerk, and A. Musk. Clinical review: Asbestos-related disease. *Intern Med J*, Feb 2011.

[13] E. T. Jaynes. Information theory and statistical mechanics. *Phys. Rev.*, 106(4):620–630, May 1957.

[14] W. Kormos. *Primary Care Medicine*, chapter Approach to the Patient With Sinusitis, pages 1402–1407. Lippincot WIlliams and WIlkins, 2009.

[15] R. Kukafka et al. Redesigning electronic health record systems to support public health. *J. of Biomedical Informatics*, 40:398–409, August 2007.

[16] G. Landau, L. Parida, and O. Weimann. Using PQ Trees for Comparative Genomics. In *Proc. CPM*, pages 128–143, 2005.

[17] R. T. Loder. The demographics of playground equipment injuries in children. *J Pediatr Surg*, 43(4):691–699, Apr 2008.

[18] J. A. Lowe, B. D. Crist, M. Bhandari, and T. A. Ferguson. Optimal treatment of femoral neck fractures according to patient's physiologic age: an evidence-based review. *Orthop Clin North Am*, 41(2):157–166, Apr 2010.

[19] T. M and L. PL. *Nasal Polyps: Origin, Etiology, Pathenogensis, and Structure*, chapter Diseases of the sinuses: diagnosis and management, pages 57–68. 2001.

[20] H. Mannila et al. Discovery of frequent episodes in event sequences. *DMKD*, 1:259–289, 1997.

[21] H. Mannila and C. Meek. Global Partial Orders from Sequential Data. In *Proc. KDD'00*, pages 161–168, 2000.

[22] L. Martino and S. Ahuja. Privacy policies of personal health records: an evaluation of their effectiveness in protecting patient information. In *Proc. of 1st ACM Intl. Health Informatics Symp.*, pages 191–200, New York, NY, USA, 2010. ACM.

[23] R. Moskovitch and Y. Shahar. Medical temporal-knowledge discovery via temporal abstraction. In *AMIA Annu Symp Proc.*, pages 452–456, 2009.

[24] A. Perotte. Using the entropy of icd9 documentation across patients to characterize using the entropy of ICD9 documentation across patients to characterize disease chronicity. AMIA Annual Symp., Nov 2010.

[25] C. Plaisant et al. Searching electronic health records for temporal patterns in patient histories: a case study with microsoft amalgaa. In *AMIA Annu Symp Proc. 2008*, pages 601–605, 2008.

[26] B. Reis et al. Longitudinal histories as predictors of future diagnoses of domestic abuse: modelling study. *BMJ*, 2009.

[27] G. Savova et al. Towards temporal relation discovery from the clinical narrative. In *AMIA Annu Symp Proc.*, pages 569–572, 2009.

[28] E. Sendtner, T. Renkawitz, P. Kramny, M. Wenzl, and J. Grifka. Fractured neck of femur–internal fixation versus arthroplasty. *Dtsch Arztebl Int*, 107(23):401–407, Jun 2010.

[29] H. Svanstrom et al. Temporal data mining for adverse events following immunization in nationwide danish healthcare databases. *Drug Saf.*, 33(11):1015–25, Nov 2010.

[30] N. Tatti. Maximum entropy based significance of itemsets. In *Proc. 7th ICDM'07*, pages 312–321, 2007.

[31] Y. Yan, G. Fung, J. G. Dy, and R. Rosales. Medical coding classification by leveraging inter-code relationships. In *Proc. 16th KDD'10*, pages 193–202, New York, NY, USA, 2010. ACM.

Understanding Atrophy Trajectories in Alzheimer's Disease Using Association Rules on MRI Images

György J. Simon
Dept. of Health Sciences Research, Mayo Clinic, Rochester, MN
simon.gyorgy@mayo.edu

Peter W. Li
Dept. of Health Sciences Research, Mayo Clinic, Rochester, MN
li.peter@mayo.edu

Clifford R. Jack Jr.
Dept. of Radiology, Mayo Clinic, Rochester, MN
jack.clifford@mayo.edu

Prashanthi Vemuri
Dept. of Radiology, Mayo Clinic, Rochester, MN
vemuri.prashanthi@mayo.edu

ABSTRACT

Alzheimer's disease (AD) is associated with progressive cognitive decline leading to dementia. The atrophy/loss of brain structure as seen on Magnetic Resonance Imaging (MRI) is strongly correlated with the severity of the cognitive impairment in AD. In this paper, we set out to find associations between predefined regions of the brain (regions of interest; ROIs) and the severity of the disease. Specifically, we use these associations to address two important issues in AD: (i) typical versus atypical atrophy patterns and (ii) the origin and direction of progression of atrophy, which is currently under debate.

We observed that each AD-related ROI is associated with a wide range of severity and that the difference between ROIs is merely a difference in severity distribution. To model differences between the severity distribution of a subpopulation (with significant atrophy in certain ROIs) and the severity distribution of the entire population, we developed the concept of Distributional Association Rules. Using the Distributional Association Rules, we clustered ROIs into disease subsystems. We define a disease subsystem as a contiguous set of ROIs that are collectively implicated in AD. AD is known to be heterogeneous in the sense that multiple sets of ROIs may be related to the disease in a population. We proposed an enhancement to the association rule mining where the algorithm only discovers association rules with ROIs that form an approximately contiguous volume. Next, we applied these association rules to infer the direction of disease progression based on the support measures of the association rules. We also developed a novel statistical test to determine the statistical significance of the discovered direction.

We evaluated the proposed method on the Mayo Clinic Alzheimer's Disease Research Center (ADRC) prospective patient cohorts. The key achievements of the methodology is that it accurately identified larger disease subsystems implicated in typical and atypical AD and it successfully mapped the directions of disease progression.

The wealth of data available in Radiology gives rise to opportunities for applying this methodology to map out the trajectory of several other diseases, e.g. other neurodegenerative diseases and cancers, most notably, breast cancer. The applicability of this method is not limited to image data, as associating predictors with severity provides valuable information in most areas of medicine as well as other industries.

KDD'11, August 21–24, 2011, San Diego, California, USA.

Categories and Subject Descriptors

H.2.8 [**Information Systems**]: Data Mining; J.3 [**Computer Applications**]: Life and Medical Sciences

General Terms: Algorithms

Keywords: spatial association analysis, continuous outcome, MRI, disease progression

1. INTRODUCTION

Alzheimer's disease (AD) is a multi faceted disease wherein cumulative brain pathology results in progressive cognitive decline, which ultimately leads to dementia. Of all the biomarkers that are being currently investigated and evaluated for AD, loss/atrophy of the brain structures as seen on structural Magnetic Resonance Imaging (MRI) appears to strongly correlate with the severity of cognitive impairment in AD [10]. In our previous works, we found that MRI images are extremely useful for separating AD from cognitively normal individuals as well as for staging the disease severity [19]. In addition, we recently established a data-mining method to use MRI to differentiate AD from other neurodegenerative diseases [18]. We implemented this method by considering 118 regions of interest (ROI) in the brain which characterize the amount of gray matter density in each of these regions. One key observation from this study was that the atrophy in AD is multi-modal in nature in a sense that multiple different sets of ROIs are predictive of AD. This observation is supported by recent literature [2, 8]. In this study we set out to investigate whether the multi-modal nature of the atrophy patterns is related to the severity of disease using spatial association rules.

The approach we took in this study was to extract the association between the atrophy in these ROIs and clinical severity of AD. Clinical severity was measured using the Clinical Dementia Rating–sum of boxes (CDR-SB) [in this paper we simply call this CDR] which assesses global functional performance in individual subjects [4]. CDR ranges from 0 to 18 in 0.5 increments with 0 representing normal functional performance. Since the relationship between atrophy and CDR is complex, we found that the relationship between gray matter in an ROI and CDR is best described by CDR distribution across patients with significant atrophy in the ROI. Our goal was to associate atrophy regions with differences in the CDR distribution between the affected population (patients with significant atrophy in the region) and the entire population. We then use the discovered associations to decipher brain loss trajectories in AD.

Evidence indicates that the pathology of AD tends to affect contiguous volumes of ROIs and the patterns of atrophy have been shown to originate at a specific ROI and to spread further away from the origin [5]. Since the ROIs are located in a three-dimensional Euclidean space, we can use spatial constraints to discover such near-contiguous sets of ROIs. We enhanced the association rule mining algorithm to only discover rules with near-contiguous sets of ROIs.

We evaluated the proposed method on the Mayo Clinic Alzheimer's Disease Research Center (ADRC) prospective patient cohorts. The subjects used in this study were 120 cognitively normal (controls), 81 mild cognitive impairment (MCI) subjects who later progressed to AD and 48 AD subjects confirmed pathologically. The MCI subjects represent the lower end of the CDR spectrum, while the pathologically confirmed AD subjects represent the mid and higher end of the spectrum.

The major contributions of this work were as follows.

1. We developed Distributional Association Rules, a method for associating ROIs with differences in the distribution of severity scores.

2. We enhance the association rule discovery by incorporating spatial constraints imposed by the requirement that the AD subsystems be near contiguous volumes. Our definition of the constraint allows for elongated volumes that may arise as a result of the how the disease is spreading.

3. We proposed a method for determining the direction of disease progression and a statistical test to assess the significance of the direction.

4. We used higher-order association rules to identify *AD subsystems*. One of the subsystems we identified is known to be consistent with atypical AD.

2. RELATED WORKS

Association rule mining has been a popular technique since its introduction in [1]. Owing to its inherent ability to handle multi-modal data, its non-greedy nature and the wealth of efficient techniques for computing the rules, it has found applications in virtually all domains, including medical imaging. Zaïane et al. [20] present a classification system for mammography images, Pan et al. [14] applied association rules to ROI detection and Sheela et al. [16] extend the well-known Classification Based on Associations (CBA) algorithm [12] to handle quantitative variables in the context of MRI image classification. While these methods are interesting, they suffer from two main drawbacks.

First, they tend to simplify the disease as a classification problem. For many diseases, just stating whether a patient is affected by the disease or not is insufficient; the degree to which the patient is affected (*severity*) often carries more importance. Predicting severity is difficult, because very often severity does not have a direct causal relationship with its predictors, it is merely correlated with them (often weakly and non-linearly). Therefore, we model disease severity as a distribution and we seek to discovery patient subpopulations whose severity distribution significantly deviates from the severity distribution of the entire population.

CDR is an ordinal categorical variable which lies between class labels (nominal categorical) and quantitative outcomes. Association between subpopulations and class labels have been considered from a statistical perspective by Brin using the χ^2-test [6] and association between subpopulations and a continuous outcome variable has been studied by Aumann et al. [3] using the Z-test. Our approach is analogous to Aumann's technique with differences dictated by (i) the non-continuous nature of CDR distribution, (ii) lack of homoscedasticity across the popopulation and (iii) detection of differences in the *shape* of the distributions.

The second drawback of the existing applications of association rule mining to the medical domain concerns the lack of incorporating known medical constraints into the mining process. Domain knowledge is mostly incorporated as features for mining or as post-discovery filtering of association rules.

2.1 Use of Spatial Constraints

A key piece of domain knowledge we have regards the pattern of how disease spreads: the pathology of AD tends to originate at a specific ROI and it spreads further away from the origin [5]. Since the ROIs in the brain are located in a 3-D Euclidean space with known distances between the ROIs, we incorporate spatial constraints into the mining process.

Although Geographic Information Systems (GIS) (see [13] for an overview) are the state of the art in incorporating spatial constraints, these systems aim to *discover* spatial knowledge rather than *use* spatial constraints to discover non-spatial (i.e. disease-related) knowledge. The most related work in using spatial constraints comes from the genomic data mining domain. Icev et al. [9] applied spatial (distance-based) constraints to find association rules involving genotypical motifs that are located close-by to each other on the genome. Our application of distance-based constraints are different in that (i) the manner in which AD spreads may result in *elongated* volumes of ROIs which our constraint accommodates and (ii) our definition of the distance constraint can be incorporated into the frequent pattern discovery process in a straight-forward fashion.

2.2 Interestingness Measures

As we discussed earlier, one of the main means of incorporating domain knowledge is filtering. Association rule mining algorithms tend to discover exponential number of rules and interestingness measures are used for discarding uninteresting rules. See [17] for an extensive list of interestingness measures. Rules that do not conform to domain knowledge can be discarded as uninteresting.

A common problem with interestingness measures is that the vast majority of them is not rooted in a rigorous statistical framework. In contrast, we filter our association rules and we infer direction of disease progression based on statistical significance.

Given a statistical model and the notion that disease progression is related to causality, a causality inference technique similar to that of Schadt et al. [15] appears applicable to progression inference. Disease progression and causality, however, possess a substantial difference that renders such a maximum likelihood-based approach inapplicable. If event A *causes* event B to occur, then A and B tend to co-occur with high probability. On the other hand, when disease progresses from ROI A to ROI B, A and B will co-occur, but not with very high probability. Our approach accounts for this crucial difference.

3. METHOD

We first provide a high-level overview of the methodology and each step will be described in detail in subsequent sections.

1. *We discover distributional association rules with spatial constraints.*

   (a) We first extract *spatial patterns* from the data set. Spatial patterns consist of ROIs of significant atrophy that form near contiguous volumes in the brain.

   (b) We form *distributional association rules* from the spatial patterns. Each *spatial pattern* applies to a subset of the patients in the sample, namely the patients with significant atrophy in each of these specific ROIs. The CDR values of these patients form a distribution. A distributional association rule is comprised of a *spatial pattern* and implies the CDR distribution of the patients the *spatial pattern* applies to. Distributional association rules are only interesting if they imply a CDR distribution that is different from the CDR distribution of the entire population.

   In the following sections, unless otherwise noted, the term 'association rules' refers to distributional associations rule with spatial patterns.

2. *We aggregate ROIs into subsystems to gain a more macroscopic view of the disease.* Evidence exists that AD affects *subsystems*, which are larger contiguous volumes consisting of multiple ROIs related to each other. High order association rules (association rules with at least 3 ROIs) are indicative of such sets of ROIs.

3. *We infer the direction of disease progression between and within the subsystems.* From the association rules consisting of pairs of ROIs, we infer whether the disease progressed from one ROI to the other. Then we combine the discovered directions of progression into a disease progression network. We enhance the interpretability of the networks by incorporating information about subsystems.

3.1 Spatial Patterns Extraction

Let X denote an observation matrix of Z-scores (standard normal quantile) indicating the amount of atrophy each patient has suffered relative to our large set of controls. X has 118 columns, one for each ROI and its rows correspond to patients. Let C denote the vector of CDR measurements. For patient j, row X_j contains the Z-scores and C_j is his CDR score.

An **item** is a predicate indicating whether patient j has suffered significant atrophy in ROI i; specifically $X_{i,j} < -1.5$. If this predicate holds, then patient j is said to **support** item i. An **itemset** is a set of **items** and hence a set of predicates. The itemset holds true if all predicates corresponding to the constituent items hold. In other words, a patient supports an itemset if he supports *all* items in the itemset. The **support (count)** of an itemset I is the number of patients that supports I. I is **frequent** if its support exceeds a user-defined minimum support threshold σ.

DEFINITION 1 (SPATIAL PATTERN). *An itemset $I = \{a, b, c\}$ is a spatial pattern with respect to a distance matrix D, if for all item i in I, there exists in another item j in I, such that $D_{i,j} < \delta$ and $i \neq j$. $D_{i,j}$ denotes the distance between ROIs i and j; and δ is a user-specified maximum distance threshold.*

Since each ROI would typically have 6 neighbors in space, we selected the 10th percentile of all distances as the threshold δ.

LEMMA 1. *If two spatial patterns I_1, I_2 of the same length differ only in one item, then their super-pattern $I_1 \cup I_2$ is also a spatial pattern.*

Let $I_1 = \{a, b, c\}$ and $I_2 = \{a, b, d\}$. Their super-pattern is $I = \{a, b, c, d\}$. If I is a spatial pattern, then for each item $i \in I$, there is another item $j \in I$, such that $D_{i,j} < \delta$. Let us consider item a. Because I_1 is a spatial pattern, $D_{a,c} < \delta$ or $D_{a,b} < \delta$ holds. Since both b and c are in I, there is at least one item in I that is within δ distance from a. The proof works analogously for items b, c and d.

The importance of Lemma 1 lies in the candidate generation of the apriori algorithm. To form candidate itemsets of length $(k+1)$, apriori joins two itemsets of length k that differ only in a single item. Therefore the apriori algorithm will generate spatial candidate patterns of length $k+1$ as long as the patterns of length k are spatial patterns.

The goal of **Spatial Pattern Extraction** is to extract *all* frequent spatial patterns from the data set that meet the minimum support threshold σ and the maximum distance threshold δ.

We utilize a modified version of the apriori algorithm to find all spatial frequent patterns. The apriori algorithm iteratively constructs the lattice structure of the items proceeding in a depth-first manner. It first considers all items and discards the ones that have insufficient support. In the second iteration, it forms pairs of items and discards the infrequent pairs. In the k-th iteration, it considers the $k-1$ patterns and combines those that differ only in one item[1].The infrequent k-itemsets are discarded.

[1]The original apriori algorithm considers two k-itemsets that differ only in their *last* item. We have consider all k-itemsets that differ in any one item, because not all subsets of a spatial pattern are spatial patterns.

3.2 Distributional Association Rules and their Statistical Significance

Let I be a frequent pattern and let P be the set of patients (rows of X) that support I. Let C_P be the CDR values corresponding to the patients in P. C_P defines a distribution of CDR values.

DEFINITION 2 (DISTRIBUTIONAL ASSOCIATION RULE). *The rule $I \rightarrow C_P$ is a distributional association rule if and only if I is a frequent pattern and C_P is the distribution of CDR values of the patients that support I. I is the* **antecedent** *and the distribution is the* **consequent** *of the rule.*

More specifically, in this paper we are interested in Distributional Association Rules with spatial patterns, that is Distributional Association Rules where I is a frequent spatial pattern.

Since both C (CDR values for the entire patient sample) and C_P represent distributions, we assess the significance of the spatial distributional association rule via the following hypothesis testing problem. The null hypothesis is that C and C_P are drawn from the same population (essentially C_P is a random sample of C); the alternative hypothesis is that C_P is associated with higher CDR values. We use the Wilcox rank test to compare the distributions. The Wilcox rank test is non-parameteric, makes no distributional assumptions and does not rely on homoscedasticity.

The majority of the population–even in the sample, where we evaluated our method–does not suffer from AD. The CDR distribution of the population is therefore heavily skewed towards 0 (subjects not affected by AD have CDR 0). Distributional association rules, for which we fail to reject the null hypothesis $H0$, show no evidence of being predictive of Alzheimer's disease. Such rules are uninformative in discovering disease subsystems or in inferring disease progression and hence they are discarded.

3.3 Disease Subsystem Discovery

In order to gain a more macroscopic view of the disease we discover disease subsystems.

DEFINITION 3 (DISEASE SUBSYSTEM). *A disease subsystem is a near contiguous set of ROIs that are significantly associated with AD. Two ROIs are* near contiguous *if their centers are within δ distance from each other.*

In practice, we approximate disease subsystems as significant association rules (with spatial patterns). The spatial pattern in the antecedent ensures the near contiguity of the ROIs and the significant difference between CDR distributions ensures that these ROIs are related to AD.

We know that AD is heterogeneous, and its heterogeneity presents itself in the existence of multiple disease subsystems. We also know that atrophy affects the left and right hemisphere of the brain symmetrically. Therefore, we aim to discover clusters of ROIs that are (i) the antecedents of an association rule highly associated with AD (low p-value w.r.t. the Wilcox test) and (ii) the left-right symmetric counterparts of the ROIs form the antecedent of an association rule we discovered and (iii) they do not overlap with other subsystems.

We find these subsystems greedily in a straightforward manner. We sort the association rules on the p-value of their distributional significance and discard all association rules where the symmetric counterpart of the ROIs in the antecedent is not the antecedent of an existing association rule we discovered. We process the rules in increasing order of the p-value and add the antecedent of the rule to the set of subsystems, if it does not overlap with any previously discovered subsystems.

3.4 Inferring the Direction of Disease Progression

Consider two ROIs R_s and R_t that co-occur in association rules. If R_s is the source of progression and R_t is the target, we initially expect to see patients with atrophy in R_s only; and in later stages of the disease, we expect to see patients with atrophy both in R_s and R_t. If R_s is indeed the source of the disease progression, then we expect

$$\Pr(R_s|R_t) > \Pr(R_t|R_s), \tag{1}$$

where $\Pr(A)$ is the probability that a randomly chosen patient has Z-score $<$ -1.5 in ROI A. In this section, we develop a statistical technique to test this hypothesis.

Moreover, if R_s is the source and R_t is the target of disease progression, then $\{R_s, R_t\}$ occurs in a later stage of the disease than R_s. Thus we expect $\{R_s, R_t\}$ to be associated with distributions that have higher severity than $\{R_s\}$. We will use this observation as an internal check to verify that the the direction inferred from Equation 1 indeed describes progression as we expected.

3.4.1 Test of Progression

We can formally infer the progression of disease through the following hypothesis testing problem.

$$H_0 \;:\; \Pr(R_s|R_t) = \Pr(R_t|R_s) \tag{2}$$

$$H_A \;:\; \Pr(R_s|R_t) > \Pr(R_t|R_s) \tag{3}$$

Under the null hypothesis

$$\frac{\Pr(R_s, R_t)}{\Pr(R_t)} = \frac{\Pr(R_s, R_t)}{\Pr(R_s)}.$$

This is only possible if

$$\Pr(R_s) = \Pr(R_t).$$

If $\Pr(R_s) = \Pr(R_t)$, then we can estimate this quantity as the *pooled probability*

$$\Pr(R_p) = \frac{\Pr(R_s) + \Pr(R_t)}{2}. \tag{4}$$

Based on the normal approximation, the $100 * (1 - \alpha)$ confidence interval of $\Pr(R_p)$ is

$$\Pr(R_p) \pm z_\alpha \sqrt{\Pr(R_p)\,(1 - \Pr(R_p))\,N^{-1}}, \tag{5}$$

where N is the sample size. Consequently, the $100(1 - \alpha)$ confidence interval of $\Pr(R_s|R_t)$ as well as $\Pr(R_t|R_s)$ under H_0 is

$$\frac{\Pr(R_s, R_t)}{\Pr(R_p) \pm z_\alpha \sqrt{\Pr(R_p)\,(1 - \Pr(R_p))\,N^{-1}}}. \tag{6}$$

H_0 is rejected if $\Pr(R_s|R_t)$ or $\Pr(R_t|R_s)$ is outside the confidence interval in Equation 6. This coincides with $\Pr(R_s)$

or $\Pr(R_t)$ falling outside the confidence interval in Equation 5. Since the null distribution is symmetric around $\Pr(R_p)$, it suffices to check whether

$$\Pr(R_t) < \Pr(R_p) - z_\alpha \sqrt{\Pr(R_p)\,(1 - \Pr(R_p))\,N^{-1}}.$$

A note on simultaneous hypothesis testing.

Since the test is carried out with respect to a large number of R_s-R_t pairs, correction for simultaneous hypothesis testing is needed. Bonferroni correction, a popular technique for correction, in this case is underestimating the true significance for the following reasons. (i) The atrophy of the brain is fairly symmetric. If a progress direction is established on one side, then it likely exists on the other side, too. (ii) If the marginally significant direction coincides with increased severity, the direction is more likely to be significant than suggested by the Bonferroni correction which is agnostic of the disease severity.

4. EVALUATION

The proposed method was evaluated on a large sample of patients coming from the Mayo Clinic Alzheimer's Disease Research Center (ADRC) prospective patient cohorts. The sample consists of three cohorts: 120 cognitively normal, 81 subjects with mild cognitive impairment (MCI) who progressed to AD and 48 pathologically confirmed AD subjects to get pathologically clean AD patients. The MCI patients represent the lower CDR spectrum, while the pathologically confirmed AD patients represent the mid to upper range of CDR spectrum. The number of MCI vs pathologically confirmed AD subjects is approximately representative of the patient population.

Gray matter density in 118 pre-defined regions of interest was used as predictors after adjusting for gender and age, standardizing to the 120 control subjects. The CDR score is available for all 249 patients.

We used all three cohorts (the controls, MCI patients and pathologically confirmed AD patients) to discover the spatial patterns and the Distributional Association Rules. We discovered 573 association rules at a minimum support count (σ) of 10. 153 of these 573 rules were found to have a CDR distribution that is significantly different from the CDR distribution of the entire sample at a Bonferroni-corrected significance level of 0.05. 37 rules contained a single ROI in their antecedent, 59 rules contained a pair of ROIs and the remaining rules had three or more ROIs. The longest rule contained 5 ROIs.

4.1 Single ROI associated with AD

Rules with a single ROI represent regions of the brain significantly associated with AD. Figure 1 depicts these ROIs with the color indicating the median severity of the effected patients. More vibrant yellow signifies higher severity. The first 6 panes represent 6 slices of the brain in axial view (view from the top) and the seventh pane is a sagittal (side) view of the brain. The sagittal view has horizontal blue lines corresponding to locations of the six slices.

The regions found to be significant are mainly in the temporo-parietal and some frontal regions which are consistent with the literature.

Figure 2 shows the CDR distribution for the individual ROIs as boxplots. ROIs are displayed on the vertical axis (e.g. ROI #37 is the hippocampus); CDR is displayed on

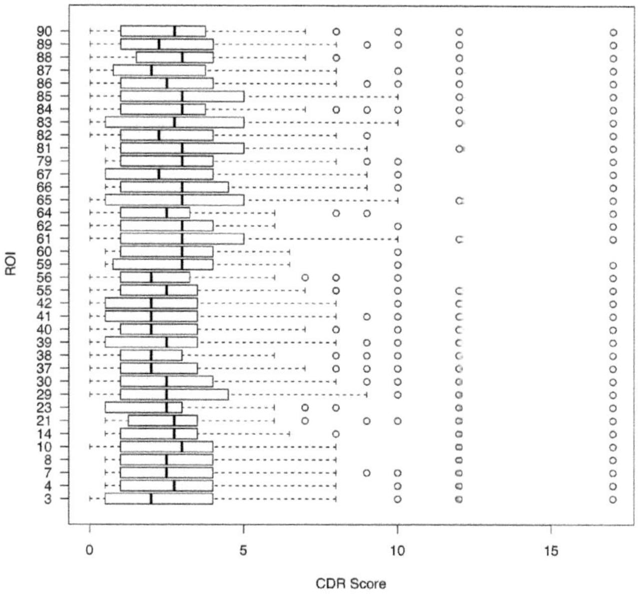

Figure 2: CDR score distribution in each of the ROIs significantly associated with AD

the horizontal axis. While the CDR ranges largely overlap across ROIs, the medians are different and differences in CDR score distribution across ROIs clearly exist. For example, ROIs in the medial temporal lobe (ROI #35-50), which have been implicated earlier in the disease, have lower CDR scores than the frontal lobe ROIs (ROI #3-30), which are affected later in the disease[2]. Such differences allow us to infer the direction of disease progression.

The large overlaps in the CDR ranges also imply that quantizing the CDR values into a relatively small number of bins would result in minimal ability to distinguish severity. Considering distributional differences is necessary.

4.2 Multi-ROI association with AD

Rules with multiple ROIs in their antecedent represent regions that commonly co-occur in AD. Due to the spatial constraint, these regions are approximately contiguous. We refer to these sets of ROIs as *subsystems*. Recall that we require subsystems to be significant (w.r.t. the Wilcox test) and to be symmetric: if a set of ROIs on one side form a subsystem, we require that corresponding set of ROIs on the symmetric side of the brain also forms a subsystem.

We discovered 3 such subsystems which we depicted in Figure 3. The subsystems can be discerned through their colors: the (left and right) hippocampal subsystems are colored blue, the subsystems containing the left and right insula are colored orange and the subsystems containing the left and right inferior parietal lobes are colored green. In the following, we will refer to these subsystems as A, B and C, respectively.

All of these subsystems are known to have elevated atro-

[2]Appearing late in the disease means appearing in only advanced stages of the disease leading to high CDR scores.

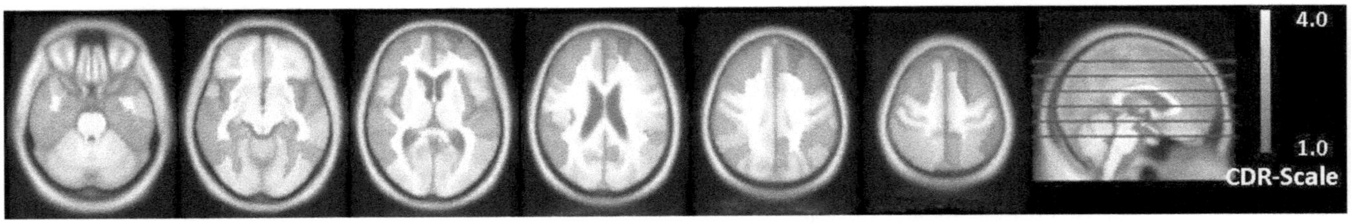

Figure 1: Median severity (CDR score) for each ROI significantly associated with AD. Yellow indicates higher severity.

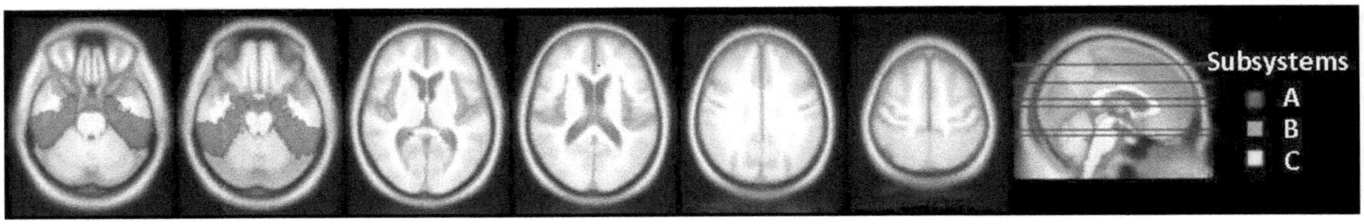

Figure 3: Three main AD subsystems. The hippocampal subsystem (A) is colored blue, the subsystem containing the insulae (B) is colored orange and the subsystem containing the parietal lobes (C) is colored green.

phy in AD. Subsystems A and B are mainly associated with typical AD, while subsystem C is known to be associated with atypical or advanced AD.

4.3 Inferring Disease Progression

Among the 153 significant rules, 59 had a pair of ROIs in the antecedent. These 59 rules were used to infer the direction of disease progression. We computed the significance of the disease progression (Equation 6) using only the MCI and the pathologically confirmed AD cases. Controls have no disease, hence they contribute no information to the disease progression. At significance level of .2, 28 of the 59 pairs of ROIs showed significant direction of progression[3].

Figure 4 depicts the patterns of AD progression we extracted from the rules. The nodes (ovals) in the figure correspond to individual ROIs and the enclosing rectangles correspond to subsystems. The black arrows going from one node (source) to the other (target) indicate the direction of the disease progression (these nodes reached significance using the test of progression). If the disease severity score of the target node is greater than the source node, the increase in the median severity scores of the patients is indicated on the black arrow. E.g. Subjects with both abnormal nodes 29 and 37 have a median severity score which is 0.51 higher than subjects with only abnormal node 37. Two nodes are connected by a gray edge when the corresponding ROIs are related but the significance of progression test failed to show significance.

We describe our findings centered around the subsystems.

[3]Type-I error (false discovery of disease progression) is easy to identify. For this reason, we were more concerned about type-II error (erroneously declaring a correct disease progression direction insignificant). This concern motivated our choice of a relatively high significance level.

In subsystem A, which originates in Nodes 37 (Left Hippocampus) and Nodes 38 (Right Hippocampus) has a disease progression pattern beginning in the hippocampus and proceeding to bilateral parahippocampal gyrus (Nodes 40 and 39) and/or bilateral fusiform (Nodes 55 and 56) with a substantial increase in the severity score of the subjects. The other ROIs there were significantly associated with hippocampal atrophy (Nodes 37 and Nodes 38) were bilateral inferior temporal ROI (Nodes 89 and 90) and bilateral amygdalae (Nodes 42 and 41). Atrophy in all the ROIs observed within this subsystem have been shown in the literature to be related to AD and the direction of disease progression concurs with the direction of tangle pathology (which is also measured by MRI) progression shown by Braak and Braak. Tangle pathology progression is used as a gold standard for AD diagnosis.

Subsystem B consisted of bilateral insulae (Nodes 29 and 30), Heschl gyrii (Nodes 79 and 80) and temporal poles (Nodes 83 and 84). The direction of disease progression was only significant on the left side with Node 29 (left insula) appearing to be the originating node for this subsystem.

Subsystem C is comprised of the bilateral inferior parietal lobes (Nodes 61 and 62), precuneus (67 and 68) and superior parietal lobes (Nodes 59 and 60). This result was very fascinating since there has been recent evidence that regions in this subsystem are affected early in disease and might occur in atypical cases [11].

5. SUMMARY AND DISCUSSION

In this paper we set out to address two important issues in Alzheimer's disease: to find typical and atypical AD presentations and to study the origin and progression of the disease. Both these topics enjoy much attention in the literature lacking a definitive answer. To achieve our goal, we proposed a technique based on distributional association rule mining with spatial constraints that allows us to asso-

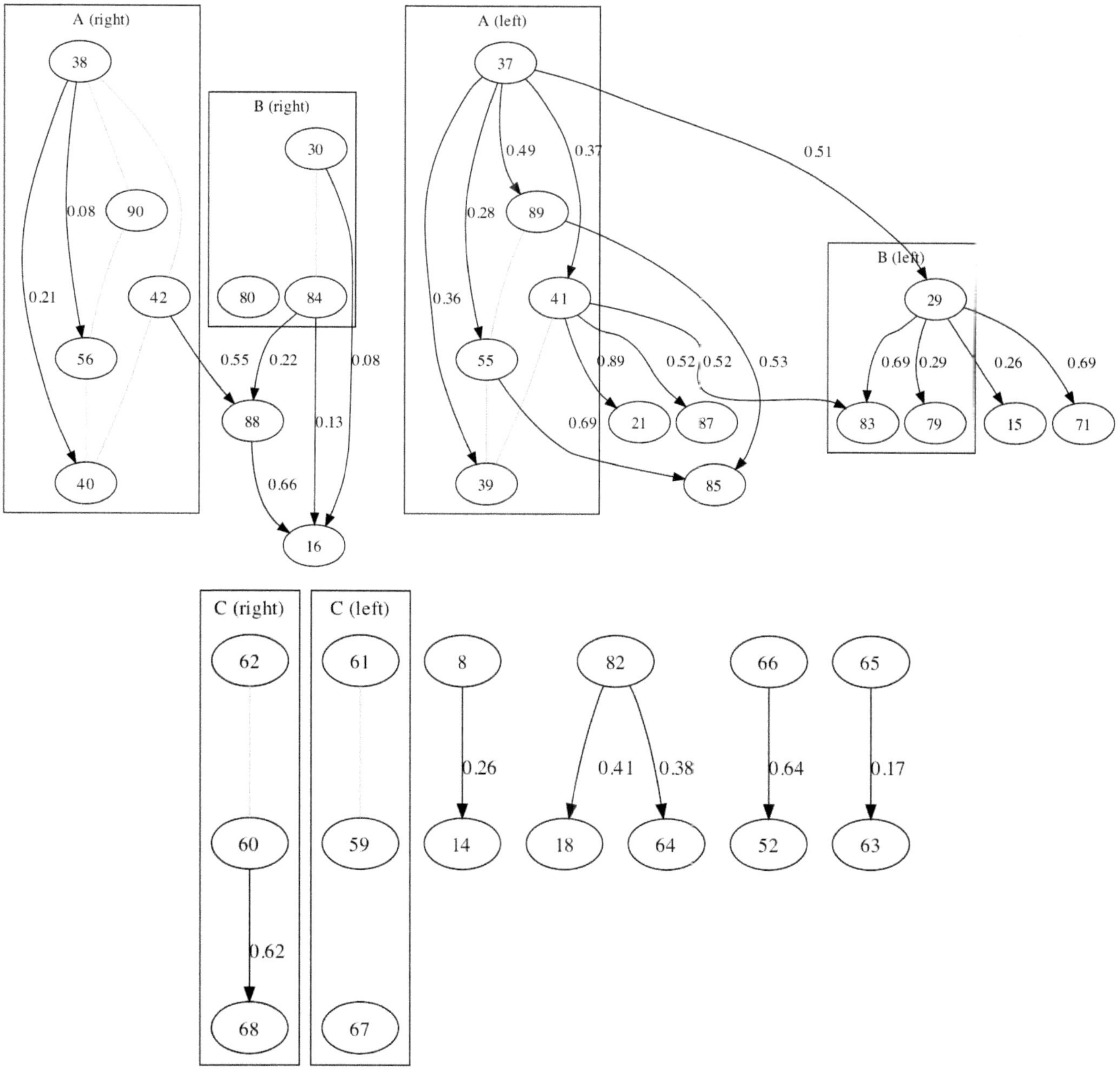

Figure 4: AD Progression. Each oval corresponds to an ROI with rectangles representing AD subsystems and arrows indicating significant directions of disease progression.

ciate brain structure atrophy in pre-defined regions of interest (ROIs) with distributional differences in disease severity. We successfully exploited these associations towards finding large subsystems of AD related to both typical and atypical disease presentations and also towards painting a clear picture of disease progression.

The association rules we mined allowed us to discover three large AD subsystems. All of these subsystems are noted in the literature, two corresponding to typical AD presentation and the third one related to atypical or advanced AD presentation.

We found that our methodology helped determine the direction of brain loss trajectories. In the AD patients, the hippocampus (both L and R) was the major originating node for the brain loss trajectory that affected the largest proportion of the study population. This is consistent with the existing literature that AD-related atrophy occurs earliest and most severely in the hippocampus. Also, the detected brain loss trajectory patterns i.e. the nodes downstream from the hippocampus were consistent with the pathological gold standard system for staging tangles proposed by Braak and Braak [5]. One key discovery was that there were different sets of originating nodes in a smaller proportion of the population supporting the evidence for atypical AD seen in some patients.

While the prevalent view of AD considers the hippocampus to be the origin of the disease, Desikan et al. [7] showed that the disease originates in the neocortical regions (specifically, parietal nodes; 61, 62, 67 and 68) and atrophy in the hippocampus is a downstream process. Our data does not support the hypothesis that hippocampal atrophy would be downstream from atrophy in the parietal regions, but we found that the disease can indeed originate in this region *independently* from the hippocampus.

An interesting implication of the hypothesis by Scahill et al. is that atrophy may progress along a very long path such as from subsystem C to subsystem A. Our current methodology is not well-suited for the discovery of such distant connections, but it can be extended by a second stage, where trajectory directions are sought among the ROIs that are present in known subsystems with no regard to the distance between them. Such an approach retain the capability of our methodology to reduce false discoveries. We will explore this direction in the future.

We found our methodology to be well-suited for finding contiguous disease-affected regions, associating these regions with disease severity and mapping out the disease progression directions. Many neurodegenerative diseases pose a similar problem and our methodology can be helpful in solving them. The applicability of the proposed methodology, however, is not limited to neurodegenerative diseases (e.g. breast cancer detection would benefit from our method), or even to image data. Our methodology can be viewed as a generic framework for associating disease severity with predictors, which offers valuable information in most medical domains as well as domains outside medicine.

6. REFERENCES

[1] R. Agrawal and R. Srikant. Fast algorithms for mining association rules. In *VLDB Conference*, 1994.

[2] S. Alladi, J. Xuereb, T. Bak, P. Nestor, J. Knibb, K. Patterson, and J. Hodges. Focal cortical presentations of alzheimer's disease. *Brain*, 130(10):2636–45, 2007.

[3] Y. Aumann and Y. Lindell. A statistical theory for quantitative association rules. In *Knowledge Discovery and Data Mining*, 1999.

[4] L. Berg. Mild senile dementia of the alzheimer type: 2. longitudinal assessment. *Annals of Neurology*, 23(477-484), 1988.

[5] H. Braak and E. Braak. Neuropathological stageing of alzheimer-related changes. *Acta Neuropathologica*, 82(4):239–259, 1991.

[6] S. Brin, R. Motvani, and C. Silverstein. Beyond market baskets: Generalizing association rules to correlations. In *ACM International Conference on Managment of Data (SIGMOD)*, 1997.

[7] R. S. Desikan, M. R. Sabuncu, N. J. Schmansky, M. Reuter, H. J. Cabral, C. P. Hess, M. W. Weiner, A. Biffi, C. D. Anderson, J. Rosand, D. H. Salat, T. L. Kemper, A. M. Dale, R. A. Sperling, B. Fischl, and Alzheimer's Disease Neuroimaging Initiative. Selective disruption of the cerebral neocortex in alzheimer's disease. *PLoS One*, 5(9):e12853, 2010.

[8] C. Galton, K. Patterson, J. Xuereb, and J. Hodges. Atypical and typical presentations of alzheimer's disease: a clinical, neuropsychological, neuroimaging and pathological study of 13 cases. *Brain*, 123(3):484–498, 2000.

[9] A. Icev, C. Ruiz, and E. F. Ryder. Distance-enhanced association rules for gene expression. In *ACM International Workshop on Data Mining in Bioinformatics*, 2007.

[10] C. Jack, D. Knopman, and W. Jagust. Hypothetical model of dynamic biomarkers of the alzheimer's pathological cascade. *Lancet Neurology*, 9, 2010.

[11] M. Lehmann, J. Rohrer, M. Clarkson, G. Ridgway, R. Scahill, M. Modat, J. Warren, S. Ourselin, J. Barnes, M. Rossor, and N. Fox. Reduced cortical thickness in the posterior cingulate gyrus is characteristic of both typical and atypical alzheimer's disease. *Journal of Alzheimer's Disease*, 20(2), 2010.

[12] B. Liu, W. Hsu, and Y. Ma. Integrating classification and association rule mining. In *ACM International Conference on Knowledge Discovery and Data Mining (KDD)*, 1998.

[13] H. J. Miller and J. Han, editors. *Geographic Data Mining and Knowledge Discovery*. Chapman and Hall, 2009.

[14] H. Pan, Q. Han, G. Yin, W. Zhang, and J. Li. Association rule mining with domain knowledge constraint. In *IEEE International Conference on Intelligent Systems and Knowledge Engineering*, 2008.

[15] E. E. Schadt, J. Lamb, X. Yang, J. Zhu, S. Edwards, D. Guhathakurta, S. K. Sieberts, S. Monks, M. Reitman, C. Zhang, P. Y. Lum, A. Leonardson, R. Thieringer, J. M. Metzger, L. Yang, J. Castle, H. Zhu, S. F. Kash, T. A. Drake, A. Sachs, and A. J. Lusis. An integrative genomics approach to infer causal associations between gene expression and disease. *Nat Genet*, 37(7):710–7, Jul 2005.

[16] L. J. Sheela and V. Shanthi. DIMAR – discovering interesting medical association rules from MRI scans. In *IEEE International Conference on Electrical Engineering/Electronics,Computer, Telecommunications and Information Technology*, 2009.

[17] P.-N. Tan, M. Steinbach, and V. Kumar. *Introduction to Data Mining*. Addison Wesley, 2005.

[18] P. Vemuri, G. Simon, K. Kantarci, J. L. Whitwell, M. L. Senjem, S. A. Przybelski, J. L. Gunter, K. A. Josephs, D. S. Knopman, B. F. Boeve, T. J. Ferman, D. W. Dickson, J. E. Parisi, R. C. Petersen, and C. R. J. Jr. Antemortem differential diagnosis of dementia pathology using structural MRI: Differential-STAND. *NeuroImage*, `http://www.ncbi.nlm.nih.gov/pubmed/21195775`, 2010.

[19] P. Vemuri, J. Whitwell, and K. Kantarci. Antemortem MRI based STructural Abnormality iNDex (STAND)-scores correlate with postmortem braak neurofibrillary tangle stage. *NeuroImage*, 42, 2008.

[20] O. R. Zaïane, M.-L. Antonie, and A. Coman. Mammography classification by an association rule-based classifier. In *International Workshop on Multimedia Data Mining*, 2002.

A Case Study in a Recommender System Based on Purchase Data

Bruno Pradel
Université Paris 6
Paris, France
pradelb@poleia.lip6.fr

Savaneary Sean
KXEN Europe
Suresnes, France
savaneary.sean@kxen.com

Julien Delporte
INSA de Rouen
Saint-Étienne-du-Rouvray, France
julien.delporte@insa-rouen.fr

Sébastien Guérif, Céline Rouveirol
Université Paris-Nord
Villetaneuse, France
surname.name@lipn.univ-paris13.fr

Nicolas Usunier
Université Paris 6
Paris, France
usunier@poleia.lip6.fr

Françoise Fogelman-Soulié
KXEN Europe
Suresnes, France
francoise.souliefogelman@kxen.com

Frédéric Dufau-Joel
La Boîte à Outils
France
frederic-dufau-joel@samse.fr

ABSTRACT

Collaborative filtering has been extensively studied in the context of ratings prediction. However, industrial recommender systems often aim at predicting a few items of immediate interest to the user, typically products that (s)he is likely to buy in the near future. In a collaborative filtering setting, the prediction may be based on the user's purchase history rather than rating information, which may be unreliable or unavailable. In this paper, we present an experimental evaluation of various collaborative filtering algorithms on a real-world dataset of purchase history from customers in a store of a French home improvement and building supplies chain. These experiments are part of the development of a prototype recommender system for salespeople in the store. We show how different settings for training and applying the models, as well as the introduction of domain knowledge may dramatically influence both the absolute and the relative performances of the different algorithms. To the best of our knowledge, the influence of these parameters on the quality of the predictions of recommender systems has rarely been reported in the literature.

Categories and Subject Descriptors

H.3.0 [**Information Storage and Retrieval**]: General; H.2.8 [**Database Applications**]: Data Mining

General Terms

Experimentation, Algorithms, Performance

Keywords

Recommender Systems, Collaborative Filtering

1. INTRODUCTION

Systems for personalized recommendation aim at predicting a few items (movies, books, ...) of interest to a particular user. They have been extensively studied in the past decade [2, 17], with a particular attention given to the collaborative filtering (CF) approach [18, 24]. In contrast to content-based recommender systems, collaborative filters rely solely on the detection of interaction patterns between users and items, where an interaction can be the rating or the purchase of an item. For instance, a system can recommend to a target user some products purchased by other users whose purchase history is similar to the target user's, making recommendation possible even if relevant descriptions of users or items are unavailable.

The development of collaborative filters has followed several, mostly independent directions. The first direction, which accounts for the majority of works in CF, is the development of different types of algorithms, such as memory-based techniques, matrix factorization algorithms, probabilistic models and ensemble methods [18, 24, 6, 14]. Almost all of these works have focused on ratings prediction on publicly available benchmark datasets such as MovieLens[1] or NetFlix[2]. A second direction is the identification of domain dependent variables that describe interactions between users and items and which may influence the recommendation performance. For instance, purchase time can be used to take into account the recency of past customer purchases for the recommendation [7, 15]. Another example is contextual variables such as the intent of a purchase (e.g. whether a book is purchased for personal or professional purposes), which allow to perform situated recommendations of potentially greater accuracy [1, 3, 5, 19]. These works generally focus on the impact of introducing domain knowledge,

[1]`http://www.grouplens.org/node/73`
[2]`http://www.netflixprize.com/`

Figure 1: Vendors in the store use a PDA which is equipped to read product bar-codes and loyalty cards. An application has been developed to receive recommendations.

and have often been evaluated on medium-scale proprietary purchase datasets with very little emphasis on performance comparisons between algorithms.

The abundance of academic papers on CF should be contrasted with many critical aspects of the design of commercial recommender systems which remain mostly undocumented. A data miner who wants to build a recommender system has to choose the appropriate algorithm to use, and probably incorporate domain knowledge to increase the recommendation quality. However, for many retailers, rating data is unavailable, or may be unreliable because ratings are purely declarative. Personalized recommendations should then be based on the customers' purchase history or other kind of implicit feedback, which is a different type of data because it does not contain *negative feedback* [10]: high and low ratings inform us about what a user likes and dislikes, but past purchases do not reliably inform us about the products which will not interest the customer in the future. The choice of the best algorithm becomes an issue as most collaborative filtering algorithms have been compared and studied in depth only on rating data. Moreover, since the algorithmic dimension is often studied independently of the introduction of domain knowledge, the relative and joint impact of these two parameters on the recommendation quality is mostly unknown.

In this paper, we present a case-study on CF recommender systems using a dataset containing the purchase history of more than 50,000 loyal customers of a home improvement store over 3 years, containing about 4.6 million transactions. We systematically evaluate three families of CF algorithms, namely item-based recommendation [16], matrix factorization [14, 26, 20] and association rule mining algorithms [22, 11] on various settings in which we introduce increasing amounts of domain knowledge. In our case, domain knowledge is inferred from purchase data in which we identify *high purchase activity* periods of the customers. This leads us first to consider the recency of the purchases in a customer's history as a critical parameter, and secondly to a clustering of the high purchase activity periods, where the categories have a meaningful interpretation in terms of contextual variables. Our main results are:

- The blind application of the algorithms leads to very low performances, which are unacceptable for an industrial recommender system. The influence of incorporating domain knowledge in the recommendation process has already been reported in the literature, even for the task of ratings prediction [13] where taking into account the changes in user tastes over time improves performances. Domain knowledge is even more important for short-term recommendation (as in our case) since the prediction task is more difficult.
- The difference in performance between the various algorithms is very small compared to what can be gained by introducing context in the recommendations. These results provide additional evidence for the need of context-aware recommender systems, in line with recent works [5, 19].
- Matrix factorizations algorithms and item-based techniques detect slightly different patterns between customers and items, as was already noticed in the context of ratings prediction [12]. On our purchase data, this leads factorization methods to mostly recommend best-sellers while item-based CF, like association rules, tends to recommend more products that are rarely bought.
- Surprisingly, the most accurate recommendations on our data are given by the simplest form of bigram association rules. This contrasts with the results on rating data where memory-based and matrix factorization are among the best performing methods [6, 14] and association rules are almost never used.

The paper is organized as follows. In Section 2, we present the dataset and the original recommendation task which lead to this study. We then describe our experimental protocol and the algorithms we evaluate in Sections 3 and 4 respectively. The results of an approach which uses no domain knowledge are reported in Section 5. We show the impact on the performance of a more business-oriented modeling in Section 6. Finally, Section 7 concludes the paper.

2. RECOMMENDATION TASK AND DATASET

This study is motivated by a need for an automatic recommender system, expressed by a French retailer, La Boîte à Outils[3] (BAO). The company possesses 27 medium and large size stores in the South-East of France, and sells products for home improvement. BAO wants to equip salespeople in the stores with tools helping them provide their customers with better and more professional answers. Very often, customers come to the store and leave, without noticing they forgot some products they will need for the job they have in mind. After that, they start working and realize they have to come back, or try a closer competitor's store. BAO thus wants to help the salespeople make sure that the customer

[3] http://www.laboiteaoutils.fr/

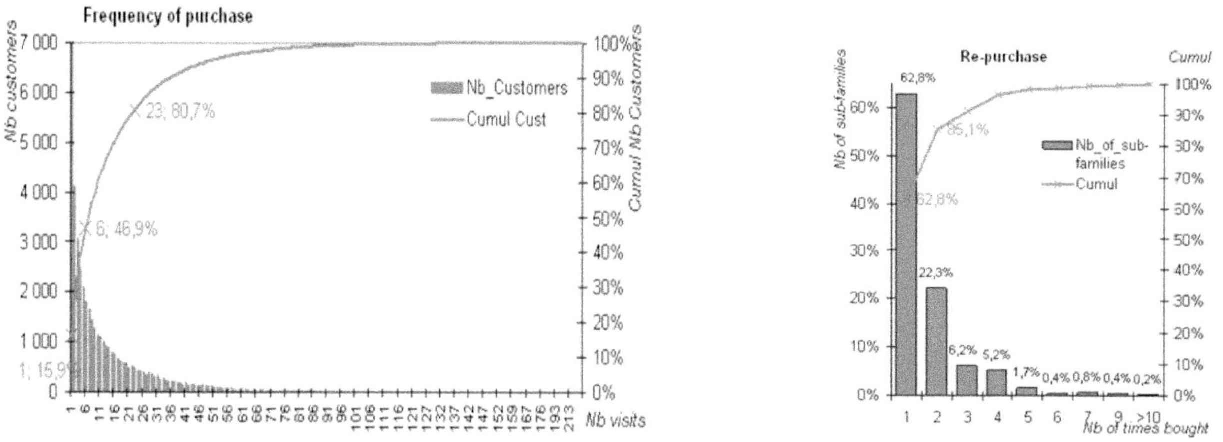

Figure 2: Frequency of purchase (left) and Re-purchase (right)

purchases the complete set of products he'll need: they can suggest missing products and show him the products in the relevant department. BAO thus launched a project to have recommendations produced in real-time for the salesperson to use in his discussion with the customer: salespeople are equipped with a PDA, which can read the loyalty card and the products bar-codes and to which the recommendations are to be sent. This scenario is represented in Figure 1. Less experienced vendors would certainly benefit more from the recommendation application, but even seasoned vendors have expressed their interest for it, saying that this could work for them as a check list of all the products needed. As can be seen, the setting for our recommender system is rather original, since most systems in the literature have been developed for on-line retailers.

The deployment scenario chosen by BAO was to first design and evaluate a recommender system on data from its major store; then to test it on the field in that store and finally deploy it throughout all the 27 stores. This paper reports on the first phase, where various techniques had to be evaluated for designing the best system, while phase 2 is presently ongoing.

The dataset we used contains all purchase history from loyal customers at BAO's major store from 2005 to 2008. As we shall see later, data from 2005 to 2007 were used for training and data for 2008 for testing. It corresponds to $43,779$ customers and $3,425,048$ transactions for training (from 2005 to 2007), and $30,784$ customers (of which $6,923$ are new customers) and $1,140,510$ transactions for testing. The items we consider are not individual products but rather groups of products or *sub-families*, because BAO decided that recommendations should be made at this level of their product hierarchy. An example of sub-family is "pipe", while individual products are pipes of varying length, color, ... This will leave more space for the salesperson's expertise and should be easier to use in the intended context. We selected only the sub-families which were sold every year of the training data, and obtained 484 sub-families.

Figure 2 shows various characteristics of the 2005-2007 data: a RFM analysis showed that 15.9% customers visited only once (and 80.7% 23 times at most) and 15% sub-families were bought at least 3 times by the same customer. Since we are working at the sub-families level, this situation should be expected in our case, as well as in a DVD retail industry for example, where customers typically buy various times at the genre – sub-family – level, yet each product once at most at the product level. This implies in particular that we need to potentially recommend an item (i.e. a sub-family) which has already been purchased by the same user.

As usual in retail contexts, data show a marked Long Tail effect [4]: 30% of the 484 sub-families (vigintiles 1 to 6) represent 81.8% of total sales (these are the *Head* sub-families); while the last 11 vigintiles (10 to 20) represent 55% of the sub-families and account for only 8.1% of sales (the *Tail*). Obviously, data are very sparse in the Tail and it will thus be harder to produce relevant recommendations in the Tail than in the Head. Being able to accurately recommend Middle or Tail items can however be an interesting property of a recommender system since it may correspond to more unexpected suggestions. We will see in our experiments that some algorithms essentially predict Head items, while some others are able to find some relevant Tail products.

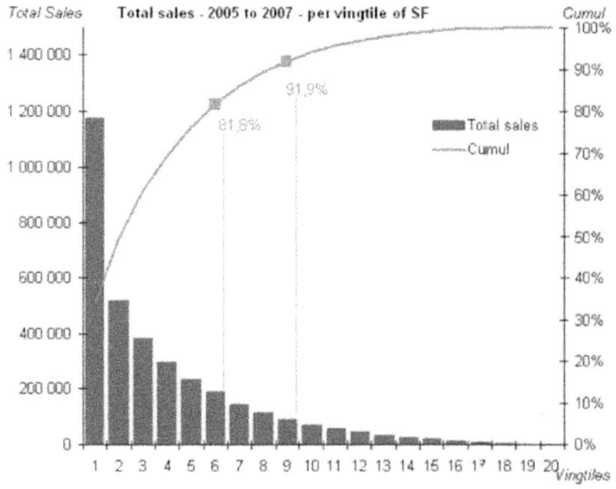

Figure 3: Total number of sales for each vigintile (5%) of sub-families.

3. GENERAL EXPERIMENTAL PROTOCOL AND EVALUATION METRICS

We now present our experimental protocol. In our setup, a CF algorithm can be seen as a black box, which takes as input a *purchase matrix*, and outputs a predictor. The purchase matrix summarizes the training data (the transactions from 2005 to 2007 in our case) as described in Subsection

3.1. A predictor can be seen as a black box as well, which takes as input a customer's purchase history and outputs a sorted list of the 484 items. The quality of the sorted list is measured by comparing the first recommended items with items bought by the same customer in a near future. Our goal is to measure the ability of the system to perform relevant recommendations when the user is in the shop. In many cases, a customer needs a product for a particular short-term project, so our evaluation has to measure the quality of the predictions in the short-term. To that end, we decompose our test data (i.e. the 2008 purchase data) into several smaller sets, each of which is based on a specific day d of 2008, and we try to predict the items purchased by a customer within 2 weeks after that day, using the customer's purchase history known at d. The construction of these test sets is detailed in Subsection 3.2, and the evaluation metrics are defined in Subsection 3.3. How we train and test each algorithm is described later in the next Section.

3.1 Purchase Matrix

The training stage of the algorithms we evaluate takes as input a *purchase matrix*, where each column corresponds to an item, and each row represents a *purchase session*. A *(purchase) session* should be understood as "the set of purchases of a given customer over a period of time". In standard collaborative filtering approaches (see e.g. [2]) and in Section 5 of this paper, a row of the purchase matrix represents the total purchase history of a specific customer. In that case, a purchase session is defined as "all known purchases of a customer" without limitation in time, but we will also consider purchase sessions defined on smaller periods of time in Section 6. In all cases, a purchase matrix, denoted $\mathbf{P}$, contains only Boolean values (0 or 1), where a 1 in the $(i, k)^{\text{th}}$ entry means that item k has been bought at least once in the i-th session (0 means the opposite). In the following, R (resp. C) will denote the number of rows (resp. columns) of $\mathbf{P}$.

3.2 Test data

As we intend to predict the future purchases of customers in the short term, we evaluate the various algorithms with a sliding window approach: for every day d of the testing period and every customer who made a purchase on that day, we predict his purchases for the next 14 days (including the *reference day* d, to predict the final purchases of the customer that day), based on his purchase history (i.e. the products bought strictly before the reference day). The window length of 14 days has been chosen by business constraints. It is motivated by the observation that most sales are *complete* within 14 days after the first purchase of this sale. In the end, there are 298 reference days and thus 298 test sets: each day of 2008 is a reference day except Sundays, holidays (when the shop is closed), and the last 13 days of 2008 (the purchases for the next 14 days are not available).

After creating the test sets, we filter some customers out of each set. For each test set, we discard all customers who did not make any purchase within 14 days before the corresponding reference day (excluded).[4] This selection is once again motivated by the fact that sales are complete within 14 days, and will allow us to compare various experimental settings on the same set of customers.

[4]Note that customers not present on the reference day are not included in the test set either, since we can only make recommendations to customers present in the store.

3.3 Evaluation Metrics

The recommendation algorithms output a sorted list of items given the purchase history of a customer at a given date. Following [9, 8], we use precision, recall and F1-score to evaluate the quality of a recommendation list. These metrics are then averaged over customers and time to provide a final performance value. In our approach, we have a set of customers for each reference day, together with a target set of products for each customer (recall that the target set contains the customer's purchases for the next 14 days, and thus depends on the reference day). For a given customer u and a given reference day d, the precision, recall and F1-score of the N first recommended items are respectively defined as:

- $prec_{u,d}@N = \dfrac{card(R_{u,d}@N \cap T_{u,d})}{N}$,
- $rec_{u,d}@N = \dfrac{card(R_{u,d}@N \cap T_{u,d})}{card(T_{u,d})}$

  where given u and d, $T_{u,d}$ is the target set and $R_{u,d}@N$ the set of top-N recommended items.
- $F1_{u,d}@N = \dfrac{2.rec_{u,d}@N.prec_{u,d}@N}{rec_{u,d}@N + prec_{u,d}@N}$.

The value of the cutoff N is chosen by business constraints. In our case, only 5 recommendations will be presented, so these measures are of greatest interest with $N = 5$.

To compute the final performance values, we first average over users for each reference day. The precision obtained for the reference day d is given by:

$$prec_d@N = \frac{\sum_{u\text{:test user for day } d} prec_{u,d}@N}{\text{nb of test users for day } d}.$$

Similar formulas are used to obtain $rec_d@N$ (resp. $F1_d@N$), the recall (resp. F1-score) for the reference day d. The final performances are then computed by averaging over all possible reference days:

$$perf@N = \frac{\sum_{d\text{:reference day}} perf_d@N}{\text{nb of reference days}} \quad \text{for } perf \in \{prec, rec, F1\}.$$

4. ALGORITHMS EVALUATED

We have selected a number of algorithms from the three main families of collaborative filtering approaches: memory-based, model-based and association rule learning. For the memory-based technique, we consider the item-based approach [16], in which the bulk of the computation is done offline. For model-based approaches, we selected two state-of-the-art matrix factorization methods, Singular Value Decomposition [23] and Non-Negative Matrix Factorization [27]. For association rule learning, we build the bigram matrix [22] (i.e. all rules of the form item i $\Rightarrow$ item j). The choices of the algorithms are arbitrary, we only intended to have representative algorithms for each of the main CF approaches.

4.1 Training the Algorithms

Item-Based Collaborative Filtering.

The item-based approach computes, on the training purchase data, a similarity matrix between products. Following Linden et al. [16], we compute the similarity between the two products k and ℓ using the cosine between their corresponding columns of the purchase matrix:

$$\mathrm{sim}(k,\ell) = \frac{\mathbf{P}_{\bullet k}^{\mathrm{T}}\mathbf{P}_{\bullet \ell}}{\sqrt{\mathbf{P}_{\bullet k}^{\mathrm{T}}\mathbf{P}_{\bullet k}}\sqrt{\mathbf{P}_{\bullet \ell}^{\mathrm{T}}\mathbf{P}_{\bullet \ell}}}$$

where $\mathbf{P}_{\bullet k}$ is the k-th column of $\mathbf{P}$, and $\mathbf{X}^{\mathrm{T}}$ is the transpose of matrix $\mathbf{X}$. The output of the training process is then the similarity matrix between products $\mathbf{S}$, where the $(k,\ell)^{\mathrm{th}}$ entry of $\mathbf{S}$ is equal to $\mathrm{sim}(k,\ell)$.

Matrix Factorization Methods.

Matrix factorization methods have shown great performance for ratings prediction [14, 26]. To apply these methods on purchase data, we use the AMAN (*all missing as negative*) reduction [20]. In this setup, matrix factorizations approximate the purchase matrix $\mathbf{P} \in \mathbb{R}^{R\times C}$ by a matrix of smaller rank r ($r \ll \mathrm{rank}(\mathbf{P})$). The approximation can be written as the product $\mathbf{U}^\star\mathbf{V}^\star$ of two matrices $\mathbf{U}^\star \in \mathbb{R}^{R\times r}$ and $\mathbf{V}^\star \in \mathbb{R}^{r\times C}$. We first evaluate the factorization which gives the best rank-r approximation of $\mathbf{P}$ in the sense of the Frobenius norm which can be found using SVD [23]:

$$\mathbf{U}^\star,\mathbf{V}^\star = \mathop{\arg\min}_{\mathbf{U}\in\mathbb{R}^{R\times r},\mathbf{V}\in\mathbb{R}^{r\times C}} \|\mathbf{P}-\mathbf{U}\mathbf{V}\|_F^2 \quad (1)$$

where $\|\mathbf{X}\|_F = \sqrt{\sum_{i,j} x_{i,j}^2}$ is the Frobenius norm of $\mathbf{X}$ and $x_{i,j}$ the $(i,j)^{\mathrm{th}}$ entry of $\mathbf{X}$. We also tried to weight missing entries as in [20], but it did not improve performances, so these results are not presented in our experiments.

We also evaluate non-negative matrix factorization (NNMF) which was shown to have good performances in CF [27]. NNMF finds an approximation of the purchase matrix with factors constrained to only have non-negative elements:

$$\mathbf{U}^\star,\mathbf{V}^\star = \mathop{\arg\min}_{\mathbf{U}\in\mathbb{R}_+^{R\times r},\mathbf{V}\in\mathbb{R}_+^{r\times C}} \|\mathbf{P}-\mathbf{U}\mathbf{V}\|_F^2 \,. \quad (2)$$

For any matrix factorization method (SVD, NNMF, or any other), the rightmost matrix $\mathbf{V}^\star$ can be seen as an *embedding matrix*, which projects every product k in $\mathbb{R}^r$ (or $\mathbb{R}_+^r$ for NNMF). Thus, the k-th column of $\mathbf{V}^\star$, $\mathbf{V}_{\bullet k}^\star$, can be interpreted as a representation of product k in the embedding space. On the other hand, $\mathbf{U}^\star$ expresses the rows of the purchase matrix as a linear combination of lines of $\mathbf{V}^\star$, and is thus representative of the training data only. Consequently, after obtaining a factorization of the training purchase matrix $\mathbf{P}$ of the form $\mathbf{U}^\star\mathbf{V}^\star$, $\mathbf{U}^\star$ is not stored. The only parameter resulting from training is matrix $\mathbf{V}^\star$.

Association Rules.

We also evaluate association rule learning for CF [22, 11]. We first consider *bigram* rules, where training simply consists in computing the following matrix on the purchase data:

$$\mathbf{B} = [b_{k,\ell}]_{\substack{k=1..C\\ \ell=1..C}} \text{ with } b_{k,\ell} = \frac{\mathbf{P}_{\bullet k}^{\mathrm{T}}\mathbf{P}_{\bullet \ell}}{\|\mathbf{P}_{\bullet k}\|_1},\ \|\mathbf{X}\|_1 = \sum_{k=1}^{C}|x_k| \quad (3)$$

$b_{k,\ell}$ is thus the confidence of rule $k \Rightarrow \ell$ (i.e. *item k is purchased* implies *item ℓ is purchased within the same session*).

Special care needs to be taken for diagonal elements $b_{k,k}$: they are all equal to 1 in (3), which does not reflect the real probability that item k was bought twice at different times within the same session. Although the true confidence of the rule $k \Rightarrow k$ cannot be computed from the purchase matrix, we compute it from the initial transactional data as follows:

$$b_{k,k} = \frac{\text{nb sessions where } k \text{ was bought at least twice}}{\text{nb of sessions where } k \text{ was bought}}\,.$$

Since bigram rules consider at most two items without any consideration of their support, we tried a more refined version of associations rules (called alpha-rules in the paper) based on the concepts of alpha Galois lattice [25] and frequent closed itemsets [21]. alpha-rule learning aims at scaling up the rule mining using domain knowledge provided as a segmentation of purchase sessions: the algorithm only finds closed itemsets and rules satisfied by at least $\alpha\%$ sessions of a given segment (the parameter α controls the complexity of the method). This method is only applicable when having a typology of purchase sessions (which will be built in Section 6), so we only present its results after Section 6.

4.2 Applying the Algorithms

At apply time, an algorithm is given a customer's purchase history (which contains all past purchases of a customer or only the most recent ones), and is required to provide a list of N recommendations for this user ($N = 5$ in our case). A purchase history is represented by a Boolean column vector $\mathbf{H} \in \{0,1\}^{1\times C}$, where 1 at the kth line means that item k has been bought by the customer at least once over the period considered for building the history. $\mathbf{H}$ contains the purchases of a single customer, so the prediction processes described below are applied to each customer of a test set. Note that our prediction processes can be applied to any customer, even if he was not seen during training.

Item-Based CF Prediction.

The recommendation list for item-based collaborative filtering is created as follows:

1. For each item k in $\mathbf{H}$ (i.e. k s.t. $h_k = 1$), select the S items which are the most similar to k using the similarity matrix $\mathbf{S}$ computed during training. We obtain $\|\mathbf{H}\|_1$ lists of items with similarity scores for each item in each list. In our experiments we use $S = 20$ as it tended to give the best results.

2. Merge the lists: concatenate the lists, and sort the items by decreasing associated score. If an item is in several lists, assign it its maximum score.

Prediction with Matrix Methods.

The inference procedure corresponds to the setting of *strong generalization* [18]. This setting allows us to make prediction for new customers or to take into account the updates (if any) of the customer's purchase history. Given the embedding matrix $\mathbf{V}^\star$ learnt on the training data, we compute a parameter vector $\mathbf{W}^\star$ such that $\mathbf{W}^{\star\mathrm{T}}\mathbf{V}^\star$ approximates best the user's purchase history $\mathbf{H}$. Depending on the method, $\mathbf{W}^\star$ is defined as follows:

- SVD: $\mathbf{W}^\star = \mathop{\arg\min}_{\mathbf{W}\in\mathbb{R}^r} \left\|\mathbf{W}^{\mathrm{T}}\mathbf{V}^\star - \mathbf{H}\right\|_F^2$ with $\mathbf{V}^\star$ given by (1),
- NNMF: $\mathbf{W}^\star = \mathop{\arg\min}_{\mathbf{W}\in\mathbb{R}_+^r} \left\|\mathbf{W}^{\mathrm{T}}\mathbf{V}^\star - \mathbf{H}\right\|_F^2$ with $\mathbf{V}^\star$ given by (2).

Both are convex quadratic problems which can be solved very efficiently at apply time. Once the parameter vector

Table 1: **Test results for the *Complete History* (left) and the 2 *Weeks History* (right) apply settings, when the algorithms are trained on the *user×item* purchase matrix. *Relative* differences of more than 5% on any metric and between any two algorithms are significant.**

	prec@5	*rec*@5	*F*1@5
item-based	6.87%	6.10%	5.62%
SVD	13.22%	12.39%	10.92%
NNMF	11.28%	9.35%	8.85%
bigram rules	10.88%	9.33%	8.64%

	prec@5	*rec*@5	*F*1@5
item-based	11.76%	9.98%	9.39%
SVD	13.20%	12.37%	10.91%
NNMF	12.27%	11.25%	10.05%
bigram rules	14.54%	13.47%	11.98%

$\mathbf{W}^\star$ is computed, all items are sorted by decreasing scores (the predicted score for item k is $\mathbf{W}^{\star T}\mathbf{V}^\star_{\bullet k}$ in both cases).

Prediction with Association Rules.

For bigram rules, we follow [22]: items k are sorted by the maximum confidence of the rules $\ell \Rightarrow k$ supported by the user history (i.e. ℓ is such that $h_\ell = 1$). The prediction with alpha-rules is similar.

5. A STANDARD APPROACH

We first evaluate what we refer to as the *standard approach.* This corresponds to the case where each row of the training purchase matrix contains all known purchases of all training customers, called the *user×item* matrix. In that case, the training purchase matrix has a sparsity coefficient of 5.7%. After training each algorithm according to Section 4.1, we evaluate 2 different *apply settings*:

Complete History In the *Complete History* apply setting, the prediction algorithms (described in Section 4.2) receive as input a purchase vector which contains *all past purchases of this customer without limitation in time.* Thus, for a given reference day and a given customer, the prediction will be based on all of this customer's purchases made strictly before the reference day.

2 Weeks History In the 2 *Weeks History* apply setting, the prediction algorithms receive as input a purchase vector containing only the customer's purchases made in the last 14 days before the reference day (excluded).

We remind to the reader that **(1)** the training procedure of the algorithms is the same for both apply settings, **(2)** thanks to the filter applied to the test sets (Subsection 3.2), the algorithms are evaluated on exactly the same customers and target sets, and finally **(3)** the reported performance for both apply settings are computed on the test data following the protocol described in Subsection 3.2.

The test performances in terms of *prec*@5, *rec*@5 and *F*1@5 for the various algorithms and the two apply settings are shown in Table 1. The rank of matrix factorization is chosen based on *F*1@5 ($r = 20$ for both methods).

The results first show that bigram association rules in the 2 weeks history apply setting obtain the best results, with relative performance gains between 8% and 10% on all metrics. However, we have to notice that in the *Complete History* apply setting, factorization methods obtain the best results. Thus the relative performances of the methods change when taking recency into account. It implies that no general conclusion can be drawn from the relative performances of each algorithm in a specific application scenario, and that testing each method for each scenario is mandatory.

When comparing the two apply settings, we see that considering only the most recent purchases has a positive impact on all performances, except for the SVD on which the difference is not significant. This suggests that only purchases made within a short period of time are strongly correlated, so that the recency of the purchase may be a critical factor for the recommendation. Similar observations have already been reported (see e.g. [14, 15]) on other datasets where users' tastes evolve with time. Even though the reason might be different in our case (see Section 6), our results give additional evidence that the recency of user feedback is an important factor in CF. In particular, it appears to be crucial for item-based CF and association rules. This is due to the aggregation scheme we chose (the max of the items similarities or rules' confidences), which is not robust to this noise. We carried out additional experiments (not reported here) where we used the *sum* of the rules' confidence (as in [11]) instead of the max for association rules. The algorithm becomes then more robust, with less than 15% relative difference in *prec*@5 between the two settings (instead of about 30% with the max as reported in Table 1). The same behavior was observed for item-based CF. The algorithms do not perform better though, because adding low confidences eventually leads to overcome the confidence of relevant rules.

In terms of absolute performance values, the best precision at 5 is lower than 15%. Acceptance of the system on the field will be hard: when the salesperson recommends 5 products to his customer, the latter will buy less than once on average. Sales staff will soon stop proposing recommendations to avoid losing the customers' confidence. We need better performances, at least 20% of precision to ensure that at least one product is bought by the customer on average.

6. A BUSINESS-ORIENTED APPROACH

The business of BAO is to sell products to customers for home improvement. This customers' activity has its specificities, one of which was highlighted in the previous section: customers have a purchasing behavior which varies a lot in time. At some periods, they only buy little, and only standard products (electric bulbs, nails, ...); while at other periods, they launch a *project* such as refurbishing the bathroom or putting a new roof. Projects requires more spending, more - very specific - products and this over a relatively short period. In this section, we try and exploit this behavior to focus on such specific activity, because it should allow us to narrow the potential choice of relevant products and thus recommend products at a given time depending on what the customer is doing at that time. From a business perspective, the recommender system should be most useful if it can help getting a complete sale for customers running a project, i.e. a sale where all the products necessary for that project are actually purchased.

We show how to detect projects periods in customers' purchase histories and automatically categorize them in Subsec-

Table 2: **Project categories found by k-means on the training data.**

Category	Bathroom	Plumbing	Exterior	Exterior improvement	Carpentry	Tiling	Isolation	Paint	Electricity	Flooring/ Paneling	Interior improvement
Nb of projects	1221	3207	14359	6136	3398	2588	1845	3221	2720	1802	1075
%	2.89	7.60	34.02	14.54	8.05	6.13	4.37	7.63	6.45	4.27	4.04
Avg nb of unique items in a project	31	15	3	8	10	11	12	10	14	14	13
Avg duration (days)	26	14	5	9	12	13	13	11	13	15	13
Nb of different items used	414	427	457	443	429	406	393	419	421	401	397

Table 3: Test results for the *Complete History* (left) and the 2 *Weeks History* (right) apply settings when the algorithms are trained on the *project×item* matrix. A relative difference of more than 5% in any metric is always statistically significant.

	prec@5	*rec@5*	*F1@5*
item-based	5.41%	4.91%	4.43%
SVD	12.85%	11.80%	10.53%
NNMF	11.08%	9.43%	8.81%
bigram rules	9.52%	8.71%	7.71%
alpha-rules	14.19%	6.65%	8.53%

	prec@5	*rec@5*	*F1@5*
item-based	10.85%	9.57%	8.77%
SVD	12.90%	11.83%	10.56%
NNMF	12.48%	11.39%	10.20%
bigram rules	15.84%	16.42%	13.67%
alpha-rules	16.10%	7.57%	9.70%

tion 6.1. We then study two strategies to integrate projects and their categories in the recommendation process.

6.1 Project Definition and Categorization

The domain experts at BAO observed that past customers' projects can be extracted from their purchase history by identifying high purchase activity periods, defined as periods where a given customer spends at least 200 € over a duration of 14 days. BAO has specialized salespeople for customers running very large projects (i.e. building a house) and wants to exclude these from the perimeter of the recommender system. We thus extracted from the 2005-2007 dataset all projects by isolating high-purchase activity periods of the customers, discarding projects that last more than 50 days or with a total expense greater than 2,000 €. We then merged projects separated by less than a week and eliminated all no-purchase days at the end of the 42,202 identified projects to calculate the real project duration. Finally, projects account for about 1/3 of all the transactions, and 50% of the customers are involved in at least one project.

We built a typology of projects using k-means[5] supervised by the number of items used in the project. We found a typology of 11 segments which were analyzed by business-owners who found a description as meaningful project categories. These categories are descriptive of the context of a purchase, such as plumbing or painting. The segments are summarized in Table 2. The two larger categories, account for 34% and 14.5% of all projects. All other categories (except for the smallest one) contain between 4% and 8% of the projects. Most categories contain projects which involve, on average, about 10 different unique items (with possibility of re-purchase), but more than 400 items are used in at least one project of each category (thus, more than 80% of the total number of items). Thus, even if the project categories contain more homogeneous sets of purchases, recommendation must cover most of the catalog.

[5]We used KXEN K2S segmentation module (KXEN AF v5.0.5, `www.kxen.com`.)

6.2 Training on Projects Only

We saw in Section 5 that considering only a short-term purchase history at prediction time increases the recommendation accuracy. Together with the analysis of projects, these results suggest that only short-term correlations between two purchases are relevant, long-term correlations being most probably accidental. We propose to integrate this additional knowledge into the training process, by learning on a modified purchase matrix which contains one row for each project detected in the period 2005-2007. We obtain a *project×item* purchase matrix of size 42,202×484. It has a higher sparsity than the *user×item* matrix (2.3% non-zero entries instead of 5.7%) but is also less noisy. Remember that the purchase matrix is only used to compute item/item similarities for item-based CF, the item projection matrix for factorization methods, and the confidence of the association rules. Thus, the models trained on this new purchase matrix are applied the same way as in Section 5. alpha-rules are trained on the *project×item* matrix like the other algorithms, but unlike them uses the categorization of projects for a faster exploration of the search space.

Recommendation performance.

The performances of the models in both the *Complete History* and the 2 *Weeks History* apply settings are shown in Table 3. The optimal rank for SVD and NNMF is still $r = 20$. alpha-rules are with $\alpha = 10\%$ and a minimal support of 1%. The differences in performances between the two apply settings are similar to those of the previous section. In the *Complete History* apply setting, the models perform worse than in the previous section, which is natural since they are trained on purchase sessions that span over shorter periods of times. In the 2 *Weeks History* apply setting, the results are similar to the previous results, except for the bigram rules which obtain significantly better performances, with a greater improvement of the recall (more than 20% relative increase). Thus, the benefit of training on the *project×item* matrix mostly concerns customers for which few items had to be predicted. alpha-rules obtain slightly better performances in terms of precision, but their

Table 4: **Proportion of recommended and purchased items in the Head, the Middle and the Tail when training on the *user×item* matrix (left) and the *project×item* matrix (right) in the 2 *Weeks History* apply setting.**

	Head	Middle	Tail
item-based	96.4%	2.5%	1.1%
SVD	98.7%	1.3%	0.0%
NNMF	99.4%	0.6%	0.0%
bigram rules	98.2%	1.1%	0.7%
alpha-rules	100%	0%	0%

	Head	Middle	Tail
item-based	93.0%	4.8%	2.2%
SVD	97%	2.7%	0.3%
NNMF	96.5%	3.2%	0.3%
bigram rules	90.8%	6.1%	3.1%
alpha-rules	95.4%	4.1%	0%

Table 5: **Test results of non-contextual (left) and contextual (right) recommendations on the subset of users running a project on the reference day, in the 2 *Weeks History* apply setting. The non-contextual *project×item* model is trained and applied as in Section 6.2. The contextual model is described in Section 6.3.**

	prec@5	*rec*@5	*F*1@5
item-based	15.08%	9.73%	10.53%
SVD	21.17%	11.21%	13.56%
NNMF	20.64%	10.97%	13.23%
bigram rules	24.15%	13.46%	15.88%
alpha-rules	25.70%	7.31%	9.40%

	prec@5	*rec*@5	*F*1@5
item-based	20.61%	12.83%	14.17%
SVD	24.30%	12.17%	15.22%
NNMF	26.26%	13.38%	16.57%
bigram rules	32.46%	17.69%	21.15%
alpha-rules	27.57%	12.81%	16.59%

recall and *F*1 is rather low. This is essentially due to the high setting of the minimal support, but decreasing it leads to very high complexity.

Recommended items.

The models trained on the *project×item* matrix produce slightly different recommendations than those trained on the *user×item* matrix. Table 4 compares these models in the 2 *Weeks History* apply setting. It shows, among the items that were recommended and actually purchased by the customer, the percentage of items belong to the Head (i.e. best-sellers), the Middle or the Tail. The Tail, which contains 55% of the items but account for only 8.1% of the sales (see Section 2) contains items that are very difficult to recommend at the right moment. Indeed, the models of the previous section are only able to make accurate recommendations in the Head (more than 95% of the correct recommendations for all models). The reason is that complete customers' purchase histories contain mostly Head items, so that Middle and Tail items are filtered out as noise by the algorithms. A larger part of the correct recommendations lies in the Middle or Tail when training on the *project×item* where short-term correlations between Middle or Tail products can be discovered. In particular, more than 9% of the bigram rules' correct recommendation are now Middle or Tail items.

6.3 Contextual Recommendation

The analysis of projects shows that a typology of more homogeneous purchase patterns can be found, and that these categories, such as "interior" or "exterior" improvement, have a clear interpretation in terms of contextual variables that describe the intent of the purchase. Following the multidimensional model of [2], we propose to evaluate the gain in predictive performance if one *knew* this context at prediction time. This is particularly relevant for our application, since we have very broad context descriptions: the context might be simply inferred by the salesperson during a normal dialogue with the customer; even asking for it has not be seen as too intrusive by professionals.

In the simplest form of the multidimensional model, given the context in which a recommendation is made, the prediction is based solely on past purchases made within the same context. In our case, this is implemented as follows:

- At training time, we train 11 models, one for each category of projects (or, equivalently, we train one model for each possible context). Each of these models is trained on a specific *project×item* purchase matrix containing one row for each project of 2005-2007 of the corresponding category.
- At apply time, we assume that we know the category of the current customer's project (i.e. we know the context of the purchase). On the test data, this is simulated by filtering out all transactions of 2008 which do not belong to a project, and by assigning to each remaining transaction the project category it belongs to. Then, for each user and each reference day, we apply the model which corresponds to the project category.

As we do not evaluate on exactly the same set of transactions as in Sections 5 and 6.2, we also provide, on this set of transactions, the results obtained by the non-contextual model of Sections 6.2 as a baseline. Note that it is exactly the same model and predictions as in Section 6.2, but we consider now only the test users and transactions that belong to a high purchase activity at the reference day. Due to lack of space, we only report the results of the models in the 2 *Weeks History* apply setting[6]. These performances are shown in Table 5. Factorization methods use a rank $r = 5$.

The non-contextual models, on this subset of transactions, have higher precision and lower recall than in general (compare Table 3 (right) and Table 5 (left)), because people running projects buy more products, artificially inflating *prec*@5 and decreasing *rec*@5. The effect of contextualization, however, is critical: item-based CF, NNMF and bigram rules show a relative increase of at least 30% in all performance values. The effect is less dramatic for SVD (which tends to be the most constant model on our data) and for alpha-rules which already used the typology in the exploration of the rules. More interestingly, bigram rules have a precision of 32%. Thus, on average, between 1 and 2 recommended products are actually bought by the customer. We also note that despite their simplicity, bigram rules perform significantly better than other methods on all measures.

Our results, in line with recent works [5, 19], provide additional evidence of the importance of the context of a recom-

[6]The performances of the algorithms in the *Complete History* apply setting, and the results of the models trained as in Section 5, are consistently worse.

mendation. Such performances are acceptable in a dialogue with a customer. Even though this only affects a part of our test data (about 1/3 of transactions), these are the transactions that involve the greater number of items, and thus for which the recommender system should be of greater interest.

When looking at which items are recommended and purchased, we see that the better performances obtained by the contextual models are due to more accurate recommendations of best-sellers: for all algorithms, at least 95% of the correct recommendations involve Head items.

7. CONCLUSION

We presented a systematic comparison of various collaborative filtering systems on a real-life purchase dataset. We showed that recommender systems can be developed on *purchase* rather than *rating* data, and that, in such cases, algorithms comparison is different from the standard rating case. In particular, on our data, the simplest algorithm based on bigram association rules obtained the best performances. We believe that such case-studies are necessary to better understand the specificities of purchase datasets and the factors that impact recommender systems for retailers.

Our results show that factors such as purchase recency and context-awareness may be at least as important as the choice or the design of a well-performing algorithm. They also show that the relative performances of the algorithms vary depending on the setting to which they are applied, so that all algorithms have to be tested at all stages of the development of the recommender system.

Acknowledgements

The authors thank A. Bordes, D. Buffoni, S. Canu, A. Spengler and G. Wisniewski for fruitful discussions. This work was partially funded by the ANR (CADI project).

8. REFERENCES

[1] G. Adomavicius, R. Sankaranarayanan, S. Sen, and A. Tuzhilin. Incorporating Contextual Information in Recommender Systems Using a Multidimensional Approach. *Trans. on Inf. Sys.*, 23(1):103–145, 2005.

[2] G. Adomavicius and A. Tuzhilin. Towards the Next Generation of Recommender Systems: A Survey of the State-of-the-Art and Possible Extensions. *IEEE Trans. on Knowledge and Data Eng.*, 17(6):734–749, 2005.

[3] G. Adomavicius and A. Tuzhilin. Context-aware Recommender Systems. In *Proc. of the 2008 ACM Conf. on Rec. Sys.*, pages 335–336, 2008.

[4] C. Anderson. *The Long Tail: Why the Future of Business Is Selling Less of More.* Hyperion, 2006.

[5] L. Baltrunas. Exploiting Contextual Information in Recommender Systems. In *Proc of the 2008 ACM Conf. on Rec. Sys.*, pages 295–298, 2008.

[6] R. Bell, Y. Koren, and C. Volinsky. Chasing 1,000,000$: How We Won the Netflix Prize. *ASA Stat. and Computing Graphics Newsletter*, 18(2), 2007.

[7] Y. Ding, X. Li, and M. E. Orlowska. Recency-based Collaborative Filtering. In *Proc. of the 17th Australasian Database Conf.*, pages 99–107, 2006.

[8] A. Gunawardana and G. Shani. A survey of accuracy evaluation metrics of recommendation tasks. *J. Mach. Learn. Res.*, 10:2935–2962, 2009.

[9] J. L. Herlocker, J. A. Konstan, L. G. Terveen, and J. T. Riedl. Evaluating Collaborative Filtering Recommender Systems. *ACM Trans. on Inf. Sys.*, 22(1):5–53, 2004.

[10] Y. Hu, Y. Koren, and C. Volinsky. Collaborative Filtering for Implicit Feedback Datasets. In *Proc. of ICDM*, pages 263–272, 2008.

[11] C. Kim and J. Kim. A Recommendation Algorithm Using Multi-Level Association Rules. In *Proc. of the 2003 IEEE/WIC Intl. Conf. on Web Intel.*, 2003.

[12] Y. Koren. Factorization Meets the Neighborhood: a Multifaceted Collaborative Filtering Model. In *Proc. of SIGKDD*, pages 426–434, 2008.

[13] Y. Koren. Collaborative filtering with temporal dynamics. *Commun. ACM*, 53(4):89–97, 2010.

[14] Y. Koren, R. Bell, and C. Volinsky. Matrix Factorization Techniques for Recommender Systems. *Computer*, 42(8):30–37, 2009.

[15] T. Q. Lee, Y. Park, and Y.-T. Park. An Empirical Study on Effectiveness of Temporal Information as Implicit Ratings. *Expert Syst. Appl.*, 36(2):1315–1321, 2009.

[16] G. Linden, B. Smith, and J. York. Amazon.com Recommendations: Item-to-Item Collaborative Filtering. *IEEE Internet Computing*, 7:76–80, 2003.

[17] J. Liu, M. Z. Q. Chen, J. Chen, F. Deng, H. Zhang, Z. Zhang, and T. Zhou. Recent Advances in Personal Recommender Systems. *J. of Inf. and Sys. Science*, 5(2):230–247, 2009.

[18] B. Marlin. Collaborative Filtering: A Machine Learning Perspective. Master's thesis, University of Toronto, 2004.

[19] C. Palmisano, A. Tuzhilin, and M. Gorgoglione. Using Context to Improve Predictive Modeling of Customers in Personalization Applications. *IEEE Trans. on Knowl. and Data Eng.*, 20(11):1535–1549, 2008.

[20] R. Pan and M. Scholz. Mind the Gaps: Weighting the Unknown in Large-Scale One-Class Collaborative Filtering. In *Proc of SIGKDD*, pages 667–676, 2009.

[21] N. Pasquier, R. Taouil, Y. Bastide, G. Stumme, and L. Lakhal. Generating a condensed representation for association rules. *J. Intell. Inf. Syst.*, 24(1):29–60, 2005.

[22] B. Sarwar, G. Karypis, J. Konstan, and J. Riedl. Analysis of Recommendation Algorithms for e-Commerce. In *Proc. of the 2nd ACM Conf. on Electronic Commerce*, pages 158–167, 2000.

[23] N. Srebro and T. Jaakkola. Weighted Low-Rank Approximations. In *Proc. of the 20th Intl. Conf. on Mach. Learn.*, pages 720–727, 2003.

[24] X. Su and T. M. Khoshgoftaar. A survey of Collaborative Filtering Techniques. *Adv. in Artif. Intell.*, 2009:2–2, 2009.

[25] V. Ventos and H. Soldano. Alpha galois lattices: An overview. In *ICFCA*, pages 299–314, 2005.

[26] M. Weimer, A. Karatzoglou, and A. J. Smola. Improving maximum margin matrix factorization. *Machine Learning*, 72(3):263–276, 2008.

[27] S. Zhang, W. Wang, J. Ford, and F. Makedon. Learning from incomplete ratings using non-negative matrix factorization. In *Proc. of SDM*, pages 549–553, 1996.

Detecting Bots via Incremental LS-SVM Learning with Dynamic Feature Adaptation

Feilong Chen
Dept. of Computer Science
Michigan State University
East Lansing, MI 48824
chenfeil@msu.edu

Supranamaya Ranjan
Narus Corporation
570 Maude Court
Sunnyvale, CA 94085
soups@narus.com

Pang-Ning Tan
Dept. of Computer Science
Michigan State University
East Lansing, MI 48824
ptan@cse.msu.edu

ABSTRACT

As botnets continue to proliferate and grow in sophistication, so does the need for more advanced security solutions to effectively detect and defend against such attacks. In particular, botnets such as Conficker have been known to encrypt the communication packets exchanged between bots and their command-and-control server, making it costly for existing botnet detection systems that rely on deep packet inspection (DPI) methods to identify compromised machines. In this paper, we argue that, even in the face of encrypted traffic flows, botnets can still be detected by examining the set of server IP-addresses visited by a client machine in the past. However there are several challenges that must be addressed. First, the set of server IP-addresses visited by client machines may evolve dynamically. Second, the set of client machines used for training and their class labels may also change over time. To overcome these challenges, this paper presents a novel incremental LS-SVM algorithm that is adaptive to both changes in the feature set and class labels of training instances. To evaluate the performance of our algorithm, we have performed experiments on two large-scale datasets, including real-time data collected from peering routers at a large Tier-1 ISP. Experimental results showed that the proposed algorithm produces classification accuracy comparable to its batch counterpart, while consuming significantly less computational resources.

Categories and Subject Descriptors

H.2.8 [**Database Management**]: Database Applications

General Terms

Algorithms

1. INTRODUCTION

Recently, many security solutions have begun using online supervised learning algorithms to address a variety of malware and spam detection problems. For instance, Wang et al. [17] presented an online support vector machine (SVM) classifier that uses "bag of keyword" features from e-mail content to label future e-mails as ham or spam. More recently, Ma et al. [8, 9] applied the online SVM and confidence-weighted (CW) algorithms to detect URLs suspected of hosting malware on the basis of the lexical and host-based features extracted from each URL.

A third application that we consider in this paper centers around the problem of detecting *botnets*, defined as a collection of machines that have been infected by malware. Some known botnets consist of tens of thousands of machines and botnets in general are responsible for launching most of the malicious attacks on the Internet including sending spam e-mails, hosting phishing sites, stealing credit card information via keyloggers, *etc.* The bot owner co-ordinates all the bot machines by sending them common commands about the next attack to launch, or sending them new spam templates. In this regards, one way of detecting botnets is by examining the command-and-control traffic exchanged between bots and the group of command-and-control servers that the bots have to obtain their instructions from.

However, some sophisticated botnets such as Conficker [12] have been known to encrypt the communication packets exchanged between the bots and the command-and-control server. This makes the detection process extremely costly for many existing botnet detection systems [6, 7] that require inspecting the encrypted packet payloads to identify compromised machines. In this paper, we argue that even in the face of encrypted traffic flows, botnets can still be detected by virtue of the fact that bots *must* communicate with command-and-control servers to obtain instructions whereas legitimate clients are unlikely to communicate with the same servers. In this regards, we position the problem of botnet detection as a binary classification problem where we label each client IP-address seen in the network as good or bad depending on a classifier built for the client machines, with features being the set of server IP-addresses that each client talks to within a certain time period. We obtain ground truth labels for a set of client IP-addresses by (*i*) consulting with IP blacklists maintained by several reputation systems such as Spamhaus, SORBS, *etc.* as well as (*ii*) consulting with an Intrusion Detection System [1] that labels a client IP-address as suspicious if it is found to exchange a traffic flow that matches a set of regular expression signatures.

A key challenge in developing an effective classifier for botnet detection is that the set of server IP-addresses used to represent the features often evolves dynamically. For instance, after a new machine gets infected, it may begin com-

KDD'11, August 21–24, 2011, San Diego, California, USA.

municating with command-and-control servers, for which we may not have seen any traffic originating to or from in the past. Even if the feature set remains the same, effects due to churn in the hosting infrastructure with new machines being infected and infected machines being cleaned up leads to changes in the importance of each feature. For instance, a newly infected machine may be elevated to the position of a command-and-control server and hence the feature weight learnt for this IP-address should be modified accordingly. Similarly, an existing command-and-control server may be taken down either by law-enforcement or due to cleaning-up of that machine by anti-virus solutions, and hence the feature weight corresponding to that IP-address should be adjusted accordingly. As a result, a supervised learning model trained on an initial feature set may not be as effective when applied to the next day's data set because it would not be able to utilize the new features present in the next day's data set. To improve its detection rate without incurring significant computational overhead, the model must be updated incrementally to take these effects into account.

Current approaches deal with this problem either via batch learning, or via online learning. Batch learning based solutions build a new model from scratch by utilizing the new data points as well as new features seen. We argue that in these class of applications, the data set size can be prohibitively large such that throwing away past computations and rebuilding from scratch may be highly compute-intensive as well as suffer from detection lags, *i.e.* attackers can get around the detector by introducing new features at a rate faster than the retraining rate. Moreover, during the classification phase, the batch learning based approachs simply apply the old model to the new data set while ignoring the new features that were encountered. Clearly, due to infrequent retraining periods and being unable to make use of new features as soon as they appear, the batch learning based approaches may not achieve a high enough detection accuracy as we will show later during our experimental evaluation. In contrast, in online learning, the model is updated with every incoming data point.

In this regards, one of the primary contributions in this paper is in the development of a botnet detection approach based on a novel online least-square support vector machine (LS-SVM) algorithm, which is incremental in terms of both evolving feature-set as well as data-points. While the problem of how to update an existing SVM model in presence of incremental data-points has been dealt with before [17], we consider our work to be the first (to the best of our knowledge) to consider the problem of updating an existing SVM model when the feature set also evolves. Towards this end, we propose a novel algorithm that achieves a time-accuracy trade-off and reduces the model update time by collapsing the old features into one feature during the retraining phase. Moreover, we constrain the (re)training time of our algorithm by constraining the number of training instances that are used, and in this regards, we introduce an approach to choose which training instances be re-used during the retraining phase.

Finally, we evaluate the performance of our proposed algorithm on two real-world datasets. First, we use the dataset evaluated in [8, 9], which considers the problem of labeling URLs as malicious. The second dataset is obtained from peering routers at a large Tier-1 ISP and provides a who-talks-to-whom graph for a one day time period. We evaluate our incremental LS-SVM approach against both the datasets and show the following. First, our dynamic feature adaptation method achieves a bounded retraining time compared to retraining from scratch and counter-intuitively, in some cases, even achieves higher detection accuracy since we bound the number of features and thereby avoid over-fitting. Second, our incremental LS-SVM with dynamic feature and data adaptation method significantly outperforms the CW algorithm [9], a state-of-the-art online classification algorithm, when applied to the large-scale botnet data from an ISP.

The rest of this paper is organized as follows. First, we provide an overview of the proposed system in Section 2. We then present the related work in Section 3. Section 4 discusses background on SVM and the various formulations of online learning. Next, Section 5 provides details about the dynamic feature adaptation part of our incremental LS-SVM approach. Section 6 discusses the approach to deal with evolving data and how we combine both the incremental feature- and incremental-data approaches. Next, we perform a comprehensive evaluation in Section 7. Finally, we conclude in Section 8.

2. SYSTEM ARCHITECTURE

As proof of concept, we develop a prototype system called *BotWatch* that passively monitors and continuously analyzes the Internet traffic in real time to detect bots. A key component of our system is an incremental LS-SVM classifier to identify emerging bots and consequently new botnets.

BotWatch relies on the following hypothesis to detect bots: the set of servers that bots communicate with are different from the set of servers that legitimate clients communicate with. This can be explained by the fact that botnet operators need to maintain communication with their bots in order to issue commands to them for the next attack to launch or to ensure that they have proper control over their bots by having the bots contact them frequently via "heart-beat" requests. However, this hypothesis can be complicated by the fact that the bot machines also communicate with legitimate servers either because the humans behind the machine are also using it or for subversion purposes. For instance, *e.g.* Conficker [12] bots first open an HTTP GET request to one from a set of over hundred legitimate servers including Google, Amazon, *etc.* to first obtain the current time of day. Regardless, as we will show later, bots can still be distinguished from legitimate clients on the basis of which unique set of machines they communicate with.

The system architecture is composed of the following components: *(i)* flow parser, *(ii)* graph feature extractor, *(iii)* external IP blacklists, and an *(iv)* an online classifier. The input to the system is traffic as obtained via the routers at an Internet Service Provider.

The flow parser reconstructs all the packets that correspond to the same traffic flow, where a flow is defined as the unique 6-tuple of client and server IP-addresses, client- and server-ports, timestamp and layer-3 protocol (TCP or UDP). On seeing each new flow, the BotWatch system updates the aggregated statistics for the pair of IP-addresses which are communicating with each other. In our implementation, we currently compute simple aggregated counts for how many flows were exchanged between the IP-pair within a pre-configured time interval. At the end of this time-interval, the following information is passed on to the online learning module: timestamp for the end of the time window, client IP-address, server IP-address and number of flows exchanged between the IP-pair.

Note that this window based updation of statistics does not have any relationship with our online algorithm which we explain in Section 5, and is only reflective of the application area of botnet detection. Essentially, in the botnet detection application, we found that gathering statistics about each IP-pair over a time window provides better detection rates than labeling each IP-pair as it is seen. Finally, the online learning module trains a classifier that is updated on each incoming IP-pair. We use an external blacklist to train the classifier, where the blacklist contains all the known bot IP addresses, and is either updated whenever the external source releases a new list, or is queried individually for each new IP address detected by the system. Due to the temporary nature of bots, as ideally users will clean their devices and remove bots, a timestamp is assigned to each entry in the list and entries are removed after a pre-configured time interval.

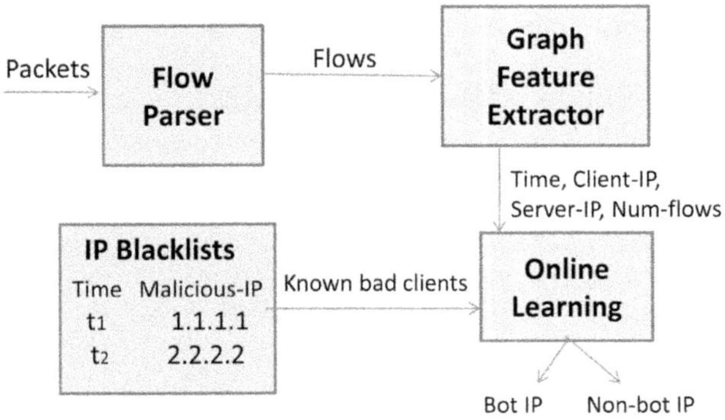

Figure 1: System Architecture

3. RELATED WORK

3.1 Botnet Detection

Botnets have emerged as one of the biggest security threats facing the Internet today. They can be broadly categorized into two types—centralized botnets and Peer-to-Peer (P2P) botnets. Centralized botnets employ one or more Command-and-Control (C&C) servers to control all infected bots and instructs them when, whom and how to attack. Most centralized botnets are based on the IRC protocol. There have been several works focusing on monitoring IRC channel traffic to detect such botnets [2, 5, 3]. Once they have been identified, the centralized botnets can be easily destroyed by blacklisting them.

Newer botnets have evolved from a centralized structure to a more distributed, P2P configuration, to make it harder for them to be detected and shut down. As P2P botnets became prevalent, more sophisticated methods are needed. Some of the recent works have focused on detecting similar communication patterns exhibited by members of the botnet ([6, 7, 10]). For instance, [11] clusters HTTP traces based on their structural similarity to detect bots. BotGrep [10] analyzes the communication graph between hosts and partitions the graph into several components based on some metrics to separate bots from non-bots. None of these approaches however employ a sophisticated online classifier such as SVM to improve their detection rate.

3.2 Online Learning Algorithms

Online learning algorithms have been developed to handle situations where the data set is extremely large and it is infeasible to load the entire data set to the main memory. A classic online learning algorithm is perceptron [13], a linear classifier that takes one data example at a time and updates the weight vector when the current classifier misclassifies the example. The perceptron is simple to implement and fast to learn but not effective when applied to nonlinearly separable problems. More recently, Ma et al. [9] applied a variety of online learning algorithms, including Passive-Aggressive (PA) and Confidence Weighted (CW), to the problem of classifying URLs as suspicious or legitimate. These algorithms were designed to minimally update the target function as new data arrives by employing different objective functions (PA minimizes a least-square loss function whereas CW uses Kullback-Leibler divergence). CW also maintains a confidence measure for each feature and updates more aggressively the weights for the features with lower confidence. However, these heuristics do not guarantee that the updated model has better generalization error. For example, if the initial model was poor, then adjusting the model minimally may not be an effective strategy. In contrast, the online LS-SVM algorithm investigated in this paper is designed to maintain a large margin to ensure good generalization performance. Though there are several online SVM classifiers proposed in the literature [16, 14], none of them were designed to adapt to new features in the data.

4. PRELIMINARIES

Let $\mathcal{D} = \mathcal{D}^{(1)}\mathcal{D}^{(2)}\cdots\mathcal{D}^{(T)}$ denote an ordered collection of labeled data sets, where each $D^{(i)} = \{(\mathbf{x}_j^{(i)}, y_j^{(i)})\}_{j=1}^{N_i}$ is a set of training instances collected during the time interval t_{i-1} and t_i. Each training instance is associated with a feature set $\mathbf{x}_j^{(i)} \in \Re^{d_i}$ and a binary class label $y_j^{(i)} \in \{-1, +1\}$. Many online learning algorithms are designed to update the classification model instantaneously, as each data example arrives (i.e., $N_i = |D^{(i)}| = 1$ for all i). However, for efficiency reasons, it may be more practical to consider the situation where the time interval is sufficiently large such that $N_i \gg 1$. Furthermore, we consider several formulations of the online classification problem:

Dynamic feature adaptation (DynF) This formulation assumes that the training instances are the same throughout the entire time period, but the feature set may grow with the addition of new features that have never been seen in the past. Furthermore, the class label of a training instance may also change over time.

Dynamic feature and data adaptation (DynFD) This formulation assumes new training instances may be collected at each time period while older instances continue to be monitored. The feature set and class labels for the training instances may evolve over time.

The classification algorithm considered in this study is the well-known support vector machine (SVM) classifier. SVM is designed to learn a linear decision surface, either in the original feature space or in a projected high-dimensional feature space, that maximizes the geometric margin of the separating hyperplanes between different classes. In this study, we consider a variation of the classifier known as least-square support vector machine (LS-SVM) [15]. Unlike regular SVM, which minimizes a hinge loss function with linear inequality constraints, LS-SVM optimizes the following least-square loss function with equality constraint:

$$\frac{1}{2}\mathbf{w}^T\mathbf{w} + \frac{\gamma}{2}\sum_{i=1}^{N} e_i^2 \tag{1}$$

$$\text{s.t.} \quad y_i\left[\mathbf{w}^T\mathbf{x}_i + b\right] = 1 - e_i, \quad \forall i \in \{1,\ldots,N\}$$

where γ is a user-specified parameter and N is the number of training instances. An appealing feature of the optimization problem for LS-SVM is that it has a closed form solution, compared to the optimization problem for regular SVM, which requires numerical methods to solve a quadratic programming problem. Previous studies have found that the generalization performance of LS-SVM is comparable to that of regular SVM [4, 19]. Furthermore, it has been theoretically proven the equivalence between linear LS-SVM and hard margin SVM with Mahalanobis distance measure [18].

The constraint optimization problem given in (1) can be cast into the following Lagrangian formulation:

$$\mathcal{L}(\mathbf{w},b,\mathbf{e},\alpha) = \frac{1}{2}\mathbf{w}^T\mathbf{w} + \frac{\gamma}{2}\sum_{i=1}^{N} e_i^2 - \sum_{i=1}^{N}\alpha_i\left\{y_i\left[\mathbf{w}^T\mathbf{x}_i + b\right] - 1 + e_i\right\}, \tag{2}$$

where $\{\alpha_i\}$ is the set of Lagrange multipliers. The optimization problem can be solved by taking its partial derivative with respect to the parameters $\mathbf{w}$, b, $\mathbf{e}$, and α and setting them to zero:

$$\begin{aligned}
\frac{\partial L}{\partial \mathbf{w}} &= \mathbf{w} - \mathbf{Z}^T\alpha = \mathbf{0}_d \\
\frac{\partial L}{\partial b} &= \alpha^T\mathbf{y} = 0 \\
\frac{\partial L}{\partial \mathbf{e}} &= \gamma\mathbf{e} - \alpha = \mathbf{0}_N \\
\frac{\partial L}{\partial \alpha} &= \mathbf{Z}\mathbf{w} + b\mathbf{y} + \mathbf{e} - \mathbf{1}_N = \mathbf{0}_N,
\end{aligned}$$

where $\mathbf{Z}$ is a rectangular matrix whose $(i,j)^{\text{th}}$ element is equal to $y_i x_{ij}$ (i.e., the product of the class label for the i-th instance and its j-th attribute value), $\mathbf{0}_p$ is a p-dimensional column vector of all zeros, and $\mathbf{1}_p$ is a p-dimensional column vector of all ones. The preceding set of linear equations can be further reduced to the following form:

$$\begin{bmatrix} \mathbf{I}_d & 0 & 0 & -\mathbf{Z}^T \\ 0 & 0 & 0 & -\mathbf{y}^T \\ 0 & 0 & \gamma\mathbf{I}_N & -\mathbf{I}_N \\ \mathbf{Z} & \mathbf{y} & \mathbf{I}_N & 0 \end{bmatrix} \begin{bmatrix} \mathbf{w} \\ b \\ \mathbf{e} \\ \alpha \end{bmatrix} = \begin{bmatrix} \mathbf{0}_d \\ 0 \\ \mathbf{0}_N \\ \mathbf{1}_N \end{bmatrix}, \tag{3}$$

where $\mathbf{I}_p$ is a $p \times p$ identity matrix. Since

$$\mathbf{I}_d\mathbf{w} - \mathbf{Z}^T\alpha = 0 \implies \mathbf{w} = \mathbf{Z}^T\alpha \tag{4}$$

$$\gamma\mathbf{I}_N\mathbf{e} - \mathbf{I}_N\alpha = 0 \implies \mathbf{e} = \gamma^{-1}\alpha, \tag{5}$$

the system of linear equations can be further simplified as follows:

$$\begin{bmatrix} 0 & \mathbf{y}^T \\ \mathbf{y} & \mathbf{Z}\mathbf{Z}^T + \gamma^{-1}\mathbf{I}_N \end{bmatrix} \begin{bmatrix} b \\ \alpha \end{bmatrix} = \begin{bmatrix} 0 \\ \mathbf{1}_N \end{bmatrix} \tag{6}$$

which leads to the following closed form solutions:

$$b = \frac{y^T(\mathbf{Z}\mathbf{Z}^T + \gamma^{-1}\mathbf{I}_N)^{-1}\mathbf{1}_N}{y^T(\mathbf{Z}\mathbf{Z}^T + \gamma^{-1}\mathbf{I}_N)^{-1}\mathbf{y}} \tag{7}$$

$$\alpha = (\mathbf{Z}\mathbf{Z}^T + \gamma^{-1}\mathbf{I}_N)^{-1}[\mathbf{1}_N - \mathbf{y}b] \tag{8}$$

Once the values for the Lagrange multipliers α are found, $\mathbf{w}$ is computed using Equation (4). Note that the solutions for α and b involve the matrix product $(\mathbf{Z}\mathbf{Z}^T)_{ij} = y_i y_j \mathbf{x}_i \cdot \mathbf{x}_j$. This suggests that we can easily turn LS-SVM into a nonlinear classifier by replacing the dot-product $\mathbf{x}_i \cdot \mathbf{x}_j$ with its corresponding kernel function, i.e., $\mathbf{A}_{ij} = y_i y_j \Phi(\mathbf{x}_i, \mathbf{x}_j)$.

Finally, having solved the equations above and obtain the model parameters, we can predict the class label for a new data instance, say $\mathbf{x}_{test}$, as $f(\mathbf{x}_{test}) = \text{sign}[\mathbf{w}^T\mathbf{x}_{test} + b]$. For nonlinear LS-SVM, this is equivalent to

$$f(\mathbf{x}_{test}) = \text{sign}\left[\sum_i y_i\alpha_i\phi(\mathbf{x}_i, \mathbf{x}_{test}) + b\right].$$

The runtime complexity for LS-SVM is $O(N^3)$, with most of the computational overhead spent on computing the matrix inverse $(\mathbf{Z}\mathbf{Z}^T + \gamma^{-1}\mathbf{I}_N)^{-1}$ in Equations (7) and (8).

5. ONLINE LS-SVM WITH DYNAMIC FEATURE ADAPTATION

Let $\mathbf{x}^t$ be the feature set at time t and $\mathbf{x}^{(t+1)} = \mathbf{x}^{(t)} \cup \hat{\mathbf{x}}^{(t+1)}$ be the expanded feature set at $t+1$, where $\hat{\mathbf{x}}^{(t+1)}$ denote the newly added features. For notational convenience, we will drop the superscript in the remainder of the paper. We begin our initial discussion with an exact formulation of online LS-SVM in the presence of dynamic features. However, the formulation makes an unrealistic assumption that the class labels are unchanged. We then discuss an efficient method for approximating the solution that allows the class labels to evolve over time.

5.1 Exact Method

Let $f(\mathbf{x}) = \mathbf{w}^T\mathbf{x} + \mathbf{v}^T\hat{\mathbf{x}} + b$ be the decision function of the LS-SVM classifier, where $\mathbf{w}$ and $\mathbf{v}$ are the weight vectors associated with the old features $(\mathbf{x})$ and new features $(\hat{\mathbf{x}})$. The weights are computed by optimizing the following objective function:

$$\mathcal{L} = \frac{1}{2}[\mathbf{w}^T\mathbf{w} + \mathbf{v}^T\mathbf{v}] + \frac{\gamma}{2}\sum_{i=1}^{N} e_i^2 - \sum_{i=1}^{N}\alpha_i\left\{y_i\left[\mathbf{w}^T\mathbf{x}_i + \mathbf{v}^T\hat{\mathbf{x}}_i + b\right] - 1 + e_i\right\}, \tag{9}$$

which is equivalent to the objective function given in (2) when the feature set consists of $\mathbf{x} \cup \hat{\mathbf{x}}$. The closed form solutions to the objective function are as follows:

$$b = \frac{y^T(\tilde{\mathbf{Z}}\tilde{\mathbf{Z}}^T + \mathbf{Z}\mathbf{Z}^T + \gamma^{-1}\mathbf{I}_N)^{-1}\mathbf{1}_N}{y^T(\tilde{\mathbf{Z}}\tilde{\mathbf{Z}}^T + \mathbf{Z}\mathbf{Z}^T + \gamma^{-1}\mathbf{I}_N)^{-1}\mathbf{y}} \tag{10}$$

$$\alpha = (\tilde{\mathbf{Z}}\tilde{\mathbf{Z}}^T + \mathbf{Z}\mathbf{Z}^T + \gamma^{-1}\mathbf{I}_N)^{-1}[\mathbf{1}_N - \mathbf{y}b]$$

$$\mathbf{w} = \mathbf{Z}^T\alpha, \quad \mathbf{v} = \tilde{\mathbf{Z}}^T\alpha,$$

where $\mathbf{Z}_{ij} = y_i x_{ij}$ and $\tilde{\mathbf{Z}}_{ij} = y_i\hat{x}_{ij}$. As can be seen from Equation (10), the exact solutions require computing the inverse of the matrix $\tilde{\mathbf{Z}}\tilde{\mathbf{Z}}^T + \mathbf{Z}\mathbf{Z}^T + \gamma^{-1}\mathbf{I}_N$, which is an $O(N^3 + N^2 d + N^2\hat{d})$ operations (where N is the number of training instances, d is the cardinality of $\mathbf{x}$ and $\hat{d}$ is the cardinality of $\hat{\mathbf{x}}$). Thus, re-computing the matrix inverse at each time period can be very expensive especially when both number of training examples and features are large.

If we assume that the class labels of the training instances do not change, i.e., $y_i^{(t+1)} = y_i^{(t)}$ ($\forall i = \{1, 2, \cdots, N\}$), or equivalently, $\mathbf{Z}^{(t+1)} = \mathbf{Z}^{(t)}$, then the matrix inverse can be computed more efficiently as follows:

LEMMA 1. *Let $\mathbf{A}$ be an invertible $N \times N$ matrix and $\hat{\mathbf{Z}}$ be an $N \times \hat{d}$ matrix (where $\hat{d} \ll N$). The inverse of the matrix $(A + \hat{\mathbf{Z}}\hat{\mathbf{Z}}^T)^{-1}$ can be computed efficiently as follows:*

$$(\mathbf{A} + \hat{\mathbf{Z}}\hat{\mathbf{Z}}^T)^{-1} = \mathbf{A}^{-1} - \mathbf{A}^{-1}\hat{\mathbf{Z}}\left(\mathbf{I}_{\hat{d}} + \hat{\mathbf{Z}}^T\mathbf{A}^{-1}\hat{\mathbf{Z}}\right)^{-1}\hat{\mathbf{Z}}^T\mathbf{A}^{-1}$$

The proof of this lemma follows from a special case of the well-known Sherman-Morrison-Woodbury formula. Although the formula requires computing the inverse of another matrix $(\mathbf{I}_{\hat{d}} + \hat{\mathbf{Z}}^T\mathbf{A}^{-1}\hat{\mathbf{Z}})$, the size of this matrix is only $\hat{d} \times \hat{d}$, which is less costly than computing the inverse of its original matrix. If $\mathbf{A}^{-1}$ is already known, then the overall cost for computing the matrix inverse using Lemma 1 reduces to $O(N^2\hat{d})$ instead of $O(N^3)$.

We can apply Lemma 1 to solve Equation (10) by setting $\mathbf{A} = \mathbf{Z}\mathbf{Z}^T + \gamma^{-1}\mathbf{I}_N$. However, the limitation of this approach is that it assumes the class labels of the training instances do not evolve over time. The next subsection presents an approximate algorithm that can overcome this limitation.

5.2 Approximate Method

This section approximates the LS-SVM objective function with the following assumption, that the weights associated with the original feature vector is modified uniformly as follows: $\mathbf{w}_{new} = \lambda\mathbf{w}_{old}$. This assumption leads to the following modified objective function:

$$\begin{aligned}\mathcal{L} &= \frac{1}{2}[\lambda^2\mathbf{w}^T\mathbf{w} + \mathbf{v}^T\mathbf{v}] + \frac{\gamma}{2}\sum_{i=1}^{l} e_i^2 \\ &- \sum_{i=1}^{l}\alpha_i\left\{y_i\left[\lambda(\mathbf{w}^T\mathbf{x}_i + b) + \mathbf{v}^T\hat{\mathbf{x}}_i + \hat{b}\right] - 1 + e_i\right\} + c\lambda^2\end{aligned}$$

where we have included a regularization term $c\lambda^2$ to constrain the magnitude of λ. For brevity, the subscript for $\mathbf{w}_{old}$ has also been omitted in the remainder of this section. As will be shown below, the parameter λ is determined automatically, based on the degree of agreement between the previous classification model and the current labels of the training instances. The more agreement there is, the larger λ will be. Furthermore, even if the uniformity assumption about the modification to $\mathbf{w}$ does not hold, any inaccuracies in the new model can be compensated by the weights associated with the new features $\hat{\mathbf{x}}$. Experimental results have suggested that the approximate model performs quite as well as its batch counterpart.

Taking the partial derivative over the model parameters and setting them to zeros yield the following:

$$\begin{bmatrix}\mathbf{I}_d & 0 & 0 & 0 & -\hat{\mathbf{Z}}^T \\ 0 & 0 & 0 & 0 & -\mathbf{y}^T \\ 0 & 0 & 0 & \gamma\mathbf{I}_N & -\mathbf{I}_N \\ 0 & 0 & c+\mathbf{w}^T\mathbf{w} & 0 & -\mathbf{g}^T \\ \hat{\mathbf{Z}} & \mathbf{y} & 0 & \mathbf{I}_N & 0\end{bmatrix}\begin{bmatrix}\mathbf{v} \\ \hat{b} \\ \lambda \\ \mathbf{e} \\ \alpha\end{bmatrix} = \begin{bmatrix}\mathbf{0}_d \\ 0 \\ \mathbf{0}_N \\ 0 \\ \mathbf{1}_N\end{bmatrix}, \quad (11)$$

where $\mathbf{g} = \mathbf{Z}\mathbf{w} + b\mathbf{y} = (\mathbf{X}\mathbf{w} + b\mathbf{1}_N) \odot \mathbf{y}$ is an N-dimensional column vector that measures the agreement between the predicted values of the previous model and the current labels of the training instances. The symbol $\odot$ denotes an element-wise vector product. After some simplification, the optimization problem reduces to solving the following system of linear equations:

$$\begin{bmatrix}0 & \mathbf{y}^T \\ \mathbf{y} & \frac{\mathbf{g}\mathbf{g}^T}{c+\mathbf{w}^T\mathbf{w}} + \hat{\mathbf{Z}}\hat{\mathbf{Z}}^T + \gamma^{-1}\mathbf{I}_N\end{bmatrix}\begin{bmatrix}\hat{b} \\ \alpha\end{bmatrix} = \begin{bmatrix}0 \\ \mathbf{1}\end{bmatrix} \quad (12)$$

There are several advantages of using this formulation. First, instead of working with the $N \times d$ matrix $\mathbf{X}$, it is sufficient to collapse the old features into a column vector $\mathbf{g}$, thereby reducing the storage requirements. This is important because the number of original features d keeps growing over time in dynamic feature adaptation. Second, the formulation may accommodate changes in the class labels of training instances in subsequent time periods. This can be accomplished by storing the vector $\tilde{\mathbf{g}} = \mathbf{X}\mathbf{w} + b\mathbf{1}_N$ instead of $\mathbf{g}$. If the class labels for some training instances have changed, we only need to update the corresponding elements in $\mathbf{y}$ to reflect these changes. The updated vector $\mathbf{g}$ is obtained by computing $\tilde{\mathbf{g}} \odot \mathbf{y}$.

Note that λ is determined automatically based on the consistency between the predictions made by the previous model and the current labels of the training instances, i.e.:

$$\lambda = \frac{\alpha^T\mathbf{g}}{\mathbf{w}^T\mathbf{w} + c} = \frac{\alpha^T[(\mathbf{X}\mathbf{w} + b\mathbf{1}) \odot \mathbf{y}]}{\mathbf{w}^T\mathbf{w} + c}.$$

This formula suggests that the value for λ is large when the predictions made by the previous model are consistent with the current labels of the training instances (especially for those instances associated with large values of α). On the other hand, if the previous model becomes outdated, then the value for λ will automatically be reduced.

5.3 Efficient Computation

The preceding formulation has to solve the system of linear equations given in (12) and performs matrix inversion on $\frac{\mathbf{g}\mathbf{g}^T}{c+\mathbf{w}^T\mathbf{w}} + \hat{\mathbf{Z}}\hat{\mathbf{Z}}^T + \gamma^{-1}\mathbf{I}_N$. The problem can be further simplified by choosing $c = 1 - \mathbf{w}^T\mathbf{w}$ (though the methodology explained below is applicable to other values of c).

LEMMA 2. *Let $S = \mathbf{g}\mathbf{g}^T + \hat{\mathbf{Z}}\hat{\mathbf{Z}}^T + \gamma^{-1}\mathbf{I}_N$, N be the number of training instances, and $\hat{d}$ be the number of new features in $\hat{\mathbf{x}}$ (where $\hat{d} \ll d$). The overall cost for solving the approximate LS-SVM formulation with dynamic feature adaptation is $O(N\hat{d}^2 + \hat{d}^3 + N^2\hat{d})$, which is independent of the number of features d in the previous time period.*

PROOF. The inverse for $\mathbf{S}$ can be computed efficiently as follows. First, we use the Sherman-Morrison-Woodbury formula (see Lemma 1) to compute the inverse of $\gamma^{-1}\mathbf{I}_N + \hat{\mathbf{Z}}\hat{\mathbf{Z}}^T$:

$$(\gamma\mathbf{I}_N + \hat{\mathbf{Z}}\hat{\mathbf{Z}}^T)^{-1} = \gamma\mathbf{I}_N - \gamma^2\hat{\mathbf{Z}}(\mathbf{I}_d + \gamma\hat{\mathbf{Z}}^T\hat{\mathbf{Z}})^{-1}\hat{\mathbf{Z}}^T \quad (13)$$

Since $(\mathbf{I}_d + \gamma\hat{\mathbf{Z}}^T\hat{\mathbf{Z}})$ is a $\hat{d} \times \hat{d}$ matrix, its inverse can be computed efficiently in $O(\hat{d}^3)$. Next, we can apply the Sherman-Morrison formula to compute the inverse of $\mathbf{S}$ as follows:

$$\mathbf{S}^{-1} = (\mathbf{J} + \mathbf{g}\mathbf{g}^T)^{-1} = \mathbf{J}^{-1} - \frac{\mathbf{J}^{-1}\mathbf{g}\mathbf{g}^T\mathbf{J}^{-1}}{1 + \mathbf{g}^T\mathbf{J}^{-1}\mathbf{g}}$$

where $\mathbf{J}$ is the inverse given in Equation (13). Since $(1 + \mathbf{g}^T\mathbf{J}^{-1}\mathbf{g})$ is a scalar, we do not need to perform any matrix inversion here. In conclusion, the overall time complexity to compute the inverse for $\mathbf{S}$ is $O(N\hat{d}^2 + \hat{d}^3 + \hat{N}^2\hat{d})$. □

6. ONLINE LS-SVM WITH DYNAMIC FEATURE AND DATA ADAPTATION

This section presents an extension to the online LS-SVM method described in the previous section to incorporate new training instances. We assume the deployed system has bounded storage capacity to store at most N training instances in memory at a time. Furthermore, since the complexity of the algorithm is proportional to N^2, maintaining the growing number of training instances would make the computation more expensive. To circumvent this problem, we present an approach that maintains the size of the training set to be N at all times. In particular, we focus on training instances that can either maintain or help improve the performance of the classifier.

First, we consider only the new labeled instances that have been misclassified by the existing model to be included in the training set. Let $\mathbf{D} = \{\mathbf{x}_1, \mathbf{x}_2, \cdots, \mathbf{x}_N\}$ be the current training set and $\mathbf{D}_2 = \{\mathbf{x}_{N+1}, \mathbf{x}_{N+2}, \cdots, \mathbf{x}_{N+m}\}$ be the misclassified new instances. In order to include the m new instances, we need to remove the same number of instances from the training set $\mathbf{D}$. In this paper, we investigate three instance removal strategies. The first strategy (**OLD**) simply removes the m oldest training examples and replaces them with the misclassified new instances. The second strategy (**MIN**) discards the m training examples with smallest values for α. The rationale behind this approach is that such examples have the least influence on the decision surface of the classifier.

Our third strategy is designed to identify training examples whose removal have minimal effect on the current model. Let $f_{\mathbf{Q}}(\mathbf{x}) = \sum_{\mathbf{x}_i \in \mathbf{Q}} y_i \alpha_i \mathbf{x}_i \cdot \mathbf{x} + b$ be the model constructed from a training set $\mathbf{Q}$ and $\mathbf{S}^* \subset \mathbf{D}$ be the set of training instances selected for removal. We formalize the problem of selecting training instances to remove as follows:

$$\begin{aligned}
\mathbf{S}^* &= \arg\min_{\mathbf{S}} E\Big[|f_{\mathbf{D}}(\mathbf{x}) - f_{\mathbf{D}\setminus\mathbf{S}}(\mathbf{x})|\Big] \\
&= \arg\min_{\mathbf{S}} E\Bigg[\Big|\sum_{\mathbf{x}_i\in\mathbf{D}} y_i\alpha_i\mathbf{x}_i\cdot\mathbf{x} - \sum_{\mathbf{x}_i\in\mathbf{D}\setminus\mathbf{S}} y_i\alpha_i\mathbf{x}_i\cdot\mathbf{x}\Big|\Bigg] \\
&= \arg\min_{\mathbf{S}} E\Bigg[\Big|\sum_{\mathbf{x}_i\in\mathbf{S}} y_i\alpha_i\mathbf{x}_i\cdot\mathbf{x}\Big|\Bigg] \\
&= \arg\min_{\mathbf{S}} E\Bigg[\Big|\Big(\sum_{\mathbf{x}_i\in\mathbf{S}} y_i\alpha_i\mathbf{x}_i\Big)\cdot\mathbf{x}\Big|\Bigg]. \qquad (14)
\end{aligned}$$

where $E[\cdot]$ denote expected value. Solving the objective function shown above can be expensive especially when the training set size is large. The **MIN** approach (strategy 2) tries to find an approximate solution by choosing

$$\mathbf{S}^* = \arg\min_{\mathbf{S}} |\sum_{\mathbf{x}_i\in\mathbf{S}} \alpha_i|$$

The limitation of this approach is that it ignores the class label of the selected training instances unlike the objective function given in Equation (14). Instead, our third strategy (**GREEDY**) is designed to select training instances that minimize the following objective function:

$$\mathbf{S}^* = \arg\min_{\mathbf{S}} |\sum_{\mathbf{x}_i\in\mathbf{S}} y_i\alpha_i$$

After we find $\mathbf{S}^*$, we can construct a new training set $\mathbf{D}^* = (\mathbf{D} \setminus \mathbf{S}^*) \cup \mathbf{D}_2$. Finally, we apply the online LS-SVM with dynamic feature adaptation approach described in the previous section to $\mathbf{D}^*$.

Table 1: Statistics of identified bots

Botnet	Regular Expression	#C&C servers	#bots
Conficker	URL ∼ `http://[0-9]+.[0-9]+.[0-9]+[0-9]+./search?q=[0-9]+`	28	1,835
Grum	URL ∼ `[a-zA-Z0-9\.]+/spm/s\_[a-zA-Z]+.php`	24	161
Pushdo	URL ∼ `[a-zA-Z0-9\.]+/40E800` || `[a-zA-Z0-9\.]+/C00000`	19	166
Sality	URL ∼ `musikrajt.sk` || `musikrajt.wz.cz` || `edmatrix.us`	10	232
Total		81	2,394

7. EXPERIMENTAL EVALUATION

We evaluated our algorithm on two real-world data sets. The first is a subset of the benchmark dataset used for detecting malicious URLs [9]. The dataset contains URLs collected over a 20-day period, each of which has 20,000 unique URLs. The features include 1,791,261 lexical features and 1,117,901 host-based features. Nearly one third of the data belongs to the positive class (i.e., malicious URL). The second is a botnet detection dataset we have collected by monitoring the HTTP network traffic at a large ISP in 24 hours. The data contains features derived from Layer-4 and Layer-7 load information, including source and destination IP-addresses, number of bytes transmitted, number of packets, *etc.* The labels are generated based on the approach described in Section 2. The botnets found in the network trace include Conficker, Grum, Pong, Pushdo, and Sality. Table 1 shows examples of the identified botnets, their statistics, and signatures used for detecting them in the data. We partition the data into four subsets, each containing all the client IP-addresses observed in a six-hourly time window. We then train the LS-SVM classifier on the first subset and incrementally update the model with new data from subsequent subsets.

7.1 Dynamic Feature Adaptation

First we evaluated the performance of our proposed dynamic feature adaptation method using the malicious URL dataset. For this experiment, we combine the data for all the days and partition them into five folds. For each fold, we designate half of the data as labeled (to be used for training and incremental model updating) and the remainder as unlabeled (to be used for testing purposes). In addition, we randomly split the feature set into ten equal-sized subsets

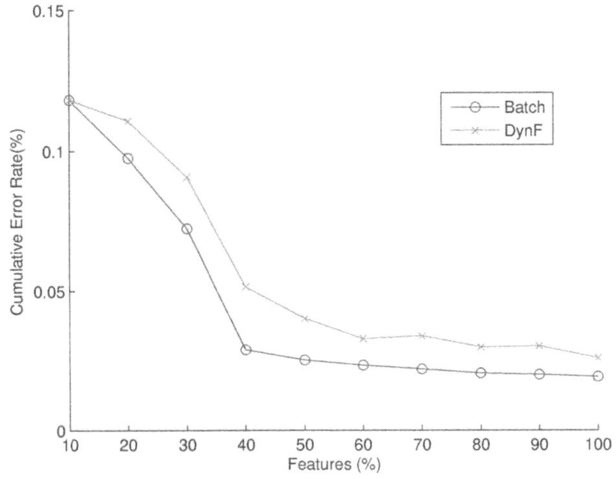

Figure 2: Comparison of classification error between batch and DynF algorithms on fold 1 data as new features are incrementally added to the classifier.

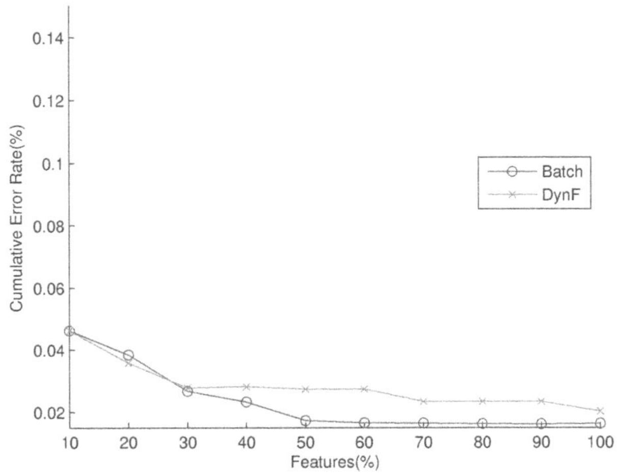

Figure 3: Comparison of classification error between batch and DynF algorithms on fold 2 data as new features are incrementally added to the classifier.

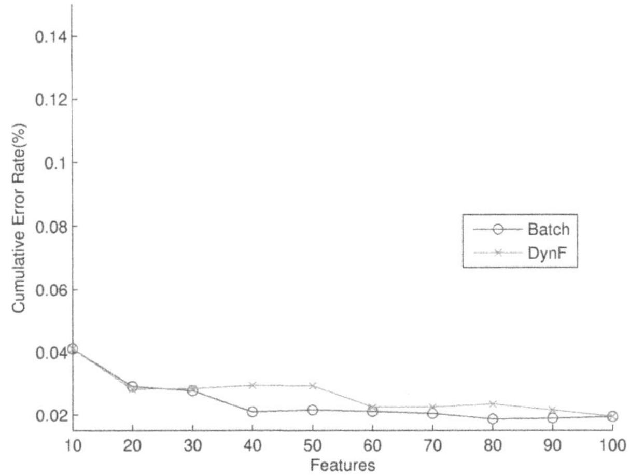

Figure 4: Comparison of classification error between batch and DynF algorithms on fold 3 data as new features are incrementally added to the classifier.

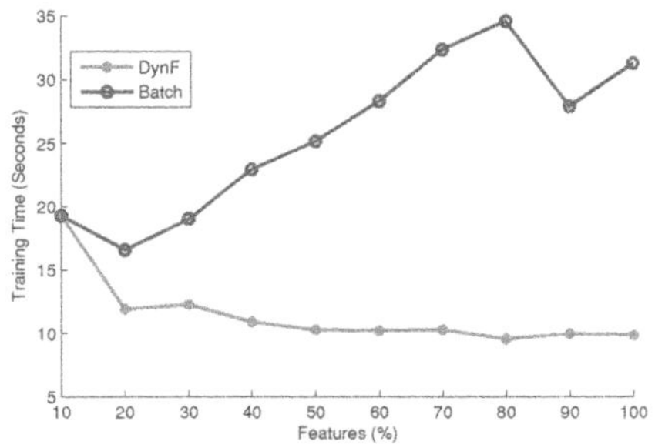

Figure 5: Comparison of training time between batch and DynF algorithms on fold 1 data as new features are incrementally added to the classifier.

and use one of them (10% of the features) for initial model building and testing. We then iteratively add another subset of features and update the model incrementally using the approach described in Section 5 (the training and test sets are assumed to be fixed throughout this experiment). This iterative update process continues until the entire feature set is included into the model. The experiment is then repeated for the remaining four folds.

We consider two metrics for evaluating the performance of our method—misclassification error rate and training time. We compared the performance of our method against the batch LS-SVM algorithm, which retrains a new model from scratch using both the old and newly augmented features. Figures 2, 3, and 4 show the classification error rates for folds 1 to 3, respectively (we omit the results for folds 4 and 5 due to lack of space, but the results are very similar). Observe that the misclassification error of our dynamic feature adaptation method (DynF) is comparable to that of the batch LS-SVM algorithm.

Figure 5 shows the training time for both batch and DynF methods. Clearly, as more features are added, the training time for the batch algorithm grows more rapidly compared to our proposed approach. In fact, the training time for DynF is somewhat stable due to the fact that the features from previous models are shrunk into a column vector $\mathbf{g}$ while the number of new features used to update the model is the same (i.e., 10% of the entire feature space). The decrease in training time for the DynF algorithm after using the first 10% features can be explained by the fact that the computational complexity for building the initial LS-SVM model is $O(N^3)$, while subsequent updates require only $O(N^2\hat{d})$.

7.2 Dynamic Feature and Data Adaptation

Next we evaluate the performance of our proposed Dynamic Feature with Data Adaptation (DynFD) algorithm. We compared the performance of our algorithm against the following baseline methods: (1) **Static**. In this approach, we train an initial model from the first time period and applies it to all subsequent time periods (without updat-

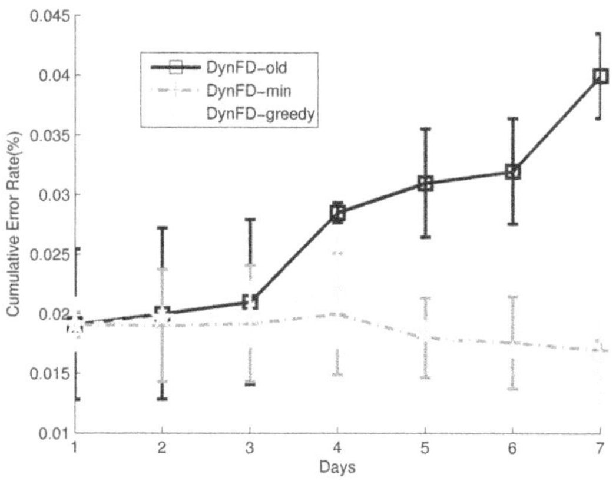

Figure 6: Cumulative error rate. The results were obtained using a benchmark suspicious URL detection dataset.

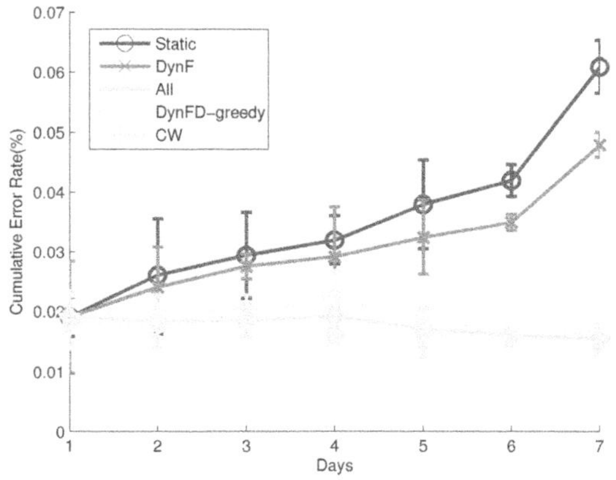

Figure 7: Cumulative error rate. The results were obtained using a benchmark suspicious URL detection dataset.

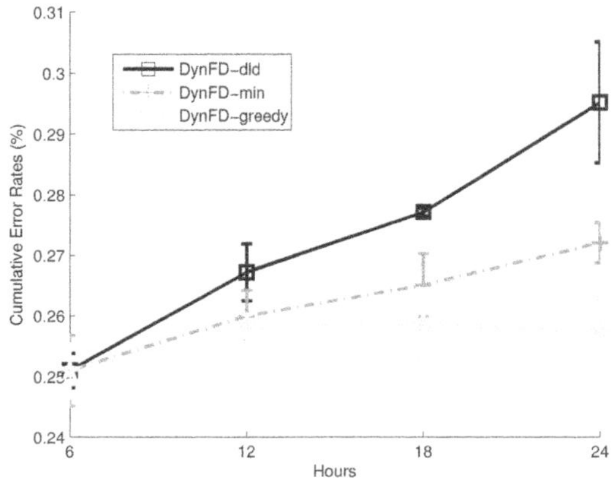

Figure 8: Cumulative error rates. The results were obtained using the botnet dataset.

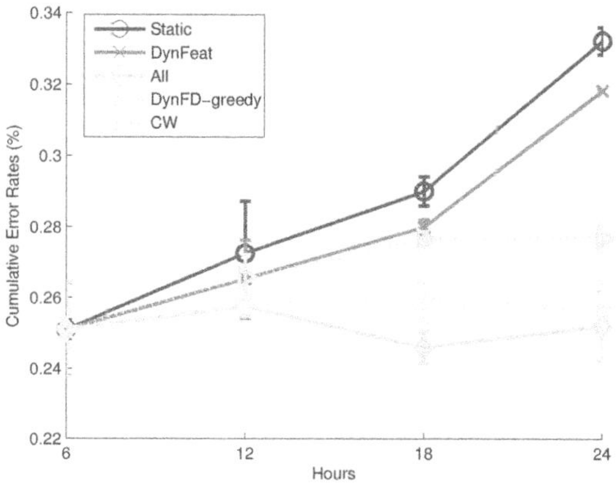

Figure 9: Cumulative error rates. The results were obtained using the botnet dataset.

ing the model). (2) **DynF**. In this approach, we train an initial model during the first time period and refines it at each subsequent time period using the *dynamic feature adaptation* approach (the training examples are assumed to be fixed). (3) **All**. In this approach, we add new features and new training examples at each iteration without removing older data examples (this approach assumes that the memory space is unbounded). (4) **CW**. This is the confidence-weighted online algorithm used in [9]. In addition to the baseline methods, we consider three variations of the proposed DynFD method: (1) **DynFD-old**. In this approach, we make room for the new training examples at each time period by removing the oldest training examples. (2) **DynFD-min**. In this approach, we accommodate the new training examples by removing training examples that have the lowest values of α. (3) **DynFD-greedy**. In this approach, we choose the older training examples to be removed according to Equation 14.

Figure 6 compares the performance of the three DynFD proposed methods on the benchmark malicious URL dataset [9]. The results suggest that both **DynFD-min** and **DynFD-greedy** achieve consistently low error rates compared to **DynFD-old**, which performed worse on datasets collected after Day 3. This is not surprising as **DynFD-old** may accidentally discard old but still useful training examples. Figure 7 compares the performance of **DynFD-greedy** against other the baseline algorithms. As shown in the figure, the method **All** which allows new examples to be added to the training set without removing other existing examples, appears to produce the best result along with the **CW** algorithm. The performance of **DynFD-greedy** is slightly worse, though the difference is not statistically significance (the error rates for all three methods are less than 2%). The other two methods, **Static** and **DynF**, appear to misclassify more test examples especially after Day 4. This is because these methods do not include newer training examples for model re-building.

Figures 8 and 9 show the performance of the seven methods on the botnet dataset. In Figure 8, we compare the three variants of the DynFD method. The results suggest **DynFD-greedy** clearly outperformed the other two methods. Furthermore, in Figure 9, we compare it against other baseline algorithms. While the **All** method once again yields the best result, our proposed **DynFD-greedy** came in close second. On this dataset, the **CW** algorithm was significantly worse than both **All** and **DynFD-greedy**. One possible explanation is that for the botnet dataset, which is noisy and harder to classify, the SVM-based methods employ the maximum-margin principle to achieve better generalization error. **Static** and **DynF** again yield the worst performance due to the fact that they do not accommodate additional training examples to rebuild the model.

8. CONCLUSIONS

This paper focuses on the problem of detecting bots in a large network using an online learning algorithm that is adaptive to both evolving features and training sets. Our assumption is that we can identify whether a client machine is a "bot" by examining the server IP-addresses they had visited in the past. Using two real-world data sets, we show that the proposed algorithm produces an accuracy comparable to its batch counterpart, while consuming significantly less computational resources. In addition, our proposed algorithm also outperformed the state-of-the-art CW algorithm when applied to large-scale botnet data obtained from an ISP.

9. ACKNOWLEDGMENTS

Feilong Chen and Pang-Ning Tan's research are supported in part by ONR grant number N00014-09-1-0663.

10. REFERENCES

[1] Snort network intrusion prevention and detection system, `http://www.snort.org`.

[2] J. R. Binkley and S. Singh. An algorithm for anomaly-based botnet detection. In *SRUTI'06: Proceedings of the 2nd Workshop on Steps to Reducing Unwanted Traffic on the Internet*, pp. 43-48, San Jose, CA, USA, 2006.

[3] E. Cooke, F. Jahanian, and D. Mcpherson. The Zombie Roundup: Understanding, Detecting, and Disrupting Botnets. In *SRUTI'05: Proceedings of the 1st Workshop on Steps to Reducing Unwanted Traffic on the Internet*, pp. 39-44, Cambridge, MA, USA, 2005.

[4] T. Gestel, J. Suykens, B. Baesens, S. Viaene, J. Vanthienen, G.Dedene, B. D. Moor, and J. Vandewalle. Benchmarking Least Square Support Vector Machine Classifiers. *Machine Learning*, 54(1):5–32, 2004.

[5] J. Goebel and T. Holz. Rishi: Identify bot contaminated hosts by IRC nickname evaluation. In *HotBots'07: Proceedings of the First Workshop on Hot Topics in Understanding Botnets*, Cambridge, MA, USA, 2007.

[6] G. Gu, P. Porras, V. Yegneswaran, M. Fong, and W. Lee. BotHunter: Detecting malware infection through IDS-driven dialog correlation. In *Proceedings of the 16th USENIX Security Symposium (Security'07)*, pp. 167-182, Boston, MA, USA, 2007.

[7] G. Gu, J. Zhang, and W. Lee. BotSniffer: Detecting botnet command and control channels in network traffic. In *NDSS'08: Proceedings of the 15th Annual Network and Distributed System Security Symposium (NDSS'08)*, San Diego, CA, USA, 2008.

[8] J. Ma, L. K. Saul, S. Savage, and G. M. Voelker. Beyond blacklists: Learning to detect malicious web sites from suspicious URLs. In *KDD'09: Proceedings of the ACM SIGKDD International Conference on Knowledge Discovery and Data Mining*, pp. 1245-1254, Paris, France, 2009.

[9] J. Ma, L. K. Saul, S. Savage, and G. M. Voelker. Identifying suspicious URLs: An application of large-scale online learning. In *ICML '09: Proceedings of the 26th Annual International Conference on Machine Learning*, Montreal, Canada, 2009.

[10] S. Nagaraja, P. Mittal, C.-Y. Hong, M. Caesar, and N. Borisov. Botgrep: finding P2P bots with structured graph analysis. In *Proceedings of the 19th USENIX conference on Security*, USENIX Security'10, Washington, DC, USA, 2010.

[11] R. Perdisci, W. Lee, and N. Feamster. Behavioral clustering of HTTP-based malware and signature generation using malicious network traces. In *NSDI'10: Proceedings of the 7th USENIX Symposium on Networked Systems Design and Implementation*, San Jose, CA, USA, 2010.

[12] P. Porras, H. Saidi, and V. Yegneswaran. An analysis of conficker's logic and rendezvous points. Technical report, SRI International, Menlo Park, CA, USA, 2009.

[13] D. E. Rumelhart, G. E. Hinton, and R. J. Williams. Learning internal representations by error propagation. *Parallel distributed processing: Explorations in the microstructure of cognition*, Vol 1, MIT Press, pp. 318–362, 1986.

[14] D. Sculley and G. M. Wachman. Relaxed online SVMs for spam filtering. In *SIGIR '07: Proceedings of the 30th International ACM SIGIR conference on Research and development in Information Retrieval*, pp. 415–422, Amsterdam, Netherlands, 2007.

[15] J. Suykens, T. Gestel, J. Brabanter, B. Moor, and J. Vandewalle. *Least Squares Support Vector Machines*. World Scientific Pub, Singapore, 2002.

[16] D. Tax and P. Laskov. Online SVM learning: from classification to data description and back. In *NNSP'03: Proceedings of the IEEE 13th Workshop on Neural Networks for Signal Processing*, pp. 499–508, Toulouse, France, 2003.

[17] Q. Wang, Y. Guan, and X. Wang. SVM-based spam filter with active and online learning. In *TREC '06: Proceedings of the 15th Text Retrieval Conference*, Gaithersburg, Maryland, USA, 2006.

[18] J. Ye and T. Xiong. SVM versus least square SVM. In *Proceedings of the 11th International Conference on Artificial Intelligence and Statistics*, pp. 644–651, San Juan, Puerto Rico, 2007.

[19] L. Zhang, J. Zhu, and T. Yao. An evaluation of statistical spam filtering techniques. In *ACM Transactions on Asian Language Information Processing*, 3(4), pp. 243-269, 2004.

Toward Personalized Care Management of Patients at Risk - The Diabetes Case Study

Hani Neuvirth, Michal Ozery-Flato,
Jonathan Laserson, Michal Rosen-Zvi
Machine Learning and Data Mining group
IBM Research
Mount Carmel, Haifa, 31905, Israel
{hani, ozery, ljon, rosen}@il.ibm.com

Jianying Hu, Martin S. Kohn,
Shahram Ebadollahi
Healthcare Transformation group
IBM Research
IBM T.J. Watson Research, Hawthorne, NY
{jyhu, marty.kohn, ebad}@us.ibm.com

ABSTRACT

Chronic diseases constitute the leading cause of mortality in the western world, have a major impact on the patients' quality of life, and comprise the bulk of healthcare costs. Nowadays, healthcare data management systems integrate large amounts of medical information on patients, including diagnoses, medical procedures, lab test results, and more. Sophisticated analysis methods are needed for utilizing these data to assist in patient management and to enhance treatment quality at reduced costs.

In this study, we take a first step towards better disease management of diabetic patients by applying state-of-the art methods to anticipate the patient's future health condition and to identify patients at high risk. Two relevant outcome measures are explored: the need for emergency care services and the probability of the treatment producing a sub-optimal result, as defined by domain experts. By identifying the high-risk patients our prediction system can be used by healthcare providers to prepare both financially and logistically for the patient needs. To demonstrate a potential downstream application for the identified high-risk patients, we explore the association between the physician treating these patients and the treatment outcome, and propose a system that can assist healthcare providers in optimizing the match between a patient and a physician.

Our work formulates the problem and examines the performance of several learning models on data from several thousands of patients. We further describe a pilot system built on the results of this analysis. We show that the risk for the two considered outcomes can be evaluated from patients' characteristics and that features of the patient-physician match improve the prediction accuracy for the treatment's success. These results suggest that personalized medicine can be valuable for high risk patients and raise interesting questions for future improvements.

Categories and Subject Descriptors

G.3 [**Mathematics of Computing**]: Probability and Statistics – *Survival analysis;* I.2.6 [**Computing Methodologies**]: Artificial Intelligence – *Learning;* J.3 [**Computer Applications**]: Life and Medical Sciences – *health, medical information systems.*

General Terms: Algorithms, Measurement, Performance

1. INTRODUCTION

Recent advances in adoption of information technology in healthcare organizations have made huge volumes of patient data available. Analysis of this data can uncover patterns for best practices and insight, which can potentially improve care delivery and make medical practices more effective. The measure of goodness of the care delivery process is ultimately obtaining optimal outcomes for the patients while reducing the costs of patient care in the long run.

Chronic diseases are known to consume the greatest majority of healthcare expenditures [4]. Chronic illness extends over many years and is often associated with acute exacerbations and progressive deterioration. One of the goals for healthcare policy is to improve chronic illness treatment and minimize the exacerbations, slow or halt deterioration, and decrease the cost of care. Diabetes is a chronic disease whose incidence is increasing and appearing in progressively younger patients. Moreover, diabetes mellitus is notoriously known for the serious complications associated with long disease duration. Thus, more patients will be dealing with diabetes and its complications for longer periods of time, making it important to improve and evaluate the quality of healthcare provided to diabetics.

An important step towards an improved diabetes treatment is to define a quantitative evaluation measure of the disease status. In this study we focus on two common methods for evaluating diabetes: blood test results and urgent care visits. The HbA1c blood test (also called glycohemoglobin) is a reliable indicator of long term diabetes management. The higher the HbA1c measure, the higher the risk of developing complications such as eye, heart, or kidney disease, nerve damage or stoke. Poorly managed diabetics will need urgent care more often and thus show an increase in the number of emergency department and urgent care visits. The number of these urgent care (UC) events can also serve as a way to measure the status of the disease.

Measurements for the time until an UC event occurs and the HbA1c lab test results can be considered labels or outcome to be predicted in a machine learning or a statistical analysis settings. The estimated probability for these outcomes can help assess the risk for disease aggravation. Determining health risks in the context of particular chronic diseases is very common in the medical literature. The seminal work of Cox in the early seventies [5] provides the most common method for prediction of disease risk and identification of the associated factors. One of the classic examples for the utility of disease risk assessment is cardiovascular disease (CVD). Assessing the risk for CVD has become a major strategy for preventing this disease and its unfavorable consequences. Over the past two decades many prediction algorithms were developed to assess CVD risk (see [6,12] for references). The vast majority of these algorithms use proportional hazards models for their prediction, most commonly the semi-parametric Cox model [5]. A few studies also applied the Cox model to the case of diabetes [3,17]. Commonly, these algorithms use the vast knowledge that has been accumulated on the disease to manually select a limited number of risk factors to be included in the model. Recent studies have proposed using machine learning methods for feature selection and dimensionality reduction combined with Cox regression for better predictions (see [13] and references therein). In this paper, we show that the best performing algorithms are those that combine Cox with various machine learning techniques.

There are very few examples of machine learning applications for personalized healthcare. Among them are prediction of risk of heart attack when consuming particular drugs [7] and prediction of treatment outcome of HIV patients [18]. Our work analyzes longitudinal operational data of patients; the data was gathered during the routine processes of a large health maintenance organization. We explore the use of classic machine learning techniques as well as common statistical methods for survival analysis to achieve the most accurate outcome prediction. Furthermore, we propose ways to use the prediction algorithms to provide better personalized care. This is carried out by employing the prediction models for identifying patients at risk and optimizing the match between those patients and the physicians who treat them to optimize the clinical condition of the patient.

The formulation of the problem includes two potential outcomes and a set of several thousand candidate features. Since the large input data is noisy, we experimented with different methods for reducing the data size, leaving only significant signals that can aid the performance of a classifier. Moreover, it is infeasible for some of the known classifiers, such as Cox, to run on hundreds of features.

There are three main approaches for feature selection. The first includes filters, where each feature is tested against the outcome and an associated score of relevancy or significance of the feature is calculated. The second approach uses wrapper algorithms, which search and select the subset of features that provide the best performance of the particular classifier being used [14]. The third is an embedded approach that incorporates feature selection directly into the learning process of a classifier. A different approach to reduce data dimensionality prior to applying a classifier is to carry out principal components analysis (PCA) of the data and then apply the classifier only on the projected data [23]. We experimented with all these approaches for feature selection and with PCA for dimensionality reduction. As part of our work, we compared the performance of three different classifiers: k-nearest neighbors, logistic regression, and Cox regression. We explored different groups of features and propose methods to increase the accuracy of the prediction by exploiting different feature selection methods and by employing an ensemble method that combines the various algorithms.

This paper describes the different features we derived from the medical data and how they are automatically selected and used to provide accurate predictions of patient status. The prediction includes both visits to urgent care departments in the following year and treatment outcome based on HbA1c results in follow-up tests. The ability to predict the future status of a chronic patient a year in advance is especially valuable for health organizations that need to manage and estimate expected expenses associated with different patients. The main contribution of this paper is the integration of the above methods into an innovative application that provides accurate predictions on the future condition of a chronic patient. This prediction has the potential to help health organizations optimize and tailor the care they provide to the individual needs of the patients.

2. METHODS

2.1 Data Organization and Problem Formulation

Our data comprises four main sources: claims, pharmacy, labs, and patient profiles, covering around 200,000 patients over a three year period. All sources have been de-identified and a unique patient id is available to link them. The key data fields in each source are:

- Claims: Patient ID, Date of Service, Diagnosis Code (ICD9), Procedure Code (CPT), ID of Physician Seen, Specialty of Physician Seen, Facility Type, Cost.
- Pharmacy: Patient ID, Date Filled, Drug Code (NDC), Dosage, Days of Supply.
- Labs: Patient ID, Test Name, Date of Test, Test Result, Unit.
- Patient Profile: Patient ID, Age, Gender, Assigned primary care provider (PCP)

Various data mapping steps were applied to make the data more amenable for extracting clinically meaningful features. For example, ICD-9 codes presented a challenge because diagnoses that are logically related in terms of risk-adjustment or clinical syndromes are often not indicated as such simply by the ICD-9 code. Consequently, several different diagnostic categorizations were employed including: HCUP-US Clinical Classifications Software (CCS) for Diagnosis (both hierarchical and single-level forms) and Hierarchical Diagnostic Categories (HDC), an IBM customized, extended variant of the Hierarchical Condition Categories (HCC) used in Medicare Risk Adjustment. Similarly, the CPT procedure codes were mapped to CCS for procedures. The Relative Value Unit (RVU) for each procedure, as defined in the Resource-Based Relative Value Scale (RBRVS) [10] is retrieved and used as an indicator of the effort level. Finally, the National Drug Code (NDC) Directory, obtained from FDA, was utilized to cross-index each NDC to its corresponding generic drug components.

2.1.1 Samples definition

For our investigation, a patient is considered to have diabetes if she had at least one hemoglobin A1c (HbA1c) test result that is higher than 6.5 [15]. Although a diagnosis of diabetes can be readily determined from the diagnosis codes, we found that such codes are not always reliable. One reason for the lack of reliability is that sometimes a patient is given a diagnosis code corresponding to diabetes to justify the prescription of an HbA1c test, even though the patient will ultimately not be diabetic.

For each patient determined to have diabetes, the day after the earliest HbA1c test result is selected as the *reference date* for the patient (Fig. 1). This reference date is used to separate the pre-reference condition evaluation period (at least 90 days), from the post-reference treatment period. Samples are further filtered to meet a requirement on the minimum number of patients treated by a physician, and on the duration of available data in the two periods.

Many patients in our data were being monitored for less than the defined follow-up period of one year. For example, consider the case in which the predicted outcome is the occurrence of an urgent care event. A patient for whom the event already occurred can be regularly analyzed. For the other "short-term" patients we have only partial information: we know that the event did not occur till a certain time. We refer to such partial data as *censored data*.

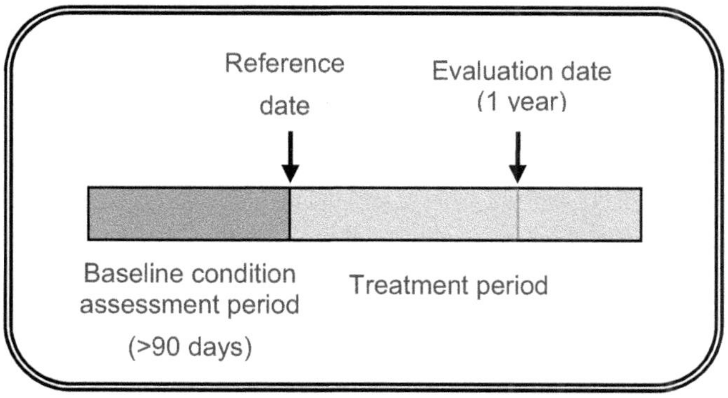

Figure 1: Formulation of a patient's longitudinal data

2.1.2 Labeling based on domain expert input

Two outcome measures are explored in this study: the occurrence of urgent care, as a surrogate measure of the degree of success in avoiding severe complications; and the control of HbA1c level, which is the outcome measure defined in most diabetes care quality metrics including the Comprehensive Diabetes Care criteria defined by National Committee for Quality Assurance (NCQA) [2].

For the first outcome measure, we checked the "Facility Type" field in the claims records. An encounter is considered emergency care if its facility type is either "Urgent Care" or "Emergency Room Hospital". In our data set, these visits account for about 4% of the total encounters. An outcome is labeled as "desirable" if the patient has no recorded emergency care encounter as defined above during the one year treatment evaluation period; otherwise it is labeled as "undesirable".

For the second outcome measure, we used widely adopted clinical ranges defined as follows [15]: HbA1c $\leq$6.4: normal; 6.5 $\leq$ HbA1c < 7: well controlled; 7$\leq$HbA1c<9: moderately controlled and 9 $\leq$HbA1c: poorly controlled. Each patient's treatment outcome is labeled by comparing the last HbA1c test result in the condition evaluation period with the one obtained after one year of treatment (allowing up to 2 months deviation). The outcome is labeled "desirable" if the HbA1c level moved into a lower range, or remained in the well controlled range, otherwise it is labeled as "undesirable".

2.1.3 Feature construction

The patient features derived from the database were used to represent patients' baseline condition. The first two features are the age and sex of the patients. Most other features are counts of records grouped by different criteria. These include the total and distinct number of CPT medical procedure codes grouped by their associated CCS code; the number of ICD-9 diagnoses codes grouped by their CCS diagnostic categorization, weighted by their HDC risk measure, or grouped and weighted by several risk categories defined by Young et al.[24]; the number of drug prescriptions and dosage for each ingredient and for each NDC drug code; the number of times each lab test was performed, and the number of visits to each facility type. Another feature weighted each CCS medical procedure category by its total effort invested for each patient as evaluated by the RVU. An advantage of all these features for medical data is that by definition, zero is a valid value, thus serving as a natural default value for cases in which some features were irrelevant for some of the patients based on medical considerations (e.g., lab tests that were not performed, as the medical condition did not require them). This also implies that many of the features are highly sparse.

In addition to the above, lab tests were also represented by the fraction of lab tests that are out of the optimal range for that patient and by the mean value of the lab test. For the latter, missing data had to be imputed. In the training and test sets, we replaced these data by the mean lab test values calculated on the training set alone.

Three types of features were derived. Patient features are described above. These features were calculated for the period prior to the reference date and were used to characterize a patient's baseline condition (Fig. 1). This set of features included 3236 different features that are used in the two analyses presented in the paper – for high-risk patient identification and for the patient-physician outcome modeling.

The features we used to characterize physicians were based on the population of their patients. These features aim to characterize a physician's treatment, and thus were derived from the period following the reference date. They were calculated by taking the mean of patient features separately on the two sets of patients that achieved desirable and undesirable outcomes. The corresponding patient for which the prediction was being performed was excluded from the mean. If one of the desirable or undesirable population set of a physician was empty, the mean over the corresponding population for the whole set of physicians was used.

The third group of features we used is patient-to-physician (P2P) features, which characterizes the match of the patient and the physician by quantifying the similarity of the patient to the characteristic population of the physician. These were calculated over the period preceding the reference date by taking the distance between patient's features and each of the two classes' population means of the physician. These means were calculated similar to the set of the physician's features above, on the baseline condition evaluation period.

To formalize the above, let $f_{pat,pre}(i), f_{pat,post}(i)$ denote a specific patient-feature of patient *i*, for the periods before and after the reference date, respectively. Let $G^{+}(j), G^{+}(j)$ denote the groups of patients treated by a physician *j* after the reference date, and who in practice achieved a desirable and undesirable outcome respectively. Then, we define the positive physician features as:

$$f^{+}_{phys,post}(i,j) = \frac{1}{|G^{+}(j)-\{i\}|} \sum_{k \in G^{+}(j)\setminus\{i\}} f_{pat,post}(k)$$

the distance between the patient and the positive set of physician patients as:

$$d^{+}_{P2P}(i,j) = | f_{pat,pre}(i,j) - f^{+}_{phys,pre}(i,j) |$$

the positive patient-to-physician features as:

$$f^{+}_{P2P}(i,j) = \exp\left(-\frac{d^{+}_{P2P}(i,j)}{Var_{i',j'}(d^{+}_{P2P}(i',j'))} \right)$$ and

correspondingly for the negative feature types derived from G^{-}_{j}.

2.2 Performance Evaluation Measures

We used two standard outcome measures to evaluate the results. The area under the receiver operating characteristic curve (AUC), and the concordance index (c-index). The c-index is a common performance measure in survival analysis; it evaluates the correspondence between the prediction and the survival times [9]. It is derived from the Willcoxon-Mann-Whitney two-sample rank test and can be regarded as an extension of the AUC to censored data. The interpretation of both measures is similar, with values around 0.5 denoting no significant predictive power and 1 indicating perfect prediction. We evaluated the performance as the mean and standard deviation on 10 different 5 fold cross-validation partitions of the dataset.

2.3 Learning Models

We evaluated and compared different analysis models following two approaches: binary classification and survival analysis. We explored two common binary classification algorithms: logistic regression (LR), and k-nearest neighbor. The survival analysis was performed with the Cox proportional hazards model. Finally, we also evaluated ensembles of the methods using a combination rule taking the mean of all predictors and the two best performing ones.

Logistic regression is a popular binary classification algorithm aiming to model the posterior probabilities of the two classes. It belongs to the classes of generalized linear models with a logit link function and a binomial distribution. Thus, the predicted outcome is the probability of a sample belonging to each class.

K-nearest neighbor (kNN) is another algorithm often used in machine learning applications. In a classification setting each test sample is classified based on its k nearest neighbors from the training set. Several variations of this algorithm exist. We used a weighted approach where the classification of a sample was a weighted mean of the k nearest neighbors with exponentially decaying weights. Specifically,

$$\hat{y}(i) = \frac{\sum_{j=1}^{k} \exp(-dist(i,j)) * y(j)}{\sum_{j=1}^{k} \exp(-dist(i,j))}$$

with *dist* denoting the Euclidean distance.

The Cox model is designed for longitudinal data in which the outcome is a pair (δ, t), where δ is an indicator for an event and t is the time in which δ was observed. In our study we formulated care services data for patients in the following way: $\delta = 1$ indicates that the patient required a care service in the following year, and t is the first time such service was given; $\delta = 0$ indicates that the patient required no service while being under study, and t is the overall time this patient has been under study.

Consider a random variable $T \in R^{+}$ representing the time till the event. The survivor function is defined by $S(t) = P(T \geq t)$. The Cox model is based on an assumption that given the features vector, **x**, the log of the survivor function can be expressed by the following equation [16]:

$$\log S(t \mid x) = \exp(\beta^{T} x) \log S_0(t)$$

where **β** is a vector of coefficients in the size of features vector **x**. This model is considered semi-parametric as the functional form of the baseline survivor function, $S_0(t)$, is not given, but determined from the data.

We trained all learning models using 5 fold cross-validation. The entire learning flow was performed over the training set, starting from data imputation, through the feature selection and the final optimization of the learner. We performed the corresponding adjustments on the test set (data imputation, feature selection and normalization) based on the training set values.

2.3.1 Feature selection

We performed two baseline feature selection procedures for all models to remove uninformative and redundant features. We removed sparse features in which 99% of the patients have identical values or the standard deviation was below 1e-6. We calculated the correlation coefficient (CC) for each pair of features and discarded one of the features in each highly correlated pair (CC > 0.9).

Next, we employed one of four feature selection and dimensionality reduction strategies:

- *Filter:* This feature selection approach is a fast pre-processing step, performed independently of the learning model. We adapted the feature selection for each model, thus binary classification methods were preceded by filters based on the p-values coming from one of two standard statistical tests: the chi square test for discreet features and the Kolmogorov-Smirnov test for continuous features, detecting features with distinguished distributions between the two classes. For the Cox regression we tested the t-test p-values for each coefficient to be different from zero in a model consisting of this single feature. We then filtered out features whose corresponding p-values were insignificant.
- *Wrapper*: This mode of feature selection is a meta-algorithm that evaluates the performance of the model under different selection of features. In this work we enhanced the Cox model by using forward stepwise feature selection with Akaike information criterion (AIC) for model evaluation.
- *Embedded optimization:* Under this scheme the feature selection is an integral part of the model. We used lasso [20], a popular method for regression that estimates the vector of coefficients, β, under a constraint that bounds $||\beta||_1$ by a constant. This method results in the shrinkage of coefficients, setting some coefficients to exactly zero, thus yielding a sparse solution. This method has been extended for generalized linear models (including logistic regression) [20] and the Cox model [21]. In our analysis we used the implementation available in the glmnet R package [8].
- *PCA:* This is a classic dimensionality reduction scheme. Features are projected on a set of orthogonal axes selected such that the first axis is aligned with the maximal variance of the data, the second axis is orthogonal to it, and is aligned

with the second largest variance axis, and so forth. Thus, selecting a subset of these axes can preserve most of the variance in the data while reducing the dimension of the data. In this work, we reduced the features to cover 90% of the variance in the data.

3. RESULTS

3.1 Data Statistics

Three datasets have been derived for each outcome. The first {Physician:All, Patients:All} is the full dataset of diabetic patients, used to construct a prediction model for patients at risk for an undesirable outcome. The other two datasets {Physician: >5 patients} are used for the secondary analysis of patient-physician match, and thus, in order to have sufficient statistics per physician, a requirement on the minimal number of patient attending each physician was added. The dataset of all the patients with the subset of the physicians seeing at least 5 patients was used to re-evaluate the patients at risk. Then, the top high-risk patients were selected to train and evaluate the patient-physician outcome model. Two contradicting considerations guided us in choosing the size of the top high-risk patients. First was to have enough information to train and evaluate the patient-physician outcome model, and second was to obtain a well characterized high-risk population. For the HbA1c outcome we selected the top 100 patients. Since in the UC model about half of the data is censored, in order to have enough samples, the top 200 patients were selected. For validation purpose we preserved the same cross-validation partition in the primary analysis identifying patients at risk and in the secondary analysis of patient-physician outcome prediction on the selected patients' subset. A more rigorous analysis would have used two embedded cross-validation partitions.

Table 1 presents the sample counts of the above datasets, providing detailed counts for the two classes of each outcome. In the UC context, the desirable outcome is the patient *not* attending emergency care services. In the HbA1c context, the desirable outcome is a reduced level of HbA1c. (See methods for details.)

Table 1. Sample counts in each of the datasets used

Outcome	**Urgent care**			**HbA1c**		
Physician	**All**	**> 5 patients**		**All**	**>5 patients**	
Patient	**All**	**All**	**At risk**	**All**	**All**	**At risk**
Desirable	2400	2374	40	1586	1412	43
Undesirable	541	531	78	666	608	57
Censored	1604	1550	82	--	--	--
Total	4545	4455	200	2152	2020	100

For some patients, censoring of UC information was before the date of the HbA1c lab test. Therefore, these individuals appear in the HbA1c dataset, but not in the UC dataset. The overlap between the datasets of the two outcomes consists of 2003 individuals, with 1462 individuals overlapping when censored data is excluded. No significant correlation was found between the two outcomes, as calculated on this overlapping subset. Thus these measures reflect complementary aspects of the disease management.

3.2 Identifying Patients-at-Risk

We compared the prediction accuracy achieved by various learning models on the two outcomes used to define patients at risk. The UC outcome is the more acute one, targeted at patients who reach emergency conditions. The common formulation of this type of data is under the framework of survival analysis. The most abundant model in the literature for this type of analysis is the Cox proportional hazards model [5]. This model is capable of handling events' time information, as well as censored data.

Table 2. Prediction performance of the high-risk patients

Outcome	**Method**	**No. Features**	**C-Index**	**AUC**
UC	Cox + LASSO	46 (±7)	0.52 (±0.07)	0.57 (±0.01)
UC	kNN(10) + filter(0.05)	41 (±1)	0.574 (±0.009)	0.63 (±0.01)
(c) UC	kNN(100) + filter(0.05)	41 (±1)	0.634 (±0.006)	0.669 (±0.008)
UC	Cox + filter(0.05)	168 (±3)	0.645 (±0.008)	0.671 (±0.009)
UC	Cox + filter(0.05) + PCA	108 (±2)	0.652 (±0.007)	0.679 (±0.008)
UC	Cox + filter(0.001) + stepwiseAIC	26 (±1)	0.652 (±0.004)	0.679 (±0.005)
UC	Cox + filter(0.001) + PCA	35 (±1)	0.653 (±0.003)	0.680 (±0.005)
(a) UC	Cox + filter(0.001)	51 (±2)	0.659 (±0.003)	0.685 (±0.004)
(b) UC	LR + filter(0.05)	41 (±1)	0.666 (±0.003)	0.713 (±0.003)
UC	Ensemble (a,b,c)	179 (±3)	0.670 (±0.003)	0.713 (±0.004)
UC	Ensemble (a,b)	71 (±2)	0.672 (±0.002)	0.714 (±0.003)
HbA1c	LR + filter(0.05)	62 (±3)	--	0.725 (±0.004)

An alternative approach we examined here for the same outcome was to formulate the data as a binary classification problem. The class labels were based on whether the patient attended UC services in the first year after the reference date. Thus, the data available for the classification approach excluded all censored samples and included only those samples having full information about the first year. This excluded 1604 samples, which represent 35% of the dataset. Also, the specific UC events time information was ignored.

Despite the limited and less informative training data available for the binary classification formulation, the logistic regression model outperforms the Cox proportional hazards model (Table 2). This is consistently reflected by both the AUC, which is calculated only on the non-censored data, and the c-index, which includes the censored data in the evaluation. This occurred despite the fact that the censored data constituted more than a third of the dataset.

One difference stands out when comparing the two classic models. Using the filter feature selection test appropriate for each algorithm with a bound of 0.05 on the p-value, the LR filter excludes significantly more features than the Cox filter. While the LR model is trained on 41 features on average, the Cox proportional hazards model is trained on a set of features about four times larger, and thus the risk of overfitting is significantly higher. Adapting the bound on the p-value to 0.001, which resulted with a similar number of features as for the LR, significantly improved the results.

To make sure the results are not biased by the different training set used, and to discard the option that the binary classification data are better in some sense, we also trained the Cox model with the 0.001 filter on the limited dataset available for the classification algorithm. This model achieved a c-index of 0.642±0.006 and an AUC of 0.526±0.006, suggesting that the utilization of the data by the LR flow model is superior.

Several enhancements of the Cox proportional hazards model have been developed in recent years. These are mainly based on sophisticated feature selection techniques. As an alternative to the naïve filter, we employed an embedded feature selection approach with the lasso optimization for Cox, and a wrapper approach running sequential feature selection to optimize the Akaike information criterion (AIC). As the performance of previous models improved when the number of parameters was 40-50, the parameter of lasso was configured to choose 50 features[1]. The stepwise feature selection was preceded with Cox-filtering with p-value bound of 0.001 in order to reduce the number of features, since running this method is infeasible when the number of features is large. Both approaches fail to improve on the simple filter approach with a p-value bound of 0.001.

An alternative strategy for reducing the number of features while preserving the information is to use dimensionality reduction techniques. PCA is one such simple, state-of-the-art technique. We employed PCA on the filtered features keeping the principal components covering 90% of the variance in the data. Using this approach the performance of the model with 0.05 feature selection bound was improved, however, no improvement on top of the strict feature selection model was observed.

The success of the logistic regression model encouraged us to explore the performance of another binary classification algorithm – k nearest neighbor. We present here the results of a variant of the algorithm using a weighted average of the neighbors' classification with weights exponentially decaying with the distance from the query point. The performance of this approach with 10 and 100 neighbors was unsatisfactory. Testing the unweighted variant completely failed learning (data not shown).

Different learning models that are trained on the same dataset can capture different properties of the data, and thus their error regions might differ. In those cases, an ensemble of the models may perform better than each of the individual models. We used a simple combination rule taking the mean of all three approaches, and another ensemble of only the two winning models (the Cox proportional hazards, and the logistic regression). The resulting prediction accuracy was slightly improved.

[1] We used the 'glmnet' R package. which allows specifying a bound on the number of features. This may yield a selection of less features than indicated by the given bound.

The HbA1c outcome is a less extreme outcome measure based on domain-experts' evaluation of the treatment quality; it compares the blood sugar levels measured by the hemoglobin A1c lab test at the reference date and 1 year ± 2 months later. The prediction accuracy for this outcome is of the same order of magnitude as the UC events. It would be interesting to compare the performance of various applications that can be utilized for these different sets of high-risk patients derived by these two different measures.

Table 3. A representative set of features that were consistently selected in 10 repetitions of 5-fold cross-validation (50 times) by the HbA1C and UC models

feature class	Feature description	HbA1C	UC
lab tests	HbA1c	50	50
	LDL	50	7
	HDL	50	14
	Cholesterol, Total	50	38
	Triglycerides	50	45
	Microalbumin/Creatinine Ratio test count	50	0
	Triglycerides test count	50	5
	% of out-of-range lab tests	50	13
drugs	Number of Insulins prescriptions	50	0
	Number of Antiypergycemic prescriptions	50	2
	Number of prescriptions for the ingredient Glyburide	50	0
diagnoses	Total HDC weighted ICD-9 codes associated with Diabetes mellitus with complications	50	0
	Number of ICD-9 codes associated with: Other diagnostic radiology and related techniques	50	29
	Number of distinct ICD-9 codes associated with: Other upper respiratory infections	0	50
	Number of distinct ICD-9 codes associated with: Other nutritional; endocrine; and metabolic disorders	1	50
medical procedures	Number of procedural codes: Microscopic examination	49	50
facility	Emergency Room Hospital	0	50
	Urgent Care	0	50
	Hospital – Outpatient	50	47

3.2.1 Selected features

Based on the results of the different high-risk identification models, we decided to use the logistic regression model to predict

UC and HbA1c outcomes in all subsequent analyses. To learn about the features being selected, we checked the consistency of the selection over the 10 repetitions of 5-fold cross-validation. Thus, every feature can potentially be selected at most 50 times by each model. We examined the features repeatedly selected by all the models. These included 16 features for the UC model and 31 features for the HbA1c model, with 6 features overlapping. Table 3 shows a representative set of 19 of these features. Many of the selected features are associated with known diabetes risk factors or consequences of the disease and its identification, supporting the clinical relevance of our models. The baseline hemoglobin A1c feature, which is the long term tracking parameter for diabetes, was selected by the two models. This was expected for the HbA1c model, which predicts the improvement in this parameter. However, it was also found significant with the UC outcome, corroborating the correlation between the severity of the diabetes and the UC events. Other features selected by the two models include the total cholesterol and triglycerides - lab tests measuring blood fats level. In particular, abnormalities in triglycerides level are known to be associated with diabetes.

The difference between the two outcomes becomes apparent when considering the differences at the feature class level. The features related to lab tests, diagnoses, and medical procedures are in agreement. The main difference lies in the drugs features, which are more significant for the HbA1c outcome, and the facility features, which have a bigger weight in the UC outcome. Indeed, it is expected that drugs would have a more significant effect on the relevant lab test, while UC events will be indicative of future events. Hence, these two feature classes are better tailored for each of the specific outcomes.

Examining the differences at the features level, those that were selected by the HbA1c model but not by the UC model include: Microalbumin/Creatinine Ratio test count - a lab test indicating diabetic kidney disease in case of abnormal values; Total HDC weighted ICD-9 codes associated with the CCS category of "Diabetes mellitus with complications" - increase in this parameter implies progression of the disease; Number of prescriptions for insulins, antihyperglycemic drugs, and glyburide – all of them are diabetic medications implying a longer history of diabetes. Features that were selected by the UC model but not by the HbA1c model include UC and emergency room visits during the baseline evaluation period, before the reference date, and the number of ICD-9 codes related to diagnoses of upper respiratory infections. These features imply poor disease management of the patient.

3.3 Patient-Physician Outcome Prediction

The first part our work shows how learning algorithms can be used to identify patients at high risk of failing their treatment. We claim that the treatment quality of these patients can be significantly enhanced by taking a personalized healthcare approach. This section presents one downstream analysis demonstrating the value of our approach. The analysis aims to predict the best physician assignment for each of the high-risk patients, based on the specific characteristics of the patient, the physician, and their match.

Similar to the high-risk patient identification analysis, patients were represented using the features derived directly from the database. Physicians were represented using the population of all their patients, excluding the index patient. These features were derived separately for their patients that reached a desirable outcome and those whose treatment failed. The patient-to-physician (P2P) match was represented by the similarity of the index patient to each of the two characteristic populations of the physician.

Assuming a hypothetical physician assignment reference date, patient and P2P features were derived from the period preceding this date, while the features characterizing the physician's treatment were derived from the period following the reference date. The labels for each patient-physician match were evaluated a year after the assignment date (see methods).

Table 4. Prediction performance of patient-physician match with the urgent care outcome

Feature Sets Used			C-Index		AUC	
Pat.	Phys.	P2P	mean	std	mean	std
0	1	0	0.51	0.06	0.52	0.11
1	1	0	0.54	0.05	0.48	0.10
1	0	0	0.56	0.04	0.48	0.05
0	0	1	0.60	0.02	0.53	0.05
0	1	1	0.60	0.02	0.53	0.05
1	1	1	0.61	0.03	0.53	0.05
1	0	1	0.61	0.02	0.54	0.05

Table 5. Prediction performance of patient-physician match with the HbA1c outcome

Feature Sets Used			AUC	
Pat.	Phys.	P2P	mean	std
1	0	0	0.45	0.02
0	1	0	0.49	0.06
1	1	0	0.49	0.06
1	0	1	0.56	0.03
0	0	1	0.56	0.03
1	1	1	0.59	0.03
0	1	1	0.59	0.03

Tables 4 and 5 present the prediction accuracy for the two outcomes used, with all possible combinations of feature classes. Having 1 in the feature set's column indicates it was used in the model, and 0 means this feature set was not used. Naturally, the patient model does not provide additional information on the treatment quality. However, features characterizing the physician and patient-physician match can further enhance the prediction up to a c-index of 0.61 ± 0.02 for the UC outcome and an AUC of 0.59 ± 0.03 for the HbA1c outcome. This implies that for this subset of patients, the personalized physician assignment plays a role in the treatment's success. In a similar analysis of the full patient population, the winning model was the one based solely on the patient features; adding physician characteristics did not affect the model's performance (data not shown).

Figure 2 presents the predicted outcome for the top 100 high-risk patients based on the HbA1c outcome. The top part of the panel shows the patients who in practice achieved a desirable outcome, while the bottom part represents patients whose treatment failed. One can see the variance of the expected outcomes of different physicians on different patients. Physicians on the right are expected to succeed for all patients, while physicians in the left columns fail more often. In addition to providing a data-driven physician assessment tool, this calls for further research on exploring the differences in treatment strategies among different physicians. A similar figure can be produced to present the predictions for the UC outcome.

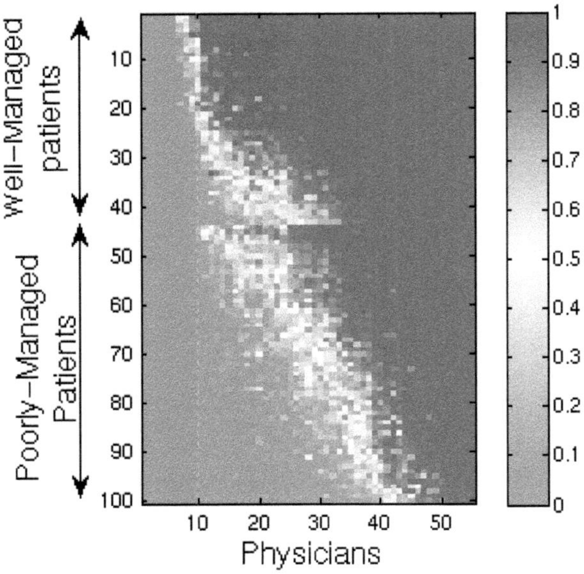

Figure 2. Predictions of treatment success probability for the high-risk patients with all possible physicians based on the HbA1c outcome. Desirable predicted outcomes appear in blue, and undesirable predicted outcome appear in red.

4. SYSTEM DEMO

The methodologies described in this paper were incorporated into a pilot system as part of a suite of analytics tools designed to support personalized decision making for both care delivery and practice management, particularly in a collaborative care or patient centered medical home (PCMH) setting. PCMH is an enhanced care model that provides comprehensive, coordinated, and timely care and payment reform, emphasizing the central role of primary care physicians [11].

Figure 3 shows a screen shot from this pilot system. The screen captures the output of the patient-physician outcome model described above for a specific index patient, and summarizes it using a sorted histogram visualization. Each potential physician is listed in a table along with a graphical bar whose length represents the predicted probability of achieving a desirable outcome for the corresponding physician. The expected outcome information is further grouped by practice location on the right side of the panel. Unlike many existing physician quality measures that evaluate physicians at aggregate levels [2], our models provide nuanced and personalized information regarding which physicians are good at managing each specific patient. In other words, the information shown on the screen is unique to each individual patient. Such a tool can be used by the medical director of a care organization to better manage high-risk patients. For example, it can be used to determine the physician or practice to which a poorly managed patient should be directed. It can also be used to guide investigations into what certain physicians do that makes them particularly successful in handling a specific type of patient. Then proper education or payment incentive programs can be put in place to improve the outcome for high-risk patients.

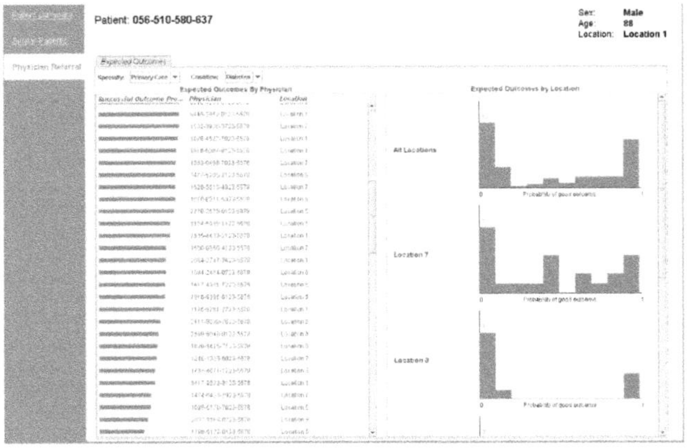

Figure 3. Screenshot of a decision support tool incorporating patient physician outcome prediction

5. DISCUSSION

This paper presents a prototype for a data-driven risk assessment system for patients with chronic diseases and its novel application for identifying physicians who can deliver optimal care to those patients. The prototype was designed and implemented for the use case of diabetes. It was evaluated on the routine operational data from approximately 4500 diabetic patients; this data was obtained from a large health maintenance organization. The prototype was incorporated into a pilot for healthcare management system that supports personalized decision making. Snapshots of the system demo, similar to the one that will be deployed for the client, are provided.

The paper describes the complete analysis process and addresses the numerous challenges encountered on the way, from data organization and feature construction to model selection and evaluation. The choices made at each of these steps may potentially have a large effect on subsequent steps and the overall system performance. One of the initial challenges faced when designing a research on medical data is defining the outcome. In this study we explored two alternative measures for a patient's outcome. These measures are fundamental in the evaluation of treatment quality for diabetes patients, and fall under two types of analytic frameworks: classification and survival analysis. Additional outcome measures should be considered in the future. The prototype system allows the end-user to interactively select the desired outcome. We tested and compared a variety of learning approaches, including the Cox proportional hazards model, a statistical method commonly used for analyzing longitudinal data, and several state-of-the-art machine learning methodologies.

Analyzing clinical records data is a highly challenging task. Part of the challenge arises from the sizable data involved, its considerable number of patients, and the vast number of features that can be derived. A second aspect is that some of the data is censored, thus providing only partial information about these patients. Moreover, missing and noisy data further increases the difficulty. Our work explored how modern feature selection approaches can be used to enhance the classic Cox proportional hazards algorithm. Through this process, we increased the analysis performance by more than 4% from 0.645±0.008 to 0.672±0.002; this is a significant amount considering the size of our data.

On our data, binary classification methods and specifically logistic regression achieved better results. This is despite the fact that censored data and time information were not utilized by the logistic regression. Since censored data may contain valuable information, there is a real need to develop new techniques that extend machine learning algorithms to handle censored data, such as those made for SVM [19,22].

The results of the personalized patient-physician match application demonstrate the advantage in focusing on high-risk patients. While chronic disease management usually follows well defined guidelines [1], these guidelines are designed to fit the majority of the population. High-risk patients are the ones for whom these guidelines may not be well-suited, thereby increasing the chance that their treatment will fail. Personalized healthcare systems that help identify these exceptional patients can eventually enhance our knowledge of the disease, particularly in the extreme edges of the population, and lead to higher quality medical care. The use of this application has the potential to further improve healthcare practice management. For example, novel financial incentive mechanisms could be adopted to improve the utility of the resources in the care delivery network to drive optimal outcomes for the patients. In conclusion, investigating patient-physician properties can reveal the patterns of best practice adopted by the high performing physicians. Such best practice patterns can then be used to educate the physician population to better treat patients with similar characteristics.

6. ACKNOWLEDGMENTS

We thank Dr. Lavi Shpigelman for fruitful discussions. Michal OF and Michal RZ were partially supported by Lithuanian Research Centre LTD.

7. REFERENCES

[1] Executive Summary: Standards of Medical Care in Diabetes—2011. Diabetes Care December 30, 2010 vol. 34 no. Supplement 1 S4-S10

[2] HEDIS 2011 Technical Specifications for Physician Measurement (Print edition), NCQA.

[3] Andersen, P.K. et al. 1985. A Cox Regression Model for the Relative Mortality and Its Application to Diabetes Mellitus Survival Data. *Biometrics*. 41, 4 (Dec. 1985), 921-932.

[4] Bodenheimer, T. et al. 2009. Confronting The Growing Burden Of Chronic Disease: Can The U.S. Health Care Workforce Do The Job? *Health Affairs*. 28, 1 (Jan. 2009), 64 -74.

[5] Cox, D.R. 1972. Regression Models and Life-Tables. *Journal of the Royal Statistical Society. Series B (Methodological)*. 34, 2 (Jan. 1972), 187-220.

[6] D'Agostino Sr, R.B. et al. 2008. General cardiovascular risk profile for use in primary care: the Framingham Heart Study. *Circulation*. 117, 6 (2008), 743.

[7] Davis, J. et al. 2008. Machine Learning for Personalized Medicine: Will This Drug Give Me a Heart Attack? *the Proceedings of International Conference on Machine Learning (ICML)* (2008).

[8] Friedman, J. et al. 2010. Regularization paths for generalized linear models via coordinate descent. *Journal of statistical software*. 33, 1 (2010), 1.

[9] Harrell, F.E. 2001. *Regression modeling strategies: with applications to linear models, logistic regression, and survival analysis*. Springer Verlag.

[10] Hsiao, W.C. et al. 1988. Estimating physicians' work for a resource-based relative-value scale. *New England Journal of Medicine*. 319, 13 (1988), 835–841.

[11] J. Adams, P. Grundy, M. S. Kohn, and E. L. Mounib, Patient-Centered Medical Home - What, why and how? [Online] Available: ftp://public.dhe.ibm.com/common/ssi/ecm/en/gbe03207usen/GBE03207USEN.PDF

[12] Jackson, R. et al. 2005. Treatment with drugs to lower blood pressure and blood cholesterol based on an individual's absolute cardiovascular risk. *The Lancet*. 365, 9457 (2005), 434–441.

[13] Khosla, A. et al. 2010. An integrated machine learning approach to stroke prediction. *Proceedings of the 16th ACM SIGKDD international conference on Knowledge discovery and data mining* (New York, NY, USA, 2010), 183–192.

[14] Kohavi, R. and John, G.H. 1997. Wrappers for feature subset selection. *Artificial intelligence*. 97, 1-2 (1997), 273–324.

[15] LabCorp: Test Menu. *https://www.labcorp.com/wps/portal/provider/testmenu.*

[16] Lawless, J.F. 2002. *Statistical Models and Methods for Lifetime Data*. Wiley-Interscience. Chapter 7.

[17] Perkins, B.A. et al. 2003. Regression of microalbuminuria in type 1 diabetes. *The New England Journal of Medicine*. 348, 23 (Jun. 2003), 2285-2293.

[18] Rosen-Zvi, M. et al. 2008. Selecting anti-HIV therapies based on a variety of genomic and clinical factors. *Bioinformatics*. 24, 13 (2008), i399.

[19] Shivaswamy, P.K. et al. 2008. A support vector approach to censored targets. *Data Mining, 2007. ICDM 2007. Seventh IEEE International Conference on* (2008), 655–660.

[20] Tibshirani, R. 1996. Regression shrinkage and selection via the lasso. *Journal of the Royal Statistical Society. Series B (Methodological)*. (1996), 267–288.

[21] Tibshirani, R. 1997. The lasso method for variable selection in the Cox model. *Statistics in Medicine*. 16, 4 (1997), 385–395.

[22] Van Belle, V. et al. 2011. Improved performance on high-dimensional survival data by application of Survival-SVM. *Bioinformatics*. 27, 1 (2011), 87.

[23] Wood, F. et al. 1987. Principal component analysis. *Chemometr. Intel. Lab. Syst.* 2, (1987), 37–52.

[24] Young, B.A. et al. 2008. Diabetes complications severity index and risk of mortality, hospitalization, and healthcare utilization. *AMERICAN JOURNAL OF MANAGED CARE*. 14, 1 (2008), 15.

Matching Unstructured Product Offers to Structured Product Specifications

Anitha Kannan
Search Labs
Microsoft Research
ankannan@microsoft.com

Inmar E. Givoni*
PSI Group
University of Toronto
inmar@psi.toronto.edu

Rakesh Agrawal
Search Labs
Microsoft Research
rakesha@microsoft.com

Ariel Fuxman
Search Labs
Microsoft Research
arielf@microsoft.com

ABSTRACT

An e-commerce catalog typically comprises of specifications for millions of products. The search engine receives millions of sales offers from thousands of independent merchants that must be matched to the right products. We describe the challenges that a system for matching unstructured offers to structured product descriptions must address, drawing upon our experience from building such a system for Bing Shopping. The heart of our system is a data-driven component that learns the matching function off-line, which is then applied at run-time for matching offers to products. We provide the design of this and other critical components of the system as well as the details of the extensive experiments we performed to assess the readiness of the system. This system is currently deployed in an experimental Commerce Search Engine and is used to match all the offers received by Bing Shopping to the Bing product catalog.

Categories and Subject Descriptors

H.2.8 [**Information Systems**]: Database Management Database applications Subjects: Data mining

General Terms

Experimentation, Measurement, Performance

Keywords

Matching, Structured data, Unstructured data, Commerce search

*Work done while author was an intern at Search Labs

1. INTRODUCTION

With the increasing widespread use of the Internet, there has been tremendous growth in the amount of commerce conducted over the web. A recent ComScore study reports record-breaking $43.4 billion in Q4 2010 U.S. retail e-commerce spending, which is up 11% from the previous year [1]. Nearly seven out of ten consumers say that the Internet has become important in providing them with information to help make buying decisions. More than 70% of consumers are likely to shop online before making an offline purchase [14].

A comprehensive product catalog is a prerequisite for the effectiveness of an e-commerce search service. Such a catalog at web-scale contains information about every product as well as sales offers from various merchants. For instance, the Bing Shopping catalog (shopping.bing.com) has information on more than five million products and more than ten million offers from upwards of tens of thousands of merchants. The product information consists of various attributes and their corresponding values, stored in a structured record comprised of attribute ⟨name, value⟩ pairs. Many products do not have universal unique identifiers. The product information is obtained from multiple product aggregators (*e.g.*, CNET, PriceGrabber), each providing only partial, but different, information. Information from different aggregators is combined to arrive at the specification for a product. However, the catalog can still have multiple data records corresponding to the same product, each somewhat different from the other.

Similarly, offers come from multiple merchants (*e.g.*, buy.com, gadgettown.com). Generally, there is very little structure in the offers. Typically, an offer consists of a concise textual description of the product for which the offer is being made. Embedded in the description are some attribute values and sometimes attribute names along with other terms, which the merchant presumes might be sufficient for the offer to be matched to the intended product. The text of the description is often not grammatically well-formed. Different merchants often use different names for the same attribute. Many offers have no identifier that could be used for matching the offer to the corresponding product. The matching is currently done using rules written manually – a costly and brittle process. Consequently, many offers are matched incorrectly and millions of offers go unmatched.

When a consumer searches for a product, the search en-

Attribute Name	Attribute Value
category	digital camera
brand	Panasonic
product line	Panasonic Lumix
model	DMC-FX07
sensor resolution	7 megapixel
color	silver
weight	132 g
width	9.4 cm
height	5.1 cm
depth	2.4 cm
display: type	LCD display
display: technology	TFT active matrix
display: diagonal size	2.5 in
audio input type	none
flash memory: form factor	memory stick
flash memory: storage capacity	8 MB
video input: still image format	JPEG
video input: digital video format	MPEG-1
lens system: optical zoom	3.6
...	

Unstructured Text (Offer-1)

Panasonic Lumix DMC-FX07 digital camera [7.2 megapixel, 2.5", 3.6x optical zoom, LCD monitor]

Unstructured Text (Offer-2)

Panasonic DMC-FX07EB digital camera silver

Unstructured Text (Offer-3)

Lumix FX07EB-S, 7.2 MP

Figure 1: Structured product record for 'Panasonic DMC-FX07 digital camera' and textual descriptions from three matching offers.

gine also shows offers paired with the product. Thus, the ability to correctly match offers to their corresponding products is of paramount importance for the success of the search engine.

Fig. 1 shows part of the structured record for a Panasonic DMC-FX07 digital camera as well as three merchant offers for this product as they appear in the Bing Shopping catalog. We observe the following:

- While Offer-1 is the most detailed one, it still contains only a small part of the information in the structured record. The phrase 'Panasonic Lumix' indicates both the brand (Panasonic) as well as the product line (Panasonic Lumix). Some of the attribute values only match approximately (7.2 megapixel *vs.* 7 megapixel, LCD monitor vs. LCD display). The only attribute name present in the offer is optical zoom (called 'lens system: optical zoom' in the structured record), with corresponding values 3.6x and 3.6, respectively.

- Information provided in Offer-2 is largely a subset of what is provided in Offer-1. This offer provides the values of the category and brand, but the value of the model has an extra suffix. It additionally provides the value of the color attribute.

- Offer-3 is even more interesting. It provides part of the value of the product line (Lumix) and a somewhat different value for the sensor resolution (7.2 MP *vs.* 7 megapixel) as well as for the model (FX07EB-S *vs.* DMC-FX07). It neither provides the category nor the brand information.

- With respect to Offer-3, note further that Panasonic also makes other 7.2 megapixel Lumix digital cameras (*e.g.*, DMC-TZ3K, DMC-LZ6, and DMC-FX12). Moreover, there is also a field controller product with model number FX07.

Clearly, we have on our hands a hard problem of matching free-text descriptions of products to their structured records for which it is desirable to have an algorithmic solution. The matching system must have high precision. Our enquiry revealed that for the system to be deployable, the precision must be at least 85%. Since a large number of offers are received on a daily basis and only a fraction of them can be shown, lower recall is not as detrimental as lower precision. In this paper, we present the design and performance of an experimental system that satisfies this desiderata.

The rest of the paper is organized as follows. Section 2 discusses related work. Section 3 gives the design of our system. Section 4 describes the datasets and metrics we used for evaluating the performance of the system. We also present experimental results in this section. We conclude with a summary and directions for future work in Section 5.

2. RELATED WORK

The problem of matching records has been studied under various topics including record linkage [13, 21, 23, 27], duplicate detection [12, 24], entity resolution [2, 3, 26], and merge/purge [15]. While our solution continues this rich lineage of work, there are distinguishing traits in our setting that call for fresh approaches and techniques. For instance, while the work of Newcombe [21] (later formalized by Fellegi and Sunter in [13]) pioneered the probabilistic approach to matching, their work (and much of the subsequent record linkage literature) tacitly assumes that the data to be matched consists of properly structured records with a well-defined schema. The work on duplicate detection, merge/purge, and entity resolution is also targeted at structured and properly segmented records.

At the other end of the spectrum, the work in natural language processing [19] focuses on the detection of mentions of the same entity in free text. In contrast, in matching offers to products, there are components from both bodies of work: the offers consist of only free text, while the products are properly structured under a given schema.

Much of the prior work has relied on the presence of values for all attributes in the data records, and the goal has been to design a similarity metric either at the entire record level [9, 20] or at the attribute level that are subsequently combined to measure record level match [5, 8]. This assumption is not valid in our setting. Since offers consist of free text, their tokens need to be mapped to attributes. However, some tokens may not map to any attribute (*e.g.*, the token 'monitor' in Offer-1 of Fig. 1), and when they do map, they can be ambiguously mapped to multiple attributes (*e.g.*, the token 'Panasonic' in Offer-1 of Fig. 1). So, unlike previous settings, the matching algorithm needs to disambiguate among the multiple possible interpretations of the offers. These problems also arise in the context of understanding queries [22, 25]. In [25], a probabilistic model is introduced to identify the annotation of a query which corresponds to best explanation of that query. In our work, we propose the notion of optimal parse which is defined with respect to a product the offer will be matched against.

The design of a matching function in prior work has focused primarily on the computation of weights for value matches and mismatches for the different fields of a record [5, 8], but the explicit modeling of missing values has not received much attention. An exception is [11], wherein a comparison feature vector is augmented to encode presence or absence of values. However, that approach does not explicitly penalize mismatches at the attribute level, and therefore does not leverage a strong signal for matching offers to products.

Additional related work includes research in assigning database entities to text documents [7, 10]. These approaches assume that the documents consist of well-formed English sentences. Closest to us is the work of Michelson and Knoblock [17], who also consider the problem of matching concise textual descriptions to structured records. Their techniques differ from ours in how blocking as well as matching are done. For blocking, they learn rules for constructing the blocks whereas we use the natural organization of products into categories for this purpose. For matching, they employ the entire unstructured text, whereas our matching function uses only those segments of the text that are deemed relevant on a per-attribute basis.

Specifically in the commerce domain, Bilenko et al. [4] proposed techniques for clustering merchant offers, but assume that the offers have structured information. Many of the challenges of matching unstructured offers to structured product specifications disappear when clustering structured offers.

3. SYSTEM DESIGN

We have a database $\mathcal{S}$ of product descriptions, represented as structured records. Every structured record $s \in \mathcal{S}$ consists of a set of attribute ⟨name, value⟩ pairs, denoted by Q_s. The attributes can be numeric or categorical. We receive as input an unstructured offer, u, which is a concise free-text description that specifies values for a subset of the attributes in $\mathcal{S}$ in an arbitrary manner. The text may also contain additional words and may be grammatically ill-formed. Our objective is to match u to one or more structured records in $\mathcal{S}$. We use the metric of precision and recall for judging the quality of the matching system.

We take a probabilistic approach and find the product $s \in \mathcal{S}$ that has the largest probability of match to the given offer, u. Our matcher is learned in an offline stage (see Algorithm 1). For this, we postulate a small training set $\mathcal{U}$ of unstructured offers. Each $u \in \mathcal{U}$ has been matched to one structured record in $\mathcal{S}$ (set $\mathcal{M}$). We also have mismatched records from $\mathcal{S}$, one for every $u \in \mathcal{U}$ (set $\mathcal{N}$).

In the subsequent online stage (Algorithm 2), new offers are matched one at a time. We first do candidate selection, and then choose the best matched product amongst the candidates by applying the learned model.

We next describe the key components required of our system:

3.1 Semantic Parsing

Our matching algorithm is based on understanding the semantics of the offer descriptions and using these semantics to aid matching. Thus, the first step in matching is the semantic parsing step. This step is performed in a three stage process consisting of *tagging* the offer with attributes, identifying *plausible parsings* based on the tags, and finally obtaining an *optimal parse*. We describe each of these steps:

Tagging: The tagging step discovers attribute names present in the offer and associates corresponding strings from the offer to them. This step is performed as follows. Let $\mathcal{A}$ represent all the attributes present in structured data available in product descriptions $\mathcal{S}$. We first build an inverted index $\mathcal{D}$ from $\mathcal{S}$ such that $\mathcal{D}(v)$ returns a set of attribute names (in $\mathcal{A}$) associated with string v. Note that multiple attributes can be associated with the same value. We perform standard preprocessing such as unit conversion and name synonymization, while building the dictionaries. Let $\mathcal{Z}_u$ represent the set of all n-grams (up to n = 4) present in u. Then, the tagging step identifies the set of all attribute ⟨name,value⟩ pairs in u:

$$\mathcal{R}_u = \Big\{\langle a, \{v | v \in \mathcal{Z}_u, a \in \mathcal{D}(v)\}\rangle | a \in \mathcal{A}\Big\} \tag{1}$$

Fig. 2(a) shows an offer for digital camera, and the output of the tagging step. A portion of the output from this step is { {brand, {'panasonic'}}, {product line, {'lumix', 'panasonic lumix'}}, where brand and product line are the two of the identified attributes, with brand having a single value 'panasonic' and product line having a set of two values {'lumix', 'panasonic lumix'}. In the same example, the value '3.6x' is associated with both optical and digital zoom: { {optical zoom, {'3.6x'}}, { {digital zoom, {'3.6x'}}

Plausible parse: Given the tagging, a plausible parse of an offer is defined to be a particular combination of all attributes identified in the tagging step such that each attribute is associated with exactly one value. Thus, if each attribute a has k_a values, then there are $\prod_a k_a$ plausible parses in the offer. Typically, k_a is small and thus, only a small number of parses are plausible.

The example in Fig. 2(a) has a single value for six of the seven identified attributes and the 'product line' attribute has two values. Thus, this offer has two plausible parses, one parse in which 'lumix' is the 'product line' and another in which 'panasonic lumix' is the 'product line'.

Multiple plausible parses arise because of ambiguities in the data. Therefore, we maintain these plausible parses until the offer is paired with a product which gives rise to the optimal parse of the offer with respect to that product.

Optimal parse: When an offer u is paired with a product s, we use the parse of u in which the maximum number of attributes agree in their values with s. We call this plausible parse *the optimal parse* of the offer with respect to the product:

$$\begin{aligned}\mathcal{R}^*_{u,s} \;=\; & \Big\{\langle a,v\rangle | \langle a,v\rangle \in \mathcal{R}_u \text{ AND } \big(\langle a,v\rangle \in Q_s \\ & \text{OR } a \text{ is numeric OR } s.val(a) = \emptyset\big)\Big\}, \end{aligned} \tag{2}$$

where $s.val(a)$ is the value of attribute a in product s. Note that in addition to keeping those attribute ⟨name, value⟩ pairs in u that match with attribute ⟨name, value⟩ pairs in s, we also retain those attribute ⟨name, value⟩ pairs for which there is no corresponding pair in s (because s has a missing

(a)

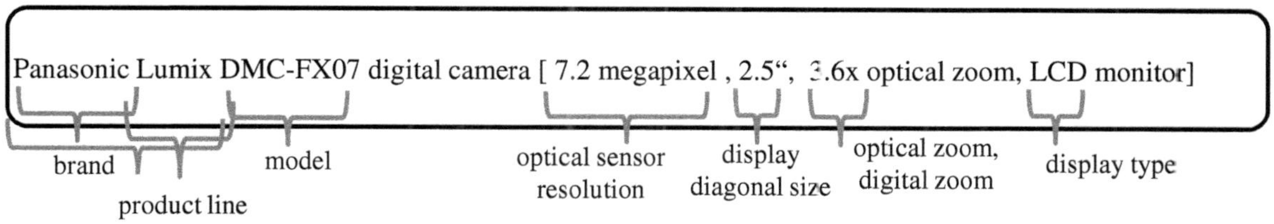

(b)

	Attribute Type	Attribute Value	Maximal Parsing of Unstructured Record (a)
s1	**brand** **product line** **model** **display diagonal size** display type	Panasonic Panasonic Lumix DMC-FX05 2.5 in LCD	Panasonic Lumix DMC-FX07 digital camera [7.2 megapixel , 2.5", 3.6x optical zoom, LCD monitor]
s2	**brand** **model** **optical sensor resolution** optical zoom	Panasonic DMC-FX07 7.2 megapixel 3.6x	Panasonic Lumix DMC-FX07 digital camera [7.2 megapixel , 2.5", 3.6x optical zoom, LCD monitor]

Figure 2: (a) An offer u with all its plausible parses, one in which 'panasonic lumix' is the product line and the other in which 'lumix' is the product line(b) Two products $s1$ and $s2$ with their structured information. Note that the optimal parse of u is different depending on the product that u is paired with.

value for that attribute) or if the attribute is numeric. As we will see momentarily, the missing values and numeric values are treated differently when we define the similarity function between offer and product. Observe that optimal parse is defined only with respect to a particular product. Different products can give rise to a different choice of plausible parse to be optimal. Continuing with our example using Fig. 2(b), the optimal parse of u corresponding to product $s1$ is the plausible parse with 'Panasonic Lumix' as the product line. When u is paired with $s2$, both plausible parses are optimal since $s2$ does not have the product line specified.

3.2 Similarity Feature Vectors

The similarity between an offer and a product is defined in terms of their similarity on the values of the attributes present in them. We consider all attributes $\mathcal{K} \subset \mathcal{A}$ that are present in at least one offer. We would like the similarity function to take into account not only the match in values of certain attributes, but also reflect mismatches or missing values in either products or offers. The function should penalize mismatches differently from missing values; in fact, a mismatched value is a stronger indicator of the corresponding offer and product mismatch. In addition, an attribute that is frequently missing reflects its lower importance for the purposes of matching.

The similarity feature vector we define in the sequel satisfies the above design considerations. Let $\mathcal{R}^*_{u,s}$ (Eq. 2) represent the optimal parse of offer u with respect to product s. Then, for the pair $\langle u, s \rangle$, we compute the similarity feature vector $\mathbf{f}$ by determining similarity levels between u and s for each attribute $k_j \in \mathcal{K}$:

$$f_j = \begin{cases} 0 & \text{if } \mathcal{R}^*_{u,s}(k_j) = \emptyset \ \text{ OR } \ s.val(k_j) = \emptyset \\ (-1)^{\mathrm{I}[\frac{|\mathcal{R}^*_{u,s}(k_j) - s.val(k_j)|}{\max(\mathcal{R}^*_{u,s}(k_j), s.val(k_j))} > \lambda]} & \text{if } k_j \text{ is numeric} \\ (-1)^{\mathrm{I}[\mathcal{R}^*_{u,s}(k_j) = s.val(k_j)]} & \text{otherwise} \end{cases} \tag{3}$$

where I[z] is the indicator function. Note that when either the optimal parse of the offer or the product has a missing value for an attribute, the corresponding feature value is 0. In addition, when the attribute values mismatch, the corresponding feature value is -1. This definition enables penalizing the matching score differently when u or s is missing an attribute value than if they disagree on that attribute.

For categorical attributes, we use binary loss rather than a string similarity measure (*c.f.* [6]). The reason for this decision was that while string similarity measure can be useful in certain situations (*e.g.,* product lines 'canon powershot' and 'powershot' are similar), we found it to be detrimental more often (*e.g.,* model numbers 'a1000' and 'a100' of Canon powershot cameras are close in string similarity but refer to distinct products). Numeric attributes, on the other hand, frequently have imprecise values because of round-off errors (*e.g.* 7 MP vs. 7.2 MP) or difference in conversion factors (1GB = 1000 MB or 1GB =1024 MB). Hence, we allow for approximation in measuring their similarity. After some experimentation, we set λ to 0.1.

3.3 Matching Function

We would like a matching function that can provide a probabilistic score of match between an offer and a product. In addition, since the number of attributes in $\mathcal{S}$ is large, and not all attributes are present in the offers, the function needs to automatically infer attributes that are required to be matched and also learn the relative importance among them.

The binary logistic regression lends itself to satisfy these criteria. Given labeled data of good and bad matches, and features that measure similarity between the attributes, it can automatically learn the relative importance between the attributes, and in turn provide a function that measures the match between an offer and product in terms of a probabilistic score. We use binary logistic regression of the form:

$$\mathcal{F}(\mathbf{w}, \mathbf{f}) = P(y = 1 | \mathbf{f}, \mathbf{w}) = \frac{1}{1 + \exp\{-(b + \mathbf{f}^T \mathbf{w})\}} \tag{4}$$

Algorithm 1 Off-line Training

Input:
$\mathcal{U} = \{u_1 \dots u_N\}$ - a set of offers
$\mathcal{S} = \{s_1 \dots s_M\}$ - a set of structured product descriptions, $M >> N$
$\mathcal{M} = \{\langle u_i, s_j \rangle_i\}_{i=1}^N, (u_i \in \mathcal{U}, s_j \in \mathcal{S})$ - pairs of correctly matched records, one for every u_i.
$\mathcal{N} = \{\langle u_i, s_k \rangle_i\}_{i=1}^N$ - similarly, pairs of mismatched records.
Output:
$\mathcal{D}$ - dictionaries,
$\mathbf{w}$ - algorithm parameters
Preprocess:
$\mathcal{D} \Leftarrow$ CreateAttributeDictionaries($\mathcal{S}$) - build dictionaries of attributes and their values using $\mathcal{S}$
Train:
for all $u \in \mathcal{U}$ **do**
  $u \Leftarrow$ SemanticParsing($u, \mathcal{D}$) - *Extract plausible parses* (Section 3.1)
end for
for all pairs $\in \mathcal{M}$ and pairs $\in \mathcal{N}$ **do**
  $\mathbf{f}_i^{\mathcal{M}} \Leftarrow$ ExtractSimFeatures(pair_i)
  $\mathbf{f}_j^{\mathcal{N}} \Leftarrow$ ExtractSimFeatures(pair_j) - *Construct similarity feature vector for matched and mismatched pairs* (Section 3.2)
end for
$\mathbf{w}^* \Leftarrow \arg\max_{\mathbf{w}}$ LearnToMatch($\mathcal{F}(\mathbf{w}, \mathbf{f}), \{\mathbf{f}_i^{\mathcal{M}}\}, \{\mathbf{f}_j^{\mathcal{N}}\}$) - *Train a function that maps feature vectors to match probability,* $\mathcal{F}(\mathbf{w}, \mathbf{f}) : \mathbf{f} \to [0, 1]$ (Section 3.3)
Return: $\mathbf{w}^*, \mathcal{D}$

The logistic regression learns a mapping from the similarity feature vector $\mathbf{f}$ to a binary label y, through the logistic function. The parameter $\mathbf{w}$ is the weight vector wherein each component w_j measures the relative importance of the feature f_j for predicting the label y.

In addition to the human-labeled matched training pairs, we construct mismatched pairs as follows. We pair each offer in the matched training pair with a small number of products(10) that are matched to offers, other than the offer under consideration. This addition of mismatched pairs introduces variability among the mismatched pairs. Some are completely different (*e.g.,* 'Canon EOS 40D camera' mismatched to 'Olympus MJU 300') while others are highly overlapping products (*e.g.,* 'Canon EOS 40D camera' mismatched to 'Canon 50D camera').

Having the matched and mismatched training pairs, let $\mathbf{f}_i = [f_{i1}, f_{i2}, \dots, f_{i|\mathcal{K}|}]$ be the feature vector for pair i. Let $\{\mathbf{F}, \mathbf{Y}\} = \{(\mathbf{f}_1, y_1), \dots, (\mathbf{f}_T, y_T)\}$ be the set of feature vectors along with their corresponding binary labels. Here, $y_i = 1$ indicates that the ith pair is a match, otherwise $y_i = 0$. Logistic regression maximizes an objective function which is the conditional log-likelihood of the training data:

$$\arg\max_{\mathbf{w}} \log P(\mathbf{Y}|\mathbf{F}, \mathbf{w}) = \arg\max_{\mathbf{w}} \sum_{i=1}^{T} \log P(y_i|\mathbf{f}_i, \mathbf{w}), \quad (5)$$

where $P(y_i = 1|\mathbf{f}_i, \mathbf{w})$ is defined by Eq. 4. Note that a feature with positive weight will affect the score by increasing the probability of match for a pair with agreement on the feature, by decreasing the score in the case of a mismatch, and by leaving the score unaffected in the case of a missing value.

Algorithm 2 Online Matching

Input:
u - offer
$\mathcal{S}, \mathcal{D}, \mathbf{w}$
Output: s^* - best matching $s \in \mathcal{S}$
$u \Leftarrow$ SemanticParsing($u, \mathcal{D}$) - (Section 3.1)
Blocking:
$k_i \Leftarrow$ Top attributes with largest weights in $\mathbf{w}$
$\mathcal{S}^* \Leftarrow$ Subset of $\mathcal{S}$ with $\cup_i(u.val(k_i) = s.val(k_i)$
for all $s_i \in \mathcal{S}^*$ **do**
  $\mathbf{f}_i \Leftarrow$ ExtractSimFeatures($\langle u, s_i \rangle, \mathcal{K}$) - (Section 3.2)
  $P(\text{match}(s_i, u)) \Leftarrow \mathcal{F}(\mathbf{w}, \mathbf{f}_i)$ - *Matching score of a pair* (Section 3.4)
end for
Return: $s^* = \arg\max_{s_i} P(\text{match}(u, s_i))$ - *Best Matching score of all pairs* (Section 3.4)

3.4 Online Matching

During the online phase, we are given a previously unseen offer u, and the goal is to identify the best matching product $s \in \mathcal{S}$.

The scoring function learned during the offline phase provides the probability of match for a pair $\langle u, s \rangle$. Naively, we can find the best match by pairing u with every $s \in \mathcal{S}$, calculating the pair match score, and choosing the s^* that results in the highest score. However, such naive pairing will cost $O(|\mathcal{S}|)$ operations for each offer.

Instead, we design a staged blocking strategy [15, 16, 27]. We note that the products are categorized into a taxonomy. Therefore, in the first stage, we use a classifier trained on product data to categorize the given offer into a category node in this taxonomy[18]. This reduces the candidate set to only those products that belong to the offer category.

Further, within the category, we would like to reduce the number of candidate products to match against the offer. For that, we make the following observation. The goal of the matching process is to match the offer to the product that has the largest matching score. To obtain this large score, a product needs to agree with the offer, especially on the values of the attributes that contribute large weights to the matching function. Using this insight, in the second stage, we further reduce the candidate set by identifying those top weighing attributes that can potentially give a matching score of at least θ in Eq. 4. Specifically, after identifying attributes in the offer using method in Section 3.1, we choose subset of attributes, $\{k_j\} \in \mathcal{K}$, in the descending order of weights until the following condition is satisfied:

$$\sum_j f_j w_j \geq \log \frac{\theta}{1 - \theta} - b \quad (6)$$

Here, θ corresponds to $P(y = 1|\mathbf{f}, \mathbf{w})$. This equation can be derived from Eq. 4 by rearranging terms and taking the log. This set of attributes $\{k_j\}$ are then used to retrieve products such that the retrieved products match on the value of at least one of the attributes in $\{k_j\}$. The union of all these products becomes the candidate set of products. Note that this candidate set is a superset of products that can potentially match to offer since we consider all products that have at least one matching value within this attribute set.

4. EVALUATION

The central goal of our work is to develop a system that can be deployed to match offers to products on a daily basis. The main requirement for us is to have, for every deployed category, at least 85% precision in matching. In general, this is a tall order for any system to achieve. In our setting, we find two main sources of difficulty that further compound this problem: First, some categories lack sufficient structured information required for matching. This prevents the matcher from performing semantic analysis effectively, and thus in turn, affects the learning of the matching function. Second, the offers are not correctly specified by the merchants, thereby contributing to reduction in matching precision. Thus, identifying error-prone categories become important. This identification enables either augmenting such a category with more structured information or reporting to the merchants about poor quality of their offers.

In this section, we discuss how we select deployable categories and describe the experiments we conducted to study the performance of our technique.

4.1 Algorithms Studied

Variants of our Algorithm

We defined the following variants of our matching function in order to study its characteristics:

1. **Equal Weights (EW):** This is the simplest version where the number of agreeing attributes between the offer u and the product s is used as the predictor for matching. The product s having the largest number of attributes in agreement with u is taken to be the best match.
2. **Learned Weights (LW):** In this version, we learn the relative importance between the attributes, but we treat missing and mismatched attributes equally. For attribute k, the value of feature $\mathbf{f}_k$ is -1 when either the values are missing or when the values are mismatched.
3. **LW with distinction between Mismatched and Missing (LWMM):** Here, relative importance between attributes is learned taking into account whether attribute values are mismatched or missing. For attribute k, the value of feature f_k for missing values is 0, and it is -1 for mismatched values. This version implements the full functionality of Algorithm 1.

Baseline

Inspired by the work in record linkage [4, 9, 20], we employ a baseline, which we call TFIDF. It uses the tf-idf weighted cosine similarity as the measure of agreement between the offers and products. Each token is associated with the tf-idf score defined as log(TF(token)+1) log(IDF(token)) [9]. Here, TF(token) is the frequency of the token in the offer/product and IDF(token) is its corresponding inverse document frequency; IDF(token) is computed across all the products in the category. Before matching, the structured specifications of a product are converted into a string representation by concatenating the content of the record.

TFIDF, instead of treating all tokens equally, weighs tokens inversely to their popularity. Thus, a token such as '40D' (corresponding to the model number of a 'Canon EOS 40D' digital camera) will have higher tf-idf score than 'digital camera' that is ubiquitous in the digital camera category. Typically, tokens that are unique such as model numbers and brands are the ones that are useful in matching. Since TFIDF can choose such unique tokens, it provides a reasonable baseline to our approach.

4.2 Performance Metrics

For evaluation purposes, we have access to a test set of offers, $u \in \mathcal{T}$. We also know the correctly matched product s^* for every u. The matcher has no knowledge about the matching product, but instead predicts the best matched product $\tilde{s}$ with probabilistic score $\gamma_{u,\tilde{s}}$. By best matched we mean that there is no other s that can match u with a higher score. Thus, instead of a standard classification task, we are considering a harder task of the matcher finding the best matching s for every offer u. We require the match score to be at least some $\eta \in [0, 1]$ before calling out a match. We define precision and recall at threshold level η as:

$$\text{Precision}(\eta) = \frac{\sum_{u \in \mathcal{U}} I[(\gamma_{u,\tilde{s}} > \eta) \text{ AND } (s^* = \tilde{s})]}{\sum_{u \in \mathcal{U}} I[\gamma_{u,\tilde{s}} > \eta]} \quad (7)$$

$$\text{Recall}(\eta) = \frac{\sum_{u \in \mathcal{U}} I[(\gamma_{u,\tilde{s}} > \eta) \text{ AND } (s^* = \tilde{s})]}{|\mathcal{T}|}, \quad (8)$$

where I[z] is the indicator function. We also combine precision and recall values into the F-measure, defined as:

$$\text{F-measure}(\eta) = \frac{2\text{Precision}(\eta)\text{Recall}(\eta)}{\text{Precision}(\eta) + \text{Recall}(\eta)}. \quad (9)$$

4.3 Dataset

The dataset comprised of 54 categories related to electronics (*e.g.*, televisions, mp3 players), computing (*e.g.*, desktop computers, laptops) and cameras and accessories (*e.g.*, digital cameras, camera accessories). We had a labeled set of 20,000 offers from these categories, each labeled with the corresponding matched products. There were on average 425 offers/category; the smallest category had 50 offers.

For each category, we randomly sampled 100 offers (20 if the number of offers is less than 200) and used them for training the matcher. We used whatever offers were left within a category as the test set for that category. Thus, the training set for each category had at most 100 samples. The test set size varied from category to category as we made use of all the available samples, but in no case was the test set smaller than 30 samples. Results are obtained using 5-fold cross validation.

Note that other than using a separate training set for each category, we do not use any category-specific features and the same code is used for different categories. We use small training set (100 offers per category), which can be curated easily from successful matches (*e.g.*, high click throughs) in a running system. We also do not have any parameters that needs to be tuned. These characteristics are critical for a solution to work at web scale.

4.4 Selecting Categories for Deployment

We use a small validation set to compute precision of matches, and select only those categories that meet our precision criteria of at least 85% precision. This enables us to do two important things required for deployment: (a) this technique can be applied at regular intervals to ensure quality control, (b) excluded categories can be analyzed for rectification, either by obtaining additional structured data

Offer Description	Products
imation 4gb nano usb 2.0 flash drive - 4gb - usb - external	imation nano flash drive usb flash drive - 4 gb imation 2gb usb 2.0 clip flash drive

Table 1: Sample offer and two products from the memory cards category.

or reporting to merchants about their data quality. In addition, after the issues are fixed, we can re-train matchers for these categories and decide whether or not to deploy.

By using the validation set, LWMM was able to select 37 categories for immediate deployment, each having the precision of at least 85% and we were able to initiate corrective action for others. We found that there was a correlation between the economic value of a category and the data quality; the higher the economic value of products in a category, the higher the data quality. Many of the categories that did not pass our filter correspond to low economic value categories (*e.g.,* accessories). An example is the 'computer memory card' category. Table 1 shows example offer and products from this category. As we can see from this example, an important attribute for this category is the capacity of the memory card. However, as this attribute is missing in all but two products (out of 7500 products), the matcher learned to ignore this attribute, and hence was not able to learn the function that can find appropriate products.

We also computed the precision achieved on the excluded categories using TFIDF. The numbers were average precision of 51% (largest precision of 70%) and 32% recall, reinforcing further that these categories are indeed error-prone.

4.5 LWMM Performance

We present precision and recall values for deployed categories. Fig. 3 shows the scatter plot of precision-recall values that the LWMM algorithm exhibits. Each circle corresponds to a category, and the area of the circle is proportional to the test set size. We have labeled some of the categories. The macro average precision is 93% while the macro average recall is 54% [1]. The corresponding micro average numbers are 93% precision and 41% recall. We studied some of these categories. The 'laptops' category has high precision and low recall. The main reason for low recall is that many of the offers have a large number of attributes that are missing, and hence the matcher decides not to match these offers to any product, so as to maintain high precision. In contrast, the 'printers' category has both high precision and recall, because a very large fraction of offers specify the attributes for matching. This difference partly arises from the nature of the categories - 'laptops' require a more detailed specification than 'printers' and hence it is easier for the merchants to include information needed for matching 'printers'.

By way of comparison, the average precision and recall values for TFIDF are 64% and 11% respectively. Fig. 4 shows the relative precision of LWMM and TFIDF. We see that LWMM performs better than TFIDF for all categories. The reason is that TFIDF weighs the relative importance

[1]The macro precision (or recall) is obtained by averaging the precision (or recall) of every categories, while the micro precision(recall) is computing the precision (recall) of all offers across all categories.

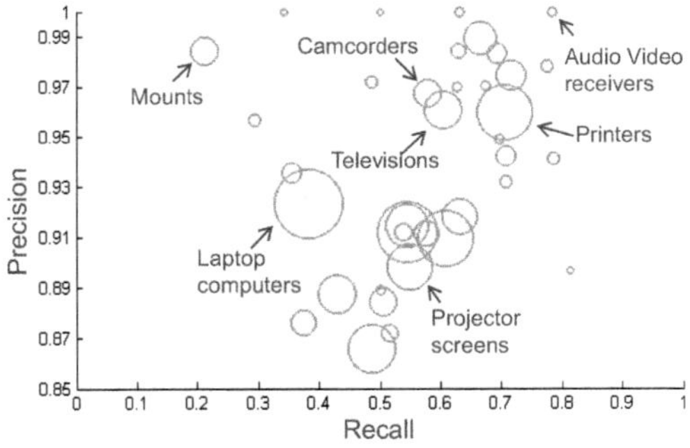

Figure 3: Performance of LWMM

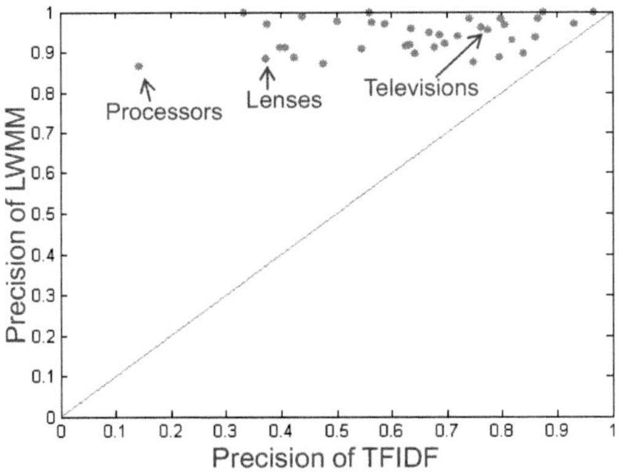

Figure 4: LWMM *v.s.* TF-IDF

of the tokens, but only as measured by the frequency of their presence in the product collection. It is not cognizant of what tokens are semantically important. As an example, the token 'canon' gets down-weighted in the 'digital cameras' category because there are many 'Canon' cameras. However, 'canon' as the brand is a very good indicator of a product identity.

4.6 Importance of Learning Weights

Fig. 5(a) shows the ratio of the LWMM's F-measure over EW's F-measure. Clearly, learning weights makes matching better. We notice that the gains are much larger for some categories than others. To understand this difference, we focus on two categories – digital cameras and televisions.

Fig. 5(b) shows the precision-recall values for digital cameras. For this category, there were seven attributes present in at least one offer during the offline training phase. These attributes were brand, model, product line, color, resolution, optical zoom, viewfinder type and video input type. EW weighs these attributes equally. At low recall, EW insists on all key attributes to agree on their values, and hence the precision becomes high. However, as we increase recall by reducing the number of agreements in attributes, precision drops. It is as expected, since certain combinations of attributes provide spurious matches (*e.g.,* agreement on color and resolution of a camera). On the other hand, by learning the relative importance of the attributes, LWMM matches a larger fraction of offers without sacrificing much precision.

The precision-recall values for televisions are shown in

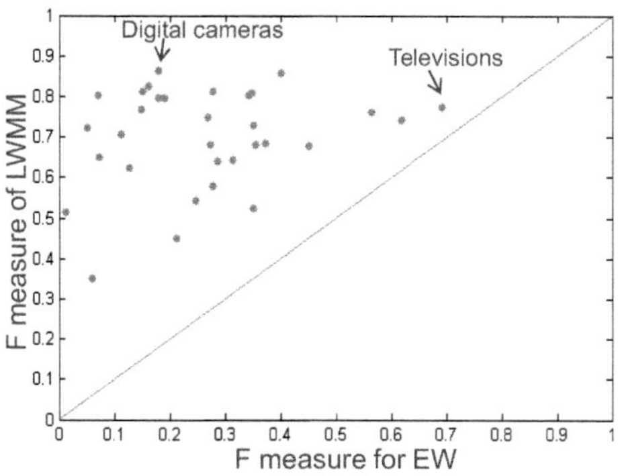

(a) LWMM *v.s.* EW

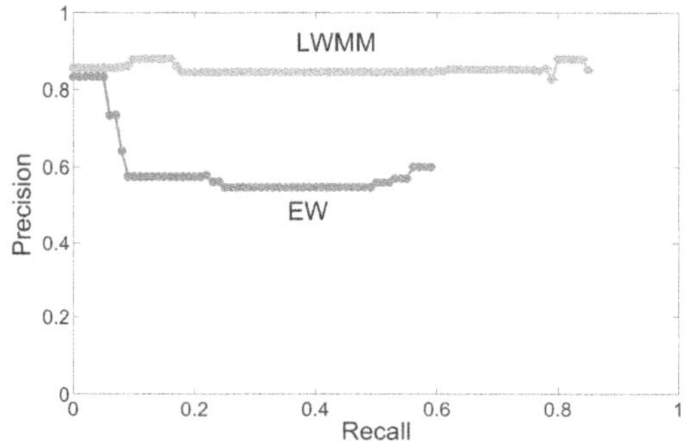

(b) LWMM *v.s.* EW (Digital Cameras)

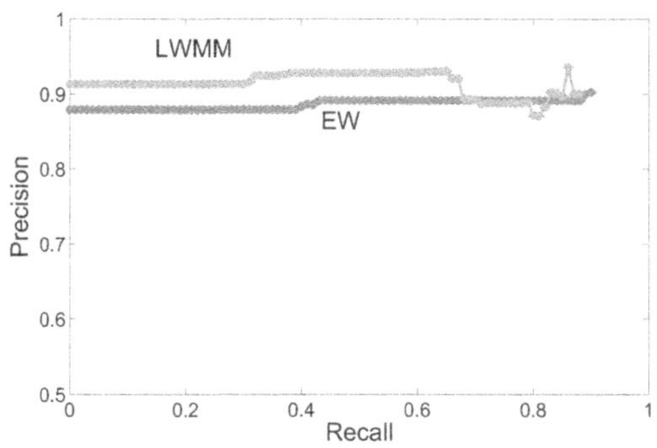

(c) LWMM *v.s.* EW (Televisions)

Figure 5: Importance of learning weights.

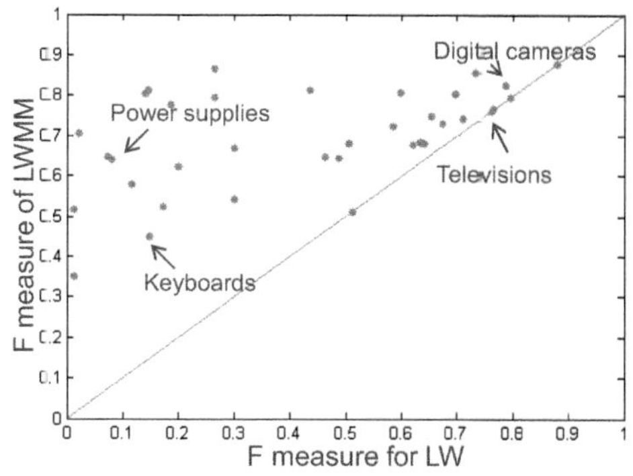

Figure 6: Treating mismatching attributes differently from missing attributes.

Fig. 5(c). For this category, only five attributes (brand, model, product line, diagonal screen size, projection display technology) are present in the offers during the offline training phase. We found that these attributes were often all present in the data and their values were generally correct. Hence, the performance of EW is quite high and it performs almost as well as its learned counterpart, LWMM.

4.7 Importance of Treating Mismatching and Missing Values Differently

Fig. 6 shows the scatter plot comparing the F-measures between LWMM and LW. We can see that there is a gain in F-measure for all categories, when we treat missing attributes differently from mismatched values. The gain is less pronounced for high economic value categories such as digital cameras than for low economic value categories such as keyboards and power supplies. The reason, we speculate, is that in the case of the former, the merchants have the incentive to provide better offer descriptions containing all the necessary attributes needed for matching. Hence, missing attributes becomes less of an issue.

4.8 Scalability

We perform staged blocking at the time of matching. In the first stage, offers are classified into categories, and then they are matched to products within that category. This substantially reduces the number of products to compare against. Subsequently, as described in Section 3.4 only a viable subset of products is selected to be matched against the given offer. Fig. 7 shows the number of candidates considered for each category. Each stem corresponds to a particular category; the length of the stem is one standard deviation of the average number of candidates across the offers in that category. We can see that the candidate set size is much smaller than the number of products in most of the categories.

5. SUMMARY AND FUTURE WORK

We described a system for matching unstructured textual descriptions to structured data records that arises in the context of matching sales offers to product specifications in e-commerce websites. The highlights of our solution include:

1. Semantic understanding of offers by leveraging structured information in the database:

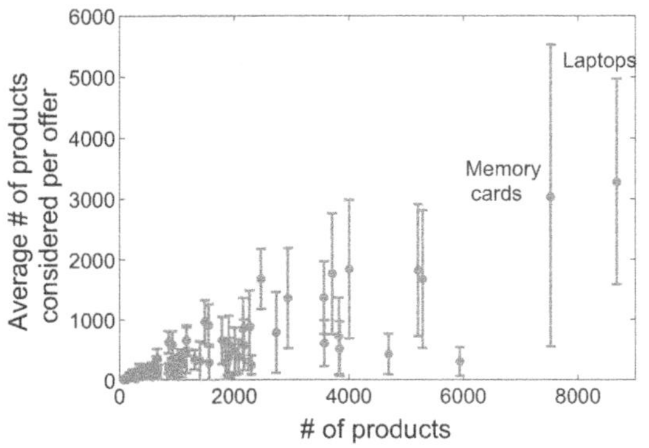

Figure 7: Scalability contributor during online matching

- The semantics is defined using plausible parses
- The same offer has different optimal parse with respect to different products, and thus no hard decision is made about the attribute ⟨name, value⟩ pairs in the offer until it is paired with a product

2. A match function based on the semantics is learned to find the product that has the largest match probability to the given offer:
   - Takes into account matches as well as mismatches in attribute values between offer-product pairs
   - Differentiates between missing attribute values and mismatch of attribute values.
   - Infers the relative importance of different attributes in the matching.
3. Built-in strategies for the solution to work at web scale:
   - Avoiding domain-specific features in the matching system
   - Reducing the candidate set of products that can potentially match a given set of offers

Extensive experiments using the Bing Shopping catalog demonstrate the effectiveness of our solution.

While presented in the context of commerce search, our system is applicable to any vertical search domain where there is the notion of an offer and a repository of structured data. As an example, in travel search there are offers for hotels (from various travel agencies) and a database with information about the hotels. Similarly, in local search, the system can be applied to match deals at restaurants against a restaurant database. As future work, we plan to apply our system to such domains.

6. REFERENCES

[1] Comscore reports record-breaking 43.4 billion in Q4 2010 U.S. retail e-commerce spending, up 11 percent vs. year ago. `http://www.comscore.com/Press_Events/Press_Releases/2011/2/comScore_Reports_Record-Breaking_43.4_Billion_in_Q4_2010_U.S._Retail_E-Commerce_Spending`, Accessed Feb 15 2011.

[2] R. Agrawal, R. Bayardo, C. Faloutsos, J. Kiernan, R. Rantzau, and R. Srikant. Auditing compliance with a hippocratic database. In *VLDB*, pages 516–527, 2004.

[3] O. Benjelloun, H. Garcia-Molina, D. Menestrina, Q. Su, S. E. Whang, and J. Widom. Swoosh: a generic approach to entity resolution. *The VLDB Journal*, 18(1):255–276, 2009.

[4] M. Bilenko, S. Basu, and M. Sahami. Adaptive product normalization: Using online learning for record linkage in comparison shopping. In *ICDM*, pages 58–65, 2005.

[5] M. Bilenko, R. Mooney, W. Cohen, P. Ravikumar, and S. Fienberg. Adaptive name matching in information integration. *IEEE Intelligent Systems*, 18(5):16–23, 2003.

[6] M. Bilenko and R. J. Mooney. Adaptive duplicate detection using learnable string similarity measures. In *KDD*, pages 39–48, 2003.

[7] V. Chakaravarthy, H. Gupta, P. Roy, and M. Mohania. Efficiently linking text documents with relevant structured information. In *VLDB*, pages 667–678, 2006.

[8] M. Cochinwala, V. Kurien, G. Lalk, and D. Shasha. Efficient data reconciliation. *Information Sciences*, 137(1-4):1–15, 2001.

[9] W. Cohen. Integration of heterogeneous databases without common domains using queries based on textual similarity. In *SIGMOD*, pages 202–212, 1998.

[10] N. Dalvi, R. Kumar, B. Pang, and A. Tomkins. Matching reviews to objects using a language model. In *EMNLP*, pages 609–618, 2009.

[11] N. S. D. DuBois. A solution to the problem of linking multivariate documents. *Journal of the American Statistical Association*, 64(325):163–174, 1969.

[12] A. K. Elmagarmid, P. G. Ipeirotis, and V. S. Verykios. Duplicate record detection: A survey. *IEEE Trans. on Knowl. and Data Eng.*, 19(1):1–16, 2007.

[13] I. P. Fellegi and A. B. Sunter. A theory for record linkage. *Journal of the American Statistical Association*, 64(328):1183–1210, 1969.

[14] G. Fulgoni. State of the U.S. Retail Economy in Q2 2009. Technical report, Comscore, August 20 2009.

[15] M. A. Hernández and S. J. Stolfo. The merge/purge problem for large databases. In *SIGMOD*, pages 127–138, 1995.

[16] A. Mccallum, K. Nigam, and H. L. Ungar. Efficient clustering of high-dimensional data sets with application to reference matching. In *In Knowledge Discovery and Data Mining*, pages 169–178, 2000.

[17] M. Michelson and C. Knoblock. Creating relational data from unstructured and ungrammatical data sources. *Journal of Artificial Intelligence Research*, 31:543–590, 2008.

[18] T. Mitchell. *Machine Learning*. McGraw Hill Higher Education, 1997.

[19] R. Mitkov. *Anaphora Resolution*. Longman, 2002.

[20] A. Monge and C. Elkan. The field-matching problem: algorithm and application. In *KDD*, 1996.

[21] H. B. Newcombe, M. J. Kennedy, S. J. Axford, and A. P. James. Automatic linkage of vital records. *Science*, 130:954–959, October 1959.

[22] K. Q. Pu and X. Yu. Keyword query cleaning. In *PVLDB*, pages 909–920, 2008.

[23] P. Ravikumar and W. W. Cohen. A hierarchical graphical model for record linkage. In *UAI*, 2004.

[24] S. Sarawagi and A. Bhamidipaty. Interactive deduplication using active learning. In *KDD*, pages 269–278, 2002.

[25] N. Sarkas, S. Paparizos, and P. Tsaparas. Structured annotations of web queries. In *SIGMOD*, pages 771–782, 2010.

[26] S. Singh, K. Schultz, and A. McCallum. Bi-directional joint inference for entity resolution and segmentation using imperatively-defined factor graphs. In *ECML-PKDD*, pages 414–429, 2009.

[27] W. E. Winkler. Overview of record linkage and current research directions. Technical report, Bureau of the Census, 2006.

Predictive Client-side Profiles for Personalized Advertising

Mikhail Bilenko
Microsoft Research
Redmond, WA 98052
mbilenko@microsoft.com

Matthew Richardson
Microsoft Research
Redmond, WA 98052
mattri@microsoft.com

ABSTRACT

Personalization is ubiquitous in modern online applications as it provides significant improvements in user experience by adapting it to inferred user preferences. However, there are increasing concerns related to issues of privacy and control of the user data that is aggregated by online systems to power personalized experiences. These concerns are particularly significant for user profile aggregation in online advertising.

This paper describes a practical, learning-driven client-side personalization approach for keyword advertising platforms, an emerging application previously not addressed in literature. Our approach relies on storing user-specific information entirely within the user's control (in a browser cookie or browser local storage), thus allowing the user to view, edit or purge it at any time (e.g., via a dedicated webpage). We develop a principled, utility-based formulation for the problem of iteratively updating user profiles stored client-side, which relies on calibrated prediction of future user activity. While optimal profile construction is NP-hard for pay-per-click advertising with bid increments, it can be efficiently solved via a greedy approximation algorithm guaranteed to provide a near-optimal solution due to the fact that keyword profile utility is submodular: it exhibits the property of diminishing returns with increasing profile size.

We empirically evaluate client-side keyword profiles for keyword advertising on a large-scale dataset from a major search engine. Experiments demonstrate that predictive client-side personalization allows ad platforms to retain almost all of the revenue gains from personalization even if they give users the freedom to opt out of behavior tracking backed by server-side storage. Additionally, we show that advertisers can potentially increase their return on investment significantly by utilizing bid increments for keyword profiles in their ad campaigns.

Categories and Subject Descriptors

H.2.8 [**Database Applications**]: Data Mining; H.3.4 [**Systems and Software**]: User profiles and alert services.

General Terms

Algorithms, Human Factors, Experimentation, Measurement

Keywords

Online advertising, client-side personalization.

KDD'11, August 21–24, 2011, San Diego, California, USA.

1. INTRODUCTION

Personalization is a core component of many web applications, where its uses vary from re-ranking search engine results to recommending items in domains such as news or online shopping. Traditional uses of personalization center on customizing the output of an information system for a given user based on attributes composing their profile. Profile attributes may be explicitly or implicitly obtained, where explicit attributes are provided by the user or computed deterministically (e.g., user-submitted demographics or IP-based location). Implicit user attributes are inferred based on the logs of the user's prior behavior, e.g., past searching, browsing, reviews or shopping transactions. A wide variety of personalization approaches have been proposed in recent years; notable examples include algorithms that leverage preference correlations across users (i.e., collaborative filtering), and methods that use past behavior to assign users to one or more pre-defined categories (i.e., "targeting segments" in online advertising).

Raw behavior logs used to infer implicit user attributes are typically stored in the online service's datacenter (*server-side*), where they are processed to compute each user profile in a compact representation chosen for the application at hand. Examples of such representations include advertiser-defined categories for behavioral targeting in display advertising [3][37] and low-dimensional latent topics in collaborative filtering methods based on matrix decomposition [24]. The resulting profiles are used in subsequent interactions with the user to adjust the output of the application to user preferences.

Server-side aggregation is being increasingly challenged by consumer and privacy advocates due to the fact that it limits users' ability to view and control data associated with their behavior, raising the need for privacy-enhanced personalization methods. In the context of personalized search, methods have been proposed for constructing category-based profiles on a user's machine (*client-side*), where they are employed to re-rank search results [34][36]. In online advertising, several alternative ad delivery architectures have been proposed based on client-side category-based profiles used to perform ad selection locally [13][10][35]. The previous approaches' reliance on broad categories for representing user interests is a significant barrier for their use in search and contextual advertising, where campaigns target highly specific intents via bids on individual keywords (short phrases that match the query or webpage exactly or approximately). Furthermore, these approaches require significant architectural changes to ad delivery pipelines and installation of additional components client-side both present significant barriers to adoption.

In this paper, we describe a novel approach to keyword-based personalization for search advertising that is practical, principled, and privacy-friendly. Based on *keyword bid increments* that allow differentiating between users with casual and long-term topical interests, the approach naturally integrates with existing ad delivery platforms, campaigns, and bid optimization frameworks, allowing advertisers to experiment with highly-granular ad personalization without significant infrastructure investments.

While highly practical, the described approach for keyword profile construction is derived from a principled utility-based framework. We demonstrate that bid-increment-based keyword profile utility is a submodular function: it has the intuitive property of diminishing returns with increasing profile size. Submodularity allows employing a simple yet highly effective approximate algorithm for profile construction. This enables real-time personalization based on client-side profile storage, avoiding server-side aggregation of user data, a major area of concern for consumer advocates.

The economic trade-offs of privacy-friendly policies are a key issue for the industry. For the proposed approach, we compare the performance of online, client-side profiling to full-history server-side profiling. Experiments on real-world large-scale datasets demonstrate that client-side profiling retains almost all revenue gains that server-side personalization yields, while allowing users to opt out of server-side logging and gain full control of their behavioral history.

Following are the paper's key contributions:

- Introducing the problem of keyword-based user profiling for online advertising, an emerging industry application that enables advertisers to customize existing search advertising campaigns based on users' prior behavior;
- Proposing a principled utility-based formulation for the client-side profile construction problem, applying it to the bid-increment setting for keyword advertising, and deriving an efficient algorithm for profile updates that does not require server-side storage of user data;
- Experimentally evaluating the trade-offs of enabling users to opt out from server-side storage of their behavioral history, and demonstrating that the corresponding "cost of privacy" for ad platforms performing personalization is minimal.

The rest of the paper is organized as follows. Section 2 describes a formal specification of the optimal profile construction problem in general, and its specialization to the client-side setting. Section 3 introduces keyword-based profiles for search advertising and validates their utility on a large real-world behavioral dataset. Section 4 describes the profile construction algorithm, while Section 5 explains the machine learning approach behind optimal profile construction. Experimental evaluation of the approach on real-world large-scale dataset from a major search engine is described in Section 6. Discussion of future work is provided Section 7. Section 8 provides an overview of related work and finishes with concluding remarks.

2. CONSTRUCTING USER PROFILES

To develop a principled foundation for deriving profile construction algorithms, we begin by formalizing the problem of profile construction for optimizing task-specific utility.

2.1 Profile Construction: Formal definition

Let $\mathcal{V}$ be the finite domain of items onto which observed user behavior is mapped, Φ be the domain of item descriptors, and $C = \mathcal{V} \times \Phi$ be the domain of observed contexts. For example, in search advertising, $\mathcal{V}$ is the set of all advertiser-bid keywords to which user queries are matched, and $\Phi = \mathbb{R}^d$ represents vectors of features associated with each query that has been mapped to the keyword. Then, every user query is represented as an observed context $c = (v, \phi)$ where $v \in \mathcal{V}$ is the most relevant ad keyword for the query, and $\phi \in \Phi$ is a vector of features that may be based on various attributes of the query and keyword, e.g., timestamp, similarity between q and v, user location, query or keyword category, etc.

Let $\mathcal{H}$ be the domain of all sequences of observed events corresponding to user behavior history, and $\mathcal{P}$ be the domain of profile representations. A *profile construction* function $f: \mathcal{H} \rightarrow \mathcal{P}$ maps a sequence of contexts observed over a time period up to t, $H = \left(c^{(t_1)}, .., c^{(t_n)}\right), t_i < t$, to a user profile $p \in \mathcal{P}$. The profile representation can be easily extended to include explicit profile attributes, e.g., demographic data.

The objective of profile construction is to maximize a utility function that captures the increase in performance for the task at hand (representing the benefits of personalization). This utility function u can be computed post-hoc by evaluating performance of the profile constructed during a preceding time interval, $u: \mathcal{H} \times \mathcal{P} \rightarrow \mathbb{R}$. Then, the optimal profile construction function f^* is one that maximizes utility:

$$f^* = \underset{f}{\operatorname{argmax}}\, \mathbb{E}\left[u\left(f(H_t), c^{(t+1)}\right)\right], \tag{1}$$

where the expectation is computed across the distribution of contexts subsequent to profile construction period.

2.2 Client-side Profile Construction

Motivated by the significant privacy concerns with server-side storage of user behavior history, we consider storing the user data employed for profile construction only on the user's machine (client-side), with the platform providing the user with a way to inspect, edit or delete it. The profile is sent to the server at interaction time along with the user request and current context (e.g., query or webpage id), updated server-side and returned to user together with the personalized response (which may be computed simultaneously or sequentially with profile update, depending on latency requirements and computational costs). The key distinction from the user privacy perspective is that no information associated with the user is retained server-side after response computation and profile update. Figure 1 illustrates the distinction between traditional server-side profiling and the client-side approach. Client-side storage of profiles is supported by current web browsers natively via cookies. While in the near future several additional mechanisms (e.g., HTML5 local storage) will provide increased client-side storage capacity, communication costs provide strong motivation for maintaining a limited-size profile.

Because client-side profiles are sent to the platform for their utilization in personalizing the user experience, this mechanism provides privacy under the assumption of compliance on behalf of the platform. However, we believe that this assumption is realistic: ad platforms already provide privacy-related guarantees to users (e.g., limiting third-party dissemination of user data and its retention over certain time limits), and both regulatory and competitive pressures strongly incentivize compliance. We note that alternative mechanisms that attempt to provide privacy guarantees by performing personalization and profile maintenance client-side [13][10][35] require users to install additional browser components, and assume significant modifications in ad platforms' delivery and reporting infrastructure, which presents a significant challenge to their implementation.

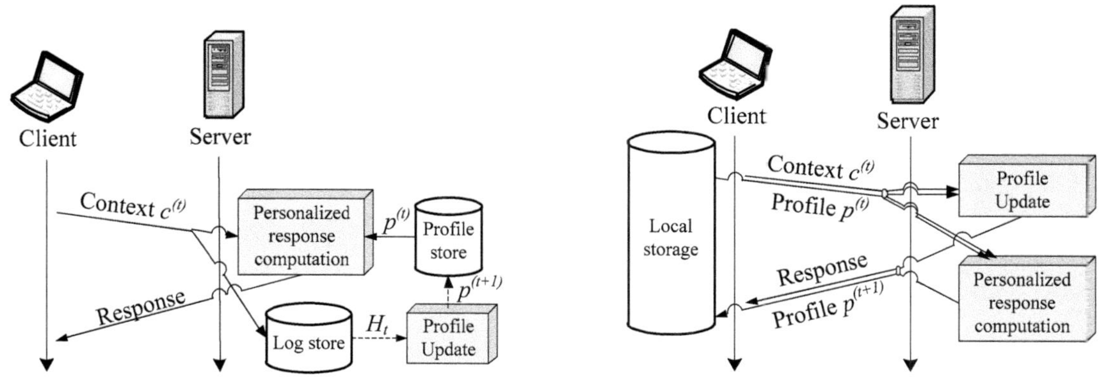

(a) Server-side profiles: The server stores user history and profiles, updating them synchronously or asynchronously.

(b) Client-side profiles: The client stores the profile, while the server only performs the profile update.

Figure 1: Comparison of personalization with server- and client-side profiles.

3. PROFILES FOR CPC ADVERTISING

3.1 Bid Increments and Keyword Profiles

Unlike display advertising platforms where inventory is sold on a pay-per-impression basis (a.k.a. CPI or CPM), search and contextual ad platforms require advertisers to submit bids on individual keywords which are matched against queries or webpage content (either exactly or approximately). If selected to be shown, advertisers are charged only when a click is observed (a.k.a. CPC), with cost assessed by discounting the bid via a second-price auction mechanism [8].

The ad inventory format impacts the choice of user profile representation that is exposed to advertisers: e.g., in display advertising where impressions are sold in large blocks, high-granularity profiles are used that are composed of such features as demographic attributes (e.g., "*Young urban males*") or broad categories (e.g., "*Car enthusiasts*").

In search and contextual ad platforms, keyword bids are inherently highly specific and can already be combined with demographic and location attributes. Hence, it is not surprising that advertisers have expressed an interest in the ability to specify keyword-specific *bid increments* by which the keyword bid is increased for users who have shown a historical interest in the keyword's narrow topic. This is the core of the emerging application setting that we address in this paper: constructing user profiles comprised of bidded keywords that trigger advertiser-specified bid increments when the user's context (query or webpage) matches the keyword in the profile (exactly or approximately).

By allowing advertisers to target keyword profiles, pay-per-click campaigns can be refined to increase bids for those users for whom they are likely to be more effective. For example, a diving equipment store may be willing to pay more for diving-keyword-related clicks of users predicted to have a long-term interest in diving, since they are more likely to purchase high-end items. We also note that bid increments are currently commonplace in display advertising, however there they are based only on explicitly known demographic attributes, or broad, loosely defined categories.

Another motivation for advertisers to employ bid increments is exploiting the variability of users' conversion rates depending on whether the keyword is in their profile or not: the following section provides analysis demonstrating the presence of this effect in real-world data.

3.2 Conversion Analysis for Profiling

To verify that keyword profiles constructed based on past searching behavior provide value to advertisers that justifies setting bid increments, we compared conversion rates for keywords that were seen in a user's past behavior, versus that for keywords that were previously not seen. Conversions are post-click events reported by advertisers that signal a user action, such as a purchase, a reservation, or answering a questionnaire, and conversion rate is defined as the fraction of ad clicks that have led to a conversion.

We analyzed 2 months of search advertising logs for a sample of 2.4 million users of Bing search engine (randomly selected from US-based active users logged in with a persistent ID over the 2-month period), and have measured the distribution of conversion rates vs. the time since the *preceding* occurrence of the keyword in the user's prior query and click behavior. Figure 2 illustrates the relative differences in conversion rate for keywords vs. time since last occurrence, where the difference is computed w.r.t. to the prior conversion probability (normalized for variability across keywords).

These results demonstrate that there is a very significant effect that previous observations of the keyword have on conversion rates: overall, conversions are more likely in the initial several hours since the previous occurrence of the keyword. Average conversion rates decline significantly after several hours, possibly representing keywords that are regular repeating queries for users (e.g., daily weather or stock ticker queries), which are arguably less likely to be converted when their ads are clicked. However, conversion rates for individual keywords show a significant variety in temporal dynamics, with many keywords showing increased conversion lift over multi-day periods.

Although conversion events represent a variety of user actions across different advertisers and hence their specific value can vary between campaigns, it is universally accepted that increases in conversion rates are desirable to advertisers, as they indicate higher user engagement for paid clicks. Thus, the results above indicate that advertisers have a strong incentive to differentiate their bids for users who have exhibited prior activity for the campaign keywords. Interestingly, this also indicates that *negative* bid increments may be of value to advertisers as well, allowing them to

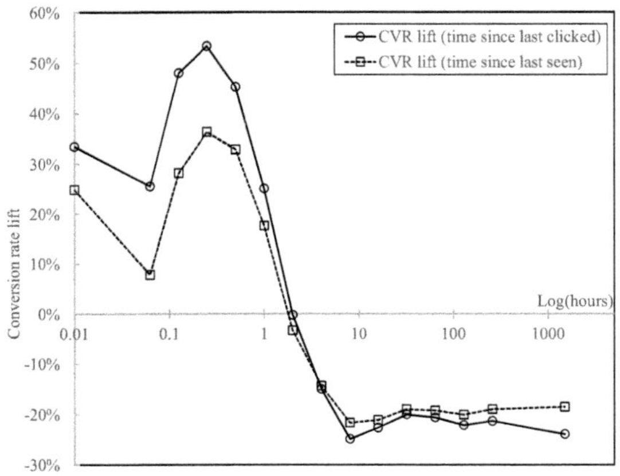

Figure 2. Conversion rate lift as a function of time since last observation of keyword in query or click.

lower bids for users whose past behavior indicates lower conversion propensity. We note that, given advertisers' bid increment amounts and known conversion curves such as those above, we can threshold inclusion of keywords by predicted conversion lift to reflect advertisers' expected ROI.

4. PROFILE CONSTRUCTION

4.1 Utility of Keyword-based Profiles

To design a profile construction policy that is optimal w.r.t. expected utility as defined by Eq.(1), we must formulate the personalization utility provided via the bid increment mechanism in pay-per-click advertising. From ad platform's perspective, personalization utility is equivalent to the gain in revenue that can be attributed to profiles. Profiles can be used in several stages of ad selection within the advertising platform, e.g., retrieval of candidate ads, CTR estimation, and ad ranking; we discuss these possibilities in Section 7 in more detail. For the present discussion, we focus on the scenario where profiles' only use is to trigger bid increments, noting that leaving other profile uses out of the analysis and experimental results, we only underestimate the potential revenue increases, and hence our results provide a lower bound on profile utility.

Then, the utility of a keyword profile $p^{(t)}$, composed of n phrases $k_1, .., k_n$, can be formulated as the revenue gain collected from future clicks that match profile components. The expectation of this gain at profile construction time t for the next ad-serving context $c^{(t+1)}$ (subsequent to profile construction) is then:

$$u(p^{(t)}) = \mathbb{E}[R(p^{(t)}, c^{(t+1)}) - R(c^{(t+1)})]$$

where the expectation is computed over the distribution of subsequent contexts $c^{(t+1)}$; $R(p^{(t)}, c^{(t+1)})$ and $R(c^{(t+1)})$ represent revenue earned in the subsequent context with the profile and without, respectively. For CPC advertising with bid increments, this expectation is equal to:

$$u(p^{(t)}) = \sum_{c^{(t+1)} \sim p^{(t)}} \Pr(c^{(t+1)}) \sum_{a \in A(c^{(t+1)})} \Pr_{click}(a) \Delta Bid(a, p^{(t)}) \quad (2)$$

where we utilize the fact that the expectation needs to be computed only over contexts (queries) that match the keywords comprising the profile (denoted as $c^{(t+1)} \sim p^{(t)}$) and hence can be enumerated, with $\Pr(c^{(t+1)})$ representing the probability of each such context, $A(c^{(t+1)})$ being the potential ads for the context, $\Pr_{click}(a)$ denoting the probability that the ad will be displayed and clicked, and $\Delta Bid(a, p^{(t)})$ is the bid increment for ad a with the given profile (which may be zero if the ad does not match the profile).

Note that this definition does not take into account auction pricing effects that are two-fold due to discounting of the bids in second-price auctions: on one hand, higher bids for incremented ads will increase the effective costs-per-click for non-incremented ads, while on the other hand, the increases in actual charged increments may be less than the full bid increments. Because these second-order effects are opposing, we consider their overall effect marginal in comparison to the first-order effects on which we focus.

4.2 Submodular Profile Construction

We note from Figure 2 that keywords observed in a recent time window exhibit a higher than expected conversion rate. This suggests maintaining a *cache* of queries that is stored client-side along with the profile, and used to enhance the pool of candidate profile keywords in addition to previous profile and current context. The size of such a cache would be determined by storage and communication limitations. We note that the cache keywords are distinct from those in the profile (though some could be in both): the cache retains keywords solely for enhancing the profile construction candidate pool, while profile keywords are selected to maximize predicted utility in Eq.(2), and may be chosen from either the cache, the previous profile or the present context. Hence, profile $p^{(t)}$ transmitted from the client in Fig.1(b) contains both actual profile keywords used for ad targeting, and cache keywords used for profile updating.

To obtain a keyword selection algorithm that optimizes the utility of Eq.(2), it must be decomposed into contributions of each individual keyword comprising the profile. However, because of approximate matching, two different keywords k_i and k_j, may share the ad inventory: $A(k_i) \cap A(k_j) \neq \emptyset$, which implies that it is not possible to decompose the utility in Eq.(2) across candidate keywords. E.g., an ad that with an approximate-match bid on keyword "*jumbo mortgage*" should also be matched to the query "*jumbo interest rates*". Such approximate matching is represented by a directed keyword graph with vertices corresponding to bidded keywords in the platform's inventory, and edges connecting keywords for which ads are approximately matched. Figure 3 below illustrates the necessity of the graph being directed: while more restrictive keywords (e.g., "*seattle mortgage*") match ads with bids for less restrictive keywords (e.g., "*home loans*"), the opposite is not true (since advertisers bidding on "*seattle mortgage*" are interested only in a small subset of all users looking for "*home loans*").

Building keyword graphs is a well-studied problem as they are a standard component for keyword ad platforms. In this work we use a large production graph with tens of millions of keyword nodes that is produced using an ensemble of data mining and machine learning algorithms that identify related keywords based on a variety of sources (query reformulations in user sessions, ad campaign co-occurrence, etc.), and rank them using a combination of supervised data and clickthrough feedback [15][16][31].

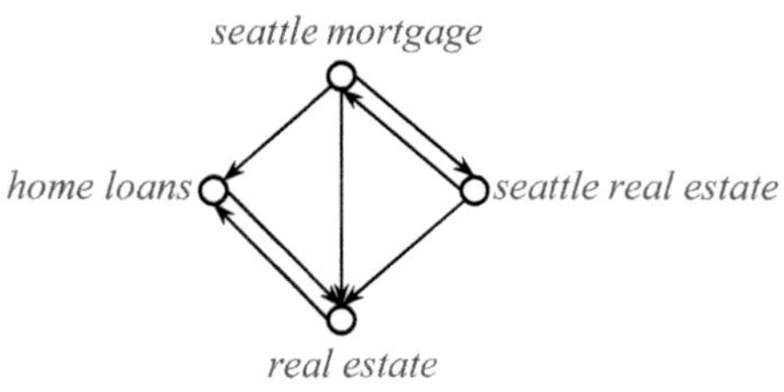

Figure 3: Sample fragment of the keyword graph

Because of the overlap in ad inventory between keywords due to approximate matching, the profile utility function in Eq.(2) is *submodular*: when a keyword k is considered for inclusion in a profile, the utility gain from including it cannot be greater than that for any subset of the profile:

$$u(p^{(t)} \cup k) - u(p^{(t)}) \leq u\left(p_{subset}^{(t)} \cup k\right) - u\left(p_{subset}^{(t)}\right)$$

for $\forall k,\ \forall p_{subset}^{(t)} \subseteq p^{(t)}$. Informally, submodularity captures the diminishing returns effect of growing the profile: as more keywords are added, they match increasingly less new ads that are not already matched by keywords selected earlier.

Limits on profile size entail that the particular submodular optimization problem to which profile construction can be reduce is *budgeted maximum coverage* [18], which is NP-hard. However, it can be solved approximately using the greedy algorithm of Nemhauser et al. [15], which is guaranteed to produce a solution that is $\left(1 - {}^{1}\!/_{e}\right) \approx 63\%$ optimal. The algorithm proceeds by starting with an empty profile and iteratively adding the keyword with maximum incremental utility gain $\Delta u(k, p^{(t)}) = u(p^{(t)} \cup k) - u(p^{(t)})$, which is:

$$\Delta u(k, p^{(t)}) = \sum_{c^{(t+1)} \sim k} \Pr\left(c^{(t+1)}\right) \sum_{\substack{a \in A\left(c^{(t+1)}\right): \\ \Delta Bid(a, p^{(t)}) = 0}} \Pr_{click}(a)\, \Delta Bid(a, k) \qquad (3)$$

This expression captures the expected revenue gain due to keyword k being added to profile $p^{(t)}$. The gain is aggregated over all approximately matched contexts, $c^{(t+1)} \sim k$, corresponding to keywords in the graph that have edges connecting them to k. For these contexts, the expected gain is aggregated over the ads $A\left(c^{(t+1)}\right)$ that are matched to the context, excluding those that are already incremented due to them being approximately matched to a keyword previously in $p^{(t)}$. Thus, the greedy approximate profile construction algorithm maximizes profile utility in Eq.(2) by iteratively adding keywords with maximum incremental utility predicted by Eq.(3). Next section describes a machine learning approach for predicting this utility.

Finally, we note that while the naïve implementation of the Nemhauser algorithm is $O(nk)$, where k is profile size and n is the candidate pool of keywords, it can be sped up dramatically by using lazy evaluation [21], and empirically can be run for hundreds to thousands of keywords within the real-time constraints of modern ad delivery platforms.

5. PROFILE UTILITY ESTIMATION

Computing incremental keyword utility given by Eq.(3) requires predicting the probability that a given context matching a given keyword will occur in the future, as well as the probability that an ad matching that context will be clicked. We employ a machine learning approach for these prediction tasks: a parameterized function is trained on past user behavior data to optimize utility estimation using observed ad impressions and clicks. Relying on past data assumes that some fraction of users choose to not opt out from server-side profiling and continue having their behavior history logged. In light of historically low opt-out rates for privacy-preserving settings in various web applications and toolbars, this assumption is reasonable.

Model training proceeds by simulating the profile construction process at an intermediate time, with the set of candidate keywords collected over the preceding time interval yielding the set of training instances. True labels (actual utilities) are obtained based on the presence of the keyword candidate in subsequent behavior. The utility is 0 if the keyword was not matched to subsequent search contexts, or if it was matched and there were no ad clicks. If the keyword was matched to a future query leading to a corresponding ad impression, and a click was observed, utility is the corresponding bid increment value. The learning algorithm then attempts to identify the predictor parameters that minimize expected error (typically, by minimizing training set error under some regularization technique that prevents overfitting).

We experimented with three different learning algorithms: max-margin averaged perceptron [6], logistic regression trained using the L-BFGS algorithm with L1 and L2 regularization [1], and boosted decision trees [11]. Section 6.3 provides a summary of results for the different learners.

5.1 Predictive Features

Features are functions of the keyword candidates considered for inclusion in the profile and/or user properties that are informative for predicting the expected utility of a keyword. We experimented with three broad feature sets that capture key signals related to the prediction task at hand. Features are computed based on known user behavior (the current user's profile information, plus historical data from other users who have not opted out of server side logging), as well as user-independent keyword properties and historical statistics.

5.1.1 User Features

A user that has searched and clicked frequently in the past is more likely to search and click in the future. Thus, we generate three features: the number of times the user queried the search engine, the number of times the user clicked on an ad, and the fraction of searches that led to clicks. The number of clicks by the user yields the most directly informative signal, but it has high variance since ad-click events are relatively rare. Thus, the number of past searches is included to provide the learner additional information it can exploit to produce a better estimate of the user's propensity to click on ads. Storing the values needed to compute and update this feature takes only a few bytes, and hence can be trivially augmented to the client-side profile.

5.1.2 Keyword Features

Some keywords are more likely to be searched for, or have higher clickthrough rates than others. Based on historical data, we compute the probability that an average user will search or click ads for a given keyword, and utilize features derived from such probabilities. Because these features are user-independent, they can be stored server-side.

5.1.3 User-Keyword Features

A user's history of past behavior in the context of a candidate keyword provides strong clues about the likelihood of its appearance in the future search and/or click behavior. These features must be stored alongside the candidate keywords in the profile, however the occurrence history for each keyword can be compressed down to just several bytes by using counts on discretized, equal-sized time windows as well as a single value indicating how recently the counts were last "moved" from one time window to older time windows. Given this discretized history, for each candidate keyword features are generated representing the number of past searches, ad impressions and clicks for a set of geometrically increasing time ranges, both as total counts for each range, as well as the differences between adjacent ranges.

An additional set of features is derived from the same past occurrence data by applying several time-decay functions – linear and logarithmic – to aggregate the counts, weighing more recent occurrences higher. These features attempt to model the fact that that predictive value of past occurrence counts decays with time yet increases with more clicks on the same keyword.

6. EXPERIMENTAL RESULTS

6.1 Methodology

The proposed approach for constructing client-side keyword profiles was evaluated using two months of search and advertising behavior logs for 2.4 million users of the Bing search engine, sampled randomly from the overall, larger pool of bot-filtered US-based active users, where active users were defined as those users who had used the search engine (issued at least one query) on at least 30 of the 60 days in the time period. The first six weeks of data was used for training the utility predictor as described in Section 5 by simulating the profile construction process and using the subsequent behavior to obtain a training label (realized utility) for every keyword that was a candidate for inclusion in the profile. With the utility predictor trained on the first six weeks, the efficacy of online profiling was evaluated by simulating profile construction over the seventh week, using behavior following the construction period to estimate utility. Section 6.2 reports results using logistic regression, trained using the L-BFGS algorithm with a combination of L1 and L2 regularization, while section 6.3 provides a comparison of different learners. Experiments utilized the actual keyword graph used by Bing's advertising system for approximate matching of related keywords.

Recall that client-side profiles contain two portions: the profile, which matches keywords and triggers bid increments, and the additional keyword cache, used to enhance the profile construction candidate pool (see Section 4.2). Whereas the profile construction uses the utility model as outlined earlier, the cache is more straightforward so we chose least-recently-used caching, a standard caching approach that typically has good performance and is efficient to compute.

Because bid increments are not currently publicly available to all advertisers, we are unable to report utility in terms of actual revenue gains. However, it is possible to report the fraction of ad clicks in post-profile-construction behavior for which the profile matched the bidded keyword, and hence would have triggered the bid increment. This metric, percentage of incremented clicks, can be viewed as the percentage of ad revenue that would be increased via increments.

6.2 Client-side vs. Server-side Profiling

Figure 4(a) presents the performance of client-side profiling for a variety of profile and additional cache sizes. All differences between profile sizes for a given cache size are statistically significant ($p < .05$). Differences in cache size, for a given profile size, are also statistically significant up to and including cache size 30 ($p < .05$).

We were able to store more than 100 keywords, including historical information necessary to compute these features, within the size limitations of Web browser cookies (4KB), with space remaining for other site-dependent uses. Since the size of the recent query cache at least partially trades off with the profile size, we evaluate the effect of the amount of available query cache on utility, comparing it to having complete past behavior history (server-side profiles) for different profile sizes. Figure 4(b) illustrates this relative performance of client-side profiles (with their limited knowledge of user history) with respect to server-side profiles for different profile sizes. The figure demonstrates that maintaining a modest cache size alongside the profiles allows achieving performance comparable to that of server-side profiling, but without the need for storing the complete user behavior history. For example, if profiles are limited to 20 keywords, utilizing a cache of the 50 most recent queries allows capturing 97% of the revenue gain achieved by server-side profiles while providing users full control of their data. Given this, these results demonstrate the practicality of allowing users to opt-out from server-side profiling with minimal revenue or performance cost.

Figure 5 compares the performance of a 20-keyword client-side profile to that of server-side profiling along with upper and lower bounds on performance. Upper bounds are represented by the server-side and client-side "oracles", which select the candidate keywords presciently (with knowledge of actual future user behavior), thus always selecting keywords that actually receive future ad clicks, when possible. The oracle is not able to match 100% of future clicks because keywords it may select are limited to candidates derived from the user's known history, mirroring the setting for the actual profile construction algorithm. The difference between the client-side and server-side oracles is that the server-side oracle has access to the user's entire history, whereas the client-side oracle has access only to the keywords contained in the user's client-side profile and cache.

The oracle results provide a bound on the overall predictability of future ad click keywords from past behavior, showing the maximum potential improvement that could be obtained with more sophisticated features or learners. Note that the client-side oracle asymptotically converges to the performance of the server-side oracle as the cache size is increased, just as the performance of actual client-side profiles converges to that of server-side profiles.

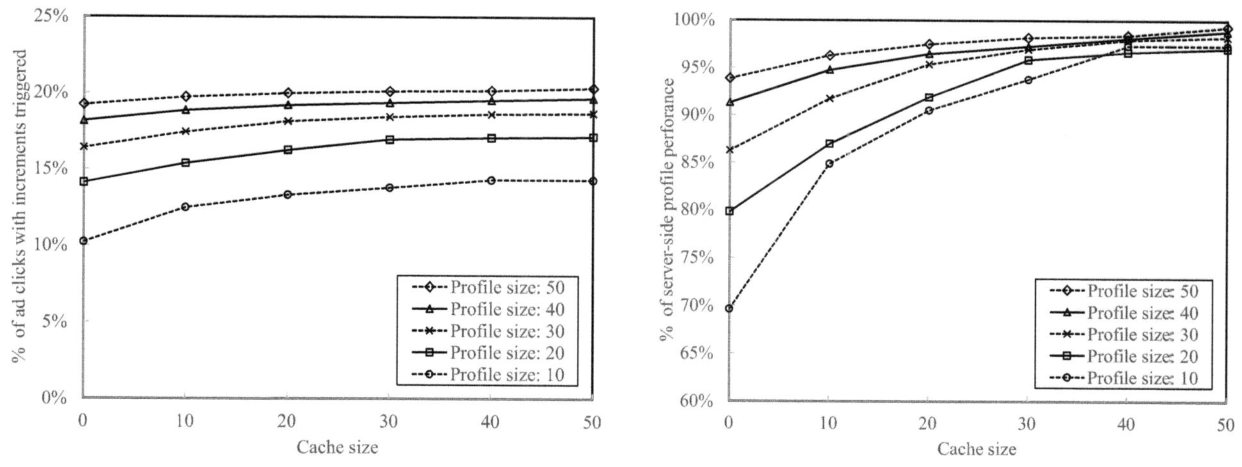

(a) Client-side profile utility (percentage of future clicks matching the profile).

(b) Relative client-side profile utility (utility as a proportion of server-side utility for profiles of the same size).

Figure 4: Client-side profile utility as a function of profile size and cache size.

Figure 5 also demonstrates that our approach to profile construction, including the scoring of keywords using machine learning and selecting the profile using submodular optimization, is able to outperform a simpler method such as using least-recently-used caching to construct the profile ("Cache as profile" in the figure). As the available pool of candidate keywords grows, the learned profile construction algorithm is able to leverage its knowledge to select those that are most likely to appear in the future, which may not even include the most recently seen keyword.

Overall, these results demonstrate that the proposed approach to constructing keyword profiles achieves a significant fraction of the maximum possible performance (e.g., 81% of oracle utility and 97% of non-oracle server-side utility for profiles of size 20). Concretely, our results imply that if advertisers opt for a 25% bid increment (an average increment seen in initial trials for select advertisers), keyword profile based personalization increases overall search engine revenue by over 4%, a sizeable gain that can be realized in a privacy-friendly way.

6.3 Learning Algorithms

To evaluate the impact of learning algorithm choice on performance, we have conducted experiments with three state-of-the-art learning algorithms: MART boosted trees, L-BFGS logistic regression, and max-margin averaged perceptron. Table 1 summarizes results obtained for 20-keyword profiles with a 50-keyword cache. Differences are statistically significant ($p < .05$).

Table 1. Impact of learning algorithm on performance.

Learning algorithm	Utility (% of future clicks with profile-triggered increments)
Boosted Decision Trees	16.63
Logistic Regression	16.86
MM-avgPerceptron	15.06

While all learners exhibit overall good results, averaged perceptron performs slightly worse. This may be due to the very significant class imbalance and overall noisy nature of the learning task at hand: because only a small fraction of keyword candidates lead to future clicks, online algorithms that optimize hinge loss (i.e., max-margin perceptron) may be less appropriate than those that optimize log-loss or exp-loss (i.e., logistic regression and boosting).

7. DISCUSSION AND FUTURE WORK

While experimental results demonstrate that client-side profiles can be almost as effective as server-side profiles in capturing users' ad-related interests from prior behavior, we have only considered their utility in the context of their use for allowing advertisers to specify bid increments to vary bids for users of interest. However, there are a number of additional search advertising platform components where keyword-based profiles can be utilized, which present very interesting opportunities for future work:

- Ad selection: how can profile keywords be used to expand the set of advertisements selected for the auction in addition to those selected by just the context alone?
- CTR prediction: what features can be computed using profile keywords to enhance the accuracy of clickthrough prediction for advertisements? Are high-granularity profiles more or less informative than previously proposed low-

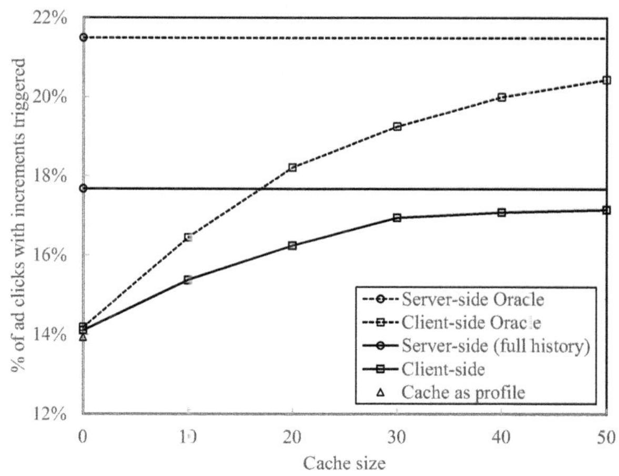

Figure 5: Comparison of client-, server-side and oracle utility (profile size 20).

granularity profiles composed of demographic and topical attributes [4][5]?
- Relevance filtering: can user profiles aid in computing ad copy and landing page relevance estimates used for filtering and ranking the selected ad candidates?
- Ranking: what are incentive-compatible auction mechanisms that can utilize information provided by user profiles for advertisers, e.g., by incrementing or reducing bids automatically to reflect adjustments in advertiser value inferred from profile information [26][12]?

The technique employed by the current paper centers on developing a principled algorithm for profile construction to optimize utility accumulated via bid increments. A sound approach to each of the above scenarios requires analogous derivation of profile utility for each task, and design of profile construction algorithms that attempt to maximize such utility, which presents an exciting array of opportunities for future work.

Finally, we note that utilizing additional signal sources, such as richer interaction data, has been shown to improve the accuracy of search intent inference [14], and may yield additional accuracy gains in the context of prediction tasks considered in this paper.

8. RELATED WORK AND CONCLUSIONS

Privacy-preserving personalization has received significant interest for a number of years from different areas of computer science; e.g., see surveys by Riedl [32] and Kobsa [19]. Advertising-specific issues at the intersection of privacy and personalization have not been considered until recently. Several architectures of personalization platforms coupled with delivery mechanisms have been designed with the goal of providing privacy guarantees [13][10][35], however, they require installation of additional client software and changes to the existing ad delivery and pricing mechanisms, and hence are not yet practical for the industry. The present paper takes a different approach and, instead of relying on theoretical privacy guarantees, provides an industry-ready method for enabling users to opt out from server-side tracking, under the assumption that advertising platforms that provide opt-out capability can be trusted, as they are legally required to comply with user agreements. Because deployment on a large, real-world ad platform was the primary motivation for this work, we believe that enabling the platform to serve personalized advertising to users who opted out of server-side logging is a key benefit of the proposed solution that makes it economically attractive.

Most previous work on personalization for advertising has focused on display advertising settings, where low-granularity profiles are employed to assign users to behavioral targeting segments: for example, Chen et al. apply a linear Poisson regression model to assign users to 450 pre-defined categories [3]. Yan et al. evaluate whether behavioral targeting provides value by clustering users into 20-160 segments and demonstrating that users in the same segment show similar CTR behavior [37]. Yan et al. also employs clustering to group users into segments based on their browsing history, assuming that users who visit the same web pages have similar interests, and thus will have an interest in similar ads [22]. In [29], Provost et al. consider a different avenue for privacy-friendly targeted display advertising: propagating user interests across inferred social networks.

As far as we are aware, only two papers considered personalization for search advertising, and both have focused on improving CTR estimates. Chen et al. [4] proposed a latent-topic model for user-dependent CTR prediction, where each user is represented by a mixture of automatically derived topics. Cheng and Cantú-Paz [5] have relied on inferred demographic features and users' historical clickthrough statistics across advertisers. In contrast, the present paper focuses on deriving a personalization approach that empowers advertisers to utilize user profiles in their campaigns, while enabling users to take control of their data. As mentioned in Section 7, there exists a number of interesting directions for hybridizing this previous work with the present paper, such as evaluating the use of keyword-based profiles for CTR prediction.

While employing user profiles in advertising is a nascent application, search result personalization has been a topic of active research for many years. Kelly and Teevan [17] provide a survey of techniques that construct profiles of users based on their past behavior. Such techniques typically rely on query history [30][33], browsing activity [24], or a combination of these [1][2][22][25][34]; see also the study of Dou et al. that compares and evaluates different search personalization strategies [7]. Because relevance improvements are the primary target of personalization in search, the corresponding utility functions differ significantly from advertising, where personalization utility is revenue-driven.

To our knowledge, this paper is first to address online construction of keyword user profiles for online advertising, as well as to consider client-side ad personalization that does not involve installing additional software or significantly changing the ad delivery infrastructure. We hope the proposed approach has significant potential not only for the personalization of advertising, but also for other information retrieval systems, such as search engines.

9. REFERENCES

[1] G. Andrew and J. Gao. Scalable training of L1-regularized log-linear models. *ICML 2007.*

[2] M. Bilenko, R. White, M. Richardson, G.C. Murray. Talking the talk vs. walking the walk: salience of information needs in querying vs. browsing. *SIGIR 2008.*

[3] Y. Chen, D. Pavlov, J. Canny. Large-scale behavioral targeting. *KDD 2009.*

[4] Y. Chen, M. Kapralov, D. Pavlov, J. Canny. Factor modeling for advertisement targeting. *NIPS 2009.*

[5] H. Cheng, E. Cantú-Paz. Personalized click prediction in sponsored search. *WSDM 2010.*

[6] M. Collins. Discriminative training methods for hidden Markov models: Theory and experiments with perceptron algorithms. *EMNLP 2002.*

[7] Z. Dou, R. Song, J.-R. Wen. A large-scale evaluation and analysis of personalized search strategies. *WWW 2007.*

[8] B. Edelman, M. Ostrovsky, M. Schwarz. Internet advertising and the generalized second-price auction: selling billions of dollars worth of keywords. *American Economic Review* 97(1):242-259, 2007.

[9] D. Fain and J. Pedersen. Sponsored search: A brief history. In *Second Workshop on Sponsored Search Auctions*, 2006.

[10] M. Fredrikson and B. Livshits. RePriv: re-envisioning in-browser privacy. *IEEE Symposium on Security and Privacy 2011.*

[11] J. H. Friedman. Greedy function approximation: A gradient boosting machine. *Annals of Statistics* 29(5): 1189-1232, 2001.

[12] A. Goel. Hybrid keyword search auctions. *WWW 2009.*

[13] S. Guha, A. Reznichenko, K. Tang, H. Haddadi, and P. Francis. Serving ads from localhost for performance, privacy, and profit. *HotNets 2009.*

[14] Q. Guo and E. Agichtein. Ready to buy or just browsing? Detecting web searcher goals from interaction data. *SIGIR 2010.*

[15] S. Gupta, M. Bilenko, M. Richardson. Catching the drift: learning broad matches from clickthrough data. *KDD 2009.*

[16] R. Jones, B. Rey, O. Madani, and W. Greiner. Generating query substitutions. *WWW 2006.*

[17] D. Kelly and J. Teevan. Implicit feedback for inferring user preference: A bibliography. *SIGIR Forum, 2003.*

[18] S. Khuller, A. Moss, and J. Noar. The budgeted maximum coverage problem. *Information Processing Letters* 70(1):39-45, 1999

[19] A. Kobsa. Privacy-enhanced personalization. *Communications of ACM* 50(8), 2007.

[20] A. Krause and E. Horvitz. A utility-theoretic approach to privacy and personalization. *AAAI 2008.*

[21] J. Leskovec, A. Krause, C. Guestrin, C. Faloutsos, J. Van-Briesen, and N. Glance. Cost-effective outbreak detection in networks. *KDD 2007.*

[22] L. Li, Z. Yang, B. Wang, and M. Kitsuregawa. Dynamic adaptation strategies for long-term and short-term user profile to personalize search. *ADWM 2007.*

[23] T. Li, N Liu, J. Yan, G. Wang, F. Bai, Z. Chen. A Markov chain model for integrating behavioral targeting into contextual advertising. *AdKDD 2009 Workshop.*

[24] B. Marlin. Modeling user rating profiles for collaborative filtering. *NIPS 2004.*

[25] N. Matthijs and F. Radlinski. Personalizing web search using long term browsing history. *WSDM 2011.*

[26] P. Milgrom and R. Weber. A Theory of auctions and competitive bidding. *Econometrica* 50:1089-1122, 1982.

[27] M. Morita and Y. Shinoda. Information filtering based on user behavior analysis and best match text retrieval. *SIGIR 1994.*

[28] G. Nemhauser, L. Wolsey, and M. Fisher. An analysis of the approximations for maximizing submodular set functions. *Mathematical Programming, 14:265-294*, 1978.

[29] F. J. Provost, B. Dalessandro, R. Hook, X. Zhang, and A. Murray. Audience selection for on-line brand advertising: privacy-friendly social network targeting. *KDD 2009.*

[30] F. Qiu and J. Cho. Automatic identification of user interest for personalized search. *WWW 2006.*

[31] F. Radlinski, A. Broder, P. Ciccolo, E. Gabrilovich, V. Josifovski, L. Riedel. Optimizing relevance and revenue in ad Search: a query substitution approach. *SIGIR 2008.*

[32] J. Riedl. Personalization and Privacy. *IEEE Internet Computing* 5(6): 29-31, 2001.

[33] K. Sugiyama, K. Hatano, and M. Yoshikawa. Adaptive web search based on user profile constructed without any efoort from users. *WWW 2004.*

[34] J. Teevan, S.T. Dumais, E. Horvitz. Personalizing search via automated analysis of interests and activities. *SIGIR 2005.*

[35] V. Toubiana, A. Narayanan, D. Boneh, H. Nissenbaum, S. Barocas. Adnostic: privacy preserving targeted advertising. *NDSS 2010.*

[36] Y. Xu, B. Zhang, Z. Chen, K. Wang. Privacy-enhancing personalized web search. *WWW 2007.*

[37] J. Yan, N. Liu, G. Wang, W. Zhang, Y. Jiang, Zh. Chen. How much can behavioral targeting help online advertising? *WWW 2009.*

Smoothing Techniques for Adaptive Online Language Models: Topic Tracking in Tweet Streams

Jimmy Lin, Rion Snow, and William Morgan
Twitter
795 Folsom St.
San Francisco, California
@lintool @rion @wm

ABSTRACT

We are interested in the problem of tracking broad topics such as "baseball" and "fashion" in continuous streams of short texts, exemplified by tweets from the microblogging service Twitter. The task is conceived as a language modeling problem where per-topic models are trained using hashtags in the tweet stream, which serve as proxies for topic labels. Simple perplexity-based classifiers are then applied to filter the tweet stream for topics of interest. Within this framework, we evaluate, both intrinsically and extrinsically, smoothing techniques for integrating "foreground" models (to capture recency) and "background" models (to combat sparsity), as well as different techniques for retaining history. Experiments show that unigram language models smoothed using a *normalized* extension of *stupid backoff* and a simple queue for history retention performs well on the task.

Categories and Subject Descriptors

H.1 [**Models and Principles**]: General

General Terms

Algorithms, Measurement, Performance

Keywords

Twitter, TDT, stream processing

1. INTRODUCTION

The rapid growth of real-time, high-volume communication on services such as Twitter has led to interesting new challenges and opportunities in tracking consistent topics across real-time streams of messages. This paper tackles the problem of tracking topics in a continuous stream of short natural language texts. Our specific application is the popular microblogging service Twitter, whereby users can send short, 140-character messages, called "tweets", that are distributed to "followers". As of Spring 2011, Twitter has over 200 million users who collectively create over one billion tweets each week. Whenever major news events happen, the service routinely achieves over 4000 tweets per second.

KDD'11, August 21–24, 2011, San Diego, California, USA.

Twitter is worthy of study from many different perspectives: its length constraint makes it distinctive in terms of language use, with substantial differences from typical texts studied by researchers in natural language processing and information retrieval such as newswire text. Tweets provide a window into users' behavior, both online and in the physical world, and provide a second-by-second update of "what's happening" in the world. Tweets capture everything from the mundane daily routines of the masses (i.e., "what I ate for breakfast") to spectacular breaking events to other messages of significant historic impact. When a US Airways jet made an emergency landing in the Hudson in January 2009, the world learned of the news via a tweet. When Iranian authorities clamped down on media coverage following the disputed presidential election in 2009, news leaked out via tweets. More recently, Twitter has been credited as an important tool that aided Egyptian protesters in toppling the Mubarak regime in February 2011—serving both as a communications platform for grassroots organization and a channel for information dissemination when other outlets were shut off. Mainstream news organizations such as CNN already consider Twitter an indispensable journalistic tool, and tweets are regularly featured on news broadcasts. Finally, researchers have shown that tweets provide a probe into the sentiments and behaviors of entire populations, enabling what has come to be known as computational social science. To give just two examples: researchers have found that tweet sentiment correlates with public opinion polls [17], and that tweets can be used to predict opening weekend box office revenues for movies [2].

Given a continuous stream of incoming tweets, we are interested in filtering and retaining only those that are relevant to a particular topic such as "American football", "Apple", and "fashion". We assume that at any given moment, there are a relatively small number of such topics (on the order of a few dozen), and for the sake of simplicity, we assume that these topics are specified in advance (for example, by editors who wish to curate the tweet stream). The problem setup naturally fits a streaming model of computation [16], in which events arrive continuously at a high rate and need to be processed in bounded space and time. An event is only encountered once and subsequently "lost" forever. Although an algorithm can "remember" previously seen events, it is assumed that the total amount of data is significantly larger than the space (i.e., memory) available to the algorithm.

The high arrival rate of events in typical streaming settings limits the amount of processing that is practical (at 1000 messages per second, a system has only one millisecond to process the message).[1] Therefore, one common approach to such problems is to

[1]Of course, we recognize that distributed stream-processing frameworks exist (e.g., [8]). However, moving to a multi-machine setup inevitably complicates the architecture from an engineering per-

eschew sophisticated models and start from the simplest technique that can possibly work. In this paper, we use simple language models (LMs) that are trained using hashtags contained in a small fraction of tweets, which serve as proxies for topic labels. These language models are adaptive in the sense that newly encountered tweets update the probability distribution in an online fashion. The LMs are then applied to filter the entire tweet stream by computing perplexity on unseen tweets: by varying the decision threshold, we can realize different precision/recall tradeoffs.

Within this general framework, we explore the design space in two dimensions:

1. different smoothing techniques for integrating "foreground" models (to capture recency) and "background" models (to combat sparsity); and,

2. different techniques for retaining history to ensure that the algorithm runs in bounded space.

We conducted both intrinsic evaluations as well as extrinsic evaluations in a topic tracking task. We find that stupid backoff [5]—an exceedingly simple smoothing technique—with a relatively short event queue works well.

The remainder of the paper is organized as follows: We begin with a discussion of related work in Section 2. Our general approach is laid out in Section 3. Data are described in Section 4, followed by results of evaluations: intrinsic (Section 5) as well as extrinsic (Section 6). We conclude in Section 7.

2. RELATED WORK

Although our problem is superficially similar to the goals of the TDT (topic detection and tracking) program [1], there are important differences. Topics in TDT are defined "to be a set of news stories that are strongly related by some seminal event that triggers the topic". Instead, we are interested in a broader definition of topics that might include a disparate collection of loosely-related events. To illustrate by example, a topic in the TDT sense might be the event "San Francisco Giants win the World Series", whereas we would define a broader topic around "baseball". Of course, the contents of the baseball topic would evolve over time and likely include the World Series story around early November 2011. Thus, topic tracking in our sense can be interpreted as the answer to the question "What's happening right now?"

Analysis of social media has attracted a lot of attention from the research community in recent years. Much work has specifically focused on Twitter, much more than can be adequately covered here. Examples include descriptive characterizations [12, 6], sentiment analysis [10, 17], entity tagging [15], influence modeling [22, 3, 4], topic modeling [19], conversation modeling [20], and modeling the diffusion of information [13, 21]. Most relevant to this study is the work of Petrović et al. [18], who examine the first-story detection problem in tweet streams. However, they adopt the narrow TDT definition of an event (i.e., a specific news event), as opposed to our broader conception, and therefore are addressing a fundamentally different problem (with a different technical approach).

Another thread of related work is the growing interest in streaming algorithms in natural language processing [14, 9, 18], highlighting the importance of time- and space-efficient algorithms in dealing with modern problems. Our work builds on this thread and contributes to this emerging area.

spective. Instead, we focus on single-machine solutions that can be trivially replicated for robustness.

3. APPROACH

Our goal is to predict the topics of interest associated with particular tweets. To make this problem more tractable, We assume that these topics of interest are denoted by hashtags, which are user-specified labels that begin with the hash character (#). It is interesting to note that hashtags were not originally part of Twitter, but evolved organically as a tool for users to organize their tweets. For example, a tweet about American football might be "annotated" with the hashtag #nfl (which stands for the National Football League, the major organization of the sport):

> Jay Glazer reports Vikings, Patriots are indeed talking trade for WR Randy Moss http://tinyurl.com/2uhbucb #NFL

Approximately a tenth of tweets contain one or more hashtags. They represent a bottom-up emergent phenomenon, as there is no authoritative source prescribing their use (or misuse). Indeed, many hashtags emerge spontaneously as cultural memes—although that process is beyond the scope of this work. Here, we focus on "persistent" hashtags that represent coherent, unambiguous topics that are (relatively) stable over time. For the sake of simplicity, we assume that the hashtags of interest (i.e., those topics we wish to track) are provided in advance. We expect that across all of Twitter, there are on the order of a few dozens of such topics, so it is not unreasonable to expect editorial (i.e., human) curation in selecting relevant hashtags.

Even though our topics of interest are generally coherent and stable over time, topical tweets may be about vastly different people, events, or entities. For example, at some point in time for the #nfl topic, Twitter users may be discussing a team that is on a long winning streak, but a short time later the focus may shift to a player who has just been traded from one team to another (as above). As another example, a topic such as #fashion is (perhaps by definition) rapidly changing.

Our approach to the topic tracking problem is to build language models (LMs) for each topic, and then apply these topic LMs to filter the entire tweet stream (including the majority of tweets that do not contain any hashtags). With language models, we explored the simplest possible classifier—based on computing the perplexity of unseen tweets. By varying the decision threshold, we can realize different tradeoffs between precision and recall. Of course, our language models need to be *adaptive* since the content of tweets for a particular topic may change rapidly. Furthermore, the language model must adapt in an online streaming fashion, since tweets are continuously arriving at a rapid rate.

The fact that topics continuously evolve introduces a tension: on the one hand, to obtain accurate term counts (that are reflective of the present state of the world) we would only want to keep track of recent tweets. However, this introduces a sparsity problem, where a large part of the event space is never encountered—leading to the well-known problem of zero-probabilities. The solution is of course *smoothing* [7, 11], whereby some probability mass is transferred from seen to unseen events: we adopt the strategy of smoothing a "foreground" model, which tracks recent term counts, with a "background" model, which provides estimates of term distributions across a much longer span of time. We empirically examine the effectiveness of different smoothing techniques (discussed in Section 3.1). The other major design decision is how to retain "history" in the foreground language model so that the algorithm will run in constant space; since vocabulary size grows unbounded with increasing amounts of text (Heap's Law), at some point in time an algorithm *must* "forget" some data. Section 3.2 discusses simple techniques for retaining history.

3.1 Smoothing Techniques

In this study, we explored both unigram and bigram language models. This section focuses on unigram language models (which are later shown to be more effective), but the description applies to bigram language models as well with standard straightforward extensions. Salient differences between the two are specifically noted.

Our basic approach involves smoothing a foreground language model with a background language model computed over a much longer period of time (one month in our case; see Section 4 for details). The purpose of the background model is to combat sparsity, since many terms may not have been observed in the foreground model (which retains limited history). In the unigram LM case, we denote the probability of a word given the background model as $P_{\mathcal{B}}(w)$. We estimate this distribution using the maximum likelihood criterion in an offline, batch setting. To restrict the vocabulary space, we discard all terms that occur ten or fewer times. The background model is itself smoothed using absolute discounting [11] (with $\delta = 0.5$). For the bigram case, we discarded bigrams that occur three or fewer times; the bigram LM was similarly smoothed using absolute discounting. For the unigram LMs, we discarded stopwords, but not for the bigram LMs. No stemming was applied in either case.

The foreground language model is defined in terms of a history, which specifies the policy under which recently-encountered terms (or bigrams) are retained. Section 3.2 describes specific history retention techniques in more detail. We use $c(w; h)$ to denote the count of word w within the history.

In this paper, we explored four different smoothing techniques to integrate the foreground and background models. Note that we excluded several well-known methods which are computationally expensive, for example, Katz backoff and Good-Turing estimation [7, 11], both of which require keeping track of frequencies of frequencies. The four smoothing techniques examined are as follows:

Absolute Discounting, where we subtract a partial count δ from each observed word and distribute the leftover probability mass to the background model. This is defined as follows, where w_n is the number of unique terms in the foreground model:

$$P(w) = \frac{\max(c(w;h) - \delta, 0)}{\sum_w c(w;h)} + \frac{\delta \cdot w_n}{\sum_w c(w;h)} P_{\mathcal{B}}(w)$$

Jelinek-Mercer smoothing, which involves a linear interpolation between the foreground and background models, parameterized by parameter λ, which controls the influence of each model:

$$P(w) = \lambda \cdot \frac{c(w;h)}{\sum_w c(w;h)} + (1 - \lambda) \cdot P_{\mathcal{B}}(w)$$

Bayesian smoothing using Dirichlet priors. A unigram language model is a multinomial, for which the conjugate prior is the Dirichlet distribution. This is defined as follows, parameterized with μ:

$$P(w) = \frac{c(w;h) + \mu \cdot P_{\mathcal{B}}(w)}{\sum_w c(w;h) + \mu}$$

Stupid backoff [5], which has been shown to be simple and effective for very large language models:

$$S(w) = \begin{cases} \frac{c(w;h)}{\sum_w c(w;h)} & \text{if } c(w;h) > 0 \\ \alpha \cdot P_{\mathcal{B}}(w) & \text{otherwise} \end{cases}$$

That is, if we have seen the term in the foreground model, we use its maximum likelihood estimate; otherwise we take the probability from the background model, scaled by α. Brants et al. [5] demonstrated that its simplicity allows the technique to be applied to larger corpora than practical with state-of-the-art techniques such as Kneser-Ney, and actually outperforms it at scale.

Note that stupid backoff does not define a valid probability distribution, which makes the score S not comparable to the other smoothing techniques. To remedy this we introduce a simple extension, *normalized* stupid backoff:

$$P(w) = \begin{cases} \frac{1}{1+\alpha} \cdot \frac{c(w;h)}{\sum_w c(w;h)} & \text{if } c(w;h) > 0 \\ \frac{\alpha}{1+\alpha} \cdot P_{\mathcal{B}}(w) & \text{otherwise} \end{cases}$$

In essence, we can renormalize stupid backoff scores into probabilities by dividing by the sum of scores. This has the nice effect of retaining all ranking properties of the scoring function.

3.2 History Retention Techniques

Orthogonal to the smoothing techniques discussed in the previous section is the method for retaining history (i.e., recently-encountered terms). In this work, we explored the following three techniques:

"Forget", the simplest possible approach, is to flush all data structures after every h events. That is, we periodically forget everything that has been observed (i.e., reset counts of all terms to zero).

"Queue" involves retaining the most recent h events in a FIFO queue. When the queue reaches capacity, newly encountered terms displace the earliest terms and counts are adjusted accordingly. This is equivalent to a fixed-width sliding window on the tweet stream. Although this technique occupies constant space, it requires remembering the entire sequence of events (as opposed to a simple counter in the "forget" approach).

"Epoch" is the approach described by Goyal et al. [9] for estimating approximate n-gram frequencies in a streaming setting. The basic approach is to delimit the incoming stream in terms of epochs (h events); after each epoch, low frequency n-grams are removed in a manner that provides theoretical guarantees on the true frequency of the remaining n-grams (see cited paper for more details). Note this is technically *not* a bounded space algorithm, although space requirements grow relatively slowly (logarithmically with respect to input size).

4. DATA

Our dataset consists of the raw (unfiltered and unsampled) tweet stream from October 1 to October 7, 2010 (inclusive) which spans an entire week. During this span, we observed an average of 93.5 million tweets per day. On average, 10.9 million tweets per day contain at least one hashtag. We manually selected 10 topics based on popularity and to obtain broad coverage of different types: sports, technology, popular culture, and general interests. These topics are shown in Table 1. Based on our experience, they represent a reasonably accurate sample cross section of typical Twitter users' interests. We discarded tweets that contained fewer than ten content words, not counting hashtags and usernames. Retweets, where users "pass on" tweets to their followers verbatim, are also discarded. The second column shows the number of tweets (that meet the above criteria) for each topic during the week span. For the background model, we used tweets from the entire month of September (2.66 billion tweets). In all cases we made no effort to perform

Topic	Tweets	Notes
1. #nfl	58913	American football
2. #mlb	39903	baseball
3. #apple	75696	Mac, iPhone, iPad, etc.
4. #android	45639	i.e., mobile phone
5. #glee	75174	TV show
6. #jerseyshore	25336	TV show
7. #teaparty	38099	political movement
8. #travel	34436	
9. #fashion	22743	
10. #health	51483	

Table 1: Topics explored in our study.

language identification and made no effort to separately tokenize or otherwise process non-English tweets.

5. INTRINSIC EVALUATION

Our first set of experiments involved intrinsic evaluation of the approach discussed in Section 3. The experimental procedure was as follows: the algorithm is initialized with the background model and an empty foreground model. Each tweet is processed in turn; tweets that do not contain the relevant hashtag or do not meet the content length requirements are discarded. For each tweet, we then remove the hashtag and compute its perplexity with respect to the current topic model, defined as:

$$\text{pow}\left[2, -\frac{1}{N}\sum_{i=1}^{n}\log_2 P(w_i)\right]$$

where the test tweet W is composed of N words $(w_1, w_2, \ldots w_n)$. Under the standard interpretation, a perplexity of k means that one is as surprised on average as guessing from k equiprobable choices at each symbol in the sequence. Finally, the foreground model is updated. This process is repeated until all tweets are consumed.

Table 2 presents the average perplexity across each topic using unigram language models under a variety of settings. We ran a large number of experiments exploring the parameter space; for space considerations, we only present the most interesting results.

The first row in the table shows the perplexity of the background model by itself, which provides the baseline. The first two blocks of the table show different smoothing techniques under the queue history retention technique ($h = \{1000, 10000\}$). The smoothing parameters represent effective settings derived from a coarse exploration of the parameter space. For Jelinek-Mercer, we found that $\lambda = \{0.3, 0.4\}$ works well in balancing the need to capture recency and to combat sparsity. With lower values we get too much influence from the background model, but with higher values we suffer from the inability to characterize rare or unseen terms in the foreground. It makes sense that a longer history calls for less weight on the background model. We noticed the following general effect when varying μ in Dirichlet smoothing: models with values too small suffer from sparsity, while those with values too large overemphasize the background model. Longer histories require a larger μ, because otherwise we are not receiving sufficient contributions from the background model. Interestingly, for absolute discounting we found that the best δ is somewhat higher than values typically reported in the literature. We explain this as follows: recall that in absolute discounting δ partial count is subtracted from every seen event; since we're only retaining limited history, the foreground vocabulary space is rather small—hence, we need a large discount to "save" enough probability mass for the background. Overall, Jelinek-Mercer appears to perform the best in terms of perplexity, although Dirichlet smoothing and absolute discounting are comparable for some topics. In nearly all cases, normalized stupid backoff is not competitive in terms of our intrinsic evaluation.

Comparing the two history sizes, it is interesting that while $h = 10000$ yields lower perplexities, we still obtain respectable perplexity values with only a tenth as much history. For certain space-constrained applications, this is a tradeoff worth considering.

In terms of absolute values, we observe large differences in perplexity, which gives an indication of how "cohesive" a topic is—and as we shall see later, this lets us quantify topic difficulty in the extrinsic task. We are able to build models with relatively low perplexity for topics such as #apple because the vocabulary is relatively restricted in terms of tweet content: terms such as iPad, iPod, etc. appear with high frequency. At the opposite extreme, a topic like #fashion is far less predictable in terms of tweet content (which makes sense).

The reduction in perplexity from adding a foreground model (compared to using only the background model) gives us a sense of how rapidly a topic changes over time. For a topic like #nfl, we observe a large decrease in perplexity—this make sense since "what's happening" in American football changes from moment to moment (e.g., successive stories on player trades, scouting reports, injury updates, etc.). At the other end of the spectrum, for a topic such as #apple there is a steady stream of discussion about popular Apple products (iPad, iPod, iPhone, etc.). There were no major new Apple products or announcements during the time considered in our study, so the content of tweets didn't differ much from the general discourse captured by the background model. Note that the "cohesiveness" of a topic appears to be orthogonal to the importance of recency effects—for example, the topic #fashion benefits from adding a foreground model, which once again seems intuitive (i.e., once a user mentions a particular item, it is more likely that other users will join in the conversation).

In the bottom block of Table 2, we fix a particular smoothing technique (Jelinek-Mercer, $\lambda = 0.4$) and history window size ($h = 10000$) and report the effects on perplexity for unigram language models using different history retention techniques (the queue, forget, and epoch methods described in Section 3.2). It is not surprising that the queue method outperforms the other two. The major weakness of the epoch approach is that it provides no mechanism to "forget" term frequencies over time, and therefore does not properly reward terms that appear recently. We are, however, somewhat surprised that the performance of the forget method is quite reasonable—for some topics, the difference in perplexity compared to the queue method is not very large. Given that the forget method requires far less space (we only need to keep track of the number of terms encountered, rather than the entire history of terms for the queue method), the higher perplexities might be a worthwhile tradeoff for some applications.

Table 3 shows perplexities of the bigram language models across all ten topics for different smoothing techniques, with the queue method ($h = 10000$). Once again, the smoothing parameters represent effective settings derived from a coarse exploration of the parameter space. For bigrams, experiments show that Jelinek-Mercer consistently has the lowest perplexity. It is no surprise to see large reductions in perplexity in moving from unigram to bigram language models. However, extrinsic evaluations show that lower perplexity does not translate into better task performance—as we shall see next. For space considerations, we omit results of additional experiments with bigram language models.

Topic	1	2	3	4	5	6	7	8	9	10
Background only	5851	5356	1676	11584	7257	3306	4442	10204	16887	7237
Queue ($h = 1000$)										
Absolute Discounting ($\delta = 0.9$)	**3754**	3578	1414	8902	4825	2798	4131	8318	9462	**3833**
Jelinek-Mercer ($\lambda = 0.3$)	3788	**3539**	**1408**	8817	**5009**	**2769**	3975	7994	**9212**	3919
Dirichlet ($\mu = 5000$)	3971	3699	1416	**8711**	5141	**2769**	**3866**	**7993**	9340	4148
Normalized Stupid Backoff ($\alpha = 1.0$)	4668	4474	1991	11865	6473	3947	5548	10225	11502	4697
Queue ($h = 10000$)										
Absolute Discounting ($\delta = 0.9$)	3696	3472	1382	8760	4538	2904	4099	8052	10595	3846
Jelinek-Mercer ($\lambda = 0.4$)	3652	3372	**1342**	**8329**	4582	**2721**	**3741**	**7595**	**9788**	3784
Dirichlet ($\mu = 10000$)	**3609**	**3336**	1353	8517	**4557**	2752	3813	7651	9969	**3738**
Normalized Stupid Backoff ($\alpha = 0.3$)	4526	4213	1778	12004	5893	3774	5311	10073	13605	4603
Jelinek-Mercer ($\lambda = 0.4, h = 10000$)										
Queue	**3652**	**3372**	**1342**	**8329**	**4582**	**2721**	**3741**	**7595**	**9788**	**3784**
Forget	3670	3421	1371	8575	4744	2762	3922	7849	9752	3790
Epoch	4772	4243	1426	9355	5428	2922	3852	7979	10800	4869

Table 2: Perplexity of unigram language models under different settings.

Topic	1	2	3	4	5	6	7	8	9	10
Background only	924	1505	150	2526	921	667	921	976	2179	1006
Queue ($h = 10000$)										
Absolute Discounting ($\delta = 0.8$)	451	573	97	1176	624	526	622	559	820	**318**
Jelinek-Mercer ($\lambda = 0.3$)	**365**	**438**	**95**	**1058**	**458**	**350**	**520**	**470**	**789**	356
Dirichlet ($\mu = 100$)	538	690	132	1518	687	562	713	674	1074	405
Normalized Stupid Backoff ($\alpha = 1.0$)	469	549	479	1366	568	431	673	638	1058	526

Table 3: Perplexity of bigram language models under different settings.

6. EXTRINSIC EVALUATION

In addition to intrinsic perplexity-based measures, we also evaluated the effectiveness of our topic language models on the task of topic tracking, conceived as a filtering problem on the tweet stream. We experimented with a simple perplexity-based classifier. For a given tweet, its perplexity with respect to the current model is computed. If the perplexity is above a certain decision threshold, we considered it relevant (i.e., on topic). By varying the decision threshold, we can realized different precision/recall tradeoffs.

A few more details about our experimental setup: To avoid the laborious task of building a test collection by hand, we focused our evaluation efforts on tweets that contained at least one hashtag. We processed all tweets with hashtags as follows: first, the ground truth label (i.e., topic of interest) is removed from the tweet. We then applied the perplexity-based classifier to obtain a classification decision. After recording the results, the foreground model is updated accordingly (if the tweet contains the ground truth label).

A few caveats on the evaluation: as with many other IR evaluations, absolute values of metrics can be misleading. For example, for the topic #nfl, there are other commonly-used tags such as #football that are roughly synonymous, or in many cases tweets are tagged with finer-grained entities such as team names. Our evaluation method would not be able to capture any of these natural variations. In many cases, it is nearly impossible to classify, even for a human, whether a tweet was topical or not. A tweet to the effect of "I'm watching #glee right now" (a popular TV show) provides little content-based signal as to the topic if the hashtag itself is removed. Finally, we perform no attempt at special processing of non-English tweets. Thus, when interpreting results, the relative effectiveness of different techniques is more important than the absolute numbers.

Figure 1 shows the precision-recall plots of our ten test topics using unigram LMs and the queue history retention approach ($h = 10000$). In each figure, we plot recall on the x-axis; since only a small fraction of tweets are topically relevant, the y-axis precision scale focuses on values close to one. In all plots, the dotted line shows the precision achievable by rejecting all tweets as non-relevant (a trivial baseline).

The striking conclusion is that although Jelinek-Mercer smoothing yields the lowest perplexities overall (from Table 2), in the extrinsic task normalized stupid backoff appears to be just as effective and in some cases more effective than the other smoothing techniques. This appears to be true for all ten topics with exception of topic 7 (#teaparty), where absolute discounting appears to perform the best. Normalized stupid backoff has the additional advantage in that it is the simplest, and hence fastest smoothing technique. We believe that the issue with Jelinek-Mercer smoothing is the λ setting, which gives relatively low weight to the foreground model—from a perplexity point of view, this allows the model to better account for background events, but this is detrimental to the extrinsic task, which requires more emphasis on recency.

Figure 2 compares the effects of different history sizes $h = \{1000, 10000\}$ with the queue method, showing absolute discounting and normalized stupid backoff for a single topic. The longer history outperforms the shorter history, as expected. We omit corresponding figures for other topics, since they are qualitatively similar and provide little additional insight.

Our final set of experiments compared unigram and bigram language models under the same conditions. Figure 3 shows results for the #nfl topic, comparing the background model and normalized stupid backoff (queue, $h = 1000$). Results from other topics look similar, and hence are omitted here. We see that unigram LMs are more effective than bigram LMs. It is perhaps not surprising,

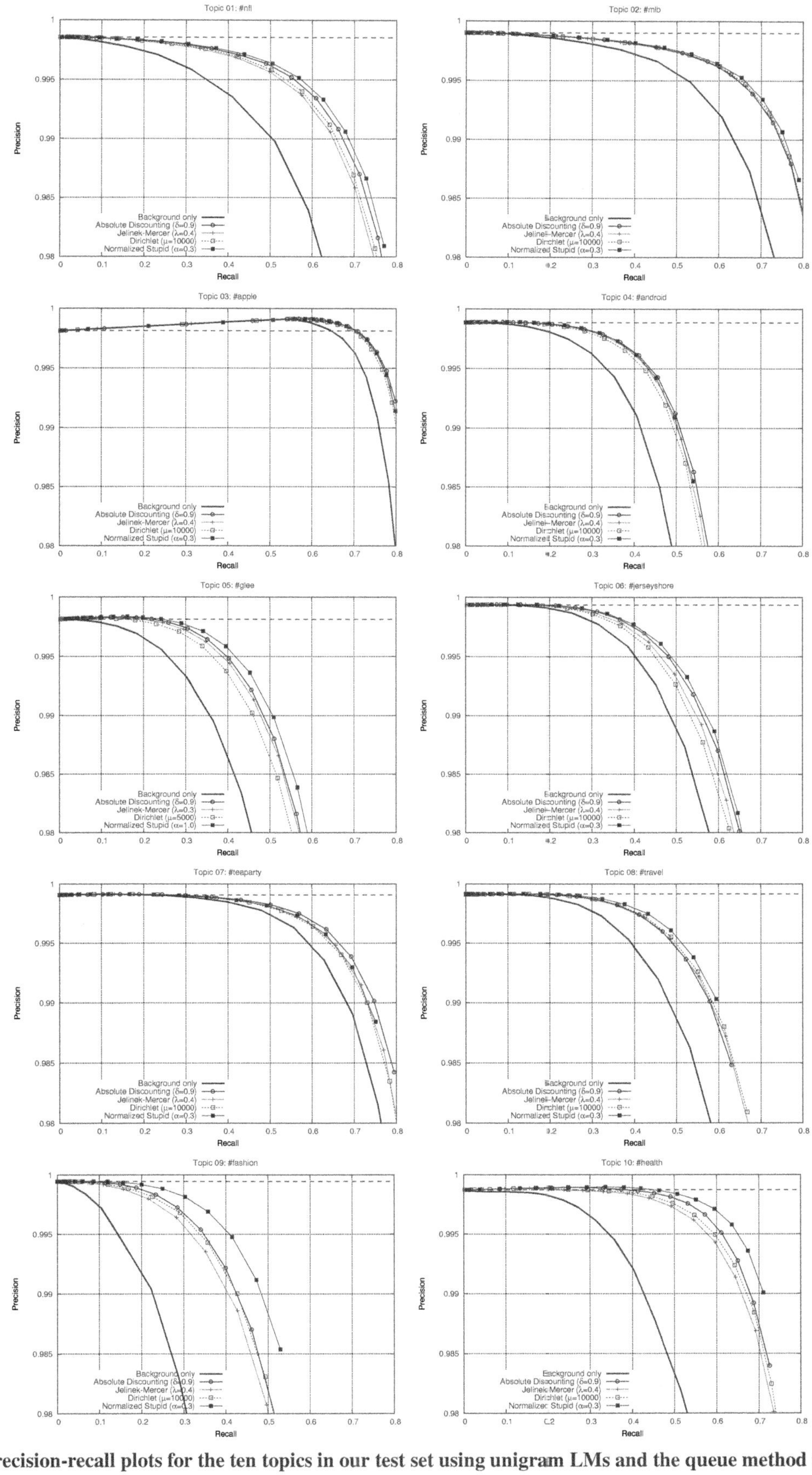

Figure 1: Precision-recall plots for the ten topics in our test set using unigram LMs and the queue method ($h = 10000$).

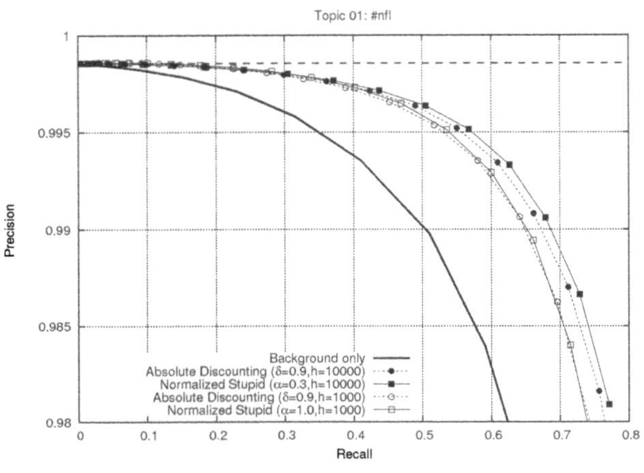

Figure 2: Comparison between different history sizes ($h = \{1000, 10000\}$), using the queue method, unigrams.

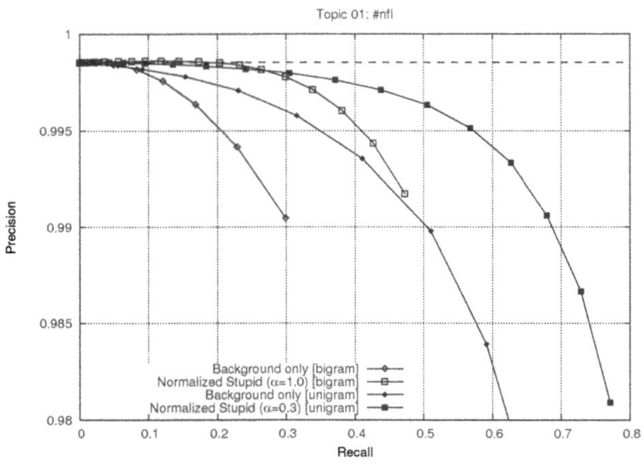

Figure 3: Comparison between unigram and bigram language models (background vs. stupid backoff).

as this conclusion is consistent with results from IR and other related tasks. Somewhat oversimplifying, topicality boils down to a problem of keyword spotting, for which unigram LMs are not only faster, but better. Based on examination of output, it appears that the bigram models are attempting to model aspects of tweet fluency (i.e., grammaticality), which is an issue completely orthogonal to topicality, the actual problem at hand. For this reason, with bigram LMs precision drops off rapidly with increasing recall: fluent tweets that are off topic are falsely classified as positive, while disfluent but topical tweets are rejected.

7. CONCLUSION

The problem of tracking topics in a continuous stream of short natural language texts, as applied to tweet streams, compels us to look for simple, efficient solutions. Our general approach is to combine a foreground model to capture "what's happening right now" with a background model to combat data sparsity. We found that stupid backoff, perhaps the simplest method to combine two probability distributions, is at least as effective as any of the more principled smoothing techniques we examined. A simple technique of retaining history in a FIFO queue was also found to be effective. The combination, applied to unigram language models, provides a good balance between maintaining recency and combating sparsity.

Beyond the immediate task, the results of this work provide more evidence that in "extreme" settings, simple approaches work well (in terms of balancing speed, effectiveness, scalability, and other real-world considerations). Brants et al. [5] demonstrated that at web-scale (i.e., extremely large datasets), stupid backoff outperforms Kneser-Ney smoothing. Here, we contribute findings along another dimension of "extreme": in rapidly evolving streams of natural language text (that, literally, change on a millisecond basis), the KISS principle remains a good starting point.

8. ACKNOWLEDGMENTS

We'd like to thank Abdur Chowdhury for helpful comments on earlier drafts of this paper. The first author is grateful to Esther and Kiri for their loving support and dedicates this work to Joshua and Jacob.

9. REFERENCES

[1] J. Allan. *Topic Detection and Tracking: Event-Based Information Organization*. Kluwer Academic Publishers, Dordrecht, The Netherlands, 2002.

[2] S. Asur and B. A. Huberman. Predicting the future with social media. Technical Report HPL-2010-53, HP Laboratories, 2010.

[3] S. Asur, B. A. Huberman, G. Szabo, and C. Wang. Trends in social media: Persistence and decay. Technical report, HP Laboratories, 2011.

[4] E. Bakshy, J. M. Hofman, W. A. Mason, and D. J. Watts. Everyone's an influencer: Quantifying influence on Twitter. In *Proceedings of the Fourth ACM International Conference on Web Search and Data Mining (WSDM 2011)*, pages 65–74, Hong Kong, China, 2011.

[5] T. Brants, A. C. Popat, P. Xu, F. J. Och, and J. Dean. Large language models in machine translation. In *Proceedings of the 2007 Joint Conference on Empirical Methods in Natural Language Processing and Computational Natural Language Learning*, pages 858–867, Prague, Czech Republic, 2007.

[6] M. Cha, H. Haddadi, F. Benevenuto, and K. P. Gummadi. Measuring user influence in Twitter: The million follower fallacy. In *Proceedings of the 4th International AAAI Conference on Weblogs and Social Media (ICWSM 2010)*, pages 10–17, Washington, D.C., 2010.

[7] S. F. Chen and J. Goodman. An empirical study of smoothing techniques for language modeling. In *Proceedings of the 34th Annual Meeting of the Association for Computational Linguistics (ACL 1996)*, pages 310–318, Santa Cruz, California, 1996.

[8] M. Cherniack, H. Balakrishnan, M. Balazinska, D. Carney, U. Çetintemel, Y. Xing, and S. B. Zdonik. Scalable distributed stream processing. In *Proceedings of the First Biennial Conference on Innovative Data Systems Research (CIDR 2003)*, Asilomar, California, 2003.

[9] A. Goyal, H. Daumé, and S. Venkatasubramanian. Streaming for large scale NLP: Language modeling. In *Proceedings of Human Language Technologies: The 2009 Annual Conference of the North American Chapter of the Association for Computational Linguistics*, pages 512–520, Boulder, Colorado, 2009.

[10] D. J. Hopkins and G. King. A method of automated nonparametric content analysis for social science. *American Journal of Political Science*, 54(1):229–247, 2010.

[11] D. Jurafsky and J. H. Martin. *Speech and Language Processing*. Pearson, Upper Saddle River, New Jersey, 2009.

[12] H. Kwak, C. Lee, H. Park, and S. Moon. What is Twitter, a social network or a news media? In *Proceedings of the 19th International World Wide Web Conference (WWW 2010)*, pages 591–600, Raleigh, North Carolina, 2010.

[13] K. Lerman and R. Ghosh. Information contagion: An empirical study of the spread of news on Digg and Twitter social networks. In *Proceedings of the 4th International AAAI Conference on Weblogs and Social Media (ICWSM 2010)*, pages 90–97, Washington, D.C., 2010.

[14] A. Levenberg and M. Osborne. Stream-based randomised language models for SMT. In *Proceedings of the 2009 Conference on Empirical Methods in Natural Language Processing (EMNLP 2009)*, pages 756–764, Singapore, 2009.

[15] X. Liu, S. Zhang, F. Wei, and M. Zhou. Recognizing named entities in tweets. In *Proceedings of the 49th Annual Meeting of the Association for Computational Linguistics: Human Language Technologies (ACL-HLT 2011)*, Portland, Oregon, 2011.

[16] S. Muthukrishnan. Data streams: Algorithms and applications. *Foundations and Trends in Computer Science*, 1(2), 2005.

[17] B. O'Connor, R. Balasubramanyan, B. R. Routledge, and N. A. Smith. From Tweets to polls: Linking text sentiment to public opinion time series. In *Proceedings of the 4th International AAAI Conference on Weblogs and Social Media (ICWSM 2010)*, pages 122–129, Washington, D.C., 2010.

[18] S. Petrović, M. Osborne, and V. Lavrenko Streaming first story detection with application to Twitter. In *Proceedings of Human Language Technologies: The 2010 Annual Conference of the North American Chapter of the Association for Computational Linguistics (HLT/NAACL 2010)*, pages 181–189, Los Angeles, California, 2010.

[19] D. Ramage, S. Dumais, and D. Liebling. Characterizing microblogs with topic models. In *Proceedings of the 4th International AAAI Conference on Weblogs and Social Media (ICWSM 2010)*, pages 130–137, Washington, D.C., 2010.

[20] A. Ritter, C. Cherry, and B. Dolan. Unsupervised modeling of Twitter conversations. In *Proceedings of Human Language Technologies: The 2010 Annual Conference of the North American Chapter of the Association for Computational Linguistics (HLT/NAACL 2010)*, pages 172–180, Los Angeles, California, 2010.

[21] D. M. Romero, B. Meeder, and J. Kleinberg. Differences in the mechanics of information diffusion across topics: Idioms, political hashtags, and complex contagion on Twitter. In *Proceedings of the 20th International World Wide Web Conference (WWW 2011)*, pages 695–704, Hyderabad, India, 2011.

[22] J. Weng, E.-P. Lim, J. Jiang, and Q. He. TwitterRank: Finding topic-sensitive influential Twitterers. In *Proceedings of the Third ACM International Conference on Web Search and Data Mining (WSDM 2010)*, pages 261–270, New York, New York, 2010.

Democrats, Republicans and Starbucks Afficionados: User Classification in Twitter

Marco Pennacchiotti
Yahoo! Labs
pennac@yahoo-inc.com

Ana-Maria Popescu
Yahoo! Labs
amp@yahoo-inc.com

ABSTRACT

More and more technologies are taking advantage of the explosion of social media (Web search, content recommendation services, marketing, ad targeting, etc.). This paper focuses on the problem of automatically constructing *user profiles*, which can significantly benefit such technologies. We describe a general and robust machine learning framework for large-scale classification of social media users according to dimensions of interest. We report encouraging experimental results on 3 tasks with different characteristics: political affiliation detection, ethnicity identification and detecting affinity for a particular business.

Categories and Subject Descriptors

H.3.5 [**Information Storage and Retrieval**]: On-line Information Services—*Web-based services*; I.2.6 [**Artificial Intelligence**]: Learning

General Terms

Algorithms, Design, Experimentation

Keywords

Microblogging, Social Media, User Profiling, Machine Learning

1. INTRODUCTION

The explosion of real-time microblogging services such as Twitter and Facebook has led to a wealth of efforts to make use of social media content as well as various social graphs. For example, major Web technology players such as Google, Bing and Yahoo! Search now incorporate microblog posts and trend analysis in their results; in addition to using social information in conjunction with existing search and retrieval models, significant efforts are dedicated to developing new applications (e.g., user and post recommendation services) for the new, real-time social realm.

In this context, a problem of significant interest is that of automatic *user classification and profiling*, i.e. mining values of various user attributes such as demographic characteristics (e.g., age, gender, ethnicity, origin), coarse- and fine-grained interests (e.g. politics, soccer, Starbucks, Glee TV series), stances on various issues (e.g. liberal, pro-choice), etc. These user models can help in multiple application scenarios, such as:

Authoritative users extraction : discovering expert users for a target topic. Bing Social, Klout [1] and other similar applications study the users' posted content and their interactions with others in order to suggest authoritative users to follow on a topic. A repository of user profiles may significantly help in estimating the authority of a user on a topic - for example, a user primarily interested in politics is more likely to be authoritative on political issues than a user whose attention is equally divided among many interests.

Post reranking in web search : reranking social media posts retrieved in response to search engine queries based on a particular quality function and the Web users' preferences. Improving and personalizing social media posts' retrieval and display would benefit from information about the authoritativeness and profile of the user writing the post, as well as from knowledge of the microblogging profile (if available) of the Web user issuing a query.

User recommendation : suggesting new interesting users to a target user. The Twitter's 'Who To Follow' and Google's 'Follow Finder' [2] applications suggest new accounts to follow to Twitter users by using exclusively the properties of a specific social network. Recently, several studies have shown the potential of user profiles to improve the quality and the coverage of those applications [16, 18]. Yet, much is still unexplored. User profile information can be used both to automatically match two users with similar profiles and to explicitly allow a user to specify the type of new "friends" he is looking for (e.g., people interested in sports).

The above applications, as well as many others, would significantly benefit from the existence of large-scale knowledge repositories of user profile attributes or classification information.

Most social network and microblog services already store profile information in the form of name, age, location and short summary of interests, but such information is often incomplete (e.g., a user may choose not to post bio details) or misleading (e.g., a user may choose to list an imaginary place - aka, "Wonderland", as her location). Furthermore, other relevant attributes, such as explicit and implicit interests or political preferences are mostly omitted. Also, Twitter *directories* such as WeFollow [3] are manually built examples of profile repositories. Such directories allow Twitter users to manually add themselves in specific categories such as 'Music' and 'Bloggers'; unfortunately they are limited in size, the categories are pre-defined and the manual addition process can be cumbersome.

In response to this shortage of user profile repositories, researchers

KDD'11, August 21–24, 2011, San Diego, California, USA.

[1] http://www.bing.com/social and http://klout.com/
[2] http://www.twitter.com and http://www.followfinder.googlelabs.com
[3] http://wefollow.com/

have experimented with automatic methods for populating values of choice attributes such a user's age and location of origin. However, a discussion of a general framework for attribute value extraction in the service of user profiling is still missing.

In this paper, we present an architecture which addresses the above problem by casting it as a **user classification** task and leveraging two types of information: *user-centric information* reflecting the linguistic content of the user's tweets, her social behaviors and likes, and; *social graph information* in the form of the distribution of the possible target class values for the people connected to the user by a social graph link. Our main contributions are:

(1) We introduce a novel architecture for social media user classification which is composed of: (i) a machine learning component that classifies users by leveraging user-centric features (profile, linguistic, behavioral, social), and; (ii) a graph-based updating component that integrates social graph information, by updating the classification result according to the class's values distribution across the social connections of the user.

(2) We show that the architecture can be instantiated and used with good results on Twitter and three different tasks (political orientation, ethnicity and business fans detection).

(3) We provide an in-depth analysis of the results, revealing that user-centric features achieve alone good classification results, while social graph information has a negligible impact on the overall performance. We also comment on the value of specific user-centric features: we show that linguistic content features are in general highly valuable, and that large-scale topic models are particularly robust, showing promise for additional user classification tasks.

The rest of the paper is organized as follows: Section 2 places our research in the context of previous work; Section 3 describes the machine learning component and its feature set; Section 4 presents the graph-based updating component; Section 5 outlines our experiments and reports an in-depth quantitative and qualitative analysis of the obtained results; Section 6 describes our conclusions and future work directions.

2. RELATED WORK

User attribute detection based on user communication streams. Previous work has explored the impact of people's profiles on the style, patterns and content of their communication streams. For example, researchers investigated the detection of *gender* from well-written, traditional text [10], blogs [4] reviews [14], e-mail [9], user search queries [12, 24] and, for the first time, Twitter [19].

Another area of focus has been understanding how the political orientation of a user is reflected in their writings: for example, [23, 13, 22] investigate congressional transcripts as well as informal user posts while [19] focuses on microblogs (we discuss the latter in more detail below). Other previously explored attributes include the user's *location* [6, 12], *location of origin* [19] and *age* [12, 19].

While such previous work has addressed blogs and other informal texts, microblogs are just starting to be explored for user classification. In the case of microblogs, we are usually interested in mining a series of short updates over a period of time for a particular user in order to infer particular user attributes.

While previous work uses a mixture of sociolinguistic features, ngram models as well as deep sentence-level analysis, we focus on aggregate features (e.g., those from large-scale topic models) in order to better exploit the user-created microblog content.

Twitter-related research and applications. Social media in general and Twitter in particular are the subject of considerable ongoing research work: spam detection research [2], tweet sentiment analysis [1], conversation modeling [20] and more.

While in the future we plan to integrate insights from a number of research directions, we focus herein on the work directly related to ours. The most relevant such paper is [19], an exploratory study of Twitter user attribute detection which uses *simple* features such as n-gram models, simple sociolinguistic features (e.g., presence of emoticons), statistics about the user's immediate network (e.g., number of followers/friends) and communication behavior (e.g., retweet frequency). In comparison, our work confirms the value of *in-depth* features which reflect a deeper understanding of the Twitter user stream and the user network structure (e.g., features derived from large-scale topic models, tweet sentiment analysis and *explicit* follower-followed links).

A second relevant paper is [18] which uses large-scale topic models to represent Twitter feeds and users, showing improved performance on tasks such as post and user recommendation. We confirm the value of large-scale topic models for a different set of tasks (user classification) and analyze their impact as part of a rich feature set.

In addition to the growing number of publications, Twitter users benefit from an entire ecosystem of applications which seek to make Twitter data easier to find and use. Of particular interest to us are *directories* such as WeFollow, whose goal is to make it easier to find users from particular categories (e.g., certain professions, political persuasions, etc.). As outlined in the previous section, our work can be used to automatically augment such already available user databases.

3. MACHINE LEARNING MODEL

Task. The goal of our work is to build a general, scalable and robust architecture for automatically computing the values of given user attributes for a large set of Twitter users.

Solution overview. We cast the problem as a classification task, and solve it using an architecture with two components: the first component is a machine learning algorithm that learns a classification model from labeled data and user-centric features. The model is then used to classify new incoming users (e.g., as being a Democrat or a Republican). The second component of the architecture is a graph-based label updating function which uses social graph information in order to revise the classification label assigned to each user by the initial machine learning component.

An important requirement for our architecture is *scalability*: as Twitter reports, the number of active Twitter users per month is in the tens of millions. We estimate that each month the number of active users increases by about 8%, and that every week 1.6M new active users join the network. [4] The post volume is also steadily increasing, amounting to about 102M tweets per day in January 2011. Our architecture adopts highly scalable algorithms and engineering solutions, in order to scale to terabytes of data, and potentially petabytes in the near future. Both our architectural components run over a Map/Reduce Hadoop system which is able to build and apply classification models on a large scale within a few hours.

The rest of this section describes in more depth the first machine learning component of the architecture, while Section 4 analyzes the updating function. The machine learning component takes as input a small training set of labeled examples for a given class (e.g. 'political affiliation') and learns a classification model which can then be used to label the large set of Twitter users. As a classification algorithm, we use the Gradient Boosted Decision Trees - GBDT framework [7], which consists of an ensemble of decision trees, fitted in a forward step-wise manner to current residuals.

[4]Statistics based on data collected between December 2010 and January 2011.

Friedman [7] shows that by drastically easing the problem of overfitting on training data (which is common in boosting algorithms), GDBT competes with state-of-the-art machine learning algorithms such as SVM with much smaller resulting models and faster decoding time [8], which is an advantage in our real-time setting. We use a distributed GBDT architecture running over Hadoop [26] which allows us to scale to the dimensionality of Twitter.

To learn the classification model, we use a large set of features, falling into four main categories (described below), according to the nature of information they aim to capture: *profile*, *messaging (tweeting) behavior*, *linguistic content of messages* and *social network information*.

3.1 Profile features

Most services (such as Twitter) publicly show by default profile information such as the user name, the location and a short bio. The Twitter API also provides access to other basic user information, such as the number of a user's friends, followers and tweets. In related work, Cheng and colleagues [6] estimated that only 26% of users report a specific *location* such as a city, while the rest provide either general locations (states, countries) or imaginary places. We conducted a pilot study in the same vein to assess the direct use of such information for basic user classification tasks, such as identifying a user's gender and ethnicity. Given a corpus of 14M users active in April 2010, we found that 48% of them provide a short bio and 80% a location. We then matched more than 30 regular expression patterns over the bio field to check if they are effective in extracting classification information, such as the following for respectively age and ethnicity classification:

```
(I|i)(m|am|'m)[0-9]+(yo|year old)
white(man|woman|boy|girl)
```

We were able to determine the *ethnicity* of less than 0.1% users; and to find the *gender* for 80%, but with very low accuracy. We then investigated the use of the profile avatar in determining the gender and ethnicity attribute values. We sampled 15,000 random users and asked a pool of editors to identify the ethnicity and gender of the user based on only the avatar picture: less than 50% of the pictures were correlated with a clear ethnicity while 57% were correlated with a specific gender. We found that pictures can often be misleading: in 20% of the cases, the editors verified that the picture was not of the account owner, but of a celebrity or of another person. The above statistics show that the profile fields do not contain enough good-quality information to be directly used for user classification purposes, though they can be effectively used for bootstrapping training material. Yet, we implemented basic profile-based features (referred as PROF in the experiments): the length of the user name, number of numeric and alphanumeric characters in the user name, different capitalization forms in the user name, use of the avatar picture, number of followers, number of friends, friends/followers ratio, date of account creation, matching of various regular expression patterns in the bio field as listed above, presence of the location field. Such features are general in nature and portable across different classification tasks.

3.2 Tweeting behavior features

Tweeting behavior is characterized by a set of statistics capturing the way the user interacts with the micro-blogging service: the average number of messages per day, number of replies, etc. Intuitively, such information is useful for constructing a model of the user; Java and colleagues [11] suggest that users who rarely post tweets but have many friends tend to be information seekers, while users who often post URLs in their tweets are most likely information providers. Rao and colleagues [19] instead suggest that tweeting behavior information is not useful for most classification tasks and that it is subsumed by linguistic features. In this paper we aim at verifying these claims, by experimenting with more than 20 tweeting behavior features (BEHAV), including: number of tweets posted by the user, number and fraction of tweets that are retweets, number and fraction of tweets that are replies, average number of hashtags and URLs per tweet, fraction of tweets that are truncated, average time and standard deviation between tweets, average number and standard deviation of tweets per day, fraction of tweets posted in each of 24 hours.

Like profile features, tweeting behavior features are fully generalizable and portable across different classification tasks.

3.3 Linguistic content features

Linguistic content information encapsulates the user's lexical usage and the main topics of interest to the user. Simple linguistic information is helpful for classifying users in several media, such as formal texts, blogs, spoken conversational transcripts or search sessions (see Section 2 for a discussion). We explore a wide variety of linguistic content features, as detailed below. Note that as far as language models are concerned, we prefer the use of Latent Dirichlet Allocation (LDA) [3] and automatically bootstrapped prototypical words over a more simple bag-of-word model, since several studies, e.g. [19], have showed that bag-of-words models are usually outperformed by more advanced linguistic ones.

Prototypical words (LING-WORD). In a classification task, classes can be described by prototypical words (hereafter 'proto words'), i.e. typical lexical expressions for people in a specific class (e.g. younger people tend to use words such as 'dude' or 'lmao') and phrases denoting typical interests of people in that class (e.g., Democrats may tend to use the expression 'health care' more than Republicans.) Rao and colleagues [19] explored this intuition by manually building a list of words that are likely to characterize socio-linguistic behaviors, e.g. emoticons and ellipses; however, their list is meant to be generic and it is not easy to translate into strong class-indicative features without manual effort. Instead, we employ a probabilistic model for automatically extracting proto words; it only needs a few seed users and it is easily portable to different tasks, similarly to what was proposed in [15].

Given n classes, each class c_i is represented by a set of seed users S_i. Each word w issued by at least one of the seed users is assigned a score for each of the classes. The score estimates the conditional probability of the class given the word as follows:

$$proto(w, c_i) = \frac{|w, S_i|}{\sum_{j=1}^{n} |w, S_j|} \qquad (1)$$

where $|w, S_i|$ is the number of times the word w is issued by all users for class c_i. For each class, we retain as proto words the highest scoring k words [5].

The $n * k$ proto words collected across all classes serve as features for representing a given user: for each proto word wp the user u is assigned the score:

$$f\_proto\_wp(u) = \frac{|u, wp|}{\sum_{w \in W_u} |u, w|} \qquad (2)$$

where $|u, wp|$ is the number of times the proto word w is issued by user u, and W_u is the set of all words issued by u. For each class, the user is also assigned an aggregated feature:

[5]In our experiment we use $k = 200$, and discard all words occurring 5 or less times, and long less than 3 characters.

$$f\_proto\_c(u) = \frac{\sum_{wp \in WP} |u, wp|}{\sum_{w \in W_u} |u, w|} \quad (3)$$

where WP is the set of proto words for class c. Table 4 reports the highest scoring proto words for the classes targeted in our paper.

Prototypical hashtags (LING-HASH). Twitter users may use hashtags (sequences of characters prefixed by '#') to denote the topic(s) of their tweet; many times, the same or similar hashtags are used by Twitter users in order to facilitate the retrieval and surfacing of information on a particular topic. We hypothesize that if users from a class are interested in the same topics, the most popular such topics can be found by collecting statistics on used hashtags. The intuition is implemented similarly to LING-WORD. Given a seed user set S_i for a class c_i, we collect all the hashtags h contained in the tweets of each seed user. We then derive the set of prototypical hashtags, by applying Eq. 1 (where w is replaced by h). Finally, we retain the highest scoring 100 hashtags for each class, and compute feature values as in Eq. 2 and 3.

Generic LDA (LING-GLDA). Our generic LDA model is an adaptation of the original LDA proposed by Blei and colleagues [3] where documents are replaced by users. Our hypothesis is that a user can be represented as a multinomial distribution over topics. This representation may help with classification: e.g., Democrats may have, on average, a higher probability of talking about social reforms, while Republicans may mention oil drilling more often. While Blei represents documents by their corresponding bag of words, we represent users by the words of their tweets.

Our generative model works as follows. Given a number U of users and a number K of topics, each user u is represented by a multinomial distribution θ_u over topics, which is drawn from a Dirichlet prior with parameter α. Also a topic is represented by a multinomial distribution β_k drawn from another Dirichlet prior with parameter η. The generative model states that each word position n in a user vocabulary is assigned a topic $z_{u,n}$ drawn from θ_u, and that the word in that position $w_{u,n}$ is drawn from the distribution $\beta_{z_{u,n}}$. The model is obtained by training an LDA parallel implementation [21] with 500 iterations over a set of 4M users, each represented by a maximum of 20,000 words collected from their tweets. As a result, we obtain 100 topics which will each be used to derive features for classification. The model is then applied to each test user in order to obtain his topic distribution, i.e. the feature values for the classification task.

Domain-specific LDA (LING-DLDA). This LDA model differs from LING-GLDA in that it is not derived from a generic set of users, but from users drawn from the training set (e.g., the training set of Democrat and Republican users is used to build the model for the political affiliation task). The intuition is that while LING-GLDA returns coarse-grained topics such as soccer, music and politics, LING-DLDA should return fine-grained topics that are more discriminative for the classification task. The model is derived as for LING-GLDA, though the smaller training set allows us to run 1000 iterations. We again use 100 topics.

Sentiment words (LING-SENT). In some cases, it is possible to identify terms or entities about which a particular user class has an overall majority opinion which is not shared by a different class (e.g., "Ronald Reagan" is generally viewed positively by Republicans and negatively by Democrats). We manually collect a small set of such terms for our classes and implement sentiment analysis techniques to find the sentiment of a user wrt the term.

Given user u, her set of tweets and each term t, we first identify the number of tweets in which a *positive*, *negative* or *neutral* sentiment is expressed wrt t by relying on Opinion Finder 1.5 [25] term lexicon for positive, negative and neutral sentiment words. For each tweet and term t, we compute the dominant sentiment in the tweet with respect to t by inspecting the phrases in a window of $k = 4$ words to the left and right of t. If more than 50% of the words in the window are neutral, or not in the OpinionFinder lexicon, the tweet is classified as neutral wrt t. Otherwise, we classify the tweet as *positive* if a majority of the terms are *positive* and *negative* otherwise (after accounting for the polarity flipping effect of simple negation modifiers such as "not" or "no"). Given the set of tweets of user u annotated with u's sentiment towards t, we retain as features the percentage of positive tweets wrt t, the percentage of negative tweets wrt t and the percentage of neutral tweets wrt t.

We also derive aggregated features indicating the overall sentiment of the user u wrt the target class, such as : the median and standard deviation of the above features across the entire term set; the number of terms t about which the user has overall, a mainly *positive*, *negative*, or *no opinion*.

3.4 Social network features

These general features explore the social connections established by the user with others he follows, to whom he replies or whose messages he retweets.

"Friend" accounts (SOC-FRIE). Intuitively, Democrats are more likely to follow the accounts of Democratic politicians and Republicans those of Republican politicians. We hypothesize that users from other classes may also share specific "friend" accounts. We use the same basic mechanism employed to bootstrap proto words (Eq. 1) in order to bootstrap a set of class-specific prototypical "friend" accounts F, by exploring the social network of users in the training set. We then derive the following *aggregate* and *individual* social network-based features for a given user u: number of accounts in F which are *friends* of u (accounts which the user is following); percentage of F accounts which are *friends of* u; percentage of all Twitter accounts followed by u which are part of F. For each prototypical "friend" account, a boolean feature is set to 1 if the user follows the account and 0 otherwise.

Prototypical replied (SOC-REP) **and retweeted** (SOC-RET) **users.** Similarly to SOC-FRIE, these two feature sets capture the idea that users from a particular class tend to reply to and retweet messages of specific accounts (e.g., young girls may tend to reply to Justin Bieber's account). These features are derived exactly as LING-WORD and LING-HASH, i.e. by first collecting accounts cited in tweets of users of a specific class, and prefixed by the reply and retweet tags ('@' and 'RT'); then discovering the 200 most significant replied/retweetd account applying Eq. 1; and, finally, deriving feature values as in Eq. 2, 3.

4. GRAPH-BASED LABEL UPDATE

In this section we describe a graph-based label updating algorithm that attempts to further improve the quality of the users' classification by taking into account social connections.

Twitter social connections are of two types: *friend* and *follower*. A user's friends are all users to whom she connected, in order to receive their messages and updates. Conversely, a user's followers are all users who have connected to her. Users with many followers and few friends are oftentimes called 'information sources' (e.g., news broadcasting organizations and celebrities), while users with many friends and few followers are called 'information seekers' (e.g., users who joined Twitter to keep up with the latest news).

Our intuition is that social connections can provide signals for correcting the errors of the machine learning component described in Section 3, by inverting the classification label. For example, a user mistakenly classified as a Democrat by the machine learning algorithm could be correctly classified as a Republican if her friends are predominantly classified as Republican.

In this paper we only experiment with users' friend connections, as they directly express the social likes of the user, and should thus intuitively provide better signal with respect to follower connections. In future work we will also explore the use of followers.

The graph-based updating algorithm is applied after the machine learning classification step, as follows. First, we collect the set of friends for each user in the original class dataset (e.g., Democrats and Republicans). We then apply the learned class-specific machine learning model on the friend set, assigning class-specific membership scores (and labels) to each friend. In a final *label updating* phase, we update the class labels for our original users based on the newly computed class-specific membership scores for their friends.

The label update function uses the classification confidence value (hereafter $score$) returned by GBDT for each user; the value is in the $[+1, -1]$ range, where positive values correspond to positively classified users, and negative values to negatively classified users. Higher absolute scores indicate a higher classification confidence.

For each user u_i in the original dataset, the function takes as input the $score(u)$ of the user and of each of her friends F_i, and returns a new updated score ($score'(u)$) for the user. If the score is positive, the user is classified as positive example, otherwise as a negative one. $score'$ is computed as follows:

$$score'(u_i) = \alpha \cdot score(u_i) + (1 - \alpha) \cdot \frac{\sum_{j \in F_i} w_{ij} \cdot score(u_j)}{|F_i|} \quad (4)$$

where $w_{ij} \in [0, 1]$ is the connection weight between user u_i and a friend u_j; $|F_i|$ is the number of friends of user u_i, and; $\alpha \in [0, 1]$ is a parameter that indicates how relevant the original ML-based user score should be. Setting $\alpha = 1$ equates to using the original machine learning model described in Section 3 without any graph-based contribution. $\alpha = 0$ updates the score using only graph-based information.

The connection weight w_{ij} models the intuitions that not all friends are equally strongly connected to a user and that some friends are overall more influential than others. For example, a user may often engage in discussion with and refer to some friends more than others. We capture this intuition by giving a higher weight to friends which are often mentioned by the user. [6] Additionally, some friends are users with a larger Twitter-wide influence (e.g., "information sources"). We combine the two components (connection strength and network-wide influence) as follows [7]:

$$w_{ij} = \frac{1}{2} \cdot \frac{|mentions_{ij}|}{\sum_{k \in F_i} |mentions_{ik}|} + \frac{1}{2} \cdot \frac{|ratioFolFriends_j|}{\sum_{k \in F_i} |ratioFolFriends_k|} \quad (5)$$

where: $|mentions_{ij}|$ is the number of times that user u_i mentions user u_j in her tweets ; $|ratioFolFriends_j|$ is a simple measure of a user's influence in form of the ratio between the number of the user's followers to the number of the user's friends.

[6]In Twitter, a user 'mentions' another user by including the tag '@' followed by the other user's name. These mentions usually correspond to replies and conversational exchanges between the two users.

[7]We experimented with a number of other combination functions, with comparable experimental results

5. EXPERIMENTAL EVALUATION

We evaluate our architecture over three binary classification tasks: detecting political affiliation, detecting a particular ethnicity, and identifying 'Starbucks fans'.

Political affiliation. The task consists in classifying users as being either Democrats (positive set) or Republicans (negative set). Political affiliation detection is a very interesting task for many applications – e.g., when employing user recommendation tools, a user may want to look for new friends with the same political ideas; social analytics applications may engage the audience by reporting opposing views on political issues or tracking the concerns and interests of a party's base.

We build the gold standard dataset by scraping lists of users who classified themselves as either Democrat or Republican in the Twitter directories WeFollow and Twellow[8]. We collect a total of 10,338 users, equally distributed in the two classes. In this paper, the datasets are balanced 50/50 in order to easily study feature behaviors. In future work we will experiment over realistic unbalanced data, by applying undersampling and skew insensitive measures. However, the real distribution for political affiliation is close to that of our sample, as shown in recent Twitter demographic studies [5]. For the graph-based component, we collect the list of friends for each user in the dataset. Overall, we found 2.7 million users, reduced to 1.2 millions by discarding those that posted less than 5 tweets in the considered Twitter corpus (see below).

Ethnicity. The ethnicity identification task consists in classifying users as either African-Americans or not. This choice is motivated by Quantcast statistics indicating that African-Americans are the most represented ethnicity among Twitter users with respect to the average internet population [17]. The statistics mean that automatically identifying users of this ethnicity can have benefits from multiple perspectives: linguistic and sociological (we can study the language, opinions or preoccupations of an important segment of the Twitter user population); for behavioral targeting applications (more focused marketing and ad targeting campaigns), if the previous analysis reveals that this segment of the user population has a set of unique interests.

We build the gold standard dataset by collecting users who explicitly mention their ethnicity in their profile, as described in Section 3.1. We then randomly sample 3000 African-American users (positive set) and 3000 users of other ethnicities (negative set). We performed a sanity check on the dataset and verified that the dataset is indeed a reliable gold standard. We then collect about 909K friends for the users in the dataset, reduced to 508K after the 5 tweets cut.

Starbucks fans. In addition to the more traditional user attribute identification tasks, we also consider the task of predicting whether a given user would likely follow a particular business. The task of identifying potential business customers is particularly attractive for ad targeting and marketing campaign design applications. For the purpose of this paper, we choose Starbucks, a business which attracts a large Twitter audience.

The gold standard dataset is composed of 5,000 positive examples, represented by a random sample of users who already follow Starbucks on Twitter, and 5000 negative examples represented by a sample of users following who do not. We finally collect about 1.9M friends for the users in the dataset, reduced to 981K after the 5 tweets cut.

Evaluation metrics. For all tasks we report Precision, Recall and F-measure. In the case of the political affiliation task, we also report the overall accuracy, since both positive and negative examples

[8]http://www.twellow.com

are classes of interest. We experiment in a 10-folds cross validation setting, to compute statistical significance.

System Configurations. We experiment with different instantiations of our architecture, as follows. ML: the architecture using only user-centric features in the machine learning component, i.e. setting $\alpha = 1$ in Eq. 4. GRAPH: the architecture using only social network information (the graph-based updating component, i.e. setting $\alpha = 0$). HYBRID: using both the machine learning component and graph updating with equal weight, i.e. $\alpha = 0.5$. These three configurations allow us to check if including graph-based information in the classification task is helpful.

The performance of the various systems is compared against two baselines. B2 is a generic reference baseline represented by our machine learning component trained only on the profile and tweeting behavior features (the basic information types readily available from Twitter). For each of the three tasks, B1 denotes a different task-specific baseline:

Political affiliation: B1 is a system which classifies as Democrats all users explicitly mentioning their Democratic/liberal political affiliation in the bio field (see Section 3.1) and proceeds the same for Republicans.

Ethnicity: B1 is an ideal system classifying users as African-Americans according to their profile picture. We simulate such a system by using the editorial annotations described in Section 3.1.

Starbucks fans: B1 is a system which classifies as Starbucks fans all the users who explicitly mention Starbucks in their bio field.

System and features setup. GBDT parameters were experimentally set as follows: number of trees=500, shrinkage= 0.01, max nodes per tree=10, sample rate=0.5. In the political affiliation task we use the full set of features. In the Starbucks and ethnicity tasks, we do not use SOC-FRIE, since these features would be intuitively difficult to apply. The set of controversial terms for LING-SENT is composed of 40 famous politicians (for the political affiliation task) and 30 popular African Americans (for the ethnicity task), semi-automatically harvested from Wikipedia. As for LING-WORD, SOC-REPL, SOC-RETW, SOC-FRIE, the list of seed users is derived from the training set of each fold. All features and models used in the experiments are computed on a Twitter firehose corpus spanning the September - October 2010 time period. All gold standard datasets described above contain users that were active in the considered time period by posting at least 5 tweets, and that posted at least 50% of their tweets in English.

5.1 Experimental results

Overall results for political affiliation, ethnicity and Starbucks fans are reported respectively in Tables 1 , 2 and 3. Table 4 reports the semi-automatically induced features, obtained by applying Eq. 1 as described in Section 3. Results show that our system generally achieves good precision and recall. However, results vary across tasks: identifying political affiliation labels can be done with very high accuracy. Classifying a user as a Starbucks fan can also be achieved with good performance, while identifying users of African-American ethnicity proves to be the most challenging task.

Political Affiliation. Our models perform best on the task of classifying a user as Democrat vs. Republican - both overall accuracy and class-specific performance measures have values above 0.80 (see Table 1). As expected, the baseline B1 has high precision but very low recall which makes the method less useful. All our system configurations largely outperform B1 in F-measure and accuracy. Also, the HYBRID system, combining the graph update function and the machine learning component using all available features, outperforms B2 in F-measure of +11% for Democrats, and +31% for Republicans. Since B2 is based only on profile and behavior features, this result suggests it is worthwhile to explore and implement sophisticated social and linguistic features, in order to obtain good classification results.

As we can see by comparing the performance of the HYBRID and ML systems, revising the ML-derived score by taking into account the scores of a test user's neighbors has a positive, but small effect on the final results; the improvements are consistent across measures and political affiliations, but not statistically significant. We attribute the magnitude of the effect to a hard-to-beat baseline (in the form of the ML system). For Democrats, the profile of the neighborhood is highly predictable - Democrats tend to consistently have a large percentage of friends with the same affiliation (as evidenced by both Figure 1 and by the precision and recall of the GRAPH system). For Republicans, the political affiliation of the neighbors is more mixed (e.g., Republican Twitter users tend to have friends - and followers - with both probable Republican and Democrat affiliations). Using the updating function alone (GRAPH) gives good performance, but significantly worse than ML, confirming that social graph information are helpful but not necessary.

Table 1 also shows that social features overall (SOC-ALL) and follower features (SOC-FRIE) in particular perform best, followed by the linguistic and profile features. Results also show that combining the high quality social features with linguistic, behavior and profile information (ML model) improves significantly over SOC-ALL alone of +2.6% accuracy, suggesting that these latter features add important value to the task. The feature importance values returned by the GBDT algorithm reveal that the 3 most discriminative features are from the SOC-FRIE set, but at the same time, among the first 20 features, 9 are linguistic and 5 behavioral/profile.

The high performance of social features is due to the typical characteristic of users interested in politics, of interacting with media or party personalities with an established Twitter presence, as those reported in the last three rows of Table 4. Linguistic features also have encouraging performance (especially, LING-DLDA, LING-WORD, LING-HASH) as different classes of users discuss either different topics or common topics in different ways, e.g., Republicans are passionate about different issues ("liberty") than Democrats ("inequality", "homophobia") and tend to use a specific vernacular ("obamacare") when discussing issues of interest to both sides (healthcare reform). Another reason for the good performance of linguistic features is the event of the November 2010 elections, which precipitated party-specific, get-out-the-vote messages and voting-related discussions showcased by the hashtag features in Table 4. We notice that class-specific topic models (LING-DLDA) outperform generic topic models (LING-GLDA); generic topic models define corse-grained topics shared by Republicans and Democrats, e.g. they inform us that users discuss the November 2010 elections (e.g, *news, delaware, o'donnell, christine*), while domain specific topics reveal items of specific interest for Republicans (*American, conservative, freedom*) vs. Democrats (*progressive, moveon, obama*), thus being more discriminative (see Table 5 for examples.)

Starbucks Fans. As seen in Table 2, deciding whether a user is a potential follower of Starbucks can be done with reasonable precision (0.764) and recall (0.756). The HYBRID system returns the best F-measure performance, though the improvement over the ML system is small and not statistically significant, this again indicating that revising the ML test user scores based on the scores is helpful to a certain extent. The correlation between the test user ML score and the scores of her neighbors for this task is not as strong as in the case of the political affiliation task, as seen both in Figure 2 and

System	Democrats			Republicans			All
	PREC	REC	F-MEAS	PREC	REC	F-MEAS	ACC
B1	**0.989**	0.183	0.308	**0.920**	0.114	0.203	0.478
B2	0.735	0.896	0.808	0.702	0.430	0.533	0.727
BEHAV-ALL	0.663	0.774†	0.714†	0.436	0.307†	0.360†	0.605†
PROF-ALL	0.728	0.808†	0.765†	0.582	0.468$^{\flat}$	0.517†	0.684†
SOC-REPL	0.671	0.988$^{\flat}$	0.799†	0.876‡	0.148†	0.252†	0.684†
SOC-RETW	0.651	0.992$^{\flat}$	0.786†	0.833‡	0.060	0.115	0.656†
SOC-FRIE	0.857‡	0.933$^{\flat}$	0.893$^{\flat}$	0.860‡	0.726$^{\flat}$	0.787$^{\flat}$	0.858$^{\flat}$
SOC-ALL	0.863‡	0.932$^{\flat}$	0.896$^{\flat}$	0.862‡	0.741$^{\flat}$	0.796$^{\flat}$	0.863$^{\flat}$
LING-HASH	0.688	0.980$^{\flat}$	0.808†	0.861‡	0.216†	0.345†	0.703†
LING-WORD	0.745	0.885†	0.808†	0.697	0.466†	0.558†	0.733†
LING-GLDA	0.723	0.790†	0.755†	0.559	0.468$^{\flat}$	0.509†	0.674†
LING-DLDA	0.798‡	0.838†	0.817†	0.688	0.627$^{\flat}$	0.656$^{\flat}$	0.761$^{\flat}$
LING-SENT	0.707	0.897†	0.791†	0.658	0.346†	0.453†	0.698†
LING-ALL	0.804‡	0.847†	0.825$^{\flat}$	0.702	0.636$^{\flat}$	0.668$^{\flat}$	0.770$^{\flat}$
ML	0.893‡	0.927$^{\flat}$	0.910$^{\flat}$	0.863‡	0.805$^{\flat}$	0.833$^{\flat}$	0.883$^{\flat}$
GRAPH	0.844‡	**0.938**$^{\flat}$	0.888$^{\flat}$	0.865‡	0.695$^{\flat}$	0.770$^{\flat}$	0.850$^{\flat}$
HYBRID	0.895‡	0.936$^{\flat}$	**0.915**$^{\flat}$	0.878‡	**0.806**$^{\flat}$	**0.840**$^{\flat}$	**0.889**$^{\flat}$

Table 1: Overall classification results for the political affiliation task. †, ‡ and ♭ respectively indicate statistical significance at the 0.95 level wrt B1 alone, B2 alone, and both B1 and B2.

System	PREC	REC	F-MEAS
B1	**0.817**	0.019	0.038
B2	0.747	0.723	0.735
BEHAV-ALL	0.583	0.613†	0.597†
PROF-ALL	0.746	0.723†	0.735†
SOC-REPL	0.511	0.979$^{\flat}$	0.671†
SOC-RETW	0.502	**0.995**$^{\flat}$	0.667†
SOC-ALL	0.532	0.885$^{\flat}$	0.613†
LING-HASH	0.528	0.950$^{\flat}$	0.678†
LING-WORD	0.585	0.660†	0.619†
LING-GLDA	0.602	0.642†	0.620†
LING-DLDA	0.614	0.660†	0.636†
LING-SENT	0.700	0.125	0.211†
LING-ALL	0.628	0.660†	0.643†
ML	0.760	0.752$^{\flat}$	0.755$^{\flat}$
GRAPH	0.706	0.702†	0.695†
HYBRID	0.764	0.756†	**0.758**$^{\flat}$

Table 2: Overall classification results for the Starbucks fan task. †, ‡ and ♭ respectively indicate statistical significance at the 0.95 level wrt B1 alone, B2 alone, and both B1 and B2.

System	PREC	REC	F-MEAS
B1	**0.878**	0.421	0.569
B2	0.579	0.633	0.604
BEHAV-ALL	0.534	0.496†	0.514
PROF-ALL	0.578	0.643†	0.609†
SOC-REPL	0.813‡	0.090	0.161
SOC-RETW	0.709‡	0.061	0.112
SOC-ALL	0.671‡	0.367	0.474
LING-HASH	0.792‡	0.127	0.218
LING-WORD	0.671‡	0.333	0.445
LING-SENT	0.597	0.254	0.355
LING-GLDA	0.625‡	0.602†	0.613†
LING-DLDA	0.645‡	0.640†	0.642$^{\flat}$
LING-ALL	0.655‡	0.641†	0.647$^{\flat}$
ML	0.629‡	**0.799**$^{\flat}$	**0.703**$^{\flat}$
GRAPH	0.604‡	0.621†	0.611†
HYBRID	0.630‡	0.753$^{\flat}$	0.686$^{\flat}$

Table 3: Overall classification results for the ethnicity task. †, ‡ and ♭ respectively indicate statistical significance at the 0.95 level wrt B1 alone, B2 alone, and both B1 and B2.

in the performance of the GRAPH system. This result is to be expected, as the preference for a particular business in itself is a very specific, low-level attribute for a user while a political affiliation label is a more encompassing, broader attribute which is a more probable basis for community building. Additionally, our graph-based update is itself affected by the quality of the scores assigned to the neighbors of a test user - this quality is not as high as in the case of the political affiliation task, introducing additional noise.

Regarding the different features of the machine learning system, results show that *profile* and *linguistic* information are the most helpful features. Profile features alone achieve performance close to the ML system. A look at the most discriminative features for GBDT reveals that the ratio between followers and friends is the most relevant feature, suggesting that Starbucks afficionados are users that follow others more than they are followed: they are mostly *information seekers*, e.g. probably people looking for deals. Both social and linguistic features do not offer performance as good as in the political affiliation task. This is probably due to the fact Starbucks fans are a very heterogeneous demographic group (as also the lists in Table 4 suggest), thus diluting the potential of prototype-based feature (e.g. LING-WORD and SOC-FRIE). Within the set of linguistic features, LING-HASH and LING-DLDA perform best overall, while sentiment features LING-SENT have the highest precision but a very low recall. This result is due to two facts: the

Dominant class	Topic words
Democrats	anti, rights, justice, protest, reform
Republicans	america, country, conservative, constitution, tea
Republicans	tax, economy, spending, cuts, stimulus
Democrats	progressive, moveon, thinkprogress, corporations

Table 5: Examples of highly discriminative topics from LING-DLDA for the political affiliation task, with the dominant class .

fact that LING-SENT look at the sentiment attached by users to the word "Starbucks"; and the nature of Twitter accounts. On average, people mention the name of a particular business only sporadically, as the focus of the communication is mostly on personal developments, news tracking and sharing, etc. Under these circumstances, features which analyze in depth the user's account become even more important (hence the good performance of PROF-ALL).

Ethnicity. The classification of African-American proves to be the most challenging task, as shown in Table 3. The ML has the best F-measure, significantly better than the HYBRID system; while the precision remains basically the same, the recall drops significantly. As we can see from the low-recall and F-measure numbers for the GRAPH system, using neighborhood information to predict the class membership of a test user is not very promising. Part of the problem is the imbalance in the real Twitter data for the target class; an additional aspect is the fact that African-American Twitter users are not a closed community, but rather connect to users of other ethnicities as well. We are again in the presence of an attribute which is not necessarily, by itself, the basis for community forming.

Regarding the different machine learning features, linguistic ones (LING-ALL) prove to perform best. Within the set of linguistic features, LING-HASH and LING-WORD have the highest precision (albeit low-recall); Table 4 shows examples of the lexical usage (e.g., "betta", "brotha") and issues or entities (e.g. "jeezy", aka "Young Jeezy") in African-American user accounts which can help our automatic classification system. However, personalities and lexical usages which were once the province of the African-American community have long gained adoption by other groups, which leads to linguistic features being useful only up to a point for our task. LDA models are once again the most balanced in P/R, showing the highest f-measure. For this classification task, topics mostly capture lexical usage, e.g. one topic is (*gettin, watchin, tryna, finna*) and popular celebrities, e.g. (*beyonce, smith, usher, kanyewest, atlanta*). We find that the task can also be helped by profile information (e.g. African Americans tend to have longer bio descriptions), but best classification performance is only achieved by combining the different classes of features.

Final observations. As a general comment, we note that the machine learning component alone achieves good performance, without the need of the social graph information embodied in the graph update function. Indeed, graph-based information seems helpful (to a small extent) only in the case of attributes such as political affiliation, for which a user may seek to connect with others which share the same conviction. Attributes such as the preference for a specific business or product and, finally, ethnicity are either too specific or too broad to alone be the basis for a connection. In such cases, graph-based information is not particularly helpful and can even hurt. Our experiments with neighborhood-based updates underscore the importance of a comprehensive ML model which can address the case of attributes not correlated with community building or the case of users with a small or inactive neighborhood. Conversely, we see that for some attributes (e.g., political affiliation), graph-based information alone can be used to confidently predict the class label for users with a shorter/sparser message history as long as they have some connections to other more active users.

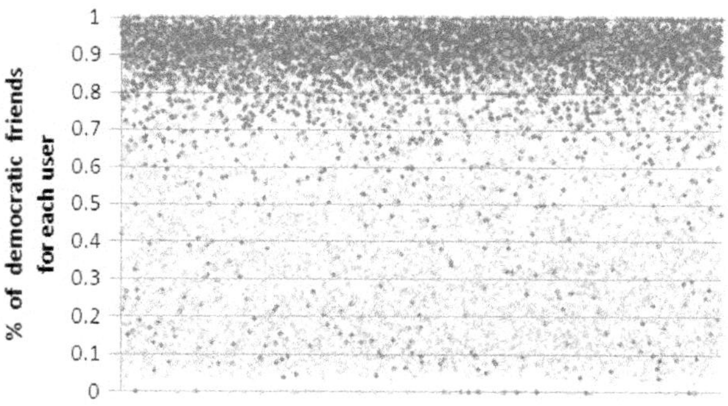

Figure 1: Percentage of friends that are Democrats for each user in the 'political affiliation' task. Black dots are Democratic users, gray dots are Republican users.

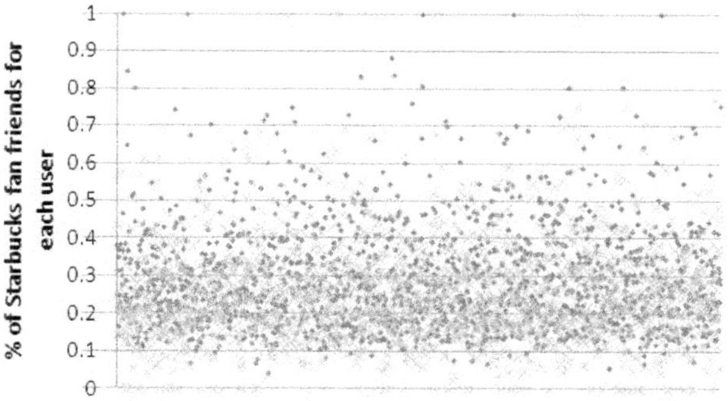

Figure 2: Percentage of friends that are Starbucks fan for each user in the 'Starbucks fan' task. Black dots are Starbucks fan users, gray dots are non Starbucks fan users.

A second important general conclusion is that linguistic features, especially topic-based LDA, are consistently reliable across all tasks, thus indicating an encouraging level of robustness and fostering further research in this area. Profile features are also quite stable across tasks, though their performance is not comparable to that of linguistic ones. Explicit social network features may be valuable in some tasks (though expensive to collect), especially when the user class of interest is rich in celebrities with which a user may connect.

6. CONCLUSIONS AND FUTURE WORK

This paper described a large-scale architecture for *user classification* in social media and extensive quantitative and qualitative results for three Twitter user classification tasks. We showed that: user classification is in general a feasible task, though results vary across different classes; a machine learning algorithm using user-centric features achieves alone good performance that is hard to improve by enriching the classification with social graph information; most machine learning features are general enough to be used in different classification and linguistic features show especially robust performance across tasks.

We are currently working on deploying and testing our models in

Features	DEMOCRATS	REPUBLICANS	AFRICAN-AMERICANS	STARBUCKS FANS
LING-WORD	inequality, homophobia, woody, socialism	obamacare, liberty, taxpayer, patriots	betta, brotha, finna, jeezy	mocha, recipes, dining, espresso
LING-HASH	#itgetsbetter, #VOTE2010, #ProgCa, #voteDem	#cagop, #ConsNC, #ObamaTVShows, #RememberNovember	#sadtweet, #pissed, #PSA, #teamdroid	#Yelp!, #iPhone, #Starbucks
SOC-REPL	txvoodoo, polipaca, liberalcrone, socratic	itsonlywords, glenasbury, RickSmall, astroterf	MonicaMyLife, serenawilliams, RayJ, MissyElliott	GoldenMiley,Heyitsmimila_, Aerocles, GoodCharlotte
SOC-RETW	ebertchicago, BarackObama, KeithOlbermann, GottaLaff	Drudge_Report, michellemalkin, fredthompson, mikepfs	WatchJ, DeRayDavis, TiaMowry, KDthunderup	TheBieberFun, Nordstrom, Starbucks, Orbitz, WholeFoods
SOC-FRIE	Michelle Malkin, Heritage Foundation, Glenn Beck, Newt Gingrich	Barack Obama, Rachel Maddow, Al Gore, Keith Olbermann		

Table 4: Example of automatically induced features LING-WORD,LING-HASH,SOC-REPL,SOC-RETW **and** SOC-FRIE.

a real-time, Twitter-based content aggregation and display application. Our user classification architecture will help in improving the user engagement with the application. An example use case involves the application being given a query (e.g., "Cairo protests") and retrieving high quality recent content from both Twitter and the Web at large about the anti-government protests in Egypt. Our architecture will help highlight content shared by users of particular political persuasions (e.g., Democrats vs. Republicans), as well as highlight authoritative users with opposing political views. Our architecture will also support the automatic analysis of the overall mood of a particular user class in conjunction with the topic at hand. In the longer term, we plan to integrate the user classification models into systems for content display personalization, which would benefit from knowing the profiles of users who create or share the displayed information.

7. REFERENCES

[1] L. Barbosa and F. J. Robust Sentiment Detection on Twitter from Biased and Noisy Data. In *Proceedings of COLING*, 2010.

[2] F. Benevenuto, G. Magno, T. Rodrigues, and V. Almeida. Detecting Spammers on Twitter. In *Proceedings of CEAS*, 2010.

[3] D. Blei, A. Ng, and M. Jordan. Latent Dirichlet Allocation. *JMLR*, (3):993–1022, 2002.

[4] J. Burger and J. Henderson. An exploration of observable features related to blogger age. In *Computational Approaches to Analyzing Weblogs*, pages 710–718, 2010.

[5] Burson-Marsteller. Press Releases Archives. In *Archive of Sept 10, 2010.*

[6] Z. Cheng, J. Caverlee, and K. Lee. You are where you tweet: A Content-based Approach to Geo-locating Twitter Users. In *Proceedings of CIKM*, 2010.

[7] J. H. Friedman. Greedy function approximation: A gradient boosting machine. *Annals of Statistics*, 29(5):1189–1232, 2001.

[8] J. H. Friedman. Recent Advances in Predictive (Machine) Learning. *Journal of Classification*, 23(2):175–197, 2006.

[9] N. Garera and D. Yarovsky. Modeling latent biographic attributes in conversational genres. In *Proceedings of CIKM*, 2007.

[10] S. Herring and J. Paolillo. Gender and genre variation in weblogs. In *Journal of Sociolinguistics*, pages 710–718, 2010.

[11] A. Java, X. Song, T. Finin, and B. Tseng. Why we twitter: understanding microblogging usage and communities. In *Proceedings of the 9th WebKDD and 1st SNA-KDD*, 2007.

[12] R. Jones, R. Kumar, B. Pang, and A. Tomkins. I Know What you Did Last Summer - Query Logs and User Privacy. In *Proceedings of CIKM*, 2007.

[13] S. Kim and E. Hovy. CRYSTAL: Analyzing Predictive Opinions on the Web. In *Proceedings of EMNLP*, 2007.

[14] J. Otterbacher. Inferring Gender of Movie Reviewers: Exploiting Writing Style, Content and Metadata. In *Proceedings of CIKM*, 2010.

[15] M. Pasca. What you seek is what you get: Extraction of class attributes from query logs. In *Proceedings of IJCAI*, 2007.

[16] M. Pennacchiotti and S. Gurumurthy. Investigating Topic Models for Social Media User Recommendation. In *Proceedings of WWW*, 2011.

[17] Quantcast. Report May 2010. In *http://www.quantcast.com/twitter.com*, 2010.

[18] D. Ramage, S. Dumais, and D. Liebling. Characterizing Microblogs with Topic Models. In *Proceedings of ICWSM*, 2010.

[19] D. Rao, Y. D., A. Shreevats, and M. Gupta. Classifying Latent User Attributes in Twitter. In *Proceedings of SMUC-10*, pages 710–718, 2010.

[20] A. Ritter, C. Cherry, and B. Dolan. Unsupervised Modeling of Twitter Conversations. In *Proceedings of HLT-NAACL*, 2010.

[21] A. Smola and S. Narayanamurthy. An architecture for parallel topic models. In *Proceedings of VLDB*, 2010.

[22] S. Somasundaran and J. Wiebe. Recognizing Stances in Ideological On-Line Debates. In *Proceedings of NAACL-HLT Workshop on Computational Approaches to Analysis and Generation of Emotion in Text*, pages 116–124, 2010.

[23] M. Thomas, B. Pang, and L. Lee. Get out the vote: determining support or opposition from congressional floor-debate transcripts. In *Proceedings of EMNLP*, 2006.

[24] I. Weber and C. Castillo. The Demographics of Web Search. In *Proceedings of SIGIR*, 2010.

[25] J. Wiebe, T. Wilson, and C. Cardie. Annotating expressions of opinions and emotions in language. In *Language Resources and Evaluation*, pages 165–210, 2005.

[26] J. Ye, C. Jyh-Herng, C. Jang, and Z. Zhaohui. Stochastic gradient boosted distributed decision trees. In *Proceedings of CIKM*, 2009.

Beyond Keyword Search: Discovering Relevant Scientific Literature

Khalid El-Arini
Computer Science Department
Carnegie Mellon University
kbe@cs.cmu.edu

Carlos Guestrin
Machine Learning Department
Carnegie Mellon University
guestrin@cs.cmu.edu

ABSTRACT

In scientific research, it is often difficult to express information needs as simple keyword queries. We present a more natural way of searching for relevant scientific literature. Rather than a string of keywords, we define a query as a small set of papers deemed relevant to the research task at hand. By optimizing an objective function based on a fine-grained notion of influence between documents, our approach efficiently selects a set of highly relevant articles. Moreover, as scientists trust some authors more than others, results are personalized to individual preferences. In a user study, researchers found the papers recommended by our method to be more useful, trustworthy and diverse than those selected by popular alternatives, such as Google Scholar and a state-of-the-art topic modeling approach.

Categories and Subject Descriptors

G.3 [**Mathematics of Computing**]: Probability and Statistics; H.3.3 [**Information Storage and Retrieval**]: Information Search and Retrieval—*query formulation,relevance feedback,retrieval models*

General Terms

Algorithms,Experimentation

Keywords

personalization, citation analysis

1. INTRODUCTION

For generations, scientists have built upon the published work of their predecessors and contemporaries in order to make new discoveries. However, as the number of publications has grown, it has become increasingly difficult for scientists to find relevant prior work for their particular research. In fact, as early as 1755, the French philosopher Denis Diderot presciently forewarned that there would come a day when "it will be almost as convenient to search for some bit of truth concealed in nature as it will be to find it hidden away in an immense multitude of bound volumes," [13]. Today, we can quantify this "immense multitude" to include tens of millions of articles published in tens of thousands of journals and conferences [43].

Currently, researchers primarily rely on keyword search of online indices such as Google Scholar and PubMed to help them combat this overload of information. While these tools are indispensable, there are many instances where a researcher's information need cannot be easily specified as a simple string of keywords. Often, such a keyword query is either overly broad, returning many articles that are at best loosely related to the researcher's specific need, or too narrow, potentially returning no articles at all. In these occasions, it may be more natural for the scientist to specify his query as a small set of papers rather than as a set of words. In particular, having already read some articles that are related to the specific task at hand, the scientist can ask, "given that these papers represent my immediate research focus, what else should I read?".

Here, we present an algorithm for discovering relevant scientific literature by responding to queries of this form. More formally, given a small set of papers $\mathcal{Q}$ that we refer to as the *query set*, we seek to return a set $\mathcal{A}$ of additional papers that are related to the concept defined by the query. Intuitively, a paper that cites all of the articles in $\mathcal{Q}$ is likely to represent related research. Likewise, a paper that is cited by every article in $\mathcal{Q}$ might contain relevant background information. However, it is restrictive to require the papers in $\mathcal{A}$ to have a direct citation to or from every article in the query set, as such papers are not guaranteed to exist. Instead, we wish to select a set $\mathcal{A}$ that maximizes a more general notion of *influence* to and from the papers in $\mathcal{Q}$.

2. MODELING SCIENTIFIC INFLUENCE

To define a notion of influence in scientific literature, we observe that the content of a publication is an amalgam of several sources, combining cited prior work with the authors' novel insights and background experience. For a given collection of articles, ideas travel *from cited papers to citing papers*, and from earlier to subsequent papers by the same author (Figure 1A). Our notion of influence should capture this transfer of ideas, modeling both the extent to which ideas travel between documents, as well as their topical matter. To achieve such fine-grained detail, we define influence with respect to the *individual concepts* found in a document collection, which could be, e.g., technical terms or informa-

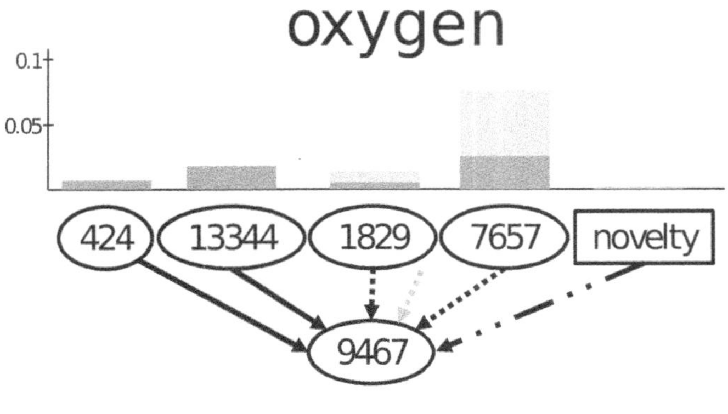

Figure 2: An example from the PNAS data set, illustrating the edge weight computation for a node in G_{oxygen}. Solid black edges indicate citations, while dotted black edges indicate common authorship. The dotted gray edge refers to a paper sharing an author with 9467, but not containing the concept "oxygen." Edge weights are assigned proportional to the bar chart, indicating the prevalence of "oxygen" in each parent node. The bars over 1829 and 7657 are shortened to one third of their original height (indicated in light gray), such that the contribution due to common authorship is equivalent to that of a single paper. The novelty node is only used to normalize the edge weights, and in this case is dominated in influence by the other articles.

tive phrases.[1] For example, we might say that the ideas transferred from one paper to another involve the concepts "energy" or "nitric oxide."

For each concept c in our vocabulary of concepts $\mathcal{C}$, we define a directed, acyclic graph G_c, where the nodes represent papers that contain c and the edges represent citations and common authorship. Figures 1B and 1C show two such graphs for a subset of articles from the Proceedings of the National Academy of Sciences (PNAS), for the concepts "plant" and "stress." While a path between two nodes in such a graph may indicate influence with respect to a particular concept, mere existence of a path does little to express the *degree* to which this influence occurs. To capture the degree of influence, we define a weight $\theta^{(c)}_{x\to y}$ for each edge (x, y) in graph G_c, representing the probability of *direct* influence from paper x to paper y with respect to concept c. We can then use these edge weights to define a probabilistic, concept-specific notion of influence between any two papers in the document collection.

2.1 Defining edge weights

Figure 2 shows an example from the PNAS data set illustrating how we define the weight $\theta^{(c)}_{x\to y}$ on each edge. Here, article 9467 cites two articles containing the concept "oxygen," $\{424, 13344\}$, indicated by the solid black edges. The dotted black edges indicate that two other articles, $\{1829, 7657\}$, contain the concept "oxygen" and share authors with 9467. (The dotted gray edge indicates that there is a third article sharing authors with 9467 that *does not* contain "oxygen.") We assume that every occurrence of the concept "oxygen" in 9467 is either a novel idea or is directly inspired by one of these sources. Thus, we view the weight $\theta^{(c)}_{x\to y}$ as the probability a random instance of concept c in paper y was directly inspired by paper x.

The bar graph over the nodes in Figure 2 illustrates the proportion of the content of each paper consisting of the "oxygen" concept. For instance, the height of the first bar on the left is $n^{(oxygen)}_{424}/N_{424}$, where $n^{(c)}_x$ is the frequency of concept c in document x, and $N_x = \sum_{c\in\mathcal{C}} n^{(c)}_x$ is the total length of document x. Additionally, the bars over 1829 and 7657 are shortened to one third of their original height (indicated in light gray), representing the intuition that an explicit citation is a more informative relationship than common authorship. The authors of 9467 have three prior publications in this example, and thus by dividing by three, the effective total contribution of these papers is that of a single paper. Finally, we represent the novelty distribution for a particular paper y as the average distribution over concepts for all papers published in the same year as y. In this case, the novelty contribution for "oxygen" is dominated by the four papers. (We note that there are no actual novelty nodes in the graph, as the associated distribution is only used for normalization.)

Here, $\theta^{(oxygen)}_{x\to 9467}$ is proportional to the height of the corresponding bar in the plot. More generally, if a paper y cites papers $\{r_1, \ldots, r_k\}$, and the authors have previously written papers $\{b_1, \ldots, b_l\}$, then the edge weights are defined as follows:

$$\theta^{(c)}_{r_i\to y} = \frac{1}{Z}\frac{n^{(c)}_{r_i}}{N_{r_i}},$$

$$\theta^{(c)}_{b_i\to y} = \frac{1}{Z}\frac{n^{(c)}_{b_i}}{l\cdot N_{b_i}},$$

with normalization constant,

$$Z = \sum_{j=1}^{k}\frac{n^{(c)}_{r_j}}{N_{r_j}} + \frac{1}{l}\sum_{j=1}^{l}\frac{n^{(c)}_{b_j}}{N_{b_j}} + novel^{(c)}_y,$$

where $novel^{(c)}_y$ is the average proportion of concept c across all papers published in the same year as y.

2.2 Calculating influence

Given a concept-specific weight for each edge in the citation graph, representing the *direct* influence between two neighboring nodes, we can now define the influence between any two papers in our collection. In particular, if we say that each edge $x \to y$ in G_c is *active* with some probability $\theta^{(c)}_{x\to y}$, we arrive at the following definition:

DEFINITION 1. *The influence between papers u and v with respect to concept c, $Influence_c(u \leftrightarrow v)$, is the probability there exists a directed path in G_c from one paper to the other, consisting only of active edges.*

While intuitive, the exact computation of this probability is intractable, as the problem of computing connectedness in a random graph belongs to the #P-complete class of computational problems [45, 37], for which there are no known polynomial-time solutions. We can overcome this computational hurdle via approximation, by employing one of two methods: 1) a simple Monte Carlo sampling procedure with theoretical guarantees; and, 2) a deterministic, linear-time

[1]For our experiments, we use a simple tf-idf heuristic to extract informative words which we use as concepts (cf. [15]).

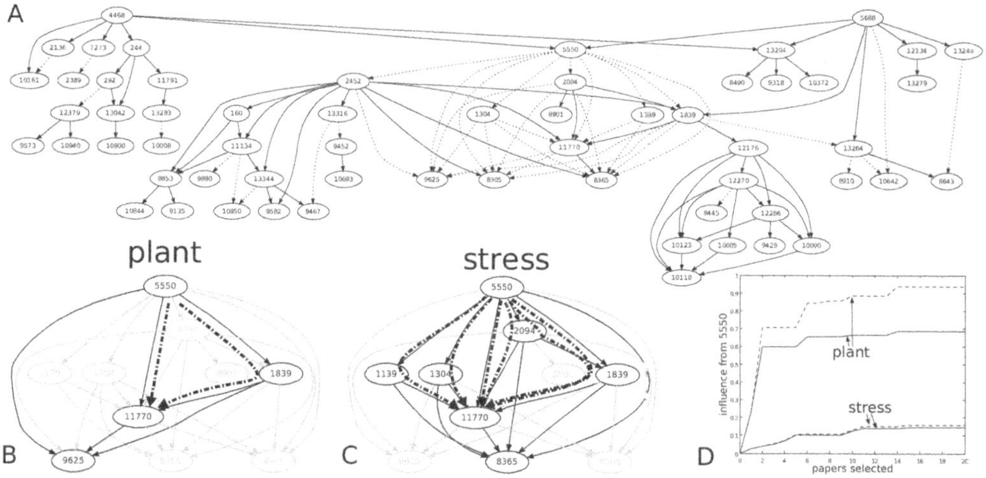

Figure 1: (A) A graph of articles from the Proceedings of the National Academy of Sciences (PNAS). Nodes represent papers, solid edges represent citations ($x \to y$ if y cites x) and dotted edges represent common authorship ($x \to y$ if x is older than y and x, y share an author). More details on the data sets used in this paper can be found in the technical report [15]. (B,C) Subgraphs of (A), limited to papers containing the concepts "plant" and "stress," respectively (other papers are grayed out). Thick dashed lines indicate paths of influence between papers 5550 and 11770. (D) Example illustrating how Equation 1 penalizes redundancy. The first two papers selected exhibit a high influence with respect to "plant," and thus subsequently adding such papers to $\mathcal{A}$ causes little increase in Equation 1 (solid lines), especially when compared to the sum of individual influences (dashed lines). The influence with respect to "stress" remains low, thus never triggering such a redundancy penalty.

dynamic programming heuristic, based on the assumption that the paths between two nodes are independent of each other.

2.2.1 *Sampling*

The simplest procedure for estimating the influence between two nodes is to generate samples directly based on the definition of influence. Each sample is generated as follows:

For each concept c:

1. Mark each edge $x \to y$ in G_c as active with probability $\theta^{(c)}_{x \to y}$.
2. For all pairs of nodes (u, v), record whether a path exists between them using only active edges.

After generating B samples, the probability that a node u influences a node v with respect to concept c is simply estimated as the proportion of the B samples for concept c in which an active path from u to v exists. A natural question to ask is, how many samples do we need for a reasonable estimate of influence? A short proof using Hoeffding's Inequality–found in the technical report [15]–shows us that the number of samples we need grows only *logarithmically* with the number of articles in the document collection.

THEOREM 1. *In order to estimate m influence values such that, with probability η, each of the m estimates is no more than δ away from its true value, a sufficient number of samples B is $\frac{2}{\delta^2}\log(2m/\delta)$.*

As the number of influence values to estimate is quadratic in the number of articles, the number of samples we need is logarithmic in the total number of articles. While this is a heartening result, we find that for large document collections, generating enough samples can still be a time-consuming process.

2.2.2 *Independence heuristic*

As an alternative to sampling, we describe an efficient dynamic programming heuristic based on the assumption that the paths between two nodes in G_c are independent of each other. For instance, in Figure 1B, the two influence paths between 5550 and 11770 with respect to the concept "plant" are completely independent of each other. Thus, the probability of at least one active path existing between the two nodes in this situation can be computed exactly:

$$\begin{aligned}
&\mathit{Influence}_{plant}(5550 \to 11770) \\
&\quad= 1 - P(\text{there is no influence between 5550 and 11770}) \\
&\quad= 1 - P(\text{there is no direct influence from 5550}) \cdot \\
&\qquad P(\text{there is no influence through 1839}) \\
&\quad= 1 - (1 - \theta^{(plant)}_{5550 \to 11770})(1 - \theta^{(plant)}_{5550 \to 1839}\theta^{(plant)}_{1839 \to 11770}).
\end{aligned}$$

The second equality follows from the independence of the two paths. On the other hand, looking at Figure 1C, we find the paths between the two nodes in G_{stress} are not independent, making such a calculation more problematic.

Based on this intuition, if we rashly assume that the paths between two nodes will *always* be independent of each other in G_c, for all c, we arrive at a simple, efficient heuristic for computing the influence between all pairs of nodes (Algorithm 1). By traversing the graph in topological order, we know that when we arrive at a node we will have already computed all the influence going to its parents. Using these influences and our independence assumption, we can then immediately compute the influence to the node itself. We note that this algorithm requires the graphs to be acyclic.[2]

[2]Based on simple chronology, one would expect a citation graph to be acyclic; after all, a researcher cannot cite a paper

Algorithm 1 Dynamic Programming Heuristic for Influence

```
N: number of documents
C: vocabulary of concepts
// Initialize to empty 3D array
// influenceEstimate[c][x][y] will contain influence
//    from x to y with respect to concept c.
influenceEstimate ← array[|C|][N][N]
for all c ∈ C do
  for all nodes y in G_c do
    // Initialize to identity
    influenceEstimate[c][y][y] ← 1
  topoOrder ← topological order of nodes in G_c
  for y ∈ topoOrder do
    // influenceEstimate[c][][x] already calculated
    //    for all x ∈ parents(y)
    if parents(y) = ∅ then
      continue
    influenceFromParents ← array[|parents(y)|]
    for all x ∈ parents(y) do
      // Influence to the parent multiplied by
      //    the edge weight
      influenceFromParents[x] ←
          influenceEstimate[c][][x] · θ^(c)_{x→y}
    // Product is element-wise
    influenceEstimate[c][][y] ←
        1−∏_{x∈parents(y)}(1−influenceFromParents[x])
```

While the independence assumption upon which this heuristic is based certainly is not true in general, we find that, nevertheless, the values we compute are close to what we would expect from sampling. (Empirical results to this effect can be found in the technical report [15].) Thus, despite not being amenable to theoretical guarantees, we find this heuristic works well in practice.

2.3 Selecting papers

As motivated in Section 1, given a query set of papers $\mathcal{Q}$, we wish to select a small set of related papers $\mathcal{A}$ that exhibit a high degree of *influence* to or from the query set. Moreover, the set of papers we select should be both *relevant* and *diverse*.

2.3.1 Relevance

The influence between the query set $\mathcal{Q}$ and the result set $\mathcal{A}$ should be focused on the concepts that are important or prevalent in both sets of documents. First, to ensure that the selected documents pertain to the concepts most prevalent in the query set, we define a weight $\gamma_q^{(c)}$ proportional to the frequency of concept c in query document q.

Likewise, from the perspective of the result set, a document d might contain a single occurrence of the concept "plant," and that single occurrence might be heavily influenced by one of the query documents q. However, as d only tangentially mentions "plant," we do not wish this strong influence to incentivize its inclusion in the result set. Thus, we define a probability $\beta_d^{(c)}$ indicating the importance of concept c in document d. Specifically, we define this as the probability a concept c is observed in a finite number ℓ of independent samples (with replacement) from the document's word distribution: $\beta_d^{(c)} = 1 - (1 - \gamma_d^{(c)})^{\ell}$. (Here, ℓ is a parameter of our model that we set to 20 in our experiments.) Figure 3 provides an illustrative example of these weights.

2.3.2 Diversity

Diversity is important in this setting as it is difficult to predict the exact information need of a researcher, and thus providing a wide variety of papers increases the likelihood of query satisfaction. As such, we define the influence between a single query paper $q \in \mathcal{Q}$ and a set of documents $\mathcal{A}$ in a manner that penalizes redundancy in the result set, thereby promoting diversity. Specifically, if we define this *set influence*, $\mathit{Influence}_c(q \leftrightarrow \mathcal{A})$, as the probability influence exists between q and *at least one* document in $\mathcal{A}$, we create a disincentive for $\mathcal{A}$ to contain multiple papers with similar influence patterns to and from q; such a redundant set $\mathcal{A}$ would exhibit less influence than one composed of a broader set of documents. Formally,

$$\mathit{Influence}_c(q \leftrightarrow \mathcal{A}) = 1 - \prod_{d \in \mathcal{A}} \left(1 - \mathit{Influence}_c(q \leftrightarrow d)\beta_d^{(c)}\right). \quad (1)$$

We note the use of the probability $\beta_d^{(c)}$ here to safeguard against selecting documents that are only tangentially related to the important concepts in the query papers.

Figure 1D shows an example illustrating how the marginal gain in set influence with respect to the concept "plant" diminishes as more papers are added to the result set $\mathcal{A}$. In particular, beyond a certain level of influence, the gain observed in Equation 1 from adding additional documents to the result set is smaller than would be expected if we were naïvely summing the individual influences. We do not see the same redundancy penalty with respect to "stress," as the result set is not sufficiently influenced with respect to this concept.

2.3.3 Optimization

Given this definition of set influence, we can now define an objective function that, when maximized, returns a diverse set of papers highly relevant to the query:

$$F_{\mathcal{Q}}(\mathcal{A}) = \sum_{q \in \mathcal{Q}} \sum_{c \in \mathcal{C}} \gamma_q^{(c)} \mathit{Influence}_c(q \leftrightarrow \mathcal{A}). \quad (2)$$

While, in general, solving such a combinatorial optimization problem is intractable, Equation 2 exhibits an intuitive diminishing returns property known as *submodularity*, allowing for efficient near-optimal solutions.

DEFINITION 2 (SUBMODULARITY). *A set function F is submodular if,* $\forall \mathcal{A} \subseteq \mathcal{B} \subseteq \mathcal{V}, \forall s \in \mathcal{V} \setminus \mathcal{B}, F(\mathcal{A} \cup \{s\}) - F(\mathcal{A}) \geq F(\mathcal{B} \cup \{s\}) - F(\mathcal{B})$.

Intuitively, this means that the utility of adding a particular paper to a result set decreases as the result set gets larger.

THEOREM 2. *Equation 2 is submodular and monotonic.*

The proof can be found in the technical report [15].

if it does not yet exist. However, this is not quite the case in practice (e.g., colleagues writing papers simultaneously may cite each other). Details on how we address this problem can be found in the technical report [15].

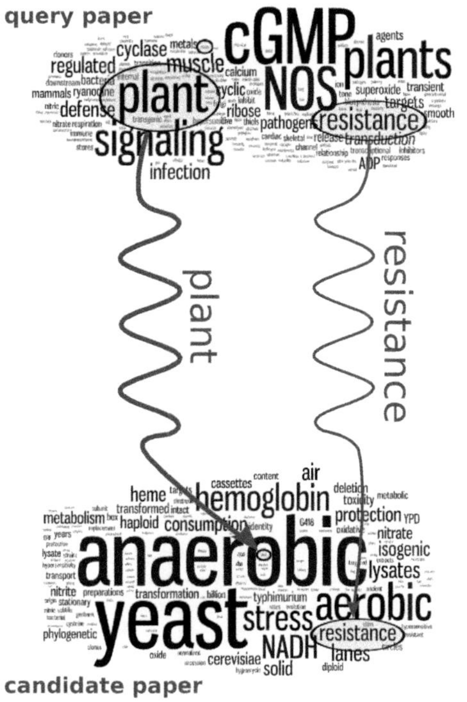

Figure 3: The top cloud represents a query paper (5550), the bottom word cloud represents a paper to be selected (11770) and the lines between them represent individual influences of varying strength. In each word cloud, the size of a word is proportional to its frequency in the corresponding article. γ is illustrated by the shaded ellipses in the top word cloud, showing a higher incentive to pick articles about "plant" or "resistance" than about "stress." However, despite its prevalence in the query document, "plant" is only tangentially present in article 11770, and thus β ensures a low degree of influence. This can be contrasted with "resistance," which is prevalent in both documents and displays a high degree of influence.

Although maximizing submodular functions is NP-hard [26], by discovering this property in our problem, we can take advantage of several efficient approximation algorithms with theoretical guarantees. For example, the classic result of Nemhauser et al. [31] shows that by simply applying a greedy algorithm to maximize our objective function, we can obtain a $(1 - \frac{1}{e})$ approximation of the optimal value. Thus, a simple greedy optimization can provide us with a near-optimal solution. However, since our set of articles is very large, a naïve greedy approach can be too costly. Therefore, we use CELF [29], which provides the same approximation guarantees, but uses lazy evaluations, often leading to dramatic speedups.

3. TRUST AND PERSONALIZATION

Considering our running example of PNAS articles (Figure 1A), we can set our query set to be $\mathcal{Q} = \{4468, 5688\}$, the parents of "Nitric Oxide in Plant Immunity" (5550). Optimizing Equation 2 for this query produces a result set of articles ranging in topics from plant biology to immunology (cf.

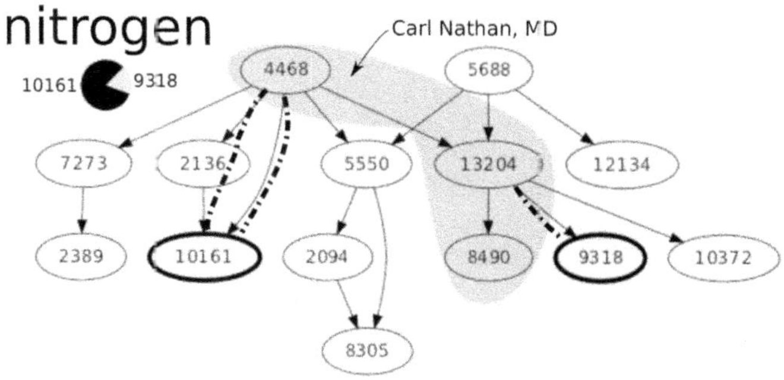

Figure 4: Example illustrating trust calculation for an immunologist asking, "How much do I trust Carl Nathan with respect to the concept 'nitrogen'?" Thick dashed lines indicate influence from Dr. Nathan to individual elements of $\mathcal{B}$, and pie chart represents relative prevalence of the word "nitrogen" in the two papers in $\mathcal{B}$.

technical report [15]). While these articles may be relevant to the query, a major shortcoming is that every researcher who submits this query will receive an identical result set. For any given topic, different researchers trust different authors and publications, and the objective in Equation 2 provides no means to express these preferences. While a long line of prior work exists on summarizing the impact of an author or publication with a single number [2], often based on citation statistics [20, 25] or eigenvector methods [27, 35, 11, 38], here we wish to capture a more detailed picture of the relationship between a researcher and the authors he cites.

In order to properly model such an individual notion of *trust* in the setting of scholarly research, we consider two motivating scenarios:

1. Different authors command different levels of respect from their research communities, e.g., a Nobel laureate versus a first-year graduate student, as an extreme case.
2. Even among distinguished scientists, a particular researcher's interests may be aligned more closely with some than others. Thus, beyond simply differentiating novices from experts, a notion of trust should also capture differences in research interests. For example, asking computer scientists to name whom they most associate with the concept "network" may yield Judea Pearl (Bayesian networks), Jon Kleinberg (social networks), Geoff Hinton (neural networks) or Van Jacobson (computer networks), depending on who is answering. All are distinguished researchers, but each is associated with a distinct subfield of computer science.

At the heart of both scenarios is a personal question that is often answered differently by different researchers: *How much do I trust this author with respect to this concept?*

By answering this question, a researcher would enable us to formally incorporate his trust preferences into our objective function, allowing us to select papers tailored specifically to his tastes. However, as researchers will not be able to provide an answer for every combination of authors and concepts, we must elicit their trust preferences in a less onerous manner. In order to do so, we assume that trust is *transitive.* For example, if Alice trusts an article, and that article is heavily influenced by Bob with respect to the concept "network," then Alice is likely to also trust Bob with respect to "network." Thus, at a fundamental level, a researcher need only specify a set of trusted papers $\mathcal{B}$, from which we can infer answers to the above question. As a shortcut, a researcher may choose to define $\mathcal{B}$ indirectly by specifying a list of trusted journals and conferences, or subsets thereof (e.g., a particular conference track or article classification). $\mathcal{B}$ could also be specified as the papers *cited by* one or more trusted authors, representing a look at one's research through the eyes of another scientist, potentially in another field. Thus, a plucky physicist could ask, "What would Steven Chu recommend I read?", and obtain a set of papers related to his query, yet tailored to the research interests and trust preferences of the Nobel laureate.

With this intuition in mind, we define $\tau^{(c)}_{a|\mathcal{B}}$, the probability a researcher trusts author a with respect to concept c, given trusted articles $\mathcal{B}$. (The "$|\mathcal{B}$" notation in this section indicates personalizing with respect to trusted set $\mathcal{B}$.) Figure 4 illustrates how we compute $\tau^{(c)}_{a|\mathcal{B}}$ for a particular example from PNAS, where the concept c is "nitrogen," the author a is Carl Nathan, MD, and the researcher has specified two immunology papers as his trusted set, $\mathcal{B} = \{10161, 9318\}$. For each paper $b \in \mathcal{B}$, we compute how much the author a influenced b with respect to concept c. As our influence is now expressed from an *author* to an article, we treat all of an author's papers as a single unit.

DEFINITION 3. *The influence from author a to article b with respect to concept c, $AuthorInfluence_c(a \to b)$, is the probability there exists a directed path in G_c from any article written by a to article b consisting only of active edges, where each edge is (independently) active with probability $\theta^{(c)}_{x\to y}$.*

As before, we employ sampling or dynamic programming to efficiently estimate this otherwise intractable computation (cf. technical report for more details [15]).

In our example, we first look at how much Dr. Nathan's papers influence 10161 with respect to "nitrogen," and again from Dr. Nathan's papers to 9318. We now weigh these two influences by the prevalence of the word "nitrogen" in each paper b (as indicated by the pie chart in Figure 4), and define $\tau^{(c)}_{a|\mathcal{B}}$ to be the weighted sum of the two.

More generally, we have:

$$\tau^{(c)}_{a|\mathcal{B}} = \begin{cases} \frac{1}{N^{(c)}_{\mathcal{B}}} \sum_{b\in\mathcal{B}} n^{(c)}_b \, AuthorInfluence_c(a \to b), & \text{if } N^{(c)}_{\mathcal{B}} > 0 \\ \tau^{(c)}_{a|\mathcal{V}}, & \text{otherwise,} \end{cases}$$

where $N^{(c)}_{\mathcal{B}}$ is the total number of occurrences of concept c in the set $\mathcal{B}$, $n^{(c)}_b$ is the frequency of concept c in paper b, and $\mathcal{V}$ is the set of all papers in the corpus. Here, the influence to each $b \in \mathcal{B}$ is weighted by the relative prevalence of concept c with respect to $\mathcal{B}$, $n^{(c)}_b / N^{(c)}_{\mathcal{B}}$. We note that if a researcher's trusted set $\mathcal{B}$ contains no occurrences of a particular concept, we assign the trust value to $\tau^{(c)}_{a|\mathcal{V}}$, as if all the papers in the corpus were trusted equally.

In order to incorporate trust into paper selection, we assume an author will trust a paper if and only if he trusts *at least one of its authors*. This intuition can be formalized by defining a modified notion of set influence, where the researcher's preferences towards the authors are directly taken into account:

$$Influence_c(q \leftrightarrow \mathcal{A}|\mathcal{B}) = 1 - \prod_{d\in\mathcal{A}} \left(1 - Influence_c(q \leftrightarrow d)\beta^{(c)}_d T^{(c)}_{d|\mathcal{B}}\right),$$

where $T^{(c)}_{d|\mathcal{B}} = 1 - \prod_{a\in authors(d)} (1 - \tau^{(c)}_{a|\mathcal{B}})$.

We can now define our *personalized* objective function as:

$$F_{\mathcal{Q}|\mathcal{B}}(\mathcal{A}) = \sum_{q\in\mathcal{Q}} \sum_{c\in\mathcal{C}} \gamma^{(c)}_q \, Influence_c(q \leftrightarrow \mathcal{A}|\mathcal{B}). \quad (3)$$

Maximizing $F_{\mathcal{Q}|\mathcal{B}}(\mathcal{A})$ subject to $|\mathcal{A}| \le k$, for some budget of k papers, leads to a personalized set of papers tailored to someone who trusts $\mathcal{B}$. This function shares the same theoretical properties as Equation 2 and can be optimized efficiently in the same manner (cf. technical report for more details [15]).

Figure 5 shows our PNAS example from before, with the same query set $\mathcal{Q} = \{4468, 5688\}$, but now incorporating the trust preferences of two hypothetical researchers: a plant biologist (A) and an immunologist (B). The figure highlights how differences in trust preferences can manifest themselves in article selection. In Figure 6, we provide another example, this time from computer science. Here, we take the famous Faloutsos, Faloutsos and Faloutsos paper, "On power-law relationships of the Internet topology" [19], and select related literature for it using the trust preferences of each author. Specifically, the visualization in the figure shows that by assuming that Michalis Faloutsos trusts SIGCOMM papers, Petros Faloutsos trusts SIGGRAPH papers, and Christos Faloutsos trusts KDD papers, we can select related work tailored to each author's perspective. While some relevant papers are common to all three points of view, other selected papers are particular to just one. For example, in Christos' data mining-focused result set, we find a few papers related to the evolution of social networks (e.g., "Microscopic evolution of social networks" by Leskovec et al.) which are not found in Michalis' and Petros' results. Moreover, these papers are not selected in the unpersonalized setting, when no trust preferences are taken into account.

4. APPROACH SUMMARY

We summarize our approach as follows:

Initialization

1. Define a vocabulary of concepts $\mathcal{C}$ (e.g., technical terms).
2. For each concept $c \in \mathcal{C}$, define a directed, acyclic graph G_c, with edge weights as in Section 2.1.
3. Compute relevance weights $\gamma^{(c)}_d$ and $\beta^{(c)}_d$, for all $c \in \mathcal{C}$ and documents d, as described in Section 2.3.1.
4. Precompute $Influence_c(u \leftrightarrow v)$ for all concepts c, and all pairs of documents u and v, using Algorithm 1.
5. Similarly, precompute $AuthorInfluence_c(a \to b)$, for all authors a, all documents b, and all $c \in \mathcal{C}$ (cf. [15]).

Per user

Given a user's trusted set of papers $\mathcal{B}$, compute $\tau^{(c)}_{a|\mathcal{B}}$ for all authors a and $c \in \mathcal{C}$.

Per query

Given query set $\mathcal{Q}$, optimize Equation 3 using CELF [29].

5. RELATED WORK

Researchers in both the library science and computer science communities have studied the shortcomings of the traditional keyword search paradigm [5, 34, 36]. In fact, our

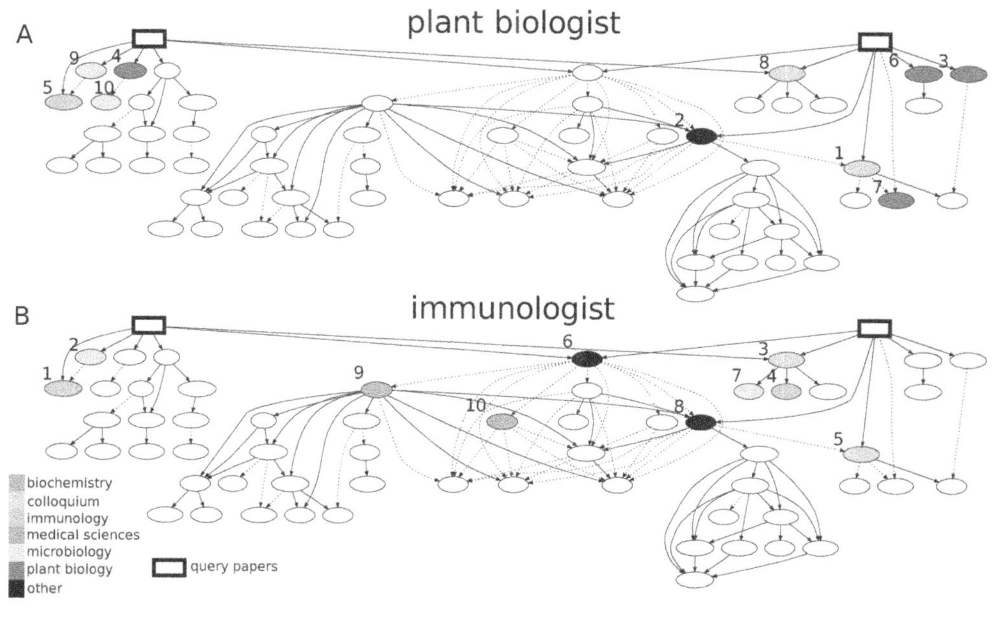

Figure 5: Top ten papers selected for $\mathcal{Q} = \{4468, 5688\}$ where $\mathcal{B}$ is defined as (A) all the plant biology papers, or (B) all the immunology papers, in the PNAS data set. Node colors correspond to article classification, as indicated by the key. (Colloquium refers to the National Academy of Sciences Colloquium on Virulence and Defense in Host-Pathogen Interactions: Common Features Between Plants and Animals. "Other" refers to unclassified papers, e.g., "From the Academy.".) Numbers indicate order of selection by optimization algorithm, roughly indicating order of importance (cf. technical report for more details [15]).

specific query model of defining a researcher's information need as a set of papers rather than as a keyword string has been described before [9, 30]. In one particularly related line of research, collaborative filtering techniques that have been successful for movie and product recommendations were adapted to the paper recommendation setting [30, 44]. Another approach uses hypothesis testing to determine the articles that most influence each paper–the paper's *Information Genealogy*–based only on article text [42]. Unlike these previous approaches, our methodology is based on a *unified* model of text and citations that places special emphasis on the different trust preferences of individual researchers.

Previous work has also considered the more general, yet related, problem of taking positive examples of membership in a set and using them to expand the set [17, 22]. While such approaches have been applied to the domain of research literature, they do not explicitly model the particular characteristics of our problem, e.g., the effect of citations, publication venues and authorship.

Moreover, it is also important to note that our algorithm is *operational* in that it describes a method for selecting papers, in contrast with many *descriptive* studies in bibliometrics, sociology and other fields [12, 39, 32, 33, 4, 40]. In particular, the large body of work on *topic modeling* in computer science and statistics focuses on fitting probabilistic models to document collections by modeling latent themes in the data [8]. While often applied to corpora of scholarly literature [18, 24, 3, 7, 41, 6, 14, 21], paper recommendation is not the primary objective of these models. Rather, our algorithm follows from a line of work that frames document selection as an explicit optimization problem (cf. [16]).

Finally, we note that the approach we describe in this paper is, in fact, agnostic to the specific definition of influence we use, and thus while we define influence to have an explicit probabilistic interpretation, other such definitions are possible. For instance, recent work by Lao and Cohen [28] provides an approach based on path-constrained random walks, which we can plug in as an alternative definition for influence.

6. EXPERIMENTAL RESULTS

While these illustrative examples provide intuition, in order to truly evaluate our methodology we must solicit feedback from real scientific researchers. To this end, we conducted a user study involving sixteen subjects (all doctoral students in computer science or related fields).

We compare two variants of our algorithm–with and without incorporating trust preferences of the participant–with three representative alternative techniques: Google Scholar [23], Information Genealogy [42] (a hypothesis testing approach based on document text), and the Relational Topic Model [10] (a state-of-the-art topic model incorporating both text and citations to model latent themes in data)[3]. For each participant, we use each of these techniques to find related work for a previously written paper–that participant's *study paper*–thereby simulating a real research scenario. We define each query set $\mathcal{Q}$ to be the references of the corresponding study paper, and we ask each participant to list up to four trusted conferences or journals, which we use to define $\mathcal{B}$.

[3]Previous work [30] has shown that Google keyword search outperforms collaborative filtering techniques for selecting useful papers, and thus we do not directly compare against these approaches.

Figure 6: A visualization of related work for Faloutsos, Faloutsos, and Faloutsos' "On power-law relationships of the Internet topology." The top word cloud represents papers selected using Equation 2, with no trust preferences. (The size of each word in the cloud is proportional to its prevalence in the selected documents.) The subsequent three word clouds represent papers selected using Equation 3 with three different trusted sets $\mathcal{B}$, one representing each author's perspective. Each word cloud visualizes the selected papers that are unique to each author's result set. For example, the bottom word cloud shows the papers found in Christos' data mining-focused results, but do not exist in Petros' or Michalis' result sets.

For Google Scholar, we ask a coauthor of each participant to provide us with the keyword query he or she would use to find related work for their paper. The Relational Topic Model and Information Genealogy approaches each use the abstract of the study paper in their paper recommendation, which our algorithm does not require. Unlike many previous studies, each participant was asked to evaluate all five comparison methods, rather than just a single technique. In total, 612 distinct papers were recommended using these five techniques across all sixteen participants. (The articles used in this study come from the ACM Digital Library [1]. More details on the study can be found in the technical report.)

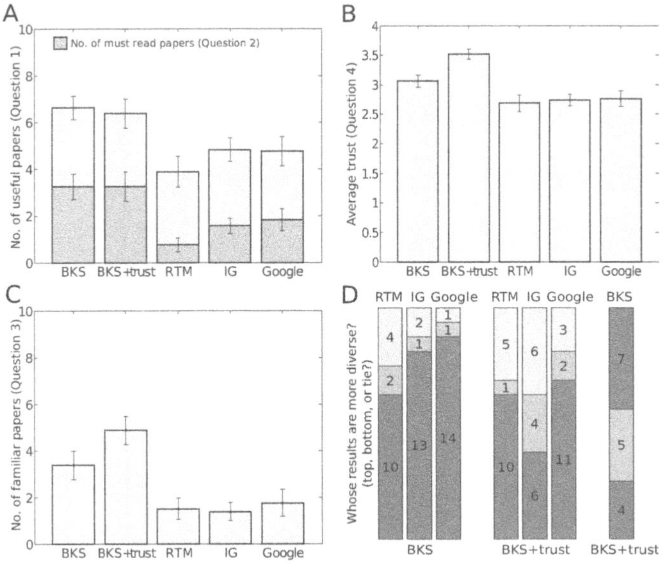

Figure 7: User study results comparing two variants of our algorithm, Beyond Keyword Search (BKS), with and without incorporating trust preferences, with the Relational Topic Model (RTM), Information Genealogy (IG) and Google Scholar. Values in bar plots (A), (B) and (C) are responses to the indicated study questions averaged over all sixteen participants, with error bars indicating one standard error. (D) shows how many participants (out of 16) found that our method produced more diverse results compared to the alternative techniques.

Each participant was presented with the recommended articles for his or her study paper in a double-blind fashion, masking the identity of the technique used to select each paper. Participants were asked to answer questions on the usefulness, novelty and trustworthiness of each paper with respect to their research. Additionally, participants were presented with entire result sets and asked to evaluate them in terms of diversity. Figure 7 shows the results of the study, from which we can glean the following main observations:

1. On average, users find the papers our algorithm selects to be more useful than those selected by the comparison techniques. The topic modeling approach performs especially poorly, with fewer than half of selected papers deemed useful.
2. Explicitly modeling the individual trust preferences of users leads to more trustworthy papers being selected. However, this comes at the expense of novelty in the selected articles, as researchers are more familiar with the work of authors they trust.
3. Our algorithm provides more diverse results than the comparison techniques, which is unsurprising, as our objective functions penalize redundancy.

7. DISCUSSION

These results illustrate the success of our approach in recommending highly relevant literature personalized to the preferences of individual researchers, acting as a promising complement to keyword search. On a personal note, employing our approach during the writing of *this article* led us to related work from another subfield of computer science that we had not discovered using more traditional search methods [30, 44]. In closing, we believe that the challenges researchers face in expressing their information needs extend beyond scientific literature to domains like patents, law and news, and the work presented herein is a significant step towards addressing this general concern.

8. ACKNOWLEDGMENTS

Research funded by NSF CNS-0625518 and ONR YIP N000140810752 and PECASE N000141010672. Word clouds generated using wordle.net. The authors are grateful to the Association for Computing Machinery for providing data from their Digital Library.

9. REFERENCES

[1] ACM Digital Library. http://portal.acm.org.

[2] R. Adler, J. Ewing, and P. Taylor. Citation statistics. *Statistical Science*, 24:1–14, 2009.

[3] E. M. Airoldi, E. A. Erosheva, S. E. Fienberg, C. Joutard, T. Love, and S. Shringarpure. Reconceptualizing the classification of PNAS articles. *Proceedings of the National Academy of Sciences USA*, 2010.

[4] A.-L. Barabási. On the topology of the scientific collaboration networks. *Physica A*, 311:590–614, 2002.

[5] M. Bates. The design of browsing and berrypicking techniques for the online search interface. *Online Review*, 13:407–424, 1989.

[6] D. M. Blei and J. Lafferty. Dynamic topic models. In *ICML*, 2006.

[7] D. M. Blei and J. Lafferty. A correlated topic model of science. *Ann. Appl. Stat.*, 1:17–35, 2007.

[8] D. M. Blei and J. Lafferty. *Topic Models.* Chapman and Hall, 2009.

[9] K. Bollacker, S. Lawrence, and C. L. Giles. Discovering relevant scientific literature on the Web. *IEEE Intelligent Systems and their Applications*, 15:42–47, 2000.

[10] J. Chang and D. M. Blei. Hierarchical relational models for document networks. *Annals of Applied Statistics*, 4:124–150, 2010.

[11] P. Chen, H. Xie, S. Maslov, and S. Redner. Finding scientific gems with Google. *Journal of Informetrics*, 1:8–15, 2007.

[12] D. J. de Solla Price. Networks of scientific papers. *Science*, 149:510:515, 1965.

[13] D. Diderot. In D. Diderot and J. d'Alembert, editors, *Encyclopedia, or a systematic dictionary of the sciences, arts and crafts*, Paris, 1755. Briasson, David, Le Breton, and Durand. (tr. from French).

[14] L. Dietz, S. Bickel, and T. Scheffer. Unsupervised prediction of citation influences. In *ICML*, 2007.

[15] K. El-Arini and C. Guestrin. Beyond keyword search: Discovering relevant scientific literature. Technical report, Carnegie Mellon University Machine Learning Department, 2011.

[16] K. El-Arini, G. Veda, D. Shahaf, and C. Guestrin. Turning down the noise in the blogosphere. In *KDD*, 2009.

[17] C. Elkan and K. Noto. Learning classifiers from only positive and unlabeled data. In *KDD*, 2008.

[18] E. A. Erosheva, S. E. Fienberg, and J. Lafferty. Mixed-membership models of scientific publications. *Proceedings of the National Academy of Sciences USA*, 101:5220–5227, 2004.

[19] M. Faloutsos, P. Faloutsos, and C. Faloutsos. On power-law relationships of the Internet topology. In *SIGCOMM*, 1999.

[20] E. Garfield. Citation analysis as a tool in journal evaluation. *Science*, 178:471–479, 1972.

[21] S. Gerrish and D. M. Blei. A language-based approach to measuring scholarly impact. In *ICML*, 2010.

[22] Z. Ghahramani and K. A. Heller. Bayesian sets. In *NIPS*, 2006.

[23] Google Scholar. http://scholar.google.com.

[24] T. Griffiths and M. Steyvers. Finding scientific topics. *Proceedings of the National Academy of Sciences USA*, 101:5228–5235, 2004.

[25] J. E. Hirsch. An index to quantify an individual's scientific research output. *Proceedings of the National Academy of Sciences USA*, 102:16569–16572, 2005.

[26] S. Khuller, A. Moss, and J. Naor. The budgeted maximum coverage problem. *Information Processing Letters*, 1999.

[27] J. Kleinberg. Authoritative sources in a hyperlinked environment. *Journal of the ACM*, 46:604–632, 1999.

[28] N. Lao and W. W. Cohen. Relational learning using a combination of path-constrained random walks. *Machine Learning*, 81(1):53–67, 2010.

[29] J. Leskovec, A. Krause, C. Guestrin, C. Faloutsos, J. VanBriesen, and N. Glance. Cost-effective outbreak detection in networks. In *KDD*, 2007.

[30] S. M. McNee, I. Albert, D. Cosley, P. Gopalkrishnan, S. K. Lam, A. M. Rashid, J. A. Konstan, and J. Riedl. On the recommending of citations for research papers. In *CSCW*, 2002.

[31] G. Nemhauser, L. Wolsey, and M. Fisher. An analysis of the approximations for maximizing submodular set functions. *Mathematical Programming*, 14:265–294, 1978.

[32] M. E. J. Newman. Scientific collaboration networks: I. network construction and fundamental results. *Phys. Rev. E*, 64:016131, 2001.

[33] M. E. J. Newman. The structure of scientific collaboration networks. *Proc. Natl. Acad. Sci. USA*, 98:404–409, 2001.

[34] C. Olston and E. H. Chi. Scenttrails: Integrating browsing and searching on the Web. *ACM Transactions on Computer-Human Interaction*, 10:177–197, 2003.

[35] L. Page, S. Brin, R. Motwani, and T. Winograd. The PageRank citation ranking: bringing order to the Web. Technical report, Stanford University InfoLab, 1999.

[36] S. Pandit and C. Olston. Navigation-aided retrieval. In *WWW*, 2007.

[37] J. S. Provan and M. O. Ball. The complexity of counting cuts and of computing the probability that a graph is connected. *SIAM J. Comput.*, 12:777–788, 1983.

[38] F. Radicchi, S. Fortunato, B. Markines, and A. Vespignani. Diffusion of scientific credits and the ranking of scientists. *Physical Review E*, 80:056103, 2009.

[39] S. Redner. How popular is your paper? an empirical study of the citation distribution. *Eur. Phys. J. B*, 4:131–134, 1998.

[40] M. Rosvall and C. T. Bergstrom. Maps of random walks on complex networks reveal community structure. *Proc. Natl. Acad. Sci. USA*, 105:1118–1123, 2008.

[41] M. Rozen-Zvi, T. Griffiths, M. Steyvers, and P. Smyth. The author-topic model for authors and documents. In *UAI*, 2004.

[42] B. Shaparenko and T. Joachims. Information genealogy: uncovering the flow of ideas in non-hyperlinked document databases. In *KDD*, 2007.

[43] Thomson Reuters Web of Knowledge. http://wokinfo.com/about/whatitis.

[44] R. Torres, S. M. McNee, M. Abel, J. A. Konstan, and J. Riedl. Enhancing digital libraries with TechLens+. In *JCDL*, 2004.

[45] L. Valiant. The complexity of enumeration and reliability problems. *SIAM J. Comput.*, 8:410–421, 1979.

Collaborative Topic Modeling for Recommending Scientific Articles

Chong Wang
Computer Science Department
Princeton University
Princeton, NJ, 08540, USA
chongw@cs.princeton.edu

David M. Blei
Computer Science Department
Princeton University
Princeton, NJ, 08540, USA
blei@cs.princeton.edu

ABSTRACT

Researchers have access to large online archives of scientific articles. As a consequence, finding relevant papers has become more difficult. Newly formed online communities of researchers sharing citations provides a new way to solve this problem. In this paper, we develop an algorithm to recommend scientific articles to users of an online community. Our approach combines the merits of traditional collaborative filtering and probabilistic topic modeling. It provides an interpretable latent structure for users and items, and can form recommendations about both existing and newly published articles. We study a large subset of data from CiteULike, a bibliography sharing service, and show that our algorithm provides a more effective recommender system than traditional collaborative filtering.

Categories and Subject Descriptors

H.3.3 [**Information Storage and Retrieval**]: Information Search and Retrieval—*information filtering*; I.2.6 [**Artificial Intelligence**]: Learning—*Parameter learning*

General Terms

Algorithms, Experimentation, Performance

Keywords

Scientific article recommendation, Topic modeling, Collaborative filtering, Latent structure interpretation

1. INTRODUCTION

Modern researchers have access to large archives of scientific articles. These archives are growing as new articles are placed online and old articles are scanned and indexed. While this growth has allowed researchers to quickly access more scientific information, it has also made it more difficult for them to find articles relevant to their interests. Modern researchers need new tools for managing what is available to them.

Historically, one way that researchers find articles is by following citations in other articles that they are interested in. This is an effective practice—and one that we should continue—but it limits researchers to specific citation communities, and it is biased towards heavily cited papers. A statistician may miss a relevant paper in economics or biology because the two literatures rarely cite each other; and she may miss a relevant paper in statistics because it was also missed by the authors of the papers that she has read. One of the opportunities of online archives is to inform researchers about literature that they might not be aware of.

A complementary method of finding articles is keyword search. This is a powerful approach, but it is also limited. Forming queries for finding new scientific articles can be difficult as a researcher may not know what to look for; search is mainly based on content, while good articles are also those that many others found valuable; and search is only good for directed exploration, while many researchers would also like a "feed" of new and interesting articles.

Recently, websites like CiteULike[1] and Mendeley[2] allow researchers to create their own reference libraries for the articles they are interested in and share them with other researchers. This has opened the door to using recommendation methods [13] as a third way to help researchers find interesting articles. In this paper, we develop an algorithm for recommending scientific articles to users of online archives. Each user has a library of articles that he or she is interested in, and our goal is to match each user to articles of interest that are not in his or her library.

We have several criteria for an algorithm to recommend scientific articles. First, recommending older articles is important. Users of scientific archives are interested in older articles for learning about new fields and understanding the foundations of their fields. When recommending old articles, the opinions of other users plays a role. A foundational article will be in many users' libraries; a less important article will be in few.

Second, recommending new articles is also important. For example, when a conference publishes its proceedings, users would like see the recommendations from these new articles to keep up with the state-of-the-art in their discipline. Since the articles are new, there is little information about which or how many other users placed the articles in their libraries, and thus traditional collaborative filtering methods has difficulties making recommendations. With new articles, a recommendation system must use their content.

Finally, exploratory variables can be valuable in online scientific archives and communities. For example, we can summarize and describe each user's preference profile based on the content of the articles that he or she likes. This lets us connect similar users to enhance the community, and indicate why we are connecting them. Further, we can describe articles in terms of what kinds of users like them. For example, we might detect that a machine learning

[1] `http://www.citeulike.org`
[2] `http://www.mendeley.com`

KDD'11, August 21–24, 2011, San Diego, California, USA.

article is of strong interest to computer vision researchers. If enough researchers use such services, these variables might also give an alternative measure of the impact of an article within a field.

With these criteria in mind, we develop a machine learning algorithm for recommending scientific articles to users in an online scientific community. Our algorithm uses two types of data—the other users' libraries and the content of the articles—to form its recommendations. For each user, our algorithm can finds both older papers that are important to other similar users and newly written papers whose content reflects the user's specific interests. Finally, our algorithm gives interpretable representations of users and articles.

Our approach combines ideas from collaborative filtering based on latent factor models [17, 18, 13, 1, 22] and content analysis based on probabilistic topic modeling [7, 8, 20, 2]. Like latent factor models, our algorithm uses information from other users' libraries. For a particular user, it can recommend articles from other users who liked similar articles. Latent factor models work well for recommending known articles, but cannot generalize to previously unseen articles.

To generalize to unseen articles, our algorithm uses topic modeling. Topic modeling provides a representation of the articles in terms of latent themes discovered from the collection. When used in our recommender system, this component can recommend articles that have similar content to other articles that a user likes. The topic representation of articles allows the algorithm to make meaningful recommendations about articles before anyone has rated them.

We combine these approaches in a probabilistic model, where making a recommendation for a particular user is akin to computing a conditional expectation of hidden variables. We will show how the algorithm for computing these expectations naturally balances the influence of the content of the articles and the libraries of the other users. An article that has not been seen by many will be recommended based more on its content; an article that has been widely seen will be recommended based more on the other users.

We studied our algorithm with data from CiteULike: $5,551$ users, $16,980$ articles, and $204,986$ bibliography entries. We will demonstrate that combining content-based and collaborative-based methods works well for recommending scientific articles. Our method provides better performance than matrix factorization methods alone, indicating that content can improve recommendation systems. Further, while traditional collaborative filtering cannot suggest articles before anyone has rated them, our method can use the content of new articles to make predictions about who will like them.

2. BACKGROUND

We first give some background. We describe two types of recommendation problems we address; we describe the classical matrix factorization solution to recommendation; and we review latent Dirichlet allocation (LDA) for topic modeling of text corpora.

2.1 Recommendation Tasks

The two elements in a recommender system are users and items. In our problem, items are scientific articles and users are researchers. We will assume I users and J items. The rating variable $r_{ij} \in \{0, 1\}$ denotes whether user i includes article j in her library [12]. If it is in the library, this means that user i is interested in article j. (This differs from some other systems where users explicitly rate items on a scale.) Note that $r_{ij} = 0$ can be interpreted into two ways. One way is that user i is not interested in article j; the other is that user i does not know about article j.

For each user, our task is to recommend articles that are not in her library but are potentially interesting. There are two types of

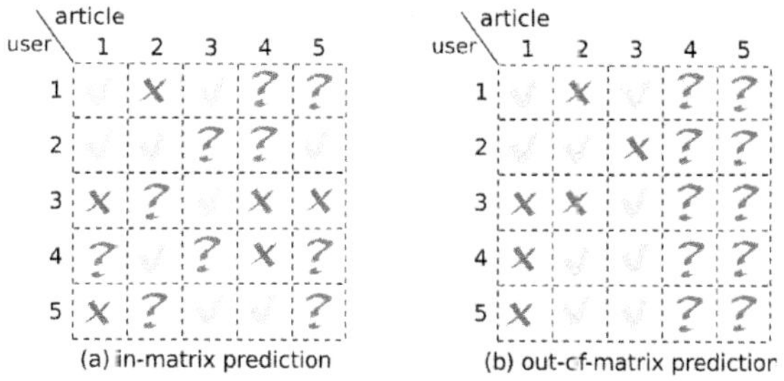

Figure 1: Illustration of the two tasks for scientific article recommendation systems, where $\surd$ indicates "like", $\times$ "dislike" and ? "unknown".

recommendation: *in-matrix prediction* and *out-of-matrix prediction*. Figure 1 illustrates the idea.

In-matrix prediction. Figure 1 (a) illustrates in-matrix prediction. This refers to the problem of making recommendations about those articles that have been rated by at least one user in the system. This is the task that traditional collaborative filtering can address.

Out-of-matrix prediction. Figure 1 (b) illustrates out-of-matrix prediction, where articles 4 and 5 have never been rated. (This is sometimes called "cold start recommendation.") Traditional collaborative filtering algorithms cannot make predictions about these articles because those algorithms only use information about other users' ratings. This task is important for online scientific archives, however, because users want to see new articles in their fields. A recommender system that cannot handle out-of-matrix prediction cannot recommend newly published papers to its users.

2.2 Recommendation by Matrix Factorization

The traditional approach to recommendation is collaborative filtering (CF), where items are recommended to a user based on other users with similar patterns of selected items. (Note that collaborative filtering does not use the content of the items.) Most successful recommendation methods are *latent factor models* [17, 18, 13, 1, 22], which provide better recommendation results than the *neighborhood methods* [11, 13]. In this paper, we focus on latent factor models.

Among latent factor methods, matrix factorization performs well [13]. In matrix factorization, we represent users and items in a shared latent low-dimensional space of dimension K—user i is represented by a latent vector $u_i \in \mathbb{R}^K$ and item j by a latent vector $v_j \in \mathbb{R}^K$. We form the prediction of whether user i will like item j with the inner product between their latent representations,

$$\hat{r}_{ij} = u_i^T v_j. \tag{1}$$

Biases for different users and items can also be incorporated [13].

To use matrix factorization, we must compute the latent representations of the users and items given an observed matrix of ratings. The common approach is to minimize the regularized squared error loss with respect to $U = (u_i)_{i=1}^I$ and $V = (v_j)_{j=1}^J$,

$$\min_{U,V} \sum_{i,j} (r_{ij} - u_i^T v_j)^2 + \lambda_u ||u_i||^2 + \lambda_v ||v_j||^2, \tag{2}$$

where λ_u and λ_v are regularization parameters.

This matrix factorization for collaborative filtering can be generalized as a probabilistic model [18]. In probabilistic matrix factorization (PMF), we assume the following generative process,

1. For each user i, draw user latent vector $u_i \sim \mathcal{N}(0, \lambda_u^{-1} I_K)$.
2. For each item j, draw item latent vector $v_j \sim \mathcal{N}(0, \lambda_v^{-1} I_K)$.

3. For each user-item pair (i,j), draw the response

$$r_{ij} \sim \mathcal{N}(u_i^T v_j, c_{ij}^{-1}), \tag{3}$$

where c_{ij} is the precision parameter for r_{ij}.

(Note that I_K is a K-dimensional identity matrix.) This is the interpretation of matrix factorization that we will build on.

When $c_{ij} = 1$, for $\forall i, j$, the maximum a posteriori estimation (MAP) of PMF corresponds to the solution in Eq. 2. Here, the precision parameter c_{ij} serves as a confidence parameter for rating r_{ij}. If c_{ij} is large, we trust r_{ij} more. As we mentioned above, $r_{ij} = 0$ can be interpreted into two ways—the user i is either not interested in item j or is unaware of it. This is thus a "one-class collaborative filtering problem," similar to the TV program and news article recommendation problems studied in [12] and [16]. In that work, the authors introduce different confidence parameters c_{ij} for different ratings r_{ij}. We will use the same strategy to set c_{ij} a higher value when $r_{ij} = 1$ than when $r_{ij} = 0$,

$$c_{ij} = \begin{cases} a, & \text{if } r_{ij} = 1, \\ b, & \text{if } r_{ij} = 0, \end{cases} \tag{4}$$

where a and b are tuning parameters satisfying $a > b > 0$.

We fit a CF model by finding a locally optimal solution of the user variables U and item variables V, usually with an iterative algorithm [12]. We then use Eq. 1 to predict the ratings of the articles outside of each user's library.

There are two main disadvantages to matrix factorization for recommendation. First, the learnt latent space is not easy to interpret; second, as mentioned, matrix factorization only uses information from other users—it cannot generalize to completely unrated items.

2.3 Probabilistic Topic Models

Topic modeling algorithms [5] are used to discover a set of "topics" from a large collection of documents, where a topic is a distribution over terms that is biased around those associated under a single theme. Topic models provide an interpretable low-dimensional representation of the documents [8]. They have been used for tasks like corpus exploration, document classification, and information retrieval. Here we will exploit the discovered topic structure for recommendation.

The simplest topic model is latent Dirichlet allocation (LDA) [7]. Assume there are K topics $\boldsymbol{\beta} = \beta_{1:K}$, each of which is a distribution over a fixed vocabulary. The generative process of LDA is as follows. For each article $\boldsymbol{w}_j$ in the corpus,

1. Draw topic proportions $\theta_j \sim \text{Dirichlet}(\alpha)$.
2. For each word n,
   (a) Draw topic assignment $z_{jn} \sim \text{Mult}(\theta_j)$.
   (b) Draw word $w_{jn} \sim \text{Mult}(\beta_{z_{jn}})$.

This process reveals how the words of each document are assumed to come from a mixture of topics: the topic proportions are document-specific, but the set of topics is shared by the corpus.

Given a collection, the posterior distribution (or maximum likelihood estimate) of the topics reveals the K topics that likely generated its documents. Unlike a clustering model, where each document is assigned to one cluster, LDA allows documents to exhibit multiple topics. For example, LDA can capture that one article might be about biology and statistics, while another might be about biology and physics. Since LDA is unsupervised, the themes of "physics" "biology" and "statistics" can be discovered from the corpus; the mixed-membership assumptions lead to sharper estimates of word co-occurrence patterns.

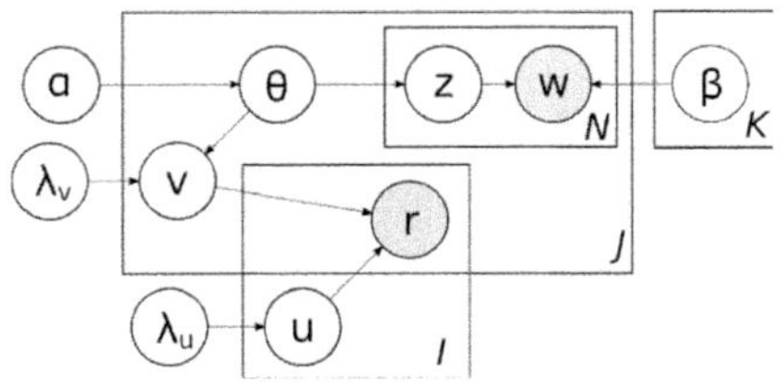

Figure 2: The graphical model for the CTR model.

Given a corpus of documents, we can use variational EM to learn the topics and decompose the documents according to them [7]. Further, given a new document, we can use variational inference to situate its content in terms of the topics. Our goal is to use topic modeling to give a content-based representation of items in a recommender system.

3. COLLABORATIVE TOPIC REGRESSION

In this section, we describe the collaborative topic regression (CTR) model. CTR combines traditional traditional collaborative filtering with topic modeling.

A first approach to combining collaborative filtering and topic modeling is to fit a model that uses the latent topic space to explain both the observed ratings and the observed words. For example, we can use the topic proportion θ_j in place of the latent item latent vector v_j in Eq. 3,

$$r_{ij} \sim \mathcal{N}(u_i^T \theta_j, c_{ij}^{-1}). \tag{5}$$

(We note that [19] proposed a similar approach to Eq. 5, but based on correlated topic models [4]. It showed modest improvement over matrix factorization on several movie recommendation datasets.)

This model suffers from the limitation that it cannot distinguish topics for explaining recommendations from topics important for explaining content. Consider two articles A and B that are both about machine learning applied to social networks. They are similar and, therefore, have similar topic proportions θ_A and θ_B. Now further suppose that these articles are interesting to different kinds of users: Article A might give an interesting machine learning algorithm that is applied to social network applications; article B uses standard machine learning techniques, but gives an important piece of data analysis on social network data.

Users that work in machine learning will prefer article A and rarely consider article B; users that work in social networks will prefer the opposite. However, using the topic proportions as in Eq. 5 will be likely to make similar recommendations for both articles to both types of users. Collaborative topic regression can detect this difference—that one type of user likes the first article and another type likes the second.

As above, collaborative topic regression (CTR) represents users with topic interests and assumes that documents are generated by a topic model. CTR additionally includes a latent variable ϵ_j that offsets the topic proportions θ_j when modeling the user ratings. As more users rate articles, we have a better idea of what this offset is. This offset variable can explain, for example, that article A is more interesting to machine learning researchers than it is to social network analysis researchers. How much of the prediction relies on content and how much it relies on other users depends on how many users have rated the article.

Figure 2 shows the graphical model. Again, assume there are K topics $\boldsymbol{\beta} = \beta_{1:K}$. The generative process of CTR is as follows,

1. For each user i, draw user latent vector $u_i \sim \mathcal{N}(0, \lambda_u^{-1} I_K)$.

2. For each item j,
   (a) Draw topic proportions $\theta_j \sim \text{Dirichlet}(\alpha)$.
   (b) Draw item latent offset $\epsilon_j \sim \mathcal{N}(0, \lambda_v^{-1} I_K)$ and set the item latent vector as $v_j = \epsilon_j + \theta_j$.
   (c) For each word w_{jn},
      i. Draw topic assignment $z_{jn} \sim \text{Mult}(\theta)$.
      ii. Draw word $w_{jn} \sim \text{Mult}(\beta_{z_{jn}})$.
3. For each user-item pair (i, j), draw the rating

$$r_{ij} \sim \mathcal{N}(u_i^T v_j, c_{ij}^{-1}). \tag{6}$$

The key property in CTR lies in how the item latent vector v_j is generated. Note that $v_j = \epsilon_j + \theta_j$, where $\epsilon_j \sim \mathcal{N}(0, \lambda_v^{-1} I_k)$, is equivalent to $v_j \sim \mathcal{N}(\theta_j, \lambda_v^{-1} I_K)$, where we assume the item latent vector v_j is close to topic proportions θ_j, but could diverge from it if it has to. Note that the expectation of r_{ij} is a linear function of θ_j,

$$\mathbb{E}[r_{ij} | u_i, \theta_j, \epsilon_j] = u_i^T(\theta_j + \epsilon_j).$$

This is why we call the model collaborative topic regression.

Learning the parameters. Given topic parameter $\boldsymbol{\beta}$, computing the full posterior of u_i, v_j and θ_j is intractable. We develop an EM-style algorithm to learn the maximum a posteriori (MAP) estimates.

Maximization of the posterior is equivalent to maximizing the complete log likelihood of U, V, $\theta_{1:J}$, and R given λ_u, λ_v and β,

$$\begin{aligned}\mathcal{L} = &-\tfrac{\lambda_u}{2} \textstyle\sum_i u_i^T u_i - \tfrac{\lambda_v}{2} \sum_j (v_j - \theta_j)^T (v_j - \theta_j) \qquad (7)\\ &+ \textstyle\sum_j \sum_n \log\left(\sum_k \theta_{jk} \beta_{k, w_{jn}}\right) - \sum_{i,j} \tfrac{c_{ij}}{2}(r_{ij} - u_i^T v_j)^2.\end{aligned}$$

We have omitted a constant and set $\alpha = 1$. We optimize this function by coordinate ascent, iteratively optimizing the collaborative filtering variables $\{u_i, v_j\}$ and the topic proportions θ_j.

For u_i and v_j, maximization follows in a similar fashion as for basic matrix factorization [12]. Given the current estimate of θ_j, taking the gradient of $\mathcal{L}$ with respect to u_i and v_j and setting it to zero leads to (recall the matrix definition $U = (u_i)_{i=1}^I$ and $V = (v_j)_{j=1}^J$)

$$u_i \leftarrow (V C_i V^T + \lambda_u I_K)^{-1} V C_i R_i \tag{8}$$

$$v_j \leftarrow (U C_j U^T + \lambda_v I_K)^{-1} (U C_j R_j + \lambda_v \theta_j). \tag{9}$$

where C_i is a diagonal matrix with $c_{ij}, j = 1 \cdots, J$ as its diagonal elements and $R_i = (r_{ij})_{j=1}^J$ for user i. For item j, C_j and R_j are similarly defined. Eq. 9 shows how topic proportions θ_j affects item latent vector v_j, where λ_v balances this effect. Finally, we note that the complexity is linear in the number of articles in the users' libraries. This follows from the special structure of c_{ij} defined in Eq. 4. (See [12] for details.)

Given U and V, we now describe how to learn the topic proportions θ_j.[3] We first define $q(z_{jn} = k) = \phi_{jnk}$. Then we separate the items that contain θ_j and apply Jensen's inequality,

$$\begin{aligned}\mathcal{L}(\theta_j) \geq &-\tfrac{\lambda_v}{2}(v_j - \theta_j)^T (v_j - \theta_j)\\ &+ \textstyle\sum_n \sum_k \phi_{jnk} \left(\log \theta_{jk} \beta_{k, w_{jn}} - \log \phi_{jnk}\right)\\ = &\ \mathcal{L}(\theta_j, \phi_j). \qquad (10)\end{aligned}$$

Let $\phi_j = (\phi_{jnk})_{n=1,k=1}^{N \times K}$. The optimal ϕ_{jnk} satisfies

$$\phi_{jnk} \propto \theta_{jk} \beta_{k, w_{jn}}. \tag{11}$$

The $\mathcal{L}(\theta_j, \phi_j)$ gives the *tight* lower bound of $\mathcal{L}(\theta_j)$. We cannot optimize θ_j analytically, so we use projection gradient [3]. We use coordinate ascent to optimize the remaining parameters, U, V, $\boldsymbol{\theta}_{1:J}$ and $\boldsymbol{\phi}_{1:J}$.

After we estimate U, V and $\boldsymbol{\phi}$, we can optimize β,

$$\beta_{kw} \propto \textstyle\sum_j \sum_n \phi_{jnk} 1[w_{jn} = w]. \tag{12}$$

Note this is the same M-step update for topics as in LDA [7].

Prediction. After all the (locally) optimal parameters U^*, V^*, $\boldsymbol{\theta}^*_{1:J}$ and $\boldsymbol{\beta}^*$ are learned, the CTR model can be used for both in-matrix and out-of-matrix prediction. Let D be the observed data, in general each prediction is estimated as

$$\mathbb{E}[r_{ij} | D] \approx \mathbb{E}[u_i \mid D]^T \left(\mathbb{E}[\theta_j \mid D] + \mathbb{E}[\epsilon_j \mid D]\right). \tag{13}$$

For in-matrix prediction, we use the point estimate of u_i, θ_j and ϵ_j to approximate their expectations,

$$r_{ij}^* \approx (u_i^*)^T (\theta_j^* + \epsilon_j^*) = (u_i^*)^T v_j^*, \tag{14}$$

where recall that $v_j = \theta_j + \epsilon_j$.

In out-of-matrix prediction the article is new, and no other ratings are available. Thus, $\mathbb{E}[\epsilon_j] = 0$ and we predict with

$$r_{ij}^* \approx (u_i^*)^T \theta_j^*. \tag{15}$$

To obtain the topic proportions θ_j^* for a new article, we optimize Eq. 10. The first term is dropped because $v_j = \theta_j$.

Related work. Several other work uses content for recommendation [15, 14, 1, 2]. Among these, the closest work to ours is fLDA by [2]. FLDA generalizes the supervised topic model (sLDA) [6], using the empirical topic proportions $\bar{z}_j = (1/N) \sum_{n=1}^N z_{jn}$ as well as several other covariates to form predictions. In our settings, where we do not have additional covariates, their approach is roughly akin to setting $v_j = \theta_j$. We show in Section 4 that a similar setting does not perform as well as the CTR model because it largely ignores the other users ratings.

Other recent work considers the related problem of using topic modeling to predict legislative votes [21, 10]. Neither of these methods introduces offset terms to account for votes (i.e., ratings). Legislative votes might be an interesting application for the CTR model.

4. EMPIRICAL STUDY

We demonstrate our model by analyzing a real-world community of researchers and their citation files.[4]

Dataset. Our data are users and their libraries of articles obtained from CiteULike.[5] At CiteUlike, registered users create personal reference libraries; each article usually has a title and abstract. (The other information about the articles, such as the authors, publications and keywords, is not used in this paper.)

We merged duplicated articles, removed empty articles, and removed users with fewer than 10 articles to obtain a data set of 5,551 users and 16,980 articles with 204,986 observed user-item pairs. (This matrix has a sparsity of 99.8%; it is highly sparse.) On average, each user has 37 articles in the library, ranging from 10 to 403. 93% of the users have fewer than 100 articles.

For each article, we concatenate its title and abstract. We remove stop words and use tf-idf to choose the top 8,000 distinct words as the vocabulary [5]. This yielded a corpus of 1.6M words. These articles were added to CiteULike between 2004 and 2010. On

[3] On our data, we found that simply fixing θ_j as the estimate from vanilla LDA gives comparable performance and saves computation.

[4] A demo of the results can be found at http://www.cs.princeton.edu/~chongw/citeulike/

[5] http://www.citeulike.org/faq/data.adp

average, each article appears in 12 users' libraries, ranging from 1 to 321. 97% of the articles appear in fewer than 40 libraries.

Evaluation. In our experiments, we will analyze a set of articles and user libraries. We will evaluate recommendation algorithms on sets of held-out articles and ratings. We will (hypothetically) present each user with M articles sorted by their predicted rating and evaluate based on which of these articles were actually in each user's library.

Two possible metrics are precision and recall. However, as we discussed earlier, zero ratings are uncertain. They may indicate that a user does not like an article or does not know about it. This makes it difficult to accurately compute precision. Rather, since ratings of $r_{ij} = 1$ are known to be true positives, we focus on recall. Recall only considers the positively rated articles within the top M—a high recall with lower M will be a better system. For each user, the definition of *recall@M* is

$$\text{recall@}M = \frac{\text{number of articles the user likes in top } M}{\text{total number of article the user likes}}.$$

The recall for the entire system can be summarized using the average recall from all users.

The recall above we defined is user-oriented. We also consider article-oriented recall for testing the system's predictive performance on a particular article. For article j, we consider the population of users that like the article and the proportion of those for whom that article appears in their top M recommended articles. This evaluates the predictive power of the system on a chosen set of articles.

As we discussed in section 2, we consider two recommendation tasks users, *in-matrix prediction* and *out-of-matrix prediction*.

In-matrix prediction. In-matrix prediction considers the case where each user has a set of articles that she has not seen, but that at least one other user has seen. We ask the question, how good is each system at rating that set of articles for each user?

As discussed in section 2.1, this task is similar to traditional collaborative filtering. We split the data into a training set and test set, ensuring that all articles in the test set have appeared in the training set. Content information is not required to perform recommendations—though we will see that it helps—and thus matrix factorization can be used.

We use 5-fold cross-validation. For every article that appears at least 5 times in the users' libraries, we evenly split their user-item pairs (both 1's and 0's) into 5 folds. We iteratively consider each fold to be a test set and the others to be the training set. For those articles that appear fewer than 5 times, we always put them into the training set. This guarantees that all articles in the test set must appear in the training set. (9% of the articles are always in the training set, since they appear fewer than 5 times.)

For each fold, we fit a model to the training set and test on the within-fold articles for each user. (Note: each user has a different set of within-fold articles.) We form predictive ratings for the test set, and generate a list of the top M recommended articles.

Out-of-matrix prediction. Out-of-matrix prediction considers the case where a new set of articles is published and no one has seen them. Again we ask, how good is each system at rating that set of articles for each user?

We again use 5-fold cross validation. First, we evenly group all articles into 5 folds. For each fold, we fit the model to the submatrix formed by the out-of-fold articles and then test the recommendations for each user on the within-fold articles. Note that in this case, each user has the same set of within-fold articles and we are guaranteed that none of these articles is in the training set for any user. Again, we form predictive ratings for the test set, and generate a list of the top M recommended articles.

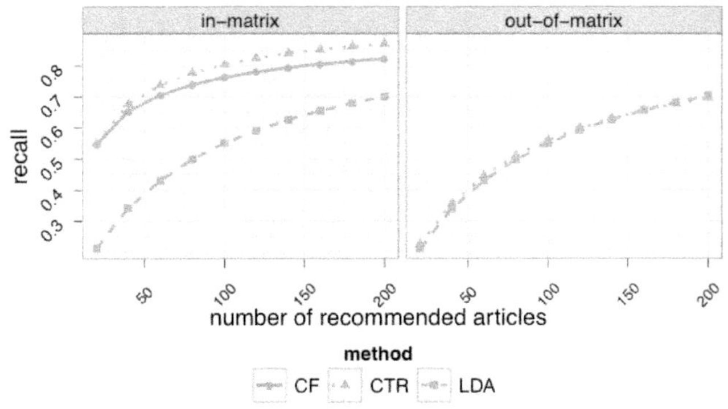

Figure 3: Recall comparison on in-matrix and out-of-matrix prediction tasks by varying the number of recommended articles. For CTR, we set $\lambda_v = 100$. Error bars are too small to show. The maximum expected recall for random recommendation is about 6%. CF can not do out-of-matrix prediction. CTR performs best.

These two experimental set-ups—in-matrix and out-of-matrix predictions—are designed to be comparable—the top M articles are computed from the same size of candidate populations.

Experimental settings. For matrix factorization for collaborative filtering (CF), we used grid search to find that $K = 200$, $\lambda_u = \lambda_v = 0.01$, $a = 1$, $b = 0.01$ gives good performance on held out recommendations. We use CF to denote this method.

For collaborative topic regression (CTR), we set the parameters similarly as for CF, $K = 200$, $\lambda_u = 0.01$, $a = 1$ and $b = 0.01$. In addition, the precision parameter λ_v balances how the article's latent vector v_j diverges from the topic proportions θ_j. We vary $\lambda_v \in \{10, 100, 1000, 10000\}$, where a larger λ_v increases the penalty of v_j diverging from θ_j.

We also compare to the model that only uses LDA-like features, as we discussed in the beginning of section 3. This is equivalent to fixing the per-item latent vector $v_j = \theta_j$ in the CTR model. This is a nearly content-only model—while the per-user vectors are fit to the ratings data, the document vectors θ_j are only based on the words of the document. We use LDA to denote this method. (Note that we use the resulting topics and proportions of LDA to initialize the CTR model.)

The baseline is the random model, where a user see M random recommended articles. We note that the expected recall for the random method from a pool of M_{tot} articles is irrelevant to library size. It is always M/M_{tot}.

Comparisons. Figure 3 shows the overall performance for in-matrix and out-of-matrix prediction, when we vary the number of returned articles $M = 20, 40, \cdots, 200$. For CTR, we pick $\lambda_v = 100$; Figure 4 shows the performs when we change λ_v for the CTR model compared with CF and LDA when we fix $M = 100$.

Figure 3 and 4 shows that matrix factorization works well for in-matrix prediction, but adding content with CTR improves performance. The improvement is greater when the number of returned documents M is larger. The reason is as follows. Popular articles are more likely to be recommended by both methods. However, when M becomes large, few user ratings are available to ensure that CF gives good recommendations; the contribution of the content becomes more important.

Compared to both CF and CTR, LDA suffers for in-matrix pre-

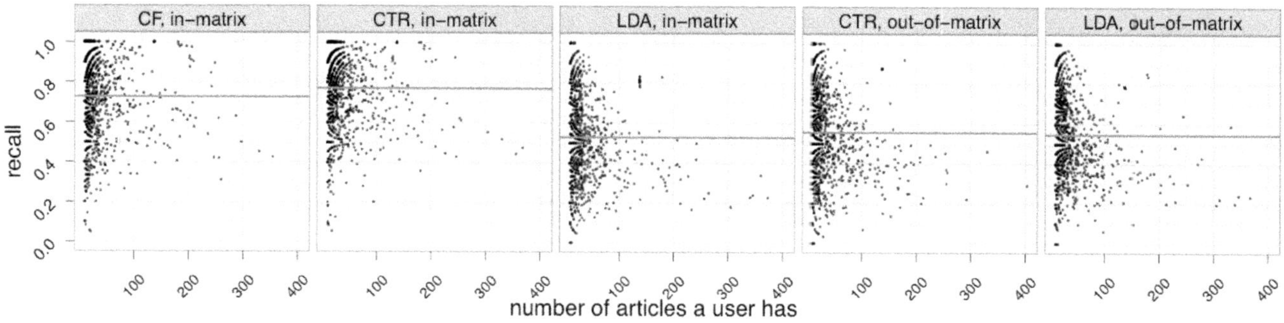

Figure 5: These scatter plots show how the number of articles a user has affects his or her recall. Red lines indicate the average. In these plots, the number of recommended articles is 100. CF can not do out-of-matrix prediction. This shows that CTR performs the best over user-oriented recall.

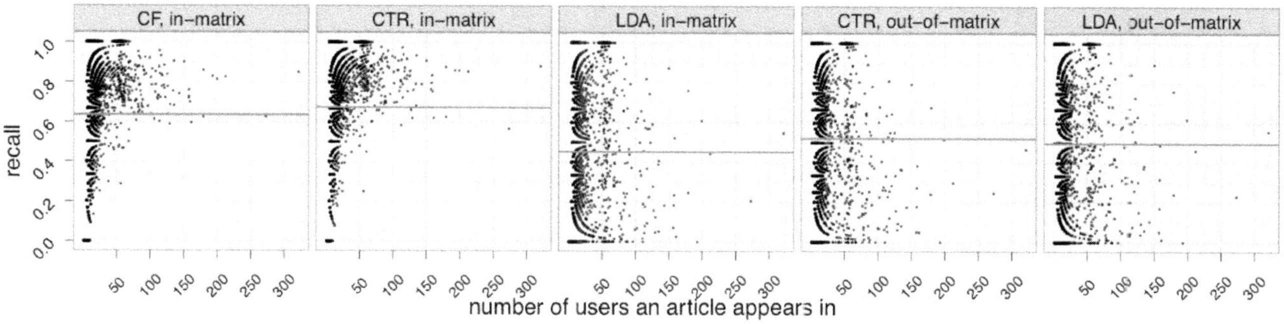

Figure 6: These scatter plots show how the number of users that like an article affects its recall. Red lines indicate the average. In these plots, the number of recommended articles is 100. CF can not do out-of-matrix prediction. This shows that CTR performs best over article-oriented recall as well.

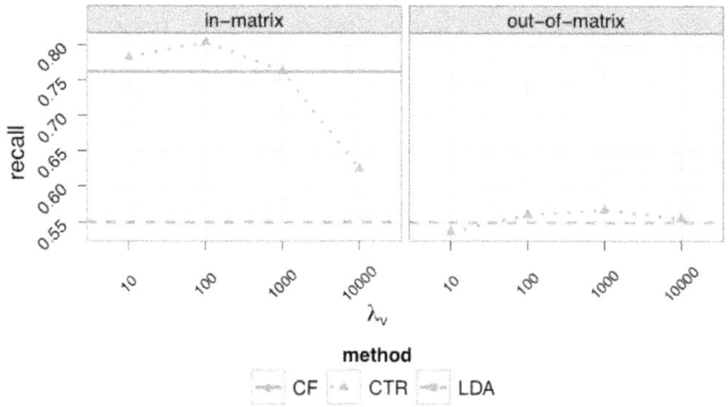

Figure 4: Recall comparison on in-matrix and out-of-matrix prediction tasks by fixing the number of recommended articles at $M = 100$. Error bars are too small to show. This shows how the precision parameter λ_v affects the performance of CTR. The expected recall of random recommendation is about 3%. CF can not do out-of-matrix prediction.

diction. It does not account enough for the users' information in forming its predicted ratings. The gap between CF and LDA is interesting—other users provide a better assessment of preferences than content alone.

Out-of-matrix prediction is a harder problem, as shown by the relatively lower recall. In this task, CTR performs slightly better than LDA. Matrix factorization cannot perform out-of-matrix prediction. (Note also that LDA performs almost the same on both in-matrix and out-of-matrix predictions. This is expected because, in both settings, it makes its recommendations almost entirely based on content.) Overall, CTR is the best model.

In Figure 4 we study the effect of the precision parameter λ_v. When λ_v is small in CTR, the per-item latent vector v_j can diverge significantly from the topic proportions θ_j. Here, CTR behaves more like matrix factorization where no content is considered. When λ_v increases, CTR is penalized for v_j diverging from the topic proportions; this brings the content into the recommendations. When λ_v is too large, v_j is nearly the same as θ_j and, consequently, CTR behaves more like LDA.

We next study the relationship, across models, between recommendation performance and properties of the users and articles. For this study we set the number of recommended articles $M = 100$ and the precision $\lambda_v = 100$. Figure 5 shows how the performance varies as a function of the number of articles in a user's library; Figure 6 shows how the performance varies as a function of the number of users that like an article.

As we see from Figure 5, for both in-matrix and out-of-matrix prediction, users with more articles tend to have less variance in their predictions. Users with few articles tend to have a diversity in the predictions, whose recall values vary around the extreme values of 0 and 1. In addition, we see that recall for users with more articles have a decreasing trend. This is reasonable because when a user has more articles then there will be more infrequent ones. As we see next, these articles are harder to predict.

From Figure 6, on in-matrix prediction for CF, CTR and LDA articles with high frequencies tend to have high recalls for in-matrix prediction and their predictions have less variance. This is because these articles have more collaborative information than infrequent ones, and, furthermore, CF and CTR make use of this information.

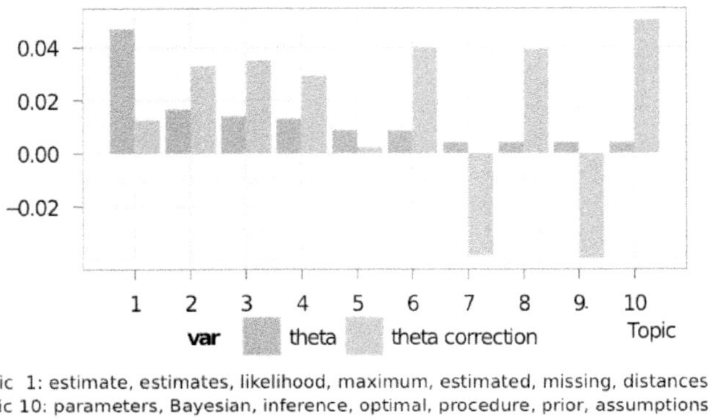

Figure 7: *Maximum likelihood from incomplete data via the EM algorithm.* **Here, "theta" denotes θ_j and "theta correction" denotes the offset ϵ_j. The 10 topics are obtained by joining the top 5 topics ranked by θ_{jk} and another top 5 topics ranked by $|\epsilon_{jk}|$, $k = 1, \cdots, K$. Under CTR, an article of wide interest is likely to exhibit more topics than its text exhibits. For example, this article brings in several other topics, including one on "Bayesian statistics" (topic 10). Note that the EM article is mainly about parameter estimation (topic 1), though is frequently referenced by Bayesian statisticians (and scholars in other fields as well).**

For LDA, this trend is much smaller. In out-of-matrix predictions, since predictions are made on new articles, these frequencies do not have an effect on training the model.

We now turn to an exploratory analysis of our results on the CTR model. (In the following, the precision $\lambda_v = 100$.)

Examining User Profiles. One advantage of the CTR model is that it can explain the user latent space using the topics learned from the data. For one user, we can find the top matched topics by ranking the entries of her latent vector u_i. Table 1 shows two example users and their top 3 matched topics along with their top 10 preferred articles as predicted by the CTR model.

The learned topics serve as a summary of what users might be interested in. For user I, we see that he or she might be a researcher working on machine learning and its applications to texts and images. Although the predicted top 10 articles don't contain a vision article, we see such articles when more articles are retrieved. For user II, he or she might be a researcher who is interested in user interfaces and collaborative filtering.

Examining the Latent Space of Articles. We can also examine the latent space of articles beyond their topic proportions. Here we inspect the articles with the largest overall offsets ϵ_j. Table 2 shows the top 10 articles with the largest offsets measured by the distance between v_j and θ_j, $\epsilon_j^T \epsilon_j = (v_j - \theta_j)^T (v_j - \theta_j)$. The last two columns show the average of predicted ratings over those users who actually have that article (avg–like) and those users who do not have that article (avg–dislike).

These articles are popular in this data. Among the top 50 articles by this measure, 94% of them have at least 50 appearances. Articles with large offsets enjoy readership from different areas, and their item latent vectors have to diverge from the topic proportions to account for this. For example, Figure 7 illustrates the article that is the main citation for the expectation-maximization algorithm, "*Maximum likelihood from incomplete data via the EM algorithm*" [9]. Its top topic (found by $k = \arg\max_k \theta_{jk}$), is shown as topic 1. It is about "parameter estimation," which is the main focus of this article. We can also examine the topics that are offset the most, $k = \arg\max_k |\epsilon_{jk}| = \arg\max_k |v_{jk} - \theta_{jk}|$. The maximum offset is for topic 10, a topic about "Bayesian statistics." Topic 10 has a low value in θ_j—the EM paper is not a Bayesian paper—but readers of Bayesian statistics typically have this paper in their library.

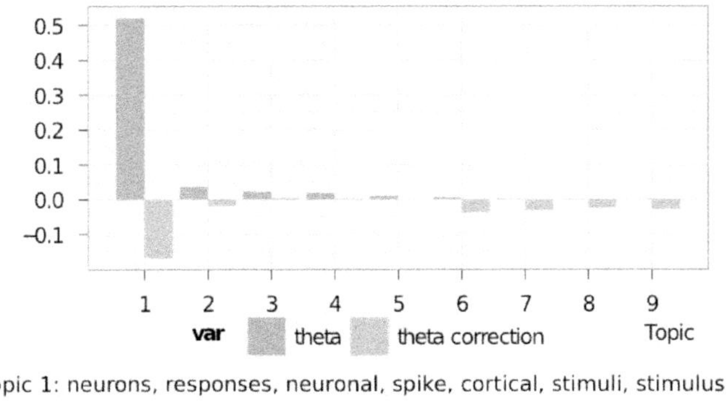

Figure 8: *Phase-of-firing coding of natural visual stimuli in primary visual cortex.* **This figure was created in the same way as Figure 7. It shows that a less popular article might also have a high offset value ϵ_j. In this case, it changes the actual magnitudes in θ_j, but does not bring in other topics.**

Examining the offset can yield the opposite kind of article. For example, consider the article "*Phase-of-firing coding of natural visual stimuli in primary visual cortex*" in Figure 8. Its most probable topic is topic 1 (about "Computational Neuroscience"). Taking into account the offset, the most probable topic does not change and nor are new topics brought in. This indicates that the offset ϵ_j only adjusts v_j so that the objective function is well minimized. This article is not as interesting to users outside of Neuroscience.

5. CONCLUSIONS AND FUTURE WORK

We proposed an algorithm for recommending scientific articles to users based on both content and other users' ratings. Our study showed that this approach works well relative to traditional matrix factorization methods and makes good predictions on completely unrated articles.

Further, our algorithm provides interpretable user profiles. Such profiles could be useful in real-world recommender systems. For example, if a particular user recognizes her profile as representing different topics, she can choose to "hide" some topics when seeking recommendations about a subject.

Acknowledgements. The authors thank anonymous reviewers for their insightful comments. Chong Wang is supported by Google PhD fellowship. David M. Blei is supported by ONR 175-6343, NSF CAREER 0745520, AFOSR 09NL202, the Alfred P. Sloan foundation, and a grant from Google.

6. REFERENCES

[1] D. Agarwal and B.-C. Chen. Regression-based latent factor models. In *Proceedings of the 15th ACM SIGKDD international conference on Knowledge discovery and data mining*, pages 19–28, New York, NY, USA, 2009. ACM.

[2] D. Agarwal and B.-C. Chen. flda: matrix factorization through latent Dirichlet allocation. In *Proceedings of the third ACM international conference on Web search and data mining*, WSDM '10, pages 91–100, New York, NY, USA, 2010. ACM.

	user I	in user's lib?
top 3 topics	1. image, measure, measures, images, motion, matching, transformation, entropy, overlap, computed, match 2. learning, machine, training, vector, learn, machines, kernel, learned, classifiers, classifier, generalization 3. sets, objects, defined, categories, representations, universal, category, attributes, consisting, categorization	
top 10 articles	1. Information theory inference learning algorithms	✓
	2. Machine learning in automated text categorization	✓
	3. Artificial intelligence a modern approach	×
	4. Data xmining: practical machine learning tools and techniques	×
	5. Statistical learning theory	×
	6. Modern information retrieval	✓
	7. Pattern recognition and machine learning, information science and statistics	✓
	8. Recognition by components: a theory of human image understanding	×
	9. Data clustering a review	✓
	10. Indexing by latent semantic analysis	✓
	user II	in user's lib?
top 3 topics	1. users, user, interface, interfaces, needs, explicit, implicit, usability, preferences, interests, personalized 2. based, world, real, characteristics, actual, exploring, exploration, quite, navigation, possibilities, dealing 3. evaluation, collaborative, products, filtering, product, reviews, items, recommendations, recommender	
top 10 articles	1. Combining collaborative filtering with personal agents for better recommendations	×
	2. An adaptive system for the personalized access to news	✓
	3. Implicit interest indicators	×
	4. Footprints history-rich tools for information foraging	✓
	5. Using social tagging to improve social navigation	✓
	6. User models for adaptive hypermedia and adaptive educational systems	✓
	7. Collaborative filtering recommender systems	✓
	8. Knowledge tree: a distributed architecture for adaptive e-learning	✓
	9. Evaluating collaborative filtering recommender systems	✓
	10. Personalizing search via automated analysis of interests and activities	✓

Table 1: Two example users. We show their position in latent space via their highest weighted topics. We list the top 10 preferred articles as predicted by CTR. The last column shows whether each article is in the user's library.

[3] D. Bertsekas. *Nonlinear Programming*. Athena Scientific, 1999.

[4] D. Blei and J. Lafferty. A correlated topic model of Science. *Annals of Applied Statistics*, 1(1):17–35, 2007.

[5] D. Blei and J. Lafferty. Topic models. In A. Srivastava and M. Sahami, editors, *Text Mining: Theory and Applications*. Taylor and Francis, 2009.

[6] D. Blei and J. McAuliffe. Supervised topic models. In *Neural Information Processing Systems*, 2007.

[7] D. Blei, A. Ng, and M. Jordan. Latent Dirichlet allocation. *Journal of Machine Learning Research*, 3:993–1022, January 2003.

[8] J. Chang, J. Boyd-Graber, S. Gerrish, C. Wang, and D. Blei. Reading tea leaves: How humans interpret topic models. In Y. Bengio, D. Schuurmans, J. Lafferty, C. K. I. Williams, and A. Culotta, editors, *Advances in Neural Information Processing Systems 22*, pages 288–296, 2009.

[9] A. Dempster, N. Laird, and D. Rubin. Maximum likelihood from incomplete data via the EM algorithm. *Journal of the Royal Statistical Society, Series B*, 39:1–38, 1977.

[10] S. M. Gerrish and D. M. Blei. Predicting legislative roll calls from text. In *Proceedings of the 28th Annual International Conference on Machine Learning*, ICML '11, 2011.

[11] J. L. Herlocker, J. A. Konstan, A. Borchers, and J. Riedl. An algorithmic framework for performing collaborative filtering. In *Proceedings of the 22nd annual international ACM SIGIR conference on Research and development in information retrieval*, SIGIR '99, pages 230–237, New York, NY, USA, 1999. ACM.

[12] Y. Hu, Y. Koren, and C. Volinsky. Collaborative filtering for implicit feedback datasets. In *Proceedings of the 2008 Eighth IEEE International Conference on Data Mining*, pages 263–272, Washington, DC, USA, 2008. IEEE Computer Society.

[13] Y. Koren, R. Bell, and C. Volinsky. Matrix factorization techniques for recommender systems. *IEEE Computer*, 42(8):30–37, 2009.

[14] P. Melville, M. R., and R. Nagaraja. Content-boosted collaborative filtering for improved recommendations. In *American Association for Artificial Intelligence*, pages 187–192, 2002.

[15] R. J. Mooney and L. Roy. Content-based book recommending using learning for text categorization. In *Proceedings of the fifth ACM conference on Digital libraries*, pages 195–204, New York, NY, USA, 2000. ACM.

[16] R. Pan, Y. Zhou, B. Cao, N. N. Liu, R. Lukose, M. Scholz, and Q. Yang. One-class collaborative filtering. In *Proceedings of the 2008 Eighth IEEE International Conference on Data Mining*, pages 502–511, Washington, DC, USA, 2008. IEEE Computer Society.

[17] R. Salakhutdinov and A. Mnih. Bayesian probabilistic matrix factorization using Markov chain Monte Carlo. In *Proceedings of the 25th International Conference on Machine learning*, pages 880–887. ACM, 2008.

[18] R. Salakhutdinov and A. Mnih. Probabilistic matrix

title	# dataset	# Google	avg–like	avg–dislike
1. The structure and function of complex networks	212	5,192	0.909	0.052
2. Emergence of scaling in random networks	193	8,521	0.899	0.058
3. R: a language and environment for statistical computing	113	837	0.827	0.047
4. A mathematical theory of communication	129	39,401	0.817	0.062
5. Maximum likelihood from incomplete data via the EM algorithm	157	22,874	0.864	0.055
6. A tutorial on hidden Markov models and selected applications in speech recognition	135	11,929	0.822	0.048
7. The structure of collaborative tagging systems	321	648	0.903	0.055
8. Why most published research findings are false	161	713	0.846	0.049
9. Phase-of-firing coding of natural visual stimuli in primary visual cortex	8	64	1.057	-0.004
10. Defrosting the digital library bibliographic tools for the next generation web	179	37	0.840	0.042

Table 2: The top 10 articles with the largest discrepancy between their item latent vector v_j and topic proportions θ_j, measured by $(v_j - \theta_j)^T(v_j - \theta_j)$. Column 2 and 3 show how often they appear in the data, as well as the number of citations (retrieved from Google Scholar on Feb 17, 2011). Most of these articles are popular. The last two columns give the average values of "predicted" ratings over those users who have the article (avg–like) in the library and those who do not (avg–dislike).

factorization. *Advances in Neural Information Processing Systems*, 20:1257–1264, 2008.

[19] H. Shan and A. Banerjee. Generalized probabilistic matrix factorizations for collaborative filtering. In *Proceedings of the 2010 IEEE International Conference on Data Mining*, pages 1025–1030, Washington, DC, USA, 2010. IEEE Computer Society.

[20] Y. Teh, M. Jordan, M. Beal, and D. Blei. Hierarchical Dirichlet processes. *Journal of the American Statistical Association*, 101(476):1566–1581, 2007.

[21] E. Wang, D. Liu, J. Silva, D. Dunson, and L. Carin. Joint analysis of time-evolving binary matrices and associated documents. In J. Lafferty, C. K. I. Williams, J. Shawe-Taylor, R. Zemel, and A. Culotta, editors, *Advances in Neural Information Processing Systems 23*, pages 2370–2378. 2010.

[22] K. Yu, J. Lafferty, S. Zhu, and Y. Gong. Large-scale collaborative prediction using a nonparametric random effects model. In *Proceedings of the 26th Annual International Conference on Machine Learning*, pages 1185–1192, New York, NY, USA, 2009. ACM.

Partially Labeled Topic Models for Interpretable Text Mining

Daniel Ramage
Computer Science Dept.
Stanford University
Stanford, California
dramage@cs.stanford.edu

Christopher D. Manning
Computer Science Dept.
Stanford University
Stanford, California
manning@cs.stanford.edu

Susan Dumais
Microsoft Research
Redmond, Washington
sdumais@microsoft.com

ABSTRACT

Much of the world's electronic text is annotated with human-interpretable labels, such as tags on web pages and subject codes on academic publications. Effective text mining in this setting requires models that can flexibly account for the textual patterns that underlie the observed labels while still discovering unlabeled topics. Neither supervised classification, with its focus on label prediction, nor purely unsupervised learning, which does not model the labels explicitly, is appropriate. In this paper, we present two new *partially* supervised generative models of labeled text, Partially Labeled Dirichlet Allocation (PLDA) and the Partially Labeled Dirichlet Process (PLDP). These models make use of the unsupervised learning machinery of topic models to discover the hidden topics within each label, as well as unlabeled, corpus-wide latent topics. We explore applications with qualitative case studies of tagged web pages from del.icio.us and PhD dissertation abstracts, demonstrating improved model interpretability over traditional topic models. We use the many tags present in our del.icio.us dataset to quantitatively demonstrate the new models' higher correlation with human relatedness scores over several strong baselines.

Categories and Subject Descriptors

H.2.8 [**Database Applications**]: Data mining; I.2.7 [**Natural Language Processing**]: Text analysis

General Terms

Algorithms, Experimentation

1. INTRODUCTION

The world's text is increasingly created and consumed electronically, providing opportunities for tools to help make sense of that text. As web technologies have evolved, the amount of human-provided annotations on that text has grown, too, becoming a source of information our text mining tools should not ignore. In this paper, we address a set of related challenges presented by such datasets. How can we understand and interpret the meaning of labels and the different ways they are used? Can we model the labels while simultaneously uncovering topics in the dataset that are not labeled? Can we discover which words in documents should be attributed to which of the documents' labels? Or to none at all? We take these challenges as examples of partially supervised text mining, in which models discover textual topics in a corpus that contains some labels, although those labels may not be the primary object of study.

This form of partially supervised learning straddles the boundary between unsupervised learning, in which models discover unmarked statistical relationships in the data, and supervised learning, which emphasizes the relationship between word features and a given space of labels for the purpose of classifying new documents. Popular unsupervised approaches like Latent Dirichlet Allocation [5], Latent Semantic Indexing [11] and related methods [20, 3] are well suited for exploratory text analysis—e.g. [13]—but most of these models do not account for the label space. When they do, it is usually to improve the quality of a shared set of latent topics—such as in [19, 4, 16, 17, 34, 23]—rather than to directly model the contents of the provided labels. As a result, practitioners face challenges in interpreting what these topics really mean, how they should be named, and to what extent trends based on them can be trusted in qualitative applications. While unsupervised topics are successful in capturing broad patterns in a document collection, the learned topics do not, in general, align with human provided labels.

In contrast, supervised learning and (multi-) label prediction explicitly model the label space for the purpose of prediction (such as in [12, 18]), but by design do not discover latent sub-structure or other latent patterns. Other learning formulations exist in the space between supervised learning and unsupervised learning, most notably semi-supervised learning [10], in which the goal is to improve label classification performance by making use of unsupervised data [35]. Another, similar learning paradigm is semi-supervised clustering—such as [2, 33]—in which some supervised information is used to improve an unsupervised task. Usually this information comes in the form of human-provided pair-wise similarity/dissimilarity scores or constraints. As a result, these approaches can be used effectively for label prediction or document clustering, but do not lend themselves to more fine-grained questions about how the terms and label space interact. By contrast, the *partially supervised* approach pursued here is explicitly designed to im-

KDD'11, August 21–24, 2011, San Diego, California, USA.

prove upon the exploratory and descriptive analyses that draw practitioners to unsupervised topic models to begin with—i.e. to discover and characterize the relationships between patterns, but with the added ability to constrain those patterns to align with label classes that are meaningful to people.

Our approach to the challenges of partially supervised text mining is through methods that make use of the unsupervised learning machinery of topic modeling, but with constraints that align some learned topics with a human-provided label. In this paper, we introduce two models, unifying and generalizing the popular unsupervised topic model, Latent Dirichlet Allocation (LDA) [5] as well as the multinomial naive Bayes supervised text classifier's event model [22] and the more recent multi-label generative model Labeled LDA [27]. As in LDA, Partially Labeled Dirichlet Allocation (PLDA), assumes that each document's words are drawn from a document-specific mixture of latent topics, where each topic is represented as a distribution over words. Unlike LDA, PLDA assumes that each document can use only those topics that are in a topic class associated with one or more of the document's labels. In particular, we introduce one class (consisting of multiple topics) for each label in the label set, as well as one latent class that applies to all documents. This construction allows PLDA to discover large-scale patterns in language usage associated with each individual label, variations of linguistic usage within a label, and background topics not associated with any label. A parallel learning and inference algorithm for PLDA allows it to scale to large document collections. Our second model, the Partially Labeled Dirichlet Process (PLDP), extends PLDA by incorporating a non-parametric Dirichlet process prior over each class's topic set, allowing the model to adaptively discover how many topics belong to each label, at the expense of parallelizability. We evaluate our approach qualitatively on PhD dissertation abstracts and quantitatively on a document-similarity task derived from tagged web pages on del.icio.us.

Related work

Recently, researchers in the topic modeling community have begun to explore new ways of incorporating meta-data and hierarchy into their models, which is the approach to partially supervised text mining that we take here. For instance, Markov Random Topic Fields [16] and Markov Topic Models [32] both allow information about document groups to influence the learned topics. There has also been a great amount of work on simultaneously modeling relationships among several variables, such as authors and topics in the Author-Topic model [28], tags and words in [29], and topics sentiment in [21]. All of these models assume a latent topic space that is influenced by external label information of some form. By contrast, we use topics to model the substructure of labels and unlabeled structure around them. Other ways to constrain and exploit topic models for text mining tasks include recent work in mining product reviews such as, Titov and McDonald [31] and later Branavan, et al. [6] who extract ratable aspects of product reviews. And recently, the Nubbi model of topics and social networks [8] introduced by Chang, et al., constrains an LDA-like topic model to learn topics that correspond to individual entities (such as heads of state in Wikipedia) and the relationships between them. Topic models that account for an extra level of topic correlation have been studied as well, with notable papers such as Blei et al.'s hierarchical topic models [3] and Li and McCallum's Pachinko Allocation [20]. These types of models assume an extra hidden layer of abstraction that models topic-topic correlation. The label classes in this work can be seen as an analogous layer, but here they are supervised, hard assignments constraining only some topics to be active depending on a document's observed labels.

The work builds upon prior work the multi-label generative model, Labeled LDA, introduced by Ramage, et al. in 2009 [27], and similar models such as the extension of Rubin et al. in [29]. Like PLDA and PLDP, Labeled LDA assumes that each document is annotated with a set of observed labels, and that these labels play a direct role in generating the document's words from per-label distributions over terms. However, Labeled LDA does not assume the existence of any latent topics (neither global nor within a label)—only the documents' distributions over their observed labels, as well as those labels' distributions over words, are inferred. Labeled LDA borrows the machinery of LDA primarily for the purpose of *credit attribution*—associating which words in each document are best associated with each of the document's labels. As a result, Labeled LDA does not support latent sub-topics within a given label nor any global latent topics. In this sense, "Labeled Latent Dirichlet Allocation" is not so latent: every output dimension is in one-to-one correspondence with the input label space. In this work, we introduce two new models, PLDA and PLDP, that by incorporating classes of latent topics extend, generalizes, and unify LDA with Labeled LDA. This simple change opens new opportunities in interpretable text mining and results in a large and surprising boost in the models' ability to correlate with human similarity judgments, as we demonstrate in Section 3.3.

2. PARTIALLY SUPERVISED MODELS

In our formalization of partially supervised text mining, we are given a collection of documents $\mathbb{D}$, each containing a multi-set of words $\vec{w}_d$ from a vocabulary $\mathbb{V}$ of size V and a set of labels Λ_d from a space of labels $\mathbb{L}$. We would like to recover a set of topics Φ that fit the observed distribution of words in the multi-labeled documents, where each topic is a multinomial distribution over words $\mathbb{V}$ that tend to co-occur with each other and some label $l \in \mathbb{L}$. Latent topics that have no associated label are optionally modeled by assuming the existence of a background *latent* label $\mathbb{L}$ that is applied to all documents in the collection. In the sections below, we define PLDA and PLDP, both of which assume that the word w at position i in each document d is generated by first picking a label l from Λ_d and then a topic z from the set of topics associated with that label. Then word w is picked from the topic indexed $\Phi_{l,z}$. In this way, both PLDA and PLDP can be used for *credit attribution* of words to labels by examining the posterior probability over labels for a particular word instance. Both PLDA and PLDP are generative probabilistic graphical models, and so for each we will use an approximate inference algorithm to re-construct the per-document mixtures over labels and topics, as well as the set of words associated with each label. By incorporating the latent class of topics in addition to the label classes, the model effectively forces each word to decide if it is better modeled by a broad, latent topic, or a topic that applies specifically to one of its document's labels.

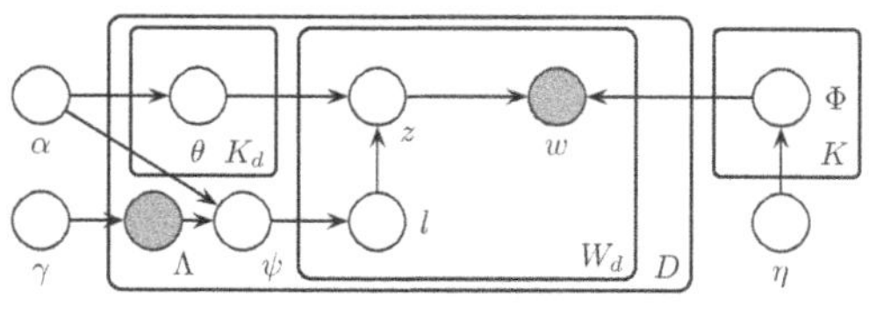

Figure 1: Graphical model for PLDA. Each document's words w and labels Λ are observed, with the per-doc label distribution ψ, per-doc-label topic distributions θ, and per-topic word distributions Φ hidden variables. Because each document's label-set Λ_d is observed, its sparse vector prior γ is unused; included for completeness.

2.1 Partially Labeled Dirichlet Allocation

Partially Labeled Dirichlet Allocation (PLDA) is a generative model for a collection of labeled documents, extending the generative story of LDA [5] to incorporate labels, and of Labeled LDA [27] to incorporate per-label latent topics. Formally, PLDA assumes the existence of a set of $\mathbb{L}$ labels (indexed by $1..L$), each of which has been assigned some number of topics $\mathbb{K}_l$ (indexed by $1..K_L$) and where each topic $\phi_{l,k}$ is represented as a multinomial distribution over all terms in the vocabulary $\mathbb{V}$ drawn from a symmetric Dirichlet prior η. One of these labels may optionally denote the shared global *latent* topic class, which can be interpreted as a label *"latent"* present on every document d. PLDA assumes that each topic takes part in exactly one label.

Figure 1 shows the Bayesian graphical model for PLDA. Each document d is generated by first drawing a document-specific subset of available label classes, represented as a sparse binary vector Λ_d from a sparse binary vector prior. A document-specific mix $\theta_{d,j}$ over topics $1..K_j$ is drawn from a symmetric Dirichlet prior α for each label $j \in \Lambda_d$ present in the document. Then, a document-specific mix of observed labels ψ_d is drawn as a multinomial of size $|\Lambda_d|$ from a Dirichlet prior $\vec{\alpha_L}$, with each element $\psi_{d,j}$ corresponding to the document's probability of using label $j \in \Lambda_d$ when selecting a latent topic for each word. For derivational simplicity, we define the element at position j of $\vec{\alpha_L}$ to be αK_j, so $\vec{\alpha_L}$ is not a free parameter. Each word w in document d is drawn from some label's topic's word distribution, i.e. it is drawn by first picking a label j from ψ_d, a topic z from $\theta_{d,l}$, and then a word w from $\phi_{l,k}$. Ultimately, this word will be picked in proportion to how much the enclosing document prefers the label l, how much that label prefers the topic z, and how much that topic prefers the word w.

We are interested in finding an efficient way to compute the joint likelihood of the observed words $\vec{w}$ with the unobserved label and topic assignments, $\vec{l}$ and $\vec{z}$, respectively: $P(\vec{w}, \vec{z}, \vec{l}|\vec{\Lambda}, \alpha, \eta, \gamma) = P(\vec{w}|\vec{z}, \eta)P(\vec{z}, \vec{l}|\vec{\Lambda}, \alpha, \gamma)$. Later, we will use this joint likelihood to derive efficient updates for the parameters Θ, Ψ, and Φ (where the capital Greek letters represent the full set of $\vec{\theta}$, $\vec{\psi}$, and $\vec{\phi}$, respectively). First, we note that the left term $P(\vec{w}|\vec{z}, \eta) = \int_\Phi P(\vec{w}|\vec{z}, \Phi)P(\Phi|\eta)d\Phi$ is the same as for standard latent Dirichlet allocation and ultimately contributes the same terms to the full conditional as well as to the sampling formula for updating individual topic assignments $z_{d,i}$, so we use the same derivation as in e.g. [13]. Using the model's independence assumptions, we consider the joint probability of the topics and labels, $P(\vec{z}, \vec{l}|\vec{\Lambda}, \alpha, \gamma) = P(\vec{z}|\vec{l}, \alpha)P(\vec{l}|\vec{\Lambda}, \gamma, \alpha)$. We will examine each half of this expression in turn. First, observe that:

$$P(\vec{z}|\vec{l}, \alpha) = \int_\Theta P(\vec{z}|\vec{l}, \Theta)P(\Theta|\alpha)d\Theta \quad (1)$$

$$P(\vec{z}|\vec{l}, \Theta) = \prod_{d=1}^{D}\prod_{i=1}^{W_d} P(z_{d,i}|l_{d,i}, \theta_{d,l_{d,i}}) \quad (2)$$

$$= \prod_{d=1}^{D}\prod_{i=1}^{W_d} \theta_{d,l_{d,i},z_{d,i}} = \prod_{d=1}^{D}\prod_{j\in\Lambda_d}\prod_{k=1}^{K_j} (\theta_{d,j,k})^{n_{d,j,k,\cdot}}$$

Here we introduce $n_{d,j,k,t}$ as the number of occurrences of label $j \in \Lambda_d$ topic $k \in \mathbb{K}_j$ within document d as applied to term $t \in \mathbb{V}$. In this notation, we sum counts using "$\cdot$" and select a vector of counts using ":", so for example $n_{d,j,k,\cdot}$ refers to $\sum_{t=1}^{V} n_{d,j,k,t}$ or the number of occurrences of label j and topic k in document d. Similarly, $n_{d,j,:,\cdot}$ selects the vector of size K_j with the term at position k equal to $n_{d,j,k,\cdot}$. After multiplying by θ's Dirichlet prior and applying the standard Dirichlet-multinomial integral, we see that $P(\vec{z}|\vec{l}, \alpha) = \prod_{d=1}^{D}\prod_{j\in\Lambda_d} \frac{\Delta(n_{d,j,:,\cdot}+\vec{\alpha})}{\Delta(\vec{\alpha})}$ making use of the notation in [14] where $\Delta(\vec{x}) = \frac{\prod_{k=1}^{\dim \vec{x}} \Gamma(x_k)}{\Gamma(\sum_{k=1}^{\dim \vec{x}} x_k)}$ and we treat $\vec{\alpha}$ as a vector of size K_j with each value equal to α. Note that because each label has its own distinct subset of topics, the topic assignment alone is sufficient to determine which label was assigned, so there is no need to represent $\vec{l}$ explicitly in order to compute $n_{d,j,:,\cdot}$.

Now let's return to the computation of $P(\vec{l}|\vec{\Lambda}, \gamma, \alpha)$, which, because $\vec{\Lambda}$ is considered observed, can be factorized into: $P(\vec{l}|\vec{\Lambda}, \Psi)P(\Psi|\alpha, \vec{\Lambda}) =$
$\int_\Phi \prod_{d=1}^{D} P(\psi_d|\alpha, \Lambda_d)\prod_{i=1}^{W_d} P(l_{d,i}|\Lambda_d, \psi_d)d\Phi$
By re-indexing over label types, and applying the standard Dirichlet prior and Dirichlet-multinomial integral to get our final probability $P(\vec{l}|\vec{\Lambda}, \vec{\alpha_L}) = \prod_{d=1}^{D}\prod_{j\in\Lambda_d} \frac{\Delta(n_{d,:,\cdot,\cdot}+\vec{\alpha_L})}{\Delta(\vec{\alpha_L})}$.

Observing that the actual values of $\vec{l}$ are never used explicitly, and because every topic takes part in only a single label, we can represent the model using a Gibbs sampler tracking only the topic assignments $\vec{z}$. We do not need to allocate memory to represent which label $\vec{l}$ is assigned to each token. After combining terms, applying Bayes rule, and folding terms into the proportionality constant, the sampling update formula for assigning a new label and topic to a word token is defined as follows:
$P(l_{d,i} = j, z_{d,i} = k|l_{\neg d,i}, z_{\neg d,i}, w_{d,i} = t; \alpha, \eta)$

$$\propto I[j \in \Lambda_d \wedge k \in 1..K_j]\left(\frac{n_{\cdot,j,k,t}^{(\neg d,i)} + \eta}{n_{\cdot,j,k,\cdot}^{(\neg d,i)} + V\eta}\right) \cdot \quad (3)$$

$$\left(\frac{n_{d,j,\cdot,\cdot}^{(\neg d,i)} + (\vec{\alpha_L})_j}{n_{d,\cdot,\cdot,\cdot}^{(\neg d,i)} + \sum_{j'\in\Lambda_d}(\vec{\alpha_L})_j}\right) \cdot \left(\frac{n_{d,j,k,\cdot}^{(\neg d,i)} + \alpha}{n_{d,j,\cdot,\cdot}^{(\neg d,i)} + K_j\alpha}\right)$$

$$\propto I[j \in \Lambda_d \wedge k \in 1..K_j]\left(\frac{n_{\cdot,j,k,t}^{(\neg d,i)} + \eta}{n_{\cdot,j,k,\cdot}^{(\neg d,i)} + V\eta}\right)\left(n_{d,j,k,\cdot}^{(\neg d,i)} + \alpha\right)$$

The notation $n^{(\neg d,i)}$ refers to the corresponding count excluding the current assignment of topic z and label l in document d position i. Here we have used the definition of $\vec{\alpha_L}$ at position j is αK_j, which allows the numerator in the second fraction to cancel the denominator in the last term. Because the denominator in the second fraction is independent of the topic and label assignment, it is folded into the proportionality constant. Interestingly, this sampler's update rule is like that of Latent Dirichlet Allocation [13] with the intuitive restriction that only those topics corresponding to the document's labels may be sampled.

The similarity of the model and the resulting sampling equations suggests some interesting contrasts to existing models. In particular, if we use PLDA in a purely unsupervised setting with no labels beyond the *latent* label class of k topics, the model reduces exactly to traditional LDA. At the other extreme, if every document has only a single label, if we have no *latent* topic class, and if we give each label's class a single topic, our model's per-class learning function becomes the same count and divide of terms within a class as used in the multinomial naive Bayes model [22]. Similarly, if we have no *latent* topic class, and if we give each label access to only a single topic by setting $K_l = 1$ for all labels l, then the model reduces to Labeled LDA [27]. Interestingly, Labeled LDA can be used to approximate PLDA by the construction of a synthetic label space where, for any given label l, we construct a class of labels of size K_l as labels "l-1 l-2 l-3 ... l-K_l" with all those labels applied to every document with label l. In this case, Labeled LDA will output multiple versions of the same label which, if symmetry is broken during initialization, may result in topics that look like our latent sub-labels in PLDA but has no theoretical guarantees as such. This construction was applied to microblogging data from Twitter with in [26] to good effect, seeding the development of the models in this paper.

Learning and Inference. An efficient Gibbs sampling algorithm can be developed for estimating the hidden parameters in PLDA based on the collapsed sampling formula in Equation 3. Efficient computation of the counts n can be done by keeping histograms over the number of times each term has been associated with each topic within each document and how often each topic has been associated with each term. The sampler loops over the corpus, re-assigning topic assignment variables z and updating the corresponding histograms. However, Gibbs sampling is inherently sequential and we would like this model scale to the size of modern web collections, so we developed a parallelizable learning and inference algorithm for PLDA based on the CVB0 variational approximation to the LDA objective as described in [1]. For each word at position i in each post d, we store a distribution $\gamma_{d,i}$ over the likelihood that each label and topic generated that word in that document using the normalized probabilities from the Gibbs sampling update formula in Equation 3. These distributions are summed into fractional counts of how often each word is paired with each topic and label globally, denoted $\#_{j,k,w}$, and how often each label appears in an each document, denoted $\#_{d,j,k}$. The algorithm alternates between assigning values to $\gamma_{d,i,j,k}$ and then summing assignments in a counts phase. The update equations are listed below. Initially, we use small random values to initialize $\#_{j,k,w}$ and $\#_{d,j,k}$.

Assign:

$$\gamma_{d,i,j,k} \propto I[j \in \Lambda_d, k \in 1..K_j] \cdot \frac{\#_{j,k,w} - \gamma_{d,i,j,k} + \eta}{\#_{j,k} - \gamma_{d,i,j,k} + W\eta} \cdot (\#_{d,j,k} - \gamma_{d,i,j,k} + \alpha)$$

Count:

$$\begin{aligned} \#_{d,j,k} &= \textstyle\sum_i \gamma_{d,i,j,k} \\ \#_{j,k,w} &= \textstyle\sum_{d,i} \gamma_{d,i,j,k} \cdot I[w_{d,i} = w] \\ \#_{j,k} &= \textstyle\sum_w \#_{j,k,w} \end{aligned}$$

The references to $\gamma_{d,i,j,k}$ on the right side of the proportionality in the assignment phase refer to the value at the previous iteration. This formulation allows for a data-parallel implementation, by distributing documents across a cluster of compute nodes. Assignments are done in parallel on all nodes based on the previous counts $\#_{d,j,k}$, $\#_{j,k,w}$ and $\#_{j,k}$ (initially small random values). The resulting assignments $\gamma_{d,i,j,k}$ are then summed in parallel across all compute nodes in a tree sum, before being distributed to all compute nodes for a new assignments phase. The process repeats until convergence. Like in [1], we find that the CVB0 learning and inference algorithm converges more quickly than the Gibbs sampler to a solution of comparable quality. In practice, we find that this algorithm scales to very large datasets—experiments on a corpus of one million PhD dissertation abstracts resulted in models that trained in less than a day on a cluster of twelve 4-core machines.

2.2 Partially Labeled Dirichlet Process

PLDA provides a great deal of flexibility in defining the space of latent topics to effectively learn latent topics both within labels and in a common background space. Unfortunately, PLDA introduces an important new parameter for each label, K_l, representing the number of topics available within each label's topic class. Fortunately, non-parametric statistical techniques can help estimate an appropriate size for each per-label topic set automatically. Concretely, we replace PLDA's per-label topic mixture θ_l with a Dirichlet process mixture model [24], which can be seen as the infinite limit of the finite mixture of topics per label used in PLDA. Formally, PLDP assumes a generative process similar to PLDA, with a multi-set of words $\vec{w}_d$ for each document and an observed set of labels Λ_d. Like in PLDA, each word $w_{d,i}$ has an associated label variable $l_{d,i}$ and topic variable $z_{d,i}$. Here, the label $l_{d,i}$ is drawn from a document-specific multinomial over labels, which for efficiency we assume is drawn from a symmetric Dirichlet prior with parameter α. To generate a topic assignment $z_{d,i}$, PLDP picks an existing topic within label $l_{d,i}$ for word $w_{d,i}$ in proportion to how often it is used, or generates a new topic with held-out mass parameter α (the same as the Dirichlet prior for the document-specific multinomial over labels). The word $w_{d,i}$, is then generated according to the topic distribution $\phi_{l_{d,i} z_{d,i}}$ as in PLDA. The Gibbs sampling formula for updating the joint label and topic assignment $l_{d,i}$ and $z_{d,i}$ in PLDP is:

$$\begin{aligned} & P(l_{d,i} = j, z_{d,i} = k | l_{\neg d,i}, z_{\neg d,i}, w_{d,i} = t; \alpha, \eta) \\ \propto\ & I[j \in \Lambda_d] \cdot \left(\frac{n^{(\neg d,i)}_{\cdot,j,k,t} + \eta}{n^{(\neg d,i)}_{\cdot,j,k,\cdot} + V\eta} \right) \left(\frac{n^{(\neg d,i)}_{d,j,\cdot,\cdot} + \alpha}{n^{(\neg d,i)}_{d,\cdot,\cdot,\cdot} + \alpha|\Lambda_d|} \right) \\ & \cdot \begin{cases} \frac{n^{(\neg d,i)}_{d,j,k,\cdot}}{n^{(\neg d,i)}_{d,j,\cdot,\cdot} + \alpha} & \text{for } k \text{ existing} \\ \frac{\alpha}{n^{(\neg d,i)}_{d,j,\cdot,\cdot} + \alpha} & \text{for } k \text{ new} \end{cases} \\ \propto\ & I[j \in \Lambda_d] \cdot \left(\frac{n^{(\neg d,i)}_{\cdot,j,k,t} + \eta}{n^{(\neg d,i)}_{\cdot,j,k,\cdot} + V\eta} \right) \cdot \begin{cases} n^{(\neg d,i)}_{d,j,k,\cdot} & \text{for } k \text{ existing} \\ \alpha & \text{for } k \text{ new} \end{cases} \end{aligned} \tag{4}$$

As in the Gibbs expression for PLDA in Equation 3, we cancel the numerator in the second fraction with the denominator in both versions of the final term. Again, the denominator in the second fraction is independent of label and topic assignments, so it is folded into the proportionality constant. The Gibbs re-assignment parameters in Equation 4, paired with data structures updated to reflect the appropriate counts of interest at reassignment, can be used to create an efficient Gibbs sampling algorithm for the Partially Labeled Dirichlet Process. Unfortunately, the embedded Dirichlet process mixture model complicates the parallelizability of learning and inference in this model.

It is worth noting that PLDP's embedding of the Dirichlet Process is, in some ways, an even more natural fit than in standard topic modeling applications such as the Hierarchical Dirichlet Process [30]. HDPs and related models discover a global set of latent topics within a corpus as a function of both the concentration parameter α and the corpus being analyzed. So for a known corpus of interest, text mining practitioners still have a single parameter to choose—instead of picking the number of topics, they pick a concentration parameter. In practice, this is often no easier than picking the number of topics directly. In contrast, for PLDP, a single DP concentration parameter α selects the number of topics for each label in $\mathbb{L}$, effectively reducing the number of model parameters related to topic cardinality from $|\mathbb{L}|$ to one, α.

3. CASE STUDIES

We illustrate applications of PLDA and PLDP to partially supervised text mining tasks on two kinds of labeled corpora with very different distributional properties: PhD dissertation abstracts annotated with subject code designations and tagged web pages from del.icio.us. Our PhD dissertation dataset contains over 1 million United States PhD dissertation abstracts from the ProQuest UMI database[1], averaging about just over 2 subject codes from a controlled vocabulary of roughly 260 codes curated by ProQuest staff. These subject codes correspond to high-level field designations such as biochemistry, public administration, cultural anthropology, etc. Each document contains 179 non-stop words on average, corresponding to about two paragraphs of text from each abstract. Our del.icio.us dataset is a subset of 3,200 popular, heavily tagged documents from the Stanford Tag Crawl Dataset [15] collected in the Summer of 2007, with an average length of 1263 words from a word vocabulary of 321,062 terms, and an average of 122 distinct tags out of a vocabulary of 344,540 tags.

These datasets have very different distributional statistics, both in terms of the underlying texts and the label spaces. The del.icio.us documents are longer and have high overlap in common tags, whereas the dissertations tend to be shorter and carefully filed in a small number of subjects. In the following subsections, we examine these datasets from the partially supervised text mining perspective, finding that, despite their differences, both datasets can be effectively modeled. Because of the size of the dissertation dataset in the case study below, we focus on qualitative results that can be achieved through our parallelized PLDA model. Because of the smaller size of the del.icio.us data, we use the del.icio.us case study to quantify our intuitions about the model's ability to approach text mining challenges and compare PLDA with PLDP. Where not otherwise specified, we used fixed hyperparameters of 0.1 for α and η.

3.1 PhD Dissertation Abstracts

Traditional digital libraries often annotate documents with a controlled vocabulary maintained by domain experts to ease indexing, searching, and browsing. While these collections represent a shrinking fraction of all the world's electronic text, they do contain some of the most focused and important content within a limited domain. One such collection is the UMI database of PhD dissertation abstracts maintained by ProQuest, the official archival agency for dissertations written in the United States as designated by the US Library of Congress. In collaboration with social scientists in Stanford's School of Education, we collected 1,023,084 PhD dissertation abstracts from the Proquest UMI database filed by US students since 1980 from any of 151 schools classified as research-intensive by the Carnegie Foundation since 1994.[2] These dissertations are an excellent basis for the study of the history academia because they reflect the entire academic output of universities, as seen through their graduating students, and do not reflect the coverage biases toward scientific or engineering publications found in most databases of academic publications, such as ISI (with a biomedicine) and CiteSeer (with computer science). A more complete study of this dataset can be found in [25] and warrants more space than is available here, so we use the PhD dissertation database as a concrete illustration of the advantages of partially supervised topic models in an active computational social science collaboration.

While the subject codes in our data cover the full range of academic fields, they are not evenly distributed in usage, reflecting real differences in field sizes. Indeed, the most common subject code in our dataset (electrical engineering) has 44,551 instances, whereas the least common (African literature) has only 1,041. Models like PLDA are a natural fit for analyzing these controlled-vocabulary document collections due to their ability to model both the text content in terms of latent usages of the known indexing vocabulary. By contrast, latent topics on this dataset collapse distinctions between small fields (folding them into a single topic) and overly emphasize the importance of larger ones, just based on the amount of support in the data. For example, one run of LDA on this dataset—using 100 latent topics—associated topics to fields in proportion to their prevalence in the data: electrical engineering was assigned three topics, whereas African literature was split between one topic related to all forms of race culture in America ("american, black, white, ethnic, african") and another on all forms of literature ("literari, novel, narr, text, writer"). By seeing which subject codes appeared in each topic, we can see that these two topics are themselves dominated by larger subjects: anthropology and political science for the former and modern and classical literature for the latter. This result is reasonable from the perspective of how much support there is for topics in the dataset. But by losing smaller subject codes in the tails of larger topics, we lose the ability to describe topic dimensions in terms of the known, human interpretable objects of study (fields) while simultaneously losing all latent sub-structure within each field.

As a modeling alternative, we could train an independent topic model on all dissertations in each subject code. However, almost all dissertations have more than one subject code. As a result, many words in the corpus will be double-counted whereas PLDA will attribute each word in each dissertation to the appropriate subject code's latent topics. As a modeling framework, PLDA further allows for the automatic construction of shared latent background topics that

[1]http://www.proquest.com/en-US/products/dissertations/

[2]http://classifications.carnegiefoundation.org/resources/

	Computer Science		Linguistics	
NB	algorithm, problem, network, design, system, method, applic, gener, comput, techniqu, present, approach, model, program, provid, propos, implement, set, structur, effici		languag, english, structur, linguist, word, chapter, verb, semant, speaker, theori, examin, present, form, subject, discours, gener, phonolog, differ, construct, syntact	
Latent sub-topics	databas queri web file access retriev storag user search document system relat process	imag object visual surfac motion algorithm shape featur segment represent	vowel speech phonet conson tone phonolog acoust word sound percept accent	phonolog rule constraint morpholog syllabl theori vowel languag stress featur
	algorithm problem graph comput optim solv solut number effici complex bound	parallel memori processor schedul comput execut architectur applic cach	languag english acquisit learner speaker second children nativ learn	claus syntact structur construct subject case propos argu phrase posit sentenc account
	design softwar user system applic environ interfac tool provid support implement	learn secur detect attack approach techniqu classif propos featur knowledg	languag linguist dialect spanish english speaker commun arab sociolinguist varieti	discours convers linguist text interact speech speaker pragmat narr languag
	network protocol rout servic commun distribut node propos applic mobil wireless	program languag gener logic specif formal semant code implement system	word languag semant linguist lexic mean grammar sentenc structur syntact	verb noun semant morpholog tens form construct aspect verbal languag
(background)	increas rate level decreas higher lower low size valu number compar reduc averag show		chapter theori discuss present concept theoret literatur approach examin question	
	abstract avail shorten librari exclus copi author umi permiss lo cambridg mit angel fax		method model simul predict techniqu estim paramet approach measur appli applic	
	chang respons activ role interact behavior influenc factor affect plai phase import condit		structur type pattern function differ characterist form similar identifi gener	
	variabl measur relationship test correl factor level sampl scale statist score differ determin		need problem provid design strategi effect goal improv success project make develop	

	del.icio.us tags
(background)	pm posted blog comments april post june great march january february comment
	file files download version click page text firefox windows window menu search make
	site free search news contact home online web read privacy information email page
	version page support using available file other system data which files source here features
programming	table database data sql mysql select query index column create tables set rows null row
	css style elements c. visual inherit layout section sheets sheet table property
	file line text command string search match number files character emacs characters
	ajax javascript page function object code asp.net element event method script var class
language	python function returns string class object module functions return type list file int
	english language spanish french nt greek learn pdf german bible chinese lessons languages
	gaelic language scottish scotland english languages unicode logo which irish code
	which language sign semiotics signs words spelling word british e.g. say english american
style	film filed movie films cinematical myyahoo under comedy trailer aol after caption stewart
	fashion manolo shoes style june bag comments dress posted vintage bags london
	class code int function line const file files header statements names type variables

Figure 2: PLDA output on dissertation abstracts (left) and del.icio.us tags (right). Computer Science and Linguistics are two subject codes. "NB" (upper, left) refers to the naive Bayes term estimates associated with each respective code, contrasted with the latent topics learned within each. The "(background)" class (for del.icio.us in upper right, dissertations in lower-left) is the latent topic class shared by all documents in the respective collection.

extract common words found in most abstracts across all per-field topics. The background topics in PLDA are explicitly labeled as such by the model and so do not need to manually identified as they would if each subject code had an independently trained model.

Examples of the topics learned by PLDA are in Figure 2. At the top, we see the most common words associated with each subject code by the simple count-and-divide multinomial naive Bayes estimate, as well as latent sub-topics discovered for each subject code. We used a distributed implementation of PLDA to learn a model with eight global latent background topics and eight latent topics per subject area, resulting in a total of 2,080 latent topics. The results shown are representative of the quality of discovered topics across all academic disciplines. Note that the major distinctions within each subject code roughly correspond to the broad areas of study within computer science and linguistics. The latent topics capture shared common structure in PhD dissertations,[3] including basic things such as variables that increase or decrease, rates of change, and structural starting points about needs, problems, and goals.

A high quality topic space with labeled groups of latent dimensions, as output by PLDA, can be used to ask and answer questions about the nature of academia. For example, we can re-run inference on any given dissertation (while allowing it to use all subject labels) in order to compute a per-dissertation distribution over fields of study—which words might the dissertation have borrowed from which other fields. This can tell us which dissertations within an area of interest are more or less interdisciplinary. Did computational biology get an earlier head start at public or private institutions? Or, at a larger-scale, we can ask which schools tend to have the most inter-disciplinary research in general, or even whether interdisciplinary dissertations are more likely to result in productive future research careers. As always, external, dataset-specific validation metrics need to be in place in order to trust the output of such analyses.

Although this section is merely descriptive, we hope it serves to illustrate the practical impact that human-interpretable topic dimensions can bring to text mining practitioners and computational social scientists. In the next section, we examine content from the social bookmarking website del.icio.us, and use that dataset's abundance of tags as the basis for extrinsic comparison between models.

[3]Note that common stopwords and very rare words were removed before training. Terms were stemmed using a Porter stemmer to further reduce the vocabulary size for memory efficiency.

3.2 Tagged web pages

Users of social bookmarking websites like del.icio.us bookmark the pages they encounter with single word tags [7]. In contrast to more traditional supervised learning problems, user-generated tags are not predetermined nor applied uniformly to all items. For example, the tag *language* on the social bookmarking site http://del.icio.us/ might be applied to web pages about human languages or programming languages. We call these variations in usage of the same tag *sub-tags*. The right half of Figure 2 summarizes some of the types of trends discovered within each tag on del.icio.us. The model was run on a randomly selected 3,200 tagged

Table 1: **HTJS within a tag (left) and within sub-tags (right). % change is relative to the .0183 score for randomly selected documents.**

Tag	Docs by tag		Docs by sub-tag	
	HTJS	Change	HTJS	Change
books	.0254	39%	.1292	605%
computer	.0362	97%	.1609	777%
culture	.0259	41%	.0780	326%
design	.0269	47%	.0510	178%
education	.0206	12%	.1784	873%
english	.0263	44%	.0531	189%
language	.0314	71%	.1996	989%
style	.0290	58%	.2244	1124%
Overall	**.0273**	**49%**	**.1191**	**550%**

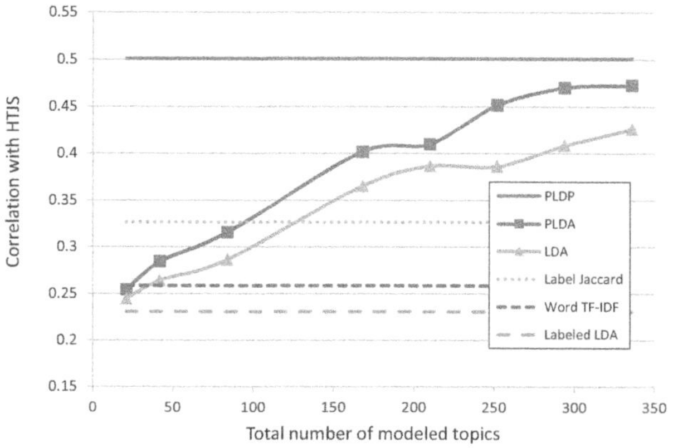

Figure 3: Correlation with HTJS for varying numbers of topic dimensions (PLDA, LDA) or as decided by model form (PLDP, Labeled LDA). Higher is better.

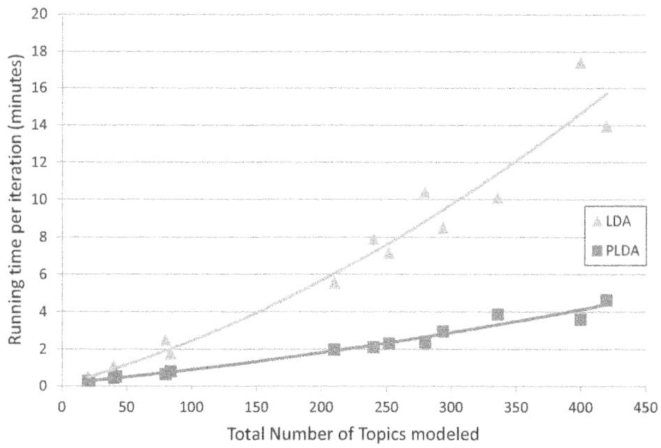

Figure 4: Average training time per iteration (in minutes) while varying the total number of latent topics for LDA (top) and PLDA (bottom) on tagged web pages. PLDA is substantially faster than LDA at a comparable number of topics because of the sparsity inherent to PLDA's sampling distribution.

web pages from [15], using 20 tags hand-selected to be relatively common but also broad in scope: reference, design, programming, internet, computer, web, java, writing, english, grammar, style, language, books, education, philosophy, politics, religion, science, history and culture. We used five latent topics and five topics for each tag. Qualitatively, the figure illustrates the model's ability to discover meaningful sub-tags, even some with a common meaning.

Because the model was trained on only a subset of all tags, we can use the remaining tags as a form of extrinsic model evaluation for computing the correlation of our model's output with a surrogate human relatedness judgment. Such an evaluation is preferable to the standard perplexity-based evaluations common in topic modeling, which have been shown to disagree with human judgments of topic quality, such as in [9]. Here, we refer to the tags not explicitly modeled as held-out tags. In our experiments, most tags are held-out (128 / 132 per document, on average). Because two related documents are more likely to be tagged the same way, overlap between their held-out tags is a natural surrogate gold-standard metric for those pages' relatedness. Formally, we measure the relatedness of a pair of documents d_1 and d_2 as their *held-out tag Jaccard score* (HTJS), defined to be the Jaccard coefficient of overlap in their held out tag sets, $G(d_1)$ and $G(d_2)$, respectively: $HTJS(d_1, d_2) = \frac{|G(d_1) \cap G(d_2)|}{|G(d_1) \cup G(d_2)|}$. To measure the average relatedness within a group of documents, we randomly select k pairs of distinct documents from within the group, with replacement. Here we set $k = 500$, finding little deviation in a set's scores across different random initializations and finding no significant impact from increasing k.

HTJS is a sensible basis for evaluating the effectiveness of our model at capturing latent sub-structure in the data. We computed HTJS on a random subset of documents in our dataset, finding the average score to be 0.0183, showing little overlap in tags of randomly chosen pages, as expected. We expect that pairs of documents that are both tagged with t will have higher held-out tag similarity than the baseline. Columns 2 and 3 in Table 1 show the improvement in HTJS scores from some of the 20 modeled tags in the dataset. Indeed, we find that documents tagged with *computer* (which is not a held-out tag) have an average HTJS score of .0362, a 97% increase over the set of all documents (.0183). On average, grouping by tag increases HTJS scores by 49%, in line with our expectation that knowing the document's tag tells us something about its other tags.

We can further utilize HTJS to quantify our model's ability to isolate coherent sub-tags within a tag. The HTJS for sub-tag s of tag t is computed on all documents labeled with tag t that use sub-tag s with at least as much probability as the sum of the other sub-tags of t. For example, the HTJS of the documents using *computer*'s first sub-tag ("security news may version update network mac") scores as high as 0.312, improving the HTJS of just knowing computer by another 31%. The right-most columns in Table 1 report the HTJS averaged across all sub-tags of the tag named in the left-most column. Not all documents tagged with t will necessarily participate in one of these subsets, as not all documents will be guaranteed to be strongly biased toward one sub-tag. The large improvements shown in Table 1 (550% relative to the baseline and 336% relative to the single tag) demonstrate PLDA's ability to model coherent sub-usages of tags.

3.3 Model comparison by HTJS Correlation

In this section we use HTJS to compare PLDA and PLDP to several strong baselines. Better performing models should have better agreement with HTJS similarity scores across a wide range of document pairs. We quantify this intuition with Pearson's correlation coefficient: for any given model, we compute the correlation of similarity scores generated by the model with HTJS scores over 5,000 randomly selected document pairs. Higher correlations mean that the similarity score implied by the model better aligns with our surrogate human judgments.

Figure 3 shows the correlation of PLDP, PLDA, LDA, Labeled LDA, and tf-idf cosine similarity with HTJS scores as the total number of latent topics changes. The way we compute similarity scores depends on the model form: the partially supervised models introduced here, like other topic models, project documents into a lower dimensional topic space through their per-document topic loadings. In the case of standard topic models such as LDA, this loading is just the per-document topic distribution θ. For PLDA and PLDP, we take a document's "θ" to be the concatenation of the documents' topic loading on all labels (even those not present in the document), resulting in a vector that is dense for topics corresponding to the document's labels and zero elsewhere. Values of these signature vectors are compared using cosine similarity, which we have found to be a stable and high performing metric in this context.

We also included two baselines: tf-idf cosine similarity (in word space) and the Jaccard score of the modeled (i.e. not held-out) tags. For all models, we used fixed hyperparameters of $\alpha = .01$ and $\eta = .01$. Along the x-axis is the total number of latent topics used by PLDA (varying the number of topics allocated per class from 1 to 16) and of LDA. Labeled LDA has a horizontal line corresponding to using 20 topics, one per class (and no latent class) and performs substantially worse than the other models because of its inability to model the sub-structure of each tag. PLDP demonstrates a higher correlation with the HTJS scores across the whole dataset by adapting to the label and word distributions in the data. PLDP's embedded Dirichlet process allows it to allocate different numbers of topics to each tag as a function of its concentration parameter α. Here, our PLDP model allocated 293 topics with substantial probability mass (and several hundred more occurring with very low frequency). These topics were allocated differentially according to the frequency of each tag and the variety of ways in which it is used—most were given to the latent class and common tags such as design, politics, and internet. Only four topics were allocated to the least common tag in the dataset (*grammar*). We experimented with several values of α for PLDP, resulting in more or fewer topics, but with similar ratios of topics allocated to each tag and similar (but not always superior) overall performance results.

As the number of topics grows, the performance of PLDA approaches that of PLDP, but with substantial computational advantages. In particular, our PLDA implementation can be parallelized in a straightforward manner and PLDA does not have the additional overhead of constructing (and possibly pruning) new topics. On average, our PLDA implementation is between 5 and 20 times faster per iteration than our (much less optimized) PLDP implementation, and takes fewer iterations to converge.

4. SCALABILITY

The expense of adding more label classes is directly proportional to how many documents each label participates in, and is always faster than modeling more global latent topics. Indeed, the impact of a label l's topics on running time appears only in computing the sampling proportions in documents with $l \in \Lambda_d$. This allows PLDA models such as those trained on the PhD dissertation dataset to scale to very large topic spaces and in an appreciably shorter period of time—indeed, training our 8 topics-per-subject PLDA model on one million abstracts ran in under a day on a small cluster of multi-core computers. Training a comparable number of latent topics (2,080) on this dataset took, on average 82 times longer per iteration and more iterations to converge. Like LDA, the running time of PLDA (for a fixed number of iterations) is linear in the size of the input data.

On collections with more common labels that have a higher degree of overlap, such as del.icio.us, incorporating more label classes or topics per class increases the computational load, but at a rate much slower than the cost of adding more global shared latent topics, as most tags are not applied to most documents. Figure 4 shows the running time per iteration (in minutes) for the collapsed variational Bayes learning algorithm on roughly twelve thousand documents from del.icio.us as the effective number of topics increases (using the same schedule of topics as in Figure 3). PLDA is substantially faster to train, and also results in a better correspondence with human similarity judgments. We note, however, that practitioners should use models like PLDA with care, choosing the set of labels modeled and topics per label depending on the statistics of the dataset. PLDP can help by automatically determining an appropriate number of topics per label class, but its flexibility comes at the expense of speed, as the model takes substantially longer to train than the Gibbs sampler for PLDA, and does not yet have a data parallel implementation.

5. CONCLUSION

This work proposes two topic models that incorporate label supervision in novel ways: PLDA and PLDP, which learn latent topic structure within the scope of observed, human-interpretable labels. The models introduce high-level constraints on latent topics that cause them to align with human provided labels, essentially "filling in the details" with the use of unsupervised machine learning. The addition of these constraints improves interpretability of the resulting topics, shortens running time, and improves correlation with similarity judgments. And because these models fit into the Bayesian framework, they can be extended to incorporate other features, such as time or sequence information.

PLDA and PLDP provide a direct solution to the problem of label ambiguity: as in linguistic word usage, labels on tagging sites like del.icio.us and social media sites like Twitter are used with different meanings in different contexts. PLDA and PLDA can tease these meanings apart into separate latent topics within each label. However, the models do not directly address the inverse problem of synonymy, where several labels may refer to the same thing. Future work could look at recognizing (partially-) synonymous labels via a post-processing step or with explicit topic sharing. However, the independence of topics across labels is central to the favorable scalability of the models, as discussed in Section 4, so care must be taken when relaxing this constraint. We believe that PLDA, PLDP, and similar future models hold promise for addressing the challenges of partially supervised learning for more interpretable text mining, where human provided labels are present but do not always align with the needs of text mining practitioners.

Acknowledgments

This work was supported by the National Science Foundation under Grant No. 0835614.

6. REFERENCES

[1] A. Asuncion, M. Welling, P. Smyth, and Y.W. Teh. On smoothing and inference for topic models. In *UAI*, 2009.

[2] S. Basu, M. Bilenko, A. Banerjee, and R. J. Mooney. *In Semi-Supervised Learning*, chapter Probabilistic Semi-Supervised Clustering with Constraints, pages 73–102. MIT Press, 2006.

[3] D. Blei, T.L. Griffiths, M.I. Jordan, and J.B. Tenenbaum. Hierarchical topic models and the nested Chinese restaurant process. In *NIPS*, 2003.

[4] D. Blei and J. McAuliffe. Supervised Topic Models. In *NIPS*, volume 21, 2007.

[5] D. M. Blei, A.Y. Ng, and M.I. Jordan. Latent Dirichlet allocation. *JMLR*, 2003.

[6] SRK Branavan, H. Chen, J. Eisenstein, and R. Barzilay. Learning document-level semantic properties from free-text annotations. *Journal of Artificial Intelligence Research*, 34(1):569–603, 2009.

[7] C. Cattuto, A. Barrat, A. Baldassarri, Schehr G., and V. Loreto. Collective dynamics of social annotation. In *PNAS*, pages 10511–10515, 2009.

[8] J. Chang, J. Boyd-Graber, and D.M. Blei. Connections between the lines: augmenting social networks with text. In *KDD*, pages 169–178. ACM, 2009.

[9] J. Chang, J. Boyd-Graber, S. Gerrish, C. Wang, and D. Blei. Reading tea leaves: How humans interpret topic models. In *Neural Information Processing Systems*. Citeseer, 2009.

[10] O. Chapelle, B. Schölkopf, and A. Zien. *Semi-supervised learning*. MIT Press, 2006.

[11] S. Deerwester, S.T. Dumais, G.W. Furnas, T.K. Landauer, and R. Harshman. Indexing by latent semantic analysis. volume 41, pages 391–407. John Wiley & Sons, 1990.

[12] O. Dekel, P.M. Long, and Y. Singer. Online learning of multiple tasks with a shared loss. *JMLR*, 8:2233–2264, 2007.

[13] T. L. Griffiths and M. Steyvers. Finding scientific topics. *PNAS*, 1:5228–35, 2004.

[14] G. Heinrich. Parameter estimation for text analysis. Technical report, 2004. *http://www.arbylon.net/publications/text-est.pdf*.

[15] P. Heymann, G. Koutrika, and H. Garcia-Molina. Can social bookmarking improve web search. In *WSDM*, 2008.

[16] H Daumé III. Markov Random Topic Fields. In *ACL*, 2009.

[17] T. Iwata, T. Yamada, and N. Ueda. Modeling Social Annotation Data with Content Relevance using a Topic Model. In *NIPS*, 2009.

[18] S. Ji, L. Tang, S. Yu, and J. Ye. Extracting shared subspace for multi-label classification. In *KDD*, pages 381–389, New York, NY, USA, 2008. ACM.

[19] S. Lacoste-Julien, F. Sha, and M. I. Jordan. DiscLDA: Discriminative learning for dimensionality reduction and classification. In *NIPS*, volume 22, 2008.

[20] Wei Li and Andrew McCallum. Pachinko allocation: Dag-structured mixture models of topic correlations. In *International conference on Machine learning*, pages 577–584, 2006.

[21] C. Lin and Y. He. Joint sentiment/topic model for sentiment analysis. In *CIKM*, pages 375–384. ACM, 2009.

[22] A. McCallum and K. Nigam. A comparison of event models for naive bayes text classification. In *AAAI-98 workshop on learning for text categorization*, volume 7, 1998.

[23] D. Mimno and A. McCallum. Expertise modeling for matching papers with reviewers. In *KDD*, pages 500–509. ACM, 2007.

[24] R. Neal. Markov chain sampling methods for Dirichlet process mixture models. *Journal of Computational and Graphical Statistics*, 9(2):249–265, June 2000.

[25] D. Ramage. *Studying People, Institutions, and the Web with Statistical Text Models*. PhD thesis, Stanford University, 2011.

[26] D. Ramage, S. Dumais, and D. Liebling. Characterizing microblogs with topic models. In *ICWSM*, 2010.

[27] D. Ramage, D. Hall, R. Nallapati, and C. D. Manning. Labeled LDA: A supervised topic model for credit attribution in multi-label corpora. In *EMNLP*, pages 248–256, 2009.

[28] M. Rosen-Zvi, T. Griffiths, M. Steyvers, and P. Smyth. The author-topic model for authors and documents. In *UAI*. AUAI Press, 2004.

[29] T.N. Rubin, UC Irvine, A. Holloway, P. Smyth, and M. Steyvers. Modeling Tag Dependencies in Tagged Documents. In *NIPS 2009 Applications for Topic Models Workshop*, 2009.

[30] Y.W. Teh, M.I. Jordan, M.J. Beal, and D.M. Blei. Hierarchical dirichlet processes. *Journal of the American Statistical Association*, 101(476):1566–1581, 2006.

[31] I. Titov and R. McDonald. Modeling online reviews with multi-grain topic models. In *WWW*, pages 111–120. ACM, 2008.

[32] C. Wang, B. Thiesson, C. Meek, and D. Blei. Markov topic models. In *AISTATS*, pages 583–590, 2009.

[33] E.P. Xing, A.Y. Ng, M.I. Jordan, and S. Russell. Distance metric learning with application to clustering with side-information. In *NIPS*, pages 521–528, 2003.

[34] J. Zhu, A. Ahmed, and E.P. Xing. MedLDA: Maximum margin supervised topic models for regression and classification. In *ICML*, pages 1257–1264. ACM, 2009.

[35] X. Zhu. Semi-Supervised Learning Literature Survey. Technical Report 1530, Computer Sciences, University of Wisconsin-Madison, 2005.

Refining Causality: Who Copied From Whom?

Tristan Snowsill
Intelligent Systems Laboratory
University of Bristol

Nick Fyson
Bristol Centre for Complexity Sciences and ISL
University of Bristol

Tijl De Bie
Intelligent Systems Laboratory
University of Bristol

Nello Cristianini
Intelligent Systems Laboratory
University of Bristol

ABSTRACT

Inferring causal networks behind observed data is an active area of research with wide applicability to areas such as epidemiology, microbiology and social science. In particular recent research has focused on identifying how information propagates through the Internet. This research has so far only used temporal features of observations, and while reasonable results have been achieved, there is often further information which can be used.

In this paper we show that additional features of the observed data can be used very effectively to improve an existing method. Our particular example is one of inferring an underlying network for how text is reused in the Internet, although the general approach is applicable to other inference methods and information sources.

We develop a method to identify how a piece of text evolves as it moves through an underlying network and how substring information can be used to narrow down where in the evolutionary process a particular observation at a node lies. Hence we narrow down the number of ways the node could have acquired the infection. Text reuse is detected using a suffix tree which is also used to identify the substring relations between chunks of reused text. We then use a modification of the NETCOVER method to infer the underlying network.

Experimental results – on both synthetic and real life data – show that using more information than just timing leads to greater accuracy in the inferred networks.

Categories and Subject Descriptors: H.2.8 Database applications: data mining

General terms: Theory

Keywords: network inference, reconstruction, text reuse, suffix tree

1. INTRODUCTION

In recent years the study of complex networks and their behaviours has become recognised as having great potential. Often the behaviour of the network is a result of the behaviours of the individual nodes under the influence of the behaviour of neighbouring nodes. The spreading of infections across a network has attracted substantial interest in the areas of outbreak detection, epidemic modelling and viral marketing.

In many cases the underlying network of relations between nodes is unknown and observation of the network is either impossible, impractical or not cost-effective, *e.g.*, epidemiological networks.

In some important cases, however, it is possible to make observations of the nodes and *infer* the underlying network. Our principal example of this is in the network of information diffusion on the Internet. When a piece of information reaches an outlet, it then behaves in a way to indicate the receipt of that information. The behaviour could be something simple, such as posting a URL, as considered in [3], or it could be something complex, such as using text which is significant in some way, *e.g.*, reproducing a speech. In this paper we describe how we can identify *text reuse* (when a sizeable chunk of text already seen at one node is reproduced by another) in a large collection of documents produced by multiple outlets which are assumed to be connected by an underlying network.

Existing methods [3, 9, 8] search for and identify markers or indicators that a node has acquired some particular infection and then use only the time of infection for inference. This essentially assumes that the underlying infection does not evolve in any way, and that the indicators may only be different due to noise. This assumption is, we believe, a waste of valuable information as we can envisage cases where infections *do evolve*. Importantly the evolution of infections will not be uniform across different branches of the propagation tree which means we can discover much more about the way infections have spread by studying the states of the infection at the nodes. This concept and an example of its power are our key contributions to the field in this paper.

In our particular example of text reuse we identify that it is only possible to copy text from another node if it already produced that text, and that the "infection" will evolve as different outlets reuse certain chunks of text and extend it. Indeed, certain nodes carrying the "infection" may share very little or no text with the node originally "infected".

This is just one example of how infections can evolve. Textual infections can evolve in other ways, *e.g.*, when short quotes are copied they may be hand-copied, resulting in transmission errors; when a news outlet reports news, the presence or absence of quotes can be an excellent indicator

KDD'11, August 21–24, 2011, San Diego, California, USA.

of the source of the information. We also reiterate that such information should benefit *all* network inference methods.

Outline of this paper.
In this paper we detail an example of how we can improve the inference of networks of outlets from text reuse data by identifying and using information about how reused text evolves. This example motivates the general approach of improving network inference by using additional features. In Sec. 2.1 we establish notation which will be used throughout the paper. In Sec. 3 we describe our method for inferring networks using text reuse and in Sec. 4 we show experimentally that the use of additional features improves network inference.

2. PRELIMINARIES

In this section we introduce notation which will help us to solve the text reuse problem which is used as an example of how network inference can be improved by using additional features of the observed data (in this case, how the text that is reused evolves as it progresses through the network). We also include Sec. 2.2, which introduces suffix trees for readers unfamiliar with them.

2.1 Memes, markers and reports

In the motivating example of this paper we are attempting to infer how online news outlets influence each other by detecting text reuse. Our notation is therefore tailored towards this application. We denote the set of outlets as $\mathcal{W}$ (from websites). Each outlet has a unique identifier. We denote the set of documents or articles as $\mathcal{D}$ (from documents). Each document similarly has a unique identifier. Each document comes from a single outlet, and so a function is defined to identify the outlet which published a document, $w : \mathcal{D} \rightarrow \mathcal{W}$.

Each document is a string of symbols drawn from an alphabet, Σ, *i.e.*, $d \in \mathcal{D}$, $d = \Sigma^{\star}$. The length or size of a document is defined as the number of symbols in the document. No limit is imposed on the size of the alphabet or of the documents. We choose the alphabet to be the set of words used (rather than the immediately obvious choice of the set of characters used).

We suppose that there is a simple underlying infection model which causes text to be copied between outlets, as adopted in, *e.g.*, [3, 9]. We additionally suppose that there is a finite set of outlets which can infect a given outlet. This leads to a network of influence between outlets. For simplicity we assume the network does not change over time. The network is described in graph notation as $G_T = (\mathcal{W}, E_T)$, where E_T is the *true* set of edges between outlets, such that if $(w_1, w_2) \in E_T$ then it is possible for w_1 to infect w_2. We assume the set of outlets is fully known and that we only need to infer the edges between outlets to produce $G_R = (\mathcal{W}, E_R)$, the *reconstructed* network. This is a formulation common to recent papers [8, 9] attempting to solve this problem.

As we do not expect the text to always be copied in the same way (small extracts may be taken, editorial comments may be injected), we say the general concept which is copied is a *meme*, which spreads from one outlet to others. It is difficult to comprehensively define a meme in this context (as it is indeed difficult to define a meme in general), so we make some simplifications.

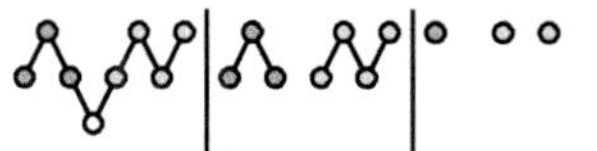

Figure 1: Setting l affects the connected-ness of the marker partial order graph, affecting what is considered a single meme

A string of n symbols drawn from Σ is termed an n-gram. We assume the reader is familiar with the substring, prefix and suffix relations.

We attempt a formal definition of a meme by stating that if one n-gram is a substring of another (and is sufficiently long that it is not a substring of numerous otherwise unrelated n-grams) then they belong to the same meme. We define *belonging to the same meme* as a transitive and symmetric relation, *e.g.*, if the n-gram x belongs to the same meme as y, and z belongs to the same meme as y, then x, y and z all belong to the same meme. A meme can be denoted as a partial order $(X, \prec)$, where X is the set of n-grams belonging to the meme and $\prec$ is the substring relation. The Hasse diagram of the partial order of a meme will be connected.

When an n-gram contained in the partial order of a meme is found in a document, we call the n-gram a *marker* because it marks that the meme has "infected" the outlet. The description of the observation is denoted a *report*.

It is necessary for us to tie down the concept of markers further. We therefore introduce two constraints which must be satisfied for an n-gram to belong to *any* meme (and hence must also be satisfied for all markers).

CONSTRAINT 1 (MINIMUM LENGTH). *The length of the n-gram must be at least l for it to belong to a meme. The number of n-grams satisfying the length constraint is monotonically decreasing for increasing values of l.*

CONSTRAINT 2 (OUTLET SUPPORT). *The n-gram must appear in documents from at least C_w outlets. The number of n-grams satisfying the outlet support constraint is monotonically decreasing for increasing values of C_w.*

There are some natural choices of constraint parameters which can be identified. One natural choice for C_w is 2, which simply ensures that there is evidence that text has been reused. The choice of l is more subjective as low values of l could result in poorly defined memes (see Fig. 1).

A further consideration is that choosing lower support constraints will increase the size of the set of markers and will therefore increase computation time.

For a given set of documents and a choice of constraint parameters there will be a corresponding set of markers. A document may contain a number of markers. The set of markers for a given set of documents is denoted $\mathcal{M} = \mathcal{M}(\mathcal{D})$. The substring partial order is defined over $\mathcal{M}$ and may be computed and represented as a directed graph. Each connected component in the undirected equivalent of this graph is a meme.

The reason why we seem so concerned about the substring relation is that it helps us to identify how a meme has evolved by using simple rules to reduce the number of possible ways an outlet could have been infected. By eliminating potential edges from our network reconstruction we improve our inference.

2.2 Suffix trees

Suffix trees [17] are a powerful data structure used frequently in combinatorial pattern matching and computational genomics [10]. Their key strength is the ability to index in linear space all the substrings of a given text, when naïve methods would require quadratic space. They can also be constructed in linear time with a constant alphabet size [12, 16], with logarithmic time complexity in the alphabet size when the alphabet size is not constant. *Generalized suffix trees* are a superimposition of multiple suffix trees to create a single tree indexing all the substrings of a set of texts, and require linear space and time to construct in the total length of texts [16]. We give a brief description of the structure of the suffix tree as it is a vital component in the text reuse detection component of our example.

The suffix tree of a text, T, is a rooted tree where edges are labelled with non-empty substrings from the text. A node in the suffix tree represents a substring of the text which is formed by concatenating the edge labels on the path from the root to the node. Each leaf node represents a suffix of the text and each suffix of the text is represented by a unique leaf node. No two edges outgoing from a node begin with the same symbol. Edge labels are stored using a pair of indices referring to the start and end positions of a substring in the text. Every substring in the text exists either as a node in the suffix tree (an *explicit node*), or partway down an edge (an *implicit node*). Many suffix tree implementations include the concept of a *suffix link*, which maps each internal node to another node in the tree whose corresponding substring in the text is the largest proper suffix of the substring of the original node, *i.e.*, following a suffix link removes the first symbol from the corresponding substring.

Suffix trees can be preprocessed [13] in linear time (independent of the alphabet size) to allow constant time *lowest common ancestor* (LCA) queries which in the context of a suffix tree give the longest common prefix of two substrings in the text.

Due to poor memory locality, suffix trees are often thought only to be appropriate for in-memory applications. These issues can, however, be mitigated even in the case where the alphabet is large and unbounded. We have implemented Ukkonen's algorithm [16] on hard-disk successfully by separating data for nodes and edges effectively to improve memory locality and using memory mapping, which allows files on hard-disk to be accessed randomly without loading them entirely into memory [15].

3. METHOD

In this section we describe our method for inferring networks of influence using text reuse. First we give an outline of our method, then we give more detailed descriptions of components of our method, including complexity analysis.

3.1 Outline

Our method attempts to infer the network of influence between text sources by identifying text reuse between the sources. We divide our method into three components: *data collection*, *text reuse detection*, and *network reconstruction*.

The data collection component handles gathering the data from the text sources and the processing necessary to turn text cluttered with markup, advertisements and site layout code into plain text. The final output of this component is plain text documents; *i.e.*, the document set, $\mathcal{D}$.

Once the document set has been collated it is passed to the component for text reuse detection. This component uses a suffix tree data structure to identify potential cases of text reuse. There is then further processing to eliminate redundant candidates until we are left with the marker set, $\mathcal{M}$. While the substring relation is defined on $\mathcal{M}$ it is not computed when $\mathcal{M}$ is found, so this must also be calculated, to produce $(\mathcal{M}, \prec)$, which is represented by the boolean matrix M, in which $m_{i,j} = true$ iff marker i is a proper superstring of marker j (note here that we are representing the superstring ordering; the substring ordering would be represented by M^{T}, the transpose of M). Finally the *coverage* of $\mathcal{M}$ in $\mathcal{D}$ is computed in the form of the boolean matrix C, in which $c_{i,j} = true$ iff marker i appears in document j.

The network reconstruction component can be further split into two subcomponents: *candidate generation* and *reconstruction method*. The candidate generation component takes M and C and produces a partially ordered set of reports, $\mathcal{R}$. The partial ordering on this set encodes whether a report can be "explained" by an earlier report and hence produces a set of candidate edges between reports for the reconstruction method. These candidate edges are specified in such a way as to indicate which edges in the outlet network could explain the presence of a marker in a document. The reconstruction method attempts to select edges for the outlet network to explain as many of the markers observed as possible. The reconstruction method is a modification of that described in [8].

3.2 Data collection

The data that needs to be collected for our method is a set of documents from multiple sources. For each document the publication time and the source must be known, as well as the full plain text of the article. There are several contexts in which this data could be found, *e.g.*, news feeds, social media, blogs, emails. In this paper we focus on the example of news feeds. Leskovec et al. [11, 9] have investigated combining news feeds and blogs by using the Spinn3r API [1], a commercial data collection service.

As part of a larger project investigating multilingual news media around the world and in Europe in particular, our research group has produced a system which regularly visits over 1 100 outlets and a total of over 3 500 RSS/Atom feeds to collect over 47 500 articles per day. Of these over 7 000 articles per day are written in English, the remainder being written in a number of European languages.

We are making four weeks of news articles written in English available to invite others to test our method independently [2]. To avoid any potential copyright infringement, however, the data is encoded using a word-to-integer mapping, which is used in our method and should not negatively impact on any attempts to apply other methods to the data.

3.3 Text reuse detection

To detect text reuse in the document set we use a *generalized suffix tree*, a data structure described in Sec. 2.2. We insert all the documents in the document set into the suffix tree. We then identify all n-grams which satisfy the constraints l and C_w in the following way:

Firstly we compute the *word depths* of all the nodes in

the suffix tree. This is done simply in linear time in the number of nodes in the suffix tree – which we will denote as n within this paper – by using a depth first search. Our algorithm uses *parent links* which are calculated by most suffix tree construction algorithms. It also requires constant time look-up for the number of children of a node, which again is available with most suffix tree implementations or can be precomputed in linear time.

We then iterate in a bottom-up fashion, starting at the leaf nodes and propagating the document and outlet IDs upwards through the tree following parent links. The outlet support of a node is monotonically increasing on the path from that node to the root. The word depth of a node is monotonically decreasing on the path from that node to the root. In this way the outlet support constraint filters out nodes from the bottom of the tree and the length constraint filters out nodes from the top of the tree.

For each node satisfying all constraints we wish to store the sets of documents and outlets in which the string corresponding to the node is found. We do not need to store these sets for nodes not meeting the constraints. Alg. 1 calculates the set of nodes corresponding to n-grams which satisfy the constraints and also calculates the *coverage* of each node (the set of documents containing the n-gram).

```
Data: T, the suffix tree of 𝒟.
Data: wordDepth, the word depths of nodes in T.
Data: l, C_w
Result: coverage
toProcess ← {};
foreach leaf ∈ T.LeafNodes() do
    parent ← T.ParentOf(leaf);
    if wordDepth(parent) < l then
        next leaf;
    toProcess ← toProcess ∪ {parent};
    increment nbChildrenProcessed(parent);
    coverage(parent) ← coverage(parent) ∪ coverage(leaf)
    delete coverage(leaf);
while toProcess ≠ ∅ do
    foreach node ∈ toProcess do
        if nbChildrenProcessed = T.NbChildren(node)
        then
            parent ← T.ParentOf(node);
            if wordDepth(parent) ≥ l then
                toProcess ← toProcess ∪ {parent};
                increment nbChildrenProcessed(parent);
                coverage(parent) ←
                coverage(parent) ∪ coverage(node)
            toProcess ← toProcess \ {node};
            if not Satisfies( coverage(node) ) then
                delete coverage(node);
```

Algorithm 1: Identify n-grams satisfying constraints

Although Alg. 1 identifies all n-grams satisfying the constraints, it also produces a set of n-grams which has some redundancy in the sense that there are likely to be n-grams which can be extended without altering the coverage. The fact that these n-grams are reused is explained entirely by a longer n-gram being used, so we filter them out. This filtering step involves simply tracing parent links and suffix links and removing redundant nodes. Tracing along parent links for redundancy removes 10–30% of candidate n-grams. Tracing along suffix links for redundancy removes a further 95–99% of candidate n-grams.

The final step in the text reuse detection component is to compute and store the substring partial order over the marker set, $\mathcal{M}$. We use the fact that if the lowest common ancestor (LCA) of two nodes in a tree is one of those nodes then that node is an ancestor of the other, and in the context of the suffix tree it corresponds to a prefix of the other node. If x is a substring of y then it must be a prefix of a suffix of y. We therefore use constant time LCA queries on all the suffixes of y which are at least as long as x to determine whether x is a substring of y and repeat this for all pairs of markers. To assist in memory locality it is also useful to use the transitive property of the substring relation to partially complete the substring partial order over $\mathcal{M}$.

3.4 Network reconstruction

The network reconstruction task is divided into *candidate generation* and the *reconstruction method*.

3.4.1 Candidate generation

Once we have identified the set of markers, $\mathcal{M}$, and the coverage of those markers, we then need to generate candidate edges for the network of outlets. We only want to provide a candidate edge from one outlet to another if there is evidence of text reuse between them and that it is possible for one outlet to have copied from the other.

As described in Sec. 2.1 we use a concept of *reports* to describe when a marker is observed in a document. A report is then a tuple of the marker and the document. The set of reports $\mathcal{R}$ is a subset of the Cartesian product of $\mathcal{M}$ and $\mathcal{D}$, *i.e.*, $\mathcal{R} \subseteq \mathcal{M} \times \mathcal{D}$. The coverage matrix gives us an obvious set of reports, $\mathcal{R}_C = \{(m,d) \mid c_{m,d} = true\}$. As well as a partial order over markers, there is a total order over documents, where $d_i > d_j$ means d_i was published *before* d_j. We can define a partial order over a given set of reports, in particular we define

$$m_1 \succeq m_2,\, d_1 \geq d_2 \Leftrightarrow r_1 = (m_1, d_1) \succeq r_2 = (m_2, d_2)\,,$$
$$m_1 = m_2,\, d_1 = d_2 \Leftrightarrow r_1 = r_2 .$$

It is assumed that if $d_i \not> d_j$ and $d_i \not< d_j$ then d_i and d_j are the same document (*i.e.*, each individual document has a unique position in the total ordering).

$\mathcal{R}$ will be used by the reconstruction method as a set of candidate edges by considering the directed graph representation of the partial order. The reconstruction method will only be able to place an edge from one outlet to another if there is at least one pair of reports which supports this.

We would like to make $\mathcal{R}$ as small as possible while still generating all candidate edges which the data suggests. The reason for this is that the reconstruction method assigns equal value to explaining each report and hence redundant reports may skew the decisions of the reconstruction method. We therefore pose a minimization problem where we attempt to make $\mathcal{R}$ optimally small while respecting the constraints which are encoded in $\mathcal{R}_C$.

In this section we show that the minimization problem can be tackled by a greedy approach and present both an algorithm to find the optimal solution (Alg. 2) and a more efficient heuristic (Alg. 3) which performs well in practice. Readers may safely skip to Sec. 3.4.2.

Formally, our aim is to find $\mathcal{R}$ satisfying the following minimization problem:

$$\min_{\mathcal{R} \subseteq \mathcal{R}_C} |\mathcal{R}| \tag{1}$$

subject to two constraints. The first constraint ensures that if a marker is observed in a document then that fact is recorded in a report. The report may have a marker which is a superstring of the report originally considered. Formally:

$$\forall r = (m, d) \in \mathcal{R}_C, \exists r' = (m', d) \in \mathcal{R} \,|\, m' \succeq m. \tag{2}$$

The second constraint ensures that if an edge between outlets could be inferred from $\mathcal{R}_C$ then it will also be inferrable from $\mathcal{R}$. Formally:

$$(\exists r_1 = (m_1, d_1), r_2 = (m_2, d_2) \in \mathcal{R}_C \,|\, r_1 \succ r_2) \rightarrow$$
$$\exists r_1' = (m_1', d_1), r_2' = (m_2', d_2) \in \mathcal{R} \,|\, r_1' \succeq r_1, r_1' \succ r_2' \succeq r_2. \tag{3}$$

We say that a report, $r = (m, d)$ is a *maximal* report if

$$\nexists r' = (m', d) \in \mathcal{R}_C \mid m' \succ m.$$

We say that a report can be safely eliminated from $\mathcal{R}$ if both Eqs. 2 and 3 hold before and after the elimination. We let $\mathcal{R}_k$ denote the set of reports after k reports have been safely eliminated, such that $\mathcal{R}_0 = \mathcal{R}_C$.

We now develop some theories to help us construct an optimal algorithm.

THEOREM 1. *Eq. 2 cannot be satisfied if maximal reports are removed.*

PROOF. A maximal report, $r = (m, d)$, is one such that there is no $r' = (m', d)$ with $m' \succ m$. So if r is removed $\nexists r'$ with $m' \succeq m$. □

THEOREM 2. *Provided edges are eliminated safely, we can replace $\mathcal{R}_C$ in Eqs. 2 and 3 with $\mathcal{R}_k$.*

PROOF. By induction. □

This means we only need to examine report pairs in Eq. 3 which remain in the current set of reports.

We now denote the set of reports which can individually be safely eliminated from $\mathcal{R}_k$ as $\mathcal{R}_k^-$, $\mathcal{R}_k^- \subset \mathcal{R}_k$.

THEOREM 3. *If $r \in \mathcal{R}_i^-$ is removed from $\mathcal{R}_i$, producing $\mathcal{R}_{i+1}$ then $\mathcal{R}_{i+1}^- = \mathcal{R}_i^- \setminus \{r\}$.*

PROOF. Clearly $r \notin \mathcal{R}_{i+1}^-$ as $r \notin \mathcal{R}_{i+1}$. Now we must show that

$$\nexists r_p \neq r \mid r_p = (m_p, d_p) \in \mathcal{R}_i^-, r_p \notin \mathcal{R}_{i+1}^-,$$

i.e., that r is the *only* report appearing in $\mathcal{R}_i^-$ not appearing in $\mathcal{R}_{i+1}^-$. There must be a $r_q = (m_q, d_q) \in \mathcal{R}_i$, $r_q \succ r_p$, such that

$$\exists (r_q', r_p') \in \mathcal{R}_i^2, r_q' = (m_q', d_q), r_p' = (m_p', d_p),$$

$$r_q' \succeq r_q, r_p' \succ r_p, r_q' \succ r_p',$$

but that $(r_q', r_p') \notin \mathcal{R}_{i+1}^2$. This means that either $r_q' = r$ or $r_p' = r$. If $r_q' = r$ then r_q' is not a maximal report and there will be a $r_q'' \succ r_q' \succeq r_q$ and hence r_p can be safely eliminated, *i.e.*, $r_p \in \mathcal{R}_{i+1}^-$. If $r_p' = r$ then as r was in $\mathcal{R}_i^-$,

$$\exists (r_q'', r_p'') \in \mathcal{R}_{i+1}^2, r_q'' \succeq r_q' \succeq r_q, r_p'' \succ r_p' \succ r_p, r_q'' \succeq r_m'',$$

therefore (r_q'', r_p'') satisfies Eq. 3, *i.e.*, $r_p \in \mathcal{R}_{i+1}^-$. For completeness one must also show that $\nexists r_p \in \mathcal{R}_{i+1}^- \mid r_p \notin \mathcal{R}_i^-$, *i.e.*, that removing a report does not increase the set of reports that can be safely eliminated; this can be shown as a result from Theorem 2. □

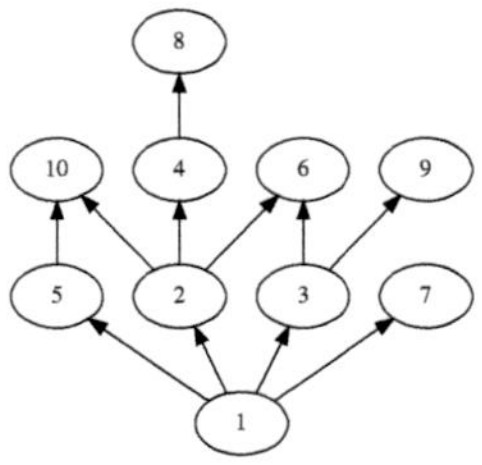

Figure 2: An example of a Hasse diagram of a partially ordered set (in this case the natural numbers up to 10 ordered by divisibility)

This means we only need to examine each report once to see whether it can be safely eliminated and that we obtain Corollary 1.

COROLLARY 1. *For a given $\mathcal{R}_C$ there is a unique minimal set $\mathcal{R}^\star \subseteq \mathcal{R}_C$ satisfying Eqs. 2 and 3.*

We briefly describe the Maximal Comparable Elements (MCE) and Lowest Greater Elements (LGE) algorithms. MCE finds the subset of elements in a partially ordered set which are comparable to a given element and maximal in the partial order. LGE finds the subset of elements in a partial order which are comparable to and strictly greater than a given element and as low in the partial order as possible. In Fig. 2, MCE(2) = {6, 8, 10} and LGE(2) = {4, 6, 10}. It is simple to devise algorithms to solve these problems, and particularly efficient algorithms are possible when the transitive reduction and transitive closure of the directed graph representing the partial order are known.

Given the theorems proved in this section it is possible to use a local examination method where each report is assessed for suitability for removal independently of the removal status of other reports. Pseudocode for such a method is presented in Alg. 2.

While Alg. 2 solves the optimization problem, it is in practice a little slow and it is possible to derive a faster heuristic.

We denote a report, $r = (m, d)$, as a *source report* if

$$\nexists (m, d') \in \mathcal{R}_C \,|\, d' > d,$$

i.e., if d is the earliest document containing m. We additionally denote a report as a *maximal source report* if it is a source report and a maximal report. If a report is not a source report then it is denoted a *carrier report*.

We can use a simple heuristic to reduce $|\mathcal{R}|$ without violating Eqs. 2 and 3, as described in Algorithm 3. This heuristic observes that non-maximal source reports can be eliminated from $\mathcal{R}_C$ without violating the contraints on $\mathcal{R}$. In a large experiment we found the heuristic ran 162 times faster than Alg. 2.

3.4.2 Reconstruction method

We now describe the way in which the partially ordered set of reports, $\mathcal{R}$, is used to infer the network of outlets. As

Data: $\mathcal{M}$, $\mathcal{D}$, $\mathcal{R}_C$
Result: $\mathcal{R}^\star \subseteq \mathcal{R}_C$, $\mathcal{R}^\star = \arg\min_{\mathcal{R}\subseteq\mathcal{R}_C} |\mathcal{R}|$

```
k ← 0;
R^(k) ← R_C;
foreach r2 = (m2, d2) ∈ R_C do
    M_d2 ← {m | (m, d2) ∈ R^(k)};
    M'2 ← LGE_{M_d2}(m2);
    if M'2 = ∅ then
        next r2;
    foreach r1 = (m1, d1) ∈ R_C | r1 ≻ r2 do
        thisSatisfied ← false;
        foreach m'2 ∈ M'2 do
            r'2 ← (m'2, d2);
            M_d1 ← {m | (m, d1) ∈ R^(k)};
            M'1 ← MCE_{M_d1}(m1);
            foreach m'1 ∈ M'1 do
                r'1 ← (m'1, d1);
                if r'1 ⪰ r'2 then
                    thisSatisfied ← true;
                    next r1;
        if not thisSatisfied then
            next r2;
    /* It is safe to eliminate r2 */
    R^(k+1) ← R^(k) \ {r2};
    k ← k + 1;
```

Algorithm 2: Algorithm to minimize $|\mathcal{R}|$

this is a development of the method in [8] we refer the reader to that paper for details and proofs.

As mentioned previously the partially ordered set of reports can be viewed as a directed graph between reports. The partial order can be found using all-pairs comparison. This directed graph will be closed under transitivity as the partial order itself is transitive. As in [8] we formulate the task of inferring the network as a set covering task. We have a universe set, $\mathcal{A} =$

$$\left\{r = (m, d) \in \mathcal{R} \mid \exists r' = (m', d') \in \mathcal{R}, m' \succeq m, d' > d\right\},$$

i.e., the set of reports which can be explained by reports from other documents. We also have a family, $\mathcal{B}$, of subsets of $\mathcal{R}$, each of which corresponds to the set of reports which will be explained if an edge is inferred between two outlets,

$$\mathcal{B} = \{B_{u,v} \mid u, v \in \mathcal{W}\}$$
$$B_{u,v} = \{r = (m, d) \in \mathcal{R} \mid \exists r' = (m', d'), r' \succeq r, w(d') = u, w(d) = v\}.$$

Our goal is to find the smallest subfamily, $\mathcal{C} \subseteq \mathcal{B}$ such that $\bigcup \mathcal{C} = \mathcal{A}$. This formulation is very similar to the formulation in [8], the principal difference being that edges must not only respect the time directionality of the relations between outlets but also the textual evolutionary directionality of those relations. This means that there are fewer candidate edges from which the algorithm can choose when trying to explain reports. The set covering problem is known to be NP-hard but is well approximated using a greedy approach [5, 14].

The reconstruction method calculates a score for each potential edge which can be added to the outlet network equal to the number of additional reports that would be explained by adding that edge to the network. These scores decrease monotonically as edges are added to the network (as adding edges cannot un-explain reports) and hence a priority queue is an ideal structure to store these scores. While there are still unexplained reports the algorithm grabs the edge with the highest score from the priority queue and adds that to the network. It then recalculates scores in a lazy manner by grabbing an edge, recalculating its score then updating its score in the priority queue. If the algorithm grabs the same edge twice in a row then that edge has the highest recalculated score in the whole queue and is added.

3.5 Overall complexity analysis

We briefly describe the complexity of the different components of our method. Table 1 gives an example of running times on data generated as in Sec. 4.1.

Building the suffix tree requires $\mathcal{O}(n \log |\Sigma|)$ time, where n is the total length of text added and $|\Sigma|$ is the size of the alphabet. Preprocessing for LCA queries takes $\mathcal{O}(n)$ time, as does computing the word depths of the suffix tree nodes. We believe that identifying the valid n-grams and calculating their coverage takes $\mathcal{O}(n \log n)$ time although we have not proved this. Removing redundant n-grams takes $\mathcal{O}(n \log |\Sigma|)$. Computing the marker partial order takes $\mathcal{O}\left(|\mathcal{M}|^2 \log(|\Sigma|) \max_{d\in\mathcal{D}} |d|\right)$ time and in practice dominates the time complexity of the entire text reuse detection component. The heuristic described in Alg. 3 takes

$$\mathcal{O}\left(\frac{|\mathcal{R}_C|^2}{|\mathcal{D}|} + |\mathcal{D}|\left(|\mathcal{M}| + |\mathcal{R}_C|\right)\right)$$

expected time. Computing the partial order over $\mathcal{R}$ takes $\mathcal{O}\left(|\mathcal{R}|^2\right)$ time. An upper bound on the time complexity of the reconstruction method is $\mathcal{O}\left(|\mathcal{R}|^4\right)$; we hope to find tighter upper bounds on this.

4. EXPERIMENTAL RESULTS

In this section we demonstrate that using substring relations greatly improves the performance of an existing network inference method. That method, described in [8], is referred to as NETCOVER within this section. Our improved method is referred to as NETCOVER+SUBSTRING.

4.1 Synthetic data

To demonstrate that taking the substring information into account significantly increases the accuracy of inferred net-

Data: $\mathcal{M}$, $\mathcal{D}$, C
Result: $\mathcal{R}' \subseteq \mathcal{R}_C$

```
R' ← {};
foreach d ∈ D do
    M_d ← {m | c_{m,d} = true};
    foreach m ∈ M_d do
        r ← (m, d);
        if IsMaximalSource(r) or IsCarrier(r) then
            R' ← R' ∪ {r};
```

Algorithm 3: Simple heuristic to reduce $|\mathcal{R}|$

Table 1: Running times (in seconds)

Nb. of nodes	100	300	1000	3000
Build tree	7	24	42	92
Preprocess for LCA queries	3	5	8	22
Calculate word depths	1	1	2	3
Alg. 1	10	50	89	180
Remove redundant nodes	1	4	5	10
Compute substring partial order over $\mathcal{M}$	17	96	342	2691
Alg. 3 and $\mathcal{R}$ partial order	3	30	212	9818

works it is necessary to compare the networks obtained to ground truth networks. In the envisaged applications there is unlikely to be a "ground truth" (although in some circumstances there may be a surrogate ground truth network – *e.g.*, we can presume that the "follow" network in Twitter will be very strongly related to the network of "retweets"), so we use synthetic data where the ground truth is known to give a demonstration of the effectiveness of our method.

4.1.1 *Generative model*

We use a model that generates a directed network of outlets and then propagates a number of memes across the network using an infection model. We use two different random network generation methods, Erdős-Rényi [6] and Bollobás [4]. We choose parameter values for each such that the expected number of edges per node is 2 (expected 1 outgoing, 1 incoming). We let the number of nodes, N, be a parameter in the experiments.

To simulate the movement of memes through the system, we use a well known Susceptible-Infected-Recovered (SIR) model of infection, in which each outlet can be in one of three states. When an outlet is susceptible and one of its neighbours is infected there is a chance that the outlet will become infected. When an outlet is infected it generates a document carrying the infection. The way in which outlets change state is similar to as described in [8] except we set $p_R = 0$ and impose a time limit on how long an infection can propagate. We start M independent infections.

For simplicity the documents are generated with a fixed length, L, where each symbol, σ_i, is drawn uniformly from a finite integer alphabet, $\Sigma = \{0, 1, \ldots, |\Sigma| - 1\}$. The first outlet to be infected (the source) generates a fully random document. Subsequent outlets which become infected copy a random section of the document from which they become infected and pad the section with further random symbols to reach the length L, as shown in Fig. 3. The length of text which is copied is drawn from a uniform distribution with a parameter, α, determining the minimum amount of text to be copied, $l \sim \mathrm{U}(\alpha L, L)$. The starting position in the original document and the new document, x_0 and x_1 respectively, are drawn uniformly randomly and independently, $x_0, x_1 \sim \mathrm{U}(0, L - l)$.

This is obviously a crude model for how text is copied – in reality a multi-modal distribution is far more likely due to the likelihood of preserving sentence and paragraph structures when copying. Also we acknowledge that words in reality are not drawn uniformly from a finite alphabet, but rather from a Zipf power law. We do not, however, believe

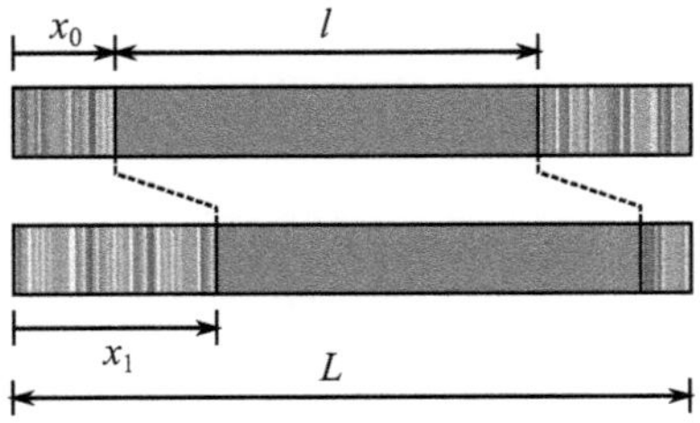

Figure 3: Generating a document when an outlet becomes infected.

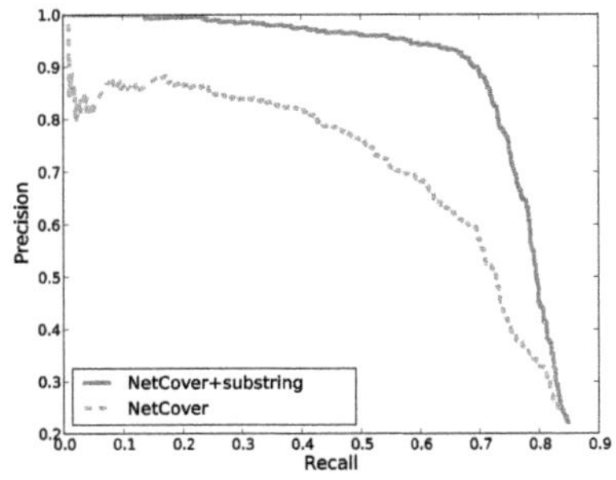

Figure 4: Precision/Recall for Erdős-Rényi graph

that these shortcomings in the generative model compromise the value of the experiments.

4.1.2 *Results*

We used the generative model to create one Erdős-Rényi graph and one Bollobás graph. Both graphs had $N = 500$ nodes. The Erdős-Rényi graph was used to generate documents for 300 markers and the Bollobás graph was used to generate documents for 1200 markers. The documents generated were processed directly as described in Sec. 3. Figs. 4 and 5 show how inference is dramatically improved by using substring information.

4.2 Real world data

We gathered data from the online mediasphere as described in Sec. 3.2 for four consecutive weeks from 3 January 2011. We chose constraint parameters for text reuse detection of $l = 100$ and $C_w = 2$.

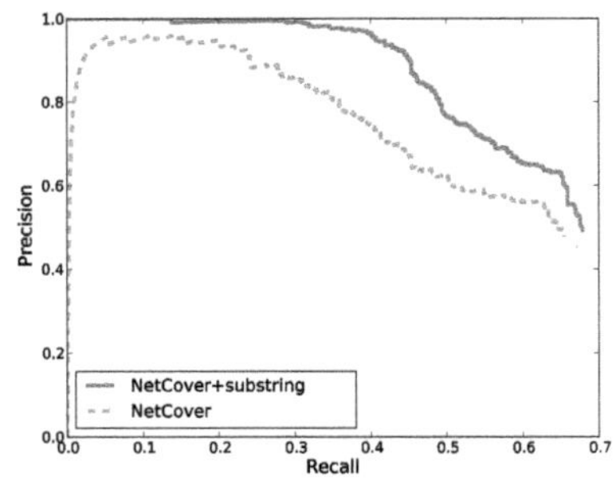

Figure 5: Precision/Recall for Bollobás graph

Table 2: Statistics of real world data

Week	1	2	3	4
Nb. of articles	121 360	128 280	124 830	124 729
Total length	57.2M	61.6M	59.5M	59.7M
$\lvert\mathcal{M}\rvert$	29 978	31 246	29 599	29 407
Articles with reports*	25 106	25 686	24 984	24 571
$\lvert\mathcal{R}_C\rvert$	103 577	106 141	97 759	98 494
$\lvert\mathcal{R}'_C\rvert$	92 481	94 981	87 393	88 311

* $\lvert\{d \mid \exists(m, d) \in \mathcal{R}_C\}\rvert$

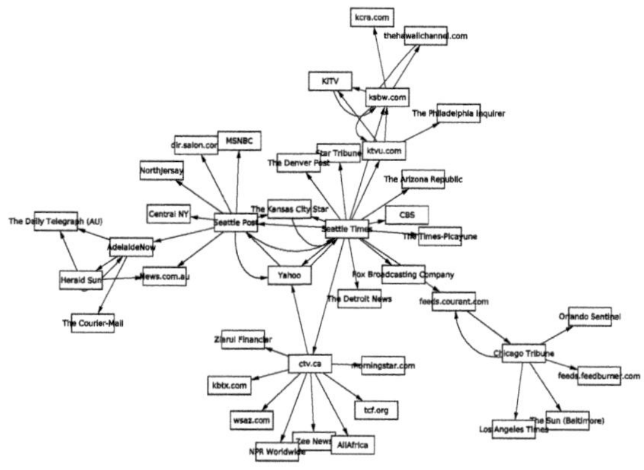

Figure 6: Largest connected component when 100 highest ranked edges are added to the reconstruction

4.2.1 *Overview of results*

Table 2 gives an overview of the data gathered and the results of detecting text reuse and generating candidate edges. Fig. 6 shows the largest connected component in the network inferred from Week 1 after 100 edges have been added, where a directed edge from A to B means the method inferred that information travelled from A to B. Further results can be found at the paper's supporting website [2].

We can see some interesting structure in the inferred network. For example, kcra.com, KITV and ksbw.com (all at the top of Fig. 6) are all Western and Pacific Region stations owned by Hearst Television Inc. The Daily Telegraph (AU), Herald Sun, news.com.au, Adelaide Now and The Courier-Mail (all on the left of Fig. 6) are all Australian newspapers owned by Rupert Murdoch's News Limited. The Chicago Tribune, feeds.courant.com (Hartford Courant), Orlando Sentinel, The Baltimore Sun, and Los Angeles Times (all in the bottom-right of Fig. 6) are all owned by the Tribune Company.

4.2.2 *Stability of the network over time*

As we do not have a ground truth network for this problem, we must demonstrate the value and the validity in a different way to in Sec. 4.1. We therefore test the stability of the network over time, as in [7].

The purpose of the test is to demonstrate that the inferred network for one week has much greater similarity to the inferred network for the previous week than would be expected by random chance. The effectiveness of this test is reliant

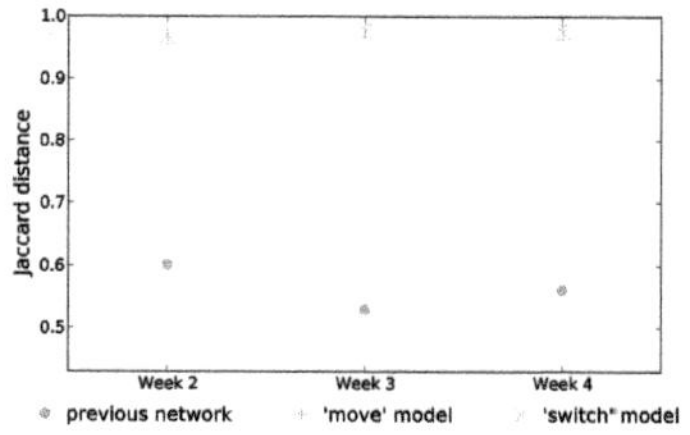

Figure 7: Network stability over time. Jaccard distance measures the distance between sets and is applied here to the set of edges.

on the underlying network itself being stable, which is an assumption of existing methods for network inference [9, 8].

To demonstrate that the network has greater similarity to the network inferred from data from the previous week than would be expected, we use two methods of randomization to produce random graphs preserving certain properties of the original network. The first method creates an Erdős-Rényi random graph with the same nodes and the same number of edges as the original network. We refer to this method as the "move model". The second method performs directed edge swaps to preserve the nodes, the number of edges and the in- and out-degree of the nodes. We refer to this method as the "switch model". We make $100 \times |E|$ swaps for each randomized network [7].

We repeated each randomization method 1000 times and the results are shown in Fig. 7. This figure shows much greater stability than would be expected by random chance and demonstrates that genuine results are being found. We also performed this test on networks generated by the original NetCover algorithm which also demonstrated greater stability than would be expected by random chance, but the Jaccard distances between networks inferred for consecutive weeks were slightly higher. This indicates that text reuse information is itself stable but that better inference is obtained using the substring information.

5. CONCLUSIONS

In this paper we have shown that existing methods for inferring networks of influence do not leverage a great deal of information which is often available and can greatly improve inference. We present an example of how we can greatly increase the effectiveness of the NetCover [8] algorithm applied to text reuse data by accounting for the way in which text is itself reused. Experiments on synthetic data showed very strong evidence for this claim. Such improvements should also be attainable by applying similar logic to other existing methods, such as NetInf [9].

We have also contributed a method for large scale text reuse detection based on the use of a suffix tree data structure, which can produce valuable observations of underlying network structures where text can be replicated.

We believe that the concept of leveraging the textual information present in observations on the Internet is a powerful one. We expect further work to identify more ways that textual information can indicate the directionality of relations between outlets.

Acknowledgements

Tristan Snowsill and Nick Fyson are supported by EPSRC grants DTG/EMAT.SB1848.6525 and EP/5011214 respectively. Nello Cristianini is supported by a Royal Society Wolfson Merit Award. This work is partially supported by EPSRC grant EP/G056447/1 amd by the European Commission through the PASCAL2 Network of Excellence (FP7-216866).

6. REFERENCES

[1] Spinn3r API. http://www.spinn3r.com/, 2008.

[2] Supporting website, https://patterns.enm.bris.ac.uk/projects/refining_causality, 2011.

[3] E. Adar and L. Adamic. Tracking information epidemics in blogspace. In *Proceedings of the 2005 IEEE/WIC/ACM International Conference on Web Intelligence*, pages 207–214. Citeseer, 2005.

[4] B. Bollobás, C. Borgs, J. Chayes, and O. Riordan. Directed scale-free graphs. In *Proceedings of the fourteenth annual ACM-SIAM symposium on Discrete algorithms*, pages 132–139. Society for Industrial and Applied Mathematics, 2003.

[5] V. Chvatal. A greedy heuristic for the set-covering problem. *Mathematics of operations research*, 4(3):233–235, 1979.

[6] P. Erdős and A. Rényi. On the evolution of random graphs. In *Publication of the Mathematical Institute of the Hungarian Academy of Sciences*, pages 17–61. 1960.

[7] I. Flaounas, M. Turchi, T. De Bie, and N. Cristianini. Inference and validation of networks. In *Machine Learning and Knowledge Discovery in Databases*, volume 5781 of *Lecture Notes in Computer Science*, pages 344–358. Springer Berlin / Heidelberg, 2009.

[8] N. Fyson, T. De Bie, and N. Cristianini. Reconstruction of Causal Networks by Set Covering. In *ICANNGA'11: International Conference on Adaptive and Natural Computing Algorithms*, Ljubljana, Slovenia, 2011.

[9] M. Gomez-Rodriguez, J. Leskovec, and A. Krause. Inferring Networks of Diffusion and Influence. In *KDD2010: The 16th ACM SIGKDD Conference on Knowledge Discovery and Data Mining*, 2010.

[10] D. Gusfield. *Algorithms on strings, trees and sequences.* Cambridge University Press, 1997.

[11] J. Leskovec, L. Backstrom, and J. Kleinberg. Meme-tracking and the Dynamics of the News Cycle. In *Proceedings of the 15th ACM SIGKDD international conference on Knowledge discovery and data mining*, pages 497–506. ACM New York, NY, USA, 2009.

[12] E. M. McCreight. A Space-Economical Suffix Tree Construction Algorithm. *Journal of the ACM*, 23(2):262–272, Apr. 1976.

[13] B. Schieber and U. Vishkin. On finding lowest common ancestors: simplification and parallelization. *SIAM Journal on Computing*, 17(6):1253–1262, 1988.

[14] P. Slavík. Improved performance of the greedy algorithm for partial cover. *Information Processing Letters*, 64(5):251–254, Dec. 1997.

[15] T. Snowsill and F. Nicart. A hard-disk based suffix tree implementation. Technical Report 133088, University of Bristol, Bristol, UK, 2011.

[16] E. Ukkonen. On-line construction of suffix trees. *Algorithmica*, 14(3):249–260, 1995.

[17] P. Weiner. Linear pattern matching algorithms. In *IEEE Conference Record of 14th Annual Symposium on Switching and Automata Theory, 1973. SWAT'08*, pages 1–11, 1973.

Conditional Topical Coding: An Efficient Topic Model Conditioned on Rich Features

Jun Zhu† Ni Lao† Ning Chen‡ Eric P. Xing†
†School of Computer Science, Carnegie Mellon University, Pittsburgh, PA 15213
‡Department of Computer Science and Technology, Tsinghua University, Beijing, China 100084
{junzhu, nlao, epxing}@cs.cmu.edu; chenn07@mails.thu.edu.cn

ABSTRACT

Probabilistic topic models have shown remarkable success in many application domains. However, a probabilistic conditional topic model can be extremely inefficient when considering a rich set of features because it needs to define a normalized distribution, which usually involves a hard-to-compute partition function. This paper presents conditional topical coding (CTC), a novel formulation of conditional topic models which is non-probabilistic. CTC relaxes the normalization constraints as in probabilistic models and learns non-negative document codes and word codes. CTC does not need to define a normalized distribution and can efficiently incorporate a rich set of features for improved topic discovery and prediction tasks. Moreover, CTC can directly control the sparsity of inferred representations by using appropriate regularization. We develop an efficient and easy-to-implement coordinate descent learning algorithm, of which each coding substep has a closed-form solution. Finally, we demonstrate the advantages of CTC on online review analysis datasets. Our results show that conditional topical coding can achieve state-of-the-art prediction performance and is much more efficient in training (one order of magnitude faster) and testing (two orders of magnitude faster) than probabilistic conditional topic models.

Categories and Subject Descriptors

I.5.1 [**Pattern Recognition**]: Models - Statistical

General Terms

Algorithms, Experimentation

Keywords

sparse coding, topic models, conditional models

1. INTRODUCTION

Probabilistic topic models, such as latent Dirichlet allocation (LDA) [4] and probabilistic latent semantic indexing (pLSI) [12], have been widely used for inferring a low dimensional representation that captures the latent semantics of text documents or images. Such low dimensional representations can be used for classifying, clustering, or structurally browsing large corpora. However, most existing topic models only consider document-word appearance (e.g., bag-of-word counts) and they are essentially not "feature-based" models. As discussed in [41], using the word information itself could be insufficient in resolving the word's meaning ambiguity. For example, in a hotel review, the word "friendly" can be used to describe a positive aspect, while it can also be used to describe a negative aspect when used with a denying word (e.g., "not"), such as in the sentence "the front desk was not very friendly". Another example is that documents are usually associated with meta-data (e.g., authors, dates and publication venues), which could serve as a rich information source for inferring semantically meaningful topical patterns [26]. Therefore, exploring a rich set of input features (e.g., non-local contextual or summary features in an article or image) can be expected to yield better models in terms of their discovered latent topics [41, 26, 29] and performance on prediction tasks (e.g., regression [41]). One can also find convincing arguments of instead preferring a feature-based model from the celebrated work on conditional random fields (CRF) [21] and their various applications on information extraction [30], gene prediction [8] and etc. However, it is non-trivial to incorporate rich features in probabilistic topic models. One reason is that a fully generative topic model specifies a joint distribution of all the introduced variables, which prevents flexible incorporation of nontrivial features in the data, because directly modeling such features as random variables would result in a prohibitively large state space that makes inference and learning very difficult, if at all possible. Recent progress has been made on developing conditional topic models [41], which can in principle incorporate arbitrary features to discover meaningful topical representations. However, due to its probabilistic nature, such a conditional topic model involves a normalization factor when defining the topic-assignment distribution given input features (please see Section 2), which can make inference and learning extremely hard in latent variable models. Various approximation techniques has been developed [41, 37, 19], but they are usually very inefficient.

Another limitation of probabilistic topic models is that they lack a mechanism to directly control the sparsity of the inferred posterior representations. Although using a sparse prior can indirectly influence the posterior sparsity, an arguably better way is to directly impose posterior regular-

KDD'11, August 21–24, 2011, San Diego, California, USA.

ization (e.g., using moment constraints [11] or entropic priors [31]). However, due to the smoothness of the entropic regularizer, such methods often do not yield truly sparse posterior representations in practice. A technical reason for the difficulty in achieving sparsity in probabilistic topic models (e.g., LDA) is that the mixing proportions or topics take the form as a normalized distribution. Thus it is unhelpful to directly use a sparsity inducing ℓ_1-regularizer as in lasso [35, 25] and sparse coding [28].

In this paper, we present conditional topical coding (CTC), a novel non-probabilistic formulation of conditional topic models. CTC is not subject to the strict normalization constraints as in probabilistic topic models and we show that it can efficiently incorporate a rich set of features for improved topic discovery and better prediction performance. Moreover, the non-probabilistic formulation can enforce a direct control on the sparsity of the inferred representations by using appropriate regularizers which have been widely studied in sparse coding [28] and lasso [35, 25] methods. In addition, the non-probabilistic CTC can be seamlessly integrated with a convex prediction loss measure (e.g., ϵ-insensitive loss [33] for learning a large-margin regression model) in order to incorporate the widely available supervised side information, such as review rating scores, for discovering predictive representations. We develop an efficient and easy-to-implement coordinate descent learning algorithm, of which each coding substep has a closed-form solution, and the feature weights and dictionary learning can be efficiently done with high-performance techniques. Finally, we extensively evaluate CTC on online review analysis data. Our results show that CTC can achieve state-of-the-art prediction performance and is much more efficient in training (one order of magnitude) and testing (two orders of magnitude faster) than probabilistic conditional topic models.

Related work: CTC represents a new extension of sparse coding (SPC) [28], which provides an elegant framework to achieve sparsity on the usually unnormalized code vectors or dictionary by using the theoretically sound ℓ_1-norm or other composite regularizers [20, 17, 16, 2]. Although much work has been done on learning a structured dictionary [17, 2], existing SPC methods typically discover flat representations, such as single-layer sparse codes of small image patches or word terms [17, 2]. In order to achieve a representation of an entire image or document, a post-processing such as average or max pooling [39] is needed. This two-step procedure can be rather sub-optimal because it lacks a channel to provide direct correlations between individual component representations [15], or to leverage the possibly available high-level weak supervision (e.g., document categories) to discover predictive representations [40] or learn a supervised dictionary [24].

The rest of the paper is structured as follows. Section 2 reviews probabilistic conditional topic models. Section 3 presents conditional topical coding together with a learning algorithm. Section 5 presents empirical studies and Section 6 concludes with future directions discussed.

2. PROBABILISTIC CONDITIONAL TOPIC MODELS

We briefly review the probabilistic conditional topic model (CdTM) [41] without Markov dependency among different topic assignments and motivate the development of CTC.

Figure 1 (a) illustrates the graphical structure of CdTM, where we have ignored the prior of θ for clarity. Let N be the number of terms in a vocabulary $V=\{1,\cdots,N\}$ and let β be a topical matrix, of which each row β_k is a unigram distribution over the terms in V, that is, $\beta_k \in \mathcal{P}_N$, where $\mathcal{P}_N$ is a $(N{-}1)$-simplex. In CdTM and standard LDA, a document is represented as a *sequence* of words $\mathbf{w}=(w_1,\cdots,w_M)$, where M is document length and w_m is the word that appears in position m of the document. Each position m is associated with a topic assignment variable Z_m, and the topics of all the words in a document are sampled from the same document-specific distribution, which is the mixing proportion θ in standard LDA. In CdTM, in order to incorporate rich features, which are denoted by A (an instance denoted by $\mathbf{a}$, e.g., POS tags or contextual features), the topic-assignment distribution is defined as a softmax function

$$p(z_m|\theta,\mathbf{a}) = \frac{1}{B(\theta)}\exp(\theta^\top \mathbf{f}(z_m,\mathbf{a})), \qquad (1)$$

where $\mathbf{f}$ is a vector of feature functions and θ is the vector of weights, which follows a prior distribution (e.g., normal prior). The normalization factor (or partition function) $B(\theta)=\sum_z \exp(\theta^\top \mathbf{f}(z,\mathbf{a}))$ is a *sum-exp* function, whose logarithm is also known as a *log-sum-exp* function [19].

Although the conditional model (1) can effectively consider rich features, the inference and learning of the resulting conditional topic model is usually hard because of the sum-exp function $B(\theta)$ especially when θ is a latent variable as in CdTM. Much research has been conducted to obtain a good approximate inference method, such as [37, 41, 19], but these methods are usually very inefficient.

Below, we present a novel non-probabilistic formulation of conditional topic models, which can efficiently incorporate a rich set of features to achieve improved topic representations and prediction performance. Another potential advantage of the non-probabilistic formulation is that it can explicitly control the sparsity of the learned representations. In contrast, a probabilistic topic model in general can be very inflexible to explicitly control the sparsity of inferred latent representations, as we have discussed in Section 1.

3. CONDITIONAL TOPICAL CODING

For clarity, we first consider the simplified CTC model without using features, which will be called sparse topical coding (STC) [42]. Slightly different from LDA and CdTM, we represent a document as a vector $\mathbf{w}=(w_1,\cdots,w_{|I|})^\top$, where I is the index set of words that appear and each w_n $(n\in I)$ represents the number of times that word n appears in this document. Like other topic models, we present STC as a technique to project the input $\mathbf{w}$ into a semantic latent space that is spanned by a set of automatically learned bases (a basis set is also called a *dictionary* [17]) and achieve a high-level representation of the entire document. To remove the strict normalization constraints, we formulate STC as regularized loss minimization [35, 25, 28]. However, purely for the ease of understanding, we start with describing a probabilistic generative procedure.

3.1 A Probabilistic Generative Process

Let β denote a dictionary with K bases. As in LDA, we assume that each row β_k is a topic, i.e., a unigram distribution over the terms in V. We will use $\beta_{.n}$ to denote the nth column of β. Graphically, STC is a hierarchical latent vari-

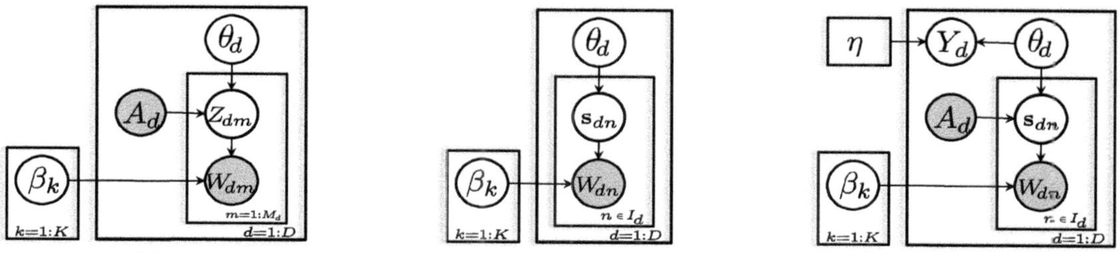

(a) (b) (c)

Figure 1: Graphical representations for (a) probabilistic conditional topic models [41]; (b) sparse topical coding; and (c) conditional topical coding with supervised information Y. We omit the priors on θ and β.

able model, as shown in Figure 1 (b), where $\theta \in \mathbb{R}^K$ is the latent representation of an entire document and $\mathbf{s}_n \in \mathbb{R}^K$ is a latent representation of the individual word n. We call $\mathbf{s}_n$ *word code* and θ *document code*. Then, a document can be described as arising from the following process

1. sample the document code θ from a prior $p(\theta)$.
2. for each observed word $n \in I$
   (a) sample the word code $\mathbf{s}_n$ from a conditional distribution $p(\mathbf{s}_n|\theta)$
   (b) sample the observed word count w_n from a distribution with the mean being $\mathbf{s}_n^\top \beta_{.n}$.

Since we have relaxed the codes θ and $\mathbf{s}$ to be real-valued vectors, we need to define a new distribution for generating word counts. Here, we adopt the ideas of sparse coding [28]. Specifically, we treat $\mathbf{s}_n$ as a coefficient vector and use the linear combination $\mathbf{s}_n^\top \beta_{.n}$ to reconstruct the observed word count w_n, under some loss measure as explained below; and the document code θ is obtained via an aggregation (e.g., truncated average) of the individual codes of all its terms. To specify a STC model, the choices of $p(\theta)$ and $p(\mathbf{s}|\theta)$ reflect our bias on the discovered latent representations and how θ and $\mathbf{s}$ are connected. We will discuss them in the next section. For the last step of generating observed data, we adopt the broad class of exponential family distributions to make STC applicable to rich forms of data. Formally, we use the linear combination $\mathbf{s}_n^\top \beta_{.n}$ as the *mean* parameter of an exponential family distribution that generates the observation w_n. In other words, we define $p(w_n|\mathbf{s}_n, \beta)$ as an exponential family distribution that satisfies

$$\mathbb{E}_{p(w_n|\mathbf{s}_n,\beta)}[T(w_n)] = \mathbf{s}_n^\top \beta_{.n}, \qquad (2)$$

where $T(w_n)$ are sufficient statistics[1] of w_n. We choose to use the linear combination as *mean* parameter instead of *natural* parameter [23] because: 1) it is natural to constrain the feasible domain of codes for good interpretation, as detailed below. As shown in [22], imposing appropriate (e.g., non-negativity for modeling word counts) constraints could result in sparser and more interpretable patterns; and 2) many distributions (e.g., Poisson and Gaussian) are commonly expressed with mean parameters. [6] uses a similar method as ours to define exponential family distributions.

3.2 STC for Sparse MAP Estimation

The generating process defines a joint distribution of codes and word counts $p(\theta, \mathbf{s}, \mathbf{w}|\beta) = p(\theta)\prod_{n\in I} p(\mathbf{s}_n|\theta)p(w_n|\mathbf{s}_n, \beta)$. By imposing a prior on β, we define STC as finding the MAP estimate on a given training set $\{\mathbf{w}_d\}$, that is, STC solves

$$\max_{\Theta} \sum_{d,n\in I_d} (\log p(w_{dn}|\mathbf{s}_{dn}, \beta) + \log p(\mathbf{s}_{dn}|\theta_d)) + \sum_d \log p(\theta_d) + \log p(\beta)$$
$$\text{s.t.}: \theta_d \geq 0,\ \forall d;\ \ \mathbf{s}_{dn} \geq 0,\ \forall d, n \in I_d;\ \ \beta_k \in \mathcal{P}_N,\ \forall k,$$

where we have used Θ to denote the parameters $(\{\theta_d\}, \{\mathbf{s}_d\}, \beta)$. Although we can have many choices, we concentrate on the following instantiation of STC for modeling word counts:

1. We define the Poisson distribution[2], i.e., $p(w_n|\mathbf{s}_n, \beta) = Poisson(w_n; \mathbf{s}_n^\top \beta_{.n})$, where $Poisson(x;\nu) = \frac{\nu^x e^{-\nu}}{x!}$.
2. We choose the Laplace prior $p(\theta) \propto \exp(-\lambda\|\theta\|_1)$, and we define $p(\mathbf{s}_n|\theta)$ as a composite distribution $p(\mathbf{s}_n|\theta) \propto \exp(-\frac{\gamma}{2}\|\mathbf{s}_n - \theta\|_2^2 - \rho\|\mathbf{s}_n\|_1)$, which is supergaussian [14]. The ℓ_1-norm will bias toward finding sparse codes.
3. We use a uniform prior of β.

The hyper-parameters (λ, γ, ρ) are non-negative and they can be selected via cross-validation or integrated out by introducing hyper-priors [7, 10]. Under such an instantiation, sparse topical coding solves the equivalent problem

$$\min_{\Theta} \sum_{d,n\in I_d} \ell(w_{dn}, \mathbf{s}_{dn}^\top \beta_{.n}) + \lambda \sum_d \|\theta_d\|_1 + \sum_{d,n\in I_d} (\frac{\gamma}{2}\|\mathbf{s}_{dn} - \theta_d\|_2^2 + \rho\|\mathbf{s}_{dn}\|_1)$$
$$\text{s.t.}: \theta_d \geq 0,\ \forall d;\ \ \mathbf{s}_{dn} \geq 0,\ \forall d, n \in I_d;\ \ \beta_k \in \mathcal{P}_N,\ \forall k, \qquad (3)$$

where $\ell(w_n, \mathbf{s}_n^\top \beta_{.n}) = -\log Poisson(w_n; \mathbf{s}_n^\top \beta_{.n})$ is a loss function. Minimizing the log-Poisson loss is actually equivalent to minimizing an unnormalized KL-divergence between observed word counts w_n and their reconstructions $\mathbf{s}_n^\top \beta_{.n}$ [34]. Since word counts are non-negative, a negative θ or $\mathbf{s}$ will lose interpretability. Therefore, we constrain θ and $\mathbf{s}$ to be non-negative as in [13]. A non-negative code can be interpreted as representing the relative importance of topics.

3.3 Conditional Topical Coding

Now, we formally present CTC, which is a novel non-probabilistic formulation of conditional topic models and is very efficient in training and inference, as we shall see. A conditional topical coding (CTC) is graphically illustrated in Figure 1 (c). To be consistent with the above generating process, we define the conditional probability

$$p(\mathbf{s}_n|\theta, \mathbf{U}, \mathbf{a}) \propto \exp\left(-\frac{\gamma}{2}(\|\mathbf{s}_n - \theta\|_2^2 + \|\mathbf{s}_n - \mathbf{U}\mathbf{f}(\mathbf{a})\|_2^2) - \rho\|\mathbf{s}_n\|_1\right),$$

where $\mathbf{f}(\mathbf{a})$ is a L-dimensional vector of real-valued feature functions; $\mathbf{U}$ is a $K \times L$ weight matrix; and $\mathbf{a}$ is again a set of

[1] In general, $\mathbf{s}_n$ will be a matrix if T is a vector.

[2] It is usually numerically safer to introduce a small offset $b \in \mathbb{R}_+$ and define $p(w_n|\mathbf{s}_n, \beta) = Poisson(w_n; \mathbf{s}_n^\top \beta_{.n} + b)$ to avoid taking the logarithm of zero. In all our experiments, we fix b at a very small positive value.

global or local features. We have omitted the normalization factor. Again, $p(\mathbf{s}_n|\theta, \mathbf{U}, \mathbf{a})$ is supergaussian [14]. We define CTC as solving the constrained problem

$$\min_{\Theta,\mathbf{U}} \sum_{d,n\in I_d} \ell(w_{dn}, \mathbf{s}_{dn}^\top \beta_{.n}) + \lambda \sum_d \|\theta_d\|_1 + \sum_{d,n\in I_d} \Big(\frac{\gamma}{2}\|\mathbf{s}_{dn} - \theta_d\|_2^2 + \frac{\gamma}{2}\|\mathbf{s}_{dn} - \mathbf{U}\mathbf{f}(\mathbf{a}_d)\|_2^2 + \rho\|\mathbf{s}_{dn}\|_1\Big)$$
$$\text{s.t.}: \theta_d \geq 0,\ \forall d;\ \mathbf{s}_{dn} \geq 0,\ \forall d, n \in I_d;\ \beta_k \in \mathcal{P}_N,\ \forall k, \quad (4)$$

which is related to but not exactly the MAP estimation because we have ignored the normalization factor of $p(\mathbf{s}_n|\theta, \mathbf{U}, \mathbf{a})$. Note that if we include the normalization factor, the non-probabilistic CTC can still be efficient (e.g., using gradient descent techniques) because we do not need to deal with the expectation of a *log-sum-exp* function, which is usually hard to compute in latent variable models [19, 41].

Supervised side information: we have presented conditional topical coding as an *unsupervised* technique that discovers latent representations. However, with the increasing availability of free on-line information, various forms of side-information such as rating scores for hotel reviews on TripAdvisor[3] and object categories for images in the LabelMe dataset[4] can potentially offer "free" supervision. This has led to a need for new models and training schemes that can make effective use of such information to achieve better results, such as more discriminative representations of documents and more accurate image classifiers. In order to incorporate such side information, we consider the general case where supervised information Y is provided in training data $\mathcal{D} = \{(\mathbf{w}_d, y_d)\}_{d=1}^D$, and we define the supervised CTC as solving the following problem for learning a prediction model η and a conditional topic discovery model $(\Theta, \mathbf{U})$

$$\min_{\Theta,\mathbf{U},\eta} h(\Theta, \mathbf{U}) + C\mathcal{R}_\mathcal{D}(\{\theta_d\}, \eta) + \frac{1}{2}\|\eta\|_2^2$$
$$\text{s.t.}: \theta_d \geq 0,\ \forall d;\ \mathbf{s}_{dn} \geq 0,\ \forall d, n \in I_d;\ \beta_k \in \mathcal{P}_N,\ \forall k, \quad (5)$$

where $h(\Theta, \mathbf{U})$ is the objective function of problem (4) and $\mathcal{R}_\mathcal{D}$ is an error measure of the prediction model η on the training data $\mathcal{D}$. Since CTC is non-probabilistic, we can seamlessly incorporate any convex loss that does not necessarily arise from a probabilistic model and thus can avoid dealing with normalization factors. Here, we consider the linear regression model (i.e., the prediction $y^* = \eta^\top\theta$) and use the ϵ-insensitive loss [33] as used in support vector regression (SVR) for large-margin learning, that is, $\mathcal{R}_\mathcal{D} = \frac{1}{D}\sum_d \max(0, |\eta^\top\theta_d - y_d| - \epsilon)$, where ϵ is a small positive precision parameter. For classification, we can use the SVM hinge loss [42], which again avoids dealing with a normalization factor that can make inference and learning hard in a probabilistic topic model (please see [37, 40] for discussions).

3.4 Optimization with Coordinate Descent

Now, we briefly present how to solve the most general problem (5), which subsumes problem (3) and problem (4). Let $f(\Theta, \mathbf{U}, \eta)$ be its objective. When using log-loss under the exponential family of distributions, $f(\Theta, \mathbf{U}, \eta)$ is bi-convex, i.e., convex over either $(\{\theta_d\}, \{\mathbf{s}_d\})$ or $(\beta, \mathbf{U}, \eta)$ when fixing the other one. Moreover, the feasible set is a convex set. A natural algorithm to solve this bi-convex problem is coordinate descent, as typically used in sparse coding methods [23, 2]. Our result relies on the following proposition

[3]http://www.tripadvisor.com/

[4]http://labelme.csail.mit.edu/

Algorithm 1 for learning supervised CTC

1: **Input:** corpus $\mathcal{D} = \{(\mathbf{w}_d, \mathbf{a}_d, y_d)\}_{d=1}^D$, regularization constants $(\lambda, \gamma, \rho, C)$ and precision parameter ϵ.
2: **Output:** codes $\{\theta_d\}_{d=1}^D$ and $\{\mathbf{s}_d\}_{d=1}^D$, dictionary β, feature weights $\mathbf{U}$ and prediction model η
3: **repeat**
4: hierarchical topical coding using Alg. 2.
5: dictionary learning by solving problem (8)
6: learning prediction model η using SVMLight
7: learning feature weights $\mathbf{U}$ using gradient descent
8: **until** convergence

Proposition 1. *Let $\psi(x)$ be a convex function on $\mathbb{R}$. If x_0 is a solution of the unconstrained problem P_0 : $\min_x \psi(x)$, then $x^\star = \max(0, x_0)$ is an optimal solution of the constrained problem P_1 : $\min_{x\geq 0} \psi(x)$.*
Proof: [Sketch] If $x_0 \geq 0$, then by definition, $x^\star$ is a solution of P_1; otherwise (i.e., $x_0 < 0$ and $x^\star = 0$), let's assume $x^\star$ is not a solution of P_1. Let x_1 be any one solution of P_1 and define $\alpha = \frac{x_1}{x_1 - x_0}$. Then, we have $x_1 > 0$, $0 < \alpha < 1$ and $0 = \alpha x_0 + (1-\alpha)x_1$. By definition, we have $\psi(x_0) \leq \psi(0)$ and $\psi(x_1) < \psi(0)$. Therefore, we can get $\alpha\psi(x_0) + (1-\alpha)\psi(x_1) < \psi(0) = \psi(\alpha x_0 + (1-\alpha)x_1)$. This contradicts the convexity of $\psi(x)$. □

Then, the procedure alternatively performs *hierarchical topical coding*, *dictionary learning*, *prediction model learning* and *feature weights learning* until convergence, as outlined in Algorithm 1 and detailed below.

Hierarchical topical coding: this step solves for the optimal codes $\{\theta_d\}$ and $\{\mathbf{s}_d\}$ when $(\beta, \mathbf{U}, \eta)$ are fixed. Since documents are not coupled, we can perform this step for each document separately by solving the ℓ_1-regularized problem

$$\min_{\theta,\mathbf{s}} \sum_{n\in I} \ell(w_n, \mathbf{s}_n^\top \beta_{.n}) + \lambda\|\theta\|_1 + \sum_{n\in I} \frac{\gamma}{2}(\|\mathbf{s}_n - \theta\|_2^2 + \|\mathbf{s}_n - \mathbf{U}\mathbf{f}(\mathbf{a})\|_2^2) + \rho\|\mathbf{s}_n\|_1))$$
$$\text{s.t.}: \theta \geq 0;\ \mathbf{s}_n \geq 0,\ \forall n \in I.$$

While previous work used either local quadratic approximation [23] or a specialized Poisson likelihood estimation method [34], we solve this problem with coordinate descent (outlined in Alg. 2), which has a closed-form at each substep. Moreover, our method have a simple structure, which is similar to the variational EM method for probabilistic LDA, as we shall see. Specifically, we alternatively solve:

Optimize over $\mathbf{s}$: when θ is fixed, $\mathbf{s}_n$ are not coupled. For each $\mathbf{s}_n$, we solve the convex problem

$$\min_{\mathbf{s}_n \geq 0} \ell(w_n, \mathbf{s}_n^\top \beta_{.n}) + \frac{\gamma}{2}(\|\mathbf{s}_n - \theta\|_2^2 + \|\mathbf{s}_n - \mathbf{U}\mathbf{f}(\mathbf{a})\|_2^2) + \rho\sum_k s_{nk}$$

where we have explicitly written the ℓ_1-norm of $\mathbf{s}_n$ under the non-negativity constraint. Let $g(\mathbf{s}_n)$ be the objective function. By Proposition 1, the solution of component k is

$$s_{nk} = \max(0, \nu_k), \quad (6)$$

where ν_k is the solution of minimizing $g(\mathbf{s}_n)$ over s_{nk} without the constraint. By setting the gradient $\nabla_{s_{nk}} g(\mathbf{s}_n)$ equal to zero, it is easy to derive that ν_k is the solution of the equation

$$\gamma\beta_{kn}\nu_k^2 + (\gamma\mu + \beta_{kn}\tau)\nu_k + \mu\tau - w_n\beta_{kn} = 0,$$

Algorithm 2 for hierarchical topical coding

```
Input: corpus D, regularization constants (λ, γ, ρ), dictionary β, feature weights U and prediction model η.
Output: codes {θ_d}_{d=1}^D and {s_d}_{d=1}^D
repeat
   for d = 1 to D do
      for each word n ∈ I_d do
         Update word code s_dn using Eq. (6).
      end for
      Update document code θ_d using Eq. (7).
   end for
until convergence
```

where $\mu = \sum_{j \neq k} s_{nj}\beta_{jn}$ and $\tau = \beta_{kn} + \rho - \gamma(\theta_k + \mathbf{U}_k \mathbf{f}(\mathbf{a}))$. Therefore, if $\beta_{kn} = 0$, the solution is $\nu_k = (\theta_k + \mathbf{U}_k\mathbf{f}(\mathbf{a})) - \frac{\rho}{\gamma}$. Otherwise (i.e., $\beta_{kn} > 0$), we need to solve a quadratic equation, which again always has real solutions because the discriminant $\nabla \triangleq (\gamma\mu + \beta_{kn}\tau)^2 - 4(\gamma\beta_{kn})(\mu\tau - w_n\beta_{kn}) = (\gamma\mu - \beta_{kn}\tau)^2 + 4\gamma w_n \beta_{kn}^2$ is guaranteed to be positive. We choose ν_k to be the larger one of the two possible solutions.

Optimize over θ: when $\mathbf{s}$ is fixed, this step solves

$$\min_{\theta \geq 0} \lambda\|\theta\|_1 + \frac{\gamma}{2}\sum_{n \in I}\|\mathbf{s}_n - \theta\|_2^2 + \frac{C}{D}\max(0, |\eta^\top\theta - y| - \epsilon).$$

We alternatively solve for each θ_k. By Proposition 1, we first solve an unconstrained one dimensional problem and then use the max operator to get the optimum solution. It is easy to show that one of the subgradient of this objective (with the ℓ_1-norm explicitly written as $\sum_k \theta_k$) is $\lambda + \gamma\sum_{n\in I}(\theta_k - s_{nk}) + \frac{C}{D}\mathbb{I}(|\eta^\top\theta - y| > \epsilon)Sign(\eta^\top\theta - y)\eta_k$. By setting the subgradient equal to zero, we have one solution

$$\forall k,\ \theta_k = \max(0, \bar{s}_k - \frac{\lambda}{\gamma|I|}), \tag{7}$$

where $\bar{s}_k = \frac{1}{|I|}\sum_{n\in I} s_{nk} - \frac{C}{D|I|}\mathbb{I}(|\eta^\top\theta - y| > \epsilon)Sign(\eta^\top\theta - y)\eta_k$ and $\mathbb{I}(\cdot)$ is an indicator function.

Dictionary learning: after we have inferred the latent codes $\{\theta_d\}$ and $\{\mathbf{s}_d\}$, we update the dictionary β by solving

$$\min_{\beta} \sum_{d,n\in I_d} \ell(w_n, \mathbf{s}_{dn}^\top \beta_{.n}),\ \text{s.t.}:\ \beta_k \in \mathcal{P}_N,\ \forall k, \tag{8}$$

which can be efficiently done with projected gradient descent. After each step of gradient descent, a projection to the simplex $\mathcal{P}_N$ is performed with a linear algorithm [9].

Learning prediction model η: when the document codes are given, we solve a standard support vector regression (SVR) problem [33], which can be efficiently done with a high-performance package, e.g., SVMLight[5].

Learning feature weights U: in practice, we need a regularization term to avoid over-fitting. Here, we constrain the ℓ_2-norm of each row to be less than a constant (e.g., 16 used in our experiments). Then, we solve for $\mathbf{U}$ using projected gradient descent.

From the update rule (7), we can see the regularization effects introduced by considering supervised side information. Specifically, if the current prediction $y^* = \eta^\top\theta$ differs much from the truth y (e.g., ℓ_1-distance is larger than ϵ), then the last term of $\bar{s}_k$ will be non-zero. Moreover, if the prediction y^* is larger than y, the last term will be of the same sign as η_k, which means the new θ will tend to be biased toward yielding a smaller new prediction. We have similar bias effects when the current prediction y^* is smaller than y. Thus we can expect to discover predictive document codes θ by considering supervised information, which usually leads to improved prediction performance as we shall see.

[5]http://svmlight.joachims.org/

3.5 Comparison with Probabilistic CdTM

Table 1 summarizes the difference between CTC and probabilistic CdTM [41]. Briefly, CdTM doesn t explicitly define word and document code. An equivalence to word code can be defined as the *empirical* word-topic assignment distribution $\tilde{p}(z(n) = k) \propto \sum_m \mathbb{I}(w_m = n)p(z_{mk} = 1|\mathbf{w})$, where $z(n)$ is the topic of word n, which needs to be inferred using variational methods [41]. Then, an equivalence to document code is the average aggregation of *empirical* word-topic assignment distributions. Second, CdTM or a probabilistic topic model in general lacks an explicit sparcification procedure on the inferred representations as discussed in Section 1.

4. EXPERIMENTS

In this section, we present empirical studies on online review data. We report quantitative evaluation on rating score prediction and time efficiency, as well as qualitative analysis of the discovered representations. Our results demonstrate that the non-probabilistic CTC can achieve state-of-the-art prediction performance and is much more efficient than probabilistic topic models. All our datasets and code are available at http://www.cs.cmu.edu/~junzhu/ctc.htm. As we have stated, STC and CTC could explicitly control the sparsity of latent representations using appropriate regularization. But a systematical analysis of the sparsity is beyond the scope of this paper. Please see the companion paper [42] for details.

4.1 Data and Features

In order to evaluate the effects of features, we use online review data, in which the documents are hotel reviews downloaded from the TripAdvisor website in 2009. Each review is associated with a global rating score and five aspect rating scores for *Value*, *Rooms*, *Location*, *Cleanliness*, and *Service*. This dataset is interesting for many data mining tasks, for example, extracting the textual mentions of each aspect [36, 18], using the guidance of side information to discover semantic information [5], or discovering latent rating aspects [38]. In these experiments, we focus on predicting the global rating score, which ranks from 1 to 5, and revealing some underlying structures.

Besides the small dataset [41], which contains 1000 reviews for each rating category or 5000 reviews in total, we also build a new dataset for evaluating the scalability of CTC, which contains 97,948 reviews in total (about 20 times larger than the small one). To avoid too short and too long reviews, we only keep those reviews whose character length is between 1000 and 6000. For each review, we use NLProcessor[6] to do part-of-speech (POS) tagging and noun phrase (NP) chunking, and we extract the following features:

- **POS-Tag**: We distinguish four types of POS tags, that is, Adjective, Noun, Adverb, and Verb. Each type includes all its subcategories, e.g., Adjective includes "JJ" (Adjective), "JJR" (comparative Adjective), and "JJS" (superlative Adjective).
- **WordNet**: WordNet[7] is a large lexical database of English.

[6]http://www.infogistics.com/textanalysis.html

[7]http://wordnet.princeton.edu/

Table 1: Comparison between CTC and probabilistic conditional topic model (CdTM) [41]

	CTC	CdTM
formulation	non-probabilistic	probabilistic
document code	$\theta \in \mathbb{R}_+^K$	no explicit definition, need to be inferred
word code	$\mathbf{s} \in \mathbb{R}_+^K$	no explicit definition, need to be inferred
dictionary	$\forall k:\ \beta_k \in \mathcal{P}_N$	$\forall k:\ \beta_k \in \mathcal{P}_N$
estimation	regularized loss minimization	(empirical) Bayesian inference
algorithm	coordinate descent	mean field dealing with expectation of log-sum-exp function [41, 19]
sparsity	direct control by using regularizers	indirect control by using sparse priors

We navigate it with some seeds of positive (e.g., good, excellent, etc) and negative (e.g., bad, painful, etc) words, and identify whether a word is positive or negative based on the synonym and antonym relationship. Words without strong relationship with the seeds are treated as neutral. For a positive or negative word, we also identify whether a denying word (e.g., not, no, etc.) appears before it within a word distance of 4.

. **NP-Chunking**: We define pairwise feature functions of conditional topical random fields (CTRF) [41] for those words that are in the same noun or verb phrase, or the conjunction "and" or "or" appears between them.

By removing a standard list of stopping words and those terms whose count frequency is less than 5, we build a dictionary with 12000 terms.

4.2 Results on the Small Dataset

We first carefully investigate the properties of CTC on the small dataset, on which a number of benchmark methods have been evaluated in [41]. For saving space, we compare the supervised CTC with other supervised topic models, including supervised CTRF [41] and CdTM [41], MedLDA [40], supervised LDA (sLDA) [3], and supervised STC (i.e., supervised CTC with none features), which usually outperform their unsupervised counterpart models as shown in various previous work [3, 37, 40, 41]. We follow the same setting as in [41] with a uniform train/test partition of the data. For hyperparameters, we set $\rho = 5e^{-4}$, $\epsilon = 1e^{-3}$ and $\lambda = \gamma$; and search for C and λ via cross-validation on training data.

4.2.1 *Prediction Performance*

Similar as in [3, 41], we take logarithm to make the response variables approximately normal and treat the problem of predicting review rating scores as a regression problem. Figure 2 shows the predictive R2 scores [3] for different models. We can see that conditional topical coding (CTC) achieves state-of-the-art prediction performance, which is comparable with the best performance of the conditional CTRF and a bit better than that of CdTM, which is a simplified CTRF without modeling the Markov dependency among topic assignments of neighboring words. As we shall see, the probabilistic CTRF and CdTM are much slower in training and testing than CTC. The reasons for this outstanding performance potentially come from three aspects. First, using the features (e.g., CTC and CdTM) can significantly improve the performance compared to the models that do not use features (e.g., STC and MedLDA). Second, the non-probabilistic formulation (e.g., STC) of topic models can potentially discover representations that have a better predictive power than the probabilistic formulation (e.g., MedLDA and sLDA). We will provide some insights about the properties of the discovered representations. Finally, the large-margin principle could potentially improve the performance, e.g., the large-margin based MedLDA achieves

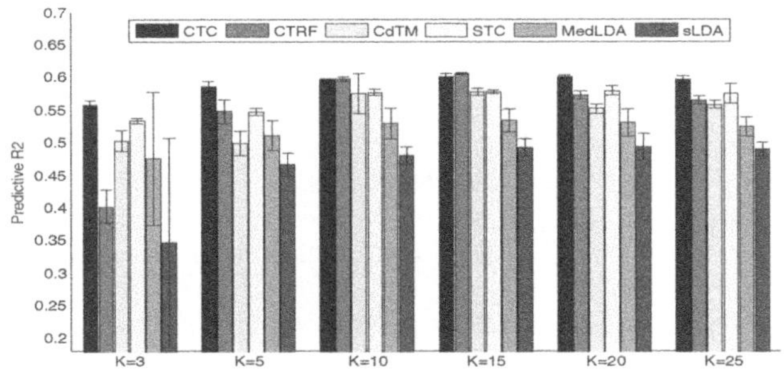

Figure 2: Predictive R2 values for different models.

slightly better results than sLDA which uses maximum likelihood estimation to learn the predictive model.

4.2.2 *Time Efficiency and Convergence*

Figure 3 (a,b) shows the averaging time and standard deviation over five randomly initialized runs. All the models are implemented in C++ language without special optimization. For probabilistic models (e.g., MedLDA and sLDA), we use variational methods [3, 40] to do inference, which has a similar structure as the coordinate descent algorithm as we have discussed. We implement these methods using the same data structure, and run the experiments on a standard desktop with 2G RAM and a 2.66 GHz processor.

We can see that in testing, the conditional CTC is about 100 times more efficient than the probabilistic conditional topic models CdTM and CTRF. In training, CTC is about 10 times more efficient than CTRF. The reason for the smaller improvement in training is that most of the training time is spent on learning large-margin SVR, whose complexity is largely dependent on the number of training samples. For the same reason, we observe that the training time of topical coding models (i.e., STC and CTC) does not change much when the topic number increases, while the training time of probabilistic models (e.g., CTRF) usually scales linearly with the topic number. This suggests that the topical coding methods have a better scalability when the number of topics is large. If we compare the models without using features, we can see that the non-probabilistic STC is about 10 times more efficient than probabilistic topic models (e.g., sLDA and MedLDA) in testing and training (when the number of topics is large, e.g., 25). The reason for the improvements is that STC (or CTC in general) is not subject to the strict constraint as made in sLDA or MedLDA that θ is a normalized mixing proportion vector. Thus, STC has one additional dimension of freedom, which usually leads to faster convergence. Moreover, probabilistic models (e.g., sLDA) need many calls to the digamma function, which can cost additional computational resources [1].

Figure 3 (c) shows the convergence curves of training CTC

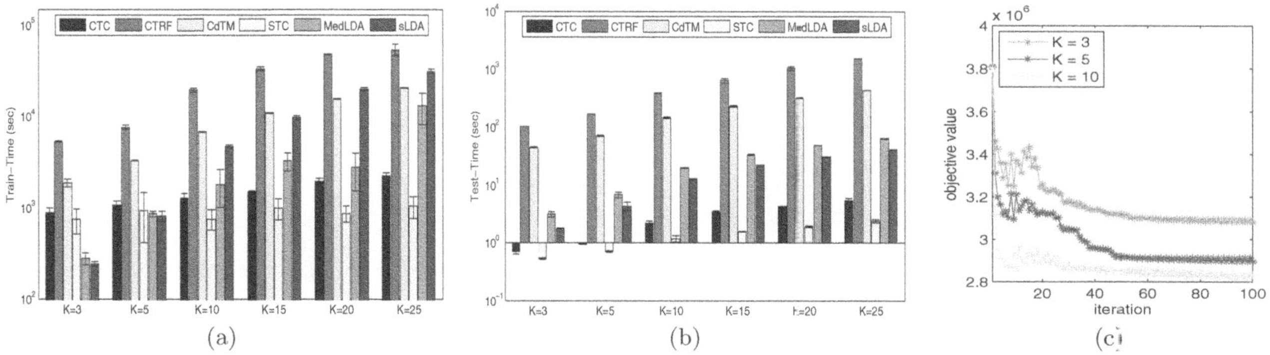

Figure 3: (a) training and (b) test time for different models on the small dataset; and (c) convergence curves of CTC with different numbers of topics.

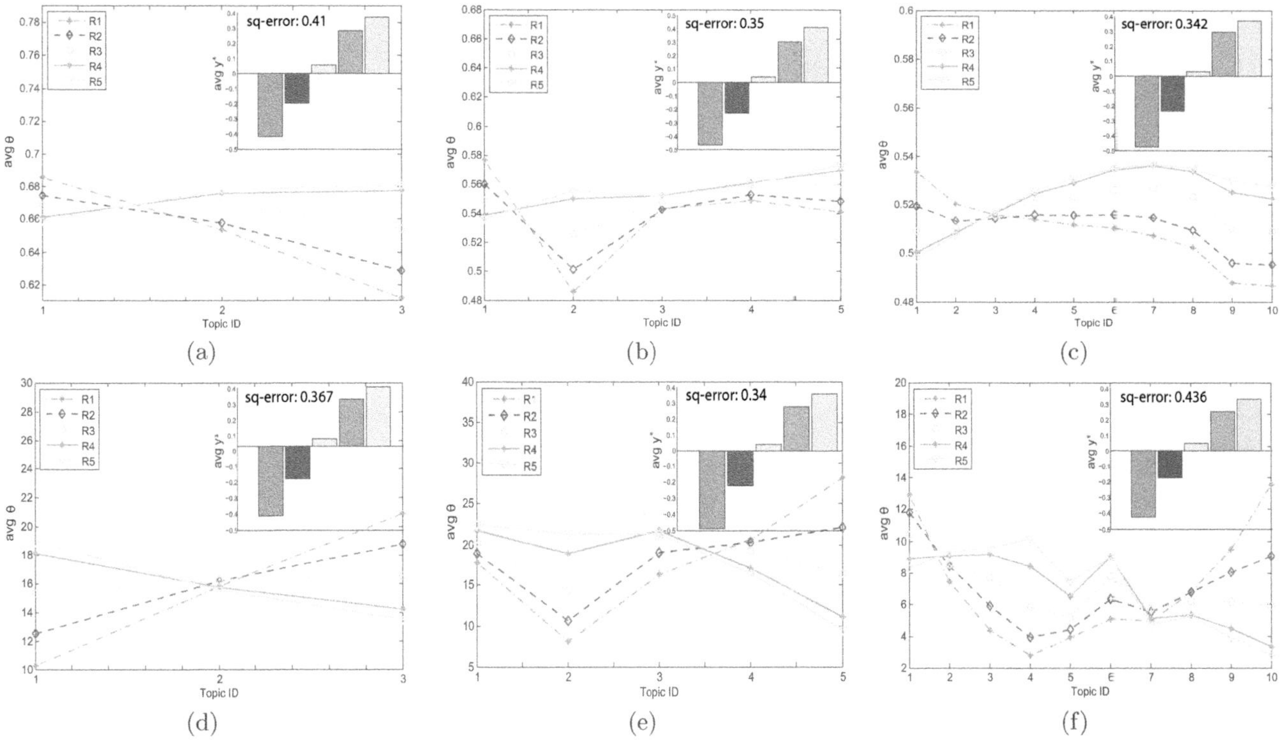

Figure 4: Average document codes discovered by (a) 3-topic CTC; (b) 5-topic CTC; (c) 10-topic CTC; (d) 3-topic STC; (e) 5-topic STC; and (f) 10-topic STC respectively. The up-right corner of each plot shows the average prediction for the documents in different rating categories together with the square distance from the true average.

Table 2: Top words in different topics by 10-topic CTC and 10-topic STC.

CTC										STC									
T1	T2	T3	T4	T5	T6	T7	T8	T9	T10	T1	T2	T3	T4	T5	T6	T7	T8	T9	T10
told	left	n't	back	resort	service	restaurant	hotel	great	n't	night	staff	good	great	make	pool	room	problem	desk	told
asked	find	food	room	place	clean	room	room	good	nice	back	day	nice	trip	dinner	beach	hotel	floor	door	asked
looked	booked	people	water	rooms	floor	hotel	beach	room	staff	stay	place	time	large	car	hotel	n't	reviews	left	called
manager	reception	small	made	night	walk	breakfast	area	hotel	good	people	breakfast	area	ocean	week	room	beds	hotels	front	manager
work	arrived	bar	hotel	bed	room	family	free	n't	front	bed	rooms	view	friendly	recommend	n't	open	person	arrived	put
bad	called	stayed	make	days	hotel	main	pool	friendly	day	bathroom	stayed	service	lovely	town	bar	internet	noise	husband	inn
inn	wanted	found	stay	dinner	lot	price	large	beautiful	view	made	days	clean	beautiful	bedroom	resort	expect	rate	looked	call
star	pay	rooms	kids	things	pool	times	restaurants	lovely	trip	morning	find	walk	pools	park	restaurant	late	needed	bad	checked
sleep	put	room	check	car	hot	children	big	plenty	bit	found	lot	water	plenty	island	food	offer	hard	gave	leave
half	money	guests	shower	coffee	desk	day	day	pools	pool	guests	experience	free	lots	year	kids	deal	cost	charge	give
phone	staying	hotel	minutes	week	evening	pool	town	lots	time	shower	food	bit	visit	property	coffee	fine	arrival	wedding	decided
returned	thought	stay	hotels	parking	night	bedroom	couple	comfortable	room	minutes	tv	location	comfortable	end	main	housekeeping	room	room	sleep
toilet	paid	door	towels	recommend	time	ocean	balcony	enjoyed	hotel	check	feel	family	drive	home	evening	standard	due	guest	phone
finally	call	experience	morning	bathroom	long	table	time	sea	perfect	reception	stay	parking	enjoyed	wife	small	fridge	number	card	toilet
card	leave	holiday	husband	room	full	area	drinks	quiet	beach	booked	eat	hot	unit	road	side	hear	business	website	returned
dirty	checked	felt	thing	side	reviews	year	location	excellent	island	towels	drink	restaurants	excellent	extra	times	helpful	order	problems	point
key	give	person	hour	open	day	end	pretty	huge	street	things	years	price	quiet	local	children	disappointed	english	cleaned	finally
cleaned	decided	expect	eat	beach	park	property	staff	wonderful	area	holiday	book	big	huge	kitchen	lobby	king	travel	review	dirty
walked	gave	drink	needed	tv	home	internet	chairs	unit	breakfast	nights	choice	balcony	enjoy	worth	full	check-in	working	rest	key
care	wait	arrival	late	lobby	part	time	buffet	fresh	shuttle	wanted	bath	street	wonderful	part	couple	issue	euros	wall	walked
smell	charge	due	return	feel	bathroom	early	road	loved	special	thing	served	chairs	loved	lunch	drinks	ready	hotel	booking	smell
poor	offered	served	years	hours	rate	nights	local	happy	helpful	long	menu	suite	fresh	places	table	decent	window	change	care
booking	point	order	guest	desk	hard	extra	suite	wine	fantastic	pay	time	buffet	dining	meal	pretty	past	entire	noticed	owner
euros	cold	review	book	hotel	fact	close	worth	views	river	money	making	close	photos	sea	early	job	weekend	cleaning	poor
window	business	rest	read	stay	front	night	airport	grounds	cabo	hours	group	small	located	house	building	tables	head	lady	move
double	room	reservation	offer	air	bed	building	lunch	ate	tip	work	stop	tub	views	walking	airport	pleasant	light	sign	management
change	website	buy	spent	noise	enjoy	wife	places	tour	san	hour	buy	taxi	grounds	quality	area	reason	previous	paying	waiting
move	working	past	wedding	walking	beds	kitchen	drive	easy	adults	staying	taking	club	ate	high	top	elevator	worked	didnt	sheets
previous	run	absolutely	door	morning	set	visit	meal	fun	sand	thought	white	vacation	hilton	spa	bus	opened	mind	charged	man
management	doors	case	bath	cost	place	top	high	perfect	resorts	rooms	simply	living	beach	return	size	eating	show	loud	moved

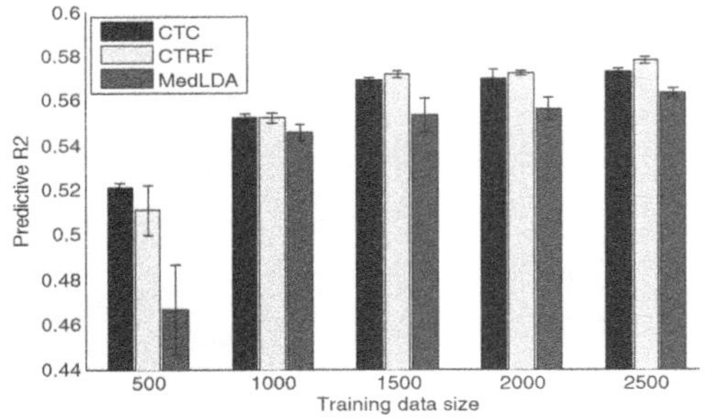

Figure 5: Predictive R2 scores for different models with 10 topical bases on the large dataset with different numbers of training data.

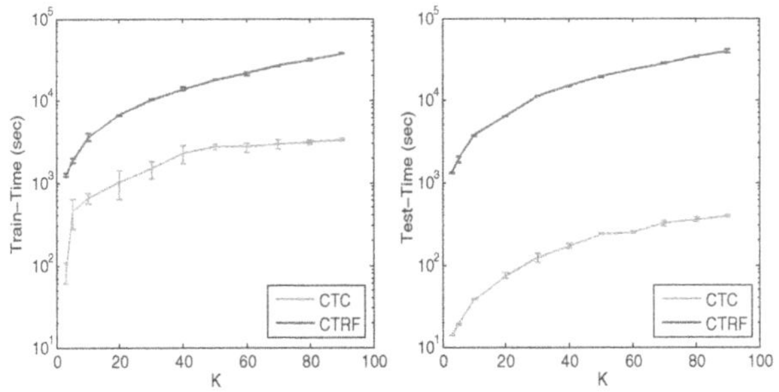

Figure 6: Training and test time for CTC and CTRF on the large dataset with different numbers of topical bases.

with different numbers of topics. We can see that the coordinate descent algorithm is quite stable and converges fast.

4.2.3 Characteristics of Code Representations

Now, we investigate the properties of the discovered representations. Figure 4 shows the average document codes θ discovered by the conditional CTC (plots a – c) and STC (plots d – f) that doesn't use features. The average document code is computed by averaging θ overall all the documents in each of the 5 rating categories, which are denoted by $R1$, $R2$, $\cdots$ and $R5$ from low to high rating values. We use lines to show the overall trend. On the up-right corner of each plot, we also show the average prediction y^* for the documents in each rating category, together with the square distance (i.e., square error) from the true average rating. Table 2 shows the top words of the learned dictionary (i.e., topics). Overall, we can see that both CTC and STC can discover very predictive code presentations (i.e., the average θ are quite different from each other), as also demonstrated by the outstanding prediction performance in Figure 2. However, using features can make CTC discover representations that are of a stronger regular pattern. For example, the documents with a high rating score (e.g., $R4$) have larger values on positive topics (e.g., T6 to T10) than the documents with a low rating score (e.g., $R2$), and the increasing trend from low rating to high rating is consistent. The reason for this strong regularity is that the discovered topics by CTC show strong positive, negative or neutral properties. For example, the topic T1 is obviously a negative topic; topics T3 to T5 tend to be neutral; while topics T6 to T10 tend to be positive, although they are about different aspects in detail. In contrast, STC which doesn't use features tends to discover topics (e.g., topic T7) that are mixtures of positive and negative words. On such topics, the corresponding average θ values usually don't show regular ordering, e.g., on topic T7 the value for $R1$ is smaller than that for $R3$, while the value for $R2$ is larger than that for $R4$.

4.3 Results on the Large Dataset

We now show the scalability of CTC on the large dataset. We compare with the conditional CTRF model and MedLDA which usually achieve better results than the other models (e.g., the standard LDA or sLDA). Also, we analyze the effect of the size of training data.

Figure 5 shows the predictive R2 scores of different models with the training set size being 500, 1000, 1500, 2000, and 2500. We build the training set from the large dataset of hotel reviews by selecting 100, 200, 300, 400 and 500 reviews from each rating category respectively. All the remaining reviews are used as test set. In this experiment, we set K at 10, which is sufficiently large for the review data, as demonstrated in Figure 2. For hyper-parameters, we fix $\rho = 5e^{-4}$, $\epsilon = 1e^{-3}$ and set $\lambda = \gamma$. Then, we select C and λ using the small dataset as validation set. We can see that the conditional models (i.e., CTC and CTRF) generally achieve better results than the unconditional model MedLDA, especially when the training set is small. For the two conditional models, again CTC and CTRF achieve comparable predictive R2 scores in all the five settings.

Finally, Figure 6 shows the training and test time on the large dataset with 2500 training samples and different numbers (e.g., $K = 3, 5, 10, 20, \cdots, 90$) of topical bases. Again, we can see that for each K CTC is about 100 times more efficient than CTRF in test and about 10 times more efficient than CTRF in training. Since the complexity of CTC in testing is linear in terms of the data size, we can expect that the efficient CTC can be scalable to very large datasets, e.g., processing tens of millions of documents in hours even when using a large number (e.g., 90) of topical bases. Moreover, the simple structure of the coordinate descent algorithm also makes it easy to be implemented in a distributed environment [32]. We leave this very large-scale implementation and evaluation as future work.

5. CONCLUSIONS AND FUTURE WORK

We have presented conditional topical coding (CTC), a novel non-probabilistic formulation of conditional topic models which can incorporate a rich set of features. By relaxing the strict normalization constraints, CTC learns non-negative code vectors and can avoid dealing with a hard-to-compute partition function. We develop an efficient and easy-to-implement coordinate descent learning algorithm. Our empirical results on online review data demonstrate that the non-probabilistic CTC can achieve state-of-the-art prediction performance and is much more efficient than probabilistic conditional topic models in both training and testing.

For future work, we plan to develop a parallel CTC and STC for very large-scale applications [27, 32] by using the simply structured coordinate descent algorithm. Also, we are interested in learning structured dictionaries [17] and extending CTC to incorporate various types of features, such as graph-based word similarity features [29] and document-level meta-data [26]. Finally, CTC raises a challenge to estimate the hyperparameters such as ρ and λ. Although the current restricted search works well in practice, it is worth of a systematical investigation to automatically estimate the hyperparameters, such as using the recent work [10, 7].

6. REFERENCES

[1] A. Asuncion, M. Welling, P. Smyth, and Y. Teh. On smoothing and inference for topic models. In *UAI*, 2009.

[2] S. Bengio, F. Pereira, Y. Singer, and D. Strelow. Group sparse coding. In *NIPS*, 2009.

[3] D. Blei and J. McAuliffe. Supervised topic models. In *NIPS*, 2007.

[4] D. Blei, A. Ng, and M. Jordan. Latent Dirichlet allocation. *JMLR*, (3):993–1022, 2003.

[5] S. Branavan, H. Chen, J. Eisenstein, and R. Barzilay. Learning document-level semantic properties from free-text annotations. In *ACL*, 2008.

[6] W. Buntine and A. Jakulin. Discrete components analysis. *Subspace, Latent Structure and Feature Selection Techniques*, 2006.

[7] G. Cawley, N. Talbot, and M. Girolami. Sparse multinomial logistic regression via bayesian ℓ_1 regularization. In *NIPS*, 2007.

[8] A. Culotta, D. Kulp, and A. McCallum. Gene prediction with conditional random fields. *Tech. Report UM-CS-2005-028, UMass, Amherst.*, 2005.

[9] J. Duchi, S. Shalev-Shwartz, Y. Singer, and T. Chandra. Efficient projections onto the ℓ_1-ball for learning in high dimensions. In *ICML*, 2008.

[10] C.-S. Foo, C. Do, and A. Ng. A majorization-minimization algorithm for (multiple) hyperparameter learning. In *ICML*, 2009.

[11] J. Graça, K. Ganchev, B. Taskar, and F. Pereira. Posterior vs. parameter sparsity in latent variable models. In *NIPS*, 2009.

[12] T. Hofmann. Probabilistic latent semantic analysis. In *UAI*, 1999.

[13] P. Hoyer. Non-negative sparse coding. In *Neural Networks for Signal Processing*, 2002.

[14] A. Hyvärinen. Sparse code shrinkage: Denoising of nongaussian data by maximum likelihood estimation. *Neural Computation*, (11):1739Ű–1768, 1999.

[15] A. Hyvärinen and P. Hoyer. A two-layer sparse coding model learns simple and complex cell receptive fields and topography from natural images. *Vision Research*, 41(18):2413–2423, 2001.

[16] L. Jacob, G. Obozinski, and J.-P. Vert. Group lasso with overlap and graph lasso. In *ICML*, 2009.

[17] R. Jenatton, J. Mairal, G. Obozinski, and F. Bach. Proximal methods for sparse hierarchical dictionary learning. In *ICML*, 2010.

[18] Y. Jo and A. Oh. Aspect and sentiment unification model for online review analysis. In *WSDM*, 2011.

[19] M. E. Khan, B. Marlin, G. Bouchard, and K. Murphy. Variational bounds for mixed-data factor analysis. In *NIPS*, 2010.

[20] S. Kim and E. P. Xing. Tree-guided group lasso for multi-task regression with structured sparsity. In *ICML*, 2010.

[21] J. Lafferty, A. McCallum, and F. Pereira. Conditional random fields: Probabilistic models for segmenting and labeling sequence data. In *ICML*, 2001.

[22] D. Lee and H. Seung. Learning the parts of objects by non-negative matrix factorization. *Nature*, 401:788 – 791, 1999.

[23] H. Lee, R. Raina, A. Teichman, and A. Ng. Exponential family sparse coding with applications to self-taught learning. In *IJCAI*, 2009.

[24] J. Mairal, F. Bach, J. Ponce, G. Sapiro, and A. Zisserman. Supervised dictionary learning. In *NIPS*, 2008.

[25] N. Meinshausen and B. Yu. Lasso-type recovery of sparse representations for high-dimensional data. *Annals of Statistics*, 37(1):246–270, 2009.

[26] D. Mimno and A. McCallum. Topic models conditioned on arbitrary features with dirichlet-multinomial regression. In *UAI*, 2008.

[27] D. Newman, A. Asuncion, P. Smyth, and M. Welling. Distributed algorithms for topic models. *JMLR*, (10):1801–1828, 2009.

[28] B. Olshausen and D. Field. Emergence of simple-cell receptive field properties by learning a sparse code for natural images. *Nature*, 381(6583):607–609, 1996.

[29] J. Petterson, A. Smola, T. Caetano, W. Buntine, and S. Narayanamurthy. Word features for latent dirichlet allocation. In *NIPS*, 2010.

[30] D. Pinto, A. McCallum, X. Wei, and W. Croft. Table extraction using conditional random fields. In *SIGIR*, 2003.

[31] M. Shashanka, B. Raj, and P. Smaragdis. Sparse overcomplete latent variable decomposition of counts data. In *NIPS*, 2007.

[32] A. Smola and S. Narayanamurthy. An architecture for parallel topic models. In *VLDB*, 2010.

[33] A. Smola and B. Schölkopf. A tutorial on support vector regression. *Statistics and Computing*, 2003.

[34] S. Sra, D. Kim, and B. Schölkopf. Non-monotonic poisson likelihood maximization. *Tech. Report, MPI for Biological Cybernetics*, 2008.

[35] R. Tibshirani. Regression shrinkage and selection via the lasso. *J. Royal. Statist. Soc.*, B(58):267–288, 1996.

[36] I. Titov and R. McDonald. A joint model of text and aspect ratings for sentiment summarization. In *ACL*, 2008.

[37] C. Wang, D. Blei, and L. Fei-Fei. Simultaneous image classification and annotation. In *CVPR*, 2009.

[38] H. Wang, Y. Lu, and C. Zhai. Latent aspect rating analysis on review text data: A rating regression approach. In *KDD*, 2010.

[39] J. Yang, K. Yu, Y. Gong, and T. Huang. Linear spatial pyramid matching using sparse coding for image classification. In *CVPR*, 2009.

[40] J. Zhu, A. Ahmed, and E. P. Xing. MedLDA: Maximum margin supervised topic models for regression and classification. In *ICML*, 2009.

[41] J. Zhu and E. P. Xing. Conditional topic random fields. In *ICML*, 2010.

[42] J. Zhu and E. P. Xing. Sparse topical coding. In *UAI*, 2011.

Tracking Trends: Incorporating Term Volume into Temporal Topic Models

Liangjie Hong† Dawei Yin† Jian Guo§ Brian D. Davison†
† Dept. of Computer Science and Engineering, Lehigh University, Bethlehem, PA, USA
§ Dept. of Statistics, University of Michigan, Ann Arbor, MI, USA
† {lih307,day207,davison}@cse.lehigh.edu, § guojian@umich.edu

ABSTRACT

Text corpora with documents from a range of time epochs are natural and ubiquitous in many fields, such as research papers, newspaper articles and a variety of types of recently emerged social media. People not only would like to know what kind of topics can be found from these data sources but also wish to understand the temporal dynamics of these topics and predict certain properties of terms or documents in the future. Topic models are usually utilized to find latent topics from text collections, and recently have been applied to temporal text corpora. However, most proposed models are general purpose models to which no real tasks are explicitly associated. Therefore, current models may be difficult to apply in real-world applications, such as the problems of tracking trends and predicting popularity of keywords. In this paper, we introduce a real-world task, tracking trends of terms, to which temporal topic models can be applied. Rather than building a general-purpose model, we propose a new type of topic model that incorporates the volume of terms into the temporal dynamics of topics and optimizes estimates of term volumes. In existing models, trends are either latent variables or not considered at all which limits the potential for practical use of trend information. In contrast, we combine state-space models with term volumes with a supervised learning model, enabling us to effectively predict the volume in the future, even without new documents. In addition, it is straightforward to obtain the volume of latent topics as a by-product of our model, demonstrating the superiority of utilizing temporal topic models over traditional time-series tools (e.g., autoregressive models) to tackle this kind of problem. The proposed model can be further extended with arbitrary word-level features which are evolving over time. We present the results of applying the model to two datasets with long time periods and show its effectiveness over non-trivial baselines.

Categories and Subject Descriptors

H.4 [**Information Systems Applications**]: Miscellaneous; H.3.3 [**Information Storage and Retrieval**]: Information Search and Retrieval—*clustering*

General Terms

Algorithms, Experimentation, Theory

Keywords

Topic models, Text mining, Temporal dynamics

1. INTRODUCTION

Text corpora with documents covering a long time-span are natural and ubiquitous in many application fields, and include such data as research papers and newspaper articles. Mining from these collections, discovering and understanding underlying topics and ideas, continues to be an important task. In addition to traditional text collections, many types of content in social media make applying machine learning techniques to these new data sources more challenging, such as forums, question answering communities and blog entries. People not only would like to know what kind of topics can be found from these data sources but also wish to understand the temporal dynamics of these topics, and hopefully predict certain properties of terms or documents in the future.

Topic models (e.g., [5]), as a class of newly developed machine learning tools, have been studied extensively in recent years. From the seminal work done by Blei et al. [5], a large body of literature about topic models has been established. Multiple disciplines of computer science, ranging from information retrieval (e.g., [24]), computer vision (e.g., [19]) to collaborative filtering (e.g., [1]) have applied topic models to their problems. For text modeling, topic models are applied to find latent topics from text collections, which is particularly useful for temporal text corpora where discovered latent topics can help researchers visualize and understand the thematic evolution of the corpora over time. This has led to the recent development of incorporating temporal dynamics into topic models (e.g., [14, 3, 21, 13, 15, 22, 20, 12, 23, 25, 2, 9, 10]). These models enable us to browse and explore datasets with temporal changes in a convenient way and open future directions for utilizing these models in a more comprehensive fashion. One drawback of these existing models is that most of them are general purpose models with which no real tasks are explicitly associated. Therefore, it might be difficult to employ these models in real-world applications, such as the problems of tracking trends and predicting popularity of keywords. As a result of the lack of a particular task, there is also no consensus on how these models should be evaluated and compared. Although perplexity is widely used in these papers, as pointed out in [6], this measure may not have correlations with the quality (e.g., coherence) of topics discovered. Furthermore, no empirical or theoretical work has been done as far as we know to show the the correlations between the low perplexity values and high performance in third-party tasks such classification, regression and clustering. In this paper, we argue that temporal topic models should be evaluated on specific real-world tasks and propose such a task to compare how they can contribute to applications. Some recent extensions of topic models (e.g., [4, 11, 26, 18]) have tried to incorporate side information, such as document-level labels and word-level features (e.g., [17]) into models in order to perform classification and regression tasks. A basic conclusion made from these attempts is that these special-purposed models, aiming to optimize particular tasks, perform better than general-purpose models, on the tasks they evaluated. We share a similar spirit in this paper, showing that temporal topic models for special tasks perform better than general-purpose models.

In this paper, we introduce a real-world task — tracking trends of terms — to which temporal topic models can be applied. Rather than building a general-purpose model, we propose a new type of topic model incorporating the volume of terms into the temporal dynamics of topics and directly optimize for the task. Unlike existing models in which trends are either latent variables or not considered at all and thus are difficult to apply in practice, we combine state-space models with term volumes in a supervised learning fashion which enables us to effectively predict volumes in the future, even without new documents. In addition, it is straightforward to obtain the volumes of latent topics as a by-product of our model, demonstrating the superiority of utilizing temporal topic models over traditional time-series tools (e.g., autoregressive models) to tackle this kind of problem. The proposed model can be further extended with arbitrary word-level features which are evolving over time. We present the results of applying the model to two datasets with long time periods and show its effectiveness over non-trivial baselines. Our contributions are threefold:

- Introduce a task — volume tracking — that can be used as a standard evaluation method for temporal topic models
- Propose a temporal topic model that directly optimizes the task introduced
- Demonstrate the effectiveness of the model as compared to state-of-the-art algorithms by experimenting on two real-world datasets

We organize the paper as follows. In Section 2, we review some related developments of topic models and existing evaluation methods for temporal topic models. In Section 3, we introduce the task of volume tracking, as a case of trend monitoring, and propose our model . In Section 4, we show how to utilize variational inference with Kalman Filter to estimate hidden parameters of the model. In Section 5, we discuss some other models that can be used in the volume tracking task. In Section 6, we demonstrate the experimental results on two datasets and conclude the paper in Section 7.

2. RELATED WORK

In this section, we review three directions of related work. First, we summarize all up-to-date topic models which try to incorporate temporal dynamics into the model. Then, we discuss the evaluation of these models and the potential to apply them in real-world applications. In the end, we present the attempts to embed side-information, or features into topic models.

To incorporate temporal dynamics into topic models, many models have been proposed. Note, as we mentioned, these attempts are general-purpose models, meaning that no real-world tasks are explicitly addressed. In general, all these models fall into two categories. The models in the first category do not impose a global distribution assumption about how topics evolve over time. In other words, these models assume that topics change over time depending on their previous conditions, effectively making "Markovian assumptions". The examples in this category are Dynamic Topic Model (DTM), proposed by Blei and Lafferty [3] and Continuous Time Dynamic Topic Models (cDTM), proposed by Wang et al. [20], embedding state-space models into topic models. Our work is inspired by this type of model. The second category of models usually imposes a global distribution of temporal dynamics. For instance, Wang et al. [21] introduce a beta distribution over timestamps and incorporate it into the standard topic model. Masada et al. [12] assume a Gaussian distribution over the whole time-line of topics. Although these models are proposed under different contexts, the drawback of this category is that the distributional assumption is hard to justify. Based on the two basic categories, other extensions are proposed. For example, Nallapati et al. [15] and Iwata et al. [9] focus on the problem of modeling topic spreading on timelines with multiple resolutions, namely how topics can be organized in a hierarchical way over time.

Table 1: Evaluation on Temporal Topic Models

(Temporal) Perplexity	[3, 15, 20, 23, 25, 2, 9, 10]
Timestamp Prediction	[21, 20, 10]
Classification/Clustering	[25]
Ad-Hoc	[21, 23, 25]

As in traditional topic models, the effectiveness of temporal topic models is difficult to evaluate in general. This is partly because these models are introduced without considering any tasks, making the process of evaluating them on third-party tasks ad-hoc. Due to a lack of evaluation tasks, comprehensive comparisons between models are seldom conducted. In order to better illustrate how temporal topic models have been evaluated, we show them in Table 1, according to the evaluation methods mentioned in papers. It is clear that temporal perplexity is a popular evaluation method. However, as pointed out in [6], perplexity may not have correlations with the quality (e.g., coherence) of latent topics. In addition, little is known, both theoretically and empirically, that a model achieving lower perplexity will perform better on real-world applications which we care about. Besides perplexity, several papers proposed some ad-hoc evaluation methods (named under "Ad-hoc" in the table) to demonstrate the potential capabilities of their models, such as the coherence of topics measured by K-L divergence, where these methods are not shared by other papers and are also not really task-driven. Nearly all papers show "anecdotal examples" of what kind of topics are found over time.

Since our model can be considered as an extension to incorporate side information, or features into topic models, we also review other similar attempts. Basically, two kinds of side information might be considered: document-level features and word-level features. For document-level features, models are proposed (e.g., [4, 11, 26, 18]) to incorporate them either conditioned on latent topic assignments or conditioned on per-document hyper-parameters. Either maximum conditional learning or max-margin learning is employed for inference. For word-level features, a recently proposed model [17] introduce a method to embed arbitrary word-level features. Unlike the ones for document-level features, this model is not a fully generative model and therefore we cannot easily infer these feature values.

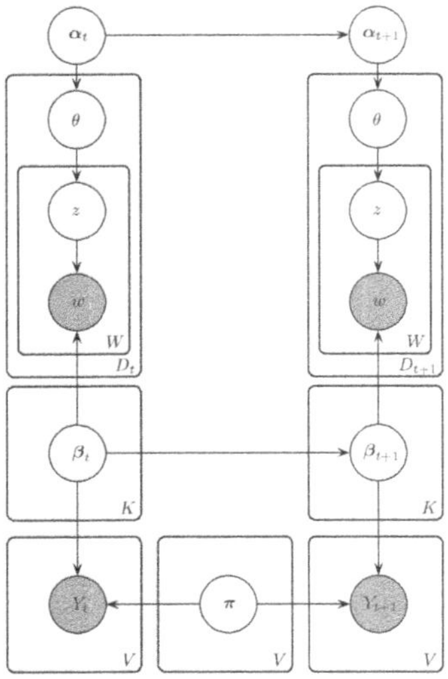

Figure 1: A graphical representation of the model with only two time epochs

3. TRACKING TRENDS BY INCORPORATING VOLUMES

In this section, we will introduce the task of volume prediction as a case of trend tracking. One reason that temporal topic models are favored is perhaps that these models can be potentially used as a tool to analyze trends and changes of keywords over time. However, these tasks are never evaluated directly or seriously in current literature.

The task of predicting the volume of terms is to predict the numeric volume of one or a set of keywords, given the historical data of these keywords in the past. This is a natural extension of tracking and monitoring keywords over time. Indeed, some commercial products provide such tools to allow users to browse and understand the rise and fall of keywords, such as `Google Trends`. One drawback of existing tools is that people usually only have a limited view of certain topics in which they are interested before they fully understand these topics. For instance, for the event of "World Cup", the phrase "World Cup" is certainly of interest. However, there are many more related terms to be explored, such as "FIFA", "South Africa" and "Ronaldo". Sometimes, users have these related terms in mind but usually they are unable to prepare them in advance. It would be great if users could track the trends (volume) of a topic as a whole and discover all those related terms at the same time. Moreover, the volume of terms in the same topic are correlated, which may help the model to find better topics. Overall, we would like to achieve three goals in tracking trends:

- Track and predict the volume of individual terms
- Obtain latent topics so that related terms can be grouped together
- Model the evolution of latent topics

The second goal will happen automatically through the modeling of topic models. The last goal can be achieved by temporal topic models, through either one of the assumptions mentioned in Section 2. The first goal is the center of this work. We believe that our work would help to track the volume of topics as a whole if the first goal can be achieved. Note, in terms of "prediction", we indicate the ability to estimate the volume of individual terms in the future where no documents are realized.

Two design issues need to be tackled when introducing term volumes into the model. First, they are word-level variables (if we treat features as random variables). Second, we need to predict values of these variables without documents. These two issues prevent these variables from being placed in the document plates, in terms of graphical modeling. This decision distinguishes our model from previous models (e.g., [4, 11, 26, 18]) where response variables are placed in document plates. Recently, Petterson et al. [17] demonstrate a technique to embed word-level features into topic models. Although our work shares similar ideas to theirs, their model is not a generative model for word features but only for words in the documents. In addition, their work is not to predict these word-level features. Since their work is for a static text corpus, it cannot be easily utilized to model temporal data. Therefore, we do not include this model in our experiments for comparison. Our model is a fully generative model for both word instantiations in documents and word-level features.

Before we further go to the formal description of our model, we discuss some intuitions behind the model. In standard topic models, each word v is associated with many latent topics $\boldsymbol{\beta}_{1:K}$. Each topic β_k is a distribution over all terms in the vocabuary V. Intuitively, the more a term appears in many topics, the more likely the term will have a high volume, such as some stop words and functional words. On the other hand, many terms only appear in a handful of topics and therefore these topics determine the volume of the term. If we think of $\boldsymbol{\beta}$ as another representation of terms, we would like to associate these latent variables with the term volumes. Following this intuition, we treat the volume of term v at time-stamp t, denoted as $Y_v^{(t)}$, as a function of latent topics $\boldsymbol{\beta}$. The simplest form of such functions is a linear function:

$$Y_v^{(t)} = \sum_{k=0}^{K} \pi_{(v,k)} \beta_{(k,v)}^{(t)} + \epsilon_v \tag{1}$$

where $\boldsymbol{\pi}_v$ is a vector of coefficients, $\beta_{(k,v)}^{(t)}$ is the probability that the term is "generated" from topic k at time stamp t, and ϵ_v is a per-term "error". In other words, the volume of a term v depends on its prevalence in all topics at that time point. If ϵ_v follows a normal distribution, namely $\epsilon_v \sim N(0, \sigma_v^2)$, we can express the generation process of $Y_V^{(t)}$ in terms of a Normal distribution as follows:

$$Y_v^{(t)} \mid \pi_{(v)}, \beta_{(*,v)}^{(t)} \sim \mathcal{N}\left(\pi_v^T \beta_{(*,v)}^{(t)}, \sigma_v^2\right) \tag{2}$$

Here, $Y_v^{(t)}$ is treated as a real valued variable. In our experiments, we use the raw counts of term v at time epoch t as $Y_v^{(t)}$.

In order to obtain Y_v at different time epochs, we need to have $\boldsymbol{\beta}$ for different time points. We mention two basic categories of approaches in Section 2 and here we adapt the first category, having a "Markovian assumption" on the evolution of topics over time. More specifically, topics $\boldsymbol{\beta}$ evolve according to a state-space model and the documents with their words are "generated" by the corresponding topics in the same time epoch. Embedding these intuitions into the model, the generative process of the model is as follows:

1. For each topic k in K:
   Draw topics $\beta_k^{(t)} \mid \beta_k^{(t-1)} \sim \mathcal{N}\left(\beta_k^{(t-1)}, \delta^2 I\right)$.
2. For each term v in V:
   Draw term volume $Y_v^{(t)} \sim \mathcal{N}\left(\pi_v^T \beta_{(*,v)}^{(t)}, \sigma^2\right)$.
3. For each document d in time epoch t:
   (a) Draw $\theta_d \sim \text{Dir}(\boldsymbol{\alpha})$

(b) For each word n:

i. Draw $z_{(d,n)} \sim \text{Multi}(\theta)$.

ii. Draw $w_{(d,n)} \sim \text{Multi}\Big(f(\beta_z^{(t)})\Big)$

where function f maps the multinomial natural parameters to mean parameters. The graphical representation of the model is shown in Figure 1. Note, the model can be easily extended in multiple ways. For instance, we can also allow the hyper-parameters of topic proportions $\boldsymbol{\alpha}$ to evolve over time, according to a different state-space model, as already mentioned in [3]. In addition, the simple state-space model can be replaced by a Brownian motion model [20], allowing arbitrary granularity of time-series. We will explore these extensions in future work.

4. VARIATIONAL INFERENCE WITH KALMAN FILTERING

The central problem in topic modeling is posterior inference, i.e., determining the distribution of the latent topic structure conditioned on the observed documents. In our case, the latent structures comprise the per-document topic proportions θ_d, per-word topic assignments $z_{(d,n)}$, the K sequences of topic distributions $\beta_k^{(t)}$ and per-term coefficient vector $\boldsymbol{\pi}_v$ for characterizing term volumes. Similar to many topic models, the true posterior is intractable [3, 20], meaning that we must appeal to an approximation.

Several approximate inference approaches have been developed for topic models. The most widely used are variational inference (e.g., [5, 3, 20]) and collapsed Gibbs sampling (e.g., [7, 21]). As noted previously by others [3, 20], collapsed Gibbs sampling is not an option in the sequential setting because the distribution of words for each topic is not conjugate to the word probabilities. Therefore, we employ variational inference for the model.

The main idea behind variational inference is to posit a simple family of distributions over the latent variables, namely variational distributions, and to find the member of that family which is closest in Kullback-Leibler divergence to the true posterior. Variational inference has been successfully adopted in temporal topic models (e.g., [3, 15, 20]).

For the model descried above, we adapt variational Kalman filtering [3] to the sequential modeling setting. We employ the following variational distribution:

$$q(\boldsymbol{\beta}_{1:T}, \boldsymbol{\theta}, \mathbf{Z} | \hat{\boldsymbol{\beta}}_{1:T}, \boldsymbol{\lambda}, \boldsymbol{\Phi}) =$$
$$\prod_{k=1}^{K} q(\beta_k^1, \cdots, \beta_k^T | \hat{\beta}_k^1, \cdots, \hat{\beta}_k^T) \times$$
$$\prod_{t=1}^{T}\Big(\prod_{d=1}^{D_t} q(\theta_d|\lambda_d) \prod_{n=1}^{N_d} q(z_{(d,n)}|\phi_{(d,n)})\Big) \quad (3)$$

The variational parameters are a Dirichlet λ_d for the per-document topic proportions, multinomials ϕ for each word's topic assignment, and $\hat{\beta}$ variables, which are "observations" to a Variational Kalman Filter. The central idea of the variational Kalman filter is that variational parameters are treated as "observations" in a common Kalman filter setting, while true parameters, here $\boldsymbol{\beta}^{(t)}$, are treated as latent states of the model. By utilizing a Kalman filter, we can effectively estimate these "latent states" through "observations".

More specifically, our state space model is:

$$\begin{aligned} \beta_k^{(t)} \mid \beta_k^{(t-1)} &\sim \mathcal{N}\Big(\beta_k^{(t-1)}, \delta^2 I\Big) \\ \hat{\beta}_k^{(t)} \mid \beta_k^{(t)} &\sim \mathcal{N}\Big(\beta_k^t, \hat{\delta}_t^2 I\Big) \end{aligned} \quad (4)$$

The variational parameters are $\hat{\beta}_k^{(t)}$ and $\hat{\delta}_t$. The key problem of Kalman filter is to derive the mean and variance for forward and backward equations, which can be used to calculate the lower bound in variational inference. Using the standard Kalman filter calculation, the forward mean and variance of the variational posterior are given by:

$$\begin{aligned} m_k^t &= \mathbb{E}[\beta_k^t | \hat{\boldsymbol{\beta}}_k^{1:t}] \\ &= \left(\frac{\hat{\delta}^2}{V_k^{t-1} + \delta^2 + \hat{\delta}^2}\right) m_k^{t-1} + \left(1 - \frac{\hat{\delta}^2}{V_k^{t-1} + \delta^2 + \hat{\delta}^2}\right) \hat{\beta}_k^t \\ V_k^t &= \mathbb{E}\Big[(\beta_k^t - m_k^t]) \mid \hat{\boldsymbol{\beta}}_k^{1:t}\Big] \\ &= \left(\frac{\hat{\delta}^2}{V_k^{t-1} + \delta^2 + \hat{\delta}^2}\right)(V_k^{t-1} + \delta^2) \end{aligned} \quad (5)$$

with initial conditions specified by fixed m^0 and V^0. The backward recursion then calculates the marginal mean and variance of β_k^t given $\hat{\boldsymbol{\beta}}_k^{1:T}$ as:

$$\begin{aligned} \widetilde{m}_k^{t-1} &= \mathbb{E}[\beta_k^{t-1} | \hat{\boldsymbol{\beta}}_k^{1:T}] \\ &= \left(\frac{\delta^2}{V_k^{t-1} + \delta^2}\right) m_k^{t-1} + \left(1 - \frac{\delta^2}{V_k^{t-1}] + \delta^2}\right) \widetilde{m}_k^t \\ \widetilde{V}_k^{t-1} &= \mathbb{E}\Big[(\beta_k^{t-1} - \widetilde{m}_k^{t-1}]) \mid \hat{\boldsymbol{\beta}}_k^{1:T}\Big] \\ &= V_k^{t-1} + \left(\frac{V_k^{t-1}}{V_k^{t-1} + \delta^2}\right)^2 \Big(\widetilde{V}_k^t - (V_k^{t-1} + \delta^2)\Big) \end{aligned} \quad (6)$$

with initial conditions $\widetilde{m}^T = m^T$ and $\widetilde{V}^T = V^T$.

With these forward and backward equations in hand, we turn to calculate the following lower bound (assuming $\boldsymbol{\Omega} = \{\boldsymbol{\alpha}, \boldsymbol{\beta}, \boldsymbol{\pi}, \sigma^2\}$) with the help of variational distributions introduced in Equation 5:

$$\begin{aligned} &\log P(\mathbf{W}, \mathbf{Y} | \boldsymbol{\Omega}) \geq \mathbb{E}_q[\log p(\boldsymbol{\beta})] + \mathbb{E}_q[\log p(\mathbf{W}, \mathbf{Z}, \boldsymbol{\theta} | \boldsymbol{\beta}, \boldsymbol{\alpha})] \\ &+ \mathbb{E}_q[\log p(\mathbf{Y} | \boldsymbol{\pi}, \boldsymbol{\beta}, \sigma^2)] + H(q) \\ &= \mathbb{E}_q[\log p(\boldsymbol{\beta})] + \mathbb{E}_q[\log p(\mathbf{W} | \mathbf{Z}, \boldsymbol{\beta})] + \mathbb{E}_q[\log p(\mathbf{Z} | \boldsymbol{\theta})] \\ &+ \mathbb{E}_q[\log p(\boldsymbol{\theta} | \boldsymbol{\alpha})] + \mathbb{E}_q[\log p(\mathbf{Y} | \boldsymbol{\pi}, \boldsymbol{\beta}, \sigma^2)] + H(q) \end{aligned} \quad (7)$$

where term $H(q)$ is the entropy. To tighten the above bound on the likelihood of the observations given by Jensen's inequality is equivalent to minimize KL-divergence. In the above bound, the term $\mathbb{E}_q[\log p(\mathbf{W}, \mathbf{Z}, \boldsymbol{\theta} | \boldsymbol{\beta}, \boldsymbol{\alpha})]$ is standard for topic models, when logistic-normal distribution is applied to represent topics (e.g., [3, 20]. The term $\mathbb{E}_q[\log p(\boldsymbol{\beta})]$ is standard for temporal topic models, which utilize the Kalman filter as a sequential modeling tool. The term $\mathbb{E}_q[\log p(\mathbf{Y} | \boldsymbol{\pi}, \boldsymbol{\beta}, \sigma^2)]$ can be calculated similarly to the document-level response variables, introduced in [4]. We will discuss these expectations in detail.

For the first term of the last line in Equation 7, we utilize the forward and backward equations introduced in Equation 6 and follow the similar steps in [3]:

$$\begin{aligned} \mathbb{E}_q[\log p(\boldsymbol{\beta})] &= -\frac{VKT}{2}(\log \delta^2 + \log 2\pi) \\ &- \frac{1}{2\delta^2} \sum_{t=1}^{T} \sum_{k=1}^{K} \left[\left(\widetilde{m}_k^t - \widetilde{m}_k^{t-1}\right)^2\right] - \frac{1}{\delta^2} \sum_{t=1}^{T} \sum_{k=1}^{K} \text{Tr}\Big(\widetilde{V}_k^t\Big) \\ &+ \frac{1}{2\delta^2} \sum_{k=1}^{K} \text{Tr}\Big(\widetilde{V}_k^T\Big) - \frac{1}{2\delta^2} \sum_{k=1}^{K} \text{Tr}\Big(\widetilde{V}_k^0\Big) \end{aligned}$$

For the second term in the same line, we have:

$$\mathbb{E}_q[\log p(\mathbf{W}|\mathbf{Z},\boldsymbol{\beta})] = \sum_{t=1}^{T}\sum_{d=1}^{D_t}\sum_{n=1}^{N_d}\Big(\sum_{k=1}^{K}\phi_{(n,k)}\widetilde{m}^t_{(k,w)}$$

$$-\sum_{k=1}^{K}\phi_{(n,k)}\mathbb{E}_q\Big[\log\sum_{w'}\exp(\beta_{(k,w')})\Big]\Big)$$

where the second line demonstrates the essential problem of non-conjugacy of using the logistic-normal distribution for topics. In order to calculate $\mathbb{E}_q\Big[\log\sum_{w'}\exp(\beta_{(k,w')})\Big]$, we further obtain a lower bound by introducing another variational parameter ζ_t and upper bound the negative log normalizer with a Taylor expansion as follows:

$$\mathbb{E}_q\Big[\log\sum_{w'}\exp(\beta_{(k,w')})\Big]\leq \zeta_t^{-1}\Big(\sum_{w'}\mathbb{E}_q[\exp(\beta_{(k,\hat{w}')})]\Big)$$

$$-1+\log(\zeta_t)$$

where the expectation $\mathbb{E}_q[\exp(\beta_{(k,w')})]$ is the mean of a log normal distribution with the mean and variance obtained from the variational parameters, essentially Kalman Filters, in our case. For the third term of the last line in Equation 7, we have:

$$\mathbb{E}_q[\log p(\mathbf{Z}|\boldsymbol{\theta})] = \sum_{t=1}^{T}\sum_{d=1}^{D_t}\sum_{n=1}^{N_d}\sum_{k=1}^{K}\phi_{(n,k)}\Big[\Psi(\lambda_{(d,k)})$$

$$-\Psi\Big(\sum_{k'=1}^{K}\lambda_{(d,k')}\Big)\Big]$$

and for the fourth term, we have:

$$\mathbb{E}_q[\log p(\boldsymbol{\theta}|\boldsymbol{\alpha})] = \sum_{t=1}^{T}\sum_{d=1}^{D_t}\Big\{\Big(\sum_{k=1}^{K}(\alpha_k-1)\Big[\Psi(\lambda_{(d,k)})$$

$$-\Psi\Big(\sum_{j=1}^{K}\lambda_{(d,j)}\Big)\Big]\Big)+\log\Gamma\Big(\sum_{k=1}^{K}\alpha_k\Big)-\sum_{k=1}^{K}\log\Gamma(\alpha_k)\Big\}$$

For the last term in the same line, we have:

$$\mathbb{E}_q[\log p(Y_v^{(t)}|\pi_v,\beta_{(,v)}^{(t)},\sigma^2)] = -\frac{1}{2}\log 2\pi - \frac{1}{2}\log\sigma^2$$

$$-\frac{\left(Y_v^{(t)}\right)^2}{2}+\frac{1}{\sigma^2}\Big[Y_v^{(t)}\sum_{k=1}^{K}\pi_{(v,k)}\widetilde{m}^t_{(k,v)}$$

$$-\frac{1}{2}\sum_{i=1}^{K}\sum_{j=1}^{K}\pi_{(v,i)}\Big(\widetilde{m}^t_{(i,v)}\widetilde{m}^t_{(j,v)}\Big)\pi_{(v,j)}\Big]$$

For the entropy term $H(q)$, we have:

$$-H(q) = \mathbb{E}_q[\log q(\boldsymbol{\beta}|\hat{\boldsymbol{\beta}})] + \mathbb{E}_q[\log q(\boldsymbol{\theta}|\boldsymbol{\lambda})] + \mathbb{E}_q[\log q(\mathbf{Z}|\boldsymbol{\Phi})]$$

$$=\sum_{t=1}^{T}\sum_{k=1}^{K}\Big(\frac{T}{2}\log 2\pi\Big)+\frac{1}{2}\sum_{t=1}^{T}\sum_{k=1}^{K}\sum_{v=1}^{V}\log\widetilde{V}^t_{(k,v)}+\sum_{t=1}^{T}\sum_{d=1}^{D_t}$$

$$\Big\{\Big(\sum_{k=1}^{K}(\lambda_{(d,k)}-1)\Big[\Psi(\lambda_{(d,k)})-\Psi\Big(\sum_{j=1}^{K}\lambda_{(d,j)}\Big)\Big]\Big)$$

$$+\log\Gamma\Big(\sum_{k=1}^{K}\lambda_{(d,k)}\Big)-\sum_{k=1}^{K}\log\Gamma(\lambda_{(d,k)})\Big\}$$

$$+\sum_{t=1}^{T}\sum_{d=1}^{D_t}\sum_{n=1}^{N_d}\sum_{k=1}^{K}\phi_{(n,k)}\log\phi_{(n,k)}$$

Algorithm 1: Variational inference with Kalman filtering.

Initialize $\hat{\boldsymbol{\beta}}$ randomly.
while *relative improvement in* $L > 0.00001$ **do**
  E step:
  for $t = 1$ **to** T **do**
    for $i = 1$ **to** D **do**
      Update λ_d according to Equation 8
      Update ϕ_d according to Equation 9
    Update ζ_t according to Equation 10
  M step:
  for $v = 1$ **to** V **do**
    Update π_v according to Equation 12
    Update σ_v^2 according to Equation 13
  Update $\hat{\beta}$ by using conjugate gradient descent

By using the expectations with respect to variational distributions, we can optimize the variational parameters as follows. For per-document parameters $\lambda_{(d,k)}$, per-word parameters ϕ_n and per time epoch parameters ζ_t, we have similar update equations as standard topic models:

$$\lambda_{(d,k)} = \alpha_k + \sum_{n=1}^{N_d}\phi_{(n,k)} \tag{8}$$

$$\phi_{(n,k)} \propto \exp\Big(\Psi(\lambda_{(d,k)}) - \Psi\Big(\sum_{k'=1}^{K}\lambda_{(d,k')}\Big)\Big)\times$$

$$\exp\Big(\widetilde{m}^t_{(k,w)} - \mathbb{E}_q\Big[\log\sum_{w'}\exp(\beta_{(k,w')})\Big]\Big) \tag{9}$$

$$\zeta_t = \frac{1}{N_t}\sum_{d=1}^{D_t}\sum_{n=1}^{N_d}\Big(\sum_{k=1}^{K}\phi_{(n,k)}\sum_{w}\exp\Big(\widetilde{m}^t_{(k,w)}$$

$$+\widetilde{V}^t_{(k,w)}/2\Big)\Big) \tag{10}$$

Since π_v is a vector of coefficients across all time epochs T, we gather the $\beta^*_{(*,v)}$ from all time epochs and form a $T\times K$ matrix X where each row is a vector of β values discussed before. We can obtain the following equation by using the notation of X:

$$\mathbb{E}_q[\mathbf{X}^T\mathbf{X}]\pi_v = \mathbb{E}_q[\mathbf{X}]^T\mathbf{Y}_v \tag{11}$$

and therefore, we have

$$\pi_v = \Big(\mathbb{E}_q[\mathbf{X}^T\mathbf{X}]\Big)^{-1}\mathbb{E}_q[\mathbf{X}]^T\mathbf{Y}_v \tag{12}$$

where the tth row of $\mathbb{E}_q[\mathbf{X}]$ is just $\mathbb{E}_q[\beta^t_{(,v)}]$. Similar to linear regression but in the expected version, we can obtain the update equation for σ_v^2 as:

$$\sigma_v^2 = \frac{1}{T}\Big(\mathbf{Y}_v^T\mathbf{Y}_v - 2\mathbf{Y}_v^T\mathbb{E}_q[\mathbf{X}]\pi_v + \pi_v^T\mathbb{E}_q[\mathbf{X}^T\mathbf{X}]\pi_v\Big) \tag{13}$$

where π_v is the new estimate value.

The real computational hurdle is to calculate the updates of $\hat{\boldsymbol{\beta}}$. Gathering all terms in the lower bound involving $\boldsymbol{\beta}$ and differenti-

Table 2: AR model on NIPS dataset

p	2007	2008	2009	Avg.
1	98.57	90.51	99.42	96.17
2	101.72	83.20	**91.06**	92.00
3	**97.66**	77.31	97.00	**90.39**
4	112.83	**75.62**	95.98	94.81
5	118.10	91.64	108.33	106.03
6	118.65	99.00	108.34	108.66
7	118.76	98.99	117.50	111.75
8	122.73	95.93	116.72	111.79
9	122.55	96.23	115.85	111.54
10	143.17	100.71	124.40	122.76

Table 3: AR model on ACL dataset

p	2005	2006	2007	2008	2009	Avg.
1	**131.85**	524.04	**39.57**	592.91	**126.29**	282.93
2	210.74	316.38	106.31	434.15	181.98	249.91
3	247.73	248.17	104.72	**381.84**	140.87	**224.65**
4	258.74	246.58	114.23	447.71	166.09	246.67
5	244.41	**223.99**	53.12	428.17	185.00	226.94
6	250.49	297.98	42.74	385.26	209.24	237.14
7	169.25	328.75	51.14	345.98	262.54	231.53
8	168.54	332.20	51.58	396.08	291.13	247.90
9	155.96	326.73	47.11	400.96	291.60	244.47
10	156.59	355.13	49.15	399.28	310.65	254.16

ating them with respect to $\hat{\beta}^t_{(k,v)}$, we have:

$$-\frac{1}{\delta^2}\sum_{t=1}^{T}\left(\widetilde{m}^t_{(k,v)} - \widetilde{m}^{t-1}_{(k,v)}\right)\left(\frac{\partial \widetilde{m}^t_{(k,v)}}{\partial \hat{\beta}^t_{(k,v)}} - \frac{\partial \widetilde{m}^{t-1}_{(k,v)}}{\partial \hat{\beta}^t_{(k,v)}}\right)$$
$$+\sum_{t=1}^{T}\Bigg(N_{(t,v)}\phi_{(v,k)} - \sum_{v=1}^{V} N_{(t,v)}\phi_{(v,k)}\zeta_t^{-1}\exp\Big(m^t_{(k,v)}$$
$$+V^t_{(k,v)}/2\Big)\Bigg)\frac{\partial \widetilde{m}^t_{(k,v)}}{\partial \hat{\beta}^t_{(k,v)}} + \frac{1}{\sigma^2}\sum_{t=1}^{T} Y^t_v \pi_{(v,k)} \frac{\partial \widetilde{m}^t_{(k,v)}}{\partial \hat{\beta}^t_{(k,v)}}$$
$$-\left[\frac{1}{2\sigma^2}\sum_{i=1}^{K}\sum_{j=1}^{K}\pi_{(v,i)}\left(\widetilde{m}^t_{(i,v)}\widetilde{m}^t_{(j,v)}\right)\pi_{(v,j)}\right]\frac{\partial \widetilde{m}^t_{(k,v)}}{\partial \hat{\beta}^t_{(k,v)}}$$

Unfortunately, no closed-form solution for $\hat{\beta}$ can be found. We adapt optimization techniques to obtain a local optimum of the $\hat{\beta}$ values. In our experiments, we utilize the conjugate gradient algorithm implemented in GSL library[1], which requires us to provide the gradients. The forward-backward equations for $\mathbb{E}_q$ can be used to derive a recurrence for the gradients. The forward recurrence is:

$$\frac{\partial m^t_{(k,v)}}{\partial \hat{\beta}^{(s)}_{(k,v)}} = \left(\frac{\hat{\delta}^2}{V_k^{t-1} + \delta^2 + \hat{\delta}^2}\right)\frac{\partial m_k^{t-1}}{\partial \hat{\beta}^s_{(k,v)}} + \left(1 - \frac{\hat{\delta}^2}{V_k^{t-1} + \delta^2 + \hat{\delta}^2}\right)\mathbb{I}[s == t]$$

with the initial condition $\partial m^0_k / \partial \hat{\beta}_k{}^s = 0$. The backward recurrence is then:

$$\frac{\partial \widetilde{m}^t_k}{\partial \hat{\beta}_k{}^s} = \left(\frac{\delta^2}{V_k^{t-1} + \delta^2}\right)\frac{\partial m_k^{t-1}}{\partial \hat{\beta}_k{}^s} + \left(1 - \frac{\delta^2}{V_k^{t-1} + \delta^2}\right)\frac{\partial m^t_k}{\partial \hat{\beta}_k{}^{(s)}}$$

with the initial condition $\partial \widetilde{m}^T_k / \partial \hat{\beta}_k{}^s = \partial m^T_k / \partial \hat{\beta}_k{}^s$. We outline the overall inference algorithm in Algorithm (1).

For prediction, since no documents are observed at test time, we initialize β values with their expected values, according to Equation 4 and then obtain the mean of the posterior distribution by the Kalman filter algorithm, as a standard problem. By using the learned $\boldsymbol{\pi}$ values, we could easily predict the volume of terms through Equation 1.

5. BASELINE MODELS

Time series analysis has been long studied in many fields. Here, we discuss the possibility to employ one traditional time series tool, autoregressive model, to track the volume of terms. In univariate autoregressive model AR(p), a response X_t can depend on its previous values, ranging from X_{t-1} to X_{t-p}:

$$X_t = w + \sum_{k=1}^{p} \pi_k X_{t-k} \tag{14}$$

where w is a constant and $\boldsymbol{\pi}$ is a vector of coefficients. Similar to linear regression, the aim of AR(p) is to learn w and $\boldsymbol{\pi}$, as well as the optimal choice of p, sometimes. If we treat the volume of each term as X, it is obvious that the volume of terms are independent with each other. A slightly more complicated model, Multivariate AutoRegressive model MAR(p), captures the correlations between M variables and preserves the simplicity of the model:

$$\mathbf{X}_t = \mathbf{w} + \sum_{k=1}^{p} \mathbf{A}_k \mathbf{X}_{t-k} \tag{15}$$

where $\mathbf{X}$ and $\mathbf{w}$ are both M dimensional vectors and each $\mathbf{A}$ is a $M \times M$ matrix, encoding the correlations. Although it first seems appealing, some limitations of the model prevent it from being applied in text mining scenarios. One of the drawbacks is that the model usually requires the number of variables to be smaller than the time stamps, which is not a problem in many traditional fields (e.g., temperature and humidity over time). However, in many text corpora, we wish to track thousands, or even millions of terms (e.g., in Twitter) while the total number of time epochs to be measured is significantly smaller (e.g., in year, months, days). In that case, it is impossible to solve the Equation 15, according to Neumaier and Schneider [16]. Therefore, we do not use MAR in our experiments.

The second baseline used in experiments is Latent Dirichlet Allocation (LDA) [5]. We run LDA for the whole dataset. For each time epoch t, we obtain empirical topic distributions on t, $\boldsymbol{\beta}^t$. For each term v, we treat $\beta_{(,v)}$ as features and $Y_v^{(t)}$ as the response, building a regression model on them. Note, this model is unrealistic because in reality, we cannot obtain empirical topic distributions from the test set due to the fact that no documents should be observed from the test set. However, we include this model in the experiments for the purpose to show that topic representations can help volume prediction. A more realistic state-of-the-art model, DTM, is also used in the experiments. Like our model, $\boldsymbol{\beta}$ values on the test time epoch are estimated by the Kalman filter algorithm. Similar to LDA, the topic distributions obtained by DTM are treated as features and we build a regression model based upon these features. The regression model used in experiments is Support Vector Regression (SVR), implemented in libSVM[2].

[1] http://www.gnu.org/software/gsl/

[2] http://www.csie.ntu.edu.tw/~cjlin/libsvm/

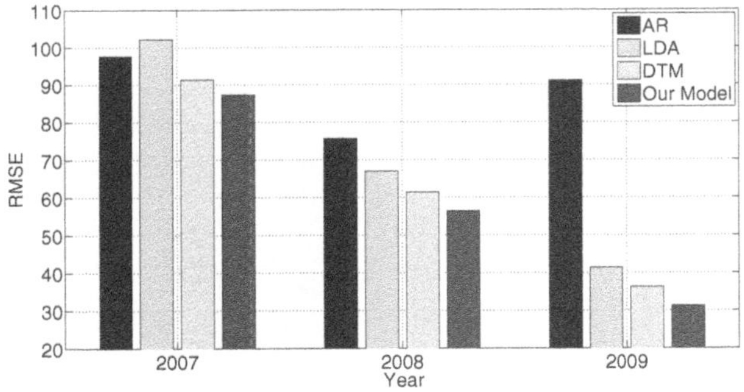

Figure 2: Performance comparison on the `NIPS` dataset. The best `RMSE` values achieved by each model are shown for the last three years.

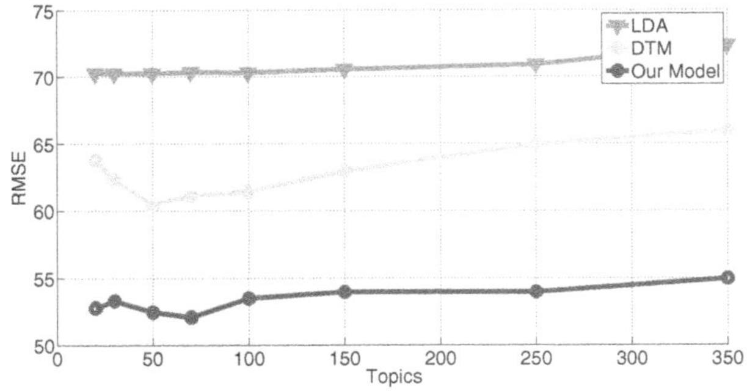

Figure 3: Performance comparison by varying the number of topics K on the `NIPS` dataset.

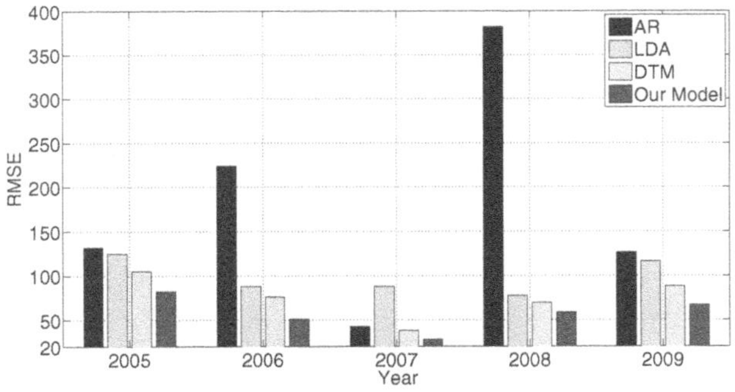

Figure 4: Performance comparison on the `ACL` dataset. The best `RMSE` values achieved by each model are shown for the last five years.

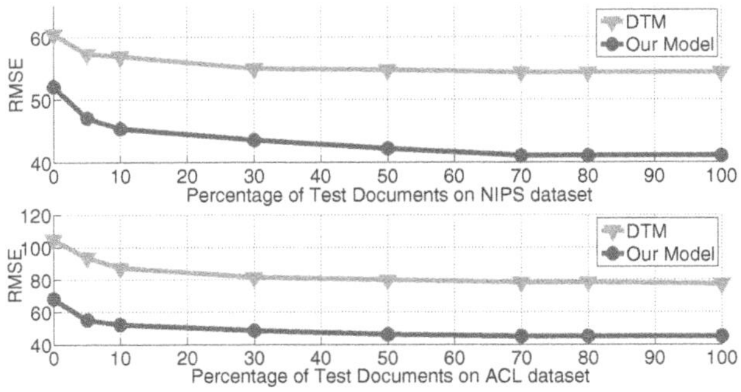

Figure 5: Performance when a fraction of the test documents is provided to the model.

6. EXPERIMENTS

Two datasets of scientific papers are used in our experiments. One is from the `NIPS` conference series. We downloaded all electronic copies of papers from online proceedings[3] and converted into text format using `pdftotext`. We tokenize the converted files and keep the terms with frequency larger than 10, resulting in to 38,029 distinct terms and 4,360 papers in total, spanning 24 years. The second dataset is from the 2009 release of The `ACL Anthology`[4], consisting of text format of papers published in the community of computational linguistics. This dataset has 14,590 papers with 74,189 distinct terms (frequency more than 10), ranging over 37 years. Both datasets have timelines that are long enough such that some topics have changed over time.

The major evaluation measure is of course the accuracy of the predicted volume of terms. In this work, we denote the estimated volume of term v at time stamp t as $\hat{Y}_v^{(t)}$. Therefore, we measure the estimation error by calculating the Root Mean Square Error (`RMSE`) between estimated values and real values:

$$\text{RMSE}_t = \sqrt{\frac{1}{V}\sum_v \left(\hat{Y}_v^{(t)} - Y_v^{(t)}\right)^2}$$

For both datasets, we adapt an "incremental" evaluation process, mimicking real application scenarios. In order to predict the volume at time t, we use the documents in all possible previous years for training. We sequentially train and test the model in multiple years and average the `RMSE` over these time periods. We conduct experiments on the last three years for the `NIPS` dataset and the last five years for the `ACL` dataset. For hyper-parameters, α is set to $50/K$, δ^2 is set to 0.1 and $\hat{\delta}^2$ is set to 1.0, similar as [3], for all experiments.

6.1 Volume Prediction

As discussed in Section 5, the first baseline we consider is the `AR` model for terms. In our case, we essentially build an `AR` model for each term. Rather than choosing the optimal p by some criteria, such as Bayesian information criterion (`BIC`)[5] or Akaike information criterion (`AIC`)[6], we simply show the predictive performance by varying p values. Therefore, it is possible that the optimal p value is out of the ranges demonstrated here. The results for the `AR` model on the `NIPS` dataset are shown in Table 2 and the results on the `ACL` dataset are shown in Table 3, where the optimal performance is in bold. Several conclusions can be made regarding these results. First, for both datasets, the optimal performance is not always obtained on $p = 1$, when the volume of terms only depends on the previous year. On average, $p = 3$ gives optimal performance on both datasets, meaning that the volume of terms in the year t depends on the previous three years. For the `NIPS` dataset, after the optimal point, the performance decreases as p increases, which indicates that for the `AR` model, no additional advantages can be obtained if we consider higher order dependencies on this particular dataset. This observation might also indicate that the latent relationships among terms, essentially topics, may change over time. Some new terms are introduced and some old concepts are outdated. For the `ACL` dataset, this is more complicated since the performance fluctuates significantly as p varies. Unlike the the

[3]http://books.nips.cc/

[4]http://clair.si.umich.edu/clair/anthology/

[5]http://en.wikipedia.org/wiki/Bayesian_information_criterion

[6]http://en.wikipedia.org/wiki/Akaike_information_criterion

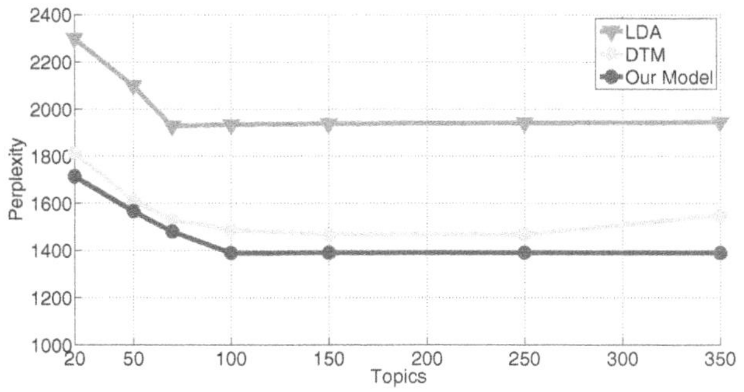

Figure 6: Perplexity comparison on NIPS dataset.

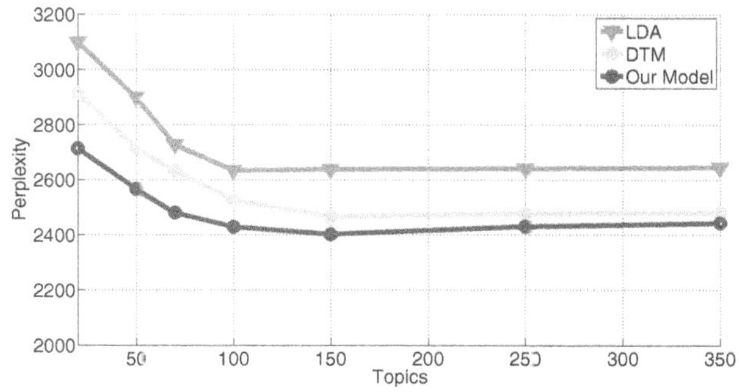

Figure 7: Perplexity comparison on ACL dataset.

NIPS dataset in which performance is relatively consistent over the recent three years, predictive performance on the ACL dataset differs significantly from year to year.

We run LDA, DTM and our model on both datasets while varying the number of topics, K. The results for the NIPS and the ACL datasets are shown in Figures 2 and 4, respectively. For each model, we only report its best performance. In addition, for both datasets, we also compare these models to the best performance achieved by the AR model. Note, as we mentioned before, LDA is unrealistic since β values for the test years are from test documents while in reality these values should be estimated from the past, assuming no documents observed in these test years. However, the purpose of showing the results from plain LDA is to demonstrate that the volume predictive performance can be greatly improved by treating topic probabilities as features if we can obtain them "correctly". For DTM and our model, these β values are estimated by the Kalman filter algorithm, mentioned in Section 3, which do not depend on the test documents at all. The first observation is that the overall performance is significantly improved over the AR model, in general. LDA is usually, but not always, better than AR in terms of average performance. For DTM and our model, which both consider temporal smoothing on topics, the performance is consistently better than both LDA and AR. Our model is also better than DTM on both datasets not only in terms of average performance but also in terms of performance on individual years.

In order to better understand the performance of topic models, we plot the performance on different K values averaged over the test years for the NIPS dataset in Figure 3. It is clear that performance is relatively stable compared to the AR model, where it is sensitive to the p value, shown in Table 2. However, for all models, as K increases, the performance slightly decreases, indicating that a higher value of K may lead models to over-fit. In any case, optimal performance is obtained from 50-70 topics for DTM and our model, which seems reasonable since NIPS is a relatively small research community and the topics are consistent over consecutive years. Similar conclusions can also be made for the ACL dataset.

Since DTM and our model prediction are performed on the year in which no documents are observed, it may be interesting to see whether performance would be improved if we partially observe the test documents. We pick the best K from the above experiments and feed a given fraction of test documents in a particular year to both models. The results are shown in Figure 5. As expected, performance improves on both datasets for both models if we observe partial data. However, when around 30% to 50% of test documents are observed, performance stabilizes.

6.2 Temporal Perplexity

Although we argue in Section 2 that perplexity may not be an appropriate evaluation method for temporal topic models, or for topic models in general, we still provide a comparison of perplexity between LDA, DTM and our model. Note, the performance on perplexity might be misleading because this measure is to evaluate how words in the documents can be assessed. Therefore, we perform the standard steps to calculate perplexity on documents in test years. As mentioned earlier, the real performance of these models should be considered when test documents are not available and how reliably the models can predict the response variables, not words. We show perplexity on the NIPS and ACL datasets in Figures 6 and 7, respectively. Overall, the perplexity values of DTM and our model are lower than LDA, for different K values, which confirms the observations in [3, 20]. In addition, perplexity decreases as K increases in general, indicating that a larger K may explain words better. However, the difference of perplexity between DTM and our model is relatively small, compared to the volume predictive performance. This is not unexpected because our model shares the same "generative" process for words in documents as DTM. Therefore, this observation also confirms that perplexity may not be appropriate to truly reflect the performance of different models, in terms of the tasks we care about. However, we do believe that a thorough study of the relationships of perplexity and the performance of third-party tasks for topic models is needed.

7. CONCLUSION

In this paper, we introduced a real-world task—tracking the volume of terms—to which temporal topic models can be applied. We proposed a new type of topic model incorporating the volumes of terms into the temporal dynamics of topics and directly optimize for the task. We combined state-space models and the volume of terms in a supervised learning fashion which enables us to effectively predict the volume in the future. The volumes of latent topics are by-products of our model, demonstrating the superiority of utilizing temporal topic models over traditional time-series tools (e.g., autoregressive models) to tackle this kind of problem. The proposed model can be further extended with arbitrary word-level features which are evolving over time. We presented the results of applying the model to two datasets with long time periods and showed its effectiveness over non-trivial baselines. Future work might include the adoption of recently developed online variational inference algorithms [8] to our model, enabling the processing of large scale datasets.

Acknowledgements

This material is based upon work supported in part by the National Science Foundation under Grant Numbers IIS-0545875 and IIS-0803605.

8. REFERENCES

[1] D. Agarwal and B.-C. Chen. fLDA: matrix factorization through Latent Dirichlet Allocation. In *Proceedings of the third ACM International Conference on Web Search and Data Mining (WSDM)*, pages 91–100, New York, NY, USA, 2010. ACM.

[2] A. Ahmed and E. P. Xing. Timeline: A dynamic hierarchical Dirichlet process model for recovering birth/death and evolution of topics in text stream. In *Proceedings of the 26th International Conference on Conference on Uncertainty in Artificial Intelligence (UAI)*, 2010.

[3] D. M. Blei and J. D. Lafferty. Dynamic topic models. In *Proceedings of the 23rd International Conference on Machine Learning (ICML)*, 2006.

[4] D. M. Blei and J. D. Mcauliffe. Supervised topic models. In *Advances in Neural Information Processing Systems 21*, 2007.

[5] D. M. Blei, A. Y. Ng, and M. I. Jordan. Latent Dirichlet Allocation. *Journal of Machine Learning Research*, 3:993–1022, 2003.

[6] J. Boyd-Graber, J. Chang, S. Gerrish, C. Wang, and D. Blei. Reading Tea Leaves: How Humans Interpret Topic Models. In *Neural Information Processing Systems (NIPS)*, 2009.

[7] T. L. Griffiths and M. Steyvers. Finding scientific topics. *Proceedings of the National Academy of Sciences of the United States of America*, 2004.

[8] M. Hoffman, D. Blei, and F. Bach. Online learning for latent dirichlet allocation. In J. Lafferty, C. K. I. Williams, J. Shawe-Taylor, R. Zemel, and A. Culotta, editors, *Advances in Neural Information Processing Systems 23*, pages 856–864, 2010.

[9] T. Iwata, T. Yamada, Y. Sakurai, and N. Ueda. Online multiscale dynamic topic models. In *Proceedings of the 16th ACM SIGKDD International Conference on Knowledge Discovery and Data Mining*, 2010.

[10] N. Kawamae and R. Higashinaka. Trend detection model. In *Proceedings of the 19th International Conference on World Wide Web (WWW)*, pages 1129–1130, New York, NY, USA, 2010. ACM.

[11] S. Lacoste-Julien, F. Sha, and M. I. Jordan. DiscLDA: Discriminative Learning for Dimensionality Reduction and Classification. In *Advances in Neural Information Processing Systems (NIPS)*, 2008.

[12] T. Masada, D. Fukagawa, A. Takasu, T. Hamada, Y. Shibata, and K. Oguri. Dynamic hyperparameter optimization for Bayesian topical trend analysis. In *Proceeding of the 18th ACM Conference on Information and Knowledge Management (CIKM)*, 2009.

[13] Q. Mei, C. Liu, H. Su, and C. Zhai. A probabilistic approach to spatiotemporal theme pattern mining on weblogs. In *Proceedings of the 15th International Conference on World Wide Web (WWW)*, 2006.

[14] Q. Mei and C. Zhai. Discovering evolutionary theme patterns from text: an exploration of temporal text mining. In *Proceedings of the eleventh ACM SIGKDD International Conference on Knowledge Discovery in Data Mining*, 2005.

[15] R. M. Nallapati, S. Ditmore, J. D. Lafferty, and K. Ung. Multiscale topic tomography. In *Proceedings of the 13th ACM SIGKDD International Conference on Knowledge Discovery and Data Mining*, 2007.

[16] A. Neumaier and T. Schneider. Estimation of parameters and eigenmodes of multivariate autoregressive models. *ACM Transactions on Mathematical Software*, 27:27–57, March 2001.

[17] J. Petterson, A. Smola, T. Caetano, W. Buntine, and S. Narayanamurthy. Word features for latent dirichlet allocation. In J. Lafferty, C. K. I. Williams, J. Shawe-Taylor, R. Zemel, and A. Culotta, editors, *Advances in Neural Information Processing Systems 23*, pages 1921–1929. 2010.

[18] D. Ramage, D. Hall, R. Nallapati, and C. D. Manning. Labeled LDA: A supervised topic model for credit attribution in multi-labeled corpora. In *Proceedings of the 2009 Conference on Empirical Methods in Natural Language Processing*, pages 248–256, Singapore, August 2009. Association for Computational Linguistics.

[19] C. Wang, D. Blei, and F.-F. Li. Simultaneous image classification and annotation. *IEEE Conference on Computer Vision and Pattern Recognition*, 0:1903–1910, 2009.

[20] C. Wang, D. M. Blei, and D. Heckerman. Continuous time dynamic topic models. In *Proceedings of the 24th Conference in Uncertainty in Artificial Intelligence (UAI)*, 2008.

[21] X. Wang and A. McCallum. Topics over time: a non-Markov continuous-time model of topical trends. In *Proceedings of the 12th ACM SIGKDD International Conference on Knowledge Discovery and Data Mining*, 2006.

[22] X. Wang, C. Zhai, X. Hu, and R. Sproat. Mining correlated bursty topic patterns from coordinated text streams. In *Proceedings of the 13th ACM SIGKDD International Conference on Knowledge Discovery and Data Mining*, 2007.

[23] X. Wang, K. Zhang, X. Jin, and D. Shen. Mining common topics from multiple asynchronous text streams. In *Proceedings of the Second ACM International Conference on Web Search and Data Mining (WSDM)*, 2009.

[24] X. Wei and W. B. Croft. LDA-based document models for ad-hoc retrieval. In *Proceedings of the 29th annual International ACM SIGIR Conference on Research and Development in Information Retrieval*, pages 178–185, New York, NY, USA, 2006. ACM.

[25] J. Zhang, Y. Song, C. Zhang, and S. Liu. Evolutionary hierarchical Dirichlet processes for multiple correlated time-varying corpora. In *Proceedings of the 16th ACM SIGKDD International Conference on Knowledge Discovery and Data Mining*, 2010.

[26] J. Zhu, A. Ahmed, and E. P. Xing. MedLDA: maximum margin supervised topic models for regression and classification. In *Proceedings of the 26th Annual International Conference on Machine Learning (ICML)*, pages 1257–1264, New York, NY, USA, 2009. ACM.

Differentially Private Data Release for Data Mining

Noman Mohammed
Concordia University
Montreal, QC, Canada
no_moham@encs.concordia.ca

Rui Chen
Concordia University
Montreal, QC, Canada
ru_che@encs.concordia.ca

Benjamin C. M. Fung
Concordia University
Montreal, QC, Canada
fung@ciise.concordia.ca

Philip S. Yu
University of Illinois at Chicago
IL, USA
psyu@cs.uic.edu

ABSTRACT

Privacy-preserving data publishing addresses the problem of disclosing sensitive data when mining for useful information. Among the existing privacy models, ϵ-*differential privacy* provides one of the strongest privacy guarantees and has no assumptions about an adversary's background knowledge. Most of the existing solutions that ensure ϵ-differential privacy are based on an *interactive* model, where the data miner is only allowed to pose aggregate queries to the database. In this paper, we propose the first anonymization algorithm for the *non-interactive* setting based on the generalization technique. The proposed solution first probabilistically generalizes the raw data and then adds noise to guarantee ϵ-differential privacy. As a sample application, we show that the anonymized data can be used effectively to build a decision tree induction classifier. Experimental results demonstrate that the proposed non-interactive anonymization algorithm is scalable and performs better than the existing solutions for classification analysis.

Categories and Subject Descriptors

H.2.7 [**Database Administration**]: [Security, integrity, and protection]; H.2.8 [**Database Applications**]: [Data mining]

General Terms

Algorithms, Performance, Security

Keywords

Differential privacy, anonymization, data mining

1. INTRODUCTION

Due to the rapid advancement in storing, processing, and networking capabilities of computing devices, there has been a tremendous growth in the collection of digital information about individuals. And the emergence of new computing paradigms, such as cloud computing, increases the possibility of large-scale distributed data collection from multiple sources. While the collected data offer tremendous opportunities for mining useful information, there is also a threat to privacy because data in raw form often contain sensitive information about individuals. *Privacy-preserving data publishing* (*PPDP*) studies how to transform raw data into a version that is immunized against privacy attacks but that still supports effective data mining tasks. In this paper, we present an anonymization algorithm to transform a raw data table into a version that satisfies ϵ-*differential privacy* [7] and supports effective classification analysis.

Defining privacy is a difficult task. One of the key challenges is how to model the background knowledge of an adversary. Simply removing explicit identifiers (e.g., name) does not preserve privacy, given that the adversary has some background knowledge about the victim. Sweeney [37] illustrates that 87% of the U.S. population can be uniquely identified based on 5-digit zip code, gender, and date of birth. These attributes are called *quasi-identifier* (*QID*) and the adversary may know these values from publicly available sources such as a voter list. An individual can be identified from published data by simply joining the QID attributes with an external data source.

To limit such disclosure, Samarati and Sweeney [36, 37] propose the k-*anonymity* privacy model, which requires that an individual should not be identifiable from a group of size smaller than k based on the QID. However, Machanavajjhala et al. [28] point out that with additional knowledge about the victim, k-anonymous data is vulnerable against background knowledge attacks. To prevent such attacks, ℓ-*diversity* requires that every QID group should contain at least ℓ "well-represented" values for the sensitive attribute. Similarly, there are a number of other partition-based privacy models such as (α, k)-*anonymity* [41], t-*closeness* [26], and (c, k)-*safety* [29] that model the adversary differently and have different assumptions about its background knowledge.

To transform a raw data table to satisfy a specified privacy requirement, one of the most popular techniques is *generalization* [36, 37]. Generalization replaces a specific value with a more general value to make the information less precise while preserving the "truthfulness" of information. Let Table 1.a be a raw data table (ignore the *class* attribute for now). Generalization can be used to create a 4-anonymous table, as shown in Table 1.b, according to the taxonomy trees given in Figure 1. A large number of anonymization

KDD'11, August 21–24, 2011, San Diego, California, USA.

Table 1: A raw data table and its anonymized versions

(a) Raw data table

Job	Age	Class
Engineer	34	Y
Lawyer	50	N
Engineer	38	N
Lawyer	33	Y
Dancer	20	Y
Writer	37	N
Writer	32	Y
Dancer	25	N

(b) 4-anonymous table

Job	Age
Professional	[18-65)
Professional	[18-65)
Professional	[18-65)
Professional	[18-65)
Artist	[18-65)
Artist	[18-65)
Artist	[18-65)
Artist	[18-65)

(c) Contingency table

Job	Age	Count
Engineer	[18-40)	2
Engineer	[40-65)	0
Lawyer	[18-40)	1
Lawyer	[40-65)	1
Dancer	[18-40)	2
Dancer	[40-65)	0
Writer	[18-40)	2
Writer	[40-65)	0

(d) Generalized contingency table

Job	Age	Count
Professional	[18-40)	3
Professional	[40-65)	1
Artist	[18-40)	4
Artist	[40-65)	0

algorithms [2, 13, 24, 23, 36], tailored for both general and specific data mining tasks, have been proposed based on generalization.

Recently, Wong et al. [39] and Zhang et al. [45] show that these algorithms are vulnerable against minimality attack and do not provide the claimed privacy guarantee. Although several fixes against minimality attack have been proposed [5, 19, 43], new attacks such as *composition attack* [14], *deFinetti attack* [21], and *foreground knowledge attack* [40] have emerged against these algorithms [2, 13, 24, 23, 36]. One way to handle these attacks is to revise the existing algorithms or propose new algorithms while keeping the current privacy models and hoping no other attack will be discovered. Another way is to choose a privacy model that is robust enough to provide a provable privacy guarantee and that is, by definition, immune against all these attacks. We adopt the latter approach in this paper.

Differential privacy [7] is a rigorous privacy model that makes no assumption about an adversary's background knowledge. A differentially-private mechanism ensures that the probability of any output (released data) is equally likely from all nearly identical input data sets and thus guarantees that all outputs are insensitive to any individual's data. In other words, an individual's privacy is not at risk because of her participation in the data set.

1.1 Motivation

Existing algorithms that provide differential privacy guarantee are based on two approaches: *interactive* and *non-interactive*. In an interactive framework, a data miner can pose aggregate queries through a private mechanism, and a database owner answers these queries in response. Most of the proposed methods for ensuring differential privacy are based on an interactive framework [6, 9, 35, 11]. In a non-interactive framework the database owner first anonymizes the raw data and then releases the anonymized version for public use. In this paper we adopt the non-interactive framework and argue that this approach has a number of advantages for data mining.

In an interactive framework privacy is ensured by adding noise to each query response. To ensure privacy a database owner can answer only a limited number of queries before she has to increase the noise level to a point that the answer is no longer useful. Thus, the database can only support a fixed number of queries for a given privacy budget. This is a big problem when there are a large number of data miners because each user (data miner) can only ask a small number of queries. Even for a small number of users, it is not possible to explore the data for testing various hypotheses.

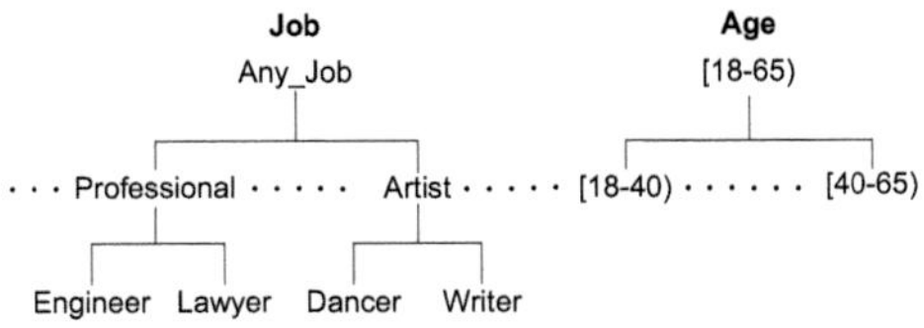

Figure 1: Taxonomy tree of attributes

On the other hand, by releasing the data all data miners get full access to the anonymized data. This gives researchers greater flexibility in performing the required data analysis, and they can fine-tune the data mining results for their research purposes.

Current techniques that adopt the non-interactive approach publish contingency tables or marginals of the raw data [9, 1, 44, 16] (see Section 2 for more discussion). The general structure of these approaches is to first derive a frequency matrix[1] of the raw data over the database domain. For example, Table 1.c shows the contingency table of Table 1.a. After that, noise is added to each count to satisfy the privacy requirement. Finally, the noisy frequency matrix is published. However, this approach is not suitable for high-dimensional data with a large domain because when the added noise is relatively large compared to the count, the utility of the data is significantly destroyed. We also confirm this point in our experimental results (Section 5).

1.2 Contributions

In this paper, we propose a novel technique for privacy-preserving data publishing that provides an ϵ*-differential privacy* [7] guarantee. While protecting privacy is a critical element in data publishing, it is equally important to preserve the utility of the published data because this is the primary reason for data release. Taking the decision tree induction classifier as an example, we show that our anonymization algorithm can be effectively tailored for preserving information for the data mining task. The contributions of this paper are summarized as follow:

1. We present the first generalization-based algorithm for differentially private data release that preserves information for classification analysis. Previous work [27] suggests that generalization technique cannot be used to achieve ϵ-differential privacy as it heavily depends on the underlying data. Yet, we show that differentially private data can be released by adding uncertainty in the generalization procedure. The proposed

[1]For a contingency table, a frequency matrix is computed over all the attributes, whereas a marginal is derived by projecting some of the attributes.

Table 2: Characteristics of PPDP algorithms

Algorithms	Dimension		Attribute Domain		Privacy Model	
	Single	Multi	Leaf Level	Hierarchical	Differential Privacy	Partition-based Privacy
Mondrian [23], TDS [13], etc.	✓	✓		✓		✓
Barak *et al.* [1]	✓	✓	✓		✓	
Hay *et al.* [16]	✓		✓	✓	✓	
Privelet [44]	✓	✓	✓		✓	
Our proposal	✓	✓	✓	✓	✓	

solution first probabilistically generates a generalized contingency table and then adds noise to the counts. For example, Table 1.d is a generalized contingency table of Table 1.a. Thus the count of each partition is typically much larger than the added noise.

2. The proposed algorithm can handle both categorical and numerical attributes. Unlike existing methods [44], it does not require the numerical attribute to be pre-discretized. The algorithm adaptively determines the split points for numerical attributes and partitions the data based on the workload, while guaranteeing ϵ-differential privacy. This is an essential requirement for getting accurate classification, as we show in Section 5. Moreover, the algorithm is very efficient and scales for large data sets.

3. It is well acknowledged that ϵ-differential privacy provides strong privacy guarantee. However, the utility aspect of the differentially-private algorithms has received much less study. Does the interactive approach offer better data mining results than the non-interactive approach? Does differentially private data provide less utility than k-anonymous data? Experimental results demonstrate that our algorithm outperforms the recently proposed differentially-private interactive algorithm for building classifier [11] and the *top-down specialization (TDS)* approach[13] that publishes k-anonymous data for classification analysis.

The rest of the paper is organized as follows. Section 2 reviews related literature. Section 3 overviews ϵ-differential privacy and generalization techniques. Our anonymization algorithm is explained in Section 4. Section 5 experimentally evaluates the performance of our solution. Section 6 concludes the paper.

2. RELATED WORK

Partition-based approach divides a given data set into disjoint groups and releases some general information about the groups. The two most popular anonymization techniques are generalization and bucketization. Generalization [2, 24, 36] makes information less precise while preserving the "truthfulness" of information. Unlike generalization, bucketization [42, 29] does not modify the QID and the sensitive attribute (SA) values but instead de-associates the relationship between the two. However, it thus also disguises the correlation between SA and other attributes and, therefore, hinders data analysis that depends on such correlation.

Many algorithms have been proposed to preserve privacy, but only a few have considered the goal for classification [12]. Iyengar [18] presents the anonymity problem for classification and proposes a genetic algorithmic solution. Bayardo and Agrawal [2] also address the classification problem using the same classification metric of [18]. Fung et al. [13] propose a top-down specialization (TDS) approach to generalize a data table. Recently, LeFevre et. al. [24] propose another anonymization technique for classification using multidimensional recoding [23]. All these algorithms adopt k-anonymity [36, 37] or its extensions [28, 38] as the underlying privacy principle and, therefore, are vulnerable to the recently discovered privacy attacks [39, 14, 21, 40]. More discussion about the partition-based approach can be found in a survey paper [12].

Differential privacy has received considerable attention recently as a substitute for partition-based privacy models for PPDP. However, most of the research on differential privacy so far concentrates on the interactive setting with the goal of reducing the magnitude of added noise [6, 9, 35], releasing certain data mining results [3, 11], or determining the feasibility and infeasibility results of differentially-private mechanisms [4, 20]. A general overview of various research works on differential privacy can be found in the recent survey [8]. Below, we briefly review the results relevant to this paper.

Barak *et al.* [1] address the problem of releasing a set of consistent marginals of a contingency table. Their method ensures that each count of the marginals is non-negative and their sum is consistent for a set of marginals. Xiao et al. [44] propose *Privelet*, a wavelet-transformation-based approach that lowers the magnitude of noise needed to ensure differential privacy to publish a multidimensional frequency matrix. Hay *et al.* [16] propose a method to publish differentially private histograms for a one-dimensional data set. Although Privelet and Hay *et al.*'s approach can achieve differential privacy by adding polylogarithmic noise variance, the latter is only limited to a one-dimensional data set.

Some works [15, 25] address how to compute the results of a number of given queries while minimizing the added noise. However, these methods require the set of queries to be given first altogether to compute the results. In contrast, our method complements the above works by determining how to partition the data adaptively so that the released data can be useful for a given data mining task. In addition, a number of recent works propose differentially-private mechanisms for different applications such as record linkage [17], and recommender systems [31]. Though closely related, all these works do not address the problem of privacy-preserving data publishing for classification analysis, the primary theme of this paper. Table 2 summaries different characteristics of the PPDP algorithms discussed above.

The most relevant work to this paper is *DiffP-C4.5* [11], an interactive algorithm for building a classifier while guaranteeing differential privacy. We have already discussed the shortcomings of an interactive framework and will experimentally compare our algorithm designed for the non-interactive setting with *DiffP-C4.5* in Section 5.

3. PRELIMINARIES

In this section, we first present an overview of ϵ-differential privacy and the core mechanisms to achieve ϵ-differential privacy. We then introduce the notion of generalization in the context of microdata publishing, followed by a problem statement.

3.1 Differential Privacy

Differential privacy is a recent privacy definition that provides a strong privacy guarantee. Partition-based privacy models ensure privacy by imposing syntactic constraints on the output. For example, the output is required to be indistinguishable among k records, or the sensitive value to be well represented in every equivalent group. Instead, differential privacy guarantees that an adversary learns nothing more about an individual, regardless of whether her record is present or absent in the data. Informally, a differentially private output is insensitive to any particular record. Therefore, from an individual's point of view, the output is computed as if from a data set that does not contain her record.

DEFINITION 3.1 (*ϵ-differential privacy*). A randomized algorithm Ag is differentially private if for all data sets D and D' where their symmetric difference contains at most one record (i.e., $|D \triangle D'| \leq 1$), and for all possible anonymized data sets $\hat{D}$,

$$\Pr[Ag(D) = \hat{D}] \leq e^{\epsilon} \times \Pr[Ag(D') = \hat{D}], \quad (1)$$

where the probabilities are over the randomness of the Ag. ∎

The parameter $\epsilon > 0$ is public and specified by a data owner. Lower values of ϵ provide a stronger privacy guarantee. Typically, the values of ϵ should be small, such as 0.01, 0.1, or in some cases $\ln 2$, or $\ln 3$ [8]. When ϵ is very small, we have $e^{\epsilon} \approx 1 + \epsilon$.

A standard mechanism to achieve differential privacy is to add random noise to the true output of a function. The noise is calibrated according to the *sensitivity* of the function. The sensitivity of a function is the maximum difference of its outputs from two data sets that differ only in one record.

DEFINITION 3.2 (*Sensitivity*). For any function $f : D \rightarrow \mathbb{R}^d$, the sensitivity of f is

$$\Delta f = \max_{D,D'} ||f(D) - f(D')||_1 \quad (2)$$

for all D, D' differing in at most one record. ∎

EXAMPLE 1. Consider the raw data set of Table 1.a. Let f be a function that counts the number of records with Age less than 40. Then, the Δf is 1 because $f(D)$ can differ at most 1 due to the addition or removal of a single record. ∎

Laplace Mechanism. Dwork et al. [9] propose the Laplace mechanism. The mechanism takes a data set D, a function f, and the parameter λ that determines the magnitude of noise as inputs. It first computes the true output $f(D)$, and then perturbs the output by adding noise. The noise is generated according to a Laplace distribution with probability density function $\Pr(x|\lambda) = \frac{1}{2\lambda}\mathtt{exp}(-|x|/\lambda)$; its variance is $2\lambda^2$ and mean is 0. The following theorem connects the sensitivity to the magnitude of noise and guarantees that perturbed output $\hat{f(D)} = f(D) + \mathtt{Lap}(\lambda)$ satisfies ϵ-differential privacy, where $\mathtt{Lap}(\lambda)$ is a random variable sampled from the Laplace distribution.

THEOREM 3.1. *[9] For any function $f : D \rightarrow \mathbb{R}^d$, the algorithm Ag that adds independently generated noise with distribution $Lap(\Delta f/\epsilon)$ to each of the d outputs satisfies ϵ-differential privacy.*

EXAMPLE 2. Continue from Example 1. The mechanism first computes the true count $f(D)$ and then outputs the noisy answer $\hat{f(D)} = f(D) + \mathtt{Lap}(1/\epsilon)$. ∎

Exponential Mechanism. McSherry and Talwar [32] propose the exponential mechanism that can choose an output $t \in \mathcal{T}$ that is close to the optimum with respect to a utility function while preserving differential privacy. The exponential mechanism takes as inputs a data set D, output range $\mathcal{T}$, privacy parameter ϵ, and a utility function $u : (D \times \mathcal{T}) \rightarrow \mathbb{R}$ that assigns a real valued score to every output $t \in \mathcal{T}$, where a higher score means better utility.

The mechanism induces a probability distribution over the range $\mathcal{T}$ and then samples an output t. Let $\Delta u = \max_{\forall t, D, D'} |u(D,t) - u(D',t)|$ be the sensitivity of the utility function. The probability associated with each output is proportional to $\mathtt{exp}(\frac{\epsilon u(D,t)}{2\Delta u})$; that is, the output with a higher score is exponentially more likely to be chosen.

THEOREM 3.2. *[32] For any function $u : (D \times \mathcal{T}) \rightarrow \mathbb{R}$, an algorithm Ag that chooses an output t with probability proportional to $exp(\frac{\epsilon u(D,t)}{2\Delta u})$ satisfies ϵ-differential privacy.*

3.2 Generalization

Let $D = \{r_1, \ldots, r_n\}$ be a multiset of records, where each record r_i represents the information of an individual with d attributes $\mathcal{A} = \{A_1, \ldots, A_d\}$. We represent the data set D in a tabular form and use the terms "data set" and "data table" interchangeably. We assume that each attribute A_i has a finite domain, denoted by $\Omega(A_i)$. The domain of D is defined as $\Omega(D) = \Omega(A_1)\times, \ldots, \times\Omega(A_d)$. To anonymize a data set D, generalization replaces a value of an attribute with a more general value. The exact general value is determined according to the attribute partition.

DEFINITION 3.3 (*Attribute Partition*). The partitions $P(A_i)$ of a numerical attribute are the intervals $\langle I_1, I_2, \ldots, I_k \rangle$ in $\Omega(A_i)$ such that $\bigcup_{j=1}^{k} I_j = \Omega(A_i)$. For categorical attribute, partitions are defined by a set of nodes from the taxonomy tree such that it covers the whole tree, and each leaf node belongs to exactly one partition. ∎

For example, *Artist* is the general value of *Dancer* according to the taxonomy tree of *Job* in Figure 1. And, *Age* 23 can be represented by the interval $[18 - 40)$. For numerical attributes, these intervals are determined adaptively from the data set.

DEFINITION 3.4 (*Generalization*). Generalization is defined by a function $\Phi = \{\phi_1, \phi_2, \ldots, \phi_d\}$, where $\phi_i : v \rightarrow p$ maps each value $v \in \Omega(A_i)$ to a $p \in P(A_i)$. ∎

Clearly, given a data set D over a set of attributes $\mathcal{A} = \{A_1, \ldots, A_d\}$, many alternative generalization functions are feasible. Each generalization function partitions the attribute domains differently. To satisfy the ϵ-differential privacy requirement the algorithm must determine a generalization function that is insensitive to the underlying data. More formally, for any two data sets D and D', where $D \triangle D' = 1$, the algorithm must ensure that the ratio of $\Pr[Ag(D) = \Phi]$ and $\Pr[Ag(D') = \Phi]$ is bounded.

One naive solution that satisfies ϵ-differential privacy is to have a fixed generalization function, irrespective of the input database. However, a proper choice of generalization function is very crucial since the data mining result varies significantly for different choices of partitioning. In Section 4 we present an efficient algorithm for determining an adaptive partitioning technique for classification analysis that guarantees ϵ-differential privacy.

3.3 Problem Statement

Suppose a data owner wants to release a data table $D(A_1^{pr}, \ldots, A_d^{pr}, A^{cls})$ to the public for classification analysis. The attributes in D are classified into three categories: (1) An *explicit identifier* A^i attribute that explicitly identifies an individual, such as *SSN*, and *Name*. These attributes are removed before releasing the data. (2) A *class* attribute A^{cls} that contains the class value, and the goal of the data miner is to build a classifier to accurately predict the value of this attribute. (3) A set of d *predictor* attributes $\mathcal{A}^{pr} = \{A_1^{pr}, \ldots, A_d^{pr}\}$, whose values are used to predict the class attribute.

We require the class attribute to be categorical, and the predictor attribute can be either numerical or categorical. Further, we assume that for each categorical-predictor attribute A_i^{pr}, a taxonomy tree is provided. The taxonomy tree of an attribute A_i^{pr} specifies the hierarchy among the values in $\Omega(A_i^{pr})$. Next, we give our problem statement.

Given a data table D and the privacy parameter ϵ, our objective is to generate an anonymized data table $\hat{D}$ such that (1) $\hat{D}$ satisfies ϵ-differential privacy, and (2) preserves as much information as possible for classification analysis.

4. THE ALGORITHM

In this section, we first present an overview of our *Diff*erentially-private anonymization algorithm based on *Gen*eralization (*DiffGen*). We then elaborate the key steps, and prove that the algorithm is ϵ-differential private. Finally, we present the implementation details and analyze the complexity of the algorithm.

4.1 Overview

Algorithm 1 first generalizes the predictor attributes $\mathcal{A}^{pr}$ and thus divides the raw data into several equivalence groups, where all the records within a group have the same attribute values. Then the algorithm publishes the noisy counts of the groups. The general idea is to anonymize the raw data by a sequence of specializations, starting from the topmost general state as shown in Figure 2. A *specialization*, written $v \rightarrow child(v)$, where $child(v)$ denotes the set of child values of v, replaces the parent value v with a child value. The specialization process can be viewed as pushing the "cut" of each taxonomy tree downwards. A *cut* of the taxonomy tree for an attribute A_i^{pr}, denoted by Cut_i, contains exactly one value on each root-to-leaf path. Figure 1 shows a solution cut indicated by the dashed curve representing the anonymous Table 1.d.

Algorithm 1 DiffGen

Input: Raw data set D, privacy budget ϵ, and number of specializations h.

Output: Generalized data set $\hat{D}$

1: Initialize every value in D to the topmost value;
2: Initialize Cut_i to include the topmost value;
3: $\epsilon' \leftarrow \frac{\epsilon}{2(|A_n^{pr}|+2h)}$;
4: Determine the split value for each $v_n \in \cup Cut_i$ with probability $\propto \exp(\frac{\epsilon'}{2\Delta u} u(D, v_n))$;
5: Compute the score for $\forall v \in \cup Cut_i$;
6: **for** $i = 1$ to h **do**
7:     Select $v \in \cup Cut_i$ with probability $\propto \exp(\frac{\epsilon'}{2\Delta u} u(D, v))$;
8:     Specialize v on D and update $\cup Cut_i$;
9:     Determine the split value for each new $v_n \in \cup Cut_i$ with probability $\propto \exp(\frac{\epsilon'}{2\Delta u} u(D, v_n))$;
10:     Update score for $v \in \cup Cut_i$;
11: **end for**
12: **return** each group with count $(C + \mathrm{Lap}(2/\epsilon))$

The specialization starts from the topmost cut and pushes down the cut iteratively by specializing some value in the current cut. Initially, all values in $\mathcal{A}^{pr}$ are generalized to the topmost value in their taxonomy trees (Line 1), and Cut_i contains the topmost value for each attribute A_i^{pr} (Line 2). At each iteration *DiffGen* probabilistically selects a candidate $v \in \cup Cut_i$ for specialization (Line 7). Candidates are selected based on their score values, and different heuristics (e.g., information gain) can be used to determine the score of the candidates. Then, the algorithm specializes v and updates $\cup Cut_i$ (Line 8). Finally, it updates the score of the affected candidates due to the specialization (Line 10). *DiffGen* terminates after a given number of specializations. The proposed algorithm can also be used to publish a contingency table by allowing the specialization to continue until it reaches the leaf level of the attribute domains.

Example 3. Consider the raw data set of Table 1.a. Initially the algorithm creates one root partition containing all the records that are generalized to $\langle$*Any_Job, [18-65)*$\rangle$. $\cup Cut_i$ includes {*Any_Job, [18-65)*}. Let the first specialization be *Any_Job* $\rightarrow$ {*Professional, Artist*}. The algorithm creates two new partitions under the root, as shown in Figure 2, and splits data records between them. $\cup Cut_i$ is updated to {*Professional, Artist, [18-65)*}. Suppose that the next specialization is *[18-65)* $\rightarrow$ {*[18-40),[40-65)*}, which creates further specialized partitions. Finally, the algorithm outputs the equivalence groups of each leaf partition along with their noisy counts. ∎

4.2 Privacy Analysis

We next elaborate the key steps of the algorithm: (1) selecting a candidate for specialization, (2) determining the split value, and (3) publishing the noisy counts. We show that each of these steps preserves privacy, and then we use the composition properties of differential privacy to guarantee that *DiffGen* is ϵ-differentially private.

(1) Candidate Selection. We use an exponential mechanism (see Section 3) to select a candidate for specialization in each round. We define two utility functions to calculate the score

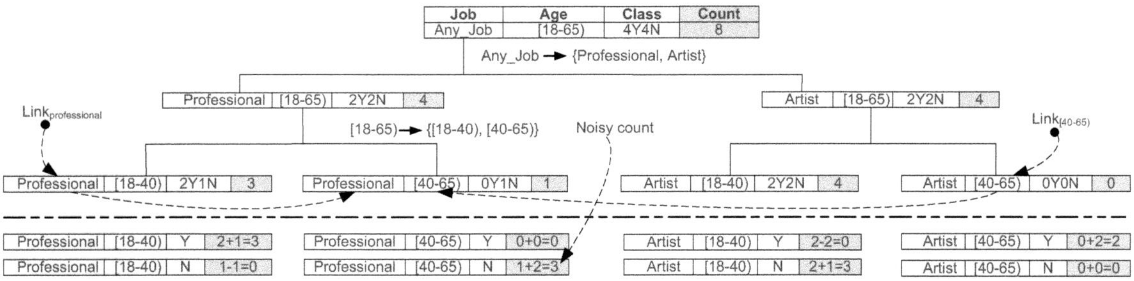

Figure 2: Tree for partitioning records

of each candidate $v \in \cup Cut_i$. The first utility function is *information gain*. Let D_v denote the set of records in D generalized to the value v. Let $|D_v^{cls}|$ denote the number of records in D_v having the class value $cls \in \Omega(A^{cls})$. Note that $|D_v| = \sum_c |D_c|$, where $c \in child(v)$. Then, we get

$$\texttt{InfoGain}(D, v) = H_v(D) - H_{v|c}(D), \tag{3}$$

where $\texttt{H}_v(D) = -\sum_{cls} \frac{|D_v^{cls}|}{|D_v|} \times \log_2 \frac{|D_v^{cls}|}{|D_v|}$ is the *entropy* of candidate v with respect to the class attribute A^{cls} and $\texttt{H}_{v|c}(D) = \sum_c \frac{|D_c|}{|D_v|}\texttt{H}_c(D)$ is the conditional entropy given the candidate is specialized. The sensitivity of $\texttt{InfoGain}(D, v)$ is $\log_2 |\Omega(A^{cls})|$, where $|\Omega(A^{cls})|$ is the domain size of the class attribute A^{cls}. It is because the value of the entropy $\texttt{H}_v(D)$ must be between 0 and $\log_2 |\Omega(A^{cls})|$. And, the value of the conditional entropy $\texttt{H}_{v|c}(D)$ lies between 0 and $\texttt{H}_v(D)$. Therefore, the maximum change of $\texttt{InfoGain}(D, v)$ due to the addition or removal of a record is bounded by $\log_2 |\Omega(A^{cls})|$.

The second utility function is:

$$\texttt{Max}(D, v) = \sum_{c \in child(v)} (\max_{cls}(|D_c^{cls}|)). \tag{4}$$

$\texttt{Max}(D, v)$ is the summation of the highest class frequencies over all child values and the sensitivity of this function is 1 because the value of $\texttt{Max}(D, v)$ can vary at most 1 due to the change of a record.

Given the scores of all the candidates, exponential mechanism selects a candidate v_i with the following probability,

$$\frac{\texttt{exp}(\frac{\epsilon'}{2\Delta u}\texttt{u}(D, v_i))}{\sum_{v \in \cup Cut_i} \texttt{exp}(\frac{\epsilon'}{2\Delta u}\texttt{u}(D, v))}, \tag{5}$$

where the $\texttt{u}(D, v)$ is either $\texttt{InfoGain}(D, v)$ or $\texttt{Max}(D, v)$ and the sensitivity of the function Δu is $\log_2 |\Omega(A^{cls})|$ and 1, respectively. Thus, from Theorem 3.2, Line 7 of Algorithm 1 satisfies ϵ'-differential privacy. The beauty of the exponential mechanism is that while it ensures privacy, it also exponentially favors a candidate with a high score.

(2) Split Value. Once a candidate is determined, *DiffGen* splits the records into child partitions. The split value of a categorical attribute is determined according to the taxonomy tree of the attribute. Since the taxonomy tree is fixed, the sensitivity of the split value is 0. Therefore, splitting the records according to the taxonomy tree does not violate differential privacy.

For numerical attributes, a split value cannot be directly chosen from the attribute values that appear in the data set D, because the probability of selecting the same split value from a different data set D' not containing this value is 0. We again use an exponential mechanism to determine the split value. We first partition the domain into intervals $I_1, \ldots, I_k$ such that all values within an interval have the same score. Then, the exponential mechanism is used to select an interval I_i with the following probability,

$$\frac{\texttt{exp}(\frac{\epsilon'}{2\Delta u}\texttt{u}(D, v_i)) \times |\Omega(I_i)|}{\sum_{j=1}^{k}(\texttt{exp}(\frac{\epsilon'}{2\Delta u}\texttt{u}(D, v_j)) \times |\Omega(I_j)|)}, \tag{6}$$

where $v_i \in \Omega(I_i)$, and $|\Omega(I_i)|$ is the length of the interval. After selecting the interval, the split value is determined by sampling a value uniformly from the interval. Thus, the probability of selecting a value $v_i \in \Omega(A_i)$ is

$$\frac{\texttt{exp}(\frac{\epsilon'}{2\Delta u}\texttt{u}(D, v_i))}{\int_{v \in \Omega(A_i)} \texttt{exp}(\frac{\epsilon'}{2\Delta u}\texttt{u}(D, v))\, dv} \tag{7}$$

This satisfies ϵ'-differential privacy because the probability of choosing any value is proportional to $\texttt{exp}(\frac{\epsilon' u(D, v_i)}{2\Delta u})$.

(3) Noisy Counts. Each leaf partition contains $|\Omega(A^{cls})|$ equivalence groups. Publishing the exact counts of these groups does not satisfy differential privacy since for a different data set D', the counts may change. This change can be easily offset by adding noise to the count of each group according to the Laplace mechanism (See Theorem 3.1). As discussed earlier, the sensitivity of count query is 1; therefore, to satisfy $\frac{\epsilon}{2}$-differential privacy, *DiffGen* adds $\texttt{Lap}(2/\epsilon)$ noise to each true count C of the groups (Line 12). We post-process the noisy counts by rounding each count to the nearest non-negative integer. Note that post-processing does not violate the differential privacy [22].

Next, we use composition properties of differential privacy to guarantee that the proposed algorithm satisfies ϵ-differential privacy as a whole.

LEMMA 4.1 (*Sequential composition* [30]). *Let each Ag_i provide ϵ_i-differential privacy. A sequence of $Ag_i(D)$ over the data set D provides $(\sum_i \epsilon_i)$-differential privacy.*

LEMMA 4.2 (*Parallel composition* [30]). *Let each Ag_i provide ϵ-differential privacy. A sequence of $Ag_i(D_i)$ over a set of disjoint data sets D_i provides ϵ-differential privacy.*

Any sequence of computations that each provides differential privacy in isolation also provides differential privacy in sequence, which is known as *sequential composition.* However, if the sequence of computations is conducted on *disjoint* data sets, the privacy cost does not accumulate but depends only on the worst guarantee of all computations. This is known as *parallel composition.*

THEOREM 4.1. *DiffGen is ϵ-differentially private.*

PROOF. (Sketch) The algorithm first determines the split value for each numerical attribute using the exponential mechanism (Line 4). Since the cost of each exponential mechanism is ϵ', Line 4 of the algorithm preserves $\epsilon'|A_n^{pr}|$-differential privacy, where $|A_n^{pr}|$ is the number of numerical attributes.

In Line 7, the algorithm selects a candidate for specialization. This step uses the exponential mechanism and thus, candidate selection step guarantees ϵ'-differential privacy for each iteration. In Line 9, the algorithm determines the split value for each new numerical candidate $v_n \in \cup Cut_i$. All records in the same partition have the same generalized values on $\mathcal{A}^{pr}$; therefore, each partition can only contain at most one candidate value v_n. Thus, determining the split value for the new candidates requires at most ϵ' privacy budget for each iteration due to the parallel composition property. Note that this step does not take place in every iteration.

Finally, the algorithm outputs the noisy count of each group (Line 12) using the Laplace mechanism and guarantees $\frac{\epsilon}{2}$-differential privacy. Therefore, for $\epsilon' = \frac{\epsilon}{2(|A_n^{pr}|+2h)}$, *DiffGen* is ϵ-differentially private. ■

4.3 Implementation

A simple implementation of *DiffGen* is to scan *all* data records to compute scores for all candidates in $\cup Cut_i$. Then scan all the records again to perform the specialization. A key contribution of this work is an efficient implementation of the proposed algorithm that computes scores based on some information maintained for candidates in $\cup Cut_i$ and provides *direct access* to the records to be specialized, instead of scanning all data records. We briefly explain the efficient implementation of the algorithm as follows.

Initial Steps (Lines 1-5). Initially, we determine split points for all numerical candidates (Line 4). First, the data is sorted with respect to the split attribute, which requires $O(|D|\log|D|)$. Then the data is scanned once to determine the score for all attribute values that appear in the data set D. An interval is represented by two successive different attribute values. Finally, the exponential mechanism is used to determine the split point. We also compute the scores for all candidates $v \in \cup Cut_i$ (Line 5). This can be done by scanning the data set once. However, for each subsequent iteration, information needed to calculate scores comes from the update of the previous iteration (Line 10). Thus the worst-case runtime of this step is $O(|\mathcal{A}^{pr}| \times |D|\log|D|)$.

Perform Specialization (Line 8). To perform a specialization $v \rightarrow child(v)$, we need to retrieve D_v, the set of data records generalized to v. To facilitate this operation we organize the records in a tree structure, with each root-to-leaf path representing a generalized record over $\mathcal{A}^{pr}$, as shown in Figure 2. Each leaf partition (node) stores the set of data records having the same generalized record for $\mathcal{A}^{pr}$ attributes. For each v in $\cup Cut_i$, P_v denotes a leaf partition whose generalized record contains v, and $Link_v$ provides direct access to all P_v partitions generalized to v.

Initially, the tree has only one leaf partition containing all data records, generalized to the topmost value on every attribute in $\mathcal{A}^{pr}$. In each iteration we perform a specialization v by refining the leaf partitions on $Link_v$. For each value $c \in child(v)$, a new partition P_c is created from P_v, and data records in P_v are split among the new partitions. This is the *only* operation in the whole algorithm that requires scanning data records. In the same scan, we also collect the following information for each c: $|D_c|$, $|D_g|$, $|D_c^{cls}|$ and $|D_g^{cls}|$, where $g \in child(c)$ and cls is a class label. These pieces of information are used in Line 10 to update scores. Thus, the total runtime of this step is $O(|D|)$.

Determine the Split Value (Line 9). If a numerical candidate v_n is selected in Line 7, then we need to determine the split points for two new numerical candidates $c_n \in child(v_n)$. This step takes time $O(|D|\log|D|)$.

Update Score (Line 10). Both `InfoGain` and `Max` scores of the other candidates $x \in \cup Cut_i$ are not affected by $v \rightarrow child(v)$, except that we need to compute the scores of each newly added value $c \in child(v)$. The scores of the new candidates are computed using the information collected in Line 8. Thus, this step can be done in constant $O(1)$ time.

Exponential Mechanism (Lines 4, 7 and 9). The cost of the exponential mechanism is proportional to the number of discrete alternatives from which it chooses a candidate. For Line 7, the cost is $O(|\cup Cut_i|)$, and for Lines 4 and 9 the cost is $O(|\mathbf{I}|)$, where $|\mathbf{I}|$ is the number of intervals. Usually both $|\cup Cut_i|$ and $|\mathbf{I}|$ are much smaller than $|D|$.

In summary, the cost of the initial steps and Lines 7-10 are $O(|\mathcal{A}^{pr}|\times|D|\log|D|)$ and $O(h\times|D|\log|D|)$, respectively. Hence, for a fixed number of attributes the total runtime of *DiffGen* is $O(h \times |D|\log|D|)$.

5. EXPERIMENTAL EVALUATION

In this section our objectives are to study the impact of enforcing differential privacy on the data quality in terms of classification accuracy, and to evaluate the scalability of the proposed algorithm for handling large data sets. We also compare *DiffGen* with *DiffP-C4.5* [11], a differentially-private interactive algorithm for building a classifier, and with the *top-down specialization (TDS)* approach [13] that publishes k-anonymous data for classification analysis.

We employ the publicly available *Adult* [10] data set, a real-life census data set that has been used for testing many anonymization algorithms [2, 13, 18, 28, 38, 33]. *Adult* has 45,222 census records with 6 numerical attributes, 8 categorical attributes, and a binary *class* column representing two income levels, ≤50K or >50K. See [13] for the description of attributes. All experiments were conducted on an Intel Core *i*7 2.7GHz PC with 12GB RAM.

Data Quality. To evaluate the impact on classification quality we divide the data into training and testing sets. First, we apply our algorithm to anonymize the training set and to determine the $\cup Cut_i$. Then, the same $\cup Cut_i$ is applied to the testing set to produce a generalized testing set. Next, we build a classifier on the anonymized training set and measure the *classification accuracy* (CA) on the generalized records of the testing set. For classification models we use the well-known C4.5 classifier [34]. To better visualize the cost and benefit of our approach we provide additional measures: *Baseline Accuracy* (BA) is the classification accuracy measured on the raw data without anonymization. $BA - CA$ represents the cost in terms of classification quality for achieving a given ϵ-differential privacy requirement. On the other extreme, we measure *Lower bound Accuracy* (LA), which is the accuracy on the raw data with all attributes (except for the *class* attribute) removed. $CA - LA$ represents the benefit of our method over the naive non-disclosure approach.

Figure 3.a depicts the classification accuracy CA for the utility function `Max`, where the privacy budget ϵ = 0.1, 0.25, 0.5, 1, and the number of specializations $4 \le h \le 16$. The BA and LA are 85.3% and 75.5%, respectively, as shown in

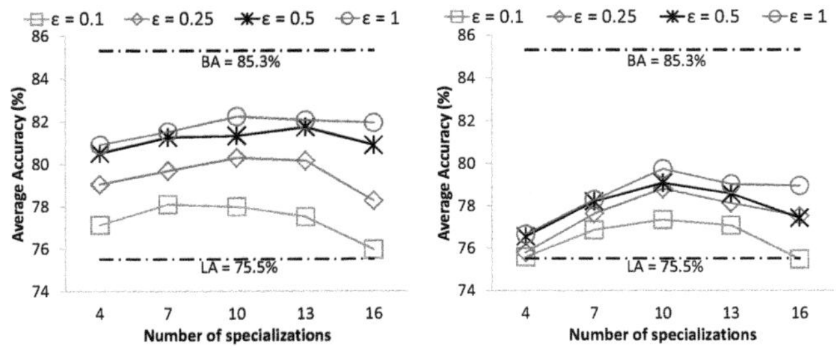

(a) Max (b) Information gain

Figure 3: Classification accuracy of *DiffGen*

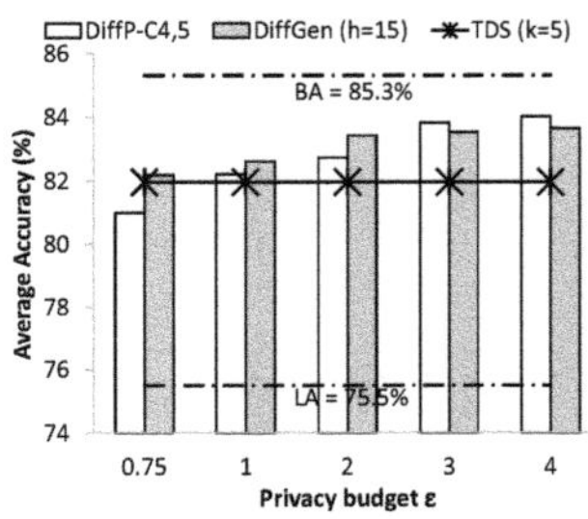

Figure 4: Comparison

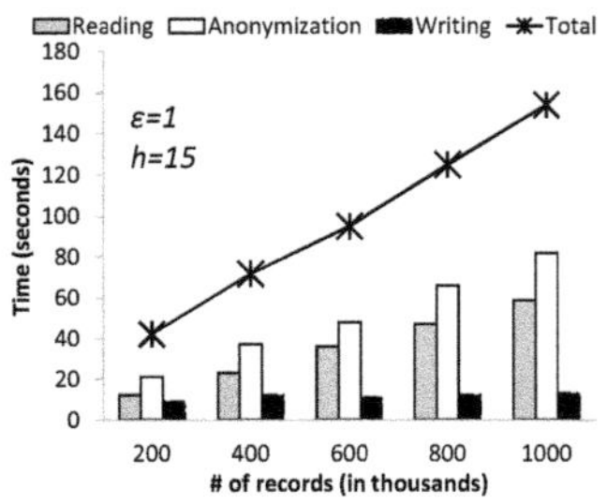

Figure 5: Scalability

the figure by the dotted lines. We use 2/3 of the records to build the classifier and measure the accuracy on the remaining 1/3 of the records. For each experiment we executed 10 runs and averaged the results over the runs. For $\epsilon = 1$ and $h = 10$, $BA - CA$ is around 3% and $CA - LA$ is 6.74%. For $\epsilon = 0.5$, $BA - CA$ spans from 3.57% to 4.8%, and $CA - LA$ spans from 5% to 6.23%. However, as ϵ decreases to 0.1, CA quickly decreases to about 78% (highest point), the cost increases to about 7%, and the benefit decreases to about 3%. These results suggest that for an acceptable privacy budget such as 1, the cost for achieving ϵ-differential privacy is small, while the benefit of our method over the naive method is large. Figure 3.b depicts the classification accuracy CA for the utility function `InfoGain`. The performance of the `InfoGain` is not as good as `Max` because the difference between the scores of a good and a bad attribute is much smaller for `InfoGain` as compared to `Max`. Therefore, exponential mechanism does not work effectively in the case of `InfoGain` as it does for `Max`.

We observe two general trends from the experiments. First, the privacy budget has a direct impact on the classification accuracy. A higher budget results in better accuracy since it ensures better attribute partitioning and lowers the magnitude of noise that is added to the count of each equivalence group. Second, the classification accuracy initially increases with the increase of the number of specializations. However, after a certain threshold the accuracy decreases with the increase of the number of specializations. This is an interesting observation. The number of equivalence groups increases quite rapidly with an increase in the number of specializations, resulting in a smaller count per group. Up to a certain threshold it has a positive impact due to more precise values; however, the influence of the Laplace noise gets stronger as the number of specializations grows. Note that if the noise is as big as the count, then the data is useless. This confirms that listing all the possible combination of values (i.e., contingency table) and then adding noise to their counts is not a good approach for high-dimensional data since the noise will be as big as the count.

Since this is a non-interactive approach, the data owner can try different values of h to find the threshold and then release the anonymized data. Determining a good value of h adaptively, given the data set and the privacy budget, is an interesting future work.

Comparison. Figure 4 shows the classification accuracy CA of *DiffGen*, *DiffP-C4.5*, and *TDS*. For *DiffGen*, we use utility function `Max` and fix the number of specializations $h = 15$. *DiffP-C4.5* also uses *Adult* data set and all the results of the *DiffP-C4.5* are taken from their paper [11]. For *TDS* we fixed the anonymity threshold $k = 5$ and conducted the experiment ourselves. Following the same setting of [11], we executed 10 runs of 10-fold cross-validation to measure the CA. 10-fold cross-validation yields higher CA since more training records are available.

The accuracy of *DiffGen* is clearly better than *DiffP-C4.5* for privacy budget $\epsilon \leq 2$. Note that the privacy budget should be typically smaller than 1 [11, 7, 8]. Even for a higher budget, the accuracy of *DiffGen* is comparable to *DiffP-C4.5*. The major advantage of our algorithm is that we publish data and the data miner has much better flexibility to perform the required data analysis. On the other hand, in *DiffP-C4.5* the classifier is built through interactive queries; therefore, the database has to be permanently shut down to satisfy the privacy requirement after generating only *one* classifier.

The experimental result also shows that *DiffGen* performs better than *TDS*. For a higher anonymity threshold k, the accuracy of *TDS* will be lower. One advantage of *DiffGen* is that, unlike *TDS*, it does not need to ensure that every equivalence group contains k records; therefore, *DiffGen* is able to provide more detailed information than *TDS*. This result demonstrates for the first time that, if designed properly, a differentially private algorithm can provide better utility than a partition-based approach.

Scalability. All the previous experiments can finish the anonymization process within 30 seconds. We further study the scalability of our algorithm over large data sets. We generate different data sets of different sizes by randomly adding records to the Adult data set. For each original record r, we create $\alpha - 1$ variations of the record by replacing some of the attribute values randomly from the same domain. Here α is the blowup scale and thus the total number of records is $\alpha \times 45,222$ after adding random records. Figure 5 depicts the runtime from 200,000 to 1 million records for $h = 15$ and $\epsilon = 1$.

6. CONCLUSIONS

This paper presents a new anonymization algorithm that achieves differential privacy and supports effective classification analysis. The proposed solution connects the classical generalization technique with output perturbation to effectively anonymize raw data. Experimental results suggest that the proposed solution provides better utility than the interactive approach and the k-anonymous data, and that it is more effective than publishing a contingency table.

7. ACKNOWLEDGMENTS

We sincerely thank the reviewers for their insightful comments. The research is supported in part by the Discovery Grants (356065-2008), Strategic Project Grants (130570020), and Canada Graduate Scholarships from the Natural Sciences and Engineering Research Council of Canada, and the NSF grant IIS-0914934.

8. REFERENCES

[1] B. Barak, K. Chaudhuri, C. Dwork, S. Kale, F. McSherry, and K. Talwar. Privacy, accuracy, and consistency too: A holistic solution to contingency table release. In *PODS*, 2007.

[2] R. J. Bayardo and R. Agrawal. Data privacy through optimal k-anonymization. In *ICDE*, 2005.

[3] R. Bhaskar, S. Laxman, A. Smith, and A. Thakurta. Discovering frequent patterns in sensitive data. In *SIGKDD*, 2010.

[4] A. Blum, K. Ligett, and A. Roth. A learning theory approach to non-interactive database privacy. In *STOC*, 2008.

[5] G. Cormode, D. Srivastava, N. Li, and T. Li. Minimizing minimality and maximizing utility: Analyzing methodbased attacks on anonymized data. In *VLDB*, 2010.

[6] I. Dinur and K. Nissim. Revealing information while preserving privacy. In *PODS*, 2003.

[7] C. Dwork. Differential privacy. In *ICALP*, 2006.

[8] C. Dwork. A firm foundation for private data analysis. *Commun. ACM*, 54(1):86–95, 2011.

[9] C. Dwork, F. McSherry, K. Nissim, and A. Smith. Calibrating noise to sensitivity in private data analysis. In *TCC*, 2006.

[10] A. Frank and A. Asuncion. UCI machine learning repository, 2010.

[11] A. Friedman and A. Schuster. Data mining with differential privacy. In *SIGKDD*, 2010.

[12] B. C. M. Fung, K. Wang, R. Chen, and P. S. Yu. Privacy-preserving data publishing: A survey of recent developments. *ACM Computing Surveys*, 42(4):1–53, June 2010.

[13] B. C. M. Fung, K. Wang, and P. S. Yu. Anonymizing classification data for privacy preservation. *IEEE TKDE*, 19(5):711–725, May 2007.

[14] S. R. Ganta, S. Kasiviswanathan, and A. Smith. Composition attacks and auxiliary information in data privacy. In *SIGKDD*, 2008.

[15] M. Hardt and K. Talwar. On the geometry of differential privacy. In *STOC*, 2010.

[16] M. Hay, V. Rastogi, G. Miklau, and D. Suciu. Boosting the accuracy of differentially private histograms through consistency. In *VLDB*, 2010.

[17] A. Inan, M. Kantarcioglu, G. Ghinita, and E. Bertino. Private record matching using differential privacy. In *EDBT*, 2010.

[18] V. S. Iyengar. Transforming data to satisfy privacy constraints. In *SIGKDD*, 2002.

[19] X. Jin, N. Zhang, and G. Das. Algorithm-safe privacy-preserving data publishing. In *EDBT*, 2010.

[20] S. P. Kasiviswanathan, M. Rudelson, A. Smith, and J. Ullman. The price of privately releasing contingency tables and the spectra of random matrices with correlated rows. In *STOC*, 2010.

[21] D. Kifer. Attacks on privacy and de finetti's theorem. In *SIGMOD*, 2009.

[22] D. Kifer and B. Lin. Towards an axiomatization of statistical privacy and utility. In *PODS*, 2010.

[23] K. LeFevre, D. J. DeWitt, and R. Ramakrishnan. Mondrian multidimensional k-anonymity. In *ICDE*, 2006.

[24] K. LeFevre, D. J. DeWitt, and R. Ramakrishnan. Workload-aware anonymization techniques for large-scale data sets. *ACM TODS*, 33(3), 2008.

[25] C. Li. M. Hay, V. Rastogi, G. Miklau, and A. McGregor. Optimizing linear counting queries under differential privacy. In *PODS*, 2010.

[26] N. Li. T. Li, and S. Venkatasubramanian. t-closeness: Privacy beyond k-anonymity and ℓ-diversity. In *ICDE*, 2007.

[27] A. Machanavajjhala, J. Gehrke, and M. Gotz. Data publishing against realistic adversaries. In *VLDB*, 2009.

[28] A. Machanavajjhala, D. Kifer, J. Gehrke, and M. Venkitasubramaniam. ℓ-diversity: Privacy beyond k-anonymity. *ACM TKDD*, 2007.

[29] D. Martin, D. Kifer, A. Machanavajjhala, J. Gehrke, and J. Halpern. Worst-case background knowledge in privacy-preserving data publishing. In *ICDE*, 2007.

[30] F. McSherry. Privacy integrated queries. In *SIGMOD*, 2009.

[31] F. McSherry and I. Mironov. Differentially private recommender systems: building privacy into the net. In *SIGKDD*, 2009.

[32] F. McSherry and K. Talwar. Mechanism design via differential privacy. In *FOCS*, 2007.

[33] N. Mohammed, B. C. M. Fung, P. C. K. Hung, and C. Lee. Anonymizing healthcare data: A case study on the blood transfusion service. In *SIGKDD*, 2009.

[34] J. R. Quinlan. *C4.5: Programs for Machine Learning*. Morgan Kaufmann, 1993.

[35] A. Roth and T. Roughgarden. Interactive privacy via the median mechanism. In *STOC*, 2010.

[36] P. Samarati. Protecting respondents' identities in microdata release. *IEEE TKDE*, 2001.

[37] L. Sweeney. k-anonymity: A model for protecting privacy. In *International Journal on Uncertainty, Fuzziness and Knowledge-based Systems*, 2002.

[38] K. Wang, B. C. M. Fung, and P. S. Yu. Handicapping attacker's confidence: An alternative to k-anonymization. *KAIS*, 11(3):345–368, April 2007.

[39] R. C. W. Wong, A. W. C. Fu, K. Wang, and J. Pei. Minimality attack in privacy preserving data publishing. In *VLDB*, 2007.

[40] R. C. W. Wong, A. W. C. Fu, K. Wang, Y. Xu, and P. S. Yu. Can the utility of anonymized data be used for privacy breaches? *ACM TKDD, to appear.*

[41] R. C. W. Wong, J. Li., A. W. C. Fu, and K. Wang. (α,k)-anonymity: An enhanced k-anonymity model for privacy preserving data publishing. In *SIGKDD*, 2006.

[42] X. Xiao and Y. Tao. Personalized privacy preservation. In *SIGMOD*, 2006.

[43] X. Xiao, Y. Tao, and N. Koudas. Transparent anonymization: Thwarting adversaries who know the algorithm. *ACM TODS*, 35(2), 2010.

[44] X. Xiao, G. Wang, and J. Gehrke. Differential privacy via wavelet transforms. In *ICDE*, 2010.

[45] L. Zhang, S. Jajodia, and A. Brodsky. Information disclosure under realistic assumptions: Privacy versus optimality. In *CCS*, 2007.

k-NN as an Implementation of Situation Testing for Discrimination Discovery and Prevention

Binh Thanh Luong
Institute for Advanced Studies
Lucca, Italy
l.thanhbinh@imtlucca.it

Salvatore Ruggieri
University of Pisa
Pisa, Italy
ruggieri@di.unipi.it

Franco Turini
University of Pisa
Pisa, Italy
turini@di.unipi.it

ABSTRACT

With the support of the legally-grounded methodology of situation testing, we tackle the problems of discrimination discovery and prevention from a dataset of historical decisions by adopting a variant of k-NN classification. A tuple is labeled as discriminated if we can observe a significant difference of treatment among its neighbors belonging to a protected-by-law group and its neighbors not belonging to it. Discrimination discovery boils down to extracting a classification model from the labeled tuples. Discrimination prevention is tackled by changing the decision value for tuples labeled as discriminated before training a classifier. The approach of this paper overcomes legal weaknesses and technical limitations of existing proposals.

Categories and Subject Descriptors

H.2.8 [**Database Applications**]: Data Mining

General Terms

Algorithms, Legal Aspects

Keywords

Discrimination discovery and prevention, k-NN classification

1. INTRODUCTION

Decisions based on categorization or social sorting may be discriminatory, in the socially negative sense of the unfair or unequal treatment of people based on membership to a category, group or minority, without regard to individual characteristics. This problem is exacerbated by the fact that increasingly sophisticated data analysis and data mining techniques support knowledge discovery from human activity data, enabling the extraction of models, patterns, profiles, and rules of human behavior in support of (automated) decision making. Human right laws [2, 9, 23, 24] prohibit discrimination against protected groups on the grounds of race, color, religion, nationality, sex, marital status, age and pregnancy; and in a number of settings, including credit and insurance; sale, rental, and financing of housing; personnel selection and wages; access to public accommodations, education, nursing homes, adoptions, and health care. Since most of the decisions in the knowledge society era are taken on the basis of historical data, there is the need of developing models, methods and technologies for modelling the processes of discrimination analysis in order to discover and prevent discrimination phenomena. *Discrimination discovery* from data consists in the actual discovery of discriminatory situations and practices hidden in a large amount of historical decision records. The process of data analysis must then be supported by tools that exploit *legally-grounded* measures and reasonings. *Discrimination prevention* in data mining consists of extracting models (typically, classifiers) that do not lead to discriminatory decisions even if trained from a dataset containing them. In fact, mining from historical data may mean to discover traditional prejudices that are endemic in reality (*taste-based discrimination* [3]), or to discover patterns of lower performances, skills or capacities of protected-by-law groups (*statistical discrimination* [10], also called *rational racism*), and to assign to such practices the status of general rules, maybe unconsciously, as these rules can be deeply hidden within a data mining classifier.

Recent data mining proposals for discrimination discovery [20, 21] and prevention [5] have followed the legal principle of *under-representation*. Unfortunately, they suffer both from legal weaknesses, due to the use of aggregation measures over undifferentiated sets of people, and technical limitations, such as the restriction to nominal attributes and decisions and to local models of discrimination. In this paper, we overcome both the legal and the technical drawbacks. Our approach is inspired by the legal experimental procedure of *situation testing*, which looks for pairs of people with similar characteristics apart from membership to a protected-by-law group. We approximate situation testing by a variant of the k-nearest neighbor (k-NN) classification, which labels each tuple in a dataset as discriminated or not. Discrimination discovery then reduces to build a classifier providing a global description of the conditions where discrimination occurs. Discrimination prevention is tackled by a pre-processing step, changing the historical decision for tuples labeled as discriminated, before training a classifier.

This paper is organized as follows. In Sect. 2 we review the legal grounds of discrimination analysis, highlighting deficiencies of the existing data mining approaches. The legal methodology of situation testing is also presented. In Sect. 3,

KDD'11, August 21–24, 2011, San Diego, California, USA.

group	benefit		
	not granted	granted	
protected	a	b	n_1
unprotected	c	d	n_2
	m_1	m_2	n

$$p_1 = a/n_1 \qquad p_2 = c/n_2 \qquad p = m_1/n$$

$$diff(c) = p_1 - p_2 \qquad slift(c) = \frac{p_1}{p_2}$$

$$elift(c) = \frac{p_1}{p} \qquad olift(c) = \frac{p_1(1-p_2)}{p_2(1-p_1)} = \frac{ad}{cb}$$

Figure 1: Discrimination measures

we recall the notion of distance functions and summarize the experimental setup. The approach based on k-NN is presented in Sect. 4, and applied in Sect. 5 to discrimination discovery, and in Sect. 6 to discrimination prevention. Finally, Sect. 7 summarizes the contributions of the paper.

2. DISCRIMINATION ANALYSIS

Discrimination analysis from data should build over the large body of existing legal and economic studies [7, 14, 18]. In this section, we review the under-representation principle that has inspired previous data mining proposals, and the situation testing methodology, which provides the legal grounds for the approach proposed in this paper.

2.1 The Under-Representation Principle

Accordingly to laws, discrimination occurs when a group is treated "less favorably" [9, 23] than others, or such that "a higher proportion of people not in the group is able to comply" [2] to a qualifying criterium. A general principle is then to consider *group under-representation* in obtaining a benefit [7, 14] as a quantitative measure of discrimination against a protected-by-law group (briefly, a *protected* group). Consider a dataset of historical decisions about granting or not a benefit (e.g., a loan, a job, a wage increase). Let p_1 (resp., p_2) be the proportion of people in the protected group (resp., not in the protected group) that were not granted the benefit, and let p be the proportion of all people (both protected and not) that were not granted the benefit. Group under-representation can be measured as the difference $p_1 - p_2$, adopted in the U.K. legislation [23]; or as the ratio p_1/p_2, called the *selection lift* and adopted in the U.S. legislation [24] (d); or as one of the measures defined in Fig. 1 over a four-fold contingency table. Higher values of those measures denote higher under-representation of the protected group.

The under-representation principle has inspired the existing approaches for discrimination discovery and prevention. [20] proposes to extract classification rules of the form $\mathbf{A}, \mathbf{B} \rightarrow \mathbf{C}$ to unveil subsets $\mathbf{B}$ of the dataset where the protected group $\mathbf{A}$ suffered from under-representation with respect to the decision $\mathbf{C}$. The approach is parametric to one of the measures in Fig. 1, and it is implemented on top of an Oracle database [21]. Another study [5] investigates three approaches for preventing discriminatory predictions in a Naïve Bayes classifier. Discrimination is measured as the difference $p_1 - p_2$ calculated on the whole set of predictions over a test set.

Unfortunately, these approaches suffer from both legal weaknesses and technical limitations. On the legal side, measuring group under-representation by aggregated values over *undifferentiated* groups is opposable in a court of law. As an example, assume a high value for $p_1 - p_2$ in a dataset of historical decisions, with women as the protected group and job hiring as the benefit. Since p_1 and p_2 are aggregated values, they mix decisions for people that may be very different as per skills required for the job. A typical legal argument is that of *genuine occupational requirement*. For the example at hand, if the job requires a special driving licence, which most of the male applicants have and most of the female applicants do not have, then the non-hiring rates p_1 and p_2 cannot be adopted for comparing people with different, legally admissible, attributes.

On the technical side, the discrimination discovery approach [20] has two limitations. First, since it relies on frequent itemset mining, it deals with nominal attributes and nominal decisions only. Interval-scaled attributes (age, income) and decisions (loan rate, wage) must be discretized as a pre-processing step. Second, the result of the knowledge discovery process is a (possibly large) set of classification rules, which provide *local* niches of possible discrimination: a *global* description of who is discriminated and who is not is lacking. The discrimination prevention approach [5] shares the same limitation on nominal attributes. In addition, it considers discrimination at top level, i.e., $p_1 - p_2$ is controlled only for the whole set of decisions. However, discrimination may still occur in some subset, e.g., as when discrimination of a bank branch manager against a minority group remains hidden in the large set of decisions of the whole bank.

2.2 Situation Testing

In the legal field, *situation testing* is a systematic research procedure for creating controlled experiments analyzing decision maker's candid responses to applicant's personal characteristics. In situation testing, pairs of research assistants undergo the same kind of selection, for example they apply for the same job, they present themselves at the same night club, and so on. Within each pair, applicant characteristics likely to be related to the situation (characteristics related to a worker's productivity on the job in the first case, look, age and the like in the second case) are made equal by selecting, training, and credentialing testers to appear equally qualified for the activity. Simultaneously, membership to a protected group is experimentally manipulated by pairing testers who differ in membership – for example, a black and a white, a male and a female, and so on. Situation testing is being experimented worldwide as one of the tools that can assist victims to establish that discrimination may have occurred [4, 19].

In this paper, we intend to exploit the idea of situation testing just inverting the point of view: given past records of decisions taken in some context, for each member of the protected group with a negative decision outcome (someone who may claim to be a victim of discrimination) we look for testers with similar, legally admissible, characteristics, apart from being or not in the protected group. If we can observe significantly different decision outcomes between the testers of the protected group and the testers of the unprotected group, we can ascribe the negative decision to a bias against the protected group. Similarity is modelled via a distance function. Testers are searched among the k-nearest neighbors. And difference is measured by one of the functions from Fig. 1 calculated over the two sets of testers.

dataset	size	No. of attributes interval	nominal	ordinal
credit	1,000	6	12	3
credit-d	1,000	0	12	9
crimes	1,994	24	0	0
adult	48,842	5	8	1
census-income	299,285	7	32	1

Table 1: Datasets: size and attribute types

3. EXPERIMENTAL SETTING

3.1 Distance Functions

Let **r** and **s** be two tuples of n attributes. A *distance function* $d()$ measures the dissimilarity between **r** and **s**. In general, $d(\mathbf{r}, \mathbf{s})$ is a non-negative real number, close to 0 when **r** and **s** are highly similar or "near" each others, and becoming larger the more they differ. We admit the unknown value in domains, syntactically represented by "?", to model missing tuple elements. In the following, we present the distance functions adopted in experiments for interval-scaled, nominal and ordinal domains. Notice that the theoretical foundations of our approach are parametric to the actual distance function adopted. Let i be an attribute index, and x, y two values in the domain of the ith attribute.

Interval-scaled values are first standardized using the z-score $z_i(x) = (x - m_i)/s_i$, where m_i is the mean value, and s_i is the mean absolute deviation. Distance between x, y is measured by the absolute difference of their z-scores: $d_i(x, y) = |z_i(x) - z_i(y)|$. We deal with unknown values by setting $|z_i(x) - z_i(y)| = 3$ if $x = ?$ or $y = ?$.

For nominal domains, distance is a binary function testing equality: $d_i(x, y) = 0$ if $x = y$, and $d_i(x, y) = 1$ otherwise. For unknown values, we set $d_i(x, y) = 1$ if $x = ?$ or $y = ?$.

Ordinal domains with ranked values $v_1, \ldots, v_M$ are first mapped into interval-scaled values $m_i(v_j) = (j-1)/(M-1)$. Distance is then computed by resorting to the absolute difference $d_i(x, y) = |m_i(x) - m_i(y)|$. We deal with unknown values by setting $d_i(x, y) = max\{m_i(x), 1 - m_i(x)\}$ if $x = ?$ and $y \neq ?$, and vice-versa; and $d_i(x, y) = 1$ if $x = y = ?$.

Finally, distance between tuples is defined as:

$$d(\mathbf{r}, \mathbf{s}) = \frac{\Sigma_{i=1}^{n} d_i(\mathbf{r}_i, \mathbf{s}_i)}{n}$$

For tuples of interval-scaled attributes only, it boils down to the Manhattan distance of z-scores (modulo division by a constant); and for tuples of nominal attributes only, it boils down to the percentage of mismatching attribute values.

3.2 Datasets

As a running example, we use the German credit dataset, which consists of 1000 records over bank account holders. It includes attributes on personal properties, past/current credits, employment status, and on personal status. The `class` attribute represents the good/bad creditor decision assigned to the bank account holder. Attributes classified by their types are the following.

Interval-scaled: duration, credit_amount, installment_commitment, age, existing_credits, num_dependents.

Nominal: credit_history, purpose, personal_status, other_parties, residence_since, property_magnitude, housing, job, other_payment_plans, own_telephone, foreign_worker, class.

Ordinal: checking_status, savings_status, employment.

We consider two versions of the dataset: *credit*, the original dataset, with interval-scaled attributes; and *credit-d*, where interval-scaled attributes are discretized into 5 bins of equal width, and the resulting attributes are assigned the ordinal type. In addition to the German credit, the larger datasets shown in Fig. 1 will be considered. Strictly speaking, they are not concerned with decisions, but rather with census information related to people income (*adult*, *census-income*) or to communities & crimes (*crimes*). Therefore, the objective of discrimination analysis on these datasets is to discover or prevent forms of statistical discrimination. All datasets are publicly available from [12]. Notice that the decision attribute is binary for all of them, apart for *crimes* where it is interval-scaled being the "total number of violent crimes per 100K population".

4. K-NN AS SITUATION TESTING

4.1 k-NN

k-nearest neighbor (k-NN) is a lazy instance-based classification method. The classification model simply consists of storing the training set. Given a tuple **r** to be classified, k-NN: (1) first searches the k tuples in the training set closest to **r** w.r.t. a distance measure $d()$, i.e., its k-nearest neighbors; (2) then assignes as class value to **r** the most frequent class value among its k-nearest neighbors.

Throughout the paper, we represent a dataset as a collection $\mathcal{R}$ of tuples with a superscript, e.g., as in $\mathbf{r}^i$ where $i \in [1, |\mathcal{R}|]$ is the tuple id. For a tuple **r**, we assign to every $\mathbf{r}^i \in \mathcal{R}$ a rank (as a neighbor of **r**) on the basis of its distance from **r** (or, for equal distances, on the tuple id). Formally, we define:

$$rank_{\mathcal{R}}(\mathbf{r}, \mathbf{r}^i) = |\{j \mid d(\mathbf{r}, \mathbf{r}^j) < d(\mathbf{r}, \mathbf{r}^i) \vee (d(\mathbf{r}, \mathbf{r}^j) = d(\mathbf{r}, \mathbf{r}^i) \wedge j \leq i\}|$$

The k-NN set for a given tuple is the set of top k tuples w.r.t. ranking. A refined version may include an additional constraint on the maximum allowable distance.

DEFINITION 4.1. *For a dataset $\mathcal{R}$, we define:*

$$kset_{\mathcal{R}}(\mathbf{r}, k) = \{\mathbf{r}^i \in \mathcal{R} \mid rank_{\mathcal{R}}(\mathbf{r}, \mathbf{r}^i) \leq k\}$$
$$kset_{\mathcal{R}}(\mathbf{r}, k, d) = \{\mathbf{r}^i \in \mathcal{R} \mid rank_{\mathcal{R}}(\mathbf{r}, \mathbf{r}^i) \leq k \wedge d(\mathbf{r}, \mathbf{r}^i) \leq d\}$$

In k-NN classification, **r** is the tuple to be classified, and $\mathcal{R}$ is the training set. In our discrimination analysis context, we take a different approach – which is closer to the situation testing methodology. Let us start by fixing some inputs.

4.2 Inputs of the Discrimination Analysis

In addition to a dataset $\mathcal{R}$, our analysis of discrimination, either for discovery or for prevention, will require the following inputs: the group under analysis, a distance function over a set of attributes, and the decision attribute.

Protected-by-law groups. Civil rights laws explicitly identify the groups to be protected against discrimination, e.g., women or black people. We assume that a protected-by-law group is specified as input of the discrimination analysis, and call it the protected group. Also, we assume that the dataset under analysis includes attributes to decide whether a tuple refers to a member of the group. Syntactically, we model this by a predicate *protected*. In the previous example, we require then that sex (resp., race) is an attribute of data, and set $protected(\mathbf{r})$ iff $\mathbf{r}[\texttt{sex}] = \texttt{female}$ (resp., $\mathbf{r}[\texttt{race}] = \texttt{black}$).

We do not impose any syntactic restriction on the definition of *protected*: for instance, in our prototype implementation, it can be any boolean expression over comparison operators $<, \leq, =, \neq, \geq, >$ for interval-scaled and ordinal attributes; and over $=, \neq$ for nominal attributes. Notice that existing approaches to discrimination analysis [5, 20] are intrinsically limited to conjunctions of equality comparisons over nominal attributes, a.k.a. to itemsets, since they rely on frequent itemset extraction or on Bayesian models.

Using *protected*, we can separate tuples of people in the protected group from those of people not in the protected group – which we call the *unprotected* group.

DEFINITION 4.2. *We define* $P(\mathcal{R}) = \{\mathbf{r}^i \in \mathcal{R} \mid protected(\mathbf{r}^i)\}$, *and* $U(\mathcal{R}) = \{\mathbf{r}^i \in \mathcal{R} \mid \neg protected(\mathbf{r}^i)\}$.

Notice that $\mathcal{R} = P(\mathcal{R}) \cup U(\mathcal{R})$ does not necessarily hold, since tuples with unknown values to be tested by *protected* are not included in $P(\mathcal{R})$ nor in $U(\mathcal{R})$, e.g., as for $\mathbf{r}[\texttt{sex}] =?$ in the previous example.

Legally-grounded attributes for distance measurement. We assume a distance function $d()$ between tuples. As in k-NN classification, distance will be used to search for neighbors of a given tuple. As in situation testing, such neighbors are searched with reference to attributes that are legally-grounded for being adopted in taking the decision. Therefore, we assume that $d()$ is defined on a subset of the attributes of the dataset, e.g., those that are legally admissible in a discrimination litigation. Additional attributes may be present in the dataset for other purposes, e.g., as shown in Sect. 5, for extracting a description of cases where discrimination occurs. Let $G \subseteq \{1, \ldots, n\}$ be the set of attribute indexes (or, equivalently, attribute names) that are legally-grounded. We write $\pi_G(\mathbf{r})$ to denote the projection of tuple $\mathbf{r}$ over attribute indexes in G, e.g., $\pi_{\{1,3\}}(\langle 3, 5, 4\rangle) = \langle 3, 4\rangle$. We make the following syntactic assumption, which helps in taking notation simple.

REMARK 4.3. *Distance is computed with reference to attributes indexes in G. In symbols, when writing* $d(\mathbf{r}, \mathbf{s})$ *we actually restrict to consider* $d(\pi_G(\mathbf{r}), \pi_G(\mathbf{s}))$.

In particular, when writing $kset_{\mathcal{R}}(\mathbf{r}, k)$ we now intend the k-NN set w.r.t. distance over attribute indexes in G.

Decision attribute. Obviously, the dataset $\mathcal{R}$ includes an attribute recording the historical decision. We write $dec(\mathbf{r})$ to denote the value for $\mathbf{r}$ of the decision attribute. Such an attribute is sometimes called the *class* attribute, because classifiers built on the dataset try and learn it as the class. As such, the decision attribute does not include unknown values. We admit nominal, interval-scaled and ordinal decision attributes. For nominal (typically binary, i.e., two-valued) decision attributes, we denote by $\ominus$ the negative decision (deny of benefit), and by $\oplus$ the positive decision (grant of benefit). Examples of interval-scaled decision attributes include wage in a dataset of personnel, and interest rate in a dataset of loans. In the rest of the paper, we will first state definitions and results for nominal decision attributes, and then describe what differs for interval-scaled ones. For lack of space, ordinal decision attributes are not explicitly commented. Basically, they are treated as interval-scaled attributes once ordinal values are mapped into interval-scaled ones using the standard mapping recalled in Sect. 3.1.

4.3 k-NN as Situation Testing

Consider a tuple $\mathbf{r}$ in the protected group $P(\mathcal{R})$. In the words of situation testing, a person feels discriminated if she observes significantly different decision outcomes for people who are similar to her apart from belonging or not to the protected group. Let us formalize this as follows. Let $\mathcal{K}_1$ be the set of k-nearest neighbors of $\mathbf{r}$ in $P(\mathcal{R}) \setminus \{\mathbf{r}\}$, where $\mathbf{r}$ has been removed in order not to be included in $\mathcal{K}_1$. Also, let $\mathcal{K}_2$ be the set of k-nearest neighbors of $\mathbf{r}$ in $U(\mathcal{R})$. $\mathcal{K}_1$ and $\mathcal{K}_2$ represent persons with attributes close to the ones of $\mathbf{r}$ apart for being in the protected group or in the unprotected group respectively. Notice that the distance function is defined on attributes that are legally-grounded, i.e., legally admissible for being adopted in taking the decision of granting or not a benefit. For a nominal decision attribute, the probability of the decision outcome for $\mathbf{r}$ can be estimated from $\mathcal{K}_1$ (resp., $\mathcal{K}_2$) as the proportion p_1 (resp., p_2) of tuples whose decision value is the same of $\mathbf{r}$. The difference between the observed values p_1 and p_2 represents then the bias of the decision for $\mathbf{r}$ due to membership to the protected group. We measure such a difference as $p_1 - p_2$, although any discrimination measure from Fig. 1 can be adopted. Let us provide a formal definition.

DEFINITION 4.4. *For* $\mathbf{r} \in P(\mathcal{R})$, *we define* $diff(\mathbf{r}) = p_1 - p_2$, *where:* $p_1 = |\{\mathbf{r}' \in kset_{P(\mathcal{R})\setminus\{\mathbf{r}\}}(\mathbf{r}, k) \mid dec(\mathbf{r}') = dec(\mathbf{r})\}|/k$ *and* $p_2 = |\{\mathbf{r}' \in kset_{U(\mathcal{R})}(\mathbf{r}, k) \mid dec(\mathbf{r}') = dec(\mathbf{r})\}|/k$.

Assume that a negative decision is assigned to $\mathbf{r}$, namely $dec(\mathbf{r}) = \ominus$. A value $diff(\mathbf{r}) = t \geq 0$ means that the decision is more frequent in the neighbors of the protected group with respect to the neighbors of the unprotected group by a percentage difference of t. This implies that the negative decision for $\mathbf{r}$ is not explainable on the basis of the legally-grounded attributes used for distance measurement, but rather it is biased by group membership. Whether the bias was intentional or not is irrelevant: laws also sanction *unintentional discrimination*. t is a measure of the strength of the discrimination bias. A value t lower than 0 means that the negative decision for $\mathbf{r}$ is not explainable by a worse treatment of the neighbors in the protected group. Hence, no discrimination conclusion can be drawn.

Conversely, assume a positive decision $dec(\mathbf{r}) = \oplus$. By reasoning as above, $diff(\mathbf{r}) \geq 0$ means a bias towards the positive decision due to group membership. This could be the result of *affirmative actions*, also called *positive actions* or *reverse discrimination*, consisting in a range of policies or quotas to overcome and to compensate for past and present discrimination [22]. Dually, $diff(\mathbf{r}) < 0$ means that the positive decision is not explainable by a general better treatment of the neighbors in the protected group.

EXAMPLE 4.5. Consider the *credit* dataset. We fix the protected group to non-single women by setting $protected(\mathbf{r})$ to $\mathbf{r}[\texttt{personal\_status}] = \texttt{female div/sep/mar}$. Also, we set the decision attribute to `class`, namely to the credit classification, with $\ominus = \texttt{bad}$ and $\oplus = \texttt{good}$. All the remaining attributes are included, for the moment, in G, i.e., they are used in distance measurement. Fig. 2 (a) shows the cumulative distribution of $diff()$ for people in the protected group that have received the bad credit classification, namely for

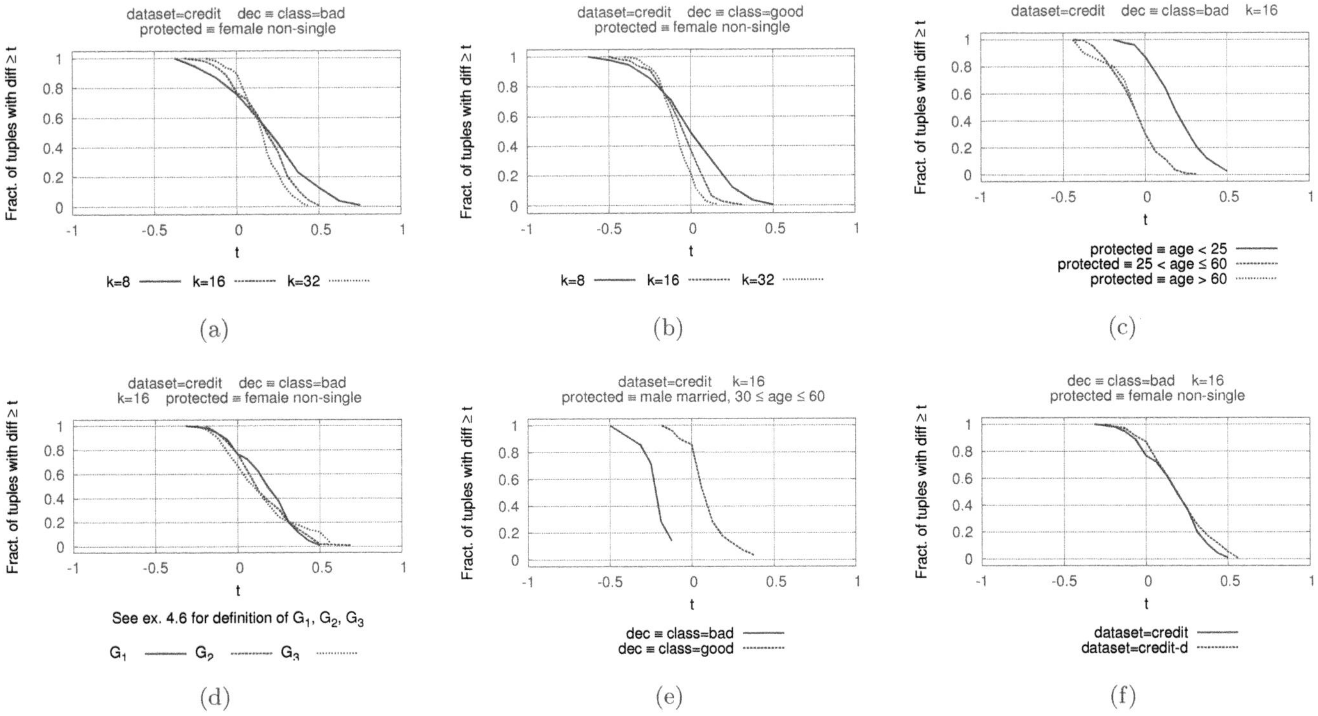

Figure 2: Cumulative distributions of *diff*() for datasets *credit* and *credit-d*

tuples $\mathbf{r}$ such that $protected(\mathbf{r})$ and $\mathbf{r}[\texttt{class}] = \texttt{bad}$. The plot shows the distributions for different values of k.

It is immediate to see that the distributions are shifted towards the positive half of the spectrum. More than 60% of the people have $diff(\mathbf{r}) \geq 0.1$, which means that bad-debtors are at least 10% more frequent among the k-most similar persons in the protected group than among the k-most similar persons in the unprotected group. Hence, the decision of classifying $\mathbf{r}$ as bad-debtor appears to be biased by her membership to the protected group.

The discrimination scenario becomes clearer if we consider the same distributions for people in the protected group having received the good-debtor decision, namely for tuples $\mathbf{r}$ such that $protected(\mathbf{r})$ and $\mathbf{r}[\texttt{class}] = \texttt{good}$. They are shown in Fig. 2 (b). Now the distributions are shifted towards the negative half of the spectrum. For $k = 16$, it turns out that $diff(\mathbf{r}) \geq 0.1$ in less than 7% of cases, which means that only a small percentage of the good-debtor classification could be attributed to a bias in favor of non-single women.

Finally, observe that the distributions in Fig. 2 (a,b) tend to shrink as k increases. This is intuitive, since for $k \to \infty$ the k-NN sets of protected and unprotected groups tend to include all the elements of the group, and then $diff(\mathbf{r}) \to \hat{p}_1 - \hat{p}_2$ where $\hat{p}_1$ (resp., $\hat{p}_2$) is the proportion of decision $dec(\mathbf{r})$ in the whole protected (resp., unprotected) group.

Example 4.6. It is worth studying how the distributions vary for different parameters in the previous example.

Fig. 2 (c) shows the cumulative distribution of *diff*() for protected groups defined on ranges of age. The plot clearly shows that youngsters suffer from a higher bias towards the bad-debtor classification than middle-age or older people.

Fig. 2 (d) shows how the distribution varies with the set G of attributes used in distance measurement (see Remark 4.3). The plot refers to three sets. G_1 includes all attributes except `sex`, used to define the protected group, and `class`, used as the decision attribute. G_1 is the set used so far. G_2 includes attributes related to credit (history, purpose, amount, existing) and to properties (savings, property, housing, third parties) – but nothing about job. Finally, G_3 includes only attributes related to credit. From the plot, we can conclude that the distributions are not dramatically sensible to the set of attributes, although by restricting the set of attributes, high values of *diff*() tend to be even higher.

Fig. 2 (e) highlights the dual concept of *favoritism*, namely discrimination in favor of a group, where the "protected" group under analysis here consists of married men in the age range between 30 and 60. Compared to Fig. 2 (a,b), the distributions for the bad and the good decision are swapped, in the sense that there is no bias *against* the group in bad-debtor classification decisions, and there is bias *in favor* of the group members in good-credit classification decisions.

Finally, Fig. 2 (f) shows the distribution of *diff*() for the *credit-d* dataset, which is obtained by discretizing interval-scaled attributes in *credit*. Protected group, decision attribute and attributes in G are kept the same as in Fig. 2 (a). Technically, discretization affects the distance function, possibly resulting in different k-NN sets. The plot, however, closely resembles the distribution of the the original dataset, with a slight shift towards higher values.

Statistical significance of the *diff*() measure should also be taken into account, and it is actually customary in legal cases [13, 16]. In our context, we can interpret the observed proportions p_1 and p_2 from Def. 4.4 as the result of an experiment. What is the chance that the observed value $p_1 - p_2$ is affected by randomness in decisions of the dataset at hand? A confidence interval provides us with a range for the true

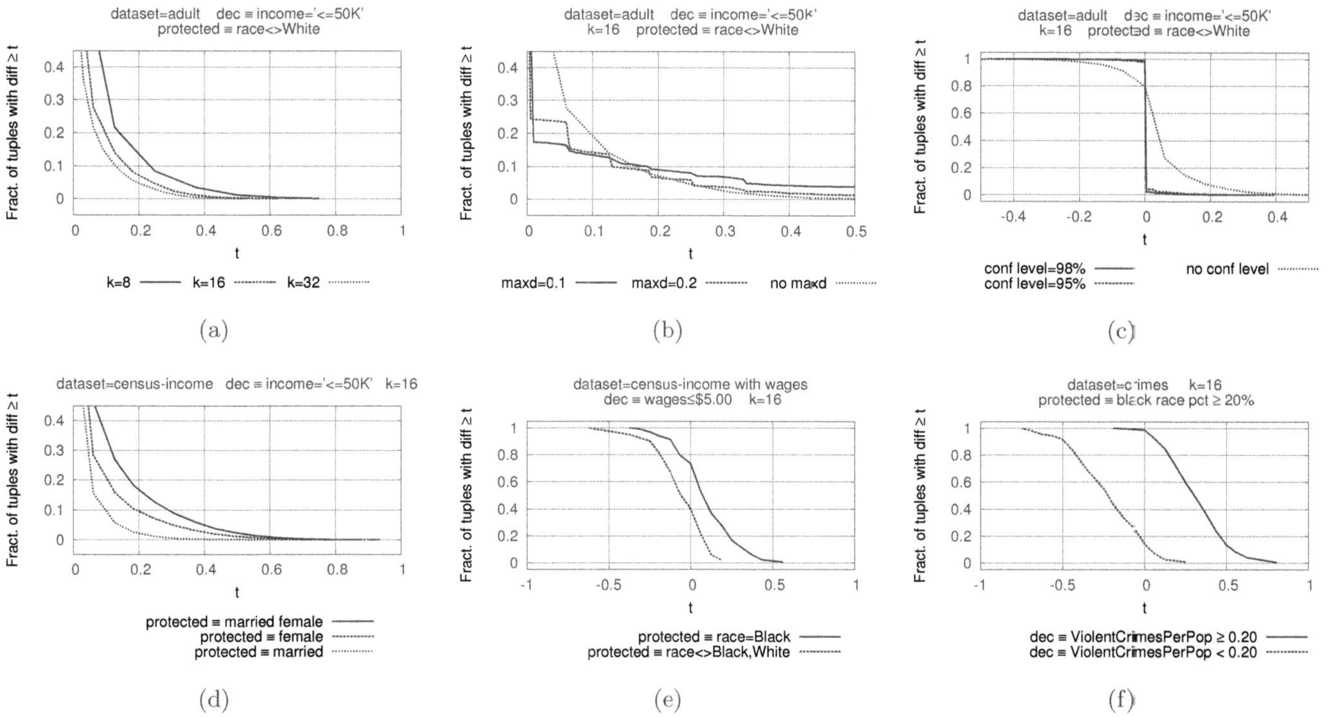

Figure 3: Cumulative distributions of *diff*() for datasets *adult*, *census-income* and *crimes*

value over the entire population (of decisions), at a certain significance level. Let us denote by π_1 and π_2 the true proportions over the protected and the unprotected neighbors. The Wald confidence interval for $\pi_1 - \pi_2$ at $100(1-\alpha)\%$ level of significance is $[(p_1 - p_2) - d, (p_1 - p_2) + d]$ where:

$$d_\alpha = Z_{1-\alpha/2}\sqrt{\frac{p_1(1-p_1)}{k} + \frac{p_2(1-p_2)}{k}}.$$

We refer the reader to [1, 11] for details, and to [15] for a comparison of several methods for interval estimation. We mention here that when k is very low, the Wald interval becomes imprecise. Exact methods have been proposed in the statistics literature, where "exact" means that the actual discrete distribution of the statistical parameter is adopted in computing the confidence intervals, instead of approximating it with a normal distribution as done in Wald intervals. In our context, we extend the *diff*() function as follows:

$$diff(\mathbf{r}, \alpha) = \begin{cases} max\{0, p_1 - p_2 - d_\alpha\} & \text{if } p_1 - p_2 \geq 0 \\ min\{0, p_1 - p_2 + d_\alpha\} & \text{otherwise} \end{cases}$$

Intuitively, non-negative values of *diff*() are corrected to the lower bound of the confidence interval, and negative values are corrected to its upper bound. $diff(\mathbf{r}, \alpha) = 0$ when the null hypothesis $\pi_1 - \pi_2 = 0$ cannot be rejected.

EXAMPLE 4.7. In the *adult* dataset the decision attribute `income` is not properly a "decision" but a range of income (lower or equal than \$50K , and higher than \$50K). Here, the objective of the discrimination analysis is to discover whether people in a protected group suffer from low income not for their own specific characteristics but rather due to membership to the group – a form of the so-called *social* discrimination. Fig. 3 (a,b,c) show the distributions of *diff*() for non-white people with low income at the variation of three parameters of the analysis: (a) the number k of nearest neighbors; (b) the additional constraint *maxd* on maximum allowable distance of the nearest neighbors (see Def. 4.1); and (c) the level of significance in statistical validation. As one would expect, the distributions tend to shrink as k increases (already observed in Ex. 4.5) and as the confidence level increases. Fig. 3 (c) shows that very few cases could be brought in a court of law with the support of strong statistical arguments. Finally, putting a maximum distance threshold when looking for neighbors results in a longer right tail distribution, as shown in Fig. 3 (b). The maximum distance parameter affects those tuples $\mathbf{r}$ that are somehow isolated (ether because of their own attributes, or by effect of the *curse of dimensionality* on the distance function) by excluding "distant neighbors" from their k-NN set.

The dataset *census-income* also contains census data, with the same decision attribute as *adult*. However, it is larger both in the number of tuples and in the number of attributes. In Fig. 3 (d) we highlight the analysis of *multiple discrimination* [8], namely discrimination on the grounds of two or more factors. The plot shows the distributions of *diff*() for the low income class of three protected groups: women, married people, and married women. As it can be readily observed, society leads married women with low income to experience a higher difference from the unprotected group (not-married or men) than the difference experienced as women (w.r.t. men) or as married people (w.r.t. not married ones) alone.

The definition of *diff*() extends to interval-scaled decision attributes by setting:

$$p_1 = |\{\mathbf{r}' \in kset_{P(\mathcal{R})\setminus\{\mathbf{r}\}}(\mathbf{r}, k) \mid dec(\mathbf{r}') \geq dec(\mathbf{r})\}|/k$$
$$p_2 = |\{\mathbf{r}' \in kset_{U(\mathcal{R})}(\mathbf{r}, k) \mid dec(\mathbf{r}') \geq dec(\mathbf{r})\}|/k \qquad (\star)$$

Assume that higher decision values mean more negative outcomes, e.g., as when the decision attribute is the interest rate to be paid for a loan or a mortgage. Intuitively, p_1 (resp., p_2) measures the proportion of the neighbors in the protected (resp., unprotected) group with a decision value higher than the one of $\mathbf{r}$. A difference $diff(\mathbf{r}) = p_1 - p_2$ greater than 0 means a negative bias due to membership to the protected group. For the interest rate example above, $diff(\mathbf{r}) = 0.3$ means that there are 30% more neighbors in the unprotected group, compared to the protected group, with a granted interest rate better[1] than $dec(\mathbf{r})$. Finally, assume that *lower* decision values mean more negative outcomes, e.g., as when the decision attribute is the percentage of salary increase. In order to have that positive values of $diff(\mathbf{r}) = p_1 - p_2$ denote bias against the protected group, the comparison predicates in ($\star$) must be changed from $\geq$ to $\leq$.

EXAMPLE 4.8. The *census-income* dataset includes the attribute `wages` recording the wage per hour. We have selected the tuples with known values of `wages`. For the resulting dataset, we can set `wages` as the (interval-scaled) decision attribute and study the distribution of *diff*(). As for nominal decision attributes, we concentrate on negative decisions. For interval-scaled attributes, the analogous of $dec(\mathbf{r}) = \ominus$ is, for some threshold value t, $dec(\mathbf{r}) \geq t$ if higher decision values mean more negative outcomes, and $dec(\mathbf{r}) \leq t$ otherwise. Fig. 3 (e) shows the distribution for `wages` up to \$5.00 for the protected groups of black people, and of other minorities (non-black & non-white people). It is readily checked that blacks with low wages observe a bias towards their group that is higher than the bias observed by the other minorities.

Finally, the decision attribute in the *crimes* dataset is `ViolentCrimesPerPop`, the number of violent crimes in a community per 100K individuals. As already observed, it is not actually a "decision" taken by someone. Rather, here the interest is to understand whether some conclusions can be drawn from the dataset that relate high values of `ViolentCrimesPerPop` to the percentage of minorities, e.g., blacks, in the community. Such conclusions could drive forms of statistical discrimination against communities with large presence of black people. Fig. 3 (f) shows the distribution of *diff*() for the protected communities having 20% or more of blacks. Those of such communities that have a high number of crimes (`ViolentCrimesPerPop`$\geq$ 0.20) observe a significant difference in crimes with communities that are similar to them apart from having less than 20% of blacks. In other words, a high number of crimes is "discriminatorily" present in communities with a high percentage of blacks! To further support this, Fig. 3 (f) shows the distribution for communities with a low number of crimes (`ViolentCrimesPerPop`$<$ 0.20). Now, communities with 20% or more of blacks and a low number of crimes observe no bias for such low number of crimes due to the high presence of blacks.

5. DISCRIMINATION DISCOVERY

In this section, we devise an approach for discovering and characterizing discrimination. From the examples of the last section, it is clear that for a tuple $\mathbf{r}$ of the protected group $diff(\mathbf{r})$ measures the discrimination bias. By assuming a non-negative threshold value for $diff(\mathbf{r})$, we can label a tuple as discriminated or not.

```
DiscoveryN(R, t) {
  L = ∅
  for r ∈ P(R) {
    if( dec(r) = ⊖ and
                 diff(r) ≥ t )
      r[disc] = yes
    else
      r[disc] = no
    L = L ∪ {r}
  }
  build a classifier on L
}
```

```
DiscoveryI(R, l, t) {
  L = ∅
  for r ∈ P(R) {
    if( dec(r) ≥ l and
                 diff(r) ≥ t )
      r[disc] = yes
    else
      r[disc] = no
    L = L ∪ {r}
  }
  build a classifier on L
}
```

Figure 4: Procedures for discrimination discovery

DEFINITION 5.1. *Let $t \in [0,1]$ be a threshold value. We say that $\mathbf{r}$ is t-discriminated, and write $disc(t, \mathbf{r})$, if $dec(\mathbf{r}) = \ominus$ and $protected(\mathbf{r})$ and $diff(\mathbf{r}) \geq t$.*

Notice that we require that $dec(\mathbf{r}) = \ominus$, namely that the decision value for $\mathbf{r}$ is negative, in order to distinguish discrimination from favoritism, such as the one resulting from affirmative actions. In fact, if $dec(\mathbf{r}) = \oplus$ and $diff(\mathbf{r}) \geq t$, then $\mathbf{r}$ and its protected neighbors were granted a benefit in higher proportion than its unprotected neighbors. Also, we require that $protected(\mathbf{r})$ holds because we are interested in characterizing under which conditions a member of the protected group was discriminated or not. Obviously, also members of the unprotected group might be discriminated (again, for instance, because of affirmative actions), but labeling both protected and unprotected group members would mix different causes of discrimination.

How should t be chosen? The answer depends on the law. For instance, the U.K. legislation [23] for sex discrimination, sets $t = 0.05$, namely a 5% difference. The U.S. legislation [24] for employment discrimination, sets a threshold (known as the "four-fifths rule") of 1.25 for the measure of selection lift *slift*(). We take a general approach, and leave t as a parameter for the analyst. We are now in the position to provide a global description of the tuples that are discriminated by reducing the discrimination discovery problem to a classification problem.

DEFINITION 5.2. *The t-labeled version of a dataset $\mathcal{R}$ is the dataset obtained: (1) by adding a binary attribute, called* `disc`*, assuming, for a tuple $\mathbf{r} \in \mathcal{R}$ the boolean value $disc(t, \mathbf{r})$; and (2) by restricting to tuples of the protected group only.*

Discrimination discovery reduces now to the extraction of an accurate classifier over a labeled version of $\mathcal{R}$ with `disc` as the class attribute. Accuracy will be evaluated with standard measures, e.g., precision and recall over the class value `disc=yes`. The intended use of the classifier is descriptive, namely to provide the analyst with a description of the conditions under which discrimination occurred. Classification models that can be interpreted clearly and easily should be adopted, such as decision trees and classification rules. The overall procedure for discrimination discovery over nominal decision attributes is shown in Fig. 4 as **DiscoveryN()**, where the t-labeled version of $\mathcal{R}$ is computed in $\mathcal{L}$.

Condition (2) in Def. 5.2 follows from the fact that for tuples not in the protected group $disc(t, \mathbf{r})$ is always false, so any classification model would derive assertions such as

[1] This statement can be better understood by observing that $diff(\mathbf{r}) = p_1 - p_2 = (1 - p_2) - (1 - p_1)$,

"if not *protected*(**r**) then `disc=no`", assuming that the model is able to express the condition defining *protected*.

EXAMPLE 5.3. Consider the *credit* dataset, with the settings of Fig. 2 (a) and $k = 32$. Using a C4.5 decision tree classifier [17], the procedure **DiscoveryN**(*credit*, 0.10) yields the following model and evaluation measures[2].

```
num_dependents <= 1
|   credit_amount <= 2631: disc=yes (59.0/9.0)
|   credit_amount > 2631: disc=no (44.0/15.0)
num_dependents > 1: disc=no (6.0)

disc=yes:  Precision  0.847   Recall  0.769
```

A pair (x, y) at a leaf node means that x tuples reach the leaf, y of which are incorrectly classified. y is omitted if it is 0. Intuitively, the bad debtor class (the decision) is *discriminatorily* assigned to a female non-single (the protected group) when she has zero or one dependents and asks for a credit amount up to $2,631. This is a concise, clear, and global characterization of the cases when discrimination occurred. It covers 77% of the protected group (recall), and it is accurate at 85 % (precision). On the same dataset, the RIPPER rule classifier [6] yields a slightly better recall.

```
(credit_amount >= 3190) => disc=no (39.0/12.0)
(installment_commitment <= 2) and (residence_since >= 3)
                                        => disc=no (10.0/2.0)
 => disc=yes (60.0/9.0)

disc=yes:  Precision  0.85   Recall  0.785
```

The model can be read as follows. Discrimination occurs in all cases, except when the credit requested is at least $3,190, or when there are up to 2 installment payments (short term loans) of a resident since at least 3 years. Of course, changing a parameter of the approach may yield different models. The following decision tree is obtained for $k = 8$.

```
num_dependents <= 1
|   installment_commitment <= 2
|   |   age <= 23: disc=no (9.0)
|   |   age > 23
|   |   |   employment = unemployed: disc=yes (1.0)
|   |   |   employment = <1: disc=no (8.0/1.0)
|   |   |   employment = 1<=X<4: disc=yes (8.0/1.0)
|   |   |   employment = 4<=X<7: disc=yes (1.0)
|   |   |   employment = >=7: disc=yes (4.0/2.0)
|   installment_commitment > 2: disc=yes (72.0/19.0)
num_dependents > 1: disc=no (6.0/1.0)

disc=yes:  Precision  0.744   Recall  0.970
```

Discrimination occurs when there are zero or one dependents and mid to long-term loans, or short term loans to applicants older than 23 that are either unemployed or employed since at least 1 year.

Finally, the overall procedure for discrimination discovery over interval-scaled decision attributes is shown in Fig. 4 as **DiscoveryI()**. A further parameter is now required, namely the threshold l such that $dec(\mathbf{r}) \geq l$ denotes the negative decision outcome (see Ex. 4.8). Notice that the class attribute `disc` in the labeled dataset $\mathcal{L}$ is still nominal, binary valued.

[2]Since the purpose of the classifier is descriptive, precision and recall are calculated over the training set. Notice that a predictive procedure simply consists of checking $disc(t, \mathbf{r})$.

PreventionN($\mathcal{T}$, $\mathcal{V}$, t) {
  $\mathcal{T}' = \emptyset$
  for $\mathbf{r} \in \mathcal{T}$ {
    $\mathbf{r}' = \mathbf{r}$
    if($dec(\mathbf{r}) = \ominus$ and
        protected($\mathbf{r}$) and
        $diff(\mathbf{r}) \geq t$)
      $\mathbf{r}'$[dec] $= \oplus$
    $\mathcal{T}' = \mathcal{T}' \cup \{\mathbf{r}'\}$
  }
  build classifiers on $\mathcal{T}$ and $\mathcal{T}'$
  compare them on $\mathcal{V}$
}

PreventionI($\mathcal{T}$, $\mathcal{V}$, l, t) {
  $\mathcal{T}' = \emptyset$
  for $\mathbf{r} \in \mathcal{T}$ {
    $\mathbf{r}' = \mathbf{r}$
    if($dec(\mathbf{r}) \geq l$ and
        protected($\mathbf{r}$) and
        $diff(\mathbf{r}) \geq t$)
      $\mathbf{r}'$[dec] $= l - \epsilon$
    $\mathcal{T}' = \mathcal{T}' \cup \{\mathbf{r}'\}$
  }
  build classifiers on $\mathcal{T}$ and $\mathcal{T}'$
  compare them on $\mathcal{V}$
}

Figure 5: Procedures for discrimination prevention

	No pre-processing		0.10-correction	
classifier	accuracy	0.10-discr.	accuracy	0.10-discr.
C4.5	85.60%	4.24%	84.94%	1.07%
Naïve Bayes	82.46%	4.06%	82.33%	2.23%
Logistic	85.28%	6.61%	84.70%	0.61%
RIPPER	84.42%	5.24%	83.98%	3.94%
PART	85.20%	12.62%	84.00%	2.3%

Table 2: Discrimination prevention on dataset *adult*

6. DISCRIMINATION PREVENTION

Starting from a dataset of historical decision records, classification models are typically extracted with the intent to learn and predict the decision $dec(\mathbf{r})$ (the class attribute) starting from the other attributes of a tuple $\mathbf{r}$. Preventing discrimination when training a classifier consists of balancing these two contrasting objectives: maximize accuracy of the extracted classification model; and minimize the number of predictions that are discriminatory. Within our framework, a prediction is discriminatory if the classified tuple is t-discriminatory, for some fixed threshold t. Why a classification model should be discriminatory? The main reason is due to *statistical discrimination*, namely the fact that the classification algorithm may recognize patterns in the data where, either directly or indirectly, the membership to a protected group is a proxy for lower performances (e.g., capacity to pay the loan installments). We now propose a simple pre-processing step, orthogonal to the classification algorithm, for tackling the discrimination prevention problem. The method consists of changing the decision value for tuples in the training set that are t-discriminated.

DEFINITION 6.1. *The t-corrected version of a training set $\mathcal{T}$ is the dataset obtained by changing $dec(\mathbf{r})$ from $\ominus$ to $\oplus$ if $disc(t, \mathbf{r})$ holds.*

Given a protected group and a threshold t, in order to evaluate the effectiveness of the pre-processing method, we build two classifiers: one on the training set $\mathcal{T}$, and the other on its t-corrected version $\mathcal{T}'$. Both classifiers are evaluated on a test set $\mathcal{V}$ with respect to two measures: accuracy, and t-discrimination. Accuracy is measured as the percentage of correct predictions. t-discrimination is measured as follows. Consider the dataset $\mathcal{V}$ where the decision attribute is set to the prediction of the classifier. t-discrimination is the percentage of tuples $\mathbf{r}$ with $diff(\mathbf{r}) \geq t$ among the tuples in the protected group with negative decision. Graphically, we look at the value of the cumulative distribution of $diff()$ (such as those in Fig. 2, 3) for the x-axis equal to t. The overall procedure is shown in Fig. 5 as **PreventionN()**.

EXAMPLE 6.2. Consider the dataset *adult* from Ex. 4.7, where the protected group consists of non-white people. By splitting the dataset into 2/3 training and 1/3 test sets, Table 2 shows accuracy and 0.10-discrimination for various types of classifiers, including decision trees (C4.5), Naïve Bayes, logistic regression, and rule induction (RIPPER and PART). If no pre-processing correction is performed, we can observe that the dataset of predictions exhibit a 0.10-discrimination measure over the test set ranging from 4.24% to 12.62%. Overall, C4.5 exhibits the best trade-off between accuracy and non-discrimination. If the training set is pre-processed by a 0.10-correction, all the classifiers have a modest decrease in accuracy and a significant gain in non-discrimination. The logistic regression model exhibits now the best trade-off.

Finally, the overall procedure for discrimination prevention over interval-scaled decision attributes is shown in Fig. 5 as **PreventionI()**. As for discrimination discovery, a threshold l, such that $dec(\mathbf{r}) \geq l$ denotes the negative decision outcome, is required as a further input. Notice that the change of the decision for t-discriminated tuples is now implemented by setting the decision value to a minimum $l - \epsilon$ that keeps the tuple below the limit of negative decisions.

7. CONCLUSIONS

We have modelled the discrimination discovery and prevention problems by a variant of k-NN classification that implements the legal methodology of situation testing. Major advancements over existing proposals consist in providing: a stronger legal ground, overcoming the weaknesses of aggregate measures over undifferentiated groups; a global description of who is discriminated and who is not in discrimination discovery; a discrimination prevention method that is independent from the classification model at hand; an approach admitting interval-scaled and ordinal attributes and decisions.

8. REFERENCES

[1] A. Agresti. *Categorical Data Analysis.* Wiley-Interscience, 2002.

[2] Australian Legislation. (a) Equal Opportunity Act – Victoria State, 2010, (b) Anti-Discrimination Act – Queensland State, 1991.

[3] G. S. Becker. *The Economics of Discrimination.* University of Chicago Press, 2nd edition, 1971.

[4] M. Bendick. Situation testing for employment discrimination in the United States of America. *Horizons Strategiques*, 5:17–39, 2007.

[5] T. Calders and S. Verwer. Three naive Bayes approaches for discrimination-free classification. *Data Mining & Knowledge Discovery*, 21(2):277–292, 2010.

[6] W. W. Cohen. Fast effective rule induction. In *Proc. of ICML 1995*, pages 115–123. Morgan Kaufmann, 1995.

[7] E. Ellis. *EU Anti-Discrimination Law.* Oxford University Press, 2005.

[8] ENAR. European Network Against Racism, Fact Sheet 33: Multiple Discrimination, 2007. http://www.enar-eu.org.

[9] European Union Legislation. (a) Race Equality Directive, 2000; (b) Employment Equality Directive, 2000; (c) Equal Treatment of Persons, 2009.

[10] H. Fang and A. Moro. Theories of statistical discrimination and affirmative action: A survey. In *Handbook of Social Economics, Vol 1B.* North-Holland, 2010.

[11] J. L. Fleiss, B. Levin, , and M. C. Paik. *Statistical Methods for Rates and Proportions.* Wiley, 2003.

[12] A. Frank and A. Asuncion. UCI machine learning repository, 2011. http://archive.ics.uci.edu/ml.

[13] J. L. Gastwirth. Statistical reasoning in the legal setting. *The American Statistician*, 46(1):55–69, 1992.

[14] N. Lerner. *Group Rights and Discrimination in International Law.* Martinus Nijhoff Publishers, 1991.

[15] R. G. Newcombe. Interval estimation for the difference between independent proportions: comparison of eleven methods. *Statistics in Medicine*, 17:873–89, 1998.

[16] M. J. Piette and P. F. White. Approaches for dealing with small sample sizes in employment discrimination litigation. *Journal of Forensic Economics*, 12:43–56, 1999.

[17] J. R. Quinlan. *C4.5: Programs for Machine Learning.* Morgan Kaufmann, San Mateo, CA, 1993.

[18] W. M. Rodgers, editor. *Handbook on the Economics of Discrimination.* Edward Elgar Publishing, 2006.

[19] I. Rorive. *Proving Discrimination Cases - the Role of Situation Testing.* Centre For Equal Rights & Migration Policy Group, 2009. http://www.migpolgroup.com.

[20] S. Ruggieri, D. Pedreschi, and F. Turini. Data mining for discrimination discovery. *ACM Trans. on Knowledge Discovery from Data*, 4(2):Article 9, 2010.

[21] S. Ruggieri, D. Pedreschi, and F. Turini. DCUBE: Discrimination discovery in databases. In *Proc. of SIGMOD 2010*, pages 1127–1130. ACM, 2010.

[22] T. Sowell, editor. *Affirmative Action Around the World: An Empirical Analysis.* Yale University Press, 2005.

[23] U.K. Legislation. (a) Sex Discrimination Act, 1975, (b) Race Relation Act, 1976.

[24] U.S. Federal Legislation. (a) Equal Credit Opportunity Act, 1974; (b) Fair Housing Act, 1968; (c) Employment Act, 1967; (d) Equal Pay Act, 1963; (e) Pregnancy Discrimination Act, 1978; (f) Civil Right Act, 1964, 1991.

Exploiting Vulnerability to Secure User Privacy on a Social Networking Site

Pritam Gundecha
Arizona State University
699 South Mill Avenue
Tempe, AZ 85281
pritam@asu.edu

Geoffrey Barbier
Arizona State University
699 South Mill Avenue
Tempe, AZ 85281
gbarbier@asu.edu

Huan Liu
Arizona State University
699 South Mill Avenue
Tempe, AZ 85281
huan.liu@asu.edu

ABSTRACT

As (one's) social network expands, a user's privacy protection goes beyond his privacy settings and becomes a social networking problem. In this research, we aim to address some critical issues related to privacy protection: Would the highest privacy settings guarantee a secure protection? Given the open nature of social networking sites, is it possible to manage one's privacy protection? With the diversity of one's social media friends, how can one figure out an effective approach to balance between vulnerability and privacy? We present a novel way to define a vulnerable friend from an individual user's perspective is dependent on whether or not the user's friends' privacy settings protect the friend and the individual's network of friends (which includes the user). As a single vulnerable friend in a user's social network might place all friends at risk, we resort to experiments and observe how much security an individual user can improve by unfriending a vulnerable friend. We also show how privacy weakens if newly accepted friends are unguarded or unprotected. This work provides a large-scale evaluation of new security and privacy indexes using a Facebook dataset. We present and discuss a new perspective for reasoning about social networking security. When a user accepts a new friend, the user should ensure that the new friend is not an increased security risk with the potential of negatively impacting the entire friend network. Additionally, by leveraging the indexes proposed and employing new strategies for unfriending vulnerable friends, it is possible to further improve security and privacy without changing the social networking site's existing architecture.

Categories and Subject Descriptors

H.2.7 [**Information Systems**]: Security, integrity, and protection; J.4 [**Social and Behavioral Sciences**]: Sociology

General Terms

Security, Experimentation

Keywords

Vulnerability, Social network, Privacy

1. INTRODUCTION

Social media [7] gives users an efficient way to communicate and network with one another on an unprecedented scale and at rates unseen in traditional media. The popularity of social media has grown exponentially resulting in evolution of social networking sites, blogs, micro-blogs, location-based social networks, wikis, social bookmarking applications, social news, media (photo, audio and video) sharing, product and business review sites, etc.

A *social networking site* [3] is a web-based service that allows web users to publish a public or semi-public profile within a bounded system, divulge a network of friends with whom they share a connection, and explore other users' profiles and friend networks. Networking through social networking sites is becoming a popular means for users to express feelings, communicate information, share thoughts, and collaborate. Social networking sites have reshaped business models [19], provided platform for communities to grow [18, 17], stimulated viral marketing [16, 9], provided trend analysis and sales prediction [15], and can be a grass-roots information source [5].

An individual user can share a large amount of personal and sometimes sensitive information with friends on a social networking site through the user's profile, status updates, messages, and status replies. Depending on individual choice, the user profile can reveal personal information to friends such as gender, birth date, relationship status, e-mail address, phone number, home address, and even political or religious affiliations. This puts an implicit responsibility on a user's social networking friends to keep shared information private and honor the implicit, and sometimes explicit, trust placed in friends by the user.

All social networking sites provide profile users a range of privacy settings to protect their personal information. These settings are often confusing and many times not well communicated to all users. Users can face a breach of privacy, unless these settings are properly used. In some cases, users' profiles are completely public, making information available and providing a communication mechanism to anyone who wants it. It is no secret that when a social networking profile is public, malicious individuals including stalkers, spammers, and hackers, can use sensitive information for their personal gain. Sometimes malevolent users can even cause physical or emotional distress to other users [13]. For example, Facebook's founder is a victim of stalking and has publicly admitted to emotional distress[1]. It is interesting to consider whether or not a completely public profile is the only risk to personal information on a social networking site. In this paper, we show that privacy settings alone are not enough to protect privacy and achieve a high level of security. Profile users can also face a breach of privacy if their friends abuse their trust. Most social networking sites do not provide adequate means to protect trust between users and their friends.

Many times social networking users are unaware that they are a threat to their friends because they are *vulnerable*. Three factors can contribute to the reduction of user's vulnerability. First, user's privacy settings are enough to protect their personal information. Second, a user has adequate means to protect their friends. Third, a user's friends must have intentions to protect the user. As we draw parallels between users and their friends, we are intrigued by questions like how vulnerable users are, how to find their vulnerable friends, what are effective mechanisms that could make users less vulnerable?

Besides helping users of a social networking site become less vulnerable, this study of vulnerability is motivated by the desire to better understand the dynamics of social networks from a security and privacy perspective. Ultimately, this may help social networking sites become more trustworthy as a medium to exchange ideas and information, better enabling sites to connect people, simplify communications, and to help them stay in touch reliably and securely.

In this paper, we address a novel problem of identifying *vulnerable friends* on a social networking site and investigate related issues and challenges. Specifically, we work to resolve the following questions:

- Are there vulnerable friends on a social networking site? Why is it important to find vulnerable them?
- What measures should be used to define vulnerable friends?
- How can a user identify his vulnerable friends? What measures can he take for effective protection?
- What is the impact of each new friend on the vulnerability of a user? Can we trust a new user?
- What role does a social networking site play towards making users less vulnerable? Is it possible to further improve security and privacy without suggesting fundamental changes to the social networking site's existing architecture?

In Section 2, we study the statistics collectible from a social networking site and define the problem of identifying vulnerable friends. We propose a methodology and measures for evaluating whether or not a user is vulnerable and how to adjust a user's network to best deal with threats presented by vulnerable friends. In Section 3, we conduct an empirical study to evaluate methods that can be manipulated to make users less vulnerable, compare the performance of an optimal algorithm with that of intuitive heuristic methods, and discuss the approach can be used to assess the impact of new friends to a user's network. We review the literature highlighting the novelty of this effort in Section 4. Finally, we discuss possible future work in Section 5.

[1]http://www.tmz.com/2011/02/07/mark-zuckerberg-restraining-order-facebook-social-network-santa-clara-county-stalker-letters-priscilla-chan/

2. VULNERABLE FRIENDS

Attributes available for every user on a social networking site can be categorized into two major types: *individual attributes* and *community attributes*. Individual attributes characterize individual user information, including personal information such as gender, birth date, phone number, home address, etc. Community attributes characterize information about friends of a user, including friends that are traceable from a user's profile (i.e., a user's friends list), tagged pictures, wall interactions, etc. Both types of attributes are always accessible to friends but may not to other users. Using privacy settings of a profile, a user can control the visibility of most individual attributes, but cannot control the visibility of most community attributes. For example, Facebook users can control traceable link information about friends but cannot control exposure of friends through photo tagging and wall interactions.

On most social networking sites, privacy related efforts have been concentrated on protecting individual attributes only. Thus, users are often left vulnerable through community attributes. We propose a mechanism that enables users to protect against vulnerability. The mechanism is tunable to accommodate individual preferences across the spectrum, from reclusive users to gregarious users.

A novel way to define a vulnerable friend from an individual user's perspective is dependent on whether or not the user's friends' privacy settings protect the friend and the individual's network of friends (which includes the user). *An individual is vulnerable if any friend in the network of friends has insufficient privacy settings to protect the entire network of friends.* Thus, whether or not an individual reciprocates privacy settings with their friends within a friend network can impact the entire network. Before presenting a formal definition of vulnerable friends, we propose four indexes, I-index, C-index, P-index, and V-index, based on individual and community attributes for each user on a social networking site. These indexes can be used to estimate user's privacy, quantify how well a user protects friends, specify how public or private user profiles are, and compute the vulnerability of individual users on a social network.

2.1 I-Index

I-index (Individual index): I-index estimates how much risk to privacy a user can incur by allowing individual attributes to be accessible or visible to other users. A user who ignores or is unaware of privacy settings is a threat to self. I-index is defined as a function of individual attributes (I-attributes). Let n be the total number of I-attributes available via a social networking site profile. I-index for a user u is given by

$$I_u = F(A_u), \tag{1}$$

where $I_u \in [0,1]$, $A_u = \{a_{u,i} : a_{u,i} = \{0,1\}; 1 \leq i \leq n\}$ is I-attribute set for user u and $a_{u,i}$ is a status of a i-th I-attribute for user u. $a_{u,i} = 1$ indicates user u has enabled i-th I-attribute to be visible otherwise non-visible (may be sensitive for a user).

Table 1 shows statistics of commonly found I-attributes on the Facebook (Refer to Section 3.1 for details on Facebook dataset consists of 2,056,646 users). The last column in the table lists the percentage of people who enable the particular attribute to be visible. For example, 7,430 (0.36%) Facebook users enabled their mobile phone numbers to be visible. We define the sensitivity (weight), of an attribute as a percentage of non-visibility. Hence, the sensitivity of a mobile phone number according to our Facebook dataset is 99.64. This means that users do not usually disclose their mobile phone number to other users. Users that do disclose phone numbers have a propensity to vulnerability because they disclose more sensitive information in their profiles.

Attributes	User Count	Percentage (%)
Total users	2,056,646	
I-attributes:		
Current City	620,401	30.17
Hometown	727,674	35.38
Gender	1,681,673	81.77
Birthday	67,834	3.30
Relationship status	539,612	26.24
Siblings	244,658	11.90
Education and work	516,848	25.13
Like and interests	1,369,080	66.57
Email	27,103	1.32
Mobile number	7,430	0.36
Website	128,776	6.26
Home address	7,580	0.37
Political Views	24,438	1.19
Religious Views	33,036	1.61
Children	86,609	4.21
Networks	284,482	13.83
Parents	73,887	3.49
Bio	199,070	9.68
Interested in	383,724	18.66
Looking for	449,498	21.86
Music	941,340	45.77
Books	281,346	13.68
Movies	574,243	27.92
Television	684,843	33.30
Activities	385,417	18.74
Interests	308,229	14.99
C-attributes:		
Friends trace (link)	1,481,472	72.03

Table 1: Attributes statistics on the Facebook

We used normalized weighted average to estimate I-index. I-index for each profile user u is given by,

$$I_u = F(A_u) = \frac{\sum_{i=1}^{n} w_i * a_{u,i}}{\sum_{i=1}^{n} w_i}, \quad (2)$$

where w_i is the sensitivity (weight) of an i-th I-attribute and $a_{u,i} = 1$ if i-th I-attribute is visible otherwise the attribute is not visible (i.e., sensitive to user u). $I_u \in [0, 1]$. $I_u = 1$ indicates user u has marked all I-attributes to be visible. On the other hand, $I_u = 0$ indicates user u has marked all I-attributes to be non-visible.

2.2 C-Index

C-index (Community index): C-index quantifies how much threat a user can pose to their friends by making community attributes accessible or visible to other users. Users who ignore and are unaware of privacy settings of community attributes can create risk to the entire community of friends. C-index is defined as a function of community attributes (C-attributes). Let m be the total number of C-attributes possible on a social networking site. C-index for a user u is given by

$$C_u = G(B_u), \quad (3)$$

where $C_u \in [0, 1]$, $B_u = \{b_{u,i} : b_{u,i} \in N; 1 \leq i \leq m\}$ is C-attributes set for user u, $b_{u,i}$ indicates the number of friends affected when a corresponding C-attribute is manifested, and N is the set of positive integers. We ignore attributes marked as non-visible. Our Facebook dataset has only one C-attribute (see Table 1) which suggests how many friends are traceable (via a friend relationship) from an individual user. 1,481,472 (72.03%) Facebook users in our dataset allowed friends to trace to other users. Thus, a large portion of users are *either not careful or not aware of the privacy concerns of their friends.*

A vulnerable user u can pose threat to his friends and the amount of the threat increases with the number of friends that are put at risk. However, the rate of the increment decreases as more friends are put at risk. To appropriately represent this threat change, we choose a convex, non-decreasing log function to estimate the threat for each user based on the number friends placed at risk by each C-attribute. Hence, C-index for a user u is calculated as

$$C_u = G(B_u) = \frac{\sum_{i=1}^{m} \log(b_{u,i})}{4 * m}, \quad (4)$$

where constant 4 is chosen because $C_u \in [0, 1]$ and none of the Facebook users in our dataset has more than 10^4 friends. $C_u > 0$ indicates user u has allowed everyone to trace friends through their own profile. On the other hand, $C_u = 0$ indicates that all the friends (except one) of a user u are non-traceable through a profile.

Figure 1(a) shows I-index and C-index for randomly chosen 100K Facebook users. Note that users are sorted in ascending order of their I-indexes. The X-axis and Y-axis indicate users and their corresponding I and C-index values, respectively.

2.3 P-index

P-index (Publicity/Visibility index): P-index shows how public (visible) or private (non-visible) a user is on a social networking site. This index also indicates how much an individual user aims to protect self as well as their friends. P-index is defined as a function of I-index and C-index. In other words, it is a function of I-attributes and C-attributes. P-index of a user u is given by

$$P_u = H(F(A_u), G(B_u)), \quad (5)$$

where $P_u \in [0, 1]$. We choose a simple, weighted average function to calculate P-index for each Facebook user in our dataset.

$$P_u = \alpha * F(A_u) + (1 - \alpha) * G(B_u), \quad (6)$$

where $\alpha \in [0, 1]$. Substituting Eq(6) with Eq(2) and Eq(4), we get

$$P_u = \alpha * \frac{\sum_{i=1}^{n} w_i * a_{u,i}}{\sum_{i=1}^{n} w_i} + (1 - \alpha) * \frac{\sum_{i=1}^{m} \log(b_{u,i})}{4 * m} \quad (7)$$

Different users may have different priorities about friends and may have different perspectives about vulnerability. Tunable parameter α can be set to address the needs of different

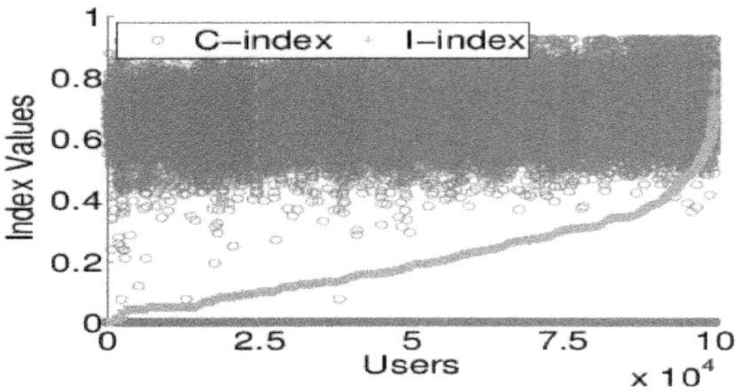

(a) I-index (red) and C-index (blue) for each User.

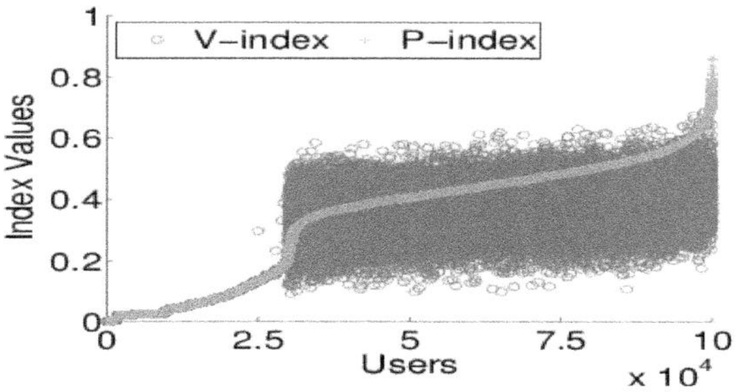

(b) P-index (red) and V-index (blue) for each User.

Figure 1: Relationship among index values for each User.

users. For example, one may choose $\alpha < 0.5$ to deemphasize the individual attributes' visibility; or one may choose $\alpha > 0.5$ to emphasize the individual attributes' visibility. For our experiments, we set $\alpha = 0.5$ to put equal weights to individual and community attributes.

2.4 V-index

V-index (Vulnerability index): V-index shows how vulnerable a user is on a social networking site. Thus far, we have provided three indexes, I-index, C-index, and P-index, for a user based on the visibility of I-attributes and C-attributes. On a social networking site, vulnerability of a user depends on privacy settings of self, friends, their friends, and so on. Intuitively, as the distance between a user and other users on a social networking site increases, the marginal risk of vulnerability decreases rapidly the further away a user is from a vulnerable user. Hence, we only consider a user and friends in estimating the vulnerability of a user. V-index of a user depends on the P-indexes of a user's friends and the user's P-index. V-index of a user u is defined as:

$$V_u = J(P_u, P_{R_u}), \tag{8}$$

where R_u is the set of friends of user u and $V_u \in [0, 1]$. A simple, weighted average function is used to calculate V-index for each user,

$$V_u = \frac{P_u + \sum_{i \in R_u} P_i}{|R_u| + 1} \tag{9}$$

P-index, P_u, of user u is also part of the V-index, V_u.

Figure 1(b) shows the P-index and V-index for 100K randomly chosen users (the same users chosen for Figure 1(a)). Note that users are sorted according to P-index. The X-axis and Y-axis indicate users and their index values respectively.

A **vulnerable friend** of a user is defined as *a friend whose removal (unfriending) will lower the V-index score of a user.* The V-index of a user u upon removing the vulnerable friend v is given by

$$V_u' = \frac{P_u + \sum_{i \in R_u - \{v\}} P_i}{|R_u|} \tag{10}$$

By definition of a vulnerable friend

$$V_u' < V_u \tag{11}$$

By substituting Eq(11) with Eq(9) and Eq(10), we can prove that

$$V_u < P_v \tag{12}$$

This means that the P-index of a vulnerable node is always greater than V-index of a user before unfriending.

The definition of vulnerable friends can be generalized to k-Vulnerable friends. **k-Vulnerable friends** *of a user are k friends whose removal (unfriending) will lower the V-index score of a user.* The V-index of a user, u, upon removing k vulnerable friends $v_1, v_2, \cdots, v_k$ is given by

$$V_u' = \frac{P_u + \sum_{i \in R_u - \{v_1, \cdots, v_k\}} P_i}{|R_u| + 1 - k} \tag{13}$$

By definition of k-Vulnerable friends

$$V_u' < V_u \tag{14}$$

By substituting Eq(14) with Eq(9) and Eq(13), we can prove that

$$V_u < \frac{\sum_{i \in \{v_1, \cdots, v_k\}} P_i}{k} \tag{15}$$

This means that the average P-index of k-vulnerable nodes is always greater than V-index of a user before unfriending.

Having formulated the problem of identifying vulnerable friends, we now demonstrate the results in next section.

3. FURTHER STUDY AND EXPERIMENTS

The proposed methods are demonstrated in practice through experiments using a dataset derived from a real social networking site. The proposed experiments address the challenge of identifying vulnerable friends. With an approach for identifying vulnerable friends, we set out to investigate the following issues:

- How effective are the P-index and V-index measures in reducing vulnerability of users? How effective is random unfriending in reducing vulnerability of users?
- What is an effective way of reducing one's vulnerability?
- Do the indexes address the dynamics of social networks? We study the impact of new friend request and its effect on vulnerability of a user.

In the next sections, we set out to use the proposed index estimation methods in an empirical study, attempt to experimentally address these issues, report preliminary results, and suggest new lines of research in finding vulnerable users.

3.1 Data Collection

Facebook users can create a profile containing personal and sometimes sensitive information. Users add other users as friends to facilitate social activity with friends. Users may also join groups organized by workplace, school, college, or other interests. As of July 2010, Facebook registered more than half billion active users[2] who returned to the site in last 30 days. To put that number in perspective, this makes Facebook users the third largest in "population" behind China (1.33 billion) and India (1.15 billion). This "population" will soon be twice the population of the United States (307 million). Facebook experiences web traffic data from 130 million[3] unique United States visitors a month. In January 2010, the amount of time the average person spent on Facebook jumped to more than seven hours per day[4]. This statistic suggests that the amount of personal information available on Facebook is richer than any other social networking site. Thus we chose a Facebook dataset for our experiments.

Facebook dataset (100K users)	Count
Non-traceable user profiles	30,391
Avg. actual friends per user	488
Avg. crawled friends per user	42
Max. actual friends per user	4,998
Min. actual friends per user	1
Max. crawled friends per user	1,590
Min. crawled friends per user	0

Table 2: Facebook dataset statistics for randomly selected 100K users from 2M+ users

The Facebook dataset is created by crawling Facebook user profiles. The dataset contains profile information for 2,056,646 users. Profile information includes attribute information for users such as age, gender, mobile phone number, address, etc. For convenience, 100K Facebook users were randomly selected from the dataset for the experiments. The findings are validated using all 2M+ users. Table 2 shows statistics for randomly selected 100K users. Out of these 100K users, around 30K users mark friends non-traceable from their profiles. The average Facebook user has 130[5] friends but our data set shows 488 actual friends per user. The dataset contains profile information for 42 friends (crawled friends) per user on average. The difference between the actual friends and crawled friends does not affect the methodology. Figure 2 shows relationships between actual friends (A-friends) and crawled friends (C-friends).

3.2 Identifying Vulnerable Friends

For the first set of experiments, we compare V-index for each of user with two optimal algorithms and six intuitive strategies for unfriending to reduce vulnerability. For each graph in Figure 3, the X-axis and Y-axis indicate users and their V-index values, respectively. For simplicity, we sort all users in ascending order based on existing V-index, and then we plot their corresponding V-index before and after unfriending. Figure 3 indicates performance of all eight al-

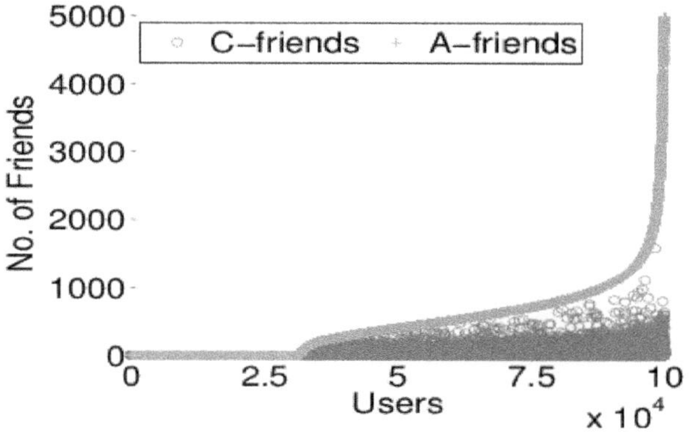

Figure 2: Actual (red) and crawled friends (blue)

gorithms which will help us to decide whether unfriending makes users more or less vulnerable. The eight algorithms are,

- *Most vulnerable friend.* For a user, the most vulnerable friend is the one whose removal lowers the V-index score the most. For each user, we first find the most vulnerable friend and then estimate the new V-index value (M1-index) after unfriending him/her. As expected, see Figure 3(a), V-index values for users decrease in comparison with V-index values before unfriending the most vulnerable friend. Unfriending the most vulnerable friend makes all users more secure.

- *Two most vulnerable friends.* If we sort all of user's vulnerable friends in ascending order based on their new V-indexes (after unfriending), the top two in the list are the two most vulnerable friends. For each user, we first find two most vulnerable friends and then estimate the new V-index value (M2-index) after unfriending them. As expected, see Figure 3(b), V-index values for all users decrease in comparison with V-index values before unfriending the two most vulnerable friends. Unfriending the two most vulnerable friends also make all users more secure.

- *Least V-friend.* For each user, we choose to unfriend the friend whose V-index is the lowest among all friends. This friend is the least V-friend. V-index values increase for 65% of 100K users, and increase for 43% of the 2M+ users, in comparison with V-index values before unfriending the least V-friend. See Figure 3(c), L-index refers to the new V-index value after unfriending the least V-friend. $V_u' > V_u$ for some users because, $P_l < V_u$ where P_l is the P-index of the least V-friend. Unfriending the least V-friend does not make all users insecure.

- *Random friend.* For each user, we randomly choose to unfriend a friend. V-index values increase for 24% of 100K users, and increase for 23.5% of the 2M+ users, in comparison with V-index values before unfriending a random friend. See Figure 3(d), R-index refers to the new V-index value after unfriending a random friend. $V_u' > V_u$ because $P_r < V_u$, where P_r is the P-index of the random friend. Unfriending a random friend does not make all users secure.

[2]http://www.facebook.com/press/info.php
[3]http://www.quantcast.com/facebook.com
[4]http://mashable.com/2010/02/16/facebook-nielsen-stats/
[5]http://www.facebook.com/press/info.php?statistics

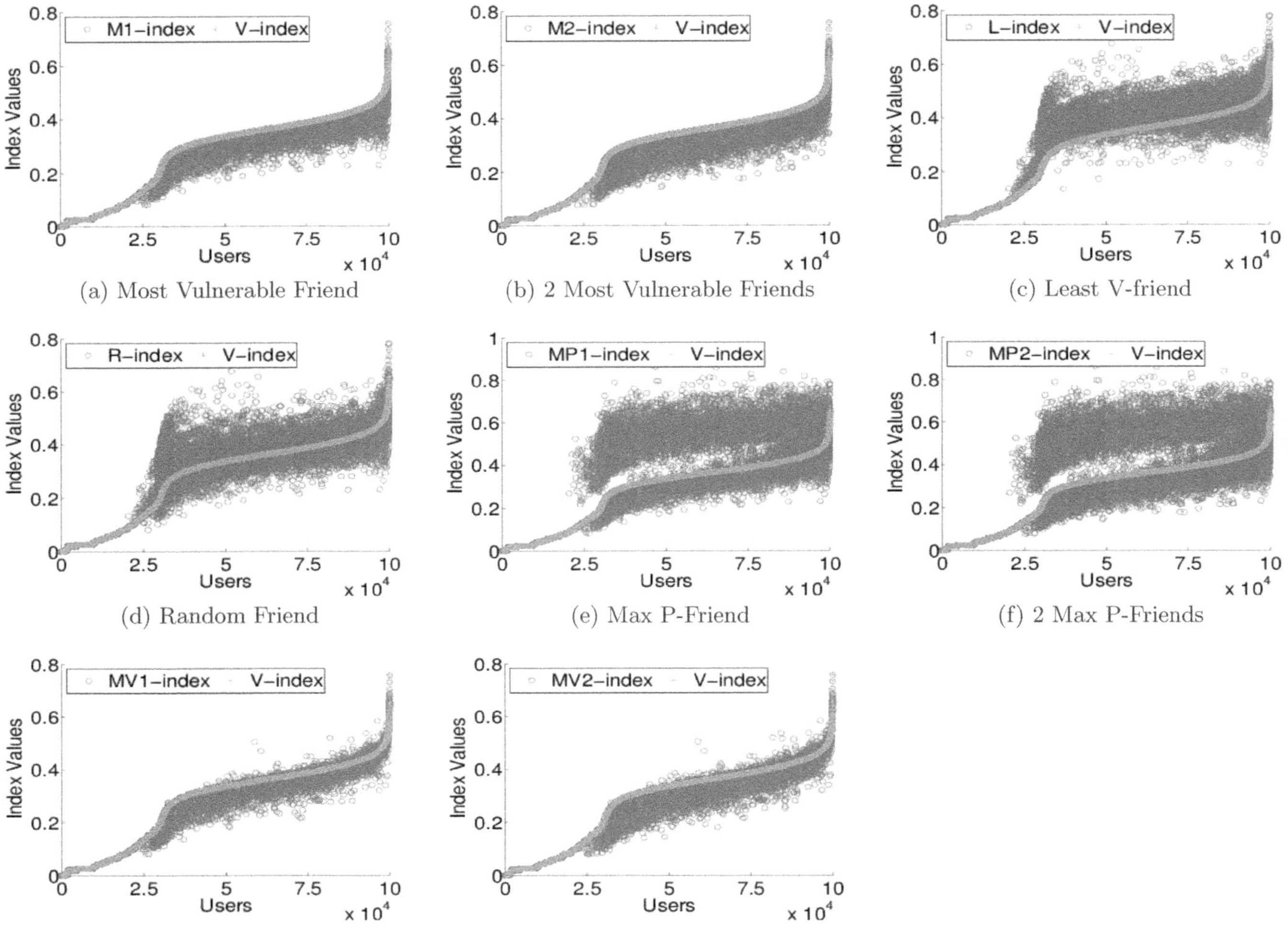

(a) Most Vulnerable Friend (b) 2 Most Vulnerable Friends (c) Least V-friend (d) Random Friend (e) Max P-Friend (f) 2 Max P-Friends (g) Max V-Friend (h) 2 Max V-Friends

Figure 3: Performance comparisons of V-indexes for each user before (red) and after (blue) unfriending based on eight different algorithms.

- *Max P-friend.* For each user, we choose to unfriend a friend whose P-index is the highest among all friends. V-index values increase for 5% of 100K users, and increase for 11% of the 2M+ users, in comparison with V-index values before unfriending the max P-friend. See Figure 3(e), MP1-index refers to the new V-index value after unfriending the max P-friend. $V_u' > V_u$ for some users because $P_{mp_1} < V_u$, where P_{mp_1} is the P-index of the max P-friend. Unfriending the max P-friend makes a majority of users more secure.

- *Two max P-friend.* For each user, we choose to unfriend two friends whose P-index is the highest and second highest among all friends. V-index values increase for 5% of 100K users, and increase for 11% of the 2M+ users, in comparison with V-index values before unfriending the two max P-friends.See Figure 3(f), MP2-index refers to the new V-index value after unfriending the two max P-friend. $V_u' > V_u$ for some users because $(P_{mp_1} + P_{mp_2})/2 < V_u$, where P_{mp1_1} and P_{mp_2} are P-indexes of the two max P-friends. Unfriending the two max P-friends makes a majority of users more secure.

- *Max V-friend.* For each user, we choose to unfriend a friend whose V-index is the highest among all friends. V-index values increase for 3.6% of 100K users, and increase for 5% of the 2M+ users, in comparison with V-index values before unfriending max V-friend. See Figure 3(g), MV1-index refers to the new V-index value after unfriending the max V-friend. $V_u' > V_u$ for some users because $P_{mv_1} < V_u$, where P_{mv_1} is the P-index of the max V-friend. Unfriending the max V-friend makes a majority of users more secure.

- *Two max V-friend.* For each user, we choose to unfriend two friends whose V-index is the highest and second highest among all friends. V-index values increase for 2.5% of 100K users, and increase for 5% of the 2M+ users, in comparison with V-index values before unfriending the two max V-friends. See Figure 3(h), GV2-index refers to the new V-index value after unfriending the two max V-friends. $V_u' > V_u$ for some users because $(P_{mv_1}+P_{mv_2})/2 < V_u$, where P_{mv_1} and P_{mv_2} are P-indexes of the two max V-friends. Unfriending the two max V-friends make a majority of users more secure.

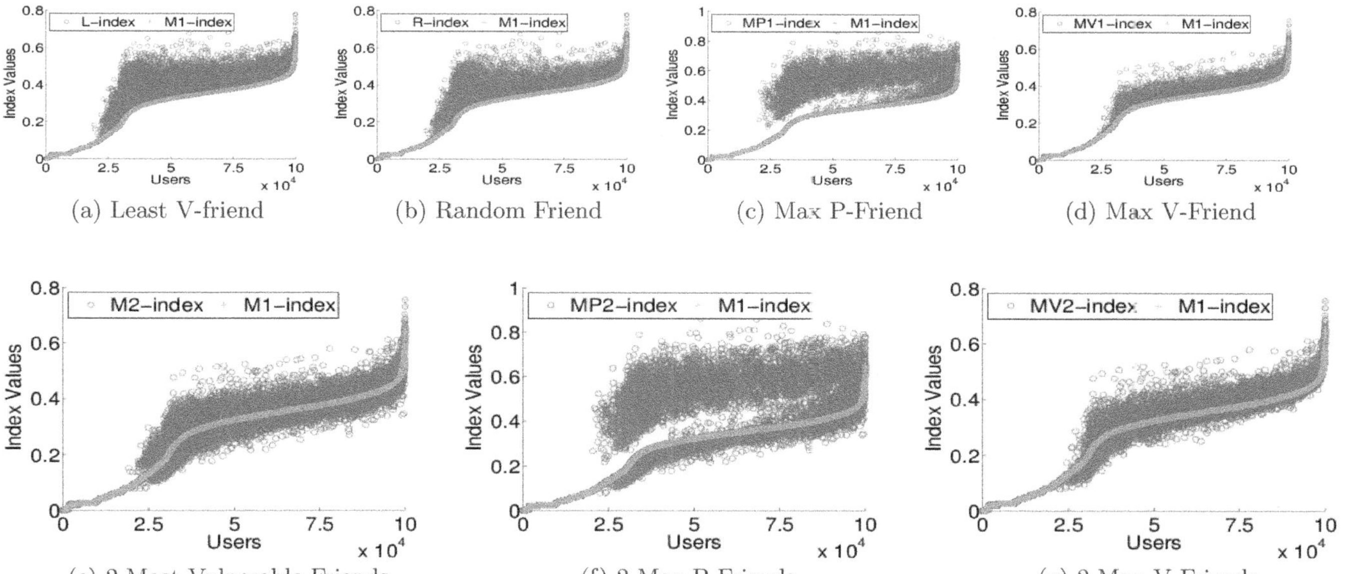

(a) Least V-friend (b) Random Friend (c) Max P-Friend (d) Max V-Friend

(e) 2 Most Vulnerable Friends (f) 2 Max P-Friends (g) 2 Max V-Friends

Figure 4: Performance comparisons of unfriending the most vulnerable friend (red) with seven different unfriending ways (blue).

In the second set of experiments, we compare the performance of unfriending most vulnerable friends with the seven intuitive unfriending strategies. For each graph in Figure 4, the X-axis and Y-axis indicate users and their associated V-index values after unfriending, respectively. We sort all users in ascending order based on V-index values after unfriending the most vulnerable friend and then plot corresponding V-index based on different unfriending strategies. We find unfriending the most vulnerable friend makes users more secure.

As expected, see Figure 4(a)-4(d), V-index values for each user based on unfriending the least V-friend, a random friend, the max P-friend, or the max V-friend increase for all users in comparison with their V-index values after unfriending the most vulnerable friend. In the case of unfriending the least V-friend, V-index values increase for 3% of users in comparison with the most vulnerable friend unfriending. Similarly, 1.7% of users increase for a random friend unfriending, 1.7% of users increase for the P-friend unfriend, and 1% of users increase for the V-friend unfriending. Thus, unfriending the most vulnerable friend makes all users more secure than all other schemes.

V-index values for each user based on unfriending the two most vulnerable friends, see Figure 4(e), do not decrease for 10% of 100K, and 21% of 2M+ users, in comparison with V-index values after unfriending the most vulnerable friend. V-index values for each user based on unfriending the two max P-friend, see Figure 4(f), do not decrease for 51% of 100K, and 81% of 2M+ users, in comparison with V-index values after unfriending the most vulnerable friend. V-index values for each user based on unfriending the two max V-friend, see Figure 4(g), do not decrease for 90% of 100K, and 75% of 2M+ users, in comparison with V-index values after unfriending the most vulnerable friend.

3.3 Impact of new friends

We now investigate the impact of new friendship on two types of secure users from vulnerable users. We select three sets of 10K users from 2M+ Facebook users: (S1) users with high V-indexes, (S2) users with low V-indexes, and (S3) C-attributes enabled users with low V-indexes. We randomly select a vulnerable user (i.e., selected from S1, 10K high V-index users) and a secure user (i.e., selected from S2, 10K low V-index users), and pair them and remove the pair from S1 and S2, respectively, until all 10K users from S1 and S2 are paired. We repeat the same with sets S1 and S3. The two sets of results are shown in Figure 5 (a) and (b). For each graph, the X- and Y-axis indicate users and their V-index values before and after the pairing of new friends, respectively. We sort all users in ascending order based on their old V-indexes. As shown in Figure 5(a), V-indexes of all users of S2 increase significantly and consistently; in Figure 5(b), V-indexes of users of S3 also increase, but vary from minor to large changes. The larger changes in the latter case occur on those users of S3 with fewer friends. The results in Figure 5 confirm that less vulnerable users can become more vulnerable if they are careless when making new friends, and reclusive users are more sensitive to the choice of new friends than less reclusive ones.

3.4 Discussions

Our experiments demonstrate different strategies for improving a user's privacy on a social networking site. It is possible to tune the index estimation methods for a wide range of individuals, from reclusive users to gregarious users.

- We choose specific functions, F, G, H, and J, to estimate the I-index, C-index, P-index and V-index. If one changes these functions, it will significantly change the criteria used to identify vulnerable friends.

- We set the tunable parameter α to 0.5. Changing the value α based on user preference will significantly change the threshold for identifying vulnerable friends.

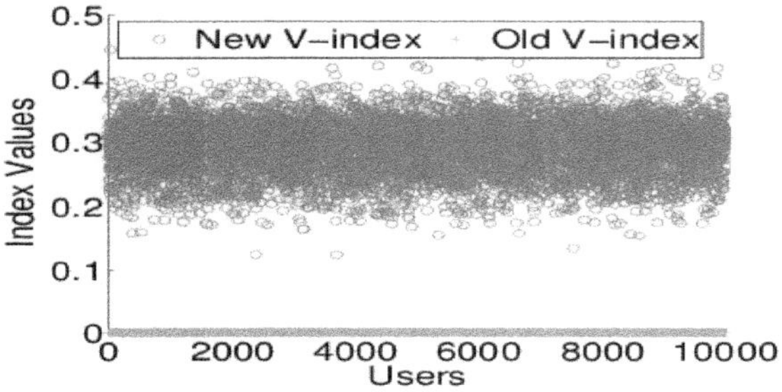

(a) C-attributes are not visible

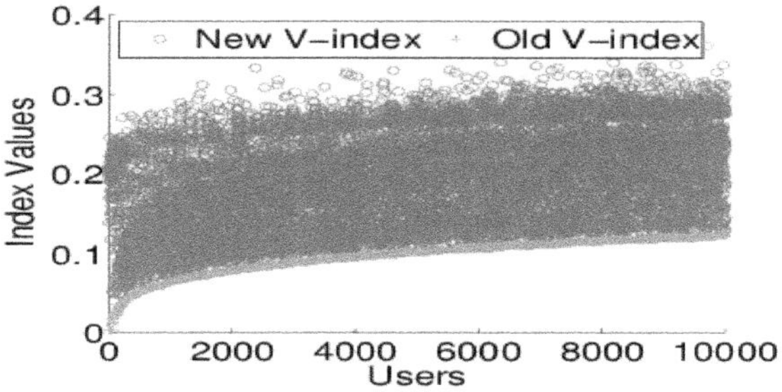

(b) C-attributes are visible

Figure 5: Impact of new friendship (blue) on users with low V-indexes (red) from users with high V-indexes

- Based on our index estimation method, unfriending the most vulnerable friend iteratively for K times should achieve at least the same vulnerability reduction as unfriending most K-vulnerable friends. Using equations 9 and 13, we can prove that additive property does not hold. Hence, unfriending most K-vulnerable friends is better than K iterative removal of most vulnerable friends.

4. RELATED WORK

Work discussed in this paper is about *identifying vulnerable friends of a user at one social networking site* and differs from most previous efforts of securing users privacy on a social networking site.

User privacy on a social networking site has received considerable attention recently. Gross and Acquisti [6] evaluate the amount of information disclosed through a social networking site and study usage of privacy settings. This work revealed that only a few users change the default privacy preferences on Facebook. Narayanan and Shmatikov [11, 12] show that users are not well protected on a social networking site by successfully deannonymizing network data solely based on network topology. They also highlight the fact that privacy laws are inadequate, confusing, and inconsistent amongst nations making social networking sites more vulnerable. Wondracek et al. [20] propose a simple deanonymization scheme which exploits the group membership information to breach users privacy.

Liu and Maes [10] point towards lack of privacy awareness and find large number of social network profiles in which people describe themselves using a rich vocabulary of their passions and interests. This fact strengthen the need for vulnerability research on a social networking site to make users aware of privacy risks. Krishnamurthy and Wills [8] discuss the problem of leakage of personally identifiable information and how it can be misused by third parties [12].

There has been some research which suggests the fundamental changes to social networking sites to achieve user privacy. Squicciarini et al. [14] introduce a novel collective privacy mechanism for better managing the shared content between the users. Fang and LeFevre [4] focus on helping users to express simple privacy settings but they have not considered additional problems such as attribute inference [22], or shared data ownership [14]. Zheleva and Getoor [22] show how an adversary can exploit an online social network with a mixture of public and private user profiles to predict the private attributes of users. Baden et al. [2] present a framework where users dictate who may access their information and based on public-private encryption-decryption algorithms. Although the proposed framework address privacy concerns, it comes at the cost of increased response time from a social networking site. Our work does not suggest any fundamental changes to social networking sites. We find users can secure user privacy by unfriending the vulnerable friends. Unfriending[6] has been studied recently but we are the first one to propose unfriending to reduce the vulnerability of a user.

5. CONCLUSIONS AND FUTURE WORK

We propose a feasible approach to a novel problem of identifying a user's vulnerable friends on a social networking site. Our work differs from existing work addressing social networking privacy by introducing a vulnerability-centered approach to a user security on a social networking site. On most social networking sites, privacy related efforts have been concentrated on protecting individual attributes only. However, users are often vulnerable through community attributes. Unfriending vulnerable friends can help protect users against the security risks. Based on our study of over 2 million users, we find that users are either not careful or not aware of security and privacy concerns of their friends. Our model clearly highlights the impact of each new friend on a user's privacy.

There are vulnerable friends on social networking sites and it is important to find vulnerable friends so that users can improve their privacy and security. Removing vulnerable friends from a user's social network might decrease the utility of the social networking service from a social perspective but this strategy improves security and helps defend privacy. We are also interested in investigating the role of user vulnerability across social networks [21] and relationship between the influential user [1] and vulnerable user.

6. ACKNOWLEDGMENTS

We thank Dr.Gabriel Fung for providing the crawled Facebook dataset for experiments. We also thank the DMML members and anonymous reviewers for their helpful comments. This research was, in part, supported by grants of ONR (N000141010091) and AFOSR (FA95500810132), and AFRL.

[6]http://www.nytimes.com/2010/10/24/fashion/24Studied.html

7. REFERENCES

[1] N. Agarwal, H. Liu, L. Tang, and P. Yu. Identifying the influential bloggers in a community. In *the first ACM International Conference on Web Search and Data Mining (WSDM)*, 2008.

[2] R. Baden, A. Bender, N. Spring, B. Bhattacharjee, and D. Starin. Persona: An online social network with user-defined privacy. *ACM SIGCOMM Computer Communication Review*, 39(4):135–146, 2009.

[3] D. M. Boyd and N. B. Ellison. Social network sites: Definition, history, and scholarship. *Journal of Computer-Mediated Communication*, 13(1):210–230, 2008.

[4] L. Fang and K. LeFevre. Privacy wizards for social networking sites. In *the 19th International World Wide Web Conference (WWW)*, 2010.

[5] R. Goolsby. Social media as crisis platform: The future of community maps/crisis maps. *ACM Trans. Intell. Syst. Technol.*, 1(1):1–11, 2010.

[6] R. Gross and A. Acquisti. Information revelation and privacy in online social networks. In *the ACM workshop on Privacy in the electronic society*, pages 71–80. ACM, 2005.

[7] A. M. Kaplan and M. Haenlein. Users of the world, unite! The challenges and opportunities of Social Media. *Business Horizons*, 53(1):59–68, 2010.

[8] B. Krishnamurthy and C. Wills. On the leakage of personally identifiable information via online social networks. *ACM SIGCOMM Computer Communication Review*, 40(1):112–117, 2010.

[9] J. Leskovec, L. Adamic, and B. Huberman. The dynamics of viral marketing. *ACM Transactions on the Web (TWEB)*, 1(1), 2007.

[10] H. Liu and P. Maes. Interestmap: Harvesting social network profiles for recommendations. *Beyond Personalization*, 2005.

[11] A. Narayanan and V. Shmatikov. Robust de-anonymization of large sparse datasets. In *the 29th IEEE Symposium on Security and Privacy*, 2008.

[12] A. Narayanan and V. Shmatikov. De-anonymizing social networks. In *the 30th IEEE Symposium on Security and Privacy*, 2009.

[13] D. Rosenblum. What anyone can know: The privacy risks of social networking sites. *IEEE Security and Privacy*, pages 40–49, 2007.

[14] A. Squicciarini, M. Shehab, and F. Paci. Collective privacy management in social networks. In *the 18th international conference on World wide web (WWW)*, 2009.

[15] J. Sterne. *Social Media Metrics*. The New Rules of Social Media. John Wiley & Sons Inc., 2010.

[16] M. R. Subramani and B. Rajagopalan. Knowledge-sharing and influence in online social networks via viral marketing. *Communications of the ACM*, 46(12):300–307, 2003.

[17] L. Tang and H. Liu. Relational learning via latent social dimensions. In *the 15th ACM SIGKDD international conference on Knowledge discovery and data mining*, 2009.

[18] L. Tang, H. Liu, J. Zhang, and Z. Nazeri. Community evolution in dynamic multi-mode networks. In *the 14th ACM SIGKDD international conference on Knowledge discovery and data mining*, 2008.

[19] G. Vaynerchuk. *Crush It!: Why Now Is the Time to Cash in on Your Passion*. HarperCollins, 1st edition, 2009.

[20] G. Wondracek, T. Holz, E. Kirda, and C. Kruegel. A practical attack to de-anonymize social network users. In *the 31st IEEE Symposium on Security and Privacy*, 2010.

[21] R. Zafarani and H. Liu. Connecting corresponding identities across communities. In *the 3rd International Conference on Weblogs and Social Media (ICWSM)*, 2009.

[22] E. Zheleva and L. Getoor. To join or not to join: the illusion of privacy in social networks with mixed public and private user profiles. In *the 18th International World Wide Web Conference (WWW)*, 2009.

On the Semantic Annotation of Places in Location-Based Social Networks

Mao Ye[1†], Dong Shou[1†], Wang-Chien Lee[1†], Peifeng Yin[1†] and Krzysztof Janowicz[2‡]
[†]Department of Computer Science & Engineering, The Pennsylvania State University, PA, USA.
[‡]Department of Geography, University of California, Santa Barbara, CA, USA.
[1]{mxy177,dus212,wlee,pzy102}@cse.psu.edu [2]{jano}@geog.ucsb.edu

ABSTRACT

In this paper, we develop a semantic annotation technique for location-based social networks to automatically annotate all places with category tags which are a crucial prerequisite for location search, recommendation services, or data cleaning. Our annotation algorithm learns a binary support vector machine (SVM) classifier for each tag in the tag space to support multi-label classification. Based on the check-in behavior of users, we extract features of places from i) *explicit patterns* (EP) of individual places and ii) *implicit relatedness* (IR) among similar places. The features extracted from EP are summarized from all check-ins at a specific place. The features from IR are derived by building a novel *network of related places* (NRP) where similar places are linked by virtual edges. Upon NRP, we determine the probability of a category tag for each place by exploring the relatedness of places. Finally, we conduct a comprehensive experimental study based on a real dataset collected from a location-based social network, *Whrrl*. The results demonstrate the suitability of our approach and show the strength of taking both EP and IR into account in feature extraction.

Categories and Subject Descriptors

I.2.6 [**Artificial Intelligence**]: Learning; J.4 [**Computer Applications**]: Social and Behavior Sciences

General Terms

Algorithms, Design, Experimentation

Keywords

Semantic Annotation, Points of Interest, User Behavior, Location-Based Social Networks

1. INTRODUCTION

With the increasing availability of GPS-enabled smart phones, rapid development of location-based services, and growing interests in on-line social networking, a number of location-based social networking (LBSN) services such as Whrrl[1], Foursquare[2] and Facebook Places[3] have emerged. These services allow users to explore places, write reviews, and share their locations and experiences with others. The number of available *places* in LBSNs is growing continuously.[4] Many places have been labeled with useful tags such as *restaurant* or *cinema*, which are crucial for assisting users in searching and exploring new places as well as for developing recommendation services [2, 12, 28]. However, based on our analysis of data collected from Whrrl and Foursquare, about 30% of all places are lacking any meaningful textual descriptions. To address this problem, we develop a novel technique, namely *semantic annotation of places* (SAP), to automatically and precisely annotate all places with *semantic tags* for LBSNs.

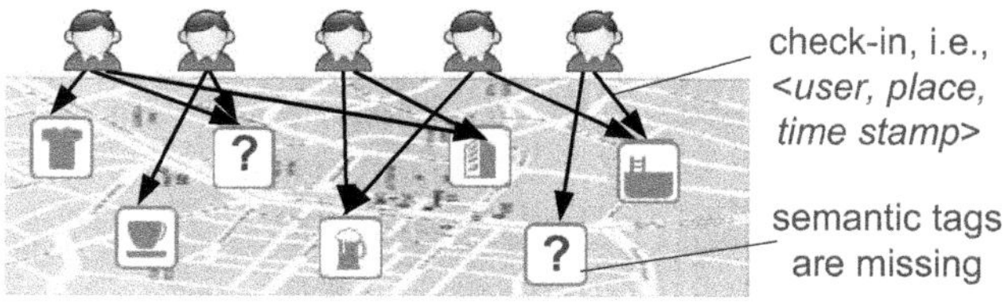

Figure 1: Users and places in an LBSN

Figure 1 shows a bipartite graph representation of the user-place relationship in an LBSN. Let U and P denote the set of all users and places in the system, respectively. Users and places are connected through a set of check-in activities $C = \{\langle u, p, h\rangle | u \in U \wedge p \in P \wedge h \in H\}$, where H is a set of time stamps. Each check-in $c \in C$ describes that "a user u has checked in a place p at time h". Note that a place p_i may be annotated by users with a set of semantic tags $T_i \subseteq T$, where T presents the tag space. Our proposed SAP technique assigns tags to places where semantic tags are missing. These targeted places are depicted with question marks in Figure 1.

The problem of *place semantic annotation* can be formulated as predicting appropriate tags for a given place. In LBSNs, a place may be associated with multiple tags. For instance, a place associated with a tag *restaurant* may also be tagged with *bar*. Hence, place semantic annotation in LBSNs may be addressed as a *multi-label classification* problem [3, 29]. While multi-label classification techniques have been developed for many applications, such as protein function classification [6], music categorization [13] and semantic scene classification [3], the problem has not been explored previously under the context of LBSNs, where we can only

[1]www.whrrl.com
[2]www.foursquare.com
[3]www.facebook.com/places
[4]*Points of Interest (POIs)* are usually referred to as *places* in LBSNs.

operate over user check-in activities (i.e., $\langle u, p, h \rangle \in C$) for certain places and time stamps.

We propose to address the place semantic annotation problem by learning a binary SVM for each tag in the tag space in order to realize the multi-label classification. To do so, a fundamental issue is to identify and extract a number of descriptive features for each place in the system. Selecting the right features is important because those features have a direct impact on the effectiveness of the classification task. As mentioned earlier, the only data resource we have is the user check-in activities at various places and times. Therefore, we explore the user behaviors and seek unique features of places captured in the check-in activities. Fortunately, human behaviors are not completely random, e.g., people usually visit restaurants for lunch at around noon. Moreover, people exhibit patterns in their activities, e.g., different places visited by the same person at the same time may be similar (e.g., having the same tags).

By leveraging the observations hinted in the above-mentioned examples, we extract features of places in two different but complementary aspects: 1) explicit patterns (EP) at individual places; and 2) implicit relatedness (IR) among similar places. Features extracted from EP, corresponding to a given place, can be derived from all check-ins at the place based on statistical analysis. In this paper, we propose to extract *population features* (e.g., number of unique visitors) and *temporal features* (e.g., distribution of check-in time) as semantic descriptions of specific places. On the other hand, we extract features from IR to capture the relatedness among places by exploiting the regularity of user check-in activities to similar places. Since only some places are tagged, we could make good use of IR by deriving descriptive features of a given place from its "related" places.

To facilitate extraction of features from IR, we develop a novel algorithm to build a *network of related places* (NRP) that captures the relatedness amongst places by exploring regularities of user check-ins to similar places. We propose a family of graph representations that capture the user-place and time-place relationships from the user check-in activities. We employ the Random Walk and Restart technique [27] on these graphs to estimate the relatedness of places in order to build an NRP. In the obtained NRP, place pairs with high relatedness values imply high similarity in the tag space and thus are linked. Accordingly, we derive the probability for a specific tag being labeled to a place (called *label probability*) from its linked (similar) places. This label probability is thus treated as a feature of IR, along with population and temporal features derived from EP, to feed the binary SVM in our SAP algorithm.

This research work has made a number of significant contributions, as summarized below.

- We propose to tackle the problem of place semantic annotation in LBSNs, which is a crucial prerequisite for effective retrieval and recommendation of POIs in LBSNs.

- We formulate the task of place semantic annotation in LBSNs as a multi-label classification problem and propose a two-phase algorithm to learn a binary SVM classifier for each tag in the entire tag space. In the proposed semantic annotation of places (SAP) algorithm, we explore explicit patterns (EP) at individual places and implicit relatedness (IR) among similar places by exploiting the user check-in activities to extract descriptive features for places. To overcome several technical challenges in realizing the proposed algorithm, we develop a number of techniques for extracting *population* and *temporal* features, building a network of related places (NRP), and deriving label probability for each place in the system.

- Through a comprehensive experimental study, using a real dataset collected from Whrrl, we validate our proposed ideas and evaluate our SAP algorithm in terms of three different feature sets: i) features extracted from EP, ii) features extracted from IR, and iii) all features (i.e., combination of i) and ii)). The experimental results show that using all features achieves the best performance among the three tested feature sets. More importantly, features derived from both EP and IR contribute significantly in unique aspects to the classification of different semantic tags. For example, features from EP are effective in labeling tags such as *restaurant* and *nightlife* because most people exhibit similar behaviors in visiting restaurants and nightlife places. On the other hand, features from IR are excellent for tagging places related to *shopping* as some people exhibit strong patterns in such activities.

The remainder of this paper is organized as follows. In Section 2, we review related works. Next, in Section 3, we give an overview of the proposed semantic annotation of places (SAP) algorithm, describe how we extract EP and IR features, and detail the realization of our SAP algorithm. In Section 4, we further discuss the issue of extracting features from IR and detail our approach. In Section 5, we conduct an empirical study using the collected Whrrl dataset and analyze our results. Finally, in Section 6, we conclude this work and point out future directions.

2. RELATED WORK

In this section, we review a number of existing works in the areas of data mining, multi-label classification, and classification of networked data.

Due to the increasing availability of location-based services and GPS-enabled devices, real traces of user locations and activities have been collected and used in several studies [1, 14, 15]. A variety of approaches for projecting user trajectories from GPS data have been proposed, including particle filtering [10], Markov models [1], Dynamic Baysian Networks [14], and Eigenbehaviors [7]. Data traces used in these studies typically do not contain explicit information regarding user activities. The LBSN data investigated in our research is unique in two aspects: i) semantic tags associated with places provide rich information about categories and activities (e.g., food, restaurant, hotel, shopping, etc.); and ii) user check-ins logged in LBSNs usually are not continual, thus revealing partial views of user activities. These differences bring several new challenges to our research. The most related work is [15], which studies people's naming preferences. The authors argue that people have different naming preferences under different contexts, and thus use a wide range of terms such as *home* and *near Liberty Bridge* to disclose their locations to others. Notice that, even though our work also explores people's naming preferences on places, we focus on enriching places with semantic tags such as *restaurant* and *cinema* for supporting location search and retrieval.

Place semantic annotation has been formulated as a multi-label classification problem in this paper. Previous studies on multi-label classification have primarily been conducted in the application domains of text classification [25, 19], protein function classification [6], music categorization [13], and semantic scene classification [3]. In [25], BoosTexer, extending AdaBoost [8], has been developed to handle multi-label text categorization. In [19], a mixture model derived by expectation maximization (EM) has been trained to select the most probable set of labels from the power set of possible classes. In [11], a set of binary SVM classifiers have been developed to realize multi-label classification for text classification. In [6], the notion of entropy has been extended to include multi-label data for gene expression in order to generate accurate rules for gene expression comprehension. In [21], geographical knowledge has been employed to help assign semantic tags to geo-tagged Flickr photos. Note that place semantic annotation for LBSNs is a new research topic that has not been studied previously.

To derive correlations amongst places from patterns of individual check-ins, we depict users and places as nodes of a bipartite graph as shown in Figure 1. We then construct a network of related places to facilitate classification. There exists some work on classifying networked data, which are generally of the same type such as web-pages or text documents connected via various explicit relations (e.g., hyperlinks [16]). Studies on simultaneously inferring interrelated values over networked data have been reported in [4, 26]. In [17], a simple univariate classifier, called the weighted-vote relational neighbor (wvRN), has been developed by obtaining a weighted average of the estimated class membership scores of the nodes' neighbors. Moreover, similar to [4], a relaxation labeling method has been proposed for collective inference [24]. In [18], a case study on learning attributes of network data has been presented. In [20], a *cautious* collective classification that adopts only top-k most confidently predicted labels has been proposed. Gallagher et al. propose *ghost edges* to create edges between nodes based on the intrinsic structure of the networks to improve the classification of sparse labels [9].

3. SEMANTIC ANNOTATION OF PLACES

We design a two-phase algorithm to address the place semantic annotation problem. The first phase takes care of the feature extraction, while the second phase handles the semantic annotation. The task of feature extraction explores two lines of ideas as discussed earlier in the Introduction. On the one hand, we explore the explicit patterns (EP) corresponding to a specific place to abstract aggregated user behaviors as *population features* and *temporal features*. On the other hand, we explore the implicit relatedness (IR) amongst places in order to formulate descriptive features of a given place from its similar places. Features derived from EP and IR are used to learn a binary SVM for each tag in the tag space in the semantic annotation phase. Given a place, the prediction by a specific SVM classifier decides whether this place belongs to the category of the corresponding semantic tag or not. After checking all SVM classifiers, we obtain all qualified semantic tags for the place under examination.

3.1 Features from EP

Our goal is to extract discriminative EP features from places with the same tag. Intuitively, users behave differently at different places due to the nature of functions and activities offered by these places. As a result, different patterns, naturally formed in aggregated behaviors of visitors to various kinds of places, are embedded in the user check-in activities which are logged in LBSNs. In a check-in record, the most important information is user and time, besides the place itself. In the following, we propose to extract several population features and temporal features to depict places as below.

- F_1 (*total number of check-ins*) - Based on the observation from the Whrrl dataset, shown in Figure 2, we find the number of check-ins to a restaurant is usually larger than the number of check-ins to a hospital. Hence the number of check-ins, which is discriminative for the classification of places such as restaurants and hospitals, is a good population feature for semantic annotation.

- F_2 (*total number of unique visitors*) - This feature focuses on the number of unique visitors. Based on our analysis on the Whrrl dataset, we find F_2 to be a similar phenomenon to F_1. Thus, we aggregate the number of unique visitors at a specific location as the second population feature extracted from EP.

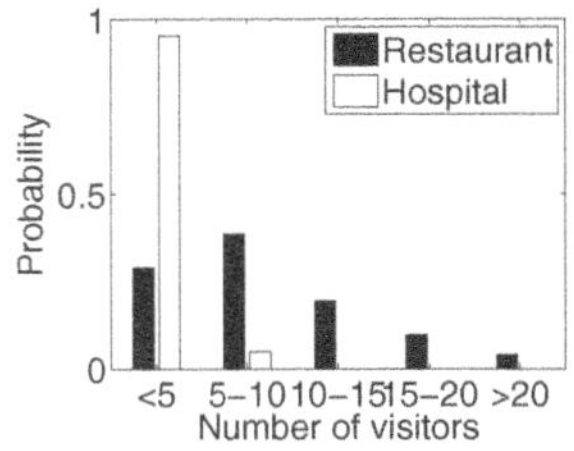

Figure 2: Distr. of # of visitors

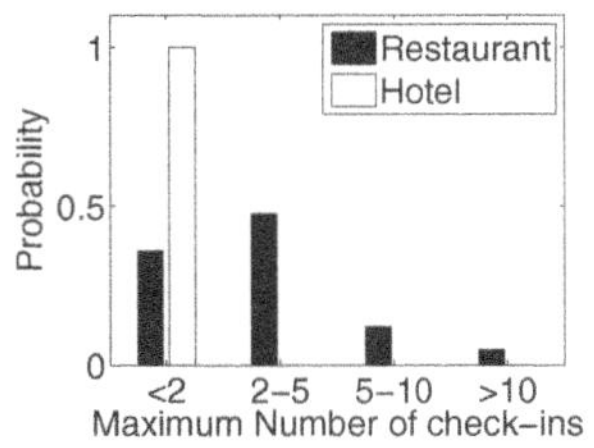

Figure 3: Distr. of Max # of check-ins by a single visitor

- F_3 (*maximum number of check-ins by a single visitor*) - As shown in Figure 3, people may check in a place tagged as restaurant for multiple times, while they may check in a hotel for only 1-2 times. Thus, the maximum number of check-ins by a single user at a place is useful to decide whether a place is a restaurant or a hotel. We use it as the third population feature extracted from EP.

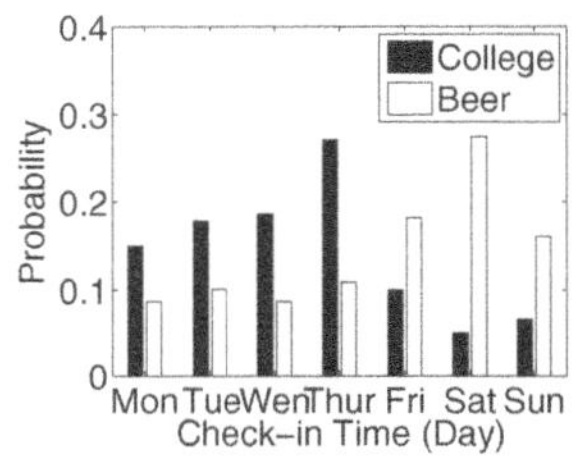

Figure 4: Distr. of check-in time (day)

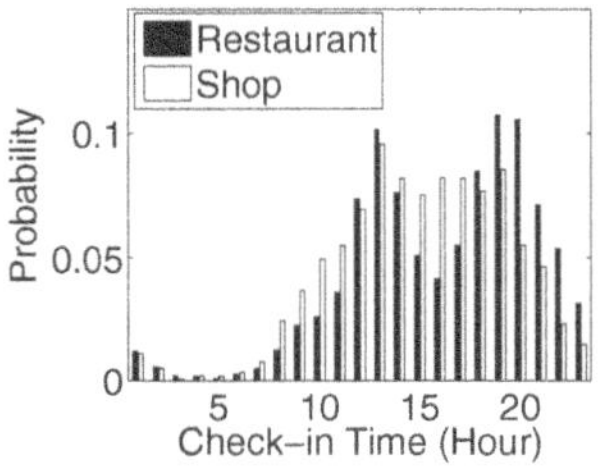

Figure 5: Distr. of check-in time (hour)

- F_4 (*distribution of check-in time in a week*) - We analyze the distribution of check-ins at different categories of places over the days of a week. As shown in Figure 4, users check in college campuses more often on weekdays than on weekends. On the contrary, they check in bars on weekends more frequently than on weekdays. Since there are different distributions of check-in days for different kinds of places, we consider the distribution to be a very useful temporal feature.

- F_5 (*distribution of check-in time in 24-hour scale*) - By plotting the distribution of check-ins in the 24-hours time scale, we show in Figure 5 two very different distribution patterns corresponding to two kinds of places (i.e., restaurant and shop). There are clearly two peak times, corresponding to lunch and dinner periods, for places associated with the tag *restaurant*. On the other hand, shopping time looks like a normal distribution with most activities between 7:00am and 8:00pm, while there is no obvious peak shopping time observed. These observations regarding the patterns of massive visitors at different kinds of places provide strong support that check-in time distributions in 24-hours time scale is a good temporal feature for semantic annotation.

Note that, besides of the aforementioned patterns, check-in activities at different places may show seasonal patterns, e.g., most people go to ski areas during winter. However, due to the limited time span in the period of data collection, we only consider F_4 and F_5 as the temporal features in this study.

3.2 Features from IR

As discussed in [7], there is regularity in people's activities. Take one of the Whrrl users as an example. We find that the user visits places in the *performing arts and entertainment* category (including museums and galleries) in the morning (at around 10:00am), visits places for food at lunch/dinner time, and usually goes shopping at around 4:00pm. Such regularity appears in certain users and thus can be used for correlating similar places. However, extracting features from implicated relatedness (IR) among similar places (e.g., checked in at the same time) is not as straightforward as extracting features from EP.

To capture the relatedness among places and extract discriminative features from IR, our approach is to build a *network of related places (NRP)*. In an NRP, places are linked based on their relatedness, measured by the information provided in user check-ins through the Random Walk and Restart technique [27]. Upon the NRP, we determine the label probability for each place by exploring the relatedness of places. As such, the label probability derived from IR serves as a feature for classification. Details of feature extraction form IR will be introduced in Section 4.

3.3 Semantic Annotation

After the feature extraction phase, features derived from both EP and IR are used as inputs for the semantic annotation phase to learn a binary SVM for each tag. We choose SVM as the binary classifier because it has shown excellent performance in similar tasks. In our approach, all places are used for each binary SVM training, i.e., an instance labeled with the specific semantic tag under examination is considered as a positive example, while places without this label serve as negative examples. For instance, places tagged *shopping* are positive examples for a classifier for shopping, but negative examples for a classifier for *nightlife*. For a place to be annotated with such a semantic tag, a binary classifier for each tag is expected to classify the place as an instance of the tag class. As a result, the place will be automatically annotated with proper semantic tags.

4. IR FEATURE EXACTION

To facilitate the extraction of features from implicit relatedness among similar places, we develop a new algorithm that builds a *network of related places* (NRP) to capture the relatedness between places, and further derive the label probability as an IR feature for each tag and each place upon the obtained NRP as follows.

4.1 Network of Related Places

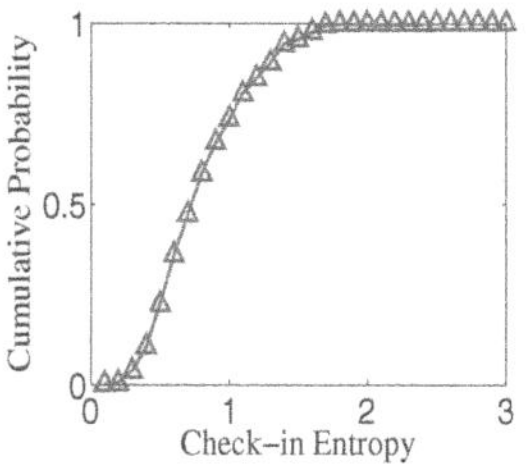

Figure 6: Entropy distribution

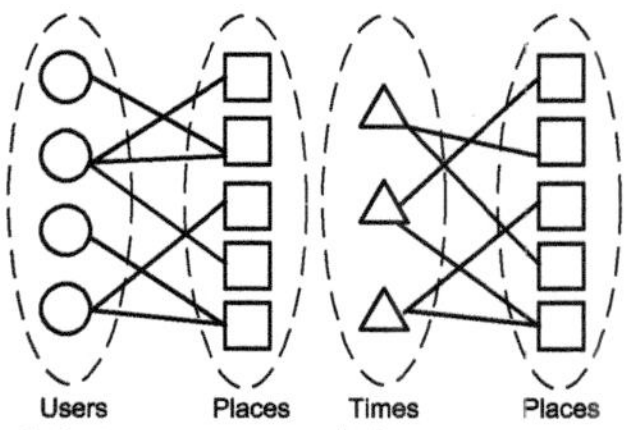

(a) UP graph (b) TP graph

Figure 7: Graph representations of LBSN data

As discussed earlier, we intend to exploit the behavior patterns of LBSN users for semantic annotation of places. By analyzing the *Whrrl* dataset, we find that the check-in activities of Whrrl users do exhibit a strong regularity that supports our idea. In the analysis, we study the diversity of places individual users visit by computing the entropy of semantic tags (in eight activity categories) in their check-ins. The result is shown in Figure 6. Smaller entropy indicates that places checked in by LBSN users usually have similar semantic tags. From the figure, we observe that about 22.07% of users have their check-in entropies smaller than 0.5 and about 75% of users have their entropies smaller than 1. In other words, a great number of Whrrl users visit similar places. Therefore, we build a *user-place (UP)* graph, which consists of users and places connected in accordance with the check-in records. Let $c(u_i, p_j, h_s) \in C$ denote a check-in record describing that user u_i has checked in place p_j at time stamp h_s, where C is the collection of all check-in records. Definition 1 gives the formal definition of the UP graph.

Definition 1. ***User-Place (UP) Graph**, denoted by $G_u(V_u, E_u)$, is an undirected bipartite graph (as illustrated in Figure 7(a)). Here $V_u = U \cup P$, where U and P are the sets of all users and places, respectively, and $E_u = \{e_{i,j} | c(u_i, p_j, \cdot) \in C\}$, where $c(u_i, p_j, \cdot)$ denotes that user u_i has visited place p_i at some time. In this graph, each edge $e_{i,j} \in E_u$ is associated with a weight $w_{i,j}$, denoting how often user u_i has visited place p_i. Formally, $w_{i,j} = \left|\{c(u_i, p_j, h_s)\}\right|$.*

On the other hand, the timing of check-ins at similar places may be similar. Therefore, we build a *temporal-place (TP)* graph, where the time space is discreterized into twenty-four hours, to capture the similarity between places in the temporal dimension. Definition 2 gives the formal definition of the TP graph.

Definition 2. ***Temporal-Place (TP) Graph**, denoted by $G_t(V_t, E_t)$, is an undirected bipartite graph (as illustrated in Figure 7(b)). Here, $V_t = H \cup P$, where H and P are the sets of all times (i.e. hours) and places, respectively, and $E_t = \{e_{j,s} | c(\cdot, p_j, h_s) \in C\}$, where $c(\cdot, p_j, h_s)$ denotes that a user has visited place p_j at time h_s. In this graph, each edge $e_{j,s} \in E_t$ is associated with a weight $w_{j,s}$, denoting how often p_j has been checked in at time h_s. Formally, $w_{j,s} = \left|\{c(u_i, p_j, h_s)\}\right|$.*

In the aforementioned graphs, places are indirectly connected through users and times. In the following, we propose to use the Random Walk and Restart method [27] to estimate the relatedness between pair-wise places in both user and time aspects in order to build a network of related places (NRP), where edges are explicitly established among places according to their relatedness values.

To construct the NRP, we need to derive the relatedness of places from the UP graph and TP graph. In our approach, we first obtain two relatedness values $r^u_{x,y}$ and $r^t_{x,y}$ for every pair of places $p_x, p_y (\in P)$ through Random Walk and Restart (RWR) over the UP and TP graphs, respectively, and then combine them into one relatedness value between place nodes in the NRP. Here we only describe how RWR proceeds on the UP graph since operations on the TP graph are similar. Given a node x, an RWR is performed by randomly following one of its links to another node y of the UP graph based on the transition probabilities of these links, in addition to a probability a to restart at node x. For the UP graph, we prepare a random walk transition matrix that consists of two zero matrices, i.e., user-user matrix (UU) and place-place matrix (PP), and a user-place matrix (actually UP) and its transpose UP^T, where the probability of transiting between a place p_j and a user u_i is proportional to $w_{i,j}$ (in Definition 1). The stationary, or steady-state, probabilities for each pair of nodes can be obtained by recursively processing Random Walk and Restart until convergence. The converged probabilities (i.e., relatedness values) give us the long-term visiting rates from any given node to any other node. In this way, we can calculate the relatedness of all pairs of location nodes, denoted by $r^p_{x,y}(\forall p_x, p_y \in P)$.

Note that the transition matrix for the TP graph can be derived in a similar way. Accordingly, we can obtain two relatedness values $r^u_{x,y}$ and $r^t_{x,y}$ for a pair of places p_x, p_y from the UP and TP graphs. Since both user and time information can help relate the semantic tags of places, we estimate the overall relatedness $r^p_{x,y}$ between place pairs p_x, p_y by integrating them as follows.

$$r^p_{x,y} = \eta r^u_{x,y} + (1-\eta) r^t_{x,y}, \forall p_x, p_y \in P$$

where η is a smoothing factor between 0 and 1. Based on the formula, places checked in by the same user at around the same time show strong relatedness because both relatedness from user and time aspects are considered.

Finally, we build a network of related places (NRP), where each place is connected to places with top-k relatedness values. More specifically, an NRP is defined as follows.

Definition 3. *A network of related places* $NRP = \{P, E\}$ *is a* directed *graph, consisting of only places. For each place* $p_i \in P$*, let* P^k_i *denote the set of top-k related places to* p_i*. Thus,* $E = \{e(x,i) | \forall p_i \in P, p_x \in P^k_i\}$*. Here* $e(x,i)$ *is a directed edge from* p_x *to* p_i*.*

4.2 Label Probability Derivation

As mentioned before, in a real LBSN, only some places have tags. The idea of extracting features from IR is to derive descriptive features of a given place from its "related" and tagged places. The network of related places (NRP) is constructed by connecting similar places together, so we aim to infer the tags of a given place by the tags of its neighbors. In order to derive an IR feature for use in the SVM, we derive the probability for a place to be labeled with a given semantic tag from its neighbors. More specifically, the label probability of a place can be estimated from the label probability of its neighbors recursively [16]. Let $\mathcal{N}_i$ be the set of immediate neighbors which have edges pointing to place p_i, and y_i be a variable denoting a tag of place p_i. For all possible tags $t \in T$, we adopt the relaxation labeling method [24] to find the final $Pr(y_i = t|\mathcal{N}_i)$ $(t \in T)$ for each place p_i. Relaxation labeling freezes the current estimations of each p_i so that, at round $n+1$, all places will be updated based on the estimations from round n. As shown below, the label probability of p_i is calculated by considering both the weighted average of the label probabilities of places in $\mathcal{N}_i$, and the current label probability of p_i itself.

$$Pr^{(n+1)}(y_i = t|\mathcal{N}_i) = \beta_t^{(n+1)} \frac{1}{Z} \sum_{p_j \in \mathcal{N}_i} r^p_{j,i} Pr^{(n)}(y_j = t|\mathcal{N}_j) + (1 - \beta_t^{(n+1)}) Pr^{(n)}(y_i = t|\mathcal{N}_i)$$

where $Z = \sum_{p_j \in \mathcal{N}_i} r^p_{j,i}$ is a normalization term and $r^p_{j,i}$ is the relatedness between places p_j and p_i, and $Pr^{(n)}(y_i = t|\mathcal{N}_i)$ denotes the estimation of $Pr(y_i = t|\mathcal{N}_i)$ at round n. Note that, we define the

$$\beta_t^{(n+1)} = \beta_t^{(n)} \alpha,$$

where $\beta_t^{(0)}$ $(t \in T)$ is a constant between 0 and 1, and α is a decay factor, i.e., $0 < \alpha < 1$. Note that in our daily activities, some of them exhibit more regularity than others (e.g., restaurants against shops). Therefore, we employ different $\beta_t^{(0)}$ values for different semantic tags. Note that different tags have different $\beta_t^{(0)}$ values, where label probability calculation with larger $\beta_t^{(0)}$ settings converges slower than the one with smaller $\beta_t^{(0)}$. More importantly, a larger $\beta_t^{(0)}$ implies that the label probability of a given place should be estimated not only according to the immediate neighbors, but also influenced by places in multi-hops away as there are multiple rounds of calculation. A smaller $\beta_t^{(0)}$ suggests that the label probability is only affected by close-by neighbors as there are very few rounds of calculation.

Here, we discuss how to initialize $Pr^{(0)}(y_i = t|\mathcal{N}_i)$ for each $p_i \in P$. Let $P_{\texttt{test}}$ denote the set of testing places, i.e., places that do not have any semantic tags. The label probability of a testing place is initialized as 0.5; while the label probability of a place already labeled with semantic tags is initialized as 1 or 0 according to the labels. Formally, the label probability is initialized as follows.

$$Pr^{(0)}(y_i = t|\mathcal{N}_i) = \begin{cases} 0.5 & \text{if } p_i \in P_{\texttt{test}} \\ 1 & \text{if } p_i \in P - P_{\texttt{test}} \text{ and } t \in T_i \\ 0 & \text{if } p_i \in P - P_{\texttt{test}} \text{ and } t \notin T_i \end{cases}$$

Once we get the label probability estimation for each possible tag on a place p_i, they are treated as IR features for SVM training. Note that features extracted from IR do not consider the explicit patterns exhibited in each individual place. Thus, in our SAP algorithm, we propose to combine features extracted from both EP and IR to address the problem of semantic annotation of places.

5. PERFORMANCE EVALUATION

In this section, we conduct a comprehensive set of experiments to validate our proposed ideas and evaluate our SAP algorithm in terms of three different feature sets: i) features extracted from EP, ii) features extracted from IR, and iii) combination of i) and ii). Here, we use one of the most popular classification toolkits, LIBSVM [5], as the binary SVM classifier. In the following, we first discuss the collected dataset and the preprocessing steps for experiments, then introduce the metrics employed to evaluate the performance, and finally analyze the experiment results.

5.1 Dataset Description

We crawled the Whrrl website, a representative LBSN, for a month to collect a dataset consisting of 5,892 users, 53,432 places and 199 types of tags.[5] Among those places, 20% of them are not specified with any semantic tags. In the vocabulary of semantic tags, we find that a lot of tag words sharing the same topic could be grouped in the same category. For example, Pizzerias, Coffee, Bakeries, Snacks, Delis, Cafes, Ice Cream and etc, all belong to the same category, namely, *Restaurant & Food*. Without loss of generality, we build a tag hierarchy based on Yelp[6] to merge those 199 semantic tags into 21 categories to simplify the task of place semantic annotation. We show the top eight major categories and their corresponding percentages in Table 1. As shown, *Restaurants & Food*, *Shopping*, *Nightlife* are the most popular check-in places in Whrrl, i.e., 74% of places are within these three categories. Furthermore, we find that about 33.5% of places belong to multiple categories in our dataset.

In order to conduct the experiments, we pre-process this raw dataset to obtain a ground-truth dataset for performance evaluation. First, places in the ground-truth dataset should have category tags, so we filter out those places without category tags. Next, since we are interested in exploring

[5]Unfortunately, we cannot obtain the check-in time in Foursquare. Thus, we conduct the performance evaluation only upon the whrrl dataset.

[6]http://www.yelp.com

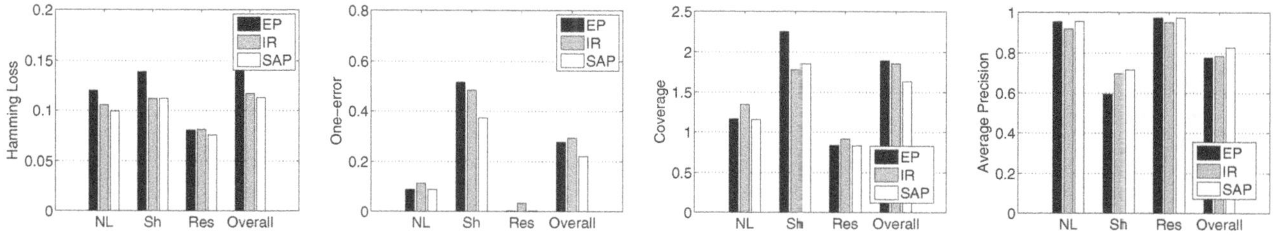

(a) Hamming loss (b) One-error (c) Coverage (d) Average precision

Figure 8: Performance comparison

Category	z%	Category	z%
Restaurants&Food	37%	Hotel & Travel	4%
Shopping	18%	Arts & Entertainment	3%
Nightlife	19%	Health and Medical	2%
Active life	5%	Beauty and Spas	2%

Table 1: Categories and their percentages (z%)

user behaviors, users who have less than 40 check-in records are not included in the ground-truth dataset. Third, we calculate the activity entropies of those users and select the users and their places with entropies less than 0.5 as the dataset to conduct performance evaluation. Moreover, we randomly remove the category tags of $x\%$ places (named testing places, and $x\% = 10\%, 20\%$ and 40% with default value 20%) over the ground-truth dataset. The SAP algorithm is used to recover the category tags for those testing places.

5.2 Performance Metrics

Given a testing place set $P_{\texttt{test}}$, we conduct a performance evaluation by measuring the following four metrics: hamming loss, one-error, coverage and average precision, as they are widely employed in previous multi-label classification studies [25, 29]. Hamming loss aims to measure the accuracy of the predicted tag set against the ground-truth tag set associated with a testing place. The other three metrics concern the ranking of tags annotated by the SAP algorithm, i.e., we consider that SAP performs well when the ground-truth tags are ranked high in the predicted ranked tag list. Note that although we define place semantic annotation as a classification problem, LIBSVM provides probability output [23] (i.e., the probability of the corresponding label), which can be used to rank the semantic tag for each place. Let $Pr(t_x|f_i)$ be the probability output for place p_i being with tag t_x ($\in T$), where f_i denotes the set of features of p_i. According to $Pr(t_x|f_i)$, we get a ranked list of semantic tags, denoted as Y_i, where semantic tags with the highest $Pr(t_x|f_i)$ are ranked at the top.

Hamming loss ($hl_{P_{\texttt{test}}}$): evaluating how many times a place-tag pair is misclassified, i.e., a tag not belonging to the place is predicted or a tag belonging to the place is not predicted. Formally, $hl_{P_{\texttt{test}}} = \frac{1}{|P_{\texttt{test}}|}\sum_{P_i\in P_{\texttt{test}}} \frac{HD(\overrightarrow{T}_i, \overrightarrow{Y}_i)}{|T|}$, where T is the whole tag space, $\overrightarrow{T}_i$ and $\overrightarrow{Y}_i$ are the ground-truth and predicted tag vectors for testing place p_i, and $HD(\overrightarrow{T}_i, \overrightarrow{Y}_i)$ is the hamming distance between $\overrightarrow{T}_i$ and $\overrightarrow{Y}_i$. In the ground-truth tag vector $\overrightarrow{T}_i$ of a place $P_{\texttt{test}}$, the vector element corresponding to a tag t is set to 1 if t is associated with $P_{\texttt{test}}$; otherwise, it is set to 0. The predicted vector $\overrightarrow{Y}_i$ is generated by the SAP algorithm accordingly.

One-error: evaluating how many times the first (or top) ranked predicted tag is not in the ground-truth tag set of the place. Formally, one-error$_{P_{\texttt{test}}} = \frac{1}{|P_{\texttt{test}}|}\sum_{p_i\in P_{\texttt{test}}} f([\arg\max_{t_x\in T} Pr(t_x|f_i)] \notin T_i)$, where for any predicate π, $f(\pi)$ equals 1 if π holds and 0 otherwise.

Coverage: evaluating how far we need, on average, to go down the list of predicted tags (Y_i) in order to recover all the ground-truth tags associated with the place p_i. Let $R(x)$ denote the rank of t_x in the ranked list Y_i generated by SAP. Formally, coverage$_{P_{\texttt{test}}} = \frac{1}{|P_{\texttt{test}}|}\sum_{p_i\in P_{\texttt{test}}} \max_{t_x\in T_i} R(x) - 1$.

Note that one-error and coverage measures are not sufficient for evaluating our SAP algorithm, which may achieve good coverage but suffer high one-error, or vice versa. Thus we introduce the average precision, which takes the ranking positions of all ground-truth tags into consideration, to evaluate the predicted ranked tag list.

Average Precision (AP): Given a place $p_i \in P_{\texttt{test}}$ and a ranked tag list Y_i generated by our SAP algorithm, the average precision for a test place p_i is defined as $AvePrec_i = \sum_{j=1}^{|T_i|} \frac{I(j)(n_j/j)}{|T_i|}$, where $|T_i|$ and n_j denote the total number of ground-truth tags and the number of ground-truth tags before the position $(j+1)$ in the tag list Y_i, respectively, and $I(j)$ is an indicator which takes value 1 if the tag at position j is a ground-truth tag and value 0 otherwise. Therefore, the overall average precision is measured as AP$_{P_{\texttt{test}}} = \frac{1}{|P_{\texttt{test}}|}\sum_{p_i\in P_{\texttt{test}}} AvePrec_i$.

5.3 Experimental Results

As mentioned earlier, we conduct a series of experiments to evaluate the proposed SAP algorithm by comparing three different feature sets. We label the results obtained using features derived from EP and IR by `EP` and `IR`, respectively, and label the results obtained using all features by `SAP`. We also perform sensitivity tests on a number of tuning parameters and different mark-off rates, as well as discreterized and continuous representations of temporal information. Note that we use $\eta = 0.2$, $k = 5$ and β as listed in Table 2 as the default parameter settings throughout the experiment.[7]

Category	β	Category	β
Restaurants&Food	0.9	Hotel & Travel	0.3
Shopping	0.1	Arts & Entertainment	0.1
Nightlife	0.9	Health and Medical	0.1
Active life	0.1	Beauty and Spas	0.1

Table 2: Optimal β settings under $\eta = 0.2$ and $k = 5$

5.3.1 *Overall Performance*

In order to evaluate the performance of our SAP algorithm in detail, we not only show the performance over the entire dataset (labeled with `overall` as show in Figure 8), but also the performance for subsets of testing places in the same category (according to the ground-truth). More specifically, we show three categories of places: *Restaurants & Food* (labeled with `Res`), *Nightlife* (labeled with `NL`) and *Shopping* (labeled with `Sh`). These categories were chosen since they constitute the majority (i.e., about 74%) of all places. As shown in Figure 8, under the default setting,

[7] β refers to $\beta_t^{(0)}$ in this experiment.

SAP shows the best performance consistently, while both EP and IR also demonstrate good strength for the task of semantic annotation in LBSNs. Note that EP performs better than IR for the places in the groups of Res and NL, particularly for the performance metrics one-error, coverage and average precision. The reason is that most people have the same routine for activities in those categories. As a result, those activities have very distinctive characteristics, such as the distribution of check-in times extracted from EP. Thus, EP is able to tag these kinds of places very well. On the other hand, IR shows great strength in labeling places with shopping tags. Regularity of shopping activities of individuals helps to discover the shopping places from other related shopping places, although different people may go shopping at different times.

5.3.2 *Tuning Parameters*

Next, we test the impact of tuning parameters, including β, η and k, on classification performance of SAP for Res, NL and Sh. Notice that the impact of each tuning parameters is tested by fixing all other parameters in default settings.

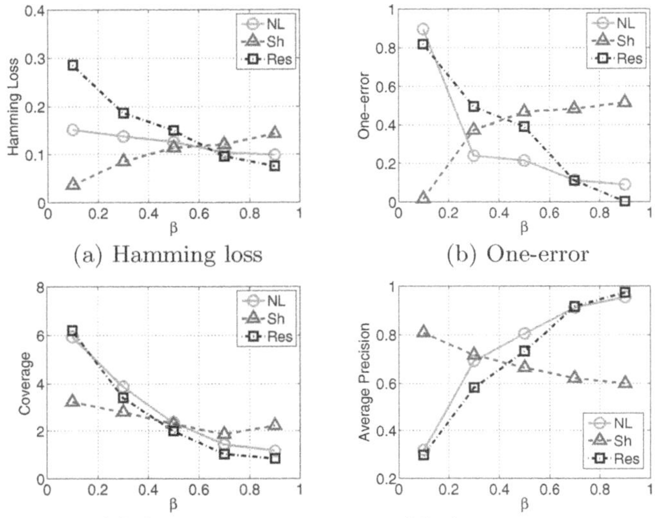

(a) Hamming loss (b) One-error

(c) Coverage (d) Average precision

Figure 9: Impact of β

As mentioned earlier, the optimal settings for the classifiers for different categories are different as shown in Table 2. Note that β tunes the influence from immediate neighboring places and places in multiple hops away. Here, we check the impact of β on the performance of classification, with particular interests in Res, NL and Sh. As shown in Figure 9, β has significant impact on the classification performance for all categories. Both Res and NL show very similar behavior with the variation of β. The best performance setting of β for Res and NL is 0.9, implying that the the label probability of a given place should be estimated not only according to its immediate neighbors but also the places in multiple hops away. The reason is that in an NRP, Res (NL) places are clustered together, thus a larger β can provide more robust and accurate estimation. On the other hand, the best β setting of Sh is 0.1, indicating that the label probability estimation of shopping places is very sensitive to the influence from their neighbors. A smaller β suggests that the label probability of a given place is only affected by immediate neighbors. We find that Sh places are usually not clustered as well as Res because the regularity of Sh activities are not as regular as Res activities. Thus, it is better to only use information from immediate neighbors to estimate label probability for Sh places.

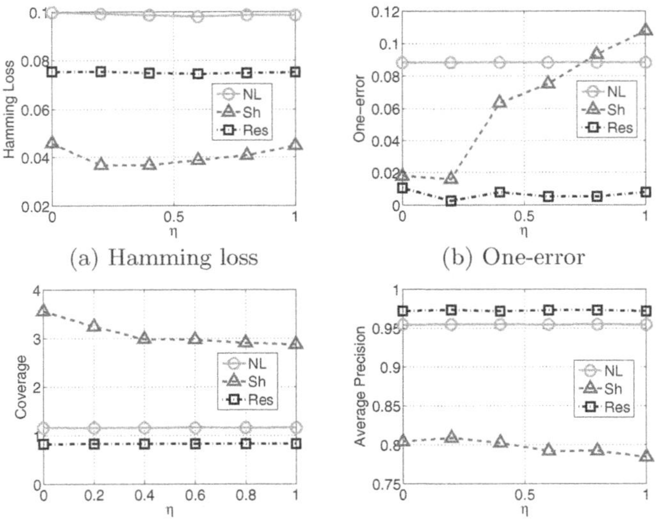

(a) Hamming loss (b) One-error

(c) Coverage (d) Average precision

Figure 10: Impact of η

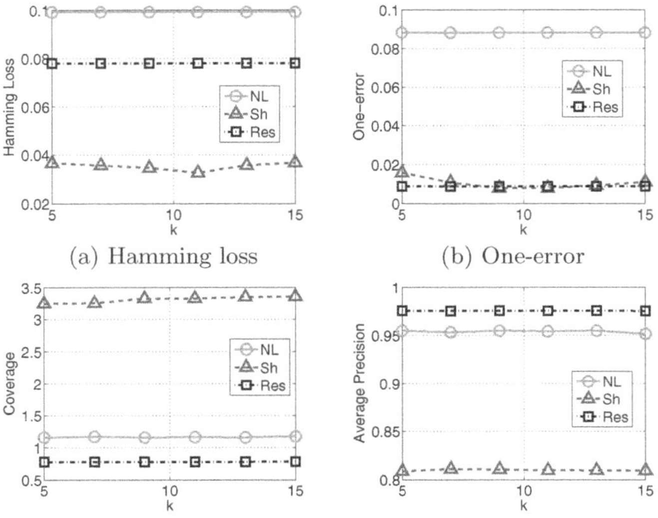

(a) Hamming loss (b) One-error

(c) Coverage (d) Average precision

Figure 11: Impact of k

In Figure 10, we show our test on the parameter η, which is used to tune the weight of place relatedness values computed from user and time aspects. As shown, we find the impact of η on classification of Res and NL places is very limited. A possible reason is that places in both Res and NL categories are well clustered according to either common users or common time. Another reason is that the default β setting for Res and NL is 0.9, which means influence from places even in multiple hops away is contributing to accurate estimation of label probability. The selection of immediate neighbors is not that sensitive to η as long as places in those categories are clustered together. Nevertheless, η does affect the performance for Sh places, as label probabilities of Sh places are mostly affected by immediate neighbors (i.e., $\beta = 0.1$ for Sh activities). As shown in Figure 10, when $\eta = 0.2$, SAP shows the best performance on classification of Sh places in terms of the metrics of hamming loss, one error and average precision; when $\eta = 0.9$, the coverage performance turns out to be the best for Sh places. Accordingly, we consider $\eta = 0.2$ as a proper parameter setting and use it as the default setting throughout the experiment. It implies that both user and time are important to discover similar places through user behavior, particularly for the classification of Sh places. Besides, as the majority of check-ins for a visitor are usually Res places, time information plays an important role to link similar Sh places through the regular behaviors of people.

We further test the tuning parameter k in Figure 11, where k determines the number of neighboring places for a given place in an NRP. Similarly, we find that the variation of k has almost no impact on the classification performance of Res and NL places since places in both categories are clustered together. However, the selection of k affects the performance of classification for Sh places. In Figure 11, the best setting of k for the classification of Sh places is different for various performance metrics. Nevertheless, we find that k should be set to a proper value, in order to avoid the noise introduced by a large number of neighboring places.

5.3.3 *Test on Mark-off Rate*

Here, we investigate the impact of different mark-off rates to the performance of EP, IR and SAP. As shown in Figure 12, the performance of algorithms with different feature sets all degrade to some extent as the mark-off rate increases. Nevertheless, SAP shows the best performance consistently over all mark-off rates as it includes all the features.

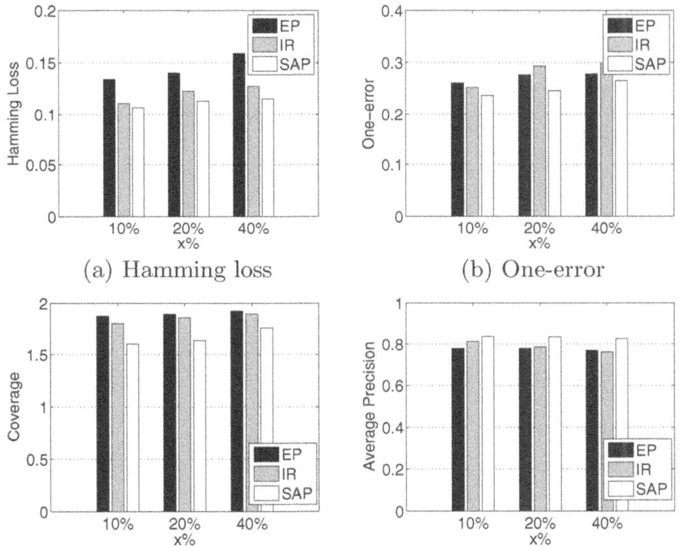

(a) Hamming loss (b) One-error

(c) Coverage (d) Average precision

Figure 12: Impact of mark-off rate, $x\%$

5.3.4 *Test on Continuity of Time*

Check-in time is continuous in the temporal dimension, even though we simplify it as discrete twenty-four hours in the initial design of TP graph. Here, we investigate the impact of the continuity of time on the performance of SAP. In order to capture the continuity of time, we propose a method to smooth hours following the intuition that a user who checks in a place at time h_s, would probably check in similar places around the times h_{s-1} and h_{s+1}, where h_{s-1} and h_{s+1} are adjacent times to h_s. More specifically, for each check-in at place p_j and time h_s, we establish additional m edges to the m most adjacent time nodes beside the time node h_s during the TP graph construction. For example, if h_s presents 20:00 and $m = 1$, we establish edges from the place to the time nodes 19:00 and 21:00, in addition to 20:00 in the construction of the TP graph.

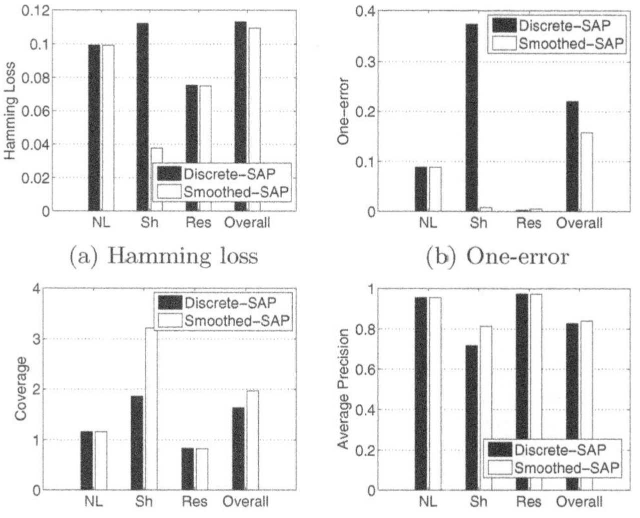

(a) Hamming loss (b) One-error

(c) Coverage (d) Average precision

Figure 13: Discrete Hours Vs. Smoothed Hours

Finally, we test the SAP algorithm, with $m = 1$ and β, η and k following the aforementioned default settings. The SAP algorithm following the initial design is denoted as Discrete-SAP, while the SAP algorithm with smoothed-hour TP graph design denoted by Smoothed-SAP. As shown in Figure 13, the impact on classification of Res and NL places are marginal, since places in those categories have been clustered together with Discrete-SAP. However, considering continuity of time does help improve the classification performance for Sh places, as shopping places checked in around the same time period (although in different hours) are possibly discovered as neighboring places in an NRP.

6. CONCLUSIONS AND FUTURE WORK

In this paper, we investigate the place semantic annotation problem, which aims to automatically annotate all places with semantic tags in location-based social networks. Such tags are a crucial pre-requisite for location search, recommendation services, or data cleaning. In order to tackle this problem, we propose a novel semantic annotation algorithm which learns a binary SVM for each tag. Based on the check-in behavior of users, we extract features of places from two aspects: explicit pattern (EP) at individual places and implicit relatedness (IR) among similar places. Specifically, we extract EP features by aggregating user check-in behaviors to the corresponding places and extract IR features by exploiting the place relatedness exhibited by regularity of user behavior. Finally, we conduct a comprehensive experimental study based on a real dataset collected from *Whrrl*. The results demonstrate the suitability of our approach and also support the assumption that both EP and IR need to be taken into account. Particularly, most people follow the same and distinctive pattern to visit restaurants and nightlife places. Thus, features extracted from EP hold very powerful discriminative capability. On the other hand, against EP, features from IR are excellent for tagging places related to shopping because some individuals exhibit strong patterns in certain shopping activities.

Through our analysis on the Whrrl dataset, we find some semantic tags usually co-occur, e.g., restaurant and bars. In the future, we plan to explore the correlation among semantic tags for the semantic annotation of places. In addition, we plan to include some alternative approaches (e.g., [22]) for comparison and to use multiple large-scale datasets to validate our proposed SAP algorithm.

7. REFERENCES

[1] D. Ashbrook and T. Starner. Using gps to learn significant locations and predict movement across multiple users. *Personal and Ubiquitous Computing*, 7(5):275–286, 2003.

[2] R. Baeza-Yztes and B.Ribeiro-Neto. *Modern Information Retrieval*. Addison Wesley, 1999.

[3] M. R. Boutell, J. Luo, X. Shen, and C. M. Brown. Learning multi-label scene classification. *Pattern Recognition*, 37(9):1757–1771, 2004.

[4] S. Chakrabarti, B. Dom, and P. Indyk. Enhanced hypertext categorization using hyperlinks. In *ACM SIGMOD International Conference on Management of Data (SIGMOD)*, pages 307–318, 1998.

[5] C.-C. Chang and C.-J. Lin. *LIBSVM: a library for support vector machines*, 2001.

[6] A. Clare and R. D. King. Knowledge Discovery in Multi-label Phenotype Data. In *European Conference on Principles and Practice of Knowledge Discovery in Databases (PKDD)*, pages 42–53, 2001.

[7] N. Eagle and A. S. Pentland. Eigenbehaviors: Identifying structure in routine. *Behavioral Ecology and Sociobiology*, 63(7):1057–1066, 2009.

[8] Y. Freund and R. E. Schapire. A Decision-Theoretic Generalization of On-Line Learning and an Application to Boosting. *Journal of Computer and System Sciences (JCSS)*, 55(1):119–139, 1997.

[9] B. Gallagher, H. Tong, T. Eliassi-Rad, and C. Faloutsos. Using ghost edges for classification in sparsely labeled networks. In *ACM SIGKDD Conference on Knowledge Discovery and Data Mining (KDD)*, pages 256–264, 2008.

[10] J. Hightower and G. Borriello. Particle filters for location estimation in ubiquitous computing: A case study. In *ACM International Conference on Ubiquitous Computing (Ubicomp)*, pages 88–106, 2004.

[11] T. Joachims. Text categorization with suport vector machines: Learning with many relevant features. In *European Conference on Machine Learning (ECML)*, pages 137–142, 1998.

[12] C. Keßler, K. Janowicz, and M. Bishr. An agenda for the next generation gazetteer: geographic information contribution and retrieval. In *ACM SIGSPATIAL International Conference on Advances in Geographic Information Systems (GIS)*, pages 91–100, 2009.

[13] T. Li and M. Ogihara. Detecting emotion in music. In *International Society for Music Information Retrieval Conference (ISMIR)*, 2003.

[14] L. Liao, D. J. Patterson, D. Fox, and H. A. Kautz. Learning and inferring transportation routines. *Artifical Intelligence*, 171(5-6):311–331, 2007.

[15] J. Lin, G. Xiang, J. I. Hong, and N. M. Sadeh. Modeling people's place naming preferences in location sharing. In *ACM International Conference on Ubiquitous Computing (UbiComp)*, pages 75–84, 2010.

[16] S. A. Macskassy. Improving learning in networked data by combining explicit and mined links. In *Conference on Artificial Intelligence (AAAI)*, pages 590–595, 2007.

[17] S. A. Macskassy and F. Provost. A simple relational classifier. In *ACM SIGKDD Conference on Knowledge Discovery and Data Mining (KDD) -Workshop (MRDM)*, pages 64–76, 2003.

[18] S. A. Macskassy and F. Provost. Classification in networked data: A toolkit and a univariate case study. *Journal of Machine Learning Research (JMLR)*, 8:935–983, 2007.

[19] A. K. McCallum. Multi-label text classification with a mixture model trained by em. In *Conference on Artificial Intelligence (AAAI) - Workshop on Text Learning*, 1999.

[20] L. McDowell, K. M. Gupta, and D. W. Aha. Cautious inference in collective classification. In *Conference on Artificial Intelligence (AAAI)*, pages 596–601, 2007.

[21] E. Moxley, J. Kleban, and B. S. Manjunath. Spirittagger: a geo-aware tag suggestion tool mined from flickr. In *ACM international conference on Multimedia information retrieval (MIR)*, pages 24–30, 2008.

[22] C. Mülligann, K. Janowicz, M. Ye, and W.-C. Lee. Analyzing spatial-semantic interaction of points of interest in volunteered geographic information. In *International Conference on Spatial Information Theory (COSIT) (to appear)*, 2011.

[23] J. C. Platt. Probabilistic outputs for support vector machines and comparisons to regularized likelihood methods. In *Advance in Large Margin Classifiers*, pages 61–74. MIT Press, 1999.

[24] A. Rosenfeld, R. Hummel, and S. Zucker. Scene labeling by relaxation operations. *IEEE Transactions on Systems, Man, and Cybernetics*, 6:420–433, 1976.

[25] R. E. Schapire and Y. Singer. Boostexter: A boosting-based systemfor text categorization. *Machine Learning*, 39:135–168, 2000.

[26] B. Taskar, E. Segal, and D. Koller. Probabilistic Classification and Clustering in Relational Data. In *International Joint Conferences on Artificial Intelligence (IJCAI)*, pages 870–878, 2001.

[27] H. Tong, C. Faloutsos, and J.-Y. Pan. Fast random walk with restart and its applications. In *Industrial Conference on Data Mining (ICDM)*, pages 613–622, 2006.

[28] M. Ye, P. Yin, W.-C. Lee, and D. L. Lee. Exploiting Geographical Influence for Collaborative Point-of-Interest Recommendation. In *Annual International ACM SIGIR Conference on Research and Development in Information Retrieval (SIGIR) (to appear)*, 2011.

[29] M.-L. Zhang and Z.-H. Zhou. A k-nearest neighbor based algorithm for multi-label classification. In *IEEE International Conference on Granular Computing (GrC)*, pages 718–721, 2005.

Sparsification of Influence Networks

Michael Mathioudakis[1*] mathiou@cs.toronto.edu
Francesco Bonchi[2] bonchi@yahoo-inc.com
Carlos Castillo[2] chato@yahoo-inc.com
Aristides Gionis[2] gionis@yahoo-inc.com
Antti Ukkonen[2] aukkonen@yahoo-inc.com

[1]Computer Science Department, University of Toronto, Canada
[2]Yahoo! Research, Barcelona, Spain

ABSTRACT

We present SPINE, an efficient algorithm for finding the "backbone" of an influence network. Given a social graph and a log of past propagations, we build an instance of the *independent-cascade model* that describes the propagations. We aim at reducing the complexity of that model, while preserving most of its accuracy in describing the data.

We show that the problem is inapproximable and we present an optimal, dynamic-programming algorithm, whose search space, albeit exponential, is typically much smaller than that of the brute force, exhaustive-search approach. Seeking a practical, scalable approach to sparsification, we devise SPINE, a greedy, efficient algorithm with practically little compromise in quality.

We claim that sparsification is a fundamental data-reduction operation with many applications, ranging from visualization to exploratory and descriptive data analysis. As a proof of concept, we use SPINE on real-world datasets, revealing the *backbone* of their influence-propagation networks. Moreover, we apply SPINE as a pre-processing step for the *influence-maximization* problem, showing that computations on sparsified models give up little accuracy, but yield significant improvements in terms of scalability.

Categories and Subject Descriptors: H.2.8 [**Database Management**]: Database Applications - *Data Mining*
General Terms: Algorithms
Keywords: Social Networks, Influence, Propagation

1. INTRODUCTION

For many scenarios of network analysis, sparsification is a fundamental data-reduction operation that equips the data analyst with the ability to visualize, explore, digest, and interpret more easily the available data. In addition, sparsification helps in reducing the noise in the data and in avoiding over-fitting, thus allowing to build more accurate models.

*Part of this work was done while the first author was visiting Yahoo! Research Barcelona, under the Yahoo! internship program.

KDD'11, August 21–24, 2011, San Diego, California, USA.

In this paper we study a sparsification framework that is appropriate for analyzing information propagation in social networks. We aim at eliminating a large number of links in the network, and preserving only the links that play an important role on how information propagates. The importance of a link is measured by its ability to explain observed propagations. Sparsifying a network with respect to a log of "information actions" can be seen as revealing the *backbone* of information propagation in the network.

A high-level description of our approach is the following. We are given a social network, that is, a set of "friendship" links or "follower-followee" links. Additionally, we assume that we are given a log of actions performed by the nodes of the network. Such actions may include posting information "memes", joining an online community or an interest group, buying a paid subscription in an on-line service, and so on. We assume that those actions have propagated in the network via the *independent cascade* model [18]. The maximum likelihood parameters of this model can be found for instance by using the EM algorithm of Saito et al. [28]. Given the parameters we formulate the sparsification problem, which is the focus of this paper: we ask to preserve the k most important links in the model, i.e., the set of k links that maximize the likelihood of the observed data. Here k might be an input parameter specified by the data analyst, or alternatively k might be set automatically following common model-selection practice.

Our framework has a number of interesting applications.

Propagation characterization: Sparsifying separately different information topics can help us answer questions such as: "What distinguishes the way important news propagate, from the way funny "memes" do?" or "Is there any structural difference between the backbone of actual news and that of false rumors?"

Feed ranking: As users in social networks receive a continuous feed of information, ranking the most interesting feeds is becoming an important problem [15]. Sparsification provides a useful feature in this ranking problem by highlighting the most important links.

Viral marketing: Finding the set of users to target in order to maximize the spread of influence is a problem that has received a lot of attention, yet there are still serious computational challenges [3, 4]. As we show in Section 7, sparsification yields significant improvement for this problem, in terms of efficiency and scalability, while sacrificing little in terms of accuracy.

Even though there has been a lot of work recently on studying information propagation, mostly devoted either to empirical analysis of real-world propagations [1, 14, 19, 22], or to devise methods for influence maximization [6, 18, 27], not much effort has been devoted to develop techniques to mine large logs of propagation traces. On the other hand, there is extensive literature on the problem of network simplification, but the scenarios assumed are different than the problem we study in this paper. We review this literature in the next section.

Our contributions are summarized as follows.

- Given a social network and a log of actions, we study the problem of pruning the network to a prefixed extent while maximizing the likelihood of generating the propagation traces in the log (Sections 3 and 4).
- We show that our problem is **NP**-hard to approximate within any multiplicative factor (Section 4).
- We show that sparsification can be decomposed into a number of subproblems equal to the number of the nodes in the network. We then present an exponential, but optimal, dynamic programming algorithm, whose search space is typically much smaller than the brute force one, but still impracticable for graphs having nodes with a large in-degree (Section 5.1).
- We devise SPINE (*Sparsification of influence networks*), a greedy algorithm that achieves efficiency with practically little compromise in quality. SPINE is structured in two phases. During the first phase it selects a set of arcs D_0 that yields a finite log-likelihood; during the second phase, it greedily seeks a solution of maximum log-likelihood. The solution returned by SPINE is guaranteed to be "close" to the optimal among the subnetworks that contain arcs D_0 (Section 5.2).
- We show that SPINE identifies efficiently sparse networks of high or even optimal likelihood (Section 6).
- We apply SPINE as a pre-processing step for the problem of *influence maximization*, showing that computations on the sparse network give up little accuracy, but yield significant improvements in terms of efficiency and scalability (Section 7).

2. RELATED WORK

The study of information diffusion in social networks has a long history in social sciences. Early work studied the adoption of medical and agricultural innovations [5, 32]. Later, marketing researchers investigated the "word-of-mouth" diffusion process for *viral marketing* [2, 9, 17, 23].

From a computational perspective, a basic problem in viral marketing is that of *influence maximization*: given a social network, find k nodes to target in order to maximize the spread of influence. The first algorithmic treatment of the problem was provided by Domingos and Richardson [6, 27], who modeled the diffusion process in terms of Markov random fields, and proposed heuristic solutions to the problem. Subsequently, Kempe et al. [18] studied the influence-maximization problem for a different family of influence models. Part of their contribution was to provide approximation algorithms for the independent cascade model, which we also adopt in this paper. Recent work [3, 4, 21] improves the efficiency of influence maximization.

Conceptually, our work can be collocated with works on network simplification, the goal of which is to identify subnetworks that preserve properties of a given network. Toivonen et al. [31, 33], for instance, prune edges while keeping the original quality of best paths between all pairs of nodes. Here, quality is defined on path-based concepts, such as shortest path or maximum flow. Misiolek and Chen [24] prune arcs while maintaining the source-to-sink flow for each pair of nodes. In the theory community, the notion of k-spanner refers to a sparse subgraph that maintains the distances in the original graph up to a factor of k. The problem is to find the sparsest k-spanner [7]. In *pathfinder networks* [26, 29] the approach is to select weighted edges that do not violate the triangular inequality. Moreover, Fung et al. [35] study *cut-sparsifiers*, i.e. subsets of edges that preserve cuts up to a multiplicative error.

Serrano et al. [30], and Foti et al. [8], focus on weighted networks and select edges that represent statistically significant deviations with respect to a null model. In a similar setting, Arenas et al. [34] select edges that preserve modularity, a measure that quantifies quality of community detection.

The approach we take in this paper is substantially different than the approach considered in the above papers. One major difference is that the problem of sparsification is defined in terms of *observed activity* in the network, and not just in terms of the structural properties of the network.

A recent line of work, perhaps the closest to ours, assumes instead that the propagations are known, but the network is not [10, 11]. In their research, Gomez-Rodriguez et al. assume that connections between nodes cannot be observed, and they use observed traces of activity to infer a sparse, "hidden" network of information diffusion. Although similar to the sparsified networks we produce, in their setting the links are only inferred and might potentially not exist in the real, but unobserved, network. Instead, in our setting, connections between nodes are explicitly declared and *known* (as in current online social network services, for example), and our goal is to find the most important connections, and to obtain the network backbone.

Papers that share our approach of simultaneously mining the social graph and network activity include the work of Goyal et al. [12], on extracting frequent patterns of influence, and the works of Goyal et al. [13] and Saito et al. [28], on learning influence models from observed activity. However, they do not consider any notion of sparsification or other summarization operation.

3. INFLUENCE MODEL

Consider a social network $G = (V, D)$, where nodes V correspond to individuals and *directed* arcs D between nodes represent social connections. For two nodes u and v in V, arc (u, v) denotes that individual v knows, is socially connected to, or *follows* individual u. Individuals perform actions, and actions can *propagate* across the network. For example, social network users who read a news story on the New York Times may decide to share the story with their friends—who, in turn, may decide to spread the news to their own friends, and so on, contributing to the propagation of the story across the network. In this paper, we assume that the propagation of actions follows the independent cascade model [18]. According to this model, every arc (u, v) in D is associated with a probability $p(u, v)$ and propagations unfold in discrete time steps.

To be specific, let us consider the propagation of one action α across the network. According to the independent cascade model, if node u performs an action α in time step

t and node v follows u, then u makes a single attempt to influence v, and succeeds with probability $p(u, v)$. The probability of success is independent of other nodes that may attempt to influence v. If it is successful, and v has not previously performed α, then v performs α in time step $(t+1)$. Note that, according to this model, several nodes may attempt to influence v, but v may perform α at most once.

Additionally, we assume that propagations are initiated by a special node $\Omega \in V$ (Figure 1(a)) that has the following two properties: *(i)* it performs α before any other node, and *(ii)* is followed by all other nodes in V. Node Ω models sources of influence that are external to the network, and thus $p(\Omega, v)$ is the probability that a propagation starts from node v.

The independent cascade model generates sequences of activations, or *traces*, as we call them. Traces of different actions are generated independently. Note that, given the trace of action α, it may not be possible to tell which node influenced a particular node v to perform α, since more than one node may have attempted to do so. In the example of Figure 1(b), for instance, one of nodes: u_1 or u_2, succeeded to influence v. We say that u_1 and u_2 *possibly influenced* v. On the other hand, neither u_3 nor u_4 could have influenced v, because then, according to the independent cascade model, v would have performed α at time t.

Every trace generated by the independent cascade model is associated with a likelihood value. Consider the trace of action α. Let $F_\alpha^+(v)$ be the set of nodes that *possibly influenced* v, and $F_\alpha^-(v)$ the set of nodes that *definitely failed to influence* v. Then, the likelihood $L_\alpha(G)$ of the trace can be written as

$$L_\alpha(G) = \prod_{v \in V} P_\alpha^+(v) \cdot P_\alpha^-(v), \tag{1}$$

where

$$P_\alpha^+(v) = \begin{cases} 1 & \text{, if } F_\alpha^+(v) = \emptyset, \\ 1 - \prod_{u \in F_\alpha^+(v)} (1 - p(u, v)) & \text{, otherwise} \end{cases}$$

expresses the likelihood that at least one of the nodes in $F_\alpha^+(v)$ succeed to influence v, and

$$P_\alpha^-(v) = \prod_{u \in F_\alpha^-(v)} (1 - p(u, v)).$$

the likelihood that all nodes in $F_\alpha^-(v)$ fail. For the rest of the paper, following common practice, we opt to work with log-likelihood, due to its better numerical behavior

$$\log L_\alpha(G) = \sum_{v \in V} \left(\log P_\alpha^+(v) + \log P_\alpha^-(v) \right). \tag{2}$$

We now describe how to estimate the probabilities $p(u, v)$ of the independent cascade model from a set of traces. Consider a set of actions $\mathcal{A}$. For each action $\alpha \in \mathcal{A}$ we observe its propagation trace, and assume that all traces are generated by the same model. Following [28], the probability values $p(u, v)$ that maximize the total log-likelihood

$$\log L(G) = \sum_{\alpha \in \mathcal{A}} \log L_\alpha(G)$$

can be computed using the following iterative formula

$$p^{(k+1)}(u, v) = \frac{p^{(k)}(u, v)}{|A_{v|u}^+| + |A_{v|u}^-|} \sum_{\alpha \in A_{v|u}^+} \frac{1}{P_\alpha^+(v)}, \tag{3}$$

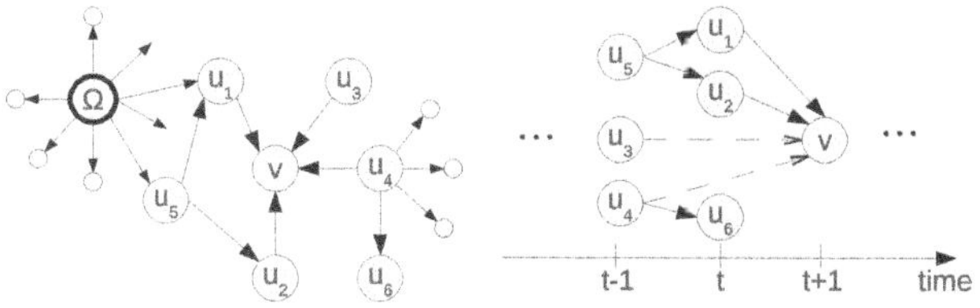

(a) Social Network (b) Trace

Figure 1: (a) Social network. An arc (u, v) indicates that v is a *follower* of u and repeats u's actions with probability $p(u, v)$. Node Ω initiates propagations of actions and influences all nodes. (b) Action trace. Solid-line arrows indicate possible influence, while dash-line arrows indicate failed influence attempts.

where actions in set

$$A_{v|u}^+ = \{\alpha \in \mathcal{A} \mid F_\alpha^+(v) \ni u\}$$

have traces where u possibly influenced v, and actions in set

$$A_{v|u}^- = \{\alpha \in \mathcal{A} \mid F_\alpha^-(v) \ni u\}$$

have traces where u definitely failed to influence v.

According to the independent cascade model, actions propagate in discrete time steps. In real-world scenarios, however, users can freely choose *when* to propagate actions of the people they follow. Therefore, to use the independent cascade model in practice and estimate probabilities $p(u, v)$ in real-world datasets, we can not rely on discrete time steps.

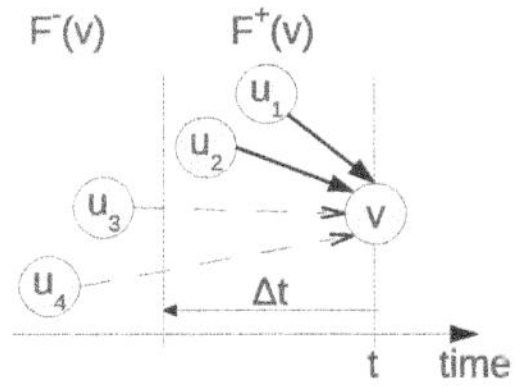

Figure 2: Delay Threshold

Instead, we may use a delay threshold Δt (Figure 2) for this purpose. Specifically, suppose that node v performs action α at time $t_\alpha(v)$. Then, the set $F_\alpha^+(v)$ of nodes that possibly influenced v are the nodes that performed action α before v and within Δt time, that is,

$$F_\alpha^+(v) = \{u : (u, v) \in D \mid t_\alpha(v) - \Delta t \leq t_\alpha(u) < t_\alpha(v)\}.$$

In the scenario of Figure 2, for example, $F_\alpha^+(v) = \{u_1, u_2\}$. The set $F_\alpha^-(v)$ of nodes that definitely failed to influence v is defined similarly:

$$F_\alpha^-(v) = \{u : (u, v) \in D \mid t_\alpha(u) < t_\alpha(v) - \Delta t\}.$$

In the scenario of Figure 2, for example, $F_\alpha^-(v) = \{u_3, u_4\}$.

Note that if v does not perform α, then we write $t_\alpha(v) = \infty$ and have $F_\alpha^+(v) = \emptyset$. Note also that, in the special case of $\Delta t = \infty$, always one of the two sets $F_\alpha^+(v)$ and $F_\alpha^-(v)$ is empty. Specifically, if v does not perform α, then $F_\alpha^+(v) = \emptyset$, while if it does, then $F_\alpha^-(v) = \emptyset$.

4. SPARSIFICATION

Given an influence model learned (as in Section 3) from a social network $G = (V, D)$ and propagation traces for a set of actions $\mathcal{A}$, our goal is to identify a "backbone" of arcs that are most important for the propagation of actions $\mathcal{A}$. Specifically, we aim to identify a sparse subnetwork G_s of G, that consists of the k arcs that are most likely to have generated the observed traces of actions $\mathcal{A}$.

Formally, we define a network $G_s = (V, D_s)$ to be a *sparse* subnetwork of $G = (V, D)$ if its arcs D_s are a subset of D, $D_s \subseteq D$, and the probabilities $p_s(u, v)$ are equal with the corresponding probabilities $p(u, v)$ of the network G, that is, $p_s(u, v) = p(u, v)$, for all (u, v) in D_s. The problem of sparsifying network G is defined as follows.

PROBLEM 1 (SPARSIFICATION). *Given a network $G = (V, D)$ with probabilities $p(u, v)$ on the arcs, a set $\mathcal{A}$ of action traces, and an integer k, find a sparse subnetwork $G_s = (V, D_s)$ of G of size $|D_s| = k$, so that the log-likelihood function $\log L(G_s)$ is maximized.*

Notice that Problem 1 is not solved by selecting the k arcs (u, v) in D with the largest probability values $p(u, v)$. As a counter-example, consider the network $G = (V, D)$ and traces of actions $\mathcal{A} = \{\alpha_1, \alpha_2, \alpha_3\}$, shown in Figure 3. Based on the three traces, we obtain the maximum likelihood estimates $p(u_1, v) = 1.0$ and $p(u_2, v) = 0.5$. Then, for $k = 3$, the best sparse model $G_s = (V, D_s)$ is the one with

$$D_s = \{(\Omega, u_1), (\Omega, u_2), (u_2, v)\} = D \setminus \{(u_1, v)\}, \quad (4)$$

even though $p(u_2, v) < p(u_1, v)$. To see why, notice that, for example, the alternative option of

$$D_s = \{(\Omega, u_1), (\Omega, u_2), (u_1, v)\} = D \setminus \{(u_2, v)\} \quad (5)$$

leads to zero likelihood ($\log L(G_s) = -\infty$). This is because the trace of action α_2 is impossible without arc (u_2, v). On the other hand, all three traces are possible in the absence of the arc (u_1, v).

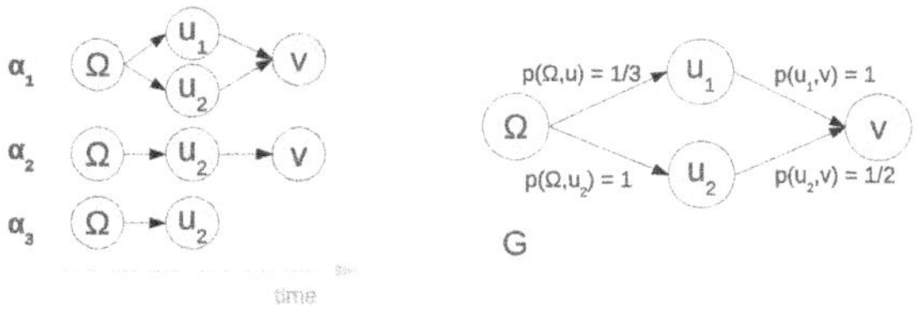

Figure 3: Sparsification is not solved by selecting the k arcs with largest probability value.

Complexity. By the definition of the independent cascade model, for a sparse network $G_s = (V, D_s)$ to have finite log-likelihood, $\log L(G_s) > -\infty$, it is necessary that the traces of all actions $\mathcal{A}$ are possible for its set of arcs D_s. This means that if node v performs an action α in $\mathcal{A}$, then D_s must include an arc from at least one of the nodes F_α^+ that possibly influenced v. Our argument is formally stated below.

LEMMA 1. *Deciding whether Problem 1 has finite solution is* **NP**-*hard.*

Proof. We obtain a reduction from the `Hitting Set` problem. We first remind the `Hitting Set` problem: Given a collection of sets $\mathcal{S} = \{S_1, \ldots, S_m\}$ over a universe of n elements $U = \{1, \ldots, n\}$ (i.e., $S_j \subseteq U$), a hitting set for $\mathcal{S}$ is a set $H \subseteq U$ that intersects all sets in $\mathcal{S}$, that is, $H \cap S_j \neq \emptyset$ for all $j = 1, \ldots, m$. Given a set collection $\mathcal{S}$ and an integer k, it is **NP**-hard to decide whether there is a hitting set H for $\mathcal{S}$ that has size at most $|H| \leq k$.

Now, consider an instance of the `Hitting Set` problem, i.e. consider a collection $\mathcal{S} = \{S_1, \ldots, S_m\}$ and an integer k. We create an instance of our problem as follows. Our graph $G = (V, D)$ has $n + 1$ nodes, namely, $V = U \cup \{n + 1\} = \{1, \ldots, n, n + 1\}$. The nodes from 0 to n have no ancestors, while the node $n + 1$ has all nodes from 0 to n as ancestors. Thus $D = \{(i, n + 1) \mid i = 1, \ldots, n\}$. For all the edges in D we set $p(i, n + 1) = 1$. Next, for each set $S_j \in \mathcal{S}$ we consider an action α that was performed by nodes $S_j \cup \{n + 1\}$.

First consider a hitting set H of $\mathcal{S}$, with $|H| \leq k$. Take the sparsified graph $G_s = (V, D_s)$ with $D_s = \{(i, n+1) \mid i \in H\}$. It is $|D_s| \leq k$. Furthermore for each action $\alpha \in \mathcal{A}$ the set D_s contains at least one edge from a parent of node $n + 1$ that is also influenced by α. Given that all arcs have probability 1 it follows that the probability $P_\alpha^+(n+1)$ is equal to 1, and consecutively the total log-likelihood is finite.

Conversely, for any sparsified graph with at most k edges and finite log-likelihood it should be the case that for each action $\alpha \in \mathcal{A}$ the set D_s contains at least one edge from a parent of node $n + 1$ that also performed α. Thus the set $H = \{i \mid (i, n + 1) \in D_s\}$ is a hitting set for $\mathcal{S}$. □

Lemma 1 leads to the following hardness results.

THEOREM 1. *Problem 1 is* **NP**-*hard.*

THEOREM 2. *Approximating Problem 1 up to any multiplicative factor is* **NP**-*hard.*

The latter Theorem follows from the simple observation that obtaining a multiplicative-factor approximation is at least as difficult as obtaining a finite solution. Theorem 1 is a special case of Theorem 2.

5. ALGORITHMS

5.1 An optimal algorithm

A brute-force approach to acquire an optimal solution to Problem 1 is to enumerate all possible subsets of arcs $D_s \subseteq D$ of size k, and select the network $G_s = (V, D_s)$ with maximum log-likelihood $\log L(G_s)$. This approach is exponential in the size of D and obviously does not scale.

Instead, we describe an optimal, dynamic programming algorithm, OPTIMALSPARSE, that makes relatively limited use of exhaustive enumeration. The algorithm is based on the observation that an optimal solution can be obtained by dividing Problem 1 into $|V|$ sub-problems, where V is the set of nodes of G, and combining their solutions. To see this, let us re-write log-likelihood as

$$\begin{aligned} \log L(G) &= \sum_{\alpha \in \mathcal{A}} \log L_\alpha(G) = \\ &= \sum_{\alpha \in \mathcal{A}} \sum_{v \in V} \left(\log P_\alpha^+(v) + \log P_\alpha^-(v)\right) \\ &= \sum_{v \in V} \sum_{\alpha \in \mathcal{A}} \left(\log P_\alpha^+(v) + \log P_\alpha^-(v)\right). \end{aligned} \quad (6)$$

Observe that the inner sum of the above formula corresponds to a single node v. Also, recall that the probabilities $P_\alpha^+(v)$ and $P_\alpha^-(v)$ are "local" to node v, meaning that they depend only on influence probabilities on arcs from the parent nodes of v in G. Denote the set of these arcs by D_v, and observe that we can compute $P_\alpha^+(v)$ and $P_\alpha^-(v)$ for an arbitrary subset $X_v \subseteq D_v$ simply by omitting probabilities on edges not present in X_v. This way we can define

$$\lambda(X_v) = \sum_{\alpha \in \mathcal{A}} \left(\log P_\alpha^+(v|X_v) + \log P_\alpha^-(v|X_v)\right), \quad (7)$$

for $X_v \subseteq D_v$. The log-likelihood of the full model can thus be written as $\log L(G) = \sum_v \lambda(D_v)$. Therefore we consider the following sub-problem for each node $v \in V$.

PROBLEM 2. *Given an integer b, identify a subset of arcs $D_v^b \subseteq D_v$ of size b, such that $\lambda(D_v^b)$ is maximized.*

Problem 2 is solved by exhaustive enumeration of subsets $D_v^b \subseteq D_v$ of size b. The solution space increases exponentially with the size of D_v, but is typically much smaller than that of the brute-force approach, which increases exponentially with the size of D.

Algorithm OPTIMALSPARSE uses dynamic programming to compute an optimal solution D_s to Problem 1 from optimal solutions of Problem 2. Specifically, let $V = \{v_1, v_2, \ldots\}$ be an enumeration of the nodes. For each node v_i, consider the solution $D_{v_i}^b$ to Problem 2 for all integers $b \in [1, k]$ (Algorithm 1, Lines 1-3). OPTIMALSPARSE then proceeds sequentially over nodes V (Algorithm 1, Line 5). At the end of the i-th step, it has processed nodes $v_1, v_2, \ldots, v_i$ and, for each integer $m \in [1, k]$ (Algorithm 1, Line 6) it identifies one number b for each node $v \in \{v_1, v_2, \ldots, v_i\}$ such that $b_1 + b_2 + \ldots + b_i = m$ and the sum

$$\Lambda(i, m) = \lambda(D_{v_1}^{b_1}) + \lambda(D_{v_2}^{b_2}) + \ldots + \lambda(D_{v_i}^{b_i})$$

is maximized (Algorithm 1, Lines 7-8). By construction, $\Lambda(|V|, k)$ contains the maximum log-likelihood value for Problem 1. The optimal solution D_s is computed with standard back-tracking (not described in Algorithm 1, in interest of brevity).

Algorithm 1 OptimalSparse

1: **for** $i = 1$ **to** $|V|$ **do**
2:   **for** $b = 1$ **to** k **do**
3:     compute optimal $D_{v_i}^b$ (Problem 2)
4: **array** Λ, **initialize** $\Lambda(0, m) = 0$; $m = 1$ **to** k
5: **for** $i = 1$ **to** $|V|$ **do**
6:   **for** $m = 1$ **to** k **do**
7:     $b_i := \arg\max\{\lambda(D_{v_i}^{b_i}) + \Lambda(i-1, m-b_i)\}$
8:     $\Lambda(i, m) := \lambda(D_{v_i}^{b_i}) + \Lambda(i-1, m-b_i)$
9: **return** $\Lambda(|V|, k)$

5.2 A greedy algorithm: SPINE

OPTIMALSPARSE follows a more sophisticated approach than brute-force, but is still prohibitively expensive for graphs that have nodes with large in-degree. In this section, we describe SPINE, a greedy algorithm for Problem 1. Although Problem 1 is inapproximable in the general case, we find experimentally that the quality of the results obtained by SPINE is comparable to the that of OPTIMALSPARSE.

SPINE produces a solution D_s to Problem 1 in k steps, adding to D_s one arc at each step. Those k steps are divided in two phases: during the first phase, SPINE aims to identify a solution D_0 of finite log-likelihood; during the second phase, it greedily seeks a solution of maximum log-likelihood. This two-phase approach is inspired by the observation that Problem 1 is at least as difficult as identifying a solution of finite log-likelihood.

First phase. Following the discussion on complexity of Problem 1 (Section 4), we look for a solution with finite $\log L$ by solving an instance of `Hitting Set` — that is, for each node $v \in V$ we seek for a hitting set of collection

$$C(v) = \{D_\alpha^+(v) \neq \emptyset \,;\, \alpha \in \mathcal{A}\}.$$

As `Hitting Set` is **NP**-hard, we employ the greedy approximation algorithm described in [16] (Algorithm 2, Lines 1-8). According to that algorithm, arcs (u, v) are ordered by the number $n(u, v)$ of actions for which u possibly influenced v

$$n(u, v) = \left|\{D_\alpha^+(v) \in C(v) \,;\, (u, v) \in D_\alpha^+(v)\}\right|. \quad (8)$$

At each step, the arc (u, v) with the maximum number $n(u, v)$ is selected (Algorithm 2, Lines 6-7) and all sets $D_\alpha^+(v)$ that contain (u, v) are ignored for the rest of this process (Algorithm 2, Line 8). The first phase ends when either the limit of k arcs is reached, or $\lambda(D_v^b)$ for $b \leq k$ selected arcs becomes finite for the first time.

Second phase. Let D_0 be the set of arcs selected by the end of the first phase, and let $G_0 = (V, D_0)$ be the associated sparse network. If $|D_0| < k$, then we still need to select $k - |D_0|$ more arcs. One viable approach to select the remaining $k - |D_0|$ arcs is to continue in a fashion similar to the OPTIMALSPARSE algorithm: divide the problem into $|V|$ subproblems, one for each node in the graph, solve optimally each subproblem for all values of $b = 1, \ldots, k - |D_0|$, and then combine the solutions of the subproblems with dynamic programming. However, due to the exhaustive search and the dynamic programming, such an approach would not be scalable. To obtain a scalable solution we propose to speed up the computation by replacing both steps – exhaustive search and the dynamic programming – with a greedy process. We choose the remaining $k - |D_0|$ arcs by selecting greedily at each step the arc that offers the largest increase in log-likelihood (Algorithm 2, Lines 9-15).

For a detailed description, let D_v and λ be defined as above, and consider a table X, where $X_v(i)$ is the subset of D_v that the greedy algorithm would add the ith step when maximizing λ. More formally, we have

$$X_v(i) = \begin{cases} \emptyset & \text{if } i = 0, \\ X_v(i-1) \cup e_v(i) & \text{otherwise,} \end{cases}$$

where $e_v(i) = \arg\max_{e \in U_v}\{\lambda(X_v(i-1) \cup e)\}$, and $U_v = D_v \setminus X_v(i-1)$. Also, let $H_v(i)$ denote the marginal gain for λ when the ith edge is added, that is, let

$$H_v(i) = \begin{cases} 0 & \text{if } i = 0, \\ \lambda(X_v(i)) - \lambda(X_v(i-1)) & \text{otherwise.} \end{cases}$$

SPINE maintains the X_v and H_v structures for every v, and at every step chooses the v^* and i^* that maximize $H_{v^*}(i^*)$ (line 13). The edge $e_{v^*}(i^*)$ will be added to the solution, and we compute $X_{v^*}(i^*+1)$ and $H_{v^*}(i^*+1)$. Computing $X_v(i+1)$ given $X_v(i)$ is an $O(|D_v|)$ operation, while inserting and extracting from Q are $O(\log|V|)$. The worst-case complexity of the 2nd phase of SPINE is thus $O\big(k(\max_v(|D_v|) + \log|V|)\big)$.

We have the following approximation guarantee.

LEMMA 2. *Let D_{opt} be a superset of D_0 that contains k arcs and that induces a subgraph $G_{\text{opt}} = (V, D_{\text{opt}})$ of G with maximum log-likelihood. Also, let D_{sp} by the set of arcs returned by* SPINE *and let $G_{\text{sp}} = (V, D_{\text{sp}})$ be the induced subgraph. That is, D_{sp} is also a superset of D_0 and it has k arcs. Then, provided that $\log L(G_0) > -\infty$, we have*

$$\log L(G_{\text{sp}}) \geq \frac{1}{e} \log L(G_0) + (1 - \frac{1}{e}) \log L(D_{\text{opt}}). \quad (9)$$

Proof. We use a well-known theorem by Nemhauser et al. [25] on maximizing submodular set functions. A set function f is submodular, when for any $S \subseteq T$ we have $f(S \cup u) - f(S) \geq f(T \cup u) - f(T)$. The theorem in [25] states that for non-negative set functions f, with $f(\emptyset) = 0$, we have $f(X_k^A) \geq (1 - 1/e) f(X_k^*)$, where X_k^* is the optimal k-sized solution, and X_k^A a solution likewise of size k that is constructed by starting from $\emptyset$, and at each step adding the item that maximizes the increase in the value of f. Observe that this greedy strategy is also used by SPINE when adding edges to the sparse model.

A direct application of this result is impossible, as log-likelihood is negative, and not equal to zero for an empty solution. However, we consider the following modification: Denote by $LL(G)$ the log-likelihood $\log L(G)$, and let

$$g(S) = LL(G_0 \cup G_S) - LL(G_0), \quad (10)$$

where $S \subset D$ is a set of edges, G_0 is the graph consisting of the edges found in the 1st phase of SPINE, and G_S is the graph corresponding to the edges in the set S. Furthermore, observe that S can be seen as the set of edges added by SPINE in the 2nd phase. Clearly $g(S)$ is non-negative, and $g(\emptyset) = 0$. We can also show the following lemma, whose proof can be found in the extended version of this paper.

LEMMA 3. *Function $g(S)$ is submodular.*

Now we apply the result of [25] directly, and have

$$g(S^A) \geq (1 - 1/e) g(S^*). \quad (11)$$

Expanding $g(S)$, inequality (11) gives

$$\begin{aligned} LL(G_{\text{sp}}) &\geq (1 - 1/e)\,(LL(G_{\text{opt}}) - LL(G_0)) + LL(G_0) \\ &= \frac{1}{e} LL(G_0) + (1 - \frac{1}{e}) LL(G_{\text{opt}}), \end{aligned}$$

where $G_{\text{sp}} = G_0 \cup G^A$ is the solution returned by SPINE, and $G_{\text{opt}} = G_0 \cup G^*$ is the optimal solution that contains G_0 as a subset, which concludes the proof of Lemma 2. □

Lemma 2 guarantees that the solution returned by SPINE is close to the optimal among the subnetworks that contain arcs D_0. Notice that this result is not a true approximation result for Problem 1. First, Lemma 2 does not associate $\log L(G_{\text{sp}})$ with $\log L(G_s)$, the log-likelihood of the optimal solution, and secondly, it is true under the provision that $\log L(G_0) > -\infty$, i.e., that the first phase of SPINE "escapes" infinite log-likelihood before the k-th step.

A note on parallelization. In practice we have observed that the total execution time of SPINE is dominated by Phase 2 by at least an order of magnitude. Therefore we only concentrate on optimizing this part of the algorithm. Note that the computationally involved part in the 2nd phase is updating the table X on line 14. In Algorithm 2 we compute entries of X on-demand, i.e., the entry $X_v(i)$ is only computed when we must find out if the ith parent of v should belong to the solution. Alternatively we could compute the entire table X in advance, and then run phase 2 of SPINE with this as the input. This approach has the advantage that the values $X_v(1), X_v(2), \ldots$ can be computed independently of other vertices for each $v \in V$, hence SPINE lends itself to easy parallelization by arbitrarily partitioning V.

Algorithm 2 SPINE

1: **{First Phase}**
2: **for** $i = 1$ **to** $|V|$ **do**
3: $\quad D_0 := \emptyset$
4: $\quad C(v) := \{D_\alpha^+(v) \neq \emptyset\ ;\ \alpha \in \mathcal{A}\}$
5: $\quad$ **while** $|D_0| < k$ **and** $\log L(G_0(V, D_0) = -\infty$ **do**
6: $\quad\quad$ **find** u **:** $(u, v) \in D$ **with max** $n(u, v)$
7: $\quad\quad D_0 := D_0 \cup \{(u, v)\}$
8: $\quad\quad C(v) := C(v) -$ **{all** $D_\alpha^+(v)$ **that contain** (u, v)**}**
9: **{Second Phase}**
10: $D_{\text{sp}} := D_0$**,** $Q :=$ **empty priority queue**
11: $\forall v \in V$ **: compute** $X_v(1)$**, insert** $H_v(1)$ **to** Q
12: **while** $|D_{\text{sp}}| \leq k$ **do**
13: $\quad$ **extract** $H_{v^*}(i^*)$ **from** Q
14: $\quad$ **compute** $X_{v^*}(i^* + 1)$**, insert** $H_{v^*}(i^* + 1)$ **to** Q
15: $\quad D_{\text{sp}} := D_{\text{sp}} \cup \{X_{v^*}(i^*) \setminus X_{v^*}(i^* - 1)\}$
16: **return** $G_{\text{sp}} = G_{\text{sp}}(V, D_{\text{sp}})$

Setting the value of k. The size k of sparse network G_s is given as input to problem 1. A natural question that arises, then, is how to specify k in a principled manner, so as to identify sparse networks that combine small size with high log-likelihood. Following common model-selection practice, one way to set k is via minimization of the *Bayesian Information Criterion* (BIC).

$$BIC(G_s) = -2 \log L(G_s) + k \log(|A|) \quad (12)$$

It is straightforward to modify our algorithms to use BIC instead of log-likelihood, and return a sparse network G_s that minimizes the BIC. Part of our experiments (Section 6) is devoted to assessing SPINE in terms of BIC.

6. EXPERIMENTS

In this section we present an evaluation of the performance of SPINE on real datasets.

6.1 Experimental framework

Datasets. We test our algorithms on samples extracted from two different datasets. The first data source, referred to as YMEME in the following, is a set of microblogging postings in Yahoo! Meme.[1] Nodes are users, actions correspond to postings (typically photos) that users share through the site, and arcs from a node u to a node v indicate that v follows u. The data source contains all posts in this platform from 2008 to early 2010.

The second data source, referred to as MTRACK in the following, is a set of phrases propagated over prominent online news sites in March 2009, obtained by Meme Tracker [20]. Nodes are mostly news portals or news blogs and actions correspond to phrases that are found by the Meme Tracker algorithm to be repeated across several sites. In absence of explicitly declared "follower-followee" relationships between

[1]http://meme.yahoo.com/

the sites, arcs from a node u to a node v indicate that the website v linked to the website u during March 2009, and thus v "follows" u. This dataset is publicly available.[2]

We used a snowball sampling procedure to obtain several subsets from these data sources. In the case of YMEME, we sampled a connected sub-graph of the social network containing the users that participated in the most reposted items. This yields very densely connected subgraphs. In the case of MTRACK, we sampled a set of highly reposted items posted by the most active sites. This yields more loosely connected subgraphs. A summary of the subsets we created is shown in Table 1.

To estimate the probabilities associated with arcs, we use the EM algorithm of [28] (Section 3). In interest of simplicity, here we show results only for delay threshold $\Delta t = \infty$ and study effects of Δt in an extended version of the paper. As explained in Section 3, $\Delta t = \infty$ means that when node v performs action α, then $F^+_\alpha(v)$ contains all nodes followed by v that performed α before v, and $F^-_\alpha(v)$ is empty. On the other hand, if v does not perform action α, then $F^+_\alpha(v)$ is empty, and $F^-_\alpha(v)$ contains all nodes followed by v that performed α and thus failed to influence v.

As a product of the maximum-likelihood estimation, it may be that some arcs are associated with zero (0) influence probability. The last column of table 1 reports the number of arcs with positive probability after estimation terminates.

Table 1: Summary of datasets used.

Dataset	Actions	Nodes	Arcs input	Arcs prob.> 0
YMEME-L	26 000	10776	1 247 711	432 613
YMEME-M	13 000	9 525	1 154 674	378 520
YMEME-S	5 000	2 573	466 284	73 396
MTRACK-L	9 000	43 865	199 153	7 788
MTRACK-M	120	35 304	110 759	1 417
MTRACK-S	780	30 300	78 302	768

Alternative algorithms. While there is no established baseline or benchmark, there are algorithms we can compare with. On one extreme, we have `OptimalSparse` that should be the most effective, at the expense of speed. We experimented with `OptimalSparse` and discovered that its running time is prohibitive for the size of datasets we use; we thus omit its performance from our results. On the other extreme, there are fast heuristic methods that may yield good solutions. One such method is `SortByProbability` that sorts the arcs in D by decreasing probability (we considered a variant that sort arcs by decreasing number of actions traversing each arc, which yields worse results than `SortByProbability` and is thus omitted). Finally, we consider algorithm `Random`, that simply permutes all edges having a non-zero probability. Please note that both heuristics use SPINE's first phase as an *initialization* procedure.

Implementation. All algorithms are implemented in Java using the COLT library implementation of sparse matrices and the Fastutils library for type-specific maps and collections.[3,4] Our experiments are performed on a single Dual-

[2]`http://snap.stanford.edu/data/memetracker9.html`
[3]`http://acs.lbl.gov/software/colt/`
[4]`http://fastutil.dsi.unimi.it/`

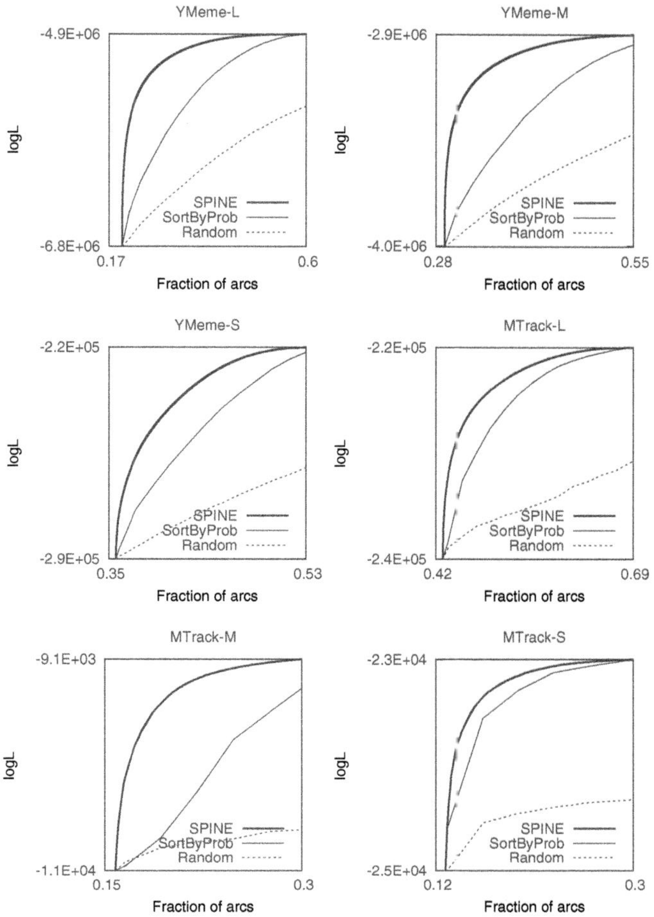

Figure 4: Log-likelihood vs fraction of non-zero-probability arcs.

Core *2530MHz Intel* processor and using less than 10GBs of memory for the largest datasets.

For efficiency reasons we create $F^+_\alpha(v)$ and $F^-_\alpha(v)$ at initialization and keep them in memory to quickly compute the log-likelihood function. Most processing time during sparsification is spent accessing these data structures to compute the likelihood for a subset of the edges incident to a node.

6.2 Results

We execute the different sparsification algorithms and measure log-likelihood at different levels of k (Figure 4).

The plots in Figure 4 demonstrate that SPINE obtains sparse graphs of high or even maximum likelihood with a fraction of the total network size. For instance, we observe that for the YMEME-L dataset, the initialization procedure produces a non-zero-likelihood solution at 17% of non-zero-probability arcs – that's about 90 000 arcs, i.e., 7% the total number of arcs. Then, SPINE achieves maximum log-likelihood at 60% of non-zero arcs – that's about 250 000 arcs, i.e., 20% of the total number of arcs. (Note that we know SPINE achieves maximum likelihood for that number of arcs, because the corresponding likelihood value remains at that level for larger values of k and is equal to the likelihood of the original network). Similar observations hold for all other datasets.

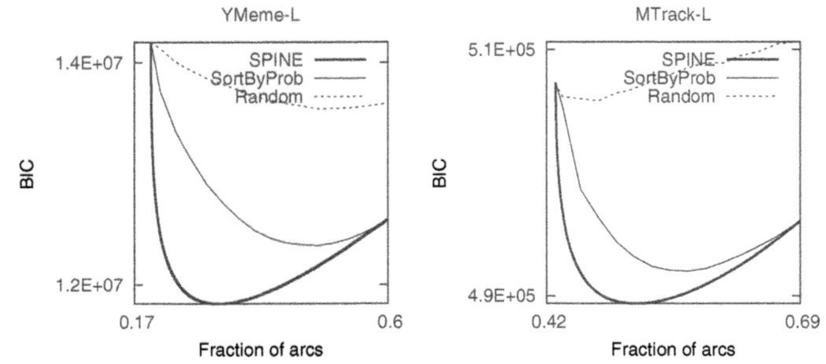

Figure 5: BIC vs fraction of non-zero-probability arcs.

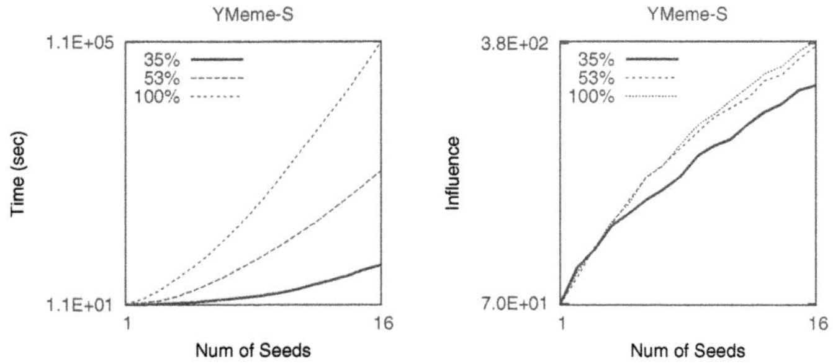

Figure 6: Seed selection running time and influence vs seed-set size, for sparse networks of different size (shown as percentage of non-zero probability arcs).

Notice also that SPINE constantly outperforms the two heuristics, `SortByProbability` and `Random`, even though they begin from the same basis, i.e., the same set of arcs of non-zero likelihood. Among the two, `SortByProbability` performs better, and in some cases achieves log-likelihood close to that of SPINE (e.g., MTRACK-S, in Figure 4).

Moreover, Figure 5 displays the BIC scores for sparse networks obtained from YMEME-L and MTRACK-L (similar plots were obtained for the rest of the datasets). We make two observations. First, there is a clear minimum, suggesting an optimal level of sparsification. Second, at that value of k, SPINE outperforms the two heuristics by a wide margin in terms of likelihood. Specifically, for YMEME-L, SPINE has its best BIC score at 39% of non-zero arcs (13% of all arcs), with log-likelihood that exceeds that of `SortByProbability` by 3×10^5. Similarly, for MTRACK-L, SPINE has its best score at 59% of non-zero arcs (2% of all arcs), with log-likelihood that exceeds that of `SortByProbability` by 8×10^2.

Running time. We experimented with SPINE over many large datasets and observed that its performance offers a vast improvement over that of `OptimalSparse`, the running time of which increases exponentially with the network size and prohibits any use in practice. As a matter of fact, `OptimalSparse` takes several days to complete for smaller datasets than the ones we report here.

Under the current implementation, the two simpler heuristics typically performed faster than Spine. In YMEME-L, the largest dataset of our experimental evaluation, the corresponding time to achieve maximum likelihood was 55 minutes for `Random` and `SortByProbability`. SPINE achieved maximum likelihood (at 260,000 arcs) in 3.5 hours and the execution time for the first phase of the algorithm was about 15 minutes. For MTRACK-S, the smallest dataset, the corresponding running time was less than 1 second. The time needed by SPINE to obtain a sparse network of maximum likelihood is reported in Table 2 for all datasets.

Table 2: SPINE – Time to reach max-likelihood

YMEME-L	3.5 hrs	MTRACK-L	10 sec
YMEME-M	35 min	MTRACK-M	1 sec
YMEME-S	1.5 min	MTRACK-S	< 1 sec

7. APPLICATION: INFLUENCE MAXIMIZATION

In Section 1 we claim that sparsification is a fundamental data-reduction operation with many applications. As a proof of concept, we apply SPINE as a pre-processing step for the *influence-maximization problem* [18], showing that computations on sparsified models give up little accuracy, but yield significant improvements in terms of scalability.

Consider a social network G with arcs annotated with probabilities of influence and assume the independent cascade model of propagation. Consider also an arbitrary set S of nodes in G (the "seed set"), and assume they are the first to perform some action α at time $t = 0$. Then, the spread of influence of that set is defined as the (expected) total number of nodes that are eventually influenced to perform α as well. Given an integer s, the problem of influence maximization consists in identifying a set S of cardinality no more than s that has maximum spread of influence.

We apply SPINE on the original network G of YMEME-S, one of our larger datasets, to identify two sparse networks G_1, G_2, of $k_1 = 25688$, $k_2 = 38899$ arcs, respectively. Network G_1 is the smallest network with non-zero likelihood identified by SPINE. Network G_2 is the smallest network of maximum likelihood.

For each of the aforementioned networks (G, G_1, G_2) we run the influence maximization greedy algorithm of [18], denoted `MaxInfl`, to identify seed-sets of size s, for different values of s. `MaxInfl` greedily selects seed nodes, every time choosing the node that leads to the biggest increase in influence spread. To estimate influence spread, `MaxInfl` performs Monte Carlo simulations of the independent cascade model. In our experiments, we perform batches of 100 simulations for every candidate seed set, and consider our estimate stable when it changes less than 10%. For each network and seed-set size s, we measure (*i*) the running time of the algorithm, and (*ii*) the influence of the identified seed set.

As shown in Figure 6, running `MaxInfl` over G_2 returns seed sets of almost optimal influence, at a considerable gain in speed in comparison with running on G, even for small seed sets. In addition, we observe that performing seed selection over G_1, the sparsest network, leads to large gains in efficiency, while returning seed sets with high influence. For example, when run over G, `MaxInfl` identifies a seed set of size $|S| = 10$ and influence $I_0 = 290$, in $t_0 = 54582$ seconds (15 hours). On the other hand, when run over G_1, it identifies a seed set of the same size and influence $I_1 = 0.88 \cdot I_0 = 255$, in $t_1 = 0.09 \cdot t_0 = 5061$ seconds (1.4 hours). As we can see, the gain from efficiency outweighs the loss in quality, especially for large sizes of S where running `MaxInfl` on G becomes excessively expensive.

8. CONCLUSIONS AND FUTURE WORK

We study the problem of sparsifying influence networks. Given a social graph and a log of propagations, we select the k arcs that best describe the propagations in terms of likelihood. We show that the problem is inapproximable within any multiplicative factor, and introduce SPINE, a greedy algorithm, to solve it efficiently.

Through experimental evaluation over real datasets, we demonstrate that SPINE identifies sparse sub-networks with practically little compromise in quality. We demonstrate examples of such sparse subnetworks, and apply sparsification as a pre-processing step to the influence maximization problem, showing that it provides significant gains in efficiency at little loss of quality.

Given the decomposition of the problem and hence its suitability to parallelization (see Section 5.2, 'A note on parallelization'), in our on-going work we are developing a Hadoop implementation of SPINE, which will allow to scale to extremely large networks.

Reproducibility. Code implementing the SPINE algorithm, along with instructions to repeat the experiments over the public MTRACK data source, is available at `http://queens.db.toronto.edu/~mathiou//spine/`.

Acknowledgements. This work was partially supported by the Spanish Centre for the Development of Industrial Technology under the CENIT program, project CEN-20101037, "Social Media" (www.cenitsocialmedia.es).

9. REFERENCES

[1] E. Adar and L. A. Adamic. Tracking information epidemics in blogspace. In *Int. Conf. on Web Intelligence (WI'05)*.

[2] F. Bass. A new product growth model for consumer durables. *Management Science*, 15:215–227, 1969.

[3] W. Chen, C. Wang, and Y. Wang. Scalable influence maximization for prevalent viral marketing in large-scale social networks. In *16th Int. Conf. on Knowledge Discovery and Data Mining (KDD'10)*.

[4] W. Chen, Y. Yuan, and L. Zhang. Scalable influence maximization in social networks under the linear threshold model. In *10th IEEE Int. Conf. on Data Mining (ICDM'10)*.

[5] J. Coleman, H. Menzel, and E. Katz. *Medical Innovations: A Diffusion Study.* Bobbs Merrill, 1966.

[6] P. Domingos and M. Richardson. Mining the network value of customers. In *7th Int. Conf. on Knowledge Discovery and Data Mining (KDD'01)*.

[7] M. Elkin and D. Peleg. Approximating k-spanner problems for $k > 2$. In *8th Conf. on Integer Programming and Combinatorial Optimization*, 2001.

[8] N. J. Foti and J. M. Hughes and D. N. Rockmore. Nonparametric Sparsification of Complex Multiscale Networks. *PLoS ONE*, 6(2), 2011.

[9] J. Goldenberg, B. Libai, and E. Muller. Talk of the network: A complex systems look at the underlying process of word-of-mouth. *Marketing Letters*, 12(3):211–223, 2001.

[10] M. Gomez-Rodriguez, D. Balduzzi, and B. Schölkopf. Uncovering the Temporal Dynamics of Diffusion Networks In *28th Int. Conf. on Machine Learning (ICML'11)*.

[11] M. Gomez-Rodriguez, J. Leskovec, and A. Krause. Inferring networks of diffusion and influence. In *16th Int. Conf. on Knowledge Discovery and Data Mining (KDD'10)*.

[12] A. Goyal, F. Bonchi, and L. Lakshmanan. Discovering leaders from community actions. In *17th Conf. on Inf. and Knowledge Management (CIKM'08)*.

[13] A. Goyal, F. Bonchi, and L. V. S. Lakshmanan. Learning influence probabilities in social networks. In *Third ACM Int. Conf. on Web Search and Data Mining (WSDM'10)*.

[14] D. Gruhl, R. V. Guha, D. Liben-Nowell, and A. Tomkins. Information diffusion through blogspace. In *13th Int. Conf. on World Wide Web, (WWW'04)*.

[15] D. Ienco, F. Bonchi, and C. Castillo. The meme ranking problem: Maximizing microblogging virality. In *SIASP 2010 workshop at ICDM*.

[16] D. S. Johnson. Approximation algorithms for combinatorial problems. In *5th Symp. on Theory of Computing (STOC'73)*.

[17] S. Jurvetson. What exactly is viral marketing? *Red Herring*, 78:110–112, 2000.

[18] D. Kempe, J. M. Kleinberg, and É. Tardos. Maximizing the spread of influence through a social network. In *9th Int. Conf. on Knowledge Discovery and Data Mining (KDD'03)*.

[19] J. Leskovec, L. A. Adamic, and B. A. Huberman. The dynamics of viral marketing. *TWEB*, 1(1), 2007.

[20] J. Leskovec, L. Backstrom, and J. M. Kleinberg. Meme-tracking and the dynamics of the news cycle. In *15th Int. Conf. on Knowledge Discovery and Data Mining (KDD'09)*.

[21] J. Leskovec, A. Krause, C. Guestrin, C. Faloutsos, J. VanBriesen, and N. S. Glance. Cost-effective outbreak detection in networks. In *13th Int. Conf. on Knowledge Discovery and Data Mining (KDD'07)*.

[22] J. Leskovec, A. Singh, and J. M. Kleinberg. Patterns of influence in a recommendation network. In *10th Pacific-Asia Conf. on Knowledge Discovery and Data Mining (PAKDD'06)*.

[23] V. Mahajan, E. Muller, and F. Bass. New product diffusion models in marketing: A review and directions for research. *Journal of Marketing*, 54(1):1–26, 1990.

[24] E. Misiolek and D. Z. Chen. Two flow network simplification algorithms. *Inf. Process. Lett.*, 97(5):197–202, 2006.

[25] G. L. Nemhauser, L. A. Wolsey, and M. L. Fisher. An analysis of approximations for maximizing submodular set functions. *Mathematical Programming*, 14(1), 1978.

[26] A. Quirin et al. A new variant of the pathfinder algorithm to generate large visual science maps in cubic time. *Inf. Process. Manage.*, 44(4), 2008.

[27] M. Richardson and P. Domingos. Mining knowledge-sharing sites for viral marketing. In *8th Int. Conf. on Knowledge Discovery and Data Mining (KDD'02)*.

[28] K. Saito, R. Nakano, and M. Kimura. Prediction of information diffusion probabilities for independent cascade model. In *12th Int. Conf. on Knowledge-Based Int. Information and Engineering Systems (KES'08)*.

[29] E. Serrano, A. Quirin, J. A. Botía, and O. Cordón. Debugging complex software systems by means of pathfinder networks. *Inf. Sci.*, 180(5):561–583, 2010.

[30] M. A. Serrano, M. Boguñá, and A. Vespignani. Extracting the multiscale backbone of complex weighted networks. *Proc. of the National Academy of Sciences*, 106(16):6483–6488, April 2009.

[31] H. Toivonen, S. Mahler, and F. Zhou. A framework for path-oriented network simplification. In *9th Int. Symp. on Advances in Intelligent Data Analysis (IDA'10)*.

[32] T. Valente. *Network Models of the Diffusion of Innovations.* Hampton Press, 1955.

[33] F. Zhou, S. Mahler, and H. Toivonen. Network simplification with minimal loss of connectivity. In *9th Int. Symp. on Advances in Intelligent Data Analysis (IDA'10)*.

[34] A. Arenas, J. Duch, A.Fernandez, and S. Gomez. Size reduction of complex networks preserving modularity. In *New Journal of Physics 9 (2007) 176*.

[35] W.S. Fung, R. Hariharan, N.J.A. Harvey, D. Panigrahi. A General Framework for Graph Sparsification. In *33th Symp. on Theory of Computing (STOC 2011)*.

Leveraging Collaborative Tagging for Web Item Design

Mahashweta Das, Gautam Das*
Department of Computer Science & Engineering
University of Texas at Arlington
mahashweta.das@mavs.uta.edu, gdas@uta.edu

Vagelis Hristidis†
School of Computing & Information Sciences
Florida International University
vagelis@cis.fiu.edu

ABSTRACT

The popularity of collaborative tagging sites has created new challenges and opportunities for designers of web items, such as electronics products, travel itineraries, popular blogs, etc. An increasing number of people are turning to online reviews and user-specified tags to choose from among competing items. This creates an opportunity for designers to build items that are likely to attract desirable tags when published. In this paper, we consider a novel optimization problem: given a training dataset of existing items with their user-submitted tags, and a query set of desirable tags, design the k best new items expected to attract the maximum number of desirable tags. We show that this problem is NP-Complete, even if simple Naive Bayes Classifiers are used for tag prediction. We present two principled algorithms for solving this problem: (a) an exact "two-tier" algorithm (based on top-k querying techniques), which performs much better than the naive brute-force algorithm and works well for moderate problem instances, and (b) a novel polynomial-time approximation algorithm with provable error bound for larger problem instances. We conduct detailed experiments on synthetic and real data crawled from the web to evaluate the efficiency and quality of our proposed algorithms.

Categories and Subject Descriptors

H.4 [**Information Systems Applications**]: Miscellaneous

General Terms

Algorithms, Performance

Keywords

collaborative tagging, item design, naive bayes, optimization

*Partially supported by NSF grants 0812601, 0915834, 1018865, a NHARP grant from the Texas Higher Education Coordinating Board, and grants from Microsoft Research and Nokia Research.

†Partially supported by NSF grants IIS-0811922, IIS-0952347, HRD-0833093 and Google Research Award.

KDD'11, August 21–24, 2011, San Diego, California, USA.

1. INTRODUCTION

Motivation: The widespread use and popularity of online collaborative tagging sites has created new challenges and opportunities for designers of "web items" such as electronics products, travel itineraries, popular blogs, etc. Various websites today (e.g., Flickr for photos, YouTube for videos, Amazon for different products) encourage users to actively participate by assigning labels or "tags" to online resources with a purpose to promote their contents and allow users to share, discover and organize them. An increasing number of people are turning to online reviews and user-specified tags to choose from among competing items. For example, a cell phone that has been tagged `lightweight` by several users is likely to influence a prospective customer decision in its favor. This creates an opportunity for designers to build items that are likely to attract desirable tags when published. In addition to traditional marketplaces like electronics, autos or apparel, tag desirability also extends to other diverse domains. For example, music websites such as `Last.fm` use social tags to guide their listeners in browsing through artists and music. An artist creating a new musical piece can leverage the tags that users have selected, in order to select the piece's attributes (e.g. acoustic and audio features) that will increase its chances of becoming popular. Similarly, a blogger can select a topic based on the tags that other popular topics have received.

Our paper investigates this novel tag maximization problem, i.e., how to decide the attribute values of new items and to return the top-k "best" items that are likely to attract the maximum number of desirable tags. We provide more details as follows.

Tag Maximization Problem: Assume we are given a set of items, each having a set of attributes and a set of user-submitted tags (e.g., cell phones on Amazon's website, each described by a set of attributes, and associated user tags). From this training data, for each distinct tag, we assume a classifier has been constructed for predicting the tag given the attributes. Tag prediction is a recent area of research (see Section 6 for discussion of related work), and the existence of such classifiers is a key assumption in our work. In addition to the item's explicitly specified attributes, other implicit factors also influence tagging behavior, such as the perceived utility and quality of an item to the user, the tagging behavior of the user's friends, etc. However, pure "content-based" tag prediction approaches are often quite effective – e.g., in the context of laptops, attributes such as smaller dimensions and the absence of a built-in DVD drive may attract tags such as `portable`.

Given a query consisting of a subset of tags that are considered "desirable", our task is to suggest a new item (i.e., a combination of attribute values) such that the expected number of desirable tags for this potential item is maximized. This can be extended to the top-k version, where the task is to suggest the k potential items with the highest expected number of desirable tags.

This information can assist web item designers in designing new items (or fine-tuning existing web content) to make them more attractive to users. Moreover, designers can explore the dataset in an interactive manner by picking and choosing different sets of desirable tags to get insight on how to build new items that target different user populations – e.g., in the context of cell phones, tags such as `lightweight` and `powerful` target professionals, whereas tags such as `cheap`, `cool` target younger users.

Novelty, Technical Challenges and Approaches: The dynamics of social tagging has been an active research area in recent years. However related literature primarily focuses on the problems of tag prediction, including cold-start recommendation to facilitate web-based activities. To our best knowledge, tags have not been studied in the context of web item design before. Of course, real-world item design is a complex task, and is an area that has been heavily studied in economics, marketing, industrial engineering and more recently in computer science. Many factors like the cost and return on investment are currently considered. We argue that the user feedback (in the form of tags of existing competing items) should be taken into consideration in the design process, especially since online user tagging is extremely widespread and offers unprecedented opportunities for understanding the collective opinion and preferences of a huge consumer base. We envision user tags to be one of the several factors in item design that can be used in conjunction with more traditional factors - e.g., our algorithms return k potential new items that maximize the number of desirable tags; and this information can assist web item designers, who can then further post-process the returned results using additional constraints such as profitability, price, resource constraints, item diversity, etc.

Solving the tag maximization problem is technically challenging. In most item sets, complex dependencies exist among the tags and items, and it is difficult to determine a combination of attribute values that maximizes the expected number of desirable tags. In this paper we consider the very popular Naive Bayes Classifier for tag prediction, although our problem framework also extends to other classifiers. As one of our first results, we show that even for this classifier (with its simplistic assumption of conditional independence), the tag maximization problem is NP-Complete. Given this intractability result, it is important to develop algorithms that work well in practice. A highlight of our paper is that we have avoided resorting to heuristics, and instead have developed principled algorithms that are practical *and at the same time* possess compelling theoretical characteristics.

Our first algorithm is a novel exact top-k algorithm **ETT** (Exact Two-Tier Top-k algorithm) that performs significantly better than the naive brute-force algorithm (which simply builds all possible items and determines the best ones), for moderate problem instances. Our algorithm is based on nontrivial adaptations of top-k query processing techniques (e.g., [4]), and has an interesting two-tier architecture. At the bottom tier, we develop a sub-system for each distinct tag, such that each sub-system has the ability to compute on demand a stream of items in order of decreasing probability of attracting the corresponding tag, *without having to pre-compute* all possible items in advance. This is achieved by partitioning the set of attributes into smaller groups (thus, each group represents a "partial" item), and running a separate merge algorithm over all the groups. The top tier considers the items retrieved from each sub-system in a round-robin manner, computes the expected number of desirable tags for each retrieved item, and stops when a threshold condition is reached. Although in the worst case this algorithm can take exponential time, for many datasets with strong correlations between attributes and tags, the stopping condition is reached much earlier.

However, although the exact algorithm performs well for moderate problem sizes, it did not easily scale to much larger sized datasets. Heuristic techniques like hill-climbing, branch and bound, etc. does not guarantee any sort of worst case behavior, either in running time or in item quality and thus we also develop a novel approximation algorithm **PA** (Poly-Time Approximation algorithm) that runs in worst case polynomial time, *and* also guarantees a provable bound on the approximation factor in item quality. The principal idea is to group the desirable tags into *constant-sized* groups, find the top-k items for each sub-group, and output the overall top-k items from among these computed items. For each sub-problem thus created, we show that it can be solved by a polynomial time approximation scheme (PTAS) given any user-defined approximation factor. The algorithm's overall running time is exponential only in the (constant) size of the groups, thus giving overall a polynomial time complexity.

We experiment with synthetic as well as real datasets crawled from the web to compare our algorithms. User study on the real dataset demonstrates that the items suggested by our algorithms appear to be meaningful. With regard to efficiency, the exact algorithm performs well on moderate problem instances, whereas the approximation algorithm scaled very well for larger datasets.

In summary, we make the following main contributions:

- We introduce the novel problem of top-k item design based on user-submitted tags and show that this problem is NP-complete, even if tag prediction is modeled using simple Naive Bayes Classifiers.
- We develop an exact two-tier algorithm (ETT) to compute the top-k best items that works well for moderate problem instances.
- We also design an approximation algorithm (PA) based on a polynomial time approximation scheme (PTAS), with provable error bounds, for larger datasets.
- We perform detailed experiments on synthetic and real datasets crawled from the web to demonstrate the effectiveness of our developed algorithms.

2. PROBLEM FRAMEWORK

Let $\mathbb{D} = \{o_1, o_2, ..., o_n\}$ be a collection of n items, where each item entry is defined over the attribute set $A = \{A_1, A_2, ..., A_m\}$ and the tag dictionary space $T = \{T_1, T_2, ..., T_r\}$. Each attribute A_i can take one of several values a_i from a multi-valued categorical domain D_i, or one of two values 0, 1 if a boolean dataset is considered. A tag T_j is a bit where a 0 implies the absence of a tag and a 1 implies the presence of a tag for item o. Each item is thus a vector of size $(m + r)$, where the first m positions correspond to a vector of attribute values, and the remaining r positions correspond to a boolean vector.[1,2]

We assume such a dataset has been used as a training set to build Naive Bayes Classifiers (NBC), that classify tags given the attribute values (one classifier per tag). The classifier for tag T_j defines the probability that a new item o is annotated by the tag T_j:

$$\begin{aligned} Pr(T_j \mid o) &= Pr(T_j \mid a_1, a_2, ..., a_m) \\ &= \frac{Pr(T_j).\Pi_{i=1}^{m} Pr(a_i \mid T_j)}{Pr(a_1, a_2, ..., a_m)} \end{aligned} \quad (1)$$

where a_i is the value of o for attribute A_i, $a_i \in D_i$. The probabilities $Pr(a_i \mid T_j)$ are computed using the dataset. In particular, $Pr(a_i \mid T_j)$ is the proportion[3] of items tagged by T_j that have $A_i = a_i$. $Pr(T_j)$ is the proportion of items in the dataset that has T_j.

Similarly, we compute the probability $Pr(T_j{}' \mid o)$ of an item o not having tag T_j:

$$Pr(T_j{}' \mid o) = \frac{Pr(T_j{}').\Pi_{i=1}^{m} Pr(a_i \mid T_j{}')}{Pr(a_1, a_2, ..., a_m)} \quad (2)$$

We know that $Pr(T_j \mid o) + Pr(T_j{}' \mid o) = 1$; hence from Equations 1, 2 we get :

$$\begin{aligned} Pr(a_1, a_2, ..., a_m) = {} & Pr(T_j).\Pi_{i=1}^{m} Pr(a_i \mid T_j) + \\ & Pr(T_j{}').\Pi_{i=1}^{m} Pr(a_i \mid T_j{}') \end{aligned} \quad (3)$$

From Equations 1, 3,

$$\begin{aligned} Pr(T_j \mid o) &= Pr(T_j \mid a_1, a_2, ..., a_m) \\ &= \frac{Pr(T_j).\Pi_{i=1}^{m} Pr(a_i \mid T_j)}{Pr(T_j).\Pi_{i=1}^{m} Pr(a_i \mid T_j) + Pr(T_j{}').\Pi_{i=1}^{m} Pr(a_i \mid T_j{}')} \\ &= \frac{1}{1 + \frac{Pr(T_j{}')}{Pr(T_j)} \Pi_{i=1}^{m} \frac{Pr(a_i \mid T_j{}')}{Pr(a_i \mid T_j)}} \end{aligned}$$

For convenience we use the notation

$$R_j = \frac{Pr(T_j{}')}{Pr(T_j)} \Pi_{i=1}^{m} \frac{Pr(a_i \mid T_j{}')}{Pr(a_i \mid T_j)} \quad (4)$$

Consider a query which picks a set of desirable tags $T^d = \{T_1, \ldots, T_z\} \subseteq T$.

The expected number of desirable tags $T_j \in T^d$ that a new item o, characterized by $(a_1, a_2, ..., a_m) \in A$ is annotated with, is given by:

$$\mathbb{E}(o, T^d) = \Sigma_{j=1}^{z} \frac{1}{1 + R_j} \quad (5)$$

We are now ready to formally define the main problem.

TAG MAXIMIZATION PROBLEM *Given a dataset of tagged items $\mathbb{D} = \{o_1, o_2, ..., o_n\}$, and a query T^d, design k new items that have the highest expected number of desirable tags they are likely to receive, given by Equation 5.*

[1]Our framework allows numeric attributes, but as is common with Naive Bayes Classifiers, we assume that they have been appropriately binned into discrete ranges.

[2]A more complex framework which leverages the frequencies of tags is left for future work.

[3]The observed probabilities are smoothened using the Bayesian m-estimate method [3]. We note that more sophisticated Bayesian methods that use an informative prior may be employed instead.

For the rest of the paper, we explain our algorithms in a boolean framework, which can be readily generalized to handle the case of categorical data. We also assume that all tags are of equal "weight"– if tags are of varying importance, Equation 5 can be re-written as a weighted sum, and all our proposed algorithms can be modified accordingly.

3. COMPLEXITY ANALYSIS AND EXACT ALGORITHMS

Our first result is on the NP-completeness of the Tag Maximization problem.

THEOREM 1. *The Tag Maximization problem is NP-Complete even for boolean datasets and for $k = 1$.*

Proof: The membership of the decision version of the problem in NP is obvious. To verify NP-hardness, we reduce the 3SAT problem to the decision version of our problem. We first reduce the 3SAT problem to the minimization version of the optimization problem, represented as $\mathbb{E}^{min}(o, T^d)$ and then reduce $\mathbb{E}^{min}(o, T^d)$ to $\mathbb{E}(A, T^d)$.

Reduction of 3SAT to decision version of $\mathbb{E}^{min}(o, T^d)$:

3SAT is the popular NP-complete boolean satisfiability problem in computational complexity theory, an instance of which concerns a boolean expression in conjunctive normal form, where each clause contains exactly 3 literals. Each clause C_j is mapped to a tag T_j in the instance of $\mathbb{E}^{min}(o, T^d)$ and each variable x_i is mapped to attribute value a_i. We make the following assignments so that if there is a boolean assignment vector $\vec{a} = [a_1, ..., a_m]$ that satisfies 3SAT, then $\mathbb{E}^{min}(o, T^d)$ equals zero (and if $\vec{a}$ does not satisfy 3SAT, then $\mathbb{E}^{min}(o, T^d)$ has a non-zero sum).

- For a variable x_i specified as positive literal in 3SAT, set $\Pr(a_i = 0 \mid T_j) = 1$
- For a variable x_i specified as negative literal in 3SAT, set $\Pr(a_i = 1 \mid T_j) = 1$
- For a particular clause and for the unspecified attributes (variables), set $\Pr(a_i = 0 \mid T_j) = \Pr(a_i = 1 \mid T_j) = 1$

For example, consider 3SAT instance $(\neg x_1 \vee x_2 \vee \neg x_3) \wedge (x_1 \vee \neg x_2 \vee \neg x_4)$. For each tag, we create two products. For instance for the first tag, x_1 (that corresponds to A_1) is negative and hence for both the first and second product it is $A_1 = 1$. x_4 is missing from the first tag, hence for the first product it is $A_4 = 0$ and for the second it is $A_4 = 1$.

Table 1: Table of boolean attributes and tags

Attributes				Tags	
A_1	A_2	A_3	A_4	T_1	T_2
1	0	1	0	1	0
1	0	1	1	1	0
0	1	0	1	0	1
0	1	1	1	0	1

Reduction of $\mathbb{E}^{min}(A, T^d)$ to $\mathbb{E}(A, T^d)$:

If we have a boolean assignment vector $\vec{a} = [a_1, ..., a_m]$ that minimizes the expected number of tags being present, we have the corresponding $\Pr(T_j{}' \mid a_1, a_2, ..., a_m)$. Hence, we get $\Pr(T_j \mid a_1, a_2, ..., a_m) = 1 - \Pr(T_j{}' \mid a_1, a_2, ..., a_m)$ that maximizes the expected number of tags being present. □

A brute-force exhaustive approach (henceforth, referred to as **Naive**) to solve the Tag Maximization problem requires us to design all possible 2^m number of items and compute $\mathbb{E}(o, T^d)$ for each possible item. Note that the number of items in the dataset is not important for the execution cost, since an initialization step can calculate all the conditional tag-attribute probabilities by a single scan of the dataset. Although general purpose pruning-based optimization techniques (such as branch-and-bound algorithms) can be used to solve the problem more efficiently than Naive, such approaches are only limited to constructing the top-1 item, and it is not clear how they can be easily extended for $k > 1$.

In the following subsection, we propose a novel exact algorithm for any k based on interesting and nontrivial adaptations of top-k query processing techniques. This algorithm is shown in practice to explore far fewer item candidates than Naive, and works well for moderate problem instances.

3.1 Exact Two-Tier Top-k Algorithm

We develop an exact *two tier* top-k algorithm (ETT) for the Tag Maximization problem. For simplicity, henceforth we refer to desirable tags as just tags. The main idea of ETT is to determine the "best" items for each individual tag in tier-1 and then match these items in tier-2 to compute the globally best items (across all tags). Both tiers use pipelined techniques to minimize the amount of accesses, as shown in Figure 1. The output of tier-1 is z unbounded buffers (one for each tag) of complete items, ordered by decreasing probability for the corresponding tag. These buffers are not fully materialized, but may be considered as "sub-systems" that can be accessed on demand in a pipelined manner.

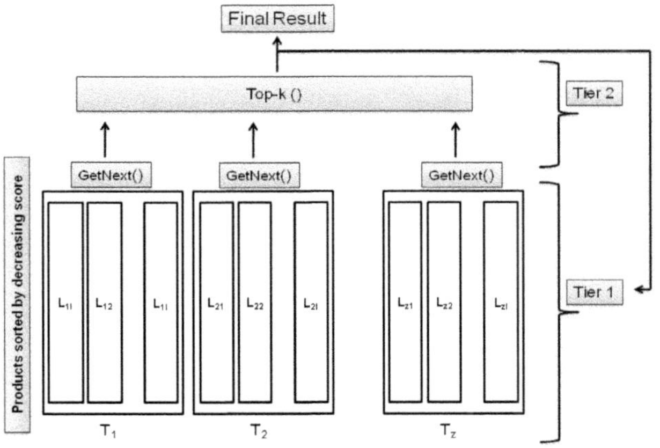

Figure 1: Two-Tier Top-K Algorithm Framework

In tier-2, the top items from the z buffers are combined in a pipelined manner to produce the global top-k items, akin the *Threshold Algorithm* (TA) [4]. In turn, tier-2 makes GetNext() requests (see Figure 1) to various buffers in tier-1 in round-robin manner. In tier-1, for each specific tag, we partition the set of attributes into subsets, and for each subset of attributes we precompute a list of all possible partial attribute value assignments, ordered by their "score" for the specific tag (the score will be defined later). The partial items are then scanned and joined, leveraging results from Rank-Join algorithms [9] that support top-k ranked join queries in relational databases, in order to feed information to tier-2. We provide more details below.

3.1.1 Tier-1

Suppose we partition the m attributes into l subsets, where each subset has $m' = \frac{m}{l}$ attributes as follows: $\{a_1, \ldots, a_{m'}\}$, $\{a_{m'+1}, \ldots, a_{2m'}\}$, ..., $\{a_{m-m'+1}, \ldots, a_m\}$. We create partial item lists $L_{j1}, \ldots, L_{jl}$ for each tag T_j. Each list L_{ji} has $2^{m'}$ entries (partial items). Consider the first list L_{j1}. The *score* of a partial item $o^p \in L_{j1}$ with attribute values $a_1, \ldots, a_{m'}$ for T_j is

$$\mathbb{E}_{partial}(o^p, \{T_j\}) = \sqrt[l]{P_j}.\Pi_{i=1}^{m'} \frac{Pr(a_i \mid T_j')}{Pr(a_i \mid T_j)} \quad (6)$$

where $P_j = \frac{Pr(T_j')}{Pr(T_j)}$. Note that the l-th root of P_j is used in order to distribute the effect of P_j from Equation 4 to the l lists, such that when they are combined using multiplication, we get P_j.

Lists L_{jl} are ordered by descending $\frac{1}{E_{partial}}$, since R_j appears on the denominator of Equation 5. The l lists are accessed in round-robin fashion and for every combination of partial items from the lists, we join them to build a complete item and resolve its exact score by Equation 5.

An item is returned as a result of GetNext() to tier-2 if its score is higher than the MPFS (*Maximum Possible Future Score*), which is the upper bound on the score of an unseen item. To compute MPFS, we assume that the current entry from a list is joined with the top entries from all other lists:

$$MPFS = \frac{1}{1 + max((s_{j1}.h_{j2}..\cdot h_{jl}), (h_{j1}.s_{j2}..\cdot h_{jl}), .., (h_{j1}.h_{j2}..\cdot s_{jl}))} \quad (7)$$

where s_{ji} and h_{ji} are the last seen and top entries from list L_{ji} respectively.

3.1.2 Tier-2

In this tier, the z unbounded buffers, one for each tag, are combined using the summation function, as shown in Equation 5. Each item from one buffer matches exactly one entry (the identical item) from each of the other buffers. Items are retrieved from each buffer using GetNext() operations, and once retrieved we directly compute its score for all other tags by running each Naive Bayes classifier, without using the process of tier-1. An item is output if its score is higher than the threshold, which is the sum of the last seen scores from all z buffers. A bounded buffer with the k best results so far is maintained. On termination, this buffer is returned as the top-k items.

The pseudocode of ETT is shown in Algorithm 1.

Table 2: Example tagged items dataset

Attribute					Tag	
ID	A_1	A_2	A_3	A_4	T_2	T_1
1	0	0	0	1	0	0
2	0	1	0	0	0	1
3	0	1	0	1	0	0
4	0	1	1	1	1	1
5	1	0	0	0	1	0
6	1	0	0	1	0	1
7	1	0	1	1	1	1
8	1	1	0	1	0	1

EXAMPLE 1. Consider the boolean dataset of 10 objects, each entry having 4 attributes and 2 tags in Table 2. We partition the 4 attributes into groups of 2 attributes: (A_1, A_2) form list L_{j1} and (A_3, A_4) form list L_{j2}. We run NBC

Algorithm 1 ETT (Naive Bayes probabilities, attributes per group m', k): top-k exact items

//Main Algorithm

Top-k-Buffer $\leftarrow \{\}$
for $j = 1$ to z **do**
  $B_j \leftarrow \{\}$ // unbounded buffer of candidate results-items per tag
  for $i = 1$ to l **do**
    $s_{ji}, h_{ji} \leftarrow$ top entry from list L_{ji}
  end for
end for
Call Threshold()

//Method Threshold() – Tier-2

while true **do**
  for $j = 1$ to z **do**
    $(o_j, score_j(o_j)) \leftarrow$ GetNext(j)
    ExactScore(o_j) $\leftarrow$ Compute for o_j by Equation 5
  end for
  Update Top-k-Buffer with new items if necessary
  MinK $\leftarrow$ lowest score in Top-k buffer
  $\alpha \leftarrow \sum_j score_j(o_j)$ // Threshold
  if MinK $\geq \alpha$ **then**
    return top-k items
  end if
end while

//Method GetNext(j) : $(o_j, score_j(o_j))$ – Tier-1

while true **do**
  Compute MPFS by Equation 7
  // $score_j(o)$ for item o is defined as $1/(1 + R_j)$ (R_j defined by Equation 4)
  if B_j has an item o with $score_j(o) > MPFS$ **then**
    return $(o, score_j(o))$ AND remove it from B_j
  end if
  Retrieve next entry o^p from a list L_{ji} in round robin and advance s_{ji}
  Join o^p with all combinations of partial items from other lists and create all items $NewItems$
  Add $NewItems$ to buffer B_j of candidate results-items
end while

and calculate all conditional tag-attribute probabilities. The algorithm framework for the running example is presented in Figure 2. List L_{11} and L_{12} under tag T_1 is sorted in decreasing order of $\frac{1}{E_{partial}}$, given by Equation 6 (and, similarly for L_{21} and L_{22} under tag T_2).

In iteration 1, call to Threshold() in tier-2 calls GetNext() for T_1 and T_2 respectively in tier-1. During GetNext(T_1), join-1 builds item 1010, whose $score_1(1010) = 0.95$ and MPFS(1010) =0.95. Since $score_1 \geq$ MPFS, (1010,0.95) is returned to tier-2. GetNext(T_2) returns (1111,0.93) to tier-2. In tier-2, call to Threshold() returns ExactScore(1010) =1.70, ExactScore(1111) =1.75. Now, top-k-buffer gets 1111; MinK=1.75 and α=1.88. Since MinK $\leq \alpha$, we continue to iteration 2. In iteration 2, we proceed similarly. GetNext(T_1) returns (1011, 0.92) and GetNext(T_2) returns (1110,0.88) to tier-2. Call to Threshold() in tier-2 gives ExactScore(1011) =1.76, ExactScore(1110) =1.77. The top-k-buffer is updated to 1110; MinK=1.77 and α=1.79. Since MinK $\leq \alpha$, we continue to iteration 3. In tier-1 of iteration 3, GetNext(T_1) returns (0010,0.89) and GetNext(T_2) returns (0111,0.84) to tier-2. Then Threshold() is called and we get ExactScore(0010) =1.76, ExactScore(0111) =1.77. The Bounded Buffer continues to be 1110; MinK=1.77 and α=1.74. We see that MinK $\geq \alpha$. Hence, ETT terminates and returns 1110 as the top-1 item. Thus, ETT returns the best item by just looking up 6 items, instead of 16 items (as in Naive algorithm). □

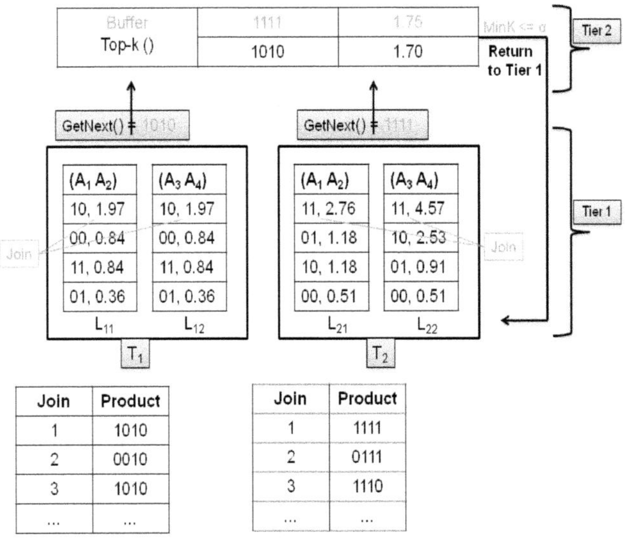

Figure 2: Iteration 1: Exact Two-Tier Top-K Algorithm for Example in Table 2

4. APPROXIMATION ALGORITHM

The exact algorithm of Section 3.1 is feasible only for moderate instances of the Tag Maximization problem. For larger problem instances, in this section we discuss a principled approximation algorithm (**PA**, or *polynomial time approximation algorithm*) that provides guarantee in the quality of the top-k results *as well as* running time.

The main idea is to group the desirable tags into *constant-sized* groups of z' tags each, find the top-k items for each subgroup, and output the overall top-k items from among these computed items.[4] For each sub-problem thus created, we show that it can be solved by a *polynomial time approximation scheme* (PTAS) [5], i.e., can be solved in polynomial time given any user-defined approximation factor ϵ (function of compression factor σ and m; details later in Theorem 2). The overall running time of the algorithm is exponential only in the (constant) size of the groups, thus giving overall a polynomial time complexity.

We now consider a sub-problem consisting of only a constant number of tags, z'. We also restrict our discussion to the case $k = 1$ (more general values of k are discussed later). We shall design a polynomial time approximation scheme (PTAS) for this sub-problem. A PTAS is defined as follows. Let $\epsilon > 0$ be any user-defined parameter. Given any instance of the sub-problem, let PTAS return the item o_a.

[4]Interestingly, we note that in this algorithm we create (z/z') sub-problems by grouping tags; in contrast in our exact ETT algorithm we create sub-problems (i.e., subsystems) by grouping attributes.

Let the optimal item be o_g. The PTAS should run in polynomial time, and $ExactScore(o_a) \geq (1-\epsilon)ExactScore(o_g)$.

In describing the PTAS, we first discuss a simple exponential time exact top-1 algorithm for the sub-problem, and then show how it can be modified to the PTAS. Given m boolean attributes and z' tags, the exponential time algorithm makes m iterations as follows: As an initial step, it produces the set S_0 consisting of the single item $\{0^m\}$ along with its z' scores, one for each tag. In the first iteration, it produces the set containing two items $S_1 = \{0^m, 10^{m-1}\}$ each accompanied by its z' scores, one for each tag. More generally, in the ith iteration, it produces the set of items $S_i = \{\{0,1\}^i \times 0^{m-1}\}$ along with their z' scores, one for each tag. Each set can be easily derived from the set computed in the previous iteration. Once m iterations have been completed, the final set S_m contains all 2^m items along with their exact scores, from which the top-1 item can be returned, which is that product for which the sum of the z' scores is the largest. However, this algorithm takes exponential time, as in each iteration the sets double in size.

The main idea of the PTAS is to not allow the sets to become exponential in size. This is done by *compressing* each set S_i produced by each iteration to another smaller set S'_i, so that they remain polynomial in size. Each item entry in S_i can be viewed as points in a z'-dimensional space,whose z' co-ordinates correspond to the item scores for z' individual tags respectively, by Equation 5. Essentially, we use a clustering algorithm in z'-dimensional space, and for each cluster, only the representative item is retained, while all other items in the cluster are deleted. The clustering has to be done in a careful way so as to guarantee that for the items that are deleted, the representative item's exact score should be close to the deleted item's exact score. Thus when the top-1 item of the final compressed set S'_m is returned, its exact score should not be too different from exact score of the top-1 item assuming no compression was done.
The pseudocode of PA is shown in Algorithm 2.

EXAMPLE 2. We execute PA on the example in Table 2 without any grouping of tags (i.e., $z = z' = 2$): Let the compression factor σ be 0.5. We start with $S'_0 = \{0000\}$. In iteration 1, $S_1 = \{0000, 1000\}$ with each item having two-dimensional co-ordinates (0.31, 0.20) and (0.51, 0.38) respectively. After compression, we get $S'_1 = \{1000\}$. In iteration 2, $S_2 = \{1000, 1100\}$ with two-dimensional co-ordinates (0.51, 0.38) and (0.31, 0.58) respectively. After compression we get $S'_2 = \{1000, 1100\}$. In iteration 3, $S_3 = \{1000, 1100, 1010, 1110\}$ with co-ordinates (0.51, 0.38), (0.31, 0.58), (0.95, 0.75) and (0.89, 0.88) respectively. After compression we get $S'_3 = \{1000, 1100, 1110\}$. In the final iteration 4, $S_4 = \{1000, 1100, 1110, 1001, 1101, 1111\}$ with co-ordinates (0.51, 0.38), (0.31, 0.58), (0.89, 0.88), (0.37, 0.52), (0.20, 0.72) and (0.82, 0.93). After compression we get $S'_4 = \{1000, 1100, 1111\}$. The top-1 approximate item is 1111 with score 1.75 while the optimal item is 1110 with score 1.77. Figure 3 shows the compression in the four iterations. The boolean items in underlined red font are the cluster representatives.□

THEOREM 2. *Given a user defined approximation factor ϵ, if we group the tags into z/z' groups of z' tags per group, and set the compression factor $\sigma = \epsilon/2m$ then*

1. *The output of PA has an exact score that is at least $\frac{z'}{z(1+\epsilon)}$ times the exact score of the optimal item*

Algorithm 2 PA (Naive Bayes probabilities, attributes per group z', compression factor σ): top-1 approximate item in polynomial time

//Main Algorithm
Partition tags T into z/z' groups $T_1, \ldots, T_{z/z'}$
for $r = 1$ to $\frac{z}{z'}$ **do**
  $o_r \leftarrow$ PTAS(T_r)
  Compute ExactScore(o_r) by Equation 5
end for
return o_r with max ExactScore

//Method $PTAS(T_r) : o$)
$S'_0 \leftarrow \{0^m\}$ // boolean vector of size m with all 0's
for $i = 1$ to m **do**
  $S_i = S'_{i-1} \cup S''_{i-1}$ // S''_{i-1} : S'_{i-1} with ith bit set to 1
  // Compress S_i to S'_i using compression factor σ
  $S'_i \leftarrow \{\}$
  repeat
    $o \leftarrow$ any selected item in S'_{i-1}
    $S'_i \leftarrow S'_i \cup \{o\}$
    Delete from S_i all items o' such that $\forall T_j \in T_r$, $|\mathbb{E}(o, \{T_j\}) - \mathbb{E}(o', \{T_j\})| \leq \sigma\mathbb{E}(o, \{T_j\})$
  until S_i is empty
end for
return item o in S'_m with largest $|\mathbb{E}(o, T_r)|$

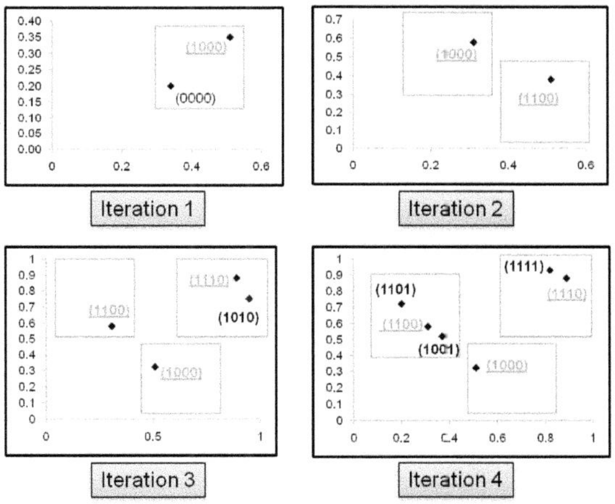

Figure 3: Compression in PA Algorithm for Example Dataset of Two Tags in Table 2

2. *PA runs in polynomial time*

Proof of Part 1: Consider any tag group T_r, and let o^{OPT} be the optimal item for this group, and o^{APP} be the item returned by PTAS. For every item o in the set S_m (assuming no compression was used in any iterations), there is an item o_a in the compressed set S'_m that satisfies

$$\mathbb{E}(o, T_r) \leq (1+\sigma)^m \mathbb{E}(o_a, T_r) \quad (8)$$

In particular, the following holds

$$\mathbb{E}(o^{OPT}, T_r) \leq (1+\sigma)^m \mathbb{E}(o^{APP}, T_r) \quad (9)$$

Since $\sigma = \epsilon/2m$, some algebraic simplifications results in:

$$\mathbb{E}(o^{OPT}, T_r) \leq (1+\epsilon)\mathbb{E}(o^{APP}, T_r) \quad (10)$$

The above analysis is for a single tag group. Since there are z/z' tag groups, it is easy to see that this introduces an additional factor of z'/z to the overall approximation factor.

Proof of Part 2 (sketch): To show that PA is a polynomial time algorithm, the main task is to show that the compressed lists are always polynomial in length. We first observe that probability quantities such as $Pr(a_i \mid T_j)$ are rational numbers, where both the numerator as well as the denominator are integers bounded by n (number of items in the dataset). If we then consider Equation 5, we can conclude that the score of any item for any single tag can be represented as a rational number, where the numerator and denominator are integers bounded by $O(n^m)$. Thus, we can normalize each such score into an integer by multiplying it with $O(n^m)$.

Next, consider a z'-dimensional cube with each side of length $L = O(n^m)$. We partition the cube into z'-dimensional *cells* as follows: Along each axis, start with the furthest value L, and then proceed towards the origin by marking the points $L/(1+\sigma)$, $L/(1+\sigma)^2$, and so on. The number of points marked along each axis is $\log_{(1+\sigma)} L = O(m \log_{(1+\sigma)} n)$ which is a polynomial in m and n. Then at each marked point we pass $(z'-1)$-dimensional hyperplanes perpendicular to the corresponding axis. Their intersections creates $O(poly(m,n)^{z'})$ cells within cube $L^{z'}$.

Due to this skewed method of partitioning cube into cells, we see that the cells that are further away from the origin are larger. Consider the ith iteration of the PTAS algorithm. Each item in S_i may be represented as a point in this cube. Though within any cell there may be several points corresponding to items of S_i, after compression *there can be at most only one* point corresponding to an item of S'_r, because two or more points could not have survived the compression process as the score between them is too small.

The length of any compressed list in the PTAS algorithm is at most $O(poly(m,n)^{z'})$. When z' is a constant, this translates to an overall polynomial running time for PA. □

Extending from Top-1 to Top-k: Our PA algorithm can be modified to return top-k items instead of just the best item. For the tag group T_r, once a set of items S_i is built, we compress to form the set S'_i. However, every time a cluster representative is selected, instead of deleting all the remaining points in the cluster, we remember $k-1$ items within the cluster and associate them with the cluster representative (and if the cluster has less than k items, we remember and associate all the items with the cluster representative).

When all the m iterations are completed, we can return the top-k items as follows: we first return the best item of S'_m along with the $k-1$ items associated with it. If the number of associated items are less than $k-1$, the second best cluster representative of S'_m and the set of items associated with it are returned, and so on.

When the approximate top-k items from all tag groups have been returned, the main algorithm returns the overall best top-k items from among them. It can be shown that this approach guarantees an approximation factor for the score of the top-k items returned.

5. EXPERIMENTS

We conduct a set of comprehensive experiments using both synthetic and real datasets for quantitative and qualitative analysis of our proposed algorithms. Our quantitative performance indicators are (a) *efficiency* of the proposed exact and approximation algorithm, and (b) *approximation factor* of results produced by the approximation algorithm. The efficiency of our algorithms is measured by the overall execution time and the number of items that are considered from the pool of all possible items, whereas approximation factor is measured as the ratio of the acquired approximate result score to the actual optimal result score. We also conduct a user study through Amazon Mechanical Turk study to qualitatively assess the results of our algorithms.

System configuration: Our prototype system is implemented in Java with JDK 5.0. All experiments were conducted on an Windows XP machine with 3.0Ghz Intel Xeon processor and 2GB RAM. The JVM size is set to 512MB. All numbers are obtained as the average over three runs.

Real Camera Dataset: We crawl a real dataset of 100 cameras[5] listed at Amazon (http://www.amazon.com). The products contain technical details (attributes), besides the tags customers associate with each product. The tags are cleaned by domain experts to remove synonyms, unintelligent and undesirable tags such as `nikon coolpix`, `quali`, `bad`, etc. Since the camera information crawled from Amazon lacks well-defined attributes, we look up Google Products (http://www.google.com/products) to retrieve a rich collection of technical specifications for each product. Each product has 40 boolean attributes, such as `self-timer`, `face-detection`, `red-eye fix`, etc; while the tag dictionary includes 40 unique keywords like `lightweight`, `advanced`, `easy`, etc.

Synthetic Dataset: We generate a large boolean matrix of dimension 10,000 (items)×100 (50 attributes + 50 tags) and randomly choose submatrices of varying sizes, based on our experimental setting. We split the 50 independent and identically distributed attributes into four groups, where the value is set to 1 with probabilities of 0.75, 0.15, 0.10 and 0.05 respectively. For each of the 50 tags, we pre-define relations by randomly picking a set of attributes that are correlated to it. A tag is set to 1 with a probability p if majority of the attributes in its pre-defined relation have boolean value 1.

We use the synthetic datasets for quantitative experiments, while the real dataset is used in the user study.

5.1 Quantitative Results: Performance

Exact Algorithm: We first compare the Naive approach with our ETT. Since the Naive algorithm can only work for small problem instances, we a pick a subset from the synthetic dataset having 1000 items, 16 attributes and 8 tags. Figures 4 and 5 compare the execution time and the number of candidate items considered, for Naive and ETT respectively, when the number of attributes (m) varies (number of items = 1000, number of tags = 8). The Naive algorithm considers all 2^m items. We used as number of attributes per group $m' = 2, 2, 4, 5, 4, 7, 4, 6$ for $m = 4, 6, 8, 10, 12, 14, 16, 18$ respectively in ETT (more analysis of m' in Figure 6). As can be seen, Naive is orders of magnitude slower than ETT.

Next, we study the behavior of attribute groupings on ETT. For a sub-sample picked from our synthetic dataset having 20 attributes, 1000 items and 8 tags, we experiment with different possible attribute groupings, m' = 1, 2, 4, 5, 10, 20. Figure 6 shows the effect of m' on the performance of ETT. The execution time and number of items considered

[5]As discussed earlier, the number of items in the dataset is not important for the execution cost; analysis in Figure 8.

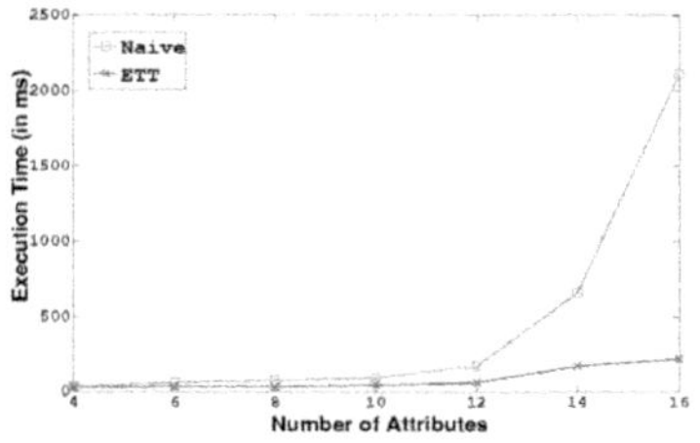

Figure 4: Execution time for varying m (Synthetic data)

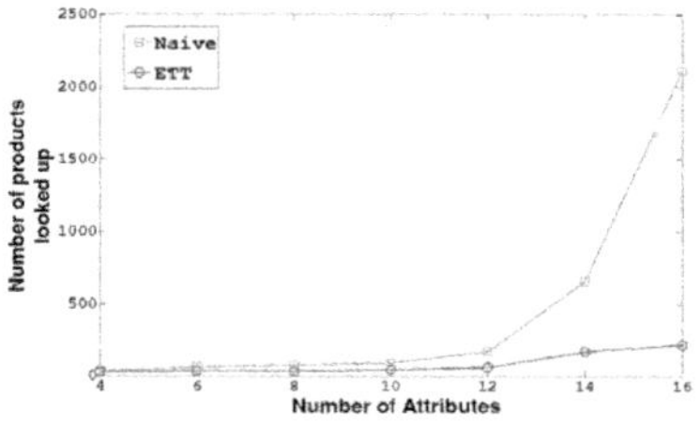

Figure 5: Number of items built for varying m (Synthetic data)

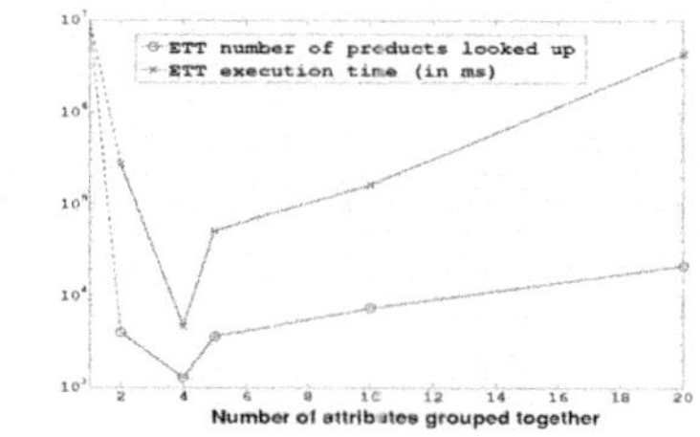

Figure 6: ETT behavior for varying m' (Synthetic data)

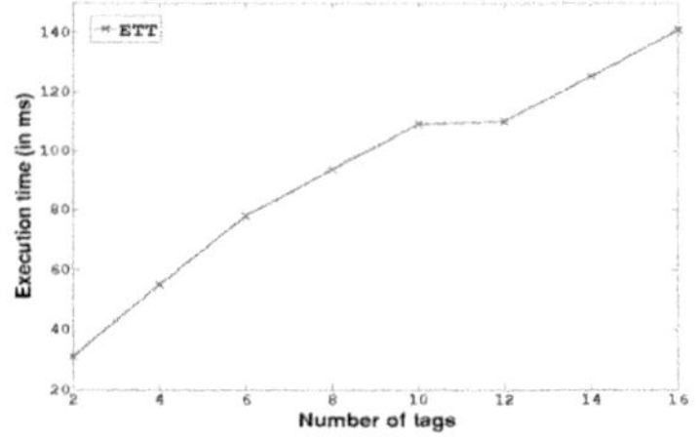

Figure 7: Execution time for varying z (Synthetic data)

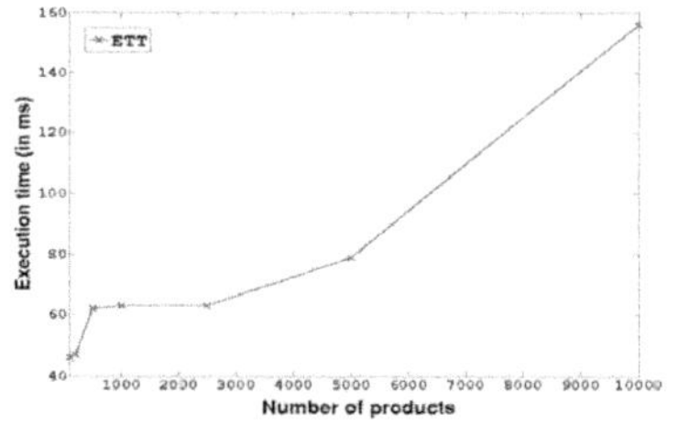

Figure 8: Execution time for varying n (Synthetic data)

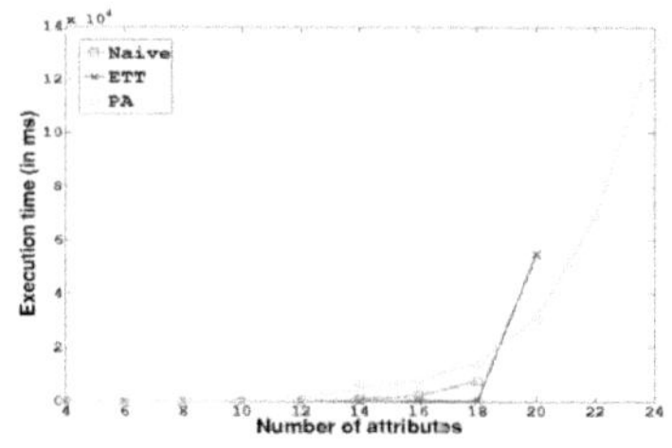

Figure 9: Execution time for varying m (Synthetic data)

for $m' = 1$ is not reported in Figure 6 as it was too slow. The trade-off of choosing m' is: a small m' means there are many short lists in tier-1, so that the cost of joining the lists is high. In contrast, a large m' indicates fewer but longer lists in tier-1 resulting in increased cost of creating the lists. We observe that the best balance is struck when $m' = 4$ attributes forming 5 lists, each having 2^4=16 items.

We also vary the number of tags z and number of items n in the dataset to study the behavior of ETT. We pick a subset from the synthetic dataset having 1000 items, 16 attributes and 16 tags, and consider further subsets of this dataset. Figure 7 reflects the change in execution time with increasing number of tags for the synthetic data (number of items = 1000, number of attributes = 12, attribute grouping = 3). The increase in number of tags increases the number of GetNext() operations in ETT, and hence the running time rises steadily. Figure 8 depicts how an increase in the number of items in the dataset (number of attributes = 12, number of tags = 8, attribute grouping = 3) barely affects the running time of ETT since an initialization step calculates all conditional tag-attribute probabilities.

Table 3: PA Performance (Synthetic data)

User-Defined Approx Factor(ϵ)	Execution Time (in ms)	Obtained Approx Factor
0.5	406.0	0.93
0.4	749.0	0.94
0.3	2796.0	0.97
0.2	41094.0	0.98

Approximation Algorithm: We observe in Figure 4 that the execution time of ETT outperforms that of Naive, for moderate data instances. Figure 9 reveals that while ETT is extremely slow beyond number of attributes (m) = 16, PA with an approximation factor ϵ=0.5, continues to return guaranteed results in reasonable time with increasing number of attributes m for a subset of the synthetic data (number of items = 1000, number of tags = 8). Therefore, PA performs better than ETT for larger datasets having many attributes and tags.

Table 3 depicts how the execution time and the obtained approximation factor vary with change in the user-defined approximation factor ϵ, for a subset of the synthetic dataset having 1000 items, 20 attributes and 8 tags . Note that, in this experimental set-up, z=z'=8 so that the number of tag groups = 1. The obtained approximation factor is the ratio of the score for top-1 item obtained by PA to the score of the optimal *item* obtained by an extended run of ETT.

5.2 Qualitative Results: User Study

We now validate how designers can leverage existing item information to design new items catering different groups of people in a user study conducted on Amazon Mechanical Turk (https://www.mturk.com) on the real camera dataset. We also consult DPreview (http://www.dpreview.com), a website about digital cameras and digital photography. There are two parts to our user study. Each part of the study involves thirty independent single-user tasks. Each task is conducted in two phases: *User Knowledge Phase* where we estimate the users' background and *User Judgment Phase* where we collect users' responses to our questions.

In the first part of our study, we build four new cameras (two digital compact and two digital slr) using our PA algorithm with an approximation factor ϵ=0.5, by considering tag sets corresponding to compact cameras and slr cameras respectively. We present these four new cameras along with four existing popular cameras (presented anonymously) and observe that 65% of users choose the new cameras, over the existing ones. For example, users overwhelmingly prefer our new compact digital camera over Nikon Coolpix L22 because the former supports both automatic and manual focus while the latter does not, thus validating how our techniques can benefit designers.

The second part of the study concerns six new cameras designed for three groups of people: young students, old retired and professional photographers. Domain experts identify and label three overlapping sets of tags from the camera dataset's complete tag vocabulary, one set for each group and we then build two potential new cameras for each of the three groups. For each of the six new cameras thus built, we ask users to assign at least five tags by looking up the complete camera tag vocabulary, provided to them. We observe that majority of the users rightly classify the six cameras into the three groups. The correctness of the classification is validated by comparing the tags received for a camera to the three tag sets identified by domain experts; we also validate the correctness by consulting data available in Dpreview. As an example, the cameras designed by leveraging tags corresponding to professional photographers draw tags like **advanced**, **high iso**, etc. while cameras designed by leveraging tags corresponding to old retired draw tags like **lightweight**, **easy**, etc. Figure 10 shows the percentage of users classifying the six cameras correctly. Thus, our technique can help designers build new items that are likely to attract desirable tags from different groups of people.

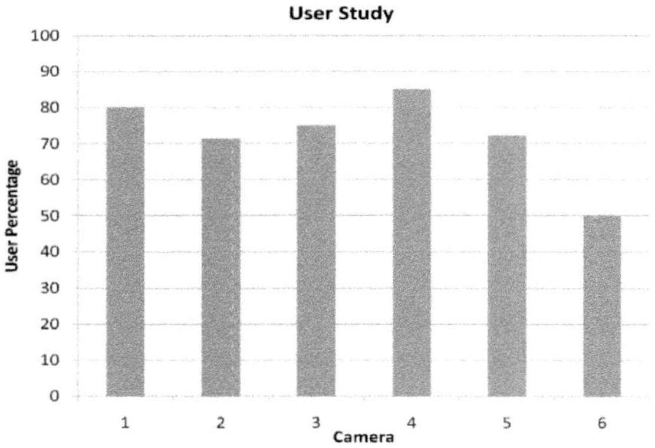

Figure 10: Users Classify Cameras Correctly

6. RELATED WORK

The dynamics of social tagging has been an active research area in recent years, with several papers focusing on the tag prediction problem. A recent work [16] proposes a probabilistic model for personalized tag prediction and employs the Naive Bayes classifier. Related research in text mining [12] found that the Naive Bayes classifier performs better than SVM and CRF in classifying blog sentiments. Another study that indirectly supports the use of Naive Bayes for tag prediction is done by Heymann et al. [7], who found that tag-based association rules can produce very high-precision predictions. The process of collaborative tagging has been studied in [6]. Other related work investigates tag suggestion, usually from a collaborative filtering and UI perspective; for example with URLs [15] and blog posts [11].

The problem of item design has been studied by many disciplines including economics, industrial engineering and computer science [13]. Optimal item design or positioning is a well studied problem in Operations Research and Marketing. Shocker *et al.* [14] first represented products and consumer preferences as points in a joint attribute space. Later, several techniques [1, 2] were developed to design/position a new item. Work in this domain requires direct involvement of consumers, who choose preferences from a set of existing alternative products. Miah et al. [10] study the problem of selecting product snippets given a user query log, in order for the designed snippet to be returned by the maximum number of queries. However, none of these works has studied the problem of item design in relation to social tagging.

Our top-k pipelined algorithm is inspired by the rich work on top-k algorithms ([4, 9]). A recent survey by Ilyas et al. [8] covers many of the important results in this area.

7. CONCLUSIONS

In this paper we consider the novel problem of leveraging online collaborative tagging in product design. We formally define the Tag Maximization problem, investigate its computational complexity, and propose several principled algorithms that are shown to work well in practice. Our work is a preliminary look at a very novel area of research, and there appear to be many exciting directions of future research. Our immediate focus is to extend our work to include tag prediction using other classifiers, such as decision trees, SVMs, and regression trees (the latter is applicable when we wish to predict the frequency of occurrence of desirable tags attracted by products). We also intend to evaluate the applicability of our proposed framework to other novel applications, e.g., guide recommender systems recommend better vacation travel itineraries by tracking tag history, help online authors write better blogs, and others.

8. REFERENCES

[1] S. Albers and K. Brockhoff. Optimal product attributes in single choice models. *Journal of the Operational Research Society, 31, 647-655*, 1980.

[2] M. D. Albritton and P. R. McMullen. Optimal product design using a colony of virtual ants. *European Journal of Operational Research*, 176(1):498–520, January 2007.

[3] B. Cestnik. Estimating probabilities: A crucial task in machine learning. In *ECAI*, pages 147–149, 1990.

[4] R. Fagin, A. Lotem, and M. Naor. Optimal aggregation algorithms for middleware. In *PODS*, 2001.

[5] M. R. Garey and D. S. Johnson. *Computers and Intractability; A Guide to the Theory of NP-Completeness.* W. H. Freeman & Co., New York, NY, USA, 1990.

[6] S. A. Golder and B. A. Huberman. Usage patterns of collaborative tagging systems. *J. Inf. Sci.*, 32(2):198–208, 2006.

[7] P. Heymann, D. Ramage, and H. Garcia-Molina. Social tag prediction. In *SIGIR*, pages 531–538, 2008.

[8] I. F. Ilyas, G. Beskales, and M. A. Soliman. A survey of top-k query processing techniques in relational database systems. *ACM Comput. Surv.*, 40(4):1–58, 2008.

[9] I. F. Ilyas, D. Martinenghi, and M. Tagliasacchi. Rank-join algorithms for search computing. In *SeCO Workshop*, pages 211–224, 2009.

[10] M. Miah, G. Das, V. Hristidis, and H. Mannila. Determining attributes to maximize visibility of objects. *IEEE Transactions on Knowledge and Data Engineering*, 21:959–973, 2009.

[11] G. Mishne. Autotag: a collaborative approach to automated tag assignment for weblog posts. In *WWW '06: Proceedings of the 15th international conference on World Wide Web*, pages 953–954, New York, NY, USA, 2006. ACM Press.

[12] A. Pak and P. Paroubek. Twitter as a corpus for sentiment analysis and opinion mining. In *LREC*, 2010.

[13] T. Selkar and W. Burlesson. Context-aware design and interaction in computer systems. *IBM Syst. J.*, 39:880–891, July 2000.

[14] A. D. Shocker and V. Srinivasan. A Consumer-Based Methodology for the Identification of New Product Ideas. *MANAGEMENT SCIENCE*, 20(6):921–937, 1974.

[15] Z. Xu, Y. Fu, J. Mao, and D. Su. Towards the semantic web: Collaborative tag suggestions. In *Proceedings of the Collaborative Web Tagging Workshop at the WWW 2006*, Edinburgh, Scotland, 2006.

[16] D. Yin, Z. Xue, L. Hong, and B. D. Davison. A probabilistic model for personalized tag prediction. In *Proceedings of the 16th ACM SIGKDD international conference on Knowledge discovery and data mining*, KDD '10, pages 959–968, New York, NY, USA, 2010. ACM.

Stackelberg Games for Adversarial Prediction Problems

Michael Brückner
Department of Computer Science
University of Potsdam, Germany
mibrueck@cs.uni-potsdam.de

Tobias Scheffer
Department of Computer Science
University of Potsdam, Germany
scheffer@cs.uni-potsdam.de

ABSTRACT

The standard assumption of identically distributed training and test data is violated when test data are generated in response to a predictive model. This becomes apparent, for example, in the context of email spam filtering, where an email service provider employs a spam filter and the spam sender can take this filter into account when generating new emails. We model the interaction between learner and data generator as a Stackelberg competition in which the learner plays the role of the leader and the data generator may react on the leader's move. We derive an optimization problem to determine the solution of this game and present several instances of the Stackelberg prediction game. We show that the Stackelberg prediction game generalizes existing prediction models. Finally, we explore properties of the discussed models empirically in the context of email spam filtering.

Categories and Subject Descriptors

I.5.1 [**Pattern Recognition**]: Models—*statistical*; H.4.3 [**Information System Applications**]: Communications Applications—*electronic mail*

General Terms

Theory, Algorithms

Keywords

Adversarial Classification, Stackelberg Competition, Prediction Game, Spam Filtering

1. INTRODUCTION

A common assumption on which most learning algorithms are based is that training and test data are governed by identical distributions. However, in a variety of applications, the distribution that governs data at application time may be influenced by an adversary whose interests conflict those of the learner. Consider, for instance, the following three scenarios. In computer and network security, scripts that control attacks are engineered with botnet and intrusion detection systems in mind. Credit card fraudsters adapt their unauthorized use of credit cards—in particular, amounts charged per transactions and per day and the type of businesses that amounts are charged from—such as not to trigger alerting mechanisms employed by credit card companies. Email spam senders design message templates that are instantiated by nodes of botnets; templates are specifically designed to produce a low spam score with current spam filters. The domain of email spam filtering will serve as a running example throughout the paper. In all of these applications, assailants factor information about countermeasures that are being employed into the process of data generation.

The interaction between learner and data generators can be modeled as a game in which one player controls the predictive model whereas another exercises some control over the process of data generation. The adversary's influence on the generation of the data can be mathematically modeled as a transformation that is imposed on the distribution that governs the data at training time. The transformed distribution then governs the data at application time. The optimization criterion of either player takes as arguments both, the predictive model chosen by the learner and the transformation carried out by the adversary.

Typically, this problem is modeled under the worst-case assumption that the adversary desires to impose the highest possible costs on the learner. This amounts to a zero-sum game in which the loss of one player is the gain of the other. In this setting, both players can maximize their expected outcome by following a minimax strategy. El Ghaoui et al. [5] derive a minimax model for input data that are known to lie within some hyper-rectangles around the training instances. Their solution minimizes the worst-case loss over all possible choices of the data in these intervals. Lanckriet et al. [10] study the minimax probability machine. This classifier minimizes the maximal probability of misclassifying new instances for a given mean and covariance matrix of each class. Geometrically, this solution corresponds to a minimax strategy with hyper-ellipsoids around the training instances, rather than hyper-rectangles. Similarly, worst-case solutions to classification games in which the adversary deletes input features or performs arbitrary feature transformation have been studied [3, 6, 7, 14, 4].

Several applications motivate problem settings in which the goals of the learner and the data generator, while still conflicting, are not necessarily entirely antagonistic. For instance, a fraudster's goal of maximizing the profit made from exploiting phished account information is not the inverse of

KDD'11, August 21–24, 2011, San Diego, California, USA.

an email service provider's goal of achieving a high spam recognition rate at close-to-zero false positives. When playing a minimax strategy, one often makes overly pessimistic assumptions about the adversary's behavior and may not necessarily obtain an optimal outcome.

For games that do not exhibit the zero-sum property, a game-theoretic model has been studied that assumes both players to commit to their actions *simultaneously* [1]; that is, without information about the opponent's course of action. When the parameter space of the learner's model and the adversary's transformation and both players' loss functions satisfy specific criteria (*e.g.*, the loss functions have to be monotonic with distinct monotonicity and twice differentiable), then the prediction game has a unique Nash equilibrium that can be found by solving a compact optimization problem [1]. The Nash equilibrium is a combination of parameters for the predictive model and the adversary's transformation which has the property that neither player benefits by unilaterally deviating from it. For the learner, playing the Nash equilibrium instead of the minimax strategy is an optimal course of action under the following sufficient conditions: First, the adversary has to be trusted to behave rationally in the sense of maximizing their profit by playing a Nash strategy, too. If the learner plays the Nash equilibrium but the adversary deviates from that equilibrium, then both players may fare arbitrarily poorly. Secondly, a unique equilibrium needs to exist, since a combination of actions from two distinct equilibria may lead to an arbitrarily poor outcome for either player. Thirdly, the adversary must not have any information about the predictive model that the learner commits to before generating the data. In practice, this assumption can be violated when the adversary is able to probe the predictive model. If the adversary violates either of the above three conditions, no guarantees on the optimality can be given and, consequently, a learner may be ill-advised to play the Nash equilibrium.

In practice, a spam sender may follow heuristics derived from past experience and experiments with the filter. Such a setting in which both players act *non-simultaneously* can be modeled as a Stackelberg competition which allows one player—the follower—to be potentially fully informed about the move of the other player—the leader. We model adversarial learning as a Stackelberg competition in which the *learner acts as leader* by committing to a predictive model in the first step. The model is then disclosed to the follower—the data generator—who then gets to transform the input distribution.

Some authors [9, 12] study the case in which the *data generator acts as leader* and the learner as follower. This reflects a setting in which the adversary discloses how the future distribution will differ from the current distribution before the learner has to commit to a model, which contradicts the intuition of an adversarial model-building problem. When the data generator acts as leader and discloses the data transformation, the learner only has to solve a simple optimization problem in order to minimize the risk on the transformed data points.

The rest of this paper is organized as follows. Section 2 introduces the problem setting. We formalize the Stackelberg prediction game, derive an optimization problem to determine the Stackelberg equilibrium, and show how to employ kernel functions in Section 3. In Section 4, we present three instances of the SPG and discuss their relation to existing prediction models. We report on experiments on email spam filtering in Section 5; Section 6 concludes.

2. PROBLEM SETTING

We study prediction games between two players: The *learner* ($v = -1$) and an adversary, the *data generator* ($v = +1$). In our running example of email spam filtering, we study the competition between recipient and senders, not competition among senders. To this end, $v = -1$ refers to the recipient whereas $v = +1$ models the entirety of all legitimate and abusive email senders as a single, amalgamated player.

In the *past*, the data generator $v = +1$ produced a sample $D = \{(x_i, y_i)\}_{i=1}^n$ of n training instances $x_i \in \mathcal{X}$ with corresponding class labels $y_i \in \mathcal{Y} = \{-1, +1\}$. These object-class pairs are drawn according to a training distribution with density function $p(x, y)$. By contrast, *future* object-class pairs, produced by the data generator at application time, are drawn from some test distribution with density $\dot{p}(x, y)$ which may differ from $p(x, y)$.

The task of the learner $v = -1$ is to select the parameters $\mathbf{w} \in \mathbb{R}^m$ of a predictive model $h(x) = \operatorname{sign} f_{\mathbf{w}}(x)$ implemented in terms of a generalized linear decision function $f_{\mathbf{w}} : \mathcal{X} \to \mathbb{R}$ with $f_{\mathbf{w}}(x) = \mathbf{w}^\mathsf{T}\phi(x)$ and feature mapping $\phi : \mathcal{X} \to \mathbb{R}^m$. The learner's theoretical *costs* at application time are given by

$$\theta_{-1}(\mathbf{w}, \dot{p}) = \sum_{\mathcal{Y}} \int_{\mathcal{X}} c_{-1}(x, y)\ell_{-1}(f_{\mathbf{w}}(x), y)\dot{p}(x, y)\mathrm{d}x,$$

where weighting function $c_{-1} : \mathcal{X} \times \mathcal{Y} \to \mathbb{R}$ and loss function $\ell_{-1} : \mathbb{R} \times \mathcal{Y} \to \mathbb{R}$ detail the *weighted loss* $c_{-1}(x, y)\ell_{-1}(f_{\mathbf{w}}(x), y)$ that the learner incurs when the predictive model classifies instance x as $h(x) = \operatorname{sign} f_{\mathbf{w}}(x)$ while the true label is y. The positive class- and instance-specific weighting factors $c_{-1}(x, y)$ with $\mathbb{E}[c_{-1}(\mathbf{X}, \mathbf{Y})] = 1$ specify the importance of minimizing the loss $\ell_{-1}(f_{\mathbf{w}}(x), y)$ for the corresponding object-class pair (x, y). For instance, in spam filtering, the correct classification of non-spam messages can be business-critical for email service providers while failing to detect spam messages runs up processing and storage costs, depending on the size of the message.

The data generator $v = +1$ can modify the data generation process for future instances. In practice, spam senders update their campaign templates which are disseminated to the nodes of botnets. Formally, the data generator transforms the training distribution with density p to the test distribution with density $\dot{p}$. The data generator incurs *transformation costs* by modifying the data generation process which is quantified by $\Omega_{+1}(p, \dot{p})$. This term acts as a regularizer on the transformation and may implicitly constrain the shift that can be imposed on the distribution, depending on the nature of the application that is to be modeled. For instance, the email sender may not be allowed to alter the training distribution for non-spam messages, or to modify the nature of the messages by changing the label from *spam* to *non-spam* or vice versa. Additionally, changing the training distribution for spam messages may run up costs depending on the extent of distortion inflicted on the informational payload.

The theoretical *costs* of the data generator at application time are the sum of the expected prediction costs and the transformation costs,

$$\theta_{+1}(\mathbf{w}, \dot{p}) = \sum_{\mathcal{Y}} \int_{\mathcal{X}} c_{+1}(x, y)\ell_{+1}(f_{\mathbf{w}}(x), y)\dot{p}(x, y)\mathrm{d}x + \Omega_{+1}(p, \dot{p}).$$

In analogy to the learner's costs, $c_{+1}(x, y)\ell_{+1}(f_{\mathbf{w}}(x), y)$ quantifies the loss that the data generator incurs when instance x is labeled as $h(x) = \operatorname{sign} f_{\mathbf{w}}(x)$ while the true label is y. The weighting factors $c_{+1}(x, y)$ with $\mathbb{E}[c_{+1}(\mathbf{X}, \mathbf{Y})] = 1$ express the significance of (x, y) from the perspective of the data generator. In our example scenario, this allows to reflect that costs of correctly or incorrectly classified instances may vary greatly across different physical senders that are aggregated into the amalgamated player.

Since the theoretical costs of both players depend on the test distribution, they can, for all practical purposes, not be calculated. Hence, we focus on a regularized, empirical counterpart of the theoretical costs based on the training sample D. The empirical counterpart $\hat{\Omega}_{+1}(D, \dot{D})$ of the data generator's regularizer $\Omega_{+1}(p, \dot{p})$ penalizes the divergence between training sample $D = \{(x_i, y_i)\}_{i=1}^n$ and a perturbated training sample $\dot{D} = \{(\dot{x}_i, y_i)\}_{i=1}^n$ that would be the outcome of applying the transformation that translates p into $\dot{p}$ to sample D. The learner's cost function, instead of integrating over $\dot{p}$, sums over the elements of the perturbated training sample $\dot{D}$. The players' empirical cost functions can still only be evaluated after the learner has committed to parameters $\mathbf{w}$ and the data generator to a transformation from training to test density function, but this transformation need only be represented in terms of the effects that it will have on the training sample D. The transformed training sample $\dot{D}$ must not be mistaken for test data; test data will be generated under $\dot{p}$ at application time after the players have committed to their actions.

The empirical costs incurred by the predictive model h with parameters $\mathbf{w}$ and the shift from p to $\dot{p}$ amount to

$$\hat{\theta}_{-1}(\mathbf{w}, \dot{D}) = \sum_{i=1}^{n} c_{-1,i}\ell_{-1}(f_{\mathbf{w}}(\dot{x}_i), y_i) + \rho_{-1}\hat{\Omega}_{-1}(\mathbf{w}), \quad (1)$$

$$\hat{\theta}_{+1}(\mathbf{w}, \dot{D}) = \sum_{i=1}^{n} c_{+1,i}\ell_{+1}(f_{\mathbf{w}}(\dot{x}_i), y_i) + \rho_{+1}\hat{\Omega}_{+1}(D, \dot{D}), \quad (2)$$

where we have replaced the weighting terms $\frac{1}{n}c_v(\dot{x}_i, y_i)$ by constant cost factors $c_{v,i} > 0$ with $\sum_i c_{v,i} = 1$. The learner's regularizer $\hat{\Omega}_{-1}(\mathbf{w})$ in (1) accounts for the fact that $\dot{D}$ does not constitute the test data itself, but is merely a training sample transformed to reflect the test distribution and then used to learn the model parameters $\mathbf{w}$. The trade-off between the empirical loss and the regularizer is controlled by each player's regularization parameter $\rho_v > 0$ for $v \in \{-1, +1\}$.

In our analysis, we estimate the transformation costs by the average squared ℓ^2-distance between x_i and $\dot{x}_i$ in feature space,

$$\hat{\Omega}_{+1}(\dot{D}, D) = \frac{1}{n}\sum_{i=1}^{n}\frac{1}{2}\|\phi(\dot{x}_i) - \phi(x_i)\|^2. \quad (3)$$

The learner's regularizer $\hat{\Omega}_{-1}$ penalizes the complexity of the predictive model $h(x) = \operatorname{sign} f_{\mathbf{w}}(x)$. For our analysis, we consider Tikhonov regularization which, for linear decision functions $f_{\mathbf{w}}$, reduces to the squared ℓ^2-norm of $\mathbf{w}$,

$$\hat{\Omega}_{-1}(\mathbf{w}) = \frac{1}{2}\|\mathbf{w}\|^2. \quad (4)$$

Note that either player's empirical costs $\hat{\theta}_v(\mathbf{w}, \dot{D})$ depend on both players' actions. The concept of an *optimal* choice of model parameters $\mathbf{w}$ regardless of the adversary's choice of a data transformation is therefore not well-defined. In the following section, we will refer to the Stackelberg model which identifies the concept of an optimal move of the leader which minimizes $\hat{\theta}_{-1}$ over $\mathbf{w}$ under the assumption that the follower will react by minimizing $\hat{\theta}_{+1}$ over $\dot{D}$ given the parameters $\mathbf{w}$ chosen by the leader.

3. STACKELBERG PREDICTION GAME

We model the prediction game as a Stackelberg competition; we refer to the resulting model as the *Stackelberg prediction game* (SPG). A Stackelberg game is one of the simplest dynamic games: In the first stage, the *leader*—in our case, the learner—decides on a predictive model $h(x) = \operatorname{sign} f_{\mathbf{w}}(x)$ with parameters $\mathbf{w}$. In the second stage, the data generator, who plays the part of the *follower*, observes the leader's decision and chooses a transformation that changes the distribution of *past* instances into the distribution of *future* instances. In this scenario, the learner has to commit to a set of parameters unilaterally whereas the data generator can take the model parameters $\mathbf{w}$ into account when preparing the data transformation.

The optimality of a *Stackelberg equilibrium* which we will now introduce rests on the assumption that the follower—the data generator—will act rationally in the sense of choosing a transformation that minimizes the resulting costs $\hat{\theta}_{+1}$ given the disclosed $\mathbf{w}$. To reach minimal costs given $\mathbf{w}$, the data generator has to identify a sample $\dot{D}$ that constitutes a global minimum of the cost function $\hat{\theta}_{+1}(\mathbf{w}, \dot{D})$. There may be several global minima with identical values of the cost function; in general, the data generator has to identify any element $\dot{D}$ from the set of optimal responses to $\mathbf{w}$,

$$\dot{\mathcal{D}}_{\mathbf{w}} = \left\{\{(\dot{x}_i, y_i)\}_{i=1}^n : \{\dot{x}_i\}_{i=1}^n \in \operatorname*{argmin}_{\dot{x}'_1,\ldots,\dot{x}'_n \in \mathcal{X}} \hat{\theta}_{+1}\left(\mathbf{w}, \{(\dot{x}'_i, y_i)\}_{i=1}^n\right)\right\}.$$

Identifying an element $\dot{D} \in \dot{\mathcal{D}}_{\mathbf{w}}$ amounts to solving a regular optimization problem because $\mathbf{w}$ can be observed before $\dot{D}$ has to be chosen. A Stackelberg equilibrium is now identified by backward induction. Assuming that the data generator will decide for any $\dot{D} \in \dot{\mathcal{D}}_{\mathbf{w}}$, the learner has to choose model parameters $\mathbf{w}^*$ that minimize the learner's cost function $\hat{\theta}_{-1}$ for any of the possible reactions $\dot{D} \in \dot{\mathcal{D}}_{\mathbf{w}}$ that are optimal for the data generator:

$$\mathbf{w}^* \in \operatorname*{argmin}_{\mathbf{w} \in \mathbb{R}^m} \max_{\dot{D} \in \dot{\mathcal{D}}_{\mathbf{w}}} \hat{\theta}_{-1}(\mathbf{w}, \dot{D}). \quad (5)$$

An action $\mathbf{w}^*$ that minimizes the learner's costs and a corresponding optimal action $\dot{D} \in \dot{\mathcal{D}}_{\mathbf{w}^*}$ of the data generator are called a *Stackelberg equilibrium*. The Stackelberg equilibrium is a special case of a subgame perfect equilibrium which is an extension of the Nash equilibrium for games that are played non-simultaneously.

3.1 Finding a Stackelberg Equilibrium

Equation 5 establishes a hierarchical mathematical program—specifically, a *bilevel optimization problem*—with upper-level objective $\hat{\theta}_{-1}$ and lower-level objective $\hat{\theta}_{+1}$.

$$\min_{\mathbf{w}\in\mathbb{R}^m} \max_{\forall i:\dot{x}_i\in\mathcal{X}} \hat{\theta}_{-1}(\mathbf{w}, \{(\dot{x}_i, y_i)\}_{i=1}^n) \quad (6)$$

$$\text{s.t.} \quad \{\dot{x}_i\}_{i=1}^n \in \operatorname*{argmin}_{\dot{x}'_1,\ldots,\dot{x}'_n\in\mathcal{X}} \hat{\theta}_{+1}(\mathbf{w}, \{(\dot{x}'_i, y_i)\}_{i=1}^n) \quad (7)$$

Bilevel programs are intrinsically hard to solve. Even the simplest instance in which all constraints and objectives are linear is known to be NP-hard [8]. The main difficulties arise from the constraints $\dot{x}'_i \in \mathcal{X}$ of the lower-level optimization problem which generally render constraint (7) of the upper-level optimization problem to be non-differentiable in $\mathbf{w}$, even if $\hat{\theta}_{+1}$ is continuously differentiable in $\mathbf{w}$ and $\dot{x}'_i$ for $i = 1, \ldots, n$.

Numerous approaches that address bilevel programs have been studied, for instance, based on gradient descent, penalty function, and trust-region methods; see, for instance, [2] for a detailed survey. Commonly, these methods reformulate the optimization problem into a mathematical program with equilibrium constraints. In this, the lower-level optimization problem is replaced by its Karush-Kuhn-Tucker (KKT) conditions. The resulting optimization problem with equilibrium constraints can be solved approximately by relaxing the complementary conditions [15]. However these methods do not necessarily converge to a (local) optimum and are applicable to small problems only.

That is why we focus on a special case of the above bilevel program. The following theorem reformulates the lower-level optimization problem into an unconstrained problem such that constraint (7) becomes continuously differentiable in $\mathbf{w}$. This requires the feature space induced by mapping ϕ, but not necessarily the input space $\mathcal{X}$, to be unrestricted and the data generator's loss function $\ell_{+1}(z, y)$ to be convex and continuously differentiable in $z \in \mathbb{R}$.

THEOREM 1. *Let the leader's cost function $\hat{\theta}_{-1}$ and the follower's cost function $\hat{\theta}_{+1}$ be defined as in (1) and (2) with regularizers $\hat{\Omega}_{-1}$ and $\hat{\Omega}_{+1}$ defined as in (4) and (3), respectively. Let feature mapping $\phi : \mathcal{X} \to \mathbb{R}^m$ be surjective, let the data generator's loss function $\ell_{+1}(z, y)$ be convex and continuously differentiable with respect to $z \in \mathbb{R}$ for any fixed $y \in \mathcal{Y}$. Now let weight vector $\mathbf{w}^* \in \mathbb{R}^m$ and factors $\tau_1^*, \ldots, \tau_n^* \in \mathbb{R}$ be a solution of the optimization problem*

$$\min_{\mathbf{w},\forall i:\tau_i} \sum_{i=1}^n c_{-1,i}\ell_{-1}\left(f_{\mathbf{w}}(x_i) + \tau_i\|\mathbf{w}\|^2, y_i\right) + \frac{\rho_{-1}}{2}\|\mathbf{w}\|^2 \quad (8)$$

$$\text{s.t.} \quad \forall i : 0 = \tau_i + \frac{n}{\rho_{+1}} c_{+1,i}\ell'_{+1}\left(f_{\mathbf{w}}(x_i) + \tau_i\|\mathbf{w}\|^2, y_i\right).$$

Then the Stackelberg prediction game in Equation 6 attains an equilibrium at $(\mathbf{w}^*, \dot{D}^*)$ with $\dot{D}^* = \{(\dot{x}_i^*, y_i)\}_{i=1}^n$ and $\dot{x}_i^* \in \{\dot{x} \in \mathcal{X} : \phi(\dot{x}) = \phi(x_i) + \tau_i^*\mathbf{w}^*\}$.

Proof. Constraint 7 says that $\{\dot{x}_i^*\}_{i=1}^n$ has to be a solution of the restricted optimization problem

$$\min_{\forall i:\dot{x}_i\in\mathcal{X}} \sum_{i=1}^n c_{+1,i}\ell_{+1}(\mathbf{w}^\mathsf{T}\phi(\dot{x}_i), y_i) + \frac{\rho_{+1}}{n}\sum_{i=1}^n \frac{1}{2}\|\phi(\dot{x}_i) - \phi(x_i)\|^2.$$

As the objective as well as the constraints are entirely defined in terms of $\dot{\mathbf{x}}_i^* = \phi(\dot{x}_i^*)$, this condition is equivalent to enforcing $\{\dot{\mathbf{x}}_i^*\}_{i=1}^n$ to be a solution of the unrestricted optimization problem

$$\min_{\forall i:\dot{\mathbf{x}}_i\in\mathbb{R}^m} \sum_{i=1}^n c_{+1,i}\ell_{+1}(\mathbf{w}^\mathsf{T}\dot{\mathbf{x}}_i, y_i) + \frac{\rho_{+1}}{n}\sum_{i=1}^n \frac{1}{2}\|\dot{\mathbf{x}}_i - \phi(x_i)\|^2. \quad (9)$$

This solution is uniquely defined for any fixed $\mathbf{w}$ as loss function $\ell_{+1}(z, y)$ is required to be convex in z, and consequently in $\dot{\mathbf{x}}_i$, and the term $\|\dot{\mathbf{x}}_i - \phi(x_i)\|^2$ is quadratic in $\dot{\mathbf{x}}_i$ and therefore strictly convex for any fixed $\phi(x_i)$. Given $\mathbf{w} \in \mathbb{R}^m$ and minimizer $\dot{\mathbf{x}}_i^* \in \mathbb{R}^m$, the set $\dot{\mathcal{X}}_{\mathbf{w}}^i = \{\dot{x}^* \in \mathcal{X} : \phi(\dot{x}^*) = \dot{\mathbf{x}}_i^*\}$ contains all instances $\dot{x}^*$ which correspond to the optimally transformed instance in feature space $\dot{\mathbf{x}}_i^*$. Since ϕ is surjective, $\dot{\mathcal{X}}_{\mathbf{w}}^i$ is guaranteed to be non-empty, and consequently, for any solution $\{\dot{\mathbf{x}}_i^*\}_{i=1}^n$, there exist at least one corresponding set of instances $\{\dot{x}_i^*\}_{i=1}^n$. As ϕ is not required to be a bijective mapping, there may exist multiple instances $\dot{x} \in \dot{\mathcal{X}}_{\mathbf{w}}^i$ which are optimal in the sense of minimizing the data generator's loss. However, since all of these instances share the same feature representation $\dot{\mathbf{x}}_i^*$, the inner maximization of the upper-level optimization problem in (6) vanishes,

$$\min_{\mathbf{w}\in\mathbb{R}^m} \max_{\forall i:\dot{x}_i\in\dot{\mathcal{X}}_{\mathbf{w}}^i} \hat{\theta}_{-1}(\mathbf{w}, \{(\dot{x}_i, y_i)\}_{i=1}^n) =$$

$$\min_{\mathbf{w}\in\mathbb{R}^m} \sum_{i=1}^n c_{-1,i}\ell_{-1}\left(\mathbf{w}^\mathsf{T}\dot{\mathbf{x}}_i^*, y_i\right) + \frac{\rho_{-1}}{2}\|\mathbf{w}\|^2, \quad (10)$$

where $\{\mathbf{x}_i^*\}_{i=1}^n$ is the solution of Optimization Problem 9. Since 9 is convex, this constraint can be replaced by its complementary conditions which are given by $\nabla_{\dot{\mathbf{x}}_i}\hat{\theta}_{+1}(\mathbf{w}, \dot{D}) = 0$ for $i = 1, \ldots, n$ where

$$\nabla_{\dot{\mathbf{x}}_i}\hat{\theta}_{+1}(\mathbf{w}, \dot{D}) = c_{+1,i}\ell'_{+1}(\mathbf{w}^\mathsf{T}\dot{\mathbf{x}}_i^*, y_i)\mathbf{w} + \frac{\rho_{+1}}{n}(\dot{\mathbf{x}}_i - \phi(x_i)).$$

The mapped instance $\dot{\mathbf{x}}_i^*$ that satisfies the i-th complementary condition is given by

$$\dot{\mathbf{x}}_i^* = \phi(x_i) + \tau_i\mathbf{w} \quad (11)$$

with

$$\begin{aligned}\tau_i &= -\frac{n}{\rho_{+1}} c_{+1,i}\ell'_{+1}\left(\mathbf{w}^\mathsf{T}\dot{\mathbf{x}}_i^*, y_i\right), \\ &= -\frac{n}{\rho_{+1}} c_{+1,i}\ell'_{+1}\left(\mathbf{w}^\mathsf{T}\phi(x_i) + \tau_i\mathbf{w}^\mathsf{T}\mathbf{w}, y_i\right), \\ &= -\frac{n}{\rho_{+1}} c_{+1,i}\ell'_{+1}\left(f_{\mathbf{w}}(x_i) + \tau_i\|\mathbf{w}\|^2, y_i\right). \quad (12)\end{aligned}$$

When replacing $\dot{\mathbf{x}}_i^*$ by (11) in the upper-level Optimization Problem 10 and enforcing Equation 12, Optimization Problem 8 follows. Hence, a solution $\mathbf{w}^*$ of (8) with corresponding $\tau_1^*, \ldots, \tau_n^*$ is also a solution of (6) with $\dot{x}_i^* \in \dot{\mathcal{X}}_{\mathbf{w}^*}^i = \{\dot{x} \in \mathcal{X} : \phi(\dot{x}) = \phi(x_i) + \tau_i^*\mathbf{w}^*\}$. □

The objective as well as the constraints of the optimization problem in Theorem 1 are generally not jointly convex in $\mathbf{w}$ and $\tau_1, \ldots, \tau_n$. However, under the assumptions of the following proposition, a locally optimal solution can still be found efficiently by standard SQP solvers.

PROPOSITION 1. *Let loss function $\ell_{-1}(z, y)$ be twice continuously differentiable and loss function $\ell_{+1}(z, y)$ be convex and thrice continuously differentiable with respect to $z \in \mathbb{R}$ for any fixed $y \in \mathcal{Y}$. Then, a point satisfying the KKT conditions of the optimization problem in Equation (8) can be obtained by* sequential quadratic programming *(SQP) methods.*

The objective as well as the constraints in (8) are twice continuously differentiable with respect to $\mathbf{w}$ and τ_i for $i = 1, \ldots, n$. Hence, the corresponding complementary conditions are continuously differentiable which is a sufficient condition to apply SQP methods; this proves Proposition 1.

3.2 Applying Kernels

Theorem 1 states that a Stackelberg equilibrium with parameter vector $\mathbf{w} \in \mathbb{R}^m$ can be obtained by solving the optimization problem in (8) which requires an explicit feature representation $\phi(x_i)$ of the training instances. However, in some applications, such a feature mapping is unwieldy or even not existing. Instead, one is often equipped with a kernel function $k : \mathcal{X} \times \mathcal{X} \to \mathbb{R}$ which measures the similarity between two instances. Generally, kernel function k is assumed to be a positive-semidefinite kernel such that it can be stated in terms of a scalar product in the corresponding reproducing kernel Hilbert space; *i.e.*, $\exists\phi$ with $k(x, x') = \phi(x)^\mathsf{T}\phi(x')$. Making use of the representer theorem [13], we can now express weight vector $\mathbf{w}$ as a linear combination of the mapped training instances; that is,

$$\mathbf{w} = \sum_{i=1}^{n} \alpha_i \phi(x_i) \tag{13}$$

where feature mapping ϕ is implicitly defined by kernel k. When substituting $\mathbf{w}$ in (8) by (13), the squared norm of $\mathbf{w}$ and decision function $f_\mathbf{w}$ can be completely expressed in terms of the kernel,

$$\|\mathbf{w}\|^2 = \sum_{j,k=1}^{n} \alpha_j \alpha_k k(x_j, x_k), \tag{14}$$

$$f_\mathbf{w}(x_i) = \sum_{j=1}^{n} \alpha_j k(x_i, x_j). \tag{15}$$

Hence, the optimization problem in (8) can be reformulated into an optimization problem over $\tau_1, \ldots, \tau_n \in \mathbb{R}$ and the dual weights $\alpha_1, \ldots, \alpha_n \in \mathbb{R}$ without the need of an explicit feature mapping ϕ. However, inferring an optimal transformed sample $\dot{D}^*$ still requires the knowledge of an explicit mapping ϕ and its inverse ϕ^{-1}. Of course, this is not a restriction as we are interested in the predictive model $f_\mathbf{w}$ rather than the transformed sample $\dot{D}^*$.

Note that for computational reasons, it may be advisable to first construct an explicit feature mapping from the kernel matrix and then to train the Stackelberg model in the primal. For instance, we can employ the kernel PCA map[1]

$$\phi : x \mapsto \mathbf{K}^{-\frac{1}{2}} \left[k(x, x_1), \ldots, k(x, x_n)\right]^\mathsf{T}, \tag{16}$$

where $\mathbf{K}$ denotes the kernel matrix with $\mathbf{K}_{ij} = k(x_i, x_j)$. Within our experiments (presented in Chapter 5) where we use linear kernels, we study all three variants: Computing the model in input space, computing the kernelized version, and computing the PCA map-induced variant. Even though all variants yield the same solution, using an explicit PCA mapping is generally fastest for reasonable n.

[1] Matrix $\mathbf{K}^{-\frac{1}{2}}$ can be computed directly from the eigenvalue decomposition of the kernel matrix $\mathbf{K}$; in case it is singular we use the pseudo-inverse of $\mathbf{K}^{\frac{1}{2}}$.

4. INSTANCES OF THE SPG

By the choice of ℓ_v, distinct instances of the Stackelberg prediction game (SPG) can be identified which, to some extent, generalize existing prediction models such as the *SVM for invariances* [14] and the *SVM with uneven margins* [11].

4.1 SPG with Worst-Case Loss

The *SPG with worst-case loss* is an instance of the Stackelberg prediction game that is characterized by an antagonicity of the (weighted) empirical costs of learner and data generator; that is, the data generator employs the loss function

$$\ell_{+1}^{\mathrm{wc}}(z, y) = -\ell_{-1}(z, y)$$

and cost factors $c_{+1,i} = c_{-1,i}$. Loss functions ℓ_{+1}^{wc} and ℓ_{-1} cannot both be convex at the same time—except for an inappropriate linear function—and so the requirements of either Theorem 1 or Proposition 1 are violated. As we cannot apply Theorem 1, we consider the original optimization problem (Equations 6-7). We substitute ℓ_{+1}^{wc} and $c_{+1,i}$ in the objective (Equation 2) of the lower-level optimization problem

$$\min_{\forall i : \dot{x}_i \in \mathcal{X}} \sum_{i=1}^{n} c_{+1,i} \ell_{+1}^{\mathrm{wc}} \left(f_\mathbf{w}(\dot{x}_i), y_i\right) + \frac{\rho_{+1}}{n} \sum_{i=1}^{n} \frac{1}{2} \|\phi(\dot{x}_i) - \phi(x_i)\|^2$$

which decouples into n maximization problems

$$\max_{\dot{x}_i \in \mathcal{X}} c_{-1,i} \ell_{-1}(f_\mathbf{w}(\dot{x}_i), y_i) - \frac{\rho_{+1}}{n} \frac{1}{2} \|\phi(\dot{x}_i) - \phi(x_i)\|^2. \tag{17}$$

An equivalent formulation of (17) is given by

$$\max_{\dot{x}_i \in \mathcal{X}_i'} \ell_{-1}(f_\mathbf{w}(\dot{x}_i), y_i) \tag{18}$$

where $\mathcal{X}_i' = \{\dot{x} \in \mathcal{X} : c_{-1,i} = \frac{\rho_{+1}'}{n} \frac{1}{2} \|\phi(\dot{x}) - \phi(x_i)\|^2\}$ are feasible sets of transformed instances. The difference between both formulations is that in (18), regularization parameter ρ_{+1}' explicitly restricts the amount of transformation of each instance x_i. As now the inner maximization of the upper-level optimization problem in (6) can be stated in terms of the solution of the lower-level optimization problem, $\ell_{-1}(f_\mathbf{w}(\dot{x}_i^*), y_i)$, the entire bilevel optimization problem reduces to the following constrained minimization problem.

$$\min_{\mathbf{w}, \forall i : \xi_i} \sum_{i=1}^{n} c_{-1,i} \xi_i + \rho_{-1} \frac{1}{2} \|\mathbf{w}\|^2 \tag{19}$$

$$\text{s.t.} \quad \forall i : \xi_i \geq 0,\ \xi_i \geq \max_{\dot{x}_i \in \mathcal{X}_i'} \ell_{-1}(f_\mathbf{w}(\dot{x}_i), y_i) \tag{20}$$

If the lower-level maximization problem (20) has a unique solution for any fixed $\mathbf{w} \in \mathbb{R}^m$, then the above optimization problem can be solved by gradient descent where in each iteration the maximization problem in (20) has to be solved for the current iterate $\mathbf{w}^k$ (see, *e.g.*, [14]). In case the learner choses the hinge loss,

$$\ell_{-1}^{\mathrm{h}}(z, y) = \max(0, 1 - yz), \tag{21}$$

the SPG with worst-case loss reduces to an instance of the *SVM for invariances* [14].

4.2 SPG with Linear Loss

A second instance of the Stackelberg prediction game is the *SPG with linear loss* in which the data generator employs a linear loss function,

$$\ell_{+1}^{\mathrm{lin}}(z, y) = z,$$

which penalizes high decision values z independently of the class. This choice is appropriate, for instance, in email spam filtering where the data generator is purely interested in the delivery of an email x which becomes unlikely for large values of z, independently of the corresponding true class y.

For the linear loss that is continuously differentiable and convex, the constraints in (8) reduce to

$$\tau_i = -\frac{n}{\rho_{+1}} c_{+1,i} \tag{22}$$

for $i = 1, \ldots, n$. When choosing the hinge loss (21) for the learner and replacing τ_i in (8) by (22) we arrive at the following minimization problem.

$$\min_{\mathbf{w}, \forall i : \xi_i} \sum_{i=1}^{n} c_{-1,i} \xi_i + \rho_{-1} \frac{1}{2} \|\mathbf{w}\|^2$$

$$\text{s.t.} \quad \forall i : \xi_i \geq 0, \ \xi_i \geq 1 - y_i \left(\mathbf{w}^\mathsf{T} \phi(x_i) - \frac{n}{\rho_{+1}} c_{+1,i} \|\mathbf{w}\|^2 \right)$$

The latter constraints can be reformulated to

$$y_i \mathbf{w}^\mathsf{T} \phi(x_i) \geq 1 + y_i \kappa_i - \xi_i$$

which amounts to the constraints of the *SVM with uneven margins* [11]. The only syntactic distinction is that $\kappa_i = \frac{n}{\rho_{+1}} c_{+1,i} \|\mathbf{w}\|^2$ is indirectly defined by ρ_{+1} and $c_{+1,i}$; however, for each choice of $\kappa_i \geq 0$ in the SVM with uneven margins, there exist appropriate parameters ρ_{+1} and $c_{+1,i}$ of an equivalent SPG with linear loss and vice versa.

Consider the special case of equal factors $c_{+1,i} = c_{+1,j}$, and consequently $\kappa = \kappa_i = \kappa_j$, for all $i, j = 1, \ldots, n$. Then the margin of negative instances becomes $1 - \kappa$ whereas the margin of positive instances is $1 + \kappa$. In our example of spam filtering, this goes with the intuition that the margin of spam instances that vary greatly has to be larger than the margin of non-spam instances that remain almost unmodified. This effect is stronger when the data generator's regularization parameter ρ_{+1} is small. By contrast, if ρ_{+1} goes to infinity, and consequently κ attains zero, then the SPG with linear loss reduces to the regular SVM.

4.3 SPG with Logistic Loss

Finally, this section introduces the *SPG with logistic loss*. This instantiation meets the preconditions of Theorem 1 and Proposition 1, and the resulting optimization criterion can be solved with standard tools. The learner may use any loss function that is convex and twice continuously differentiable (Equation 23 details the loss function used in our experiments) while the data generator uses the logistic loss

$$\ell_{+1}^{\log}(z, y) = \log(1 + e^z)$$

which again penalizes large decision values z. The rationale behind this loss function is that the data generator experiences costs when the learner blocks an event, *i.e.*, produces a high decision function value for an instance. For instance, a legitimate sender experiences costs when a legitimate email is erroneously blocked just like an abusive sender, also amalgamated into the *data generator*, experiences costs when spam messages are blocked. Cost function $\ell_{+1}^{\log}$ approaches zero for small values of the decision function. Now, the constraints in (8) resolve to $g_i(\mathbf{w}, \tau_i) = 0$ for $i = 1, \ldots, n$ with

$$g_i(\mathbf{w}, \tau_i) = \tau_i \left(1 + e^{-f_{\mathbf{w}}(x_i) - \tau_i \|\mathbf{w}\|^2}\right) + \frac{n}{\rho_{+1}} c_{+1,i}.$$

Functions $g_i(\mathbf{w}, \tau_i)$ are not jointly convex in $\mathbf{w}$ and τ_i. However, as they are smooth (*i.e.*, infinitely differentiable) in both arguments, their roots can be obtained efficiently and, consequently, the resulting optimization problem

$$\min_{\mathbf{w}, \forall i : \tau_i} \sum_{i=1}^{n} c_{-1,i} \ell_{-1} \left(f_{\mathbf{w}}(x_i) + \tau_i \|\mathbf{w}\|^2, y_i \right) + \frac{\rho_{-1}}{2} \|\mathbf{w}\|^2$$

$$\text{s.t.} \quad \forall i : 0 = g_i(\mathbf{w}, \tau_i)$$

can be solved by standard SQP solvers.

5. EXPERIMENTAL EVALUATION

The goal of this section is to explore the relative strengths and weaknesses of the discussed instances of Stackelberg prediction games and existing baseline methods in the context of email spam filtering. We compare a regular *support vector machine* (SVM), *logistic regression* (LogReg), the *SVM for invariances* with feature scaling (Invar-SVM, [14]), *Nash logistic regression* (Nash, [1]), and the Stackelberg instances *SPG with worst-case loss* (SPG^{wc}, *cf.* Section 4.1), *SPG with linear loss* (SPG^{lin}, *cf.* Section 4.2), and the *SPG with logistic loss* (SPG^{log}, *cf.* Section 4.3). For all Stackelberg instances we choose the logistic loss function

$$\ell_{-1}^{\log}(z, y) = \log\left(1 + e^{-yz}\right) \tag{23}$$

for the learner which is convex and smooth, and consequently satisfies Proposition 1. In the absence of prior knowledge on the instance-specific costs, we set $c_{v,i} = \frac{1}{n}$ for all $v \in \{-1, +1\}$, $i = 1, \ldots, n$ and train all methods in the PCA map induced feature space. To solve the nonlinear program of the SPG with logistic loss we use the Ipopt solver [16].

We use four email corpora detailed in Table 1: The first data set contains emails of an email service provider (*ESP*) collected between 2007 and 2010. The second (*Mailinglist*) is a collection of emails from publicly available mailing lists augmented by spam emails from Bruce Guenter's spam trap of the same time period. The third corpus (*Private*) contains newsletters and spam and non-spam emails of the authors. The last corpus is the NIST *TREC 2007* spam corpus. All emails are tokenized, converted into binary bag-of-word vectors, and sorted chronologically.

Table 1: Data sets used in the experiments.

data set	*instances*	*features*	*delivery period*
ESP	169,612	541,713	01/06/2007 - 27/04/2010
Mailinglist	128,117	266,378	01/04/1999 - 31/05/2006
Private	108,178	582,100	01/08/2005 - 31/03/2010
TREC 2007	75,496	214,839	04/08/2007 - 07/06/2007

Our evaluation protocol is as follows. We use the 4,000 oldest emails as training portion and set the remaining emails aside as test instances. We use the F-measure—that is, the harmonic mean of precision and recall—as evaluation measure and train all methods 20 times on a stratified subset of 200 spam and 200 non-spam messages sampled from the training portion. In order to tune the regularization parameters we perform a 5-fold cross validation on the training sample within each repetition of an experiment and for each method separately.

In the first experiment, we evaluate all methods *into the future* by processing the test set in chronological order. Each test sample is split into 20 disjoint subsets. We average

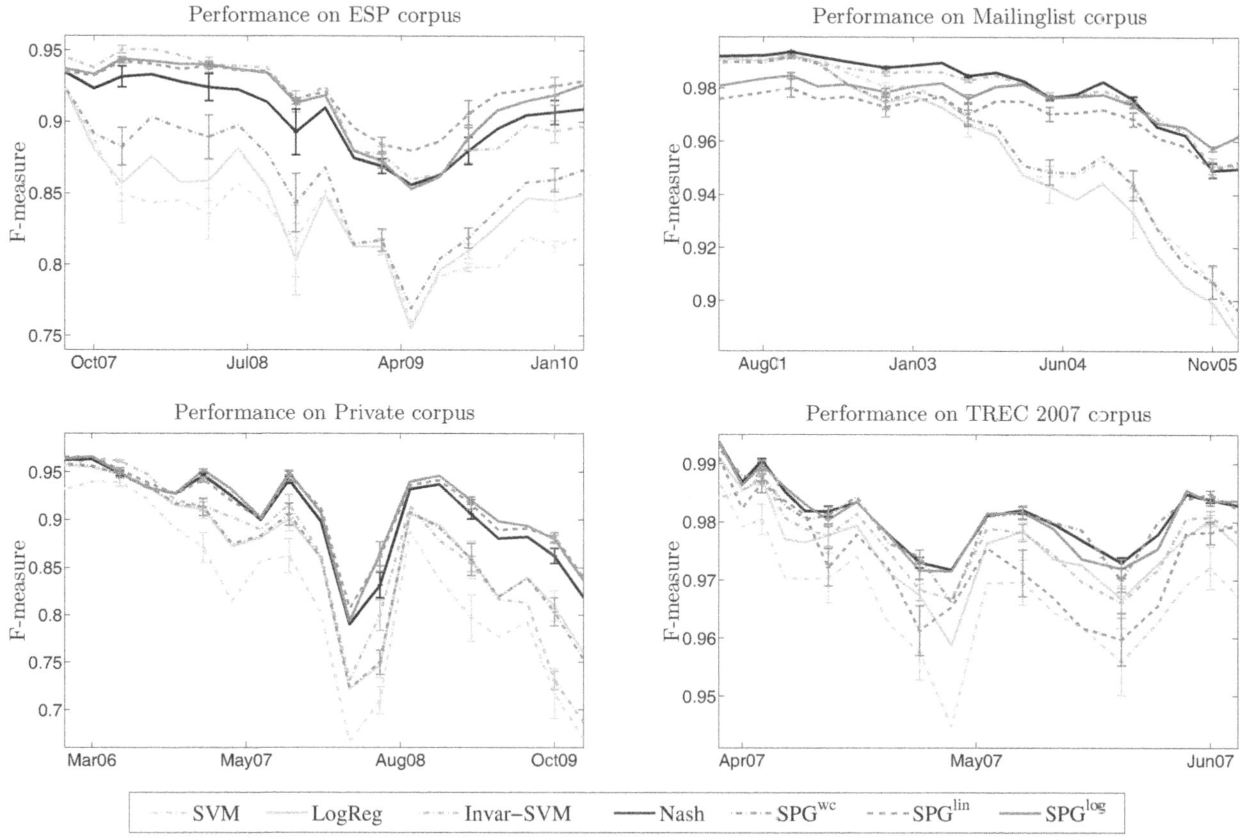

Figure 1: F-measure of predictive models. Error bars indicate standard errors.

the F-measure on each of those subsets over the 20 models (trained on different samples drawn from the training portion) for each method and perform a paired t-test.

Figure 1 shows that, for all data sets, the Stackelberg prediction games with linear loss and with logistic loss outperform the regular SVM and logistic regression that do not explicitly factor the adversary into the optimization criterion. On the ESP corpus, the SPG with linear loss is slightly better than the SPG with logistic loss whereas for the Mailinglist corpus the SPG with logistic loss outperforms the SPG with linear loss. On the TREC 2007 data set, most of the methods behave comparably with a slight advantage for the Nash logistic regression and the SPG instances with logistic loss and linear loss. The period over which the TREC 2007 data have been collected is very short; therefore we believe that the training and test instances are governed by nearly identical distributions. Consequently the game-theoretic models do not gain a significant advantage over logistic regression that assumes *iid* samples. For the other three data sets, the game-theoretical models outperform the *iid* baselines.

Table 2 shows aggregated results over all four data sets. For each point in each of the diagrams of Figure 1, we conduct a pairwise comparison of all methods based on a paired t-test at a confidence level of $\alpha = 0.05$. When a difference is significant, we count this as a win for the method that achieves a higher F-measure. Each line of Table 2 details the wins and, set in italics, the *losses* of one method against all other methods. The Stackelberg prediction game with logistic loss has more wins than it has losses against each of the other methods. The Stackelberg prediction game with linear loss has more wins than losses against each of the other methods except for the SPG with logistic loss and the Nash logistic regression. The ranking continues with the Invar-SVM, the SPG with worst-case loss, logistic regression, and the regular SVM which loses more frequently than it wins against all other methods.

To study the predictive performance as well as running time behavior with respect to the size of the data set, we train the baselines and the three SPG instances for a varying number of training examples. We report on the results for the representative ESP data set in Figure 2. Except for SPG^{wc}, the game models significantly outperform the trivial baseline methods SVM and logistic regression, especially for small corpus sizes. However, this comes at the price of considerably higher computational cost. For the game models, the Stackelberg instance SPG^{lin} clearly outperforms all reference methods with respect to efficiency. Though, the larger the size of the data set, the stronger the computational differences, where at the same time the discrepancy of the predictive performance diminishes.

The data generator's regularizer that we use in the experiments does not distinguish between modifications of spam and non-spam messages. In reality, most senders of legitimate messages do not deliberately change their writing behavior such as to bypass spam filters, perhaps with the exception of senders of legitimate newsletters who must be careful not to trigger filtering mechanisms. In a final exper-

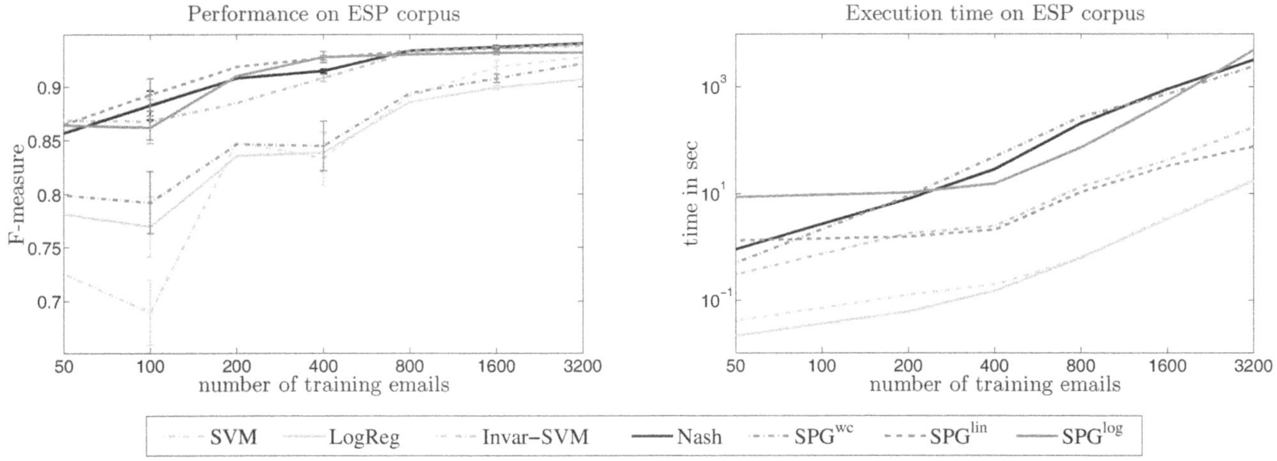

Figure 2: Predictive performance (left) and execution time (right) for varying sizes of the training data set.

Table 2: Results of paired t-test over all corpora: Number of trials in which each method (row) has significantly outperformed each other *method (column)* vs. number of times it *was outperformed*.

method vs. *method*	*SVM*	*LogReg*	*Invar-SVM*	*Nash*	SPG^{wc}	SPG^{lin}	SPG^{log}
SVM	0:*0*	6:*44*	2:*64*	0:*72*	8:*50*	6:*54*	6:*69*
LogReg	44:*6*	0:*0*	3:*41*	0:*72*	0:*29*	6:*48*	5:*57*
Invar-SVM	64:*2*	41:*3*	0:*0*	6:*40*	39:*10*	20:*23*	18:*30*
Nash	72:*0*	72:*0*	40:*6*	0:*0*	57:*2*	33:*17*	14:*16*
SPG^{wc}	50:*8*	29:*0*	10:*39*	2:*57*	0:*0*	17:*46*	9:*48*
SPG^{lin}	54:*6*	48:*6*	23:*20*	17:*33*	46:*17*	0:*0*	10:*23*
SPG^{log}	69:*6*	57:*5*	30:*18*	16:*14*	48:*9*	23:*10*	0:*0*

iment, we want to study whether the Stackelberg model reflects this aspect of reality. Table 3 shows the average number of modifications—*i.e.*, word additions and deletions—performed by the sender per spam and per non-spam email depending on the sender's regularization parameter ρ_{+1} for fixed ρ_{-1}.

Table 3: Average number of word additions and deletions per instance for SPG^{log}.

ρ_{+1}	non-spam		spam	
	additions	*deletions*	*additions*	*deletions*
4	1.4	1.6	14.6	17.6
16	0.3	0.3	9.9	11.6
64	0.0	0.0	7.1	8.7
256	0.0	0.0	2.4	2.8
1024	0.0	0.0	0.8	0.9

As expected, the number of transformations increases inversely proportional to the regularization parameter. Even for equal cost factors $c_{v,i}$, non-spam messages are rarely modified because the interests of sender and recipient are coherent for legitimate messages.

6. CONCLUSIONS

We model adversarial prediction problems as a game in which a learner has to commit to a predictive model using past data whereas the data generator may choose a transformation function after the predictive model has been disclosed which then defines the test distribution. This model reflects applications such as the detection of network attacks and spam filtering in which an assailant can probe the filter. The cost functions of learner and data generator are generally conflicting but are not constrained to be perfectly antagonistic. Playing the Stackelberg equilibrium instead of a worst-case strategy based on a zero-sum model is advisable when the data generator can be assumed to behave rational in the sense of minimizing a cost function. However, in contrast to the Nash strategy, the Stackelberg model does not rely on the existence of a unique equilibrium and the assumptions that the adversary has no information about the predictive model and is able to identify and follow the equilibrial strategy.

We derived a compact optimization problem that determines the solution of the resulting Stackelberg prediction game. We showed that the Stackelberg model generalizes existing prediction models such as SVM with uneven margins and SVM for invariances. We evaluated spam filters resulting from a regular SVM, logistic regression, existing game-theoretical models, and three instances of the Stackelberg game on several spam-filtering data sets. The relative performance of the distinct game-theoretic models varies, but we observe that when compared to any other model, the Stackelberg model with logistic loss has more wins than it has losses against each of the baseline methods.

Acknowledgments

This work was supported by the German Science Foundation DFG under grant SCHE 540/12-1 and by STRATO AG.

7. REFERENCES

[1] M. Brückner and T. Scheffer. Nash equilibria of static prediction games. In *Advances in Neural Information Processing Systems*. MIT Press, 2009.

[2] B. Colson, P. Marcotte, and G. Savard. An overview of bilevel optimization. *Annals of Operations Research*, 153(1):235–256, 2007.

[3] O. Dekel and O. Shamir. Learning to classify with missing and corrupted features. In *Proceedings of the International Conference on Machine Learning*, pages 216–223. ACM, 2008.

[4] O. Dekel, O. Shamir, and L. Xiao. Learning to classify with missing and corrupted features. *Machine Learning*, 81(2):149–178, 2010.

[5] L. E. Ghaoui, G. R. G. Lanckriet, and G. Natsoulis. Robust classification with interval data. Technical Report UCB/CSD-03-1279, EECS Department, University of California, Berkeley, 2003.

[6] A. Globerson and S. T. Roweis. Nightmare at test time: robust learning by feature deletion. In *Proceedings of the International Conference on Machine Learning*. ACM, 2006.

[7] A. Globerson, C. H. Teo, A. J. Smola, and S. T. Roweis. *Dataset Shift in Machine Learning*, chapter An adversarial view of covariate shift and a minimax approach, pages 179–198. MIT Press, 2009.

[8] R. Jeroslow. The polynomial hierarchy and a simple model for competitive analysis. *Mathematical Programming*, 32:146–164, 1985.

[9] M. Kantarcioglu, B. Xi, and C. Clifton. Classifier evaluation and attribute selection against active adversaries. *Data Mining and Knowledge Discovery*, 22(1-2):291–335, 2011.

[10] G. R. G. Lanckriet, L. E. Ghaoui, C. Bhattacharyya, and M. I. Jordan. A robust minimax approach to classification. *Journal of Machine Learning Research*, 3:555–582, 2002.

[11] Y. Li and J. Shawe-Taylor. The SVM with uneven margins and chinese document categorization. In *Proceedings of the Pacific Asia Conference on Language, Information and Computation*, pages 216–227, 2003.

[12] W. Liu and S. Chawla. A game theoretical model for adversarial learning. In *ICDM Workshops*, pages 25–30. IEEE Computer Society, 2009.

[13] B. Schölkopf, R. Herbrich, and A. J. Smola. A generalized representer theorem. In *COLT: Proceedings of the Workshop on Computational Learning Theory, Morgan Kaufmann Publishers*, 2001.

[14] C. H. Teo, A. Globerson, S. T. Roweis, and A. J. Smola. Convex learning with invariances. In *Advances in Neural Information Processing Systems*. MIT Press, 2007.

[15] S. Veelken. *A New Relaxation Scheme for Mathematical Programs with Equilibrium Constraints: Theory an Numerical Experience*. PhD thesis, Technische Universität München, 2009.

[16] A. Wächter and L. T. Biegler. On the implementation of an interior-point filter line-search algorithm for large-scale nonlinear programming. *Mathematical Programming*, 106:25–57, 2006.

Leakage in Data Mining: Formulation, Detection, and Avoidance

Shachar Kaufman
School of Electrical Engineering
Tel-Aviv University
69978 Tel-Aviv, Israel
shachark@post.tau.ac.il

Saharon Rosset
School of Mathematical Sciences
Tel-Aviv University
69978 Tel-Aviv, Israel
saharon@post.tau.ac.il

Claudia Perlich
Media6Degrees
37 East 18th Street, 9th floor
New York, NY 10003
claudia@media6degrees.com

ABSTRACT

Deemed "one of the top ten data mining mistakes", leakage is essentially the introduction of information about the data mining target, which should not be legitimately available to mine from. In addition to our own industry experience with real-life projects, controversies around several major public data mining competitions held recently such as the INFORMS 2010 Data Mining Challenge and the IJCNN 2011 Social Network Challenge are evidence that this issue is as relevant today as it has ever been. While acknowledging the importance and prevalence of leakage in both synthetic competitions and real-life data mining projects, existing literature has largely left this idea unexplored. What little has been said turns out not to be broad enough to cover more complex cases of leakage, such as those where the classical i.i.d. assumption is violated, that have been recently documented. In our new approach, these cases and others are explained by explicitly defining modeling goals and analyzing the broader framework of the data mining problem. The resulting definition enables us to derive general methodology for dealing with the issue. We show that it is possible to avoid leakage with a simple specific approach to data management followed by what we call a learn-predict separation, and present several ways of detecting leakage when the modeler has no control over how the data have been collected.

Categories and Subject Descriptors

H.2.8 [Database Management]: Database Applications – *Data mining*. I.5.2 [Pattern Recognition]: Design Methodology – *Classifier design and evaluation*.

General Terms

Theory, Algorithms.

Keywords

Data mining, Leakage, Statistical inference, Predictive modeling.

1. INTRODUCTION

Deemed "one of the top ten data mining mistakes" [7], leakage in data mining (henceforth, *leakage*) is essentially the introduction of information about the target of a data mining problem, which should not be legitimately available to mine from. A trivial example of leakage would be a model that uses the target itself as an input, thus concluding for example that 'it rains on rainy days'. In practice, the introduction of this illegitimate information is unintentional, and facilitated by the data collection, aggregation and preparation process. It is usually subtle and indirect, making it very hard to detect and eliminate. Leakage is undesirable as it may lead a *modeler*, someone trying to solve the problem, to learn a suboptimal solution, which would in fact be outperformed in deployment by a leakage-free model that could have otherwise been built. At the very least leakage leads to overestimation of the model's performance. A *client* for whom the modeling is undertaken is likely to discover the sad truth about the model when performance in deployment is found to be systematically worse than the estimate promised by the modeler. Even then, identifying leakage as the reason might be highly nontrivial.

Existing literature, which we survey in Section 2, mentions leakage and acknowledges its importance and prevalence in both synthetic competitions and real-life data mining projects [e.g. 2, 7]. However these discussions lack several key ingredients. First, they do not present a general and clear theory of what constitutes leakage. Second, these sources do not suggest practical methodologies for leakage detection and avoidance that modelers could apply to their own statistical inference problems. This gap in theory and methodology could be the reason that several major data mining competitions held recently such as KDD-Cup 2008, or the INFORMS 2010 Data Mining Challenge, though judiciously organized by capable individuals, suffered from severe leakage. In many cases, attempts to fix leakage resulted in the introduction of new leakage which is even harder to deal with. Other competitions such as KDD-Cup 2007 and IJCNN 2011 Social Network Challenge were affected by a second form of leakage which is specific to competitions. Leakage from available external sources undermined the organizers' implicit true goal of encouraging submissions that would actually be useful for the domain. These cases, in addition to our own experience with leakage in the industry and as competitors in and organizers of data mining challenges, are examined in more detail also in Section 2. We revisit them in later sections to provide a more concrete setting for our discussion.

The major contribution of this paper, that is, aside from raising awareness to an important issue which we believe is often overlooked, is a proposal in Section 3 for a formal definition of leakage. This definition covers both the common case of leaking features and more complex scenarios that have been encountered in predictive modeling competitions. We use this formulation to facilitate leakage avoidance in Section 4, and suggest in Section 5 methodology for detecting leakage when we have limited or no

KDD'11, August 21 – 24, 2011, San Diego, California, USA.
Copyright 2011 ACM 978-1-4503-0813-7/11/08...$10.00.

control over how the data have been collected. This methodology should be particularly useful for practitioners in predictive modeling problems, as well as for prospective competition organizers.

2. LEAKAGE IN THE KDD LITERATURE

The subject of leakage has been visited by several data mining textbooks as well as a few papers. Most of the papers we refer to are related to KDD-Cup competitions, probably due to authors of works outside of competitions locating and fixing leakage issues without reporting the process. We shall give a short chronological review here while collecting examples to be used later as case studies for our proposed definition of leakage.

Pyle [9, 10, 11] refers to the phenomenon which we call here leakage, in the context of predictive modeling, as *Anachronisms* (something that is out of place in time), and says that "too good to be true" performance is "a dead giveaway" of its existence. The author suggests turning to *exploratory data analysis* in order to find and eliminate leakage sources, which we will also discuss in Section 5. Nisbet *et al.* [7] refer to the issue as "leaks from the future" and claim it is "one of the top 10 data mining mistakes". They repeat the same basic insights, but also do not suggest a general definition or methodology to correct and prevent leakage. These titles provide a handful of elementary but common examples of leakage. Two representative ones are: (i) An "account number" feature, for the problem of predicting whether a potential customer would open an account at a bank. Obviously, assignment of such an account number is only done after an account has been opened. (ii) An "interviewer name" feature, in a cellular company churn prediction problem. While the information "who interviewed the client when they churned" appears innocent enough, it turns out that a specific salesperson was assigned to take over cases where customers had already notified they intend to churn.

Kohavi *et al.* [2] describe the introduction of leaks in data mining competitions as giveaway attributes that predict the target because they are downstream in the data collection process. The authors give an example in the domain of retail website data analytics where for each page viewed the prediction target is whether the user would leave or stay to view another page. A leaking attribute is the "session length", which is the total number of pages viewed by the user during this visit to the website. This attribute is added to each page-view record at the end of the session. A solution is to replace this attribute with "page number in session" which describes the session length up to the current page, where prediction is required.

Subsequent work by Kohavi *et al.* [3] presents the common business analysis problem of characterizing big spenders among customers. The authors explain that this problem is prone to leakage since immediate triggers of the target (*e.g.* a large purchase or purchase of a diamond) or consequences of the target (*e.g.* paying a lot of tax) are usually available in collected data and need to be manually identified and removed. To show how correcting for leakage can become an involved process, the authors also discuss the more complex situation where removing the information "total purchase in jewelry" caused information of "no purchases in any department" to become fictitiously predictive. This is because each customer found in the database is there in the first place due to some purchase, and if this purchase is not in any department (still available), it has to be jewelry (which has been removed). They suggest defining analytical questions that should suffer less from leaks – such as characterizing a "migrator" (a user who is a light spender but will become a heavy one) instead of characterizing the "heavy spender". The idea is that it is better to ask analytical questions that have a clear temporal cause-and-effect structure. Of course leaks are still possible, but much harder to introduce by accident and much easier to identify. We return to this idea in Section 3. A later paper by the authors [4] reiterates the previous discussion, and adds the example of the "use of free shipping", where a leak is introduced when free shipping is provided as a special offer with large purchases.

Rosset *et al.* [11] discuss leakage encountered in the 2007 KDD-Cup competition. In that year's contest there were two related challenges concerning movie viewers' reviews from the famous Netflix database. The first challenge, "Who Reviewed What", was to predict whether each user would give a review for each title in 2006, given data up to 2005. The second challenge, "How Many Reviews", was to predict the number of reviews each title would receive in 2006, also using data given up to 2005. For the first challenge, a test set with actual reviews from 2006 was provided. Although disjoint sets of titles were used to construct the data sets for these two challenges, Rosset *et al.*'s winning submission managed to use the test set for the first problem as the target in a supervised-learning modeling approach for the second problem. This was possible due to a combination of two facts. First, up to a scaling factor and noise, the expected number of user/review pairs in the first problem's test set in which a title appears is equal to the total number of reviews which that titled received in 2006. This is exactly the target for the second problem, only on different titles. Second, the titles are similar enough to share statistical properties, so from the available dynamics for the first group of titles one can infer the dynamics of the second group's. We shall revisit this complex example in Section 3, where this case will motivate us to extend our definition of leakage beyond leaking features.

Two medical data mining contests held the following year and which also exhibited leakage are discussed in [7, 13]. KDD-Cup 2008 dealt with cancer detection from mammography data. Analyzing the data for this competition, the authors point out that the "Patient ID" feature (ignored by most competitors) has tremendous and unexpected predictive power. They hypothesize that multiple clinical study, institution or equipment sources were used to compile the data, and that some of these sources were assigned their population with prior knowledge of the patient's condition. Leakage was thus facilitated by assigning consecutive patient IDs for data from each source, that is, the merge was done without obfuscating the source. The INFORMS Data Mining Challenge 2008 competition held the same year, addressed the problem of pneumonia diagnosis based on patient information from hospital records. The target was originally embedded as a special value of one or more features in the data given to competitors. The organizers removed these values, however it was possible to identify traces of such removal, constituting the source of leakage in this example (*e.g.* a record with all condition codes missing, similarly to Kohavi's jewelry example).

Also in the recent work by Rosset *et al.* [13], the concept of identifying and harnessing leakage has been openly addressed as one of three key aspects for winning data mining competitions. This work provides the intuitive definition of leakage as "The unintentional introduction of predictive information about the target by the data collection, aggregation and preparation process". The authors mention that leakage might be the cause of many failures of data mining applications, and give the illustrative example of predicting people who are likely to be sick by looking at how many work days they would end up missing. They also describe a real-life business intelligence project at IBM where potential customers for certain products were identified, among other things, based on keywords found on their websites. This turned out to be leakage since the website content used for training had been sampled at the point in time where the potential customer has already become a customer, and where the website contained traces of the IBM products purchased, such as the word "Websphere" (*e.g.* in a press release about the purchase or a specific product feature the client uses).

The latest INFORMS and IJCNN competitions held in late 2010 and early 2011 are fresh examples of how leakage continues to plague predictive modeling problems and competitions in particular. The INFORMS 2010 Data Mining Challenge required participants to develop a model that predicts stock price movements, over a fixed one-hour horizon, at five minute intervals. Competitors were provided with intraday trading data showing stock prices, sectoral data, economic data, experts' predictions and indices. The data were segmented to a training database, on which participants were expected to build their predictive models, and a test database which was used by the organizers to evaluate submissions. The surprising results were that about 30 participating groups achieved more than 0.9 AUC, with the best model surpassing 0.99 AUC. Had these models been legitimate they would've indeed made a "big impact on the finance industry" as the organizers had hoped, not to mention making their operators very wealthy individuals. Unfortunately, however, it became clear that although some steps had been taken to prevent competitors from "looking up the answers" (the underlying target stock's identity was not revealed, and the test set did not include the variable being predicted), it was still possible to build models that rely on data from the future. Having data from the future for the explanatory variables, some of which are highly cointegrated with the target (*e.g.* a second stock within the same sector as the target stock), and having access to publicly available stock data such as Yahoo/Google Finance (which allows finding at least good candidates for the identity of the target stock, consequently revealing all test values) was the true driver of success for these models. The organizers held two rankings of competitors, one where future information was allowed and another where it was forbidden, however in the end they had to admit that verifying future information was not used was impossible, and that it was probable that all models were tainted, as all modelers had been exposed to the test set.

The IJCNN 2011 Social Network Challenge presented participants with anonymized 7,237,983 edges from an undisclosed online social network and asked to predict which of an additional set of 8,960 potential edges are in fact realized on the network as well. The winners have recently reported [3] they had been able to recognize, through sophisticated analysis, that the social network in question was Flickr and then to de-anonymize the majority of the data. This allowed them to use edges available from the on-line Flickr network to correctly predict over 60% of edges which were identified, while the rest had to be handled classically using legitimate prediction. Similarly to other cases that have been mentioned, these rogue solutions are sometimes so elegant and insightful that they carry merit in their own right. The problem is that they do not answer the original question presented by the organizers.

Clearly, then, the issue of leakage has been observed in various contexts and problem domains, with a natural focus on predictive modeling. However, none of the discussions that we could find has addressed the issue in a general way, or suggested methodology for handling it. In the following section we make our attempt to derive a definition of leakage.

3. FORMULATION

3.1 Preliminaries and Legitimacy

In our discussion of leakage we shall define the roles of client and modeler as in Section 1, and consider the standard statistical inference framework of supervised learning and its generalizations, where we can discuss examples, targets and features. We assume the reader is familiar with these concepts. For a complete reference see [1]. Let us just lay out our notation and say that in our framework we receive from an axiomatic data preparation stage a multivariate random *process* $\mathcal{W} = (\mathcal{X}, \mathcal{Y})$. $\mathcal{Y}$ is the outcome or target generating process with samples y target *instances*. Values or *realizations* of the random variable y are denoted $\boldsymbol{y}$ (in bold). Similarly, $\mathcal{X}$, X and $\boldsymbol{X}$ are the feature-vector generating process, an instance and realization. For individual feature generating processes, instances and realizations we use $x \in \mathcal{X}$, $x \in X$ and $\boldsymbol{x} \in \boldsymbol{X}$. Specific instances x_0 and y_0 taken from the same instance of $\mathcal{W}$ are said to be $\mathcal{W}$-related. The modeler's goal is to statistically infer a target instance, from its associated feature-vector instance in $\mathcal{W}$ and from a separate group of samples of $\mathcal{W}$, called the training examples $\boldsymbol{W_{tr}}$. The solution to this problem is a model $\hat{y} = \mathbb{M}(X, \boldsymbol{W_{tr}})$. We say that the model's *observational inputs* for predicting y are X and $\boldsymbol{W_{tr}}$, and this relation between the various elements in the framework is the base for our discussion.

Models containing leaks are a subclass of the broader concept of illegitimate or unacceptable models. At this level, *legitimacy*, which is a key concept in our formulation of leakage, is completely abstract. Every modeling problem sets its own rules for what constitutes a legitimate or acceptable solution and different problems, even if using the same data, may have wildly different views on legitimacy. For example a solution could be considered illegitimate if it is too complex – say if it uses too many features or if it is not linear in its features.

However our focus here is on leakage, which is a specific form of illegitimacy that is an intrinsic property of the observational inputs of a model. This form of illegitimacy remains partly abstract, but could be further defined as follows: Let u be some random variable. We say a second random variable v is u-legitimate if v is observable to the client for the purpose of inferring u. In this case we write $v \in legit\{u\}$.

A fully concrete meaning of legitimacy is built-in to any specific inference problem. The trivial legitimacy rule, going back to the first example of leakage given in Section 1, is that the target itself must never be used for inference:

$$y \notin legit\{y\}. \quad (1)$$

We could use this rule if we wanted to disqualify the winning submission to the IJCNN 2011 Social Network Challenge, for it, however cleverly, eventually uses some of the targets themselves for inference. This condition should be abided by all problems, and we refrain from explicitly mentioning it for the remaining examples we shall discuss.

Naturally, a model contains leaks with respect to a target instance y if one or more of its observational inputs are y-illegitimate. We say that the model *inherits* the illegitimacy property from the features and training examples it uses. The discussion proceeds along these two possible sources of leakage for a model: features and training examples.

3.2 Leaking Features

We begin with the more common case of *leaking features*. First we must extend our abstract definition of legitimacy to the case of random processes: Let $\mathcal{u}$ be some random process. We say a second random process $\mathcal{v}$ is $\mathcal{u}$-legitimate if, for every pair of instances of $\mathcal{u}$ and $\mathcal{v}$, u and v respectively, which are $\mathcal{W}$-related, v is u-legitimate. We use the same notation as we did for random variables in 3.1, and write that $\mathcal{v} \in legit\{\mathcal{u}\}$.

Leaking features are then covered by a simple condition for the absence of leakage:

$$\forall x \in \mathcal{X}, x \in legit\{\mathcal{Y}\}. \quad (2)$$

That is, any feature made available by the data preparation process is deemed legitimate by the precise formulation of the modeling problem at hand, instance by instance w.r.t. its matching target.

The prevailing example for this type of leakage is what we call the *no-time-machine* requirement. In the context of predictive modeling, it is implicitly required that a legitimate model only build on features with information from a time earlier (or sometimes, no later) than that of the target. Formally, $\mathcal{x}$ and $\mathcal{y}$, made scalar for the sake of simplicity, are random processes over some time axis t (not necessarily physical time). Prediction is required by the client for the target process $\mathcal{y}$ at times $t_{\mathcal{y}}$, and their $\mathcal{W}$-related feature process $\mathcal{x}$ is observable to the client at times $t_{\mathcal{x}}$. We then have:

$$legit\{\mathcal{y}\} \subseteq \{x \in \mathcal{X} | t_x < t_{\mathcal{y}}\}. \quad (3)$$

Such a rule should be read: Any legitimate feature w.r.t. the target process is a member of the right hand side set of features. In this case the right hand side is the set of all features whose every instance is observed earlier than its $\mathcal{W}$-related target instance. We are assuming with this notation that $\mathcal{X}$ contains all possible features, and use "$\subseteq$" to express that additional legitimacy constraints might also apply (otherwise "$=$" could be used).

While the simple no-time-machine requirement is indeed the most common case, one could think of additional scenarios which are still covered by condition (2). A simple extension is to require features to be observable a sufficient period of time prior to $t_{\mathcal{y}}$ as in (4) below in order to preclude any information that is an immediate trigger of the target. One reason why this might be necessary is that sometimes it is too limiting to think of the target as pertaining to a point-in-time, only to a rough interval. Using data observable close to $t_{\mathcal{y}}$ makes the problem uninteresting. Such is the case for the "heavy spender" example from [3]. With legitimacy defined as (3) (or as (4) when $\tau = 0$) a model may be built that uses the purchase of a diamond to conclude that the customer is a big spender but with τ sufficiently large this is not allowed. This transforms the problem from identification of "heavy spenders" to the suggested identification of "migrators".

$$legit\{\mathcal{y}\} \subseteq \{x \in \mathcal{X} | t_x < t_{\mathcal{y}} - \tau\}. \quad (4)$$

Another example, using the same random process notation, is a memory limitation, where a model may not use information *older* than a time relative to that of the target:

$$legit\{\mathcal{y}\} \subseteq \{x \in \mathcal{X} | t_{\mathcal{y}} - \tau < t_x < t_{\mathcal{y}}\}. \quad (5)$$

We can think of a requirement to use exactly n features from a specified pool $\mathcal{X}_p$ of preselected features:

$$legit\{\mathcal{y}\} \subseteq \{[x_1, \ldots, x_n] | \forall k\ x_k \in \mathcal{X}_p, k\ unique\}, \quad (6)$$

and so on. In fact, there is a variant of example (6) which is very common: only the features $\mathcal{X}_p$ selected for a specific provided dataset are considered legitimate. Sometimes this rule allows free use of the entire set:

$$legit\{\mathcal{y}\} \subseteq \mathcal{X}_p. \quad (7)$$

Usually however this rule is combined with (3) to give:

$$legit\{\mathcal{y}\} \subseteq \{x \in \mathcal{X}_p | t_x < t_{\mathcal{y}}\}. \quad (8)$$

Most documented cases of leakage mentioned in Section 2 are covered by condition (2) in conjunction with a no-time-machine requirement as in (3). For instance, in the trivial example of predicting rainy days, the target is an illegitimate feature since its value is not observable to the client when the prediction is required (say, the previous day). As another example, the pneumonia detection database in the INFORMS 2008 challenge discussed in [8, 13] implies that a certain combination of missing diagnosis code and some other features is highly informative of the target. However this feature is illegitimate, as the patient's condition is still being studied.

It is easy to see how conditions (2) and (3) similarly apply to the account number and interviewer name examples from [10], the session length of [2] (while the corrected "page number in session" is fine), the immediate and indirect triggers described in [3, 4], the remaining competitions described in [8, 13], and the website based features used by IBM and discussed in [13]. However not all examples fall under condition (2).

Let us examine the case mentioned earlier of KDD-Cup 2007 as discussed in [11]. While clearly taking advantage of information from reviews given to titles during 2006 (the mere fact of using data from the future is proof, but we can also see it in action by the presence of measurable leakage – the fact that this model performed significantly better both in internal tests and the final competition), the final delivered model $\mathbb{M}$ does not include any illegitimate feature[1]. To understand what has transpired, we must address the issue of *leakage in training examples*.

3.3 Leakage in Training Examples

Let us first consider the following synthetic but illustrative example. Suppose we are trying to predict the level of a white noise process $\mathcal{y}_t$ for $t = [101, 102, \ldots, 200]$, clearly a hopeless task. Suppose further that for the purpose of predicting $\mathcal{y}_t$, t itself is a legitimate feature but otherwise, as in (3), only past information is deemed legitimate – so obviously we cannot cheat. Now consider a model trained on examples $\boldsymbol{W_{tr}}$ taken from $t = [1, 2, \ldots, 200]$. The proposed model is $\hat{y}_t = \mathbb{M}(\mathrm{t}, \boldsymbol{W_{tr}})$, a table containing for each $\boldsymbol{t}$ the target's realized value $\boldsymbol{y_t}$. Strictly speaking, the only

[1] In fact the use of external sources that are not rolled-back to 2005, such as using current (2007) IMDB data, is simple leakage just like in the IBM example. However this is not the major source of leakage in this example.

feature used by this model, t, is legitimate. Hence the model has no leakage as defined by condition (2), however it clearly has perfect prediction performance for the evaluation set in the example. We would naturally like to capture this case under a complete definition of leakage for this problem.

In order to tackle this case, we suggest adding to (2) the following condition for the absence of leakage: For all $y \in Y_{ev}$,

$$\forall X \in X_{tr}, X \in legit\{y\} \land \forall \tilde{y} \in Y_{tr}, \tilde{y} \in legit\{y\} \quad (9)$$

where Y_{ev} is the set of evaluation[2] target instances, and Y_{tr}, X_{tr} are the sets of training targets and feature-vectors respectively whose realizations make up the set of training examples $\boldsymbol{W}_{tr}$.

One way of interpreting this condition is to think of the information presented for training as constant features embedded into the model, and added to every feature-vector instance the model is called to generate a prediction for.

For modeling problems where the usual i.i.d. instances assumption is valid, and when without loss of generality considering all information specific to the instance being predicted as features rather than examples, condition (9) simply reduces to condition (2) since irrelevant observations can always be considered legitimate. In contrast, when dealing with problems exhibiting non-stationarity, a.k.a. concept-drift [15], and more specifically the case when samples of the target (or, within a Bayesian framework, the target/feature) are not mutually independent, condition (9) cannot be reduced to condition (2). Such is the case of KDD-Cup 2007. Available information about the number of reviews given to a group of titles for the "who reviewed what" task is not statistically independent of the number of reviews given to the second group of titles which is the target in the "how many ratings" task. The reason for this is that these reviews are all given by the same population of users over the same period in 2006, and thus are mutually affected by shared causal ancestors such as viewing and participation trends (*e.g.* promotions, similar media or event that gets a lot of exposure and so on). Without proper conditioning on these shared ancestors we have potential dependence, and because most of these ancestors are unobservable, and difficult to find observable proxies for, dependence is bound to occur.

3.4 Discussion

It is worth noting that leakage in training examples is not limited to the explicit use of illegitimate examples in the training process. A more dangerous way in which illegitimate examples may creep in and introduce leakage is through *design decisions*. Suppose for example that we have access to illegitimate data about the deployment population, but there is no evidence in training data to support this knowledge. This might prompt us to use a certain modeling approach that otherwise contains no leakage in training examples but is still illegitimate. Examples could be: (i) selecting or designing features that will have predictive power in deployment, but don't show this power on training examples, (ii) algorithm or parametric model selection, and (iii) meta-parameter value choices. This form of leakage is perhaps the most dangerous as an evaluator may not be able to identify it even when she knows what she is looking for. The exact same design could have been brought on by theoretic rationale, in which case it would have been completely legitimate. In some domains such as time series prediction, where typically only a single history measuring the phenomenon of interest is available for analysis, this form of leakage is endemic and commonly known as *data snooping / dredging* [5].

Regarding concretization of legitimacy for a new problem: Arguably, more often than not the modeler might find it very challenging to define, together with the client, a complete set of such legitimacy guidelines prior to any modeling work being undertaken, and specifically prior to performing preliminary evaluation. Nevertheless it should usually be rather easy to provide a coarse definition of legitimacy for the problem, and a good place to start is to consider model use cases. The specification of any modeling problem is really incomplete without laying out these ground rules of what constitutes a legitimate model.

As a final point on legitimacy, let us mention that once it has been clearly defined for a problem, the major challenge becomes preparing the data in such a way that ensures models built on this data would be leakage free. Alternatively, when we do not have full control over data collection or when it is simply given to us, a methodology for detecting when a large number of seemingly innocent pieces of information are in fact plagued with leakage is required. This shall be the focus of the following two sections.

4. AVOIDANCE

4.1 Methodology

Our suggested methodology for avoiding leakage is a two stage process of tagging every observation with *legitimacy tags* during collection and then observing what we call a *learn-predict separation*. We shall now describe these stages and then provide some examples.

At the most basic level suitable for handling the more general case of leakage in training examples, legitimacy tags (or hints) are ancillary data attached to every pair (x, y) of observational input instance x and target instance y, sufficient for answering the question "is x legitimate for inferring y" under the problem's definition of legitimacy. With this tagged version of the database it is possible, for every example being studied, to roll back the state of

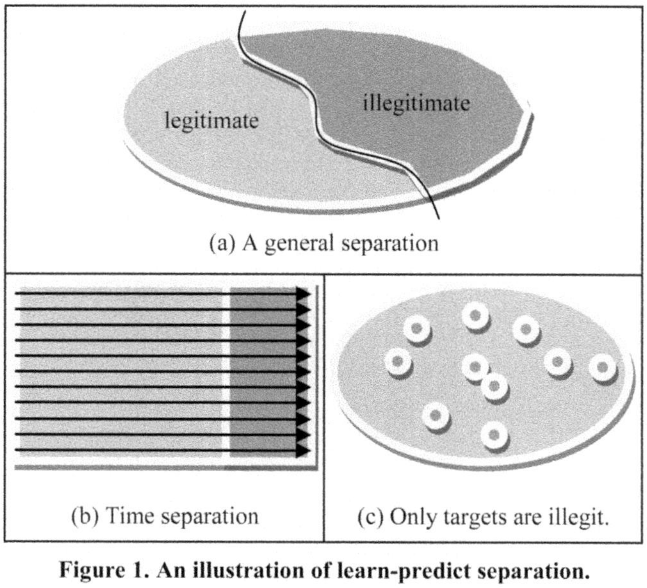

Figure 1. An illustration of learn-predict separation.

[2] We use the term *evaluation* as it could play the classic role of either validation or testing.

the world to a legitimate decision state, eliminating any confusion that may arise from only considering the original raw data.

In the learn-predict separation paradigm (illustrated in Figure 1) the modeler uses the raw but tagged data to construct training examples in such a way that (i) for each target instance, only those observational inputs which are purely legitimate for predicting it are included as features, and (ii) only observational inputs which are purely legitimate with all evaluation targets may serve as examples. This way, by construction, we directly take care of the two types of leakage that make up our formulation, respectively leakage in features (2) and in training examples (9). To completely prevent leakage by design decisions, the modeler has to be careful not to even get exposed to information beyond the separation point, for this we can only prescribe self-control.

As an example, in the common no-time-machine case where legitimacy is defined by (3), legitimacy tags are time-stamps with sufficient precision. Legitimacy tagging is implemented by time-stamping every observation. Learn-predict separation is implemented by a cut at some point in time that segments training from evaluation examples. This is what has been coined in [13] *prediction about the future*. Interestingly enough, this common case does not sit well with the equally common way databases are organized. Updates to database records are usually not time-stamped and not stored separately, and at best whole records end up with one time-stamp. Records are then translated into examples, and this loss of information is often the source of all evil that allows leakage to find its way into predictive models.

The original data for the INFORMS 2008 Data Mining Challenge, lacked proper time-stamping, causing observations taken before *and* after the target's time-stamp to end up as components of examples. This made time-separation impossible, and models built on this data did not perform prediction about the future. On the other hand, the data for KDD-Cup 2007's "How Many Reviews" task in itself was (as far as we are aware) well time-stamped and separated. Training data provided to competitors was sampled prior to 2006, while test data was sampled after and including 2006, and was not given. The fact that training data exposed by the organizers for the separate "Who Reviewed What" task contained leakage was due to an external source of leakage, an issue related with data mining competitions which we shall discuss next.

4.2 External Leakage in Competitions

Our account of leakage avoidance, especially in light of our recurring references to data mining competitions in this paper, would be incomplete without mentioning the case of *external leakage*. This happens when some data source other than what is simply given by the client (organizer) for the purpose of performing inference, contains leakage and is accessible to modelers (competitors). Examples for this kind of leakage include the KDD-Cup 2007 "How Many Reviews" task, the INFORMS 2010 financial forecasting challenge, and the IJCNN 2011 Social Network Challenge[3].

In these cases, it would seem that even a perfect application of the suggested avoidance methodology breaks down by considering the additional source of data. Indeed, separation only prevents leakage from the data actually separated. The fact that other data are even considered is indeed a competition issue, or in some cases an issue of a project organized like a competition (*i.e.* projects within large organizations, outsourcing or government issued projects). Sometimes this issue stems from a lack of an auditing process for submissions, however most of the time, it is introduced to the playground on purpose.

Competition organizers, and some project clients, have an ulterior conflict of interest. On the one hand they do not want competitors to cheat and use illegitimate data. On the other hand they would welcome insightful competitors suggesting new ideas for sources of information. This is a common situation, but the two desires or tasks are often conflicting: when one admits not knowing which sources could be used, one also admits she can't provide an air-tight definition of what she accepts as legitimate. She may be able to say something about legitimacy in her problem, but would intentionally leave room for competitors to maneuver.

The solution to this conflict is to separate the task of suggesting broader legitimacy definitions for a problem from the modeling task that fixes the current understanding of legitimacy. Competitions should just choose one task, or have two separate challenges: one to suggest better data, and one to predict with the given data only. The two tasks require different approaches to competition organization, a thorough account of which is beyond the scope of this paper. One approach for the first task that we will mention is *live prediction*.

When the legitimacy definition for a data mining problem is isomorphic to the no-time-machine legitimacy definition (3) of predictive modeling, we can sometimes take advantage of the fact that a learn-predict separation over time is physically impossible to circumvent. We can then ask competitors to literally predict targets in the future (that is, a time after submission date) with whatever sources of data they think might be relevant, and they will not be able to cheat in this respect. For instance the IJCNN Social Network Challenge could have asked to predict new edges in the network graph a month in advance, instead of synthetically removing edges from an existing network which left traces and the online original source for competitors to find.

5. DETECTION

Often the modeler doesn't have control over the data collection process. When the data are not properly tagged, the modeler cannot pursue a learn-predict separation as in the previous section. One important question is how to detect leakage when it happens in given data, as the ability to detect that there is a problem can help mitigate its effects. In the context of our formulation from Section 3, detecting leakage boils down to pointing out how conditions (2) or (9) fail to hold for the dataset in question. A brute-force solution to this task is often infeasible because datasets will always be too large. We propose the following methods for filtering leakage candidates.

Exploratory data analysis (EDA) can be a powerful tool for identifying leakage. EDA [14] is the good practice of getting more intimate with the raw data, examining it through basic and interpretable visualization or statistical tools. Prejudice free and methodological, this kind of examination can expose leakage as patterns in the data that are *surprising*. In the INFORMS 2008 breast cancer example, for instance, the fact that the "patient id" is so strongly correlated with the target is surprising, if we expect ids to be given with little or no knowledge of the patient's diagnosis, for instance on an arrival time basis. Of course some surprising

[3] Although it is entirely possible that internal leakage was also present in these cases (e.g. forum discussions regarding the IJCNN 2011 competition on http://www.kaggle.com).

facts revealed by the data through basic analysis could be legitimate, for the same breast cancer example it might be the case that family doctors direct their patients to specific diagnosis paths (which issue patient IDs) based on their initial diagnosis, which is a legitimate piece of information. Generally however, as most worthy problems are highly nontrivial, it is reasonable that only few surprising candidates would require closer examination to validate their legitimacy.

Initial EDA is not the only stage of modeling where surprising behavior can expose leakage. The "IBM Websphere" example discussed in Section 1 is an excellent example that shows how the surprising behavior of a feature in the fitted model, in this case a high entropy value (the word "Websphere"), becomes apparent only after the model has been built. Another approach related to critical examination of modeling results comes from observing overall surprising model performance. In many cases we can come to expect, from our own experience or from prior/competing documented results, a certain level of performance for the problem at hand. A substantial divergence from this expected performance is surprising and merits testing the most informative observations the model is based on more closely for legitimacy. The results of many participants in the INFORMS 2010 financial forecasting Challenge are an example of this case because they contradict prior evidence about the efficiency of the stock market.

Finally, perhaps the best approach but possibly also the one most expensive to implement, is early in-the-field testing of initial models. Any substantial leakage would be reflected as a difference between estimated and realized out-of-sample performance. However, this is in fact a sanity check of the model's generalization capability, and while this would work well for many cases, other issues can make it challenging or even impossible to isolate the cause of such performance discrepancy as leakage: classical over-fitting, tangible concept-drift, issues with the design of the field-test such a sampling bias and so on.

A fundamental problem with the methods for leakage detection suggested in this section is that they all require some degree of domain knowledge: For EDA one needs to know if a good predictor is reasonable; comparison of model performance to alternative models or prior state-of-art models requires knowledge of the previous results; and the setup for early in-the-field evaluation is obviously very involved. The fact that these methods still rely on domain knowledge places an emphasis on leakage avoidance during data collection, where we have more control over the data.

6. (NOT) FIXING LEAKAGE

Once we have detected leakage, what should we do about it? In the best-case scenario, one might be able to take a step back, get access to raw data with intact legitimacy tags, and use a learn-predict separation to reconstruct a leakage-free version of the problem. The second-best scenario happens when intact data is not available but the modeler can afford to fix the data collection process and postpone the project until leakage-free data become available. In the final scenario, one just has to make do with that which is available.

Because of structural constraints at work, leakage can be somewhat localized in samples. This is true in both INFORMS 2008 and INFORMS 2009 competitions mentioned above, and also in the IBM Websphere example. When the model is used in the field, by definition all observations are legitimate and there can be no active leaks. So to the extent that most training examples are also leakage-free, the model may perform worse in deployment than in the pilot evaluation – but would still be better than random guessing and possibly competitive with models built with no leakage. This is good news as it means that, for some problems, living with leakage without attempting to fix it could work.

What happens when we do try to fix leakage? Without explicit legitimacy tags in the data, it is often impossible to figure out the legitimacy of specific observations and/or features even if it is obvious that leakage has occurred. It may be possible to partly plug the leak but not to seal it completely, and it is not uncommon that an attempt to fix leakage only makes it worse.

Usually, where there is one leaking feature, there are more. Removing the "obvious" leaks that are detected may exacerbate the effect of undetected ones. In the e-commerce example from [4], one might envision to simply remove the obvious 'free shipping' field, however this kind of *feature removal* succeeds only in very few and simple scenarios to completely eradicate leaks. In particular, in this example you are still left with the 'no purchase in any department' signature. Another example for this is KDD-Cup 2008 breast cancer prediction competition, where the patient ID contained an obvious leak. It is by no means obvious that removing this feature would leave a leakage-free dataset, however. Assuming different ID ranges correspond to different health care facilities (in different geographical locations, with different equipment), there may be additional traces of this in the data. If for instance the imaging equipment's grey scale is slightly different and in particular grey levels are higher in the location with high cancer rate, the model without ID could pick up this leaking signal from the remaining data, and the performance estimate would still be optimistic (the winners show evidence of this in their report [8]).

Similar arguments can be made about *feature modification* performed in INFORMS 2008 in an attempt to plug obvious leaks, which clearly created others; and *instance removal* in organization of INFORMS 2009, which also left some unintended traces [16].

In summary, further research into general methodology for leakage correction is indeed required. Lacking such methodology, our experience is that fully fixing leakage without learn-predict separation is typically very hard, perhaps impossible, and that modeling with the remaining leakage is often the preferred alternative to futile leakage removal efforts.

7. CONCLUSION

It should be clear by now that modeling with leakage is undesirable on many levels: it is a source for poor generalization and overestimation of expected performance. A rich set of examples from diverse data mining domains given throughout this paper add to our own experience to suggest that in the absence of methodology for handling it, leakage could be the cause of many failures of data mining applications.

In this paper we have described leakage as an abstract property of the relationship of observational inputs and target instances, and showed how it could be made concrete for various problems. In light of this formulation an approach for preventing leakage during data collection was presented that adds legitimacy tags to each observation. Also suggested were three ways for zooming in on potentially leaking features: EDA, ex-post analysis of modeling results and early field-testing. Finally, problems with fixing leakage have been discussed as an area where further research is required.

Many cases of leakage happen when in selecting the target variable from an existing dataset, the modeler neglects to consider the legitimacy definition imposed by this selection, which makes other related variables illegitimate (e.g. large purchases vs. free shipping). In other cases, the modeler is well aware of the implications of his selection, but falters when facing the tradeoff between removing potentially important predictive information and ensuring no leakage. Most instances of internal leakage in competitions were in fact of this nature and have been created by the organizers despite best attempts to avoid it.

We hope that the case studies and suggested methodology described in this paper can help save projects and competitions from falling in the leakage trap and allow them to encourage models and modeling approaches that would be relevant in their domains.

8. REFERENCES

[1] Hastie T., Tibshirani, R. and Friedman, J. H. 2009. *The Elements of Statistical Learning: Data Mining, Inference, and Prediction*. Second Edition. Springer.

[2] Kohavi, R., Brodley, C., Frasca, B., Mason, L., and Zheng, Z. 2000. KDD-cup 2000 organizers' report: peeling the onion. *ACM SIGKDD Explorations Newsletter*. 2(2).

[3] Kohavi, R. and Parekh, R. 2003. Ten supplementary analyses to improve e-commerce web sites. In *Proceedings of the Fifth WEBKDD Workshop*.

[4] Kohavi, R., Mason L., Parekh, R. and Zheng Z. 2004. Lessons and challenges from mining retail e-commerce data. *Machine Learning*. 57(1-2).

[5] Lo, A.W. and MacKinlay A.C. 1990. Data-snooping biases in tests of financial asset pricing models. *Review of Financial Studies*. 3(3) 431-467.

[6] Narayanan, A., Shi, E., and Rubinstein, B. 2011. Link Prediction by De-anonymization: How We Won the Kaggle Social Network Challenge. *Proceedings of the 2011 International Joint Conference on Neural Networks (IJCNN). Preprint.*

[7] Nisbet, R., Elder, J. and Miner, G. 2009. *Handbook of Statistical Analysis and Data Mining Applications*. Academic Press.

[8] Perlich C., Melville P., Liu Y., Swirszcz G., Lawrence R., Rosset S. 2008. Breast cancer identification: KDD cup winner's report. *SIGKDD Explorations Newsletter*. 10(2) 39-42.

[9] Pyle, D. 1999. *Data Preparation for Data Mining*. Morgan Kaufmann Publishers.

[10] Pyle, D. 2003. *Business Modeling and Data Mining*. Morgan Kaufmann Publishers.

[11] Pyle, D. 2009. *Data Mining: Know it All*. Ch. 9. Morgan Kaufmann Publishers.

[12] Rosset. S., Perlich, C. and Liu, Y. 2007. Making the most of your data: KDD-Cup 2007 "How Many Ratings" Winner's Report *ACM SIGKDD Explorations Newsletter*. 9(2).

[13] Rosset. S., Perlich, C., Swirszcz, G., Liu. Y., and Prem, M. 2010. Medical data mining: lessons from winning two competitions. *Data Mining and Knowledge Discovery*. 20(3) 439-468.

[14] Tukey, J. 1977. *Exploratory Data Analysis*. Addison-Wesley.

[15] Widmer, G. and Kubat, M. 1996. Learning in the presence of concept drift and hidden contexts. *Machine Learning*. 23(1).

[16] Xie, J. and Coggeshall, S. 2010. Prediction of transfers to tertiary care and hospital mortality: A gradient boosting decision tree approach. *Statistical Analysis and Data Mining*, 3: 253–258.

An Information Theoretic Framework for Data Mining

Tijl De Bie
University of Bristol, Intelligent Systems Laboratory
MVB, Woodland Road
Bristol, UK
tijl.debie@gmail.com

ABSTRACT

We formalize the data mining process as a process of information exchange, defined by the following key components. The data miner's state of mind is modeled as a probability distribution, called the background distribution, which represents the uncertainty and misconceptions the data miner has about the data. This model initially incorporates any prior (possibly incorrect) beliefs a data miner has about the data. During the data mining process, properties of the data (to which we refer as patterns) are revealed to the data miner, either in batch, one by one, or even interactively. This acquisition of information in the data mining process is formalized by updates to the background distribution to account for the presence of the found patterns.

The proposed framework can be motivated using concepts from information theory and game theory. Understanding it from this perspective, it is easy to see how it can be extended to more sophisticated settings, e.g. where patterns are probabilistic functions of the data (thus allowing one to account for noise and errors in the data mining process, and allowing one to study data mining techniques based on subsampling the data). The framework then models the data mining process using concepts from information geometry, and I-projections in particular.

The framework can be used to help in designing new data mining algorithms that maximize the efficiency of the information exchange from the algorithm to the data miner.

Categories and Subject Descriptors

H.2.8 [**Database Management**]: Database applications—*Data mining*

General Terms

Algorithms, Theory

Keywords

Data mining framework, subjective interestingness, MaxEnt

1. INTRODUCTION

Loosely speaking, we would define data mining as the process of extracting patterns present in data that are ideally interesting to a user, the data miner. There has been considerable debate about the difference and added value of data mining when compared to related disciplines. We believe the distinctiveness of the field of data mining is hidden in the word *interesting*: at its heart is the task of quantifying how interesting patterns are. This has proved to be a hard problem, and attempts to solve it wholly or partially are numerous. For example, the number of clustering objectives is practically uncountable. The number of measures of interest used in frequent pattern mining and association analysis is in the order of a hundred. Even in a setting as well-defined as supervised classification, the accuracy objective can be meaningfully quantified in a large number of ways. The practitioner trying to find her way in this jungle is not to be envied.

Partly in recognition of this problem, and to define the boundaries of this relatively young field, efforts have been made to come up with theoretical frameworks for data mining. A very insightful paper [22] on this topic suggested a list of properties such a theoretical framework for data mining should satisfy. In particular, the paper argues it must encompass all or most typical data mining tasks, have a probabilistic nature, be able to talk about inductive generalizations, deal with different types of data, recognize the data mining process as an interactive and iterative process, and account for background knowledge in deciding what is an interesting discovery.

In [22] various attempts at achieving subsets of these criteria are surveyed, such as reducing data mining to multivariate statistics or to machine learning; regarding it as a probabilistic modeling or as a compression effort; formalizing it from a microeconomic viewpoint with an externally defined utility function; or regarding data mining research as the development of a query language on so-called inductive databases.

The purpose of this paper is to suggest a new framework that usefully defines the boundaries of data mining as different from statistics, machine learning, and probabilistic modeling.[1] In particular, the subject of our framework is data mining as defined as follows.

DEFINITION 1.1 (DATA MINING). *Data mining is a process of information transmission from an algorithm (called the data mining algorithm) that has access to data, to a data miner who is interested in understanding the data but who has an information processing capacity that is too limited to access it directly. The information transmitted is in the form of patterns of a type or syntax specified by the data miner. Here,* pattern *is broadly defined, as a quantifiable property of the data. The transmission of a pattern results in a reduction of the data miner's uncertainty and misconceptions about the data, and the stronger this reduction, the more interesting the pattern is deemed to be. The data mining process can be iterative, such that patterns are communicated one by one. It can also be interactive, allowing the data miner to influence the data mining algorithm in the course of the process, e.g. steering it toward patterns of a certain syntax or complexity.*

From this definition, it should be clear that we focus on the data miner as much as on the data. Indeed, we contend that *postulating* which patterns are interesting and which ones are not in an 'objective' way, as is common practice, is bound to be of limited practical use. Instead, we believe that what makes a pattern interesting should be part of the object of study of data mining research. The framework we propose in this paper will serve that goal: studying the interaction between the data and the data miner in order to quantify the subjective level of interest in a pattern (see [28, 25] for remarkably early and significant steps in this direction).

Before we embark on the details of our framework for data mining defined in this way, let us point out what our framework is not, and which questions it does not attempt to answer. In doing this, we contrast our framework with the possible frameworks considered in [22].

Our setting is distinctly different from the machine learning setting, in that *interesting* patterns in data may allow one to *predict*, but do not need to do so. To derive PAC-style learning theoretic results [30], statistical assumptions about the source of the data need to be made. As this is done adequately in the machine learning literature, we would rather not make these assumptions and leave it to machine learning studies to do this. Even stronger, in the general setting we regard *the data* as a monolithic entity, not necessarily composed of similar constituent parts typically called *data points*. This is important e.g. in relational data mining (if one wants to avoid using techniques such as propositionalization), where such a reduction is often nontrivial and not unique.

Similarly, our framework is philosophically different from probabilistic modeling. In particular, we consider situations where the data miner's primary concern is understanding the data itself, rather than the stochastic source that generated it. Whenever we consider a probabilistic model for the data, this represents the data miner's belief about what the value of the data may be, rather than a probability distribution from which the data might have been sampled.

Our formalism also differs in important respects from the view of data mining as compression [10, 27]. This popular and powerful view suffers from a few problems. A theoretical problem is its philosophical dependence on the Kolmogorov complexity of the data, which is uncomputable. A more serious practical problem is that, at least in its common form, it is ignorant of the user or her prior information or beliefs about the data.

The microeconomic view of data mining [19] is highly dissimilar but complementary to our framework. It is useful in different settings, namely when the data mining utility function can be formally specified. However, we contend that in many cases it is impractical to specify such a utility function.

Also the inductive database view (e.g. [21, 26]) could possibly be united and lead to synergies with our framework. However, we will not utilize the terminology common in that area of research, as we are not concerned with the inductive learning aspects, nor the query aspects, as much as with the information theoretic aspects of the data mining process.

Probably the key difference of our framework with all theoretical frameworks surveyed by [22] is its primary focus on the user, rather than on the data. Some early papers have taken a similar approach, e.g. [28, 25], but unfortunately the fraction of papers that aim to define interestingness in a subjective manner is small. Still, we believe this is critical to the very identity of data mining, as a field concerned with defining which patterns are interesting, and we consider it crucial to enhance the successful adoption of data mining in practice, especially of exploratory data mining techniques.

The present paper results from various ideas that were published earlier, or are currently under review [11, 12, 4, 5, 6, 8, 20, 7]. Furthermore, relations exist with various prior work [28, 25, 17, 27, 29, 24, 23, 14], but for space reasons we postpone a detailed discussion of these connections to a forthcoming paper. For information theory and information geometry references related to this paper, see e.g. [15, 3, 1].

2. THE USER'S PERSPECTIVE AND A DATA MINING FORMALISM

2.1 A bird's eye view on the framework

We regard data mining as a process that decreases a user's uncertainty or misconceptions about the value of the data $x \in \mathcal{X}$ (see Def. 1.1). This data mining process can be more or less efficient, depending on which patterns are being communicated and the prior beliefs of the data miner. In this sense, a pattern that reduces the data miner's uncertainty more strongly is subjectively more interesting. A central component of our framework is thus a representation of the uncertainty of the data miner about the data (as believed by the data miner).

In this initial simplified bird's eye view, let us assume that the data miner is able to formalize her beliefs in a *background distribution*, denoted P^*. Her interest is to get to know the data x in as cheap a way as possible. A simple approach could be to agree a code with the algorithm, and request the entire data to be sent over encoded in this way. For

[1]Note that the purpose of this paper is fundamentally different from the purpose of [9], which introduces a different kind of framework for data mining. Whereas the purpose of [9] appears to be the establishment of a common taxonomy and language to formalize data mining processes as they are usually implemented today, the purpose of the current paper is to propose a framework for how data mining could and perhaps sometimes should be done differently from this standard practice.

convenience, we will assume the code is an optimal code where Kraft's inequality is an equality, which means that the code lengths can be specified by means of a probability distribution P as $-\log(P(x))$ for data x. We will also refer to such code as a Shannon code with respect to P. It is in the data miner's interest to design the code lengths in this code (or equivalently the probability distribution P) so as to minimize her expectation of the code length, equal to $E_{X\sim P^*}\{-\log(P(X))\}$. It is easy to show that this function is minimized for $P = P^*$, and the expected code length is equal to the entropy $H(P^*) = -E_{X\sim P^*}\{\log(P^*(X))\}$ of P^*. Note that a small entropy does not guarantee that the code length $-\log(P^*(x))$ for the actual data x is small: this depends on the accuracy of the prior beliefs as formalized in P^*. The entropy of P^* could be small due to the data miner being overly confident.

The result of the communication of a pattern to the data miner is that she will update her beliefs about the data, resulting in a new background distribution $P^{*\prime}$. Correspondingly, to ensure efficient communication of the data, the data miner may update the code to be used for communicating the data such that the new code word length for $x \in \mathcal{X}$ is equal to $-\log(P'(x))$ for some distribution P' (again, assuming that Kraft's inequality can be an equality). A rational choice to determine these new code word lengths (or equivalently the distribution P') would be to maximize the expected reduction in code length, equal to $E_{X\sim P^{*\prime}}\{\log(P'(X)) - \log(P^*(X))\}$. It is easy to show that the maximum is achieved for $P' = P^{*\prime}$, and the expected reduction in code length is then equal to the *Kullback-Leibler (KL) divergence* $KL(P^{*\prime}||P^*) = E_{X\sim P^{*\prime}}\{\log(P^{*\prime}(X)) - \log(P^*(X))\}$ between the initial and updated background distributions P^* and $P^{*\prime}$. It is quite fitting that the KL-divergence is also known as the *information gain.*

Then, good data mining algorithms are those that are able to pinpoint those patterns that lead to a large information gain.[2] Simultaneously, an interesting pattern needs to be easy to describe, itself. Describing a pattern requires a code as well, which should also be defined by the data miner. This code provides the data miner with a way to steer the search toward patterns of a certain syntactical complexity or form. It is then the trade-off between the information gain due to the revealing of a pattern in the data, and the description length of the pattern, that should define a pattern's interest to the data miner.

We have not touched upon how the background distributions P^* and $P^{*\prime}$ are determined, or how they become known to the algorithm so that it could work out the Shannon code lengths. Typically, the data miner will not be able to specify these distributions explicitly, as it would be too laborious or the introspective exercise may be prohibitively hard. In the rest of this Section we will discuss how this can be handled, and we will further detail some of the other aspects of the framework.

2.2 The data miner and prior beliefs

We assume that a data miner is interested in getting to know as much as possible about the data at hand, at as little a description cost as possible. If the data miner did not have prior beliefs, this would amount to data compression, e.g. using a universal compression scheme (such as Lempel-Ziv). See e.g. [27, 10] for a discussion of the compression view.

Prior beliefs allow one to specify a compression scheme that reflects the data's complexity as perceived by the data miner. Let us assume that the prior beliefs of the data miner can be summarized using a background distribution P^*. Then we have argued that the optimal code to be used for communicating the data has code word lengths equal to $-\log(P^*(x))$ for $x \in \mathcal{X}$. The more probable the data miner judges the data to be, the shorter the code describing it would be. The code length for x is effectively a measure of the subjective complexity of the data x.

Ideally, the data miner directly formalizes her prior beliefs by specifying P^*. However, while we postulate the existence of P^* somewhere deep in the mind of the data miner, requiring her to fully specify it is bound to be impractical. More manageable would be to allow the data miner to just specify (some of) her beliefs in the form of *constraints* the background distribution must satisfy, or equivalently a set $\mathcal{P}$ of distributions P^* must belong to. For example, the data miner could state that the expected value of a certain property of the data is equal to a given value. The resulting $\mathcal{P}$ would be a convex set, as we will assume in the sequel.

Not knowing the exact background distribution, it is unclear then how the code for the data should be designed, i.e. how to choose the distribution P that defines the code lengths as $-\log(P(x))$ for $x \in \mathcal{X}$. We argue it makes most sense to choose the distribution $P \in \mathcal{P}$ of maximum entropy, and we call this the ME (Maximum Entropy) distribution, i.e.:

$$P = \arg\max_{P\in\mathcal{P}} -E_{X\sim P}\{\log(P(X))\}.$$

It should be acknowledged that typically $P \neq P^*$. However, as we will argue in two different ways, P is a good surrogate for P^* for the design of a code for the data.

The first argument is that in the absence of any other constraints, the best estimate for P^* is the ME distribution from $\mathcal{P}$. The motivation of this Maximum Entropy Principle is that any distribution from $\mathcal{P}$ with lower entropy than the ME distribution effectively injects additional knowledge, reducing the uncertainty in undue ways. After estimating the background distribution as the ME distribution P, we can repeat the reasoning from Sec. 2.1 and set the code lengths equal to $-\log(P(x))$ in order to minimize (an estimate of) the expected code length.

The second argument is a game-theoretic one. For a Shannon code with respect to P, the expected code length according to P^* is equal to $-E_{X\sim P^*}\{\log(P(X))\}$. Of course, this quantity cannot be evaluated when P^* is incompletely specified. As fully specifying it is impractical, the data miner and the data mining algorithm could instead agree to play safe and choose P so as to minimize the expected code length *in the worst case* over all possible $P^* \in \mathcal{P}$. Then, P is found as:

$$P = \arg\min_{P}\max_{P^*\in\mathcal{P}} -E_{X\sim P^*}\{\log(P(X))\}.$$

It is well-known that for convex $\mathcal{P}$ the solution P is equal to the ME distribution from $\mathcal{P}$. Hence, in this argument, we do not try to estimate P^*, but instead we design the code

[2]Note that ideally, rather than the *expected* reduction in code length for the data, it should be the *actual* reduction that guides the search for patterns. However, we will show below that focusing on the information gain is equivalent with focusing on the actual reduction in code length.

lengths defined by P in the safest possible way given the prior beliefs specified by the data miner.

In summary, at the start of the data mining process, the most sensible way to quantify the subjective complexity of the data is using the code length in an optimal Shannon code with respect to the ME model P. We will also refer to this distribution as the *surrogate background distribution*.

2.3 Patterns and conditioning

In a data mining process, the data mining algorithm reveals a pattern to the data miner (see Sec. 2.6 for pattern *sets*). For concreteness, let us narrow down our definition of a pattern to mean any property of the data that restricts the set of possible values of the data to a subset of its domain. Then a pattern can be formalized as a constraint $x \in \mathcal{X}'$ for some $\mathcal{X}' \subseteq \mathcal{X}$. Although not fully general, we believe that many data mining algorithms can be studied using this definition of pattern. Nevertheless, in Sec. 4.2 we will outline how the framework could be generalized to include other types of pattern as well.

The result of revealing a pattern to the data miner is that the data miner's beliefs adapt, and thus the background distribution P^* turns into an adapted background distribution $P^{*\prime}$. To exploit this, also the code describing the data should be reconsidered to minimize the expected code length.

As is the case for P^* at the start of the data mining process, the data miner cannot be expected to specify $P^{*\prime}$. All we know about it is that $P^{*\prime}(x) = 0$ for all $x \notin \mathcal{X}'$, as the pattern has revealed to the data miner that $x \in \mathcal{X}'$. To exploit this, it should be possible to update the code describing the data, making it more efficient (at least in expectation, but it would be even better if it is deterministically more efficient, irrespective of the actual value of the data).

We argue that the new code should have Shannon code lengths with respect to a distribution P' that is defined as the distribution P conditioned on the information that the data x belongs to the new support $\mathcal{X}' \subseteq \mathcal{X}$. Formally:

$$\begin{aligned} P'(x) &= P(x|x \in \mathcal{X}'), \\ &= \begin{cases} 0 & \text{for } x \notin \mathcal{X}', \\ \frac{1}{P(X\in\mathcal{X}')} \cdot P(x) & \text{for } x \in \mathcal{X}'. \end{cases} \end{aligned}$$

The reduction in code length (and thus also the reduction in expected description length, called the information gain in Sec. 2.1) of the data achieved by encoding the data w.r.t. P' instead of P is then equal to $-\log(P(X \in \mathcal{X}'))$. We refer to this quantity as the *self-information* of the pattern. In the discussion below, we will refer to the distribution P' as the *updated surrogate background distribution*.

As for choosing P as the ME distribution, there are again two arguments for choosing the updated surrogate background distribution P' as the conditional of P on the fact that $x \in \mathcal{X}'$.

In the first argument, we attempt to estimate the new background distribution $P^{*\prime}$ by P'. In the absence of any other information, it seems sensible to let P' be as similar to P as possible, while incorporating the new information that $x \in \mathcal{X}'$. This difference between the updated and original distributions P' and P can be quantified using the KL divergence $KL(P'||P) = E_{X\sim P'}\{\log(P'(X)) - \log(P(X))\}$. Thus, with $\mathcal{P}'$ the set of distributions that assign zero probability to the set of all $x \notin \mathcal{X}'$, P' can be estimated as:

$$P' = \arg\min_{P'\in\mathcal{P}'} E_{X\sim P'}\{\log(P'(X)) - \log(P(X))\}.$$

This principle of choosing P' is known as the Minimum Discrimination Information Principle, and is a generalization of the Maximum Entropy Principle. For the particular choice of $\mathcal{P}'$, it can be shown that the optimum is indeed achieved for P' as the conditioning of P on the new domain $\mathcal{X}'$, i.e. $P'(x) = P(x|x \in \mathcal{X}')$. After estimating $P^{*\prime}$ as P', it is again easy to show that the shortest code in expectation is the Shannon code with respect to P'.[3]

The second argument is again a game-theoretic one, and avoids the need to estimate the new background distribution $P^{*\prime}$. All we assume about it is that $\sum_{x\notin\mathcal{X}'} P^{*\prime}(x) = 0$, i.e. that $P^{*\prime} \in \mathcal{P}'$, as the pattern revealed to the data miner specifies that $x \in \mathcal{X}'$. We want to find a distribution P' and the associated Shannon code lengths for describing the data, for which the data miner's expectation of the reduction in description length is maximal. This expected reduction in description length is equal to the expected value with respect to $P^{*\prime}$ of the difference between the code length using P and using P', i.e. $E_{X\sim P^{*\prime}}\{\log(P'(X)) - \log(P(X))\}$. It is impossible to maximize this directly, as $P^{*\prime}$ is unspecified. However, we can maximize it in the worst-case over all $P^{*\prime} \in \mathcal{P}'$:

$$P' = \arg\max_{P'} \min_{P^{*\prime}\in\mathcal{P}'} E_{X\sim P^{*\prime}}\{\log(P'(X)) - \log(P(X))\}. \quad (1)$$

It can be shown that the optimum P' is P conditioned on the new domain $\mathcal{X}'$, as suggested (see also Sec. 4.2).

Note that the initial set of prior beliefs may not be true anymore in the updated background distribution $P^{*\prime}$, i.e. it may be that $P^{*\prime} \notin \mathcal{P}$. As a result, also the updated surrogate background distribution P' may not belong to $\mathcal{P}$. This is desirable, as the revealed patterns may help the data miner to fine-tune the prior beliefs, or even to correct outright misconceptions.

REMARK 2.1. *Note that although the description length of the data is reduced by the self-information of the pattern after conditioning the surrogate background distribution, the expected description length may actually increase. This is due to more information becoming available, such that the description length can be estimated more accurately. Thus, patterns that lead the data miner to revise her background distribution in such a way that the expected description length increases are not to be avoided for that reason. We should just be concerned by the amount by which a pattern reduces the description length of the actual data, which is its self-information.*

Data mining could thus be formalized as the process of revealing aspects of the data in the form of patterns that allow the data miner to revise her beliefs in such a way that the data becomes more plausible (i.e. less complex to describe). For patterns defined as constraints of the form $x \in \mathcal{X}'$ for some $\mathcal{X}' \subseteq \mathcal{X}$, this means reducing the set of possible values of the data to a subset of the domain of the data. In doing so, the remaining uncertainty of the data miner is reduced, as reflected in a reduction in the data's description length. Without knowing the data x it would

[3]Note that $KL(P'||P)$ is then equal to the expected difference in coding length using a Shannon code based on P and a Shannon code based on P', where the expectation is taken with respect to the new estimated P'. This should corroborate the choice for the KL-divergence as a way to quantify the difference between P and P'.

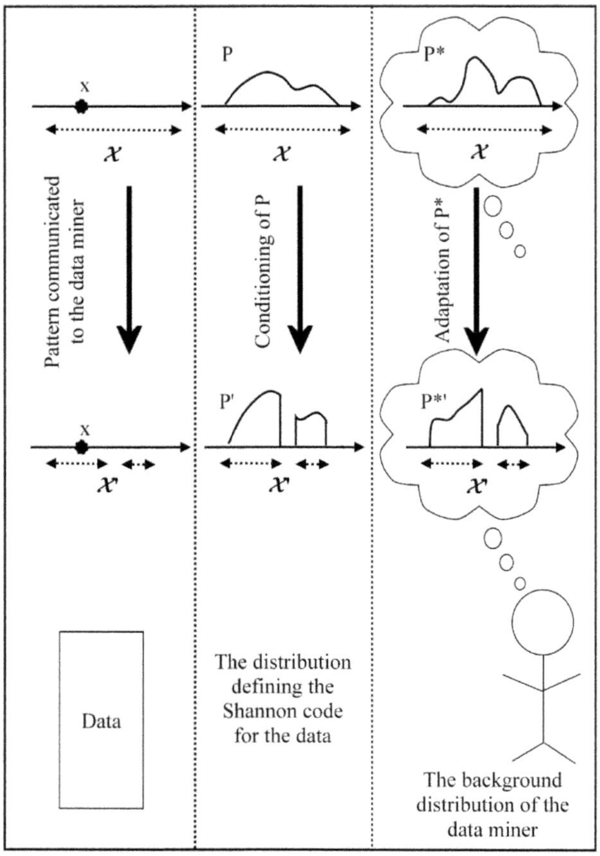

Figure 1: A schematic illustration of the effect of the communication of a pattern reducing the set of possible values for x from $\mathcal{X}$ to $\mathcal{X}' \subseteq \mathcal{X}$. The surrogate background distribution P used to determine the code lengths is conditioned on this new reduced domain, leading to an updated surrogate background distribution P' and associated set of code lengths. The unknown new background distribution $P^{*\prime}$ could be anything consistent with the requirement that it assigns zero probability to $\mathcal{X} \backslash \mathcal{X}'$.

seem we can only reason about the information gain due to a pattern, i.e. the *expected* reduction in code length. However, it turns out that by defining P' as the conditional of P on the presence of the revealed pattern, the reduction in description length is independent of the value of the data x, and equal to the self-information of the revealed pattern. Patterns can then be considered more interesting if their self-information is larger. This is equivalent to what we suggested in Sec. 2.1, considering patterns more interesting if they lead to a larger information gain.

A schematic illustration of the essential components of the data mining process is given in Fig. 1. This Figure shows what may happen to the true (unknown) background background distribution when it is revealed that the data x belongs to $\mathcal{X}' \subseteq \mathcal{X}$. In particular, all $P^{*\prime}$ needs to satisfy is that its domain is restricted to $\mathcal{X}'$. Also shown is how P', which defines the code lengths for the data after observing the pattern, is obtained from the ME distribution P, simply conditioning it on the reduced domain $\mathcal{X}'$.

2.4 The cost of a pattern

Instead of just being concerned with encoding the data given that a pattern is known to be present, we should be concerned with the length of the joint description of the data and the pattern. Indeed, also with the communication of a pattern to the data miner a description cost is associated.

The code length of each possible pattern should be specified in advance by the data miner. It should reflect the subjective complexity of a pattern, and can be used to favour patterns of a certain syntax or complexity over others by assigning them a smaller code word.

2.5 Effective data mining as a specific type of compression, and subjective level of interest of a pattern

The above completes the essence of our framework for data mining. Given this framework, we can reason about the efficiency of the process. In particular, we believe it should be the goal of a data mining algorithm to search for the pattern that strikes the right balance between the self-information (and hence the reduction in description length of the data) on the one hand, and the description cost for the pattern on the other. There may be various ways to trade-off these two aspects.

For example, assume that the data miner has a certain processing capacity, defined as an upper bound on the pattern description length she can cope with. Then the level of interest of the pattern should be defined by its self-information, as long as its description length under the user-specified code (see Sec. 2.4) is smaller than that upper bound.

On the other hand, if the data miner is truly interested in fully knowing the data (which we believe is less common), it is the overall compression of the data that is of interest. Then the measure of interest should be defined by the reduction in overall coding length achieved, taking into account the need to also encode the pattern. I.e., then the difference between the self-information (the gain in the description length of the data) and the description length of the pattern would be of interest, as it represents the gain in total description length.

2.6 Pattern set mining, iterative data mining, and interactive data mining

In the above, we have assumed that only one pattern is revealed to the data miner. Here, a pattern was defined as anything that reduces the set of possible values for the data from the entire domain $\mathcal{X}$ down to $\mathcal{X}'_i \subseteq \mathcal{X}$. Note that we introduced a subscript i here, which is an index running over the set of patterns of potential interest to the data miner (i.e. those the data miner assigned a finite code word length). Obviously, this implies that a *pattern set* is a pattern itself—for the discussion below let us call this a composite pattern (even though this is a rather badly defined notion). Indeed, a composite pattern defined by a set of patterns with indices i in a set $\mathcal{I}$, corresponds to a constraint $x \in \mathcal{X}'_{\mathcal{I}}$ with $\mathcal{X}'_{\mathcal{I}} = \bigcap_{i \in I} \mathcal{X}'_i$. Clearly, since the intersection operation is commutative and associative, it does not matter in which order patterns are revealed.

Note that the conditioning operator applied to distributions is commutative and associative as well. This means that the conditioning of the surrogate background distribution based on a composite pattern is the same as the iterative conditioning on the atomic (as opposed to composite) constituent patterns. The framework thus describes pattern set mining in a sound and natural way. Patterns can be combined, leading to the definition of new (composite) patterns.

As such, the notion of a pattern set becomes theoretically less relevant as it can be regarded as a single pattern of different kind. Indeed, the aim of iterative data mining is simply to search for a single composite pattern with a maximal self-information $-\log(P(X \in \mathcal{X}'_{\mathcal{I}}))$, while its description should not be too long. Here, the description length of a composite pattern is the sum of the description lengths of the atomic constituent patterns.

However, from a practical algorithmic perspective, *pattern set mining* remains important as a concept. Interestingly, pattern set mining formalized in this way always boils down to a *weighted set coverage problem* of some kind. Indeed, consider the domain $\mathcal{X}$ of the data as the universe, each element $x \in \mathcal{X}$ of which is assigned a weight $P(x)$ equal to the probability under the initial surrogate background distribution. Furthermore, associate with each pattern a subset of this universe, namely the set $\mathcal{X}\backslash\mathcal{X}'_i$ of elements from the data domain it rides out. Also associate a cost with each pattern, equal to its description length. Then, the search for a pattern set with indices $\mathcal{I}$ such that the union of subsets from the data space associated to the patterns in the pattern set have the largest cumulative weight is equivalent with searching for the pattern set for which $\bigcup_{i\in I}\mathcal{X}\backslash\mathcal{X}'_i = \mathcal{X}\backslash\bigcap_{i\in I}\mathcal{X}'_i = \mathcal{X}\backslash\mathcal{X}'_{\mathcal{I}}$ has the largest total probability under P. This in turn is equivalent to searching for the pattern set with indices $\mathcal{I}$ for which $\mathcal{X}'_{\mathcal{I}}$ has the smallest total probability, i.e. for which $P(X \in \mathcal{X}'_{\mathcal{I}})$ is minimal, or hence for which self-information $-\log(P(X \in \mathcal{X}'_{\mathcal{I}}))$ is maximal, as we aim to do in pattern set mining under our framework.

This shows that pattern set mining can be reduced to a weighted set coverage problem. With an additional upper bound on the overall description length of the pattern set, it is a budgeted version of the weighted set coverage problem. These problems are known to be hard to solve exactly, but can be approximated well using an iterative greedy search approach [18]. In the present context, this amounts to using *iterative data mining* approaches to pattern set mining.

Ideally, the iterative data mining process should be *interactive*, allowing the data miner to change her 'prior' beliefs (a specific pattern may lead to a more global insight or belief), or to change the focus of the search. Both can easily be modeled in our framework: the former by updating the background model (e.g. using I-projections, see below), the latter by adapting the description lengths assigned to the atomic patterns in the course of the iterative data mining process.

2.7 Practical aspects

To allow this framework to be practically useful, algorithmic challenges will need to be overcome. We will touch upon this very briefly in the context of some of the special cases discussed below.

More fundamentally, the framework would loose most of its appeal if mechanisms to allow the data miner to specify prior beliefs, or coding lengths for patterns, were impractical. We believe, however, that such mechanisms do often exist. This will also be demonstrated briefly for the special cases discussed in Sec. 3.

In particular, such prior beliefs and coding lengths can often be specified at a generic intentional level. Also, in many typical scenarios the number of prior beliefs could be very limited (e.g. just on the mean or variance of certain aspects of the data). Even when it is impractical to specify all prior beliefs, the iterative data mining approach would only initially return uninteresting patterns, until the unspecified prior beliefs have been covered by the discovered patterns.

With regards to the coding lengths the data miner needs to specify, let us point out a connection between these coding lengths and a regularization function in machine learning. Both bias the search in a certain direction. In machine learning, the regularizer has been used conveniently and effectively to bias the search toward certain solutions, e.g. to ensure sparsity.

3. SPECIAL CASES

In [22] the author argues that a framework for data mining should be able to describe important existing methods. Equally important is that it provides us with additional insights on such methods, providing an opportunity to improve their usability. Below we will argue at a high level that this is indeed the case for a number of important examples.

3.1 Clustering and alternative clustering

An example of a clustering pattern is one that specifies that the data can be clustered at a certain cost around a specified set of cluster centres. This cost could for example be the average squared distance to the nearest cluster centre, or the likelihood of the maximum likelihood Gaussian mixture distribution. Alternatively, a cluster pattern can be specified by the subset of points belonging to the cluster along with its mean. Clearly, knowing that such a pattern is present reduces the set of possible values for the data.

The degree to which a clustering is of interest to a data miner will strongly depend on prior beliefs the data miner has. For example, for data that is elongated along one dimension, K-means clustering will typically return a result that partitions the data along this dimension. If the data miner had prior knowledge about the overall data shape, this would be a pattern of little interest to the user, and indeed it would have a small self-information.

Recently there has been considerable interest in alternative clustering (see e.g. [2]). This is the task of generating a set of different clusterings, each of which reveals different aspects of the data. A key challenge here is quantifying the redundancy between two alternative clusterings. In our setting, this redundancy could be captured by computing the self-information of the composite pattern composed of the two clustering patterns, and comparing it with the self-information of the two atomic patterns for the two clusterings by themselves. If there is a small difference only, the clusterings are redundant. Alternatively, we could assess the self-information of the second clustering under the updated background model conditioned on the first clustering pattern. If the clusterings are redundant, this self-information will be small.

Note that the user can inject a preference for a specific number of clusters, by ensuring that the coding length for clustering patterns with the specified number of clusters is small.

We have not touched upon computational cost, and we acknowledge that developing practical algorithms to implement the above may be challenging for some types of patterns. Thus, as a proof of concept and a useful result in its own right, we have developed an alternative clustering algorithm based on this framework, for cluster patterns that specify the mean of a specified subset of the data points belonging to the cluster. After working out the details of the framework for this type of pattern, we end up with an algorithm that bears similarities with K-Means clustering and spectral clustering, while it is more flexible in that it can take prior beliefs on the data into account to ensure the clusters are subjectively interesting to the data miner. See [7] for more details of this application of the framework.

3.2 Dimensionality reduction

Principal Component Analysis (PCA) [16] can be described as a method implementing our framework. Imagine prior beliefs of a data miner in the form of the expected value of each of the features (i.e. the mean of all data points), and an isotropic variance of say 1. This gives a ME model equal to an isotropic multivariate normal distribution centred at the assumed data mean $\boldsymbol{\mu}$. With data matrix $\mathbf{X} \in \mathbb{R}^{n \times d}$ containing the d-dimensional data points $\mathbf{x}_i$ as its n rows, the background distribution is thus:[4]

$$P(\mathbf{X}) = \frac{1}{\sqrt{(2\pi)^{dn}}} \exp\left(-\frac{1}{2}\sum_{i=1}^{n}(\mathbf{x}_i - \boldsymbol{\mu})'(\mathbf{x}_i - \boldsymbol{\mu})\right).$$

In PCA, the type of patterns sought specify the values of the centered data points' projections onto a weight vector $\mathbf{w}$ (we assume, without loss of generality, that $\mathbf{w}'\mathbf{w} = 1$). I.e., such patterns are constraints of the form $(\mathbf{X} - \mathbf{1}\boldsymbol{\mu}')\mathbf{w} = \mathbf{z}$, and there is a possible pattern for each possible weight vector. Clearly, given a pattern for a certain weight vector, the set of possible values of the data is reduced. A priori, none of these patterns is to be preferred, so they should all be given the same coding cost.[5]

It can be shown that the probability density of a pattern $(\mathbf{X} - \mathbf{1}\boldsymbol{\mu}')\mathbf{w} = \mathbf{z}$ under the above background model is given by:

$$P((\mathbf{X} - \mathbf{1}\boldsymbol{\mu}')\mathbf{w} = \mathbf{z}) = \frac{1}{\sqrt{(2\pi)^{n}}} \exp\left(-\frac{1}{2}\mathbf{z}'\mathbf{z}\right).$$

The self-information of the pattern is thus given by:

$$-\log\left(P((\mathbf{X} - \mathbf{1}\boldsymbol{\mu}')\mathbf{w} = \mathbf{z})\right) = \frac{n}{2}\log(2\pi) + \frac{1}{2}\mathbf{z}'\mathbf{z}.$$

Thus, the pattern with the largest self-information is the one that maximizes the sum of squares of the projections of the centered data points onto the corresponding weight vector $\mathbf{w}$—i.e. the one that maximizes the variance of the projections (assuming mean $\boldsymbol{\mu}$) and thus the PCA objective.

A similar reasoning shows that the k patterns with weight vectors equal to the k dominant principal components form a set of k patterns with maximal self-information. Interestingly, the marginal probability densities for patterns corresponding to orthogonal weight vectors are independent, as fixing the values of the projections of all data points on one weight vector does not constrain the possible values of the projections on an orthogonal weight vector. Thus, the self-information of a composite pattern consisting of a set of PCA patterns with orthogonal weight vectors, is equal to the sum of the self-informations of the individual patterns. This is the reason that the greedy set coverage approach (i.e. selecting principal components by a method of deflation of the covariance matrix) is optimal, as is well-known.

Understanding PCA in this way may shed some new light on what PCA is doing. However, the true power is in the framework's ability to show how to adapt PCA for other settings where the prior beliefs may be different (e.g. an anisotropic covariance matrix or an altogether different distribution).

3.3 Frequent pattern mining

In previous work, we and others have already applied the ideas from the suggested framework to searching for interesting tiles and interesting sets of tiles in binary databases. We also pointed out ways to set up ME models for more complex databases and prior beliefs, including for non-binary databases. We also actually implemented the iterative greedy data mining approach, and demonstrated its use on a number of text data sets. For details we refer to the relevant papers [4, 5, 6, 8, 20].

3.4 Community detection

When networks are represented as binary adjacency matrices, community detection is very similar to frequent pattern mining, in particular to the tile mining discussed above. The presented framework may be useful in designing community detection methods that take into account prior knowledge on certain topological properties of the network, such as an a priori known cluster structure, degree distribution, etc.

3.5 Variations on the framework: subgroup discovery and supervised learning

With a minor modification, the framework can be extended to incorporate subgroup discovery (and in a sense supervised learning, although we should reemphasize that investigating generalization is not a goal of our framework).

The modification required is that the background model should be a distribution for the labels conditioned on the actual input data. The prior beliefs are beliefs on the labels conditioned on the input data, such as: "Given that x has a certain property, the expected value of y is equal to bla". Typically, patterns would be expressed in a conditional way as well, i.e. specifying the label as a function of the value of the input data (at least for a subset of the data points). Such a pattern reduces the set of possible values of the set of the labels for the given input data. The effect of observing a pattern is similar to the basic framework: it would lead to a conditioning of the surrogate background distribution.

[4] Note that this is a density function as the domain is continuous, while in the exposition of the framework we focused on distributions on discrete domains. However, the ideas carry over without serious problems.

[5] In this case, the set of patterns is uncountable. As usual in encoding real-valued data, we could therefore discretize the space, and consider a pattern for each of the discretized weight vectors.

4. BROADER CONTEXT AND GENERALIZATIONS OF THE FRAMEWORK

4.1 Significant patterns

In recent years, data mining research, and in particular (frequent) pattern mining research (with 'pattern' defined narrowly here), has made increasing use of the notion of a p-value to quantify interest to a data miner (see e.g. [13, 24, 11, 12, 14]. Here, the null hypothesis is taken to be a distribution not unlike our background distribution, representing any prior beliefs the data miner has.

It is easy to see that this approach is a special case of our framework, for a special choice of pattern, with 'pattern' defined in the general way used in the rest of this paper. In particular, choose a test statistic (e.g. the support of a specific itemset), and define a pattern as the fact that this test statistic in the given data is larger than or equal to a certain value (typically its actual support). Then the probability against the background distribution of this pattern being present in the data is, by definition, equal to the p-value associated to the value of the test statistic, with the surrogate background distribution as null hypothesis. Hence, selecting such patterns based on small p-value is equivalent to selecting them based on large self-information.

We believe it has not been fully clear how to iteratively mine for low p-value itemsets, and heuristic approaches have been developed to update the null hypothesis (surrogate background distribution) to take prior selected patterns into account (see e.g. [12]). Interestingly, our framework suggests how it should be done in a theoretically meaningful way, although it must be admitted that it does not guarantee computational feasibility.

4.2 Generalizing the framework

In motivating the choice for conditioning the surrogate background distribution to take a seen pattern into account, we made use of a game-theoretic argument, leading to Eq. (1). We considered patterns that constrain the updated background distribution $P^{*\prime}$ to the set $\mathcal{P}'$ containing distributions that assign probability zero outside some region $\mathcal{X}' \subseteq \mathcal{X}$. For such patterns, the solution of Eq. (1), i.e. the updated surrogate background distribution P', is equal to the initial surrogate background distribution P conditioned on the new domain $\mathcal{X}'$.

However, in information geometry Eq. (1) is studied more generally [15, 3, 1]. In particular, it is known that for any closed convex set $\mathcal{P}'$, the optimum P' of Eq. (1) is the I-projection of P onto $\mathcal{P}'$. Thus, our framework also applies to pattern types that constrain the updated background distribution to any closed convex set of distributions, not just to the set of distributions restricted to a specified domain.

In other words, the conditioning of P in Sec. 2.3 is a special case of an I-projection. We introduced our framework for this special case for reasons of clarity, and also because we believe it is sufficiently general to be applicable to many data mining settings. However, the more general result can be of genuine interest. For example, for computational reasons patterns could be searched for by the algorithm on a subsample of the data, such that they only have a (known) probabilistic relation with the actual data. Interestingly, if this is the case, an I-projection amounts to a Bayes update of the background distribution, rather than a conditioning. Other pattern types could be imagined, with I-projections taking into account the presence of such patterns, possibly amounting to yet different operations on the background distribution.

4.3 Alternative interpretation

We have set up the framework in terms of prior beliefs. Then, patterns are more interesting if they contrast more strongly with these prior beliefs, as quantified using simple information theoretic concepts.

An alternative interpretation of the background distribution P^* is that it models all aspects of the data the data miner is not interested in. A special case of an aspect in which a data miner is not interested is an aspect implied by a prior belief; hence, this alternative interpretation of the background model is in a sense more general.

4.4 Data mining and machine learning

To set out we strongly insisted on distinguishing data mining and machine learning, the former being concerned with identifying interesting patterns, the latter with quantifying predictive performance and designing algorithms that guarantee generalization.

That said, we contend that our framework may be easily integrated with machine learning paradigms—they would simply study different aspects of the same practical problem. For example, we have already highlighted a strong similarity between the description cost (coding length) of a pattern and a regularization cost in machine learning. In fact, all that is needed to add on a learning element would be to make additional statistical assumptions about the data, such as i.i.d.-ness.

5. CONCLUSIONS

In this paper, we introduced a general framework for data mining. It emphatically takes a user perspective, following and modeling the user's state of mind throughout the data mining process, and allowing one to guide the data mining process so as to maximally reduce the data miner's uncertainty and misconceptions about the data. The framework naturally formalizes pattern set mining, iterative data mining, as well as interactive data mining.

By taking a user perspective, fully accounting for any prior beliefs a user may have, we believe our framework is able to capture what is truly of interest to a data miner. Considering the data miner as part of the study object of data mining research, our framework allows to define subjective level of interest of patterns in a formal way.

We argued that various existing methods can be regarded as implementations of this framework, such as PCA, our prior work related to tile mining in binary databases, and our recent work on alternative clustering. We also pointed out that it could be used with great potential in new contexts, such as in subgroup discovery.

We observed that iterative data mining in this framework always amounts to a greedy algorithm for a set coverage type problem attempting to select the best pattern set. However, importantly we did not go into the algorithmic details. As such, our framework is mostly a theoretical ideal, with a few practical instances as indications of its potential. It remains to be investigated if it can be implemented efficiently for more interesting problems. This, and the further development of these ideas for various data mining problems, is subject of our current research.

Acknowledgements

The author is grateful to the anonymous reviewers for useful suggestions, and to Akis Kontonasios, Eirini Spyropoulou and the organizers and participants of the Mining Patterns and Subgroups workshop in Leiden, 2010, for many useful and insightful discussions and critiques related to this work. This work is supported by the EPSRC grant EP/G056447/1.

6. REFERENCES

[1] S.-I. Amari and H. Nagaoka. *Methods of information geometry.* The American Mathematical Society, Oxford University Press, 2000.

[2] E. Bae and J. Bailey. Coala: A novel approach for the extraction of an alternate clustering of high quality and high dissimilarity. In *Proceedings of the International Conference on Data Mining (ICDM)*, 2006.

[3] I. Csiszár and P. C. Shields. *Information theory and statistics: a tutorial.* now Publishers Inc., Delft, The Netherlands, 2004.

[4] T. De Bie. Explicit probabilistic models for databases and networks. Technical report, University of Bristol TR-123931, arXiv:0906.5148v1, 2009.

[5] T. De Bie. Finding interesting itemsets using a probabilistic model for binary databases. Technical report, University of Bristol TR-123930, 2009.

[6] T. De Bie. Maximum entropy models and subjective interestingness: an application to tiles in binary databases. *Data Mining and Knowledge Discovery*, 2010.

[7] T. De Bie. Subjectively interesting alternative clusters. Technical report, University of Bristol TR-133090, 2011.

[8] T. De Bie, K.-N. Kontonasios, and E. Spyropoulou. A framework for mining interesting pattern sets. *SIGKDD Explorations*, 12(2), 2010.

[9] S. Dzeroski. Towards a general framework for data mining. In *Lecture Notes in Computer Science volume 4747*, pages 259–300. springer, 2006.

[10] C. Faloutsos and V. Megalooikonomou. On data mining, compression, and kolmogorov complexity. *Data Mining and Knowledge Discovery*, 15:3–20, 2007.

[11] A. Gallo, T. De Bie, and N. Cristianini. MINI: Mining informative non-redundant itemsets. In *Proceedings of Principles and Practice of Knowledge Discovery in Databases (PKDD)*, 2007.

[12] A. Gallo, A. Mammone, T. De Bie, M. Turchi, and N. Cristianini. From frequent itemsets to informative patterns. Technical report, University of Bristol TR 123936, 2009.

[13] A. Gionis, H. Mannila, T. Mielikäinen, and P. Tsaparas. Assessing data mining results via swap randomization. *ACM Transactions on Knowledge Discovery from Data*, 1(3):14, 2007.

[14] S. Hanhijarvi, M. Ojala, N. Vuokko, K. Puolamäki, N. Tatti, and H. Mannila. Tell me something I don't know: Randomization strategies for iterative data mining. In *Proc. of the 15th ACM SIGKDD International Conference on Knowledge Discovery and Data Mining (KDD09)*, pages 379–388, 2009.

[15] P. Harremoës and F. Topsøe. Maximum entropy fundamentals. *Entropy*, 2001.

[16] H. Hotelling. Analysis of a complex of statistical variables into principal components. *Journal of Educational Psychology*, 24:417–441, 1933.

[17] S. Jaroszewicz and D. A. Simovici. Interestingness of frequent itemsets using bayesian networks as background knowledge. In *Proc. of the 10th ACM SIGKDD International Conference on Knowledge Discovery and Data Mining (KDD04)*, pages 178–186, 2004.

[18] S. Khuller, A. Moss, and J. Naor. The budgeted maximum coverage problem. *Information Processing Letters*, 70, 1999.

[19] J. Kleinberg, C. Papadimitriou, and P. Raghavan. A microeconomic view of data mining. *Data Mining and Knowledge Discovery*, 2(4), 1998.

[20] K.-N. Kontonasios and T. De Bie. An information-theoretic approach to finding informative noisy tiles in binary databases. In *Proceedings of the 2010 SIAM International Conference on Data Mining*, 2010.

[21] H. Mannila. Inductive databases and condensed representations for data mining. In *Proceedings of the 1997 International Symposium on Logic Programming*, pages 21–30, 1997.

[22] H. Mannila. Theoretical frameworks for data mining. *SIGKDD Explorations*, 2000.

[23] H. Mannila. Randomization techniques for data mining methods. In *Proc. of the 12th East European Conference on Advances in Databases and Information Systems (ADBIS08)*, page 1, 2008.

[24] M. Ojala, N. Vuokko, A. Kallio, N. Haiminen, and H. Mannila. Randomization of real-valued matrices for assessing the significance of data mining results. In *Proc. of the 2008 SIAM International Conference on Data Mining (SDM08)*, pages 494–505, 2008.

[25] B. Padmanabhan and A. Tuzhilin. A belief-driven method for discovering unexpected patterns. In *Proc. of the 4th ACM SIGKDD International Conference on Knowledge Discovery and Data Mining (KDD98)*, pages 94–100, 1998.

[26] L. D. Raedt. A perspective on inductive databases. *SIGKDD Explorations*, 4(2):69–77, 2002.

[27] A. Siebes, J. Vreeken, and M. van Leeuwen. Item sets that compress. In *SIAM Conference on Data Mining*, 2006.

[28] A. Silberschatz and A. Tuzhilin. On subjective measures of interestingness in knowledge discovery. In *Proc. of the 1st ACM SIGKDD International Conference on Knowledge Discovery and Data Mining (KDD95)*, pages 275–281, 1995.

[29] N. Tatti. Maximum entropy based significance of itemsets. *Knowledge and Information Systems*, 17(1):57–77, 2008.

[30] L. Valiant. A theory of the learnable. *Communications of the ACM*, 27, 1984.

Tell Me What I Need to Know: Succinctly Summarizing Data with Itemsets

Michael Mampaey Nikolaj Tatti Jilles Vreeken

Department of Mathematics and Computer Science
Universiteit Antwerpen
{firstname.lastname}@ua.ac.be

ABSTRACT

Data analysis is an inherently iterative process. That is, what we know about the data greatly determines our expectations, and hence, what result we would find the most interesting. With this in mind, we introduce a well-founded approach for succinctly summarizing data with a collection of itemsets; using a probabilistic maximum entropy model, we iteratively find the most interesting itemset, and in turn update our model of the data accordingly. As we only include itemsets that are surprising with regard to the current model, the summary is guaranteed to be both descriptive and non-redundant. The algorithm that we present can either mine the top-k most interesting itemsets, or use the Bayesian Information Criterion to automatically identify the model containing only the itemsets most important for describing the data. Or, in other words, it will 'tell you what you need to know'. Experiments on synthetic and benchmark data show that the discovered summaries are succinct, and correctly identify the key patterns in the data. The models they form attain high likelihoods, and inspection shows that they summarize the data well with increasingly specific, yet non-redundant itemsets.

Categories and Subject Descriptors

H.2.8 [**Database management**]: Database applications-*Data mining*

General Terms

Theory, Algorithms, Experimentation

1. INTRODUCTION

Knowledge discovery from data is an inherently iterative process. That is, what we already know about the data greatly determines our expectations, and therefore, which results we would find interesting and/or surprising. Early on in the process of analyzing a database, for instance, we are happy to learn about the generalities underlying the data, while later on we will be more interested in the specifics that build upon these concepts. Essentially, this process comes down to summarization: we want to know what is interesting in the data, and we want this to be reported succinctly and without redundancy.

As a simple example, consider supermarket basket analysis. Say, we just learned that *pasta* and *tomatoes* are very often sold together, and that we already know that many people buy *wine*. Then it is not very interesting to find out that the combination of these three items is also sold frequently. Even if we cannot predict this frequency exactly, we can say that this pattern is redundant. At the same time, at this stage of the analysis we are probably also not interested in highly detailed patterns, e.g., an itemset representing the many ingredients of an elaborate Italian dinner. While its frequency may be surprising, it is also very specific, and may well be better explained by some more general patterns. Still, this itemset might be regarded as highly interesting further on in the discovery process, after we have learned those more general patterns, and if this is the case, we would like it to be reported at that time. Consequently, this is the approach we adopt in this paper; we incrementally adjust our model as we discover new patterns, to obtain a non-redundant summary.

As natural as it may seem to update a knowledge model during the discovery process, few pattern mining techniques actually follow such a dynamic approach of discovering patterns that are surprising with regard to what we have learned so far. That is, while many techniques provide a series of patterns in order of interestingness, most score these patterns using a static model; during this process the model, and hence the itemset scores, are not updated with the knowledge gained from previously discovered patterns. For instance, Tan et al. study 21 of the most well-known interestingness measures, all of which are static, and most of which are based on the independence model [24]. The static approach gives rise to the typical problem of traditional pattern mining: overwhelmingly large and highly redundant collections of patterns.

Our objective is to find a succinct summary of a binary dataset, that is, to obtain a small, yet high-quality set of itemsets that describes key characteristics of the data at hand, in order to gain useful insights. This is motivated by the fact that many existing algorithms often return too large collections of patterns with considerable redundancy, as discussed above. The view that we take in this paper on succinctness and non-redundancy is therefore a fairly strict one.

To model the data, we use the powerful and versatile class of maximum entropy models. We construct a maximum entropy distribution that allows us to directly calculate the expected frequencies of itemsets. Then, at each iteration, we return the itemset that provides the most information, i.e., for which our frequency estimate was most off. We update our model with this new knowledge, and continue the process. The non-redundant model that contains the most important information is thus automatically identified. Therefore, we paraphrase our method as 'tell me what I need to know'.

While solving the maximum entropy model is infeasible in general, we show that in our setting it can be solved efficiently, depending on the amount of overlap between the selected patterns.

Similarly, we give an efficient method for estimating frequencies from the model. Further, we provide an efficient convex heuristic for pruning the search space for the most informative itemsets. This approach allows us to mine our collection of itemsets on the fly, instead of picking them from a larger candidate set which would have to be mined and stored beforehand. Our approach is parameter-free: no maximal error threshold needs to be provided, nor a minimum support or a significance level. The best model can automatically be determined through the Bayesian Information Criterion (BIC); alternatively, we can also mine the top-k most interesting itemsets. Finally, the user can easily infuse background knowledge into the model (in the form of itemset frequencies), to avoid redundancy with regard to what the user already knows.

2. RELATED WORK

Selecting or ranking interesting patterns is a well-studied field in data mining. Existing techniques can roughly be split in two groups.

The first group consists of techniques that measure how *surprising* the support of an itemset is compared against some null hypothesis: the more the observed frequency deviates from the expected value, the more interesting it is. The simplest null hypothesis is the independence model [1,2]. More flexible models have been suggested, for example, Bayesian Networks [14]. The major caveat of these approaches is that the null hypothesis is static and hence we keep rediscovering the same information. As a result, this will lead to pattern collections with high levels of redundancy. The alternative approach is to select itemsets using a dynamic hypothesis. That is, when a new itemset is discovered, the model is updated such that we take the already discovered information into account.

The use of maximum entropy models in pattern mining has been proposed by several authors [15,26,28,30]. Discovering an itemset collection with a good BIC score was suggested by Tatti and Heikinheimo [28]. Alternatively, Tatti [27] samples collections and bases the significance of an itemset on its occurrence in the discovered collections. However, in order to guarantee that the score can be computed, the authors restrict themselves to downward closed and decomposable collections. The method of Tatti [26] uses local models, that is, to compute the support of an itemset X, we are only allowed to use sub-itemsets of X, and it outputs a p-value. A threshold is needed to determine whether X is important. Related, Webb [31] defines itemsets as *self-sufficient*, if their support differs significantly from what can be inferred from their sub- and supersets; therefore such a model is also local. Wang and Parthasarathy [30] incrementally build a maximum entropy model by adding itemsets that deviate more than a given error threshold. The approach ranks and adds itemsets in level-wise batches. This may still, however, lead to redundancy within a batch of itemsets. The method introduced by Kontonasios and De Bie [15] uses row and column margins to construct a maximum entropy model of the data, from which noisy tiles [9] are then discovered, using an MDL-based information score. An important difference, however, is that the data is treated as a single sample from the space of datasets, whereas we consider distributions of transactions.

An alternative approach, called swap randomization, has been suggested by Gionis et al. [10] and Hanhijärvi et al. [13]. The former approach ranks itemsets using a static hypothesis, the latter uses a dynamic hypothesis. Here as well, the authors treat the whole data as a sample from the space of datasets, having the same certain set of statistics, including row and column margins. The authors use an MCMC approach to sample datasets and compute empirical p-values. In both approaches, the framework needs a threshold for deciding which itemsets are significant.

The MINI algorithm by Gallo et al. [7] similarly uses row and column margins to rank itemsets. It first orders all potentially interesting itemsets by computing their p-value according to these margins. Then, as subsequent itemsets are added, the p-values are recomputed, and the itemsets are re-ordered according to their new p-values. This method, however, does not allow querying.

The method of Yan et al. [32] summarizes a collection of itemsets by clustering them, and then representing each cluster as a *profile*. The approach is different from ours, in that it summarizes a given set of patterns, rather than the data itself.

KRIMP, by Siebes et al. [23], employs the MDL principle to select those itemsets that together compress the data best. As such, patterns that essentially describe the same part of the data are rejected. The models it finds are not probabilistic, and therefore cannot easily be used to calculate probabilities. Further, while non-redundant from a compression point of view, many of the patterns it selects are variations of the same theme. Other differences to our method are that KRIMP considers its candidates in a static order, and that it is not trivial to make it consider background knowledge.

It should be noted that in contrast to the algorithm that we propose here, most of the above methods require the user to set one or several parameters, such as a maximum error threshold or a significance level. Many also cannot easily be used to estimate the frequency of an itemset. Further, all of them are two-phase algorithms, i.e., they require that the user provides a collection of candidate (frequent) itemsets to the algorithm, which must be completely mined and stored first, before running the actual algorithm.

3. PRELIMINARIES AND NOTATION

This section provides some preliminaries and the notation that we will use throughout the paper.

By a *transaction* we mean a binary vector of size N generated by some unknown distribution. The ith element in a random transaction corresponds to an *attribute* or an *item* a_i, a Bernoulli random variable. We denote the set of all items by $A = \{a_1, \ldots, a_N\}$. We denote the set of all possible transactions by $\mathcal{T} = \{0,1\}^N$.

The input of our method is a *binary dataset* D, which is simply a sample of $|D|$ (not necessarily distinct) transactions. Given the data D we define an empirical distribution

$$q_D(a_1 = v_1, \ldots, a_N = v_N) = |\{t \in D \mid t = v\}| / |D| \ .$$

An *itemset* X is a subset of A. For notational convenience, given a distribution p, an itemset $X = \{x_1, \ldots, x_L\}$, and a binary vector v of length L, we often use $p(X = v)$ to denote $p(x_1 = v_1, \ldots, x_L = v_L)$. If v consists entirely of 1's, then we use the notation $p(X = 1)$. Given the data D, the *frequency* of an itemset X is defined $fr(X) = q_D(X = 1)$. An *indicator function* $S_X : \mathcal{T} \to \{0,1\}$ of an itemset X maps a transaction t to a binary value such that $S_X(t) = 1$ if and only if t contains X.

The *entropy* of a distribution p over $\mathcal{T}$ is defined as

$$H(p) = -\sum_{t \in \mathcal{T}} p(A = t) \log p(A = t) \ ,$$

where the base of the logarithm is 2, and by convention $0 \log 0 = 0$.

4. IDENTIFYING THE BEST SUMMARY

Our goal is to discover the set of itemsets $\mathcal{C}$ that provides the most important information about the data, while containing as little redundancy as possible. Here, we regard information as whether we are able to reliably predict the data using these itemsets and their frequencies. By non-redundancy, we mean that any subset of $\mathcal{C}$ provides a significantly different description of the data. This is equivalent to requiring that the frequency of an itemset $X \in \mathcal{C}$ should be surprising with respect to $\mathcal{C} \setminus X$. In other words, we do not want $\mathcal{C}$ as a collection to be unnecessarily complex, or capture spurious information. We want it to contain only those itemsets that we really need.

Informally, assume that we have a score $s(\mathcal{C})$ which measures the quality of an itemset collection $\mathcal{C}$. Then our aim is to find that $\mathcal{C}$ with the best score $s(\mathcal{C})$. Analogously, if we only want to know k itemsets, we look for the set $\mathcal{C}$ of size at most k, with the best $s(\mathcal{C})$.

Next, we will detail how we define our models, how we define this score, provide theoretical evidence why it is a good choice, and discuss how to compute it efficiently.

EXAMPLE 1. *As a running example, assume we have a transaction dataset D with eight items, a to h. Furthermore, consider the set of itemsets $\mathcal{C} = \{abc, cd, def\}$ with frequencies 0.5, 0.4 and 0.8, respectively. Assume for the moment that based on $\mathcal{C}$, our method predicts that the frequency of the itemset agh is 0.19. Now, if we observe in the data that $fr(agh) = 0.18$, then we can safely say that agh is redundant because it does not contribute a lot. On the other hand, if $fr(agh) = 0.7$, then the frequency of agh is surprising, and therefore $\mathcal{C} \cup \{agh\}$ would give an improved description of D.*

4.1 Maximum Entropy Model

In our approach we make use of maximum entropy models. This is a class of probabilistic models that are identified by the Maximum Entropy principle [4] as those models that make optimal use of the provided information. That is, they rely only on this information and are fully unbiased otherwise. This property makes these models very suited for identifying good patterns: by using maximum entropy models to measure the quality of a set of patterns, we know that our measurement only relies on the provided frequencies of the patterns, and that it will not be thrown off due to some spurious structure in the data. These models have a number of theoretically appealing properties, which we will discuss after a formal introduction.

Assume that we are given a set of itemsets $\mathcal{C} = \{X_1, \ldots, X_k\}$. Each itemset X_i has a frequency $fr(X_i)$ in the data. We are interested in distributions that satisfy these frequencies, that is, let us consider the following set of distributions

$$\mathcal{P} = \{p \mid p(X_i = 1) = fr(X_i), i = 1, \ldots, k\} .$$

Among these distributions we are interested in only one, namely the unique distribution that maximizes the entropy,

$$p^*_{\mathcal{C}} = \arg\max_p \{H(p) \mid p \in \mathcal{P}\} .$$

For notational convenience we will omit $\mathcal{C}$ from p^* whenever it is clear from the context. Although we restrict ourselves to itemset frequencies here, many other patterns or count statistics that can be expressed as linear combinations of transactions could be used, e.g., transaction lengths [29], association rule confidence, etc. Computing the maximum entropy model, however, is far from trivial, and is treated in Section 4.5.

4.2 Model Scoring

First we discuss how we will measure the quality of a model. A natural first choice would be to directly measure the goodness of fit, using the log-likelihood of the maximum entropy model, that is, $\log p^*(D) = \sum_{t \in D} \log p^*(A = t)$. However, this choice suffers from overfitting: larger collections of itemsets will always provide more information, hence allow for better estimates, and therefore have a better log-likelihood. Consequently, we need to prevent our method from overfitting. Therefore, we use the well-founded Bayesian Information Criterion (BIC), which favors models that fit the data well with few parameters. It has a strong theoretical support in Bayesian model selection [22] as well as through the Minimum Description Length principle [12]. The BIC score of a collection $\mathcal{C}$ is defined as

$$s(\mathcal{C}) = -\log p^*_{\mathcal{C}}(D) + 1/2\, |\mathcal{C}| \log |D| .$$

The smaller this score, the better the model. The first term is simply the negative log-likelihood of the model, while the second term is a penalty on the number of parameters—the number of itemsets in our case. Consequently, the best model is identified as the model that provides a good balance between high likelihood and low complexity. Moreover, we automatically avoid redundancy, since models with redundant itemsets are penalized for being too complex, without sufficiently improving the likelihood.

4.3 Properties of the Model

In this subsection we discuss some properties of the quality measure and the maximum entropy model.

We begin by stating a famous theorem that the maximum entropy model has an exponential form.

THEOREM 2 (THEOREM 3.1 IN [4]). *Given a collection of itemsets $\mathcal{C} = \{X_i\}_{i=1}^k$ with frequencies $fr(X_i)$, let us define $\mathcal{P} = \{p \mid p(X_i = 1) = fr(X_i)\}$. If there is a distribution in $\mathcal{P}$ that has only non-zero entries, then the maximum entropy distribution p^* can be written as*

$$p^*(A = t) = u_0 \prod_{X \in \mathcal{C}} u_X^{S_X(t)} ,$$

where $u_X \in \mathbb{R}$, and u_0 is a normalization factor.

This form will help us to discover the model and compute the likelihood term in the scoring function.

COROLLARY 3 (OF THEOREM 2). *The log-likelihood of the maximum entropy distribution p^* for a set of itemsets $\mathcal{C}$ is equal to*

$$\log p^*(D) = |D|(\log u_0 + \sum_{X \in \mathcal{C}} fr(X) \log u_X) = -|D| H(p^*) .$$

Thus, to calculate the BIC score $s(\mathcal{C})$, it suffices to compute the parameters u_X and u_0 of the distribution p^*.

4.4 Reducing Redundancy

Here we show that our score favors itemset collections with low redundancy, and make a theoretical link with some existing redundancy reduction techniques for pattern mining.

A baseline technique for ranking itemsets is to compare the observed frequency against the expected value of some null hypothesis. The next theorem shows that if the observed frequency of an itemset X agrees with the expected value $p^*(X = 1)$, then X is redundant.

THEOREM 4. *Let $\mathcal{C}$ be a collection of itemsets and let p^* be the corresponding maximum entropy model. Let $X \notin \mathcal{C}$ be an itemset such that $fr(X) = p^*(X = 1)$. Then $s(\mathcal{C} \cup \{X\}) > s(\mathcal{C})$.*

PROOF. We will prove the theorem by showing that the likelihood terms for both collections are equal. Define the collection $\mathcal{C}_1 = \mathcal{C} \cup \{X\}$ and let $\mathcal{P}_1$ be the corresponding set of distributions. Let p^*_1 be the distribution maximizing the entropy in $\mathcal{P}_1$. Note that since $\mathcal{C} \subset \mathcal{C}_1$, we have $\mathcal{P}_1 \subseteq \mathcal{P}$ and hence $H(p^*_1) \leq H(p^*)$. On the other hand, the assumption in the theorem implies that $p^* \in \mathcal{P}_1$ and so $H(p^*) \leq H(p^*_1)$. Thus, $H(p^*) = H(p^*_1)$ and since the distribution maximizing the entropy is unique, we have $p^* = p^*_1$. This shows that the likelihood terms in $s(\mathcal{C})$ and $s(\mathcal{C}_1)$ are equal. The BIC penalty term is larger in $s(\mathcal{C}_1)$ which concludes the proof. □

Algorithm 1: ITERATIVESCALING($\mathcal{C}$)

input : itemset collection $\mathcal{C} = \{X_1, \ldots, X_k\}$, frequencies $fr(X_1), \ldots, fr(X_k)$

output : parameters u_X and u_0 of the maximum entropy distribution $p^*_{\mathcal{C}}$ satisfying $p^*_{\mathcal{C}}(X_i) = fr(X_i)$ for all i

1 initialize p;
2 **while** p has not converged **do**
3   **for each** X in $\mathcal{C}$ **do**
4   compute $p(X = 1)$;
5         $u_X \leftarrow u_X \frac{fr(X)}{p(X=1)} \frac{1-p(X=1)}{1-fr(X)}$;
6         $u_0 \leftarrow u_0 \frac{1-fr(X)}{1-p(X=1)}$;
7 **return** p;

Theorem 4 states that adding an itemset X to $\mathcal{C}$ improves the score only if its observed frequency deviates from the expected value. The amount of deviation required is determined by the penalty term. This gives us a convenient advantage over methods that are based solely on deviation, since they require a user-specified threshold.

Two corollaries stated below follow directly from Theorem 4. The first relates our approach to *closed* itemsets [21]. An itemset is closed if all of its supersets have a strictly lower support. An itemset is a *generator* if all of its subsets have a strictly higher support. The second corollary provides a similar relation with *non-derivable* itemsets [3]. An itemset is called derivable if its support can be inferred exactly from the supports of all of its proper subsets.

COROLLARY 5 (OF THEOREM 4). *Let $\mathcal{C}$ be a collection of itemsets. Assume that $X, Y \in \mathcal{C}$ such that $X \subset Y$ and $fr(X) = fr(Y) \neq 0$. Assume that $Z \notin \mathcal{C}$ such that $X \subset Z \subset Y$. Then $s(\mathcal{C} \cup \{Z\}) > s(\mathcal{C})$.*

COROLLARY 6 (OF THEOREM 4). *Let $\mathcal{C}$ be a collection of itemsets. Assume that $X \notin \mathcal{C}$ is a derivable itemset and all sub-itemsets of X are included in $\mathcal{C}$. Then $s(\mathcal{C} \cup \{X\}) > s(\mathcal{C})$.*

Corollaries 5 and 6 connect our approach with popular techniques that losslessly remove redundancy—so-called *condensed representations*. The advantage of our method is that it does not have to be exact. For example, in Corollary 5, $fr(X)$ does not have to equal $fr(Y)$ exactly in order to reject Z from $\mathcal{C}$. This allows us to prune redundancy more aggressively.

4.5 Efficiently Computing the Model

Computing the maximum entropy model comes down to finding the u_0 and u_X parameters from Theorem 2. To achieve this, we use the well-known Iterative Scaling procedure [5], which is given as Algorithm 1. Simply put, it iteratively updates the parameters of the distribution, until it converges to the maximum entropy distribution p^* which satisfies a given set of constraints—itemset frequencies in our case. The distribution is initialized with the uniform distribution, which is done by setting the u_X parameters to 1, and $u_0 = 2^{-N}$ to normalize. Then, for each itemset $X \in \mathcal{C}$, we adjust the corresponding parameter u_X to enforce $p(X = 1) = fr(X)$ (line 5,6). This process is repeated in a round robin fashion until p converges, and it can be shown [5] that p always converges to the maximum entropy distribution p^*. Typically the number of iterations required for convergence is low (usually < 10 in our experiments).

EXAMPLE 7. *In our running example, with $\mathcal{C} = \{abc, cd, def\}$, the maximum entropy model has three parameters u_1, u_2, u_3, and a normalization factor u_0. Initially we set $u_1 = u_2 = u_3 = 1$ and $u_0 = 2^{-N} = 2^{-8}$. Then we iteratively loop over the itemsets and scale the parameters. For instance, for the first itemset abc with frequency 0.5, we first compute its current estimate to be $2^{-3} = 0.125$. Thus, we update the first parameter $u_1 = 1 \cdot (0.5/2^{-3}) \cdot ((1 - 2^{-3})/0.5) = 7$. The normalization factor becomes $u_0 = 2^{-8} \cdot 0.5/(1 - 2^{-3}) \approx 2.2 \cdot 10^{-3}$. Next, we do the same for cd, and so on. After a few iterations, the model parameters converge to $u_1 = 28.5$, $u_2 = 0.12$, $u_3 = 85.4$, and $u_0 = 3 \cdot 10^{-4}$.*

The main bottleneck of this procedure is the inference of an itemset's probability on line 4 of the algorithm,

$$p(X = 1) = \sum_{t \in \mathcal{T}; S_X(t)=1} p(A = t) \; .$$

Since this sum ranges over all possible transactions containing X, it is infeasible to do this in a brute force manner for any non-trivial number of items N. In fact, it has been shown that querying the maximum entropy model is **PP**-hard [25].

Therefore, in order to be able to query the model efficiently, we introduce a partitioning scheme, which makes use of the observation that many transactions have the same probability. Remark that an itemset collection $\mathcal{C}$ partitions $\mathcal{T}$ into blocks of transactions that contain the same set of itemsets. That is, two transactions t_1 and t_2 belong to the same block T if and only if $S_X(t_1) = S_X(t_2)$ for all X in $\mathcal{C}$. Hence, from Theorem 2 we know $p(A = t_1) = p(A = t_2)$. This allows us to define $S_X(T) = S_X(t)$ for any $t \in T$ and $X \in \mathcal{C}$. We denote the partition of $\mathcal{T}$ induced by $\mathcal{C}$ as $\mathcal{T}_{\mathcal{C}}$. Now we can compute the probability of an itemset as

$$p(X = 1) = \sum_{T \in \mathcal{T}_{\mathcal{C}}; S_X(T)=1} p(A \in T) \; .$$

The sum has been reduced to a sum over blocks of transactions, and the inference problem has been moved from the transaction space $\mathcal{T}$ to the block space $\mathcal{T}_{\mathcal{C}}$. In our setting we will see that $|\mathcal{T}_{\mathcal{C}}| \ll |\mathcal{T}|$, which makes inference a lot more feasible. In the worst case, this partition may contain $2^{|\mathcal{C}|}$ blocks, however, through the interplay of the itemsets, it can be as low as $|\mathcal{C}| + 1$. As explained further on, we can exploit, or even choose to limit, the structure of $\mathcal{C}$, such that practical computation is guaranteed.

All we must do now is obtain the block probabilities $p(A \in T)$. Since all transactions t in a block T have the same probability $p(A = t) = u_0 \prod_{X \in \mathcal{C}} u_X^{S_X(t)}$, it suffices to compute the number of transactions in T to get $p(A \in T)$. So, let us define $e(T)$ to be the number of transactions in T, then

$$p(A \in T) = \sum_{t \in T} p(A = t) = e(T)\, u_0 \prod_{X \in \mathcal{C}} u_X^{S_X(T)} \; .$$

Algorithm 2 describes COMPUTEBLOCKSIZES. In order to compute the block sizes $e(T)$, we introduce a partial order on $\mathcal{T}_{\mathcal{C}}$. Let

$$sets(T; \mathcal{C}) = \{X \in \mathcal{C} \mid S_X(T) = 1\}$$

be the itemsets in $\mathcal{C}$ that occur in the transactions of T. Note that every block corresponds to a unique subset of $\mathcal{C}$, but conversely not every subset of $\mathcal{C}$ corresponds to a (nonempty) transaction block. We can now define the partial order on $\mathcal{T}_{\mathcal{C}}$ as follows,

$$T_1 \subseteq T_2 \quad \text{if and only if} \quad sets(T_1; \mathcal{C}) \subseteq sets(T_2; \mathcal{C}) \; .$$

In order to compute the size $e(T)$ of a block, we first compute its *cumulative* size,

$$c(T) = \sum_{T' \supseteq T} e(T') \; ,$$

Algorithm 2: ComputeBlockSizes($\mathcal{C}$)

input : itemset collection $\mathcal{C} = \{X_1, \ldots, X_k\}$
output : block sizes $e(T)$ for each T in $\mathcal{T}_\mathcal{C}$

for T in $\mathcal{T}_\mathcal{C}$ **do**
  $I \leftarrow \bigcup\{X \mid X \in sets(T;\mathcal{C})\}$;
  $c(T) \leftarrow 2^{N-|I|}$;
sort the blocks in $\mathcal{T}_\mathcal{C}$;
for T_i in $\mathcal{T}_\mathcal{C}$ **do**
  $e(T_i) \leftarrow c(T_i)$;
  for T_j in $\mathcal{T}_\mathcal{C}$, with $j < i$ **do**
    if $T_i \subset T_j$ **then**
      $e(T_i) \leftarrow e(T_i) - e(T_j)$;
return $\mathcal{T}_\mathcal{C}$;

which is the number of transactions that contain *at least* all the itemsets in $sets(T;\mathcal{C})$. Let $I = \bigcup\{X \mid X \in sets(T;\mathcal{C})\}$. That is, I are the items that occur in all transactions of T. Then it holds that $c(T) = 2^{N-|I|}$, where N is the total number of items. Finally, to extract the block sizes $e(T)$ from the cumulative sizes $c(T)$, we use the inclusion-exclusion principle. To that end, we topologically sort the blocks such that if $T_2 \subset T_1$, then T_1 occurs before T_2 (which can easily be ensured when constructing $\mathcal{T}_\mathcal{C}$). Then we simply iterate over the blocks in reverse, and subtract the sizes of their super-blocks,

$$e(T) = c(T) - \sum_{T' \supsetneq T} e(T') \ .$$

Example 8. *Assume again that we have a dataset with eight items (a to h), and an itemset collection containing three itemsets $\mathcal{C} = \{abc, cd, def\}$ with frequencies 0.5, 0.4 and 0.8.*

Table 1 shows the sizes of the transaction blocks. Note that while there are 256 transactions in $\mathcal{T}$, there are only 7 blocks in $\mathcal{T}_\mathcal{C}$, whose sizes and probabilities are to be computed. (The eighth combination, abc and def but not cd, is clearly impossible.)

Let us compute the sizes of the first three blocks. For the first block, $I = abcdef$ and therefore $c(T) = 4$, for the second block $I = abcd$, and for the third block $I = abc$. Since the first block is the maximum with respect to the order $\subseteq$, its cumulative size is simply its size, so $e(T) = 4$. For the second block, we subtract the first block, and obtain $e(T) = 16 - 4 = 12$. From the third block we subtract the first two blocks, and we have $e(T) = 32 - 12 - 4 = 16$. Now, to compute, say, $p(abc = 1)$, we simply need the sizes of the blocks containing abc, and the current model parameters,

$$p(abc = 1) = 4(u_0u_1u_2u_3) + 12(u_0u_1u_2) + 16(u_0u_1).$$

Table 1: Transaction blocks for the running example above, with $X_1 = abc$, $X_2 = cd$, and $X_3 = def$.

X_1	X_2	X_3	$c(T)$	$e(T)$	$p(A = t)$
1	1	1	4	4	$u_0u_1u_2u_3$
1	1	0	16	12	$u_0u_1u_2$
1	0	0	32	16	u_0u_1
0	1	1	16	12	$u_0u_2u_3$
0	1	0	64	36	u_0u_2
0	0	1	32	16	u_0u_3
0	0	0	256	160	u_0

Lastly, the algorithm can be significantly optimized as follows. Assume that we can divide $\mathcal{C}$ into two disjoint groups $\mathcal{C}_1$ and $\mathcal{C}_2$, such that if $X_1 \in \mathcal{C}_1$ and $X_2 \in \mathcal{C}_2$, then $X_1 \cap X_2 = \emptyset$. Let $B = \bigcup \mathcal{C}_1$ be the set of items occurring in $\mathcal{C}_1$. Theorem 2 implies that $p^*(A) = p^*(B)p^*(A \setminus B)$. In other words, the maximum entropy distribution can be factorized into two *independent* distributions, namely $p^*(B)$ and $p^*(A \setminus B)$, more importantly, the factor $p^*(B)$ depends only on $\mathcal{C}_1$. Consequently, if we wish to compute the probability $p^*(X = 1)$ such that $X \in B$, we can ignore all variables outside B and all itemsets outside $\mathcal{C}_1$. The number of computations to perform by ComputeBlockSizes can now be greatly reduced, since in the case of independence $|\mathcal{T}_\mathcal{C}| = |\mathcal{T}_{\mathcal{C}_1}| \times |\mathcal{T}_{\mathcal{C}_2}|$, and we can simply compute the block sizes for $\mathcal{T}_{\mathcal{C}_1}$ and $\mathcal{T}_{\mathcal{C}_2}$ separately. Naturally, this decomposition can also be applied when there are more than two of such disjoint groups of itemsets.

Further, in order to *guarantee* that we can apply the above separation, we could reduce the solution space slightly by imposing a limit on the number of items or itemsets per group, such that the number of blocks remains small. Alternatively, we could first partition the items of the dataset into smaller, approximately independent groups [16], and then apply the algorithm for each group separately.

4.6 Including Frequencies of Individual Items

Often it is useful to inspect the frequencies of the individual items (i.e., the column margins) in a dataset, since they supply basic, yet intuitive and easily calculable information about the data. For instance, they say which combinations of items are more (or less) likely to occur together frequently. However, in our method we cannot add the set of all singleton itemsets $\mathcal{I}$ to a collection $\mathcal{C}$, since the number of transaction blocks would become $|\mathcal{T}_{\mathcal{C}\cup\mathcal{I}}| = |\mathcal{T}| = 2^N$, by which we would be back at square one. We sketch (due to space restrictions) how this can be solved easily. Let $\mathcal{C}' = \mathcal{C} \cup \mathcal{I}$. We continue working with $\mathcal{T}_\mathcal{C}$ rather than $\mathcal{T}_{\mathcal{C}'}$. As before, the maximum entropy model has an exponential form: $p^*_{\mathcal{C}'}(A = t) = u_0 \prod_{X\in\mathcal{C}} u_X^{S_X(t)} \prod_{i\in\mathcal{I}} v_i^{S_i(t)}$. The second product defines an independence distribution $v = v_0 \prod_i v_i^{S_i(t)}$. Then $p^*_{\mathcal{C}'}(A \in T) = v(A \in T)\frac{u_0}{v_0} \prod_{X\in\mathcal{C}} u_X^{S_X(T)}$. Thus, we simply need to compute $v(A \in T)$, which is computed very similar to $e(A \in T)$ with ComputeBlockSizes—note that $e(A = t)$ is basically the uniform distribution multiplied with 2^N. Hence, we can include the item frequencies at an only marginal additional cost.

4.7 Querying the Model

We have seen how we can efficiently query the probability of an itemset $X \in \mathcal{C}$ when given the maximum entropy distribution p^*. In order to compute the probability of an arbitrary itemset Y that is not a member of $\mathcal{C}$, we do the following. We first set $\mathcal{G} = \mathcal{C} \cup \{Y\}$ and compute the block probabilities $e(T)$ or $v(A \in T)$ for T in $\mathcal{T}_\mathcal{G}$ by calling ComputeBlockSizes. Then, we can simply use the parameters of p^* to compute $p^*(Y = 1)$,

$$p^*(Y = 1) = \sum_{\substack{T\in\mathcal{T}_\mathcal{G} \\ S_Y(T)=1}} v(A \in T)\frac{u_0}{v_0} \prod_{X\in\mathcal{C}} u_X^{S_X(T)} \ .$$

Thus, to obtain the probability of an itemset, it suffices to compute the block probabilities in $\mathcal{T}_\mathcal{G}$, for which we know that $|\mathcal{T}_\mathcal{G}| \leq 2|\mathcal{T}_\mathcal{C}|$.

4.8 Computational Complexity

Let us analyze the complexity of IterativeScaling. To this end, we define $ps(\mathcal{C}) = |\mathcal{T}_\mathcal{C}|$ as the number of blocks in a partition. Note that $ps(\mathcal{C}) \leq \min\left(2^{|\mathcal{C}|}, 2^N\right)$. The computational complexity of ComputeBlockSizes is $O(ps(\mathcal{C})^2)$ for a given

Algorithm 3: MTV(D)

input : binary dataset D, background knowledge itemsets $\mathcal{B}$, integer k if mining top-k
output : itemset collection $\mathcal{C}$

$\mathcal{I} \leftarrow$ items in D;
$\mathcal{C} \leftarrow \mathcal{B}$;
while $s(\mathcal{C})$ decreases **and** $|\mathcal{C}| < k$ **do**
  $X \leftarrow$ FINDBESTITEMSET$(\emptyset, \mathcal{I}, \emptyset)$;
  $\mathcal{C} \leftarrow \mathcal{C} \cup \{X\}$;
  $p^*_{\mathcal{C}} \leftarrow$ ITERATIVESCALING$(\mathcal{C})$;
  compute $s(\mathcal{C})$;
return $\mathcal{C}$;

collection $\mathcal{C}$. Assume now that we can partition $\mathcal{C}$ into L disjoint parts $\mathcal{C} = \mathcal{C}_1 \cup \cdots \cup \mathcal{C}_L$, such that if $X \in \mathcal{C}_i$ and $Y \in \mathcal{C}_j$ then $X \cap Y = \emptyset$. As mentioned in Section 4.5, we can now simply compute L independent distributions at a lower total cost. Denoting $B_i = \bigcup_{X \in \mathcal{C}_i} X$, it holds that $ps(\mathcal{C}_i) \leq \min\left(2^{|\mathcal{C}_i|}, 2^{|B_i|}\right)$. If $\mathcal{C}_i$ cannot be partitioned further, this usually means that either $|\mathcal{C}_i|$ is small, or the itemsets in $\mathcal{C}_i$ overlap a lot and $ps(\mathcal{C}_i) \ll 2^{|\mathcal{C}_i|}$. The total execution time of ITERATIVESCALING is $O(K \sum_{i=1}^{L} ps(\mathcal{C}_i)^2)$, where K is the number of iterations, which is usually low. The complexity of estimating the frequency of an itemset requires running COMPUTEBLOCKSIZES once and hence equals $O(\sum_{i=1}^{L} ps(\mathcal{C}_i)^2)$.

5. PROBLEM STATEMENT

In this section we formally state the problem we intend to solve, based on the theory introduced above.

THE PROBLEM. *Given a collection of itemsets $\mathcal{B}$ that represents our background knowledge of a dataset D, a collection of potentially interesting itemsets $\mathcal{F}$, and an integer k, find the subset $\mathcal{C} \subseteq \mathcal{F}$ of size at most k, such that $s(\mathcal{B} \cup \mathcal{C})$ is minimal.*

Note that $\mathcal{F}$ can simply consist of all itemsets, or e.g., be restricted to a collection of frequent itemsets. If we do not wish to constrain the size of $\mathcal{C}$, and essentially disregard k, we can simply set $k = \infty$. Also note that the problem statement does not require $\mathcal{F}$ to be explicitly available beforehand, i.e., it does not have to be mined or materialized in advance (we postpone the details to Section 6.2).

6. MINING SUCCINCT SUMMARIES

In Section 4 we described how to compute the maximum entropy model and its BIC score *given* a set of itemsets. Finding the optimal collection as stated in Section 5, however, is clearly infeasible. The size of the search space is $\sum_{j=0}^{k} \binom{|\mathcal{F}|}{j} \leq 2^{|\mathcal{F}|}$. If we do not restrict the candidate itemsets, then the number of all non-singleton itemsets is $|\mathcal{F}| = 2^N - N - 1$. Moreover, the score function is not monotonic, which prevents us from straightforwardly exploring the search space.

Therefore, we resort to using a heuristic, greedy approach. Starting with a set of itemsets representing our background knowledge—for instance the singletons—we incrementally construct our summary by iteratively adding the itemset that reduces the BIC score the most. The algorithm stops either when k interesting itemsets are found, or when the score no longer decreases. The pseudo-code for our MTV algorithm, which mines Maximally informaTiVe summaries, is given as Algorithm 3.

6.1 A Heuristic for Scoring Itemsets

Finding the best itemset to add to the current collection is practically infeasible, since it involves solving the maximum entropy model for each and every candidate. This remains infeasible even if we restrict the search space (for example, using only frequent itemsets). Therefore, instead of selecting the candidate that optimizes the BIC score directly, we select the candidate that maximizes a heuristic which expresses the divergence between its frequency and its estimate. To derive and motivate this heuristic we first need the following theorem.

THEOREM 9. *Given an itemset collection $\mathcal{C}$, it holds that*

$$\begin{aligned} \arg\min_X s(\mathcal{C} \cup \{X\}) &= \arg\max_X KL\left(p^*_{\mathcal{C} \cup \{X\}} \,\|\, p^*_{\mathcal{C}}\right) \\ &= \arg\min_X KL\left(q_D \,\|\, p^*_{\mathcal{C} \cup \{X\}}\right) \end{aligned}$$

where KL is the Kullback-Leibler divergence between two distributions, defined as $KL(p \,\|\, q) = \sum_x p(x) \log \frac{p(x)}{q(x)}$, and q_D is the empirical distribution of the data.

PROOF. Let us write $\mathcal{G} = \mathcal{C} \cup \{X\}$. Corollary 3 states that $-\log p^*_{\mathcal{G}}(D) = |D| H(p^*_{\mathcal{G}})$. In addition, we can show with a straightforward calculation that $KL(p^*_{\mathcal{G}} \,\|\, p^*_{\mathcal{C}}) = H(p^*_{\mathcal{C}}) - H(p^*_{\mathcal{G}})$. Therefore, minimizing $s(\mathcal{G})$ is equivalent to maximizing the divergence $KL(p^*_{\mathcal{G}} \,\|\, p^*_{\mathcal{C}})$. The second equality follows similarly. □

Thus, we search for the itemset X such that the new distribution diverges maximally from the previous one, or equivalently, brings us as close to the empirical distribution as possible. The heuristic that we use is an approximation of the KL divergence, where we group the terms containing X in one term, and the terms not containing X into another term. We define $h : [0,1] \times [0,1] \rightarrow \mathbb{R}^+$ as

$$h(x,y) = x \log \frac{x}{y} + (1-x) \log \frac{1-x}{1-y} .$$

We then pick the itemset maximizing $h(fr(X), p^*(X=1))$, which we will denote simply as $h(X)$ when fr and p^* are clear from the context. To compute this heuristic, we only need the frequency of X, and its estimate according to the current p^* distribution. This gives us a measure of the divergence between $fr(X)$ and $p^*(X=1)$, i.e., its surprisingness given the current model.

The following theorem gives and indication of how KL and h relate to one another.

THEOREM 10. *For an itemset collection $\mathcal{C}$ and itemset X, it holds that*

$$0 \leq h(X) \leq KL\left(p^*_{\mathcal{C} \cup \{X\}} \,\|\, p^*_{\mathcal{C}}\right) .$$

Moreover, $h(X) = 0$ if and only if $KL\left(p^*_{\mathcal{C} \cup \{X\}} \,\|\, p^*_{\mathcal{C}}\right) = 0$, i.e., when $fr(X) = p^*(X=1)$.

PROOF. The second inequality follows from the log-sum inequality. The equality to zero is trivially verified. □

6.2 Looking for the Best Itemset

In order to find the itemset maximizing h, we take a depth-first branch-and-bound approach. We exploit the fact that h is convex, and employ the bound introduced by Nijssen et al. [20] to prune large parts of the search space as follows. Say that for a candidate itemset X in the search space, its maximal possible extension in the branch below it is $X \cup Y$ (denoted XY), then for any itemset W such that $X \subseteq W \subseteq XY$, it holds that

$$h(W) \leq \max\left\{h\left(fr(X), p^*(XY)\right), h\left(fr(XY), p^*(X)\right)\right\} .$$

If this bound is lower than the best value of h seen so far, we know that no (local) extension W of X can ever become the best itemset with respect to h, and therefore we can safely prune the branch of the search space below X. The algorithm is given in Algorithm 4.

Algorithm 4: FINDBESTITEMSET(X, Y, Z)

```
   input  : itemset X, remaining items Y, currently best set Z
   output : itemset between X and XY maximizing h, or Z
1  compute fr(X) and p*(X);
2  if h(X) = h(fr(X), p*(X)) > h(Z) then
3  |  Z ← X;
4  compute fr(XY) and p*(XY);
5  b ← max{h(fr(X), p*(XY)), h(fr(XY), p*(X))};
6  if b > h(Z) then
7  |  for y ∈ Y do
8  |  |  Y ← Y \ {y};
9  |  |  Z ← FINDBESTITEMSET(X ∪ {y}, Y, Z);
10 return Z;
```

Table 2: Synthetic and real datasets used in the experiments.

	$\|A\|$	$\|D\|$	$minsup$	$\|\mathcal{F}\|$
Independent	50	100 000	15%	25 110
Markov	20	100 000	5%	8 748
Mosaic	50	100 000	10%	12 256
Abstracts	3 933	859	1%	101 673
Chess (kr-k)	58	28 056	0.1%	19 620
DNA Amplification	391	4 590	0.5%	672 345
Mammals	121	2 183	20%	2 169 624
Mushroom	119	8 124	5%	3 755 512
Paleo	139	124	2%	635 496

An advantage of this approach is that we do not need to collect the frequencies of all candidate itemsets beforehand. Instead, we just compute them on the fly as we need them (line 1). For instance, if we wish to pick itemsets from a collection $\mathcal{F}$ of frequent itemsets for some minimum support threshold, we can integrate the support counting in the depth-first traversal of the algorithm, rather than first mining and storing $\mathcal{F}$ in its entirety. Since mining real datasets with non-trivial minimal support thresholds can easily yield billions of frequent itemsets, this is indubitably a great benefit.

7. EXPERIMENTS

In this section we experimentally evaluate our method and empirically validate the quality of the returned summaries. We implemented a prototype of our algorithm in C++, and provide the source code for research purposes.[1] All experiments were executed on a six-core Intel Xeon machine with 12GB of memory, running Linux.

We evaluate our method on three synthetic datasets, as well as on six real datasets. Their basic characteristics are given in Table 2. The *Independent* data has independent items with random frequencies between 0.2 and 0.8. In the *Markov* dataset each item is a noisy copy of the previous one, with a random copy probability between 0.2 and 0.8. The *Mosaic* dataset is generated by randomly planting five itemsets of size 5 with random frequencies between 0.2 and 0.5, in a database with 1% noise. The *Abstracts* dataset contains the abstracts of all accepted papers at the ICDM conference up to 2007, where words have been stemmed and stop words removed. The *Chess (kr-k)* dataset was obtained from the UCI ML Repository [6], and converted into binary form. The *DNA* data contains information on DNA copy number amplifications. Such copies activate oncogenes and are hallmarks of nearly all advanced tumors [19]. The *Mammals* presence data consists of presence records of European mammals within geographical areas of 50×50 km^2 [17, 18]. The *Mushroom* dataset was obtained from the FIMI dataset repository [11]. Finally, *Paleo* is a dataset of fossil records.

Our method is inherently parameter-free. That is, given enough time, it can select the best set of itemsets from the complete space of possible itemsets. However, although our algorithm is quite efficient, in practice it may not always be feasible to consider *all* itemsets for dense or large datasets. In general, choosing a larger candidate space, yields better models. In our experiments we therefore consider collections of frequent itemsets $\mathcal{F}$ mined at support thresholds as low as feasible. The actual thresholds and corresponding size of $\mathcal{F}$ are depicted in Table 2. Note that the minsup threshold is used to limit the size of $\mathcal{F}$, and is strictly speaking not a parameter of the algorithm itself. For the synthetic datasets, we let the algorithm decide on the best summary size, that is, we set $k = \infty$. As for the real datasets, we do impose a maximum of k itemsets that our algorithm may select. We set k such that the runtime remains within one hour. In all experiments, we initialize $\mathcal{C}$ with the singleton itemsets, i.e., we start from the independence model.

7.1 Model BIC Scores

In Table 3 we give the scores of top-k summaries, the time required to compute them, and for comparison we include the score of the independence model. We see that for most datasets the BIC score (and thus relatedly the negative log-likelihood) decreases a lot, which implies that the summaries we find are of high quality. For very structured datasets, such as *DNA*, this improvement is very large, while it only takes a handful of itemsets to achieve this.

7.2 Summary Evaluation

Here we inspect the discovered data summaries in closer detail.

For the *Independent* dataset we see that the first itemset that the algorithm tries to add immediately increases the BIC score. Therefore, the summary contains only singleton itemsets, which correctly corresponds to the independence model.

With the *Markov* data we notice that the itemsets in the summary are all quite small, and consist of consecutive items. This is in line with expectations, since the items form a Markov chain. The algorithm finds that together with the individual items, a summary of 21 itemsets suffices.

The summary of the *Mosaic* data contains the itemsets that were used to construct the dataset. Figure 1 depicts the evolution of the BIC score. We see that as the five embedded itemsets are discovered, the BIC score is drastically reduced. Afterwards, some additional itemsets are discovered, which contain items from two or more of the generating itemsets. However, they are not noise, and are needed to

Table 3: The BIC scores of the discovered models, compared to the independence model. (Lower scores are better.)

	k	time	$s(\mathcal{C})$	$s(indep)$
Independent	0	10 s	4 494 656	4 494 656
Markov	21	4 834 s	1 826 576	2 000 143
Mosaic	19	686 s	812 792	2 168 276
Abstracts	24	2 774 s	254 974	256 937
Chess (kr-k)	15	3 104 s	774 899	787 078
DNA Amplification	132	3 303 s	91 125	185 499
Mammals	13	1 826 s	107 268	120 132
Mushroom	15	1 817 s	343 367	441 903
Paleo	13	2 307 s	7 787	8 822

[1] http://www.adrem.ua.ac.be/implementations

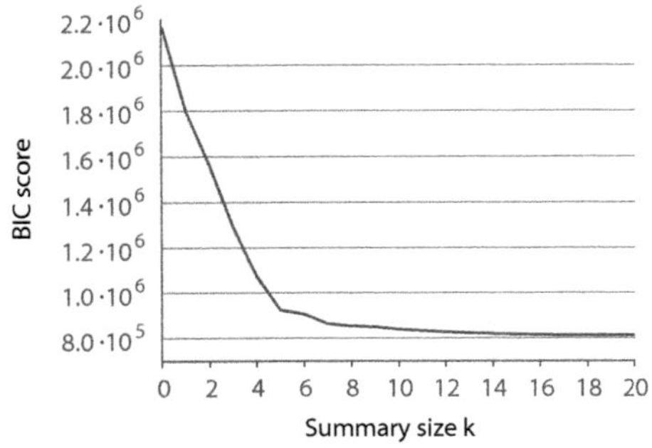

Figure 1: BIC scores for the *Mosaic* dataset for increasing k. The minimum BIC score is attained at $k = 19$.

explain the overlapping behavior of some of the generating itemsets. When k reaches 20, the BIC score increases, and the algorithm stops. (Due to the scale of the plot this is not clearly visible in Figure 1.) Therefore, the algorithm decides that the dataset can be best described with 19 itemsets, of which 5 (the generating itemsets) clearly provide the most information.

The transactions in the *Mammals* data represent geographical areas of 50×50 km^2 in Europe. The itemsets discovered here represent sets of mammals that co-exist in these regions. Investigating the areas where these sets of mammals are present, reveals that many of them form contiguous geographically sound territories, e.g., Scandinavia, the Iberian peninsula, or Eastern Europe. (Pictures are not shown here due to lack of space.)

In the case of the *DNA* data, our algorithm reached more than 100 iterations within one hour. As this dataset is banded, it contains a lot of structure [8]. Our method correctly discovers these bands, i.e., blocks of consecutive items corresponding to related genes, lying on the same chromosomes. The first few dozen sets are large, and describe the general structure of the data. Then, as we continue, we start to encounter smaller itemsets, which describe more detailed nuances in the correlations between the genes. Figure 2 depicts a detail of the *DNA* dataset (note that the figure is transposed), together with a few of the itemsets from the discovered summary.

7.3 Comparison with Other Methods

In Table 4, we give the top-10 itemsets in the *Abstracts* dataset, as discovered by our method (top left), KRIMP [23] (top right), Kontonasios and De Bie's method [15] (bottom left), and Tiling [9] (bottom right). We see that our algorithm discovers recognizable

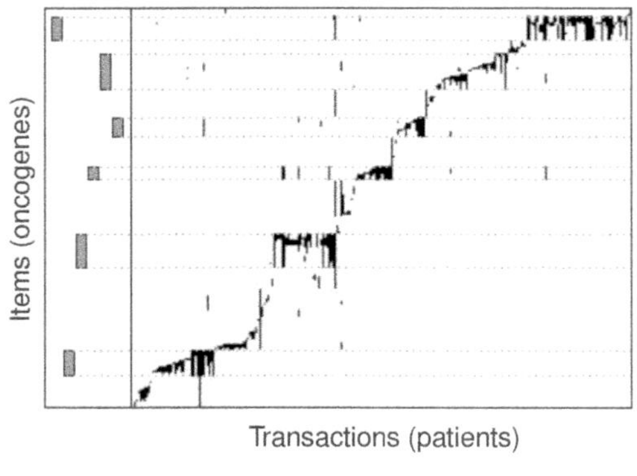

Figure 2: Detail of the *DNA* dataset (right), along with some of the discovered itemsets (left). (Figure is rotated to the left.)

Table 4: Top-10 itemsets of the *Abstracts* dataset for our method (top left), KRIMP [23] (top right), Kontonasios and De Bie [15] (bottom left), and Tiling [9] (bottom right).

machin support svm vector	algorithm experiment result set
associ mine rule	demonstr space
algorithm frequent mine pattern	larg databas
analysi discrimin lda linear	consid problem
algorithm cluster dimension high	knowledg discoveri
nearest neighbor	demonstr experiment
bay naiv	rule mine associ databas
frequent itemset mine	algorithm base approach cluster
analysi compon princip	state art
dimension high real subspac synthet	global local
vector machin support	algorithm mine
discov frequent effici pattern mine algorithm	algorithm base
associ rule database mine algorithm	result set
train learn classifi perform set	approach problem
frequent itemset	method propos
dimensional high cluster mine	result experiment
synthetic real	algorithm perform
seri time	base model
decis tree classifi	set method
experiment propos problem approach result	algorithm gener

data mining topics such as *support vector machines*, *frequent itemset mining* and *principle component analysis*. Further, there is little overlap between the itemsets, and there is no variations-on-the-same-theme type of redundancy present.

For KRIMP we depict the itemsets from the code table which have the highest usage. From a compression point of view, the items in these sets co-occur often, and thus result in small codes for the itemsets. Arguably, this does not necessarily make them the most interesting, however, and we observe that some rather general terms such as *state [of the] art* or *consider problem* are ranked highly. The results of Kontonasios and De Bie's algorithm, based on the Information Ratio of tiles, are different from ours, but seem to be more or less similar in quality for this particular dataset. Finally, for Tiling we provide the top-10 itemsets of size at least two. Without this size restriction, only singletons are returned, which, although having the largest area, are not very informative. Still, the largest discovered tiles are of size two, and contain quite some redundancy, for instance, the top-10 contains only 13 (out of 20) distinct items.

8. DISCUSSION

The approach introduced in this paper fulfills several intuitive expectations one might have about summarization, such as succinctness, providing a characteristic description of the data, and having little redundancy. The experiments show that quantitatively we can achieve good BIC scores with only a handful of itemsets, and that these results are highly qualitative and meaningful; moreover, we can discover them in a relatively short amount of time.

In this paper we consider data mining as an iterative process. By starting off with what we already know, we can identify those patterns that are the most surprising. Simply finding the itemset that is most surprising, is a problem that Hanhijärvi et al. summarize as 'tell me something I don't know'. When we repeat this process, in the end, we will have identified a group of itemsets that 'tell me all there is to know' about the data. Clearly, this group strongly overfits the data. This is where BIC provides a solution, as it automatically identifies the most informative group. Hence, we paraphrase our approach as 'tell me what I need to know'.

The view that we take here on succinctness and non-redundancy is fairly strict. Arguably, there are settings conceivable where limited redundancy (at the cost of brevity) can give some robustness to a technique, or provide alternative insights by restating facts differently. However, this is not the intention of this paper, and we furthermore argue that to this end our method can perfectly be complemented by techniques such as redescription mining [33].

There are a number of possible improvements for our method. We are interested in refining the penalty in our score. Our current score only penalizes the *number* of elements in $\mathcal{C}$, not their complexity (e.g., their size). Such a refinement would make it more strict, and could provide better results. Another problem setting in which our method is applicable, is that of finding the best specialization of a given itemset X. That is, to identify the superset Y of X that provides the best score $s(\mathcal{C} \cup \{Y\})$. This setup allows experts to interactively discover interesting itemsets. As part of future work, we are currently investigating this in practice for finding patterns in proteomics and mass-spectrometry data.

9. CONCLUSION

In this paper we introduced a well-founded method for iteratively mining a non-redundant collection of interesting itemsets from transaction data. We employ the Maximum Entropy principle to build a probabilistic model of the data, use this model to iteratively identify the most surprising itemsets, and then update our model accordingly. As such, unlike static interestingness models, our approach does not return patterns that are redundant with regard to what we have learned, and keeps the result set succinct yet informative.

Experiments show that we discover succinct summaries, which correctly identify important patterns in the data. The resulting models attain high log-likelihoods, and are easy to interpret.

Acknowledgements

Michael Mampaey is supported by the Institute for the Promotion of Innovation through Science and Technology in Flanders (IWT-Vlaanderen), Nikolaj Tatti and Jilles Vreeken are supported by Post-Doctoral Fellowships of the Research Foundation—Flanders (FWO).

10. REFERENCES

[1] C. C. Aggarwal and P. S. Yu. A new framework for itemset generation. In *Proc. PODS'98*, pages 18–24, 1998.

[2] S. Brin, R. Motwani, and C. Silverstein. Beyond market baskets: Generalizing association rules to correlations. In *Proc. ACM SIGMOD'97*, pages 265–276, 1997.

[3] T. Calders and B. Goethals. Non-derivable itemset mining. *Data Min. Knowl. Disc.*, 14(1):171–206, 2007.

[4] I. Csiszár. I-divergence geometry of probability distributions and minimization problems. *The Annals of Probability*, 3(1):146–158, Feb. 1975.

[5] J. Darroch and D. Ratcliff. Generalized iterative scaling for log-linear models. *The Annals of Mathematical Statistics*, 43(5):1470–1480, 1972.

[6] A. Frank and A. Asuncion. UCI machine learning repository. http://archive.ics.uci.edu/ml, 2010.

[7] A. Gallo, N. Cristianini, and T. De Bie. MINI: Mining informative non-redundant itemsets. In *Proc. PKDD'07*, pages 438–445, 2007.

[8] G. C. Garriga, E. Junttila, and H. Mannila. Banded structure in binary matrices. In *Proc. ACM SIGKDD'08*, pages 292–300, 2008.

[9] F. Geerts, B. Goethals, and T. Mielikäinen. Tiling databases. In *Proc. DS'04*, pages 278–289, 2004.

[10] A. Gionis, H. Mannila, T. Mielikäinen, and P. Tsaparas. Assessing data mining results via swap randomization. *Trans. Knowl. Disc. Data*, 1(3), 2007.

[11] B. Goethals and M. Zaki. Frequent itemset mining dataset repository. http://fimi.ua.ac.be/.

[12] P. D. Grünwald. *The Minimum Description Length Principle*. MIT Press, 2007.

[13] S. Hanhijärvi, M. Ojala, N. Vuokko, K. Puolamäki, N. Tatti, and H. Mannila. Tell me something I don't know: randomization strategies for iterative data mining. In *Proc. ACM SIGKDD'09*, pages 379–388, 2009.

[14] S. Jaroszewicz and D. A. Simovici. Interestingness of frequent itemsets using bayesian networks as background knowledge. In *Proc. ACM SIGKDD'04*, pages 178–186, 2004.

[15] K.-N. Kontonasios and T. De Bie. An information-theoretic approach to finding noisy tiles in binary databases. In *Proc. SDM'10*, pages 153–164, 2010.

[16] M. Mampaey and J. Vreeken. Summarising data by clustering items. In *Proc. ECML PKDD'10*, pages 321–336, 2010.

[17] A. Mitchell-Jones, G. Amori, W. Bogdanowicz, B. Krystufek, P. H. Reijnders, F. Spitzenberger, M. Stubbe, J. Thissen, V. Vohralik, and J. Zima. *The Atlas of European Mammals*. Academic Press, 1999.

[18] T. Mitchell-Jones. Societas europaea mammalogica. http://www.european-mammals.org.

[19] S. Myllykangas, J. Himberg, T. Böhling, B. Nagy, J. Hollmén, and S. Knuutila. DNA copy number amplification profiling of human neoplasms. *Oncogene*, 25(55):7324–7332, 2006.

[20] S. Nijssen, T. Guns, and L. De Raedt. Correlated itemset mining in ROC space: a constraint programming approach. In *Proc. ACM SIGKDD'09*, pages 647–656, 2009.

[21] N. Pasquier, Y. Bastide, R. Taouil, and L. Lakhal. Discovering frequent closed itemsets for association rules. In *Proc. ICDT'99*, pages 398–416, 1999.

[22] G. Schwarz. Estimating the dimension of a model. *Annals of Statistics*, 6(2):461–464, 1978.

[23] A. Siebes, J. Vreeken, and M. van Leeuwen. Item sets that compress. In *Proc. SDM'06*, pages 393–404, 2006.

[24] P. Tan, V. Kumar, and J. Srivastava. Selecting the right interestingness measure for association patterns. In *Proc. ACM SIGKDD'02*, pages 32–41. ACM, 2002.

[25] N. Tatti. Computational complexity of queries based on itemsets. *Inf. Proc. Letters*, pages 183–187, 2006.

[26] N. Tatti. Maximum entropy based significance of itemsets. *Knowl. Inf. Sys.*, 17(1):57–77, 2008.

[27] N. Tatti. Probably the best itemsets. In *Proc. ACM SIGKDD'10*, pages 293–302. ACM, 2010.

[28] N. Tatti and H. Heikinheimo. Decomposable families of itemsets. In *Proc. ECMLPKDD'08*, pages 472–487, 2008.

[29] N. Tatti and M. Mampaey. Using background knowledge to rank itemsets. *Data Min. Knowl. Disc.*, 21(2):293–309, 2010.

[30] C. Wang and S. Parthasarathy. Summarizing itemset patterns using probabilistic models. In *Proc. ACM SIGKDD'06*, pages 730–735, 2006.

[31] G. I. Webb. Self-sufficient itemsets: An approach to screening potentially interesting associations between items. *Trans. Knowl. Disc. Data*, 4(1), 2010.

[32] X. Yan, H. Cheng, J. Han, and D. Xin. Summarizing itemset patterns: a profile-based approach. In *Proc. ACM SIGKDD'05*, pages 314–323, 2005.

[33] M. J. Zaki and N. Ramakrishnan. Reasoning about sets using redescription mining. In *Proc. ACM SIGKDD'05*, pages 364–373, New York, NY, USA, 2005. ACM Press.

Direct Local Pattern Sampling by Efficient Two-Step Random Procedures

Mario Boley
Fraunhofer IAIS and
University of Bonn
mario.boley@iais.fhg.de

Claudio Lucchese
I.S.T.I.-C.N.R. Pisa
claudio.lucchese@isti.cnr.it

Daniel Paurat
University of Bonn
daniel.paurat@uni-bonn.de

Thomas Gärtner
Fraunhofer IAIS and
University of Bonn
thomas.gaertner@iais.fhg.de

ABSTRACT

We present several exact and highly scalable local pattern sampling algorithms. They can be used as an alternative to exhaustive local pattern discovery methods (e.g, frequent set mining or optimistic-estimator-based subgroup discovery) and can substantially improve efficiency as well as controllability of pattern discovery processes. While previous sampling approaches mainly rely on the Markov chain Monte Carlo method, our procedures are direct, i.e., non process-simulating, sampling algorithms. The advantages of these direct methods are an almost optimal time complexity per pattern as well as an exactly controlled distribution of the produced patterns. Namely, the proposed algorithms can sample (item-)sets according to frequency, area, squared frequency, and a class discriminativity measure. Experiments demonstrate that these procedures can improve the accuracy of pattern-based models similar to frequent sets and often also lead to substantial gains in terms of scalability.

Categories and Subject Descriptors: H.2.8 [Database Management]: Database Applications—*Data Mining*

General Terms: Algorithms, Theory

Keywords: Local pattern discovery, Sampling, Pattern-based classification, Frequent sets

1. INTRODUCTION

This paper presents simple yet effective procedures for local pattern discovery [20] that attack the task from a different algorithmic angle than the standard search approach—namely, by directly generating individual patterns as the outcome of a random experiment. Local patterns such as association rules [1] or emerging patterns [12] are used in various application contexts from exploratory data analysis where they constitute units of discovered knowledge to predictive model construction where patterns act as binary features [9, 10, 13]. What all applications have in common is that usually only a few patterns can be effectively utilized—either due to the limited attention of a data analyst or because too many features can reduce the comprehensibility and performance of a global model. Standard local pattern discovery algorithms, however, are based on exhaustive search within huge pattern spaces (e.g., frequent set miners [19, 26], or optimistic-estimator-based subgroup and association discovery [17, 23]). Consequently, they tend to either produce a vast amount of output patterns or at least enumerate them internally.

This motivates the invention of algorithms that only sample a representative set of patterns without explicitly searching in the pattern space. Such algorithms exist in the literature [2, 6, 8] but they provide either no control over the distribution of their output or only asymptotic control by simulating a stochastic process on the pattern space using the Markov chain Monte Carlo method (MCMC). In addition to only offering approximate sampling, MCMC methods have a scalability problem: the number of required process simulation steps is often large and, even more critical, individual simulation steps typically involve expensive support counting operations. Hence, these algorithms are often infeasible for large input datasets. Therefore, we present novel pattern generation methods that sample patterns exactly and directly, i.e., without simulating time-consuming stochastic processes. More precisely, given a dataset $\mathcal{D}$ and a number of desired patterns k, the procedures

- produce exactly k patterns each of which is generated exactly according to a distribution proportional to either frequency, squared frequency, area (i.e., frequency times size), or discriminativity (i.e., frequency in positive data portion times negative frequency in negative data portion);
- use time $O(\|\mathcal{D}\| + kn)$ for frequency and area or time $O(\|\mathcal{D}\|^2 + kn)$ for squared frequency and discriminativity, where n denotes the number of items and $\|\mathcal{D}\|$ the size of the dataset, i.e., the sum of all data record sizes[1].

That is, after a linear or quadratic preprocessing phase each pattern is produced in a time linear in the number of items.

[1]This assumes that $\exp(n) > |\mathcal{D}|$; the actual complexities are $O(\|\mathcal{D}\| + k(n + \ln |\mathcal{D}|))$ and $O(\|\mathcal{D}\|^2 + k(n + \ln^2 |\mathcal{D}|))$.

This time complexity appears to be almost optimal, because only reading the data once requires $O(\|\mathcal{D}\|)$ and just printing k patterns without any further computation requires time $O(kn)$.

After giving some more background on the idea of controlled repeated pattern sampling and reviewing other pattern sampling algorithms, the remainder of this paper is structured as follows. We define formal and notational background (Sec. 2) followed by a detailed description of the sampling procedures (Sec 3). Then we report experimental results showing that sampled patterns are equally useful for pattern-based classification as frequent sets and that pattern sampling can easily outperform exhaustive listing on large datasets (Sec. 4). Finally, we give a summarizing discussion of all results (Sec. 5).

1.1 Pattern Sampling

The data mining literature contains several local pattern discovery algorithms that can efficiently produce large output families. Here, efficiency is defined in an output-sensitive way (see, e.g., [16]), that is for instance amortized polynomial time per pattern, which is a useful notion assuming that the produced pattern collections are the final output. When viewed from a global (application-driven) perspective though, the enumerated patterns are usually only an intermediate result, from which a final—often much smaller—pattern collection is selected. That is, enumeration is only one step within a surrounding local pattern discovery process. This two phase approach, which we refer to as "exhaustive search" is illustrated in Figure 1(a): during the enumeration step part of the implicitly defined pattern space is physically constructed—we refer to that part as "enumeration space"—and then, during the selection step, the most valuable patterns from this enumeration space are collected with respect to some interestingness measure.

An example for this paradigm is listing frequent sets of an input dataset, but subsequently using only those sets that provide rules with a large value of some measure that reflects the primary user interest (e.g., lift). A further example is optimistic-estimator-based pruning for subgroup or association discovery. There the enumeration space is the family of all sets having a large enough optimistic estimate of their interestingness, and the patterns that are selected for the result family are those with a large value of the actual interestingness measure. Note that, in this example, enumeration and selection are algorithmically interweaved, i.e., sets are already selected during the enumeration phase. Many more examples emerge from the LeGo approach to data mining [22] where patterns are selected according to their utility for constructing global models.

Two reasons usually motivate this two phase approach: either there is no efficient algorithm that directly optimizes the measure of primary interest or this measure is not known in advance (this happens in exploratory settings where interestingness can be user-specific). In either case, the enumeration step can constitute a severe bottleneck. Even if enumeration is performed by an amortized polynomial time algorithm, its computation time is essentially unpredictable: the size of the enumeration space cannot be directly controlled and its explicit construction takes time at least proportional to that size. On the other hand, if one enforces a maximum computation time by aborting the execution at a certain point, one ends up with an uncontrolled subset of the enumeration space, which depends on the internal search order of the enumeration algorithm.

In contrast, suppose we can access the pattern space $\mathcal{L}$ by an efficient sampling procedure simulating a distribution $\pi : \mathcal{L} \to [0, 1]$ that is defined proportional to some function that either is our primary interestingness measure or a function that correlates with it. Then, for any designated number of patterns (or corresponding designated computation time) it is possible to efficiently generate a collection of exactly that many patterns that is representative of the distribution π. Consequently, since π has a semantic connection to the underlying notion of interestingness, a meaningful allocation of computational resources is guaranteed for any limited time budget.

Figure 1(b) illustrates this alternative approach, which we want to refer to as "controlled repeated pattern sampling". A potentially positive side-effect of this paradigm is that instead of the usual hard constraints it utilizes parameter-free soft constraints [5]. Hence, the user is freed of the often troublesome task of finding appropriate hard threshold parameters such as a minimum frequency threshold.

1.2 Related Work

In contrast to sampling from the input database (see, e.g., [25, 28]), it is a relatively new development in local pattern discovery to sample from the pattern space. In the context of maximal frequent subgraph mining, Chaoji et al. [8] describes a random process that stops after a certain number of steps that is bounded by the maximum number of edges present in an input graph and produces a maximal frequent subgraph. A similar process is already applied in Gunopoulos et al. [18] within a Las Vegas variant of the Dualize and Advance algorithm. More precisely, it is used for the internal randomization of an algorithm with an otherwise deterministic output (all maximal frequent and minimal infrequent sets of a given input database). When applied for the final pattern discovery, however, this random process has the weakness that it provides no control over the generation probabilities of individual patterns.

Several papers propose to overcome this weakness by applying the MCMC method. Boley and Grosskreutz [7] proposes frequent set sampling to approximate the effect of specific minimum frequency thresholds. The proposed algorithm simulates a simple Glauber dynamic on the frequent set lattice: starting with the empty set, in each subsequent time step a single item is either removed or added to the current set. A similar MCMC method is used in Zaki and Al Hasan [2] for generating a representative set of graph patterns. These MCMC methods provide limited control of the generation probabilities, namely of the infinite limit of the state distribution. The worst-case convergence can, however, be exponentially slow in the size of the input database. For sampling from the family of frequent patterns, this problem appears to be inherent: almost uniform frequent pattern sampling can be used for approximate frequent pattern counting, which one can show to be intractable under reasonable complexity assumptions (see [7]). Similar conclusions can be drawn for enumeration spaces defined by linearly scaled versions of the frequency measure such as the standard optimistic estimator for the binomial test quality function in subgroup discovery [27].

In order to avoid this implication of hard-constraint-based pattern discovery (e.g., using a hard frequency threshold),

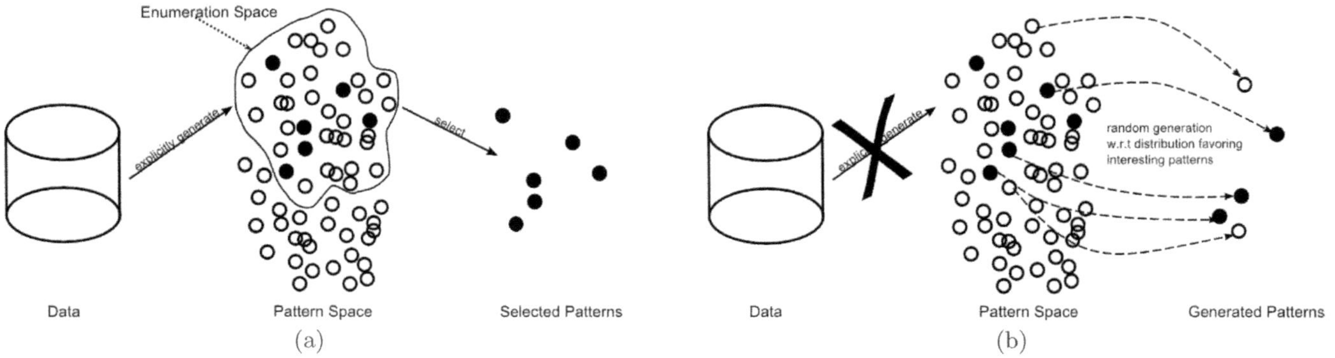

Figure 1: (a) *Exhaustive search*: involves complete generation of an enumeration space guaranteed to contain all interesting patterns; however, size of that space usually has no reasonable bound w.r.t. to input size and is hard to predict. (b) *Controlled pattern sampling*: no explicit construction of uncontrolled, potentially huge, part of pattern space; instead random generation of designated number of patterns; no guarantee of finding patterns satisfying hard interestingness threshold, but control over time, output size, and distribution.

Boley et al. [6] combines pattern space sampling with soft-constraint-based pattern discovery [5]—resulting in the pattern sampling paradigm described in Section 1.1 above. Still, the underlying method is again MCMC-based, and, despite using a more sophisticated chain defined on the closed set lattice of the input database, it shares the practical weaknesses of this technique. The present paper retains the idea of controlled pattern sampling without hard constraints, but proposes novel pattern generation methods that are exact and direct, i.e., they do not involve MCMC process simulation. Consequently, the resulting pattern discovery processes are efficient not only theoretically but also on a wide range of real-world benchmark datasets.

2. PRELIMINARIES

Before going into technical details, we introduce some basic notions and notation. For a finite set X we denote by $\mathcal{P}(X)$ its power set and by $u(X)$ the uniform probability distribution on X. Moreover, for positive weights $w: X \to \mathbb{R}^+$ let $w(X)$ denote the distribution on X arising from normalizing w, i.e., the distribution described by $x \mapsto w(x)/\sum_{x' \in X} w(x)$—assuming that there is an $x \in X$ with $w(x) > 0$.

A binary **dataset** $\mathcal{D}$ over some finite **ground set** E is a bag (multiset) of sets, called **data records**, $D_1, \ldots, D_m$ each of which is a subset of $E = \{e, \ldots, e_n\}$. The **size** of $\mathcal{D}$, denoted by $\|\mathcal{D}\|$, is defined as the sum of all its data record sizes $\sum_{D \in \mathcal{D}} = |D|$. Inspired by the application of market basket analysis the elements of E are often referred to as "items". More generally, one can think of E as a set of binary features describing the data records. In particular, a categorical data table can easily be represented as a binary dataset by choosing the ground set as consisting of all attribute/value equality expressions that can be formed from the table. More precisely, a **categorical data table** T consisting of m data row vectors $d_1, \ldots, d_m$ with $d_i = (d_i(1), \ldots, d_i(n))$ can be represented by the dataset $\mathcal{D}_T = \{D_1, \ldots, D_m\}$ with $D_i = \{(j, v) : d_i(j) = v\}$ over ground set

$$E_T = \{(j, d_i(j)) \colon 1 \leq i \leq m, 1 \leq j \leq n\} \ .$$

For a given dataset $\mathcal{D}$ over E, the **pattern space** (or pattern *language*) $\mathcal{L}(\mathcal{D})$ considered in this paper is the power set $\mathcal{P}(E)$ of the features and its elements are interpreted conjunctively. That is, the *local* data portion described by a set $F \subseteq E$, called the **support (set)** of F in $\mathcal{D}$ and denoted $\mathcal{D}[F]$, is defined as the multiset of all data records from $\mathcal{D}$ that contain *all* elements of F, i.e., $\mathcal{D}[F] = \{D \in \mathcal{D} \colon D \supseteq F\}$.

An **interestingness measure** for a pattern language $\mathcal{L}(\cdot)$ is a function

$$q \colon \{(\mathcal{D}, x) \colon \mathcal{D} \text{ a binary dataset}, x \in \mathcal{L}(\mathcal{D})\} \to \mathbb{R} \ .$$

However, often there is a fixed dataset that is clear from the context. In such cases—and if we want to simplify the notation—we just write q as a unary function $q(\cdot) = q(\mathcal{D}, \cdot)$ and omit the first argument. The most basic measures for set patterns are the **support (count)**, i.e., the size of its support set $q_{\text{supp}}(\mathcal{D}, F) = |\mathcal{D}[F]|$ and the **frequency**, i.e., the relative size of its support with respect to the total number of data records $q_{\text{freq}}(\mathcal{D}, F) = |\mathcal{D}[F]| / |\mathcal{D}|$. For a frequency threshold $t \in [0, 1]$ a set is called ***t*-frequent** (w.r.t. $\mathcal{D}$) if $q_{\text{freq}}(\mathcal{D}, F) \geq t$. A further measure considered here is the **area function** [15] $q_{\text{area}}(\mathcal{D}, F) = |F| \, |\mathcal{D}[F]|$. Intuitively, the area of a set corresponds to the number of 1 entries of the submatrix (of the binary matrix representation of $\mathcal{D}$) consisting of the columns corresponding to F and the rows corresponding to $\mathcal{D}[F]$.

All measures defined so far are unsupervised measures in the sense that they rely on no further information but the dataset itself. In contrast, there are so-called supervised descriptive rule induction techniques that rely on additional information in the form of **class labels** $l(D) \in C = \{c_1, \ldots, c_k\}$ associated to each data record $D \in \mathcal{D}$. For $c \in C$ we denote by $\mathcal{D}_c$ the data portion labeled c, i.e., $\mathcal{D}_c = \{D \in \mathcal{D} \colon l(D) = c\}$. Examples for this setting are emerging pattern mining [12] and contrast set mining [3], where one is interested in patterns having a high support difference between the positive and the negative portion of the data records, or subgroup discovery [27], where one searches for patterns with a high distributional unusualness of these labels on their support set. An important special case is the case of binary labels, i.e., $C = \{\oplus, \ominus\}$. For this case we consider the following **discriminativity measure**

$$q_{\text{disc}}(F) = |\mathcal{D}_{\oplus}[F]| \, |\mathcal{D}_{\ominus} \setminus \mathcal{D}_{\ominus}[F]| \enspace .$$

A further measure for the discriminative power of a pattern is the **Fisher score** q_{fish}, which is defined for datasets with arbitrary labels C. Intuitively, it measures the relation of the inter-class variance of a feature to its intra-class variances, i.e.,

$$q_{\text{fish}}(F) = \frac{\sum_{c \in C} |\mathcal{D}_c| \, (q_{\text{freq}}(\mathcal{D}_c, F) - q_{\text{freq}}(\mathcal{D}, F))^2}{\sum_{c \in C} \sum_{D \in \mathcal{D}_c} (\delta(D \supseteq F) - q_{\text{freq}}(\mathcal{D}_c, F))^2}$$

where $\delta(D \supseteq F)$ is 1 if $D \supseteq F$ and 0 otherwise. This paper does not present a sampling algorithm for this measure. However, the Fisher score is used for post-processing generated patterns in the context of constructing global classification models.

3. SAMPLING ALGORITHMS

After the introduction of set patterns and interestingness measures, we can now present our sampling procedures. A naive approach for sampling a pattern according to a distribution π is to generate a list $F_1, \ldots, F_N$ of all patterns with $\pi(F) > 0$, draw an $x \in [0,1]$ uniformly at random, and then return the unique set F_k with $\sum_{i=1}^{k-1} \pi(F_i) \leq x < \sum_{i=1}^{k} \pi(F_i)$. However, the exhaustive enumeration of any non-constant part of the pattern space is precisely what we want to avoid. That is, we are interested in *non-enumerative* sampling algorithms.

Below we give such algorithms for four quality functions: frequency and squared frequency as well as area and discriminativity. The algorithms are inspired by the elementary procedures used in Karp et al. [21] (for estimating the number of satisfying assignments of a DNF formula): in a first step one element of a suitably constructed set of base objects is drawn, and in a second step a sub-object is drawn that is induced by that base object; hence the term "two-step random procedures".

Note that, in contrast to the frequency measures, for the latter two quality functions it is **NP**-hard to find optimal patterns: Finding a set of maximum area for a given input dataset is equivalent to the **NP**-hard problem of computing a biclique with maximum number of edges from a given bipartite graph (see [15]). The same hardness result holds for the discriminativity measure because optimizing area can be linearly reduced to optimizing discriminativity: by setting $\mathcal{D}_{\oplus}$ to $\mathcal{D}$ and $\mathcal{D}_{\ominus}$ to $\{E \setminus \{e\} \colon e \in E\}$ we get

$$q_{\text{disc}}(\mathcal{D}_{\oplus} \cup \mathcal{D}_{\ominus}, F) = |\mathcal{D}[F]| \, (|E| - |E| + |F|) = q_{\text{area}}(\mathcal{D}, F)$$

for all $F \subseteq E$ because with this construction of the negative data portion we have $|\mathcal{D}_{\ominus}[F]| = |E| - |F|$.

3.1 Frequency and Area

Algorithm 1 Frequency-based Sampling

Require: dataset $\mathcal{D}$ over ground set E,
Returns: random set $R \sim q_{\text{freq}}(\mathcal{P}(E)) = q_{\text{supp}}(\mathcal{P}(E))$

1. **let** weights w be defined by $w(D) = 2^{|D|}$ for all $D \in \mathcal{D}$
2. **draw** $D \sim w(\mathcal{D})$
3. **return** $R \sim u(\mathcal{P}(D))$

We start with sampling according to frequency and area, both of which can be achieved by very similar linear time algorithms. The key insight for frequency-based sampling, i.e., $\pi = q_{\text{freq}}(\mathcal{P}(E))$, is that random experiments are good in reproducing frequent events. Namely, if we look at a pattern that is supported by a random data record we are likely to observe a pattern that is supported by many data records altogether. This intuition leads to a two-step non-enumerative sampling routine (see Algorithm 1), which is as fast as it is simple: First select a data record of the input dataset randomly with a probability proportional to the size of its power set. Then return a uniformly sampled subset of that data record. Using the size of the power set in the first step is important, as otherwise the sampling routine would be biased towards sets occurring in small data records. As noted in Proposition 1 below, the random set resulting from combining both steps follows the desired distribution.

Regarding the computational complexity of the sampling algorithm we can observe that it is indeed efficient: if one has knowledge of the numbers $|D|$ for all data records $D \in \mathcal{D}$ and, moreover, has index access to all data records, a single random set can be produced in time $O(\log |\mathcal{D}| + |E|)$ (the two terms correspond to producing a random number for drawing a data record in step 1 and to drawing one of its subsets in step 2, respectively). Both requirements can be achieved via a single initial pass over the dataset. Thus, we have the following proposition.

Proposition 1. *On input dataset $\mathcal{D}$ over E, a family of k realizations of the random set $\mathbf{R} \sim q_{\text{freq}}(\mathcal{P}(E))$ can be generated in time $O(\|\mathcal{D}\| + k(|E| + \ln |\mathcal{D}|))$.*

Proof. Let Z be the normalizing constant $\sum_{F \subseteq E} |\mathcal{D}[F]|$ and $\mathbf{D}$ denote the random data record that is drawn in step 2 of the algorithm. For the probability distribution of the returned random set we have

$$\begin{aligned} \mathbb{P}[\mathbf{R} = R] &= \sum_{D \in \mathcal{D}} \mathbb{P}[\mathbf{R} = R \wedge \mathbf{D} = D] \\ &= \sum_{D \in \mathcal{D}[R]} \frac{1}{2^{|D|}} \frac{2^{|D|}}{Z} \\ &= \frac{|\mathcal{D}[R]|}{Z} = \frac{q_{\text{supp}}(\mathcal{D}, R)}{Z} \end{aligned}$$

with a normalizing $Z = \sum_{D \in \mathcal{D}} 2^{|D|}$ (which is equal to the desired $\sum_{F \subseteq E} |\mathcal{D}[F]|$). □

Algorithm 2 Area-based Sampling

Require: dataset $\mathcal{D}$ over ground set E with $\|\mathcal{D}\| > 0$,
Returns: random set $R \sim q_{\text{area}}(\mathcal{P}(E))$

1. **let** weights w be defined for all $D \in \mathcal{D}$ by

   $$w(D) = |D| \, 2^{|D|-1}$$

2. **draw** $D \sim w(\mathcal{D})$
3. **return** $R \sim s(\mathcal{P}(D))$ with $s(F) = |F|$

Sampling according to area, i.e., $\pi = q_{\text{area}}(\mathcal{P}(E))$, can be achieved via a slight modification of frequency-based sampling: in step two, instead of drawing a subset uniformly from a data record, draw a subset with probability proportional to its size. The latter step can be implemented, e.g., by first drawing a size s with probability proportional to $\binom{|D|}{s}$ and then by uniformly drawing from D a subset of size s. As a side effect, this modification affects the normalization constants and in particular the data record weights of step one. Since for the sum of all subset sizes of a data record D we have

$$\sum_{F \subseteq D} |F| = |D| \, 2^{|D|-1} \ ,$$

the data record weights need to be modified accordingly. The resulting pseudo-code is given in Algorithm 2. Again, after all weights have been computed via an initial pass over the data, an arbitrary number of random sets can be produced in time $O(\log |\mathcal{D}| + |E|)$. Hence, with a similar proof as for Proposition 1 we can conclude:

PROPOSITION 2. *On input dataset $\mathcal{D}$ over E, a family of k realizations of the random set $\boldsymbol{R} \sim q_{\text{area}}(\mathcal{P}(E))$ can be generated in time $O(\|\mathcal{D}\| + k(|E| + \ln |\mathcal{D}|))$.*

It is important to note that area can be replaced by *weighted* area relatively easy without changing the asymptotic complexity—where weighted area is defined as

$$q_{\text{ware}}(F) = \left(\sum_{e \in F} w(e)\right)\left(\sum_{D \in \mathcal{D}[F]} w(D)\right)$$

for a set of positive weights $w \colon (E \cup \mathcal{D}) \to \mathbb{R}_+$. The same holds for weighted frequency. In this paper, however, for the sake of simplicity we only consider the unweighted case.

3.2 Discriminativity and Squared Frequency

Algorithm 3 Discriminativity-based Sampling

Require: binary labeled dataset $\mathcal{D}$ over ground set E such that there is an $F \subseteq E$ with $q_{\text{disc}}(F) > 0$
Returns: random set $R \sim q_{\text{disc}}(\mathcal{P}(E))$

1. **let** weights w be defined by
$$w(D_\oplus, D_\ominus) = (2^{|D_\oplus \setminus D_\ominus|} - 1) 2^{|D_\oplus \cap D_\ominus|}$$
for all $(D_\oplus, D_\ominus) \in \mathcal{D}_\oplus \times \mathcal{D}_\ominus$
2. **draw** $(D_\oplus, D_\ominus) \sim w(\mathcal{D}_\oplus \times \mathcal{D}_\ominus)$
3. **return** $R = (F \cup F')$ with
$$F \sim u(\mathcal{P}(D_\oplus \setminus D_\ominus) \setminus \emptyset) \text{ and } F' \sim u(\mathcal{P}(D_\oplus \cap D_\ominus))$$

In order to design a sampling procedure for discriminativity, i.e., $\pi = q_{\text{disc}}(\mathcal{P}(E))$, we can lift the principle of frequency-based sampling to a random experiment that is a little more complicated and has the following intuition: if we look at a pattern that is supported by a random positive data record and *not* supported by a random negative data record, we are likely to observe a pattern that is altogether supported by many positive data records and only few negative data records, i.e., we are likely to observe a pattern with a relatively high discriminativity score. Again, in order to control the resulting distribution, it is necessary to consider a pair of data records $(D_\oplus, D_\ominus)$ with a probability equal to the number of sets $F \subseteq E$ with $F \subseteq D_\oplus$ and $F \not\subseteq D_\ominus$. This implies that the increased expressivity of discriminativity compared to frequency comes at a price: due to the necessity of weight computation for all pairs of positive and negative data records, we end up with a quadratic preprocessing phase. Algorithm 3 contains all the details of the resulting sampling procedure and leads to the following result.

PROPOSITION 3. *Let $\mathcal{D}$ be a binary labeled input dataset over ground set E such that there is a set $F \subseteq E$ with $q_{\text{disc}}(\mathcal{D}, F) > 0$. A family of k realizations of the random set $\boldsymbol{R} \sim q_{\text{disc}}(\mathcal{P}(E))$ can be generated in time $O(\|\mathcal{D}\|^2 + k(|E| + \ln^2 |\mathcal{D}|))$.*

PROOF. Let $\mathbf{R}$ denote the random set returned in step 3 of the algorithm and $\mathbf{D}_\oplus$, $\mathbf{D}_\ominus$ the data records drawn in step 2. Moreover, for $D \in \mathcal{D}_\oplus$ and $D' \in \mathcal{D}_\ominus$ let $\delta(D, D')$ denote the family of all sets $F \subseteq E$ that are supported by D but not supported by D'. We can rewrite this definition as

$$\begin{aligned} &\delta(D, D') \\ =&\{F \subseteq E \colon F \subseteq D, F \not\subseteq D'\} \\ =&\{F \cup F' : \emptyset \subset F \subseteq (D \setminus D'), F' \subseteq (D \cap D')\} \ . \end{aligned}$$

This form shows that the weights $w(\cdot, \cdot)$ assigned in step 1 are equivalent to $|\delta(\cdot, \cdot)|$ and, moreover, that $\mathbf{R}$ is a set drawn uniformly from $\delta(\mathbf{D}_\oplus, \mathbf{D}_\ominus)$. With this we can conclude similar to the previous algorithms that

$$\begin{aligned} \mathbb{P}[\mathbf{R} = F] &= \sum_{D \in \mathcal{D}_\oplus} \sum_{D' \in \mathcal{D}_\ominus} \mathbb{P}[\mathbf{R} = F, \mathbf{D}_\oplus = D, \mathbf{D}_\ominus = D'] \\ &= \sum_{D, D' \in \delta^{-1}[F]} \frac{1}{|\delta(D, D')|} \frac{w(D, D')}{Z} \\ &= \frac{1}{Z} \left|\{(D, D') \in \mathcal{D}_\oplus \times \mathcal{D}_\ominus \colon D \supseteq F, D' \not\supseteq F\}\right| \\ &= \frac{1}{Z} |\mathcal{D}_\oplus[F]| \left(|\mathcal{D}_\ominus| - \mathcal{D}_\ominus[F]\right) \end{aligned}$$

with $Z = \sum_{D, D' \in \mathcal{D}_\oplus \times \mathcal{D}_\ominus} |\delta(D, D')| = \sum_{F \subseteq E} q_{\text{disc}}(F)$ as required. □

Algorithm 4 Squared-frequency-based Sampling

Require: dataset $\mathcal{D}$ over ground set E,
Returns: random set $F \sim q^2_{\text{freq}}(\mathcal{P}(E)) = q^2_{\text{supp}}(\mathcal{P}(E))$

1. **let** weights w be defined by
$$w(D_1, D_2) = 2^{|D_1 \cap D_2|}$$
for all $(D_1, D_2) \in \mathcal{D} \times \mathcal{D}$
2. **draw** $(D_1, D_2) \sim w(\mathcal{D} \times \mathcal{D})$
3. **return** $F \sim u(\mathcal{P}(D_1 \cap D_2))$

It is straightforward to see that the approach of drawing two data records can also be used to implement other potentially interesting distributions that can be expressed as the product of two support counts. A basic example is squared frequency. In order to achieve this distribution, one can consider a uniformly[2] drawn subset of two random data records, i.e., a subset of their intersection. The resulting pseudo-code

[2]For sampling according to the squared area function, draw a subset with probabilities proportional to its squared size instead of uniformly.

with appropriate pairwise weights is given in Algorithm 4. Closely following the proof of Proposition 3 this algorithm can be used to show another proposition.

PROPOSITION 4. *On input dataset $\mathcal{D}$ over E, a family of k realizations of the random set $\boldsymbol{R} \sim q^2_{\mathrm{freq}}(\mathcal{P}(E))$ can be generated in time $O(\|\mathcal{D}\|^2 + k(|E| + \ln^2 |\mathcal{D}|))$.*

In principle, one can design sampling algorithms for an abitrary power c of the frequency measure by drawing a subset from c random data records. However, the resulting time complexity for computing the weights for each c-tuple of data records gets out of hand quickly.

4. EVALUATION

The sampling procedures presented in the previous section are provably efficient and correct, i.e., their randomized output follows the specified distributions. Beside their practical scalability, it remains to be evaluated how useful these distributions are in the context of local pattern discovery. It is inherently difficult to evaluate pattern discovery methods for exploratory data analysis. There one aims to find *interesting* patterns based on notions of interestingness that are often user-subjective. Hence, a sophisticated experimental design would be required. Here we resort to the other branch of local pattern discovery applications, i.e., pattern-based global model construction, which allows us to simply use Fisher score as primary interestingness measure and accuracy as objective evaluation metric for the overall process.

dataset	class	nm/ct	items	rows	density
autos	7	15/10	135	205	0.190
balance-scale	3	4/0	20	625	0.250
breast-cancer	2	0/9	51	286	0.195
colic	3	7/15	84	366	0.271
credit-a	2	6/9	71	690	0.223
diabetes	2	8/0	40	768	0.225
glass	7	9/0	45	214	0.222
heart-c	5	6/7	49	303	0.285
heart-h	5	6/7	46	294	0.246
heart-statlog	2	13/0	55	270	0.254
hepatitis	2	6/13	55	155	0.344
hypothyroid	4	7/22	78	3772	0.364
iris	3	4/0	20	150	0.250
lymph	4	3/15	57	148	0.333
prim.-tumor	22	0/17	37	339	0.468
sonar	2	60/0	300	208	0.203
tic-tac-toe	2	0/9	27	958	0.370
vehicle	4	18/0	90	846	0.211
zoo	7	1/16	135	101	0.133

Table 1: Benchmark datasets with basic statistics: number of *classes* $|C|$, number of numerical and categorical columns (*nm/ct*), number $|E_T|$ of *items* in corresponding binary dataset, number of *rows*, *density* $|\mathcal{D}_T|\,|E_T|\,/\|\mathcal{D}_T\|$.

In our experiments we use a variety of databases from the UCI machine learning repository [14] listed in Table 1. In order to apply the pattern discovery algorithms, binary datasets are created from these databases by first converting them into categorical datatables using five bucket frequency discretization of all numeric data columns, and then by considering the corresponding binary datasets (using attribute / value pairs of categorical attributes as items; see Section 2). Implementations of the sampling algorithms are available in the software section of `http://www-kd.iai.uni-bonn.de`.

4.1 Predictive Performance

We start with experiments evaluating the sampling algorithms in the context of pattern-based classification. Here one aims to improve classification accuracy by enriching given labeled training data with pattern-based features. We closely follow the framework of Cheng et al. [9]. In a nutshell it consists of three basic steps: extraction of a collection of patterns (which are subsequently considered as features of the data records supporting them), feature selection based on Fisher score and pattern redundancy, and classification, for which we use a linear support vector machine.

In more detail, for an input data table T with corresponding binary dataset $\mathcal{D}_T = \mathcal{D}$ and class labels $C = \{1, \ldots, c\}$ we consider **pattern collections** $\mathcal{C}$, $\mathcal{R}_{\mathrm{frq}}$, $\mathcal{R}_{\mathrm{sfr}}$, $\mathcal{R}_{\mathrm{dcr}}$ that are based on deterministic top-k frequent closed sets (these can be efficiently produced, e.g., by the algorithm of Pietracaprina and Vandin [24]) and sampling according to frequency, squared frequency, and discriminativity, respectively. Area-based sampling is not considered here, because it is not designed to provide good features for classification. Each pattern collection $\mathcal{P}$ is the union of c collections $\mathcal{P}_i$ based on the class labels $i \in C$ where the size of $\mathcal{P}_i$ is proportional to the number of training examples of that class, i.e., $|\mathcal{P}_i| = \alpha\,|\mathcal{D}_i|$. Consequently, the size of the complete collection is $\alpha\,|\mathcal{D}|$, which is linear in the input size. The parameter α is set to 32 independently of the method and the dataset. This setting is a compromise between efficiency and stability of the pattern selection process (described below) as captured by the average Fisher score of finally selected features. See Figure 2 for an illustration on three exemplary datasets.

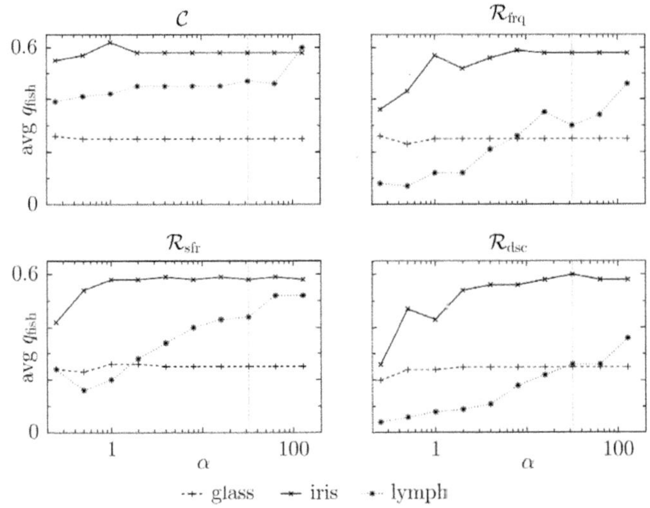

Figure 2: Average Fisher score of collections produced by methods for increasing values of α.

The **feature selection** step for a pattern collection $\mathcal{P}$ is then performed as follows: initialize $\mathcal{P}_0 = \emptyset$ and consider all sets $F_1, \ldots, F_l \in \mathcal{P}$ having $q_{\mathrm{freq}}(\mathcal{D}, \cdot) \geq 0.05$ in descending order of their Fisher score $q_{\mathrm{fish}}(\mathcal{D}, \cdot)$. Select a pattern F_i if the number of previously uncovered data records that it covers is at least 1% of the dataset, i.e.,

$$\left| \mathcal{D}[F_i] \setminus \bigcup_{F \in \mathcal{P}_{i-1}} \mathcal{D}[F] \right| \geq 0.01\, |\mathcal{D}|$$

where $\mathcal{P}_{i-1}$ is the family of sets already selected when considering F_i. The selection process is stopped either after all patterns have been considered or if $\mathcal{P}_i$ covers the dataset completely, i.e., $\bigcup_{F \in \mathcal{P}_i} \mathcal{D}[F] = \mathcal{D}$. This is a very simple instantiation of the framework of Cheng et al. with the condition of 1% coverage improvement acting as binary redundancy measure. A further deviation is that in our case the remaining patterns are not reordered after each selection step. While the original procedure constructs potentially more powerful feature collections, this simplified version is much faster: the time complexity is only linear instead of quadratic in the number of input features. For the final pattern collection $\mathcal{P}'$ the original data table T is then augmented by binary attributes corresponding to the elements of $F_1, \ldots, F_k \in \mathcal{P}'$. That is, the augmented table T' has $n + |\mathcal{P}'|$ columns with rows defined by

$$t'_i(j) = \begin{cases} t_i(j), & \text{if } j \leq n \\ 1, & \text{if } j > n \text{ and } D_i \supseteq F_{j-n} \\ 0, & \text{otherwise} \end{cases}$$

where D_i is the data record of $\mathcal{D}_T$ corresponding the the i-th row of T.

dataset	plain	$\mathcal{C}$	q_{freq}	q^2_{freq}	q_{disc}
autos	76.31	75.79	75.26	74.74	75.79
balance-scale	85.09	85.09	85.09	85.09	85.09
breast-cancer	70.37	**71.48**	**72.59**	**72.22**	**72.96**
colic	65.71	**67.14**	**67.43**	**66.86**	**66.00**
credit-a	85.44	84.56	85.00	85.15	85.00
diabetis	74.40	**75.20**	73.87	73.87	73.87
glass	63.00	**64.00**	**65.50**	**68.00**	**68.50**
heart-c	81.73	79.66	**82.76**	**82.76**	**82.07**
heart-h	82.50	81.79	81.43	81.43	81.79
heart-statlog	81.16	80.39	**83.08**	**83.46**	**82.69**
hepatitis	80.71	80.71	80.71	**85.00**	79.29
hypothyroid	97.55	97.53	97.50	**97.63**	**97.58**
iris	89.29	88.57	**91.43**	**91.43**	**91.43**
lymph	83.08	**85.39**	**85.39**	**83.85**	**84.62**
primary-tumor	40.94	**44.38**	**45.94**	**47.50**	**47.81**
sonar	78.42	77.37	78.42	78.42	78.42
tic-tac-toe	76.28	**92.55**	**96.60**	**96.60**	**94.15**
vehicle	67.95	**70.48**	**69.64**	**69.64**	**70.24**
zoo	91.11	91.11	**93.33**	91.11	**92.22**

Table 2: Accuracy of SVM classification on plain database and with feature enrichment based on frequent sets and sampled pattern collections (bold face indicates outperformed baseline).

The linear SVM of the LIBSVM software is used as **classifier**—wrapped in an optimization layer for its regularization parameter c. That is, the training set is first used to determine the optimal regularization parameter $c \in \{2^i : i = -5, -3, \ldots, 14\}$ using 5-fold cross-validation and then a model is trained with the optimal parameter using the whole training set. The complete workflow is validated using 10-fold cross-validation for all pattern collections simultaneously.

Table 2 contains the **results**. As one can observe, for some of the datasets pattern-based classification provides a substantial accuracy boost compared to the plain SVM baseline ("tic-tac-toe", "primary-tumor", "glass"). For others there is still an improvement but to a lesser extend, or the results are roughly identical. Most importantly, the sampling methods perform stronger than exhaustive top-k mining on a majority of datasets. A Wilcoxon signed ranks test (see [11]) for our $N = 19$ databases reveals that pattern-based classification with each of the random set collections outperforms the plain SVM significantly at the 5%-level (t-values of 42, 28.5, and 45.5 respectively; critical value 46). Moreover, although all random set collections are lying ahead of the frequent set collection on our test databases, it is not significantly outperformed by any of them. We can conclude that pattern-based classification based on all tested sampling algorithms is likely to outperform the plain SVM, and is unlikely to be inferior to standard frequent-pattern-based classification.

4.2 Scalability and Effectivity

Having evaluated the quality of the sampled patterns we now turn to scalability and effectivity studies.[3] The theoretical potential of the direct sampling procedures is already indicated by the guarantees of Propositions 1-4. In particular for frequency and area-based sampling they suggest applicability on larger to large-scale datasets. Below we investigate to what degree this potential can be realized in practice.

The practical advantages of direct pattern sampling over the MCMC pattern sampling algorithms are very clear: while for instance the closed set Markov chain simulation [6] takes seven minutes to sample a closed set from a 30K row subset of the US census dataset, frequency-based direct sampling takes only 0.067 seconds to draw the first sample including preprocessing—afterwards additional samples can be produced in milliseconds.

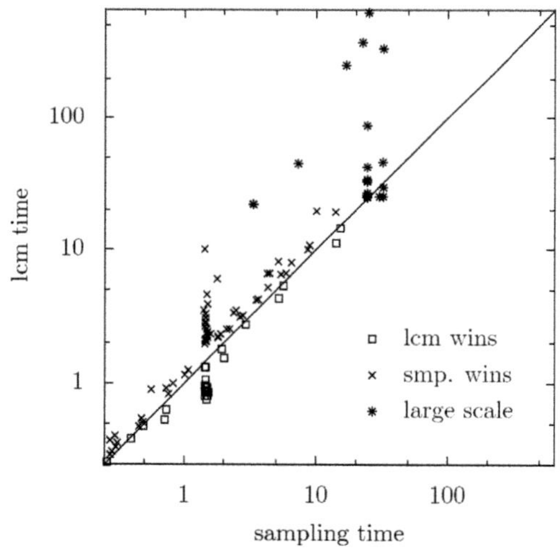

Figure 4: Time of lcm versus time of frequency-based sampling for an identical number of patterns.

For comparing direct sampling to exhaustive search algorithms there is a very large number of possible contenders in the literature, and, in principle, each of them requires an individual comparative study. For this paper we resort to

[3]Used hardware was a 2.67GHz 2 core CPU with 8GB RAM.

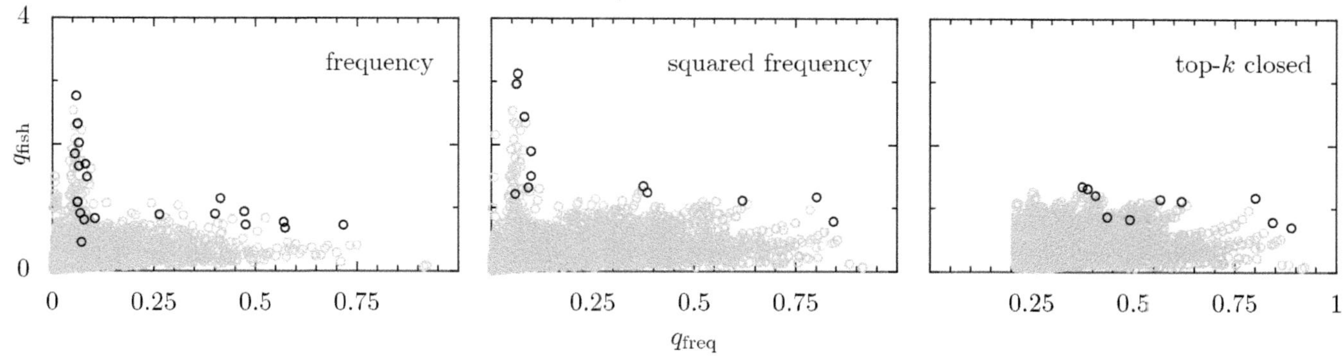

Figure 3: Pattern collections generated for "primary-tumor" by frequency-based sampling, squared-frequency-based sampling, and top-k closed frequent set listing; plotted according to frequency (x-axis) and Fisher score (y-axis); highlighted patterns are selected by feature selection procedure.

a rather general setting: we compare the computation time of the sampling algorithms with that of the linear closed frequent set mining algorithm (lcm) of Uno et al. [26] *per pattern*. For direct sampling this constitutes a worst-case setting because within the group of exhaustive methods frequent set mining algorithms usually produce the largest output per time unit and lcm is known to be among the fastest of them (winner of the FIMI contest [4]). In addition to the datasets used for the predictive performance study, we also consider several of the larger benchmark datasets of the FIMI workshop, including the 1GB sized "webdocs", and a 500MB random dataset.

The results are presented as log/log scatter-plot in Figure 4. One can observe that for most configurations lcm and the frequency-based sampling generate their patterns in approximately equal time with the majority of wins going to the sampling. However, focusing on the configurations with large-scale datasets (star symbol) reveals that the sampling algorithm can substantially outperform lcm. For "webdocs" this includes a speed-up factor of 10, for the random dataset even one of 25. We can conclude that frequency-based sampling can substantially outperform (closed) frequent set listing on large datasets and it performs equally well with slight advantage on small-scale data.

While the time performance of frequency-based sampling is also representative for area-based sampling, this is not true for the two sampling procedures with quadratic time weight computation phase. For almost all of the relatively small datasets of Tab. 1, this weight computation time is only marginal, i.e., less than 0.2 seconds. For large-scale datasets, however, the quadratic complexity is prohibitive; as already indicated on the 3772 row dataset "hypothyroid" where weight computation takes 13 seconds. After data record weights are computed, the performance is essentially equal to frequency-based sampling.

	$\mathcal{C}$	q_{freq}	q^2_{freq}
diabetes	**0.023** (0.066)	**0.023** (0.066)	**0.023** (0.066)
hypo.	0.016 (0.0190)	0.356 (3.613)	**0.414** (5.420)
lymph	**0.446** (0.580)	0.148 (0.352)	0.372 (0.580)
tumor	1.035 (1.270)	1.552 (3.630)	**1.725** (4.336)

Table 3: Average (maximum) Fisher score of features selected from pattern collections.

The scalability experiments above compared computation times for an equal number of generated patterns. This leads to the question of effectivity, i.e., what can be said about the quality per pattern? To this end, we again use the feature selection procedure from Section 4.1 and consider the quality of features within top-k frequent closed sets and random set families of the same size with respect to our measure of primary interest, the Fisher score; again using the setting of $k = 32\|\mathcal{D}\|$. This time we do not split the datasets according to the label, in order to avoid different values for global and local frequency of patterns (hence, we ignore discriminativity, which inherently requires splits). Table 3 shows the results of four datasets that are representative for different constellations: For datasets that contain high-frequency patterns with high discriminative power, as for instance for "lymph", the top-k paradigm is highly effective. Often, however, the patterns with high Fisher score are of relatively low frequency and are hidden (from the perspective of top-k frequent set listing) underneath a large pattern set of high frequency but low discriminativity. Such a constellation can for instance be observed for "primary-tumor" (see also Fig. 3).

5. CONCLUSION

We introduced four simple direct sampling procedures that generate random set patterns distributed according to frequency, squared frequency, area, and a discriminativity measure for binary labels. All procedures come with tight theoretical performance guarantees. Moreover, we described experimental studies demonstrating that the produced patterns are as useful as frequent pattern collections for pattern-based classification, and that direct sampling can compete with and often even outperform the fastest exhaustive mining algorithms when generating an equal number of patterns.

In the context of pattern-based classification there is a large amount of pattern discovery approaches that range from optimistic-estimator-based best-first-search algorithms [23] to methods interweaving model training and pattern discovery [10, 13]. Although such algorithms typically traverse much less patterns per time unit as lcm, their search is more directed towards high quality patterns. This motivates an in-depth comparative study with such methods potentially leading to more sophisticated usage of the sampling algorithms (e.g., applying it within model training just as the cited approaches do with exhaustive mining).

That said, pattern sampling as a paradigm is in no way restricted to pattern-based classification, and should also be evaluated for other in particular unsupervised model construction tasks as well as for exploratory data analysis. This is likely to motivate further variants of pattern sampling procedures. An example is the introduction of column and row weights to the interestingness measure in order to model subjective interest in certain parts of the input data or to decrease the probability of re-discovering redundant patterns.

Acknowledgments

Part of this work was supported by the German Science Foundation (DFG) under 'GA 1615/1-1' as well as by the European Commission under 'ICT-FP7-LIFT-255951' and 'EU-FP7-250527'. The authors would like to thank Andrea Pietracaprina and Fabio Vandin for providing the top-k closed frequent set mining software.

6. REFERENCES

[1] R. Agrawal, H. Mannila, R. Srikant, H. Toivonen, and A. I. Verkamo. Fast discovery of association rules. In *Advances in Knowl. Disc. and Data Min.*, pp. 307–328. 1996.

[2] M. Al Hasan and M. J. Zaki. Output space sampling for graph patterns. *PVLDB*, 2(1):730–741, 2009.

[3] S. D. Bay and M. J. Pazzani. Detecting group differences: Mining contrast sets. *Data Min. Knowl. Discov.*, 5(3):213–246, 2001.

[4] R. Bayardo, B. Goethals, and M. J. Zaki, editors. *Proc. IEEE ICDM Workshop on Frequent Itemset Mining Implementations, 2004*, vol. 126 of *CEUR Workshop Proc.*.

[5] S. Bistarelli and F. Bonchi. Soft constraint based pattern mining. *Data and Knowl. Engineering*, 62(1):118–137, 2007.

[6] M. Boley, T. Gärtner, and H. Grosskreutz. Formal concept sampling for counting and threshold-free local pattern mining. In *Proc. SIAM Int. Conf. on Data Mining (SDM 2010)*, pp. 177–188, 2010.

[7] M. Boley and H. Grosskreutz. Approximating the number of frequent sets in dense data. *Knowl. Inf. Syst.*, 21(1):65–89, 2009.

[8] V. Chaoji, M. A. Hasan, S. Salem, J. Besson, and M. J. Zaki. Origami: A novel and effective approach for mining representative orthogonal graph patterns. *Stat. Anal. Data Min.*, 1(2):67–84, 2008.

[9] H. Cheng, X. Yan, J. Han, and C.-W. Hsu. Discriminative frequent pattern analysis for effective classification. In *Proc. 23rd Int. Conf. on Data Engineering (ICDE 2007)*, pp. 716–725, 2007.

[10] H. Cheng, X. Yan, J. Han, and P. S. Yu. Direct discriminative pattern mining for effective classification. In *Proc. 24th Int. Conf. on Data Engineering (ICDE 2008)*, pp. 169–178, 2008.

[11] J. Demsar. Statistical comparisons of classifiers over multiple data sets. *J. of Mach. Learn. Res.*, 7:1–30, 2006.

[12] G. Dong and J. Li. Efficient mining of emerging patterns: Discovering trends and differences. In *Proc. 5th ACM SIGKDD Int. Conf. on Knowl. Disc. and Data Mining (KDD '99)*, pp. 43–52. ACM, 1999.

[13] W. Fan, K. Zhang, H. Cheng, J. Gao, X. Yan, J. Han, P. S. Yu, and O. Verscheure. Direct mining of discriminative and essential frequent patterns via model-based search tree. In *Proc. 14th Int. Conf. on Knowl. Disc. and Data Mining (KDD '08*, pp. 230–238, 2008.

[14] A. Frank and A. Asuncion. UCI machine learning repository, 2010.

[15] F. Geerts, B. Goethals, and T. Mielikäinen. Tiling databases. In *Proc. 7th Int. Disc. Science Conf.*, vol. 3245 of *LNCS*, pp. 278–289. Springer, 2004.

[16] L. A. Goldberg. *Efficient algorithms for listing combinatorial structures.* Cambridge University Press, New York, NY, USA, 1993.

[17] H. Grosskreutz, S. Rüping, and S. Wrobel. Tight optimistic estimates for fast subgroup discovery. In *Proc. European Conf. on Machine Learning and Knowl. Disc. in Databases (ECML/PKDD 2008), Part I*, vol. 5211 of *LNCS*, pp. 440–456, 2008.

[18] D. Gunopulos, H. Mannila, and S. Saluja. Discovering all most specific sentences by randomized algorithms. In *Proc. 6th Int. Conf. of Database Theory (ICDT '97)*, vol. 1186 of *LNCS*, pp. 215–229, 1997.

[19] J. Han, J. Pei, Y. Yin, and R. Mao. Mining frequent patterns without candidate generation: A frequent-pattern tree approach. *Data Min. Knowl. Discov.*, 8(1):53–87, 2004.

[20] D. J. Hand. Pattern detection and discovery. In *Proc. ESF Workshop on Pattern Detection and Disc.*, vol. 2447 of *LNCS*, pp. 1–12. Springer, 2002.

[21] R. M. Karp, M. Luby, and N. Madras. Monte-carlo approximation algorithms for enumeration problems. *J. Algorithms*, 10(3):429–448, 1989.

[22] A. J. Knobbe, B. Crémilleux, J. Fürnkranz, and M. Scholz. From local patterns to global models: the lego approach to data mining. In *From Local Patterns to Global Models: Proc. ECML/PKDD 2008 Workshop (LEGO '08)*, 2008.

[23] S. Morishita and J. Sese. Traversing itemset lattice with statistical metric pruning. In *Proc. 19th ACM SIGMOD-SIGACT-SIGART Symp. on Principles of Database Systems (PODS)*, pp. 226–236, 2000.

[24] A. Pietracaprina and F. Vandin. Efficient incremental mining of top-k frequent closed itemsets. In *Proc. 10th Int. Disc. Science Conf. (DS 2007)*, pp. 275–280, 2007.

[25] T. Scheffer and S. Wrobel. Finding the most interesting patterns in a database quickly by using sequential sampling. *J. of Mach. Learn. Res.*, 3:833–862, 2002.

[26] T. Uno, T. Asai, Y. Uchida, and H. Arimura. An efficient algorithm for enumerating closed patterns in transaction databases. In *Proc. 7th Int. Disc. Science Conf. (DS 2004)*, vol. 3245 of *LNCS*, pp. 16–31. Springer, 2004.

[27] S. Wrobel. An algorithm for multi-relational discovery of subgroups. In *Proc. 1st Euro. Symp. on Principles of Data Mining and Knowl. Disc. (PKDD '97)*, vol. 1263 of *LNCS*, pp. 78–87. Springer, 1997.

[28] M. J. Zaki, S. Parthasarathy, W. Li, and M. Ogihara. Evaluation of sampling for data mining of association rules. In *Proc. 7th Workshop on Research Issues in Data Engineering (RIDE)*, 1997.

Mining Frequent Closed Graphs on Evolving Data Streams

Albert Bifet, Geoff Holmes, and Bernhard Pfahringer
University of Waikato
Hamilton, New Zealand
{abifet,geoff,bernhard}@cs.waikato.ac.nz

Ricard Gavaldà
LARCA Research Group
UPC-Barcelona Tech
Barcelona, Catalonia
gavalda@lsi.upc.edu

ABSTRACT

Graph mining is a challenging task by itself, and even more so when processing data streams which evolve in real-time. Data stream mining faces hard constraints regarding time and space for processing, and also needs to provide for concept drift detection. In this paper we present a framework for studying graph pattern mining on time-varying streams. Three new methods for mining frequent closed subgraphs are presented. All methods work on coresets of closed subgraphs, compressed representations of graph sets, and maintain these sets in a batch-incremental manner, but use different approaches to address potential concept drift. An evaluation study on datasets comprising up to four million graphs explores the strength and limitations of the proposed methods. To the best of our knowledge this is the first work on mining frequent closed subgraphs in non-stationary data streams.

Categories and Subject Descriptors

H.2.8 [**Database applications**]: Database Applications—*Data Mining*

General Terms

Algorithms

Keywords

Data streams, closed mining, graphs, concept drift

1. INTRODUCTION

Graph mining is a challenging task that extracts novel and useful knowledge from graph data [19, 4]. Due to novel applications in social networks, chemical informatics, bioinformatics, communication networks, computer vision, video indexing and the Web [21], more and more large-scale graphs and sets of graphs are becoming available for analysis. Frequent pattern mining on graphs is one of the ways to obtain useful patterns, e.g. for discriminating graphs in classification and clustering tasks.

Conventional graph mining methods assume that the amount of data is limited and that it is therefore possible to store all data in memory or local secondary storage. There is no limitation on processing time, either. In the *Data Stream* model, we have space and time restrictions. Fundamentally, these restrictions imply the use of incremental techniques. Furthermore, as the data source is not necessarily stationary, methods must be able to adapt to changes over time in the data as well.

As the number of possible subgraphs is exponential, we propose to use *coresets* or compressed representations of the graphs based on closed patterns. Closed patterns are powerful representatives of frequent patterns, since they eliminate redundant information. A frequent pattern is *closed* for a dataset if none of its proper superpatterns has the same support as itself. Other possible definitions of a frequent closed pattern are the following:

- a frequent pattern is closed if it is one of the intersections of all transactions that contain it.
- a frequent pattern is closed if no superpattern is contained in exactly the same transactions as itself.

Generally, there are many fewer frequent closed graphs than frequent ones. In fact, we can obtain all frequent subgraphs with their support from the set of frequent closed subgraphs with their support. So, the set of frequent closed subgraphs maintains the same information as the set of all frequent subgraphs.

There are many methods for computing frequent closed itemsets (see [21]), frequent closed sequences [31, 28], and trees [18, 6, 26, 5], but only two for frequent closed graphs [30, 13], and none for frequent closed graphs on data streams.

We propose the first general methodology to identify closed graphs in a data stream. We develop three closed graph algorithms: IncGraphMiner, an incremental closed graph mining algorithm; WinGraphMiner, a sliding window-based closed graph mining algorithm; and finally AdaGraphMiner, an adaptive closed graph mining algorithm. "Adaptive" means that the model maintains at all times the closed graphs that are frequent in the current state of the data stream, that is, since the latest change in distribution was detected.

The rest of the paper is organised as follows. Sections 2 and 3 give background and present the novel weighted frequent closed pattern setting. Section 4 introduces a new coreset structure and its properties. Section 5 details the handling of concept drift and Section 6 introduces the general mining framework. Experimental results are given in Section 7, and conclusions are drawn in Section 8.

1.1 Related Work

There is a large body of work on itemset mining from data streams; see the survey [23] and the references therein. We can divide these data stream methods into two different classes depending on whether they use a landmark window, containing all the examples seen so far, or a sliding window. Only a small fraction of these methods deal with frequent closed mining. *Moment* [17], *CFI-Stream* [24] and *IncMine* [22] are state-of-the-art algorithms for mining frequent closed itemsets over a sliding window. *CFI-Stream* stores only closed itemsets in memory, but maintains all closed itemsets as it does not apply a minimum support threshold, with the corresponding memory penalty. *Moment* stores much more information besides the current frequent closed itemsets, but it has a minimum support threshold to reduce the number of patterns found. *IncMine* proposes a notion of semi-FCIs that increases the minimum support threshold for an itemset as it is retained longer in the window.

For trees, the work in [8] shows a general methodology to identify closed patterns in a data stream, using Galois Lattice Theory. This approach is based on an efficient representation of trees and a low complexity notion of relaxed closed trees, and presents an online strategy and an adaptive sliding window technique for dealing with changes over time. The approach is different to the one presented in this paper, as it does not use coresets, or weighted frequent mining techniques.

In terms of graphs, two main algorithms exist for mining frequent closed graphs:

- CloseGraph [30]: based on gSpan [29], a miner for finding frequent subgraphs, based on depth-first search (DFS)
- MoSS [13]: an extension to MoFa [11] based on breadth-first search (BFS).

Aggarwal et al. [3] present a mining methodology to find frequent and dense patterns in graph streams. Their notion of density is based both on node-occurrence and edge density, and they present an approach based on finding an approximation of the exact method with the use of a min-hash approach.

To the best of our knowledge the work presented here is the first work dealing with mining frequent closed graphs in streaming data that evolve with time.

2. PRELIMINARIES

We are interested in (possibly infinite) sets of graphs, endowed with a partial order relation $\preceq$ among these graphs. The set of all graphs will be denoted by $\mathcal{G}$, but actually all our developments will proceed in some finite subset of $\mathcal{G}$ which will act as our universe of discourse.

Given two graphs g and g', we say that g is a *subgraph* of g', or g' is a *super-graph* of g, if $g \preceq g'$. Two graphs g, g' are said to be *comparable* if $g \preceq g'$ or $g' \preceq g$. Otherwise, they are incomparable. Also we write $g \prec g'$ if g is a proper subgraph of g' (that is, $g \preceq g'$ and $g \neq g'$).

The input to our data mining process is a dataset $\mathcal{D}$ of weighted transactions, where each transaction $s \in \mathcal{D}$ consists of a transaction identifier *tid*, and a graph. The dataset is a finite set in the standard setting, and a potentially infinite sequence in the data stream setting. Tids are supposed to run sequentially from 1 to the size of $\mathcal{D}$.

Transaction Id	Graph	Weight
1	O | C - C - S - N | O	1
2	O | C - C - S - N | C	1
3	O | C - S - N | C	1
4	N || C - C - S - N	1
5	N || C - S - N	1
6	N || C - S - O	1

Table 1: Example of graph weighted transaction dataset.

Following standard usage, we say that a transaction s *supports* a graph g if g is a subgraph of the graph in transaction s. The number of transactions in the dataset $\mathcal{D}$ that support g is called the *support* of the graph g. A subgraph g is called *frequent* if its support is greater than or equal to a given threshold *min_sup*. The frequent subgraph mining problem is to find all frequent subgraphs in a given dataset. Any subgraph of a frequent graph is also frequent and, therefore, any supergraph of a infrequent graph is also infrequent (the *antimonotonicity* property).

We define a graph g to be *closed* (implicitly, w.r.t. to $\mathcal{D}$) if none of its proper supergraphs has the same support as g has in $\mathcal{D}$.

In this paper we focus our examples and experiments on molecular graphs, but our approach is general enough to be applied to any type of graph.

3. FREQUENT CLOSED WEIGHTED GRAPH MINING

In this section we introduce an extension to the frequent closed graph mining problem which enables the use of compressed graph representations in our adaptive methods: the frequent *weighted* closed graph mining problem. This problem differs from standard frequent closed graph mining in that each input graph has a weight, and this weight is used to compute its weighted support.

The input into the data mining process is a dataset $\mathcal{D}$ of weighted transactions, where each transaction $s \in \mathcal{D}$ consists of a transaction identifier, *tid*, a graph, and a weight value.

Graph	Relative Support	Support
N	-2	6
C - S	-3	6
C - C - S - N	3	3
O | C - S - N	3	3
N ‖ C - S	3	3
C - S - O	1	4
C - S - N	-1	5

Table 2: Example of a coreset with minimum support 50% and $\delta = 0$ for the transaction dataset of Table 1.

Table 1 shows an example of a weighted dataset with six molecule graphs [11].

The sum of the weights of transactions in the dataset $\mathcal{D}$ that supports g is called the *weighted support* of the graph g. For brevity, weighted support will be abbreviated to just *support*. A subgraph g is called *frequent* if its weighted support is greater than or equal to a given threshold *min_sup*.

We define a graph g to be *closed* if none of its proper supergraphs has the same weighted support as it has. A graph g is *maximal* if none of its proper supergraphs is frequent. All maximal graphs are closed but not necessarily otherwise. We define a graph g to be *δ-tolerance closed* [16, 25] if none of its proper frequent supergraphs has a weighted support larger than or equal to $(1-\delta)\cdot support(g)$. Note that a maximal graph is a 1-tolerance closed graph, and a closed graph is a 0-tolerance closed graph. Note that, from [8] we have the following propositions:

PROPOSITION 1. *Adding a transaction with pattern g to a dataset of patterns $\mathcal{D}$ where g is closed does not modify the number of closed patterns for $\mathcal{D}$.*

PROPOSITION 2. *Deleting a pattern transaction that is repeated in a dataset of patterns $\mathcal{D}$ does not modify the number of closed patterns for $\mathcal{D}$.*

Using these propositions we can observe that when adding to or removing from the weights of transactions, we are not modifying the number of closed patterns provided they remain frequent.

4. CORESETS OF CLOSED GRAPHS

A *coreset* [2] of a set P with respect to some problem is a small subset that approximates the original set P, in the sense that solving the problem for the coreset provides an approximate solution for the problem on the original set P. This notion was introduced in computational geometry to denote a small subset of points that can be used to obtain approximate solutions with theoretical guarantees.

For example, for clustering [1], a coreset for a set is a small set, such that for any set of cluster centers the clustering cost of the coreset is an approximation for the clustering cost of the original set with small relative error.

Graph	Relative Support	Support
C - C - S - N	3	3
O | C - S - N	3	3
N ‖ C - S	3	3

Table 3: Example of a coreset with minimum support 50% and $\delta = 1$ for the graph dataset of Table 1.

The main advantage of coresets is that we can apply any fast approximation algorithm on the usually much smaller coreset to compute an approximate solution for the original set more efficiently.

Here we use the set of frequent closed subgraphs as a smaller subset of the frequent subgraphs maintaining the same information but using less space. We define the *relative support* of a closed graph as the support of a graph minus the relative support of its closed supergraphs. We define the relative support in this way to exploit the fact that the sum of the closed supergraphs' relative supports of a graph is equal to its own support.

We define a *(s,δ)-coreset* for the problem of computing closed graphs as a weighted multiset of frequent δ-tolerance closed graphs with minimum support s using their relative support as a weight. Table 2 shows a (50%,0)-coreset for the dataset in Table 1 and Table 3 shows a (50%,1)-coreset for the same dataset.

Note that given a graph dataset D, its $(s,0)$-coreset is the set of frequent closed graphs, and its $(s,1)$-coreset contains the frequent maximal graphs. As the set of maximal graphs is contained in the set of closed graphs for a minimum support s, the set of graphs in the $(s,1)$-coreset is also a subset of the graphs in the $(s,0)$-coreset. For example, the set of graphs in the (50%,1)-coreset of Table 3 is a subset of the graphs in the (50%,0)-coreset of Table 2.

For two minimum supports s_L and s_H where $s_L < s_H$, the set of graphs in its (s_H,δ)-coreset is a subset of the graphs in the (s_L,δ)-coreset.

A coreset is a "compressed representation" of the original dataset. This compression is two-dimensional:

- Minimum support excludes infrequent graphs
- δ-tolerance excludes supergraphs with very similar support

In this paper we focus only on $(s,0)$-coresets, i.e., frequent closed graphs, as they are the only coresets that can guarantee the recovery of all frequent and frequent closed graphs with minimum support s. To show that this $(s,0)$-coreset outputs all the frequent subgraphs with minimum support s, we need the following proposition.

PROPOSITION 3. *Let $\mathcal{D}1$ and $\mathcal{D}2$ be two datasets of graphs. Let $C1$ and $C2$ be the $(s,0)$-coresets of closed graphs for $\mathcal{D}1$ and $\mathcal{D}2$. The set of closed graphs of $C1 \cup C2$ is exactly the set of closed graphs of $\mathcal{D}1 \cup \mathcal{D}2$.*

First, we note that the support of a graph in $C1$ and $C2$ is the same support of a graph in $\mathcal{D}1$ and $\mathcal{D}2$, due to the fact that the support of a graph in $C1$ and $C2$ is the sum of all relative supports. As the support of a closed graph in $\mathcal{D}1$ and $\mathcal{D}2$ is the same support as in $C1$ and $C2$, we can obtain from them the same closed subgraphs, using relative support instead of support.

PROPOSITION 4. *Let $\mathcal{D}1$ and $\mathcal{D}2$ be two datasets of graphs. Let $C1$ and $C2$ be the $(s,0)$-coresets of closed graphs for $\mathcal{D}1$ and $\mathcal{D}2$. The set of frequent graphs of $C1 \cup C2$ is exactly the set of frequent graphs of $\mathcal{D}1 \cup \mathcal{D}2$.*

To show that we can also obtain the frequent ones, we see that the frequent non-closed graphs have the support of their closure, so we obtain the same frequent graphs.

PROPOSITION 5. *Let $\mathcal{D}1$, $\mathcal{D}2$ and $\mathcal{D}$ be three datasets of graphs with $\mathcal{D} = \mathcal{D}1 \cup \mathcal{D}2$. Let $C1$, $C2$ and C be the $(s,0)$-coresets of closed graphs for $\mathcal{D}1$, $\mathcal{D}2$ and $\mathcal{D}$. The set of frequent graphs for $C1 = C \backslash C2 = C \cup \overline{C2}$ obtained using relative support for $C1$ and negative relative support for $C2$, is exactly the set of frequent graphs for $\mathcal{D}1 = \mathcal{D} \backslash \mathcal{D}2$.*

As the support of a graph in $C1$ is the support of the graph in C minus its support in $C2$, we can obtain the closed graphs in $C1$ by adding the closed graphs in $C2$, with negated relative support, to C.

In general terms, using $(s,0)$-coresets we can obtain all frequent, closed and maximal graphs with minimum support s without losing any information. Using (s,δ)-coresets we get more compact representations of the original dataset, and we can still obtain the maximal graphs, but we cannot completely recover all frequent closed graphs of minimum support s.

5. ESTIMATING FREQUENCIES ADAPTIVELY

To deal with concept drift, our methods have to be able to adapt to changes in the input distribution. Keeping a sliding window of recent elements is an option, however, it has the cost of maintaining it in memory. In this paper, we propose to use ADWIN to estimate frequencies of graphs with theoretical guarantees.

ADWIN (ADaptive sliding WINdow) [7] is a change detector and estimation algorithm. It solves, in a well-specified way, the problem of tracking the average of a stream of bits or real-valued numbers. ADWIN keeps a variable-length window of recently seen items, with the property that the window has the maximal length statistically consistent with the hypothesis "there has been no change in the average value inside the window".

More precisely, an older fragment of the window is dropped if and only if there is enough evidence that its average value differs from that of the rest of the window. This has two consequences: one, change is reliably detected whenever the window shrinks; and two, at any time the average over the existing window can be used as a reliable estimate of the current average in the stream (barring a very small or recent change that is not yet statistically significant).

The inputs to ADWIN are a confidence value $\delta \in (0,1)$ and a (possibly infinite) sequence of real values $x_1, x_2, x_3, \ldots, x_t, \ldots$ The value of x_t is available only at time t. Each x_t is generated according to some distribution D_t, independently for every t. We denote with μ_t the expected value of x_t when it is drawn according to D_t. We assume that x_t is always in $[0,1]$; rescaling deals with cases where $a \leq x_t \leq b$. No further assumption is being made about the distribution D_t; in particular, μ_t is unknown for all t.

ADWIN is parameter- and assumption-free in the sense that it automatically detects and adapts to the current rate of change. Its only parameter is a confidence bound δ, indicating how confident we want to be in the algorithm's output, inherent to all algorithms dealing with random processes.

It is important to note that ADWIN does not maintain the window explicitly, but compresses it using a variant of the exponential histogram technique [20]. This means that it keeps a window of length W using only $O(\log W)$ memory and $O(\log W)$ processing time per item, rather than the $O(W)$ one expects from a naïve implementation.

The main technical result in [7] about the performance of ADWIN is the following theorem, that provides bounds on the rate of false positives and false negatives:

THEOREM 1. *With ϵ_{cut} defined as*

$$\epsilon_{cut} = \sqrt{\frac{1}{2m} \cdot \ln \frac{4|W|}{\delta}}$$

where for some partition of W in two parts W_0W_1 (where W_1 contains the most recent items), and m is the harmonic mean of $|W_0|$ and $|W_1|$, at every time step we have:

1. (False positive rate bound). *If μ_t has remained constant within W, the probability that ADWIN shrinks the window at this step is at most δ.*

2. (False negative rate bound). *Suppose that for some partition of W in two parts W_0W_1 we have $|\mu_{W_0} - \mu_{W_1}| > 2\epsilon_{cut}$. Then with probability $1-\delta$ ADWIN shrinks W to W_1, or shorter.*

6. FREQUENT GRAPH MINING ON DATA STREAMS

In this section we present new graph mining methods for data streams using the results discussed in previous sections. We start by reviewing non-incremental basic methods, and then present the incremental miner INCGRAPHMINER, the sliding-window based miner WINGRAPHMINER, and the adaptive miner ADAGRAPHMINER.

6.1 Non-Incremental Graph Mining

[29, 30] presents two algorithms for computing frequent and closed graphs from a dataset of graphs, in a non incremental way. They represent the potential subgraphs to be checked for, being frequent and closed on the dataset, in such a way that extending them by one single node, in all possible ways, corresponds to a clear and simple operation on the representation. The completeness of the procedure is assured, that is, all graphs can be obtained in this way. This allows them to avoid extending graphs that have already been found to be infrequent.

The pseudocode of CLOSEGRAPH is presented in Figure 1. Note that the first line of the algorithm is a canonical representative check. Such checks are used frequently in tree and graph mining. The use of the right-most extension approach in CLOSEGRAPH, based on depth-first search, guarantees that all possible graphs are reached, but reduces the generation of duplicate graphs. CLOSEGRAPH selects the minimum DFS code based on a DFS lexicographical order as the canonical representative.

In MoSS [12], Borgelt et al. present a different method to perform frequent closed graph mining using breadth-first search instead of using the right-most extension approach.

```
CLOSEGRAPH(g, D, min_sup, S)
    Input: A graph g, a graph dataset D, min_sup.
    Output: The frequent graph set S.

if g ≠ CANONICAL_REPRESENTATIVE(g)
    then return S
isClosed ← TRUE
C ← ∅
for each g' that is a one step right-most
      extension of g
    do if support(g') ≥ min_sup
          then insert g' into C
       if support(g') = support(g)
          then isClosed ← FALSE
if isClosed = TRUE
    then insert g into S
for each g' in C
    do S ← CLOSEGRAPH(g', D, min_sup, S)
return S
```

Figure 1: The CloseGraph algorithm

```
INCGRAPHMINER(D, min_sup)
    Input: A graph dataset D, and min_sup.
    Output: The frequent graph set G.

G ← ∅
for every batch b_t of graphs in D
    do C ← CORESET(b_t, min_sup)
       G ← CORESET(G ∪ C, min_sup)
return G
```

```
CORESET(b_t, min_sup)
    Input: A graph dataset b_t, and min_sup.
    Output: The coreset C.

C ← CLOSEGRAPH(b_t, min_sup)
C ← COMPUTE_RELATIVE_SUPPORT(C)
return C
```

Figure 2: The INCGRAPHMINER algorithm

6.2 Incremental Mining

The incremental setting is different. Suppose that the data arrives in batches of graphs. We consider every batch of graphs b_t as a small finite dataset $\mathcal{D}_b$ of transactions, where each transaction $s \in \mathcal{D}_b$ consists of a transaction identifier, *tid*, a graph and a weight value. We maintain a set of graphs G and we update this set every time a new batch of graphs $\mathcal{D}_b$ arrives. We compute the coreset of the batch b_t, and then we use it to update the graph set G.

Note that using this methodology we can transform non-incremental methods into incremental ones by extending them to use weights and coresets of graphs. Figure 2 shows the pseudocode of INCGRAPHMINER.

```
WINGRAPHMINER(D, W, min_sup)
    Input: A graph dataset D, a size window W and min_sup.
    Output: The frequent graph set G.

G ← ∅
for every batch b_t of graphs in D
    do C ← CORESET(b_t, min_sup)
       Store C in sliding window
       if sliding window is full
          then R̄ ← Oldest C stored in sliding window,
                   negate all support values
          else R̄ ← ∅
       G ← CORESET(G ∪ C ∪ R̄, min_sup)
return G
```

Figure 3: The WINGRAPHMINER algorithm

6.3 Erroneous omission or inclusion bounds

When working on batches of graphs at a time, there is a possibility that the current batch does not contain enough occurrences of a frequent pattern, and it might also contain more than *min_sup* occurrences of an otherwise infrequent pattern. The probabilities for these two types of errors, erroneous omission or inclusion, can be bounded in the following way. Given a fixed batch size n, every *min_sup* value is equivalent to a probability p of finding a specific pattern in any given graph. Then, if the global true probability for some pattern is $p + \Delta$, and if we approximate the binomial distribution with the normal distribution $N(n * (p + \Delta), n * (p + \Delta) * (1 - p - \Delta)$, the following bound can be derived:

$$p_{discard}(\Delta, n) \leq \frac{1}{\sqrt{2\pi}} \cdot \int_{-\infty}^{-2\Delta\sqrt{n}} e^{-\frac{t^2}{2}}\, dt \qquad (1)$$

If $\Delta = 0$, then half of the patterns will be missed, but reasonably small values for Δ will already result in acceptable probabilities: if $n = 10000$, then $\Delta = 0.01$ results in less than 5% erroneous omissions or inclusions, and for $\Delta = 0.02$ this percentage is already very close to zero.

This type of argument is a heuristic that can be made formal (at the expense of worse figures) by the use of rigorous Hoeffding bounds, which underlie e.g. the `ADWIN` algorithm.

6.4 Mining with a Sliding Window

We present WINGRAPHMINER as a learner that maintains a sliding window. Its main important parameter is the size of the window W. The difference to INCGRAPHMINER lies in the management of the items in the sliding window. We update the recent frequent closed graphs, using the coresets of the new batches that arrive. When the window is full, we delete the oldest batch on the sliding window using negative relative support (Proposition 5).

Figure 3 shows the pseudocode of WINGRAPHMINER. When a new batch b_t arrives, the method performs as INCGRAPH-MINER, while the sliding window is not full. Once the window is full, the oldest coreset C is removed. The new coreset for G is computed in one step from the coresets of G and b_t, and C with negated relative support.

```
AdaGraphMiner(D, Mode, min_sup)
    Input: A graph dataset D, mode Mode and min_sup.
    Output: The frequent graph set G.

G ← ∅
Init ADWIN
for every batch b_t of graphs in D
     do C ← Coreset(b_t, min_sup)
        R̄ ← ∅
        if Mode is Sliding Window
           then Store C in sliding window
                if ADWIN detected change
                   then R̄ ← Batches to remove
                            in sliding window
                            with negative support
        G ← Coreset(G ∪ C ∪ R̄, min_sup)
        if Mode is Sliding Window
           then Insert # closed graphs into ADWIN
           else for every g in G update g's ADWIN
return G
```

Figure 4: The AdaGraphMiner algorithm

6.5 Adaptive Mining

Finally, we present AdaGraphMiner, an extension to the previous methods that is able to adapt to changes on the stream, maintaining only the *currently* frequent closed graphs.

We present two versions of this method. One uses an adaptive sliding window to maintain the batches of graphs. The other uses a separate ADWIN instance for managing the support of every single frequent closed subgraph.

Figure 4 shows the pseudocode of AdaGraphMiner, where the *Sliding Window* test distinguishes between the two methods.

Assume a scenario where at each time t the t-th element of the stream is a graph taken independently from a distribution D_t over a fixed universe $\mathcal{G}$ of graphs. Then, changes in the D_t's over time t are modelling the evolution in the stream. In particular, we say that "the stream is stationary between times $t1$ and $t2$" (for $t1 < t2$) if

$$D_{t1} = D_{t1+1} = \cdots = D_{t2-1} = \cdots = D_{t2}.$$

For a graph g, let $f_t(g)$ be the probability of g under distribution D_t, and $\hat{f}_t(g)$ the observed probability of g at time t (the number of times g has appeared in the window at time t divided by the length of the window). Since $\hat{f}_t(g)$ is our estimate of the current support of t, we would like it to be close enough to $f_t(g)$ to reliably decide whether g is frequent.

We can prove the following theorem:

Theorem 2. *Suppose the* ADWIN*'s in Algorithm* AdaGraphMiner *are initialized with parameter δ. For every time step $t1$, $t2$ such that $t1 < t2$, if the stream is stationary between $t1$ and $t2$, then for every $g \in \mathcal{G}$ we have with probability at least $1 - 2\delta$*

$$|f_{t2}(g) - \hat{f}_{t2}(g)| \leq \sqrt{\frac{1}{t2 - t1} \ln \frac{4W}{\delta}}$$

That is, if the stream remains stationary for T steps, the estimates of graph frequencies tend to the their value at a rate of roughly $O(1/\sqrt{T})$, which tends to 0 as $T \to \infty$. Observe that this is the best convergence rate obtainable by sampling even on a totally stationary stream. That is, the algorithm is able to effectively forget previous history, and converge at an optimal rate on stationary periods. Note that, if instead of ADWIN, we keep a simple sliding window of fixed size W the approximation will not tend to zero, but remain at about $1/\sqrt{W}$. The dependence on $\ln(W)$ in the theorem is to a large extent an artifact of the proof of ADWIN's guarantees, and in practice, slightly increasing the leading constant in the bound suffices for accurate results.

Proof. (Note: this proof uses both the definition of the ADWIN algorithm as well as Theorem 1 stating false positive and false negative ratios; see [7]).

Fix $t1 < t2$. We will show the following statement: For every fixed graph $g \in \mathcal{G}$, with probability at least $1 - 2\delta$ we have

$$|f_{t2}(g) - \hat{f}_{t2}(g)| \leq \sqrt{\frac{1}{t2 - t1} \ln \frac{4W}{\delta}}. \qquad (2)$$

Now also fix a graph $g \in \mathcal{G}$. If g is not present in the set G kept by the algorithm, then $\hat{f}_{t2}(g) = 0$ and an application of the Hoeffding bound shows that (2) holds for g. Otherwise, g is in the set G, so it has an associated instance of ADWIN, A. Say that, at time $t2$, A keeps a window of size W. Because the stream is stationary between $t1$ and $t2$, by Theorem 1, part (1), we know that $W \geq t2 - t1$ (i.e., the element gathered at $t1$ has not been cut out from A's window) with probability at least $1 - \delta$.

Let $t0$ be the oldest element present in the window, so that $t0 = t2 - W \leq t1$. Now let $\hat{\mu}_0$ (resp., $\hat{\mu}_1$) be the observed frequence of g in the window $[t0..t1-1]$ (resp., in the window $[t1..t2]$); observe that $E[\mu_1] = f_{t2}(g)$. Observe also that by the definition of ADWIN, if the interval $[t0..t1-1]$ has *not* been cut out from the window, we must have $|\hat{\mu}_0 - \hat{\mu}_1| \leq \epsilon_{cut}$, where

$$\epsilon_{cut} = \sqrt{\frac{1}{2}\left(\frac{1}{t2 - t1} + \frac{1}{t1 - t0}\right) \ln \frac{4W}{\delta}}.$$

The estimate produced by A at time $t2$ is the average of the elements in the window of length W, which is

$$\begin{aligned} \hat{f}_{t2}(g) &= \hat{\mu}_1 \cdot \frac{t2 - t1}{W} + \hat{\mu}_0 \cdot \frac{t1 - t0}{W} \\ &= \hat{\mu}_1 \cdot \frac{t2 - t1}{W} + (\hat{\mu}_1 \pm \epsilon_{cut}) \cdot \frac{t1 - t0}{W} \\ &= \hat{\mu}_1 \pm \epsilon_{cut} \cdot \frac{t1 - t0}{W}. \end{aligned}$$

Now using $W = t2 - t0$ and some simple algebra one can see

$$\begin{aligned} \epsilon_{cut} \cdot \frac{t1 - t0}{W} &\leq \sqrt{\frac{t1 - t0}{2(t2 - t1)(t2 - t0)} \ln \frac{4W}{\delta}} \\ &\leq \sqrt{\frac{1}{2(t2 - t1)} \ln \frac{4W}{\delta}}. \end{aligned}$$

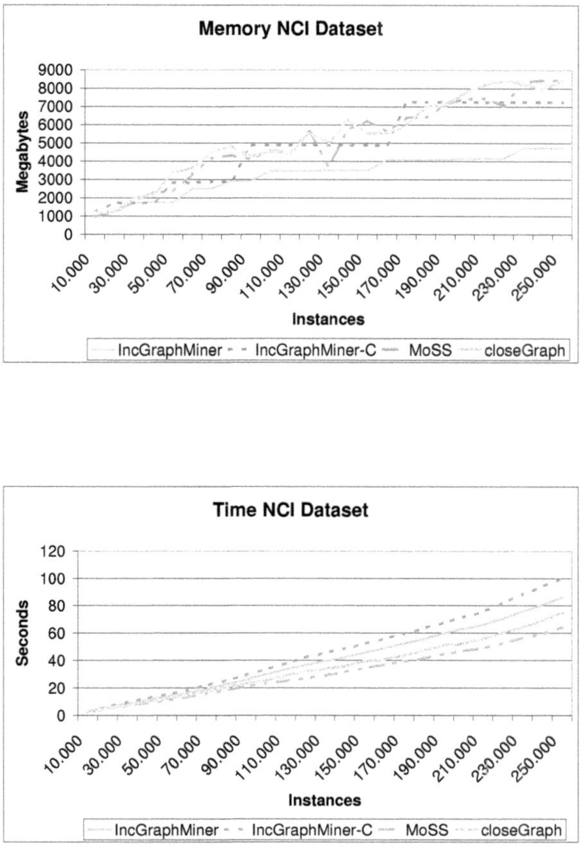

Figure 5: Memory and time used on Open NCI database with minimal support of 40%.

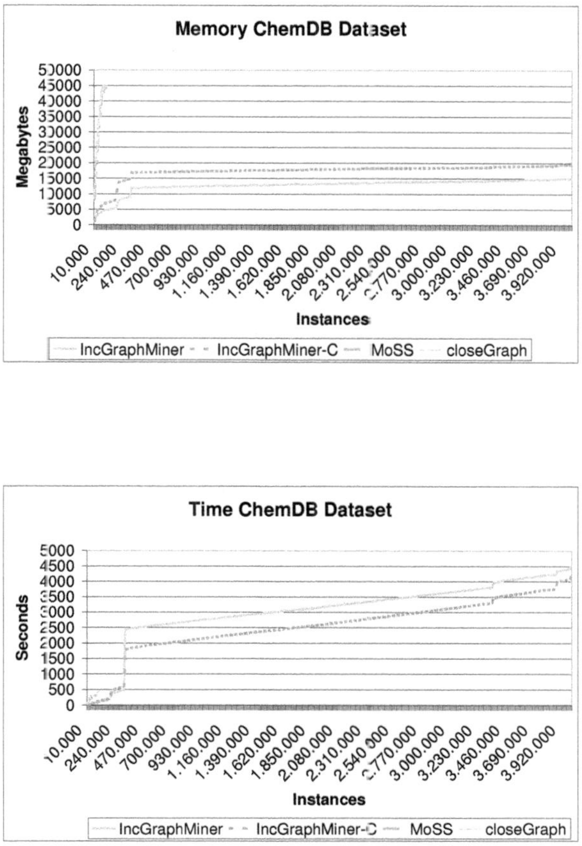

Figure 6: Memory and time used on ChemDB dataset with minimal support of 40%.

and by the Hoeffding bound and $E[\mu_1] = f_{t2}(g)$ we have

$$\Pr\left[|\hat{\mu}_1 - f_{t2}(g)| \leq \sqrt{\frac{1}{2(t2-t1)}\ln\frac{2}{\delta}}\right] \leq \delta.$$

Putting all of this together we conclude that, with probability at least $1-2\delta$,

$$\begin{aligned} |f_{t2}(g) - \hat{f}_{t2}(g)| &\leq \sqrt{\frac{1}{2(t2-t1)}\ln\frac{4W}{\delta}} + \\ &\quad \sqrt{\frac{1}{2(t2-t1)}\ln\frac{2}{\delta}} \\ &\leq \sqrt{\frac{1}{t2-t1}\ln\frac{4W}{\delta}}. \end{aligned}$$

as was to be proved. □

7. EXPERIMENTAL EVALUATION

We tested our algorithms on synthetic and real datasets. First, we compare our new incremental strategy with *closeGraph* and *MoSS* as non incremental methods to show the benefits in memory and time. Second, we perform experiments on data streams with synthetic concept drift to show the performance of our adaptive strategy.

We run our experiments extending MOA [10] using MoSS [12]. All experiments were performed on a 2.66 GHz Core 2 Duo machine with 64 GB of memory main memory, running CentOS 5.5.

Massive **O**nline **A**nalysis (MOA) [10] is a framework for online learning from continuous supplies of examples, such as data streams. It comprises online classification and clustering methods as well as tools for both offline and online evaluation.

MoSS is a batch framework for finding frequent molecular substructures and discriminative fragments in a database of molecule descriptions. MoSS is not restricted to molecular data sets, it can mine arbitrary data sets of attributed graphs. Apart from the default MoSS/MoFa algorithm, this framework also contains the gSpan [29] and CloseGraph [30] algorithms as special processing modes.

For our experiments we use the following real datasets:

ChemDB dataset ChemDB [14, 15] is a public dataset of approximately 4 million molecules built using the digital catalogs of over a hundred vendors and other public

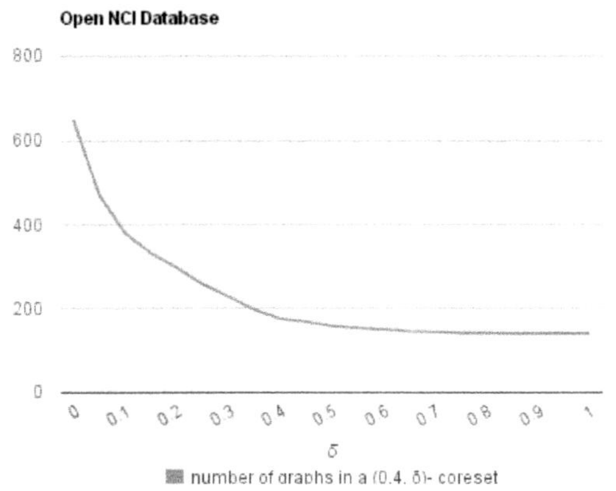

Figure 7: Number of graphs in $(40\%, \delta)$ for NCI.

sources. It is annotated with information derived from these sources as well as from computational methods, such as predicted solubility and 3D structure. It supports multiple molecular formats and is periodically updated, automatically whenever possible. It is maintained by the Institute for Genomics and Bioinformatics at the University of California, Irvine.

Open NCI Database The open National Cancer Institute (NCI) dataset [27] consists of approximately 250,000 structures. It is based on a large NCI database, built using samples from organic synthesis submitted to NCI for testing. While about half of the NCI database is not accessible, the other half of the structural data is free of any disclosure and usage restrictions and therefore termed "open". This data is public domain and often referred to as the "Open NCI Database".

First, we compare the runtime and memory usage of the incremental method IncGraphMiner to the non-incremental ones. As all methods are implemented in Java, the memory shown is the memory allocated by the Java Virtual Machine.

The results of our experiments using batches of $10,000$ instances, minimum support of 40%, $\delta = 0$, and 50 Gigabytes of maximum memory are shown in Figures 5 and 6. We test two incremental methods, IncGraphMiner based on MoSS, and IncGraphMiner-C based on closeGraph as batch learners. For the Open NCI database, which is the smaller dataset, we see that our new incremental methods need more time but less memory. However, for the larger ChemDB dataset, the non-incremental methods can only process about 110,000 instances before running out of memory (50 Gigabytes). Surprisingly, the incremental methods also outperform the non-incremental ones both in terms of runtime and memory usage for smaller subsets of ChemDB. Note that in Figure 6 there is a sudden bump in time used, since the graphs in this part of the stream are much larger.

Figure 7 shows the size of the coreset $(40\%, \delta)$ on the Open NCI database. For $\delta = 0$ there are 649 frequent closed graphs, and for $\delta = 1$ there are 140 frequent maximal graphs.

The next experiment shows how the new methods are able to adapt to changes in the distribution of graphs in an evolving stream scenario. Figure 8 shows the number of closed

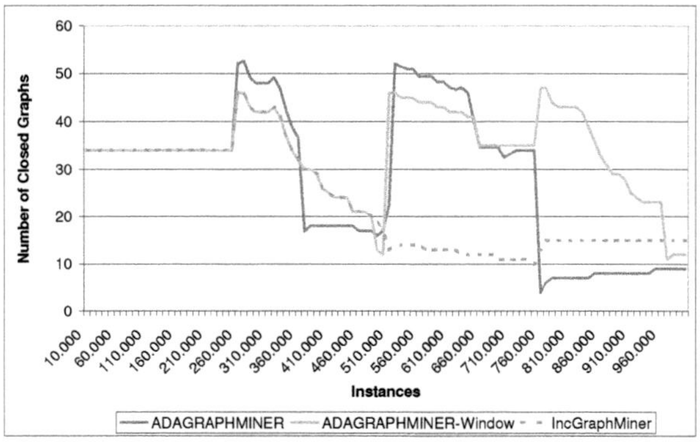

Figure 8: Number of frequent closed graphs on Open NCI database with minimal support of 40% with artificial concept drift.

graphs detected using the incremental method IncGraphMiner, and the two adaptive methods. AdaGraphMiner-Window uses a sliding window monitored only by one `ADWIN` instance, and AdaGraphMiner uses one `ADWIN` instance for each graph to monitor its support. In this experiment, the data stream exhibits artificial concept drift, as it is a concatenation of parts of two different streams. One is the Open NCI database and the other is an artificial data stream with exactly 15 frequent closed graphs generated artificially. Concept drift occurs three times, after 250,000, 500,000, and 750,000 examples, respectively. We follow the methodology in [9] to combine two data streams into one in order to create artificial drift. We observe that the incremental method is the slowest to adapt, as it does not have any forgetting mechanism. Comparing the adaptive ones, we see that AdaGraphMiner-Window, which only maintains one global `ADWIN` instance for change detection, shows a slower response to concept change. AdaGraphMiner, on the hand, can detect and respond to change faster, as it maintains a separate `ADWIN` instance for each graph.

8. CONCLUSIONS

We have presented the first efficient algorithms for mining frequent closed graphs on evolving data streams.

If the distribution of the graph dataset is stationary, the best method to use is IncGraphMiner, as no past transactions need to be forgotten. If the distribution evolves, then a sliding window method is more appropriate. If the right size of the sliding window is known in advance, then WinGraphMineris the method of choice, otherwise AdaGraphMiner is the preferred option.

Future work will analyze the impact of the size of batches and apply these new adaptive frequent mining techniques to discriminative graph feature generation for classification and clustering. Another ambitious direction for future work would be going beyond batch-incremental methods of graph mining, to develop methods that are fully instance-incremental. It is currently unclear how this could be done efficiently.

9. ACKNOWLEDGMENTS

UPC research is partially supported by the Spanish Ministry of Science and Technology TIN-2008-06582-C03-01 (SESAAME), by the Generalitat de Catalunya 2009-SGR-1428 (LARCA), and by the EU PASCAL2 Network of Excellence (FP7-ICT-216886).

The authors would like to thank Christian Borgelt for making his MoSS graph software available and for helpful discussions.

10. REFERENCES

[1] M. R. Ackermann, C. Lammersen, M. Märtens, C. Raupach, C. Sohler, and K. Swierkot. StreamKM++: A Clustering Algorithm for Data Streams. In *Proceedings of the Workshop on Algorithm Engineering and Experiments (ALENEX '10)*, 2010.

[2] P. K. Agarwal, S. Har-Peled, and K. Varadarajan. Geometric approximation via coresets. In J. E. Goodman, J. Pach, and E. Welzl, editors, *Combinatorial and computational geometry*, pages 1–30. Cambridge University Press., 2005.

[3] C. C. Aggarwal, Y. Li, P. S. Yu, and R. Jin. On dense pattern mining in graph streams. *PVLDB*, 3(1):975–984, 2010.

[4] C. C. Aggarwal and H. Wang. *Managing and Mining Graph Data*. Springer Publishing Company, Incorporated, 1st edition, 2010.

[5] H. Arimura and T. Uno. An output-polynomial time algorithm for mining frequent closed attribute trees. In *ILP*, pages 1–19, 2005.

[6] J. L. Balcázar, A. Bifet, and A. Lozano. Mining frequent closed rooted trees. *Machine Learning*, 78(1-2):1–33, 2010.

[7] A. Bifet and R. Gavaldà. Learning from time-changing data with adaptive windowing. In *SIAM International Conference on Data Mining*, 2007.

[8] A. Bifet and R. Gavaldà. Mining adaptively frequent closed unlabeled rooted trees in data streams. In *14th ACM SIGKDD*, pages 34–42, 2008.

[9] A. Bifet, G. Holmes, B. Pfahringer, R. Kirkby, and R. Gavaldà. New ensemble methods for evolving data streams. In *15th ACM SIGKDD*, pages 139–148, 2009.

[10] A. Bifet, G. Holmes, B. Pfahringer, P. Kranen, H. Kremer, T. Jansen, and T. Seidl. MOA: Massive Online Analysis, a Framework for Stream Classification and Clustering. *Journal of Machine Learning Research - Proceedings Track*, 11:44–50, 2010.

[11] C. Borgelt and M. R. Berthold. Mining molecular fragments: Finding relevant substructures of molecules. In ICDM '02, pages 51–, Washington, DC, USA, 2002. IEEE Computer Society.

[12] C. Borgelt, T. Meinl, and M. Berthold. Moss: a program for molecular substructure mining. In OSDM '05, pages 6–15, New York, NY, USA, 2005. ACM.

[13] C. Borgelt, T. Meinl, and M. R. Berthold. Advanced pruning strategies to speed up mining closed molecular fragments. In *IEEE Conf. on Systems, Man and Cybernetics (SMC 2004)*. IEEE Press, 2004.

[14] J. Chen, S. J. J. Swamidass, Y. Dou, J. Bruand, and P. Baldi. ChemDB: a public database of small molecules and related chemoinformatics resources. *Bioinformatics*, September 2005.

[15] J. H. Chen, E. Linstead, S. J. Swamidass, D. Wang, and P. Baldi. ChemDB update full-text search and virtual chemical space. *Bioinformatics*, 23(17):2348–2351, September 2007.

[16] J. Cheng, Y. Ke, W. Ng, and A. Lu. Fg-index: towards verification-free query processing on graph databases. In *SIGMOD Conference*, pages 857–872, 2007.

[17] Y. Chi, H. Wang, P. S. Yu, and R. R. Muntz. Moment: Maintaining closed frequent itemsets over a stream sliding window. In *Proceedings of the 2004 IEEE International Conference on Data Mining (ICDM'04)*, November 2004.

[18] Y. Chi, Y. Xia, Y. Yang, and R. Muntz. Mining closed and maximal frequent subtrees from databases of labeled rooted trees. *Fundamenta Informaticae*, XXI:1001–1038, 2001.

[19] D. J. Cook and L. B. Holder. *Mining Graph Data*. Wiley-Interscience, 2006.

[20] M. Datar, A. Gionis, P. Indyk, and R. Motwani. Maintaining stream statistics over sliding windows. *SIAM Journal on Computing*, 14(1):27–45, 2002.

[21] J. Han, H. Cheng, D. Xin, and X. Yan. Frequent pattern mining: current status and future directions. *Data Mining and Knowledge Discovery*, 15:55–86, 2007.

[22] Y. K. James Cheng and W. Ng. Maintaining frequent closed itemsets over a sliding window. *Journal of Intelligent Information Systems*, 2007.

[23] Y. K. James Cheng and W. Ng. A survey on algorithms for mining frequent itemsets over data streams. *Knowledge and Information Systems*, 2007.

[24] N. Jiang and L. Gruenwald. Cfi-stream: mining closed frequent itemsets in data streams. In *KDD '06*, pages 592–597, New York, NY, USA, 2006. ACM.

[25] I. Takigawa and H. Mamitsuka. Efficiently mining δ-tolerance closed frequent subgraphs. *Machine Learning*, 82(2):95–121, 2011.

[26] A. Termier, M.-C. Rousset, M. Sebag, K. Ohara, T. Washio, and H. Motoda. DryadeParent, an efficient and robust closed attribute tree mining algorithm. *IEEE Trans. Knowl. Data Eng.*, 20(3):300–320, 2008.

[27] J. H. Voigt, B. Bienfait, S. Wang, and M. C. Nicklaus. Comparison of the nci open database with seven large chemical structural databases. *Journal of Chemical Information and Computer Sciences*, 41(3):702–712, 2001.

[28] J. Wang and J. Han. Bide: Efficient mining of frequent closed sequences. In *ICDE*, pages 79–90. IEEE Computer Society, 2004.

[29] X. Yan and J. Han. gSpan: Graph-based substructure pattern mining. In *ICDM '02*, page 721, Washington, DC, USA, 2002. IEEE Computer Society.

[30] X. Yan and J. Han. CloseGraph: mining closed frequent graph patterns. In *KDD '03*, pages 286–295, 2003.

[31] X. Yan, J. Han, and R. Afshar. Clospan: Mining closed sequential patterns in large databases. In *SDM*, 2003.

Latent Topic Feedback for Information Retrieval

David Andrzejewski
Lawrence Livermore National Laboratory
Livermore, CA 94550
andrzejewski1@llnl.gov

David Buttler
Lawrence Livermore National Laboratory
Livermore, CA 94550
buttler1@llnl.gov

ABSTRACT

We consider the problem of a user navigating an unfamiliar corpus of text documents where document metadata is limited or unavailable, the domain is specialized, and the user base is small. These challenging conditions may hold, for example, within an organization such as a business or government agency. We propose to augment standard keyword search with user feedback on latent topics. These topics are automatically learned from the corpus in an unsupervised manner and presented alongside search results. User feedback is then used to reformulate the original query, resulting in improved information retrieval performance in our experiments.

Categories and Subject Descriptors

H.3.3 [**Information Storage and Retrieval**]: Information Search and Retrieval—*query formulation, relevance feedback*

General Terms

Algorithms, Experimentation

Keywords

latent topic models, user feedback

1. INTRODUCTION

This work addresses the problem of ad-hoc information retrieval and text corpus navigation under the following conditions. First, document metadata may be limited, unreliable, or nonexistent. Second, the domain of the text documents is specialized, using vocabulary ill-covered by general web documents or lexical resources such as WordNet [10]. Finally, while the text corpus itself may be large, the set of users accessing the corpus is not. This is an important problem because these conditions can preclude the use of effective information retrieval techniques such as faceted search or query log mining. These conditions are different from those encountered in general web or e-commerce search, but are realistic *within* organizations which are trying make sense of large quantities of text, such as private enterprises or government agencies.

A central problem in ad-hoc information retrieval is that users may not be able to formulate the "right" keyword combination in order to retrieve the most relevant documents. Techniques such as real-time query expansion [34] have been developed to directly attack this problem, but often rely upon a dataset of previously submitted queries, which may be sparse without a large user base. Another approach is to solicit alternative types of user input. Faceted document navigation [29] allows users to select documents based on different attributes (e.g., publication venues or hierarchical subject categories) and has emerged as a powerful complement to traditional keyword search. However, the standard assumption is that the facets are manually defined, and that facet values for each document are known.

Because of the challenging scenario we have defined, it is important to exploit all available data. Latent topic models such as Latent Dirichlet Allocation (LDA) [4] provide a means to take advantage of the statistical structure of the corpus itself. LDA assumes that observed documents have been generated by weighted mixtures of unobserved (latent) topics. These topics are learned from the documents and often correspond to meaningful semantic themes present in the corpus. LDA and its extensions have found interesting applications in fields such as natural language processing, computer vision, and social networks analysis [2].

The contribution of this work is a new method for obtaining and exploiting user feedback at the *latent topic* level. Our approach is to learn latent topics from the corpus and construct meaningful representations of these topics. At query time, we then decide *which* latent topics are potentially relevant and present the appropriate topic representations alongside keyword search results. When a user selects a latent topic, the vocabulary terms most strongly associated with that topic are then used to augment the original query. Our experiments with simulated user feedback show improved information retrieval performance. The presentation of relevant topics alongside search results also has the additional benefit of helping the user to understand corpus themes related to the original keyword query.

KDD'11, August 21–24, 2011, San Diego, California, USA.

Table 1: Example learned topic-word multinomials ϕ from three different datasets (see Table 5). For each topic ϕ_t, the five highest-probability words w are shown.

FT - Topic 1		WSJ - Topic 8		LA - Topic 94	
Word w	$P(w\|z)$	Word w	$P(w\|z)$	Word w	$P(w\|z)$
court	0.080	technology	0.094	gun	0.058
case	0.025	research	0.054	weapons	0.052
legal	0.024	high	0.025	assault	0.034
ruling	0.018	development	0.023	guns	0.029
appeal	0.018	cray	0.020	rifles	0.018

2. RELATED WORK

Our approach is partially motivated by the successes of faceted search [35]. Castanet [29] and related systems [9] aim to *automatically* construct facet hierarchies, but these techniques depend crucially on the existence of a rich lexical resource such as WordNet [10]. While specialized ontologies or controlled vocabularies have been constructed for some domains such as Gene Ontology (GO) [31] and Medical Subject Headings (MeSH) [5], the constraints of our setting prohibit us from assuming the existence of such a resource.

In light of this issue, topic models such as LDA have the advantage of relying upon corpus statistics alone. Indeed, previous analysis [23] of the digital library of the Open Content Alliance (OCA) directly posited the analogy between latent topics and faceted subjects, although specific mechanisms for exploiting this insight were not explored. The Rexa academic search engine[1] also displays relevant latent topics as tags for a given research article, allowing further investigation of the topics themselves. Another interesting topic modeling approach uses seed words to learn facet-oriented topics which can then be used to construct informative summaries [18].

LDA has previously been used in information retrieval for both document language model smoothing [33, 20] and query expansion [27]. These techniques both exploit the dimensionality reduction provided by LDA "behind the scenes" in order to improve performance, but do not leverage explicit user feedback in the way that our approach does. The approach we propose in this work can be viewed as complementary to these existing enhancements.

The BYU Topic Browser [11] provides an environment for rich explorations of learned LDA topics and how they relate to words and documents within a corpus. However, the tasks supported are more appropriate for advanced analysis by a relatively sophisticated user, as opposed to a general search setting.

3. OUR APPROACH

We propose to present automatically learned topics alongside keyword search results, allowing the user to provide feedback at the latent topic level. While it is well-known that we can learn latent topics with LDA, incorporating these topics into an information retrieval system requires us to address several questions. First, how should these topics be presented? Previous user studies [29] have found that users can become frustrated by raw LDA output. Second, which topics should be presented for a given query? To avoid overwhelming the user, we clearly cannot present all latent topics (potentially hundreds or greater) for every query. Furthermore, not all learned topics truly correspond to meaningful semantic concepts, and the presence of these incoherent topics will not be appreciated by users either. Third, how can we incorporate user latent topic feedback into search results? Ideally, the mechanism used should be simple and easy to integrate with existing search technologies. Finally, can this type of feedback improve information retrieval performance, as measured by standard metrics?

We now describe our approach, beginning with a brief review of latent topic modeling concepts and moving on to address the above questions. All examples shown are actual learned topics from the experimental datasets described in Table 5. In Section 4, experimental results demonstrate that our approach can indeed achieve performance gains.

3.1 Latent Dirichlet Allocation (LDA)

In LDA [4], it is assumed that observed words in each document are generated by a document-specific mixture of corpus-wide latent topics. We define our corpus of length N with the flat word vector $\mathbf{w} = w_1 \ldots w_N$. At corpus position i, the element d_i in $\mathbf{d} = d_1 \ldots d_N$ designates the document containing observed word w_i. Similarly, the vector $\mathbf{z} = z_1 \ldots z_N$ defines the hidden topic assignments of each observed word. The number of latent topics is fixed to some T, and each topic $t = 1 \ldots T$ is associated with a topic-word multinomial ϕ_t over the W-word vocabulary. Each ϕ multinomial is generated by a conjugate Dirichlet prior with parameter β. Each document $j = 1 \ldots D$ is associated with a multinomial θ_j over T topics, which is also generated by a conjugate Dirichlet prior with parameter α. The full generative model is then given by

$$P(\mathbf{w}, \mathbf{z}, \phi, \theta \mid \alpha, \beta, \mathbf{d}) \propto \left(\prod_t^T p(\phi_t|\beta)\right) \left(\prod_j^D p(\theta_j|\alpha)\right) \left(\prod_i^N \phi_{z_i}(w_i)\theta_{d_i}(z_i)\right),$$

where $\phi_{z_i}(w_i)$ is the w_i-th element in vector ϕ_{z_i}, and $\theta_{d_i}(z_i)$ is the z_i-th element in vector θ_{d_i}. Given an observed corpus $(\mathbf{w}, \mathbf{d})$ and model hyperparameters (α, β), the typical modeling goal is to infer the latent variables $(\mathbf{z}, \phi, \theta)$.

While exact LDA inference is intractable, a variety of approximate schemes have been developed [24, 4, 30]. In this work, we use Markov Chain Monte Carlo (MCMC) inference, specifically collapsed Gibbs sampling [12]. This approach iteratively re-samples a new value for each latent topic assignment z_i, conditioned on the current values of all

[1]http://rexa.info/

Table 2: Features used to determine "best topic word" labels for each topic. The topic-word posterior $P(z = t|w)$ is computed using Bayes Rule and a uniform prior over topics.

Description	Score
Word probability	$f_1(w) = P(w\|z = t)$
Topic posterior	$f_2(w) = P(z = t\|w)$
PMI	$f_3(w) = \sum_{w' \in W_t \setminus w} PMI(w, w')$
Conditional 1	$f_4(w) = \sum_{w' \in W_t \setminus w} P(w\|w')$
Conditional 2	$f_5(w) = \sum_{w' \in W_t \setminus w} P(w'\|w)$

other z values. After running this chain for a fixed number of iterations, we estimate the topic-word multinomials ϕ and the document-topic mixture weights θ from the final $\mathbf{z}$ sample, using the means of their posteriors given by

$$\phi_t(w) \propto n_{tw} + \beta$$
$$\theta_j(t) \propto n_{jt} + \alpha$$

where n_{tw} is the number of times word w is assigned to topic t, and n_{jt} is the number of times topic t is used in document j, with both counts being taken with respect to the final sample $\mathbf{z}$. The topic-word multinomials ϕ_t for each topic t are our learned topics; each document-topic multinomial θ_d represents the prevalence of topics within document d.

3.2 Topic representation

Typically, each learned topic-word multinomial ϕ_t is presented as a "Top N" list of the most probable words for that topic, as shown for three example learned topics in Table 1. We define the k-argmax operator to yield the k arguments which result in the k largest values for the given function. We use this operator to define the ten most probable words for topic t as W_t, given by the following expression with $k = 10$

$$W_t = \underset{w}{\text{k-argmax}}\, \phi_t(w)$$

We apply techniques from recent topic modeling research to improve on this basic representation. Our post-processing of the learned topics has three components: label generation, n-gram identification, and capitalization recovery.

For topic labeling, we assume the availability of a *reference corpus* containing themes similar to the target retrieval corpus. Since only raw text is required, this should be considerably easier to obtain than a full ontology, even for specialized domains. For example, a user exploring a corpus related infectious disease outbreaks could obtain a suitable reference corpus by crawling web resources from the United States Centers for Disease Control and Prevention. Since our experiments use general newswire corpora for evaluation, we use Wikipedia[2] as our reference corpus.

We label each topic using a simplified variant of the "Best Topic Word" [15] method. For a given topic t, this method selects a single word label from the top ten most probable words W_t, using features designed to test how representative each word is of the topic as a whole. We deviate slightly from Lau et al. to avoid relying upon WordNet, selecting the label word by majority vote among five features shown in Table 2 where each feature f_i casts its vote for the highest scoring word and ties are broken arbitrarily. Several of these features are computed from co-occurrence frequencies among words in W_t, counted within ten-word sliding windows taken over the reference corpus. Specifically, we compute the pointwise mutual information (PMI) and conditional occurrence probabilities between each pair of words (w, w') as

$$PMI(w, w') = \log \frac{P(w, w')}{P(w)P(w')}$$
$$P(w|w') = \frac{P(w, w')}{P(w')}$$

where $P(w, w')$ is the probability of jointly observing w and w' within a given sliding window, and $P(w)$ is the probability of observing w within a sliding window. Several example labels can be seen in the "label" column of Table 3.

Table 3: Topic representations for example high-PMI (coherent) and low-PMI (incoherent) topics.

PMI	Label	n-grams
3.09	jurors	Deputy Dist Atty
		cross examination, closing arguments
		trial, jury, case, testified
1.68	Petroleum	state oil company
		North Sea, natural gas
		production, exploration, field, energy
-0.09	things	(no trigrams found)
		pretty good, years ago
		ve, ll, time, don
-0.03	sales	(no trigrams found)
		year earlier, Feb Feb
		December, March, month, rose

We then identify statistically significant bigrams and trigrams (e.g., "White House", "President Barack Obama") for each topic using an approach based on the Turbo Topics [3] algorithm. This approach considers adjacent word pairs (w_i, w_{i+1}) occurring in the same document and assigned to the same topic (i.e., $d_i = d_{i+1}$ and $z_i = z_{i+1}$) and identifies pairs which occur much more often than we would expect by chance alone, proceeding similarly for trigrams. For each topic, we show the topic label along with the most significant trigram, the two most significant bigrams and the four most probable unigrams. Example latent topic representations are shown in Table 3.

Finally, we restore capitalization to the topic n-grams before presenting them to the user. As a pre-processing step, all text is converted to lower-case before doing LDA inference. However, the information conveyed by capitalization can ease user interpretation of topics (e.g., by making proper names obvious). For each n-gram, we simply count all occurrences of each possible capitalization occurring in the original documents, and present the most frequent version to the user.

[2]http://www.wikipedia.org

3.3 Topic selection

It will typically be necessary to learn at least hundreds of latent topics in order to get suitably fine-grained topics for user feedback. This makes it impractical to present all topics to the user after every query; we therefore must decide which topics to present.

We use the idea of pseudo-relevance feedback [6] by assuming that the top two documents returned by the original query q, which we call D_q, are relevant. For each of these documents, we consider the top $k = 2$ topics as determined by the topic weights θ to be *enriched* topics for the user query. This constitutes a natural set of candidates for latent topic feedback, and can be defined as

$$E = \bigcup_{d \in D_q} \text{k-argmax}_t \ \theta_d(t).$$

However, we also show the user topics that are *related* to the enriched topic set E, but which may themselves not be present in the highly ranked documents. We identify related topics by looking for topics highly likely to co-occur with the enriched topics E, using the $T \times T$ topic covariance matrix Σ of the estimated $D \times T$ document-topic θ matrix. Letting $\Sigma(t_1, t_2)$ be the covariance between $P(z = t_1|d)$ and $P(z = t_2|d)$ computed over all documents $d = 1, \ldots, D$, we take the $k = 2$ topics with the highest covariance with each of our enriched topics in E. We define this *related* topic set as

$$R = \bigcup_{t \in E} \text{k-argmax}_{t' \notin E} \ \Sigma(t, t').$$

The candidate topics for feedback are the union of the enriched and related topics $E \cup R$, but we perform a final filter before presenting these topics to the user.

One hazard of presenting automatically discovered latent topics to the user is the threat of incoherent "junk" topics which do not seem to have a single clear theme. We filter out these topics using a recently developed topic evaluation method [26, 25] which has been shown to predict human topic quality judgments at nearly the inter-annotator agreement rate. Similar to the topic labeling technique, this method uses PMI values computed over a reference corpus (again, we use Wikipedia), except that we now apply these scores to the topics themselves. We compute the PMI score of a topic t as the average PMI between all pairs of words within the top $k = 10$ most probable words W_t

$$PMI(t) = \frac{1}{k(k-1)} \sum_{(w,w') \in W_t} PMI(w, w').$$

Table 3 shows example high-PMI (coherent) and low-PMI (incoherent) latent topics.

We can use these PMI values to avoid confusing users with incoherent topics. Letting PMI_{25} be the 25th percentile PMI score among all learned topics, we define our set of "dropped" topics D as

$$D = \{t | t \in E \cup R \text{ and } PMI(t) < PMI_{25}\}.$$

We present the topics in $\{E \cup R\} \setminus D$ to the user alongside the returned documents for the original keywords query q. Note that the union operations and final filtering mean that the number of topics actually presented to the user may vary from query to query. Since we consider the top two topics within the top two documents, along with each of their top two related topics, we will present a maximum of $(2 \times 2) + (2 \times 2 \times 2) = 12$ topics, minus set overlaps and PMI-filtered topics.

3.4 Query expansion

If the user selects a topic as relevant, we reformulate the query by combining the top ten most probable words W_t for that topic with the original query q. To preserve the intent of the original query, we use the Indri [22] `#weight()` operator to form a weighted combination of the original query keywords and the highly probable latent topic words. The weight parameter $\gamma \in [0, 1]$ controls the trade-off between the original query keywords and the latent topic words. A larger γ value places more weight on the new latent topic words, while setting $\gamma = 0$ is equivalent to the original keyword query.

Each of the N_q words in the original query is given weight $(1 - \gamma)/N_q$ and each new topic t word w is given weight $\gamma * \tilde{\phi}_t(w)$, where $\tilde{\phi}$ is the re-normalized topic-word probability

$$\tilde{\phi}_t(w) = \frac{\phi_t(w)}{\sum_{w' \in W_t} \phi_t(w')}.$$

While our implementation uses the Indri query language, it would be straightforward to achieve similar results in other information retrieval systems and frameworks (e.g., by using term boosting in Apache Lucene[3]).

3.5 Example

We now walk through an example query for a corpus of news articles from the Financial Times (FT). The query is "euro opposition", and it targets documents discussing opposition to the introduction of the single European currency. The corpus, query, and relevance judgments used here are drawn from our experimental dataset which will be used in Section 4. The number of topics used is $T = 500$.

The *enriched* topics E shown in Table 5a consist of three distinct topics: two topics related to the euro debate within the United Kingdom and Denmark, and a confusing topic vaguely centered around "business" which is *dropped* by our PMI filtering. Within this topic, the interesting trigram "PERSONAL FILE Born" arises from brief biographies sometimes found at the bottom of the articles.

High θ covariance with topics in E is then used to identify the five *related* topics R shown in Table 5b, which deal with various aspects of business and politics. However the appearance of "economic monetary union" and "Europe" in the topic 79 representation appear highly related to the euro currency union, and indeed selecting this topic as feedback improves retrieval results. Selecting topic 79 as user feedback and setting the feedback weight $\gamma = 0.25$, our approach produces an expanded query containing the most probable words from topic 79

```
#weight(0.375 euro, 0.375 opposition,
        0.031 European, ..., 0.015 Emu).
```

[3]http://lucene.apache.org/

Table 4: A detailed example of our approach for the query "euro opposition" on the Financial Times (FT) corpus. The strikethrough topic 466 is not presented to the user due to low PMI coherence score. The bolded topic 79 results in improved information retrieval performance versus the baseline query: NDCG15 increases 0.22, NDCG increases 0.07, and MAP increases 0.02. The prominent term "Emu" appears to be an alternate form of the acronym "EMU" commonly used in Financial Times articles.

Enriched topic	Terms
196 (debate)	Tory Euro sceptics
	social chapter, Liberal Democrat
	mps, Labour, bill, Commons
404 (ratification)	ratification Maastricht treaty
	Poul Schluter, Poul Rasmussen
	Danish, vote, Denmark, ec
~~466 (business)~~	PERSONAL FILE Born
	years ago, past years
	man, time, job, career

(a) Enriched topics E.

Related topic	Terms
79 (Emu)	economic monetary union
	Maastricht treaty, member states
	European, Europe, Community, Emu
377 (George)	President George Bush, White House
	Mr Clinton, administration
	Democratic, Republican, Washington
115 (powers)	de regulation bill
	Sunday trading, Queen Speech
	law, legislation, government, act
446 (years)	chairman chief executive
	managing director, finance director
	Sir, board, group, company
431 (cabinet)	Mr John Major
	prime minister, Mr Major
	party, tory, government, Conservative

(b) Related topics R.

Using ground truth document relevance judgments, we can see that documents returned by this expanded query have superior performance on standard information retrieval measures as described in the caption of Table 4. Figure 1 shows the receiver operating characteristic (ROC) curves for the baseline query (dotted) and the expanded topic 79 query (solid). Points on the ROC curve correspond to the true positive rates (TPR) and false positive rates (FPR) for sets of documents returned at different ranking thresholds. Here we consider the true positive (TP) set to be the union of relevant documents found within the top 500 documents returned by both queries. This plot visually depicts a clear improvement in the ranking of relevant documents. An additional benefit is that users are given the opportunity to see and explore different aspects of "euro opposition" such as the political dimension with respect to the United Kingdom.

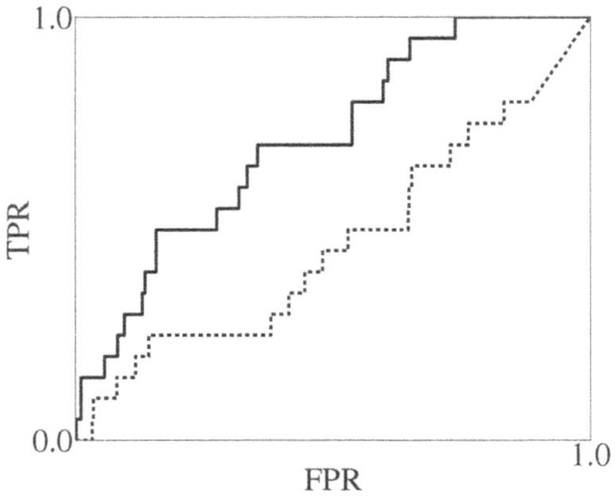

Figure 1: ROC curve of baseline (dashed) versus topic 79 feedback (solid) for the example query "euro opposition".

4. EXPERIMENTS

To our knowledge there has been no attempt to use latent topics as a user feedback mechanism in the way we have described. To determine whether our approach could be genuinely useful in practice, we must answer several questions. First, can query expansion with latent topic feedback improve the results of actual queries? While previous work has found that latent topics align well with existing document subject categories [23], it may be that these categories are more "topically coherent" than the relevant result sets for ad-hoc queries, and therefore more suitable for topic modeling. Second, assuming that for a given query there exists some latent topic which would improve retrieval results, will the topic selection approach described in Section 3.3 present it to the user? Finally, there is a third question which we do not address in this work: if presented with a helpful topic, will a user actually select it? For the following experiments we make the simplifying assumption that the user will always select the most helpful topic (with respect to the information retrieval measure of interest) among those presented. If no topic feedback will improve the set of returned documents, we assume the user will not provide topic feedback.

4.1 Experiment setup

While the ultimate goal of this work is to improve search and navigation under the specialized conditions described in Section 1, we evaluate our approach by conducting information retrieval experiments on several benchmark datasets from the Text REtrieval Conference (TREC) [32], using Wikipedia as a reference corpus. Each datasets consists of a corpus of text documents, a set of queries, and relevance judgments for each query. For each query, the individual words in the the title field are used as the baseline keyword query (e.g., "Industrial Espionage" is broken up into "Industrial", "Espionage"). Table 5 shows dataset details.

For each corpus, we first apply the LDA model to learn a set of latent topics, using the MALLET topic modeling toolkit [21]. We pre-process documents by downcasing, removing numbers and punctuation, applying a standard stopword list, and finally filtering out rarely occurring terms to yield vocabulary sizes of between 10,000 and 20,000 terms. We run parallelized collapsed Gibbs inference for 1,000 samples, re-estimating the document-topic hyperparameter α

Table 5: TREC datasets and queries (known within TREC as "topics") used in experimental evaluations. The number of documents D is given in thousands and Q denotes the number of queries.

Corpus	Abbrev	D	Q	TREC topics
Associated Press	AP	243	100	51-150
Financial Times	FT	210	200	251-450
Los Angeles Times	LA	128	150	301-450
Wall Street Journal	WSJ	173	100	51-100 151-200
Federal Register	FR	37	150	301-450
Foreign Broadcast Information Service	FBIS	127	150	301-450

every 25 samples. We learn $T = 500$ topics for each corpus in our experimental dataset, except $T = 250$ for the significantly smaller Federal Register (FR) corpus.

For all queries, we use the Galago [8] information retrieval system with default settings to retrieve 500 documents. Galago uses a query language and retrieval model based on Indri [22]. For the topic-expanded queries we set $\gamma = 0.25$, based on trial-and-error experimentation on held-aside preliminary development datasets.

4.2 Results

We calculate improvement over the baseline query with respect to three information retrieval measures [8]: mean average precision (MAP), normalized discounted cumulative gain (NDCG), and NDCG calculated with the first 15 results only (NDCG15). These quantitative results are shown in Table 6, along with the average number of feedback candidate topics shown to the user by our topic selection technique (fewer than eight topics per query).

We now return to the experimental questions we had set out to answer. These results demonstrate that latent topic feedback can indeed improve information retrieval results. Across evaluation measures, the results of approximately 40% of queries can be improved by latent topic feedback. However, these gains are irrelevant if we cannot identify potentially helpful topics and present them to the user. Again across measures, we see that our topic selection approach is able present a helpful topic for more than 40% of the queries for which there exists at least one helpful topic. Doing the rough arithmetic, this means that for about 16% of the queries in our experiment the user would be presented with at least one latent topic which would improve the relevance of the returned documents. Furthermore, we stress that even for the "missed" queries where presented topics do not provide quantitative relevance improvement, the corpus theme information conveyed may still be beneficial.

To give a better feel for the nature of these results, Figure 2 shows six queries along with helpful topics which were selected for presentation by our approach. In all cases, the connection between the topic and the query is fairly clear, resulting in gains across retrieval performance measures and visible improvement on ROC curves.

4.3 Analysis

First, we observe that for most queries (roughly 60%), there did not exist a single latent topic for which feedback would enhance information retrieval results. From manual inspection, this can occur because either no learned topic is well-aligned with the relevant documents, or because the results of the original query are good and difficult to improve upon.

Second, for queries where there exists one or more topics which *would* improve results, roughly 60% of the time our topic selection approach fails to select them. Minor variations on our topic selection method (i.e., showing more topics) did not correct this – many of the "missed" topics are not even close to making the cutoff. Manual investigations reveal that, interestingly, these topics often appear to be helpful *because* they are somewhat "distant" from the original query and the top few baseline documents returned. Attempts to predict topic feedback gain using linear or logistic regression and features such as $P(\text{query}|\phi_t)$ were unsuccessful, although more sophisticated approaches or richer features could possibly be applied.

It is also instructive to further examine the impact of two key aspects of our topic selection procedure: the inclusion of related topics and the exclusion of incoherent topics. For simplicity we will discuss NDCG15 measurements, but similar results hold for MAP and NDCG. Our selection approach recovers helpful topics for 133 out of 850 queries (15.6%) while presenting an average of 7.76 topics to the user for each query.

If we do *not* use PMI to filter out topics suspected of being incoherent, the number of topics shown per query rises to 9.79, but the number of queries for which helpful topics are presented only increases to 143 out of 850 (16.8%). The presence of incoherent topics may also impose cognitive burdens on the user, and it is uncertain whether users would be able to successfully identify incoherent topics for feedback.

If we were to omit the related topics R, it would decrease the average number of topics shown to 2.70, but it would decrease substantially the number of queries for which a helpful topic is presented, down to 93 out of 850 (10.9%). Also, we note that the presentation of related topics is potentially useful for exploratory corpus search, giving the user information about corpus themes "adjacent" to the topics present in returned documents.

Taken together, these findings suggest that our topic selection procedure is reasonable. The inclusion of related topics considerably increases the number of queries for which we present helpful topics while presenting novel and possibly interesting corpus themes. The filtering of suspect low-PMI topics does not discard many helpful topics, and should spare users the ordeal of interpreting ill-defined topics.

5. DISCUSSION

In this work we have developed a novel technique for improving text corpus search and navigation in difficult settings where we do not have access to metadata, rich lexical resources, or large user populations. This is an important problem because these conditions make information retrieval more difficult, and are applicable within organizations that have large quantities of *internal* text documents which they wish to explore, analyze, and exploit.

Table 6: Improvement from simulated latent topic feedback calculated only over queries where feedback improves performance. The "avg shown" column indicates the average number of topics actually shown to the user as a result of the topic selection procedure described in Section 3.3. For each query and evaluation measure, the "imprv" column shows the number of queries for which there *exists* at least one latent topic which improves performance, "found" shows the number of queries for which a helpful topic is *actually presented* to the user by our selection scheme, and "avg gain" shows the mean improvement when a helpful topic is presented to the user.

			NCDG15			NCDG			MAP		
Corpus	Q	avg shown	imprv	found	avg gain	imprv	found	avg gain	imprv	found	avg gain
AP	100	7.79	32	16	0.165	32	21	0.093	31	20	0.037
FT	200	7.47	97	43	0.238	138	80	0.134	137	72	0.041
LA	150	8.65	79	27	0.090	81	27	0.070	82	29	0.027
WSJ	100	7.73	29	16	0.205	30	18	0.050	29	18	0.026
FR	150	7.22	26	10	0.131	39	13	0.034	39	11	0.024
FBIS	150	7.78	62	21	0.163	64	25	0.037	67	29	0.024

To enhance search and exploration capabilities in this scenario, we have developed an approach that gives users the ability to provide feedback at the latent topic level. We leverage recent advances in latent topic modeling in order to construct meaningful representations of latent topics while filtering out incoherent "junk topics". We propose a mechanism for deciding on a manageably small set of topics to present to the user, as well as a method for constructing expanded queries based on user topic feedback. Quantitative results on benchmark TREC datasets show that this technique can result in major improvements for a non-trivial proportion of queries. Furthermore, the presentation of enriched and related topics alongside search results can help to deliver insights about corpus themes, which may be beneficial for knowledge discovery as well.

One potential obstacle to this approach is the scalability bottleneck presented by LDA topic inference. However, two factors act to ameliorate these concerns. First, topics can be inferred "offline" in advance; we do not need to do any expensive inference at query-time. Second, there have been significant recent advances along multiple fronts in scalable LDA inference. A distributed system developed at Yahoo! is reported to process 42,000 documents per hour [28]. Alternatively, an online inference algorithm for LDA [13] promises both improved scalability and a principled means of updating topics to reflect new documents. In practice, a hybrid system could update topics in an online fashion as documents are received, periodically performing distributed batch inference to refresh the learned topics.

6. FUTURE WORK

There are several promising directions in which to extend this approach. Two obvious areas for improvement are increasing the proportion of queries for which a helpful topic exists and improving the selection method for presenting helpful topics to the user.

It may be possible to improve the alignment between learned topics and user queries by the use of more sophisticated topic models such as the Pachinko Allocation Model (PAM) [16]. While these models were *not* found to be helpful for document smoothing [36], rich hierarchical topics may be beneficial when combined with the *explicit* user feedback present in our approach. Our approach could also exploit prior information such as predefined concepts by using topic model variants which can incorporate domain knowledge [7, 1].

However, learning finer-grained topics can only increase the importance of carefully choosing which topics to show the user. Here it may be instructive to consider the large body of research on "learning to rank" [19], as well as recent work in facet selection [17, 14].

The query expansion mechanism is another potential target for extension. If our underlying information retrieval system supports phrase search terms (e.g., "White House"), it may be helpful to directly use discovered n-grams as well.

Further work could also compare the use of topics for explicit feedback in this work versus the implicit use of topics to improve document language models in prior work [33]. It may be that the two techniques could be combined profitably, with some topics being more suitable for explicit feedback while others are better used for smoothing.

Finally, another important step is to validate our user model assumptions. One approach may be to directly evaluate information retrieval performance using actual user feedback, for example via Amazon Mechanical Turk [37]. It may also be interesting to explore the relationship between topic presentation (e.g., topic labeling strategies, whether to display n-grams) and user behavior.

7. ACKNOWLEDGMENTS

This work was performed under the auspices of the U.S. Department of Energy by Lawrence Livermore National Laboratory under Contract DE-AC52-07NA27344 (LLNL-CONF-471258).

8. REFERENCES

[1] D. Andrzejewski, X. Zhu, and M. Craven. Incorporating domain knowledge into topic modeling via Dirichlet forest priors. In *ICML*, pages 25–32. Omnipress, 2009.

[2] D. Blei, L. Carin, and D. Dunson. Probabilistic topic models. *Signal Processing Magazine, IEEE*, 27(6):55 –65, 2010.

[3] D. Blei and J. Lafferty. Visualizing topics with multi-word expressions. Technical report, 2009. `arXiv:0907.1013v1 [stat.ML]`.

[4] D. Blei, A. Ng, and M. Jordan. Latent Dirichlet allocation. *JMLR*, 3:993–1022, 2003.

FBIS query 426 "law enforcement dogs"
Topic 321 (heroin) seized kg cocaine drug traffickers, kg heroin police, arrested, drugs, marijuana

NDCG15	NDCG	MAP
+0.299	+0.065	+0.046

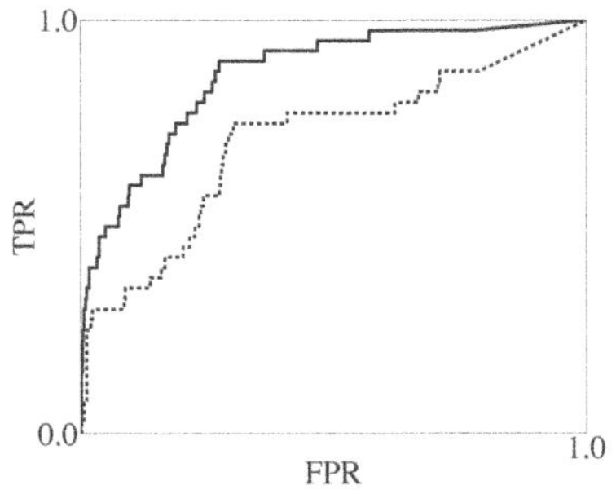

FBIS query 450 "King Hussein, peace"
Topic 293 (Amman) Majesty King Husayn al Aqabah, peace process Jordan, Jordanian, Amman, Arab

NDCG15	NDCG	MAP
+0.708	+0.175	+0.171

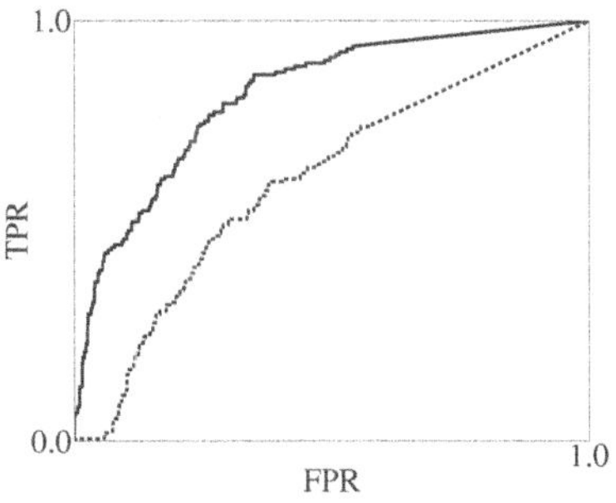

WSJ query 86 "bank failures"
Topic 444 (FDIC) Federal Deposit Insurance William Seidman, Insurance Corp banks, bank, FDIC, banking

NDCG15	NDCG	MAP
+0.602	+0.121	+0.110

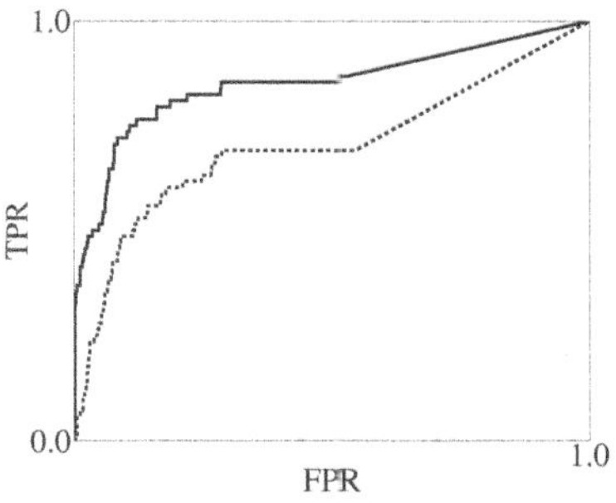

AP query 127 "U.S.-U.S.S.R. Arms Control Agreements"
Topic 232 (missile) Strategic Defense Initiative United States, arms control treaty, nuclear, missiles, range

NDCG15	NDCG	MAP
+0.296	+0.209	+0.105

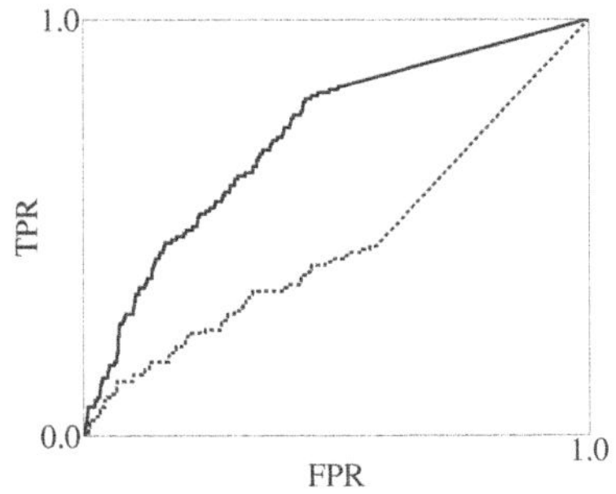

AP query 135 "Possible Contributions of Gene Mapping to Medicine"
Topic 325 (called) British journal Nature immune system, genetically engineered cells, research, researchers, scientists

NDCG15	NDCG	MAP
+0.147	+0.040	+0.019

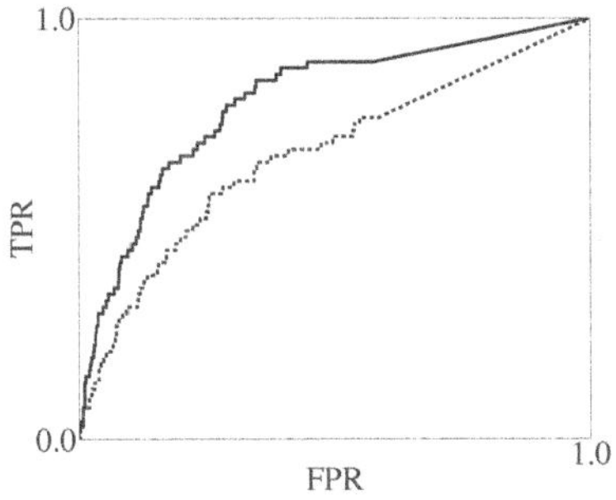

AP query 113 "New Space Satellite Applications"
Topic 237 (communications) European Space Agency Air Force, Cape Canaveral satellite, launch, rocket, satellites

NDCG15	NDCG	MAP
+0.237	+0.033	+0.007

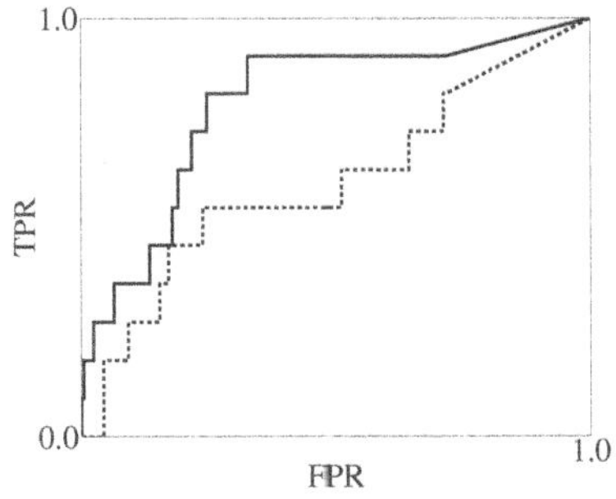

Figure 2: Six example queries with helpful topics and ROC curves. For each ROC curve, the set of true positive (TP) relevant documents is considered to be the union of the relevant documents discovered (i.e., ranked within the top 500) by the baseline query (dashed line) and the expanded query that incorporates latent topic feedback (solid line).

[5] O. Bodenreider. The Unified Medical Language System (UMLS): integrating biomedical terminology. *Nucleic Acids Research*, 32(suppl 1):D267–D270, 2004.

[6] C. Buckley, G. Salton, J. Allan, and A. Singhal. Automatic query expansion using SMART: TREC 3. In *TREC*, pages 69–80. NIST, 1994.

[7] C. Chemudugunta, A. Holloway, P. Smyth, and M. Steyvers. Modeling documents by combining semantic concepts with unsupervised statistical learning. In *ISWC*, pages 229–244. Springer, 2008.

[8] B. Croft, D. Metzler, and T. Strohman. *Search*

Engines: Information Retrieval in Practice. Addison-Wesley, 2010.

[9] W. Dakka, P. G. Ipeirotis, and K. R. Wood. Automatic construction of multifaceted browsing interfaces. In *CIKM*, pages 768–775. ACM, 2005.

[10] C. Fellbaum. *WordNet : an Electronic Lexical Database.* MIT Press, 1998.

[11] M. J. Gardner, J. Lutes, J. Lund, J. Hansen, D. Walker, E. Ringger, and K. Seppi. The topic browser: An interactive tool for browsing topic models. In *NIPS Workshop on Challenges of Data Visualization.* MIT Press, 2010.

[12] T. L. Griffiths and M. Steyvers. Finding scientific topics. *PNAS*, 101(Suppl 1):5228–5235, 2004.

[13] M. Hoffman, D. Blei, and F. Bach. Online learning for latent Dirichlet allocation. In *NIPS*, pages 856–864. MIT Press, 2010.

[14] J. Koren, Y. Zhang, and X. Liu. Personalized interactive faceted search. In *WWW*, pages 477–486, New York, NY, USA, 2008. ACM.

[15] J. H. Lau, D. Newman, S. Karimi, and T. Baldwin. Best topic word selection for topic labelling. In *Coling 2010: Posters*, pages 605–613. Coling 2010 Organizing Committee, 2010.

[16] W. Li and A. McCallum. Pachinko allocation: DAG-structured mixture models of topic correlations. In *ICML*, pages 577–584. ACM, 2006.

[17] S. Liberman and R. Lempel. Approximately optimal facet selection. In *(submission)*, 2011.

[18] X. Ling, Q. Mei, C. Zhai, and B. Schatz. Mining multi-faceted overviews of arbitrary topics in a text collection. In *KDD*, pages 497–505. ACM, 2008.

[19] T.-Y. Liu. Learning to rank for information retrieval. In *SIGIR Tutorials*, page 904, 2010.

[20] Y. Lu, Q. Mei, and C. Zhai. Investigating task performance of probabilistic topic models: an empirical study of PLSA and LDA. *Information Retrieval*, pages 1–26, 2010.

[21] A. K. McCallum. Mallet: A machine learning for language toolkit. http://mallet.cs.umass.edu, 2002.

[22] D. Metzler and W. B. Croft. Combining the language model and inference network approaches to retrieval. *Inf. Process. Manage.*, 40:735–750, 2004.

[23] D. M. Mimno and A. McCallum. Organizing the OCA: learning faceted subjects from a library of digital books. In *JCDL*, pages 376–385. ACM, 2007.

[24] T. Minka and J. Lafferty. Expectation-propagation for the generative aspect model. In *UAI*, pages 352–359. Morgan Kaufmann, 2002.

[25] D. Newman, J. H. Lau, K. Grieser, and T. Baldwin. Automatic evaluation of topic coherence. In *HLT-NAACL*, pages 100–108, Morristown, NJ, USA, 2010. ACL.

[26] D. Newman, Y. Noh, E. Talley, S. Karimi, and T. Baldwin. Evaluating topic models for digital libraries. In *JCDL*, pages 215–224. ACM, 2010.

[27] L. A. Park and K. Ramamohanarao. The sensitivity of latent Dirichlet allocation for information retrieval. In *ECML PKDD*, pages 176–188. Springer-Verlag, 2009.

[28] A. Smola and S. Narayanamurthy. An architecture for parallel topic models. *Proc. VLDB Endow.*, 3:703–710, 2010.

[29] E. Stoica, M. Hearst, and M. Richardson. Automating creation of hierarchical faceted metadata structures. In *HLT-NAACL*, pages 244–251, Rochester, New York, April 2007. ACL.

[30] Y. W. Teh, D. Newman, and M. Welling. A collapsed variational Bayesian inference algorithm for latent Dirichlet allocation. In *In NIPS*. MIT Press, 2007.

[31] The Gene Ontology Consortium. Gene Ontology: Tool for the unification of biology. *Nature Genetics*, 25:25–29, 2000.

[32] E. M. Voorhees and D. K. Harman. *TREC: Experiment and Evaluation in Information Retrieval.* MIT Press, 2005.

[33] X. Wei and W. B. Croft. LDA-based document models for ad-hoc retrieval. In *SIGIR*, pages 178–185. ACM, 2006.

[34] R. W. White and G. Marchionini. Examining the effectiveness of real-time query expansion. *Inf. Process. Manage.*, 43:685–704, 2007.

[35] K.-P. Yee, K. Swearingen, K. Li, and M. Hearst. Faceted metadata for image search and browsing. In *CHI*, pages 401–408. ACM, 2003.

[36] X. Yi and J. Allan. A comparative study of utilizing topic models for information retrieval. In *ECIR*, pages 29–41. Springer-Verlag, 2009.

[37] L. Zhang and Y. Zhang. Interactive retrieval based on faceted feedback. In *SIGIR*, pages 363–370. ACM, 2010.

Localized Factor Models for Multi-Context Recommendation

Deepak Agarwal, Bee-Chung Chen and Bo Long
Yahoo! Labs
Sunnyvale, CA
{dagarwal,beechun,bolong}@yahoo-inc.com

ABSTRACT

Combining correlated information from multiple contexts can significantly improve predictive accuracy in recommender problems. Such information from multiple contexts is often available in the form of several incomplete matrices spanning a set of entities like users, items, features, and so on. Existing methods simultaneously factorize these matrices by sharing a single set of factors for entities across all contexts. We show that such a strategy may introduce significant bias in estimates and propose a new model that ameliorates this issue by positing *local*, context-specific factors for entities. To avoid over-fitting in contexts with sparse data, the local factors are connected through a *shared* global model. This sharing of parameters allows information to flow across contexts through multivariate regressions among local factors, instead of enforcing exactly the same factors for an entity, everywhere. Model fitting is done in an EM framework, we show that the E-step can be fitted through a fast multi-resolution Kalman filter algorithm that ensures scalability. Experiments on benchmark and real-world Yahoo! datasets clearly illustrate the usefulness of our approach. Our model significantly improves predictive accuracy, especially in cold-start scenarios.

Categories and Subject Descriptors

H.3.3 [**Information Search and Retrieval**]: Information filtering; G.3 [**Mathematics of Computing**]: Probability and Statistics

General Terms

Algorithms, Design, Experimentation

1. INTRODUCTION

Amalgamating information from multiple related contexts to improve predictive accuracy is important in several large scale recommender problems, especially those where severe data sparsity is typical. For instance, user affinity to different kinds of news categories inferred from prior visits to Yahoo! News may help in improving article recommendation when users visit the Yahoo! Front Page and vice-versa. User activity on different Yahoo! verticals like Sports, MyYahoo!, Finance, and others can potentially be combined to improve content recommendation on every single page that the user visits on Yahoo! . A content module on the Yahoo! Front Page maybe syndicated and displayed in other contexts like MyYahoo! Yahoo! Mail — interchanging the role of users and items, one can potentially leverage enormous amounts of feedback received on Front Page module articles to improve performance of the same module on MyYahoo! which is a significantly lower volume site with a different user population. Similar issues arise in other recommender applications like movie recommendation, advertising, and so on.

Abstractly, multi-context data in recommender problems consists of the following: (1) user-item interaction matrices in different contexts (e.g. Yahoo! Front Page, Yahoo! News) measuring some response (clicks, ratings, etc), where the response is typically available only for a small subset of all possible user-item pairs; (2) user-feature and item-feature matrices in different contexts, some features are declared (e.g. user age, movie genre, zip code, etc) while others are inferred (user affinity to news type). For the inferred features, associating different weights to capture uncertainty is important. It is routine to see matrices with different degrees of data sparsity and different user (item) populations across contexts. Users (items) that have no or little data (cold-start) in the prediction context of interest may have data in other contexts that could be leveraged to improve performance.

Loosely speaking, predicting user-item response in a context of interest could improve if information available from other contexts are used as *predictors* (especially in cold-start and small sample size scenarios.) While true, constructing such predictors is a challenging task in recommender problems due to several reasons. Interaction and feature matrices are often noisy and highly incomplete. Entries are often not missing at random since occurrence distribution of items served in a recommender systems tends to be heavy-tailed; hence, imputation is difficult. The amount of overlap in user (item) population for different contexts may vary, and the amount of data in different contexts can have large variation. If predictors are not constructed and used appropriately, there is a danger of high volume contexts having excessive influence and even deteriorating predictions in sparse contexts.

KDD'11, August 21–24, 2011, San Diego, California, USA.

For the sake of concreteness, consider a scenario with data from three contexts: (1) user-item response matrix from a module on Yahoo! Front Page, (2) user-item response matrix on Yahoo! News, and (3) user-category inferred feature matrix based on articles read by users in the past. There is no overlap in the items for these contexts; the only overlap that exists is for users. A natural approach to deal with missing entries and noise in such scenarios is to extract sufficient statistics that capture user-item interactions in each context. Matrix factorization is a popular approach whereby the incomplete matrix Y_k in context k is approximated as $f(Z_k B_k')$, where Z_k and B_k are dense user and item factors respectively, and f is some function (linear or non-linear) depending on the response type. Given user factors in all three contexts, one can build regression models to predict factors in each context by using the estimated factors in the other two contexts as predictors (or features) for the common user population. For example, Z_1 may be predicted by using Z_2 and Z_3 as predictors. If such a regression relationship (or correlation) is strong among contexts, we can obtain a better estimate of Z_1 by exploiting the information in Z_2 and Z_3, especially when the response matrix in context 1 is sparse, because the data in contexts 2 and 3 is implicitly used to *smooth* the estimate of Z_1. This is the main idea of our localized matrix factorization (LMF) approach — we produce *local* factors in each context that are *smoothed* by borrowing strength from factor estimates in other contexts. However, regressions to share factor information across contexts cannot be learnt using point estimates of factors since these are subject to different degrees of uncertainty; this may lead to biased regression estimates due to measurement error in the predictors [12]. To see this, consider a simple linear regression $y = a + bx + \text{error}$, where $x = z + \text{error}$. When predictor x is subject to error, performing a linear regression of y on a noisy version of the true predictor z leads to downward bias in the estimate of b. It is easy to visualize this geometrically, a relatively tight straight line of y on z incurs more scatter when z is measured with error through x and the slope shrinks towards zero. Incorporating the measurement error in z through a model reduces this bias in estimating b. Figure 1 shows an illustration. Further, the set of users in

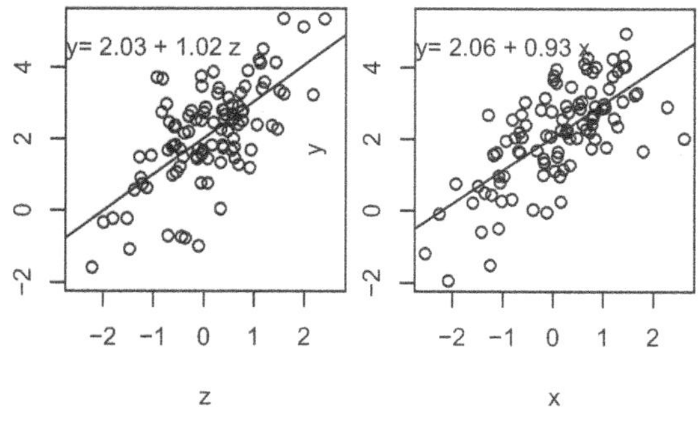

Figure 1: ***Attenuation bias in estimating regression line with measurement error in predictor. Data simulated using $y = 2.0 + 1.0x + error$, left panel is regression fit from exact predictor, right panel has error in the predictor.***

different contexts have different degrees of overlaps. A naive regression approach using estimated factors may not be suitable for combining information, especially when the number of contexts is large. Hence we borrow information across contexts through a multi-level hierarchical model where the observed response matrix in a context is generated from a distribution centered around a context-specific local factorization, and the latent context-specific local factors are assumed to be drawn from a common prior distribution. Such sharing of local factors induces factor correlations that are estimated from the data, which facilitates information sharing that depends on the strength of inter-context correlations. Other than reducing bias due to measurement error in the factors, joint modeling also helps in utilizing overlaps across multiple contexts in a principled way to improve the estimates of all local factors. For instance, assume there are users in context 1 that overlap with users in context 2 but not with the users in context 3. Then estimation of Z_1 can naturally benefit from data in context 2 because of the overlap. Furthermore, if users in context 2 overlap with some users in context 3, the estimation of Z_1 can also benefit from data in context 3, even if there is no direct overlap between contexts 1 and 3. Such transitivity becomes important in the presence of many contexts that are correlated; naive regressions on estimated factors do not have the flexibility to fully utilize such information.

Existing approaches in the literature do not posit local factors; instead, they are too constrained and assume same factors per user (item) across contexts. We shall refer to this as collective matrix factorization (CMF) as in [40]. In our example, this approach assumes a common global user factor matrix Z for all contexts, which gets estimated by optimizing the joint multi-context likelihood (with suitably regularized factors). Since the likelihood of contexts with large amounts of data would have more influence on global factor estimates, such an approach may introduce significant bias for sparse and skewed contexts. To mitigate this issue, a weighted geometric mean of the likelihoods that balance the information entering in estimating the common global factors is used. Such an approach requires careful tweaking of the geometric weights that gets difficult and formidable with a large number of contexts. Also, separate tweakings of weights may have to be done for each prediction task. This makes it an unattractive approach compared to our LMF mode that provides a relaxation of factors locally and eliminates the need to tweak influence of information from different contexts.

Although LMF provides additional flexibility through factor localization, scalable model-fitting is an important consideration. As typical with most multi-level hierarchical models, fitting can be done through an EM algorithm. In our case, we show the E-step can be computed through a fast multi-resolution Kalman filter [23, 13, 22] algorithm, this makes the fitting procedure scalable to large applications.

Our **contributions** are as follows. We propose a novel method LMF to enhance predictions in multi-context recommender problems through a localized latent factor model. Our method posits local user (item) factors in each context, and then borrows strength across contexts by positing a second stage prior which assumes local factors are centered around a global factor with some variance. In fact, our second stage prior can be interpreted as performing a multivariate regression for all local factors through a reduced-rank model; one could also interpret this as estimating local factor covariances parametrized through outer products of low-rank matrices. Our LMF approach removes several deficiencies of existing approaches that learn from different contexts by using the same factors for each entity. We illustrate the deficiencies of CMF and the flexibility of LMF on benchmark data sets and a new Yahoo! multi-context data set from Yahoo! Front Page and Yahoo! News.

2. MODEL

We provide modeling details for the localized matrix factorization model (LMF). Although the model is general and can combine information for both items and users that are common across contexts, we make some simplifying assumptions for ease of exposition and to avoid notational clutter. We assume only user-ids have possible overlaps across contexts, item populations are distinct with no overlaps. Hence, we only describe the joint learning of user factors, joint learning of both user and/or item factors follow a straightforward generalization. We begin with notations.

Notations: We consider K different contexts, each of which may represent a recommendation application or a collection of features. Let $\mathcal{I}$ denote the set of all users from the union of all contexts. We use y_{ijk} to denote the rating that user i gives to item j in context k, or user i's feature value on feature j in context k. Since features play the same role as ratings in the model, to simplify notations and terms, we call a feature an item, and call a rating and a feature value the response. As stated before, we assume each context has a different set of items for simplicity. Let $\mathcal{K}_i$ denote the set of contexts that include data of user i. Let $\mathcal{J}_{ik}$ denote the set of items in context k with response from user i. Note that some users do not have any observed response in some contexts. Our goal is to simultaneously *impute* the missing response values for all (or some selected) contexts of interest.

Localized matrix factorization model (LMF): We assume that the response y_{ijk} of a (user i, item j) pair in context k is generated according to a *local latent profile* vector $\boldsymbol{z}_{ik}$. (Recall that we use the term "response" to refer to both user's ratings and features.) Then, the distribution of response conditional on latent factors is denoted by

$$p(y_{ijk}|f(\boldsymbol{z}_{ik})),$$

where $f(.)$ is a known function, and p is a generic symbol used to denote probability distributions. For computational ease, we assume $f(.)$ is a linear function of latent factor $\boldsymbol{z}_{ik}$. We consider two response distributions — normal distribution for continuous response and Bernoulli distribution for binary response. Hence we have the following two response distributions conditional on latent factors.

$$y_{ijk} \mid \boldsymbol{z}_{ik} \sim N(\boldsymbol{\beta}'_{jk}\boldsymbol{z}_{ik} + \alpha_{jk},\ \sigma^2_{y,k} w_{ijk}), \text{ or}$$
$$y_{ijk} \mid \boldsymbol{z}_{ik} \sim \text{Bernoulli}((1 + \exp\{-(\boldsymbol{\beta}'_{jk}\boldsymbol{z}_{ik} + \alpha_{jk})\})^{-1})$$

Note that:

- $\boldsymbol{\beta}_{jk}$ and α_{jk} are the regression weight vector and the bias term for item j in context k, respectively.
- w_{ijk} is a known weight attached to response y_{ijk}, in many scenarios $w_{ijk} = 1$ for each response. One can also set w_{ijk} based on the known uncertainty associated with each response.
- $\sigma^2_{y,k}$ is the variance of the response in context k, which will be estimated from data.

To transfer knowledge cross different contexts, we assume the local profiles of user i are generated according to a *global latent profile* vector $\boldsymbol{u}_i$, which captures a user's deeper taste across multiple contexts. The conditional distribution capturing this is denoted by

$$p(\boldsymbol{z}_{ik}|g(\boldsymbol{u}_i)),$$

where $g(.)$ is a known function. Again, for computational ease, we assume $g(.)$ is a linear function of $\boldsymbol{u}_i$ and the conditional distribution of local factors $\boldsymbol{z}_{ik}$ is normal. Furthermore, we assume standard normal distribution for the global latent user profile $\boldsymbol{u}_i$. The complete specification of the generative model for latent user profiles is given as

$$\boldsymbol{z}_{ik} \mid \boldsymbol{u}_i \sim N(A_k \boldsymbol{u}_i,\ \sigma^2_{z,k} I)$$
$$\boldsymbol{u}_i \sim N(\mathbf{0},\ I).$$

Note that:

- A_k is a linear transformation matrix that transform the global profile to the local profile in context k. A_k will be learnt from data.
- $\sigma^2_{z,k}$ is the variance that determines the strength of correlation between local and global factors for context k. $\sigma^2_{z,k}$ will also be estimated from data.

For ease of exposition, we use the following notations:

- $\mathbf{y} = \{y_{ijk}\}_{\forall i \in \mathcal{I}, k \in \mathcal{K}_i, j \in \mathcal{J}_{ik}}$ denotes all observed response.
- $\mathbf{z} = \{\boldsymbol{z}_{ik}\}_{\forall i \in \mathcal{I}, k \in \mathcal{K}_i}$ denotes all local profile vectors.
- $\mathbf{u} = \{\boldsymbol{u}_i\}$ denotes all global profile vectors.
- $\mathbf{y}_k$ and $\mathbf{z}_k$ denote response and factors for context k.
- B_k denotes the matrix created by stacking the β_{jk}s together for items in application k.
- Let $\boldsymbol{\Theta} = (\boldsymbol{\alpha}, \boldsymbol{\beta}, \mathbf{A}, \boldsymbol{\sigma}^2)$, where $\boldsymbol{\alpha} = \{\alpha_{jk}\}$, $\boldsymbol{\beta} = \{\boldsymbol{\beta}_{jk}\}$, $\mathbf{A} = \{A_k\}$, and $\boldsymbol{\sigma}^2 = \{\sigma^2_{\cdot,k}\}$ denote all the model parameters that needs to be estimated from data.

Our goal is to obtain $E[y_{ijk} \mid \mathbf{y}]$, for (i, j, k) triples such that $k \notin \mathcal{K}_i$ or $j \notin \mathcal{J}_{ik}$.

Discussion: Our multi-level hierarchical model LMF provides a number of advantages over existing methods. To simplify discussion, assume two contexts, i.e., $K = 2$. Existing methods assume $z_{i1} = z_{i2} = z_i$ for each i. We note that this is a special case of our LMF that arises by assuming $A_1 = A_2 = I$ and $\sigma^2_{z,k} = 0$. To see this, consider a Gaussian response, then negative log-likelihood of $\mathbf{y}$ is (ignoring regularization terms)

$$|\mathbf{y}_1 - B_1 Z|^2/\sigma^2_{y,1} + |\mathbf{y}_2 - B_2 Z|^2/\sigma^2_{y,2} + const \qquad (1)$$

The common user factor matrix Z is obtained by minimizing the loss function in Equation 1 (after adding L_2 regularizers for B_1, B_2, Z). This is referred to as collective matrix factorization in the literature [40], we shall call this CMF. However in CMF, the weighting attached to loss functions in different contexts are assumed known and in general obtained through cross-validation, in our case the weights $\sigma^2_{y,k}$s are obtained through an EM algorithm. This is attractive and necessary for large K where it gets unwieldy to determine a large number of such parameters through cross-validation. One of the datasets on Epinions we analyze in section 4.4 has 10 contexts, automatic estimation of weights attached to likelihood of different contexts is essential in such scenarios.

However, estimating such weighting parameters automatically when common factors are shared across contexts may cause problems. For instance, if the first context is a sparse response matrix that needs to be predicted and the second context is a dense matrix represents user feature vectors, the sparse response matrix will force the common user factors to be influenced more by features and may result in inferior performance. By assuming $Z_1 \neq Z_2$ in LMF but rather correlated, we avoid this problem inherent in CMF. In fact, it is easy to see that a-priori, the covariance matrix Σ_{12} of (z_{i1}, z_{i2}) is given by

$$\Sigma_{12} = \begin{pmatrix} A_1A_1' + \sigma^2_{z,1}I & A_1A_2' \\ A_2A_1' & A_2A_2' + \sigma^2_{z,2}I \end{pmatrix}$$

Thus, LMF provides more flexibility by assuming local factors per context but avoids over-fitting by connecting the parameters through a joint multivariate normal distribution with covariance estimated through a reduced rank structure. For Gaussian response, the posterior distribution is also Gaussian and hence the local factors across contexts are smoothed through cross-context global covariance. If a user is new in context 1 but have been seen in context 2, one could predict the local factor z_1 through the conditional posterior of $z_1|z_2$. This is how LMF transfers information from one context to the other without getting overly influenced by contexts merely due to large sample size. The simpler approach of performing factorization separately in each context and then using the estimated factors as features does not account for the uncertainty in estimated factors. By obtaining a joint posterior, our LMF provides a principled way of learning across contexts.

To provide further intuition on how LMF learns across contexts, consider the Gaussian model and our two-context example. Then, the predicted rating for a new user-item pair (i, j) in context k is given as $\beta'_{jk}\hat{z}_{ik}$, where $\hat{z}_{ik}$ is the estimated posterior mean. For two contexts, the posterior mean estimate is obtained from the joint posterior as $E_{z_{i2}}[E(z_{i1}|z_{i2})]$, i.e., we average out the conditional expectation of $z_{i1}|z_{i2}$ w.r.t. the marginal distribution of z_{i2}. This is referred to as Rao-Blackwellization in the literature [7] and is known to reduce variance in estimators. Hence our LMF can also be thought of as a Rao-Blackwellization procedure to obtain low-variance estimates by leveraging data across contexts.

3. FITTING ALGORITHM

We take an *empirical bayes* approach to model fitting by treating $\mathbf{\Theta} = (\boldsymbol{\alpha}, \boldsymbol{\beta}, \mathbf{A}, \boldsymbol{\sigma}^2)$ as model parameters, and $\mathbf{u}$ and $\mathbf{z}$ as hidden variables. Our goal is to first obtain the maximum likelihood estimate of $\mathbf{\Theta}$; i.e.,

$$\hat{\mathbf{\Theta}} = \arg\max_{\mathbf{\Theta}} \Pr[\mathbf{y} \mid \mathbf{\Theta}] = \arg\max_{\mathbf{\Theta}} \int \Pr[\mathbf{y}, \mathbf{u}, \mathbf{z} \mid \mathbf{\Theta}]\, d\mathbf{u}\, d\mathbf{z},$$

and then obtain the posterior distribution of the hidden variables. Because all the distributions are normal, the marginal distribution is available in closed form, but quite complicated. In the following, we provide the details for the Gaussian model. For the Logistic model, we use variational approximation [25]. This approximation converts the logistic into a weighted Gaussian by obtaining a quadratic approximation to the logistic loss.

EM algorithm: Iteratively, we can solve the problem using the EM algorithm [19]. Let q_k and r denote the lengths of vectors $\boldsymbol{z}_{ik}$ and $\boldsymbol{u}_i$ respectively. Let n denote the total number of users. The complete data (including the hidden variables) log likelihood is $L(\mathbf{\Theta}, \mathbf{u}, \mathbf{z}; \mathbf{y})$, given in Table 1. Let $\hat{\mathbf{\Theta}}_t$ denote the current estimated value of $\mathbf{\Theta}$ at the beginning of the tth iteration. In the tth iteration, the EM algorithm update $\mathbf{\Theta}$ to get a new estimate

$$\hat{\mathbf{\Theta}}_{t+1} = \arg\max_{\mathbf{\Theta}} E_{(\mathbf{u},\mathbf{z} \mid \mathbf{y}, \hat{\mathbf{\Theta}}_t)}[L(\mathbf{\Theta}, \mathbf{u}, \mathbf{z}; \mathbf{y})], \tag{2}$$

where $\hat{\mathbf{\Theta}}_t$ is constant; $\mathbf{\Theta}$ is the variable to optimize; $\mathbf{u}$ and $\mathbf{z}$ are the random variables to take expectation over; and the expectation is taken over the posterior distribution of $(\mathbf{u}, \mathbf{v} \mid \mathbf{y}, \hat{\mathbf{\Theta}}_t)$, which is Gaussian; and $E_{(\mathbf{u},\mathbf{z} \mid \mathbf{y}, \hat{\mathbf{\Theta}}_t)}[L(\mathbf{\Theta}, \mathbf{u}, \mathbf{z}; \mathbf{y})]$ is given in Table 1. Note that, in the rest of this section, we consider the computation in a single EM iteration, thus dropping subscript t in the following notations: Let $\hat{\boldsymbol{u}}_i = E[\boldsymbol{u}_i \mid \mathbf{y}, \hat{\mathbf{\Theta}}_t]$, $\hat{\boldsymbol{z}}_{ik} = E[\boldsymbol{z}_{ik} \mid \mathbf{y}, \hat{\mathbf{\Theta}}_t]$, $\hat{V}[\boldsymbol{u}_i] = Var[\boldsymbol{u}_i \mid \mathbf{y}, \hat{\mathbf{\Theta}}_t]$, $\hat{V}[\boldsymbol{z}_{ik}] = Var[\boldsymbol{z}_i \mid \mathbf{y}, \hat{\mathbf{\Theta}}_t]$ and $\hat{V}[\boldsymbol{z}_{ik}, \boldsymbol{u}_i] = Cov[\boldsymbol{z}_{ik}, \boldsymbol{u}_i \mid \mathbf{y}, \hat{\mathbf{\Theta}}_t]$. Let $A_{k,\ell}$ denote the ℓth row of A_k.

3.1 E-step

In the E-step, we compute $\hat{\boldsymbol{u}}_i$, $\hat{\boldsymbol{z}}_{ik}$, $\hat{V}[\boldsymbol{u}_i]$, $\hat{V}[\boldsymbol{z}_{ik}]$ and $\hat{V}[\boldsymbol{z}_{ik}, \boldsymbol{u}_i]$ using the multi-resolution Kalman filter algorithm. It is safe to skip this section without loss of continuity but it is crucial to understand the implementation of fitting algorithm. The Kalman filter algorithm provides an essentially linear time algorithm (for small number of latent factors) to obtain state estimates that are connected linearly in a hierarchical fashion (see [23, 13] for more discussion). As such, it is important to scale our fitting to large datasets. At a high-level, the algorithm consists of two steps: (1) **Bottom-up filtering** where information is transmitted from observed data to local factors $\boldsymbol{z}_{ik}$, and from local factors $\boldsymbol{z}_{ik}$ to the global factors $\boldsymbol{u}_i$. (2) **Top-down smoothing** which transmits information from global factors to the local factors and facilitates cross-context learning. Detailed derivation of formulas for a general hierarchical linear state-space model is provided in [23]; we provide the details in the context of our model. For ease of exposition, if $\boldsymbol{a}_1, ..., \boldsymbol{a}_n$ are n column vectors, each has length m, then $[\boldsymbol{a}_1, ..., \boldsymbol{a}_n]$ denotes a $m \times n$ matrix that binds them together. We use (HC Eq n) to denote Equation n in [23], and the following notation.

$$\begin{aligned}
\boldsymbol{d}'_{ik} &= [(y_{ijk} - \alpha_{jk}) : \forall j \in \boldsymbol{\mathcal{J}}_{ik}] \\
C'_{ik} &= [\boldsymbol{\beta}_{jk} : \forall j \in \boldsymbol{\mathcal{J}}_{ik}] \\
D_{ik} &= \text{diag}([\sigma^2_{y,k} w_{ijk} : \forall j \in \boldsymbol{\mathcal{J}}_{ik}]) \\
\Sigma_{ik} &= Var[\boldsymbol{z}_{ik}] = \sigma^2_u A_k A'_k + \sigma^2_{z,k} I \quad \text{(independent of } i\text{)} \\
E_{ik} &= C_{ik}\Sigma_{ik}C'_{ik} + D_{ik} \\
F_{ik} &= \Sigma^{-1}_{ik} + C'_{ik}D^{-1}_{ik}C_{ik} \\
H_{ik} &= \sigma^2_u A'_k \Sigma^{-1}_{ik} \\
R_{ik} &= \sigma^2_u I - \sigma^4_u A'_k \Sigma^{-1}_{ik} A_k
\end{aligned}$$

Note that with this notation, we have

$$\boldsymbol{d}_{ik} \mid \boldsymbol{z}_{ik} \sim N(C_{ik}\boldsymbol{z}_{ik}, D_{ik})$$

$$\text{Marginally, } \boldsymbol{d}_{ik} \sim N(\mathbf{0}, E_{ik}) \quad \text{(they are not } iid\text{)}$$

$$E^{-1}_{ik} = D^{-1}_{ik} - D^{-1}_{ik}C_{ik}F^{-1}_{ik}C'_{ik}D^{-1}_{ik}$$

$$\boldsymbol{u}_i = H_{ik}\boldsymbol{z}_{ik} + \boldsymbol{\xi}_{ik}, \quad \boldsymbol{\xi}_{ik} \sim N(\mathbf{0}, R_{ik})$$

Filtering: By (HC Eq 1.4) and (HC Eq 1.5), we obtain

Complete data log-likelihood: $L(\boldsymbol{\Theta}, \mathbf{u}, \mathbf{z}; \mathbf{y}) = \Pr[\mathbf{u}, \mathbf{z}, \mathbf{y} \mid \boldsymbol{\Theta}] =$ some constant

$$-\frac{1}{2}\sum_i \sum_{k\in\mathcal{K}_i^y} \sum_{j\in\mathcal{J}_{ik}} \left(\log\sigma_{y,k}^2 + \frac{(y_{ijk} - \boldsymbol{\beta}_{jk}'\boldsymbol{z}_{ik} - \alpha_{jk})^2}{\sigma_{y,k}^2 w_{ijk}}\right) - \frac{1}{2}\sum_i \sum_{k\in\mathcal{K}_i}\left(q_k \log\sigma_{z,k}^2 + \frac{\|\boldsymbol{z}_{ik} - A_k\boldsymbol{u}_i\|^2}{\sigma_{z,k}^2}\right) - \frac{1}{2}\sum_i \frac{\|\boldsymbol{u}_i\|^2}{\sigma_u^2} - \frac{1}{2}nr\log\sigma_u^2$$

Expected log-likelihood: $E_{(\mathbf{u},\mathbf{z}\,|\,\mathbf{y},\hat{\boldsymbol{\Theta}}_t)}[L(\boldsymbol{\Theta}, \mathbf{u}, \mathbf{z}; \mathbf{y})] =$ some constant

$$-\frac{1}{2}\sum_i \sum_{k\in\mathcal{K}_i^y} \sum_{j\in\mathcal{J}_{ik}} \left(\log\sigma_{y,k}^2 + \frac{(y_{ijk} - \boldsymbol{\beta}_{jk}'\hat{\boldsymbol{z}}_{ik} - \alpha_{jk})^2 + \boldsymbol{\beta}_{jk}'\hat{V}[\boldsymbol{z}_{ik}]\boldsymbol{\beta}_{jk}}{\sigma_{y,k}^2 w_{ijk}}\right) - \frac{1}{2}\sum_i\sum_\ell \frac{\hat{u}_{i,\ell}^2 + \hat{V}[u_{i,\ell}]}{\sigma_u^2} - \frac{1}{2}nr\log\sigma_u^2$$

$$-\frac{1}{2}\sum_i\sum_{k\in\mathcal{K}_i}\left(q_k\log\sigma_{z,k}^2 + \sum_\ell \frac{(\hat{z}_{ik,\ell} - A_{k,\ell}\hat{\boldsymbol{u}}_i)^2 + A_{k,\ell}\hat{V}[\boldsymbol{u}_i]A_{k,\ell}' - 2A_{k,\ell}\hat{V}[z_{ik,\ell}, \boldsymbol{u}_i] + \hat{V}[z_{ik,\ell}]}{\sigma_{z,k}^2}\right)$$

Note that $A_{k,\ell}$ denotes the ℓth rows of A_k; $\hat{a}$ and $\hat{V}[a]$ denote the posterior mean and variance of variable a.

Table 1: Log likelihood formulas

$$\begin{aligned}
\hat{\boldsymbol{z}}_{ik|ik} &= E[\boldsymbol{z}_{ik} \mid \boldsymbol{d}_{ik}] = \gamma_{ik}\Sigma_{ik}C_{ik}'E_{ik}^{-1}\boldsymbol{d}_{ik} \\
&= \gamma_{ik}(\Sigma_{ik}C_{ik}'D_{ik}^{-1}\boldsymbol{d}_{ik} - \Sigma_{ik}C_{ik}'D_{ik}^{-1}C_{ik}F_{ik}^{-1}C_{ik}'D_{ik}^{-1}\boldsymbol{d}_{ik}), \\
\Gamma_{ik|ik} &= Var[\boldsymbol{z}_{ik} \mid \boldsymbol{d}_{ik}] = \Sigma_{ik} - \gamma_{ik}\Sigma_{ik}C_{ik}'E_{ik}^{-1}C_{ik}\Sigma_{ik} \\
&= \Sigma_{ik} - \gamma_{ik}(\Sigma_{ik}C_{ik}'D_{ik}^{-1}C_{ik}\Sigma_{ik} \\
&\quad - \Sigma_{ik}C_{ik}'D_{ik}^{-1}C_{ik}F_{ik}^{-1}C_{ik}'D_{ik}^{-1}C_{ik}\Sigma_{ik}),
\end{aligned}$$

where $\gamma_{ik} = 1$ if $k \in \mathcal{K}_i$; otherwise, $\gamma_{ik} = 0$. Here, $\hat{\boldsymbol{z}}_{ik|ik}$ and $\Gamma_{ik|ik}$ are the posterior mean and covariances of $\boldsymbol{z}_{ik}$ for user i using data only in context k. Letting $\boldsymbol{d}_i = \{\boldsymbol{d}_{ik}\}_{\forall k}$, by (HC Eq 1.8) and (HC Eq 1.9), we obtain

$$\begin{aligned}
\hat{\boldsymbol{u}}_i &= E[\boldsymbol{u}_i \mid \boldsymbol{d}_i] = \hat{V}[\boldsymbol{u}_i]\textstyle\sum_k \Gamma_{i|ik}^{-1}H_{ik}\hat{\boldsymbol{z}}_{ik|ik} \\
\hat{V}[\boldsymbol{u}_i] &= Var[\boldsymbol{u}_i \mid \boldsymbol{d}_i] = \left(I/\sigma_u^2 + \textstyle\sum_k(\Gamma_{i|ik}^{-1} - I/\sigma_u^2)\right)^{-1} \\
\Gamma_{i|ik} &= \hat{V}[\boldsymbol{u}_i|\boldsymbol{z}_{ik}] = H_{ik}\Gamma_{ik|ik}H_{ik}' + R_{ik}
\end{aligned}$$

Here, the global factors are estimated by combining information across all contexts through local factors, the weighting depends crucially on $\Gamma_{i|ik}$, posterior covariance of global factor when one uses information only from context k. Note the summation $\sum_k$ in the above formulas. We consider two options: (1) $\sum_{k\in\mathcal{K}_i}$; (2) $\sum_{k\in \text{ all applications}}$ (as Huang and Cressie suggest).

Smoothing: Finally, by (HC Eq 1.13) and (HC Eq 1.14), we obtain

$$\begin{aligned}
\hat{\boldsymbol{z}}_{ik} &= E[\boldsymbol{z}_{ik} \mid \boldsymbol{d}_i] \\
&= \hat{\boldsymbol{z}}_{ik|ik} + \Gamma_{ik|ik}H_{ik}'\Gamma_{i|ik}^{-1}(\hat{\boldsymbol{u}}_i - H_{ik}\hat{\boldsymbol{z}}_{ik|ik}) \\
\hat{V}[\boldsymbol{z}_{ik}] &= Var[\boldsymbol{z}_{ik} \mid \boldsymbol{d}_i] \\
&= \Gamma_{ik|ik} + \Gamma_{ik|ik}H_{ik}'\Gamma_{i|ik}^{-1}(\hat{V}[\boldsymbol{u}_i] - \Gamma_{i|ik})\Gamma_{i|ik}^{-1}H_{ik}\Gamma_{ik|ik} \\
\hat{V}[\boldsymbol{z}_{ik}, \boldsymbol{u}_i] &= Cov[\boldsymbol{z}_{ik}, \boldsymbol{u}_i \mid \boldsymbol{d}_i] = \Gamma_{ik|ik}H_{ik}'\Gamma_{i|ik}^{-1}\hat{V}[\boldsymbol{u}_i]
\end{aligned}$$

Notice how information collected by the global factors from all contexts are now being transmitted to each individual local factors to facilitate cross-context learning. Such learning depends crucially on the matrices H_{ik} that are functions of the global correlation model parameters A_ks.

3.2 M-step

In the M-step, we compute $\hat{\boldsymbol{\Theta}}_{t+1}$. In fact, we solve two instances of the following optimization problem:

$$\begin{aligned}
&\text{Let loss}(\boldsymbol{\eta}; o, \boldsymbol{s}, V, \boldsymbol{v}, w, c, \mathcal{I}) \\
&= \textstyle\sum_{i\in\mathcal{I}} \frac{(o_i - \boldsymbol{\eta}'\boldsymbol{s}_i)^2 + \boldsymbol{\eta}'V_i\boldsymbol{\eta} - 2\boldsymbol{\eta}'\boldsymbol{v}_i + c_i}{w_i} \\
&= \boldsymbol{\eta}'\left(\textstyle\sum_i \frac{V_i + \boldsymbol{s}_i\boldsymbol{s}_i'}{w_i}\right)\boldsymbol{\eta} - 2\left(\textstyle\sum_i \frac{\boldsymbol{s}_i o_i + \boldsymbol{v}_i}{w_i}\right)\boldsymbol{\eta} + \textstyle\sum_i \frac{o_i^2 + c_i}{w_i} \\
\hat{\boldsymbol{\eta}} &= \arg\min_{\boldsymbol{\eta}} \text{ loss}(\boldsymbol{\eta}; o, \boldsymbol{s}, V, \boldsymbol{v}, w, c, \mathcal{I}) \\
&= \left(\textstyle\sum_i \frac{V_i + \boldsymbol{s}_i\boldsymbol{s}_i'}{w_i}\right)^{-1}\left(\textstyle\sum_i \frac{\boldsymbol{s}_i o_i + \boldsymbol{v}_i}{w_i}\right),
\end{aligned}$$

Estimating A_k and $\sigma_{z,k}^2$: For each context k and each row ℓ of A_k, solve the regression problem by letting $\boldsymbol{\eta}' = A_{k,\ell}$, $\boldsymbol{s}_i = \hat{\boldsymbol{u}}_i$, $c_i = \hat{z}_{ik,\ell}$, $V_i = \hat{V}[\boldsymbol{u}_i]$, $\boldsymbol{v}_i = \hat{V}[z_{ik,\ell}, \boldsymbol{u}_i]$, $w_i = 1$, $c_i = \hat{V}[z_{ik,\ell}]$ and $\mathcal{I} = \{i : k \in \mathcal{K}_i\}$. Let $\text{loss}_{k,\ell}$ denote the corresponding loss. Then, for each k,

$$\hat{\sigma}_{z,k} = \frac{\sum_\ell \text{loss}_{k,\ell}}{q_k \cdot |\{i : k\in\mathcal{K}_i\}|}.$$

Estimating α_{jk}, $\boldsymbol{\beta}_{jk}$ and $\sigma_{y,k}^2$: For each context k and each item j, solve the regression problem by letting $\boldsymbol{\eta}' = [\alpha_{jk}, \boldsymbol{\beta}_{jk}]$, $\boldsymbol{s}_i' = [1, \hat{\boldsymbol{z}}_{ik}']$, $o_i = y_{ijk}$, $V_i = I_0(\hat{V}[\boldsymbol{z}_{ik}])$, $\boldsymbol{v}_i = 0$, $w_i = w_{ijk}$, $c_i = 0$ and $\mathcal{I} = \{i : k \in \mathcal{K}_i \text{ and } j \in \mathcal{J}_{ik}\}$. Note that $I_0(X)$ is a function that adds a row and a column of all zeros to matrix X; the added row and column are the first row and first column of $I_0(X)$. Let $\text{loss}_{j,k}$ denote the corresponding loss. Then, for each k,

$$\hat{\sigma}_{y,k} = \frac{\sum_j \text{loss}_{j,k}}{\sum_j |\{i : k\in\mathcal{K}_i \text{ and } j\in\mathcal{J}_{ik}\}|}.$$

4. EXPERIMENTS

We begin with an example that shows how LMF can be used to perform linear/logistic regression when features have missing values for a large fraction of records. Although not directly related to recommender problems, it is interesting to note that this is a special case of LMF. It also provides an interesting benchmark dataset for future research in this area.

4.1 UCI Ad data

To illustrate the use of LMF for correcting the effects of missing feature values in regression, we use the Ad data available from the UCI repository. This dataset represents a set of possible advertisements on Internet pages. The features encode the geometry of the image (if available) as well as phrases occuring in the URL, the image's URL and alt text, the anchor text, and words occuring near the anchor text. The task is to predict whether an image is an advertisement ("ad") or not ("nonad"). Previous approach to this problem using C4.5 achieved more than 97% accuracy [29], so this is a relatively simple classification problem. There are 3279 instances, of which 458 are ads. We build a logistic regression by using only 3 continuous attributes — height, width and aspect ratio. There are about 28% missing attribute values, so a correction for missing attribute values may lead to good results. In addition to 3 attributes, we also include 3 second order interactions among the variables. The vanilla logistic regression is run by encoding missing values for an attribute as a separate binary indicator (missing or not), we fit LMF by assuming the response matrix has one item and each record is a user. In other words, $y_{i1} \sim \text{logistic}(\boldsymbol{\beta}' \boldsymbol{z}_i)$ and features $x_{ij} \sim N(B\boldsymbol{z}_i, \sigma_x^2)$, $j = 1, \cdots, 6$. Since this is a regression problem, it makes sense to assume a common factor for both feature and response.Thus, $\boldsymbol{z}_i \sim MVN(\mathbf{0}, \sigma_z^2 I)$. We fit this model with 6 factors, note that factorization on the feature matrix is possible with missing values. To compare the performance of LMF with vanilla logistic regression, we report area under the ROC curve (AUC) based on leave-one-out model fitting. This involves fitting LMF 3279 times, which is fast due to our Kalman filtering based model fitting procedure. The AUC for vanilla logistic regression is 82% but LMF obtains an AUC of 99%. This is remarkable since we are able to achieve such high accuracy by using only 3 features through corrections on missing attribute values.

Next, we illustrate the difference between CMF and LMF in the presence of additional feature information in recommender problems. In particular, we show that using the same user factors both for the response and feature matrices can lead to biased estimates, relaxing the factors to be local and using feature information through multivariate regression in the latent space leads to better performance. In fact, the flexibility provided by locality prevents the user factors from being overwhelmed by information in other contexts when response information is sparse.

4.2 Movielens Data

We experiment with the benchmark Movielens dataset, Netflix was not considered since it did not have user features. Our goal here is to compare the behavior of CMF and LMF on response (movie rating) prediction in the presence of different amounts of feature information. In this experiment, we study the impact on predictive performance for different models in the presence of weak and noisy features. To facilitate such a comparison, we consider the top 100 out of approximately 5k movies. The pruned dataset has 6040 users and approximately 182k ratings. We do a 75:25 split sorted by event timestamp into training and test sets respectively. The test set has approximately 900 new users (not seen in the training set), roughly 25% of test set ratings belong to these new users. We construct a feature matrix for users using their gender, age-groups, occupation and first two digits of zipcode. Each level of these categorical variables are considered as separate binary predictors, this gives us a total of 129 distinct binary features.

We fit both CMF and LMF by varying the amount of feature information available during the training period. In fact, we randomly sample features of f% users where f varies from 0 (no feature) to 1 (consider all user features). Since the model performance depends on initial parameter values, we perform 100 replications of our model fitting procedure for each value of f. Note that both CMF and LMF are fitted on a simulated dataset for a given f in each replication. In Figure 2(a), we show the mean value of test RMSE across different replications for each value of f; we also plotted the two-sample t-test statistic between CMF and LMF for each f using 100 replications(see Figure 2(b)). Both figures clearly show the performance of CMF deteriorates with increase in number of sampled users with feature information. However, after a certain threshold (approximately .75) there is an interesting point of inflexion where the deterioration gets smaller. Further inspection revealed that this happens due to the presence of a large number of cold-start users, obtaining feature information for these users through a factorization slightly improves performance. However, performance of LMF does not deteriorate with addition of features, in fact it improves slightly. For this application, the feature information is noisy and does not help much in improving predictive performance, but CMF gets impacted by noise while LMF is able to learn the weak correlation of features with response and avoids getting affected.

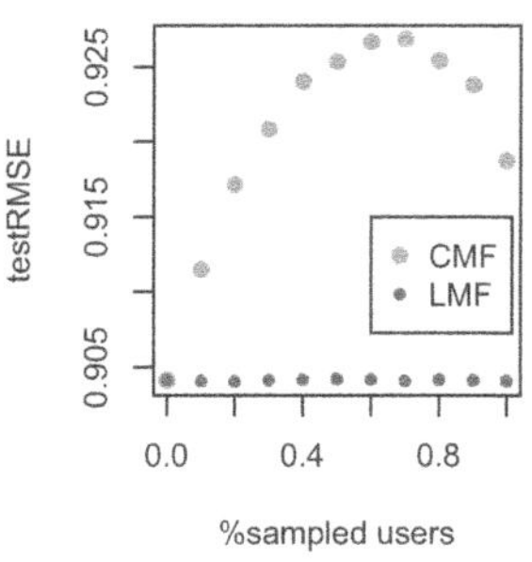

(a) Mean test RMSE

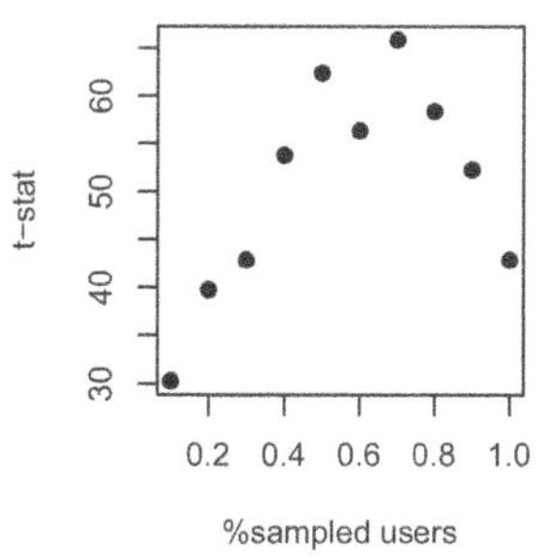

(b) t-statistic

Figure 2: Performance of CMF and LMF with varying amount of feature information. A t-statistics > 3 is highly significant.

4.3 Yahoo! Warm Start Data

We now illustrate the bias problem of CMF on a proprietary Yahoo! data. We study the impact on predictive performance when one of the contexts has sparse response while others have relatively large amounts of data. This dataset also illustrates the use of our model on binary response through variational approximation.

The task is to predict click-rates (CTR) on two content modules: (1) The today module on Yahoo! Front Page [2] and (2) the top stories module that display links to articles on the top-right when a user is reading some news article on Yahoo! News. The goal of the Top stories module is to prolong the stay of a user on Yahoo! News and increase engagement. For instance, a user may click on a news link about "Egyptian revolution" somewhere outside Yahoo! News and get routed to the main article page of the topic on Yahoo! News. The Top stories module on this article page may show an article about Obama which the user may click and end up reading another news story. We collected click event stream for a subset of heavy users on Today module and Top stories for a period of 6 weeks. Overall there were 10k users in the dataset we used for this experiment, there was 55% overlap in the News and Front Page user population. In addition, we constructed profile features for users in News by using all the News pages they read during the time period under study. Each news article was classified into a topic category and a user topic profile is defined as affinity to different categories. Our data had 460 news categories, the procedure for estimating user-category affinity is described below.

Profile construction: Let n_{ij} denote the number of articles read by user i in category j $(i = 1, \cdots, N, j = 1, \cdots, M)$. Let p_{+j} denote the overall probability of reading articles in category j in the heavy user population in News, we estimate this as $\hat{p}_{+j} = n_{+j}/n_{++}$, the "pluses" in the suffix denote marginalization over the corresponding dimension. Then user affinity λ_{ij} is estimated from the following model

$$n_{ij} \sim \text{Poisson}(n_{i+}\hat{p}_{+j}\lambda_{ij}) \quad (3)$$
$$\lambda_{ij} \sim \text{Gamma}(\text{mean} = 1, \text{var} = 1/a)$$

The parameter a can be interpreted as additional psuedo clicks added to the cells. For this Gamma-Poisson model one could obtain a method-of-moments estimator of a given as

$$\hat{a} = (\bar{e_{ij}}/(\mathcal{X}^2 - 1))$$

where $e_{ij} = n_{i+}\hat{p}_{+j}$ is the expected number of reads under baseline model of no affinity and

$$\mathcal{X}^2 = \text{mean}(n_{ij} - e_{ij})^2/e_{ij}.$$

Higher values of $\mathcal{X}^2$ indicates more deviation from baseline (and stronger affinity signal), when $\mathcal{X}^2 < 1$ we assume $\hat{a} = \inf$ and hence there is no affinity in the data. For our data, we obtained $\hat{a} = 0.22$ which indicates high variation in data. Given $\hat{a}$, the posterior of $\lambda_{ij} \sim \text{Gamma}(\text{mean} = \hat{\lambda}_{ij} = (n_{ij} + \hat{a})/(e_{ij} + \hat{a}), \text{var} = \hat{\lambda}_{ij}/(e_{ij} + \hat{a}))$. To work with a Guassian predictor in our framework we consider $\ell\lambda_{ij} = log(\lambda_{ij})$ with approximate mean and variance given by given by $\ell\hat{\lambda}_{ij} = log(\lambda_{ij})$ and $w_{ij} = 1/(e_{ij} + \hat{a})$ respectively(from second order Taylor series expansion). To reduce noise we only retain observations with z-statistic $(|\ell\hat{\lambda}_{ij}|/\sqrt{w_{ij}})$ exceeding the threshold of 1.

Prediction task: For both today module and top stories clickstream our prediction task is based on splitting the data at the item level. In fact we sort the events for each item by timestamp and perform a training-test split. Although this is not exactly the scenario in our actual system where the set of articles in the content pool change over time, it is a realistic setting to study the predictive power of different methods that play an important role in determining the quality of our recommendations. We consider the task of predicting test set response for both today module and top stories by utilizing user feature information available from pages read by users on News. We performed a 25:75 and and 75:25 training-test split on today module and top stories clickstream respectively. For today module this gave us a training set with 171K events, the test set had 514k events. For top stories the training data consisted of 2.16M events while the test set contained 719K events. The feature matrix in News contained 1.47M feature values for roughly 9.6K users. Our goal here is to study the impact CMF has on predictions in today module in the presence of large amounts of data on top stories compared to today module. Such asymmetric data distributions are common in context specific learning for recommender problems, large amounts of additional data from different contexts should not bias predictions for response in a smaller context.

Method	News	Today
CMF (Feature)	.757	.614
CMF (No Feature)	.708	.662
LMF (Feature)	.753	.661
LMF (No Feature)	.709	.664
SMF (No Feature)	.703	.666

Table 2: AUC on different model variations for Yahoo! warm start data.

Table 2 shows the area under the ROC curves (AUC) for three different methods:

- CMF (Feature, No Feature) shares same user factors for all three matrices (for the Feature case) or two matrices (for the No Feature case).
- SMF (separate matrix factorization) fits two models, one for today module and the other for News, separately.
- LMF (Feature, No Feauture) fits localized factors for all three or two matrices jointly.

Since there is little cold-start in this data, matrix factorization done separately has comparable performance to LMF on the today module. On the top stories module, adding feature matrix improves performance significantly for both CMF and LMF, this is because the category affinity of users are strongly correlated to click-rates on top stories articles. However, using CMF deteriorates performance on today module significantly due to the bias induced on user factors. Since the amount of data available on top stories is significantly larger, the user factors are swamped by it and this leads to inferior performance on today module. On the other hand, LMF does not suffer from this problem due to the flexibility of having local user factors in each application, it is able to exploit information from all three sources to obtain good performance on both today module and top stories. Further scrutiny on both lift due to category features and deterioration in today module performance was done by splitting the user population in test according to the total clicks in the training period. Both improvement and deterioration was uniform across all user populations. This clearly shows the ability of LMF to exploit large amounts of additional data from other contexts to improve performance everywhere, even in contexts that are sparse where CMF suffers.

4.4 Epinions Data

We now use the Epinions dataset [34] to show the superior performance of LMF over CMF and the baseline method SMF (separate matrix factorization). This dataset consists of ratings that users of epinions.com gave to reviews in several different verticals on the site. We take the top 10 verticals (each of which contains more than 0.5M ratings) as 10 contexts. Here we consider a user recommendation problem — we want to recommend review authors for users to follow. Thus each (vertical, author) pair is an item. We only consider items that received at least 100 ratings and users

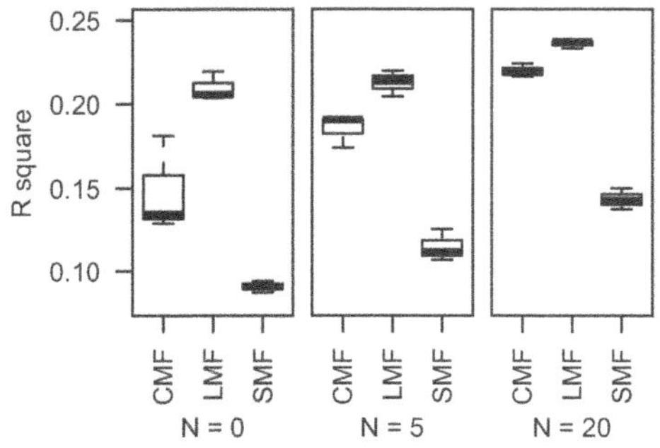

Figure 3: Accuracy of different models on the Epinions dataset with different levels of sparseness

who rated at least 30 items. We compare different methods using R^2 as the accuracy measure; a higher R^2 number means better performance. Five-fold cross validation is used to compute the R^2 of each method. In particular, we use one fold to select the best number of user factors for each method and report the R^2 numbers of the other four folds. The selected numbers of factors are 3 for LMF, 3 for CMF, and 1 for SMF. Instead of averaging the R^2 numbers for each method, we show a boxplot. To understand how different methods perform in cold start, when we compute the R^2 numbers, we only consider the test-set (user,context) pairs, each of which receives $\leq N$ ratings in the training set. We show R^2 of different methods for $N = 0, 5, 20$ in Figure 3. As expected, all the methods perform better in warm start ($N = 20$) than in cold start ($N = 0$). In all three scenarios ($N = 0, 5, 20$) LMF is significantly better than CMF which is significantly better than SMF. Notice that no boxes overlap in any boxplot. The difference between LMF and CMF shrinks as N goes up. Interestingly the $R^2$of LMF for $N = 0$ is still comparable to that of CMF for $N = 20$. This shows the strong performance of LMF over CMF.

5. RELATED WORK

In this section, we discuss related work and describe how LMF is different from prior work.

Matrix factorization: One major motivation for LMF is to perform collaborative filtering in multiple contexts. In recent years, matrix factorization (MF) has gained great popularity since it usually outperforms more traditional methods [21, 42] It has achieved the state-of-the-art performance particularly on large scale recommendation tasks [28]. However, most MF approaches focus on learning latent factors from a single rating matrix. A few recent work extends MF to jointly modeling multiple matrices [1, 41, 40]. Specifically, in [1, 41], user and item feature matrices are used to improve the factorization of the rating matrix. The major difference between [1, 41] and LMF is that the former assumes the features are all known withouth any uncertainty, while LMF allows the feature values to be uncertain or missing. Collective matrix factorization (CMF) [40] jointly factorizes the rating matrix and other feature matrices by assuming user factors are the same in both the rating and feature matrices. The main advantage of LMF over CMF is that LMF defines a different user factor vectors for each matrix and then connects these factors through a regression prior.

Multi-task learning: Multi-context recommendation is closely related to the field of multi-task learning [37], which learns multiple related tasks simultaneously to take advantage of knowledge transfer cross the tasks. Multi-task learning can be broadly summarized into four classes. First class of multi-task learning approaches aims to uncover the common (latent) features that can benefit each individual task [9, 38, 33, 14, 3, 4, 5, 31, 40]. Those methods are most related to our approaches; however they have again follow the spirit of collective matrix factorization where some shared factors are assumed to be the same across different tasks. The second class of of multi-task learning approaches are based on parameter-sharing [39, 30, 20, 11, 44, 45], which assumes that the source tasks and the target tasks share some parameters or priors of their models. Of those methods, hierarchial Bayesian approaches, such as [44], are close to our LMF approach in the sense of multi-level structure, however they do not learn low-dimensional local and global latent factors, which are critical for multi-context recommendation. The third and fourth classes of multi-task learning based on instance re-weighting [6, 26, 15, 32, 8, 24, 17, 43, 16] and relational knowledge transfer [36, 18, 35], individually. Those two classes of approaches are not as relevant as first two class of approaches to our approach.

Multi-view learning: Another related field is multiple view learning introduced by [10] and [27] in the semi-supervised setting. They propose the co-training approach to train a classifier from two representations with both labeled and unlabeled instances. The idea of the co-training approach is to train one learner on each view of the labeled instances and then to iteratively let each learner label the unlabeled instances it predicts with the highest confidence. Given independence between the learners, newly labeled examples from one learner may give the other learner new information to improve its model. In our approach, we assume dependence among different contexts, that is crucial for learning across contexts.

6. CONCLUSION

Learning from multiple contexts is an effective strategy to ameliorate cold-start problems in recommender systems. In this paper, we presented a new methodology called LMF that provides a flexible modeling framework to estimate cross-context correlations and use them to enhance local factor estimates across all contexts. We clearly illustrated the pitfalls of using the current practice of sharing exactly the same factors across contexts for each entity. On a large benchmark dataset we clearly showed the superior performance of LMF, especially for cold-start scenarios.

Our LMF assumes local factors are linear functions of a global factor a-priori, this is equivalent to assuming a low-rank covariance matrix for local factors. Relaxing this assumption to incorporate richer class of covariance functions is an interesting research direction. Moving away from the low rank structure would require new computational fitting algorithms that are scalable since the multi-resolution Kalman filter fails to work in the absence of linearity.

7. REFERENCES

[1] D. Agarwal and B.-C. Chen. Regression-based latent factor models. In *KDD*, 2009.

[2] D. Agarwal and B.-C. Chen, et al. Online models for content optimization. In *NIPS*, 2008.

[3] R. Ando and T. Zhang. A high-performance semi-supervised learning method for text chunking. In *ACL*, 2005.
[4] A. Argyriou, T. Evgeniou, and M. Pontil. Multi-task feature learning. In *NIPS*, 2007.
[5] A. Argyriou, C. Micchelli, M. Pontil, and Y. Ying. A spectral regularization framework for multi-task structure learning. *NIPS*, 2008.
[6] S. Bickel, M. Brückner, and T. Scheffer. Discriminative learning for differing training and test distributions. In *ICML*, 2007.
[7] D. Blackwell. Conditional expectation and unbiased sequential estimation. *Annals of Math. Stat.*, 1947.
[8] J. Blitzer, K. Crammer, A. Kulesza, F. Pereira, and J. Wortman. Learning bounds for domain adaptation. *NIPS*, 2008.
[9] J. Blitzer, R. McDonald, and F. Pereira. Domain adaptation with structural correspondence learning. In *EMNLP*, 2006.
[10] A. Blum and T. Mitchell. Combining labeled and unlabeled data with co-training. In *COLT*, 1998.
[11] E. Bonilla, K. Chai, and C. Williams. Multi-task gaussian process prediction. *NIPS*, 2007.
[12] R. Carroll, D. Ruppert, L. Stefanski, and C. Crainiceanu. *Measurement Error in Nonlinear Models*. Chapman and Hall, 2008.
[13] K. C. Chou, A. S. Willsky, and R. Nikoukhah. Multiscale systems, Kalman filters, and Ricatti equations. *IEEE Trans. on Automatic Control*, 1994.
[14] W. Dai, G. Xue, Q. Yang, and Y. Yu. Co-clustering based classification for out-of-domain documents. In *KDD*, 2007.
[15] W. Dai, Q. Yang, G. Xue, and Y. Yu. Boosting for transfer learning. In *ICML*, 2007.
[16] H. Daumé. Cross-task knowledge-constrained self training. In *EMNLP*, 2008.
[17] H. Daume III and D. Marcu. Domain adaptation for statistical classifiers. *Journal of Artificial Intelligence Research*, 2006.
[18] J. Davis and P. Domingos. Deep transfer via second-order markov logic. In *AAAI Workshop on Transfer Learning for Complex Tasks*, 2008.
[19] A. P. Dempster, N. M. Laird, and D. B. Rubin. Maximum likelihood from incomplete data via the EM algorithm. *J. of the Royal Statistical Society, Series B*, 1977.
[20] T. Evgeniou and M. Pontil. Regularized multi-task learning. In *KDD*, 2004.
[21] J. L. Herlocker, J. A. Konstan, A. Borchers, and J. Riedl. An algorithmic framework for performing collaborative filtering. In *SIGIR*, 1999.
[22] H. Huang and N. Cressie. Fast spatial prediction of global processes from satellite data. *SIAM J. on Scientific Computing*, 2000.
[23] H. Huang and N. Cressie. Multiscale graphical modeling in space: Applications to command and control. In *Spatial Statistics Workshop*, 2000.
[24] J. Huang, A. Smola, A. Gretton, K. Borgwardt, and B. Scholkopf. Correcting sample selection bias by unlabeled data. *NIPS*, 2007.
[25] T. Jaakkola and M. Jordan. Bayesian logistic regression: a variational approach. *Statistics and Computing*, 2000.
[26] J. Jiang and C. Zhai. Instance weighting for domain adaptation in NLP. In *ACL*, 2007.
[27] H. Kaji and Y. Morimoto. Unsupervised word sense disambiguation using bilingual comparable corpora. In *COLIN*, 2002.
[28] Y. Koren, R. Bell, and C. Volinsky. Matrix factorization techniques for recommender systems. *Computer*, 2009.
[29] N. Kushmerick. Learning to remove internet advertisements. In *Int. Conf. Autonomous Agents*, 1999.
[30] N. Lawrence and J. Platt. Learning to learn with the informative vector machine. In *ICML*, 2004.
[31] S. Lee, V. Chatalbashev, D. Vickrey, and D. Koller. Learning a meta-level prior for feature relevance from multiple related tasks. In *ICML*, 2007.
[32] X. Liao, Y. Xue, and L. Carin. Logistic regression with an auxiliary data source. In *ICML*, 2005.
[33] X. Ling, W. Dai, G.-R. Xue, Q. Yang, and Y. Yu. Spectral domain-transfer learning. In *KDD*, 2008.
[34] P. Massa and P. Avesani. Trust metrics in recommender systems. In *Computing with Social Trust*, 2009.
[35] L. Mihalkova, T. Huynh, and R. Mooney. Mapping and revising markov logic networks for transfer learning. In *AAAI*, 2007.
[36] L. Mihalkova and R. Mooney. Transfer learning by mapping with minimal target data. In *AAAI Workshop on Transfer Learning for Complex Tasks*, 2008.
[37] S. J. Pan and Q. Yang. A survey on transfer learning. Technical Report HKUST-CS08-08, Hong Kong University of Science and Technology, 2008.
[38] R. Raina, A. Battle, H. Lee, B. Packer, and A. Ng. Self-taught learning: Transfer learning from unlabeled data. In *ICML*, 2007.
[39] A. Schwaighofer, V. Tresp, and K. Yu. Learning Gaussian process kernels via hierarchical Bayes. *NIPS*, 2005.
[40] A. P. Singh and G. J. Gordon. Relational learning via collective matrix factorization. In *KDD*, 2008.
[41] D. H. Stern, R. Herbrich, and T. Graepel. Matchbox: large scale online bayesian recommendations. In *WWW*, 2009.
[42] X. Su and T. M. Khoshgoftaar. A survey of collaborative filtering techniques. *Adv. in Artif. Intell.*, 2009.
[43] M. Sugiyama, S. Nakajima, H. Kashima, P. von Bunau, and M. Kawanabe. Direct importance estimation with model selection and its application to covariate shift adaptation. *NIPS*, 2008.
[44] K. Yu and V. Tresp. Learning to learn and collaborative filtering. In *In NIPS Workshop on Inductive Transfer: 10 Years Later*, 2005.
[45] S. Yu, K. Yu, V. Tresp, and H.-P. Kriegel. Collaborative ordinal regression. In *ICML*, 2006.

Latent Aspect Rating Analysis without Aspect Keyword Supervision

Hongning Wang, Yue Lu, ChengXiang Zhai
Department of Computer Science
University of Illinois at Urbana-Champaign
Urbana IL, 61801 USA
{wang296, yuelu2, czhai}@cs.uiuc.edu

ABSTRACT

Mining detailed opinions buried in the vast amount of review text data is an important, yet quite challenging task with widespread applications in multiple domains. *Latent Aspect Rating Analysis* (LARA) refers to the task of inferring both opinion ratings on topical aspects (e.g., location, service of a hotel) and the relative weights reviewers have placed on each aspect based on review content and the associated overall ratings. A major limitation of previous work on LARA is the assumption of pre-specified aspects by keywords. However, the aspect information is not always available, and it may be difficult to pre-define appropriate aspects without a good knowledge about what aspects are actually commented on in the reviews.

In this paper, we propose a unified generative model for LARA, which does not need pre-specified aspect keywords and simultaneously mines 1) latent topical aspects, 2) ratings on each identified aspect, and 3) weights placed on different aspects by a reviewer. Experiment results on two different review data sets demonstrate that the proposed model can effectively perform the *Latent Aspect Rating Analysis* task without the supervision of aspect keywords. Because of its generality, the proposed model can be applied to explore all kinds of opinionated text data containing overall sentiment judgments and support a wide range of interesting application tasks, such as aspect-based opinion summarization, personalized entity ranking and recommendation, and reviewer behavior analysis.

Categories and Subject Descriptors

H.3.3 [**Information Search and Retrieval**]: Text Mining

General Terms

Algorithms, Experimentation

Keywords

Aspect Identification, Latent Rating Analysis, Review Mining

KDD'11, August 21–24, 2011, San Diego, California, USA.

1. INTRODUCTION

In the era of Web 2.0, more and more people express their opinions on all kinds of entities, including products and services, which in turn help not only customers make informed decisions but also merchants improve their services. The rapid growth of such opinionated text data on the web, such as user reviews, raises interesting new challenges for text mining communities and leads to many studies on extracting information from reviews [4, 20, 17], sentiment analysis [19, 18, 11] and opinion summarization [6, 8, 14].

To help users efficiently and accurately digest a large number of online reviews about a particular entity (e.g., mp3 player), it is necessary to reveal detailed opinions on multiple topical aspects of the entity (e.g., battery life of mp3 player). To this end, recent work on opinion mining has attempted to perform fine-grained sentiment analysis: in most work (e.g., [21, 25, 6, 7]), the proposed algorithms are able to identify sentiment orientation or ratings on specific topical aspects, leading to useful detailed opinion summaries.

However, decomposing an overall rating into ratings on specific aspects is still not informative enough from a user's perspective. For example, a hotel with a five-star rating on the "*value*" aspect may actually be quite expensive by common standard if the reviewer emphasizes much more on the "*service*" of the hotel than the "*value*" (e.g., for a business trip), though it could also be indeed cheap if the reviewer really cares much more about the price than about other aspects of a hotel (e.g., for a casual vacation).

Figure 1: A sample output of LARA.

To further differentiate such different meanings of the same aspect rating, in our previous work [23], we went beyond aspect rating prediction to also infer the relative emphasis placed by a reviewer on different aspects, and introduced a new opinion mining problem named *Latent Aspect Rating Analysis* (LARA). The task of LARA is to take as input a set of review text documents about an entity with overall ratings and generate as output 1) ratings on a set of predefined aspects of the entity, and 2) relative weights placed by a reviewer on each aspect when writing the review.

For example, Figure 1 shows a sample result of LARA on a hotel review where we see that LARA not only decomposes the overall rating into ratings on each of the four topical aspects (e.g., three stars on "*value*" and two stars on "*room*"), but also infers that the reviewer has placed a much higher weight on "*value*" than other aspects (thus the actual price of this hotel is likely indeed cheap). The inferred aspect weights of reviewers can be very useful. For example, to help a current user who also cares much about "*room*", we could selectively emphasize more on the reviews written by reviewers who have a similar taste to the current user (i.e., also placing a very high weight on "*room*") to recommend hotels, achieving personalized ranking of hotels. The inferred weights can also be used to analyze the rating behavior of reviewers with applications in business intelligence as shown in [23].

However, a major limitation of [23] is that the aspects must be given through keywords specified by users, restricting its usefulness in applications. Indeed, such supervision of specifying aspects with keywords requires manual work and is not always available. More importantly, in many cases, it is often unclear what are the aspects actually commented on in the reviews, thus it is very difficult, if not impossible, to pre-specify the aspects beforehand.

To address this limitation and enable LARA on arbitrary review data without explicit aspect keyword supervision, in this paper, we propose a unified generative Latent Aspect Rating Analysis Model (LARAM), which simultaneously identifies: 1) latent topical aspects, 2) ratings on each identified aspect, and 3) weights placed on different aspects by a reviewer. LARAM is a fully generative model for both the review text and the companion overall rating. Specifically, it is assumed that the text content describing a particular aspect is generated by sampling words from a topic model (i.e., a multinomial word distribution) corresponding to the latent aspect, the latent rating on an aspect is determined based on the words describing each aspect with latent sentiment polarities, and the overall rating is generated based on a weighted combination of aspect ratings where the (latent) weights reflect the relative emphasis on each aspect by the reviewer.

LARAM can be regarded as an extension of the Latent Rating Regression (LRR) model proposed in [23] to perform both aspect segmentation and aspect rating prediction in a unified framework (in contrast, the two tasks were performed separately in [23] with segmentation done based on user-provided keywords).

Experiment results on a hotel review data set crawled from TripAdvisor (`www.tripadvisor.com`) and a product review data set crawled from Amazon (`www.amazon.com`) show that the proposed LARAM can effectively perform Latent Aspect Rating Analysis task without requiring the supervision of aspect keywords. Since LARAM is a general framework, it can be applied to analyze any kind of review text data with overall sentiment judgment to discover opinionated latent topical aspects, decompose overall opinion into sentiment specific topical aspects, and infer relative weights placed by reviewers on different topical aspects; such detailed opinion analysis can support many interesting applications such as aspect-based opinion summarization, personalized opinion-based ranking of entities, and reviewer behavior analysis.

2. RELATED WORK

The closest work to this study is our previous work [23], which introduced the problem of Latent Aspect Rating Analysis (LARA) and proposed a two-stage approach: in the first stage, keywords specified by users are used in a bootstrapping algorithm to identify the aspects and segment the review content; in the second stage, a generative Latent Rating Regression (LRR) model is applied to infer aspect ratings and weights in a review. However, this previous work requires a user to specify aspect keywords in advance, which requires manual work and is often very hard to achieve without knowing well about the opinions buried in the target review text. In this paper, we overcome this limitation, and propose a new generative model (i.e., LARAM) that can be regarded as an extension of LRR to perform aspect segmentation and aspect rating prediction simultaneously in a unified framework, thus enabling LARA without needing keyword specification from users.

The proposed LARAM is a hybrid generative model containing both aspect modeling and rating prediction, thus it is also related to the work of using topic modeling techniques to extract aspects and associated opinions. Mei et al. incorporated two additional sentiment language models into topic models to extract the facets and positive/negative opinions in weblogs [16]. Later, some work further introduced aspect-specific sentiment models in different ways, e.g., using supervision from sentiment priors [12, 9] or supervision from labeled sentences [24]. In [21], Titov and McDonald extended their multi-grain topic model [22] to discover topics that are representative of ratable aspects. Their regression module requires "ground truth" user ratings on the pre-defined aspects, which are not always available. In contrast, the proposed LARAM does not require aspect ratings from users and can decompose overall ratings into the ratings on the discovered aspects. More importantly, none of the work in this line is able to identify a reviewer's relative emphasis on different aspects, which is required for accurate interpretation of aspect ratings as we discussed in Section 1.

Other work on finer granularity analysis of opinions expressed in review text content is mostly to analyze the aspect-level opinion orientations [25, 6, 7, 20, 4, 15]. However, these methods can only identify the opinions associated with each individual aspect, but they cannot infer the reviewer's relative emphasis on different aspects, which the proposed LARAM is designed to achieve.

3. LATENT ASPECT RATING ANALYSIS

As a text mining problem, Latent Aspect Rating Analysis (LARA) [23] is to take as input a set of reviews of some interesting entities with companion overall ratings, and discover: 1) latent topical aspects that are commented on in the reviews; 2) ratings on each individual latent aspects; and 3) relative weights placed on different aspects by a reviewer when generating the overall rating.

Formally, the input can be represented as $D = \{d_1, d_2, \cdots, d_{|D|}\}$, a set of review text documents for a particular entity, where each review $d \in D$ is associated with a numerical overall rating r. A review d is modeled as a bag of words $\mathbf{W}$ in a fixed vocabulary $V = \{v_1, v_2, \ldots, v_{|V|}\}$.

The desired output of LARA consists of the following three kinds of detailed information about opinions buried in the reviews: 1) k topical aspects that are frequently commented on in all the review data: $\{A_1, A_2, \ldots, A_k\}$, where each aspect A_i is characterized by a topic model, i.e., multinomial word distribution $p(w|A_i)$, where $w \in V$; 2) for each review d, a k dimensional aspect rating vector $\mathbf{s}$, where $\mathbf{s}_i$ is the predicted rating for aspect A_i in the review; and 3) for each review d, an aspect weight vector α, where α_i is the relative weight (emphasis) placed by the reviewer on aspect A_i when writing the review. In the following discussions, we will use "aspect" and "topic" interchangeably unless noted otherwise.

Note that a main difference between our definition of LARA here and that in our previous work [23] is that in the previous definition, all the aspects are explicitly specified with keywords provided by a user, thus while the aspect ratings are latent, the aspects are not really latent, whereas here, both aspect ratings and the aspects themselves are latent, which we need to infer from the data. Naturally, such a definition of the problem is more challenging, but it is also more general. If we can solve such a problem setup, it would enable a much wider scope of future applications.

Because the aspects are assumed to be latent, the previously proposed Latent Rating Regression (LRR) model cannot solve the new problem setup directly. Below, we present an extension of the LRR model that can simultaneously discover latent aspects, decompose overall ratings into aspect ratings, and infer weights on different aspects.

4. A GENERATIVE MODEL FOR LARA

A main challenge in solving LARA without the aspect keywords supervision is to properly associate the words with those meaningful aspects corresponding to the major opinions. To address this challenge, our basic idea is to use topic modeling techniques which provide a convenient way of segmenting the review contents by exploiting the word co-occurrence patterns in the data. The main technical contribution of this work is to incorporate topic modeling technique into the Latent Rating Regression (LRR) model proposed in [23] to obtain a more "complete" generative model called Latent Aspect Rating Analysis Model (LARAM), which can model the generation of both text data and the overall ratings in a unified framework. As a result, by fitting LARAM to the review data, we can identify latent topical aspects from the review contents as well as discover the latent ratings and weights for each aspect in a review.

The basic assumption in LARAM is that the latent aspects of a particular entity are characterized by a set of coherent topics, which are shared across different reviews discussing the same entity (e.g., "*service*" and "*location*" for a hotel). The topics can be used to identify aspect text segments which contribute to the observed overall ratings in each review via the latent aspect ratings and weights. Along this line, we propose a fully generative framework to capture such dependency between the review contents and overall sentiment ratings.

Based on the notations in Section 3, our generative assumption of a reviewer's rating behavior is as follows: to generate an opinionated review d, the reviewer would first decide the set of aspects $\{A_i\}$ she wants to comment on, and then for each aspect, the reviewer would choose the words with appropriate sentiment polarities to reflect her opinions on the aspects which are characterized by the aspect ratings $\mathbf{s}$. Finally the reviewer would assign an overall rating r based on a weighted sum of all the aspect ratings in her mind, where the weight α reflects the relative emphasis she has placed on each aspect.

According to this generative assumption, we define and combine two components: 1) an aspect modeling module based on statistical topic modeling is introduced to discover the topical aspects from the review contents, and 2) a rating analysis module similar to the Latent Rating Regression Model (LRR) used in [23], is employed to infer the latent aspect ratings and weights based on the aspect segmented review contents.

In the aspect modeling part, we assume an aspect A_i is characterized by a multinomial word distribution $Mul(\epsilon_i)$ over the vocabulary V. The proportion of aspects θ being discussed in each review d is drawn from a Dirichlet distribution $Dir(\gamma)$, where γ postulates the prior distribution of aspects in the whole corpus. Then, a review is treated as a mixture over the latent aspects, and the joint probability of observed word contents $\mathbf{W}$, latent aspect assignments $\{z_n\}_{n=1}^{|d|}$ and aspect proportion θ is defined as follows:

$$p(\mathbf{W}, \mathbf{z}, \theta|\gamma, \epsilon) = p(\theta|\gamma) \prod_{n=1}^{|d|} p(w_n|z_n, \epsilon)p(z_n|\theta) \qquad (1)$$

where z_n is an indicator variable representing the latent aspect from which the word w_n is drawn.

In the rating analysis part, aspect rating $\mathbf{s}_i$ is assumed to be determined by the aggregated sentiment over the text segments discussing aspect A_i:

$$\mathbf{s}_i = \sum_{n=1}^{|d|} \beta_{ij} \mathbf{\Delta}[w_n = v_j, z_n = i] \qquad (2)$$

where $\beta_{ij} \in \Re$ represents the word j's sentiment polarity on aspect A_i, and $\mathbf{\Delta}[w_n = v_j, z_n = i]$ is an indicator function representing the nth word in review d, which is the jth entry in vocabulary V, is discussing aspect A_i. When we have each aspect's rating, the overall rating r is assumed to be drawn from a Normal distribution with fixed variance δ^2 and mean value as the weighted sum of aspect ratings, i.e., $\alpha^T\mathbf{s} = \sum_{i=1}^{k} \alpha_i \mathbf{s}_i$. Plugging in $\mathbf{s}_i$ defined in Eq (2), we have:

$$r \sim N(\sum_{i=1}^{k} \alpha_i \sum_{n=1}^{|d|} \beta_{ij} \mathbf{\Delta}[w_n = v_j, z_n = i], \delta^2) \qquad (3)$$

In order to further capture the diversity of different reviewers' preferences over different aspects and the dependency among the aspects, we employ a multivariate Normal distribution as the prior for aspect weight α, i.e., $\alpha \sim N(\mu, \mathbf{\Sigma})$. As a whole, the probability of observing the overall rating r and aspect weight α given the aspect segments in review d is defined as:

$$p(r, \alpha|\mathbf{W}, \mu, \mathbf{\Sigma}, \delta^2) \qquad (4)$$
$$= p(\alpha|\mu, \mathbf{\Sigma})p(r|\sum_{i=1}^{k} \alpha_i \sum_{n=1}^{|d|} \beta_{ij} \mathbf{\Delta}[w_n = v_j, z_n = i], \delta^2)$$

We can find from the above description of the two components that the dependency between review text content

$\mathbf{W}$ and the latent aspect ratings $\mathbf{s}$ is bridged by the aspect assignment $\{z_n\}_{n=1}^{|d|}$. More specifically, we introduce the latent aspect assignments to associate the appropriate word descriptions with the corresponding aspect, so that the rating regression model can exploit such association to infer the latent aspect ratings/weights. Compared with the previous two-stage approach in [23], where a bootstrapping algorithm is used to generate a hard association, in the unified model, such correspondence is determined by the probabilistic aspect assignments.

Combining the two components, the joint probability of the observed text content $\mathbf{W}$ and overall rating r in a given review d can thus be defined as:

$$\begin{aligned} & P(r, \mathbf{W}|\epsilon, \gamma, \beta, \mu, \mathbf{\Sigma}, \delta^2) \qquad (5) \\ =& P(\mathbf{W}|\epsilon, \gamma) \times P(r|\mathbf{W}, \beta, \mu, \mathbf{\Sigma}, \delta^2) \\ =& \iint \prod_{n=1}^{|d|} \sum_{z_n=1}^{k} p(w_n|z_n)p(z_n|\theta)p(\theta|\gamma)d\theta \times \\ & p(r|\sum_{i=1}^{k} \alpha_i \sum_{n=1}^{|d|} \beta_{ij} \mathbf{\Delta}[w_n = v_j, z_n = i], \delta^2)p(\alpha|\mu, \Sigma)d\alpha \end{aligned}$$

where we denote $\mathbf{\Theta} = (\epsilon, \gamma, \beta, \mu, \mathbf{\Sigma}, \delta^2)$ as the set of *corpus-level* model parameters, which do not depend on individual reviews. A graphical model illustration of the unified LARAM is shown in Figure 2.

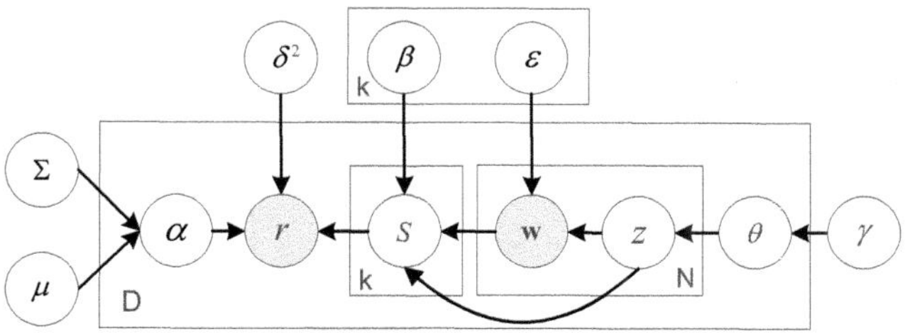

Figure 2: Graphical model representation of LARAM. The outer box represents reviews, while the inner box represents the composition of latent aspect rating regression and word generation within a review.

As illustrated in Figure 2, the word usage patterns embedded in the review text collection are captured by the aspect modeling part; the latent aspect assignments $\{z_n\}_{n=1}^{|d|}$ associate such word clusters with the corresponding aspect, and based on such probabilistic aspect segmentations, the latent aspect ratings and weights are discovered accordingly. We want to emphasize that the aim of the proposed LARAM is not to predict the overall ratings; instead, we are more interested in leveraging the observed general sentiment polarities from overall ratings to identify the opinions in each detailed latent aspect.

We should also note the proposed LARAM is not a trivial replacement of previous keyword-based bootstrapping method in [23] with topic models. Instead, it naturally bridges the gap between the aspect segmentation and sentiment analysis procedure in the previously used two-stage approach. There are two important factors distinguishing the proposed LARAM from the previous LRR model. First, in the current model, the latent aspect rating is a random variable, or more specifically, sum of a set of random variables (because each word's aspect assignment is a probability distribution over all the aspects), while in LRR model, it is treated as a fixed response variable of a rating regression module based on the given aspect segments. This difference enables us to model the uncertainty from the aspect segmentation part as well. Second, the latent rating analysis part provides informative feedback for the aspect segmentation part in the new model. Intuitively, in LARAM, we should assign the word w_j to a proper aspect A_i, in which the word's sentiment orientation β_{ij} is the most consistent with the identified orientation $\mathbf{s}_i$, or in other words, to be consistent with other words in its segment. In the previous LRR model, such segmentation is fixed once the set of aspect keywords is determined.

It would be also interesting to compare LARAM with sLDA introduced in [2]. sLDA is a topic modeling based regression method, which aims at modeling the labeled data in the projected latent topic space. One obvious difference between LARAM and sLDA is that sLDA is designed to predict the overall response for the given input; it can not discover the latent aspect ratings, since it assumes the observed overall response is directly generated from the weighted combination of the latent topic factors. Our LARAM further assumes that the overall rating is determined based on a set of latent ratings over different topical aspects, naturally modeling the latent aspect ratings.

4.1 Posterior Inference

Given the model parameters $\mathbf{\Theta} = (\epsilon, \gamma, \beta, \mu, \mathbf{\Sigma}, \delta^2)$, the key step of applying the proposed LARAM is to infer the posterior distribution of the latent aspect assignment $\{z_n\}_{n=1}^{|d|}$ and aspect weight α in a given review d. Once this is done, the aspect ratings can be easily derived from Eq (2). In this work, we use the variational inference method [10] due to its computational efficiency. The key idea behind variational approximation is to optimize the free parameters of a distribution over the latent variables so that the approximated distribution is close to the true posterior by Kullback-Leibler divergence.

More specifically, we introduce a family of factorized variational distribution for the hidden variables (z, θ, α) in each review d,

$$q(\mathbf{z}, \theta, \alpha|\phi, \eta, \lambda, \sigma^2) = q(\theta|\eta) \prod_n q(z_n|\phi_n)q(\alpha|\lambda, \sigma^2) \qquad (6)$$

where the aspect assignment z for each word in d is specified by a k-dimensional multinomial distribution $Mul(\phi)$, aspect proportion θ is governed by a k-dimensional Dirichlet distribution $Dir(\eta)$, and aspect weight α is determined by a k-dimensional multivariate Normal distribution $N(\lambda, \sigma^2)$ with a diagonal covariance matrix to simplify the computation.

Based on the introduced variational distribution, the lower bound of the log-likelihood in review d can be approximated as follows:

$$\begin{aligned} & \log p(r, \mathbf{W}|\epsilon, \gamma, \beta, \mu, \mathbf{\Sigma}, \delta^2) \qquad (7) \\ =& \log p(\mathbf{W}|\epsilon, \gamma) + \log p(r|\mathbf{W}, \beta, \mu, \mathbf{\Sigma}, \delta^2) \\ \geq& E_q[\log p(\mathbf{z}, \theta, \mathbf{W}|\epsilon, \gamma)] - E_q[\log q(\mathbf{z}, \theta|\phi, \eta)] \\ &+ E_q\big[\log p(r, \alpha, \mathbf{z}|\mathbf{W}, \beta, \mu, \mathbf{\Sigma}, \delta^2)\big] - E_q[\log q(\alpha, \mathbf{z}|\epsilon, \gamma, \phi, \eta)] \end{aligned}$$

where the bound is derived from the Jensen's inequality for convex function. In the following discussions, we will use

$\mathcal{L}_d(\phi, \eta, \lambda, \sigma^2)$ to represent the lower bound defined by a set of variational parameters $(\phi, \eta, \lambda, \sigma^2)$ in review d.

The explanation for this lower bound is quite intuitive: the first part of $\mathcal{L}_d(\phi, \eta, \lambda, \sigma^2)$ represents the objective of aspect modeling module, which aims at finding the optimal aspect assignments $\{z_n\}_{n=1}^{|d|}$ and the corresponding aspect proportion θ for the observed review contents; the second part explains the objective of rating analysis module, which tunes both $\{z_n\}_{n=1}^{|d|}$ and α to fit the overall ratings. These two parts are not independently separated but connected by the common aspect assignments $\{z_n\}_{n=1}^{|d|}$. Both parts attempt to allocate proper aspect assignments to better accommodate the observed text contents and overall rating, respectively.

Details for calculating the expectation of the first part can be found in [3]. The expectation of the complete-data log-likelihood function for the rating analysis module under the variational distribution is derived as:

$$
\begin{aligned}
&E_q\big[\log p(r, \alpha, \mathbf{z}|\mathbf{W}, \beta, \mu, \mathbf{\Sigma}, \delta^2)\big] \\
&= -\frac{(\lambda^T\bar{\mathbf{s}} - r)^2}{2\delta^2} - \frac{1}{2\delta^2}\sum_{i=1}^{k}\Big\{(\lambda_i^2 + \sigma_i^2)Var[\mathbf{s}_i] + \sigma_i^2\bar{\mathbf{s}_i}^2\Big\} \\
&-\frac{1}{2}(\lambda - \mu)^T\Sigma^{-1}(\lambda - \mu) - \frac{1}{2}Tr\big(diag(\sigma^2)\Sigma^{-1}\big) - \frac{1}{2}\log\delta^2 - \frac{1}{2}\log|\Sigma|
\end{aligned}
$$

where $\bar{\mathbf{s}}_i = \sum_{n=1}^{|d|}\beta_{ij}w_n^j\phi_{ni}$, $Var[\mathbf{s}_i] = \sum_{n=1}^{|d|}(\beta_{ij}w_n^j)^2\phi_{ni}(1-\phi_{ni})$ (w_n^j is a short for the indicator function $\mathbf{\Delta}[w_n = j]$).

Once the expectations in $\mathcal{L}_d(\phi, \eta, \lambda, \sigma^2)$ are analytically determined, an iterative fixed-point method is employed to find the set of variational parameters $(\phi, \eta, \lambda, \sigma^2)$ in order to maximize the lower bound of the original log-likelihood, which in turn would minimize the KL divergency between the variational posterior and true posterior in each review. In particular, we compute the derivative of $\mathcal{L}_d(\phi, \eta, \lambda, \sigma^2)$ with respect to the variational parameters accordingly, and use them to find the optimal setting for each variational parameter.

In the aspect modeling part, the variational parameter η can be easily estimated as

$$
\hat{\eta}_i = \gamma_i + \sum_{n=1}^{|d|}\phi_{ni} \tag{8}
$$

Due to the involvement of rating analysis part, it is hard for us to get a closed-form solution for ϕ as in [3]. Therefore, we appeal to the gradient-based optimization procedure to obtain the optimal solution:

$$
\begin{aligned}
\hat{\phi}_n = \arg\max_{\phi_n}\sum_{i=1}^{k}w_n^j\phi_{ni}\Big[\psi(\eta_i) - \psi(\sum_{j=1}^{k}\eta_j) + w_n^j\log\epsilon_{ij} - \log\phi_{ni}\Big] \\
-\frac{1}{2\delta^2}(\lambda^T\bar{\mathbf{s}} - r)^2 - \frac{1}{2\delta^2}\sum_{i=1}^{k}\Big[(\lambda_i^2 + \sigma_i^2)Var[\mathbf{s}_i] + \sigma_i^2\bar{\mathbf{s}_i}^2\Big] \quad (9)
\end{aligned}
$$

s.t. $\forall$ i, $0 \le \phi_{ni} \le 1$ and $\sum_{i=1}^{k}\phi_{ni} = 1$

In the rating analysis part, to make it comparable across different aspects within the same review, we need to force the aspect weight α to satisfy the constraint that $\forall$ i, $0 \le \alpha_i \le 1$ and $\sum_{i=1}^{k}\alpha_i = 1$. This would postulate additional constraints on the optimization procedures for $\mathcal{L}_d(\phi, \eta, \lambda, \sigma^2)$ with respect to variational parameter λ. We use posterior constrained expectation maximization [5] to address this problem. Gradient-based searching algorithm is utilized to find the optimal solution:

$$
\begin{aligned}
\hat{\lambda} = \arg\min_{\lambda}\Big\{\frac{1}{2\delta^2}\Big[\sum_{i=1}^{k}\lambda_i^2Var[\mathbf{s}_i] + (\lambda^T\bar{\mathbf{s}} - r)^2\Big] + \\
\frac{1}{2}(\lambda - \mu)^T\Sigma^{-1}(\lambda - \mu)\Big\} \quad (10)
\end{aligned}
$$

s.t. $\forall$ i, $0 \le \lambda_i \le 1$ and $\sum_i^k\lambda_i = 1$.

Finally, σ^2 could be easily calculated as,

$$
\sigma_i^2 = \frac{\delta^2}{Var[\mathbf{s}_i] + \bar{\mathbf{s}}_i^2 + \delta^2\Sigma_{ii}^{-1}} \tag{11}
$$

The interaction between the aspect modeling module and latent rating analysis module is now clearly stated in the above inference procedures: an optimal aspect assignments $\{z_n\}_{n=1}^{|d|}$ should not only fit the observed review contents as much as possible, but also minimize the overall rating prediction error and the variance of each aspect rating prediction; in other words, the rating prediction part can be considered as a regularization factor for the aspect assignments. Meanwhile, the rating analysis part should also consider the variance of each inferred aspect rating, i.e., we should not put too much emphasis on any single aspect, which is highly uncertain.

4.2 Model Estimation

In the previous section, we have discussed how to infer the latent aspect assignments $\{z_n\}_{n=1}^{|d|}$ and aspect weight α in each review d when given the model $\mathbf{\Theta} = (\epsilon, \gamma, \beta, \mu, \mathbf{\Sigma}, \delta^2)$. In this section, we discuss how to estimate these *corpus-level* parameters using the Expectation Maximization (EM) algorithm by maximizing the expectation of observing review contents and the overall ratings in a given review document collection.

As defined in Eq (7), we can approximate the log-likelihood in each individual review d by the introduced variational distribution $q(z, \theta, \alpha|\phi, \eta, \lambda, \sigma^2)$. Since the variational inference is carried out independently for each review in the collection, the log-likelihood over the whole collection D is simply a summation over the lower bound of each review:

$$
\mathcal{L}(D) = \sum_{d\in D}\mathcal{L}_d(\phi, \eta, \lambda, \sigma^2) \tag{12}
$$

Following similar procedures used in Section 4.1, we maximize Eq (12) by finding the optimal *corpus-level* model parameters $\mathbf{\Theta} = (\epsilon, \gamma, \beta, \mu, \mathbf{\Sigma}, \delta^2)$.

The detailed procedures for updating the parameters in the aspect modeling part is the same as derived in [3], so we only list them here:

$$
\epsilon_{ij} \propto \sum_{d}^{D}\sum_{n}^{N_d}\phi_{dni}w_{dn}^j \tag{13}
$$

$$
\frac{\partial\mathcal{L}(\gamma)}{\partial\gamma_i} = D\Big[\psi(\sum_j\gamma_j) - \psi(\gamma_i)\Big] + \sum_d^D\Big[\psi(\eta_{di}) - \psi(\sum_j\eta_{dj})\Big] \tag{14}
$$

$$
\frac{\partial^2\mathcal{L}(\gamma)}{\partial\gamma_i\partial\gamma_j} = D\big[\psi'(\sum_j\gamma_j) - \sigma(i,j)\psi'(\gamma_i)\big] \tag{15}
$$

The updating equations for the aspect weight prior $(\mu, \mathbf{\Sigma})$, and overall rating prediction variance δ^2 in the rating analysis part can be easily obtained from their sufficient statistics accordingly:

$$\hat{\mu} = \frac{1}{D}\sum_{d=1}^{D}\lambda_d \quad (16)$$

$$\hat{\Sigma} = \frac{1}{D}\sum_{d=1}^{D}[(\lambda_d - \hat{\mu})(\lambda_d - \hat{\mu})^T + diag(\sigma_d^2)] \quad (17)$$

$$\hat{\delta}^2 = \frac{1}{D}\sum_{d=1}^{D}\Big\{(r_d - \lambda_d^T \bar{\mathbf{s}}_d)^2 + \sum_{i=1}^{k}[(\lambda_{di}^2 + \sigma_{di}^2)Var[\mathbf{s}_{di}] + \sigma_{di}^2\bar{\mathbf{s}}_{di}^2]\Big\} \quad (18)$$

However a closed-form updating formula for the term weight matrix β is hard to write out:

$$\hat{\beta} = \arg\min_{\beta}\sum_{d}^{D}\Big\{(\lambda_d^T\bar{\mathbf{s}}_d - r_d)^2 + \sum_{i=1}^{k}[(\lambda_{di}^2 + \sigma_i^2)Var[\mathbf{s}_{di}] + \sigma_{di}^2\bar{\mathbf{s}}_{di}^2]\Big\} \quad (19)$$

We apply the gradient-based optimization technique to find the optimal solution of β with the following gradients:

$$\frac{\partial \mathcal{L}(\beta_i)}{\partial \beta_{ij}} =$$

$$\sum_{d}^{D}\Big[(\lambda_d^T\bar{\mathbf{s}}_d - r_d)\lambda_{di} + \sigma_{di}^2\bar{\mathbf{s}}_{di} + (\lambda_{di}^2 + \sigma_{reviewi}^2)\beta_{ij}w_{dn}^j(1-\phi_{dni})\Big]\phi_{dni}w_{dn}^j$$

From the above equation, we can find another evidence of the interaction between aspect modeling module and rating analysis module: an optimal word sentiment polarity setting should not only ensure the sentiment orientation expressed in the review content consist with the observed overall sentiment judgment, but also reduce the uncertainty on each latent aspect's opinion prediction, which would help the model allocate the aspect assignment for each word more accurately.

All the parameters are first randomly initialized to obtain $\Theta_{(0)}$ (subscript indicates the iteration step) and then the following EM algorithm is applied to iteratively update and improve the parameters by alternatively executing the *E-step* and *M-step* in each iteration until the log-likelihood defined in Eq (12) converges.

E-Step: For each review d in the corpus, infer aspect weight α and topic assignments $\{z_n\}_{n=1}^{|d|}$ based on the current parameter $\Theta_{(t)}$ by using Eq (8) to Eq (11) and compute aspect rating $\mathbf{s}$ by Eq (2).

M-Step: Given the sufficient statistics collected from each review in ***E-Step***, find the updated model parameters $\Theta_{(t+1)}$ by using Eq (13) to Eq (19).

5. EXPERIMENT RESULTS

In this section, we first describe the review data sets we used for evaluation purpose, and then discuss both qualitative and quantitative experiment results.

5.1 Data Sets and Preprocessing

We include two review data sets in our experiments: a hotel review data set originally used in [23], and an MP3 player review data set crawled from `www.amazon.com`. In the hotel data, in addition to the overall ratings, reviewers are also asked to provide ratings on 7 pre-defined aspects in each review: *value, room, location, cleanliness, check in/front desk, service, business service* ranging from 1 star to 5 stars. This can serve as the ground-truth for quantitative evaluation of both aspect identification and latent aspect rating prediction. In the MP3 data set, there is only one overall rating in each review, ranging from 1 star to 5 stars. Both data sets are available at `http://timan.cs.uiuc.edu/downloads.html`.

Table 1: Statistics of data sets

	#Item	#Review	#Reviewer	Avg Len	Rating
Hotel	2,232	37,181	34,187	96.5	3.92±1.23
MP3	686	16,680	15,004	87.3	3.76±1.41

Table 2: Topical aspects learned on MP3 reviews

Low Overall Ratings			High Overall Ratings		
unit	jack	service	files	player	vision
usb	headphone	charge	format	music	video
battery	warranty	problem	included	download	player
charger	replacement	support	easy	headphones	quality
reset	problem	hours	convert	button	great
time	player	months	mp3	set	product
hours	back	weeks	videos	hours	sound
work	months	back	file	buds	radio
thing	buy	customer	wall	volume	accessory
wall	amazon	time	hours	ear	fm

We first perform simple pre-processing on these two data sets: 1) remove the reviews with any missing aspect rating or document length less than 50 words (to keep the content coverage of all possible aspects); 2) convert all the words into lower cases; and 3) removing punctuations, stop words defined in [1], and the terms occurring in less than 10 reviews in the collection. After the pre-processing, we have 37,181 hotel reviews and 16,680 MP3 reviews; the detailed statistics are listed in Table 1.

5.2 Aspect Identification

Automatic Adaptation of Aspects: In Amazon reviews, the reviewers are only asked to give an overall rating, so they would have more freedom, or less guidance to write the comments. In this case, it is *very difficult* to pre-specify aspects in keywords. Here, we will qualitatively demonstrate that our unified model, LARAM, can automatically identify meaningful aspects based on the data characteristics. We separate the reviews into two subsets, one with low overall ratings (at most 3 stars) and the other with high overall ratings (at least 4 stars), and run LARAM to extract 20 aspects on each subset. It is expected that users usually comment on different aspects in positive reviews and negative reviews. In Table 2, we show the top 10 words of the highest generation probability for the three aspects with the highest aspect weight prior μ which can be considered as contributing most to the overall ratings. We can see that LARAM automatically adapts to such different data characteristics: in the negative reviews, the most complained aspects are about warranty and service while positive reviews emphasize the good product features such as flexible file format and great video quality.

Next, we quantitatively compare our model with existing methods on the quality of identified topical aspects.

Algorithms for Comparison: Since we depend on the topic modeling techniques to discover the aspects, we compare LARAM with two different topic models: unsupervised **LDA** model and supervised **sLDA** model. LDA behaves similarly as our aspect modeling module, but it can only fit the word co-occurrence patterns in the review content. sLDA extends LDA by adding a regression module to model the observed overall response, so that it uses the same input as our model. However, since sLDA and LARAM employ

Table 3: KL divergence between the align aspects

	LDA	sLDA	LARAM
7 topics	**5.675**	14.878	5.827
14 topics	8.819	19.074	**8.356**
21 topics	12.745	22.411	**11.167**

different generation assumption for the overall response, it would be interesting to compare these two models.

Measure: In the hotel data set, since TripAdvisor asks reviewers to rate the predefined 7 aspects, it is reasonable to assume those are the major aspects most reviewers comment about. Thus, we use the full set of keywords (in total 309 words) generated by the bootstrapping method used in [23] as a prior to train a LDA model on this data set, and treat the learned topics as the "ground-truth" aspect descriptions. Then we train all the three models *without* any supervision of aspect keywords, find the optimal alignment between the learned topics with "ground-truth" aspects by Kuhn-Munkres algorithm [13] and quantitatively measure the quality of the identified aspects using KL divergence:

$$D(p||q) = \sum_x p(x) \log \frac{p(x)}{q(x)}$$

where p(x) is the "ground-truth" word distribution, and q(x) is the word distribution learned by a given model.

Result Analysis: We train these three models with 7, 14 and 21 topics (since we already know there are 7 aspects) on the hotel data set separately and list the results in Table 3. From the results, we can find that compared with the unsupervised LDA model, the aspects identified by LARAM are closer to the ground-truth aspects when we have more topics (i.e., smaller KL divergence); sLDA's performance is the worst, even though it has additional information from the overall ratings. From the comparison we can see that the inferred aspect ratings from LARAM help the aspect model to better allocate the words across different aspects, which would not be easily distinguished solely from the co-occurrence patterns (LARAM versus LDA). The sLDA model assumes that the topics (aspects) directly characterize the overall ratings, rather than the words' sentiment polarities in the specific aspects as we assumed in LARAM, so it prefers rating sentiment sensitive words than those general content words. As a result, the word distribution under each topic learned by sLDA is quite different from the keyword specified aspects. Besides, we can observe that when we use more topics, KL divergence gets larger. The reason is that with more topics, all the models will then have more freedom to distinguish the aspects in a finer granularity, which is not covered by the predefined aspect keywords.

5.3 Aspect Rating Prediction

Although LARAM is designed to infer ratings on any discovered topical aspects, we can only quantitatively evaluate the predicted ratings on the collection where we have ground-truth aspect ratings from the users. In this experiment, we use the hotel review data set as the testing corpus. In order to ensure our discovered aspects are aligned with the pre-defined aspects, we use the full set of keywords as prior to guide the aspect modeling part.

Algorithms for Comparison: As an alternative method to the proposed unified method **LARAM**, we can take a two-stage approach: apply topic models (e.g., LDA or sLDA) or bootstrapping to identify the aspect segments and then apply LRR to predict aspect ratings. Therefore we include three methods for the comparison purpose, i.e., **LDA+LRR**, **sLDA+LRR**, and **Bootstrap+LRR**.

Table 4: Aspect rating prediction performance on reviews

	LDA+LRR	sLDA+LRR	LARAM
MSE	2.130	2.360	**1.234**
ρ_{aspect}	0.080	0.079	**0.228**
Mis_{aspect}	0.439	0.439	**0.387**
$nDCG_{aspect}$	0.860	0.886	**0.901**
ρ_{hotel}	0.558	0.450	**0.622**
MAP_{hotel}@10	0.427	**0.437**	0.436

Measures: We quantitatively evaluate the algorithms using six different measures, including: (1) Mean Square Error (MSE_{aspect}) of the predicted aspect ratings compared with the ground-truth aspect ratings; (2) Pearson correlation inside reviews (ρ_{aspect}) measures how well the predicted aspect ratings can preserve the relative order of aspects within a review given by their ground-truth ratings; (3) percentage of mis-ordered aspects inside reviews (Mis_{aspect}) measures the cases when the predicted aspect ratings confuse the best and worst aspects within reviews (if they are different as in ground-truth); (4) nDCG of aspect ranking inside reviews ($nDCG_{aspect}$) evaluates the model's ranking accuracy of aspects inside reviews, where the ground truth aspect ratings are used as the graded relevance in the measure; (5) Pearson correlation across hotels (ρ_{hotel}) measures how well the predicted aspect ratings (average over the predicted aspect ratings of all the reviews commenting on this hotel) can preserve the relative order of hotels by their ground-truth ratings; and (6) Mean Average Precision (MAP_{hotel}@10) evaluates the model's ranking accuracy of hotels. We treat each aspect as a query, the top 10% of hotels ranked by the ground-truth aspect ratings as the relevant answers, and test whether we would be able to rank these top 10 hotels on the top, if we use the predicted aspect ratings to rank them. Those measurements can be categorized into two different groups: aspect-level evaluation, including the first four metrics, which are averaged over all the reviews, and hotel-level evaluation, including the last two metrics, which are averaged over all the aspects.

Result Analysis (1): Since we are only interested in predicting the latent aspect ratings, we used all the data for both training and testing. We report the performance of running different models on individual reviews in Table 4, where we highlight the best performance in each metric. We did not include Bootstrap+LRR in this table, because only a small subset of reviews can be tagged with all 7 aspects using the bootstrapping method, but the second-stage LRR requires all reviews to be tagged with 7 aspects as input.

In general, LARAM outperforms other methods in all measures except that its MAP_{hotel}@10 performance is basically the same as sLDA+LRR. The top part of the table shows MSE, which directly measures the difference between the predicted aspect ratings and ground truth ratings. The middle part shows the performance of ranking different aspects inside reviews. The absolute values of ρ_{aspect} are generally low because this measure is over-penalizing all numerical regression methods which produce ratings in real value while ground-truth ratings are all integers. This bias is eliminated in $nDCG_{aspect}$ which also measures the aspect ranking accuracy but handles the integer tie cases well. Mis_{aspect} only looks at the most confident cases where reviewers show explicit preference of one aspect to another. All three measures show superior performance of the proposed unified model in aspect ranking inside reviews which can answer questions like "Do the reviewer like the *location* better than *cleanliness* of hotel XXX?". Finally, the bottom part of the table demonstrates the model's ranking capability of hotels based on the predicted aspect ratings. Since we average the aspect ratings from individual reviews to get aspect ratings for the same hotel, which are in real value, there is no bias in the ρ_{hotel} measure.

Table 5: Aspect rating prediction performance on h-reviews

	Bootstrap+LRR	LARAM	LARAM+LRR
MSE	1.617	1.589	**0.947**
ρ_{aspect}	0.322	0.197	**0.445**
Mis_{aspect}	0.298	0.318	**0.239**
$nDCG_{aspect}$	0.889	0.905	**0.947**
ρ_{hotel}	0.697	**0.767**	0.764
$MAP_{hotel}@10$	0.599	**0.627**	0.590

Result Analysis (2): In order to compare with Bootstrap+LRR, we perform another set of experiments where we concatenate all the reviews commenting on the same hotel together as a new review (we call it "h-review") and average the overall/aspect ratings over them as the ground-truth ratings for this hotel.

The results are shown in Table 5. We observe mixed results when comparing Bootstrap+LRR with our unified LARAM model: LARAM is worse in the middle part which measures the aspect ranking performance within reviews while better in MSE_{aspect} (top part) and hotel ranking (bottom part). To explain this behavior, we analyzed the results from aspect modeling component of LARAM and found that the bag-of-words assumption affected the aspect tagging results of general sentiment words a lot[1]. For example, if a word like "nice" appears in a review, LARAM can hardly associate it with the correct aspect with regard to the local context, or mistakenly assign it to a fixed aspect only because they co-occur more often. And the situation gets even worse when we concatenate different reviews together. In contrast, by considering the adjacency of words or sentence boundaries, we will know that "nice" should contribute to the aspect "*location*" if they are in the same sentence. To test this hypothesis, we first use the topics learned using LARAM to annotate sentences and then apply LRR on the tagged sentences. We call this method LARAM+LRR and show its performance on the last column in Table 5, where the highlighted numbers are the best results on each measure. We can see that by tagging each whole sentence with one aspect, LARAM+LRR provides the best performance in almost all measures. It also validates that the topical aspects discovery by LARAM are effective.

[1]A sample annotation result can be found in `http://sifaka.cs.uiuc.edu/~wang296/Data/annotation.html`

5.4 Aspect Weights Prediction

As we discussed before, a significant advantage of our unified model over existing joint models of aspect and sentiment is that we can infer the relative wights that reviewers have placed on different aspects, i.e., α. Unfortunately, it is infeasible to evaluate the inferred aspect weights directly because we cannot obtain the ground-truth weights from the reviewers. As a result, we choose to evaluate the weights indirectly through clustering the reviewers based on their weights on different aspects.

More specifically, we apply k-means on the aggregated aspect weights of each reviewer over all her reviews to get 10 clusters, where reviewers in the same cluster are expected to share similar taste if the clustering based on the inferred weights is meaningful. In other words, we assume reviewers who share similar aspect preference tend to give the same entity (hotel/MP3 player) similar overall ratings. We test this hypothesis by looking at two sets of standard deviations of ground-truth overall ratings: the first set is for reviewers in the same cluster who also reviewed the same entity while the second control set is for all the reviewers who reviewed the same entity. To make the comparison stable and accurate, we filter out the entities with less than 10 reviews and get 884 hotels with 23,870 reviews and 222 MP3 players with 11,012 reviews in the testing set.

In Figure 3, we show the scatter plot of the two sets of standard deviations. It is clear that most standard deviations of the first set (reviewers from the same cluster on the same entity) are smaller than those of the second control set (all the reviewers on the same entity). Furthermore, two-sample Kolmogorov-Smirnov (KS) test of the samples in the two sets of standard deviations indicates that the difference between the two groups is statistically significant with p-value of e^{-10} for both data sets. This means that reviewers clustered together based on similar aspect weights tend to give more similar overall ratings to the same entity. It also indirectly suggests that the aspect weights learned by our unified model capture the taste of different reviewers.

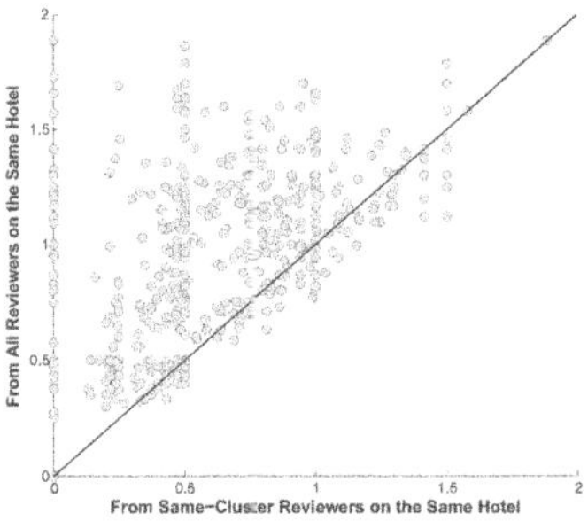

(a) Hotel

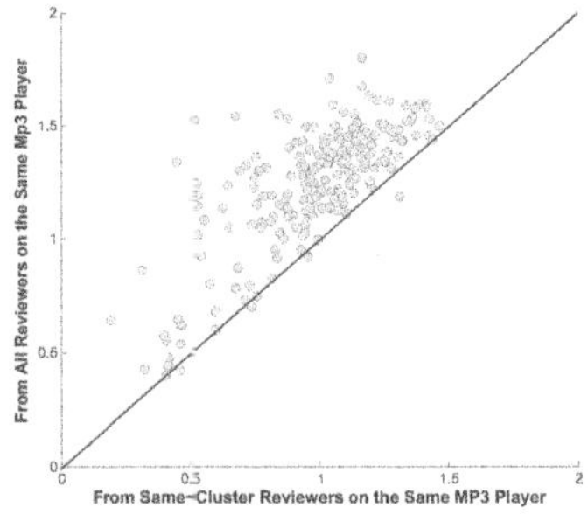

(b) MP3

Figure 3: Scatter plot of standard deviations of overall ratings

6. CONCLUSIONS

In this paper, we propose a unified generative Latent Aspect Rating Analysis Model (LARAM) which can explore review text data with companion overall ratings to simultaneously discover: 1) latent topical aspects, 2) latent ratings on each identified aspect, and 3) latent weights placed on different aspects by a reviewer. It is a fully generative model for both the review text and the overall rating, and enables LARA task on arbitrary review data without needing aspect keyword supervision. Our empirical experiments on a hotel review data set and an MP3 player review data set show that the proposed LARAM can effectively solve the problem of LARA, including automatically identifying meaningful topical aspects, inferring interesting differences in aspect ratings within reviews, and modeling users' preferences with the inferred relative emphasis on different aspects. Such detailed analysis of opinions at the level of topical aspects enabled by LARAM can support multiple application tasks, including aspect opinion summarization, ranking of entities based on aspect ratings, and analysis of reviewers rating behavior.

As we have observed in the detailed experiment results, the bag-of-words assumption seriously hampers the model's aspect segmentation capability, which provides inaccurate segments for the later rating analysis part. For our future work, we are interested in restricting the naive bag-of-words assumption by adding sentence boundary and proximity information into the model for better associating general sentiment words with the appropriate aspect, which will lead to better aspect rating prediction performance. Also, it would be interesting to study how to alleviate the data sparseness problem because reviewers usually do not comment on all the aspects for a given entity. In this situation, borrowing some ideas from the collaborative filtering problem would be beneficial.

7. ACKNOWLEDGMENTS

This material is based upon work supported by the National Science Foundation under Grant Numbers IIS-0713581 and CNS 1028381, and by an AFOSR MURI Grant FA9550-08-1-0265.

8. REFERENCES

[1] Onix text retrieval toolkit stopword list. `http://www.lextek.com/manuals/onix/stopwords1.html`.

[2] D. Blei and J. McAuliffe. Supervised topic models. *Advances in Neural Information Processing Systems*, 20:121–128, 2008.

[3] D. Blei, A. Ng, and M. Jordan. Latent dirichlet allocation. *The Journal of Machine Learning Research*, 3:993–1022, 2003.

[4] X. Ding, B. Liu, and L. Zhang. Entity discovery and assignment for opinion mining applications. In *Proceedings of the 15th KDD*, pages 1125–1134. ACM, 2009.

[5] J. Graça, K. Ganchev, and B. Taskar. Expectation maximization and posterior constraints. In *Advances in Neural Information Processing Systems*, volume 20. MIT Press, 2007.

[6] M. Hu and B. Liu. Mining and summarizing customer reviews. In *Proceedings of the 10th KDD*, pages 168–177. ACM, 2004.

[7] M. Hu and B. Liu. Mining opinion features in customer reviews. In *AAAI*, pages 755–760. AAAI Press / The MIT Press, 2004.

[8] N. Jindal and B. Liu. Identifying comparative sentences in text documents. In *Proceedings of 29th SIGIR*, 2006.

[9] Y. Jo and A. H. Oh. Aspect and sentiment unification model for online review analysis. In *Proceedings of the fourth ACM international conference on Web search and data mining*, 2011.

[10] M. Jordan, Z. Ghahramani, T. Jaakkola, and L. Saul. An introduction to variational methods for graphical models. *Machine learning*, 37(2):183–233, 1999.

[11] S. Kim and E. Hovy. Determining the sentiment of opinions. In *Proceedings of the 20th international conference on Computational Linguistics*, pages 1367–1373. Association for Computational Linguistics, 2004.

[12] C. Lin and Y. He. Joint sentiment/topic model for sentiment analysis. In *Proceeding of the 18th CIKM*, pages 375–384, New York, NY, USA, 2009. ACM.

[13] L. Lovász and M. Plummer. *Matching theory*. Elsevier Science Ltd, 1986.

[14] Y. Lu and C. Zhai. Opinion integration through semi-supervised topic modeling. In *Proceeding of the 17th WWW*, pages 121–130. ACM, 2008.

[15] Y. Lu, C. Zhai, and N. Sundaresan. Rated aspect summarization of short comments. In *Proceedings of the 18th WWW*, pages 131–140, 2009.

[16] Q. Mei, X. Ling, M. Wondra, H. Su, and C. Zhai. Topic sentiment mixture: modeling facets and opinions in weblogs. In *Proceedings of the 16th WWW*, pages 171–180. ACM, 2007.

[17] S. Morinaga, K. Yamanishi, K. Tateishi, and T. Fukushima. Mining product reputations on the web. In *Proceeding of the 8th KDD*, pages 341–349, 2002.

[18] B. Pang and L. Lee. Seeing stars: Exploiting class relationships for sentiment categorization with respect to rating scales. In *Proceedings of the 43rd ACL*, pages 115–124, 2005.

[19] B. Pang, L. Lee, and S. Vaithyanathan. Thumbs up? Sentiment classification using machine learning techniques. In *Proceedings of the 2002 Conference on Empirical Methods in Natural Language Processing*, pages 79–86, 2002.

[20] A.-M. Popescu and O. Etzioni. Extracting product features and opinions from reviews. In *HLT '05*, pages 339–346, Morristown, NJ, USA, 2005.

[21] I. Titov and R. T. McDonald. A joint model of text and aspect ratings for sentiment summarization. In *Proceedings of the 46th ACL*, pages 308–316, 2008.

[22] I. Titov and R. T. McDonald. Modeling online reviews with multi-grain topic models. In *Proceeding of the 17th WWW*, pages 111–120, 2008.

[23] H. Wang, Y. Lu, and C. Zhai. Latent aspect rating analysis on review text data: a rating regression approach. In *Proceedings of the 16th KDD*, pages 783–792. ACM, 2010.

[24] W. X. Zhao, J. Jiang, H. Yan, and X. Li. Jointly modeling aspects and opinions with a maxent-lda hybrid. In *Proceedings of the 2010 Conference on Empirical Methods in Natural Language Processing*, EMNLP '10, 2010.

[25] L. Zhuang, F. Jing, and X.-Y. Zhu. Movie review mining and summarization. In *Proceedings of the 15th ACM international conference on Information and knowledge management*, 2006.

Density Estimation Trees

Parikshit Ram
Georgia Institute of Technology
Atlanta GA, 30332
p.ram@gatech.edu

Alexander G. Gray
Georgia Institute of Technology
Atlanta GA, 30332
agray@cc.gatech.edu

ABSTRACT

In this paper we develop *density estimation trees* (DETs), the natural analog of classification trees and regression trees, for the task of density estimation. We consider the estimation of a joint probability density function of a d-dimensional random vector X and define a piecewise constant estimator structured as a decision tree. The integrated squared error is minimized to learn the tree. We show that the method is nonparametric: under standard conditions of nonparametric density estimation, DETs are shown to be asymptotically consistent. In addition, being decision trees, DETs perform automatic feature selection. They empirically exhibit the interpretability, adaptability and feature selection properties of supervised decision trees while incurring slight loss in accuracy over other nonparametric density estimators. Hence they might be able to avoid the curse of dimensionality if the true density is sparse in dimensions. We believe that density estimation trees provide a new tool for exploratory data analysis with unique capabilities.

Categories and Subject Descriptors

I.5 [**Pattern Recognition**]: Models; G.3 [**Probability and Statistics**]: Nonparametric statistics

General Terms

Algorithms, Experimentation

Keywords

Decision trees, density estimation, data analysis

1. INTRODUCTION

Three most fundamental tasks of machine learning are classification, regression, and density estimation. Classification and regression are instances of supervised data analysis where a training set of examples is provided. The learning task is to estimate a function using the training set which also performs well on a test set. The third task, density estimation, is an instance of unsupervised learning. This is generally harder because one does not have any instance of the ground truth regarding the quantity being estimated. Decision trees [1] have been widely used in the supervised setting for classification and regression. *In this paper we introduce, derive, and explore the natural analog of classification trees and regression trees for the unsupervised task of density estimation.* To our knowledge this analogy has never been explored rigorously, though several other ideas for density estimation involving hierarchical schemes have been proposed. Our hope is that the unique advantages of decision trees in the supervised setting will transfer to the unsupervised setting, to give rise to a new nonparametric density estimation method with interesting capabilities.

Density estimation. The problem of density estimation can be defined as estimating an unknown distribution f on $\mathcal{X}^1$ with a close approximation $\hat{f}\colon \mathcal{X} \to \mathbb{R}_+$ given a set of N IID (independent and identically distributed) observations $\{X_1, X_2, \ldots, X_N\} \subset \mathcal{X}$ drawn from f. Estimating the probability density of the given data is a fundamental task in multivariate statistics. It often appears as a subroutine in other inference – for example, in classification, one is required to find $\hat{P}(C|X) = \frac{\hat{p}(X|C)P(C)}{\hat{p}(X)}$, where C is one of the possible K classes and $\hat{p}(X|C)$ is the class-conditional density of the data X [2, 3, 4]. It is also widely used for conducting exploratory analyses such as outlier or cluster detection.

Decision trees. Decision trees [1] were developed for classification [5] and regression [6]. They are primarily used for the purpose of supervised learning and have been widely and successfully used in nonparametric classification and regression. The piecewise constant estimators and the simplistic model of univariate binary splits of the data in decision trees lead to relatively *less accurate* estimators with unknown convergence rates [7]. Techniques such as bagging are used to boost this accuracy. More sophisticated methods with better accuracies and clearer asymptotic properties such as local linear regression [8] and support vector machines [9] exist for regression and classification respectively.

Nonetheless, anecdotally, decision trees remain one of the more widely used methods in practice [7], possibly even the most widely used. This is due to the inherent *intuitiveness*, *adaptability* and *interpretability* of the models learned. Moreover, they are capable of dealing with *mixed* categorical, discrete and continuous variables within one unified framework. They also perform *feature selection* and are easy to implement. These properties come at the cost of accuracy in prediction but still make decision trees very desirable and

[1]If all the attributes of the data are continuous then $\mathcal{X} \subset \mathbb{R}^d$

Table 1: Characteristics of Methods for Density Estimation

METHODS	np	Accuracy	Interpretability			Adaptability		Speed	
			COD	VI	Rules	ABD	AWD	Training	Query
MoG	×	low	✓	×	×	×	×	fast EM algorithm	very fast $O(d^2)$
Histogram	✓	low	×	×	×	×	×	fast $O(MdN)$	very fast $O(d)$
KDE (FBW)	✓	medium	×	×	×	×	×	slow $O(HdN^2)$	slow $O(dN)$
KDE* (FBW)	✓	medium	×	×	×	×	×	fast $O(HdN)$	medium $O(d \log N)$
KDE (VBW)	✓	highest	×	×	×	✓	✓	very slow $O(H^d dN)/q$	slow $O(dN)$
KDE* (VBW)	✓	high	×	×	×	✓	✓	slow $O(H^d d \log N)/q$	medium $O(d \log N)$
local r-KDE	✓	very high	×	×	×	✓	✓	fast CV step/q	slow $O(dN)$
global r-KDE	✓	medium/high	×	×	×	✓	×	t fast CV steps	slow $O(dN)$
DET	✓	medium	✓	✓	✓	✓	✓	slow LOO-CV	fast $O(D_T)$

practical. Another advantage of decision trees is the *efficient test querying* once the model (in this case a tree) has been trained.

Decision trees trade some accuracy for a simple, interpretable model. Considering that density estimation is widely used in exploratory analysis, giving up accuracy (which is not a useful concept in the absence of the ground truth) for understanding is acceptable.

1.1 Nonparametric Density Estimators

Histograms and kernel density estimators (KDEs) [10] are simpler nonparametric (np) techniques, whereas variants of KDEs such as rodeo-KDEs [11] and wavelet based methods [8] are more complex nonparametric estimators. A number of nonparametric Bayesian methods have also been developed for the task of density estimation [12]. Mixtures of Gaussians (MoGs) are widely used parametric density estimators. Even though the nonparametric methods have been shown to be significantly more accurate than the parametric methods and require fewer assumptions on the data than parametric methods, MoGs are widely used because of their interpretability as clusters (as well as their simple implementation).

Adaptability and Speed. Adaptability has two implications in density estimation: (1) *adaptable between dimensions (ABD)* – the estimation process should treat dimensions differently depending on their influence on the density (for example, addition of unimportant dimensions of uniform noise should not affect the estimator) (2) *adaptable within a dimension (AWD)* – determining regions of interest for a given dimension and adjusting the estimator to the local behavior of the density in that dimension (for example, regions with fast changing density vs. regions with flat densities).

MoGs are not known to adapt between or within dimensions. Fixed-bandwidth KDEs (FBW) are accurate nonparametric estimators but are not adaptable between or within dimensions because of the restriction of using a multivariate kernel with the same bandwidth in every dimension (spherical kernel) for every point. The bandwidth is chosen through leave-one-out cross-validation (LOO-CV) by picking the one with the best CV loss among the H different values tried. A significantly high value of H is required to obtain accurate results. LOO-CV for the naïve implementation of KDE takes $O(HdN^2)$. Spatial partitioning tree data structures have been used for fast-approximate computation of KDEs (KDE*s) [13, 14]. For cover-trees [15], this process requires $O(HdN)$ time [16].

Various KDEs with adaptive bandwidths have been developed but are complicated in practice. The nearest-neighbor KDEs [10] are locally adaptive by choosing bandwidths based on their k^{th}-nearest-neighbor distance. However, they are not adaptive over dimensions since they still use a spherical multivariate kernel. Moreover, the estimate does not represent a probability density function (pdf), and is discontinuous and heavy tailed. A truly adaptive (ABD) KDE would require an optimal bandwidth for each dimension (VBW). This means the kernel used would be elliptical, adapting to the density of the data. This makes the VBW-KDEs adaptable between dimensions. If H bandwidths are tried in *each* dimension, the training time required for the naïve implementation of KDEs would be $O(H^d dN)$. To make this locally adaptive for each dimension(AWD), the bandwidth estimation would be required for each query q. Even the faster methods (KDE*) would require $O(H^d d \log N)$ training time for each query. This makes the computational cost of CV for VBW-KDEs intractable even in medium dimensions.

A recent algorithm [11] uses *rodeo* [17] to greedily select adaptive bandwidths for a KDE in each dimension. Under certain sparsity conditions on the unknown density function, the resulting estimator is shown to empirically perform well and obtain near optimal convergence rate for KDEs. The local version (local r-KDE) of this estimator computes the optimal bandwidth in every dimension for every query point. The paper demonstrates rodeo's adaptability – implicitly identifying the dimensions of interest during the process of bandwidth selection as well as identifying regions of interest within a single dimension, selecting smaller bandwidths where the density varies more rapidly. However, this technique is expensive, requiring a rodeo step for every single query. The rodeo step is iterative and we are not aware of its runtime bound. However, it is empirically faster than LOO-CV for VBW-KDEs. The global-rodeo [11] (global r-KDE) improves efficiency by using a fixed bandwidth within each dimension, and estimating it by averaging the estimated bandwidths for t training points in every dimension. Hence, the resulting estimator loses local adaptability within a dimension (property 2 of adaptability). The training time now involves t rodeo steps instead of a rodeo step for each query. The accuracy of the estimate obviously depends on the t (larger number training queries imply more accurate estimates and slower training).

KDEs can be made adaptable, however, at the cost of computational complexity. Moreover, given the estimated bandwidths, the time taken for a single query using the naïve implementation of a KDE is $O(dN)$. The cover-tree data structure provides an approximate estimate in $O(d \log N)$ query time. For $O(N)$ queries, the query cost can be amortized over the queries using a tree-data-structure over the queries, requiring a total time of $O(dN)$ [16][2].

Decision trees are known for their adaptability over the data (over features by implicit feature selection and within dimensions by choosing different leaf size in different regions). In this paper, we will demonstrate their adaptability for the task of density estimation. However, training decision trees using LOO-CV is an expensive step involving the growing of the tree, and the subsequent cost-complexity pruning [1, 7]. However this cost is amortized over the multiple empirically efficient queries. The query time for a decision tree estimator is $O(D_T)$ where D_T is the depth of a decision tree T. The worst case upper bound for D_T is $O(N)$, but is empirically seen to be much tighter in practice (much more closer to $O(\log N)$). Hence decision trees also bring efficiency to nonparametric density estimation at the cost of some accuracy. Histograms are also fast nonparametric estimators during training as well as query time. They require $O(MdN)$ training time for trying M different bin-widths and choosing the one with the best CV error. The query time is a blazing $O(d)$. However, they lack the adaptability of decision trees, and become prohibitively inaccurate as the number of dimensions increases.

Interpretability. We also propose the use of decision trees for density estimation to introduce interpretability in the nonparametric setting. The decision trees provide an interesting overlap between the accuracy of nonparametric methods and the simplicity and interpretability of parametric methods. Interpretability in density estimation can be useful in the providing the following information about the density of the data: (1) *detecting clusters and outliers (COD)* (2) *providing relative variable/dimension importance (VI)* – identifying dimensions that significantly affect the density (3) *providing simple univariate rules* – these simple rules can be used, for example, for directly specifying some chunk of a huge data set which sits on a DBMS database. In the case of a DET, this chunk might represent a cluster.

MoGs are known to detect clusters but are incapable of imparting any interpretability regarding the dimensions. The aforementioned method using rodeo [11] implicitly does identify dimensions of interest. However, it is hard to obtain relative importance of dimensions by just looking at the values of the estimated bandwidths. Moreover, cluster and outlier detection is complicated with KDEs – an exhaustive scan of the whole space provides regions of high (clusters) and low density (outliers). So KDEs are not interpretable density estimators. When accuracy is required with no concern over computation time, adaptive-KDEs are the method of choice. However, they might be too costly for exploratory analysis.

We attempt to achieve the properties of interpretability, while retaining adaptability, by using the CART-style univariate splits which gives rise to the uniquely readable rule structure of decision trees. This key property is not shared by the several other methods for density estimation involving hierarchical schemes which have been proposed over the years. Determining dimensions of interest is a direct by-product of the decision tree framework via the measure of *relative importance* of predictor variables [1][3]. While linear models such as linear regression and linear SVMs yield such a capability via examination of the linear coefficients, this capability is harder to find in nonparametric methods. A sorted list of the leaves of a DET can easily identify the clusters and the outliers in the data.

All the aforementioned properties of these estimators are summarized in Table 1. We further motivate the desirability of interpretability of a decision tree in the following example:

Motivating example. Consider the density estimates for the **Iris** data set (150×4)[4] as a set of rules depicted in Figure 1. Each leaf node contains the piecewise constant density estimate. More explicitly, $\hat{f}(x) = 0.026\ \forall x \in R_1$ (say). Here the leaf $R_1 = \{x\colon x_4 \leq 0.2\ \&\ x_3 \leq 1.5\}$. We have also listed the class memberships of the points in the leaf nodes[5]. This figure also presents the relative importance of the attributes.

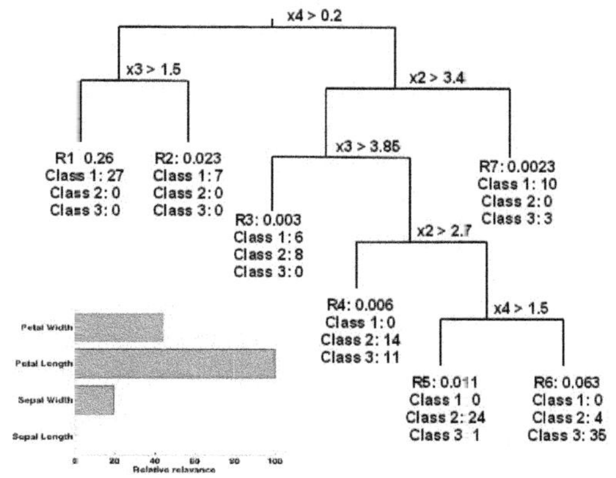

Figure 1: Density estimate in form of a decision tree and the relative variable importance.

The tree representation lets us easily find regions of relatively high (R_1) and low densities (R_3). The subtree corresponding to the regions R_1 and R_2 contains purely class 1, representing the well-known linearly separable class in the Iris data. The chart containing the relative importance of the predictor variables implies that the *petal length* has the highest importance with regards to the density, whereas, the *sepal length* has no influence on the density (example of feature deletion).

Thus we see that density estimation in the decision tree framework provides much more information about the data than just the density estimates. There are several other cases where it would be useful to get this kind of information about the data: (1)*Astronomy* – performing density estimation on quasar data is a common task in astronomy [18]. Common features in the data are colors. The feature-importance analysis corresponding to the density will indicate the unimportant color features. This information can be useful in deciding which filters are useful in future analyses, thereby, conserving resources. (2)*Bioinformatics* – consider a metabolomics data set containing pa-

[2]It is important to note that the spatial partitioning tree building has a one-time cost of $O(dN \log N)$.

[3]We will define this measure in the technical section of the paper.

[4]We will continue to represent the size of data sets with N point with d attributes/dimensions in the form $(N \times d)$ throughout this paper.

[5]We intend to perform density estimation only on the points in the unsupervised setting. However, we provide class memberships of the points in the node to motivate a well known property of the Iris data set.

tient information with over 20000 features, where the task is to differentiate cancer patients from healthy patients [19]. Density estimation performed over all patients' profiles can reveal which features are responsible for the main variation within, say, cancer patients, or within healthy patients. This is different from feature selection for classification which would select features which most differentiate the patients with cancer from the rest. In addition, cluster and outlier detection performed on this data set will produce interesting and possibly crucial information.

Moreover, a representative partition of the state space by itself sheds light on the underlying structure of the distribution. Such information is particularly valuable in high dimensional problems where direct visualization of the data is difficult.

Remark. DETs are similar to variable bin-width histograms, but are restricted only to a hierarchical partitioning of the data (hence possibly having lower accuracy than the best possible variable bin-width histogram, although our experiments suggest otherwise).

1.2 Overview

The focus of this paper is to develop a rigorous decision-tree-structured density estimator and demonstrate the usefulness and interpretability of the same.

In Section 2, we discuss existing connections between density estimation and decision trees. In the following section, we define an estimator based on the decision tree and apply the decision-tree framework for density estimation using this estimator. We also provide certain asymptotic properties of the decision-tree-structured estimator. Section 4 contains experimental results displaying the performance of DETs with some comparisons with histograms and KDEs. The adaptability of DETs is demonstrated by using some synthetic data sets. High dimensional image data sets are used to demonstrate the DETs' interpretability and their application to classification. Training and querying time of DETs are compared with the fastest training and querying method for KDEs (KDE*s). In the final section, conclusions are discussed along with certain open questions.

2. FURTHER RELATED WORK

Decision trees have been used alongside density estimation in earlier works. For example, Kohavi, 1996 [20] and Smyth et al., 1995 [21] use decision trees for the supervised task of classification, and density estimation (with naïve Bayes classifiers and KDEs respectively) is used solely for the purpose of obtaining a smoother and more accurate classification and class-conditional probabilities in contrast to the piecewise constant non-smooth estimates of the standard classification trees. Decision trees been used for the task of diagnosing extrapolation [22] by building a classification tree differentiating the given data set from a random sample from a uniform distribution in the support of the data set. This tree provides a way to compute a measure for extrapolation. This measure can be indirectly used to compute the density, but the tree still performs classification. Decision trees have also been used in the supervised setting for estimating the joint probability (of the data and the label of the training examples) [23] for censored data by replacing the standard loss function (for example 0-1 loss or Gini-index) with the negative loglikelihood of the joint density.

The idea of having a nested hierarchy of partitions of the support of the data has been used for dicretization of univariate data [24]. The set of observations are partitioned on the basis of the density using the loglikelihood loss function. But the focus is solely on univariate data. Decision trees have also been used in an unsupervised setting to perform hierarchical clustering [25] but do not trivially translate to density estimation. Siedl et al., 2009 [26] propose a novel method for indexing the density model in the form of a tree (called Bayes tree) for fast access with desired level of accuracy. This tree is grown bottom-up from the estimate of a KDE for the whole data set. The Bayes tree uses MoGs to index the density at the intermediate levels (increasing the number of Gaussians with the depth). This tree successfully locates clusters in the data. However, being a MoG, it fails to determine relative relevance of the dimensions. Pólya trees [27] are hierarchical spatial partitioning trees but used as a prior for probability measures over the data space. Density estimation is done either by computing the posterior mean density given this prior or "learning" a fixed tree topology and computing the piecewise constant estimate conditional on this topology.

DETs are related in spirit, however, they will be learned by directly minimizing the density estimation loss and the estimates are finally obtained directly from the tree. Moreover, the aforementioned methods, though hierarchical in nature, do not share the interpretability and feature selection properties of decision trees, which are based on univariate splits.

3. DENSITY ESTIMATION TREE

This section provides the road map to perform density estimation using decision trees. We define an estimator and the corresponding loss function to be minimized during the training of the decision tree for continuous and mixed data. Following that, we explain the process of learning the optimal decision tree over the given sample and provide an asymptotic property of the DET.

3.1 Continuous Features

DEFINITION 1. *The piecewise constant density estimate of the decision tree T built on a set $\mathcal{S}$ of N observations in $\mathbb{R}^d$ is defined as*

$$\hat{f}_N(x) = \sum_{l \in \tilde{T}} \frac{|l|}{NV_l} \mathbb{I}(x \in l) \tag{1}$$

where $\tilde{T}$ is the set of leaves of the decision tree T representing the partitions of the data space, $|l|$ is the number of observations of $\mathcal{S}$ in the leaf l, V_l is the volume of the leaf l within the d dimensional bounding box of $\mathcal{S}$ and $\mathbb{I}(\cdot)$ is the indicator function.

A decision tree T requires a notion of a loss function $R(T)$ which is minimized using a greedy algorithm to construct a tree on the set of observations. For the unsupervised task of density estimation, we consider the Integrated Squared Error (ISE) loss function [10]. The ISE gives a notion of overall distance between the estimated and the true density and is a favored choice in nonparametric density estimation for its inherent robustness in comparison to maximum-likelihood-based loss functions [8]. However, other distance functions such as the KL-divergence can be used as the loss function. We will explore this in the longer version of the paper.

The task of learning a DET would involve solving the following optimization problem:

$$\min_{\hat{f}_N \in \mathcal{F}_N} \int_X \left(\hat{f}_N(x) - f(x)\right)^2 dx \tag{2}$$

where $\mathcal{F}_N$ is the class of estimators of form in Definition 1 that can learned with any set of N observations. After expanding the square and the following Monte-Carlo substitution $\int_X \hat{f}_N(x) f(x) dx \approx \frac{1}{N}\sum_{i=1}^N \hat{f}_N(X_i)$ (where $\{X_i\}_{i=1}^N$ is the training set), the objective function in Eq. 2 is replaced by the following consistent plug-in estimator of the ISE [10][6]:

$$\min_{\hat{f}_N \in \mathcal{F}_N} \left\{ \int_X \left(\hat{f}_N(x)\right)^2 dx - \frac{2}{N}\sum_{i=1}^{N} \hat{f}_N(X_i) \right\} \tag{3}$$

Using the piecewise constant estimator from Definition 1 (which is constant within each leaf l), the objective function in Eq. 3 is replaced with the following:

$$\sum_{l \in \tilde{T}} \left\{ \int_l \left(\frac{|l|}{NV_l}\right)^2 dx - \frac{2}{N}\frac{|l|}{NV_l} \cdot |l| \right\} \tag{4}$$

by substituting

$$\hat{f}_N^2(x) = \sum_{l \in \tilde{T}} \left(\frac{|l|}{NV_l}\right)^2 \mathbb{I}(x \in l)$$

(since the cross terms in the expansion of $\hat{f}_N^2(x)$ vanish because of the indicator function) and simple calculation shows that

$$\sum_{i=1}^{N} \hat{f}_N(X_i) = \sum_{i=1}^{N}\sum_{l \in \tilde{T}} \frac{|l|}{NV_l} \cdot \mathbb{I}(X_i \in l) = \sum_{l \in \tilde{T}} \frac{|l|}{NV_l} \cdot |l|$$

By making the following substitution

$$\int_l \left(\frac{|l|}{NV_l}\right)^2 dx = \left(\frac{|l|}{NV_l}\right)^2 \int_l dx = \left(\frac{|l|}{NV_l}\right)^2 \cdot V_l,$$

the estimator of the ISE for DET has the following form:

$$\sum_{l \in \tilde{T}} \left\{ -\frac{|l|^2}{N^2 V_l} \right\} \tag{5}$$

Defining Eq. 5 as the error $R(T)$ of the tree, the greedy surrogate of the error for any node t (internal or otherwise) can be defined as

$$R(t) = -\frac{|t|^2}{N^2 V_t}. \tag{6}$$

The tree is grown in a top down manner by maximizing the reduction in this greedy surrogate of the error over the given observations.

3.2 Mixed Features

For density estimation over data with mixed features, we define a novel density estimator and a loss function involving ordinal and categorical data along with continuous data that can be used to learn DETs with mixed data:

[6]The term $\int_X (f(x))^2 dx$ is removed from the objective function since it is independent of the estimate and hence doesn't affect the optimum.

DEFINITION 2. *Let $\mathcal{S} \subset \mathbb{R}^d \times \mathbb{Z}^{d'} \times \mathbb{C}^{d''}$ with d real features, d' ordinal features and d'' categorical features. The piecewise constant density estimator of the decision tree T built on $\mathcal{S}$ is defined as*

$$\hat{f}_N(x) = \sum_{l \in \tilde{T}} \frac{|l| \cdot \mathbb{I}(x \in l)}{N \cdot V_{l_d} \cdot \prod_{j=1}^{d'_l} R_{l_j} \cdot \prod_{i=1}^{d''_l} M_{l_i}} \tag{7}$$

where V_{l_d} is the volume of the leaf l within the d dimensional bounding box of the real part of $\mathcal{S}$, R_{l_j} is the range of the ordinal values in the jth of the d'_l ordinal dimensions present in l and M_{l_i} is the number of categories present in l for the ith of the d''_l categorical dimensions present in l.

The error at a node t corresponding to the ISE is then obtained as

$$R(t) = -\frac{|t|^2}{N^2 \cdot V_{t_d} \cdot \prod_{j=1}^{d'_t} R_{t_j} \cdot \prod_{i=1}^{d''_t} M_{t_i}} \tag{8}$$

where V_{t_d} is the volume of the node t in the d real dimensions, R_{t_j} is the range of the ordinal values in the jth of the d'_t ordinal dimensions present in t and M_{t_i} is the number of categories present in t for the ith of the d''_t categorical dimensions present in t.

3.3 Tree Construction

We use the tree learning algorithm presented in Breiman, et al.,1984 [1]. The splitting, pruning and the cross-validation procedures are modified to work with this new loss function and for the unsupervised task of density estimation.

Splitting. For growing the tree, each node is split into two children. Let S be the set of all univariate splits.

DEFINITION 3. *[1] The best split s^* of a node t is the split in the set of splits S which maximally reduces $R(T)$.*

This is done by greedily reducing $R(t)$ for all the terminal nodes t of the current tree. Hence, for any currently terminal node, we need to find a split s^* for a node t into t_L and t_R such that

$$s^* = \arg\max_{s \in S}\{R(t) - R(t_L) - R(t_R)\} \tag{9}$$

where $|t| = |t_L| + |t_R|$. For continuous and ordinal dimensions, this optimization is performed by trying every $|t| - 1$ possible splits of the data in each of the dimensions. For categorical dimensions, the splits are performed in the manner similar to the CART model [1]. The splitting is stopped when the node size $|t|$ goes below a certain threshold (say $N_{\min}$).

Pruning. To avoid overfitting, we use the minimal cost-complexity pruning [1]. The regularized error of a subtree rooted at a node t is defined as

$$R_\alpha(t) = R(\tilde{t}) + \alpha \cdot |\tilde{t}| \tag{10}$$

where α is a regularization parameter (to be estimated through cross-validation) and $\tilde{t}$ is the set of leaves in the subtree rooted at t. The value of α is gradually increased and a subtree rooted at t is pruned for the value of α where $R_\alpha(t) = R_\alpha(\{t\})$, the regularized error of the pruned subtree. Since the size of the initial tree constructed by the splitting algorithm described previously is finite, the number of possible values of α at which a prune occurs is finite and can be calculated efficiently. Hence we only need to select the optimal α from a finite set of values (See Section 3.3 in Breiman, et al., 1984 [1] for complete details).

Cross-validation. The leave-one-out cross-validation (LOO-CV) estimator of the density estimation loss function in Eq. 3 is given by

$$\hat{J}(\alpha) = \int_X \left(\hat{f}_N^\alpha(x)\right)^2 dx - \frac{2}{N}\sum_{i=1}^{N} \hat{f}_{(-i)}^\alpha(X_i) \qquad (11)$$

where $\hat{f}_N^\alpha$ is the estimator with the decision tree T pruned with a regularization parameter α, and $\hat{f}_{(-i)}^\alpha$ is the estimator with the decision tree $T_{(-i)}$ built without the training example X_i pruned with the regularization parameter α. This LOO-CV estimator is obtained from Silverman, 1986 [10] by switching the regularization parameter (replacing the bandwidth with α). The best sized tree is the tree T pruned with the parameter α^* such that:

$$\alpha^* = \arg\min_\alpha \hat{J}(\alpha) \qquad (12)$$

3.4 Asymptotic Properties

We show that the method is *nonparametric* – it is consistent under mild assumptions on the model class of the input distribution f. Consistency is typically shown [28] for a nonparametric estimator $\hat{f}_N$ obtained from a set of N observations by showing that

$$\Pr\left(\lim_{N\to\infty} \int_X \left(\hat{f}_N(x) - f(x)\right)^2 dx = 0\right) = 1. \qquad (13)$$

We prove the consistency of DETs on data with continuous features. The proof of consistency of the density estimator proposed in Definition 1 follows arguments similar to those used to show the consistency of regression trees [1] .

THEOREM 1. *The estimator $\hat{f}_N$ defined in Definition 1 satisfies Eq. 13.*

PROOF. Given a fixed positive integer d_1, let $\mathcal{B}$ denote the collection of all sets $t \subset X$ that can be described as the solution set to a system of d_1 inequalities, each of the form $b^T x \leq c$ for $b \in \mathbb{R}^d$ and $c \in \mathbb{R}$. Now in a decision tree T, every leaf $l \in \tilde{T}$ is the solution set of a system of d_1 inequalities of the form $b^T x \leq c$ with $b \in \mathbb{R}^d$ with just one entry equal to 1 and the rest of the entries equal to 0. Therefore, $\tilde{T} \subset \mathcal{B}$.

Let X_n, $n \geq 1$, be a random sample from a density function f on X. For $N \geq 1$, let $\hat{F}_N$ denote the empirical distribution of $X_n, 1 \leq n \leq N$, defined on a set $t \subset X$ by

$$\hat{F}_N(t) = \frac{1}{N}\sum_{n=1}^{N} \mathbb{I}(X_n \in t) = \frac{|t|}{N} = \int_t \hat{f}_N(x)dx \qquad (14)$$

where $|t|$ is the number of random samples in the set $t \cap \{X_n\}_{n=1}^N$ and $\hat{f}_N(x)$ is the estimator given in Definition 1.

According to a general version of the Glivenko-Cantelli theorem [29],

$$\Pr\left(\lim_{N\to\infty} \sup_{t\in\mathcal{B}} |\hat{F}_N(t) - \int_t f(x)dx| = 0\right) = 1. \qquad (15)$$

By Eq.14 and 15, we get

$$\Pr\left(\lim_{N\to\infty} \sup_{t\in\mathcal{B}} |\int_t \hat{f}_N(x)dx - \int_t f(x)dx| = 0\right) = 1$$

$$\Rightarrow \Pr\left(\lim_{N\to\infty} \sup_{t\in\mathcal{B}} \int_t |\hat{f}_N(x) - f(x)|dx \geq 0\right) = 1.$$

Assuming that $\lim_{N\to\infty} \Pr(\text{diameter}(t) \geq \epsilon) = 0$, hence $\Pr\left(\lim_{N\to\infty} \int_t dx = 0\right) = 1$, we get the following with probability 1

$$\begin{aligned}\lim_{N\to\infty} \sup_{t\in\mathcal{B}} \int_t |\hat{f}_N(x) - f(x)|dx &\leq \\ \lim_{N\to\infty} |\hat{f}_N(x') - f(x')| \cdot \int_t dx \text{ for some } x' \in t &= 0\end{aligned}$$

This assumption is commonly used for the consistency of data-partitioning estimators [30] and is justified since as $N \to \infty$, the diameter of any leaf node would become smaller and smaller since the leaf node can only have a bounded number of points. Hence

$$\Pr\left(\lim_{N\to\infty} \sup_{t\in\mathcal{B}} \int_t |\hat{f}_N(x) - f(x)|dx = 0\right) = 1$$

$$\Rightarrow \Pr\left(\lim_{N\to\infty} \int_X \left(\hat{f}_N(x) - f(x)\right)^2 dx = 0\right) = 1.$$

Hence $\hat{f}_N$ satisfies Eq. 13. □

4. EXPERIMENTS

In this section, we demonstrate the performance of DETs under different conditions using synthetic and real data sets. Estimation accuracies of DETs are compared with existing nonparametric estimators. We exhibit the interpretability of DETs with two real data sets. Furthermore, density estimates of DETs are applied to classification and subsequent labelling accuracies are presented. Finally, the speed of training and querying DETs are presented on several real data sets and compared with an existing method. We only consider continuous and ordinal data in this paper for the lack of space. Experiments with categorical and mixed data will be presented in the longer version of the paper.

4.1 Estimation Accuracy: Synthetic Examples

For the unsupervised task of density estimation, estimation accuracy can only be computed on synthetic data sets. We choose the best-sized tree through LOO-CV. To compute estimation error on synthetic data for density queries, we use 2 measures: *Root Mean Squared Error* (RMSE) and *Hellinger Distance* (HD). We compare DETs only with other nonparametric density estimators since parametric estimators would involve choosing the model class (like choosing the number of Gaussians in MoGs). We report the comparison between DETs, histograms (bin-width selected by LOO-CV) and KDEs (using the Gaussian kernel) with the bandwidth selected by unbiased LOO-CV using the ISE criterion (FBW) and by local rodeo (local r-KDE) (VBW) on synthetic data sets.

Example 1. (Strongly skewed distribution in one dimension) This distribution is defined as

$$X \sim \sum_{i=0}^{7} \frac{1}{8}\mathcal{N}\left(3\left(\left(\frac{2}{3}\right)^i - 1\right), \left(\frac{2}{3}\right)^{2i}\right).$$

Figure 2 shows the estimated density functions by a DET, a histogram and two KDEs for a sample size $N = 1000$. Because of the high skewness of the density function, the KDE (FBW) and the histogram fail to fit the very smooth

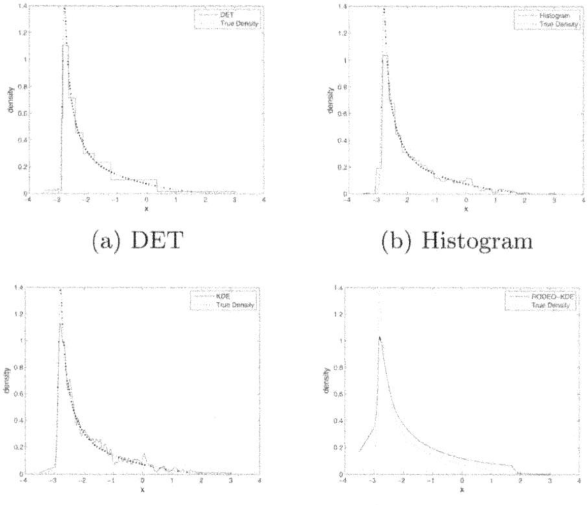

(a) DET (b) Histogram (c) KDE (FBW) (d) local r-KDE

Figure 2: The density estimates obtained with 1000 points for Example 1 using DET, Histogram and KDEs compared to the true density.

Table 2: Estimation errors for Histograms, KDEs and DETs with increasing number of observations

Type	N	Hist	KDE(FBW)	local r-KDE	DET
RMSE	10^2	0.2213	0.1748	0.1318	0.2548
	10^3	0.1158	0.0949	0.1339	0.1090
	10^4	0.0565	0.0235	0.0596	0.0527
HD	10^2	0.1292	0.2365	0.0967	0.1187
	10^3	0.0832	0.0684	0.2343	0.0278
	10^4	0.01	0.0130	0.1634	0.0072

tail. The fixed bandwidth/binwidth results in a highly wiggly estimate of the very smooth tail. The DET provides a piecewise constant estimate, but it adjusts to the different parts of the density function by varying the leaf size – the tree has small leaves closer to the spike where the density function changes rapidly, having larger leaves where the density function does not change rapidly. This demonstrates the adaptability of DETs within the same dimension. The local r-KDE exhibits the same adaptability by obtaining different bandwidths at different regions, hence capturing the smooth tail of the true density.

Table 2 provides the estimation errors with increasing sample sizes for the different methods. The RMSE values are fairly close and the HD values for the DETs are in fact better than that of KDE using unbiased LOO-CV. This can be attributed to the adaptive nature of DET with respect to the leaf sizes. The error values of local r-KDE are better than DET when the data set size is small (in case of larger data sets, the local method might be overfitting over this instance of the data set). The accuracies of the histogram estimators and DETs are comparable in this univariate example. But we will demonstrate in the next example that the performance of histograms decline with increasing dimensions.

Example 2. (Two dimensional data – Mixture of Beta distributions in one dimension, uniform in the other dimension) We create a (600×2) data set by sampling one dimension as a mixture of Beta distributions and the other dimension as a uniform distribution

$$X_1 \sim \frac{2}{3}\mathcal{B}(1,2) + \frac{1}{3}\mathcal{B}(10,10); X_2 \sim \mathcal{U}(0,1).$$

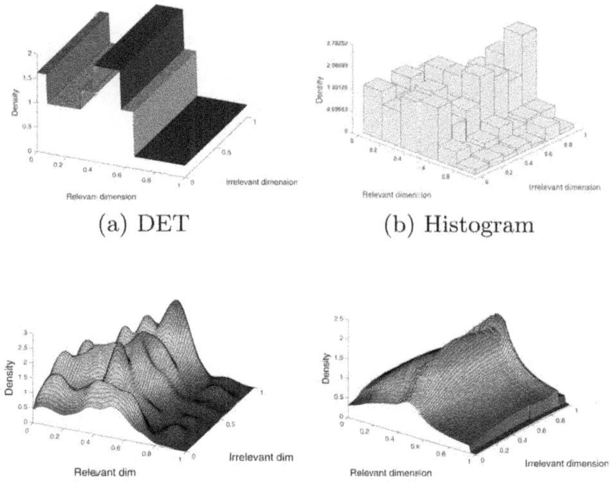

(a) DET (b) Histogram (c) KDE (FBW) (d) local r-KDE

Figure 3: Perspective plots of the density estimates for a DET, a Histogram and two KDEs on the data set in Example 2.

Figure 3 shows the 2-dimensional density estimates of a DET, a histogram and two KDEs. The DET fits the irrelevant uniform dimension perfectly, while closely approximating the mixture of Beta distributions in the relevant dimension. The KDE with fixed bandwidth and the histogram estimator completely fail to fit the irrelevant dimension. The local r-KDE does a better job of fitting the irrelevant dimension compared to the KDE (FBW), but still does not entirely capture the uniform density.

4.2 Interpretability: Variable Importance

The decision-tree framework defines a *measure of relevance* for each of the predictor variables [1] as following:

DEFINITION 4. *The measure of relevance $\mathcal{I}_d(T)$ for each attribute X_d (the dth attribute) in a decision tree T is defined as*

$$\mathcal{I}_d(T) = \sum_{t=1}^{|\tilde{T}|-1} \hat{\iota}_t^2 \mathbb{I}(d(t) = d) \tag{16}$$

where the summation is over the $|\tilde{T}| - 1$ internal nodes of the tree T, and the attribute $d(t)$ used to partition node t obtains $\hat{\iota}_t^2$ improvement in squared error over the constant fit in node t.

We use this measure to present the interpretability of the DETs on two real data sets.

Example 3. (Iris data set) We perform density estimation on this 4 dimensional data set and compute variable importance for each of the dimensions. Figure 1 displays the tree and the relative variable importance. The interpretation has been explained in Section 1.1.

Example 4. (MNIST digits – image data) Each image has 28-by-28 pixels providing a 784-dimensional data set. We perform density estimation on the 5851 images of the digit 8 (left panel of Figure 4). This is also an instance of performing density estimation with *ordinal data* since the pixel values are discrete. We compute the variable importance of each of the dimensions (pixels in this case). The right panel of Figure 4 displays the results obtained. The black pixels indicate pixels with zero variable importance in density

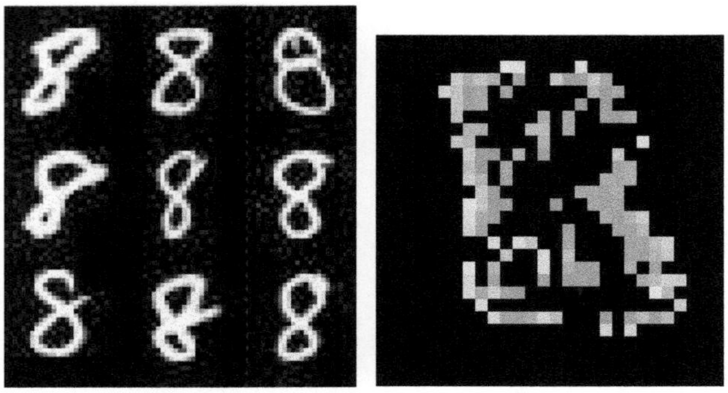

(a) Originals (b) Variable Importance

Figure 4: Relative importance of the predictor variables (pixels in this case) in density estimation for images of digit 8.

Table 3: Classification Accuracy: r-KDE vs. DET

Case	# Train	# Test	r-KDE	DET
1v7	240	121	0.93	0.91
2v7	237	119	0.97	0.87
3v8	238	119	0.81	0.81
5v8	237	119	0.86	0.72
8v9	236	118	0.75	0.77
All	1347	450	0.70	0.73

estimation. For the pixels with non-zero variable importance, the color transitions for green (indicating low relative variable importance) to red (indicating high relative variable importance). The marginal densities of many pixels are close to point masses. Hence the density does not vary at all in those dimensions, and the relative variable importance depicted in Figure 4 indicates that the DET is capable of capturing this property of the data.

4.3 Classification

As mentioned earlier, density estimation is a common subroutine in classification where the class-conditional density $\hat{p}(x|C)$ is to be estimated for the query point x using the training set X. The estimated class $\hat{C}(x) = \arg\max_C P(x|C) \cdot P(C)$. We compare the accuracy of classification between the density estimates computed by DETs and local r-KDEs.

Example 5. (Opt-digits – image data (1797×64) [31]) We conduct binary as well as multi-class classification. For binary classification, we consider the following cases: 1 vs. 7, 2 vs. 7, 3 vs. 8, 5 vs. 8, 8 vs. 9. We perform multi-class classification using all the classes (0-9). Table 3 lists the classification accuracies for the different tasks. In most cases, the accuracies are close for the two methods of density estimation, with the r-KDEs being more accurate than the DETs. But in the last two cases, the DETs outperform the r-KDEs. Moreover, the whole experiment (training and testing) with the DETs is much faster than the one using the local r-KDEs. For example, in the last experiment performing multi-class classification required ~ 8 seconds using DETs and ~ 500 seconds using r-KDEs[7].

4.4 Speed

We compare DETs to KDE*s(FBW) using the fast approximate dual-tree algorithm [32] with *kd*-trees. We use LOO-CV to estimate the optimal bandwidth for the KDE*s

[7]The DET is implemented in C++ and the rodeo-KDE is implemented using MATLAB on the same machine.

Table 4: Timings (in seconds) for training(T) and all queries(Q) with KDE*s and DETs

Data set	T(KDE*)	T(DET)	Q(KDE*)	Q(DET)
sj2	93.77	485.77	11.79	0.0026
Colors	101.68	427.02	12.11	0.0022
Bio	421.22	1213.84	5.7	0.0069
Pall7	1240.75	1719.26	10.67	0.0046
psf	18039.27	32456.43	77.48	0.975

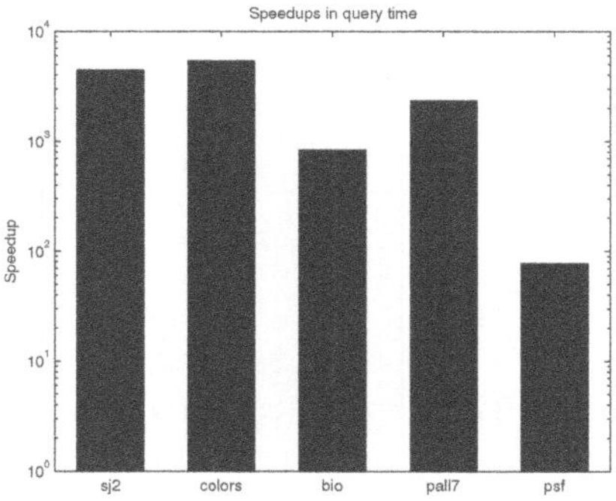

Figure 5: Query Time speedup for the DTE over the KDE. Note that the KDE is faster than the DTE in case of training.

(FBW). Real world data sets drawn from the SDSS repository [33] (SJ2 (50000×2), PSF (3000000×2)) and the UCI Machine Learning Repository [31] (Colors (50000×2), dimension reduced version of the Bio dataset (100000×5), Pall7 (100000×7)) are used. The query set is same as the training set in all the experiments and the KDE*s provide the leave-one-out estimates.

For the KDE*, we use around $H \approx 10$ bandwidths and chose the one with the best CV error. Usually, a much larger number of bandwidths are tried and the training times scale linearly with H. For the DETs, we use 10-fold cross-validation since we were not able to find an efficient way to conduct LOO-CV with decision trees and it would require prohibitively long time for these large data sets. This is one major limitation of this method. However, for sufficiently large data sets, our experiments indicate that DETs trained with LOO-CV are only slightly more accurate than those with 10-fold CV.

The absolute timing values (in seconds) for training(T) and querying(Q) are given in Table 4. The speedups of the DETs over the KDE*s in test/query time are shown in Figure 5. As can be seen from the results, the training time for the decision tree algorithm is significantly larger than the LOO-CV for the KDE*s, but the DETs provide up to 3.5 orders of magnitude speedup in query time. The KDE*s are fast to train, but their work comes at test time. This experiment demonstrates the efficient querying of decision trees while also indicating that the task of training decision trees using LOO-CV is quite challenging.

5. DISCUSSION AND CONCLUSIONS

This framework of decision-tree-structured density estimation provides a new way to estimate the density of a given set of observations in the form of a simple set of rules which are inherently intuitive and interpretable. This framework has the capability of easily dealing with categorical, discrete as well as continuous variables and performs automatic feature selection. On having these rules, the density of a new test point can be computed cheaply. All these features stem from the fact that the density estimation is performed in the form of a decision tree. Along with that, the DETs are easily implementable like supervised decision trees. Although these advantages come with the loss of accuracy, the DETs are shown to be consistent, and hence are quite reliable in the presence of enough data.

Future directions of improvement include the reduction of the discontinuities in the density estimate because of the piecewise constant estimator and the boundary bias since the DETs put no mass outside the span of the data. Boundary bias is a common problem for almost all density estimators. One possible remedy is to use a normalized KDE at each of the leaves instead of using the piecewise constant estimator (similar to the approach in Smyth et.al. [21].

An analysis of the convergence rate of the DETs would quantify the amount of loss of accuracy to account for the simplicity of the estimator. Being effectively a variable bin-width histogram, we conjecture that the convergence rate for the DETs would be $o(N^{-2/3})$ for univariate data and better than histograms in higher dimensions since we demonstrate that the DETs can effectively model uninformative dimensions easily without requiring that extra number of points as imposed by the curse of dimensionality. Moreover, we are actively working on obtaining density dependent bounds on the depth of the DETs to quantify the runtimes for training and test query.

Overall, this method for density estimation has immediate application to various fields of data analysis (for example, outlier and anomaly detection)[8] and machine learning due to its simple and interpretable solution to the fundamental task of density estimation.

6. REFERENCES

[1] L. Breiman, J. H. Friedman, R. A. Olshen, and C. J. Stone. *Classification and Regression Trees.* Wadsworth, 1984.

[2] C. Bishop. *Neural Networks for Pattern Recognition.* Oxford University Press, 1995.

[3] C. M. Bishop. *Pattern recognition and machine learning.* Springer, 2006.

[4] R. O. Duda and P. E. Hart. *Pattern Classification and Scene Analysis.* Wiley New York, 1973.

[5] J. H. Friedman. A Recursive Partitioning Decision Rule for Nonparametric Classification. *Transactions on Computers*, 1977.

[6] J. H. Friedman. A tree-structured approach to nonparametric multiple regression. *Smoothing Techniques for Curve Estimation*, 1979.

[7] T. Hastie, R. Tibshirani, and J. Friedman. *The Elements of Statistical Learning: Data Mining, Inference, and Prediction.* Springer, 2001.

[8] L. Wasserman. *All of Nonparametric Statistics.* Physica-Verlag, 2006.

[9] C. Cortes and V. N. Vapnik. Support vector networks. *Machine Learning*, 1995.

[10] B. W. Silverman. *Density Estimation for Statistics and Data Analysis.* Chapman & Hall/CRC, 1986.

[11] H. Liu, J. Lafferty, and L. Wasserman. Sparse Nonparametric Density Estimation in High Dimensions Using the Rodeo. In *AISTATS*, 2007.

[12] P. Müller and F.A. Quintana. Nonparametric Bayesian data analysis. *Statistical Science*, 2004.

[13] A. G. Gray and A. W. Moore. Nonparametric density estimation: Toward computational tractability. In *SIAM Data Mining*, 2003.

[14] D. Lee and A. G. Gray. Fast high-dimensional kernel summations using the monte carlo multipole method. In *Advances in NIPS*, 2008.

[15] A. Beygelzimer, S. Kakade, and J.C. Langford. Cover Trees for Nearest Neighbor. *ICML*, 2006.

[16] P. Ram, D. Lee, W. March, and A. Gray. Linear-time algorithms for pairwise statistical problems. In *Advances in NIPS*. 2009.

[17] J. Lafferty and L. Wasserman. Rodeo: Sparse Nonparametric Regression in High Dimensions. *Arxiv preprint math.ST/0506342*, 2005.

[18] R. Riegel, A. G. Gray, and G. Richards. Massive-Scale Kernel Discriminant Analysis: Mining for Quasars. In *SIAM Data Mining (SDM)*, 2008.

[19] W. Guan, M. Zhou, C. Y. Hampton, B. B. Benigno, L. D. Walker, A. G. Gray, J. F. McDonald, and F. M. Fernandez. Ovarian Cancer Detection from Metabolomic Liquid Chromatography/Mass Spectrometry Data by Support Vector Machines. *BMC Bioinformatics Journal*, 2009.

[20] R. Kohavi. Scaling up the accuracy of naive-Bayes classifiers: A decision-tree hybrid. In *KDD*, 1996.

[21] P. Smyth, A. G. Gray, and U. M. Fayyad. Retrofitting decision tree classifiers using kernel density estimation. In *ICML*, 1995.

[22] G. Hooker. Diagnosing extrapolation: Tree-based density estimation. In *SIGKDD*, 2004.

[23] A.M. Molinaro, S. Dudoit, and M.J. Van der Laan. Tree-based multivariate regression and density estimation with right-censored data. *Journal of Multivariate Analysis*, 2004.

[24] G. Schmidberger and E. Frank. Unsupervised discretization using tree-based density estimation. *Lecture Notes in Computer Science*, 2005.

[25] J. Basak and R. Krishnapuram. Interpretable hierarchical clustering by constructing an unsupervised decision tree. *IEEE transactions on knowledge and data engineering*, 2005.

[26] T. Seidl, I. Assent, P. Kranen, R. Krieger, and J. Herrmann. Indexing density models for incremental learning and anytime classification on data streams. In *ICEDT: Advances in Database Technology*, 2009.

[27] W.H. Wong and L. Ma. Optional Pólya tree and Bayesian inference. *The Annals of Statistics*, 2010.

[28] E. Parzen. On the estimation of a probability density function and mode. *Annals of Mathematical Statistics*, pages 1065–1076, 1962.

[29] V. N. Vapnik and A. Y. Chervonenkis. On the uniform convergence of relative frequencies of events to their probabilities. *Theory of Probability and its Applications*, 1971.

[30] L. Devroye, L. Györfi, and G. Lugosi. *A probabilistic theory of pattern recognition.* Springer Verlag, 1996.

[31] C.L. Blake and C.J. Merz. UCI repository of machine learning databases. 1998.

[32] A. G. Gray and A. W. Moore. 'n-body' problems in statistical learning. In *Advances in NIPS*, 2000.

[33] R. Lupton, J.E. Gunn, Z. Ivezic, G.R. Knapp, S. Kent, and N. Yasuda. The SDSS Imaging Pipelines. *Arxiv preprint astro-ph/0101420*, 2001.

[8] We will demonstrate these applications in the longer version of the paper.

Unsupervised Clustering of Multidimensional Distributions using Earth Mover Distance

David Applegate
david@research.att.com

Tamraparni Dasu
tamr@research.att.com

Shankar Krishnan
krishnas@research.att.com

Simon Urbanek
urbanek@research.att.com

AT&T Labs - Research
180 Park Ave
Florham Park, NJ 07932

ABSTRACT

Multidimensional distributions are often used in data mining to describe and summarize different features of large datasets. It is natural to look for distinct classes in such datasets by clustering the data. A common approach entails the use of methods like k-means clustering. However, the k-means method inherently relies on the Euclidean metric in the embedded space and does not account for additional topology underlying the distribution.

In this paper, we propose using Earth Mover Distance (EMD) to compare multidimensional distributions. For a n-bin histogram, the EMD is based on a solution to the transportation problem with time complexity $O(n^3 \log n)$. To mitigate the high computational cost of EMD, we propose an approximation that reduces the cost to linear time. Given the large size of our dataset a fast approximation is crucial for this application.

Other notions of distances such as the information theoretic Kullback-Leibler divergence and statistical χ^2 distance, account only for the correspondence between bins with the same index, and do not use information across bins, and are sensitive to bin size. A cross-bin distance measure like EMD is not affected by binning differences and meaningfully matches the perceptual notion of "nearness".

Our technique is simple, efficient and practical for clustering distributions. We demonstrate the use of EMD on a real-world application of analyzing 411,550 anonymous mobility usage patterns which are defined as distributions over a manifold. EMD allows us to represent inherent relationships in this space, and enables us to successfully cluster even sparse signatures.

Categories and Subject Descriptors

I.5.3 [**Pattern Recognition**]: Clustering

General Terms

Algorithms, Similarity measures

Keywords

Earth mover distance (EMD), clustering, signatures, distributions

1. INTRODUCTION

Massive data sets are often summarized using *signatures* that capture important characteristics of the data. Signatures are compact representations that can be used for further mining tasks such as clustering and anomaly detection. For example, Cortes *et al* [3] discuss the use of signatures for mining massive telecommunications data to find communities of interest, and for detecting fraud. In [19], Wong *et al* demonstrate the use of data signatures for visualizing complex scientific data sets.

In many instances, signatures are multidimensional distributions that represent the distribution of probability mass over a manifold. An important data mining task involves measuring distances between such distributions, which are then used for subsequent tasks such as clustering, change detection or alerting. For instance, clustering usage signatures of telecommunications customers identifies canonical patterns of usage that can be used to provide better service and for network load balancing tasks.

While clustering algorithms like k-means are frequently used to cluster distributions, they can lead to misleading results. Consider the following example of a population of cell phone users with different types of usage behavior. Figure 1 shows examples of different usage signatures. We defer a detailed explanation to Section 5.1, but for now let us treat them as heat maps that show the density of usage for voice calls and text messages aggregated over two months across "hour of the day" (rows in the heat map) by "day of the week" (columns). The signature in Figure 1 (left) is representative of users with a moderately high volume of calls and texts, distributed across the bins corresponding to working days. The signature in Figure 1 (right), on the other hand, is representative of users with lower usage. Such users generate very few calls or text messages, their signatures are quite sparse, typically consisting of isolated spikes. Any method that relies on a distance that treats bins separately is bound to fail on such data. To demonstrate, we applied a k-means clustering algorithm to a sample of 5,000 signatures from the bottom quartile of the usage distribution. The centers of the resulting 8 clusters are shown in Figure 2. Regardless of the choice of the number of clusters, k, the clustering scheme always resulted in one large cluster and many small clusters consisting entirely of individual bins from the

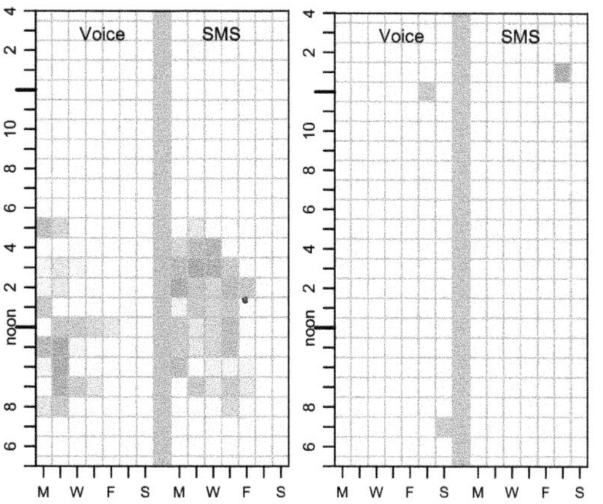

Figure 1: Two examples of a mobile usage distributions created by binning usage by hour of day, day of the week and type of activity. Color scale of the counts in bins ranges from light yellow (zero) to red (high density). Columns of each matrix correspond to days of week, rows correspond to hours of day. Left: Moderately high usage, mostly during work hours on working days. Right: Sparse usage. For privacy reasons the examples do not match any actual, individual user's signature in the data.

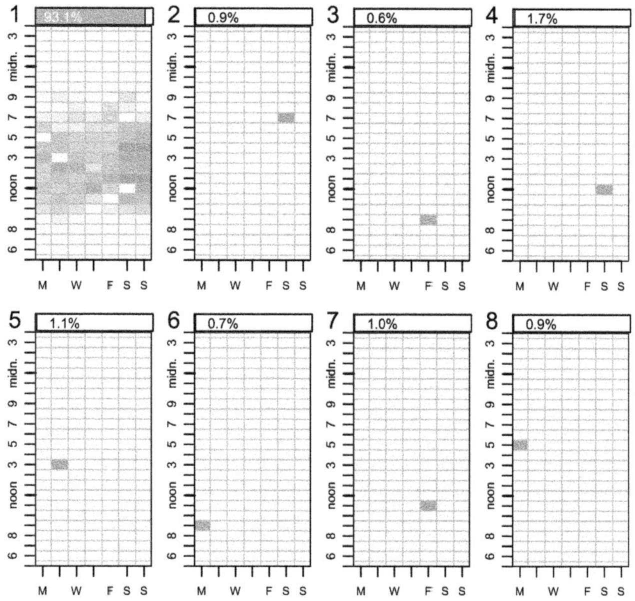

Figure 2: Cluster centers of low voice usage signatures using k-means clustering for $k = 8$. The bold number on top represents cluster number (id), top bar represents relative cluster size. Regardless of the value of k, the number of clusters, the method is unable to separate any clusters other than individual bins of the histogram. The location of the bins is random, based entirely on the initial cluster seeds.

distribution. The location of those small clusters is determined by the initial seeds of cluster centers, quite unrelated to any underlying structure in the data and therefore conveys no meaningful information. This is an example of a real world application where k-means would result in arbitrary clusters. For comparison purposes, Figure 3 shows the clustering obtained with EMD as the underlying similarity measure. Even with very sparse signatures, EMD is capable of separating them into coherent groups such as weekday (Clusters 1-5) weekend (Clusters 6-8), or time of the day (Clusters 2,3).

The reason for such odd clusters is that the k-means method inherently relies on the Euclidean metric in the embedded space and does not take into account any additional topology of the bins. This is not surprising, because in such a high-dimensional space, all sparse signatures are roughly equidistant from each other. Distributions lie on the probability simplex, and the right distance metric must be applied to the clustering framework to find meaningful clusters. More specifically, in order to cluster distributions, we need a notion of similarity or distance between distributions.

1.1 Distance Between Distributions

There are numerous *statistical distances* that measure the distance between distributions. Many of them are not true metrics because they violate one or more of the three requirements of a metric, that of non-negativity, symmetry and triangular inequality. We briefly describe some well know distances below.

A prominent class of distances known as f-divergences, is based on the expected value of a convex function of the ratio of the two distributions. If P and Q are two probability distributions over $\mathbb{R}^d$ such that P and Q are continuous with respect to each other, and f is a convex function such that $f(1) = 0$, then the f-divergence is given by:

$$D_f(P, Q) = E_Q\left(f\left(\frac{P}{Q}\right)\right) \tag{1}$$

where the subscript Q refers to the expectation E taken over the distribution Q. This class of distributions is known by the names Csiszar's f-divergence [4], Csiszar-Morimoto divergences or Ali-Silvey family of distances [1]. Depending on the form of f, distances in this family include the Kullback Leibler distance, Hellinger distance, total variational divergence, χ^2 divergence and alpha-divergence. Gibbs *et al.* [5] provide an overview of choosing appropriate probability metrics, including whether the metric has an interpretation with respect to the problem at hand. This is critical, since the results of clustering are heavily dependent on the choice of the metric. Liese *et al.* [11] describe a novel approach characterizing distances and their relationships, and the derivation of new properties with respect to desirable statistical properties like sufficiency.

Other popular distributional distances include Jensen Shannon divergence which is a symmetricized version of KL-divergence, Bhattacharya distance used to measure separability of classes, and Wasserstein's metric.

In this paper, we focus on Wasserstein's metric, popularized in computer vision and image retrieval community by the name Earth Mover Distance or EMD. The major drawback of the Kullback-Leibler divergence and statistical χ^2 distance is that they account only for the correspondence between bins with the same index, and do not use infor-

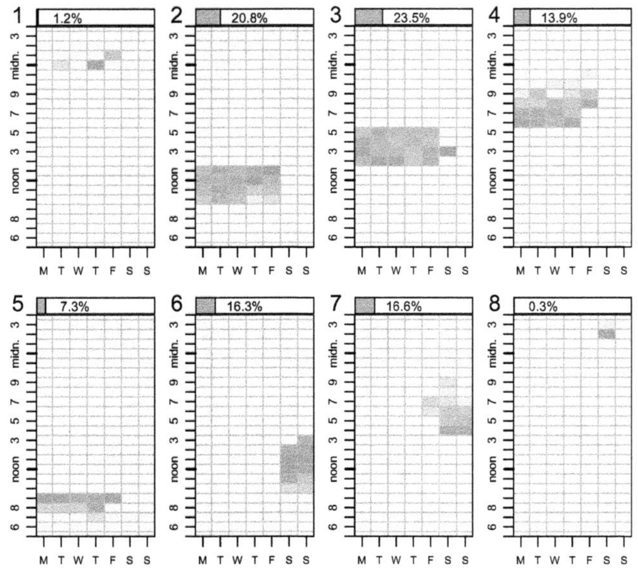

Figure 3: Cluster centers of the same low voice usage signature data as Figure 2, but using hierarchical clustering with EMD. Even with very sparse signatures, EMD is capable of separating them into coherent groups such as weekday (Clusters 1-5) weekend (Clusters 6-8), or time of the day (Clusters 2,3).

mation across bins, or distributions with different binning schemes. They are also sensitive to bin size. A binning that is too coarse will not have sufficient discriminative power, while a binning that is too fine will place similar features in different bins which will never be matched. EMD is a cross-bin distance and is not affected by binning differences. It meaningfully matches the perceptual notion of "nearness" and hence its popularity in image matching and retrieval.

EMD has not found widespread application outside the computer vision community due to its prohibitive computational cost. A lone exception has been the work of Zhou *et al.* [20], who propose the use of Mallows distance for comparing clusters.

By generalizing the wavelet approximation proposed in [17] to any general manifold we create a fast approximation to EMD that is applicable in any general domain. This allows us to apply it specifically to signatures that are defined on a manifold, not limited to flat feature spaces.

The rest of the paper is organized as follows. We define the problem, outline our approach and describe our contributions in Section 2. In Section 3 we discuss the Earth Mover Distance and its relationship to other distances like the Mallows distance. Section 4 describes an efficient, linear time approximation to EMD, which makes it feasible on very large data. In Section 5, we conduct experiments on a massive real-world application involving anonymized mobility data. Finally, we present our conclusions and outline directions for future research in Section 6.

2. OUR APPROACH

In this paper, we address the problem of clustering distributional signatures derived from massive multidimensional data. Extant approaches typically rely on methods such as k-means that are based on the Euclidean distance. However, signatures are not mere points in a metric space, they are defined over a distinct topology of the underlying domain. While well known distributional divergences can be used for clustering distributions, the advantages of EMD discussed in Section 3 make it an ideal candidate for clustering distributional signatures. EMD has not found widespread use due to its computational cost. Our approximation makes it feasible, and to the best of our knowledge, we introduce the notion of EMD for data mining.

We make three contributions.

- While wavelet-based approximations to EMD have been proposed for Euclidean spaces, we generalize it to any manifold, thus making it widely applicable to topologies that include probability distributions on manifolds. This novel generalization allows us to apply EMD to distributional signatures, and on a previously infeasible scale.
- We use the Earth Mover Distance for the unsupervised clustering of multi-dimensional data distributions.
- We demonstrate the efficacy of the method and showcase its properties using a compelling real world application of mobility data patterns.

We start with a brief introduction to EMD in the next section.

3. EARTH MOVER DISTANCE

Rubner *et al.* [15, 16] introduced EMD to the computer vision community as a technique for image retrieval. It is also known as the Mallows distance [10] or Wasserstein distance in statistical literature. EMD is a distance measure between two distributions. We start by introducing some terminology to define EMD.

Distributions can generally be described as functions over an underlying (feature) domain. In the rest of the paper, we will assume that multidimensional distributions are defined as histograms by partitioning the underlying domain into bins with a mass associated with each bin. Defining a distance between two distributions requires a notion of distance between points in the underlying domain defining the distributions. This distance is called the *ground distance*. EMD is a natural and intuitive metric between histograms if we think of them as piles of sand sitting on the ground (underlying domain). Each grain of sand is an observed sample. To quantify the difference between two distributions, we measure how far the grains of sand have to be moved so that the two distributions coincide exactly. EMD is the minimal total ground distance travelled weighted by the amount of sand moved (called flow). For perceptually meaningful ground distances, EMD agrees with perceptual dissimilarity better than other measures [16, 17]. Further, if the ground distance is a metric and the distributions all have the same mass (this is true in the case of probability distributions), EMD is a metric as well. There are several advantages of using EMD over other distribution dissimilarity measures. For example, it does not suffer from arbitrary quantization problems due to rigid binning strategies. Therefore, it is robust to errors in transformation that take raw data into feature space.

We provide a formal definition for EMD by using the same notation as proposed in Rubner *et al.* [16]. Let $\mathcal{F}$ be the underlying (feature) space over which the distributions are defined, endowed with a distance function $d : \mathcal{F} \times \mathcal{F} \rightarrow \mathbb{R}^+$. Rubner *et al.* describe a distribution using *signatures* - a sparse representation of a histogram. Specifically, a signature is defined as a vector of tuples, $P = \{< \mathbf{p}_1, w_{p_1} >, < \mathbf{p}_2, w_{p_2} >, \ldots, < \mathbf{p}_m, w_{p_m} >\}$, where $\mathbf{p} \in \mathcal{F}$ is a point in the feature space and w_p is the weight. Let P and Q be two distributions of the form

$$P = \{(\mathbf{p}_1, w_{p_1}), (\mathbf{p}_2, w_{p_2}), \ldots, (\mathbf{p}_m, w_{p_m})\} \quad (2)$$

$$Q = \{(\mathbf{q}_1, w_{q_1}), (\mathbf{q}_2, w_{q_2}), \ldots, (\mathbf{q}_n, w_{q_n})\}, \quad (3)$$

and let $D = [d_{ij}]$ be the ground distance between points $\mathbf{p}_i$ and $\mathbf{q}_j$. We want to find a flow, $F = [f_{ij}]$, where f_{ij} is the flow between points $\mathbf{p}_i$ and $\mathbf{q}_j$, that minimizes the overall cost

$$W(P, Q, F) = \sum_{i=1}^{m} \sum_{j=1}^{n} f_{ij} d_{ij} \quad (4)$$

The flow f_{ij} must satisfy the following linear constraints:

$$f_{ij} \geq 0, \qquad \forall i \in 1, \ldots, m, j \in 1, \ldots, n \quad (5)$$

$$\sum_{j=1}^{n} f_{ij} \leq w_{p_i} \qquad \forall i \in 1, \ldots, m \quad (6)$$

$$\sum_{i=1}^{n} f_{ij} \leq w_{q_j} \qquad \forall j \in 1, \ldots, n \quad (7)$$

$$\sum_{i=1}^{m} \sum_{j=1}^{n} f_{ij} = min\left(\sum_{i=1}^{m} w_{p_i}, \sum_{j=1}^{n} w_{q_j}\right) \quad (8)$$

The first constraint limits the flow to move from P to Q and not the other way around. The next two constraints limit the flow from exceeding the weights in the corresponding bins, and the final constraint sets a lower bound on the flow. Let $[f_{ij}^*]$ be the optimal flow that minimizes Equation 4. Then, the Earth Mover Distance is defined to be

$$EMD(P, Q) = \frac{\sum_{i=1}^{m} \sum_{j=1}^{n} f^*{}_{ij} d_{ij}}{\sum_{i=1}^{m} \sum_{j=1}^{n} f^*{}_{ij}} \quad (9)$$

The optimization problem above is essentially a linear program. However, it can be formulated as an uncapacitated minimum cost flow problem and can be solved optimally by using Orlin's algorithm [9] in $O(n^3 \log n)$, where n is the number of bins in the two histograms. The biggest drawback of using EMD for clustering distributions is its high computational complexity. When dealing with large datasets (with each distribution potentially having a large number of bins) as in our case, the exact computation of EMD becomes impractical. To alleviate this problem, we propose a modified version of an algorithm proposed by Shirdhonkar *et al.* [17] that works on arbitrary ground spaces.

4. APPROXIMATION TO EMD

In order to mitigate the high computational cost of EMD, several approximation schemes have been proposed in the literature. Ling and Okada [12] empirically showed that EMD could be computed in $O(n^2)$ time if an L_1 ground distance is used instead of the usual Euclidean distance. Indyk and Thaper [7] use a randomized multiscale embedding of histograms into a space equipped with the L_1 norm. The multiscale hierarchy is obtained by a series of random shifting and dyadic merging of bins. The histogram levels are weighted by powers of 2, with more weight at the coarser levels. They show that the L_1 norm computed in this space, averaged over all random shifts, is equivalent to the EMD. Their approach runs in roughly $O(ndk)$ time, where d is the histogram dimension and k is the number of times randomized embedding is performed. Shirdhonkar and Jacobs [17] present a linear time algorithm for approximating the EMD for low dimensional histograms using the sum of absolute values of the weighted wavelet coefficients of the difference histogram. The weighted wavelet transform is computed in time linear in the number of histogram bins. One main restriction in the methods of Indyk *et al.* and Shirdhonkar *et al.* is that the underlying (feature) space must be flat (for example, Euclidean).

In the context of our work, the distributions are embedded in a manifold-like space. In these cases, the above approximation strategies are not applicable. Inspired by the work of Shirdhonkar *et al.*, we modify their approach to extend it to the case where manifolds can be the underlying space. We model manifolds as weighted graphs and apply wavelets on these graphs using spectral graph theory [6].

We start our description of the approximate EMD computation by describing the theory behind the approach of Shirdhonkar *et al.*. The connection becomes apparent when we look at the continuous version of the EMD problem known as the Kantorovich-Rubinstein transshipment problem. Let $S \subset \mathbb{R}^d$ be a compact space, and let P_1 and P_2 be probability distributions with densities p_1 and p_2, respectively, defined on S, endowed with a continuous cost function $d : S \times S \rightarrow \mathbb{R}^+$. Let $0 < s \leq 1$ be a fixed parameter. Then the transshipment problem is to find

$$\mu_d = \inf_q \int d(x, y)^s q(x, y) dx dy,$$

where the infimum is over all joint probability densities q on $S \times S$. q is analogous to the flow in the discrete setting. The joint distribution must satisfy a mass conservation constraint of the form

$$p_1(u) - p_2(u) = \int q(u, y) dy - \int q(x, u) dx$$

Here $p := p_1 - p_2$ is the difference distribution with the property that $\int p = 0$. The Kantorovich-Rubinstein theorem states that the above problem admits a dual representation

$$\mu_d = \sup_f \int f(x) p(x) dx \quad (10)$$

The supremum is over all bounded continuous functions f on S satisfying the order s Hölder continuity condition $f(x) - f(y) \leq d(x, y)^s$, for all $x, y \in S$. In the special case of $S = \mathbb{R}^d$, and $d(x, y) = \| x - y \|$, Shirdhonkar *et al.* observed that the dual objective function is the maximum inner product between the potential function and the difference histogram, which can be easily represented in the wavelet domain (since orthonormal wavelets preserve inner products). Their formulation in the wavelet domain has the explicit solution:

$$\mu^*(p_1, p_2) = \sum_{\lambda} 2^{-j(1+n/2)} |p_\lambda|, \quad (11)$$

where p is the n-dimensional difference histogram and p_λ are its wavelet coefficients. The main result of their paper states that, depending on the wavelet used, there exist constants C_L and C_U such that $C_L\mu^* \leq \mu_d \leq C_U\mu^*$. We refer the reader to their paper for more details.

Diffusion wavelets [13, 18] generalize classical wavelets, allowing for multiscale analysis on general structures, such as manifolds, graphs and point clouds in Euclidean space. They allow us to perform signal processing tasks on functions on these spaces. We are interested in preserving dot products; hence we rely on orthonormal wavelets. The diffusion wavelets were designed specifically to be orthonormal, and applicable to smooth manifolds as well as graphs. Their construction interacts with the underlying graph or manifold space through repeated applications of a diffusion operator T (like the heat operator on graphs). The orthogonality of the wavelets is achieved by running a localized orthogonalization procedure after applying dyadic powers of T at each scale to yield nested approximation spaces. Wavelets are then produced by locally orthogonalizing vectors spanning the difference of these approximation spaces.

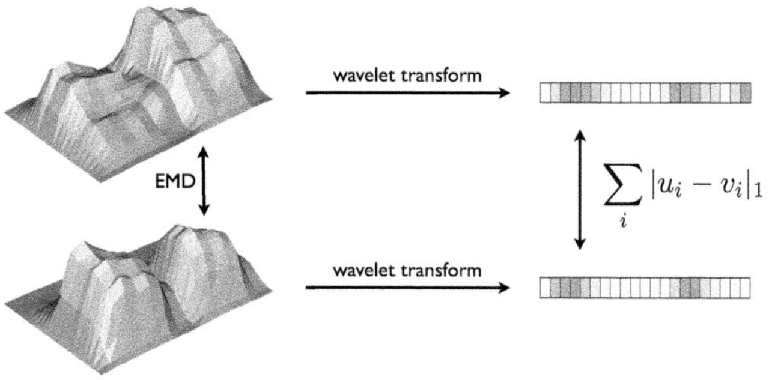

Figure 4: Illustration of the EMD approximation process

We generate a weighted graph to reflect the underlying topology of our space (a product space of a torus and real line), and perform the wavelet computation once. This wavelet replaces the simpler wavelets used by Shirdhonkar *et al.*. All the results directly extend to this wavelet except for the specific values of C_L and C_U. The rest of the computation remains exactly the same. In order to perform the approximate computation, we compute the weighted wavelet transform (as in Equation 11) of each distribution independently. Once the coefficients are obtained as a sparse vector, the approximate EMD is essentially the L_1 norm of the difference of transform coefficients. Figure 4 illustrates the process of approximating EMD using wavelet transforms on a simple domain and the main steps of the algorithm are described in Algorithm 1.

4.1 Accuracy and Performance of Approximate EMD

We compare the results of exact EMD and our approximation on a simulated example and real data. For the simulation, we generate uniformly distributed vectors of size 16^3 using a sparsity factor ρ. From this vector we generate two histograms: one with all positive entries and one with absolute values of only the negative entries. We then compute the EMD between those histograms using exact computation (using the code provided by Rubner[16]) and our approximation. We repeat this process 1000 times varying ρ linearly between 0 and 1. The resulting scatterplot of the exact values vs approximations is shown in Figure 5(a).

Algorithm 1: Approximate EMD(p_1, p_2)
Input: Two distributions p_1 and p_2 over a compact space $S \subset \mathbb{R}^d$
Output: ApproxEMD(p_1, p_2)

Discretize the compact space S by sampling bin locations
Construct a weighted graph G reflecting manifold metric
Construct diffusion wavelets for G (Maggioni *et al.* [13])
Let wd_1 (wd_2) be the weighted diffusion wavelet descriptor (Eq. 11) of p_1 (p_2)
$D^* = L_1\text{-dist}(wd_1, wd_2)$
return D^*

We also used data from the application described in section 5.1 to perform the same comparison. Here, we calculated the EMD of a random non-sparse signature from 5,000 random signatures. The result is shown in Figure 5(b). Our experiments validate the theoretical guarantees provided by the algorithm.

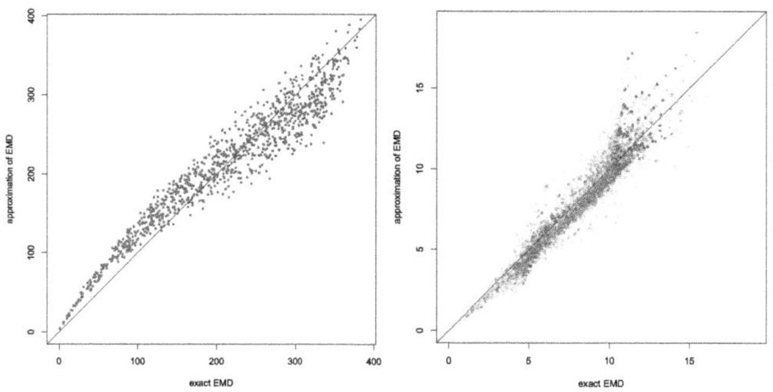

(a) simulated vectors (b) mobility application

Figure 5: Comparison of EMD distances based on exact EMD (x−axis) vs wavelet approximation (y−axis).

In order to measure the performance of the approximate algorithm we picked 50 histogram sizes varying from 25 to 1600. For each histogram size, we generated 25 random histograms and performed pairwise distance computations between them. The timing reported is the average over the 300 distance computations for each histogram size. Figure 6 shows the performance of our algorithm with respect to the exact method. The timing measurements were performed on a Linux machine with 2.27GHz Intel Xeon CPU with 12GB of RAM.

5. A REAL WORLD APPLICATION

In this section, we demonstrate the use of EMD based clustering of signatures of cell phone usage data, and compare conventional clustering based on Euclidean distances with clusters derived using the EMD. We hypothesize that while k-means might provide a reasonable approximation in situations where the signature distributions are fairly smooth, it will struggle when the distributions have spikes e.g. when the density is concentrated in a few bins such as when the signatures are sparse as shown in Figure 1 (right). We have already discussed in Section 1 that k-means results in ar-

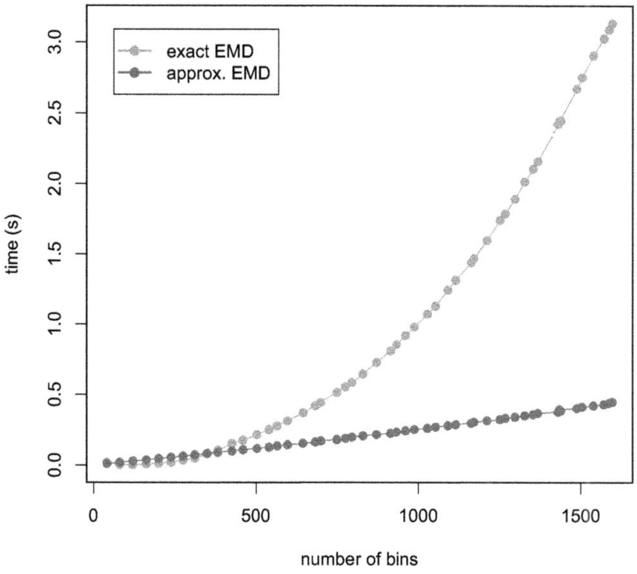

Figure 6: Timing comparison of the exact EMD algorithm (red) vs our approximate algorithm (blue). The timing measurements were performed on a Linux machine with 2.27GHz Intel Xeon CPU with 12GB of RAM.

bitrary clusters determined entirely by the initial seeds, illustrated by cluster centers shown in Figure 2. We will see in Section 5.1 that such extreme situations do arise in real world data making it imperative that the proper distance metric be used for clustering distributional signatures.

5.1 Mobility Usage Signatures

Given the ubiquity of cellphones and their constant use, cell phone calling patterns have been used extensively to study the location and movements of large numbers of people for urban planning, event management and traffic monitoring. In addition, aggregated cell phone usage data find application for traditional network management and monitoring tasks. Isaacman *et al* [8] show by using anonymized, aggregated statistics based on hundreds of thousands of cell phone calls in New York and Los Angeles, that the commuting patterns, travel distances and times are very different for New Yorkers and Los Angelenos. Similarly, by clustering anonymized aggregates of cell phone calls in a small town, Becker *et al* [2] identify interesting clusters of users with distinct behavior such as commuters and students.

In general, we are interested in analyzing mobile phone usage signatures in order to find common patterns, detect outliers, and identify trouble spots in the network. We describe below our experiments with the use of EMD for clustering mobile usage signatures. There exist many more applications of EMD to signatures, like clustering network traffic patterns and detecting changes in traffic distributions, but for the purpose of this paper, we confine ourselves to clustering usage signatures.

5.2 Data Description

The data consisted of 411,550 unique handsets that generated around 15 million voice calls and 26 million text messages collected over a 60 day period from 35 cell towers located within a radius of 5 miles.

Given the sensitivity of the data, we took several steps to ensure the privacy of individuals. First, only anonymous records were used in this study. The data was collected and anonymized by a third party not involved in the data analysis. We worked only on usage aggregates by hour and day of week. Second, all our results are presented as aggregates. That is, no individual anonymous identifier was singled out for the study. By observing and reporting only on the aggregates, we protect the privacy of individuals.

For each user, we aggregated the calls and text messages separately over the 24×7 grid of "hour of day" vs. "day of the week" resulting in 168 bins. We had two such grids, one for voice and one for text message activity. The voice minutes and text message counts were made comparable by normalizing them so that they have the same global mean, resulting in one SMS corresponding to approximately 1.5 minutes of a voice call. The two usage vectors for each handset were concatenated to form one vector of $2 \times 24 \times 7 = 336$ elements. This vector was further normalized to have a total sum of one. The distribution of cell phone usage across 336 bins defines our signature. Examples of such distributions were presented in Figure 1, visualized as heat maps of the underlying voice and SMS matrices each consisting of 24 rows and 7 columns.

5.3 Clustering the Signatures

The size of our data set consists of 411,550 signatures which poses a challenge for clustering algorithms. Distance-based methods typically require a distance matrix consisting of $(n^2 - n)/2$ entries, which in our case implies more than 84 billion distances. Although our proposed EMD approximation algorithm reduces the computational cost to linear time, the estimated duration for the computation of the 8.4×10^{10} distances was 6 days, therefore we decided to use a random sample of 50,000 signatures to perform the clustering. We can then use EMD to compute distances from cluster centers to the entire data set, allowing for both outlier detection and cluster assignment. The computation of EMD distances to each of the cluster centers for the entire large set is highly feasible and is completed in a matter of minutes.

A major advantage of using our novel approximation to EMD is that it allows us to define a topology on the bins, and introduce the notion of nearness of bins. Since the boundaries of bins by hour are in a sense arbitrary, we would consider neighboring bins in time as 'close'. For example, we would consider users exhibiting activities at 12:45pm and 1:15pm more similar than those active at 7am and 11pm. Also typically human activities follow a daily cycle, so that there is a certain similarity between different days of the week at the same time. Finally, we have two types of activities – voice and SMS – which are distinct, so we model them as being at a constant distance from each other over the space of time. EMD allows us to specify such complex relationship between the bins.

To model the "time of day" and "day of week" relationship, we use a torus as the underlying geometry for the time and day of week space since the torus is defined as the product of two circles. By using a uniform helix on the torus we have a structure that wraps around at the end from one day to another and also from the end of the week to the beginning

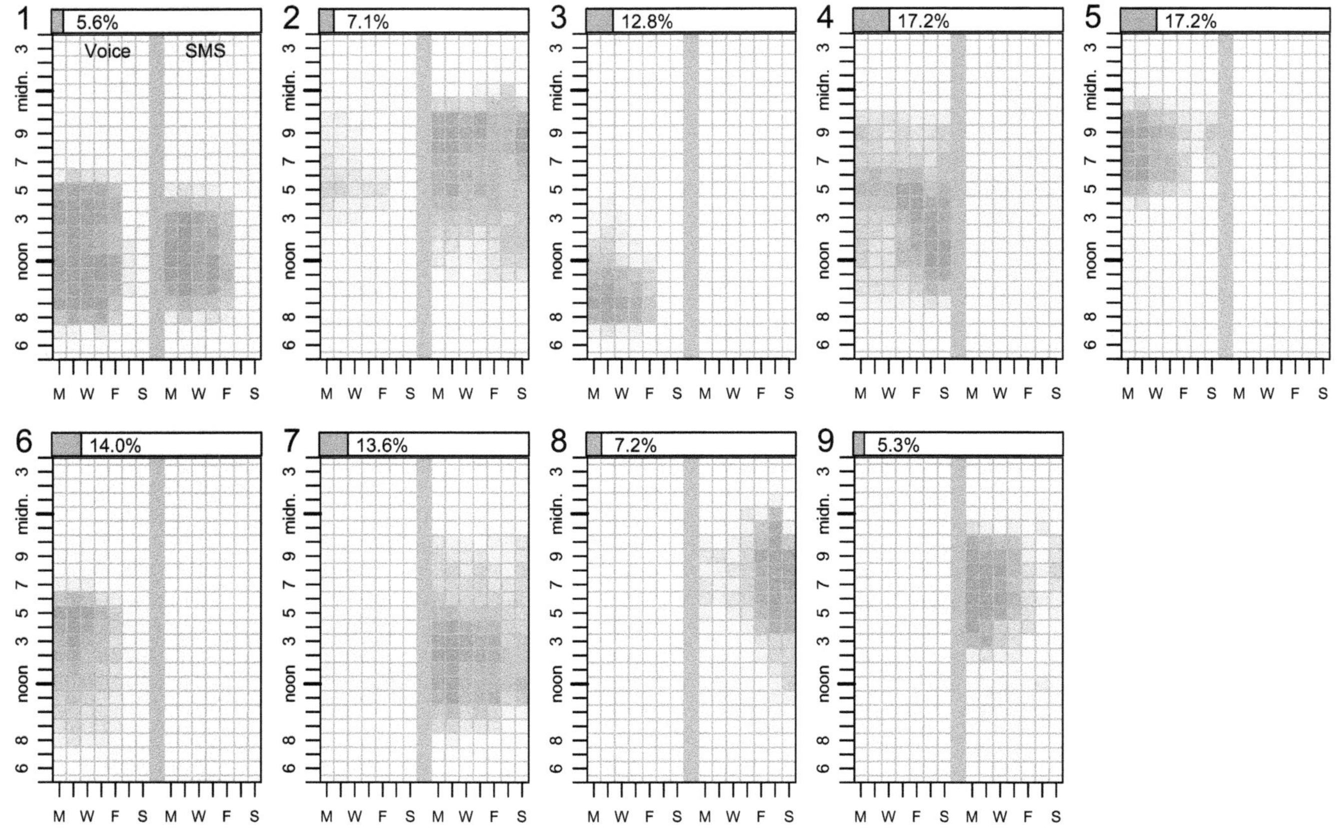

Figure 7: Aggregate usage per cluster for clusters obtained using hierarchical clustering with EMD on a random sample of 50,000 signatures drawn from the full range of signatures including sparse ones, . The clusters capture distinct patterns, such as mixed activity during work hours (Cluster 1), morning voice call activity (Cluster 3), or exclusive texting (Clusters 8 and 9).

of the week. Finally we add the activity type as a product with $\mathbb{R}$.

In our experiments, we used *complete linkage hierarchical clustering*[14] given Earth Mover Distances. Figure 7 shows the result of the clustering. It was run on a random sample of 50,000 cases from the dataset, including a large portion of low usage signatures. We plot the aggregate signatures based on all members in each cluster. The cluster number is at the top left corner of each plot. The blue bar on top of each signature represents the relative size of the cluster. Since we are interested in detection of general patterns, the exact number of clusters is not critical for our application. We selected the number of clusters taking into account within-cluster variance and cluster size.

The EMD clusters show distinct patterns. Cluster 1 corresponds to a mixed usage of both voice and SMS, predominantly during working hours. In contrast, Cluster 2 represents mostly SMS usage on evenings and into the weekend. Similar structure but limited to voice calls can be seen in Cluster 4. Clusters 3-6 separate signatures with almost no SMS activity whereas Clusters 7-9 have predominantly SMS usage. The clustering allows us to identify groups with similar usage patterns and their relative sizes, which can be used in many applications such as optimization of the operation of the cellular network, or on a local scale, to help in urban planning by identifying spatial groupings.

Once the clusters have been formed, their signature distribution can be used to compute EMD for new data. This operation is computationally far less expensive than computing a full pairwise distance matrix. This is useful for several purposes. We can compare the resulting distances with the within-cluster distances to find outliers with respect to the existing data and clusters. In addition, we can use this information to assign new data into clusters.

Figure 8 shows cluster signatures based on the entire dataset. We assigned each of the 411,550 signatures into clusters by taking the cluster with the closest center as determined by EMD. We see only a slight shift of the cluster size distribution between clusters compared to the clustering result on the subset of 50,000. The resulting signatures are consistent with the cluster centers, with some patterns standing out even more sharply. Weekends are more strongly represented in Clusters 4 and 8, and Cluster 7 is more clearly focused on SMS during working hours. This allows us to extend our identification of patterns to the entire dataset.

In the same way that we used cluster signatures for comparison, any set of target distributions could be used, allowing supervised clustering applications on a large scale as well. In our example, we used a fixed time frame, but if new data are obtained periodically, it allows for comparison of cluster evolution over time.

Alternatively, it is also possible to compare the evolution

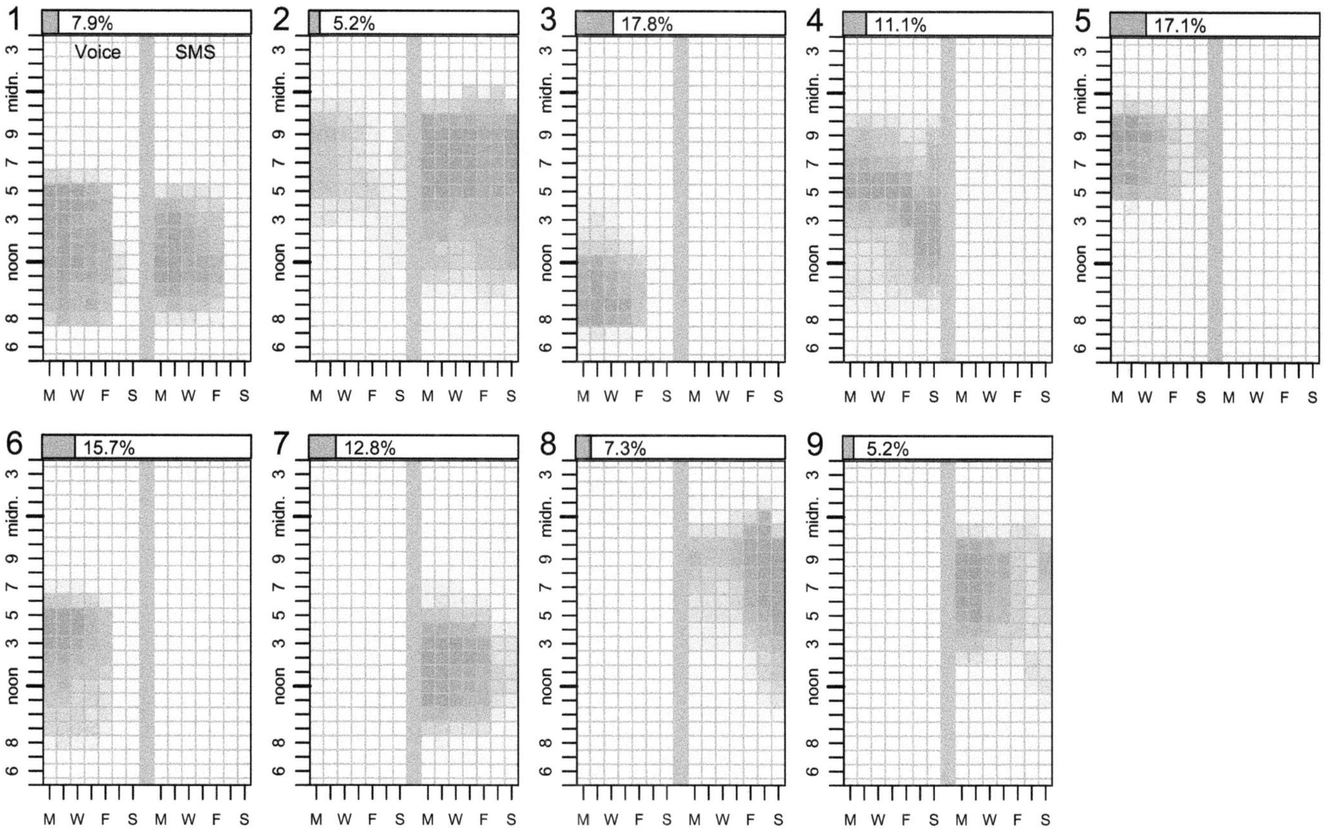

Figure 8: Aggregate signatures of clusters for all 411,550 data points. Cases are assigned to clusters according to their proximity to cluster centers derived using EMD on a random sample of 50,000 signatures.

of signatures in linear time using our proposed EMD approximation by measuring the distance between distributions of subsequent signature in time. There are numerous application for EMD based analysis in change detection and spatio-temporal clustering.

6. CONCLUSION

In this paper, we proposed the use of the Earth Mover Distance for clustering distributions and signatures. EMD is inherently meaningful since it takes into account the underlying topology of the distributions unlike clustering methods like k-means that simply use the Euclidean metric defined over the point space. It allows for cross-bin comparisons creating a similarity measure that matches the perceptual notion of nearness and is tolerant to heterogeneous binning strategies.

EMD runs in $O(n^3 \log n)$ time, but we proposed a novel generalization of a well-known wavelet-based approximation algorithm that enables us to apply EMD to massive data for general topologies including distributional signatures.

We applied EMD based clustering to a massive real world mobile phone usage data set of 411,550 users by computing full pairwise distances, clustering a sample subset of 50,000, and extending the results to the entire population by assigning to clusters using EMD. The results of EMD based clustering are meaningful in every part of the usage distribution while k-means fails in clustering sparsely populated signatures.

6.1 Future Research

An interesting problem for further research involves clustering multivariate time series. Existing techniques represent time series as signatures and cluster them as was done in this paper, or impose artificial windows that capture slices of the time series and treat them as multi-dimensional vectors that are clustered in a routine way. While we ignore the temporal aspect in signatures, EMD can be used to cluster multivariate time series by defining similarity on the time space. Because of its notion of 'nearness' in the time domain, it recognizes small shifts in the time series as being similar enough to belong to the same cluster.

The wavelet-based approximation transforms the calculation of EMD into a computation of the L_1 norm between vectors in a sparse high-dimensional space. This space lends itself to dimensionality reduction techniques like locality sensitive hashing to further optimize the clustering algorithm without the need to compute the complete distance matrix.

7. REFERENCES

[1] S. M. Ali and S. D. Silvey. A general class of coefficients of divergence of one distribution from another. *Journal of the Royal Statistical Society. Series B (Methodological)*, 28(1):131–142, 1966.

[2] R. Becker, R. Cáceres, K. Hanson, J. M. Loh, S. Urbanek, A. Vasharsvky, and C. Volinsky. A tale of one city: Using cellular network data for urban planning. *In Review*, 2011.

[3] C. Cortes and D. Pregibon. Signature-based methods for data streams. *Data Mining and Knowledge Discovery*, 5(3):167–182, 2001-07-01.

[4] I. Csiszar. Information-type measures of difference of probability distributions and indirect observations. *Studia Sci. Math. Hungar.*, 2:299–318, 1967.

[5] A. L. Gibbs and F. E. Su. On choosing and bounding probability metrics. *International Statistical Review*, 70(3):419–435, 2002.

[6] D. K. Hammond, P. Vandergheynst, and R. Gribonval. Wavelets on graphs via spectral graph theory. Dec. 2009.

[7] P. Indyk and N. Thaper. Fast image retrieval via embeddings. In *3rd International Workshop on Statistical and Computational Theories of Vision*. ICCV, 2003.

[8] S. Isaacman, R. Becker, R. Cáceres, S. Kobourov, J. Rowland, and A. Varshavsky. Ranges of human mobility in los angeles and new york. In *Proc. of 8th International Workshop on Managing Ubiquitous Communications and Services (MUCS)*, 2011.

[9] B. Korte and J. Vygen. *Combinatorial Optimization: Theory and Algorithms*. Springer Publishing Company, Incorporated, 4th edition, 2007.

[10] E. Levina and P. Bickel. The earth mover's distance is the mallows distance: Some insights from statistics. In *ICCV 2001*, pages 251–256, 2001.

[11] F. Liese and I. Vajda. On divergences and informations in statistics and information theory. *Information Theory, IEEE Transactions on*, 52(10):4394 -4412, October 2006.

[12] H. Ling and K. Okada. An efficient earth mover's distance algorithm for robust histogram comparison. *IEEE Trans. Pattern Anal. Mach. Intell.*, 29:840–853, May 2007.

[13] M. Maggioni, J. C. Bremer, R. R. Coifman, and A. D. Szlam. Biorthogonal diffusion wavelets for multiscale representations on manifolds and graphs. volume 5914. Proc. SPIE Wavelet XI, 2005.

[14] F. Murtagh. Multidimensional clustering algorithms. In *COMPSTAT Lectures 4*, Wuerzburg, 1985. Physica-Verlag.

[15] Y. Rubner, C. Tomasi, and L. J. Guibas. A metric for distributions with applications to image databases. In *Proceedings of the Sixth International Conference on Computer Vision*, ICCV '98, pages 59–, Washington, DC, USA, 1998. IEEE Computer Society.

[16] Y. Rubner, C. Tomasi, and L. J. Guibas. The earth mover's distance as a metric for image retrieval. *Int. J. Comput. Vision*, 40:99–121, November 2000.

[17] S. Shirdhonkar and D. W. Jacobs. Approximate earth mover's distance in linear time. *Computer Vision and Pattern Recognition, IEEE Computer Society Conference on*, 0:1–8, 2008.

[18] A. D. Szlam, M. Maggioni, R. R. Coifman, and J. C. Bremer. Diffusion-driven multiscale analysis on manifolds and graphs: top-down and bottom-up constructions. volume 5914, 2005.

[19] P. C. Wong, H. Foote, R. Leung, D. Adams, and J. Thomas. Data signatures and visualization of scientific data sets. *IEEE Computer Graphics and Applications*, 20:12–15, 2000.

[20] D. Zhou, J. Li, and H. Zha. A new mallows distance based metric for comparing clusterings. In *Proceedings of the 22nd international conference on Machine learning*, ICML '05, pages 1028–1035, New York, NY, USA, 2005. ACM.

Online Heterogeneous Mixture Modeling with Marginal and Copula Selection

Ryohei Fujimaki
NEC Laboratories America
Media Analytics Department
NEC Laboratories America
rfujimaki@sv.nec-labs.com

Yasuhiro Sogawa*
The Institute of Scientific and Industrial Research
Osaka University
sogawa@ar.sanken.osaka-u.ac.jp

Satoshi Morinaga
Information and Media Processing Research Labs.
NEC Corporation
morinaga@cw.jp.nec.com

ABSTRACT

This paper proposes an online mixture modeling methodology in which individual components can have different marginal distributions and dependency structures. Mixture models have been widely studied and applied to various application areas, including density estimation, fraud/failure detection, image segmentation, etc. Previous research has been almost exclusively focused on mixture models having components of a single type (e.g., a Gaussian mixture model.) However, recent growing needs for complicated data modeling necessitate the use of more flexible mixture models (e.g., a mixture of a lognormal distribution for medical costs and a Gaussian distribution for blood pressure, for medical analytics.) Our key ideas include: 1) separating marginal distributions and their dependencies using copulas and 2) online extension of a recently-developed "expectation minimization of description length," which enable us to efficiently learn types of both marginal distributions and copulas as well as their parameters. The proposed method provides not only good performance in applications, but also scalable, automatic model selection, which greatly reduces the intensive modeling costs in data mining processes. We show that the proposed method outperforms state-of-the-art methods in application to density estimation and to anomaly detection.

Categories and Subject Descriptors

H.2.8 [**Database Management**]: Database applications—*Data Mining*; I.2.6 [**Artificial Intelligence**]: Learning

General Terms

Algorithms

*Under internship program of NEC Corporation.

1. INTRODUCTION

Mixture models have been widely studied and applied in a variety of areas, including topic analysis [15], fraud detection [27], image segmentation [25], and speech recognition [20]. Previous research has been almost exclusively focused on mixture models having single types of distributions (e.g., a Gaussian mixture model, a Bernoulli mixture model, etc.) However, in many real applications, the assumption that all variables have the same distribution type will not be satisfied, and the estimation/prediction performance of such models will consequently degrade. In medical analytics [6], for examples medical costs and blood pressure usually have, respectively, a log normal distribution (or a mixture of lognormal and normal distributions) and a (skewed) normal distribution.

Fig. 1 presents the concept of the issue dealt with in this paper. "Component 1" has (lognormal, Gaussian) marginal distributions, and they have negative dependency. "Component 2" has (Gaussian, Gaussian) marginal distributions, and they have positive dependency. The learning problem with such models includes selection of the number of components and types of marginal distributions and their dependency structures as well as parameter estimation. A brute-force search with such classical statistical information criteria as Akaike's information criterion [1] or the minimum description length principle (MDL) [21] might be expected to suffer from a combinatorial scalability problem with respect to types of components.

Recently, Fujimaki et al. [9] have proposed the concept of "heterogeneous mixture models," in which individual components can have different types. The algorithm, "expectation minimization of description length (EMDL)," addresses the model selection issue for heterogeneous mixture models in which types of components, as well as the number of components and their parameters, are optimized. Their model and EMDL have two limitations w.r.t. our problem: Limitation 1) it is difficult to define joint distributions for individual components having different types of marginal distributions[1], and Limitation 2) the number of component candidates will become prohibitively large with increasing data dimensionality D if we allow different variables to have different types of marginal distributions[2].

[1]Let us consider the case where random variables X_1 and X_2 have different types of marginal distributions. The pdf $p(X_1|X_2)$ or $P(X_2|X_1)$ will not generally be obvious.

[2]Let us assume that we have two marginal candidates,

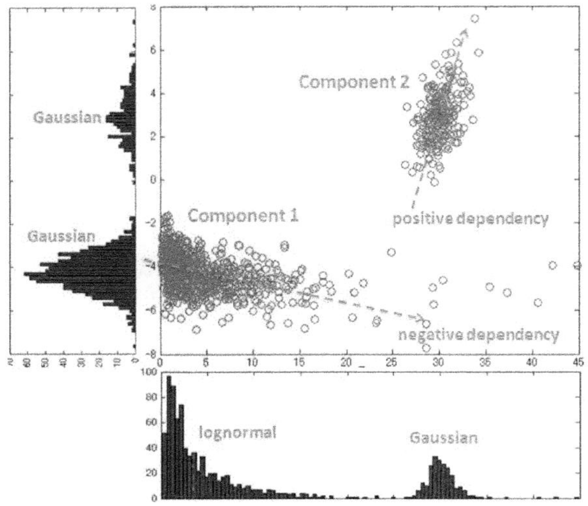

Figure 1: Concept of our problem. The goal is to specify all of the number of components, types of marginal distributions, dependency structures, and their parameters.

The goal of this study is to construct a mixture modeling methodology for the simultaneous model selection and parameter estimation described above. In addition to achievement of good estimation/prediction performance using a flexible model, we address computational scalability and modeling automation issues, which are essential for reduction of the total cost of data mining processes.

Our key ideas and contributions may be summarized as:

Heterogeneous Marginals and Copulas.

We separate, for individual components, marginal distributions and their dependency structures using copulas [17] to address Limitation 1. Our model here, which we refer to as a "mixture model with heterogeneous marginals and copulas" (MHMC), allows us to use both heterogeneous types of marginal distributions and heterogeneous types of dependencies among variables (i.e., copulas), and it provides a powerful tool of modeling complicated data. From the viewpoint of computational and modeling costs, this direct incorporation of copulas into the heterogeneous mixture model actually contributes importantly to the efficiency of our learning algorithm (we can separately optimize individual marginal distributions and copulas.)

Online Model Selection Algorithm.

We propose an online EMDL algorithm for MHMC which automatically optimizes the number of components, types of marginal distributions, types of copulas, and their parameters. By combining MHMC and (online) EMDL, we can avoid the combinatorial scalability issue involved in selecting marginal and copula types (Limitation 2). Further, MHMC with online EMDL, which we abbreviate as OMHMC, addresses the scalability issue for large datasets, and it is also expected to have good convergence properties, on the basis of an analogy with the EM algorithm [5] and the incremental EM algorithm[3] [16].

Gaussian and lognormal. Then we have 2^D candidates for marginal combinations for each component: i.e., (Gaussian, Gaussian), (Gaussian, lognormal), (lognormal, Gaussian), (lognormal, lognormal) for $D = 2$.

	Batch	Online	Nonstationary
Parameter	EM algorithm[5]	incremental EM[16]	Sequential Discounting EM[27]
Component Number	Variational Bayes Model Selection[4] Dirichlet Process Mixture[12,18] AIC[1], MDL[21] Cross Validation	Online VB Model Selection[22]	Dynamic Model Selection[15,28]
Component Type	EMDL[9]	OMHMC	
Marginal and Copula Type			

Figure 2: Related work

To the best of our knowledge, OMHMC is the first online model selection algorithm which is capable of optimizing types of components (further, OMHMC is capable of optimizing marginal distributions and copulas for individual components.) Fig.2 lists a number of studies for parameter estimation and model selection of the number of component algorithms [1, 4, 5, 12, 18, 21] and their online/nonstationary learning extensions [16, 15, 22, 27, 28], including OMHMC.

We summarize the notation in Section 6. It is rather complicated because we must distinguish a large number of variables and parameters (marginal distributions of individual variables, copulas for individual components, and their parameters.)

2. MIXTURE MODEL WITH HETEROGENEOUS MARGINALS AND COPULAS

2.1 Copulas

Copulas [17] separate a dependency structure among variables from their marginal distributions. Intuitively speaking, their joint distribution can be represented as the product of the marginals of individual variables and a copula. Historically, copulas have been actively studied in financial engineering [13, 17] in order to model dependencies among different types of risks. Recently, data mining and machine learning communities have also noticed their powerful and useful properties, and a number of studies have been conducted [7, 26].

Let $X = (X_1, \ldots, X_D)$ be a random variable. Let $F(x) = P(X_1 \leq x_1, \ldots, X_D \leq x_D)$ and $F_d(x_d) = P_d(X_d \leq x_d)$ be cumulative distribution functions (cdfs), respectively.

A copula function is formally defined as follows:

Definition 1 (Copula). *Let $U = (U_1, \ldots, U_D)$ and $u = (u_1, \ldots, u_D)$ be, respectively, random variables uniformly distributed on $[0,1]^D$ and its realization. Copula function $Q : [0,1]^D \to [0,1]$ is a joint distribution function represented as follows:*

$$Q(u) = P(U_1 \leq u_1, \ldots, U_D \leq u_D). \quad (1)$$

Sklar's theorem [24] provides theoretical support of copulas:

[3] We were unable to confirm that our online EMDL had better convergence than the batch EMDL because a numerical error resulted in non-convergence of the batch algorithm. Briefly, $x \neq \zeta^{-1}(\zeta(x))$, where ζ and ζ^{-1} are, respectively, a cumulative distribution function and its inverse.

THEOREM 1 (SKLAR'S THEOREM). *There exists a copula function such that*

$$F(x) = Q(F_1(x_1), \ldots, F_D(x_D)). \quad (2)$$

If $F_1, \ldots, F_D$ are all continuous, then Q is unique.

Let us denote joint and marginal probabilistic density functions (pdfs) as $f(X) = \frac{\partial^D F(X)}{\partial X_1 \cdots \partial X_D}$ and $f_d(X_d) = \frac{\partial F_d(X_d)}{\partial X_d}$, respectively. Then, using the chain rule, we have,

$$f(X) = \frac{\partial^D Q(F_1(X_1), \ldots, F_D(X_D))}{\partial F_1(X_1) \cdots \partial F_D(X_D)} \prod_{d=1}^{D} f_d(X_d)$$
$$= q(F_1(X_1), \ldots, F_D(X_D)) \prod_{d=1}^{D} f_d(X_d), \quad (3)$$

where $q(F_1(X_1), \ldots, F_D(X_D))$ is referred to as the "copula density function."

2.2 Heterogeneous Mixture Modeling

Let us define "component candidates" as $\mathcal{S} = \{\mathcal{S}_j | j = 1, \ldots, |\mathcal{S}|\}$, where $| \circ |$ represents the number of elements in a set $\circ$. If $\mathcal{S}_j$ is Gaussian, $p(X; \boldsymbol{\phi}(\mathcal{S}_j), \mathcal{S}_j)$ is the Gaussian distribution having parameter $\boldsymbol{\phi}(\mathcal{S}_j)$. For notational simplicity, we denote $\boldsymbol{\phi}(\mathcal{S}_j)$ as $\boldsymbol{\phi}$ alone, so long as there is no fear of confusion.

For given component candidates $\mathcal{S}$, a heterogeneous mixture model is defined as follows [9]:

$$p(X; \boldsymbol{\theta}, \boldsymbol{S}, C) = \sum_{c=1}^{C} \alpha_c p_c(X; \boldsymbol{\phi}_c, S_c). \quad (4)$$

We denote the number of components, types of components, and parameters of components as C, $\boldsymbol{S} = (S_1, \ldots, S_C)$ ($S_c \in \mathcal{S}$) and $\boldsymbol{\theta} = (\boldsymbol{\alpha}, \phi_1, \ldots, \phi_C)$, respectively. $\boldsymbol{\alpha} = (\alpha_1, \ldots, \alpha_C)$ is the mixture coefficient.

This paper proposes a mixture model with heterogeneous marginals and copulas (MHMC) in order to address Limitations 1) and 2) for (4). Let us define "marginal candidates" and "copula candidates" as $\mathcal{M} = \{\mathcal{M}_j | j = 1, \ldots, |\mathcal{M}|\}$ and $\mathcal{Q} = \{\mathcal{Q}_j | j = 1, \ldots, |\mathcal{Q}|\}$, respectively. MHMC is defined by replacing the pdf of each component in (4) with the product of marginal distributions and a copula as follows:

$$p_c(X; \boldsymbol{\phi}_c, S_c) = q_c(\boldsymbol{\psi}_c; \boldsymbol{\xi}_c, Q_c) \prod_{d=1}^{D} p_{cd}(X_d; \boldsymbol{\phi}_{cd}, M_{cd}). \quad (5)$$

$p_{cd}(X_d; \boldsymbol{\phi}_{cd}, M_{cd})$ and $\boldsymbol{\phi}_{cd}$ are the marginal distribution and its parameter[4] specified by $M_{cd} \in \mathcal{M}$. $\psi_{cd} = F_{cd}(X_d)$ is the cdf. of $p_{cd}(X_d; \boldsymbol{\phi}_{cd}, M_{cd})$ where $\boldsymbol{\psi}_c = (\psi_{c1}, \ldots, \psi_{cD})$. $q_c(\boldsymbol{\psi}_c; \boldsymbol{\xi}_c, Q_c)$ and $\boldsymbol{\xi}_c$ are, respectively, the copula density function and its parameter[5] specified by $Q_c \in \mathcal{Q}$. We redefine the component types and the parameter in (4) as $S_c = (M_{c1}, \ldots, M_{cD}, Q_c)$ and $\boldsymbol{\theta} = (\boldsymbol{\alpha}, \phi_{11}, \ldots, \phi_{CD}, \boldsymbol{\xi}_1, \ldots, \boldsymbol{\xi}_C)$, respectively.

A copula plugged into each component naturally addresses Limitation 1). In addition, by separating the marginal distributions and dependencies among them using copulas, we can avoid the combinatorial issue (Limitation 2)) and can efficiently learn the model.

[4]For example, if M_{cd} is Gaussian, p_{cd} is a one dimensional Gaussian distribution and $\boldsymbol{\phi}_{cd}$ is mean and variance.

[5]For example, if Q_c is Gaussian, q is a Gaussian copula and $\boldsymbol{\xi}_c$ is a correlation matrix.

3. ONLINE MIXTURE MODELING

3.1 Expectation Minimization of Description Length

For MHMC, we must specify the number of components C, the types of marginal distributions M_{cd}, and the types of copulas Q_c as well as their parameters $\boldsymbol{\theta}$. This is a issue of "model selection for heterogeneous models," and an efficient batch learning framework, "expectation minimization of description length" (EMDL), has been proposed [9].

Let $\boldsymbol{x}^N = \boldsymbol{x}_1, \ldots, \boldsymbol{x}_N$ be N observed data of X. Let us denote latent variables as $\boldsymbol{z}^N = \boldsymbol{z}_1, \ldots, \boldsymbol{z}_N$, where $\boldsymbol{z}_n = (z_{n1}, \ldots, z_{nC})$. $\boldsymbol{z}_n$ indicates the component assignment of $\boldsymbol{x}_n$ and $z_{nc} = 1$ if $\boldsymbol{x}_n$ is generated from the c-th component and $z_{nc} = 0$ otherwise. A pair $(\boldsymbol{x}^N, \boldsymbol{z}^N)$ is called "complete data" while $\boldsymbol{x}^N$ by itself is called "incomplete data."

Like the EM algorithm [5], for the fixed number of components C, EMDL iterates the EM steps by optimizing the types of components S_c and their parameter $\boldsymbol{\theta}_c = (\alpha_c, \boldsymbol{\phi}_{c1}, \ldots, \boldsymbol{\phi}_{cD}, \boldsymbol{\xi}_C)$ for $\forall c$. This procedure for MHMC is described below. In the t-th E step, we calculate the posterior of latent variables as follows:

$$p(z_{nc}|\boldsymbol{x}^N, \boldsymbol{\theta}_c^{(t-1)}, S_c^{(t-1)}) \propto \alpha_c^{(t-1)} \prod_{d=1}^{D} p_{cd}(x_{nd}; \boldsymbol{\phi}_{cd}^{(t-1)}, M_{cd}^{(t-1)})$$
$$\times q_c(\boldsymbol{\psi}_c^{(t-1)}; \boldsymbol{\xi}_c^{(t-1)}, Q_c^{(t-1)}), \quad (6)$$

where superscription (t) represents the t-th EM step. Then, in the t-th M step, for individual components, we optimize S_c and $\boldsymbol{\phi}_c$ as follows:

$$S_c^{(t)}, \boldsymbol{\theta}_c^{(t)} = \arg\min_{S_c, \boldsymbol{\theta}_c} E_Z^{(t)}\Big[J(\boldsymbol{x}^N, \boldsymbol{z}^N; \alpha_c, \boldsymbol{\phi}_c, S_c)\Big], \quad (7)$$

$$J(\boldsymbol{x}^N, \boldsymbol{z}^N; \boldsymbol{\theta}_c, S_c) = \sum_{n=1}^{N} -z_{nc}\Big(\sum_{d=1}^{D} \log p_{cd}(x_{nd}; \boldsymbol{\phi}_{cd}, M_{cd})$$
$$+ \log q_c(\boldsymbol{\psi}_{nc}; \boldsymbol{\xi}_c, Q_c) + \log \alpha_c\Big)$$
$$+ \frac{\sum_{d=1}^{D} \beta(M_{cd}) + \beta(Q_c)}{2} \log\Big(\sum_{n=1}^{N} z_{nc}\Big),$$

where $\boldsymbol{\psi}_{nc} = (\psi_{nc1}, \ldots, \psi_{ncD})$, $\psi_{ncd} = F_{cd}(x_{nd})$ and $\boldsymbol{\phi}_c = (\phi_{c1}, \ldots, \phi_{cD}, \boldsymbol{\xi}_c)$. The objective $J(\boldsymbol{x}^N, \boldsymbol{z}^N; \boldsymbol{\theta}_c, S_c)$ is the expected description length of complete data w.r.t. the c-th component. $E_Z^{(t)}[\bullet]$ is the expectation of $\bullet$ w.r.t. the posterior (6). $\beta(\bullet)$ is the dimensionality of $\bullet$, i.e., $\beta(M_{cd}) = 2$ if M_{cd} is Gaussian.

Fujimaki et al. [9] show that it is possible to efficiently calculate the second order approximation[6] of $E_Z^{(t)}[\log(\sum_{n=1}^{N} z_{nc})]$ for the last term in (7) as follows:

$$E_Z^{(t)}[\log(\sum_{n=1}^{N} z_{nc})] \approx \log\Big(\sum_{n=1}^{N} E_Z^{(t)}[z_{nc}]\Big)$$
$$- \frac{\sum_{n=1}^{N} E_Z^{(t)}[z_{nc}] - \sum_{n=1}^{N} (E_Z^{(t)}[z_{nc}])^2}{2(\sum_{n=1}^{N} E_Z^{(t)}[z_{nc}])^2}. \quad (8)$$

The number of components is determined on the basis of

[6]We can calculate the higher order approximations with $\mathcal{O}(N)$ computational cost.

MDL [21] as follows:

$$\hat{C} = \arg\min_{C}\Big\{-\sum_{n=1}^{N}\log p(\boldsymbol{x}_n;\hat{\boldsymbol{\theta}},\hat{\boldsymbol{S}},C)+\frac{\beta(\boldsymbol{S})+C-1}{2}\log N\Big\}, \tag{9}$$

where $\hat{\boldsymbol{\theta}}$ and $\hat{\boldsymbol{S}}$ are the estimated parameters and the component types for C through the EM procedure.

The key to MHMC in EMDL is that the M step can be separated into optimizations of individual marginals and copulas for individual components, and therefore we can avoid the combinatorial issue for component types. Otherwise, a naive modeling of the joint distribution of each component would suffer from a drastic increase in the number of component candidates (i.e., the combination of marginal distributions.) even if we made use of EMDL for Limitation 2). Further, in order to address the scalability issue for large scale data, we next propose our online learning algorithm.

3.2 Online EMDL for MHMC

We design the online EMDL with reference to two existing algorithms: an incremental EM algorithm [16] and an inference functions for marginals (IFM) [10]. The incremental EM algorithm estimates a mixture model by incrementally updating sufficient statistics with respect to complete data. Neal and Hinton [16] show that incremental learning provides faster convergence than the standard batch EM algorithm. For a joint distribution having a single component, IFM estimates the marginal parameters first and then estimates the copula parameter among them because the simultaneous estimation of marginals and a copula is generally prohibitively difficult.

3.2.1 Online Update Procedure

Let us assume that the number of components C is fixed (C is optimized in (21).) The online EMDL sequentially updates the model and sufficient statistics on the basis of input dataset $\mathcal{X}_t = \boldsymbol{x}_{K_0+K(t-1)+1},\dots,\boldsymbol{x}_{K_0+Kt}$, where K_0 and K are the numbers of initial data $\mathcal{X}_0$ and sequential dataset $\mathcal{X}_t$ ($\mathcal{X}_0 = \boldsymbol{x}_1,\dots,\boldsymbol{x}_{K_0}$.) Though the cases $K=1$ and $K>1$ are usually called "online" and "mini-batch", respectively, we do not distinguish them.

The update procedure for each component consists of the four steps summarized below. Let us redefine the superscription (t) as the notation of the t-th online update.

Latent Variable Update.

The latent variable update corresponds to the E step in EMDL. First, we calculate the posterior expectation of the latent variable $E_Z^{(t)}[z_{nc}]$ ($n = K_0+K(t-1)+1,\dots,K_0+Kt$), which calculation is identical to that of the posterior distribution of z_{nc}, as follows:

$$E_Z^{(t)}[z_{nc}] = \frac{\alpha_c^{(t-1)}p_c(\boldsymbol{x}_n;\boldsymbol{\phi}_c^{(t-1)},S_c^{(t-1)})}{\sum_{c=1}^{C}\alpha_c^{(t-1)}p_c(\boldsymbol{x}_n;\boldsymbol{\phi}_c^{(t-1)},S_c^{(t-1)})}. \tag{10}$$

For sufficient statistics, we update the r-th order moment of latent variables as follows:

$$\mathcal{U}_{rc}^{(t)} = \mathcal{U}_{rc}^{(t-1)} + \sum_{n=K_0+K(t-1)+1}^{K_0+Kt}(E_Z^{(t)}[z_{nc}])^r \quad (r=1,\dots,R_z), \tag{11}$$

where R_z is set[7] to $R_z=2$. The first order moment is used in (19) and (12), and moments of higher order than one are used in (12). We can calculate the complexity term of the c-th component in the t-th update as follows:

$$\mathcal{E}_c^{(t)} = \log(\mathcal{U}_{1c}^{(t)}) - (\mathcal{U}_{1c}^{(t)} - \mathcal{U}_{2c}^{(t)})/2(\mathcal{U}_{1c}^{(t)})^2, \tag{12}$$

where $\mathcal{E}_c^{(t)}$ is used in (15) and (18).

Marginal Update.

This update step, corresponding to the M step of EMDL, updates moments of individual marginal distributions and optimizes types of marginals and their parameters. As for sufficient statistics, we update the r-th order moment of observed variables as follows:

$$\mathcal{V}_{rcd}^{(t)} = \mathcal{V}_{rcd}^{(t-1)} + \sum_{n=K_0+K(t-1)+1}^{K_0+Kt}E_Z^{(t)}[z_{nc}](x_{nd})^r \quad (r=1,\dots,R_x). \tag{13}$$

For a given marginal candidate $\bar{\mathcal{M}} \in \mathcal{M}$, we obtain the moment-matching estimator[8] $\bar{\phi}_{cd}(\bar{\mathcal{M}},\mathcal{V}_{cd}^{(t)})$ of ϕ_{cd}, where $\mathcal{V}_{cd}^{(t)} = (\mathcal{V}_{1cd}^{(t)},\dots,\mathcal{V}_{Rcd})$. Using moment-matching estimation, we need to memorize only moments. This is an advantage over other estimation methods, such as maximum likelihood estimation, which memorizes parameters for all marginal candidates. We set R_x to a value sufficient for moment-matching estimation (Here, $R_x = 2$. See the next section for more detail.)

We then update the (negative) expected complete likelihood of the marginal distribution $\bar{\mathcal{M}}$ as follows:

$$\mathcal{I}_{cd}^{(t)}(\bar{\mathcal{M}},\mathcal{V}_{cd}^{(t)}) = \mathcal{I}_{cd}^{(t-1)}(\bar{\mathcal{M}},\mathcal{V}_{cd}^{(t-1)}) - \sum_{n=K_0+K(t-1)+1}^{K_0+Kt}E_Z^{(t)}[z_{nc}]\log p_{cd}\Big(x_{cd};\bar{\phi}_{cd}(\bar{\mathcal{M}},\mathcal{V}_{cd}^{(t)}),\bar{\mathcal{M}}\Big), \tag{14}$$

using the moment-matching estimator $\bar{\phi}_{cd}(\bar{\mathcal{M}},\mathcal{V}_{cd}^{(t)})$. The optimal types of marginals and their parameters are obtained by solving the following optimization problem:

$$M_{cd}^{(t)},\phi_{cd}^{(t)} = \arg\min_{\bar{\mathcal{M}}\in\mathcal{M},\bar{\phi}_{cd}}\Big\{\mathcal{I}_{cd}^{(t)}(\bar{\mathcal{M}},\mathcal{V}_{cd}^{(t)}) + \frac{\beta(\bar{\mathcal{M}})}{2}\mathcal{E}_c^{(t)}\Big\}. \tag{15}$$

Copula Update.

This update step, updating moments of copulas and optimizing types and parameters of copulas, also corresponds to the M step in EMDL. As with IFM, the types and parameters of marginals are fixed in this step. In order to avoid notational confusion, we here explain the update procedure for the Gaussian type of copulas which this paper implements (Section 4.) Other types of copulas, such as t-copulas and Archimedean copulas [17], can be implemented in a similar manner.

[7]To obtain more accurate approximation than (8), we could set a higher value of R_z but this would scarcely have a practical impact.

[8]For a Gaussian distribution, the first and second order moment-matching estimator is consistent with the maximum likelihood estimator. The same holds for the first order moment-matching estimator in an exponential distribution.

For sufficient statistics, we update the moment for copulas as follows:

$$\mathcal{W}_c^{(t)} = \mathcal{W}_c^{(t-1)} + \sum_{n=K_0+K(t-1)+1}^{K_0+Kt} E_Z^{(t)}[z_{nc}]\zeta^{-1}(\boldsymbol{\psi}_{nc}^{(t)})\zeta^{-1}(\boldsymbol{\psi}_{nc}^{(t)})^{\dagger}, \quad (16)$$

where $\zeta^{-1}(\boldsymbol{\psi}_{nc}) = (\zeta^{-1}(\psi_{nc1}), \ldots, \zeta^{-1}(\psi_{ncD}))$. ζ^{-1} is the inverse cdf of the standard Gaussian distribution. The superscription $\dagger$ represents the vector/matrix transpose operation.

We then update the (negative) expected complete likelihood of the copula $\bar{\mathcal{Q}}$ as follows:

$$\mathcal{J}_c^{(t)}(\bar{\mathcal{Q}}, \mathcal{W}_c^{(t)}) = \mathcal{J}_c^{(t-1)}(\bar{\mathcal{Q}}, \mathcal{W}_c^{(t-1)}) - \quad (17)$$
$$\sum_{n=K_0+K(t-1)+1}^{K_0+Kt} E_Z^{(t)}[z_{nc}] \log q_c(\boldsymbol{\psi}_{nc}^{(t)}; \boldsymbol{\xi}_c(\mathcal{W}_c^{(t)}, \bar{\mathcal{Q}}), \bar{\mathcal{Q}}),$$

where $\bar{\mathcal{Q}} \in \mathcal{Q}$. We use the moment-matching estimator $\boldsymbol{\xi}_c(\mathcal{W}_c^{(t)}$ of $\boldsymbol{\xi}_c$ as in the case of the marginal update. The optimal types of copulas and their parameters are obtained by solving the following optimization problem:

$$Q_c^{(t)}, \boldsymbol{\xi}_c^{(t)} = \arg\min_{\bar{\mathcal{Q}} \in \mathcal{Q}, \boldsymbol{\xi}_c} \left\{ \mathcal{J}_c^{(t)}(\bar{\mathcal{Q}}, \mathcal{W}_c^{(t)}) + \frac{\beta(\bar{\mathcal{Q}})}{2} \mathcal{E}_c^{(t)} \right\}. \quad (18)$$

In the marginal update and the copula update, we can separately optimize the individual marginal distributions and copulas for individual components, and therefore can address the combinatorial scalability issue (Limitation 2). This is an important advantage in our modeling, in which the joint distributions of individual components are divided into marginal distributions and copulas (5).

Other Updates.

At the end of the t-th update procedure, we update the number of data, the mixture ratio, and the negative incomplete likelihood as follows:

$$N^{(t)} = N^{(t-1)} + K, \quad \alpha_c^{(t)} = \mathcal{U}_{1c}^{(t)}/N^{(t)}, \quad (19)$$

$$\mathcal{L}^{(t)}(C) = \mathcal{L}^{(t-1)}(C) - \sum_{n=K_0+K(t-1)+1}^{K_0+Kt} \log p(\boldsymbol{x}_n; \boldsymbol{\theta}^{(t)}, \boldsymbol{S}^{(t)}, C), \quad (20)$$

where both $\boldsymbol{\theta}^{(t)}$ and $\boldsymbol{S}^{(t)}$ are functions of C. We can then select the number of components which will minimize the value of MDL as follows:

$$C^{(t)} = \arg\min_{1 \le C \le C_{\max}} \left\{ \mathcal{L}^{(t)}(C) + \frac{\beta(\boldsymbol{S}^{(t)}) + C - 1}{2} \log N^{(t)} \right\}, \quad (21)$$

where $C_{\max}$ is the predetermined maximum component size. Through these online update procedures, we optimize the number of components (21), types and parameters of marginal distributions (15), and types and parameters of copulas (18).

3.2.2 *Initialization Procedure*

For the initialization ($t = 0$), we randomly set $E_Z^{(0)}[z_{nc}]$ ($n = 1, \ldots, K_0$). Then we execute the same procedure with (11)-(21), where the terms having superscription $(t-1)$ are set to zero.

3.2.3 *Whole Algorithm Description*

The whole process of Online EMDL for MHMC (OMHMC) is described in Algorithms 1 and 2. Let us define $\mathcal{A}$ as all moments $\mathcal{A} = \mathcal{U}_{rc}, \mathcal{V}_{qcd}, \mathcal{W}_c, \mathcal{I}_{cd}, \mathcal{J}_c, \mathcal{L}, N$ (for all $c = 1, \ldots, C, d = 1, \ldots, D, r = 1, \ldots, R_z, q = 1, \ldots, R_x$.)

Algorithm 1 Online EMDL for MHMC

input : $\{\mathcal{X}_0, \mathcal{X}_1, \ldots, \mathcal{X}_T\}$, $C_{\max}$, $\mathcal{M}$, $\mathcal{Q}$
output : $C^{(T)}$, $\boldsymbol{S}^{(T)}$, $\hat{\boldsymbol{\theta}}^{(T)}$, $\mathcal{A}^{(T)}$
1: **for** $C = 1, \ldots, C_{\max}$ **do**
2: $(\boldsymbol{S}^{(0)}, \boldsymbol{\theta}^{(0)}, \mathcal{A}^{(0)}) = \mathit{Initialization}(\mathcal{X}_0, C, \mathcal{M}, \mathcal{Q})$
3: **end for**
4: **for** $t = 1, \ldots, T$ **do**
5: **for** $C = 1, \ldots, C_{\max}$ **do**
6: $(\boldsymbol{S}^{(t)}, \boldsymbol{\theta}^{(t)}, \mathcal{A}^{(t)}) = \mathit{updateModel}(\mathcal{X}_t, C, \mathcal{M}, \mathcal{Q}, \boldsymbol{S}^{(t-1)}, \boldsymbol{\theta}^{(t-1)}, \mathcal{A}^{(t-1)})$
7: **end for**
8: Select $C^{(t)}$, $\boldsymbol{S}^{(t)}$, $\boldsymbol{\theta}^{(t)}$ by solving (21)
9: **end for**

Algorithm 2 updateModel

input : $\mathcal{X}_t, C, \mathcal{M}, \mathcal{Q}, \boldsymbol{S}^{(t-1)}, \boldsymbol{\theta}^{(t-1)}, \mathcal{A}^{(t-1)}$
output : $\boldsymbol{S}^{(t)}, \boldsymbol{\theta}^{(t)}, \mathcal{A}^{(t)}$
1: Calculate $E_Z^{(t)}[z_nc]$ and update $\mathcal{U}_{rc}^{(t)}$ and $\mathcal{E}_c^{(t)}$ ((10)-(12))
2: **for** $c = 1 \ldots C$ **do**
3: **for** $d = 1 \ldots D$ **do**
4: Update $\mathcal{V}_{rcd}^{(t)}$ based on (13)
5: **for** $\bar{\mathcal{M}} \in \mathcal{M}$ **do**
6: Calculate $\bar{\phi}_{cd}^{(t)}(\bar{\mathcal{M}}, \mathcal{V}_{cd}^{(t)})$ using the moment-matching method for $\bar{\mathcal{M}}$
7: Update $\mathcal{I}_{cd}^{(t)}(\bar{\mathcal{M}}, \mathcal{V}_{cd}^{(t)})$ (14)
8: **end for**
9: Select $M_{cd}^{(t)}$ and $\phi_{cd}^{(t)}$ based on (15)
10: **end for**
11: Update $\mathcal{W}_c^{(t)}$ based on (16)
12: **for** $\bar{\mathcal{Q}} \in \mathcal{W}$ **do**
13: Calculate $\boldsymbol{\xi}_c(\mathcal{W}_c^{(t)}, \bar{\mathcal{Q}})$
14: Update $\mathcal{J}_c^{(t)}(\bar{\mathcal{Q}}, \mathcal{W}_c^{(t)})$ based on (17)
15: **end for**
16: Select $Q_c^{(t)}$ and $\boldsymbol{\xi}_c^{(t)}$ based on (18)
17: **end for**

First, the initialization (steps 1-3 in Algorithm 1) is executed for each component on the basis of the initialization procedure described in Section 3.2.2. For the t-th update with the fixed number of components C (steps 4-9 in Algorithm 1), we update the corresponding model on the basis of Algorithm 2. In Algorithm 2, we first execute the latent variable update (step 1). Then, for each component, marginal updates (step 3-10) and a copula update (steps 11-16) are executed, and we obtain the updated model and parameters $\boldsymbol{S}^{(t)}, \boldsymbol{\theta}^{(t)}, \mathcal{A}^{(t)}$. In step 8 of Algorithm 1, we select the number of components $C^{(t)}$.

3.3 Implemented Model

In this paper, we implement MHMCs in which $\mathcal{M}$ is a set of (Gaussian, exponential, lognormal) and $\mathcal{Q}$ is a set of sparse Gaussian copulas.

Gaussian Marginal.

The Gaussian marginal distribution described as

$$p_{cd}(X_d; \phi_{cd}, M_{cd}) = \frac{1}{\sqrt{2\pi(\sigma_{cd})^2}} \exp\left(\frac{-(X_d - \mu_{cd})^2}{2(\sigma_{cd})^2} \right) \quad (22)$$

has two parameters, mean μ_{cd} and variance $(\sigma_{cd})^2$, and the moment-matching estimator is obtained as follows:

$$\bar{\phi}_{cd}^{(t)} = (\bar{\mu}_{cd}^{(t)}, (\sigma_{cd}^{(t)})^2) = (\mathcal{V}_{1cd}^{(t)}/\mathcal{U}_{1c}^{(t)}, (\mathcal{V}_{2cd}^{(t)} - (\mathcal{V}_{1cd}^{(t)})^2)/\mathcal{U}_{1c}^{(t)}), \tag{23}$$

The parameter dimensionality $\beta(M_{cd})$ is 2.

Exponential Marginal.

The exponential marginal distribution described as

$$p_{cd}(X_d; \phi_{cd}, M_{cd}) = \frac{1}{\lambda_{cd}} \exp(-X_d/\lambda_{cd}) \tag{24}$$

has one scale parameter, λ_{cd}, and the moment-matching estimator is obtained as follows:

$$\bar{\phi}_{cd}^{(t)} = (\bar{\lambda}_{cd}^{(t)}) = (\mathcal{V}_{1cd}^{(t)}/\mathcal{U}_{1c}^{(t)}), \tag{25}$$

The parameter dimensionality $\beta(M_{cd})$ is 1.

Lognormal Marginal.

The lognormal marginal distribution described as

$$p_{cd}(X_d; \phi_{cd}, M_{cd}) = \frac{1}{\sqrt{2\pi(\rho_{cd})^2} X_d} \exp\Big(\frac{-(\log(X_d) - \nu_{cd})^2}{2(\rho_{cd})^2}\Big) \tag{26}$$

has two parameters, log-mean ν_{cd} and log-variance $(\rho_{cd})^2$, and the moment-matching estimator is obtained as follows:

$$\begin{aligned}\bar{\phi}_{cd}^{(t)} &= (\bar{\nu}_{cd}^{(t)}, (\rho_{cd}^{(t)})^2) \qquad (27)\\ &= (\log(\mathcal{V}_{1cd}^{(t)}) - (\sigma_{cd}^{(t)})^2/2, 1 + \log(\mathcal{V}_{2cd}^{(t)}/(\mathcal{V}_{1cd}^{(t)})^2) - 1),\end{aligned}$$

The parameter dimensionality $\beta(M_{cd})$ is 2.

Sparse Gaussian Copula.

The sparse Gaussian copula, having sparse correlation parameter $\boldsymbol{\xi}_c = \boldsymbol{\Sigma}_c(\tau)$, is described as:

$$q_c(\boldsymbol{\psi}_c; \boldsymbol{\xi}_c, Q_c) = \frac{\mathcal{N}(\boldsymbol{\psi}_c; \mathbf{0}, \boldsymbol{\Sigma}_c(\tau_c))}{\prod_{d=1}^{D} \mathcal{N}(\psi_{cd}; 0, 1)}, \tag{28}$$

where $\mathbf{0}$ is a zero vector and $\mathcal{N}(\bullet; *, \star)$ is the multivariate Gaussian distribution of $\bullet$ with mean $*$ and correlation $\star$ (diagonal elements of $\star$ are one). The moment-matching estimator is obtained as follows:

$$[\bar{\boldsymbol{\xi}}_c^{(t)}]_{ij} = [\bar{\boldsymbol{\Sigma}}_c(\tau_c)]_{ij} = \begin{cases} 1 & \text{if } i = j \\ c_{ij}^{(t)} & \text{if } i \neq j \quad |c_{ij}^{(t)}| > \tau_c \\ 0 & \text{if } i \neq j \quad |c_{ij}^{(t)}| \leq \tau_c \end{cases} \tag{29}$$

$$c_{ij} = [\mathcal{W}_c^{(t)}]_{ij} / \sqrt{[\mathcal{W}_c^{(t)}]_{ii} [\mathcal{W}_c^{(t)}]_{jj}}, \tag{30}$$

where $[\bullet]_{ij}$ represents the (i, j)-th element of a matrix $\bullet$. If τ_c is 0, the sparse Gaussian copula will be consistent with the regular Gaussian copula. Candidates for sparse Gaussian copulas can be defined as those having different values of τ. The parameter dimensionality $\beta(Q_c)$ is the number of non-diagonal, non-zero elements divided by two.

4. EXPERIMENTS AND DISCUSSION

We conducted experiments with respect to two basic investigations and two applications. The former consisted of evaluations of 1) model selection performance and 2) scalability and update scheduling. The applications were 3) density estimation and 4) anomaly detection, both of which are important applications for mixture modeling.

For OMHMC, the hyperparameters are set to $C_{\max} = 10$, $\mathcal{M} = \{gaussian, lognormal, exponetial\}$, $\mathcal{Q} = \{\tau = 0, \tau = 0.05, \tau = 0.1, \tau = 0.2\}$, $K_0 = 10, T = 100$ (therefore, K takes different values for different data). All results represent the averages of ten runs (or ten-fold cross validation.) In Tables 1 and 2, the best value for each dataset is highlighted in boldface.

4.1 Model Selection

In this evaluation, we investigated the basic model selection performance of OMHMC, especially focusing on selection of marginal and copulas types. Hereafter, superscription $*$ represents the true model.

Experimental Settings.

We first evaluated marginal selection error and copula selection error, which are calculated[9] as:

$$ERR_M = \frac{1}{C^* D} \sum_{c=1}^{C^*} \sum_{d=1}^{D} (M_{cd}^* \neq M_{cd}^{(T)}), \tag{31}$$

$$ERR_C = \frac{1}{C^* D(D-1)} \sum_{c=1}^{C^*} ||B(\boldsymbol{\xi}_c^*) - B(\boldsymbol{\xi}_c^{(T)})||_F, \tag{32}$$

where $[B(\bullet)]_{ij} = 0$ if $[\bullet]_{ij} = 0$, and $[B(\bullet)]_{ij} = 1$ otherwise. $|\bullet|_F$ is the Frobenius norm of $\bullet$. ERR_C is the ratio of non-diagonal elements of $[B(\boldsymbol{\xi}_c^*)]_{ij} \neq [B(\boldsymbol{\xi}_c^{(T)})]_{ij}$. Note that both ERR_M and ERR_C are zero if $M_{cd}^* = M_{cd}^{(T)}$ and $\boldsymbol{\xi}_c^* = \boldsymbol{\xi}_c^{(T)}$ for all c and d. Since there is no previously-reported algorithm which can optimize marginal and copula types, we only evaluated them for OMHMC.

We also evaluated the Kullback-Leibler (KL) divergence between the true pdf and the estimated pdf, which was approximated as[10]:

$$KL = \sum_{n=1}^{N_{KL}} p(\boldsymbol{x}_n^{KL}; \boldsymbol{\theta}^*, \boldsymbol{S}^*, C^*) \log \frac{p(\boldsymbol{x}_n^{KL}; \boldsymbol{\theta}^*, \boldsymbol{S}^*, C^*)}{p(\boldsymbol{x}_n^{KL}; \boldsymbol{\theta}^{(T)}, \boldsymbol{S}^{(T)}, C^{(T)})},$$

where $\boldsymbol{x}_n^{KL}$ are samples for the KL calculation. We compared OMHMC with a state-of-the-art variational Dirichlet process Gaussian mixture model[11] [12] (VDPGMM).

We artificially generated the true model on the basis of Algorithm 3. Here we only explain the results for $C^* = 5$ because of space limitations (in fact, results show that the value of C^* scarcely affected basic behaviors.) In step 1, parameters for marginal distributions were sampled from $\mu_{cd}^* \sim [-5, 5]$, $(\sigma_{cd}^*)^2 \sim [0.5, 1.5]$, $\lambda_{cd}^* \sim (0, 1]$, $\nu_{cd}^* \sim (0, 1.5]$ and $(\rho_{cd}^*)^2 \sim [0.5, 1.0]$. In step 2, τ_c^* was sampled from $[0, 0.5]$ and $\boldsymbol{\xi}_c^*$ were generated using the "gallery" function in MATLAB. In step 3, α_c^* was sampled from $(0, 1]$.

Results and Discussion.

Fig. 3 presents ERR_M and ERR_C over the number of data and the data dimensionality. The marginal selection

[9]We had to identify the correspondence between the estimated components and the true components. For this purpose, we calculated Kullback-Leibler divergences between all component pairs and determined the correspondence which minimizes the sum of KL divergence.

[10]We set $N_{KL} = 10000$ in our experiments.

[11]We used the implementation of Kenichi Kurihara at `http://sites.google.com/site/kenichikurihara/`, and also used the default hyperparameter values in the software.

Algorithm 3 Data Generation Recipe

input : C^* and D

1: Randomly select M^*_{cd} from (Gaussian, lognormal, exponential), and set their parameters ϕ^*_{cd}.
2: Randomly set τ^*_c for Q^*_c and generate correlation matrices $\boldsymbol{\xi}^*_c$. The non-diagonal elements of $\boldsymbol{\xi}^*_c$ smaller than τ^*_c are set to be zero.
3: Randomly set α^*_c. Normalize α^*_c so that $\sum_{c=1}^{C^*} \alpha^*_c = 1$.

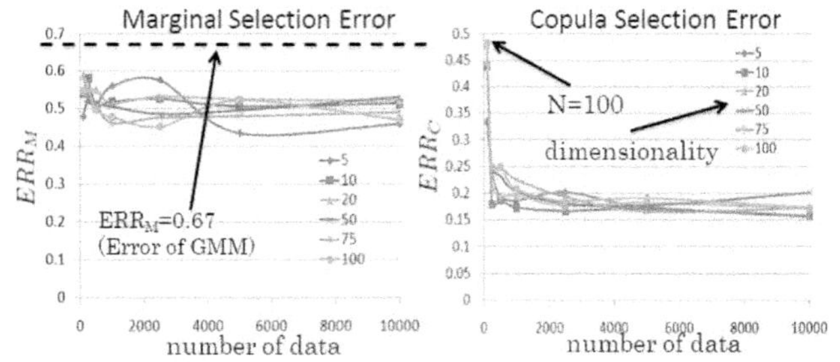

Figure 3: Marginal selection error (left) and copula selection error (right) for OMHMC.

errors are distributed around $ERR_M = 0.5$ and are better than the marginal error of the usual Gaussian mixture model[12] (GMM). Because there are parameter ranges for which it is difficult (or unnecessary) to distinguish (Gaussian, lognormal, exponential) distributions, ERR_M did not decrease over N (in the other settings, we observed that ERR_M decreased over N.) The copula selection errors EMM_C converged over N around $EMM_C = 0.2$, and OMHMC succeeded in its sparse dependency discovery. Since the correlation between different types of marginal distributions is no longer "linear," this results indicate that OMHMC can discover nonlinear dependency structures among variables (further, different components can have different nonlinearities[13].) With respect to both ERR_M and ERR_C, the data dimensionality ($D = 5 \sim 100$) scarcely affected the model selection performance, while it will degrade in higher dimensional spaces due to the curse of dimensionality.

Fig. 4 presents a comparison of the KL between OMHMC and VDPGMM. The KL of OMHMC (left) decreased over N, while the KL of VDPGMM did not markedly decrease. At high dimensionality ($D = 50, 75, 100$), OMHMC greatly outperformed VDPGMM.

4.2 Scalability and Update Scheduling

OMHMC has two important predetermined parameters: initial data size K_0 and the number of updates T (or size of mini-batch data $\mathcal{X}_t$, i.e., $K = (N^{(T)} - K_0)/T$.) These update-scheduling parameters determine the scalability and stability of OMHMC.

To investigate the behavior of OMHMC over K_0 and T, we evaluated: 1) CPU time (scalability), and 2) MDL value per data item, $\mathcal{L}^{(T)}/N^{(T)}$ (convergence and stability). Here, we employed the KDDCUP99 network intrusion dataset, which has 976158 data in total (see Section 4.4 for more detail.)

[12]Since we randomly selected M^*_{cd} from (Gaussian, exponential, lognormal), ERR_M of GMM is 0.67.

[13]For example, the correlation between Gaussian and lognormal distributions has different nonlinearity from that of the correlation between two lognormal distributions.

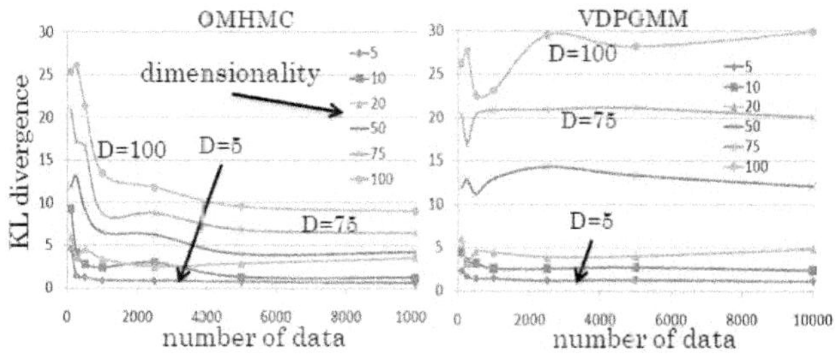

Figure 4: KL divergences between the true model and the estimated model (left: OMHMC, right: VDPGMM).

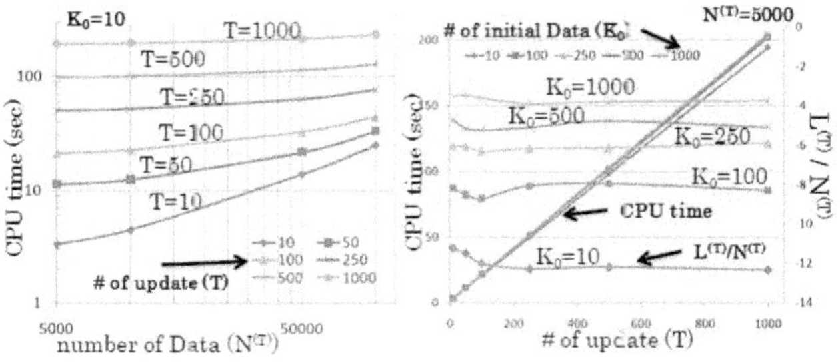

Figure 5: CPU time and $\mathcal{L}^{(T)}/N^{(T)}$. The left figure ($K_0 = 10$) shows CPU time over $N^{(T)}$ (double log plot). The right figure ($N^{(T)} = 5000$) shows CPU time (left axis) and $\mathcal{L}^{(T)}/N^{(T)}$ (right axis) over T.

First, we observed that the impact of $N^{(T)}$ on CPU time was only linear (Fig. 5, left.) In fact, the difference between the cases of $N^{(T)} = 5000$ and $N^{(T)} = 100000$ is only about 20 sec, with little relation to T. Second, with $T = 100$, $\mathcal{L}^{(T)}/N^{(T)}$ nearly converged, with little relation to K_0 (Fig. 5, right.) On the other hand, CPU time grew linearly with T. We have obtained the significant insight that the choice of a relatively small value of T has a great advantage in scalability, with little performance degradation. We further observed that the smaller value of K_0 showed better performance w.r.t. $\mathcal{L}^{(T)}/N^{(T)}$. All components were initialized to closely similar values of moments and parameters when K_0 was large, and they had little difference through the updates in OMHMC. On the other hand, a small value of K_0 generated differences among components. In summary, both T and K_0 will preferrably be set to small values to obtain both good scalability and performance. The CPU time for all data ($N^{(T)} = 976158, K_0 = 10, T = 100$) was 242.6 sec in total.

4.3 Density Estimation

Density estimation is the most basic and significant application of mixture modeling, and a number of unsupervised methods, such as topic modeling [15], image segmentation [25], and speech recognition [20], are based on it.

We compared OMHMC with VDPGMM on the basis of the predictive likelihood (likelihood of test data) per data item. We used the seven datasets from the UCI data repository [8] that are shown in Table 1.

As Table 1 shows, for the well-known iris data, VDPGMM outperformed OMHMC, partly because iris data can be well modeled by a Gaussian mixture (therefore OMHMC is likely

Table 1: Predictive likelihood per data.

Data[14]	N	D	OMHMC	VDPGMM
iris	150	4	-4.60±3.41	**-2.00 ± 0.99**
FF	466	11	**-21.51 ± 2.90**	-24.78 ± 0.23
yeast	1255	8	**31.77 ± 3.49**	2.081 ± 2.91
YQ	5848	11	**-3.76 ± 0.66**	-5.68 ± 1.73
CT	61236	16	**16.16 ± 0.90**	15.50 ± 0.86
CM	68040	9	-7.51 ± 0.62	**-7.45 ± 0.64**
YPMSD	463811	12	**13.59 ± 0.09**	**13.59 ± 0.12**

to be overfitted), and partly because $N = 150$ is too small for the online learning algorithm. With increasing N, OMHMC outperformed VDPGMM, except for the Color Moment data. This result indicates that the "Gaussian assumption" is not satisfied with real data, which our modeling with heterogeneous marginal distributions and copulas fit well. Since VDPGMM also has strong expressiveness, the density estimation performance of the two methods was competitive for large scale data (YPMSD).

4.4 Anomaly Detection

Anomaly detection is also a significant application. On the basis of the assumption that the number of anomaly data is much smaller than that of normal data, mixture-model-based anomaly detectors [27] are used to detect anomalous data having low log-likelihood (or high negative log-likelihood.) We employed datasets from the Rätsch's benchmark repository [19] (Dataset 1) and the KDDCUP99 network intrusion dataset[15]. The sample size and data dimensionality of each dataset are shown in Table 2.

For each dataset in Dataset 1, to satisfy the small sample size assumption for anomaly data, we randomly selected 10% of the anomaly data in each run. Further, for KDDCUP99, we generated normal (normal access) and anomaly (intrusion success) data on the basis of generation recipe in [27]. Briefly, we chose (duration, src_bytes, dst_bytes) attributes and picked up all 972781 normal samples and 3377 intrusions whose logged_in attributes were positive. Then, for each run, we randomly selected 50% of the samples.

We compared OMHMC-based anomaly detection with state-of-the-art anomaly detectors: VDPGMM [12], i-forest [14], and one-class support vector machine (OSVM) [23] with a Gaussian kernel[16] and local outlier factor (LOF) [2]. For a comparison with another mixture modeling method, we applied VDPGMM on the basis of "log-likelihood" scoring, as with OMHMC, while the original VDPGMM has not been applied to anomaly detection. The performance was measured using Area Under the ROC Curve (AUC), which is widely used in the domain of anomaly detection.

Table 2 shows a comparison of AUCs. OMHMC, VDPGMM, and i-forest worked in large scale datasets where OSVM and LOF were not available because of computational time/memory issues. OMHMC and i-forest outperformed the others, and their performance was similar (both of them took first place for four datasets.) Since estimation performance increases with an increased number of data, OMHMC has tended to perform well with comparatively large datasets. OSVM and LOF were sensitive to parameter changes, and we do not have systematic ways to choose their parameters (cross validation is not available in anomaly detection.)

[14]FF:forest fire, WQ: wine quality, CT: Cooc Texture, CM: Color Moment

[15]`http://www.sigkdd.org/kddcup/index.php`

[16]We use the libsvm [3] for implementation of OSVM.

5. SUMMARY

This paper has addressed the data mining issue for mixture modeling with complicated data having heterogeneous marginal distributions and dependencies among variables. The proposed OMHMC provides a powerful, scalable model selection tool that can execute fully-automatic model selection of types of marginal distributions and copulas as well as parameter estimations. Our experimental results confirm the scalability and performance of OMHMC in application to density estimation and anomaly detection.

We have two challenges for future study. First, as seen in Fig. 2, a nonstationary extension of OMHMC remains as an open problem. It should be addressed by incorporating a time-discounting concept into OMHMC. Second, mixture models have been employed for classification/regression problems (e.g., a mixture of experts [11]), and OMHMC might be usable for help in their model selections.

6. NOTATION

We summarize here the notations used in this paper.

c : component number n : data number d : dimension number r : the order of the indexed moment t : update number $*$: true model
N : data size D : data dimensionality
X and $\boldsymbol{x}_n$: random variable in $\mathbb{R}^D$ and its observation $\boldsymbol{z}_n$: latent variable of $\boldsymbol{x}_n$
p : pdf of whole model p_c : pdf of component p_{cd} : pdf of marginal q_c : pdf of copula
$\mathcal{M}$: possible candidates of marginal distribionts $\mathcal{Q}$: possible candidates of copulas
C : # of component M_{cd} : type of marginal distribution Q_c : type of copula $\boldsymbol{\alpha}$: mixture ratio ϕ_{cd} : parameter of M_{cd} ψ_{cd} : cdf. corresponding to $p_{cd}(\bullet; \phi_{cd}, M_{cd})$ $\boldsymbol{\xi}_c$: parameter of Q_c S_c : $(M_{c1}, \ldots, M_{cD}, Q_c)$ $\boldsymbol{\theta}$: $(\boldsymbol{\alpha}, \boldsymbol{\phi}_{11}, \ldots, \boldsymbol{\phi}_{CD}, \boldsymbol{\xi}_1, \ldots, \boldsymbol{\xi}_C))$ $\boldsymbol{\theta}_c$: $(\alpha_c, \boldsymbol{\phi}_c, \boldsymbol{\xi}_C)$ and $\boldsymbol{\phi}_c = (\phi_{c1}, \ldots, \phi_{cD})$
$\mathcal{U}_{rc}$: the r-th order momnent of latent variables $\mathcal{V}_{rcd}$: the r-th order moment of observed variables $\mathcal{V}_{cd}$: $(\mathcal{V}_{1cd}, \ldots, \mathcal{V}_{R_x cd})$ $\mathcal{W}_c$: moment for copula
T : the number of update K_0 : initial data size K : mini-batch data size
$\beta(\bullet)$: dimensionality of $\bullet$ $E_Z[\bullet]$: expectation of $\bullet$ w.r.t. latent variables' posterior $[\bullet]_{ij}$: the (i,j)-th element of $\bullet$

Table 2: AUC values (N/A represents "not available" because of computational time/memory issues.)

Dataset	# of normal / total anomalies	dim D	OMHMC	VDPGMM	i-forest	OSVM	LOF	
							$k=5$	$k=30$
bcancer	186/77	9	0.61 ± 0.09	$\mathbf{0.70 \pm 0.10}$	$\mathbf{0.70 \pm 0.07}$	0.61 ± 0.05	0.53 ± 0.08	0.67 ± 0.01
heart	150/120	13	0.78 ± 0.07	0.73 ± 0.05	$\mathbf{0.83 \pm 0.05}$	0.56 ± 0.03	0.47 ± 0.10	0.76 ± 0.06
diabetis	500/268	8	$\mathbf{0.73 \pm 0.03}$	0.68 ± 0.04	0.72 ± 0.04	0.67 ± 0.05	0.60 ± 0.05	0.67 ± 0.05
twonorm	3697/3703	20	$\mathbf{0.87 \pm 0.01}$	0.73 ± 0.01	0.84 ± 0.01	0.57 ± 0.01	0.56 ± 0.02	0.62 ± 0.02
ringnorm	3736/3664	20	$\mathbf{1.00 \pm 0.00}$	$\mathbf{1.00 \pm 0.00}$	$\mathbf{1.00 \pm 0.00}$	0.80 ± 0.00	$\mathbf{1.00 \pm 0.00}$	$\mathbf{1.00 \pm 0.00}$
shuttle	45586/3511	9	0.99 ± 0.00	0.99 ± 0.00	$\mathbf{1.00 \pm 0.01}$	0.78 ± 0.01	N/A	N/A
KDDCUP	972781/3377	3	$\mathbf{0.89 \pm 0.02}$	0.87 ± 0.04	0.85 ± 0.00	N/A	N/A	N/A

7. REFERENCES

[1] H. Akaike. Information theory and an extension of the maximum likelihood principle. In B. N. Petrov and F. Caski, editors, *Proceedings of the 2nd International Symposium on Information Theory*, pages 267–281, 1973.

[2] M. M. Breunig, H. P. Kriegel, R. T. Ng, and J. Sander. LOF: identifying density-based local outliers. *Sigmod Record*, 29(2):93–104, 2000.

[3] C.-C. Chang and C.-J. Lin. LIBSVM: a library for support vector machines. `http://www.csie.ntu.edu.tw/~cjlin/libsvm`, 2001.

[4] A. Corduneanu and C. Bishop. Variational bayesian model selection for mixture distributions. In *Proceedings of the Eighth International Workshop on Artificial Intelligence and Statistics*, 2001.

[5] A. P. Dempster, N. M. Laird, and D. B. Rubin. Maximum likelihood from imcomplete data via the em algorithm. *Journal of the Royal Statistical Society*, B39(1):1–38, 1977.

[6] P. Diehr, D. Yanez, A. S. Ash, M. Hornbrook, , and D. Y. Lin. Methods for analyzing health care utilization and costs. *Annual Review of Public Health*, 20:125–144, 1999.

[7] G. Elidan. Copula bayesian networks. In *Advances in Neural Information Processing Systems 23*, pages 559–567, 2010.

[8] A. Frank and A. Asuncion. UCI machine learning repository. `http://archive.ics.uci.edu/ml`, 2010. University of California, Irvine, School of Information and Computer Sciences.

[9] R. Fujimaki, S. Morinaga, M. Momma, K. Aoki, and T. Nakata. Linear time model selection for mixture of heterogeneous components. In *Proceedings of the 1st Asian Conference on Machine Learning*, pages 82–97, 2009.

[10] H. Joe, editor. *Multivariate Models and Dependence Concepts*. Chapman & Hall, 1997.

[11] M. I. Jordan and R. A. Jacobs. Hierarchical mixtures of experts and the EM algorithm. *Neural Computation*, 6:181–214, 1994.

[12] K. Kurihara, M. Welling, and N. Vlassis. Accelerated variational dirichlet mixture models. In *Advances in Neural Information Processing Systems 19*, pages 761–768. MIT Press, 2006.

[13] D. X. Li. On default correlation: A copula function approach. *Journal of Fixed Income*, 9(4):43–54, 1999.

[14] F. T. Liu, K. M. Ting, and Z. H. Zhou. Isolation Forest. In *Proceedings of the 2008 Eighth IEEE International Conference on Data Mining*, pages 413–422, 2008.

[15] S. Morinaga and K. Yamanishi. Tracking dynamics of topic trends using a finite mixture model. In *Proceedings of the tenth ACM SIGKDD international conference on Knowledge discovery and data mining*, pages 811–816. ACM Press, 2004.

[16] R. Neal and G. E. Hinton. A view of the EM algorithm that justifies incremental, sparse, and other variants. In *Learning in Graphical Models*, pages 355–368, 1998.

[17] R. B. Nelsen, editor. *An Introduction to Copulas*. Springer Series in Statistics, 2006.

[18] C. E. Rasmussen. The infinite gaussian mixture model. In *In Advances in Neural Information Processing Systems 12*, pages 554–560, 2000.

[19] G. Rätsch, T. Onoda, and K. Müller. Soft margins for AdaBoost. *Machine Learning*, 42(3):287–320, 2001.

[20] D. A. Reynolds, T. F. Quatieri, and R. B. Dunn. Speaker verification using adapted gaussian mixture models. *Digital Signal Processing*, 10(1):19–41, 2000.

[21] J. Rissanen. Modeling by shortest data description. *Automatica*, 14:465–471, 1978.

[22] M. Sato. On-line model selection based on the variational bayes. *Neural Computation*, 13:1649–1681, 2001.

[23] B. Scholkopf, J. C. Platt, J. Shawe-Taylor, A. J. Smola, and R. C. Williamson. Estimating the support of a high-dimensional distribution. *Neural computation*, 13(7):1443–1471, 2001.

[24] A. Sklar. Fonctions de repartition a n dimensions et leurs marges. Technical report, Publications de l'Institut de Statistique de L'Universite de Paris, 1959.

[25] C. Stauffer and W. E. L. Grimson. Adaptive background mixture models for real-time tracking. In *IEEE Computer Society Conference on Computer Vision and Pattern Recognition*, pages 246–252, 1999.

[26] A. Wilson and Z. Ghahramani. Copula processes. In *Advances in Neural Information Processing Systems 23*, pages 2460–2468, 2010.

[27] K. Yamanishi, J. ichi Takeuchi, G. Williams, and P. Milne. On-line unsupervised outlier detection using finite mixtures with discounting learning algorithms. *Data Mining and Knowledge Discovery*, 8(3):275–300, 2004.

[28] K. Yamanishi and Y. Maruyama. Dynamic model selection with its applications to novelty detection. *IEEE Transactions on Information Theory*, 53:2180–2189, 2007.

Dual Active Feature and Sample Selection for Graph Classification

Xiangnan Kong
University of Illinois at Chicago
Chicago, IL, USA
xkong4@uic.edu

Wei Fan
IBM T. J. Watson Research
Hawthorn, NY, USA
weifan@us.ibm.com

Philip S. Yu
University of Illinois at Chicago
Chicago, IL, USA
psyu@cs.uic.edu

ABSTRACT

Graph classification has become an important and active research topic in the last decade. Current research on graph classification focuses on mining discriminative subgraph features under supervised settings. The basic assumption is that a large number of labeled graphs are available. However, labeling graph data is quite expensive and time consuming for many real-world applications. In order to reduce the labeling cost for graph data, we address the problem of how to select the most important graph to query for the label. This problem is challenging and different from conventional active learning problems because there is no predefined feature vector. Moreover, the subgraph enumeration problem is NP-hard. The active sample selection problem and the feature selection problem are *correlated* for graph data. Before we can solve the active sample selection problem, we need to find a set of optimal subgraph features. To address this challenge, we demonstrate how one can simultaneously estimate the usefulness of a query graph and a set of subgraph features. The idea is to maximize the dependency between subgraph features and graph labels using an active learning framework. We propose a branch-and-bound algorithm to search for the optimal query graph and optimal features simultaneously. Empirical studies on nine real-world tasks demonstrate that the proposed method can obtain better accuracy on graph data than alternative approaches.

Categories and Subject Descriptors

H.2.8 [**Database Management**]: Database Applications-Data Mining

General Terms

Algorithm, Experimentation, Performance

Keywords

Active Learning, Feature Selection, Graph Classification, Subgraph Pattern, Data Mining, Feature Construction

1. INTRODUCTION

Graphs arise naturally in a wide range of application domains. Examples include chemical compounds, XML documents and program flows. There is a great need for building models to classify graph objects. For example, in chemoinformatics, researchers would like to predict the anticancer activities of chemical compounds in order to find new drugs for cancer or chronic diseases [26, 17]; in software engineering, researchers are interested in studying how to automatically identify bugs in program flows [5]. Motivated by these challenges, *graph classification* has received considerable attention in the last decade.

Graph classification has been studied extensively in the literature [18, 24, 3]. Conventional approaches focus on mining discriminative subgraph features [28] under supervised settings. They assume explicitly or implicitly that a large number of labeled graphs are available. However, in many real-world applications, labeling graph data can be very expensive and time consuming. For example, in molecular medicine, it is very expensive to test the anticancer activity by preclinical studies and clinical trials; in software engineering, human experts have to examine a program flow carefully in order to find software bugs. The labeling cost for graph data can be significantly reduced by training a model that can select the most important graph to query for the label. This setting is also known as *active learning* or *active query selection.* It aims to exploit unlabeled data effectively by selecting important examples to query for labels. Thus, active learning approaches can usually achieve performance comparable to supervised approaches, while using less labeled data. Active learning has been shown to be useful in many real-world applications [25, 29].

Formally, the active learning problem for graph data corresponds to learning a model to select important graphs to obtain class labels. Active learning is particularly challenging in graph data. Conventional active learning approaches estimate the importance of unlabeled examples, and assume that all useful features are given. However, in graph data the useful features are not available. Thus, additional steps of subgraph feature mining and selection are required to estimate the usefulness of subgraphs. What makes this problem even more interesting and challenging is that subgraph enumeration and graph isomorphism testing problems are NP-

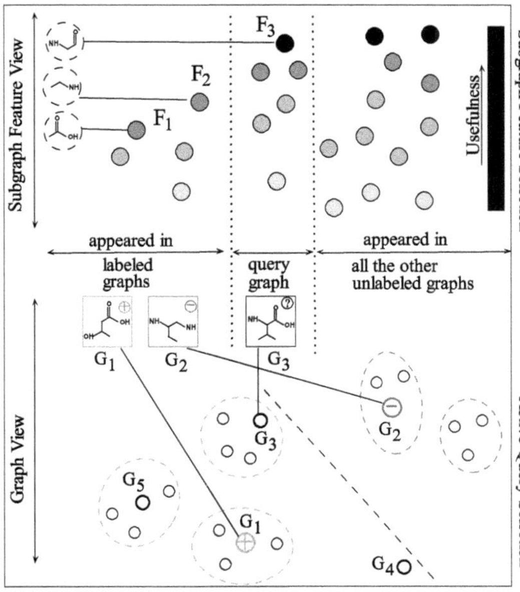

Figure 1: An example of dual active feature and sample selection in graph data.

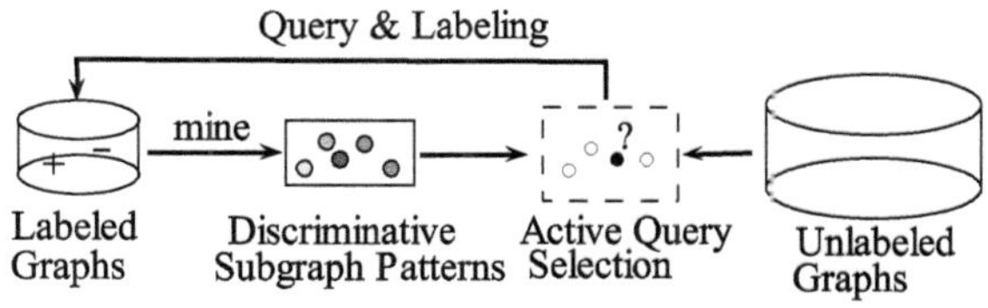

Figure 2: Two-stage active learning in graph data

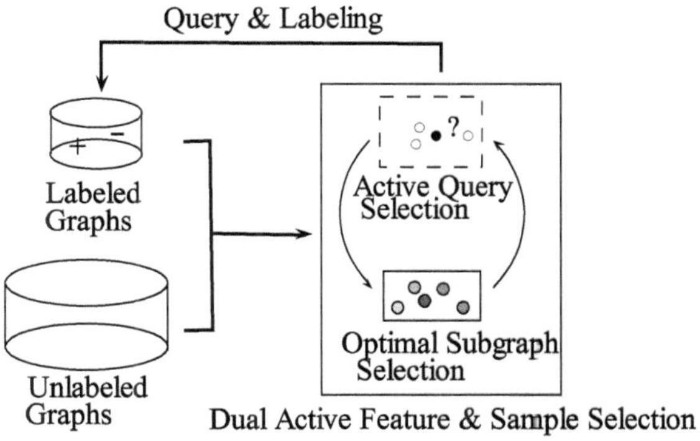

Figure 3: Dual active feature and sample selection

complete. Thus, it is impossible to enumerate all subgraph features and adopt existing approaches for active learning.

In active learning for graph data, the active query selection problem and the subgraph feature selection problem are closely related to each other. The reasons are summarized as follows:

- In active query selection, we need to estimate the importance of each unlabeled graph in order to select the most important graph to query for the label. However, before the most important graph can be determined, we need to find a set of useful subgraph features. Graph data are not directly represented in a meaningful feature space. The performance of the active sample selection directly depends on the quality of the subgraph features mined from the graph dataset. For example, in Figure 1, G_3 is the most important graph which we want to query for the label. G_3 is close to the class boundary like graph G_4. Moreover, G_3 is representative of a cluster of unlabeled graphs. However, the informativeness and representativeness of a graph object depends on which feature set is used. The better the feature set we use, the better we will be able to estimate the importance of the query graphs.

- In the subgraph feature selection problem, we also need to select a set of important subgraph features for the graph classification task. Conventional feature selection approaches for graph data focus on supervised settings [26, 17]. The feature evaluation strategies strictly follow the assumption that a large number of labeled graphs are available. However, in the active learning settings, we can only afford to query a small number of unlabeled graphs and obtain their labels. The performance of the feature selection process depends strongly on the quality of the queried graphs in the active sample selection process. For example, in Figure 1, suppose we are given two labeled graphs (G_1 and G_2). Only a small number of the useful subgraph features (F_1 and F_2) appear in the labeled graphs. If we query the graph G_3 that is both representative and informative, we are more likely to find new features like F_3. The process of query selection can assist the process of feature selection in finding useful subgraph features. In other words, the better the query graph we select, the more effectively we can discover the useful subgraph features.

Thus, the active sample selection problem and the subgraph feature selection problem are correlated and should be considered simultaneously. The combined problem is referred to as *dual active feature and sample selection for graph classification*. This problem can be summarized as follows: in order to minimize the labeling cost in graph classification, we need to determine how one can actively select the most important graph to obtain the class label.

To the best of our knowledge, the dual active feature and sample selection for graph classification has not been studied in this context. A straightforward solution to this problem would be the two-stage active learning framework as shown in Figure 2. In this framework, the feature selection problem and the active sample selection problem are considered in two separate steps. In the first step, we select a set of subgraph features based upon the labeled graphs. In the second step, we estimate the importance of query graphs based upon the feature set selected in the first step. Obviously, only the subgraph features that appear in the label graphs can be found in the first step. The useful features that only appear in the unlabeled graphs can not be found. Thus, when we only use the features found in the first step, the estimation of the importance of query graphs will not be accurate.

In this paper we introduce a novel framework for the above problems by exploiting useful subgraph features and optimal query graphs simultaneously. Our framework is illustrated

Table 1: Important Notations.

Symbol	Definition
$\mathcal{D} = \{G_1, \cdots, G_n\}$	given graph dataset, G_i denotes the i-th graph in the dataset.
n_ℓ, n_a and n_u	number of labeled graphs, unlabeled graphs including and excluding the query graph in $\mathcal{D}$
$l = \{1, \cdots, n_\ell\}$	index set for labeled graphs in $\mathcal{D}$
s and u	index of selected graph and the index set of the other unlabeled candidate graphs in $\mathcal{D}$.
$a = \{n_\ell + 1, \cdots, n\}$	index set for all unlabeled graphs in the pool including the selected graph. $a = \{s\} \cup u$
$\mathbf{y} = [y_1, \cdots, y_n]^\top$	class label vector for graphs in $\mathcal{D}$, $y_i \in \{+1, -1, 0\}$
$\mathcal{S} = \{g_1, \cdots, g_m\}$	set of all subgraph patterns in the graph dataset $\mathcal{D}$.
$\mathbf{x}_i = [x_i^1, \cdots, x_i^m]^\top$	binary vector for G_i using subgraph features in $\mathcal{S}$, $x_i^k \in \{0, 1\}$ and $x_i^k = 1$ i ff$g_k \subseteq G_i$
$\mathbf{f}_i = [f_i^1, \cdots, f_i^n]^\top$	binary vector for subgraph pattern g_i in the $\mathcal{D}$
$X = [X_{ij}]_{(m \times n)}$	matrix of all binary feature vectors in the dataset, $X = [\mathbf{x}_1, \cdots, \mathbf{x}_n] = [\mathbf{f}_1, \cdots, \mathbf{f}_m]^\top$
$\mathcal{T}$	set of selected subgraph patterns, $\mathcal{T} \subset \mathcal{S}$
$\mathbf{K}(\mathcal{T}) = [K_{ij}]_{(n \times n)}$	kernel matrix of all graphs using the selected subgraph features $\mathcal{T}$
$\mathbf{L}(y_s, \mathbf{y}_\ell) = [L_{ij}]_{(n \times n)}$	label kernel matrix of all graphs based upon the class labels
$\mathbf{H} = [H_{ij}]_{(n \times n)}$	centering matrix, $H_{ij} = \delta_{ij} - n^{-1}$. ($\delta_{ij} = 1$ i ff$i = j$, otherwise 0)
$D_\mathcal{T}$	an $m \times m$ diagonal matrix indicating which features are selected from $\mathcal{S}$ into $\mathcal{T}$
Π_ℓ, Π_u andΠ_s	mapping matrices,$\Pi_\ell \in \{0,1\}^{(n_\ell \times n)}$, $\Pi_s \in \{0,1\}^{(1 \times n)}$, $\Pi_u \in \{0,1\}^{(n_u \times n)}$ and $[\Pi_\ell^\top, \Pi_s^\top, \Pi_u^\top] = \mathbf{I}_n$

in Figure 3. Unlike the two-stage active learning method, the proposed approach, called gActive, can estimate the usefulness of a query graph and effectiveness of subgraph features simultaneously. The gActive method maximizes the dependence between subgraph features and graph labels based upon an active learning framework. Furthermore, we propose a branch-and-bound algorithm to search for optimal features efficiently by pruning the subgraph search space. Empirical studies on real-world tasks demonstrate that the proposed method can obtain promising results using fewer labeled graphs than alternative approaches.

2. PROBLEM FORMULATION

Suppose we are given a graph dataset $\mathcal{D} = \{G_1, \cdots, G_n\}$ that consists of n graphs. $\mathbf{y} = [y_1, \cdots, y_n]^\top$ denotes the vector of labels, where $y_i \in \{+1, 0, -1\}$ is the label of G_i. $y_i = 0$ implies that G_i is unlabeled. Active learning in graph data is the task of selecting one graph G_s from the pool of unlabeled graphs to query for its label. For convenience, we partition the graph dataset into three parts: the labeled graphs $\mathcal{D}_\ell$, the query graph G_s, and the remaining unlabeled graphs D_u. $\mathcal{D}_a = \mathcal{D}_u \cup \{G_s\}$ denotes all unlabeled graphs. The vector $\mathbf{y}$ is partitioned as follows:

$$\mathbf{y} = \begin{bmatrix} \mathbf{y}_\ell \\ y_s \\ \mathbf{y}_u \end{bmatrix} = \begin{bmatrix} \mathbf{y}_\ell \\ \mathbf{y}_a \end{bmatrix} \quad \text{and} \quad \mathbf{y}_a = \begin{bmatrix} y_s \\ \mathbf{y}_u \end{bmatrix}$$

where $\mathbf{y}_\ell$, y_s and $\mathbf{y}_u$ represent the class labels assigned to the graphs in $\mathcal{D}_\ell$, $\{G_s\}$ and $\mathcal{D}_u$ respectively. We denote the number of labeled graphs by n_ℓ. n_u is the number of unlabeled graphs excluding the query graph, and n_a is the number of all unlabeled graphs. $n_a = n_u + 1$. We assume the first n_ℓ graphs in the dataset $\mathcal{D}$ are labeled.

Definition 1 (Graph). *A graph is represented as $G = (\mathcal{V}, E, \mathcal{L}, l)$. $\mathcal{V}$ is the set of vertices, and $\mathcal{V} = \{v_1, \cdots, v_{n_v}\}$. $E \subseteq \mathcal{V} \times \mathcal{V}$ is the set of edges. $\mathcal{L}$ is the set of labels for the vertices and edges. $l : \mathcal{V} \cup E \to \mathcal{L}$ is the function assigning labels to the vertices and edges.*

We focus on using subgraph patterns to define the feature space of graph classification. It is assumed that a graph object G_i is represented as a binary vector $\mathbf{x}_i = [x_i^1, \cdots, x_i^m]^\top$ associated with a set of subgraph patterns $\{g_1, \cdots, g_m\}$. Here, $x_i^k \in \{0, 1\}$ is the binary feature of G_i corresponding to the subgraph pattern g_k. $x_i^k = 1$ i ffg_k is a subgraph of G_i. Now suppose the full set of subgraph features in the graph dataset $\mathcal{D}$ is $\mathcal{S} = \{g_1, \cdots, g_m\}$, which we use to predict the class labels of the graph objects. The full feature set $\mathcal{S}$ is very large. Only a subset of the features ($\mathcal{T} \subseteq \mathcal{S}$) is relevant to the graph classification task. Let X denote the matrix consisting of the binary feature vectors based on $\mathcal{S}$ to represent the graph dataset $\mathcal{D}$. $X = [\mathbf{x}_1, \mathbf{x}_2, \cdots, \mathbf{x}_n] = [\mathbf{f}_1, \mathbf{f}_2, \cdots, \mathbf{f}_m]^\top \in \{0, 1\}^{m \times n}$, where $X = [X_{ij}]_{m \times n}$, $X_{ij} = 1$ iff $g_i \subseteq G_j$. We briefly summarize the notations used in this paper in Table 1.

Definition 2 (Subgraph). *Let $G' = (\mathcal{V}', E', \mathcal{L}', l')$ and $G = (\mathcal{V}, E, \mathcal{L}, l)$ be graphs. G' is a subgraph of G ($G' \subseteq G$) iff there exists an injective function $\psi : \mathcal{V}' \to \mathcal{V}$. $\forall v \in \mathcal{V}'$, $l'(v) = l(\psi(v))$. $\forall (u, v) \in E'$, $(\psi(u), \psi(v)) \in E$ and $l'(u, v) = l(\psi(u), \psi(v))$. If G' is a subgraph of G, then G is a supergraph of G'.*

The key issue of *dual active feature and sample selection* is to find the most important query graph and a set of optimal subgraph patterns simultaneously. The problems studied in this paper are as follows:
1) How can one estimate the importance of a query graph among unlabeled graphs?
2) How can one estimate the usefulness of a set of features for the graph classification task?
3) How can one determine the optimal subgraph features within a reasonable amount of time, and avoid the exhaustive enumeration of all features?

2.1 Optimization Framework

We propose an optimization framework to select the optimal query graph by maximizing the minimum score of an evaluation function.

$$G_s^* = \arg\max_{G_s \in \mathcal{D}_a} \min_{y_s \in \{\pm 1\}} \mathcal{E}(G_s, y_s, \mathcal{D}, \mathbf{y}_\ell) \tag{1}$$

where $\mathcal{D}_a$ denotes the pool of all unlabeled graphs. $\mathcal{E}$ denotes the evaluation function for querying a graph G_s in $\mathcal{D}_a$. Because the label of the selected graph G_s can be either 1 or -1, we need to consider both alternatives and select the worst case to maximize. In this max-min view of active learning, it guarantees that the selected graph G_s will lead to a large value for the function $\mathcal{E}(G_s, y_s, \mathcal{D}, \mathbf{y}_\ell)$.

Note that in graph data the useful features are not given. We need to make use of the label information to select a subset of optimal subgraph features. If we know the class label

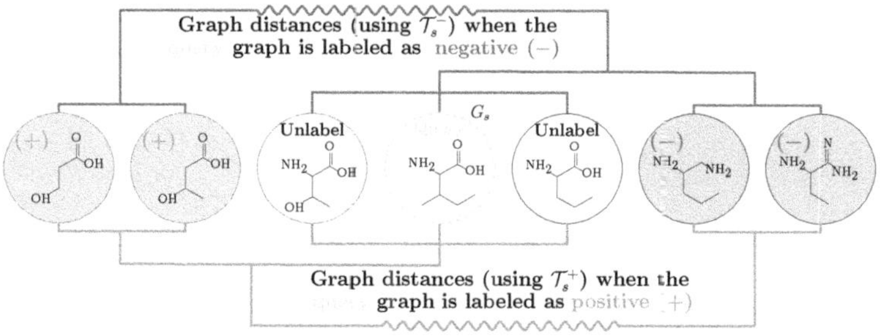

Figure 4: Graph distances using two optimal feature sets ($\mathcal{T}_s^+$ and $\mathcal{T}_s^-$) respectively depending on the label of the query graph.

of the selected query graph G_s, we can select the optimal feature set by maximizing the following function.

$$\mathcal{E}(G_s, y_s, \mathcal{D}, \mathbf{y}_\ell) = \max_{\mathcal{T}\subseteq\mathcal{S}, |\mathcal{T}|=t} J(G_s, y_s, \mathcal{D}, \mathbf{y}_\ell, \mathcal{T}) \quad (2)$$

We select a subset of subgraph features $\mathcal{T}$ from $\mathcal{S}$, such that the feature selection evaluation function $J(G_s, y_s, \mathcal{D}, \mathbf{y}_\ell, \mathcal{T})$ is maximized.

2.1.1 The Intuition

Now, we show the key ideas of this paper from the following views.

Query Selection View: from the active query selection view, we assume that the optimal query graph should satisfy the following properties:

(a) Dependence maximization: based upon a feature set $\mathcal{T}$, the query graph G_s should be able to maximize the dependence between features of graphs and labels in a max-min view as in Eq. 1.

(b) Informative and representative: the selected query graph should be both informative and representative among the pool of unlabeled graphs. The query graph G_s should be close to some of the unlabeled graphs in the dataset, such that G_s is likely to be representative of a group of unlabeled graphs instead of being an outlier. The query graph G_s should also be far from the labeled graphs in $\mathcal{D}_\ell$, such that the label of G_s is unlikely to be redundant.

Feature Selection View: from the subgraph feature selection view, the optimal feature set can be very different depending on which graph we query, and what class label we get from the domain expert. For example, in Figure 4, we have a graph dataset with seven graph objects. Suppose the selected query graph is G_s. We denote the optimal feature set as $\mathcal{T}_s^+$, when G_s is positive. $\mathcal{T}_s^-$ represents the optimal feature set, when G_s is negative. From the feature selection perspective, the optimal subgraph features should also satisfy the following properties:

(a) Dependence maximization: graphs with the same class labels should have similar subgraph features, and be close to each other; while graphs with different labels should have different features and be far away from each other.

(b) Informative and representative: the query graph G_s should be close to the other unlabeled graphs, and be far from the existing labeled graphs.

2.1.2 The Solution

Many criteria can be used to evaluate the dependence between subgraph features and graph labels. In this paper we adopt the Hilbert-Schmidt Independence Criterion (HSIC) [12] for subgraph evaluation. HSIC measures the dependence between two variables (X, Y) in the kernel space. We briefly review the definition of HSIC. Suppose we have two reproducing kernel Hilbert spaces (RKHS) of functions $\mathcal{G}$ and $\mathcal{F}$. Let a covariance operator be

$$C = \mathrm{E}\{[p(X) - \mathrm{E}(p(X))][q(Y) - \mathrm{E}(q(Y))]\}, \ \forall p \in \mathcal{G}, q \in \mathcal{F}$$

Then the HSIC is defined as the Hilbert-Schmidt norm of the operator C, *i.e.*, $\|C\|_{HS}^2$. Given a data sample, HSIC has an empirical estimator HSIC $= \mathrm{tr}(\mathbf{K}\ \mathbf{H}\ \mathbf{L}\ \mathbf{H})$. Here, $\mathrm{tr}(\cdot)$ is the trace of a matrix. $\mathbf{H} = [H_{ij}]_{n\times n}$, where $H_{ij} = \delta_{ij} - 1/n$. δ_{ij} is the indicator function. $\delta_{ij} = 1$ iff $i = j$, otherwise $\delta_{ij} = 0$. $\mathbf{K}$ and $\mathbf{L}$ are kernel matrices on the samples.

Based upon the HSIC measure, we propose the following evaluation function for active feature selection:

$$\begin{aligned} J(G_s, y_s, \mathcal{D}, \mathbf{y}_\ell, \mathcal{T}) =& \mathrm{tr}\left[\ \mathbf{K}(\mathcal{T})\ \mathbf{H}\ \mathbf{L}(y_s, \mathbf{y}_\ell)\ \mathbf{H}\ \right] \\ &+ \alpha\frac{\mathbf{1}^\top\mathbf{K}_{u,s}(\mathcal{T})}{n_u} - \beta\frac{\mathbf{1}^\top\mathbf{K}_{l,s}(\mathcal{T})}{n_\ell} \end{aligned} \quad (3)$$

where $\mathbf{K}(\mathcal{T}) = [K_{ij}]_{(n\times n)}$ denotes the kernel matrix of graphs based upon a subgraph feature $\mathcal{T}$. $K_{ij} = \langle D_\mathcal{T}\mathbf{x}_i, D_\mathcal{T}\mathbf{x}_j\rangle$. $D_\mathcal{T} = diag(\mathbf{d}_\mathcal{T})$ is a diagonal matrix, where $\mathbf{d}_\mathcal{T} = [d(\mathcal{T})_i]_{(m\times 1)}$ and $d(\mathcal{T})_i = I(g_i \in \mathcal{T}) \in \{0, 1\}$. $\mathbf{L}(y_s, \mathbf{y}_\ell) = [L_{ij}]_{(n\times n)} = \mathbf{y}\mathbf{y}^\top$ denotes the kernel matrix based upon the labels of the graphs, where $\mathbf{y} = [\ \mathbf{y}_\ell^\top, y_s, \mathbf{y}_u^\top\ ]^\top$. $L_{ij} = \langle y_i, y_j\rangle$ is used in our current implementation. Other kernels can also be directly used in this formulation. α and β are two parameters that control the weights of the three terms in the evaluation function. The first term denotes the dependence between the features and labels of the graphs. The second term represents the average similarity between the query graph and the unlabeled graphs. The third term represents the average similarity between the query graph and the labeled graphs.

The evaluation function in Eq. 3 can be simplified as follows:

$$\begin{aligned} \mathrm{tr}\left(\mathbf{K}(\mathcal{T})\mathbf{H}\mathbf{y}\mathbf{y}^\top\mathbf{H}\right) &= \mathrm{tr}\left(X^\top D_\mathcal{T} D_\mathcal{T} X\ \mathbf{H}\ \mathbf{y}\mathbf{y}^\top\ \mathbf{H}\right) \\ &= \mathrm{tr}\left(D_\mathcal{T} X\ \mathbf{H}\ \mathbf{y}\mathbf{y}^\top\ \mathbf{H}\ X^\top D_\mathcal{T}\right) \\ &= \sum_{g_i\in\mathcal{T}}\left(\mathbf{f}_i^\top\mathbf{H}\ \mathbf{y}\mathbf{y}^\top\ \mathbf{H}\ \mathbf{f}_i\right) \end{aligned}$$

Input:
$\mathcal{D}$: the graph dataset $\{G_1, \cdots, G_n\}$ t: the maximum number of features.
$\mathbf{y}_\ell$: the vector of class labels for labeled graphs, min_sup: the minimum frequency.
Initialize:
- Construct the feature evaluation functions $h(g, \mathbf{M})$ and initialize candidate feature lists:
1. Calculate $2 \times n_a$ matrices using Eq. 4 by considering each case for G_s and y_s as follows:
$\mathbf{M}_i^+ = \mathbf{H}\ \mathbf{L}(y_i = +1, \mathbf{y}_\ell)\ \mathbf{H}\ + \frac{\alpha}{n_u}\ \Pi_i \mathbf{1}^\top \Pi_u^\top - \frac{\beta}{n_\ell}\ \Pi_i \mathbf{1}^\top \Pi_\ell^\top$, $(\forall\ i,\ n_\ell < i \leq n)$
$\mathbf{M}_i^- = \mathbf{H}\ \mathbf{L}(y_i = -1, \mathbf{y}_\ell)\ \mathbf{H}\ + \frac{\alpha}{n_u}\ \Pi_i \mathbf{1}^\top \Pi_u^\top - \frac{\beta}{n_\ell}\ \Pi_i \mathbf{1}^\top \Pi_\ell^\top$, $(\forall\ i,\ n_\ell < i \leq n)$
2. Initialize $2 \times n_a$ empty lists for candidate subgraph features as follows:
$\forall\ i\ (n_\ell < i \leq n)$, let $\mathcal{T}_i^+ = \mathcal{T}_i^- = \emptyset$ with maximum size t, and pruning thresholds $\theta_i^+ = \theta_i^- = -\infty$

Recursive Feature Mining:
- Depth-first search the gSpan's code tree and update the feature lists as follows:
1. Update each of the candidate feature lists using the current subgraph feature g_c:
$\forall\ i$, if $h(g_c, \mathbf{M}_i^+)$ is larger than the worst feature in $\mathcal{T}_i^+$, replace it and update $\theta_i^+ = \min_{g \in \mathcal{T}_i^+} h(g, \mathbf{M}_i^+)$
$\forall\ i$, if $h(g_c, \mathbf{M}_i^-)$ is larger than the worst feature in $\mathcal{T}_i^-$, replace it and update $\theta_i^- = \min_{g \in \mathcal{T}_i^-} h(g, \mathbf{M}_i^-)$
2. Test pruning criteria for the sub-tree rooted from node g as follows:
if $freq(g_c) < min\_sup$, prune the sub-tree of g_c
if $\forall\ i\ (n_\ell < i \leq n)$, $\widetilde{h}(g_c, \mathbf{M}_i^+) \leq \theta_i^+$ and $\widetilde{h}(g_c, \mathbf{M}_i^-) \leq \theta_i^-$, prune the sub-tree of g_c
3. Recursion: Depth-first search the sub-tree rooted from node g_c

Active Query Selection:
- Select the query graph using Eq. 5

Output:
G_s: The selected query graph.
$\mathcal{T}_s^+$: the optimal subgraph features if G_s is labeled as a positive graph.
$\mathcal{T}_s^-$: the optimal subgraph features if G_s is labeled as a negative graph.

Figure 5: The gActive algorithm

We can rewrite $J(G_s, y_s, \mathcal{D}, \mathbf{y}_\ell, \mathcal{T})$ in Eq. 2 as

$$\begin{aligned} & J(G_s, y_s, \mathcal{D}, \mathbf{y}_\ell, \mathcal{T}) \\ &= \sum_{g_i \in \mathcal{T}} \mathbf{f}_i^\top \left(\mathbf{H}\ \mathbf{y}\mathbf{y}^\top\ \mathbf{H}\ + \frac{\alpha}{n_u}\ \Pi_s \mathbf{1}^\top \Pi_u^\top - \frac{\beta}{n_\ell}\ \Pi_s \mathbf{1}^\top \Pi_\ell^\top \right) \mathbf{f}_i \\ &= \sum_{g_i \in \mathcal{T}} \mathbf{f}_i^\top\ \mathbf{M}\ \mathbf{f}_i \end{aligned}$$

whereΠ_ℓ andΠ_u are projection matrices. $X_\ell = X\Pi_\ell$, $X_u = X\Pi_u$ and $\mathbf{x}_s = X\Pi_s$.

$$\mathbf{M} = \mathbf{H}\ \mathbf{y}\mathbf{y}^\top\ \mathbf{H}\ + \frac{\alpha}{n_u}\ \Pi_s \mathbf{1}^\top \Pi_u^\top - \frac{\beta}{n_\ell}\ \Pi_s \mathbf{1}^\top \Pi_\ell^\top \quad (4)$$

Given the evaluation function $h(g_i, G_s, y_s, \mathcal{D}, \mathbf{y}_\ell) = \mathbf{f}_i^\top\ \mathbf{M}\ \mathbf{f}_i$, we can define the optimization problem of dual active feature and sample selection as follows:

$$G_s^* = \arg\max_{G_s \in \mathcal{D}_a}\ \min_{y_s \in \{\pm 1\}}\ \max_{\mathcal{T} \subseteq \mathcal{S}, |\mathcal{T}| = t} \sum_{g_i \in \mathcal{T}} h(g_i, G_s, y_s, \mathcal{D}, \mathbf{y}_\ell) \quad (5)$$

DEFINITION 3 (gFScore). *Let $\mathcal{D} = \{G_1, \cdots, G_n\}$ denote a graph dataset, with first n_ℓ graphs labeled as $y_1, \cdots, y_{n_\ell}$. Suppose we have a query graph G_s with its potential label y_s. We define a quality criterion $h(g_i, G_s, y_s, \mathcal{D}, \mathbf{y}_\ell) = h(g_i, \mathbf{M}) = \mathbf{f}_i^\top\ \mathbf{M}\ \mathbf{f}_i$, called gFScore, for a subgraph feature g_i. $\mathbf{M}$ is a matrix defined in Eq. 4.*

The optimal solution to Eq. 5 can be found by the following method: we go through each unlabeled graph one by one. Suppose G_s is the currently selected graph. We need to go through a positive case ($y_s = 1$) and a negative case ($y_s = -1$). In each case, we mine the top-t best subgraph features according to the gFScore. As shown in Figure 6, we need to mine $2 \times n_a$ optimal feature sets from the graph dataset. $\mathcal{T}_i^+$ denotes the optimal feature set, when the i-th graph is queried and labeled as a positive graph. $\mathcal{T}_i^-$ denotes the optimal feature set, when G_i is queried and labeled as negative. Then, we can directly use Eq. 5 to find the optimal query graph.

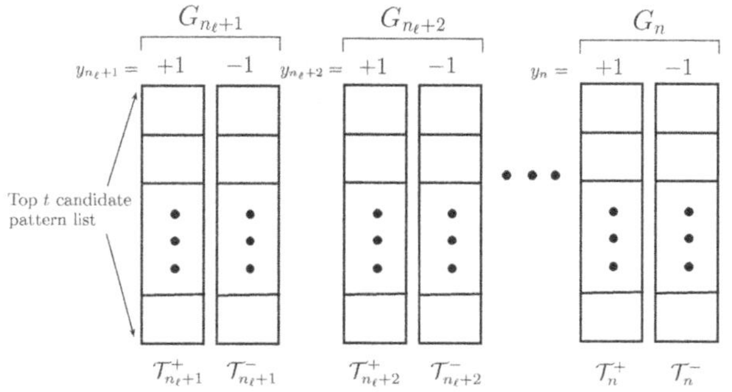

Figure 6: Candidate subgraph pattern lists

2.1.3 *Upper Bound of gFScore*

Now we address the problem on how to mine the optimal feature sets without exhaustive enumeration of all subgraphs. Note that the number of subgraphs in a graph dataset can be extremely large. It grows at an exponential rate as the size of the graphs increases. Thus, it is computationally intractable to enumerate all subgraphs in the graph dataset.

Some recent graph classification approaches [26, 24, 18] incorporate constraints to prune the search space of gSpan [27]. In this paper we derive a new constraint to prune the search space in the DFS-code tree. A straightforward upper-bound of gFScore is defined as follows:

THEOREM 1 (UPPER BOUND OF GFSCORE). *Suppose we have two subgraph patterns $g_i, g_j \in \mathcal{S}$, and g_j is a supergraph of g_i*

$(g_j \supseteq g_i)$. *The gFScore value of* g_j *is bounded by* $\widetilde{h}(g_i, \mathbf{M})$, *i.e.*, $h(g_j, \mathbf{M}) \leq \widetilde{h}(g_i, \mathbf{M})$. $\widetilde{h}(g_i, \mathbf{M})$ *is defined as follows:*

$$\widetilde{h}(g_i, \mathbf{M}) \triangleq \mathbf{f}_i{}^\top \widetilde{\mathbf{M}} \mathbf{f}_i \tag{6}$$

where the matrix $\widetilde{\mathbf{M}}$ *is defined as* $\widetilde{M}_{pq} \triangleq \max(0, M_{pq})$.

PROOF.

$$h(g_j, \mathbf{M}) = \mathbf{f}_j{}^\top \mathbf{M} \mathbf{f}_j = \sum_{p,q:G_p,G_q \in \mathcal{D}(g_j)} M_{pq} \tag{7}$$

where $\mathcal{D}(g_j) \triangleq \{G_k | g_j \subseteq G_k, 1 \leq k \leq n\}$. Since g_j is a supergraph of g_i $(g_j \supseteq g_i)$, we have $\mathcal{D}(g_j) \subseteq \mathcal{D}(g_i)$ according to the anti-monotonic property. $\widetilde{M}_{pq} \triangleq \max(0, M_{pq})$. We have $\widetilde{M}_{pq} \geq M_{pq}$ and $\widetilde{M}_{pq} \geq 0$. Thus,

$$\begin{aligned} h(g_j, \mathbf{M}) &= \sum_{p,q:G_p,G_q \in \mathcal{D}(g_j)} M_{pq} \leq \sum_{p,q:G_p,G_q \in \mathcal{D}(g_j)} \widetilde{M}_{pq} \\ &\leq \sum_{p,q:G_p,G_q \in \mathcal{D}(g_i)} \widetilde{M}_{pq} = \widetilde{h}(g_i, \mathbf{M}) \end{aligned} \tag{8}$$

For any $g_j \supseteq g_i$, $h(g_j, \mathbf{M}) \leq \widetilde{h}(g_i, \mathbf{M})$. □

We now utilize the upper bound to prune the DFS-code tree in gSpan by the branch-and-bound pruning. The top-t best features are maintained in $2 \times n_a$ candidate lists. Figure 6 shows an example of the candidate lists. During the course of the subgraph pattern mining, we calculate the upper-bound of each subgraph pattern in the search tree. If a subgraph pattern node with its children nodes cannot update any of the candidate feature lists, we can prune the subtree of gSpan rooted from this node. It is guaranteed by the upper-bound that we will not miss any better features for any of the candidate feature lists. Thus, the subgraph feature mining process can be speeded up without loss of performance. The algorithm of gActive is summarized in Figure 5.

3. EXPERIMENTS

Data Collection: in order to evaluate the performance of the proposed approach for graph classification, we tested our algorithm on nine real-world datasets as summarized in Table 2.

1) *Anti-cancer activity prediction (NCI)*: the first eight benchmark datasets are collected from the *PubChem* website[1]. The datasets contain records of anticancer activities for more than 20,000 chemical compounds against eight types of cancer. Each chemical compound is represented as a graph. We collected eight graph data sets with *active* and *inactive* labels from the *PubChem* website. The original datasets are unbalanced, where the percentage of positive compounds is around 5%. We randomly sampled 500 inactive compounds and 500 active compounds from each dataset for performance evaluation.

2) *AIDS anti-virus prediction (HIV)*: the last benchmark dataset is collected from the AIDS anti-viral screening program[2]. The dataset consists of screening records of more than 7700 chemical compounds. Each compound is described by its activity against HIV, which is one of the following categories: confirmed active (CA), confirmed moderately active (CM) and confirmed inactive (CI). We treat CA+CM as the *positive* label, and CI as the *negative* label. This is the same setting used in [9]. The original data set is unbalanced, where the percentage of positive compounds is around 3%. We randomly sampled 266 inactive compounds and used the original 266 active compounds for performance evaluation.

[1]http://pubchem.ncbi.nlm.nih.gov

[2]http://dtp.nci.nih.gov/

Table 2: Summary of experimental datasets. "# Pos" denotes the number of active graphs in the dataset.

Dataset	# Pos	# Graph	Details
NCI1	2040	40526	Lung Cancer
NCI33	1636	40209	Melanoma
NCI41	1561	27585	Prostate Cancer
NCI47	2011	40447	Central Nerve System
NCI81	1396	40700	Colon Cancer
NCI83	2276	27992	Breast Cancer
NCI123	3112	40152	Leukemia
NCI145	1940	40164	Renal Cancer
AIDS	266	7781	HIV Anti-virus

Comparative Methods: in order to demonstrate the effectiveness of the proposed approach, we compare our method against four baseline methods. These baseline methods include both supervised and unsupervised feature selection approaches combined with active sample selection approaches. The compared methods are summarized as follows:

- *Dual Active Feature and Sample Selection (gActive)*: the proposed method in this paper. The default parameter setting for the gActive method is $\alpha = \beta = 10^{-3}$.
- *Supervised Feature Selection + Random Sampling (IG + Random)*: we compare with a supervised feature selection method combined with random sampling. A set of frequent subgraphs within the graph dataset is first mined. Then a supervised feature selection method based upon Information Gain (IG) is used to select a subset of discriminative features from the frequent subgraphs. We randomly select query graphs from the pool. Note that discriminative features are recomputed after each iteration of feature and graph selection.
- *Supervised Feature Selection + Margin (IG + Margin)*: we compare with a two-stage active learning approach. A supervised feature selection method is combined with a margin-based active learning method. In this approach, a set of frequent subgraphs within the graph dataset are first mined. Then we iteratively use information gain to select a subset of discriminative features from the frequent subgraphs. We use a margin-based active learning approach [25] to select informative graphs to query for labels.
- *Unsupervised Feature Selection + Random Sampling (Top-k + Random)*: we compare with an unsupervised feature selection method combined with random sampling. In this approach, we use the top-k frequent subgraph features in the pool dataset. Then we randomly select query graphs from the pool.
- *Unsupervised Feature Selection + Margin (Top-k + Margin)*: we compare with an unsupervised feature selection method combined with a margin-based active

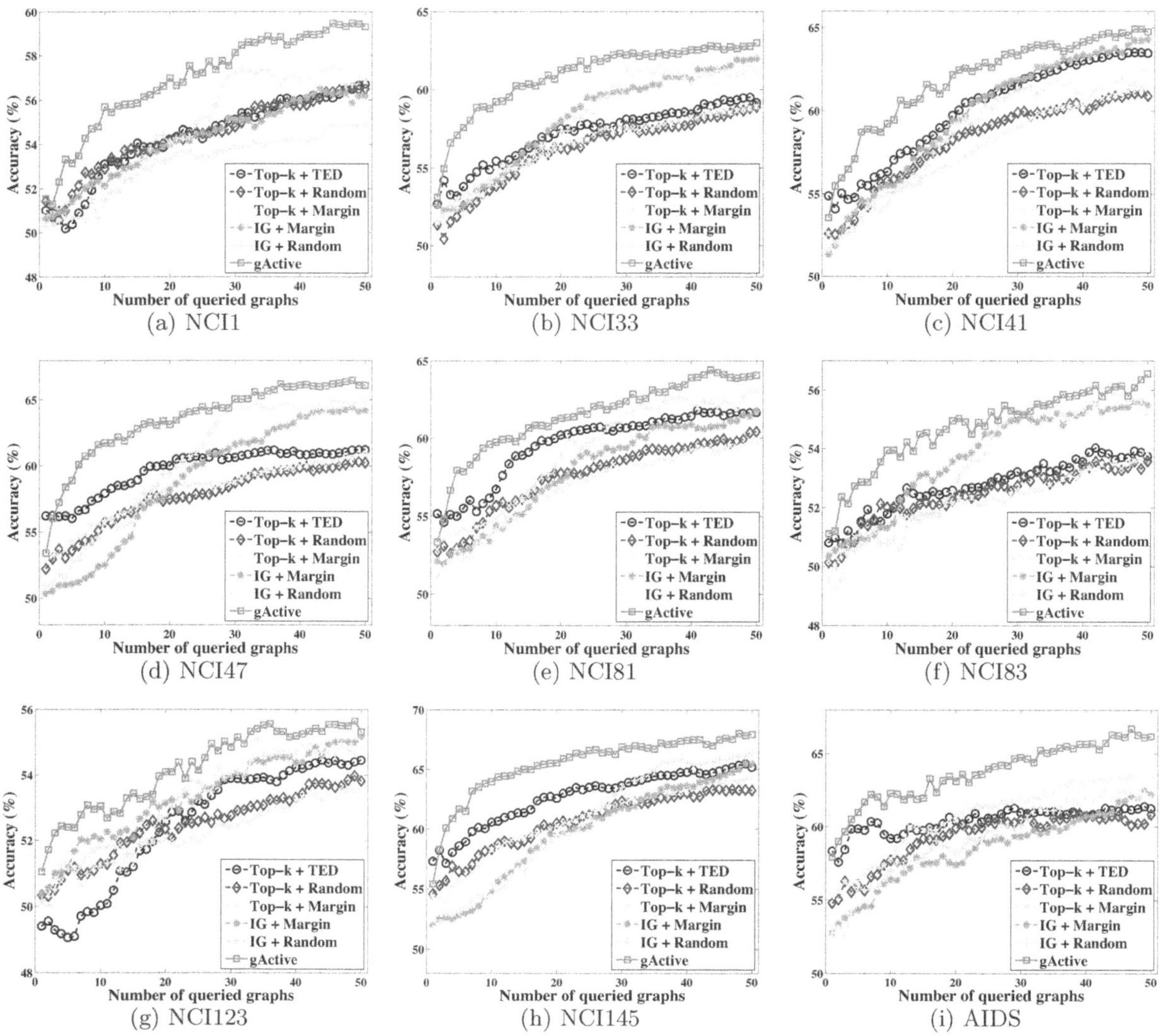

(a) NCI1 (b) NCI33 (c) NCI41 (d) NCI47 (e) NCI81 (f) NCI83 (g) NCI123 (h) NCI145 (i) AIDS

Figure 7: Graph classification accuracy after different number of graphs being queried.

learning method. In this approach, we use the top-k most frequent subgraphs in the pool dataset. Then margin-based active learning is used to select informative graphs to query.

- *Unsupervised Feature Selection + Sequential TED (Top-k + TED)*: we compare with an unsupervised feature selection method combined with experimental designs. In this approach, we use the top-k most frequent subgraphs in the pool dataset. Then the sequential transductive experimental design [30] is used to select representative graphs from the pool dataset.

All experiments are conducted on machines with Intel Xeon^{TM} Quad-Core CPUs of 2.27 GHz and 24 GB RAM. LibSVM [4] with the linear kernel is used as the base classifier for all compared methods. min_sup =10% in the gSpan. The default number of selected features in all compared methods is set as 500.

3.1 Performance on Graph Classification

In our experiments, we first randomly sample two labeled graphs, *i.e.*, one positive and one negative graph. They are used as the initial training set. Then we partition the remaining graphs into two groups with equal size: one group is used as the pool dataset; the other group is used as the testing dataset for performance evaluation. In each iteration, the active learner selects one unlabeled graph in the pool dataset and queries the label. Then, the queried graph is put into the training set, and the base classifier is trained to classify the testing graphs. We report the average results of 50 runs on randomly sampled graph datasets.

The results of all compared methods are summarized in Figure 7. We run each of the methods for 50 iterations and compare the learning curves. In all datasets, the proposed dual active feature and sample selection algorithm (gActive) consistently outperforms other baseline methods. Note that in the NCI33 and NCI145 datasets, all the baselines with margin-based active learning (IG + Margin and Top-k + Margin) are unable to achieve better performance than randomized baselines (IG + Random and Top-k + Random). However, our method can achieve substantially better performance than other baselines. This result supports the intuition of this paper: the feature selection problem and the active query selection problem are correlated, and should be considered simultaneously. Moreover, we notice that in the NCI41 dataset, all the baselines using margin-based active learning can improve the performance over randomized baselines. In this dataset, the improvements by the proposed gActive method can be even more significant.

3.2 Parameter Settings

In the proposed model, different weights can be assigned to the three terms in Equation 3. If we use different settings for the two parameters, α and β, we can perform the dual active feature and sample selection with different weights for the three constraints: *dependence maximization*, *representativeness* and *informativeness*. To be precise, α represents how much we weight the *representativeness*, and β denotes how much we weight the *informativeness*. The larger the value of α is, the closer the query graph is with other unlabeled graphs. The larger the value of β is, the further away the query graph is from the other labeled graphs. We test α and β with values among $\{100, 10, 1, 0.1, 0.01, 0.001, 0\}$ separately. The average results for our model in the first 50 iterations are reported. As shown in Figure 8, the performance of our model using α and β with similar values is often better than other settings. In these real-world graph classification tasks, the constraints for *informativeness* and *representativeness* are equally important for our active feature and sample selection problem.

In Figure 8(a), we find that the best parameter setting for NCI47 dataset is $\alpha = 0.001$, $\beta = 0.001$, and the accuracy is 63.5%. This setting is the same as our default parameter setting. The best parameter setting for NCI145 dataset is $\alpha = 0$, $\beta = 0.001$, and the resulting accuracy is 65.5%. Under our default setting, the accuracy is 65.4%. We find that the performance of our gActive model with the default setting is satisfactory. If we try to optimize the selection of α and β values, the accuracy improvement over other baselines will be even larger.

We also compare gActive models with and without pruning in the subgraph search space as summarized in Figure 9. The average CPU time with different *min_sup* during the first iteration is reported. gActive can improve the efficiencies by pruning the subgraph search space.

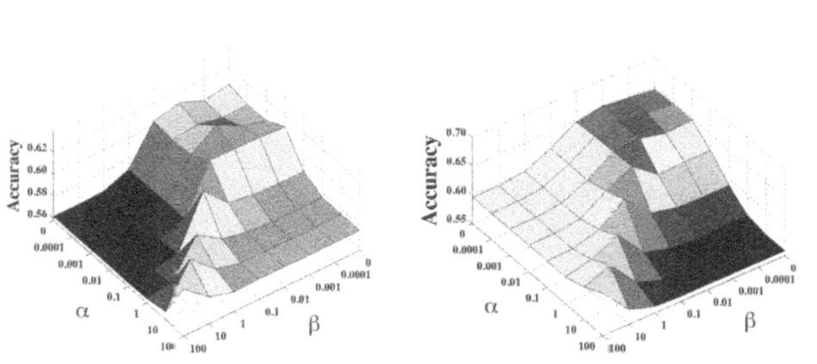

(a) NCI47 (b) NCI145

Figure 8: gActive accuracies with different α and β.

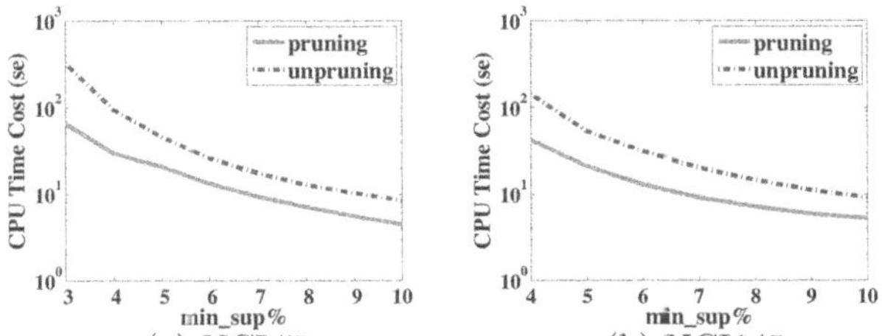

(a) NCI47 (b) NCI145

Figure 9: CPU time with/without pruning.

4. RELATED WORK

In this section, we discuss some related work. Active learning aims at reducing the labeling cost by querying the most informative example. Many methods have been proposed based upon different active learning settings. Please see [23] for a detailed survey. Conventional active learning approaches focus on data in vector space. One approach is to query the most informative instance. The active learners select the uncertain instances based upon a single classifier [25, 1] or a committee of classifiers [6, 10, 22]. The problems with this approach are that it can be sensitive to outliers or noise, and can not exploit the structures of unlabeled data. The alternative approach is to query the most representative instance. The active learners exploit the structure of unlabeled data using clustering methods [20, 7] or optimal experimental design approaches [30]. The major problems are that this approach is unsupervised and can not use the labeled data. Some work has also been done to combine informativeness and representativeness measures to find the optimal query examples [8, 15].

Mining subgraph features from graph data has also been studied in recent years [19]. The aim of these approaches is to extract useful subgraph features from a set of graphs by adopting some filtering criteria. Depending on if the label information is considered in the feature mining process, the existing methods can roughly be classified into two types: unsupervised and supervised. In the unsupervised setting, the frequency of each subgraph is used as the criterion for feature selection. To discover frequent subgraphs, Yan and Han developed a depth-first search algorithm, gSpan [27], which builds a lexicographic order among graphs, and maps each graph to a unique minimum DFS code as its canonical label. The gSpan algorithm adopts a depth-first search in the DFS code tree to mine frequent subgraphs efficiently. There are also many other frequent subgraph feature mining approaches that have been developed recently, *e.g.*, AGM [16], FSG [19], MoFa [2], FFSM [14], and Gaston [21]. Supervised subgraph feature mining approaches have also been proposed in the literature, such as LEAP [26], CORK [24] and MbT [9], where the focus is on discovering discriminative features for graph classifications. In addition, gSSC [18] addresses the problem of feature selection for graph classification under semi-supervised settings. Some other graph classification approaches based upon graph kernels have also been proposed [11, 13].

5. CONCLUSIONS

In this paper we studied the dual active feature and sample selection problem for graph classification. The objective was to minimize the labeling efforts in graph classification. We demonstrated how to find a useful query graph and a set of optimal features simultaneously. We proposed to maximize the dependence between subgraph features and labels based upon an active learning framework. Our approach can find the most representative and informative graph and an optimal feature set. Then a branch-and-bound algorithm was proposed to prune the subgraph search space efficiently.

6. ACKNOWLEDGEMENTS

The work is supported in part by NSF through grants IIS-0905215, DBI-0960443, OISE-0968341 and OIA-0963278.

7. REFERENCES

[1] M. F. Balcan, A. Z. Broder, and T. Zhang. Margin based active learning. In *COLT*, pages 35–50, 2007.

[2] C. Borgelt and M. Berthold. Mining molecular fragments: Finding relevant substructures of molecules. In *ICDM*, pages 211–218, 2002.

[3] K. M. Borgwardt. *Graph Kernels*. PhD thesis, Ludwig-Maximilians-University Munich, 2007.

[4] C.-C. Chang and C.-J. Lin. *LIBSVM: a library for support vector machines*, 2001. Software available at `http://www.csie.ntu.edu.tw/~cjlin/libsvm`.

[5] H. Cheng, D. Lo, Y. Zhou, X. Wang, and X. Yan. Identifying bug signatures using discrimative graph mining. In *ISSTA*, pages 141–152, 2009.

[6] I. Dagan and S. P. Engenlson. Committee-based sampling for training probabilistic classifiers. In *ICML*, pages 150–157, 1995.

[7] S. Dasgupta and D. Hsu. Hierarchical sampling for active learning. In *ICML*, pages 208–215, 2008.

[8] P. Donmez, J. G. Carbonell, and P. N. Bennett. Dual strategy active learning. In *ECML*, pages 116–127, 2007.

[9] W. Fan, K. Zhang, H. Cheng, J. Gao, X. Yan, J. Han, P. S. Yu, and O. Verscheure. Direct mining of discriminative and essential frequent patterns via model-based search tree. In *KDD*, pages 230–238, 2008.

[10] Y. Freund, E. S. H. S. Seung, and N. Tishby. Selective sampling using the query by committee algorithm. *Machine Learning*, 28(2-3):133–168, 1997.

[11] T. Gärtner, P. A. Flach, and S. Wrobel. On graph kernels: Hardness results and efficient alternatives. In *COLT/Kernel*, 2003.

[12] A. Gretton, O. Bousquet, A. Smola, and B. Schölkopf. Measuring statistical dependence with Hilbert-Schmidt norms. In *ALT*, pages 63–77, Singapore, 2005.

[13] T. Horvath, T. Gärtner, and S. Wrobel. Cyclic pattern kernels for predictive graph mining. In *KDD*, 2004.

[14] J. Huan, W. Wang, and J. Prins. Efficient mining of frequent subgraph in the presence of isomorphism. In *ICDM*, pages 549–552, 2003.

[15] S.-J. Huang, R. Jin, and Z.-H. Zhou. Active learning by querying informative and representative examples. In *NIPS*. 2011.

[16] A. Inokuchi, T. Washio, and H. Motoda. An apriori-based algorithm for mining frequent substructures from graph data. In *PKDD*, pages 13–23, 2000.

[17] N. Jin, C. Young, and W. Wang. GAIA: graph classification using evolutionary computation. In *SIGMOD*, pages 879–890, 2010.

[18] X. Kong and P. S. Yu. Semi-supervised feature selection for graph classification. In *KDD*, pages 793–802, 2010.

[19] M. Kuramochi and G. Karypis. Frequent subgraph discovery. In *ICDM*, pages 313–320, 2001.

[20] H. T. Nguyen and A. W. M. . Smeulders. Active learning using pre-cluster. In *ICML*, pages 623–630, 2004.

[21] S. Nijssen and J. Kok. A quickstart in frequent structure mining can make a difference. In *KDD*, pages 647–652, 2004.

[22] M. Opper, H. S. Seung, and H. Sompolinsky. Query by committee. In *COLT*, pages 287–294, 1992.

[23] B. Settles. Active learning literature survey. Computer Sciences Technical Report 1648, University of Wisconsin–Madison, 2009.

[24] M. Thoma, H. Cheng, A. Gretton, J. Han, H. Kriegel, A. Smola, L. Song, P. Yu, X. Yan, and K. Borgwardt. Near-optimal supervised feature selection among frequent subgraphs. In *SDM*, pages 1075–1086, 2009.

[25] S. Tong and D. Koller. Support vector machine active learning with applications to text classification. In *ICML*, pages 999–1006, 2000.

[26] X. Yan, H. Cheng, J. Han, and P. Yu. Mining significant graph patterns by leap search. In *SIGMOD*, pages 433–444, 2008.

[27] X. Yan and J. Han. gSpan: Graph-based substructure pattern mining. In *ICDM*, pages 721–724, 2002.

[28] X. Yan, P. S. Yu, and J. Han. Graph indexing based on discriminative frequent struture analysis. *ACM Transactions on Database Systems*, 30(4):960–993, 2005.

[29] B. Yang, J. Sun, T. Wang, and Z. Chen. Effective multi-label active learning for text classification. In *KDD*, pages 917–926, 2009.

[30] K. Yu, J. Bi, and V. Tresp. Active learning via transductive experimental design. In *ICML*, pages 1081–1088, 2006.

It's Who You Know: Graph Mining Using Recursive Structural Features

Keith Henderson
Lawrence Livermore Lab
keith@llnl.gov

Brian Gallagher
Lawrence Livermore Lab
bgallagher@llnl.gov

Lei Li & Leman Akoglu
Carnegie Mellon University
{leili,lakoglu}@cs.cmu.edu

Tina Eliassi-Rad
Rutgers University
eliassi@cs.rutgers.edu

Hanghang Tong
IBM Watson
htong@us.ibm.com

Christos Faloutsos
Carnegie Mellon University
christos@cs.cmu.edu

ABSTRACT

Given a graph, how can we extract good features for the nodes? For example, given two large graphs from the same domain, how can we use information in one to do classification in the other (i.e., perform across-network classification or transfer learning on graphs)? Also, if one of the graphs is anonymized, how can we use information in one to de-anonymize the other? The key step in all such graph mining tasks is to find effective node features. We propose ReFeX (Recursive Feature eXtraction), a novel algorithm, that recursively combines local (node-based) features with neighborhood (egonet-based) features; and outputs regional features – capturing "behavioral" information. We demonstrate how these powerful regional features can be used in within-network and across-network classification and de-anonymization tasks – without relying on homophily, or the availability of class labels. The contributions of our work are as follows: (a) ReFeX is scalable and (b) it is effective, capturing regional ("behavioral") information in large graphs. We report experiments on real graphs from various domains with over 1M edges, where ReFeX outperforms its competitors on typical graph mining tasks like network classification and de-anonymization.

Categories and Subject Descriptors

H.2.8 [**Database Applications**]: Data mining; E.1 [**Data Structures**]: Graphs and networks

General Terms

Algorithms, Design, Performance, Experimentation.

Keywords

Graph mining, feature extraction, network classification, identity resolution

1. INTRODUCTION

Extracting effective features for nodes of a given graph is a key step for many data mining tasks, such as outlier detection (i.e., nodes with strange feature combinations), or mining across different graphs from the same domain. For example, given IP communication graphs from different days or different enterprise networks, can we train a classifier on one day (say Monday) and use the same classifier to accurately predict traffic on another day (say Thursday) without any labels on the latter graph? Here, the key step is to extract effective and transferrable features from each node that would best capture node characteristics, so that we can distinguish and classify the nodes (or edges). Another example is the following: given an anonymized social network (say Twitter's who-follows-whom graph) and a non-anonymized communication graph (say Twitter's who-mentions-whom graph), can we find node features that will help de-anonymize (or re-identify) the people in the social network?

Here, we propose a novel solution, *ReFeX* (Recursive Feature eXtraction) to these graph mining tasks. *ReFeX* recursively combines local (node-based) features, with neighborhood (egonet-based) features, and outputs regional features that capture "behavioral" information. These regional features represent the *kind* of nodes to which a given node is connected (e.g., connected to rich people), as opposed to the *identity* of those nodes (e.g., connected to Bill Gates) – i.e., it is who you know at the type-level that matters in mining across different graphs. In empirical studies, we demonstrate how these powerful regional features can be used in within- and across-network classification and de-anonymization tasks – without relying on homophily, or the availability of class labels.

Thus, the problem is defined as follows. Given a graph G, compute a node-feature matrix F with the following properties:

- *Structural*: The construction of F should not require additional attribute information on nodes or links.
- *Effective*: Good node-features should (1) help us predict node attributes, when such attributes are available (as in the case of IP traffic that we discuss next), and (2) be transferable across graphs (e.g., when the graph changes over time).

The ideal features should help with data mining tasks. Typical tasks include node classification (after we are given some labels), de-anonymization of the nodes of a graph, and transfer learning.

Figure 1 gives a quick overview of (a) the intuition behind *ReFeX* and (b) a preview of its classification accuracy. In (a), we show egonets of nodes from different days in an IP network, where node size and edge size are proportional to the traffic. The main point is that the characteristics of the neighbors are valuable and help us characterize the center node (manually labeled as 'web', 'dns-server' and 'p2p', respectively for each column). Figure 1(b) shows the classification accuracy of *ReFeX* (in blue bars) vs competitors - higher is better; *ReFeX* wins consistently.

KDD'11, August 21–24, 2011, San Diego, California, USA.
Copyright 2011 ACM 978-1-4503-0813-7/11/08 ...$10.00.

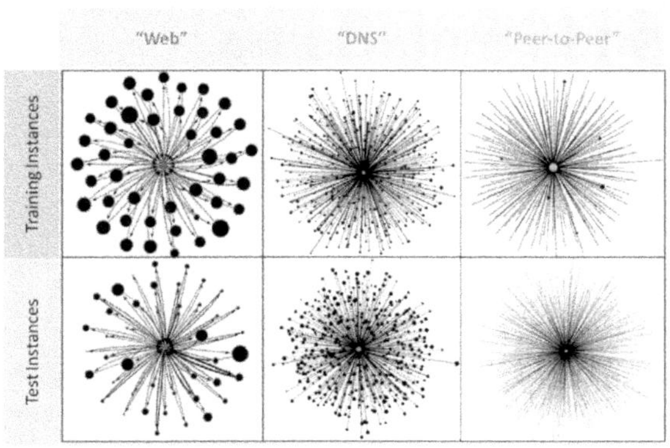

(a) Intuition (neighbors matter)

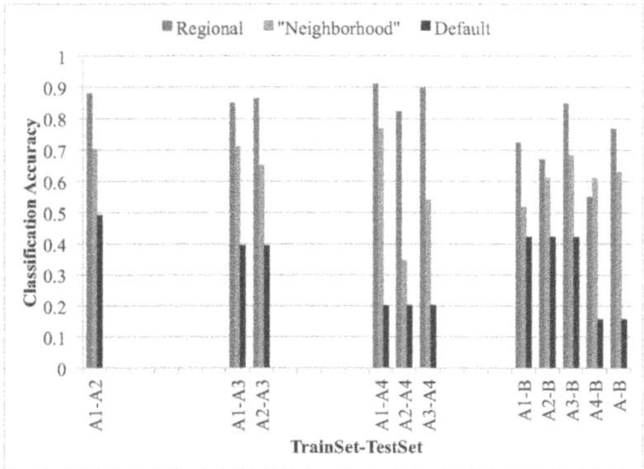

(b) Performance preview (blue bars: highest - win)

Figure 1: (a) Intuition behind *ReFeX*: Six IP hosts from different days of an enterprise network trace and (manually) labeled by their primary traffic type. Node and edge size indicate communication volume relative to the central node in each frame. Regional structure, i.e. the *types* of neighbors that a given host connects to, are vital. (b) classification accuracy of *ReFeX* with respect to transfer learning, in blue bars (higher is better) - see Figure (4) for more details.

The contributions of our work are as follows:

- *Novel Design*: We propose *ReFeX*, a scalable algorithm that computes regional features capturing "behavioral" information on large graphs.
- *Effectiveness*: *ReFeX*'s regional features perform well for several graph mining tasks, like transfer learning (across-network classification) and node de-anonymization on large graphs.

The rest of the paper is organized as follows: the proposed strategies are presented in Section 2; the experiments are presented in Sections 3 and 4. In Section 5, we review the related work; and we conclude the paper in Section 6.

2. PROPOSED ALGORITHM

Our algorithm *ReFeX* aggregates existing feature values of a node and uses them to generate new *recursive* features. The initial set of features used to seed the recursive feature generation can be structural information from the network or attributes from an external source. Here, we focus on tasks where only structural information is available. We separate structural attributes into three types: *local*, *egonet*, and *recursive* features. Local and egonet features together are called *neighborhood* features, and all three together are called *regional* features.

2.1 Neighborhood Features

The base features that seed the recursive *ReFeX* process are *local* and *egonet* features. These can be computed quickly for a given node. We call the set of local and egonet features together *neighborhood* features.

Local features are all essentially measures of the node degree. If the graph is directed, they include in- and out-degree as well as total degree. For weighted graphs, they contain weighted versions of each local feature.

Egonet features are computed for each node based on the node's ego network (a.k.a. egonet). The egonet includes the node, its neighbors, and any edges in the induced subgraph on these nodes. Egonet features include the number of within-egonet edges, as well as the number of edges entering and leaving the egonet. Strictly speaking, the latter are not in the egonet but they can be counted without looking at non-egonet nodes. As with local features, we compute directed and/or weighted versions of these features if the edges are directed and/or weighted.

2.2 Recursive Features

We broadly define a recursive feature as any aggregate computed over a feature value among a node's neighbors.

2.2.1 Generating Recursive Features

Currently *ReFeX* collects two types of recursive features: means and sums.[1] As a typical example, one recursive feature is defined as the mean value of the feature *unweighted degree* among all neighbors of a node. The features that can be aggregated are not restricted to neighborbood features, or even to structural features. The aggregates can be computed over any real-valued feature (including other recursive features). We compute the means and sums of all feature values. Moreover, when applicable, we compute these for incoming and outgoing edges separately.

2.2.2 Pruning Recursive Features

Clearly, the number of possible recursive features is infinite and grows exponentially with each recursive iteration. To reduce the number of generated features, a variety of pruning techniques can be employed. A simple example is to look for pairs of features that are highly correlated. In this example case, the pruning strategy is to eliminate one of the features whenever two features are correlated above a user-defined threshold.

For computational reasons, *ReFeX* uses a simplified version of this approach. Specifically, feature values are mapped to small integers via *vertical logarithmic binning*, then *ReFeX* looks for pairs of features whose values never disagree by more than a threshold. For details on the threshold, see Section 2.3 below.

First, each feature's values are transformed into *vertical logarithmic bins* of size p (where $0 < p < 1$). The process is as

[1]We selected sum and mean as aggregate functions heuristically. These simple measures capture the dominant trends among a node's neighbors w.r.t. each feature. Other functions, such as maximum, minimum, and variance could easily be added to *ReFeX*. In our experiments, sum and mean were sufficient to provide good empirical performance on data mining tasks with a reasonable runtime.

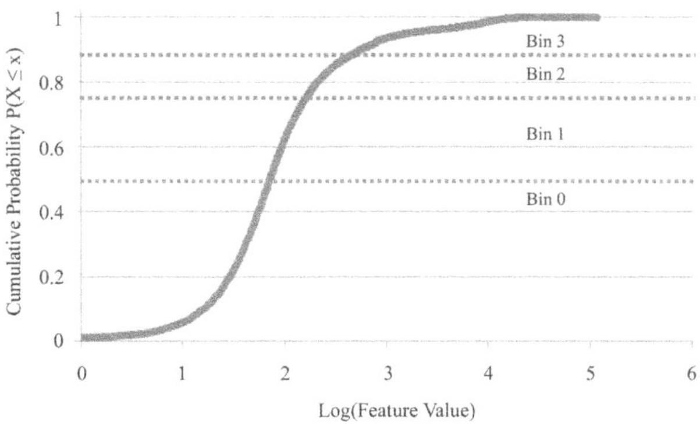

Figure 2: Vertical logarithmic binning of a feature value.

follows. For feature f_i, the $p|V|$ nodes with the lowest f_i value are reassigned f_i value 0. If there are ties, it may be necessary to include more than $p|V|$ nodes. Next, p fraction of the remaining nodes are assigned f_i value 1, and p of the remaining nodes after this are assigned value 2. This is repeated until all f_i values have been replaced by integer values between 0 and $log_{p^{-1}}(|V|)$ (see Figure 2).

We choose logarithmic binning for all features based on the observation that many graph properties exhibit power law distributions [1]. In particular, logarithmic binning always places most of the discriminatory power among sets of nodes with large feature values. This is reasonable, given that we expect to be able to make better predictions about active nodes for which we have many observations than nodes for which we only have a few.

Once a set of features has been generated and binned, *ReFeX* looks for pairs of features that do *not* disagree at any vertex by more than a threshold s. We call such a pair of features s-friends. To eliminate redundant features, we construct a *feature-graph*, whose nodes are features and whose links are s-friend relations. Each connected component of this graph is replaced by a single feature. When possible, we retain "simpler" features, i.e. features generated using fewer recursive iterations.[2]

If a recursive iteration results in no retained features, *ReFeX* halts and reports the retained feature values from each of the previous iterations. Note that a feature retained in iteration k may not be retained in iteration $k+1$, due to recursive features connecting them in the feature-graph. In this case, we still record and output the feature because it was retained at some iteration.

2.3 Parameters

ReFeX requires two parameters: p, which is the fraction of nodes placed in each logarithmic bin, and s, which is the feature similarity threshold.

The parameter p takes a value between 0 and 1, inclusive. Increasing p too close to 1 reduces the number of bins and increases the effective pruning aggressiveness, which can lead to a loss of discriminatory power. Decreasing p to near 0 can generate many bins and retain many features during pruning, which can increase runtime significantly. In our experiments, we found $p = 0.5$ to be a sensible choice – with each bin containing the bottom half of the remaining nodes. We also found that the results were not sensitive to the value of p as long as its value was not near 0 or 1.

For s, *ReFeX* uses *relaxation* at each iteration. For small graphs ($\leq 100K$ nodes), *ReFeX* uses $s = 0$ for the initial iteration (to generate neighborhood features). This effectively retains any feature that does not totally agree with another feature in logarithmic bin values. For larger graphs ($> 100K$ nodes), the initial value of s may be increased if computational resources are insufficient to generate the full set. On each subsequent iteration, *ReFeX* increased s by 1. This ensures that the process will halt after no more than $log_{p^{-1}}(|V|)$ iterations, since the maximum value of any feature is s at that point.

[2]It may be the case that two features are not similar enough to be joined in the feature graph, but reside in the same component because of a chain of similar features between them. We examined feature graphs for a number of data sets and found that this does occur. However, any other choice of criterion for joining features (cliques, community discovery algorithms, etc.) would be similarly heuristic and probably include outside cases that are unsatisfactory. Any of these criteria could be used in place of the connected-components criterion, however; we use connectedness for its simplicity and ease of computation.

2.4 Computational Complexity

Let n be the number of nodes, m be number of edges, M = maximum degree, f = number of features, and d_i = degree of node i. Computational complexity of *ReFeX* can be divided into two steps: (1) computation of neighborhood features, and (2) computation at each subsequent iteration. Computation of neighborhood features is expected to take $O(n)$ for real-world graphs. See Lemma 1 for details. At each subsequent iteration, *ReFeX* takes $O(f(m+nf))$ time, where $f \ll n$. The space requirement is $O(m+nf)$.

Lemma 1. The computation of neighborhood features takes $O(nM^{\epsilon})$.

Proof. For brevity, we only give a sketch of the proof:
$\sum_{(u \to v) \in E} degree(u) \approx \int_1^M n * d_i^{(\epsilon-1)} \partial d_i \approx nM^{\epsilon}$.
$\epsilon = 3 - \alpha$ for real-world graph with power-law degree distributions with exponent α. However, since α is typically in the range $2 < \alpha < 3$ for real-world graphs [3], $0 < \epsilon < 1$. ■

3. FEATURE EFFECTIVENESS ON NETWORK CLASSIFICATION

We describe experiments on within- and across-network classification using features from *ReFeX*.

3.1 Data

IP-A and IP-B are real network-trace data sets collected roughly one year apart on separate enterprise networks. The nodes are IP addresses and the links are communications between the IPs. The IP-A trace begins at midnight on day 1 and continues up to 12pm on day 5. The IP-B trace begins at midnight on day 1 and continues up to ≈5pm on day 6.

For days 1-4 of the IP-A dataset (IP-A1 to IP-A4), we extract flows in the period from 12pm-1pm. We exclude day 5 because the trace ended at 12pm. For IP-B, we extract flows from 12pm-1pm for day 3 only. We then label all flows using a payload signature-based classification tool. Once network flows are labeled, we transfer labels to hosts by selecting the most frequent class labels from among the host's flows. The payload classifier can distinguish between over 15 classes of traffic (e.g., Web, DNS, SMTP, P2P). However, since we found that 3 classes (namely, Web, DNS, and P2P) made up the dominant traffic type for over 90% of the labeled hosts, we remove all other labels and focus on the 3-class classification problem. Table 1 summarizes the data that we extracted.

3.2 Classifiers

To test the predictive ability of *ReFeX*'s features, we use the logForest model described by Gallagher et al. [11]. The logForest is a bagged model, composed of a set of logistic regression (LR) clas-

	IP-A1	IP-A2	IP-A3	IP-A4	IP-B
Nodes	81450	57415	154103	206704	181267
(labeled)	29868	16112	30955	67944	27649
Links	968138	432797	1266341	1756082	1945215
(unique)	206112	137822	358851	465869	397925
Web	32%	38%	38%	18%	42%
DNS	36%	49%	39%	20%	42%
P2P	32%	12%	23%	62%	16%

Table 1: Extracted data

sifiers, where each is given a subset of $\log(f) + 1$ of the f total features. For our experiments, we use a logForest of 500 LR classifiers. Like Gallagher et al. [11], we found that the overall performance of logForest was superior to standard logistic regression. In addition, as a baseline, we include a standard homophily-based relational neighbor classifier: wvRN (short for weighted-vote Relational Neighbor) [23]. The wvRN classifier has been shown to have excellent performance across a range of tasks. The classifiers we compare are:

- *wnRN+RL* - a relational neighbor model, which uses wvRN and relaxation labeling for collective classification
- *Neighborhood* - a logForest model, which uses the neighborhood features only
- *Regional* - a logForest model, which uses the regional features (i.e., neighborhood + recursive)

3.3 Feature Effectiveness on Within-Network Classification

3.3.1 Methodology

Each data set contains a set of core nodes for which we have ground-truth (i.e., we know the true class labels). In all cases, classifiers have access to the entire data graph during both training and testing.[3] However, not all of the core nodes are labeled. We vary the proportion of labeled core nodes from 10% to 90%. Classifiers are trained on all labeled core nodes and evaluated on all unlabeled core nodes.

Our methodology is as follows. For each proportion of core nodes labeled, we run 10 trials and report the average performance. For each trial and proportion labeled, we choose a class-stratified random-sample containing (1.0 - proportion labeled)% of the core instances as the test set and the remaining core instances become the training set. Note that proportion labeled less than 0.9 (or greater than 10 trials) means that a single instance will necessarily appear in multiple test sets. The test sets cannot be made to be independent because of this overlap. However, we carefully choose the test sets to ensure that each instance in our data set occurs in the same number of test sets over the course of our experiments. This ensures that each instance carries the same weight in the overall evaluation regardless of the proportion labeled. Labels are kept on the training instances and removed from the test instances. We use identical train/test splits for each classifier. Our experimental framework sits on top of the open source Weka system [28]. We implement our own network data representation and experimental code, which handles tasks such as splitting the data into training and test sets, labeling and unlabeling of data, and converting network fragments into a Weka-compatible form. We rely on Weka for the implementation of logistic regression and for measuring classifier performance on individual training/test trials.

[3]This is the norm in within-network classification.

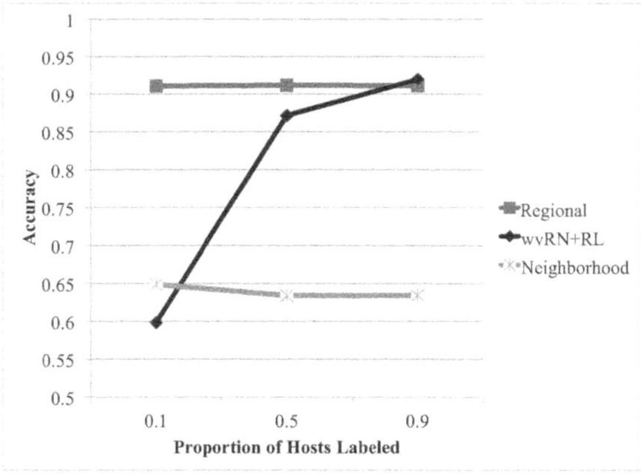

Figure 3: Within-network classification with wvRN+RL, neighborhood, and regional classifiers. The regional classifier dominates when labels are sparse.

3.3.2 Results

Figure 3 demonstrates the performance of the *wnRN+RL*, *Neighborhood* and *Regional* classifiers on a within-network classification task on the IP-A3 data set. We repeated this task on each of the IP-A data sets with essentially equivalent results. The within-network classification setting is the sweet spot for homophily-based models like wvRN. So, it is no surprise that wvRN+RL performs well on this task with 90% of nodes in the network labeled. However, the performance of wvRN+RL degrades quickly as labels become more sparse. The Regional and Neighborhood classifiers are less sensitive to the availability of labeled data since they do not rely on labeled neighbors to make accurate classifications. As a result, the Regional classifier outperforms wvRN+RL when labeled data are sparse. The dramatic difference in performance between Neighborhood and Regional demonstrates that the recursive feature generation process leads to more expressive features that are able to represent important concepts that cannot be captured by the neighborhood features alone.

3.4 Feature Effectiveness on Across-Network Transfer Learning

3.4.1 Methodology

For each experiment, the training graph has all known labels available. The test graph is *completely* unlabeled. Each classifier is evaluated on all known ground truth labels in the test graph. We use an identical set of features for all data sets. This set of features comes from running *ReFeX* on the IP-A1 data set. Table 2 summarizes the across-network experiments.

3.4.2 Results

Figure 4 demonstrates the performance of *Neighborhood* and *Regional* on a series of across-network transfer learning tasks. Here, we train on one network, where all known labels are available, and test on a separate network that is completely unlabeled. We emphasize the difficulty of these tasks given the (sometime extreme) differences in class distributions between data sets (see Table 1). The performance of the *Default* classifier is a good indicator of the difficulty of each task since this model makes predictions based

Train Graph	Test Graph: IP-A2	IP-A3	IP-A4	IP-B
IP-A1	✓	✓	✓	✓
IP-A2		✓	✓	✓
IP-A3			✓	✓
IP-A4				✓
IP-A1 to IP-A4				✓

Table 2: Across-network experiments performed

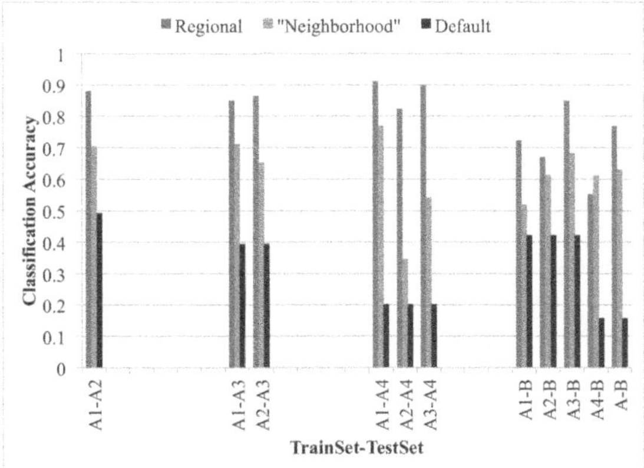

Figure 4: Across-network transfer learning with neighborhood and regional features. Regional demonstrates consistently high accuracy on difficult transfer learning tasks.

solely on the most frequent class from the training set. We also note that *wnRN+RL* is not applicable for these tasks since it relies on the availability of some known class labels to seed the inference process.

As in the within-network setting, the Regional classifier is the best overall performer on the across-network tasks, achieving 82% - 91% accuracy training and testing on separate days of IP-A and 77% accuracy training on all days of IP-A and testing on IP-B. The performance of Regional applied to IP-A4 is particularly impressive, given the extreme differences in class distribution between IP-A4 and the other data sets (see Table 1). We note that Regional is somewhat less successful training on IP-A4. In fact, training on IP-A4 and testing on IP-B is the one case where Regional underperforms Neighborhood. However, the difference in performance is small (<5%). Finally, and not surprisingly, we see a benefit to training on a number of diverse data sets instead of a single data set. Specifically, we achieve 77% training on all of the IP-A data sets and testing on IP-B, whereas we see a lot of variation (55% - 85%) training on individual days from IP-A.

4. FEATURE EFFECTIVENESS ON IDENTITY RESOLUTION

To demonstrate that regional features capture meaningful and informative behaviors of nodes, we present a collection of identity resolution tasks. In each task, we compute a set of regional features on a pair of networks whose node-sets overlap. Our hypothesis is that a node's feature values will be similar across graphs. We present an experimental framework that allows us to test this empirically. In our experiments, we will demonstrate how this method can be used to perform "de-anonymization"on social network datasets when external non-anonymized data is available.

4.1 Problem Statement

For a pair of graphs whose node-sets overlap, but whose edge-sets can be distinct (or even represent a totally different type of observation), can we use network structure alone to map nodes in one network to nodes in the other? More realistically, can we reduce the entropy associated with each node in one graph, with respect to its possible identity among nodes in the second graph? For a given method, we will measure success at this task by counting how many "incorrect" nodes the method guesses before it finds the correct node in the second graph.

4.2 Methodology

We are given two graphs, G_{target} and $G_{reference}$, and a vertex v_{test} which exists in both graphs. To test a given identity resolution strategy, we allow the strategy to guess reference vertices $\langle v_1^{guess}, v_2^{guess}, \ldots, v_k^{guess}\rangle$ until it correctly guesses v_{test}. The score associated with this strategy is k, the number of guesses required to find the node. The baseline method is to guess at random; for this strategy we assume the expected score $|V_{reference}|/2$.

The strategies we test experimentally use structural features to compute guesses. We present results for (1) Local features only, (2) Neighborhood features only, and (3) Regional features. The features are computed using *ReFeX* on G_{target}. The same features are then computed on $G_{reference}$. For a given strategy, the guesses are generated in order of increasing Euclidian distance from V_{target} in feature space. Our hypothesis is that Regional will score lower (i.e. better) than Local or Neighborhood.

To compare the overall performances of strategies, we compute scores across a set $S_{overlap}$ of all vertices that exist in both graphs. When it is not computationally feasible to analyze every node in $S_{overlap}$, we select a set of vertices $S_{test} \subset S_{overlap}$ and report all scores for nodes in S_{test}. In these experiments, we select S_{test} by taking the 1000 vertices in V_{target} with the highest degree, and keeping only those vertices that are also in $S_{overlap}$.

There are a number of ways to compare performance on a given test set. For example, the mean score across all target instances is a measure of success, with lower mean scores indicating better performance. We can also compute the fraction of target instances that score less than a given threshold; here a larger fraction is better. For example, we can report the fraction of target vertices whose score is less than 1% of $|V_{reference}|$.[4]

4.3 Data

Table 3 outlines the data sets used in this set of experiments. The first is a pair of Twitter networks from 2008, including a who-follows-whom network and a who-mentions-whom network. The second is an SMS communication network. The third is a collection of 28 days of Yahoo IM events. The fourth is IP traffic on two separate enterprise networks, observed at several different times. We described the IP network in details in Section 3.1.

Yahoo! IM Networks. Each graph here is a collection of IM

[4]If we combine the latter across all thresholds, we can treat it as the cumulative distribution function of $p(score(x))$, the empirical probability distribution over scores for this strategy. This presentation is harder to interpret, however, since one strategy may perform better in some regions and worse in others, and we are generally concerned with the lowest possible scores.

Data Graph	Source	# Nodes	# Edges	Weighted?	Directed?	# Local Features	# Nbrhood Features	# Regional Features	# Recursive Iterations
Twitter (T)	Who-follows-whom	465K	845K	Yes	No	3	8	45	6
Twitter (R)	Who-mentions-whom-1st	840K	1.4M	Yes	No	3	8	45	–
SMS (T)	04/01/2008	144K	580K	Yes	Yes	7	21	53	3
SMS (R)	04/02/2008	128K	505K	Yes	Yes	7	21	53	–
Yahoo! IM (T)	Day 1	50K	123K	Yes	Yes	3	12	79	5
Yahoo! IM (R)	Day 2-28	29K-100K	80K-280K	Yes	Yes	3	12	79	–
IP Comm. (T)	IP-A1	81K	206K	Yes	Yes	7	22	373	4
IP Comm. (R)	IP-A2, -A3, -A4, IP-B	57K-206K	137K-466K	Yes	Yes	7	22	373	–

Table 3: Data sets used in the identity resolution task. (R) refers to the Reference Graph. (T) refers to the Target Graph. The features are generated on the Target Graph are used to compute feature values in the Reference Graph.

events taken from one of 28 days of observation.[5] Each node is an IM user, and each link is a communication event on a given day. In some cases, multiple events are reported for a given pair of users on a given day; when this happens the links are given weights according to how many events are reported.

We use the IMs from day 1 as G_{target}, and compute scores for the other days (2 - 28) as $G_{reference}$. The task here is to take an IM user from day 1 and locate him in later days. Figure 5 shows that the similarity in node-sets and edge-sets with G_{target} is low for all $G_{reference}$ graphs. However, in most cases there is a significant overlap with the 1000 nodes in the test set S_{test}.

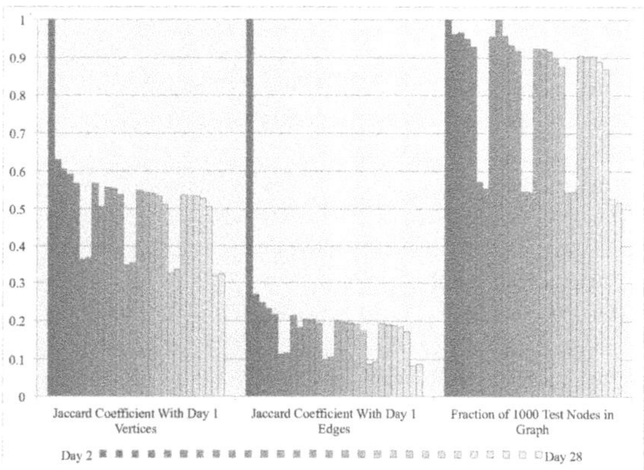

Figure 5: Yahoo! IM graphs across 28 days. The similarity between G_{target} on Day 1 and $G_{reference}$ on Days 2 to 28 is low but there is significant overlap in most cases with the test nodes.

Enterprise Network Traces. We describe these IP networks in detail in Section 3.1. The target graph comes from IP-A1. There are four reference graphs total: IP-A2, IP-A3, IP-A4, and IP-B. The task is to identify an external IP address from one day to the next or one IP network to the next. A potential application of this task is to de-anonymize a network trace where the IP addresses are hidden; one could observe a non-anonymized enterprise trace and use structural information to guess the identities of the anonymized IPs.

Twitter Relationships. This dataset consists of two graphs taken from Twitter in 2008.[6] One is a social "who-follows-whom" network that was generated by starting with a few seed users (all famous people with verified accounts) and crawling "follows" links for a few iterations. The other is taken from actual tweets observed during a year. The users whose tweets are observed are the same as the users in the social network.

To construct a graph from tweets, we generate "mentions-first" edges. That is, if a tweet by $user1$ contains a username (e.g. @$user2$), we add a link between $user1$ and $user2$ in the network, but only if $user2$ is the first user mentioned in the tweet. We do not include self-mentions.

For this experiment, we use the social network as G_{target} and the mentioning network as $G_{reference}$. Success at this task indicates that one could de-anonymize a social network by using publicly available text data, so long as usernames can be parsed from the text. This has important implications with respect to privacy of users in published "anonymized" social networks.

SMS Messages. SMS-Message dataset is constructed from short messages in a mobile phone operator at Asia. Each node corresponds to a mobile phone client. The reference and the target graphs encode the number of short messages among those nodes, extracted at two different days. We also eliminate those pairs of less active users with only one message exchange between them.

4.4 Feature Effectiveness Results

We present results for each of the four datasets. The first three demonstrate the effectiveness of regional features for identity resolution, and the fourth serves as a practitioner's note regarding test-set selection.

Yahoo! IM Networks. Figure 6 shows the average score for each of the 27 reference graphs, as a percentage of the expected score in the baseline strategy (recall that the baseline strategy scores $\frac{|V_{reference}|}{2}$ on average). All feature-based strategies outperform the baseline strategy, but performance of all strategies suffers on weekends when the graphs are significantly different. In general, expected scores are much better (lower) for Neighborhood than Local, and somewhat better for Regional than Neighborhood.

Figure 7 provides another view of the performance. Each data point here shows the fraction of test nodes that scored better than 1% of the maximum possible score $|V_{reference}|$. A higher fraction here indicates better performance, as the distribution of scores is higher near the minimum score 1. Again, Regional outperforms the other strategies in most instances. This improvement decreases on the weekends, and in one case (Day 27) Regional does no better than Local.

Poor performance on the weekends is not unexpected, and strength-

[5]http://sandbox.yahoo.com/

[6]http://www.public.asu.edu/ mdechoud/datasets.html

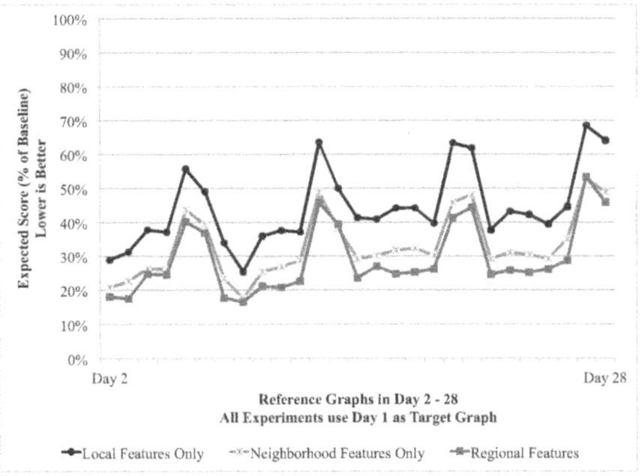

Figure 6: Yahoo! IM: Regional is consistently better (lower average score) at tracking test nodes across several weeks of IM traffic.

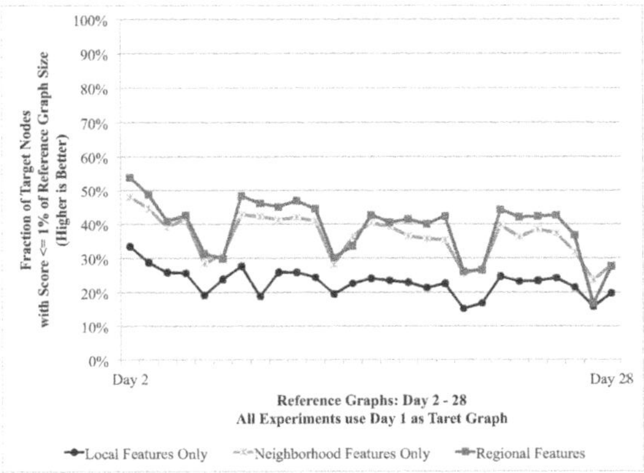

Figure 7: Yahoo! IM: Regional is consistently able to identify more test nodes within the first 1% of guesses (higher is better). It dips in performance corresponding to weekends, when the graph structure is very different.

ens our belief that structural features are capturing behavior. Recall from Figure 5 that the set of active users is significantly different on the weekends, as is the set of observed communications. Intuitively, it is an obvious fact that many users behave differently both in general and specifically with respect to IM communication on the weekend than during the weekdays. Regional is especially susceptible to errors in this case, because these changes in behavior are amplified during recursive feature generation.

Enterprise Network Traces. Regional is very effective at tracking external IP addresses over time, as seen Figure 8. It dominates the performance of Local and Neighborhood in all tests, with over 45% of S_{test} scoring in the top 1% of possible scores even a year after the communications in G_{target} are observed. Note that S_{test} is significantly smaller after a year due to decreased overlap; the reported results are fractions of $|S_{test}|$. Even though the traces were collected from separate networks, common external nodes (e.g., google.com) will be included in both.

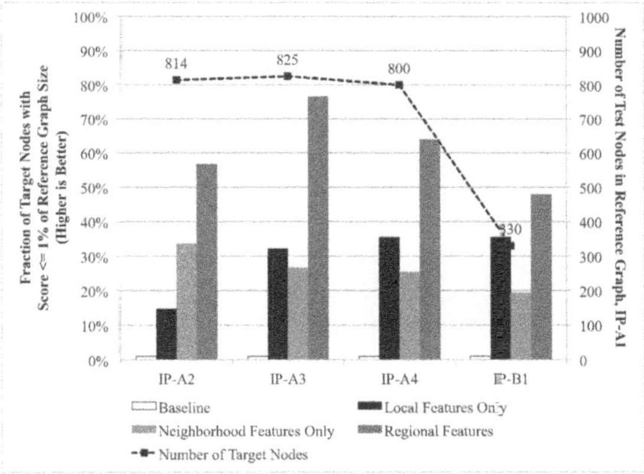

Figure 8: IP Communication: Regional is the best strategy for tracking IP addresses (higher is better). Even in the IP-B1 graph, which was observed on a different enterprise network, Regional locates nearly 50% of test nodes in the first 1% of its guesses.

In this task, average scores were inconsistent, with Local outperforming Regional in some instances. Analysis of the distributions of scores here shows that Regional outperforms Local for a majority of the test instances, but there is a small subset of test nodes for which Regional performs extremely poorly (near baseline).

Twitter Relationships. This experiment is the "hardest", in that G_{target} and $G_{reference}$ are generated by different processes altogether. G_{target} is a social network of users following other users, while $G_{reference}$ is generated by users mentioning each other in tweets. Surprisingly, our method is still able to do well at resolving some users here.

For this experiment, we applied each strategy to several different test sets, rather than just taking the top 1000 nodes by degree. In particular, we tested separately on each vertical logarithmic bin (see Section 2.2.2). For bins with over 1000 users, we sampled 1000 users uniformly at random.

Figure 9 shows the expected scores of each strategy. The ten highest-degree bins, taken together, correspond roughly to the top 1000 nodes by degree. Regional features outperform other strategies in this range, although their performance drops off in the lower degree bins.

All three strategies perform less well on these graphs than on the other datasets, but they are still able to reduce the entropy significantly for the most active users. For example, the highest degree user is BarackObama, and Regional achieved a score of 5 on that instance (the four wrong guesses were AddToAny, MrTweet, tferriss, and THE_REAL_SHAQ). Local and Neighborhood each scored 24 for BarackObama.

For the lowest-degree nodes, all methods perform worse than baseline. This drop-off is expected; less active nodes are harder to identify because (1) they have fewer observed behaviors to leverage and (2) there are more nodes that are very similar to them.

SMS Messages. This dataset serves to point out a case in which Regional does not perform best, but also a practitioner's note that

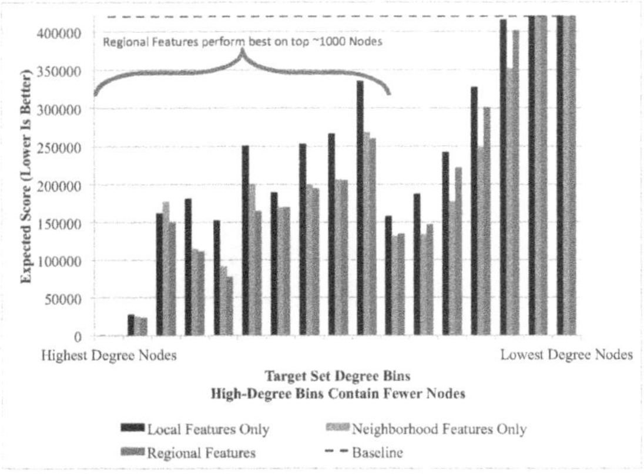

Figure 9: Twitter: Regional features are able to de-anonymize more active nodes (lower is better).

often allows for improved results when performing identity resolution outside of an experimental setting.

Figure 10 shows that the performance with respect to nodes scoring better than 1% of $|V_{reference}|$ can depend on the elements of S_{test}. When S_{test} consists of the top 1000 nodes by degree, each method scores better than 1% on $60-65\%$ of the test nodes, and Regional performs worst. However, if each strategy is allowed to "hand-pick" a test set by taking the top 1000 nodes by feature-vector magnitude (in that strategy's feature space), performance improves across the board. Regional improves the most, and is the top performer in this case.

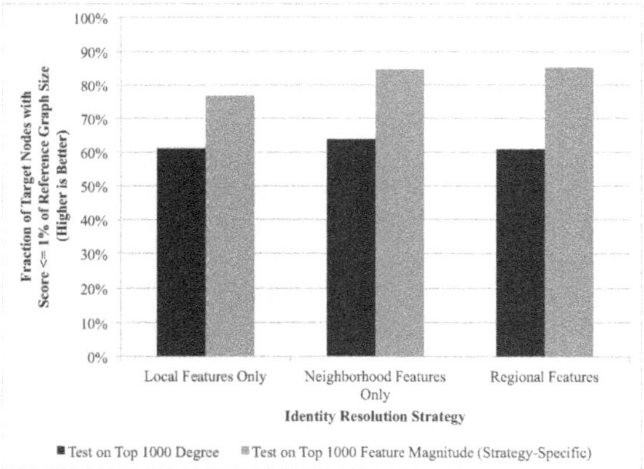

Figure 10: SMS: When allowed to suggest test nodes, Neighborhood and Regional locate near 85% of test nodes in the top 1% of guesses. Without test set selection, all strategies perform equally well.

By allowing each strategy to select its test set, we leverage the fact that a high-degree node may be less distinctive than a low-degree node that has other large feature values. However, as an experiment to compare strategies this approach is not "fair" because the set of test instances is different for each strategy.

We tested the other datasets to determine whether feature magnitude is always better than degree for selecting test nodes. While this is true in general, there are cases in which performance degrades when using feature magnitudes. This is often due to different sizes in the overlap between the 1000 proposed test nodes and $V_{reference}$.

With respect to runtime, our largest graph (Twitter Mentions graph with 840K nodes and 1.4M edges) ran in about 5 hours on a commodity processor. Graphs with fewer than 100K nodes run in an hour or less.

5. RELATED WORK

Feature Engineering in Graph data. There has been comprehensive work studying both global and local structural features of real graphs. For example, at global scale, graph diameter has been observed to be small [2] and to shrink over time [20]. It has also been reported that the number of edges in a time-varying graph grows super-linearly with the number of nodes, following a power-law relation [20]. Moreover, the principal (largest) eigenvalue of the graph is shown to be informative as a vulnerability measure of the graph [27]. Other local and community-level observations show that degree distributions in many graphs follow power-laws [5, 7, 17, 24] and that graphs exhibit modular structure, with nodes forming groups, and groups within groups [9, 14]. This body of work has informed our selection of a set of neighborhood features, upon which we then build recursive features.

Feature Extraction for Data Mining. There also exists related work which exploits feature extraction from graphs for several data mining tasks. One study approaches link prediction as a supervised learning problem [21]. They extract topological features for node pairs and show that the features boost prediction performance and that the supervised approach outperforms unsupervised methods. Another recent study [16] develops a multi-level framework to detect anomalies in time-varying graphs based on graph, subgraph, and node level features. The algorithms rely on extracting graph-level (global) features and tracking these metrics over time. The time points identified as interesting or suspicious are passed to finer levels where more complex tools inspect node and community features to spot regions of interests and flag abnormal nodes. Another study extracts egonet features and patterns in order to detect anomalous nodes in weighted graphs[1]. There has also been work on using local and global structural features to improve the performance of network classifiers[10]. In our work, we introduce methods for *recursive feature extraction.* Our results show that recursive features yield better performance in several data mining tasks, such as transfer learning and identity resolution, compared to their non-recursive counterparts.

Another body of related work uses frequent sub-graphs as structural features for classification of graphs [18, 8] and anomaly detection [26, 22]. These methods, however, assume that the nodes in given graphs have labels. On the other hand, our feature extraction procedures exploit the structure of the graphs, without any assumption on the availability of labels.

Transfer Learning. Transfer learning (i.e., domain adaption) has been a very active research area in recent years. Representative work includes multi-label text classification [30, 13], cross-domain sentiment prediction [4, 6, 15], intrusion detection [12], verb argument classification [19], cross-lingual classification [25], and cross-domain relation extraction [29]. In all of these scenarios, the features are *given* as the input of their algorithms (e.g. the word frequency of the documents) and the goal is to leverage the given features to boost performance in the target domain. In this paper, we aim to answer an orthogonal question: *what kind of features are effective in transferring the knowledge from the source domain to the target domain?* Our case studies show that the proposed recursive features are indeed effective for across-network classification and identity resolution, especially when there are few or no labels in the target domain, or homophily among class labels does not hold. We expect the proposed recursive features to have wide applicability for transfer learning tasks.

6. CONCLUSIONS

We described a novel algorithm *ReFeX*, which extracts regional features from nodes based on their neighborhood connectivity. These regional features capture behavior in terms of the the kind of nodes to which a given node is connected as opposed to the identity of those nodes. We showed that *ReFeX* was scalable and effective in various graph mining tasks including within- and across-network classification and identity resolution tasks.

Future work includes using the regional features generated by *ReFeX* for other mining tasks such as clustering, anomaly detection, and network comparison.

7. ACKNOWLEDGEMENTS

We thank Danai Koutra for all her help on this paper. This work was performed under the auspices of the U.S. Department of Energy by Lawrence Livermore National Laboratory under Contract No. DE-AC52-07NA27344 (LLNL-CONF-479453) and partially supported by Army Research Laboratory (ARL) under Cooperative Agreement No. W911NF-09-2-0053. The U.S. Government is authorized to reproduce and distribute reprints for Government purposes notwithstanding any copyright annotation thereon. The views and conclusions contained herein are those of the authors and should not be interpreted as necessarily representing the official policies or endorsements, either expressed or implied, of ARL or the U.S. Government.

8. REFERENCES

[1] L. Akoglu, M. McGlohon, and C. Faloutsos. Oddball: Spotting anomalies in weighted graphs. In *PAKDD*, pages 410–421, 2010.

[2] R. Albert, H. Jeong, and A.-L. Barabasi. Diameter of the world wide web. *Nature*, (401):130–131, 1999.

[3] A.-L. Barabasi, R. Albert, and H. Jeong. Scale-free characteristics of random networks: the topology of the world-wide web. *Physica A: Statistical Mechanics and its Applications*, 281(1-4):69 – 77, 2000.

[4] J. Blitzer, M. Dredze, and F. Pereira. Biographies, bollywood, boom-boxes and blenders: Domain adaptation for sentiment classification. In *ACL*, 2007.

[5] D. Chakrabarti, Y. Zhan, and C. Faloutsos. R-MAT: A recursive model for graph mining. In *SDM*, Apr. 2004.

[6] W. Dai, Q. Yang, G.-R. Xue, and Y. Yu. Boosting for transfer learning. In *ICML*, pages 193–200, 2007.

[7] M. Faloutsos, P. Faloutsos, and C. Faloutsos. On power-law relationships of the internet topology. *SIGCOMM*, pages 251–262, Aug-Sept. 1999.

[8] H. Fei and J. Huan. Structure feature selection for graph classification. In *CIKM*, pages 991–1000, 2008.

[9] G. Flake, S. Lawrence, C. L. Giles, and F. Coetzee. Self-organization and identification of web communities. *IEEE Computer*, 35(3), Mar. 2002.

[10] B. Gallagher and T. Eliassi-Rad. Leveraging label-independent features for classification in sparsely labeled networks: An empirical study. *Lecture Notes in Computer Science*, 5498:1–19, 2010.

[11] B. Gallagher, H. Tong, T. Eliassi-Rad, and C. Faloutsos. Using ghost edges for classification in sparsely labeled networks. In *KDD*, pages 256–264, 2008.

[12] J. Gao, W. Fan, J. Jiang, and J. Han. Knowledge transfer via multiple model local structure mapping. In *KDD*, pages 283–291, 2008.

[13] N. Ghamrawi and A. McCallum. Collective multi-label classification. In *CIKM*, pages 195–200, 2005.

[14] M. Girvan and M. E. J. Newman. Community structure in social and biological networks. *PNAS*, 99:7821, 2002.

[15] J. He, Y. Liu, and R. D. Lawrence. Graph-based transfer learning. In *CIKM*, pages 937–946, 2009.

[16] K. Henderson, T. Eliassi-Rad, C. Faloutsos, L. Akoglu, L. Li, K. Maruhashi, B. A. Prakash, and H. Tong. Metric forensics: a multi-level approach for mining volatile graphs. In *KDD*, pages 163–172, 2010.

[17] J. M. Kleinberg, R. Kumar, P. Raghavan, S. Rajagopalan, and A. S. Tomkins. The Web as a graph: Measurements, models and methods. *Lecture Notes in Computer Science*, 1627:1–17, 1999.

[18] X. Kong and P. S. Yu. Multi-label feature selection for graph classification. In *ICDM*, pages 274–283, 2010.

[19] S.-I. Lee, V. Chatalbashev, D. Vickrey, and D. Koller. Learning a meta-level prior for feature relevance from multiple related tasks. In *ICML*, pages 489–496, 2007.

[20] J. Leskovec, J. Kleinberg, and C. Faloutsos. Graphs over time: densification laws, shrinking diameters and possible explanations. In *KDD*, pages 177–187, 2005.

[21] R. N. Lichtenwalter, J. T. Lussier, and N. V. Chawla. New perspectives and methods in link prediction. In *KDD*, pages 243–252, 2010.

[22] C. Liu, X. Yan, H. Yu, J. Han, and P. S. Yu. Mining behavior graphs for "backtrace" of noncrashing bugs. In *SDM*, 2005.

[23] S. A. Macskassy and F. Provost. A simple relational classifier. In *Proc. of the 2nd Workshop on Multi-Relational Data Mining (MRDM) at KDD*, pages 64–76, 2003.

[24] M. E. J. Newman. Power laws, Pareto distributions and Zipf's law. *Contemporary Physics*, 46:323–351, 2005.

[25] X. Ni, J.-T. Sun, J. Hu, and Z. Chen. Cross lingual text classification by mining multilingual topics from wikipedia. In *WSDM*, pages 375–384, 2011.

[26] C. C. Noble and D. J. Cook. Graph-based anomaly detection. In *KDD*, pages 631–636, 2003.

[27] H. Tong, B. A. Prakash, C. E. Tsourakakis, T. Eliassi-Rad, C. Faloutsos, and D. H. Chau. On the vulnerability of large graphs. In *ICDM*, pages 1091–1096, 2010.

[28] I. H. Witten and E. Frank. *Data Mining: Practical Machine Learning Tools and Techniques, Second Edition (Morgan Kaufmann Series in Data Management Systems)*. Morgan Kaufmann Publishers Inc., San Francisco, CA, USA, 2005.

[29] L. Yao, S. Riedel, and A. McCallum. Collective cross-document relation extraction without labelled data. In *EMNLP*, pages 1013–1023, 2010.

[30] J. Zhang, Z. Ghahramani, and Y. Yang. Learning multiple related tasks using latent independent component analysis. In *NIPS*, 2005.

Triangle Listing in Massive Networks and Its Applications

Shumo Chu
Nanyang Technological University, Singapore
shumo.chu@acm.org

James Cheng
Nanyang Technological University, Singapore
j.cheng@acm.org

ABSTRACT

Triangle listing is one of the fundamental algorithmic problems whose solution has numerous applications especially in the analysis of complex networks, such as the computation of clustering coefficient, transitivity, triangular connectivity, etc. Existing algorithms for triangle listing are mainly in-memory algorithms, whose performance cannot scale with the massive volume of today's fast growing networks. When the input graph cannot fit into main memory, triangle listing requires random disk accesses that can incur prohibitively large I/O cost. Some streaming and sampling algorithms have been proposed but these are approximation algorithms. We propose an I/O-efficient algorithm for triangle listing. Our algorithm is exact and avoids random disk access. Our results show that our algorithm is scalable and outperforms the state-of-the-art local triangle estimation algorithm.

Categories and Subject Descriptors

H.2.8 [**DATABASE MANAGEMENT**]: Database Applications—*Data mining*
; G.2.2 [**DISCRETE MATHEMATICS**]: Graph Theory—*Graph algorithms*

General Terms

Algorithms, Experimentation, Performance

Keywords

Triangle Listing, Triangle Counting, Clustering Coefficient, Large Graphs, Massive Networks

1. INTRODUCTION

We study the problem of **triangle listing** in a simple undirected graph G, that is, *listing all triangles in* G. Our focus is to design efficient algorithm for triangle listing when G is too large to fit into main memory and is disk-resident.

Triangles are one of the fundamental types of small subgraphs most commonly used in the analysis of complex graphs/networks. In particular, a triangle is also the shortest non-trivial cycle (i.e., a cycle of length 3) and the smallest non-trivial clique (i.e., a clique of size 3). The concept of triangle is at the heart of the definition of many important measures for network analysis, such as the clustering coefficient (of a single vertex and of the entire network) [36], transitivity [35, 28], triangular connectivity [8], etc. All these measures can be directly computed from the result of triangle listing.

The aforementioned triangle-centered measures have a large number of important applications. In addition, triangle listing also has a broad range of applications in other areas such as in the discovery of dense subgraphs [34], in the detection of spamming activities [9], in the study of motif occurrences [27], in the uncovering of hidden thematic relationships in the Web [15], etc. In all these applications, triangle listing plays a vital role in their computation.

Although many algorithms have been proposed for triangle listing, these existing algorithms [22, 23, 4, 7, 30, 29, 26, 16] all fall into the category of *in-memory algorithms*. The best existing in-memory algorithms require space that is asymptotically linear in the size of the input graph. Unfortunately, many real-world networks have grown exceedingly large in recent years and are continuing to grow at a steady rate. For example, the Web graph has over 1 trillion webpages (by Google in 2008), most social networks (e.g., Facebook, MSN) have millions to billions of users, many citation networks (e.g., DBLP, Citeseer) have millions of publications, other networks such as phone-call networks, email networks, stock-market networks, etc., are also massively large.

For handling large graphs that cannot fit into main memory, a number of approximation algorithms have been proposed [3, 6, 14, 10, 9, 33]. However, all these algorithms are restricted to approximation of *triangle counting*, i.e., estimating the number of triangles in a graph or that formed at each vertex. Algorithms for estimating the total number of triangles in a graph only are more accurate [3, 6, 14, 10, 33], but their applications are also much more limited than those of triangle listing. Algorithms for estimating the number of triangles formed at each vertex in a graph, also called *local triangle counting*, have a wider range of applications but the state-of-the-art algorithm [9] is still not accurate enough. Moreover, the set of applications of triangle counting is only a small subset of that of triangle listing, as the result of triangle counting is directly obtainable from that of triangle listing.

We propose an I/O-efficient algorithm for exact triangle listing. Designing such an algorithm is difficult because triangle listing requires to access the neighbors of the neighbor of a vertex, which may appear arbitrarily in any position in the graph. Thus, random access to the graph stored on disk is required, which incurs huge I/O cost.

Our algorithm iteratively partitions the input graph G into a set of subgraphs that fit into memory and processes triangle listing in each local subgraph. To ensure the correctness and completeness of the final result computed iteratively from the local subgraphs, we categorize the triangles into three types. We devise an mechanism that lists all Type 1 and Type 2 triangles, and then converts the remaining Type 3 triangles into Types 1 and 2 by a new partition at the next iteration. To limit the total number of iterations, we show that we can remove all edges in each subgraph at the end of each iteration, thus shrinking G until it becomes empty. We propose two effective algorithms for graph partitioning for the task of triangle listing in our framework, one achieving high efficiency in practice while the other giving theoretical bound on the total number of iterations (also efficient in practice).

We evaluate our algorithm on large real datasets with up to 106 million vertices and 1,877 million edges, by comparing with the state-of-the-art in-memory algorithm [26] and the most related approximation algorithm [9]. Our algorithm achieves comparable performance with the in-memory algorithm when the graph can fit into memory. For large graphs that cannot fit into memory, the error rate of the approximation algorithm [9] can be as large as 95% to 133% while ours returns exact result, with comparable running time and memory. When we attempt to attain a lower error rate, e.g., at 50%, the approximation algorithm is already orders of magnitude slower than our exact algorithm.

Paper Organization. Section 2 gives the notations and problem definition. Section 3 describes an in-memory algorithm. Section 4 discusses our main algorithm. Section 5 presents two applications of our algorithm. Section 6 reports the experimental results. Section 7 gives the related work. Section 8 concludes the paper.

2. NOTATIONS AND PROBLEM DEFINITION

Let $G = (V_G, E_G)$ be a simple undirected graph, where V_G is the set of vertices and E_G is the set of edges. We define the set of *adjacent vertices* (or *neighbors*) of a vertex v in G as $adj_G(v) = \{u : (u, v) \in E_G\}$, and the *degree* of v in G as $deg_G(v) = |adj_G(v)|$. We assume that the graph is stored in the adjacency list representation, with vertices ordered according to their ID.

Given three distinct vertices, $u, v, w \in V_G$, we say that u, v and w form a *triangle* in G if $(u, v), (u, w), (v, w) \in E_G$. We use $\triangle_{uvw}$ to denote the triangle formed by the vertices u, v and w.

The set of triangles that consist of a vertex v, denoted by $\triangle(v)$, is defined as

$$\triangle(v) = \{\triangle_{uvw} : u, w \in adj_G(v), (u, w) \in E_G\}. \quad (1)$$

The *triangle number* of v, denoted by $N_\triangle(v)$, is defined as $N_\triangle(v) = |\triangle(v)|$.

Let $\triangle(G)$ be the set of all triangles in G. Then, $\triangle(G)$ is given by

$$\triangle(G) = \bigcup_{v \in V_G} \triangle(v). \quad (2)$$

The number of triangles in G, denoted by $N_\triangle(G)$, is defined as $N_\triangle(G) = |\triangle(G)|$, which is also given as follows

$$N_\triangle(G) = \frac{1}{3} \sum_{v \in V_G} N_\triangle(v). \quad (3)$$

Equation 3 holds because every triangle $\triangle_{uvw}$ is counted three times for the three vertices u, v and w.

Given a vertex $v \in V_G$, we say that u, v and w form an *open triangle* centered at v if $u, w \in adj_G(v)$. An open triangle is considered as a potential triangle. A triangle $\triangle_{uvw}$ may be regarded as a *closed triangle* and by definition, $\triangle_{uvw}$ contains three open triangles, centered at u, v, and w, respectively.

Table 1: Notations

Symbol	Description
$G = (V_G, E_G)$	A simple undirected graph
$adj_G(v)$	The set of adjacent vertices of v in G
$deg_G(v)$	Degree of v in G
$\triangle_{uvw}$	A triangle formed by u, v and w
$\triangle(v)$	The set of triangles that contains v (Eq. 1)
$N_\triangle(v)$	The triangle number of v, $N_\triangle(v) = \lvert\triangle(v)\rvert$
$\triangle(G)$	The set of all triangles in G (Eq. 2)
$N_\triangle(G)$	The number of triangles in G (Eq. 3)
$N_\vee(v)$	The number of open triangles centered at v (Eq. 4)
M	Available main memory size
B	Disk block size
$scan(N)$	$\Theta(N/B)$ I/Os
$sort(N)$	$\Theta(\frac{N}{B} \log_{M/B} \frac{N}{B})$ I/Os

The number of open triangles centered at v, denoted by $N_\vee(v)$, is defined as

$$N_\vee(v) = \frac{1}{2} deg_G(v)(deg_G(v) - 1). \quad (4)$$

Intuitively, $N_\vee(v)$ defines the maximum number of triangles that can be potentially formed from v.

The following example illustrates the concepts.

Example 1. Let G be the graph given in Figure 1. Consider the vertices b and e, we have $\triangle(b) = \{\triangle_{abc}, \triangle_{bcg}, \triangle_{bgi}\}$ and $\triangle(e) = \{\triangle_{cej}, \triangle_{efh}\}$. Thus, $N_\triangle(b) = 3$ and $N_\triangle(e) = 2$. By Equation 4, $N_\vee(b) = 6$ and $N_\vee(e) = 6$ since $deg_G(b) = 4$ and $deg_G(e) = 4$. We can also easy find $\triangle(G) = \{\triangle_{abc}, \triangle_{bcg}, \triangle_{bgi}, \triangle_{dej}, \triangle_{efh}, \triangle_{jkl}\}$ and $N_\triangle(G) = |\triangle(G)| = 6$. □

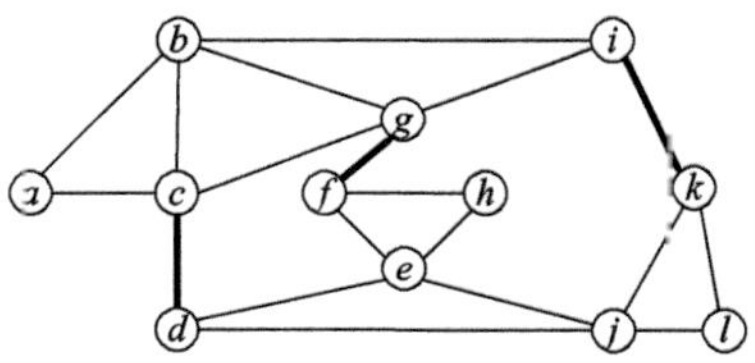

Figure 1: A Graph G

Problem Definition. This paper studies the problem of **triangle listing** defined as follows. Given a graph $G = (V_G, E_G)$, output $\triangle(G)$. In particular, we design I/O-efficient algorithms when G cannot fit into main memory, i.e., $(|V_G| + |E_G|) > M$, where M is the size of available main memory.

For the complexity analysis of I/O-efficient algorithms, we use the standard I/O model [2] with the following parameters: M is the available main memory size and B is the disk block size, where $1 \ll B \leq M/2$.

We also use the following standard I/O complexity notations: $scan(N)$=$\Theta(N/B)$ I/Os and $sort(N)$=$\Theta(\frac{N}{B} \log_{M/B} \frac{N}{B})$ I/Os, where N is the amount of data being read or written from/to disk.

Table 1 gives the frequently-used notations in the paper.

3. IN-MEMORY TRIANGLE LISTING

In this section, we first present an in-memory algorithm for triangle listing and use it to highlight the difficulty for triangle listing when main memory is insufficient.

We sketch the algorithm in Algorithm 1. Assume that the input graph G is in its adjacency-list representation and the vertices are

Algorithm 1 *In-Memory Triangle Listing*

Input: A graph $G = (V_G, E_G)$
Output: $\triangle(G)$

1. $\triangle(G) \leftarrow \emptyset$;
2. **for each** $u \in V_G$ **do**
3. **for each** $v \in adj_G(u)$, where $v > u$, **do**
4. **for each** $w \in (adj_G(u) \cap adj_G(v))$, where $w > v$, **do**
5. $\triangle(G) \leftarrow (\triangle(G) \cup \{\triangle_{uvw}\})$;
6. **return** $\triangle(G)$;

ordered in ascending order of their vertex ID, which is the most common format used for graph storage. The algorithm intersects the adjacency-list of each vertex u with the adjacency-list of u's neighbor v. Clearly, each vertex w as the result of the intersection is a neighbor of both u and v, and as u and v are also neighbors, we obtain a triangle $\triangle_{uvw}$.

A naive algorithm for triangle listing processes every neighbor v in $adj_G(u)$, and intersects the entire $adj_G(u)$ and $adj_G(v)$. This involves much redundant processing. In Algorithm 1, we only process a neighbor v that is ordered after u (Line 3), because if v is ordered before u, i.e., $v < u$, then v has been processed before u and hence the triangle $\triangle_{vuw}$ must have been already listed (note that $\triangle_{vuw} = \triangle_{uvw}$). For the intersection between $adj_G(u)$ and $adj_G(v)$ (Line 4), we also skip those vertices that are ordered before v (hence also u) in $adj_G(u)$ and $adj_G(v)$. The above process is similar to the state-of-the-art in-memory algorithm for triangle listing [26], except that their work orders the vertices in non-increasing order of their degree, which requires pre-processing.

When G cannot fit into main memory, however, the I/O cost becomes a bottleneck. Most existing in-memory algorithms [22, 23, 4, 7, 29, 26, 16] require random access to each $adj_G(v)$ for each $v \in adj_G(u)$ (as in Line 4 for the intersection). Note that each $adj_G(u)$ in Algorithm 1 is read sequentially as we read G, but $adj_G(v)$ can be in an arbitrary position on disk where G is stored. Others [30] use an additional array for each vertex in G and the total size of these arrays is in the order of the size of the input graph; thus these arrays need to be stored on disk and random access is again inevitable.

When G cannot fit into main memory, Algorithm 1 requires $O(|E_G| \cdot scan(d_{max}))$ I/Os in the worst case, where d_{max} is the maximum vertex degree in G, since we need to randomly access $adj_G(v)$ for each edge $(u, v) \in E_G$ and $deg_G(v) = O(d_{max})$. This I/O cost can be prohibitively large especially when G is large.

4. I/O-EFFICIENT TRIANGLE LISTING

In this section, we first sketch the framework of our algorithm and then present the details of the algorithm.

4.1 Algorithm Framework

When the input graph G cannot fit into memory, we could only load a portion (i.e., a subgraph) of G that can fit into memory each time. Thus, our algorithm iteratively performs triangle listing in a subgraph of G that fits in memory. We outline the framework of our algorithm as follows.

- Each iteration:
  - Partition G into a set of subgraphs, $\mathcal{P} = \{G_1, \ldots, G_i, \ldots, G_p\}$, such that each G_i can fit into memory;
  - Load each G_i into memory and perform triangle listing in G_i;
  - Remove from G those edges of G_i that can no longer contribute to triangle listing.
- Repeat the above iteration until G becomes empty.

The main idea of our algorithm is to iteratively partition the graph and perform triangle listing in each local subgraph G_i separately, as to avoid random access to arbitrary vertices (and their adjacency-list) in the graph.

The concept is simple but there are a number of challenging technical issues: (1) ensuring the correctness and completeness of the final result obtained from the iterative local computations; (2) an effective and efficient partitioning algorithm for triangle listing; and (3) bounding the overall I/O complexity of the algorithm (i.e., the I/O complexity at each step and the number of iterations). We discuss the above three issues in each of the following subsections.

4.2 Correctness and Global-Completeness of Local Triangle Listing

We first propose an algorithm that ensures the correctness of triangle listing in each local subgraph of G as well as the completeness of the global result obtained from all local computations.

The design of our algorithm is based on the following Lemma.

LEMMA 1. *Let $\mathcal{P} = \{G_1, \ldots, G_i, \ldots, G_p\}$ be a partition of G, where $\cup_{1 \le i \le p} V_{G_i} = V_G$ and $V_{G_i} \cap V_{G_j} = \emptyset$ for $1 \le i < j \le p$. Then, $\triangle(G) = \triangle 1 \cup \triangle 2 \cup \triangle 3$, where $\triangle 1$, $\triangle 2$, and $\triangle 3$ are disjoint sets defined as follows.*

- $\triangle 1 = \cup_{1 \le i \le p} \{\triangle_{uvw} : u, v, w \in V_{G_i}\}$.
- $\triangle 2 = \cup_{1 \le i,j \le p \,\wedge\, i \ne j} \{\triangle_{uvw} : u, v \in V_{G_i}, w \in V_{G_j}\}$.
- $\triangle 3 = \cup_{1 \le i < j < k \le p} \{\triangle_{uvw} : u \in V_{G_i}, v \in V_{G_j}, w \in V_{G_k}\}$.

PROOF. First, $(\triangle 1 \cup \triangle 2 \cup \triangle 3) \subseteq \triangle(G)$, since the elements in $\triangle 1$, $\triangle 2$, and $\triangle 3$ are triangles in G.

Next we show $\triangle(G) \subseteq (\triangle 1 \cup \triangle 2 \cup \triangle 3)$. For any triangle $\triangle_{uvw} \in \triangle(G)$, there are only three cases where u, v, and w can be located: (1) they are all in the same subgraph G_i; (2) two of them are in the same subgraph G_i while the other in another different subgraph G_j (WLOG, we may assume that $u, v \in V_{G_i}, w \in V_{G_j}, i \ne j$); (3) they are in three different subgraphs G_i, G_j, and G_k (WLOG, we may assume that $u \in V_{G_i}, v \in V_{G_j}, w \in V_{G_k}, i < j < k$). The three cases correspond to the three types $\triangle 1$, $\triangle 2$, and $\triangle 3$, and thus $\triangle(G) \subseteq (\triangle 1 \cup \triangle 2 \cup \triangle 3)$. □

We call triangles in $\triangle 1$, $\triangle 2$, and $\triangle 3$, *Type 1*, *Type 2*, and *Type 3* triangles. The following example illustrates the concept of the three types of triangles.

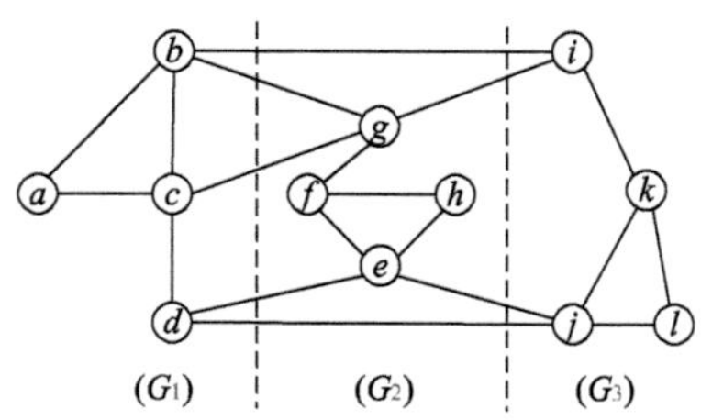

Figure 2: A partition of G in Figure 1: $\mathcal{P} = \{G_1, G_2, G_3\}$

Example 2. Figure 2 shows a partition, $\mathcal{P} = \{G_1, G_2, G_3\}$, of the graph shown in Figure 1. In the figure, $\triangle_{abc}$, $\triangle_{efh}$ and $\triangle_{jkl}$

are Type 1 triangles because all the three vertices of each triangle are in the same subgraph. We only have one Type 2 triangle, $\triangle_{bcg}$, because its vertices are in two subgraphs in $\mathcal{P}$. We have two Type 3 triangles, $\triangle_{bgi}$ and $\triangle_{dej}$, because all the three vertices of each triangle are in three different subgraphs in $\mathcal{P}$. □

According to Lemma 1, a triangle $\triangle_{uvw}$ can be listed by searching any subgraph G_i alone only if u, v and w are all in G_i (i.e., Type 1 triangles). However, the number of Type 1 triangles may be limited. More critically, we cannot remove any edge (and hence any vertex) of G_i from G even after we list all Type 1 triangles, because an edge (u,v) in $\triangle_{uvw}$ may form another triangle $\triangle_{uvx}$ with a vertex x in another subgraph G_j.

To enable the removal of edges after all triangles containing these edges are listed, and at same time to ensure the completeness of the global result, we introduce the notion of *extended subgraph*.

Definition 1 (EXTENDED SUBGRAPH). *Let $H = (V_H, E_H)$ be a subgraph of G. An* extended subgraph *of H in G, denoted by H^+, is a* directed *subgraph defined as $H^+ = (V_{H^+}, E_{H^+})$, where $V_{H^+} = V_H \cup \{v : u \in V_H, v \in V_G \backslash V_H, (u,v) \in E_G\}$ and $E_{H^+} = \{(u,v) : (u,v) \in E_G, u \in V_H\}$.*

Intuitively, an extended subgraph of H is a subgraph obtained by adding (to H) those directed edges from the vertices in H to those vertices not in H. In this paper, we assume that if $V_H = \{v\}$, for any $v \in V$, then the corresponding H^+ fits into memory. We give an example of extended subgraph as follows.

Example 3. Figure 3 depicts the extended subgraphs of G_1, G_2, and G_3 in Figure 2. The shaded vertices are the vertices in each G_i, while the directed edges show the extension to vertices outside each G_i. □

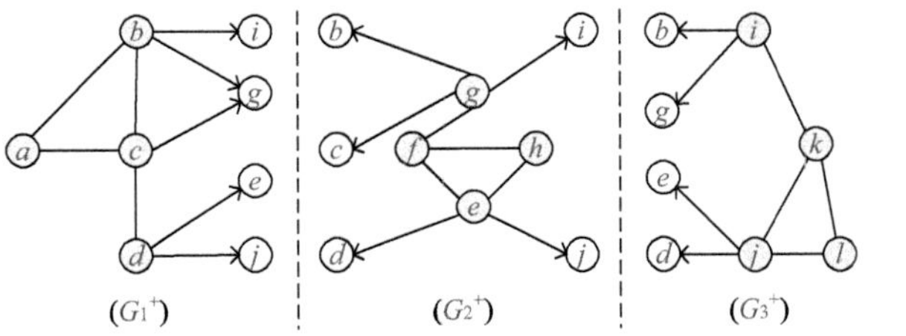

Figure 3: The extended subgraphs of G_1, G_2, G_3 in Figure 2

Based on Definition 1, we have the following lemma for triangle listing in an extended subgraph.

LEMMA 2. *Let H^+ be an extended subgraph of a subgraph H of G. Then:*

- *Let $\triangle 1(H^+) = \{\triangle_{uvw} : \triangle_{uvw} \in \triangle 1,\ u,v,w \in V_H\}$. Then, $\forall \triangle_{uvw} \in \triangle 1(H^+)$, $\triangle_{uvw}$ can be listed by searching H^+ alone.*
- *Let $\triangle 2(H^+) = \{\triangle_{uvw} : \triangle_{uvw} \in \triangle 2,\ u,v \in V_H\}$. Then, $\forall \triangle_{uvw} \in \triangle 2(H^+)$, $\triangle_{uvw}$ can be listed by searching H^+ alone.*

In addition, for any edge $(u,v) \in E_H$, (u,v) does not exist in any triangle in $\triangle(G) \backslash (\triangle 1(H^+) \cup \triangle 2(H^+))$.

PROOF. First, $\forall \triangle_{uvw} \in \triangle 1(H^+)$, $\triangle_{uvw}$ can be listed by searching H^+ alone because all the three edges (u,v) (u,w), and (v,w) of $\triangle_{uvw}$ are in H and hence also in H^+. Second, $\forall \triangle_{uvw} \in \triangle 2(H^+)$, $\triangle_{uvw}$ can be listed by searching H^+ alone because $u, v \in V_H$, $u \in adj_{H^+}(v)$, $w \in adj_{H^+}(v)$, and $\triangle_{uvw}$ can be found by intersecting $adj_{H^+}(u)$ and $adj_{H^+}(v)$.

Finally, for any edge $(u,v) \in E_H$, (u,v) does not exist in any triangle in $\triangle(G) \backslash (\triangle 1(H^+) \cup \triangle 2(H^+))$ because any triangle containing (u,v) must be in either $\triangle 1(H^+)$ or $\triangle 2(H^+)$. □

Algorithm 2 *I/O-Efficient Triangle Listing*

Input: A graph $G = (V_G, E_G)$
Output: A listing of $\triangle(G)$

1. **while**(G is not empty)
2. Partition G into $\mathcal{P} = \{G_1, \ldots, G_i, \ldots, G_p\}$;
3. **for each** extended subgraph G_i^+ of $G_i \in \mathcal{P}$ **do**
4. List all triangles in $\triangle 1(G_i^+)$ and $\triangle 2(G_i^+)$ (by Algorithm 3);
5. Remove all edges in G_i from G;

Algorithm 3 *Triangle Listing in Extended Subgraph*

Input: An extended subgraph $H^+ = (V_{H^+}, E_{H^+})$
Output: A listing of $\triangle 1(H^+)$ and $\triangle 2(H^+)$

1. **for each** $u \in V_H$ **do**
2. **for each** $v \in adj_H(u)$, where $v > u$, **do**
3. **for each** $w \in (adj_{H^+}(u) \cap adj_{H^+}(v))$ **do**
4. **if**($w > v$ or $w \notin V_H$)
5. List $\triangle_{uvw}$;

Lemma 2 implies that we can list all Type 1 and Type 2 triangles from the extended subgraph G_i^+ of each subgraph G_i in the partition $\mathcal{P}$ of G. More importantly, after listing the two types of triangles in each G_i^+, we can remove all edges in G_i (i.e., those bi-directed edges in G_i^+), since all triangles containing these edges have been already listed.

The above scheme lists all Type 1 and Type 2 triangles but still misses all Type 3 triangles. We devise an efficient algorithm that iteratively converts Type 3 triangles into Type 1 and Type 2 triangles so that all triangles can be listed, while at the same time reducing the size of the graph to reduce the I/O cost. We outline our algorithm in Algorithm 2.

Algorithm 2 is essentially an iterative computation of $\triangle 1(G_i^+)$ and $\triangle 2(G_i^+)$ from the extended subgraph G_i^+ of each $G_i \in \mathcal{P}$, as defined in Lemma 2, where $\mathcal{P}$ is the new partition of G at each iteration. (G_i^+ can be easily obtained along with the computation of $\mathcal{P}$, which we discuss in Section 4.3.)

At the end of each iteration, we remove all edges in each G_i in the current $\mathcal{P}$ and obtain a shrunk new graph. Then, at the beginning of the next iteration, we re-partition the new shrunk graph. The new partition $\mathcal{P}$ defines new sets of $\triangle 1(G_i^+)$ and $\triangle 2(G_i^+)$ for the G_i^+ of each $G_i \in \mathcal{P}$. Thus, Algorithm 2 iteratively converts the old set of Type 3 triangles in the previous iteration into Type 1 and Type 2 triangles with respect to the new partition at the current iteration. This process continues until all edges in G are removed.

Note that another purpose of graph partition is to make sure that each subgraph in $\mathcal{P}$ is small enough to fit into main memory, so as to avoid random disk access for triangle listing. Meanwhile, we also want to take full utilization of the available memory and hence each $G_i \in \mathcal{P}$ should be as big as possible under the condition that $(|V_{G_i}| + |E_{G_i}|) \leq M$. Thus, if G at any iteration is small enough to fit into memory, Step 2 of Algorithm 2 computes a partition consisting of only one element, i.e., $\mathcal{P} = \{G\}$, after which the algorithm terminates since all edges in G will be removed at the end of the iteration.

Step 4 of Algorithm 2 invokes Algorithm 3 to compute $\triangle 1(G_i^+)$

and $\triangle 2(G_i^+)$ from G_i^+, i.e., H^+ in Algorithm 3. Algorithm 3 is an in-memory algorithm similar to Algorithm 1. The only difference is that the extended graph H^+ contains two sets of vertices, V_H and $V_{H^+} \backslash V_H$. Algorithm 3 only intersects the adjacency-lists of those vertices in V_H. Let w be a vertex found in $(adj_{H^+}(u) \cap adj_{H^+}(v))$, where $u, v \in V_H$. If $w \in V_H$, we also require $w > v$ (and hence also $w > u$) in order to avoid duplicate listing of the triangle $\triangle_{uvw}$. If $w \notin V_H$, then we simply list $\triangle_{uvw}$ since it cannot be listed elsewhere.

We now prove the correctness and completeness of Algorithm 2.

THEOREM 1. *Given a graph $G = (V_G, E_G)$, Algorithm 2 lists all triangles in G and no false or duplicate triangle is listed.*

PROOF. Lemma 2 ensures that (1) all triangles containing a removed edge are listed, (2) all edges of any triangle not yet listed are still in the current G, and (3) the already listed triangles will not be listed again in future iterations because at least one of their edges has been removed from G. By (1) and (2), all triangles in G are listed because G becomes empty when Algorithm 2 terminates. Since Algorithm 3 does not list any duplicate triangle due to the enforced vertex ordering, by (3) Algorithm 2 does not list any duplicate triangle. Finally, since all triangles listed by Algorithm 3 are real triangles in G, Algorithm 2 does not list any false triangle. □

4.3 Graph Partitioning for Triangle Listing

The objectives of graph partitioning for the task of triangle listing are: (1) each subgraph in the partition should fill the available memory as much as possible; and (2) each subgraph should contain as many intra-partition edges (i.e., edges within the same subgraph) as possible. The first objective is to fully utilize memory, while the second objective is to remove as many edge as possible at each iteration of Algorithm 2 in order to reduce the number of total iterations.

Graph partitioning that fulfills the above two objectives, however, is known to be APX-hard [5] when the number of subgraphs in the partition is more than 2. There have been a number of approximation algorithms proposed [25, 19, 24, 17, 18, 1], but they are in-memory algorithms that are not suitable for triangle listing in massive networks that cannot fit into memory. Instead, we need an efficient algorithm that partitions a large graph with limited memory consumption. We devise two efficient graph partitioning algorithms that require only one scan or two scans of the input graph and has linear CPU time complexity.

4.3.1 Sequential Graph Partitioning

Sequential graph partitioning is a simple but very efficient algorithm, which works as follows: we sequentially read the input graph G from disk, whenever the available memory is filled up, the portion of G being read in memory forms a subgraph in the partition. Note that this subgraph is actually an extended subgraph, because each vertex v being read is associated with its adjacency-list $adj_G(v)$.

After we scan G once, we obtain a partition with approximately $(|V_G|+|E_G|)/M$ subgraphs in it. Since the algorithm scans G only once, it requires only $O(scan(|V_G| + |E_G|))$ I/Os and $O(|V_G| + |E_G|)$ CPU time. Furthermore, since the subgraphs in the partition is obtained sequentially one after another as we read G, it allows pipelining such that we can process triangle listing for each subgraph as soon as it is produced, rather than starting triangle listing until the entire partitioning process finishes.

Sequential graph partitioning is effective when graphs exhibit high locality, i.e., vertices are naturally clustered according to the sequential order by which the graph is stored. For example, in a road network proximate vertices are assigned consecutive vertex IDs and they are stored sequentially in nearby positions in the adjacency-list graph representation. In social network graphs, local communities may also be stored together.

Procedure 4 *DominatingSet(G)*

1. Create a bit array A of size $|V_G|$ and set each bit to 0;
2. **for each** v in G, where $A[v] = 0$, **do**
3. Add v to D and mark v and all v's neighbors as 1 in A;
4. **return** D;

Algorithm 5 *Dominating-Set-based Graph Partitioning*

Input: A graph $G = (V_G, E_G)$
Output: A partition of G, $\mathcal{P} = \{G_1, \ldots, G_i, \ldots, G_p\}$

1. Compute a dominating set D of G by invoking *DominatingSet*(G);
2. Divide D into p disjoint subsets of roughly the same size;
3. Create p subgraphs for $\mathcal{P}$ out of the p subsets of D;
4. **for each** $v \in V_G$, where $v \notin D$, **do**
5. Add v (and $adj_G(v)$) to the smallest subgraph in $\mathcal{P}$ that has at least $(deg_{\mathcal{P}}(v)/p)$ neighbors of v;
6. **return** $\mathcal{P}$;

4.3.2 Dominating-Set-based Graph Partitioning

Sequential graph partitioning may be efficient in practice but it gives no guarantee on the number of iterations Algorithm 2 may take. To this end, we propose another graph partitioning algorithm based on the concept of *dominating set.*

A dominating set of a graph G is a subset of vertices $D \subseteq V_G$ such that every vertex in G is either in D or a neighbor of some vertex in D. Computing the minimum dominating set is known to be NP-hard. However, for our purpose of graph partitioning, we do not require a minimum dominating set. More specifically, we devise a one-pass algorithm to compute a dominating set for G as shown in Procedure 4.

In Procedure 4, we first initialize a bit array A of size $|V_G|$ and set each bit to 0. Then, we read G from disk sequentially and for each vertex v (together with $adj_G(v)$) read, we add v to D only if $A[v] = 0$. If v is added to D, then we also set v and all v's neighbors to 1 in A. Thus, all vertices in $V_G \backslash D$ are neighbors of some vertex in D.

We then use D to compute a partition of G, as outlined in Algorithm 5. For triangle listing, we want the vertices in the same subgraph in the partition to be highly connected with each other. We divide D into $p = O((|V_G| + |E_G|)/M)$ subsets and create p initial subgraphs in $\mathcal{P}$. Then, we use the dominating vertices in each subset as seeds to grow each of the p subgraphs by attracting their neighbors. Again, we read G sequentially from disk. For each vertex v (together with $adj_G(v)$) read, let $deg_{\mathcal{P}}(v)$ be the *current* total number of neighbors of v in all the subgraphs in the *current* $\mathcal{P}$, which can be easily obtained by scanning $adj_G(v)$. We choose the subgraph that has at least $(deg_{\mathcal{P}}(v)/p)$ neighbors of v currently, and add v to that subgraph. If there are more than one such subgraph, we add v to the subgraph with the smallest size so far. Upon adding v, we also add $adj_G(v)$ to the subgraph, so that the resultant subgraph is an extended subgraph ready for triangle listing in Algorithm 2.

Whenever the size of a subgraph becomes greater than B (i.e., the block size), we write a block of the subgraph to disk. Thus, we need extra I/Os to first write all subgraphs in $\mathcal{P}$ to disk and then read each subgraph in $\mathcal{P}$ into memory for triangle listing in Algorithm 2. However, the asymptotic I/O complexity of Algorithm 5 is still $O(scan(|V_G| + |E_G|))$. The CPU time complexity is $O(|V_G| + |E_G|)$ since we only need to scan $adj_G(v)$ for each v. But to compute $deg_{\mathcal{P}}(v)$ efficiently we need a look-up table of size $(|V_G| \log_2 p)$ bits. However, in this case, the algorithm is considered as a semi-external-memory algorithm.

Dominating-set-based graph partitioning not only groups neighborhood vertices together, but more importantly it gives a lower bound on the number of intra-partition edges, i.e., edges that can be removed at the end of each iteration of Algorithm 2.

LEMMA 3. *Let $\mathcal{P} = \{G_1, \ldots, G_i, \ldots, G_p\}$ be a partition of G computed by Algorithm 5. Then, the number of intra-partition edges of $\mathcal{P}$ (i.e., edges that are incident on vertices within the same subgraph in $\mathcal{P}$) is at least $|E_G|/p$.*

PROOF. Let $P_{t(v)}$ be the current partition P at the time when a vertex v is added to P at Step 5 of Algorithm 5. For each vertex v, v is added to the smallest subgraph in $\mathcal{P}_{t(v)}$ that has at least $(deg_{\mathcal{P}(v)_{t(v)}}/p)$ neighbors of v. First, there must exist such a subgraph in $\mathcal{P}_{t(v)}$ when v is being added, because v is the neighbor of at least one vertex in D. Thus, the total number of intra-partition edges is at least $\sum_{v \in V_G \setminus D}(deg_{\mathcal{P}_{t(v)}}(v)/p)$. We have $\sum_{v \in V_G \setminus D} deg_{\mathcal{P}_{t(v)}}(v) = |E_G|$ because each edge is counted once by one of its end vertices and no edge exists between any two vertices in D according to Procedure 4. The result thus follows. □

We further show that Lemma 3 implies an upper bound on the total number of iterations required for Algorithm 2 in Lemma 4 in the following subsection.

4.4 Bounding I/O Complexity

We now analyze the overall complexity of our algorithm. As discussed in Section 4.3, graph partitioning at each iteration of Algorithm 2 requires $O(scan(|V_G|+|E_G|))$ I/Os. For triangle listing at each iteration, we only read once the extended subgraph of each subgraph in the partition into memory. Thus, the overall I/O complexity for each iteration is $O(scan(|V_G|+|E_G|))$ (for a shrinking G). Note that both partitioning algorithms in Section 4.3 actually output the extended subgraphs.

From the above analysis, the overall I/O complexity of Algorithm 2 depends on the total number of iterations needed. If we use sequential graph partitioning, the number of iterations depends largely on the locality of the graph data, which varies for different datasets. If we use dominating-set-based graph partitioning, then we can obtain an upper bound on the number of iterations (but require $|V_G| \log_2 p$ bits of memory) for Algorithm 2 as follows.

LEMMA 4. *If Algorithm 2 partitions G by Algorithm 5, then the number of iterations in Algorithm 2 is $O(|E_G|/M)$.*

PROOF. According to Lemma 3, the number of intra-partition edges of $\mathcal{P}$ is at least $|E_G|/p$, which means that at least $|E_G|/p \approx |E_G|/(|E_G|/M) = M$ edges can be removed at the end of each iteration since $p = O((|V_G|+|E_G|)/M) \approx |E_G|/M$. Thus, the total number of iterations in Algorithm 2 is approximately $|E_G|/M$. □

THEOREM 2. *If Algorithm 2 partitions G by Algorithm 5, then Algorithm 2 requires $O(\frac{|E_G|}{M} scan(|V_G| + |E_G|) - (\frac{|E_G|}{M})^2 M)$ I/Os, where $(|V_G|+|E_G|)$ is the original size of the input graph G.*

PROOF. According to Lemma 4, at least M edges are removed from G at the end of each iteration of Algorithm 2. Thus, at the start of the i-th iteration, $(i-1)M$ edges have been removed from the original G. Summing up, the overall complexity of Algorithm 2 is $O(\sum_{i=1}^{|E_G|/M}(scan(|V_G| + |E_G|) - (i-1)M)) = O(\frac{|E_G|}{M} scan(|V_G| + |E_G|) - (\frac{|E_G|}{M})^2 M)$. □

Algorithm 6 *Triangle Counting, Clustering Coeff., and Transitivity*

Input: A graph $G = (V_G, E_G)$
Output: $N_\triangle(v)$ and $\mathcal{C}(v)$ for each $v \in V_G$, $\mathcal{C}(G)$, and $\mathcal{T}(G)$

1. $\forall v \in V_G, N_\triangle(v) \leftarrow 0$;
2. $\mathcal{C}(G) \leftarrow 0$; $N_\triangle(G) \leftarrow 0$; $N_\vee(G) \leftarrow 0$;
3. **for each** triangle $\triangle_{uvw}$ listed by Algorithm 2 **do**
4. $N_\triangle(x) \leftarrow N_\triangle(x) + 1$, for $x \in \{u, v, w\}$;
5. **for each** $v \in V_G$ **do**
6. $\mathcal{C}(v) \leftarrow 2N_\triangle(v)/deg_G(v)(deg_G(v) - 1)$;
7. $\mathcal{C}(G) \leftarrow \mathcal{C}(G) + \mathcal{C}(v)$;
8. $N_\triangle(G) \leftarrow N_\triangle(G) + N_\triangle(v)$;
9. $N_\vee(G) \leftarrow N_\vee(G) + deg_G(v)(deg_G(v) - 1)/2$;
10. $\mathcal{C}(G) \leftarrow \mathcal{C}(G)/|V_G|$;
11. $\mathcal{T}(G) \leftarrow 3N_\triangle(G)/N_\vee(G)$;

Finally, we remark that the CPU time complexity for triangle listing at each iteration of Algorithm 2 is the same as that of the counter-part in-memory algorithm with the same input graph. We thus refer the readers to the related work [26] for details.

5. APPLICATIONS OF TRIANGLE LISTING

Triangle listing has many important applications. Here, we focus on a few popular ones and demonstrate how our algorithm can be applied to benefit these applications in massive networks that cannot fit into main memory.

5.1 Triangle Counting, Clustering Coefficients, and Transitivity

Our algorithm can be readily applied to compute triangle counting, clustering coefficients, and transitivity. For completeness, we first give the definition of the concepts.

Clustering coefficient [36], which is a popular index for network analysis, is defined as follows.

Definition 2 (CLUSTERING COEFFICIENT). *The clustering coefficient of a vertex $v \in V_G$, where $deg_G(v) > 1$, denoted by $\mathcal{C}(v)$, is defined as*

$$\mathcal{C}(v) = \frac{N_\triangle(v)}{N_\vee(v)}. \tag{5}$$

When $deg_G(v) \leq 1$, we define $\mathcal{C}(v) = 0$.
The clustering coefficient of G, denoted by $\mathcal{C}(G)$, is defined as

$$\mathcal{C}(G) = \frac{1}{|V_G|} \sum_{v \in V_G} \mathcal{C}(v). \tag{6}$$

Transitivity [35, 28] is defined as follows.

Definition 3 (TRANSITIVITY). *The transitivity of a graph G, denoted by $\mathcal{C}(G)$, is defined as*

$$\mathcal{T}(G) = \frac{N_\triangle(G)}{\frac{1}{3}\sum_{v \in V_G} N_\vee(v)}. \tag{7}$$

Instead of first computing all triangles and performing a post-processing, our algorithm can be pipelined to compute all the above measures as shown in Algorithm 6. The algorithm is self-explanatory.

Lines 5-9 of Algorithm 6 requires another scan of G, but the asymptotic I/O complexity of the algorithm is the same as Algorithm 2. Updating $N_\triangle(v)$ for all $v \in V_G$ may require $O(|V_G|)$ space, but this can be avoided by writing $N_\triangle(v)$ after processing each extended subgraph and then merging the results of all extended subgraphs. The asymptotic I/O complexity still remains the same since the size of $N_\triangle(v)$ for all v in an extended subgraph is bounded by the size of the subgraph.

5.2 Triangular Vertex Connectivity

Triangular vertex connectivity (also called *3-gonal connectivity*) defines stronger connectivity in a network than single link connectivity, since edges that are in short cyclic component (e.g., triangles) are considered as strong ties [21, 8]. Triangular vertex connectivity is formally defined as follows [29].

Definition 4 (TRIANGULAR-VERTEX-CONNECTIVITY). *Two vertices u and v are* triangularly vertex connected *if there exists a sequence of triangles $\langle \triangle_1, \ldots, \triangle_n \rangle$ such that u is in $\triangle_1$, v is in $\triangle_n$, and either (1) $n = 1$, or (2) for $1 \le i < n$, $\triangle_i$ and $\triangle_{i+1}$ share at least one common vertex.*

Intuitively, if u and v are connected by a single path, then they become disconnected if any edge on the path is removed. On the contrary, if u and v are connected by a sequence of triangles, then removing any edge does not disconnect them.

Triangular vertex connectivity is important in many applications [15, 20, 32, 36]. It defines an equivalence relation $\mathcal{V}^{\triangle}$ on V_G. Two vertices u and v belong to the same equivalence class if they are triangularly vertex connected. The following example further explains the concept.

Example 4. In the graph in Figure 1, there are two equivalence classes defined by triangular vertex connectivity, $\{a, b, c, g, i\}$ and $\{d, e, f, h, j, k, l\}$, which can be obtained by removing the three edges (in bold lines) that are not part of any triangle. Removing any edge from the induced subgraph by any class does not disconnect the vertices in the class, which shows a stronger connectivity. □

The existing algorithm for computing the equivalence classes of $\mathcal{V}^{\triangle}$ is based on triangle listing [8]. However, the algorithm requires random disk access when the graph is stored in disk.

The result of Algorithm 2 can be easily pipelined to compute the equivalence classes of $\mathcal{V}^{\triangle}$. Upon processing each extended subgraph, we first mark the directed edges (u, v), (u, w), (v, w), where $u < v < w$, for each triangle $\triangle_{uvw}$ listed. Then, we write these marked edges to disk. When Algorithm 2 terminates, we read the marked edges one by one to find which equivalent class each $v \in V_G$ belongs to. This can be done by using two lookup tables, C and A, where $C[j] = i$ indicates that i is the smallest class ID that Class j is connected to, and $A[v] = i$ indicates v belongs to Class i. Initially, $C[i] = i$ and $A[v] = \infty$. We keep a counter c which is initialized to 0. For each marked edge (u, v) read, we do the following: (1) if $A[u] = A[v] = \infty$, we set $A[u] = A[v] = c$ and increment c; (2) if $A[u] \neq A[v]$, WLOG assuming $A[u] < A[v]$, we set $C[A[v]] = min(C[A[v]], A[u])$ and $A[v] = A[u]$; (3) otherwise, do nothing. Finally, we scan C once to update each $C[i]$ to the small class ID that Class i is connected to, and update $A[v] = C[A[v]]$, which indicates the class v belongs to.

Since the number of marked edges written to disk for each extended subgraph cannot exceed the size of the subgraph, the asymptotic I/O complexity of computing the equivalence classes of $\mathcal{V}^{\triangle}$ by the above algorithm is the same as Algorithm 2.

6. EXPERIMENTAL RESULTS

We compare our algorithms with the semi-streaming local triangle estimating algorithm (denoted by **Semi-stream**) [9] and the state-of-the-art in-memory triangle listing algorithm (denoted by **In-mem**) [26]. We run the experiments on a machine with an Intel Xeno 2.67GHz CPU and 4GB RAM, and we use g++ 4.4.5 compiler on CentOS 5.4.

Dataset. We use four real datasets: *LiveJournal* (**LJ**), *U.S. road network* (**USRD**), *World Wide Web of UK* (**WebUK**), and *Billion Triple Challenge* (**BTC**). LJ is a social network (http://www.livejournal.com, http://snap.stanford.edu), where vertices are members and edges represent friendship between members. USRD is the road network of United States, where vertices represent intersections and endpoints, and edges represent the roads connecting these intersections or road endpoints. WebUK is obtained from the YAHOO webspam dataset (http://barcelona.research.yahoo.net), where vertices are pages and edges are hyperlinks. BTC is a semantic graph converted from the Billion Triple Challenge 2009 RDF dataset (http://vmlion25.deri.ie), where each vertex represents an object such as a person, a document, and an event, and each edge represents the relationship between two vertices such as "has-author", "links-to", and "has-title". We give the number of vertices and edges, and the storage size on disk, of the datasets in Table 2.

Table 2: Datasets

	LJ	USRD	WebUK	BTC
$\lvert V_G \rvert$	4.8M	24M	106M	165M
$\lvert E_G \rvert$	69M	58M	1,877M	773M
Disk size	809.1MB	969.6MB	20.3GB	10.0GB

6.1 Effectiveness of Partitioning Algorithms

We first show the effectiveness of two graph partitioning algorithms, *sequential graph partitioning* (**Seq**) and *dominating-set-based graph partitioning* (**DS**). We set the available memory size M for partitioning to be $512MB$, $1GB$, $2GB$, and $4GB$, respectively. Table 3 reports the number of iterations Algorithm 2 takes by adopting Seq or DS, on the two large datasets BTC and WebUK. The theoretical upper bound on the number of iterations by adopting DS is also shown.

Table 3: Number of Iterations of Algorithm 2

	M=512MB	M=1GB	M=2GB	M=4GB
BTC (Seq)	$\to \infty$	7	2	1
BTC (DS)	6	3	2	1
BTC (Theoretical)	19	10	5	3
WebUK (Seq)	3	2	2	1
WebUK (DS)	3	2	2	1
WebUK (Theoretical)	29	15	7	4

The result shows that Seq is effective in practice. The number of iterations of Algorithm 2 by adopting Seq is as small as that by adopting DS in most cases, but as shown in Table 4 in Section 6.2 adopting Seq is more efficient than adopting DS since DS requires two more scans of G at each iteration of Algorithm 2.

However, when the available memory becomes smaller (M = 512MB), adopting Seq does not terminate since there is a point that all triangles are Type 3 triangles w.r.t. the partition; thus no more edges can be removed. Such a situation may also happen to other datasets that exhibit low locality. In this case, DS shows its advantage as it gives a guaranteed upper bound on the number of iterations, while our result shows that it indeed has consistent performance. The result also shows that in all cases, the actual number of iterations needed by adopting DS is always less than its theoretical upper bound.

6.2 Triangle Listing

We now report the performance of Algorithm 2 by adopting Seq (denoted by **TL-Seq**) and by adopting DS (denoted by **TL-DS**), compared with In-mem and Semi-stream. We set the available memory size to be 2GB.

Table 4 reports the running time of the different algorithms. We do not report the memory consumption since the smaller datasets

LJ and USRD can fit in memory and all algorithms use roughly the same memory (less than 1GB), while our algorithms and Semi-stream use all available memory for BTC and WebUK. In-mem runs out of memory for BTC and WebUK (BTC and WebUK requires about 10GB and 20GB of memory).

Table 4: Running time (wall-clock time in seconds)

	LJ	USRD	BTC	WebUK
TL-Seq	29.63	6.24	350	2411
TL-DS	29.43	12.46	412	2503
In-mem	32.98	6.68	N.A.	N.A.
Semi-stream ($\overline{\sigma}(N_\triangle(v)) \approx 0.8$)	306	321	3402	7032
Semi-stream ($\overline{\sigma}(N_\triangle(v)) \approx 0.5$)	1275	1683	13711	34722

The result shows that the performance of our algorithms is very competitive. When the graphs can fit into memory, our algorithms have comparable performance compared with In-mem. When the graphs are too large to fit into memory, our algorithms demonstrate great advantage over Semi-stream, which makes multiple passes over the data as do our algorithms.

Let $\overline{\sigma}(N_\triangle(v))$ be the *average approximation error rate* for $N_\triangle(v)$, defined as (|approximate value − exact value|/exact value) averaged over all vertices. We find that Semi-stream takes prohibitively long time to obtain a low $\overline{\sigma}(N_\triangle(v))$. Table 4 reports the running time for Semi-stream by setting $\overline{\sigma}(N_\triangle(v)) \approx 0.8$ and $\overline{\sigma}(N_\triangle(v)) \approx 0.5$. The result shows that Semi-stream is many times slower than both our algorithms for $\overline{\sigma}(N_\triangle(v)) \approx 0.8$ and up to orders of magnitude slower for $\overline{\sigma}(N_\triangle(v)) \approx 0.5$.

From another angle of comparison, if we choose a setting for Semi-stream that it takes slightly longer time than our algorithm TL-Seq, we also report its error rate in Table 5. The result shows that at comparable time, the error rate $\overline{\sigma}(N_\triangle(v))$ of Semi-stream increases significantly.

Table 5: Error rate of Semi-stream at comparable time as TL-Seq

LJ	USRD	BTC	WebUK
97.6%	133.6%	115.4%	95.0%

6.3 Performance on Applications

When the graphs are too large to fit into memory, our algorithm shows significant advantages over approximation algorithms. Table 6 reports the error rate of clustering coefficient of a network and of transitivity approximated by Semi-stream, denoted by $\sigma(\mathcal{C}(G))$ and $\sigma(\mathcal{T}(G))$, respectively. The result shows that, although the error rate of Semi-stream is not too large for those global measures, we obtain exact results at comparable time.

Table 6: Error rate of Semi-stream for $\sigma(\mathcal{C}(G))$ and $\sigma(\mathcal{T}(G))$

BTC ($\sigma(\mathcal{C}(G))$)	**BTC** ($\sigma(\mathcal{T}(G))$)	**WebUK** ($\sigma(\mathcal{C}(G))$)	**WebUK** ($\sigma(\mathcal{T}(G))$)
26.5%	40.2%	12.7%	15.3%

We also assess the performance of using our algorithm for computing triangular-vertex-connectivity-based equivalence classes, compared with the state-of-the-art in-memory algorithm [8] (also denoted by **In-mem** here for simplicity).

Table 7 shows that the running time of our algorithm is comparable with In-mem for LJ and USRD. But for the larger datasets, BTC and WebUK, In-mem runs out of memory while our algorithm still records high efficiency. The result again demonstrates our algorithms are I/O-efficient for processing large graphs.

Table 7: Triangular Vertex Connectivity

	LJ	USRD	BTC	WebUK
TL-Seq	173.1	11.5	380.2	3670.3
In-mem	138.1	9.0	N.A.	N.A.

7. RELATED WORK

The algorithms for triangle listing or counting can be categorized into *exact* algorithms and *approximation* algorithms.

The first non-trivial exact algorithm was a spanning-tree-based algorithm [22, 23], which achieves a running time of $O(|E_G|^{1.5})$. The asymptotic complexity of in-memory exact triangle listing has not been improved since then. However, a number of practical fast algorithms have been proposed that use vertex ordering and efficient data structures such as lookup tables to facilitate the intersection of the adjacency-lists of the neighboring vertices [30, 29, 26]. For triangle counting, the number of triangles can be counted in $O(|E_G|^{1.41})$ time with a fast matrix multiplication algorithm [4]. The basic triangle listing algorithm was also extended to count triads (directed subgraph with three vertices) in directed graph [7]. Maintaining the number of triangles in a dynamic graph was discussed in [16]. All the aforementioned algorithms are in-memory algorithm and require at least $O(|V_G| + |E_G|)$ space.

Approximation algorithms have been proposed for triangle counting in large graphs that cannot fit in memory. Accurate streaming algorithms [3, 6, 14, 10] and sampling algorithm [33] have been proposed to estimate the total number of triangles in a graph. More closely related to estimate the number of triangles formed locally at each vertex in a graph. All these algorithms, however, cannot handle triangle listing, which has a broader range of applications.

Very recently, a parallel algorithm for triangle counting using MapReduce framework [31] has been proposed. Their algorithm is exact and do not require to keep the entire input graph in memory at each individual machine. Algorithms for listing more complex subgraphs are also studied in [13, 12].

8. CONCLUSIONS

We propose an I/O-efficient algorithm for exact triangle listing. To avoid random disk access, we partition the input graph and only process one subgraph in the partition each time. By carefully extracting the subgraphs, we prove that triangle listing in those local subgraphs gives globally correct and complete result. We devise two effective partitioning strategies, one achieving high efficiency in practice while the other bounding the I/O complexity theoretically. Our experimental results on large graphs with up to 106 million vertices and 1,877 million edges show that our algorithm is significantly more efficient than the state-of-the-art approximation algorithm for local triangle counting [9]: at comparable running time and memory, their algorithm records a very high error rate while ours returns the exact result. We also demonstrate the efficiency of applying our algorithm on computing various network measures such as clustering coefficients and transitivity, as well as equivalence classes of the graph based on triangular vertex connectivity. Thus, we believe that our work can benefit many other applications in processing large graphs.

For future work, we plan to study the relationship between the triangles and the k-cores [11] for analyzing massive networks.

Acknowledgment

The authors would like to thank the reviewers for their constructive comments. This research is supported in part by the AcRF Tier-1 Grant (M52020092) from Ministry of Education of Singapore.

9. REFERENCES

[1] A. Abou-Rjeili and G. Karypis. Multilevel algorithms for partitioning power-law graphs. In *IPDPS*, 2006.

[2] A. Aggarwal and S. Vitter, Jeffrey. The input/output complexity of sorting and related problems. *Commun. ACM*, 31(9):1116–1127, 1988.

[3] N. Alon, Y. Matias, and M. Szegedy. The space complexity of approximating the frequency moments. *J. Comput. Syst. Sci.*, 58(1):137–147, 1999.

[4] N. Alon, R. Yuster, and U. Zwick. Finding and counting given length cycles. *Algorithmica*, 17(3):354–364, 1997.

[5] K. Andreev and H. Racke. Balanced graph partitioning. In *SPAA*, pages 120–124, 2004.

[6] Z. Bar-Yossef, K. Hildrum, and F. Wu. Incentive-compatible online auctions for digital goods. In *SODA*, pages 964–970, 2002.

[7] V. Batagelj and A. Mrvar. A subquadratic triad census algorithm for large sparse networks with small maximum degree. *Social Networks*, 23(3):237–243, 2001.

[8] V. Batagelj and M. Zaveršnik. Short cycle connectivity. *Discrete Mathematics*, 307(3-5):310 - 318, 2007.

[9] L. Becchetti, P. Boldi, C. Castillo, and A. Gionis. Efficient semi-streaming algorithms for local triangle counting in massive graphs. In *KDD*, pages 16–24, 2008.

[10] L. S. Buriol, G. Frahling, S. Leonardi, A. Marchetti-Spaccamela, and C. Sohler. Counting triangles in data streams. In *PODS*, pages 253–262, 2006.

[11] J. Cheng, Y. Ke, S. Chu, and M. T. Özsu. Efficient core decomposition in massive networks. In *ICDE*, pages 51–62, 2011.

[12] J. Cheng, Y. Ke, A. W.-C. Fu, J. X. Yu, and L. Zhu. Finding maximal cliques in massive networks. *ACM Transactions on Database Systems.*

[13] J. Cheng, Y. Ke, A. W.-C. Fu, J. X. Yu, and L. Zhu. Finding maximal cliques in massive networks by h*-graph. In *SIGMOD Conference*, pages 447–458, 2010.

[14] D. Coppersmith and R. Kumar. An improved data stream algorithm for frequency moments. In *SODA*, pages 151–156, 2004.

[15] J.-P. Eckmann and E. Moses. Curvature of co-links uncovers hidden thematic layers in the world wide web. *PNAS*, 99:5825–5829, 2002.

[16] D. Eppstein and E. S. Spiro. The *h*-index of a graph and its application to dynamic subgraph statistics. In *WADS*, pages 278–289, 2009.

[17] U. Feige and R. Krauthgamer. A polylogarithmic approximation of the minimum bisection. In *FOCS*, pages 105–115, 2000.

[18] U. Feige, R. Krauthgamer, and K. Nissim. Approximating the minimum bisection size (extended abstract). In *STOC*, pages 530–536, 2000.

[19] C. M. Fiduccia and R. M. Mattheyses. A linear time heuristic for improving network partitions. In *IEEE Design Automation Conference*, 1982.

[20] B. Fritzke. A self-organizing network for unsupervised learning. *TR-03-026*, 42, 1993.

[21] M. Granovetter. The strength of weak ties. *American Journal of Sociology*, 78(6):1360–1380, 1973.

[22] A. Itai and M. Rodeh. Finding a minimum circuit in a graph. In *STOC*, pages 1–10, 1977.

[23] A. Itai and M. Rodeh. Finding a minimum circuit in a graph. *SIAM J. Comput.*, 7(4):413–423, 1978.

[24] G. Karypis and V. Kumar. Parallel multilevel k-way partitioning for irregular graphs. *SIAM Review*, 41(2):278–300, 1999.

[25] B. W. Kernigham and S. Lin. An efficient heuristic procedure for partitioning graphs. *Bell System Technical Journal*, pages 291–308, 1970.

[26] M. Latapy. Main-memory triangle computations for very large (sparse (power-law)) graphs. *Theor. Comput. Sci.*, 407(1-3):458–473, 2008.

[27] R. Milo, S. Shen-Orr, S. Itzkovitz, N. Kashtan, D. Chklovskii, and U. Alon. Network Motifs: Simple Building Blocks of Complex Networks. *Science*, 298(5594):824–827, 2002.

[28] M. E. J. Newman, D. J. Watts, and S. H. Strogatz. Random graph models of social networks. *PNAS*, 99:2566–2572, 2002.

[29] T. Schank. Algorithmic aspects of triangle-based network analysis. *Ph.D. Dissertation, Universität Karlsruhe, Fakultät für Informatik*, 2007.

[30] T. Schank and D. Wagner. Finding, counting and listing all triangles in large graphs, an experimental study. In *WEA*, pages 606–609, 2005.

[31] S. Suri and S. Vassilvitskii. Counting triangles and the curse of the last reducer. In *WWW*, pages 607–614, 2011.

[32] G. Taubin and J. Rossignac. Geometric compression through topological surgery. *ACM Trans. Graph.*, 17(2):84–115, 1998.

[33] C. E. Tsourakakis, U. Kang, G. L. Miller, and C. Faloutsos. Doulion: counting triangles in massive graphs with a coin. In *KDD*, pages 837–846, 2009.

[34] N. Wang, J. Zhang, K.-L. Tan, and A. K. H. Tung. On triangulation-based dense neighborhood graphs discovery. *PVLDB*, 4(2):58–68, 2010.

[35] S. Wasserman and K. Faust. Social network analysis: Methods and applications. *Cambridge University Press*, 1994.

[36] D. J. Watts and S. H. Strogatz. Collective dynamics of 'small-world' networks. *Nature*, 393(6684):440–442, 1998.

Fast Clustering using MapReduce*

(Extended Abstract)†

Alina Ene‡
University of Illinois
Urbana, IL, USA
ene1@illinois.edu

Sungjin Im§
University of Illinois
Urbana, IL, USA
im3@illinois.edu

Benjamin Moseley¶
University of Illinois
Urbana, IL, USA
bmosele2@illinois.edu

ABSTRACT

Clustering problems have numerous applications and are becoming more challenging as the size of the data increases. In this paper, we consider designing clustering algorithms that can be used in MapReduce, the most popular programming environment for processing large datasets. We focus on the practical and popular clustering problems, k-center and k-median. We develop fast clustering algorithms with constant factor approximation guarantees. From a theoretical perspective, we give the first analysis that shows several clustering algorithms are in $\mathcal{MRC}^0$, a theoretical MapReduce class introduced by Karloff et al. [26]. Our algorithms use sampling to decrease the data size and they run a time consuming clustering algorithm such as local search or Lloyd's algorithm on the resulting data set. Our algorithms have sufficient flexibility to be used in practice since they run in a constant number of MapReduce rounds. We complement these results by performing experiments using our algorithms. We compare the empirical performance of our algorithms to several sequential and parallel algorithms for the k-median problem. The experiments show that our algorithms' solutions are similar to or better than the other algorithms' solutions. Furthermore, on data sets that are sufficiently large, our algorithms are faster than the other parallel algorithms that we tested.

Categories and Subject Descriptors

F.2.2 [**Analysis of Algorithms and Problem Complexity**]: Non-numerical Algorithms and Problems

*All authors are first authors.

†This is an extended abstract without proofs. A full version of the paper will be made available on arXiv.

‡Partially supported by NSF grants CCF-0728782 and CCF-1016684.

§Partially supported by NSF grants CCF-0728782, CCF-1016684, and a Samsung Fellowship.

¶Partially supported by NSF grants CCF-0728782 and CCF-1016684.

KDD'11, August 21–24, 2011, San Diego, California, USA.

General Terms

Algorithms, Theory, Experimentation

Keywords

Clustering Algorithms, Approximation Algorithms, Parallel Algorithms, MapReduce, k-center, k-median

1. INTRODUCTION

Clustering data is a fundamental problem in a variety of areas of computer science and related fields. Machine learning, data mining, pattern recognition, networking, and bioinformatics use clustering for data analysis. Consequently, there is a vast amount of research focused on the topic [3, 29, 14, 13, 4, 32, 10, 17, 9, 31]. In the clustering problems that we consider in this paper, the goal is to partition the data into subsets, called clusters, such that the data points assigned to the same cluster are similar according to some metric.

In several applications, it is of interest to classify or group web pages according to their content or cluster users based on their online behavior. One such example is finding communities in social networks. Communities consist of individuals that are closely related according to some relationship criteria. Finding these communities is of interest for applications such as predicting buying behavior or designing targeted marking plans and is an ideal application for clustering. However, the size of the web graph and social network graphs can be quite large; for instance, the web graph consists of a trillion edges [30]. When the amount of data is this large, it is difficult or even impossible for the data to be stored on a single machine, which renders sequential algorithms unusable. In situations where the amount of data is prohibitively large, the MapReduce [16] programming paradigm is used to overcome this obstacle. MapReduce and its open source counterpart Hadoop [33] are distributed computing frameworks designed to process massive data sets.

The MapReduce model is quite novel, since it interleaves sequential and parallel computation. Succinctly, MapReduce consists of several *rounds* of computation. There is a set of machines, each of which has a certain amount of memory available. The memory on each machine is limited, and there is no communication between the machines during a round. In each round, the data is distributed among the machines. The data assigned to a single machine is constrained to be sub-linear in the input size. This restriction is motivated by the fact that the input size is assumed to be very large [26, 15]. After the data is distributed, each of the machines performs some computation on the data that is available to them. The output of these computations is either the final result or it becomes the input of another MapReduce round. A more precise overview of the MapReduce model is given in Section 1.1.

Problems: In this paper, we are concerned with designing clustering algorithms that can be implemented using MapReduce. In particular, we focus on two well-studied problems: metric k-median and k-center. In both of these problems, we are given a set V of n points, together with the distances between any pair of points; we give a precise description of the input representation below. The goal is to choose k of the points. Each of the k chosen points represents a cluster and is referred to as a *center*. Every data point is assigned to the closest center and all of the points assigned to a given point form a cluster. In the k-center problem, the goal is to choose the centers such that the maximum distance between a center and a point assigned to it is minimized. In the k-median problem the objective is to minimize the sum of the distances from the centers to each of the points assigned to the centers. Both of the problems are known to be NP-Hard. Thus previous work has focused on finding approximation algorithms [23, 5, 12, 11, 4, 21, 8]. Many of the existing algorithms are inherently sequential and, with the exception of the algorithms of [8, 20], they are difficult to adapt to a parallel computing setting. We discuss the algorithms of [20] in more detail later.

Input Representation: Let $d : V \times V \rightarrow \mathbb{R}_+$ denote the distance function. The distance function d is a metric, i.e., it has the following properties: (1) $d(x, y) = 0$ if and only if $x = y$, (2) $d(x, y) = d(y, x)$ for all x, y, and (3) $d(x, z) \leq d(x, y) + d(y, z)$ for all x, y, z. The third property is called the triangle inequality; we note that our algorithms only rely on the fact that the distances between points satisfy the triangle inequality.

Now we discuss how the distance function is given to our algorithms. In some settings, the distance function has an implicit compact representation; for example, if the distances between points are shortest path distances in a sparse graph, the graph represents the distance function compactly. However, currently there does not exist a MapReduce algorithm that computes shortest paths in a constant number of rounds, even if the graph is unweighted. This motivates the assumption that we are given the distance function *explicitly* as a set of $\Theta(n^2)$ distances, one for each pair of points, or we are given access to an *oracle* that takes as input two points and returns the distance between them. Throughout this paper, we assume that the distance function is given explicitly. More precisely, we assume that the input is a *weighted complete graph* $G = (V, E)$ that has an edge xy between any two points in V, and the weight of the edge xy is $d(x, y)$[1]. Moreover, we assume that k is at most $O(n^{1-\delta})$ for some constant $\delta > 0$, and the distance between any pair of points is upper bounded by some polynomial in n. These assumptions are justified in part by the fact that the number of points is very large, and by the memory constraints of the MapReduce model; we discuss the MapReduce model in more detail in Section 1.1.

Contributions: We introduce the *first* approximate metric k-median and k-center algorithms designed to run on MapReduce. More precisely, we show the following results.

THEOREM 1.1. *There is a randomized constant approximation algorithm for the k-center problem that, with high probability, runs in $O(\frac{1}{\delta})$ MapReduce rounds and uses memory at most $O(k^2n^\delta)$ on each of the machines for any constant $\delta > 0$.*

THEOREM 1.2. *There is a randomized constant approximation algorithm for the k-median problem that, with high probability, runs in $O(\frac{1}{\delta})$ MapReduce rounds and uses memory at most $O(k^2n^\delta)$ on each of the machines for any constant $\delta > 0$.*

To complement these results, we run our algorithms on randomly generated data sets. For the k-median problem we compare our algorithm to a parallelized implementation of Lloyd's algorithm [28, 7, 1], arguably the most popular clustering algorithm used in practice (see [2, 22] for example), the local search algorithm [4, 21], the best known approximation algorithm for the k-median problem and a partitioning based algorithm that can parallelize any sequential clustering algorithm (see Section 4). Our algorithms achieve a speed-up of 1000x over the local search algorithm and 20x over the parallelized Lloyd's algorithm, a significant improvement in running time. Further, our algorithm's objective is similar to Lloyd's algorithm and the local search algorithm. For the partitioning based algorithm, we show that our algorithm achieves faster running time when the number of points is large. Thus for the k-median problem our algorithms are fast with a small loss in performance. For the k-center problem we compare our algorithm to the well known algorithm of [17, 19], which is the best approximation algorithm for the problem and is quite efficient. Unfortunately, for the k-center problem our algorithm's objective is a factor four worse in some cases. This is due to the sensitivity of the k-center objective to sampling.

Our algorithms show that the k-center and k-median problem belong to the theoretical MapReduce class $\mathcal{MRC}^0$ that was introduced by Karloff et al. [26][2]. Let N denote the total size of the input, and let $0 < \epsilon < 1$ be a fixed constant. A problem is in the MapReduce class $\mathcal{MRC}^0$ if it can be solved using a constant number of rounds and an $O(N^{1-\epsilon})$ number of machines, where each machine has $O(N^{1-\epsilon})$ memory available [26]. Differently said, the problem has an algorithm that uses a sub-linear amount of memory on each machine and a sub-linear number of machines. One of the main motivations for these restrictions is that a typical MapReduce input is very large and it might not be possible to store the entire input on a single machine. Moreover, the size of the input might be much larger than the number of machines available. We discuss the theoretical MapReduce model in Section 1.1. Our assumptions on the size of k and the point distances are needed in order to show that the memory that our algorithms use on each machine is sub-linear in the total input size. For instance, without the assumption on k, we will not be able to fit k points in the memory available on a machine.

Adapting Existing Algorithms to MapReduce: Previous work on designing algorithms for MapReduce are generally based on the following approach. Partition the input and assign each partition to a unique machine. On each machine, we perform some computation that eliminates a large fraction of the input. We collect the results of this computations on a single machine, which can store the data since the data has been sparsified. On this machine, we perform some computation and we return the final solution. We can use a similar approach for the k-center and k-median problems. We partition the points across the machines. We cluster each of the partitions. We select one point from each cluster and put all of the selected points on a single machine. We cluster these points and output the solution. Indeed, a similar algorithm was considered by Guha et al. [20] for the k-median problem in the streaming model. We give the details of how to implement this algorithm in

[1]We note that some of the techniques in this paper extend to the setting in which the distance function is given as an oracle.

[2]Recall that we only consider instances of the problems in which k is sub-linear in the number of points, and the distances between points are upper bounded by some polynomial in n.

MapReduce in Section 4 along with an analysis of the algorithm's approximation guarantees. Unfortunately, the total running time for the algorithm can be quite large, since it runs a costly clustering algorithm on $\Omega(k\sqrt{n/k})$ points. Further, this algorithm requires $\Omega(kn)$ memory on each of the machines.

Another strategy for developing algorithms for k-center and k-median that run in MapReduce is to try to adapt existing parallel algorithms. To the best of our knowledge, the only parallel algorithms known with provable guarantees were given by Blelloch and Tangwongsan [8]; Blelloch and Tangwongsan [8] give the first PRAM algorithms for k-center and k-median. Unfortunately, these algorithms assume that the number of machines available is $\Omega(N^2)$, where N is the total input size, and there is some memory available in the system that can be accessed by all of the machines. These assumptions are too strong for the algorithms to be in used in MapReduce. Indeed, the requirements that the machines have a limited amount of memory and that there is no communication between the machines is what differentiates the MapReduce model from standard parallel computing models. Another approach is to try to adapt algorithms that were designed for the streaming model. Guha et al. [20] have given a k-median algorithm for the streaming model; with some work, we can adapt one of the algorithms in [20] to the MapReduce model. However, this algorithm's approximation ratio degrades exponentially in the number of rounds.

Related Work: There has been a large amount of work on the metric k-median and k-center problems. Due to space constraints, we focus only on closely related work that we have not already mentioned. Both problems are known to be NP-Hard. Bartal [6, 5] gave an algorithm for the k-median problem that achieves an $O(\log n \log\log n)$ approximation ratio. Later Charikar et al. gave the first constant factor approximation of $6+\frac{2}{3}$ [12]. This approach was based on LP rounding techniques. The best known approximation algorithm achieves a $3+\frac{2}{c}$ approximation in $O(n^c)$ time [4, 21]; this algorithm is based on the local search technique. On the other hand, Jain et al. [24] have shown that there does not exist an $1+(2/e)$ approximation for the k-median problem unless NP $\subseteq$ DTIME$(n^{O(\log\log n)})$. For the k-center problem, two simple algorithms are known which achieve a 2-approximation [23, 17, 19] and this approximation ratio is tight assuming that P $\neq$ NP.

MapReduce has received a significant amount of attention recently. Most previous work has been on designing practical heuristics to solve large scale problems [25, 27]. Recent papers [26, 18] have focused on developing computational models that abstract the power and limitations of MapReduce. Finally, there has been work on developing algorithms and approximation algorithms that fit into the MapReduce model [26, 15]. This line of work has shown that problems such as minimum spanning tree, maximum coverage, and connectivity can be solved efficiently using MapReduce.

1.1 MapReduce Overview

In this section we give a high-level overview of the MapReduce model; for a more detailed description, see [26]. The data is represented as $\langle key; value\rangle$ pairs. The key acts as an address of the machine to which the $value$ needs to be sent to. A MapReduce round consists of three stages: map, shuffle, and reduce. The map phase processes the data as follows. The algorithm designer specifies a map function μ, which we refer to as a *mapper*. The mapper takes as input a $\langle key; value\rangle$ pair, and it outputs a sequence of $\langle key; value\rangle$ pairs. Intuitively, the mapper maps the data stored in the $\langle key; value\rangle$ pair to a machine. In the map phase, the map function is applied to all $\langle key; value\rangle$ pairs. In the shuffle phase, all $\langle key; value\rangle$ pairs with a given key are sent to the same machine; this is done automatically by the underlying system. The reduce phase processes the $\langle key; value\rangle$ pairs created in the map phase as follows. The algorithm designer specifies a reduce function ρ, which we refer to as a *reducer*. The reducer takes as input all the $\langle key; value\rangle$ pairs that have the same key, and it outputs a sequence of $\langle key; value\rangle$ pairs which have the same key as the input pairs; these pairs are either the final output, or they become the input of the next MapReduce round. Intuitively, the reducer performs some sequential computation on all the data that is stored on a machine. The mappers and reducers are constrained to run in time that is polynomial in the size of the initial input, and not their input.

The theoretical $\mathcal{MRC}$ class was introduced in [26]. The class is designed to capture the practical restrictions of MapReduce as faithfully as possible; a detailed justification of the model can be found in [26]. In addition to the constraints on the mappers and reducers, there are three types of restrictions in $\mathcal{MRC}$: constraints on the number of machines used, on the memory available on each of the machines, and on the number of rounds of computation. If the input to a problem is of size N then an algorithm is in $\mathcal{MRC}$ if it uses at most $N^{1-\epsilon}$ machines, each with at most $N^{1-\epsilon}$ memory for some constant $\epsilon > 0$[3]. Notice that this implies that the total memory available is $O(N^{2-2\epsilon})$. Thus the difficulty of designing algorithms for the MapReduce model does not come from the lack of total memory. Rather, it stems from the fact that the memory available on each machine is limited; in particular, the entire input does not fit on a single machine. Not allowing the entire input to be placed on a single machine makes designing algorithms difficult, since a machine is only aware of a subset of the input. Indeed, because of this restriction, it is currently not known whether fundamental graph problems such as shortest paths or maximum matchings can be computed in a constant number of rounds, even if the graphs are unweighted.

In the following, we state the precise restrictions on the resources available to an algorithm for a problem in the class $\mathcal{MRC}^0$.

- **Memory**: The total memory used on a specific machine is at most $O(N^{1-\epsilon})$.
- **Machines**: The total number of machines used is $O(N^{1-\epsilon})$.
- **Rounds**: The number of rounds is constant.

2. ALGORITHMS

In this section we describe our clustering algorithms `MapReduce-kCenter` and `MapReduce-kMedian`. For both of our algorithms, we will parameterize the amount of memory needed on a machine. For the MapReduce setting, the amount of memory our algorithms require on each of the machines is parameterized by $\delta > 0$ and we assume that the memory is $\Omega(k^2 n^\delta)$. It is further assumed that the number of machines is large enough to store all of the input data across the machines. Both algorithms use `Iterative-Sample` as a subroutine which uses sampling ideas from [32]. The role of `Iterative-Sample` is to get a substantially smaller subset of points that represents all of the points well. To achieve this, `Iterative-Sample` performs the following computation iteratively: in each iteration, it adds a small sample of points to the final sample, it determines which points are "well represented" by the sample, and it recursively considers only the points that are not well represented. More precisely, after sampling, `Iterative-Sample` discards most points that are close to the current sample, and it recurses on the remaining (unsampled) points. The algorithm repeats this procedure until the number of points that are still unrepresented is small and all such points are added to the sample. Once we have a good sample, we

[3]The algorithm designer can choose ϵ.

run a clustering algorithm on just the sampled points. Knowing that the sampling represents all unsampled points well, a good clustering of the sampled points will also be a good clustering of all of the points. Here the clustering algorithm used will depend on the problem considered. In the following section, we show how `Iterative-Sample` can be implemented in the sequential setting to highlight the high level ideas. Then we show how to extend the algorithms to the MapReduce setting.

2.1 Sampling Sequentially

In this section, the sequential version of the sampling algorithm is discussed. When we mention the distance of a point x to a set S, we mean the minimum distance between x and any point in S. Our algorithm is parameterized by a constant $0 < \epsilon < \frac{\delta}{2}$ whose value can be changed depending on the system specifications. Simply, the value of ϵ determines the sample size. For each of our algorithms there is a natural trade-off between the sample size and the running time of the algorithm.

Algorithm 1 `Iterative-Sample`(V, E, k, ϵ):

1: Set $S \leftarrow \emptyset$, $R \leftarrow V$.
2: **while** $|R| > \frac{4}{\epsilon}kn^{\epsilon} \log n$ **do**
3: Add each point in R with probability $\frac{9kn^{\epsilon}}{|R|} \log n$ independently to S.
4: Add each point in R with probability $\frac{4n^{\epsilon}}{|R|} \log n$ independently to H.
5: $v \leftarrow$ `Select`(H, S)
6: Find the distance of each point $x \in R$ to S. Remove x from R if this distance is smaller than the distance of v to S.
7: **end while**
8: Output $C := S \cup R$

Algorithm 2 `Select`(H, S):

1: For each point $x \in H$, find the distance of x to S.
2: Order the points in H according to their distance to S from farthest to smallest.
3: Let v be the point that is in the $8 \log n$th position in the ordering.
4: Return v.

The algorithm `Iterative-Sample` maintains a set of sampled points S and a set of points R that contains the set of points that are not well represented by the current sample. The algorithm repeately adds new points to the sample. By adding more points to the sample, S will represent more points well. More points are added to S until the number of remaining points decreases below the threshold given in line 2. The point v chosen in line 5 serves as the pivot to determine which points are well represented: if a point x is closer to the sample S than the pivot v, the point x is considered to be well represented by S and dropped from R. Finally, `Iterative-Sample` returns the union of S and R. Note that R must be returned since R is not well represented by S even at the end of the while loop.

2.2 MapReduce Algorithms

First we show a MapReduce version of `Iterative-Sample` and then we give MapReduce algorithms for the k-center and k-median problems. For these algorithms we assume that for any set S and parameter η, the set S can be arbitrarily partitioned into sets of size $|S|/\eta$ by the mappers. To see that this is the case, we refer the reader to [26].

Algorithm 3 `MapReduce-Iterative-Sample`(V, E, k, ϵ):

1: Set $S \leftarrow \emptyset$, $R \leftarrow V$.
2: **while** $|R| > \frac{4}{\epsilon}kn^{\epsilon} \log n$ **do**
3: The mappers arbitrarily partition R into $\lceil |R|/n^{\epsilon} \rceil$ sets of size at most $\lceil n^{\epsilon} \rceil$. Each of these sets is mapped to a unique reducer.
4: For a reducer i, let R^i denote the points assigned to the reducer. Reducer i adds each point in R^i to a set S^i independently with probability $\frac{9kn^{\epsilon}}{|R|} \log n$ and also adds each point in R^i to a set H^i independently with probability $\frac{4n^{\epsilon}}{|R|} \log n$.
5: Let $H := \bigcup_{1 \leq i \leq \lceil n^{\epsilon} \rceil} H^i$ and $S := S \cup (\bigcup_{1 \leq i \leq \lceil n^{\epsilon} \rceil} S^i)$. The mappers assign H and S to a single machine along with all edge distances from each point in H to each point in S.
6: The reducer whose input is H and S sets $v \leftarrow$ `Select`(H, S).
7: The mappers arbitrarily partition the points in R into $\lceil n^{1-\epsilon} \rceil$ subsets, each of size at most $\lceil |R|/n^{1-\epsilon} \rceil$. Let R^i for $1 \leq i \leq \lceil n^{1-\epsilon} \rceil$ denote these sets. Let v, R^i, S, the distances between each point in R^i and each point in S be assigned to reducer i.
8: Reducer i finds the distance of each point $x \in R^i$ to S. The point x is removed from R^i if this distance is smaller than the distance of v to S.
9: Let $R := \bigcup_{i \in [\eta]} R^i$.
10: **end while**
11: Output $C := S \cup R$

The following propositions give the theoretical guarantees of the algorithm; these propositions can also serve as a guide for choosing an appropriate value for the parameter ϵ. If the probability of an event is $1 - O(1/n)$, we say that the event occurs with high probability, which we abbreviate as w.h.p. The first two propositions follow from the fact that, w.h.p., each iteration of `Iterative-Sample` decreases the number of remaining points — i.e., the size of the set R — by a factor of $\Theta(n^{\epsilon})$. We give the proofs of these propositions in the next section. Note that the propositions imply that our algorithm belongs to $\mathcal{MRC}^0$.

PROPOSITION 2.1. *The number of iterations of the while loop of* `Iterative-Sample` *is at most* $O(\frac{1}{\epsilon})$ *w.h.p.*

PROPOSITION 2.2. *The set returned by* `Iterative-Sample` *has size* $O(\frac{1}{\epsilon}kn^{\epsilon} \log n)$ *w.h.p.*

PROPOSITION 2.3. `MapReduce-Iterative-Sample` *is a MapReduce algorithm that requires* $O(\frac{1}{\epsilon})$ *rounds when machines have memory* $O(kn^{\delta})$ *for a constant* $\delta > 2\epsilon$ *w.h.p.*

PROOF. Consider a single iteration of the while loop. Each iteration takes a constant number of MapReduce rounds. By Proposition 2.1, the number of iterations of this loop is $O(\frac{1}{\epsilon})$, and therefore the number of rounds is $O(\frac{1}{\epsilon})$. The memory needed on a machine is dominated by the memory required by Step (7). The size of S is $O(\frac{1}{\epsilon}kn^{\epsilon} \log n)$ by Proposition 2.2. Further, the size of R^i is at most $n/n^{1-\epsilon} = n^{\epsilon}$. Let η be the maximum number of bits needed to represent the distance from one point to another. Thus the total memory needed on a machine is $O(\frac{1}{\epsilon}kn^{\epsilon} \log n \cdot n^{\epsilon} \cdot \eta)$, the memory needed to store the distances from points in R^i to points in S. By assumption $\eta = O(\log n)$, thus the total memory needed on a machine is upper bounded by $O(\frac{1}{\epsilon}kn^{2\epsilon} \log^2 n)$. By setting δ to be a constant slightly larger than 2ϵ, the proposition follows. □

Once we have this sampling algorithm, our algorithm `MapReduce-kCenter` for the k-center problem is fairly straightforward. This is the algorithm considered in Theorem 1.1. The memory needed by the algorithm is dominated by storing the pairwise distances between points in C on a single machine. By Proposition 2.2 and the assumption that the maximum distance between any two points can be represented using $O(\log n)$ bits, w.h.p. the memory needed is $O((\frac{1}{\epsilon}kn^{\epsilon}\log n)^2 \cdot \log n) = O(n^{\delta}k^2)$, where δ is a constant greater than 2ϵ.

Algorithm 4 `MapReduce-kCenter`(V, E, k, ϵ):

1: Let $C \leftarrow$ `Iterative-Sample`(V, E, k, ϵ).
2: Map C and all of pairwise distances between points in C to a reducer.
3: The reducer runs a k-center clustering algorithm $\mathcal{A}$ on C.
4: Return the set constructed by $\mathcal{A}$.

However, for the k-median problem, the sample must contain more information than just the set of sampled points. This is because the k-median objective considers the sum of the distances to the centers. To ensure that we can map a good solution for the points in the sample to a good solution for all of the points, for each unsampled point x, we select the sampled point that is closest to x (if there are several points that are closest to x, we pick one arbitrarily). Additionally, we assign a weight to each sampled point y that is equal to the number of unsampled points that picked y as its closest point. This is done so that, when we cluster the sampled points on a single machine, we can take into account the effect of the unsampled points on the objective. For a point x and a set of points A, let $d(x, A)$ denote the minimum distance from the point $x \in V$ to a point in A, i.e., $d(x, A) = \min_{y \in A} d(x, y)$. The algorithm `MapReduce-kMedian` is the following.

Algorithm 5 `MapReduce-kMedian`(V, E, k, ϵ):

1: Let $C \leftarrow$ `MapReduce-Iterative-Sample`(V, E, k, ϵ)
2: The mappers arbitrarily partition V into $\lceil n^{1-\epsilon} \rceil$ sets of size at most $\lceil n^{\epsilon} \rceil$. Let V^i for $1 \le i \le \lceil n^{1-\epsilon} \rceil$ be the partitioning.
3: The mappers assign V^i, C and all distances between points in V^i and C to reducer i for all $1 \le i \le \lceil n^{1-\epsilon} \rceil$.
4: Each reducer i, for each $y \in C$, computes $w^i(y) = |\{x \in V^i \setminus C \mid d(x, y) = d(x, C)\}|$.
5: Map all of the weights $w^i(\cdot)$, C and the pairwise distances between all points in C to a single reducer.
6: The reducer computes $w(y) = \sum_{i \in [m]} w^i(y) + 1$ for all $y \in C$.
7: The reducer runs a weighted k-median clustering algorithm $\mathcal{A}$ on that machine with $\langle C, w, k \rangle$ as input.
8: Return the set constructed by $\mathcal{A}$.

The `MapReduce-kMedian` algorithm performs additional rounds to give a weight to each point in the sample C. We remark that these additional rounds can be easily removed by gradually performing this operation in each iteration of `MapReduce-Iterative-Sample`. The maximum memory used by a machine in `MapReduce-kMedian` is bounded similarly as `MapReduce-kCenter`. The proof of all propositions and theorems will be given in the next section. The algorithm `MapReduce-kMedian` is the algorithm considered in Theorem 1.2. Notice that both `MapReduce-kMedian` and `MapReduce-kCenter` use some clustering algorithm as a subroutine. The running times of these clustering algorithms depend on the size of the sample and therefore there is a trade-off between the running times of these algorithms and the number of MapReduce rounds.

3. ANALYSIS

3.1 Subroutine: Iterative-Sample

This section is devoted to the analysis of `Iterative-Sample`, the main subroutine of our clustering algorithms. Before we give the analysis, we introduce some notation. Let S^* denote any set. We will show several lemmas and theorems that hold for any set S^*, and in the final step, we will set S^* to be the optimal set of centers. The reader may read the lemmas and theorems assuming that S^* is the optimal set of centers. We assign each point $x \in V$ to its closest point in S^*, breaking ties arbitrarily but consistently. Let x^{S^*} be the point in S^* to which x is assigned; if x is in S^*, we assign x to itself. Let $S^*(x)$ be the set of all points assigned to $x \in S^*$.

We say that a point x is *satisfied* by S with respect to S^* if $d(S, x^{S^*}) \le d(x, x^{S^*})$. If S and S^* are clear from the context, we will simply say that x is satisfied. We say that x is *unsatisfied* if it is not satisfied. Throughout the analysis, for any point x in V and any subset $S \subseteq V$, we will let x^S denote the point in S that is closest to x.

We now explain the intuition behind the definition of "satisfied". Our sampling subroutine's output C may not include each center in S^*. However, a point x could be "satisfied", even though $x^{S^*} \notin C$, by including a point in C that is closer to x than x^{S^*}. Intuitively, if all points are satisfied, our sampling algorithm returned a very representative sample of all points, and our clustering algorithms will perform well. However, we cannot guarantee that all points are satisfied. Instead, we will show that the number of unsatisfied points is small and their contribution to the clustering cost is negligible compared to the satisfied points' contribution. This will allow us to upper bound the distance between the unsatisfied points and the final solution constructed by our algorithm by the cost of the optimal solution.

Since the sets described in `Iterative-Sample` change in each iteration, for the purpose of the analysis, we let R_ℓ, S_ℓ, and H_ℓ denote the sets R, S, and H at the beginning of iteration ℓ. Note that $R_1 = V$ and $S_1 = \emptyset$. Let D_ℓ denote the set of points that are removed (deleted) during iteration ℓ. Note that $R_{\ell+1} = R_\ell - D_\ell$. Let U_ℓ denote the set of points in R_ℓ that are not satisfied by $S_{\ell+1}$ with respect to S^*. Let C denote the set of points that `Iterative-Sample` returns. Let U denote the set of all unsatisfied points by C with respect to S^*. If one point is satisfied by S_ℓ with respect to S^* then it is also satisfied by C with respect to S^*, and therefore $U \subseteq \bigcup_{\ell \ge 1} U_\ell$.

We start by upper bounding $|U_\ell|$, the number of unsatisfied points at the end of iteration ℓ.

LEMMA 3.1. *Let S^* be any set with no more than k points. Consider iteration ℓ of `Iterative-Sample`, where $\ell \ge 1$. Then* $\textbf{\textit{Pr}}\left[|U_\ell| \ge \frac{|R_\ell|}{3n^{\epsilon}}\right] \le \frac{1}{n^2}$.

Recall that we selected a threshold point v to discard the points that are well represented by the current sample S. Let $\mathrm{rank}_{R_\ell}(v)$ denote the number of points x in R_ℓ such that the distance from x to S is greater than the distance from v to S. The proof of the following lemma follows easily from the Chernoff inequality.

LEMMA 3.2. *Let S^* be any set with no more than k points. Consider any ℓ-th iteration of the while loop of*

Iterative-Sample. *Let* v_ℓ *denote the threshold in the current iteration, i.e. the* $(8\log n)$*-th farthest point in* H_ℓ *from* $S_{\ell+1}$*. Then we have* $\textbf{Pr}[\frac{|R_\ell|}{n^\epsilon} \le rank(v_\ell) \le \frac{4|R_\ell|}{n^\epsilon}] \ge 1 - \frac{2}{n^2}$.

COROLLARY 3.3. *Consider any* ℓ*-th iteration of the while loop of* Iterative-Sample. *Then* $\textbf{Pr}[\frac{|R_\ell|}{n^\epsilon} \le |R_{\ell+1}| \le \frac{4|R_\ell|}{n^\epsilon}] \ge 1 - \frac{2}{n^2}$.

The above corollary immediately implies Proposition 2.1 and 2.2. Now we show how to map each unsatisfied point to a satisfied point such that no two unsatisfied points are mapped to the same satisfied point; that is, the map is injective. Such a mapping will allow us to bound the cost of unsatisfied points by the cost of the optimal solution. The following theorem is the core of our analysis. The theorem defines a mapping $p : U \to V$; for each point x, we refer to $p(x)$ as the *proxy* point of x.

THEOREM 3.4. *Consider any set* $S^* \subseteq V$*. Let* C *be the set of points returned by* Iterative-Sample*. Let* U *be the set of all points in* $V - C$ *that are unsatisfied by* C *with respect to* S^**. Then w.h.p., there exists an injective function* $p : U \to V \setminus U$ *such that, for any* $x \in U$, $d(p(x), S^*) \ge d(x, C)$.

3.2 MapReduce-KCenter

This section is devoted to proving Theorem 1.1. For the sake of analysis, we will consider the following variant of the k-center problem. In the kCenter(V, T) problem, we are given two sets V and $T \subseteq V$ of points in a metric space, and we want to select a subset $S^* \subseteq T$ such that $|S^*| \le k$ and S^* minimizes $\max_{x \in V} d(x, S)$ among all sets $S \subseteq T$ with at most k points. For notational simplicity, we let OPT(V, T) denote the optimal solution for the problem kCenter(V, T). Depending on the context, OPT(V, T) may denote the cost of the solution. Since we are interested eventually in OPT(V, V), we let OPT := OPT(V, V).

PROPOSITION 3.5. *Let* C *be the set of centers returned by* Iterative-Sample*. Then w.h.p. we have that for any* $x \in V$, $d(x, C) \le 2$OPT.

PROPOSITION 3.6. *Let* C *be the set of centers returned by* Iterative-Sample*. Then w.h.p. we have* OPT$(C, C) \le$ OPT$(V, C) \le$ OPT.

THEOREM 3.7. *If* $\mathcal{A}$ *is an algorithm that achieves an* α*-approximation for the* k *center problem, then w.h.p. the algorithm* MapReduce-kCenter *achieves a* $(4\alpha + 2)$*-approximation for the* k *center problem.*

By setting the algorithm $\mathcal{A}$ to be the 2-approximation of [17, 19], we complete the proof Theorem 1.1.

3.3 MapReduce-KMedian

In the following, we will consider the following variants of the k-median problem similar to the variant of the k-center problem considered in the previous section. In the kMedian(V, T) problem, we are given two sets V and $T \subseteq V$ of points in a metric space, and we want to select a subset $S^* \subseteq T$ such that $|S^*| \le k$ and S^* minimizes $\sum_{x \in V} d(x, S)$ among all sets $S \subseteq T$ with at most k points. We let OPT(V, T) denote a fixed optimal solution for kMedian(V, T) or the optimal cost depending on the context. Note that we are interested in obtaining a solution that is comparable to OPT(V, V). Hence, for notational simplicity, we let OPT := OPT(V, V). In the Weighted-kMedian(V, w) problem, we are given a set V of points in a metric space such that each point x has a weight $w(x)$, and we want to select a subset $S^* \subseteq V$ such that $|S^*| \le k$ and S^* minimizes $\sum_{x \in V} w(x) d(x, S)$ among all sets $S \subseteq V$ with at most k points. Let OPT$^w(V, w)$ denote a fixed optimal solution for a Weighted-kMedian(V, w).

Recall that MapReduce-kMedian computes an approximate k-medians on C with each point x in C having a weight $w(x)$. Hence we first show that we can obtain a good approximate k-medians using only the points in C.

PROPOSITION 3.8. *Let* $S^* :=$ OPT*. Let* C *be the set of centers returned by* Iterative-Sample*. Then w.h.p., we have that* $\sum_{x \in V} d(x, C) \le 3$OPT.

PROPOSITION 3.9. *Let* C *be the set returned by* Iterative-Sample*. Then w.h.p.,* OPT$(V, C) \le 5$OPT.

So far we have shown that we can obtain a good approximate solution for the kMedian(V, V) even when we are restricted to C. However, we need a stronger argument, since MapReduce-kMedian only sees the weighted points in C and not the entire point set V.

PROPOSITION 3.10. *Consider any subset of points* $C \subseteq V$*. For each point* $y \in C$*, let* $w(y) = |\{x \in V - C \mid x^C = y\}| + 1$*. Then we have* OPT$^w(C, w) \le 2OPT(V, C)$.

THEOREM 3.11. *If* $\mathcal{A}$ *is an algorithm that achieves an* α*-approximation for* Weighted-kMedian*, w.h.p. the algorithm* MapReduce-kMedian *achieves a* $(10\alpha + 3)$*-approximation for* kMedian.

Recall that there is a $(3 + 2/c)$ approximation algorithm for k-median that runs in $O(n^c)$ time [4, 21]. In order to complete the proof of Theorem 1.2, we pick a constant c and we use the $(3 + 2/c)$-approximation algorithm.

4. EXPERIMENTS

In this section we give an experimental study of the algorithms introduced in this paper. The focus for this section is on the k-median objective because this is where our algorithm gives the largest increase in performance. Unfortunately, our sampling algorithm does not perform well for the k-center metric. This is because the k-center objective is quite sensitive to sampling. Since the maximum distance from a point to a center is considered in the objective, if the sampling algorithm misses even one important point then the objective can substantially increase. From now on, we only consider the k-median problem. In the following, we describe the algorithms we tested and we give an overview of the experiments and the results.

4.1 Implemented Algorithms

We compare our algorithm MapReduce-kMedian to several algorithms. Recall that MapReduce-kMedian uses Iterative-Sample as a sub-procedure and we have shown that MapReduce-kMedian gives a constant approximation when the local search algorithm [4, 21] is applied on the sample that was obtained by Iterative-Sample. We also consider Lloyd's algorithm together with the sampling procedure Iterative-Sample; that is, in MapReduce-kMedian, the algorithm $\mathcal{A}$ is Lloyd's algorithm and it takes as input the sample constructed by Iterative-Sample. Note that Lloyd's algorithm does not give an approximation guarantee. However, it is the most popular algorithm for clustering in practice and therefore it is worth testing its performance. We will use

	Number of points	10,000	20,000	40,000	100,000	200,000	400,000	1,000,000
cost	Parallel-Lloyd	1.000	1.000	1.000	1.000	1.000	1.000	1.000
	Divide-Lloyd	1.030	1.088	1.132	1.033	1.051	0.994	1.023
	Divide-LocalSearch	0.999	1.024	1.006	0.999	1.008	0.999	1.010
	Sampling-Lloyd	1.086	1.165	1.051	1.138	1.068	1.095	1.132
	Sampling-LocalSearch	1.018	1.019	1.011	1.006	1.024	1.025	1.029
	LocalSearch	0.948	0.964	0.958	N/A	N/A	N/A	N/A
time	Parallel-Lloyd	0.0	3.3	6.0	18.0	29.3	52.7	205.7
	Divide-Lloyd	0.0	0.3	0.3	1.3	1.0	1.0	2.7
	Divide-LocalSearch	5.0	5.0	5.0	6.0	9.0	19.0	70.7
	Sampling-Lloyd	0.3	0.0	0.3	0.7	1.3	3.0	4.0
	Sampling-LocalSearch	1.7	2.3	3.0	4.3	6.0	8.3	11.0
	LocalSearch	666.7	943.0	2569.3	N/A	N/A	N/A	N/A

Figure 1: The relative cost and running time of clustering algorithms when the number of points is not too large. The costs are normalized to that of `Parallel-Lloyd`. The running time is given in seconds.

	Number of points	2,000,000	5,000,000	10,000,000
cost	Parallel-Lloyd	1.000	1.000	1.000
	Divide-Lloyd	1.018	1.036	1.000
	Sampling-Lloyd	1.064	1.106	1.073
	Sampling-LocalSearch	1.027	1.019	1.015
time	Parallel-Lloyd	458.0	1333.3	702.3
	Divide-Lloyd	8.3	24.7	50.7
	Sampling-Lloyd	8.0	18.3	38.0
	Sampling-LocalSearch	16.3	29.3	86.3

Figure 2: The relative cost and running time of the scalable algorithms when the number of points are large. The costs were normalized to that of `Parallel-Lloyd`. The running time is given in seconds.

`Sampling-LocalSearch` to refer to `MapReduce-kMedian` with the local search algorithm as $\mathcal{A}$ and we will use `Sampling-Lloyd` to refer to `MapReduce-kMedian` with Lloyd's algorithm as $\mathcal{A}$. Note that the only difference between `Sampling-LocalSearch` and `Sampling-Lloyd` is the clustering algorithm chosen as $\mathcal{A}$ in `MapReduce-kMedian`.

We also implement the local search algorithm and Lloyd's algorithm without sampling. The local search algorithm, denoted as `LocalSearch`, is the only sequential algorithm among all algorithms that we implemented [4, 21]. We implement a parallelized version of Lloyd's algorithm, `Parallel-Lloyd` [28, 7, 1]. This implementation of Lloyd's algorithm parallelizes a sub-procedure of the sequential Lloyd's algorithm. The parallel version of Lloyd's gives the same solution as the sequential version of Lloyd's; the only difference between the two implementations is the parallelization. We give a more formal description of the parallel Lloyd's algorithm below.

Finally, we implement clustering algorithms based on a simple partitioning scheme used to adapt sequential algorithms to the parallel setting. In the partition scheme `MapReduce-Divide-kMedian` we consider, points are partitioned into ℓ sets of size $\lceil \frac{n}{\ell} \rceil$. In parallel, centers are computed for each of the partitions. Then all of the centers computed are combined into a single set and the centers are clustered. We formalize this in the algorithm `MapReduce-Divide-kMedian`. We evaluated the local search algorithm and Lloyd's algorithm coupled with this partition scheme. Throughout this section, we use `Divide-LocalSearch` for the local search together with this partition scheme. We call Lloyd's algorithm coupled with the partition scheme as `Divide-Lloyd`. We give the details of the partition framework `MapReduce-Divide-kMedian` shortly.

The following is a summary of the algorithms we implemented:

- `LocalSearch`: Local Search
- `Parallel-Lloyd`: Parallel Lloyd's
- `Sampling-LocalSearch`: Sampling and Local Search
- `Sampling-Lloyd`: Sampling and Lloyd's
- `Divide-LocalSearch`: Partition and Local Search
- `Divide-Lloyd`: Partition and Lloyd's

A careful reader may note that Lloyd's algorithm is generally used for the k-means objective and not for k-median. Lloyd's algorithm is more commonly used for k-means, but it can be used for k-median as well, and it is one of the most popular clustering algorithms in practice. We note that the parallelized version of Lloyd's algorithm we introduce only works with points in Euclidean space.

Parallel Lloyd's Algorithm: We give a sketch of parallelized implementation of Lloyd's algorithm used in the experiments. More details can be found in [7, 1]. The algorithm begins by partitioning the points evenly across the machines and these points will remain on the machines. The algorithm initializes the k centers to an arbitrary set of points. In each iteration, the algorithm improves the centers as follows. The mapper sends the k centers to each of the machines. On each machine, the reducer clusters the points on the machine by assigning each point to its closest center. For each cluster, the average[4] of the points in the cluster is computed along with the number of points assigned to the center. The mappers map all this information to a single machine. For each center, the mappers aggregate the points assigned to the center over all partitions along with the centers, and then the reducers update the center to be the average of these points. It is important to note that the solution

[4]Recall that the input to Lloyd's algorithm is a set of points in Euclidean space. The average of the points is the point in Euclidean space whose coordinates are the average of the coordinates of the points.

computed by the algorithm is the same as the sequential version of Lloyd's algorithm.

Partitioning Based Scheme: We describe the partition scheme `MapReduce-Divide-kMedian` that is used for the `Divide-LocalSearch` and `Divide-Lloyd` algorithms. The algorithm `MapReduce-Divide-kMedian` is a partitioning-based parallelization of any arbitrary sequential clustering algorithm. We note that this algorithm and the following analysis have also been considered by Guha et al. [20] in the streaming model.

Algorithm 6 `MapReduce-Divide-kMedian`(V, E, k, ℓ):

1: Let $n = |V|$.
2: The mappers arbitrarily partition V into disjoint sets $S_1, \cdots, S_\ell$, each of size $\Theta(n/\ell)$.
3: **for** $i = 1$ to ℓ **do**
4: The mapper assigns S_i and all the distances between points in S_i to reducer i.
5: Reducer i runs a k-median clustering algorithm $\mathcal{A}$ with $\langle S_i, k\rangle$ as input to find a set $C_i \subseteq S_i$ of k centers.
6: Reducer i computes, for each $y \in C_i$, $w(y) = |\{x \in S^i \setminus C_i \mid d(x, y) = d(x, C_i)\}| + 1$.
7: **end for**
8: Let $C = \bigcup_{i=1}^{\ell} C_i$.
9: The mapper sends C, the pairwise distances between points in C and the numbers $w(\cdot)$ to a single reducer.
10: The reducer runs a `Weighted-kMedian` algorithm $\mathcal{A}$ with $\langle C, w, k\rangle$ as input.
11: Return the set constructed by $\mathcal{A}$.

It is straightforward to verify that setting $\ell = \sqrt{n/k}$ minimizes the maximum memory needed on a machine; in the following, we assume that $\ell = \sqrt{n/k}$. The total memory used by the algorithm is $O(kn \log n)$. (Recall that we assume that the distance between two points can be represented using $O(\log n)$ bits.) Additionally, the memory needed is also $\Omega(kn)$, since in Step (9), $\Theta(\sqrt{n/k})$ sets of k points are sent to a single machine along with their pairwise distances. The following proposition follows from the algorithm description.

PROPOSITION 4.1. *`MapReduce-Divide-kMedian` runs in $O(1)$ MapReduce rounds.*

From the analysis given in [20], we have the following theorem which can be used to bound the approximation factor of `MapReduce-Divide-kMedian`.

THEOREM 4.2 (THEOREM 2.2 IN [20]). *Consider any set of n points arbitrarily partitioned into disjoint sets $S_1, \cdots, S_\ell$. The sum of the optimum solution values for the k-median problem on the ℓ sets of points is at most twice the cost of the optimum k-median problem solution for all n points, for any $\ell > 0$.*

COROLLARY 4.3 ([20]). *If the algorithm $\mathcal{A}$ achieves an α-approximation for the k-median problem, the algorithm `MapReduce-Divide-kMedian` achieves a 3α-approximation for the k-median problem.*

By this Corollary, note that `Divide-LocalSearch` is a constant factor approximation.

4.2 Experiment Overview

We generate a random set of points in $\mathbb{R}^3$. Our data set consists of k centers and randomly generated points around the centers to create clusters. The k centers are randomly positioned in a unit cube. The number of points generated within a cluster is sampled from a Zipf distribution. More precisely, let $\{C_i\}_{1 \le i \le k}$ be the set of clusters. Given a fixed number of points, a unique point is assigned to the cluster C_i with probability $i^\alpha / \sum_{i=1}^{k} i^\alpha$ where α is the parameter of the Zipf distribution. Notice that when $\alpha = 0$, all clusters will have almost the same size and, as α grows, the sizes of the clusters become more non-uniform. The distance between a point and its center is sampled from a normal distribution with a fixed global standard deviation σ. Each experiment with the same parameter set was repeated three times and the average was calculated. When running the local search or Lloyd's algorithm, the seed centers were chosen arbitrarily.

All experiments were performed on a single machine. When running MapReduce algorithms, we simulated each machine used by the algorithm. For a given round, we recorded the time it takes for the machine that ran the longest in the round. Then we summed this time over all the rounds to get the final running time of the parallel algorithms. In these experiments, the communication cost was ignored. More precisely, we ignored the time needed to move data to a different machine. The specifications of the machine were Intel(R) Core(TM) i7 CPU 870 @ 2.93GHz and the memory available was 8GB. We used the standard `clock()` function to measure the time for each experiment. All parallel algorithms were simulated assuming that there are 100 machines. For the algorithm `MapReduce-kMedian` the value of ϵ was set to .1 for the sampling probability.

4.3 Results

Because of the space constraints, we only give a brief summary of our results. The data can be found in Figures 1 and 2. For the data in the figures, the number of points is the only variable, and other parameters are fixed: $\sigma = 0.1$, $\alpha = 0$ and $k = 25$. The cost of the algorithms' objectives is normalized to the cost of `Parallel-Lloyd` in the figures. Figure 1 summarizes the results of the experiments on data sets with at most 10^6 points, and Figure 2 summarizes the results of the experiments on data sets with at most 10^7 points.

Our experiments show that `Sampling-Lloyd` and `Sampling-LocalSearch` achieve a significant speedup over `Parallel-Lloyd` (about 20x), a speedup of more than ten times over `Divide-LocalSearch` and a significant speedup over `LocalSearch` (over 1000x) as seen in Figure 1. The speedup increases very fast as the number of points increases. Further, this speedup is achieved with negligible loss in performance; our algorithm's objective performs close to the `Parallel-Lloyd` and `LocalSearch` when the number of points is sufficiently large.

Finally, we compare the performance of `Sampling-LocalSearch` and `Sampling-Lloyd` with the performance of `Divide-Lloyd` on the largest data sets; the results are summarized in Figure 2. These algorithms were chosen because they are the most scalable and perform well; as shown in Figure 1, `LocalSearch` is far from scalable. Although `Divide-LocalSearch`'s running times are similar to `Parallel-Lloyd`'s, we were not able to run additional experiments with `Divide-LocalSearch` because it takes a very long time to simulate on a single machine. These additional experiments show that, for data sets consisting of 5×10^6 points, the running time of `Sampling-LocalSearch` is slightly larger than `Divide-Lloyd`'s and the clustering cost of `Sampling-LocalSearch` is similar to the cost of `Divide-Lloyd`. The algorithm `Sampling-Lloyd` achieves a speedup of about 25% over `Divide-Lloyd` when the number of points is 10^7. Overall the experiments show that, when coupled with Lloyd's algorithm, our sampling algorithm runs faster than any previously known algorithm that we considered, and this speedup is achieved at a very small loss in performance. We also ran experiments with different settings for the parameters α, k, and σ, and the results were similar; we omit these results from this version of the paper.

5. CONCLUSION

In this paper we give the first approximation algorithms for the k-center and k-median problems that run in a constant number of MapReduce rounds. We note that we have preliminary evidence that the analysis used for the k-median problem can be extended to the k-means problem in Euclidean space; for this problem, our analysis also gives a MapReduce algorithm that runs in a constant number of rounds and achieves a constant factor approximation.

Acknowledgments: We thank Kyle Fox for his help with the implementation of the algorithms and several discussions. We thank Chandra Chekuri for helpful comments on an earlier draft of this paper. We thank Ravi Kumar and Sergei Vassilvitskii for helpful comments on the problems considered. We thank Jeff Erickson for his advice on how to improve the presentation.

6. REFERENCES

[1] Google: Cluster computing and mapreduce. *http://code.google.com/edu/submissions/mapreduce-minilecture/listing.html.*

[2] P. K. Agarwal and N. H. Mustafa. k-means projective clustering. In *PODS*, pages 155–165, 2004.

[3] D. Arthur and S. Vassilvitskii. k-means++: the advantages of careful seeding. In *SODA*, pages 1027–1035, 2007.

[4] V. Arya, N. Garg, R. Khandekar, A. Meyerson, K. Munagala, and V. Pandit. Local search heuristics for k-median and facility location problems. *SIAM J. Comput.*, 33(3):544–562, 2004.

[5] Y. Bartal. Probabilistic approximations of metric spaces and its algorithmic applications. In *FOCS*, pages 184–193, 1996.

[6] Y. Bartal. On approximating arbitrary metrices by tree metrics. In *STOC*, pages 161–168, 1998.

[7] M. Berry. Mapreduce and k-means clustering. *http://blog.data-miners.com/2008/02/mapreduce-and-k-means-clustering.html,* 2008.

[8] G. E. Blelloch and K. Tangwongsan. Parallel approximation algorithms for facility-location problems. In *SPAA*, pages 315–324, 2010.

[9] M. Charikar, C. Chekuri, T. Feder, and R. Motwani. Incremental clustering and dynamic information retrieval. *SIAM J. Comput.*, 33(6):1417–1440, 2004.

[10] M. Charikar, C. Chekuri, A. Goel, and S. Guha. Rounding via trees: Deterministic approximation algorithms for group steiner trees and k-median. In *STOC*, pages 114–123, 1998.

[11] M. Charikar and S. Guha. Improved combinatorial algorithms for the facility location and k-median problems. In *FOCS*, pages 378–388, 1999.

[12] M. Charikar, S. Guha, É. Tardos, and D. B. Shmoys. A constant-factor approximation algorithm for the k-median problem. *J. Comput. Syst. Sci.*, 65(1):129–149, 2002.

[13] K. Chen. On k-median clustering in high dimensions. In *SODA*, pages 1177–1185, 2006.

[14] K. Chen. A constant factor approximation algorithm for k-median clustering with outliers. In *SODA*, pages 826–835, 2008.

[15] F. Chierichetti, R. Kumar, and A. Tomkins. Max-cover in map-reduce. In *WWW*, pages 231–240, 2010.

[16] J. Dean and S. Ghemawat. MapReduce: Simplified data processing on large clusters. In *Proceedings of OSDI*, pages 137–150, 2004.

[17] M. E. Dyer and A. M. Frieze. A simple heuristic for the p-centre problem. *Operations Research Letters*, 3(6):285 – 288, 1985.

[18] J. Feldman, S. Muthukrishnan, A. Sidiropoulos, C. Stein, and Z. Svitkina. On distributing symmetric streaming computations. *ACM Transactions on Algorithms*, 6(4), 2010.

[19] T. F. Gonzalez. Clustering to minimize the maximum intercluster distance. *Theoretical Computer Science*, 38:293 – 306, 1985.

[20] S. Guha, A. Meyerson, N. Mishra, R. Motwani, and L. O'Callaghan. Clustering data streams: Theory and practice. *IEEE Trans. Knowl. Data Eng.*, 15(3):515–528, 2003.

[21] A. Gupta and K. Tangwongsan. Simpler analyses of local search algorithms for facility location. *CoRR*, abs/0809.2554, 2008.

[22] R. Herwig, A. J. Poustka, C. Müller, C. Bull, H. Lehrach, and J. O'Brien. Large-Scale Clustering of cDNA-Fingerprinting Data. *Genome Research*, 9(11):1093–1105, November 1999.

[23] D. S. Hochbaum and D. B. Shmoys. A best possible heuristic for the k-center problem. *Mathematics of Operations Research*, 10(2):180–184, May 1985.

[24] K. Jain, M. Mahdian, and A. Saberi. A new greedy approach for facility location problems. In *STOC*, pages 731–740. ACM, 2002.

[25] U. Kang, C. Tsourakakis, A. P. Appel, C. Faloutsos, and J. Leskovec. Hadi: Fast diameter estimation and mining in massive graphs with hadoop. Technical report, School of Computer Science, Carnegie Mellon University Pittsburgh, December 2008.

[26] H. J. Karloff, S. Suri, and S. Vassilvitskii. A model of computation for mapreduce. In *SODA*, pages 938–948, 2010.

[27] J. Lin and C. Dyer. *Data-Intensive Text Processing with MapReduce*. Synthesis Lectures on Human Language Technologies. Morgan & Claypool Publishers, 2010.

[28] S. P. Lloyd. Least squares quantization in PCM. *IEEE Transactions on Information Theory*, 28(2):129–136, 1982.

[29] A. Ma and I. K. Sethi. Distributed k-median clustering with application to image clustering. In *PRIS*, pages 215–220, 2007.

[30] G. Malewicz, M. H. Austern, A. J. C. Bik, J. C. Dehnert, I. Horn, N. Leiser, and G. Czajkowski. Pregel: a system for large-scale graph processing. In *SIGMOD Conference*, pages 135–146, 2010.

[31] R. M. McCutchen and S. Khuller. Streaming algorithms for k-center clustering with outliers and with anonymity. In *APPROX-RANDOM*, pages 165–178, 2008.

[32] M. Thorup. Quick k-median, k-center, and facility location for sparse graphs. *SIAM J. Comput.*, 34(2):405–432, 2004.

[33] T. White. *Hadoop: The Definitive Guide*. O'Reilly Media, 2009.

Clustering Very Large Multi-dimensional Datasets with MapReduce*

Robson L. F. Cordeiro
CS Department - ICMC,
University of São Paulo - Brazil
robson@icmc.usp.br

Caetano Traina Jr.
CS Department - ICMC,
University of São Paulo - Brazil
caetano@icmc.usp.br

Agma J. M. Traina
CS Department - ICMC,
University of São Paulo - Brazil
agma@icmc.usp.br

Julio López
SCS, Carnegie Mellon
University - USA
jclopez@andrew.cmu.edu

U Kang
SCS, Carnegie Mellon
University - USA
ukang@cs.cmu.edu

Christos Faloutsos
SCS, Carnegie Mellon
University - USA
christos@cs.cmu.edu

ABSTRACT

Given a *very large* moderate-to-high dimensionality dataset, how could one cluster its points? For datasets that don't fit even on a single disk, parallelism is a first class option. In this paper we explore MapReduce for clustering this kind of data. The main questions are (a) how to minimize the I/O cost, taking into account the *already existing* data partition (e.g., on disks), and (b) how to minimize the network cost among processing nodes. Either of them may be a bottleneck. Thus, we propose the ***Best of both Worlds – BoW*** method, that automatically spots the bottleneck and chooses a good strategy. Our main contributions are: (1) We propose *BoW* and carefully derive its cost functions, which dynamically choose the best strategy; (2) We show that *BoW* has numerous desirable features: it can work with most serial clustering methods as a plugged-in clustering subroutine, it balances the cost for disk accesses and network accesses, achieving a very good tradeoff between the two, it uses no user-defined parameters (thanks to our reasonable defaults), it matches the clustering quality of the serial algorithm, and it has near-linear scale-up; and finally, (3) We report experiments on real and synthetic data with *billions* of points, using up to 1,024 cores in parallel. To the best of our knowledge, our *Yahoo! web* is the *largest real dataset ever reported* in the database *subspace clustering* literature. Spanning 0.2 TB of multi-dimensional data, it took only 8 minutes to be clustered, using 128 cores.

Categories and Subject Descriptors

H.2.8 [**Database Applications**]: Data mining; D.1.3 [**Concurrent Programming**]: Parallel programming

General Terms

Algorithms, Design, Performance, Experimentation.

* Work performed during Mr. Cordeiro's visit to the Carnegie Mellon University.

KDD'11, August 21–24, 2011, San Diego, California, USA.

1. INTRODUCTION

Given a *very large* dataset of moderate-to-high dimensional elements, how could one cluster them? Numerous successful, serial *subspace clustering* algorithms for data in five or more dimensions exist in literature. See [14] for a recent survey. However, the existing algorithms are impractical for datasets spanning Terabytes and Petabytes (e.g., Twitter crawl: > 12 TB, Yahoo! operational data: 5 *Petabytes* [10]). In such cases, the data are *already* stored on multiple disks, since the largest modern disks are 1-2TB. Just to read a single Terabyte of data (at 5GB/min on a single modern eSATA disk) one takes more than 3 hours! Thus, parallelism is not another option – it is by far the best choice. Nevertheless, good, serial clustering algorithms and strategies are still extremely valuable, because we can (and should) use them as 'plug-ins' for parallel clustering. Naturally, the best algorithm is the one that combines (a) a fast, scalable serial algorithm and (b) makes it run efficiently in parallel. This is exactly what our proposed method does.

Examples of applications with Terabytes of data in five or more dimensions abound: weather monitoring systems and climate change models, where we want to record wind speed, temperature, rain, humidity, pollutants, etc; social networks like Facebook TM, with millions of nodes, and several attributes per node (gender, age, number of friends, etc); astrophysics data, such as the SDSS (Sloan Digital Sky Survey), with billions of galaxies and attributes like red-shift, diameter, spectrum, etc.

This paper focuses on the problem of finding *subspace clusters* in *very large* moderate-to-high dimensional data, that is, having typically more than 5 axes. Our method uses MapReduce, and can treat as plug-in most of the serial clustering methods. The major research challenges addressed are (a) how to minimize the I/O cost, taking into account the *already existing* data partition (e.g., on disks), and (b) how to minimize the network cost among processing nodes. Any of them may be a bottleneck. So, we propose the ***Best of both Worlds – BoW*** method, that automatically spots the bottleneck and picks a good strategy. Our main contributions are:

1. *Algorithm design and analysis*: we propose *BoW*, a novel, adaptive method to automatically pick the best of two strategies and proper parameters for it, one of the strategies uses a novel *sampling-and-ignore* idea to shrink the network traffic;
2. *Effectiveness, scalability and generality*: we show that *BoW* can work with most serial clustering methods as a plugged-in clustering subroutine, it balances the cost for disk accesses and network accesses, achieving a very good tradeoff between the two, it uses no user defined parameters (thanks

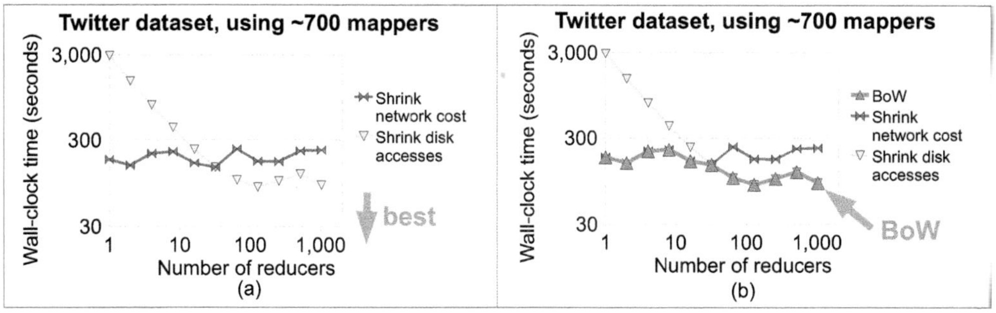

Figure 1: Results on real data from Twitter. Time vs. # of machines (`MapReduce` reducers), in log-log scale. $\sim$ 700 `MapReduce` mappers used for all runs. Left: the upcoming *ParC* (yellow down-triangles) and *SnI* (dark-green butterflies) approaches. The latter uses our *sampling-and-ignore* idea; Right: the same, *including BoW* (in red up-triangles). *BoW* uses cost-based optimization to pick the winning method and proper parameters for it, and thus practically over-writes the respective curve on the graph.

to our defaults), and it maintains the serial clustering quality, with near-linear scale-up;

3. *Experiments*: we report experiments on real and synthetic data of *billions* of points, using up to $1,024$ cores in parallel.

Figure 1 shows an example of *BoW*'s results on real data. It plots the wall-clock-time versus the number of machines (`MapReduce` reducers), in log-log scales. The data consists of the top 10 eigenvectors of the adjacency matrix of the Twitter (http://twitter.com/) graph, which represents $\sim$ 62 million users and their relationships. The eigenvectors span $\sim 14GB$. The full details are in Section 5. Figure 1(a) shows the results for two of the best approaches we studied: the first, in yellow down-triangles, processes the whole dataset, while the second, in dark-green 'butterfly' glyphs, uses our proposed *sampling-and-ignore* idea. Notice that there is no universal winner, with a cross-over point at about 30 machines for this setting. Figure 1(b) shows exactly the same results, this time *including* the wall-clock time of our *BoW*, in red up-triangles. Notice that *BoW* locks onto the best of the two alternatives, hence its name *'Best of both Worlds'*. This is due to our upcoming cost-estimation formulas (Eq. (4) and (5)), which help *BoW* to pick the best alternative and set proper parameters for the chosen environment, while requiring nimble computational effort. Furthermore, notice that the two curves in Figure 1(a) intersect at a narrow angle, which means that the optimal curve has a *smooth plateau*, and thus the cost is rather *robust* wrt small variations of the environment parameters (like effective network bandwidth, disk transfer rate, file size, etc.).

We report experiments on real and synthetic, large datasets, including the *Yahoo! web* one.[1] To the best of our knowledge, the Yahoo! web is the largest real dataset for which results have ever been reported in the database clustering literature for data in five or more axes. Although spanning 0.2 TB of multi-dimensional data, *BoW* took only 8 minutes to cluster it, using 128 cores. We also report experiments using $1,024$ cores, the highest such number in the clustering literature for moderate-to-high dimensional data.

Notice that *BoW* is *tailored to subspace clustering* and can handle most serial algorithms as plug-ins, since the only required API is that the serial algorithm should return clusters of points in hyper-rectangles, which we shall refer to as β-clusters. Subspace clustering methods spot clusters that exist only in subspaces of the original, d-dimensional space (i.e., spaces formed by subsets of the original axes or linear combinations thereof). Thus, the *natural* shape of the clusters in the original space facilitates their representation with hyper-rectangles, as the points of each cluster spread linearly through several irrelevant axes (original axes or linear combinations thereof) in the original space. For that reason, many serial, subspace clustering methods (e.g., CLIQUE [5], FPC/CFPC [19], MrCC [8], P3C [17] and STATPC [16]) return clusters in hyper-rectangles, and adapting others to work with *BoW* tends to be facilitated by the clusters' natural shape. Nevertheless, besides focusing on subspace clustering and moderate-to-high dimensional data, *BoW* also works with traditional clustering methods and low dimensional data, if the plug-in returns clusters in hyper-rectangles.

The remaining of the paper comprises: related work (Section 2); proposed techniques (Sections 3 and 4); experiments (Section 5) and conclusions (Section 6). Table 1 lists the used symbols.

Table 1: Table of symbols.

Symbols	Definitions
${}^dS$	A d-dimensional dataset.
d	Dimensionality of dataset ${}^dS$.
η	Cardinality of dataset ${}^dS$. $\eta = \lvert {}^dS \rvert$
k	Number of clusters in dataset ${}^dS$.
r	Number of reducers for parallel run.
m	Number of mappers for parallel run.
F_s	Database file size in bytes.
D_s	Disk transfer rate in bytes/sec.
N_s	Network transfer rate in bytes/sec.
D_r	Dispersion ratio.
R_r	Reduction ratio.
S_r	Sampling ratio.
$start\_up\_cost(t)$	Start-up cost for t `MapReduce` tasks.
$plug\_in\_cost(s)$	Serial clustering cost wrt the data size s.

2. RELATED WORK

2.1 Subspace Clustering

Clustering methods for data in five or more dimensions, known as *subspace clustering* methods, usually follow one of two approaches: density-based and k-means-based. A recent survey is found in [14]. Density-based methods assume that a cluster is a data space region in which the element distribution is dense. Each region may have an arbitrary shape and the elements inside it may be arbitrarily distributed. A cluster is separated from the others by regions of low density, whose points are considered as noise. The algorithms use own heuristics to identify dense and non-dense regions, usually relying on user-defined density thresholds. Examples of such algorithms are CLIQUE [5], COPAC [1], P3C [17], 4C [6], FIRES [13], FPC/CFPC [19], STATPC [16] and MrCC [8].

[1] Provided by Yahoo! Research (www.yahoo.com).

Methods like k-means start by picking k space positions as clusters centroids, selected either by own heuristics or randomly. Clustering is achieved by an iterative process that assigns each point to its closest center, constantly improving the centers according to the points assigned to each cluster. The process stops when a quality criterion is satisfied or when a maximum number of iterations is achieved. Some of these methods are: PROCLUS [4], ORCLUS [3], PkM [2], CURLER [18] and LWC/CLWC [7].

Despite the several desirable properties found in existent methods, currently no *subspace clustering* algorithm is able to handle *very large* datasets in feasible time, and interesting datasets span way over the existing method's limits (e.g., Twitter crawl: > 12 TB, Yahoo! operational data: 5 *Petabytes* [10]). For data that do not fit even on a single disk, parallelism is mandatory, and thus we must re-think, re-design and re-implement existing serial algorithms in order to allow for parallel processing.

2.2 MapReduce

`MapReduce` is a programming framework [9] to process large-scale data in a massively parallel way. `MapReduce` has two major advantages: the programmer is oblivious of the details related to the data storage, distribution, replication, load balancing, etc.; and furthermore, it adopts the familiar concept of functional programming. The programmer must specify only two functions, a *map* and a *reduce*. The typical framework is as follows [15]: (a) the *map* stage passes over the input file and outputs (key, value) pairs; (b) the *shuffling* stage transfers the mappers' output to the reducers based on the key; (c) the *reduce* stage processes the received pairs and outputs the final result. Due to its scalability, simplicity and the low cost to build large clouds of computers, `MapReduce` is a very promising tool for large scale data analysis, something already reflected in academia (see [12] [11] for examples).

3. PROPOSED MAIN IDEAS – REDUCING BOTTLENECKS

The major research problems for clustering *very large* datasets with `MapReduce` are: (a) how to minimize the I/O cost, and (b) how to minimize the network cost among processing nodes. *Should we split the data points at random, across machines? What should each node do, and how should we combine the results? Do we lose accuracy (if any), compared to a serial algorithm on a huge-memory machine?*

Our proposed method answers all these questions, by careful design and by adaptively trading-off disk delay and network delay.

In a nutshell, our proposed method *BoW* is a hybrid between two methods that we propose next: the *ParC* method and the *SnI*. The former does data partitioning and merges the results; the latter does some sampling first, to reduce communication cost at the expense of higher I/O cost. Next, we describe each proposal in detail.

3.1 Parallel Clustering – ParC

The *ParC* algorithm has three steps: (1) appropriately partition the input data and assign each data partition to one machine, (2) each machine finds clusters in its assigned partition, named as β-clusters, and, (3) merge the β-clusters found to get the final clusters.

We considered three options for data partitioning, shortly described as follows due to space limitations: (a) *random data partitioning*: elements are assigned to machines at random, striving for load balance; (b) *address-space data partitioning*: eventually, nearby elements in the data space often end up in the same machine, trading-off load balance to achieve better merging of the β-clusters; and (c) *arrival order or 'file-based' data partitioning*: the first several elements in the collection go to one machine, the next batch goes to the second, and so on, achieving perfect load balance. The rationale is that it may *also* facilitate the merging of the β-clusters, because data elements that are stored consecutively on the disk, may also be nearby in address space, due to locality: For example, galaxy records from the Sloan Digital Sky Survey (SDSS) are scanned every night with smooth moves of the telescope, and thus galaxies close in (2-d) address space, often result in records that are stored in nearby locations on the disk.

Notice one observation: we performed an extensive experimental evaluation of the three partitioning approaches, which is omitted here due to space limitations. The *file-based data partitioning* was the fastest approach in our evaluation, still providing highly accurate results. Thus, the *file-based* approach is considered and used as the default strategy for the rest of this paper. Notice, however, that our methods work with the three partitioning approaches described, and, *potentially*, work with any user-defined partitioning strategy.

As described in Section 2.2, a `MapReduce`-based application has at least two modules: the map and the reduce. Our *ParC* method partitions the data through `MapReduce` mappers and does the clustering in `MapReduce` reducers. The final merging is performed serially, since it only processes the clusters descriptions, which consist of a tiny amount of data and processing. Figure 2a (2b will be explained latter) illustrates the process. It starts in phase **P1** with m mappers reading the data in parallel from the `MapReduce` distributed file system. In this phase, each mapper receives a data element at a time, computes its key, according to the data partition strategy used, and outputs a pair $\langle key, point \rangle$. All elements with the same key are forwarded in phase **P2** to be processed together, by the same reducer, and the elements with distinct keys are processed apart, by distinct reducers.

In phase **P3**, each reducer receives its assigned set of elements and normalizes them to a unitary hyper-cube. Each reducer then applies the plugged-in serial clustering algorithm over the normalized elements, aiming to spot β-clusters. For each β-cluster found, the reducer outputs, in phase **P4**, a pair $\langle key, cluster\_description \rangle$. The key concatenates the reducer identification and a cluster identification. The reducer identification is the input key. The cluster identification is a sequential number according to the order in which the β-cluster was found in the corresponding reducer. A β-cluster description consists of the unnormalized minimum/maximum bounds of the cluster in each dimension, defining a hyper-rectangle in the data space. Notice that this is a tiny amount of data, amounting to two float values per axis, per β-cluster.

The final phase **P5** is performed serially, as it processes only the tiny amount of data (β-clusters' bounds) received from phase **P4**, and *not* the data elements themselves. Phase **P5** merges all β-clusters pairs that overlap in the data space. Checking if two β-clusters overlap refers to checking if two hyper-rectangles overlap in a d-dimensional space.

3.2 Sample-and-Ignore – SnI

The first algorithm, ParC, reads the dataset once, aimed at minimizing disk accesses, which is the most common strategy used by serial algorithms to shrink computational costs. However, this strategy does not address the issue of minimizing the network traffic: in the shuffle phase of the *ParC* algorithm (phase **P2** of Figure 2a), almost all of the records have to be shipped over the network, to the appropriate reducer. *How can we reduce this network traffic?*

Our main idea is to exploit the skewed distribution of cluster sizes that typically appears in real datasets: Most of the elements usually belong to a few large clusters, and these are exactly the elements that we try to *avoid* processing. Thus, we propose *SnI*, a

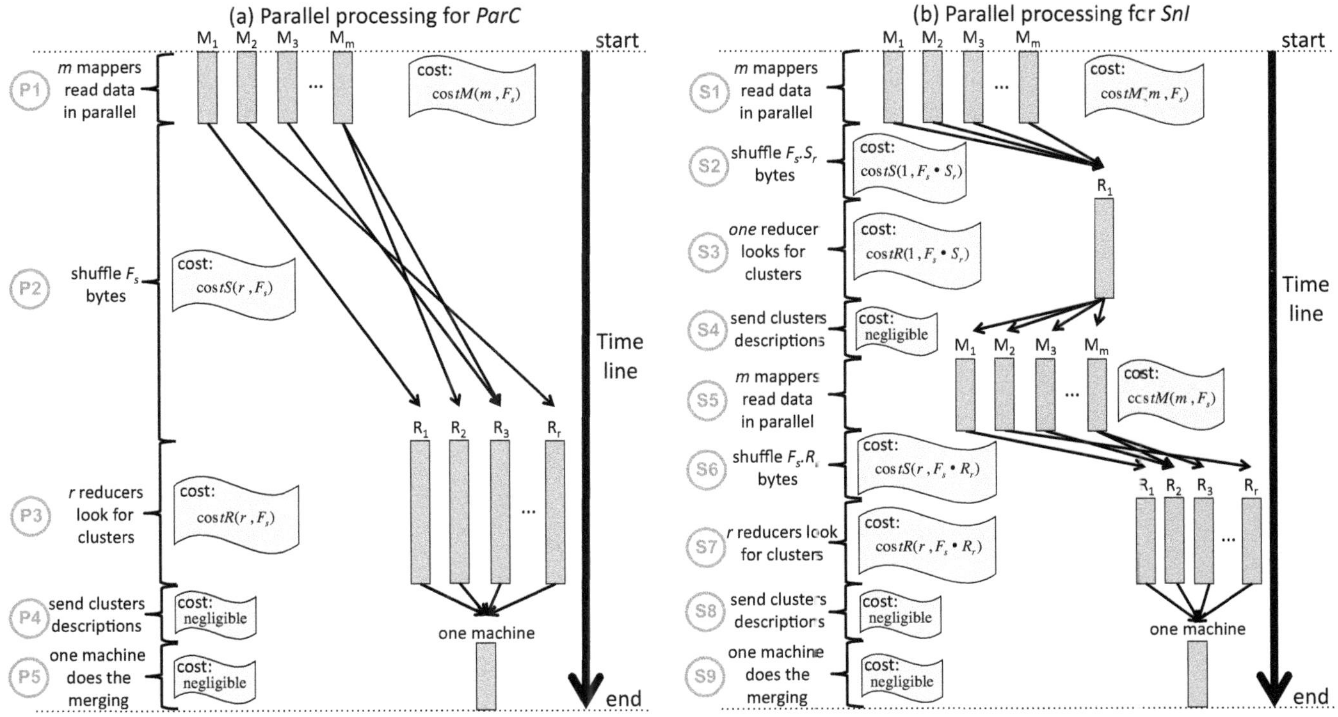

Figure 2: *Which one is best?* **Parallel run overview for *ParC* (left) and *SnI* (right - with sampling). *ParC* executes the map (*P1*), shuffle (*P2*) and reduce (*P3*) phases once, on the full dataset. *SnI* uses sampling (phases *S1-S4*) to get rough cluster estimates and then uses phases *S5-S9* to cluster the remaining points (see section 3.2 for details). Their clustering qualities are similar (see Section 5). The winning approach depends on the environment; *BoW* uses cost-based optimization to automatically pick the best.**

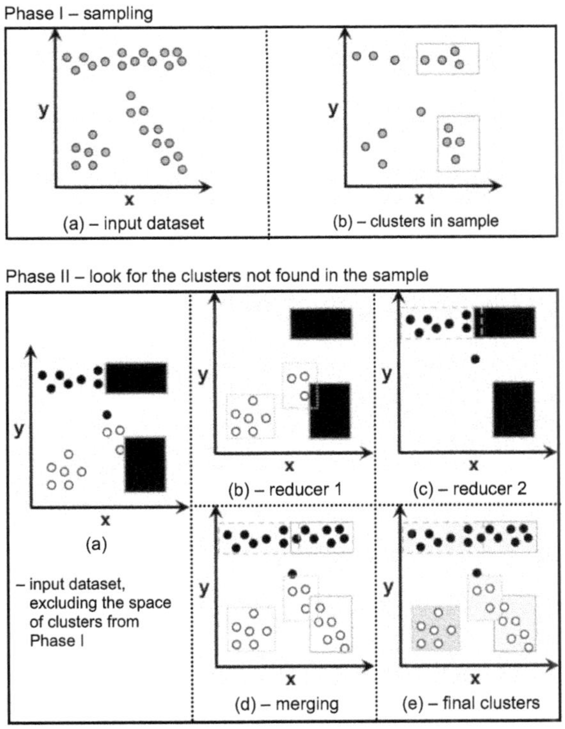

Figure 3: Multi-phase Sample-and-Ignore (SnI) Method. Phase-I finds clusters on a sample of the input data. Phase-II ignores elements that fall within any previously found cluster and finds clusters using the remaining elements only.

parallel clustering algorithm that consists of: (a) a novel *sample-and-ignore* preprocessing step; and (b) the *ParC* algorithm from Section 3.1. The *sample-and-ignore* step works on a small dataset sample, spots the major clusters and ignores their members in the follow-up steps. It significantly reduces the amount of data moved in the shuffling phases of *SnI*, with consequent savings for the network traffic, as well as the I/O cost for the intermediate results and processing cost for the receiving reduce tasks. Notice one point: the proposed *sample-and-ignore* idea is an alternative general strategy that can improve many clustering methods, and not only *ParC*.

The *SnI* method is defined in Algorithm 1 and the process is illustrated in Figure 2b. At a high-level, in Phase I (steps **S1-S4** in the figure, and lines **1-3** in the algorithm) the method *samples* the input data and builds an initial set of clusters. In the second phase (steps **S5-S9** in the figure, and lines **4-8** in the algorithm) , the input data is filtered, so that we only include *unclassified* elements, that is, those that do not belong to any of the clusters found in Phase I. These unclassified elements are then clustered using *ParC*.

Figure 3 illustrates the *SnI* approach over a toy dataset, assuming that we have $r = 2$ reducers available for parallel processing. The top part of the figure shows Phase-I. First, in Phase-I (a) the input dataset is read in parallel by m map tasks, each mapper passes the input elements to the same reducer with some probability, for example, 0.5 for the case shown in the figure. A single reducer builds clusters using the sample elements in Phase-I (b). In this case two clusters were found and are denoted by the gray boxes around the elements. The summary descriptors of the clusters found in Phase-I, i.e., the minimum/maximum limits of the clusters wrt each dimension, are passed to Phase-II. In Phase-II (a), m mappers perform a second pass over the data, this time filtering out elements that fall in the clusters found in Phase-I, which are denoted by the black boxes. The elements that do not fall into clusters are passed to the two reducers available, as shown in Phase-II (b) and (c), in which we assume that the used partitioning strategy divided the elements into 'black points' and 'white points'. Each reducer finds new clusters, denoted by the points surrounded by dotted boxes. In Phase-II (d), the clusters found by the reducers are merged with the clusters from the sampling phase using the same merging strategies used in *ParC*. The global set of clusters, with three clusters represented in Phase-II (e) by distinct gray levels, is the final output.

The main benefit of the *SnI* approach is realized in the shuffle/reduce stages. In Phases **S2** and **S3** of Figure 2b, only a small sample is shuffled and processed by a receiving reducer. In Phases **S6** and **S7** of Figure 2b, only the *non-ignored* elements may need to be shuffled through the network to other machines and processed. This means that most elements belonging to the major clusters spotted in the sample are ignored, *never* being shuffled through the network nor processed by a reducer. Compared to the *ParC* algorithm, *SnI* significantly minimizes the network cost and the reducers processing, at the cost of reading the whole dataset twice. In other words, *ParC* does a single pass over the data, but almost all of the records have to be shipped over the network (phase **P2** of Figure 2a), to the appropriate reducer. On the other hand, *SnI* minimizes the shuffle/reduce cost, at the expense of reading the data one extra time. *What approach is the best?* The answer is given in Section 4.

Algorithm 1 : Multi-phase Sample-and-Ignore (SnI) Method.

Input: dataset ${}^dS$; sampling ratio S_r;
Output: $clusters$;
1: // Phase 1 – Sample
2: m mappers read the data and send the elements to one reducer with probability S_r;
3: one reducer uses plug-in to find clusters in $\sim \eta.S_r$ received elements, and passes clusters descriptions to m mappers;
4: // Phase 2 – Ignore
5: m mappers read the data, ignore the elements from the clusters found in the sample and send the rest to r reducers, according to the data partition approach used;
6: r reducers use the plug-in to find clusters in the received elements, and send the clusters descriptions to one machine;
7: one machine merges the clusters received and the ones from the sample, let the merged result be $clusters$;
8: **return** $clusters$

4. PROPOSED COST-BASED OPTIMIZATION

We propose an adaptive, hybrid method named *BoW (**B**est of both **W**orlds)* that exploits the advantages of the previously described approaches, *ParC* and *SnI*, taking the best of them. There is no universal winner, since it depends on the environment and on the data characteristics. See Figure 1 and Section 5 for a complete explanation. Therefore, the main question here is: *When should our sampling-and-ignore idea be used and when should it be avoided?* *ParC* runs the map, shuffle and reduce phases only once on the whole dataset. *SnI* reduces the amount of data to be shipped to and processed by the reducers, at the cost of a second pass on the input data (in the map phase). We propose a cost-based optimization that uses analytics models to estimate the running time of each clustering strategy. *BoW* picks the one with the lowest estimated cost.

The environmental parameters required by *BoW* are presented in Table 2. They describe the hardware characteristics (i.e., the specs of the available MapReduce cluster), the total amount of data to be processed, and the cost estimate for the plugged-in serial clustering method. Setting the value for F_s is straightforward. D_s, N_s and $start\_up\_cost(t)$ are inferred by analyzing the cloud of computers' logs, while $plug\_in\_cost(s)$ is defined based on the plugged-in method's original time complexity analysis and/or experiments, or measured by the user in a simple experiment. Notice: each machine in the cloud may run many MapReduce tasks (mappers and/or reducers) in parallel, *sharing* the machine's disks and network connection. So, N_s and D_s are expected to be *smaller* than the effective network bandwidth and disk transfer rate respectively.

Table 2: Environmental parameters

Parameter	Meaning	Explanation
F_s	data file size (bytes)	Size of the dataset to be clustered.
D_s	disk speed (bytes/sec.)	Average bytes/sec. that a MapReduce task (mapper or reducer) can read from local disks.
N_s	network speed (bytes/sec.)	Average bytes/sec. that a MapReduce task (mapper or reducer) can read from other computers in the cloud.
$start\_up\_cost(t)$	start-up cost (seconds)	Average time to start-up t MapReduce tasks (mappers or reducers).
$plug\_in\_cost(s)$	plug-in cost (seconds)	Average time to run the plugged-in serial method over s data bytes on a standard computer in the cloud.

Two other parameters are used, shown in Table 3. We provide reasonable default values for them based on empirical evaluation. Notice one *important* observation: As is the common knowledge in database query optimization, at the cross-over point of two strategies, the wall-clock-time performances usually create *flat plateaus*, being not much sensitive to parameter variations. This occurs in our setting, and the results in Figures 1a, 7a and 7d exemplify it (notice the log-log scale). Thus, tuning exact values to our parameters barely affects *BoW*'s results and the suggested values are expected to work well in most cases.

Table 3: Other parameters

Param.	Meaning	Explanation	Our defaults
D_r	dispersion ratio	Ratio of data transferred in the shuffling through the network relative to the total amount of data involved.	0.5
R_r	reduction ratio	Ratio of data that does not belong to the major clusters found in the sampling phase of *SnI* relative to the full data size F_s.	0.1

The following lemmas and proofs define the equations of our cost-based optimization. First, we give the expected costs for the map, shuffle and reduce phases wrt the number of mappers and/or reducers available and to the data size involved. Then, we infer the costs for: *ParC*, that minimizes disk accesses, and; *SnI*, that aims at shrinking the network cost. For clarity, consider again Figure 2 that provides a graphical overview of the parallel execution of both methods, as well as their expected cost equations.

LEMMA 1. *Map Cost – the expected cost for the map phase of the parallel clustering approaches is a function of the number of mappers m used and the involved data size s, given by:*

$$costM(m, s) = start\_up\_cost(m) + \frac{s}{m}.\frac{1}{D_s} \quad (1)$$

PROOF. In the map phase, m mappers are started-up at the cost of $start\_up\_cost(m)$. The majority of the extra time spent is related to reading the input data from disk. s bytes of data will be read in parallel by m mappers, which are able to read D_s bytes per second each. Thus, the total reading time is given by: $\frac{s}{m}.\frac{1}{D_s}$. □

LEMMA 2. *Shuffle Cost – the expected shuffle cost is a function of the number of reducers r to receive the data and the amount of data to be shuffled s, which is given by:*

$$costS(r, s) = \frac{s.D_r}{r}.\frac{1}{N_s} \quad (2)$$

PROOF. The majority of the shuffling cost is related to shipping the data between distinct machines through the network. Whenever possible, MapReduce minimizes this cost by assigning reduce tasks to the machines that already have the required data in local disks. D_r is the ratio of data actually shipped between distinct machines relative to the total amount of data processed. Thus, the total amount of data to be shipped is $s.D_r$ bytes. The data will be received in parallel by r reducers, each one receiving in average N_s bytes per second. Thus, the total cost is given by: $\frac{s.D_r}{r}.\frac{1}{N_s}$. □

LEMMA 3. *Reduce Cost – the expected cost for the reduce phase is a function of the number of reducers r used for parallel processing and the size s of the data involved, which is given by:*

$$costR(r, s) = start\_up\_cost(r) + \frac{s}{r}.\frac{1}{D_s} + plug\_in\_cost(\frac{s}{r}) \quad (3)$$

PROOF. In the reduce phase, r reducers are started-up at cost $start\_up\_cost(r)$. After the start-up process, the reducers will read from disk s bytes in parallel at the individual cost of D_s bytes per second. Thus, the total reading time is $\frac{s}{r}.\frac{1}{D_s}$. Finally, the plugged-in serial clustering method will be executed in parallel over partitions of the data, whose average sizes are $\frac{s}{r}$. Therefore, the approximate clustering cost is $plug\_in\_cost(\frac{s}{r})$. □

LEMMA 4. *ParC Cost – the expected cost for* ParC *is:*

$$costC = costM(m, F_s) + costS(r, F_s) + costR(r, F_s) \quad (4)$$

PROOF. The parallel processing for *ParC* is: (i) m mappers process F_s bytes of data in the map phase; (ii) F_s bytes of data are shuffled to r reducers in the shuffling phase; (iii) F_s bytes of data are analyzed in the reduce phase by r reducers, and; (iv) a single machine merges all the β-clusters found. The last step has negligible cost, as it performs simple computations over data amounting to two float values per β-cluster, per dimension. Thus, summing the costs of the three initial phases leads to the expected cost. □

LEMMA 5. *SnI Cost – the expected cost for* SnI *is:*

$$costCs = 2\ .\ costM(m, F_s) + costS(1, F_s.S_r) + costR(1, F_s.S_r) + costS(r, F_s.R_r) + costR(r, F_s.R_r) \quad (5)$$

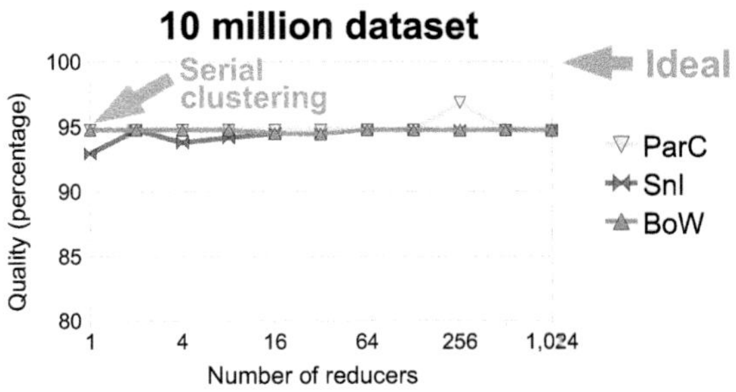

Figure 4: All our variants give top quality results. 10 million dataset; quality vs. number r of reducers, for *ParC*, *SnI* and *BoW*. All methods match the quality of the serial clustering method (top left), for all values of r, like 1,024.

PROOF. *SnI* runs two complete map, shuffle and reduce phases. In both map phases, the full dataset is processed by m mappers, at combined cost: $2\ .\ costM(m, F_s)$. In the first shuffle phase, a data sample of size $F_s.S_r$ bytes is shuffled to a single reducer, at cost $costS(1, F_s.S_r)$. The reduce cost to process this sample is: $costR(1, F_s.S_r)$. R_r is the ratio of data that does not belong to the major clusters, the ones found in the sampling phase, relative to F_s. That is, $F_s.(1 - R_r)$ bytes are *ignored* in the Second Phase of *SnI*, while $F_s.R_r$ bytes of data are *not ignored*, being processed after clustering the sample. Also, both second shuffle and reduce phases involve r reducers. Thus, their combined costs are: $costS(r, F_s.R_r) + costR(r, F_s.R_r)$. The costs for shipping and processing β-clusters descriptions is negligible, since the involved amount of data and processing is extremely small. □

Notice one observation: when our algorithms are executed, the number of distinct key values to be sorted by the MapReduce framework is tiny; it is *always* the number r of reducers used only. Each reducer handles a single key, so it does not need to do sorting. Thus, the sorting cost is negligible for our approaches. The I/O and network costs are the real bottlenecks. The wall-clock time results in all of our experiments (see Section 5) confirm this assertion.

Algorithm 2 describes the main steps of *BoW*. In summary, *ParC* executes the map, shuffle and reduce phases once, involving the full dataset. *SnI* runs these phases twice, but involving less data. *What is the fastest approach?* It depends on your environment. *BoW* takes the environment description as input and uses cost-based optimization to automatically choose the fastest, prior to the real execution. Provided that the clustering accuracies are similar for both approaches (see Section 5 for a complete explanation), *BoW* actually picks the *'Best of both Worlds'*.

Algorithm 2 : The ***Best of both Worlds – BoW*** method.

Input: dataset ^dS; environmental parameters (Table 2); other parameters (Table 3); number of reducers r; number of mappers m; sampling ratio S_r;
Output: $clusters$;
1: compute $costC$ from Equation 4;
2: compute $costCs$ from Equation 5;
3: **if** $costC > costCs$ **then**
4: $clusters$ = result of *SnI* for ^dS; // use *sampling-and-ignore*
5: **else** $clusters$ = result of *ParC* for ^dS; // use no sampling
6: **end if**
7: **return** $clusters$

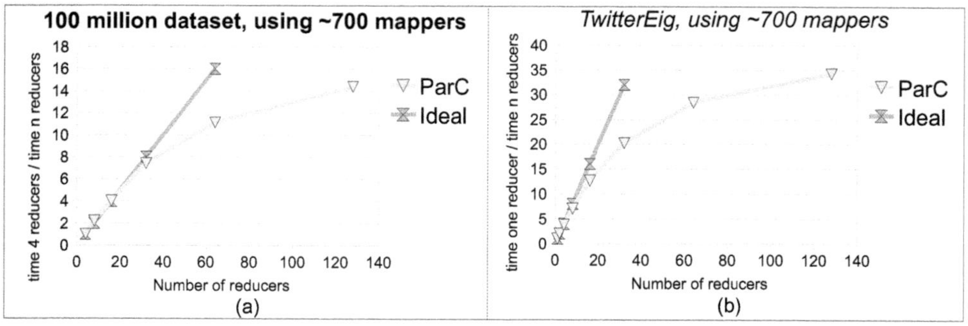

Figure 5: Near-linear scale-up wrt the number of reducers. Expected behavior: our method starts with near-linear scale-up, and then flattens. 100 **million dataset (left);** `TwitterEig` **(right). X-axes:** $\#$ **of reducers, Y-axes: the relative performance with** r **reducers compared to that with** 1 **reducer (right) or** 4 **reducers (left).** $r = 1$ **in the left case needs prohibitively long time.** ~ 700 **mappers used.**

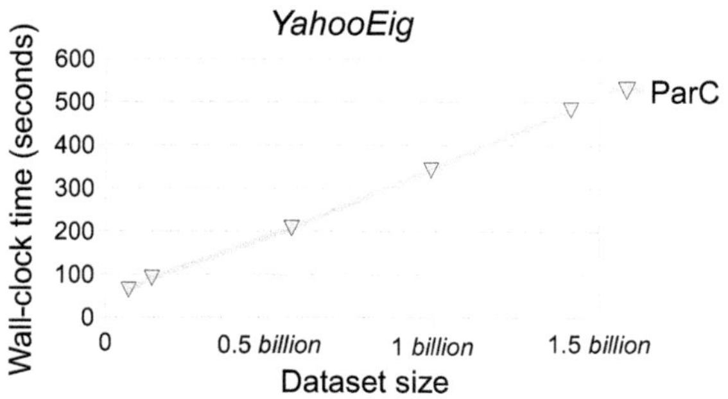

Figure 6: Linear scale-up on db size: wall-clock time vs. data size. Random samples from `YahooEig`**, up to** 1.4 *billion* **points. Fixed numbers of reducers** (128) **and mappers** ($\sim$ 700)**.**

5. EXPERIMENTAL RESULTS

In this section, we describe the experiments performed. We aimed at answering the following questions:

Q1 How much (if at all) parallelism affects the cluster's quality?

Q2 How does our method scale-up?

Q3 How accurate are our cost-based optimization equations?

All experiments were done using the `Hadoop`[2] implementation for the `MapReduce` framework, on two `Hadoop` clusters: M45 by Yahoo! and DISC/Cloud by Parallel Data Lab in CMU. M45 is one of the top 50 supercomputers in the world totaling 400 machines (3,200 cores), 1.5 PB of storage and 3.5 TB of main memory. DISC/Cloud has 512 cores, distributed in 64 machines, 1TB of RAM and 256 TB of raw disk storage. We used the real and synthetic datasets described in Table 4, which are detailed as follows.

- `YahooEig`: The top 6 eigenvectors from the adjacency matrix of one of the largest web graphs. The web graph was crawled by Yahoo! [3] in 2002 and contains 1.4 *billion* nodes and 6.6 *billion* edges. The eigenvectors amount to 0.2 *TB*.
- `TwitterEig`: The top 10 eigenvectors from the adjacency matrix of the Twitter [4] graph, that represents 62 million users and their relationships. Eigenvectors amount to 0.014 TB.
- `Synthetic`: A group of datasets with sizes varying from 100 thousand up to 100 million 15-dimensional points, containing 10 clusters each. We created clusters following standard procedures used by most of the clustering algorithms cited in Section 2, including the plugged-in serial method used in our experiments. All clusters follow normal distributions with random means and random standard deviations in at least 50% of the axes, spreading through at most 15% of these axes domains. In other axes, all clusters have uniform distribution, spreading through the whole axes domains.

[2] www.hadoop.com

[3] www.yahoo.com

[4] http://twitter.com/

Table 4: Summary of datasets. TB: TeraBytes

Dataset	# of Points	# of Axes	File Size
`YahooEig`	1.4 *billion*	6	0.2 *TB*
`TwitterEig`	62 million	10	0.014 TB
`Synthetic`	up to 100 million	15	up to 0.014 TB

As our real world datasets have 6 and 10 axes, we chose the MrCC algorithm as the serial clustering method for the plug-in in all experiments. MrCC is one state-of-the-art clustering method for medium-dimensionality data. Its original code was used.

Notice one observation: to evaluate how much (if at all) parallelism affects the serial clustering quality, the ideal strategy is to use as ground truth the clustering results obtained by running the plugged-in algorithm serially on any dataset, synthetic or real, and to compare these results to the ones obtained with parallel processing. But, for most of our large datasets, to run a serial algorithm (MrCC or, potentially, any other clustering method for moderate-to-high dimensionality data) is an impractical task – it would require impractical amounts of main memory and/or take a very long time. Thus, in practice, the `Synthetic` datasets are the only ones from which we have clustering ground truth, and they were used to evaluate the quality of all tested techniques in all experiments.

For a fair comparison with the plugged-in serial algorithm, the quality is computed following the same procedure used in its original publication. That is, the quality is computed by comparing the results provided by a technique to the ground truth, based on the averaged precision and recall of all clusters.

The *file-based data partitioning* strategy used may provide distinct quality results wrt the order in which the input data is physically stored. Obviously, the best results appear when the data is totally ordered, i.e., the elements of each cluster are sequentially stored in the data file. On the other hand, when the elements are randomly positioned in the file, the qualities are similar to the ones obtained when using the *random data partitioning*. For a fair analysis, we built each dataset from the `Synthetic` group considering an average case, i.e., 50% of the elements from the totally ordered case were randomly repositioned throughout the data file.

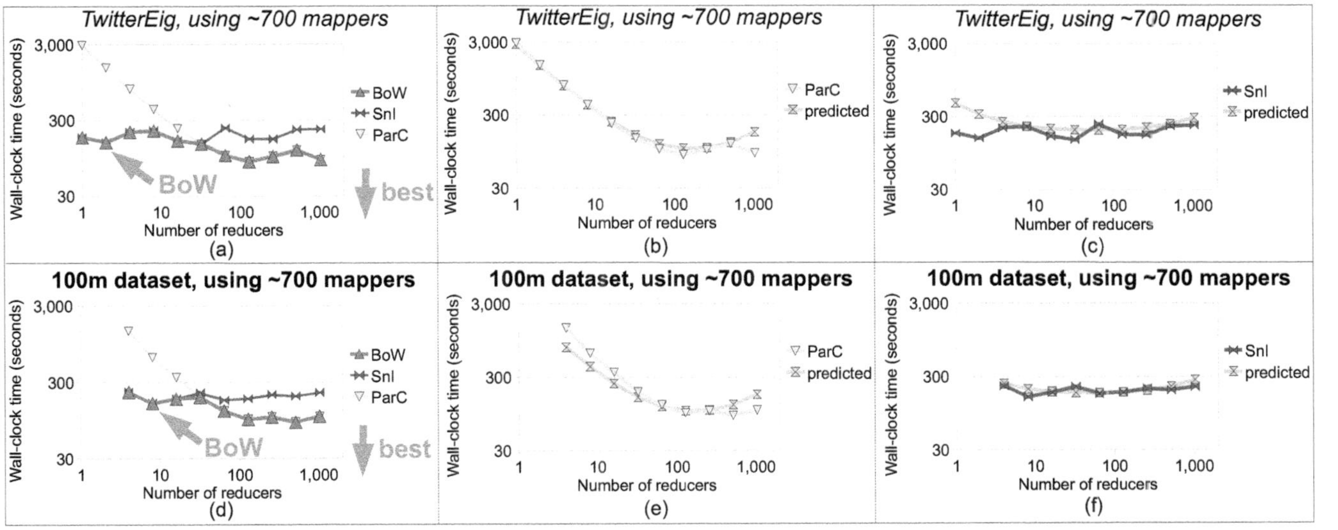

Figure 7: Top: `TwitterEig`; Bottom: `Synthetic`, 100 million. Time vs. # of reducers, in log-log scale. $\sim$ 700 mappers always. Left column: *BoW*'s ability to pick the winner, among *ParC* (yellow down-triangles) and *SnI* (dark-green butterflies). *BoW* (red up-triangles) gets the best of both, always picks the winning strategy, and thus practically over-writes the winner's curve. Middle/right columns: accuracy of our Equations 4 and 5; In all cases, the light-green hour-glass shapes stand for our formulas; Notice how close they are to the actual measurements (*ParC* in yellow triangles and *SnI* in dark-green butterflies).

The following values were used for the environmental parameters: F_s: the data file size; D_s: $40MB/sec$; N_s: $20MB/sec$; $start\_up\_cost(t)$: $0.1t$; $plug\_in\_cost(s)$: $1.4E^{-7}s$. They were measured by experiments on the M45 machines and on the serial plug-in to represent the environment employed. Details on this procedure are not shown due to space limitation. All experiments involving *BoW* used these parameters and the M45 machines.

The results on quality and wall-clock time shown for all experiments are averages of 10 *distinct runs*. All experiments used a sample size of $\sim 1\ million$, i.e., $S_r = \frac{1\ million}{\eta}$, and, in all cases, the number of mappers m used was automatically chosen by `Hadoop`.

5.1 Quality of results

This section intends to answer question $Q1$: How much (if at all) does the parallelism affect the clustering quality? Figure 4 shows the quality results obtained by *ParC*, *SnI* and *BoW* over our `Synthetic` dataset with 10 million elements. All tested methods presented top quality, even for large numbers of reducers, like 1,024. Notice, that the serial execution quality of the plugged-in clustering method is the one obtained when using a single reducer ($r = 1$, extreme left in the plot). Similar results were observed with the other `Synthetic` datasets, not shown for brevity.

An interesting observation is that the quality may decrease for small datasets, when using a large number of reducers. The obvious reason is that, in those cases, we are partitioning a small amount of data through a large number of reducers, which actually receive too little data, not enough to represent the main data patterns. This fact was confirmed in all our experiments, and they lead us to recommend at least $\sim 150k$ points per reducer in average, i.e., $r \leq \frac{\eta}{150k}$.

Thus, based on our experiments, the answer to question $Q1$ is: as long as you have enough data, parallelism barely affects the accuracy, even for large numbers of reducers, like 1,024. *BoW* found top quality clusters in little time from all our *very large* datasets.

5.2 Scale-up results

This section intends to answer question $Q2$: How does our method scale-up? Scale-up results with different numbers of reducers are in Figure 5. Here we used the `TwitterEig` eigenvectors and the `Synthetic` dataset with 100 million points. The plots show X-axes as the number of reducers r, and the Y-axes as the relative performance with n reducers compared to that with 1 reducer (`TwitterEig`) or 4 reducers (`Synthetic`). A fixed number of mappers $m = \sim 700$ was used. The results shown are the average of 10 distinct runs. We picked 4 reducers for our `Synthetic` dataset, as the running time for one reducer was impractical. Notice that our method achieves near-linear scale-up.

The scale-up results with different data sizes are in Figure 6. The `YahooEig` dataset is used. Random samples of the data with increasing sizes, up to the full dataset (1.4 *billion* elements) were generated to perform this experiment. We plot wall clock time vs. data size. The wall-clock time shown is the average time of 10 distinct runs. Fixed numbers of reducers and mappers ($r = 128$ and $m = \sim 700$) were used. As shown, our method has desired scalability, scaling-up linearly with the data size.

It took only $\sim$ 8 *minutes* to cluster the full dataset, which amounts to 0.2 *TB*! Let's provide some context to this result by characterizing the time taken at different stages in the process: (a) the mappers took 47 seconds to read the data from disks; (b) 65 seconds were taken to shuffle the data; and (c) the reduce stage took 330 seconds. To estimate the time taken by the serial method in item (c), we clustered a random sample of the `YahooEig` dataset, of size $\frac{F_s}{r} = \frac{0.2\ TB}{128}$, by running the plug-in on a single machine (one core), similar to the ones of the used cloud of computes. The serial clustering time was 192 seconds. This indicates that the plug-in took $\sim 43\%$ of the total time, being the main bottleneck.

Similar scale-up results were obtained for all other datasets, not shown here due to the space limitation.

5.3 Accuracy of our cost equations

Here we refer to question Q3, by checking *BoW*'s ability to pick the correct alternative and the accuracy of our cost formulas, (Eq. (4) and (5)) from Section 4. The results for the `TwitterEig` and `Synthetic` (with 100 million points) datasets are shown in the top and bottom lines of Figure 7, respectively. The six plots give the wall-clock time (average of 10 runs) versus the number of reducers r, in log-log scales. The left column ((a) and (d)) shows that *BoW*, in red up-triangles, consistently picks the winning strategy among the two alternatives: *ParC* (yellow down-triangles) and *SnI* (dark-green butterflies), that uses our *sample-and-ignore* idea. For both datasets, *BoW* gives results so close to the winner, that its curve practically overwrites the winner's curve; the only overhead of *BoW* is the CPU time required to run the cost equations, which is negligible. The next two columns of Figure 7 illustrate the accuracy of our cost formulas. Light-green hour-glasses refer to our theoretical prediction; yellow triangles stand for *ParC* (middle column), and dark-green butterflies stand for *SnI* (right column). Notice: the theory and the measurements usually agree very well. All other datasets gave similar results, omitted for brevity.

6. CONCLUSIONS

Given a *very large* moderate-to-high dimensionality dataset, how could one cluster its points? For data that don't fit even on a single disk, parallelism is mandatory. The bottlenecks are then: I/O cost and network cost. Our main contributions are:

1. *Algorithm design and analysis*: We proposed *BoW* and carefully derived its cost functions that allow the automatic, dynamic trade-off between disk delay and network delay;
2. *Effectiveness, scalability and generality*: We showed that *BoW* has many desirable features: it can work with most serial methods as a plugged-in clustering subroutine (the only API: clusters described by hyper-rectangles), it balances the cost for disk accesses and network accesses, achieving a very good tradeoff between the two, it uses no user defined parameters (thanks to our defaults) and it matches the serial algorithm's clustering accuracy with near-linear scale-up;
3. *Experiments*: We report experiments on real and synthetic data of *billions* of points, using up to $1,024$ cores in parallel.

To the best of our knowledge, the *Yahoo! web* is the *largest real dataset ever reported* in the database *subspace clustering* literature. *BoW* clustered its $0.2TB$ in only 8 minutes, with 128 cores!

Finally, notice that *BoW* is a hard-clustering method and, as well as any other method of this type, it may not be the best solution for data with many overlapping clusters. So, we report an idea for future work: to extend *BoW*'s merging stage to return soft-clustering results, allowing any data point to belong to two or more clusters. In our opinion, soft-clustering is a promising idea, but there are several issues involved, which are out of the scope of this paper.

7. ACKNOWLEDGMENTS

This material is based upon work supported by FAPESP (São Paulo State Research Foundation), CAPES (Brazilian Coordination for Improvement of Higher Level Personnel), CNPq (Brazilian National Council for Supporting Research), Microsoft Research, the National Science Foundation (NSF), under award CCF-1019104, the Qatar National Fund, under award NPRP 09-1114-1-172 in the QCloud project, the Gordon and Betty Moore Foundation, in the eScience project, the Defense Threat Reduction Agency, accomplished under contract No. HDTRA1-10-1-0120, and the Army Research Laboratory, accomplished under Cooperative Agreement Number W911NF-09-2-0053. The views and conclusions contained in this document are those of the authors and should not be interpreted as representing the official policies, either expressed or implied, of the Army Research Laboratory, the U.S. Government, the National Science Foundation, or other funding parties. The U.S. Government is authorized to reproduce and distribute reprints for Government purposes notwithstanding any copyright notation here on. We also thank the member companies of the PDL Consortium (including APC, EMC, Facebook, Google, HP Labs, Hitachi, IBM, Intel, Microsoft Research, NEC Labs, NetApp, Oracle, Panasas, Riverbed, Samsung, Seagate, STEC, Symantec, and VMware) for their interest, insights, feedback, and support.

8. REFERENCES

[1] E. Achtert, C. Böhm, H.-P. Kriegel, P. Kröger, and A. Zimek. Robust, complete, and efficient correlation clustering. In *SDM, USA*, 2007.

[2] P. K. Agarwal and N. H. Mustafa. k-means projective clustering. In *PODS*, pages 155–165, Paris, France, 2004. ACM.

[3] C. Aggarwal and P. Yu. Redefining clustering for high-dimensional applications. *IEEE TKDE*, 14(2):210–225, 2002.

[4] C. C. Aggarwal, J. L. Wolf, P. S. Yu, C. Procopiuc, and J. S. Park. Fast algorithms for projected clustering. *SIGMOD Rec.*, 28(2):61–72, 1999.

[5] R. Agrawal, J. Gehrke, D. Gunopulos, and P. Raghavan. Automatic subspace clustering of high dimensional data for data mining applications. *SIGMOD Rec.*, 27(2):94–105, 1998.

[6] C. Böhm, K. Kailing, P. Kröger, and A. Zimek. Computing clusters of correlation connected objects. In *SIGMOD*, pages 455–466, NY, USA, 2004.

[7] H. Cheng, K. A. Hua, and K. Vu. Constrained locally weighted clustering. *PVLDB*, 1(1):90–101, 2008.

[8] R. L. F. Cordeiro, A. J. M. Traina, C. Faloutsos, and C. Traina Jr. Finding clusters in subspaces of very large, multi-dimensional datasets. In *ICDE*, pages 625–636, 2010.

[9] J. Dean and S. Ghemawat. Mapreduce: Simplified data processing on large clusters. *OSDI*, 2004.

[10] U. Fayyad. A data miner's story – getting to know the grand challenges. In *Invited Innovation Talk, KDD*, 2007: Slide 61. Available at: http://videolectures.net/kdd07_fayyad_dms/.

[11] U. Kang, C. Tsourakakis, A. P. Appel, C. Faloutsos, and J. Leskovec. Radius plots for mining tera-byte scale graphs: Algorithms, patterns, and observations. *SDM*, 2010.

[12] U. Kang, C. Tsourakakis, and C. Faloutsos. Pegasus: A peta-scale graph mining system - implementation and observations. *ICDM*, 2009.

[13] H.-P. Kriegel, P. Kröger, M. Renz, and S. Wurst. A generic framework for efficient subspace clustering of high-dimensional data. In *ICDM*, pages 250–257, USA, 2005.

[14] H.-P. Kriegel, P. Kröger, and A. Zimek. Clustering high-dimensional data: A survey on subspace clustering, pattern-based clustering, and correlation clustering. *ACM TKDD*, 3(1):1–58, 2009.

[15] R. Lämmel. Google's mapreduce programming model – revisited. *Science of Computer Programming*, 70:1–30, 2008.

[16] G. Moise and J. Sander. Finding non-redundant, statistically significant regions in high dimensional data: a novel approach to projected and subspace clustering. In *KDD*, pages 533–541, 2008.

[17] G. Moise, J. Sander, and M. Ester. Robust projected clustering. *Knowl. Inf. Syst.*, 14(3):273–298, 2008.

[18] A. K. H. Tung, X. Xu, and B. C. Ooi. Curler: finding and visualizing nonlinear correlation clusters. In *SIGMOD*, pages 467–478, New York, NY, USA, 2005.

[19] M. L. Yiu and N. Mamoulis. Iterative projected clustering by subspace mining. *IEEE TKDE*, 17(2):176–189, Feb. 2005.

Selective Block Minimization for Faster Convergence of Limited Memory Large-Scale Linear Models

Kai-Wei Chang and Dan Roth
Dept. of Computer Science
University of Illinois at Urbana-Champaign, IL USA
{kchang10, danr}@illinois.edu

ABSTRACT

As the size of data sets used to build classifiers steadily increases, training a linear model efficiently with limited memory becomes essential. Several techniques deal with this problem by loading blocks of data from disk one at a time, but usually take a considerable number of iterations to converge to a reasonable model. Even the best block minimization techniques [1] require many block loads since they treat all training examples uniformly. As disk I/O is expensive, reducing the amount of disk access can dramatically decrease the training time.

This paper introduces a selective block minimization (SBM) algorithm, a block minimization method that makes use of selective sampling. At each step, SBM updates the model using data consisting of two parts: (1) new data loaded from disk and (2) a set of informative samples already in memory from previous steps. We prove that, by updating the linear model in the dual form, the proposed method fully utilizes the data in memory and converges to a globally optimal solution on the entire data. Experiments show that the SBM algorithm dramatically reduces the number of blocks loaded from disk and consequently obtains an accurate and stable model quickly on both binary and multi-class classification.

Categories and Subject Descriptors

I.5.2 [**Pattern Recognition**]: Design Methodology—*Classifier design and evaluation*

General Terms

Algorithms, Performance, Experimentation

1. INTRODUCTION

In the past few years, the size of data sets used to build classifiers has steadily increased. Significantly larger amounts of annotated data are available now (e.g., for web applications such as spam filtering), and it has been argued that using more samples and adding more features (e.g, using n-gram in a bag-of-words model) actually boosts performance [2]. In some applications, unlimited amounts of annotated data can be generated (e.g., see Sec. 7). Linear classification models have been shown to handle large amounts of data well, and several optimization techniques (e.g., [3, 4, 5]) have been applied to efficiently train linear models. However, when the data cannot fit into memory, batch learners, which load the entire data during the training process, suffer severely due to disk swapping [1]. In these cases, training techniques that deal well with memory limitations become crucial.

A popular scheme that addresses the memory problem processes the data in an online fashion in multiple rounds (e.g., [6, 7, 4, 8]). However, an online learner, which performs a simple weight update over a single training example at a time, usually requires a large number of iterations to converge. Therefore, when an online learner loads data from disk at each step, disk I/O overhead becomes the bottleneck of the training process. Sec. 7 shows an example where the online learner MIRA [9] takes more than one hour loading data but spends less than one minute updating the model. As discussed in [1], training time consists of (1) the time used to update the model's parameters given the data in memory and (2) the time needed to load data from disk. The machine learning literature focuses on the first issue and neglects the second. Consequently, most algorithms aim at reducing CPU time and the number of passes over the data required to obtain an accurate model (e.g, [4, 5]). However, the cost of disk access could be orders of magnitude higher. *In this paper, we focus on the second issue – saving I/O time by reducing disk access.* To our knowledge, this is the first work that targets minimizing disk access when training a linear model.

There are two ways to reduce the expensive I/O overhead. One is by applying data compression to reduce loading time. The other, orthogonal direction, is algorithmic. It suggests placing more effort on learning from data that is already in memory (e.g, [7, 8]). Recently, [1] proposed a block minimization framework which makes progress in both directions. Their solver splits the data into blocks and stores them in compressed files. By loading and training on a block of samples at a time, it employs a better weight update scheme and achieves faster convergence than online algorithms. However, they assume that all training samples are equally important and treat them uniformly. Consequently, their proposed block minimization method still requires a considerable number of iterations to converge to a reasonable model.

KDD'11, August 21–24, 2011, San Diego, CA, USA.

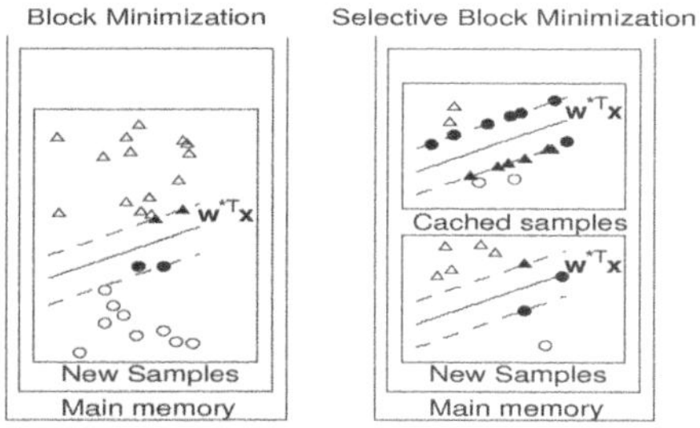

Figure 1: The figure illustrates how a block minimization method wastes resources by considering a lot of unimportant samples (blank circles/triangles), while the selective block minimization (SBM) algorithm focuses on training on informative samples (solid circles/triangles) by caching. The circles/triangles represent the samples drawn from the entire data set. We treat samples closer to the final separator ($\boldsymbol{w}^*$) as more informative (see Sec. 2.2).

This paper develops the selective block minimization (SBM) algorithm, which is shown to significantly improve the I/O cost. SBM can be applied to various linear models, such as SVM and Logistic Regression, when the model can be learned in the dual form. At each step, the proposed algorithm solves the minimization problem on a block of data consisting of new samples loaded from disk along with samples that are already stored in memory, selected from previous steps. The cached samples are selected based on gradient information computed while solving the sub-problem. Figure 1 illustrates the comparison between the proposed algorithm and the block minimization framework (details are given in Sec. (2)). By caching informative samples in memory, the selective block minimization algorithm fully utilizes the memory capacity. The proposed method enjoys the following properties:

- SBM caches informative samples in memory, thus requiring fewer data loads before reaching a given level of performance relative to existing approaches. For example, in one document classification experiment (Sec. 7.2), SBM obtained a model that was as accurate as the optimal one with just a single pass over the data set. For the same data, the current best method [1] requires loading the data from disk 10 times to reach the same performance. That is, SBM saves I/O access by reducing the number of required iterations.
- SBM caches data selectively and thus treats samples non-uniformly, but it still keeps the convergence properties of the block minimization approach.

We present experimental results that exhibit the dramatic reduction in training time achieved by SBM when solving large binary and multi-class problems with limited memory. Moreover, when SBM is required to load each sample into memory once, it is shown to outperform online learners.

The rest of this paper is organized as follows. The selective block minimization algorithm is presented in Sec. 2. Extensions to multi-class classification and streaming data are discussed in Sec. 3 and 4. We address implementation issues in Sec. 5 and analyze SBM's relations with other algorithms for learning with large scale data in Sec. 6. Experimental results are presented in Sec. 7, and Sec. 8 concludes with some discussion. Proofs, additional experiments, and code can be found at
`http://cogcomp.cs.illinois.edu/page/publication_view/660.`

Algorithm 1 A Selective Block Minimization Algorithm for Linear Classification

1. Split data D into subsets $B_j, j = 1 \ldots m$.
2. Initialize $\boldsymbol{\alpha} = \mathbf{0}$.
3. Set cache set $\Omega^{1,1} = \emptyset$.
4. For $t = 1, 2, \ldots$ (outer iteration)
   For $j = 1, \ldots, m$ (inner iteration)
   (a) Read $B_j = (\boldsymbol{x}_i, y_i)_{i=1\ldots m_D}$ from disk.
   (b) Obtain $d^{t,j}$ by exactly or loosely solving (3) on $W^{t,j} = B_j \cup \Omega^{t,j}$, where $\Omega^{t,j}$ is cache.
   (c) Update $\boldsymbol{\alpha}$ by (4).
   (d) *Select cached data $\Omega^{t,j+1}$ for next round from $W^{t,j}$ (see Sec. 2.2).*

2. SELECTIVE BLOCK MINIMIZATION

In this section, we describe the selective block minimization method by exemplifying it in the context of a L1-loss linear SVM for binary classification. Given a sequence of data $D = \{(\boldsymbol{x}_i, y_i)\}_{i=1}^{l}, \boldsymbol{x}_i \in R^n, y_i = \{1, -1\}$, linear SVM considers the following minimization problem:

$$\min_{\boldsymbol{w}} 1/2\|\boldsymbol{w}\|^2 + C \sum\nolimits_{i=1}^{l} \max(1 - y_i \boldsymbol{w}^T \boldsymbol{x}_i, 0), \quad (1)$$

where $C > 0$ is a penalty parameter. Instead of solving (1), in this paper we solve its equivalent dual problem:

$$\begin{aligned} \min_{\boldsymbol{\alpha}} \quad & f(\boldsymbol{\alpha}) = (1/2)\boldsymbol{\alpha}^T Q \boldsymbol{\alpha} - \boldsymbol{e}^T \boldsymbol{\alpha} \\ \text{subject to} \quad & 0 \le \alpha_i \le C, i = 1, \ldots, l, \end{aligned} \quad (2)$$

where $\boldsymbol{e} = [1, \ldots, 1]^T$ and $Q_{ij} = y_i y_j \boldsymbol{x}_i^T \boldsymbol{x}_j$. Eq. (2) is a box constraint optimization problem, and each variable corresponds to one training instance. Let $\boldsymbol{\alpha}^*$ be the optimal solution of (2). We call an instance $(\boldsymbol{x}_i, y_i)$ a support vector if the corresponding parameter satisfies $\alpha_i^* > 0$, and an instance i is an unbounded support vector if $0 < \alpha_i^* < C$. We show in Sec. 2.2 that unbounded support vectors are more important during the training process.

With abundant memory, one can load the entire data set and solve (1) or (2) with a batch learner. However, when memory is limited, only part of the data can be considered at a given time. [1] applies a block minimization technique to deal with this situation. We first introduce their method for solving (2). In [1] the data is split into subsets $B_j, j = 1 \ldots m$, and a two-level iterative procedure is considered, as follows. Initializing $\boldsymbol{\alpha}$ to zero vectors, the block minimization algorithm generates a sequence of solutions $\{\boldsymbol{\alpha}^{t,j}\}_{t=1\ldots\infty, j=1\ldots m}$. We refer to the step from $\boldsymbol{\alpha}^t = \boldsymbol{\alpha}^{t,1}$ to $\boldsymbol{\alpha}^{t+1} = \boldsymbol{\alpha}^{t,m+1}$ as an *outer* iteration, and $\boldsymbol{\alpha}^{t,j}$ to $\boldsymbol{\alpha}^{t,j+1}$ as an *inner* iteration. For updating from $\boldsymbol{\alpha}^{t,j}$ to $\boldsymbol{\alpha}^{t,j+1}$, [1] considers solving a sub-problem on B_j. After the sub-problem is solved, they update the models and removed all the samples $i, i \in B_j$ from memory, and then load another block into it. As each sample only appears in one B_j, their process treats all the samples equally. Since informative samples are likely to be present in different blocks, the solver wastes time on unimportant samples.

Intuitively, we should select only informative samples and use them to update the model. However, trying to select only informative samples and using only them in training may be too sensitive to noise and initialization and does not yield the appropriate convergence result we show later. Instead, we propose a selective block minimization algorithm. On one hand, as we show, our method maintains the convergence property of block minimization by loading a block of new data B_j from disk at each iteration. On the other hand, it maintains a cache set $\Omega^{t,j}$, such that informative samples are kept in memory. At each inner iteration, SBM solves the following sub-problem in the dual on $W^{t,j} = B_j \cup \Omega^{t,j}$:

$$\begin{aligned} \mathbf{d}^{j,t} &= \arg\min_{\mathbf{d}} \quad f(\boldsymbol{\alpha}+\mathbf{d}) \\ &\quad \text{subject to } \mathbf{d}_{\bar{W}^{t,j}} = 0, 0 \le \alpha_i + d_i \le C, \forall i, \end{aligned} \tag{3}$$

where $\bar{W}^{t,j} = \{1 \dots l\} \setminus W^{t,j}$. Then it updates the model by

$$\boldsymbol{\alpha}^{t,j+1} = \boldsymbol{\alpha}^{t,j} + \mathbf{d}^{t,j}. \tag{4}$$

In other words, it updates α_W, while fixing $\alpha_{\bar{W}}$. [1] shows that, by maintaining a temporary vector $\mathbf{w} \in R^n$, solving equation (3) only involves the training samples in $W^{t,j}$. After updating the model, SBM selects samples from $W^{t,j}$ to the cache $\Omega^{t,j+1}$ for the next round.

We discuss the cache selection in Sec. 2.2 and show that by solving the sub-problem mentioned above with coordinate descent methods, SBM reduces to a dual coordinate descent method [3] and converges to the global solution of (2), regardless of the cache selection strategy. Note that the samples in cache $\Omega^{t,j+1}$ are only chosen from $W^{t,j}$ and are already in memory. If a sample is important, though, it may stay in the cache for many rounds, as $\Omega^{t,j} \subset W^{t,j}$. Algorithm 1 summarizes the procedure.

We assume here that the cache size and the data partition are fixed. One can adjust the ratio between $|\Omega|$ and $|W|$ during the training procedure. However, if the partition varies during training, we lose the advantage of storing B_j in a compressed file. In the rest of this section, we discuss the design details of the selective block minimization method.

2.1 Solving using Dual Coordinate Decent

While [1] considers solving the linear SVM both in the primal and in the dual forms, here we only consider solving it in the dual form. The reason is that primal methods directly update $\mathbf{w}$, which corresponds to the entire data set [4], so they usually assume that samples are treated uniformly. In Algorithm 1, a cached sample appears in several sub-problems within an outer iteration. Therefore, primal methods cannot directly apply to our model. In the dual, on the other hand, each α_i corresponds to a sample. Therefore, it allows us to put emphasis on informative samples, and train the corresponding α_i.

Following the discussion in [1], we use LIBLINEAR [10] as the solver for the sub-problem. LIBLINEAR implements a dual coordinate descent method [3], which iteratively updates variables in $W^{t,j}$ to solve (3) until the stopping condition is satisfied. The following theorem shows the convergence of $\{\boldsymbol{\alpha}^{t,j}\}$ in Algorithm 1:

Theorem 1
Assume that a coordinate descent method is applied to solving (3). For each inner iteration (t, j) assume that

- *the number of updates, $\{t^{t,j}\}$, used in solving the sub-problem is uniformly bounded, and*
- *each $\alpha_i, fori \in W^{t,j}$, is updated at least once.*

Then, the vector $\{\boldsymbol{\alpha}^{t,j}\}$ generated by algorithm 1 globally converges to an optimal solution $\boldsymbol{\alpha}^*$ at a linear rate or better. That is, there exist $0 < \mu < 1$ and k_0 such that

$$f(\boldsymbol{\alpha}^{k+1}) - f(\boldsymbol{\alpha}^*) \le \mu \left(f(\boldsymbol{\alpha}^k) - f(\boldsymbol{\alpha}^*) \right), \forall k \ge k_0.$$

The proof can be modified from [1, Theorem 1].

Sec. 3.1 and Sec. 3.2 in [1] show that the sub-problem can be solved tightly until the gradient-based stopping condition holds, or solved loosely by going through the samples in $W^{t,j}$ a fixed number of rounds. Either way, the first condition in Theorem 1 holds (see [1, Theorem 2]). Moreover, as LIBLINEAR goes through all the data at least once at its first iteration, the second condition is satisfied too. Therefore, Theorem 1 implies the convergence of Algorithm 1. Notice that Theorem 1 holds regardless of the cache selection strategy used.

2.2 Selecting Cached Data

The idea of training on only informative samples appears in the selective sampling literature [11], in active set methods for non-linear SVM (see Sec. 6), and in shrinking techniques in optimization [12]. In this section we discuss our strategy for selecting $\Omega^{t,j}$ from $W^{t,j}$.

During the training, some α_is may stay on the boundary ($\alpha_i = 0$ or $\alpha_i = C$) until the end of the optimization process. Shrinking techniques consider fixing such α_is, thus solving a problem with fewer variables. In the following, we show that those unbounded support vectors with $0 < \alpha_i^* < C$ are more important during the training process. We first show in the following theorem that, if we have an oracle of support vectors, solving a sub-problem using only the support vectors provides the same result as if training is done on the entire data.

Theorem 2
Let $\boldsymbol{\alpha}^*$ be the optimal solution of (2), $V = \{i \mid \alpha_i^* = 0\}$ and $\bar{V} = \{1 \dots l\} \setminus V$. If $\boldsymbol{\alpha}'$ is the optimal solution of the following problem:

$$\begin{aligned} &\min_{\boldsymbol{\alpha}} \ (1/2)\boldsymbol{\alpha}^T Q \boldsymbol{\alpha} - \mathbf{e}^T \boldsymbol{\alpha} \\ &\textit{subject to } \boldsymbol{\alpha}_{\bar{V}} = 0, 0 \le \alpha_i \le C, i = 1, \dots, l, \end{aligned}$$

then $f(\boldsymbol{\alpha}') = f(\boldsymbol{\alpha}^*)$ and $\boldsymbol{\alpha}'$ is an optimal solution of (2).

The proof is omitted due to space limitations. Similarly, if we know in advance that $\alpha_i^* = C$, we can solve a smaller problem by fixing $\alpha_i = C$. Therefore, those unbounded support vectors are more important and should be kept in memory. However, we do not know the unbounded support vectors before we solve (2). Therefore, we consider caching unbounded variables ($0 < \alpha_i < C$), which are more likely to eventually be unbounded support vectors.

In dual coordinate descent, α_i is updated in the direction of $-\nabla_i f(\boldsymbol{\alpha})$. Therefore, if $\alpha_i = 0$ and $\nabla_i f(\boldsymbol{\alpha}) > 0$ or if $\alpha_i = C$, and $\nabla_i f(\boldsymbol{\alpha}) < 0$, then α_i is updated toward the boundary. Theorem 2 in [3] implies such α_i will probably stay on the boundary until convergence.

Based on the shrinking strategy proposed in [3], we define the following score to indicate such situations:

$$g(\alpha_i) = \begin{cases} -\nabla_i f(\boldsymbol{\alpha}) & \alpha_i = 0, \nabla_i f(\boldsymbol{\alpha}) > 0, \\ \nabla_i f(\boldsymbol{\alpha}) & \alpha_i = C, \nabla_i f(\boldsymbol{\alpha}) < 0, \\ 0 & \text{Otherwise.} \end{cases}$$

$g(\alpha_i)$ is a non-positive score with the property that the lower its value is, the higher the probability is that the corresponding α_i stays on the boundary. We calculate $g(\alpha_i)$ for each sample i, and select the l_c samples with the higher scores into $\Omega^{t,j+1}$, where l_c is the cache size.

In some situations, there are many unbounded variables, so we further select those with the higher gradient value:

$$g(\alpha_i) = \begin{cases} -\nabla_i f(\alpha) & \alpha_i = 0, \\ \nabla_i f(\alpha) & \alpha_i = C \\ |\nabla_i f(\alpha)| & \text{Otherwise.} \end{cases}$$

To our knowledge, this is the first work that applies a shrinking strategy at the disk level. Our experimental results indicate that our selection strategy significantly improves the performance of a block minimization framework.

3. MULTI-CLASS CLASSIFICATION

Multi-class classification is important in a large number of applications. A multi-class problem can be solved by either training several binary classifiers or by directly optimizing a multi-class formulation [13]. One-versus-all takes the first approach and trains a classifier $\boldsymbol{w}^i$ for each class i to separate it from the union of the other labels. To minimize disk access, [1] proposed an implementation that updates $\boldsymbol{w}^1, \boldsymbol{w}^2 \dots \boldsymbol{w}^k$ simultaneously when B_j is loaded into memory. With a similar technique, Algorithm 1 can be adapted to multi-class problems and maintain separate caches $\Omega_u, u = 1 \dots k$ for each sub-problem. In one-versus-all, the k binary classifiers are trained independently and the training process can be easily parallelized in a multi-core machine. However, in this case there is no shared information among the k binary classifiers so the solver has little global information when selecting the cache. In the following, we investigate an approach that applies SBM in solving a direct multi-class formulation [14] in the dual:

$$\min_{\boldsymbol{\alpha}} \quad f_M(\boldsymbol{\alpha}) = 1/2 \sum_{u=1}^{k} \|\boldsymbol{w}^u\|^2 + \sum_{i=1}^{l} \sum_{u=1}^{k} e_i^u \alpha_i^u$$

$$\text{subject to} \quad \sum_{u=1}^{k} \alpha_i^u = 0, \forall i = 1, \dots, l \qquad (5)$$

$$\alpha_i^u \leq C_{y_i}^u, \forall i = 1, \dots, l, u = 1, \dots, k, \text{ where}$$

$$\boldsymbol{w}^u = \sum_{i=1}^{l} \alpha_i^u \boldsymbol{x}_i, \; C_{y_i}^u = \begin{cases} 0 & \text{if } y_i \neq u, \\ C & \text{if } y_i = u, \end{cases} \; e_i^u = \begin{cases} 1 & \text{if } y_i \neq u, \\ 0 & \text{if } y_i = u. \end{cases}$$

The decision function is

$$\arg\max_{u=1,\dots,k} (\boldsymbol{w}^u)^T \boldsymbol{x}.$$

The superscript u denotes the class label, and the underscript i represents the sample index. Each sample corresponds to k variables $\alpha_i^1 \dots \alpha_i^k$, and each $\boldsymbol{w}^u$ corresponds to one class. Similar to Algorithm 1, we first split data into m blocks. Then, at each step, we load a data block B_j and train a sub-problem on $W^{t,j} = B_j \cup \Omega^{t,j}$

$$\min_{\boldsymbol{d}} \quad f(\boldsymbol{\alpha} + \boldsymbol{d})$$

$$\text{subject to} \quad \sum_{u=1}^{k} (\alpha_i^u + d_i^u) = 0, \; (\alpha_i^u + d_i^u) \leq C_{y_i}^u, \forall i, u$$

$$d_i^u = 0, \text{ if } i \notin W^{t,j}, \qquad (6)$$

and update the $\boldsymbol{\alpha}$ by

$$\boldsymbol{\alpha} \leftarrow \boldsymbol{\alpha} + \boldsymbol{d},$$

To apply SBM, we need to solve (6) only with the data block $W^{t,j}$. [15] proposed a sequential dual method to solve (5). The method sequentially picks a sample i and solves for the corresponding k variables $\alpha_i^u, u = 1, 2, \dots, k$. In their update, i is the only sample needed. Therefore, their methods can be applied in SBM. We use the implementation of [15] in LIBLINEAR.

In Sec. 2.2, we mentioned the relationship between shrinking and cache selection. For multi-class SBM, [10, Appendix E.5] describes a shrinking technique implemented in LIBLINEAR. If α_i^u is on the boundary (i.e., $\alpha_i^u = C_i^u$) and satisfies certain conditions, then it is shrunken. To select a cache set, we consider a sample 'informative' if a small fraction of its corresponding variables $\alpha_i^u, u = 1, 2, \dots, k$ are shrunken. We keep such samples in the cache $\Omega^{t,j}$. Sec. 7 demonstrates the performance of SBM in solving (5).

4. LEARNING FROM STREAMING DATA

Learning over streaming data is important in many applications when the amount of data is just too large to keep in memory; in these cases, it is difficult to process the data in multiple passes and it is often treated as a stream that the algorithm needs to process in an online manner. However, online learners make use of a simple update rule, and a single pass over the samples is typically insufficient to obtain a good model. In the following, we introduce a variant of SBM that considers Algorithm 1 with only one iteration. Unlike existing approaches, we accumulate the incoming samples as a block, and solve the optimization problem one data block at a time. This strategy allows SBM to fully utilize its resources (learning time and memory capacity) and to obtain a significantly more accurate model than in standard techniques that load each sample from disk only once.

When SBM collects a block of samples B from the incoming data, it sets the corresponding $\alpha_i, i \in B$ to 0. Then, as in Algorithm 1, it updates the model by solving (3) on $W = B \cup \Omega$, where Ω is the cache set collected from the previous step. In Sec. 2, we described SBM as processing the data multiple times to solve Eq. (2) exactly. This required maintaining the whole $\boldsymbol{\alpha}$. When the number of instances is large, storing $\boldsymbol{\alpha}$ becomes a problem (see Sec. 5.2). However, when dealing with streaming data each sample is loaded once. Therefore, if a sample i is removed from memory, the corresponding α_i will not be updated later, and keeping $\alpha_i, i \in W$ is sufficient. Without the need to store the whole $\boldsymbol{\alpha}$, the solver is able to keep more data in memory.

The SBM for streaming data thus obtains a feasible solution that approximately solves (2). Compared to other approaches for streaming data, SBM has two advantages:

- By adjusting the cache size and the tightness of solving the sub-problems, we can obtain models with different accuracy levels. Therefore, the solver can adjust to the available resources.
- As we update the model on both a set of incoming samples and a set of cached samples, the model is more stable than the model learned by other online learners.

We study its performance experimentally in Sec. 7.2.

5. IMPLEMENTATION ISSUES

[1] introduces several techniques to speed up block minimization algorithms. Some techniques such as data compression and loading blocks in a random order can also be applied to Algorithm 1. In the following, we further discuss implementation issues that are relevant to SBM.

5.1 Storing Cached Samples in Memory

In Step 4(d) of Algorithm 1, we update the cache set $\Omega^{t,j}$ to $\Omega^{t,j+1}$ by selecting samples from $W^{t,j}$. As memory is limited, non-cached samples $i \notin \Omega^{t,j+1}$ are removed from memory. If data is stored in a continuous array[1] we need a careful design to avoid duplicating samples.

Assume that $W^{t,j}$ is stored in a continuous memory chunk MEM_W. The lower part of MEM_W, MEM_Ω, stores the samples in $\Omega^{t,j}$, and the higher part stores B_j. In the following we discuss a way to update the samples in MEM_Ω from $W^{t,j} = \Omega^{t,j} \cup B_j$ to $W^{t,j+1} = \Omega^{t,j+1} \cup B_{j+1}$ without using extra memory. We want to update MEM_W and store

[1]This operation can be performed easily if the data is stored in a linked list. However, accessing data in a linked list is slower than in an array.

$\Omega^{t,j+1}$ in its lower part. However, as $\Omega^{t,j+1}$ is selected from $\Omega^{t,j} \cup B_j$, which is currently in Mem_W, we need to move the samples in such an order that the values of samples in $\Omega^{t,j+1}$ will not be covered. Moreover, as data is stored in a sparse format, the memory consumption for storing each sample is different. We cannot directly swap the samples in memory. To deal with this problem, we first sort the samples in $\Omega^{t,j+1}$ by their memory location. Then, we sequentially move each sample in $\Omega^{t,j+1}$ to a lower address of MEM_W and cover those non-cached samples. This way, we form a continuous memory chunk $\Omega^{t,j+1}$. Finally, we load B_{j+1} after the last cached sample in $\Omega^{t,j+1}$; MEM_W stores $W^{t,j+1}$ now.

5.2 Dealing with a Large α

When the number of examples is huge, storing $\boldsymbol{\alpha}$ becomes a problem. This is especially the case in multi-class classification, as the size of $\boldsymbol{\alpha}$ grows rapidly since each sample corresponds to k elements in $\boldsymbol{\alpha}$. In the following we introduce two approaches to cope with this situation.

1. Storing $\alpha_i, i \notin W$ in a hash table: In real world applications, the number of support vectors is sometimes much less than the number of samples. In these situations, many α_is will stay at 0 during the whole training process. Therefore, we can store the α_is in a sparse format. That is, we store non-zero $\alpha_i > 0$ in a hash table. We can keep a copy of the current working $\alpha_i, i \in W$ in an array, as accessing data from a hash table is slower than from an array. The hash strategy is widely used in developing large scale learning systems. For example, VW uses a hash table to store the model $\boldsymbol{w}$ when n is huge.

2. Storing $\alpha_i, i \notin W$ in disk: In solving a sub-problem, $\alpha_i, i \notin W^{t,j}$ are fixed. Therefore, we can store them in disk and load them when the corresponding samples $B_j, i \in B_j$ are loaded. We maintain m files to save those α_is which are not involved in the current sub-problem. Then, we save the α_i to the jth file when the corresponding sample $i \in B_j$ is removed from memory. To minimize disk access, the α_is can be stored in a sparse format, and only the α_is with non-zero value are stored.

6. RELATIONS WITH OTHER METHODS

In Sec. 1 and Sec. 2 we discussed the differences between the block minimization framework and our Algorithm 1. In the following, we review other approaches to large scale classification and their relations to Algorithm 1.

Online learning: Online learning is a popular approach to learning from huge data sets. An online learner iteratively goes over the entire data and updates the model as it goes. A commonly held view was that online learners efficiently deal with large data sets due to their simplicity. In the following, we show that the issues are different when the data does not fit in memory. At each step, an online learner performs a simple update on a single data instance. The update done by an online learner is usually cheaper than the one done by a batch learner (e.g., Newton-type method). Therefore, even though an online learner takes a large number of iterations to converge, it could obtain a reasonable model quickly [16, 17]. However, when the data cannot fit into memory, we need to access each sample from disk again every round. An online method thus requires large I/O due to the large number of iterations required. One may consider a block of data at a time to reduce the number of iterations.

Some online learning algorithms have considered solving a block of data at a time. For example, Pegasos [4] allows a block-size update when solving (1) with projected stochastic gradient descent. However, as they assume data points are randomly drawn from the entire data, they cannot do multiple updates on one block. Therefore, it still cannot fully utilize the data in memory. Some online learning methods have considered a caching technique. [18] suggested periodically updating the model on samples the model gets wrong. However, their caching technique is ad-hoc and has no convergence guarantees. To our knowledge, SBM is the first method that uses caching and *provably converges* to (1).

Parallelizing batch algorithm: Although parallel algorithms such as [19, 20] can scale up to huge problems, the communication across machines still incurs a large overhead. Moreover, the aforementioned algorithms still require that training is done on a single machine, so we do not consider parallel solutions in this work. Recently there have been proposals for solving large problems by parallelizing online methods using multi-core machines [21]. However, these methods only shorten the learning time and do not solve the I/O problem.

Reducing data size: Sub-sampling and feature pruning techniques as in [22, 23] reduce the size of the data. In some situations, training on a subset of the data is sufficient to generate a reasonable model. But in other situations, the huge amount of data is already preprocessed and further pruning may degrade the performance. In fact, in SBM we start from a model trained on a randomly drawn data block, and iteratively improve the model by loading other sample blocks. Therefore, its performance should be at least as good as random sub-sampling.

Bagging models trained on a subset of the data: Bagging [24] is an algorithm that improves test performance by combining models trained on subsets of data. To train on large data, a bagging algorithm randomly picks k-subsets of the entire data, and trains k models $\{w^1, w^2, \ldots, w^k\}$ separately on each subset. The final model is obtained by averaging the k models. Some analysis was provided recently in [25]. Although a bagging algorithm can sometimes learn a good model, it does not solve Eq. (1). Therefore, in practice, it is not clear if a bagging model can obtain as good a classifier as obtained by solving (1).

Selective sampling: Selective sampling and active learning methods select informative samples for learning a model [26, 27]. Even though their goal is different, these methods can be applied when training on large data sets (See Sec. 6 in [22]). Starting from a subset of the data, selective sampling methods iteratively select the samples that are close to the current margin, and update the model on those samples. To compute the margin accurately, a selective sub-sampling method may require access to the entire data from disk, which is expensive. In contrast, SBM loads a data block not only for selection but also for training. It selects samples into the cache only if they are already in memory. Therefore, it suffers a very small overhead when selecting samples. Moreover, selective sampling is not guaranteed to converge to (1), while SBM converges linearly.

Related methods for non-linear models: In solving non-linear models, data is usually mapped into a high dimensional feature space via a kernel trick. When the kernel matrix goes beyond memory capacity, an active set method (e.g., [28, 29, 30]) maintains an active set A and updates only the variables $\alpha_i, i \in A$ each time. If $|A|$ is small, the

Table 1: Data statistics: We assume data is stored in a sparse representation. Each feature with non-zero value takes 16 bytes on a 64-bit machine due to data structure alignment. l, n, and #nonzeros are number of instances, features, and non-zero values in each training set, respectively. l_t is the number of instances in the test set. Memory is the memory consumption needed to store the entire data. #nBSV shows the number of unbounded support vectors ($0 < \alpha_i < C$) in the optimal solution. #classes is the number of class labels.

Data set	l	l_t	n	#nonzeros	Memory (Bytes)	C	#nBSV	#classes
webspam	280,000	70,000	16,609,143	1,043,792,623	16,700,681,968	64	7071	2
kddcup10	19,264,093	748,401	29,890,095	566,345,790	9,061,532,640	0.1	2,775,946	2
prep	60,000,000	5,710,649	11,148,531	918,704,364	14,699,269,824	0.1	-	10

corresponding kernel entries can be stored in memory and the active set method yields fast training. Active set methods are related to our work as they also select samples during training. However, the memory problem of dealing with non-linear models is different from the one we face. Non-linear solvers usually assume that samples are stored in memory, while the entire kernel cannot be stored. Therefore, there is no restriction on accessing data. In our case, the samples can only be loaded sequentially from disk.

Another algorithm, Forgetron [31], is related to our work. However, the focus there is different. When training a model with a non-linear kernel, the model is represented by some samples (support vectors). When they have too many samples to store in memory, Forgetron selects the samples which can represent the current model best. In the linear case, $\boldsymbol{w}$ can be directly stored. In our case, on the other hand, the selection process is done in order to speed up the training rather than to just represent the model more concisely.

7. EXPERIMENTAL STUDY

In this section, we first show that SBM provides an improvement over the block minimization algorithm (BMD) in [1]. Then, we demonstrate that SBM converges faster than an online learner. Finally, we investigate the setting in which each sample is loaded from disk only once and show that SBM deals better with streaming data.

We consider two large binary classification data sets, webspam and kddcup10, and one multi-class data set, prep. webspam is a document collection; kddcup10 is taken from educational applications and has been used in the data mining challenge.[2] prep is a 10-classes classification task, aiming at predicting the correct preposition in an English sentence with a bag-of-words model [32].[3] In kddcup10 and webspam, the feature vectors are scaled to unit length, so that $\forall i, \|\boldsymbol{x}_i\| = 1$. prep takes binary features, and we prune the features which appear less than 5 times in all samples. Table 1 lists the data statistics. As shown in [33], applying sub-sampling or bagging downgrades the test performance on kddcup10 and webspam. Each data set is stored as an ASCII file before the training process.

We tune the penalty parameter C using a five-fold cross-validation on the training data and report the performance of solving (2) with the best parameter. This setting allows SBM for linear SVM to be compared with other learning packages such as VW. The implementation of BMD and SBM is in C/C++[4] with double precision in a 64-bit machine. We restrict each process to use at most 2GB memory.

7.1 Training Time and Testing Accuracy

Comparison between SBM and BMD: We compare SBM with the block minimization algorithm in the dual (BMD) [1], as both the algorithms consider a block of data at a time. For a fair comparison, we take the largest block size ($|D_{\text{BM}}| = \max_j |B_j|$) in BMD as a reference, and adjust SBM to use the same amount of memory during training. We consider three variants of Algorithm 1: SBM-1/2, SBM-1/3, and SBM-1/2-rand. SBM-1/2 and SBM-1/2-rand load half the memory with new data and the rest is kept for the cache ($|B_j| = |\Omega| = 1/2|D_{\text{BM}}|$). SBM-1/3 reserves 1/3 of the memory capacity for cache and loads the rest with new data ($|\Omega| = 1/3|D_{\text{BM}}|$ and $|B_j| = 2|\Omega|$). Both SBM-1/2 and SBM-1/3 select the cached sample using the gradient information as described in Sec. 2.2 and 3. SBM-1/2-rand selects the cached sample by picking randomly from the samples in memory (W). All sub-problems in BMD and SBM-* are solved by a dual coordinate method with 10 rounds ($t^{i,j} = 10$). We split both webspam and kddcup10 into 12 blocks ($m = 12$)[5] and split prep into 15 blocks in BMD. The cache size and block size of SBM-* are adjusted according to BMD. Each block is stored in a compressed file. The compression introduces additional cost in storing compressed files but it reduces the load time of each block (see [1, Sec. 5.1]). We report the *wall clock* time in all experiments including the initial time to generate the compressed files (the time to read data from an ASCII file, split it, and store the compressed data in disk.)

The number of α_i^us in prep is 600 million. Therefore, storing all α_i^u takes 4.8GB memory which exceeds the memory restriction. Following the discussion in Sec. 5.2, we store the unused α_i^u in files for BMD and SBM-*.

To check the convergence speed of each method, we compare the relative difference between the dual objective function value (2) and the optimum ($f(\boldsymbol{\alpha}^*)$),

$$|(f(\boldsymbol{\alpha}) - f(\boldsymbol{\alpha}^*))/f(\boldsymbol{\alpha})|, \tag{7}$$

over time. We are also interested in the time it takes each method to obtain a reasonable and stable model. Therefore, we compare the difference between the performance of the current model (acc($\boldsymbol{w}$)) and the best test accuracy among all methods (acc*)

$$(\text{acc}^* - \text{acc}(\boldsymbol{w}))\%. \tag{8}$$

Note that tightly solving (1) is not guaranteed to have the best test performance. Some solvers may reach a higher accuracy before the model converges.

[2] kddcup10 is preprocessed from the second data set in KDD Cup 2010. webspam and kddcup10 can be downloaded at http://www.csie.ntu.edu.tw/~cjlin/libsvmtools/datasets/.

[3] prep is extracted from Wikipedia and New York Times. As the annotation can be automatically generated from articles (assuming the given text is correct), the supervised data can be very large.

[4] The experimental code is modified from [1] http://www.csie.ntu.edu.tw/~cjlin/liblinear/exp.html.

[5] Although the data size of webspam is larger than kddcup10. kddcup10 has a huge number of samples and features, and it takes about 500MB to store the model.

Convergence to optimum. Testing performance.

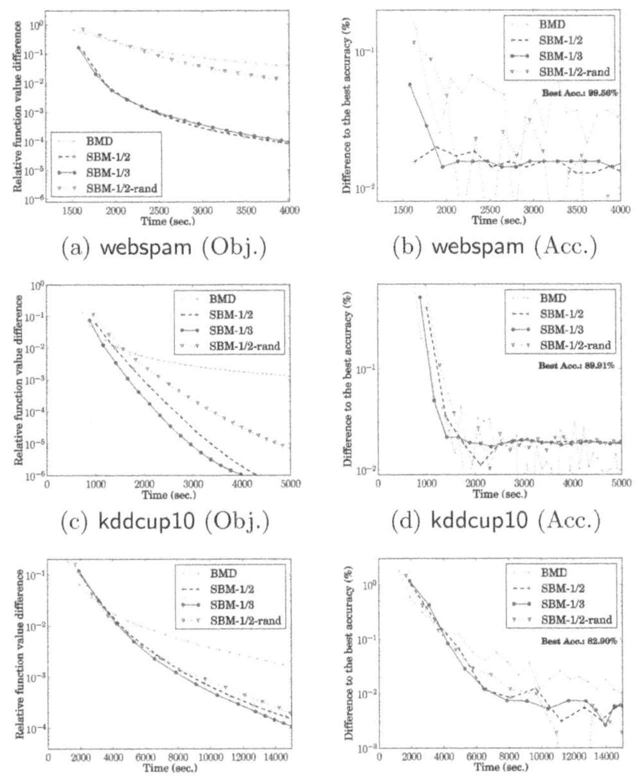

(a) webspam (Obj.) (b) webspam (Acc.)

(c) kddcup10 (Obj.) (d) kddcup10 (Acc.)

(e) prep (Obj.) (f) prep (Acc.)

Figure 2: Comparison between the proposed methods (SBM-*) and the block minimization algorithm (BMD) [1]. Left column: the relative function value difference (7) to the minimum of (2). Right column: the test accuracy difference (8) from the best achievable accuracy. Time is in seconds, and the y-axis is in log-scale. Each marker indicates one outer iteration. As all the solvers access all samples from disk once at each outer iteration, the markers indicate the amount of disk access. It is shown that SBM-* converges faster and obtains a more accurate and stabler model quickly.

Figure 2 shows that all the SBM-* outperform BMD significantly. By selecting cached samples using the gradient information, our key methods, SBM-1/2 and SBM-1/3 perform even better. In particular, when the unbounded support vectors can fit into memory, SBM-1/2 and SBM-1/3 keep most of them in cache during the training process and thus enjoy fast convergence.[6] Consequently, the models generated are more stable in test. The performance of SBM-1/2 and SBM-1/3 are similar. This indicates that the model is not sensitive to the ratio between block size and cache size. Note that SBM is more general than BMD, as it is reduced to BMD when the cache size is zero.

It's interesting to note that even when the cached set is selected randomly, SBM-1/2-rand is still faster than BMD. One possible reason is that partitioning the data affects the performance of the solver. BMD uses a fixed partition $B_j, \forall j$, throughout the training process. For SBM, although, $\forall j, B_j$ is fixed as well, the cached set Ω varies at each iteration.

[6]E.g., in figure 2(a), more than 98% of the unbounded support vectors are stored in cache after 2 iterations.

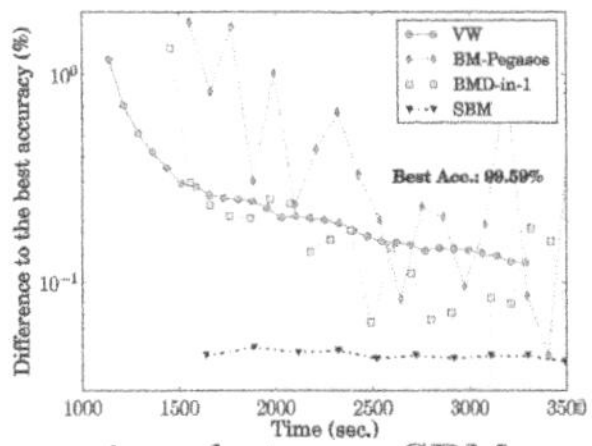

Figure 3: A comparison between SBM and online learning algorithms on webspam. We show the difference between test performance and the best accuracy achievable (8). Time is in seconds. The markers indicate the time it takes each solver to access data from disk once. Except for VW, each solver takes about 90 sec. in each round to load data from the compressed files.

Therefore, SBM avoids wasting time on a bad data block. When the number of bounded support vectors is large, the selection of Ω is less important since drawing a sample randomly already has a high probability of including bounded support vectors in the cache (see figure 2(e)). SBM-* works better in binary classification than in multi-class classification, as sub-problems of the multi-class formulation take more learning time. Thus, the I/O overhead plays a smaller role at training time.

Comparison between SBM and online learners: In Sec. 6, we mentioned that people in the community believe that online learners are fast for large data sets since they make use of a simple update rule. However, as we show, online learners use more I/O time when the data is not in memory. We compare the following solvers:

- VW[7]: an online learning package (version 5.1).[8] It implements a stochastic gradient descent method [34].
- BM-Pegasos: A version of Pegasos implemented under a block minimization framework [1, 4].
- BMD-in-1: Similar to BMD but the inner solver goes through the samples in each sub-problem only once.
- SBM: The same as SBM-1/2 in the previous experiment.

We implemented Pegasos under the block minimization framework such that it saves considerable I/O time by loading data from a compressed file. Although VW also considers a hinge loss function, it does not converge to (2). Therefore, its final accuracy is different from that of the others. Except for SBM, all the methods update the model on each sample once per outer iteration. BMD-in-1 takes the same update rule as the passive-aggressive online algorithm [9], but it keeps α and its solution converges to (2). Except for VW, all methods take about 90 seconds to access each sample from the compressed files. VW has a faster implementation[9] for loading data and takes about 70 seconds per outer iteration.

Figure 3 shows the test performance over time (8) on webspam. SBM converges faster than other online methods to the final performance. *The reason is that an online learner spends most of its time loading data instead of learning a*

[7] https://github.com/JohnLangford/vowpal_wabbit

[8]We use the latest version 5.1, and set the parameter as -b 24 --loss_function hinge --initial_t 80000 --power_t 0.5 -l 1000 --compressed as the author suggested.

[9] VW uses single floating point precision while our implementations use double precision. Although using single precision reduces the training time, numerical inaccuracy may occur. In addition, VW is a multi-threaded program. It uses one thread for loading data and another thread for learning.

Table 2: Training time (*wall clock time*) and testing accuracy for each solver *when each sample is loaded into memory only once.* We show both the loading time (the time to read data from an ASCII file) and the learning time. The reference model is obtained by solving (1) until it converges (see text). We show that by updating the model on one data block at a time, SBM obtains an accurate model for streaming data. Note that the time reported here is different from the time required to finish the first iteration in Figure 2 (see text). Some entries in the table are missing. BM-Pegasos and VW do not support multi-class classification. Also, it is difficult to access the I/O and learning time of VW since it is a multi-threaded program. The top three methods are implemented in Java, and the rest are in C/C++.

Method	webspam				kddcup10				prep			
	Training Time (sec.)			Acc.	Training Time (sec.)			Acc.	Training Time (sec.)			Acc.
	I/O	Learning	Total		I/O	Learning	Total		I/O	Learning	Total	
Perceptron	5078	31	5108	98.66	1403	42	1448	84.93	1843	903	2753	76.10
MIRA [9]	5392	27	5419	98.73	1265	44	1312	86.14	1829	816	2652	76.81
CW [8, 35]	4698	59	4757	99.49	1439	99	1535	89.07	1820	1121	2949	77.70
VW	-	-	507	98.42	-	-	223	85.25	-	-	-	-
BM-Pegasos	470	9	479	97.87	187	20	207	87.48	-	-	-	-
BMD	472	60	532	99.48	181	201	382	88.62	265	649	914	80.06
SBM-in-3	484	81	565	**99.55**	181	151	332	89.54	321	778	1099	81.61
SBM	473	177	650	**99.55**	180	442	634	**89.67**	354	1956	2310	**81.80**
Reference	-	-	-	99.55	-	-	-	89.90	-	-	-	82.90

model (see Sec. 6). For example, BM-Pegasos spends only 15 seconds updating the model. Therefore, it spends 85% of the training time loading data. In contrast, the learning time per iteration in SBM is 180 seconds. Thus, SBM uses 2/3 of the training time to update the model and consequently converges faster.

7.2 Experiments on Streaming Data

In Sec. 4, we introduced a variation of SBM that deals with streaming data. Now we investigate its performance.

In addition to the solvers BMD, SBM, BM-Pegasos and VW introduced in previous experiments, we further compare them to the implementations in [35].[10] The package currently supports the following solvers for data streams:

- MIRA: an online learning algorithm proposed in [9].
- CW: a confidences weighted online algorithm [8, 35].
- Perceptron: an online learning algorithm.

In addition, we consider a setting of SBM, SBM-in-3, in which we only allow 3 rounds when solving each sub-problem (the general setting allows 10 rounds). The training time of this version of SBM is similar to the training time of BMD. Note that MIRA, CW and Perceptron are implemented in JAVA, and the rest of the solvers are implemented in C/C++. For multi-class problems, we used the top-1 approach [35] in MIRA, CW and Perceptron.

Table 2 lists the training time and test accuracy when each sample is loaded from disk only once. To see if loading data once can achieve a result similar to running over the data multiple times, we show a reference model in the table, which solves Eq. (1) until the model converges. We provide both the time to load data from an ASCII file (I/O) and the update time of the model (Learning). For each solver we focus on the ratio of loading to learning time rather than on comparing the absolute times across different solvers. Note that the time reported in Table 2 is different from the time to complete the first round in Figure 2. Figure 2 includes the time it takes to generate compressed files from an ASCII file. However, for streaming data, each sample is loaded into memory once and there is no need to store data in compressed files, resulting in shorter I/O time.

The results show that SBM is able to utilize the memory capacity and spend more learning time to achieve an accurate model. It even achieves a model that is almost as accurate as the reference model on webspam. As the I/O is expensive, for all the methods, the loading time takes a large fraction of the total training time. Online methods such as MIRA and Perceptron use a simple update rule. Their learning time is indeed small, but the model learned with a single pass over the samples is far from converging. CW uses a better update rule and achieves a more accurate model, but the performance is still limited. In contrast, both SBM and BMD are able to update on a data block at a time, thus taking more information into account. Therefore, they achieve a better result. Comparing SBM-in-3 to BMD we see that SBM-in-3 has a similar training time to that of BMD, but learns a model with better accuracy. As shown, by keeping informative samples in memory, SBM utilizes the memory storage better. When the resources are limited, users can adjust the test performance of SBM by adjusting the memory usage and the accuracy level of solving the sub-problems.

8. DISCUSSION AND CONCLUSION

In summary, we presented a selective block minimization algorithm for training large-scale linear classifiers under memory restrictions. We also analyzed the proposed algorithm and provided extensive experimental results. To reduce the amount of disk access, we suggested caching informative samples in memory and updating the model on the important data more frequently. We show that, even though the proposed method treats data points non-uniformly, it provably converges to the global optimum on the entire data. Our experimental results on binary, multi-class and streaming data, show the significant advantage of SBM over block minimization and online algorithms. SBM converges quicker to a more accurate and stable model.

We note that these methods can be applied more broadly. For example, it can be applied for solving L2-loss SVM, regularized least square problems, and logistic regression, by

[10] `http://www.cs.jhu.edu/~mdredze/`. The original package takes a very long time to train on the webspam data set. It might be due to the deep class hierarchy in the package. We fixed the problem and sped up the package.

applying the corresponding dual solvers [3, 36]. Moreover, note that in this work we considered sparse data stored in row format. Therefore, we could split the data into blocks and access particular instances. When data is stored in a column format, splitting can only be done feature by feature. It would be interesting to investigate how to extend our method to this scenario.

Acknowledgments This research is supported by the Defense Advanced Research Projects Agency (DARPA) Machine Reading Program under Air Force Research Laboratory (AFRL) prime contract no. FA8750-09-C-0181 and by the DARPA under the Bootstrap Learning Program. Any opinions, findings, and conclusion or recommendations expressed in this material are those of the author(s) and do not necessarily reflect the view of the DARPA, AFRL, ARL or the US government.

9. REFERENCES

[1] H.-F. Yu, C.-J. Hsieh, K.-W. Chang, and C.-J. Lin, "Large linear classification when data cannot fit in memory," in *ACM KDD*, 2010.

[2] G. Loosli, S. Canu, and L. Bottou, "Training invariant support vector machines using selective sampling," in *Large Scale Kernel Machines* (L. Bottou, O. Chapelle, D. DeCoste, and J. Weston, eds.), pp. 301–320, Cambridge, MA.: MIT Press, 2007.

[3] C.-J. Hsieh, K.-W. Chang, C.-J. Lin, S. S. Keerthi, and S. Sundararajan, "A dual coordinate descent method for large-scale linear SVM," in *ICML*, 2008.

[4] S. Shalev-Shwartz, Y. Singer, and N. Srebro, "Pegasos: primal estimated sub-gradient solver for SVM," in *ICML*, 2007.

[5] T. Joachims, "Training linear SVMs in linear time," in *ACM KDD*, 2006.

[6] J. Langford, L. Li, and T. Zhang, "Sparse online learning via truncated gradient," *JMLR*, vol. 10, pp. 771–801, 2009.

[7] P. Rai, H. Daumé III, and S. Venkatasubramanian, "Streamed learning: One-pass SVMs," in *IJCAI*, 2009.

[8] M. Dredze, K. Crammer, and F. Pereira, "Confidence-weighted linear classification," in *ICML*, 2008.

[9] K. Crammer, O. Dekel, J. Keshet, S. Shalev-Shwartz, and Y. Singer, "Online passive-aggressive algorithms," *JMLR*, 2006.

[10] R.-E. Fan, K.-W. Chang, C.-J. Hsieh, X.-R. Wang, and C.-J. Lin, "LIBLINEAR: A library for large linear classification," *JMLR*, vol. 9, pp. 1871–1874, 2008.

[11] G. Loosli, S. Canu, and L. Bottou, "Training invariant support vector machines using selective sampling," in *Large Scale Kernel Machines*, pp. 301–320, Cambridge, MA.: MIT Press, 2007.

[12] T. Joachims, "Making large-scale SVM learning practical," in *Advances in Kernel Methods - Support Vector Learning*, MIT Press, 1998.

[13] S. Har-Peled, D. Roth, and D. Zimak, "Constraint classification for multiclass classification and ranking," in *NIPS*, 2003.

[14] K. Crammer and Y. Singer, "On the learnability and design of output codes for multiclass problems," in *COLT*, 2000.

[15] S. S. Keerthi, S. Sundararajan, K.-W. Chang, C.-J. Hsieh, and C.-J. Lin, "A sequential dual method for large scale multi-class linear SVMs," in *ACM KDD*, 2008.

[16] L. Bottou and Y. L. Cun, "Large scale online learning," in *NIPS*, 2004.

[17] S. Shalev-Shwartz and N. Srebro, "SVM optimization: inverse dependence on training set size," in *ICML*, 2008.

[18] M. Collins and B. Roark, "Incremental parsing with the perceptron algorithm," in *ACL*, 2004.

[19] K. Woodsend and J. Gondzio, "Hybrid mpi/openmp parallel linear support vector machine training," *JMLR*, vol. 10, pp. 1937–1953, 2009.

[20] E. Chang, K. Zhu, H. Wang, H. Bai, J. Li, Z. Qiu, and H. Cui, "Parallelizing support vector machines on distributed computers," in *NIPS*, 2007.

[21] J. Langford, A. J. Smola, and M. Zinkevich, "Slow learners are fast," in *NIPS*, 2009.

[22] H. Yu, J. Yang, and J. Han, "Classifying large data sets using SVMs with hierarchical clusters," in *ACM KDD*, 2003.

[23] J. L. Balcázar, Y. Dai, and O. Watanabe, "A random sampling technique for training support vector machines," in *ALT*, 2001.

[24] L. Breiman, "Bagging predictors," *Machine Learning*, vol. 24, pp. 123–140, August 1996.

[25] M. Zinkevich, M. Weimer, A. Smola, and L. Li, "Parallelized stochastic gradient descent," in *NIPS*, 2010.

[26] F. Pérez-Cruz, A. R. Figueiras-Vidal, and A. Artés-Rodríguez, "Double chunking for solving SVMs for very large datasets," in *Proceedings of Learning 2004, Spain*, 2004.

[27] S. Tong and D. Koller, "Support vector machine active learning with applications to text classification," *JMLR*, vol. 2, pp. 45–66, 2002.

[28] S. V. N. Vishwanathan, A. J. Smola, and M. N. Murty, "Simplesvm," in *ICML*, 2003.

[29] K. Scheinberg, "An efficient implementation of an active set method for svms," *JMLR*, vol. 7, pp. 2237–2257, 2006.

[30] A. Bordes, S. Ertekin, J. Weston, and L. Bottou, "Fast kernel classifiers with online and active learning," *JMLR*, vol. 6, pp. 1579–1619, 2005.

[31] O. Dekel, S. Shalev-Shwartz, and Y. Singer, "The forgetron: A kernel-based perceptron on a budget," *SIAM Journal on Computing*, vol. 37, pp. 1342–1372, January 2008.

[32] A. Rozovskaya and D. Roth, "Generating confusion sets for context-sensitive error correction," in *EMNLP*, 2010.

[33] H.-F. Yu, C.-J. Hsieh, K.-W. Chang, and C.-J. Lin, "Large linear classification when data cannot fit in memory," tech. rep., National Taiwan University, 2011. `http://www.csie.ntu.edu.tw/~r96050/papers/bm.pdf`.

[34] Y. Freund, R. E. Schapire, Y. Singer, and M. K. Warmuth, "Using and combining predictors that specialize," in *STOC*, 1997.

[35] K. Crammer, M. Dredze, and A. Kulesza, "Multi-class confidence weighted algorithms," in *EMNLP*, 2009.

[36] H.-F. Yu, F.-L. Huang, and C.-J. Lin, "Dual coordinate descent methods for logistic regression and maximum entropy models," *Machine Learning*, 2011. To appear.

Bounded Coordinate-Descent for Biological Sequence Classification in High Dimensional Predictor Space

Georgiana Ifrim
Cork Constraint Computation Centre (4C)
University College Cork
Cork, Ireland
g.ifrim@4c.ucc.ie

Carsten Wiuf
Bioinformatics Research Centre (BiRC)
C.F. Møllers Allé 8
DK-8000 Aarhus C, Denmark
wiuf@cs.au.dk

ABSTRACT

We present a framework for discriminative sequence classification where linear classifiers work directly in the explicit high-dimensional predictor space of all subsequences in the training set (as opposed to kernel-induced spaces). This is made feasible by employing a gradient-bounded coordinate-descent algorithm for efficiently selecting discriminative subsequences without having to expand the whole space. Our framework can be applied to a wide range of loss functions, including binomial log-likelihood loss of logistic regression and squared hinge loss of support vector machines. When applied to protein remote homology detection and remote fold recognition, our framework achieves comparable performance to the state-of-the-art (e.g., kernel support vector machines). In contrast to state-of-the-art sequence classifiers, our models are simply lists of weighted discriminative subsequences and can thus be interpreted and related to the biological problem – a crucial requirement for the bioinformatics and medical communities.

Categories and Subject Descriptors

H.3 [**Information Storage and Retrieval**]: Content Analysis and Indexing; I.2.6 [**Artificial Intelligence**]: Learning

General Terms

Algorithms, Performance, Experimentation

Keywords

Greedy Coordinate-Descent, Sequence Classification, String Classification, Logistic Regression, Support Vector Machines

1. INTRODUCTION

Many problems in biology today require accurate computational prediction of properties. For example, the primary DNA sequence is a main determinant of functional and structural protein properties, yet little is known about this relationship and we must therefore turn to computational prediction for advancing our understanding. Likewise, accurate gene and motif prediction is of crucial importance for the annotation of recently sequenced genomes. To achieve this goal, we need machine learning techniques that are fast, highly scalable and preferably treat feature selection as an integral part of the learning algorithm. The latter requirement means that neither time nor expertise is invested in pre-processing the original data (e.g., for defining features) and no potentially hard to validate assumptions are made about data distribution. Recent advances in developing efficient machine learning tools such as fast logistic regression [7, 27, 28] and support vector machines [16, 9, 36, 35] enable learning of classifiers in very large predictor spaces, thus reducing the need for pre-processing the data. Nevertheless, most of these techniques are typically designed to exploit the sparsity of the training set (i.e., many features occur sparsely in the training data) which holds for many applications, such as text categorization [27, 9]. This assumption unfortunately does not hold for biological sequences, where many subsequences often occur very frequently.

We present an efficient coordinate-descent algorithm for optimizing regularized fitting of classification loss in high dimensional predictor space. Our approach does not rely on feature sparsity assumptions. In our framework, the feature space is spanned by all subsequences present in the training set. Furthermore, the features can have a flexible number of wildcard matches, which allows us to model complex biological processes such as substitutions, insertions and deletions. The optimization proceeds coordinate-wise by iteratively selecting the feature with maximum (absolute) gradient value, following the Gauss-Southwell rule [30, 37]. In order to select the best features quickly, we provide bounds on the gradient value of any subsequence based on its prefix. This drastically reduces the search space. We discuss the tightness of the proposed bounds as well as the convergence of the algorithm.

Our learning technique is applicable to both unregularized and regularized loss functions. In this paper we show bounds for the more complex case of *elastic-net* regularized loss [10]. By adding an explicit elastic-net penalty (a convex combination of $l1$ and $l2$ regularizers) to the loss function, we allow the user to directly trade-off $l1$-regularization (encouraging model sparsity) for $l2$-regularization (correcting for correlations) [8, 10, 6]. As can be observed in our experiments this positively affects the prediction quality. We present applications of our learning algorithm to protein remote homology detection and fold recognition. In order to compare to previously published results, we work with standard protein benchmarks. For homology detection we use SCOP1.59 [15, 22, 24, 19], and for fold recognition we use the challenging dataset of [3]. The classification problems associated with these datasets are hard and the training data is rather small scale (2,800 and 300 sequences respectively). In order to further analyse the scalability of our technique, we present a large scale experiment on the latest version of the Silva-LSUPARC102 database (150,000 unique sequences). We compare our algorithm to state-of-the-art sequence classifiers, support vector machines with spectrum kernel [24], mismatch kernel [22, 21], and the recent sparse spatial sample kernel [19, 20]. Besides being fast and highly accurate, our classification models are easily interpretable, an important advantage for the bioinformatics and medical communities.

The remainder of this paper proceeds as follows. Section 2 addresses related work. Section 3 presents our learning framework. Section 4 and 5 analyse the experimental setup and results. We conclude with pointers to future work in Section 6.

2. RELATED WORK

Working in high dimensional predictor space and regularizing is statistically preferable to a two-step procedure of first reducing the dimension, then fitting a model in the reduced space [32]. Recently, efficient regularized learning algorithms for logistic regression and support vector machines (SVM) were proposed for fitting classifiers in high dimensional predictor space [27, 9]. In order to scale, most of these techniques restrict the allowed features (i.e., use k-mers, for fixed and reasonably small k) and exploit the feature space sparsity. For some applications, such as text categorization, where the features occur sparsely in the training instances, existing techniques perform very well [12]. However, this is not the case for applications involving biological sequence classification where the feature space is dense (i.e., many subsequences occur in many of the training sequences), thus challenging the running time and memory requirements of existing methods.

Recent work on efficiently computing string kernels for SVM [22, 24, 19, 33, 36] addressed some of the computational challenges associated with this type of techniques. Nevertheless, the kernels proposed still restrict the set of features to subsequences of certain length (e.g, $k = 10$) or format (e.g., allowing some mismatches) in order to scale. In this paper we work with the space of all (unrestricted-length) subsequences in the training set and allow wildcard matches.

A popular class of models used for sequence classification is the generative classifier family, such as profile Hidden Markov Models [4]. Generative models only learn from positive training examples, while discriminative techniques (such as SVM and those proposed in this paper) directly focus on separating the positive and negative training examples. Previous work has shown that discriminative approaches outperform generative approaches for sequence classification [2, 22, 17].

In this paper we propose learning linear classifiers directly in the explicit high dimensional feature space rather than using an implicit mapping via a string kernel as in kernel-SVM. The computational trick in our algorithm is to use coordinate descent coupled with bounding the search for the best coordinate. The idea of using branch-and-bound to efficiently search the feature space has been proposed for graph boosting [18]. Boosting approximately minimizes its l1-regularized loss criterion [32]. Our generic algorithm can be used for *exact* regularized fitting of a range of classification loss functions, such as exponential loss, binomial log-likelihood loss of logistic regression, gaussian loss and the squared hinge-loss of SVM [8]. This work is an extension of [14] which focused on (unregularized) logistic regression applied to text categorization. Here, we extend the bounds of [14] to a class of regularized loss functions, discuss the tightness of the proposed bounds and focus on the aspect of dense feature spaces characteristic of biological applications.

3. METHOD PROPOSED

In this section we present our generic learning algorithm and its concrete implementation for logistic regression and support vector machines.

3.1 Preliminaries and Basic Notation

We first introduce the theoretical framework and some basic notation. Assume we have a training set of instance-label pairs $\{x_i, y_i\}_{i=1}^N$, with $y_i \in \{-1, +1\}$. The training instances x_i are sequences, e.g., biological sequences $x_i = AGTCAACTGGAA....$, text sequences $x_i = ABCD...$, sequences of rankings $x_i = A < B < C < D < \ldots$, sequences of tasks $x_i = ABCD\ldots$. Let d be the number of distinct subsequences in the feature space. We formally represent the training sequences as binary vectors in the space of all subsequences of the training set: $x_i = (x_{i1}, \ldots x_{ij}, \ldots x_{id})^T$, $x_{ij} \in \{0, 1\}$, $i = \overline{1, N}$. Let $\beta = (\beta_1, \ldots, \beta_j, \ldots, \beta_d)$ be a parameter vector (defining a linear classifier).

The goal is to learn a mapping, also called classification model, $f : X \to \{-1, +1\}$ from the given training set such that given a new sample $x \in X$, we can predict a label $y \in \{-1, +1\}$.

Let

$$L(\beta) = \sum_{i=1}^{N} \xi(y_i, x_i, \beta) + CR_\alpha(\beta) \quad (1)$$

be the regularized classification loss criterion. Here, $\xi(y_i, x_i, \beta)$ is a classification loss function, C is a constant and $R_\alpha(\beta)$ is a regularizer. Learning a classification model is achieved by finding the parameter vector β that minimizes the regularized classification loss on the training set

$$\hat{\beta} = \text{argmin}_\beta L(\beta).$$

In Equations (2)–(5) we list a few examples of commonly used classification loss functions.

$$Exponential\ loss : \xi(y_i, x_i, \beta) = e^{-y_i\beta^t x_i} \quad (2)$$

$$Binomial\ loglikelihood\ loss : \xi(y_i, x_i, \beta) = \log(1+e^{-y_i\beta^t x_i}) \quad (3)$$

$$Squared\ hinge\ loss : \xi(y_i, x_i, \beta) = \max(1 - y_i\beta^t x_i, 0)^2 \quad (4)$$

$$Gaussian\ loss^1 : \xi(y_i, x_i, \beta) = \log \frac{1}{\Phi(y_i\beta^t x_i)} \quad (5)$$

The penalty weight $C \geq 0$ controls the amount of regularization of the parameter vector β. A large C means more

[1] Φ is the cdf of the standard normal distribution.

penalty on the β parameters. The regularization term can take various forms, the most common being the $l1$ and the $l2$ (Equation (6)). In our work $R_\alpha(\beta)$ is the elastic-net regularizer [10, 6] (defined in Equation (7)), which is a compromise between the $l2$ ($\alpha = 0$) and the $l1$ ($\alpha = 1$).

$$l1 = \sum_{j=1}^{d} |\beta_j|, \qquad l2 = \frac{1}{2}\sum_{j=1}^{d} \beta_j^2 \tag{6}$$

$$R_\alpha(\beta) = \alpha \sum_{j=1}^{d} |\beta_j| + (1-\alpha)\frac{1}{2}\sum_{j=1}^{d} \beta_j^2 \tag{7}$$

Depending on the type of regularization, increasing the weight C of the penalty term results in many zero β_j (for $l1$-regularization) or shrinking the coefficients β_j of correlated predictors (for $l2$-regularization). The elastic-net regularizer allows balancing the two effects.

3.2 Gradient-Bounded Coordinate-Descent Algorithm

In this section we describe our learning algorithm and characterize the properties of loss functions to which it can be applied. Assume the following properties for the loss function:

1. ξ depends on y_i, x_i and β only through the classification margin $m_i = y_i \beta^t x_i$. Note that x_i is correctly classified if the margin m_i is positive and the higher the margin the higher the classification confidence. We write $\xi(y, x, \beta) = \xi(m)$.
2. ξ is a monotone decreasing function of the margin: $\xi'(m) \leq 0$.
3. ξ is convex and continuously differentiable.

Properties 1-2 are required for the bounding strategy (Theorem 1), while property 3 is required for the convergence result (Theorem 2). The gradient of $L(\beta)$ (defined in Equation (1)) with respect to a coordinate β_j is

$$\frac{\partial L}{\partial \beta_j}(\beta) = \sum_{i=1}^{N} y_i x_{ij} \xi'(y_i \beta^t x_i) + C[\alpha \text{ sign}(\beta_j) + (1-\alpha)\beta_j]$$

or using the margin notation

$$\frac{\partial L}{\partial \beta_j}(\beta) = \sum_{i=1}^{N} y_i x_{ij} \xi'(m_i) + C R'_\alpha(\beta_j).$$

If $R_\alpha(\beta)$ is not differentiable in $\beta = 0$ we use the left-right derivatives. We proceed minimizing $L(\beta)$ by coordinate-wise gradient descent in the feature space of all subsequences. In each iteration we update only the coordinate corresponding to the subsequence with the largest gradient magnitude, following the Gauss-Southwell rule [30]:

$$j = \text{argmax}_l \left| \frac{\partial L}{\partial \beta_l}(\beta) \right|$$

This results in a greedy advance towards the optimum of the objective function, without having to explicitly generate the full space of subsequences. All we need is an efficient way to find the best coordinate (i.e., feature) in each iteration. We summarize the steps of our generic coordinate-descent algorithm in Algorithm 1. The core part of the algorithm is a search routine (line 2(a) in Algorithm 1) that quickly returns the best feature in each iteration. The search procedure relies on bounding the gradient value of any subsequence early on, by only looking at its prefix. This looks difficult at first glance since the prefix may be a poor feature, while its extension can be highly discriminative. The intuition behind our bound is based on two observations: the gradient is determined by class-wise feature frequency and the subsequence space has structure (that we can exploit to bound the per-class frequency). More concretely, a feature has high gradient value if its frequent in one class and infrequent in the other. Per class, the frequency of a given feature is bounded by the frequency of its prefix. Thus, class-wise, we can bound the gradient of a given subsequence based on its prefix, and then build a global bound from the class-wise bounds. Using this bound we can discard large parts of the search space during the search for the best subsequence, making the whole search process efficient, both time-wise (fast running time) and space-wise (low memory). Once we found the best feature, we do an adapted Armijo rule line search [37, 12] to compute the feature weight and guarantee convergence.

Algorithm 1 Generic coordinate-descent algorithm

1. Set $\beta^{(0)} = 0$
2. For t=1:T
   (a) Find $j_t = \text{argmax}_j \left| \frac{\partial L}{\partial \beta_{j_t}}(\beta^{(t-1)}) \right|$ (using Theorem 1)
   (b) Use line search to set the step length ϵ_t for coordinate j_t
   (c) Set $\beta_{j_t}^{(t)} = \beta_{j_t}^{(t-1)} - \epsilon_t \frac{\partial L}{\partial \beta_{j_t}}(\beta^{(t-1)})$ and $\beta_k^{(t)} = \beta_k^{(t-1)}, k \neq j_t$

Let j be a coordinate corresponding to a given subsequence s_j, and l be a coordinate corresponding to a super sequence of s_j, s_l, i.e. s_j is a prefix of s_l. We write $s_j \in x_i$ to denote $x_{ij} \neq 0$.

The following theorem gives a *tight* upper bound on the gradient value of any subsequence.

THEOREM 1. *For any loss function ξ satisfying properties 1-2 and any subsequence $s_l \supseteq s_j$, $j = 1, \ldots, d$,*

$$\left| \frac{\partial L}{\partial \beta_l}(\beta) \right| \leq \max \left\{ \left| \sum_{\{i | \mathbf{s_j} \in \mathbf{x_i}, y_i = +1\}} \xi'(m_i) + C R'_\alpha(\beta_l) \right|, \left| \sum_{\{i | \mathbf{s_j} \in \mathbf{x_i}, y_i = -1\}} -\xi'(m_i) + C R'_\alpha(\beta_l) \right| \right\}. \tag{8}$$

PROOF. *We split the analysis in two parts, the first part focuses on deriving a bound within the negative class, and the second part focuses on the positive class. Recall that*

$\xi'(m) \leq 0$. *Then,*

$$\begin{aligned}
\frac{\partial L}{\partial \beta_l}(\beta) &= \sum_{\{i|s_l \in x_i\}} y_i x_{il} \xi'(m_i) + CR'_\alpha(\beta_l) \qquad (9)\\
&\leq \sum_{\{i|s_l \in x_i, y_i=-1\}} y_i x_{il} \xi'(m_i) + CR'_\alpha(\beta_l)\\
&\leq \sum_{\{i|s_j \in x_i, y_i=-1\}} y_i x_{ij} \xi'(m_i) + CR'_\alpha(\beta_l)\\
&= \sum_{\{i|s_j \in x_i, y_i=-1\}} -\xi'(m_i) + CR'_\alpha(\beta_l)
\end{aligned}$$

The last inequality in Equation (9) holds because of the anti-monotonicity property $\{i|s_l \in x_i, y_i = -1\} \subseteq \{i|s_j \in x_i, y_i = -1\}$. *Similarly, we can show for the positive class that*

$$\frac{\partial L}{\partial \beta_l}(\beta) \geq \sum_{\{i|s_j \in x_i, y_i=+1\}} \xi'(m_i) + CR'_\alpha(\beta_l)$$

Thus we obtain the lower and upper bounds

$$\begin{aligned}
\sum_{\{i|s_j \in x_i, y_i=+1\}} \xi'(m_i) + CR'_\alpha(\beta_l) \leq \frac{\partial L}{\partial \beta_l}(\beta) \qquad (10)\\
\leq \sum_{\{i|s_j \in x_i, y_i=-1\}} -\xi'(m_i) + CR'_\alpha(\beta_l).
\end{aligned}$$

We are interested in an upper bound on the absolute magnitude of the gradient at a given coordinate, thus we write more conveniently

$$\left|\frac{\partial L}{\partial \beta_l}(\beta)\right| \leq \max \left\{ \left| \sum_{\{i|s_j \in x_i, y_i=+1\}} \xi'(m_i) + CR'_\alpha(\beta_l) \right|, \left| \sum_{\{i|s_j \in x_i, y_i=-1\}} -\xi'(m_i) + CR'_\alpha(\beta_l) \right| \right\}.$$

□

The main property on which Theorem 1 relies on (last inequality in Equation (9)) is *anti-monotonicity*: the prefix frequency is higher than that of its extension subsequence. This means that the same bound holds for *any* weight x_j as long as $x_j \geq x_l$. This observation is useful for example if we want to integrate prior biological knowledge about the target problem, such as the fact that some amino acids in protein sequences are more useful than others. We could encode this information by giving weights $w_a \in (0, 1)$ to individual amino acids and still have the property that $x_j = \Pi_a w_a \geq x_l$.

As we can observe from Equation (8), without explicit regularization of the loss function, the upper bound on the gradient of a subsequence s_l solely depends on the frequency of its prefix s_j. This means that we can decide not to expand the s_j prefix further, without inspecting the longer feature s_l. If we use a regularizer, we have the term β_l in the bound which depends on the longer subsequence, rather than the prefix alone. Thus, we have to take care to compute the correct bound whenever $\beta_l \neq 0$. Since at start all β_j are zero, during the iterations we only need to check those features that have non-zero β_l because they were selected in the model in previous iterations. In practice, as supported by our experiments, this part is fairly fast due to the sparsity of the final model learned by this algorithm.

The bound presented in Theorem 1 is tight since we can construct examples for which the inequality is an equality. Consider the simple case of a training set with positive examples of the type $AAAAAAA$, and negative examples of the type $BBBBBB$. Whenever the subsequence set of occurrences is the same as that of its prefix, the inequality becomes equality.

The iterates generated by Algorithm 1 converge to the optimal solution of the objective function given in Equation (1). Based on results from [37] characterizing the convergence of iterates generated by coordinate-descent using the Gauss-Southwell rule for l1-regularized convex minimization we have:

THEOREM 2. *Let* $\beta^{(t)}$ *be a sequence of iterates generated by Algorithm 1. Then* $\beta^{(t)}$ *converges to the optimal solution of (1).*

In the next subsections we describe the specific bounds used to design learning algorithms in the style of Algorithm 1 for logistic regression and support vector machines. We choose these popular classifiers for concrete implementations because their loss functions satisfy the properties 1-3 and they are margin maximizing [32]. The latter property typically translates into good generalization ability in practice.

3.3 Logistic Regression

Let

$$L(\beta) = \sum_{i=1}^{N} \log(1 + e^{-y_i \beta^t x_i}) + CR_\alpha(\beta)$$

be the elastic-net-regularized binomial log-likelihood loss [8]. The gradient of $L(\beta)$ with respect to a coordinate j at a given parameter vector β is:

$$\frac{\partial L}{\partial \beta_j}(\beta) = \sum_{i=1}^{N} y_i x_{ij} \underbrace{\left(\frac{-1}{1 + e^{y_i \beta^t x_i}}\right)}_{\xi'(m_i)} + CR'_\alpha(\beta_l)$$

COROLLARY 1. *For binomial log-likelihood loss and any subsequence* $s_l \supseteq s_j$, $j = 1, \ldots, d$,

$$\left|\frac{\partial L}{\partial \beta_l}(\beta)\right| \leq \max \left\{ \left| \sum_{\{i|s_j \in x_i, y_i=+1\}} \frac{-1}{1 + e^{\beta^t x_i}} + CR'_\alpha(\beta_l) \right|, \left| \sum_{\{i|s_j \in x_i, y_i=-1\}} \frac{1}{1 + e^{-\beta^t x_i}} + CR'_\alpha(\beta_l) \right| \right\}.$$

3.4 Support Vector Machines

Let

$$L(\beta) = \sum_{i=1}^{N} \max(1 - y_i \beta^t x_i, 0)^2 - CR_\alpha(\beta)$$

be the elastic-net-regularized squared hinge loss [1]. We can rewrite $L(\beta)$ in the equivalent form

$$L(\beta) = \sum_{\{i|1 - y_i \beta^t x_i > 0\}} (1 - y_i \beta^t x_i)^2 + CR_\alpha(\beta)$$

The gradient of $L(\beta)$ with respect to a coordinate j at a given parameter vector β is:

$$\frac{\partial L}{\partial \beta_j}(\beta) = \sum_{\{i|1 - y_i \beta^t x_i > 0\}} y_i x_{ij} \underbrace{2(y_i \beta^t x_i - 1)}_{\xi'(m_i)} + CR'_\alpha(\beta_l)$$

COROLLARY 2. *For squared hinge loss and any subsequence* $s_l \supseteq s_j$, $j = 1, \ldots, d$,

$$\left|\frac{\partial L}{\partial \beta_l}(\beta)\right| \le \max\left\{ \left| \sum_{\{i | s_j \in x_i, 1-\beta^t x_i > 0, y_i = +1\}} 2(\beta^t x_i - 1) + C R'_\alpha(\beta_l) \right|, \left| \sum_{\{i | s_j \in x_i, 1+\beta^t x_i > 0, y_i = -1\}} 2(1 + \beta^t x_i) + C R'_\alpha(\beta_l) \right| \right\}.$$

3.5 Algorithmic Details

In this section we give some details on using the bound of Theorem 1 to prune the search space.

Before starting the optimization iterations we build an inverted index on all the distinct unigrams in the training set, i.e., a list of document ids and positions of occurrence for each unigram. In each iteration we start the process of searching for the best feature from the level of unigrams.

We implement two strategies of prefix-expansion. The breadth-first-search (BFS) expands all unigrams to bi-grams, then all bi-grams to tri-grams, etc. For each unigram, we compute the gradient value, we keep track of the best gradient/feature seen so far and we compare the bound to the current best gradient. If the bound is lower than the current best gradient value, no subsequence starting with this unigram can improve the current optimum and we prune this part of the search space (i.e., we discard this prefix). Then we move on to the next level of expansion, and repeat this process. The depth-first-search (DFS) strategy expands the unigram to its longest subsequence until the pruning condition is met, and it then backtracks to the longest valid prefix and re-attempts to expand. Depending on the sequence tokenization used, word-level or character-level, the two strategies have different benefits. For word-level tokenization, such as in text categorization, short subsequences are more likely to be useful than long ones (e.g., phrases of 2-3 words are typically good discriminators), and therefore BFS may be a better expansion strategy. For character-level tokenization, such as for biological sequences, longer subsequences tend to be more useful than shorter ones (e.g., subsequences of length 3 or less may occur in all the sequences), so DFS is a better expansion choice. For the experiments in this paper we have used DFS. In order to keep track of the occurrences of all active prefixes (e.g., subsequences that could not be pruned using Theorem 1), we expand the inverted index on-demand. The inverted index does not grow excessively due to the effectiveness of the bound. After selecting the feature with the best gradient in a given iteration, we do a line search to compute the final feature weight [12]. We stop the optimization iterations based on a threshold on the change of predicted scores [12].

The worst-case complexity of each iteration is $O(dN)$, where d is the number of features and N is the number of training samples. In practice, our algorithm drastically prunes the search space and is thus very fast. For example, for the classification task *Scorpion-toxin like* (presented in detail in Section 5) we have observed the following behaviour. There are 23 distinct unigrams in the training set (22 amino acids and we add the wildcard as an additional unigram). The longest sequence in the training set has length 892, and the average sequence lenght is ~ 50. Even if we were to restrict the maximum k-mer size to $k = 50$, the number of features d is $O(23^{50})$ (all the subsequences up to size $k = 50$ created using the 23 unigrams; in practice, there are 6.5 million such features in the training set). For finding the best feature in the first iteration using SVM loss and unrestricted k, our algorithm checks the pruning bound 1,113 times, and prunes the space 1,104 times (i.e., discards 1,104 prefixes out of the total 1,113 analysed). The algorithm stops in 3 seconds, after 77 iterations. In the last iteration, it checks the bound 14,077 times and prunes the space 13,952 times. Thus, the bound in Theorem 1 efficiently prunes the huge search space. For future work we will focus on quantitative measures of index growth as a function of the alphabet size and number of training examples.

For simplifying the implementation we currently prune the space using a prefix-expansion strategy. Theorem 1 however can be used for pruning all features that contain a given subsequence, not necessarily in the start position as a prefix. This observation could be used to further speed up the training process.

4. EXPERIMENTS

We implement the generic coordinate-descent algorithm in our machine learning tool SEQL (**SEQ**uence **L**earner), available from `http://www.daimi.au.dk/~ifrim/seql` (v2.0). For now, SEQL implements the two elastic-net-regularized classifiers presented in the previous section: logistic regression and support vector machines. In this section we describe the datasets, the techniques compared and the methodology for designing experiments.

4.1 Datasets

In order to compare our results to the state-of-the-art we compare directly to published results and perform experiments on the same benchmarks.

For **protein remote homology detection** we use the benchmark SCOP1.59 [22, 24, 38, 19]. This is an expert-curated database of protein domains organized heirarchically into folds, superfamilies and families. Protein sequences belonging to different families, but the same superfamily, are considered to be remote homologs in SCOP. This dataset contains 2,862 labeled sequences organized into 54 binary classification problems simulating homology detection by predicting the super-family using a hold-one-family-out strategy. No pair of sequences shares more than 95% identity. The positive training sets are quite small and the learning task is challenging. For more details on this benchmark see [15, 24, 38].

For **protein remote fold recognition** we use the benchmark published by [3]. This dataset consists of sequences from 27 folds divided into two independent sets such that the training and test sequences share less than 35% sequence identities and within the training set, no sequences share more than 40% sequence identities. There are 311 training sequences and 383 test sequences.

In order to analyze the **scalability** of our method in a large scale experiment, we have downloaded the latest **ribosomal RNA** (rRNA) database Silva-LSUParc[2] [31], version 102 (released in February 2010.) The LSUParc102 database contains 180,344 rRNA sequences. After removing duplicate sequences we obtain a dataset of 150,780 unique sequences organized in 3 (one-vs-all) binary classification tasks

[2]Silva-LSUParc database: http://www.arb-silva.de/documentation/background/release-102/.

according to the Bacteria, Archaea and Eukarya domains. The distribution by domain is dominated by Eukarya with 141,601 sequences, followed by Bacteria with 8,967 and Archaea with 212 sequences. All datasets are available from http://www.daimi.au.dk/~ifrim/seql/data.

4.2 Techniques Compared

Previous studies have shown that discriminative approaches for sequence classification (such as kernel-SVM) outperform generative approaches (such as profile HMM) by a large margin [2, 17, 22, 26].

We compare our algorithms to the latest sequence kernels for SVM: the spectrum kernel, the mismatch kernel [22, 24, 29], and the recent sparse spatial sample kernel (SSSK) [20, 19]. All these methods aim at computing similarity for all pairs of sequences (the kernel matrix) in a particular feature space. Due to computational challenges, these techniques typically restrict the length and expressive power of the subsequences used as features. For example, the spectrum-k kernel [23] implicitly compares sequences in the space of all k-mers, where the length k of subsequence-features is a parameter of the model. The mismatch kernel [22] generalizes the spectrum-k kernel by allowing up to m mismatches or substitutions to accomodate mutations. The sparse spatial sample kernel (SSSK) further generalizes the mismatch kernel by sampling the sequences at different resolutions and comparing the resulting spectra [19]. SSSK has 3 parameters, (k, t, d), where k is the probe size, t is the number of probes and d is the number of *maximum* allowed positions between the probes. Our learning algorithm SEQL uses all (unrestricted-length) subsequences in the training set as features. Furthermore, we also allow mismatches or so called wildcard matches, by a parameter that controls the *maximum* number of *consecutive* wildcards allowed. This allows us to model complex biological processes such as substitutions, insertions and deletions. Figure 1 gives examples of the types of features implicitly used by the above described kernels, as compared to the features used by our technique.

One advantage of kernel techniques is their ability to integrate unlabeled data during kernel computation to relax labeled data requirements [19]. However, computing all-pair similarities for large datasets (resulting from the addition of unlabeled sequences) remains computationally very challenging for kernel methods both time and memory-wise. For example, we couldn't apply any of the above mentioned kernel methods on our large dataset (150,000 sequences) since this would require more than 90GByte memory. In contrast, by exploiting the feature space structure, SEQL can use more expresive features and still be able to scale.

For completion we also report the results of a technique published by [26] which applies SVM using an empirical kernel map based on pairwise Smith-Waterman sequence alignment scores (SVM-pairwise in Table1).

We use SEQL-LR and SEQL-SVM to denote the logistic regression and support vector machines implementations of our generic learning algorithm.

4.3 Methodology

Previous studies on biological sequence classification have extensively used the AUC (area under the ROC curve) and AUC50 for evaluation [5, 24, 34]. AUC describes the ranking of prediction scores rather then being dependent on a fixed classification threshold. The ROC curve is obtained by plotting the fraction of true positives versus the fraction of false positives for a binary classifier as its discrimination threshold is varied [5]. A common aggregate measure is to report the area under the ROC curve (AUC) where an area of 1 represents a perfect ranking of all positives above all negatives and an area close to 0.5 represents a random classifier. The AUC50 focuses on top ranked examples and is defined as the normalized area under the ROC curve computed for up to 50 true negatives [34]. It is typically used to evaluate classifiers on datasets where the number of positives is much lower than the number of negatives. While for a complete test set the AUC is betwen 0.5 and 1, the AUC values for truncated top lists are between 0 and 1. The shorter the top list is, the smaller the AUC values [34]. In some studies instead of AUC or AUC50 only the balanced-error-rate (BER) is reported. To compare our results to the state-of-the-art, we also show the balanced-error (Equation (11)) which measures the average of the errors on each class for a fixed classification threshold. It can equivalently be interpreted in terms of Specificity and Sensitivity [25].

$$BER = \frac{1}{2}\left(\underbrace{\frac{FN}{TP+FN}}_{1-\text{Sensitivity}} + \underbrace{\frac{FP}{FP+TN}}_{1-\text{Specificity}}\right) \quad (11)$$

The benchmarks for remote homology detection and fold recognition have pre-defined training and test splits. We use the same data for experiments for all methods compared, and for the prior techniques *we report directly the results published in the original papers*. For the large scale experiment on ribosomal RNA, we show 5-fold cross-validation results on the full dataset. Since the prior techniques required more than the available memory, for the large dataset we only report results using our method.

All experiments were run on a Linux laptop with 2.5GByte memory and 2.8GHz Intel CPU.

5. RESULTS AND DISCUSSION

In this section we present the results of applying SEQL-LR and SEQL-SVM to protein remote homology detection and fold recognition. Furthermore, to evaluate the scalability of our approach, we present a large-scale experiment on the latest release of the Silva-LSUParc database [31].

5.1 Comparison to State-of-the-Art

We first compare the performance of SEQL-LR and SEQL-SVM to that of kernel-SVM techniques on two protein classification tasks.

5.1.1 *Protein remote homology detection*

In Table 1 we show results on the SCOP1.59 benchmark for all compared methods. The numbers in brackets next to the name of each method refer to their explicit parameters as discussed in the previous section (e.g., length k of subsequences used as features or maximum number of wildcards). The results are averaged over all 54 binary classification tasks which correspond to superfamilies.

For SEQL-LR and SEQL-SVM we do grid search to set d (the maximum allowed number of consecutive wildcards, $d \in \{0, 1, 2, .., 5\}$), and the regularization parameters C and α of the elastic-net penalty ($C \in \{0, 0.001, 0.01, .., 100\}$, $\alpha \in \{0, 0.1, 0.2, .., 1\}$). We show the most accurate results across

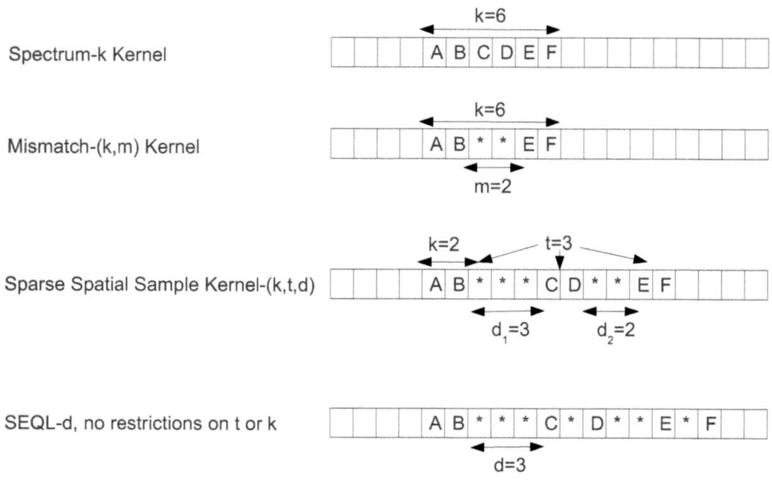

Figure 1: Features employed by state-of-the-art kernels versus our method SEQL. Spectrum-k Kernel, k is the length of features. Mismatch-(k,m) Kernel, k is the length of features, m is the maximum number of mismatches. Sparse Spatial Sample-(k,t,d) Kernel, k is the probe size, t is the number of probes and d is the number of maximum allowed positions between the probes. SEQL-d, d is the maximum number of consecutive wildcards.

Method	AUC	AUC50	BER
SVM-SPECTRUM(2)	0.8581	0.3583	-
SVM-SPECTRUM(3)	0.8723	0.4037	-
SVM-MISMATCH(5,1)	0.8749	0.4167	-
SVM-SSSK(1,2,5)	0.8901	0.4629	-
SVM-SSSK(1,3,3)	0.9148	0.5118	-
SVM-pairwise	0.8930	0.4340	-
SEQL-LR(5)	**0.9155**	**0.5184**	**0.4477**
SEQL-SVM(5)	**0.9220**	**0.5237**	**0.4158**

Table 1: Remote homology detection on the Scop1.59 dataset. The average AUC, AUC50 and BER scores over the 54 target superfamilies. Results for kernel-SVM methods cited directly from [24, 19]. SEQL-LR and SEQL-SVM are the methods proposed in this paper.

the parameter values tried. We observe that our techniques are comparable to the state-of-the-art methods regarding classification quality. We believe it is important to allow flexible features, (e.g., allowing wildcards and not restricting the feature lenght in advance), although here the training sets are quite small and the gain is not large. We note that SEQL-SVM has slightly better AUC and AUC50 than SEQL-LR. Learning SEQL classifiers on this dataset took a few seconds per topic and about 80MByte memory. The computational requirements of SEQL are mainly influenced by the maximum allowed number of consecutive wildcards.

Figure 2 shows a graphic comparison of some of the methods (for which we had access to published per class AUC50 scores) by plotting the total number of superfamilies above an AUC50 score threshold, as a function of the threshold value. The threshold is changed so as to generate the next AUC50 value in the ranked list of AUC50 scores of the respective method. The numerical integral of this cumulative

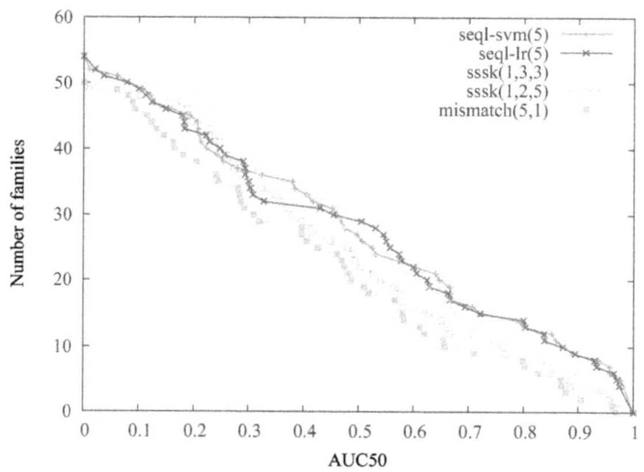

Figure 2: Comparison of mismatch-SVM, SSSK-SVM, SEQL-LR and SEQL-SVM on SCOP1.59. The total number of superfamilies for which a given method exceeds an AUC50 score threshold.

AUC50 curve is the arithmetic average of the AUC50 values shown in Table 1 [34]. SVM with sparse-sample-spatial kernel (SSSK-SVM) behaves best among the prior techniques. Even though the features employed by SSSK-SVM are quite flexible (see Figure 1), we observe we can gain some performance by imposing less restrictions on features.

[19] analyzed the biological relevance of features learned by SSSK-SVM taking the *Scorpion toxin-like* superfamily as an example. This classification task has 16 members of this superfamily as positive training examples, 1067 non-members as negative examples and the *short-chain scorpion toxin* family as a test case. SSSK-SVM(1,2,5) achieved an AUC50 of 0.7661 for this task [19]. In their work [19] present the schematic representation of the *short-chain scorpion toxin*

family obtained from PROSITE [11]. The PROSITE database consists of a large collection of manually-curated biologically meaningful signatures that are described as patterns or profiles [11]. In Figure 3 we show the PROSITE representation. The scheme shows that these type of toxins contain six

```
       +---------------------+
       |                     |
       |     xxxxxxxxxxxxxxxxxxxxxxxx
*******C*****C***C***********C****C*C***
             |   |                |  |
             |   +----------------|-+
             +--------------------+

'C': conserved cysteine involved in a disulfide bond.
'x': position of the consensus pattern
```

Figure 3: Schematic representation of the *short-chain scorpion toxins* family from PROSITE.

conserved cysteines (C) residues involved in disulfide bonds. PROSITE also lists a consensus pattern present in all the members of this family shown as well in Figure 3 (marked with 'X'). We focus here on the same superfamily and look at the features learned by SEQL-SVM(5). In Table 2 we show

Positive Features	
Weight	Feature
0.0460	SG*C
0.0450	N**C***C
0.0415	C*C**L
0.0410	C***C***G
0.0340	C*C
0.0329	G**G*C
0.0326	C*****C***C
0.0308	GYC
0.0308	C***C
0.0307	G***G*C

Negative Features	
Weight	Feature
-0.0329	G
-0.0313	A
-0.0292	S
-0.0541	Q
-0.0502	E
-0.0462	A*****K
-0.0217	K
-0.0216	CP
-0.0206	C**G
-0.0205	C**C

Table 2: Top-10 positive and negative SEQL-SVM features on the SCOP.1.59 Scorpion-toxin-like superfamily.

the top-10 positive and top-10 negative features selected by SEQL-SVM on this superfamily.

SEQL-SVM(5) has an AUC50 of 0.9573 on this task. [19] analyzed the support vectors of their method and observed that the feature C***C had the highest weight. Similarly, SEQL-SVM(5) selects the feature C***C in top-10, but ranks features such as SG*C and N**C***C higher. In order to understand the effect of these features on the AUC50 score, we took a closer look at the quality of some of the selected features. We observed that although C***C occurs in all positive examples, it is also present in many negatives and is thus less useful than SG*C, which occurs in most positive examples, but in very few negative examples.

5.1.2 Protein remote fold recognition

In this section we show an application of SEQL-LR and SEQL-SVM to protein remote fold recognition on the dataset published by [3]. They proposed a technique based on building an SVM classifier using features deemed biologically relevant for this problem, such as percentage composition of the 20 amino acids, predicted secondary structure, polarity. In Table 3 we show results comparing the technique of [3], denoted by SVM(D&D), with published results of kernel-SVM methods and with our SEQL-LR and SEQL-SVM algorithms. Recall that lower BER means better classification quality.

Method	AUC	AUC50	BER
SVM (D&D)	-	-	0.5650
SVM-MISMATCH(5,1)	-	-	0.5322
SVM-SSSK(1,2,5)	-	-	0.4619
SVM-SSSK(1,3,3)	-	-	0.4499
SEQL-LR(5)	**0.7882**	**0.3551**	**0.4412**
SEQL-SVM(5)	**0.7982**	**0.3742**	**0.4222**

Table 3: Remote fold recognition on the D&D dataset. The average AUC, AUC50 and BER over the 27 target folds. Results for SVM(D&D) and other kernel-SVM methods cited from [3, 19].

Even if we don't use any domain-specific knowledge in this experiment, we observe that our techniques have better classification quality than the method of [3] which relies on deep biological insight. We believe this advantage results from having feature selection as a part of the learning algorithm and allowing for a large degree of flexibility in the features. SEQL-LR and SEQL-SVM outperform the state-of-the-art techniques in terms of balanced-error-rate on this benchmark.

5.2 Large-Scale Experiment

In this section we analyze the scalability of our method on a ribosomal RNA (rRNA) domain-prediction task.

5.2.1 Ribosomal RNA Domain-Prediction

The dataset used for this task contains 150,780 unique rRNA sequences. It is estimated that based on the new capacity for cheap and rapid sequencing there is a steady flow of about 10,000 rRNA sequences per month into the public sequence databases [31]. Furthermore, many sequences are derived from cultivation independent biodiversity surveys, which rely on rapid pattern- or clone-based approaches that often generate partial rRNA sequences [31] (problematic for sequence alignment).

We show the average results of SEQL-LR and SEQL-SVM over 5-fold cross-validation splits for fixed parameter values. We set the amount of regularization $C = 1.0$, we balance $l1$ and $l2$ regularization by setting $\alpha = 0.5$ and allow no wildcards by setting the maximum number of consecutive wildcards $d = 0$.

In Table 4 we show classification quality, training time and memory resources required by SEQL-LR and SEQL-SVM. We

Method	AUC	AUC50	BER	Time	Memory
SEQL-LR	0.9992	0.9745	0.0095	30 min	2GByte
SEQL-SVM	0.9986	0.9744	0.0118	25 min	2GByte

Table 4: Ribosomal RNA domain-prediction on Silva-LSUParc102.

note that both SEQL-based techniques have high classification quality. Additionally, they only take about half-an-hour running-time and a reasonable 2GByte memory instead of 90GByte required by a kernel matrix computation. Instead of building sequence classifiers by costly multiple sequence alignment as currently done for sequence retrieval in this database, we could directly learn domain SEQL-classifiers from the original input sequences in the respective domains.

6. CONCLUSION

In this paper we present a new learning algorithm for sequence classification in high dimensional predictor space. Our framework has at its core a gradient-bounded coordinate-descent strategy to quickly retrieve high quality features. The generic learning algorithm works with a wide range of loss functions, including that of logistic regression and support vector machines. When applied to protein remote homology detection and fold recognition, as well as large-scale domain-prediction for ribosomal RNA, our techniques are comparable to the state-of-the-art in terms of classification quality. In addition, the techniques presented are highly scalable and the resulting classification models can easily be interpreted and connected to biologically relevant facts. Furthermore, the same gradient-bounding strategy can be used for tackling sequence regression [13]. Finally, our algorithm can be applied to more complex structured data such as trees and graphs which follow the anti-monotonicity property required by our theoretical framework. We plan to investigate these research directions in our future work.

7. ACKNOWLEDGMENTS

This work was supported by the Danish Cancer Society and Science Foundation Ireland Grant 10/IN.1/I303.

8. REFERENCES

[1] K.-W. Chang, C.-J. Hsieh, and C.-J. Lin. Coordinate descent method for large-scale l2-loss linear support vector machines. *J. Mach. Learn. Res.*, 9:1369–1398, 2008.

[2] J. Cheng and P. Baldi. A machine learning information retrieval approach to protein fold recognition. *Bioinformatics*, 22(12):1456–1463, 2006.

[3] C. H. Ding and I. Dubchak. Multi-class protein fold recognition using support vector machines and neural networks . *Bioinformatics*, 17(4):349–358, 2001.

[4] S. R. Eddy. Profile hidden markov models. *Bioinformatics*, 14(9):755–763, 1998.

[5] T. Fawcett. Roc graphs: Notes and practical considerations for researchers, 2004.

[6] J. H. Friedman, T. Hastie, and R. Tibshirani. Regularization paths for generalized linear models via coordinate descent. *Journal of Stat. Soft.*, 33(1):1–22, 2010.

[7] A. Genkin, D. Lewis, , and D. Madigan. Large-scale bayesian logistic regression for text categorization. *Technometrics*, 49(3):291–304, 2007.

[8] T. Hastie, R. Tibshirani, and J. Friedman. *The Elements of Statistical Learning.* Springer Series in Statistics, 2003.

[9] C.-J. Hsieh, K.-W. Chang, C.-J. Lin, S. S. Keerthi, and S. Sundararajan. A dual coordinate descent method for large-scale linear SVM. In *ICML*, 2008.

[10] Z. Hui and T. Hastie. Regularization and variable selection via the elastic net. *Journal of the Royal Stat. Soc. Series*, 67(2):301–320, 2005.

[11] N. Hulo, A. Bairoch, V. Bulliard, L. Cerutti, E. De Castro, P. S. Langendijk-Genevaux, M. Pagni, and C. J. A. Sigrist. The prosite database. *Nucl. Acids Res.*, 34(1):227–230, 2006.

[12] G. Ifrim. *Statistical Learning Techniques for Text Categorization with Sparse Labeled Data.* PhD thesis, Universität des Saarlandes, 2009.

[13] G. Ifrim. Gradient-bounded coordinate-descent for sequence regression. www.4c.ucc.ie/ ifrim/seql/data, 2010.

[14] G. Ifrim, G. Bakir, and G. Weikum. Fast logistic regression for text categorization with variable-length n-grams. In *KDD*, pages 354–362, USA, 2008.

[15] T. Jaakkola, M. Diekhans, and D. Haussler. Using the fisher kernel method to detect remote protein homologies. In *ICISMB*, pages 149–158. AAAI Press, 1999.

[16] T. Joachims. Training linear SVMs in linear time. In *KDD*, pages 217–226, USA, 2006. ACM Press.

[17] R. Kuang, E. Ie, K. Wang, K. Wang, M. Siddiqi, Y. Freund, and C. Leslie. Profile-based string kernels for remote homology detection and motif extraction. In *CSBC*, pages 152–160, USA, 2004. IEEE Computer Society.

[18] T. Kudo, E. Maeda and Y. Matsumoto. An Application of Boosting to Graph Classification. In *NIPS*, 2004.

[19] P. Kuksa, P. H. Huang, and V. Pavlovic. A fast, semi-supervised learning method for protein sequence classification. In *International Workshop on Data Mining in Bioinformatics*, pages 29–37, 2008.

[20] P. Kuksa, P. H. Huang, and V. Pavlovic. Scalable algorithms for string kernels with inexact matching. In *NIPS*, 2008.

[21] C. Leslie, E. Eskin, A. Cohen, J. Weston, and W. S. Noble. Mismatch string kernels for discriminative protein classification. *Bioinformatics*, 20(4):467–476, 2004.

[22] C. Leslie, E. Eskin, and W. Noble. Mismatch string kernels for svm protein classification. In *NIPS*, 2002.

[23] C. Leslie, E. Eskin, and W. Noble. The spectrum kernel: a string kernel for svm protein classification. In *Pacific Biocomputing Symposium*, pages 564–575, 2002.

[24] C. Leslie and R. Kuang. Fast string kernels using inexact matching for protein sequences. *J. Mach. Learn. Res.*, 5:1435–1455, 2004.

[25] I. Levner, V. Bulitko, and G. Lin. Feature extraction for classification of proteomic mass spectra: A comparative study. *Studies in Fuzziness and Soft Computing*, 207:607–624, 2006.

[26] L. Liao and W. S. Noble. Combining pairwise sequence similarity and support vector machines for remote protein homology detection. In *ICCB*, pages 225–232, USA, 2002.

[27] C.-J. Lin, R. C. Weng, and S. S. Keerthi. Trust region Newton method for large-scale logistic regression. *J. Mach. Learn. Res.*, 9:627–650, 2008.

[28] J. Liu, J. Chen, and J. Ye. Large-scale sparse logistic regression. In *KDD*, pages 547–556, USA, 2009.

[29] H. Lodhi, C. Saunders, J. Shawe-Taylor, N. Cristianini, and C. Watkins. Text classification using string kernels. *J. Mach. Learn. Res.*, 2:419–444, 2002.

[30] D. Luenberger. *Linear and Nonlinear Programming.* Addison-Wesley Publishing Co.: Reading Mass, 1984.

[31] E. Pruesse, C. Quast, K. Knittel, B. M. Fuchs, W. Ludwig, J. Peplies, and F. O. Glockner. SILVA: a comprehensive online resource for quality checked and aligned ribosomal RNA sequence data compatible with ARB. *Nucl. Acids Res.*, 35(21):7188–7196, 2007.

[32] S. Rosset, J. Zhu, and T. Hastie. Boosting as a regularized path to a maximum margin classifier. *J. Mach. Learn. Res.*, 5:941–973, 2004.

[33] Q. Shi, J. Petterson, G. Dror, J. Langford, A. Smola, and S. Vishwanathan. Hash kernels for structured data. *J. Mach. Learn. Res.*, 10:2615–2637, 2009.

[34] P. Sonego, A. Kocsor, and S. Pongor. ROC analysis: applications to the classification of biological sequences and 3D structures. *Brief. in Bioinf.*, 9(3):198–209, 2008.

[35] S. Sonnenburg and V. Franc. Coffin : A computational framework for linear svms. In *ICML*, 2010.

[36] S. Sonnenburg, G. Rätsch, S. Henschel, C. Widmer, J. Behr, A. Zien, F. de Bona, A. Binder, C. Gehl, and V. Franc. The SHOGUN machine learning toolbox. *J. Mach. Learn. Res.*, 11:1799–1802, 2010.

[37] P. Tseng and S. Yun. A coordinate gradient descent method for nonsmooth separable minimization. *Mathematical Programming*, 117:387–423, 2009.

[38] J. Weston, C. Leslie, E. Ie, D. Zhou, A. Elisseeff, and W. S. Noble. Semi-supervised protein classification using cluster kernels. *Bioinformatics*, 21(15):3241–3247, 2005.

Multi-Source Domain Adaptation and Its Application to Early Detection of Fatigue

Rita Chattopadhyay [1], Jieping Ye [1,2], Sethuraman Panchanathan [1], Wei Fan [3], Ian Davidson [4]
[1]Computer Science and Engineering, Arizona State University, AZ 85287
[2]Center for Evolutionary Medicine and Informatics, The Biodesign Institute, Arizona State University, AZ 85287
[3]IBM T.J.Watson Research, Hawthorne, NY 10532
[4]Department of Computer Science, University of California, Davis, CA 95616

ABSTRACT

We consider the characterization of muscle fatigue through noninvasive sensing mechanism such as surface electromyography (SEMG). While changes in the properties of SEMG signals with respect to muscle fatigue have been reported in the literature, the large variation in these signals across different individuals makes the task of modeling and classification of SEMG signals challenging. Indeed, the variation in SEMG parameters from subject to subject creates differences in the data distribution. In this paper, we propose a transfer learning framework based on the multi-source domain adaptation methodology for detecting different stages of fatigue using SEMG signals, that addresses the distribution differences. In the proposed framework, the SEMG data of a subject represent a domain; data from multiple subjects in the training set form the multiple source domains and the test subject data form the target domain. SEMG signals are predominantly different in conditional probability distribution across subjects. The key feature of the proposed framework is a novel weighting scheme that addresses the conditional probability distribution differences across multiple domains (subjects). We have validated the proposed framework on Surface Electromyogram signals collected from 8 people during a fatigue-causing repetitive gripping activity. Comprehensive experiments on the SEMG data set demonstrate that the proposed method improves the classification accuracy by 20% to 30% over the cases without any domain adaptation method and by 13% to 30% over the existing state-of-the-art domain adaptation methods.

Categories and Subject Descriptors

H.2.8 [**Database Management**]: Database Applications - Data Mining

General Terms

Algorithm

Keywords

Multi-source domain adaption, transfer learning, surface electromyogram, subject based variability

1. INTRODUCTION

Daily life activities such as typing on the keyboard, dusting, brooming, ironing, as well as the use of hand tools such as scissors and knives, repetitive work in assembly lines, repetitive lifting, involve repetitive movements of the different parts of the body. It has been proved that repetitive task makes work particularly hazardous as it is the primary cause of muscle fatigue [28, 13, 30]. According to the US Bureau of Labor Statistics, in 2002, there were more than 345,000 on the job back injuries, due to muscle fatigue, which required time off from work. According to the Bureau of Labor Statistics (2004), annual direct cost of occupational injuries due to slip and fall caused due to muscle fatigue is expected to exceed $43.8 billion by the year 2020 in the US.

These accidents and the consequential loss in work hours and lifes, besides the high medical cost, can be avoided if one can intervene such fatigue inducing repetitive activities at an early stage by intelligent devices having the capability for detecting different stages of fatigue. Technologies for detecting muscle fatigue at an early stage can also be used to remove the cause of fatigue by altering the environmental ergonomics where possible [1].

There are a number of techniques that can be used to objectively determine the level of fatigue in a subject. Electromyography (EMG) is a method for biosignal recording of skeletal muscle activity. Surface Electromyography (SEMG) allows for noninvasive recording of these biosignals. Researchers have observed that certain aspects of SEMG signals change as a muscle becomes fatigued. Localized muscle fatigue has been correlated with a shift in the power spectral density of SEMG signals, root mean square (rms), instantaneous frequency, zero crossing rate, mean-frequency, median-frequency, etc. However, there is a large variation in the values of these measures across different subjects, due to variances in their SEMG power spectrum and their shifts. These generally unpredictable and wide variations make the task of modeling SEMG difficult, and the task of automating the process of signal classification as a generalized tool challenging. The variation in SEMG parameters from subject to subject creates differences in the data distribution. Figure 1 shows the distribution of the data over four stages of a fatigue-causing activity, done with varying speed, for three different subjects (subjects 1, 2, 4). The data distribution shown in Figure 1 is of factor scores obtained as a

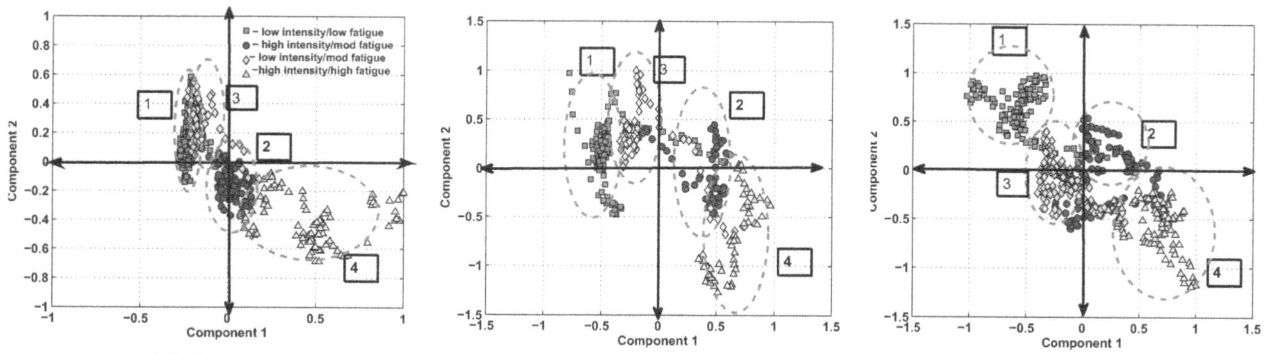

(a) Subject 1 (b) Subject 2 (c) Subject 4

Figure 1: Three sample subjects (subjects 1, 2, 4) with four classes (four physiological stages) in our SEMG data set: SEMG signals are predominantly different in conditional probability distribution across subjects.

result of factor analysis [2] applied on the twelve dimensional feature vectors derived from raw SEMG signals[1]. The four physiological stages corresponding to four classes, shown in the figure, are (1) *low intensity of activity and low fatigue*, (2) *high intensity of activity and moderate fatigue*, (3) *low intensity of activity and moderate fatigue* and (4) *high intensity of activity and high fatigue*. We observe that the data distribution during each stage or class varies from subject to subject. This variation leads to predominantly conditional probability differences across subjects.

Traditional data mining algorithms assume that training data and test data are drawn from the same distribution, and they may not be effective if the assumption is violated as in the case of SEMG data over multiple subjects. One effective approach is domain adaptation which enables transfer of knowledge between the source and target domains [22]. It has been applied successfully in various applications [6, 11, 10, 20] including text classification (parts of speech tagging, webpage tagging, etc), video concept detection across different TV channels, sentiment analysis (identifying positive and negative reviews across domains), WiFi Localization (locating device location depending upon the signal strengths from various access points.

In this paper we present a successful case study of application of multi-source domain adaptation techniques for detecting different stages of fatigue based on the Surface Electromyogram signals across multiple subjects. The proposed framework addresses the subject based variability, predominantly the distribution differences in conditional probabilities in Surface Electromyogram signals. Specifically, a classifier is learnt to distinguish the four classes as shown in Figure 1 on the basis of some labeled and unlabeled data from the target domain (or subject). The unlabeled data are labeled using a weighting scheme that measures the similarities in conditional probabilities between the source and target domain data; the key of the proposed weighting scheme is a joint optimization framework based on smoothness assumption on the probability distribution of the target domain data. To the best of our knowledge, this is the first systematic analysis of subject based variability in SEMG signals. We have applied the proposed algorithm to Surface Electromyogram signals collected from 8 people during a fatigue-causing repetitive gripping activity. Our extensive experiments on the SEMG data set demonstrate that the proposed method improves the subject independent classification accuracy by 20% to 30% over the cases without any domain adaptation method and by 13% to 30% over the existing state-of-the-art domain adaptation methods.

[1]More details on the twelve features derived, the factor analysis results and a real time deployment of fatigue grading framework can be found in our earlier papers [8, 9].

2. PROPOSED FRAMEWORK

The proposed domain adaptation framework focuses on learning from multiple auxiliary sources related to the target data, e.g., multiple subject data having different distributions, collected under similar physiological conditions. Specifically, we consider the problem of detecting different stages of fatigue in a subject for whom we have very few labeled samples available in the training data. The training data also includes data from many other subjects collected under similar physiological conditions. The test subject data forms target domain data and the multiple subject data in the training domain form multiple auxiliary sources.

2.1 Problem Setting and Motivation

Assume that there are k subjects in the source domain. The s-th subject in the source domain is characterized by a sample set $D^s = (x_i^s, y_i^s)|_{i=1}^{n_s}$, where x_i^s is the feature vector, y_i^s is the corresponding label, and n_s is the total number of samples for the subject s. The target domain consists of a few labeled data $D_l^T = (x_i^T, y_i^T)|_{i=1}^{n_l}$ and plenty of unlabeled data $D_u^T = x_i^T|_{i=n_l+1}^{n_l+n_u}$ where n_l and n_u are numbers of labeled and unlabeled target domain samples respectively, $D^T = D_l^T \bigcup D_u^T$, and $n_T = n_l + n_u$. The goal is to develop a target classifier f^T that can predict the labels of the unlabeled data in the target domain, using the multi-source domain data and a few labeled target domain data.

One simple approach for predicting the labels of the target domain data is to combine the training samples from all subjects and build a single classifier based on the pooled training samples. However, this simple approach will not work well in our application as there are significant conditional probability differences across subjects in the SEMG data. A better alternative is to learn individual models for each subject in the source domain, and then combine the hypothesis generated by each of these source models, on the basis of some similarity measures between the source and target domains. The similarity measures are commonly computed by considering each source domain data separately. This procedure has two potential limitations. First, it minimizes the loss with respect to the probability distribution $P_s(x, y|D^s)$ on the source domain which will not generally coincide with the minimal loss on the distribution $P_T(x, y|D^T)$ on the target domain. Second, it assumes all sources are independent when computing the similarity measures, thus it does not fully exploit the interaction among multiple sources.

Thus one of the important issues is to choose the right similarity measure between the source and target domains depending upon the nature of differences in the distribution. There are predominantly conditional probability differences in our multi-subject SEMG data as shown in Figure 1. In addition, we observe from the figure that different classes vary differently over subjects. For example, subjects 1 and 2 have similar data distributions of classes 1 and 3, and subjects 1 and 4 have similar data distributions of class 4. Hence computing a single similarity measure for an auxiliary source with respect to target data does not capture the differences at the class level. The proposed approach presented below addresses all these challenges.

2.2 Proposed Approach

We learn a classifier f^T for the target domain data, using a few labeled samples and a large number of unlabeled samples from the target domain. The key of our proposed approach is a novel weighting scheme that integrates multiple source domain data using a set of weights, one for each source domain. We use these weights to compute the labels of the unlabeled target domain data, called "pseudo labels". The target domain prediction model is then learnt from both labeled and pseudo labeled target domain samples in a regularized framework. Specifically, the proposed multi-source domain adaptation framework is given as follows:

$$\min_{f^T \in H_K} \gamma_A \|f^T\|_K^2 + \frac{1}{n_l}\sum_{i=1}^{n_l} V(x_i, y_i, f^T) + \Omega_r(f_u^T) + \Omega_m(f^T) \tag{1}$$

The first term controls the complexity of the classifier f^T in the Reproducing Kernel Hilbert Space (RKHS) H_K, γ_A controls the penalty factor, the second term is the empirical error of the target classifier f^T on the few labeled target domain data D_l^T, and n_l is the number of labeled target domain data. The empirical error on the unlabeled target data, labeled using a conditional probability based weighting scheme, forms the third term. This regularizer enforces the target classifier f^T to have similar decision values to the auxiliary source which has similar conditional probability distribution, explained in detail in Subsection 2.3. The fourth term is a manifold based regularizer based on the smoothness assumption [4] on target domain data: if two points x_i and x_j are close to each other in the intrinsic geometry of marginal distribution then they are most likely to have similar conditional probabilities, i.e., $f^T(x_i)$ should be similar to $f^T(x_j)$. The *manifold based regularizer* is defined as in [4]:

$$\Omega_m(f^T) = \frac{\gamma_I}{n_T^2} f^{T'} L f^T. \tag{2}$$

where L is the graph Laplacian matrix constructed on D^T, $f^T = [f^T(x_1), \cdots, f^T(x_{n_T})]$, γ_I controls the complexity of the function f^T in the intrinsic geometry of the marginal probability of x and the normalizing coefficient $\frac{1}{n_T^2}$ is the natural scale factor for the empirical estimate of the Laplace operator, and the symbol $'$ is used to represent the matrix or vector *transpose* operation.

2.3 Multi-Source Weighting

Let $f_u^T = [f_{n_l+1}^T \cdots f_{n_T}^T]'$ be the decision values of the target classifier f^T for the unlabeled target domain data and let $f_u^s = [f_{n_l+1}^s \cdots f_{n_T}^s]'$ be the decision values of the s-th auxiliary classifier for the same unlabeled target domain data. Let γ_s be the measure of relevance or similarity between the distributions of the s-th source and the target data, and let $f_j^T = f^T(x_j)$ be the decision value of target classifier on the target domain data x_j and $f_j^s = f^s(x_j)$ be the decision value of the s-th auxiliary source classifier on x_j. We use a weighted combination of the k source domain classifiers f^s to estimate the target classifier. Specifically, the estimated label $(\hat{y}_j)$ of the unlabeled target data x_j based on the k source domain classifiers f^s is given by

$$\hat{y}_j = \sum_{s=1}^{k} \gamma_s f_j^s, \tag{3}$$

where $\gamma_s > 0$ is the weight for the s-th source. We assume that the weights are normalized, that is, $\sum_s \gamma_s = 1$. The auxiliary classifier f^s for the s-th source is pre-computed based on its respective data. The auxiliary classifiers f^s and the target classifier f^T can be trained using different kernels or even different learning methods. The resulting regularizer, $\Omega_r(f_u^T)$, named as *relevance based regularizer* measures the difference between the target classifier decision value and the estimation based on multiple source data, and is defined as follows:

$$\Omega_r(f_u^T) = \frac{\theta}{2}\sum_{j=n_l+1}^{n_T} \|f_j^T - \sum_{s=1}^{k}\gamma_s f_j^s\|^2, \tag{4}$$

where $\theta > 0$ is a constant.

The weight γ_s which provides a measure of relevance between the s-th auxiliary source domain and the target domain is computed on the basis of a *Conditional Probability based Weighting Scheme*, which evaluates the similarities in distributions between the source and target domains predominantly based on conditional probability differences.

Next, we show how to estimate the weights γ_s's. The proposed weighting scheme evaluates the similarities between auxiliary source data and the target domain data considering the similarities in their conditional probabilities.

Let $F_i^S = [f_i^1 \cdots f_i^k]$ be the $1 \times k$ vector of predicted labels of k auxiliary source models for the i-th sample of target domain data. Let $\gamma = [\gamma_1 \cdots \gamma_k]^T$ be the $k \times 1$ weight vector, where γ_s is the weight corresponding to the s-th auxiliary source. Following (3), the predicted label for the i-th sample of target domain data is

$$\hat{y}_i = \sum_{s=1}^{k} \gamma_s f_i^s = F_i^S \gamma. \tag{5}$$

This motivates us to estimate the weight vector γ based on the smoothness assumption on the conditional probability distribution: we compute the optimal weight vector γ by minimizing the difference in predicted labels between two nearby points in the target domain. Specifically, the proposed weighting framework solves the following problem:

$$\min_{\gamma:\gamma' e=1,\gamma\geq 0} \sum_{i,j=n_l+1}^{n_l+n_u} (F_i^S\gamma - F_j^S\gamma)^2 W_{ij} \quad (6)$$

where $F_i^S\gamma$ and $F_j^S\gamma$ are the predicted labels for i-th and j-th samples of target domain data and W_{ij} is the edge weight between the two samples. We can rewrite the minimization problem as follows:

$$\min_{\gamma:\gamma' e=1,\gamma\geq 0} \gamma' \left(F^S\right)' L_u F^S \gamma \quad (7)$$

where F^S is an $n_u \times k$ matrix with each row of F^S being the $1 \times k$ vector of k predicted labels for a sample of target domain data and L_u is graph Laplacian associated with the target domain data D_u^T, given by $L_u = D - W$, where W is the adjacency graph defining edge weights between the samples in the target domain data, and D is the diagonal matrix given by $D_{ii} = \sum_{j=1}^{n} W_{ij}$.

The minimization problem in (7) is a standard quadratic problem and can be solved by applying many existing solvers. We simply use the 'quadprog' function in MATLAB. With the computed weights, the labels for the unlabeled target domain data, called *psuedo labels*, are computed using (3), and are substituted into the regulariser in (4).

Intuitively, by enforcing that nearby points in the marginal distribution of the target data have similar class labels (or conditional probability) via the optimization in (7), the proposed weighting scheme is likely to give higher weights to those sources with the conditional probability distribution similar to the target data. This is verified in our empirical study on both SEMG and synthetic data. If a source has a conflicting conditional distribution as the target, it is likely to get a low or even zero weight. In addition, different from many existing weight schemes which compute the weights by considering each source independently, the proposed weighting scheme computes the optimal value of γ or the optimal weights of all the k sources simultaneously, thus taking the potential interaction among multiple subjects in the source domain into account.

2.4 Proposed Algorithm

Using the least square error and substituting the regularizers we can rewrite (1) as follows:

$$\min_{f^T\in H_K} \gamma_A \|f^T\|_K^2 + \frac{1}{n_l}\sum_{i=1}^{n_l}(f_i^T - y_i^T)^2$$
$$+\frac{\theta}{2}\sum_{j=n_l+1}^{n_T} \|f_j^T - \sum_{s=1}^{k}\gamma_s f_j^s\|^2 + \frac{\gamma_I}{n_T^2} f^{T'} L f^T \quad (8)$$

By the Representer theorem [24], we can find an optimal solution of (8), which is a linear expansion of the kernel function K, over both the labeled D_l^T and the pseudo labeled target domain data D_u^T given as follows:

$$f^T(x) = \sum_{i=1}^{n_l+n_u} \alpha_i K(x_i, x). \quad (9)$$

Substituting this into (8), we can obtain the optimal $\alpha = [\alpha_1 \cdots\cdots\cdots \alpha_{n_l+n_u}]^T$ by solving the following optimization problem:

$$\min_{\alpha} \frac{1}{n_l+\theta n_u}(Y - K\alpha)' J(Y - K\alpha)$$
$$+\gamma_A \alpha' K\alpha + \frac{\gamma_I}{(n_u+n_l)^2}\alpha' KLK\alpha \quad (10)$$

where K is the $(n_l+n_u)\times(n_l+n_u)$ kernel Gram matrix over the target domain data, Y is the label vector over labeled and pseudo labeled target domain data points given by:

$$\left[y_1 \cdots y_{n_l} \sum_s \gamma_{s(n_l+1)} f^s_{(n_l+1)} \cdots \sum_s \gamma_{s(n_l+n_u)} f^s_{(n_l+n_u)}\right] \quad (11)$$

L is the graph Laplacian defined over labeled and pseudo labeled target domain data, and J is a diagonal matrix of size $(n_l + n_u) \times (n_l + n_u)$ given by $J = diag(1, \cdots 1, \theta, \cdots \theta)$ with the first n_l diagonal entries as 1 and the rest as θ. θ is assigned a number between 0 and 1, thus the pseudo labels of the target domain data get smaller weights compared to the labels of the labeled target domain data. From (10), the optimal α^* is given by:

$$\alpha^* = \left(JK + \gamma_A(n_l + \theta n_u)I + \frac{\gamma_I(n_l+\theta n_u)}{(n_u+n_l)^2}LK\right)^{-1} JY.$$

With the computed α^*, the prediction of any unseen test data x is given by:

$$f^T(x) = \sum_{i=1}^{n_l+n_u} \alpha_i^* K(x_i, x). \quad (12)$$

Since the proposed domain adaptation framework is based on multiple sources whose similarities to target domain data or weights are computed based on a conditional probability based weighting scheme, we refer the proposed framework as *Conditional Probability based Multi-Source Domain Adaptation (CP-MDA)*.

3. RELATED WORK

Most of the existing methods measure the similarity between a particular source and the target domain based on the similarity of their marginal probabilities. Shimodaira *et al.* [27] biased the training samples by their test-to-training ratio to match the marginal distribution of the test data. Sugiyama *et al.* [29] proposed to reduce the gap in marginal probabilities by minimizing the KL-divergence between test and weighted training data and Bickel *et al.* [5] discriminated training against test data with a probabilistic model that accounts for the marginal probability difference between training and test distribution. There are several other methods which are also based on marginal probability differences using Maximum Mean Discrepancy [7] as a measure such as Kernel Mean Matching [14] and Transfer Component Analysis [20]. The proposed domain adaptation framework CP-MDA, differs from all these methods in two ways: (1) it is predominantly based on conditional probability differences, and (2) it is based on multiple source domains.

Several algorithms have been developed in past to combine knowledge from multiple sources. Luo *et al.* used consensus maximization as the basis of combining multiple source data [18]. Mansour *et al.* based the transferability of knowledge on a distribution weighted combination of the hypothesis generated by the independent sources [19]. The theoretical proof of both frameworks are based on strong assumptions on the predictive power of the individual source domains on the target domain data. In [26], a clustering based knowledge transfer was proposed for applications with different class labels across source and target domains, unlike the application addressed in this paper.

The proposed framework is related to two multi-source domain adaptation frameworks including Domain Adaptation Machine (DAM) [11] and Locally Weighted Ensemble (LWE) [12]. The proposed framework differs from DAM in the way the weights are computed for different auxiliary sources. In DAM, the weight assigned to each auxiliary source is obtained by measuring the marginal probability distribution difference between the target domain and the particular auxiliary source only, using an empirical estimate of the difference based on the Maximum Mean Discrepancy measure [7]. The proposed framework however computes weights for the auxiliary source data considering predominantly conditional probability distribution of the target data. The weights for all sources are computed in a joint optimization framework, which takes the interaction among multiple auxiliary sources into account.

The proposed framework differs from LWE [12] in that in LWE, the label y of an unlabeled target domain data x is computed using a local weighting ensemble (LWE) scheme:

$$P(y|x) = \sum_{i=1}^{k} w_{M_i,x} P(y|M_i, x) \tag{13}$$

where $P(y|M_i, x)$ is the prediction made by one of the k models M_i for target data point x and $w_{M_i,x}$ is the weight of the model M_i at point x computed by comparing the similarity graphs of the source and target data around point x. Different from the proposed weighting scheme where we compute all weights in a joint framework, the weight for each auxiliary classifier is computed independently [12].

We also compare our framework with representative single-source domain adaptation algorithms such as Kernel Mean Matching (KMM) proposed by Huang *et al.* [14], Transfer Component Analysis (TCA) proposed by Pan *et al.* [21] and KMapEnsemble (KE) proposed by Zhong *et al.* [31]. KMM re-weights the samples in the source domain so as to minimize the marginal probability difference between the source and target domain using Maximum Mean Discrepancy (MMD) as the measure. TCA is based on feature mapping so as to reduce the marginal probability differences between the source and target distributions again using MMD as the measure. KE differs from the first two algorithms, in which it addresses the conditional probability differences by sample selection after performing a feature mapping step to reduce the marginal probability differences.

There was some classification work dealing with physiological signals using neural networks [17] and linear discriminant analysis [15]; they achieved moderate generalization performance across subjects. To the best of our knowledge we report the first systematic empirical analysis of domain adaptation methods to address the distribution differences due to the subject based variability in physiological signals.

4. EXPERIMENTS

The proposed algorithm has been evaluated on a synthetic dataset and on real-world SEMG data collected from 8 different subjects during a fatigue-causing exercise.

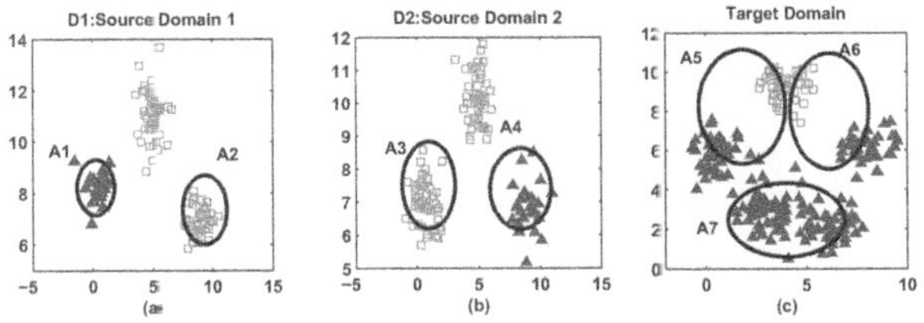

Figure 2: The synthetic dataset includes two source domains (D1 and D2) and one target domain with conflicting conditional probabilities.

4.1 Experimental Setup

4.1.1 *Synthetic data*

The synthetic data set consisting of two source domains D1 and D2 and a target domain as shown in Figure 2, are generated from several Gaussian distributions with different mean and variances. Source domain D1 has 20 positive and 90 negative examples and source domain D2 has 25 positive and 100 negative examples. There are conflicting conditional probabilities between D1 and D2 as shown in four regions (A1, A2, A3 and A4) in Figure 2. The target domain has 180 positive and 60 negative examples. Region A5 of the target domain is similar to D1, while region A6 is similar to D2. Thus the data exhibits conflicting and varied difference in conditional probability between the source domains and the target domain.

4.1.2 *SEMG data*

The SEMG data was collected during a repetitive gripping action performed by the forearm. Figure 3 shows the subject with surface EMG differential electrodes on the extensor carpi radialis muscle to record the SEMG signal. The subject performs a cycle of flexion-extension of forearm as shown in Figure 3 at two different speeds, i.e., low speed (1 cycles/sec) and high speed (2 cycles/sec) repetitively for about 4 minutes. The cycles of low and high speed are alternated after every minute to form four phases (or classes) as discussed in the introduction.

The raw SEMG activity was recorded by Grass Model 8-16C at 1000Hz and passed through a band pass filter of 20Hz to 500Hz. The data was collected and saved by the LabView software (from National Instruments) running on a PC. Data of the order of 1.92 Million samples ($1000 \times 4 \times 60 \times 8$), was collected from 8 subjects including male and female of the age group of 25 years to 45 years. A set of twelve amplitude and frequency domain features including mean frequency, median frequency, spectral energy, spectral entropy, root mean square, number of zero crossings, to mention a few are derived from running windows of 1000 time samples with 50% overlap [16].

Each subject data consists of around 280 to 400 samples of 12 dimensional feature vectors, belonging to four classes with around 70 to 100 samples per class (some subjects who got fatigued sooner and hence could not maintain the required uniform speed for 1 minute the time period was reduced to 30 to 45 secs per phase, hence the number of samples varies between different subjects).

4.1.3 *Experimental Procedure*

To evaluate the effectiveness of the proposed method, we compare the results with four baseline methods, including

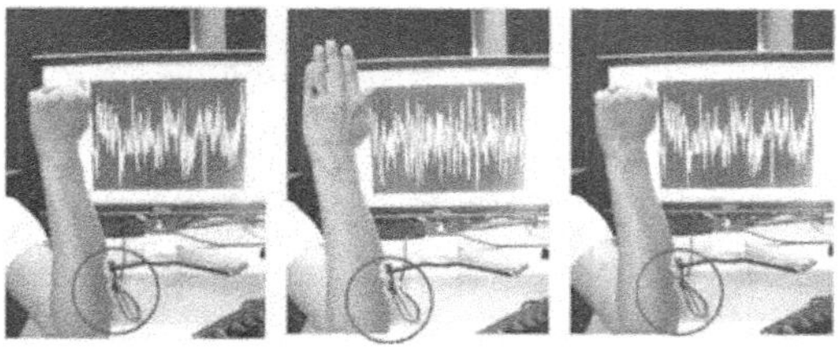

Figure 3: SEMG data collection during a repetitive gripping activity

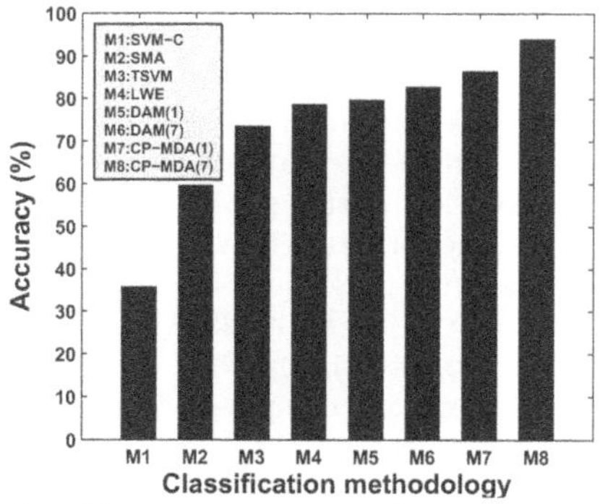

Figure 4: Comparative performance of different methods on the synthetic data - Accuracy (%)

SVM-C, SVM-M, SMA, and TSVM (Transductive SVM), and two recently proposed multi-source learning methods, including Locally Weighted Ensemble (LWE) [12] and Domain Adaptation Machine (DAM) [11]. More details on LWE and DAM are given in Section 3.

SVM-C refers to *all but one* method where the training data comprises of data from seven subjects and the test data is the data from the remaining subject. SVM-M, refers to the *majority voting* based ensemble framework. The class y assigned to each unlabeled test data x is $\max_y NV(y|x)$ where $NV(y|x)$ is the number of votes given for class y for a particular test sample x by the seven auxiliary sources. SMA refers to *simple model averaging*, which provides equal weight to all the classifiers learned on each auxiliary source domain in an weighted ensemble framework used to generate the label for the target domain data. TSVM refers to Transductive SVM [3] implemented in the svmlight package. It is a semi-supervised method where the training data consists of labeled data from all seven subjects from the source domain and unlabeled data from the target subject.

We vary the number of labeled samples per class in the target domain. DAM(1) and DAM(7) refer to the DAM framework with 1 and 7 target domain labeled samples per class respectively. The proposed CP-MDA method is also implemented using 1 and 7 labeled data from target domain, referred as CP-MDA(1) and CP-MDA(7) respectively. For both cases the unlabeled data from the target domain, is fixed at 10% of the target domain data. The weights of the auxiliary sources computed by the proposed method are also based on this 10% unlabeled target domain data. The rest of the target domain data is treated as unseen target domain data. All the methods are tested on the same pool of *unseen* unlabeled target domain data. The accuracies are computed in a subject independent manner.

We mention here briefly some of the parameters used in implementing the existing and the proposed method. The values of γ_A and γ_I were kept as 0.014 and 0.01 respectively, as suggested in [4]. The Laplacian graph matrix used in calculating the weights was set as 'binary' type based on the N nearest neighbors with $N = 10$. The value of Θ was estimated via 5-fold cross validation on the set $\{i10^{-2}|i = 0, 1, \cdots, 100\}$.

4.2 Results and Analysis

4.2.1 Synthetic data

Figure 4 shows the classification accuracies of different methods on the synthetic dataset. The classification accuracies on the target domain data when the SVM classifier is applied on the source data D1 or D2 without using any transfer learning methodologies are 62.97% and 72.61%, respectively.

We observe that SVM-C and SMA perform poorly. This may be attributed to the conflicting conditional probabilities between the two training sets, that degrade the performance of the classifier when learned on the combined data. In addition, there is a conditional probability difference with the test data, hence the brute-force use of knowledge without evaluating similarities between the source and the target data degrades the performance of the classifier in the target domain [25] related to *negative transfer* [23].

We also observe that CP-MDA(1) improves the classification accuracy by 20% to 50% over the baseline methods without any transfer learning and by 11% over LWE. We also observe that CP-MDA(1) outperforms DAM(7). Since the target classifier is learned using some labeled and some pseudo labeled data, which is labeled using the proposed weighting scheme, hence higher classification accuracy verifies the effectiveness of the proposed weighting scheme in Section 2.3.

To further evaluate the effectiveness of the proposed weighting scheme, we compared three different weighting schemes using the weighted ensemble methodology of LWE in (13). MMD-WE refers to the method when weights are computed based on MMD, and CP-MDA-WE refers to the method when weights are computed based on the proposed framework in (7). The accuracies using LWE, MMD-WE, and CP-MDA-WE are 78.6%, 72.75%, and 80.54%, respectively. To examine why the proposed method outperforms the other two, we report the predictive power of each of the two source data (D1, D2) as well as the weights obtained by different methods. The classification accuracies obtained using the source data D1 and D2 individually are 62.97% and 72.61%, respectively. The weights for D1 and D2 obtained by MMD-WE are 0.93 and 0.06, respectively; the weights for D1 and D2 obtained by CP-MDA-WE are 0.08 and 0.91, respectively. Thus, the weights obtained by the proposed method match the predictive powers of the source data better than MMD-WE.

4.2.2 SEMG data

We compare different methods including SVM-C, SVM-M, SMA, TSVM, LWE, DAM and the proposed CP-MDA. The results are summarized in Table 1. The first column of the table indicates the subject data under test (target domain). The training data (source domain) consists of the data from the remaining seven subjects. Similar to the results obtained in the case of synthetic data we see that

Table 1: Comparative performance of different methods on SEMG data - Accuracy (%)

Test Sub	SVM-C	SVM-M	SMA	TSVM	LWE	DAM(1)	DAM(7)	CP-MDA(1)	CP-MDA(7)
1	70.76	33.9	44.96	49.09	67.44	74.83	77.43	81.93	85.25
2	43.69	50.76	44.61	55.68	77.54	81.36	83.35	84.73	87.7
3	50.11	56.85	56.84	65.09	75.55	74.77	78.99	82.45	85.06
4	59.65	47.93	49.67	56.98	81.22	80.63	84.32	81.27	86.4
5	40.37	44.79	50.15	62.5	52.48	76.74	81.14	80.74	86.62
6	59.21	61.45	60.33	71.32	65.77	59.21	74.28	83.12	88.09
7	47.13	46.91	45.76	60.73	60.32	74.27	83.31	81.57	86.4
8	69.85	64.53	74.46	68.55	72.81	84.55	86.6	88.5	90.56
Average	55.09	50.85	53.34	61.24	69.14	75.79	81.18	**83.04**	**87.01**

Table 2: Comparison of SVM-T, DAM, and CP-MDA on Subject 6 (top) and Subject 7 (bottom) in terms of accuracy (%) when the number of labeled target domain data per class varies.

	Number of labeled data per class					
Method	1	2	3	4	6	7
SVM-T	4.26	4.26	49.09	73.63	84.69	85.67
DAM	59.12	59.21	59.35	59.59	65.03	74.28
CP-MDA	**83.12**	83.12	85.45	87.58	87.77	88.09
SVM-T	10.59	45.5	77.79	83.25	85.48	84.97
DAM	74.27	75.11	79.10	81.19	82.43	83.3
CP-MDA	**81.57**	83.99	85.81	86.24	86.32	86.4

SVM-C, SVM-M, SMA, and TSVM perform very poorly. We observe significant improvement in classification accuracy when domain adaptation methodologies are employed. The proposed method CP-MDA(1) provides a 20% to 30% improvement over the baseline methods including SVM-C, SVM-M, SMA and TSVM. The classification accuracies of the proposed method are in average 13% higher than LWE. It is also observed as in the case of synthetic data that CP-MDA(1) performs not only better than DAM(1) but also better than DAM(7) in 5 out of 8 cases. These results verify the effectiveness of the proposed method.

Next, we evaluate the performance of CP-MDA when the number of labeled target domain data varies. We compare CP-MDA with DAM and SVM-T. SVM-T refers to an SVM classifier trained on the labeled target domain data. The results for two subjects are summarized in Table 2; we obtain similar results for the other six subjects and the results are omitted. We can observe from the table that when the number of labeled target domain data per class is small, e.g., 1 to 4 samples per class, both domain adaptation methods perform much better than SVM-T. But with an increasing number of labeled data from the target domain the accuracies become comparable. However the proposed method always performs better than the other two methods. This result demonstrates that domain adaption is especially useful when the amount of labeled target domain data is small.

Similar to the synthetic data case, we compare the performance of the weighting schemes used in LWE, DAM and CP-MDA. Table 3 summarizes the results for different test cases. We observe that CP-MDA-WE performs better than the other methods in 6 out of 8 cases, and LWE performs better in the remaining 2 cases. Recall that like CP-MDA-WE, LWE computes weights for the auxiliary source domain based on the conditional probability differences between the source and target domains, while MMD-WE computes the weights based on the marginal probability differences only. Since SEMG data has significant conditional probability differences, CP-MDA-WE and LWE are expected to outperform DAM-WE.

Table 3: Comparison of different weighting schemes for different test subjects - Accuracy (%).

Test Sub	LWE	MMD-WE	CP-MDA-WE
1	67.44	68.27	75.12
2	77.54	69.48	83.23
3	75.55	71.84	75.68
4	81.22	62.65	81.09
5	52.48	68.32	78.16
6	65.77	58.91	76.11
7	60.32	67.75	75.07
8	72.81	66.11	78.71
Average	69.14%	66.66%	**77.89%**

The proposed algorithm CP-MDA computes weights for each class for each of the auxiliary source domain data, thus exploiting the similarities and dissimilarities at the class level. Table 4 shows the weights for four different classes assigned to each training subject in the source domain for test subject 1 in the target domain. We observe that the proposed weighting scheme assigns different weights to different auxiliary source domain data (subject data) for different classes. Subjects 5 and 8 get higher weights for class 1, subject 7 gets a higher weight for class 2, subject 5 gets a higher weight for class 3, and for class 4 subject 4 gets a higher weight. We observe from Figure 1 that the data distribution of class 4 of subject 1 is very similar to that of class 4 of subject 4.

Table 4: Weights computed by CP-MDA for four different classes for each of the source domain subjects 2-8 for test target subject 1.

Class	Target subject						
	2	3	4	5	6	7	8
1	0	0	0.02	0.50	0.48	0	0
2	0	0.01	0.03	0	0.11	0.74	0.11
3	0	0.02	0.12	0.75	0	0.01	0.11
4	0.09	0.02	0.66	0.11	0.11	0.01	0

One of the key advantage of the proposed algorithm is that it exploits the information from multiple source domains for classifying the target data. It will be interesting to study how the number of sources used in the training set affects the classification. Figure 5 presents the error rates

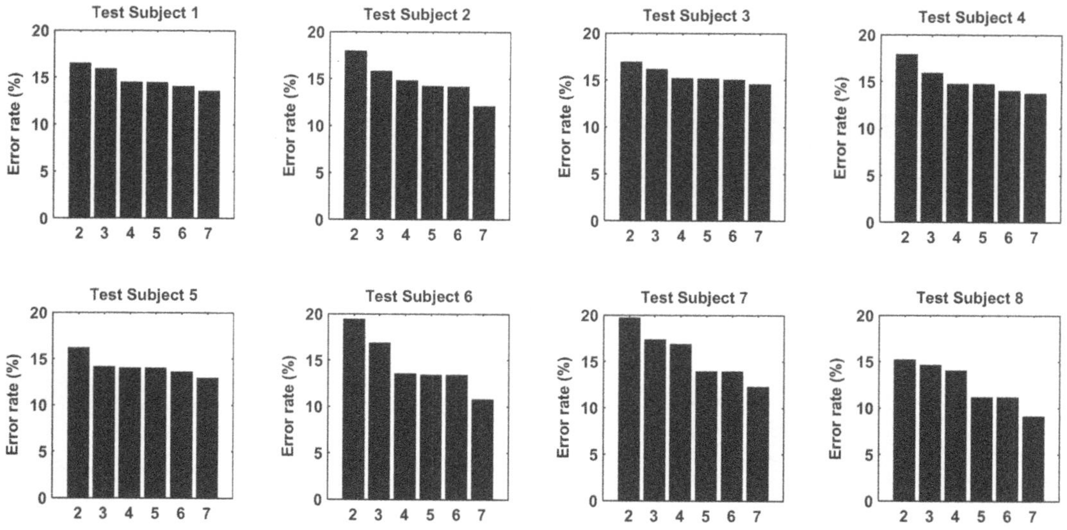

Figure 5: The effect of the number of auxiliary source domains (horizontal axis) in the training set on the proposed CP-MDA algorithm in terms of the classification error rates (%) for all eight subjects.

obtained for each test subject when the number of subjects in the source domain varies (from 1 to 7); we simply keep adding subjects to the training set in increasing order of the subject number. We observe that for all subjects, the error rate decreases monotonically when the number of subjects increases. These results demonstrate the effectiveness of the proposed algorithm for extracting useful information from multiple sources.

Table 5: Comparison of CP-MDA with three single source domain adaptation algorithms (KMM, TCA, and KE) - Accuracy(%).

Test Sub	CP-MDA(7)	KMM	TCA	KE
1	85.25	65.15	45.15	71.85
2	87.7	46.96	68.93	74.62
3	85.06	59.55	56.78	74.79
4	86.4	73.38	52.68	69.35
5	86.62	45.31	60.15	73.44
6	88.09	70.62	76.92	83.92
7	86.4	51.13	55.64	77.97
8	90.56	42.79	67.24	79.48
Average	**87.01**	56.86	53.84	75.67

To evaluate the benefit of a multi-source domain adaption framework for addressing subject based variability, we compare the proposed algorithm with three representative single-source domain adaption algorithms discussed in Section 3. Table 5 summarizes the classification accuracies obtained by different methods for each of the test subjects. The target data is from the subject shown in column 1 and the source data consists of the combined data from the remaining seven subject. Classification results were averaged over 10 runs with different sets of randomly selected 7 labeled samples per class from the target domain data. We can observe from the table that combining all the subject data and forming a single domain degrades the performance. We also observe that among the three single domain adaption algorithms, KMM or TCA which consider the marginal probability differences only perform worse than KE. These results are expected as SEMG data has significant conditional probability differences. Our results demonstrate the effectiveness of the proposed multi-domain framework for dealing with subject based variability in SEMG data.

5. CONCLUSION

We consider the characterization of muscle fatigue through noninvasive sensing mechanism such as surface electromyography (SEMG). The variation in SEMG parameters from subject to subject creates a difference in the data distribution, thus traditional data mining algorithms may not be effective. In this paper, we propose a transfer learning framework based on the multi-source domain adaptation methodology for detecting different stages of fatigue using SEMG signals. The proposed CP-MDA framework differs from most existing work in domain adaption in that it addresses the conditional probability distribution differences across domains based on a novel weighting scheme. We have validated the proposed framework using a synthetic dataset and real-world SEMG data collected from eight different subjects during a fatiguing exercise. Our comprehensive experiments demonstrate the effectiveness of the proposed framework and suggest that it is possible to develop a generalized framework with SEMG data. This increases the scope of application of SEMG data for fatigue detection in a larger scale beyond training and rehabilitation settings for monitoring during daily life and industrial work, as it alleviates the need for subject specific calibration for assessing the physiological state across subjects.

We plan to extend the proposed framework to applications involving other types of physiological signals for developing generalized models across subjects for emotion and health monitoring in everyday life, industrial work and geriatric care [17, 15]. In addition, we plan to study the generalization performance of the proposed framework.

6. ACKNOWLEDGEMENTS

We acknowledge Dr. Arthur Gretton, Dr. Yishay Mansour, Dr. Lixin Duan, Dr. Jing Gao, Dr. Erheng Zhong, Dr. Luo Ping, Dr. Sinno Jialin Pan, and Dr. Masashi Sugiyama for providing codes and other supporting materials. This research is sponsored in part by NSF IIS-0953662, CCF-1025177, and ONR N00014-11-1-0108.

7. REFERENCES

[1] http://www.environmental-ergonomics.org/.

[2] http://en.wikipedia.org/wiki/Factor_analysis.

[3] http://svmlight.joachims.org/.

[4] M. Belkin, P. Niyogi, and V. Sindhwani. Manifold regularization: A geometric framework for learning from labeled and unlabeled examples. *JMLR*, 7:2399–2434, 2006.

[5] S. Bickel, M. Brückner, and T. Scheffer. Discriminative learning under covariate shift. *JMLR*, 10:2137–2155, 2009.

[6] J. Blitzer, M.Dredze, and F. Pereira. Biographies, bollywood, boom-boxes and blenders: Domain adaptation for sentiment classification. In *ACL*, 2007.

[7] K. Borgwardt, A. Gretton, M. Rasch, H. Kriegel, Schölkopf, and A. J. Smola. Integrating structured biological data by kernel maximum mean discrepancy. *Bioinformatics*, 22(14):49–57, 2006.

[8] R. Chattopadhyay, P. Gaurav, and P. Sethuraman. A generalized machine learning framework for continuous monitoring of physiological conditions based on fatigue and intensity of activity in daily living. In *WIML, NIPS*, 2009.

[9] R. Chattopadhyay, P. Sethuraman, and P. Gaurav. Towards fatigue and intensity measurement framework during continuous repetitive activities. In *I2MTC*, 2010.

[10] H. Daumé III. Frustratingly easy domain adaptation. In *ACL*, 2007.

[11] L. Duan, I. W. Tsang, D. Xu, and T. S. Chua. Domain adaptation from multiple sources via auxiliary classifiers. In *ICML*, pages 289–296, 2009.

[12] J. Gao, W. Fan, J. Jiang, and J. Han. Knowledge transfer via multiple model local structure mapping. In *KDD*, pages 283–291, 2008.

[13] P. Higgs. Upper extremity impairment in workers performing repetitive tasks. *Plastic and reconstructive surgery*, 90:614, 1992.

[14] J. Huang, A. J. Smola, A. Gretton, K. Borgwardt, and B. Schölkopf. Correcting sample selection bias by unlabeled data. In *NIPS*, 2007.

[15] J. Kim and E. Andre. Emotion recognition based on physiological changes in music listening. *IEEE Transactions on Pattern Analysis and Machine Intelligence*, 30(12):2067–2083, 2008.

[16] M. Knaflitz and P. Bonato. Time-frequency methods applied to muscle fatigue assessment during dynamic contractions. 9(5):337–350, Oct. 1999.

[17] E. Leon, G. Clarke, V. Callaghan, and F. Sepulveda. A user independent real time emotion recognition system for software agents in domestic environment. *Engineering Applications of Artificial Intelligence*, 20(3):337–345, 2007.

[18] P. Luo, F. Zhuang, H. Xiong, Y. Xiong, and Q. He. Transfer learning from multiple source domains via consensus regularization. In *CIKM*, 2008.

[19] Y. Mansour, M. Mohri, and A. Rostamizadeh. Domain adaptation with multiple sources. In *NIPS*, 2009.

[20] S. J. Pan, J. T. Kwok, and Q. Yang. Transfer learning via dimensionality reduction. In *AAAI*, 2008.

[21] S. J. Pan, I. W. Tsang, J. T. Kwok, and Q. Yang. Domain adaptation via transfer component analysis. In *IJCAI*, 2009.

[22] S. J. Pan and Q. Yang. A survey on transfer learning. *IEEE Transactions on Knowledge and Data Engineering*, 2009.

[23] M. Rosenstein, Z. Marx, and L. Kaelbling. To transfer or not to transfer. In *NIPS 2005 Workshop on Inductive Transfer: 10 Years Later*, 2005.

[24] B. Schölkopf and A. J. Smola. *Learning with Kernels Support Vector Machines, Regularization, Optimization and Beyond.* The MIT Press, 2002.

[25] G. Schweikert, C. Widmer, B. Schölkopf, and G. Rätsch. An empirical analysis of domain adaptation algorithms for genomic sequence analysis. In *NIPS*, 2009.

[26] X. Shi, W. Fan, Q. Yang, and J. Ren. Relaxed transfer of different classes via spectral partition. In *KDD*, 2009.

[27] H. Shimodaira. Improving predictive inference under covariate shift by weighting the log-likelihood function. In *JSPI*, 2000.

[28] B. Silverstein, L. Fine, and T. Armstrong. Hand wrist cumulative trauma disorders in industry [1351-0711]. *Occupational and Environmental Medicine*, 43:779, 1986.

[29] M. Sugiyama, S. Nakajima, H. Kashima, P. V. Buenau, and M. Kawanabe. Direct importance estimation with model selection and its application to covariate shift adaptation. In *NIPS*, 2008.

[30] V. L. Young, M. K. Seaton, C. A. Feely, C. Arfken, D. F. Edwards, C. M. Baum, and S. Logan. Detecting cumulative trauma disorders in workers performing repetitive tasks. In *AJIM*, 1995.

[31] E. Zhong, W. Fan, J. Peng, K. Zhang, J. Ren, D. Turaga, and O. Verscheure. Cross domain distribution adaptation via kernel mapping. In *KDD*, 2009.

Author Index

www.ingramcontent.com/pod-product-compliance
Ingram Content Group UK Ltd.
Pitfield, Milton Keynes, MK11 3LW, UK
UKHW051455290926
15471UKWH00008B/1210

9 781450 312578